ANNUAL STATEMENT STUDIES

FINANCIAL RATIO BENCHMARKS

Volume I

2024 2025

RMA
Annual Statement Studies®
Copyright, Ordering, Licensing, and Use of Data Information

All of the information contained herein is obtained from sources believed to be accurate and reliable.

ALL REPRESENTATIONS CONTAINED HEREIN ARE BELIEVED BY RMA TO BE AS ACCURATE AS THE DATA AND METHODOLOGIES WILL ALLOW. HOWEVER, BECAUSE OF THE POSSIBILITIES OF HUMAN AND MECHANICAL ERROR, AS WELL AS UNFORESEEN FACTORS BEYOND RMA'S CONTROL, THE INFORMATION IN THIS BOOK IS PROVIDED "AS IS" WITHOUT WARRANTY OF ANY KIND. RMA MAKES NO REPRESENTATIONS OR WARRANTIES EXPRESS OR IMPLIED TO A SUBSCRIBER OR LICENSEE OR ANY OTHER PERSON OR ENTITY AS TO THE ACCURACY, TIMELINESS, COMPLETENESS, MERCHANTABILITY OR FITNESS FOR ANY PARTICULAR PURPOSE OF ANY OF THE INFORMATION CONTAINED IN THIS BOOK. MOREOVER, INFORMATION IS SUPPLIED WITHOUT WARRANTY ON THE UNDERSTANDING THAT ANY PERSON WHO ACTS UPON IT OR OTHERWISE CHANGES POSITION IN RELIANCE THEREON DOES SO ENTIRELY AT SUCH PERSON'S OWN RISK.

This Annual Statement Studies® book and information is not intended to provide loan advice or recommendations of any kind. The information contained herein is intended for educational, informational, and research purposes only. Accordingly, RMA does not offer any advice regarding the suitability of any loan, of any debtor or of any other business determination related to the information contained in this Annual Statement Studies® book. You use this book and information at your own risk, and RMA assumes no responsibility or liability for any advice or other guidance that you may take from this book or the information contained therein. Prior to making any business decisions, you should conduct all necessary due diligence as may be appropriate under the circumstances, and RMA assumes no responsibility or liability for any business decisions, including but not limited to loan decisions, or other services rendered by you based upon the Statement Studies® data or results obtained therefrom.

The Annual Statement Studies®:
Financial Ratio Benchmarks, 2024-2025
is a copyrighted product of RMA.
All rights reserved.
No part of this product may be copied, reproduced, replicated, disseminated, or distributed in any form or by any means, electronic or mechanical, without the express written permission of RMA.

To **obtain permission** to copy, quote, reproduce, replicate, disseminate, or distribute the Statement Studies® data/material please fax or email a brief letter stating who you are and how you intend to use the Statement Studies® data to: Statement Studies Information Products at fax number 215-446-4101 or via email to estatementstudies@rmahq.org. Depending on the requested use, RMA may require a license agreement and royalty fee.

A **License Agreement is required** if you wish to use or incorporate any portion of the data, in whole or in part in other products that will in turn be sold to others, such as in software oriented or derived products, scholarly publications, or training materials.

To **purchase** a copy, or additional copies, of the Statement Studies® data in book or online format, contact RMA's Customer Relations at 1-800-677-7621. Regional data presented in the same fashion as you see in this book is only available in eStatement Studies.

If you have a **question regarding the data** please reference the detailed explanatory notes provided in the Introduction section of the enclosed product. If you are unable to find the answer to your question, please contact us by e-mail at: estatementstudies@rmahq.org. Be sure to include your detailed question along with your telephone number, fax number, and email address.

The Risk Management Association
2005 Market Street, 36th Floor
Philadelphia, PA 19103
© 2024 by RMA
ISBN# 978-1-57070-365-2

TABLE OF CONTENTS

Information on Copyright, Ordering, Licensing, and use of Data iii
List of Participating Institutions vi
Introduction to Statement Studies and Organization of Content viii
Definition of Ratios x
Explanation of Noncontractor Balance Sheet and Income Data xix
Explanation of Contractor—Percentage-of-Completion Basis of Accounting xx
IDP Sample Report xxiii
NAICS Codes Appearing in the Statement Studies 27
Full Descriptions of Industries Appearing in the Statement Studies 31

	Description Index	Data Set Begins On
Agriculture, Forestry, Fishing and Hunting	31	85
Mining	32	125
Utilities	33	141
Construction—General Industries Format*	33	157
Manufacturing	36	219
Wholesale Trade	50	587
Retail Trade	54	715
Transportation and Warehousing	57	797
Information	60	863
Finance and Insurance	61	893
Real Estate and Rental and Leasing	63	939
Professional, Scientific and Technical Services	64	983
Management of Companies and Enterprises	68	1059
Administrative and Support and Waste Management and Remediation Services	68	1065
Educational Services	71	1129
Health Care and Social Assistance	72	1149
Arts, Entertainment and Recreation	76	1225
Accommodation and Food Services	77	1257
Other Services (Except Public Administration)	78	1285
Public Administration	81	1345
Construction—Percentage of Completion Basis of Accounting*	82	1369

Supplemental Information:

Text—Key Word Index of Industries Appearing in the Statement Studies I
Construction Financial Management Association Data VII
RMA's Credit & Lending Dictionary XVII

*General Industries Format means that a valid construction NAICS was assigned to the subject companies contained in the sample; however, the financial statements were prepared using a general or traditional manufacturing or service industries presentation of results versus using a percentage-of-completion method of accounting. Industries found in the percentage-of-completion presentation follow the presentation used by RMA in the past.

About Risk Management Association (RMA)

Founded in 1914, the Risk Management Association is a not-for-profit, member-driven professional association whose sole purpose is to advance the use of sound risk management principles in the financial services industry, including the farm credit sector. RMA promotes an enterprise approach to risk management that focuses on credit risk, market risk, and operational risk. Headquartered in Philadelphia, Pennsylvania, RMA has 1,600 institutional members that include banks of all sizes as well as nonbank financial institutions. They are represented in the Association by 35,000 individuals located throughout North America, Europe, Australia, and Asia/Pacific.

Guided by RMA's mission of advancing sound risk management principles, RMA brings financial institutions high-quality, cost-effective model risk management services delivered by a team of industry practitioners with more than 25 advanced degrees.

RMA ACKNOWLEDGES AND THANKS THE FOLLOWING INSTITUTIONS, CONTRIBUTORS TO THE 2024 STATEMENT STUDIES DATA SUBMISSION PROGRAM.

ARKANSAS
Legacy National Bank

CALIFORNIA
Banc of California
Pinnacle Bank

CONNECTICUT
Dime Bank
Jewett City Savings Bank

FLORIDA
Axiom Bank National Association
Community Bank NA
EverBank

HAWAII
American Savings Bank

IDAHO
Washington Trust Bank

ILLINOIS
First Merchants Bank

INDIANA
1st Source Bank
First Merchants Bank

IOWA
MidWestOne Bank
Northwest Bank
The Security National Bank of Sioux City

KANSAS
Emprise Bank
Fidelity Bank, N.A.
Vintage Bank Kansas

KENTUCKY
Community Trust Bank, Inc.

LOUISIANA
b1Bank
Hancock Whitney Bank

MAINE
Bangor Savings Bank

MARYLAND
Harford Bank

MASSACHUSETTS
BankFive
Community Bank, N.A.
Eastern Bank
Enterprise Bank & Trust Co.
Pittsfield Cooperative Bank

MICHIGAN
Comerica Bank
Commercial Bank
First Merchants Bank
First National Bank of Michigan
First State Bank
Huron Community Bank
Mercantile Bank

MINNESOTA
Bremer Bank, NA
Community Resource Bank
First Minnetonka City Bank
Minnwest Bank
New Market Bank
Scale Bank

MISSISSIPPI
Cadence Bank
Hancock Whitney Bank
The Peoples Bank, Boloxi

MISSOURI
Academy Bank

MONTANA
First Interstate Bank

NEBRASKA
Union Bank and Trust

NEW HAMPSHIRE
Community Bank, N.A.

NEW JERSEY
The First National Bank of Elmer

NEW YORK
Community Bank, N.A.
Lake Shore Savings Bank
M&T Bank
NBT Bank, NA
The Adirondack Trust Company
TSB

NORTH CAROLINA
First Citizens Bank
HomeTrust Bank
Truist Financial Corporation

NORTH DAKOTA
Bell State Bank & Trust

OHIO
Community Bank NA
Fifth Third Bank
First Merchants Bank
First National Bank
Huntington National Bank

OKLAHOMA
First United Bank & Trust
Oklahoma Fidelity Bank, N.A.

OREGON
Bank of the Pacific
Washington Trust Bank

PENNSYLVANIA
1st SUMMIT BANK
Community Bank
Community Bank, N.A.
First Columbia Bank & Trust Co.
Fulton Bank
PNC Bank, National Association
QNB Bank
Somerset Trust Company
Washington Financial Bank

RHODE ISLAND
Citizens Financial Group
The Washington Trust Company

SOUTH CAROLINA
Southern First Bank
United Community

SOUTH DAKOTA
First PREMIER Bank
The First National Bank in Sioux Falls

TENNESSEE
First Horizon Bank
Pinnacle Bank

TEXAS
American Bank of Commerce
American National Bank of Texas
Frost Bank
Independent Financial
Southside Bank
Woodforest National Bank

UTAH
Cache Valley Bank

VERMONT
Union Bank

VIRGINIA
Atlantic Union Bank
First Community Bank
TowneBank
United Bank
Virginia National Bank

WASHINGTON
1st Security Bank of Washington
Bank of the Pacific
Banner Bank
HomeStreet Bank
Mountain Pacific Bank
Washington Trust Bank

WEST VIRGINIA
Wesbanco Bank Wheeling

WISCONSIN
Associated Bank N.A.
Bank Five Nine
Johnson Financial Group

Introduction to Annual Statement Studies: Financial Ratio Benchmarks, 2024-2025 and General Organization of Content

The notes below will explain the presentation of *Annual Statement Studies: Financial Ratio Benchmarks*, describe how the book is organized, and answer most of your questions.

The Quality You Expect from RMA: RMA is the most respected source of objective, unbiased information on issues of importance to credit risk professionals. In its 105th year, RMA's *Annual Statement Studies®* has been the industry standard for comparison financial data. Material contained in today's *Annual Statement Studies* was first published in the March 1919 issue of the *Federal Reserve Bulletin*. In the days before computers, the *Annual Statement Studies* data was recorded in pencil on yellow ledger paper! Today, it features data for over 645 industries derived <u>directly</u> from more than 182,000 statements of financial institutions' borrowers and prospects.

- **Data That Comes Straight from Original Sources:** The more than 182,000 statements used to produce the composites presented here come directly from RMA member institutions and represent the financials from their commercial customers and prospects. RMA does not know the names of the individual entities. In fact, to ensure confidentiality, company names are removed before the data is even delivered to RMA. The raw data making up each composite is not available to any third party.

- **Data Presented in Common Size:** *Annual Statement Studies: Financial Ratio Benchmarks* contains composite financial data. Balance sheet and income statement information is shown in common size format, with each item a percentage of total assets and sales. RMA computes common size statements for each individual statement in an industry group, then aggregates and averages all the figures. In some cases, because of computer rounding, the figures to the right of the decimal point do not balance exactly with the totals shown. A minus sign beside the value indicates credits and losses.

- **Includes the Most Widely Used Ratios:** Nineteen of the most widely used ratios in the financial services industry accompany the balance sheet information, including various types of liquidity, coverage, leverage, and operating ratios.

- **Organized by the NAICS for Ease of Use:** This edition is organized according to the 2022 North American Industry Classification System (NAICS), a product of the U.S. Office of Management and Budget. At the top of each page of data, you will find the NAICS. Please note, the NAICS catalog is revised every FIVE years, in which industries may change code, description, or may be removed completely, while other industries may be added. For more information on the NAICS, visit the RMA site or: https://www.census.gov/naics/

- **Twenty Sections Outline Major Types of Businesses:** To provide further delineation, the book is divided into 20 sections outlining major lines of businesses. If you know the NAICS number you are looking for, use the NAICS-page guide provided in the front of this book. In general, the book is arranged in ascending NAICS numerical order. For your convenience, full descriptions of each NAICS are presented in this book. In addition, you will find a text-based index near the end of the book.

- **If You Do Not Know the NAICS Code You Are Looking for…** If you do not know the precise industry NAICS you are looking for, contact the Census Bureau at 1-888-75NAICS or naics@census.gov. Describe the activity of the establishment for which you need an industry code and you will receive a reply. Another source to help you assign the correct NAICS industry name and number can be found at https://www.census.gov/naics/ .

- **Can't Find the Industry You Want?** There are a number of reasons you may not find the industry you are looking for (i.e., you know you need industry xxxxxx but it is not in the product). Many times we have information on an industry, but it is not published because the sample size was too small or there were significant questions concerning the data. (For an industry to be displayed in the *Annual Statement Studies: Financial Ratio Benchmarks*, there must be at least 30 valid statements submitted to RMA.) In other instances, we simply do not have the data. Generally, most of what we receive is published.

- **Composite Data Not Shown?** When there are fewer than 10 financial statements in a particular asset or sales size category, the composite data is not shown because a sample this small is not considered representative and could be misleading. However, all the data for that industry is shown in the All Sizes column. The total number of statements for each size category is shown in bold print at the top of each column. In addition, the number of statements used in a ratio array will differ from the number of statements in a sample because certain elements of data may not be present in all financial statements. In these cases, the number of statements used is shown in parentheses to the left of the array.

- **Presentation of the Data on Each Page-Spread:** For all non-contracting spread statements, the data for a particular industry appears on both the left and right pages. The heading Current Data Sorted by Assets is in the five columns on the left side. The center section of the double-page presentation contains the Comparative Historical Data, with the All Sizes column for the current year shown under the heading 4/1/23-3/31/24. Comparable data from past editions of the *Annual Statement Studies: Financial Ratio Benchmarks* also appears in this section. Current Data Sorted by Sales is displayed in the five columns to the far right.

- **Companies with Less than $250 Million in Total Assets:** In our presentation, we used companies having less than $250 million in total assets—except in the case of contractors who use the percentage-of-completion method of accounting. *The section for contractors using the percentage-of-completion method of accounting contains data only sorted by revenue.* There is no upper limit placed on revenue size for any industry. Its information is found on only one page.

- **Page Headers:** The information shown at the top of each page includes the following: 1) the identity of the industry group; 2) its North American Industry Classification System (NAICS); 3) a breakdown by size categories of the types of financial statements reported; 4) the number of statements in each category; 5) the dates of the statements used; and 6) the size categories. For instance, 16 (4/1-9/30/23) means that 16 statements with fiscal dates between April 1 and September 30, 2023, make up part of the sample.

- **Page Footers:** At the bottom of each page, we have included the sum of the sales (or revenues) and total assets for all the financial statements in each size category. This data allows recasting of the common size statements into dollar amounts. To do this, divide the number at the bottom of the page by the number of statements in that size category. Then multiply the result by the percentages in the common size statement. Please note: The dollar amounts will be an approximation because RMA computes the balance sheet and income statement percentages for each individual statement in an industry group, then aggregates and averages all the figures.

- **Our Thanks to CFMA:** RMA appreciates the cooperation of the Construction Financial Management Association in permitting us to reproduce excerpts from its *Construction Industry Annual Financial Survey*. This data complements the RMA contractor industry data. For more details on this data, please visit www.cfma.org.

- **Recommended for Use as General Guidelines:** RMA recommends you use *Annual Statement Studies: Financial Ratio Benchmarks* data only as general guidelines and not as absolute industry norms. There are several reasons why the data may not be fully representative of a given industry:

1. **Data Not Random** — The financial statements used in the *Annual Statement Studies: Financial Ratio Benchmarks* are not selected by any random or statistically reliable method. RMA member banks voluntarily submit the raw data they have available each year with no limitation on company size.

2. **Categorized by Primary Product Only** — Many companies have varied product lines; however, the *Annual Statement Studies: Financial Ratio Benchmarks* categorizes them by their primary product NAICS number only.

3. **Small Samples** — Some of the industry samples are small in relation to the total number of firms for a given industry. A relatively small sample can increase the chances that some composites do not fully represent an industry.

4. **Extreme Statements** — An extreme or outlier statement can occasionally be present in a sample, causing a disproportionate influence on the industry composite. This is particularly true in a relatively small sample.

5. **Operational Differences** — Companies within the same industry may differ in their method of operations, which in turn can directly influence their financial statements. Since they are included in the sample, these statements can significantly affect the composite calculations.

6. **Additional Considerations** — There are other considerations that can result in variations among different companies engaged in the same general line of business. These include different labor markets, geographical location, different accounting methods, quality of products handled, sources and methods of financing, lease classification held by a lessee or lessor, and terms of sale.

For these reasons, RMA does not recommend using the *Annual Statement Studies: Financial Ratio Benchmarks* figures as absolute norms for a given industry. Rather, you should use the figures only as general guidelines and as a supplement to the other methods of financial analysis. RMA makes no claim regarding how representative the figures printed in this book are.

DEFINITION OF RATIOS

Introduction

On each data page, below the common size balance sheet and income statement information, you will find a series of ratios computed from the financial statement data.

Here is how these figures are calculated for any given ratio:

1. The ratio is computed for each financial statement in the sample.

2. These values are arrayed (listed) in an order from the strongest to the weakest. In interpreting ratios, the "strongest" or "best" value is not always the largest numerical value, nor is the "weakest" always the lowest numerical value. (For certain ratios, there may be differing opinions as to what constitutes a strong or a weak value. RMA follows general banking guidelines consistent with sound credit practice to resolve this problem.)

3. The array of values is divided into four groups of equal size. The description of each ratio appearing in the *Statement Studies* provides details regarding the arraying of the values.

What Are Quartiles?

Each ratio has three points, or "cutoff values," that divide an array of values into four equal-sized groups called quartiles, as shown below. The quartiles include the upper quartile, upper-middle quartile, lower-middle quartile, and the lower quartile. The upper quartile is the cutoff value where one-quarter of the array of ratios falls between it and the strongest ratio. The median is the midpoint—that is, the middle cutoff value where half of the array falls above it and half below it. The lower quartile is the point where one-quarter of the array falls between it and the weakest ratio. In many cases, the average of two values is used to arrive at the quartile value. You will find the median and quartile values on all *Statement Studies* data pages in the order indicated in the chart below.

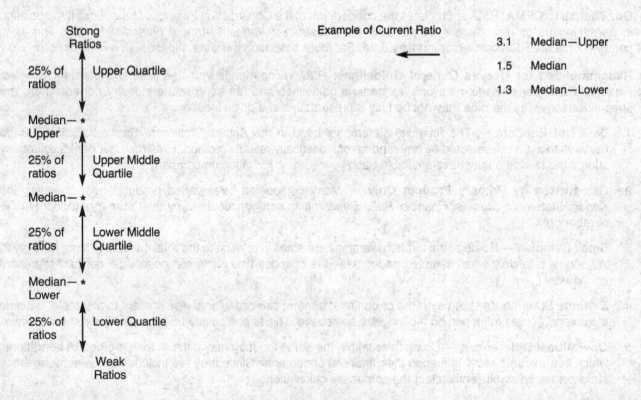

Why Use Medians/Quartiles Instead of the Average?

There are several reasons why medians and quartiles are used instead of an average. Medians and quartiles eliminate the influence of an "outlier" (an extremely high or low value compared to the rest of the values). They also more accurately reflect the ranges of ratio values than a straight averaging method would.

It is important to understand that the spread (range) between the upper and lower quartiles represents the middle 50% of all the companies in a sample. Therefore, ratio values greater than the upper quartile or less than the lower quartile may begin to approach "unusual" values.

Nonconventional Values:

For some ratio values, you will occasionally see an entry that is other than a conventional number. These entries are defined as follows:

(1) <u>UND</u> — This stands for "undefined," the result of the denominator in a ratio calculation approaching zero.

(2) <u>NM</u> — This may occasionally appear as a quartile or median for the ratios sales/working capital, debt/worth, and fixed/worth. It stands for "no meaning" in cases where the dispersion is so small that any interpretation is meaningless.

(3) <u>999.8</u> — When a ratio value equals 1,000 or more, it also becomes an "unusual" value and is given the "999.8" designation. This is considered to be a close enough approximation to the actual unusually large value.

Linear versus Nonlinear Ratios:

An array that is ordered in ascending sequence or in descending sequence is linear. An array that deviates from true ascending or true descending when its values change from positive to negative (low to high positive, followed by high to low negative) is non-linear.

A specific example of a nonlinear ratio would be the Sales/Working Capital ratio. In other words, when the Sales/Working Capital ratio is positive, then the top quartile would be represented by the *lowest positive* ratio. However, if the ratio is negative, the top quartile will be represented by the *highest negative* ratio! In a nonlinear array such as this, the median could be either positive or negative because it is whatever the middle value is in the particular array of numbers.

Nonlinear Ratios
Sales/Working Capital
Fixed/Worth
Debt/Worth

Linear Ratios
Current Ratio
Quick Ratio
Sales Receivables
Days' Receivables
Cost of Sales/Inventory
Days' Inventory
Cost of Sales/Payables
Days' Payables
EBIT/Interest
Net Profit + Deprec, Depletion, Amort/Current Maturities Long-Term Debt
% Profits Before Taxes/Tangible Net Worth
% Profits Before Taxes/Total Assets
Sales/Net Fixed Assets
Sales/Total Assets
% Depreciation, Depletion, Amortization/Sales
% Officers', Directors', Owners' Compensation/Sales

Important Notes on Ratios:

Turnover Ratios — For certain ratios (sales/receivables, cost of sales/inventory, cost of sales/payables) you will see two numbers, one in **BOLD** and one in regular type. These ratios are generally called turnover ratios. The number in **BOLD** represents **the number of days** and the number in regular type is **the number of times**. Please see the definition of sales/receivables on the following pages for a more complete description of the two types of calculations and what each means.

Inventory Presentations — **Inventory presentations** are based on fiscal year-end point-in-time balances, not averages. In addition, our data capture does not permit us to know what method of inventory accounting (LIFO or FIFO, for instance) was used.

The following ratios contained in the *Statement Studies* are grouped into five principal categories: liquidity, coverage, leverage, operating, and specific expense items.

LIQUIDITY RATIOS

Liquidity is a measure of the quality and adequacy of current assets to meet current obligations as they come due. In other words, can a firm quickly convert its assets to cash — without a loss in value — in order to meet its immediate and short-term obligations? For firms such as utilities that can readily and accurately predict their cash inflows, liquidity is not nearly as critical as it is for firms like airlines or manufacturing businesses that can have wide fluctuations in demand and revenue streams. These ratios provide a level of comfort to lenders in case of liquidation.

1. Current Ratio

How to Calculate: Divide total current assets by total current liabilities.

$$\frac{\text{Total Current Assets}}{\text{Total Current Liabilities}}$$

How to Interpret: This ratio is a rough indication of a firm's ability to service its current obligations. Generally, the higher the current ratio, the greater the "cushion" between current obligations and a firm's ability to pay them. While a stronger ratio shows that the numbers for current assets exceed those for current liabilities, the composition and quality of current assets are critical factors in the analysis of an individual firm's liquidity.

The ratio values are arrayed from the highest positive to the lowest positive.

2. Quick Ratio

How to Calculate: Add cash and equivalents to trade receivables. Then, divide by total current liabilities.

$$\frac{\text{Cash \& Equivalents + Trade Receivables (net)}}{\text{Total Current Liabilities}}$$

How to Interpret: Also known as the "acid test" ratio, this is a stricter, more conservative measure of liquidity than the current ratio. This ratio reflects the degree to which a company's current liabilities are covered by its most liquid current assets, the kind of assets that can be converted quickly to cash and at amounts close to book value. Inventory and other less liquid current assets are removed from the calculation. Generally, if the ratio produces a value that's less than 1 to 1, it implies a "dependency" on inventory or other "less" current assets to liquidate short-term debt.

The ratio values are arrayed from the highest positive to the lowest positive.

3. Sales/Receivables

How to Calculate: Divide net sales by trade receivables.

$$\frac{\text{Net Sales}}{\text{Trade Receivables (net)}}$$

Please note — In the contractor section, both accounts receivable-progress billings and accounts receivable-current retention are included in the receivables figure used in calculating the revenues/receivables and receivables/payables ratios.

How to Interpret: This ratio measures the number of times trade receivables turn over during the year. The higher the turnover of receivables, the shorter the time between sale and cash collection.

> For example, a company with sales of $720,000 and receivables of $120,000 would have a sales/receivables ratio of 6.0. This means receivables turn over six times a year. If a company's receivables appear to be turning more slowly than the rest of the industry, further research is needed and the quality of the receivables should be examined closely.

Cautions — A problem with this ratio is that it compares one day's receivables, shown at statement date, to total annual sales and does not take into consideration seasonal fluctuations. An additional problem in interpretation may arise when there is a large proportion of cash sales to total sales.

When the receivables figure is zero, the quotient will be undefined (UND) and represents the best possible ratio. The ratio values are therefore arrayed starting with undefined (UND) and then from the numerically highest value to the numerically lowest value. The only time a zero will appear in the array is when the sales figure is low and the quotient rounds off to zero. By definition, this ratio cannot be negative.

4. Days' Receivables

The sales/receivables ratio will have a figure printed in bold type directly to the left of the array. This figure is the days' receivables.

How to Calculate the Days' Receivables: Divide the sales/receivables ratio into 365 (the number of days in one year).

$$\frac{365}{\text{Sales/Receivable ratio}}$$

How to Interpret the Days' Receivables: This figure expresses the average number of days that receivables are outstanding. Generally, the greater the number of days outstanding, the greater the probability of delinquencies in accounts receivable. A comparison of a company's daily receivables may indicate the extent of a company's control over credit and collections.

Please note — You should take into consideration the terms offered by a company to its customers because these may differ from terms within the industry.

> *For example*, using the sales/receivable ratio calculated above, 365 ÷ 6 = 61 (i.e., the average receivable is collected in 61 days).

5. Cost of Sales/Inventory

How to Calculate: Divide cost of sales by inventory.

$$\frac{\text{Cost of Sales}}{\text{Inventory}}$$

How to Interpret: This ratio measures the number of times inventory is turned over during the year.

High Inventory Turnover — On the positive side, high inventory turnover can indicate greater liquidity or superior merchandising. Conversely, it can indicate a shortage of needed inventory for sales.

Low Inventory Turnover — Low inventory turnover can indicate poor liquidity, possible overstocking, or obsolescence. On the positive side, it could indicate a planned inventory buildup in the case of material shortages.

Cautions — A problem with this ratio is that it compares one day's inventory to cost of goods sold and does not take seasonal fluctuations into account. When the inventory figure is zero, the quotient will be undefined (UND) and represents the best possible ratio. The ratio values are arrayed starting with undefined (UND) and then from the numerically highest value to the numerically lowest value. The only time a zero will appear in the array is when the figure for cost of sales is very low and the quotient rounds off to zero.

Please note — For service industries, the cost of sales is included in operating expenses. In addition, please note that the data collection process does not differentiate the method of inventory valuation.

6. Days' Inventory

The days' inventory is the figure printed in bold directly to the left of the cost of sales/inventory ratio.

How to Calculate the Days' Inventory: Divide the cost of sales/inventory ratio into 365 (the number of days in one year).

$$\frac{365}{\text{Cost of Sales/Inventory ratio}}$$

How to Interpret: Dividing the inventory turnover ratio into 365 days yields the average length of time units are in inventory.

7. Cost of Sales/Payables

How to Calculate: Divide cost of sales by trade payables.

$$\frac{\text{Cost of Sales}}{\text{Trade Payables}}$$

Please note — In the contractor section, both accounts payable-trade and accounts payable-retention are included in the payables figure used in calculating the cost of revenues/payables and receivables/payables ratios.

How to Interpret: This ratio measures the number of times trade payables turn over during the year. The higher the turnover of payables, the shorter the time between purchase and payment. If a company's payables appear to be turning more slowly than the industry, then the company may be experiencing cash shortages, disputing invoices with suppliers, enjoying extended terms, or deliberately expanding its trade credit. The ratio comparison of company to industry suggests the existence of these or other possible causes. If a firm buys on 30-day terms, it is reasonable to expect this ratio to turn over in approximately 30 days.

Cautions — A problem with this ratio is that it compares one day's payables to cost of goods sold and does not take seasonal fluctuations into account. When the payables figure is zero, the quotient will be undefined (UND) and represents the best possible ratio. The ratio values are arrayed starting with undefined (UND) and then from the numerically highest to the numerically lowest value. The only time a zero will appear in the array is when the figure for cost of sales is very low and the quotient rounds off to zero.

8. Days' Payables

The days' payables is the figure printed in bold type directly to the left of the cost of sales/payables ratio.

How to Calculate the Days' Payables: Divide the cost of sales/payables ratio into 365 (the number of days in one year).

$$\frac{365}{\text{Cost of Sales/Payables ratio}}$$

How to Interpret: Division of the payables turnover ratio into 365 days yields the average length of time trade debt is outstanding.

9. Sales/Working Capital

How to Calculate: Divide net sales by net working capital (current assets less current liabilities equals net working capital).

$$\frac{\text{Net Sales}}{\text{Net Working Capital}}$$

How to Interpret: Because it reflects the ability to finance current operations, working capital is a measure of the margin of protection for current creditors. When you relate the level of sales resulting from operations to the underlying working capital, you can measure how efficiently working capital is being used.

Low ratio (close to zero) — A low ratio may indicate an inefficient use of working capital.

High ratio (high positive or high negative) — A very high ratio often signifies overtrading, which is a vulnerable position for creditors.

Please note — The sales/working capital ratio is a nonlinear array. In other words, it is an array that is NOT ordered from highest positive to highest negative as is the case for linear arrays. The ratio values are arrayed from the lowest positive to the highest positive, to undefined (UND), and then from the highest negative to the lowest negative. If working capital is zero, the quotient is undefined (UND).

If the sales/working capital ratio is positive, then the top quartile would be represented by the lowest positive ratio. However, if the ratio is negative, the top quartile will be represented by the highest negative ratio! In a nonlinear array such as the sales/working capital ratio, the median could be either positive or negative because it is whatever the middle value is in the particular array of numbers.

Cautions — When analyzing this ratio, you need to focus on working capital, not on the sales figure. Although sales cannot be negative, working capital can be. If you have a large, positive working capital number, the ratio will be small *and* positive — which is good. Because negative working capital is bad, if you have a large, negative working capital number, the sales/working capital ratio will be small *and* negative — which is NOT good. Therefore, the lowest positive ratio is the best and the lowest negative ratio is the worst. If working capital is a small negative number, the ratio will be large, which is the best of the negatives.

COVERAGE RATIOS

Coverage ratios measure a firm's ability to service its debt. In other words, how well does the flow of a company's funds cover its short-term financial obligations? In contrast to liquidity ratios that focus on the possibility of liquidation, coverage ratios seek to provide lenders a comfort level based on the belief the firm will remain a viable enterprise.

1. Earnings Before Interest and Taxes (EBIT)/Interest

How to Calculate: Divide earnings (profit) before annual interest expense and taxes by annual interest expense.

$$\frac{\text{Earnings Before Interest \& Taxes}}{\text{Annual Interest Expense}}$$

How to Interpret: This ratio measures a firm's ability to meet interest payments. A high ratio may indicate that a borrower can easily meet the interest obligations of a loan. This ratio also indicates a firm's capacity to take on additional debt.

Please note — Only statements reporting annual interest expense were used in the calculation of this ratio. The ratio values are arrayed from the highest positive to the lowest positive and then from the lowest negative to the highest negative.

2. Net Profit + Depreciation, Depletion, Amortization/Current Maturities Long-Term Debt

How to Calculate: Add net profit to depreciation, depletion, and amortization expenses. Then, divide by the current portion of long-term debt.

$$\frac{\text{Net Profit + Depreciation, Depletion, Amortization Expenses}}{\text{Current Portion of Long-Term Debt}}$$

How to Interpret: This ratio reflects how well cash flow from operations covers current maturities. Because cash flow is the primary source of debt retirement, the ratio measures a firm's ability to service principal repayment and take on additional debt. Even though it is a mistake to believe all cash flow is available for debt service, this ratio is still a valid measure of the ability to service long-term debt.

Please note — Only data for corporations with the following items was used:

(1) Profit or loss after taxes (positive, negative, or zero).

(2) A positive figure for depreciation/depletion/amortization expenses.

(3) A positive figure for current maturities of long-term debt.

Ratio values are arrayed from the highest to the lowest positive and then from the lowest to the highest negative.

LEVERAGE RATIOS

How much protection do a company's assets provide for the debt held by its creditors? Highly leveraged firms are companies with heavy debt in relation to their net worth. These firms are more vulnerable to business downturns than those with lower debt-to-worth positions. While leverage ratios help measure this vulnerability, keep in mind that these ratios vary greatly depending on the requirements of particular industry groups.

1. Fixed/Worth

How to Calculate: Divide fixed assets (net of accumulated depreciation) by tangible net worth (net worth minus intangibles).

$$\frac{\text{Net Fixed Assets}}{\text{Tangible Net Worth}}$$

How to Interpret: This ratio measures the extent to which owner's equity (capital) has been invested in plant and equipment (fixed assets). A lower ratio indicates a proportionately smaller investment in fixed assets in relation to net worth and a better "cushion" for creditors in case of liquidation. Similarly, a higher ratio would indicate the opposite situation. The presence of a substantial number of fixed assets that are leased — and not appearing on the balance sheet — may result in a deceptively lower ratio.

Fixed assets may be zero, in which case the quotient is zero. If tangible net worth is zero, the quotient is undefined (UND). If tangible net worth is negative, the quotient is negative.

Please note — Like the sales/working capital ratio discussed above, this fixed/worth ratio is a nonlinear array. In other words, it is an array that is NOT ordered from highest positive to highest negative as a linear array would be. The ratio values are arrayed from the lowest positive to the highest positive, to undefined (UND), and then from the highest negative to the lowest negative.

If the Fixed/Worth ratio is positive, then the top quartile would be represented by the lowest positive ratio. However, if the ratio is negative, the top quartile will be represented by the highest negative ratio! In a nonlinear array such as this, the median could be either positive or negative because it is whatever the middle value is in the particular array of numbers.

2. Debt/Worth

How to Calculate: Divide total liabilities by tangible net worth.

$$\frac{\text{Total Liabilities}}{\text{Tangible Net Worth}}$$

How to Interpret: This ratio expresses the relationship between capital contributed by creditors and that contributed by owners. Basically, it shows how much protection the owners are providing creditors. The higher the ratio, the greater the risk being assumed by creditors. A lower ratio generally indicates greater long-term financial safety. Unlike a highly leveraged firm, a firm with a low debt/worth ratio usually has greater flexibility to borrow in the future.

Tangible net worth may be zero, in which case the ratio is undefined (UND). Tangible net worth may also be negative, which results in the quotient being negative. The ratio values are arrayed from the lowest to highest positive, to undefined, and then from the highest to lowest negative.

Please note — Like the sales/working capital ratio discussed above, this debt/worth ratio is a nonlinear array. In other words, it is an array that is NOT ordered from highest positive to highest negative as a linear array would be. The ratio values are arrayed from the lowest positive to the highest positive, to undefined (UND), and then from the highest negative to the lowest negative.

If the debt/worth ratio is positive, then the top quartile would be represented by the *lowest positive* ratio. However, if the ratio is negative, the top quartile will be represented by the *highest negative* ratio! In a nonlinear array such as this, the median could be either positive or negative because it is whatever the middle value is in the particular array of numbers.

OPERATING RATIOS

Operating ratios are designed to assist in the evaluation of management performance.

1. % Profits Before Taxes/Tangible Net Worth

How to Calculate: Divide profit before taxes by tangible net worth. Then, multiply by 100.

$$\frac{\text{Profit Before Taxes}}{\text{Tangible Net Worth}} \times 100$$

How to Interpret: This ratio expresses the rate of return on tangible capital employed. While it can serve as an indicator of management performance, you should always use it in conjunction with other ratios. Normally associated with effective management, a high return could actually point to an undercapitalized firm. Conversely, a low return that's usually viewed as an indicator of inefficient management performance could actually reflect a highly capitalized, conservatively operated business.

This ratio has been multiplied by 100 because it is shown as a percentage.

Profit before taxes may be zero, in which case the ratio is zero. Profits before taxes may be negative, resulting in negative quotients. Firms with negative tangible net worth have been omitted from the ratio arrays. Negative ratios will therefore only result in the case of negative profit before taxes. If the tangible net worth is zero, the quotient is undefined (UND). If there are fewer than 10 ratios for a particular size class, the result is not shown. The ratio values are arrayed starting with undefined (UND), then from the highest to the lowest positive values, and finally from the lowest to the highest negative values.

2. % Profits Before Taxes/Total Assets

How to Calculate: Divide profit before taxes by total assets and multiply by 100.

$$\frac{\text{Profit Before Taxes}}{\text{Total Assets}} \times 100$$

How to Interpret: This ratio expresses the pre-tax return on total assets and measures the effectiveness of management in employing the resources available to it. If a specific ratio varies considerably from the ranges found in this book, the analyst will need to examine the makeup of the assets and take a closer look at the earnings figure. A heavily depreciated plant and a large amount of intangible assets or unusual income or expense items will cause distortions of this ratio.

This ratio has been multiplied by 100 since it is shown as a percentage. If profit before taxes is zero, the quotient is zero. If profit before taxes is negative, the quotient is negative. These ratio values are arrayed from the highest to the lowest positive and then from the lowest to the highest negative.

3. Sales/Net Fixed Assets

How to Calculate: Divide net sales by net fixed assets (net of accumulated depreciation).

$$\frac{\text{Net Sales}}{\text{Net Fixed Assets}}$$

How to Interpret: This ratio is a measure of the productive use of a firm's fixed assets. Largely depreciated fixed assets or a labor-intensive operation may cause a distortion of this ratio.

If the net fixed figure is zero, the quotient is undefined (UND). The only time a zero will appear in the array will be when the net sales figure is low and the quotient rounds off to zero. These ratio values cannot be negative.

They are arrayed from undefined (UND) and then from the highest to the lowest positive values.

4. Sales/Total Assets

How to Calculate: Divide net sales by total assets.

$$\frac{\text{Net Sales}}{\text{Total Assets}}$$

How to Interpret: This ratio is a general measure of a firm's ability to generate sales in relation to total assets. It should be used only to compare firms within specific industry groups and in conjunction with other operating ratios to determine the effective employment of assets.

The only time a zero will appear in the array will be when the net sales figure is low and the quotient rounds off to zero. The ratio values cannot be negative. They are arrayed from the highest to the lowest positive values.

EXPENSE TO SALES RATIOS

The following two ratios relate specific expense items to net sales and express this relationship as a percentage. Comparisons are convenient because the item, net sales, is used as a constant. Variations in these ratios are most pronounced between capital- and labor-intensive industries.

1. % Depreciation, Depletion, Amortization/Sales

How to Calculate: Divide annual depreciation, amortization, and depletion expenses by net sales and multiply by 100.

$$\frac{\text{Depreciation, Amortization, Depletion Expenses}}{\text{Net Sales}} \times 100$$

2. % Officers', Directors', Owners' Compensation/Sales

How to Calculate: Divide annual officers', directors', owners' compensation by net sales and multiply by 100. Include total salaries, bonuses, commissions, and other monetary remuneration to all officers, directors, and/or owners of the firm during the year covered by the statement. This includes drawings of partners and proprietors.

$$\frac{\text{Officers', Directors', Owners' Compensation}}{\text{Net Sales}} \times 100$$

Only statements showing a positive figure for each of the expense categories shown above were used. The ratios are arrayed from the lowest to highest positive values.

Explanation of Noncontractor Balance Sheet and Income Data

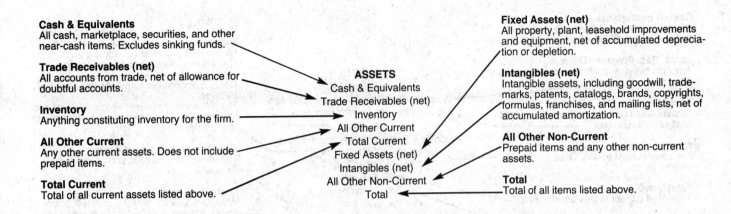

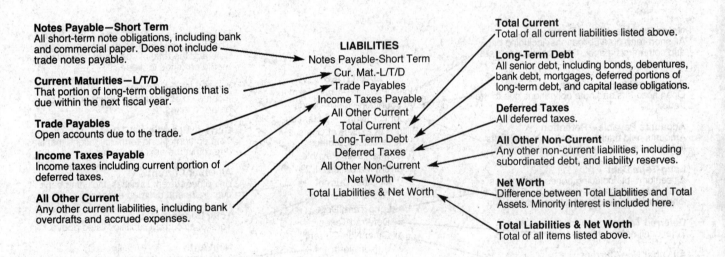

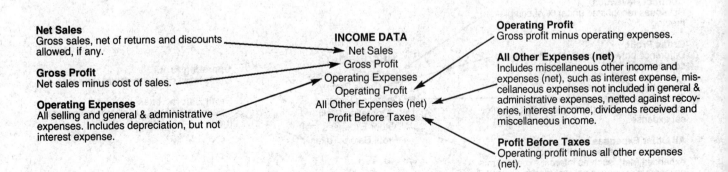

For further analysis, please refer to *Industry Default Probabilities and Cash Flow Measures*

If you think *Financial Ratio Benchmarks* is a valuable resource, wait until you see its companion study. Now in its twenty-third year and bigger than ever, *Industry Default Probabilities and Cash Flow Measures* is a major expansion of our *Annual Statement Studies*. These benchmarks add substantial value to the critical analysis of cash flow for private companies.

The latest edition of *Industry Default Probabilities and Cash Flow Measures* includes many new industries, stronger statements, five years of historical data sorted by assets and sales. In short, it is more like our traditional *Statement Studies*.

Industry Default Probabilities and Cash Flow Measures includes:
- Cash flow measures on a common-size percentage scale. Ratios include:
  - Cash from Trading
  - Cash after Operations
  - Net Cash after Operations
  - Cash after Debt Amortization
  - Debt Service P&I Coverage
  - Interest Coverage (Operating Cash)
- Change in position, normalized, year over year, for eight financial statement line items. Ratios include:
  - Change in Inventory
  - Total Current Assets (TCA)
  - Total Assets (TA)
  - Retained Earnings (RE)
  - Net Sales (NS)
  - Cost of Goods Sold (CGS)
  - Profit before Interest & Taxes (PBIT)
  - Depreciation/Depletion/Amortization (DDA)
- Trend data available for the past five years.
- Other ratios:
  - Sustainable Growth Rate
  - Funded Debt/EBITDA
- Data arrayed by asset and sales size.

Access to the Industry Default Probabilities and Cash Flow Measures is only available in the eStatement Studies online database. A copy of a sample report can be found on the next page. For more information on how to upgrade to eStatement Studies, please see the inside back cover, or contact us at 1-800-677-7621.

INDUSTRY DEFAULT PROBABILITIES AND CASH FLOW MEASURES SAMPLE REPORT

AGRICULTURE—Soybean Farming NAICS 111110

Current Data Sorted by Assets							Type of Statement	Comparative Historical Data	
		1	4	1	1		Unqualified	10	20
	2	3	3				Reviewed	5	19
	2	1					Compiled	5	12
6	8	6	1				Tax Returns	25	30
2	5	9	3	2			Other	33	52
	7 (4/1-9/30/17)		53 (10/1/17-3/31/18)					4/1/13-	4/1/14-
0-500M	500M-2MM	2-10MM	10-50MM	50-100MM	100-250MM		Assets Size	3/31/14	3/31/15
8	17	20	11	3	1		Number of Statements	ALL 78	ALL 133
%	%	%	%	%	%			%	%

							CASH FLOW MEASURES		
							%	%	
							Cash from Trading/Sales		
	17.2	38.9	25.1				Cash after Operations/Sales	25.3	26.4
	6.5	19.3	9.7					(76) 10.5	10.0
	-16.9	3.9	-1.7					4.8	3.2
	16.7	28.1	23.8				Net Cash after Operations/Sales	25.8	26.3
	5.3	15.0	9.0					(76) 10.7	11.7
	-.3	2.6	2.1					5.3	3.9
	12.6	5.6	4.9				Net Cash after Debt Amortization/Sales	12.5	8.7
(16)	5.7	.9	-2.2					(76) 4.1	2.2
	-3.0	-11.2	-6.7					-2.3	-2.6
	14.7	2.4	29.3				Debt Service P&I Coverage	7.1	6.0
(14)	9.6	(16) 1.3	(10) 2.2					(68) 2.8	(120) 2.4
	-.2	.1	.0					.8	1.1
	51.9	22.1	59.6				Interest Coverage (Operating Cash)	18.4	24.1
(13)	8.3	(16) 5.7	(10) 16.3					(66) 5.1	(118) 7.0
	-3.3	.5	2.2					1.3	2.5
		48.0					Δ Inventory	31.5	22.9
	(10)	-.5						(43) 6.0	(66) 4.1
		-17.4						-6.6	-5.9
	28.6	31.7	4.9				Δ Total Current Assets	47.0	49.4
	2.8	10.5	-6.2					14.1	9.1
	-35.1	-20.4	-26.1					-13.4	-12.6
	36.3	20.8	8.3				Δ Total Assets	26.9	24.1
	3.1	3.1	-1.9					6.1	4.9
	-5.8	-7.7	-5.7					-3.5	-3.7
	111.1	32.9	6.6				Δ Retained Earnings	82.3	36.6
(15)	10.8	(19) 4.2	-15.0					(76) 17.1	(131) 10.1
	-72.0	-38.7	-91.3					-.8	-4.3
	34.7	13.8	16.5				Δ Net Sales	27.9	23.3
	-2.5	6.9	5.4					10.0	3.2
	-11.7	.3	-7.8					-2.3	-6.3
							Δ Cost of Goods Sold		
	96.1	88.0	73.5				Δ Profit before Int. & Taxes	120.8	82.7
(16)	-.7	13.6	-7.4					35.5	(131) 14.9
	-44.8	-34.1	-47.6					-18.0	-35.3
	67.7	12.6	100.7				Δ Depr./Depl./Amort.	11.3	21.1
(12)	-21.3	(18) 2.3	7.7					(69) -4.7	(110) .0
	-81.6	-15.8	-31.1					-33.6	-16.3
	64.9	50.4	12.5				**RATIOS** Sustainable Growth Rate	16.1	26.3
	.0	17.7	-.1					(77) .1	(131) 5.6
	-39.7	-.2	-11.5					-17.7	-7.9
	.0	.6	.5				Funded Debt/EBITDA	.5	.6
	1.0	1.4	8.2					2.1	2.2
	3.4	8.3	15.4					5.9	7.6
9580M	42882M	289548M	468863M	141379M	56029M		Net Sales ($)	1170146M	3006125M
2078M	21645M	95307M	207335M	218849M	105246M		Total Assets ($)	874532M	1601154M

M = $ thousand   MM = $ million

© RMA 2018

AGRICULTURE—Soybean Farming NAICS 111110

Comparative Historical Data			Type of Statement	Current Data Sorted by Sales					
14	6	7	Unqualified		1				5
13	5	8	Reviewed		1		3	2	2
9	8	3	Compiled		1			1	
31	23	21	Tax Returns	5	12	2	2		
50	40	21	Other	5	4		2	4	5
4/1/15-3/31/16 ALL	4/1/16-3/31/17 ALL	4/1/17-3/31/18 ALL			7 (4/1-9/30/17)		53 (10/1/17-3/31/18)		
			Sales Size	0-1MM	1-3MM	3-5MM	5-10MM	10-25MM	25MM & OVER
117	82	60	Number of Statements	10	19	4	8	7	12
%	%	%		%	%	%	%	%	%

%	%	%	**CASH FLOW MEASURES**	%	%	%	%	%	%
			Cash from Trading/Sales						
25.2	18.7	22.0		98.9	22.7				9.8
10.0	5.0	6.7	Cash after Operations/Sales	19.0	18.9				6.3
3.6	-2.1	-1.9		-15.4	3.6				1.9
24.1	18.4	20.4		90.5	27.2				9.6
(116) 10.0	5.8	7.5	Net Cash after Operations/Sales	1.0	17.1				7.1
4.5	.0	1.1		-19.1	4.9				1.9
14.5	5.7	8.8		3.0	11.8				3.7
(116) 2.7	(81) .7	(59) .0	Net Cash after Debt Amortization/Sales	-15.4	8.8				-1.0
-3.5	-6.0	-6.7		-65.5	-2.6				-5.4
8.9	8.9	11.9			13.4				13.1
(95) 2.6	(70) 1.9	(50) 1.7	Debt Service P&I Coverage	(16) 7.4				(11) 2.4	
.7	.0	.0		.5				.6	
21.5	22.4	23.9			42.8				30.4
(90) 6.0	(64) 5.8	(49) 5.1	Interest Coverage (Operating Cash)	(15) 10.9				(11) 13.1	
2.2	.0	.0		1.8				1.2	
13.8	25.6	38.4							
(49) .0	(42) -1.0	(27) 1.6	Δ Inventory						
-17.5	-19.5	-15.4							
47.1	38.8	23.3		-15.8	39.4				11.7
4.4	3.7	2.1	Δ Total Current Assets	-49.2	13.7				.5
-15.0	-17.3	-25.0		-80.4	-26.1				-10.4
27.3	16.8	21.0		34.7	33.9				9.3
3.3	-.4	2.4	Δ Total Assets	-7.1	8.3				-2.8
-4.0	-9.0	-7.7		-61.7	-5.6				-5.5
45.7	44.3	35.5		28.5	135.5				5.6
(112) 8.3	(80) 4.1	(57) 4.5	Δ Retained Earnings	11.8	(16) 10.6				-12.3
-9.3	-24.5	-39.5		-52.3	-.3				-51.2
17.7	19.2	14.5		7.8	49.8				30.1
.2	4.5	6.0	Δ Net Sales	-.6	11.8				9.7
-14.7	-9.5	-4.9		-30.2	-3.1				-.8
			Δ Cost of Goods Sold						
90.4	85.5	101.7		101.4	188.1				55.8
(116) 11.9	12.0	(59) 6.5	Δ Profit before Int. & Taxes	15.5	(18) 30.3				-25.6
-44.7	-46.3	-44.8		-72.9	-10.1				-68.9
29.4	28.5	36.4			30.6				43.8
(89) .0	(70) -5.6	(49) .0	Δ Depr./Depl./Amort.		(16) -15.8			(10)	21.4
-34.0	-55.5	-26.8			-37.5				-17.1
			RATIOS						
24.5	19.8	27.4		4.5	42.7				22.3
6.5	(81) 1.4	.3	Sustainable Growth Rate	-.9	2.2				.6
-7.0	-7.0	-13.8		-32.4	-24.5				-17.0
.3	.3	.3		2.7	.2				.5
2.4	2.1	2.3	Funded Debt/EBITDA	9.0	1.0				1.9
6.7	10.5	9.1		NM	2.8				10.2
2343689M	1692251M	1008281M	Net Sales ($)	5415M	34506M	17030M	56364M	130791M	764155M
1662679M	922447M	650460M	Total Assets ($)	24514M	51377M	12629M	44808M	123974M	393158M

© RMA 2018 M = $ thousand   MM = $ million

NAICS CODES APPEARING IN THE STATEMENT STUDIES

NAICS Codes	Page	NAICS Codes	Page	NAICS Codes	Page
111110	86-87	238290	200-201	323113	310-311
111211	88-89	238310	202-203, 1386	324121	312-313
111219	90-91	238320	204-205	324191	314-315
111331	92-93	238330	206-207, 1387	325180	316-317
111332	94-95	238340	208-209	325199	318-319
111335	96-97	238350	210-211	325211	320-321
111421	98-99	238390	212-213	325314	322-323
111998	100-101	238910	214-215, 1388	325320	324-325
112111	102-103	238990	216-217, 1389	325411	326-327
112112	104-105	311111	220-221	325412	328-329
112120	106-107	311119	222-223	325510	330-331
113110	108-109	311211	224-225	325520	332-333
113310	110-111	311412	226-227	325611	334-335
115111	112-113	311421	228-229	325612	336-337
115112	114-115	311511	230-231	325620	338-339
115114	116-117	311513	232-233	325998	340-341
115116	118-119	311520	234-235	326111	342-343
115210	120-121	311611	236-237	326112	344-345
115310	122-123	311612	238-239	326122	346-347
211120	126-127	311710	240-241	326140	348-349
211130	128-129	311811	242-243	326150	350-351
212312	130-131	311812	244-245	326160	352-353
212319	132-133	311919	246-247	326199	354-355
212321	134-135	311920	248-249	326220	356-357
213111	136-137	311942	250-251	326299	358-359
213112	138-139	311991	252-253	327215	360-361
221112	142-143	311999	254-255	327320	362-363
221114	144-145	312111	256-257	327331	364-365
221115	146-147	312120	258-259	327390	366-367
221118	148-149	312130	260-261	327991	368-369
221122	150-151	312140	262-263	331110	370-371
221210	152-153	313210	264-265	331210	372-373
221310	154-155	313310	266-267	331221	374-375
236115	158-159, 1370	314110	268-269	331314	376-377
236116	160-161, 1371	314999	270-271	331318	378-379
236117	162-163, 1372	315210	272-273	331523	380-381
236118	164-165, 1373	315250	274-275	332111	382-383
236210	166-167, 1374	315990	276-277	332119	384-385
236220	168-169, 1375	316990	278-279	332216	386-387
237110	170-171, 1376	321113	280-281	332311	388-389
237120	172-173	321211	282-283	332312	390-391
237130	174-175, 1377	321911	284-285	332313	392-393
237210	176-177	321918	286-287	332321	394-395
237310	178-179, 1378	321920	288-289	332322	396-397
237990	180-181, 1379	321992	290-291	332323	398-399
238110	182-183, 1380	321999	292-293	332420	400-401
238120	184-185, 1381	322120	294-295	332439	402-403
238130	186-187	322211	296-297	332510	404-405
238140	188-189	322212	298-299	332613	406-407
238150	190-191, 1382	322220	300-301	332618	408-409
238160	192-193, 1383	322230	302-303	332710	410-411
238190	194-195	322291	304-305	332721	412-413
238210	196-197, 1384	322299	306-307	332722	414-415
238220	198-199, 1385	323111	308-309	332811	416-417

NAICS CODES APPEARING IN THE STATEMENT STUDIES

NAICS Codes	Page
332812	418-419
332813	420-421
332911	422-423
332912	424-425
332919	426-427
332991	428-429
332994	430-431
332996	432-433
332999	434-435
333111	436-437
333112	438-439
333120	440-441
333131	442-443
333132	444-445
333241	446-447
333248	448-449
333310	450-451
333413	452-453
333414	454-455
333415	456-457
333511	458-459
333514	460-461
333515	462-463
333517	464-465
333519	466-467
333912	468-469
333914	470-471
333922	472-473
333923	474-475
333924	476-477
333992	478-479
333993	480-481
333994	482-483
333998	484-485
334111	486-487
334118	488-489
334220	490-491
334290	492-493
334310	494-495
334412	496-497
334413	498-499
334418	500-501
334419	502-503
334511	504-505
334513	506-507
334516	508-509
334519	510-511
335132	512-513
335311	514-515
335312	516-517
335313	518-519
335314	520-521
335999	522-523
336110	524-525

NAICS Codes	Page
336211	526-527
336212	528-529
336214	530-531
336310	532-533
336320	534-535
336360	536-537
336370	538-539
336390	540-541
336411	542-543
336412	544-545
336413	546-547
336611	548-549
336612	550-551
336991	552-553
336999	554-555
337110	556-557
337121	558-559
337126	560-561
337127	562-563
337212	564-565
337215	566-567
339112	568-569
339113	570-571
339114	572-573
339910	574-575
339920	576-577
339950	578-579
339991	580-581
339992	582-583
339999	584-585
423110	588-589
423120	590-591
423130	592-593
423140	594-595
423210	596-597
423220	598-599
423310	600-601
423320	602-603
423330	604-605
423390	606-607
423420	608-609
423430	610-611
423440	612-613
423450	614-615
423490	616-617
423510	618-619
423610	620-621
423620	622-623
423690	624-625
423710	626-627
423720	628-629
423730	630-631
423740	632-633
423810	634-635

NAICS Codes	Page
423820	636-637
423830	638-639
423840	640-641
423850	642-643
423860	644-645
423910	646-647
423920	648-649
423930	650-651
423940	652-653
423990	654-655
424110	656-657
424120	658-659
424130	660-661
424210	662-663
424310	664-665
424340	666-667
424350	668-669
424410	670-671
424420	672-673
424430	674-675
424440	676-677
424450	678-679
424460	680-681
424470	682-683
424480	684-685
424490	686-687
424510	688-689
424590	690-691
424610	692-693
424690	694-695
424710	696-697
424720	698-699
424810	700-701
424820	702-703
424910	704-705
424930	706-707
424940	708-709
424990	710-711
425120	712-713
441110	716-717
441120	718-719
441210	720-721
441222	722-723
441227	724-725
441330	726-727
441340	728-729
444110	730-731
444140	732-733
444180	734-735
444230	736-737
444240	738-739
445110	740-741
445131	742-743
445240	744-745

NAICS CODES APPEARING IN THE STATEMENT STUDIES

NAICS Codes	Page	NAICS Codes	Page	NAICS Codes	Page
445291	746-747	493120	856-857	532310	970-971
445298	748-749	493130	858-859	532411	972-973
445320	750-751	493190	860-861	532412	974-975
449110	752-753	512110	864-865	532420	976-977
449121	754-755	512131	866-867	532490	978-979
449129	756-757	512230	868-869	533110	980-981
449210	758-759	513130	870-871	541110	984-985
455219	760-761	513210	872-873	541199	986-987
456110	762-763	516110	874-875	541211	988-989
456120	764-765	516120	876-877	541213	990-991
456191	766-767	516210	878-879	541214	992-993
456199	768-769	517111	880-881	541219	994-995
457110	770-771	517112	882-883	541310	996-997
457120	772-773	517121	884-885	541320	998-999
457210	774-775	517810	886-887	541330	1000-1001
458110	776-777	518210	888-889	541370	1002-1003
458210	778-779	519290	890-891	541380	1004-1005
458310	780-781	522220	894-895	541410	1006-1007
459110	782-783	522291	896-897	541420	1008-1009
459140	784-785	522292	898-899	541430	1010-1011
459410	786-787	522299	900-901	541490	1012-1013
459420	788-789	522310	902-903	541511	1014-1015
459510	790-791	522320	904-905	541512	1016-1017
459910	792-793	522390	906-907	541513	1018-1019
459999	794-795	523150	908-909	541519	1020-1021
481111	798-799	523910	910-911	541611	1022-1023
481211	800-801	523940	912-913	541612	1024-1025
481219	802-803	523991	914-915	541613	1026-1027
483111	804-805	523999	916-917	541614	1028-1029
483211	806-807	524114	918-919	541618	1030-1031
484110	808-809	524126	920-921	541620	1032-1033
484121	810-811	524128	922-923	541690	1034-1035
484122	812-813	524130	924-925	541714	1036-1037
484210	814-815	524210	926-927	541715	1038-1039
484220	816-817	524292	928-929	541720	1040-1041
484230	818-819	524298	930-931	541810	1042-1043
485410	820-821	525910	932-933	541820	1044-1045
485510	822-823	525920	934-935	541850	1046-1047
485999	824-825	525990	936-937	541860	1048-1049
488119	826-827	531110	940-941	541890	1050-1051
488190	828-829	531120	942-943	541910	1052-1053
488210	830-831	531130	944-945	541940	1054-1055
488310	832-833	531190	946-947	541990	1056-1057
488320	834-835	531210	948-949	551112	1060-1061
488330	836-837	531311	950-951	551114	1062-1063
488390	838-839	531312	952-953	561110	1066-1067
488410	840-841	531390	954-955	561210	1068-1069
488490	842-843	532111	956-957	561311	1070-1071
488510	844-845	532112	958-959	561312	1072-1073
488991	846-847	532120	960-961	561320	1074-1075
488999	848-849	532210	962-963	561330	1076-1077
492110	850-851	532283	964-965	561422	1078-1079
492210	852-853	532284	966-967	561440	1080-1081
493110	854-855	532289	968-969	561499	1082-1083

NAICS CODES APPEARING IN THE STATEMENT STUDIES

NAICS Codes	Page
561510	1084-1085
561520	1086-1087
561599	1088-1089
561612	1090-1091
561621	1092-1093
561710	1094-1095
561720	1096-1097
561730	1098-1099
561740	1100-1101
561790	1102-1103
561910	1104-1105
561920	1106-1107
561990	1108-1109
562111	1110-1111
562119	1112-1113
562211	1114-1115
562212	1116-1117
562219	1118-1119
562910	1120-1121
562920	1122-1123
562991	1124-1125
562998	1126-1127
611110	1130-1131
611310	1132-1133
611430	1134-1135
611512	1136-1137
611519	1138-1139
611610	1140-1141
611620	1142-1143
611699	1144-1145
611710	1146-1147
621111	1150-1151
621112	1152-1153
621210	1154-1155
621310	1156-1157
621320	1158-1159
621330	1160-1161
621340	1162-1163
621391	1164-1165
621399	1166-1167
621420	1168-1169
621491	1170-1171
621492	1172-1173
621493	1174-1175
621498	1176-1177
621511	1178-1179
621512	1180-1181
621610	1182-1183
621910	1184-1185
621991	1186-1187
621999	1188-1189
622110	1190-1191
622210	1192-1193
622310	1194-1195
623110	1196-1197
623210	1198-1199
623220	1200-1201
623311	1202-1203
623312	1204-1205
623990	1206-1207
624110	1208-1209
624120	1210-1211
624190	1212-1213
624210	1214-1215
624221	1216-1217
624229	1218-1219
624310	1220-1221
624410	1222-1223
711110	1226-1227
711211	1228-1229
711310	1230-1231
711510	1232-1233
712110	1234-1235
712130	1236-1237
713110	1238-1239
713210	1240-1241
713290	1242-1243
713910	1244-1245
713920	1246-1247
713930	1248-1249
713940	1250-1251
713950	1252-1253
713990	1254-1255
721110	1258-1259
721120	1260-1261
721191	1262-1263
721199	1264-1265
721211	1266-1267
721214	1268-1269
721310	1270-1271
722310	1272-1273
722320	1274-1275
722410	1276-1277
722511	1278-1279
722513	1280-1281
722515	1282-1283
811111	1286-1287
811114	1288-1289
811121	1290-1291
811191	1292-1293
811192	1294-1295
811198	1296-1297
811210	1298-1299
811310	1300-1301
811490	1302-1303
812112	1304-1305
812199	1306-1307
812210	1308-1309
812310	1310-1311
812320	1312-1313
812331	1314-1315
812910	1316-1317
812930	1318-1319
812990	1320-1321
813110	1322-1323
813211	1324-1325
813212	1326-1327
813219	1328-1329
813312	1330-1331
813319	1332-1333
813410	1334-1335
813910	1336-1337
813920	1338-1339
813930	1340-1341
813990	1342-1343
921110	1346-1347
921120	1348-1349
921130	1350-1351
921140	1352-1353
921190	1354-1355
922160	1356-1357
923110	1358-1359
923120	1360-1361
925110	1362-1363
925120	1364-1365
926110	1366-1367

DESCRIPTION OF INDUSTRIES INCLUDED IN THE STATEMENT STUDIES

AGRICULTURE, FORESTRY, FISHING AND HUNTING

NAICS #		Page
111110	**Soybean Farming.** This industry comprises establishments primarily engaged in growing soybeans and/or producing soybean seeds.	86-87
111211	**Potato Farming.** This U.S. industry comprises establishments primarily engaged in growing potatoes and/or producing seed potatoes (except sweet potatoes).	88-89
111219	**Other Vegetable (except Potato) and Melon Farming.** This U.S. industry comprises establishments primarily engaged in one or more of the following: (1) growing melons and/or vegetables (except potatoes; dry peas; dry beans; field, silage, or seed corn; and sugar beets); (2) producing vegetable and/or melon seeds; and (3) growing vegetable and/or melon bedding plants.	90-91
111331	**Apple Orchards.** This U.S. industry comprises establishments primarily engaged in growing apples.	92-93
111332	**Grape Vineyards.** This U.S. industry comprises establishments primarily engaged in growing grapes and/or growing grapes to sun dry into raisins.	94-95
111335	**Tree Nut Farming.** This U.S. industry comprises establishments primarily engaged in growing tree nuts.	96-97
111421	**Nursery and Tree Production.** This U.S. industry comprises establishments primarily engaged in (1) growing nursery products, nursery stock, shrubbery, bulbs, fruit stock, sod, and so forth, under cover or in open fields and/or (2) growing short rotation woody trees with a growth and harvest cycle of 10 years or less for pulp or tree stock.	98-99
111998	**All Other Miscellaneous Crop Farming.** This U.S. industry comprises establishments primarily engaged in one of the following: (1) growing crops (except oilseeds and/or grains; vegetables and/or melons; fruits and/or tree nuts; greenhouse, nursery and/or floriculture products; tobacco; cotton; sugarcane; hay; sugar beets; or peanuts); (2) growing a combination of crops (except a combination of oilseed(s) and grain(s); and a combination of fruit(s) and tree nut(s)) with no one crop or family of crop(s) accounting for one-half of the establishment's agricultural production (i.e., value of crops for market); or (3) gathering tea or maple sap.	100-101
112111	**Beef Cattle Ranching and Farming.** This U.S. industry comprises establishments primarily engaged in raising cattle (including cattle for dairy herd replacements).	102-103
112112	**Cattle Feedlots.** This U.S. industry comprises establishments primarily engaged in feeding cattle for fattening.	104-105
112120	**Dairy Cattle and Milk Production.** This U.S. industry comprises establishments primarily engaged in milking dairy cattle.	106-107
113110	**Timber Tract Operations.** This industry comprises establishments primarily engaged in the operation of timber tracts for the purpose of selling standing timber.	108-109
113310	**Logging.** This industry comprises establishments primarily engaged in one or more of the following: (1) cutting timber; (2) cutting and transporting timber; and (3) producing wood chips in the field.	110-111
115111	**Cotton Ginning.** This U.S. industry comprises establishments primarily engaged in ginning cotton.	112-113
115112	**Soil Preparation, Planting, and Cultivating.** This U.S. industry comprises establishments primarily engaged in performing a soil preparation activity or crop production service, such as plowing, fertilizing, seed bed preparation, planting, cultivating, and crop protecting services.	114-115
115114	**Postharvest Crop Activities (except Cotton Ginning).** This U.S. industry comprises establishments primarily engaged in performing services on crops, subsequent to their harvest, with the intent of preparing them for market or further processing. These establishments provide postharvest activities, such as crop cleaning, sun drying, shelling, fumigating, curing, sorting, grading, packing, and cooling.	116-117

MINING

NAICS # Page

115116 **Farm Management Services.** This U.S. industry comprises establishments primarily engaged in providing farm management services on a contract or fee basis usually to citrus groves, orchards, or vineyards. These establishments always provide management and may arrange or contract for the partial or the complete operations of the farm establishment(s) it manages. Operational activities may include cultivating, harvesting, and/or other specialized agricultural support activities. 118-119

115210 **Support Activities for Animal Production.** This industry comprises establishments primarily engaged in performing support activities related to raising livestock (e.g., cattle, goats, hogs, horses, poultry, sheep). These establishments may perform one or more of the following: (1) breeding services for animals, including companion animals (e.g., cats, dogs, pet birds); (2) pedigree record services; (3) boarding horses; (4) dairy herd improvement activities; (5) livestock spraying; and (6) sheep dipping and shearing. 120-121

115310 **Support Activities for Forestry.** This industry comprises establishments primarily engaged in performing particular support activities related to timber production, wood technology, forestry economics and marketing, and forest protection. These establishments may provide support activities for forestry, such as estimating timber, forest firefighting, forest pest control, and consulting on wood attributes and reforestation. 122-123

MINING

211120 **Crude Petroleum Extraction.** This industry comprises establishments primarily engaged in (1) the exploration, development, and/or the production of petroleum from wells in which the hydrocarbons will initially flow or can be produced using normal or enhanced drilling and extraction techniques or (2) the production of crude petroleum from surface shales or tar sands or from reservoirs in which the hydrocarbons are semisolids. Establishments in this industry operate oil wells on their own account or for others on a contract or fee basis. 126-127

211130 **Natural Gas Extraction.** This industry comprises establishments primarily engaged in (1) the exploration, development, and/or the production of natural gas from wells in which the hydrocarbons will initially flow or can be produced using normal or enhanced drilling and extraction techniques or (2) the recovery of liquid hydrocarbons from oil and gas field gases. Establishments primarily engaged in sulfur recovery from natural gas are included in this industry. . . 128-129

212312 **Crushed and Broken Limestone Mining and Quarrying.** This U.S. industry comprises (1) establishments primarily engaged in developing the mine site, mining or quarrying crushed and broken limestone (including related rocks, such as dolomite, cement rock, marl, travertine, and calcareous tufa); and (2) preparation plants primarily engaged in beneficiating limestone (e.g., grinding or pulverizing). 130-131

212319 **Other Crushed and Broken Stone Mining and Quarrying.** This U.S. industry comprises: (1) establishments primarily engaged in developing the mine site and/or mining or quarrying crushed and broken stone (except limestone and granite); (2) preparation plants primarily engaged in beneficiating (e.g., grinding and pulverizing) stone (except limestone and granite); and (3) establishments primarily engaged in mining or quarrying bituminous limestone and bituminous sandstone. 132-133

212321 **Construction Sand and Gravel Mining.** This U.S. industry comprises establishments primarily engaged in one or more of the following: (1) operating commercial grade (i.e., construction) sand and gravel pits; (2) dredging for commercial grade sand and gravel; and (3) washing, screening, or otherwise preparing commercial grade sand and gravel. 134-135

213111 **Drilling Oil and Gas Wells.** This U.S. industry comprises establishments primarily engaged in drilling oil and gas wells for others on a contract or fee basis. This industry includes contractors that specialize in spudding in, drilling in, redrilling, and directional drilling. 136-137

213112 **Support Activities for Oil and Gas Operations.** This U.S. industry comprises establishments primarily engaged in performing support activities on a contract or fee basis for oil and gas operations (except site preparation and related construction activities). Services included are exploration (except geophysical surveying and mapping); excavating slush pits and cellars, well surveying; running, cutting, and pulling casings, tubes, and rods; cementing wells, shooting wells; perforating well casings; acidizing and chemically treating wells; and cleaning out, bailing, and swabbing wells. 138-139

CONSTRUCTION-GENERAL

NAICS # | Page

UTILITIES

221112 **Fossil Fuel Electric Power Generation.** This U.S. industry comprises establishments primarily engaged in operating fossil fuel powered electric power generation facilities. These facilities use fossil fuels, such as coal, oil, or gas, in internal combustion or combustion turbine conventional steam process to produce electric energy. The electric energy produced in these establishments are provided to electric power transmission systems or to electric power distribution systems. 142-143

221114 **Solar Electric Power Generation.** This U.S. industry comprises establishments primarily engaged in operating solar electric power generation facilities. These facilities use energy from the sun to produce electric energy. The electric energy produced in these establishments is provided to electric power transmission systems or to electric power distribution systems. ... 144-145

221115 **Wind Electric Power Generation.** This U.S. industry comprises establishments primarily engaged in operating wind electric power generation facilities. These facilities use wind power to drive a turbine and produce electric energy. The electric energy produced in these establishments is p... 146-147

221118 **Other Electric Power Generation.** This U.S. industry comprises establishments primarily engaged in operating electric power generation facilities (except hydroelectric, fossil fuel, nuclear, solar, wind, geothermal, biomass). These facilities convert other forms of energy, such as tidal power, into electric energy. The electric energy produced in these establishments is provided to electric power transmission systems or to electric power distribution systems. ... 148-149

221122 **Electric Power Distribution.** This U.S. industry comprises electric power establishments primarily engaged in either (1) operating electric power distribution systems (i.e., consisting of lines, poles, meters, and wiring) or (2) operating as electric power brokers or agents that arrange the sale of electricity via power distribution systems operated by others. 150-151

221210 **Natural Gas Distribution.** This industry comprises: (1) establishments primarily engaged in operating gas distribution systems (e.g., mains, meters); (2) establishments known as gas marketers that buy gas from the well and sell it to a distribution system; (3) establishments known as gas brokers or agents that arrange the sale of gas over gas distribution systems operated by others; and (4) establishments primarily engaged in transmitting and distributing gas to final consumers. 152-153

221310 **Water Supply and Irrigation Systems.** This industry comprises establishments primarily engaged in operating water treatment plants and/or operating water supply systems. The water supply system may include pumping stations, aqueducts, and/or distribution mains. The water may be used for drinking, irrigation, or other uses. 154-155

CONSTRUCTION—GENERAL

236115 **New Single-Family Housing Construction (except For-Sale Builders).** This U.S. industry comprises general contractor establishments primarily respon-sible for the entire construction of new single-family housing, such as single-family detached houses and town houses or row houses where each housing unit (1) is separated from its neighbors by a ground-to-roof wall and (2) has no housing units constructed above or below. This industry includes general contractors responsible for the on-site assembly of modular and prefabricated houses. Single-family housing design-build firms and single-family construction management firms acting as general contractors are included in this industry. 158-159

236116 **New Multifamily Housing Construction (except For-Sale Builders).** This U.S. industry comprises general contractor establishments responsible for the construction of new multifamily residential housing units (e.g., high-rise, garden, and town house apartments and condominiums where each unit is not separated from its neighbors by a ground-to-roof wall). Multifamily design-build firms and multifamily housing construction management firms acting as general contractors are included in this industry. 160-161

236117 **New Housing For-Sale Builders.** This U.S. industry comprises operative builders primarily responsible for the entire construction of new houses and other residential buildings, single-family and multifamily, on their own account for sale. Operative builders are also known as speculative or merchant builders. 162-163

CONSTRUCTION-GENERAL

NAICS #		Page
236118	**Residential Remodelers.** This U.S. industry comprises establishments primarily responsible for the remodeling construction (including additions, alterations, reconstruction, maintenance and repair work) of houses and other residential buildings, single-family and multifamily. Included in this industry are remodeling general contractors, operative remodelers, remodeling design-build firms, and remodeling project construction management firms.	164-165
236210	**Industrial Building Construction.** This industry comprises establishments primarily responsible for the construction (including new work, additions, alterations, maintenance, and repairs) of industrial buildings (except warehouses). The construction of selected additional structures, whose production processes are similar to those for industrial buildings (e.g., incinerators, cement plants, blast furnaces, and similar nonbuilding structures), is included in this industry. Included in this industry are industrial building general contractors, industrial building operative builders, industrial building design-build firms, and industrial building construction management firms.	166-167
236220	**Commercial and Institutional Building Construction.** This industry comprises establishments primarily responsible for the construction (including new work, additions, alterations, maintenance, and repairs) of commercial and institutional buildings and related structures, such as stadiums, grain elevators, and indoor swimming pools. This industry includes establishments responsible for the on-site assembly of modular or prefabricated commercial and institutional buildings. Included in this industry are commercial and institutional building general contractors, commercial and institutional building operative builders, commercial and institutional building design-build firms, and commercial and institutional building project construction management firms.	168-169
237110	**Water and Sewer Line and Related Structures Construction.** This industry comprises establishments primarily engaged in the construction of water and sewer lines, mains, pumping stations, treatment plants and storage tanks. The work performed may include new work, reconstruction, rehabilitation, and repairs. Specialty trade contractors are included in this group if they are engaged in activities primarily related to water and sewer line and related structures construction. All structures (including buildings) that are integral parts of water and sewer networks (e.g., storage tanks, pumping stations, water treatment plants, and sewage treatment plants) are included in this industry.	170-171
237120	**Oil and Gas Pipeline and Related Structures Construction.** This industry comprises establishments primarily engaged in the construction of oil and gas lines, mains, refineries, and storage tanks. The work performed may include new work, reconstruction, rehabilitation, and repairs. Specialty trade contractors are included in this group if they are engaged in activities primarily related to oil and gas pipeline and related structures construction. All structures (including buildings) that are integral parts of oil and gas networks (e.g., storage tanks, pumping stations, and refineries) are included in this industry.	172-173
237130	**Power and Communication Line and Related Structures Construction.** This industry comprises establishments primarily engaged in the construction of power lines and towers, power plants, and radio, television, and telecommunications transmitting/receiving towers. The work performed may include new work, reconstruction, rehabilitation, and repairs. Specialty trade contractors are included in this group if they are engaged in activities primarily related to power and communication line and related structures construction. All structures (including buildings) that are integral parts of power and communication networks (e.g., transmitting towers, substations, and power plants) are included.	174-175
237210	**Land Subdivision.** This industry comprises establishments primarily engaged in servicing land and subdividing real property into lots, for subsequent sale to builders. Servicing of land may include excavation work for the installation of roads and utility lines. The extent of work may vary from project to project. Land subdivision precedes building activity and the subsequent building is often residential, but may also be commercial tracts and industrial parks. These establishments may do all the work themselves or subcontract the work to others. Establishments that perform only the legal subdivision of land are not included in this industry.	176-177
237310	**Highway, Street, and Bridge Construction.** This industry comprises establishments primarily engaged in the construction of highways (including elevated), streets, roads, airport runways, public sidewalks, or bridges. The work performed may include new work, reconstruction, rehabilitation, and repairs. Specialty trade contractors are included in this group if they are engaged in activities primarily related to highway, street, and bridge construction (e.g., installing guardrails on highways).	178-179

CONSTRUCTION-GENERAL

NAICS #   **Page**

237990   **Other Heavy and Civil Engineering Construction.** This industry comprises establishments primarily engaged in heavy and engineering construction projects (excluding highway, street, bridge, and distribution line construction). The work performed may include new work, reconstruction, rehabilitation, and repairs. Specialty trade contractors are included in this group if they are engaged in activities primarily related to engineering construction projects (excluding highway, street, bridge, distribution line, oil and gas structure, and utilities building and structure construction). Construction projects involving water resources (e.g., dredging and land drainage), development of marine facilities, and projects involving open space improvement (e.g., parks and trails) are included in this industry. 180-181

238110   **Poured Concrete Foundation and Structure Contractors.** This industry comprises establishments primarily engaged in pouring and finishing concrete foundations and structural elements. This industry also includes establishments performing grout and shotcrete work. The work performed may include new work, additions, alterations, maintenance, and repairs. 182-183

238120   **Structural Steel and Precast Concrete Contractors.** This industry comprises establishments primarily engaged in: (1) erecting and assembling structural parts made from steel or precast concrete (e.g., steel beams, structural steel components, and similar products of precast concrete); and/or (2) assembling and installing other steel construction products (e.g., steel rods, bars, rebar, mesh, and cages) to reinforce poured-in-place concrete. The work performed may include new work, additions, alterations, maintenance, and repairs. 184-185

238130   **Framing Contractors.** This industry comprises establishments primarily engaged in structural framing and sheathing using materials other than structural steel or concrete. The work performed may include new work, additions, alterations, maintenance, and repairs. 186-187

238140   **Masonry Contractors.** This industry comprises establishments primarily engaged in masonry work, stone setting, brick laying, and other stone work. The work performed may include new work, additions, alterations, maintenance, and repairs. 188-189

238150   **Glass and Glazing Contractors.** This industry comprises establishments primarily engaged in installing glass panes in prepared openings (i.e., glazing work) and other glass work for buildings. The work performed may include new work, additions, alterations, maintenance, and repairs. 190-191

238160   **Roofing Contractors.** This industry comprises establishments primarily engaged in roofing. This industry also includes establishments treating roofs (i.e., spraying, painting, or coating) and installing skylights. The work performed may include new work, additions, alterations, maintenance, and repairs. 192-193

238190   **Other Foundation, Structure, and Building Exterior Contractors.** This industry comprises establishments primarily engaged in building foundation and structure trades work (except poured concrete, structural steel, precast concrete, framing, masonry, glass and glazing, roofing, and siding). The work performed may include new work, additions, alterations, maintenance, and repairs. 194-195

238210   **Electrical Contractors and Other Wiring Installation Contractors.** This industry comprises establishments primarily engaged in installing and servicing electrical wiring and equipment. Electrical contractors included in this industry may include both the parts and labor when performing work. Electrical contractors may perform new work, additions, alterations, maintenance, and repairs. 196-197

238220   **Plumbing, Heating, and Air-Conditioning Contractors.** This industry comprises establishments primarily engaged in installing and servicing plumbing, heating, and air-conditioning equipment. Contractors in this industry may provide both parts and labor when performing work. The work performed may include new work, additions, alterations, maintenance, and repairs. 198-199

238290   **Other Building Equipment Contractors.** This industry comprises establishments primarily engaged in installing or servicing building equipment (except electrical; plumbing; heating, cooling, or ventilation equipment). The repair and maintenance of miscellaneous building equipment is included in this industry. The work performed may include new work, additions, alterations, maintenance, and repairs. 200-201

238310   **Drywall and Insulation Contractors.** This industry comprises establishments primarily engaged in drywall, plaster work, and building insulation work. Plaster work includes applying plain or ornamental plaster, and installation of lath to receive plaster. The work performed may include new work, additions, alterations, maintenance, and repairs. 202-203

MANUFACTURING

NAICS #		Page
238320	**Painting and Wall Covering Contractors.** This industry comprises establishments primarily engaged in interior or exterior painting or interior wall covering. The work performed may include new work, additions, alterations, maintenance, and repairs.	204-205
238330	**Flooring Contractors.** This industry comprises establishments primarily engaged in the installation of resilient floor tile, carpeting, linoleum, and hard wood flooring. The work performed may include new work, additions, alterations, maintenance, and repairs.	206-207
238340	**Tile and Terrazzo Contractors.** This industry comprises establishments primarily engaged in setting and installing ceramic tile, stone (interior only), and mosaic and/or mixing marble particles and cement to make terrazzo at the job site. The work performed may include new work, additions, alterations, maintenance, and repairs.	208-209
238350	**Finish Carpentry Contractors.** This industry comprises establishments primarily engaged in finish carpentry work. The work performed may include new work, additions, alterations, maintenance, and repairs.	210-211
238390	**Other Building Finishing Contractors.** This industry comprises establishments primarily engaged in building finishing trade work (except drywall, plaster and insulation work; painting and wall covering work; flooring work; tile and terrazzo work; and finish carpentry work). The work performed may include new work, additions, alterations, or maintenance and repairs.	212-213
238910	**Site Preparation Contractors.** This industry comprises establishments primarily engaged in site preparation activities, such as excavating and grading, demolition of buildings and other structures, septic system installation, and house moving. Earth moving and land clearing for all types of sites (e.g., building, nonbuilding, mining) is included in this industry. Establishments primarily engaged in construction equipment rental with operator (except cranes) are also included.	214-215
238990	**All Other Specialty Trade Contractors.** This industry comprises establishments primarily engaged in specialized trades (except foundation, structure, and building exterior contractors; building equipment contractors; building finishing contractors; and site preparation contractors). The specialty trade work performed includes new work, additions, alterations, maintenance, and repairs.	216-217

MANUFACTURING

311111	**Dog and Cat Food Manufacturing.** This U.S. industry comprises establishments primarily engaged in manufacturing dog and cat food from ingredients, such as grains, oilseed mill products, and meat products.	220-221
311119	**Other Animal Food Manufacturing.** This U.S. industry comprises establishments primarily engaged in manufacturing animal food (except dog and cat) from ingredients, such as grains, oilseed mill products, and meat products.	222-223
311211	**Flour Milling.** This U.S. industry comprises establishments primarily engaged in (1) milling flour or meal from grains (except rice) or vegetables and/or (2) milling flour and preparing flour mixes or doughs.	224-225
311412	**Frozen Specialty Food Manufacturing.** This U.S. industry comprises establishments primarily engaged in manufacturing frozen specialty foods (except seafood), such as frozen dinners, entrees, and side dishes; frozen pizza; frozen whipped topping; and frozen waffles, pancakes, and french toast.	226-227
311421	**Fruit and Vegetable Canning.** This U.S. industry comprises establishments primarily engaged in manufacturing canned, pickled, and brined fruits and vegetables.	228-229
311511	**Fluid Milk Manufacturing.** This U.S. industry comprises establishments primarily engaged in (1) manufacturing processed milk products, such as pasteurized milk or cream and sour cream and/or (2) manufacturing fluid milk dairy substitutes from soybeans and other nondairy substances.	230-231
311513	**Cheese Manufacturing.** This U.S. industry comprises establishments primarily engaged in (1) manufacturing cheese products (except cottage cheese) from raw milk and/or processed milk products and/or (2) manufacturing cheese substitutes from soybean and other nondairy substances.	232-233

MANUFACTURING

NAICS #		Page
311520	**Ice Cream and Frozen Dessert Manufacturing.** This industry comprises establishments primarily engaged in manufacturing ice cream, frozen yogurts, frozen ices, sherbets, frozen tofu, and other frozen desserts (except bakery products).	234-235
311611	**Animal (except Poultry) Slaughtering.** This U.S. industry comprises establishments primarily engaged in slaughtering animals (except poultry and small game). Establishments that slaughter and prepare meats are included in this industry.	236-237
311612	**Meat Processed from Carcasses.** This U.S. industry comprises establishments primarily engaged in processing or preserving meat and meat byproducts (except poultry and small game) from purchased meats. This industry includes establishments primarily engaged in assembly cutting and packing of meats (i.e., boxed meats) from purchased meats.	238-239
311710	**Seafood Product Preparation and Packaging.** This industry comprises establishments primarily engaged in one or more of the following: (1) canning seafood (including soup); (2) smoking, salting, and drying seafood; (3) eviscerating fresh fish by removing heads, fins, scales, bones, and entrails; (4) shucking and packing fresh shellfish; (5) processing marine fats and oils; and (6) freezing seafood. Establishments known as "floating factory ships" that are engaged in the gathering and processing of seafood into canned seafood products are included in this industry.	240-241
311811	**Retail Bakeries.** This U.S. industry comprises establishments primarily engaged in retailing bread and other bakery products not for immediate consumption made on the premises from flour, not from prepared dough.	242-243
311812	**Commercial Bakeries.** This U.S. industry comprises establishments primarily engaged in manufacturing fresh and frozen bread and bread-type rolls and other fresh bakery (except cookies and crackers) products.	244-245
311919	**Other Snack Food Manufacturing.** This U.S. industry comprises establishments primarily engaged in manufacturing snack foods (except roasted nuts and peanut butter).	246-247
311920	**Coffee and Tea Manufacturing.** This industry comprises establishments primarily engaged in one or more of the following: (1) roasting coffee; (2) manufacturing coffee and tea concentrates (including instant and freeze-dried); (3) blending tea; (4) manufacturing herbal tea; and (5) manufacturing coffee extracts, flavorings, and syrups.	248-249
311942	**Spice and Extract Manufacturing.** This U.S. industry comprises establishments primarily engaged in (1) manufacturing spices, table salt, seasonings, flavoring extracts (except coffee and meat), and natural food colorings and/or (2) manufacturing dry mix food preparations, such as salad dressing mixes, gravy and sauce mixes, frosting mixes, and other dry mix preparations.	250-251
311991	**Perishable Prepared Food Manufacturing.** This U.S. industry comprises establishments primarily engaged in manufacturing perishable prepared foods, such as salads, sandwiches, prepared meals, fresh pizza, fresh pasta, and peeled or cut vegetables.	252-253
311999	**All Other Miscellaneous Food Manufacturing.** This U.S. industry comprises establishments primarily engaged in manufacturing food (except animal food; grain and oilseed milling; sugar and confectionery products; preserved fruits, vegetables, and specialties; dairy products; meat products; seafood products; bakeries and tortillas; snack foods; coffee and tea; flavoring syrups and concentrates; seasonings and dressings; and perishable prepared food). Included in this industry are establishments primarily engaged in mixing purchased dried and/or dehydrated ingredients including those mixing purchased dried and/ or dehydrated ingredients for soup mixes and bouillon.	254-255
312111	**Soft Drink Manufacturing.** This U.S. industry comprises establishments primarily engaged in manufacturing soft drinks and artificially carbonated waters.	256-257
312120	**Breweries.** This industry comprises establishments primarily engaged in brewing beer, ale, malt liquors, and nonalcoholic beer.	258-259
312130	**Wineries.** This industry comprises establishments primarily engaged in one or more of the following: (1) growing grapes and manufacturing wine and brandies; (2) manufacturing wine and brandies from grapes and other fruits grown elsewhere; and (3) blending wines and brandies.	260-261
312140	**Distilleries.** This industry comprises establishments primarily engaged in one or more of the following: (1) distilling potable liquors (except brandies); (2) distilling and blending liquors; and (3) blending and mixing liquors and other ingredients.	262-263

MANUFACTURING

NAICS #		Page
313210	**Broadwoven Fabric Mills.** This industry comprises establishments primarily engaged in weaving broadwoven fabrics and felts (except tire fabrics and rugs). Establishments in this industry may weave only, weave and finish, or weave, finish, and further fabricate fabric products.	264-265
313310	**Textile and Fabric Finishing Mills.** This industry comprises (1) establishments primarily engaged in finishing of textiles, fabrics, and apparel, and (2) establishments of converters who buy fabric goods in the grey, have them finished on contract, and sell at wholesale. Finishing operations include: bleaching, dyeing, printing (e.g., roller, screen, flock, plisse), stonewashing, and other mechanical finishing, such as preshrinking, shrinking, sponging, calendering, mercerizing, and napping; as well as cleaning, scouring, and the preparation of natural fibers and raw stock.	266-267
314110	**Carpet and Rug Mills.** This industry comprises establishments primarily engaged in (1) manufacturing woven, tufted, and other carpets and rugs, such as art squares, floor mattings, needlepunch carpeting, and door mats and mattings, from textile materials or from twisted paper, grasses, reeds, sisal, jute, or rags and/or (2) finishing carpets and rugs.	268-269
314999	**All Other Miscellaneous Textile Product Mills.** This U.S. industry comprises establishments primarily engaged in manufacturing textile products (except carpets and rugs; curtains and linens; textile bags and canvas products; rope, cordage, and twine; and tire cords and tire fabrics) from purchased materials.	270-271
315210	**Cut and Sew Apparel Contractors.** This industry comprises establishments commonly referred to as contractors primarily engaged in (1) cutting materials owned by others for apparel and accessories and/or (2) sewing materials owned by others for apparel and accessories.	272-273
315250	**Cut and Sew Apparel Manufacturing (except Contractors).** This industry comprises establishments primarily engaged in manufacturing cut and sew apparel from purchased fabric. Clothing jobbers, who perform entrepreneurial functions involved in apparel manufacture, including buying raw materials, designing and preparing samples, arranging for apparel to be made from their materials, and marketing finished apparel, are included.	274-275
315990	**Apparel Accessories and Other Apparel Manufacturing.** This industry comprises establishments primarily engaged in manufacturing apparel and accessories (except apparel knitting mills, cut and sew apparel contractors, men's and boys' cut and sew apparel, women's and girls' cut and sew apparel, and other cut and sew apparel). Jobbers, who perform entrepreneurial functions involved in apparel accessories manufacture, including buying raw materials, designing and preparing samples, arranging for apparel accessories to be made from their materials, and marketing finished apparel accessories, are included. Examples of products made by these establishments are belts, caps, gloves (except medical, sporting, safety), hats, and neckties.	276-277
316990	**Other Leather and Allied Product Manufacturing.** This industry comprises establishments primarily engaged in manufacturing leather products (except footwear and apparel) from purchased leather or leather substitutes (e.g., fabric, plastics).	278-279
321113	**Sawmills.** This U.S. industry comprises establishments primarily engaged in sawing dimension lumber, boards, beams, timbers, poles, ties, shingles, shakes, siding, and wood chips from logs or bolts. Sawmills may plane the rough lumber that they make with a planing machine to achieve smoothness and uniformity of size.	280-281
321211	**Hardwood Veneer and Plywood Manufacturing.** This U.S. industry comprises establishments primarily engaged in manufacturing hardwood veneer and/or hardwood plywood.	282-283
321911	**Wood Window and Door Manufacturing.** This U.S. industry comprises establishments primarily engaged in manufacturing window and door units, sash, window and door frames, and doors from wood or wood clad with metal or plastics.	284-285
321918	**Other Millwork (including Flooring).** This U.S. industry comprises establishments primarily engaged in manufacturing millwork (except wood windows, wood doors, and cut stock).	286-287
321920	**Wood Container and Pallet Manufacturing.** This industry comprises establishments primarily engaged in manufacturing wood pallets, wood box shook, wood boxes, other wood containers, and wood parts for pallets and containers.	288-289
321992	**Prefabricated Wood Building Manufacturing.** This U.S. industry comprises establishments primarily engaged in manufacturing prefabricated wood buildings and wood sections and panels for prefabricated wood buildings.	290-291

MANUFACTURING

NAICS #		Page
321999	**All Other Miscellaneous Wood Product Manufacturing.** This U.S. industry comprises establishments primarily engaged in manufacturing wood products (except establishments operating sawmills and preservation facilities; establishments manufacturing veneer, engineered wood products, millwork, wood containers, pallets, and wood container parts; and establishments making manufactured homes (i.e., mobile homes) and prefabricated buildings and components).	292-293
322120	**Paper Mills.** This industry comprises establishments primarily engaged in manufacturing paper from pulp. These establishments may manufacture or purchase pulp. In addition, the establishments may convert the paper they make. The activity of making paper classifies an establishment into this industry regardless of the output.	294-295
322211	**Corrugated and Solid Fiber Box Manufacturing.** This U.S. industry comprises establishments primarily engaged in laminating purchased paper or paperboard into corrugated or solid fiber boxes and related products, such as pads, partitions, pallets, and corrugated paper without manufacturing paperboard. These boxes are generally used for shipping.	296-297
322212	**Folding Paperboard Box Manufacturing.** This U.S. industry comprises establishments primarily engaged in converting paperboard (except corrugated) into folding paperboard boxes without manufacturing paper and paperboard.	298-299
322220	**Paper Bag and Coated and Treated Paper Manufacturing.** This industry comprises establishments primarily engaged in one or more of the following: (1) cutting and coating paper and paperboard; (2) cutting and laminating paper, paperboard, and other flexible materials (except plastics film to plastics film); (3) manufacturing bags, multiwall bags, sacks of paper, metal foil, coated paper, laminates, or coated combinations of paper and foil with plastics film; (4) manufacturing laminated aluminum and other converted metal foils from purchased foils; and (5) surface coating paper or paperboard.	300-301
322230	**Stationery Product Manufacturing.** This industry comprises establishments primarily engaged in converting paper or paperboard into products used for writing, filing, art work, and similar applications.	302-303
322291	**Sanitary Paper Product Manufacturing.** This U.S. industry comprises establishments primarily engaged in converting purchased sanitary paper stock or wadding into sanitary paper products, such as facial tissues and handkerchiefs, table napkins, toilet paper, towels, disposable diapers, sanitary napkins, and tampons.	304-305
322299	**All Other Converted Paper Product Manufacturing.** This U.S. industry comprises establishments primarily engaged in converting paper or paperboard into products (except containers, bags, coated and treated paper, stationery products, and sanitary paper products) or converting pulp into pulp products, such as egg cartons, food trays, and other food containers from molded pulp.	306-307
323111	**Commercial Printing (except Screen and Books).** This U.S. industry comprises establishments primarily engaged in gravure printing without publishing (except books, grey goods, and manifold business forms). This industry includes establishments engaged in gravure printing on purchased stock materials, such as stationery, letterhead, invitations, labels, and similar items, on a job order basis.	308-309
323113	**Commercial Screen Printing.** This U.S. industry comprises establishments primarily engaged in screen printing without publishing (except books, grey goods, and manifold business forms). This industry includes establishments engaged in screen printing on purchased stock materials, such as stationery, invitations, labels, and similar items, on a job order basis. Establishments primarily engaged in printing on apparel and textile products, such as T-shirts, caps, jackets, towels, and napkins, are included in this industry.	310-311
324121	**Asphalt Paving Mixture and Block Manufacturing.** This U.S. industry comprises establishments primarily engaged in manufacturing asphalt and tar paving mixtures and blocks from purchased asphaltic materials.	312-313
324191	**Petroleum Lubricating Oil and Grease Manufacturing.** This U.S. industry comprises establishments primarily engaged in blending or compounding refined petroleum to make lubricating oils and greases and/or rerefining used petroleum lubricating oils.	314-315

MANUFACTURING

NAICS #		Page
325180	**Other Basic Inorganic Chemical Manufacturing.** This industry comprises establishments primarily engaged in manufacturing basic inorganic chemicals (except industrial gases and synthetic dyes and pigments). This industry comprises establishments primarily engaged in manufacturing basic inorganic chemicals (except industrial gases and synthetic dyes and pigments).	316-317
325199	**All Other Basic Organic Chemical Manufacturing.** This U.S. industry comprises establishments primarily engaged in manufacturing basic organic chemical products (except aromatic petrochemicals, industrial gases, synthetic organic dyes and pigments, gum and wood chemicals, cyclic crudes and intermediates, and ethyl alcohol).	318-319
325211	**Plastics Material and Resin Manufacturing.** This U.S. industry comprises establishments primarily engaged in (1) manufacturing resins, plastics materials, and nonvulcanizable thermoplastic elastomers and mixing and blending resins on a custom basis and/or (2) manufacturing noncustomized synthetic resins.	320-321
325314	**Fertilizer (Mixing Only) Manufacturing.** This U.S. industry comprises establishments primarily engaged in mixing ingredients made elsewhere into fertilizers.	322-323
325320	**Pesticide and Other Agricultural Chemical Manufacturing.** This industry comprises establishments primarily engaged in the formulation and preparation of agricultural and household pest control chemicals (except fertilizers).	324-325
325411	**Medicinal and Botanical Manufacturing.** This U.S. industry comprises establishments primarily engaged in (1) manufacturing uncompounded medicinal chemicals and their derivatives (i.e., generally for use by pharmaceutical preparation manufacturers) and/or (2) grading, grinding, and milling uncompounded botanicals.	326-327
325412	**Pharmaceutical Preparation Manufacturing.** This U.S. industry comprises establishments primarily engaged in manufacturing in-vivo diagnostic substances and pharmaceutical preparations (except biological) intended for internal and external consumption in dose forms, such as ampoules, tablets, capsules, vials, ointments, powders, solutions, and suspensions.	328-329
325510	**Paint and Coating Manufacturing.** This industry comprises establishments primarily engaged in (1) mixing pigments, solvents, and binders into paints and other coatings, such as stains, varnishes, lacquers, enamels, shellacs, and water repellant coatings for concrete and masonry, and/or (2) manufacturing allied paint products, such as putties, paint and varnish removers, paint brush cleaners, and frit.	330-331
325520	**Adhesive Manufacturing.** This industry comprises establishments primarily engaged in manufacturing adhesives, glues, and caulking compounds.	332-333
325611	**Soap and Other Detergent Manufacturing.** This U.S. industry comprises establishments primarily engaged in manufacturing and packaging soaps and other detergents, such as laundry detergents; dishwashing detergents; toothpaste gels, and tooth powders; and natural glycerin.	334-335
325612	**Polish and Other Sanitation Good Manufacturing.** This U.S. industry comprises establishments primarily engaged in manufacturing and packaging polishes and specialty cleaning preparations.	336-337
325620	**Toilet Preparation Manufacturing.** This industry comprises establishments primarily engaged in preparing, blending, compounding, and packaging toilet preparations, such as perfumes, shaving preparations, hair preparations, face creams, lotions (including sunscreens), and other cosmetic preparations.	338-339
325998	**All Other Miscellaneous Chemical Product and Preparation Manufacturing.** This U.S. industry comprises establishments primarily engaged in manufacturing chemical products (except basic chemicals, resins, synthetic rubber; cellulosic and noncellulosic fiber and filaments; pesticides, fertilizers, and other agricultural chemicals; pharmaceuticals and medicines; paints, coatings and adhesives; soap, cleaning compounds, and toilet preparations; printing inks; explosives; custom compounding of purchased resins; and photographic films, papers, plates, and chemicals).	340-341
326111	**Plastics Bag and Pouch Manufacturing.** This U.S. industry comprises establishments primarily engaged in (1) converting plastics resins into plastics bags or (2) forming, coating or laminating plastics film and sheet into single wall or multiwall plastics bags. Establishments in this industry may print on the bags they manufacture.	342-343

MANUFACTURING

NAICS #		Page
326112	**Plastics Packaging Film and Sheet (including Laminated) Manufacturing.** This U.S. industry comprises establishments primarily engaged in converting plastics resins into plastics packaging (flexible) film and packaging sheet.	344-345
326122	**Plastics Pipe and Pipe Fitting Manufacturing.** This U.S. industry comprises establishments primarily engaged in converting plastics resins into rigid plastics pipes and pipe fittings.	346-347
326140	**Polystyrene Foam Product Manufacturing.** This industry comprises establishments primarily engaged in manufacturing polystyrene foam products.	348-349
326150	**Urethane and Other Foam Product (except Polystyrene) Manufacturing.** This industry comprises establishments primarily engaged in manufacturing plastics foam products (except polystyrene).	350-351
326160	**Plastics Bottle Manufacturing.** This industry comprises establishments primarily engaged in manufacturing plastics bottles.	352-353
326199	**All Other Plastics Product Manufacturing.** This U.S. industry comprises establishments primarily engaged in manufacturing plastics products (except film, sheet, bags, profile shapes, pipes, pipe fittings, laminates, foam products, bottles, plumbing fixtures, and resilient floor coverings).	354-355
326220	**Rubber and Plastics Hoses and Belting Manufacturing.** This industry comprises establishments primarily engaged in manufacturing rubber hose and/or plastics (reinforced) hose and belting from natural and synthetic rubber and/or plastics resins. Establishments manufacturing garden hoses from purchased hose are included in this industry.	356-357
326299	**All Other Rubber Product Manufacturing.** This U.S. industry comprises establishments primarily engaged in manufacturing rubber products (except tires; hoses and belting; and molded, extruded, and lathecut rubber goods for mechanical applications) from natural and synthetic rubber.	358-359
327215	**Glass Product Manufacturing Made of Purchased Glass.** This U.S. industry comprises establishments primarily engaged in coating, laminating, tempering, or shaping purchased glass.	360-361
327320	**Ready-Mix Concrete Manufacturing.** This industry comprises establishments, such as batch plants or mix plants, primarily engaged in manufacturing concrete delivered to a purchaser in a plastic and unhardened state. Ready-mix concrete manufacturing establishments may mine, quarry, or purchase sand and gravel.	362-363
327331	**Concrete Block and Brick Manufacturing.** This U.S. industry comprises establishments primarily engaged in manufacturing concrete block and brick.	364-365
327390	**Other Concrete Product Manufacturing.** This industry comprises establishments primarily engaged in manufacturing concrete products (except block, brick, and pipe).	366-367
327991	**Cut Stone and Stone Product Manufacturing.** This U.S. industry comprises establishments primarily engaged in cutting, shaping, and finishing granite, marble, limestone, slate, and other stone for building and miscellaneous uses. Stone product manufacturing establishments may mine, quarry, or purchase stone.	368-369
331110	**Iron and Steel Mills and Ferroalloy Manufacturing.** This industry comprises establishments primarily engaged in one or more of the following: (1) direct reduction of iron ore; (2) manufacturing pig iron in molten or solid form; (3) converting pig iron into steel; (4) making steel; (5) making steel and manufacturing shapes (e.g., bar, plate, rod, sheet, strip, wire); (6) making steel and forming pipe and tube; and (7) manufacturing electrometallurgical ferroalloys. Ferroalloys add critical elements, such as silicon and manganese for carbon steel and chromium, vanadium, tungsten, titanium, and molybdenum for low- and high-alloy metals. Ferroalloys include iron-rich alloys and more pure forms of elements added during the steel manufacturing process that alter or improve the characteristics of the metal being made.	370-371
331210	**Iron and Steel Pipe and Tube Manufacturing from Purchased Steel.** This industry comprises establishments primarily engaged in manufacturing welded, riveted, or seamless pipe and tube from purchased iron or steel.	372-373
331221	**Rolled Steel Shape Manufacturing.** This U.S. industry comprises establishments primarily engaged in rolling or drawing shapes (except wire), such as plate, sheet, strip, rod, and bar, from purchased steel.	374-375

MANUFACTURING

NAICS #		Page
331314	**Secondary Smelting and Alloying of Aluminum.** This U.S. industry comprises establishments primarily engaged in (1) recovering aluminum and aluminum alloys from scrap and/or dross (i.e., secondary smelting) and making billet or ingot (except by rolling) and/or (2) manufacturing alloys, powder, paste, or flake from purchased aluminum.	376-377
331318	**Other Aluminum Rolling, Drawing, and Extruding.** This U.S. industry comprises establishments primarily engaged in (1) rolling, drawing, or extruding shapes (except flat rolled sheet, plate, foil, and welded tube) from purchased aluminum and/or (2) recovering aluminum from scrap and rolling, drawing, or extruding shapes (except flat rolled sheet, plate, foil, and welded tube) in integrated mills.	378-379
331523	**Nonferrous Metal Die-Casting Foundries.** This U.S. industry comprises establishments primarily engaged in introducing molten nonferrous metal, under high pressure, into molds or dies to make nonferrous metal die-castings. Establishments in this industry purchase nonferrous metals made in other establishments.	380-381
332111	**Iron and Steel Forging.** This U.S. industry comprises establishments primarily engaged in manufacturing iron and steel forgings from purchased iron and steel by hammering mill shapes. Establishments making iron and steel forgings and further manufacturing (e.g., machining, assembling) a specific manufactured product are classified in the industry of the finished product. Iron and steel forging establishments may perform surface finishing operations, such as cleaning and deburring, on the forgings they manufacture.	382-383
332119	**Metal Crown, Closure, and Other Metal Stamping (except Automotive).** This U.S. industry comprises establishments primarily engaged in (1) stamping metal crowns and closures, such as bottle caps and home canning lids and rings; and/or (2) manufacturing other unfinished metal stampings and spinning unfinished metal products (except automotive and coins). Establishments making metal stampings and metal spun products and further manufacturing (e.g. machining, assembling) a specific product are classified in the industry of the finished product. Metal stamping and metal spun products establishments may perform surface finishing operations, such as cleaning and deburring, on the products they manufacture.	384-385
332216	**Saw Blade and Handtool Manufacturing.** This U.S. industry comprises establishments primarily engaged in (1) manufacturing saw blades, all types (including those for power sawing machines) and/or (2) manufacturing nonpowered hand and edge tools.	386-387
332311	**Prefabricated Metal Building and Component Manufacturing.** This U.S. industry comprises establishments primarily engaged in manufacturing prefabricated metal buildings, panels, and sections.	388-389
332312	**Fabricated Structural Metal Manufacturing.** This U.S. industry comprises establishments primarily engaged in fabricating structural metal products, such as concrete reinforcing bars and fabricated bar joists.	390-391
332313	**Plate Work Manufacturing.** This industry comprises establishments primarily engaged in manufacturing fabricated metal plate work by cutting, punching, bending, shaping, and welding purchased metal plate.	392-393
332321	**Metal Window and Door Manufacturing.** This U.S. industry comprises establishments primarily engaged in manufacturing metal framed windows (i.e., typically using purchased glass) and metal doors.	394-395
332322	**Sheet Metal Work Manufacturing.** This U.S. industry comprises establishments primarily engaged in manufacturing sheet metal work (except stampings).	396-397
332323	**Ornamental and Architectural Metal Work Manufacturing.** This U.S. industry comprises establishments primarily engaged in manufacturing ornamental and architectural metal work, such as staircases, metal open steel flooring, fire escapes, railings, and scaffolding.	398-399
332420	**Metal Tank (Heavy Gauge) Manufacturing.** This industry comprises establishments primarily engaged in cutting, forming, and joining heavy gauge metal to manufacture tanks, vessels, and other containers.	400-401
332439	**Other Metal Container Manufacturing.** This U.S. industry comprises establishments primarily engaged in manufacturing metal (light gauge) containers (except cans).	402-403
332510	**Hardware Manufacturing.** This industry comprises establishments primarily engaged in manufacturing metal hardware, such as metal hinges, metal handles, keys, and locks (except coin-operated time locks).	404-405

MANUFACTURING

NAICS #		Page
332613	**Spring Manufacturing.** This U.S. industry comprises establishments primarily engaged in manufacturing springs from purchased wire, strip, or rod.	406-407
332618	**Other Fabricated Wire Product Manufacturing.** This U.S. industry comprises establishments primarily engaged in manufacturing fabricated wire products (except springs) made from purchased wire.	408-409
332710	**Machine Shops.** This industry comprises establishments known as machine shops primarily engaged in machining metal parts on a job or order basis. Generally machine shop jobs are low volume using machine tools, such as lathes (including computer numerically controlled); automatic screw machines; and machines for boring, grinding, and milling.	410-411
332721	**Precision Turned Product Manufacturing.** This U.S. industry comprises establishments known as precision turned manufacturers primarily engaged in machining precision products of all materials on a job or order basis. Generally precision turned product jobs are large volume using machines, such as automatic screw machines, rotary transfer machines, computer numerically controlled (CNC) lathes, or turning centers.	412-413
332722	**Bolt, Nut, Screw, Rivet, and Washer Manufacturing.** This U.S. industry comprises establishments primarily engaged in manufacturing metal bolts, nuts, screws, rivets, and washers, and other industrial fasteners using machines, such as headers, threaders, and nut forming machines.	414-415
332811	**Metal Heat Treating.** This U.S. industry comprises establishments primarily engaged in heat treating, such as annealing, tempering, and brazing, metals and metal products for the trade.	416-417
332812	**Metal Coating, Engraving (except Jewelry and Silverware), and Allied Services to Manufacturers.** This U.S. industry comprises establishments primarily engaged in one or more of the following: (1) enameling, lacquering, and varnishing metals and metal products; (2) hot dip galvanizing metals and metal products; (3) engraving, chasing, or etching metals and metal products (except jewelry; personal goods carried on or about the person, such as compacts and cigarette cases; precious metal products (except precious plated flatware and other plated ware); and printing plates); (4) powder coating metals and metal products; and (5) providing other metal surfacing services for the trade.	418-419
332813	**Electroplating, Plating, Polishing, Anodizing, and Coloring.** This U.S. industry comprises establishments primarily engaged in electroplating, plating, anodizing, coloring, buffing, polishing, cleaning, and sandblasting metals and metal products for the trade.	420-421
332911	**Industrial Valve Manufacturing.** This U.S. industry comprises establishments primarily engaged in manufacturing industrial valves and valves for water works and municipal water systems.	422-423
332912	**Fluid Power Valve and Hose Fitting Manufacturing.** This U.S. industry comprises establishments primarily engaged in manufacturing fluid power valves and hose fittings.	424-425
332919	**Other Metal Valve and Pipe Fitting Manufacturing.** This U.S. industry comprises establishments primarily engaged in manufacturing metal valves (except industrial valves, fluid power valves, fluid power hose fittings, and plumbing fixture fittings and trim).	426-427
332991	**Ball and Roller Bearing Manufacturing.** This U.S. industry comprises establishments primarily engaged in manufacturing ball and roller bearings of all materials.	428-429
332994	**Small Arms, Ordnance, and Ordnance Accessories Manufacturing.** This U.S. industry comprises establishments primarily engaged in manufacturing small firearms that are carried and fired by the individual.	430-431
332996	**Fabricated Pipe and Pipe Fitting Manufacturing.** This U.S. industry comprises establishments primarily engaged in fabricating, such as cutting, threading and bending metal pipes and pipe fittings made from purchased metal pipe.	432-433
332999	**All Other Miscellaneous Fabricated Metal Product Manufacturing.** This U.S. industry comprises establishments primarily engaged in manufacturing fabricated metal products (except forgings and stampings, cutlery and handtools, architectural and structural metals, boilers, tanks, shipping containers, hardware, spring and wire products, machine shop products, turned products, screws, nuts and bolts, metal valves, ball and roller bearings, ammunition, small arms and other ordnances, fabricated pipes and pipe fittings, industrial patterns, and enameled iron and metal sanitary ware).	434-435

MANUFACTURING

NAICS #		Page
333111	**Farm Machinery and Equipment Manufacturing.** This U.S. industry comprises establishments primarily engaged in manufacturing agricultural and farm machinery and equipment, and other turf and grounds care equipment, including planting, harvesting, and grass mowing equipment (except lawn and garden-type).	436-437
333112	**Lawn and Garden Tractor and Home Lawn and Garden Equipment Manufacturing.** This U.S. industry comprises establishments primarily engaged in manufacturing powered lawnmowers, lawn and garden tractors, and other home lawn and garden equipment, such as tillers, shredders, and yard vacuums and blowers.	438-439
333120	**Construction Machinery Manufacturing.** This industry comprises establishments primarily engaged in manufacturing construction machinery, surface mining machinery, and logging equipment.	440-441
333131	**Mining Machinery and Equipment Manufacturing.** This U.S. industry comprises establishments primarily engaged in (1) manufacturing underground mining machinery and equipment, such as coal breakers, mining cars, core drills, coal cutters, rock drills and (2) manufacturing mineral beneficiating machinery and equipment used in surface or underground mines.	442-443
333132	**Oil and Gas Field Machinery and Equipment Manufacturing.** This U.S. industry comprises establishments primarily engaged in (1) manufacturing oil and gas field machinery and equipment, such as oil and gas field drilling machinery and equipment; oil and gas field production machinery and equipment; and oil and gas field derricks and (2) manufacturing water well drilling machinery.	444-445
333241	**Food Product Machinery Manufacturing.** This U.S. industry comprises establishments primarily engaged in manufacturing food and beverage manufacturing-type machinery and equipment, such as dairy product plant machinery and equipment (e.g., homogenizers, pasteurizers, ice cream freezers), bakery machinery and equipment (e.g., dough mixers, bake ovens, pastry rolling machines), meat and poultry processing and preparation machinery, and other commercial food products machinery (e.g., slicers, choppers, and mixers).	446-447
333248	**All Other Industrial Machinery Manufacturing.** This U.S. industry comprises establishments primarily engaged in manufacturing industrial machinery (except agricultural and farm-type; construction and mining machinery; food manufacturing-type machinery; semiconductor making machinery; and sawmill, woodworking, and paper making machinery).	448-449
333310	**Commercial and Service Industry Machinery Manufacturing.** This industry comprises establishments primarily engaged in manufacturing commercial and service industry machinery, such as optical instruments and lenses (except ophthalmic), photographic and photocopying equipment, automatic vending machinery, commercial laundry and drycleaning machinery, office machinery, automotive maintenance equipment (except mechanics' handtools), and commercial-type cooking equipment.	450-451
333413	**Industrial and Commercial Fan and Blower and Air Purification Equipment Manufacturing.** This U.S. industry comprises establishments primarily engaged in (1) manufacturing stationary air purification equipment, such as industrial dust and fume collection equipment, electrostatic precipitation equipment, warm air furnace filters, air washers, and other dust collection equipment and/or (2) manufacturing attic fans and industrial and commercial fans and blowers, such as commercial exhaust fans and commercial ventilating fans.	452-453
333414	**Heating Equipment (except Warm Air Furnaces) Manufacturing.** This U.S. industry comprises establishments primarily engaged in manufacturing heating equipment (except electric and warm air furnaces), such as heating boilers, heating stoves, floor and wall furnaces, and wall and baseboard heating units.	454-455
333415	**Air-Conditioning and Warm Air Heating Equipment and Commercial and Industrial Refrigeration Equipment Manufacturing.** This U.S. industry comprises establishments primarily engaged in (1) manufacturing air-conditioning (except motor vehicle) and warm air furnace equipment and/or (2) manufacturing commercial and industrial refrigeration and freezer equipment.	456-457
333511	**Industrial Mold Manufacturing.** This U.S. industry comprises establishments primarily engaged in manufacturing industrial molds for casting metals or forming other materials, such as plastics, glass, or rubber.	458-459
333514	**Special Die and Tool, Die Set, Jig, and Fixture Manufacturing.** This U.S. industry comprises establishments, known as tool and die shops, primarily engaged in manufacturing special tools and fixtures, such as cutting dies and jigs.	460-461

MANUFACTURING

NAICS #		Page
333515	**Cutting Tool and Machine Tool Accessory Manufacturing.** This U.S. industry comprises establishments primarily engaged in manufacturing accessories and attachments for metal cutting and metal forming machine tools.	462-463
333517	**Machine Tool Manufacturing.** This U.S. industry comprises establishments primarily engaged in (1) manufacturing metal cutting machine tools (except handtools) and/or (2) manufacturing metal forming machine tools (except handtools), such as punching, sheering, bending, forming, pressing, forging and die-casting machines.	464-465
333519	**Rolling Mill and Other Metalworking Machinery Manufacturing.** This U.S. industry comprises establishments primarily engaged in manufacturing rolling mill machinery and equipment and/or other metal working machinery (except industrial molds; special dies and tools, die sets, jigs, and fixtures; cutting tools and machine tool accessories; and machine tools).	466-467
333912	**Air and Gas Compressor Manufacturing.** This U.S. industry comprises establishments primarily engaged in manufacturing general purpose air and gas compressors, such as reciprocating compressors, centrifugal compressors, vacuum pumps (except laboratory), and nonagricultural spraying and dusting compressors and spray gun units.	468-469
333914	**Measuring, Dispensing, and Other Pumping Equipment Manufacturing.** This U.S. industry comprises establishments primarily engaged in (1) manufacturing measuring and dispensing pumps, such as gasoline pumps and lubricating oil measuring and dispensing pumps and/or (2) manufacturing general purpose pumps and pumping equipment (except fluid power pumps and motors), such as reciprocating pumps, turbine pumps, centrifugal pumps, rotary pumps, diaphragm pumps, domestic water system pumps, oil well and oil field pumps, and sump pumps.	470-471
333922	**Conveyor and Conveying Equipment Manufacturing.** This U.S. industry comprises establishments primarily engaged in manufacturing conveyors and conveying equipment, such as gravity conveyors, trolley conveyors, tow conveyors, pneumatic tube conveyors, carousel conveyors, farm conveyors, and belt conveyors.	472-473
333923	**Overhead Traveling Crane, Hoist, and Monorail System Manufacturing.** This U.S. industry comprises establishments primarily engaged in manufacturing overhead traveling cranes, hoists, and monorail systems.	474-475
333924	**Industrial Truck, Tractor, Trailer, and Stacker Machinery Manufacturing.** This U.S. industry comprises establishments primarily engaged in manufacturing industrial trucks, tractors, trailers, and stackers (i.e., truck-type), such as forklifts, pallet loaders and unloaders, and portable loading docks.	476-477
333992	**Welding and Soldering Equipment Manufacturing.** This U.S. industry comprises establishments primarily engaged in manufacturing welding and soldering equipment and accessories (except transformers), such as arc, resistance, gas, plasma, laser, electron beam, and ultrasonic welding equipment; welding electrodes; coated or cored welding wire; and soldering equipment (except handheld).	478-479
333993	**Packaging Machinery Manufacturing.** This U.S. industry comprises establishments primarily engaged in manufacturing packaging machinery, such as wrapping, bottling, canning, and labeling machinery.	480-481
333994	**Industrial Process Furnace and Oven Manufacturing.** This U.S. Industry comprises establishments primarily engaged in manufacturing industrial process furnaces, ovens, induction and dielectric heating equipment, and kilns (except cement, chemical, wood).	482-483
333998	**All Other Miscellaneous General Purpose Machinery Manufacturing.** This U.S. industry comprises establishments primarily engaged in manufacturing general purpose machinery (except ventilating, heating, air-conditioning, and commercial refrigeration equipment; metalworking machinery; engines, turbines, and power transmission equipment; pumps and compressors; material handling equipment; power-driven handtools; welding and soldering equipment; packaging machinery; industrial process furnaces and ovens; fluid power cylinders and actuators; and fluid power pumps and motors).	484-485

MANUFACTURING

NAICS #		Page
334111	**Electronic Computer Manufacturing.** This U.S. industry comprises establishments primarily engaged in manufacturing and/or assembling electronic computers, such as mainframes, personal computers, workstations, laptops, and computer servers. Computers can be analog, digital, or hybrid. Digital computers, the most common type, are devices that do all of the following: (1) store the processing program or programs and the data immediately necessary for the execution of the program; (2) can be freely programmed in accordance with the requirements of the user; (3) perform arithmetical computations specified by the user; and (4) execute, without human intervention, a processing program that requires the computer to modify its execution by logical decision during the processing run. Analog computers are capable of simulating mathematical models and contain at least analog, control, and programming elements. The manufacture of computers includes the assembly or integration of processors, coprocessors, memory, storage, and input/output devices into a user-programmable final product.	486-487
334118	**Computer Terminal and Other Computer Peripheral Equipment Manufacturing.** This U.S. industry comprises establishments primarily engaged in manufacturing computer terminals and other computer peripheral equipment (except storage devices).	488-489
334220	**Radio and Television Broadcasting and Wireless Communications Equipment Manufacturing.** This industry comprises establishments primarily engaged in manufacturing radio and television broadcast and wireless communications equipment. Examples of products made by these establishments are: transmitting and receiving antennas, cable television equipment, GPS equipment, pagers, cellular phones, mobile communications equipment, and radio and television studio and broadcasting equipment.	490-491
334290	**Other Communications Equipment Manufacturing.** This industry comprises establishments primarily engaged in manufacturing communications equipment (except telephone apparatus, and radio and television broadcast, and wireless communications equipment).	492-493
334310	**Audio and Video Equipment Manufacturing.** This industry comprises establishments primarily engaged in manufacturing electronic audio and video equipment for home entertainment, motor vehicle, public address and musical instrument amplifications. Examples of products made by these establishments are video cassette recorders, televisions, stereo equipment, speaker systems, household-type video cameras, jukeboxes, and amplifiers for musical instruments and public address systems.	494-495
334412	**Bare Printed Circuit Board Manufacturing.** This U.S. industry comprises establishments primarily engaged in manufacturing bare (i.e., rigid or flexible) printed circuit boards without mounted electronic components. These establishments print, perforate, plate, screen, etch, or photoprint interconnecting pathways for electric current on laminates.	496-497
334413	**Semiconductor and Related Device Manufacturing.** This U.S. industry comprises establishments primarily engaged in manufacturing semiconductors and related solid state devices.	498-499
334418	**Printed Circuit Assembly (Electronic Assembly) Manufacturing.** This U.S. industry comprises establishments primarily engaged in loading components onto printed circuit boards or who manufacture and ship loaded printed circuit boards. Also known as printed circuit assemblies, electronics assemblies, or modules, these products are printed circuit boards that have some or all of the semiconductor and electronic components inserted or mounted and are inputs to a wide variety of electronic systems and devices.	500-501
334419	**Other Electronic Component Manufacturing.** This U.S. industry comprises establishments primarily engaged in manufacturing electronic components (except electron tubes; bare printed circuit boards; semiconductors and related devices; electronic capacitors; electronic resistors; coils, transformers and other inductors; connectors; and loaded printed circuit boards).	502-503
334511	**Search, Detection, Navigation, Guidance, Aeronautical, and Nautical System and Instrument Manufacturing.** This U.S. industry comprises establishments primarily engaged in manufacturing search, detection, navigation, guidance, aeronautical, and nautical systems and instruments.	504-505
334513	**Instruments and Related Products Manufacturing for Measuring, Displaying, and Controlling Industrial Process Variables.** This U.S. industry comprises establishments primarily engaged in manufacturing instruments and related devices for measuring, displaying, indicating, recording, transmitting, and controlling industrial process variables. These instruments measure, display or control (monitor, analyze, and so forth) industrial process variables, such as temperature, humidity, pressure, vacuum, combustion, flow, level, viscosity, density, acidity, concentration, and rotation.	506-507

MANUFACTURING

NAICS #		Page

334516 **Analytical Laboratory Instrument Manufacturing.** This U.S. industry comprises establishments primarily engaged in manufacturing instruments and instrumentation systems for laboratory analysis of the chemical or physical composition or concentration of samples of solid, fluid, gaseous, or composite material. 508-509

334519 **Other Measuring and Controlling Device Manufacturing.** This U.S. industry comprises establishments primarily engaged in manufacturing measuring and controlling devices (except search, detection, navigation, guidance, aeronautical, and nautical instruments and systems; automatic environmental controls for residential, commercial, and appliance use; instruments for measurement, display, and control of industrial process variables; totalizing fluid meters and counting devices; instruments for measuring and testing electricity and electrical signals; analytical laboratory instruments; watches, clocks, and parts; irradiation equipment; and electromedical and electrotherapeutic apparatus). 510-511

335132 **Commercial, Industrial, and Institutional Electric Lighting Fixture Manufacturing.** This U.S. industry comprises establishments primarily engaged in manufacturing commercial, industrial, and institutional electric lighting fixtures. 512-513

335311 **Power, Distribution, and Specialty Transformer Manufacturing.** This U.S. industry comprises establishments primarily engaged in manufacturing power, distribution, and specialty transformers (except electronic components). Industrial-type and consumer-type transformers in this industry vary (e.g., step up or step down) voltage but do not convert alternating to direct or direct to alternating current. 514-515

335312 **Motor and Generator Manufacturing.** This U.S. industry comprises establishments primarily engaged in manufacturing electric motors (except internal combustion engine starting motors), power generators (except battery charging alternators for internal combustion engines), and motor generator sets (except turbine generator set units). This industry includes establishments rewinding armatures on a factory basis. 516-517

335313 **Switchgear and Switchboard Apparatus Manufacturing.** This U.S. industry comprises establishments primarily engaged in manufacturing switchgear and switchboard apparatus. 518-519

335314 **Relay and Industrial Control Manufacturing.** This U.S. industry comprises establishments primarily engaged in manufacturing relays, motor starters and controllers, and other industrial controls and control accessories. 520-521

335999 **All Other Miscellaneous Electrical Equipment and Component Manufacturing.** This U.S. industry comprises establishments primarily engaged in manufacturing industrial and commercial electric apparatus and other equipment (except lighting equipment, household appliances, transformers, motors, generators, switchgear, relays, industrial controls, batteries, communication and energy wire and cable, wiring devices, and carbon and graphite products). This industry includes power converters (i.e., AC to DC and DC to AC), power supplies, surge suppressors, and similar equipment for industrial-type and consumer-type equipment. 522-523

336110 **Automobile and Light Duty Motor Vehicle Manufacturing.** This industry comprises establishments primarily engaged in (1) manufacturing complete automobiles and light duty motor vehicles (i.e., body and chassis or unibody) or (2) manufacturing automobile and light duty motor vehicle chassis only. Vehicles made include passenger cars, light duty trucks, light duty vans, pick-up trucks, minivans, and sport utility vehicles. 524-525

336211 **Motor Vehicle Body Manufacturing.** This U.S. industry comprises establishments primarily engaged in manufacturing truck and bus bodies and cabs and automobile bodies. The products made may be sold separately or may be assembled on purchased chassis and sold as complete vehicles. 526-527

336212 **Truck Trailer Manufacturing.** This U.S. industry comprises establishments primarily engaged in manufacturing truck trailers, truck trailer chassis, cargo container chassis, detachable trailer bodies, and detachable trailer chassis for sale separately. 528-529

336214 **Travel Trailer and Camper Manufacturing.** This U.S. industry comprises establishments primarily engaged in one or more of the following: (1) manufacturing travel trailers and campers designed to attach to motor vehicles; (2) manufacturing pickup coaches (i.e., campers) and caps (i.e., covers) for mounting on pickup trucks; and (3) manufacturing automobile, utility and light-truck trailers. Travel trailers do not have their own motor but are designed to be towed by a motor unit, such as an automobile or a light truck. 530-531

MANUFACTURING

NAICS #		Page

336310   **Motor Vehicle Gasoline Engine and Engine Parts Manufacturing.** This industry comprises establishments primarily engaged in (1) manufacturing and/or rebuilding motor vehicle gasoline engines and engine parts and/or (2) manufacturing and/or rebuilding carburetors, pistons, piston rings, and engine valves, whether or not for vehicular use. 532-533

336320   **Motor Vehicle Electrical and Electronic Equipment Manufacturing.** This industry comprises establishments primarily engaged in manufacturing and/or rebuilding electrical and electronic equipment for motor vehicles and internal combustion engines. The products made can be used for all types of transportation equipment (i.e., aircraft, automobiles, trucks, trains, ships) or stationary internal combustion engine applications. 534-535

336360   **Motor Vehicle Seating and Interior Trim Manufacturing.** This industry comprises establishments primarily engaged in manufacturing motor vehicle seating, seats, seat frames, seat belts, and interior trimmings. 536-537

336370   **Motor Vehicle Metal Stamping.** This industry comprises establishments primarily engaged in manufacturing motor vehicle stampings, such as fenders, tops, body parts, trim, and molding. 538-539

336390   **Other Motor Vehicle Parts Manufacturing.** This industry comprises establishments primarily engaged in manufacturing and/or rebuilding motor vehicle parts and accessories (except motor vehicle gasoline engines and engine parts, motor vehicle electrical and electronic equipment, motor vehicle steering and suspension components, motor vehicle brake systems, motor vehicle transmissions and power train parts, motor vehicle seating and interior trim, and motor vehicle stampings). 540-541

336411   **Aircraft Manufacturing.** This U.S. industry comprises establishments primarily engaged in one or more of the following: (1) manufacturing or assembling complete aircraft; (2) developing and making aircraft prototypes; (3) aircraft conversion (i.e., major modifications to systems); and (4) complete aircraft overhaul and rebuilding (i.e., periodic restoration of aircraft to original design specifications). 542-543

336412   **Aircraft Engine and Engine Parts Manufacturing.** This U.S. industry comprises establishments primarily engaged in one or more of the following: (1) manufacturing aircraft engines and engine parts; (2) developing and making prototypes of aircraft engines and engine parts; (3) aircraft propulsion system conversion (i.e., major modifications to systems); and (4) aircraft propulsion systems overhaul and rebuilding (i.e., periodic restoration of aircraft propulsion system to original design specifications). 544-545

336413   **Other Aircraft Parts and Auxiliary Equipment Manufacturing.** This U.S. industry comprises establishment primarily engaged in (1) manufacturing aircraft parts or auxiliary equipment (except engines and aircraft fluid power subassemblies) and/or (2) developing and making prototypes of aircraft parts and auxiliary equipment. Auxiliary equipment includes such items as crop dusting apparatus, armament racks, inflight refueling equipment, and external fuel tanks. 546-547

336611   **Ship Building and Repairing.** This U.S. industry comprises establishments primarily engaged in operating a shipyard. Shipyards are fixed facilities with drydocks and fabrication equipment capable of building a ship, defined as watercraft typically suitable or intended for other than personal or recreational use. Activities of shipyards include the construction of ships, their repair, conversion and alteration, the production of prefabricated ship and barge sections, and specialized services, such as ship scaling. 548-549

336612   **Boat Building.** This U.S. industry comprises establishments primarily engaged in building boats. Boats are defined as watercraft not built in shipyards and typically of the type suitable or intended for personal use. 550-551

336991   **Motorcycle, Bicycle, and Parts Manufacturing.** This U.S. industry comprises establishments primarily engaged in manufacturing motorcycles, bicycles, tricycles and similar equipment, and parts. 552-553

336999   **All Other Transportation Equipment Manufacturing.** This U.S. industry comprises establishments primarily engaged in manufacturing transportation equipment (except motor vehicles, motor vehicle parts, boats, ships, railroad rolling stock, aerospace products, motorcycles, bicycles, armored vehicles and tanks). 554-555

MANUFACTURING

NAICS #		Page
337110	**Wood Kitchen Cabinet and Countertop Manufacturing.** This industry comprises establishments primarily engaged in manufacturing wood or plastics laminated on wood kitchen cabinets, bathroom vanities, and countertops (except freestanding). The cabinets and counters may be made on a stock or custom basis.	556-557
337121	**Upholstered Household Furniture Manufacturing.** This U.S. industry comprises establishments primarily engaged in manufacturing upholstered household-type furniture. The furniture may be made on a stock or custom basis.	558-559
337126	**Household Furniture (except Wood and Upholstered) Manufacturing.** This U.S. industry comprises establishments primarily engaged in manufacturing nonupholstered household-type furniture of materials other than wood, such as metal, plastics, reed, rattan, wicker, and fiberglass. The furniture may be partially upholstered (e.g., chairs with upholstered seats or backs), made on a stock or custom basis, and may be assembled or unassembled (i.e., knockdown).	560-561
337127	**Institutional Furniture Manufacturing.** This U.S. industry comprises establishments primarily engaged in manufacturing institutional-type furniture (e.g., library, school, theater, and church furniture). The furniture may be made on a stock or custom basis and may be assembled or unassembled (i.e., knockdown).	562-563
337212	**Custom Architectural Woodwork and Millwork Manufacturing.** This U.S. industry comprises establishments primarily engaged in manufacturing custom designed interiors consisting of architectural woodwork and fixtures utilizing wood, wood products, and plastics laminates. All of the industry output is made to individual order on a job shop basis and requires skilled craftsmen as a labor input. A job might include custom manufacturing of display fixtures, gondolas, wall shelving units, entrance and window architectural detail, sales and reception counters, wall paneling, and matching furniture.	564-565
337215	**Showcase, Partition, Shelving, and Locker Manufacturing.** This U.S. industry comprises establishments primarily engaged in manufacturing wood and nonwood office and store fixtures, shelving, lockers, frames, partitions, and related fabricated products of wood and nonwood materials, including plastics laminated fixture tops. The products are made on a stock basis and may be assembled or unassembled (i.e., knockdown). Establishments exclusively making furniture parts (e.g., frames) are included in this industry.	566-567
339112	**Surgical and Medical Instrument Manufacturing.** This U.S. industry comprises establishments primarily engaged in manufacturing medical, surgical, ophthalmic, and veterinary instruments and apparatus (except electrotherapeutic, electromedical and irradiation apparatus). Examples of products made by these establishments are syringes, hypodermic needles, anesthesia apparatus, blood transfusion equipment, catheters, surgical clamps, and medical thermometers.	568-569
339113	**Surgical Appliance and Supplies Manufacturing.** This U.S. industry comprises establishments primarily engaged in manufacturing surgical appliances and supplies. Examples of products made by these establishments are orthopedic devices, prosthetic appliances, surgical dressings, crutches, surgical sutures, and personal industrial safety devices (except protective eyewear).	570-571
339114	**Dental Equipment and Supplies Manufacturing.** This U.S. industry comprises establishments primarily engaged in manufacturing dental equipment and supplies used by dental laboratories and offices of dentists, such as dental chairs, dental instrument delivery systems, dental hand instruments, and dental impression material and dental cements.	572-573
339910	**Jewelry and Silverware Manufacturing.** This industry comprises establishments primarily engaged in one or more of the following: (1) manufacturing, engraving, chasing, or etching jewelry; (2) manufacturing, engraving, chasing, or etching metal personal goods (i.e., small articles carried on or about the person, such as compacts or cigarette cases); (3) manufacturing, engraving, chasing, or etching precious metal solid, precious metal clad, or pewter flatware and other hollowware; (4) stamping coins; (5) manufacturing unassembled jewelry parts and stock shop products, such as sheet, wire, and tubing; (6) cutting, slabbing, tumbling, carving, engraving, polishing, or faceting precious or semiprecious stones and gems; (7) recutting, repolishing, and setting gem stones; and (8) drilling, sawing, and peeling cultured and costume pearls. This industry includes establishments primarily engaged in manufacturing precious solid, precious clad, and precious plated jewelry and personal goods.	574-575
339920	**Sporting and Athletic Goods Manufacturing.** This industry comprises establishments primarily engaged in manufacturing sporting and athletic goods (except apparel and footwear).	576-577

WHOLESALE

NAICS #		Page
339950	**Sign Manufacturing.** This industry comprises establishments primarily engaged in manufacturing signs and related displays of all materials (except printing paper and paperboard signs, notices, displays).	578-579
339991	**Gasket, Packing, and Sealing Device Manufacturing.** This U.S. industry comprises establishments primarily engaged in manufacturing gaskets, packing, and sealing devices of all materials.	580-581
339992	**Musical Instrument Manufacturing.** This U.S. industry comprises establishments primarily engaged in manufacturing musical instruments (except toys).	582-583
339999	**All Other Miscellaneous Manufacturing.** This U.S. industry comprises establishments primarily engaged in miscellaneous manufacturing (except medical equipment and supplies, jewelry and flatware, sporting and athletic goods, dolls, toys, games, office supplies (except paper), musical instruments, fasteners, buttons, needles, pins, brooms, brushes, mops, and burial caskets).	584-585

WHOLESALE TRADE

423110	**Automobile and Other Motor Vehicle Merchant Wholesalers.** This industry comprises establishments primarily engaged in the merchant wholesale distribution of new and used passenger automobiles, trucks, trailers, and other motor vehicles, such as motorcycles, motor homes, and snowmobiles.	588-589
423120	**Motor Vehicle Supplies and New Parts Merchant Wholesalers.** This industry comprises establishments primarily engaged in the merchant wholesale distribution of motor vehicle supplies, accessories, tools, and equipment; and new motor vehicle parts (except new tires and tubes).	590-591
423130	**Tire and Tube Merchant Wholesalers.** This industry comprises establishments primarily engaged in the merchant wholesale distribution of new and/or used tires and tubes for passenger and commercial vehicles.	592-593
423140	**Motor Vehicle Parts (Used) Merchant Wholesalers.** This industry comprises establishments primarily engaged in the merchant wholesale distribution of used motor vehicle parts (except used tires and tubes) and establishments primarily engaged in dismantling motor vehicles for the purpose of selling the parts.	594-595
423210	**Furniture Merchant Wholesalers.** This industry comprises establishments primarily engaged in the merchant wholesale distribution of furniture (except hospital beds, medical furniture, and drafting tables).	596-597
423220	**Home Furnishing Merchant Wholesalers.** This industry comprises establishments primarily engaged in the merchant wholesale distribution of home furnishings and/or housewares.	598-599
423310	**Lumber, Plywood, Millwork, and Wood Panel Merchant Wholesalers.** This industry comprises establishments primarily engaged in the merchant wholesale distribution of lumber; plywood; reconstituted wood fiber products; wood fencing; doors and windows and their frames (all materials); wood roofing and siding; and/or other wood or metal millwork.	600-601
423320	**Brick, Stone, and Related Construction Material Merchant Wholesalers.** This industry comprises establishments primarily engaged in the merchant wholesale distribution of stone, cement, lime, construction sand, and gravel; brick; asphalt and concrete mixtures; and/or concrete, stone, and structural clay products.	602-603
423330	**Roofing, Siding, and Insulation Material Merchant Wholesalers.** This industry comprises establishments primarily engaged in the merchant wholesale distribution of nonwood roofing and nonwood siding and insulation materials.	604-605
423390	**Other Construction Material Merchant Wholesalers.** This industry comprises (1) establishments primarily engaged in the merchant wholesale distribution of manufactured homes (i.e., mobile homes) and/or prefabricated buildings and (2) establishments primarily engaged in the merchant wholesale distribution of construction materials (except lumber, plywood, millwork, wood panels, brick, stone, roofing, siding, electrical and wiring supplies, and insulation materials).	606-607
423420	**Office Equipment Merchant Wholesalers.** This industry comprises establishments primarily engaged in the merchant wholesale distribution of office machines and related equipment (except computers and computer peripheral equipment).	608-609

WHOLESALE

NAICS #		Page
423430	**Computer and Computer Peripheral Equipment and Software Merchant Wholesalers.** This industry comprises establishments primarily engaged in the merchant wholesale distribution of computers, computer peripheral equipment, loaded computer boards, and/or computer software.	610-611
423440	**Other Commercial Equipment Merchant Wholesalers.** This industry comprises establishments primarily engaged in the merchant wholesale distribution of commercial and related machines and equipment (except photographic equipment and supplies; office equipment; and computers and computer peripheral equipment and software) generally used in restaurants and stores.	612-613
423450	**Medical, Dental, and Hospital Equipment and Supplies Merchant Wholesalers.** This industry comprises establishments primarily engaged in the merchant wholesale distribution of professional medical equipment, instruments, and supplies (except ophthalmic equipment and instruments and goods used by ophthalmologists, optometrists, and opticians).	614-615
423490	**Other Professional Equipment and Supplies Merchant Wholesalers.** This industry comprises establishments primarily engaged in the merchant wholesale distribution of professional equipment and supplies (except ophthalmic goods and medical, dental, and hospital equipment and supplies).	616-617
423510	**Metal Service Centers and Other Metal Merchant Wholesalers.** This industry comprises establishments primarily engaged in the merchant wholesale distribution of products of the primary metals industries. Service centers maintain inventory and may perform functions, such as sawing, shearing, bending, leveling, cleaning, or edging, on a custom basis as part of sales transactions.	618-619
423610	**Electrical Apparatus and Equipment, Wiring Supplies, and Related Equipment Merchant Wholesalers.** This industry comprises establishments primarily engaged in the merchant wholesale distribution of electrical construction materials; wiring supplies; electric light fixtures; light bulbs; and/or electrical power equipment for the generation, transmission, distribution, or control of electric energy.	620-621
423620	**Household Appliances, Electric Housewares, and Consumer Electronics Merchant Wholesalers.** This industry comprises establishments primarily engaged in the merchant wholesale distribution of household-type electrical appliances, room air-conditioners, gas and electric clothes dryers, and/or household-type audio or video equipment.	622-623
423690	**Other Electronic Parts and Equipment Merchant Wholesalers.** This industry comprises establishments primarily engaged in the merchant wholesale distribution of electronic parts and equipment (except electrical apparatus and equipment, wiring supplies and construction material; and electrical appliances, television and radio sets).	624-625
423710	**Hardware Merchant Wholesalers.** This industry comprises establishments primarily engaged in the merchant wholesale distribution of hardware, knives, or handtools.	626-627
423720	**Plumbing and Heating Equipment and Supplies (Hydronics) Merchant Wholesalers.** This industry comprises establishments primarily engaged in the merchant wholesale distribution of plumbing equipment, hydronic heating equipment, house-hold- type gas appliances (except gas clothes dryers), and/or supplies.	628-629
423730	**Warm Air Heating and Air-Conditioning Equipment and Supplies Merchant Wholesalers.** This industry comprises establishments primarily engaged in the merchant wholesale distribution of warm air heating and air-conditioning equipment and supplies.	630-631
423740	**Refrigeration Equipment and Supplies Merchant Wholesalers.** This industry comprises establishments primarily engaged in the merchant wholesale distribution of refrigeration equipment (except household-type refrigerators, freezers, and air-conditioners).	632-633
423810	**Construction and Mining (except Oil Well) Machinery and Equipment Merchant Wholesalers.** This industry comprises establishments primarily engaged in the merchant wholesale distribution of specialized machinery, equipment, and related parts generally used in construction, mining (except oil well) and logging activities.	634-635
423820	**Farm and Garden Machinery and Equipment Merchant Wholesalers.** This industry comprises establishments primarily engaged in the merchant wholesale distribution of specialized machinery, equipment, and related parts generally used in agricultural, farm, and lawn and garden activities.	636-637

WHOLESALE

NAICS #		Page
423830	**Industrial Machinery and Equipment Merchant Wholesalers.** This industry comprises establishments primarily engaged in the merchant wholesale distribution of specialized machinery, equipment, and related parts generally used in manufacturing, oil well, and warehousing activities.	638-639
423840	**Industrial Supplies Merchant Wholesalers.** This industry comprises establishments primarily engaged in the merchant wholesale distribution of supplies for machinery and equipment generally used in manufacturing, oil well, and warehousing activities.	640-641
423850	**Service Establishment Equipment and Supplies Merchant Wholesalers.** This industry comprises establishments primarily engaged in the merchant wholesale distribution of specialized equipment and supplies of the type used by service establishments (except specialized equipment and supplies used in offices, stores, hotels, restaurants, schools, health and medical facilities, photographic facilities, and specialized equipment used in transportation and construction activities).	642-643
423860	**Transportation Equipment and Supplies (except Motor Vehicle) Merchant Wholesalers.** This industry comprises establishments primarily engaged in the merchant wholesale distribution of transportation equipment and supplies (except marine pleasure craft and motor vehicles).	644-645
423910	**Sporting and Recreational Goods and Supplies Merchant Wholesalers.** This industry comprises establishments primarily engaged in the merchant wholesale distribution of sporting goods and accessories; billiard and pool supplies; sporting firearms and ammunition; and/or marine pleasure craft, equipment, and supplies.	646-647
423920	**Toy and Hobby Goods and Supplies Merchant Wholesalers.** This industry comprises establishments primarily engaged in the merchant wholesale distribution of games, toys, fireworks, playing cards, hobby goods and supplies, and/or related goods.	648-649
423930	**Recyclable Material Merchant Wholesalers.** This industry comprises establishments primarily engaged in the merchant wholesale distribution of automotive scrap, industrial scrap, and other recyclable materials. Included in this industry are auto wreckers primarily engaged in dismantling motor vehicles for the purpose of wholesaling scrap.	650-651
423940	**Jewelry, Watch, Precious Stone, and Precious Metal Merchant Wholesalers.** This industry comprises establishments primarily engaged in the merchant wholesale distribution of jewelry, precious and semiprecious stones, precious metals and metal flatware, costume jewelry, watches, clocks, silverware, and/or jewelers' findings.	652-653
423990	**Other Miscellaneous Durable Goods Merchant Wholesalers.** This industry comprises establishments primarily engaged in the merchant wholesale distribution of durable goods (except motor vehicle and motor vehicle parts and supplies; furniture and home furnishings; lumber and other construction materials; professional and commercial equipment and supplies; metals and minerals (except petroleum); electrical goods; hardware, and plumbing and heating equipment and supplies; machinery, equipment and supplies; sporting and recreational goods and supplies; toy and hobby goods and supplies; recyclable materials; and jewelry, watches, precious stones and precious metals).	654-655
424110	**Printing and Writing Paper Merchant Wholesalers.** This industry comprises establishments primarily engaged in the merchant wholesale distribution of bulk printing and/or writing paper generally on rolls for further processing.	656-657
424120	**Stationery and Office Supplies Merchant Wholesalers.** This industry comprises establishments primarily engaged in the merchant wholesale distribution of stationery, office supplies and/or gift wrap.	658-659
424130	**Industrial and Personal Service Paper Merchant Wholesalers.** This industry comprises establishments primarily engaged in the merchant wholesale distribution of kraft wrapping and other coarse paper, paperboard, converted paper (except stationery and office supplies), and/or related disposable plastics products.	660-661
424210	**Drugs and Druggists' Sundries Merchant Wholesalers.** This industry comprises establishments primarily engaged in the merchant wholesale distribution of biological and medical products; botanical drugs and herbs; and pharmaceutical products intended for internal and external consumption in such forms as ampoules, tablets, capsules, vials, ointments, powders, solutions, and suspensions.	662-663

WHOLESALE

NAICS #		Page
424310	**Piece Goods, Notions, and Other Dry Goods Merchant Wholesalers.** This industry comprises establishments primarily engaged in the merchant wholesale distribution of piece goods, fabrics, knitting yarns (except industrial), thread and other notions, and/or hair accessories.	664-665
424340	**Footwear Merchant Wholesalers.** This industry comprises establishments primarily engaged in the merchant wholesale distribution of footwear (including athletic) of leather, rubber, and other materials.	666-667
424350	**Clothing and Clothing Accessories Merchant Wholesalers.** This industry comprises establishments primarily engaged in the merchant wholesale distribution of clothing and clothing accessories.	668-669
424410	**General Line Grocery Merchant Wholesalers.** This industry comprises establishments primarily engaged in the merchant wholesale distribution of a general line (wide range) of groceries.	670-671
424420	**Packaged Frozen Food Merchant Wholesalers.** This industry comprises establishments primarily engaged in the merchant wholesale distribution of packaged frozen foods (except dairy products).	672-673
424430	**Dairy Product (except Dried or Canned) Merchant Wholesalers.** This industry comprises establishments primarily engaged in the merchant wholesale distribution of dairy products (except dried or canned).	674-675
424440	**Poultry and Poultry Product Merchant Wholesalers.** This industry comprises establishments primarily engaged in the merchant wholesale distribution of poultry and/or poultry products (except canned and packaged frozen).	676-677
424450	**Confectionery Merchant Wholesalers.** This industry comprises establishments primarily engaged in the merchant wholesale distribution of confectioneries; salted or roasted nuts; popcorn; potato, corn, and similar chips; and/or fountain fruits and syrups.	678-679
424460	**Fish and Seafood Merchant Wholesalers.** This industry comprises establishments primarily engaged in the merchant wholesale distribution of fish and seafood (except canned or packaged frozen).	680-681
424470	**Meat and Meat Product Merchant Wholesalers.** This industry comprises establishments primarily engaged in the merchant wholesale distribution of meats and meat products (except canned and packaged frozen) and/or lard.	682-683
424480	**Fresh Fruit and Vegetable Merchant Wholesalers.** This industry comprises establishments primarily engaged in the merchant wholesale distribution of fresh fruits and vegetables.	684-685
424490	**Other Grocery and Related Products Merchant Wholesalers.** This industry comprises establishments primarily engaged in the merchant wholesale distribution of groceries and related products (except a general line of groceries; packaged frozen food; dairy products (except dried and canned); poultry products (except canned); confectioneries; fish and seafood (except canned); meat products (except canned); and fresh fruits and vegetables). Included in this industry are establishments primarily engaged in the bottling and merchant wholesale distribution of spring and mineral waters processed by others.	686-687
424510	**Grain and Field Bean Merchant Wholesalers.** This industry comprises establishments primarily engaged in the merchant wholesale distribution of grains, such as corn, wheat, oats, barley, and unpolished rice; dry beans; and soybeans and other inedible beans. Included in this industry are establishments primarily engaged in operating country or terminal grain elevators primarily for the purpose of wholesaling.	688-689
424590	**Other Farm Product Raw Material Merchant Wholesalers.** This industry comprises establishments primarily engaged in the merchant wholesale distribution of farm products (except grain and field beans, livestock, raw milk, live poultry, and fresh fruits and vegetables).	690-691
424610	**Plastics Materials and Basic Forms and Shapes Merchant Wholesalers.** This industry comprises establishments primarily engaged in the merchant wholesale distribution of plastics materials and resins, and unsupported plastics film, sheet, sheeting, rod, tube, and other basic forms and shapes.	692-693
424690	**Other Chemical and Allied Products Merchant Wholesalers.** This industry comprises establishments primarily engaged in the merchant wholesale distribution of chemicals and allied products (except agricultural and medicinal chemicals, paints and varnishes, fireworks, and plastics materials and basic forms and shapes).	694-695

RETAIL

NAICS #		Page
424710	**Petroleum Bulk Stations and Terminals.** This industry comprises establishments with bulk liquid storage facilities primar-ily engaged in the merchant wholesale distribution of crude petroleum and petroleum products, including liquefied petroleum gas.	696-697
424720	**Petroleum and Petroleum Products Merchant Wholesalers (except Bulk Stations and Terminals).** This industry comprises establishments primarily engaged in the merchant wholesale distribution of petroleum and petroleum products (except from bulk liquid storage facilities).	698-699
424810	**Beer and Ale Merchant Wholesalers.** This industry comprises establishments primarily engaged in the merchant wholesale distribution of beer, ale, porter, and other fermented malt beverages.	700-701
424820	**Wine and Distilled Alcoholic Beverage Merchant Wholesalers.** This industry comprises establishments primarily engaged in the merchant wholesale distribution of wine, distilled alcoholic beverages, and/or neutral spirits and ethyl alcohol used in blended wines and distilled liquors.	702-703
424910	**Farm Supplies Merchant Wholesalers.** This industry comprises establishments primarily engaged in the merchant wholesale distribution of farm supplies, such as animal feeds, fertilizers, agricultural chemicals, pesticides, plant seeds, and plant bulbs.	704-705
424930	**Flower, Nursery Stock, and Florists' Supplies Merchant Wholesalers.** This industry comprises establishments primarily engaged in the merchant wholesale distribution of flowers, florists' supplies, and/or nursery stock (except plant seeds and plant bulbs).	706-707
424940	**Tobacco Product and Electronic Cigarette Merchant Wholesalers.** This industry comprises establishments primarily engaged in the merchant wholesale distribution of tobacco products, such as cigarettes, snuff, cigars, and pipe tobacco.	708-709
424990	**Other Miscellaneous Nondurable Goods Merchant Wholesalers.** This industry comprises establishments primarily engaged in the merchant wholesale distribution of nondurable goods (except printing and writing paper; stationery and office supplies; industrial and personal service paper; drugs and druggists' sundries; apparel, piece goods, and notions; grocery and related products; farm product raw materials; chemical and allied products; petroleum and petroleum products; beer, wine, and distilled alcoholic beverages; farm supplies; books, periodicals and newspapers; flower, nursery stock and florists' supplies; tobacco and tobacco products; and paint, varnishes, wallpaper, and supplies).	710-711
425120	**Wholesale Trade Agents and Brokers.** This industry comprises wholesale trade agents and brokers acting on behalf of buyers or sellers in the wholesale distribution of goods, including those that use the Internet or other electronic means to bring together buyers and sellers. Agents and brokers do not take title to the goods being sold but rather receive a commission or fee for their service. Agents and brokers for all durable and nondurable goods are included in this industry.	712-713

RETAIL TRADE

441110	**New Car Dealers.** This industry comprises establishments primarily engaged in retailing new automobiles and light trucks, such as sport utility vehicles, and passenger and cargo vans, or retailing these new vehicles in combination with activities, such as repair services, retailing used cars, and selling replacement parts and accessories.	716-717
441120	**Used Car Dealers.** This industry comprises establishments primarily engaged in retailing used automobiles and light trucks, such as sport utility vehicles, and passenger and cargo vans.	718-719
441210	**Recreational Vehicle Dealers.** This industry comprises establishments primarily engaged in retailing new and/ or used recreational vehicles commonly referred to as RVs or retailing these new vehicles in combination with activities, such as repair services and selling replacement parts and accessories.	720-721
441222	**Boat Dealers.** This U.S. industry comprises establishments primarily engaged in (1) retailing new and/or used boats or retailing new boats in combination with activities, such as repair services and selling replacement parts and accessories, and/or (2) retailing new and/or used outboard motors, boat trailers, marine supplies, parts, and accessories.	722-723

RETAIL

NAICS #		Page
441227	**Motorcycle, ATV, and All Other Motor Vehicle Dealers.** This U.S. industry comprises establishments primarily engaged in retailing new and/or used motorcycles, motor scooters, motorbikes, mopeds, off-road all-terrain vehicles (ATV), personal watercraft, utility trailers, and other motor vehicles (except automobiles, light trucks, recreational vehicles, and boats) or retailing these new vehicles in combination with activities, such as repair services and selling replacement parts and accessories.	724-725
441330	**Automotive Parts and Accessories Retailers.** This industry comprises establishments primarily engaged in retailing new, used, and/or rebuilt automotive parts and accessories, with or without repairing automobiles; and/or establishments primarily engaged in retailing and installing automotive accessories.	726-727
441340	**Tire Dealers.** This industry comprises establishments primarily engaged in retailing new and/or used tires and tubes or retailing new tires in combination with automotive repair services.	728-729
444110	**Home Centers.** This industry comprises establishments known as home centers primarily engaged in retailing a general line of new home repair and improvement materials and supplies, such as lumber, plumbing goods, electrical goods, tools, housewares, hardware, and lawn and garden supplies, with no one merchandise line predominating. The merchandise lines are normally arranged in separate departments.	730-731
444140	**Hardware Retailers.** This industry comprises establishments primarily engaged in retailing a general line of new hardware items, such as tools and builders' hardware.	732-733
444180	**Other Building Material Dealers.** This industry comprises establishments (except home centers, paint and wallpaper retailers, and hardware retailers) primarily engaged in retailing specialized lines of new building materials, such as lumber, fencing, glass, doors, plumbing fixtures and supplies, electrical supplies, prefabricated buildings and kits, and kitchen and bath cabinets and countertops to be installed.	734-735
444230	**Outdoor Power Equipment Retailers.** This industry comprises establishments primarily engaged in retailing new outdoor power equipment or retailing new outdoor power equipment in combination with activities, such as repair services and selling replacement parts.	736-737
444240	**Nursery, Garden Center, and Farm Supply Retailers.** This industry comprises establishments primarily engaged in retailing nursery and garden products, such as trees, shrubs, plants, seeds, bulbs, and sod, that are predominantly grown elsewhere. These establishments may sell a limited amount of a product they grow themselves. Also included in this industry are establishments primarily engaged in retailing farm supplies, such as animal (except pet) feed, fertilizers, agricultural chemicals, and pesticides.	738-739
445110	**Supermarkets and Other Grocery Retailers (except Convenience Retailers).** This industry comprises establishments generally known as supermarkets and grocery stores primarily engaged in retailing a general line of food, such as canned and frozen foods; fresh fruits and vegetables; and fresh and prepared meats, fish, and poultry. Included in this industry are delicatessen-type establishments primarily engaged in retailing a general line of food.	740-741
445131	**Convenience Retailers.** This U.S. industry comprises establishments primarily engaged in retailing a limited line of groceries that generally includes milk, bread, soda, and snacks, such as convenience stores or food marts (except those operating fuel pumps).	742-743
445240	**Meat Retailers.** This industry comprises establishments primarily engaged in retailing fresh, frozen, or cured meats and poultry not for immediate consumption. Delicatessen-type establishments primarily engaged in retailing fresh meat are included in this industry.	744-745
445291	**Baked Goods Retailers.** This U.S. industry comprises establishments primarily engaged in retailing baked goods not for immediate consumption and not made on the premises.	746-747
445298	**All Other Specialty Food Retailers.** This U.S. industry comprises establishments primarily engaged in retailing miscellaneous specialty foods (except fruit and vegetables, meat, fish, seafood, confections, nuts, popcorn, and baked goods) not for immediate consumption and not made on the premises.	748-749
445320	**Beer, Wine, and Liquor Retailers.** This industry comprises establishments primarily engaged in retailing packaged alcoholic beverages, such as ale, beer, wine, and liquor.	750-751

RETAIL

NAICS #		Page
449110	**Furniture Retailers.** This industry comprises establishments primarily engaged in retailing new furniture, such as household furniture (e.g., baby furniture, box springs, and mattresses) and outdoor furniture; office furniture (except sold in combination with office supplies and equipment); and/or furniture sold in combination with major appliances, home electronics, home furnishings, or floor coverings.	752-753
449121	**Floor Covering Retailers.** This U.S. industry comprises establishments primarily engaged in retailing new floor coverings, such as rugs and carpets, laminate and vinyl floor coverings, linoleum flooring, and floor tile (except ceramic tile or hardwood floor coverings only); or retailing new floor coverings in combination with installation and repair services.	754-755
449129	**All Other Home Furnishings Retailers.** This U.S. industry comprises establishments primarily engaged in retailing new home furnishings (except furniture, floor coverings, and window treatments).	756-757
449210	**Electronics and Appliance Retailers.** This industry comprises establishments primarily engaged in one of the following: (1) retailing an array of new household-type appliances and consumer-type electronic products, such as televisions, computers, electronic tablets, and cameras; (2) specializing in retailing a single line of new consumer-type electronic products; (3) retailing these new products in combination with repair and support services; (4) retailing new prepackaged or downloadable computer software (without publishing); and/or (5) retailing prerecorded audio and video media, such as downloadable digital music and video files (without production or publishing), CDs, and DVDs.	758-759
455219	**All Other General Merchandise Retailers.** This U.S. industry comprises establishments primarily engaged in retailing new and used general merchandise (except department stores, warehouse clubs, superstores, and supercenters). These establishments retail a general line of new and used merchandise, such as apparel, automotive parts, dry goods, groceries, hardware, housewares or home furnishings, and other lines in limited amounts, with none of the lines predominating. This industry also includes establishments primarily engaged in retailing a general line of new and used merchandise on an auction basis.	760-761
456110	**Pharmacies and Drug Retailers.** This industry comprises establishments generally known as pharmacies and drug retailers engaged in retailing prescription or nonprescription drugs and medicines.	762-763
456120	**Cosmetics, Beauty Supplies, and Perfume Retailers.** This industry comprises establishments primarily engaged in retailing cosmetics, perfumes, toiletries, and personal grooming products.	764-765
456191	**Food (Health) Supplement Retailers.** This U.S. industry comprises establishments primarily engaged in retailing food supplement products, such as vitamins, nutrition supplements, and body enhancing supplements.	766-767
456199	**All Other Health and Personal Care Retailers.** This U.S. industry comprises establishments primarily engaged in retailing specialized lines of health and personal care merchandise (except drugs, medicines, cosmetics, beauty supplies, perfumes, optical goods, and food supplement products).	768-769
457110	**Gasoline Stations with Convenience Stores.** This industry comprises establishments primarily engaged in retailing automotive fuels (e.g., gasoline, diesel fuel, gasohol, alternative fuels) in combination with a limited line of groceries. These establishments can either be in a convenience store (i.e., food mart) setting or a gasoline station setting. These establishments may also provide automotive repair services.	770-771
457120	**Other Gasoline Stations.** This industry comprises establishments generally known as gasoline stations (except those with convenience stores) or truck stops primarily engaged in (1) retailing automotive fuels (e.g., gasoline, diesel fuel, gasohol, alternative fuels) or (2) retailing these fuels in combination with activities, such as providing repair services; selling automotive oils, replacement parts, and accessories; and/or providing food services.	772-773
457210	**Fuel Dealers.** This industry comprises establishments primarily engaged in retailing heating oil, liquefied petroleum (LP) gas, and other fuels via direct selling (i.e., home delivery).	774-775
458110	**Clothing and Clothing Accessories Retailers.** This industry comprises establishments primarily engaged in retailing general or specialized lines of new clothing and clothing accessories, such as hats and caps, costume jewelry, gloves, handbags, ties, wigs, toupees, and belts. These establishments may provide basic alterations, such as hemming, taking in or letting out seams, or lengthening or shortening sleeves.	776-777

TRANSPORTATION

NAICS #		Page
458210	**Shoe Retailers.** This industry comprises establishments primarily engaged in retailing all types of new footwear (except hosiery and specialty sports footwear, such as golf shoes, bowling shoes, and cleated shoes). Establishments primarily engaged in retailing new tennis shoes or sneakers are included in this industry.	778-779
458310	**Jewelry Retailers.** This industry comprises establishments primarily engaged in retailing one or more of the following items: (1) new jewelry (except costume jewelry); (2) new sterling and plated silverware; and (3) new watches and clocks. Also included are establishments retailing these new products in combination with lapidary work and/or repair services.	780-781
459110	**Sporting Goods Retailers.** This industry comprises establishments primarily engaged in retailing new sporting goods, such as bicycles and bicycle parts; camping equipment; exercise and fitness equipment; athletic uniforms; specialty sports footwear; and other sporting goods, equipment, and accessories.	782-783
459140	**Musical Instrument and Supplies Retailers.** This industry comprises establishments primarily engaged in retailing new musical instruments, sheet music, and related supplies; or retailing these new products in combination with musical instrument repair, rental, or music instruction.	784-785
459410	**Office Supplies and Stationery Retailers.** This industry comprises establishments primarily engaged in one or more of the following: (1) retailing new office supplies, stationery, and school supplies; (2) retailing a combination of new office equipment, furniture, and supplies; and (3) retailing new office equipment, furniture, and supplies in combination with selling new computers.	786-787
459420	**Gift, Novelty, and Souvenir Retailers.** This industry comprises establishments primarily engaged in retailing new gifts, novelty merchandise, souvenirs, greeting cards, seasonal and holiday decorations, and curios.	788-789
459510	**Used Merchandise Retailers.** This industry comprises establishments primarily engaged in retailing used merchandise, antiques, and secondhand goods (except motor vehicles, such as automobiles, RVs, motorcycles, and boats; motor vehicle parts; tires; and mobile homes). This industry includes establishments retailing used merchandise on an auction basis.	790-791
459910	**Pet and Pet Supplies Retailers.** This industry comprises establishments primarily engaged in retailing pets, pet foods, and pet supplies.	792-793
459999	**All Other Miscellaneous Retailers.** This U.S. industry comprises establishments primarily engaged in retailing miscellaneous specialized lines of merchandise (except motor vehicle and parts dealers; building material and garden equipment and supplies dealers; food and beverage retailers; furniture, home furnishings, electronics, and appliance retailers; general merchandise retailers; health and personal care retailers; gasoline stations and fuel dealers; clothing, clothing accessories, shoe, and jewelry retailers; sporting goods, hobby, and musical instrument retailers; book retailers and news dealers; florists; office supplies, stationery, and gift retailers; used merchandise retailers; pet and pet supplies retailers; art dealers; manufactured (mobile) home dealers; and tobacco, electronic cigarette, and other smoking supplies retailers).	794-795

TRANSPORTATION AND WAREHOUSING

481111	**Scheduled Passenger Air Transportation.** This U.S. industry comprises establishments primarily engaged in providing air transportation of passengers or passengers and freight over regular routes and on regular schedules. Establishments in this industry operate flights even if partially loaded. Scheduled air passenger carriers including commuter and helicopter carriers (except scenic and sightseeing) are included in this industry.	798-799
481211	**Nonscheduled Chartered Passenger Air Transportation.** This U.S. industry comprises establishments primarily engaged in providing air transportation of passengers or passengers and cargo with no regular routes and regular schedules.	800-801
481219	**Other Nonscheduled Air Transportation.** This U.S. industry comprises establishments primarily engaged in providing air transportation with no regular routes and regular schedules (except nonscheduled chartered passenger and/or cargo air transportation). These establishments provide a variety of specialty air transportation or flying services based on individual customer needs using general purpose aircraft.	802-803

TRANSPORTATION

NAICS #		Page
483111	**Deep Sea Freight Transportation.** This U.S. industry comprises establishments primarily engaged in providing deep sea transportation of cargo to or from foreign ports.	804-805
483211	**Inland Water Freight Transportation.** This U.S. industry comprises establishments primarily engaged in providing inland water transportation of cargo on lakes, rivers, or intracoastal waterways (except on the Great Lakes System).	806-807
484110	**General Freight Trucking, Local.** This industry comprises establishments primarily engaged in providing local general freight trucking. General freight establishments handle a wide variety of commodities, generally palletized and transported in a container or van trailer. Local general freight trucking establishments usually provide trucking within a metropolitan area which may cross state lines. Generally the trips are same-day return.	808-809
484121	**General Freight Trucking, Long-Distance, Truckload.** This U.S. industry comprises establishments primarily engaged in providing long-distance general freight truckload (TL) trucking. These long-distance general freight truckload carrier establishments provide full truck movement of freight from origin to destination. The shipment of freight on a truck is characterized as a full single load not combined with other shipments.	810-811
484122	**General Freight Trucking, Long-Distance, Less Than Truckload.** This U.S. industry comprises establishments primarily engaged in providing long-distance, general freight, less than truckload (LTL) trucking. LTL carriage is characterized as multiple shipments combined onto a single truck for multiple deliveries within a network. These establishments are generally characterized by the following network activities: local pickup, local sorting and terminal operations, line-haul, destination sorting and terminal operations, and local delivery.	812-813
484210	**Used Household and Office Goods Moving.** This industry comprises establishments primarily engaged in providing local or long-distance trucking of used household, used institutional, or used commercial furniture and equipment. Incidental packing and storage activities are often provided by these establishments.	814-815
484220	**Specialized Freight (except Used Goods) Trucking, Local.** This industry comprises establishments primarily engaged in providing local, specialized trucking. Local trucking establishments provide trucking within a metropolitan area that may cross state lines. Generally the trips are same-day return.	816-817
484230	**Specialized Freight (except Used Goods) Trucking, Long-Distance.** This industry comprises establishments primarily engaged in providing long-distance specialized trucking. These establishments provide trucking between metropolitan areas that may cross North American country borders.	818-819
485410	**School and Employee Bus Transportation.** This industry comprises establishments primarily engaged in providing buses and other motor vehicles to transport pupils to and from school or employees to and from work.	820-821
485510	**Charter Bus Industry.** This industry comprises establishments primarily engaged in providing buses for charter. These establishments provide bus services to meet customers' road transportation needs and generally do not operate over fixed routes and on regular schedules.	822-823
485999	**All Other Transit and Ground Passenger Transportation.** This U.S. industry comprises establishments primarily engaged in providing ground passenger transportation (except urban transit systems; interurban and rural bus transportation, taxi and/or limousine services (except shuttle services), school and employee bus transportation, charter bus services, and special needs transportation). Establishments primarily engaged in operating shuttle services and vanpools are included in this industry. Shuttle services establishments generally provide travel on regular routes and on regular schedules between hotels, airports, or other destination points.	824-825
488119	**Other Airport Operations.** This U.S. industry comprises establishments primarily engaged in (1) operating international, national, or civil airports, or public flying fields or (2) supporting airport operations, such as rental of hangar space, and providing baggage handling and/or cargo handling services.	826-827
488190	**Other Support Activities for Air Transportation.** This industry comprises establishments primarily engaged in providing specialized services for air transportation (except air traffic control and other airport operations).	828-829

TRANSPORTATION

NAICS #		Page
488210	**Support Activities for Rail Transportation.** This industry comprises establishments primarily engaged in providing specialized services for railroad transportation including servicing, routine repairing (except factory conversion, overhaul or rebuilding of rolling stock), and maintaining rail cars; loading and unloading rail cars; and operating independent terminals.	830-831
488310	**Port and Harbor Operations.** This industry comprises establishments primarily engaged in operating ports, harbors (including docking and pier facilities), or canals.	832-833
488320	**Marine Cargo Handling.** This industry comprises establishments primarily engaged in providing stevedoring and other marine cargo handling services (except warehousing).	834-835
488330	**Navigational Services to Shipping.** This industry comprises establishments primarily engaged in providing navigational services to shipping. Marine salvage establishments are included in this industry.	836-837
488390	**Other Support Activities for Water Transportation.** This industry comprises establishments primarily engaged in providing services to water transportation (except port and harbor operations; marine cargo handling services; and navigational services to shipping).	838-839
488410	**Motor Vehicle Towing.** This industry comprises establishments primarily engaged in towing light or heavy motor vehicles, both local and long distance. These establishments may provide incidental services, such as storage and emergency road repair services.	840-841
488490	**Other Support Activities for Road Transportation.** This industry comprises establishments primarily engaged in providing services (except motor vehicle towing) to road network users.	842-843
488510	**Freight Transportation Arrangement.** This industry comprises establishments primarily engaged in arranging transportation of freight between shippers and carriers. These establishments are usually known as freight forwarders, marine shipping agents, or customs brokers and offer a combination of services spanning transportation modes.	844-845
488991	**Packing and Crating.** This U.S. industry comprises establishments primarily engaged in packing, crating, and otherwise preparing goods for transportation.	846-847
488999	**All Other Support Activities for Transportation.** This U.S. industry comprises establishments primarily engaged in providing support activities to transportation (except for air transportation; rail transportation; water transportation; road transportation; freight transportation arrangement; and packing and crating).	848-849
492110	**Couriers and Express Delivery Services.** This industry comprises establishments primarily engaged in providing air, surface, or combined courier delivery services of parcels generally between metropolitan areas or urban centers. The establishments of this industry form a network including courier local pick-up and delivery to serve their customers' needs.	850-851
492210	**Local Messengers and Local Delivery.** This industry comprises establishments primarily engaged in providing local messenger and delivery services of small items within a single metropolitan area or within an urban center. These establishments generally provide point-to-point pickup and delivery and do not operate as part of an intercity courier network.	852-853
493110	**General Warehousing and Storage.** This industry comprises establishments primarily engaged in operating merchandise warehousing and storage facilities. These establishments generally handle goods in containers, such as boxes, barrels, and/or drums, using equipment, such as forklifts, pallets, and racks. They are not specialized in handling bulk products of any particular type, size, or quantity of goods or products.	854-855
493120	**Refrigerated Warehousing and Storage.** This industry comprises establishments primarily engaged in operating refrigerated warehousing and storage facilities. Establishments primarily engaged in the storage of furs for the trade are included in this industry. The services provided by these establishments include blast freezing, tempering, and modified atmosphere storage services.	856-857
493130	**Farm Product Warehousing and Storage.** This industry comprises establishments primarily engaged in operating bulk farm product warehousing and storage facilities (except refrigerated). Grain elevators primarily engaged in storage are included in this industry.	858-859
493190	**Other Warehousing and Storage.** This industry comprises establishments primarily engaged in operating warehousing and storage facilities (except general merchandise, refrigerated, and farm product warehousing and storage).	860-861

INFORMATION

NAICS #   Page

INFORMATION

512110   **Motion Picture and Video Production.** This industry comprises establishments primarily engaged in producing, or producing and distributing motion pictures, videos, television programs, or television commercials. 864-865

512131   **Motion Picture Theaters (except Drive-Ins).** This U.S. industry comprises establishments primarily engaged in operating motion picture theaters (except drive-ins) and/or exhibiting motion pictures or videos at film festivals, and so forth. 866-867

512230   **Music Publishers.** This industry comprises establishments primarily engaged in acquiring and registering copyrights for musical compositions in accordance with law and promoting and authorizing the use of these compositions in recordings, radio, television, motion pictures, live performances, print, or other media. Establishments in this industry represent the interests of the songwriter or other owners of musical compositions to produce revenues from the use of such works, generally through licensing agreements. These establishments may own the copyright or act as administrator of the music copyrights on behalf of copyright owners. Publishers of music books and sheet music are included in this industry. 868-869

513130   **Book Publishers.** This industry comprises establishments known as book publishers. Establishments in this industry carry out design, editing, and marketing activities necessary for producing and distributing books. These establishments may publish books in print, electronic, or audio form, including exclusively on the Internet. 870-871

513210   **Software Publishers.** This industry comprises establishments primarily engaged in software publishing. Establishments in this industry carry out operations necessary for producing and distributing computer software, such as designing, providing documentation, assisting in installation, and providing support services to software purchasers. These establishments may design, develop, and publish, or publish only. These establishments may publish and distribute software through subscriptions and/or downloads. 872-873

516110   **Radio Broadcasting Stations.** This industry comprises establishments primarily engaged in broadcasting aural programs by radio to the public. These establishments operate radio broadcasting studios and facilities for the programming and transmission of programs to the public. Programming may originate in their own studio, from an affiliated network, or from external sources. 874-875

516120   **Television Broadcasting Stations.** This industry comprises establishments primarily engaged in broadcasting images together with sound. These establishments operate television broadcasting studios and facilities for the programming and transmission of programs to the public. Programming may originate in their own studio, from an affiliated network, or from external sources. 876-877

516210   **Media Streaming Distribution Services, Social Networks, and Other Media Networks and Content Providers.** This industry comprises establishments primarily providing media streaming distribution services, operating social network sites, operating media broadcasting and cable television networks, and supplying information, such as news reports, articles, pictures, and features, to the news media. These establishments distribute textual, audio, and/or video content of general or specific interest. 878-879

517111   **Wired Telecommunications Carriers.** This U.S. industry comprises establishments primarily engaged in operating, maintaining, and/or providing access to transmission facilities and infrastructure that they own and/or lease for the transmission of voice, data, text, sound, and video using wired telecommunications networks. Transmission facilities may be based on a single technology or a combination of technologies. Establishments in this industry use the wired telecommunications network facilities that they operate to provide a variety of services, such as wired telephony services, including VoIP services; wired (cable) audio and video programming distribution; and wired broadband Internet services. By exception, establishments providing satellite television distribution services using facilities and infrastructure that they operate are included in this industry. 880-881

517112   **Wireless Telecommunications Carriers (except Satellite).** This U.S. industry comprises establishments primarily engaged in operating and maintaining switching and transmission facilities to provide communications via the airwaves. Establishments in this industry have spectrum licenses and provide services using that spectrum, such as cellular phone services, paging services, wireless Internet access, and wireless video services. 882-883

FINANCE

NAICS #		Page
517121	**Telecommunications Resellers.** This U.S. industry comprises establishments engaged in purchasing access and network capacity from owners and operators of telecommunications networks and reselling wired and wireless telecommunications services to businesses and households (except satellite telecommunications and agents for wireless telecommunications services). Establishments in this industry resell telecommunications; they do not operate transmission facilities and infrastructure.	884-885
517810	**All Other Telecommunications.** This industry comprises establishments primarily engaged in providing specialized telecommunications services, such as satellite tracking, communications telemetry, and radar station operation. This industry also includes establishments primarily engaged in providing satellite terminal stations and associated facilities connected with one or more terrestrial systems and capable of transmitting telecommunications to, and receiving telecommunications from, satellite systems. Establishments providing Internet services or Voice over Internet protocol (VoIP) services via client-supplied telecommunications connections are also included in this industry. Establishments in this industry do not operate as telecommunications carriers.	886-887
518210	**Computing Infrastructure Providers, Data Processing, Web Hosting, and Related Services.** This industry comprises establishments primarily engaged in providing infra-structure for hosting or data processing services. These establishments may provide specialized hosting activities, such as Web hosting, streaming services or application hosting, provide application service provisioning, or may provide general time-share mainframe facilities to clients. Data processing establishments provide complete processing and specialized reports from data supplied by clients or provide automated data processing and data entry services.	888-889
519290	**Web Search Portals and All Other Information Services.** This industry comprises establishments primarily engaged in operating Web sites that use a search engine to generate and maintain extensive databases of Internet addresses and content in an easily searchable format (and known as Web search portals) or providing other information services not elsewhere classified. Establishments known as Web search portals often provide additional Internet services, such as email, connections to other Web sites, auctions, news, and other limited content.	890-891

FINANCE AND INSURANCE

522220	**Sales Financing.** This industry comprises establishments primarily engaged in sales financing or sales financing in combination with leasing. Sales financing establishments are primarily engaged in lending money for the purpose of providing collateralized goods through a contractual installment sales agreement, either directly from or through arrangements with dealers.	894-895
522291	**Consumer Lending.** This U.S. industry comprises establishments primarily engaged in making unsecured cash loans to consumers.	896-897
522292	**Real Estate Credit.** This U.S. industry comprises establishments primarily engaged in lending funds with real estate as collateral.	898-899
522299	**International, Secondary Market, and All Other Nondepository Credit Intermediation.** This U.S. industry comprises (1) establishments primarily engaged in providing working capital funds to U.S. exporters, lending funds to foreign buyers of U.S. goods, and/or lending funds to domestic buyers of imported goods; (2) establishments primarily engaged in buying, pooling, and repackaging loans for sale to others on the secondary market; and (3) establishments primarily providing other nondepository credit (except credit card issuing, sales financing, consumer lending, and real estate credit). Examples of types of lending in this industry are short-term inventory credit, agricultural lending (except real estate and sales financing), and consumer cash lending secured by personal property.	900-901
522310	**Mortgage and Nonmortgage Loan Brokers.** This industry comprises establishments primarily engaged in arranging loans by bringing borrowers and lenders together on a commission or fee basis.	902-903
522320	**Financial Transactions Processing, Reserve, and Clearinghouse Activities.** This industry comprises establishments primarily engaged in providing one or more of the following: (1) financial transaction processing (except central bank); (2) reserve and liquidity services (except central bank); and/or (3) check or other financial instrument clearinghouse services (except central bank).	904-905

FINANCE

NAICS #		Page
522390	**Other Activities Related to Credit Intermediation.** This industry comprises establishments primarily engaged in facilitating credit intermediation (except mortgage and loan brokerage; and financial transactions processing, reserve, and clearinghouse activities).	906-907
523150	**Investment Banking and Securities Intermediation.** This industry comprises establishments primarily engaged in underwriting, originating, and/or maintaining markets for issues of securities, or acting as agents (i.e., brokers) between buyers and sellers in buying or selling securities on a commission or transaction fee basis. Investment bankers act as principals (i.e., investors who buy or sell on their own account) in firm commitment transactions or act as agents in best effort and standby commitments. This industry also includes establishments acting as principals in buying or selling securities generally on a spread basis, such as securities dealers or stock option dealers.	908-909
523910	**Miscellaneous Intermediation.** This industry comprises establishments primarily engaged in acting as principals (except investment bankers, securities dealers, and commodity contracts dealers) in buying or selling of financial contracts generally on a spread basis. Principals are investors that buy or sell for their own account.	910-911
523940	**Portfolio Management and Investment Advice.** This industry comprises establishments primarily engaged in managing the portfolio assets (i.e., funds) of others on a fee or commission basis and/or providing customized investment advice to clients on a fee basis. Establishments providing portfolio management have the authority to make investment decisions, and they derive fees based on the size and/or overall performance of the portfolio. Establishments providing investment advice provide financial planning advice and investment counseling to meet the goals and needs of specific clients, but do not have the authority to execute trades.	912-913
523991	**Trust, Fiduciary, and Custody Activities.** This U.S. industry comprises establishments primarily engaged in providing trust, fiduciary, and custody services to others, as instructed, on a fee or contract basis, such as bank trust offices and escrow agencies (except real estate).	914-915
523999	**Miscellaneous Financial Investment Activities.** This U.S. industry comprises establishments primarily engaged in acting as agents and/or brokers (except securities brokerages and commodity contracts brokerages) in buying or selling financial contracts and those providing financial investment services (except securities and commodity exchanges; portfolio management; investment advice; and trust, fiduciary, and custody services) on a fee or commission basis.	916-917
524114	**Direct Health and Medical Insurance Carriers.** This U.S. industry comprises establishments primarily engaged in initially underwriting (i.e., assuming the risk and assigning premiums) health and medical insurance policies. Group hospitalization plans and HMO establishments (except those providing health care services) that provide health and medical insurance policies without providing health care services are included in this industry.	918-919
524126	**Direct Property and Casualty Insurance Carriers.** This U.S. industry comprises establishments primarily engaged in initially underwriting (i.e., assuming the risk and assigning premiums) insurance policies that protect policyholders against losses that may occur as a result of property damage or liability.	920-921
524128	**Other Direct Insurance (except Life, Health, and Medical) Carriers.** This U.S. industry comprises establishments primarily engaged in initially underwriting (e.g., assuming the risk, assigning premiums) insurance policies (except life, disability income, accidental death and dismemberment, health and medical, property and casualty, and title insurance policies).	922-923
524130	**Reinsurance Carriers.** This industry comprises establishments primarily engaged in assuming all or part of the risk associated with existing insurance policies originally underwritten by other insurance carriers.	924-925
524210	**Insurance Agencies and Brokerages.** This industry comprises establishments primarily engaged in acting as agents (i.e., brokers) in selling annuities and insurance policies.	926-927
524292	**Pharmacy Benefit Management and Other Third Party Administration of Insurance and Pension Funds.** This U.S. industry comprises establishments primarily engaged in providing third party administration services of insurance and pension funds, such as claims processing and other administrative services to insurance carriers, employee-benefit plans, and self-insurance funds.	928-929
524298	**All Other Insurance Related Activities.** This U.S. industry comprises establishments primarily engaged in providing insurance services on a contract or fee basis (except insurance agencies and brokerages, claims adjusting, and third party administration). Insurance advisory services and insurance ratemaking services are included in this industry.	930-931

REAL ESTATE

NAICS #		Page
525910	**Open-End Investment Funds.** This industry comprises legal entities (i.e., open-end investment funds) organized to pool assets that consist of securities or other financial instruments. Shares in these pools are offered to the public in an initial offering with additional shares offered continuously and perpetually and redeemed at a specific price determined by the net asset value.	932-933
525920	**Trusts, Estates, and Agency Accounts.** This industry comprises legal entities, trusts, estates, or agency accounts, administered on behalf of the beneficiaries under the terms of a trust agreement, will, or agency agreement.	934-935
525990	**Other Financial Vehicles.** This industry comprises legal entities (i.e., funds (except insurance and employee benefit funds; open-end investment funds; trusts, estates, and agency accounts; and Real Estate Investment Trusts (REITs)).	936-937

REAL ESTATE AND RENTAL AND LEASING

531110	**Lessors of Residential Buildings and Dwellings.** This industry comprises establishments primarily engaged in acting as lessors of buildings used as residences or dwellings, such as single-family homes, apartment buildings, and town homes. Included in this industry are owner-lessors and establishments renting real estate and then acting as lessors in subleasing it to others. The establishments in this industry may manage the property themselves or have another establishment manage it for them.	940-941
531120	**Lessors of Nonresidential Buildings (except Miniwarehouses).** This industry comprises establishments primarily engaged in acting as lessors of buildings (except miniwarehouses and self-storage units) that are not used as residences or dwellings. Included in this industry are: (1) owner-lessors of nonresidential buildings; (2) establishments renting real estate and then acting as lessors in subleasing it to others; and (3) establishments providing full service office space, whether on a lease or service contract basis. The establishments in this industry may manage the property themselves or have another establishment manage it for them.	942-943
531130	**Lessors of Miniwarehouses and Self-Storage Units.** This industry comprises establishments primarily engaged in renting or leasing space for self-storage. These establishments provide secure space (i.e., rooms, compartments, lockers, containers, or outdoor space) where clients can store and retrieve their goods.	944-945
531190	**Lessors of Other Real Estate Property.** This industry comprises establishments primarily engaged in acting as lessors of real estate (except buildings), such as manufactured home (i.e., mobile home) sites, vacant lots, and grazing land.	946-947
531210	**Offices of Real Estate Agents and Brokers.** This industry comprises establishments primarily engaged in acting as agents and/or brokers in one or more of the following: (1) selling real estate for others; (2) buying real estate for others; and (3) renting real estate for others.	948-949
531311	**Residential Property Managers.** This U.S. industry comprises establishments primarily engaged in managing residential real estate for others.	950-951
531312	**Nonresidential Property Managers.** This U.S. industry comprises establishments primarily engaged in managing nonresidential real estate for others.	952-953
531390	**Other Activities Related to Real Estate.** This industry comprises establishments primarily engaged in performing real estate related services (except lessors of real estate, offices of real estate agents and brokers, real estate property managers, and offices of real estate appraisers).	954-955
532111	**Passenger Car Rental.** This industry comprises establishments primarily engaged in renting passenger cars without drivers, generally for short periods of time.	956-957
532112	**Passenger Car Leasing.** This industry comprises establishments primarily engaged in leasing passenger cars without drivers, generally for long periods of time.	958-959
532120	**Truck, Utility Trailer, and RV (Recreational Vehicle) Rental and Leasing.** This industry comprises establishments primarily engaged in renting or leasing, without drivers, one or more of the following: trucks, truck tractors or buses: semitrailers, utility trailers, or RVs (recreational vehicles).	960-961

PROFESSIONAL SERVICES

NAICS #		Page
532210	**Consumer Electronics and Appliances Rental.** This industry comprises establishments primarily engaged in renting consumer electronics equipment and appliances, such as televisions, stereos, and refrigerators. Included in this industry are appliance rental centers.	962-963
532283	**Home Health Equipment Rental.** This U.S. industry comprises establishments primarily engaged in renting home-type health and invalid equipment, such as wheel chairs, hospital beds, oxygen tanks, walkers, and crutches.	964-965
532284	**Recreational Goods Rental.** This U.S. industry comprises establishments primarily engaged in renting recreational goods, such as bicycles, canoes, motorcycles, skis, sailboats, beach chairs, and beach umbrellas.	966-967
532289	**All Other Consumer Goods Rental.** This U.S. industry comprises establishments primarily engaged in renting consumer goods and products (except consumer electronics and appliances; formal wear and costumes; prerecorded video tapes and discs for home electronic equipment; home health furniture and equipment; and recreational goods). Included in this industry are furniture rental centers and party rental supply centers.	968-969
532310	**General Rental Centers.** This industry comprises establishments primarily engaged in renting a range of consumer, commercial, and industrial equipment. Establishments in this industry typically operate from conveniently located facilities where they maintain inventories of goods and equipment that they rent for short periods of time. The type of equipment that establishments in this industry provide often includes, but is not limited to: audio visual equipment, contractors' and builders' tools and equipment, home repair tools, lawn and garden equipment, moving equipment and supplies, and party and banquet equipment and supplies.	970-971
532411	**Commercial Air, Rail, and Water Transportation Equipment Rental and Leasing.** This U.S. industry comprises establishments primarily engaged in renting or leasing off-highway transportation equipment without operators, such as aircraft, railroad cars, steamships, or tugboats.	972-973
532412	**Construction, Mining, and Forestry Machinery and Equipment Rental and Leasing.** This U.S. industry comprises establishments primarily engaged in renting or leasing heavy equipment without operators that may be used for construction, mining, or forestry, such as bulldozers, earthmoving equipment, well-drilling machinery and equipment, or cranes.	974-975
532420	**Office Machinery and Equipment Rental and Leasing.** This industry comprises establishments primarily engaged in renting or leasing office machinery and equipment, such as computers, office furniture, duplicating machines (i.e., copiers), or facsimile machines.	976-977
532490	**Other Commercial and Industrial Machinery and Equipment Rental and Leasing.** This industry comprises establishments primarily engaged in renting or leasing nonconsumer-type machinery and equipment (except heavy construction, transportation, mining, and forestry machinery and equipment without operators; and office machinery and equipment). Establishments in this industry rent or lease products, such as manufacturing equipment; metalworking, telecommunications, motion picture, or theatrical machinery and equipment; institutional (i.e., public building) furniture, such as furniture for schools, theaters, or buildings; or agricultural equipment without operators.	978-979
533110	**Lessors of Nonfinancial Intangible Assets (except Copyrighted Works).** This industry comprises establishments primarily engaged in assigning rights to assets, such as patents, trademarks, brand names, and/or franchise agreements for which a royalty payment or licensing fee is paid to the asset holder.	980-981

PROFESSIONAL, SCIENTIFIC, AND TECHNICAL SERVICES

541110	**Offices of Lawyers.** This industry comprises offices of legal practitioners known as lawyers or attorneys (i.e., counselors-at-law) primarily engaged in the practice of law. Estab-lishments in this industry may provide expertise in a range or in specific areas of law, such as criminal law, corporate law, family and estate law, patent law, real estate law, or tax law.	984-985
541199	**All Other Legal Services.** This U.S. industry comprises establishments of legal practitioners (except offices of lawyers and attorneys, settlement offices, and title abstract offices). These establishments are primarily engaged in providing specialized legal or paralegal services.	986-987

PROFESSIONAL SERVICES

NAICS #		Page
541211	**Offices of Certified Public Accountants.** This U.S. industry comprises establishments of accountants that are certified to audit the accounting records of public and private organizations and to attest to compliance with generally accepted accounting practices. Offices of certified public accountants (CPAs) may provide one or more of the following accounting services: (1) auditing financial statements; (2) designing accounting systems; (3) preparing financial statements; (4) developing budgets; and (5) providing advice on matters related to accounting. These establishments may also provide related services, such as bookkeeping, tax return preparation, and payroll processing.	988-989
541213	**Tax Preparation Services.** This U.S. industry comprises establishments (except offices of CPAs) engaged in providing tax return preparation services without also providing accounting, bookkeeping, billing, or payroll processing services. Basic knowledge of tax law and filing requirements is required.	990-991
541214	**Payroll Services.** This U.S. industry comprises establishments (except offices of CPAs) engaged in the following without also providing accounting, bookkeeping, or billing services: (1) collecting information on hours worked, pay rates, deductions, and other payroll- related data from their clients and (2) using that information to generate paychecks, payroll reports, and tax filings. These establishments may use data processing and tabulating techniques as part of providing their services.	992-993
541219	**Other Accounting Services.** This U.S. industry comprises establishments (except offices of CPAs) engaged in providing accounting services (except tax return preparation services only or payroll services only). These establishments may also provide tax return preparation or payroll services. Accountant (except CPA) offices, bookkeeper offices, and billing offices are included in this industry.	994-995
541310	**Architectural Services.** This industry comprises establishments primarily engaged in planning and designing residential, institutional, leisure, commercial, and industrial buildings and structures by applying knowledge of design, construction procedures, zoning regulations, building codes, and building materials.	996-997
541320	**Landscape Architectural Services.** This industry comprises establishments primarily engaged in planning and designing the development of land areas for projects, such as parks and other recreational areas; airports; highways; hospitals; schools; land subdivisions; and commercial, industrial, and residential areas, by applying knowledge of land characteristics, location of buildings and structures, use of land areas, and design of landscape projects.	998-999
541330	**Engineering Services.** This industry comprises establishments primarily engaged in applying physical laws and principles of engineering in the design, development, and utilization of machines, materials, instruments, structures, processes, and systems. The assignments undertaken by these establishments may involve any of the following activities: provision of advice, preparation of feasibility studies, preparation of preliminary and final plans and designs, provision of technical services during the construction or installation phase, inspection and evaluation of engineering projects, and related services.	1000-1001
541370	**Surveying and Mapping (except Geophysical) Services.** This industry comprises establishments primarily engaged in performing surveying and mapping services of the surface of the earth, including the sea floor. These services may include surveying and mapping of areas above or below the surface of the earth, such as the creation of view easements or segregating rights in parcels of land by creating underground utility easements.	1002-1003
541380	**Testing Laboratories and Services.** This industry comprises establishments primarily engaged in performing physical, chemical, and other analytical testing services, such as acoustics or vibration testing, assaying, biological testing (except medical and veterinary), calibration testing, electrical and electronic testing, geotechnical testing, mechanical testing, nondestructive testing, or thermal testing. The testing may occur in a laboratory or on-site.	1004-1005
541410	**Interior Design Services.** This industry comprises establishments primarily engaged in planning, designing and administering projects in interior spaces to meet the physical and aesthetic needs of people using them, taking into consideration building codes, health and safety regulations, traffic patterns and floor planning, mechanical and electrical needs, and interior fittings and furniture. Interior designers and interior design consultants work in areas, such as hospitality design, health care design, institutional design, commercial and corporate design, and residential design. This industry also includes interior decorating consultants engaged exclusively in providing aesthetic services associated with interior spaces.	1006-1007

PROFESSIONAL SERVICES

NAICS #		Page
541420	**Industrial Design Services.** This industry comprises establishments primarily engaged in creating and developing designs and specifications that optimize the use, value, and appearance of their products. These services can include the determination of the materials, construction, mechanisms, shape, color, and surface finishes of the product, taking into consideration human characteristics and needs, safety, market appeal, and efficiency in production, distribution, use, and maintenance. Establishments providing automobile or furniture industrial design services or industrial design consulting services are included in this industry.	1008-1009
541430	**Graphic Design Services.** This industry comprises establishments primarily engaged in planning, designing, and managing the production of visual communication in order to convey specific messages or concepts, clarify complex information, or project visual identi-ties. These services can include the design of printed materials, packaging, advertising, signage systems, and corporate identification (logos). This industry also includes commercial artists engaged exclusively in generating drawings and illustrations requiring technical accuracy or interpretative skills.	1010-1011
541490	**Other Specialized Design Services.** This industry comprises establishments primarily engaged in providing professional design services (except architectural, landscape architecture, engineering, interior, industrial, graphic, and computer system design).	1012-1013
541511	**Custom Computer Programming Services.** This U.S. industry comprises establishments primarily engaged in writing, modifying, testing, and supporting software to meet the needs of a particular customer.	1014-1015
541512	**Computer Systems Design Services.** This U.S. industry comprises establishments primarily engaged in planning and designing computer systems that integrate computer hardware, software, and communication technologies. The hardware and software components of the system may be provided by this establishment or company as part of integrated services or may be provided by third parties or vendors. These establishments often install the system and train and support users of the system.	1016-1017
541513	**Computer Facilities Management Services.** This U.S. industry comprises establishments primarily engaged in providing onsite management and operation of clients' computer systems and/or data processing facilities. Establishments providing computer systems or data processing facilities support services are included in this industry.	1018-1019
541519	**Other Computer Related Services.** This U.S. industry comprises establishments primarily engaged in providing computer related services (except custom programming, systems integration design, and facilities management services). Establishments providing computer disaster recovery services or software installation services are included in this industry.	1020-1021
541611	**Administrative Management and General Management Consulting Services.** This U.S. industry comprises establishments primarily engaged in providing operating advice and assistance to businesses and other organizations on administrative management issues, such as financial planning and budgeting, equity and asset management, records management, office planning, strategic and organizational planning, site selection, new business startup, and business process improvement. This industry also includes establishments of general management consultants that provide a full range of administrative; human resource; marketing; process, physical distribution, and logistics; or other management consulting services to clients.	1022-1023
541612	**Human Resources Consulting Services.** This U.S. industry comprises establishments primarily engaged in providing advice and assistance to businesses and other organizations in one or more of the following areas: (1) human resource and personnel policies, practices, and procedures; (2) employee benefits planning, communication, and administration; (3) compensation systems planning; (4) wage and salary administration; and (5) executive search and recruitment.	1024-1025
541613	**Marketing Consulting Services.** This U.S. industry comprises establishments primarily engaged in providing operating advice and assistance to businesses and other organizations on marketing issues, such as developing marketing objectives and policies, sales forecasting, new product developing and pricing, licensing and franchise planning, and marketing planning and strategy.	1026-1027

PROFESSIONAL SERVICES

| NAICS # | | Page |

541614 **Process, Physical Distribution, and Logistics Consulting Services.** This U.S. industry comprises establishments primarily engaged in providing operating advice and assistance to businesses and other organizations in areas, such as: (1) manufacturing operations improvement; (2) productivity improvement; (3) production planning and control; (4) quality assurance and quality control; (5) inventory management; (6) distribution networks; (7) warehouse use, operations, and utilization; (8) transportation and shipment of goods and materials; and (9) materials management and handling. 1028-1029

541618 **Other Management Consulting Services.** This U.S. industry comprises establishments primarily engaged in providing management consulting services (except administrative and general management consulting; human resources consulting; marketing consulting; or process, physical distribution, and logistics consulting). Establishments providing telecommunications or utilities management consulting services are included in this industry. 1030-1031

541620 **Environmental Consulting Services.** This industry comprises establishments primarily engaged in providing advice and assistance to businesses and other organizations on environmental issues, such as the control of environmental contamination from pollutants, toxic substances, and hazardous materials. These establishments identify problems (e.g. inspect buildings for hazardous materials), measure and evaluate risks, and recommend solutions. They employ a multidisciplined staff of scientists, engineers, and other technicians with expertise in areas, such as air and water quality, asbestos contamination, remediation, and environmental law. Establishments providing sanitation or site remediation consulting services are included in this industry. 1032-1033

541690 **Other Scientific and Technical Consulting Services.** This industry comprises establishments primarily engaged in providing advice and assistance to businesses and other organizations on scientific and technical issues (except environmental). 1034-1035

541714 **Research and Development in Biotechnology (except Nanobiotechnology).** This U.S. industry comprises establishments primarily engaged in conducting biotechnology (except nanobiotechnology) research and experimental development. Biotechnology (except nanobiotechnology) research and experimental development involves the study of the use of microorganisms and cellular and biomolecular processes to develop or alter living or non-living materials. This research and development in biotechnology (except nanobiotechnology) may result in development of new biotechnology (except nanobiotechnology) processes or in prototypes of new or genetically-altered products that may be reproduced, utilized, or implemented by various industries. 1036-1037

541715 **Research and Development in the Physical, Engineering, and Life Sciences (except Nanotechnology and Biotechnology).** This U.S. industry comprises establishments primarily engaged in conducting research and experimental development (except nanotechnology and biotechnology research and experimental development) in the physical, engineering, and life sciences, such as agriculture, electronics, environmental, biology, botany, computers, chemistry, food, fisheries, forests, geology, health, mathematics, medicine, oceanography, pharmacy, physics, veterinary and other allied subjects. 1038-1039

541720 **Research and Development in the Social Sciences and Humanities.** This industry comprises establishments primarily engaged in conducting research and analyses in cognitive development, sociology, psychology, language, behavior, economic, and other social science and humanities research. 1040-1041

541810 **Advertising Agencies.** This industry comprises establishments primarily engaged in creating advertising campaigns and placing such advertising in periodicals, newspapers, radio and television, or other media. These establishments are organized to provide a full range of services (i.e., through in-house capabilities or subcontracting), including advice, creative services, account management, production of advertising material, media planning, and buying (i.e., placing advertising). 1042-1043

541820 **Public Relations Agencies.** This industry comprises establishments primarily engaged in designing and implementing public relations campaigns. These campaigns are designed to promote the interests and image of their clients. Establishments providing lobbying, political consulting, or public relations consulting are included in this industry. 1044-1045

ADMIN & WASTE MANAGEMENT SERVICES

NAICS #		Page
541850	**Indoor and Outdoor Display Advertising.** This industry comprises establishments primarily engaged in creating and designing public display advertising, campaign materials, such as printed, painted, or electronic displays, and/or placing such displays on indoor or outdoor billboards and panels, or on or within transit vehicles or facilities, shopping malls, retail (in-store) displays, and other display structures or sites.	1046-1047
541860	**Direct Mail Advertising.** This industry comprises establishments primarily engaged in (1) creating and designing advertising campaigns for the purpose of distributing advertising materials (e.g., coupons, flyers, samples) or specialties (e.g., key chains, magnets, pens with customized messages imprinted) by mail or other direct distribution; and/ or (2) preparing advertising materials or specialties for mailing or other direct distribution. These establishments may also compile, maintain, sell, and rent mailing lists.	1048-1049
541890	**Other Services Related to Advertising.** This industry comprises establishments primarily engaged in providing advertising services (except advertising agency services, public relations agency services, media buying agency services, media representative services, display advertising services, direct mail advertising services, advertising material distribution services, and marketing consulting services).	1050-1051
541910	**Marketing Research and Public Opinion Polling.** This industry comprises establishments primarily engaged in systematically gathering, recording, tabulating, and presenting marketing and public opinion data.	1052-1053
541940	**Veterinary Services.** This industry comprises establishments of licensed veterinary practitioners primarily engaged in the practice of veterinary medicine, dentistry, or surgery for animals; and establishments primarily engaged in providing testing services for licensed veterinary practitioners.	1054-1055
541990	**All Other Professional, Scientific, and Technical Services.** This industry comprises establishments primarily engaged in the provision of professional, scientific, or technical services (except legal services; accounting, tax preparation, bookkeeping, and related services; architectural, engineering, and related services; specialized design services; computer systems design and related services; management, scientific, and technical consulting services; scientific research and development services; advertising and related services; market research and public opinion polling; photographic services; translation and interpretation services; and veterinary services).	1056-1057

MANAGEMENT OF COMPANIES AND ENTERPRISES

551112	**Offices of Other Holding Companies.** This U.S. industry comprises legal entities known as holding companies (except bank holding) primarily engaged in holding the securities of (or other equity interests in) companies and enterprises for the purpose of owning a controlling interest or influencing the management decisions of these firms. The holding companies in this industry do not administer, oversee, and manage other establishments of the company or enterprise whose securities they hold.	1060-1061
551114	**Corporate, Subsidiary, and Regional Managing Offices.** This U.S. industry comprises establishments (except government establishments) primarily engaged in administering, overseeing, and managing other establishments of the company or enterprise. These establishments normally undertake the strategic or organizational planning and decisionmaking role of the company or enterprise. Establishments in this industry may hold the securities of the company or enterprise.	1062-1063

ADMINISTRATIVE AND SUPPORT AND WASTE MANAGEMENT AND REMEDIATION SERVICES

561110	**Office Administrative Services.** This industry comprises establishments primarily engaged in providing a range of day-to-day office administrative services, such as financial planning; billing and recordkeeping; personnel; and physical distribution and logistics for others on a contract or fee basis. These establishments do not provide operating staff to carry out the complete operations of a business.	1066-1067

ADMIN & WASTE MANAGEMENT SERVICES

NAICS #		Page
561210	**Facilities Support Services.** This industry comprises establishments primarily engaged in providing operating staff to perform a combination of support services within a client's facilities. Establishments in this industry typically provide a combination of services, such as janitorial; maintenance; trash disposal; guard and security; mail routing; reception; laundry; and related services to support operations within facilities. These establishments provide operating staff to carry out these support activities; but, are not involved with or responsible for the core business or activities of the client. Establishments providing facilities (except computer and/or data processing) operation support services and establishments operating correctional facilities (i.e., jails) on a contract or fee basis are included in this industry.	1068-1069
561311	**Employment Placement Agencies.** This U.S. industry comprises establishments primarily engaged in listing employment vacancies and in referring or placing applicants for employment. The individuals referred or placed are not employees of the employment agencies.	1070-1071
561312	**Executive Search Services.** This U.S. industry comprises establishments primarily engaged in providing executive search, recruitment, and placement services for clients with specific executive and senior management position requirements. The range of services provided by these establishments may include developing a search strategy and position specification based on the culture and needs of the client; researching, identifying, screening, and interviewing candidates; verifying candidate qualifications; and assisting in final offer negotiations and assimilation of the selected candidate. The individuals identified, recruited, or placed are not employees of the executive search services establishments.	1072-1073
561320	**Temporary Help Services.** This industry comprises establishments primarily engaged in supplying workers to clients' businesses for limited periods of time to supplement the working force of the client. The individuals provided are employees of the temporary help service establishment. However, these establishments do not provide direct supervision of their employees at the clients' work sites.	1074-1075
561330	**Professional Employer Organizations.** This industry comprises establishments primarily engaged in providing human resources and human resource management services to client businesses. Establishments in this industry operate in a coemployment relationship with client businesses or organizations and are specialized in performing a wide range of human resource and personnel management duties, such as payroll, payroll tax, benefits administration, workers' compensation, unemployment, and human resource administration. Professional employer organizations (PEOs) are responsible for payroll, including withholding and remitting employment-related taxes, for some or all of the employees of their clients, and also serve as the employer of those employees for benefits and related purposes.	1076-1077
561422	**Telemarketing Bureaus and Other Contact Centers.** This U.S. industry comprises establishments primarily engaged in providing telemarketing services on a contract or fee basis for others, such as: (1) promoting clients' products or services by telephone, (2) taking orders for clients by telephone, and (3) soliciting contributions or providing information for clients by telephone. These establishments never own the product or provide the services they are representing and generally can originate and/or receive calls for others.	1078-1079
561440	**Collection Agencies.** This industry comprises establishments primarily engaged in collecting payments for claims and remitting payments collected to their clients.	1080-1081
561499	**All Other Business Support Services.** This U.S. industry comprises establishments primarily engaged in providing business support services (except secretarial and other document preparation services; telephone answering and telemarketing services; private mail services or document copying services conducted as separate activities or in conjunction with other office support services; monetary debt collection services; credit reporting services; repossession services; and court reporting and stenotype recording services).	1082-1083
561510	**Travel Agencies.** This industry comprises establishments primarily engaged in acting as agents in selling travel, tour, and accommodation services to the general public and commercial clients.	1084-1085
561520	**Tour Operators.** This industry comprises establishments primarily engaged in arranging and assembling tours. The tours are sold through travel agencies or tour operators. Travel or wholesale tour operators are included in this industry.	1086-1087
561599	**All Other Travel Arrangement and Reservation Services.** This U.S. industry comprises establishments (except travel agencies, tour operators, and convention and visitors bureaus) primarily engaged in providing travel arrangement and reservation services.	1088-1089

ADMIN & WASTE MANAGEMENT SERVICES

NAICS #		Page
561612	**Security Guards and Patrol Services.** This U.S. industry comprises establishments primarily engaged in providing guard and patrol services, such as bodyguard, guard dog, and parking security services.	1090-1091
561621	**Security Systems Services (except Locksmiths).** This U.S. industry comprises establishments primarily engaged in (1) selling security alarm systems, such as burglar and fire alarms, along with installation, repair, or monitoring services or (2) remote monitoring of electronic security alarm systems.	1092-1093
561710	**Exterminating and Pest Control Services.** This industry comprises establishments primarily engaged in exterminating and controlling birds, mosquitoes, rodents, termites, and other insects and pests (except for crop production and forestry production). Establishments providing fumigation services are included in this industry.	1094-1095
561720	**Janitorial Services.** This industry comprises establishments primarily engaged in cleaning building interiors, interiors of transportation equipment (e.g., aircraft, rail cars, ships), and/or windows.	1096-1097
561730	**Landscaping Services.** This industry comprises (1) establishments primarily engaged in providing landscape care and maintenance services and/or installing trees, shrubs, plants, lawns, or gardens and (2) establishments primarily engaged in providing these services along with the design of landscape plans and/or the construction (i.e., installation) of walkways, retaining walls, decks, fences, ponds, and similar structures.	1098-1099
561740	**Carpet and Upholstery Cleaning Services.** This industry comprises establishments primarily engaged in cleaning and dyeing used rugs, carpets, and upholstery.	1100-1101
561790	**Other Services to Buildings and Dwellings.** This industry comprises establishments primarily engaged in providing services to buildings and dwellings (except exterminating and pest control; janitorial; landscaping care and maintenance; and carpet and upholstery cleaning).	1102-1103
561910	**Packaging and Labeling Services.** This industry comprises establishments primarily engaged in packaging client-owned materials. The services may include labeling and/or imprinting the package.	1104-1105
561920	**Convention and Trade Show Organizers.** This industry comprises establishments primarily engaged in organizing, promoting, and/or managing events, such as business and trade shows, conventions, conferences, and meetings (whether or not they manage and provide the staff to operate the facilities in which these events take place).	1106-1107
561990	**All Other Support Services.** This industry comprises establishments primarily engaged in providing day-to-day business and other organizational support services (except office administrative services, facilities support services, employment services, business support services, travel arrangement and reservation services, security and investigation services, services to buildings and other structures, packaging and labeling services, and convention and trade show organizing services).	1108-1109
562111	**Solid Waste Collection.** This U.S. industry comprises establishments primarily engaged in one or more of the following: (1) collecting and/or hauling nonhazardous solid waste (i.e., garbage) within a local area; (2) operating nonhazardous solid waste transfer stations; and (3) collecting and/or hauling mixed recyclable materials within a local area.	1110-1111
562119	**Other Waste Collection.** This U.S. industry comprises establishments primarily engaged in collecting and/or hauling waste (except nonhazardous solid waste and hazardous waste) within a local area. Establishments engaged in brush or rubble removal services are included in this industry.	1112-1113
562211	**Hazardous Waste Treatment and Disposal.** This U.S. industry comprises establishments primarily engaged in (1) operating treatment and/or disposal facilities for hazardous waste or (2) the combined activity of collecting and/or hauling of hazardous waste materials within a local area and operating treatment or disposal facilities for hazardous waste.	1114-1115
562212	**Solid Waste Landfill.** This U.S. industry comprises establishments primarily engaged in (1) operating landfills for the disposal of nonhazardous solid waste or (2) the combined activity of collecting and/or hauling nonhazardous waste materials within a local area and operating landfills for the disposal of nonhazardous solid waste.	1116-1117

EDUCATION

NAICS #		Page
562219	**Other Nonhazardous Waste Treatment and Disposal.** This U.S. industry comprises establishments primarily engaged in (1) operating nonhazardous waste treatment and disposal facilities (except landfills, combustors, incinerators and sewer systems or sewage treatment facilities) or (2) the combined activity of collecting and/or hauling of nonhazardous waste materials within a local area and operating waste treatment or disposal facilities (except landfills, combustors, incinerators and sewer systems, or sewage treatment facilities). Compost dumps are included in this industry.	1118-1119
562910	**Remediation Services.** This industry comprises establishments primarily engaged in one or more of the following: (1) remediation and cleanup of contaminated buildings, mine sites, soil or ground water; (2) integrated mine reclamation activities, including demolition, soil remediation, waste water treatment, hazardous material removal, contouring land and revegetation; and (3) asbestos, lead paint and other toxic material abatement.	1120-1121
562920	**Materials Recovery Facilities.** This industry comprises establishments primarily engaged in (1) operating facilities for separating and sorting recyclable materials from nonhazardous waste streams (i.e., garbage) and/or (2) operating facilities where commingled recyclable materials, such as paper, plastics, used beverage cans, and metals are sorted into distinct categories.	1122-1123
562991	**Septic Tank and Related Services.** This U.S. industry comprises establishments primarily engaged in (1) pumping (i.e., cleaning) septic tanks and cesspools and/or (2) renting and/or servicing portable toilets.	1124-1125
562998	**All Other Miscellaneous Waste Management Services.** This U.S. industry comprises establishments primarily engaged in providing waste management services (except waste collection, waste treatment and disposal, remediation, operation of materials recovery facilities, septic tank pumping and related services, and waste management consulting services).	1126-1127

EDUCATIONAL SERVICES

611110	**Elementary and Secondary Schools.** This industry comprises establishments primarily engaged in furnishing academic courses and associated course work that comprise a basic preparatory education. A basic preparatory education ordinarily constitutes kindergarten through 12th grade. This industry includes school boards and school districts.	1130-1131
611310	**Colleges, Universities, and Professional Schools.** This industry comprises establishments primarily engaged in furnishing academic courses and granting degrees at baccalaureate or graduate levels. The requirement for admission is at least a high school diploma or equivalent general academic training. Instruction may be provided in diverse settings, such as the establishment's or client's training facilities, educational institutions, the workplace, or the home, and through correspondence, television, Internet, or other means.	1132-1133
611430	**Professional and Management Development Training.** This industry comprises establishments primarily engaged in offering an array of short duration courses and seminars for management and professional development. Training for career development may be provided directly to individuals or through employers' training programs; and courses may be customized or modified to meet the special needs of customers. Instruction may be provided in diverse settings, such as the establishment's or client's training facilities, educational institutions, the workplace, or the home, and through correspondence, television, Internet, or other means.	1134-1135
611512	**Flight Training.** This U.S. industry comprises establishments primarily engaged in offering aviation and flight training. These establishments may offer vocational training, recreational training, or both.	1136-1137
611519	**Other Technical and Trade Schools.** This U.S. industry comprises establishments primarily engaged in offering job or career vocational or technical courses (except cosmetology and barber training, aviation and flight training, and apprenticeship training). The curriculums offered by these schools are highly structured and specialized and lead to job-specific certification.	1138-1139
611610	**Fine Arts Schools.** This industry comprises establishments primarily engaged in offering instruction in the arts, including dance, art, drama, and music.	1140-1141
611620	**Sports and Recreation Instruction.** This industry comprises establishments, such as camps and schools, primarily engaged in offering instruction in athletic activities to groups of individuals. Overnight and day sports instruction camps are included in this industry.	1142-1143

HEALTH CARE

NAICS #		Page
611699	**All Other Miscellaneous Schools and Instruction.** This U.S. industry comprises establishments primarily engaged in offering instruction (except business, computer, management, technical, trade, fine arts, athletic, language instruction, tutoring, and automobile driving instruction). Also excluded from this industry are academic schools, colleges, and universities.	1144-1145
611710	**Educational Support Services.** This industry comprises establishments primarily engaged in providing noninstructional services that support educational processes or systems.	1146-1147

HEALTH CARE AND SOCIAL ASSISTANCE

621111	**Offices of Physicians (except Mental Health Specialists).** This U.S. industry comprises establishments of health practitioners having the degree of M.D. (Doctor of medicine) or D.O. (Doctor of osteopathy) primarily engaged in the independent practice of general or specialized medicine (except psychiatry or psychoanalysis) or surgery. These practitioners operate private or group practices in their own offices (e.g., centers, clinics) or in the facilities of others, such as hospitals or HMO medical centers.	1150-1151
621112	**Offices of Physicians, Mental Health Specialists.** This U.S. industry comprises establishments of health practitioners having the degree of M.D. (Doctor of medicine) or D.O. (Doctor of osteopathy) primarily engaged in the independent practice of psychiatry or psychoanalysis. These practitioners operate private or group practices in their own offices (e.g., centers, clinics) or in the facilities of others, such as hospitals or HMO medical centers.	1152-1153
621210	**Offices of Dentists.** This industry comprises establishments of health practitioners having the degree of D.M.D. (Doctor of dental medicine), D.D.S. (Doctor of dental surgery), or D.D.Sc. (Doctor of dental science) primarily engaged in the independent practice of general or specialized dentistry or dental surgery. These practitioners operate private or group practices in their own offices (e.g., centers, clinics) or in the facilities of others, such as hospitals or HMO medical centers. They can provide either comprehensive preventive, cosmetic, or emergency care, or specialize in a single field of dentistry.	1154-1155
621310	**Offices of Chiropractors.** This industry comprises establishments of health practitioners having the degree of D.C. (Doctor of chiropractic) primarily engaged in the independent practice of chiropractic. These practitioners provide diagnostic and therapeutic treatment of neuromusculoskeletal and related disorders through the manipulation and adjustment of the spinal column and extremities, and operate private or group practices in their own offices (e.g., centers, clinics) or in the facilities of others, such as hospitals or HMO medical centers.	1156-1157
621320	**Offices of Optometrists.** This industry comprises establishments of health practitioners having the degree of O.D. (Doctor of optometry) primarily engaged in the independent practice of optometry. These practitioners provide eye examinations to determine visual acuity or the presence of vision problems and to prescribe eyeglasses, contact lenses, and eye exercises. They operate private or group practices in their own offices (e.g., centers, clinics) or in the facilities of others, such as hospitals or HMO medical centers, and may also provide the same service as opticians, such as selling and fitting prescription eyeglasses and contact lenses.	1158-1159
621330	**Offices of Mental Health Practitioners (except Physicians).** This industry comprises establishments of independent mental health practitioners (except physicians) primarily engaged in (1) the diagnosis and treatment of mental, emotional, and behavioral disorders and/or (2) the diagnosis and treatment of individual or group social dysfunction brought about by such causes as mental illness, alcohol and substance abuse, physical and emotional trauma, or stress. These practitioners operate private or group practices in their own offices (e.g., centers, clinics) or in the facilities of others, such as hospitals or HMO medical centers.	1160-1161
621340	**Offices of Physical, Occupational and Speech Therapists, and Audiologists.** This industry comprises establishments of independent health practitioners primarily engaged in one of the following: (1) administering medically prescribed physical therapy treatment for patients suffering from injuries or muscle, nerve, joint, and bone disease; (2) planning and administering educational, recreational, and social activities designed to help patients or individuals with disabilities, regain physical or mental functioning or to adapt to their disabilities; and (3) diagnosing and treating speech, language, or hearing problems. These practitioners operate private or group practices in their own offices (e.g., centers, clinics) or in the facilities of others, such as hospitals or HMO medical centers.	1162-1163

HEALTH CARE

NAICS #		Page

621391 **Offices of Podiatrists.** This U.S. industry comprises establishments of health practitioners having the degree of D.P. (Doctor of podiatry) primarily engaged in the independent practice of podiatry. These practitioners diagnose and treat diseases and deformities of the foot and operate private or group practices in their own offices (e.g., centers, clinics) or in the facilities of others, such as hospitals or HMO medical centers. 1164-1165

621399 **Offices of All Other Miscellaneous Health Practitioners.** This U.S. industry comprises establishments of independent health practitioners (except physicians; dentists; chiropractors; optometrists; mental health specialists; physical, occupational, and speech therapists; audiologists; and podiatrists). These practitioners operate private or group practices in their own offices (e.g., centers, clinics) or in the facilities of others, such as hospitals or HMO medical centers. 1166-1167

621420 **Outpatient Mental Health and Substance Abuse Centers.** This industry comprises establishments with medical staff primarily engaged in providing outpatient services related to the diagnosis and treatment of mental health disorders and alcohol and other substance abuse. These establishments generally treat patients who do not require inpatient treatment. They may provide a counseling staff and information regarding a wide range of mental health and substance abuse issues and/or refer patients to more extensive treatment programs, if necessary. 1168-1169

621491 **HMO Medical Centers.** This U.S. industry comprises establishments with physicians and other medical staff primarily engaged in providing a range of outpatient medical services to the health maintenance organization (HMO) subscribers with a focus generally on primary health care. These establishments are owned by the HMO. Included in this industry are HMO establishments that both provide health care services and underwrite health and medical insurance policies. 1170-1171

621492 **Kidney Dialysis Centers.** This U.S. industry comprises establishments with medical staff primarily engaged in providing outpatient kidney or renal dialysis services. 1172-1173

621493 **Freestanding Ambulatory Surgical and Emergency Centers.** This U.S. industry comprises establishments with physicians and other medical staff primarily engaged in (1) providing surgical services (e.g., orthoscopic and cataract surgery) on an outpatient basis or (2) providing emergency care services (e.g., setting broken bones, treating lacerations, or tending to patients suffering injuries as a result of accidents, trauma, or medical conditions necessitating immediate medical care) on an outpatient basis. Outpatient surgical establishments have specialized facilities, such as operating and recovery rooms, and specialized equipment, such as anesthetic or X-ray equipment. 1174-1175

621498 **All Other Outpatient Care Centers.** This U.S. industry comprises establishments with medical staff primarily engaged in providing general or specialized outpatient care (except family planning centers, outpatient mental health and substance abuse centers, HMO medical centers, kidney dialysis centers, and freestanding ambulatory surgical and emergency centers). Centers or clinics of health practitioners with different degrees from more than one industry practicing within the same establishment (i.e., Doctor of medicine and Doctor of dental medicine) are included in this industry. 1176-1177

621511 **Medical Laboratories.** This U.S. industry comprises establishments known as medical laboratories primarily engaged in providing analytic or diagnostic services, including body fluid analysis, generally to the medical profession or to the patient on referral from a health practitioner. 1178-1179

621512 **Diagnostic Imaging Centers.** This U.S. industry comprises establishments known as diagnostic imaging centers primarily engaged in producing images of the patient generally on referral from a health practitioner. 1180-1181

621610 **Home Health Care Services.** This industry comprises establishments primarily engaged in providing skilled nursing services in the home, along with a range of the following: personal care services; homemaker and companion services; physical therapy; medical social services; medications; medical equipment and supplies; counseling; 24-hour home care; occupation and vocational therapy; dietary and nutritional services; speech therapy; audiology; and high-tech care, such as intravenous therapy. 1182-1183

621910 **Ambulance Services.** This industry comprises establishments primarily engaged in providing transportation of patients by ground or air, along with medical care. These services are often provided during a medical emergency but are not restricted to emergencies. The vehicles are equipped with lifesaving equipment operated by medically trained personnel. 1184-1185

HEALTH CARE

NAICS # | Page

621991 **Blood and Organ Banks.** This U.S. industry comprises establishments primarily engaged in collecting, storing, and distributing blood and blood products and storing and distributing body organs. 1186-1187

621999 **All Other Miscellaneous Ambulatory Health Care Services.** This U.S. industry comprises establishments primarily engaged in providing ambulatory health care services (except offices of physicians, dentists, and other health practitioners; outpatient care centers; medical and diagnostic laboratories; home health care providers; ambulances; and blood and organ banks). ... 1188-1189

622110 **General Medical and Surgical Hospitals.** This industry comprises establishments known and licensed as general medical and surgical hospitals primarily engaged in providing diagnostic and medical treatment (both surgical and nonsurgical) to inpatients with any of a wide variety of medical conditions. These establishments maintain inpatient beds and provide patients with food services that meet their nutritional requirements. These hospitals have an organized staff of physicians and other medical staff to provide patient care services. These establishments usually provide other services, such as outpatient services, anatomical pathology services, diagnostic X-ray services, clinical labora-tory services, operating room services for a variety of procedures, and phar-macy services... 1190-1191

622210 **Psychiatric and Substance Abuse Hospitals.** This industry comprises establishments known and licensed as psychiatric and substance abuse hospitals primarily engaged in providing diagnostic, medical treatment, and monitoring services for inpatients who suffer from mental illness or substance abuse disorders. The treatment often requires an extended stay in the hospital. These establishments maintain inpatient beds and provide patients with food services that meet their nutritional requirements. They have an organized staff of physicians and other medical staff to provide patient care services. Psychiatric, psychological, and social work services are available at the facility. These hospitals usually provide other services, such as outpatient services, clinical laboratory services, diagnostic X-ray services, and electroencephalograph services... 1192-1193

622310 **Specialty (except Psychiatric and Substance Abuse) Hospitals.** This industry consists of establishments known and licensed as specialty hospi-tals primarily engaged in providing diagnostic and medical treatment to inpatients with a specific type of disease or medical condition (except psychiatric or substance abuse). Hospitals providing long-term care for the chronically ill and hospitals providing rehabilitation, restorative, and adjustive services to physically challenged or disabled people are included in this industry. These establishments maintain inpatient beds and provide patients with food services that meet their nutritional requirements. They have an organized staff of physicians and other medical staff to provide patient care services. These hospitals may provide other services, such as outpatient services, diagnostic X-ray services, clinical laboratory services, operating room services, physical therapy services, educational and vocational services, and psychological and social work services. 1194-1195

623110 **Nursing Care Facilities (Skilled Nursing Facilities).** This industry comprises establishments primarily engaged in providing inpatient nursing and rehabilitative services. The care is generally provided for an extended period of time to individuals requiring nursing care. These establishments have a permanent core staff of registered or licensed practical nurses who, along with other staff, provide nursing and continuous personal care services. 1196-1197

623210 **Residential Intellectual and Developmental Disability Facilities.** This industry comprises establishments (e.g. group homes, hospitals, intermediate care facilities) primarily engaged in providing residential care services for persons diagnosed with mental retardation. These facilities may provide some health care, though the focus is on room, board, protective supervision, and counseling. 1198-1199

623220 **Residential Mental Health and Substance Abuse Facilities.** This industry comprises establishments primarily engaged in providing residential care and treatment for patients with mental health and substance abuse illnesses. These establishments provide room, board, supervision, and counseling services. Although medical services may be available at these establishments, they are incidental to the counseling, mental rehabilitation, and support services offered. These establishments generally provide a wide range of social services in addition to counseling. ... 1200-1201

HEALTH CARE

NAICS #		Page

623311 **Continuing Care Retirement Communities.** This U.S. industry comprises establishments primarily engaged in providing a range of residential and personal care services with on-site nursing care facilities for (1) the elderly and other persons who are unable to fully care for themselves and/or (2) the elderly and other persons who do not desire to live independently. Individuals live in a variety of residential settings with meals, housekeeping, social, leisure, and other services available to assist residents in daily living. Assistedliving facilities with on-site nursing care facilities are included in this industry. 1202-1203

623312 **Assisted Living Facilities for the Elderly.** This U.S. industry comprises establishments primarily engaged in providing residential and personal care services (i.e., without on-site nursing care facilities) for (1) the elderly or other persons who are unable to fully care for themselves and/or (2) the elderly or other persons who do not desire to live independently. The care typically includes room, board, supervision, and assistance in daily living, such as housekeeping services. 1204-1205

623990 **Other Residential Care Facilities.** This industry comprises establishments primarily engaged in providing residential care (except residential mental retardation facilities, residential health and substance abuse facilities, continuing care retirement communities, and homes for the elderly). These establishments also provide supervision and personal care services. 1206-1207

624110 **Child and Youth Services.** This industry comprises establishments primarily engaged in providing nonresidential social assistance services for children and youth. These establishments provide for the welfare of children in such areas as adoption and foster care, drug prevention, life skills training, and positive social development. 1208-1209

624120 **Services for the Elderly and Persons with Disabilities.** This industry comprises establishments primarily engaged in providing nonresidential social assistance services to improve the quality of life for the elderly, persons diagnosed with mental retardation, or persons with disabilities. These establishments provide for the welfare of these individuals in such areas as day care, nonmedical home care or homemaker services, social activities, group support, and companionship. 1210-1211

624190 **Other Individual and Family Services.** This industry comprises establishments primarily engaged in providing nonresidential individual and family social assistance services (except those specifically directed toward children, the elderly, persons diagnosed with mental retardation, or persons with disabilities). 1212-1213

624210 **Community Food Services.** This industry comprises establishments primarily engaged in the collection, preparation, and delivery of food for the needy. Establishments in this industry may also distribute clothing and blankets to the poor. These establishments may prepare and deliver meals to persons who by reason of age, disability, or illness are unable to prepare meals for themselves; collect and distribute salvageable or donated food; or prepare and provide meals at fixed or mobile locations. Food banks, meal delivery programs, and soup kitchens are included in this industry. 1214-1215

624221 **Temporary Shelters.** This U.S. industry comprises establishments primarily engaged in providing (1) short term emergency shelter for victims of domestic violence, sexual assault, or child abuse and/or (2) temporary residential shelter for homeless individuals or families, runaway youth, and patients and families caught in medical crises. These establishments may operate their own shelters or may subsidize housing using existing homes, apartments, hotels, or motels. 1216-1217

624229 **Other Community Housing Services.** This U.S. industry comprises establishments primarily engaged in providing one or more of the following community housing services: (1) transitional housing to low-income individuals and families; (2) volunteer construction or repair of lowcost housing, in partnership with the homeowner who may assist in the construction or repair work; and (3) the repair of homes for elderly or disabled homeowners. These establishments may subsidize housing using existing homes, apartments, hotels, or motels or may require a low-cost mortgage or sweat equity. These establishments may also provide low-income families with furniture and household supplies. 1218-1219

ENTERTAINMENT

NAICS #		Page

624310 **Vocational Rehabilitation Services.** This industry comprises (1) establishments primarily engaged in providing vocational rehabilitation or habilitation services, such as job counseling, job training, and work experience, to unemployed and underemployed persons, persons with disabilities, and persons who have a job market disadvantage because of lack of education, job skill, or experience and (2) establishments primarily engaged in providing training and employment to persons with disabilities. Vocational rehabilitation job training facilities (except schools) and sheltered workshops (i.e., work experience centers) are included in this industry. 1220-1221

624410 **Child Care Services.** This industry comprises establishments primarily engaged in providing day care of infants or children. These establishments generally care for preschool children, but may care for older children when they are not in school and may also offer prekindergarten educational programs. 1222-1223

ARTS, ENTERTAINMENT, AND RECREATION

711110 **Theater Companies and Dinner Theaters.** This industry comprises (1) companies, groups, or theaters primarily engaged in producing the following live theatrical presentations: musicals; operas; plays; and comedy, improvisational, mime, and puppet shows and (2) establishments, commonly known as dinner theaters, engaged in producing live theatrical productions and in providing food and beverages for consumption on the premises. Theater groups or companies may or may not operate their own theater or other facility for staging their shows. 1226-1227

711211 **Sports Teams and Clubs.** This U.S. industry comprises professional or semiprofessional sports teams or clubs primarily engaged in participating in live sporting events, such as baseball, basketball, football, hockey, soccer, and jai alai games, before a paying audience. These establishments may or may not operate their own arena, stadium, or other facility for presenting these events. 1228-1229

711310 **Promoters of Performing Arts, Sports, and Similar Events with Facilities.** This industry comprises establishments primarily engaged in (1) organizing, promoting, and/or managing live performing arts productions, sports events, and similar events, such as state fairs, county fairs, agricultural fairs, concerts, and festivals, held in facilities that they manage and operate and/or (2) managing and providing the staff to operate arenas, stadiums, theaters, or other related facilities for rent to other promoters. 1230-1231

711510 **Independent Artists, Writers, and Performers.** This industry comprises independent (i.e., freelance) individuals primarily engaged in performing in artistic productions, in creating artistic and cultural works or productions, or in providing technical expertise necessary for these productions. This industry also includes athletes and other celebrities exclusively engaged in endorsing products and making speeches or public appearances for which they receive a fee. ... 1232-1233

712110 **Museums.** This industry comprises establishments primarily engaged in the preservation and exhibition of objects of historical, cultural, and/or educational value. 1234-1235

712130 **Zoos and Botanical Gardens.** This industry comprises establishments primarily engaged in the preservation and exhibition of live plant and animal life displays. 1236-1237

713110 **Amusement and Theme Parks.** This industry comprises establishments, known as amusement or theme parks, primarily engaged in operating a variety of attractions, such as mechanical rides, water rides, games, shows, theme exhibits, refreshment stands, and picnic grounds. These establishments may lease space to others on a concession basis. 1238-1239

713210 **Casinos (except Casino Hotels).** This industry comprises establishments primarily engaged in operating gambling facilities that offer table wagering games along with other gambling activities, such as slot machines and sports betting. These establishments often provide food and beverage services. Included in this industry are floating casinos (i.e., gambling cruises, riverboat casinos). 1240-1241

713290 **Other Gambling Industries.** This industry comprises establishments primarily engaged in operating gambling facilities (except casinos or casino hotels) or providing gambling services. ... 1242-1243

713910 **Golf Courses and Country Clubs.** This industry comprises (1) establishments primarily engaged in operating golf courses (except miniature) and (2) establishments primarily engaged in operating golf courses, along with dining facilities and other recreational facilities that are known as country clubs. These establishments often provide food and beverage services, equipment rental services, and golf instruction services. 1244-1245

RESTAURANT/LODGING

NAICS #   Page

713920   **Skiing Facilities.** This industry comprises establishments primarily engaged in (1) operating downhill, cross-country, or related skiing areas and/or (2) operating equipment, such as ski lifts and tows. These establishments often provide food and beverage services, equipment rental services, and ski instruction services. Four season resorts without accommodations are included in this industry. ... 1246-1247

713930   **Marinas.** This industry comprises establishments, commonly known as marinas, engaged in operating docking and/or storage facilities for pleasure craft owners, with or without one or more related activities, such as retailing fuel and marine supplies; and repairing, maintaining, or renting pleasure boats. ... 1248-1249

713940   **Fitness and Recreational Sports Centers.** This industry comprises establishments primarily engaged in operating fitness and recreational sports facilities featuring exercise and other active physical fitness conditioning or recreational sports activities, such as swimming, skating, or racquet sports. ... 1250-1251

713950   **Bowling Centers.** This industry comprises establishments engaged in operating bowling centers. These establishments often provide food and beverage services. ... 1252-1253

713990   **All Other Amusement and Recreation Industries.** This industry comprises establishments (except amusement parks and arcades; gambling industries; golf courses and country clubs; skiing facilities; marinas; fitness and recreational sports centers; and bowling centers) primarily engaged in providing recreational and amusement services. ... 1254-1255

ACCOMMODATION AND FOOD SERVICES

721110   **Hotels (except Casino Hotels) and Motels.** This industry comprises establishments primarily engaged in providing short-term lodging in facilities known as hotels, motor hotels, resort hotels, and motels. The establishments in this industry may offer food and beverage services, recreational services, conference rooms and convention services, laundry services, parking, and other services. ... 1258-1259

721120   **Casino Hotels.** This industry comprises establishments primarily engaged in providing short-term lodging in hotel facilities with a casino on the premises. The casino on premises includes table wagering games and may include other gambling activities, such as slot machines and sports betting. These establishments generally offer a range of services and amenities, such as food and beverage services, entertainment, valet parking, swimming pools, and conference and convention facilities. ... 1260-1261

721191   **Bed-and-Breakfast Inns.** This U.S. industry comprises establishments primarily engaged in providing short-term lodging in facilities known as bed-and-breakfast inns. These establishments provide short-term lodging in private homes or small buildings converted for this purpose. Bed-and-breakfast inns are characterized by a highly personalized service and inclusion of a full breakfast in a room rate. ... 1262-1263

721199   **All Other Traveler Accommodation.** This U.S. industry comprises establishments primarily engaged in providing short-term lodging (except hotels, motels, casino hotels, and bed-and-breakfast inns). ... 1264-1265

721211   **RV (Recreational Vehicle) Parks and Campgrounds.** This U.S. industry comprises establishments primarily engaged in operating sites to accommodate campers and their equipment, including tents, tent trailers, travel trailers, and RVs (recreational vehicles). These establishments may provide access to facilities, such as washrooms, laundry rooms, recreation halls and playgrounds, stores, and snack bars. ... 1266-1267

721214   **Recreational and Vacation Camps (except Campgrounds).** This U.S. industry comprises establishments primarily engaged in operating overnight recreational camps, such as children's camps, family vacation camps, hunting and fishing camps, and outdoor adventure retreats that offer trail riding, white-water rafting, hiking, and similar activities. These establishments provide accommodation facilities, such as cabins and fixed campsites, and other amenities, such as food services, recreational facilities and equipment, and organized recreational activities. ... 1268-1269

OTHER SERVICES

NAICS #		Page

721310 **Rooming and Boarding Houses, Dormitories, and Workers' Camps.** This industry comprises establishments primarily engaged in operating rooming and boarding houses and similar facilities, such as fraternity houses, sorority houses, off-campus dormitories, residential clubs, and workers' camps. These establishments provide temporary or longer-term accommodations which, for the period of occupancy, may serve as a principal residence. These establishments also may provide complementary services, such as housekeeping, meals, and laundry services. 1270-1271

722310 **Food Service Contractors.** This industry comprises establishments primarily engaged in providing food services at institutional, governmental, commercial, or industrial locations of others based on contractual arrangements with these type of organizations for a specified period of time. The establishments of this industry provide food services for the convenience of the contracting organization or the contracting organization's customers. The contractual arrangement of these establishments with contracting organizations may vary from type of facility operated (e.g., cafeteria, restaurant, fast-food eating place), revenue sharing, cost structure, to providing personnel. Management staff is always provided by the food service contractors. . . . 1272-1273

722320 **Caterers.** This industry comprises establishments primarily engaged in providing single event-based food services. These establishments generally have equipment and vehicles to transport meals and snacks to events and/or prepare food at an off-premise site. Banquet halls with catering staff are included in this industry. Examples of events catered by establishments of this industry are graduation parties, wedding receptions, business or retirement luncheons, and trade shows. 1274-1275

722410 **Drinking Places (Alcoholic Beverages).** This industry comprises establishments known as bars, taverns, nightclubs, or drinking places primarily engaged in preparing and serving alcoholic beverages for immediate consumption. These establishments may also provide limited food services. 1276-1277

722511 **Full-Service Restaurants.** This U.S. industry comprises establishments primarily engaged in providing food services to patrons who order and are served while seated (i.e., waiter/waitress service) and pay after eating. These establishments may provide this type of food service to patrons in combination with selling alcoholic beverages, providing carryout services, or presenting live nontheatrical entertainment. 1278-1279

722513 **Limited-Service Restaurants.** This U.S. industry comprises establishments primarily engaged in providing food services (except snack and nonalcoholic beverage bars) where patrons generally order or select items and pay before eating. Food and drink may be consumed on premises, taken out, or delivered to the customer's location. Some establishments in this industry may provide these food services in combination with selling alcoholic beverages. 1280-1281

722515 **Snack and Nonalcoholic Beverage Bars.** This U.S. industry comprises establishments primarily engaged in (1) preparing and/or serving a specialty snack, such as ice cream, frozen yogurt, cookies, or popcorn or (2) serving nonalcoholic beverages, such as coffee, juices, or sodas for consumption on or near the premises. These establishments may carry and sell a combination of snack, nonalcoholic beverage, and other related products (e.g., coffee beans, mugs, coffee makers) but generally promote and sell a unique snack or nonalcoholic beverage. 1282-1283

OTHER SERVICES (EXCEPT PUBLIC ADMINISTRATION)

811111 **General Automotive Repair.** This U.S. industry comprises establishments primarily engaged in providing (1) a wide range of mechanical and electrical repair and maintenance services for automotive vehicles, such as passenger cars, trucks, and vans, and all trailers or (2) engine repair and replacement. 1286-1287

811114 **Specialized Automotive Repair.** This U.S. industry comprises establishments primarily engaged in providing specialized mechanical or electrical repair and maintenance services (except engine repair and replacement) for automotive vehicles, such as passenger cars, trucks, and vans, and all trailers. 1288-1289

811121 **Automotive Body, Paint, and Interior Repair and Maintenance.** This U.S. industry comprises establishments primarily engaged in repairing or customizing automotive vehicles, such as passenger cars, trucks, and vans, and all trailer bodies and interiors; and/or painting automotive vehicles and trailer bodies. 1290-1291

OTHER SERVICES

NAICS #		Page

811191 **Automotive Oil Change and Lubrication Shops.** This U.S. industry comprises establishments primarily engaged in changing motor oil and lubricating the chassis of automotive vehicles, such as passenger cars, trucks, and vans. 1292-1293

811192 **Car Washes.** This U.S. industry comprises establishments primarily engaged in cleaning, washing, and/or waxing automotive vehicles, such as passenger cars, trucks, and vans, and trailers. 1294-1295

811198 **All Other Automotive Repair and Maintenance.** This U.S. industry comprises establishments primarily engaged in providing automotive repair and maintenance services (except mechanical and electrical repair and maintenance; body, paint, interior, and glass repair; motor oil change and lubrication; and car washing) for automotive vehicles, such as passenger cars, trucks, and vans, and all trailers. 1296-1297

811210 **Electronic and Precision Equipment Repair and Maintenance.** This industry comprises establishments primarily engaged in repairing and maintaining one or more of the following: (1) consumer electronic equipment; (2) computers; (3) office machines; (4) communication equipment; and (5) other electronic and precision equipment and instruments, without retailing these products as new. Establishments in this industry repair items, such as microscopes, radar and sonar equipment, televisions, stereos, video recorders, computers, fax machines, photocopying machines, two-way radios, cellular telephones, and other communications equipment, scientific instruments, and medical equipment. 1298-1299

811310 **Commercial and Industrial Machinery and Equipment (except Automotive and Electronic) Repair and Maintenance.** This industry comprises establishments primarily engaged in the repair and maintenance of commercial and industrial machinery and equipment. Establishments in this industry either sharpen/install commercial and industrial machinery blades and saws or provide welding (e.g., automotive, general) repair services; or repair agricultural and other heavy and industrial machinery and equipment (e.g., forklifts and other materials handling equipment, machine tools, commercial refrigeration equipment, construction equipment, and mining machinery). 1300-1301

811490 **Other Personal and Household Goods Repair and Maintenance.** This industry comprises establishments primarily engaged in repairing and servicing personal or household-type goods without retailing new personal and household-type goods (except home and garden equipment, appliances, furniture, and footwear and leather goods). Establishments in this industry repair items, such as garments; watches; jewelry; musical instruments; bicycles and motorcycles; motorboats, canoes, sailboats, and other recreational boats. 1302-1303

812112 **Beauty Salons.** This U.S. industry comprises establishments (except those known as barber shops or men's hair stylist shops) primarily engaged in one or more of the following: (1) cutting, trimming, shampooing, weaving, coloring, waving, or styling hair; (2) providing facials; and (3) applying makeup (except permanent makeup). 1304-1305

812199 **Other Personal Care Services.** This U.S. industry comprises establishments primarily engaged in providing personal care services (except hair, nail, facial, nonpermanent makeup, or nonmedical diet and weight reducing services). 1306-1307

812210 **Funeral Homes and Funeral Services.** This industry comprises establishments primarily engaged in preparing the dead for burial or interment and conducting funerals (i.e., providing facilities for wakes, arranging transportation for the dead, selling caskets and related merchandise). Funeral homes combined with crematories are included in this industry. 1308-1309

812310 **Coin-Operated Laundries and Drycleaners.** This industry comprises (1) establishments primarily engaged in operating facili-ties with coin-operated or similar self-service laundry and drycleaning equipment for customer use on the premises and (2) establishments primarily engaged in supplying and servicing coin-operated or similar self-service laundry and drycleaning equipment for customer use in places of business operated by others, such as apartments and dormitories. 1310-1311

812320 **Drycleaning and Laundry Services (except Coin-Operated).** This industry comprises establishments primarily engaged in one or more of the following: (1) providing drycleaning services (except coin-operated); (2) providing laundering services (except linen and uniform supply or coin-operated); (3) providing dropoff and pickup sites for laundries and/or drycleaners; and (4) providing specialty cleaning services for specific types of garments and other textile items (except carpets and upholstery), such as fur, leather, or suede garments; wedding gowns; hats; draperies; and pillows. These establishments may provide all, a combination of, or none of the cleaning services on the premises. 1312-1313

OTHER SERVICES

NAICS #		Page
812331	**Linen Supply.** This U.S. industry comprises establishments primarily engaged in supplying, on a rental or contract basis, laundered items, such as table and bed linens; towels; diapers; and uniforms, gowns, or coats of the type used by doctors, nurses, barbers, beauticians, and waitresses.	1314-1315
812910	**Pet Care (except Veterinary) Services.** This industry comprises establishments primarily engaged in providing pet care services (except veterinary), such as boarding, grooming, sitting, and training pets.	1316-1317
812930	**Parking Lots and Garages.** This industry comprises establishments primarily engaged in providing parking space for motor vehicles, usually on an hourly, daily, or monthly basis and/or valet parking services.	1318-1319
812990	**All Other Personal Services.** This industry comprises establishments primarily engaged in providing personal services (except personal care services, death care services, drycleaning and laundry services, pet care services, photofinishing services, or parking space and/or valet parking services).	1320-1321
813110	**Religious Organizations.** This industry comprises (1) establishments primarily engaged in operating reli-gious organizations, such as churches, religious temples, and monasteries and/or (2) establishments primarily engaged in administering an organized religion or promoting religious activities.	1322-1323
813211	**Grantmaking Foundations.** This U.S. industry comprises establishments known as grantmaking foundations or charitable trusts. Establishments in this industry award grants from trust funds based on a competitive selection process or the preferences of the foundation managers and grantors; or fund a single entity, such as a museum or university.	1324-1325
813212	**Voluntary Health Organizations.** This U.S. industry comprises establishments primarily engaged in raising funds for health related research, such as disease (e.g., heart, cancer, diabetes) prevention, health education, and patient services.	1326-1327
813219	**Other Grantmaking and Giving Services.** This U.S. industry comprises establishments (except voluntary health organizations) primarily engaged in raising funds for a wide range of social welfare activities, such as educational, scientific, cultural, and health.	1328-1329
813312	**Environment, Conservation and Wildlife Organizations.** This U.S. industry comprises establishments primarily engaged in promoting the preservation and protection of the environment and wildlife. Establishments in this industry address issues, such as clean air and water; global warming; conserving and developing natural resources, including land, plant, water, and energy resources; and protecting and preserving wildlife and endangered species. These organizations may solicit contributions and offer memberships to support these causes.	1330-1331
813319	**Other Social Advocacy Organizations.** This U.S. industry comprises establishments primarily engaged in social advocacy (except human rights and environmental protection, conservation, and wildlife preservation). Establishments in this industry address issues, such as peace and international understanding; community action (excluding civic organizations); or advancing social causes, such as firearms safety, drunk driving prevention, drug abuse awareness. These organizations may solicit contributions and offer memberships to support these causes.	1332-1333
813410	**Civic and Social Organizations.** This industry comprises establishments primarily engaged in promoting the civic and social interests of their members. Establishments in this industry may operate bars and restaurants for their members.	1334-1335
813910	**Business Associations.** This industry comprises establishments primarily engaged in promoting the business interests of their members. These establishments may conduct research on new products and services; develop market statistics; sponsor quality and certification standards; lobby public officials; or publish newsletters, books, or periodicals for distribution to their members.	1336-1337
813920	**Professional Organizations.** This industry comprises establishments primarily engaged in promoting the professional interests of their members and the profession as a whole. These establishments may conduct research; develop statistics; sponsor quality and certi-fication standards; lobby public officials; or publish newsletters, books, or periodicals for distribution to their members.	1338-1339
813930	**Labor Unions and Similar Labor Organizations.** This industry comprises establishments primarily engaged in promoting the interests of organized labor and union employees.	1340-1341

PUBLIC ADMINISTRATION

NAICS #		Page
813990	**Other Similar Organizations (except Business, Professional, Labor, and Political Organizations).** This industry comprises establishments (except religious organizations, social advocacy organizations, civic and social organizations, business associations, professional organizations, labor unions, and political organizations) primarily engaged in promoting the interest of their members.	1342-1343

PUBLIC ADMINISTRATION

921110	**Executive Offices.** This industry comprises government establishments serving as offices of chief executives and their advisory committees and commissions. This industry includes offices of the president, governors, and mayors, in addition to executive advisory commissions.	1346-1347
921120	**Legislative Bodies.** This industry comprises government establishments serving as legislative bodies and their advisory committees and commissions. Included in this industry are legislative bodies, such as Congress, state legislatures, and advisory and study legislative commissions.	1348-1349
921130	**Public Finance Activities.** This industry comprises government establishments primarily engaged in public finance, taxation and monetary policy. Included are financial administration activities, such as monetary policy; tax administration and collection; custody and disbursement of funds; debt and investment administration; auditing activities; and government employee retirement trust fund administration.	1350-1351
921140	**Executive and Legislative Offices, Combined.** This industry comprises government establishments serving as councils and boards of commissioners or supervisors and such bodies where the chief executive (e.g., county executive or city mayor) is a member of the legislative body (e.g., county or city council) itself.	1352-1353
921190	**Other General Government Support.** This industry comprises government establishments primarily engaged in providing general support for government. Such support services include personnel services, election boards, and other general government support establishments that are not classified elsewhere in public administration.	1354-1355
922160	**Fire Protection.** This industry comprises government establishments primarily engaged in fire fighting and other related fire protection activities. Government establishments providing combined fire protection and ambulance or rescue services are classified in this industry.	1356-1357
923110	**Administration of Education Programs.** This industry comprises government establishments primarily engaged in the central coordination, planning, supervision and administration of funds, policies, intergovernmental activities, statistical reports and data collection, and centralized programs for educational administration. Government scholarship programs are included in this industry.	1358-1359
923120	**Administration of Public Health Programs.** This industry comprises government establishments primarily engaged in the planning, administration, and coordination of public health programs and services, including environmental health activities, mental health, categorical health programs, health statistics, and immunization services. Government establishments primarily engaged in conducting public health-related inspections are included in this industry.	1360-1361
925110	**Administration of Housing Programs.** This industry comprises government establishments primarily engaged in the administration and planning of housing programs.	1362-1363
925120	**Administration of Urban Planning and Community and Rural Development.** This industry comprises government establishments primarily engaged in the administration and planning of the development of urban and rural areas. Included in this industry are government zoning boards and commissions.	1364-1365
926110	**Administration of General Economic Programs.** This industry comprises government establishments primarily engaged in the administration, promotion and development of economic resources, including business, industry, and tourism. Included in this industry are government establishments responsible for the development of general statistical data and analyses and promotion of the general economic well-being of the governed area.	1366-1367

CONSTRUCTION—PERCENTAGE OF COMPLETION

NAICS #		Page
236115	**New Single-Family Housing Construction (except For-Sale Builders).** This U.S. industry comprises general contractor establishments primarily responsible for the entire construction of new single-family housing, such as single-family detached houses and town houses or row houses where each housing unit (1) is separated from its neighbors by a ground-to-roof wall and (2) has no housing units constructed above or below. This industry includes general contractors respon-sible for the on-site assembly of modular and prefabricated houses. Single-family housing design-build firms and single-family construction management firms acting as general contractors are included in this industry.	1370
236116	**New Multifamily Housing Construction (except For-Sale Builders).** This U.S. industry comprises general contractor establishments responsible for the construction of new multifamily residential housing units (e.g., high-rise, garden, and town house apartments and condominiums where each unit is not separated from its neighbors by a ground-to-roof wall). Multifamily design-build firms and multifamily housing construction management firms acting as general contractors are included in this industry.	1371
236117	**New Housing For-Sale Builders.** This U.S. industry comprises operative builders primarily responsible for the entire construction of new houses and other residential buildings, single-family and multifamily, on their own account for sale. Operative builders are also known as speculative or merchant builders.	1372
236118	**Residential Remodelers.** This U.S. industry comprises establishments primarily responsible for the remodeling construction (including additions, alterations, reconstruction, maintenance and repair work) of houses and other residential buildings, single-family and multifamily. Included in this industry are remodeling general contractors, operative remodelers, remodeling design-build firms, and remodeling project construction management firms.	1373
236210	**Industrial Building Construction.** This industry comprises establishments primarily responsible for the construction (including new work, additions, alterations, maintenance, and repairs) of industrial buildings (except warehouses). The construction of selected additional structures, whose production processes are similar to those for industrial buildings (e.g., incinerators, cement plants, blast furnaces, and similar nonbuilding structures), is included in this industry. Included in this industry are industrial building general contractors, industrial building operative builders, industrial building design-build firms, and industrial building construction management firms.	1374
236220	**Commercial and Institutional Building Construction.** This industry comprises establishments primarily responsible for the construction (including new work, additions, alterations, maintenance, and repairs) of commercial and institutional buildings and related structures, such as stadiums, grain elevators, and indoor swimming pools. This industry includes establishments responsible for the on-site assembly of modular or prefabricated commercial and institutional buildings. Included in this industry are commercial and institutional building general contractors, commercial and institutional building operative builders, commercial and institutional building design-build firms, and commercial and institutional building project construction management firms.	1375
237110	**Water and Sewer Line and Related Structures Construction.** This industry comprises establishments primarily engaged in the construction of water and sewer lines, mains, pumping stations, treatment plants and storage tanks. The work performed may include new work, reconstruction, rehabilitation, and repairs. Specialty trade contractors are included in this group if they are engaged in activities primarily related to water and sewer line and related structures construction. All structures (including buildings) that are integral parts of water and sewer networks (e.g., storage tanks, pumping stations, water treatment plants, and sewage treatment plants) are included in this industry.	1376
237130	**Power and Communication Line and Related Structures Construction.** This industry comprises establishments primarily engaged in the construction of oil and gas lines, mains, refineries, and storage tanks. The work performed may include new work, reconstruction, rehabilitation, and repairs. Specialty trade contractors are included in this group if they are engaged in activities primarily related to oil and gas pipeline and related structures construction. All structures (including buildings) that are integral parts of oil and gas networks (e.g., storage tanks, pumping stations, and refineries) are included in this industry.	1377

CONSTRUCTION-% OF COMPLETION

NAICS #		Page
237310	**Highway, Street, and Bridge Construction.** This industry comprises establishments primarily engaged in the construction of highways (including elevated), streets, roads, airport runways, public sidewalks, or bridges. The work performed may include new work, reconstruction, rehabilitation, and repairs. Specialty trade contractors are included in this group if they are engaged in activities primarily related to highway, street, and bridge construction (e.g., installing guardrails on highways).	1378
237990	**Other Heavy and Civil Engineering Construction.** This industry comprises establishments primarily engaged in heavy and engineering construction projects (excluding highway, street, bridge, and distribution line construction). The work performed may include new work, reconstruction, rehabilitation, and repairs. Specialty trade contractors are included in this group if they are engaged in activities primarily related to engineering construction projects (excluding highway, street, bridge, distribution line, oil and gas structure, and utilities building and structure construction). Construction projects involving water resources (e.g., dredging and land drainage), development of marine facilities, and projects involving open space improvement (e.g., parks and trails) are included in this industry.	1379
238110	**Poured Concrete Foundation and Structure Contractors.** This industry comprises establishments primarily engaged in pouring and finishing concrete foundations and structural elements. This industry also includes establishments performing grout and shotcrete work. The work performed may include new work, additions, alterations, maintenance, and repairs.	1380
238120	**Structural Steel and Precast Concrete Contractors.** This industry comprises establishments primarily engaged in: (1) erecting and assembling structural parts made from steel or precast concrete (e.g., steel beams, structural steel components, and similar products of precast concrete); and/or (2) assembling and installing other steel construction products (e.g., steel rods, bars, rebar, mesh, and cages) to reinforce poured-in-place concrete. The work performed may include new work, additions, alterations, maintenance, and repairs.	1381
238150	**Glass and Glazing Contractors.** This industry comprises establishments primarily engaged in installing glass panes in prepared openings (i.e., glazing work) and other glass work for buildings. The work performed may include new work, additions, alterations, maintenance, and repairs.	1382
238160	**Roofing Contractors.** This industry comprises establishments primarily engaged in roofing. This industry also includes establishments treating roofs (i.e., spraying, painting, or coating) and installing skylights. The work performed may include new work, additions, alterations, maintenance, and repairs.	1383
238210	**Electrical Contractors and Other Wiring Installation Contractors.** This industry comprises establishments primarily engaged in installing and servicing electrical wiring and equipment. Electrical contractors included in this industry may include both the parts and labor when performing work. Electrical contractors may perform new work, additions, alterations, maintenance, and repairs.	1384
238220	**Plumbing, Heating, and Air-Conditioning Contractors.** This industry comprises establishments primarily engaged in installing and servicing plumbing, heating, and air-conditioning equipment. Contractors in this industry may provide both parts and labor when performing work. The work performed may include new work, additions, alterations, maintenance, and repairs.	1385
238310	**Drywall and Insulation Contractors.** This industry comprises establishments primarily engaged in drywall, plaster work, and building insulation work. Plaster work includes applying plain or ornamental plaster, and installation of lath to receive plaster. The work performed may include new work, additions, alterations, maintenance, and repairs.	1386
238330	**Flooring Contractors.** This industry comprises establishments primarily engaged in the installation of resilient floor tile, carpeting, linoleum, and hard wood flooring. The work performed may include new work, additions, alterations, maintenance, and repairs.	1387
238910	**Site Preparation Contractors.** This industry comprises establishments primarily engaged in site preparation activities, such as excavating and grading, demolition of buildings and other structures, septic system installation, and house moving. Earth moving and land clearing for all types of sites (e.g., building, nonbuilding, mining) is included in this industry. Establishments primarily engaged in construction equipment rental with operator (except cranes) are also included.	1388

CONSTRUCTION-% OF COMPLETION

NAICS #		Page
238990	**All Other Specialty Trade Contractors.** This industry comprises establishments primarily engaged in specialized trades (except foundation, structure, and building exterior contractors; building equipment contractors; building finishing contractors; and site preparation contractors). The specialty trade work performed includes new work, additions, alterations, maintenance, and repairs.	1389

AGRICULTURE, FORESTRY, FISHING AND HUNTING

AGRICULTURE—Soybean Farming NAICS 111110

Current Data Sorted by Assets | **Comparative Historical Data**

0-500M	500M-2MM	2-10MM	10-50MM	50-100MM	100-250MM	Type of Statement		4/1/19-3/31/20 ALL	4/1/20-3/31/21 ALL
						Unqualified		8	16
		2	1	3		Reviewed		2	7
		2		1		Compiled		5	6
4	4	1		1		Tax Returns		16	34
4	6	13	7	2	2	Other		48	76
	11 (4/1-9/30/23)		42 (10/1/23-3/31/24)			NUMBER OF STATEMENTS		79	139
8	10	18	8	7	2				
%	%	%	%	%	%	ASSETS		%	%
	17.2	24.1				Cash & Equivalents		9.2	22.9
	4.2	16.6				Trade Receivables (net)		14.0	13.5
	2.8	16.3				Inventory		10.2	12.7
	16.1	5.3				All Other Current		8.5	5.3
	40.2	62.3				Total Current		41.9	54.4
	53.7	31.5				Fixed Assets (net)		45.4	31.4
	.0	2.0				Intangibles (net)		2.9	6.1
	6.0	4.1				All Other Non-Current		9.7	8.1
	100.0	100.0				Total		100.0	100.0
						LIABILITIES			
	47.1	7.4				Notes Payable-Short Term		11.8	8.2
	1.5	3.0				Cur. Mat.-L.T.D.		7.8	4.5
	3.4	7.4				Trade Payables		8.5	8.9
	.0	.0				Income Taxes Payable		.1	.1
	15.0	22.0				All Other Current		13.9	19.4
	67.0	39.8				Total Current		42.2	41.0
	60.1	28.2				Long-Term Debt		29.1	20.4
	.0	.0				Deferred Taxes		.2	.0
	3.6	1.5				All Other Non-Current		3.7	4.3
	-30.6	30.5				Net Worth		24.8	34.3
	100.0	100.0				Total Liabilities & Net Worth		100.0	100.0
						INCOME DATA			
	100.0	100.0				Net Sales		100.0	100.0
						Gross Profit			
	91.3	95.2				Operating Expenses		87.5	89.9
	8.7	4.8				Operating Profit		12.5	10.1
	6.6	1.2				All Other Expenses (net)		2.8	.9
	2.1	3.7				Profit Before Taxes		9.7	9.2
						RATIOS			
	3.9	2.9						2.9	3.9
	.4	1.8				Current		1.1	1.9
	.1	1.0						.5	1.1
	3.3	2.0						1.6	2.6
	.2	1.1				Quick		.5	1.2
	.0	.1						.2	.5
0	UND	0	UND				0	UND	0	UND
0	UND	8	45.3			Sales/Receivables	17	22.0	18	19.8
15	24.3	42	8.7				60	6.1	43	8.5
						Cost of Sales/Inventory			
						Cost of Sales/Payables			
	10.9	3.9						6.1	3.6
	-4.9	9.9				Sales/Working Capital		33.7	7.3
	-1.8	NM						-5.4	38.0
		17.6						10.4	26.1
	(13)	1.2				EBIT/Interest	(65)	3.7	(108)	5.7
		-.6						1.1	1.8
						Net Profit + Depr., Dep., Amort./Cur. Mat. L/T/D			8.0
								(12)	3.9
									1.0
	.4	.0						.5	.1
	8.4	.6				Fixed/Worth		1.2	.7
	-.9	NM						-12.6	2.2
	1.5	.7						.6	.6
	NM	1.6				Debt/Worth		2.7	1.3
	-1.8	NM						-19.9	5.5
		57.8				% Profit Before Taxes/Tangible Net Worth		59.9	50.3
	(14)	19.3					(57)	23.6	(117)	24.3
		8.2						4.5	4.7
	60.3	16.6				% Profit Before Taxes/Total Assets		15.5	22.7
	-.2	6.9						5.2	7.3
	-13.8	-.9						.3	.9
	47.4	109.2						19.1	66.5
	2.7	19.9				Sales/Net Fixed Assets		3.9	9.2
	.3	1.8						1.2	2.3
	4.6	2.9						3.2	2.8
	1.3	1.9				Sales/Total Assets		1.2	1.7
	.3	.6						.6	.7
		.3						1.3	.8
	(11)	.6				% Depr., Dep., Amort./Sales	(56)	3.6	(94)	3.4
		15.9						9.3	7.9
						% Officers', Directors' Owners' Comp/Sales		1.2	1.1
							(17)	2.1	(43)	3.8
								5.7	8.0
24539M	27847M	618576M	234698M	853589M	315233M	Net Sales ($)		2597923M	3785323M
1728M	12460M	89866M	169481M	431175M	224478M	Total Assets ($)		1617524M	3286186M

M = $ thousand   MM = $ million
See Pages viii through xx for Explanation of Ratios and Data

© RMA 2024

AGRICULTURE—Soybean Farming NAICS 111110

Comparative Historical Data | Current Data Sorted by Sales

						Type of Statement						
		15		8		4	Unqualified			1		3
		7		1		3	Reviewed		1			2
		2		3		2	Compiled		1	1		
		25		17		10	Tax Returns	2	5	3		
		52		38		34	Other	4	4	4	3	9	10
		4/1/21-3/31/22 ALL		4/1/22-3/31/23 ALL		4/1/23-3/31/24 ALL			11 (4/1-9/30/23)			42 (10/1/23-3/31/24)	
								0-1MM	1-3MM	3-5MM	5-10MM	10-25MM	25MM & OVER
		101		67		53	NUMBER OF STATEMENTS	6	11	7	5	9	15
		%		%		%	ASSETS	%	%	%	%	%	%
		20.9		17.9		23.3	Cash & Equivalents		24.5				23.3
		12.3		14.4		12.5	Trade Receivables (net)		8.6				20.9
		11.3		11.8		10.7	Inventory		1.7				14.9
		4.0		6.6		8.2	All Other Current		10.7				6.0
		48.5		50.7		54.8	Total Current		45.5				65.1
		37.4		27.9		32.9	Fixed Assets (net)		45.2				14.7
		5.0		8.8		5.6	Intangibles (net)		.0				13.3
		9.1		12.5		6.7	All Other Non-Current		9.3				6.9
		100.0		100.0		100.0	Total		100.0				100.0
							LIABILITIES						
		8.6		16.1		22.1	Notes Payable-Short Term		37.6				1.7
		4.9		3.7		4.5	Cur. Mat.-L.T.D.		3.6				8.7
		8.1		7.9		6.3	Trade Payables		1.1				8.5
		.1		.0		.4	Income Taxes Payable		.0				1.0
		18.5		16.8		21.3	All Other Current		6.9				22.2
		40.2		44.4		54.6	Total Current		49.2				42.1
		35.0		20.9		41.8	Long-Term Debt		39.7				9.1
		.0		.0		.0	Deferred Taxes		.0				.0
		1.9		5.9		8.9	All Other Non-Current		4.8				5.3
		22.8		28.8		-5.4	Net Worth		6.3				43.6
		100.0		100.0		100.0	Total Liabilties & Net Worth		100.0				100.0
							INCOME DATA						
		100.0		100.0		100.0	Net Sales		100.0				100.0
							Gross Profit						
		87.9		90.4		87.3	Operating Expenses		83.0				82.5
		12.1		9.6		12.7	Operating Profit		17.0				17.5
		-.3		.6		1.5	All Other Expenses (net)		2.8				.5
		12.4		9.1		11.3	Profit Before Taxes		14.2				16.9
							RATIOS						
		3.7		2.8		2.9			5.8				2.9
		1.7		1.4		1.4	Current		2.7				1.6
		.9		.5		.4			.0				1.0
		2.6		1.8		2.0			3.8				1.4
		1.0		.6		.6	Quick		.4				1.1
		.5		.2		.2			.0				.3
	0	UND	0	UND	0	UND		0	UND			1	658.0
	7	51.9	15	24.8	5	67.4	Sales/Receivables	0	UND			17	21.2
	38	9.7	49	7.5	32	11.3		18	19.9			47	7.8
							Cost of Sales/Inventory						
							Cost of Sales/Payables						
		3.3		5.3		4.6			2.4				3.9
		9.7		35.7		31.6	Sales/Working Capital		29.4				15.6
		-46.8		-7.0		-8.1			-1.6				563.1
		24.7		21.2		27.0							82.6
(70)		8.9	(51)	7.5	(37)	5.7	EBIT/Interest					(12)	15.1
		2.7		2.7		1.0							4.8
							Net Profit + Depr., Dep., Amort./Cur. Mat. L/T/D						
		.2		.1		.1			.0				.0
		.9		.8		1.1	Fixed/Worth		1.3				.6
		3.5		84.8		-11.2			-2.3				1.3
		.5		.6		.8			.6				.9
		1.2		2.1		2.8	Debt/Worth		1.8				3.0
		13.8		-13.4		-11.5			-3.6				4.8
		45.3		76.8		93.1							267.3
(80)		20.9	(50)	23.5	(37)	33.5	% Profit Before Taxes/Tangible Net Worth					(14)	93.1
		6.6		8.3		10.1							28.9
		24.3		17.3		30.4			49.0				22.8
		10.2		8.5		8.9	% Profit Before Taxes/Total Assets		6.5				15.2
		3.3		2.5		.2			.2				9.1
		40.7		106.4		88.5			180.9				208.5
		5.5		15.4		13.0	Sales/Net Fixed Assets		2.2				18.6
		1.9		2.3		2.0			.5				9.9
		2.3		3.1		4.3			8.4				4.2
		1.5		1.6		1.9	Sales/Total Assets		.6				2.0
		.7		.7		.8			.4				1.7
		.6		.8		.5							.4
(71)		3.6	(41)	2.7	(29)	2.0	% Depr., Dep., Amort./Sales					(10)	.6
		12.3		11.0		11.5							3.7
		1.1		1.2		1.1							
(21)		2.5	(14)	1.7	(11)	3.0	% Officers', Directors' Owners' Comp/Sales						
		8.6		5.5		4.9							
		3327245M		2381824M		2074482M	Net Sales ($)	2655M	21004M	27508M	40495M	123763M	1859057M
		2442413M		1355251M		929188M	Total Assets ($)	5054M	87009M	12982M	29010M	94872M	700261M

M = $ thousand   MM = $ million

© RMA 2024

See Pages viii through xx for Explanation of Ratios and Data

AGRICULTURE—Potato Farming NAICS 111211

Current Data Sorted by Assets

							Type of Statement		Comparative Historical Data	
					3	1	Unqualified		1	1
				2			Reviewed		11	6
		1	2	6			Compiled		10	4
	1	2	1				Tax Returns		5	2
1	4 (4/1-9/30/23)	3	17 (10/1/23-3/31/24)				Other		13	10
0-500M	500M-2MM	2-10MM	10-50MM	50-100MM	100-250MM				4/1/19-3/31/20 ALL	4/1/20-3/31/21 ALL
1	1	6	9	3	1		NUMBER OF STATEMENTS		40	23
%	%	%	%	%	%		ASSETS		%	%
							Cash & Equivalents		4.5	8.3
							Trade Receivables (net)		12.7	17.5
							Inventory		17.2	17.2
							All Other Current		3.2	7.2
							Total Current		37.6	50.2
							Fixed Assets (net)		50.6	34.0
							Intangibles (net)		1.6	1.3
							All Other Non-Current		10.2	14.5
							Total		100.0	100.0
							LIABILITIES			
							Notes Payable-Short Term		28.9	25.1
							Cur. Mat.-L.T.D.		3.7	3.9
							Trade Payables		8.0	7.1
							Income Taxes Payable		.1	.2
							All Other Current		3.7	6.2
							Total Current		44.4	42.6
							Long-Term Debt		23.9	26.1
							Deferred Taxes		.4	.6
							All Other Non-Current		2.3	5.1
							Net Worth		29.1	25.5
							Total Liabilities & Net Worth		100.0	100.0
							INCOME DATA			
							Net Sales		100.0	100.0
							Gross Profit			
							Operating Expenses		90.7	91.2
							Operating Profit		9.3	8.8
							All Other Expenses (net)		2.3	-.5
							Profit Before Taxes		7.0	9.3
							RATIOS			
							Current		1.6	3.8
									1.1	1.1
									.7	.9
							Quick		.7	1.0
									.5	.7
									.1	.2
							Sales/Receivables	0	UND	0	UND
								34	10.7	31	11.6
								55	6.6	70	5.2
							Cost of Sales/Inventory			
							Cost of Sales/Payables			
							Sales/Working Capital		6.5	3.2
									30.9	11.7
									-13.2	-22.7
							EBIT/Interest		4.8	6.6
								(37)	2.6	(18)	4.4
									.9	1.1
							Net Profit + Depr., Dep., Amort./Cur. Mat. L/T/D			
							Fixed/Worth		1.0	.9
									1.4	1.5
									2.2	3.5
							Debt/Worth		1.1	1.0
									2.3	3.4
									3.6	9.0
							% Profit Before Taxes/Tangible Net Worth		29.2	47.8
								(36)	14.9	(20)	23.5
									2.4	1.2
							% Profit Before Taxes/Total Assets		10.0	13.2
									4.7	10.3
									.2	.5
							Sales/Net Fixed Assets		5.3	13.7
									2.7	4.0
									.9	2.2
							Sales/Total Assets		2.0	2.4
									1.1	1.3
									.6	.6
							% Depr., Dep., Amort./Sales		3.6	3.9
								(35)	4.8	(16)	4.7
									8.2	10.2
							% Officers', Directors' Owners' Comp/Sales			
674M	4397M	54456M	231066M	236296M	159655M		Net Sales ($)		1877465M	531301M
398M	1016M	25791M	185280M	204512M	151547M		Total Assets ($)		1562350M	676594M

© RMA 2024   M = $ thousand   MM = $ million
See Pages viii through xx for Explanation of Ratios and Data

AGRICULTURE—Potato Farming NAICS 111211

Comparative Historical Data				Current Data Sorted by Sales					
			Type of Statement						
1	4	4	Unqualified				1	1	4
3	7	3	Reviewed			1			1
1	1	4	Compiled			1	1	1	2
7	5	10	Tax Returns	1		1	3	2	3
4/1/21-3/31/22 ALL	4/1/22-3/31/23 ALL	4/1/23-3/31/24 ALL	Other	0-1MM	4 (4/1-9/30/23) 1-3MM	3-5MM	17 (10/1/23-3/31/24) 5-10MM	10-25MM	25MM & OVER
12	17	21	**NUMBER OF STATEMENTS**	1		1	4	3	10
%	%	%	**ASSETS**	%	%	%	%	%	%
13.0	4.8	19.1	Cash & Equivalents						17.0
11.6	7.3	7.2	Trade Receivables (net)		D				9.4
14.0	20.6	12.5	Inventory		A				22.7
4.5	5.5	2.6	All Other Current		T				5.0
43.1	38.1	41.4	Total Current		A				54.1
38.4	43.6	40.1	Fixed Assets (net)						34.0
1.9	2.3	7.6	Intangibles (net)		N				4.1
16.6	16.0	10.9	All Other Non-Current		O				7.8
100.0	100.0	100.0	Total		T				100.0
			LIABILITIES		A				
24.7	29.3	31.7	Notes Payable-Short Term		V				43.2
3.4	4.2	3.5	Cur. Mat.-L.T.D.		A				2.1
5.0	3.6	6.9	Trade Payables		I				13.2
.4	.0	.0	Income Taxes Payable		L				.0
1.3	1.6	2.5	All Other Current		A				3.6
34.7	38.7	44.6	Total Current		B				62.0
21.4	36.4	42.5	Long-Term Debt		L				20.8
.0	.3	.0	Deferred Taxes		E				.1
1.4	6.3	1.9	All Other Non-Current						.6
42.4	18.4	10.9	Net Worth						16.4
100.0	100.0	100.0	Total Liabilities & Net Worth						100.0
			INCOME DATA						
100.0	100.0	100.0	Net Sales						100.0
			Gross Profit						
98.6	97.1	89.9	Operating Expenses						95.0
1.4	2.9	10.1	Operating Profit						5.0
-1.3	1.0	2.2	All Other Expenses (net)						1.8
2.7	1.9	7.9	Profit Before Taxes						3.2
			RATIOS						
3.2	1.3	4.9							3.7
1.1	1.1	1.8	Current						1.2
.7	.6	.4							.4
1.1	.5	4.2							1.6
.7 (16)	.3 (20)	.5	Quick						.4
.4	.2	.2							.1
0 UND	0 UND	0 UND							0 UND
31 11.7	23 15.6	1 662.1	Sales/Receivables						30 12.1
69 5.3	46 7.9	34 10.6							39 9.3
			Cost of Sales/Inventory						
			Cost of Sales/Payables						
4.0	9.3	3.7							3.9
49.5	37.6	13.7	Sales/Working Capital						14.3
-12.0	-9.1	-10.4							-7.4
19.9	9.9	10.7							11.5
(11) 3.2	2.1 (20)	2.8	EBIT/Interest						2.1
1.0	.3	1.5							.7
			Net Profit + Depr., Dep., Amort./Cur. Mat. L/T/D						
.5	.6	.7							.6
1.0	1.9	2.0	Fixed/Worth						1.4
2.1	-5.6	-2.3							NM
.7	1.1	.7							.9
1.3	3.3	2.6	Debt/Worth						2.1
3.9	-7.8	-4.5							NM
34.1	33.3	28.3	% Profit Before Taxes/Tangible Net Worth						11.7
(11) 11.7	(12) 11.9	(14) 17.4							3.4
-.1	5.9	5.1							-1.8
14.5	9.7	18.8	% Profit Before Taxes/Total Assets						11.7
6.3	3.8	7.8							3.4
.2	-.9	2.2							-1.8
9.0	6.3	11.5	Sales/Net Fixed Assets						13.1
4.0	3.1	4.3							4.5
2.8	1.0	1.3							3.8
1.8	1.5	2.1	Sales/Total Assets						2.9
1.2	1.0	1.4							1.7
1.0	.7	.9							1.1
2.5	2.0	1.9	% Depr., Dep., Amort./Sales						
(10) 5.7	(15) 5.7	(16) 2.5							
8.6	10.7	4.7							
			% Officers', Directors' Owners' Comp/Sales						
394856M	453170M	686544M	Net Sales ($)	674M		11449M	28087M	53677M	592657M
277320M	466805M	568544M	Total Assets ($)	398M		6869M	23529M	92449M	445299M

M = $ thousand   MM = $ million
See Pages viii through xx for Explanation of Ratios and Data

© RMA 2024

AGRICULTURE—Other Vegetable (except Potato) and Melon Farming NAICS 111219

Current Data Sorted by Assets | Comparative Historical Data

0-500M	500M-2MM	2-10MM	10-50MM	50-100MM	100-250MM	Type of Statement		4/1/19-3/31/20 ALL		4/1/20-3/31/21 ALL
1	2	5	6		1	Unqualified		3		1
1		6	4	2		Reviewed		10		3
			11		7	Compiled		9		1
	7 (4/1-9/30/23)		40 (10/1/23-3/31/24)	1		Tax Returns		11		5
						Other		37		16
2	2	11	21	3	8	NUMBER OF STATEMENTS		70		26
%	%	%	%	%	%	ASSETS		%		%
		25.9	5.1			Cash & Equivalents		9.2		13.2
		23.4	14.0			Trade Receivables (net)		18.0		12.3
		9.2	14.8			Inventory		11.6		9.0
		1.5	1.6			All Other Current		7.0		3.8
		60.1	35.5			Total Current		45.8		38.2
		28.0	49.2			Fixed Assets (net)		40.1		48.7
		5.9	4.0			Intangibles (net)		3.1		5.0
		6.0	11.3			All Other Non-Current		11.0		8.1
		100.0	100.0			Total		100.0		100.0
						LIABILITIES				
		8.7	17.0			Notes Payable-Short Term		16.6		21.3
		1.8	2.2			Cur. Mat.-L.T.D.		5.3		2.9
		2.0	6.4			Trade Payables		11.5		11.3
		.0	.0			Income Taxes Payable		.1		.2
		21.1	17.5			All Other Current		6.7		6.8
		33.7	43.2			Total Current		40.3		42.5
		11.9	17.8			Long-Term Debt		24.5		25.5
		.0	.0			Deferred Taxes		.5		1.0
		.4	6.8			All Other Non-Current		9.8		.1
		54.1	32.3			Net Worth		24.8		30.4
		100.0	100.0			Total Liabilties & Net Worth		100.0		100.0
						INCOME DATA				
		100.0	100.0			Net Sales		100.0		100.0
						Gross Profit				
		99.3	99.9			Operating Expenses		93.1		96.5
		.7	.1			Operating Profit		6.9		3.5
		-1.1	-.7			All Other Expenses (net)		1.7		-2.0
		1.9	.8			Profit Before Taxes		5.2		5.5
						RATIOS				
		23.9	2.0					3.0		2.3
		1.9	1.1			Current		1.4		1.1
		.3	.4					.9		.5
		23.9	1.2					1.5		1.2
		1.3	.5			Quick		.7		.7
		.3	.3					.4		.3
		0 UND	5 68.2					5 78.2		0 UND
		34 10.6	29 12.7			Sales/Receivables		31 11.8		21 17.8
		78 4.7	45 8.2					58 6.3		38 9.7
						Cost of Sales/Inventory				
						Cost of Sales/Payables				
		2.8	9.3					4.3		6.7
		6.9	365.8			Sales/Working Capital		13.4		62.4
		-3.6	-3.8					-29.4		-11.6
			4.8					21.6		18.2
		(16) 2.3				EBIT/Interest	(59)	5.7	(22)	9.2
			1.1					.2		1.7
						Net Profit + Depr., Dep., Amort./Cur. Mat. L/T/D		11.6		
							(11)	2.7		
								1.4		
		.1	.5					.4		.7
		.2	3.0			Fixed/Worth		.9		1.2
		2.5	NM					4.0		NM
		.0	1.0					.4		.8
		1.2	2.9			Debt/Worth		1.4		1.7
		2.8	NM					6.5		-66.8
		25.6	20.5					35.1		65.2
		.8	(16) 7.8			% Profit Before Taxes/Tangible Net Worth	(55)	14.7	(19)	19.0
		-22.0	-5.9					2.1		4.0
		9.4	7.0					14.0		14.7
		.7	1.5			% Profit Before Taxes/Total Assets		7.3		6.7
		-5.6	-2.2					-1.0		.0
		111.8	8.9					14.5		9.3
		8.3	7.2			Sales/Net Fixed Assets		5.9		4.0
		2.3	.8					2.2		2.1
		3.1	2.5					3.5		3.4
		1.3	1.6			Sales/Total Assets		1.7		2.4
		1.0	.7					.7		.9
			1.8					1.5		1.1
		(16)	4.5			% Depr., Dep., Amort./Sales	(57)	3.2	(18)	3.1
			6.2					5.1		7.9
								.7		
						% Officers', Directors' Owners' Comp/Sales	(11)	1.6		
								2.2		
8188M	14075M	106140M	753573M	117472M	1874460M	Net Sales ($)		3599651M		1772626M
398M	3039M	58292M	406953M	224586M	1324463M	Total Assets ($)		2484798M		991786M

© RMA 2024   M = $ thousand   MM = $ million
See Pages viii through xx for Explanation of Ratios and Data

AGRICULTURE—Other Vegetable (except Potato) and Melon Farming NAICS 111219

Comparative Historical Data / Current Data Sorted by Sales

					Type of Statement						
	1		3		Unqualified				1	1	5
	5		7		7	Reviewed			3	4	4
	3		3		11	Compiled			1	1	
	9		9		3	Tax Returns					
	14		25		26	Other	1	1	7	4	12
	4/1/21-3/31/22 ALL		4/1/22-3/31/23 ALL		4/1/23-3/31/24 ALL		1	2	7 (4/1-9/30/23)	40 (10/1/23-3/31/24)	
							0-1MM	1-3MM	3-5MM	5-10MM	10-25MM	25MM & OVER
	32		47		47	NUMBER OF STATEMENTS	2	3	11	10	21
	%		%		%	ASSETS	%	%	%	%	%	%
	17.5		13.8		9.7	Cash & Equivalents			10.3	15.8	4.4
	11.8		21.2		15.7	Trade Receivables (net)	D		11.1	23.6	14.3
	11.7		10.6		15.2	Inventory	A		19.3	7.7	19.9
	1.5		3.6		2.5	All Other Current	T		.7	2.3	4.2
	42.6		49.2		43.1	Total Current	A		41.4	49.4	42.8
	41.2		34.7		41.8	Fixed Assets (net)			48.4	31.2	38.3
	6.8		4.1		5.0	Intangibles (net)	N		4.2	17.3	.7
	9.5		12.0		10.1	All Other Non-Current	O		6.0	2.1	18.2
	100.0		100.0		100.0	Total	T		100.0	100.0	100.0
						LIABILITIES	A				
	12.9		15.6		16.4	Notes Payable-Short Term	V		8.4	19.8	18.9
	2.8		2.8		2.3	Cur. Mat.-L.T.D.	A		1.0	2.1	3.1
	6.1		7.0		6.5	Trade Payables	I		2.3	3.9	7.1
	.2		.0		.0	Income Taxes Payable	L		.0	.0	.0
	9.3		20.6		15.7	All Other Current	A		32.6	5.5	7.6
	31.2		46.0		40.9	Total Current	B		44.4	31.3	36.7
	46.5		28.1		20.8	Long-Term Debt	L		13.3	11.5	18.8
	.1		.7		.5	Deferred Taxes	E		.0	.0	1.2
	1.0		5.1		3.8	All Other Non-Current			2.2	7.3	3.9
	21.0		20.2		33.9	Net Worth			40.2	49.9	39.5
	100.0		100.0		100.0	Total Liabilties & Net Worth			100.0	100.0	100.0
						INCOME DATA					
	100.0		100.0		100.0	Net Sales			100.0	100.0	100.0
						Gross Profit					
	85.7		89.6		97.3	Operating Expenses			99.0	97.8	94.6
	14.3		10.4		2.7	Operating Profit			1.0	2.2	5.4
	1.4		.7		-.6	All Other Expenses (net)			.4	-2.5	.2
	12.9		9.7		3.3	Profit Before Taxes			.6	4.7	5.2
						RATIOS					
	2.6		3.7		2.8				2.0	16.5	2.8
	1.6		1.6		1.2	Current			1.2	2.0	1.2
	.8		.6		.5				.1	1.3	.7
	1.8		2.3		1.3				1.0	14.3	1.2
	.8		.7		.5	Quick			.3	1.3	.5
	.4		.3		.3				.0	.5	.4
0	UND	0	999.8	4	99.2		0	UND	0	UND	17	21.8
26	14.0	30	12.1	23	15.9	Sales/Receivables	11	33.4	60	6.1	27	13.4
46	7.9	49	7.5	54	6.8		43	8.4	94	3.9	49	7.4
						Cost of Sales/Inventory					
						Cost of Sales/Payables					
	3.6		5.9		5.1				6.1	2.2	5.2
	10.7		17.3		19.3	Sales/Working Capital			189.2	7.9	19.3
	-47.0		-33.7		-8.0				-1.0	NM	-14.9
	16.6		46.2		11.9						11.6
(24)	6.3	(39)	12.6	(38)	3.5	EBIT/Interest				(20)	2.8
	2.5		4.1		1.2						1.3
						Net Profit + Depr., Dep., Amort./Cur. Mat. L/T/D					
	.3		.2		.3				.2	.2	.4
	1.2		.9		1.0	Fixed/Worth			2.5	.6	.9
	-1.8		4.1		5.2				5.2	NM	6.5
	.7		.5		.5				.9	.1	.5
	1.8		1.7		1.8	Debt/Worth			2.3	1.1	1.4
	-4.0		4.8		4.9				4.9	NM	9.2
	66.4		65.2		24.3				44.1		19.9
(21)	25.3	(39)	28.6	(39)	9.6	% Profit Before Taxes/Tangible Net Worth	(10)	4.9	(17)	9.6
	8.3		11.2		.3				-13.5		1.4
	29.3		23.3		9.4				12.1	11.5	8.3
	8.1		10.8		3.6	% Profit Before Taxes/Total Assets			1.2	6.1	4.6
	5.0		3.0		-2.0				-5.6	-5.2	.4
	19.7		26.1		10.5				28.3	45.3	8.9
	4.1		6.0		5.6	Sales/Net Fixed Assets			2.3	8.0	5.6
	1.8		3.2		1.5				.7	3.1	3.0
	2.4		4.2		2.7				2.7	3.8	2.5
	1.4		2.1		1.6	Sales/Total Assets			1.2	1.5	2.0
	.6		1.1		.8				.5	1.0	1.0
	3.2		.8		1.7						2.3
(18)	6.5	(29)	3.0	(33)	3.6	% Depr., Dep., Amort./Sales				(13)	3.4
	9.3		4.8		5.5						4.6
						% Officers', Directors', Owners' Comp/Sales					
	997076M		2737490M		2873908M	Net Sales ($)		4404M	11885M	85571M	152873M	2619175M
	827965M		1614960M		2017731M	Total Assets ($)		4858M	35741M	102730M	164324M	1710078M

© RMA 2024   M = $ thousand   MM = $ million
See Pages viii through xx for Explanation of Ratios and Data

AGRICULTURE—Apple Orchards NAICS 111331

Current Data Sorted by Assets | **Comparative Historical Data**

						Type of Statement		
				1	1	Unqualified	4	1
			1	1		Reviewed	6	3
			4			Compiled	5	4
		1	2			Tax Returns	3	3
1	2	1	4	2	1	Other	13	13
1	1 (4/1-9/30/23)		21 (10/1/23-3/31/24)				4/1/19-	4/1/20-
0-500M	500M-2MM	2-10MM	10-50MM	50-100MM	100-250MM		3/31/20	3/31/21
2	2	2	10	4	2	**NUMBER OF STATEMENTS**	31 ALL	24 ALL
%	%	%	%	%	%	**ASSETS**	%	%
			6.7			Cash & Equivalents	4.9	6.6
			14.4			Trade Receivables (net)	8.4	11.8
			22.0			Inventory	11.9	13.5
			2.3			All Other Current	5.0	2.2
			45.4			Total Current	30.2	34.1
			42.2			Fixed Assets (net)	56.2	55.2
			.1			Intangibles (net)	3.7	2.9
			12.3			All Other Non-Current	10.0	7.8
			100.0			Total	100.0	100.0
						LIABILITIES		
			20.0			Notes Payable-Short Term	18.2	13.3
			2.9			Cur. Mat.-L.T.D.	3.9	2.7
			7.7			Trade Payables	6.4	6.0
			.0			Income Taxes Payable	.0	.0
			11.4			All Other Current	7.3	3.2
			42.0			Total Current	35.7	25.3
			16.1			Long-Term Debt	31.6	33.0
			.5			Deferred Taxes	.9	.4
			1.8			All Other Non-Current	1.1	6.2
			39.7			Net Worth	30.7	35.4
			100.0			Total Liabilties & Net Worth	100.0	100.0
						INCOME DATA		
			100.0			Net Sales	100.0	100.0
						Gross Profit		
			91.3			Operating Expenses	100.0	95.0
			8.7			Operating Profit	.0	5.0
			2.6			All Other Expenses (net)	5.0	.0
			6.1			Profit Before Taxes	-5.0	5.0
						RATIOS		
			1.5				1.5	2.1
			1.3			Current	1.0	1.5
			1.0				.6	1.0
			.8				.6	1.4
			.5			Quick	.4	.7
			.1				.1	.1
			0 UND				0 999.8	0 UND
			56 6.5			Sales/Receivables	33 10.9	50 7.3
			140 2.6				68 5.4	135 2.7
						Cost of Sales/Inventory		
						Cost of Sales/Payables		
			3.6				4.2	2.8
			9.1			Sales/Working Capital	-67.9	5.0
			NM				-2.9	UND
							2.1	5.1
						EBIT/Interest	(28) -.1	(22) 1.8
							-1.2	.0
						Net Profit + Depr., Dep., Amort./Cur. Mat. L/T/D		
			.4				1.2	1.0
			1.1			Fixed/Worth	1.6	1.6
			1.7				4.3	5.8
			1.0				.9	.8
			1.6			Debt/Worth	1.9	2.0
			2.9				7.3	7.7
			44.3				8.2	26.2
			7.5			% Profit Before Taxes/Tangible Net Worth	(25) -5.5	(19) 4.2
			-20.7				-13.9	1.0
			22.7				1.8	8.7
			2.8			% Profit Before Taxes/Total Assets	-2.2	1.5
			-6.6				-4.5	-2.0
			UND				2.2	1.6
			1.3			Sales/Net Fixed Assets	1.0	1.0
			1.0				.8	.5
			.7				1.1	.7
			.6			Sales/Total Assets	.7	.6
			.5				.4	.3
							4.4	6.5
						% Depr., Dep., Amort./Sales	(30) 7.5	(20) 10.4
							10.9	13.8
						% Officers', Directors' Owners' Comp/Sales		
1289M	5234M	16655M	178028M	127475M	149373M	Net Sales ($)	1085613M	503700M
291M	2413M	11632M	220336M	311983M	371265M	Total Assets ($)	1770147M	1047407M

© RMA 2024 M = $ thousand MM = $ million
See Pages viii through xx for Explanation of Ratios and Data

AGRICULTURE—Apple Orchards NAICS 111331

Comparative Historical Data | Current Data Sorted by Sales

				Type of Statement						
	1	3	2	Unqualified						2
	2	5	5	Reviewed				1	2	2
	3		3	Compiled				3		
	3	3	3	Tax Returns	1	1	1			
	13	8	9	Other	1			3	2	3
	4/1/21-	4/1/22-	4/1/23-			1 (4/1-9/30/23)		21 (10/1/23-3/31/24)		
	3/31/22	3/31/23	3/31/24							
	ALL	ALL	ALL		0-1MM	1-3MM	3-5MM	5-10MM	10-25MM	25MM & OVER
	22	19	22	NUMBER OF STATEMENTS	2	1	1	7	4	7
	%	%	%	ASSETS	%	%	%	%	%	%
	10.2	4.4	10.2	Cash & Equivalents						
	9.7	9.1	11.4	Trade Receivables (net)						
	16.4	12.5	15.3	Inventory						
	5.1	13.2	6.9	All Other Current						
	41.4	39.3	43.8	Total Current						
	46.7	48.0	43.1	Fixed Assets (net)						
	1.4	5.3	1.4	Intangibles (net)						
	10.5	7.5	11.7	All Other Non-Current						
	100.0	100.0	100.0	Total						
				LIABILITIES						
	12.7	9.1	22.1	Notes Payable-Short Term						
	5.5	2.3	3.0	Cur. Mat.-L.T.D.						
	3.0	6.9	6.6	Trade Payables						
	.0	.1	.0	Income Taxes Payable						
	25.8	16.0	7.0	All Other Current						
	47.1	34.5	38.7	Total Current						
	24.4	26.1	33.5	Long-Term Debt						
	.0	.6	.2	Deferred Taxes						
	15.2	10.0	7.3	All Other Non-Current						
	13.3	28.9	20.4	Net Worth						
	100.0	100.0	100.0	Total Liabilities & Net Worth						
				INCOME DATA						
	100.0	100.0	100.0	Net Sales						
				Gross Profit						
	100.2	98.7	99.1	Operating Expenses						
	-.2	1.3	.9	Operating Profit						
	-2.9	.6	3.4	All Other Expenses (net)						
	2.8	.7	-2.5	Profit Before Taxes						
				RATIOS						
	2.1	2.6	1.9							
	1.7	1.5	1.4	Current						
	.8	1.0	1.1							
	1.2	1.1	1.4							
	.6	.6	.7	Quick						
	.2	.2	.3							
	0 UND	0 999.8	0 UND							
	25 14.4	33 11.0	54 6.7	Sales/Receivables						
	78 4.7	111 3.3	111 3.3							
				Cost of Sales/Inventory						
				Cost of Sales/Payables						
	2.6	2.4	3.6							
	4.4	6.5	5.9	Sales/Working Capital						
	-27.9	34.7	124.3							
	5.4	4.0	4.0							
(20)	2.8	(18) 2.1	(18) 1.1	EBIT/Interest						
	-.9	-1.2	-5.7							
				Net Profit + Depr., Dep., Amort./Cur. Mat. L/T/D						
	.8	.9	.9							
	1.1	1.3	1.1	Fixed/Worth						
	NM	11.0	2.4							
	1.0	.5	1.3							
	1.4	1.4	2.3	Debt/Worth						
	NM	16.7	5.2							
	27.5	26.3	35.4							
(17)	12.4	(16) 4.7	(18) 4.4	% Profit Before Taxes/Tangible Net Worth						
	-1.2	-8.0	-23.4							
	9.9	4.4	15.2							
	4.8	1.4	-.2	% Profit Before Taxes/Total Assets						
	-1.7	-3.4	-10.6							
	6.2	2.0	16.1							
	2.4	1.2	1.4	Sales/Net Fixed Assets						
	.9	.7	.8							
	1.9	.9	1.8							
	.9	.5	.7	Sales/Total Assets						
	.5	.3	.4							
	3.6	5.6	3.2							
(20)	9.3	(16) 10.7	(17) 6.5	% Depr., Dep., Amort./Sales						
	14.1	12.6	11.4							
				% Officers', Directors', Owners' Comp/Sales						
	522215M	611571M	478054M	Net Sales ($)	1289M	1121M	4113M	52319M	63294M	355918M
	915331M	1269081M	917920M	Total Assets ($)	291M	666M	1747M	102774M	172048M	640394M

M = $ thousand   MM = $ million

© RMA 2024

AGRICULTURE—Grape Vineyards NAICS 111332

Current Data Sorted by Assets

0-500M	500M-2MM	2-10MM	10-50MM	50-100MM	100-250MM
1	2	1	1		
	3	1	2		
		1	1		
		5	3	2	1
1 (4/1-9/30/23)			23 (10/1/23-3/31/24)		
1 %	5 %	7 %	8 %	2 %	1 %

Comparative Historical Data

Type of Statement	4/1/19-3/31/20 ALL	4/1/20-3/31/21 ALL
Unqualified	3	2
Reviewed	14	2
Compiled		2
Tax Returns	26	7
Other	54	12
NUMBER OF STATEMENTS	97	25
ASSETS	%	%
Cash & Equivalents	9.6	10.5
Trade Receivables (net)	12.3	10.9
Inventory	8.1	16.1
All Other Current	5.1	3.5
Total Current	35.1	41.1
Fixed Assets (net)	55.1	47.2
Intangibles (net)	4.2	5.4
All Other Non-Current	5.6	6.3
Total	100.0	100.0
LIABILITIES		
Notes Payable-Short Term	20.0	12.5
Cur. Mat.-L.T.D.	3.9	4.0
Trade Payables	3.4	4.5
Income Taxes Payable	.0	.0
All Other Current	3.2	2.6
Total Current	30.6	23.6
Long-Term Debt	38.0	36.3
Deferred Taxes	.2	.0
All Other Non-Current	5.6	7.4
Net Worth	25.7	32.6
Total Liabilties & Net Worth	100.0	100.0
INCOME DATA		
Net Sales	100.0	100.0
Gross Profit		
Operating Expenses	91.3	84.1
Operating Profit	8.7	15.9
All Other Expenses (net)	5.9	5.6
Profit Before Taxes	2.8	10.2
RATIOS		
Current	2.5	4.6
	1.4	1.7
	.6	.9
Quick	1.7	1.2
	.7 (24)	.6
	.2	.2
Sales/Receivables	0 UND	0 UND
	42 8.6	12 31.6
	101 3.6	85 4.3
Cost of Sales/Inventory		
Cost of Sales/Payables		
Sales/Working Capital	2.8	1.9
	9.5	4.1
	-8.3	-19.9
EBIT/Interest	6.2	13.7
	(84) 1.2	(21) 2.9
	-.4	-.2
Net Profit + Depr., Dep., Amort./Cur. Mat. L/T/D	5.8	
	(19) 1.6	
	-.3	
Fixed/Worth	.9	.4
	2.0	1.5
	NM	30.0
Debt/Worth	.7	.5
	2.3	2.1
	-532.2	80.7
% Profit Before Taxes/Tangible Net Worth	20.2	53.2
	(72) 3.5	(20) 13.3
	-11.9	-6.2
% Profit Before Taxes/Total Assets	9.0	15.6
	1.1	2.6
	-3.9	-3.0
Sales/Net Fixed Assets	4.8	10.4
	1.0	1.1
	.5	.6
Sales/Total Assets	1.2	1.0
	.6	.6
	.3	.3
% Depr., Dep., Amort./Sales	3.1	1.9
	(81) 6.3	(19) 6.5
	13.3	10.7
% Officers', Directors' Owners' Comp/Sales	1.5	
	(12) 2.9	
	12.9	

0-500M	500M-2MM	2-10MM	10-50MM	50-100MM	100-250MM		ALL	ALL
1236M	6649M	19655M	99157M	89520M	115399M	Net Sales ($)	2083257M	333543M
393M	7108M	32990M	134143M	160728M	223511M	Total Assets ($)	3091860M	527319M

© RMA 2024   M = $ thousand   MM = $ million
See Pages viii through xx for Explanation of Ratios and Data

AGRICULTURE—Grape Vineyards NAICS 111332

Comparative Historical Data | Current Data Sorted by Sales

				Type of Statement						
	2	5	1	Unqualified				1		
	5	4	2	Reviewed				1	1	
	2	1	2	Compiled					2	
	13	6	5	Tax Returns		3		1	1	
	30	35	14	Other	2	7	1	1		3
	4/1/21-	4/1/22-	4/1/23-			1 (4/1-9/30/23)		23 (10/1/23-3/31/24)		
	3/31/22	3/31/23	3/31/24							
	ALL	ALL	ALL		0-1MM	1-3MM	3-5MM	5-10MM	10-25MM	25MM & OVER
	52	51	24	NUMBER OF STATEMENTS	3	10	1	3	4	3
	%	%	%	ASSETS	%	%	%	%	%	%
	12.1	15.8	11.6	Cash & Equivalents		22.2				
	13.1	12.5	10.7	Trade Receivables (net)		3.9				
	11.3	8.5	14.3	Inventory		7.9				
	4.2	2.1	3.0	All Other Current		.1				
	40.8	38.9	39.6	Total Current		34.1				
	51.8	45.9	44.6	Fixed Assets (net)		52.7				
	.9	4.5	8.5	Intangibles (net)		9.0				
	6.5	10.7	7.3	All Other Non-Current		4.2				
	100.0	100.0	100.0	Total		100.0				
				LIABILITIES						
	24.8	25.8	9.2	Notes Payable-Short Term		14.2				
	2.1	1.8	1.4	Cur. Mat.-L.T.D.		1.8				
	4.0	4.5	7.2	Trade Payables		6.0				
	.0	.0	.0	Income Taxes Payable		.0				
	5.0	6.3	5.2	All Other Current		2.9				
	35.9	38.4	23.0	Total Current		25.0				
	58.6	50.1	24.5	Long-Term Debt		25.5				
	.1	.1	.0	Deferred Taxes		.0				
	4.3	5.8	8.7	All Other Non-Current		7.6				
	1.1	5.6	43.7	Net Worth		42.0				
	100.0	100.0	100.0	Total Liabilities & Net Worth		100.0				
				INCOME DATA						
	100.0	100.0	100.0	Net Sales		100.0				
				Gross Profit						
	84.4	92.8	82.8	Operating Expenses		80.3				
	15.6	7.2	17.2	Operating Profit		19.7				
	2.1	4.0	4.6	All Other Expenses (net)		3.2				
	13.5	3.2	12.5	Profit Before Taxes		16.5				
				RATIOS						
	9.8	7.0	14.2			149.7				
	2.3	1.6	1.6	Current		2.3				
	.9	.7	1.1			.4				
	5.8	5.2	8.2			144.6				
	1.1	.8	1.1	Quick		2.3				
	.3	.3	.2			.3				
0	UND	0	UND	0	UND			0	UND	
22	16.6	20	18.7	10	36.9	Sales/Receivables		0	UND	
101	3.6	63	5.8	96	3.8			9	40.9	
				Cost of Sales/Inventory						
				Cost of Sales/Payables						
	2.2	4.1	1.8			1.7				
	4.3	7.0	5.0	Sales/Working Capital		15.0				
	-26.6	-6.8	23.4			-3.0				
	18.1	8.9	34.4							
(46)	6.1	(42)	1.8	(15)	6.3	EBIT/Interest				
	2.3		.2		2.5					
				Net Profit + Depr., Dep.,						
				Amort./Cur. Mat. L/T/D						
	.7	.4	.4			.6				
	2.4	1.5	1.0	Fixed/Worth		1.4				
	-5.3	-2.5	3.4			NM				
	1.1	1.0	.1			.2				
	3.6	2.4	1.1	Debt/Worth		1.2				
	-8.1	-6.2	5.0			NM				
	38.8	28.7	31.4	% Profit Before Taxes/Tangible						
(34)	17.0	(33)	4.3	(20)	16.9	Net Worth				
	6.1		-2.2		.8					
	22.1	12.8	12.8	% Profit Before Taxes/Total		13.0				
	8.1	1.8	8.2	Assets		10.6				
	2.4	-2.0	.3			3.2				
	7.6	12.5	7.3			3.8				
	1.2	1.9	1.5	Sales/Net Fixed Assets		1.5				
	.7	.7	.6			.5				
	1.4	1.7	1.3			1.3				
	.6	1.1	.5	Sales/Total Assets		.5				
	.4	.4	.3			.4				
	4.9	2.1	2.7							
(39)	8.3	(30)	5.3	(13)	8.9	% Depr., Dep., Amort./Sales				
	14.5	11.9	19.1							
			1.3	% Officers', Directors'						
		(12)	2.3	Owners' Comp/Sales						
			8.4							
	1422892M	2503400M	331616M	Net Sales ($)	1059M	17660M	3819M	20672M	66043M	222363M
	1196930M	1612499M	558873M	Total Assets ($)	7775M	46936M	10502M	141006M	51676M	300978M

© RMA 2024

M = $ thousand   MM = $ million
See Pages viii through xx for Explanation of Ratios and Data

AGRICULTURE—Tree Nut Farming NAICS 111335

Current Data Sorted by Assets						Type of Statement	Comparative Historical Data	
		3	4	1	3	Unqualified	3	1
			4	2	1	Reviewed	11	
1	2	4	7			Compiled	5	
	1					Tax Returns	19	3
		3	7	2	1	Other	38	3
0-500M	8 (4/1-9/30/23) 500M-2MM	2-10MM	38 (10/1/23-3/31/24) 10-50MM	50-100MM	100-250MM		4/1/19-3/31/20 ALL	4/1/20-3/31/21 ALL
1	3	10	22	5	5	NUMBER OF STATEMENTS	76	7
%	%	%	%	%	%	ASSETS	%	%
		13.8	7.5			Cash & Equivalents	8.6	
		18.3	15.9			Trade Receivables (net)	11.1	
		.8	7.4			Inventory	4.9	
		1.8	3.1			All Other Current	3.3	
		34.7	34.0			Total Current	27.9	
		37.2	58.2			Fixed Assets (net)	59.4	
		19.6	6.0			Intangibles (net)	3.2	
		8.4	1.8			All Other Non-Current	9.5	
		100.0	100.0			Total	100.0	
						LIABILITIES		
		3.9	10.8			Notes Payable-Short Term	15.7	
		2.0	2.1			Cur. Mat.-L.T.D.	3.6	
		1.0	8.7			Trade Payables	2.8	
		.0	.0			Income Taxes Payable	.0	
		.7	2.3			All Other Current	6.0	
		7.7	23.9			Total Current	28.1	
		12.9	32.3			Long-Term Debt	39.4	
		1.0	.8			Deferred Taxes	.1	
		6.2	8.5			All Other Non-Current	3.6	
		72.3	34.4			Net Worth	28.8	
		100.0	100.0			Total Liabilities & Net Worth	100.0	
						INCOME DATA		
		100.0	100.0			Net Sales	100.0	
						Gross Profit		
		65.6	90.9			Operating Expenses	85.4	
		34.4	9.1			Operating Profit	14.6	
		11.6	7.0			All Other Expenses (net)	6.9	
		22.8	2.2			Profit Before Taxes	7.7	
						RATIOS		
		45.2	4.0				2.8	
		3.2	1.1			Current	1.4	
		1.3	.7				.6	
		43.0	3.8				2.0	
		2.8	.6			Quick	.7	
		1.1	.2				.2	
		0 UND	0 UND				0 UND	
		34 10.6	107 3.4			Sales/Receivables	7 53.8	
		304 1.2	215 1.7				122 3.0	
						Cost of Sales/Inventory		
						Cost of Sales/Payables		
		.6	2.3				3.9	
		3.0	21.1			Sales/Working Capital	17.1	
		NM	-3.3				-8.1	
			3.5				4.2	
			(17) 1.7			EBIT/Interest	(61) 2.6	
			-.1				1.6	
						Net Profit + Depr., Dep., Amort./Cur. Mat. L/T/D		
		.2	.8				.9	
		.8	3.3			Fixed/Worth	1.9	
		1.6	NM				7.4	
		.1	.3				.7	
		.3	3.2			Debt/Worth	1.8	
		1.4	NM				13.3	
			21.4				42.1	
		(17)	10.2			% Profit Before Taxes/Tangible Net Worth	(62) 11.1	
			-1.5				3.1	
		14.1	6.5				10.0	
		7.2	1.9			% Profit Before Taxes/Total Assets	3.0	
		3.4	-1.4				.8	
		2.0	2.3				4.1	
		1.4	.5			Sales/Net Fixed Assets	1.0	
		.6	.3				.3	
		.5	.8				1.5	
		.4	.3			Sales/Total Assets	.6	
		.1	.2				.2	
			4.1				2.3	
		(19)	9.2			% Depr., Dep., Amort./Sales	(54) 6.4	
			13.1				11.8	
							1.1	
						% Officers', Directors' Owners' Comp/Sales	(12) 3.0	
							6.7	
3764M	2374M	13907M	259579M	209792M	749089M	Net Sales ($)	940080M	144654M
213M	4343M	46008M	418424M	391062M	696999M	Total Assets ($)	1409143M	110816M

© RMA 2024   M = $ thousand   MM = $ million
See Pages viii through xx for Explanation of Ratios and Data

AGRICULTURE—Tree Nut Farming NAICS 111335

Comparative Historical Data | Current Data Sorted by Sales

Comparative Historical Data			Type of Statement	Current Data Sorted by Sales					
2	8	11	Unqualified		2	1	2		6
2	7	7	Reviewed		1	1	1	2	2
4	10	14	Compiled	4	6	2	1	1	
7	10	1	Tax Returns	1					
20	15	13	Other	1	2	3	1	1	5
4/1/21-3/31/22 ALL	4/1/22-3/31/23 ALL	4/1/23-3/31/24 ALL		0-1MM	8 (4/1-9/30/23) 1-3MM	3-5MM	38 (10/1/23-3/31/24) 5-10MM	10-25MM	25MM & OVER
35	50	46	NUMBER OF STATEMENTS	6	11	7	5	4	13
%	%	%	ASSETS	%	%	%	%	%	%
6.6	8.9	8.3	Cash & Equivalents		6.9				9.3
14.7	12.6	13.7	Trade Receivables (net)		14.5				18.6
6.7	9.1	9.3	Inventory		3.0				23.5
4.4	5.7	3.0	All Other Current		2.6				2.1
32.4	36.4	34.3	Total Current		27.0				53.6
51.7	48.9	52.6	Fixed Assets (net)		62.1				38.9
2.0	3.5	9.4	Intangibles (net)		9.5				4.9
13.9	11.4	3.7	All Other Non-Current		1.3				2.6
100.0	100.0	100.0	Total		100.0				100.0
			LIABILITIES						
15.4	12.1	12.8	Notes Payable-Short Term		17.5				13.8
2.2	1.9	2.2	Cur. Mat.-L.T.D.		2.4				1.6
7.6	7.1	6.4	Trade Payables		1.9				17.4
.1	.0	.0	Income Taxes Payable		.0				.0
6.5	4.4	6.7	All Other Current		18.3				6.3
31.7	25.5	28.1	Total Current		40.1				39.1
37.3	32.5	29.9	Long-Term Debt		21.0				35.0
.0	.5	.6	Deferred Taxes		.9				.0
6.6	3.9	6.6	All Other Non-Current		8.4				3.8
24.4	37.4	34.7	Net Worth		29.7				22.1
100.0	100.0	100.0	Total Liabilities & Net Worth		100.0				100.0
			INCOME DATA						
100.0	100.0	100.0	Net Sales		100.0				100.0
89.9	93.1	88.3	Gross Profit / Operating Expenses		91.1				93.9
10.1	6.9	11.7	Operating Profit		8.9				6.1
3.0	5.8	7.9	All Other Expenses (net)		7.8				3.6
7.1	1.1	3.8	Profit Before Taxes		1.1				2.5
			RATIOS						
4.0	7.1	3.9			34.8				2.1
1.5	1.4	1.3	Current		1.5				1.2
.6	.8	.9			.7				1.0
3.2	4.5	3.1			33.9				1.1
.9	.7	.9	Quick		1.5				.7
.1	.1	.2			.0				.3
0 UND	0 UND	0 UND			0 UND			25	14.4
33 10.9	33 10.9	51 7.1	Sales/Receivables		159 2.3			47	7.7
192 1.9	140 2.6	182 2.0			243 1.5			94	3.9
			Cost of Sales/Inventory						
			Cost of Sales/Payables						
2.4	2.9	2.0			1.3				3.4
13.0	9.9	12.5	Sales/Working Capital		10.7				13.5
-11.9	-40.0	-33.4			-1.6				177.9
15.0	5.8	3.4							2.7
(31) 3.5	(38) 2.7	(35) 1.9	EBIT/Interest						2.1
1.1	-.4	.4							1.0
		3.2	Net Profit + Depr., Dep., Amort./Cur. Mat. L/T/D						
	(11)	1.4							
		.4							
.8	.5	.8			.4				1.1
2.3	1.2	2.3	Fixed/Worth		1.2				2.3
5.3	31.6	NM			3.7				-8.2
.5	.2	.3			.3				2.2
2.1	2.1	2.7	Debt/Worth		.4				4.7
20.7	144.4	NM			3.1				-17.0
40.9	35.2	19.5	% Profit Before Taxes/Tangible Net Worth						
(27) 16.9	(41) 7.5	(35) 9.7							
3.5	-8.3	-1.8							
11.9	7.8	6.5	% Profit Before Taxes/Total Assets		9.5				3.2
3.5	2.3	2.1			-.1				2.0
.2	-4.2	-1.4			-1.9				.1
8.7	7.6	2.5			1.7				4.8
1.7	1.9	1.0	Sales/Net Fixed Assets		1.1				2.7
.5	.5	.4			.1				.8
2.1	1.9	.8			.6				1.7
.6	.6	.4	Sales/Total Assets		.3				1.1
.4	.3	.2			.1				.4
3.8	1.9	3.9			7.0				1.5
(22) 8.1	(38) 6.7	(38) 8.1	% Depr., Dep., Amort./Sales	(10)	13.4			(10)	2.6
14.3	15.3	15.3			17.9				5.3
2.5	1.9								
(11) 4.4	(13) 4.4		% Officers', Directors' Owners' Comp/Sales						
10.5	11.8								
646657M	1593519M	1238505M	Net Sales ($)	2723M	19102M	28516M	30323M	59511M	1098330M
834510M	1270517M	1557049M	Total Assets ($)	24542M	100567M	85101M	155185M	101529M	1090125M

© RMA 2024
M = $ thousand   MM = $ million
See Pages viii through xx for Explanation of Ratios and Data

AGRICULTURE—Nursery and Tree Production NAICS 111421

Current Data Sorted by Assets | Comparative Historical Data

Type of Statement								
						Unqualified	8	2
		1	1			Reviewed	19	7
		3	7			Compiled	13	6
	2	2	2	1		Tax Returns	15	12
1	4	7		1		Other	39	25
	9 (4/1-9/30/23)		8 (10/1/23-3/31/24)	5	1		4/1/19-	4/1/20-
0-500M	500M-2MM	2-10MM	10-50MM	50-100MM	100-250MM		3/31/20	3/31/21
1	6	13	18	7	1	NUMBER OF STATEMENTS	94 ALL	52 ALL
%	%	%	%	%	%	ASSETS	%	%
		5.5	8.2			Cash & Equivalents	8.9	21.6
		13.7	6.8			Trade Receivables (net)	9.8	6.8
		36.0	37.8			Inventory	32.3	33.1
		.5	.4			All Other Current	3.3	1.4
		55.8	53.2			Total Current	54.2	62.9
		35.3	30.0			Fixed Assets (net)	35.4	26.9
		3.2	6.9			Intangibles (net)	1.9	4.2
		5.8	10.0			All Other Non-Current	8.5	6.0
		100.0	100.0			Total	100.0	100.0
						LIABILITIES		
		9.1	5.8			Notes Payable-Short Term	17.4	8.4
		1.8	3.4			Cur. Mat.-L.T.D.	3.8	4.4
		12.6	6.9			Trade Payables	7.5	5.3
		.0	.0			Income Taxes Payable	.2	.1
		16.1	8.9			All Other Current	10.1	10.4
		39.5	24.9			Total Current	38.9	28.5
		19.3	17.5			Long-Term Debt	24.1	25.9
		.0	1.7			Deferred Taxes	.9	.9
		2.9	4.6			All Other Non-Current	4.6	4.8
		38.2	51.3			Net Worth	31.6	39.9
		100.0	100.0			Total Liabilities & Net Worth	100.0	100.0
						INCOME DATA		
		100.0	100.0			Net Sales	100.0	100.0
		33.0	30.0			Gross Profit	41.4	44.3
		26.4	25.5			Operating Expenses	36.9	36.9
		6.6	4.5			Operating Profit	4.4	7.4
		1.4	-.7			All Other Expenses (net)	.8	-1.8
		5.1	5.2			Profit Before Taxes	3.6	9.1
						RATIOS		
		3.0	5.1				3.2	6.6
		1.8	2.6			Current	1.5	3.2
		.8	1.3				.8	1.3
		1.1	1.1				1.0	2.2
		.6	.5			Quick	.4	1.1
		.1	.3				.2	.4
		9 39.1	4 90.5				5 68.4	1 268.5
		13 29.1	14 26.7			Sales/Receivables	15 24.8	9 42.6
		33 10.9	42 8.7				35 10.3	19 19.2
		45 8.2	60 6.1				5 69.5	2 176.2
		85 4.3	174 2.1			Cost of Sales/Inventory	99 3.7	101 3.6
		192 1.9	281 1.3				228 1.6	281 1.3
		10 36.5	7 54.3				1 639.7	0 999.8
		25 14.7	22 16.6			Cost of Sales/Payables	20 18.4	10 37.9
		66 5.5	42 8.7				47 7.8	29 12.5
		4.1	2.1				3.1	2.4
		8.6	3.3			Sales/Working Capital	8.6	4.8
		-13.6	18.5				-39.0	120.4
		15.7	31.6				8.6	28.9
	(12)	6.2	(17) 3.7			EBIT/Interest	(89) 3.1	(44) 12.1
		3.1	1.3				1.1	4.8
						Net Profit + Depr., Dep.,		3.8
						Amort./Cur. Mat. L/T/D	(14) 1.8	
							.8	
		.4	.3				.3	.2
		.9	.5			Fixed/Worth	.9	.6
		NM	1.0				2.5	2.3
		.6	.3				.7	.4
		2.1	1.3			Debt/Worth	1.8	1.3
		NM	2.3				7.3	7.4
		56.5	20.1			% Profit Before Taxes/Tangible	32.5	54.6
	(10)	14.4	(17) 10.1			Net Worth	(79) 11.1	(43) 30.0
		6.6	1.6				2.2	11.8
		17.5	9.3				14.3	24.2
		8.7	5.1			% Profit Before Taxes/Total Assets	5.0	14.4
		4.8	1.5				.2	4.5
		17.0	6.8				15.1	17.2
		7.8	4.2			Sales/Net Fixed Assets	6.0	7.8
		3.2	2.7				2.8	4.2
		2.8	1.5				2.9	2.7
		1.9	1.0			Sales/Total Assets	1.6	1.8
		1.6	.7				.9	1.0
		1.1	1.7				1.3	1.1
	(11)	2.4	(17) 2.4			% Depr., Dep., Amort./Sales	(84) 2.4	(36) 2.2
		4.2	5.7				4.7	4.1
						% Officers', Directors'		1.6 1.5
						Owners' Comp/Sales	(29) 4.2	(21) 3.6
							7.4	6.2
1097M	13580M	198697M	586009M	363060M	115059M	Net Sales ($)	3122125M	1000999M
428M	7490M	101181M	462017M	479019M	146184M	Total Assets ($)	2159300M	739022M

M = $ thousand   MM = $ million
See Pages viii through xx for Explanation of Ratios and Data

© RMA 2024

AGRICULTURE—Nursery and Tree Production NAICS 111421

Comparative Historical Data | Current Data Sorted by Sales

				Type of Statement						
				Unqualified					4	2
1	5	2		Reviewed				4	4	4
8	6	8		Compiled		2		1	1	2
5	4	6		Tax Returns		3	1	8	8	1
7	10	4		Other	1	9 (4/1-9/30/23)	4	37 (10/1/23-3/31/24)		9
37	28	26			0-1MM	1-3MM	3-5MM	5-10MM	10-25MM	25MM & OVER
4/1/21-3/31/22 ALL	4/1/22-3/31/23 ALL	4/1/23-3/31/24 ALL								
58	53	46		NUMBER OF STATEMENTS	1	5	1	8	13	18
%	%	%		ASSETS	%	%	%	%	%	%
15.3	7.9	7.8		Cash & Equivalents					7.6	6.1
7.7	8.2	8.8		Trade Receivables (net)					5.7	14.4
31.3	30.2	32.0		Inventory					37.7	38.9
2.5	1.7	1.5		All Other Current					.6	2.9
56.8	48.0	50.1		Total Current					51.5	62.3
31.2	36.7	34.1		Fixed Assets (net)					38.8	29.2
7.3	5.6	8.7		Intangibles (net)					4.3	2.9
4.7	9.8	7.2		All Other Non-Current					5.4	5.6
100.0	100.0	100.0		Total					100.0	100.0
				LIABILITIES						
8.9	8.8	6.4		Notes Payable-Short Term					9.4	5.5
2.9	2.2	3.3		Cur. Mat.-L.T.D.					1.9	3.1
5.9	6.2	7.7		Trade Payables					5.6	9.4
.0	.1	.0		Income Taxes Payable					.0	.0
6.6	5.9	11.6		All Other Current					13.6	9.6
24.4	23.1	29.1		Total Current					30.5	27.7
21.0	25.0	21.9		Long-Term Debt					17.4	17.8
.4	.5	.7		Deferred Taxes					.5	1.2
9.6	3.3	5.5		All Other Non-Current					4.7	2.3
44.6	48.1	42.9		Net Worth					46.9	51.1
100.0	100.0	100.0		Total Liabilities & Net Worth					100.0	100.0
				INCOME DATA						
100.0	100.0	100.0		Net Sales					100.0	100.0
42.4	42.3	36.5		Gross Profit					33.6	31.0
33.6	35.7	29.9		Operating Expenses					26.9	23.0
8.8	6.6	6.6		Operating Profit					6.7	8.1
-1.9	-.1	.7		All Other Expenses (net)					-.2	1.0
10.7	6.7	5.9		Profit Before Taxes					7.0	7.0
				RATIOS						
5.3	6.7	3.4							3.1	3.7
2.9	2.4	1.8		Current					1.7	2.3
1.8	1.6	1.1							1.0	1.7
1.9	2.9	1.1							.6	1.0
1.3	.7	.5		Quick					.4	.6
.5	.3	.2							.2	.4
3	120.3	2	173.5	6	62.2		Sales/Receivables		7	48.8	8	44.3
11	32.0	12	30.2	13	29.0				11	33.3	16	22.6
24	15.0	30	12.1	32	11.5				23	15.8	51	7.2
0	UND	3	113.5	37	9.9		Cost of Sales/Inventory		65	5.6	52	7.0
99	3.7	122	3.0	130	2.8				166	2.2	166	2.2
243	1.5	261	1.4	228	1.6				261	1.4	215	1.7
1	265.1	4	103.1	5	79.1		Cost of Sales/Payables		4	87.5	18	20.0
16	23.2	11	32.5	22	16.8				13	28.6	26	14.2
33	11.2	39	9.4	54	6.7				47	7.7	38	9.6
2.4	2.8	2.8		Sales/Working Capital					3.1	2.2
4.9	4.6	6.0							4.4	4.3
14.9	15.8	NM							NM	8.7
45.5	20.6	14.0		EBIT/Interest					20.8	24.0
(51) 16.6	(51) 9.3	(43) 5.6							5.8	10.0
8.3	3.4	1.6							2.7	1.9
14.8	8.7	6.0		Net Profit + Depr., Dep., Amort./Cur. Mat. L/T/D						
(10) 5.8	(12) 5.9	(12) 1.6								
.8	2.6	.3								
.2	.3	.3		Fixed/Worth					.6	.3
.6	.6	.7							.9	.4
1.6	1.6	2.7							1.9	1.1
.4	.3	.5		Debt/Worth					.6	.4
.9	.9	1.5							1.4	1.0
2.9	2.6	32.6							3.0	2.1
75.9	29.5	23.2		% Profit Before Taxes/Tangible Net Worth					26.1	26.4
(50) 27.0	(45) 12.7	(37) 10.5						(12)	10.5	(17) 12.6
13.8	5.0	5.4							7.5	8.0
29.1	15.2	14.0		% Profit Before Taxes/Total Assets					14.8	16.6
14.9	7.6	6.7							6.5	8.2
7.8	3.0	2.3							2.7	3.6
14.8	7.7	8.0		Sales/Net Fixed Assets					7.4	7.1
7.1	4.7	4.3							3.9	5.0
3.3	3.1	2.4							2.5	2.6
2.5	2.4	2.0		Sales/Total Assets					2.0	2.0
1.5	1.4	1.3							1.5	1.4
1.1	.9	.8							.8	.8
1.4	2.0	1.6		% Depr., Dep., Amort./Sales					1.8	1.8
(48) 3.0	(38) 3.4	(37) 3.0						(11)	4.3	2.6
5.4	4.1	5.7							6.2	5.8
1.4	.8	1.1		% Officers', Directors' Owners' Comp/Sales						
(19) 3.4	(14) 6.8	(13) 1.5								
7.4	9.7	5.6								
1075639M	1451622M	1277502M		Net Sales ($)	904M	8469M	3739M	56555M	214459M	993376M
910532M	1285759M	1196319M		Total Assets ($)	921M	5126M	12552M	151054M	179235M	847431M

M = $ thousand   MM = $ million
See Pages viii through xx for Explanation of Ratios and Data

© RMA 2024

AGRICULTURE—All Other Miscellaneous Crop Farming   NAICS 111998

Current Data Sorted by Assets / Comparative Historical Data

							Type of Statement				
		1	1	4	1	1	Unqualified		7		5
		1	2	5	3	1	Reviewed		20		13
		1	4	6			Compiled		28		16
	4	4	10	3			Tax Returns		52		37
	3	6	5	3		3	Other		68		59
		6 (4/1-9/30/23)		66 (10/1/23-3/31/24)					4/1/19-		4/1/20-
	0-500M	500M-2MM	2-10MM	10-50MM	50-100MM	100-250MM			3/31/20		3/31/21
	7	12	22	21	5	5	NUMBER OF STATEMENTS		175 ALL		130 ALL
	%	%	%	%	%	%	**ASSETS**		%		%
		14.1	17.3	6.8			Cash & Equivalents		7.5		9.0
		.0	7.8	12.0			Trade Receivables (net)		8.8		10.6
		1.0	9.4	15.1			Inventory		11.1		12.8
		13.8	3.2	5.7			All Other Current		5.9		3.2
		29.1	37.7	39.6			Total Current		33.3		35.7
		52.0	46.6	46.9			Fixed Assets (net)		51.0		54.7
		3.1	4.8	1.3			Intangibles (net)		4.0		2.1
		15.8	10.9	12.2			All Other Non-Current		11.7		7.5
		100.0	100.0	100.0			Total		100.0		100.0
							LIABILITIES				
		6.6	14.7	14.5			Notes Payable-Short Term		20.7		24.2
		2.1	5.3	3.3			Cur. Mat.-L.T.D.		4.0		7.5
		.8	7.6	4.9			Trade Payables		3.1		5.9
		.0	.1	.3			Income Taxes Payable		.2		.1
		3.0	9.7	3.0			All Other Current		4.3		3.9
		12.5	37.4	26.0			Total Current		32.4		41.5
		49.2	25.2	21.6			Long-Term Debt		32.9		29.7
		.0	.9	.9			Deferred Taxes		.5		.4
		16.8	.8	5.7			All Other Non-Current		9.6		3.4
		21.4	35.7	45.8			Net Worth		24.6		24.9
		100.0	100.0	100.0			Total Liabilities & Net Worth		100.0		100.0
							INCOME DATA				
		100.0	100.0	100.0			Net Sales		100.0		100.0
							Gross Profit				
		77.1	96.4	86.8			Operating Expenses		90.8		89.1
		22.9	3.6	13.2			Operating Profit		9.2		10.9
		10.8	1.2	2.0			All Other Expenses (net)		3.5		.9
		12.1	2.4	11.1			Profit Before Taxes		5.7		10.0
							RATIOS				
		23.3	2.7	2.5					2.9		3.0
		.6	1.7	1.4			Current		1.3		1.3
		.2	.3	.8					.5		.7
		1.9	2.4	1.1					1.6		1.9
		.6	.7	.6			Quick		.5		.5
		.2	.2	.3					.1		.2
	0 UND	0 UND	0 UND					0 UND		0 UND	
	0 UND	2 223.2	19 19.4				Sales/Receivables	7 53.2		14 25.7	
	0 UND	31 11.9	96 3.8					55 6.6		72 5.1	
							Cost of Sales/Inventory				
							Cost of Sales/Payables				
		3.9	7.3	2.2					3.3		3.0
		-87.4	10.8	5.7			Sales/Working Capital		16.4		11.4
		-7.0	-4.2	-22.5					-10.0		-11.8
			7.0	12.5					7.3		10.7
		(20)	.2	(20) 1.9			EBIT/Interest	(151)	2.6	(96)	3.0
			-3.6	.9					.6		.7
							Net Profit + Depr., Dep.,		4.2		
							Amort./Cur. Mat. L/T/D	(29)	2.0		
									.9		
		.3	.4	.4					.8		.7
		2.3	1.0	1.5			Fixed/Worth		1.4		1.1
		-.7	4.1	2.1					64.2		3.0
		.1	.4	.5					.6		.4
		1.5	1.4	1.1			Debt/Worth		1.6		1.1
		-3.1	7.5	3.1					107.2		5.6
			9.0	14.9			% Profit Before Taxes/Tangible		24.0		24.1
		(18)	1.2	(20) 6.2			Net Worth	(133)	9.4	(104)	11.0
			-18.2	-.2					-.3		2.2
		32.1	5.5	8.7					9.6		14.0
		6.1	-1.1	2.5			% Profit Before Taxes/Total Assets		3.9		5.3
		-3.2	-5.2	-.1					-1.1		.4
		6.6	12.0	3.4					5.8		4.8
		3.2	4.8	1.7			Sales/Net Fixed Assets		2.1		1.2
		1.3	.8	.7					.8		.6
		2.5	3.7	.9					1.8		1.5
		1.5	1.2	.5			Sales/Total Assets		.8		.7
		.5	.6	.3					.5		.4
			2.4	2.7					3.3		4.6
		(15)	5.2	(18) 5.9			% Depr., Dep., Amort./Sales	(139)	7.0	(81)	9.8
			12.6	9.7					12.1		16.7
							% Officers', Directors'		1.3		1.2
							Owners' Comp/Sales	(36)	3.5	(23)	2.3
									7.1		5.3
	12081M	17037M	197919M	378991M	256051M	666089M	Net Sales ($)		3073134M		1712026M
	2140M	13190M	114655M	555742M	352979M	762257M	Total Assets ($)		3773501M		2066331M

© RMA 2024   M = $ thousand   MM = $ million
See Pages viii through xx for Explanation of Ratios and Data

AGRICULTURE—All Other Miscellaneous Crop Farming NAICS 111998

Comparative Historical Data | Current Data Sorted by Sales

Comparative Historical Data			Type of Statement	Current Data Sorted by Sales					
6	9	7	Unqualified			1	1	2	4
14	21	12	Reviewed		1	3	3	3	5
9	7	11	Compiled	1	2	3	3	3	1
24	44	21	Tax Returns	3	10	1	1	3	
54	59	21	Other	4	5	1	3	3	5
4/1/21-3/31/22 ALL	4/1/22-3/31/23 ALL	4/1/23-3/31/24 ALL		0-1MM	6 (4/1-9/30/23) 1-3MM	3-5MM	66 (10/1/23-3/31/24) 5-10MM	10-25MM	25MM & OVER
107	140	72	NUMBER OF STATEMENTS	8	17	7	11	14	15
%	%	%	ASSETS	%	%	%	%	%	%
7.5	10.5	13.9	Cash & Equivalents	18.2	17.5		9.7		9.2
8.6	7.2	7.6	Trade Receivables (net)	.2	10.8		14.5		14.0
15.2	12.1	9.9	Inventory	2.0	10.4		18.1		19.2
2.1	6.3	5.6	All Other Current	7.2	6.6		3.7		4.0
33.4	36.1	37.0	Total Current	27.6	45.3		46.0		46.5
54.5	51.2	45.7	Fixed Assets (net)	49.6	40.4		38.4		30.5
3.9	1.6	4.8	Intangibles (net)	.7	3.9		6.2		11.9
8.2	11.0	12.5	All Other Non-Current	22.1	10.4		9.3		11.2
100.0	100.0	100.0	Total	100.0	100.0		100.0		100.0
			LIABILITIES						
17.6	24.9	14.2	Notes Payable-Short Term	14.5	13.0		16.0		13.4
3.2	4.0	6.9	Cur. Mat.-L.T.D.	7.4	2.0		7.2		2.6
3.7	3.5	5.0	Trade Payables	.0	9.9		4.0		10.9
.0	.1	.3	Income Taxes Payable	.0	.0		.1		.4
2.4	3.6	7.5	All Other Current	16.5	3.6		3.7		6.0
26.9	36.1	33.9	Total Current	38.4	28.6		30.9		33.2
32.1	37.4	29.1	Long-Term Debt	41.2	21.2		19.1		14.9
.3	.3	.5	Deferred Taxes	.0	2.6		.6		.1
3.9	6.0	9.6	All Other Non-Current	27.0	.3		5.7		5.1
36.8	20.2	26.9	Net Worth	-6.5	47.3		43.7		46.6
100.0	100.0	100.0	Total Liabilties & Net Worth	100.0	100.0		100.0		100.0
			INCOME DATA						
100.0	100.0	100.0	Net Sales	100.0	100.0		100.0		100.0
			Gross Profit						
88.9	90.9	89.7	Operating Expenses	94.8	92.5		93.7		96.6
11.1	9.1	10.3	Operating Profit	5.2	7.5		6.3		3.4
.7	2.0	3.0	All Other Expenses (net)	.1	1.3		1.4		1.0
10.4	7.1	7.3	Profit Before Taxes	5.1	6.1		4.9		2.4
			RATIOS						
3.3	3.8	2.5		4.9	2.5		4.5		2.4
1.6	1.4	1.3	Current	2.0	1.5		1.8		1.2
.8	.8	.6		.2	1.2		.8		1.0
1.4	1.7	1.8		2.2	1.8		2.7		1.5
.7	.6	.6	Quick	.3	1.0		.7		.6
.2	.1	.2		.1	.6		.2		.3
0 UND	0 UND	0 UND		0 UND	0 UND		0 UND		19 19.4
8 43.9	0 UND	3 138.3	Sales/Receivables	0 UND	33 11.1		25 14.6		40 9.2
62 5.9	35 10.4	41 8.8		0 UND	101 3.6		72 5.1		51 7.2
			Cost of Sales/Inventory						
			Cost of Sales/Payables						
3.3	3.9	4.3		4.2	3.7		2.3		4.2
10.3	13.8	12.4	Sales/Working Capital	86.5	8.7		10.8		16.0
-20.8	-15.8	-10.0		-7.3	11.4		-27.4		484.9
15.8	9.0	9.6		12.6			16.0		9.8
(87) 4.7	(111) 3.0	(63) 2.2	EBIT/Interest	(16) 3.8		(13)	1.6	(14)	1.9
2.5	.8	.0		-1.0			.1		-.1
2.9	9.0	16.0	Net Profit + Depr., Dep.,						
(15) 2.0	(10) 2.7	(14) 1.6	Amort./Cur. Mat. L/T/D						
1.3	.1	.8							
.7	.7	.4		.2	.5		.3		.2
1.3	1.3	1.1	Fixed/Worth	1.4	1.0		1.6		.8
2.2	3.1	2.7		-.7	2.0		6.9		1.2
.4	.4	.4		.4	.6		.3		.7
1.0	1.5	1.4	Debt/Worth	2.2	1.4		.9		1.6
3.3	14.5	6.5		-2.5	3.1		15.4		3.2
31.9	32.2	33.1	% Profit Before Taxes/Tangible	58.6	33.1		10.6		23.0
(89) 12.4	(111) 12.5	(59) 4.8	Net Worth	(12) 4.5	-.9	(12)	4.8	(14)	14.5
5.5	2.6	-5.1		-19.8	-16.7		-1.4		-9.1
12.6	12.5	11.2	% Profit Before Taxes/Total	42.8	6.4		8.3		10.0
6.1	4.0	2.9	Assets	2.7	-.3		2.3		3.0
2.6	-.2	-2.9		-9.4	-3.0		-.5		-5.5
4.4	6.8	9.4		20.6	7.6		9.0		13.4
1.5	2.0	2.4	Sales/Net Fixed Assets	5.5	4.7		2.2		3.4
.6	.7	1.1		1.5	1.1		1.1		1.6
1.5	2.3	2.3		5.1	2.7		2.7		1.8
.6	.9	.9	Sales/Total Assets	1.7	1.5		.8		1.2
.4	.5	.4		.8	.3		.5		.6
3.5	3.1	3.1					2.7		1.2
(78) 7.7	(88) 6.4	(50) 5.9	% Depr., Dep., Amort./Sales			(10)	6.0	(12)	3.5
13.2	15.2	13.1					9.4		6.7
.9	1.2	1.0	% Officers', Directors'						
(28) 2.6	(37) 2.2	(10) 3.3	Owners' Comp/Sales						
4.7	3.9	7.1							
1419973M	2177151M	1528168M	Net Sales ($)	4917M	32812M	26165M	85179M	217512M	1161583M
1624830M	2859423M	1800963M	Total Assets ($)	23921M	72677M	43685M	169443M	281099M	1210138M

© RMA 2024
M = $ thousand   MM = $ million
See Pages viii through xx for Explanation of Ratios and Data

AGRICULTURE—Beef Cattle Ranching and Farming NAICS 112111

Current Data Sorted by Assets | Comparative Historical Data

						Type of Statement		
						Unqualified	2	
				4		Reviewed	7	3
	1		3			Compiled	16	2
5	10	2	1			Tax Returns	37	19
	2	6	3		1	Other	23	12
	4 (4/1-9/30/23)		34 (10/1/23-3/31/24)				4/1/19-3/31/20	4/1/20-3/31/21
0-500M	500M-2MM	2-10MM	10-50MM	50-100MM	100-250MM		ALL	ALL
5	13	8	11		1	NUMBER OF STATEMENTS	85	36
%	%	%	%	%	%	ASSETS	%	%
	5.3		10.7			Cash & Equivalents	3.4	7.3
	8.3		4.4			Trade Receivables (net)	6.4	3.2
	50.2		42.0			Inventory	25.9	22.4
	3.2		1.0			All Other Current	5.4	1.7
	66.9		58.1	DATA		Total Current	41.1	34.6
	23.1		33.8	NOT		Fixed Assets (net)	48.1	47.8
	.0		1.9	AVAILABLE		Intangibles (net)	3.0	9.2
	10.0		6.3			All Other Non-Current	7.8	8.4
	100.0		100.0			Total	100.0	100.0
						LIABILITIES		
	26.3		20.9			Notes Payable-Short Term	34.2	23.0
	.1		1.7			Cur. Mat.-L.T.D.	2.1	3.3
	6.6		1.3			Trade Payables	2.6	2.1
	.0		.9			Income Taxes Payable	.5	.3
	7.5		9.7			All Other Current	7.2	7.4
	40.5		34.6			Total Current	46.5	36.0
	16.2		20.6			Long-Term Debt	32.4	36.4
	.0		.1			Deferred Taxes	.0	.0
	9.7		1.9			All Other Non-Current	2.4	3.6
	33.6		42.8			Net Worth	18.6	24.0
	100.0		100.0			Total Liabilities & Net Worth	100.0	100.0
						INCOME DATA		
	100.0		100.0			Net Sales	100.0	100.0
						Gross Profit		
	94.9		95.0			Operating Expenses	95.2	94.0
	5.1		5.0			Operating Profit	4.8	6.0
	1.1		1.4			All Other Expenses (net)	4.3	3.5
	4.1		3.5			Profit Before Taxes	.5	2.5
						RATIOS		
	9.7		2.2				2.1	1.8
	1.9		1.5			Current	.9	.8
	1.4		1.2				.5	.3
	2.0		2.1				.6	.6
	.4		.2			Quick	(83) .1	(35) .1
	.0		.1				.0	.0
	0 UND		0 UND				0 UND	0 UND
	0 UND		4 101.3			Sales/Receivables	0 UND	0 UND
	1 531.5		25 14.7				22 16.6	1 484.9
						Cost of Sales/Inventory		
						Cost of Sales/Payables		
	2.6		2.8				7.0	5.2
	6.1		3.9			Sales/Working Capital	-36.3	-74.4
	20.6		31.4				-5.4	-5.1
	6.2		5.9				5.6	5.5
	(12) 1.6		1.9			EBIT/Interest	(73) 1.7	(28) 1.4
	.4		1.1				-.4	-.2
						Net Profit + Depr., Dep., Amort./Cur. Mat. L/T/D		
	.0		.2				.5	.4
	1.1		.6			Fixed/Worth	1.3	1.5
	NM		2.3				5.2	NM
	.3		.4				.6	.8
	1.8		1.8			Debt/Worth	1.8	1.9
	NM		5.4				51.2	-7.1
	39.4		26.0				17.1	16.7
	(10) 16.8		(10) 9.9			% Profit Before Taxes/Tangible Net Worth	(65) 3.4	(25) 2.9
	1.1		2.3				-6.8	-.4
	16.4		12.7				7.1	6.1
	1.7		2.2			% Profit Before Taxes/Total Assets	1.6	1.4
	-2.5		.4				-3.3	-1.2
	UND		11.6				15.7	18.2
	21.7		2.3			Sales/Net Fixed Assets	1.8	1.9
	6.0		1.4				.5	.4
	3.2		1.3				2.2	1.9
	2.0		.9			Sales/Total Assets	.8	.7
	.9		.5				.3	.3
			1.0				1.6	4.9
			(10) 3.1			% Depr., Dep., Amort./Sales	(59) 8.1	(22) 6.4
			8.4				22.5	16.7
							1.3	.3
						% Officers', Directors' Owners' Comp/Sales	(25) 5.5	(10) 1.3
							12.9	3.1
8826M	25689M	44255M	273900M		936864M	Net Sales ($)	1431284M	296865M
1390M	12649M	44523M	242822M		193859M	Total Assets ($)	1223639M	377693M

© RMA 2024 M = $ thousand   MM = $ million
See Pages viii through xx for Explanation of Ratios and Data

AGRICULTURE—Beef Cattle Ranching and Farming NAICS 112111

Comparative Historical Data | Current Data Sorted by Sales

				Type of Statement						
		1		Unqualified		1			3	3
5	5		4	Reviewed						
3	8		4	Compiled		11		2	1	
17	18		18	Tax Returns	3	4	3	2	3	2
25	17		12	Other	1			3	3	
4/1/21-	4/1/22-		4/1/23-			4 (4/1-9/30/23)		34 (10/1/23-3/31/24)		
3/31/22	3/31/23		3/31/24		0-1MM	1-3MM	3-5MM	5-10MM	10-25MM	25MM & OVER
ALL	ALL		ALL							
50	49		38	NUMBER OF STATEMENTS	4	16	3	3	7	5
%	%		%	ASSETS	%	%	%	%	%	%
8.9	8.9		11.3	Cash & Equivalents		15.1				
4.7	7.3		4.8	Trade Receivables (net)		.6				
28.3	30.0		34.2	Inventory		35.0				
5.7	3.2		3.5	All Other Current		3.0				
47.6	49.4		53.8	Total Current		53.7				
43.4	37.5		35.5	Fixed Assets (net)		32.6				
3.4	3.7		3.2	Intangibles (net)		4.9				
5.5	9.4		7.5	All Other Non-Current		8.7				
100.0	100.0		100.0	Total		100.0				
				LIABILITIES						
24.9	24.8		27.2	Notes Payable-Short Term		37.5				
2.5	1.9		1.5	Cur. Mat.-L.T.D.		.6				
4.5	4.2		4.6	Trade Payables		3.8				
.0	.3		.3	Income Taxes Payable		.0				
5.4	15.6		17.1	All Other Current		6.5				
37.4	46.7		50.7	Total Current		48.3				
18.5	25.7		20.3	Long-Term Debt		20.0				
.2	.2		.0	Deferred Taxes						
6.4	16.2		16.3	All Other Non-Current		30.4				
37.5	11.2		12.7	Net Worth		1.3				
100.0	100.0		100.0	Total Liabilities & Net Worth		100.0				
				INCOME DATA						
100.0	100.0		100.0	Net Sales		100.0				
				Gross Profit						
92.5	95.6		97.4	Operating Expenses		96.2				
7.5	4.4		2.6	Operating Profit		3.8				
1.2	3.1		.6	All Other Expenses (net)		.3				
6.2	1.3		1.9	Profit Before Taxes		3.5				
				RATIOS						
3.0	2.0		2.6			3.3				
1.7	1.3		1.5	Current		1.4				
.7	.6		.6			.3				
.7	.7		1.0			.4				
(49) .2	.2		.2	Quick		.0				
.0	.0		.0			.0				
0 UND	0 UND		0 UND			0 UND				
0 UND	0 UND		0 UND	Sales/Receivables		0 UND				
7 52.7	19 18.9		6 57.7			0 UND				
				Cost of Sales/Inventory						
				Cost of Sales/Payables						
2.4	4.4		3.0			6.9				
10.6	14.1		14.2	Sales/Working Capital		17.9				
-6.2	-5.8		-12.9			-10.3				
9.6	6.3		5.2			6.2				
(42) 4.9	(43) 2.4	(35)	1.8	EBIT/Interest	(13)	1.8				
1.2	.1		.6			1.0				
				Net Profit + Depr., Dep., Amort./Cur. Mat. L/T/D						
.3	.3		.1			.1				
.9	.8		1.2	Fixed/Worth		1.3				
2.2	3.0		NM			-.6				
.3	.7		.5			.5				
1.1	1.3		2.0	Debt/Worth		2.3				
NM	11.5		NM			-2.9				
18.0	16.2		32.7			50.2				
(38) 9.5	(38) 6.8	(29)	9.0	% Profit Before Taxes/Tangible Net Worth	(11)	18.5				
2.0	-1.1		1.0			4.1				
10.1	6.8		11.9			41.6				
5.0	1.3		1.4	% Profit Before Taxes/Total Assets		3.7				
.1	-1.9		-1.8			.0				
19.3	21.4		88.0			688.0				
2.8	6.5		7.6	Sales/Net Fixed Assets		17.6				
.6	.9		1.4			2.0				
1.9	2.6		3.4			4.5				
.8	1.2		1.3	Sales/Total Assets		2.3				
.4	.4		.8			.9				
2.1	1.1		1.0							
(30) 5.9	(34) 4.2	(26)	5.1	% Depr., Dep., Amort./Sales						
13.4	14.6		18.3							
1.2	.6		1.2							
(14) 3.2	(13) 1.4	(12)	2.5	% Officers', Directors' Owners' Comp/Sales						
6.7	2.3		4.5							
566498M	960351M		1289534M	Net Sales ($)	2468M	35448M	10077M	24463M	110859M	1106219M
592541M	528344M		495243M	Total Assets ($)	2361M	29147M	7315M	30622M	139654M	286144M

M = $ thousand   MM = $ million
See Pages viii through xx for Explanation of Ratios and Data

© RMA 2024

AGRICULTURE—Cattle Feedlots NAICS 112112

Current Data Sorted by Assets

	0-500M	500M-2MM	2-10MM	10-50MM	50-100MM	100-250MM
Type of Statement						
Unqualified				1	2	1
Reviewed				2	1	
Compiled			2	1		
Tax Returns		3	3			
Other		10 (4/1-9/30/23)		17 (10/1/23-3/31/24)		
				2	4	2
NUMBER OF STATEMENTS		3	8	6	7	3

Data Not Available for 0-500M column.

Comparative Historical Data

	4/1/19-3/31/20 ALL	4/1/20-3/31/21 ALL
Type of Statement		
Unqualified	11	7
Reviewed	14	4
Compiled	12	6
Tax Returns	20	5
Other	37	13
NUMBER OF STATEMENTS	94	35

ASSETS	%	%
Cash & Equivalents	7.3	10.0
Trade Receivables (net)	12.6	14.1
Inventory	41.0	33.1
All Other Current	6.0	9.4
Total Current	67.0	66.6
Fixed Assets (net)	26.9	25.9
Intangibles (net)	1.3	3.5
All Other Non-Current	4.8	3.9
Total	100.0	100.0

LIABILITIES		
Notes Payable-Short Term	24.6	19.7
Cur. Mat.-L.T.D.	3.8	3.3
Trade Payables	5.6	5.5
Income Taxes Payable	.2	.8
All Other Current	6.8	7.8
Total Current	41.0	37.1
Long-Term Debt	9.8	11.8
Deferred Taxes	.3	.1
All Other Non-Current	6.2	.3
Net Worth	42.8	50.7
Total Liabilities & Net Worth	100.0	100.0

INCOME DATA		
Net Sales	100.0	100.0
Gross Profit		
Operating Expenses	97.3	96.5
Operating Profit	2.7	3.5
All Other Expenses (net)	.5	-1.2
Profit Before Taxes	2.1	4.7

RATIOS		
Current	2.6	3.4
	1.5	2.0
	1.2	1.1
Quick	1.0	1.8
	(92) .5	.8
	.1	.1
Sales/Receivables	0 UND	1 258.8
	16 23.3	16 22.6
	47 7.8	40 9.1
Cost of Sales/Inventory		
Cost of Sales/Payables		
Sales/Working Capital	2.7	2.7
	5.5	6.4
	13.8	14.2
EBIT/Interest	11.1	32.2
	(85) 3.5	(32) 7.7
	.8	2.4
Net Profit + Depr., Dep., Amort./Cur. Mat. L/T/D	24.9	
	(11) 11.3	
	1.9	
Fixed/Worth	.2	.1
	.4	.4
	1.2	1.0
Debt/Worth	.5	.5
	1.2	.9
	3.1	3.3
% Profit Before Taxes/Tangible Net Worth	18.4	39.8
	(83) 8.7	(33) 19.3
	-.5	7.8
% Profit Before Taxes/Total Assets	8.8	13.2
	3.4	10.5
	-.8	2.2
Sales/Net Fixed Assets	23.7	41.5
	6.9	7.9
	3.9	4.9
Sales/Total Assets	2.0	2.3
	1.4	1.3
	1.0	1.1
% Depr., Dep., Amort./Sales	.9	1.1
	(74) 1.8	(31) 1.7
	3.5	3.7
% Officers', Directors' Owners' Comp/Sales	.4	
	(15) 1.2	
	1.9	

	0-500M	500M-2MM	2-10MM	10-50MM	50-100MM	100-250MM		4/1/19-3/31/20	4/1/20-3/31/21
Net Sales ($)		55544M	252262M	284746M	691261M	657146M		6012199M	2170700M
Total Assets ($)		2556M	31809M	137269M	531565M	453307M		4173773M	1438094M

M = $ thousand MM = $ million
See Pages viii through xx for Explanation of Ratios and Data

© RMA 2024

AGRICULTURE—Cattle Feedlots NAICS 112112

Comparative Historical Data / Current Data Sorted by Sales

Comparative Historical Data			Type of Statement	Current Data Sorted by Sales					
3	9	4	Unqualified						4
5	6	3	Reviewed						3
7	5	3	Compiled						3
4	7	6	Tax Returns	1	1	1	2		1
21	13	11	Other				1		7
4/1/21-3/31/22 ALL	4/1/22-3/31/23 ALL	4/1/23-3/31/24 ALL		0-1MM	10 (4/1-9/30/23) 1-3MM	3-5MM	3 17 (10/1/23-3/31/24) 5-10MM	10-25MM	25MM & OVER
40	40	27	NUMBER OF STATEMENTS	1	1	2	5		18
%	%	%	ASSETS	%	%	%	%	%	%
9.2	10.1	9.3	Cash & Equivalents						10.7
15.3	12.7	11.3	Trade Receivables (net)					D	13.1
36.2	35.6	30.9	Inventory					A	30.3
4.9	10.5	7.4	All Other Current					T	10.4
65.6	68.9	58.9	Total Current					A	64.4
28.8	25.0	28.7	Fixed Assets (net)						23.4
3.0	.4	.1	Intangibles (net)					N	.1
2.6	5.7	12.3	All Other Non-Current					O	12.1
100.0	100.0	100.0	Total					T	100.0
			LIABILITIES					A	
17.0	22.0	18.6	Notes Payable-Short Term					V	21.9
2.5	1.5	1.6	Cur. Mat.-L.T.D.					A	1.1
7.3	8.8	7.2	Trade Payables					I	7.0
.6	.0	.0	Income Taxes Payable					L	.0
4.6	14.9	8.6	All Other Current					A	7.6
31.9	47.3	36.0	Total Current					B	37.6
11.2	8.2	11.4	Long-Term Debt					L	7.8
.0	.0	.0	Deferred Taxes					E	.0
1.1	2.1	1.9	All Other Non-Current						.7
55.7	42.4	50.7	Net Worth						53.9
100.0	100.0	100.0	Total Liabilities & Net Worth						100.0
			INCOME DATA						
100.0	100.0	100.0	Net Sales						100.0
			Gross Profit						
92.9	95.6	91.2	Operating Expenses						94.1
7.1	4.4	8.8	Operating Profit						5.9
1.9	-.2	1.0	All Other Expenses (net)						.1
5.1	4.6	7.8	Profit Before Taxes						5.8
			RATIOS						
4.3	2.4	2.1							2.3
2.1	1.6	1.6	Current						1.6
1.4	1.2	1.3							1.3
1.5	1.4	1.2							1.6
.9	.4	.4	Quick						.8
.3	.1	.1							.3
4 87.8	0 943.4	0 UND						1	471.6
28 13.1	8 46.2	5 73.2	Sales/Receivables					16	22.9
52 7.0	32 11.3	39 9.3						32	11.3
			Cost of Sales/Inventory						
			Cost of Sales/Payables						
2.2	5.0	3.1							5.6
5.3	8.2	7.6	Sales/Working Capital						7.4
10.7	23.1	18.2							14.3
31.8	17.6	13.2							22.7
(31) 13.3	(36) 4.8	(26) 5.2	EBIT/Interest					(17)	5.3
3.9	1.3	2.3							3.0
			Net Profit + Depr., Dep., Amort./Cur. Mat. L/T/D						
.3	.3	.1							.2
.4	.5	.5	Fixed/Worth						.4
.7	.9	.8							.6
.2	.6	.5							.4
.7	1.1	1.1	Debt/Worth						.9
2.9	3.4	2.2							2.3
35.8	30.6	26.3	% Profit Before Taxes/Tangible Net Worth						26.3
(39) 18.5	(38) 13.7	16.9							20.3
10.4	1.8	9.4							10.8
17.8	15.8	16.3	% Profit Before Taxes/Total Assets						16.5
10.4	4.8	8.0							8.3
3.6	1.1	3.5							4.3
20.0	32.1	27.2							29.9
7.9	11.4	8.3	Sales/Net Fixed Assets						8.7
4.1	4.4	4.7							5.1
2.5	3.1	2.8							3.6
1.5	2.0	1.9	Sales/Total Assets						1.8
1.0	1.3	1.2							1.3
1.1	1.1	1.1							.9
(38) 1.9	(36) 1.6	(24) 1.5	% Depr., Dep., Amort./Sales					(17)	1.3
3.8	2.2	3.9							2.2
			% Officers', Directors' Owners' Comp/Sales						
2510546M	3397361M	1940959M	Net Sales ($)	217M	1600M	8359M	37334M		1893449M
1399661M	1774945M	1156506M	Total Assets ($)	764M	2715M	4813M	48751M		1099463M

© RMA 2024
M = $ thousand   MM = $ million
See Pages viii through xx for Explanation of Ratios and Data

AGRICULTURE—Dairy Cattle and Milk Production NAICS 112120

Current Data Sorted by Assets | Comparative Historical Data

						Type of Statement		
						Unqualified	4	2
		7	34	10	4	Reviewed	152	35
		1	1	1		Compiled	34	5
3	2	6	1	1		Tax Returns	18	9
	3	6	1	1		Other	67	13
		6 (4/1-9/30/23)		81 (10/1/23-3/31/24)			4/1/19-3/31/20	4/1/20-3/31/21
0-500M	500M-2MM	2-10MM	10-50MM	50-100MM	100-250MM		ALL	ALL
3	5	19	40	15	5	NUMBER OF STATEMENTS	275	64
%	%	%	%	%	%	ASSETS	%	%
		2.6	1.3	.9		Cash & Equivalents	2.7	3.0
		3.3	6.5	5.8		Trade Receivables (net)	8.7	12.4
		13.6	15.7	11.6		Inventory	11.6	11.8
		4.4	1.8	2.3		All Other Current	2.4	2.1
		23.9	25.4	20.5		Total Current	25.4	29.1
		65.4	57.1	68.8		Fixed Assets (net)	62.3	59.0
		2.3	.5	1.6		Intangibles (net)	2.9	.9
		8.4	17.0	9.0		All Other Non-Current	9.5	11.0
		100.0	100.0	100.0		Total	100.0	100.0
						LIABILITIES		
		9.0	14.8	14.2		Notes Payable-Short Term	11.8	9.1
		3.5	3.3	4.5		Cur. Mat.-L.T.D.	4.6	3.0
		4.3	4.4	3.6		Trade Payables	4.6	5.1
		.0	.0	.0		Income Taxes Payable	.1	.1
		1.8	4.0	4.1		All Other Current	4.9	3.9
		18.7	26.6	26.4		Total Current	26.0	21.2
		41.9	24.9	25.7		Long-Term Debt	31.6	32.4
		.0	.0	.0		Deferred Taxes	.1	.2
		12.9	1.8	1.1		All Other Non-Current	5.4	2.7
		26.6	46.7	46.8		Net Worth	37.0	43.5
		100.0	100.0	100.0		Total Liabilities & Net Worth	100.0	100.0
						INCOME DATA		
		100.0	100.0	100.0		Net Sales	100.0	100.0
						Gross Profit		
		89.2	101.2	98.9		Operating Expenses	88.7	87.5
		10.8	-1.2	1.1		Operating Profit	11.3	12.5
		7.8	1.8	2.9		All Other Expenses (net)	5.9	4.5
		3.0	-3.1	-1.8		Profit Before Taxes	5.4	8.0
						RATIOS		
		2.4	1.9	1.4			1.5	2.0
		.9	.9	1.1		Current	1.1	1.3
		.2	.6	.5			.7	.8
		.7	.5	.7			.7	1.3
		.2	.3	.2		Quick	.4	.6
		.1	.1	.1			.2	.2
		0 UND	16 23.1	13 27.3			17 21.7	15 24.3
		11 32.6	27 13.4	23 16.2		Sales/Receivables	28 13.2	31 11.6
		22 16.4	47 7.8	70 5.2			59 6.2	79 4.6
						Cost of Sales/Inventory		
						Cost of Sales/Payables		
		4.7	4.8	6.6			7.3	4.4
		-29.4	-29.1	20.8		Sales/Working Capital	56.9	14.3
		-6.3	-6.2	-2.9			-9.9	-21.8
		6.1	1.6	1.2			5.5	15.4
		(16) 1.3	(39) -1.0	.6		EBIT/Interest	(258) 3.0	(62) 5.7
		-.9	-2.6	-.1			1.2	1.7
						Net Profit + Depr., Dep., Amort./Cur. Mat. L/T/D		9.8
							(15) 2.9	
							1.6	
		1.2	1.0	1.0			1.1	.8
		1.9	1.5	1.6		Fixed/Worth	1.6	1.4
		5.1	1.9	2.2			2.7	2.3
		.5	.7	.6			.8	.6
		1.0	1.5	1.1		Debt/Worth	1.5	1.3
		6.1	2.2	1.9			3.3	2.3
		7.7	4.1	2.9		% Profit Before Taxes/Tangible Net Worth	17.3	25.7
		(17) 3.5	-6.0	-3.8			(251) 8.2	(60) 12.7
		-25.9	-21.0	-9.3			1.7	3.9
		3.9	1.8	.5		% Profit Before Taxes/Total Assets	7.4	12.0
		2.0	-2.6	-1.9			3.3	5.7
		-7.5	-8.3	-3.8			.3	1.6
		2.4	1.7	1.1			1.7	2.5
		1.2	1.2	.8		Sales/Net Fixed Assets	1.1	1.3
		.6	.9	.6			.7	.7
		1.6	1.0	.7			.9	1.2
		.7	.7	.5		Sales/Total Assets	.7	.8
		.4	.6	.4			.5	.5
		6.3	6.1	3.9			6.2	4.5
		(18) 9.3	(38) 7.4	8.6		% Depr., Dep., Amort./Sales	(258) 8.5	(61) 7.8
		13.8	8.8	9.5			11.6	10.0
			.7				.6	.5
			(11) .9			% Officers', Directors' Owners' Comp/Sales	(90) 1.2	(11) 1.4
			1.4				2.2	5.7
2230M	5331M	94574M	740071M	540615M	908526M	Net Sales ($)	6108233M	2113639M
1064M	7542M	119508M	949265M	1003204M	744694M	Total Assets ($)	7686921M	1831052M

M = $ thousand   MM = $ million
See Pages viii through xx for Explanation of Ratios and Data

© RMA 2024

AGRICULTURE—Dairy Cattle and Milk Production NAICS 112120

Comparative Historical Data | Current Data Sorted by Sales

Comparative Historical Data				Type of Statement	Current Data Sorted by Sales					
	2			Unqualified				12	23	16
62	70	55		Reviewed	1		3		1	1
4	4	2		Compiled					1	2
15	11	13		Tax Returns	5	2	2	1	1	2
10	17	17		Other	6	1	1	1	3	5
4/1/21-3/31/22 ALL	4/1/22-3/31/23 ALL	4/1/23-3/31/24 ALL			0-1MM	1-3MM	3-5MM	5-10MM	10-25MM	25MM & OVER
						6 (4/1-9/30/23)		81 (10/1/23-3/31/24)		
91	104	87		NUMBER OF STATEMENTS	12	3	6	14	28	24
%	%	%		ASSETS	%	%	%	%	%	%
3.3	2.9	1.9		Cash & Equivalents	3.6			1.3	1.9	.5
9.4	11.6	5.5		Trade Receivables (net)	.2			6.1	7.1	6.4
12.2	12.6	14.2		Inventory	2.0			17.6	14.7	14.8
3.8	3.5	2.7		All Other Current	2.8			.2	2.9	1.2
28.7	30.5	24.2		Total Current	8.6			25.2	26.7	23.0
55.8	56.2	62.1		Fixed Assets (net)	87.0			62.3	59.1	59.3
2.0	1.8	1.3		Intangibles (net)	.1			.0	1.1	1.7
13.5	11.5	12.4		All Other Non-Current	4.3			12.4	13.1	16.0
100.0	100.0	100.0		Total	100.0			100.0	100.0	100.0
				LIABILITIES						
13.2	13.3	13.4		Notes Payable-Short Term	10.1			11.8	11.3	20.9
3.2	3.8	3.4		Cur. Mat.-L.T.D.	2.7			3.9	3.5	3.4
4.4	6.0	4.2		Trade Payables	.0			5.1	4.8	5.4
.0	.0	.0		Income Taxes Payable	.0			.0	.0	.0
3.4	3.7	3.8		All Other Current	3.6			3.0	3.7	5.0
24.3	26.8	24.9		Total Current	16.4			23.8	23.3	34.7
39.8	31.9	30.3		Long-Term Debt	46.9			43.8	26.4	19.7
.0	.0	.0		Deferred Taxes	.0			.0	.0	.0
3.0	2.8	6.3		All Other Non-Current	17.9			16.4	2.0	1.0
32.9	38.4	38.6		Net Worth	18.8			15.9	48.2	44.6
100.0	100.0	100.0		Total Liabilities & Net Worth	100.0			100.0	100.0	100.0
				INCOME DATA						
100.0	100.0	100.0		Net Sales	100.0			100.0	100.0	100.0
				Gross Profit						
92.5	86.2	97.6		Operating Expenses	74.6			103.5	103.7	98.8
7.5	13.8	2.4		Operating Profit	25.4			-3.5	-3.7	1.2
2.8	2.4	3.3		All Other Expenses (net)	14.6			3.1	.0	2.5
4.7	11.4	-.9		Profit Before Taxes	10.9			-6.6	-3.7	-1.3
				RATIOS						
2.2	2.0	1.9			.7			2.1	1.9	1.4
1.1	1.2	.9		Current	.2			.9	1.1	.8
.7	.6	.5			.1			.8	.7	.3
1.0	1.0	.6			.4			.5	.7	.3
.4	.4	.2		Quick	.1			.3	.3	.2
.2	.2	.1			.0			.2	.2	.1
18 20.7	17 21.7	11 32.6			0 UND			17 21.0	14 25.2	14 26.1
32 11.5	38 9.7	19 19.4		Sales/Receivables	0 UND			22 16.8	28 12.9	19 19.1
87 4.2	78 4.7	35 10.3			0 UND			53 6.9	55 6.6	29 12.6
				Cost of Sales/Inventory						
				Cost of Sales/Payables						
3.7	4.5	5.7			-41.1			7.3	4.1	12.5
18.9	27.3	-45.3		Sales/Working Capital	-6.1			-74.9	30.7	-10.7
-11.4	-13.1	-6.4			-3.3			-7.8	-9.8	-2.7
5.2	12.0	3.3						.8	2.1	1.6
(85) 2.0	(94) 5.5	(83) .4		EBIT/Interest				-.9	-.3	.5
-1.0	2.7	-1.7						-3.5	-2.5	-.5
				Net Profit + Depr., Dep., Amort./Cur. Mat. L/T/D						
.9	.9	1.0			1.5			1.3	1.0	.9
1.4	1.4	1.5		Fixed/Worth	1.9			1.5	1.5	1.5
2.3	2.3	2.2			NM			3.8	2.0	2.0
.6	.7	.6			.7			.7	.6	.7
1.4	1.5	1.4		Debt/Worth	1.2			1.6	1.3	1.5
2.9	2.8	2.5			NM			5.0	2.5	2.1
9.1	27.3	5.1						-.8	5.2	4.2
(83) 3.2	(96) 18.0	(82) -2.5		% Profit Before Taxes/Tangible Net Worth	(13) -20.2			-39.3	-3.8	-4.1
-6.8	8.1	-16.0						-39.3	-16.9	-9.6
4.3	11.2	3.1			10.9			-1.1	1.9	1.7
1.5	7.5	-1.7		% Profit Before Taxes/Total Assets	2.8			-7.1	-1.8	-2.1
-3.1	3.1	-6.4			-1.1			-12.0	-8.3	-3.9
1.9	2.2	1.7			1.2			1.3	1.7	1.8
1.2	1.4	1.1		Sales/Net Fixed Assets	.4			1.1	1.3	1.1
.8	.9	.7			.1			.8	.8	.7
1.0	1.1	.9			.8			.8	.9	1.0
.7	.8	.7		Sales/Total Assets	.3			.7	.7	.7
.5	.6	.5			.1			.5	.5	.5
6.3	4.9	5.9			1.9			7.4	6.1	2.7
(84) 8.4	(98) 6.3	(80) 7.9		% Depr., Dep., Amort./Sales	(11) 21.0	(13)		8.8 (27)	7.5 (21)	7.2
9.9	8.2	10.0			54.9			9.6	10.0	9.0
.8	.7	.8							.7	
(18) 1.4	(17) 1.1	(20) 1.3		% Officers', Directors' Owners' Comp/Sales				(10)	1.0	
1.9	2.1	3.0							1.7	
1733935M	3367106M	2291347M		Net Sales ($)	7752M	8153M	25565M	107260M	474657M	1667960M
2336982M	3654869M	2825277M		Total Assets ($)	47197M	8289M	34522M	187621M	790635M	1757013M

© RMA 2024   M = $ thousand   MM = $ million
See Pages viii through xx for Explanation of Ratios and Data

AGRICULTURE—Timber Tract Operations NAICS 113110

Current Data Sorted by Assets | **Comparative Historical Data**

0-500M	4 (4/1-9/30/23) 500M-2MM	2-10MM	26 (10/1/23-3/31/24) 10-50MM	50-100MM	100-250MM			Type of Statement		4/1/19-3/31/20 ALL	4/1/20-3/31/21 ALL
		1	1	2	1			Unqualified		8	3
	1	1	2	1				Reviewed			3
		1	4					Compiled		9	4
1		4	7	4	3			Tax Returns		15	14
								Other		21	18
1	2	12	8	6	1			NUMBER OF STATEMENTS		53	42
%	%	%	%	%	%			ASSETS		%	%
		13.0						Cash & Equivalents		8.3	13.2
		21.1						Trade Receivables (net)		7.3	6.8
		13.6						Inventory		15.1	15.5
		6.2						All Other Current		1.7	4.1
		53.9						Total Current		32.4	39.6
		17.3						Fixed Assets (net)		48.6	42.8
		9.6						Intangibles (net)		3.2	4.2
		19.2						All Other Non-Current		15.8	13.3
		100.0						Total		100.0	100.0
								LIABILITIES			
		15.3						Notes Payable-Short Term		9.9	12.5
		3.5						Cur. Mat.-L.T.D.		5.9	7.3
		5.9						Trade Payables		4.7	3.3
		.1						Income Taxes Payable		.3	.1
		16.5						All Other Current		8.0	6.8
		41.3						Total Current		28.8	30.0
		8.4						Long-Term Debt		26.7	34.9
		.0						Deferred Taxes		.0	.1
		.6						All Other Non-Current		1.8	3.3
		49.8						Net Worth		42.6	31.7
		100.0						Total Liabilities & Net Worth		100.0	100.0
								INCOME DATA			
		100.0						Net Sales		100.0	100.0
		95.0						Gross Profit			
		5.0						Operating Expenses		87.8	93.6
		-.5						Operating Profit		12.2	6.4
		5.5						All Other Expenses (net)		2.0	.4
								Profit Before Taxes		10.2	6.0
								RATIOS			
		3.2								3.2	2.0
		1.3					Current				1.1	1.2
		.7								.5	.6
		1.6								1.6	1.6
		.8					Quick				.7	.6
		.3								.1	.3
	0	UND							0	UND	0	UND
	16	23.0					Sales/Receivables		4	89.7	10	35.0
	33	11.0							18	20.2	20	18.5
								Cost of Sales/Inventory			
								Cost of Sales/Payables			
		6.3								9.2	13.2
		71.2					Sales/Working Capital			135.4	33.8
		-33.3								-9.1	-24.8
										11.7	6.1
								EBIT/Interest		(44) 4.3	(38) 3.4
										.8	.6
								Net Profit + Depr., Dep., Amort./Cur. Mat. L/T/D			
		.0								.4	.7
		.3					Fixed/Worth			1.1	1.8
		2.8								3.0	5.3
		.5								.4	.8
		2.4					Debt/Worth			1.4	2.2
		5.2								8.0	NM
		81.5								54.5	34.4
		13.8					% Profit Before Taxes/Tangible Net Worth		(46) 11.6	(32) 5.7
		-16.2								.2	-2.0
		13.5								15.1	12.3
		6.2					% Profit Before Taxes/Total Assets			3.4	4.5
		-2.2								.0	-.9
		UND								41.3	36.6
		63.7					Sales/Net Fixed Assets			4.6	7.0
		14.9								.8	1.3
		6.3								4.8	3.3
		4.5					Sales/Total Assets			2.1	1.9
		2.4								.3	.3
										1.6	2.5
								% Depr., Dep., Amort./Sales		(35) 3.2	(27) 10.7
										14.7	16.6
										1.4	.9
								% Officers', Directors' Owners' Comp/Sales		(16) 2.4	(13) 2.0
										3.9	3.8
15M	9251M	248867M	241035M	477038M	111439M			Net Sales ($)		749841M	631328M
1M	2295M	58539M	202546M	378613M	102002M			Total Assets ($)		1158857M	735619M

M = $ thousand   MM = $ million
See Pages viii through xx for Explanation of Ratios and Data

© RMA 2024

AGRICULTURE—Timber Tract Operations NAICS 113110

Comparative Historical Data | Current Data Sorted by Sales

Comparative Historical Data					Current Data Sorted by Sales					
4	7	5	Type of Statement							5
1	3	2	Unqualified							
3	6	3	Reviewed							3
6	12	5	Compiled					1	2	2
18	13	15	Tax Returns			1		1	6	3
4/1/21-	4/1/22-	4/1/23-	Other		2	4 (4/1-9/30/23)	1	3	26 (10/1/23-3/31/24)	
3/31/22	3/31/23	3/31/24			0-1MM	1-3MM	3-5MM	5-10MM	10-25MM	25MM & OVER
ALL	ALL	ALL	NUMBER OF STATEMENTS		2		2	4	8	13
32	41	30			%	%	%	%	%	%
%	%	%	**ASSETS**							
11.8	10.8	9.3	Cash & Equivalents							5.8
7.9	9.4	13.5	Trade Receivables (net)							12.3
12.3	16.9	15.3	Inventory							13.5
4.1	2.1	4.7	All Other Current							8.7
36.1	39.2	42.8	Total Current							40.3
39.1	41.9	38.3	Fixed Assets (net)							45.6
9.7	4.4	7.0	Intangibles (net)							5.3
15.2	14.5	11.9	All Other Non-Current							8.8
100.0	100.0	100.0	Total							100.0
			LIABILITIES							
13.6	10.0	14.8	Notes Payable-Short Term							14.3
1.7	3.9	4.4	Cur. Mat.-L.T.D.							5.0
2.2	3.3	4.0	Trade Payables							4.5
.2	.0	.1	Income Taxes Payable							.1
10.0	11.7	10.5	All Other Current							12.7
27.7	28.9	33.8	Total Current							36.8
30.7	21.0	15.1	Long-Term Debt							12.1
.0	.0	.0	Deferred Taxes							.0
3.4	2.5	3.3	All Other Non-Current							2.3
38.2	47.5	47.8	Net Worth							48.8
100.0	100.0	100.0	Total Liabilities & Net Worth							100.0
			INCOME DATA							
100.0	100.0	100.0	Net Sales							100.0
			Gross Profit							
82.6	82.5	93.1	Operating Expenses							100.9
17.4	17.5	6.9	Operating Profit							-.9
-.1	5.2	2.6	All Other Expenses (net)							.3
17.5	12.4	4.4	Profit Before Taxes							-1.2
			RATIOS							
3.0	3.1	2.7								1.6
1.3	1.5	1.3	Current							1.2
.6	.8	.7								.7
2.2	2.6	1.5								.9
1.0	1.0	.4	Quick							.3
.3	.2	.3							.2
0 UND	0 UND	0 UND							6	60.8
5 73.6	5 69.3	13 27.1	Sales/Receivables						15	25.0
21 17.7	24 15.0	24 14.9							26	14.0
			Cost of Sales/Inventory							
			Cost of Sales/Payables							
9.6	6.0	6.9								8.9
28.1	22.7	30.9	Sales/Working Capital							31.0
-50.9	-24.9	-21.1								-51.0
17.8	15.7	8.8								4.8
(26) 8.8	(34) 5.2	(23) 3.2	EBIT/Interest						(11)	2.0
3.2	2.1	.4								.1
			Net Profit + Depr., Dep., Amort./Cur. Mat. L/T/D							
.1	.2	.5								.8
1.1	1.0	1.1	Fixed/Worth							.9
3.3	1.8	2.3								1.5
.8	.5	.6								.7
1.9	1.2	1.2	Debt/Worth							1.0
7.5	2.8	3.9								2.0
102.0	53.7	64.9	% Profit Before Taxes/Tangible Net Worth							8.0
(26) 32.1	(39) 10.3	(29) 7.6								3.5
9.8	.9	-6.2								-17.9
37.2	14.9	12.7	% Profit Before Taxes/Total Assets							4.8
13.7	5.1	3.5								1.8
2.3	.4	-2.1								-4.4
71.6	90.3	57.5	Sales/Net Fixed Assets							13.8
10.1	4.1	7.0								3.7
3.6	.5	2.1								2.3
5.2	3.6	5.6	Sales/Total Assets							4.9
2.3	1.3	2.4								1.7
.4	.1	1.2								1.2
1.5	1.5	1.2	% Depr., Dep., Amort./Sales							1.7
(22) 4.6	(27) 3.6	(23) 4.3								4.4
14.6	8.2	6.2								6.2
1.0	1.4		% Officers', Directors' Owners' Comp/Sales							
(10) 2.1	(15) 2.6									
5.0	9.3									
607099M	889556M	1087645M	Net Sales ($)		883M	2881M	6190M	29291M	136936M	911464M
773113M	1070844M	743996M	Total Assets ($)		11506M	53094M	87014M	53399M	53430M	485553M

M = $ thousand   MM = $ million
See Pages viii through xx for Explanation of Ratios and Data

© RMA 2024

AGRICULTURE—Logging NAICS 113310

Current Data Sorted by Assets

							Comparative Historical Data	
			1	2		Type of Statement		
		1	1	1		Unqualified	4	
	1	3	1	1		Reviewed	4	6
3	5	1				Compiled	13	3
	6	6				Tax Returns	25	17
	7 (4/1-9/30/23)		30 (10/1/23-3/31/24)		1	Other	54	32
0-500M	500M-2MM	2-10MM	10-50MM	50-100MM	100-250MM		4/1/19-3/31/20	4/1/20-3/31/21
3	12	11	5	5	1	NUMBER OF STATEMENTS	100 ALL	58 ALL
%	%	%	%	%	%	ASSETS	%	%
	29.6	36.4				Cash & Equivalents	13.0	14.9
	3.2	7.2				Trade Receivables (net)	7.1	7.4
	3.0	3.2				Inventory	7.3	8.6
	.0	11.7				All Other Current	3.1	2.3
	35.8	58.5				Total Current	30.5	33.2
	59.7	30.1				Fixed Assets (net)	57.2	51.4
	.0	7.0				Intangibles (net)	4.0	2.7
	4.5	4.5				All Other Non-Current	8.3	12.7
	100.0	100.0				Total	100.0	100.0
						LIABILITIES		
	2.9	2.1				Notes Payable-Short Term	6.1	22.7
	12.4	18.8				Cur. Mat.-L.T.D.	8.6	7.4
	.8	6.6				Trade Payables	5.5	3.7
	.1	.0				Income Taxes Payable	.2	.0
	8.6	4.1				All Other Current	8.0	10.4
	24.8	31.7				Total Current	28.5	44.2
	69.6	34.7				Long-Term Debt	43.4	43.5
	.0	.0				Deferred Taxes	.6	.4
	.4	5.7				All Other Non-Current	6.2	5.2
	5.2	27.9				Net Worth	21.4	6.6
	100.0	100.0				Total Liabilties & Net Worth	100.0	100.0
						INCOME DATA		
	100.0	100.0				Net Sales	100.0	100.0
	46.6	33.2				Gross Profit	36.4	40.8
	45.6	30.8				Operating Expenses	29.9	37.4
	1.0	2.5				Operating Profit	6.4	3.5
	-3.2	-.7				All Other Expenses (net)	1.0	-.4
	4.3	3.2				Profit Before Taxes	5.4	3.8
						RATIOS		
	28.0	4.6					2.4	2.1
	3.2	1.9				Current	1.1	1.1
	.4	1.0					.5	.4
	23.1	3.1					1.7	1.7
	3.2	1.1				Quick	.7	.6
	.2	.5					.3	.2
	0 UND	2 198.3					0 UND	0 UND
	0 UND	10 37.3				Sales/Receivables	6 64.5	7 53.2
	0 UND	14 26.3					19 19.5	17 22.1
	0 UND	0 UND					0 UND	0 UND
	0 UND	0 UND				Cost of Sales/Inventory	0 UND	0 UND
	0 UND	0 999.8					21 17.3	39 9.4
	0 UND	3 130.0					0 UND	0 UND
	0 UND	8 44.9				Cost of Sales/Payables	8 46.7	2 173.1
	1 527.5	17 22.1					24 15.0	21 17.8
	7.1	4.8					10.1	8.3
	35.3	6.5				Sales/Working Capital	85.0	48.2
	-28.3	-999.8					-13.5	-10.6
	8.3	12.8					9.8	13.6
(11)	2.9	1.8				EBIT/Interest	(90) 4.3	(54) 4.0
	1.5	.8					1.0	1.2
						Net Profit + Depr., Dep., Amort./Cur. Mat. L/T/D	1.6	
							(11) 1.2	
							.6	
	.4	.2					1.0	1.1
	15.9	1.1				Fixed/Worth	2.4	2.1
	-2.7	-7.0					28.4	-4.9
	.9	1.1					1.2	1.1
	20.9	1.5				Debt/Worth	2.6	5.1
	-5.2	-60.5					60.3	-7.7
						% Profit Before Taxes/Tangible Net Worth	65.2	39.0
							(78) 27.0	(36) 14.2
							1.2	.2
	26.5	16.5				% Profit Before Taxes/Total Assets	16.4	19.4
	7.1	5.1					6.9	8.4
	1.3	-.6					.0	1.2
	18.4	52.0					10.6	17.2
	4.4	16.8				Sales/Net Fixed Assets	3.2	4.1
	4.0	3.8					2.0	2.0
	4.0	3.4					3.1	3.6
	3.6	2.9				Sales/Total Assets	1.9	2.0
	2.5	1.3					1.1	1.3
							2.5	1.8
						% Depr., Dep., Amort./Sales	(75) 7.9	(43) 6.7
							14.0	12.9
							1.2	1.4
						% Officers', Directors' Owners' Comp/Sales	(49) 1.9	(31) 3.0
							3.7	6.2
2067M	48256M	178234M	174400M	941441M	236423M	Net Sales ($)	1739018M	1031133M
604M	14230M	56115M	105851M	346565M	100382M	Total Assets ($)	1099843M	706518M

M = $ thousand   MM = $ million
See Pages viii through xx for Explanation of Ratios and Data

© RMA 2024

AGRICULTURE—Logging NAICS 113310

Comparative Historical Data / Current Data Sorted by Sales

Comparative Historical Data			Type of Statement	Current Data Sorted by Sales					
3	1	3	Unqualified				1	1	3
	4	2	Reviewed			1	2	2	3
18	6	6	Compiled	2	3	2	1	1	
23	27	9	Tax Returns		2	2	5	2	
4/1/21-	19	17	Other	1					5
3/31/22	4/1/22-	4/1/23-			7 (4/1-9/30/23)		30 (10/1/23-3/31/24)		
ALL	3/31/23	3/31/24		0-1MM	1-3MM	3-5MM	5-10MM	10-25MM	25MM & OVER
	ALL	ALL	NUMBER OF STATEMENTS						
44	57	37		3	5	5	7	6	11
%	%	%	ASSETS	%	%	%	%	%	%
18.4	18.8	28.0	Cash & Equivalents						19.2
9.5	5.6	5.5	Trade Receivables (net)						8.7
9.6	7.8	5.5	Inventory						10.8
5.7	3.2	8.0	All Other Current						8.5
43.2	35.4	47.0	Total Current						47.3
44.6	53.8	44.1	Fixed Assets (net)						38.7
2.2	.9	2.2	Intangibles (net)						1.0
9.9	9.8	6.7	All Other Non-Current						12.9
100.0	100.0	100.0	Total						100.0
			LIABILITIES						
8.0	10.3	4.0	Notes Payable-Short Term						6.7
8.8	9.0	13.7	Cur. Mat.-L.T.D.						14.2
4.0	5.1	5.0	Trade Payables						9.7
.1	.1	.1	Income Taxes Payable						.0
11.9	4.1	6.2	All Other Current						5.6
32.9	28.6	28.9	Total Current						36.3
58.8	46.2	41.8	Long-Term Debt						27.2
.4	.3	.5	Deferred Taxes						1.7
8.5	4.5	4.7	All Other Non-Current						1.9
-.7	20.3	24.1	Net Worth						33.0
100.0	100.0	100.0	Total Liabilities & Net Worth						100.0
			INCOME DATA						
100.0	100.0	100.0	Net Sales						100.0
42.8	42.1	36.1	Gross Profit						18.3
37.3	37.2	35.1	Operating Expenses						18.8
5.5	4.9	.9	Operating Profit						-.5
-1.5	-.8	-1.3	All Other Expenses (net)						-.4
7.0	5.7	2.3	Profit Before Taxes						-.1
			RATIOS						
3.7	2.6	5.5							1.5
1.6	.9	1.3	Current						1.0
.7	.5	.9							.9
1.9	2.0	4.5							1.2
1.0	.7	.9	Quick						.7
.3	.3	.3							.1
0 UND	0 UND	0 UND						5	69.2
9 41.4	2 164.4	5 69.2	Sales/Receivables					7	49.0
21 17.5	12 29.4	16 23.0						24	15.2
0 UND	0 UND	0 UND						0	999.8
0 UND	0 UND	0 UND	Cost of Sales/Inventory					6	59.2
50 7.3	17 21.0	8 43.2						33	11.0
0 UND	0 UND	0 UND						9	39.2
3 106.9	3 113.3	8 45.2	Cost of Sales/Payables					11	34.3
17 21.2	17 21.8	16 22.4						22	16.3
6.5	7.8	6.1							10.4
25.6	-293.8	41.0	Sales/Working Capital						999.8
-17.2	-12.2	-58.2							-74.8
17.9	12.1	7.4							2.2
(40) 10.0	(53) 5.1	(36) 1.7	EBIT/Interest						.4
1.2	1.7	.1							.1
			Net Profit + Depr., Dep., Amort./Cur. Mat. L/T/D						
.7	.6	.5							.8
1.3	1.7	1.4	Fixed/Worth						1.4
NM	34.2	NM							3.4
1.2	.7	1.1							.7
3.0	2.3	1.9	Debt/Worth						1.9
-31.3	NM	NM							3.5
124.3	50.8	34.2	% Profit Before Taxes/Tangible Net Worth						
(32) 47.0	(43) 19.3	(28) 6.4							
23.4	6.6	-6.1							
24.5	19.1	9.4	% Profit Before Taxes/Total Assets						3.5
14.9	7.1	2.1							-2.1
2.6	2.5	-2.2							-2.9
25.4	8.4	19.3							14.5
5.5	4.2	6.6	Sales/Net Fixed Assets						7.0
2.5	2.4	4.0							6.3
3.6	3.4	3.8							3.5
2.5	2.3	2.9	Sales/Total Assets						2.4
1.5	1.6	1.8							2.1
2.5	4.3	3.9							
(26) 7.3	(40) 8.3	(21) 8.1	% Depr., Dep., Amort./Sales						
16.8	14.2	13.4							
1.9	1.7	1.6	% Officers', Directors' Owners' Comp/Sales						
(22) 2.4	(26) 3.9	(15) 2.4							
5.3	5.0	5.9							
530467M	1081298M	1580821M	Net Sales ($)	1887M	9672M	21160M	51779M	93670M	1402653M
296177M	532108M	623747M	Total Assets ($)	1424M	3871M	8320M	26026M	57308M	526798M

M = $ thousand   MM = $ million
See Pages viii through xx for Explanation of Ratios and Data
© RMA 2024

AGRICULTURE—Cotton Ginning NAICS 115111

Current Data Sorted by Assets

						Type of Statement		
						Unqualified		
		1	1			Reviewed		
		1	1			Compiled		
		2	1			Tax Returns		
3	1	2	1			Other		
1	1	5						
	7 (4/1-9/30/23)		14 (10/1/23-3/31/24)					
0-500M	500M-2MM	2-10MM	10-50MM	50-100MM	100-250MM	NUMBER OF STATEMENTS		
4	2	11	4					
%	%	%	%	%	%	ASSETS		
		11.2				Cash & Equivalents		
		10.7		D	D	Trade Receivables (net)		
		17.4		A	A	Inventory		
		8.3		T	T	All Other Current		
		47.6		A	A	Total Current		
		36.0				Fixed Assets (net)		
		7.2		N	N	Intangibles (net)		
		9.3		O	O	All Other Non-Current		
		100.0		T	T	Total		
						LIABILITIES		
		6.2		A	A	Notes Payable-Short Term		
		6.3		V	V	Cur. Mat.-L.T.D.		
		15.5		A	A	Trade Payables		
		.0		I	I	Income Taxes Payable		
		5.7		L	L	All Other Current		
		33.7		A	A	Total Current		
		12.8		B	B	Long-Term Debt		
		.1		L	L	Deferred Taxes		
		2.5		E	E	All Other Non-Current		
		51.0				Net Worth		
		100.0				Total Liabilities & Net Worth		
						INCOME DATA		
		100.0				Net Sales		
						Gross Profit		
		89.5				Operating Expenses		
		10.5				Operating Profit		
		.2				All Other Expenses (net)		
		10.3				Profit Before Taxes		
						RATIOS		
		3.2						
		2.1				Current		
		.6						
		1.4						
		.6				Quick		
		.4						
	2	219.4						
	6	57.9				Sales/Receivables		
	13	28.6						
						Cost of Sales/Inventory		
						Cost of Sales/Payables		
		5.0						
		12.8				Sales/Working Capital		
		-14.6						
						EBIT/Interest		
						Net Profit + Depr., Dep., Amort./Cur. Mat. L/T/D		
		.2						
		1.1				Fixed/Worth		
		2.7						
		.3						
		1.4				Debt/Worth		
		3.7						
		64.0				% Profit Before Taxes/Tangible Net Worth		
		2.9						
		-4.1						
		17.5				% Profit Before Taxes/Total Assets		
		1.7						
		-.5						
		54.3				Sales/Net Fixed Assets		
		6.8						
		1.8						
		4.1				Sales/Total Assets		
		1.9						
		1.0						
						% Depr., Dep., Amort./Sales		
						% Officers', Directors' Owners' Comp/Sales		
6774M	32541M	152891M	196534M			Net Sales ($)		
1317M	2690M	56143M	80199M			Total Assets ($)		

Comparative Historical Data

2		
3		1
4		3
7		4
8		3
4/1/19-3/31/20 ALL		4/1/20-3/31/21 ALL
24		11
%		%
11.7		12.4
12.1		18.7
23.7		15.5
2.2		.6
49.8		47.1
40.3		47.1
2.7		.8
7.2		4.9
100.0		100.0
21.2		9.3
3.3		3.2
6.3		7.9
.2		.0
4.6		11.9
35.6		32.2
23.1		25.6
1.0		.0
2.9		3.9
37.4		38.2
100.0		100.0
100.0		100.0
91.8		95.3
8.2		4.7
.9		-.5
7.3		5.2
4.3		1.8
1.4		1.2
1.1		1.0
2.2		1.7
1.0		1.0
.1		.3
0 UND	6	61.4
17 21.9	29	12.8
72 5.1	72	5.1
3.3		4.4
7.4		11.5
21.7		-30.7
18.7		12.6
(21) 3.5		6.8
-.9		2.7
.6		.8
.8		1.7
1.6		4.4
.4		.8
1.3		2.3
2.0		13.1
26.1		177.1
(20) 10.6		13.3
-2.8		5.4
19.5		15.3
6.4		4.7
-2.0		2.0
6.5		12.8
2.8		1.5
1.7		1.2
1.4		2.1
1.2		.9
.8		.8
3.2		
(19) 4.9		
11.6		
201883M		101767M
195860M		73460M

M = $ thousand   MM = $ million
See Pages viii through xx for Explanation of Ratios and Data

© RMA 2024

AGRICULTURE—Cotton Ginning NAICS 115111

Comparative Historical Data			Type of Statement	Current Data Sorted by Sales					
4	2	2	Unqualified				1		1
2	2	2	Reviewed				1	1	1
3	1	3	Compiled			1	1		1
2	5	7	Tax Returns	1	2	1		1	2
2	5	7	Other	1	1		3	1	1
4/1/21-3/31/22 ALL	4/1/22-3/31/23 ALL	4/1/23-3/31/24 ALL		7 (4/1-9/30/23)		14 (10/1/23-3/31/24)			
				0-1MM	1-3MM	3-5MM	5-10MM	10-25MM	25MM & OVER
13	15	21	NUMBER OF STATEMENTS	2	3	2	5	3	6
%	%	%	ASSETS	%	%	%	%	%	%
18.7	19.6	19.4	Cash & Equivalents						
12.3	12.0	10.7	Trade Receivables (net)						
16.4	17.1	11.4	Inventory						
2.7	.4	7.4	All Other Current						
50.2	49.2	48.9	Total Current						
37.1	45.2	39.4	Fixed Assets (net)						
3.7	1.8	4.7	Intangibles (net)						
9.0	3.8	7.1	All Other Non-Current						
100.0	100.0	100.0	Total						
			LIABILITIES						
1.1	2.1	7.3	Notes Payable-Short Term						
8.6	6.5	9.2	Cur. Mat.-L.T.D.						
14.1	9.1	13.9	Trade Payables						
.0	.0	.0	Income Taxes Payable						
13.0	11.9	11.5	All Other Current						
36.9	29.6	41.9	Total Current						
30.0	32.5	16.0	Long-Term Debt						
.1	.0	.0	Deferred Taxes						
.7	4.0	4.6	All Other Non-Current						
32.3	33.9	37.4	Net Worth						
100.0	100.0	100.0	Total Liabilities & Net Worth						
			INCOME DATA						
100.0	100.0	100.0	Net Sales						
			Gross Profit						
87.5	90.4	92.3	Operating Expenses						
12.5	9.6	7.7	Operating Profit						
-.7	-2.0	.2	All Other Expenses (net)						
13.2	11.6	7.4	Profit Before Taxes						
			RATIOS						
2.0	3.0	2.3							
1.4	1.6	1.6	Current						
1.1	1.1	.7							
1.7	1.9	1.6							
.8	1.6	.7	Quick						
.5	.7	.3							
0 UND	0 UND	0 UND							
18 20.7	23 15.9	6 64.7	Sales/Receivables						
28 13.1	51 7.1	15 24.3							
			Cost of Sales/Inventory						
			Cost of Sales/Payables						
5.3	2.7	9.2							
20.2	13.3	24.4	Sales/Working Capital						
22.7	188.5	-22.8							
20.9	18.5	12.0							
6.5 (14)	3.8 (16)	3.2	EBIT/Interest						
1.6	.1	1.0							
			Net Profit + Depr., Dep., Amort./Cur. Mat. L/T/D						
.5	.7	.3							
.9	1.4	1.1	Fixed/Worth						
2.0	6.9	2.7							
1.0	.4	.7							
1.4	1.4	1.7	Debt/Worth						
2.5	8.2	4.6							
124.1	57.3	38.6	% Profit Before Taxes/Tangible Net Worth						
(12) 35.4	(14) 22.9	(19) 9.1							
8.1	-2.9	-.3							
20.4	31.2	14.8	% Profit Before Taxes/Total Assets						
8.3	4.9	4.8							
2.0	-1.5	.8							
14.7	13.9	22.4							
4.3	2.5	10.1	Sales/Net Fixed Assets						
1.8	1.5	3.2							
3.1	4.7	4.4							
1.2	1.0	2.4	Sales/Total Assets						
1.0	.8	1.2							
2.2	2.5	1.2							
(12) 3.1	(10) 8.4	(14) 2.4	% Depr., Dep., Amort./Sales						
6.4	20.9	8.5							
			% Officers', Directors' Owners' Comp/Sales						
514689M	137861M	388740M	Net Sales ($)	1916M	4452M	7385M	33646M	45571M	295770M
415914M	81561M	140349M	Total Assets ($)	824M	5662M	3932M	31371M	25458M	73102M

M = $ thousand   MM = $ million

© RMA 2024

AGRICULTURE—Soil Preparation, Planting, and Cultivating NAICS 115112

Current Data Sorted by Assets | Comparative Historical Data

							Type of Statement		
		1					Unqualified	1	
	2	1	2				Reviewed	5	2
2	7	13	3		1		Compiled	4	4
	3	8	1	2	1		Tax Returns	25	10
	4 (4/1-9/30/23)		33 (10/1/23-3/31/24)				Other	30	20
0-500M	500M-2MM	2-10MM	10-50MM	50-100MM	100-250MM			4/1/19-3/31/20 ALL	4/1/20-3/31/21 ALL
2	12	13	6	2	2		NUMBER OF STATEMENTS	65	36
%	%	%	%	%	%		ASSETS	%	%
	26.9	13.5					Cash & Equivalents	19.6	23.5
	1.6	15.2					Trade Receivables (net)	12.9	14.8
	4.4	4.9					Inventory	12.8	8.6
	.8	2.2					All Other Current	4.1	4.6
	33.6	35.8					Total Current	49.4	51.4
	52.2	41.5					Fixed Assets (net)	38.6	38.6
	2.0	7.6					Intangibles (net)	5.7	3.9
	12.3	15.2					All Other Non-Current	6.3	6.1
	100.0	100.0					Total	100.0	100.0
							LIABILITIES		
	3.3	4.4					Notes Payable-Short Term	12.0	5.3
	11.0	3.0					Cur. Mat.-L.T.D.	11.3	10.0
	4.8	8.1					Trade Payables	8.7	5.6
	.1	.0					Income Taxes Payable	.1	.3
	4.5	10.5					All Other Current	8.8	7.8
	23.7	26.0					Total Current	40.9	29.0
	61.8	22.1					Long-Term Debt	26.7	54.9
	.0	.0					Deferred Taxes	.2	.2
	5.8	2.0					All Other Non-Current	4.4	2.8
	8.7	50.0					Net Worth	27.7	13.1
	100.0	100.0					Total Liabilities & Net Worth	100.0	100.0
							INCOME DATA		
	100.0	100.0					Net Sales	100.0	100.0
							Gross Profit		
	96.9	83.6					Operating Expenses	93.9	88.5
	3.1	16.4					Operating Profit	6.1	11.5
	-2.2	-1.4					All Other Expenses (net)	1.4	1.2
	5.4	17.8					Profit Before Taxes	4.7	10.2
							RATIOS		
	14.4	3.1						3.5	3.5
	1.6	1.5					Current	1.6	1.8
	.7	.7						.9	.9
	13.9	2.5						2.1	2.7
	1.3	1.4					Quick	1.1	1.3
	.5	.4						.4	.5
0	UND	3	123.9					0	UND	0	UND
0	UND	27	13.5				Sales/Receivables	16	22.9	22	16.4
3	126.8	83	4.4					40	9.1	53	6.9
							Cost of Sales/Inventory		
							Cost of Sales/Payables		
	7.7	3.9						4.6	4.6
	19.5	24.7					Sales/Working Capital	12.3	11.5
	-29.1	-13.1						-63.5	-71.2
	11.0	13.0						12.7	31.6
	4.2	(11) 8.9					EBIT/Interest	(58) 3.5	(34) 11.1
	1.8	1.3						.7	1.9
							Net Profit + Depr., Dep., Amort./Cur. Mat. L/T/D	8.6	
								(10) 5.0	
								1.9	
	2.3	.3						.2	.5
	NM	1.4					Fixed/Worth	.9	1.2
	-5.2	1.8						UND	NM
	3.3	.8						.5	.5
	NM	1.4					Debt/Worth	2.2	1.7
	-7.9	2.1						-54.8	NM
		55.1						50.3	66.1
	(12)	38.5					% Profit Before Taxes/Tangible Net Worth	(48) 14.0	(27) 32.8
		4.7						3.3	17.2
	27.0	33.0						11.5	31.0
	11.7	14.8					% Profit Before Taxes/Total Assets	6.0	14.0
	2.6	.9						-.2	4.2
	10.3	11.3						22.2	14.8
	5.4	3.6					Sales/Net Fixed Assets	8.2	6.1
	2.0	1.1						2.7	3.0
	3.5	2.0						3.0	2.8
	2.6	1.3					Sales/Total Assets	1.8	2.0
	1.4	.5						1.2	1.3
								1.8	1.9
							% Depr., Dep., Amort./Sales	(44) 3.4	(30) 3.1
								12.8	9.0
	5.5							2.4	2.9
	(10) 6.6						% Officers', Directors' Owners' Comp/Sales	(25) 4.9	(17) 9.2
	8.2							11.3	13.9
836M	30040M	82771M	164036M	531179M	342421M		Net Sales ($)	1456161M	1785171M
425M	11648M	62816M	81112M	147109M	256579M		Total Assets ($)	991377M	846681M

M = $ thousand   MM = $ million
See Pages viii through xx for Explanation of Ratios and Data

© RMA 2024

AGRICULTURE—Soil Preparation, Planting, and Cultivating NAICS 115112

Comparative Historical Data | Current Data Sorted by Sales

Comparative Historical Data				Type of Statement	Current Data Sorted by Sales					
1	1		1	Unqualified		1				3
1	5		6	Reviewed		3		1	5	1
8	7		15	Compiled	2	6		1	1	3
13	15		15	Tax Returns	1	6	3	1	1	
17	30			Other						
4/1/21-	4/1/22-		4/1/23-			4 (4/1-9/30/23)		33 (10/1/23-3/31/24)		
3/31/22	3/31/23		3/31/24							
ALL	ALL		ALL		0-1MM	1-3MM	3-5MM	5-10MM	10-25MM	25MM & OVER
40	57		37	NUMBER OF STATEMENTS	3	15	3	3	6	7
%	%		%	**ASSETS**	%	%	%	%	%	%
15.9	20.5		18.6	Cash & Equivalents		20.9				
12.2	10.5		9.7	Trade Receivables (net)		2.5				
13.4	14.5		12.8	Inventory		1.8				
2.2	5.1		3.5	All Other Current		.9				
43.8	50.6		44.5	Total Current		26.1				
46.0	37.5		41.2	Fixed Assets (net)		58.2				
3.3	2.2		3.8	Intangibles (net)		1.6				
6.9	9.6		10.5	All Other Non-Current		14.1				
100.0	100.0		100.0	Total		100.0				
				LIABILITIES						
4.5	4.0		7.0	Notes Payable-Short Term		3.0				
6.4	5.0		5.8	Cur. Mat.-L.T.D.		9.4				
5.4	6.0		8.2	Trade Payables		.2				
.0	.0		.0	Income Taxes Payable		.0				
10.1	10.1		8.2	All Other Current		6.1				
26.4	25.0		29.3	Total Current		18.6				
37.6	37.3		34.3	Long-Term Debt		52.7				
.0	.1		.0	Deferred Taxes		.0				
4.1	9.6		6.2	All Other Non-Current		5.1				
31.8	28.1		30.3	Net Worth		23.6				
100.0	100.0		100.0	Total Liabilities & Net Worth		100.0				
				INCOME DATA						
100.0	100.0		100.0	Net Sales		100.0				
				Gross Profit						
89.7	90.8		90.6	Operating Expenses		86.7				
10.3	9.2		9.4	Operating Profit		13.3				
-.6	.3		.0	All Other Expenses (net)		-.7				
10.9	8.9		9.4	Profit Before Taxes		14.0				
				RATIOS						
2.9	4.8		3.7			14.4				
1.8	2.5		1.6	Current		1.5				
.8	1.3		.9			.7				
2.3	3.3		2.7			13.3				
1.1	1.5		1.1	Quick		1.5				
.5	.5		.4			.3				
0 UND	0 UND		0 UND			0 UND				
17 21.0	19 19.7		4 101.6	Sales/Receivables		0 UND				
40 9.1	45 8.2		35 10.3			4 101.6				
				Cost of Sales/Inventory						
				Cost of Sales/Payables						
6.3	3.9		5.4			5.5				
13.2	8.3		14.3	Sales/Working Capital		21.6				
-23.1	26.5		-63.8			-17.4				
21.6	28.8		11.3			11.0				
(34) 9.9	(52) 6.3		(33) 4.8	EBIT/Interest	(13)	5.5				
3.6	2.5		1.0			1.9				
				Net Profit + Depr., Dep., Amort./Cur. Mat. L/T/D						
.4	.4		.4			1.5				
1.3	1.3		1.5	Fixed/Worth		3.4				
19.1	9.7		14.4			-5.9				
.6	.8		1.1			.9				
1.4	2.0		2.2	Debt/Worth		3.4				
19.9	12.0		21.8			-8.3				
67.0	71.0		54.3	% Profit Before Taxes/Tangible Net Worth		56.3				
(35) 41.1	(48) 20.7		(29) 30.6		(10)	29.7				
12.5	7.3		-.5			.7				
29.5	16.6		25.7	% Profit Before Taxes/Total Assets		27.7				
12.9	7.6		10.5			10.5				
4.1	1.0		-.1			2.4				
32.3	15.4		12.5	Sales/Net Fixed Assets		8.2				
5.0	5.2		5.2			3.3				
1.2	1.7		2.1			.9				
2.9	2.9		2.7	Sales/Total Assets		2.8				
1.9	1.5		1.7			1.7				
1.0	.9		.9			.5				
1.5	1.8		1.9	% Depr., Dep., Amort./Sales						
(27) 4.3	(38) 6.6		(24) 6.4							
10.3	11.9		21.1							
.8	1.2		1.2	% Officers', Directors' Owners' Comp/Sales						
(19) 4.7	(18) 2.5		(20) 3.4							
9.6	5.0		7.6							
613636M	740642M		1151283M	Net Sales ($)	1427M	28855M	10792M	25514M	93748M	990947M
423567M	551364M		559689M	Total Assets ($)	1289M	41995M	8811M	16114M	46620M	444860M

© RMA 2024
M = $ thousand   MM = $ million
See Pages viii through xx for Explanation of Ratios and Data

AGRICULTURE—Postharvest Crop Activities (except Cotton Ginning) NAICS 115114

Current Data Sorted by Assets | Comparative Historical Data

0-500M	500M-2MM	2-10MM	10-50MM	50-100MM	100-250MM	Type of Statement	4/1/19-3/31/20 ALL	4/1/20-3/31/21 ALL
		3	5	1	4	Unqualified	18	6
	3	3	6	6		Reviewed	27	18
		24 (4/1-9/30/23)	3	1		Compiled	16	10
1	3		6	2	3	Tax Returns	21	7
			12	6	11	Other	49	34
0-500M	500M-2MM	2-10MM	10-50MM	50-100MM	100-250MM			
1	6	14	43 (10/1/23-3/31/24) 22	10	14	NUMBER OF STATEMENTS	131	75
%	%	%	%	%	%	ASSETS	%	%
		19.0	7.3	4.1	1.9	Cash & Equivalents	10.5	13.0
		24.6	16.5	18.4	15.1	Trade Receivables (net)	18.0	16.9
		17.2	29.6	18.9	19.6	Inventory	16.0	16.6
		.8	2.9	4.9	5.3	All Other Current	5.9	5.7
		61.5	56.3	46.2	41.9	Total Current	50.4	52.3
		34.0	31.3	32.5	39.3	Fixed Assets (net)	42.0	39.3
		1.3	1.8	5.7	8.6	Intangibles (net)	2.0	2.4
		3.2	10.6	15.6	10.2	All Other Non-Current	5.7	6.0
		100.0	100.0	100.0	100.0	Total	100.0	100.0
						LIABILITIES		
		4.9	11.0	8.0	13.3	Notes Payable-Short Term	8.9	8.1
		5.4	2.4	2.0	5.2	Cur. Mat.-L.T.D.	3.8	3.6
		23.2	17.6	9.8	10.6	Trade Payables	13.8	13.7
		.2	.0	.0	.0	Income Taxes Payable	.2	.1
		7.7	14.3	8.1	7.7	All Other Current	11.3	8.2
		41.4	45.3	27.9	36.7	Total Current	37.9	33.5
		14.2	14.4	12.6	27.9	Long-Term Debt	22.4	20.9
		.4	.2	.0	.1	Deferred Taxes	.4	.6
		2.1	3.5	8.2	6.3	All Other Non-Current	5.5	6.6
		41.9	36.6	51.3	29.1	Net Worth	33.7	38.3
		100.0	100.0	100.0	100.0	Total Liabilities & Net Worth	100.0	100.0
						INCOME DATA		
		100.0	100.0	100.0	100.0	Net Sales	100.0	100.0
		93.8	95.6	91.7	93.3	Gross Profit	91.7	92.4
		6.2	4.4	8.3	6.7	Operating Expenses	8.3	7.6
		-.2	.7	-1.0	2.7	Operating Profit	1.7	1.0
		6.4	3.8	9.3	4.0	All Other Expenses (net)	6.6	6.6
						Profit Before Taxes		
						RATIOS		
		1.9	2.2	3.5	1.3		2.1	2.6
		1.5	1.5	2.1	1.1	Current	1.4	1.6
		.9	1.1	1.3	1.0		.9	1.1
		1.5	1.3	1.7	.6		1.2	1.7
		.9	.6	1.0	.5	Quick	.7	.9
		.5	.2	.6	.3		.4	.4
	5	76.7	23 16.1	29 12.8	47 7.7		15 23.9	19 18.9
	20	18.5	38 9.7	47 7.7	58 6.3	Sales/Receivables	39 9.4	34 10.7
	54	6.8	43 8.4	65 5.6	73 5.0		62 5.9	58 6.3
						Cost of Sales/Inventory		
						Cost of Sales/Payables		
		8.2	5.3	4.1	8.6		4.3	4.5
		23.9	12.5	7.0	34.6	Sales/Working Capital	13.3	10.6
		-178.1	37.7	11.7	-47.1		-66.4	101.0
		35.9	4.6	88.0	4.0		13.6	13.5
	(11)	3.0	(20) 1.5	4.8	2.4	EBIT/Interest	(123) 5.4	(67) 5.5
		-.4	1.3	2.5	.5		1.4	1.7
						Net Profit + Depr., Dep., Amort./Cur. Mat. L/T/D	9.7	5.7
							(30) 2.8	(19) 2.2
							1.3	1.5
		.0	.3	.5	1.0		.5	.5
		1.2	.9	.8	2.1	Fixed/Worth	1.0	1.0
		1.8	2.1	1.1	NM		2.1	2.5
		.7	.6	.4	1.6		.8	.7
		1.3	2.1	1.0	3.3	Debt/Worth	2.0	1.9
		2.9	6.1	2.2	NM		5.6	4.9
		81.4	17.8	23.5	24.5		35.1	37.0
	(13)	12.2	(20) 8.1	(11) 11.7	11.4	% Profit Before Taxes/Tangible Net Worth	(120) 17.4	(69) 16.3
		-7.2	1.4	5.6	-18.6		2.3	4.0
		25.1	6.2	11.4	7.1		13.8	12.3
		5.1	2.0	5.5	3.2	% Profit Before Taxes/Total Assets	5.5	5.7
		-1.9	.4	2.2	-1.8		.6	1.4
		580.8	26.7	7.0	5.2		9.8	8.5
		9.6	7.0	3.1	3.3	Sales/Net Fixed Assets	4.5	4.2
		2.0	2.7	1.9	.9		1.7	1.5
		6.3	2.3	2.4	1.3		2.2	2.3
		1.9	1.4	1.1	.9	Sales/Total Assets	1.4	1.3
		1.0	.9	.7	.4		.8	.8
			.6	2.7	2.4		1.9	2.4
		(20) 2.0	4.2	(12) 4.1	% Depr., Dep., Amort./Sales	(116) 3.7	(61) 3.9
			3.4	6.1	11.4		8.0	7.1
						% Officers', Directors' Owners' Comp/Sales	1.1	1.1
							(21) 2.1	(12) 1.7
							5.2	6.3
1189M	27290M	228583M	1137535M	1208449M	2221254M	Net Sales ($)	6196531M	4332365M
245M	6302M	65010M	589260M	718943M	2396091M	Total Assets ($)	5034568M	3292511M

M = $ thousand   MM = $ million
See Pages viii through xx for Explanation of Ratios and Data

© RMA 2024

AGRICULTURE—Postharvest Crop Activities (except Cotton Ginning) NAICS 115114

Comparative Historical Data | **Current Data Sorted by Sales**

Comparative Historical			Type of Statement	0-1MM	1-3MM	3-5MM	5-10MM	10-25MM	25MM & OVER
3	12	8	Unqualified					1	8
11	15	6	Reviewed					2	5
9	5	6	Compiled				2	2	1
12	7	8	Tax Returns	3	1	1	2	4	1
40	42	39	Other			3		4	25
4/1/21-3/31/22	4/1/22-3/31/23	4/1/23-3/31/24			24 (4/1-9/30/23)			43 (10/1/23-3/31/24)	
ALL	ALL	ALL							
75	81	67	NUMBER OF STATEMENTS	3	1	5	7	11	40
%	%	%	ASSETS	%	%	%	%	%	%
13.0	10.9	9.3	Cash & Equivalents					21.3	4.8
17.0	19.5	18.7	Trade Receivables (net)					17.4	20.5
18.3	23.1	21.0	Inventory					18.1	24.2
3.7	4.5	4.3	All Other Current					.7	4.5
52.0	57.9	53.3	Total Current					57.6	54.0
36.3	32.1	34.1	Fixed Assets (net)					34.4	29.6
2.0	2.1	3.5	Intangibles (net)					1.3	4.2
9.7	7.8	9.1	All Other Non-Current					6.6	12.2
100.0	100.0	100.0	Total					100.0	100.0
			LIABILITIES						
11.5	9.7	9.1	Notes Payable-Short Term					10.3	10.9
3.2	2.9	4.7	Cur. Mat.-L.T.D.					2.4	2.9
14.3	13.4	14.9	Trade Payables					20.0	15.2
.1	.1	.1	Income Taxes Payable					.1	.0
7.7	14.0	11.1	All Other Current					2.8	13.3
36.9	40.1	39.9	Total Current					35.4	42.3
21.4	17.7	17.0	Long-Term Debt					15.9	16.9
.3	.4	.2	Deferred Taxes					.5	.2
2.3	4.1	4.1	All Other Non-Current					4.6	5.0
38.9	37.7	38.8	Net Worth					43.4	35.6
100.0	100.0	100.0	Total Liabilities & Net Worth					100.0	100.0
			INCOME DATA						
100.0	100.0	100.0	Net Sales					100.0	100.0
			Gross Profit					96.6	93.5
92.9	95.7	93.0	Operating Expenses					3.4	6.5
7.1	4.3	7.0	Operating Profit					.3	1.1
-.1	.5	1.2	All Other Expenses (net)					3.1	5.4
7.3	3.8	5.8	Profit Before Taxes						
			RATIOS						
2.7	2.2	2.5						2.7	1.9
1.4	1.4	1.4	Current					1.5	1.3
1.0	1.1	1.0						1.1	1.0
1.5	1.4	1.5						1.8	1.1
.9	.7	.7	Quick					1.2	.6
.4	.4	.3						.3	.3
17	21.4	24	14.9	22	16.3		Sales/Receivables					11	32.0	27	13.4
35	10.3	43	8.5	41	9.0							24	15.4	42	8.6
59	6.2	66	5.5	61	6.0							38	9.7	60	6.1
			Cost of Sales/Inventory						
			Cost of Sales/Payables						
4.6	3.9	6.0	Sales/Working Capital					8.5	6.6
10.3	8.3	13.4						23.8	13.2
50.5	37.5	41.9						31.4	40.5
16.9	14.6	6.5	EBIT/Interest						4.7
(62) 6.0	(70) 4.2	(61) 2.8						(38) 2.6
1.9	.9	1.3							1.3
6.8	4.5	3.4	Net Profit + Depr., Dep., Amort./Cur. Mat. L/T/D						3.7
(17) 3.8	(23) 2.6	(14) 1.9						(10) 2.7
1.6	1.1	.7							1.7
.3	.3	.4	Fixed/Worth					.1	.5
.8	.9	1.1						1.2	.9
1.7	1.6	2.1						2.1	2.5
.8	.7	.7	Debt/Worth					.5	.9
1.7	1.7	1.6						1.9	1.8
5.8	4.4	4.1						3.3	6.3
40.9	29.1	21.7	% Profit Before Taxes/Tangible Net Worth					18.9	22.6
(67) 19.9	(73) 8.7	(60) 9.5						9.4	(35) 8.6
5.8	1.8	1.8						-5.3	2.8
15.6	10.6	9.5	% Profit Before Taxes/Total Assets					9.4	8.7
5.9	3.4	3.2						2.5	2.9
.5	-.3	.4						-1.4	.5
13.6	14.8	18.4	Sales/Net Fixed Assets					286.6	16.2
4.4	5.7	4.6						10.9	4.7
2.1	1.9	2.0						1.3	2.5
2.1	2.2	2.5	Sales/Total Assets					9.7	2.2
1.3	1.4	1.3						2.3	1.3
.8	.6	.8						.8	.9
2.1	1.3	1.5	% Depr., Dep., Amort./Sales						1.9
(58) 3.3	(66) 2.7	(55) 3.2						(35) 3.0
8.8	6.6	6.5							4.5
.9	.9	.6	% Officers', Directors' Owners' Comp/Sales						
(17) 2.0	(16) 1.2	(10) 1.0							
5.8	10.5	2.1							
2565161M	3931940M	4824300M	Net Sales ($)	1948M	1189M	19386M	52221M	212016M	4537540M
2330663M	3206290M	3775851M	Total Assets ($)	2556M	245M	32197M	100278M	139857M	3500718M

M = $ thousand MM = $ million
See Pages viii through xx for Explanation of Ratios and Data
© RMA 2024

AGRICULTURE—Farm Management Services NAICS 115116

Current Data Sorted by Assets | Comparative Historical Data

							Type of Statement			
		2			4		Unqualified		3	1
	1	1	1				Reviewed		5	1
		4					Compiled		2	2
1	4		1				Tax Returns		10	6
1	7 (4/1-9/30/23)	3	17 (10/1/23-3/31/24)	1			Other		20	12
0-500M	500M-2MM	2-10MM	10-50MM	50-100MM	100-250MM				4/1/19-3/31/20	4/1/20-3/31/21
2	5	10	2	1	4		NUMBER OF STATEMENTS		ALL 40	ALL 22
%	%	%	%	%	%		ASSETS		%	%
		18.3					Cash & Equivalents		15.0	12.1
		22.1					Trade Receivables (net)		16.0	18.4
		3.2					Inventory		10.6	22.3
		4.7					All Other Current		4.8	4.6
		48.3					Total Current		46.3	57.5
		36.8					Fixed Assets (net)		37.2	33.4
		8.1					Intangibles (net)		6.4	2.1
		6.8					All Other Non-Current		10.1	7.0
		100.0					Total		100.0	100.0
							LIABILITIES			
		.3					Notes Payable-Short Term		8.5	15.6
		8.2					Cur. Mat.-L.T.D.		4.6	3.2
		9.2					Trade Payables		10.4	13.9
		.0					Income Taxes Payable		.3	.4
		9.2					All Other Current		8.5	9.6
		26.9					Total Current		32.2	42.6
		14.4					Long-Term Debt		22.4	22.0
		.0					Deferred Taxes		.4	.5
		2.2					All Other Non-Current		2.2	3.1
		56.5					Net Worth		42.8	31.8
		100.0					Total Liabilities & Net Worth		100.0	100.0
							INCOME DATA			
		100.0					Net Sales		100.0	100.0
							Gross Profit			
		97.9					Operating Expenses		88.0	99.6
		2.1					Operating Profit		12.0	.4
		-1.5					All Other Expenses (net)		.6	-.4
		3.7					Profit Before Taxes		11.4	.8
							RATIOS			
		7.2							3.1	2.4
		1.3					Current		1.6	1.2
		.6							.6	.9
		4.6							1.8	1.4
		1.3					Quick		1.2	1.0
		.5							.4	.3
		0 UND							0 UND	4 87.9
		36 10.2					Sales/Receivables		17 20.9	29 12.8
		52 7.0							61 6.0	62 5.9
							Cost of Sales/Inventory			
							Cost of Sales/Payables			
		1.7							3.8	3.3
		35.1					Sales/Working Capital		13.2	9.7
		-17.6							-35.2	-307.9
									90.5	10.7
							EBIT/Interest	(35)	10.5	(21) 2.7
									5.6	1.5
							Net Profit + Depr., Dep., Amort./Cur. Mat. L/T/D			
		.0							.1	.4
		.7					Fixed/Worth		.8	.7
		1.5							4.0	3.4
		.1							.5	1.1
		.7					Debt/Worth		1.4	2.6
		2.0							5.5	8.7
									71.0	37.0
							% Profit Before Taxes/Tangible Net Worth	(35)	39.6	(20) 15.7
									15.9	2.6
		18.0							28.7	8.4
		4.4					% Profit Before Taxes/Total Assets		13.6	4.4
		-4.9							3.7	1.3
		UND							27.6	48.7
		5.8					Sales/Net Fixed Assets		8.9	8.6
		1.0							3.0	1.8
		4.3							3.5	2.8
		1.1					Sales/Total Assets		1.9	1.7
		.5							1.0	.8
									2.0	.7
							% Depr., Dep., Amort./Sales	(28)	2.8	(17) 1.6
									8.3	6.6
									.4	
							% Officers', Directors' Owners' Comp/Sales	(12)	3.9	
									5.5	
8889M	12921M	123357M	30364M	115475M	421951M		Net Sales ($)		838192M	502174M
944M	5045M	46530M	51035M	65192M	590836M		Total Assets ($)		861536M	496173M

© RMA 2024

M = $ thousand   MM = $ million
See Pages viii through xx for Explanation of Ratios and Data

AGRICULTURE—Farm Management Services NAICS 115116

Comparative Historical Data / Current Data Sorted by Sales

				Type of Statement						
	1		3	6	Unqualified		1	1		4
	2		4	2	Reviewed				1	1
	2		4	5	Compiled		1		1	2
	7		5	1	Tax Returns	1	1			
	15		16	10	Other		1	3	2	1
	4/1/21-3/31/22 ALL		4/1/22-3/31/23 ALL	4/1/23-3/31/24 ALL		0-1MM	7 (4/1-9/30/23) 1-3MM	3-5MM	17 (10/1/23-3/31/24) 5-10MM 10-25MM	25MM & OVER
	27		32	24	NUMBER OF STATEMENTS	2	6	4	2	2	8
	%		%	%		%	%	%	%	%	%
					ASSETS						
	10.9		9.7	20.1	Cash & Equivalents						
	15.6		12.0	19.8	Trade Receivables (net)						
	16.4		12.4	5.1	Inventory						
	5.4		4.9	7.8	All Other Current						
	48.4		39.0	52.7	Total Current						
	35.6		46.2	32.7	Fixed Assets (net)						
	3.8		8.4	5.4	Intangibles (net)						
	12.2		6.4	9.2	All Other Non-Current						
	100.0		100.0	100.0	Total						
					LIABILITIES						
	11.7		9.2	4.2	Notes Payable-Short Term						
	3.1		2.9	3.6	Cur. Mat.-L.T.D.						
	16.6		12.1	10.3	Trade Payables						
	.1		.0	.1	Income Taxes Payable						
	8.2		6.7	15.6	All Other Current						
	39.7		30.9	33.8	Total Current						
	32.4		26.6	20.0	Long-Term Debt						
	.0		.3	.1	Deferred Taxes						
	2.5		1.6	2.6	All Other Non-Current						
	25.3		40.6	43.5	Net Worth						
	100.0		100.0	100.0	Total Liabilities & Net Worth						
					INCOME DATA						
	100.0		100.0	100.0	Net Sales						
					Gross Profit						
	97.3		92.1	100.8	Operating Expenses						
	2.7		7.9	-.8	Operating Profit						
	-1.7		-.4	-1.6	All Other Expenses (net)						
	4.4		8.2	.7	Profit Before Taxes						
					RATIOS						
	3.0		2.8	6.8							
	1.5		1.8	1.7	Current						
	.6		1.0	.9							
	1.4		2.3	3.8							
	.7		1.2	1.2	Quick						
	.3		.3	.5							
0	UND	0	UND	15	24.4						
27	13.4	24	15.3	37	9.9	Sales/Receivables					
47	7.8	47	7.7	61	6.0						
					Cost of Sales/Inventory						
					Cost of Sales/Payables						
	4.6		4.8	2.0							
	13.2		14.3	6.9	Sales/Working Capital						
	-41.3		169.2	NM							
	21.3		26.8	34.7							
(25)	4.2	(26)	6.4	(18)	2.2	EBIT/Interest					
	-1.7		2.0	-.9							
					Net Profit + Depr., Dep., Amort./Cur. Mat. L/T/D						
	.2		.5	.1							
	.7		1.1	1.0	Fixed/Worth						
	3.2		2.0	3.5							
	.6		.7	.3							
	2.0		1.4	.8	Debt/Worth						
	38.1		4.0	49.0							
	49.2		36.4	32.8	% Profit Before Taxes/Tangible Net Worth						
(21)	19.9	(27)	9.3	(19)	9.5						
	-6.1		4.2	-9.7							
	15.8		16.2	11.9							
	4.3		4.1	7.0	% Profit Before Taxes/Total Assets						
	-6.8		1.9	-4.1							
	30.1		12.1	57.3							
	6.7		4.6	10.1	Sales/Net Fixed Assets						
	3.0		.8	1.3							
	3.3		2.6	3.0							
	2.1		1.8	1.7	Sales/Total Assets						
	1.0		.4	.5							
	.8		1.0	1.1							
(17)	1.9	(19)	3.3	(15)	5.5	% Depr., Dep., Amort./Sales					
	8.9		12.6	19.2							
	.6										
(10)	3.7				% Officers', Directors' Owners' Comp/Sales						
	7.0										
	483151M		1327137M	712957M	Net Sales ($)	682M	11020M	14020M	14606M	29868M	642761M
	455519M		969372M	759582M	Total Assets ($)	2810M	45000M	8910M	5072M	10990M	686800M

M = $ thousand   MM = $ million
See Pages viii through xx for Explanation of Ratios and Data

© RMA 2024

AGRICULTURE—Support Activities for Animal Production NAICS 115210

Current Data Sorted by Assets | **Comparative Historical Data**

0-500M	500M-2MM	2-10MM	10-50MM	50-100MM	100-250MM		Type of Statement				
				1			Unqualified		1		4
1		1					Reviewed		1		1
2		2					Compiled		7		2
2	3	3					Tax Returns		19		12
	5	6					Other		23		15
	4 (4/1-9/30/23)		24 (10/1/23-3/31/24)						4/1/19-		4/1/20-
0-500M	500M-2MM	2-10MM	10-50MM	50-100MM	100-250MM				3/31/20		3/31/21
5	8	12		1			NUMBER OF STATEMENTS		51 ALL		34 ALL
%	%	%	%	%	%		ASSETS		%		%
		5.8					Cash & Equivalents		18.5		23.6
		23.1					Trade Receivables (net)		17.3		14.1
		14.2	D				Inventory		13.2		18.2
		1.1	A				All Other Current		3.5		4.0
		44.2	T				Total Current		52.5		59.9
		39.7	A				Fixed Assets (net)		30.7		26.5
		1.5					Intangibles (net)		6.0		2.8
		14.6	N				All Other Non-Current		10.8		10.8
		100.0	O				Total		100.0		100.0
			T				LIABILITIES				
		12.0					Notes Payable-Short Term		15.7		9.2
		.9	A				Cur. Mat.-L.T.D.		6.1		2.9
		11.8	V				Trade Payables		5.5		8.5
		.0	A				Income Taxes Payable		.0		.1
		12.3	I				All Other Current		11.6		12.8
		37.1	L				Total Current		39.0		33.4
		33.6	A				Long-Term Debt		22.5		38.5
		.0	B				Deferred Taxes		.1		.5
		.4	L				All Other Non-Current		7.6		4.2
		28.8	E				Net Worth		30.8		23.4
		100.0					Total Liabilities & Net Worth		100.0		100.0
							INCOME DATA				
		100.0					Net Sales		100.0		100.0
							Gross Profit				
		87.5					Operating Expenses		92.8		93.9
		12.5					Operating Profit		7.2		6.1
		5.2					All Other Expenses (net)		1.2		.5
		7.3					Profit Before Taxes		5.9		5.6
							RATIOS				
		2.5							2.9		3.5
		1.2					Current		1.2		1.5
		.4							.8		1.2
		1.4							2.3		1.9
	(11)	.8					Quick		.8	(33)	1.0
		.4							.4		.4
	2	155.5						0	999.8	0	UND
	15	24.9					Sales/Receivables	22	16.9	16	23.2
	89	4.1						53	6.9	49	7.5
							Cost of Sales/Inventory				
							Cost of Sales/Payables				
		7.4							4.9		3.8
		48.4					Sales/Working Capital		16.6		7.0
		-9.7							-31.8		67.7
		21.4							21.3		13.0
	(10)	4.1					EBIT/Interest	(36)	3.4	(27)	4.7
		2.3							.6		1.4
							Net Profit + Depr., Dep., Amort./Cur. Mat. L/T/D				
		.1							.2		.3
		.9					Fixed/Worth		1.0		.8
		3.7							61.5		5.5
		2.0							.3		.7
		2.7					Debt/Worth		1.7		2.8
		15.9							212.5		9.6
		73.4							93.4		73.9
	(11)	23.3					% Profit Before Taxes/Tangible Net Worth	(40)	27.8	(29)	17.9
		3.8							3.9		6.9
		15.4							21.0		23.1
		5.2					% Profit Before Taxes/Total Assets		7.4		10.4
		2.8							-2.0		.7
		758.2							27.2		27.7
		6.6					Sales/Net Fixed Assets		12.7		8.5
		1.0							5.5		3.2
		3.3							4.1		3.5
		1.6					Sales/Total Assets		2.2		2.2
		.4							1.5		.6
									.8		1.0
							% Depr., Dep., Amort./Sales	(36)	1.7	(17)	2.6
									3.3		6.7
									1.4		
							% Officers', Directors' Owners' Comp/Sales	(20)	3.2		
									3.7		
3169M	21819M	177985M	66363M		795255M		Net Sales ($)		1217266M		503166M
966M	9223M	58382M	42866M		445017M		Total Assets ($)		636068M		418671M

M = $ thousand   MM = $ million
See Pages viii through xx for Explanation of Ratios and Data

© RMA 2024

AGRICULTURE—Support Activities for Animal Production NAICS 115210

Comparative Historical Data | Current Data Sorted by Sales

Comparative Historical Data				Type of Statement	Current Data Sorted by Sales					
1	1	1		Unqualified						1
1	1	1		Reviewed						1
3	4	3		Compiled			1		1	
16	15	8		Tax Returns	1	3		2	1	
16	25	15		Other	2	4	1	1		4
4/1/21-	4/1/22-	4/1/23-			6					
3/31/22	3/31/23	3/31/24				4 (4/1-9/30/23)		24 (10/1/23-3/31/24)		
ALL	ALL	ALL			0-1MM	1-3MM	3-5MM	5-10MM	10-25MM	25MM & OVER
37	46	28		NUMBER OF STATEMENTS	9	7	1	3	2	6
%	%	%		ASSETS	%	%	%	%	%	%
20.5	12.0	15.6		Cash & Equivalents						
15.9	19.8	21.1		Trade Receivables (net)						
11.6	15.6	10.8		Inventory						
4.9	5.3	5.1		All Other Current						
52.8	52.7	52.5		Total Current						
32.5	38.6	34.8		Fixed Assets (net)						
6.5	2.3	1.9		Intangibles (net)						
8.1	6.4	10.8		All Other Non-Current						
100.0	100.0	100.0		Total						
				LIABILITIES						
11.1	15.4	16.4		Notes Payable-Short Term						
2.3	2.7	1.9		Cur. Mat.-L.T.D.						
8.3	7.8	7.0		Trade Payables						
.1	.0	.1		Income Taxes Payable						
10.2	12.4	13.6		All Other Current						
32.1	38.3	38.9		Total Current						
24.3	29.5	23.3		Long-Term Debt						
.0	.0	.0		Deferred Taxes						
2.9	3.0	1.0		All Other Non-Current						
40.7	29.2	36.8		Net Worth						
100.0	100.0	100.0		Total Liabilities & Net Worth						
				INCOME DATA						
100.0	100.0	100.0		Net Sales						
				Gross Profit						
93.6	90.9	90.5		Operating Expenses						
6.4	9.1	9.5		Operating Profit						
-1.2	.1	4.2		All Other Expenses (net)						
7.6	9.0	5.3		Profit Before Taxes						
				RATIOS						
6.1	2.3	3.2								
1.9	1.3	1.2		Current						
.6	.8	.5								
3.4	1.7	1.4								
(36) 1.4	(45) .8	(27) .8		Quick						
.4	.3	.3								
0 UND	0 UND	0 UND								
14 25.4	21 17.6	15 24.9		Sales/Receivables						
28 13.2	35 10.3	66 5.5								
				Cost of Sales/Inventory						
				Cost of Sales/Payables						
6.9	7.7	6.0								
11.4	29.8	22.8		Sales/Working Capital						
-23.5	-49.1	-7.6								
37.4	25.9	21.4								
(28) 10.6	(35) 6.9	(22) 6.4		EBIT/Interest						
4.3	2.3	2.2								
				Net Profit + Depr., Dep., Amort./Cur. Mat. L/T/D						
.1	.3	.1								
.5	1.0	.7		Fixed/Worth						
5.8	6.2	3.7								
.3	.9	.6								
1.6	3.0	2.2		Debt/Worth						
NM	8.8	11.2								
67.1	78.7	73.1		% Profit Before Taxes/Tangible Net Worth						
(28) 43.9	(37) 44.4	(25) 27.2								
14.0	12.2	5.5								
35.6	23.6	20.8		% Profit Before Taxes/Total Assets						
14.3	11.2	7.4								
2.0	2.1	1.7								
148.6	34.6	881.2		Sales/Net Fixed Assets						
11.9	9.2	11.3								
4.6	4.3	1.8								
4.4	4.0	3.7		Sales/Total Assets						
2.8	2.1	2.1								
1.3	1.5	.6								
.5	.6	.9		% Depr., Dep., Amort./Sales						
(19) 2.3	(23) 1.3	(13) 2.3								
4.6	8.5	11.7								
1.6	1.2			% Officers', Directors' Owners' Comp/Sales						
(15) 2.7	(23) 2.7									
16.6	12.2									
420732M	1096651M	1064591M		Net Sales ($)	4118M	11664M	4927M	24642M	28020M	991220M
139668M	442623M	556454M		Total Assets ($)	10971M	8740M	8631M	7369M	10742M	510001M

M = $ thousand   MM = $ million
See Pages viii through xx for Explanation of Ratios and Data

© RMA 2024

AGRICULTURE—Support Activities for Forestry NAICS 115310

Current Data Sorted by Assets

							Type of Statement		
				2			Unqualified	2	
			1	1			Reviewed	2	1
		4					Compiled		
1	1	1	2	8			Tax Returns	7	3
	1 (4/1-9/30/23)			19 (10/1/23-3/31/24)			Other	6	13
0-500M	500M-2MM	2-10MM	10-50MM	50-100MM	100-250MM			4/1/19-3/31/20 ALL	4/1/20-3/31/21 ALL
1	5	3	11				NUMBER OF STATEMENTS	17	17
%	%	%	%	%	%		ASSETS	%	%
			14.6				Cash & Equivalents	17.8	17.5
			15.1	D	D		Trade Receivables (net)	15.4	16.8
			7.7	A	A		Inventory	5.4	10.9
			3.5	T	T		All Other Current	5.6	1.2
			40.8	A	A		Total Current	44.1	46.4
			39.7				Fixed Assets (net)	44.4	41.5
			5.1	N	N		Intangibles (net)	1.0	5.0
			14.4	O	O		All Other Non-Current	10.4	7.1
			100.0	T	T		Total	100.0	100.0
							LIABILITIES		
			5.2	A	A		Notes Payable-Short Term	8.4	10.2
			4.2	V	V		Cur. Mat.-L.T.D.	6.2	5.6
			4.7	A	A		Trade Payables	7.6	5.0
			.0	I	I		Income Taxes Payable	.2	.0
			4.4	L	L		All Other Current	11.2	7.2
			18.5	A	A		Total Current	33.6	28.0
			17.2	B	B		Long-Term Debt	30.3	30.9
			1.4	L	L		Deferred Taxes	.6	.0
			2.0	E	E		All Other Non-Current	1.3	1.1
			61.0				Net Worth	34.2	39.9
			100.0				Total Liabilities & Net Worth	100.0	100.0
							INCOME DATA		
			100.0				Net Sales	100.0	100.0
							Gross Profit		
			89.1				Operating Expenses	95.6	75.9
			10.9				Operating Profit	4.4	24.1
			-.9				All Other Expenses (net)	.6	-.3
			11.8				Profit Before Taxes	3.8	24.4
							RATIOS		
			8.8					2.4	5.1
			1.9				Current	1.5	1.9
			1.2					.7	1.0
			8.8					1.8	5.0
			1.3				Quick	.8	1.0
			.5					.5	.5
		15	23.7					9	40.6	15	24.3
		21	17.6				Sales/Receivables	18	20.1	29	12.8
		57	6.4					50	7.3	57	6.4
							Cost of Sales/Inventory		
							Cost of Sales/Payables		
			3.5					6.0	4.7
			5.6				Sales/Working Capital	22.9	10.0
			21.0					-27.2	93.4
			154.8					22.2	37.8
			(10) 23.9				EBIT/Interest	(16) 4.6	(15) 14.0
			1.9					.1	7.3
							Net Profit + Depr., Dep., Amort./Cur. Mat. L/T/D		
			.3					.3	.6
			.7				Fixed/Worth	.9	.9
			.9						
			1.9					6.1	4.0
			.2					.7	.9
			.6				Debt/Worth	1.5	1.7
			2.2					7.7	4.4
			47.7					35.2	93.7
			(10) 23.5				% Profit Before Taxes/Tangible Net Worth	(16) 15.0	(14) 70.9
			3.9					-24.0	42.3
			21.7					24.4	35.3
			13.6				% Profit Before Taxes/Total Assets	6.9	27.2
			-.9					-2.6	16.2
			9.9					16.7	12.2
			2.4				Sales/Net Fixed Assets	6.9	4.6
			1.5					1.8	1.9
			1.5					6.5	2.4
			1.1				Sales/Total Assets	2.3	1.5
			.8					1.1	1.0
									1.8
							% Depr., Dep., Amort./Sales	(14) 4.5	
									8.6
							% Officers', Directors' Owners' Comp/Sales		
732M	19938M	44417M	304591M				Net Sales ($)	543227M	182266M
160M	6122M	18006M	240333M				Total Assets ($)	401850M	126247M

© RMA 2024 M = $ thousand   MM = $ million
See Pages viii through xx for Explanation of Ratios and Data

AGRICULTURE—Support Activities for Forestry NAICS 115310

Comparative Historical Data | Current Data Sorted by Sales

	1			1		2	**Type of Statement**							1			1
					3		Unqualified										
	2			3		2	Reviewed								2		
	4			7		4	Compiled										
	11			10		12	Tax Returns	1		1		1		1	5		4
	4/1/21-3/31/22			4/1/22-3/31/23		4/1/23-3/31/24	Other	1	1 (4/1-9/30/23)					2	19 (10/1/23-3/31/24)		
	ALL			ALL		ALL		0-1MM	1-3MM		3-5MM		5-10MM		10-25MM		25MM & OVER
	18			24		20	**NUMBER OF STATEMENTS**	2	1		1		4		7		5
	%			%		%	**ASSETS**	%	%		%		%		%		%
	33.7			23.4		17.9	Cash & Equivalents										
	11.5			15.6		17.5	Trade Receivables (net)										
	3.7			5.9		7.9	Inventory										
	7.0			5.4		5.0	All Other Current										
	55.9			50.2		48.2	Total Current										
	33.3			32.5		40.1	Fixed Assets (net)										
	2.7			5.9		3.6	Intangibles (net)										
	8.1			11.3		8.0	All Other Non-Current										
	100.0			100.0		100.0	Total										
							LIABILITIES										
	9.8			4.7		7.4	Notes Payable-Short Term										
	4.9			7.4		6.7	Cur. Mat.-L.T.D.										
	7.6			8.3		4.5	Trade Payables										
	.0			.8		.3	Income Taxes Payable										
	5.1			8.0		4.0	All Other Current										
	27.4			29.2		23.0	Total Current										
	25.7			27.2		26.1	Long-Term Debt										
	.0			.3		.7	Deferred Taxes										
	3.9			2.1		1.1	All Other Non-Current										
	43.0			41.1		49.1	Net Worth										
	100.0			100.0		100.0	Total Liabilities & Net Worth										
							INCOME DATA										
	100.0			100.0		100.0	Net Sales										
							Gross Profit										
	90.1			98.1		92.8	Operating Expenses										
	9.9			1.9		7.2	Operating Profit										
	.7			1.1		-.9	All Other Expenses (net)										
	9.1			.7		8.1	Profit Before Taxes										
							RATIOS										
	6.6			3.7		10.6											
	2.5			1.4		2.4	Current										
	.8			1.0		1.2											
	5.7			3.0		8.0											
	1.5			1.0		1.5	Quick										
	.4			.6		.6											
0	UND		0	UND		10	35.2										
5	72.9		8	47.2		21	17.8	Sales/Receivables									
42	8.7		34	10.6		54	6.8										
							Cost of Sales/Inventory										
							Cost of Sales/Payables										
	3.5			7.0		3.9											
	10.1			21.9		7.8	Sales/Working Capital										
	-152.1			NM		34.1											
	54.0			14.5		53.6											
(15)	12.6		(22)	5.7		(18)	4.6	EBIT/Interest									
	2.6			-.7		-.4											
							Net Profit + Depr., Dep., Amort./Cur. Mat. L/T/D										
	.3			.3		.3											
	.8			1.0		1.0	Fixed/Worth										
	2.2			25.1		1.9											
	.2			.3		.1											
	.9			1.0		.6	Debt/Worth										
	4.7			40.5		2.1											
	61.1			50.0		36.7	% Profit Before Taxes/Tangible Net Worth										
(15)	33.2		(19)	28.6		(17)	10.4										
	.0			.5		-5.7											
	40.8			16.4		21.1											
	22.0			5.7		5.3	% Profit Before Taxes/Total Assets										
	.5			-3.4		-10.2											
	54.7			23.9		15.4											
	13.1			11.5		6.5	Sales/Net Fixed Assets										
	2.7			5.7		2.0											
	5.5			4.3		2.7											
	2.5			2.4		1.5	Sales/Total Assets										
	1.1			1.7		1.0											
						2.6		4.5										
			(13)	4.1	(13)	8.6	% Depr., Dep., Amort./Sales										
						14.5		15.2										
							% Officers', Directors' Owners' Comp/Sales										
	164107M			296633M		369678M	Net Sales ($)	1671M	1545M		3546M		29642M		98701M		234573M
	266405M			332470M		264621M	Total Assets ($)	1067M	953M		1464M		27175M		72924M		161038M

M = $ thousand   MM = $ million
See Pages viii through xx for Explanation of Ratios and Data
© RMA 2024

MINING

MINING—Crude Petroleum Extraction NAICS 211120

		Current Data Sorted by Assets					Comparative Historical Data	
						Type of Statement		
				1	9	9	12	Unqualified	28	19
					1			Reviewed	1	1
			1	1	2	1		Compiled	9	2
		1	1					Tax Returns	7	1
		8	11	11	3	10	Other	67	50
0-500M	11 (4/1-9/30/23) 500M-2MM	2-10MM	70 (10/1/23-3/31/24) 10-50MM	50-100MM	100-250MM		4/1/19-3/31/20 ALL	4/1/20-3/31/21 ALL
	9	14	23	13	22	NUMBER OF STATEMENTS	112	73
%	%	%	%	%	%	ASSETS	%	%
		9.0	8.9	12.8	6.6	Cash & Equivalents	11.2	11.8
D		9.4	8.6	6.8	7.9	Trade Receivables (net)	9.4	4.7
A		.3	3.7	.3	1.3	Inventory	1.5	.5
T		5.3	9.8	1.6	2.4	All Other Current	2.9	4.6
A		23.9	31.1	21.5	18.2	Total Current	25.1	21.6
N		65.7	47.5	66.4	76.9	Fixed Assets (net)	58.9	67.7
O		.2	1.4	3.5	1.5	Intangibles (net)	1.6	.4
T		10.2	20.0	8.7	3.4	All Other Non-Current	14.4	10.2
		100.0	100.0	100.0	100.0	Total	100.0	100.0
A						LIABILITIES		
V		5.0	4.5	5.0	2.0	Notes Payable-Short Term	11.3	11.4
A		5.4	2.6	2.5	.3	Cur. Mat.-L.T.D.	2.5	2.5
I		3.4	8.4	7.2	4.7	Trade Payables	10.6	4.7
L		.0	.0	.0	.0	Income Taxes Payable	.0	.0
A		5.8	8.7	11.1	9.5	All Other Current	9.1	5.9
B		19.6	24.3	25.8	16.6	Total Current	33.5	24.5
L		9.8	9.8	4.6	11.8	Long-Term Debt	18.7	21.3
E		.0	.1	.0	.2	Deferred Taxes	.4	.5
		13.3	9.5	5.3	5.4	All Other Non-Current	6.3	4.7
		57.3	56.4	64.4	66.0	Net Worth	41.2	49.1
		100.0	100.0	100.0	100.0	Total Liabilties & Net Worth	100.0	100.0
						INCOME DATA		
		100.0	100.0	100.0	100.0	Net Sales	100.0	100.0
		72.1	56.4	69.7	64.8	Gross Profit	55.2	54.9
		34.7	36.1	38.9	35.6	Operating Expenses	42.5	45.7
		37.4	20.3	30.8	29.2	Operating Profit	12.7	9.1
		2.5	1.7	-.9	.9	All Other Expenses (net)	3.4	4.3
		34.8	18.5	31.7	28.3	Profit Before Taxes	9.3	4.8
						RATIOS		
		4.3	2.7	13.1	2.9		2.6	4.0
		.7	1.8	1.1	1.3	Current	1.0	1.3
		.2	1.0	.4	.8		.3	.4
		3.2	2.2	12.8	1.5		2.0	2.9
		.4	1.2	.9	1.0	Quick	.8	1.1
		.1	.5	.3	.4		.2	.3
	0 UND	0 999.8	23 15.7	22 16.6			0 788.3	0 UND
	0 UND	33 11.1	34 10.8	38 9.7		Sales/Receivables	31 11.7	30 12.2
	23 15.8	55 6.6	83 4.4	72 5.1			68 5.4	70 5.2
	0 UND	0 UND	0 UND	0 UND			0 UND	0 UND
	0 UND	0 UND	0 UND	0 UND		Cost of Sales/Inventory	0 UND	0 UND
	0 UND	4 94.6	0 UND	8 46.3			0 UND	0 UND
	0 UND	1 342.6	9 39.7	0 UND			3 128.9	2 201.1
	31 11.8	34 10.8	96 3.8	35 10.3		Cost of Sales/Payables	46 7.9	49 7.5
	96 3.8	79 4.6	243 1.5	87 4.2			203 1.8	107 3.4
		6.3	4.7	4.3	6.1			4.2	2.0
		-24.9	11.2	21.0	12.2	Sales/Working Capital	343.8	14.4
		-3.8	-6.7	-1.5	-39.1		-2.1	-2.4
			51.9	19.0	74.8		14.1	7.4
		(20) 14.2	(10) 6.6	(18) 10.6	EBIT/Interest	(94) 3.1	(59) 1.4
			2.3	1.1	2.8		-.3	-3.5
						Net Profit + Depr., Dep., Amort./Cur. Mat. L/T/D		
		.6	.3	.8	1.0		.7	.8
		1.0	.9	1.1	1.3	Fixed/Worth	1.4	1.3
		1.8	1.6	2.1	1.5		2.3	3.1
		.1	.1	.0	.2		.3	.2
		.4	.7	.6	.5	Debt/Worth	1.0	.6
		1.4	2.5	1.3	.8		3.4	2.7
		72.6	45.9	37.7	32.9		21.4	11.7
	(13)	50.2	(20) 26.5	(11) 23.9	17.0	% Profit Before Taxes/Tangible Net Worth	(98) 5.8	(64) .7
		10.0	.2	8.7	2.6		-2.9	-6.2
		59.5	24.3	22.8	18.8		10.9	6.5
		27.8	14.9	15.2	10.1	% Profit Before Taxes/Total Assets	3.1	.4
		5.2	-.6	4.6	1.7		-2.7	-4.6
		4.9	4.6	1.1	1.1		3.0	1.0
		.8	1.7	.6	.5	Sales/Net Fixed Assets	.8	.4
		.4	.6	.4	.3		.3	.3
		2.2	.9	.6	.6		.8	.4
		.7	.5	.5	.4	Sales/Total Assets	.4	.3
		.3	.3	.3	.3		.3	.2
			2.7	11.7			3.4	5.9
		(19)	9.3	(10) 20.0		% Depr., Dep., Amort./Sales	(51) 11.0	(36) 15.9
			17.8	26.0			38.5	37.1
						% Officers', Directors' Owners' Comp/Sales		
	29003M	101814M	451925M	438585M	2626374M	Net Sales ($)	3300373M	1626695M
	13070M	63865M	557310M	865854M	3523262M	Total Assets ($)	5625693M	4784011M

© RMA 2024 M = $ thousand MM = $ million
See Pages viii through xx for Explanation of Ratios and Data

MINING—Crude Petroleum Extraction NAICS 211120

Comparative Historical Data				Type of Statement	Current Data Sorted by Sales					
29	29	31		Unqualified	2	2	2	5	20	
		1		Reviewed				1		
4	1	4		Compiled				2		
4	1	2		Tax Returns	1		1			
48	49	43		Other	6	6	3	5	11	12
4/1/21-	4/1/22-	4/1/23-			0-1MM	1-3MM	3-5MM	5-10MM	10-25MM	25MM & OVER
3/31/22	3/31/23	3/31/24				11 (4/1-9/30/23)			70 (10/1/23-3/31/24)	
ALL	ALL	ALL								
85	80	81		NUMBER OF STATEMENTS	7	8	7	8	19	32
%	%	%		ASSETS	%	%	%	%	%	%
14.0	12.2	11.3		Cash & Equivalents					9.7	8.1
14.7	13.2	8.6		Trade Receivables (net)					11.1	10.3
1.0	1.8	1.5		Inventory					1.3	2.8
3.7	6.7	5.2		All Other Current					4.9	2.9
33.5	33.9	26.6		Total Current					27.0	24.2
52.0	57.6	60.3		Fixed Assets (net)					56.7	67.2
1.1	1.2	1.6		Intangibles (net)					.4	2.8
13.4	7.2	11.5		All Other Non-Current					15.9	5.8
100.0	100.0	100.0		Total					100.0	100.0
				LIABILITIES						
19.4	7.1	4.3		Notes Payable-Short Term					5.0	2.8
3.3	2.2	2.2		Cur. Mat.-L.T.D.					3.0	1.4
8.9	11.3	7.6		Trade Payables					5.2	8.1
.0	.0	.0		Income Taxes Payable					.0	.0
11.8	12.1	9.4		All Other Current					6.1	9.1
43.4	32.8	23.5		Total Current					19.3	21.4
18.3	10.3	9.6		Long-Term Debt					8.5	9.0
.3	.1	.1		Deferred Taxes					.1	.1
6.8	6.7	7.3		All Other Non-Current					6.9	6.3
31.3	50.0	59.5		Net Worth					65.2	63.2
100.0	100.0	100.0		Total Liabilties & Net Worth					100.0	100.0
				INCOME DATA						
100.0	100.0	100.0		Net Sales					100.0	100.0
65.2	64.7	63.0		Gross Profit					68.7	58.9
37.9	33.0	35.4		Operating Expenses					37.3	30.9
27.3	31.7	27.6		Operating Profit					31.4	28.1
5.5	2.8	1.0		All Other Expenses (net)					.0	.4
21.8	28.9	26.7		Profit Before Taxes					31.4	27.6
				RATIOS						
2.8	2.4	4.1		Current					22.4	2.7
1.2	1.2	1.5							2.6	1.3
.5	.6	.6							.9	.7
2.6	2.0	3.2		Quick					22.3	1.7
.9	1.0	1.0							1.5	1.0
.4	.3	.4							.4	.4
1 589.0	0 977.7	0 999.8		Sales/Receivables					0 999.8	23 15.6
48 7.6	36 10.1	30 12.2							34 10.8	35 10.4
85 4.3	69 5.3	61 6.0							69 5.3	64 5.7
0 UND	0 UND	0 UND		Cost of Sales/Inventory					0 UND	0 UND
0 UND	0 UND	0 UND							0 UND	0 UND
0 UND	0 UND	0 UND							0 UND	7 49.8
6 63.4	0 805.7	0 UND		Cost of Sales/Payables					1 342.6	0 UND
48 7.6	44 8.3	39 9.4							41 8.9	41 9.0
159 2.3	182 2.0	96 3.8							140 2.6	96 3.8
5.3	4.8	5.4		Sales/Working Capital					3.9	6.6
37.1	46.6	13.4							5.9	13.1
-2.9	-6.5	-5.2							-31.7	-20.3
44.9	47.2	44.1		EBIT/Interest					90.0	66.6
(68) 8.1	(65) 21.3	(61) 11.5							(15) 13.6	(28) 12.2
4.0	4.9	2.7							2.6	5.3
				Net Profit + Depr., Dep., Amort./Cur. Mat. L/T/D						
.4	.6	.8		Fixed/Worth					.6	.8
1.1	1.1	1.1							1.0	1.2
2.6	1.8	1.6							1.5	1.5
.3	.4	.2		Debt/Worth					.0	.3
1.0	.7	.5							.5	.6
3.5	2.1	1.3							.8	1.2
46.1	65.2	46.6		% Profit Before Taxes/Tangible Net Worth					68.3	38.0
(75) 19.9	(72) 36.9	(72) 24.2							(17) 26.4	(31) 22.9
4.9	12.2	8.2							7.0	10.0
24.0	31.0	24.6		% Profit Before Taxes/Total Assets					48.8	22.6
10.1	19.1	13.2							17.1	14.4
1.9	5.4	2.1							3.6	6.8
9.1	7.0	3.1		Sales/Net Fixed Assets					4.1	1.7
.9	1.1	.7							1.1	.7
.4	.5	.4							.6	.5
1.3	1.4	.9		Sales/Total Assets					1.6	1.0
.5	.6	.5							.5	.5
.3	.4	.3							.3	.4
5.4	3.9	4.9		% Depr., Dep., Amort./Sales					5.9	1.2
(35) 10.8	(47) 9.2	(43) 13.1							(15) 13.1	(13) 13.1
21.9	14.8	20.6							25.8	19.4
				% Officers', Directors' Owners' Comp/Sales						
3423788M	7715338M	3647701M		Net Sales ($)	5366M	16745M	27527M	62337M	329859M	3205867M
6225572M	5529277M	5023361M		Total Assets ($)	26994M	42490M	103993M	290604M	683088M	3876192M

M = $ thousand MM = $ million
See Pages viii through xx for Explanation of Ratios and Data

© RMA 2024

MINING—Natural Gas Extraction NAICS 211130

Current Data Sorted by Assets

			3	2	6	Type of Statement		
				1		Unqualified		
	1					Reviewed		
	6 (4/1-9/30/23)	1	5	2	2	Compiled		
			17 (10/1/23-3/31/24)			Tax Returns	1	2
						Other	4/1/19-	6
0-500M	500M-2MM	2-10MM	10-50MM	50-100MM	100-250MM		3/31/20	4/1/20-
							ALL	3/31/21
	1	1	8	5	8	NUMBER OF STATEMENTS	1	ALL
%	%	%	%	%	%	ASSETS	%	8
						Cash & Equivalents		%
D						Trade Receivables (net)		
A						Inventory		
T						All Other Current		
A						Total Current		
						Fixed Assets (net)		
N						Intangibles (net)		
O						All Other Non-Current		
T						Total		
						LIABILITIES		
A						Notes Payable-Short Term		
V						Cur. Mat.-L.T.D.		
A						Trade Payables		
I						Income Taxes Payable		
L						All Other Current		
A						Total Current		
B						Long-Term Debt		
L						Deferred Taxes		
E						All Other Non-Current		
						Net Worth		
						Total Liabilities & Net Worth		
						INCOME DATA		
						Net Sales		
						Gross Profit		
						Operating Expenses		
						Operating Profit		
						All Other Expenses (net)		
						Profit Before Taxes		
						RATIOS		
						Current		
						Quick		
						Sales/Receivables		
						Cost of Sales/Inventory		
						Cost of Sales/Payables		
						Sales/Working Capital		
						EBIT/Interest		
						Net Profit + Depr., Dep., Amort./Cur. Mat. L/T/D		
						Fixed/Worth		
						Debt/Worth		
						% Profit Before Taxes/Tangible Net Worth		
						% Profit Before Taxes/Total Assets		
						Sales/Net Fixed Assets		
						Sales/Total Assets		
						% Depr., Dep., Amort./Sales		
						% Officers', Directors' Owners' Comp/Sales		
	2248M	8490M	127922M	285590M	691312M	Net Sales ($)	55360M	147061M
	1420M	4926M	179528M	425720M	1290801M	Total Assets ($)	161983M	475813M

© RMA 2024   M = $ thousand   MM = $ million
See Pages viii through xx for Explanation of Ratios and Data

MINING—Natural Gas Extraction NAICS 211130

Comparative Historical Data | Current Data Sorted by Sales

						Type of Statement						
		9		8		11	Unqualified					8
						1	Reviewed					1
							Compiled					
							Tax Returns	1	1	1		
		9		11		11	Other					
		4/1/21-		4/1/22-		4/1/23-			6 (4/1-9/30/23)		17 (10/1/23-3/31/24)	4
		3/31/22		3/31/23		3/31/24				3	3	
		ALL		ALL		ALL		0-1MM	1-3MM	3-5MM	5-10MM	10-25MM	25MM & OVER
		18		19		23	NUMBER OF STATEMENTS	1	1	4	4	13
		%		%		%	ASSETS	%	%	%	%	%	%
		10.2		11.1		6.7	Cash & Equivalents						3.9
		6.8		10.6		8.0	Trade Receivables (net)						7.7
		.0		.7		1.7	Inventory						2.3
		.9		3.2		4.1	All Other Current	DATA NOT AVAILABLE					5.1
		18.0		25.6		20.5	Total Current						19.0
		74.5		68.7		69.2	Fixed Assets (net)						74.0
		3.6		3.1		4.3	Intangibles (net)						1.2
		3.9		2.6		6.0	All Other Non-Current						5.9
		100.0		100.0		100.0	Total						100.0
							LIABILITIES						
		1.2		1.4		1.9	Notes Payable-Short Term						1.0
		.4		1.2		.5	Cur. Mat.-L.T.D.						.5
		4.4		4.0		4.5	Trade Payables						3.2
		.0		.0		.0	Income Taxes Payable						.0
		9.2		10.4		8.7	All Other Current						6.2
		15.2		17.0		15.6	Total Current						10.9
		23.4		21.8		20.1	Long-Term Debt						23.8
		.0		.0		.3	Deferred Taxes						.0
		15.6		13.6		11.4	All Other Non-Current						9.0
		45.8		47.5		52.6	Net Worth						56.2
		100.0		100.0		100.0	Total Liabilties & Net Worth						100.0
							INCOME DATA						
		100.0		100.0		100.0	Net Sales						100.0
		64.1		54.1		44.4	Gross Profit						47.7
		35.9		26.0		30.2	Operating Expenses						27.1
		28.2		28.1		14.1	Operating Profit						20.6
		10.9		4.4		3.3	All Other Expenses (net)						4.8
		17.3		23.8		10.8	Profit Before Taxes						15.8
							RATIOS						
		1.6		2.1		3.2							3.1
		.8		1.4		1.7	Current						1.8
		.4		.6		.9							.9
		1.5		2.1		1.8							1.9
		.6		.9		1.1	Quick						1.1
		.4		.5		.5							.5
17	21.0	23	15.6	17	21.0						22	16.5
42	8.6	35	10.5	37	9.8	Sales/Receivables					37	9.8
49	7.4	72	5.1	52	7.0						51	7.1
0	UND	0	UND	0	UND						0	UND
0	UND	0	UND	0	UND	Cost of Sales/Inventory					0	UND
0	UND	0	UND	1	594.4						0	UND
0	UND	0	UND	0	UND						0	UND
52	7.0	38	9.6	24	15.4	Cost of Sales/Payables					23	15.6
130	2.8	65	5.6	68	5.4						44	8.3
		7.4		10.5		5.2							5.3
		-19.7		22.9		13.3	Sales/Working Capital						10.4
		-7.2		-7.4		-14.8							-20.2
		17.4		13.6		10.9							10.9
		7.9	(16)	10.8	(19)	5.4	EBIT/Interest					(11)	5.4
		2.9		7.9		2.1							2.8
							Net Profit + Depr., Dep., Amort./Cur. Mat. L/T/D						
		1.4		1.0		1.1							1.2
		1.8		1.7		1.3	Fixed/Worth						1.3
		2.5		1.9		1.8							1.6
		.7		.6		.5							.5
		1.1		.9		.8	Debt/Worth						.8
		2.6		1.4		1.6							1.3
		32.8		49.3		44.4							43.2
(17)	22.0	(17)	32.1	(21)	15.5	% Profit Before Taxes/Tangible Net Worth						15.1
		6.3		21.3		2.4							2.4
		12.9		25.4		17.1							17.1
		10.4		14.1		6.9	% Profit Before Taxes/Total Assets						6.9
		1.3		7.4		-1.5							1.4
		.9		6.3		2.6							1.8
		.5		.7		.6	Sales/Net Fixed Assets						.6
		.4		.4		.4							.4
		.7		1.4		.9							1.0
		.4		.6		.5	Sales/Total Assets						.5
		.4		.4		.4							.4
		13.1		7.2		12.3							
(12)	15.9	(15)	9.2	(13)	16.4	% Depr., Dep., Amort./Sales						
		25.7		13.3		19.4							
							% Officers', Directors' Owners' Comp/Sales						
		677526M		813369M		1115562M	Net Sales ($)	2248M	4857M	34311M	58196M	1015950M
		1529326M		1511472M		1902395M	Total Assets ($)	1420M	11593M	80722M	130846M	1677814M

© RMA 2024   M = $ thousand   MM = $ million
See Pages viii through xx for Explanation of Ratios and Data

MINING—Crushed and Broken Limestone Mining and Quarrying NAICS 212312

Current Data Sorted by Assets | Comparative Historical Data

0-500M	500M-2MM	2-10MM	10-50MM	50-100MM	100-250MM	Type of Statement	4/1/19-3/31/20 ALL	4/1/20-3/31/21 ALL
			3		4	Unqualified	5	2
	1		5	1	1	Reviewed	6	3
			1			Compiled	3	
		1				Tax Returns	2	2
	1	5	3	2	4	Other	21	11
	9 (4/1-9/30/23)		23 (10/1/23-3/31/24)					
1	1	7	12	3	9	NUMBER OF STATEMENTS	37	18
%	%	%	%	%	%	ASSETS	%	%
			14.6			Cash & Equivalents	16.9	9.2
D			11.1			Trade Receivables (net)	14.0	9.9
A			8.8			Inventory	11.2	13.5
T			1.4			All Other Current	2.2	1.0
A			36.0			Total Current	44.3	33.6
			47.7			Fixed Assets (net)	48.5	52.0
N			8.8			Intangibles (net)	2.8	4.7
O			7.6			All Other Non-Current	4.4	9.7
T			100.0			Total	100.0	100.0
						LIABILITIES		
A			3.1			Notes Payable-Short Term	4.2	6.3
V			8.9			Cur. Mat.-L.T.D.	3.4	9.0
A			4.5			Trade Payables	7.4	4.3
I			.0			Income Taxes Payable	.1	.0
L			8.9			All Other Current	4.8	6.2
A			25.5			Total Current	19.9	25.8
B			22.6			Long-Term Debt	14.5	15.8
L			1.6			Deferred Taxes	1.1	.9
E			4.3			All Other Non-Current	2.9	3.4
			46.0			Net Worth	61.6	54.1
			100.0			Total Liabilties & Net Worth	100.0	100.0
						INCOME DATA		
			100.0			Net Sales	100.0	100.0
			29.8			Gross Profit	30.0	32.1
			12.1			Operating Expenses	19.4	23.9
			17.7			Operating Profit	10.6	8.1
			1.1			All Other Expenses (net)	.6	-2.1
			16.7			Profit Before Taxes	10.0	10.3
						RATIOS		
			3.0				7.6	3.6
			1.7			Current	2.7	1.7
			.6				1.5	1.0
			2.0				4.7	2.8
			1.2			Quick	1.7	1.1
			.4				.7	.4
			27 13.5				31 11.8	24 15.1
			32 11.5			Sales/Receivables	41 8.8	41 9.0
			46 8.0				54 6.7	55 6.6
			24 15.5				17 21.3	44 8.3
			39 9.3			Cost of Sales/Inventory	49 7.4	81 4.5
			68 5.4				99 3.7	107 3.4
			7 52.2				14 25.3	16 22.9
			16 23.2			Cost of Sales/Payables	23 16.2	21 17.0
			23 16.0				36 10.0	33 11.0
			4.0				2.9	3.8
			12.0			Sales/Working Capital	4.6	13.9
			-5.3				12.3	277.4
			23.1				41.4	23.4
			8.5			EBIT/Interest	(30) 7.5	(15) 6.2
			2.6				1.5	2.7
						Net Profit + Depr., Dep.,		62.4	
						Amort./Cur. Mat. L/T/D	(13) 5.3	
							2.6	
			.7				.5	.6
			1.1			Fixed/Worth	.8	1.1
			3.6				1.4	1.7
			.3				.2	.2
			.8			Debt/Worth	.4	.5
			5.7				1.7	3.7
			54.9				36.0	25.7
			(10) 29.9			% Profit Before Taxes/Tangible Net Worth	(34) 17.5	(15) 11.5
			16.7				3.4	4.8
			22.3				18.5	16.2
			12.2			% Profit Before Taxes/Total Assets	11.7	6.8
			3.8				1.3	3.8
			3.3				4.3	3.2
			2.2			Sales/Net Fixed Assets	2.8	2.2
			1.2				1.5	1.0
			1.3				1.5	1.1
			1.0			Sales/Total Assets	1.1	1.0
			.5				.8	.7
			4.4				4.2	5.8
			7.9			% Depr., Dep., Amort./Sales	(32) 6.0	(13) 9.6
			11.1				9.5	15.1
						% Officers', Directors' Owners' Comp/Sales		
434M	51459M	344077M	148414M	892010M		Net Sales ($)	1437353M	936807M
1887M	44056M	344830M	234959M	1247133M		Total Assets ($)	1812492M	1048408M

M = $ thousand   MM = $ million
See Pages viii through xx for Explanation of Ratios and Data
© RMA 2024

MINING—Crushed and Broken Limestone Mining and Quarrying   NAICS 212312

Comparative Historical Data | Current Data Sorted by Sales

									Type of Statement												
		4			7			7	Unqualified									3			4
		5			5			8	Reviewed					1				3			4
		1			3			1	Compiled												1
								1	Tax Returns							1					
		12			14			15	Other		1		1	4		1		23			8
		4/1/21-3/31/22			4/1/22-3/31/23			4/1/23-3/31/24			0-1MM		9 (4/1-9/30/23) 1-3MM			3-5MM		10/1/23-3/31/24) 5-10MM		10-25MM	25MM & OVER
		ALL 22			ALL 29			ALL 32	NUMBER OF STATEMENTS		1		1	4		1		5		7	17
		%			%			%	ASSETS		%		%	%		%		%		%	%
		17.0			10.8			13.9	Cash & Equivalents												13.5
		13.0			14.3			9.6	Trade Receivables (net)												10.9
		12.2			9.4			10.0	Inventory												9.4
		2.0			2.0			1.1	All Other Current												1.1
		44.3			36.5			34.6	Total Current												34.9
		41.1			54.9			50.2	Fixed Assets (net)												54.8
		2.5			3.8			5.1	Intangibles (net)												3.2
		12.2			4.8			10.2	All Other Non-Current												7.1
		100.0			100.0			100.0	Total												100.0
									LIABILITIES												
		3.4			1.0			3.6	Notes Payable-Short Term												2.5
		4.1			4.9			5.3	Cur. Mat.-L.T.D.												4.3
		5.0			6.8			4.0	Trade Payables												5.1
		.0			.0			.0	Income Taxes Payable												.1
		5.0			5.6			6.6	All Other Current												4.4
		17.4			18.4			19.6	Total Current												16.4
		20.6			26.1			17.3	Long-Term Debt												7.8
		.7			.7			1.1	Deferred Taxes												1.7
		2.4			2.3			2.9	All Other Non-Current												1.9
		58.9			52.5			59.2	Net Worth												72.1
		100.0			100.0			100.0	Total Liabilties & Net Worth												100.0
									INCOME DATA												
		100.0			100.0			100.0	Net Sales												100.0
		38.6			38.6			32.0	Gross Profit												24.4
		24.1			29.9			17.4	Operating Expenses												11.4
		14.5			8.7			14.6	Operating Profit												13.0
		-1.2			.0			-.2	All Other Expenses (net)												-.9
		15.7			8.7			14.8	Profit Before Taxes												13.9
									RATIOS												
		5.8			4.1			3.2													6.4
		2.5			2.8			1.5	Current												1.4
		1.7			.9			.8													1.0
		5.2			3.4			2.1													4.5
		1.8			1.0			.9	Quick												.9
		.7			.5			.5													.5
33		11.1	29		12.4	29		12.4												35	10.3
41		8.8	41		8.9	38		9.7	Sales/Receivables											39	9.3
51		7.1	57		6.4	45		8.1												51	7.1
36		10.2	2		240.0	22		16.9												22	16.5
61		6.0	31		11.7	45		8.2	Cost of Sales/Inventory											45	8.1
111		3.3	107		3.4	78		4.7												66	5.5
14		25.4	16		22.7	11		32.2												13	28.5
23		15.6	25		14.5	19		19.2	Cost of Sales/Payables											22	16.8
51		7.2	37		9.9	28		12.9												31	11.9
		1.8			2.3			2.5													2.7
		3.9			4.3			12.1	Sales/Working Capital												8.7
		9.5			-93.4			-37.4													-109.6
		40.9			33.4			24.6													47.3
(20)		11.3	(25)		12.1	(27)		8.9	EBIT/Interest											(14)	13.6
		3.6			3.5			4.0													3.7
								11.7	Net Profit + Depr., Dep.,												
						(10)		4.0	Amort./Cur. Mat. L/T/D												
								1.2													
		.4			.6			.4													.5
		.7			1.0			.9	Fixed/Worth												.9
		1.1			2.3			1.5													1.3
		.3			.3			.2													.1
		.7			.7			.6	Debt/Worth												.3
		1.4			2.1			1.2													.8
		56.6			41.4			33.8	% Profit Before Taxes/Tangible												24.9
(21)		24.9	(27)		10.0	(30)		15.4	Net Worth												11.8
		5.7			5.2			7.9													6.9
		25.2			12.8			18.6	% Profit Before Taxes/Total												16.2
		11.9			7.3			11.3	Assets												10.9
		2.2			2.4			3.7													4.0
		3.5			2.7			3.0													3.2
		2.8			1.7			2.0	Sales/Net Fixed Assets												1.5
		1.6			1.3			1.2													1.0
		1.3			1.4			1.2													1.1
		.9			1.0			.7	Sales/Total Assets												.7
		.6			.7			.6													.6
		4.2			4.0			4.0													1.6
(20)		7.2	(25)		7.9	(26)		8.1	% Depr., Dep., Amort./Sales											(13)	8.0
		10.6			9.8			11.6													11.2
									% Officers', Directors' Owners' Comp/Sales												
		828136M			1107095M			1436394M	Net Sales ($)		434M		2965M	4848M		43646M		120051M			1264450M
		1119173M			1217482M			1872865M	Total Assets ($)		1887M		4628M	7011M		32417M		169732M			1657190M

© RMA 2024   M = $ thousand   MM = $ million
See Pages viii through xx for Explanation of Ratios and Data

MINING—Other Crushed and Broken Stone Mining and Quarrying NAICS 212319

Current Data Sorted by Assets | Comparative Historical Data

0-500M	500M-2MM	2-10MM	10-50MM	50-100MM	100-250MM	Type of Statement			
			3	1	1	Unqualified		6	2
		1	1			Reviewed		7	1
		2				Compiled		1	1
1		6	8	3	1	Tax Returns		4	5
4 (4/1-9/30/23)			24 (10/1/23-3/31/24)			Other		15	20
								4/1/19-	4/1/20-
								3/31/20	3/31/21
	1	9	12	4	2	NUMBER OF STATEMENTS		ALL 33	ALL 29
%	%	%	%	%	%	ASSETS		%	%
			13.1			Cash & Equivalents		11.0	17.0
D			13.9			Trade Receivables (net)		12.2	12.7
A			9.0			Inventory		16.4	15.1
T			8.4			All Other Current		1.7	1.0
A			44.3			Total Current		41.3	45.7
			49.6			Fixed Assets (net)		43.2	43.7
N			.8			Intangibles (net)		9.4	4.0
O			5.3			All Other Non-Current		6.1	6.6
T			100.0			Total		100.0	100.0
A						LIABILITIES			
V			.6			Notes Payable-Short Term		5.3	5.3
A			4.9			Cur. Mat.-L.T.D.		5.2	7.0
I			8.8			Trade Payables		7.1	5.9
L			.2			Income Taxes Payable		.2	.0
A			4.7			All Other Current		11.3	6.4
B			19.2			Total Current		29.1	24.6
L			24.3			Long-Term Debt		20.4	37.3
E			.9			Deferred Taxes		.9	.5
			11.0			All Other Non-Current		4.1	8.8
			44.5			Net Worth		45.5	28.8
			100.0			Total Liabilities & Net Worth		100.0	100.0
						INCOME DATA			
			100.0			Net Sales		100.0	100.0
			31.6			Gross Profit		26.0	34.1
			22.5			Operating Expenses		15.3	26.2
			9.0			Operating Profit		10.7	7.8
			2.1			All Other Expenses (net)		.1	1.1
			6.9			Profit Before Taxes		10.5	6.7
						RATIOS			
			3.2					5.2	5.8
			2.1			Current		1.8	2.7
			1.7					1.0	1.3
			2.5					3.4	4.3
			1.2			Quick		1.1	1.4
			.8					.4	.6
		28	13.1				26	13.8	21 17.6
		45	8.1			Sales/Receivables	37	9.8	41 9.0
		56	6.5				54	6.8	66 5.5
		4	86.8				16	23.4	10 36.3
		28	13.1			Cost of Sales/Inventory	54	6.8	46 7.9
		101	3.6				104	3.5	111 3.3
		17	20.9				13	27.9	9 42.2
		34	10.6			Cost of Sales/Payables	22	16.8	20 18.3
		57	6.4				31	11.7	37 9.8
			2.3					2.8	2.3
			4.9			Sales/Working Capital		5.9	5.5
			9.4					-142.5	15.5
			11.6					17.4	35.2
		(11)	6.8			EBIT/Interest	(29)	7.4	(26) 12.9
			4.1					2.7	2.2
						Net Profit + Depr., Dep., Amort./Cur. Mat. L/T/D			
			.6					.6	.5
			1.2			Fixed/Worth		1.0	.9
			1.9					2.2	5.6
			.4					.4	.4
			.6			Debt/Worth		1.2	1.6
			2.6					5.0	6.9
			22.4					29.2	30.6
		(10)	16.9			% Profit Before Taxes/Tangible Net Worth	(28)	17.1	(23) 20.9
			12.7					7.5	9.3
			12.2					11.6	15.6
			9.0			% Profit Before Taxes/Total Assets		6.3	7.9
			7.5					2.6	3.9
			3.0					4.9	5.2
			2.4			Sales/Net Fixed Assets		2.4	2.4
			1.3					1.2	1.3
			1.2					1.2	1.5
			1.0			Sales/Total Assets		1.0	.9
			.7					.7	.7
			4.6					4.1	4.7
			7.2			% Depr., Dep., Amort./Sales	(26)	6.5	(24) 7.7
			9.5					10.1	10.8
						% Officers', Directors' Owners' Comp/Sales			
	4306M	81725M	268882M	343110M	399556M	Net Sales ($)		1053684M	1064278M
	1964M	54554M	282844M	240112M	385352M	Total Assets ($)		1382785M	1130769M

M = $ thousand   MM = $ million
See Pages viii through xx for Explanation of Ratios and Data

© RMA 2024

MINING—Other Crushed and Broken Stone Mining and Quarrying NAICS 212319

Comparative Historical Data | Current Data Sorted by Sales

					Type of Statement						
	1		1		2	Unqualified					2
	3		5		3	Reviewed				3	
	3		3		2	Compiled			1	1	
	3		4		3	Tax Returns		1		1	
	10		8		18	Other	1	1	2	5	8
	4/1/21-3/31/22 ALL		4/1/22-3/31/23 ALL		4/1/23-3/31/24 ALL		0-1MM	4 (4/1-9/30/23) 1-3MM	3-5MM	24 (10/1/23-3/31/24) 5-10MM 10-25MM	25MM & OVER
	20		21		28	NUMBER OF STATEMENTS	2	3	3	10	10
	%		%		%	ASSETS	%	%	%	%	%	%
	20.1		13.8		13.3	Cash & Equivalents					10.5	12.8
	13.6		11.7		15.1	Trade Receivables (net)					22.5	13.0
	20.1		15.3		14.2	Inventory					17.7	13.8
	.7		.8		5.4	All Other Current					2.6	1.0
	54.6		41.6		47.9	Total Current					53.4	40.7
	36.7		51.7		44.8	Fixed Assets (net)					43.2	49.0
	3.3		.8		2.1	Intangibles (net)	DATA NOT AVAILABLE				.1	2.2
	5.4		5.9		5.3	All Other Non-Current					3.4	8.1
	100.0		100.0		100.0	Total					100.0	100.0
						LIABILITIES						
	7.3		5.0		1.7	Notes Payable-Short Term					2.4	.2
	3.4		5.8		4.9	Cur. Mat.-L.T.D.					4.8	4.6
	6.5		5.4		8.4	Trade Payables					12.8	3.8
	.0		.4		.1	Income Taxes Payable					.1	.0
	3.9		5.4		8.2	All Other Current					6.4	7.4
	21.1		21.9		23.4	Total Current					26.5	16.1
	22.9		20.3		21.7	Long-Term Debt					28.9	18.0
	.3		.4		.6	Deferred Taxes					.5	1.1
	12.4		3.5		5.9	All Other Non-Current					3.5	4.2
	43.4		53.9		48.5	Net Worth					40.6	60.6
	100.0		100.0		100.0	Total Liabilities & Net Worth					100.0	100.0
						INCOME DATA						
	100.0		100.0		100.0	Net Sales					100.0	100.0
	32.0		28.2		33.4	Gross Profit					32.5	26.8
	18.8		20.1		19.9	Operating Expenses					18.2	18.7
	13.2		8.2		13.4	Operating Profit					14.2	8.1
	-.3		-.6		1.1	All Other Expenses (net)					1.4	.4
	13.5		8.7		12.3	Profit Before Taxes					12.9	7.6
						RATIOS						
	5.6		5.3		3.9						2.8	4.8
	3.9		2.1		2.2	Current					1.8	2.5
	1.9		1.0		1.2						1.5	1.5
	4.2		3.6		2.5						1.9	2.8
	2.1		1.5		1.4	Quick					1.2	2.0
	1.3		.6		.5						.8	.3
38	9.7	29	12.8	24	15.1					39	9.4	19	19.1
46	8.0	36	10.2	38	9.6	Sales/Receivables				46	8.0	29	12.5
56	6.5	70	5.2	54	6.7					63	5.8	55	6.6
24	14.9	7	51.6	4	86.8					13	27.7	19	19.4
59	6.2	60	6.1	38	9.5	Cost of Sales/Inventory				41	9.0	43	8.5
182	2.0	140	2.6	111	3.3					91	4.0	130	2.8
12	30.8	14	26.2	12	29.8					26	13.9	10	36.5
23	15.8	23	16.1	19	18.8	Cost of Sales/Payables				40	9.2	13	27.3
39	9.3	38	9.5	50	7.3					53	6.9	17	21.3
	2.0		2.4		2.4						3.3	2.4
	2.7		3.9		5.5	Sales/Working Capital					6.9	4.9
	7.9		NM		46.9						22.2	NM
	34.1		24.1		35.3							67.5
(18)	10.8	(20)	6.4	(25)	8.3	EBIT/Interest						8.5
	4.4		2.8		4.8							5.1
						Net Profit + Depr., Dep., Amort./Cur. Mat. L/T/D						
	.4		.6		.5						.5	.5
	.8		1.0		1.1	Fixed/Worth					1.2	.8
	1.8		1.9		2.1						NM	1.6
	.4		.3		.4						.4	.3
	.7		.9		.6	Debt/Worth					.7	.5
	5.8		2.1		2.7						NM	1.7
	38.0		24.7		34.3							16.5
(17)	26.1		11.9	(25)	19.4	% Profit Before Taxes/Tangible Net Worth						12.6
	8.1		3.9		12.6							7.7
	22.5		11.4		18.9						23.6	9.8
	14.3		5.5		10.2	% Profit Before Taxes/Total Assets					11.8	7.8
	4.6		2.6		7.7						8.6	5.3
	5.8		2.9		6.4						40.6	5.7
	2.5		2.0		2.4	Sales/Net Fixed Assets					2.6	2.0
	1.3		1.2		1.3						1.1	1.5
	1.5		1.3		1.7						2.0	1.4
	1.0		.9		1.0	Sales/Total Assets					1.1	1.1
	.8		.7		.7						.8	.9
	4.7		3.8		4.3							
(16)	7.9	(18)	6.9	(23)	6.5	% Depr., Dep., Amort./Sales						
	13.7		13.1		9.5							
						% Officers', Directors' Owners' Comp/Sales						
	538299M		890707M		1097579M	Net Sales ($)	3374M	12821M	22651M	168650M	890083M
	643051M		814848M		964826M	Total Assets ($)	7277M	23498M	18437M	153067M	762547M

© RMA 2024   M = $ thousand   MM = $ million
See Pages viii through xx for Explanation of Ratios and Data

MINING—Construction Sand and Gravel Mining NAICS 212321

Current Data Sorted by Assets / Comparative Historical Data

							Type of Statement		
		3		3			Unqualified	8	6
		6	2	7	3		Reviewed	11	7
	3		4	1	1		Compiled	9	5
	6	3	3	2			Tax Returns	15	7
1	3	12	12	23	6	5	Other	61	27
	12 (4/1-9/30/23)			77 (10/1/23-3/31/24)				4/1/19-3/31/20	4/1/20-3/31/21
0-500M	500M-2MM	2-10MM	10-50MM	50-100MM	100-250MM			ALL	ALL
1	12	21	37	12	6		NUMBER OF STATEMENTS	104	52
%	%	%	%	%	%		ASSETS	%	%
	16.4	13.2	10.7	18.4			Cash & Equivalents	13.7	19.5
	15.5	18.9	16.5	15.0			Trade Receivables (net)	17.8	11.3
	15.7	8.5	7.7	6.8			Inventory	7.2	7.8
	3.2	11.5	4.3	.7			All Other Current	1.3	1.5
	50.8	52.1	39.1	40.9			Total Current	40.0	40.1
	29.0	36.8	48.0	52.1			Fixed Assets (net)	48.4	48.8
	.3	1.3	4.8	.8			Intangibles (net)	5.0	3.9
	19.8	9.8	8.0	6.1			All Other Non-Current	6.6	7.2
	100.0	100.0	100.0	100.0			Total	100.0	100.0
							LIABILITIES		
	2.5	1.4	2.4	2.3			Notes Payable-Short Term	2.7	2.4
	2.2	5.1	4.9	5.0			Cur. Mat.-L.T.D.	4.5	5.3
	22.0	9.6	6.5	6.8			Trade Payables	9.7	5.6
	.0	.0	.0	.0			Income Taxes Payable	.0	.0
	24.9	10.5	4.1	8.1			All Other Current	7.7	4.9
	51.5	26.6	17.8	22.2			Total Current	24.6	18.4
	24.1	22.1	23.2	23.0			Long-Term Debt	26.2	28.6
	.0	.0	.4	.8			Deferred Taxes	.5	.4
	1.1	11.4	6.2	2.0			All Other Non-Current	4.8	7.6
	23.3	39.9	52.3	52.1			Net Worth	43.9	45.1
	100.0	100.0	100.0	100.0			Total Liabilities & Net Worth	100.0	100.0
							INCOME DATA		
	100.0	100.0	100.0	100.0			Net Sales	100.0	100.0
	34.3	37.9	30.1	34.6			Gross Profit	39.0	43.9
	27.3	27.6	18.4	19.8			Operating Expenses	28.3	31.2
	7.0	10.3	11.7	14.9			Operating Profit	10.7	12.8
	-.7	-.4	1.1	-1.5			All Other Expenses (net)	.0	-.4
	7.6	10.7	10.7	16.4			Profit Before Taxes	10.8	13.1
							RATIOS		
	5.4	5.1	4.0	7.9				3.7	3.6
	2.2	2.0	1.8	1.4			Current	2.0	2.4
	.6	1.2	1.2	1.1				1.1	1.3
		3.3	3.2	3.4				3.0	3.1
	5.1	1.5	1.2	1.0			Quick	1.6	1.7
	1.3	.6	.6	.5				.6	.9
	.4								
9	42.6	21 17.0	24 15.3	33 11.2				25 14.5	20 18.3
30	12.1	26 14.2	41 8.8	42 8.7			Sales/Receivables	41 8.9	28 13.1
41	8.9	51 7.1	51 7.1	56 6.5				56 6.5	49 7.4
0	UND	0 UND	0 22.2	13 28.1				0 UND	0 UND
14	25.4	2 151.5	16 5.3	27 13.3			Cost of Sales/Inventory	18 19.8	21 17.5
55	6.6	36 10.2	69	66 5.5				73 5.0	72 5.1
6	56.9	3 120.3	12 30.3	18 20.4				12 30.6	7 49.9
22	16.5	14 25.6	20 17.9	27 13.5			Cost of Sales/Payables	26 13.9	16 22.2
89	4.1	29 12.6	31 11.8	52 7.0				44 8.3	45 8.1
	4.6	3.2	3.7	2.7				3.9	3.2
	11.9	6.7	7.9	9.9			Sales/Working Capital	7.6	6.6
	-7.4	25.2	25.0	47.2				42.2	15.3
	27.7	30.9	24.1	18.3				25.7	26.3
(10)	7.1	(17) 6.2	(34) 5.3	(11) 7.3			EBIT/Interest	(96) 9.3	(49) 10.4
	-.9	2.2	2.9	2.1				1.9	2.7
							Net Profit + Depr., Dep.,	5.2	
							Amort./Cur. Mat. L/T/D	(17) 2.6	
								1.0	
	.2	.2	.6	.6				.6	.6
	.7	1.2	1.1	1.3			Fixed/Worth	1.0	1.2
	-.7	2.1	1.9	2.0				2.2	2.5
	.2	.6	.4	.3				.4	.4
	1.0	1.1	.8	1.3			Debt/Worth	.9	.9
	-2.9	5.9	2.2	2.2				3.4	4.5
		57.1	36.5	33.7			% Profit Before Taxes/Tangible	40.9	43.2
	(19)	23.3	(33) 23.3	17.8			Net Worth	(88) 22.7	(44) 27.6
		8.8	7.3	11.4				6.7	13.1
	23.6	23.4	19.0	20.0			% Profit Before Taxes/Total	20.2	23.1
	12.5	9.4	8.2	10.1			Assets	10.8	14.6
	-.4	2.9	3.7	3.3				2.2	3.8
	16.9	18.7	3.6	7.4				5.5	5.3
	12.2	6.3	2.4	2.2			Sales/Net Fixed Assets	2.5	2.4
	2.9	2.0	1.6	1.0				1.3	1.3
	3.4	2.7	1.7	1.4				1.7	1.6
	1.8	1.5	1.2	.9			Sales/Total Assets	1.1	1.2
	1.0	1.1	.6	.6				.7	.7
		3.4	4.7					4.0	4.4
	(14)	7.1	(32) 9.0				% Depr., Dep., Amort./Sales	(85) 6.3	(40) 8.7
		10.9	11.2					13.4	12.8
							% Officers', Directors',	1.4	.9
							Owners' Comp/Sales	(26) 3.3	(17) 1.6
								6.3	7.7
1528M	33943M	206719M	1274907M	833751M	901265M		Net Sales ($)	2698495M	987610M
389M	15040M	114743M	952228M	897636M	757413M		Total Assets ($)	2613447M	996781M

© RMA 2024   M = $ thousand   MM = $ million
See Pages viii through xx for Explanation of Ratios and Data

MINING—Construction Sand and Gravel Mining NAICS 212321

Comparative Historical Data | Current Data Sorted by Sales

Comparative Historical Data			Type of Statement	Current Data Sorted by Sales					
5	8	6	Unqualified					1	5
8	12	10	Reviewed				3	3	4
6	10	14	Compiled		2	2	2	4	4
10	12	9	Tax Returns	1	3	1	3	1	
44	49	50	Other	2	3	4	7	9	25
4/1/21-3/31/22 ALL	4/1/22-3/31/23 ALL	4/1/23-3/31/24 ALL		0-1MM	1-3MM	12 (4/1-9/30/23) 3-5MM	5-10MM	77 (10/1/23-3/31/24) 10-25MM	25MM & OVER
73	91	89	NUMBER OF STATEMENTS	3	8	7	15	18	38
%	%	%	ASSETS	%	%	%	%	%	%
15.6	15.0	14.0	Cash & Equivalents				10.8	16.9	14.2
18.2	15.0	17.1	Trade Receivables (net)				10.6	14.6	21.9
8.2	9.4	9.0	Inventory				7.0	3.4	8.4
2.8	3.0	5.2	All Other Current				13.5	5.9	3.0
44.8	42.4	45.3	Total Current				41.9	40.9	47.5
41.1	45.6	42.3	Fixed Assets (net)				45.2	44.8	43.7
3.8	3.5	2.8	Intangibles (net)				4.0	3.3	3.0
10.4	8.5	9.6	All Other Non-Current				8.8	11.0	5.9
100.0	100.0	100.0	Total				100.0	100.0	100.0
			LIABILITIES						
4.0	1.9	2.0	Notes Payable-Short Term				1.0	.7	2.8
3.6	5.0	4.5	Cur. Mat.-L.T.D.				4.7	5.7	4.5
11.3	7.1	9.2	Trade Payables				14.1	4.1	8.2
.1	.2	.0	Income Taxes Payable				.0	.1	.0
8.1	6.5	9.0	All Other Current				17.2	4.4	6.1
27.1	20.8	24.7	Total Current				37.0	14.9	21.6
21.8	22.8	22.1	Long-Term Debt				16.9	29.1	15.6
.6	.3	.3	Deferred Taxes				.0	.1	.5
9.5	4.1	5.7	All Other Non-Current				12.2	7.9	2.1
41.0	51.9	47.3	Net Worth				33.9	48.1	60.2
100.0	100.0	100.0	Total Liabilities & Net Worth				100.0	100.0	100.0
			INCOME DATA						
100.0	100.0	100.0	Net Sales				100.0	100.0	100.0
32.7	38.5	33.5	Gross Profit				31.0	35.0	27.3
24.0	28.3	22.2	Operating Expenses				21.7	27.0	15.7
8.7	10.3	11.3	Operating Profit				9.3	7.9	11.6
-1.4	-.2	.1	All Other Expenses (net)				.1	.9	-1.7
10.1	10.4	11.2	Profit Before Taxes				9.2	7.1	13.3
			RATIOS						
5.0	4.2	5.1					8.8	6.4	3.9
2.3	2.1	2.0	Current				1.7	3.0	1.8
1.3	1.1	1.2					.7	1.5	1.3
4.2	3.5	3.6					4.0	5.2	3.6
1.6	1.3	1.3	Quick				.6	1.9	1.2
.6	.6	.7					.1	.9	.8
27 13.4	24 15.2	24 15.1		15 24.6	22 16.6	37 9.9			
39 9.4	41 8.9	38 9.7	Sales/Receivables	23 15.9	31 11.6	46 7.9			
57 6.4	56 6.5	53 6.9		52 7.0	47 7.7	61 6.0			
0 UND	0 UND	0 UND		0 UND	0 UND	3 104.5			
13 28.0	29 12.6	17 20.9	Cost of Sales/Inventory	13 27.6	5 70.9	22 16.8			
49 7.4	79 4.6	65 5.6		94 3.9	33 11.1	54 6.7			
11 33.1	12 30.9	10 36.3		13 27.7	3 135.5	16 22.8			
23 15.8	25 14.8	20 17.9	Cost of Sales/Payables	23 15.6	14 26.8	21 17.1			
41 9.0	39 9.3	35 10.4		55 6.6	24 15.4	33 11.0			
2.6	3.4	3.2					3.2	3.0	3.4
6.4	6.2	7.5	Sales/Working Capital				11.7	6.8	7.7
20.8	42.9	25.0					-12.3	14.2	16.8
33.5	24.3	25.1					7.3	19.5	37.0
(66) 14.0	(78) 4.7	(78) 6.9	EBIT/Interest	(12) 2.8	(16) 3.9	(35) 13.1			
3.0	.3	2.7					-5.1	1.0	4.2
16.5	9.6	5.1	Net Profit + Depr., Dep.,						6.9
(12) 4.5	(15) 3.2	(19) 2.9	Amort./Cur. Mat. L/T/D					(12)	3.2
3.5	1.0	2.3							2.3
.4	.4	.4					1.0	.3	.4
.9	1.0	1.0	Fixed/Worth				1.3	1.2	.9
2.1	1.8	1.6					3.2	2.9	1.3
.3	.4	.4					.6	.5	.3
.9	.9	.8	Debt/Worth				1.5	1.2	.8
3.3	2.2	2.3					5.5	3.6	1.5
38.5	38.6	38.1					48.9	53.1	38.6
(62) 25.7	(86) 17.2	(79) 23.3	% Profit Before Taxes/Tangible Net Worth			(12) 12.2	(17) 23.5	27.5	
8.5	4.4	10.5					3.2	3.0	13.4
19.6	17.5	20.3					12.1	22.1	23.6
11.6	9.0	9.7	% Profit Before Taxes/Total Assets				3.2	8.3	17.0
3.2	.0	3.5					-3.0	3.3	5.7
10.2	6.0	10.2					11.6	8.5	7.0
2.6	2.1	2.9	Sales/Net Fixed Assets				3.4	3.7	2.6
1.4	1.4	1.8					1.5	1.5	2.0
1.7	1.6	1.9					2.1	2.7	1.7
1.2	1.1	1.2	Sales/Total Assets				1.1	1.3	1.3
.8	.7	.8					.5	.7	1.0
2.8	3.7	3.9					3.5	5.0	3.7
(53) 6.6	(70) 7.6	(68) 6.6	% Depr., Dep., Amort./Sales			(12) 7.1	(14) 8.2	(31) 6.1	
12.9	11.9	10.6					13.6	11.1	9.3
1.0	1.3	1.4	% Officers', Directors'						
(19) 1.6	(19) 2.6	(22) 3.1	Owners' Comp/Sales						
3.2	7.7	4.7							
2008804M	2525066M	3252113M	Net Sales ($)	2187M	14051M	26829M	103197M	295931M	2809918M
2378550M	2263585M	2737449M	Total Assets ($)	5080M	23896M	40238M	188905M	337455M	2141875M

© RMA 2024   M = $ thousand   MM = $ million
See Pages viii through xx for Explanation of Ratios and Data

MINING—Drilling Oil and Gas Wells NAICS 213111

Current Data Sorted by Assets

				2	3	Type of Statement
			2	1		Unqualified
2	1	3	1			Reviewed
2	3	9	8	3	2	Compiled
	1 (4/1-9/30/23)		39 (10/1/23-3/31/24)			Tax Returns
0-500M	500M-2MM	2-10MM	10-50MM	50-100MM	100-250MM	Other
4	4	12	11	4	5	NUMBER OF STATEMENTS

Comparative Historical Data

7	4	Unqualified
3	1	Reviewed
3	3	Compiled
6	3	Tax Returns
38	25	Other
4/1/19-	4/1/20-	
3/31/20	3/31/21	
ALL	ALL	
57	36	NUMBER OF STATEMENTS

0-500M	500M-2MM	2-10MM	10-50MM	50-100MM	100-250MM		4/1/19-3/31/20 ALL	4/1/20-3/31/21 ALL
%	%	%	%	%	%	**ASSETS**	%	%
		5.5	6.5			Cash & Equivalents	10.2	12.9
		33.0	20.5			Trade Receivables (net)	21.2	21.5
		2.1	12.2			Inventory	3.0	5.3
		8.2	2.9			All Other Current	5.3	3.5
		48.8	42.1			Total Current	39.7	43.2
		30.0	41.1			Fixed Assets (net)	45.6	45.7
		14.5	.9			Intangibles (net)	7.4	4.0
		6.7	16.0			All Other Non-Current	7.4	7.0
		100.0	100.0			Total	100.0	100.0
						LIABILITIES		
		3.4	5.1			Notes Payable-Short Term	6.3	7.2
		2.4	2.0			Cur. Mat.-L.T.D.	3.0	4.2
		14.7	9.7			Trade Payables	11.2	9.0
		.0	.3			Income Taxes Payable	.1	.5
		3.8	13.1			All Other Current	10.4	14.1
		24.4	30.2			Total Current	31.0	35.0
		33.3	44.1			Long-Term Debt	22.7	32.5
		.0	.2			Deferred Taxes	.2	.4
		4.9	4.0			All Other Non-Current	3.6	6.6
		37.4	21.5			Net Worth	42.5	25.5
		100.0	100.0			Total Liabilties & Net Worth	100.0	100.0
						INCOME DATA		
		100.0	100.0			Net Sales	100.0	100.0
						Gross Profit		
		98.2	80.8			Operating Expenses	90.2	102.8
		1.8	19.2			Operating Profit	9.8	-2.8
		.0	12.2			All Other Expenses (net)	3.8	2.0
		1.8	6.9			Profit Before Taxes	6.0	-4.8
						RATIOS		
		5.0	2.3				2.3	3.8
		2.4	2.0			Current	1.4	1.3
		1.6	1.1				.8	.8
		4.5	1.6				1.9	3.5
		2.0	1.1			Quick	1.1	1.1
		1.0	.3				.6	.5
		30 12.3	41 9.0				30 12.3	24 14.9
		53 6.9	53 6.9			Sales/Receivables	47 7.7	46 7.9
		118 3.1	72 5.1				70 5.2	89 4.1
						Cost of Sales/Inventory		
						Cost of Sales/Payables		
		3.1	2.6				5.5	3.0
		7.6	13.5			Sales/Working Capital	18.4	17.2
		42.9	63.9				-15.9	-11.2
		71.6					21.2	5.9
		4.3				EBIT/Interest	(52) 3.6	(30) -.6
		-7.8					.4	-10.6
						Net Profit + Depr., Dep., Amort./Cur. Mat. L/T/D		
		.2	.0				.5	.6
		.6	1.1			Fixed/Worth	1.0	1.8
		11.1	2.3				2.1	NM
		.4	.4				.4	.4
		2.9	2.4			Debt/Worth	1.2	1.7
		17.7	3.6				4.2	NM
		40.5	32.1			% Profit Before Taxes/Tangible Net Worth	46.9	10.5
		(10) 9.1	(10) 19.8				(49) 18.2	(27) -5.7
		-188.7	-.2				2.3	-33.3
		19.6	12.8			% Profit Before Taxes/Total Assets	15.3	5.1
		6.9	10.1				6.1	-3.5
		-17.4	.5				-1.2	-14.3
		13.4	186.9				8.4	8.9
		5.5	4.8			Sales/Net Fixed Assets	2.6	3.3
		4.3	1.9				.8	.9
		3.2	2.0				2.4	2.1
		1.5	1.5			Sales/Total Assets	.8	.8
		1.2	.5				.5	.4
							2.2	5.9
						% Depr., Dep., Amort./Sales	(33) 9.5	(23) 13.4
							18.0	22.2
						% Officers', Directors' Owners' Comp/Sales		
5514M	9901M	138060M	370091M	250642M	669980M	Net Sales ($)	1727866M	525721M
1286M	4193M	65036M	302188M	252796M	890502M	Total Assets ($)	2489222M	928456M

© RMA 2024   M = $ thousand   MM = $ million
See Pages viii through xx for Explanation of Ratios and Data

MINING—Drilling Oil and Gas Wells NAICS 213111

Comparative Historical Data | Current Data Sorted by Sales

						Type of Statement							
	1		3		5	Unqualified		1					4
	3		2			Reviewed							
	1		2		2	Compiled						1	1
	3		7		6	Tax Returns	2			2		2	
	22		21		27	Other	1	6	3	3	5		9
	4/1/21-3/31/22		4/1/22-3/31/23		4/1/23-3/31/24			1 (4/1-9/30/23)			39 (10/1/23-3/31/24)		
	ALL		ALL		ALL		0-1MM	1-3MM	3-5MM	5-10MM	10-25MM		25MM & OVER
	30		35		40	NUMBER OF STATEMENTS	3	7	3	5	8		14
	%		%		%	ASSETS	%	%	%	%	%		%
	8.1		13.5		11.1	Cash & Equivalents							6.9
	17.7		28.2		22.6	Trade Receivables (net)							24.3
	6.4		6.6		7.1	Inventory							12.7
	5.6		8.0		5.5	All Other Current							4.2
	37.8		56.3		46.2	Total Current							48.0
	38.4		32.5		36.5	Fixed Assets (net)							42.7
	8.1		2.4		7.0	Intangibles (net)							3.4
	15.7		8.8		10.3	All Other Non-Current							6.0
	100.0		100.0		100.0	Total							100.0
						LIABILITIES							
	16.6		6.5		3.1	Notes Payable-Short Term							4.1
	5.0		2.8		2.4	Cur. Mat.-L.T.D.							3.2
	11.2		13.2		10.9	Trade Payables							10.9
	.0		.0		.1	Income Taxes Payable							.0
	14.4		6.6		10.8	All Other Current							6.3
	47.2		29.2		27.3	Total Current							24.5
	21.8		23.4		27.2	Long-Term Debt							12.6
	.5		.3		.2	Deferred Taxes							.5
	5.4		11.7		7.5	All Other Non-Current							6.4
	25.1		35.4		37.9	Net Worth							56.0
	100.0		100.0		100.0	Total Liabilities & Net Worth							100.0
						INCOME DATA							
	100.0		100.0		100.0	Net Sales							100.0
						Gross Profit							
	94.4		89.7		90.2	Operating Expenses							87.0
	5.6		10.3		9.8	Operating Profit							13.0
	4.5		1.2		4.2	All Other Expenses (net)							2.4
	1.1		9.1		5.6	Profit Before Taxes							10.6
						RATIOS							
	2.3		5.2		3.5								3.0
	1.1		1.9		2.2	Current							1.9
	.6		1.1		1.2								1.2
	1.5		4.2		2.6								1.9
	.8		1.2		1.6	Quick							1.2
	.4		.8		.8								.9
30	12.1	28	13.1	24	14.9							40	9.1
65	5.6	54	6.7	50	7.3	Sales/Receivables						50	7.3
89	4.1	74	4.9	79	4.6							70	5.2
						Cost of Sales/Inventory							
						Cost of Sales/Payables							
	4.5		3.7		3.3								4.0
	28.2		9.0		7.9	Sales/Working Capital							7.7
	-5.5		47.7		60.9								32.3
	9.5		25.9		17.0								13.4
(24)	1.0	(29)	10.2	(32)	5.7	EBIT/Interest						(12)	6.1
	-1.8		2.8		-2.9								3.2
						Net Profit + Depr., Dep., Amort./Cur. Mat. L/T/D							
	.6		.3		.2								.2
	1.4		.9		.8	Fixed/Worth							.9
	-1.6		2.2		2.2								1.3
	1.0		.7		.4								.4
	2.5		2.3		1.0	Debt/Worth							.9
	-6.9		5.6		4.5								1.6
	40.5		64.0		53.4								61.1
(20)	6.1	(31)	40.0	(35)	21.7	% Profit Before Taxes/Tangible Net Worth							32.6
	-.1		4.8		-2.7								10.7
	5.8		23.6		18.8								25.1
	.0		11.9		7.2	% Profit Before Taxes/Total Assets							11.8
	-7.3		1.1		-1.0								6.9
	10.2		15.0		16.4								50.5
	2.2		6.9		5.1	Sales/Net Fixed Assets							5.2
	1.2		2.7		3.0								1.5
	1.6		2.8		2.5								2.0
	.8		1.5		1.5	Sales/Total Assets							1.3
	.3		.6		.8								.7
	3.9		3.1		2.6								
(18)	10.8	(19)	4.1	(19)	4.7	% Depr., Dep., Amort./Sales							
	14.8		12.8		9.1								
						% Officers', Directors' Owners' Comp/Sales							
	895880M		2263864M		1444188M	Net Sales ($)	1704M	12377M	12339M	42464M	140119M		1235185M
	1296179M		1681992M		1516001M	Total Assets ($)	1354M	53397M	64122M	23080M	103812M		1270236M

© RMA 2024   M = $ thousand   MM = $ million
See Pages viii through xx for Explanation of Ratios and Data

MINING—Support Activities for Oil and Gas Operations NAICS 213112

Current Data Sorted by Assets | **Comparative Historical Data**

							Type of Statement		
		1	4	18	19	15	Unqualified	35	16
			5	8	1		Reviewed	21	8
		2	5	4			Compiled	26	9
	1	6	9	2			Tax Returns	24	11
	3	29	70	62	31	22	Other	312	171
		40 (4/1-9/30/23)			277 (10/1/23-3/31/24)			4/1/19-3/31/20	4/1/20-3/31/21
	0-500M	500M-2MM	2-10MM	10-50MM	50-100MM	100-250MM	NUMBER OF STATEMENTS	ALL	ALL
	4	38	93	94	51	37		418	215
	%	%	%	%	%	%	ASSETS	%	%
		17.3	15.3	8.9	5.0	3.7	Cash & Equivalents	12.1	14.6
		27.0	32.7	28.3	29.9	22.8	Trade Receivables (net)	26.2	20.5
		9.3	8.5	10.6	8.8	15.8	Inventory	7.5	7.2
		4.2	3.8	6.3	4.8	2.1	All Other Current	3.4	3.9
		57.8	60.3	54.0	48.6	44.4	Total Current	49.2	46.2
		34.0	28.5	31.7	36.6	39.3	Fixed Assets (net)	39.4	42.5
		2.3	2.9	3.9	7.6	9.0	Intangibles (net)	5.1	5.3
		5.9	8.3	10.3	7.3	7.3	All Other Non-Current	6.3	6.1
		100.0	100.0	100.0	100.0	100.0	Total	100.0	100.0
							LIABILITIES		
		7.8	6.7	7.3	5.0	5.0	Notes Payable-Short Term	11.1	9.4
		1.0	2.0	3.2	3.7	4.1	Cur. Mat.-L.T.D.	4.5	4.9
		13.8	12.1	11.4	15.2	8.7	Trade Payables	9.8	9.2
		.1	.2	.1	.1	.1	Income Taxes Payable	.1	.1
		8.7	10.6	8.6	9.5	8.2	All Other Current	8.6	8.2
		31.4	31.7	30.6	33.5	26.1	Total Current	34.0	31.8
		25.3	22.9	14.1	19.6	18.6	Long-Term Debt	21.6	25.1
		.0	.0	.5	.4	.3	Deferred Taxes	.3	.1
		14.7	4.0	5.8	7.0	7.2	All Other Non-Current	5.9	5.3
		28.5	41.3	49.0	39.4	47.6	Net Worth	38.2	37.7
		100.0	100.0	100.0	100.0	100.0	Total Liabilities & Net Worth	100.0	100.0
							INCOME DATA		
		100.0	100.0	100.0	100.0	100.0	Net Sales	100.0	100.0
							Gross Profit		
		88.5	89.0	91.6	92.8	86.7	Operating Expenses	91.8	98.4
		11.5	11.0	8.4	7.2	13.3	Operating Profit	8.2	1.6
		1.5	2.0	1.9	2.4	3.3	All Other Expenses (net)	3.1	2.6
		10.0	9.0	6.5	4.9	10.0	Profit Before Taxes	5.1	-1.0
							RATIOS		
		3.7	4.0	3.6	2.4	2.0		3.1	3.3
		2.0	2.1	2.0	1.5	1.7	Current	1.7	1.9
		.8	1.1	1.2	1.1	1.3		.9	.9
		3.2	2.9	2.8	1.8	1.6		2.4	2.7
		1.3	1.7	1.2	1.1	.9	Quick	1.2	1.4
		.5	.9	.9	.7	.8		.6	.5
	0 UND	33 11.0	40 9.1	46 8.0	45 8.2			32 11.5	31 11.8
	43 8.5	48 7.6	55 6.6	59 6.2	58 6.3		Sales/Receivables	51 7.1	51 7.2
	69 5.3	73 5.0	78 4.7	76 4.8	78 4.7			73 5.0	76 4.8
							Cost of Sales/Inventory		
							Cost of Sales/Payables		
		3.4	4.2	3.5	4.9	4.8		5.2	3.6
		12.4	7.1	7.5	10.1	8.6	Sales/Working Capital	9.9	7.4
		-134.0	41.1	31.0	56.5	20.2		-80.0	-21.2
		18.4	21.1	36.0	6.1	9.4		16.9	11.0
	(22)	4.3	(77) 5.0	(82) 5.8	(48) 3.6	(35) 4.9	EBIT/Interest	(364) 3.4	(183) 1.2
		-3.5	.7	-1.2	1.5	2.0		.0	-4.2
					7.3			7.5	2.9
				(12)	3.0		Net Profit + Depr., Dep., Amort./Cur. Mat. L/T/D	(46) 2.3	(24) 1.6
					1.4			.6	-.3
		.1	.1	.2	.6	.2		.3	.5
		.7	.6	.8	.9	.7	Fixed/Worth	1.0	1.1
		16.0	2.7	1.2	1.8	1.9		2.9	2.7
		.3	.4	.4	.8	.8		.5	.5
		1.0	1.0	1.0	2.5	1.4	Debt/Worth	1.2	1.3
		-17.1	6.1	2.3	5.4	2.5		5.7	5.3
		66.6	76.5	45.9	49.6	46.3		54.0	27.7
	(28)	30.3	(79) 40.0	(85) 17.9	(47) 17.1	(34) 28.4	% Profit Before Taxes/Tangible Net Worth	(345) 17.2	(186) 1.0
		-.8	8.7	-3.4	.7	10.5		-1.6	-18.1
		39.1	29.5	18.4	11.4	18.1		18.6	8.9
		10.0	11.5	6.7	6.6	9.7	% Profit Before Taxes/Total Assets	5.8	-.1
		-6.8	.3	-1.7	.0	2.9		-2.3	-9.9
		76.0	45.6	17.5	10.4	18.5		24.3	12.3
		13.0	10.6	6.9	5.1	6.8	Sales/Net Fixed Assets	5.1	3.3
		2.8	4.5	2.7	1.2	1.0		1.7	1.0
		4.0	3.0	2.3	2.2	2.3		2.7	2.0
		2.0	2.0	1.6	1.4	1.2	Sales/Total Assets	1.7	1.2
		.8	1.3	1.0	.8	.4		.9	.6
		.6	1.1	2.2	2.2	.2		1.6	2.6
	(12)	2.2	(49) 2.8	(74) 4.8	(37) 5.9	(15) 1.6	% Depr., Dep., Amort./Sales	(250) 5.3	(141) 6.2
		5.4	7.9	8.2	11.8	13.8		11.4	15.3
		1.7	.5					1.1	1.0
	(10)	5.8	(23) 1.1				% Officers', Directors' Owners' Comp/Sales	(68) 2.7	(35) 1.7
		7.3	4.3					5.8	6.8
	4258M	133491M	1155472M	4584713M	9057217M	12085485M	Net Sales ($)	20387437M	8019499M
	720M	47450M	519069M	2419880M	3495228M	6329509M	Total Assets ($)	15678932M	7997711M

M = $ thousand   MM = $ million
See Pages viii through xx for Explanation of Ratios and Data

© RMA 2024

MINING—Support Activities for Oil and Gas Operations NAICS 213112

Comparative Historical Data | Current Data Sorted by Sales

Comparative Historical Data			Type of Statement	Current Data Sorted by Sales					
32	51	57	Unqualified	2	1	2	6	46	
5	11	14	Reviewed				6	8	
7	5	11	Compiled		1	3	4	3	
13	22	18	Tax Returns	1	4	3	8	3	
131	203	217	Other	16	14	17	32	43	95
4/1/21-3/31/22 ALL	4/1/22-3/31/23 ALL	4/1/23-3/31/24 ALL			40 (4/1-9/30/23)			277 (10/1/23-3/31/24)	
				0-1MM	1-3MM	3-5MM	5-10MM	10-25MM	25MM & OVER
188	292	317	NUMBER OF STATEMENTS	16	21	18	40	67	155
%	%	%	ASSETS	%	%	%	%	%	%
12.1	11.3	10.9	Cash & Equivalents	14.4	16.3	8.5	18.6	14.2	6.8
24.7	26.4	28.9	Trade Receivables (net)	11.0	26.2	25.1	25.5	30.2	31.8
8.2	7.7	10.0	Inventory	4.9	15.0	3.8	8.2	11.0	10.7
5.5	5.2	4.6	All Other Current	6.8	6.8	5.9	2.5	2.4	5.5
50.5	50.6	54.5	Total Current	37.2	64.3	43.1	54.7	57.8	54.7
37.7	36.8	32.4	Fixed Assets (net)	45.3	20.9	50.8	30.6	30.1	32.0
5.4	4.4	4.6	Intangibles (net)	7.7	.7	2.0	2.2	4.2	5.8
6.5	8.2	8.5	All Other Non-Current	9.2	14.0	4.1	12.5	7.9	7.5
100.0	100.0	100.0	Total	100.0	100.0	100.0	100.0	100.0	100.0
			LIABILITIES						
10.0	6.2	6.8	Notes Payable-Short Term	6.4	18.0	10.5	3.8	4.5	6.6
4.2	3.3	2.8	Cur. Mat.-L.T.D.	1.0	1.6	5.0	1.5	2.5	3.4
10.6	11.2	12.1	Trade Payables	4.6	15.5	11.0	11.3	11.0	13.2
.1	.2	.1	Income Taxes Payable	.0	.1	.0	.2	.1	.1
9.4	9.4	9.3	All Other Current	12.4	8.2	9.2	7.9	8.6	9.7
34.4	30.3	31.1	Total Current	24.5	43.5	35.7	24.6	26.8	33.1
24.3	23.2	19.5	Long-Term Debt	25.7	23.3	12.2	25.8	23.0	16.0
.3	.2	.2	Deferred Taxes	.0	.2	.3	.0	.4	.3
7.2	7.3	6.6	All Other Non-Current	10.5	15.7	7.3	6.4	5.1	5.7
33.8	38.9	42.5	Net Worth	38.7	17.4	44.6	43.2	44.7	44.9
100.0	100.0	100.0	Total Liabilities & Net Worth	100.0	100.0	100.0	100.0	100.0	100.0
			INCOME DATA						
100.0	100.0	100.0	Net Sales	100.0	100.0	100.0	100.0	100.0	100.0
			Gross Profit						
92.3	87.1	89.8	Operating Expenses	65.3	83.2	92.4	90.9	91.0	92.1
7.7	12.9	10.2	Operating Profit	34.7	16.8	7.6	9.1	9.0	7.9
1.6	2.0	2.1	All Other Expenses (net)	8.5	5.3	1.6	1.1	1.4	1.6
6.1	10.9	8.1	Profit Before Taxes	26.2	11.4	6.0	8.0	7.5	6.3
			RATIOS						
3.3	3.3	3.4		2.8	4.0	3.9	4.1	3.9	2.7
1.8	2.0	1.9	Current	1.2	1.7	2.0	2.2	2.3	1.7
1.0	1.2	1.1		.2	.9	.5	1.1	1.3	1.1
2.5	2.7	2.5		2.6	3.5	2.1	3.3	3.0	2.1
1.2	1.3	1.3	Quick	.9	1.0	1.2	1.8	1.7	1.1
.7	.7	.7		.1	.5	.5	1.0	1.0	.7
32 11.4	36 10.1	35 10.4		0 UND	0 UND	24 15.2	33 11.1	34 10.8	43 8.5
61 6.0	62 5.9	54 6.8	Sales/Receivables	6 56.2	39 9.4	42 8.6	54 6.8	51 7.2	58 6.3
85 4.3	83 4.4	76 4.8		118 3.1	99 3.7	68 5.4	72 5.1	73 5.0	76 4.8
			Cost of Sales/Inventory						
			Cost of Sales/Payables						
4.0	3.8	4.2		.8	2.4	4.5	3.3	4.0	4.9
8.2	7.7	8.4	Sales/Working Capital	7.7	5.3	16.0	6.5	6.5	9.2
NM	26.0	45.4		-2.9	NM	-4.4	43.6	16.2	52.5
21.0	38.3	18.0		15.7	17.9	18.3	36.1	15.2	
(157) 4.7	(240) 8.3	(267) 4.8	EBIT/Interest	(13) 3.6	(13) 4.7	(30) 5.5	(57) 5.0	(146) 4.6	
-.5	1.8	.7		-2.5	-.7	-.6	.6	.9	
5.1	10.7	8.5	Net Profit + Depr., Dep.,						7.8
(24) 2.6	(34) 3.6	(27) 2.8	Amort./Cur. Mat. L/T/D					(23) 2.8	
.8	1.7	.5							.5
.3	.3	.2		.1	.0	.5	.1	.2	.2
1.0	.8	.7	Fixed/Worth	1.0	.6	.8	.6	.7	.8
3.1	2.1	1.8		6.9	NM	1.9	2.1	2.8	1.5
.5	.5	.5		.3	.7	.4	.4	.3	.6
1.4	1.2	1.2	Debt/Worth	1.1	2.3	.6	.8	1.0	1.3
6.1	5.3	4.0		7.5	-7.4	2.2	3.4	6.1	3.0
45.3	59.8	56.1	% Profit Before Taxes/Tangible	62.1	69.4	59.6	78.4	64.3	48.2
(155) 12.7	(249) 28.8	(277) 26.5	Net Worth	(13) 5.2	(14) 54.3	(15) 23.1	(36) 38.6	(57) 29.1	(142) 21.9
.8	6.4	3.4		.8	2.2	1.4	4.1	6.2	2.2
17.2	25.4	22.0	% Profit Before Taxes/Total	17.2	41.2	36.6	32.8	27.9	17.7
5.0	9.8	9.2	Assets	4.2	11.5	6.7	14.0	11.3	8.5
-2.0	1.5	-.3		-1.4	-4.3	-5.8	.4	.0	-.1
21.5	15.3	26.4		19.4	825.2	14.0	27.9	27.6	23.4
4.1	5.0	8.0	Sales/Net Fixed Assets	1.1	23.1	3.6	7.2	10.3	7.7
1.3	1.8	2.8		.2	3.4	1.0	2.8	3.5	3.0
2.6	2.4	2.8		.7	3.2	3.9	2.8	3.0	2.7
1.2	1.4	1.7	Sales/Total Assets	.3	1.1	1.5	1.7	2.0	1.8
.6	.7	.9		.1	.7	.5	1.2	1.0	1.1
2.4	1.8	1.1					.7	1.8	.8
(115) 7.0	(179) 5.6	(189) 3.7	% Depr., Dep., Amort./Sales			(24) 3.2	(42) 4.3	(102) 3.6	
15.6	9.6	8.3					8.4	8.4	7.2
1.1	1.2	.8	% Officers', Directors'				2.4	.8	.1
(24) 2.8	(40) 3.6	(45) 2.4	Owners' Comp/Sales		(11) 3.0	(15) 1.2	(10) .7		
6.2	7.0	6.1					6.3	4.3	1.4
9157888M	18992553M	27020636M	Net Sales ($)	7337M	43384M	75985M	297957M	1126537M	25469436M
7721822M	13119712M	12811856M	Total Assets ($)	31956M	93414M	100250M	300871M	960718M	11324647M

© RMA 2024   M = $ thousand   MM = $ million
See Pages viii through xx for Explanation of Ratios and Data

UTILITIES

UTILITIES—Fossil Fuel Electric Power Generation NAICS 221112

Current Data Sorted by Assets / **Comparative Historical Data**

							Type of Statement		
			1	1	1	5	Unqualified	3	1
							Reviewed		
						1	Compiled	2	1
							Tax Returns	2	
	1	3	3	4	11	Other	10	18
	11 (4/1-9/30/23)		20 (10/1/23-3/31/24)				4/1/19- 3/31/20	4/1/20- 3/31/21
0-500M	500M-2MM	2-10MM	10-50MM	50-100MM	100-250MM		ALL	ALL
	1				17	NUMBER OF STATEMENTS	17	20
%	%	%	%	%	%	ASSETS	%	%
					5.0	Cash & Equivalents	4.3	3.7
D					3.2	Trade Receivables (net)	6.1	2.8
A					3.3	Inventory	9.0	.8
T					2.7	All Other Current	2.4	2.3
A					14.3	Total Current	21.8	9.6
					60.3	Fixed Assets (net)	57.7	61.5
N					15.9	Intangibles (net)	6.6	15.0
O					9.6	All Other Non-Current	13.9	13.9
T					100.0	Total	100.0	100.0
						LIABILITIES		
A					1.3	Notes Payable-Short Term	2.4	.0
V					7.5	Cur. Mat.-L.T.D.	10.9	10.6
A					2.5	Trade Payables	8.3	.5
I					.0	Income Taxes Payable	.0	.3
L					4.8	All Other Current	5.6	3.8
A					16.1	Total Current	27.2	15.3
B					59.9	Long-Term Debt	17.1	47.0
L					.0	Deferred Taxes	.6	.0
E					3.6	All Other Non-Current	8.8	9.0
					20.3	Net Worth	46.4	28.7
					100.0	Total Liabilities & Net Worth	100.0	100.0
						INCOME DATA		
					100.0	Net Sales	100.0	100.0
						Gross Profit		
					68.1	Operating Expenses	84.0	64.4
					31.9	Operating Profit	16.0	35.6
					15.1	All Other Expenses (net)	8.5	30.7
					16.8	Profit Before Taxes	7.5	4.9
						RATIOS		
					1.9		1.9	1.0
					1.2	Current	1.0	.7
					.5		.7	.3
					1.0		.9	.8
					.6	Quick	.5	.4
					.3		.2	.2
				11 32.6		20 18.0	8 43.1
				30 12.0	Sales/Receivables	30 12.2	34 10.6
				34 10.7		54 6.8	51 7.1
						Cost of Sales/Inventory		
						Cost of Sales/Payables		
					4.8		12.8	NM
					15.5	Sales/Working Capital	237.0	-8.5
					-6.7		-8.9	-2.2
							7.5	6.4
						EBIT/Interest	(13) 3.1	(10) 3.8
							-9.9	1.6
						Net Profit + Depr., Dep., Amort./Cur. Mat. L/T/D		
					1.2		.5	1.2
					9.6	Fixed/Worth	1.5	3.8
					-1.3		11.5	-3.7
					1.6		.5	.9
					10.7	Debt/Worth	1.1	5.2
					-2.8		12.5	-5.1
							17.3	22.5
						% Profit Before Taxes/Tangible Net Worth	(14) 5.0	(12) 9.8
							-3.5	4.5
					18.0		10.2	7.9
					2.4	% Profit Before Taxes/Total Assets	1.3	1.6
					.7		-2.6	-3.3
					1.3		4.4	.9
					.6	Sales/Net Fixed Assets	.4	.3
					.5		.3	.2
					.7		.9	.3
					.4	Sales/Total Assets	.3	.2
					.3		.2	.1
					4.3		5.7	14.1
				(10)	9.9	% Depr., Dep., Amort./Sales	(13) 14.1	(10) 21.4
					18.5		24.3	41.7
						% Officers', Directors' Owners' Comp/Sales		
	3161M	30257M	72066M	892373M	1750555M	Net Sales ($)	533356M	583993M
	664M	20145M	95933M	398721M	3227877M	Total Assets ($)	1760453M	3022054M

M = $ thousand   MM = $ million
See Pages viii through xx for Explanation of Ratios and Data

© RMA 2024

UTILITIES—Fossil Fuel Electric Power Generation NAICS 221112

Comparative Historical Data			Type of Statement	Current Data Sorted by Sales				
4	2	8	Unqualified	1	1	1		5
1		1	Reviewed					1
			Compiled					
			Tax Returns					
5	9	22	Other		3	1	3	15
4/1/21-3/31/22 ALL	4/1/22-3/31/23 ALL	4/1/23-3/31/24 ALL		0-1MM	11 (4/1-9/30/23) 1-3MM	3-5MM	20 (10/1/23-3/31/24) 5-10MM 10-25MM	25MM & OVER
10	11	31	NUMBER OF STATEMENTS	4	2	1	3	21
%	%	%	ASSETS	%	%	%	%	%
3.3	9.1	8.3	Cash & Equivalents					7.4
5.7	9.8	6.2	Trade Receivables (net)	DATA				7.8
1.5	10.5	4.8	Inventory					6.6
1.2	2.4	2.7	All Other Current					3.0
11.8	31.7	22.1	Total Current	NOT				24.8
58.7	43.9	54.7	Fixed Assets (net)					59.4
13.8	1.4	12.4	Intangibles (net)	AVAILABLE				10.8
15.7	23.0	10.7	All Other Non-Current					5.0
100.0	100.0	100.0	Total					100.0
			LIABILITIES					
3.2	.3	1.0	Notes Payable-Short Term					1.1
9.3	2.7	5.4	Cur. Mat.-L.T.D.					7.3
1.0	6.8	3.2	Trade Payables					3.8
.1	.2	.0	Income Taxes Payable					.0
4.2	9.6	5.7	All Other Current					5.7
17.7	19.5	15.3	Total Current					17.9
27.0	28.2	47.1	Long-Term Debt					52.6
1.1	2.4	.9	Deferred Taxes					.0
11.5	13.5	12.7	All Other Non-Current					14.9
42.7	36.4	24.0	Net Worth					14.7
100.0	100.0	100.0	Total Liabilities & Net Worth					100.0
			INCOME DATA					
100.0	100.0	100.0	Net Sales					100.0
			Gross Profit					
67.1	83.3	76.1	Operating Expenses					73.4
32.9	16.7	23.9	Operating Profit					26.6
8.6	5.9	10.8	All Other Expenses (net)					10.7
24.3	10.8	13.1	Profit Before Taxes					15.9
			RATIOS					
1.5	2.4	2.8						3.4
.7	1.7	1.3	Current					1.3
.2	1.1	.6						.5
.9	1.6	2.2						2.2
.4	.9	.6	Quick					.6
.1	.5	.4						.3
13 27.4	28 13.1	20 18.5					11 34.0
36 10.1	39 9.3	30 12.0	Sales/Receivables				29 12.5
76 4.8	65 5.6	36 10.2					33 11.1
			Cost of Sales/Inventory					
			Cost of Sales/Payables					
14.5	3.5	4.9						5.5
-11.7	9.4	13.0	Sales/Working Capital					9.4
-1.9	44.3	-8.4						-6.7
		8.1						17.5
	(19)	4.9	EBIT/Interest				(14)	6.3
		1.6						2.9
			Net Profit + Depr., Dep., Amort./Cur. Mat. L/T/D					
1.0	.0	.8						.8
2.1	1.8	3.7	Fixed/Worth					4.7
NM	2.3	-1.6						-1.4
.7	1.2	.9						.7
2.8	1.8	3.8	Debt/Worth					5.3
NM	2.4	-3.6						-2.8
	72.9	32.3	% Profit Before Taxes/Tangible Net Worth					54.1
	7.0	(20) 9.3					(12)	19.2
	2.2	3.0						.9
15.6	17.9	17.2	% Profit Before Taxes/Total Assets					19.6
4.4	2.4	3.1						5.6
1.2	.4	.8						.8
1.8	388.0	8.5						7.0
.4	1.4	.9	Sales/Net Fixed Assets					1.0
.3	.4	.5						.6
.5	1.7	1.2						1.8
.2	.4	.4	Sales/Total Assets					.5
.1	.2	.3						.3
		3.4						2.6
	(20)	7.5	% Depr., Dep., Amort./Sales				(12)	4.5
		16.7						14.1
			% Officers', Directors' Owners' Comp/Sales					
677023M	367807M	2748412M	Net Sales ($)	6605M	6195M	8696M	51036M	2675880M
1763567M	715436M	3743340M	Total Assets ($)	21333M	11344M	65027M	408702M	3236934M

© RMA 2024 M = $ thousand MM = $ million
See Pages viii through xx for Explanation of Ratios and Data

UTILITIES—Solar Electric Power Generation NAICS 221114

Current Data Sorted by Assets | Comparative Historical Data

						Type of Statement		
	2	3	27	18	25	Unqualified	20	25
		1	6			Reviewed	6	3
	1	3	2		3	Compiled	2	
	4	2				Tax Returns	3	2
5	25	41	45	20	31	Other	46	30
	40 (4/1-9/30/23)		224 (10/1/23-3/31/24)				4/1/19-3/31/20	4/1/20-3/31/21
0-500M	500M-2MM	2-10MM	10-50MM	50-100MM	100-250MM		ALL	ALL
5	32	50	80	38	59	NUMBER OF STATEMENTS	77	60
%	%	%	%	%	%	ASSETS	%	%
	24.3	19.3	6.4	4.5	3.4	Cash & Equivalents	6.8	9.5
	17.8	25.3	11.5	2.8	3.2	Trade Receivables (net)	7.5	8.1
	5.6	7.8	5.0	4.5	1.7	Inventory	1.9	3.1
	.8	2.9	4.1	2.0	4.4	All Other Current	6.4	6.6
	48.4	55.3	27.0	13.8	12.8	Total Current	22.6	27.1
	32.3	34.7	52.5	70.2	72.7	Fixed Assets (net)	65.4	58.4
	7.8	3.0	5.8	3.1	4.9	Intangibles (net)	3.5	8.8
	11.5	7.1	14.6	12.9	9.6	All Other Non-Current	8.5	5.7
	100.0	100.0	100.0	100.0	100.0	Total	100.0	100.0
						LIABILITIES		
	10.6	7.6	3.0	.5	2.3	Notes Payable-Short Term	2.9	1.8
	5.2	3.5	3.4	2.6	5.5	Cur. Mat.-L.T.D.	2.8	4.5
	15.7	12.1	7.0	1.3	3.2	Trade Payables	5.3	7.0
	.0	.0	.2	.0	.0	Income Taxes Payable	.0	.0
	29.6	16.2	12.4	9.6	5.6	All Other Current	9.3	9.3
	61.0	39.4	26.2	14.0	16.5	Total Current	20.3	22.6
	29.7	17.7	30.4	36.8	24.1	Long-Term Debt	30.4	30.9
	.0	.0	.1	.0	.1	Deferred Taxes	.0	.1
	2.9	5.7	4.7	8.3	8.2	All Other Non-Current	6.9	6.9
	6.4	37.2	38.7	40.9	51.1	Net Worth	42.4	39.5
	100.0	100.0	100.0	100.0	100.0	Total Liabilities & Net Worth	100.0	100.0
						INCOME DATA		
	100.0	100.0	100.0	100.0	100.0	Net Sales	100.0	100.0
						Gross Profit		
	82.9	91.2	80.9	79.1	78.8	Operating Expenses	77.0	75.9
	17.1	8.8	19.1	20.9	21.2	Operating Profit	23.0	24.1
	5.8	6.2	15.4	20.6	16.2	All Other Expenses (net)	20.0	16.3
	11.3	2.6	3.7	.2	5.1	Profit Before Taxes	2.9	7.8
						RATIOS		
	1.6	4.0	1.7	1.9	1.3		2.1	2.0
	.9	1.3	1.0	1.0	.7	Current	1.2	1.0
	.6	.6	.4	.4	.2		.6	.4
	1.5	3.1	1.2	1.5	1.0		1.4	1.5
	.9	.9	.6	.8	.4	Quick	.7	.7
	.5	.5	.2	.2	.1		.2	.3
0	UND	1	318.7	13	28.3	23	15.6	16	23.1		9	40.4	14	26.7
3	136.0	33	10.9	28	13.0	34	10.8	23	15.7	Sales/Receivables	27	13.7	27	13.3
20	18.1	54	6.7	62	5.9	62	5.9	44	8.3		46	8.0	53	6.9
						Cost of Sales/Inventory		
						Cost of Sales/Payables		
	26.0	8.4	6.3	3.4	11.3		5.6	4.0
	-452.5	26.3	NM	NM	-10.7	Sales/Working Capital	19.8	NM
	-15.6	-12.3	-3.5	-3.6	-3.5		-5.8	-2.9
	245.8	57.5	26.0		45.6		42.9	29.4
(21)	19.1	(37) 10.0	(36) 4.0		(24) 7.5	EBIT/Interest	(34) 5.9	(33) 5.9
	-3.6	.8	-1.2		1.6		.8	2.3
						Net Profit + Depr., Dep., Amort./Cur. Mat. L/T/D		
	.4	.1	.7	1.2	1.0		.9	.6
	2.8	.8	1.5	1.9	1.6	Fixed/Worth	1.7	1.7
	-.3	2.8	4.7	6.1	4.5		2.6	5.5
	.5	.4	.6	.7	.3		.6	.7
	4.2	1.3	1.5	1.4	1.2	Debt/Worth	1.3	1.7
	-4.3	6.7	5.9	6.3	4.0		4.2	7.7
	114.7	60.9	51.3	6.5	5.3		19.9	31.7
(18)	99.2	(39) 41.3	(65) 3.9	(36) -.2	(57) 1.0	% Profit Before Taxes/Tangible Net Worth	(67) 1.3	(49) 4.3
	7.0	5.0	-1.5	-3.2	-1.9		-3.2	-1.7
	62.8	39.5	6.1	1.7	4.1		6.7	10.4
	24.8	11.7	.9	-.1	.4	% Profit Before Taxes/Total Assets	.5	2.1
	.4	-2.4	-1.2	-1.1	-1.0		-1.6	-.9
	477.0	97.2	17.5	.2	.2		12.0	14.8
	56.8	19.6	.1	.1	.1	Sales/Net Fixed Assets	.1	.2
	9.5	.6	.1	.1	.1		.1	.1
	14.8	5.3	1.6	.1	.1		1.0	1.3
	7.5	2.9	.1	.1	.1	Sales/Total Assets	.1	.1
	.8	.4	.1	.1	.1		.1	.1
	.1	.4	1.7	33.0	31.1		4.4	3.5
(15)	.9	(30) 4.0	(64) 37.4	(37) 44.8	(48) 46.3	% Depr., Dep., Amort./Sales	(63) 35.9	(46) 34.4
	31.0	62.9	52.5	59.5	57.1		56.9	52.8
		.5				% Officers', Directors' Owners' Comp/Sales		
	(10)	1.9						
		5.7						
11489M	331597M	761571M	1743010M	1307959M	3585078M	Net Sales ($)	2445446M	2589019M
1267M	43525M	277146M	2321555M	2626123M	9940547M	Total Assets ($)	5136136M	4383893M

© RMA 2024

M = $ thousand   MM = $ million
See Pages viii through xx for Explanation of Ratios and Data

UTILITIES—Solar Electric Power Generation NAICS 221114

Comparative Historical Data / Current Data Sorted by Sales

				Type of Statement						
	27	39	75	Unqualified	5	20	10	14	15	11
	4	3	7	Reviewed					2	5
	2	2	9	Compiled		3		2	1	3
	4	3	6	Tax Returns	1			1	4	
	62	72	167	Other	20	24	16	29	41	37
	4/1/21-3/31/22 ALL	4/1/22-3/31/23 ALL	4/1/23-3/31/24 ALL		40 (4/1-9/30/23)			224 (10/1/23-3/31/24)		
					0-1MM	1-3MM	3-5MM	5-10MM	10-25MM	25MM & OVER
	99	119	264	NUMBER OF STATEMENTS	26	47	26	46	63	56
	%	%	%	ASSETS	%	%	%	%	%	%
	9.6	6.9	10.7	Cash & Equivalents	10.0	4.5	2.6	12.3	11.8	17.2
	8.9	10.6	11.8	Trade Receivables (net)	3.5	1.2	4.6	11.9	16.7	22.1
	2.2	7.5	4.8	Inventory	1.3	1.1	.0	2.0	4.5	14.5
	3.9	5.5	3.2	All Other Current	.3	1.8	.8	2.3	2.6	8.1
	24.5	30.5	30.5	Total Current	15.1	8.7	8.0	28.5	35.7	61.8
	59.3	56.0	53.1	Fixed Assets (net)	78.1	70.9	80.9	59.9	48.1	13.8
	5.7	4.0	4.9	Intangibles (net)	1.0	3.4	1.6	2.8	4.7	11.3
	10.4	9.5	11.5	All Other Non-Current	5.7	16.9	9.5	8.8	11.4	13.0
	100.0	100.0	100.0	Total	100.0	100.0	100.0	100.0	100.0	100.0
				LIABILITIES						
	2.1	3.0	5.1	Notes Payable-Short Term	1.2	2.6	2.7	5.7	7.3	7.0
	4.7	4.1	4.0	Cur. Mat.-L.T.D.	5.0	4.7	5.7	2.2	2.4	5.4
	5.9	6.0	7.3	Trade Payables	1.1	.7	1.1	4.1	9.4	18.9
	.0	.2	.1	Income Taxes Payable	.0	.0	.0	.0	.0	.3
	9.7	14.8	13.2	All Other Current	14.1	6.6	5.0	9.7	11.9	26.3
	22.4	28.2	29.6	Total Current	21.3	14.6	14.4	21.9	31.0	58.0
	36.7	30.2	27.5	Long-Term Debt	46.9	44.1	43.2	21.7	22.0	8.3
	.0	.0	.1	Deferred Taxes	.0	.0	.1	.1	.0	.1
	6.8	7.8	5.9	All Other Non-Current	6.2	3.4	6.3	8.8	7.8	3.0
	34.1	33.8	36.9	Net Worth	25.6	37.8	36.0	47.6	39.2	30.6
	100.0	100.0	100.0	Total Liabilities & Net Worth	100.0	100.0	100.0	100.0	100.0	100.0
				INCOME DATA						
	100.0	100.0	100.0	Net Sales	100.0	100.0	100.0	100.0	100.0	100.0
				Gross Profit						
	78.4	80.4	82.2	Operating Expenses	79.5	75.9	72.5	81.8	83.6	92.0
	21.6	19.6	17.8	Operating Profit	20.5	24.1	27.5	18.2	16.4	8.0
	8.6	11.5	13.1	All Other Expenses (net)	22.4	19.7	24.9	12.7	8.6	3.3
	13.0	8.1	4.7	Profit Before Taxes	-1.9	4.4	2.6	5.5	7.8	4.7
				RATIOS						
	1.4	1.9	1.8		1.2	1.6	1.5	3.9	2.2	1.7
	.7	1.1	1.0	Current	.6	.8	.7	1.3	1.1	1.3
	.4	.6	.5		.2	.2	.2	.5	.6	.8
	1.0	1.3	1.3		1.0	1.0	1.2	3.1	1.7	1.2
	.7	.7	.7	Quick	.6	.4	.6	.9	.9	.7
	.3	.3	.2		.2	.2	.1	.2	.3	.4
13	28.9	14 25.9	6 60.0		0 UND	4 85.2	18 20.5	4 88.0	5 74.1	9 42.7
27	13.3	26 13.9	25 14.7	Sales/Receivables	17 20.9	23 15.9	54 6.7	27 13.6	27 13.4	23 16.0
48	7.6	51 7.1	54 6.8		58 6.3	39 9.4	78 4.7	55 6.6	54 6.8	45 8.2
				Cost of Sales/Inventory						
				Cost of Sales/Payables						
	11.7	7.0	7.9		20.5	4.0	8.5	4.0	9.7	9.5
	-7.7	90.9	NM	Sales/Working Capital	-5.2	-8.4	-4.4	27.2	146.7	30.1
	-3.0	-3.9	-4.3		-.4	-1.6	-.4	-5.6	-6.6	-31.0
	18.2	57.0	49.2		5.4	7.0		223.0	116.5	37.0
(55)	4.3	(60) 8.1	(130) 5.3	EBIT/Interest	(11) -.8	(11) 3.7		(17) 5.6	(43) 14.4	(43) 13.8
	1.9	.7	-.3		-1.0	-3.4		1.7	1.6	-2.2
			4.1	Net Profit + Depr., Dep.,						
		(14)	1.7	Amort./Cur. Mat. L/T/D						
			-.9							
	.6	.7	.6		1.3	1.2	1.6	.5	.7	.1
	2.0	1.4	1.5	Fixed/Worth	1.8	1.6	2.2	1.4	1.8	.6
	5.3	5.2	5.8		-91.1	4.6	16.9	4.6	18.0	7.5
	.7	.4	.5		.5	.4	.8	.3	.4	1.1
	2.1	2.4	1.4	Debt/Worth	1.4	1.1	2.5	.8	1.4	2.2
	9.5	12.4	6.1		-116.4	4.2	16.8	4.2	19.7	39.0
	31.9	41.5	49.4		7.6	3.9	5.7	29.0	62.7	101.1
(83)	6.6	(96) 4.2	(217) 4.0	% Profit Before Taxes/Tangible Net Worth	(19) -2.7	(40) .4	(24) .6	(42) 2.1	(48) 6.0	(44) 60.3
	1.0	-.9	-1.5		-4.3	-2.9	-1.2	-.8	-.6	18.2
	9.8	9.4	13.5		5.4	2.5	1.1	18.8	29.4	33.0
	2.6	2.0	1.3	% Profit Before Taxes/Total Assets	-.2	.4	.1	.9	3.1	12.8
	.3	-.9	-1.0		-2.7	-1.7	-.4	-.7	-1.1	-1.9
	19.1	24.2	33.0		.2	.2	.1	43.4	67.9	448.6
	.2	.2	.2	Sales/Net Fixed Assets	.1	.1	.1	.1	8.2	31.8
	.1	.1	.1		.1	.1	.1	.1	.1	16.0
	.8	2.0	2.8		.2	.1	.1	2.9	4.7	4.6
	.1	.1	.1	Sales/Total Assets	.1	.1	.1	.1	.9	2.9
	.1	.1	.1		.1	.0	.1	.1	.1	1.5
	4.2	.8	1.5		32.1	36.7	38.0	37.4	.5	.3
(75)	36.7	(93) 23.8	(195) 40.2	% Depr., Dep., Amort./Sales	(22) 57.7	(41) 52.8	(22) 42.7	(31) 48.3	(39) 32.0	(40) .6
	53.8	51.5	56.5		84.8	65.8	49.7	59.7	50.3	1.6
		.2	.5	% Officers', Directors', Owners' Comp/Sales						
		(11) .7	(19) 1.0							
			1.8 3.0							
	3781642M	5281402M	7740704M	Net Sales ($)	14215M	99814M	99432M	343895M	1029787M	6153561M
	5969182M	8654913M	15210163M	Total Assets ($)	167333M	1464932M	1826987M	3269126M	5392014M	3089771M

© RMA 2024   M = $ thousand   MM = $ million
See Pages viii through xx for Explanation of Ratios and Data

UTILITIES—Wind Electric Power Generation NAICS 221115

Current Data Sorted by Assets

0-500M	3 (4/1-9/30/23) 500M-2MM	3 2-10MM	2 5 28 (10/1/23-3/31/24) 10-50MM	1 1 50-100MM	7 12 100-250MM	Type of Statement	Comparative Historical Data 8 14 4/1/19-3/31/20 ALL	3 1 9 4/1/20-3/31/21 ALL
						Unqualified		
						Reviewed		
						Compiled		
						Tax Returns		
						Other		
		3	7	2	19	NUMBER OF STATEMENTS	22	13
%	%	%	%	%	%	ASSETS	%	%
D	D				1.9	Cash & Equivalents	3.4	1.9
A	A				1.1	Trade Receivables (net)	2.7	1.1
T	T				.3	Inventory	2.6	.2
A	A				1.9	All Other Current	.9	1.3
					5.1	Total Current	9.6	4.4
N	N				76.0	Fixed Assets (net)	81.7	64.1
O	O				14.4	Intangibles (net)	1.7	3.2
T	T				4.5	All Other Non-Current	7.1	28.3
					100.0	Total	100.0	100.0
A	A					LIABILITIES		
V	V				.0	Notes Payable-Short Term	.4	.0
A	A				3.0	Cur. Mat.-L.T.D.	2.3	2.9
I	I				.5	Trade Payables	5.3	.1
L	L				.0	Income Taxes Payable	.0	.0
A	A				1.4	All Other Current	1.9	5.6
B	B				4.9	Total Current	9.8	8.5
L	L				31.9	Long-Term Debt	53.2	52.2
E	E				.0	Deferred Taxes	.0	.0
					7.1	All Other Non-Current	12.7	6.7
					56.1	Net Worth	24.3	32.5
					100.0	Total Liabilities & Net Worth	100.0	100.0
						INCOME DATA		
					100.0	Net Sales	100.0	100.0
						Gross Profit		
					91.3	Operating Expenses	83.4	67.4
					8.7	Operating Profit	16.6	32.6
					16.7	All Other Expenses (net)	21.4	38.1
					-7.9	Profit Before Taxes	-4.7	-5.5
						RATIOS		
					3.1		5.0	1.4
					1.1	Current	1.4	.6
					.6		.6	.3
					1.8		2.5	.6
					.7	Quick	.9	.4
					.2		.4	.1
				20	17.9		9 40.1	24 15.1
				37	9.9	Sales/Receivables	27 13.7	34 10.7
				48	7.6		41 8.8	42 8.6
						Cost of Sales/Inventory		
						Cost of Sales/Payables		
					3.8		4.1	5.6
					20.8	Sales/Working Capital	16.6	-5.4
					-5.4		-5.2	-1.2
						EBIT/Interest		
						Net Profit + Depr., Dep., Amort./Cur. Mat. L/T/D		
					1.0		1.4	.5
					1.4	Fixed/Worth	2.7	1.4
					-2.0		NM	4.7
					.1		1.0	.8
					.6	Debt/Worth	2.7	4.3
					-3.4		NM	NM
					1.2		10.0	12.4
				(13)	-1.5	% Profit Before Taxes/Tangible Net Worth	(17) -.9	(10) 1.4
					-3.3		-7.6	-2.0
					1.0		2.8	1.8
					-1.5	% Profit Before Taxes/Total Assets	-.3	-.1
					-3.2		-2.2	-3.3
					.3		.7	UND
					.1	Sales/Net Fixed Assets	.2	.2
					.1		.1	.1
					.1		.3	.1
					.1	Sales/Total Assets	.1	.1
					.1		.1	.1
					39.0		29.6	
				(10)	45.4	% Depr., Dep., Amort./Sales	(16) 52.4	
					62.1		56.9	
						% Officers', Directors' Owners' Comp/Sales		
		18611M	50341M	23026M	385610M	Net Sales ($)	444565M	190060M
		11538M	262129M	183380M	3528177M	Total Assets ($)	1732407M	1507516M

M = $ thousand   MM = $ million
See Pages viii through xx for Explanation of Ratios and Data

© RMA 2024

UTILITIES—Wind Electric Power Generation NAICS 221115

Comparative Historical Data			Type of Statement	Current Data Sorted by Sales					
3	5	10	Unqualified		1	2	6	1	
1			Reviewed						
2			Compiled						
			Tax Returns						
			Other		4	1	2	10	4
14	10	21		3 (4/1-9/30/23)				28 (10/1/23-3/31/24)	
4/1/21-3/31/22	4/1/22-3/31/23	4/1/23-3/31/24		0-1MM	1-3MM	3-5MM	5-10MM	10-25MM	25MM & OVER
ALL	ALL	ALL							
20	15	31	NUMBER OF STATEMENTS	4	2	4	4	16	5
%	%	%	ASSETS	%	%	%	%	%	%
7.0	3.7	4.0	Cash & Equivalents					1.7	
3.8	7.0	4.5	Trade Receivables (net)	D				6.7	
.2	.6	1.2	Inventory	A				1.8	
3.5	4.3	2.1	All Other Current	T				1.4	
14.6	15.6	11.8	Total Current	A				11.8	
72.7	72.1	68.6	Fixed Assets (net)					68.0	
3.0	.1	12.4	Intangibles (net)	N				11.1	
9.8	12.2	7.1	All Other Non-Current	O				9.2	
100.0	100.0	100.0	Total	T				100.0	
			LIABILITIES	A					
.0	2.2	1.0	Notes Payable-Short Term	V				2.0	
11.9	5.4	4.0	Cur. Mat.-L.T.D.	A				2.5	
2.6	3.2	2.5	Trade Payables	I				4.6	
.0	.0	.0	Income Taxes Payable	L				.0	
2.7	2.5	3.0	All Other Current	A				4.7	
17.2	13.2	10.6	Total Current	B				13.8	
54.0	31.4	38.7	Long-Term Debt	L				23.1	
.0	.0	.0	Deferred Taxes	E				.0	
6.7	12.4	6.0	All Other Non-Current					6.3	
22.1	43.0	44.7	Net Worth					56.8	
100.0	100.0	100.0	Total Liabilities & Net Worth					100.0	
			INCOME DATA						
100.0	100.0	100.0	Net Sales					100.0	
			Gross Profit					90.5	
65.4	75.3	80.5	Operating Expenses					9.5	
34.6	24.7	19.5	Operating Profit					11.5	
15.7	7.1	15.4	All Other Expenses (net)					-2.0	
18.9	17.5	4.1	Profit Before Taxes						
			RATIOS						
2.2	3.5	2.9						3.0	
1.1	1.2	1.1	Current					1.1	
.6	.9	.5						.5	
1.5	1.3	1.8						1.6	
.6	.7	.7	Quick					.6	
.3	.2	.2						.2	
1 302.8	8 45.0	20 17.9						16 23.1	
31 11.9	33 11.1	37 9.9	Sales/Receivables					38 9.5	
48 7.6	56 6.5	51 7.2						62 5.9	
			Cost of Sales/Inventory						
			Cost of Sales/Payables						
3.7	2.0	3.8						5.1	
188.4	12.7	20.8	Sales/Working Capital					109.7	
-4.0	-11.1	-5.4						-4.3	
6.7	15.2	16.9							
(11) 3.5	(10) 2.9	(11) 2.8	EBIT/Interest						
1.2	1.7	-.4							
			Net Profit + Depr., Dep., Amort./Cur. Mat. L/T/D						
1.1	1.0	1.0						1.0	
2.0	1.5	1.4	Fixed/Worth					1.1	
NM	3.7	-2.0						-1.8	
1.1	.2	.1						.1	
4.7	2.2	.8	Debt/Worth					.4	
-20.9	3.3	-3.4						-8.3	
31.3	14.0	2.8						2.4	
(14) 6.8	(13) 6.8	(20) -.5	% Profit Before Taxes/Tangible Net Worth					(11) -1.4	
-1.5	1.8	-2.7						-1.8	
8.8	7.1	5.9						7.0	
4.0	3.0	-.4	% Profit Before Taxes/Total Assets					-1.1	
-.1	.8	-1.9						-3.1	
.5	.3	.3						.3	
.3	.2	.2	Sales/Net Fixed Assets					.1	
.1	.1	.1						.1	
.3	.2	.2						.1	
.2	.2	.1	Sales/Total Assets					.1	
.1	.1	.1						.1	
35.2	12.9	32.4						32.2	
(10) 40.6	(10) 40.6	(19) 44.9	% Depr., Dep., Amort./Sales					(10) 44.8	
48.7	54.3	55.1						56.4	
			% Officers', Directors' Owners' Comp/Sales						
409544M	234101M	477588M	Net Sales ($)		8375M	9350M	35870M	259766M	164227M
1834162M	1363979M	3985224M	Total Assets ($)		115297M	52833M	420069M	2388808M	1008217M

© RMA 2024 M = $ thousand MM = $ million
See Pages viii through xx for Explanation of Ratios and Data

UTILITIES—Other Electric Power Generation NAICS 221118

Current Data Sorted by Assets

0-500M	500M-2MM	2-10MM	10-50MM	50-100MM	100-250MM		Comparative Historical Data		
						Type of Statement		21	13
			2			Unqualified		1	2
		1	1		11	Reviewed		2	2
		1		1		Compiled		2	1
	2	6	16	6	11	Tax Returns		16	18
	6 (4/1-9/30/23)		54 (10/1/23-3/31/24)			Other		4/1/19-3/31/20 ALL	4/1/20-3/31/21 ALL
		2-10	10-50MM		100-250MM	**NUMBER OF STATEMENTS**		42	36
2	2	10	19	7	22				
%	%	%	%	%	%	**ASSETS**		%	%
		20.7	15.1		6.9	Cash & Equivalents		7.3	12.5
D		19.1	14.9		3.2	Trade Receivables (net)		12.8	12.3
A		12.8	3.9		4.8	Inventory		3.8	5.0
T		5.6	7.9		1.9	All Other Current		2.0	2.3
A		58.3	41.8		16.8	Total Current		26.0	32.1
		31.4	38.9		63.5	Fixed Assets (net)		66.4	53.1
N		2.7	8.6		5.5	Intangibles (net)		4.8	5.1
O		7.7	10.7		14.2	All Other Non-Current		2.9	9.8
T		100.0	100.0		100.0	Total		100.0	100.0
						LIABILITIES			
A		2.7	2.8		.0	Notes Payable-Short Term		2.8	1.9
V		1.4	1.1		2.0	Cur. Mat.-L.T.D.		1.9	3.1
A		4.9	7.2		3.6	Trade Payables		4.4	6.0
I		.4	.5		.0	Income Taxes Payable		.0	.0
L		20.0	10.1		3.7	All Other Current		15.0	12.7
A		29.4	21.8		9.2	Total Current		24.2	23.8
B		20.0	19.4		40.4	Long-Term Debt		23.0	34.3
L		1.3	.0		.3	Deferred Taxes		.9	1.2
E		7.1	3.9		4.4	All Other Non-Current		7.9	9.0
		42.2	54.8		45.7	Net Worth		44.0	31.7
		100.0	100.0		100.0	Total Liabilities & Net Worth		100.0	100.0
						INCOME DATA			
		100.0	100.0		100.0	Net Sales		100.0	100.0
						Gross Profit			
		86.3	84.6		77.5	Operating Expenses		85.0	89.9
		13.7	15.4		22.5	Operating Profit		15.0	10.1
		5.2	5.5		20.8	All Other Expenses (net)		7.6	4.9
		8.6	9.9		1.8	Profit Before Taxes		7.4	5.2
						RATIOS			
		5.6	3.3		3.9			3.0	2.7
		1.6	1.3		1.9	Current		1.4	1.3
		1.0	1.0		1.1			.7	.5
		5.3	3.1		2.9			1.9	2.5
		1.2	.9		1.1	Quick		1.0	.9
		.3	.6		.5			.5	.2
	20	18.6	22 16.6	16	22.8		17	21.5	17 21.1
	55	6.6	51 7.2	33	11.1	Sales/Receivables	31	11.6	35 10.3
	76	4.8	57 6.4	45	8.1		41	8.9	58 6.3
						Cost of Sales/Inventory			
						Cost of Sales/Payables			
		3.1	3.1		1.8			6.0	3.5
		8.6	12.6		5.9	Sales/Working Capital		16.9	15.3
		-143.6	-91.8		NM			-10.3	-5.1
			39.6					18.3	7.3
		(14)	3.5			EBIT/Interest	(21)	3.7	(29) 2.7
			1.2					1.7	1.6
						Net Profit + Depr., Dep., Amort./Cur. Mat. L/T/D			
		.2	.2		.8			.9	.4
		.5	.6		1.3	Fixed/Worth		1.0	2.0
		3.9	1.9		2.9			2.3	3.3
		.4	.4		.2			.1	.6
		2.6	1.6		.9	Debt/Worth		.9	1.5
		34.1	2.4		3.3			2.2	5.4
			53.1		15.2			9.2	42.0
			10.2	(20)	-.7	% Profit Before Taxes/Tangible Net Worth	(37)	2.4	(30) 6.5
			.5		-2.6			-.4	-.1
		23.2	16.6		7.3			6.0	13.7
		10.2	4.2		-.2	% Profit Before Taxes/Total Assets		1.8	1.9
		.8	.3		-1.6			-1.0	-.9
		65.0	22.3		3.4			10.9	10.8
		19.2	4.2		.2	Sales/Net Fixed Assets		.2	.7
		.4	.3		.1			.1	.4
		1.9	1.7		.4			1.7	1.6
		1.5	1.1		.1	Sales/Total Assets		.1	.6
		.3	.2		.1			.1	.2
			1.6		7.7			9.4	5.1
		(13)	5.4	(13)	30.7	% Depr., Dep., Amort./Sales	(34)	34.9	(30) 11.5
			21.6		63.7			51.3	26.1
						% Officers', Directors' Owners' Comp/Sales			
2801M		81330M	567492M	239356M	1497720M	Net Sales ($)		1273865M	1509195M
2481M		58750M	459079M	533007M	3820421M	Total Assets ($)		3563883M	2270876M

© RMA 2024   M = $ thousand   MM = $ million
See Pages viii through xx for Explanation of Ratios and Data

UTILITIES—Other Electric Power Generation NAICS 221118

Comparative Historical Data | Current Data Sorted by Sales

Comparative Historical Data						Current Data Sorted by Sales					
7		23		15	**Type of Statement**		2	3	2	4	4
3		1		1	Unqualified						
2		1		2	Reviewed			1		1	
1		1		1	Compiled				1		
10		24		41	Tax Returns	1	5	2	2	15	16
4/1/21-		4/1/22-		4/1/23-	Other		6 (4/1-9/30/23)			54 (10/1/23-3/31/24)	
3/31/22		3/31/23		3/31/24		0-1MM	1-3MM	3-5MM	5-10MM	10-25MM	25MM & OVER
ALL		ALL		ALL							
23		50		60	**NUMBER OF STATEMENTS**	1	7	6	6	20	20
%		%		%	**ASSETS**	%	%	%	%	%	%
10.1		6.1		13.9	Cash & Equivalents					15.2	14.4
12.2		11.0		11.0	Trade Receivables (net)					13.5	14.0
6.7		5.6		6.1	Inventory					3.5	10.9
7.1		4.7		4.7	All Other Current					5.3	7.0
36.1		27.3		35.7	Total Current					37.5	46.4
54.6		55.8		47.4	Fixed Assets (net)					50.3	35.9
3.9		6.3		6.1	Intangibles (net)					3.9	10.1
5.7		10.5		10.8	All Other Non-Current					8.3	7.6
100.0		100.0		100.0	Total					100.0	100.0
					LIABILITIES						
1.1		1.2		2.0	Notes Payable-Short Term					2.1	3.5
2.7		1.8		2.0	Cur. Mat.-L.T.D.					1.9	2.8
6.1		5.4		4.7	Trade Payables					3.6	8.8
.0		.3		.2	Income Taxes Payable					.2	.0
12.4		10.5		9.1	All Other Current					7.8	10.9
22.4		19.1		18.1	Total Current					15.6	25.9
36.2		20.5		29.2	Long-Term Debt					18.9	30.1
.4		.9		.3	Deferred Taxes					.0	.3
3.1		5.7		4.6	All Other Non-Current					6.0	2.3
37.6		53.8		47.7	Net Worth					59.5	41.3
100.0		100.0		100.0	Total Liabilities & Net Worth					100.0	100.0
					INCOME DATA						
100.0		100.0		100.0	Net Sales					100.0	100.0
					Gross Profit						
86.5		88.6		83.8	Operating Expenses					91.8	83.4
13.5		11.4		16.2	Operating Profit					8.2	16.6
1.7		3.5		11.6	All Other Expenses (net)					5.3	6.0
11.8		7.8		4.7	Profit Before Taxes					3.0	10.6
					RATIOS						
2.7		4.2		3.8						3.8	3.7
1.5		1.2		1.7	Current					2.0	1.8
1.0		.8		1.0						.8	1.3
1.5		2.1		3.0						3.3	2.9
.9		.7		1.0	Quick					1.1	.9
.3		.4		.4						.5	.5
11	33.3	11	33.4	20	18.7					33	11.0	20	18.4
39	9.4	31	11.8	46	8.0	Sales/Receivables				46	8.0	43	8.5
54	6.8	66	5.5	61	6.0					74	4.9	57	6.4
					Cost of Sales/Inventory						
					Cost of Sales/Payables						
4.0		4.0		2.6						2.6	3.6
8.4		23.0		7.2	Sales/Working Capital					5.9	6.1
-253.4		-11.0		-385.7						-25.0	17.8
	22.1		15.0		19.2						38.1		20.9
(19)	5.2	(28)	2.8	(36)	3.9	EBIT/Interest				(11)	2.7	(15)	5.9
	3.4		-1.8		.8						.3		.7
					Net Profit + Depr., Dep., Amort./Cur. Mat. L/T/D						
.7		.6		.3						.2	.3
1.7		1.0		1.0	Fixed/Worth					1.0	.6
3.6		2.4		2.3						1.6	1.4
.5		.2		.4						.3	.4
2.6		1.4		1.0	Debt/Worth					.7	1.2
3.4		3.6		3.0						1.8	4.2
	42.0		14.3		22.8						44.4		42.2
(20)	15.6	(45)	2.1	(55)	9.7	% Profit Before Taxes/Tangible Net Worth					3.8	(17)	17.9
	6.4		-1.2		-.9						-2.3		8.1
11.8		5.9		13.1						14.8	14.9
7.2		1.6		2.6	% Profit Before Taxes/Total Assets					2.4	8.5
3.0		-1.0		-.9						-1.4	-1.0
7.6		5.9		18.4						16.9	25.5
.6		.4		1.5	Sales/Net Fixed Assets					1.5	3.9
.3		.1		.2						.1	.5
1.6		1.2		1.4						1.6	1.9
.5		.3		.4	Sales/Total Assets					.5	1.1
.2		.1		.1						.1	.4
	2.2		3.6		1.6						1.6		.8
(20)	10.1	(38)	18.8	(41)	7.2	% Depr., Dep., Amort./Sales				(15)	7.2	(11)	2.0
	14.6		44.8		49.9						57.5		3.4
					% Officers', Directors' Owners' Comp/Sales						
1029007M		2069523M		2388699M	Net Sales ($)	371M	10394M	23907M	38817M	343077M	1972133M
1699002M		4471904M		4873738M	Total Assets ($)	2013M	199943M	329373M	477360M	1688467M	2176582M

© RMA 2024
M = $ thousand MM = $ million
See Pages viii through xx for Explanation of Ratios and Data

UTILITIES—Electric Power Distribution NAICS 221122

Current Data Sorted by Assets

0-500M	500M-2MM	2-10MM	10-50MM	50-100MM	100-250MM		Comparative Historical Data	
						Type of Statement		
		1	5	9	24	Unqualified	39	35
						Reviewed	4	5
				1		Compiled		3
						Tax Returns	3	1
1		9	7	3	12	Other	34	28
	23 (4/1-9/30/23)		50 (10/1/23-3/31/24)				4/1/19-3/31/20	4/1/20-3/31/21
							ALL	ALL
1		10	13	13	36	**NUMBER OF STATEMENTS**	80	72
%	%	%	%	%	%	**ASSETS**	%	%
		18.6	13.4	13.2	7.4	Cash & Equivalents	10.8	9.6
		31.8	12.3	10.6	4.9	Trade Receivables (net)	11.1	9.9
	D	5.7	2.3	2.0	2.3	Inventory	4.6	4.4
	A	11.3	12.2	1.1	3.2	All Other Current	3.6	3.0
	T	67.3	40.3	26.9	17.7	Total Current	30.1	27.0
	A	10.3	33.7	43.1	64.2	Fixed Assets (net)	53.0	52.8
		13.1	4.9	7.8	5.1	Intangibles (net)	4.3	5.5
	N	9.3	21.1	22.3	13.0	All Other Non-Current	12.6	14.7
	O	100.0	100.0	100.0	100.0	Total	100.0	100.0
	T					**LIABILITIES**		
		1.1	19.0	2.1	.6	Notes Payable-Short Term	6.0	2.4
	A	1.5	.4	8.0	3.4	Cur. Mat.-L.T.D.	2.3	2.3
	V	7.4	10.9	5.9	4.6	Trade Payables	6.5	4.9
	A	.1	.0	.0	.0	Income Taxes Payable	.1	.1
	I	15.3	22.0	3.0	4.7	All Other Current	10.1	7.8
	L	25.5	52.2	19.1	13.4	Total Current	25.0	17.5
	A	11.2	8.8	18.8	31.7	Long-Term Debt	33.7	27.7
	B	.0	.0	2.2	.0	Deferred Taxes	1.1	.7
	L	18.6	16.4	15.8	9.2	All Other Non-Current	7.9	7.3
	E	44.7	22.5	44.1	45.7	Net Worth	32.3	46.7
		100.0	100.0	100.0	100.0	Total Liabilities & Net Worth	100.0	100.0
						INCOME DATA		
		100.0	100.0	100.0	100.0	Net Sales	100.0	100.0
						Gross Profit		
		87.3	80.1	88.7	87.6	Operating Expenses	89.6	89.0
		12.7	19.9	11.3	12.4	Operating Profit	10.4	11.0
		1.2	5.8	-.1	4.3	All Other Expenses (net)	4.0	2.5
		11.5	14.2	11.5	8.1	Profit Before Taxes	6.5	8.5
						RATIOS		
		11.6	4.3	5.4	2.1		2.2	2.5
		3.4	2.9	2.0	1.1	Current	1.1	1.2
		1.5	1.0	.9	.8		.7	.8
		7.1	4.1	5.3	1.4		1.6	1.9
		2.4	2.3	1.7	.6	Quick	.8	.9
		1.3	.5	.5	.3		.5	.5
		16 22.5	3 129.4	30 12.1	21 17.5		23 16.2	22 16.6
		57 6.4	24 15.0	48 7.6	28 13.0	Sales/Receivables	32 11.4	35 10.5
		85 4.3	61 6.0	68 5.4	38 9.5		41 8.9	46 8.0
						Cost of Sales/Inventory		
						Cost of Sales/Payables		
		2.2	3.4	1.4	4.6		4.5	5.5
		5.4	9.4	9.1	60.4	Sales/Working Capital	62.5	27.5
		16.4	NM	NM	-15.5		-16.9	-18.2
			40.4	13.2	4.7		7.5	11.5
		(10)	6.9	6.5	(28) 2.3	EBIT/Interest	(66) 3.4	(62) 3.8
			1.3	2.4	1.4		2.4	2.3
						Net Profit + Depr., Dep.,	6.2	11.4
						Amort./Cur. Mat. L/T/D	(11) 4.7	(12) 4.0
							1.9	1.7
		.0	.0	.6	1.0		.6	.7
		.2	1.0	1.2	1.6	Fixed/Worth	1.6	1.5
		.6	1.6	3.0	2.8		2.4	2.5
		.3	.4	.7	.6		.9	.6
		2.1	.9	1.5	1.5	Debt/Worth	1.6	1.3
		NM	11.1	6.9	3.5		2.7	2.1
			38.0	11.6	9.5	% Profit Before Taxes/Tangible	16.2	17.9
		(11)	10.1	(11) 7.2	(34) 5.7	Net Worth	(72) 9.5	(67) 8.8
			.7	3.9	2.4		4.7	5.2
		42.9	22.1	5.5	4.1	% Profit Before Taxes/Total	5.7	7.6
		24.6	3.4	4.1	2.2	Assets	3.8	3.4
		5.3	.3	2.4	.9		2.0	2.0
		UND	478.6	7.3	1.1		15.4	10.5
		110.0	23.8	1.5	.7	Sales/Net Fixed Assets	.9	.7
		18.7	.9	.6	.4		.5	.5
		2.5	2.4	1.1	.7		1.5	1.2
		2.0	.9	.6	.4	Sales/Total Assets	.6	.5
		1.2	.6	.3	.3		.3	.3
				5.3	5.9		4.1	4.8
			(12)	6.3	(31) 8.9	% Depr., Dep., Amort./Sales	(68) 6.9	(60) 7.7
				12.2	12.0		11.5	11.0
						% Officers', Directors'		
						Owners' Comp/Sales		
392M		100616M	616130M	665777M	3338685M	Net Sales ($)	6222421M	3813566M
255M		46886M	301774M	911563M	6249127M	Total Assets ($)	7374316M	5993297M

M = $ thousand   MM = $ million
See Pages viii through xx for Explanation of Ratios and Data

© RMA 2024

UTILITIES—Electric Power Distribution NAICS 221122

Comparative Historical Data

						Type of Statement							
	27		47		39	Unqualified	1		1	1	9	27
	4		2			Reviewed						1
	1		2		1	Compiled						
	1				1	Tax Returns				1		
	26		29		32	Other	2	1	1	2	9	17
	4/1/21-3/31/22 ALL		4/1/22-3/31/23 ALL		4/1/23-3/31/24 ALL		0-1MM	23 (4/1-9/30/23) 1-3MM	3-5MM	5-10MM	50 (10/1/23-3/31/24) 10-25MM	25MM & OVER

Current Data Sorted by Sales

	59		80		73	NUMBER OF STATEMENTS	3	1	2	4	18	45
	%		%		%	ASSETS	%	%	%	%	%	%
	9.4		9.7		12.3	Cash & Equivalents					8.0	10.6
	12.1		9.2		10.9	Trade Receivables (net)					15.2	8.6
	2.4		2.3		2.7	Inventory					4.0	2.4
	3.4		5.4		5.5	All Other Current					6.1	5.7
	27.3		26.6		31.3	Total Current					33.4	27.3
	57.4		55.7		46.8	Fixed Assets (net)					39.0	51.1
	3.1		3.8		6.6	Intangibles (net)					15.0	4.7
	12.2		13.9		15.4	All Other Non-Current					12.6	16.9
	100.0		100.0		100.0	Total					100.0	100.0
						LIABILITIES						
	1.2		5.1		4.2	Notes Payable-Short Term					1.5	6.3
	1.9		1.9		3.4	Cur. Mat.-L.T.D.					2.0	4.4
	5.9		7.2		6.3	Trade Payables					4.9	7.2
	.1		.1		.0	Income Taxes Payable					.0	.0
	6.9		8.4		8.9	All Other Current					8.9	9.7
	15.9		22.8		22.8	Total Current					17.3	27.6
	28.0		28.1		22.3	Long-Term Debt					20.6	23.5
	1.5		.6		.4	Deferred Taxes					.6	.3
	9.3		10.4		12.8	All Other Non-Current					12.7	11.6
	45.3		38.2		41.7	Net Worth					48.8	37.0
	100.0		100.0		100.0	Total Liabilities & Net Worth					100.0	100.0
						INCOME DATA						
	100.0		100.0		100.0	Net Sales					100.0	100.0
						Gross Profit						
	84.5		87.9		86.8	Operating Expenses					75.8	93.1
	15.5		12.1		13.2	Operating Profit					24.2	6.9
	4.3		4.3		3.3	All Other Expenses (net)					3.1	1.2
	11.2		7.8		9.9	Profit Before Taxes					21.1	5.7
						RATIOS						
	2.8		2.3		3.8						5.6	2.5
	1.4		1.4		1.6	Current					1.6	1.3
	.8		.8		.9						1.1	.8
	2.1		2.1		3.0						3.5	1.9
	.9		.8		1.2	Quick					1.5	.9
	.4		.5		.4						.4	.3
23	15.6	21	17.2	20	17.9						16 23.2	21 17.3
35	10.3	36	10.1	29	12.7	Sales/Receivables					29 12.5	29 12.7
45	8.2	53	6.9	54	6.8						91 4.0	48 7.6
						Cost of Sales/Inventory						
						Cost of Sales/Payables						
	4.2		3.2		3.4						3.4	4.7
	17.3		13.9		11.5	Sales/Working Capital					11.5	27.8
	-18.3		-17.1		-32.3						172.5	-16.9
	8.2		7.0		10.9						43.9	6.8
(51)	3.5	(70)	3.0	(61)	3.2	EBIT/Interest				(13)	11.0 (41)	2.6
	2.5		1.8		1.4						4.9	1.4
	31.2		6.4		7.2	Net Profit + Depr., Dep.,						
(10)	4.6	(13)	4.4	(10)	2.7	Amort./Cur. Mat. L/T/D						
	2.6		2.0		.4							
	.8		.8		.6						.2	.9
	1.5		1.4		1.2	Fixed/Worth					1.0	1.4
	2.3		2.1		2.4						NM	2.4
	.7		.7		.6						.5	.7
	1.4		1.3		1.5	Debt/Worth					3.3	1.5
	2.2		2.3		5.2						NM	3.5
	14.7		12.2		23.9						148.1	10.5
(55)	10.6	(74)	6.0	(65)	7.0	% Profit Before Taxes/Tangible Net Worth				(14)	17.2 (42)	6.0
	5.0		3.1		2.5						2.5	2.5
	5.1		4.7		7.6	% Profit Before Taxes/Total Assets					34.0	4.4
	3.8		2.7		2.9						6.8	2.5
	1.7		1.0		.7						2.2	.7
	8.7		1.9		14.8						132.7	6.4
	.7		.7		1.1	Sales/Net Fixed Assets					1.5	1.0
	.4		.4		.5						.2	.6
	1.1		.7		1.3						2.1	.9
	.5		.5		.6	Sales/Total Assets					.7	.6
	.3		.3		.3						.1	.4
	5.3		4.9		4.8						6.0	4.8
(52)	7.6	(67)	7.2	(56)	7.5	% Depr., Dep., Amort./Sales				(13)	12.6 (39)	6.3
	12.1		12.3		10.9						27.0	8.9
						% Officers', Directors' Owners' Comp/Sales						
	2623781M		4292241M		4721600M	Net Sales ($)	1630M	1659M	9356M	30971M	269660M	4408324M
	4667385M		8112558M		7509605M	Total Assets ($)	13971M	2155M	124892M	98579M	1153286M	6116722M

© RMA 2024
M = $ thousand   MM = $ million
See Pages viii through xx for Explanation of Ratios and Data

UTILITIES—Natural Gas Distribution NAICS 221210

Current Data Sorted by Assets | Comparative Historical Data

							Type of Statement		
			2	7	3	4	Unqualified	23	16
			4	2			Reviewed	2	2
							Compiled	4	2
		1	1	1			Tax Returns	3	7
1	2	3	8		6	10	Other	42	29
	14 (4/1-9/30/23)			41 (10/1/23-3/31/24)				4/1/19-3/31/20	4/1/20-3/31/21
0-500M	500M-2MM	2-10MM	10-50MM	50-100MM		100-250MM		ALL	ALL
1	3	10	18	9		14	NUMBER OF STATEMENTS	74	56
%	%	%	%	%		%	ASSETS	%	%
		9.4	17.3			11.4	Cash & Equivalents	14.6	15.2
		27.1	17.4			14.6	Trade Receivables (net)	15.8	12.0
		9.8	4.3			7.3	Inventory	5.0	3.6
		4.1	5.9			9.3	All Other Current	3.9	7.8
		50.4	44.9			42.7	Total Current	39.3	38.5
		32.6	43.3			44.1	Fixed Assets (net)	47.7	47.5
		6.7	2.9			8.6	Intangibles (net)	4.1	6.3
		10.3	8.9			4.7	All Other Non-Current	8.9	7.7
		100.0	100.0			100.0	Total	100.0	100.0
							LIABILITIES		
		6.0	2.2			3.8	Notes Payable-Short Term	3.0	2.9
		1.3	1.1			2.6	Cur. Mat.-L.T.D.	3.9	2.0
		18.7	15.1			13.9	Trade Payables	12.1	7.8
		.2	.1			.5	Income Taxes Payable	.4	.3
		9.8	8.7			7.2	All Other Current	9.2	10.7
		35.9	27.1			27.9	Total Current	28.6	23.7
		8.4	12.1			22.6	Long-Term Debt	19.8	19.9
		2.8	1.6			1.0	Deferred Taxes	2.3	1.8
		11.4	2.7			3.5	All Other Non-Current	6.6	7.2
		41.4	56.4			45.0	Net Worth	42.7	47.5
		100.0	100.0			100.0	Total Liabilities & Net Worth	100.0	100.0
							INCOME DATA		
		100.0	100.0			100.0	Net Sales	100.0	100.0
							Gross Profit		
		83.6	90.2			83.5	Operating Expenses	88.3	88.8
		16.4	9.8			16.5	Operating Profit	11.7	11.2
		.6	2.1			8.5	All Other Expenses (net)	3.3	2.4
		15.8	7.7			8.1	Profit Before Taxes	8.5	8.8
							RATIOS		
		3.0	3.0			2.1		2.4	2.7
		1.1	1.5			1.5	Current	1.2	1.7
		.9	.9			.8		.6	.9
		1.8	2.3			1.6		1.8	2.1
		1.0	1.2			1.0	Quick	.9	1.2
		.3	.8			.4		.4	.6
	7	53.3	9 40.9		14	25.2		18 20.0	20 18.1
	25	14.8	28 12.9		23	15.6	Sales/Receivables	30 12.0	33 11.2
	53	6.9	51 7.2		38	9.7		50 7.3	51 7.2
							Cost of Sales/Inventory		
							Cost of Sales/Payables		
		6.2	6.9			5.0		5.6	4.3
		56.5	19.6			20.0	Sales/Working Capital	35.1	11.4
		UND	NM			-16.5		-12.8	-28.5
			19.8			13.4		18.8	32.9
		(11)	3.9		(11)	2.0	EBIT/Interest	(60) 5.3	(45) 4.2
			.9			1.8		1.6	1.9
							Net Profit + Depr., Dep.,		9.4
							Amort./Cur. Mat. L/T/D	(15) 2.7	
								1.3	
		.0	.0			.0		.3	.2
		.8	.7			1.4	Fixed/Worth	1.1	1.2
		3.1	1.5			2.1		2.3	2.6
		.5	.2			.9		.5	.5
		1.0	.8			1.4	Debt/Worth	1.4	1.3
		UND	1.7			2.3		2.9	2.9
			61.7			18.3		28.2	27.0
		(17)	10.0		(13)	4.7	% Profit Before Taxes/Tangible Net Worth	(68) 12.9	(49) 9.8
			.7			3.7		4.4	3.2
		38.0	17.9			5.9		13.7	9.0
		10.4	5.5			1.9	% Profit Before Taxes/Total Assets	5.2	3.6
		3.7	.2			1.7		1.7	1.2
		UND	204.9			999.8		35.8	13.1
		32.7	2.2			.8	Sales/Net Fixed Assets	1.7	1.0
		1.5	.5			.3		.4	.5
		3.3	4.0			5.3		3.0	2.1
		1.7	1.5			.6	Sales/Total Assets	.9	.6
		1.0	.5			.2		.3	.3
			.3			1.0		1.3	4.0
		(15)	6.8		(11)	8.3	% Depr., Dep., Amort./Sales	(57) 6.5	(41) 8.5
			10.3			9.7		12.8	13.5
							% Officers', Directors' Owners' Comp/Sales		
2555M	15648M	124520M	1189299M	1441166M		6801010M	Net Sales ($)	5560339M	2503447M
64M	3329M	50993M	499388M	624627M		2241871M	Total Assets ($)	3814662M	2685134M

© RMA 2024   M = $ thousand   MM = $ million
See Pages viii through xx for Explanation of Ratios and Data

UTILITIES—Natural Gas Distribution NAICS 221210

Comparative Historical Data | Current Data Sorted by Sales

				Type of Statement							
	19		17	Unqualified			1		5		10
	3		6	Reviewed				3	1		2
			2	6 Compiled							
	3		4	3 Tax Returns			1	2			
	32		25	30 Other		2	4	3	4		17
	4/1/21-		4/1/22-	4/1/23-		14 (4/1-9/30/23)			41 (10/1/23-3/31/24)		
	3/31/22		3/31/23	3/31/24	0-1MM	1-3MM	3-5MM	5-10MM	10-25MM		25MM & OVER
	ALL		ALL	ALL							
	57		54	55	**NUMBER OF STATEMENTS**	2	6	8	10		29
	%		%	%	**ASSETS**	%	%	%	%	%		%
	14.2		14.1	15.0	Cash & Equivalents					9.4		16.3
	15.5		19.6	18.9	Trade Receivables (net)					11.7		25.0
	4.9		8.3	6.1	Inventory					8.6		6.7
	4.8		6.4	6.5	All Other Current					2.5		10.2
	39.4		48.5	46.4	Total Current					32.2		58.2
	49.9		40.5	39.1	Fixed Assets (net)					51.2		29.6
	4.0		3.9	4.8	Intangibles (net)					9.2		3.9
	6.7		7.1	9.7	All Other Non-Current					7.4		8.3
	100.0		100.0	100.0	Total					100.0		100.0
					LIABILITIES		DATA NOT AVAILABLE				
	3.9		2.7	3.1	Notes Payable-Short Term					1.9		4.6
	1.9		2.3	3.5	Cur. Mat.-L.T.D.					2.1		1.5
	11.6		14.7	14.9	Trade Payables					8.7		18.9
	.5		.2	.2	Income Taxes Payable					.3		.2
	9.1		10.7	10.2	All Other Current					5.3		9.7
	27.0		30.6	31.9	Total Current					18.3		35.0
	18.9		13.1	16.1	Long-Term Debt					19.5		9.2
	2.0		2.5	1.6	Deferred Taxes					2.0		1.3
	3.8		7.8	5.7	All Other Non-Current					2.4		5.5
	48.4		46.0	44.8	Net Worth					57.8		49.0
	100.0		100.0	100.0	Total Liabilities & Net Worth					100.0		100.0
					INCOME DATA						
	100.0		100.0	100.0	Net Sales					100.0		100.0
					Gross Profit						
	88.3		90.2	87.8	Operating Expenses					83.7		92.9
	11.7		9.8	12.2	Operating Profit					16.3		7.1
	1.6		1.0	3.0	All Other Expenses (net)					4.2		1.3
	10.1		8.9	9.1	Profit Before Taxes					12.1		5.8
					RATIOS						
	2.6		2.5	2.5						3.0		2.2
	1.2		1.6	1.5	Current					1.5		1.5
	.9		1.0	1.0						.7		1.0
	1.5		1.7	1.9						1.8		1.5
	.9		1.0	1.1	Quick					1.2		1.1
	.6		.6	.6						.4		.7
26	14.3	25	14.8	15	24.4					12	30.4	15	24.9
38	9.5	37	9.9	26	14.1	Sales/Receivables				51	7.1	26	14.3
53	6.9	49	7.5	42	8.6					78	4.7	35	10.3
					Cost of Sales/Inventory						
					Cost of Sales/Payables						
	3.2		3.0	7.0						1.8		10.0
	26.0		15.9	18.8	Sales/Working Capital					9.5		21.1
	-25.7		NM	999.8						-12.7		UND
	35.6		57.0	19.8								18.5
(49)	8.9	(47)	15.1	(39)	4.9	EBIT/Interest						(21)	3.7
	2.5		3.5	1.8								1.7
	12.6		11.0									
(12)	5.9	(10)	4.0			Net Profit + Depr., Dep., Amort./Cur. Mat. L/T/D						
	1.5		1.6									
	.6		.1	.0						.6		.0
	1.3		.9	.9	Fixed/Worth					1.0		.5
	2.2		1.4	2.0						2.6		1.4
	.5		.4	.5						.4		.7
	1.3		1.3	1.1	Debt/Worth					.7		1.2
	2.5		2.5	2.1						2.3		1.6
	28.0		30.2	61.1						41.3		60.4
(54)	14.5	(50)	12.5	(50)	8.9	% Profit Before Taxes/Tangible Net Worth					8.5	(27)	9.0
	7.0		4.2	4.0						4.7		.8
	9.7		11.4	17.5						12.3		18.2
	5.3		5.0	5.3	% Profit Before Taxes/Total Assets					4.5		4.3
	2.4		2.8	1.8						1.9		.3
	7.2		235.9	664.3						169.3		999.8
	1.2		2.4	4.9	Sales/Net Fixed Assets					.5		70.5
	.5		.8	.6						.3		1.7
	1.7		2.9	4.3						2.7		5.9
	.6		1.0	1.8	Sales/Total Assets					.4		3.3
	.3		.5	.4						.2		.8
	2.6		1.2	.3								.0
(47)	6.8	(44)	4.9	(40)	6.2	% Depr., Dep., Amort./Sales						(21)	1.0
	11.0		9.3	10.1								8.6
					% Officers', Directors' Owners' Comp/Sales						
	4200452M		5725167M	9574198M	Net Sales ($)	3869M	24257M	64575M	180410M		9301087M
	2896284M		2509250M	3420272M	Total Assets ($)	4114M	148636M	111596M	536325M		2619601M

© RMA 2024
M = $ thousand   MM = $ million
See Pages viii through xx for Explanation of Ratios and Data

UTILITIES—Water Supply and Irrigation Systems NAICS 221310

Current Data Sorted by Assets / Comparative Historical Data

							Type of Statement		
			10	18	1	10	Unqualified	35	39
			4	3			Reviewed	6	5
		1	3	2			Compiled	7	3
	1	6	3	1			Tax Returns	15	5
	4	10	14	10	3	1	Other	46	34
		34 (4/1-9/30/23)		71 (10/1/23-3/31/24)				4/1/19-3/31/20	4/1/20-3/31/21
0-500M	500M-2MM	2-10MM	10-50MM	50-100MM	100-250MM			ALL	ALL
5	17	34	34	4	11		NUMBER OF STATEMENTS	109	86
%	%	%	%	%	%		ASSETS	%	%
	24.2	22.8	22.8		11.6		Cash & Equivalents	18.2	22.7
	11.3	23.2	6.7		4.7		Trade Receivables (net)	12.4	8.3
	14.7	7.1	3.4		1.4		Inventory	7.1	5.6
	7.6	4.0	2.3		.4		All Other Current	2.2	1.8
	57.8	57.1	35.2		18.0		Total Current	39.9	38.5
	23.2	33.7	49.5		58.2		Fixed Assets (net)	48.1	53.5
	2.6	.8	8.7		11.9		Intangibles (net)	5.2	2.7
	16.3	8.4	6.6		11.8		All Other Non-Current	6.8	5.4
	100.0	100.0	100.0		100.0		Total	100.0	100.0
							LIABILITIES		
	4.6	2.0	1.6		.0		Notes Payable-Short Term	4.6	2.8
	4.3	1.7	2.1		1.8		Cur. Mat.-L.T.D.	2.1	2.6
	5.7	9.7	3.2		2.3		Trade Payables	5.8	3.8
	.0	.2	.0		.0		Income Taxes Payable	.0	.1
	16.3	7.7	5.8		2.1		All Other Current	8.3	4.2
	30.9	21.3	12.7		6.2		Total Current	20.9	13.5
	44.0	13.8	17.3		24.9		Long-Term Debt	22.9	28.1
	.0	.3	.2		.1		Deferred Taxes	.2	.2
	3.4	6.7	7.3		2.0		All Other Non-Current	10.6	6.4
	21.7	57.9	62.4		66.9		Net Worth	45.3	51.7
	100.0	100.0	100.0		100.0		Total Liabilities & Net Worth	100.0	100.0
							INCOME DATA		
	100.0	100.0	100.0		100.0		Net Sales	100.0	100.0
							Gross Profit		
	90.7	88.9	88.2		84.1		Operating Expenses	85.8	83.6
	9.3	11.1	11.8		15.9		Operating Profit	14.2	16.4
	1.5	.3	.2		-1.7		All Other Expenses (net)	3.1	2.0
	7.8	10.8	11.6		17.6		Profit Before Taxes	11.1	14.3
							RATIOS		
	7.1	13.2	9.2		7.1			4.7	9.2
	2.3	3.0	3.5		2.5		Current	2.2	3.7
	1.0	2.0	1.7		1.4			1.0	1.6
	3.2	13.0	8.7		6.7			4.0	8.5
	1.6	2.8	3.1		2.4		Quick	1.6	3.2
	.5	1.1	1.1		1.2			.8	1.1
2	231.8	31 11.9	12 29.8		36 10.0			7 50.6	8 43.2
14	26.9	43 8.5	31 11.7		41 8.9		Sales/Receivables	28 13.2	30 12.1
40	9.2	65 5.6	49 7.4		56 6.5			46 7.9	47 7.7
							Cost of Sales/Inventory		
							Cost of Sales/Payables		
	3.4	1.7	.7		.7			1.9	.9
	8.3	5.1	2.3		2.4		Sales/Working Capital	6.4	2.6
	NM	8.2	5.9		8.4			170.2	11.1
	19.0	28.3	13.6					13.0	16.9
	(10) 7.8	(26) 12.1	(28) 5.0				EBIT/Interest	(86) 5.4	(60) 5.5
	.4	5.3	1.8					2.2	1.9
							Net Profit + Depr., Dep.,	14.7	
							Amort./Cur. Mat. L/T/D	(10) 5.0	
								2.0	
	.0	.2	.6		.8			.5	.5
	.2	.5	1.0		1.0		Fixed/Worth	1.1	1.0
	NM	1.0	1.4		1.5			2.6	1.4
	.5	.2	.3		.2			.4	.2
	1.1	.6	.7		.5		Debt/Worth	.9	.7
	-6.1	1.7	1.3		5.7			3.2	1.9
	27.2	57.2	11.8		13.3		% Profit Before Taxes/Tangible	32.7	16.0
	(11) 11.5	(33) 15.7	(31) 4.6	(10)	5.1		Net Worth	(92) 8.4	(79) 6.6
	3.7	1.3	1.1		1.5			3.8	2.0
	25.9	22.6	10.4		4.3		% Profit Before Taxes/Total	14.3	10.4
	10.7	11.6	3.1		3.1		Assets	4.1	3.3
	-1.3	1.1	.7		1.0			1.2	1.3
	UND	29.0	4.2		.4			16.7	10.2
	37.9	10.2	.5		.2		Sales/Net Fixed Assets	2.8	.4
	4.2	.6	.3		.1			.3	.2
	3.4	2.8	.6		.2			2.3	1.6
	1.7	1.8	.3		.2		Sales/Total Assets	.7	.3
	.7	.4	.2		.1			.2	.2
		1.2	4.0		10.8			1.8	4.8
	(23)	2.7	(27) 12.9		15.2		% Depr., Dep., Amort./Sales	(85) 8.7	(65) 12.8
		11.1	20.0		24.3			15.4	21.3
								1.7	.6
							% Officers', Directors'	(26) 4.2	(11) 1.9
							Owners' Comp/Sales	6.8	8.5
3348M	45837M	324516M	396401M	109964M	396162M		Net Sales ($)	1271892M	672154M
1107M	17622M	190275M	793015M	313959M	1647884M		Total Assets ($)	2766183M	2126352M

© RMA 2024 M = $ thousand   MM = $ million
See Pages viii through xx for Explanation of Ratios and Data

UTILITIES—Water Supply and Irrigation Systems NAICS 221310

Comparative Historical Data | Current Data Sorted by Sales

				Type of Statement						
34		37	39	Unqualified	1	7	7	7	11	6
4		10	7	Reviewed			2	1	2	2
9		8	6	Compiled		1			3	
12		13	11	Tax Returns	2	1	2	1	3	
41		43	42	Other	4	1	2	1	3	7
4/1/21-		4/1/22-	4/1/23-		7	7	5	8	8	
3/31/22		3/31/23	3/31/24			34 (4/1-9/30/23)			71 (10/1/23-3/31/24)	
ALL		ALL	ALL		0-1MM	1-3MM	3-5MM	5-10MM	10-25MM	25MM & OVER
100		111	105	NUMBER OF STATEMENTS	14	16	16	17	27	15
%		%	%	ASSETS	%	%	%	%	%	%
17.8		18.1	21.6	Cash & Equivalents	25.6	22.3	29.9	23.4	19.9	9.0
11.1		14.2	12.8	Trade Receivables (net)	3.4	9.6	8.4	12.9	19.0	18.2
6.0		7.3	6.7	Inventory	7.3	10.5	6.3	5.1	3.6	10.0
3.2		4.6	3.3	All Other Current	7.2	.2	3.5	2.1	2.4	6.0
38.1		44.1	44.4	Total Current	43.4	42.7	48.0	43.6	44.9	43.3
50.5		45.9	40.5	Fixed Assets (net)	37.3	55.0	45.1	38.6	40.8	24.8
3.5		3.6	5.6	Intangibles (net)	.6	.2	1.7	11.1	1.5	21.4
8.0		6.4	9.5	All Other Non-Current	18.7	2.1	5.2	6.8	12.8	10.4
100.0		100.0	100.0	Total	100.0	100.0	100.0	100.0	100.0	100.0
				LIABILITIES						
5.0		3.4	2.4	Notes Payable-Short Term	4.9	1.7	5.3	2.3	.9	.6
1.6		2.8	2.7	Cur. Mat.-L.T.D.	5.0	1.9	1.6	1.1	3.5	3.0
5.3		6.6	5.5	Trade Payables	6.1	2.7	2.2	5.7	6.2	10.0
.0		.1	.1	Income Taxes Payable	.0	.0	.0	.0	.3	.0
4.8		9.1	9.4	All Other Current	17.3	9.8	9.4	5.5	6.0	12.0
16.8		22.0	20.1	Total Current	33.3	16.1	18.6	14.5	16.9	25.6
22.6		21.7	23.8	Long-Term Debt	51.4	23.2	9.5	18.0	24.1	20.0
.1		.1	.2	Deferred Taxes	.0	.0	.0	.0	.5	.5
3.6		6.7	5.9	All Other Non-Current	6.2	.9	7.6	5.5	9.2	3.7
56.9		49.5	50.0	Net Worth	9.1	59.8	64.2	62.0	49.4	50.3
100.0		100.0	100.0	Total Liabilties & Net Worth	100.0	100.0	100.0	100.0	100.0	100.0
				INCOME DATA						
100.0		100.0	100.0	Net Sales	100.0	100.0	100.0	100.0	100.0	100.0
				Gross Profit						
85.2		86.1	88.0	Operating Expenses	76.1	90.3	86.3	90.6	89.1	93.9
14.8		13.9	12.0	Operating Profit	23.9	9.7	13.7	9.4	10.9	6.1
3.6		1.6	.3	All Other Expenses (net)	3.1	2.8	-.9	.9	-1.7	-1.1
11.2		12.3	11.7	Profit Before Taxes	20.8	6.8	14.6	8.5	12.6	7.2
				RATIOS						
7.1		5.6	6.9		11.1	13.3	16.1	8.4	5.9	2.6
2.3		2.4	3.1	Current	1.7	4.3	3.8	4.7	2.9	1.8
1.5		1.3	1.5		.9	2.4	1.3	2.0	1.7	1.4
6.7		4.5	6.2		6.1	13.1	15.3	7.8	5.4	2.1
2.0		1.8	2.4	Quick	1.4	3.8	3.7	2.8	2.8	1.2
.9		.8	.9		.3	2.3	1.0	1.1	1.3	.7
17 21.0		16 23.1	15 24.7		0 UND	11 32.3	18 20.3	11 34.1	21 17.6	24 15.0
34 10.8		32 11.5	36 10.1	Sales/Receivables	16 22.5	34 10.7	34 10.8	31 11.9	41 9.0	43 8.4
51 7.2		63 5.8	50 7.3		51 7.2	49 7.5	50 7.3	41 8.9	56 6.5	59 6.2
				Cost of Sales/Inventory						
				Cost of Sales/Payables						
1.4		1.8	1.4		1.3	.9	.8	.8	2.5	3.6
5.0		4.9	4.9	Sales/Working Capital	5.5	1.7	2.1	3.3	5.1	6.7
11.3		17.3	10.7		NM	6.0	15.5	13.3	8.2	15.6
16.6		14.7	15.5			16.9	18.7	9.6	17.7	30.2
(73) 7.7		(90) 6.0	(78) 5.8	EBIT/Interest	(12) 6.8	(13) 5.5	(12) 3.9	(23) 9.1	(13) 5.8	
2.6		2.5	2.6			1.2	3.4	-7.4	4.4	1.9
			12.0	Net Profit + Depr., Dep.,						
		(13) 5.6		Amort./Cur. Mat. L/T/D						
			2.1							
.4		.4	.2		.0	.6	.1	.3	.2	.2
.9		1.0	.8	Fixed/Worth	.3	1.0	.8	.9	.6	1.0
1.5		1.9	1.3		NM	1.6	1.3	2.0	1.2	1.2
.2		.3	.3		.2	.1	.2	.2	.4	.6
.7		.9	.7	Debt/Worth	1.3	.5	.3	.7	.7	1.4
1.8		2.6	1.9		-6.7	1.0	1.0	1.8	1.5	9.3
30.4		33.1	32.3		9.8	16.8	22.2	41.2	82.0	
(94) 10.0		(103) 9.1	(91) 7.4	% Profit Before Taxes/Tangible Net Worth	(15) 4.1	(14) 6.7	(15) 3.9	(26) 9.1	(12) 52.2	
2.8		4.6	1.2			-3.0	3.0	-11.3	1.5	6.5
15.8		11.7	17.1		35.5	9.2	15.8	14.7	21.1	21.0
4.9		6.1	4.3	% Profit Before Taxes/Total Assets	9.8	2.6	4.1	2.7	4.9	4.3
.8		1.8	.9		1.1	-1.1	1.2	-6.0	.9	1.7
9.7		17.4	25.5		UND	14.1	91.8	25.9	24.5	22.4
.9		1.4	3.6	Sales/Net Fixed Assets	4.3	.5	.5	2.5	7.5	12.9
.3		.3	.4		.5	.2	.4	.5	.3	3.6
1.7		2.1	2.0		1.1	2.3	1.3	1.7	3.0	1.9
.5		.6	.6	Sales/Total Assets	.7	.4	.3	.5	1.8	1.4
.2		.2	.2		.3	.1	.2	.2	.2	.5
4.4		2.9	2.5		8.1	7.7	2.1	1.4	1.2	
(74) 9.7		(80) 10.7	(71) 8.0	% Depr., Dep., Amort./Sales	(10) 15.2	(10) 13.3	(10) 14.2	(21) 3.3	(12) 3.3	
17.8		16.8	18.9			30.8	20.5	22.1	14.7	9.5
1.6		1.2	2.2	% Officers', Directors' Owners' Comp/Sales						
(15) 6.9		(23) 6.0	(18) 3.9							
11.8		13.5	9.3							
777006M		2052060M	1276228M	Net Sales ($)	7890M	29153M	62451M	124534M	403351M	648849M
1764819M		3610277M	2963862M	Total Assets ($)	19264M	110384M	196777M	396919M	1199812M	1040706M

© RMA 2024   M = $ thousand   MM = $ million
See Pages viii through xx for Explanation of Ratios and Data

CONSTRUCTION—GENERAL INDUSTRIES FORMAT*

CONSTRUCTION-GENERAL—New Single-Family Housing Construction (except For-Sale Builders) NAICS 236115

Current Data Sorted by Assets | **Comparative Historical Data**

							Type of Statement				
		1	1	3	12	7	Unqualified		37		24
		10	17	8	4	Reviewed		44		31
2	3	7	6		1	Compiled		45		27
27	39	54	23	3	1	Tax Returns		274		203
28	38	94	85	19	10	Other		401		344
	29 (4/1-9/30/23)		474 (10/1/23-3/31/24)				4/1/19-3/31/20		4/1/20-3/31/21	
0-500M	500M-2MM	2-10MM	10-50MM	50-100MM	100-250MM	NUMBER OF STATEMENTS	ALL		ALL	
57	81	166	134	42	23		801		629	
%	%	%	%	%	%	ASSETS	%		%	
32.6	24.6	14.3	10.2	8.9	7.8	Cash & Equivalents	15.9		17.3	
9.2	12.3	13.7	11.2	13.1	6.5	Trade Receivables (net)	9.6		9.3	
10.7	20.4	39.8	51.5	49.9	60.3	Inventory	43.6		41.8	
8.5	8.7	7.8	7.2	8.9	9.2	All Other Current	6.5		6.3	
60.9	66.0	75.6	80.1	80.8	83.9	Total Current	75.6		74.6	
29.6	22.9	16.0	10.8	10.7	8.6	Fixed Assets (net)	15.3		15.4	
1.1	2.5	.9	2.0	1.8	.7	Intangibles (net)	1.3		1.5	
8.1	8.7	7.5	7.1	6.7	6.8	All Other Non-Current	7.8		8.5	
100.0	100.0	100.0	100.0	100.0	100.0	Total	100.0		100.0	
						LIABILITIES				
33.0	16.0	22.9	26.9	25.6	22.4	Notes Payable-Short Term	28.8		26.4	
10.2	4.2	4.5	2.8	5.9	4.6	Cur. Mat.-L.T.D.	3.1		3.0	
9.4	10.4	10.2	10.3	13.0	5.7	Trade Payables	9.4		9.2	
.0	.0	.1	.1	.0	.1	Income Taxes Payable	.1		.1	
23.0	10.5	15.7	12.8	9.2	17.9	All Other Current	14.4		13.4	
75.7	41.0	53.4	53.0	53.6	50.7	Total Current	55.8		52.1	
32.7	24.3	13.4	7.5	9.9	9.4	Long-Term Debt	15.9		18.1	
.0	.0	.0	.0	.0	.0	Deferred Taxes	.0		.1	
6.1	3.6	3.6	4.6	17.7	4.8	All Other Non-Current	4.9		6.7	
-14.4	31.1	29.6	34.9	18.7	35.0	Net Worth	23.4		23.0	
100.0	100.0	100.0	100.0	100.0	100.0	Total Liabilties & Net Worth	100.0		100.0	
						INCOME DATA				
100.0	100.0	100.0	100.0	100.0	100.0	Net Sales	100.0		100.0	
28.0	28.7	20.9	19.1	20.5	23.4	Gross Profit	21.2		20.4	
21.0	23.7	14.3	11.4	10.9	12.8	Operating Expenses	14.3		13.2	
7.0	5.0	6.7	7.7	9.6	10.6	Operating Profit	6.8		7.2	
.5	.3	1.3	.7	1.3	.5	All Other Expenses (net)	.9		.1	
6.5	4.6	5.4	7.0	8.3	10.1	Profit Before Taxes	5.9		7.1	
						RATIOS				
3.8	4.0	2.2	2.2	2.1	2.3		2.5		2.8	
1.3	1.9	1.4	1.5	1.5	1.5	Current	1.4		1.5	
.5	1.2	1.1	1.1	1.1	1.3		1.0		1.1	
2.2	2.6	1.2	.9	.7	.7		1.1		1.3	
.8	1.1	.3	.2	.3	.1	Quick	.3		.4	
.4	.2	.1	.1	.1	.1		.1		.1	
0 UND	0 UND	0 UND	0 UND	0 UND	1 714.2		0 UND		0 UND	
0 UND	0 UND	0 999.8	1 256.2	2 150.6	2 151.7	Sales/Receivables	0 999.8		0 999.8	
0 UND	14 26.9	23 15.6	24 15.5	43 8.5	14 26.1		11 32.9		14 26.2	
0 UND	0 UND	0 UND	5 71.0	0 UND	135 2.7		0 UND		0 UND	
0 UND	0 UND	74 4.9	182 2.0	192 1.9	243 1.5	Cost of Sales/Inventory	96 3.8		104 3.5	
0 UND	55 6.6	243 1.5	281 1.3	365 1.0	332 1.1		243 1.5		215 1.7	
0 UND	0 UND	0 999.8	4 97.2	9 40.1	10 37.6		0 UND		0 UND	
0 UND	2 180.8	11 33.0	14 25.3	18 20.8	16 23.2	Cost of Sales/Payables	10 37.7		10 38.0	
10 36.4	17 20.9	25 14.6	31 11.6	53 6.9	31 11.7		26 13.8		25 14.8	
12.1	4.5	4.1	2.8	2.1	2.4		4.1		3.8	
170.9	14.8	11.4	6.8	4.4	3.6	Sales/Working Capital	12.0		9.5	
-25.4	61.5	66.6	17.0	31.5	15.5		183.0		45.8	
30.8	33.0	34.6	34.2	89.3	12.4		26.7		42.3	
(40) 8.0	(63) 6.7	(126) 6.0	(108) 8.0	(35) 8.9	(22) 5.4	EBIT/Interest	(613) 6.6		(464) 11.2	
2.4	.7	1.5	2.7	3.7	3.1		2.1		3.8	
					6.4				11.0	12.2
			(10) 2.0			Net Profit + Depr., Dep., Amort./Cur. Mat. L/T/D	(15) 1.5		(16) 4.8	
					1.2				.5	1.9
.1	.1	.0	.0	.0	.0		.0		.0	
.8	.5	.1	.1	.1	.1	Fixed/Worth	.1		.1	
-.6	2.9	1.1	.4	.6	.3		1.2		1.1	
.7	.6	1.1	1.1	1.0	1.2		1.2		1.0	
2.2	1.5	2.8	2.4	2.2	1.7	Debt/Worth	3.1		2.6	
-3.4	24.1	9.0	5.6	5.7	2.9		15.5		10.5	
199.0	77.6	63.6	56.0	49.6	54.1		81.8		85.5	
(36) 64.6	(63) 45.0	(146) 27.6	(131) 29.2	(38) 27.5	28.6	% Profit Before Taxes/Tangible Net Worth	(679) 37.8		(540) 41.4	
38.4	7.0	6.6	13.3	16.0	14.0		14.1		18.1	
80.5	45.1	19.3	15.6	17.7	19.9		20.7		22.6	
35.8	14.0	7.3	8.7	8.6	8.6	% Profit Before Taxes/Total Assets	8.8		11.6	
6.8	.7	1.4	2.7	3.6	2.8		2.2		4.2	
902.4	252.8	999.8	456.6	205.2	157.4		691.3		999.8	
65.7	25.1	77.9	68.2	51.6	40.5	Sales/Net Fixed Assets	90.9		74.9	
17.6	6.2	10.6	16.6	19.2	12.8		17.1		12.8	
15.3	5.4	3.3	2.2	2.1	1.5		3.6		3.1	
9.1	2.7	1.8	1.5	1.3	1.3	Sales/Total Assets	1.8		1.9	
4.1	1.6	1.0	.9	.9	1.0		1.2		1.2	
.3	.4	.1	.1	.1	.2		.2		.2	
(24) 1.6	(30) 1.3	(66) .5	(63) .3	(32) .2	(17) .2	% Depr., Dep., Amort./Sales	(354) .6		(250) .5	
4.1	3.2	1.6	.8	.4	.7		1.7		1.6	
2.6	2.1	1.1	.3				1.1		.9	
(29) 4.0	(38) 3.4	(68) 1.8	(32) .6			% Officers', Directors' Owners' Comp/Sales	(311) 2.1		(222) 2.0	
7.5	5.9	4.0	1.3				4.7		4.3	
154156M	431528M	1892124M	5132380M	7074826M	4465409M	Net Sales ($)	24567347M		16985714M	
12734M	97107M	863239M	3125270M	2913335M	3556133M	Total Assets ($)	12288488M		9159752M	

M = $ thousand   MM = $ million
See Pages viii through xx for Explanation of Ratios and Data

© RMA 2024

CONSTRUCTION-GENERAL—New Single-Family Housing Construction (except For-Sale Builders) NAICS 236115

Comparative Historical Data | Current Data Sorted by Sales

Comparative Historical Data				Type of Statement	Current Data Sorted by Sales					
27	26		24	Unqualified			2	4	2	22
50	36		39	Reviewed					8	27
22	28		19	Compiled	2	1	3	3	4	6
244	222		147	Tax Returns	16	32	21	34	24	20
304	320		274	Other	10	43	24	43	64	90
4/1/21-3/31/22 ALL	4/1/22-3/31/23 ALL		4/1/23-3/31/24 ALL		29 (4/1-9/30/23)			474 (10/1/23-3/31/24)		
					0-1MM	1-3MM	3-5MM	5-10MM	10-25MM	25MM & OVER
647	632		503	**NUMBER OF STATEMENTS**	28	76	48	84	102	165
%	%		%	**ASSETS**	%	%	%	%	%	%
18.0	17.3		16.2	Cash & Equivalents	13.2	19.2	23.7	17.6	18.6	11.0
9.7	11.4		11.9	Trade Receivables (net)	1.6	9.9	13.0	5.2	16.7	14.8
42.2	38.0		38.3	Inventory	29.0	26.3	24.9	44.3	34.8	48.3
5.8	7.5		8.0	All Other Current	12.6	5.6	6.2	9.1	6.9	9.0
75.7	74.0		74.4	Total Current	56.3	60.9	67.9	76.1	77.0	83.1
15.3	16.2		16.5	Fixed Assets (net)	29.8	27.9	25.8	14.3	14.5	8.6
1.0	1.5		1.5	Intangibles (net)	.0	.8	3.4	1.1	1.8	1.6
7.9	8.3		7.6	All Other Non-Current	13.2	10.5	2.9	8.4	6.7	6.7
100.0	100.0		100.0	Total	100.0	100.0	100.0	100.0	100.0	100.0
				LIABILITIES						
23.1	23.0		24.2	Notes Payable-Short Term	33.0	24.6	28.9	25.6	17.3	24.7
3.2	3.1		4.8	Cur. Mat.-L.T.D.	2.2	9.3	6.3	4.2	3.1	4.0
8.7	10.9		10.2	Trade Payables	9.9	4.7	5.3	6.1	11.2	15.7
.0	.1		.0	Income Taxes Payable	.0	.0	.0	.0	.1	.1
14.6	13.6		14.5	All Other Current	9.3	16.8	18.9	14.6	14.4	13.0
49.6	50.6		53.7	Total Current	54.4	55.3	59.4	50.5	46.1	57.6
15.5	16.5		15.3	Long-Term Debt	33.2	24.8	27.9	10.6	14.0	7.4
.1	.0		.0	Deferred Taxes	.0	.0	.0	.0	.0	.0
6.6	5.9		5.4	All Other Non-Current	10.6	2.1	4.4	5.7	4.2	6.9
28.2	27.0		25.6	Net Worth	1.9	17.8	8.3	33.2	35.7	28.1
100.0	100.0		100.0	Total Liabilities & Net Worth	100.0	100.0	100.0	100.0	100.0	100.0
				INCOME DATA						
100.0	100.0		100.0	Net Sales	100.0	100.0	100.0	100.0	100.0	100.0
21.9	22.9		22.6	Gross Profit	36.5	28.0	28.6	23.4	18.2	18.2
14.5	15.7		15.5	Operating Expenses	31.4	20.3	21.4	15.5	12.7	10.5
7.3	7.3		7.1	Operating Profit	5.1	7.7	7.2	8.0	5.6	7.8
-.3	.3		.8	All Other Expenses (net)	2.6	.9	1.0	1.2	.2	.7
7.6	6.9		6.3	Profit Before Taxes	2.5	6.8	6.2	6.7	5.4	7.0
				RATIOS						
3.3	3.3		2.6	Current	3.2	4.1	2.7	2.7	3.2	1.9
1.6	1.5		1.5		1.3	1.7	1.3	1.5	1.7	1.4
1.1	1.1		1.1		.6	.8	1.1	1.1	1.2	1.1
1.5	1.4		1.2	Quick	1.1	2.4	2.0	.9	1.8	1.0
.4	(629) .4		.4		.4	.6	.7	.3	.7	.3
.1	.1		.1		.0	.1	.1	.1	.2	.1
0 UND	0 UND		0 UND	Sales/Receivables	0 UND	0 UND	0 UND	0 UND	0 UND	0 UND
0 999.8	0 999.8		0 999.8		0 UND	0 UND	0 UND	0 UND	3 110.8	3 137.0
10 35.3	18 20.2		22 16.8		0 UND	5 72.0	11 32.3	3 118.7	34 10.7	30 12.3
0 UND	0 UND		0 UND	Cost of Sales/Inventory	0 UND	0 UND	0 UND	0 UND	0 UND	0 UND
99 3.7	60 6.1		57 6.4		0 UND	0 UND	0 UND	118 3.1	38 9.7	152 2.4
243 1.5	261 1.4		243 1.5		521 .7	215 1.7	261 1.4	281 1.3	215 1.7	261 1.4
0 UND	0 UND		0 UND	Cost of Sales/Payables	0 UND	0 UND	0 UND	0 862.7	1 449.5	7 54.1
10 36.3	10 36.4		10 36.7		10 36.4	0 UND	1 670.0	8 47.7	16 23.2	16 22.4
28 12.9	25 14.7		25 14.8		58 6.3	18 20.6	18 20.6	20 18.2	24 15.0	31 11.7
3.8	3.7		3.4	Sales/Working Capital	1.7	3.3	5.1	3.7	3.3	3.6
9.0	10.8		9.9		5.0	17.8	18.0	7.9	10.3	9.4
44.5	50.1		47.4		-12.2	-25.4	151.5	38.8	36.8	30.1
51.8	41.1		31.8	EBIT/Interest	4.8	20.3	35.3	17.3	38.2	41.0
(484) 14.2	(465) 12.0		(394) 7.3		(19) 1.5	(55) 4.9	(38) 10.1	(65) 5.1	(79) 7.9	(138) 9.6
4.8	3.6		2.1		-7.0	1.5	1.4	1.3	2.2	3.6
19.3	11.9		13.0	Net Profit + Depr., Dep., Amort./Cur. Mat. L/T/D						14.3
(20) 5.3	(19) 2.6		(24) 2.3						(16)	5.3
2.6	.7		.8							1.9
.0	.0		.0	Fixed/Worth	.0	.0	.0	.0	.0	.0
.2	.1		.2		.7	.6	.8	.1	.2	.1
1.1	1.0		1.0		NM	7.6	NM	1.0	.9	.4
1.0	1.0		1.0	Debt/Worth	1.3	.6	1.6	.9	.8	1.2
2.6	2.7		2.3		4.0	1.7	3.6	2.0	2.3	2.2
9.1	8.1		8.3		-7.3	-36.0	NM	8.1	4.7	5.5
89.5	96.5		65.0	% Profit Before Taxes/Tangible Net Worth	50.0	68.0	199.7	73.1	62.5	61.0
(573) 44.5	(567) 44.7		(437) 32.4		(20) 6.5	(56) 32.9	(36) 50.4	(76) 19.2	(93) 31.8	(156) 33.9
18.8	19.1		11.3		-12.0	12.4	18.0	3.2	9.6	20.9
22.2	25.4		23.2	% Profit Before Taxes/Total Assets	13.2	34.5	40.0	22.8	24.4	20.7
11.4	11.7		9.3		1.9	8.3	17.2	7.8	9.4	11.6
3.9	3.5		2.8		-3.0	2.4	2.3	1.5	3.4	4.6
832.5	754.9		495.0	Sales/Net Fixed Assets	UND	754.8	259.7	999.8	425.4	430.2
85.7	69.9		57.2		18.5	24.3	41.5	72.7	58.6	89.0
14.3	13.4		12.4		3.5	4.2	7.6	12.4	15.2	24.5
3.1	3.6		3.6	Sales/Total Assets	4.0	5.0	7.0	3.1	4.2	3.0
1.8	1.9		1.9		1.0	2.0	2.4	1.7	2.1	1.8
1.1	1.0		1.1		.4	1.0	.9	1.0	1.3	1.1
.2	.2		.2	% Depr., Dep., Amort./Sales	3.3	.4	.1	.2	.2	.1
(284) .5	(270) .5		(232) .4		(11) 5.2	(28) 1.7	(23) 1.1	(25) .6	(46) .4	(99) .2
1.3	1.3		1.4		9.1	3.3	1.6	1.9	1.2	.6
1.1	1.0		1.0	% Officers', Directors', Owners' Comp/Sales		2.5	1.9	1.3	.9	.2
(240) 2.2	(233) 2.1		(179) 1.9		(34) 3.6	(24) 3.5	(37) 1.8	(34) 1.7	(42) .7
4.1	4.4		4.5			5.8	5.8	4.0	2.3	1.5
19039470M	19374597M		19150423M	Net Sales ($)	14596M	144587M	186656M	614657M	1678853M	16511074M
11023389M	11252671M		10567818M	Total Assets ($)	23342M	137695M	131657M	547514M	1077778M	8649832M

© RMA 2024 M = $ thousand MM = $ million
See Pages viii through xx for Explanation of Ratios and Data

CONSTRUCTION-GENERAL—New Multifamily Housing Construction (except For-Sale Builders) NAICS 236116

Current Data Sorted by Assets | **Comparative Historical Data**

0-500M	500M-2MM	2-10MM	10-50MM	50-100MM	100-250MM	Type of Statement		4/1/19-3/31/20 ALL	4/1/20-3/31/21 ALL
1			12	5	4	Unqualified		18	15
	6		5	1	1	Reviewed		18	7
	1				1	Compiled		7	4
1	5	3	3			Tax Returns		21	19
2	6	7	20	8	4	Other		50	42
4	12 (4/1-9/30/23) 11	17	84 (10/1/23-3/31/24) 40	14	10	NUMBER OF STATEMENTS		114	87
%	%	%	%	%	%	ASSETS		%	%
28.8	16.2	17.5	14.7	12.2		Cash & Equivalents		20.5	23.4
19.6	33.9	43.7	53.4	32.7		Trade Receivables (net)		36.2	28.9
2.2	10.2	7.7	2.5	.2		Inventory		10.3	13.1
22.8	13.1	12.2	14.9	11.2		All Other Current		7.3	8.4
73.5	73.3	81.1	85.5	56.3		Total Current		74.4	73.8
16.0	16.2	10.8	2.6	18.9		Fixed Assets (net)		14.7	12.7
.2	5.9	2.1	.8	1.6		Intangibles (net)		1.9	3.1
10.3	4.6	5.9	11.1	23.3		All Other Non-Current		9.1	10.3
100.0	100.0	100.0	100.0	100.0		Total		100.0	100.0
						LIABILITIES			
11.2	6.7	3.4	.1	.0		Notes Payable-Short Term		10.5	12.0
1.1	.8	2.7	5.1	1.1		Cur. Mat.-L.T.D.		1.4	1.9
10.1	26.3	28.7	43.6	29.5		Trade Payables		26.8	24.8
.0	.0	.0	.0	.0		Income Taxes Payable		.0	.1
10.1	11.5	21.6	30.0	12.6		All Other Current		15.1	15.7
32.5	45.3	56.4	78.8	43.3		Total Current		53.8	54.5
20.4	17.3	15.4	3.3	25.8		Long-Term Debt		11.0	9.9
.0	.0	.2	.0	.1		Deferred Taxes		.1	.1
2.2	3.9	3.6	4.2	9.1		All Other Non-Current		3.6	11.1
44.9	33.4	24.4	13.7	21.8		Net Worth		31.5	24.4
100.0	100.0	100.0	100.0	100.0		Total Liabilities & Net Worth		100.0	100.0
						INCOME DATA			
100.0	100.0	100.0	100.0	100.0		Net Sales		100.0	100.0
32.1	18.0	15.9	6.6	12.4		Gross Profit		19.2	20.0
23.7	11.7	12.3	4.9	10.8		Operating Expenses		12.2	15.9
8.4	6.3	3.6	1.7	1.6		Operating Profit		7.0	4.1
.0	.6	1.6	-.6	-1.2		All Other Expenses (net)		.3	-.3
8.4	5.7	2.0	2.3	2.8		Profit Before Taxes		6.7	4.3
						RATIOS			
13.8	3.6	2.3	1.3	1.6				2.1	2.1
2.0	1.7	1.3	1.1	1.3		Current		1.3	1.3
1.4	1.3	1.1	1.0	1.1				1.1	1.1
2.4	3.4	1.7	1.1	1.4				1.5	1.5
1.3	1.3	1.2	.9	1.1		Quick		1.1	1.0
1.1	.4	.9	.7	.9				.7	.5
0 UND	1 502.7	34 10.6	54 6.8	33 10.9				4 84.8	0 999.8
1 405.2	44 8.3	54 6.7	66 5.5	50 7.3		Sales/Receivables		47 7.8	39 9.4
65 5.6	83 4.4	81 4.5	83 4.4	69 5.3				74 4.9	63 5.8
0 UND	0 UND	0 UND	0 UND	0 UND				0 UND	0 UND
0 UND	0 UND	0 UND	0 UND	0 UND		Cost of Sales/Inventory		0 UND	0 UND
0 UND	3 139.9	0 UND	0 UND	0 UND				0 864.6	0 999.8
0 UND	10 36.8	20 18.5	40 9.1	45 8.2				9 38.7	47.1
13 28.7	33 11.1	39 9.4	60 6.1	53 6.9		Cost of Sales/Payables		35 10.3	30 12.3
66 5.5	62 5.9	54 6.7	85 4.3	66 5.5				66 5.5	65 5.6
4.1	3.8	5.5	16.8	7.7				7.1	6.5
13.7	7.8	14.2	30.1	16.9		Sales/Working Capital		13.4	14.9
64.4	28.3	42.6	-135.9	30.6				53.1	43.0
	175.0	57.6						112.6	69.3
(13)	16.5	(32) 16.1				EBIT/Interest		(81) 27.1	(49) 17.6
	.7	2.1						6.5	6.3
								47.6	
						Net Profit + Depr., Dep., Amort./Cur. Mat. L/T/D		(14) 10.0	
								3.5	
.0	.0	.1	.0	.0				.0	.0
.0	.1	.2	.2	.6		Fixed/Worth		.2	.1
.4	.5	.5	.4	NM				.5	.5
.6	1.0	1.1	3.2	3.2				1.1	1.2
.9	2.4	4.2	5.4	5.8		Debt/Worth		2.6	2.8
2.0	4.7	9.9	21.7	NM				6.1	7.7
186.3	83.0	62.4	102.3					73.3	80.7
(10) 90.6	(15) 33.2	(35) 32.6	(13) 60.7			% Profit Before Taxes/Tangible Net Worth		(102) 36.3	(79) 43.1
31.8	15.1	8.2	34.9					14.2	18.4
60.5	21.6	12.2	12.5	8.5				26.0	22.2
38.9	9.0	5.6	6.9	5.6		% Profit Before Taxes/Total Assets		9.2	10.6
8.6	4.6	1.4	1.9	2.1				3.7	4.4
UND	967.0	329.6	466.1	178.4				615.1	479.0
76.0	96.9	80.4	133.7	26.3		Sales/Net Fixed Assets		58.5	97.2
7.6	10.4	21.5	75.1	3.7				18.4	15.5
5.4	3.9	3.9	3.7	3.7				3.8	3.8
3.4	2.4	2.9	3.2	1.8		Sales/Total Assets		2.7	2.7
1.4	1.4	1.8	2.8	.9				1.7	1.7
			.1	.0				.1	.1
		(25) .2	(10) .1			% Depr., Dep., Amort./Sales		(78) .5	(48) .2
			.8	.2				1.1	.8
								.9	.7
						% Officers', Directors', Owners' Comp/Sales		(35) 1.5	(29) 1.9
								4.1	5.2
4502M	78297M	273944M	2740090M	2930779M	3386104M	Net Sales ($)		8530519M	6398866M
1116M	12975M	81808M	950892M	983571M	1848255M	Total Assets ($)		3620204M	2463403M

© RMA 2024   M = $ thousand   MM = $ million
See Pages viii through xx for Explanation of Ratios and Data

CONSTRUCTION-GENERAL—New Multifamily Housing Construction (except For-Sale Builders) NAICS 236116

Comparative Historical Data / Current Data Sorted by Sales

				Type of Statement						
11	16	22		Unqualified	1			1	1	20
13	13	13		Reviewed					5	7
4	5	2		Compiled				1		2
18	15	12		Tax Returns	3		3	4	2	2
45	45	47		Other	9	3	3	5	2	27
4/1/21-3/31/22 ALL	4/1/22-3/31/23 ALL	4/1/23-3/31/24 ALL			12 (4/1/23-9/30/23)			84 (10/1/23-3/31/24)		
					0-1MM	1-3MM	3-5MM	5-10MM	10-25MM	25MM & OVER
91	94	96		NUMBER OF STATEMENTS	1	12	3	7	15	58
%	%	%		ASSETS	%	%	%	%	%	%
24.5	18.2	18.4		Cash & Equivalents		18.0			20.0	17.9
29.3	31.2	38.8		Trade Receivables (net)		17.6			34.2	47.1
17.2	9.9	6.2		Inventory		20.6			2.8	2.1
8.1	13.2	13.6		All Other Current		9.3			18.7	14.3
79.1	72.4	76.9		Total Current		65.5			75.7	81.4
8.6	12.7	11.9		Fixed Assets (net)		16.5			19.1	8.4
2.3	2.9	2.3		Intangibles (net)		6.9			2.9	1.3
10.0	12.0	8.9		All Other Non-Current		11.0			2.4	8.9
100.0	100.0	100.0		Total		100.0			100.0	100.0
				LIABILITIES						
9.4	5.6	4.3		Notes Payable-Short Term		10.0			2.1	3.0
1.7	2.7	2.3		Cur. Mat.-L.T.D.		1.0			8.5	1.2
24.1	24.4	28.3		Trade Payables		10.6			19.6	37.0
.2	.0	.0		Income Taxes Payable		.0			.0	.0
16.2	17.9	19.5		All Other Current		20.5			10.3	24.1
51.7	50.6	54.4		Total Current		42.1			40.4	65.3
10.5	14.1	15.3		Long-Term Debt		29.2			20.5	8.7
.0	.0	.1		Deferred Taxes		.0			.5	.1
4.8	5.2	4.4		All Other Non-Current		3.4			3.4	4.6
33.0	30.0	25.8		Net Worth		25.3			35.2	21.3
100.0	100.0	100.0		Total Liabilities & Net Worth		100.0			100.0	100.0
				INCOME DATA						
100.0	100.0	100.0		Net Sales		100.0			100.0	100.0
18.3	22.6	16.7		Gross Profit		32.8			25.5	10.1
12.8	16.0	12.7		Operating Expenses		23.3			19.9	7.7
5.5	6.6	4.0		Operating Profit		9.5			5.6	2.4
-.7	.4	.5		All Other Expenses (net)		1.3			-.9	-.1
6.2	6.2	3.5		Profit Before Taxes		8.2			6.4	2.5
				RATIOS						
2.3	2.5	2.3				4.2			4.1	1.6
1.5	1.4	1.4		Current		1.9			2.0	1.2
1.2	1.1	1.1				.7			1.3	1.1
1.7	1.6	1.7				2.1			4.1	1.4
1.2	1.1	1.1		Quick		1.2			1.7	1.1
.8	.7	.9				.2			.6	.9
1 377.4	4 103.1	26 14.3			0 UND			0 UND	34 10.7	
35 10.4	40 9.1	54 6.8		Sales/Receivables	0 UND			57 6.4	54 6.8	
66 5.5	58 6.3	79 4.6			78 4.7			96 3.8	74 4.9	
0 UND	0 UND	0 UND			0 UND			0 UND	0 UND	
0 UND	0 UND	0 UND		Cost of Sales/Inventory	0 UND			0 UND	0 UND	
24 14.9	0 UND	0 UND			107 3.4			1 267.5	0 UND	
4 97.5	11 33.4	19 18.9			0 UND			9 38.6	30 12.3	
29 12.5	35 10.5	42 8.7		Cost of Sales/Payables	20 18.1			40 9.1	49 7.5	
61 6.0	54 6.7	64 5.7			51 7.1			68 5.4	64 5.7	
	5.0	5.9	5.9			2.6			3.7	13.2
	11.6	16.6	17.2	Sales/Working Capital		12.0			7.0	24.6
	26.5	63.8	44.5			NM			17.3	59.2
	196.7	64.3	77.7						209.2	123.2
(60)	27.5	(66) 24.6	(72) 17.2	EBIT/Interest		(12) 36.0			(45) 22.4	
	3.7	5.9	2.1						6.8	2.1
			18.7							15.5
		(12) 5.5		Net Profit + Depr., Dep., Amort./Cur. Mat. L/T/D					(10) 5.0	
			2.8							2.1
.0	.0	.0				.0			.0	.0
.1	.2	.2		Fixed/Worth		.4			.2	.2
.3	.6	.6				-1.9			.6	.5
1.1	1.2	1.1				.6			.3	2.3
2.5	3.2	4.1		Debt/Worth		7.8			2.3	5.1
6.9	8.7	9.9				-10.0			3.4	9.8
	112.0	78.3	79.5						78.3	79.0
(85)	49.3	(87) 44.4	(83) 39.6	% Profit Before Taxes/Tangible Net Worth		(13) 50.5			(53) 39.6	
	14.7	18.1	15.2						15.2	14.3
27.9	26.9	17.7				38.4			27.1	11.5
11.1	11.4	7.7		% Profit Before Taxes/Total Assets		12.0			15.0	6.2
4.1	3.6	2.4				-2.1			3.6	1.9
920.0	566.0	543.2				361.6			106.9	403.6
117.9	91.0	93.2		Sales/Net Fixed Assets		54.9			19.3	112.1
32.2	20.8	21.2				5.8			4.1	33.4
3.7	4.1	3.8				3.4			3.0	4.1
2.6	2.8	2.8		Sales/Total Assets		1.7			2.2	3.2
1.4	1.7	1.8				.6			1.5	2.5
.1	.1	.1								.0
(53) .2	(50) .3	(52) .2		% Depr., Dep., Amort./Sales					(41) .2	
.6	1.3	.7								.4
1.1	.9	.3								
(31) 2.5	(33) 2.6	(18) 1.0		% Officers', Directors' Owners' Comp/Sales						
5.6	5.6	2.6								
5310894M	5710700M	9413716M		Net Sales ($)	389M	21414M	11178M	47521M	265299M	9067915M
2382971M	2355129M	3878617M		Total Assets ($)	143M	27544M	47889M	34075M	193521M	3575445M

M = $ thousand   MM = $ million
See Pages viii through xx for Explanation of Ratios and Data

© RMA 2024

CONSTRUCTION-GENERAL—New Housing For-Sale Builders NAICS 236117

Current Data Sorted by Assets

						Type of Statement
1	1		9	8	9	Unqualified
6	6		36	12	3	Reviewed
3	10		24	4	3	Compiled
14	18	49	30	4	1	Tax Returns
25	21	95	165	47	38	Other
	67 (4/1-9/30/23)		575 (10/1/23-3/31/24)			
0-500M	500M-2MM	2-10MM	10-50MM	50-100MM	100-250MM	
49	39	161	264	75	54	NUMBER OF STATEMENTS

Comparative Historical Data

48	41
74	45
67	42
193	118
435	347
4/1/19-3/31/20	4/1/20-3/31/21
ALL	ALL
817	593

Combined Table

0-500M	500M-2MM	2-10MM	10-50MM	50-100MM	100-250MM		4/1/19-3/31/20 ALL	4/1/20-3/31/21 ALL
%	%	%	%	%	%	**ASSETS**	%	%
21.3	20.1	13.5	12.6	11.7	9.9	Cash & Equivalents	12.3	13.7
4.1	7.6	2.3	2.4	2.6	1.3	Trade Receivables (net)	3.2	2.3
59.5	46.3	64.4	64.2	70.3	69.5	Inventory	65.4	65.1
2.4	9.3	4.1	5.1	3.6	2.5	All Other Current	3.0	3.6
87.3	83.3	84.3	84.3	88.1	83.2	Total Current	84.0	84.8
7.9	9.8	8.9	7.5	3.5	4.5	Fixed Assets (net)	8.1	8.9
.8	.7	.8	1.6	.7	2.6	Intangibles (net)	.6	1.0
4.0	6.2	6.1	6.7	7.7	9.7	All Other Non-Current	7.2	5.3
100.0	100.0	100.0	100.0	100.0	100.0	Total	100.0	100.0
						LIABILITIES		
40.6	21.1	29.2	33.1	38.6	27.0	Notes Payable-Short Term	38.6	32.8
1.2	2.6	2.4	1.5	3.5	2.3	Cur. Mat.-L.T.D.	2.1	2.1
4.5	10.3	4.9	6.2	5.5	5.3	Trade Payables	6.1	6.0
2.2	.2	.0	.0	.0	.1	Income Taxes Payable	.0	.1
19.2	19.4	12.7	10.6	9.6	8.8	All Other Current	13.9	8.8
67.7	53.6	49.2	51.5	57.2	43.4	Total Current	60.8	49.7
8.8	13.5	11.1	7.5	4.9	7.2	Long-Term Debt	7.8	11.0
.0	.0	.0	.0	.0	.0	Deferred Taxes	.0	.0
5.1	1.4	6.4	4.2	4.3	2.6	All Other Non-Current	3.2	5.9
18.3	31.4	33.3	36.8	33.6	46.8	Net Worth	28.1	33.3
100.0	100.0	100.0	100.0	100.0	100.0	Total Liabilities & Net Worth	100.0	100.0
						INCOME DATA		
100.0	100.0	100.0	100.0	100.0	100.0	Net Sales	100.0	100.0
23.4	19.7	18.8	20.2	19.0	20.7	Gross Profit	18.5	19.0
14.9	10.7	10.3	10.4	10.5	9.5	Operating Expenses	11.6	10.1
8.5	9.0	8.5	9.8	8.4	11.2	Operating Profit	6.9	9.0
.4	.7	1.2	.6	.5	-.2	All Other Expenses (net)	.8	.3
8.1	8.3	7.3	9.2	7.9	11.5	Profit Before Taxes	6.1	8.7
						RATIOS		
2.9	3.2	3.3	2.3	1.9	2.8		1.9	2.6
1.7	1.5	1.7	1.6	1.5	1.8	Current	1.4	1.6
1.3	1.0	1.2	1.3	1.3	1.5		1.1	1.3
.6	1.4	.7	.5	.4	.5		.4	.6
.3	.5	.3	.2	.1	.2	Quick	.2	.2
.1	.1	.1	.1	.1	.1		.1	.1
0 UND	0 UND	0 UND	0 UND	0 UND	0 UND		0 UND	0 UND
0 UND	0 UND	0 UND	0 UND	0 UND	0 999.8	Sales/Receivables	0 UND	0 UND
0 UND	0 937.0	0 999.8	2 239.3	1 290.2	2 152.7		2 221.5	1 292.3
0 UND	0 UND	85 4.3	135 2.7	182 2.0	192 1.9		99 3.7	114 3.2
203 1.8	74 4.9	174 2.1	228 1.6	243 1.5	243 1.5	Cost of Sales/Inventory	203 1.8	192 1.9
365 1.0	159 2.3	304 1.2	332 1.1	332 1.1	332 1.1		332 1.1	304 1.2
0 UND	0 UND	0 UND	5 80.5	4 90.9	9 41.2		0 999.8	1 415.9
11 33.0	2 150.8	6 66.3	14 26.8	11 32.1	15 24.2	Cost of Sales/Payables	11 33.0	11 32.1
25 14.8	23 16.1	20 18.6	24 15.5	18 20.2	22 16.5		24 15.3	23 15.9
2.1	3.5	2.7	2.4	3.1	2.5		3.6	2.8
4.3	9.3	5.4	4.5	4.6	3.3	Sales/Working Capital	6.7	5.2
17.5	996.0	16.8	9.7	7.5	4.7		23.6	10.0
23.2	37.6	37.3	37.9	73.7	72.5		28.1	35.7
(20) 3.5	(26) 5.1	(107) 5.6	(184) 8.7	(54) 17.3	(41) 25.8	EBIT/Interest	(570) 7.7	(412) 10.4
2.0	2.0	2.1	3.5	3.6	5.3		2.5	4.3
			35.0				10.3	
		(12) 16.3				Net Profit + Depr., Dep., Amort./Cur. Mat. L/T/D	(10) 3.1	
		1.1					.1	
.0	.0	.0	.0	.0	.0		.0	.0
.0	.0	.0	.0	.0	.0	Fixed/Worth	.0	.0
.1	.5	.3	.2	.1	.1		.2	.3
.5	1.0	1.0	1.0	1.3	.8		1.3	1.1
1.3	2.6	2.3	2.1	2.1	1.5	Debt/Worth	2.5	2.0
3.6	8.8	6.0	3.7	3.8	2.0		6.3	4.0
58.2	116.8	62.2	59.5	49.3	46.5		61.0	66.7
(42) 29.0	(33) 62.5	(148) 32.2	(261) 34.8	(74) 29.5	(53) 30.8	% Profit Before Taxes/Tangible Net Worth	(748) 31.3	(551) 40.5
11.0	16.0	13.8	19.1	15.7	18.0		12.1	21.7
35.1	40.0	20.5	19.4	15.9	21.9		16.5	20.1
13.0	15.6	10.7	11.3	9.2	11.1	% Profit Before Taxes/Total Assets	7.6	12.2
2.9	3.9	3.2	5.5	4.2	7.4		2.8	5.7
UND	UND	UND	999.8	734.1	353.9		UND	999.8
UND	152.6	470.0	169.2	159.8	141.9	Sales/Net Fixed Assets	223.9	198.3
47.6	37.3	18.8	38.0	52.1	48.1		42.3	32.1
6.6	4.0	2.3	1.9	1.7	1.6		2.3	2.3
1.6	2.5	1.6	1.4	1.3	1.3	Sales/Total Assets	1.6	1.6
1.0	1.6	.9	.9	1.0	1.0		1.0	1.1
		.1	.1	.1	.1		.1	.1
	(41) .4	(112) .2	(38) .1	(30) .2	% Depr., Dep., Amort./Sales	(310) .3	(197) .2
		1.4	.4	.3	.3		.6	.6
2.5	2.0	1.0	.4	.3			.9	.6
(10) 8.6	(13) 3.0	(56) 1.8	(65) 1.0	(17) .5		% Officers', Directors', Owners' Comp/Sales	(251) 2.0	(149) 1.5
32.6	6.0	3.1	2.5	1.1			3.5	3.0
56583M	157879M	1540468M	11733515M	9242217M	11252063M	Net Sales ($)	25686971M	23687533M
6431M	49053M	863493M	6589798M	5403898M	8421477M	Total Assets ($)	18518188M	15168860M

© RMA 2024   M = $ thousand   MM = $ million
See Pages viii through xx for Explanation of Ratios and Data

CONSTRUCTION-GENERAL—New Housing For-Sale Builders NAICS 236117

Comparative Historical Data | Current Data Sorted by Sales

Comparative Historical Data			Type of Statement	Current Data Sorted by Sales						
32	29	28	Unqualified	1			5	5	22
49	63	63	Reviewed	6	1		10	41
46	51	44	Compiled	3	3		3	11	24
87	148	116	Tax Returns	9	17	19	22	30	19
425	535	391	Other	30	17	29	49	74	192
4/1/21-3/31/22	4/1/22-3/31/23	4/1/23-3/31/24		67 (4/1-9/30/23)			575 (10/1/23-3/31/24)		
ALL	ALL	ALL		0-1MM	1-3MM	3-5MM	5-10MM	10-25MM	25MM & OVER
639	826	642	NUMBER OF STATEMENTS	49	38	48	79	130	298
%	%	%	**ASSETS**	%	%	%	%	%	%
13.9	13.1	13.6	Cash & Equivalents	11.4	21.9	13.1	16.0	11.9	13.1
3.3	3.4	2.8	Trade Receivables (net)	.3	5.5	4.0	2.6	2.4	2.8
64.9	62.5	63.9	Inventory	66.3	43.7	56.8	63.4	65.5	66.7
3.4	3.8	4.5	All Other Current	4.8	8.0	4.5	3.3	4.4	4.3
85.4	82.8	84.8	Total Current	82.8	79.0	78.4	85.3	84.2	87.0
8.2	9.7	7.3	Fixed Assets (net)	12.2	10.0	10.8	11.2	8.0	4.3
.8	.4	1.2	Intangibles (net)	1.1	.0	2.2	.6	1.7	1.2
5.6	7.0	6.7	All Other Non-Current	4.0	10.9	8.6	2.9	6.1	7.5
100.0	100.0	100.0	Total	100.0	100.0	100.0	100.0	100.0	100.0
			LIABILITIES						
33.8	33.2	32.1	Notes Payable-Short Term	37.0	22.7	26.9	31.6	33.4	32.9
1.7	2.3	2.1	Cur. Mat.-L.T.D.	.5	3.4	2.5	2.4	1.7	2.2
6.8	6.3	5.8	Trade Payables	4.3	6.7	1.7	5.2	6.5	6.5
.0	.1	.2	Income Taxes Payable	.0	.0	.0	1.4	.1	.0
10.9	14.4	12.1	All Other Current	5.5	34.2	11.3	13.2	10.1	11.0
53.3	56.4	52.3	Total Current	47.4	66.9	42.5	53.8	51.7	52.7
8.2	9.2	8.5	Long-Term Debt	7.5	18.8	19.0	8.2	8.1	6.0
.0	.0	.0	Deferred Taxes	.0	.0	.0	.0	.0	.0
4.2	3.8	4.5	All Other Non-Current	3.2	4.5	4.2	11.0	4.0	3.3
34.4	30.6	34.6	Net Worth	41.7	9.8	34.3	27.2	36.2	38.0
100.0	100.0	100.0	Total Liabilties & Net Worth	100.0	100.0	100.0	100.0	100.0	100.0
			INCOME DATA						
100.0	100.0	100.0	Net Sales	100.0	100.0	100.0	100.0	100.0	100.0
20.4	20.6	20.0	Gross Profit	27.6	21.6	23.1	18.9	18.2	19.0
10.3	11.3	10.7	Operating Expenses	15.8	14.5	13.3	10.1	9.9	9.4
10.1	9.3	9.3	Operating Profit	11.8	7.2	9.7	8.8	8.3	9.6
-.1	.3	.6	All Other Expenses (net)	.4	1.6	1.1	1.2	.7	.3
10.2	9.0	8.6	Profit Before Taxes	11.4	5.6	8.6	7.7	7.6	9.3
			RATIOS						
2.3	2.3	2.6	Current	2.8	3.3	3.9	3.4	2.9	2.2
1.6	1.5	1.6		1.7	1.4	1.7	1.7	1.6	1.6
1.3	1.1	1.3		1.3	1.0	1.1	1.1	1.3	1.3
.6	.6	.6	Quick	.5	1.7	1.5	.7	.7	.5
.2	.2	.2		.2	.2	.2	.3	.2	.2
.1	.1	.1		.1	.1	.0	.1	.1	.1
0 UND	0 UND	0 UND	Sales/Receivables	0 UND	0 UND	0 UND	0 UND	0 UND	0 UND
0 UND	0 UND	0 UND		0 UND	0 UND	0 UND	0 UND	0 UND	0 999.8
2 231.2	2 209.3	1 283.8		0 UND	1 272.4	2 195.5	0 835.3	1 498.5	2 225.9
114 3.2	89 4.1	114 3.2	Cost of Sales/Inventory	159 2.3	0 UND	73 5.0	81 4.5	107 3.4	135 2.7
203 1.8	203 1.8	215 1.7		281 1.3	81 4.5	182 2.0	203 1.8	228 1.6	215 1.7
332 1.1	332 1.1	332 1.1		406 .9	456 .8	730 .5	365 1.0	332 1.1	281 1.3
2 171.6	0 999.8	2 197.9	Cost of Sales/Payables	0 UND	0 UND	0 UND	0 UND	4 82.3	5 80.3
13 27.5	10 36.5	11 32.4		14 27.0	0 UND	3 138.6	7 48.8	14 26.3	12 30.5
26 14.2	23 15.8	22 16.7		26 14.3	23 16.2	15 24.5	27 13.5	26 14.2	20 18.5
2.8	2.9	2.6	Sales/Working Capital	1.7	2.0	1.5	2.1	2.4	2.9
5.2	5.7	4.5		3.5	7.1	4.3	4.1	4.4	4.8
11.6	18.1	10.6		5.9	NM	25.6	53.2	13.2	9.0
68.0	74.0	42.5	EBIT/Interest	3.6	12.1	38.5	25.9	40.2	62.7
(438) 16.4	(548) 18.0	(432) 8.0		(16) 2.5	(24) 2.5	(37) 4.4	(54) 5.2	(84) 10.5	(217) 13.5
6.2	5.3	2.7		.3	1.3	1.7	2.0	2.5	4.2
120.8	37.2	35.0	Net Profit + Depr., Dep., Amort./Cur. Mat. L/T/D						38.3
(10) 28.5	(19) 19.8	(20) 11.6						(17) 21.5
4.6	1.4	1.1							3.6
.0	.0	.0	Fixed/Worth	.0	.0	.0	.0	.0	.0
.0	.0	.0		.0	.1	.0	.0	.0	.1
.2	.3	.1		.2	.7	.6	.3	.2	.1
1.0	1.1	1.0	Debt/Worth	.6	1.4	.7	.9	1.0	1.1
2.1	2.3	2.0		1.4	2.8	1.7	3.0	2.3	1.8
4.2	5.6	3.9		3.1	18.1	8.2	6.3	4.3	3.0
69.8	69.9	59.9	% Profit Before Taxes/Tangible Net Worth	41.3	81.6	69.0	70.7	58.3	59.3
(602) 42.4	(776) 40.7	(611) 33.7		(47) 25.5	(32) 23.1	(44) 24.3	(72) 26.7	(121) 36.1	(295) 36.5
23.0	19.0	16.1		2.3	4.3	9.3	11.4	14.0	22.9
23.1	20.9	20.4	% Profit Before Taxes/Total Assets	15.6	22.1	15.1	21.0	20.8	20.8
13.0	11.3	11.0		7.1	4.8	5.3	10.5	10.5	13.2
6.3	5.1	4.5		.0	.7	2.4	2.2	3.5	7.8
999.8	999.8	UND	Sales/Net Fixed Assets	UND	UND	UND	UND	UND	926.9
171.2	152.4	191.9		UND	57.8	214.4	159.5	492.8	172.2
35.6	29.2	40.0		21.0	13.6	4.5	16.5	51.3	55.2
2.2	2.2	2.1	Sales/Total Assets	1.6	2.5	1.9	2.3	2.2	2.1
1.5	1.5	1.5		1.0	1.5	1.1	1.5	1.4	1.6
1.0	1.0	1.0		.6	.5	.4	.9	.9	1.1
.1	.1	.1	% Depr., Dep., Amort./Sales			.3	.2	.1	.1
(240) .2	(261) .2	(232) .2		(11) 1.3	(19) .7	(38) .2	(150) .2
.4	.5	.5				4.8		1.7	.9	.3
.6	.7	.6	% Officers', Directors' Owners' Comp/Sales	1.8	2.1	1.3	.9	.4
(151) 1.5	(216) 1.5	(166) 1.4		(12) 3.2	(16) 3.2	(25) 2.1	(42) 1.4	(65) .7
3.0	3.4	3.1		6.1	4.3	3.2	2.7	1.2
30664991M	36591446M	33982725M	Net Sales ($)	10442M	83160M	190202M	544166M	2117602M	31037153M
20435333M	25666489M	21334150M	Total Assets ($)	34726M	116689M	412379M	459857M	1904123M	18406376M

M = $ thousand   MM = $ million
See Pages viii through xx for Explanation of Ratios and Data.

© RMA 2024

CONSTRUCTION-GENERAL—Residential Remodelers NAICS 236118

Current Data Sorted by Assets | Comparative Historical Data

						Type of Statement		
			1		1	Unqualified	6	4
			7			Reviewed	10	7
1	1	3				Compiled	13	5
14	15	5	1			Tax Returns	72	58
24	28	11	19	2	2	Other	104	76
	14 (4/1-9/30/23)	43	165 (10/1/23-3/31/24)				4/1/19-3/31/20	4/1/20-3/31/21
0-500M	500M-2MM	2-10MM	10-50MM	50-100MM	100-250MM		ALL	ALL
39	45	62	28	2	3	NUMBER OF STATEMENTS	205	150
%	%	%	%	%	%	**ASSETS**	%	%
30.9	25.9	21.5	21.1			Cash & Equivalents	24.0	30.5
12.4	19.3	28.3	26.2			Trade Receivables (net)	22.6	22.0
4.1	4.8	7.1	7.0			Inventory	9.5	9.5
3.4	9.1	11.5	6.7			All Other Current	6.3	8.6
50.9	59.1	68.3	61.0			Total Current	62.4	70.5
31.1	25.8	15.7	13.0			Fixed Assets (net)	20.9	17.8
7.3	4.0	6.1	10.7			Intangibles (net)	3.8	4.9
10.8	11.1	9.9	15.3			All Other Non-Current	12.8	6.7
100.0	100.0	100.0	100.0			Total	100.0	100.0
						LIABILITIES		
25.4	7.7	7.2	5.6			Notes Payable-Short Term	19.5	15.5
5.6	2.6	2.3	2.2			Cur. Mat.-L.T.D.	3.3	4.6
12.7	13.6	15.7	9.4			Trade Payables	14.9	10.6
.5	.1	.1	.1			Income Taxes Payable	.1	.1
21.9	17.5	22.3	16.1			All Other Current	22.5	12.4
66.0	41.5	47.6	33.3			Total Current	60.4	43.3
42.8	15.9	15.1	16.8			Long-Term Debt	18.9	29.4
.0	.0	.1	.1			Deferred Taxes	.0	.0
1.2	7.7	5.1	5.7			All Other Non-Current	5.0	4.7
-9.8	35.0	32.1	44.1			Net Worth	15.7	22.5
100.0	100.0	100.0	100.0			Total Liabilities & Net Worth	100.0	100.0
						INCOME DATA		
100.0	100.0	100.0	100.0			Net Sales	100.0	100.0
34.4	40.5	34.2	37.4			Gross Profit	35.0	38.4
28.7	30.9	26.8	27.8			Operating Expenses	27.3	31.2
5.7	9.6	7.4	9.5			Operating Profit	7.7	7.3
.7	1.1	.1	.6			All Other Expenses (net)	.5	-.6
4.9	8.4	7.3	9.0			Profit Before Taxes	7.2	7.9
						RATIOS		
1.6	7.0	5.0	3.4				2.5	5.7
.9	2.6	1.5	1.9			Current	1.4	2.0
.4	1.2	.8	1.4				.7	1.1
1.2	5.3	4.7	2.6				2.0	3.9
.9	2.0	1.0	1.4			Quick	.9	1.5
.3	.9	.5	.9				.3	.7
0 UND	0 UND	2 181.0	25 14.7				0 UND	0 UND
0 UND	5 67.3	34 10.7	46 7.9			Sales/Receivables	12 31.1	11 33.3
15 24.5	35 10.4	63 5.8	65 5.6				42 8.7	54 6.8
0 UND	0 UND	0 UND	0 UND				0 UND	0 UND
0 UND	0 UND	0 UND	0 UND			Cost of Sales/Inventory	0 UND	0 UND
0 UND	1 247.1	12 29.8	9 41.2				3 111.3	2 222.5
0 UND	0 UND	4 103.5	5 67.9				0 UND	0 UND
0 UND	5 78.5	18 20.6	17 21.8			Cost of Sales/Payables	10 38.1	3 106.7
13 28.9	29 12.4	46 7.9	39 9.4				25 14.6	29 12.5
36.0	5.8	4.3	4.0				7.8	4.8
-182.0	12.5	12.8	9.3			Sales/Working Capital	30.4	12.0
-33.0	39.5	-30.7	25.4				-31.3	148.4
13.7	63.9	115.8	43.7				43.1	81.3
(29) 5.2	(32) 16.4	(51) 13.6	(22) 14.5			EBIT/Interest	(158) 10.1	(112) 23.4
1.4	5.6	4.5	4.2				2.8	3.9
						Net Profit + Depr., Dep., Amort./Cur. Mat. L/T/D	(10) 23.1	7.8
								2.5
.6	.1	.1	.0				.1	.1
2.9	.5	.4	.2			Fixed/Worth	.5	.4
-1.1	1.8	-29.0	.8				-9.9	5.3
1.7	.4	.6	.9				.8	.7
13.0	1.1	2.3	1.9			Debt/Worth	2.1	2.2
-2.9	8.3	-29.8	3.2				-30.7	79.5
216.9	128.0	73.2	88.5				125.4	157.7
(23) 65.9	(40) 54.1	(44) 39.4	(24) 48.8			% Profit Before Taxes/Tangible Net Worth	(149) 61.7	(116) 66.5
29.3	25.0	19.9	11.5				21.9	25.3
57.5	43.4	33.5	26.7				50.3	54.4
16.7	17.5	16.8	15.8			% Profit Before Taxes/Total Assets	21.4	21.1
6.3	10.4	6.9	9.1				5.6	5.8
229.6	69.0	165.8	71.5				143.4	180.8
39.7	18.1	49.9	25.5			Sales/Net Fixed Assets	43.0	47.9
18.3	7.1	12.9	11.4				17.2	13.6
11.4	5.5	3.9	2.9				7.1	6.4
6.3	3.1	2.7	1.7			Sales/Total Assets	4.0	3.4
3.8	2.2	1.9	1.0				2.4	2.0
	.3	.7	.1				.5	.3
(15)	.9	(25) 1.5	(18) .8			% Depr., Dep., Amort./Sales	(101) 1.0	(67) .9
	2.5	2.0	2.6				1.8	1.9
3.5	2.1	1.0	.6				1.8	2.0
(18) 5.4	(15) 3.8	(20) 1.8	(10) .9			% Officers', Directors' Owners' Comp/Sales	(102) 3.1	(79) 3.4
7.9	5.0	4.7	1.9				5.8	6.4
90001M	200690M	994818M	1275016M	249530M	1733572M	Net Sales ($)	7500501M	2512460M
9855M	50121M	308705M	618637M	184601M	562139M	Total Assets ($)	1750817M	1011614M

© RMA 2024

M = $ thousand   MM = $ million
See Pages viii through xx for Explanation of Ratios and Data

CONSTRUCTION-GENERAL—Residential Remodelers NAICS 236118

Comparative Historical Data / Current Data Sorted by Sales

				Type of Statement						
2	4	2		Unqualified		1		4	2	
8	8	11		Reviewed	1			1	5	
7	9	7		Compiled	2		1	5	3	
57	45	41		Tax Returns	6	10	10	9	3	1
95	107	118		Other	10	18	11	34	20	25
4/1/21-	4/1/22-	4/1/23-				14 (4/1-9/30/23)		165 (10/1/23-3/31/24)		
3/31/22	3/31/23	3/31/24			0-1MM	1-3MM	3-5MM	5-10MM	10-25MM	25MM & OVER
ALL	ALL	ALL		NUMBER OF STATEMENTS						
169	173	179			16	31	22	44	30	36
%	%	%		ASSETS	%	%	%	%	%	%
27.8	28.3	24.4		Cash & Equivalents	21.2	32.7	26.8	19.8	25.9	21.6
19.5	26.2	21.8		Trade Receivables (net)	5.9	13.0	15.8	25.4	29.3	29.6
9.7	6.0	5.8		Inventory	6.8	5.4	4.5	6.5	4.4	6.6
6.9	6.8	8.6		All Other Current	4.5	6.5	8.3	9.3	8.0	12.2
63.9	67.3	60.6		Total Current	38.4	57.6	55.5	60.9	67.5	69.9
22.7	18.1	21.2		Fixed Assets (net)	35.3	28.0	25.0	21.6	15.9	10.6
5.6	5.4	7.0		Intangibles (net)	14.2	5.4	3.0	7.2	5.3	8.5
7.8	9.1	11.3		All Other Non-Current	12.0	8.9	16.6	10.2	11.2	11.0
100.0	100.0	100.0		Total	100.0	100.0	100.0	100.0	100.0	100.0
				LIABILITIES						
14.5	12.0	11.2		Notes Payable-Short Term	18.3	17.5	16.5	9.2	5.5	6.6
3.9	2.1	3.1		Cur. Mat.-L.T.D.	4.9	2.8	4.4	3.6	1.7	2.6
8.5	11.7	13.3		Trade Payables	2.5	12.7	8.2	11.9	24.6	14.0
.1	.6	.2		Income Taxes Payable	.0	.1	.0	.4	.0	.2
14.1	21.0	20.1		All Other Current	19.3	13.7	13.4	16.2	35.7	22.0
41.1	47.4	47.9		Total Current	44.9	46.8	42.5	41.4	67.5	45.3
27.3	23.1	22.3		Long-Term Debt	29.2	22.6	41.0	22.8	10.7	16.6
.0	.1	.0		Deferred Taxes	.0	.0	.0	.1	.1	.0
8.0	6.2	5.1		All Other Non-Current	11.5	.8	5.2	3.6	6.6	6.4
23.6	23.2	24.7		Net Worth	14.9	29.8	11.3	32.1	15.1	31.7
100.0	100.0	100.0		Total Liabilities & Net Worth	100.0	100.0	100.0	100.0	100.0	100.0
				INCOME DATA						
100.0	100.0	100.0		Net Sales	100.0	100.0	100.0	100.0	100.0	100.0
37.6	34.9	37.0		Gross Profit	46.0	37.0	35.7	34.5	33.8	39.7
29.6	28.4	29.0		Operating Expenses	37.5	26.7	29.7	28.6	25.3	30.2
8.0	6.5	8.1		Operating Profit	8.5	10.3	5.9	5.9	8.5	9.6
-.7	.2	.6		All Other Expenses (net)	3.3	.6	.6	.0	.1	.6
8.7	6.3	7.4		Profit Before Taxes	5.2	9.7	5.3	5.9	8.4	8.9
				RATIOS						
4.9	3.6	4.0			1.7	5.2	3.0	5.6	4.5	2.4
1.9	1.7	1.6		Current	1.0	1.7	1.7	2.0	1.7	1.4
1.0	1.0	.9			.5	.6	.9	.7	.7	1.2
3.8	2.9	2.8			1.4	4.2	2.4	5.2	4.4	2.1
1.3	1.3	1.2		Quick	1.0	1.3	1.3	1.3	1.5	1.2
.5	.6	.5			.2	.6	.4	.4	.5	.7
0 UND	0 UND	0 UND			0 UND	0 UND	0 UND	3 120.3	10 36.9	
14 26.0	17 21.5	16 23.4		Sales/Receivables	0 UND	2 211.5	0 UND	23 16.1	38 9.5	32 11.5
39 9.3	64 5.7	48 7.6			28 13.2	29 12.7	24 15.4	51 7.1	63 5.8	63 5.8
0 UND	0 UND	0 UND			0 UND	0 UND	0 UND	0 UND	0 UND	0 UND
0 UND	0 UND	0 UND		Cost of Sales/Inventory	0 UND	0 UND	0 UND	0 UND	0 UND	0 UND
2 189.2	2 241.3	2 162.6			0 UND	1 370.0	0 UND	4 93.2	0 927.3	18 20.2
0 UND	0 UND	0 UND			0 UND	0 UND	0 UND	0 999.8	8 43.9	5 67.9
5 80.7	10 34.8	12 30.9		Cost of Sales/Payables	0 UND	5 71.0	0 UND	14 26.0	20 18.0	17 21.8
21 17.1	27 13.3	34 10.6			8 43.4	26 13.9	21 17.0	36 10.0	42 8.7	36 10.2
	6.0	5.7			47.6	4.7	11.0	5.0	4.2	5.5
12.7	17.6	15.5		Sales/Working Capital	UND	15.1	29.5	14.7	8.6	14.6
-548.7	-170.6	-122.1			-18.6	-43.9	-190.2	-100.3	-17.6	26.9
	67.4	40.1	56.1		15.0	45.2	42.3	89.6	136.1	73.9
(130) 14.6	(132) 11.3	(138) 11.5		EBIT/Interest	(11) 2.7	(24) 10.3	(17) 8.3	(32) 12.4	(27) 30.5	(27) 11.6
4.6	2.0	3.3			.5	3.8	2.1	1.4	6.6	3.3
		5.9		Net Profit + Depr., Dep.,						
	(11) 3.1			Amort./Cur. Mat. L/T/D						
		2.5								
.1	.0	.1			.7	.1	.2	.1	.1	.1
.6	.4	.6		Fixed/Worth	UND	.7	.9	.5	.5	.2
NM	2.7	46.4			-1.5	6.0	UND	9.9	-9.1	.9
.7	.6	.6			.5	.6	.6	.6	.5	1.2
2.1	2.3	2.3		Debt/Worth	UND	1.5	3.1	2.0	2.7	2.1
-60.7	-42.7	-136.2			-3.7	13.6	UND	NM	-4.9	4.2
						92.2	175.8	101.4	62.3	90.0
115.4	100.0	96.7		% Profit Before Taxes/Tangible	(25) 41.6	(17) 58.1	(33) 45.6	(20) 40.0	(30) 53.3	
(123) 57.6	(128) 51.5	(134) 48.9		Net Worth		27.8		22.1	18.5	20.0	26.0
24.0	19.1	22.6								
49.4	34.1	36.9		% Profit Before Taxes/Total	32.0	49.8	32.0	41.1	33.1	45.5
20.5	15.7	17.2		Assets	7.0	17.2	15.6	15.1	20.7	18.6
5.5	4.3	7.4			-1.8	7.6	9.8	6.1	12.2	10.6
106.9	271.2	133.0			622.5	60.9	50.2	155.8	115.5	102.3
31.4	44.9	31.4		Sales/Net Fixed Assets	6.9	21.6	25.7	39.3	51.5	39.7
10.7	12.2	10.9			3.5	7.5	12.2	11.8	8.5	19.8
5.8	6.0	5.4			3.9	5.7	8.8	5.8	4.3	4.7
3.3	3.3	3.0		Sales/Total Assets	2.8	3.1	4.7	3.3	2.9	3.1
2.0	1.9	2.0			1.5	2.0	2.2	1.9	1.9	2.0
.6	.4	.4						.5	.3	.4
(73) 1.3	(75) 1.0	(67) 1.3		% Depr., Dep., Amort./Sales		(16) 1.9	(13) 1.4	(20) .7		
2.8	2.7	2.2						2.6	1.8	1.6
1.4	1.3	1.6				3.6	3.2	1.7	.9	
(90) 3.7	(81) 3.1	(63) 3.2		% Officers', Directors' Owners' Comp/Sales	(13) 4.3	(11) 3.9	(11) 2.1	(13) 1.7		
6.5	5.3	5.4				5.5	5.2	3.3	3.7	
2849132M	3421340M	4543627M		Net Sales ($)	7705M	62911M	86751M	318851M	486586M	3580823M
1270257M	1357631M	1734058M		Total Assets ($)	4296M	25612M	27380M	130261M	198015M	1348494M

© RMA 2024   M = $ thousand   MM = $ million
See Pages viii through xx for Explanation of Ratios and Data

CONSTRUCTION-GENERAL—Industrial Building Construction NAICS 236210

Current Data Sorted by Assets | **Comparative Historical Data**

		3	25	5	4	Type of Statement			
		14	21	3		Unqualified	38	25	
	1	1				Reviewed	47	25	
3	7	7	5		1	Compiled	9	4	
8	17	39	38	10	9	Tax Returns	43	29	
	36 (4/1-9/30/23)		185 (10/1/23-3/31/24)			Other	90	100	
0-500M	500M-2MM	2-10MM	10-50MM	50-100MM	100-250MM		4/1/19-3/31/20 ALL	4/1/20-3/31/21 ALL	
11	25	64	89	18	14	NUMBER OF STATEMENTS	227	183	
%	%	%	%	%	%	ASSETS	%	%	
62.2	28.1	23.0	21.6	22.8	14.2	Cash & Equivalents	21.9	23.0	
14.3	37.2	41.9	44.2	41.3	36.3	Trade Receivables (net)	42.8	40.3	
2.2	1.0	1.8	2.5	3.0	3.9	Inventory	2.7	4.8	
.3	3.8	9.2	9.0	11.6	12.2	All Other Current	9.0	7.6	
78.9	70.0	75.9	77.3	78.8	66.6	Total Current	76.4	75.7	
11.4	22.7	14.9	15.2	15.6	14.6	Fixed Assets (net)	15.2	16.9	
.0	2.3	1.7	2.5	.7	5.7	Intangibles (net)	1.8	3.3	
9.7	5.0	7.5	5.0	4.9	13.1	All Other Non-Current	6.6	4.1	
100.0	100.0	100.0	100.0	100.0	100.0	Total	100.0	100.0	
						LIABILITIES			
22.9	11.1	4.6	2.6	.9	6.1	Notes Payable-Short Term	5.6	6.4	
.7	1.7	1.6	1.8	2.1	1.6	Cur. Mat.-L.T.D.	2.1	1.9	
2.6	21.1	25.3	30.0	31.8	22.4	Trade Payables	26.0	22.9	
.0	.4	.1	.0	.1	.3	Income Taxes Payable	.2	.3	
14.7	15.8	15.7	18.8	19.0	16.8	All Other Current	18.9	18.6	
40.9	50.1	47.2	53.1	53.8	47.2	Total Current	52.9	50.1	
28.6	16.2	10.5	8.4	7.9	6.7	Long-Term Debt	9.4	12.8	
.0	.2	.0	.1	.0	.7	Deferred Taxes	.4	.1	
23.2	4.0	1.3	.8	3.2	4.8	All Other Non-Current	1.5	2.2	
7.4	29.6	41.0	37.6	35.1	40.7	Net Worth	35.9	34.8	
100.0	100.0	100.0	100.0	100.0	100.0	Total Liabilities & Net Worth	100.0	100.0	
						INCOME DATA			
100.0	100.0	100.0	100.0	100.0	100.0	Net Sales	100.0	100.0	
37.5	27.8	22.4	15.3	11.8	14.8	Gross Profit	18.8	19.9	
29.9	22.4	16.4	9.9	8.5	8.6	Operating Expenses	13.7	16.1	
7.6	5.4	6.1	5.3	3.2	6.2	Operating Profit	5.1	3.7	
.2	-.2	.3	-.4	-.1	.2	All Other Expenses (net)	.2	-.7	
7.5	5.5	5.7	5.7	3.3	6.1	Profit Before Taxes	4.9	4.4	
						RATIOS			
6.7	3.3	3.0	2.0	2.3	1.9		2.3	2.6	
2.6	1.6	1.6	1.4	1.3	1.5	Current	1.5	1.5	
1.1	.9	1.2	1.2	1.1	1.1		1.2	1.2	
6.7	3.3	2.4	1.7	1.7	1.7		1.9	2.2	
2.5	1.4	1.4	1.2	1.2	1.1	Quick	1.2	1.3	
1.1	.7	.9	1.0	1.0	.9		1.0	1.0	
0 UND	9 39.4	32 11.5	42 8.7	49 7.5	52 7.0		32 11.4	30 12.3	
4 84.8	38 9.5	47 7.8	64 5.7	72 5.1	68 5.4	Sales/Receivables	51 7.1	54 6.8	
17 21.8	58 6.3	79 4.6	87 4.2	101 3.6	81 4.5		72 5.1	78 4.7	
0 UND	0 UND	0 UND	0 UND	0 UND	0 UND		0 UND	0 UND	
0 UND	0 UND	0 UND	0 UND	0 UND	2 232.0	Cost of Sales/Inventory	0 UND	0 UND	
0 UND	0 UND	0 UND	0 UND	2 200.3	14 25.3		0 999.8	0 999.8	
0 UND	0 UND	21 17.0	24 15.2	26 14.0	29 12.6		14 26.8	11 34.1	
0 UND	19 19.0	35 10.5	44 8.3	66 5.5	42 8.7	Cost of Sales/Payables	34 10.8	32 11.4	
10 38.0	45 8.2	51 7.2	69 5.3	83 4.4	65 5.6		51 7.2	52 7.0	
6.3	7.8	5.5	6.2	5.0	6.1		7.2	5.5	
13.8	23.4	10.9	11.0	10.1	10.5	Sales/Working Capital	13.8	10.4	
86.1	-67.5	27.7	24.7	17.9	29.6		34.7	25.8	
	16.8	99.0	107.3	125.9	65.6		99.5	71.7	
(20)	5.1	(57) 13.6	(69) 21.0	(14) 22.1	(12) 26.7	EBIT/Interest	(189) 23.1	(134) 18.2	
	-.4	2.4	5.4	1.8	7.7		4.9	4.4	
			69.9				21.7	22.6	
		(11) 5.7				Net Profit + Depr., Dep., Amort./Cur. Mat. L/T/D	(39) 8.2	(18) 7.1	
			2.4				3.1	2.2	
.0	.1	.1	.1	.2	.2		.1	.1	
.2	.9	.2	.3	.3	.4	Fixed/Worth	.3	.3	
-1.3	5.6	.9	.7	.7	.6		.8	1.0	
.4	.4	.6	.9	.7	.9		.8	.7	
.7	2.2	1.8	1.9	2.9	1.5	Debt/Worth	1.8	2.0	
-3.4	NM	4.0	4.0	4.6	3.1		4.5	5.4	
	106.3	78.8	54.6	42.9	44.9		69.1	59.7	
(19)	60.7	(62) 26.5	(84) 32.3	25.1	(13) 22.2	% Profit Before Taxes/Tangible Net Worth	(212) 32.7	(169) 31.9	
	-1.8	8.6	16.1	11.8	15.5		12.0	10.0	
94.4	43.6	22.2	20.3	12.4	17.9		20.3	20.0	
51.7	15.3	12.1	12.1	6.1	10.1	% Profit Before Taxes/Total Assets	9.5	7.6	
12.7	-3.6	3.8	4.8	2.2	5.3		3.6	2.3	
UND	632.9	101.0	162.8	65.9	71.9		113.5	125.3	
319.1	23.2	38.1	35.6	28.0	30.6	Sales/Net Fixed Assets	39.5	26.6	
29.1	11.5	18.2	7.3	5.0	6.7		14.2	10.5	
15.8	6.4	4.4	3.2	2.6	3.1		4.1	3.6	
7.7	4.2	2.8	2.4	2.0	1.9	Sales/Total Assets	3.1	2.6	
3.0	1.9	2.0	1.9	1.5	1.2		2.3	1.8	
	.1	.3	.2	.2	.3		.3	.3	
(11)	.7	(42) .5	(73) .7	(17) .4	(11) .6	% Depr., Dep., Amort./Sales	(170) .6	(129) .9	
	3.7	1.2	2.6	1.8	1.6		1.6	2.3	
	.9	.9	.3				.7	1.1	
(10)	1.7	(22) 1.5	(17) .6			% Officers', Directors' Owners' Comp/Sales	(74) 2.0	(55) 1.9	
	5.4	2.5	1.7				3.7	4.0	
33920M	232481M	1118475M	5539288M	2541534M	4997482M	Net Sales ($)	13401435M	11340419M	
2736M	32396M	369229M	2060632M	1221634M	2432337M	Total Assets ($)	4731445M	4406278M	

© RMA 2024

M = $ thousand   MM = $ million
See Pages viii through xx for Explanation of Ratios and Data

CONSTRUCTION-GENERAL—Industrial Building Construction NAICS 236210

Comparative Historical Data | Current Data Sorted by Sales

Comparative Historical Data			Type of Statement	Current Data Sorted by Sales						
28	27	37	Unqualified				4	33	
30	35	38	Reviewed				3	10	25
7	7	2	Compiled			1	1		
37	25	23	Tax Returns	1	3	7	4	2	13
87	112	121	Other	4	9	16	16	30	55
4/1/21-3/31/22	4/1/22-3/31/23	4/1/23-3/31/24		36 (4/1-9/30/23)			185 (10/1/23-3/31/24)		
ALL	ALL	ALL		0-1MM	1-3MM	3-5MM	5-10MM	10-25MM	25MM & OVER
189	206	221	NUMBER OF STATEMENTS	5	12	8	24	46	126
%	%	%	ASSETS	%	%	%	%	%	%
23.7	21.6	24.4	Cash & Equivalents	44.8	17.1		24.2	22.7	
39.0	39.8	40.5	Trade Receivables (net)	16.8	43.4		41.7	43.7	
4.8	3.8	2.2	Inventory	.9	2.6		3.5	1.9	
9.0	11.1	8.4	All Other Current	.9	5.2		8.6	10.0	
76.4	76.3	75.6	Total Current	63.4	68.3		78.0	78.3	
16.7	14.6	15.7	Fixed Assets (net)	31.6	16.3		13.6	14.2	
1.9	2.4	2.2	Intangibles (net)	2.8	.8		2.9	2.3	
5.1	6.6	6.5	All Other Non-Current	2.2	14.6		5.5	5.3	
100.0	100.0	100.0	Total	100.0	100.0		100.0	100.0	
			LIABILITIES						
5.9	6.2	5.2	Notes Payable-Short Term	7.8	16.4		5.3	2.9	
2.0	1.1	1.7	Cur. Mat.-L.T.D.	1.5	2.3		1.8	1.6	
24.8	24.0	25.9	Trade Payables	5.3	22.6		25.0	30.7	
.3	.1	.1	Income Taxes Payable	.8	.2		.0	.1	
16.8	17.9	17.2	All Other Current	10.8	19.0		14.7	18.8	
49.8	49.3	50.2	Total Current	26.2	60.5		46.9	53.9	
11.5	10.8	10.7	Long-Term Debt	25.2	14.8		11.3	8.2	
.1	.2	.1	Deferred Taxes	.2	.0		.0	.1	
5.0	2.0	2.9	All Other Non-Current	21.9	2.5		1.3	1.7	
33.6	37.7	36.2	Net Worth	26.5	22.2		40.4	36.1	
100.0	100.0	100.0	Total Liabilities & Net Worth	100.0	100.0		100.0	100.0	
			INCOME DATA						
100.0	100.0	100.0	Net Sales	100.0	100.0		100.0	100.0	
19.7	20.3	19.5	Gross Profit	36.3	28.5		18.7	14.8	
14.6	14.1	14.0	Operating Expenses	24.9	26.2		12.8	9.8	
5.1	6.2	5.5	Operating Profit	11.3	2.4		6.0	5.0	
-1.5	-.3	-.1	All Other Expenses (net)	1.8	-.5		-.5	-.1	
6.6	6.5	5.6	Profit Before Taxes	9.5	2.8		6.4	5.1	
			RATIOS						
2.9	2.6	2.5		5.5	2.1		3.2	1.9	
1.5	1.7	1.5	Current	3.3	1.3		1.7	1.4	
1.2	1.2	1.2		2.1	.9		1.3	1.2	
2.1	2.0	2.0		5.1	1.8		3.0	1.7	
1.3	1.2	1.3	Quick	2.9	1.2		1.4	1.2	
1.0	.9	1.0		1.5	.8		1.0	1.0	
27 13.4	30 12.1	32 11.5		0 UND	31 11.7		35 10.5	38 9.5	
53 6.9	56 6.5	55 6.6	Sales/Receivables	14 26.6	49 7.5		54 6.7	60 6.1	
85 4.3	78 4.7	81 4.5		65 5.6	91 4.0		78 4.7	83 4.4	
0 UND	0 UND	0 UND		0 UND	0 UND		0 UND	0 UND	
0 UND	0 UND	0 UND	Cost of Sales/Inventory	0 UND	0 UND		0 UND	0 UND	
0 775.1	1 544.4	0 UND		0 UND	0 UND		0 999.8	0 999.8	
15 24.8	15 24.4	19 19.5		0 UND	13 27.3		22 16.7	24 15.2	
33 10.9	36 10.2	36 10.0	Cost of Sales/Payables	0 UND	38 9.5		34 10.7	41 8.8	
59 6.2	58 6.3	62 5.9		44 8.3	57 6.4		57 6.4	69 5.3	
	5.4	6.1		2.4	8.9		3.8	7.1	
5.2 9.4	8.7	11.1	Sales/Working Capital	5.9	19.8		8.0	11.3	
23.5	25.0	28.0		16.7	-81.5		25.2	27.8	
84.1	103.3	79.6			10.5		95.7	105.2	
(141) 21.7	(149) 25.1	(177) 15.6	EBIT/Interest	(19) 1.2	(39) 13.6	(101) 24.6			
7.2	6.5	3.5			-7.7		2.1	6.5	
35.2	15.9	22.4	Net Profit + Depr., Dep.,					14.8	
(20) 8.2	(30) 7.1	(29) 5.6	Amort./Cur. Mat. L/T/D					(20) 5.6	
3.3	3.3	1.5						1.8	
.1	.1	.1		.2	.1		.1	.1	
.3	.3	.3	Fixed/Worth	.6	.4		.4	.2	
.8	.8	.9		NM	1.9		1.3	.7	
.8	.8	.7		.4	.7		.5	1.0	
2.0	1.9	1.9	Debt/Worth	.6	2.8		1.9	2.0	
4.6	4.8	4.4		-12.3	28.3		6.8	4.1	
66.2	68.0	64.2	% Profit Before Taxes/Tangible		78.2		81.1	61.4	
(174) 35.8	(187) 33.4	(202) 32.3	Net Worth	(19) 33.9	(42) 23.5	(120) 34.1			
15.6	15.7	14.6			-14.6		8.1	17.6	
23.8	20.3	21.9	% Profit Before Taxes/Total	42.0	20.1		24.5	20.3	
12.0	11.3	11.9	Assets	12.3	9.3		10.7	11.9	
5.2	4.7	3.9		2.8	-8.0		2.8	4.9	
126.7	110.0	129.4		249.0	73.7		103.5	158.0	
36.0	33.2	36.0	Sales/Net Fixed Assets	11.4	25.2		45.7	41.7	
12.2	12.5	11.0		1.7	14.6		12.6	11.1	
3.5	3.6	3.7		7.1	5.3		3.4	3.5	
2.6	2.5	2.7	Sales/Total Assets	2.2	3.6		2.6	2.7	
1.8	1.8	1.9		.7	1.7		2.0	2.0	
.3	.3	.2			.1		.3	.2	
(142) .7	(151) .7	(157) .6	% Depr., Dep., Amort./Sales	(13) 1.1	(34) .6	(102) .4			
1.9	1.8	1.9			2.1		2.1	1.7	
.9	.8	.6					.9	.3	
(64) 2.0	(53) 2.0	(53) 1.3	% Officers', Directors'		(16) 1.7	(22) .6			
3.7	4.8	2.7	Owners' Comp/Sales					2.4	1.2
8365464M	16842848M	14463180M	Net Sales ($)	2426M	22096M	31417M	173312M	785120M	13448809M
3563976M	6018691M	6118964M	Total Assets ($)	2289M	17961M	28653M	86468M	380023M	5603570M

M = $ thousand MM = $ million
See Pages viii through xx for Explanation of Ratios and Data

© RMA 2024

CONSTRUCTION-GENERAL—Commercial and Institutional Building Construction NAICS 236220

Current Data Sorted by Assets | Comparative Historical Data

0-500M	500M-2MM	2-10MM	10-50MM	50-100MM	100-250MM		4/1/19-3/31/20 ALL	4/1/20-3/31/21 ALL
1	2	16	81	50	58	Type of Statement		
1	9	74	122	10	6	Unqualified	194	128
2	2	12	8	1	1	Reviewed	310	153
14	22	44	18			Compiled	26	17
25	60	152	159	46	28	Tax Returns	158	78
	164 (4/1-9/30/23)		860 (10/1/23-3/31/24)			Other	475	345
43	95	298	388	107	93	NUMBER OF STATEMENTS	1163	721
%	%	%	%	%	%	ASSETS	%	%
35.5	23.8	22.7	22.8	26.3	22.6	Cash & Equivalents	23.4	28.7
15.7	39.3	43.8	48.4	45.1	47.6	Trade Receivables (net)	43.8	40.7
5.5	1.7	2.3	2.2	1.2	1.0	Inventory	2.6	2.4
3.2	6.5	10.0	10.6	9.6	11.6	All Other Current	9.4	9.5
59.9	71.2	78.7	84.0	82.2	82.8	Total Current	79.2	81.2
29.0	18.0	12.3	9.4	8.5	10.2	Fixed Assets (net)	13.1	10.8
2.1	4.4	2.4	1.5	3.2	2.7	Intangibles (net)	2.0	2.9
8.9	6.4	6.6	5.1	6.1	4.3	All Other Non-Current	5.8	5.1
100.0	100.0	100.0	100.0	100.0	100.0	Total	100.0	100.0
						LIABILITIES		
13.6	5.8	3.8	2.1	1.5	1.2	Notes Payable-Short Term	5.5	5.6
7.2	1.9	1.7	1.6	1.2	1.4	Cur. Mat.-L.T.D.	1.7	2.1
10.8	22.2	26.7	38.8	38.6	43.9	Trade Payables	32.0	30.4
.0	.2	.5	.1	.1	.1	Income Taxes Payable	.2	.1
16.8	15.2	15.7	18.6	23.6	22.3	All Other Current	17.3	17.1
48.3	45.3	48.3	61.2	64.9	68.8	Total Current	56.6	55.3
22.5	15.8	9.7	5.3	6.8	5.6	Long-Term Debt	7.5	9.4
.0	.0	.2	.1	.1	.2	Deferred Taxes	.2	.2
5.6	4.6	1.9	2.1	1.9	4.2	All Other Non-Current	2.1	2.6
23.4	34.3	39.8	31.3	26.2	21.2	Net Worth	33.6	32.6
100.0	100.0	100.0	100.0	100.0	100.0	Total Liabilities & Net Worth	100.0	100.0
						INCOME DATA		
100.0	100.0	100.0	100.0	100.0	100.0	Net Sales	100.0	100.0
39.4	28.0	21.6	13.0	12.5	9.5	Gross Profit	17.9	17.2
31.6	22.5	15.3	8.4	7.7	6.1	Operating Expenses	13.1	13.2
7.8	5.5	6.3	4.6	4.7	3.4	Operating Profit	4.8	4.0
-.6	.1	-.1	-.3	-.1	.0	All Other Expenses (net)	.1	-.9
8.3	5.4	6.4	4.9	4.9	3.4	Profit Before Taxes	4.8	4.9
						RATIOS		
6.0	3.5	2.6	1.7	1.4	1.3		1.9	2.1
2.6	1.7	1.7	1.3	1.2	1.2	Current	1.3	1.4
.5	1.1	1.2	1.2	1.1	1.1		1.1	1.2
3.8	2.8	2.3	1.5	1.2	1.2		1.7	1.8
1.7	1.5	1.4	1.2	1.1	1.0	Quick	1.2	1.2
.4	1.0	1.0	1.0	.9	.9		.9	1.0
0 UND	2 218.0	35 10.4	49 7.5	52 7.0	53 6.9		33 11.2	31 11.8
0 UND	34 10.7	56 6.5	65 5.6	64 5.7	72 5.1	Sales/Receivables	54 6.8	51 7.2
19 19.3	70 5.2	81 4.5	83 4.4	81 4.5	87 4.2		74 4.9	73 5.0
0 UND	0 UND	0 UND	0 UND	0 UND	0 UND		0 UND	0 UND
0 UND	0 UND	0 UND	0 UND	0 UND	0 UND	Cost of Sales/Inventory	0 UND	0 UND
0 UND	0 UND	0 UND	0 UND	0 999.8	0 996.7		0 UND	0 UND
0 UND	0 886.6	22 16.8	38 9.7	44 8.3	51 7.1		21 17.1	21 17.6
0 UND	21 17.8	35 10.3	57 6.4	61 6.0	69 5.3	Cost of Sales/Payables	41 8.8	41 8.9
6 57.1	52 7.0	60 6.1	76 4.8	78 4.7	83 4.4		64 5.7	61 6.0
13.0	7.2	5.1	6.8	10.3	13.9		7.9	6.5
33.0	15.0	10.2	13.4	17.1	22.7	Sales/Working Capital	15.3	12.6
-33.3	80.1	25.5	24.6	28.7	47.6		34.3	26.7
56.2	60.3	91.1	128.0	156.5	72.3		91.8	105.0
(28) 15.5	(70) 13.1	(221) 25.1	(278) 35.0	(75) 50.3	(65) 19.6	EBIT/Interest	(885) 22.7	(516) 30.0
-1.8	4.5	6.4	9.3	7.5	7.1		5.4	5.5
		24.4	27.2	21.7	18.8	Net Profit + Depr., Dep.,	18.9	20.0
	(34) 9.6	(92) 8.4	(36) 8.0	(18) 4.4		Amort./Cur. Mat. L/T/D	(176) 7.1	(93) 5.8
		4.1	3.3	2.6	2.2		2.8	1.6
.1	.1	.1	.1	.1	.1		.1	.1
.7	.3	.2	.2	.2	.2	Fixed/Worth	.2	.2
2.8	1.1	.5	.5	.5	1.0		.6	.5
.4	.6	.7	1.3	2.0	3.0		1.0	1.0
2.0	1.7	1.4	2.5	3.4	5.1	Debt/Worth	2.2	2.3
48.8	10.1	4.2	4.8	6.2	9.7		4.7	4.5
443.7	92.3	73.9	60.3	71.1	65.4		64.6	65.8
(35) 140.4	(75) 43.8	(272) 41.2	(371) 35.6	(101) 48.1	(85) 36.0	% Profit Before Taxes/Tangible Net Worth	(1072) 33.5	(666) 36.3
30.1	12.2	14.5	14.6	22.2	16.1		13.3	12.8
105.4	30.1	26.7	17.2	15.6	10.9		21.7	21.5
40.8	12.2	13.9	9.6	9.8	6.1	% Profit Before Taxes/Total Assets	10.5	9.7
7.8	2.5	3.8	3.5	4.9	3.1		3.5	3.4
379.5	199.3	135.8	144.8	182.5	194.8		168.4	209.8
43.7	57.5	42.3	57.3	67.9	64.6	Sales/Net Fixed Assets	55.3	63.1
20.8	15.1	16.9	22.9	17.8	15.0		18.7	20.1
15.6	6.5	3.9	3.4	3.3	3.1		4.1	3.9
9.1	4.2	2.7	2.7	2.6	2.7	Sales/Total Assets	3.0	3.0
4.3	2.1	1.9	2.0	1.9	1.9		2.3	2.2
.5	.3	.2	.1	.1	.1		.2	.2
(11) 1.1	(46) .7	(194) .6	(316) .3	(94) .2	(79) .2	% Depr., Dep., Amort./Sales	(867) .4	(514) .4
2.4	1.2	1.4	.7	.8	.8		1.2	1.1
2.5	1.5	.8	.4	.2			.7	.9
(20) 5.0	(38) 3.1	(112) 1.3	(102) .8	(21) .4		% Officers', Directors' Owners' Comp/Sales	(402) 1.5	(223) 1.8
9.5	6.2	2.7	1.4	.7			3.0	4.4
102602M	584255M	5069724M	24912560M	19034334M	35554319M	Net Sales ($)	76651039M	50008839M
10064M	122771M	1706944M	9039588M	7267073M	14129454M	Total Assets ($)	26413100M	17461696M

© RMA 2024

M = $ thousand MM = $ million
See Pages viii through xx for Explanation of Ratios and Data

CONSTRUCTION-GENERAL—Commercial and Institutional Building Construction NAICS 236220

Comparative Historical Data / Current Data Sorted by Sales

Comparative Historical Data			Type of Statement	Current Data Sorted by Sales					
152	180	208	Unqualified		1	1	5	8	193
194	221	222	Reviewed	1	2	2	16	52	149
14	20	26	Compiled	2		1	2	12	9
83	122	98	Tax Returns	3	11	14	24	27	19
357	442	470	Other	15	32	29	54	104	236
4/1/21-3/31/22 ALL	4/1/22-3/31/23 ALL	4/1/23-3/31/24 ALL		164 (4/1-9/30/23)			860 (10/1/23-3/31/24)		
				0-1MM	1-3MM	3-5MM	5-10MM	10-25MM	25MM & OVER
800	985	1024	NUMBER OF STATEMENTS	21	46	47	101	203	606
%	%	%	ASSETS	%	%	%	%	%	%
25.4	23.9	23.7	Cash & Equivalents	18.6	27.9	24.0	22.4	24.5	23.5
41.4	42.7	44.4	Trade Receivables (net)	23.1	24.5	36.0	37.7	41.3	49.5
2.7	2.5	2.1	Inventory	.1	7.5	3.5	4.2	2.7	1.1
10.4	10.8	9.7	All Other Current	5.9	3.8	7.1	8.5	10.4	10.4
79.8	79.8	80.0	Total Current	47.7	63.7	70.6	72.9	78.9	84.6
12.1	11.6	11.8	Fixed Assets (net)	35.6	21.6	17.0	16.5	12.3	8.9
2.6	2.7	2.4	Intangibles (net)	3.9	7.5	3.0	2.9	2.1	1.9
5.5	5.9	5.8	All Other Non-Current	12.6	7.2	9.4	7.7	6.7	4.7
100.0	100.0	100.0	Total	100.0	100.0	100.0	100.0	100.0	100.0
			LIABILITIES						
3.9	5.8	3.3	Notes Payable-Short Term	1.9	9.3	8.9	7.2	2.8	1.9
1.6	1.6	1.8	Cur. Mat.-L.T.D.	1.4	5.5	2.5	3.0	2.2	1.2
31.3	31.0	33.0	Trade Payables	9.3	11.5	19.1	20.6	26.7	40.8
.1	.2	.2	Income Taxes Payable	.0	.1	.1	.2	.6	.1
18.3	18.1	18.2	All Other Current	19.9	15.3	11.1	13.6	17.1	20.0
55.2	56.7	56.5	Total Current	32.6	41.7	41.8	44.6	49.4	64.0
7.4	9.5	8.4	Long-Term Debt	23.2	18.7	18.5	13.8	9.7	5.1
.2	.2	.1	Deferred Taxes	.0	.0	.2	.2	.2	.1
2.6	1.5	2.6	All Other Non-Current	.0	8.2	4.8	1.8	1.6	2.6
34.6	32.1	32.3	Net Worth	43.8	31.5	34.8	39.7	39.2	28.2
100.0	100.0	100.0	Total Liabilities & Net Worth	100.0	100.0	100.0	100.0	100.0	100.0
			INCOME DATA						
100.0	100.0	100.0	Net Sales	100.0	100.0	100.0	100.0	100.0	100.0
16.4	17.0	17.6	Gross Profit	49.1	42.9	26.0	28.2	19.3	11.7
12.7	13.0	12.4	Operating Expenses	33.7	33.5	21.5	22.2	13.5	7.4
3.7	4.0	5.2	Operating Profit	15.4	9.4	4.5	6.0	5.8	4.2
-1.6	-.3	-.2	All Other Expenses (net)	.3	.3	-.2	-.3	-.2	-.2
5.3	4.3	5.4	Profit Before Taxes	15.1	9.1	4.7	6.3	6.0	4.4
			RATIOS						
2.0	2.1	2.0		4.0	4.7	3.8	3.5	2.4	1.6
1.4	1.4	1.4	Current	1.9	2.9	1.8	1.7	1.7	1.3
1.2	1.1	1.1		.7	1.0	1.3	1.2	1.2	1.1
1.7	1.7	1.7		3.0	3.9	3.4	2.7	2.2	1.4
1.2	1.2	1.2	Quick	1.6	2.3	1.5	1.5	1.4	1.1
1.0	.9	1.0		.6	.6	.9	1.0	1.0	1.0
36 10.0	35 10.4	40 9.1		0 UND	0 UND	8 46.5	33 10.9	29 12.4	48 7.6
56 6.5	56 6.5	60 6.1	Sales/Receivables	43 8.5	15 24.8	59 6.2	57 6.4	54 6.7	63 5.8
76 4.8	81 4.5	81 4.5		96 3.8	74 4.9	111 3.3	78 4.7	79 4.6	81 4.5
0 UND	0 UND	0 UND		0 UND	0 UND	0 UND	0 UND	0 UND	0 UND
0 UND	0 UND	0 UND	Cost of Sales/Inventory	0 UND	0 UND	0 UND	0 UND	0 UND	0 UND
0 UND	0 UND	0 UND		0 UND	0 UND	0 UND	0 UND	0 UND	0 UND
26 14.0	21 17.3	25 14.4		0 UND	0 UND	2 164.5	12 29.9	21 17.7	38 9.7
46 8.0	45 8.1	49 7.4	Cost of Sales/Payables	1 272.5	8 43.9	31 11.7	31 11.8	36 10.2	57 6.4
69 5.3	69 5.3	73 5.0		47 7.8	51 7.2	66 5.5	65 5.6	62 5.9	76 4.8
6.4	6.7	6.9		2.9	3.9	3.5	5.1	5.5	9.2
12.1	13.2	14.4	Sales/Working Capital	7.5	12.4	9.1	10.6	10.2	16.2
26.1	32.6	30.5		-18.4	NM	33.0	26.7	27.4	30.2
120.4	106.4	104.0		40.1	42.2	32.4	50.4	80.8	148.2
(573) 31.2	(704) 25.1	(737) 27.9	EBIT/Interest	(10) 10.2	(29) 9.7	(38) 10.5	(76) 18.3	(157) 20.9	(427) 38.7
7.6	5.3	6.7		3.4	-1.6	1.0	5.3	7.0	8.9
30.1	24.2	22.7						28.0	23.1
(108) 9.2	(133) 9.2	(182) 8.1	Net Profit + Depr., Dep., Amort./Cur. Mat. L/T/D				(25) 8.3	(150) 8.1
3.0	2.8	2.9						3.4	2.5
.1	.1	.1		.2	.0	.0	.1	.1	.1
.2	.2	.2	Fixed/Worth	1.0	.4	.3	.3	.2	.2
.5	.6	.6		3.8	1.5	1.8	.9	.7	.5
1.0	1.0	1.0		.3	.3	.5	.5	.7	1.6
2.1	2.2	2.5	Debt/Worth	1.1	1.4	1.9	1.4	1.4	3.1
4.3	5.2	5.5		6.5	22.0	14.0	3.2	4.2	5.9
61.2	61.5	72.1		100.0	145.0	110.0	84.3	79.7	64.7
(754) 33.4	(893) 31.4	(939) 40.2	% Profit Before Taxes/Tangible Net Worth	(19) 18.6	(37) 37.6	(38) 19.0	(87) 35.6	(188) 42.7	(570) 39.7
13.5	10.2	15.5		5.1	7.2	7.0	8.8	21.5	18.0
20.1	18.7	20.8	% Profit Before Taxes/Total Assets	19.2	44.6	21.8	26.6	27.7	16.4
10.2	8.9	10.7		11.3	16.9	7.6	11.1	15.3	9.5
3.6	3.0	4.1		1.7	-.3	2.1	3.5	5.2	4.1
166.5	173.4	161.3		31.8	199.4	379.5	105.8	128.4	169.5
50.3	54.9	55.6	Sales/Net Fixed Assets	9.1	43.3	45.0	31.9	46.3	64.7
16.8	17.9	19.2		1.1	14.7	18.8	10.8	18.7	24.8
3.5	3.7	3.7		2.9	7.0	6.4	4.3	4.0	3.5
2.7	2.8	2.8	Sales/Total Assets	1.2	2.7	2.3	2.6	2.7	2.9
2.0	2.1	2.0		.4	1.3	1.4	1.7	2.0	2.2
.2	.1	.1		.8	.3	.4	.3	.1	
(607) .4	(677) .4	(740) .4	% Depr., Dep., Amort./Sales	(17) 1.1	(20) .8	(54) .9	(139) .6	(503) .3
1.2	1.1	.9		2.8	1.8	2.7	1.3	.7	
.7	.7	.6			3.1	2.1	1.1	.9	.3
(242) 1.6	(284) 1.5	(297) 1.2	% Officers', Directors' Owners' Comp/Sales	(14) 5.6	(22) 3.1	(46) 2.2	(73) 1.3	(136) .6
3.9	2.9	2.6			10.3	5.4	5.1	2.2	.7
58863448M	69617938M	85257794M	Net Sales ($)	8748M	92941M	185571M	755317M	3465566M	80749651M
21502595M	25339279M	32275894M	Total Assets ($)	40855M	50344M	95249M	400533M	1392982M	30295931M

M = $ thousand   MM = $ million
See Pages viii through xx for Explanation of Ratios and Data

© RMA 2024

CONSTRUCTION-GENERAL—Water and Sewer Line and Related Structures Construction   NAICS 237110

Current Data Sorted by Assets | Comparative Historical Data

0-500M	500M-2MM	2-10MM	10-50MM	50-100MM	100-250MM	Type of Statement	4/1/19-3/31/20 ALL	4/1/20-3/31/21 ALL
1		7	15	13	11	Unqualified	40	26
		16	24	3	3	Reviewed	60	25
	1	2	5			Compiled	16	5
2	3	12	3		1	Tax Returns	34	18
4	12	35	53	10	17	Other	140	90
7	**46 (4/1-9/30/23) 16**	**72**	**207 (10/1/23-3/31/24) 100**	**26**	**32**	**NUMBER OF STATEMENTS**	**290**	**164**
%	%	%	%	%	%	**ASSETS**	%	%
	23.9	18.7	13.9	13.2	12.2	Cash & Equivalents	15.6	20.7
	24.2	30.8	36.2	33.3	27.9	Trade Receivables (net)	36.1	29.4
	6.2	1.6	1.6	1.6	.8	Inventory	2.7	1.8
	12.0	7.8	12.8	14.0	12.7	All Other Current	9.6	9.1
	66.3	58.9	64.6	62.2	53.7	Total Current	64.0	61.0
	29.1	33.2	27.8	26.2	26.9	Fixed Assets (net)	28.1	29.9
	.7	2.8	1.6	6.8	15.0	Intangibles (net)	2.9	4.9
	3.9	5.1	6.0	4.7	4.4	All Other Non-Current	5.0	4.2
	100.0	100.0	100.0	100.0	100.0	Total	100.0	100.0
						LIABILITIES		
	8.7	2.5	2.8	1.8	2.9	Notes Payable-Short Term	4.9	5.9
	4.3	4.4	4.3	3.4	7.8	Cur. Mat.-L.T.D.	4.8	4.3
	7.1	12.1	14.7	14.5	12.6	Trade Payables	16.5	11.7
	.0	.6	.1	.0	.1	Income Taxes Payable	.2	.1
	16.2	8.9	17.0	18.2	14.0	All Other Current	13.8	11.3
	36.2	28.5	38.9	37.9	37.4	Total Current	40.2	33.4
	20.4	17.5	12.6	14.1	22.4	Long-Term Debt	15.6	21.1
	.4	.3	.8	.1	1.1	Deferred Taxes	.5	.3
	.0	2.0	1.4	2.6	3.6	All Other Non-Current	3.3	2.8
	42.9	51.7	46.3	45.3	35.5	Net Worth	40.3	42.4
	100.0	100.0	100.0	100.0	100.0	Total Liabilities & Net Worth	100.0	100.0
						INCOME DATA		
	100.0	100.0	100.0	100.0	100.0	Net Sales	100.0	100.0
	43.5	36.4	22.7	22.0	24.9	Gross Profit	24.9	29.9
	37.0	25.8	14.1	15.1	19.1	Operating Expenses	18.2	21.8
	6.5	10.6	8.6	6.9	5.9	Operating Profit	6.7	8.1
	-1.0	.9	-.4	.6	1.6	All Other Expenses (net)	.2	-.4
	7.5	9.7	9.0	6.3	4.3	Profit Before Taxes	6.5	8.5
						RATIOS		
	5.3	4.3	2.3	2.3	2.0		2.4	3.2
	1.7	2.3	1.7	1.8	1.6	Current	1.6	2.0
	1.0	1.3	1.3	1.3	1.2		1.2	1.4
	5.3	3.6	1.9	1.9	1.5		2.1	2.4
	1.4	1.8	1.5	1.2	1.1	Quick	1.3	1.6
	.4	1.1	1.0	1.0	.8		.9	1.1
0	UND	30	12.3	54	6.8	49	7.5	46	7.9		46	8.0	37	9.8
14	27.0	59	6.2	73	5.0	70	5.2	72	5.1	Sales/Receivables	61	6.0	61	6.0
72	5.1	81	4.5	96	3.8	94	3.9	85	4.3		85	4.3	79	4.6
0	UND	0	UND	0	UND	0	UND	0	UND		0	UND	0	UND
0	UND	0	UND	0	UND	0	UND	0	UND	Cost of Sales/Inventory	0	UND	0	UND
0	UND	0	UND	1	291.8	2	169.5	6	61.4		3	105.4	3	109.7
0	UND	10	34.8	23	16.2	24	15.1	30	12.1		19	19.2	15	23.9
4	91.0	27	13.4	35	10.5	33	11.2	40	9.2	Cost of Sales/Payables	34	10.6	28	13.2
16	22.3	44	8.3	50	7.3	57	6.4	66	5.5		52	7.0	46	7.9
	5.1	3.6	4.4	4.3	5.5		5.1	4.1
	15.1	6.4	7.0	5.9	7.5	Sales/Working Capital	9.0	6.6
	315.3	23.9	14.7	9.5	17.0		24.3	12.0
		78.1	54.6	60.0	20.1		34.2	44.9
	(64)	14.2	(88)	15.7	(22)	17.0	(29)	9.1	EBIT/Interest	(264)	12.3	(147)	14.0
		4.4	5.5	9.0	3.6		3.4	3.3
		15.6	10.3	20.6			9.1	5.8
	(16)	6.8	(32)	6.0	(11)	4.7		Net Profit + Depr., Dep., Amort./Cur. Mat. L/T/D	(69)	4.1	(29)	3.6
		3.2	2.3	3.0			1.8	1.4
	.0	.3	.3	.3	.6		.3	.3
	.4	.6	.6	.5	1.3	Fixed/Worth	.6	.6
	1.5	1.2	1.2	1.2	-9.1		1.2	1.3
	.2	.4	.7	.8	1.1		.7	.7
	.7	.9	1.1	1.2	2.9	Debt/Worth	1.3	1.2
	15.0	1.8	2.1	3.0	-17.8		2.9	2.6
	63.9	68.9	44.0	47.8	49.3		52.9	54.9
(14)	38.8	(68)	33.1	(98)	27.5	31.8	(21)	32.5	% Profit Before Taxes/Tangible Net Worth	(265)	24.5	(147)	30.5
	3.0	11.6	15.8	15.5	22.7		12.4	15.1
	38.1	29.2	21.1	14.7	14.7		20.0	26.5
	10.5	16.4	12.9	11.4	9.5	% Profit Before Taxes/Total Assets	10.2	12.5
	1.9	5.3	6.5	5.4	.5		3.7	4.2
	114.8	18.8	15.2	16.4	10.4		18.7	15.6
	11.4	7.3	7.6	6.8	6.4	Sales/Net Fixed Assets	8.7	6.3
	4.5	3.2	4.5	4.4	4.0		4.5	4.0
	3.9	2.5	2.2	2.1	1.9		2.7	2.3
	2.8	1.9	1.8	1.7	1.5	Sales/Total Assets	2.1	1.8
	1.3	1.3	1.4	1.2	1.1		1.5	1.3
		1.8	1.6	1.4	1.9		1.3	1.9
	(48)	3.4	(87)	2.6	(24)	2.7	(15)	2.8	% Depr., Dep., Amort./Sales	(235)	2.6	(131)	3.5
		7.3	4.3	5.2	4.6		4.9	5.5
		1.8	.9				1.2	1.2
	(27)	3.2	(23)	2.0			% Officers', Directors' Owners' Comp/Sales	(105)	2.4	(63)	2.7
		5.3	2.6				4.4	5.7
14058M	71388M	750762M	4582796M	3076740M	8112568M	Net Sales ($)	13228294M	6728451M
1686M	18740M	373998M	2566806M	1906358M	5279799M	Total Assets ($)	6847263M	3872080M

© RMA 2024   M = $ thousand   MM = $ million
See Pages viii through xx for Explanation of Ratios and Data

CONSTRUCTION-GENERAL—Water and Sewer Line and Related Structures Construction   NAICS 237110

Comparative Historical Data / Current Data Sorted by Sales

						Type of Statement						
	27		41		47	Unqualified			1	1	8	37
	33		40		46	Reviewed	1	2	4	13	26	
	5		10		8	Compiled			1	1	5	
	23		23		21	Tax Returns	3	1	9	6	2	
	96		107		131	Other	5	8	9	17	23	69
	4/1/21-3/31/22 ALL		4/1/22-3/31/23 ALL		4/1/23-3/31/24 ALL			46 (4/1-9/30/23)			207 (10/1/23-3/31/24)	
							0-1MM	1-3MM	3-5MM	5-10MM	10-25MM	25MM & OVER
	184		221		253	NUMBER OF STATEMENTS	6	13	12	32	51	139
	%		%		%	ASSETS	%	%	%	%	%	%
	18.0		18.0		16.0	Cash & Equivalents	22.6	26.9	22.0	16.9	13.2	
	30.0		30.3		32.4	Trade Receivables (net)	9.0	25.0	30.6	36.0	34.7	
	2.9		2.4		1.8	Inventory	1.1	1.7	1.5	1.3	1.5	
	8.4		9.6		11.2	All Other Current	4.8	5.8	4.2	11.0	13.7	
	59.4		60.3		61.4	Total Current	37.5	59.4	58.3	65.1	63.1	
	32.3		31.6		29.1	Fixed Assets (net)	50.2	32.8	35.1	27.8	25.5	
	4.1		2.9		4.2	Intangibles (net)	3.3	.3	1.8	2.7	5.9	
	4.2		5.2		5.3	All Other Non-Current	9.0	7.4	4.8	4.3	5.4	
	100.0		100.0		100.0	Total	100.0	100.0	100.0	100.0	100.0	
						LIABILITIES						
	4.2		5.3		3.1	Notes Payable-Short Term	5.6	6.3	2.6	3.6	2.6	
	3.9		4.0		5.5	Cur. Mat.-L.T.D.	22.2	4.3	5.6	3.4	4.9	
	15.2		14.2		13.3	Trade Payables	4.2	11.7	7.5	14.0	15.3	
	.1		.1		.2	Income Taxes Payable	.0	.0	1.2	.1	.1	
	12.4		10.8		14.6	All Other Current	15.7	8.9	9.7	12.6	16.4	
	35.8		34.4		36.7	Total Current	47.6	31.2	26.6	33.8	39.3	
	20.0		20.4		16.1	Long-Term Debt	37.1	17.0	17.3	14.8	14.5	
	.5		.5		.6	Deferred Taxes	.0	1.6	.0	.2	.8	
	1.9		2.1		1.9	All Other Non-Current	.1	.2	1.6	2.0	2.2	
	41.9		42.7		44.7	Net Worth	15.1	50.1	54.5	49.2	43.1	
	100.0		100.0		100.0	Total Liabilties & Net Worth	100.0	100.0	100.0	100.0	100.0	
						INCOME DATA						
	100.0		100.0		100.0	Net Sales	100.0	100.0	100.0	100.0	100.0	
	30.1		28.6		28.8	Gross Profit	49.0	41.6	35.5	34.7	20.9	
	24.2		22.8		20.3	Operating Expenses	39.1	31.2	25.2	24.9	13.8	
	5.8		5.8		8.5	Operating Profit	10.0	10.4	10.3	9.9	7.1	
	-2.0		.0		.3	All Other Expenses (net)	-.5	.1	.7	.3	.0	
	7.8		5.8		8.2	Profit Before Taxes	10.5	10.3	9.6	9.6	7.1	
						RATIOS						
	2.6		3.3		2.6		6.4	11.1	4.5	3.1	2.2	
	1.7		1.8		1.8	Current	1.2	2.2	2.4	2.0	1.7	
	1.2		1.3		1.3		.3	1.1	1.4	1.3	1.3	
	2.3		2.7		2.3		4.3	7.7	4.3	2.9	1.7	
	1.2	(220)	1.4		1.5	Quick	1.2	1.7	2.1	1.6	1.3	
	.9		1.0		1.0		.1	1.0	1.2	1.0	.9	
41	8.9	36	10.0	45	8.1		0 UND	5 70.2	15 24.8	40 9.2	52 7.0	
57	6.4	59	6.2	66	5.5	Sales/Receivables	0 UND	46 7.9	52 7.0	72 5.1	70 5.2	
85	4.3	85	4.3	89	4.1		61 6.0	85 4.3	83 4.4	96 3.8	89 4.1	
0	UND	0	UND	0	UND		0 UND	0 UND	0 UND	0 UND	0 UND	
0	UND	0	UND	0	UND	Cost of Sales/Inventory	0 UND	0 UND	0 UND	0 UND	0 UND	
6	59.0	1	459.1	1	348.7		0 UND	8 45.4	0 999.8	0 UND	3 132.1	
18	20.6	13	28.0	17	21.8		0 UND	2 225.2	2 219.2	22 16.6	25 14.6	
36	10.0	30	12.3	33	11.1	Cost of Sales/Payables	4 96.9	21 17.4	16 22.8	36 10.1	35 10.3	
54	6.7	50	7.3	50	7.3		15 23.9	68 5.4	27 13.3	46 7.9	56 6.5	
	4.9		4.7		4.3		4.1	3.4	3.6	3.8	4.9	
	8.3		8.1		7.0	Sales/Working Capital	25.5	6.5	6.0	6.1	7.0	
	19.9		17.7		18.2		-14.3	74.5	29.8	19.2	14.2	
	56.1		40.1		52.2		12.0		88.3	55.7	53.7	
(168)	15.5	(190)	12.7	(216)	13.7	EBIT/Interest	(10) 3.9		(29) 9.1	(43) 16.8	(123) 15.7	
	4.5		3.2		4.6		2.0		4.4	7.0	5.4	
	6.4		6.5		11.9	Net Profit + Depr., Dep.,				8.4	13.9	
(30)	3.6	(44)	3.1	(65)	5.2	Amort./Cur. Mat. L/T/D			(14) 5.0	(44) 5.2		
	1.7		1.5		2.3					2.8	2.1	
	.4		.3		.3		.5	.2	.1	.2	.3	
	.7		.7		.6	Fixed/Worth	1.5	.4	.6	.5	.6	
	2.0		1.3		1.3		NM	2.2	1.2	1.2	1.4	
	.7		.6		.6		.5	.3	.3	.5	.8	
	1.5		1.3		1.2	Debt/Worth	1.4	.8	.9	1.0	1.3	
	3.3		2.8		2.8		NM	2.5	1.7	2.0	3.0	
	59.7		46.8		52.6		77.1	74.0	77.5	57.6	48.3	
(165)	28.5	(205)	23.1	(232)	31.4	% Profit Before Taxes/Tangible Net Worth	(10) 18.0	(11) 31.8	(31) 34.4	(49) 32.1	(126) 31.3	
	11.4		9.0		15.1		8.6	2.9	10.8	12.5	18.2	
	23.6		19.8		23.7		47.0	41.5	31.3	25.2	19.5	
	12.3		9.4		13.0	% Profit Before Taxes/Total Assets	18.5	11.7	16.4	15.2	12.3	
	3.3		2.8		5.3		5.5	-4.0	5.4	5.4	6.0	
	11.7		14.7		15.8		13.8	12.6	22.9	23.7	14.7	
	6.4		6.8		7.7	Sales/Net Fixed Assets	4.2	7.8	6.4	8.6	7.7	
	3.8		4.1		4.4		1.7	3.3	2.7	4.1	4.8	
	2.4		2.5		2.3		6.0	2.6	2.6	2.5	2.2	
	1.8		1.9		1.8	Sales/Total Assets	2.0	1.6	2.0	1.8	1.8	
	1.3		1.5		1.3		.7	1.2	1.3	1.4	1.5	
	1.8		1.6		1.7				2.0	1.7	1.7	
(137)	3.4	(167)	3.1	(181)	2.8	% Depr., Dep., Amort./Sales		(20)	(35) 3.2	(109) 3.5	2.5	
	5.8		5.3		4.9				5.8	4.3	3.9	
	1.4		1.5		.9				2.7	.9	.4	
(71)	2.7	(75)	2.7	(71)	2.3	% Officers', Directors' Owners' Comp/Sales		(14)	(20) 3.2	(24) 1.6	1.1	
	4.4		4.8		4.0				5.9	2.9	2.4	
	7161347M		10801372M		16608312M	Net Sales ($)	2593M	26487M	47826M	230194M	869390M	15431822M
	4542526M		6263508M		10147387M	Total Assets ($)	5439M	20645M	31308M	130788M	601028M	9358179M

M = $ thousand   MM = $ million
See Pages viii through xx for Explanation of Ratios and Data

© RMA 2024

CONSTRUCTION-GENERAL—Oil and Gas Pipeline and Related Structures Construction NAICS 237120

Current Data Sorted by Assets | **Comparative Historical Data**

						Type of Statement		
		1				Unqualified	16	12
	1	2	4	5		Reviewed	5	3
		7				Compiled	5	2
	2	2				Tax Returns	9	1
	6	11	1	13	1	4	Other	40	39
	14 (4/1-9/30/23)		47 (10/1/23-3/31/24)				4/1/19-	4/1/20-
0-500M	500M-2MM	2-10MM	10-50MM	50-100MM	100-250MM		3/31/20	3/31/21
	9	14	23	6	9	NUMBER OF STATEMENTS	75 ALL	57 ALL
%	%	%	%	%	%		%	%

D		6.5	15.9			**ASSETS**		
A		6.5	15.9			Cash & Equivalents	16.2	21.3
T		43.7	31.2			Trade Receivables (net)	35.7	27.2
A		5.5	5.9			Inventory	3.6	3.8
		8.5	7.1			All Other Current	6.5	6.8
N		64.3	60.0			Total Current	62.0	59.0
O		23.4	25.5			Fixed Assets (net)	27.1	30.3
T		3.0	4.4			Intangibles (net)	6.5	3.8
		9.4	10.1			All Other Non-Current	4.5	6.9
A		100.0	100.0			Total	100.0	100.0
V						**LIABILITIES**		
A		8.4	7.0			Notes Payable-Short Term	5.9	7.3
I		10.0	7.0			Cur. Mat.-L.T.D.	3.4	4.7
L		10.8	15.4			Trade Payables	11.7	9.7
A		.2	.0			Income Taxes Payable	.1	.2
B		12.3	13.7			All Other Current	10.6	10.1
L		41.7	43.1			Total Current	31.8	32.0
E		14.4	9.6			Long-Term Debt	15.1	18.7
		.1	.3			Deferred Taxes	.6	.4
		3.9	1.0			All Other Non-Current	2.2	10.3
		39.9	46.0			Net Worth	50.3	38.5
		100.0	100.0			Total Liabilities & Net Worth	100.0	100.0
						INCOME DATA		
		100.0	100.0			Net Sales	100.0	100.0
		89.8	93.9			Gross Profit		
		89.8	93.9			Operating Expenses	91.5	92.5
		10.2	6.1			Operating Profit	8.5	7.5
		.9	.8			All Other Expenses (net)	.8	.8
		9.3	5.3			Profit Before Taxes	7.7	6.7
						RATIOS		
		3.2	4.2				3.2	3.2
		1.6	1.3			Current	2.0	2.3
		1.1	.9				1.5	1.3
		1.7	2.3				2.8	2.8
		1.3	1.3			Quick	1.6	1.8
		.8	.5				1.1	.8
	49	7.4	37	9.9			39	9.4	27	13.5
	69	5.3	57	6.4		Sales/Receivables	57	6.4	50	7.3
	83	4.4	76	4.8			74	4.9	70	5.2
						Cost of Sales/Inventory		
						Cost of Sales/Payables		
		4.0	4.1				5.2	4.7
		11.7	17.8			Sales/Working Capital	7.7	7.0
		NM	-12.9				13.0	18.3
		58.3	27.4				38.4	33.5
	(12)	9.8	(20)	8.7		EBIT/Interest	(70)	9.1	(48)	8.2
		1.9	1.6				2.4	-2.3
						Net Profit + Depr., Dep.,	12.2	5.1
						Amort./Cur. Mat. L/T/D	(14)	2.5	(12)	1.9
							.7	-.1
		.1	.2				.3	.3
		.8	.9			Fixed/Worth	.6	.7
		1.7	4.0				1.4	1.4
		.7	.3				.6	.6
		1.3	1.0			Debt/Worth	.9	1.2
		2.3	9.2				2.5	3.2
		83.8	44.7				63.8	61.5
	(12)	25.9	(20)	18.1		% Profit Before Taxes/Tangible Net Worth	(68)	30.3	(51)	25.7
		9.8	5.5				12.1	-2.5
		26.3	19.9				26.4	30.0
		11.5	9.7			% Profit Before Taxes/Total Assets	12.6	7.8
		2.8	2.9				2.7	-5.1
		49.8	14.6				24.0	22.5
		14.0	7.7			Sales/Net Fixed Assets	11.5	8.9
		5.6	5.4				5.9	4.0
		2.5	2.7				3.1	3.0
		2.2	2.0			Sales/Total Assets	2.3	2.0
		1.8	1.5				1.5	1.3
			2.3				1.0	1.3
		(13)	3.8			% Depr., Dep., Amort./Sales	(51)	2.0	(36)	2.8
			4.9				3.7	5.7
						% Officers', Directors' Owners' Comp/Sales	1.6	.9
							(12)	1.7	(11)	3.0
							3.7	6.1
35177M	195175M	942013M	841255M	2245771M		Net Sales ($)	7438261M	3752389M
13314M	87191M	477939M	453225M	1255610M		Total Assets ($)	3521415M	2245314M

M = $ thousand   MM = $ million
See Pages viii through xx for Explanation of Ratios and Data

© RMA 2024

CONSTRUCTION-GENERAL—Oil and Gas Pipeline and Related Structures Construction   NAICS 237120

Comparative Historical Data | Current Data Sorted by Sales

					Type of Statement						
	6		15	10	Unqualified				1	1	9
	8		10	10	Reviewed				2	2	6
	1		3	2	Compiled				1	1	1
	5		2	4	Tax Returns			1	2	2	
	30		29	35	Other	2	2		9	9	16
	4/1/21-3/31/22		4/1/22-3/31/23	4/1/23-3/31/24			14 (4/1-9/30/23)			47 (10/1/23-3/31/24)	
	ALL		ALL	ALL		0-1MM	1-3MM	3-5MM	5-10MM	10-25MM	25MM & OVER
	50		59	61	NUMBER OF STATEMENTS	2	3	1	8	15	32
	%		%	%	ASSETS	%	%	%	%	%	%
	14.6		15.8	11.7	Cash & Equivalents					12.7	9.0
	30.7		32.0	33.7	Trade Receivables (net)					29.7	36.1
	4.2		5.1	5.4	Inventory					7.1	3.6
	8.2		5.0	7.6	All Other Current					8.7	8.6
	57.8		58.0	58.4	Total Current					58.2	57.3
	27.8		26.8	28.2	Fixed Assets (net)					26.4	29.5
	6.2		4.3	3.4	Intangibles (net)					1.9	5.5
	8.2		10.9	10.0	All Other Non-Current					13.6	7.7
	100.0		100.0	100.0	Total					100.0	100.0
					LIABILITIES						
	6.2		6.3	7.0	Notes Payable-Short Term					6.4	6.3
	3.6		4.9	6.8	Cur. Mat.-L.T.D.					8.6	7.6
	11.2		13.1	11.5	Trade Payables					12.1	13.6
	.1		.2	.1	Income Taxes Payable					.0	.0
	13.0		8.8	11.7	All Other Current					13.0	12.4
	34.1		33.2	37.0	Total Current					40.2	39.9
	16.7		18.7	15.9	Long-Term Debt					13.0	15.7
	.9		.3	.2	Deferred Taxes					.0	.4
	3.1		3.5	2.2	All Other Non-Current					4.4	1.3
	45.3		44.3	44.7	Net Worth					42.3	42.7
	100.0		100.0	100.0	Total Liabilities & Net Worth					100.0	100.0
					INCOME DATA						
	100.0		100.0	100.0	Net Sales					100.0	100.0
	94.6		93.2	90.9	Gross Profit					92.6	94.2
	5.4		6.8	9.1	Operating Expenses					7.4	5.8
	-1.2		-.1	1.3	Operating Profit					2.3	.1
	6.6		6.9	7.8	All Other Expenses (net)					5.1	5.8
					Profit Before Taxes						
					RATIOS						
	3.6		3.3	3.1						4.3	2.5
	1.9		1.8	1.8	Current					1.8	1.4
	1.3		1.1	1.1						.9	1.1
	2.7		2.8	2.3						2.6	2.0
	1.6		1.4	1.4	Quick					1.3	1.2
	.9		.8	.8						.7	.7
31	11.9	37	9.8	36 10.2					42	8.7	41 8.9
54	6.8	57	6.4	58 6.3	Sales/Receivables				68	5.4	64 5.7
73	5.0	83	4.4	76 4.8					79	4.6	81 4.5
					Cost of Sales/Inventory						
					Cost of Sales/Payables						
	4.8		4.9	4.4						2.9	5.8
	8.4		9.3	8.0	Sales/Working Capital					6.7	17.2
	29.3		27.4	46.5						-22.8	95.8
	33.1		20.1	31.4						25.7	25.7
(46)	8.3	(55)	7.6	(54) 9.0	EBIT/Interest				(13)	2.6	(30) 8.7
	1.4		2.2	1.9						1.0	1.3
	9.2		4.2	7.2	Net Profit + Depr., Dep.,						
(10)	5.4	(12)	2.4	(10) 3.5	Amort./Cur. Mat. L/T/D						
	2.0		1.2	1.9							
	.3		.2	.3						.2	.5
	.6		.5	.7	Fixed/Worth					.8	.8
	1.7		1.2	1.6						1.7	3.6
	.5		.6	.6						.4	.7
	1.3		1.2	1.0	Debt/Worth					1.2	1.4
	3.2		3.0	3.1						1.8	8.2
	70.1		43.9	60.9	% Profit Before Taxes/Tangible					47.2	48.3
(46)	34.2	(53)	21.1	(53) 23.9	Net Worth				(13)	14.6	(27) 23.9
	5.7		5.0	10.0						6.0	9.6
	21.8		20.5	22.2	% Profit Before Taxes/Total					13.8	20.5
	11.2		8.4	10.5	Assets					10.3	9.6
	-2.4		2.0	3.3						2.2	3.6
	26.8		30.0	19.9						13.9	15.9
	9.0		8.4	8.5	Sales/Net Fixed Assets					6.5	7.6
	4.9		4.5	4.4						4.3	4.3
	2.7		2.7	2.8						2.3	2.9
	2.0		1.7	2.0	Sales/Total Assets					1.8	2.1
	1.5		1.1	1.5						1.5	1.5
	1.2		1.4	1.7						1.3	1.6
(33)	2.1	(40)	2.9	(36) 3.1	% Depr., Dep., Amort./Sales				(11)	3.2	(19) 3.1
	6.7		6.5	4.8						4.5	4.8
					% Officers', Directors'						
					Owners' Comp/Sales						
	2854958M		4217296M	4259391M	Net Sales ($)	1188M	5224M	3237M	57258M	276154M	3916330M
	1328153M		2501295M	2287279M	Total Assets ($)	3964M	3352M	980M	26826M	253093M	1999064M

© RMA 2024   M = $ thousand   MM = $ million
See Pages viii through xx for Explanation of Ratios and Data

CONSTRUCTION-GENERAL—Power and Communication Line and Related Structures Construction NAICS 237130

Current Data Sorted by Assets | Comparative Historical Data

						Type of Statement		
	1		4	5	3	Unqualified	15	12
	1	6	10	1	1	Reviewed	23	13
		2	2	1	1	Compiled	9	3
1	3	6	1			Tax Returns	19	5
1	5	24	31	11	11	Other	82	52
	26 (4/1-9/30/23)		106 (10/1/23-3/31/24)				4/1/19-3/31/20 ALL	4/1/20-3/31/21 ALL
0-500M	500M-2MM	2-10MM	10-50MM	50-100MM	100-250MM			
2	10	38	48	18	16	NUMBER OF STATEMENTS	148	85
%	%	%	%	%	%	ASSETS	%	%
	15.6	17.8	15.7	10.9	12.5	Cash & Equivalents	13.8	17.2
	25.0	32.3	26.9	25.4	26.8	Trade Receivables (net)	32.3	30.4
	5.7	3.0	2.3	2.4	5.4	Inventory	2.9	3.0
	6.4	6.2	9.4	13.1	7.7	All Other Current	8.6	8.5
	52.7	59.3	54.4	51.9	52.4	Total Current	57.6	59.0
	35.0	35.0	32.6	20.5	21.4	Fixed Assets (net)	27.5	28.6
	11.5	.8	5.9	22.5	22.4	Intangibles (net)	7.9	7.1
	.8	4.9	7.2	5.1	3.7	All Other Non-Current	7.0	5.3
	100.0	100.0	100.0	100.0	100.0	Total	100.0	100.0
						LIABILITIES		
	8.9	6.6	5.0	2.9	.4	Notes Payable-Short Term	7.0	6.1
	3.4	3.9	5.0	5.1	4.1	Cur. Mat.-L.T.D.	5.8	3.7
	5.2	8.8	9.3	7.8	9.3	Trade Payables	11.7	9.5
	.0	.0	.0	.0	.2	Income Taxes Payable	.2	.3
	13.7	5.0	6.7	14.4	11.4	All Other Current	10.0	12.5
	31.2	24.4	26.1	30.4	25.4	Total Current	34.7	32.1
	22.9	23.5	20.4	29.7	26.7	Long-Term Debt	21.9	22.9
	.0	.0	.8	.4	.7	Deferred Taxes	.5	.6
	.0	1.3	2.2	6.5	3.8	All Other Non-Current	3.5	4.2
	45.8	50.8	50.5	33.0	43.3	Net Worth	39.4	40.2
	100.0	100.0	100.0	100.0	100.0	Total Liabilities & Net Worth	100.0	100.0
						INCOME DATA		
	100.0	100.0	100.0	100.0	100.0	Net Sales	100.0	100.0
	66.0	39.6	30.3	27.9	27.5	Gross Profit	32.7	35.0
	52.5	31.5	20.7	18.7	18.6	Operating Expenses	24.2	27.7
	13.5	8.2	9.6	9.2	8.9	Operating Profit	8.5	7.3
	1.2	-.3	1.4	3.7	1.1	All Other Expenses (net)	1.1	-.1
	12.3	8.4	8.3	5.5	7.8	Profit Before Taxes	7.5	7.4
						RATIOS		
	4.2	3.5	3.6	2.6	3.0		3.3	3.8
	1.7	2.6	1.8	1.8	2.0	Current	1.8	1.9
	.9	1.6	1.4	1.4	1.7		1.2	1.2
	3.8	3.3	2.9	1.8	2.1		2.5	3.3
	1.6	2.2	1.5	1.3	1.5	Quick	1.4	1.5
	.3	1.4	1.0	1.0	1.2		.9	.9
	0 UND	24 15.0	37 9.8	45 8.2	40 9.2		33 10.9	30 12.0
	20 17.9	47 7.7	50 7.3	56 6.5	60 6.1	Sales/Receivables	61 6.0	54 6.7
	111 3.3	76 4.8	76 4.8	69 5.3	79 4.6		79 4.6	78 4.7
	0 UND	0 UND	0 UND	0 UND	0 UND		0 UND	0 UND
	0 UND	0 UND	0 UND	0 UND	3 142.3	Cost of Sales/Inventory	0 UND	0 UND
	35 10.3	0 UND	10 38.2	1 257.3	34 10.8		5 76.7	6 63.1
	0 UND	1 280.2	8 44.3	14 26.1	20 18.4		9 39.1	9 38.7
	0 UND	21 17.0	23 15.7	19 19.1	28 13.0	Cost of Sales/Payables	23 16.1	20 18.1
	37 9.8	43 8.5	42 8.6	31 11.7	41 8.9		43 8.5	33 11.1
	4.5	4.2	4.3	5.1	3.4		5.1	3.9
	20.2	7.6	7.8	9.3	6.0	Sales/Working Capital	9.0	7.1
	-187.4	13.7	21.0	12.9	8.8		23.1	20.6
		91.6	28.1	15.6	19.1		36.7	32.2
	(33)	16.3 (43)	5.7 (15)	3.0 (15)	5.3	EBIT/Interest	(138) 10.1	(75) 15.2
		1.6	1.1	1.4	.9		2.8	3.2
			5.9				6.7	14.4
		(15) 2.3				Net Profit + Depr., Dep., Amort./Cur. Mat. L/T/D	(17) 2.9	(19) 4.5
			.9				1.3	1.9
	.4	.3	.3	.2	.5		.3	.3
	.9	.7	.8	NM	1.0	Fixed/Worth	.7	.7
	NM	1.8	1.8	-1.0	-2.2		1.8	2.2
	.6	.4	.5	.6	1.0		.7	.5
	1.6	.8	1.1	NM	2.3	Debt/Worth	1.6	1.7
	NM	2.5	2.9	-3.4	-12.2		7.9	6.1
		61.3	48.3		41.4		72.2	61.1
	(36)	25.6 (45)	26.0	(10)	26.0	% Profit Before Taxes/Tangible Net Worth	(124) 38.8	(68) 39.3
		.6	9.0		8.1		13.4	15.7
	57.7	37.1	25.3	20.5	16.1		25.3	23.7
	24.1	12.3	9.5	9.9	11.3	% Profit Before Taxes/Total Assets	12.6	12.7
	-2.5	.3	1.4	.4	1.0		3.8	6.3
	29.2	15.7	13.6	13.6	17.6		24.7	17.1
	6.6	7.3	6.6	9.0	10.5	Sales/Net Fixed Assets	8.9	8.6
	2.3	4.6	3.2	6.6	4.4		4.5	4.6
	3.3	3.2	2.2	1.9	2.1		2.8	2.4
	2.0	2.3	1.7	1.7	1.4	Sales/Total Assets	1.9	1.9
	1.3	1.7	1.3	1.3	1.0		1.4	1.4
		1.6	2.6	1.1			1.7	1.5
	(23)	3.3 (41)	3.8 (13)	4.2		% Depr., Dep., Amort./Sales	(106) 3.7	(62) 3.3
		6.1	5.6	7.0			6.7	6.5
		1.9	.7				1.1	.6
	(15)	2.5 (11)	1.7			% Officers', Directors' Owners' Comp/Sales	(46) 2.8	(22) 3.0
		4.1	1.9				5.1	5.9
1004M	43391M	564964M	2138251M	1952666M	3924307M	Net Sales ($)	9152920M	5921619M
381M	12914M	213767M	1206025M	1215923M	2824342M	Total Assets ($)	5284993M	3421929M

M = $ thousand   MM = $ million
See Pages viii through xx for Explanation of Ratios and Data

© RMA 2024

CONSTRUCTION-GENERAL—Power and Communication Line and Related Structures Construction NAICS 237130

Comparative Historical Data / Current Data Sorted by Sales

				Type of Statement						
	6	15	13	Unqualified				1	1	11
	10	17	19	Reviewed		1		2	3	12
	4	8	6	Compiled						4
	12	9	11	Tax Returns	1	1		4	3	2
	68	77	83	Other	2	4	3	9	17	48
	4/1/21-3/31/22 ALL	4/1/22-3/31/23 ALL	4/1/23-3/31/24 ALL		0-1MM	26 (4/1-9/30/23) 1-3MM	3-5MM	106 (10/1/23-3/31/24) 5-10MM	10-25MM	25MM & OVER
	100	126	132	NUMBER OF STATEMENTS	3	7	5	15	25	77
	%	%	%	ASSETS	%	%	%	%	%	%
	18.0	13.8	15.5	Cash & Equivalents				20.4	20.3	14.2
	31.2	31.9	28.1	Trade Receivables (net)				35.0	28.4	28.1
	2.5	2.5	3.1	Inventory				2.3	1.1	3.0
	6.5	9.4	8.4	All Other Current				2.2	8.4	10.4
	58.2	57.6	55.1	Total Current				59.9	58.2	55.6
	27.1	29.2	30.3	Fixed Assets (net)				33.0	35.7	25.7
	8.2	7.5	9.1	Intangibles (net)				1.7	1.2	13.6
	6.5	5.6	5.6	All Other Non-Current				5.4	4.9	5.1
	100.0	100.0	100.0	Total				100.0	100.0	100.0
				LIABILITIES						
	5.9	6.2	5.5	Notes Payable-Short Term				6.1	3.2	4.3
	4.9	5.0	4.5	Cur. Mat.-L.T.D.				3.9	5.3	4.5
	7.9	10.4	8.6	Trade Payables				6.6	10.7	9.1
	.3	.1	.0	Income Taxes Payable				.0	.0	.1
	9.6	8.5	8.3	All Other Current				8.5	4.5	9.5
	28.7	30.3	27.0	Total Current				25.1	23.8	27.5
	21.9	24.3	23.4	Long-Term Debt				12.2	29.6	23.1
	.4	.6	.4	Deferred Taxes				.0	1.0	.4
	2.0	3.1	2.5	All Other Non-Current				1.7	1.2	2.9
	47.1	41.7	46.7	Net Worth				61.0	44.5	46.0
	100.0	100.0	100.0	Total Liabilities & Net Worth				100.0	100.0	100.0
				INCOME DATA						
	100.0	100.0	100.0	Net Sales				100.0	100.0	100.0
	35.1	31.1	35.6	Gross Profit				48.3	39.5	28.0
	27.3	23.3	26.2	Operating Expenses				35.3	33.0	19.5
	7.8	7.8	9.4	Operating Profit				13.1	6.5	8.5
	-1.6	.1	1.1	All Other Expenses (net)				-1.0	.8	1.5
	9.4	7.6	8.2	Profit Before Taxes				14.1	5.7	7.0
				RATIOS						
	3.6	3.3	3.3					3.3	5.1	3.1
	2.3	2.0	1.9	Current				2.7	1.9	1.9
	1.5	1.3	1.5					1.7	1.5	1.6
	3.2	2.7	2.8					3.3	4.2	2.6
	2.0	1.4	1.6	Quick				2.3	1.9	1.5
	1.2	1.0	1.1					1.5	1.3	1.1
29	12.5	29 12.4	31 11.7		29	12.5	38 9.7	36 10.0		
59	6.2	55 6.6	52 7.0	Sales/Receivables	53	6.9	50 7.3	54 6.7		
76	4.8	73 5.0	76 4.8		85	4.3	89 4.1	73 5.0		
0	UND	0 UND	0 UND		0	UND	0 UND	0 UND		
0	UND	0 UND	0 UND	Cost of Sales/Inventory	0	UND	0 UND	0 UND		
1	287.3	4 86.2	4 100.1		0	UND	0 UND	10 37.3		
4	85.3	8 48.2	7 50.0		3	118.1	4 103.1	14 26.5		
18	19.8	21 17.4	22 16.3	Cost of Sales/Payables	28	12.9	30 12.2	21 17.0		
31	11.7	36 10.0	40 9.1		47	7.7	55 6.6	34 10.8		
	4.3	5.1	4.3					3.5	4.0	5.0
	6.8	8.3	7.8	Sales/Working Capital				6.1	8.2	8.3
	16.8	25.7	14.5					8.2	23.5	12.0
	54.8	35.7	28.7					175.4	39.4	23.7
(84)	14.5	(112) 12.7	(115) 5.8	EBIT/Interest	(14)	27.5	(22) 9.1	(69) 5.3		
	4.3	2.9	1.2					3.8	-.4	1.6
	7.8	4.6	5.0	Net Profit + Depr., Dep.,						5.1
(15)	4.8	(27) 2.2	(26) 2.3	Amort./Cur. Mat. L/T/D					(21) 2.3	
	2.8	1.6	1.0							.7
	.3	.3	.3					.3	.3	.3
	.7	.7	.8	Fixed/Worth				.5	.9	.9
	2.3	1.9	3.0					.8	2.3	3.8
	.5	.5	.6					.3	.4	.7
	1.0	1.3	1.3	Debt/Worth				.7	1.7	1.4
	6.2	4.8	4.3					.9	3.8	5.8
	78.1	73.5	58.7	% Profit Before Taxes/Tangible				58.1	58.5	65.6
(83)	44.4	(107) 38.3	(109) 31.2	Net Worth	(14)	27.2	(23) 21.1	(60) 31.9		
	19.3	15.6	9.0					2.3	-10.2	10.9
	32.5	28.1	26.7	% Profit Before Taxes/Total				33.1	35.5	24.5
	15.3	12.8	11.5	Assets				24.0	8.2	11.8
	6.9	4.3	1.4					4.1	-3.2	1.8
	20.8	18.1	15.2					15.6	14.3	18.9
	9.2	8.6	7.7	Sales/Net Fixed Assets				6.5	7.2	8.8
	4.3	4.3	4.1					4.8	4.1	4.9
	2.8	2.8	2.6					2.9	2.8	2.4
	1.9	2.2	1.8	Sales/Total Assets				2.2	1.9	1.8
	1.3	1.5	1.3					1.1	1.4	1.4
	1.7	1.8	1.8						1.5	1.9
(67)	3.5	(95) 3.1	(90) 3.4	% Depr., Dep., Amort./Sales				(20) 3.0	(54) 3.3	
	5.6	5.3	5.6						6.3	5.0
	1.6	.9	.8							.5
(27)	3.2	(36) 3.2	(30) 2.0	% Officers', Directors' Owners' Comp/Sales					(11) .8	
	6.6	5.7	3.8							1.9
	5521765M	7299336M	8624583M	Net Sales ($)	1812M	14797M	19445M	115232M	427246M	8046051M
	3512088M	3564908M	5473352M	Total Assets ($)	1095M	15730M	40389M	73054M	246301M	5096783M

M = $ thousand   MM = $ million
See Pages viii through xx for Explanation of Ratios and Data

© RMA 2024

CONSTRUCTION-GENERAL—Land Subdivision NAICS 237210

Current Data Sorted by Assets | Comparative Historical Data

							Type of Statement		
			1	2	2	6	Unqualified	21	6
		1	1	2	1	1	Reviewed	7	3
	1	4	4	1	2		Compiled	12	7
4	4	13	7	7	3		Tax Returns	60	31
2	17	35	36		6	7	Other	144	104
	15 (4/1-9/30/23)		143 (10/1/23-3/31/24)					4/1/19-	4/1/20-
0-500M	500M-2MM	2-10MM	10-50MM	50-100MM	100-250MM			3/31/20	3/31/21
								ALL	ALL
6	22	54	48	14	14	NUMBER OF STATEMENTS	244	151
%	%	%	%	%	%	ASSETS	%	%
	14.4	10.2	6.5	5.4	14.3	Cash & Equivalents	7.7	12.4
	7.1	8.1	8.3	3.5	11.3	Trade Receivables (net)	4.7	4.4
	22.0	27.3	30.9	38.6	15.4	Inventory	37.3	23.4
	11.5	3.5	4.2	.2	2.9	All Other Current	2.8	7.8
	55.0	49.2	49.8	47.7	43.9	Total Current	52.5	48.1
	36.6	37.7	35.8	26.8	21.4	Fixed Assets (net)	29.9	34.9
	1.4	1.3	3.0	1.7	7.4	Intangibles (net)	1.8	2.8
	7.1	11.9	11.4	23.8	27.3	All Other Non-Current	15.8	14.2
	100.0	100.0	100.0	100.0	100.0	Total	100.0	100.0
						LIABILITIES		
	6.8	12.0	8.7	10.9	11.5	Notes Payable-Short Term	13.9	13.4
	6.0	3.6	1.1	3.6	2.0	Cur. Mat.-L.T.D.	1.8	1.5
	2.1	2.5	4.2	2.4	5.4	Trade Payables	3.2	4.0
	.8	.0	.1	.0	.0	Income Taxes Payable	.0	.0
	7.7	9.3	13.8	12.2	14.0	All Other Current	19.3	12.2
	23.4	27.4	27.8	29.1	32.9	Total Current	38.2	31.1
	42.9	20.5	24.5	38.0	15.7	Long-Term Debt	23.6	24.1
	.0	.1	.0	.0	1.2	Deferred Taxes	.1	.1
	14.0	7.9	2.8	4.9	7.5	All Other Non-Current	7.0	9.0
	19.7	44.1	44.9	28.0	42.6	Net Worth	31.1	35.8
	100.0	100.0	100.0	100.0	100.0	Total Liabilities & Net Worth	100.0	100.0
						INCOME DATA		
	100.0	100.0	100.0	100.0	100.0	Net Sales	100.0	100.0
						Gross Profit		
	71.7	69.0	75.4	70.6	90.4	Operating Expenses	79.1	72.1
	28.3	31.0	24.6	29.4	9.6	Operating Profit	20.9	27.9
	10.6	6.5	6.1	5.9	4.3	All Other Expenses (net)	5.8	5.0
	17.6	24.5	18.5	23.5	5.3	Profit Before Taxes	15.1	22.9
						RATIOS		
	7.4	6.4	6.5	3.2	3.8		2.9	5.6
	1.8	2.3	1.8	1.4	1.4	Current	1.4	1.8
	1.0	.8	.9	.4	1.0		.8	1.0
	2.0	3.4	1.7	.9	2.3		1.2	2.5
	.7	.7	.6	.1	1.1	Quick	.3	.7
	.3	.1	.1	.0	.3		.0	.1
0	UND	0	UND	0	UND		0	UND	0	UND
0	UND	0	UND	4	101.0	0	UND	4	94.9	Sales/Receivables	0	UND	0	UND
10	35.9	16	23.2	21	17.8	1	250.3	83	4.4		7	51.6	9	40.3
						Cost of Sales/Inventory		
						Cost of Sales/Payables		
	2.4	.8	.8	1.1	1.7		1.1	1.3
	10.3	3.6	3.7	2.2	7.5	Sales/Working Capital	5.7	5.5
	NM	-13.0	-34.4	-9.6	NM		-13.9	337.2
	59.4		15.8	24.6		13.1		13.6	42.6
(13)	20.5	(31)	4.3	(26)	7.5		(10)	3.9	EBIT/Interest	(144)	4.6	(87)	9.4
	3.0		1.4	3.4		1.3		1.6	3.2
						Net Profit + Depr., Dep.,		
						Amort./Cur. Mat. L/T/D		
	.0	.0	.0	.0	.1		.0	.0
	1.2	.5	.8	.3	.3	Fixed/Worth	.2	.4
	54.7	2.1	2.5	2.4	1.6		2.4	2.2
	.2	.5	.4	1.2	.8		.9	.4
	4.6	1.2	1.3	3.3	1.6	Debt/Worth	2.3	1.6
	230.8	3.0	3.7	7.0	4.8		13.0	7.5
	222.2		52.9	35.2		33.3		28.7		41.7	47.5
(18)	59.5	(50)	15.6	(41)	17.7	(13)	29.2	(13)	6.6	% Profit Before Taxes/Tangible Net Worth	(208)	15.0	(131)	22.4
	12.9		1.6	4.1		7.8		1.2		2.6	7.1
	50.4	16.4	16.5	10.5	6.4		10.9	19.0
	9.3	7.1	5.4	6.2	2.6	% Profit Before Taxes/Total Assets	3.9	7.6
	2.6	.8	.4	2.9	.3		.2	2.3
	UND	UND	137.1	UND	269.7		UND	UND
	9.3	3.2	4.8	5.0	5.8	Sales/Net Fixed Assets	24.7	7.5
	1.1	.3	.3	.4	1.1		.6	.6
	2.9	.9	.9	.8	1.3		.9	1.1
	1.1	.3	.4	.3	.5	Sales/Total Assets	.4	.5
	.2	.1	.2	.1	.1		.2	.2
			1.4	.3				.6	.2
		(15)	9.2	(23)	1.8			% Depr., Dep., Amort./Sales	(89)	2.9	(59)	1.6
			23.7	9.0				10.5	7.3
						% Officers', Directors'	.8	1.5
						Owners' Comp/Sales	(20)	2.8	(21)	3.8
							12.3	7.0
3450M	45493M	215883M	812440M	465875M	1542763M	Net Sales ($)	2839275M	2163955M
1766M	26775M	304371M	1251864M	1002809M	2035037M	Total Assets ($)	5108954M	3850338M

© RMA 2024

M = $ thousand   MM = $ million
See Pages viii through xx for Explanation of Ratios and Data

CONSTRUCTION-GENERAL—Land Subdivision NAICS 237210

Comparative Historical Data | Current Data Sorted by Sales

Comparative Historical Data			Type of Statement	Current Data Sorted by Sales					
8	12	11	Unqualified	1				4	6
4	10	5	Reviewed			1			4
8	6	8	Compiled	2	2	1	1	1	2
48	48	31	Tax Returns	8	8	4	5	4	2
96	109	103	Other	24	21	11	21	14	12
4/1/21-3/31/22 ALL	4/1/22-3/31/23 ALL	4/1/23-3/31/24 ALL		15 (4/1-9/30/23)			143 (10/1/23-3/31/24)		
				0-1MM	1-3MM	3-5MM	5-10MM	10-25MM	25MM & OVER
164	185	158	NUMBER OF STATEMENTS	35	31	15	28	23	26
%	%	%	ASSETS	%	%	%	%	%	%
11.9	11.7	9.5	Cash & Equivalents	5.1	9.7	9.7	8.0	14.1	12.6
4.0	4.2	8.3	Trade Receivables (net)	7.0	6.3	7.3	3.3	11.7	15.1
30.7	35.2	27.1	Inventory	20.9	33.2	16.5	31.9	29.1	27.3
6.1	5.4	4.4	All Other Current	3.8	5.3	.8	6.4	3.0	5.2
52.8	56.6	49.2	Total Current	36.8	54.4	34.4	49.6	57.9	60.1
29.6	28.4	35.3	Fixed Assets (net)	53.9	35.7	42.8	35.1	20.4	18.6
2.4	1.1	2.3	Intangibles (net)	.2	1.0	4.9	.7	5.7	4.1
15.3	13.9	13.2	All Other Non-Current	9.2	8.9	18.0	14.5	16.0	17.2
100.0	100.0	100.0	Total	100.0	100.0	100.0	100.0	100.0	100.0
			LIABILITIES						
10.5	12.6	13.3	Notes Payable-Short Term	13.9	26.8	8.6	6.3	9.7	10.1
2.0	1.3	3.3	Cur. Mat.-L.T.D.	5.2	1.0	1.2	2.6	6.5	2.3
3.3	4.3	3.2	Trade Payables	1.8	1.8	1.3	1.4	3.6	9.5
.1	.0	.1	Income Taxes Payable	.0	.5	.0	.0	.1	.0
12.5	12.1	10.8	All Other Current	3.7	7.8	20.8	16.9	6.7	15.2
28.4	30.3	30.7	Total Current	24.6	38.0	32.0	27.2	26.6	37.2
26.4	26.8	26.0	Long-Term Debt	27.5	36.7	25.6	25.6	15.0	21.3
.1	.0	.1	Deferred Taxes	.0	.1	.0	.3	.2	.1
7.3	4.4	6.8	All Other Non-Current	9.2	7.9	.6	8.6	3.1	7.0
37.9	38.4	36.4	Net Worth	38.6	17.4	41.8	38.2	55.0	34.4
100.0	100.0	100.0	Total Liabilities & Net Worth	100.0	100.0	100.0	100.0	100.0	100.0
			INCOME DATA						
100.0	100.0	100.0	Net Sales	100.0	100.0	100.0	100.0	100.0	100.0
77.8	77.5	73.6	Gross Profit						
22.2	22.5	26.4	Operating Expenses	58.7	70.4	75.1	72.6	81.7	90.8
3.2	4.8	6.9	Operating Profit	41.3	29.6	24.9	27.4	18.3	9.2
19.0	17.7	19.5	All Other Expenses (net)	15.3	6.3	4.1	6.5	3.5	1.0
			Profit Before Taxes	26.0	23.4	20.8	20.9	14.8	8.2
			RATIOS						
8.4	6.0	5.7		3.2	13.8	6.7	5.6	7.6	4.5
2.4	2.0	1.7	Current	1.8	2.7	.8	1.6	3.1	1.5
1.1	1.0	.9		.4	1.0	.2	.3	1.4	1.0
2.5	2.0	2.3		1.9	1.6	1.7	2.3	6.5	1.4
(163) .9	(183) .5	.6	Quick	.5	.5	.3	.2	1.6	.8
.2	.1	.1		.2	.1	.2	.1	.2	.3
0 UND	0 UND	0 UND		0 UND	0 UND	0 UND	0 UND	0 UND	0 UND
0 UND	0 UND	0 UND	Sales/Receivables	0 UND	0 UND	0 UND	0 UND	8 45.3	6 59.4
10 36.5	4 92.4	14 26.5		18 20.4	0 UND	13 27.3	6 58.7	42 8.7	64 5.7
			Cost of Sales/Inventory						
			Cost of Sales/Payables						
.9	1.1	1.1		.6	.4	10.2	.9	1.2	2.7
3.4	3.6	4.8	Sales/Working Capital	4.3	3.3	-15.0	8.8	2.0	9.3
55.6	248.6	-30.6		-4.6	43.4	-.5	-3.3	5.1	39.7
40.5	28.7	24.0		5.6	10.8		26.6	39.3	25.7
(101) 10.3	(111) 6.7	(90) 5.9	EBIT/Interest	(16) 2.8	(13) 3.0		(18) 7.0	(15) 15.8	(20) 10.1
1.8	2.0	1.8		1.4	1.0		1.5	1.8	4.5
			Net Profit + Depr., Dep., Amort./Cur. Mat. L/T/D						
.0	.0	.0		.0	.0	.0	.0	.0	.0
.3	.2	.6	Fixed/Worth	1.2	.7	.6	1.2	.1	.3
2.2	1.8	3.0		5.2	7.8	5.2	3.6	1.4	1.5
.5	.5	.5		.7	.3	.6	1.0	.1	1.1
1.8	1.7	1.5	Debt/Worth	1.6	1.3	1.6	1.8	.8	1.8
8.5	5.8	4.6		8.1	6.8	5.4	3.9	1.7	7.4
50.5	51.3	43.0		40.7	44.1	61.1	62.8	34.4	48.3
(142) 21.9	(162) 20.7	(139) 19.1	% Profit Before Taxes/Tangible Net Worth	(31) 9.4	(26) 14.3	(12) 17.6	(25) 24.3	(22) 21.0	(23) 30.5
4.8	5.0	3.9		.4	2.9	2.8	8.4	.3	19.7
18.9	15.1	15.2		7.6	12.5	18.9	33.5	27.0	20.0
6.4	6.5	5.8	% Profit Before Taxes/Total Assets	3.5	5.0	5.3	9.2	7.6	8.6
.6	.6	.8		.4	-1.6	1.1	.3	.3	4.3
UND	UND	761.6		UND	UND	UND	114.0	144.2	798.1
11.0	13.5	4.3	Sales/Net Fixed Assets	.2	2.6	.7	9.6	20.2	12.7
.8	1.1	.4		.1	.3	.3	.5	1.3	5.4
1.0	1.3	1.2		.2	1.2	.6	1.1	1.2	2.1
.5	.5	.3	Sales/Total Assets	.1	.3	.3	.5	.6	1.2
.2	.2	.2		.1	.2	.2	.2	.3	.8
.3	.2	1.1		.2	1.2	.6	.3	.2	.9
(65) 1.7	(75) 1.6	(66) 4.2	% Depr., Dep., Amort./Sales	(15) 16.8	(10) 4.5		(13) 1.2	(11) 1.2	(13) 1.8
8.5	10.8	12.6		25.0	13.6		12.6	9.6	4.5
.6	1.5	1.0							
(18) 2.0	(20) 2.5	(14) 2.3	% Officers', Directors' Owners' Comp/Sales						
4.3	5.0	9.2							
2949718M	3339548M	3085904M	Net Sales ($)	15466M	57916M	57735M	192840M	348885M	2413062M
3688111M	4768650M	4622622M	Total Assets ($)	115579M	285415M	390490M	783271M	843446M	2204421M

© RMA 2024
M = $ thousand   MM = $ million
See Pages viii through xx for Explanation of Ratios and Data

CONSTRUCTION-GENERAL—Highway, Street, and Bridge Construction NAICS 237310

Current Data Sorted by Assets / Comparative Historical Data

0-500M	500M-2MM	2-10MM	10-50MM	50-100MM	100-250MM	Type of Statement	ALL 4/1/19-3/31/20	ALL 4/1/20-3/31/21
1	2	17	48	29	34	Unqualified	183	126
	3	21	53	8	3	Reviewed	129	58
2	12	6	5	1		Compiled	23	15
5	12	13	7			Tax Returns	60	26
	67 (4/1-9/30/23)	46	71	26	29	Other	317	157
			387 (10/1/23-3/31/24)				4/1/19-3/31/20	4/1/20-3/31/21
7	30	103	184	64	66	**NUMBER OF STATEMENTS**	712	382
%	%	%	%	%	%	**ASSETS**	%	%
	27.8	23.1	21.4	18.9	22.0	Cash & Equivalents	18.4	24.3
	23.6	32.5	29.3	29.1	23.4	Trade Receivables (net)	27.8	24.1
	2.4	2.9	4.4	3.2	4.1	Inventory	3.6	3.4
	2.3	7.4	7.3	8.1	6.5	All Other Current	6.2	6.5
	56.1	65.9	62.4	59.3	56.0	Total Current	55.9	58.2
	36.5	26.8	29.4	32.6	32.8	Fixed Assets (net)	35.7	33.9
	1.0	1.7	1.5	2.0	4.5	Intangibles (net)	2.4	2.4
	6.3	5.6	6.7	6.1	6.7	All Other Non-Current	6.0	5.5
	100.0	100.0	100.0	100.0	100.0	Total	100.0	100.0
						LIABILITIES		
	7.9	4.0	3.0	2.1	1.0	Notes Payable-Short Term	4.1	4.1
	4.7	4.1	3.9	4.5	3.7	Cur. Mat.-L.T.D.	4.8	4.6
	9.7	14.5	14.3	13.7	12.3	Trade Payables	13.6	10.8
	.1	.2	.3	.1	.3	Income Taxes Payable	.2	.1
	11.4	11.0	12.7	13.9	15.3	All Other Current	10.1	10.1
	33.8	33.9	34.2	34.2	32.6	Total Current	32.9	29.7
	30.1	14.3	12.0	13.5	10.9	Long-Term Debt	15.5	17.6
	.0	.2	.7	1.0	.9	Deferred Taxes	.8	.8
	.4	1.1	2.4	1.4	3.8	All Other Non-Current	2.9	3.5
	35.7	50.6	50.7	49.7	51.8	Net Worth	47.9	48.4
	100.0	100.0	100.0	100.0	100.0	Total Liabilities & Net Worth	100.0	100.0
						INCOME DATA		
	100.0	100.0	100.0	100.0	100.0	Net Sales	100.0	100.0
	39.1	24.8	19.8	17.6	15.7	Gross Profit	21.0	22.5
	34.7	17.6	12.2	9.4	7.9	Operating Expenses	15.1	16.5
	4.4	7.2	7.5	8.1	7.8	Operating Profit	5.9	6.0
	-.2	-.5	-.2	-.4	-.5	All Other Expenses (net)	.1	-1.1
	4.6	7.7	7.8	8.5	8.3	Profit Before Taxes	5.8	7.1
						RATIOS		
	4.8	3.8	2.8	2.4	2.3		2.7	3.3
	1.8	2.0	1.9	1.7	1.7	Current	1.7	2.0
	.9	1.4	1.4	1.3	1.3		1.3	1.4
	4.5	2.9	2.3	2.0	1.9		2.3	2.8
	1.7	1.7	1.5	1.4	1.2	Quick	1.4	1.6
	.9	1.2	1.1	1.1	1.0		1.0	1.1
0 UND	31 11.7	35 10.3	42 8.6	38 9.6			29 12.7	26 14.0
30 12.2	53 6.9	54 6.8	56 6.5	52 7.0		Sales/Receivables	49 7.5	42 8.6
56 6.5	81 4.5	76 4.8	85 4.3	65 5.6			70 5.2	66 5.5
0 UND	0 UND	0 UND	0 UND	0 UND			0 UND	0 UND
0 UND	0 UND	0 999.8	3 120.2	4 85.2		Cost of Sales/Inventory	1 620.8	0 999.8
3 132.0	4 88.4	13 28.2	12 31.0	20 18.7			10 35.5	11 33.0
0 UND	9 38.5	15 23.8	24 15.3	21 17.8			15 24.2	10 35.4
8 44.0	23 16.0	31 11.9	32 11.3	31 11.7		Cost of Sales/Payables	27 13.6	23 16.1
39 9.4	42 8.7	49 7.5	41 9.0	39 9.3			42 8.6	40 9.1
	5.1	4.4	4.1	4.6	4.0		5.0	3.6
	8.8	6.9	6.9	7.4	8.1	Sales/Working Capital	9.1	6.5
	-141.3	15.1	12.8	13.4	17.1		22.4	14.3
	7.9	67.0	42.6	75.7	73.2		30.1	40.8
(24)	2.9 (95)	16.5 (162)	14.9 (59)	17.6 (62)	24.6	EBIT/Interest	(637) 8.9	(334) 12.9
	-.2	6.1	4.3	5.1	7.5		3.1	4.7
		9.1	6.9	13.2	14.5		6.7	6.8
	(18)	4.5 (51)	3.5 (26)	4.4 (11)	5.5	Net Profit + Depr., Dep., Amort./Cur. Mat. L/T/D	(178) 3.3	(74) 3.1
		2.5	1.7	2.7	2.5		1.7	1.6
	.1	.2	.4	.4	.4		.4	.4
	.8	.5	.6	.6	.7	Fixed/Worth	.7	.7
	1.9	1.0	.9	1.0	1.1		1.2	1.1
	.5	.4	.5	.6	.5		.5	.5
	1.2	.8	.9	1.0	.9	Debt/Worth	1.1	1.0
	4.9	2.0	1.8	1.8	2.3		2.1	2.0
	60.0	57.9	44.2	35.3	34.5		38.9	38.8
(25)	13.1 (94)	24.6 (180)	24.2 (63)	26.9 (61)	23.9	% Profit Before Taxes/Tangible Net Worth	(676) 20.8	(362) 22.8
	-9.2	12.1	10.3	13.9	15.2		7.9	8.9
	28.4	30.8	20.8	17.6	17.8		18.3	18.1
	7.9	12.7	11.2	12.5	11.5	% Profit Before Taxes/Total Assets	9.6	10.8
	-4.4	4.6	4.2	5.6	5.9		3.1	3.9
	50.0	27.2	12.8	8.6	8.7		10.4	10.3
	9.2	8.9	6.6	5.7	5.0	Sales/Net Fixed Assets	6.0	6.0
	4.2	4.8	4.2	3.5	3.7		3.6	3.5
	4.0	2.9	2.2	2.0	1.8		2.6	2.3
	2.8	2.1	1.8	1.7	1.6	Sales/Total Assets	1.9	1.8
	1.7	1.6	1.4	1.3	1.2		1.4	1.3
	1.5	1.0	1.8	2.4	1.9		2.2	2.3
(19)	4.6 (72)	2.6 (163)	3.0 (61)	3.3 (35)	2.5	% Depr., Dep., Amort./Sales	(601) 3.7	(295) 3.8
	9.5	4.8	4.4	5.2	3.8		5.6	5.9
	3.9	1.3	.7	.4			.8	.9
(11)	4.7 (40)	1.9 (54)	1.3 (14)	1.3		% Officers', Directors' Owners' Comp/Sales	(224) 1.8	(102) 2.3
	9.9	3.0	2.0	3.0			3.7	4.7
12972M	109408M	1282426M	7943167M	7890044M	16430461M	Net Sales ($)	45593047M	22500206M
1952M	38268M	569745M	4231445M	4457025M	10607798M	Total Assets ($)	26227318M	13525883M

M = $ thousand MM = $ million
See Pages viii through xx for Explanation of Ratios and Data

© RMA 2024

CONSTRUCTION-GENERAL—Highway, Street, and Bridge Construction NAICS 237310

Comparative Historical Data | Current Data Sorted by Sales

110		124		129		**Type of Statement**						
66		87		87		Unqualified	1	1	4	6	19	104
18		19		15		Reviewed		2	4	7	26	48
23		34		34		Compiled			4	4	5	4
180		214		189		Tax Returns		6	8	8	8	4
4/1/21-3/31/22 ALL		4/1/22-3/31/23 ALL		4/1/23-3/31/24 ALL		Other	2	9	7	17	43	111
								67 (4/1-9/30/23)		387 (10/1/23-3/31/24)		
							0-1MM	1-3MM	3-5MM	5-10MM	10-25MM	25MM & OVER
397		478		454		**NUMBER OF STATEMENTS**	3	18	19	42	101	271
%		%		%		**ASSETS**	%	%	%	%	%	%
19.8		18.1		21.9		Cash & Equivalents	17.2	36.3	20.5	25.1	20.2	
26.6		28.1		28.7		Trade Receivables (net)	32.9	14.4	29.3	29.0	29.2	
3.8		3.5		3.7		Inventory	.6	5.9	4.2	3.1	3.9	
7.5		8.1		6.9		All Other Current	1.2	2.8	7.3	7.3	7.4	
57.7		57.8		61.1		Total Current	51.9	59.4	61.3	64.5	60.7	
34.7		32.9		30.4		Fixed Assets (net)	40.0	28.4	29.3	28.5	30.6	
2.0		2.4		2.0		Intangibles (net)	.6	1.8	3.1	1.2	2.3	
5.6		6.9		6.4		All Other Non-Current	7.5	10.5	6.2	5.8	6.4	
100.0		100.0		100.0		Total	100.0	100.0	100.0	100.0	100.0	
						LIABILITIES						
3.2		3.6		3.2		Notes Payable-Short Term	6.9	4.1	6.9	3.0	2.3	
4.5		4.4		4.2		Cur. Mat.-L.T.D.	3.4	3.8	6.7	4.1	3.9	
12.5		12.9		13.6		Trade Payables	11.8	7.2	10.6	13.9	14.5	
.1		.2		.2		Income Taxes Payable	.2	.1	.1	.4	.2	
10.0		11.7		12.9		All Other Current	6.9	16.1	15.0	9.2	14.3	
30.4		32.7		34.1		Total Current	29.2	31.2	39.4	30.6	35.2	
13.8		14.7		14.3		Long-Term Debt	30.4	29.1	20.5	13.3	11.6	
.9		.5		.6		Deferred Taxes	.0	.1	.2	.3	.9	
3.1		2.0		2.2		All Other Non-Current	.8	.2	1.2	2.5	2.2	
51.8		50.1		48.8		Net Worth	39.6	39.5	38.7	53.3	50.0	
100.0		100.0		100.0		Total Liabilities & Net Worth	100.0	100.0	100.0	100.0	100.0	
						INCOME DATA						
100.0		100.0		100.0		Net Sales	100.0	100.0	100.0	100.0	100.0	
21.0		20.4		21.5		Gross Profit	35.9	34.2	30.4	24.4	17.2	
15.3		14.9		14.3		Operating Expenses	32.4	28.6	24.4	15.6	9.8	
5.8		5.5		7.2		Operating Profit	3.5	5.7	6.0	8.8	7.4	
-2.2		-.4		-.3		All Other Expenses (net)	-.6	.3	-.5	-.6	-.2	
8.0		5.9		7.5		Profit Before Taxes	4.0	5.4	6.5	9.4	7.6	
						RATIOS						
	3.0		2.7		2.9			5.2	4.8	4.1	3.4	2.4
	2.0		1.8		1.8	Current		1.8	2.1	1.8	2.3	1.7
	1.4		1.3		1.3			.6	1.1	1.1	1.5	1.3
	2.6		2.2		2.4			5.2	4.4	3.2	2.9	2.0
	1.6		1.4		1.5	Quick		1.7	2.1	1.5	2.0	1.4
	1.1		1.0		1.1			.5	.9	.8	1.2	1.1
31	11.9	31	11.6	34	10.8		10	35.8	0 UND	21 17.3	33 10.9	37 9.9
51	7.1	53	6.9	52	7.0	Sales/Receivables	42	8.6	32 11.4	54 6.8	52 7.0	53 6.9
74	4.9	74	4.9	74	4.9		118	3.1	62 5.9	76 4.8	76 4.8	74 4.9
0	UND	0	UND	0	UND		0	UND	0 UND	0 UND	0 UND	0 UND
1	293.6	0	999.8	0	UND	Cost of Sales/Inventory	0	UND	0 UND	0 UND	0 UND	1 271.2
12	30.3	10	37.5	11	32.4		0	UND	16 23.2	12 30.5	4 85.1	13 28.9
15	24.4	14	25.4	15	24.4		4	91.1	0 UND	4 85.8	11 33.1	19 18.9
27	13.7	26	14.2	28	13.0	Cost of Sales/Payables	17	21.4	6 58.1	14 25.7	29 12.5	31 11.9
44	8.3	42	8.7	43	8.4		55	6.6	42 8.7	36 10.1	50 7.3	41 8.8
	4.1		4.9		4.4			3.4	5.1	4.5	3.3	5.2
	6.6		7.9		7.3	Sales/Working Capital		5.8	6.7	7.3	5.6	7.9
	13.6		15.4		14.5			-63.9	16.3	NM	11.2	14.5
	59.4		40.7		46.3			8.3	28.3	39.5	65.4	52.8
(349)	18.2	(417)	11.6	(407)	14.8	EBIT/Interest	(14)	1.9	(18) 5.3	(41) 8.6	(90) 18.0	(243) 17.1
	5.5		3.5		4.6			-10.8	-.2	1.9	7.1	5.7
	9.4		8.1		9.5	Net Profit + Depr., Dep.,					12.6	9.9
(87)	3.9	(95)	3.7	(106)	4.4	Amort./Cur. Mat. L/T/D				(22) 6.0	(76) 4.4
	2.3		1.8		2.1						2.4	2.1
	.4		.4		.4			.0	.2	.2	.3	.4
	.7		.7		.6	Fixed/Worth		.9	.7	.5	.5	.7
	1.1		1.1		1.0			1.8	1.2	3.0	.9	.9
	.5		.5		.5			.5	.4	.4	.5	.5
	.9		.9		.9	Debt/Worth		1.2	.7	.8	.8	1.0
	1.7		1.7		2.0			NM	3.9	7.9	1.4	2.0
	40.1		37.9		44.4			32.2	22.0	65.0	51.1	42.0
(383)	24.4	(450)	20.9	(427)	24.3	% Profit Before Taxes/Tangible Net Worth	(14) 16.8	(17) 12.4	(34) 19.7	(97) 24.8	(263) 26.1
	9.4		7.4		11.3			-2.2	-8.0	6.6	11.6	14.3
	21.1		18.2		21.0			14.5	20.0	23.6	28.2	19.4
	11.9		9.0		11.6	% Profit Before Taxes/Total Assets		5.6	3.4	9.4	14.4	11.8
	3.9		2.6		4.4			-6.7	-2.4	2.8	7.0	5.4
	9.2		11.2		13.7			UND	25.4	27.9	17.2	10.2
	5.2		5.8		6.6	Sales/Net Fixed Assets		5.6	7.7	9.8	6.3	6.2
	3.4		3.8		4.1			2.2	4.0	4.7	4.3	4.1
	2.2		2.4		2.3			2.6	3.9	2.9	2.3	2.2
	1.8		1.8		1.8	Sales/Total Assets		1.8	2.2	2.1	1.8	1.8
	1.3		1.4		1.4			1.2	1.1	1.5	1.3	1.5
	2.2		2.1		1.8				1.5	1.5	1.5	1.9
(321)	3.9	(373)	3.5	(352)	3.0	% Depr., Dep., Amort./Sales	(12) 5.2	(30) 3.2	(79) 3.1	(220) 2.9
	5.9		5.3		4.8				6.7	4.7	5.4	4.2
	.8		.7		.8					1.5	1.1	.5
(101)	1.6	(132)	1.7	(131)	1.5	% Officers', Directors' Owners' Comp/Sales		(22) 2.8	(33) 1.8	(64) 1.1
	3.5		3.2		2.9					3.5	2.9	1.8
25573254M		33392830M		33668478M		Net Sales ($)	1476M	36207M	74412M	314152M	1753201M	31489030M
15680001M		19338614M		19906233M		Total Assets ($)	805M	23289M	48730M	167668M	1082343M	18583398M

© RMA 2024 M = $ thousand MM = $ million
See Pages viii through xx for Explanation of Ratios and Data

CONSTRUCTION-GENERAL—Other Heavy and Civil Engineering Construction NAICS 237990

Current Data Sorted by Assets | Comparative Historical Data

				Type of Statement		
		7	22	14	14	Unqualified	53	25
	1	20	26	4	2	Reviewed	69	21
	1	3	1			Compiled	8	9
4	3	10			1	Tax Returns	42	32
2	10	46	50	18	18	Other	149	98
	36 (4/1-9/30/23)		241 (10/1/23-3/31/24)				4/1/19-3/31/20	4/1/20-3/31/21
0-500M	500M-2MM	2-10MM	10-50MM	50-100MM	100-250MM		ALL	ALL
6	15	86	99	36	35	NUMBER OF STATEMENTS	321	185

%	%	%	%	%	%	ASSETS	%	%
	17.1	13.9	13.9	14.8	9.0	Cash & Equivalents	16.2	20.0
	20.6	33.9	32.1	28.9	28.7	Trade Receivables (net)	29.9	27.2
	1.5	2.2	3.2	2.2	.8	Inventory	3.0	4.0
	6.6	6.8	9.2	8.3	9.7	All Other Current	6.8	7.4
	45.8	56.7	58.4	54.2	48.3	Total Current	55.9	58.6
	46.5	35.2	32.7	30.0	35.8	Fixed Assets (net)	34.2	31.8
	1.3	1.7	2.6	7.4	7.5	Intangibles (net)	4.3	4.2
	6.4	6.4	6.3	8.4	8.4	All Other Non-Current	5.5	5.4
	100.0	100.0	100.0	100.0	100.0	Total	100.0	100.0
						LIABILITIES		
	4.0	6.2	2.8	3.5	4.1	Notes Payable-Short Term	6.4	6.7
	3.7	4.2	5.4	4.3	4.5	Cur. Mat.-L.T.D.	5.0	5.2
	10.8	15.7	13.3	15.6	15.8	Trade Payables	14.7	13.4
	.0	.1	.4	.0	.1	Income Taxes Payable	.2	.1
	15.9	11.6	13.1	16.0	15.4	All Other Current	11.8	13.2
	34.5	37.8	34.9	39.5	40.0	Total Current	38.1	38.7
	39.1	23.4	14.0	14.0	19.6	Long-Term Debt	18.3	22.6
	.0	.3	.4	.0	1.0	Deferred Taxes	.4	.4
	2.9	1.9	2.3	4.9	3.7	All Other Non-Current	3.6	5.2
	23.6	36.6	48.5	41.6	35.6	Net Worth	39.7	33.2
	100.0	100.0	100.0	100.0	100.0	Total Liabilities & Net Worth	100.0	100.0
						INCOME DATA		
	100.0	100.0	100.0	100.0	100.0	Net Sales	100.0	100.0
	44.1	34.9	23.3	20.9	22.0	Gross Profit	28.8	31.5
	37.1	25.6	15.9	12.6	14.3	Operating Expenses	21.3	25.6
	7.0	9.3	7.5	8.3	7.7	Operating Profit	7.5	5.8
	-.2	.9	-.3	-.5	.8	All Other Expenses (net)	.3	-1.3
	7.3	8.4	7.8	8.7	6.9	Profit Before Taxes	7.2	7.1
						RATIOS		
	2.7	2.9	2.3	1.9	1.6		2.6	2.7
	1.8	1.6	1.7	1.4	1.2	Current	1.6	1.6
	1.0	1.0	1.3	1.0	1.0		1.1	1.2
	1.9	2.8	1.9	1.6	1.2		2.1	2.2
	1.3	1.3	1.3	1.1	1.0	Quick	1.3	1.4
	.9	.9	.9	.9	.7		.8	.9
7	52.0	34	10.8	46	8.0	47	7.7	55	6.6		33	11.0	24	15.0
23	16.2	62	5.9	65	5.6	76	4.8	73	5.0	Sales/Receivables	54	6.7	49	7.5
47	7.8	91	4.0	81	4.5	96	3.8	89	4.1		81	4.5	78	4.7
0	UND	0	UND	0	UND	0	UND	0	UND		0	UND	0	UND
0	UND	0	UND	0	UND	0	UND	0	UND	Cost of Sales/Inventory	0	UND	0	UND
0	UND	0	UND	3	106.7	6	62.3	3	121.1		3	137.6	2	153.4
3	109.4	14	26.0	21	17.4	26	13.8	33	11.1		13	27.6	12	29.5
16	23.2	31	11.7	30	12.0	38	9.5	38	9.5	Cost of Sales/Payables	30	12.2	26	13.9
50	7.3	53	6.9	45	8.2	60	6.1	66	5.5		47	7.7	47	7.7
	8.0		5.1		4.4		4.4		8.3			5.5		5.2
	11.6		10.4		8.6		9.5		15.9	Sales/Working Capital		9.8		9.6
	-252.9		135.1		16.4		91.4		92.1			56.6		30.9
	71.5		30.8		48.9		56.9		23.2			39.9		31.8
(13)	15.3	(75)	8.5	(87)	12.4	(33)	16.2	(34)	7.3	EBIT/Interest	(285)	10.3	(154)	11.3
	2.3		1.8		5.6		5.3		3.6			3.0		4.4
			15.0		4.6							6.0		9.7
		(13)	8.5	(19)	2.6					Net Profit + Depr., Dep., Amort./Cur. Mat. L/T/D	(70)	3.0	(22)	3.6
			2.3		1.4							1.2		2.8
	.6		.5		.4		.4		.5			.4		.4
	1.6		1.0		.7		.9		1.5	Fixed/Worth		.8		.8
	4.2		2.5		1.1		1.6		2.4			1.4		1.6
	1.0		.7		.6		.9		1.4			.6		.8
	2.6		1.8		1.0		1.5		2.0	Debt/Worth		1.4		1.6
	4.8		4.7		1.9		3.3		5.4			3.0		4.2
	117.2		73.6		52.0		39.0		45.3			47.0		49.3
(12)	56.1	(75)	36.6	(94)	26.5	(31)	24.3	(31)	32.0	% Profit Before Taxes/Tangible Net Worth	(280)	25.8	(156)	27.1
	44.2		15.2		13.4		18.2		20.2			12.0		13.3
	35.2		25.9		21.1		15.9		13.6			22.5		20.9
	23.7		11.2		12.0		11.7		8.7	% Profit Before Taxes/Total Assets		9.7		9.4
	9.5		3.1		6.1		5.0		6.7			4.1		3.7
	12.9		16.8		10.8		12.0		11.5			17.5		17.1
	6.5		6.7		5.7		4.8		4.7	Sales/Net Fixed Assets		6.7		6.7
	2.8		3.2		3.3		3.0		1.9			3.2		3.5
	3.1		3.0		2.1		2.0		1.8			2.7		2.6
	2.7		1.9		1.8		1.5		1.5	Sales/Total Assets		1.9		1.9
	2.0		1.3		1.3		1.1		.9			1.3		1.4
			1.3		1.8		1.9		1.6			1.5		1.9
		(61)	2.5	(93)	3.4	(34)	3.5	(21)	3.7	% Depr., Dep., Amort./Sales	(257)	3.3	(127)	3.7
			6.3		5.8		6.3		5.2			5.9		6.3
			.7		.8							1.2		1.9
		(24)	1.6	(18)	1.3					% Officers', Directors', Owners' Comp/Sales	(114)	2.3	(59)	3.5
			2.9		2.5							5.0		5.6
14205M	53734M	1019403M	4346940M	3960144M	9468643M	Net Sales ($)	16356048M	7701280M
1751M	20812M	467746M	2519919M	2600674M	5579310M	Total Assets ($)	9772347M	5138257M

© RMA 2024

M = $ thousand MM = $ million
See Pages viii through xx for Explanation of Ratios and Data

CONSTRUCTION-GENERAL—Other Heavy and Civil Engineering Construction NAICS 237990

Comparative Historical Data | Current Data Sorted by Sales

				Type of Statement						
28		41	57	Unqualified	1	1			6	49
35		51	53	Reviewed			1	5	21	26
9		3	5	Compiled		1	1	2		1
24		30	18	Tax Returns	3	4	2	2	6	1
95		114	144	Other	1	8	11	18	28	78
4/1/21-3/31/22 ALL		4/1/22-3/31/23 ALL	4/1/23-3/31/24 ALL		36 (4/1-9/30/23)			241 (10/1/23-3/31/24)		
					0-1MM	1-3MM	3-5MM	5-10MM	10-25MM	25MM & OVER
191		239	277	NUMBER OF STATEMENTS	5	14	15	27	61	155
%		%	%	ASSETS	%	%	%	%	%	%
18.9		15.2	14.0	Cash & Equivalents		15.7	10.6	19.7	15.0	13.0
29.1		29.7	30.8	Trade Receivables (net)		16.9	26.6	26.0	34.7	32.2
2.1		2.7	2.3	Inventory		2.5	1.7	2.6	2.0	2.4
7.4		8.6	8.1	All Other Current		6.5	2.6	4.5	8.7	9.5
57.5		56.2	55.2	Total Current		41.6	41.4	52.7	60.5	57.1
34.3		34.5	34.4	Fixed Assets (net)		49.9	50.8	36.8	31.4	31.0
1.7		1.8	3.4	Intangibles (net)		.2	2.2	2.4	1.9	4.7
6.6		7.4	6.9	All Other Non-Current		8.3	5.5	8.0	6.2	7.2
100.0		100.0	100.0	Total		100.0	100.0	100.0	100.0	100.0
				LIABILITIES						
5.5		4.5	4.2	Notes Payable-Short Term		4.2	6.6	4.4	5.7	3.2
4.6		3.7	4.8	Cur. Mat.-L.T.D.		5.4	4.2	4.9	5.0	4.8
12.8		13.7	14.2	Trade Payables		5.5	14.9	10.8	15.7	15.4
.2		.1	.2	Income Taxes Payable		.0	.1	.0	.1	.3
9.9		11.7	13.7	All Other Current		10.1	11.9	7.3	12.2	15.3
33.0		33.7	37.1	Total Current		25.3	37.6	27.5	38.8	38.9
19.4		20.7	20.3	Long-Term Debt		56.2	36.3	38.9	13.2	14.9
.5		.5	.4	Deferred Taxes		.0	.0	.0	.6	.4
3.0		2.7	2.8	All Other Non-Current		5.4	2.2	1.3	1.4	3.4
44.0		42.4	39.4	Net Worth		13.2	23.9	32.4	46.1	42.4
100.0		100.0	100.0	Total Liabilties & Net Worth		100.0	100.0	100.0	100.0	100.0
				INCOME DATA						
100.0		100.0	100.0	Net Sales		100.0	100.0	100.0	100.0	100.0
32.1		29.1	28.5	Gross Profit		61.1	44.5	40.6	26.6	21.4
24.4		22.4	20.3	Operating Expenses		49.5	37.5	31.6	17.7	14.2
7.6		6.7	8.2	Operating Profit		11.6	7.0	8.9	8.9	7.3
-1.6		-.5	.2	All Other Expenses (net)		1.1	-.4	.8	.2	-.1
9.2		7.3	8.0	Profit Before Taxes		10.5	7.4	8.2	8.7	7.4
				RATIOS						
						4.5	2.0	7.2	2.8	1.9
3.4		2.7	2.3							
1.9		1.7	1.5	Current		2.1	1.3	2.3	1.7	1.5
1.2		1.2	1.1			1.3	.7	1.0	1.1	1.2
2.8		2.3	1.9			4.3	1.7	7.0	2.6	1.6
1.6		1.4	1.2	Quick		1.7	1.1	2.3	1.3	1.2
1.0		.9	.9			.9	.7	1.0	.9	.9
36 10.2	33	11.0	42 8.6		0 UND	30 12.0	27 13.5	42 8.6	47 7.8	
57 6.4	61	6.0	65 5.6	Sales/Receivables	25 14.8	53 6.9	64 6.7	64 5.7	69 5.3	
85 4.3	85	4.3	87 4.2		104 3.5	96 3.8	94 3.9	89 4.1	83 4.4	
0 UND	0	UND	0 UND		0 UND	0 UND	0 UND	0 UND	0 UND	
0 UND	0	UND	0 UND	Cost of Sales/Inventory	0 UND	0 UND	0 UND	0 UND	0 UND	
3 125.1	3	127.5	2 198.6		0 UND	1 623.0	0 UND	1 453.1	3 140.1	
13 27.3	16	22.7	19 19.6		0 UND	23 15.6	7 51.0	16 23.1	24 14.9	
33 11.2	32	11.5	33 11.0	Cost of Sales/Payables	0 UND	50 7.3	31 11.7	29 12.7	34 10.6	
52 7.0	49	7.5	50 7.3		53 6.9	79 4.6	52 7.0	52 7.0	47 7.8	
4.4		4.6	5.5			6.0	7.1	3.8	4.6	5.7
6.9		7.2	10.3	Sales/Working Capital		8.8	22.0	7.0	9.4	10.3
19.5		24.9	41.7			23.9	-14.7	135.1	114.9	26.6
49.2		37.9	41.2			39.3	10.3	30.5	90.8	41.6
(166) 14.7	(213)	12.0	(246) 10.7	EBIT/Interest	(12) 6.3	(11) 7.5	(23) 8.5	(56) 11.8	(139) 13.0	
4.0		3.1	3.6			2.5	1.9	1.8	3.1	4.5
6.1		7.4	8.5						10.3	7.6
(32) 2.7	(37)	3.0	(47) 3.2	Net Profit + Depr., Dep., Amort./Cur. Mat. L/T/D				(11) 7.7	(32) 3.1	
1.8		1.6	1.7						2.0	1.8
.3		.4	.5			1.3	.9	.4	.4	.4
.7		.8	.9	Fixed/Worth		2.2	2.3	.8	.8	.8
1.4		1.5	1.7			UND	-80.9	1.9	1.4	1.5
.5		.6	.7			1.7	1.6	.3	.5	.9
1.1		1.2	1.5	Debt/Worth		2.9	4.4	1.3	1.1	1.5
2.4		2.5	3.2			UND	-141.1	3.6	2.4	2.8
55.5		44.4	53.7			540.2	105.7	90.2	52.7	50.5
(175) 29.7	(216)	21.0	(246) 32.9	% Profit Before Taxes/Tangible Net Worth	(11) 102.2	(11) 52.3	(23) 35.9	(56) 30.2	(141) 31.1	
12.4		6.9	17.1			28.4	37.5	17.7	10.7	15.9
26.5		20.8	20.8			27.6	23.7	29.0	26.1	17.6
13.0		8.5	11.8	% Profit Before Taxes/Total Assets		11.8	14.9	13.6	10.9	11.8
4.5		2.5	4.9			3.9	2.6	6.0	3.8	6.2
13.9		11.8	12.3			10.6	4.9	13.1	18.1	11.7
5.9		5.7	5.7	Sales/Net Fixed Assets		2.6	3.1	6.7	7.4	5.7
3.0		3.4	3.1			1.2	2.8	3.1	3.7	3.3
2.3		2.4	2.3			4.4	2.0	2.8	2.9	2.1
1.7		1.8	1.7	Sales/Total Assets		1.3	1.7	1.6	1.9	1.7
1.3		1.3	1.3			.8	1.6	1.3	1.3	1.3
2.2		1.7	1.6					1.5	1.3	1.8
(133) 3.7	(175)	3.4	(218) 3.2	% Depr., Dep., Amort./Sales		(17) 2.9	(53) 2.8	(131) 3.2		
6.5		5.8	5.8					5.7	6.3	4.9
1.5		1.0	.8						.7	.6
(57) 2.5	(66)	1.8	(54) 1.5	% Officers', Directors' Owners' Comp/Sales				(22) 1.2	(19) 1.0	
5.1		4.6	3.2						3.0	2.2
8056090M		9802165M	18863069M	Net Sales ($)	2586M	28842M	60015M	204985M	983392M	17583249M
5480834M		6392218M	11190212M	Total Assets ($)	9630M	24309M	36384M	130080M	643715M	10346094M

© RMA 2024
M = $ thousand   MM = $ million
See Pages viii through xx for Explanation of Ratios and Data

CONSTRUCTION-GENERAL—Poured Concrete Foundation and Structure Contractors NAICS 238110

Current Data Sorted by Assets

						Type of Statement	Comparative Historical Data	
1	1	2	18	3	5	Unqualified	19	11
		14	32	1		Reviewed	56	23
	3	5	2	1		Compiled	16	7
7	20	15	4	1	1	Tax Returns	54	29
13	28	53	53	13	4	Other	187	122
0-500M	500M-2MM	2-10MM	10-50MM	50-100MM	100-250MM		4/1/19-3/31/20 ALL	4/1/20-3/31/21 ALL
	45 (4/1-9/30/23)		255 (10/1/23-3/31/24)					
21	52	89	109	19	10	NUMBER OF STATEMENTS	332	192
%	%	%	%	%	%	ASSETS	%	%
33.6	27.5	17.8	13.5	13.6	11.7	Cash & Equivalents	14.1	20.1
15.2	27.4	38.3	42.6	32.8	41.1	Trade Receivables (net)	36.9	32.3
3.9	1.1	3.0	4.3	2.9	1.6	Inventory	2.9	2.8
1.9	3.4	5.0	7.1	11.8	15.1	All Other Current	5.8	5.3
54.6	59.4	64.1	67.5	61.0	69.5	Total Current	59.8	60.6
35.3	30.9	26.2	26.5	28.8	23.3	Fixed Assets (net)	30.6	30.7
4.4	4.2	3.0	1.0	6.6	1.8	Intangibles (net)	3.6	2.4
5.6	5.6	6.7	5.0	3.6	5.4	All Other Non-Current	6.0	6.4
100.0	100.0	100.0	100.0	100.0	100.0	Total	100.0	100.0
						LIABILITIES		
7.8	3.9	3.3	4.7	4.2	1.8	Notes Payable-Short Term	7.7	5.5
6.1	3.5	4.7	4.1	3.5	4.3	Cur. Mat.-L.T.D.	4.2	4.2
7.5	10.5	15.5	17.5	15.3	19.1	Trade Payables	16.3	14.5
.0	.1	.2	.1	.1	.0	Income Taxes Payable	.2	.5
19.6	7.6	8.9	10.9	11.1	20.1	All Other Current	10.7	10.5
41.0	25.5	32.5	37.3	34.2	45.3	Total Current	39.0	35.3
52.0	31.2	16.2	13.6	13.0	18.1	Long-Term Debt	21.2	27.1
.0	.0	.3	.3	.8	1.1	Deferred Taxes	.2	.3
7.0	2.8	1.4	4.9	3.5	3.5	All Other Non-Current	3.4	2.9
.0	40.5	49.6	43.9	48.5	32.0	Net Worth	36.2	34.4
100.0	100.0	100.0	100.0	100.0	100.0	Total Liabilities & Net Worth	100.0	100.0
						INCOME DATA		
100.0	100.0	100.0	100.0	100.0	100.0	Net Sales	100.0	100.0
48.4	43.7	30.7	25.6	23.2	17.0	Gross Profit	31.0	32.6
41.7	34.2	21.5	18.2	14.6	11.9	Operating Expenses	23.6	25.5
6.7	9.5	9.1	7.4	8.6	5.1	Operating Profit	7.3	7.1
-.3	1.4	.2	.0	1.2	.1	All Other Expenses (net)	.7	-1.3
6.9	8.1	8.9	7.3	7.3	5.0	Profit Before Taxes	6.7	8.4
						RATIOS		
6.6	9.8	5.1	2.8	2.1	1.8		2.8	3.3
2.7	3.3	2.2	1.8	1.5	1.4	Current	1.6	1.9
.7	.9	1.5	1.3	1.4	1.2		1.1	1.2
6.5	9.5	4.7	2.4	1.8	1.3		2.4	2.9
2.3	3.0	1.9	1.6	1.3	1.2	Quick	1.4	1.5
.5	.9	1.3	1.1	.9	1.0		.8	1.1
0 UND	0 UND	31 11.9	45 8.1	40 9.1	47 7.8		27 13.7	24 15.1
2 152.8	22 16.7	56 6.5	70 5.2	62 5.9	74 4.9	Sales/Receivables	54 6.7	47 7.7
27 13.5	51 7.1	83 4.4	91 4.0	78 4.7	81 4.5		78 4.7	70 5.2
0 UND	0 UND	0 UND	0 UND	0 UND	0 UND		0 UND	0 UND
0 UND	0 UND	0 UND	0 UND	3 119.0	0 999.8	Cost of Sales/Inventory	0 UND	0 UND
0 UND	0 UND	2 235.1	7 53.7	15 24.7	4 92.0		3 143.7	1 370.6
0 UND	0 UND	12 31.0	19 19.5	22 16.3	25 14.8		8 47.3	7 54.7
0 UND	6 66.0	24 15.3	31 11.9	31 11.6	33 11.0	Cost of Sales/Payables	25 14.5	26 14.2
2 165.8	39 9.3	43 8.4	51 7.1	41 9.0	52 7.0		45 8.2	42 8.7
9.4	4.7	4.1	4.5	5.8	8.2		6.6	5.3
18.4	10.5	7.0	6.8	9.2	12.7	Sales/Working Capital	12.9	9.2
-49.7	-168.0	16.8	14.3	17.1	19.3		80.4	33.1
36.6	44.2	69.3	55.5	35.1	24.4		38.7	60.6
(18) 8.2	(36) 8.9	(79) 23.1	(102) 10.7	(18) 4.0	15.9	EBIT/Interest	(292) 10.9	(163) 18.4
3.6	1.0	4.5	3.0	2.5	6.2		3.1	5.8
			8.9	19.4			7.4	15.1
		(33) 4.7	(11) 3.9		Net Profit + Depr., Dep.,	(52) 3.8	(23) 4.5
			1.4	1.3		Amort./Cur. Mat. L/T/D	1.9	2.5
.3	.1	.1	.2	.4	.4		.3	.3
.6	.7	.4	.5	.9	.9	Fixed/Worth	.6	.7
-2.0	3.0	.9	1.1	1.3	1.4		1.9	1.9
.4	.4	.5	.6	.6	1.2		.6	.7
2.4	1.1	.9	1.3	1.3	2.5	Debt/Worth	1.5	1.2
-3.1	20.4	2.0	2.6	3.5	3.4		5.1	5.0
365.8	107.7	71.5	55.4	61.8	86.4		70.3	84.3
(14) 78.1	(42) 59.6	(82) 40.8	(107) 31.0	23.3	37.8	% Profit Before Taxes/Tangible Net Worth	(285) 36.9	(163) 45.4
12.1	9.3	13.2	12.3	8.6	18.7		15.0	21.3
61.1	48.5	32.4	23.4	27.9	19.8		29.7	31.2
29.3	20.0	19.7	12.6	9.8	10.7	% Profit Before Taxes/Total Assets	12.6	17.3
8.3	.6	5.4	4.2	1.9	7.2		4.8	7.6
88.8	108.5	35.2	26.4	40.4	26.2		30.4	27.3
23.8	17.6	12.2	11.4	9.5	9.1	Sales/Net Fixed Assets	12.7	10.9
7.9	7.2	5.3	5.1	4.1	5.5		5.1	4.5
9.4	5.3	3.2	3.0	2.5	3.5		3.6	3.4
5.5	3.1	2.3	2.0	2.1	2.3	Sales/Total Assets	2.7	2.4
3.2	2.1	1.8	1.6	1.6	1.5		1.9	1.8
	1.4	1.1	1.0	.7			1.1	.9
(20) 4.1	(55) 2.2	(93) 1.9	(17) 2.0		% Depr., Dep., Amort./Sales	(219) 2.4	(130) 2.2
	7.2	5.5	3.6	4.3			5.0	4.9
	1.6	1.1	.6				1.4	1.1
(19) 4.0	(41) 1.9	(19) 1.1		% Officers', Directors' Owners' Comp/Sales	(128) 2.6	(72) 2.6
	7.0	3.0	2.5				4.5	5.8
33959M	216640M	1202216M	5122496M	2884374M	3728348M	Net Sales ($)	8498319M	6010987M
5702M	56637M	462093M	2385516M	1403477M	1485805M	Total Assets ($)	3762569M	2687963M

© RMA 2024 M = $ thousand MM = $ million
See Pages viii through xx for Explanation of Ratios and Data

CONSTRUCTION-GENERAL—Poured Concrete Foundation and Structure Contractors NAICS 238110

Comparative Historical Data			Type of Statement	Current Data Sorted by Sales					
12	22	30	Unqualified		2		2	2	24
23	40	47	Reviewed		1	2	17	27	
13	18	11	Compiled		1	3	3	3	4
43	58	48	Tax Returns	5	6	7	13	12	5
114	198	164	Other	6	25	12	22	34	65
4/1/21-3/31/22 ALL	4/1/22-3/31/23 ALL	4/1/23-3/31/24 ALL		45 (4/1-9/30/23)			255 (10/1/23-3/31/24)		
				0-1MM	1-3MM	3-5MM	5-10MM	10-25MM	25MM & OVER
205	336	300	NUMBER OF STATEMENTS	11	34	23	39	68	125
%	%	%	ASSETS	%	%	%	%	%	%
18.0	17.8	18.6	Cash & Equivalents	28.5	28.6	25.0	20.4	16.3	14.4
32.0	35.5	36.1	Trade Receivables (net)	7.6	24.1	30.4	35.1	33.2	44.8
3.3	2.7	3.1	Inventory	1.4	2.9	.1	2.2	4.7	3.4
5.8	6.6	6.1	All Other Current	4.4	2.7	2.2	3.1	5.8	8.9
59.0	62.5	63.8	Total Current	42.0	58.3	57.7	60.8	59.9	71.5
31.2	28.1	27.8	Fixed Assets (net)	44.0	30.6	35.5	28.4	30.9	22.4
3.3	3.1	2.8	Intangibles (net)	.0	4.7	4.8	2.9	2.8	2.0
6.4	6.3	5.6	All Other Non-Current	14.1	6.4	2.0	7.9	6.4	4.1
100.0	100.0	100.0	Total	100.0	100.0	100.0	100.0	100.0	100.0
			LIABILITIES						
7.9	6.9	4.2	Notes Payable-Short Term	9.0	4.4	3.8	3.2	3.5	4.6
4.1	3.3	4.3	Cur. Mat.-L.T.D.	7.0	3.5	4.1	3.3	6.6	3.3
14.0	14.2	14.9	Trade Payables	2.2	10.5	7.7	13.6	13.4	19.8
.0	.2	.1	Income Taxes Payable	.3	.0	.0	.2	.1	.2
9.0	13.3	10.7	All Other Current	5.1	12.3	7.0	10.3	10.0	11.8
35.0	37.9	34.2	Total Current	23.6	30.7	22.7	30.6	33.5	39.7
26.2	19.6	20.2	Long-Term Debt	26.0	44.1	28.3	21.2	19.6	11.7
.2	.2	.3	Deferred Taxes	.0	.0	.5	.0	.3	.5
4.3	3.5	3.5	All Other Non-Current	1.8	6.7	1.5	1.3	3.4	3.9
34.3	38.7	41.8	Net Worth	48.6	18.5	47.1	46.9	43.2	44.3
100.0	100.0	100.0	Total Liabilities & Net Worth	100.0	100.0	100.0	100.0	100.0	100.0
			INCOME DATA						
100.0	100.0	100.0	Net Sales	100.0	100.0	100.0	100.0	100.0	100.0
30.0	31.1	31.4	Gross Profit	62.7	45.4	36.0	38.4	31.2	21.9
24.2	24.1	23.2	Operating Expenses	42.3	37.6	27.3	28.5	23.4	15.0
5.9	6.9	8.2	Operating Profit	20.4	7.8	8.7	9.8	7.8	6.9
-1.6	-.1	.4	All Other Expenses (net)	7.3	.4	-.2	.1	.1	.2
7.4	7.0	7.8	Profit Before Taxes	13.1	7.4	8.9	9.7	7.7	6.7
			RATIOS						
3.4	4.2	3.8	Current	33.5	7.3	11.7	6.6	3.8	2.6
1.9	2.0	2.0		3.3	2.9	3.2	2.8	1.9	1.8
1.2	1.3	1.3		1.2	.8	1.5	1.1	1.2	1.3
2.8	3.6	3.4	Quick	18.5	7.3	11.7	5.5	3.6	2.1
1.5	1.6	1.7		2.3	2.4	2.8	2.8	1.6	1.5
1.0	1.0	1.0		1.1	.6	1.5	.8	1.0	1.1
18 20.2	23 16.0	30 12.3	Sales/Receivables	0 UND	2 190.6	0 UND	19 18.9	31 11.7	43 8.5
47 7.8	54 6.8	52 7.0		2 152.8	19 18.9	45 8.1	47 7.7	53 6.9	70 5.2
78 4.7	81 4.5	79 4.6		48 7.6	47 7.7	89 4.1	73 5.0	87 4.2	89 4.1
0 UND	0 UND	0 UND	Cost of Sales/Inventory	0 UND	0 UND	0 UND	0 UND	0 UND	0 UND
0 UND	0 UND	0 UND		0 UND	0 UND	0 UND	1 401.5	5 67.4	5 79.6
2 157.2	2 169.7	2 168.2		0 UND	0 UND	0 UND	4 86.4	9 41.8	21 17.0
4 93.4	4 93.1	9 42.8	Cost of Sales/Payables	4 90.3	1 418.8	13 28.7	20 17.9	23 15.6	31 11.7
21 17.5	22 16.8	25 14.6		62 5.9	26 14.1	34 10.6	41 8.8	49 7.5	47 7.7
41 8.9	41 9.0	43 8.5							
5.3	5.5	4.7	Sales/Working Capital	.9	5.7	4.1	4.7	4.2	4.9
9.6	8.8	8.0		5.7	11.6	9.3	7.9	7.3	7.8
41.3	21.2	23.1		96.2	-44.4	30.2	79.8	28.4	14.3
63.6	56.3	47.1	EBIT/Interest		22.8	37.1	65.5	43.7	54.5
(184) 14.8	(289) 15.5	(263) 12.3		(25) 8.1	(18) 6.4	(35) 25.3	(63) 9.1	(118) 14.7	
4.4	4.1	3.1			2.2	.9	11.4	3.0	3.5
16.0	8.5	9.0	Net Profit + Depr., Dep., Amort./Cur. Mat. L/T/D					18.1	7.3
(25) 6.6	(42) 2.7	(59) 4.5					(10) 5.3	(43) 4.5	
3.3	1.4	1.6						.8	1.6
.3	.2	.2	Fixed/Worth	.0	.1	.2	.2	.2	.2
.7	.5	.5		.6	1.0	.5	.5	.5	.5
2.7	1.5	1.4		2.5	NM	1.4	1.5	1.5	1.0
.5	.5	.5	Debt/Worth	.1	.4	.4	.5	.5	.6
1.3	1.1	1.1		.8	2.0	1.1	.9	1.1	1.3
6.6	3.4	2.7		38.4	-16.9	2.1	3.1	2.2	2.7
63.8	70.3	68.8	% Profit Before Taxes/Tangible Net Worth		123.6	69.9	103.8	50.9	63.6
(165) 37.5	(302) 37.7	(274) 36.0		(24) 55.5	(20) 41.3	(36) 61.6	(62) 32.5	(123) 32.0	
14.6	14.0	12.8			8.1	14.8	26.6	11.8	14.8
32.7	32.0	30.6	% Profit Before Taxes/Total Assets	35.9	50.9	38.2	47.8	24.7	25.7
14.8	14.5	16.0		17.6	17.1	19.0	26.1	14.3	14.0
5.4	4.8	4.3		-1.8	5.0	.1	15.8	4.4	5.2
27.0	33.2	39.9	Sales/Net Fixed Assets	UND	109.2	42.3	37.7	28.0	39.8
10.4	14.1	12.8		14.8	23.1	12.1	14.9	8.5	13.9
5.1	5.4	5.5		1.7	7.1	3.5	5.6	4.7	6.7
3.4	3.5	3.4	Sales/Total Assets	5.2	4.5	5.1	3.6	3.1	3.1
2.5	2.5	2.4		1.6	3.2	2.5	2.7	2.1	2.4
1.8	1.8	1.7		.4	2.3	1.6	2.1	1.7	1.7
1.2	1.1	1.2	% Depr., Dep., Amort./Sales		.8		1.2	1.3	.8
(144) 2.4	(214) 2.6	(195) 2.2		(12) 3.9		(19) 2.8	(50) 2.6	(101) 1.7	
4.9	5.3	4.9			5.6		6.1	5.9	2.9
1.3	.9	.9	% Officers', Directors' Owners' Comp/Sales		5.2		1.4	1.0	.4
(89) 3.1	(129) 2.2	(95) 2.0		(11) 7.1		(18) 2.1	(28) 1.8	(27) .7	
5.4	3.9	4.0			9.5		3.2	3.3	2.3
5999176M	11617556M	13188033M	Net Sales ($)	6783M	63082M	88154M	287279M	1153010M	11589725M
2778091M	5153556M	5799230M	Total Assets ($)	11607M	23524M	40080M	109549M	656887M	4957583M

M = $ thousand   MM = $ million
See Pages viii through xx for Explanation of Ratios and Data

© RMA 2024

CONSTRUCTION-GENERAL—Structural Steel and Precast Concrete Contractors NAICS 238120

Current Data Sorted by Assets | Comparative Historical Data

0-500M	500M-2MM	2-10MM	10-50MM	50-100MM	100-250MM	Type of Statement	4/1/19-3/31/20 ALL	4/1/20-3/31/21 ALL
		11	5 13	5	3	Unqualified	24	10
		4			1	Reviewed	35	13
1		2	2	1		Compiled	13	7
3	7	19	16	3	2	Tax Returns	14	7
	15 (4/1-9/30/23)		83 (10/1/23-3/31/24)			Other	43	30
4	7	36	36	9	6	**NUMBER OF STATEMENTS**	129	67
%	%	%	%	%	%	**ASSETS**	%	%
		13.7	15.4			Cash & Equivalents	14.1	17.0
		46.5	46.1			Trade Receivables (net)	43.9	39.0
		4.7	3.7			Inventory	4.8	8.0
		10.0	8.5			All Other Current	7.3	6.6
		74.8	73.7			Total Current	70.1	70.6
		17.0	18.0			Fixed Assets (net)	24.3	21.2
		3.6	2.3			Intangibles (net)	2.3	3.3
		4.5	5.9			All Other Non-Current	3.4	4.9
		100.0	100.0			Total	100.0	100.0
						LIABILITIES		
		2.7	3.8			Notes Payable-Short Term	6.9	7.3
		1.9	1.6			Cur. Mat.-L.T.D.	2.5	2.0
		18.2	15.0			Trade Payables	14.9	16.2
		.4	.1			Income Taxes Payable	.1	.1
		9.2	12.5			All Other Current	11.8	9.5
		32.4	33.0			Total Current	36.3	35.0
		12.4	7.8			Long-Term Debt	11.0	14.9
		.2	.1			Deferred Taxes	.4	.2
		2.3	3.6			All Other Non-Current	1.7	1.5
		52.7	55.4			Net Worth	50.7	48.4
		100.0	100.0			Total Liabilities & Net Worth	100.0	100.0
						INCOME DATA		
		100.0	100.0			Net Sales	100.0	100.0
		30.0	26.5			Gross Profit	26.7	26.3
		22.7	16.3			Operating Expenses	19.1	20.2
		7.3	10.2			Operating Profit	7.6	6.1
		-.2	.0			All Other Expenses (net)	.2	-.8
		7.5	10.2			Profit Before Taxes	7.5	6.9
						RATIOS		
		3.6	4.8				3.5	3.3
		2.4	2.1			Current	2.0	2.2
		1.9	1.5				1.4	1.5
		3.1	4.0				3.1	2.7
		2.0	1.8			Quick	1.6	1.6
		1.4	1.2				1.0	1.1
	41	8.8	65 5.6				50 7.3	46 7.9
	66	5.5	83 4.4			Sales/Receivables	73 5.0	70 5.2
	91	4.0	111 3.3				96 3.8	91 4.0
		0 UND	0 UND				0 UND	0 UND
		0 UND	3 142.3			Cost of Sales/Inventory	0 UND	2 162.3
		4 98.0	11 34.1				9 42.0	29 12.4
		8 46.1	17 21.0				10 34.9	16 22.8
		35 10.4	32 11.5			Cost of Sales/Payables	24 15.4	31 11.6
		49 7.4	55 6.6				45 8.1	49 7.4
		4.0	3.2				4.2	3.4
		6.3	5.2			Sales/Working Capital	7.2	5.9
		11.5	9.4				15.2	10.8
		116.0	45.0				52.6	45.0
		(31) 17.0	(33) 28.2			EBIT/Interest	(115) 11.2	(54) 15.2
		5.3	11.9				3.8	2.4
			24.0			Net Profit + Depr., Dep.,	15.0	
		(10)	6.4			Amort./Cur. Mat. L/T/D	(19) 6.0	
			1.5				3.1	
		.1	.1				.2	.2
		.3	.3			Fixed/Worth	.4	.4
		.5	.5				.8	.8
		.6	.4				.4	.5
		.9	.9			Debt/Worth	1.0	1.0
		1.8	1.7				2.3	2.3
		67.2	48.1			% Profit Before Taxes/Tangible	54.3	73.2
		(35) 26.5	34.7			Net Worth	(125) 28.0	(63) 34.6
		11.6	13.3				9.4	10.8
		32.2	27.1				26.9	24.5
		13.9	18.1			% Profit Before Taxes/Total	13.3	15.5
		6.0	9.1			Assets	4.0	2.8
		69.1	25.2				30.7	41.8
		28.2	14.1			Sales/Net Fixed Assets	13.5	15.2
		9.6	6.2				5.8	5.3
		3.4	2.5				3.1	2.6
		2.7	1.9			Sales/Total Assets	2.3	2.1
		2.1	1.5				1.7	1.5
		.7	.6				.7	.6
		(28) 1.4	(31) 1.6			% Depr., Dep., Amort./Sales	(110) 1.4	(54) 1.4
		2.0	3.0				3.2	3.0
		1.4	.2				.9	1.4
		(14) 2.4	(11) .9			% Officers', Directors'	(53) 1.7	(23) 3.4
		3.5	2.5			Owners' Comp/Sales	3.0	5.3
13528M	31825M	549355M	1533011M	1332581M	1626338M	Net Sales ($)	5973565M	1974302M
1417M	8854M	198838M	809095M	665098M	917793M	Total Assets ($)	3102734M	1077943M

M = $ thousand   MM = $ million
See Pages viii through xx for Explanation of Ratios and Data

© RMA 2024

CONSTRUCTION-GENERAL—Structural Steel and Precast Concrete Contractors   NAICS 238120

Comparative Historical Data | Current Data Sorted by Sales

Comparative Historical Data			Type of Statement	Current Data Sorted by Sales					
8	15	13	Unqualified				1	1	12
18	22	25	Reviewed				2	10	13
5	6	5	Compiled			1		3	1
10	15	5	Tax Returns					3	1
43	48	50	Other	1	6	2	5	18	19
4/1/21-3/31/22 ALL	4/1/22-3/31/23 ALL	4/1/23-3/31/24 ALL		0-1MM	15 (4/1-9/30/23) 1-3MM	3-5MM	5-10MM	83 (10/1/23-3/31/24) 10-25MM	25MM & OVER
84	106	98	**NUMBER OF STATEMENTS**	1	6	2	7	35	46
%	%	%	**ASSETS**	%	%	%	%	%	%
18.7	16.9	16.7	Cash & Equivalents					15.3	16.2
37.2	37.2	43.2	Trade Receivables (net)					45.3	45.8
6.2	7.5	4.4	Inventory					1.7	5.4
8.5	8.4	8.4	All Other Current					11.7	8.3
70.5	70.0	72.7	Total Current					74.0	75.7
20.8	19.0	19.0	Fixed Assets (net)					15.4	17.1
3.4	4.1	2.6	Intangibles (net)					3.2	2.3
5.3	6.8	5.7	All Other Non-Current					7.3	5.0
100.0	100.0	100.0	Total					100.0	100.0
			LIABILITIES						
5.5	4.6	3.0	Notes Payable-Short Term					2.5	3.4
2.4	1.7	1.9	Cur. Mat.-L.T.D.					1.6	1.5
14.4	13.5	15.8	Trade Payables					16.7	16.8
.0	.2	.2	Income Taxes Payable					.4	.1
10.9	12.0	11.7	All Other Current					10.4	15.6
33.2	32.0	32.6	Total Current					31.5	37.4
16.8	11.9	11.4	Long-Term Debt					10.6	8.5
.3	.1	.1	Deferred Taxes					.2	.1
3.4	3.3	3.0	All Other Non-Current					2.8	3.4
46.3	52.8	52.9	Net Worth					54.9	50.5
100.0	100.0	100.0	Total Liabilities & Net Worth					100.0	100.0
			INCOME DATA						
100.0	100.0	100.0	Net Sales					100.0	100.0
25.2	28.1	28.3	Gross Profit					31.6	21.9
20.0	21.9	19.9	Operating Expenses					22.7	13.4
5.3	6.2	8.3	Operating Profit					8.9	8.6
-3.1	-.5	.0	All Other Expenses (net)					-.2	-.1
8.4	6.8	8.3	Profit Before Taxes					9.2	8.7
			RATIOS						
4.2	3.9	3.7						3.7	3.0
2.1	2.4	2.2	Current					2.4	1.9
1.4	1.5	1.6						1.8	1.5
2.9	2.9	3.2						3.7	2.2
1.6	1.7	1.8	Quick					2.0	1.6
1.1	1.0	1.3						1.6	1.2
45 8.1	40 9.1	47 7.7						44 8.3	59 6.2
74 4.9	63 5.8	72 5.1	Sales/Receivables					68 5.4	78 4.7
99 3.7	91 4.0	96 3.8						91 4.0	99 3.7
0 UND	0 UND	0 UND						0 UND	0 UND
1 263.6	2 162.5	0 847.6	Cost of Sales/Inventory					0 UND	4 91.3
21 17.1	27 13.7	9 39.7						1 499.7	15 23.6
13 27.6	8 43.5	13 28.6						8 46.9	20 18.0
31 11.6	26 14.2	31 11.9	Cost of Sales/Payables					24 15.1	35 10.5
51 7.1	47 7.7	51 7.2						50 7.3	53 6.9
3.4	3.5	3.8						3.4	3.6
6.1	5.9	6.5	Sales/Working Capital					6.1	6.7
13.1	13.2	11.5						12.0	9.8
81.5	68.9	90.8						118.1	54.8
(67) 16.9	(84) 19.6	(84) 19.9	EBIT/Interest					(30) 48.3	(39) 24.3
5.6	5.0	5.5						9.0	6.7
21.3	30.3	17.9							19.4
(16) 7.1	(19) 5.5	(22) 5.9	Net Profit + Depr., Dep., Amort./Cur. Mat. L/T/D					(12) 5.9
2.6	2.3	2.5							2.8
.2	.1	.1						.1	.1
.4	.3	.3	Fixed/Worth					.3	.3
1.0	.7	.6						.5	.6
.4	.4	.5						.4	.5
1.2	.8	.9	Debt/Worth					.9	.9
2.3	1.8	1.8						1.8	1.9
76.6	45.3	59.9	% Profit Before Taxes/Tangible Net Worth					67.6	54.7
(77) 28.7	(97) 28.6	(97) 34.3						(34) 36.2	33.9
9.8	8.9	11.6						17.9	12.1
26.0	26.1	28.6	% Profit Before Taxes/Total Assets					33.0	27.3
13.0	12.4	15.3						17.7	14.7
3.8	4.2	5.6						8.6	6.0
31.4	36.8	48.1						72.8	48.1
14.2	16.7	16.1	Sales/Net Fixed Assets					20.4	16.1
5.5	5.8	7.5						8.9	7.6
2.6	2.7	3.2						3.4	2.8
1.9	2.0	2.2	Sales/Total Assets					2.4	2.1
1.5	1.4	1.7						1.9	1.6
.7	.9	.7						.8	.5
(64) 1.7	(75) 1.6	(76) 1.4	% Depr., Dep., Amort./Sales					(26) 1.4	(41) .9
3.3	3.2	2.4						2.0	2.7
1.3	1.2	.9						1.2	
(31) 1.8	(40) 2.3	(28) 1.8	% Officers', Directors' Owners' Comp/Sales					(14) 2.4	
5.6	4.2	3.4						3.5	
4054342M	4558804M	5086638M	Net Sales ($)	685M	13990M	11256M	52309M	586504M	4421894M
2357768M	2519974M	2601095M	Total Assets ($)	101M	6432M	8345M	28203M	258228M	2299786M

M = $ thousand   MM = $ million
See Pages viii through xx for Explanation of Ratios and Data

© RMA 2024

CONSTRUCTION-GENERAL—Framing Contractors NAICS 238130

Current Data Sorted by Assets

0-500M	500M-2MM	2-10MM	10-50MM	50-100MM	100-250MM
		5 (4/1-9/30/23)	30 (10/1/23-3/31/24)		
			1	1	
		2	4		1
4	6	2	1		
	2	6	1		
			5		1
4	8	10	11		2

Comparative Historical Data

Type of Statement	4/1/19-3/31/20 ALL	4/1/20-3/31/21 ALL
Unqualified	5	2
Reviewed	11	5
Compiled	1	2
Tax Returns	12	2
Other	20	14
NUMBER OF STATEMENTS	49	25

0-500M %	500M-2MM %	2-10MM %	10-50MM %	50-100MM	100-250MM %		ALL %	ALL %
						ASSETS		
		12.8	39.4			Cash & Equivalents	20.4	24.7
		38.3	37.2			Trade Receivables (net)	34.3	36.7
		2.9	2.9	D		Inventory	6.0	8.2
		4.8	10.2	A		All Other Current	9.0	8.4
		58.9	89.7	T		Total Current	69.8	78.0
		27.3	2.8	A		Fixed Assets (net)	17.8	10.3
		2.0	2.9			Intangibles (net)	6.6	4.4
		11.8	4.6	N		All Other Non-Current	5.9	7.4
		100.0	100.0	O		Total	100.0	100.0
				T		**LIABILITIES**		
		14.1	1.8			Notes Payable-Short Term	7.5	7.1
		1.3	.3	A		Cur. Mat.-L.T.D.	2.2	.9
		14.9	14.5	V		Trade Payables	16.5	13.5
		.1	.2	A		Income Taxes Payable	.3	.0
		19.2	13.5	I		All Other Current	11.3	10.5
		49.5	30.3	L		Total Current	37.8	32.0
		7.6	5.1	A		Long-Term Debt	12.6	9.9
		.0	.0	B		Deferred Taxes	.2	.0
		.0	1.8	L		All Other Non-Current	3.3	5.5
		43.0	62.8	E		Net Worth	46.0	52.6
		100.0	100.0			Total Liabilities & Net Worth	100.0	100.0
						INCOME DATA		
		100.0	100.0			Net Sales	100.0	100.0
		26.3	19.3			Gross Profit	25.6	26.0
		15.7	8.6			Operating Expenses	18.3	18.3
		10.6	10.7			Operating Profit	7.3	7.7
		.4	.0			All Other Expenses (net)	-.2	-1.2
		10.2	10.6			Profit Before Taxes	7.5	8.9
						RATIOS		
		2.1	4.6				3.5	4.9
		1.1	3.7			Current	2.0	2.4
		.5	2.0				1.3	1.6
		1.9	4.5				2.8	3.8
		1.0	2.7			Quick	1.4	2.2
		.5	1.7				1.0	1.1
	16	22.9	29 12.5				6 57.5	12 29.9
	58	6.3	35 10.5			Sales/Receivables	45 8.2	43 8.5
	89	4.1	70 5.2				68 5.4	65 5.6
	0	UND	0 UND				0 UND	0 UND
	0	UND	0 UND			Cost of Sales/Inventory	0 UND	0 999.8
	5	76.8	9 42.0				4 103.7	41 8.9
	0	UND	12 29.4				4 87.3	2 146.0
	14	25.2	22 16.3			Cost of Sales/Payables	19 19.3	14 26.0
	36	10.0	31 11.9				33 11.0	38 9.6
		13.3	4.2				5.3	3.9
		NM	5.8			Sales/Working Capital	9.9	7.0
		-6.0	8.2				47.0	21.6
							65.9	144.9
						EBIT/Interest	(37) 21.2	(21) 23.3
							4.5	9.3
						Net Profit + Depr., Dep., Amort./Cur. Mat. L/T/D		
		.1	.0				.1	.0
		.5	.0			Fixed/Worth	.3	.2
		1.6	.1				.9	.4
		.8	.3				.4	.3
		1.3	.7			Debt/Worth	1.3	1.2
		3.1	1.1				3.9	2.6
		63.4	85.5				110.5	109.3
		34.6	64.1			% Profit Before Taxes/Tangible Net Worth	(44) 51.8	48.8
		7.7	11.3				23.2	21.8
		30.1	49.9				41.6	45.4
		10.5	39.8			% Profit Before Taxes/Total Assets	24.6	18.8
		5.2	7.3				3.5	9.3
		87.3	582.3				103.1	271.7
		31.5	208.2			Sales/Net Fixed Assets	29.9	44.8
		6.2	60.1				14.2	16.4
		4.3	5.7				5.1	4.4
		2.1	2.7			Sales/Total Assets	3.5	3.2
		1.8	1.9				2.4	1.9
							.4	.4
						% Depr., Dep., Amort./Sales	(31) .8	(18) 1.1
							1.5	2.6
							.8	1.3
						% Officers', Directors' Owners' Comp/Sales	(21) 3.0	(10) 4.2
							5.5	8.1
6301M	52220M	143188M	587192M		369975M	Net Sales ($)	1315853M	1141082M
657M	8907M	52382M	167114M		310147M	Total Assets ($)	604200M	435643M

© RMA 2024

M = $ thousand   MM = $ million
See Pages viii through xx for Explanation of Ratios and Data

CONSTRUCTION-GENERAL—Framing Contractors NAICS 238130

Comparative Historical Data					Current Data Sorted by Sales					
				Type of Statement						
		3	1	Unqualified					1	1
4	3	3	7	Reviewed				1	6	
3	1	1	1	Compiled					1	
7	4	4	13	Tax Returns	3	3	2	1	3	1
19	22	13		Other	1	1		2	5	4
4/1/21-3/31/22 ALL	4/1/22-3/31/23 ALL	4/1/23-3/31/24 ALL			0-1MM	5 (4/1-9/30/23) 1-3MM	3-5MM	30 (10/1/23-3/31/24) 5-10MM	10-25MM	25MM & OVER
33	33	35		**NUMBER OF STATEMENTS**	4	4	2	3	9	13
%	%	%		**ASSETS**	%	%	%	%	%	%
23.3	25.8	25.2		Cash & Equivalents						28.7
36.6	30.7	26.8		Trade Receivables (net)						40.3
6.4	6.9	4.4		Inventory						5.0
11.2	9.2	7.9		All Other Current						10.9
77.4	72.6	64.3		Total Current						84.9
15.9	16.9	24.0		Fixed Assets (net)						5.0
2.8	7.3	5.2		Intangibles (net)						2.5
3.9	3.3	6.5		All Other Non-Current						7.5
100.0	100.0	100.0		Total						100.0
				LIABILITIES						
5.9	4.2	7.6		Notes Payable-Short Term						2.0
1.2	1.1	1.6		Cur. Mat.-L.T.D.						.6
15.6	13.5	13.7		Trade Payables						18.4
.0	.1	.3		Income Taxes Payable						.0
21.5	12.7	13.7		All Other Current						18.6
44.3	31.6	36.9		Total Current						39.6
9.5	16.6	7.2		Long-Term Debt						2.7
.0	.0	.0		Deferred Taxes						.0
1.3	3.9	3.3		All Other Non-Current						3.4
44.8	47.9	52.9		Net Worth						54.4
100.0	100.0	100.0		Total Liabilities & Net Worth						100.0
				INCOME DATA						
100.0	100.0	100.0		Net Sales						100.0
26.0	24.3	29.8		Gross Profit						23.7
19.6	17.1	20.4		Operating Expenses						13.6
6.4	7.2	9.4		Operating Profit						10.2
-1.5	.0	.4		All Other Expenses (net)						-.1
7.9	7.2	9.0		Profit Before Taxes						10.2
				RATIOS						
4.7	5.5	4.0								3.7
2.3	2.8	2.0		Current						2.0
1.2	1.4	.9								1.5
3.7	5.0	3.3								2.8
1.6	2.0	1.4		Quick						1.7
1.0	1.0	.6								1.2
14 26.5	2 158.6	0 UND							27	13.3
46 8.0	33 11.1	28 12.9		Sales/Receivables					35	10.5
64 5.7	61 6.0	76 4.8							73	5.0
0 UND	0 UND	0 UND							0	UND
0 999.8	0 UND	0 UND		Cost of Sales/Inventory					7	55.0
15 24.7	22 16.4	8 45.1							14	25.3
0 UND	2 180.4	0 UND							13	27.8
12 29.5	16 23.5	14 26.3		Cost of Sales/Payables					22	16.3
35 10.4	23 15.7	31 11.9							38	9.7
4.6	5.6	5.8								4.8
7.6	7.1	10.2		Sales/Working Capital						7.9
33.9	17.6	-103.8								9.5
146.8	80.5	386.3								999.8
(24) 25.4	(28) 29.9	(28) 25.8		EBIT/Interest					(11)	192.3
.5	13.9	3.7								20.5
				Net Profit + Depr., Dep., Amort./Cur. Mat. L/T/D						
.1	.1	.0								.0
.2	.2	.2		Fixed/Worth						.1
.5	1.0	1.1								.2
.3	.5	.4								.4
.8	.8	1.0		Debt/Worth						1.0
2.4	3.5	2.4								1.5
104.0	71.8	85.6		% Profit Before Taxes/Tangible Net Worth						95.6
(30) 57.8	(29) 36.5	(34) 48.3								74.3
14.3	13.6	14.2								13.2
61.8	38.7	47.8		% Profit Before Taxes/Total Assets						48.9
25.5	19.9	25.8								27.0
6.8	4.0	7.3								5.9
139.9	235.9	265.1								314.1
25.2	40.2	53.7		Sales/Net Fixed Assets						83.2
15.1	15.4	11.8								35.4
5.2	4.4	5.8								5.7
3.6	3.3	2.7		Sales/Total Assets						3.0
2.4	2.4	1.9								2.0
.2	.1	.3								.1
(25) .8	(22) .5	(23) .7		% Depr., Dep., Amort./Sales					(12)	.3
1.5	1.4	1.6								.7
.8	.6	.8								
(15) 1.5	(11) .9	(13) 1.2		% Officers', Directors' Owners' Comp/Sales						
4.8	4.4	3.3								
1162349M	2648895M	1158876M		Net Sales ($)	2388M	6874M	8210M	19578M	150865M	970961M
356232M	1010908M	539207M		Total Assets ($)	5000M	2224M	1550M	10270M	54032M	466131M

M = $ thousand   MM = $ million
See Pages viii through xx for Explanation of Ratios and Data
© RMA 2024

CONSTRUCTION-GENERAL—Masonry Contractors NAICS 238140

Current Data Sorted by Assets

0-500M	500M-2MM	2-10MM	10-50MM	50-100MM	100-250MM		Type of Statement	4/1/19-3/31/20 ALL	4/1/20-3/31/21 ALL
	1	1	6				Unqualified	4	2
	2	13	9	2			Reviewed	36	18
			1				Compiled	6	4
4	7	7	1				Tax Returns	30	15
3	15	19	18	2			Other	57	41
	14 (4/1-9/30/23)		97 (10/1/23-3/31/24)						
8	25	39	35	4			NUMBER OF STATEMENTS	133	80
%	%	%	%	%	%		**ASSETS**	%	%
	25.6	13.4	16.9				Cash & Equivalents	14.9	23.1
	33.1	49.5	41.1				Trade Receivables (net)	39.8	29.9
	3.3	4.4	3.4				Inventory	4.4	5.9
	1.3	5.7	11.9		D		All Other Current	6.3	6.3
	63.3	73.0	73.3		A		Total Current	65.3	65.1
	19.3	17.5	13.5		T		Fixed Assets (net)	24.0	23.7
	4.8	2.6	10.2		A		Intangibles (net)	3.6	4.1
	12.6	6.9	2.9				All Other Non-Current	7.1	7.1
	100.0	100.0	100.0		N		Total	100.0	100.0
					O		**LIABILITIES**		
	7.5	7.1	2.6		T		Notes Payable-Short Term	12.2	11.0
	3.1	2.9	1.4				Cur. Mat.-L.T.D.	3.5	3.9
	9.4	16.0	12.0		A		Trade Payables	12.5	10.6
	.0	.2	.0		V		Income Taxes Payable	.2	.0
	18.9	16.0	14.8		A		All Other Current	17.6	11.0
	39.0	42.3	30.8		I		Total Current	45.9	36.7
	19.8	9.6	9.1		L		Long-Term Debt	21.9	23.0
	.0	.6	.1		A		Deferred Taxes	.5	.2
	1.7	1.3	1.2		B		All Other Non-Current	2.5	6.0
	39.6	46.2	58.7		L		Net Worth	29.1	34.1
	100.0	100.0	100.0		E		Total Liabilities & Net Worth	100.0	100.0
							INCOME DATA		
	100.0	100.0	100.0				Net Sales	100.0	100.0
	37.5	31.5	26.2				Gross Profit	30.1	33.0
	31.8	22.0	18.7				Operating Expenses	23.7	28.5
	5.8	9.5	7.6				Operating Profit	6.4	4.5
	-.1	.3	-1.0				All Other Expenses (net)	.7	-1.4
	5.9	9.2	8.6				Profit Before Taxes	5.7	6.0
							RATIOS		
	3.0	3.5	4.1					3.0	3.3
	1.7	2.2	2.3				Current	1.8	2.0
	1.1	1.1	1.7					1.1	1.3
	2.8	3.5	3.5					2.7	2.9
	1.4	2.0	1.8				Quick	1.5	1.8
	1.0	.9	1.2					.9	1.0
0	UND	45	8.1	68	5.4			22	16.5	24	15.0
26	14.1	69	5.3	85	4.3		Sales/Receivables	59	6.2	51	7.2
56	6.5	96	3.8	114	3.2			87	4.2	85	4.3
0	UND	0	UND	0	UND			0	UND	0	UND
0	UND	0	UND	0	UND		Cost of Sales/Inventory	0	UND	0	UND
0	999.8	2	173.1	2	234.5			1	264.2	17	21.2
0	UND	12	30.6	17	22.0			7	55.1	11	33.5
9	41.1	25	14.4	28	13.0		Cost of Sales/Payables	17	21.8	19	18.8
24	15.4	43	8.4	42	8.7			32	11.3	32	11.3
	8.0	4.0	3.0					4.7	4.6
	26.3	7.7	4.3				Sales/Working Capital	9.3	7.1
	97.5	34.6	6.5					39.0	21.6
	40.6	53.0	82.6					38.1	59.0
(17)	10.4	(33)	18.1	(29)	34.9		EBIT/Interest	(112)	10.6	(65)	13.0
	1.2	7.0	7.8					2.9	3.2
							Net Profit + Depr., Dep., Amort./Cur. Mat. L/T/D		22.6		18.1
								(17)	3.7	(11)	4.7
								2.2	-5.5
	.1	.1	.1					.2	.2
	.5	.4	.2				Fixed/Worth	.4	.4
	3.7	.7	.4					1.2	2.4
	.4	.3	.4					.5	.5
	1.7	.8	.7				Debt/Worth	1.2	1.2
	12.2	2.3	1.4					4.0	8.9
	121.0	65.6	43.9					56.8	62.1
(21)	26.7	(34)	45.0	(32)	25.7		% Profit Before Taxes/Tangible Net Worth	(111)	33.3	(66)	31.1
	8.7	21.5	12.5					12.0	11.6
	36.2	31.1	24.5					27.2	25.3
	17.3	20.1	12.2				% Profit Before Taxes/Total Assets	14.3	12.8
	2.2	8.5	3.2					3.0	2.3
	150.2	62.3	28.3					55.2	23.5
	33.0	18.9	15.0				Sales/Net Fixed Assets	18.2	13.7
	11.9	7.8	8.7					9.1	7.3
	7.5	3.5	2.3					4.0	2.7
	3.9	2.6	2.0				Sales/Total Assets	2.8	2.2
	2.7	2.0	1.4					2.0	1.7
	.5	1.1	1.1					.8	1.5
(13)	2.4	(24)	1.5	(29)	1.7		% Depr., Dep., Amort./Sales	(90)	1.6	(60)	2.4
	5.0	2.5	2.5					2.9	3.7
	2.0	1.2	1.0					1.9	3.0
(17)	3.1	(12)	2.4	(11)	1.2		% Officers', Directors' Owners' Comp/Sales	(60)	4.2	(28)	5.0
	4.2	4.9	2.7					7.9	10.0
12550M	141377M	503292M	1438974M	711247M			Net Sales ($)	1979703M	1088056M
2021M	29424M	190410M	768908M	291426M			Total Assets ($)	834124M	570967M

M = $ thousand   MM = $ million
See Pages viii through xx for Explanation of Ratios and Data

© RMA 2024

CONSTRUCTION-GENERAL—Masonry Contractors NAICS 238140

Comparative Historical Data					Current Data Sorted by Sales					
3	4	10	Type of Statement		1		1		1	7
18	25	24	Unqualified							7
2	3	1	Reviewed		1		5		11	
13	19	19	Compiled							1
46	55	57	Tax Returns		2	1	3	9	3	1
4/1/21-3/31/22 ALL	4/1/22-3/31/23 ALL	4/1/23-3/31/24 ALL	Other		1	8	7	20	20	13
					0-1MM	14 (4/1-9/30/23) 1-3MM	3-5MM	97 (10/1/23-3/31/24) 5-10MM	10-25MM	25MM & OVER
82	106	111	NUMBER OF STATEMENTS		4	9	12	22	35	29
%	%	%	ASSETS		%	%	%	%	%	%
22.5	20.7	18.9	Cash & Equivalents				22.1	22.2	15.7	18.8
33.9	38.2	40.6	Trade Receivables (net)				29.2	36.9	50.2	41.3
2.0	2.0	3.9	Inventory				8.5	4.8	3.0	3.0
8.1	8.6	6.3	All Other Current				1.1	3.0	6.8	12.9
66.5	69.5	69.8	Total Current				61.0	66.8	75.6	76.0
22.9	18.3	17.5	Fixed Assets (net)				25.2	18.8	14.2	13.6
4.0	3.9	5.9	Intangibles (net)				7.4	4.4	4.0	6.9
6.5	8.3	6.8	All Other Non-Current				6.3	10.0	6.2	3.6
100.0	100.0	100.0	Total				100.0	100.0	100.0	100.0
			LIABILITIES							
7.0	5.7	5.5	Notes Payable-Short Term				4.8	10.2	6.2	2.5
2.3	3.3	3.0	Cur. Mat.-L.T.D.				3.4	1.5	3.1	2.2
11.5	11.8	12.6	Trade Payables				4.0	12.2	18.4	11.9
.1	.2	.1	Income Taxes Payable				.0	.2	.1	.0
18.4	14.8	15.9	All Other Current				17.1	19.4	14.1	15.7
39.4	35.7	37.1	Total Current				29.4	43.5	41.8	32.3
15.5	15.9	13.1	Long-Term Debt				23.2	11.5	12.8	8.6
.2	.4	.2	Deferred Taxes				.0	.2	.6	.1
5.2	2.3	1.4	All Other Non-Current				2.9	1.8	.9	1.1
39.7	45.7	48.2	Net Worth				44.6	43.0	43.9	58.0
100.0	100.0	100.0	Total Liabilities & Net Worth				100.0	100.0	100.0	100.0
			INCOME DATA							
100.0	100.0	100.0	Net Sales				100.0	100.0	100.0	100.0
31.1	31.2	32.2	Gross Profit				41.7	31.7	30.1	22.3
24.3	25.6	24.4	Operating Expenses				33.7	26.2	20.2	15.3
6.9	5.6	7.8	Operating Profit				8.0	5.5	9.9	6.9
-1.1	-.5	-.2	All Other Expenses (net)				.5	.1	-.2	-1.2
7.9	6.1	8.0	Profit Before Taxes				7.6	5.4	10.1	8.1
			RATIOS							
4.8	3.7	3.7					8.9	3.2	3.7	3.7
2.3	2.1	2.1	Current				1.9	1.8	1.9	2.3
1.3	1.4	1.3					.9	.9	1.3	1.8
4.3	3.3	3.3					7.1	3.0	3.6	3.2
1.9	1.7	1.8	Quick				1.6	1.7	1.8	1.9
1.1	1.1	1.1					.7	.8	1.1	1.2
19 19.4	21 17.1	27 13.3			0 UND	23 16.1	32 11.3	51 7.1		
62 5.9	61 6.0	65 5.6	Sales/Receivables		25 14.4	61 6.0	72 5.1	73 5.0		
85 4.3	87 4.2	87 4.2			57 6.4	99 3.7	104 3.5	89 4.1		
0 UND	0 UND	0 UND			0 UND	0 UND	0 UND	0 UND		
0 UND	0 UND	0 UND	Cost of Sales/Inventory		0 UND	0 UND	0 999.8	0 UND		
2 191.3	1 273.8	2 217.4			14 26.3	0 UND	2 173.1	1 271.5		
4 95.5	9 40.5	11 34.0			0 UND	8 44.8	15 24.1	15 24.9		
16 22.9	18 19.8	24 15.5	Cost of Sales/Payables		2 195.7	25 14.7	24 14.9	28 13.0		
34 10.8	36 10.2	36 10.1			17 21.8	43 8.4	42 8.7	36 10.1		
3.5	4.2	4.0					9.4	4.3	3.8	3.5
6.4	7.1	6.8	Sales/Working Capital				12.8	7.4	9.1	4.8
20.5	14.7	27.2					NM	-52.4	27.2	6.5
87.4	47.9	50.8					46.9		56.3	84.1
(65) 22.6	(83) 13.3	(88) 18.7	EBIT/Interest			(19)	14.4	(28) 19.0	(24) 34.9	
4.8	2.0	5.6					6.4	8.2	6.5	
20.1	11.1	13.6	Net Profit + Depr., Dep.,							
(13) 11.0	(16) 4.4	(17) 4.3	Amort./Cur. Mat. L/T/D							
7.3	2.8	1.8								
.1	.1	.1					.1	.3	.1	.1
.4	.3	.4	Fixed/Worth				.6	.4	.3	.2
1.1	.6	.8					4.2	3.1	.6	.4
.3	.4	.4					.2	.4	.4	.4
.8	.9	.9	Debt/Worth				1.5	.8	1.0	.7
2.7	2.3	2.5					21.6	11.0	2.5	1.4
66.2	63.9	60.2	% Profit Before Taxes/Tangible				167.9	49.0	72.2	44.8
(71) 26.0	(96) 29.7	(98) 36.3	Net Worth		(10)	57.7	(18) 26.7	(31) 54.3	(28) 25.7	
12.5	6.4	14.6					21.0	11.8	26.1	12.8
32.9	31.4	32.1	% Profit Before Taxes/Total				61.2	23.2	39.0	28.0
16.0	11.8	17.3	Assets				26.6	16.5	21.2	13.0
6.2	1.7	4.4					2.0	4.2	10.3	3.3
36.1	59.2	62.3					78.5	88.3	140.0	28.1
15.3	18.7	19.0	Sales/Net Fixed Assets				28.4	11.2	24.4	18.5
7.8	10.0	9.1					11.6	7.5	10.7	9.6
3.2	3.6	3.5					5.4	3.7	3.7	2.7
2.2	2.4	2.5	Sales/Total Assets				3.1	2.4	2.7	2.1
1.6	1.8	1.9					2.5	1.9	1.8	1.8
1.0	.7	1.1						2.0	1.1	1.0
(54) 2.1	(67) 1.7	(73) 1.7	% Depr., Dep., Amort./Sales			(13)	2.4	(21) 1.4	(26) 1.5	
3.3	3.2	2.7						3.1	1.8	2.5
1.9	2.3	1.2					1.1	.6		
(29) 3.2	(45) 3.9	(45) 2.8	% Officers', Directors' Owners' Comp/Sales			(12)	2.4	(11) 1.3		
7.7	7.0	4.5					3.6	5.1		
1840125M	1899493M	2807440M	Net Sales ($)		2071M	21384M	43586M	161450M	603208M	1975741M
925149M	857229M	1282189M	Total Assets ($)		803M	14657M	12498M	72912M	248130M	933189M

© RMA 2024

M = $ thousand   MM = $ million
See Pages viii through xx for Explanation of Ratios and Data

CONSTRUCTION-GENERAL—Glass and Glazing Contractors NAICS 238150

Current Data Sorted by Assets | Comparative Historical Data

			4	1	1	**Type of Statement**			
		9	13			Unqualified		6	2
	1	6				Reviewed		38	16
3	3	11				Compiled		5	5
6	10	14	15	2		Tax Returns		24	10
	22 (4/1-9/30/23)		77 (10/1/23-3/31/24)			Other		54	38
0-500M	500M-2MM	2-10MM	10-50MM	50-100MM	100-250MM			4/1/19-3/31/20 ALL	4/1/20-3/31/21 ALL
9	14	40	32	3	1	**NUMBER OF STATEMENTS**		127	71
%	%	%	%	%	%	**ASSETS**		%	%
	16.6	19.6	14.2			Cash & Equivalents		16.5	25.8
	33.7	47.1	42.4			Trade Receivables (net)		43.0	40.5
	10.4	4.1	6.1			Inventory		7.6	6.3
	2.5	4.8	11.2			All Other Current		7.4	5.9
	63.1	75.6	73.9			Total Current		74.5	78.5
	12.6	16.4	15.4			Fixed Assets (net)		13.9	13.1
	9.2	5.2	4.6			Intangibles (net)		5.8	2.8
	15.1	2.8	6.2			All Other Non-Current		5.8	5.6
	100.0	100.0	100.0			Total		100.0	100.0
						LIABILITIES			
	7.4	5.5	7.6			Notes Payable-Short Term		8.4	10.7
	3.4	1.1	1.6			Cur. Mat.-L.T.D.		2.7	2.3
	14.9	12.9	14.5			Trade Payables		16.0	14.9
	.1	.3	.1			Income Taxes Payable		.2	.2
	11.6	14.1	17.1			All Other Current		20.9	21.2
	37.3	33.9	40.9			Total Current		48.1	49.3
	44.1	13.1	9.6			Long-Term Debt		12.7	15.9
	.0	.2	.4			Deferred Taxes		.3	.2
	8.7	2.1	6.5			All Other Non-Current		4.9	2.7
	9.9	50.7	42.6			Net Worth		33.9	32.0
	100.0	100.0	100.0			Total Liabilities & Net Worth		100.0	100.0
						INCOME DATA			
	100.0	100.0	100.0			Net Sales		100.0	100.0
	42.0	29.9	22.2			Gross Profit		32.3	33.8
	37.9	27.5	17.4			Operating Expenses		24.9	28.1
	4.1	2.4	4.9			Operating Profit		7.4	5.6
	.0	-.1	-.5			All Other Expenses (net)		.5	-1.3
	4.0	2.5	5.4			Profit Before Taxes		6.8	7.0
						RATIOS			
	4.0	3.6	2.9					2.8	5.0
	1.8	2.3	1.8			Current		1.7	2.1
	1.0	1.6	1.4					1.2	1.4
	3.2	2.9	2.5					2.4	4.0
	1.3	2.1	1.4			Quick		1.4	1.8
	.6	1.4	1.1					.9	1.2
0	UND	46	8.0	60	6.1		34	10.6	41	8.8
30	12.1	87	4.2	91	4.0	Sales/Receivables	61	6.0	59	6.2
51	7.2	114	3.2	107	3.4		89	4.1	83	4.4
0	UND	0	UND	0	UND		0	UND	0	UND
5	75.9	2	224.4	3	138.4	Cost of Sales/Inventory	3	111.5	2	214.2
14	25.3	18	20.3	29	12.5		20	17.9	26	14.2
0	UND	11	33.8	17	21.8		13	28.7	10	36.2
19	19.3	27	13.7	31	11.6	Cost of Sales/Payables	24	15.4	23	15.8
37	9.9	42	8.6	52	7.0		45	8.2	42	8.6
	7.2	3.6	3.1					5.1	3.2
	11.3	4.9	6.8			Sales/Working Capital		8.3	5.3
	NM	9.7	9.1					23.0	12.9
	27.9	46.1	13.8					47.2	152.0
	4.1	(31) 13.4	(27) 7.5			EBIT/Interest	(102)	13.8	(55) 31.7
	.5	1.8	2.1					3.5	4.0
			13.5			Net Profit + Depr., Dep.,		20.8	
		(10) 5.7				Amort./Cur. Mat. L/T/D	(26)	7.7	
			2.7					1.9	
	.1	.1	.1					.1	.1
	.4	.2	.2			Fixed/Worth		.3	.2
	NM	.5	.8					1.3	.5
	.9	.5	.6					.6	.4
	2.5	.9	2.0			Debt/Worth		1.7	1.1
	-6.6	2.1	3.8					5.5	2.3
	102.4	39.4	50.5					61.8	61.9
(10)	16.1	(37) 15.3	(31) 23.4			% Profit Before Taxes/Tangible Net Worth	(106)	38.4	(64) 37.6
	-6.1	3.2	6.7					14.8	17.2
	35.9	23.0	19.6					26.2	31.8
	8.3	7.8	5.5			% Profit Before Taxes/Total Assets		15.1	19.9
	-1.2	1.3	2.2					4.3	5.3
	138.7	43.2	51.2					69.5	77.0
	40.8	24.4	22.2			Sales/Net Fixed Assets		29.3	27.9
	20.7	9.9	7.9					14.3	13.2
	4.5	3.0	2.1					3.7	2.9
	3.2	2.0	1.8			Sales/Total Assets		2.6	2.5
	2.3	1.6	1.5					1.9	1.9
		.5	.6					.5	.3
	(31)	1.0	(23) 1.0			% Depr., Dep., Amort./Sales	(87)	1.0	(47) .8
		1.7	1.3					1.6	2.0
		1.4						1.8	2.6
	(24)	2.6				% Officers', Directors' Owners' Comp/Sales	(61)	3.1	(32) 3.9
		3.6						6.2	5.9
20420M	56713M	454111M	1374022M	321071M	141997M	Net Sales ($)		2939513M	1366181M
3069M	15323M	202876M	761326M	205038M	125532M	Total Assets ($)		1434762M	713696M

M = $ thousand   MM = $ million
See Pages viii through xx for Explanation of Ratios and Data

© RMA 2024

CONSTRUCTION-GENERAL—Glass and Glazing Contractors NAICS 238150

Comparative Historical Data | Current Data Sorted by Sales

Comparative Historical Data			Type of Statement	Current Data Sorted by Sales					
12	4 21	6 22	Unqualified				4 1	10 6	6 8
4	9	7	Reviewed						
19	18	17	Compiled	1	4	1	6	5	
48	46	47	Tax Returns	3	9	3	10	6	16
4/1/21-3/31/22	4/1/22-3/31/23	4/1/23-3/31/24	Other	22 (4/1-9/30/23)			77 (10/1/23-3/31/24)		
ALL	ALL	ALL		0-1MM	1-3MM	3-5MM	5-10MM	10-25MM	25MM & OVER
83	98	99	NUMBER OF STATEMENTS	4	13	4	21	27	30
%	%	%	ASSETS	%	%	%	%	%	%
21.3	21.0	18.9	Cash & Equivalents	26.1			20.8	20.3	11.5
39.3	37.4	40.6	Trade Receivables (net)	19.5			46.2	44.0	48.4
7.0	5.2	5.6	Inventory	2.1			3.8	4.3	7.0
7.1	6.7	6.9	All Other Current	2.0			4.6	7.7	10.9
74.8	70.2	71.9	Total Current	49.8			75.4	76.4	77.7
14.1	16.3	15.5	Fixed Assets (net)	17.1			16.8	16.3	11.6
3.6	5.2	6.6	Intangibles (net)	13.4			5.4	3.7	4.3
7.4	8.2	6.0	All Other Non-Current	19.7			2.3	3.6	6.4
100.0	100.0	100.0	Total	100.0			100.0	100.0	100.0
			LIABILITIES						
6.3	5.5	7.3	Notes Payable-Short Term	6.6			9.4	3.9	9.6
1.8	1.4	1.5	Cur. Mat.-L.T.D.	2.4			1.4	1.1	1.4
11.9	11.3	13.0	Trade Payables	5.7			13.6	14.7	16.3
.4	.5	.2	Income Taxes Payable	.1			.1	.5	.0
11.3	13.4	14.4	All Other Current	4.1			14.0	13.4	20.4
31.6	32.1	36.4	Total Current	18.9			38.4	33.6	47.7
11.8	12.5	16.0	Long-Term Debt	31.6			9.3	10.1	8.5
.1	.1	.2	Deferred Taxes	.0			.3	.4	.1
5.9	3.9	5.0	All Other Non-Current	6.8			.7	3.8	6.8
50.7	51.4	42.4	Net Worth	42.7			51.3	52.1	36.9
100.0	100.0	100.0	Total Liabilities & Net Worth	100.0			100.0	100.0	100.0
			INCOME DATA						
100.0	100.0	100.0	Net Sales	100.0			100.0	100.0	100.0
35.3	30.8	29.5	Gross Profit	42.0			29.1	31.0	21.0
30.1	25.9	24.9	Operating Expenses	40.5			24.2	25.1	17.2
5.2	4.9	4.5	Operating Profit	1.5			5.0	5.9	3.8
-2.2	-.8	-.3	All Other Expenses (net)	.2			-.6	.2	-.5
7.4	5.7	4.8	Profit Before Taxes	1.3			5.5	5.7	4.3
			RATIOS						
5.4	5.1	3.7		11.7			4.4	3.0	2.4
2.6	2.3	2.1	Current	9.3			2.3	2.4	1.5
1.4	1.5	1.4		1.0			1.5	1.8	1.3
4.1	3.8	2.9		10.2			3.8	2.7	1.9
2.3	1.8	1.9	Quick	9.2			2.1	2.0	1.2
1.3	1.2	1.2		.9			1.4	1.4	.9
37 9.8	30 12.3	33 11.1		0 UND			42 8.7	33 11.1	61 6.0
62 5.9	66 5.5	74 4.9	Sales/Receivables	19 19.2			66 5.5	85 4.3	91 4.0
94 3.9	99 3.7	107 3.4		49 7.4			99 3.7	111 3.3	111 3.3
0 UND	0 UND	0 UND		0 UND			0 UND	0 UND	0 UND
4 103.7	1 564.8	2 163.0	Cost of Sales/Inventory	0 UND			1 415.9	3 112.0	5 78.7
22 16.3	13 28.1	17 20.9		4 95.0			7 51.7	19 19.0	34 10.8
8 48.5	6 64.2	11 33.8		0 UND			7 55.5	21 17.4	17 20.9
17 21.0	16 22.3	26 14.0	Cost of Sales/Payables	1 372.5			23 15.9	30 12.0	32 11.4
43 8.4	43 8.5	45 8.1		23 16.2			38 9.5	47 7.7	59 6.2
3.1	3.8	3.8		5.7			3.7	3.4	3.8
4.6	6.2	6.8	Sales/Working Capital	15.3			5.3	4.5	8.1
14.1	15.0	12.6		NM			10.0	8.0	12.7
90.5	64.9	41.0		43.3			85.7	67.2	17.8
(59) 17.9	(76) 16.1	(81) 7.8	EBIT/Interest	(11) 5.9			(17) 9.9	(22) 11.5	(27) 7.8
4.0	2.3	1.8		1.3			1.7	3.9	.4
	14.2	10.7	Net Profit + Depr., Dep.,						
(18)	6.6	(17) 5.2	Amort./Cur. Mat. L/T/D						
	2.9	2.0							
.1	.1	.1		.0			.1	.1	.1
.2	.3	.2	Fixed/Worth	.3			.2	.2	.2
.5	.7	.8		NM			.4	.5	.8
.3	.4	.5		.1			.3	.5	1.1
.9	1.0	1.3	Debt/Worth	1.4			.6	.9	2.4
3.0	2.5	3.8		-7.3			3.0	2.0	4.1
63.0	52.6	52.5					100.9	38.0	51.4
(78) 32.2	(92) 20.2	(88) 22.0	% Profit Before Taxes/Tangible Net Worth	(19) 14.6		(26)	15.5	(28) 24.8	
16.5	2.7	3.7					3.4	8.6	4.0
26.8	21.8	24.6	% Profit Before Taxes/Total Assets	45.1			37.4	21.0	18.2
14.5	8.7	7.9		16.1			9.6	7.7	6.7
8.8	1.5	1.4		-4.5			1.4	2.8	.2
74.2	82.2	52.6		102.9			81.0	42.0	66.9
23.2	24.4	25.9	Sales/Net Fixed Assets	42.9			24.4	23.6	31.6
13.4	11.2	10.5		18.0			6.9	9.7	15.7
2.9	3.0	3.0		6.1			3.2	3.0	2.2
2.4	2.0	2.0	Sales/Total Assets	4.0			2.1	2.0	1.8
1.7	1.6	1.6		2.0			1.7	1.6	1.5
.6	.5	.7					.4	.8	.3
(53) .9	(60) 1.1	(66) 1.0	% Depr., Dep., Amort./Sales			(16)	1.1	(21) 1.0	(21) .9
1.7	2.0	1.5					1.7	1.5	1.2
2.2	1.8	1.4	% Officers', Directors' Owners' Comp/Sales				2.2	1.1	
(39) 3.9	(42) 3.6	(42) 2.4				(13)	3.1	(14) 1.6	
7.5	6.6	3.8					3.7	2.6	
1265542M	1942767M	2368334M	Net Sales ($)	2459M	23122M	16576M	162419M	428048M	1735710M
646554M	1139178M	1313164M	Total Assets ($)	3375M	10353M	5501M	71200M	211488M	1011247M

© RMA 2024   M = $ thousand   MM = $ million
See Pages viii through xx for Explanation of Ratios and Data

CONSTRUCTION-GENERAL—Roofing Contractors NAICS 238160

Current Data Sorted by Assets | **Comparative Historical Data**

							Type of Statement		
1	2	23	8	6	3		Unqualified	11	11
2	4	4	26	2			Reviewed	55	40
9	13	12	1				Compiled	7	13
16	27	54	2				Tax Returns	48	23
			29	5	3		Other	136	88
	29 (4/1-9/30/23)		219 (10/1/23-3/31/24)					4/1/19-3/31/20	4/1/20-3/31/21
0-500M	500M-2MM	2-10MM	10-50MM	50-100MM	100-250MM			ALL	ALL
28	42	93	66	13	6		**NUMBER OF STATEMENTS**	257	175
%	%	%	%	%	%		**ASSETS**	%	%
41.1	34.9	20.0	22.2	10.9			Cash & Equivalents	20.1	27.2
14.9	25.9	41.2	42.5	33.7			Trade Receivables (net)	41.1	33.3
.0	3.9	6.8	5.0	1.6			Inventory	3.9	3.2
9.4	2.3	9.3	9.8	15.0			All Other Current	6.0	6.6
65.4	66.9	77.2	79.5	61.1			Total Current	71.2	70.4
25.6	19.2	14.8	9.6	10.8			Fixed Assets (net)	18.2	18.6
1.9	7.3	3.9	1.8	21.5			Intangibles (net)	3.1	3.8
7.1	6.6	4.1	9.1	6.6			All Other Non-Current	7.5	7.2
100.0	100.0	100.0	100.0	100.0			Total	100.0	100.0
							LIABILITIES		
13.3	8.4	6.9	3.0	1.5			Notes Payable-Short Term	10.7	9.2
3.8	1.2	1.6	1.4	.9			Cur. Mat.-L.T.D.	2.4	2.3
8.7	13.6	15.5	12.7	12.4			Trade Payables	18.1	14.6
.0	.1	.2	.2	.7			Income Taxes Payable	.1	.2
18.2	13.9	13.1	19.3	19.4			All Other Current	14.0	15.3
44.0	37.2	37.2	36.7	34.8			Total Current	45.3	41.5
20.2	17.7	10.2	4.5	11.2			Long-Term Debt	11.5	20.6
.0	.0	.3	.4	.2			Deferred Taxes	.2	.3
5.0	4.9	.7	3.1	5.4			All Other Non-Current	3.0	4.7
30.8	40.1	51.6	55.2	48.3			Net Worth	40.0	32.8
100.0	100.0	100.0	100.0	100.0			Total Liabilities & Net Worth	100.0	100.0
							INCOME DATA		
100.0	100.0	100.0	100.0	100.0			Net Sales	100.0	100.0
38.8	38.4	30.8	28.4	29.7			Gross Profit	30.8	33.4
27.5	31.6	22.4	17.4	22.0			Operating Expenses	23.7	25.6
11.3	6.8	8.4	11.0	7.7			Operating Profit	7.1	7.8
1.5	.2	.3	-.2	.9			All Other Expenses (net)	.2	-1.2
9.8	6.5	8.0	11.2	6.8			Profit Before Taxes	6.9	9.0
							RATIOS		
13.0	4.4	3.8	3.8	2.1				3.1	3.5
3.0	1.9	2.3	2.2	1.7			Current	1.7	2.2
.6	1.3	1.4	1.5	1.3				1.1	1.3
13.0	4.4	3.1	3.2	1.6				2.7	2.9
1.3	1.8	1.8	1.7	1.2			Quick	1.5	1.8
.4	1.2	1.0	1.2	1.0				1.0	1.1
0 UND	0 UND	27 13.7	54 6.8	28 12.9				23 15.7	10 35.5
0 UND	17 21.4	54 6.7	69 5.3	78 4.7			Sales/Receivables	49 7.5	46 8.0
15 24.2	42 8.6	81 4.5	83 4.4	94 3.9				74 4.9	68 5.4
0 UND	0 UND	0 UND	0 UND	0 UND				0 UND	0 UND
0 UND	0 UND	3 143.1	4 89.1	2 173.4			Cost of Sales/Inventory	0 999.8	0 999.8
0 UND	3 108.8	18 20.5	13 27.5	6 56.9				6 62.5	6 61.2
0 UND	0 UND	7 48.8	15 24.3	15 23.6				9 41.5	5 67.5
0 UND	15 25.1	21 17.3	28 13.0	33 11.0			Cost of Sales/Payables	24 14.9	19 19.6
4 81.3	31 11.9	43 8.5	37 9.9	48 7.6				41 8.8	33 11.0
8.3	8.2	4.4	3.3	4.7				6.4	4.7
23.3	15.8	6.8	5.8	8.8			Sales/Working Capital	11.8	9.0
-32.5	42.1	15.8	10.3	21.2				49.8	28.2
56.0	57.0	127.8	229.7	188.7				63.9	81.5
(19) 21.2	(31) 11.4	(76) 17.6	(52) 60.3	(11) 4.9			EBIT/Interest	(215) 20.6	(135) 25.2
4.6	1.3	6.7	13.2	2.1				5.1	6.5
			63.7					16.4	16.9
		(19) 16.2					Net Profit + Depr., Dep., Amort./Cur. Mat. L/T/D	(30) 4.5	(23) 5.9
		4.9						1.9	2.5
.1	.1	.1	.1	.1				.1	.1
.5	.4	.2	.1	.6			Fixed/Worth	.3	.4
UND	1.3	.7	.3	NM				.7	.8
.2	.5	.4	.4	.8				.5	.5
1.2	1.3	.8	.8	1.2			Debt/Worth	1.3	1.2
UND	3.9	2.9	1.7	NM				3.4	3.7
292.5	132.4	67.6	69.2	64.5				82.2	95.2
(22) 102.3	(35) 57.7	(87) 47.0	42.9	(10) 39.0			% Profit Before Taxes/Tangible Net Worth	(229) 43.6	(152) 38.8
37.2	13.3	16.5	27.3	14.9				21.9	18.2
91.7	48.5	38.4	35.6	22.9				38.0	44.5
45.4	22.2	19.4	22.9	12.4			% Profit Before Taxes/Total Assets	19.3	20.7
8.3	1.2	6.3	14.5	2.4				6.3	8.0
809.2	121.1	56.7	61.1	48.1				65.3	73.1
46.6	31.3	26.4	29.9	29.5			Sales/Net Fixed Assets	25.9	26.3
13.1	16.7	14.4	16.2	13.5				13.9	11.6
12.2	6.3	3.6	2.7	2.5				4.5	4.3
6.6	4.4	2.8	2.2	2.0			Sales/Total Assets	3.0	2.9
3.0	3.1	2.2	1.9	1.4				2.4	2.2
.7	.3	.8	.5	.4				.5	.8
(10) 2.8	(15) 1.3	(58) 1.2	(52) .9	(10) 1.2			% Depr., Dep., Amort./Sales	(177) 1.0	(105) 1.4
5.2	2.5	1.9	1.3	1.3				1.7	2.3
2.8	1.8	1.4	.8					1.3	1.7
(11) 6.8	(18) 3.0	(33) 2.0	(16) 1.1				% Officers', Directors' Owners' Comp/Sales	(108) 2.6	(61) 2.8
18.7	5.9	3.2	2.7					6.2	5.4
57655M	237827M	1405085M	3361699M	1649512M	1393424M		Net Sales ($)	7061246M	5480189M
7646M	48500M	473674M	1418512M	851747M	865272M		Total Assets ($)	2323066M	1802487M

M = $ thousand   MM = $ million
See Pages viii through xx for Explanation of Ratios and Data

© RMA 2024

CONSTRUCTION-GENERAL—Roofing Contractors NAICS 238160

Comparative Historical Data					Current Data Sorted by Sales					
			Type of Statement							
9	10	17	Unqualified							17
45	51	54	Reviewed		1	1	7	21	24	
9	8	7	Compiled				1	3	2	
31	34	36	Tax Returns	1	3	7	15	5	3	
92	138	134	Other	10	12	12	21	42	37	
4/1/21-3/31/22 ALL	4/1/22-3/31/23 ALL	4/1/23-3/31/24 ALL		29 (4/1-9/30/23)			219 (10/1/23-3/31/24)			
				0-1MM	1-3MM	3-5MM	5-10MM	10-25MM	25MM & OVER
186	241	248	NUMBER OF STATEMENTS	14	16	20	44	71	83
%	%	%	ASSETS	%	%	%	%	%	%
24.4	22.5	24.7	Cash & Equivalents	33.9	33.6	32.9	30.5	23.2	17.6
36.2	36.2	35.5	Trade Receivables (net)	17.2	21.1	31.7	28.6	40.0	42.1
4.9	5.6	4.7	Inventory	.9	.7	3.7	6.6	5.1	4.9
9.2	10.0	8.5	All Other Current	13.4	5.1	2.1	7.9	8.4	10.3
74.8	74.3	73.3	Total Current	65.3	60.5	70.4	73.6	76.6	74.9
17.3	14.8	15.0	Fixed Assets (net)	17.4	22.6	21.2	17.5	14.7	10.5
2.4	2.7	5.4	Intangibles (net)	9.1	4.8	5.2	4.0	3.4	7.3
5.6	8.2	6.3	All Other Non-Current	8.2	12.2	3.2	4.8	5.3	7.3
100.0	100.0	100.0	Total	100.0	100.0	100.0	100.0	100.0	100.0
			LIABILITIES						
9.2	9.1	6.5	Notes Payable-Short Term	5.6	15.9	16.3	6.1	5.5	3.5
2.1	2.3	1.7	Cur. Mat.-L.T.D.	3.1	3.1	2.5	1.8	1.3	1.4
15.3	14.6	13.4	Trade Payables	3.6	12.3	9.4	15.2	15.0	14.0
.2	.1	.2	Income Taxes Payable	.0	.0	.2	.0	.2	.3
12.8	14.4	15.9	All Other Current	6.5	35.8	10.1	12.5	12.2	19.9
39.6	40.6	37.6	Total Current	18.8	67.1	38.5	35.6	34.2	39.0
13.1	11.1	11.6	Long-Term Debt	31.5	16.4	16.9	13.8	8.3	7.7
.3	.3	.2	Deferred Taxes	.0	.0	.0	.3	.3	.3
2.2	3.1	2.9	All Other Non-Current	4.2	.5	8.3	3.1	1.5	2.9
44.8	44.9	47.6	Net Worth	45.6	16.1	36.4	47.2	55.8	50.0
100.0	100.0	100.0	Total Liabilties & Net Worth	100.0	100.0	100.0	100.0	100.0	100.0
			INCOME DATA						
100.0	100.0	100.0	Net Sales	100.0	100.0	100.0	100.0	100.0	100.0
30.9	31.4	32.2	Gross Profit	48.0	38.7	38.2	33.3	29.9	28.3
24.7	23.7	23.2	Operating Expenses	29.4	29.7	31.9	27.3	20.9	18.5
6.3	7.7	9.1	Operating Profit	18.6	9.0	6.3	6.0	9.0	9.8
-2.0	-.4	.4	All Other Expenses (net)	3.0	.5	-.1	.2	.5	.0
8.3	8.1	8.7	Profit Before Taxes	15.6	8.5	6.4	5.8	8.5	9.8
			RATIOS						
3.8	3.4	3.9		23.9	2.0	6.7	4.3	3.7	2.6
2.2	2.0	2.1	Current	6.3	1.0	1.9	2.5	2.4	1.9
1.5	1.3	1.4		1.7	.5	1.1	1.3	1.6	1.3
3.2	2.6	3.3		23.9	1.6	6.6	4.1	3.3	2.3
1.7	1.5	1.6	Quick	4.9	.9	1.7	1.9	2.0	1.5
1.1	1.0	1.0		.8	.4	1.0	1.0	1.2	1.1
22 16.3	21 17.7	18 19.9		0 UND	0 UND	0 UND	0 800.5	27 13.7	43 8.5
46 7.9	53 6.9	53 6.9	Sales/Receivables	0 UND	0 UND	40 9.2	30 12.2	60 6.1	68 5.4
73 5.0	76 4.8	76 4.8		63 5.8	35 10.4	60 6.1	62 5.9	81 4.5	79 4.6
0 UND	0 UND	0 UND		0 UND	0 UND	0 UND	0 UND	0 UND	0 UND
1 421.6	1 425.0	1 543.0	Cost of Sales/Inventory	0 UND	0 UND	0 UND	0 UND	2 155.2	3 129.0
12 30.3	13 28.0	11 31.9		0 UND	0 UND	6 63.8	14 25.9	19 19.3	12 30.5
7 55.4	3 130.5	4 87.2		0 UND	0 UND	0 UND	1 457.5	10 37.4	13 27.1
25 14.5	20 18.5	19 18.8	Cost of Sales/Payables	0 UND	0 UND	15 24.2	13 28.5	24 14.9	26 14.1
40 9.1	40 9.1	37 9.9		11 34.3	17 21.1	35 10.4	43 8.4	38 9.7	37 9.9
4.9	4.6	4.6		3.2	14.1	7.8	4.1	3.7	4.6
7.6	7.6	8.3	Sales/Working Capital	6.4	UND	13.4	8.7	6.6	7.7
19.0	19.4	20.5		18.4	-16.3	163.4	33.5	14.4	13.3
107.7	106.8	106.3			57.0	55.5	62.0	206.1	143.0
(144) 38.3	(190) 27.0	(195) 21.3	EBIT/Interest	(11) 16.1	(17) 11.4	(32) 11.6	(59) 34.7	(68) 38.2	
9.3	6.7	5.0			4.6	.4	2.3	4.4	7.1
22.3	20.7	57.9	Net Profit + Depr., Dep.,					39.8	87.0
(28) 10.9	(34) 11.8	(33) 16.6	Amort./Cur. Mat. L/T/D				(10) 12.0	(21) 16.6	
3.4	4.7	5.1						2.0	7.3
.1	.1	.1		.0	.2	.1	.1	.1	.1
.3	.2	.3	Fixed/Worth	.3	.9	.4	.2	.2	.2
.6	.5	.7		24.7	UND	NM	1.1	.5	.5
.5	.5	.5		.1	.6	.3	.4	.4	.6
.9	1.1	.9	Debt/Worth	.4	3.0	1.5	1.0	.7	1.0
2.0	2.4	2.8		84.7	UND	NM	4.4	1.6	2.4
90.6	78.5	93.7	% Profit Before Taxes/Tangible Net Worth	288.9	248.2	138.3	132.4	67.0	69.7
(170) 41.6	(220) 41.8	(223) 47.5		(12) 102.3	(12) 97.6	(15) 43.1	(39) 35.3	(69) 44.7	(76) 50.9
13.4	17.5	22.8		44.3	43.3	26.8	7.1	15.0	31.6
46.4	36.3	40.1	% Profit Before Taxes/Total Assets	89.8	61.7	45.0	42.4	38.9	34.2
22.6	18.2	21.3		46.3	27.7	19.4	12.4	21.3	21.9
6.4	6.1	7.9		12.8	16.0	2.4	1.5	4.9	12.5
66.8	65.4	69.2		UND	111.9	76.0	84.3	62.9	56.8
26.2	33.4	29.3	Sales/Net Fixed Assets	56.9	48.1	35.7	30.7	23.8	29.5
13.4	16.1	16.0		10.7	10.7	18.3	18.3	14.5	16.4
4.6	4.3	3.9		7.9	7.5	6.7	5.3	3.7	3.0
2.8	2.9	2.8	Sales/Total Assets	3.0	3.7	3.6	3.2	2.7	2.3
2.2	2.1	2.1		1.4	2.9	2.2	2.3	2.1	2.1
.7	.6	.6					.7	.7	.5
(114) 1.2	(134) 1.0	(146) 1.0	% Depr., Dep., Amort./Sales				(24) 1.1	(49) 1.2	(58) .9
1.9	1.9	1.6						2.7 1.8	1.3
1.1	1.4	1.2					1.7	1.2	.6
(58) 2.5	(82) 2.1	(79) 2.4	% Officers', Directors' Owners' Comp/Sales			(23) 2.7	(23) 2.3	(17) 1.1	
6.3	4.3	4.4					6.0	3.0	2.6
7559759M	7392978M	8105202M	Net Sales ($)	9018M	29844M	78704M	319285M	1171731M	6496620M
2032786M	2654088M	3665351M	Total Assets ($)	3917M	7634M	24152M	100064M	478278M	3051306M

© RMA 2024 M = $ thousand   MM = $ million
See Pages viii through xx for Explanation of Ratios and Data

CONSTRUCTION-GENERAL—Other Foundation, Structure, and Building Exterior Contractors NAICS 238190

Current Data Sorted by Assets | Comparative Historical Data

						Type of Statement				
			2	1	1	Unqualified			7	5
	2	6	8			Reviewed			14	10
						Compiled			5	2
4	5	2	1			Tax Returns			21	13
3	7	22	14	1	2	Other			41	46
	12 (4/1-9/30/23)		69 (10/1/23-3/31/24)						4/1/19-3/31/20	4/1/20-3/31/21
0-500M	500M-2MM	2-10MM	10-50MM	50-100MM	100-250MM				ALL	ALL
7	14	30	25	2	3	NUMBER OF STATEMENTS			88	76
%	%	%	%	%	%	ASSETS			%	%
	28.7	14.2	19.9			Cash & Equivalents			18.2	24.5
	23.0	44.1	31.3			Trade Receivables (net)			33.5	30.1
	12.7	4.9	4.9			Inventory			4.7	5.2
	7.7	6.2	12.1			All Other Current			7.5	5.4
	72.0	69.5	68.3			Total Current			63.9	65.3
	17.5	19.6	21.9			Fixed Assets (net)			27.5	25.6
	3.0	3.4	7.1			Intangibles (net)			3.0	5.1
	7.5	7.5	2.7			All Other Non-Current			5.7	4.0
	100.0	100.0	100.0			Total			100.0	100.0
						LIABILITIES				
	9.9	3.7	4.6			Notes Payable-Short Term			8.8	7.7
	1.5	2.2	3.1			Cur. Mat.-L.T.D.			2.6	3.6
	11.0	16.0	13.8			Trade Payables			14.7	8.9
	.0	.3	.1			Income Taxes Payable			.2	.2
	13.7	9.1	11.5			All Other Current			10.4	9.2
	36.2	31.3	33.0			Total Current			36.7	29.5
	13.1	13.8	8.7			Long-Term Debt			17.2	33.3
	.0	.0	.1			Deferred Taxes			.1	.0
	1.3	5.2	4.3			All Other Non-Current			4.7	4.2
	49.4	49.7	53.8			Net Worth			41.2	33.0
	100.0	100.0	100.0			Total Liabilities & Net Worth			100.0	100.0
						INCOME DATA				
	100.0	100.0	100.0			Net Sales			100.0	100.0
	41.3	34.3	31.2			Gross Profit			33.9	36.7
	33.4	26.1	19.2			Operating Expenses			25.9	28.0
	8.0	8.1	12.0			Operating Profit			8.0	8.7
	1.6	-.1	.5			All Other Expenses (net)			.6	-1.1
	6.4	8.3	11.5			Profit Before Taxes			7.4	9.8
						RATIOS				
	4.6	3.6	3.8						3.5	4.2
	2.4	2.4	2.0			Current			1.8	2.5
	1.4	1.7	1.2						1.2	1.5
	3.7	3.1	2.8						3.1	3.4
	2.1	2.0	1.6			Quick			1.5	2.1
	.7	1.4	1.0						.9	1.1
0	UND	40	9.1	27	13.4		16	22.7	16	22.6
15	24.6	76	4.8	65	5.6	Sales/Receivables	46	8.0	54	6.8
43	8.5	107	3.4	85	4.3		68	5.4	79	4.6
0	UND	0	UND	0	UND		0	UND	0	UND
1	662.7	0	UND	4	95.3	Cost of Sales/Inventory	0	UND	0	UND
29	12.6	11	33.8	26	14.2		7	50.8	7	49.3
0	UND	9	42.7	17	22.1		3	140.3	1	471.5
9	39.9	31	11.7	30	12.1	Cost of Sales/Payables	20	18.3	17	21.4
30	12.2	59	6.2	42	8.7		44	8.3	31	11.9
	5.2	3.8	3.5						5.6	3.6
	13.3	5.2	6.2			Sales/Working Capital			10.5	5.6
	25.9	9.7	19.3						44.4	15.8
	165.5	74.3	143.3						35.4	74.5
	(10) 69.2	(27) 11.8	22.8			EBIT/Interest	(73)	8.4	(65)	14.5
	2.4	3.3	5.0						4.0	5.5
						Net Profit + Depr., Dep., Amort./Cur. Mat. L/T/D			11.3	
							(14)		3.5	
									1.2	
	.1	.1	.2						.2	.2
	.2	.4	.6			Fixed/Worth			.5	.4
	.8	.8	1.1						1.6	1.6
	.4	.5	.4						.6	.8
	1.2	1.0	.8			Debt/Worth			1.4	1.4
	3.2	2.2	2.4						3.1	3.7
	92.7	64.7	86.8						73.7	76.4
	66.1	36.8	(23) 43.1			% Profit Before Taxes/Tangible Net Worth	(80)	36.2	(66)	44.2
	8.1	7.2	12.2						17.6	19.6
	51.9	31.8	35.1						35.9	33.2
	18.9	17.0	16.3			% Profit Before Taxes/Total Assets			15.0	22.0
	4.2	1.6	6.6						5.8	6.0
	202.4	39.9	26.3						48.6	40.6
	25.9	15.0	11.8			Sales/Net Fixed Assets			16.2	18.4
	7.9	7.5	4.3						6.8	6.0
	5.5	2.8	2.4						4.2	3.5
	3.2	2.3	1.9			Sales/Total Assets			2.6	2.3
	2.6	1.6	1.1						1.9	1.7
		.3	.6						.5	.7
		(16) 1.2	(18) 2.1			% Depr., Dep., Amort./Sales	(57)	1.3	(45)	1.4
		3.4	3.5						4.1	4.7
		2.1							1.6	1.4
		(11) 2.9				% Officers', Directors' Owners' Comp/Sales	(32)	3.4	(29)	3.2
		5.9							5.2	6.7
19432M	63540M	336536M	963336M	396529M	1212015M	Net Sales ($)			2650750M	1910753M
2032M	16137M	139991M	543407M	152449M	500934M	Total Assets ($)			1198617M	866388M

M = $ thousand   MM = $ million
See Pages viii through xx for Explanation of Ratios and Data

© RMA 2024

CONSTRUCTION-GENERAL—Other Foundation, Structure, and Building Exterior Contractors NAICS 238190

Comparative Historical Data | Current Data Sorted by Sales

	5		5		4	**Type of Statement**						1		3	
	9		10		16	Unqualified					3	2		7	
	5					Reviewed							4		
	12		13		12	Compiled	2	4	1	3	1				
	39		42		49	Tax Returns	3	3	3	11	14	15			
	4/1/21-		4/1/22-		4/1/23-	Other									
	3/31/22		3/31/23		3/31/24			12 (4/1-9/30/23)			69 (10/1/23-3/31/24)				
	ALL		ALL		ALL		0-1MM	1-3MM	3-5MM	5-10MM	10-25MM	25MM & OVER			
	70		70		81	**NUMBER OF STATEMENTS**	5	7	7	16	20	26			
	%		%		%	**ASSETS**	%	%	%	%	%	%			
	26.0		19.4		20.8	Cash & Equivalents				12.8	20.1	20.0			
	28.1		35.7		33.0	Trade Receivables (net)				43.0	35.6	33.0			
	5.7		4.4		5.6	Inventory				5.4	4.9	4.6			
	6.8		7.2		9.3	All Other Current				8.8	5.8	13.8			
	66.6		66.7		68.7	Total Current				70.1	66.4	71.4			
	21.5		23.6		18.8	Fixed Assets (net)				18.4	22.2	17.1			
	5.5		2.9		4.6	Intangibles (net)				4.9	3.0	7.6			
	6.5		6.8		7.9	All Other Non-Current				6.6	8.5	3.9			
	100.0		100.0		100.0	Total				100.0	100.0	100.0			
						LIABILITIES									
	6.3		6.1		5.0	Notes Payable-Short Term				8.2	3.7	3.6			
	2.3		3.7		2.2	Cur. Mat.-L.T.D.				2.7	1.2	2.7			
	13.2		15.3		14.0	Trade Payables				12.4	12.8	18.0			
	.0		.1		.1	Income Taxes Payable				.3	.0	.1			
	13.5		8.7		12.5	All Other Current				9.5	9.5	15.0			
	35.3		33.8		33.8	Total Current				33.1	27.2	39.4			
	22.4		18.3		12.4	Long-Term Debt				17.5	9.4	7.9			
	.0		.2		.1	Deferred Taxes				.0	.0	.1			
	1.7		4.8		5.2	All Other Non-Current				5.2	3.0	6.1			
	40.6		43.0		48.5	Net Worth				44.2	60.4	46.5			
	100.0		100.0		100.0	Total Liabilities & Net Worth				100.0	100.0	100.0			
						INCOME DATA									
	100.0		100.0		100.0	Net Sales				100.0	100.0	100.0			
	32.8		31.1		34.8	Gross Profit				35.5	32.9	28.1			
	25.1		23.9		25.4	Operating Expenses				26.6	23.7	18.0			
	7.7		7.2		9.4	Operating Profit				9.0	9.2	10.0			
	-2.0		-.4		.4	All Other Expenses (net)				.8	-.2	.5			
	9.7		7.6		9.0	Profit Before Taxes				8.2	9.4	9.6			
						RATIOS									
	4.7		3.6		4.0					3.4	5.4	3.3			
	2.2		1.9		2.2	Current				2.4	2.3	1.9			
	1.4		1.4		1.3					1.6	1.5	1.2			
	3.7		2.6		3.1					3.1	4.2	2.3			
	1.7		1.6		1.8	Quick				1.9	2.0	1.3			
	1.0		1.0		1.0					1.4	1.4	.9			
9	38.9	17	22.0	17	20.9					33	10.9	32	11.5	24	14.9
46	8.0	54	6.8	49	7.4	Sales/Receivables				70	5.2	54	6.8	55	6.6
79	4.6	85	4.3	87	4.2					107	3.4	91	4.0	81	4.5
0	UND	0	UND	0	UND					0	UND	0	UND	0	UND
0	UND	0	UND	0	UND	Cost of Sales/Inventory				0	UND	0	UND	1	574.2
6	64.5	4	84.8	13	28.7					12	31.6	9	40.8	14	26.1
3	126.1	2	177.6	8	47.0					15	24.7	2	194.2	17	21.0
16	23.4	21	17.6	27	13.6	Cost of Sales/Payables				32	11.3	21	17.8	30	12.2
42	8.6	41	9.0	45	8.1					46	7.9	33	11.1	51	7.2
	4.0		4.2		4.0						4.2		3.7		3.9
	8.7		9.2		7.8	Sales/Working Capital					6.1		7.1		8.1
	20.7		26.7		20.5						13.7		17.7		29.1
	101.1		83.9		89.8						50.9		210.2		121.2
(58)	19.0	(58)	31.9	(69)	21.2	EBIT/Interest				(13)	9.8	(17)	50.8	(25)	22.8
	8.3		4.6		3.9						2.9		11.8		5.0
	19.2					Net Profit + Depr., Dep.,									
(10)	4.6					Amort./Cur. Mat. L/T/D									
	3.5														
	.1		.1		.1						.1		.2		.1
	.4		.3		.3	Fixed/Worth					.2		.3		.4
	1.1		.9		1.0						.9		.8		1.1
	.5		.6		.5						.7		.3		.5
	1.1		1.3		1.0	Debt/Worth					1.4		.7		1.3
	3.0		2.9		2.9						4.8		1.0		5.9
	99.2		85.2		80.9						67.6		71.2		86.8
(61)	40.8	(63)	39.0	(77)	43.6	% Profit Before Taxes/Tangible Net Worth					39.7		38.4	(23)	51.0
	18.7		11.0		14.1						18.3		13.3		12.2
	46.4		39.4		34.8						29.0		37.0		35.0
	17.4		16.9		17.1	% Profit Before Taxes/Total Assets					17.7		22.8		14.3
	8.9		5.0		6.1						7.3		9.3		5.1
	79.4		96.3		57.9						157.0		44.7		51.8
	22.9		20.2		20.1	Sales/Net Fixed Assets					25.3		15.2		22.6
	7.3		7.8		8.0						8.1		6.3		7.4
	4.2		4.0		3.2						4.1		3.5		2.6
	2.6		2.6		2.3	Sales/Total Assets					2.5		2.3		2.2
	1.4		1.8		1.7						1.6		1.6		1.7
	.5		.3		.4								.5		.4
(42)	1.2	(34)	1.4	(47)	1.5	% Depr., Dep., Amort./Sales				(13)	2.3	(19)	1.2		
	3.8		2.6		2.9								4.7		2.2
	.8		.9		2.1										
(27)	2.5	(28)	2.0	(27)	2.8	% Officers', Directors', Owners' Comp/Sales									
	4.3		4.1		5.3										
	2525223M		2761931M		2991388M	Net Sales ($)	3103M	16124M	28262M	121425M	313932M	2508542M			
	1249582M		1121000M		1354950M	Total Assets ($)	5457M	4942M	11646M	52369M	171796M	1108740M			

M = $ thousand   MM = $ million
See Pages viii through xx for Explanation of Ratios and Data

© RMA 2024

CONSTRUCTION-GENERAL—Electrical Contractors and Other Wiring Installation Contractors NAICS 238210

Current Data Sorted by Assets | Comparative Historical Data

							Type of Statement		
		3	8	34	13	20	Unqualified	79	46
1	3	3	68	87	8	2	Reviewed	196	120
1	3	3	12	3			Compiled	39	14
20	26	28	11	1	1		Tax Returns	173	85
24	51	124	88	28	23		Other	405	263
		112 (4/1-9/30/23)		579 (10/1/23-3/31/24)				4/1/19- 3/31/20	4/1/20- 3/31/21
0-500M	500M-2MM	2-10MM	10-50MM	50-100MM	100-250MM			ALL	ALL
46	86	240	223	50	46		NUMBER OF STATEMENTS	892	528
%	%	%	%	%	%		ASSETS	%	%
32.6	26.9	19.4	17.9	12.2	13.3		Cash & Equivalents	18.7	24.9
20.4	34.7	44.3	41.6	44.5	39.6		Trade Receivables (net)	43.6	37.5
2.7	5.2	4.6	3.5	1.7	2.6		Inventory	4.3	4.3
9.1	2.9	8.7	14.1	12.2	14.2		All Other Current	7.5	7.5
64.8	69.6	77.0	77.0	70.7	69.7		Total Current	74.1	74.3
20.5	16.9	13.5	13.9	15.3	13.2		Fixed Assets (net)	17.2	16.7
5.7	3.0	3.4	3.6	6.1	9.5		Intangibles (net)	2.6	4.0
9.0	10.4	6.1	5.4	7.9	7.6		All Other Non-Current	6.1	4.9
100.0	100.0	100.0	100.0	100.0	100.0		Total	100.0	100.0
							LIABILITIES		
22.9	8.7	5.1	3.3	3.4	.8		Notes Payable-Short Term	10.3	10.8
3.7	2.6	1.5	2.2	3.6	2.4		Cur. Mat.-L.T.D.	2.7	3.0
7.9	8.4	15.8	13.7	15.0	12.3		Trade Payables	16.2	12.3
.2	.1	.1	.1	.2	.3		Income Taxes Payable	.2	.3
21.3	11.8	15.8	19.9	26.6	29.6		All Other Current	17.2	16.2
56.0	31.6	38.4	39.2	48.8	45.3		Total Current	46.6	42.7
42.2	19.7	9.5	8.2	9.0	16.3		Long-Term Debt	12.6	16.3
.0	.1	.2	.4	.3	.1		Deferred Taxes	.3	.3
1.7	3.8	3.8	4.0	3.8	5.2		All Other Non-Current	3.7	4.4
.2	44.9	48.2	48.3	38.2	33.0		Net Worth	36.8	36.2
100.0	100.0	100.0	100.0	100.0	100.0		Total Liabilities & Net Worth	100.0	100.0
							INCOME DATA		
100.0	100.0	100.0	100.0	100.0	100.0		Net Sales	100.0	100.0
50.8	41.9	32.6	24.2	20.7	20.8		Gross Profit	31.5	32.3
43.1	33.8	24.9	16.5	15.2	14.2		Operating Expenses	25.3	27.1
7.6	8.1	7.7	7.8	5.5	6.6		Operating Profit	6.3	5.2
.8	.3	.0	-.2	.3	1.4		All Other Expenses (net)	.3	-1.6
6.8	7.8	7.7	7.9	5.2	5.1		Profit Before Taxes	6.0	6.8
							RATIOS		
3.5	6.7	3.9	2.7	1.9	1.9			2.9	3.3
1.8	3.1	2.2	2.0	1.6	1.6		Current	1.8	2.1
1.0	1.6	1.4	1.4	1.3	1.2			1.3	1.4
2.9	6.0	3.1	2.2	1.5	1.6			2.4	2.6
1.4	2.7	1.9	1.5	1.2	1.1		Quick	1.4	1.6
.6	1.3	1.1	1.0	1.0	.9			1.0	1.1
0 UND	1 363.4	42 8.7	55 6.6	63 5.8	62 5.9			38 9.6	33 11.0
0 UND	46 8.0	65 5.6	76 4.8	78 4.7	83 4.4		Sales/Receivables	63 5.8	54 6.7
34 10.7	76 4.8	87 4.2	96 3.8	96 3.8	96 3.8			83 4.4	76 4.8
0 UND	0 UND	0 UND	0 UND	0 UND	0 UND			0 UND	0 UND
0 UND	0 UND	0 909.9	1 554.9	0 UND	1 285.6		Cost of Sales/Inventory	0 999.8	0 794.3
0 UND	5 70.5	10 37.6	8 48.4	3 106.6	8 45.3			7 51.2	10 36.5
0 UND	0 UND	13 27.2	17 21.3	21 17.8	21 17.8			11 34.5	9 38.9
0 UND	10 36.3	26 14.0	29 12.7	34 10.6	31 11.7		Cost of Sales/Payables	24 15.4	22 16.3
15 25.0	29 12.7	48 7.6	45 8.1	46 7.9	39 9.3			41 8.8	34 10.6
9.4	4.4	4.1	3.6	5.7	5.6			5.4	4.7
25.6	8.1	5.8	5.9	7.7	7.8		Sales/Working Capital	9.1	7.2
-847.0	21.3	13.0	11.5	13.0	17.1			22.0	15.2
	30.6	57.3	89.1	88.0	32.3	75.7		54.1	64.9
(35) 7.0	(73) 15.8	(196) 27.2	(183) 24.0	(41) 13.1	(39) 8.9		EBIT/Interest	(746) 14.9	(441) 18.3
3.5	2.3	5.9	5.2	5.6	2.4			4.1	4.4
			14.6	30.0	19.1	24.2	Net Profit + Depr., Dep.,	19.4	26.7
		(26) 7.7	(60) 7.9	(21) 7.5	(16) 6.5		Amort./Cur. Mat. L/T/D	(130) 6.0	(79) 6.3
		3.0	2.1	3.3	2.4			2.8	2.1
.1	.1	.1	.1	.1	.2			.1	.1
.6	.2	.2	.2	.3	.4		Fixed/Worth	.3	.3
NM	.9	.6	.5	.9	15.9			.8	1.0
1.0	.3	.5	.5	1.0	1.5			.6	.7
3.3	.9	1.0	1.1	1.4	2.7		Debt/Worth	1.3	1.4
-26.1	4.5	2.6	2.3	2.9	156.0			3.2	3.5
291.0	102.5	69.3	54.9	42.2	50.3		% Profit Before Taxes/Tangible	64.9	73.5
(34) 118.7	(75) 56.8	(225) 35.5	(214) 32.0	(46) 25.6	(36) 25.5		Net Worth	(789) 33.4	(456) 42.0
45.9	12.8	13.9	13.2	15.3	13.4			15.2	16.0
90.5	41.9	31.0	25.9	15.8	16.8		% Profit Before Taxes/Total	27.4	30.5
38.8	22.6	15.9	13.7	9.5	9.3		Assets	14.1	17.3
14.6	4.8	6.5	4.6	6.2	2.5			4.6	4.4
494.1	98.4	65.4	42.5	43.5	40.2			61.2	55.2
44.9	45.6	24.5	22.6	17.2	16.9		Sales/Net Fixed Assets	26.0	25.3
19.2	10.6	14.3	11.5	9.5	8.8			13.2	12.5
8.7	4.6	3.1	2.6	2.3	2.3			3.9	3.6
5.7	3.1	2.5	2.1	2.0	1.8		Sales/Total Assets	2.8	2.6
3.9	1.8	1.9	1.6	1.7	1.5			2.1	2.0
1.1	.8	.5	.5	.6	.5			.5	.6
(10) 2.5	(30) 1.6	(163) 1.1	(187) .9	(45) .9	(31) .8		% Depr., Dep., Amort./Sales	(636) 1.1	(363) 1.1
6.0	3.6	2.2	1.7	1.8	1.2			1.9	1.9
2.2	2.3	1.5	.6	.7			% Officers', Directors'	1.5	1.4
(23) 7.5	(52) 3.8	(108) 2.2	(74) 1.3	(11) 1.7			Owners' Comp/Sales	(373) 3.0	(211) 3.5
9.6	6.1	4.1	2.6	2.2				5.8	7.2
98905M	466105M	3144186M	10237583M	6895174M	13984192M		Net Sales ($)	35147082M	18481091M
12347M	113777M	1227398M	4905650M	3416482M	7645672M		Total Assets ($)	13626011M	7942646M

© RMA 2024

M = $ thousand   MM = $ million
See Pages viii through xx for Explanation of Ratios and Data

CONSTRUCTION-GENERAL—Electrical Contractors and Other Wiring Installation Contractors NAICS 238210

Comparative Historical Data / Current Data Sorted by Sales

Comparative Historical Data			Type of Statement	Current Data Sorted by Sales					
58	70	78	Unqualified		1		2	10	65
123	168	169	Reviewed		1	3	19	62	84
15	18	19	Compiled	1	1	2	4	9	2
103	138	87	Tax Returns	7	17	12	17	19	15
315	416	338	Other	11	29	34	57	80	127
4/1/21-3/31/22 ALL	4/1/22-3/31/23 ALL	4/1/23-3/31/24 ALL		112 (4/1-9/30/23)			579 (10/1/23-3/31/24)		
				0-1MM	1-3MM	3-5MM	5-10MM	10-25MM	25MM & OVER
614	810	691	NUMBER OF STATEMENTS	19	49	51	99	180	293
%	%	%	ASSETS	%	%	%	%	%	%
22.7	20.7	19.8	Cash & Equivalents	30.1	26.4	22.9	23.3	20.2	16.0
39.2	39.5	40.3	Trade Receivables (net)	23.8	26.6	40.0	40.0	43.1	42.2
5.0	5.4	3.8	Inventory	6.3	3.2	4.9	4.8	4.4	3.0
9.2	9.8	10.4	All Other Current	2.0	5.5	4.1	6.5	11.2	13.6
76.1	75.3	74.3	Total Current	62.2	61.8	71.9	74.6	78.9	74.7
15.1	14.7	14.6	Fixed Assets (net)	25.5	20.3	14.6	15.0	12.1	14.4
3.5	4.1	4.2	Intangibles (net)	5.9	4.0	4.6	2.4	4.3	4.5
5.3	5.9	6.8	All Other Non-Current	6.3	13.9	8.8	7.9	4.7	6.3
100.0	100.0	100.0	Total	100.0	100.0	100.0	100.0	100.0	100.0
			LIABILITIES						
6.5	8.1	5.7	Notes Payable-Short Term	21.5	12.0	15.5	4.6	4.5	3.2
1.8	2.0	2.2	Cur. Mat.-L.T.D.	1.4	3.0	3.1	1.6	1.6	2.7
13.7	14.4	13.4	Trade Payables	10.2	5.5	9.9	11.1	16.6	14.3
.1	.2	.2	Income Taxes Payable	.6	.1	.1	.1	.1	.2
15.0	15.7	18.7	All Other Current	29.3	14.6	9.1	11.3	17.9	23.3
37.1	40.3	40.2	Total Current	63.1	35.1	37.6	28.6	40.6	43.6
13.5	14.0	12.9	Long-Term Debt	31.1	36.8	11.7	15.1	8.6	9.9
.4	.2	.2	Deferred Taxes	.0	.0	.1	.2	.4	.2
3.5	3.3	3.8	All Other Non-Current	4.9	2.7	2.1	1.7	4.8	4.3
45.5	42.1	42.9	Net Worth	1.3	25.3	48.5	54.4	45.5	42.0
100.0	100.0	100.0	Total Liabilities & Net Worth	100.0	100.0	100.0	100.0	100.0	100.0
			INCOME DATA						
100.0	100.0	100.0	Net Sales	100.0	100.0	100.0	100.0	100.0	100.0
30.9	30.9	30.6	Gross Profit	49.7	52.1	39.2	38.4	28.9	22.8
25.2	24.5	23.1	Operating Expenses	43.3	43.8	30.9	30.0	21.4	15.7
5.7	6.4	7.5	Operating Profit	6.4	8.2	8.3	8.4	7.5	7.1
-2.2	-.3	.2	All Other Expenses (net)	1.1	.2	1.1	-.4	.0	.2
7.8	6.7	7.4	Profit Before Taxes	5.4	8.0	7.2	8.8	7.5	6.9
			RATIOS						
3.8	3.5	3.3	Current	3.9	7.1	4.4	4.9	3.6	2.2
2.2	2.1	1.9		1.7	2.5	2.3	2.9	2.2	1.7
1.5	1.4	1.4		.9	1.3	1.6	1.8	1.3	1.4
3.1	3.0	2.9	Quick	3.9	5.7	4.4	4.3	2.9	1.8
1.8	1.6	1.6		1.6	2.0	2.1	2.3	1.7	1.3
1.2	1.0	1.0		.5	1.1	1.3	1.3	1.1	1.0
37 9.9	36 10.1	41 8.8	Sales/Receivables	0 UND	0 UND	32 11.4	32 11.5	45 8.2	55 6.6
62 5.9	64 5.7	68 5.4		24 14.9	33 11.0	61 6.0	61 6.0	69 5.3	74 4.9
83 4.4	85 4.3	89 4.1		69 5.3	83 4.4	83 4.4	76 4.8	89 4.1	91 4.0
0 UND	0 UND	0 UND	Cost of Sales/Inventory	0 UND	0 UND	0 UND	0 UND	0 UND	0 UND
0 983.9	0 999.8	0 999.8		0 UND	0 UND	0 UND	1 491.9	0 UND	1 569.7
9 41.0	11 33.3	7 49.3		20 18.5	0 UND	6 65.1	17 21.7	9 42.0	6 64.4
10 35.4	11 34.4	12 30.6	Cost of Sales/Payables	0 UND	0 UND	1 379.5	5 73.1	14 26.0	18 20.7
25 14.4	26 14.1	25 14.8		9 39.6	2 190.0	14 26.7	22 16.4	27 13.3	29 12.8
40 9.2	41 8.9	43 8.5		41 8.8	21 17.5	34 10.7	37 9.8	52 7.0	43 8.5
3.9	4.2	4.2	Sales/Working Capital	5.2	4.2	4.4	3.7	3.8	4.6
6.4	7.2	6.9		12.6	11.1	6.0	5.1	5.7	7.3
11.8	15.1	14.0		-213.5	39.1	13.6	12.6	14.4	12.9
97.7	75.5	70.9	EBIT/Interest	8.5	45.6	85.6	82.1	93.2	78.1
(498) 27.6	(644) 19.4	(567) 18.5		(11) 3.7	(40) 9.4	(41) 12.0	(85) 29.4	(141) 26.2	(249) 17.8
6.3	3.7	4.8		-.1	2.3	1.7	5.2	6.0	5.5
23.8	17.7	21.0	Net Profit + Depr., Dep., Amort./Cur. Mat. L/T/D					19.0	21.8
(72) 10.3	(118) 5.2	(124) 7.5					(27) 9.3	(89) 7.0
3.2	2.0	2.3						5.0	2.2
.1	.1	.1	Fixed/Worth	.2	.1	.1	.1	.1	.1
.3	.2	.3		1.0	.5	.3	.2	.2	.3
.6	.7	.7		-.9	2.0	.8	.5	.6	.7
.5	.5	.6	Debt/Worth	.6	.7	.3	.4	.5	.8
1.0	1.1	1.2		3.0	1.9	.9	.7	1.0	1.4
2.4	3.2	3.0		-5.1	18.2	3.4	1.9	2.9	3.0
65.2	64.1	68.3	% Profit Before Taxes/Tangible Net Worth	177.9	166.7	76.0	77.9	64.9	56.7
(557) 40.8	(715) 31.4	(630) 35.4		(14) 100.5	(41) 70.9	(43) 30.6	(98) 39.7	(163) 35.9	(271) 31.3
16.0	10.7	14.1		7.1	12.7	4.9	10.2	15.7	16.6
31.9	28.6	29.7	% Profit Before Taxes/Total Assets	50.0	55.4	40.3	37.3	30.2	23.4
18.2	13.4	15.1		24.8	23.4	15.7	20.1	15.9	13.0
6.6	3.6	5.2		1.5	3.9	2.5	6.5	6.2	5.1
56.5	82.4	57.6	Sales/Net Fixed Assets	59.5	62.3	78.2	90.2	78.4	44.0
27.1	29.4	25.0		15.2	27.6	28.4	22.7	27.2	22.6
12.3	13.7	11.8		5.5	8.6	8.1	11.7	15.4	11.4
3.3	3.3	3.1	Sales/Total Assets	5.1	6.0	3.7	3.5	3.1	2.7
2.5	2.4	2.3		3.8	3.2	2.5	2.6	2.4	2.2
1.9	1.9	1.8		1.9	1.5	1.7	2.0	1.8	1.7
.5	.5	.5	% Depr., Dep., Amort./Sales		1.2	.9	.4	.4	.5
(429) 1.1	(520) 1.0	(466) 1.0		(15) 2.7	(24) 2.8	(52) 1.3	(125) 1.0	(242) .8
2.1	1.9	2.1			4.6	4.4	2.7	1.7	1.5
1.4	1.4	1.3	% Officers', Directors', Owners' Comp/Sales	5.1	3.2	2.3	1.9	1.3	.6
(258) 2.7	(325) 2.9	(272) 2.2		(10) 8.7	(27) 6.6	(27) 3.5	(53) 2.5	(74) 1.9	(81) 1.5
5.3	5.2	4.3		12.0	9.4	5.0	4.4	3.8	2.4
22372803M	35499850M	34826145M	Net Sales ($)	11651M	95250M	204817M	738922M	2963852M	30811653M
9989222M	16338717M	17321326M	Total Assets ($)	6223M	43995M	89545M	323101M	1360574M	15497888M

© RMA 2024   M = $ thousand   MM = $ million
See Pages viii through xx for Explanation of Ratios and Data

CONSTRUCTION-GENERAL—Plumbing, Heating, and Air-Conditioning Contractors NAICS 238220

Current Data Sorted by Assets

							Type of Statement		
		1	8	34	8	12	Unqualified		
	1	3	50	67	3	2	Reviewed		
	3	16	14	5		1	Compiled		
	19	53	44	7		1	Tax Returns		
	55	68	152	112	28	10	Other		
		130 (4/1-9/30/23)		647 (10/1/23-3/31/24)					
0-500M	500M-2MM	2-10MM	10-50MM	50-100MM	100-250MM				

Comparative Historical Data

									50	43
									223	114
									57	36
									235	136
									444	315
									4/1/19-3/31/20 ALL	4/1/20-3/31/21 ALL

0-500M	500M-2MM	2-10MM	10-50MM	50-100MM	100-250MM					
78	141	268	225	39	26	NUMBER OF STATEMENTS			1009	644
%	%	%	%	%	%	ASSETS			%	%
31.6	29.2	19.5	20.2	12.8	16.5	Cash & Equivalents			18.5	28.7
16.7	23.5	38.8	42.8	40.8	31.4	Trade Receivables (net)			40.8	32.0
5.5	7.3	6.7	4.9	4.2	9.8	Inventory			6.4	5.8
4.3	3.8	6.6	8.9	9.0	9.3	All Other Current			5.9	5.0
58.1	63.9	71.6	76.8	66.8	67.0	Total Current			71.6	71.6
33.5	22.4	16.4	12.4	13.0	12.0	Fixed Assets (net)			18.5	17.3
3.0	6.5	4.4	4.5	15.7	13.6	Intangibles (net)			3.7	4.7
5.5	7.2	7.6	6.3	4.5	7.5	All Other Non-Current			6.2	6.5
100.0	100.0	100.0	100.0	100.0	100.0	Total			100.0	100.0
						LIABILITIES				
23.7	6.8	3.2	2.7	3.8	6.0	Notes Payable-Short Term			7.9	7.8
4.1	3.1	2.7	1.8	2.4	2.0	Cur. Mat.-L.T.D.			3.2	3.2
12.3	10.5	18.1	18.1	19.7	14.5	Trade Payables			18.9	14.6
.2	.1	.1	.1	.0	.0	Income Taxes Payable			.2	.1
27.2	15.1	14.7	22.5	24.4	22.3	All Other Current			15.9	13.9
67.5	35.6	38.9	45.2	50.3	44.8	Total Current			46.2	39.6
47.2	27.6	14.0	8.0	13.2	10.0	Long-Term Debt			17.3	24.4
.0	.0	.2	.2	.1	.0	Deferred Taxes			.3	.1
2.4	3.8	4.6	3.1	10.6	4.5	All Other Non-Current			3.8	4.7
-17.0	33.0	42.4	43.5	25.9	40.7	Net Worth			32.4	31.2
100.0	100.0	100.0	100.0	100.0	100.0	Total Liabilities & Net Worth			100.0	100.0
						INCOME DATA				
100.0	100.0	100.0	100.0	100.0	100.0	Net Sales			100.0	100.0
50.7	43.6	33.3	26.5	25.0	27.0	Gross Profit			33.1	34.2
44.6	35.9	26.6	19.6	18.5	18.1	Operating Expenses			27.5	29.3
6.1	7.7	6.8	6.9	6.5	8.9	Operating Profit			5.6	4.9
.6	.5	.2	-.3	1.4	.6	All Other Expenses (net)			.3	-1.5
5.5	7.3	6.5	7.1	5.1	8.3	Profit Before Taxes			5.3	6.4
						RATIOS				
4.1	5.3	3.5	2.3	1.6	1.9				2.6	3.1
2.1	2.1	2.0	1.8	1.3	1.4	Current			1.7	2.0
.5	1.1	1.4	1.3	1.2	1.2				1.2	1.4
3.5	4.4	2.7	2.0	1.4	1.4				2.2	2.7
1.6	1.8	1.6	1.4	1.1	1.1	Quick			1.4	1.7
.4	.8	1.1	1.0	.8	.8				.9	1.1

0	UND	0	UND	26	13.9	53	6.9	69	5.3	24	15.1	Sales/Receivables	22	16.3	13	27.3
2	190.5	12	29.8	54	6.8	73	5.0	87	4.2	59	6.2		51	7.1	45	8.1
24	15.2	49	7.5	81	4.5	91	4.0	99	3.7	76	4.8		76	4.8	68	5.4
0	UND	0	UND	0	UND	0	UND	0	UND	0	UND	Cost of Sales/Inventory	0	UND	0	UND
0	UND	0	999.8	3	117.9	3	121.7	1	323.6	6	59.4		2	183.2	2	174.0
5	77.9	14	26.9	19	19.0	16	23.5	11	32.7	25	14.6		13	27.4	14	25.4
0	UND	0	UND	15	23.8	23	15.6	29	12.7	20	18.6	Cost of Sales/Payables	14	26.1	11	32.6
2	231.4	12	30.1	27	13.3	32	11.4	43	8.5	27	13.7		27	13.6	23	16.0
22	16.5	30	12.1	47	7.8	49	7.5	62	5.9	41	9.0		43	8.5	38	9.7

9.1	6.4	4.9	4.6	7.6	6.8	Sales/Working Capital			6.3	5.0
23.9	13.0	8.2	6.9	12.9	12.4				11.4	8.7
-23.6	76.3	17.7	13.0	20.4	24.4				36.9	19.6
21.0	42.1	66.0	128.9	22.7	202.0	EBIT/Interest			43.3	62.5
(57) 6.7	(122) 11.6	(232) 20.6	(187) 27.2	(36) 6.0	(23) 21.5		(877)		13.8	(532) 18.8
.1	2.3	4.2	7.0	1.1	2.7				3.4	3.7
		18.0	20.6	10.5	28.0	Net Profit + Depr., Dep., Amort./Cur. Mat. L/T/D			14.7	13.8
	(41)	6.0 (66)	7.5 (10)	2.1 (10)	15.9		(145)		4.7	(69) 5.9
		1.6	2.7	-.1	1.9				1.9	1.8
.3	.1	.1	.1	.2	.2	Fixed/Worth			.2	.1
1.1	.5	.3	.2	.8	.3				.4	.4
-1.0	4.4	.8	.5	-1.1	1.1				1.3	1.5
.6	.5	.5	.7	1.5	1.3	Debt/Worth			.7	.8
5.2	1.5	1.2	1.4	3.5	2.2				1.6	1.8
-2.9	10.8	2.9	3.4	-7.1	3.5				5.5	6.9
176.6	105.3	67.7	60.4	56.0	53.5	% Profit Before Taxes/Tangible Net Worth			68.3	79.0
(45) 86.2	(110) 53.3	(241) 39.1	(214) 32.4	(24) 34.1	(22) 33.6		(854)		36.1	(536) 44.4
22.7	22.1	12.6	17.0	24.8	17.1				14.5	15.6
62.7	46.6	30.5	23.6	15.0	20.0	% Profit Before Taxes/Total Assets			28.3	31.3
23.9	22.4	15.2	14.1	8.7	9.3				13.4	15.0
.0	4.4	4.4	5.1	.7	5.4				4.2	3.6
75.2	79.5	55.6	52.9	42.5	38.3	Sales/Net Fixed Assets			58.7	64.3
21.3	24.8	23.0	27.5	24.2	24.2				25.5	26.3
10.1	10.5	12.3	13.4	8.7	11.9				13.0	12.6
10.6	5.4	3.6	2.8	2.4	2.7	Sales/Total Assets			4.3	3.8
6.3	3.4	2.7	2.2	2.0	2.3				3.1	2.9
3.3	2.5	2.1	1.8	1.1	1.5				2.4	2.1
1.0	.7	.6	.4	.5	.4	% Depr., Dep., Amort./Sales			.5	.5
(35) 2.5	(75) 1.7	(175) 1.2	(187) .7	(30) .7	(20) .6		(722)		1.0	(443) 1.1
5.1	3.5	2.2	1.4	1.7	1.1				1.9	2.1
3.0	2.2	1.5	.6			% Officers', Directors' Owners' Comp/Sales			1.7	1.9
(41) 5.1	(79) 3.8	(128) 2.5	(78) 1.5				(478)		3.5	(310) 3.5
10.5	4.7	4.0	2.6						6.3	6.0
138382M	721331M	3787296M	11285407M	5161208M	9868876M	Net Sales ($)			27487458M	13708904M
19611M	168636M	1320347M	5028909M	2823909M	3904123M	Total Assets ($)			10688440M	5772034M

M = $ thousand   MM = $ million
See Pages viii through xx for Explanation of Ratios and Data

© RMA 2024

CONSTRUCTION-GENERAL—Plumbing, Heating, and Air-Conditioning Contractors NAICS 238220

Comparative Historical Data | Current Data Sorted by Sales

				Type of Statement						
41		53	63	Unqualified			3	2	5	53
117		146	126	Reviewed	1	1	3	16	34	71
47		48	39	Compiled	1	3	6	16	9	4
148		179	124	Tax Returns	8	26	18	36	21	15
365		453	425	Other	22	56	32	63	106	146
4/1/21-3/31/22 ALL		4/1/22-3/31/23 ALL	4/1/23-3/31/24 ALL		130 (4/1-9/30/23)			647 (10/1/23-3/31/24)		
718		879	777	NUMBER OF STATEMENTS						
					0-1MM	1-3MM	3-5MM	5-10MM	10-25MM	25MM & OVER
					32	86	62	133	175	289
%		%	%	ASSETS	%	%	%	%	%	%
26.5		22.3	22.2	Cash & Equivalents	35.1	24.8	30.6	22.9	21.8	18.2
31.7		33.6	34.8	Trade Receivables (net)	15.1	18.6	23.1	33.3	39.6	42.2
6.8		6.6	6.1	Inventory	4.8	7.3	9.0	4.8	5.8	6.1
6.5		7.1	6.7	All Other Current	4.0	4.7	3.9	4.9	7.6	8.6
71.5		69.5	70.0	Total Current	58.9	55.4	66.7	66.0	74.9	75.1
17.5		18.5	17.7	Fixed Assets (net)	33.2	30.4	20.1	20.9	13.6	12.7
5.5		6.0	5.6	Intangibles (net)	2.9	6.1	6.2	6.3	4.1	6.1
5.4		6.0	6.8	All Other Non-Current	5.0	8.1	7.0	6.8	7.4	6.1
100.0		100.0	100.0	Total	100.0	100.0	100.0	100.0	100.0	100.0
				LIABILITIES						
5.7		6.7	5.9	Notes Payable-Short Term	23.8	11.6	6.0	6.9	3.5	3.1
3.7		2.3	2.6	Cur. Mat.-L.T.D.	3.2	3.3	3.4	3.0	2.4	2.1
14.5		15.2	16.1	Trade Payables	5.6	10.5	13.0	13.1	19.5	19.0
.1		.1	.1	Income Taxes Payable	.1	.1	.1	.2	.1	.1
13.3		15.2	19.0	All Other Current	21.8	19.7	13.8	16.6	15.7	22.7
37.3		39.4	43.7	Total Current	54.4	45.2	36.3	39.8	41.2	47.0
18.9		19.1	17.9	Long-Term Debt	38.5	44.2	28.4	17.8	11.1	9.6
.2		.2	.1	Deferred Taxes	.0	.0	.1	.2	.2	.2
2.9		3.3	4.1	All Other Non-Current	3.1	2.8	4.5	3.1	2.9	5.7
40.7		38.0	34.2	Net Worth	4.2	7.8	30.7	39.1	44.6	37.5
100.0		100.0	100.0	Total Liabilities & Net Worth	100.0	100.0	100.0	100.0	100.0	100.0
				INCOME DATA						
100.0		100.0	100.0	Net Sales	100.0	100.0	100.0	100.0	100.0	100.0
34.5		34.2	34.3	Gross Profit	52.1	49.7	43.7	38.2	31.7	25.6
28.6		28.4	27.4	Operating Expenses	42.2	43.3	35.1	31.4	24.6	19.2
5.9		5.9	7.0	Operating Profit	10.0	6.4	8.7	6.8	7.2	6.4
-2.2		-.1	.2	All Other Expenses (net)	1.3	1.1	.4	.1	.1	.1
8.1		6.0	6.7	Profit Before Taxes	8.7	5.3	8.3	6.8	7.1	6.3
				RATIOS						
3.3		3.5	3.0		8.1	4.9	6.2	3.5	3.6	2.2
2.1		1.9	1.8	Current	3.1	2.2	2.2	2.1	1.9	1.6
1.4		1.3	1.2		1.0	.8	1.2	1.3	1.4	1.2
2.8		3.0	2.5		4.4	3.6	4.5	2.9	2.8	1.7
(717) 1.6	(878)	1.5	1.4	Quick	2.5	1.5	1.9	1.7	1.6	1.3
1.0		1.0	1.0		.7	.4	1.0	1.0	1.0	.9
12 30.3	11	32.7	13 27.2		0 UND	0 UND	0 UND	7 50.8	30 12.0	44 8.3
42 8.6	47	7.7	54 6.8	Sales/Receivables	1 721.5	11 34.3	16 22.8	47 7.7	52 7.0	69 5.3
69 5.3	76	4.8	81 4.5		47 7.7	40 9.1	51 7.1	72 5.1	81 4.5	91 4.0
0 UND	0	UND	0 UND		0 UND	0 UND	0 UND	0 UND	0 UND	0 999.8
3 145.0	2	147.6	2 209.8	Cost of Sales/Inventory	0 UND	0 UND	5 81.0	1 621.8	2 150.0	4 101.4
17 21.7	16	22.3	15 23.6		2 151.3	17 21.9	25 14.7	11 34.2	15 25.0	16 22.8
10 36.3	9	41.7	13 28.6		0 UND	0 UND	0 UND	8 45.6	16 23.5	22 16.5
24 15.1	25	14.8	26 13.8	Cost of Sales/Payables	0 UND	9 40.3	18 20.3	24 14.9	30 12.2	31 11.7
39 9.4	42	8.7	45 8.2		21 17.1	40 9.1	31 11.8	38 9.5	49 7.5	47 7.8
5.1		5.3	5.3		4.5	5.8	5.1	5.4	4.9	5.3
7.9		9.0	9.5	Sales/Working Capital	11.8	15.5	10.6	9.5	8.2	8.9
19.9		21.9	24.3		NM	-37.9	44.8	32.1	16.0	17.5
78.4		59.5	70.4		21.9	15.3	63.6	47.8	81.7	94.8
(569) 25.9	(702)	15.0	(657) 17.3	EBIT/Interest	(18) 6.7	(68) 3.5	(53) 10.1	(120) 18.6	(152) 24.2	(246) 21.2
6.8		3.4	3.3		1.0	-.2	2.2	3.2	5.6	5.6
17.1		14.7	19.0					11.4	19.4	22.7
(72) 8.1	(119)	6.2	(133) 6.6	Net Profit + Depr., Dep., Amort./Cur. Mat. L/T/D			(17) 5.2	(27) 5.4	(84) 8.0	
3.2		1.2	1.8					.9	1.5	2.1
.1		.1	.1		.2	.2	.1	.1	.1	.1
.3		.3	.3	Fixed/Worth	.7	1.5	.4	.4	.2	.3
1.0		1.3	1.1		-.9	-1.4	2.9	1.4	.5	.7
.6		.6	.6		.2	.7	.4	.5	.6	.9
1.2		1.4	1.5	Debt/Worth	1.0	3.7	1.5	1.4	1.1	1.8
3.9		4.6	4.4		-3.3	-4.4	21.4	3.5	2.6	4.0
85.1		68.8	73.2		96.6	86.7	121.2	74.6	77.1	60.4
(615) 49.1	(744)	34.8	(656) 38.2	% Profit Before Taxes/Tangible Net Worth	(20) 45.6	(55) 38.7	(49) 77.3	(116) 38.3	(161) 43.1	(255) 33.7
24.2		12.5	16.5		12.5	15.5	23.1	12.8	14.8	17.9
35.7		29.6	30.7		46.8	42.2	51.0	34.2	31.4	23.5
21.4		13.5	14.9	% Profit Before Taxes/Total Assets	21.5	14.1	21.5	14.2	17.0	12.9
7.9		3.8	4.6		3.2	-.1	3.9	5.7	5.0	5.0
60.8		61.0	56.3		62.2	52.4	69.3	55.1	71.6	52.9
25.0		24.2	24.4	Sales/Net Fixed Assets	14.5	15.6	21.6	20.8	32.7	26.6
12.8		11.6	12.1		4.4	8.4	11.4	9.9	16.4	13.6
3.9		4.0	3.7		6.8	5.2	5.4	3.8	4.0	3.0
2.8		2.8	2.6	Sales/Total Assets	3.1	3.0	3.2	2.9	2.8	2.3
2.1		2.0	2.0		1.9	1.9	2.1	2.2	2.1	1.9
.7		.5	.5		1.0	1.0	.6	.8	.5	.4
(458) 1.2	(549)	1.1	(522) 1.0	% Depr., Dep., Amort./Sales	(16) 4.3	(47) 2.5	(29) 1.5	(81) 1.7	(112) 1.0	(237) .7
2.2		2.0	2.1		5.9	4.0	3.7	3.1	1.7	1.3
1.6		1.5	1.5		3.1	3.2	2.5	1.9	1.2	.6
(345) 3.2	(390)	2.8	(329) 2.6	% Officers', Directors' Owners' Comp/Sales	(14) 5.6	(46) 4.6	(37) 4.1	(68) 3.0	(75) 2.2	(89) 1.5
5.6		5.0	4.5		15.6	7.6	6.1	4.6	3.3	2.6
17592222M		24166250M	30962500M	Net Sales ($)	20208M	158770M	251073M	947296M	2864302M	26720851M
7532760M		10995450M	13265535M	Total Assets ($)	7743M	77699M	89816M	398353M	1301901M	11390023M

© RMA 2024   M = $ thousand   MM = $ million
See Pages viii through xx for Explanation of Ratios and Data

CONSTRUCTION-GENERAL—Other Building Equipment Contractors NAICS 238290

Current Data Sorted by Assets | Comparative Historical Data

						Type of Statement		
	1		4	2	3	Unqualified	9	8
1	1	9	11	1		Reviewed	25	12
	1	4	3	1		Compiled	13	8
5	3	10	1			Tax Returns	37	26
1	6	25	15	7	5	Other	63	45
	13 (4/1-9/30/23)		106 (10/1/23-3/31/24)				4/1/19-3/31/20	4/1/20-3/31/21
0-500M	500M-2MM	2-10MM	10-50MM	50-100MM	100-250MM	NUMBER OF STATEMENTS	147 ALL	99 ALL
7	11	48	34	11	8			
%	%	%	%	%	%	ASSETS	%	%
	13.1	16.4	12.3	10.9		Cash & Equivalents	17.8	21.8
	34.8	37.7	38.4	23.5		Trade Receivables (net)	35.1	33.4
	7.8	12.8	9.1	7.7		Inventory	10.5	11.6
	11.7	4.5	8.7	6.2		All Other Current	4.0	7.0
	67.5	71.4	68.5	48.3		Total Current	67.4	73.7
	17.9	16.6	16.7	29.8		Fixed Assets (net)	22.0	13.7
	6.1	6.0	6.3	10.5		Intangibles (net)	5.0	5.2
	8.5	6.1	8.5	11.5		All Other Non-Current	5.7	7.4
	100.0	100.0	100.0	100.0		Total	100.0	100.0
						LIABILITIES		
	12.6	5.2	3.9	1.3		Notes Payable-Short Term	10.9	7.8
	6.6	3.5	3.7	5.0		Cur. Mat.-L.T.D.	3.1	4.4
	11.2	13.7	13.7	11.2		Trade Payables	14.0	11.7
	.1	.1	.1	1.1		Income Taxes Payable	.1	.1
	40.8	18.3	16.5	13.5		All Other Current	14.7	14.8
	71.2	40.8	38.0	32.0		Total Current	42.7	38.8
	35.8	15.7	13.7	21.9		Long-Term Debt	14.6	14.1
	.0	.4	.4	.2		Deferred Taxes	.5	.2
	11.1	3.9	7.2	2.9		All Other Non-Current	5.8	5.4
	-18.2	39.1	40.7	43.1		Net Worth	36.4	41.5
	100.0	100.0	100.0	100.0		Total Liabilities & Net Worth	100.0	100.0
						INCOME DATA		
	100.0	100.0	100.0	100.0		Net Sales	100.0	100.0
	33.8	36.2	31.5	28.9		Gross Profit	36.6	34.6
	33.8	28.6	23.3	18.7		Operating Expenses	30.3	28.7
	-.1	7.7	8.2	10.2		Operating Profit	6.2	5.9
	-.6	.4	-.3	1.0		All Other Expenses (net)	.3	-1.4
	.5	7.3	8.5	9.2		Profit Before Taxes	6.0	7.3
						RATIOS		
	2.2	2.6	3.2	3.8			2.8	5.0
	1.9	1.8	1.8	1.6		Current	1.8	2.1
	.8	1.3	1.3	1.0			1.2	1.4
	1.8	2.3	2.2	3.1			2.2	3.3
	1.4	1.4	1.5	1.3		Quick	1.5 (98)	1.7
	.5	.9	.8	.6			.8	.9
4	86.8	22 16.6	54 6.7	55 6.6			18 19.8	19 19.1
54	6.7	61 6.0	72 5.1	70 5.2		Sales/Receivables	51 7.1	47 7.8
70	5.2	94 3.9	85 4.3	87 4.2			69 5.3	72 5.1
0	UND	0 UND	0 UND	0 UND			0 UND	0 UND
3	127.0	8 43.9	7 53.9	0 999.8		Cost of Sales/Inventory	4 84.3	3 109.9
18	20.6	36 10.1	56 6.5	8 44.8			33 11.0	36 10.1
0	UND	16 23.1	19 18.8	3 112.3			7 52.8	4 83.9
25	14.7	29 12.8	31 11.6	42 8.6		Cost of Sales/Payables	20 18.1	20 18.5
42	8.7	51 7.2	51 7.2	50 7.3			39 9.3	37 9.8
	6.3	5.2	3.8	3.2			5.3	4.7
	9.9	7.6	7.1	8.6		Sales/Working Capital	9.3	6.3
	-21.4	16.0	10.9	999.8			39.1	18.6
		44.8	62.8	22.8			33.7	58.0
	(40)	10.8	(30) 11.3	(10) 8.5		EBIT/Interest	(126) 10.8	(77) 17.1
		4.6	2.1	-2.5			3.8	3.9
						Net Profit + Depr., Dep., Amort./Cur. Mat. L/T/D	6.9	11.4
							(23) 3.6	(11) 5.3
							2.2	.6
	.2	.1	.1	.6			.1	.0
	.9	.2	.4	.8		Fixed/Worth	.5	.3
	-6.9	1.0	1.0	-.5			1.2	.9
	4.0	.9	.7	.4			.6	.6
	6.3	1.5	1.2	.8		Debt/Worth	1.4	1.6
	-6.7	4.0	8.7	-4.5			5.4	5.2
		70.6	58.9				61.8	87.3
	(41)	44.6	(29) 44.0			% Profit Before Taxes/Tangible Net Worth	(123) 35.3	(85) 42.1
		16.6	24.7				14.1	17.8
	21.5	38.6	22.4	20.0			26.1	33.2
	9.0	15.5	14.3	8.4		% Profit Before Taxes/Total Assets	13.0	16.4
	.8	5.7	4.0	-7.9			4.2	5.0
	39.2	122.6	31.6	18.4			58.3	149.3
	13.8	32.6	14.1	10.8		Sales/Net Fixed Assets	24.2	34.0
	9.5	12.2	7.0	1.6			8.8	14.8
	3.3	3.4	2.4	1.6			3.7	3.9
	2.7	2.4	1.8	1.1		Sales/Total Assets	2.7	2.7
	1.9	1.7	1.3	.8			1.9	1.8
		.4	.6				.6	.6
	(28)	1.2	(27) 1.8			% Depr., Dep., Amort./Sales	(93) 1.4	(57) 1.4
		2.9	2.6				3.5	3.2
		1.1					1.7	1.5
	(19)	2.3				% Officers', Directors' Owners' Comp/Sales	(63) 3.5	(39) 3.1
		4.8					7.5	5.3
12185M	46644M	672720M	1359412M	906700M	2183523M	Net Sales ($)	2744288M	2245298M
644M	17141M	254757M	762647M	754185M	1311687M	Total Assets ($)	1253368M	1055104M

M = $ thousand   MM = $ million
See Pages viii through xx for Explanation of Ratios and Data

© RMA 2024

CONSTRUCTION-GENERAL—Other Building Equipment Contractors NAICS 238290

Comparative Historical Data | Current Data Sorted by Sales

Comparative Historical Data			Type of Statement	Current Data Sorted by Sales										
6	9	9	Unqualified				3	2	7					
12	18	23	Reviewed	1	1		3	7	11					
8	7	9	Compiled				2	3	4					
19	29	19	Tax Returns	2	2	4	5	3	3					
47	55	59	Other	1	4	5	10	11	28					
4/1/21-3/31/22 ALL	4/1/22-3/31/23 ALL	4/1/23-3/31/24 ALL		13 (4/1-9/30/23)			106 (10/1/23-3/31/24)							
				0-1MM	1-3MM	3-5MM	5-10MM	10-25MM	25MM & OVER					
92	118	119	NUMBER OF STATEMENTS	4	7	9	20	26	53					
%	%	%	ASSETS	%	%	%	%	%	%					
19.6	20.1	17.5	Cash & Equivalents				15.5	19.8	14.3					
29.8	32.6	33.6	Trade Receivables (net)				34.5	39.2	34.6					
10.0	10.9	10.0	Inventory				11.7	10.8	10.3					
6.7	5.8	6.3	All Other Current				6.2	4.9	7.4					
66.0	69.5	67.4	Total Current				67.9	74.6	66.5					
22.2	18.8	18.9	Fixed Assets (net)				14.6	15.5	17.8					
5.0	5.4	6.2	Intangibles (net)				10.9	3.4	6.9					
6.7	6.3	7.6	All Other Non-Current				6.6	6.5	8.8					
100.0	100.0	100.0	Total				100.0	100.0	100.0					
			LIABILITIES											
5.5	6.4	7.0	Notes Payable-Short Term				8.6	5.2	2.5					
2.6	3.3	3.8	Cur. Mat.-L.T.D.				4.9	2.1	4.0					
9.2	10.4	12.4	Trade Payables				12.2	14.2	13.8					
.1	.1	.2	Income Taxes Payable				.0	.2	.3					
11.2	13.9	19.8	All Other Current				16.8	15.9	19.6					
28.6	34.1	43.3	Total Current				42.4	37.6	40.3					
15.9	21.7	19.7	Long-Term Debt				36.2	13.1	13.0					
.3	.2	.3	Deferred Taxes				.1	.6	.4					
12.4	7.1	5.2	All Other Non-Current				6.4	4.1	4.4					
42.8	36.9	31.4	Net Worth				14.8	44.6	42.0					
100.0	100.0	100.0	Total Liabilities & Net Worth				100.0	100.0	100.0					
			INCOME DATA											
100.0	100.0	100.0	Net Sales				100.0	100.0	100.0					
31.8	34.7	34.4	Gross Profit				37.4	33.0	28.9					
26.8	27.8	26.6	Operating Expenses				28.4	25.6	20.4					
5.0	6.8	7.8	Operating Profit				9.1	7.5	8.5					
-1.7	-.1	.2	All Other Expenses (net)				.9	.2	.1					
6.7	6.9	7.7	Profit Before Taxes				8.2	7.3	8.4					
			RATIOS											
5.0	4.6	2.6					3.3	3.2	2.5					
2.6	2.2	1.7	Current				1.8	1.8	1.6					
1.7	1.5	1.3					.9	1.5	1.3					
3.6	3.6	2.1					2.6	2.9	2.0					
1.7	1.6	1.3	Quick				1.1	1.5	1.3					
1.0	.8	.8					.6	1.0	.8					
26 14.0	26 14.2	35 10.3		8 44.7			34 10.6		46 7.9					
51 7.2	55 6.6	63 5.8	Sales/Receivables	54 6.8			72 5.1		70 5.2					
76 4.8	87 4.2	87 4.2		126 2.9			96 3.8		83 4.4					
0 UND	0 UND	0 UND		0 UND			0 UND		0 999.8					
3 121.9	4 92.1	3 108.0	Cost of Sales/Inventory	18 20.0			3 130.1		4 82.6					
45 8.2	46 8.0	37 9.9		33 11.0			34 10.6		44 8.3					
6 58.5	4 92.2	13 27.6		18 19.8			16 22.5		15 24.6					
19 19.7	21 17.4	29 12.6	Cost of Sales/Payables	35 10.5			29 12.8		32 11.5					
35 10.4	41 8.9	49 7.4		49 7.5			54 6.7		48 7.6					
3.8	3.6	4.7					3.7	5.4	4.8					
5.0	6.0	8.4	Sales/Working Capital				8.1	7.5	7.9					
11.6	16.6	27.5					-52.8	11.3	14.2					
53.6	45.2	38.4					28.5	84.8	52.7					
(77) 18.0	(103) 11.4	(100) 9.4	EBIT/Interest	(19) 4.4			(20) 12.2		(46) 13.5					
2.8	2.2	2.8					2.4	5.4	3.6					
9.4	9.3	11.3							21.7					
(17) 4.7	(19) 3.7	(22) 2.9	Net Profit + Depr., Dep., Amort./Cur. Mat. L/T/D						(13) 2.9					
1.9	1.5	1.4							1.7					
.2	.1	.1					.0	.2	.1					
.5	.4	.6	Fixed/Worth				.2	.4	.6					
.9	1.5	1.4					-3.7	.7	1.0					
.5	.5	.8					1.1	.6	.8					
1.1	1.4	1.6	Debt/Worth				4.9	1.6	1.2					
3.2	7.6	10.1					-6.0	2.7	5.3					
52.0	52.8	68.0					187.1	65.7	66.0					
(81) 27.1	(95) 29.5	(97) 39.5	% Profit Before Taxes/Tangible Net Worth	(12) 44.9			(24) 44.8		(48) 37.6					
9.8	11.5	19.3					13.2	29.4	20.3					
25.3	23.0	26.4					24.1	36.8	25.1					
11.5	11.9	15.2	% Profit Before Taxes/Total Assets				10.7	22.5	16.6					
3.6	1.9	4.1					3.7	6.7	4.6					
39.1	57.7	59.7					580.4	41.7	45.1					
18.5	18.2	22.8	Sales/Net Fixed Assets				25.2	19.0	18.4					
8.1	9.9	8.3					10.9	9.1	6.6					
3.2	3.2	3.0					2.6	3.1	2.7					
2.2	2.3	2.1	Sales/Total Assets				2.1	2.5	1.9					
1.3	1.6	1.4					1.3	1.8	1.3					
.8	.7	.6					.9	.2	.5					
(57) 1.9	(81) 1.5	(81) 1.6	% Depr., Dep., Amort./Sales				(12) 1.2	(18) 1.4	(38) 1.9					
3.0	2.6	2.9					2.1	2.9	3.2					
1.7	1.0	.9							.6					
(33) 3.3	(47) 3.1	(33) 2.3	% Officers', Directors', Owners' Comp/Sales						(10) 1.4					
6.9	5.6	4.5							2.7					
1941837M	3628585M	5181184M	Net Sales ($)	1502M	13290M	36374M	145295M	420074M	4564649M					
1275526M	1970175M	3101061M	Total Assets ($)	71M	16729M	16238M	98605M	195326M	2774092M					

© RMA 2024   M = $ thousand   MM = $ million

CONSTRUCTION-GENERAL—Drywall and Insulation Contractors NAICS 238310

Current Data Sorted by Assets | Comparative Historical Data

							Type of Statement				
		1	4	6	1	1	Unqualified		14		7
	1	1	24	27			Reviewed		55		33
		2	6	2		1	Compiled		10		8
8	10	12	2				Tax Returns		54		23
6	11	29	23	5	3		Other		91		53
	27 (4/1-9/30/23)		158 (10/1/23-3/31/24)						4/1/19-3/31/20		4/1/20-3/31/21
0-500M	500M-2MM	2-10MM	10-50MM	50-100MM	100-250MM		NUMBER OF STATEMENTS		ALL		ALL
14	25	75	60	6	5				224		124
%	%	%	%	%	%		ASSETS		%		%
48.6	25.4	20.3	18.7				Cash & Equivalents		16.3		26.0
1.6	37.3	49.9	49.3				Trade Receivables (net)		50.4		42.4
.9	4.4	4.1	3.1				Inventory		4.8		5.8
.0	5.0	8.3	10.7				All Other Current		6.8		6.3
51.1	72.1	82.6	81.8				Total Current		78.4		80.5
41.7	16.1	10.9	7.8				Fixed Assets (net)		12.0		10.8
.1	.9	1.4	1.6				Intangibles (net)		2.2		2.0
7.0	10.9	5.1	8.8				All Other Non-Current		7.5		6.7
100.0	100.0	100.0	100.0				Total		100.0		100.0
							LIABILITIES				
21.8	4.2	4.6	4.2				Notes Payable-Short Term		9.1		8.3
4.2	4.7	2.6	2.0				Cur. Mat.-L.T.D.		2.2		3.1
5.1	11.8	10.9	13.8				Trade Payables		12.3		10.3
.0	.0	.1	.0				Income Taxes Payable		.2		.1
15.3	7.6	16.9	20.7				All Other Current		17.1		17.6
46.4	28.3	35.0	40.8				Total Current		40.8		39.4
31.5	22.3	8.6	5.0				Long-Term Debt		13.7		12.8
.0	.0	.3	.0				Deferred Taxes		.3		.3
1.8	1.0	2.8	2.8				All Other Non-Current		4.4		5.8
20.2	48.4	53.3	51.5				Net Worth		40.8		41.7
100.0	100.0	100.0	100.0				Total Liabilties & Net Worth		100.0		100.0
							INCOME DATA				
100.0	100.0	100.0	100.0				Net Sales		100.0		100.0
39.5	35.2	27.5	20.9				Gross Profit		28.2		31.4
32.9	24.6	19.5	12.7				Operating Expenses		21.6		24.9
6.7	10.5	8.0	8.3				Operating Profit		6.7		6.5
-.2	-.1	-.1	.1				All Other Expenses (net)		.2		-1.5
6.9	10.6	8.1	8.2				Profit Before Taxes		6.4		8.0
							RATIOS				
8.4	5.3	4.7	3.4						3.3		4.4
2.8	2.8	2.4	2.2				Current		2.1		2.4
.8	1.9	1.7	1.5						1.4		1.5
8.4	4.3	3.5	2.8						2.9		3.6
2.8	2.0	2.1	1.9				Quick	(223)	1.8		1.9
.8	1.4	1.4	1.2						1.2		1.2
0 UND	11 32.3	50 7.3	58 6.3					40	9.2	40	9.2
0 UND	31 11.8	64 5.7	78 4.7				Sales/Receivables	66	5.5	66	5.5
0 UND	65 5.6	89 4.1	101 3.6					89	4.1	85	4.3
0 UND	0 UND	0 UND	0 UND					0	UND	0	UND
0 UND	0 UND	0 UND	0 UND				Cost of Sales/Inventory	0	UND	1	657.6
0 UND	3 138.1	8 45.8	5 77.5					5	70.6	10	35.6
0 UND	0 UND	6 56.9	14 26.3					7	55.2	8	47.6
0 UND	13 27.7	17 21.1	20 18.0				Cost of Sales/Payables	17	21.3	15	23.9
0 UND	31 11.7	24 15.2	35 10.3					27	13.4	28	12.9
32.5	5.4	3.8	3.7						4.7		4.2
97.0	8.3	5.8	5.1				Sales/Working Capital		7.5		5.9
-758.8	15.0	9.3	11.1						16.0		12.1
20.9	68.6	90.4	389.9						70.3		95.1
(11) 13.9	(20) 34.0	(62) 17.7	(46) 32.3				EBIT/Interest	(184)	19.6	(93)	23.2
6.0	8.4	6.6	7.4						6.4		7.9
			139.3						35.4		42.5
		(10) 25.7					Net Profit + Depr., Dep., Amort./Cur. Mat. L/T/D	(28)	5.1	(16)	5.9
			4.0						.9		1.9
.3	.0	.0	.0						.0		.0
.8	.2	.1	.1				Fixed/Worth		.1		.2
NM	.5	.3	.2						.4		.6
.4	.3	.3	.4						.5		.5
.9	.7	.9	1.1				Debt/Worth		1.1		1.0
-3.0	2.4	2.0	1.7						2.6		4.0
289.8	118.6	65.5	60.5						66.0		90.5
(10) 91.4	(23) 64.3	(73) 32.5	(57) 39.6				% Profit Before Taxes/Tangible Net Worth	(202)	40.2	(109)	41.5
60.0	39.6	14.4	21.9						12.9		19.7
165.8	62.3	31.7	33.9						32.4		36.8
57.5	43.6	17.2	18.9				% Profit Before Taxes/Total Assets		17.8		20.2
32.7	22.8	7.2	10.9						6.6		7.4
UND	512.1	131.0	98.5						175.0		133.7
38.2	48.6	39.1	45.0				Sales/Net Fixed Assets		48.8		43.8
12.7	14.7	16.3	24.1						23.5		21.4
26.8	5.4	3.4	2.8						4.1		4.0
17.2	4.3	2.6	2.4				Sales/Total Assets		3.0		2.6
6.9	2.8	2.0	1.9						2.4		1.9
	.4	.3	.2						.2		.3
	(12) 1.0	(48) .6	(47) .4				% Depr., Dep., Amort./Sales	(153)	.5	(85)	.6
	2.3	1.3	.6						1.1		1.3
	1.5	.9	1.0						1.4		1.2
(15)	2.5	(32) 2.1	(14) 1.6				% Officers', Directors' Owners' Comp/Sales	(102)	2.5	(61)	2.9
	5.4	4.2	1.8						4.8		6.0
55926M	136693M	1111811M	2900729M	946628M	1590833M		Net Sales ($)		7779516M		2964649M
3655M	28476M	398021M	1176859M	430975M	794858M		Total Assets ($)		2773855M		1326919M

M = $ thousand   MM = $ million
See Pages viii through xx for Explanation of Ratios and Data

© RMA 2024

CONSTRUCTION-GENERAL—Drywall and Insulation Contractors NAICS 238310

Comparative Historical Data					Current Data Sorted by Sales					
6	12	13	**Type of Statement**		2	1	4	6		
36	41	52	Unqualified		1	4	22	25		
9	9	11	Reviewed	2	2	3	3	3		
29	38	32	Compiled	3	5	11	7	4		
63	85	77	Tax Returns	2	4	16	20	30		
4/1/21-3/31/22 ALL	4/1/22-3/31/23 ALL	4/1/23-3/31/24 ALL	Other	27 (4/1-9/30/23)		158 (10/1/23-3/31/24)				
				0-1MM	1-3MM	3-5MM	5-10MM	10-25MM	25MM & OVER	
143	185	185	**NUMBER OF STATEMENTS**	2	12	12	35	56	68	
%	%	%	**ASSETS**	%	%	%	%	%	%	
22.3	19.9	21.9	Cash & Equivalents	28.0	34.4	26.3	20.2	17.6		
39.0	43.7	44.2	Trade Receivables (net)	19.6	38.9	37.0	49.3	50.0		
5.4	5.2	3.5	Inventory	8.4	2.2	3.2	2.7	3.7		
8.8	9.7	8.3	All Other Current	2.4	3.7	6.6	9.8	10.1		
75.5	78.5	77.9	Total Current	58.4	79.2	73.2	82.0	81.4		
16.3	12.4	12.9	Fixed Assets (net)	32.0	15.3	17.9	8.1	9.2		
2.8	2.2	1.9	Intangibles (net)	1.1	.8	1.7	.8	3.2		
5.5	6.9	7.3	All Other Non-Current	8.4	4.7	7.3	9.1	6.2		
100.0	100.0	100.0	Total	100.0	100.0	100.0	100.0	100.0		
			LIABILITIES							
6.0	8.1	5.7	Notes Payable-Short Term	20.4	7.9	5.1	5.0	3.8		
4.1	2.4	2.8	Cur. Mat.-L.T.D.	3.7	.7	2.0	4.3	2.3		
11.4	14.3	11.4	Trade Payables	5.9	6.4	8.5	13.1	13.7		
.1	.1	.0	Income Taxes Payable	.0	.0	.0	.1	.0		
13.5	14.7	17.2	All Other Current	17.5	6.5	12.8	19.2	20.3		
35.1	39.6	37.2	Total Current	47.5	21.5	28.4	41.5	40.1		
11.2	13.4	11.1	Long-Term Debt	48.6	7.9	12.3	6.8	7.3		
.0	.2	.1	Deferred Taxes	.0	.0	.4	.2	.0		
3.9	2.6	2.7	All Other Non-Current	.0	2.2	1.6	3.6	2.9		
49.8	44.3	48.9	Net Worth	3.8	68.3	57.4	47.9	49.7		
100.0	100.0	100.0	Total Liabilities & Net Worth	100.0	100.0	100.0	100.0	100.0		
			INCOME DATA							
100.0	100.0	100.0	Net Sales	100.0	100.0	100.0	100.0	100.0		
27.0	28.5	26.8	Gross Profit	45.1	35.9	29.8	24.1	21.3		
21.1	22.9	18.6	Operating Expenses	33.0	28.0	21.2	17.6	12.7		
5.9	5.7	8.2	Operating Profit	12.1	7.9	8.7	6.5	8.6		
-2.0	-.4	-.1	All Other Expenses (net)	.2	-1.3	-.6	.6	-.1		
7.9	6.1	8.3	Profit Before Taxes	11.9	9.2	9.3	5.9	8.7		
			RATIOS							
5.2	3.9	3.9		4.7	21.8	5.6	3.2	3.3		
2.5	2.2	2.3	Current	1.4	4.6	2.8	2.3	2.1		
1.7	1.4	1.5		.9	2.5	1.9	1.6	1.5		
4.1	3.1	3.1		2.5	20.5	5.1	2.8	2.5		
2.1	1.8	1.9	Quick	1.1	4.4	2.2	2.0	1.7		
1.2	1.1	1.3		.6	2.2	1.5	1.3	1.2		
34 10.8	31 11.8	32 11.3		0 UND	1 265.9	1 495.5	52 7.0	46 8.0		
55 6.6	63 5.8	64 5.7	Sales/Receivables	0 UND	34 10.6	52 7.0	70 5.2	72 5.1		
81 4.5	91 4.0	89 4.1		53 6.9	99 3.7	83 4.4	101 3.6	91 4.0		
0 UND	0 UND	0 UND		0 UND	0 UND	0 UND	0 UND	0 UND		
0 UND	0 742.9	0 UND	Cost of Sales/Inventory	0 UND	0 UND	0 UND	0 UND	1 480.9		
9 38.7	8 44.1	5 74.3		12 30.0	6 58.5	3 113.6	1 245.5	6 60.0		
7 54.8	8 44.2	7 54.0		0 UND	0 UND	0 999.8	11 32.9	14 25.8		
17 21.1	18 20.2	17 21.3	Cost of Sales/Payables	2 166.9	5 68.3	13 28.5	21 17.6	20 18.4		
30 12.1	40 9.1	28 13.1		22 16.6	15 23.6	21 17.4	34 10.7	31 11.8		
4.0	4.3	4.1		5.9	3.9	4.1	3.9	4.2		
5.8	6.6	6.2	Sales/Working Capital	12.4	5.6	7.7	5.5	6.5		
14.4	16.1	13.1		NM	14.7	17.0	9.8	12.0		
105.8	101.1	105.7				131.9	54.9	463.5		
(109) 30.5	(142) 20.0	(150) 18.9	EBIT/Interest		(28) 32.6	(44) 14.5	(58) 32.3			
6.7	3.4	7.2			8.4	5.3	8.2			
24.3	9.3	75.4						37.6		
(19) 8.3	(29) 3.4	(18) 7.0	Net Profit + Depr., Dep., Amort./Cur. Mat. L/T/D				(11) 8.1			
3.2	.5	3.2						3.6		
.1	.0	.0		.2	.0	.0	.0	.1		
.2	.1	.1	Fixed/Worth	1.0	.2	.2	.1	.1		
.6	.4	.4		NM	.5	.6	.3	.3		
.4	.4	.4		.6	.2	.3	.4	.5		
.7	1.0	.9	Debt/Worth	2.1	.5	.6	1.1	1.1		
2.0	3.2	2.0		-3.2	.8	1.1	2.6	1.8		
69.7	60.8	73.6	% Profit Before Taxes/Tangible Net Worth		97.8	76.7	57.7	74.1		
(130) 39.7	(164) 30.8	(172) 40.9			41.9	(33) 57.7	(54) 30.2	(63) 46.1		
16.0	12.7	19.9			26.6	15.0	10.8	24.1		
36.7	31.4	40.4	% Profit Before Taxes/Total Assets		90.1	63.0	52.7	27.7	36.0	
16.7	13.8	20.8			43.0	30.7	23.8	14.2	20.0	
5.9	3.9	9.6			21.0	16.0	8.9	5.5	11.0	
92.1	162.1	126.0			196.9	187.2	182.4	141.8	100.7	
32.4	47.4	39.1	Sales/Net Fixed Assets		18.9	42.0	30.6	53.6	38.7	
13.9	19.1	19.1			7.5	11.1	17.1	31.0	20.6	
3.6	3.7	3.5			7.0	5.1	5.1	3.4	3.2	
2.7	2.7	2.6	Sales/Total Assets		2.9	2.8	2.9	2.5	2.6	
2.0	2.1	2.1			2.5	2.0	2.5	1.9	2.2	
.3	.3	.3				.6	.3	.2		
(97) .6	(119) .6	(120) .6	% Depr., Dep., Amort./Sales		(17) 1.1	(36) .5	(51) .4			
1.5	1.4	1.1				1.9	.8	.6		
1.2	1.1	1.1				1.6	.9	.7		
(54) 2.5	(90) 2.3	(70) 2.1	% Officers', Directors' Owners' Comp/Sales		(16) 2.9	(26) 1.6	(14) 1.2			
5.8	5.3	4.4				5.3	3.5	1.7		
3304725M	5460297M	6742620M	Net Sales ($)	1209M	23873M	46554M	242675M	925165M	5503144M	
1334136M	2215784M	2832844M	Total Assets ($)	601M	7432M	16915M	88193M	393381M	2326322M	

© RMA 2024 M = $ thousand MM = $ million
See Pages viii through xx for Explanation of Ratios and Data

CONSTRUCTION-GENERAL—Painting and Wall Covering Contractors NAICS 238320

Current Data Sorted by Assets / Comparative Historical Data

							Type of Statement				
				4	1		Unqualified		5		4
			10	10			Reviewed		28		11
		1	4				Compiled		6		7
	14	8	5	1			Tax Returns		24		9
	8	10	20	10	1	1	Other		59		45
		7 (4/1-9/30/23)		101 (10/1/23-3/31/24)					4/1/19-3/31/20		4/1/20-3/31/21
	0-500M	500M-2MM	2-10MM	10-50MM	50-100MM	100-250MM	NUMBER OF STATEMENTS		ALL		ALL
	22	19	39	25	2	1			122		76
	%	%	%	%	%	%	ASSETS		%		%
	44.6	20.5	18.3	13.5			Cash & Equivalents		21.6		29.3
	10.3	31.8	45.1	49.6			Trade Receivables (net)		43.2		36.9
	3.8	1.3	1.2	1.5			Inventory		.9		2.0
	6.8	1.3	8.3	12.5			All Other Current		7.1		4.4
	65.5	54.9	72.9	77.0			Total Current		72.9		72.6
	19.3	21.2	15.1	11.5			Fixed Assets (net)		16.6		14.4
	8.0	10.1	3.6	3.8			Intangibles (net)		4.9		3.8
	7.2	13.7	8.5	7.7			All Other Non-Current		5.6		9.3
	100.0	100.0	100.0	100.0			Total		100.0		100.0
							LIABILITIES				
	33.9	12.6	9.4	5.3			Notes Payable-Short Term		14.7		9.8
	2.4	3.2	1.5	2.7			Cur. Mat.-L.T.D.		2.0		3.5
	5.8	6.3	9.0	13.8			Trade Payables		9.2		9.7
	.0	.0	.1	.2			Income Taxes Payable		.1		.2
	9.5	6.9	11.0	18.7			All Other Current		13.0		15.0
	51.5	28.9	31.0	40.7			Total Current		39.0		38.3
	101.6	28.0	6.9	10.3			Long-Term Debt		16.3		23.8
	.0	.0	.1	.3			Deferred Taxes		.1		.0
	.0	5.6	1.9	3.3			All Other Non-Current		1.8		2.5
	-53.1	37.5	60.1	45.4			Net Worth		42.7		35.5
	100.0	100.0	100.0	100.0			Total Liabilties & Net Worth		100.0		100.0
							INCOME DATA				
	100.0	100.0	100.0	100.0			Net Sales		100.0		100.0
	53.8	41.4	33.5	29.1			Gross Profit		36.9		36.3
	43.3	32.6	25.4	22.3			Operating Expenses		28.6		29.5
	10.6	8.8	8.1	6.7			Operating Profit		8.3		6.7
	1.4	.2	.4	.1			All Other Expenses (net)		.4		-1.6
	9.1	8.6	7.7	6.6			Profit Before Taxes		7.9		8.4
							RATIOS				
	12.8	5.4	5.1	2.6					4.3		5.0
	1.8	2.0	2.5	1.9			Current		2.5		2.5
	.8	.8	1.5	1.3					1.4		1.5
	7.8	4.1	5.1	2.4					4.1		4.9
	1.8	2.0	2.1	1.5			Quick		2.1		2.4
	.7	.8	1.1	1.2					1.3		1.4
0	UND	0 UND	50 7.3	56 6.5				31	11.8	20	18.3
0	UND	31 11.8	72 5.1	87 4.2			Sales/Receivables	57	6.4	57	6.4
3	132.4	62 5.9	87 4.2	96 3.8				79	4.6	79	4.6
0	UND	0 UND	0 UND	0 UND				0	UND	0	UND
0	UND	0 UND	0 UND	0 UND			Cost of Sales/Inventory	0	UND	0	UND
0	UND	0 999.8	3 131.3	3 104.9				0	999.8	1	372.6
0	UND	0 UND	3 142.1	16 22.4				3	132.9	2	153.9
0	UND	0 UND	16 23.3	26 13.9			Cost of Sales/Payables	11	32.7	14	25.8
1	645.5	20 18.2	24 15.4	36 10.1				24	15.1	24	14.9
	16.3	7.7	3.3	4.7					5.0		4.1
	44.8	14.7	6.0	6.0			Sales/Working Capital		8.8		8.2
	-41.6	-90.3	13.1	15.0					18.5		19.6
	50.3	60.7	28.9	84.7					99.5		75.1
(18)	3.7	(15) 14.8	(30) 12.7	33.3			EBIT/Interest	(99)	13.8	(50)	26.8
	1.8	-.1	4.3	3.8					3.6		2.9
							Net Profit + Depr., Dep.,		20.2		20.4
							Amort./Cur. Mat. L/T/D	(16)	2.9	(10)	5.6
									.8		2.4
	.0	.1	.1	.1					.1		.1
	.4	.6	.2	.2			Fixed/Worth		.3		.2
	-.3	4.0	.5	.9					.8		.9
	.6	.5	.2	.6					.4		.3
	5.3	2.7	.6	1.2			Debt/Worth		.8		1.0
	-1.5	7.2	1.7	3.3					3.6		3.3
	186.1	123.6	56.5	78.0			% Profit Before Taxes/Tangible		79.7		93.3
(12)	104.4	(15) 44.7	(38) 30.8	(22) 28.9			Net Worth	(105)	40.4	(65)	45.6
	21.0	-22.2	6.1	11.2					18.5		9.4
	115.2	64.5	34.6	32.7			% Profit Before Taxes/Total		39.8		45.7
	28.3	23.3	12.8	11.5			Assets		20.7		18.6
	5.3	-3.7	4.8	6.0					5.1		3.2
	UND	98.5	85.1	38.3					93.8		58.2
	240.1	41.8	25.6	22.3			Sales/Net Fixed Assets		27.6		32.8
	29.0	16.7	11.8	15.1					14.3		13.8
	17.2	5.6	3.3	2.9					4.3		4.1
	8.0	3.8	2.8	2.5			Sales/Total Assets		3.1		2.9
	3.3	2.6	2.0	1.6					2.4		2.2
		.3	.6	.4					.6		.6
	(12)	.8	(24) 1.1	(21) 1.0			% Depr., Dep., Amort./Sales	(80)	1.1	(51)	1.0
		1.9	2.0	1.6					1.8		2.2
	2.0		1.4						2.0		2.5
(16)	4.9	(13)	2.5				% Officers', Directors'	(62)	3.8	(33)	4.3
	12.0		5.6				Owners' Comp/Sales		7.0		8.3
	65522M	89700M	518321M	1098111M	473106M	153639M	Net Sales ($)		2313637M		704553M
	5720M	21976M	198228M	469451M	148707M	127769M	Total Assets ($)		758667M		298477M

© RMA 2024 M = $ thousand MM = $ million
See Pages viii through xx for Explanation of Ratios and Data

CONSTRUCTION-GENERAL—Painting and Wall Covering Contractors NAICS 238320

Comparative Historical Data | Current Data Sorted by Sales

Comparative Historical Data				Type of Statement	Current Data Sorted by Sales					
4	8	5		Unqualified					2	3
12	17	20		Reviewed				5	5	10
5	7	5		Compiled			1		4	
16	20	28		Tax Returns	4	7	4	7	5	1
59	67	50		Other	5	6	4	15	8	12
4/1/21-3/31/22 ALL	4/1/22-3/31/23 ALL	4/1/23-3/31/24 ALL				7 (4/1-9/30/23)			101 (10/1/23-3/31/24)	
					0-1MM	1-3MM	3-5MM	5-10MM	10-25MM	25MM & OVER
96	119	108		NUMBER OF STATEMENTS	9	13	9	27	24	26
%	%	%		ASSETS	%	%	%	%	%	%
27.3	25.9	22.4		Cash & Equivalents	20.9	20.4	20.3	12.6		
32.9	34.6	36.6		Trade Receivables (net)		24.3		38.8	39.1	53.0
2.0	2.4	1.9		Inventory		8.0		1.2	1.7	.8
7.5	9.7	7.8		All Other Current		1.5		6.5	9.6	14.2
69.7	72.5	68.7		Total Current		54.7		66.9	70.7	80.6
17.0	14.0	16.3		Fixed Assets (net)		15.3		18.6	14.2	11.3
6.1	6.4	5.9		Intangibles (net)		11.0		5.1	7.3	2.5
7.1	7.1	9.1		All Other Non-Current		19.0		9.4	7.8	5.6
100.0	100.0	100.0		Total		100.0		100.0	100.0	100.0
				LIABILITIES						
10.6	10.4	14.3		Notes Payable-Short Term		8.0		26.0	5.5	9.4
2.5	1.7	2.2		Cur. Mat.-L.T.D.		2.5		2.7	2.1	2.0
6.7	8.6	9.0		Trade Payables		5.2		8.2	7.6	15.9
.1	.1	.1		Income Taxes Payable		.2		.0	.1	.1
12.4	13.6	11.9		All Other Current		7.4		8.9	13.3	19.3
32.3	34.4	37.6		Total Current		23.3		45.8	28.6	46.8
23.0	15.3	30.8		Long-Term Debt		38.8		20.4	8.9	8.6
.2	.1	.1		Deferred Taxes		.3		.0	.2	.2
3.6	3.9	2.7		All Other Non-Current		5.1		3.5	2.5	2.7
40.9	46.3	28.8		Net Worth		32.5		30.3	59.9	41.7
100.0	100.0	100.0		Total Liabilities & Net Worth		100.0		100.0	100.0	100.0
				INCOME DATA						
100.0	100.0	100.0		Net Sales		100.0		100.0	100.0	100.0
37.5	35.6	37.7		Gross Profit		42.5		37.3	30.2	27.5
31.0	29.4	29.5		Operating Expenses		40.3		31.4	24.2	19.6
6.4	6.2	8.3		Operating Profit		2.2		5.9	6.0	8.0
-2.6	-.1	.5		All Other Expenses (net)		.8		.2	-.3	.8
9.1	6.3	7.8		Profit Before Taxes		1.4		5.7	6.3	7.2
				RATIOS						
5.4	4.0	5.0				6.5		5.3	5.0	2.3
2.3	2.2	2.0		Current		3.2		1.9	2.5	1.7
1.4	1.6	1.2				1.8		1.1	1.6	1.3
4.5	3.0	3.7				3.7		5.3	4.4	2.1
1.9	1.8	1.6		Quick		2.0		1.3	2.2	1.3
1.1	1.2	1.0				1.0		.9	1.4	1.0
5 79.0	9 40.5	0 UND			0 UND		0 UND	50 7.3	57 6.4	
47 7.8	51 7.2	56 6.5		Sales/Receivables	16 22.9		49 7.4	69 5.3	74 4.9	
78 4.7	76 4.8	85 4.3			51 7.1		81 4.5	91 4.0	91 4.0	
0 UND	0 UND	0 UND			0 UND		0 UND	0 UND	0 UND	
0 UND	0 UND	0 UND		Cost of Sales/Inventory	0 UND		0 UND	0 UND	0 UND	
0 UND	2 231.5	1 674.5			2 228.2		2 164.7	3 145.7	2 159.2	
0 852.7	0 UND	0 UND			0 UND		0 UND	3 116.3	18 20.8	
11 34.4	13 28.0	15 24.6		Cost of Sales/Payables	0 UND		14 25.8	14 25.6	25 14.7	
20 18.7	26 14.0	26 13.9			27 13.4		22 16.4	22 16.4	39 9.4	
3.9	4.6	4.8			4.3		4.3	3.9	5.4	
8.7	7.6	10.7		Sales/Working Capital	10.6		14.6	6.0	9.8	
47.8	21.0	32.4			25.3		999.8	12.9	17.0	
154.0	42.5	50.8					41.8	107.5	53.6	
(75) 38.7	(87) 10.1	(91) 14.7		EBIT/Interest	(23) 15.8		(21) 10.7	(24) 21.5		
8.3	2.6	2.8					2.2	1.2	4.4	
66.3	23.1	20.7		Net Profit + Depr., Dep.,						
(10) 6.4	(17) 4.9	(16) 7.4		Amort./Cur. Mat. L/T/D						
4.0	2.3	2.5								
.1	.1	.1			.0		.1	.1	.1	
.3	.2	.2		Fixed/Worth	.4		.3	.2	.2	
1.8	.8	1.1			NM		1.7	.7	.6	
.3	.4	.4			.8		.3	.2	.7	
.9	.9	1.1		Debt/Worth	1.1		1.0	.6	1.4	
7.9	2.3	5.1			NM		5.5	3.0	3.0	
94.1	64.2	79.1			75.8		77.8	49.1	79.6	
(78) 42.2	(103) 37.8	(90) 34.3	% Profit Before Taxes/Tangible	(10) 7.3		(23) 38.6	(22) 26.8	(24) 38.1		
24.0	13.4	8.5		Net Worth	-60.5		8.5	6.5	21.1	
54.1	33.3	38.4		% Profit Before Taxes/Total	28.4		43.0	29.7	33.4	
26.5	16.4	15.1		Assets	3.5		23.3	9.1	13.2	
11.5	3.7	4.7			-19.2		4.8	3.6	7.7	
118.9	101.9	133.5			133.6		111.1	38.2	70.2	
30.5	30.1	29.2		Sales/Net Fixed Assets	31.5		47.9	23.1	27.5	
14.9	15.0	14.4			17.7		16.7	9.6	17.3	
5.8	4.7	4.2			5.8		5.8	3.1	3.2	
3.1	2.8	3.0		Sales/Total Assets	3.3		3.8	2.3	2.7	
2.0	2.0	2.1			1.6		2.7	1.5	2.2	
.7	.6	.5					.7	.5	.4	
(52) 1.3	(72) 1.2	(62) 1.1	% Depr., Dep., Amort./Sales			(12) .7	(19) 1.1	(22) 1.0		
3.0	2.2	1.8					2.1	1.6	1.6	
2.3	2.0	1.6					1.4	1.0		
(37) 5.4	(56) 3.7	(46) 3.9	% Officers', Directors',			(10) 4.5	(11) 2.2			
7.9	6.8	8.5		Owners' Comp/Sales			5.5	4.5		
964602M	1849004M	2398399M		Net Sales ($)	4203M	27321M	33861M	203893M	422075M	1707046M
438567M	810472M	971851M		Total Assets ($)	4310M	13745M	7281M	60158M	219518M	666839M

M = $ thousand   MM = $ million
See Pages viii through xx for Explanation of Ratios and Data

© RMA 2024

CONSTRUCTION-GENERAL—Flooring Contractors NAICS 238330

Current Data Sorted by Assets / Comparative Historical Data

							Type of Statement			
				3	1	1	Unqualified		2	2
1	1	13	10			Reviewed		22	15
1	4	8	1			Compiled		10	8
6	10	10	1			Tax Returns		34	20
13	14	39	11	1	2	Other		72	51
0-500M	17 (4/1-9/30/23) 500M-2MM	2-10MM	134 (10/1/23-3/31/24) 10-50MM	50-100MM	100-250MM			4/1/19-3/31/20 ALL	4/1/20-3/31/21 ALL
21	29	70	26	2	3	NUMBER OF STATEMENTS		140	96
%	%	%	%	%	%	**ASSETS**		%	%
20.7	21.0	13.8	11.4			Cash & Equivalents		17.9	21.1
22.8	35.6	39.0	43.3			Trade Receivables (net)		38.2	34.0
14.2	9.4	10.4	15.4			Inventory		10.7	12.0
.4	4.4	9.6	11.8			All Other Current		6.4	6.9
58.2	70.5	72.8	82.0			Total Current		73.2	74.0
20.4	15.5	13.1	10.5			Fixed Assets (net)		16.6	14.3
15.8	11.4	5.1	3.7			Intangibles (net)		3.8	5.3
5.6	2.5	9.0	3.8			All Other Non-Current		6.3	6.4
100.0	100.0	100.0	100.0			Total		100.0	100.0
						LIABILITIES			
22.4	6.3	4.9	8.3			Notes Payable-Short Term		12.7	11.4
3.0	1.8	1.2	1.2			Cur. Mat.-L.T.D.		3.7	1.5
19.7	17.5	9.7	13.0			Trade Payables		14.2	12.3
.0	.0	.1	.0			Income Taxes Payable		.1	.1
18.2	11.4	17.2	14.6			All Other Current		12.9	14.3
63.2	37.0	33.1	37.0			Total Current		43.7	39.6
36.7	20.1	11.8	8.4			Long-Term Debt		13.3	14.3
.0	.0	.1	.0			Deferred Taxes		.1	.1
26.6	2.4	3.4	2.6			All Other Non-Current		2.5	1.8
-26.4	40.5	51.6	52.0			Net Worth		40.5	44.2
100.0	100.0	100.0	100.0			Total Liabilities & Net Worth		100.0	100.0
						INCOME DATA			
100.0	100.0	100.0	100.0			Net Sales		100.0	100.0
35.1	32.7	28.7	26.1			Gross Profit		31.5	32.6
30.8	26.0	23.0	18.7			Operating Expenses		25.8	27.7
4.3	6.7	5.7	7.4			Operating Profit		5.7	4.9
.5	.6	.2	.0			All Other Expenses (net)		.3	-.6
3.8	6.2	5.5	7.4			Profit Before Taxes		5.3	5.5
						RATIOS			
2.7	5.0	3.8	4.0					3.1	3.4
1.3	2.5	2.3	2.0			Current		1.9	2.1
.5	1.1	1.6	1.6					1.2	1.5
2.0	3.8	2.9	2.2					2.5	2.7
.7	1.6	1.5	1.3			Quick		1.5	1.4
.2	.9	1.1	1.1					.9	1.0
0 UND	15 24.2	36 10.1	46 8.0					9 39.6	15 23.6
7 50.7	46 8.0	59 6.2	69 5.3			Sales/Receivables		44 8.3	42 8.6
35 10.4	64 5.7	76 4.8	94 3.9					74 4.9	69 5.3
0 UND	0 UND	0 UND	1 521.6					0 UND	0 UND
0 UND	11 33.6	5 76.3	25 14.5			Cost of Sales/Inventory		4 90.2	9 39.0
8 43.9	32 11.5	34 10.7	42 8.6					26 14.2	32 11.3
0 UND	7 53.6	8 43.5	12 30.3					6 58.6	7 51.9
2 149.0	16 22.8	15 24.7	21 17.2			Cost of Sales/Payables		16 22.8	18 20.7
23 15.9	30 12.2	26 14.3	39 9.4					30 12.2	31 11.9
10.8	5.2	4.2	3.8					5.8	5.0
43.7	10.1	6.6	5.2			Sales/Working Capital		10.0	7.4
-16.7	68.5	14.3	8.6					41.3	21.5
15.8	45.1	35.0	71.2					43.5	37.8
(16) 6.0	(24) 11.0	(56) 9.9	(21) 14.3			EBIT/Interest		(119) 11.9	(73) 9.8
-9.8	.8	2.3	6.8					3.2	1.9
						Net Profit + Depr., Dep., Amort./Cur. Mat. L/T/D		38.5 (12) 14.6 5.2	
.0	.1	.1	.1					.1	.1
.7	.3	.1	.2			Fixed/Worth		.2	.2
UND	1.4	.4	.3					.7	.7
1.6	.4	.5	.4					.5	.6
309.0	2.1	.9	1.2			Debt/Worth		1.2	1.2
-2.5	NM	1.7	1.8					3.9	4.1
999.8	87.9	41.8	46.9					67.7	73.8
(13) 157.6	(22) 44.7	(66) 22.6	34.4			% Profit Before Taxes/Tangible Net Worth		(119) 27.3	(85) 37.2
5.5	11.0	11.6	23.5					12.3	7.5
70.2	42.9	24.5	24.0					32.4	31.8
28.6	18.9	10.2	14.9			% Profit Before Taxes/Total Assets		12.5	15.9
-28.9	1.8	3.5	11.3					4.9	2.2
UND	159.4	93.6	101.9					122.6	142.5
101.8	44.8	43.2	37.7			Sales/Net Fixed Assets		48.2	41.8
21.5	11.5	15.7	9.8					19.1	15.3
9.9	4.3	3.4	3.1					5.0	3.8
5.5	3.0	2.6	2.3			Sales/Total Assets		3.3	2.8
2.6	2.0	2.0	1.8					2.5	2.2
	.2	.3	.3					.3	.4
(18)	1.2	(49) .5	(22) .3			% Depr., Dep., Amort./Sales		(90) .6	(60) .8
	2.4	1.2	.6					1.3	1.6
2.7	1.9		2.1					1.9	2.0
(10) 5.1	(10) 4.8	(29)	3.5			% Officers', Directors' Owners' Comp/Sales		(67) 3.5	(46) 3.7
8.7	6.5		4.7					7.0	7.0
50066M	134386M	846444M	1438609M	254756M	1406101M	Net Sales ($)		2906626M	1477593M
6968M	39863M	321601M	548399M	113003M	624865M	Total Assets ($)		910885M	523020M

© RMA 2024   M = $ thousand   MM = $ million
See Pages viii through xx for Explanation of Ratios and Data

CONSTRUCTION-GENERAL—Flooring Contractors NAICS 238330

Comparative Historical Data / Current Data Sorted by Sales

			Type of Statement						
3	1	5	Unqualified				5	9	5
18	18	25	Reviewed				5	4	11
9	20	14	Compiled		3	1	5	4	1
15	22	27	Tax Returns	1	5	1	14	6	14
61	71	80	Other	5	13	7	23	18	
4/1/21-	4/1/22-	4/1/23-			17 (4/1-9/30/23)		134 (10/1/23-3/31/24)		
3/31/22	3/31/23	3/31/24							
ALL	ALL	ALL		0-1MM	1-3MM	3-5MM	5-10MM	10-25MM	25MM & OVER
106	132	151	**NUMBER OF STATEMENTS**	6	21	9	47	37	31
%	%	%	**ASSETS**	%	%	%	%	%	%
20.6	17.5	15.3	Cash & Equivalents		20.4		18.1	14.8	8.7
40.2	37.2	36.5	Trade Receivables (net)		29.1		34.5	46.1	40.6
10.2	9.4	12.0	Inventory		11.2		10.5	10.2	14.9
8.6	8.3	7.5	All Other Current		2.3		5.7	11.3	11.5
79.6	72.4	71.4	Total Current		63.0		68.8	82.4	75.6
10.5	13.4	14.3	Fixed Assets (net)		25.4		16.8	7.8	11.1
5.3	6.2	7.7	Intangibles (net)		8.3		6.4	2.4	6.0
4.6	7.9	6.6	All Other Non-Current		3.3		7.9	7.4	7.3
100.0	100.0	100.0	Total		100.0		100.0	100.0	100.0
			LIABILITIES						
10.7	11.3	8.4	Notes Payable-Short Term		15.7		8.1	5.8	8.0
1.2	.9	1.7	Cur. Mat.-L.T.D.		2.0		2.3	.9	1.8
12.2	11.7	13.2	Trade Payables		12.2		8.2	14.7	12.2
.2	.2	.0	Income Taxes Payable		.0		.0	.1	.0
10.5	13.6	15.4	All Other Current		13.8		13.4	18.6	14.9
34.7	37.6	38.7	Total Current		43.8		32.0	40.1	37.0
18.1	14.1	16.6	Long-Term Debt		37.1		14.8	6.6	8.9
.1	.1	.1	Deferred Taxes		.0		.0	.0	.2
1.6	1.9	6.5	All Other Non-Current		1.1		4.0	1.1	5.2
45.4	46.2	38.2	Net Worth		17.9		49.1	52.3	48.7
100.0	100.0	100.0	Total Liabilities & Net Worth		100.0		100.0	100.0	100.0
			INCOME DATA						
100.0	100.0	100.0	Net Sales		100.0		100.0	100.0	100.0
30.3	31.0	29.9	Gross Profit		36.2		30.7	25.1	26.4
25.4	25.7	23.9	Operating Expenses		31.1		24.6	19.9	19.9
5.0	5.2	6.0	Operating Profit		5.1		6.1	5.2	6.5
-1.8	-.5	.3	All Other Expenses (net)		.7		.1	-.2	.4
6.8	5.7	5.7	Profit Before Taxes		4.4		6.0	5.4	6.1
			RATIOS						
4.1	4.5	3.7			4.6		5.1	3.8	2.7
2.8	2.5	2.1	Current		1.4		2.3	2.3	1.9
1.8	1.4	1.4			.8		1.4	1.5	1.6
3.5	3.5	2.6			3.0		3.9	2.6	1.7
2.0	1.8	1.4	Quick		1.3		1.7	1.5	1.2
1.3	1.0	.8			.6		.9	1.1	1.0
28 12.9	22 16.7	26 14.3		0 UND		16 22.5	38 9.6	35 10.5	
51 7.1	54 6.7	53 6.9	Sales/Receivables	31 11.8		53 6.9	72 5.1	59 6.2	
78 4.7	73 5.0	76 4.8		73 5.0		70 5.2	89 4.1	79 4.6	
0 UND	0 UND	0 UND		0 UND		0 UND	1 298.4	2 169.0	
4 81.9	5 70.7	6 63.0	Cost of Sales/Inventory	0 UND		6 63.1	5 79.4	23 15.7	
34 10.8	33 11.0	35 10.3		31 11.6		33 11.0	34 10.6	40 9.1	
9 39.9	7 49.7	7 53.1		0 UND		3 142.0	13 27.9	10 34.8	
18 20.6	16 22.8	16 22.9	Cost of Sales/Payables	14 25.6		11 34.5	22 16.8	19 19.6	
30 12.3	30 12.3	28 13.0		23 15.6		24 14.9	31 11.7	29 12.6	
4.4	4.6	4.5		6.9		4.5	4.3	4.5	
5.9	7.0	7.9	Sales/Working Capital	20.1		8.0	5.9	7.8	
11.6	15.3	23.1		-26.0		17.5	16.1	11.2	
	64.5	41.2	38.5		10.8		59.5	29.5	56.2
(77) 28.2	(104) 16.0	(122) 8.5	EBIT/Interest	(16) 2.3		(44) 11.5	(24) 9.9	(26) 13.2	
	6.1	4.7	2.8		-4.4		2.4	3.3	5.9
	77.4	70.7	7.8	Net Profit + Depr., Dep.,						
(12) 14.2	(16) 11.4	(13) 3.4	Amort./Cur. Mat. L/T/D						
	6.8	3.9	1.3							
.0	.1	.1			.0		.1	.0	.1
.1	.2	.2	Fixed/Worth		.6		.3	.1	.1
.4	.6	.7			NM		.9	.3	.6
.3	.4	.6			.8		.4	.4	.7
.8	1.1	1.3	Debt/Worth		7.3		1.1	.9	1.3
2.2	3.4	5.7			-3.9		4.1	1.6	2.2
	59.6	57.8	60.9		178.8		62.0	41.6	60.7
(94) 36.3	(115) 31.8	(132) 31.2	% Profit Before Taxes/Tangible Net Worth	(13) 36.8		(44) 28.7	(35) 23.7	34.7	
	16.7	12.0	12.5		3.2		9.7	11.7	21.5
31.1	26.1	29.1		33.8		35.8	21.2	23.3	
17.9	13.9	12.2	% Profit Before Taxes/Total Assets	3.6		15.0	10.9	13.6	
10.0	4.8	3.5		-21.1		3.2	6.3	8.7	
148.9	118.9	105.1		844.4		101.1	195.4	86.4	
54.5	43.1	44.8	Sales/Net Fixed Assets	23.5		35.3	64.3	57.5	
23.9	15.0	13.7		6.3		11.7	25.0	10.8	
3.9	4.0	3.9		5.0		4.0	3.9	3.4	
3.0	2.8	2.6	Sales/Total Assets	2.5		2.9	2.6	2.4	
2.3	2.1	2.0		1.9		2.3	2.3	2.1	
	.3	.3	.2				.3	.2	.3
(66) .6	(90) .8	(101) .5	% Depr., Dep., Amort./Sales		(29) .7		(28) .3	(28) .3	
	1.1	1.4	1.3				1.7	.7	.6
	1.7	1.4	1.8	% Officers', Directors' Owners' Comp/Sales		2.4		1.1		
(42) 2.9	(58) 2.9	(55) 3.5			(25) 4.2	(11) 2.2			
	5.9	4.6	5.5				5.3	3.2	
1820800M	2663479M	4130362M	Net Sales ($)	3591M	34842M	34986M	336144M	577596M	3143203M
775448M	1020344M	1654699M	Total Assets ($)	2445M	17320M	16077M	136137M	219442M	1263278M

M = $ thousand   MM = $ million
See Pages viii through xx for Explanation of Ratios and Data
© RMA 2024

CONSTRUCTION-GENERAL—Tile and Terrazzo Contractors NAICS 238340

Current Data Sorted by Assets | Comparative Historical Data

						Type of Statement		
		3	1			Unqualified	2	3
	1		1			Reviewed	5	5
3	7	4				Compiled	1	1
4	8	10	4	1		Tax Returns	11	3
	3 (4/1-9/30/23)		44 (10/1/23-3/31/24)			Other	32	18
0-500M	500M-2MM	2-10MM	10-50MM	50-100MM	100-250MM		4/1/19-3/31/20 ALL	4/1/20-3/31/21 ALL
7	16	17	6	1		NUMBER OF STATEMENTS	51	30
%	%	%	%	%	%	ASSETS	%	%
	30.8	13.8				Cash & Equivalents	11.8	16.6
	19.4	30.9				Trade Receivables (net)	35.5	28.9
	12.9	12.5			D	Inventory	10.7	18.6
	2.6	9.7			A	All Other Current	6.6	4.9
	65.7	66.9			T	Total Current	64.6	69.1
	16.4	26.1			A	Fixed Assets (net)	22.4	14.7
	4.9	.2				Intangibles (net)	3.4	8.1
	12.9	6.8			N	All Other Non-Current	9.7	8.0
	100.0	100.0			O	Total	100.0	100.0
					T	LIABILITIES		
	7.6	6.6				Notes Payable-Short Term	11.3	5.7
	3.5	1.5			A	Cur. Mat.-L.T.D.	2.7	3.0
	5.6	11.2			V	Trade Payables	17.2	13.7
	.0	.0			A	Income Taxes Payable	.0	.1
	9.8	10.0			I	All Other Current	15.6	13.7
	26.5	29.3			L	Total Current	46.8	36.1
	20.3	22.4			A	Long-Term Debt	15.6	23.6
	.0	.0			B	Deferred Taxes	.1	.4
	3.1	9.2			L	All Other Non-Current	1.0	5.0
	50.0	39.1			E	Net Worth	36.5	35.0
	100.0	100.0				Total Liabilties & Net Worth	100.0	100.0
						INCOME DATA		
	100.0	100.0				Net Sales	100.0	100.0
	38.1	29.6				Gross Profit	36.9	33.6
	33.9	23.1				Operating Expenses	29.9	30.5
	4.3	6.4				Operating Profit	7.1	3.2
	-.1	.7				All Other Expenses (net)	.8	-2.1
	4.4	5.7				Profit Before Taxes	6.3	5.2
						RATIOS		
	15.1	4.3					2.2	3.1
	3.1	2.5				Current	1.6	2.0
	1.2	2.0					1.1	1.5
	16.6	4.1					1.6	1.9
	(15) 2.4	2.3				Quick	1.0	1.4
	1.1	.9					.6	.8
	0 UND	0 UND					23 15.8	19 19.7
	15 24.5	40 9.2				Sales/Receivables	46 7.9	43 8.5
	41 8.8	78 4.7					78 4.7	78 4.7
	0 UND	0 UND					0 UND	0 UND
	11 34.7	0 UND				Cost of Sales/Inventory	9 40.7	14 26.3
	44 8.3	46 7.9					32 11.3	96 3.8
	0 UND	0 UND					13 27.2	8 46.1
	3 118.8	12 30.8				Cost of Sales/Payables	26 14.1	27 13.3
	14 26.0	35 10.3					57 6.4	38 9.6
	4.6	3.5					7.2	4.1
	11.4	6.7				Sales/Working Capital	13.3	6.4
	227.2	9.2					36.3	12.9
	64.8	37.7					36.4	25.9
	(13) 15.0	4.2				EBIT/Interest	(46) 11.9	(25) 5.7
	2.3	-.1					1.5	.7
						Net Profit + Depr., Dep., Amort./Cur. Mat. L/T/D		
	.0	.2					.1	.0
	.1	.6				Fixed/Worth	.4	.3
	5.8	3.8					1.3	-8.3
	.2	.5					.8	.8
	.5	1.0				Debt/Worth	1.5	2.2
	10.3	8.4					3.2	-19.7
	52.3	49.4					91.2	58.2
	(14) 28.2	(15) 18.2				% Profit Before Taxes/Tangible Net Worth	(44) 39.2	(21) 44.0
	19.6	-4.7					9.2	17.5
	24.6	23.7					29.2	25.3
	19.0	8.1				% Profit Before Taxes/Total Assets	13.7	10.8
	13.3	-2.9					.3	-.7
	156.5	43.8					45.1	112.2
	47.6	14.0				Sales/Net Fixed Assets	17.5	22.9
	18.5	6.1					9.6	9.0
	6.2	3.1					3.9	2.7
	4.4	2.1				Sales/Total Assets	2.3	2.3
	2.1	1.8					1.9	1.8
		.5					.9	.3
	(10)	1.5				% Depr., Dep., Amort./Sales	(30) 1.6	(18) 1.0
		2.4					2.5	2.6
	2.0						2.4	1.8
	(11) 3.2					% Officers', Directors' Owners' Comp/Sales	(21) 3.1	(14) 3.5
	8.8						5.5	7.0
5191M	94649M	181921M	245927M	25165M		Net Sales ($)	521791M	632650M
959M	20538M	70699M	145707M	77202M		Total Assets ($)	255056M	365765M

© RMA 2024   M = $ thousand   MM = $ million
See Pages viii through xx for Explanation of Ratios and Data

CONSTRUCTION-GENERAL—Tile and Terrazzo Contractors NAICS 238340

Comparative Historical Data | Current Data Sorted by Sales

Comparative Historical Data				Type of Statement	Current Data Sorted by Sales					
1	2			Unqualified			1		2	1
	3			Reviewed					1	
			2	Compiled			1	5	4	
7	12	14		Tax Returns	2	2	8	3	5	5
15	28	27		Other	2	4				
4/1/21-3/31/22 ALL	4/1/22-3/31/23 ALL	4/1/23-3/31/24 ALL			3 (4/1-9/30/23)			44 (10/1/23-3/31/24)		
					0-1MM	1-3MM	3-5MM	5-10MM	10-25MM	25MM & OVER
23	45	47		NUMBER OF STATEMENTS	4	6	10	9	12	6
%	%	%		ASSETS	%	%	%	%	%	%
21.0	15.2	22.5		Cash & Equivalents			17.8		27.2	
20.0	27.4	20.7		Trade Receivables (net)			20.7		33.9	
20.3	16.0	13.3		Inventory			13.3		12.7	
4.7	7.4	6.0		All Other Current			2.8		5.0	
66.1	66.1	62.5		Total Current			54.6		78.7	
19.2	22.1	22.7		Fixed Assets (net)			38.6		10.7	
4.8	3.2	4.8		Intangibles (net)			1.1		3.1	
9.9	8.7	10.0		All Other Non-Current			5.7		7.5	
100.0	100.0	100.0		Total			100.0		100.0	
				LIABILITIES						
9.0	8.9	5.6		Notes Payable-Short Term			12.5		4.3	
1.9	2.9	8.1		Cur. Mat.-L.T.D.			3.6		2.5	
9.9	11.1	9.1		Trade Payables			4.2		13.3	
.0	.3	.0		Income Taxes Payable			.0		.0	
11.0	13.6	11.1		All Other Current			15.2		6.2	
31.9	36.8	33.9		Total Current			35.4		26.2	
27.6	24.6	21.3		Long-Term Debt			22.3		10.9	
.0	.1	.1		Deferred Taxes			.0		.0	
2.9	8.1	5.1		All Other Non-Current			5.0		8.9	
37.6	30.5	39.6		Net Worth			37.3		54.0	
100.0	100.0	100.0		Total Liabilities & Net Worth			100.0		100.0	
				INCOME DATA						
100.0	100.0	100.0		Net Sales			100.0		100.0	
37.0	36.4	37.5		Gross Profit			38.5		26.8	
31.5	32.6	31.4		Operating Expenses			34.5		22.3	
5.5	3.9	6.2		Operating Profit			4.0		4.5	
-.3	-.5	.7		All Other Expenses (net)			.5		.2	
5.8	4.4	5.5		Profit Before Taxes			3.5		4.3	
				RATIOS						
6.4	4.5	4.3					22.2		5.0	
3.1	2.1	2.3		Current			2.6		3.9	
1.6	1.1	1.1					.7		2.2	
6.0	3.1	3.9					20.9		4.8	
(22) 1.6	(46) 1.6	1.6		Quick			2.3		2.8	
.7	.8	.7					.3		1.3	
0 UND	0 UND	0 UND					0 UND		13 27.2	
14 25.7	31 11.9	18 20.6		Sales/Receivables			14 26.6		39 9.3	
60 6.1	73 5.0	55 6.6					60 6.1		69 5.3	
0 UND	0 UND	0 UND					0 UND		0 UND	
26 14.0	5 75.3	3 131.0		Cost of Sales/Inventory			0 UND		4 86.9	
79 4.6	64 5.7	49 7.5					21 17.1		47 7.7	
0 UND	0 UND	0 UND					0 UND		10 36.6	
19 19.3	20 17.9	12 30.8		Cost of Sales/Payables			0 UND		13 27.5	
30 12.0	36 10.2	33 10.9					8 46.0		26 13.8	
4.5	3.9	3.9					3.6		3.5	
6.6	9.7	9.4		Sales/Working Capital			7.2		8.4	
9.3	57.7	225.5					-9.9		14.7	
27.3	34.7	55.8							51.1	
(18) 6.3	(40) 9.5	(43) 9.1		EBIT/Interest					8.0	
1.6	1.6	.7							-.1	
				Net Profit + Depr., Dep., Amort./Cur. Mat. L/T/D						
.1	.1	.1					.2		.1	
.5	.5	.4		Fixed/Worth			1.5		.2	
1.8	6.7	6.2					NM		.5	
.6	.7	.5					.4		.5	
1.6	1.8	1.3		Debt/Worth			1.4		.8	
25.7	50.0	10.3					NM		2.3	
90.5	97.6	53.5							69.1	
(18) 18.8	(35) 32.0	(39) 26.2		% Profit Before Taxes/Tangible Net Worth					20.1	
6.3	9.6	11.8							-10.3	
19.7	22.9	28.9					16.1		27.2	
6.6	7.6	13.5		% Profit Before Taxes/Total Assets			9.9		10.8	
2.4	.7	-.7					-3.0		-3.1	
116.5	47.1	76.4					21.1		95.0	
15.8	19.5	21.7		Sales/Net Fixed Assets			8.7		31.1	
10.1	9.9	8.3					2.6		16.6	
3.4	3.8	4.5					3.5		6.5	
2.5	2.7	2.6		Sales/Total Assets			2.3		3.5	
1.9	1.9	1.8					1.8		2.1	
.6	.5	.4								
(11) 2.6	(33) 1.1	(25) 1.8		% Depr., Dep., Amort./Sales						
4.5	2.7	2.5								
1.9	2.7	1.8								
(11) 3.9	(18) 6.2	(24) 3.8		% Officers', Directors' Owners' Comp/Sales						
8.8	10.7	8.8								
199013M	826896M	552853M		Net Sales ($)	1897M	8005M	39081M	59413M	189876M	254581M
81857M	445934M	315105M		Total Assets ($)	496M	3672M	17300M	21465M	60528M	211644M

M = $ thousand MM = $ million
See Pages viii through xx for Explanation of Ratios and Data

© RMA 2024

CONSTRUCTION-GENERAL—Finish Carpentry Contractors NAICS 238350

Current Data Sorted by Assets | Comparative Historical Data

0-500M	500M-2MM	2-10MM	10-50MM	50-100MM	100-250MM				
1	2	5	1	2		Type of Statement		4	3
	1	1				Unqualified		9	9
1	9	5				Reviewed		5	5
9	9	5	1			Compiled		31	17
7	8	23	13	1		Tax Returns		52	46
	7 (4/1-9/30/23)		82 (10/1/23-3/31/24)			Other		4/1/19-3/31/20	4/1/20-3/31/21
17	21	34	14	3		NUMBER OF STATEMENTS		101 ALL	80 ALL
%	%	%	%	%	%	ASSETS		%	%
28.8	29.9	20.6	21.3		D	Cash & Equivalents		16.3	25.6
18.3	23.3	34.0	25.7		A	Trade Receivables (net)		38.7	29.0
9.5	10.6	10.5	18.5		T	Inventory		9.4	9.9
3.9	4.5	7.0	4.3		A	All Other Current		5.0	6.6
60.4	68.3	72.1	69.8			Total Current		69.5	71.1
22.5	17.2	17.4	11.8		N	Fixed Assets (net)		19.7	16.0
6.6	5.4	3.5	10.6		O	Intangibles (net)		2.7	6.5
10.5	9.0	6.9	7.8		T	All Other Non-Current		8.1	6.4
100.0	100.0	100.0	100.0			Total		100.0	100.0
					A	LIABILITIES			
5.7	7.0	5.1	1.1		V	Notes Payable-Short Term		11.9	10.3
7.3	2.7	1.8	1.4		A	Cur. Mat.-L.T.D.		2.3	3.5
14.6	16.4	11.3	9.0		I	Trade Payables		17.9	9.8
.1	.0	.2	.6		L	Income Taxes Payable		.1	.0
24.2	21.1	19.2	22.1		A	All Other Current		17.5	15.4
51.8	47.1	37.6	34.3		B	Total Current		49.7	39.1
40.4	13.7	15.1	13.1		L	Long-Term Debt		17.7	27.8
.0	.0	.0	.4		E	Deferred Taxes		.1	.0
5.7	.0	1.8	1.3			All Other Non-Current		3.9	5.3
2.1	39.2	45.4	51.0			Net Worth		28.7	27.8
100.0	100.0	100.0	100.0			Total Liabilities & Net Worth		100.0	100.0
						INCOME DATA			
100.0	100.0	100.0	100.0			Net Sales		100.0	100.0
49.0	42.2	39.0	35.0			Gross Profit		33.8	37.0
44.3	33.5	29.7	29.0			Operating Expenses		29.2	30.8
4.7	8.7	9.3	6.1			Operating Profit		4.6	6.2
.0	-.6	.3	-.1			All Other Expenses (net)		.2	-1.3
4.7	9.3	9.0	6.2			Profit Before Taxes		4.4	7.6
						RATIOS			
5.1	4.1	4.2	4.2					2.5	4.3
1.8	1.5	2.1	2.0			Current		1.7	2.2
.5	.9	1.3	1.3					1.0	1.2
3.8	3.1	3.0	2.8					2.2	3.3
1.8	1.0	1.3	1.1			Quick		1.2	1.5
.3	.6	.8	.9					.7	1.0
0 UND	0 UND	26 14.1	25 14.5				9	39.5	4 101.0
0 UND	21 17.4	43 8.5	47 7.8			Sales/Receivables	48	7.6	29 12.5
19 19.0	54 6.8	69 5.3	63 5.8				73	5.0	62 5.9
0 UND	0 UND	0 UND	16 22.8				0	UND	0 UND
2 211.7	0 UND	12 30.4	40 9.1			Cost of Sales/Inventory	3	140.1	5 78.2
8 43.6	42 8.7	41 9.0	57 6.4				19	19.2	26 14.3
0 UND	2 171.0	11 34.2	15 24.8				7	55.0	1 577.9
3 134.3	19 19.7	22 16.8	20 18.3			Cost of Sales/Payables	20	18.2	12 30.5
27 13.5	50 7.3	36 10.0	30 12.0				38	9.6	26 13.9
5.6	6.6	4.6	3.9					7.4	5.3
22.9	16.8	7.3	7.1			Sales/Working Capital		14.7	9.4
-78.0	NM	17.8	14.4					-431.7	44.1
55.5	42.6	127.8	71.0					38.0	44.1
(14) 15.7	(16) 23.0	(29) 27.7	(11) 14.9			EBIT/Interest	(87)	14.9	(67) 15.2
-.2	12.9	2.0	4.5					1.9	2.5
						Net Profit + Depr., Dep., Amort./Cur. Mat. L/T/D	(10)	11.5 3.5 .8	
.0	.1	.1	.1					.1	.1
.4	.4	.3	.2			Fixed/Worth		.5	.4
NM	3.3	1.1	1.8					4.1	2.4
.4	.4	.4	.3					.7	.8
3.5	1.9	1.5	1.6			Debt/Worth		1.8	2.2
-4.1	145.4	3.3	6.3					27.6	92.1
291.2	143.3	97.7	47.9					92.4	115.6
(12) 80.4	(18) 83.0	(33) 41.9	(12) 32.0			% Profit Before Taxes/Tangible Net Worth	(79)	43.0	(61) 46.0
41.1	44.7	20.2	15.5					10.7	19.5
39.4	45.8	37.0	21.2					41.5	41.4
20.7	35.2	17.8	9.2			% Profit Before Taxes/Total Assets		13.9	21.5
-6.1	11.7	4.5	4.8					.8	4.6
UND	159.3	81.9	60.6					121.1	218.2
36.0	33.7	23.1	25.2			Sales/Net Fixed Assets		37.9	38.5
18.0	12.1	8.6	11.3					14.4	12.7
11.1	4.9	3.7	2.8					5.9	4.6
5.8	3.6	2.8	2.1			Sales/Total Assets		3.8	3.3
3.6	3.3	1.7	1.5					2.3	2.1
			.3					.4	.3
	(23)	.7				% Depr., Dep., Amort./Sales	(61)	1.0	(41) .8
			3.1					2.4	2.4
3.0	1.8	1.6						1.8	1.8
(11) 5.9	(12) 3.4	(16) 2.4				% Officers', Directors' Owners' Comp/Sales	(52) 3.1	(38) 3.2
9.3	8.6	2.6						6.8	6.4
30805M	101492M	464743M	454827M	837587M		Net Sales ($)		1420644M	1301750M
4669M	23340M	169782M	234358M	219611M		Total Assets ($)		483280M	415356M

© RMA 2024 M = $ thousand   MM = $ million
See Pages viii through xx for Explanation of Ratios and Data

CONSTRUCTION-GENERAL—Finish Carpentry Contractors NAICS 238350

Comparative Historical Data | Current Data Sorted by Sales

Comparative Historical Data			Type of Statement	Current Data Sorted by Sales										
1	2	1	Unqualified			1							
6	4	10	Reviewed			1		2		5		2	
5	6	3	Compiled			1		2		2			
18	29	23	Tax Returns			9		3		3		12	
34	41	52	Other	2		5		9		18			
4/1/21-3/31/22 ALL	4/1/22-3/31/23 ALL	4/1/23-3/31/24 ALL		3		7 (4/1-9/30/23)		82 (10/1/23-3/31/24)					
				0-1MM		1-3MM		3-5MM		5-10MM		10-25MM	25MM & OVER
64	82	89	NUMBER OF STATEMENTS	5		16		12		16		26	14
%	%	%	ASSETS	%		%		%		%		%	%
24.3	28.0	24.9	Cash & Equivalents			37.3		18.1		23.1		21.3	27.5
26.7	27.1	27.2	Trade Receivables (net)			18.6		20.3		29.1		32.5	30.5
7.7	14.6	11.4	Inventory			6.8		16.0		12.5		12.3	13.9
6.0	4.5	5.7	All Other Current			6.2		4.3		1.9		7.0	7.8
64.7	74.2	69.3	Total Current			68.9		58.7		66.6		73.1	79.7
21.2	15.6	17.0	Fixed Assets (net)			21.7		18.9		20.4		14.2	7.0
5.9	4.4	5.6	Intangibles (net)			4.7		4.6		4.4		5.0	6.5
8.2	5.8	8.1	All Other Non-Current			4.7		17.8		8.6		7.8	6.8
100.0	100.0	100.0	Total			100.0		100.0		100.0		100.0	100.0
			LIABILITIES										
5.0	4.0	4.9	Notes Payable-Short Term			7.4		3.0		5.4		5.1	1.2
2.6	3.2	2.9	Cur. Mat.-L.T.D.			1.3		10.1		3.2		1.9	1.5
10.2	13.7	12.6	Trade Payables			13.3		23.7		10.5		11.1	11.0
.0	.1	.2	Income Taxes Payable			.1		.0		.1		.2	.6
15.7	18.5	21.9	All Other Current			24.2		15.7		15.7		28.4	24.8
33.5	39.5	42.6	Total Current			46.4		52.5		34.9		46.6	39.0
17.5	21.4	18.8	Long-Term Debt			20.4		46.4		17.7		8.1	10.5
.0	.0	.1	Deferred Taxes			.0		.0		.0		.1	.2
7.0	11.5	2.0	All Other Non-Current			6.3		.0		.6		1.9	1.1
42.1	27.6	36.6	Net Worth			26.9		1.1		46.8		43.2	49.2
100.0	100.0	100.0	Total Liabilities & Net Worth			100.0		100.0		100.0		100.0	100.0
			INCOME DATA										
100.0	100.0	100.0	Net Sales			100.0		100.0		100.0		100.0	100.0
37.6	37.2	40.9	Gross Profit			41.8		33.0		51.4		33.5	32.6
31.6	29.7	32.8	Operating Expenses			33.0		28.4		40.4		25.5	24.6
6.0	7.6	8.1	Operating Profit			8.8		4.7		11.0		8.0	8.0
-2.4	-.1	-.1	All Other Expenses (net)			-.1		-1.2		.1		.7	-.8
8.4	7.7	8.1	Profit Before Taxes			8.9		5.8		10.9		7.3	8.8
			RATIOS										
3.8	4.8	4.2				4.9		2.8		4.6		3.4	3.8
2.3	2.2	1.8	Current			2.4		1.3		2.9		1.5	2.0
1.3	1.4	1.1				1.1		.6		1.0		1.1	1.4
3.1	3.2	2.9				4.5		1.8		4.4		2.0	2.6
1.6	1.5	1.2	Quick			2.0		.7		2.1		1.1	1.4
.9	.9	.7				.7		.4		.5		.8	1.0
3 112.8	6 57.3	8 43.7		0	UND	0	UND	23	15.6	15	25.1	25 14.5
29 12.5	26 13.8	33 10.9	Sales/Receivables	12	30.6	10	35.1	41	9.0	49	7.5	35 10.3
58 6.3	59 6.2	54 6.8		53	6.9	35	10.3	58	6.3	63	5.8	54 6.8
0 UND	0 UND	0 UND		0	UND	0	UND	0	UND	0	UND	7 53.5
5 67.3	15 23.6	9 39.8	Cost of Sales/Inventory	4	90.8	10	37.9	18	19.8	3	111.3	22 16.4
31 11.8	43 8.4	41 9.0		22	16.9	22	16.8	42	8.6	39	9.3	51 7.2
2 155.0	3 136.7	6 56.4		3	131.9	0	821.9	7	52.0	11	32.1	13 28.3
18 20.8	15 23.7	17 21.0	Cost of Sales/Payables	16	22.6	11	34.4	18	20.5	17	21.7	19 19.7
35 10.5	33 11.2	32 11.5		39	9.4	39	9.3	40	9.1	30	12.0	24 15.5
5.2	5.0	4.9				4.4		13.0		4.5		6.4	4.2
8.8	8.8	9.7	Sales/Working Capital			9.5		104.6		6.6		10.5	7.1
33.4	22.6	80.5				514.9		-57.5		433.4		33.1	16.6
86.3	119.6	71.0				57.0				106.4		108.2	154.9
(54) 29.9	(64) 11.2	(71) 20.8	EBIT/Interest	(11)	28.4			(13)	13.3	(23)	30.7	(10) 35.9
6.6	3.4	4.3				15.1				3.8		3.2	5.8
			Net Profit + Depr., Dep., Amort./Cur. Mat. L/T/D										
.1	.0	.1				.0		.0		.1		.1	.1
.4	.2	.3	Fixed/Worth			.4		.5		.4		.3	.1
1.5	1.2	1.4				1.4		NM		1.7		1.1	.5
.5	.4	.4				.3		1.2		.3		.4	.4
1.4	1.8	1.8	Debt/Worth			2.0		22.0		1.3		2.2	1.3
4.5	19.1	6.5				8.1		-3.6		3.6		5.3	3.5
100.4	105.5	106.7				202.0				97.3		105.4	75.3
(52) 48.6	(63) 48.1	(78) 51.2	% Profit Before Taxes/Tangible Net Worth	(15)	59.9	(14)		49.9	(25)	36.5	(12)	47.1
20.0	12.2	25.4				38.4				24.9		19.9	20.2
46.9	41.6	39.8				45.0		47.7		38.4		29.8	47.3
21.8	21.3	18.8	% Profit Before Taxes/Total Assets			23.2		10.4		27.8		16.8	21.6
8.8	3.9	5.8				10.9		-5.2		9.7		3.9	6.5
108.7	308.2	88.8				UND		UND		62.5		122.7	181.6
24.0	46.2	30.1	Sales/Net Fixed Assets			31.9		48.0		25.7		25.1	47.4
8.9	16.5	12.1				10.0		12.5		10.5		10.8	27.2
4.4	5.1	4.4				5.5		12.1		3.6		4.3	4.0
3.2	3.1	3.3	Sales/Total Assets			3.5		5.0		3.2		2.8	2.8
1.9	2.2	2.1				2.3		3.3		1.9		1.7	2.5
.5	.2	.4								.4		.3	
(35) 1.0	(46) .6	(51) 1.4	% Depr., Dep., Amort./Sales						(10)	1.3	(17)	.7	
3.3	1.5	2.7								2.3		2.7	
2.2	1.9	1.9						2.0				1.7	
(31) 5.5	(39) 3.2	(42) 3.2	% Officers', Directors' Owners' Comp/Sales			(10)	2.7			(10)	2.3	
7.0	7.6	7.3						4.5				3.5	
1439327M	2006220M	1889454M	Net Sales ($)	3696M		27985M		48346M		108691M		425839M	1274897M
574912M	702885M	651760M	Total Assets ($)	1097M		10260M		13304M		47492M		166789M	412818M

© RMA 2024   M = $ thousand   MM = $ million
See Pages viii through xx for Explanation of Ratios and Data

CONSTRUCTION-GENERAL—Other Building Finishing Contractors NAICS 238390

Current Data Sorted by Assets | **Comparative Historical Data**

						Type of Statement		
		1		5	1	1	Unqualified	4	5
		1	8	12	1		Reviewed	26	13
	1	5	2	1			Compiled	6	7
7	5	5	6	1			Tax Returns	24	19
8	3	3	28	12	2		Other	74	57
		12 (4/1-9/30/23)		93 (10/1/23-3/31/24)				4/1/19- 3/31/20	4/1/20- 3/31/21
0-500M	500M-2MM	2-10MM	10-50MM	50-100MM	100-250MM			ALL	ALL
15	10	44	31	4	1	NUMBER OF STATEMENTS	134	101
%	%	%	%	%	%	ASSETS	%	%
32.4	23.6	16.1	14.6			Cash & Equivalents	19.8	28.9
8.9	24.7	36.9	42.4			Trade Receivables (net)	36.5	31.3
2.1	7.4	12.3	3.4			Inventory	5.2	4.9
5.3	.9	8.9	8.9			All Other Current	7.1	6.0
48.6	56.5	74.1	69.2			Total Current	68.6	71.1
24.7	27.8	15.0	12.6			Fixed Assets (net)	18.3	16.5
6.8	9.5	4.4	6.0			Intangibles (net)	4.6	5.9
19.9	6.2	6.6	12.2			All Other Non-Current	8.6	6.5
100.0	100.0	100.0	100.0			Total	100.0	100.0
						LIABILITIES		
30.6	3.9	4.5	3.4			Notes Payable-Short Term	8.1	10.1
3.5	.7	1.3	1.4			Cur. Mat.-L.T.D.	2.9	2.5
1.8	16.4	16.2	13.4			Trade Payables	15.2	11.0
.0	.0	.2	.0			Income Taxes Payable	.3	.2
22.6	6.5	13.8	20.3			All Other Current	17.2	14.4
58.5	27.5	36.1	38.4			Total Current	43.7	38.2
55.7	16.3	11.6	9.9			Long-Term Debt	19.7	23.6
.0	.0	.2	.8			Deferred Taxes	.4	.1
.2	4.8	4.2	6.7			All Other Non-Current	4.0	4.3
-14.4	51.4	47.9	44.1			Net Worth	32.1	33.9
100.0	100.0	100.0	100.0			Total Liabilities & Net Worth	100.0	100.0
						INCOME DATA		
100.0	100.0	100.0	100.0			Net Sales	100.0	100.0
35.9	39.0	33.3	26.9			Gross Profit	35.1	32.7
32.5	31.4	25.5	18.8			Operating Expenses	28.2	26.7
3.3	7.6	7.7	8.2			Operating Profit	6.9	6.0
.7	-.2	.1	.1			All Other Expenses (net)	.3	-1.1
2.7	7.8	7.6	8.1			Profit Before Taxes	6.6	7.1
						RATIOS		
5.3	12.7	3.5	3.0				3.2	4.9
1.5	2.6	1.8	1.9			Current	1.7	2.2
.5	1.0	1.3	1.3				1.1	1.3
2.7	12.6	2.9	2.3				2.8	4.4
1.5	1.1	1.6	1.7			Quick	1.4	1.9
.4	1.0	.8	1.1				.8	1.0
0 UND	0 UND	27 13.5	49 7.5				17 21.4	7 50.6
0 UND	0 UND	46 7.9	85 4.3			Sales/Receivables	47 7.8	45 8.2
1 614.7	45 8.1	83 4.4	107 3.4				79 4.6	74 4.9
0 UND	0 UND	0 UND	0 UND				0 UND	0 UND
0 UND	0 UND	5 77.5	0 UND			Cost of Sales/Inventory	0 UND	0 UND
0 UND	0 UND	53 6.9	21 17.2				13 27.5	10 36.9
0 UND	0 UND	18 20.8	13 28.5				8 48.5	1 295.3
0 UND	3 144.6	26 14.2	23 16.2			Cost of Sales/Payables	20 18.0	18 20.6
0 999.8	42 8.6	54 6.8	40 9.2				41 8.8	35 10.4
30.6	6.5	3.9	4.4				6.0	4.5
40.8	24.9	7.1	6.6			Sales/Working Capital	10.7	8.0
-66.5	NM	16.7	14.9				58.8	26.5
22.8		82.9	110.6				58.1	102.7
(10) 11.1	(39)	(27) 20.6	19.7			EBIT/Interest	(113) 11.3	(82) 19.4
-5.0		4.2	4.3				4.1	2.5
						Net Profit + Depr., Dep., Amort./Cur. Mat. L/T/D	23.1 (18) 5.9 1.0	
.0	.0	.1	.1				.1	.1
1.0	.5	.2	.2			Fixed/Worth	.3	.4
UND	NM	.7	.9				1.3	1.7
1.1	.3	.4	.6				.7	.4
3.6	1.2	1.2	1.6			Debt/Worth	1.7	1.5
-2.8	NM	3.2	4.7				5.6	8.2
UND		55.0	85.7				87.0	83.7
(10) 77.7	(40)	36.4	(27) 28.3			% Profit Before Taxes/Tangible Net Worth	(117) 39.2	(80) 35.1
23.1		18.2	5.4				17.4	10.6
143.8	49.6	25.1	24.1				32.3	34.0
25.0	34.1	15.0	11.5			% Profit Before Taxes/Total Assets	18.5	15.5
-7.6	20.4	6.9	1.1				6.1	3.2
UND	UND	62.5	59.1				68.0	93.1
54.1	58.3	31.3	25.6			Sales/Net Fixed Assets	30.3	37.3
8.5	6.2	10.5	9.7				12.2	11.2
16.6	5.9	3.5	3.0				4.0	4.0
6.1	4.0	2.4	1.8			Sales/Total Assets	3.0	2.9
3.6	3.4	1.6	1.4				2.1	1.8
		.2	.4				.6	.3
	(26)	.7	(24) .8			% Depr., Dep., Amort./Sales	(82) .9	(63) .8
		1.8	2.2				2.2	2.5
		1.5					1.6	1.9
	(19)	2.0				% Officers', Directors' Owners' Comp/Sales	(63) 3.2	(42) 3.5
		3.8					6.1	5.2
31004M	42671M	664101M	1557213M	646775M	479386M	Net Sales ($)	4347224M	3945387M
3139M	8060M	250310M	766313M	277108M	164237M	Total Assets ($)	1424992M	1342826M

© RMA 2024

M = $ thousand   MM = $ million
See Pages viii through xx for Explanation of Ratios and Data

CONSTRUCTION-GENERAL—Other Building Finishing Contractors NAICS 238390

Comparative Historical Data | Current Data Sorted by Sales

Comparative Historical Data			Type of Statement	Current Data Sorted by Sales					
5	4	7	Unqualified					7	7
16	20	22	Reviewed		1	1	1	13	
1	6	4	Compiled			1	1	2	
21	39	19	Tax Returns	4	5	4	4	2	
44	76	53	Other	2	5	6	8	17	15
4/1/21-3/31/22 ALL	4/1/22-3/31/23 ALL	4/1/23-3/31/24 ALL		0-1MM	12 (4/1-9/30/23) 1-3MM	3-5MM	93 (10/1/23-3/31/24) 5-10MM	10-25MM	25MM & OVER
87	145	105	NUMBER OF STATEMENTS	6	10	11	14	27	37
%	%	%	ASSETS	%	%	%	%	%	%
25.4	25.4	18.6	Cash & Equivalents	32.2	14.4	13.8	17.9	16.7	
33.7	30.2	32.8	Trade Receivables (net)	10.8	28.3	28.8	33.8	44.7	
9.0	8.4	7.5	Inventory	2.6	17.3	12.6	8.0	4.8	
5.8	8.2	7.9	All Other Current	2.0	6.6	4.3	11.7	9.5	
73.8	72.3	66.7	Total Current	47.6	66.6	59.5	71.5	75.7	
16.2	15.9	17.0	Fixed Assets (net)	31.4	22.6	10.5	14.0	12.3	
2.8	3.6	6.3	Intangibles (net)	2.0	1.2	9.2	6.8	5.9	
7.2	8.1	10.0	All Other Non-Current	19.0	9.5	20.8	7.7	6.1	
100.0	100.0	100.0	Total	100.0	100.0	100.0	100.0	100.0	
			LIABILITIES						
6.8	5.0	8.0	Notes Payable-Short Term	11.5	3.5	28.0	2.9	4.7	
1.2	2.2	1.7	Cur. Mat.-L.T.D.	.0	2.4	1.4	.9	1.6	
12.9	12.8	13.0	Trade Payables	1.9	14.3	13.5	17.9	13.5	
.2	.7	.1	Income Taxes Payable	.0	.0	.0	.3	.0	
13.9	19.2	16.4	All Other Current	12.1	31.1	13.3	11.5	20.2	
35.0	39.9	39.2	Total Current	25.5	51.3	56.2	33.4	40.0	
13.9	19.8	18.2	Long-Term Debt	57.0	17.3	27.5	9.1	9.8	
.1	.1	.3	Deferred Taxes	.0	.7	.0	.1	.6	
2.7	4.3	4.4	All Other Non-Current	6.5	1.2	7.3	2.1	6.1	
48.2	35.7	37.9	Net Worth	11.0	29.5	9.0	55.3	43.4	
100.0	100.0	100.0	Total Liabilities & Net Worth	100.0	100.0	100.0	100.0	100.0	
			INCOME DATA						
100.0	100.0	100.0	Net Sales	100.0	100.0	100.0	100.0	100.0	
33.9	34.0	31.9	Gross Profit	39.5	40.4	36.6	26.5	28.0	
28.1	28.2	24.8	Operating Expenses	37.7	33.3	26.7	18.8	20.8	
5.8	5.8	7.1	Operating Profit	1.8	7.2	9.8	7.7	7.1	
-2.2	-.1	.2	All Other Expenses (net)	-.1	.5	1.5	-.9	.6	
8.0	5.9	6.9	Profit Before Taxes	2.0	6.7	8.3	8.5	6.6	
			RATIOS						
6.3	4.2	3.5		19.0	4.1	2.7	3.5	3.2	
3.0	2.0	1.7	Current	4.0	1.2	1.2	1.7	2.0	
1.4	1.4	1.3		.9	.5	.6	1.3	1.4	
4.5	3.5	2.6		15.7	1.3	1.7	3.0	2.5	
1.7	1.6	1.5	Quick	3.9	1.0	.7	1.6	1.7	
1.1	1.0	.8		.8	.3	.4	.9	1.2	
17 21.5	3 119.6	20 18.7		0 UND	0 UND	20 18.1	27 13.5	35 10.3	
46 8.0	34 10.6	47 7.8	Sales/Receivables	0 UND	44 8.3	36 10.2	47 7.8	63 5.8	
79 4.6	70 5.2	83 4.4		33 11.0	53 6.9	87 4.2	83 4.4	101 3.6	
0 UND	0 UND	0 UND		0 UND	0 UND	0 UND	0 UND	0 UND	
1 390.7	0 999.8	0 UND	Cost of Sales/Inventory	0 UND	0 UND	2 223.2	4 83.9	0 UND	
27 13.6	23 15.7	22 16.4		0 UND	83 4.4	104 3.5	29 12.6	18 19.8	
7 49.0	0 787.5	6 65.9		0 UND	0 UND	19 19.0	20 18.7	9 41.0	
18 20.7	15 24.0	20 18.2	Cost of Sales/Payables	0 UND	63.6	35 10.4	25 14.5	20 18.6	
34 10.8	35 10.4	38 9.6		8 46.3	65 5.6	53 6.9	63 5.8	33 11.0	
4.0	4.9	4.6		7.8	4.6	3.7	3.9	4.6	
6.4	9.1	10.0	Sales/Working Capital	16.9	27.5	25.4	6.6	7.3	
14.8	21.8	36.7		-771.2	-17.2	-52.5	15.0	17.1	
172.0	69.4	56.3			66.8	25.6	104.1	98.9	
(75) 49.6	(108) 16.1	(90) 18.7	EBIT/Interest	(10)	29.9	11.1	(23) 25.0	(33) 18.6	
6.9	3.0	4.0			3.4	1.7	15.8	2.9	
	7.7	57.1	Net Profit + Depr., Dep.,						
	(16) 3.6	(12) 6.8	Amort./Cur. Mat. L/T/D						
	1.5	3.0							
.1	.1	.1		.3	.0	.1	.1	.1	
.2	.3	.3	Fixed/Worth	5.5	.2	.2	.2	.2	
.8	.9	1.2		UND	5.0	-1.2	.5	1.5	
.4	.5	.5		.6	.4	.5	.4	.6	
.8	1.4	1.5	Debt/Worth	8.4	2.0	3.4	.9	1.6	
2.6	4.0	5.0		UND	5.2	-4.0	1.9	3.0	
76.5	89.0	78.1					50.3	79.5	
(79) 37.2	(125) 38.1	(89) 35.5	% Profit Before Taxes/Tangible Net Worth				(26) 33.5	(32) 29.5	
19.3	9.9	15.2					23.5	5.2	
42.6	38.4	31.4		75.6	29.6	61.7	26.1	26.3	
20.0	14.9	15.5	% Profit Before Taxes/Total Assets	10.4	13.7	19.3	17.1	11.6	
5.4	2.0	4.0		-27.9	2.2	2.6	11.5	.9	
89.1	107.5	72.6		UND	999.8	476.8	82.8	60.1	
33.5	39.5	30.8	Sales/Net Fixed Assets	20.0	30.0	33.2	32.5	29.5	
10.2	15.8	9.1		5.8	6.3	14.4	9.7	13.0	
4.1	4.6	4.0		7.7	4.5	4.9	3.5	3.5	
2.8	3.0	2.8	Sales/Total Assets	4.0	3.3	2.2	2.4	2.6	
1.9	2.1	1.6		3.2	1.4	1.2	1.6	1.7	
.3	.4	.3					.2	.3	
(56) .7	(84) .9	(64) 1.0	% Depr., Dep., Amort./Sales				(21) .4	(26) .6	
1.4	1.8	2.3					2.1	1.3	
1.8	1.4	1.1	% Officers', Directors',					.7	
(40) 3.3	(73) 2.8	(43) 2.4	Owners' Comp/Sales				(10) 1.4		
7.8	5.7	4.6						3.1	
1526066M	3694309M	3421150M	Net Sales ($)	3175M	18811M	43137M	105850M	447616M	2802561M
577619M	1413949M	1469167M	Total Assets ($)	487M	5611M	27728M	53007M	234960M	1147374M

© RMA 2024
M = $ thousand MM = $ million
See Pages viii through xx for Explanation of Ratios and Data

CONSTRUCTION-GENERAL—Site Preparation Contractors NAICS 238910

Current Data Sorted by Assets

Type of Statement	0-500M	500M-2MM	2-10MM	10-50MM	50-100MM	100-250MM
Unqualified		3	9	32	15	11
Reviewed	2	2	58	67	13	6
Compiled	2	2	12	11	2	1
Tax Returns	20	32	33	9	1	
Other	14	50	98	112	16	14
		78 (4/1-9/30/23)		567 (10/1/23-3/31/24)		
NUMBER OF STATEMENTS	36	89	210	231	47	32

ASSETS (%)

	0-500M	500M-2MM	2-10MM	10-50MM	50-100MM	100-250MM
Cash & Equivalents	19.3	23.0	13.7	14.4	15.9	15.0
Trade Receivables (net)	16.7	20.3	32.9	32.6	30.3	28.5
Inventory	1.9	2.0	1.3	1.9	1.8	2.9
All Other Current	5.4	5.9	5.8	7.8	11.0	7.2
Total Current	43.3	51.2	53.7	56.7	58.9	53.5
Fixed Assets (net)	43.4	38.8	37.2	37.2	31.4	38.0
Intangibles (net)	2.7	4.4	2.1	1.5	3.9	2.0
All Other Non-Current	10.7	5.6	7.0	4.6	5.8	6.4
Total	100.0	100.0	100.0	100.0	100.0	100.0

LIABILITIES

	0-500M	500M-2MM	2-10MM	10-50MM	50-100MM	100-250MM
Notes Payable-Short Term	10.6	6.4	5.6	2.8	1.0	3.6
Cur. Mat.-L.T.D.	7.4	7.1	5.8	5.5	5.7	4.8
Trade Payables	7.2	7.2	10.6	14.8	14.9	10.6
Income Taxes Payable	.0	.0	.1	.2	.1	.3
All Other Current	14.9	8.7	8.1	10.5	15.5	14.8
Total Current	40.1	29.5	30.3	33.8	37.1	34.2
Long-Term Debt	45.5	35.4	19.4	15.5	15.1	13.3
Deferred Taxes	.1	.0	.3	.5	1.1	1.0
All Other Non-Current	7.8	3.9	2.1	1.5	2.5	1.9
Net Worth	6.5	31.3	48.0	48.7	44.2	49.7
Total Liabilities & Net Worth	100.0	100.0	100.0	100.0	100.0	100.0

INCOME DATA

	0-500M	500M-2MM	2-10MM	10-50MM	50-100MM	100-250MM
Net Sales	100.0	100.0	100.0	100.0	100.0	100.0
Gross Profit	49.5	48.8	35.8	25.2	17.3	21.5
Operating Expenses	43.1	37.8	27.3	16.0	10.9	11.3
Operating Profit	6.4	11.1	8.5	9.2	6.4	10.2
All Other Expenses (net)	.8	1.2	-.1	-.1	-.2	-.1
Profit Before Taxes	5.6	9.9	8.5	9.3	6.7	10.3

RATIOS

	0-500M	500M-2MM	2-10MM	10-50MM	50-100MM	100-250MM
Current	4.6	10.7	3.6	2.5	2.3	2.1
	1.1	2.1	2.0	1.6	1.6	1.5
	.5	.7	1.1	1.2	1.2	1.2
Quick	4.6	6.1	3.3	2.1	1.8	1.8
	1.0	2.0	1.6	1.4	1.3	1.3
	.2	.7	.9	1.0	.9	.9
Sales/Receivables	0 UND / 0 UND / 22 16.6	0 UND / 25 14.8 / 48 7.6	33 10.9 / 55 6.6 / 83 4.4	47 7.7 / 70 5.2 / 91 4.0	47 7.7 / 72 5.1 / 99 3.7	60 6.1 / 70 5.2 / 89 4.1
Cost of Sales/Inventory	0 UND / 0 UND / 0 UND	0 UND / 0 UND / 0 UND	0 UND / 0 UND / 0 UND	0 UND / 0 UND / 2 238.5	0 UND / 0 999.8 / 4 90.3	0 UND / 1 315.2 / 9 42.1
Cost of Sales/Payables	0 UND / 0 UND / 11 34.6	0 UND / 1 272.1 / 25 14.5	8 45.8 / 21 17.2 / 41 8.9	20 18.3 / 37 9.9 / 56 6.5	23 15.6 / 38 9.6 / 64 5.7	25 14.7 / 35 10.3 / 49 7.5
Sales/Working Capital	9.1 / 88.6 / -16.5	5.4 / 11.9 / -67.3	4.6 / 7.8 / 37.3	4.5 / 8.0 / 21.2	4.2 / 8.1 / 18.8	4.5 / 6.6 / 20.1
EBIT/Interest	15.0 / (28) 5.9 / .7	43.3 / (74) 8.8 / 2.0	29.8 / (188) 11.2 / 3.2	46.3 / (218) 14.3 / 4.2	34.9 / (41) 9.2 / 4.2	62.3 / (30) 23.8 / 9.1
Net Profit + Depr., Dep., Amort./Cur. Mat. L/T/D		(23) 2.7	7.5 / (60) 3.4 / 1.1	7.5 / (15) 2.9 / 1.8	5.1 / (11) 3.5 / 1.9	6.5 / 3.5 / 1.5
Fixed/Worth	.6 / 2.2 / -2.8	.3 / .9 / 13.5	.4 / .8 / 1.6	.5 / .8 / 1.2	.3 / 1.0 / 1.4	.5 / .8 / 1.2
Debt/Worth	1.0 / 6.6 / -4.7	.4 / 1.7 / 35.9	.5 / 1.0 / 2.1	.5 / 1.1 / 2.0	.7 / 1.3 / 2.3	.6 / 1.0 / 1.7
% Profit Before Taxes/Tangible Net Worth	99.8 / (20) 58.9 / 29.2	102.8 / (71) 55.0 / 14.4	51.5 / (192) 28.4 / 10.6	46.3 / (222) 28.1 / 14.3	38.4 / (44) 22.6 / 12.8	35.6 / (31) 27.8 / 17.0
% Profit Before Taxes/Total Assets	33.7 / 15.7 / -1.6	41.6 / 20.9 / -5.0	24.5 / 13.5 / 2.9	22.9 / 12.5 / 5.6	16.1 / 9.5 / 3.2	17.7 / 11.2 / 6.2
Sales/Net Fixed Assets	102.7 / 13.8 / 5.3	22.0 / 8.1 / 3.5	11.7 / 5.9 / 3.0	9.2 / 4.7 / 2.8	10.5 / 5.4 / 2.9	6.1 / 4.2 / 2.0
Sales/Total Assets	7.2 / 3.8 / 2.6	4.0 / 2.7 / 1.7	2.7 / 1.9 / 1.4	2.1 / 1.6 / 1.3	1.8 / 1.6 / 1.2	1.7 / 1.5 / .9
% Depr., Dep., Amort./Sales	2.0 / (14) 6.1 / 10.9	1.8 / (43) 5.1 / 12.3	2.2 / (138) 4.3 / 7.6	2.7 / (201) 4.6 / 6.9	2.4 / (42) 3.8 / 5.5	2.3 / (18) 4.2 / 5.8
% Officers', Directors' Owners' Comp/Sales	3.8 / (18) 6.7 / 8.4	3.1 / (42) 4.7 / 6.3	1.2 / (83) 2.9 / 4.4	.6 / (67) 1.3 / 2.1		
Net Sales ($)	47458M	301600M	2170736M	9587323M	5115345M	7110463M
Total Assets ($)	10019M	94809M	1099225M	5585716M	3391344M	5074335M

Comparative Historical Data

Type of Statement	4/1/19-3/31/20 ALL	4/1/20-3/31/21 ALL
Unqualified	71	47
Reviewed	159	85
Compiled	33	18
Tax Returns	151	93
Other	381	225
NUMBER OF STATEMENTS	795	468

ASSETS (%)

	4/1/19-3/31/20	4/1/20-3/31/21
Cash & Equivalents	13.5	21.1
Trade Receivables (net)	31.5	25.4
Inventory	2.9	3.0
All Other Current	5.6	4.7
Total Current	53.4	54.3
Fixed Assets (net)	37.6	36.8
Intangibles (net)	3.0	3.2
All Other Non-Current	6.0	5.6
Total	100.0	100.0

LIABILITIES

	4/1/19-3/31/20	4/1/20-3/31/21
Notes Payable-Short Term	6.5	7.8
Cur. Mat.-L.T.D.	5.9	5.5
Trade Payables	13.5	10.4
Income Taxes Payable	.2	.1
All Other Current	10.3	10.7
Total Current	36.4	34.7
Long-Term Debt	23.7	29.0
Deferred Taxes	.6	.5
All Other Non-Current	4.3	3.4
Net Worth	34.9	32.4
Total Liabilities & Net Worth	100.0	100.0

INCOME DATA

	4/1/19-3/31/20	4/1/20-3/31/21
Net Sales	100.0	100.0
Gross Profit	31.6	36.0
Operating Expenses	24.3	29.2
Operating Profit	7.3	6.9
All Other Expenses (net)	.4	-1.5
Profit Before Taxes	6.9	8.4

RATIOS

	4/1/19-3/31/20	4/1/20-3/31/21
Current	2.3 / 1.6 / 1.1	3.5 / 1.9 / 1.2
Quick	2.1 / (794) 1.3 / .9	3.2 / 1.6 / 1.0
Sales/Receivables	30 12.3 / 57 6.4 / 85 4.3	17 21.5 / 47 7.7 / 73 5.0
Cost of Sales/Inventory	0 UND / 0 UND / 3 132.0	0 UND / 0 UND / 2 153.3
Cost of Sales/Payables	9 39.5 / 28 13.2 / 49 7.5	6 64.1 / 23 15.8 / 41 8.9
Sales/Working Capital	6.2 / 11.3 / 63.4	4.6 / 8.0 / 33.5
EBIT/Interest	26.1 / (734) 8.9 / 2.8	40.3 / (412) 11.7 / 3.4
Net Profit + Depr., Dep., Amort./Cur. Mat. L/T/D	5.7 / (137) 3.1 / 1.6	10.3 / (56) 3.0 / 1.3
Fixed/Worth	.5 / .9 / 2.2	.5 / .9 / 2.1
Debt/Worth	.7 / 1.5 / 4.0	.6 / 1.3 / 4.9
% Profit Before Taxes/Tangible Net Worth	54.7 / (694) 27.4 / 11.2	66.2 / (401) 32.8 / 11.4
% Profit Before Taxes/Total Assets	22.9 / 10.7 / 3.2	26.8 / 14.0 / 3.9
Sales/Net Fixed Assets	14.8 / 5.6 / 3.1	15.5 / 5.6 / 2.9
Sales/Total Assets	2.8 / 1.9 / 1.4	2.8 / 1.8 / 1.3
% Depr., Dep., Amort./Sales	2.3 / (599) 4.6 / 7.3	2.8 / (314) 4.8 / 8.0
% Officers', Directors' Owners' Comp/Sales	1.4 / (313) 2.8 / 5.2	1.6 / (180) 3.2 / 5.4
Net Sales ($)	22366454M	9566707M
Total Assets ($)	12720794M	5973001M

M = $ thousand MM = $ million

© RMA 2024

CONSTRUCTION-GENERAL—Site Preparation Contractors NAICS 238910

Comparative Historical Data | Current Data Sorted by Sales

Comparative Historical Data				Type of Statement	Current Data Sorted by Sales					
34	56	70		Unqualified		2	2	3	9	54
98	148	146		Reviewed		5	4	18	50	69
23	28	30		Compiled	2	3	2	2	10	11
83	125	95		Tax Returns	11	19	20	14	20	11
259	303	304		Other	14	34	38	46	65	107
4/1/21-3/31/22	4/1/22-3/31/23	4/1/23-3/31/24			78 (4/1-9/30/23)			567 (10/1/23-3/31/24)		
ALL	ALL	ALL			0-1MM	1-3MM	3-5MM	5-10MM	10-25MM	25MM & OVER
497	660	645		NUMBER OF STATEMENTS	27	63	66	83	154	252
%	%	%		ASSETS	%	%	%	%	%	%
18.6	15.4	15.8		Cash & Equivalents	15.4	23.0	17.7	13.5	13.1	15.9
25.9	28.6	29.8		Trade Receivables (net)	20.6	14.9	24.2	29.9	33.4	33.6
2.9	2.9	1.8		Inventory	4.6	.9	1.3	1.6	1.8	1.8
6.5	6.6	6.9		All Other Current	5.0	3.0	7.5	6.5	6.3	8.5
53.8	53.5	54.2		Total Current	45.7	41.8	50.7	51.5	54.5	59.9
37.7	37.4	37.4		Fixed Assets (net)	48.6	45.8	37.7	37.8	38.8	33.0
2.8	3.0	2.4		Intangibles (net)	.7	3.7	4.4	2.5	1.6	2.1
5.7	6.1	6.0		All Other Non-Current	5.1	8.7	7.2	8.3	5.0	5.1
100.0	100.0	100.0		Total	100.0	100.0	100.0	100.0	100.0	100.0
				LIABILITIES						
5.0	5.2	4.6		Notes Payable-Short Term	10.3	6.9	8.1	5.0	4.4	2.4
5.2	5.7	5.9		Cur. Mat.-L.T.D.	5.4	7.4	7.1	6.0	5.9	5.3
10.5	11.8	11.8		Trade Payables	7.0	6.7	6.2	9.6	11.6	15.8
.2	.1	.1		Income Taxes Payable	.0	.0	.1	.2	.0	.2
8.9	10.8	10.3		All Other Current	12.2	8.9	8.6	9.1	7.3	13.1
29.8	33.7	32.7		Total Current	35.0	29.9	30.1	29.9	29.2	36.8
25.8	25.8	21.0		Long-Term Debt	29.5	43.1	31.3	21.1	16.7	14.6
.5	.4	.4		Deferred Taxes	.0	.0	.0	.4	.6	.6
2.4	2.9	2.5		All Other Non-Current	2.0	5.4	3.9	3.4	1.8	1.5
41.4	37.3	43.4		Net Worth	33.5	21.6	34.7	45.2	51.7	46.6
100.0	100.0	100.0		Total Liabilities & Net Worth	100.0	100.0	100.0	100.0	100.0	100.0
				INCOME DATA						
100.0	100.0	100.0		Net Sales	100.0	100.0	100.0	100.0	100.0	100.0
33.9	32.2	32.5		Gross Profit	59.6	52.6	41.3	39.1	30.2	21.4
26.7	25.1	23.6		Operating Expenses	47.5	40.7	34.4	29.3	21.6	13.3
7.2	7.1	8.9		Operating Profit	12.1	12.0	6.9	9.9	8.7	8.1
-2.0	-.2	.1		All Other Expenses (net)	1.5	1.3	.0	.4	-.2	-.2
9.2	7.4	8.8		Profit Before Taxes	10.6	10.7	6.9	9.5	8.8	8.3
				RATIOS						
3.6	2.8	2.9			10.8	6.3	6.3	4.0	3.4	2.3
2.0	1.8	1.7		Current	1.2	2.0	1.9	1.7	2.1	1.6
1.3	1.2	1.1			.5	.5	.7	1.1	1.3	1.2
3.0	2.5	2.6			2.3	5.3	5.8	3.5	2.8	1.9
(496) 1.6	(659) 1.4	1.4		Quick	1.1	2.0	1.4	1.5	1.8	1.3
1.0	.9	.9			.3	.5	.6	.9	1.0	1.0
27 13.6	27 13.3	32 11.4			0 UND	0 UND	0 UND	28 13.0	38 9.5	48 7.6
53 6.9	56 6.5	60 6.1		Sales/Receivables	20 18.7	18 20.7	37 9.8	54 6.7	62 5.9	68 5.4
74 4.9	79 4.6	85 4.3			72 5.1	45 8.1	62 5.9	85 4.3	89 4.1	89 4.1
0 UND	0 UND	0 UND			0 UND	0 UND	0 UND	0 UND	0 UND	0 UND
0 UND	0 UND	0 UND		Cost of Sales/Inventory	0 UND	0 UND	0 UND	0 UND	0 UND	0 UND
3 124.8	2 155.0	1 339.9			9 42.0	0 UND	0 UND	1 389.5	2 193.2	3 141.5
7 51.3	8 45.4	9 41.0			0 UND	0 UND	0 UND	8 48.4	12 30.1	23 15.8
25 14.5	25 14.8	26 13.9		Cost of Sales/Payables	0 UND	9 41.1	6 65.3	19 19.2	25 14.4	37 9.9
44 8.3	45 8.1	48 7.6			21 17.0	31 11.7	36 10.0	42 8.6	45 8.2	55 6.6
4.2	4.9	4.8			4.9	5.0	4.6	5.0	4.3	4.8
8.1	9.0	8.8		Sales/Working Capital	84.4	16.9	10.6	9.5	6.8	8.3
19.7	37.0	36.6			-10.4	-11.6	-29.8	31.8	17.8	21.1
50.9	38.6	36.8			10.3	14.9	35.4	23.6	33.1	57.8
(437) 16.8	(594) 12.7	(579) 11.9		EBIT/Interest	(16) 5.3	(58) 8.8	(56) 5.3	(71) 8.4	(144) 13.8	(234) 16.5
4.7	3.1	3.4			1.0	1.4	1.8	3.0	4.5	5.2
10.1	7.3	6.5		Net Profit + Depr., Dep.,					6.1	7.4
(84) 4.0	(104) 3.8	(109) 3.4		Amort./Cur. Mat. L/T/D				(27) 3.3	(73) 3.5	
2.2	2.0	1.7							1.1	1.9
.4	.4	.4			.3	.6	.2	.3	.4	.4
.9	.9	.8		Fixed/Worth	2.1	1.6	.8	1.0	.7	.8
1.7	1.8	1.6			14.5	-8.5	4.5	1.9	1.2	1.2
.6	.6	.5			.6	.7	.3	.5	.4	.6
1.2	1.2	1.1		Debt/Worth	2.4	2.0	1.6	1.2	.7	1.2
3.1	3.0	2.6			14.8	-9.6	7.3	2.3	1.5	2.2
57.1	59.2	53.8			99.6	85.1	78.9	57.3	48.6	46.1
(452) 32.0	(573) 28.9	(580) 29.5		% Profit Before Taxes/Tangible Net Worth	(21) 26.8	(44) 49.4	(57) 28.6	(72) 31.0	(146) 28.2	(240) 28.6
14.7	10.6	13.1			3.5	11.5	4.8	13.6	11.1	15.9
25.5	23.8	24.6			22.6	35.3	32.7	27.6	23.8	21.7
14.5	12.3	13.4		% Profit Before Taxes/Total Assets	12.4	15.9	15.9	15.4	13.9	12.1
4.9	3.6	4.7			1.2	.9	1.7	5.2	5.0	5.8
11.0	12.9	11.5			16.5	11.8	27.3	11.7	10.4	10.3
4.9	5.3	5.5		Sales/Net Fixed Assets	3.5	5.5	6.5	6.3	4.8	5.7
2.9	3.0	3.0			1.9	2.7	2.8	2.9	2.9	3.3
2.6	2.5	2.6			3.1	3.6	3.7	2.7	2.5	2.1
1.8	1.8	1.8		Sales/Total Assets	1.7	2.4	2.2	1.9	1.7	1.7
1.2	1.4	1.4			.9	1.4	1.3	1.3	1.4	1.4
2.6	2.5	2.5			5.5	2.7	1.2	2.6	2.8	2.4
(344) 4.8	(450) 4.6	(456) 4.5		% Depr., Dep., Amort./Sales	(12) 14.0	(30) 5.7	(37) 5.1	(48) 4.0	(117) 4.9	(212) 4.0
7.9	7.4	7.2			24.5	12.9	8.2	8.8	7.3	6.2
1.1	1.2	1.0		% Officers', Directors', Owners' Comp/Sales	3.8	2.6	1.2	1.2	.4	.4
(187) 2.5	(255) 2.7	(221) 2.2			(35) 5.6	(31) 3.9	(32) 3.1	(56) 2.0	(60) 1.0	
5.3	4.9	4.6			7.8	5.3	4.3	3.6	1.6	
17212341M	23695165M	24332925M		Net Sales ($)	16821M	125839M	263316M	617590M	2397168M	20912191M
9729618M	14102651M	15255448M		Total Assets ($)	12936M	79390M	162121M	373160M	1485157M	13142684M

M = $ thousand   MM = $ million
See Pages viii through xx for Explanation of Ratios and Data
© RMA 2024

CONSTRUCTION-GENERAL—All Other Specialty Trade Contractors NAICS 238990

Current Data Sorted by Assets | **Comparative Historical Data**

							Type of Statement		
		7	25	13	8		Unqualified	54	31
2	12	51	39	4	4		Reviewed	127	61
2	7	14	5	1			Compiled	48	31
36	47	41	9				Tax Returns	237	146
27	83	172	97	22	20		Other	451	303
	82 (4/1-9/30/23)		666 (10/1/23-3/31/24)					4/1/19-3/31/20	4/1/20-3/31/21
0-500M	500M-2MM	2-10MM	10-50MM	50-100MM	100-250MM			ALL	ALL
67	149	285	175	40	32		NUMBER OF STATEMENTS	917	572
%	%	%	%	%	%		ASSETS	%	%
30.9	27.4	17.5	15.9	11.5	9.3		Cash & Equivalents	19.0	24.8
18.8	24.3	34.4	31.5	33.2	27.9		Trade Receivables (net)	32.1	27.9
4.8	7.3	6.8	5.5	5.2	2.4		Inventory	7.0	6.0
5.4	5.1	6.9	7.3	9.8	6.0		All Other Current	5.3	4.8
59.9	64.1	65.6	60.2	59.7	45.7		Total Current	63.4	63.5
29.8	21.0	23.3	26.6	22.9	34.1		Fixed Assets (net)	26.2	25.7
3.5	6.5	4.4	6.5	11.7	13.4		Intangibles (net)	4.2	4.8
6.8	8.4	6.7	6.7	5.7	6.9		All Other Non-Current	6.2	6.0
100.0	100.0	100.0	100.0	100.0	100.0		Total	100.0	100.0
							LIABILITIES		
17.6	10.3	5.0	3.1	3.6	5.0		Notes Payable-Short Term	9.4	9.4
7.3	4.1	2.8	3.9	3.0	5.2		Cur. Mat.-L.T.D.	3.8	4.4
10.2	10.6	11.8	12.7	11.7	12.6		Trade Payables	13.4	10.2
.1	.0	.3	.1	.0	.2		Income Taxes Payable	.2	.2
17.3	12.5	10.9	12.8	16.5	12.6		All Other Current	12.1	11.1
52.6	37.4	30.8	32.7	34.8	35.6		Total Current	38.9	35.3
45.7	29.3	16.8	15.1	20.7	23.6		Long-Term Debt	19.0	24.6
.0	.0	.2	.2	.3	1.1		Deferred Taxes	.3	.2
5.3	4.6	2.2	3.9	3.1	3.3		All Other Non-Current	3.5	4.0
-3.6	28.7	50.1	48.1	41.1	36.4		Net Worth	38.3	35.9
100.0	100.0	100.0	100.0	100.0	100.0		Total Liabilities & Net Worth	100.0	100.0
							INCOME DATA		
100.0	100.0	100.0	100.0	100.0	100.0		Net Sales	100.0	100.0
44.8	44.4	36.9	28.6	26.1	26.0		Gross Profit	36.4	36.8
40.2	36.0	27.4	18.6	17.1	18.4		Operating Expenses	28.9	29.4
4.6	8.4	9.5	10.0	9.0	7.7		Operating Profit	7.5	7.4
.3	.1	-.1	.6	1.4	3.0		All Other Expenses (net)	.5	-1.0
4.3	8.3	9.6	9.4	7.7	4.7		Profit Before Taxes	7.0	8.4
							RATIOS		
5.3	5.2	4.6	3.1	2.4	1.9			3.3	4.1
1.2	2.1	2.4	1.8	1.6	1.2		Current	1.8	2.1
.7	1.0	1.4	1.3	1.3	.9			1.1	1.3
4.2	4.2	3.7	2.4	2.0	1.5			2.8	3.4
1.1	1.8	1.9	1.4	1.2	1.0		Quick	1.4	1.7
.4	.7	1.1	.9	.9	.8			.8	1.0
0 UND	0 UND	25 14.6	36 10.1	51 7.1	51 7.2			15 24.5	12 30.6
0 UND	16 22.6	50 7.3	61 6.0	66 5.5	66 5.5		Sales/Receivables	44 8.3	41 8.9
23 16.2	51 7.1	74 4.9	83 4.4	81 4.5	85 4.3			72 5.1	69 5.3
0 UND	0 UND	0 UND	0 UND	0 UND	0 UND			0 UND	0 UND
0 UND	0 UND	1 628.8	1 246.0	6 63.5	7 55.8		Cost of Sales/Inventory	0 UND	0 UND
1 411.0	7 50.1	21 17.1	18 20.4	16 23.3	14 26.1			16 22.4	14 26.0
0 UND	0 UND	7 55.5	13 28.0	16 22.6	17 21.1			6 64.3	2 159.8
0 UND	6 59.3	18 20.8	25 14.5	26 13.9	30 12.0		Cost of Sales/Payables	21 17.2	16 22.6
13 28.4	33 10.9	38 9.6	46 8.0	41 8.8	47 7.7			40 9.2	33 11.2
9.0	5.2	4.4	4.0	4.7	7.0			6.0	4.8
53.8	11.9	6.8	7.5	7.6	14.1		Sales/Working Capital	11.5	8.8
-48.8	451.2	19.4	19.1	15.7	-186.7			60.4	27.9
33.3	43.7	62.8	50.6	23.3	9.4			42.0	46.3
(49) 11.3	(120) 9.8	(239) 18.0	(147) 15.3	(35) 6.4	(29) 3.6		EBIT/Interest	(791) 12.6	(465) 14.3
2.5	2.4	4.2	5.2	2.3	.0			3.5	3.7
		14.2	21.1	14.2				11.0	12.4
	(33) 6.0	(38) 8.2	(11) 5.8			Net Profit + Depr., Dep., Amort./Cur. Mat. L/T/D	(107) 3.5	(47) 3.6
		2.0	2.6	1.9				1.5	1.6
.2	.1	.1	.2	.3	.5			.2	.2
.9	.5	.4	.5	.8	1.6		Fixed/Worth	.6	.6
-2.5	7.0	1.2	1.3	4.7	4.9			1.7	1.8
.9	.5	.4	.6	.9	1.2			.5	.6
4.9	1.8	.9	1.2	2.0	3.4		Debt/Worth	1.3	1.3
-3.5	510.5	2.9	2.2	11.7	44.7			4.4	5.5
118.2	147.0	70.8	57.4	87.9	54.4			77.0	85.1
(40) 64.0	(113) 66.1	(259) 39.5	(161) 33.9	(34) 40.8	(26) 19.4		% Profit Before Taxes/Tangible Net Worth	(787) 42.2	(487) 45.1
25.9	18.2	17.4	17.2	18.6	-2.8			17.7	16.6
66.1	52.7	32.1	25.5	18.0	11.9			34.1	35.6
24.8	23.3	17.9	15.5	8.9	5.9		% Profit Before Taxes/Total Assets	16.5	18.0
6.5	5.7	7.1	7.2	4.7	-2.0			5.9	5.7
206.4	120.0	51.4	29.2	22.0	21.6			49.0	44.5
41.0	29.0	16.4	9.1	8.5	4.0		Sales/Net Fixed Assets	16.0	15.2
12.4	9.7	6.6	4.7	4.6	1.5			6.3	5.8
10.7	5.1	3.3	2.5	2.4	1.9			4.3	3.7
5.1	3.4	2.4	1.9	1.6	1.4		Sales/Total Assets	2.8	2.5
2.8	2.3	1.8	1.3	1.2	.7			1.9	1.7
.8	.5	.5	1.0	.8	.5			.8	.9
(33) 1.4	(60) 1.2	(191) 1.2	(139) 2.4	(33) 2.1	(13) 1.5		% Depr., Dep., Amort./Sales	(582) 2.0	(356) 2.3
4.2	2.6	3.4	4.4	4.4	3.2			3.9	4.5
2.5	1.9	1.2	.5					1.7	1.8
(34) 5.2	(74) 4.3	(137) 2.2	(39) .9			% Officers', Directors' Owners' Comp/Sales	(410) 3.2	(233) 3.4
10.1	6.3	3.4	1.7					5.8	5.7
131646M	752818M	3891665M	7912747M	5358357M	7152991M		Net Sales ($)	23968145M	12013953M
17881M	173179M	1419452M	4121402M	2994204M	5050508M		Total Assets ($)	9765536M	6086735M

M = $ thousand   MM = $ million
See Pages viii through xx for Explanation of Ratios and Data

© RMA 2024

CONSTRUCTION-GENERAL—All Other Specialty Trade Contractors NAICS 238990

Comparative Historical Data | Current Data Sorted by Sales

			Type of Statement						
34	58	53	Unqualified			1	12	40	
76	97	112	Reviewed	2	2	11	17	34	46
35	68	29	Compiled		5	2	8	10	4
176	216	133	Tax Returns	15	31	26	29	22	10
346	484	421	Other	22	41	37	77	119	125
4/1/21-3/31/22 ALL	4/1/22-3/31/23 ALL	4/1/23-3/31/24 ALL		82 (4/1-9/30/23)			666 (10/1/23-3/31/24)		
				0-1MM	1-3MM	3-5MM	5-10MM	10-25MM	25MM & OVER
667	923	748	NUMBER OF STATEMENTS	39	79	76	132	197	225
%	%	%	ASSETS	%	%	%	%	%	%
23.5	19.2	19.6	Cash & Equivalents	19.8	22.0	25.4	24.1	18.7	14.9
26.1	29.1	30.0	Trade Receivables (net)	22.2	23.0	21.5	32.6	30.7	34.5
7.0	7.7	6.1	Inventory	6.1	7.4	8.0	5.3	6.7	5.0
6.2	6.0	6.6	All Other Current	4.0	5.3	7.0	4.1	7.9	7.8
62.7	62.0	62.3	Total Current	52.0	57.8	61.9	66.0	64.0	62.3
26.1	25.7	24.6	Fixed Assets (net)	34.8	27.2	24.4	22.6	23.9	23.9
4.0	4.4	6.0	Intangibles (net)	3.4	7.1	9.4	5.2	3.8	7.3
7.2	7.8	7.0	All Other Non-Current	9.8	8.0	4.4	6.1	8.3	6.5
100.0	100.0	100.0	Total	100.0	100.0	100.0	100.0	100.0	100.0
			LIABILITIES						
8.6	6.7	6.7	Notes Payable-Short Term	15.8	9.0	10.4	6.3	5.7	4.2
3.6	3.2	3.8	Cur. Mat.-L.T.D.	4.2	4.1	5.0	3.7	3.6	3.5
11.1	11.6	11.6	Trade Payables	13.8	8.2	8.3	9.1	12.4	14.4
.2	.1	.2	Income Taxes Payable	.1	.1	.0	.0	.5	.1
11.4	11.6	12.6	All Other Current	13.0	13.4	9.5	12.3	11.4	14.5
34.8	33.2	34.9	Total Current	46.9	34.7	33.3	31.5	33.5	36.7
22.4	22.0	22.0	Long-Term Debt	41.5	37.5	31.1	20.0	16.6	15.9
.2	.2	.2	Deferred Taxes	.0	.0	.0	.1	.3	.3
3.9	3.8	3.4	All Other Non-Current	9.8	5.1	1.7	2.7	2.9	3.3
38.6	40.7	39.5	Net Worth	1.9	22.7	33.8	45.7	46.7	43.8
100.0	100.0	100.0	Total Liabilities & Net Worth	100.0	100.0	100.0	100.0	100.0	100.0
			INCOME DATA						
100.0	100.0	100.0	Net Sales	100.0	100.0	100.0	100.0	100.0	100.0
37.0	36.2	36.1	Gross Profit	49.3	51.5	41.7	40.5	34.0	25.8
29.6	28.3	27.2	Operating Expenses	40.6	41.3	34.8	30.8	24.9	17.3
7.4	8.0	8.9	Operating Profit	8.7	10.2	6.9	9.6	9.0	8.5
-1.9	-.1	.4	All Other Expenses (net)	1.3	.2	.2	-.1	.2	.7
9.3	8.1	8.5	Profit Before Taxes	7.4	10.1	6.7	9.7	8.8	7.8
			RATIOS						
4.2	4.2	3.9		3.6	6.8	5.5	5.6	4.1	2.5
2.1	2.1	2.0	Current	1.1	2.1	2.6	2.7	2.1	1.7
1.3	1.3	1.2		.5	1.0	1.2	1.4	1.2	1.2
	3.6	3.4	3.2		2.6	6.3	4.1	4.5	3.3	2.0
(665)	1.6	1.6	1.5	Quick	1.1	1.6	1.8	2.1	1.6	1.4
	.8	.9	.9		.4	.5	.9	1.1	.9	1.0
3	137.5	11	34.6	15	23.7		0	UND	0	UND	0	UND	13	28.2	23	15.8	38	9.5
40	9.1	45	8.2	47	7.7	Sales/Receivables	15	24.1	17	21.3	29	12.7	43	8.5	47	7.7	60	6.1
72	5.1	73	5.0	74	4.9		70	5.2	58	6.3	64	5.7	66	5.5	74	4.9	79	4.6
0	UND	0	UND	0	UND		0	UND	0	UND	0	UND	0	UND	0	UND	0	UND
0	UND	0	UND	0	UND	Cost of Sales/Inventory	0	UND	0	UND	0	UND	0	UND	2	181.3	1	623.5
15	24.5	18	20.3	16	22.4		13	27.1	25	14.7	28	13.1	13	27.6	22	16.8	14	26.2
1	644.0	2	169.1	5	77.9		0	UND	0	UND	0	UND	4	409.1	7	55.3	15	25.0
18	20.3	18	20.7	18	19.9	Cost of Sales/Payables	5	73.0	5	66.6	9	41.4	13	27.4	19	19.4	25	14.5
39	9.4	36	10.2	37	9.9		36	10.1	34	10.7	33	11.0	34	10.7	38	9.5	44	8.3
	4.8	4.5	4.7		4.8	4.0	4.6	4.1	4.6	5.6
	8.6	9.1	8.7	Sales/Working Capital	28.5	8.9	10.2	7.5	7.2	9.3
	40.9	30.0	44.2		-14.4	-352.0	56.6	24.6	36.6	26.2
	59.8	45.0	44.4		15.0	41.0	32.5	65.3	59.0	56.7
(529)	20.4	(768)	13.4	(619)	12.5	EBIT/Interest	(27)	9.3	(59)	11.6	(73)	5.7	(101)	17.9	(162)	16.1	(197)	13.3
	5.6	3.7	3.5		1.1	2.7	-.6	7.3	3.6	4.3
	20.9	10.5	14.5	Net Profit + Depr., Dep.,					22.5	14.2
(49)	6.5	(101)	4.7	(93)	6.0	Amort./Cur. Mat. L/T/D				(29)	6.0	(52)	6.1
	3.2	2.1	2.0						2.0	1.8
	.1	.1	.1		.3	.1	.2	.1	.1	.2
	.5	.5	.5	Fixed/Worth	1.0	.6	.8	.4	.3	.5
	1.9	1.5	1.8		-3.1	10.1	NM	1.3	1.5	1.5
	.5	.5	.5		.9	.3	.4	.4	.4	.7
	1.3	1.2	1.3	Debt/Worth	4.2	1.4	2.4	.9	1.1	1.4
	4.0	3.7	4.4		-7.3	-3.5	-23.2	3.7	2.5	3.6
	79.6	67.5	78.1	% Profit Before Taxes/Tangible	79.1	115.3	150.6	94.7	63.6	67.9
(567)	43.4	(808)	33.8	(633)	39.9	Net Worth	(26)	39.2	(57)	58.0	(56)	31.4	(115)	55.2	(179)	29.2	(200)	37.3
	21.8	13.5	17.0		16.5	16.7	-1.2	24.8	13.8	17.4
	37.7	30.0	32.7	% Profit Before Taxes/Total	24.8	48.1	44.0	46.5	32.2	26.7
	20.0	14.8	16.7	Assets	12.3	21.3	11.5	24.6	16.4	14.3
	7.5	4.6	6.3		1.2	5.0	-1.5	10.8	6.4	5.7
	66.5	54.5	54.7		57.0	79.4	67.9	83.3	42.8	49.7
	15.3	15.7	15.1	Sales/Net Fixed Assets	10.3	20.1	16.6	25.3	14.2	12.6
	5.4	5.9	6.2		4.3	6.3	6.6	8.7	6.7	5.2
	3.6	3.6	3.5		3.9	4.5	4.4	4.5	3.3	3.0
	2.5	2.3	2.4	Sales/Total Assets	2.3	2.6	2.6	2.8	2.4	2.2
	1.7	1.6	1.7		1.1	1.8	1.7	1.9	1.8	1.5
	.9	.9	.6		1.4	.9	.8	.4	.7	.5
(403)	2.1	(564)	2.0	(469)	1.6	% Depr., Dep., Amort./Sales	(20)	3.1	(34)	1.4	(41)	1.4	(74)	1.4	(136)	1.5	(164)	1.7
	4.9	4.5	3.5		7.8	3.5	3.4	3.9	3.5	3.4
	1.5	1.3	1.1		6.5	2.4	2.3	1.8	1.0	.4
(288)	3.1	(375)	2.7	(294)	2.4	% Officers', Directors', Owners' Comp/Sales	(15)	10.2	(38)	5.0	(41)	3.7	(60)	3.0	(86)	1.7	(54)	.7
	6.3	4.7	4.6		13.3	7.4	5.8	4.6	3.1	1.5
13401458M	21922000M	25200224M	Net Sales ($)	23925M	166487M	296531M	967271M	3199734M	20546276M
7314538M	11522267M	13776626M	Total Assets ($)	22071M	81434M	128984M	419044M	1595510M	11529583M

M = $ thousand   MM = $ million

© RMA 2024
See Pages viii through xx for Explanation of Ratios and Data

MANUFACTURING

MANUFACTURING—Dog and Cat Food Manufacturing NAICS 311111

Current Data Sorted by Assets

0-500M	500M-2MM	2-10MM	10-50MM	50-100MM	100-250MM
2	1	1	1	1	1
1	1	1	1		
		1			
		3	4	4	5
			20 (10/1/23-3/31/24)		
7 (4/1-9/30/23)					
3	2	6	5	5	6
%	%	%	%	%	%

Comparative Historical Data

Type of Statement	4/1/19-3/31/20 ALL	4/1/20-3/31/21 ALL
Unqualified	5	3
Reviewed	1	
Compiled	2	1
Tax Returns	7	1
Other	21	15
NUMBER OF STATEMENTS	36	20
	%	%
ASSETS		
Cash & Equivalents	7.5	16.5
Trade Receivables (net)	17.5	16.3
Inventory	21.0	21.6
All Other Current	1.9	.9
Total Current	47.9	55.3
Fixed Assets (net)	34.8	23.5
Intangibles (net)	13.6	13.4
All Other Non-Current	3.8	7.8
Total	100.0	100.0
LIABILITIES		
Notes Payable-Short Term	7.6	2.3
Cur. Mat.-L.T.D.	3.7	5.2
Trade Payables	8.9	13.8
Income Taxes Payable	.2	.2
All Other Current	8.7	20.7
Total Current	29.1	42.2
Long-Term Debt	19.7	16.6
Deferred Taxes	.0	.0
All Other Non-Current	10.6	13.3
Net Worth	40.6	27.8
Total Liabilities & Net Worth	100.0	100.0
INCOME DATA		
Net Sales	100.0	100.0
Gross Profit	32.2	31.8
Operating Expenses	22.9	28.2
Operating Profit	9.3	3.6
All Other Expenses (net)	2.7	2.0
Profit Before Taxes	6.7	1.7
RATIOS		
Current	2.7	4.0
	1.6	2.4
	1.2	1.3
Quick	1.5	1.8
	.7	1.3
	.5	.8
Sales/Receivables	24 15.3	18 20.7
	36 10.0	36 10.1
	43 8.5	45 8.1
Cost of Sales/Inventory	35 10.5	36 10.2
	55 6.6	52 7.0
	85 4.3	85 4.3
Cost of Sales/Payables	12 31.7	19 19.4
	19 18.9	29 12.5
	32 11.5	41 8.9
Sales/Working Capital	6.8	4.3
	12.3	7.0
	27.9	55.1
EBIT/Interest	12.1	13.7
	(31) 5.7	(18) 4.8
	.9	-.1
Net Profit + Depr., Dep., Amort./Cur. Mat. L/T/D		
Fixed/Worth	.5	.1
	1.1	1.1
	2.6	5.4
Debt/Worth	.7	.4
	1.9	1.8
	5.1	12.6
% Profit Before Taxes/Tangible Net Worth	67.9	89.4
	(28) 32.7	(16) 11.8
	2.2	1.6
% Profit Before Taxes/Total Assets	26.6	14.5
	9.7	4.3
	.8	-3.4
Sales/Net Fixed Assets	16.2	29.9
	5.3	9.8
	2.6	4.9
Sales/Total Assets	2.8	3.2
	1.6	1.9
	1.2	1.1
% Depr., Dep., Amort./Sales	1.3	1.0
	(29) 3.8	(13) 1.9
	4.6	5.7
% Officers', Directors' Owners' Comp/Sales		

3892M	13380M	60543M	153147M	918548M	2355802M	Net Sales ($)	2739250M	1314453M
786M	1784M	26740M	161272M	376567M	1084326M	Total Assets ($)	1997766M	857309M

M = $ thousand   MM = $ million
See Pages viii through xx for Explanation of Ratios and Data

© RMA 2024

MANUFACTURING—Dog and Cat Food Manufacturing NAICS 311111

Comparative Historical Data / Current Data Sorted by Sales

							Type of Statement							
							Unqualified					1		2
							Reviewed					1		
							Compiled							1
		1		2		3	Tax Returns		3		1			
		2		1		1	Other		1	2		3		12
		2		12		4			7 (4/1-9/30/23)		20 (10/1/23-3/31/24)			
		16		12		18		0-1MM	1-3MM	3-5MM	5-10MM	10-25MM		25MM & OVER
		4/1/21-3/31/22 ALL		4/1/22-3/31/23 ALL		4/1/23-3/31/24 ALL								
		21		15		27	NUMBER OF STATEMENTS	4		2	1	6		14
		%		%		%	ASSETS	%	%	%	%	%		%
		18.4		12.0		9.0	Cash & Equivalents	D						4.3
		15.8		21.6		20.0	Trade Receivables (net)	A						18.1
		24.6		36.1		21.7	Inventory	T						18.5
		.9		3.4		2.8	All Other Current	A						.9
		59.7		73.2		53.5	Total Current							41.9
		23.9		18.3		20.8	Fixed Assets (net)	N						24.8
		14.9		5.8		14.0	Intangibles (net)	O						15.7
		1.5		2.8		11.7	All Other Non-Current	T						17.5
		100.0		100.0		100.0	Total							100.0
							LIABILITIES	A						
		5.3		6.5		4.5	Notes Payable-Short Term	V						.9
		1.4		.6		1.9	Cur. Mat.-L.T.D.	A						2.8
		12.1		15.8		10.9	Trade Payables	I						11.5
		.7		.0		.0	Income Taxes Payable	L						.0
		4.6		7.6		7.3	All Other Current	A						6.8
		24.1		30.5		24.6	Total Current	B						21.9
		47.7		18.7		23.0	Long-Term Debt	L						20.5
		.0		.2		.3	Deferred Taxes	E						.2
		11.6		7.5		8.2	All Other Non-Current							10.1
		16.6		43.1		43.9	Net Worth							47.2
		100.0		100.0		100.0	Total Liabilties & Net Worth							100.0
							INCOME DATA							
		100.0		100.0		100.0	Net Sales							100.0
		34.2		28.9		25.3	Gross Profit							19.3
		27.3		29.2		20.8	Operating Expenses							14.6
		6.9		-.4		4.5	Operating Profit							4.6
		1.0		.8		2.3	All Other Expenses (net)							2.8
		5.9		-1.1		2.2	Profit Before Taxes							1.8
							RATIOS							
		6.6		4.1		3.1								3.0
		3.3		2.1		2.3	Current							2.6
		1.8		1.6		1.5								1.9
		4.2		2.5		1.8								1.9
		2.0		.9		1.3	Quick							1.7
		.8		.4		.8								.8
9		40.2	27	13.6	20	17.9							25	14.4
34		10.6	41	8.9	30	12.0	Sales/Receivables						31	11.9
49		7.4	48	7.6	49	7.4							41	8.9
40		9.1	65	5.6	27	13.7							26	13.9
55		6.6	74	4.9	41	9.0	Cost of Sales/Inventory						37	9.8
107		3.4	118	3.1	69	5.3							59	6.2
14		25.3	19	18.9	17	22.1							19	19.4
23		15.6	22	16.3	24	14.9	Cost of Sales/Payables						23	15.7
36		10.2	83	4.4	36	10.1							31	11.6
		3.1		4.2		6.5								6.4
		5.9		6.4		8.4	Sales/Working Capital							8.3
		11.5		10.2		13.9								19.8
		28.4		19.9		18.7								13.3
(17)		2.6	(13)	3.6	(23)	4.7	EBIT/Interest						(13)	4.7
		.2		-1.9		.5								-.2
							Net Profit + Depr., Dep., Amort./Cur. Mat. L/T/D							
		.1		.0		.1								.1
		.6		.4		.7	Fixed/Worth							.8
		NM		1.2		3.0								2.5
		.6		.7		.5								.5
		1.7		.9		1.4	Debt/Worth							1.0
		-6.8		3.5		5.5								4.4
		80.1		38.5		56.2								48.9
(15)		18.6	(13)	11.7	(22)	15.2	% Profit Before Taxes/Tangible Net Worth						(12)	14.2
		3.2		-13.8		6.9								-.9
		35.9		17.2		23.2								13.3
		4.6		1.7		7.1	% Profit Before Taxes/Total Assets							7.8
		-3.2		-3.0		-1.3								-2.6
		64.1		340.6		63.6								34.9
		9.1		9.7		12.9	Sales/Net Fixed Assets							9.4
		5.5		6.8		5.4								5.5
		3.1		2.8		3.5								2.7
		1.9		2.2		2.4	Sales/Total Assets							2.2
		1.0		1.8		1.1								1.1
		1.3				.6								.7
(11)		1.9	(19)			1.4	% Depr., Dep., Amort./Sales						(12)	1.6
		4.8				2.9								5.8
							% Officers', Directors' Owners' Comp/Sales							
		1099082M		1726603M		3505312M	Net Sales ($)	6244M	7275M	8687M	94291M			3388815M
		892925M		798743M		1651475M	Total Assets ($)	1449M	6733M	2587M	65887M			1574819M

M = $ thousand   MM = $ million
See Pages viii through xx for Explanation of Ratios and Data

© RMA 2024

MANUFACTURING—Other Animal Food Manufacturing NAICS 311119

Current Data Sorted by Assets / Comparative Historical Data

							Type of Statement				
			2	4		4	Unqualified		10		10
			1	2			Reviewed		4		3
			2	2			Compiled		5		3
		1	3				Tax Returns		15		1
1	1	1	8	16	4	2	Other		55		39
0-500M	500M-2MM	22 (4/1-9/30/23) 2-10MM		31 (10/1/23-3/31/24) 10-50MM	50-100MM	100-250MM			4/1/19-3/31/20		4/1/20-3/31/21
1	2	16		24	4	6	NUMBER OF STATEMENTS		89 ALL		56 ALL
%	%	%		%	%	%	ASSETS		%		%
		11.7		7.8			Cash & Equivalents		8.7		10.9
		12.7		23.0			Trade Receivables (net)		22.2		21.3
		27.2		27.8			Inventory		22.8		23.3
		4.8		1.9			All Other Current		4.0		3.6
		56.3		60.5			Total Current		57.6		59.1
		35.8		23.6			Fixed Assets (net)		32.9		29.6
		2.8		4.8			Intangibles (net)		3.6		2.7
		5.1		11.1			All Other Non-Current		5.9		8.7
		100.0		100.0			Total		100.0		100.0
							LIABILITIES				
		6.0		11.0			Notes Payable-Short Term		13.1		6.4
		3.4		3.2			Cur. Mat.-L.T.D.		2.1		2.6
		9.5		14.8			Trade Payables		14.1		13.5
		.0		.1			Income Taxes Payable		.1		.0
		13.0		4.5			All Other Current		9.3		9.1
		31.9		33.6			Total Current		38.7		31.7
		19.7		9.8			Long-Term Debt		17.2		15.6
		.4		.2			Deferred Taxes		.4		.5
		6.2		4.1			All Other Non-Current		3.7		2.8
		41.8		52.4			Net Worth		40.0		49.4
		100.0		100.0			Total Liabilities & Net Worth		100.0		100.0
							INCOME DATA				
		100.0		100.0			Net Sales		100.0		100.0
		24.4		27.0			Gross Profit		23.2		22.1
		20.1		19.0			Operating Expenses		18.4		17.6
		4.3		8.0			Operating Profit		4.8		4.6
		.6		1.8			All Other Expenses (net)		.5		-.4
		3.7		6.2			Profit Before Taxes		4.3		5.0
							RATIOS				
		2.7		3.7					2.6		3.5
		1.6		2.3			Current		1.7		1.9
		1.4		1.4					1.2		1.4
		1.1		1.7					1.6		2.0
		.6		1.1			Quick		.9		1.1
		.5		.5					.5		.7
		4 84.7	17	21.3				17	22.1	18	20.1
		21 17.1	29	12.7			Sales/Receivables	29	12.8	29	12.4
		33 10.9	44	8.3				38	9.6	40	9.2
		28 12.9	35	10.4				17	21.2	23	16.1
		62 5.9	50	7.3			Cost of Sales/Inventory	35	10.5	36	10.0
		99 3.7	114	3.2				76	4.8	74	4.9
		7 53.2	13	28.1				12	30.5	12	30.5
		17 21.6	21	17.4			Cost of Sales/Payables	21	17.2	19	18.9
		30 12.2	53	6.9				34	10.7	32	11.3
		7.5		3.9					6.2		5.9
		11.0		11.2			Sales/Working Capital		12.4		9.5
		23.1		18.0					50.3		20.9
		18.9		23.3					13.4		33.5
		(15) 4.5	(20)	6.0			EBIT/Interest	(74)	6.4	(47)	7.6
		2.6		2.0					2.7		3.0
											10.5
							Net Profit + Depr., Dep., Amort./Cur. Mat. L/T/D			(10)	3.6
											1.9
		.6		.2					.4		.2
		1.0		.5			Fixed/Worth		.8		.7
		1.7		.7					1.6		1.0
		.8		.3					.5		.4
		1.2		.9			Debt/Worth		1.2		1.0
		3.9		2.4					2.7		2.3
		54.1		36.8					41.7		40.6
		(15) 12.7	(22)	26.2			% Profit Before Taxes/Tangible Net Worth	(79)	21.9	(53)	22.3
		5.5		13.2					7.6		11.7
		15.6		22.1					16.0		16.6
		5.5		12.4			% Profit Before Taxes/Total Assets		9.2		10.6
		2.3		4.1					2.4		4.3
		13.3		34.6					19.1		18.4
		6.3		10.0			Sales/Net Fixed Assets		9.1		9.9
		3.7		4.8					4.4		5.3
		2.8		3.1					3.5		3.4
		2.3		2.2			Sales/Total Assets		2.6		2.4
		1.5		1.6					1.7		2.1
		1.6		.8					.9		1.0
		(15) 2.2	(15)	1.2			% Depr., Dep., Amort./Sales	(79)	1.7	(47)	1.6
		3.4		3.5					3.0		2.2
									1.2		
							% Officers', Directors' Owners' Comp/Sales	(22)	2.5		
									4.0		
850M	12025M	258461M		1361126M	818719M	3021209M	Net Sales ($)		6497209M		4934195M
290M	2873M	89148M		534889M	228547M	1054574M	Total Assets ($)		2663220M		1827981M

© RMA 2024

M = $ thousand   MM = $ million
See Pages viii through xx for Explanation of Ratios and Data

MANUFACTURING—Other Animal Food Manufacturing NAICS 311119

Comparative Historical Data				Current Data Sorted by Sales					
			Type of Statement					1	8
5	13	10	Unqualified					2	1
5	6	3	Reviewed					3	1
3	5	4	Compiled				1	1	
5	4	4	Tax Returns			1	4	4	21
33	23	32	Other	1	22 (4/1-9/30/23)	4	2		
4/1/21-	4/1/22-	4/1/23-						31 (10/1/23-3/31/24)	
3/31/22	3/31/23	3/31/24		0-1MM	1-3MM	3-5MM	5-10MM	10-25MM	25MM & OVER
ALL	ALL	ALL							
51	51	53	**NUMBER OF STATEMENTS**	1		6	4	11	31
%	%	%	**ASSETS**	%		%	%	%	%
8.8	9.4	9.7	Cash & Equivalents					11.8	7.4
21.5	21.7	19.7	Trade Receivables (net)		D			13.2	23.9
24.2	26.9	26.6	Inventory		A			26.5	27.2
2.8	2.2	3.7	All Other Current		T			5.4	2.6
57.2	60.1	59.7	Total Current		A			56.9	61.1
30.9	29.3	26.1	Fixed Assets (net)					33.2	23.5
4.0	5.5	5.6	Intangibles (net)		N			1.8	6.0
7.9	5.1	8.5	All Other Non-Current		O			8.1	9.4
100.0	100.0	100.0	Total		T			100.0	100.0
			LIABILITIES		A				
7.5	5.2	7.9	Notes Payable-Short Term		V			5.5	8.2
2.1	1.9	3.2	Cur. Mat.-L.T.D.		A			2.2	3.3
14.0	16.9	13.5	Trade Payables		I			9.2	17.8
.1	.1	.1	Income Taxes Payable		L			.1	.1
10.7	9.4	7.3	All Other Current		A			9.1	6.9
34.5	33.5	31.9	Total Current		B			26.1	36.2
11.6	15.1	14.7	Long-Term Debt		L			12.9	11.9
.3	.3	.2	Deferred Taxes		E			.4	.1
6.8	4.0	4.4	All Other Non-Current					6.2	4.1
46.9	47.1	48.6	Net Worth					54.4	47.7
100.0	100.0	100.0	Total Liabilties & Net Worth					100.0	100.0
			INCOME DATA						
100.0	100.0	100.0	Net Sales					100.0	100.0
22.9	19.9	23.5	Gross Profit					27.7	19.7
16.7	14.4	17.3	Operating Expenses					21.3	13.3
6.2	5.5	6.2	Operating Profit					6.4	6.4
-.5	.4	1.1	All Other Expenses (net)					.9	.4
6.7	5.1	5.1	Profit Before Taxes					5.5	6.0
			RATIOS						
2.8	2.6	3.5						3.8	3.2
1.7	2.0	1.9	Current					1.9	1.6
1.3	1.3	1.4						1.4	1.4
1.8	1.5	1.7						1.5	1.7
.9	.9	.9	Quick					.7	1.0
.6	.5	.5						.6	.6
20 18.2	18 20.8	16 23.1					4	84.7	16 22.4
27 13.5	26 13.8	26 14.3	Sales/Receivables				31	11.7	26 14.3
40 9.2	35 10.5	37 9.9					46	8.0	34 10.6
22 16.5	24 15.2	25 14.5					43	8.5	20 18.0
45 8.2	46 7.9	46 7.9	Cost of Sales/Inventory				62	5.9	39 9.3
81 4.5	73 5.0	87 4.2					99	3.7	52 7.0
9 40.0	14 26.0	12 29.2					7	49.5	14 25.3
20 18.1	24 15.4	18 19.8	Cost of Sales/Payables				22	16.5	21 17.5
32 11.3	33 11.1	32 11.4					30	12.0	47 7.7
5.7	5.8	4.9						3.5	6.8
12.6	10.8	11.2	Sales/Working Capital					9.0	16.2
19.8	21.0	19.4						13.4	25.2
30.0	23.9	16.0						21.1	20.2
(45) 15.1	(44) 7.9	(46) 5.9	EBIT/Interest					(27) 10.6	(27) 5.8
4.3	2.0	2.4						6.1	2.5
			Net Profit + Depr., Dep., Amort./Cur. Mat. L/T/D						
.3	.3	.3						.3	.3
.7	.7	.6	Fixed/Worth					.7	.5
1.0	1.2	1.4						1.0	1.2
.6	.8	.5						.5	.4
.9	1.2	1.1	Debt/Worth					.8	1.7
1.9	3.1	3.4						1.2	3.3
56.0	53.8	42.6						30.8	45.0
(47) 31.8	(50) 23.6	(49) 23.8	% Profit Before Taxes/Tangible Net Worth					15.5	(29) 26.5
11.7	7.1	10.5						5.7	15.6
22.3	17.1	17.9						16.3	19.7
13.6	7.6	9.4	% Profit Before Taxes/Total Assets					8.5	11.2
4.3	1.5	3.4						4.8	4.6
20.7	16.5	28.8						13.9	35.2
8.6	10.4	11.1	Sales/Net Fixed Assets					6.0	13.3
4.5	5.3	5.0						3.7	7.0
3.3	4.2	3.3						2.5	3.7
2.6	2.7	2.5	Sales/Total Assets					2.1	2.9
1.8	1.8	1.6						1.5	2.1
1.0	.6	.9							.5
(41) 2.0	(39) 1.6	(38) 1.6	% Depr., Dep., Amort./Sales					(21)	1.1
3.0	2.8	2.9							1.6
1.0	.6		% Officers', Directors' Owners' Comp/Sales						
(11) 1.6	(11) 1.4								
3.5	2.2								
5043610M	7135056M	5472390M	Net Sales ($)	850M	26118M	31245M	182049M	5232128M	
2018386M	2803094M	1910321M	Total Assets ($)	290M	27539M	16582M	96327M	1769583M	

M = $ thousand   MM = $ million
See Pages viii through xx for Explanation of Ratios and Data
© RMA 2024

MANUFACTURING—Flour Milling NAICS 311211

Current Data Sorted by Assets / Comparative Historical Data

						Type of Statement		
			1	1	3	Unqualified	11	4
	1		1			Reviewed	1	2
		1				Compiled	4	1
						Tax Returns	2	
	10 (4/1-9/30/23)		5 (10/1/23-3/31/24)	3	3	Other	8	10
0-500M	500M-2MM	2-10MM	10-50MM	50-100MM	100-250MM		4/1/19-3/31/20	4/1/20-3/31/21
		2	8	4	6	NUMBER OF STATEMENTS	26 ALL	17 ALL
%	%	%	%	%	%	ASSETS	%	%
DATA NOT AVAILABLE	DATA NOT AVAILABLE					Cash & Equivalents	8.2	10.2
						Trade Receivables (net)	19.5	12.2
						Inventory	23.9	19.9
						All Other Current	2.0	3.3
						Total Current	53.5	45.6
						Fixed Assets (net)	41.3	47.3
						Intangibles (net)	2.3	1.6
						All Other Non-Current	2.9	5.4
						Total	100.0	100.0
						LIABILITIES		
						Notes Payable-Short Term	6.4	7.0
						Cur. Mat.-L.T.D.	2.0	2.6
						Trade Payables	9.5	6.6
						Income Taxes Payable	.1	.0
						All Other Current	6.8	6.7
						Total Current	24.8	23.0
						Long-Term Debt	18.0	18.1
						Deferred Taxes	1.3	2.2
						All Other Non-Current	2.8	1.9
						Net Worth	53.1	54.9
						Total Liabilities & Net Worth	100.0	100.0
						INCOME DATA		
						Net Sales	100.0	100.0
						Gross Profit	23.4	31.4
						Operating Expenses	18.6	26.5
						Operating Profit	4.7	4.9
						All Other Expenses (net)	.8	-1.5
						Profit Before Taxes	4.0	6.4
						RATIOS		
						Current	4.7	4.3
							2.1	2.0
							1.5	1.2
						Quick	2.4	1.7
							1.2	1.0
							.8	.5
						Sales/Receivables	26 14.1	18 20.2
							37 9.9	26 14.0
							46 7.9	37 9.8
						Cost of Sales/Inventory	31 11.9	35 10.5
							46 8.0	49 7.5
							99 3.7	107 3.4
						Cost of Sales/Payables	10 36.7	8 46.9
							19 19.3	20 18.0
							30 12.0	31 11.8
						Sales/Working Capital	4.3	4.5
							10.1	9.2
							16.1	46.4
						EBIT/Interest	22.1	14.9
							(24) 7.2	(14) 6.5
							1.3	1.9
						Net Profit + Depr., Dep., Amort./Cur. Mat. L/T/D		
						Fixed/Worth	.5	.4
							.9	1.0
							1.5	1.4
						Debt/Worth	.4	.3
							1.1	.7
							2.0	2.0
						% Profit Before Taxes/Tangible Net Worth	24.9	27.5
							9.8	15.9
							3.4	2.7
						% Profit Before Taxes/Total Assets	12.7	11.9
							4.5	8.0
							1.2	1.4
						Sales/Net Fixed Assets	6.9	6.9
							4.6	3.0
							2.6	2.1
						Sales/Total Assets	2.4	2.4
							1.8	1.5
							1.5	1.2
						% Depr., Dep., Amort./Sales	1.4	1.4
							(24) 2.3	(12) 2.2
							4.2	4.0
						% Officers', Directors' Owners' Comp/Sales		
		24774M	340491M	295605M	1164131M	Net Sales ($)	2959108M	1875655M
		15221M	188884M	242200M	981054M	Total Assets ($)	1735101M	1153564M

M = $ thousand MM = $ million
See Pages viii through xx for Explanation of Ratios and Data

© RMA 2024

MANUFACTURING—Flour Milling NAICS 311211

Comparative Historical Data | Current Data Sorted by Sales

			Type of Statement						
3	5	5	Unqualified					2	5
1	1	2	Reviewed						1
2	3	1	Compiled						
1			Tax Returns				1	3	8
8	4	12	Other						
4/1/21-	4/1/22-	4/1/23-			10 (4/1-9/30/23)		10 (10/1/23-3/31/24)		
3/31/22	3/31/23	3/31/24		0-1MM	1-3MM	3-5MM	5-10MM	10-25MM	25MM & OVER
ALL	ALL	ALL							
15	13	20	NUMBER OF STATEMENTS				1	5	14
%	%	%	ASSETS	%	%	%	%	%	%
8.6	4.8	5.0	Cash & Equivalents						5.1
17.5	16.8	14.8	Trade Receivables (net)	D	D	D			18.3
23.2	25.9	25.8	Inventory	A	A	A			15.5
2.8	2.7	1.7	All Other Current	T	T	T			2.3
52.0	50.2	47.4	Total Current	A	A	A			41.2
36.6	38.9	43.6	Fixed Assets (net)						47.6
3.0	5.5	5.4	Intangibles (net)	N	N	N			6.5
8.3	5.4	3.6	All Other Non-Current	O	O	O			4.7
100.0	100.0	100.0	Total	T	T	T			100.0
			LIABILITIES	A	A	A			
6.2	13.3	6.4	Notes Payable-Short Term	V	V	V			2.1
2.2	2.2	2.8	Cur. Mat.-L.T.D.	A	A	A			2.7
10.7	8.9	7.2	Trade Payables	I	I	I			6.8
.0	.1	.0	Income Taxes Payable	L	L	L			.0
7.1	6.2	7.4	All Other Current	A	A	A			7.7
26.1	30.7	23.8	Total Current	B	B	B			19.4
16.8	21.3	19.3	Long-Term Debt	L	L	L			23.2
.5	1.0	1.1	Deferred Taxes	E	E	E			1.5
4.2	4.5	5.9	All Other Non-Current						6.6
52.4	42.5	50.0	Net Worth						49.3
100.0	100.0	100.0	Total Liabilties & Net Worth						100.0
			INCOME DATA						
100.0	100.0	100.0	Net Sales						100.0
23.4	16.3	17.9	Gross Profit						14.1
21.6	12.8	13.3	Operating Expenses						9.7
1.8	3.5	4.6	Operating Profit						4.4
-.4	1.1	2.1	All Other Expenses (net)						2.3
2.2	2.5	2.5	Profit Before Taxes						2.1
			RATIOS						
2.8	2.0	2.6							3.4
2.0	1.6	2.1	Current						2.1
1.4	1.3	1.6							1.5
1.2	1.4	1.4							1.6
1.0	.8	.9	Quick						1.3
.6	.4	.5							.9
27 13.6	17 22.1	20 18.6						29	12.4
34 10.8	33 11.0	34 10.7	Sales/Receivables					43	8.4
43 8.5	39 9.4	51 7.2						60	6.1
42 8.6	37 9.9	35 10.5						34	10.8
52 7.0	57 6.4	54 6.7	Cost of Sales/Inventory					40	9.2
79 4.6	81 4.5	111 3.3						62	5.9
16 23.3	9 42.2	12 29.6						10	35.6
21 17.0	20 18.3	21 17.3	Cost of Sales/Payables					15	23.6
40 9.2	31 11.6	36 10.0						36	10.1
6.4	5.8	3.5							5.7
7.8	9.5	5.9	Sales/Working Capital						6.6
19.2	18.5	7.4							10.6
42.8	13.7	9.6							9.4
(13) 2.1	(11) 6.4	(18) 4.1	EBIT/Interest					(12)	3.7
.7	-.5	.5							.8
			Net Profit + Depr., Dep., Amort./Cur. Mat. L/T/D						
.4	.6	.6							.9
.7	.8	1.1	Fixed/Worth						1.2
1.5	1.9	1.4							1.4
.5	.8	.7							.7
.9	1.5	1.1	Debt/Worth						1.0
1.3	3.0	1.4							1.5
16.2	36.5	19.3	% Profit Before Taxes/Tangible Net Worth						18.4
(14) 4.9	(12) 18.0	(19) 6.0						(13)	5.6
-6.3	-5.0	-.3							1.5
9.4	12.7	10.7	% Profit Before Taxes/Total Assets						8.9
1.9	8.8	3.4							2.8
-1.7	-3.1	-.8							-.5
10.4	11.0	3.9							4.7
4.9	4.9	3.2	Sales/Net Fixed Assets						2.7
2.5	2.3	2.0							1.8
2.8	2.7	1.9							2.0
1.5	1.4	1.1	Sales/Total Assets						1.2
1.1	.9	.9							1.0
1.3	1.2	1.2							1.9
1.9	2.2	2.3	% Depr., Dep., Amort./Sales						2.5
4.3	3.3	3.3							3.6
			% Officers', Directors' Owners' Comp/Sales						
836961M	2055104M	1825001M	Net Sales ($)				5445M	73801M	1745755M
686088M	1019840M	1427359M	Total Assets ($)				5968M	65340M	1356051M

M = $ thousand   MM = $ million

© RMA 2024

MANUFACTURING—Frozen Specialty Food Manufacturing NAICS 311412

Current Data Sorted by Assets | Comparative Historical Data

Type of Statement									
			4	1	4	Unqualified		6	5
		2	3			Reviewed		6	2
	1		2			Compiled		3	
1		3		3	8	Tax Returns		4	1
	9 (4/1-9/30/23)		9 (10/1/23-3/31/24)			Other		38	24
0-500M	500M-2MM	2-10MM	10-50MM	50-100MM	100-250MM			4/1/19-3/31/20 ALL	4/1/20-3/31/21 ALL
1	1	7	16	4	12	NUMBER OF STATEMENTS		57	32
%	%	%	%	%	%	ASSETS		%	%
			16.9		4.4	Cash & Equivalents		9.5	12.8
			19.0		19.8	Trade Receivables (net)		19.9	21.2
			16.9		19.2	Inventory		23.0	22.2
			2.0		5.5	All Other Current		1.9	1.3
			54.7		48.9	Total Current		54.3	57.5
			35.2		32.9	Fixed Assets (net)		34.5	32.8
			5.3		4.0	Intangibles (net)		7.5	5.2
			4.8		14.1	All Other Non-Current		3.7	4.5
			100.0		100.0	Total		100.0	100.0
						LIABILITIES			
			.2		6.8	Notes Payable-Short Term		9.6	5.2
			4.7		6.2	Cur. Mat.-L.T.D.		2.4	2.0
			9.3		10.0	Trade Payables		13.3	12.4
			.1		.4	Income Taxes Payable		.0	.1
			9.1		7.0	All Other Current		9.1	12.4
			23.5		30.4	Total Current		34.4	32.2
			14.6		26.4	Long-Term Debt		22.1	20.0
			1.1		.1	Deferred Taxes		.7	.4
			1.5		10.7	All Other Non-Current		4.8	5.6
			59.3		32.3	Net Worth		37.9	41.9
			100.0		100.0	Total Liabilities & Net Worth		100.0	100.0
						INCOME DATA			
			100.0		100.0	Net Sales		100.0	100.0
			28.7		30.4	Gross Profit		28.0	28.0
			20.7		22.8	Operating Expenses		22.2	20.2
			8.0		7.6	Operating Profit		5.8	7.7
			.8		1.2	All Other Expenses (net)		1.1	.7
			7.2		6.3	Profit Before Taxes		4.7	7.0
						RATIOS			
			3.4		2.2			3.4	3.0
			2.8		1.4	Current		1.6	1.8
			1.8		1.3			1.1	1.5
			2.4		1.0			1.7	1.9
			1.9		.6	Quick		1.0	1.1
			1.1		.5			.6	.7
		26	14.1	29	12.4		23	16.2	23	15.7
		29	12.7	32	11.5	Sales/Receivables	29	12.5	30	12.2
		34	10.6	37	9.8		38	9.6	41	8.9
		30	12.1	29	12.4		30	12.0	30	12.0
		38	9.7	48	7.6	Cost of Sales/Inventory	48	7.6	39	9.4
		49	7.4	70	5.2		70	5.2	66	5.5
		13	28.0	22	16.7		17	21.0	13	28.9
		15	24.6	24	14.9	Cost of Sales/Payables	23	15.9	25	14.4
		30	12.1	35	10.5		29	12.4	33	11.0
			4.2		5.8			5.4	5.9
			7.1		16.2	Sales/Working Capital		11.7	10.4
			11.7		25.6			67.3	16.1
			21.6		13.4			19.0	27.4
		(13)	8.3		8.7	EBIT/Interest	(52)	4.8	(27)	10.3
			3.3		3.0			1.6	1.9
						Net Profit + Depr., Dep.,		4.4	
						Amort./Cur. Mat. L/T/D	(13)	2.4	
								1.6	
			.4		.7			.6	.5
			.8		1.1	Fixed/Worth		1.0	.9
			1.0		1.2			1.9	1.4
			.5		1.5			.8	.8
			.6		2.1	Debt/Worth		1.6	1.4
			1.3		2.8			5.7	3.2
			65.0		38.3			45.9	77.6
		(15)	23.2	(10)	19.4	% Profit Before Taxes/Tangible Net Worth	(48)	22.6	(28)	20.3
			12.9		12.7			3.0	1.8
			24.7		17.8			18.5	26.7
			13.8		9.6	% Profit Before Taxes/Total Assets		8.8	12.7
			6.7		3.7			1.1	1.2
			9.9		8.2			13.3	20.3
			7.4		6.5	Sales/Net Fixed Assets		6.1	6.4
			3.7		3.9			3.8	3.7
			3.0		2.5			2.9	3.4
			2.3		1.8	Sales/Total Assets		2.2	2.3
			1.4		1.5			1.6	1.4
			1.3		1.9			1.7	1.7
		(13)	2.4	(11)	2.3	% Depr., Dep., Amort./Sales	(46)	2.6	(24)	2.9
			2.8		2.7			3.7	3.8
								.8	
						% Officers', Directors' Owners' Comp/Sales	(10)	1.3	
								2.7	
28M	1801M	94358M	1137792M	537731M	3741724M	Net Sales ($)		4022420M	3300270M
7M	679M	37545M	520212M	291561M	1893951M	Total Assets ($)		2025530M	1492221M

M = $ thousand   MM = $ million
See Pages viii through xx for Explanation of Ratios and Data

© RMA 2024

MANUFACTURING—Frozen Specialty Food Manufacturing NAICS 311412

Comparative Historical Data | Current Data Sorted by Sales

Comparative Historical Data						Current Data Sorted by Sales					
				Type of Statement							
	4	9	9	Unqualified					1	2	9
	3	5	5	Reviewed						1	2
		3		Compiled							1
	3	3	3	Tax Returns			1		2	1	1
	29	29	24	Other	1	9 (4/1-9/30/23)			32 (10/1/23-3/31/24)		20
	4/1/21-	4/1/22-	4/1/23-								
	3/31/22	3/31/23	3/31/24								
	ALL	ALL	ALL		0-1MM	1-3MM	3-5MM	5-10MM	10-25MM	25MM & OVER	
	39	49	41	NUMBER OF STATEMENTS	1	1		3	4	32	
	%	%	%	ASSETS	%	%	%	%	%	%	
	13.6	8.7	12.4	Cash & Equivalents						11.5	
	18.1	18.6	19.9	Trade Receivables (net)						20.5	
	19.4	27.1	20.1	Inventory			DATA			18.4	
	1.7	3.6	2.8	All Other Current						3.1	
	52.8	57.9	55.3	Total Current						53.5	
	35.2	28.7	31.6	Fixed Assets (net)			NOT			32.1	
	6.9	6.8	4.3	Intangibles (net)						4.3	
	5.1	6.6	8.8	All Other Non-Current			AVAILABLE			10.1	
	100.0	100.0	100.0	Total						100.0	
				LIABILITIES							
	4.3	6.7	3.8	Notes Payable-Short Term						3.3	
	4.6	3.4	4.3	Cur. Mat.-L.T.D.						5.0	
	11.5	15.4	12.2	Trade Payables						10.7	
	.0	.1	.2	Income Taxes Payable						.2	
	6.1	9.0	8.0	All Other Current						9.4	
	26.5	34.7	28.4	Total Current						28.7	
	25.4	23.4	20.9	Long-Term Debt						18.6	
	.6	.4	.5	Deferred Taxes						.5	
	5.5	6.1	5.4	All Other Non-Current						5.5	
	42.0	35.5	44.7	Net Worth						46.8	
	100.0	100.0	100.0	Total Liabilities & Net Worth						100.0	
				INCOME DATA							
	100.0	100.0	100.0	Net Sales						100.0	
	28.6	26.0	32.5	Gross Profit						30.1	
	22.2	22.1	24.6	Operating Expenses						21.8	
	6.4	3.9	7.9	Operating Profit						8.4	
	.1	.4	.9	All Other Expenses (net)						.9	
	6.3	3.5	7.1	Profit Before Taxes						7.4	
				RATIOS							
	4.1	2.9	3.3							2.9	
	2.5	1.9	1.9	Current						1.8	
	1.6	1.3	1.3							1.3	
	2.8	1.1	2.1							2.0	
	1.3	.8	1.2	Quick						1.0	
	.7	.6	.6							.6	
20	18.2	23 15.9	26 14.2						26	13.9	
29	12.5	30 12.0	30 12.2	Sales/Receivables					31	11.8	
35	10.4	37 9.9	38 9.6						38	9.6	
26	14.1	34 10.8	30 12.0						30	12.1	
41	9.0	54 6.8	47 7.7	Cost of Sales/Inventory					40	9.2	
60	6.1	89 4.1	68 5.4						64	5.7	
16	22.3	19 19.3	16 23.5						15	24.8	
23	16.1	29 12.6	26 14.2	Cost of Sales/Payables					23	15.6	
32	11.3	40 9.2	37 9.8						35	10.3	
	4.8	5.2	5.1							5.9	
	8.3	10.3	8.6	Sales/Working Capital						10.0	
	15.3	26.7	17.1							17.5	
	23.9	12.7	21.6							19.6	
(35)	11.9	(44) 6.5	(37) 8.3	EBIT/Interest					(29)	8.4	
	3.9	2.7	3.0							3.2	
		11.2	4.7	Net Profit + Depr., Dep.,						4.7	
	(15)	6.0	(15) 1.2	Amort./Cur. Mat. L/T/D					(14)	1.5	
		3.5	.8							1.0	
	.6	.6	.5							.4	
	1.0	1.3	.9	Fixed/Worth						.9	
	1.4	2.9	1.2							1.2	
	.7	.7	.5							.5	
	1.2	2.7	1.3	Debt/Worth						1.3	
	3.4	6.3	2.6							2.4	
	52.3	45.2	51.5							48.6	
(35)	32.1	(39) 24.7	(36) 23.2	% Profit Before Taxes/Tangible Net Worth					(29)	23.2	
	21.1	10.6	11.6							13.0	
	20.6	15.4	20.3							19.1	
	14.4	8.9	12.6	% Profit Before Taxes/Total Assets						11.7	
	5.5	2.0	5.1							6.0	
	11.2	14.9	9.9							9.7	
	6.8	7.8	7.5	Sales/Net Fixed Assets						7.4	
	3.3	4.1	3.7							3.8	
	3.3	3.1	3.0							2.8	
	2.1	2.3	2.1	Sales/Total Assets						2.1	
	1.6	1.5	1.5							1.5	
	1.1	1.2	1.5							1.5	
(28)	1.9	(39) 2.2	(33) 2.4	% Depr., Dep., Amort./Sales					(28)	2.4	
	3.5	3.1	2.9							2.8	
				% Officers', Directors', Owners' Comp/Sales							
	4538430M	6260771M	5513434M	Net Sales ($)	28M	1801M		25039M	66904M	5419662M	
	2222492M	3178571M	2743955M	Total Assets ($)	7M	679M		20930M	36996M	2685343M	

M = $ thousand   MM = $ million
See Pages viii through xx for Explanation of Ratios and Data
© RMA 2024

MANUFACTURING—Fruit and Vegetable Canning NAICS 311421

Current Data Sorted by Assets / Comparative Historical Data

							Type of Statement				
			1	3	2	3	Unqualified		11		2
			1	2	1	1	Reviewed		3		3
		1	1	2			Compiled		3		3
	1		4	1			Tax Returns		4		1
3	3	3		6	6	9	Other		26		25
0-500M	14 (4/1-9/30/23) 500M-2MM	2-10MM	10-50MM	35 (10/1/23-3/31/24)	50-100MM	100-250MM			4/1/19- 3/31/20		4/1/20- 3/31/21
3	4	6	14		9	13	NUMBER OF STATEMENTS		47 ALL		34 ALL
%	%	%	%		%	%	ASSETS		%		%
			15.5			4.1	Cash & Equivalents		3.4		9.7
			16.5			13.8	Trade Receivables (net)		13.6		14.7
			33.2			37.4	Inventory		40.1		32.9
			1.1			2.4	All Other Current		2.6		1.1
			66.2			57.8	Total Current		59.7		58.4
			29.2			34.8	Fixed Assets (net)		33.1		30.6
			1.0			2.2	Intangibles (net)		3.0		6.2
			3.5			5.2	All Other Non-Current		4.1		4.8
			100.0			100.0	Total		100.0		100.0
							LIABILITIES				
			2.4			10.8	Notes Payable-Short Term		14.3		4.4
			2.0			2.5	Cur. Mat.-L.T.D.		2.1		3.5
			15.8			10.0	Trade Payables		15.4		16.0
			.1			.1	Income Taxes Payable		.2		.3
			7.8			9.2	All Other Current		5.5		9.9
			28.1			32.6	Total Current		37.6		34.1
			16.0			23.7	Long-Term Debt		15.6		15.8
			.2			.0	Deferred Taxes		.2		.4
			3.8			4.2	All Other Non-Current		2.0		3.3
			51.9			39.6	Net Worth		44.6		46.2
			100.0			100.0	Total Liabilities & Net Worth		100.0		100.0
							INCOME DATA				
			100.0			100.0	Net Sales		100.0		100.0
			21.9			18.2	Gross Profit		17.2		23.4
			16.6			12.6	Operating Expenses		15.8		17.9
			5.4			5.5	Operating Profit		1.4		5.4
			.4			1.6	All Other Expenses (net)		1.0		.2
			5.0			4.0	Profit Before Taxes		.4		5.2
							RATIOS				
			4.7			2.8			2.5		2.6
			2.4			1.6	Current		1.6		1.7
			1.6			1.3			1.1		1.2
			1.7			.7			.7		1.0
			1.0			.4	Quick		.5		.7
			.6			.3			.3		.5
		18 20.5		27 13.6				21 17.1		22 16.3	
		27 13.3		29 12.7			Sales/Receivables	30 12.3		27 13.4	
		35 10.4		32 11.3				39 9.3		35 10.3	
		50 7.3		69 5.3				69 5.3		56 6.5	
		76 4.8		99 3.7			Cost of Sales/Inventory	99 3.7		89 4.1	
		101 3.6		146 2.5				146 2.5		135 2.7	
		19 19.5		8 44.9				23 16.2		24 15.1	
		24 15.0		24 15.0			Cost of Sales/Payables	32 11.3		35 10.4	
		47 7.8		43 8.4				55 6.6		58 6.3	
			3.6			4.4			4.6		5.2
			4.8			7.2	Sales/Working Capital		8.8		7.9
			10.7			15.7			68.6		18.0
			26.2			12.0			10.0		21.2
			(11) 5.9			3.1	EBIT/Interest	(46) 2.3		(30) 9.0	
			3.5			.8			.0		2.6
							Net Profit + Depr., Dep., Amort./Cur. Mat. L/T/D		5.9		
								(22)	2.8		
									1.5		
			.4			.4			.6		.4
			.6			1.0	Fixed/Worth		.8		.8
			.9			2.1			1.5		1.2
			.4			.9			.6		.5
			.9			1.5	Debt/Worth		1.7		1.3
			1.7			3.2			2.6		3.1
			26.4			36.3			20.5		45.4
			(13) 15.9			18.2	% Profit Before Taxes/Tangible Net Worth	(46) 10.5		(32) 22.6	
			10.9			-4.2			-5.0		12.1
			14.9			16.1			7.8		15.8
			6.7			8.8	% Profit Before Taxes/Total Assets		2.6		10.2
			3.7			-.9			-1.8		4.1
			9.1			12.3			7.1		9.6
			7.1			5.7	Sales/Net Fixed Assets		5.1		6.0
			5.1			2.6			3.2		3.7
			2.4			2.0			2.1		2.3
			2.1			1.6	Sales/Total Assets		1.6		1.9
			1.4			1.3			1.2		1.3
			.9			1.2			1.6		1.3
			1.9		(10)	1.7	% Depr., Dep., Amort./Sales	(41) 2.4		(25) 2.0	
			3.6			2.2			3.6		2.9
							% Officers', Directors' Owners' Comp/Sales				
3031M	18529M	55604M	641128M	972658M		3142915M	Net Sales ($)		5844264M		3357559M
619M	5125M	28975M	335603M	639087M		1831149M	Total Assets ($)		4094925M		1915066M

M = $ thousand   MM = $ million
See Pages viii through xx for Explanation of Ratios and Data

© RMA 2024

MANUFACTURING—Fruit and Vegetable Canning NAICS 311421

Comparative Historical Data | **Current Data Sorted by Sales**

	7		12		9	Type of Statement							1	8
	3		2		4	Unqualified						2	2	2
	2		3		3	Reviewed								2
			3		3	Compiled			1					1
					2	Tax Returns						1		21
	17		24		31	Other	2	3		1	35			
	4/1/21-		4/1/22-		4/1/23-									
	3/31/22		3/31/23		3/31/24		0-1MM	1-3MM	3-5MM	5-10MM	10-25MM		25MM & OVER	
	ALL		ALL		ALL		14 (4/1-9/30/23)			35 (10/1/23-3/31/24)				
	29		42		49	NUMBER OF STATEMENTS	2	4	1	3	5		34	
	%		%		%	ASSETS	%	%	%	%	%		%	
	9.2		9.3		14.6	Cash & Equivalents							7.5	
	13.8		15.3		13.5	Trade Receivables (net)							14.4	
	30.1		33.7		34.3	Inventory							37.5	
	1.7		2.1		3.0	All Other Current							1.9	
	54.9		60.4		65.4	Total Current							61.2	
	38.1		29.4		27.2	Fixed Assets (net)							31.0	
	1.1		2.9		3.0	Intangibles (net)							1.7	
	5.8		7.3		4.4	All Other Non-Current							6.0	
	100.0		100.0		100.0	Total							100.0	
						LIABILITIES								
	6.2		8.5		9.1	Notes Payable-Short Term							7.4	
	3.8		4.2		2.3	Cur. Mat.-L.T.D.							2.5	
	11.2		16.7		10.7	Trade Payables							11.7	
	.1		.1		.1	Income Taxes Payable							.1	
	11.1		7.1		10.0	All Other Current							7.9	
	32.5		36.5		32.2	Total Current							29.5	
	20.7		12.5		19.2	Long-Term Debt							17.5	
	.5		.7		.5	Deferred Taxes							.8	
	5.6		6.1		2.6	All Other Non-Current							3.3	
	40.8		44.2		45.5	Net Worth							48.9	
	100.0		100.0		100.0	Total Liabilties & Net Worth							100.0	
						INCOME DATA								
	100.0		100.0		100.0	Net Sales							100.0	
	25.0		23.9		26.7	Gross Profit							20.8	
	15.4		20.5		19.6	Operating Expenses							14.7	
	9.6		3.3		7.1	Operating Profit							6.0	
	.2		-.2		.7	All Other Expenses (net)							.9	
	9.4		3.5		6.3	Profit Before Taxes							5.1	
						RATIOS								
	3.4		2.7		3.9								3.4	
	1.8		1.6		2.4	Current							1.9	
	1.2		1.3		1.5								1.5	
	1.5		.9		1.6								1.1	
	.7		.6		.7	Quick							.6	
	.4		.3		.4								.4	
19	19.5	20	18.1	18	19.8							24	15.2	
28	13.0	28	13.0	27	13.5	Sales/Receivables						29	12.8	
35	10.4	41	8.9	33	11.1							33	10.9	
49	7.4	47	7.8	49	7.4							72	5.1	
74	4.9	96	3.8	83	4.4	Cost of Sales/Inventory						91	4.0	
111	3.3	130	2.8	140	2.6							135	2.7	
16	23.1	17	21.2	11	33.0							16	23.3	
30	12.3	35	10.4	24	15.5	Cost of Sales/Payables						24	15.0	
38	9.6	64	5.7	37	9.8							36	10.2	
	4.2		4.7		3.4								3.8	
	7.2		8.0		5.5	Sales/Working Capital							5.9	
	24.4		12.2		10.6								10.5	
	27.8		25.8		22.3								14.5	
(24)	6.9	(39)	5.3	(42)	6.6	EBIT/Interest						(31)	5.9	
	2.1		1.9		2.0								2.0	
			16.9		14.0	Net Profit + Depr., Dep.,							12.4	
		(16)	7.7	(18)	8.1	Amort./Cur. Mat. L/T/D						(16)	8.1	
					1.3								3.8	4.4
	.4		.3		.3								.4	
	.8		.8		.6	Fixed/Worth							.7	
	2.3		1.2		1.3								1.1	
	.4		.6		.5								.6	
	2.1		1.2		1.0	Debt/Worth							1.1	
	3.2		2.8		2.2								1.9	
	31.7		28.2		32.6	% Profit Before Taxes/Tangible							29.9	
(25)	22.0	(39)	14.3	(45)	16.7	Net Worth						(33)	15.8	
	9.3		3.7		8.8								8.4	
	18.0		13.8		17.4	% Profit Before Taxes/Total							15.3	
	10.6		5.7		8.7	Assets							6.7	
	5.4		1.5		3.6								3.5	
	8.7		13.4		13.4								10.1	
	4.9		6.4		6.8	Sales/Net Fixed Assets							6.1	
	3.0		3.4		4.6								3.8	
	2.3		2.4		2.3								2.2	
	1.8		1.6		1.9	Sales/Total Assets							1.6	
	1.0		1.2		1.3								1.3	
	1.3		1.0		1.2								1.4	
(24)	2.3	(35)	1.9	(38)	2.0	% Depr., Dep., Amort./Sales						(30)	2.0	
	4.0		3.5		3.1								3.3	
					.8	% Officers', Directors'								
				(10)	1.5	Owners' Comp/Sales								
					3.8									
	2623036M		4169682M		4833865M	Net Sales ($)	989M	8672M	4601M	25125M	86168M		4708310M	
	1632641M		2625840M		2840558M	Total Assets ($)	185M	5567M	1916M	8551M	41631M		2782708M	

M = $ thousand   MM = $ million
See Pages viii through xx for Explanation of Ratios and Data
© RMA 2024

MANUFACTURING—Fluid Milk Manufacturing NAICS 311511

Current Data Sorted by Assets

	0-500M	5 (4/1-9/30/23) 500M-2MM	2-10MM	1 1 1 3 15 (10/1/23-3/31/24) 10-50MM	1 1 3 4 50-100MM	3 6 100-250MM
	%	%	2 %	5 %	4 %	9 %

Comparative Historical Data

Type of Statement		
Unqualified	9	3
Reviewed	3	2
Compiled	1	
Tax Returns	4	2
Other	18	8
	4/1/19- 3/31/20 ALL	4/1/20- 3/31/21 ALL
NUMBER OF STATEMENTS	35	15
ASSETS	%	%
Cash & Equivalents	9.0	11.2
Trade Receivables (net)	23.0	22.7
Inventory	11.8	14.0
All Other Current	2.9	1.2
Total Current	46.6	49.2
Fixed Assets (net)	42.5	35.7
Intangibles (net)	5.6	4.2
All Other Non-Current	5.3	11.0
Total	100.0	100.0
LIABILITIES		
Notes Payable-Short Term	6.7	3.5
Cur. Mat.-L.T.D.	3.2	8.9
Trade Payables	15.8	11.2
Income Taxes Payable	.3	.0
All Other Current	8.6	17.5
Total Current	34.6	41.1
Long-Term Debt	16.3	23.1
Deferred Taxes	.3	.1
All Other Non-Current	7.4	4.8
Net Worth	41.4	30.9
Total Liabilties & Net Worth	100.0	100.0
INCOME DATA		
Net Sales	100.0	100.0
Gross Profit	25.3	20.1
Operating Expenses	23.8	19.7
Operating Profit	1.5	.4
All Other Expenses (net)	.5	-.2
Profit Before Taxes	1.0	.6
RATIOS		
Current	2.1	2.1
	1.3	1.1
	1.1	.7
Quick	1.3	1.2
	1.0	.8
	.5	.4

Data Not Available for columns 0-500M and 500M-2MM.

Ratio		Historical 1		Historical 2
Sales/Receivables	23	16.2	21	17.5
	28	12.9	24	15.2
	35	10.5	36	10.1
Cost of Sales/Inventory	9	40.2	6	59.3
	21	17.0	20	18.3
	37	9.9	33	11.1
Cost of Sales/Payables	12	31.6	8	43.8
	21	17.3	13	27.7
	36	10.0	32	11.5
Sales/Working Capital		11.6		16.9
		31.6		140.5
		82.3		-15.4
EBIT/Interest		11.6		10.8
	(32)	2.2	(14)	4.9
		-.1		-7.5
Net Profit + Depr., Dep., Amort./Cur. Mat. L/T/D		4.7		
	(13)	2.7		
		1.6		
Fixed/Worth		.7		.5
		1.3		1.2
		2.1		9.1
Debt/Worth		.6		1.3
		1.5		2.4
		6.0		10.6
% Profit Before Taxes/Tangible Net Worth		15.6		43.4
	(29)	7.6	(13)	20.3
		-9.5		-34.2
% Profit Before Taxes/Total Assets		5.8		10.3
		2.5		6.0
		-2.8		-6.4
Sales/Net Fixed Assets		10.1		34.5
		5.7		9.6
		3.8		3.9
Sales/Total Assets		3.5		5.5
		2.8		3.3
		1.9		1.6
% Depr., Dep., Amort./Sales		1.4		.3
	(29)	2.4	(13)	1.4
		4.5		2.1
% Officers', Directors' Owners' Comp/Sales				

	2-10MM	10-50MM	50-100MM	100-250MM		Historical 1	Historical 2
Net Sales ($)	18566M	927423M	1296287M	4020056M		6245927M	2686859M
Total Assets ($)	7459M	117438M	271796M	1802756M		2177147M	664125M

M = $ thousand   MM = $ million
See Pages viii through xx for Explanation of Ratios and Data

© RMA 2024

MANUFACTURING—Fluid Milk Manufacturing NAICS 311511

Comparative Historical Data / Current Data Sorted by Sales

						Type of Statement							
		3		7	4	Unqualified				1	1	4	
		4		1	2	Reviewed							
		1		1	1	Compiled					1		
		11		8	13	Tax Returns						13	
		4/1/21-		4/1/22-	4/1/23-	Other							
		3/31/22		3/31/23	3/31/24			5 (4/1-9/30/23)		15 (10/1/23-3/31/24)			
		ALL		ALL	ALL		0-1MM	1-3MM	3-5MM	5-10MM	10-25MM	25MM & OVER	
		19		17	20	NUMBER OF STATEMENTS				1	2	17	
		%		%	%	ASSETS	%	%	%	%	%	%	
		7.1		4.9	8.1	Cash & Equivalents						8.4	
		25.7		27.8	23.1	Trade Receivables (net)	D	D	D			24.5	
		14.6		12.4	10.5	Inventory	A	A	A			9.8	
		1.3		2.1	1.2	All Other Current	T	T	T			1.3	
		48.7		47.2	42.9	Total Current	A	A	A			43.9	
		39.5		35.5	30.9	Fixed Assets (net)						25.3	
		2.8		5.0	14.8	Intangibles (net)	N	N	N			17.4	
		9.0		12.3	11.5	All Other Non-Current	O	O	O			13.4	
		100.0		100.0	100.0	Total	T	T	T			100.0	
						LIABILITIES	A	A	A				
		3.6		7.4	3.4	Notes Payable-Short Term	V	V	V			3.7	
		2.9		3.3	2.2	Cur. Mat.-L.T.D.	A	A	A			1.6	
		19.0		13.9	14.6	Trade Payables	I	I	I			16.1	
		.0		.0	.0	Income Taxes Payable	L	L	L			.1	
		10.9		11.1	9.2	All Other Current	A	A	A			9.1	
		36.4		35.7	29.5	Total Current	B	B	B			30.5	
		22.8		22.6	21.9	Long-Term Debt	L	L	L			19.2	
		.1		.0	.0	Deferred Taxes	E	E	E			.0	
		2.4		6.3	5.1	All Other Non-Current						6.0	
		38.3		35.4	43.4	Net Worth						44.3	
		100.0		100.0	100.0	Total Liabilities & Net Worth						100.0	
						INCOME DATA							
		100.0		100.0	100.0	Net Sales						100.0	
		17.6		24.9	20.9	Gross Profit						20.2	
		16.0		23.2	17.4	Operating Expenses						17.7	
		1.6		1.7	3.5	Operating Profit						2.5	
		-.7		-.5	.6	All Other Expenses (net)						.4	
		2.3		2.2	2.9	Profit Before Taxes						2.1	
						RATIOS							
		1.8		1.8	2.2							2.2	
		1.3		1.1	1.4	Current						1.4	
		1.1		1.0	1.2							1.1	
		1.1		1.1	1.6							1.6	
		.9		.8	1.1	Quick						1.1	
		.9		.5	.8							.9	
	23	16.0	17	21.6	18	20.2						19	18.8
	26	14.2	30	12.0	24	15.0	Sales/Receivables					24	14.9
	27	13.4	35	10.5	31	11.8						30	12.1
	8	43.8	10	36.8	5	75.5						4	84.5
	26	14.3	21	17.2	10	35.7	Cost of Sales/Inventory					9	39.5
	32	11.5	54	6.7	31	11.9						14	25.5
	10	36.7	12	29.5	11	32.5						12	31.4
	25	14.8	19	18.9	18	19.9	Cost of Sales/Payables					19	19.0
	36	10.0	33	10.9	26	14.0						25	14.4
		14.8		18.6		12.0							12.3
		33.2		61.5		24.6	Sales/Working Capital						29.1
		85.8		298.7		89.7							125.9
		8.6		20.3		15.5							14.8
		4.5	(15)	4.5	(18)	5.4	EBIT/Interest					(15)	4.4
		1.4		-1.6		2.1							1.0
						Net Profit + Depr., Dep.,							
						Amort./Cur. Mat. L/T/D							
		.6		.7		.5							.5
		1.1		1.2		.7	Fixed/Worth						.6
		1.7		2.0		2.9							2.2
		1.0		1.4		.7							.7
		1.4		2.2		1.3	Debt/Worth						1.2
		3.3		4.6		4.5							5.1
		39.0		23.3		32.6							32.3
(17)		16.8		8.4	(17)	23.7	% Profit Before Taxes/Tangible Net Worth					(14)	21.3
		3.2		-13.3		15.3							12.8
		11.6		8.0		13.7							12.7
		4.8		1.4		6.5	% Profit Before Taxes/Total Assets						6.0
		1.2		-2.3		1.0							.4
		17.5		18.6		24.6							36.8
		8.5		11.5		10.1	Sales/Net Fixed Assets						11.7
		4.1		3.2		5.4							8.8
		5.8		4.8		4.8							5.1
		2.9		2.4		2.9	Sales/Total Assets						3.8
		2.0		1.3		1.4							1.4
		1.1		.8		.6							.4
(17)		2.0	(14)	1.8	(15)	1.9	% Depr., Dep., Amort./Sales					(12)	1.5
		2.9		3.1		3.0							2.0
						% Officers', Directors' Owners' Comp/Sales							
		5515930M		4680872M		6262332M	Net Sales ($)				6705M	26482M	6229145M	
		1534557M		1530076M		2199449M	Total Assets ($)				3226M	14599M	2181624M	

M = $ thousand   MM = $ million
See Pages viii through xx for Explanation of Ratios and Data

© RMA 2024

MANUFACTURING—Cheese Manufacturing NAICS 311513

Current Data Sorted by Assets | **Comparative Historical Data**

0-500M	6 (4/1-9/30/23) 500M-2MM	2-10MM	16 (10/1/23-3/31/24) 10-50MM	50-100MM	100-250MM	Type of Statement		27 4/1/19-3/31/20 ALL		19 4/1/20-3/31/21 ALL
			3			Unqualified		9		5
			2	3		Reviewed		5		5
			1		1	Compiled		5		5
			1			Tax Returns		2		2
		2	7	2		Other		6		2
		5	11	5	1	NUMBER OF STATEMENTS		49		31
%	%	%	%	%	%	ASSETS		%		%
D	D		5.3			Cash & Equivalents		8.3		11.0
A	A		16.5			Trade Receivables (net)		16.0		20.2
T	T		24.9			Inventory		19.7		22.0
A	A		2.6			All Other Current		2.5		3.6
			49.4			Total Current		46.6		56.8
N	N		40.9			Fixed Assets (net)		41.4		30.1
O	O		3.0			Intangibles (net)		9.3		11.5
T	T		6.7			All Other Non-Current		2.7		1.7
			100.0			Total		100.0		100.0
A	A					LIABILITIES				
V	V		3.8			Notes Payable-Short Term		8.6		8.3
A	A		2.5			Cur. Mat.-L.T.D.		3.1		2.5
I	I		10.7			Trade Payables		11.6		15.2
L	L		.0			Income Taxes Payable		.0		.2
A	A		5.4			All Other Current		5.4		6.5
B	B		22.3			Total Current		28.8		32.6
L	L		45.3			Long-Term Debt		22.2		16.5
E	E		.1			Deferred Taxes		.9		.9
			9.7			All Other Non-Current		4.1		2.1
			22.6			Net Worth		44.1		48.0
			100.0			Total Liabilities & Net Worth		100.0		100.0
						INCOME DATA				
			100.0			Net Sales		100.0		100.0
			18.0			Gross Profit		22.6		21.5
			13.0			Operating Expenses		19.3		16.2
			5.0			Operating Profit		3.3		5.3
			1.1			All Other Expenses (net)		1.3		.4
			3.9			Profit Before Taxes		1.9		4.8
						RATIOS				
			3.9					2.9		2.5
			2.6			Current		1.3		1.5
			2.1					1.0		1.2
			1.5					1.4		1.3
			1.1			Quick		.7		.8
			.6					.4		.5
		22	16.7				25	14.6	23	15.6
		26	14.3			Sales/Receivables	28	13.1	27	13.7
		28	13.0				36	10.0	42	8.6
		19	19.3				23	16.1	21	17.1
		59	6.2			Cost of Sales/Inventory	41	8.9	29	12.6
		104	3.5				83	4.4	58	6.3
		13	27.4				17	21.8	16	23.5
		20	18.5			Cost of Sales/Payables	26	13.8	24	15.5
		23	15.7				37	9.8	37	9.9
			4.6					3.9		8.5
			9.9			Sales/Working Capital		19.1		12.1
			11.9					-186.6		26.1
			97.2					10.8		21.8
			6.3			EBIT/Interest	(48)	2.7	(25)	6.3
			2.4					.3		1.4
						Net Profit + Depr., Dep.,		3.8		
						Amort./Cur. Mat. L/T/D	(11)	3.5		
								1.3		
			.6					.7		.6
			-71.8			Fixed/Worth		1.4		1.1
			-5.0					4.5		13.7
			.5					.8		.5
			-137.0			Debt/Worth		1.9		1.9
			-10.5					5.9		35.1
						% Profit Before Taxes/Tangible		18.9		53.1
						Net Worth	(42)	9.2	(25)	24.7
								-3.0		16.2
			16.7			% Profit Before Taxes/Total		9.6		22.9
			8.3			Assets		3.0		9.1
			5.1					-1.9		2.1
			14.8					9.0		15.2
			5.4			Sales/Net Fixed Assets		4.6		9.2
			2.8					2.7		5.2
			3.4					2.7		3.7
			2.3			Sales/Total Assets		1.8		2.6
			1.5					.9		1.2
								1.9		1.1
						% Depr., Dep., Amort./Sales	(39)	3.2	(20)	2.0
								7.1		3.6
						% Officers', Directors'		.7		
						Owners' Comp/Sales	(11)	1.0		
								3.3		
		100999M	1055397M	789835M	157502M	Net Sales ($)		5040723M		3880853M
		31877M	416244M	381792M	138094M	Total Assets ($)		2863164M		1923364M

M = $ thousand   MM = $ million
See Pages viii through xx for Explanation of Ratios and Data

© RMA 2024

MANUFACTURING—Cheese Manufacturing NAICS 311513

Comparative Historical Data | **Current Data Sorted by Sales**

				Type of Statement						
2		4	5	Unqualified					2	5
4		3	5	Reviewed						3
			2	Compiled						1
			1	Tax Returns					2	
20		17	11	Other						9
4/1/21-3/31/22 ALL		4/1/22-3/31/23 ALL	4/1/23-3/31/24 ALL		0-1MM	6 (4/1-9/30/23) 1-3MM	3-5MM	5-10MM	16 (10/1/23-3/31/24) 10-25MM	25MM & OVER
26		26	22	NUMBER OF STATEMENTS					4	18
%		%	%	ASSETS	%	%	%	%	%	%
6.3		7.3	7.7	Cash & Equivalents	D	D	D	D		6.0
18.4		20.8	15.9	Trade Receivables (net)	A	A	A	A		16.0
27.0		25.2	25.0	Inventory	T	T	T	T		24.7
1.9		1.6	2.0	All Other Current	A	A	A	A		1.8
53.6		54.8	50.5	Total Current						48.5
35.0		39.4	39.0	Fixed Assets (net)	N	N	N	N		41.3
8.7		1.5	5.1	Intangibles (net)	O	O	O	O		3.7
2.6		4.3	5.4	All Other Non-Current	T	T	T	T		6.5
100.0		100.0	100.0	Total						100.0
				LIABILITIES	A	A	A	A		
4.8		4.7	4.2	Notes Payable-Short Term	V	V	V	V		4.1
2.8		1.6	2.4	Cur. Mat.-L.T.D.	A	A	A	A		2.5
11.6		17.9	11.6	Trade Payables	I	I	I	I		9.9
.1		.2	.0	Income Taxes Payable	L	L	L	L		.0
3.9		7.7	7.2	All Other Current	A	A	A	A		5.2
23.3		32.2	25.4	Total Current	B	B	B	B		21.7
22.8		25.8	30.0	Long-Term Debt	L	L	L	L		34.5
.6		.0	.3	Deferred Taxes	E	E	E	E		.4
.8		2.4	9.0	All Other Non-Current						7.8
52.5		39.7	35.3	Net Worth						35.6
100.0		100.0	100.0	Total Liabilties & Net Worth						100.0
				INCOME DATA						
100.0		100.0	100.0	Net Sales						100.0
20.4		18.6	19.0	Gross Profit						17.3
14.8		14.8	13.7	Operating Expenses						12.3
5.6		3.8	5.3	Operating Profit						5.0
-.4		.4	1.0	All Other Expenses (net)						1.2
6.0		3.4	4.2	Profit Before Taxes						3.8
				RATIOS						
4.1		2.8	3.9							3.9
2.4		2.1	2.4	Current						2.5
1.6		1.5	1.4							1.7
1.8		1.3	1.6							1.6
1.0		.9	.9	Quick						1.0
.6		.6	.6							.6
23 15.9		21 17.3	21 17.0						22	16.5
29 12.6		28 13.2	25 14.8	Sales/Receivables					26	14.2
40 9.2		35 10.3	28 13.0						28	13.0
27 13.4		23 15.7	26 13.9						24	15.5
55 6.6		49 7.4	48 7.6	Cost of Sales/Inventory					51	7.2
87 4.2		76 4.8	87 4.2						99	3.7
16 23.4		19 19.2	15 25.1						14	25.9
23 15.9		30 12.1	19 19.0	Cost of Sales/Payables					19	19.0
31 11.7		40 9.2	30 12.0						24	14.9
3.9		5.2	4.5							4.5
7.9		8.7	9.9	Sales/Working Capital						8.7
13.5		24.3	19.3							12.1
22.9		16.7	57.5							63.9
(23) 11.2		(22) 4.6	(18) 5.5	EBIT/Interest					(17)	5.8
2.0		-.1	2.3							2.1
				Net Profit + Depr., Dep., Amort./Cur. Mat. L/T/D						
.3		.6	.6							.7
.9		.9	1.4	Fixed/Worth						1.4
1.7		3.7	-7.2							-7.2
.4		.5	.5							.5
1.0		1.2	4.6	Debt/Worth						1.9
2.7		8.4	-13.6							-13.6
32.2		30.3	45.0	% Profit Before Taxes/Tangible Net Worth						42.9
(21) 25.8		(21) 17.3	(14) 13.9						(11)	10.2
19.2		6.1	7.3							3.5
17.9		16.3	14.8							14.1
11.4		8.3	8.1	% Profit Before Taxes/Total Assets						6.6
3.5		-1.3	2.8							1.8
14.3		9.8	15.0							15.0
6.4		6.0	5.4	Sales/Net Fixed Assets						4.9
3.6		4.2	2.8							2.8
2.7		3.0	3.4							3.4
2.0		2.5	2.2	Sales/Total Assets						2.1
1.4		1.5	1.6							1.5
2.0		1.1	1.5							1.5
(22) 3.2		(23) 2.4	(19) 2.0	% Depr., Dep., Amort./Sales					(16)	2.3
3.6		3.5	3.4							3.4
				% Officers', Directors' Owners' Comp/Sales						
2759677M		2898976M	2103733M	Net Sales ($)					75059M	2028674M
1468642M		1169768M	968007M	Total Assets ($)					25436M	942571M

© RMA 2024

M = $ thousand   MM = $ million
See Pages viii through xx for Explanation of Ratios and Data

MANUFACTURING—Ice Cream and Frozen Dessert Manufacturing NAICS 311520

Current Data Sorted by Assets | Comparative Historical Data

0-500M	6 (4/1-9/30/23) 500M-2MM	2-10MM	19 (10/1/23-3/31/24) 10-50MM	50-100MM	100-250MM	Type of Statement	22 4/1/19-3/31/20 ALL	8 4/1/20-3/31/21 ALL
			1	1	3	Unqualified		
		1	1			Reviewed	1	1
		2				Compiled	7	3
		5	1			Tax Returns	1	2
1			7	2	1	Other	22	8
1	%	8	9	3	4	NUMBER OF STATEMENTS	31	14
%	%	%	%	%	%	ASSETS	%	%
						Cash & Equivalents	6.4	22.2
	D					Trade Receivables (net)	17.0	16.3
	A					Inventory	24.3	25.7
	T					All Other Current	1.7	.3
	A					Total Current	49.4	64.4
						Fixed Assets (net)	35.0	26.6
	N					Intangibles (net)	11.3	2.3
	O					All Other Non-Current	4.3	6.7
	T					Total	100.0	100.0
						LIABILITIES		
	A					Notes Payable-Short Term	9.9	4.6
	V					Cur. Mat.-L.T.D.	3.0	3.5
	A					Trade Payables	17.3	9.1
	I					Income Taxes Payable	.0	.2
	L					All Other Current	10.8	6.4
	A					Total Current	41.2	23.7
	B					Long-Term Debt	26.0	20.2
	L					Deferred Taxes	.1	.3
	E					All Other Non-Current	13.7	4.7
						Net Worth	19.0	51.1
						Total Liabilities & Net Worth	100.0	100.0
						INCOME DATA		
						Net Sales	100.0	100.0
						Gross Profit	34.9	37.3
						Operating Expenses	30.7	28.7
						Operating Profit	4.2	8.6
						All Other Expenses (net)	2.4	-.3
						Profit Before Taxes	1.8	8.9
						RATIOS		
						Current	2.0 / 1.4 / .9	6.9 / 2.7 / 1.7
						Quick	1.2 / .6 / .3	3.6 / 1.6 / 1.0
						Sales/Receivables	17 21.8 / 21 17.0 / 32 11.5	12 31.2 / 19 19.1 / 38 9.5
						Cost of Sales/Inventory	33 11.1 / 51 7.1 / 70 5.2	23 15.9 / 52 7.0 / 73 5.0
						Cost of Sales/Payables	16 22.2 / 26 14.0 / 42 8.7	7 52.7 / 17 22.0 / 29 12.8
						Sales/Working Capital	8.8 / 21.6 / -70.9	4.7 / 6.7 / 13.3
						EBIT/Interest	12.4 / (28) 3.8 / .6	52.3 / (12) 9.8 / 3.6
						Net Profit + Depr., Dep., Amort./Cur. Mat. L/T/D	7.0 / (11) 4.7 / 2.2	
						Fixed/Worth	.7 / 1.6 / -10.7	.3 / .5 / 1.2
						Debt/Worth	1.1 / 3.3 / -5.1	.5 / 1.1 / 2.1
						% Profit Before Taxes/Tangible Net Worth	74.1 / (22) 28.1 / .0	64.2 / 30.9 / 13.4
						% Profit Before Taxes/Total Assets	18.0 / 5.6 / -.9	33.6 / 15.4 / 7.0
						Sales/Net Fixed Assets	17.5 / 6.3 / 4.1	22.8 / 10.7 / 6.9
						Sales/Total Assets	3.8 / 2.5 / 1.5	3.1 / 2.7 / 2.0
						% Depr., Dep., Amort./Sales	1.5 / (24) 3.1 / 5.0	1.5 / (10) 2.3 / 3.5
						% Officers', Directors' Owners' Comp/Sales		
20M		89953M	468190M	366694M	1219838M	Net Sales ($)	1586930M	934783M
22M		35464M	243804M	165547M	763536M	Total Assets ($)	900066M	392100M

M = $ thousand   MM = $ million
See Pages viii through xx for Explanation of Ratios and Data

© RMA 2024

MANUFACTURING—Ice Cream and Frozen Dessert Manufacturing NAICS 311520

Comparative Historical Data | Current Data Sorted by Sales

			Type of Statement						
1	1	3	Unqualified						3
1	2	2	Reviewed						2
1	1	1	Compiled					1	
1	4	3	Tax Returns				1		2
8	12	16	Other	1	6 (4/1-9/30/23)	1	19 (10/1/23-3/31/24)	2	10
4/1/21-3/31/22 ALL	4/1/22-3/31/23 ALL	4/1/23-3/31/24 ALL		0-1MM	1-3MM	3-5MM	5-10MM	10-25MM	25MM & OVER
12	20	25	NUMBER OF STATEMENTS	1	1	1	2	3	17
%	%	%	ASSETS	%	%	%	%	%	%
11.0	12.1	13.8	Cash & Equivalents						15.7
18.1	15.1	16.9	Trade Receivables (net)						15.5
16.7	23.2	20.7	Inventory						23.1
.4	2.1	1.1	All Other Current						.8
46.2	52.5	52.5	Total Current						55.1
42.6	31.2	34.4	Fixed Assets (net)						32.1
7.4	6.6	4.8	Intangibles (net)						6.8
3.7	9.6	8.4	All Other Non-Current						6.0
100.0	100.0	100.0	Total						100.0
			LIABILITIES						
5.4	6.5	10.0	Notes Payable-Short Term						3.1
2.6	5.0	1.7	Cur. Mat.-L.T.D.						1.8
10.3	11.8	12.8	Trade Payables						11.8
.2	.1	.2	Income Taxes Payable						.3
6.5	18.3	20.0	All Other Current						8.4
24.9	41.7	44.6	Total Current						25.3
39.1	23.0	26.4	Long-Term Debt						27.1
.2	.6	.5	Deferred Taxes						.8
4.7	10.1	2.0	All Other Non-Current						3.0
31.1	24.6	26.2	Net Worth						43.8
100.0	100.0	100.0	Total Liabilities & Net Worth						100.0
			INCOME DATA						
100.0	100.0	100.0	Net Sales						100.0
26.7	39.3	37.3	Gross Profit						31.8
23.2	33.8	33.5	Operating Expenses						28.6
3.5	5.5	3.8	Operating Profit						3.2
.1	.7	.6	All Other Expenses (net)						1.0
3.4	4.8	3.2	Profit Before Taxes						2.2
			RATIOS						
3.1	3.1	3.8							3.1
1.5	1.7	2.2	Current						2.1
1.1	.8	1.6							1.6
1.7	1.5	2.7							2.1
.9	.9	1.4	Quick						1.2
.5	.1	.7							.7
23 16.0	8 43.3	18 19.9						19	19.1
28 13.0	24 15.3	29 12.7	Sales/Receivables					29	12.5
38 9.7	36 10.1	34 10.8						36	10.2
42 8.7	23 15.6	37 9.8						41	8.9
54 6.8	60 6.1	56 6.5	Cost of Sales/Inventory					59	6.2
66 5.5	107 3.4	83 4.4						73	5.0
19 19.1	0 UND	15 23.7						17	22.0
26 14.2	14 25.3	22 16.6	Cost of Sales/Payables					22	16.6
48 7.6	29 12.8	35 10.3						35	10.3
7.6	6.0	5.5							4.8
11.9	10.6	6.7	Sales/Working Capital						6.1
111.0	-46.5	12.3							12.3
15.0	57.1	43.0							40.0
(10) 9.3	(16) 4.0	(24) 7.9	EBIT/Interest						7.8
4.0	-2.1	1.5							2.7
		17.9	Net Profit + Depr., Dep.,						18.7
	(11) 9.5	Amort./Cur. Mat. L/T/D					(10)	13.5
		3.9							3.9
.4	.2	.3							.3
3.9	.7	.6	Fixed/Worth						.6
6.0	3.3	1.9							3.1
.8	1.0	.3							.5
5.0	1.7	.8	Debt/Worth						.9
6.8	4.0	5.0							5.0
40.0	51.3	30.4	% Profit Before Taxes/Tangible						30.3
(10) 28.4	(16) 17.6	(21) 20.9	Net Worth					(14)	19.8
15.2	2.0	9.3							10.2
17.4	14.8	16.0	% Profit Before Taxes/Total						14.8
7.2	4.6	8.3	Assets						8.6
4.1	-3.7	2.0							3.0
11.6	31.6	19.6							11.7
8.6	10.2	6.6	Sales/Net Fixed Assets						6.6
1.0	4.2	3.3							3.3
3.3	3.5	2.9							2.6
1.6	2.1	2.4	Sales/Total Assets						2.4
.7	1.3	1.1							1.4
	1.1	.7							.7
	(10) 2.0	(19) 1.6	% Depr., Dep., Amort./Sales					(14)	1.7
	2.9	4.7							3.1
			% Officers', Directors' Owners' Comp/Sales						
861581M	641367M	2144695M	Net Sales ($)	20M	2211M	4394M	14702M	43121M	2080247M
867826M	460562M	1208373M	Total Assets ($)	22M	5724M	7649M	4459M	9159M	1181360M

M = $ thousand   MM = $ million
See Pages viii through xx for Explanation of Ratios and Data

© RMA 2024

MANUFACTURING—Animal (except Poultry) Slaughtering NAICS 311611

Current Data Sorted by Assets

					1	1
			1		1	
			2	1	5	2	7
0-500M	3 (4/1-9/30/23) 500M-2MM	2-10MM	18 (10/1/23-3/31/24) 10-50MM	50-100MM	100-250MM	
%	%	3 %	8 %	2 %	8 %	

Type of Statement row (under Comparative Historical):
- Unqualified: 1
- Reviewed: 1
- Compiled: 1
- Tax Returns: 2, 1, 5, 2
- Other: 18, 7

DATA NOT AVAILABLE (for 0-500M and 500M-2MM columns)

Comparative Historical Data

Type of Statement	4/1/19-3/31/20 ALL	4/1/20-3/31/21 ALL
Unqualified	3	3
Reviewed	2	
Compiled	3	2
Tax Returns	7	2
Other	20	9
NUMBER OF STATEMENTS	35	16
	%	%
ASSETS		
Cash & Equivalents	10.1	14.9
Trade Receivables (net)	24.9	13.6
Inventory	15.5	18.4
All Other Current	1.7	2.1
Total Current	52.2	49.0
Fixed Assets (net)	40.0	42.7
Intangibles (net)	3.7	6.0
All Other Non-Current	4.0	2.3
Total	100.0	100.0
LIABILITIES		
Notes Payable-Short Term	5.9	5.5
Cur. Mat.-L.T.D.	6.3	4.1
Trade Payables	11.6	6.7
Income Taxes Payable	.1	.1
All Other Current	5.1	6.3
Total Current	28.8	22.8
Long-Term Debt	24.4	23.6
Deferred Taxes	.5	.7
All Other Non-Current	1.7	4.0
Net Worth	44.5	48.9
Total Liabilities & Net Worth	100.0	100.0
INCOME DATA		
Net Sales	100.0	100.0
Gross Profit	23.8	25.9
Operating Expenses	19.6	21.3
Operating Profit	4.2	4.6
All Other Expenses (net)	1.1	-.1
Profit Before Taxes	3.1	4.7
RATIOS		
Current	3.7	4.2
	1.8	2.5
	1.0	1.0
Quick	2.2	3.3
	1.1	1.1
	.5	.5
Sales/Receivables	12 29.8	11 33.5
	16 22.8	16 23.4
	22 16.7	21 17.7
Cost of Sales/Inventory	6 60.2	11 32.6
	15 23.7	24 15.4
	23 15.9	38 9.5
Cost of Sales/Payables	3 145.3	3 105.8
	8 47.7	12 29.8
	18 20.7	16 22.6
Sales/Working Capital	13.1	7.0
	26.1	10.2
	999.8	NM
EBIT/Interest	10.8	20.4
	(31) 3.2	(15) 6.9
	2.2	1.2
Net Profit + Depr., Dep., Amort./Cur. Mat. L/T/D		
Fixed/Worth	.4	.6
	1.1	.9
	2.8	2.2
Debt/Worth	.6	.4
	1.2	1.4
	4.6	2.6
% Profit Before Taxes/Tangible Net Worth	26.2	39.1
	(32) 17.4	(15) 12.8
	7.3	3.7
% Profit Before Taxes/Total Assets	11.1	14.7
	6.2	7.8
	3.1	.5
Sales/Net Fixed Assets	37.1	13.3
	11.4	7.2
	5.6	4.8
Sales/Total Assets	7.9	3.4
	4.3	2.5
	2.4	2.2
% Depr., Dep., Amort./Sales	.7	.6
	(26) 2.0	(13) 2.4
	3.6	4.5
% Officers', Directors' Owners' Comp/Sales		
Net Sales ($)	6532703M	2770554M
Total Assets ($)	1529104M	833341M

Current Data totals (bottom row):
2-10MM	10-50MM	50-100MM	100-250MM
24588M	566674M	423769M	2421837M
9792M	158004M	129550M	1084621M

M = $ thousand   MM = $ million
See Pages viii through xx for Explanation of Ratios and Data

© RMA 2024

MANUFACTURING—Animal (except Poultry) Slaughtering NAICS 311611

Comparative Historical Data | Current Data Sorted by Sales

				Type of Statement						
4	4	2		Unqualified						2
	1	1		Reviewed						1
3	4			Compiled						
	3	2		Tax Returns					1	1
10	12	16		Other			1	1		14
4/1/21-3/31/22 ALL	4/1/22-3/31/23 ALL	4/1/23-3/31/24 ALL			0-1MM	3 (4/1-9/30/23) 1-3MM	3-5MM	5-10MM	18 (10/1/23-3/31/24) 10-25MM	25MM & OVER
17	24	21	NUMBER OF STATEMENTS				1	1	1	18
%	%	%	ASSETS	%	%	%	%	%	%	%
11.5	9.1	14.0	Cash & Equivalents	D	D					11.6
20.6	14.9	16.8	Trade Receivables (net)	A	A					14.3
13.9	16.8	17.6	Inventory	T	T					19.4
2.0	1.7	3.1	All Other Current	A	A					3.6
48.0	42.5	51.5	Total Current							48.9
35.5	41.7	36.6	Fixed Assets (net)	N	N					38.1
8.2	12.9	4.6	Intangibles (net)	O	O					5.4
8.4	2.8	7.2	All Other Non-Current	T	T					7.6
100.0	100.0	100.0	Total							100.0
			LIABILITIES	A	A					
6.1	9.6	6.6	Notes Payable-Short Term	V	V					7.7
3.3	1.8	1.6	Cur. Mat.-L.T.D.	A	A					1.9
7.3	6.7	7.7	Trade Payables	I	I					8.6
.1	.1	.0	Income Taxes Payable	L	L					.0
6.3	7.3	7.9	All Other Current	A	A					6.4
23.0	25.5	23.8	Total Current	B	B					24.5
27.8	20.9	15.5	Long-Term Debt	L	L					17.3
.6	.4	.3	Deferred Taxes	E	E					.3
4.2	2.5	7.0	All Other Non-Current							8.2
44.4	50.8	53.4	Net Worth							49.7
100.0	100.0	100.0	Total Liabilities & Net Worth							100.0
			INCOME DATA							
100.0	100.0	100.0	Net Sales							100.0
20.5	29.9	22.5	Gross Profit							19.2
15.2	26.0	19.9	Operating Expenses							17.2
5.3	3.9	2.6	Operating Profit							2.0
.1	.0	-.1	All Other Expenses (net)							.7
5.1	3.9	2.7	Profit Before Taxes							1.4
			RATIOS							
4.9	3.5	4.1								3.7
1.9	1.6	1.8	Current							1.6
1.4	1.1	1.2								1.1
4.1	2.1	2.8								2.5
.9	.8	.9	Quick							.8
.6	.6	.3								.3

11	34.6	4	85.7	14	26.9						13	28.7
18	20.0	11	34.5	18	20.2	Sales/Receivables					18	20.4
23	15.6	24	14.9	27	13.3						23	16.2
7	49.0	6	58.9	6	56.3						8	47.3
10	37.6	24	15.3	27	13.3	Cost of Sales/Inventory					31	11.6
26	14.0	43	8.5	49	7.4						56	6.5
3	107.6	3	135.6	6	60.6						6	58.9
7	49.6	9	38.5	12	31.1	Cost of Sales/Payables					12	30.1
17	21.9	17	21.7	19	19.7						18	20.4
	8.4		9.0		6.3							6.6
	18.7		21.0		12.2	Sales/Working Capital						16.2
	32.4		154.6		27.0							32.5
	40.9		25.8		20.0							15.9
(16)	13.7	(20)	7.9	(20)	5.0	EBIT/Interest						4.5
	2.8		1.2		-.3							-1.2
						Net Profit + Depr., Dep., Amort./Cur. Mat. L/T/D						
	.4		.5		.4							.5
	1.0		1.1		.9	Fixed/Worth						1.0
	2.0		1.6		1.5							1.9
	.6		.5		.3							.4
	1.2		.9		1.0	Debt/Worth						1.2
	2.6		3.6		2.5							3.8
	77.6		47.7		24.4							23.0
(15)	34.9	(21)	18.3	(18)	14.8	% Profit Before Taxes/Tangible Net Worth					(15)	14.5
	15.2		.5		-8.4							-8.6
	27.7		25.1		14.8							13.7
	9.4		7.6		10.1	% Profit Before Taxes/Total Assets						7.9
	3.1		.4		-4.1							-5.3
	34.7		18.1		16.8							15.6
	8.9		7.9		11.4	Sales/Net Fixed Assets						10.3
	3.9		3.5		3.7							3.8
	6.0		3.6		4.4							4.6
	2.9		2.8		3.0	Sales/Total Assets						2.9
	2.3		1.9		1.5							1.5
	.7		.8		.6							.6
(11)	2.1	(16)	1.8	(14)	2.4	% Depr., Dep., Amort./Sales					(12)	2.4
	4.2		4.6		3.5							2.9
						% Officers', Directors' Owners' Comp/Sales						
	2298887M		4101434M		3436868M	Net Sales ($)		4783M	9745M	10060M		3412280M
	715293M		1465684M		1381967M	Total Assets ($)		5085M	2342M	2365M		1372175M

© RMA 2024 M = $ thousand MM = $ million
See Pages viii through xx for Explanation of Ratios and Data

MANUFACTURING—Meat Processed from Carcasses NAICS 311612

Current Data Sorted by Assets

						Type of Statement		
			3	5	4	Unqualified		
			6			Reviewed		
	1	2	5			Compiled		
1	2	7				Tax Returns		
2	1	6	22	8	9	Other		
0-500M	18 (4/1-9/30/23) 500M-2MM	2-10MM	66 (10/1/23-3/31/24) 10-50MM	50-100MM	100-250MM			
3	4	15	36	13	13	NUMBER OF STATEMENTS		
%	%	%	%	%	%	ASSETS		
		19.3	11.6	7.9	2.8	Cash & Equivalents		
		21.2	23.0	17.3	16.4	Trade Receivables (net)		
		25.1	23.7	29.7	20.2	Inventory		
		.6	1.2	1.5	4.9	All Other Current		
		66.1	59.5	56.4	44.3	Total Current		
		25.9	28.4	30.2	32.6	Fixed Assets (net)		
		2.5	4.0	9.1	18.1	Intangibles (net)		
		5.4	8.1	4.3	5.0	All Other Non-Current		
		100.0	100.0	100.0	100.0	Total		
						LIABILITIES		
		6.0	10.3	11.6	7.4	Notes Payable-Short Term		
		1.8	2.3	2.8	2.8	Cur. Mat.-L.T.D.		
		12.9	12.3	8.5	9.9	Trade Payables		
		.0	.0	.3	.0	Income Taxes Payable		
		4.0	7.1	5.9	5.1	All Other Current		
		24.7	32.1	29.1	25.3	Total Current		
		23.8	14.2	14.8	16.4	Long-Term Debt		
		.5	.0	.4	.0	Deferred Taxes		
		5.4	6.9	8.5	2.9	All Other Non-Current		
		45.6	46.8	47.1	55.4	Net Worth		
		100.0	100.0	100.0	100.0	Total Liabilities & Net Worth		
						INCOME DATA		
		100.0	100.0	100.0	100.0	Net Sales		
		24.8	15.8	21.4	17.2	Gross Profit		
		19.8	11.2	15.5	12.6	Operating Expenses		
		5.0	4.6	5.9	4.6	Operating Profit		
		.1	.6	.0	.8	All Other Expenses (net)		
		4.8	4.0	5.9	3.8	Profit Before Taxes		
						RATIOS		
		5.6	4.4	4.0	2.2			
		2.6	2.0	2.2	1.7	Current		
		2.0	1.1	1.3	1.0			
		5.1	2.0	1.3	1.2			
		1.6	1.0	.8	.7	Quick		
		.5	.6	.5	.5			
	12	29.3	16 22.9	18 19.8	14 26.5			
	23	15.9	18 20.6	25 14.6	23 15.7	Sales/Receivables		
	32	11.4	24 14.9	34 10.6	27 13.3			
	12	30.8	14 25.6	30 12.3	18 20.5			
	26	13.9	20 18.2	41 8.8	31 11.8	Cost of Sales/Inventory		
	81	4.5	33 11.1	111 3.3	42 8.7			
	5	68.7	8 47.0	7 54.0	12 29.8			
	12	29.5	12 30.9	12 29.9	17 22.0	Cost of Sales/Payables		
	22	16.3	15 23.8	25 14.5	19 19.7			
		6.2	6.4	5.0	10.5			
		8.3	17.2	11.0	15.7	Sales/Working Capital		
		15.8	78.3	18.3	-720.8			
		23.3	36.4	13.1	19.7			
	(12)	7.8	(35) 9.3	(12) 4.9	5.2	EBIT/Interest		
		3.0	1.7	1.8	.5			
			18.3			Net Profit + Depr., Dep.,		
		(10)	3.9			Amort./Cur. Mat. L/T/D		
			-2.2					
		.2	.2	.3	.4			
		1.2	.6	.6	1.1	Fixed/Worth		
		1.5	1.6	2.0	2.2			
		.6	.6	.5	.6			
		2.0	1.3	1.0	1.0	Debt/Worth		
		2.9	2.9	5.5	4.5			
		67.8	55.7	54.3	45.2			
		37.3	(33) 31.2	(11) 26.4	(11) 33.8	% Profit Before Taxes/Tangible Net Worth		
		7.6	5.3	1.0	11.9			
		24.0	23.6	17.8	21.9			
		10.1	13.6	13.4	7.3	% Profit Before Taxes/Total Assets		
		2.4	1.6	1.8	-1.4			
		81.6	31.3	20.5	19.7			
		8.7	14.5	10.4	9.1	Sales/Net Fixed Assets		
		5.7	8.1	5.4	3.7			
		4.0	5.6	3.0	4.5			
		3.0	4.1	2.4	2.6	Sales/Total Assets		
		2.2	2.5	1.3	1.2			
		.9	.6	.7	.5			
	(10)	2.3	(31) .9	1.3	(10) 1.2	% Depr., Dep., Amort./Sales		
		3.6	1.8	2.9	6.9			
			.4			% Officers', Directors' Owners' Comp/Sales		
		(11)	1.0					
			1.5					
1926M	9901M	375876M	4219258M	1993362M	5422169M	Net Sales ($)		
967M	4882M	80062M	981235M	825778M	1921218M	Total Assets ($)		

Comparative Historical Data

	14		10	Unqualified
	15		10	Reviewed
	8		3	Compiled
	11		2	Tax Returns
	47		31	Other
	4/1/19-3/31/20 ALL		4/1/20-3/31/21 ALL	
	95		56	NUMBER OF STATEMENTS
	%		%	ASSETS
	9.0		16.3	Cash & Equivalents
	21.5		18.0	Trade Receivables (net)
	20.4		18.7	Inventory
	1.3		2.9	All Other Current
	52.3		56.0	Total Current
	35.2		35.4	Fixed Assets (net)
	7.3		6.3	Intangibles (net)
	5.2		2.4	All Other Non-Current
	100.0		100.0	Total
				LIABILITIES
	9.7		4.5	Notes Payable-Short Term
	3.0		3.5	Cur. Mat.-L.T.D.
	11.8		9.6	Trade Payables
	.3		.1	Income Taxes Payable
	9.6		6.8	All Other Current
	34.3		24.5	Total Current
	19.7		22.4	Long-Term Debt
	.3		.3	Deferred Taxes
	7.3		4.9	All Other Non-Current
	38.5		47.9	Net Worth
	100.0		100.0	Total Liabilities & Net Worth
				INCOME DATA
	100.0		100.0	Net Sales
	20.6		23.5	Gross Profit
	15.1		17.6	Operating Expenses
	5.5		5.9	Operating Profit
	.7		.1	All Other Expenses (net)
	4.8		5.7	Profit Before Taxes
				RATIOS
	3.2		3.4	
	1.7		2.2	Current
	1.2		1.6	
	1.8		2.4	
	1.0		1.3	Quick
	.6		.7	
17	21.7	16	22.8	
22	16.5	20	18.4	Sales/Receivables
29	12.7	27	13.5	
17	21.5	16	22.9	
25	14.6	24	15.0	Cost of Sales/Inventory
41	8.9	36	10.2	
8	46.3	6	58.1	
12	29.7	13	28.5	Cost of Sales/Payables
22	16.6	19	18.8	
	8.7		6.4	
	18.2		9.8	Sales/Working Capital
	56.4		23.0	
	18.9		51.7	
(86)	9.3	(47)	20.6	EBIT/Interest
	3.3		6.9	
	5.8		7.9	Net Profit + Depr., Dep., Amort./Cur. Mat. L/T/D
(21)	4.1	(17)	4.7	
	1.6		2.6	
	.4		.4	
	.8		.7	Fixed/Worth
	1.6		1.7	
	.6		.4	
	1.3		1.1	Debt/Worth
	5.1		2.2	
	45.0		78.1	
(85)	28.0	(52)	41.1	% Profit Before Taxes/Tangible Net Worth
	12.5		22.5	
	20.2		29.5	
	12.3		19.2	% Profit Before Taxes/Total Assets
	5.6		10.0	
	22.4		20.4	
	9.5		9.1	Sales/Net Fixed Assets
	4.9		4.8	
	4.9		4.3	
	2.9		2.9	Sales/Total Assets
	2.0		2.3	
	.8		.8	
(78)	1.6	(47)	1.4	% Depr., Dep., Amort./Sales
	2.8		2.2	
	.4		.7	% Officers', Directors' Owners' Comp/Sales
(28)	1.2	(16)	1.3	
	2.0		3.0	
	11378234M		6435719M	Net Sales ($)
	3971092M		2256776M	Total Assets ($)

M = $ thousand   MM = $ million
See Pages viii through xx for Explanation of Ratios and Data

© RMA 2024

MANUFACTURING—Meat Processed from Carcasses NAICS 311612

Comparative Historical Data | Current Data Sorted by Sales

				Type of Statement						
7	12	12		Unqualified						12
8	12	6		Reviewed						6
3	3	8		Compiled	1			1		6
1	4	10		Tax Returns	2	1		2	4	1
33	40	48		Other	2			1	6	39
4/1/21-3/31/22 ALL	4/1/22-3/31/23 ALL	4/1/23-3/31/24 ALL			0-1MM	1-3MM	18 (4/1-9/30/23) 3-5MM	5-10MM	66 (10/1/23-3/31/24) 10-25MM	25MM & OVER
52	71	84		NUMBER OF STATEMENTS	5	1		4	10	64
%	%	%		ASSETS	%	%	%	%	%	%
11.9	12.8	12.3		Cash & Equivalents					13.5	10.1
21.6	21.6	19.5		Trade Receivables (net)					16.4	21.2
24.3	23.0	23.1		Inventory					32.7	23.9
2.0	2.0	2.0		All Other Current			DATA		.9	1.9
59.8	59.3	56.8		Total Current					63.5	57.2
30.6	31.0	29.5		Fixed Assets (net)			NOT		24.7	29.5
5.2	5.7	6.9		Intangibles (net)					9.2	6.9
4.4	4.0	6.8		All Other Non-Current			AVAILABLE		2.6	6.4
100.0	100.0	100.0		Total					100.0	100.0
				LIABILITIES						
8.4	7.3	9.2		Notes Payable-Short Term					8.4	9.8
2.4	2.5	2.3		Cur. Mat.-L.T.D.					1.8	2.4
11.1	11.2	10.8		Trade Payables					11.0	11.5
.0	.1	.1		Income Taxes Payable					.1	.1
6.4	6.7	5.8		All Other Current					2.1	6.6
28.3	27.8	28.2		Total Current					23.3	30.4
15.6	20.0	18.5		Long-Term Debt					32.3	14.2
.3	.2	.1		Deferred Taxes					.7	.1
3.0	4.7	5.7		All Other Non-Current					7.4	6.2
52.8	47.3	47.5		Net Worth					36.3	49.1
100.0	100.0	100.0		Total Liabilities & Net Worth					100.0	100.0
				INCOME DATA						
100.0	100.0	100.0		Net Sales					100.0	100.0
17.8	19.8	22.3		Gross Profit					22.5	16.7
13.9	16.0	17.8		Operating Expenses					18.5	11.9
3.9	3.7	4.5		Operating Profit					4.0	4.8
-.7	.4	.1		All Other Expenses (net)					1.3	.3
4.6	3.3	4.4		Profit Before Taxes					2.8	4.4
				RATIOS						
5.1	4.0	3.7		Current					9.4	3.6
2.3	2.1	2.1							2.4	2.0
1.3	1.3	1.2							1.2	1.2
3.2	2.9	2.2		Quick					6.5	1.6
1.2	1.0	1.0							.7	.9
.6	.6	.6							.4	.6
17 20.9	14 27.0	15 24.9		Sales/Receivables					15 25.0	16 22.9
22 16.3	19 19.6	19 19.1							24 15.4	19 19.1
28 13.2	27 13.7	28 12.9							29 12.4	27 13.5
20 18.1	14 25.4	16 23.4		Cost of Sales/Inventory					20 18.4	16 23.4
26 13.9	25 14.6	27 13.7							36 10.1	26 13.8
48 7.6	43 8.5	45 8.1							87 4.2	43 8.4
8 46.3	8 45.1	8 47.8		Cost of Sales/Payables					2 195.6	8 46.0
12 29.8	12 31.6	12 29.4							16 22.6	12 29.5
18 20.6	19 19.6	19 19.2							28 13.2	17 22.0
6.6	6.8	5.9		Sales/Working Capital					5.6	6.4
9.7	10.9	11.6							7.8	14.0
26.2	33.6	40.9							NM	49.8
45.0	38.6	18.4		EBIT/Interest						18.5
(42) 19.1	(62) 12.4	(78) 7.8							(61) 9.2
5.6	1.9	1.7								1.7
13.1	9.4	5.7		Net Profit + Depr., Dep., Amort./Cur. Mat. L/T/D						4.9
(12) 6.4	(13) 5.6	(20) 3.9							(19) 3.7
1.7	4.0	1.6								1.6
.3	.2	.2		Fixed/Worth					.3	.3
.6	.6	.7							1.5	.6
1.1	1.2	1.8							2.0	1.8
.5	.4	.6		Debt/Worth					1.5	.6
1.0	1.1	1.3							2.7	1.1
1.8	3.2	3.1							16.7	3.0
70.1	50.2	53.6		% Profit Before Taxes/Tangible Net Worth						53.5
(51) 37.1	(64) 31.5	(75) 31.2							(58) 31.3
14.2	10.1	5.9								5.6
26.4	22.2	19.7		% Profit Before Taxes/Total Assets					16.3	22.0
17.2	12.7	12.3							8.4	13.4
5.0	2.7	1.4							1.8	1.6
26.4	29.5	31.3		Sales/Net Fixed Assets					76.6	26.5
12.5	14.7	12.0							17.4	12.1
5.7	5.3	5.7							5.0	6.6
4.5	5.3	4.8		Sales/Total Assets					3.5	5.2
3.3	3.2	2.9							2.8	3.2
2.3	2.4	2.0							2.1	2.1
.6	.5	.7		% Depr., Dep., Amort./Sales						.6
(43) 1.2	(59) 1.0	(68) 1.2							(54) 1.1
2.4	2.5	2.8								1.9
.4	.5	.5		% Officers', Directors' Owners' Comp/Sales						.4
(15) .9	(20) 1.1	(22) 1.4							(12) 1.1
1.6	3.9	3.0								1.5
9215620M	12252797M	12022492M		Net Sales ($)	3715M	2432M		25594M	153615M	11837136M
2748363M	3540075M	3814142M		Total Assets ($)	2946M	1035M		13702M	76315M	3720144M

M = $ thousand   MM = $ million
See Pages viii through xx for Explanation of Ratios and Data

© RMA 2024

MANUFACTURING—Seafood Product Preparation and Packaging NAICS 311710

Current Data Sorted by Assets | Comparative Historical Data

							Type of Statement		
			1		2		Unqualified	10	3
		3	2		1		Reviewed	5	3
	1	1					Compiled	1	3
		3	11	1	3		Tax Returns	5	1
1	13 (4/1-9/30/23)		18 (10/1/23-3/31/24)				Other	32	12
0-500M	500M-2MM	2-10MM	10-50MM	50-100MM	100-250MM			4/1/19-3/31/20 ALL	4/1/20-3/31/21 ALL
1	1	7	14	2	6		NUMBER OF STATEMENTS	53	22
%	%	%	%	%	%		ASSETS	%	%
			5.5				Cash & Equivalents	4.8	12.1
			20.5				Trade Receivables (net)	19.3	22.4
			28.0				Inventory	32.5	24.6
			3.6				All Other Current	2.6	5.2
			57.6				Total Current	59.2	64.3
			29.8				Fixed Assets (net)	25.8	21.9
			6.2				Intangibles (net)	9.4	7.7
			6.4				All Other Non-Current	5.6	6.1
			100.0				Total	100.0	100.0
							LIABILITIES		
			11.6				Notes Payable-Short Term	19.0	7.2
			2.8				Cur. Mat.-L.T.D.	1.9	1.7
			11.8				Trade Payables	9.3	11.4
			.0				Income Taxes Payable	.1	.1
			10.4				All Other Current	9.4	11.5
			36.7				Total Current	39.7	31.9
			16.2				Long-Term Debt	15.5	15.3
			.0				Deferred Taxes	.7	.3
			4.0				All Other Non-Current	4.3	4.1
			43.1				Net Worth	39.9	48.4
			100.0				Total Liabilities & Net Worth	100.0	100.0
							INCOME DATA		
			100.0				Net Sales	100.0	100.0
			14.6				Gross Profit	16.5	18.0
			13.3				Operating Expenses	15.3	13.2
			1.2				Operating Profit	1.2	4.9
			-.2				All Other Expenses (net)	.7	-.5
			1.4				Profit Before Taxes	.4	5.4
							RATIOS		
			2.0					2.5	4.4
			1.5				Current	1.6	2.3
			1.2					1.1	1.3
			.9					1.1	2.4
			.7				Quick	.5	1.3
			.4					.4	.6
			18 20.5					22 16.7	16 22.3
			29 12.7				Sales/Receivables	32 11.3	30 12.0
			39 9.3					46 8.0	38 9.6
			26 13.9					36 10.0	17 21.1
			54 6.8				Cost of Sales/Inventory	74 4.9	40 9.1
			63 5.8					114 3.2	89 4.1
			9 42.5					9 42.8	7 50.8
			16 22.5				Cost of Sales/Payables	15 24.7	11 34.1
			26 14.0					26 13.8	22 16.3
			7.4					5.0	3.5
			18.2				Sales/Working Capital	11.2	8.0
			32.7					65.9	35.2
			7.0					8.2	13.4
			2.4				EBIT/Interest	(52) 2.4	(20) 7.8
			.0					-.2	2.4
							Net Profit + Depr., Dep., Amort./Cur. Mat. L/T/D	6.6	
								(10) 1.1	
								.2	
			.6					.3	.2
			.8				Fixed/Worth	.8	.5
			1.7					1.8	1.1
			.8					.7	.5
			2.3				Debt/Worth	1.7	1.3
			4.2					13.5	2.8
			26.3					13.9	59.3
			3.4				% Profit Before Taxes/Tangible Net Worth	(44) 5.0	(20) 19.9
			-15.2					-3.3	2.7
			14.8					6.7	22.4
			2.1				% Profit Before Taxes/Total Assets	2.0	11.6
			-2.8					-1.4	1.9
			18.0					28.9	81.5
			10.9				Sales/Net Fixed Assets	10.6	16.2
			4.2					3.1	5.5
			3.1					2.8	4.1
			2.8				Sales/Total Assets	2.0	2.1
			2.2					1.2	1.7
			1.2					.9	.4
			(12) 1.7				% Depr., Dep., Amort./Sales	(38) 1.7	(17) .9
			2.5					2.4	2.0
							% Officers', Directors' Owners' Comp/Sales	.8	
								(11) 1.1	
								2.3	
2156M	2383M	160373M	1036670M	398197M	1448111M		Net Sales ($)	5350029M	1398807M
198M	853M	29355M	395604M	155312M	657370M		Total Assets ($)	3393544M	555809M

© RMA 2024

M = $ thousand   MM = $ million
See Pages viii through xx for Explanation of Ratios and Data

MANUFACTURING—Seafood Product Preparation and Packaging NAICS 311710

Comparative Historical Data / Current Data Sorted by Sales

Comparative Historical Data			Type of Statement	Current Data Sorted by Sales					
1	7	4	Unqualified						4
2	5	3	Reviewed					3	3
2	1	3	Compiled						
2	3	2	Tax Returns		1		2	1	
14	18	19	Other		1		18		15
4/1/21-3/31/22 ALL	4/1/22-3/31/23 ALL	4/1/23-3/31/24 ALL		0-1MM	13 (4/1-9/30/23) 1-3MM	3-5MM	18 (10/1/23-3/31/24) 5-10MM	10-25MM	25MM & OVER
21	34	31	NUMBER OF STATEMENTS	2	2		2	5	22
%	%	%	ASSETS	%	%	%	%	%	%
20.3	8.0	11.1	Cash & Equivalents						5.7
22.5	27.7	22.9	Trade Receivables (net)						23.6
19.8	31.8	28.9	Inventory						33.9
3.9	3.9	4.3	All Other Current	DATA NOT AVAILABLE	DATA NOT AVAILABLE				4.6
66.5	71.3	67.2	Total Current						67.8
21.0	17.8	21.5	Fixed Assets (net)						22.3
4.6	3.5	6.1	Intangibles (net)						3.9
7.9	7.4	5.2	All Other Non-Current						5.9
100.0	100.0	100.0	Total						100.0
			LIABILITIES						
9.6	13.6	10.7	Notes Payable-Short Term						13.7
2.3	.8	1.8	Cur. Mat.-L.T.D.						1.8
9.3	14.3	10.8	Trade Payables						12.5
.3	.1	.1	Income Taxes Payable						.1
7.5	11.1	8.0	All Other Current						8.7
28.8	39.9	31.5	Total Current						36.7
12.9	15.0	15.3	Long-Term Debt						15.5
.3	.2	.2	Deferred Taxes						.3
5.4	4.4	4.9	All Other Non-Current						4.7
52.7	40.5	48.1	Net Worth						42.7
100.0	100.0	100.0	Total Liabilities & Net Worth						100.0
			INCOME DATA						
100.0	100.0	100.0	Net Sales						100.0
21.0	18.1	16.3	Gross Profit						14.3
13.8	15.2	14.1	Operating Expenses						11.1
7.2	2.9	2.2	Operating Profit						3.2
-1.0	-.1	.4	All Other Expenses (net)						.8
8.3	3.0	1.8	Profit Before Taxes						2.3
			RATIOS						
4.3	2.8	4.2	Current						3.2
2.5	1.7	2.0							1.7
1.2	1.3	1.5							1.3
2.9	1.4	1.7	Quick						1.4
1.3	.8	.9							.8
.7	.4	.5							.4
18 20.6	21 17.1	18 20.3	Sales/Receivables						21 17.0
32 11.4	30 12.3	32 11.3							33 11.1
39 9.4	40 9.1	39 9.4							41 8.9
15 24.5	20 18.0	16 22.6	Cost of Sales/Inventory						26 13.9
21 17.2	45 8.1	41 8.9							54 6.8
57 6.4	79 4.6	64 5.7							87 4.2
4 88.7	10 35.0	8 45.3	Cost of Sales/Payables						12 30.2
12 30.5	22 16.5	14 25.6							18 20.2
28 12.9	30 12.1	26 14.3							28 13.2
3.4	6.1	4.8	Sales/Working Capital						4.5
11.8	11.8	10.0							9.2
24.3	24.9	27.5							27.9
41.4	17.0	6.5	EBIT/Interest						6.5
(20) 9.8	(33) 6.9	(30) 3.5							3.1
3.7	2.1	.2							.9
			Net Profit + Depr., Dep., Amort./Cur. Mat. L/T/D						
.0	.0	.1	Fixed/Worth						.1
.4	.5	.3							.7
.7	1.0	1.1							1.0
.4	.7	.6	Debt/Worth						1.0
1.2	1.6	1.3							1.5
2.1	3.4	4.0							4.0
54.9	47.8	30.0	% Profit Before Taxes/Tangible Net Worth						29.0
(20) 26.4	(31) 23.0	11.3							10.6
21.1	10.7	-9.1							-1.0
22.7	20.2	14.1	% Profit Before Taxes/Total Assets						13.4
14.4	10.3	5.6							4.8
6.3	3.8	-1.7							.0
UND	189.6	43.9	Sales/Net Fixed Assets						36.6
15.3	20.8	18.2							17.4
5.0	7.4	7.8							8.1
4.8	4.1	3.6	Sales/Total Assets						3.3
2.5	2.8	2.8							2.7
1.7	1.8	2.2							1.9
.3	.3	.5	% Depr., Dep., Amort./Sales						.5
(11) 1.0	(26) .9	(25) 1.2						(20)	1.3
3.1	2.1	2.2							2.1
			% Officers', Directors', Owners' Comp/Sales						
1544451M	3077999M	3047890M	Net Sales ($)		4539M		13116M	91499M	2938736M
888116M	1161712M	1238692M	Total Assets ($)		1051M		12383M	17521M	1207737M

© RMA 2024 M = $ thousand MM = $ million
See Pages viii through xx for Explanation of Ratios and Data

MANUFACTURING—Retail Bakeries NAICS 311811

Current Data Sorted by Assets

						Type of Statement	
		1			2	Unqualified	
	1		1	1		Reviewed	
5	6	3			1	Compiled	
6	10	7	6	4	1	Tax Returns	
	7 (4/1-9/30/23)		48 (10/1/23-3/31/24)			Other	
0-500M	500M-2MM	2-10MM	10-50MM	50-100MM	100-250MM		
11	17	11	7	5	4	NUMBER OF STATEMENTS	

Comparative Historical Data

	1	3
		1
	4	
	10	6
	24	19
	4/1/19-3/31/20	4/1/20-3/31/21
	ALL	ALL
	39	29

%	%	%	%	%	%	ASSETS	%	%
51.6	23.4	15.6				Cash & Equivalents	19.1	31.5
4.4	4.4	11.2				Trade Receivables (net)	10.0	6.1
6.7	2.3	9.0				Inventory	6.9	10.0
2.9	.6	4.6				All Other Current	.9	2.6
65.5	30.8	40.4				Total Current	36.9	50.2
28.3	46.6	41.8				Fixed Assets (net)	37.4	40.0
4.1	16.7	9.1				Intangibles (net)	10.7	7.1
2.2	5.9	8.7				All Other Non-Current	15.1	2.6
100.0	100.0	100.0				Total	100.0	100.0
						LIABILITIES		
3.8	9.7	5.0				Notes Payable-Short Term	8.6	6.2
3.5	.7	1.7				Cur. Mat.-L.T.D.	5.1	10.1
3.3	3.4	10.8				Trade Payables	9.3	6.8
.0	.3	.1				Income Taxes Payable	.0	.1
12.0	20.7	3.5				All Other Current	13.3	15.4
22.6	34.9	21.1				Total Current	36.4	38.7
12.3	27.4	25.6				Long-Term Debt	28.9	42.0
.0	.0	.1				Deferred Taxes	.2	.0
2.8	19.9	.4				All Other Non-Current	2.9	10.2
62.4	17.8	52.8				Net Worth	31.7	8.8
100.0	100.0	100.0				Total Liabilties & Net Worth	100.0	100.0
						INCOME DATA		
100.0	100.0	100.0				Net Sales	100.0	100.0
61.9	55.0	45.9				Gross Profit	55.8	55.1
49.5	49.9	41.7				Operating Expenses	50.9	53.3
12.4	5.2	4.2				Operating Profit	4.9	1.8
-.7	2.0	.9				All Other Expenses (net)	.8	-.8
13.1	3.2	3.3				Profit Before Taxes	4.1	2.6
						RATIOS		
17.9	2.7	3.9					1.7	3.1
3.5	.6	2.2				Current	1.0	1.4
1.4	.3	1.5					.6	.9
17.2	2.5	2.2					1.4	2.8
3.4	.5	1.5				Quick	.6	1.2
1.4	.2	.6					.4	.5
0 UND	0 UND	0 999.8					0 UND	0 UND
0 UND	0 UND	3 108.7				Sales/Receivables	5 74.9	4 90.3
2 189.0	2 173.5	27 13.3					21 17.8	12 29.4
0 UND	0 UND	10 37.4					4 99.4	4 93.4
1 333.0	5 68.6	24 15.3				Cost of Sales/Inventory	15 24.1	24 15.0
7 55.4	13 27.8	33 11.0					29 12.5	40 9.1
0 UND	0 UND	8 48.3					2 203.0	0 UND
0 UND	0 UND	21 17.5				Cost of Sales/Payables	20 18.1	19 19.6
2 190.0	26 14.3	39 9.3					36 10.2	34 10.7
6.5	11.9	6.6					21.1	8.6
10.9	-250.4	14.5				Sales/Working Capital	-999.8	19.2
42.5	-4.5	19.7					-15.8	-37.3
	24.8						16.1	32.2
(13)	4.3					EBIT/Interest	(30) 3.1	(23) 6.2
	-.9						-.1	-1.4
						Net Profit + Depr., Dep., Amort./Cur. Mat. L/T/D		
.1	1.1	.3					.6	.9
.4	6.5	1.0				Fixed/Worth	2.3	4.7
.8	-.3	6.6					-3.8	-2.1
.1	.4	.2					.7	1.5
.3	8.4	1.3				Debt/Worth	2.9	7.7
.4	-2.3	10.2					-8.8	-6.5
389.6	100.7	42.0					129.0	136.6
(10) 70.3	(11) 53.1	(10) 2.6				% Profit Before Taxes/Tangible Net Worth	(25) 41.4	(17) 70.2
45.4	21.6	-19.5					.1	17.8
223.1	27.2	14.6					35.6	26.2
52.7	11.7	2.6				% Profit Before Taxes/Total Assets	7.5	14.2
15.9	-3.0	-4.7					-1.4	-4.9
116.9	19.1	31.2					28.6	24.9
17.6	5.5	6.3				Sales/Net Fixed Assets	7.6	5.5
11.0	2.2	1.8					4.2	3.1
14.5	5.0	3.8					4.6	5.2
5.2	2.1	2.1				Sales/Total Assets	3.2	2.6
3.5	1.1	1.3					2.0	1.6
	2.1						.9	1.2
(10)	4.4					% Depr., Dep., Amort./Sales	(29) 1.8	(15) 2.5
	8.6						3.6	4.7
							2.1	
						% Officers', Directors' Owners' Comp/Sales	(16) 2.6	
							7.4	
18819M	55062M	130793M	179698M	526918M	3799565M	Net Sales ($)	1342060M	1731889M
2362M	18639M	56480M	134800M	394413M	682342M	Total Assets ($)	538928M	497447M

M = $ thousand   MM = $ million
See Pages viii through xx for Explanation of Ratios and Data

© RMA 2024

MANUFACTURING—Retail Bakeries   NAICS 311811

Comparative Historical Data | Current Data Sorted by Sales

					Type of Statement						
	1		5	4	Unqualified		1				3
			1	2	Reviewed					1	1
	1		3		Compiled						
	7		8	15	Tax Returns	3	4	3	2	2	1
	15		21	34	Other	4	8	2	5	6	9
	4/1/21-		4/1/22-	4/1/23-		7 (4/1-9/30/23)			48 (10/1/23-3/31/24)		
	3/31/22		3/31/23	3/31/24		0-1MM	1-3MM	3-5MM	5-10MM	10-25MM	25MM & OVER
	ALL		ALL	ALL							
	24		38	55	NUMBER OF STATEMENTS	7	13	5	7	9	14
	%		%	%	ASSETS	%	%	%	%	%	%
	30.2		27.1	23.6	Cash & Equivalents		35.9				11.2
	4.9		6.9	7.1	Trade Receivables (net)		7.1				11.7
	7.0		9.0	5.4	Inventory		2.6				7.3
	3.5		3.1	2.5	All Other Current		1.2				3.4
	45.7		46.2	38.6	Total Current		46.9				33.6
	35.5		34.7	39.4	Fixed Assets (net)		34.7				38.3
	13.4		13.0	13.5	Intangibles (net)		16.5				12.7
	5.3		6.0	8.4	All Other Non-Current		1.9				15.4
	100.0		100.0	100.0	Total		100.0				100.0
					LIABILITIES						
	17.5		8.4	5.4	Notes Payable-Short Term		5.2				2.3
	1.2		8.0	2.6	Cur. Mat.-L.T.D.		2.4				4.7
	8.2		9.6	6.0	Trade Payables		2.1				9.0
	.2		.2	.1	Income Taxes Payable		.3				.0
	10.8		10.7	12.4	All Other Current		14.5				11.7
	37.9		36.8	26.5	Total Current		24.5				27.7
	36.9		36.1	24.3	Long-Term Debt		21.4				27.5
	.0		.3	.0	Deferred Taxes		.0				.0
	15.9		17.2	10.7	All Other Non-Current		5.1				12.8
	9.3		9.6	38.5	Net Worth		48.9				32.0
	100.0		100.0	100.0	Total Liabilties & Net Worth		100.0				100.0
					INCOME DATA						
	100.0		100.0	100.0	Net Sales		100.0				100.0
	61.6		53.9	52.6	Gross Profit		61.9				45.4
	54.6		51.6	45.6	Operating Expenses		47.4				39.9
	6.9		2.3	7.1	Operating Profit		14.5				5.5
	-4.3		-1.0	1.2	All Other Expenses (net)		1.1				.9
	11.3		3.3	5.9	Profit Before Taxes		13.5				4.6
					RATIOS						
	5.8		4.4	3.5			9.2				3.0
	3.5		1.8	1.6	Current		3.0				1.5
	.9		.7	.6			1.0				.5
	4.7		4.4	2.7			8.4				1.9
	2.1		1.1	1.3	Quick		2.7				1.1
	.7		.4	.4			.8				.4
0	UND	0	UND	0 UND		0 UND				17	21.6
2	193.6	4	98.1	2 205.6	Sales/Receivables	0 UND				24	15.4
10	37.4	26	13.9	23 16.1		3 115.5				29	12.4
9	38.9	0	UND	2 242.0		0 UND				16	23.5
24	15.2	17	21.5	14 26.8	Cost of Sales/Inventory	5 70.6				22	16.7
29	12.6	42	8.6	22 16.3		13 27.8				36	10.2
0	UND	0	UND	0 UND		0 UND				16	23.5
17	21.0	21	17.5	11 34.2	Cost of Sales/Payables	0 UND				34	10.8
40	9.1	49	7.4	33 11.2		3 109.0				59	6.2
	6.5		7.8	9.3			6.3				9.0
	10.9		15.8	16.6	Sales/Working Capital		11.4				23.4
	NM		-31.4	-43.1			NM				-11.1
	63.7		11.5	21.8							60.5
(18)	10.6	(30)	2.4	(42) 5.7	EBIT/Interest						4.7
	-.4		-2.5	.8							1.0
					Net Profit + Depr., Dep., Amort./Cur. Mat. L/T/D						
	.5		.3	.4			.2				.7
	1.4		3.2	1.6	Fixed/Worth		.8				2.6
	NM		-.8	-9.7			NM				-7.3
	.4		.6	.3			.3				.6
	3.3		8.4	2.0	Debt/Worth		.5				7.4
	-3.8		-3.6	-24.9			NM				-19.4
	159.5		107.5	88.7	% Profit Before Taxes/Tangible Net Worth		168.6				93.3
(17)	77.4	(21)	53.1	(41) 39.3		(10) 75.8				(10)	39.7
	39.0		-2.2	12.3			45.2				28.0
	47.5		34.4	24.5	% Profit Before Taxes/Total Assets		49.0				17.3
	26.4		7.7	11.7			23.4				6.9
	-.2		-6.5	.6			12.0				.1
	23.6		34.7	17.6	Sales/Net Fixed Assets		18.8				12.5
	9.0		10.7	6.3			11.0				5.0
	4.2		4.6	3.2			3.4				3.3
	4.0		4.5	4.3	Sales/Total Assets		7.0				3.3
	2.6		2.5	2.1			2.3				1.5
	1.8		1.3	1.2			1.3				1.1
	1.9		2.0	1.1	% Depr., Dep., Amort./Sales						1.1
(17)	3.7	(26)	2.5	(37) 3.9						(12)	2.9
	5.5		5.6	6.4							5.7
	2.7		1.7	1.0	% Officers', Directors' Owners' Comp/Sales						
(14)	6.6	(15)	4.6	(23) 3.0							
	7.5		7.0	6.2							
	333859M		1363684M	4710855M	Net Sales ($)	4059M	22391M	20297M	47626M	126731M	4489751M
	181280M		708339M	1289036M	Total Assets ($)	3213M	12181M	6347M	14179M	83759M	1169357M

© RMA 2024   M = $ thousand   MM = $ million
See Pages viii through xx for Explanation of Ratios and Data

MANUFACTURING—Commercial Bakeries NAICS 311812

Current Data Sorted by Assets | Comparative Historical Data

						Type of Statement		
			1	10	3	3	Unqualified	23	9
			3	3	1		Reviewed	14	3
1	1		4	1	1		Compiled	7	6
		2	5				Tax Returns	15	11
5	4	18 (4/1-9/30/23)	16	20	12	8	Other	70	55
0-500M	500M-2MM	2-10MM	10-50MM	50-100MM	100-250MM		4/1/19-3/31/20	4/1/20-3/31/21
6	7	29	34	17	11	NUMBER OF STATEMENTS	ALL 129	ALL 84
%	%	%	%	%	%	ASSETS	%	%
			15.4	8.2	5.9	14.1	Cash & Equivalents	12.4	18.6
			18.8	17.7	12.0	13.5	Trade Receivables (net)	15.9	14.3
			11.5	9.1	11.3	9.4	Inventory	9.1	9.8
			2.4	2.1	3.0	.7	All Other Current	1.8	1.9
			48.1	37.1	32.2	37.8	Total Current	39.1	44.5
			36.2	39.9	38.2	39.3	Fixed Assets (net)	45.2	41.0
			7.0	8.2	18.9	9.1	Intangibles (net)	6.3	7.7
			8.7	14.7	10.7	13.8	All Other Non-Current	9.5	6.7
			100.0	100.0	100.0	100.0	Total	100.0	100.0
							LIABILITIES		
			8.3	4.1	3.6	2.9	Notes Payable-Short Term	6.3	6.8
			2.1	3.6	2.5	5.6	Cur. Mat.-L.T.D.	3.6	4.6
			14.0	11.8	9.4	8.7	Trade Payables	13.3	10.5
			.0	.0	.2	.1	Income Taxes Payable	.1	.0
			6.7	10.3	7.4	8.8	All Other Current	6.6	9.0
			31.0	29.8	23.1	26.0	Total Current	29.9	30.9
			39.4	23.6	29.9	17.5	Long-Term Debt	27.0	29.5
			.1	.0	.5	.6	Deferred Taxes	.5	.6
			6.1	9.9	8.3	7.1	All Other Non-Current	8.6	9.5
			23.4	36.7	38.2	48.7	Net Worth	34.1	29.5
			100.0	100.0	100.0	100.0	Total Liabilities & Net Worth	100.0	100.0
							INCOME DATA		
			100.0	100.0	100.0	100.0	Net Sales	100.0	100.0
			42.5	29.7	27.0	28.5	Gross Profit	34.5	35.7
			40.4	25.7	22.8	22.5	Operating Expenses	29.9	32.2
			2.1	4.1	4.2	6.0	Operating Profit	4.7	3.6
			.7	1.1	.8	.9	All Other Expenses (net)	1.1	.5
			1.4	3.0	3.4	5.1	Profit Before Taxes	3.6	3.1
							RATIOS		
			3.0	1.8	2.1	2.6		2.6	3.2
			1.7	1.2	1.7	1.6	Current	1.3	1.6
			.9	.9	1.1	1.0		.9	.9
			2.4	1.4	1.5	1.7		1.8	2.4
			1.1	.9	.9	1.1	Quick	1.0	1.2
			.6	.5	.5	.6		.5	.6
			10 38.1	22 16.3	23 15.8	23 15.9		13 28.9	13 27.8
			18 20.3	28 13.1	27 13.4	29 12.7	Sales/Receivables	24 15.1	21 17.0
			34 10.7	42 8.7	35 10.3	34 10.6		32 11.4	29 12.5
			6 65.8	13 27.2	28 13.2	14 25.9		7 54.7	9 41.7
			15 24.1	24 15.3	38 9.5	21 17.5	Cost of Sales/Inventory	18 20.8	20 18.7
			33 11.0	36 10.2	46 7.9	47 7.8		31 11.6	32 11.3
			14 26.3	19 19.0	19 19.6	23 16.0		17 21.6	13 28.4
			24 15.4	31 11.8	30 12.0	25 14.5	Cost of Sales/Payables	25 14.6	20 17.9
			52 7.0	45 8.2	46 7.9	33 11.2		35 10.4	33 10.9
			7.2	10.1	9.0	6.1		9.6	6.5
			13.1	57.2	14.1	14.3	Sales/Working Capital	29.1	17.1
			-143.5	-53.3	92.1	-164.1		-59.3	-59.9
			13.1	15.5	5.8	17.2		11.0	17.2
		(28) 5.5	(32) 4.9	(15) 2.7	4.2	EBIT/Interest	(121) 4.0	(76) 3.8
			-.4	.2	-1.8	1.1		.2	-1.8
				5.8				4.9	4.1
			(14) 3.9			Net Profit + Depr., Dep., Amort./Cur. Mat. L/T/D	(35) 2.4	(11) 2.5
			1.3				.8	1.8
			.4	.8	.7	.5		.8	.6
			1.4	1.4	1.1	.8	Fixed/Worth	1.5	1.9
			NM	3.6	14.1	6.3		7.1	36.0
			.8	.9	.7	.4		.7	.8
			1.8	2.3	1.2	1.0	Debt/Worth	2.0	2.4
			NM	5.8	24.5	7.0		13.7	NM
			63.6	49.4	30.5			56.5	50.9
		(22) 28.7	(30) 20.3	(14) 10.7		% Profit Before Taxes/Tangible Net Worth	(101) 17.8	(63) 18.2
			.0	-15.9	-13.3			.9	-2.0
			22.3	15.7	15.7	13.0		14.6	22.3
			12.9	6.3	2.8	9.8	% Profit Before Taxes/Total Assets	5.9	5.0
			-4.9	-3.2	-4.8	.5		-.3	-5.5
			32.4	11.3	6.8	6.8		10.9	11.0
			9.0	5.5	5.1	5.6	Sales/Net Fixed Assets	5.8	6.4
			4.7	2.9	2.4	2.6		3.2	3.3
			3.6	2.4	2.0	1.8		3.6	3.2
			3.1	2.0	1.4	1.7	Sales/Total Assets	2.5	2.3
			2.4	1.3	.6	1.1		1.6	1.5
			.4	1.6	2.2			1.9	2.2
		(23) 1.4	(33) 2.8	(11) 3.5		% Depr., Dep., Amort./Sales	(108) 2.9	(61) 2.9
			3.6	5.4	5.1			4.1	4.4
			1.0					1.1	1.6
		(13) 2.4				% Officers', Directors', Owners' Comp/Sales	(39) 2.5	(25) 3.6
			7.4					4.2	7.0
9691M	30149M	375676M	1681643M	2005403M	2752641M	Net Sales ($)	8115467M	4484814M
2056M	7725M	129218M	896411M	1332105M	1684451M	Total Assets ($)	3890044M	2378063M

© RMA 2024   M = $ thousand   MM = $ million
See Pages viii through xx for Explanation of Ratios and Data

MANUFACTURING—Commercial Bakeries NAICS 311812

Comparative Historical Data | Current Data Sorted by Sales

Type of Statement								
				Unqualified				2	15
7	10	17	Reviewed			1	2	4
9	10	7	Compiled		1	3	2	2
6	5	8	Tax Returns			1	3	3
4	9	7	Other	3	3	3	3	16	37
41	61	65			18 (4/1-9/30/23)		86 (10/1/23-3/31/24)	
4/1/21-	4/1/22-	4/1/23-						
3/31/22	3/31/23	3/31/24						
ALL	ALL	ALL		0-1MM	1-3MM	3-5MM	5-10MM	10-25MM	25MM & OVER
67	95	104	NUMBER OF STATEMENTS	3		4	10	25	58

%	%	%	ASSETS	%	%	%	%	%	%
18.0	13.8	12.9	Cash & Equivalents				19.6	14.9	9.0
12.7	17.5	16.4	Trade Receivables (net)				25.9	17.9	16.2
8.7	13.2	10.2	Inventory				10.5	10.9	10.0
.7	2.3	2.0	All Other Current				1.2	2.3	2.3
40.1	46.9	41.4	Total Current				57.1	46.0	37.4
42.1	35.6	37.4	Fixed Assets (net)				24.9	37.2	37.8
9.7	6.6	10.5	Intangibles (net)				8.8	10.1	10.4
8.1	10.9	10.7	All Other Non-Current				9.2	6.7	14.3
100.0	100.0	100.0	Total				100.0	100.0	100.0

			LIABILITIES						
4.7	7.6	6.5	Notes Payable-Short Term				14.2	6.8	3.9
4.0	3.9	3.9	Cur. Mat.-L.T.D.				3.0	3.0	3.4
9.8	13.3	11.5	Trade Payables				16.1	14.3	11.0
.0	.1	.0	Income Taxes Payable				.0	.0	.1
7.1	7.2	10.1	All Other Current				8.6	6.3	9.7
25.6	32.0	32.0	Total Current				41.8	30.5	28.1
27.6	32.0	32.5	Long-Term Debt				51.6	37.5	24.2
.5	.4	.2	Deferred Taxes				.0	.1	.3
6.4	4.7	9.8	All Other Non-Current				1.7	7.9	8.9
40.0	30.9	25.5	Net Worth				4.9	24.1	38.5
100.0	100.0	100.0	Total Liabilities & Net Worth				100.0	100.0	100.0

			INCOME DATA						
100.0	100.0	100.0	Net Sales				100.0	100.0	100.0
32.6	32.6	35.1	Gross Profit				42.7	42.4	27.1
29.3	30.8	31.9	Operating Expenses				43.7	38.9	22.6
3.3	1.8	3.2	Operating Profit				-1.0	3.5	4.5
-.8	.5	1.0	All Other Expenses (net)				.7	.9	.8
4.1	1.4	2.2	Profit Before Taxes				-1.6	2.6	3.7

			RATIOS						
3.4	2.7	2.5	Current				3.2	3.0	2.1
1.6	1.5	1.4					1.7	1.3	1.3
1.2	.9	.9					.8	.8	1.0
2.6	1.9	1.8	Quick				3.0	2.4	1.5
1.2	1.1	1.0					.9	.9	.9
.6	.5	.5					.6	.4	.5
15 23.7	17 21.3	17 21.9	Sales/Receivables			1 372.1	10 38.1	24 15.5
24 15.5	25 14.5	26 14.3				27 13.4	17 21.3	28 12.9
35 10.4	32 11.4	36 10.2				47 7.7	29 12.4	40 9.2
8 46.5	10 34.9	11 32.7	Cost of Sales/Inventory			0 UND	9 39.5	16 22.8
22 16.8	24 15.3	22 16.5				15 24.4	15 24.7	28 13.1
35 10.4	43 8.5	38 9.7				36 10.2	35 10.5	40 9.2
12 29.6	17 21.7	15 24.7	Cost of Sales/Payables			4 84.7	14 27.0	21 17.1
24 14.9	28 13.1	26 14.3				20 18.0	24 14.9	30 12.1
38 9.7	38 9.7	36 10.2				66 5.5	60 6.1	34 10.6
7.1	6.7	8.5	Sales/Working Capital				9.1	7.5	8.7
12.8	15.6	18.8					13.4	35.9	23.8
46.8	-140.4	-153.0					-31.0	-96.1	NM
27.9	11.4	13.6	EBIT/Interest				15.0	15.7
(62) 8.2	(87) 3.4	(95) 3.9					(23) 6.6	(55) 4.2
.5	-2.1	-.2					.5	.3
9.6	4.1	6.7	Net Profit + Depr., Dep.,					6.0
(15) 5.8	(20) 3.5	(21) 4.6	Amort./Cur. Mat. L/T/D					(19) 4.6
3.0	2.5	1.6						1.6
.6	.5	.6	Fixed/Worth				.2	.4	.6
1.4	1.2	1.4					1.0	1.1	1.2
4.2	3.5	12.0					-1.0	-3.6	3.6
.6	.7	.8	Debt/Worth				1.0	.4	.8
1.8	2.0	1.8					1.7	3.1	1.5
6.7	7.4	16.2					-3.0	-15.5	6.4
55.6	35.1	48.6	% Profit Before Taxes/Tangible Net Worth				75.1	39.3
(56) 31.2	(76) 12.3	(81) 20.6					(18) 34.4	(50) 19.5
7.7	-8.4	-2.9						-1.5	-5.2
26.0	12.6	17.5	% Profit Before Taxes/Total Assets				13.5	23.3	15.7
10.9	4.3	6.3					-.7	14.2	6.3
-1.4	-3.9	-3.5					-16.8	-3.7	-1.7
8.2	11.1	12.8	Sales/Net Fixed Assets				94.1	32.4	9.0
5.2	6.6	6.6					26.5	10.1	5.6
3.1	4.0	3.4					4.2	4.7	2.9
2.8	3.3	3.2	Sales/Total Assets				8.2	3.7	2.4
2.0	2.2	2.1					2.9	3.3	1.7
1.3	1.8	1.3					1.8	2.4	1.3
2.0	1.5	1.4	% Depr., Dep., Amort./Sales					.4	1.7
(60) 4.0	(79) 2.5	(83) 2.4					(20) 1.3	(48) 2.6
5.5	4.5	5.0						5.4	5.0
.6	1.5	1.1	% Officers', Directors', Owners' Comp/Sales					1.0
(15) 1.9	(22) 4.2	(23) 2.4					(10) 2.4
5.4	6.0	4.3						7.1
3872210M	5659056M	6855203M	Net Sales ($)	1814M	6378M	14134M	66761M	398282M	6367834M
2312816M	3057175M	4051966M	Total Assets ($)	1720M	2950M	10939M	24743M	166299M	3845315M

M = $ thousand   MM = $ million
See Pages viii through xx for Explanation of Ratios and Data

© RMA 2024

MANUFACTURING—Other Snack Food Manufacturing NAICS 311919

Current Data Sorted by Assets

						Type of Statement		
				3		Unqualified		
				2	3	Reviewed		
						Compiled		
			1	2		Tax Returns		
	2	6	7	3	1	Other		
0-500M	8 (4/1-9/30/23) 500M-2MM	2-10MM	22 (10/1/23-3/31/24) 10-50MM	50-100MM	100-250MM			
	2	7	14	6	1	NUMBER OF STATEMENTS		
%	%	%	%	%	%	ASSETS		

Current Data							Comparative Historical Data	
							4/1/19-3/31/20 ALL 53	4/1/20-3/31/21 ALL 24
							%	%
DATA NOT AVAILABLE			8.0			Cash & Equivalents	8.9	9.7
			12.1			Trade Receivables (net)	24.5	20.7
			23.9			Inventory	19.0	26.2
			2.1			All Other Current	1.5	1.5
			46.1			Total Current	54.0	58.2
			43.2			Fixed Assets (net)	30.5	34.7
			4.4			Intangibles (net)	8.8	.8
			6.3			All Other Non-Current	6.8	6.4
			100.0			Total	100.0	100.0
						LIABILITIES		
			2.3			Notes Payable-Short Term	10.9	8.4
			2.7			Cur. Mat.-L.T.D.	2.5	2.5
			8.1			Trade Payables	19.4	20.8
			.1			Income Taxes Payable	.0	.0
			6.5			All Other Current	8.2	5.8
			19.7			Total Current	41.1	37.4
			24.4			Long-Term Debt	20.1	18.2
			.6			Deferred Taxes	.4	.5
			3.2			All Other Non-Current	13.0	3.9
			52.0			Net Worth	25.6	40.0
			100.0			Total Liabilities & Net Worth	100.0	100.0
						INCOME DATA		
			100.0			Net Sales	100.0	100.0
			31.5			Gross Profit	31.8	30.6
			26.5			Operating Expenses	27.9	30.0
			5.0			Operating Profit	3.9	.6
			1.6			All Other Expenses (net)	1.4	-.5
			3.5			Profit Before Taxes	2.4	1.1
						RATIOS		
			4.1				2.4	3.0
			2.7			Current	1.5	1.7
			1.1				.9	1.2
			1.6				1.3	1.5
			1.1			Quick	.8	.8
			.5				.6	.5
		21	17.6				26 13.8	17 21.5
		31	11.6			Sales/Receivables	34 10.6	21 17.0
		36	10.2				44 8.3	29 12.4
		43	8.4				19 19.1	29 12.4
		83	4.4			Cost of Sales/Inventory	31 11.7	51 7.1
		118	3.1				51 7.1	78 4.7
		18	20.5				21 17.2	18 20.3
		27	13.5			Cost of Sales/Payables	32 11.5	29 12.5
		38	9.6				51 7.1	41 9.0
			3.9				6.9	6.1
			6.2			Sales/Working Capital	17.1	10.3
			42.4				-93.9	39.4
			21.7				9.9	14.4
		(13)	5.0			EBIT/Interest	(49) 4.5	(20) 4.9
			.4				-.5	1.3
						Net Profit + Depr., Dep., Amort./Cur. Mat. L/T/D	4.6	
							(10) 3.8	
							2.3	
			.3				.3	.5
			.9			Fixed/Worth	1.0	.8
			1.9				6.7	2.2
			.5				.9	.5
			1.0			Debt/Worth	2.0	1.5
			1.7				-48.0	3.5
			23.2				33.0	47.0
		(13)	13.3			% Profit Before Taxes/Tangible Net Worth	(39) 19.7	(20) 23.0
			-1.3				5.4	9.1
			9.4				13.9	21.8
			6.3			% Profit Before Taxes/Total Assets	7.1	7.7
			.2				-3.5	2.3
			14.4				38.4	24.7
			4.2			Sales/Net Fixed Assets	9.2	7.1
			1.2				4.3	5.2
			2.8				3.3	3.5
			1.3			Sales/Total Assets	2.4	2.5
			.8				1.9	1.9
			1.0				.9	1.3
		(12)	3.7			% Depr., Dep., Amort./Sales	(38) 2.3	(21) 3.3
			5.9				3.9	5.6
						% Officers', Directors' Owners' Comp/Sales		
	3188M	90514M	593260M	815668M	284158M	Net Sales ($)	3482125M	1366250M
	2230M	41754M	358417M	377605M	229167M	Total Assets ($)	1614978M	558670M

© RMA 2024   M = $ thousand   MM = $ million
See Pages viii through xx for Explanation of Ratios and Data

MANUFACTURING—Other Snack Food Manufacturing NAICS 311919

Comparative Historical Data | Current Data Sorted by Sales

Comparative Historical Data			Type of Statement	Current Data Sorted by Sales						
1	5	6	Unqualified						6
2	3	2	Reviewed						2
2	2		Compiled						
5	5	3	Tax Returns					2	1
14	15	19	Other		2		5	5	7
4/1/21-3/31/22 ALL	4/1/22-3/31/23 ALL	4/1/23-3/31/24 ALL		0-1MM	8 (4/1-9/30/23) 1-3MM	3-5MM	22 (10/1/23-3/31/24) 5-10MM	10-25MM	25MM & OVER
24	30	30	NUMBER OF STATEMENTS		2		5	7	16
%	%	%	ASSETS	%	%	%	%	%	%
9.2	8.7	8.6	Cash & Equivalents	D		D			10.0
16.9	16.7	17.8	Trade Receivables (net)	A		A			19.5
30.8	27.5	25.0	Inventory	T		T			29.3
1.1	3.2	2.6	All Other Current	A		A			2.3
58.0	56.1	54.0	Total Current						61.2
31.1	27.7	32.8	Fixed Assets (net)	N		N			29.3
7.3	6.5	7.2	Intangibles (net)	O		O			2.2
3.6	9.7	6.0	All Other Non-Current	T		T			7.3
100.0	100.0	100.0	Total						100.0
			LIABILITIES	A		A			
8.6	9.2	9.9	Notes Payable-Short Term	V		V			4.8
1.5	2.7	2.4	Cur. Mat.-L.T.D.	A		A			2.0
13.9	19.0	10.2	Trade Payables	I		I			13.1
.3	.1	.1	Income Taxes Payable	L		L			.1
6.3	6.3	9.6	All Other Current	A		A			5.7
30.5	37.3	32.2	Total Current	B		B			25.7
21.1	21.9	20.7	Long-Term Debt	L		L			15.0
.7	.4	.3	Deferred Taxes	E		E			.3
9.5	11.2	9.2	All Other Non-Current						5.2
38.2	29.1	37.7	Net Worth						53.8
100.0	100.0	100.0	Total Liabilities & Net Worth						100.0
			INCOME DATA						
100.0	100.0	100.0	Net Sales						100.0
31.9	24.9	27.0	Gross Profit						23.0
27.3	27.0	25.1	Operating Expenses						20.2
4.6	-2.2	1.9	Operating Profit						2.9
.7	1.0	.9	All Other Expenses (net)						.5
3.8	-3.2	1.0	Profit Before Taxes						2.4
			RATIOS						
3.2	2.2	3.3							3.8
1.9	1.8	2.5	Current						2.9
1.3	1.0	1.1							1.3
1.6	1.1	1.7							2.1
.9	.7	1.0	Quick						1.4
.5	.4	.5							.6
15 24.0	22 16.9	24 15.0						22	16.5
25 14.8	28 12.9	34 10.7	Sales/Receivables					34	10.7
41 8.8	38 9.6	45 8.2						44	8.3
35 10.5	27 13.4	38 9.7						27	13.4
68 5.4	65 5.6	55 6.6	Cost of Sales/Inventory					60	6.1
114 3.2	89 4.1	94 3.9						89	4.1
19 19.3	23 15.7	17 21.2						18	20.6
30 12.2	41 8.8	26 13.8	Cost of Sales/Payables					28	13.1
45 8.1	79 4.6	42 8.7						41	8.8
3.8	5.6	4.3							4.0
8.5	12.9	6.8	Sales/Working Capital						6.3
28.1	80.3	43.1							21.7
27.5	12.5	26.2							73.2
(22) 6.4	(27) .9	(27) 3.6	EBIT/Interest						21.7
-1.4	-4.9	-2.6							-1.8
			Net Profit + Depr., Dep., Amort./Cur. Mat. L/T/D						
.5	.3	.3							.3
.9	1.0	1.0	Fixed/Worth						.5
NM	-34.0	1.9							1.0
.6	.8	.5							.5
1.9	2.5	1.5	Debt/Worth						.6
NM	-61.6	3.4							1.7
48.5	11.8	36.6	% Profit Before Taxes/Tangible Net Worth						37.1
(18) 23.4	(21) 5.4	(26) 14.6							18.1
-10.0	-11.7	-12.4							-2.9
20.3	5.8	12.7	% Profit Before Taxes/Total Assets						20.1
3.8	-.3	5.7							7.1
-5.4	-14.5	-4.4							-1.9
33.1	33.2	21.7							20.9
7.7	8.7	7.0	Sales/Net Fixed Assets						10.0
4.8	4.9	2.4							3.9
2.9	2.8	2.7							2.9
2.0	1.9	1.7	Sales/Total Assets						2.3
1.3	1.5	1.2							1.4
.7	.8	1.0							.9
(18) 1.8	(23) 3.3	(23) 3.2	% Depr., Dep., Amort./Sales					(15)	1.5
3.8	4.4	5.4							4.9
			% Officers', Directors' Owners' Comp/Sales						
800201M	1493414M	1786788M	Net Sales ($)		3188M		39220M	117718M	1626662M
584254M	952080M	1009173M	Total Assets ($)		2230M		28950M	121368M	856625M

M = $ thousand   MM = $ million
See Pages viii through xx for Explanation of Ratios and Data

© RMA 2024

MANUFACTURING—Coffee and Tea Manufacturing NAICS 311920

Current Data Sorted by Assets | Comparative Historical Data

						Type of Statement		
		1	1			Unqualified	3	5
			3	1	1	Reviewed	6	
		1	1			Compiled	5	
1	1	3				Tax Returns	7	4
3	3	13	13	2	7	Other	32	18
	9 (4/1-9/30/23)		46 (10/1/23-3/31/24)				4/1/19-3/31/20	4/1/20-3/31/21
0-500M	500M-2MM	2-10MM	10-50MM	50-100MM	100-250MM		ALL	ALL
4	5	18	17	3	8	NUMBER OF STATEMENTS	53	27
%	%	%	%	%	%	**ASSETS**	%	%
		11.6	4.9			Cash & Equivalents	11.8	22.2
		12.1	11.8			Trade Receivables (net)	14.4	10.5
		20.2	18.2			Inventory	26.3	17.1
		1.8	1.2			All Other Current	2.2	1.5
		45.7	36.2			Total Current	54.8	51.3
		31.6	45.2			Fixed Assets (net)	30.9	30.0
		8.0	6.2			Intangibles (net)	7.6	7.7
		14.7	12.3			All Other Non-Current	6.8	10.9
		100.0	100.0			Total	100.0	100.0
						LIABILITIES		
		6.8	8.4			Notes Payable-Short Term	7.1	17.6
		2.7	3.7			Cur. Mat.-L.T.D.	3.0	1.3
		10.1	13.0			Trade Payables	13.1	10.6
		.1	.1			Income Taxes Payable	.1	.1
		16.7	7.4			All Other Current	10.6	13.6
		36.5	32.5			Total Current	33.9	43.3
		29.6	29.9			Long-Term Debt	13.5	24.1
		.8	.3			Deferred Taxes	.3	.6
		5.4	14.0			All Other Non-Current	5.3	3.6
		27.7	23.2			Net Worth	47.0	28.4
		100.0	100.0			Total Liabilities & Net Worth	100.0	100.0
						INCOME DATA		
		100.0	100.0			Net Sales	100.0	100.0
		45.9	29.6			Gross Profit	40.0	43.4
		40.8	30.3			Operating Expenses	33.1	43.3
		5.1	-.7			Operating Profit	6.9	.1
		.2	2.2			All Other Expenses (net)	1.1	-.1
		4.9	-2.8			Profit Before Taxes	5.9	.2
						RATIOS		
		3.3	1.6				3.5	2.3
		1.7	1.4			Current	2.0	1.5
		1.0	.9				1.1	.8
		1.2	.9				1.4	1.7
		.6	.6			Quick	.9	1.0
		.4	.4				.5	.4
		9 40.4	19 19.2				13 29.1	9 38.5
		16 22.5	27 13.6			Sales/Receivables	26 13.9	21 17.0
		23 15.7	35 10.3				34 10.8	34 10.6
		41 9.0	48 7.6				45 8.2	38 9.6
		60 6.1	59 6.2			Cost of Sales/Inventory	64 5.7	66 5.5
		85 4.3	72 5.1				87 4.2	94 3.9
		13 27.8	26 14.1				13 28.9	21 17.4
		33 11.2	35 10.5			Cost of Sales/Payables	25 14.5	39 9.4
		40 9.2	42 8.6				43 8.4	62 5.9
		8.0	11.1				5.4	5.7
		15.7	26.5			Sales/Working Capital	9.6	9.3
		-81.9	-513.5				35.1	-23.7
		10.5	2.9				24.7	95.1
		4.2	(16) 1.0			EBIT/Interest	(46) 9.7	(20) 2.4
		1.1	-3.3				1.5	-4.3
							12.8	
						Net Profit + Depr., Dep., Amort./Cur. Mat. L/T/D	(13) 3.3	
							2.1	
		.5	1.7				.3	.4
		1.3	2.9			Fixed/Worth	.7	1.4
		NM	8.5				1.8	55.8
		1.3	2.2				.5	.8
		3.6	4.5			Debt/Worth	1.0	1.9
		NM	22.3				5.6	99.2
		149.6	38.6				40.5	43.5
		(14) 19.5	(14) 1.1			% Profit Before Taxes/Tangible Net Worth	(44) 14.5	(21) 5.4
		2.0	-29.1				5.8	-21.6
		18.3	6.2				17.4	13.7
		6.9	-1.9			% Profit Before Taxes/Total Assets	9.3	-1.6
		.3	-9.2				1.7	-12.9
		13.1	5.1				19.7	12.6
		7.5	3.8			Sales/Net Fixed Assets	8.3	7.5
		5.0	2.6				4.2	3.2
		2.8	1.7				3.2	2.6
		2.5	1.5			Sales/Total Assets	2.3	2.0
		1.7	1.3				1.5	1.1
		2.8	3.0				1.5	.9
		(12) 3.1	3.7			% Depr., Dep., Amort./Sales	(40) 2.2	(16) 2.6
		5.0	5.0				4.6	5.4
							1.8	
						% Officers', Directors' Owners' Comp/Sales	(14) 3.1	
							5.0	
4209M	9326M	210079M	750022M	310546M	1956860M	Net Sales ($)	2611690M	1168977M
493M	6222M	95045M	473224M	239833M	1446930M	Total Assets ($)	1641453M	974416M

M = $ thousand   MM = $ million
See Pages viii through xx for Explanation of Ratios and Data

© RMA 2024

MANUFACTURING—Coffee and Tea Manufacturing NAICS 311920

Comparative Historical Data / Current Data Sorted by Sales

Comparative Historical Data				Type of Statement	Current Data Sorted by Sales					
4	6	4		Unqualified		1		1		2
3	1	3		Reviewed					1	2
	1	2		Compiled					1	1
5	14	5		Tax Returns	1		1	1	2	
10	24	41		Other	1	5		5	12	18
4/1/21-3/31/22 ALL	4/1/22-3/31/23 ALL	4/1/23-3/31/24 ALL			0-1MM	9 (4/1-9/30/23) 1-3MM	3-5MM	46 (10/1/23-3/31/24) 5-10MM	10-25MM	25MM & OVER
22	46	55		NUMBER OF STATEMENTS	2	6	1	7	16	23
%	%	%		ASSETS	%	%	%	%	%	%
16.2	17.2	11.1		Cash & Equivalents					8.0	5.9
8.6	9.2	11.5		Trade Receivables (net)					7.8	13.9
24.6	23.1	19.7		Inventory					16.0	22.1
2.3	3.6	2.3		All Other Current					1.2	3.4
51.7	53.1	44.7		Total Current					32.9	45.2
35.8	30.0	33.2		Fixed Assets (net)					39.5	35.4
6.1	7.0	8.7		Intangibles (net)					9.2	5.5
6.1	9.9	13.4		All Other Non-Current					18.5	14.0
100.0	100.0	100.0		Total					100.0	100.0
				LIABILITIES						
10.2	8.6	7.6		Notes Payable-Short Term					3.9	7.0
4.4	1.2	3.1		Cur. Mat.-L.T.D.					2.1	2.9
10.9	9.0	10.5		Trade Payables					10.2	12.4
.0	.0	.1		Income Taxes Payable					.1	.1
11.5	6.8	13.9		All Other Current					9.1	9.7
37.0	25.6	35.2		Total Current					25.3	32.1
42.2	37.3	29.2		Long-Term Debt					28.5	25.1
.3	.1	.4		Deferred Taxes					.2	.2
5.0	6.6	7.5		All Other Non-Current					10.5	9.4
15.2	30.4	27.8		Net Worth					35.6	33.2
100.0	100.0	100.0		Total Liabilities & Net Worth					100.0	100.0
				INCOME DATA						
100.0	100.0	100.0		Net Sales					100.0	100.0
38.9	45.3	40.1		Gross Profit					40.2	30.6
38.3	41.9	37.8		Operating Expenses					38.4	29.5
.7	3.4	2.2		Operating Profit					1.8	1.0
-2.1	.6	1.6		All Other Expenses (net)					.5	2.5
2.8	2.9	.6		Profit Before Taxes					1.3	-1.5
				RATIOS						
2.8	7.5	1.8							3.1	2.1
1.4	3.5	1.5		Current					1.6	1.5
.9	1.5	1.0							1.0	1.1
1.7	3.8	1.1							1.1	1.0
.8	1.3	.6		Quick					.6	.6
.4	.5	.4							.4	.4
4 87.6	0 UND	6 59.0						6 65.1	23 15.7	
17 21.1	16 22.3	23 16.1		Sales/Receivables				12 31.6	32 11.3	
25 14.5	31 11.6	33 10.9						24 15.4	44 8.3	
32 11.5	37 9.9	38 9.6						28 13.0	51 7.1	
60 6.1	69 5.3	60 6.1		Cost of Sales/Inventory				54 6.7	64 5.7	
94 3.9	118 3.1	85 4.3						64 5.7	101 3.6	
2 230.4	2 210.1	16 22.7						15 23.6	23 15.8	
25 14.4	18 20.7	34 10.8		Cost of Sales/Payables				32 11.3	37 9.8	
49 7.4	46 8.0	43 8.5						43 8.4	51 7.2	
5.6	3.9	7.6							9.1	6.8
16.2	7.0	16.3		Sales/Working Capital					22.2	12.7
-118.1	15.7	-999.8							NM	30.0
19.2	14.6	7.4							8.1	4.0
(21) 8.4	(41) 5.2	(51) 2.3		EBIT/Interest				(15) 1.2	(22) 2.7	
-1.9	.1	-.2							-.2	-1.8
		5.0		Net Profit + Depr., Dep.,						
	(10)	2.8		Amort./Cur. Mat. L/T/D						
		.6								
.6	.4	.5							.7	.5
1.5	.9	1.5		Fixed/Worth					1.7	1.5
78.5	NM	21.5							3.8	7.5
1.2	.7	1.1							1.3	.8
3.3	2.2	3.6		Debt/Worth					3.4	2.6
219.0	NM	-24.1							7.0	19.2
61.9	49.2	41.9		% Profit Before Taxes/Tangible					19.5	38.6
(18) 28.2	(35) 16.1	(41) 11.4		Net Worth				(13) .0	(19) 11.0	
-10.6	3.1	-9.2							-15.7	-27.6
28.4	15.7	11.0							10.2	7.5
6.5	6.4	4.2		% Profit Before Taxes/Total Assets					.2	4.6
-12.7	-2.0	-4.3							-4.2	-14.3
15.4	13.0	11.5							9.0	5.8
7.9	8.1	5.8		Sales/Net Fixed Assets					4.9	4.2
3.3	3.9	3.8							3.9	3.3
3.2	2.9	2.5							2.7	1.8
2.1	2.0	1.7		Sales/Total Assets					1.6	1.6
1.4	1.4	1.4							1.4	1.2
2.1	1.5	2.6							2.8	2.5
(16) 3.2	(35) 2.5	(38) 3.1		% Depr., Dep., Amort./Sales				(14) 3.5	(19) 3.1	
5.1	3.9	4.3							5.3	3.8
	1.5			% Officers', Directors'						
	(13) 3.9			Owners' Comp/Sales						
		4.3								
1111547M	2037360M	3241042M		Net Sales ($)	726M	9668M	3141M	58967M	231501M	2937039M
815429M	1470413M	2261747M		Total Assets ($)	81M	5300M	1334M	23701M	133949M	2097382M

M = $ thousand   MM = $ million
See Pages viii through xx for Explanation of Ratios and Data

© RMA 2024

MANUFACTURING—Spice and Extract Manufacturing NAICS 311942

Current Data Sorted by Assets | Comparative Historical Data

					3	2	Type of Statement				
				3	2		Unqualified		11		5
			4	2			Reviewed		3		5
		1					Compiled		5		1
	1	3	10	12	8	5	Tax Returns		5		2
		19 (4/1-9/30/23)		35 (10/1/23-3/31/24)			Other		21		13
	0-500M	500M-2MM	2-10MM	10-50MM	50-100MM	100-250MM			4/1/19-3/31/20 ALL		4/1/20-3/31/21 ALL
	1	4	14	17	11	7	NUMBER OF STATEMENTS		45		26
	%	%	%	%	%	%	ASSETS		%		%
			11.8	11.3	.4		Cash & Equivalents		9.4		9.6
			25.8	15.5	20.6		Trade Receivables (net)		20.0		23.0
			40.7	29.8	41.4		Inventory		26.9		30.8
			3.2	3.5	7.2		All Other Current		1.1		1.8
			81.5	60.2	69.5		Total Current		57.4		65.1
			6.0	29.7	11.8		Fixed Assets (net)		30.8		26.7
			9.5	.9	1.6		Intangibles (net)		7.5		4.8
			2.9	9.2	17.1		All Other Non-Current		4.2		3.4
			100.0	100.0	100.0		Total		100.0		100.0
							LIABILITIES				
			13.2	6.8	8.5		Notes Payable-Short Term		6.9		7.2
			.2	2.1	3.8		Cur. Mat.-L.T.D.		2.4		1.9
			21.4	10.5	14.1		Trade Payables		11.9		14.4
			.0	.0	.0		Income Taxes Payable		.1		.7
			12.4	7.4	17.4		All Other Current		5.4		6.8
			47.2	26.9	43.8		Total Current		26.7		31.1
			12.4	15.4	15.9		Long-Term Debt		14.5		10.7
			.5	.1	.0		Deferred Taxes		.5		.5
			4.9	8.4	58.8		All Other Non-Current		2.8		2.6
			35.0	49.2	-18.5		Net Worth		55.5		55.0
			100.0	100.0	100.0		Total Liabilities & Net Worth		100.0		100.0
							INCOME DATA				
			100.0	100.0	100.0		Net Sales		100.0		100.0
			40.5	35.0	29.1		Gross Profit		35.6		33.1
			37.0	33.4	24.6		Operating Expenses		27.1		23.1
			3.4	1.5	4.5		Operating Profit		8.5		10.0
			.2	.5	7.0		All Other Expenses (net)		1.0		1.6
			3.2	1.1	-2.5		Profit Before Taxes		7.5		8.4
							RATIOS				
			4.0	3.9	1.6				3.9		3.7
			1.6	2.2	1.5		Current		2.4		2.6
			1.2	1.3	1.4				1.3		1.8
			2.9	2.6	.6				2.2		2.1
			.5	.7	.4		Quick		1.1		1.5
			.4	.4	.4				.5		.7
			26 14.3	24 14.9	28 12.9				21 17.8		25 14.6
			35 10.4	32 11.3	31 11.7		Sales/Receivables		32 11.3		39 9.3
			49 7.5	41 9.0	36 10.0				43 8.4		54 6.8
			43 8.5	64 5.7	83 4.4				38 9.5		45 8.2
			79 4.6	96 3.8	87 4.2		Cost of Sales/Inventory		59 6.2		64 5.7
			140 2.6	166 2.2	101 3.6				91 4.0		140 2.6
			34 10.8	22 16.7	26 14.0				19 19.2		22 16.8
			44 8.3	30 12.3	34 10.7		Cost of Sales/Payables		26 13.9		26 13.9
			58 6.3	49 7.4	37 9.8				36 10.1		53 6.9
			2.7	2.1	8.9				4.2		3.1
			10.1	7.0	10.0		Sales/Working Capital		8.1		5.0
			26.9	13.2	10.8				19.6		10.2
			184.9	12.4	1.7				38.6		109.9
		(13)	4.0	4.8	.3		EBIT/Interest	(40)	9.8	(24)	30.3
			1.3	-1.7	.1				4.1		4.7
							Net Profit + Depr., Dep., Amort./Cur. Mat. L/T/D		9.8		
								(12)	4.7		
									3.1		
			.0	.3	4.5				.3		.2
			.1	.6	-.1		Fixed/Worth		.6		.4
			NM	1.3	-.1				1.4		.7
			.4	.5	5.4				.4		.4
			10.8	1.4	-3.9		Debt/Worth		.7		.6
			-37.9	2.6	-3.5				2.6		2.1
			220.7	18.1					47.6		57.4
		(10)	26.8	8.8			% Profit Before Taxes/Tangible Net Worth	(40)	34.2	(25)	39.4
			17.7	-5.6					21.0		10.4
			16.0	10.0	6.5				21.0		28.1
			11.4	3.5	-3.2		% Profit Before Taxes/Total Assets		15.9		14.6
			2.7	-3.2	-19.4				8.0		5.0
			999.8	13.5	64.7				15.6		24.4
			140.6	5.3	55.3		Sales/Net Fixed Assets		9.2		10.6
			24.8	3.0	18.1				3.6		3.1
			3.7	2.3	2.6				2.9		2.8
			2.4	1.5	2.5		Sales/Total Assets		2.2		1.5
			1.5	.9	2.0				1.4		1.3
				.7	.6				1.0		.8
				1.4	.7		% Depr., Dep., Amort./Sales	(37)	1.9	(21)	1.9
				3.0	1.2				3.2		3.2
									1.9		
							% Officers', Directors' Owners' Comp/Sales	(13)	2.6		
									5.5		
2675M	17205M	175355M	514587M	1954973M	1328635M		Net Sales ($)		3678112M		1418436M
473M	6070M	80128M	351551M	883919M	1195664M		Total Assets ($)		2095801M		1064876M

M = $ thousand   MM = $ million
See Pages viii through xx for Explanation of Ratios and Data

© RMA 2024

MANUFACTURING—Spice and Extract Manufacturing NAICS 311942

Comparative Historical Data / Current Data Sorted by Sales

Comparative Historical Data				Type of Statement		Current Data Sorted by Sales				
3	6	5		Unqualified						5
4	5	3		Reviewed					3	3
2	5	6		Compiled			1			2
1	3	1		Tax Returns			1		3	
12	17	39		Other		2	4	3	10	20
4/1/21-3/31/22	4/1/22-3/31/23	4/1/23-3/31/24				19 (4/1-9/30/23)		35 (10/1/23-3/31/24)		
ALL	ALL	ALL			0-1MM	1-3MM	3-5MM	5-10MM	10-25MM	25MM & OVER
22	36	54		NUMBER OF STATEMENTS		2	3	6	13	30
%	%	%		ASSETS	%	%	%	%	%	%
11.9	9.8	8.8		Cash & Equivalents					14.6	5.3
19.7	20.9	18.7		Trade Receivables (net)	D				25.7	17.5
33.0	32.7	33.7		Inventory	A				33.1	30.9
6.0	5.2	5.1		All Other Current	T				3.5	6.2
70.6	68.6	66.4		Total Current	A				76.9	59.9
22.5	19.7	17.1		Fixed Assets (net)					10.7	22.8
2.7	6.2	7.8		Intangibles (net)	N				9.5	6.8
4.2	5.5	8.7		All Other Non-Current	O				2.9	10.6
100.0	100.0	100.0		Total	T				100.0	100.0
				LIABILITIES	A					
11.4	5.1	8.9		Notes Payable-Short Term	V				15.1	6.4
1.0	3.5	2.2		Cur. Mat.-L.T.D.	A				.1	3.2
16.7	15.4	14.2		Trade Payables	I				17.9	10.9
.1	.1	.0		Income Taxes Payable	L				.0	.1
4.6	8.4	11.2		All Other Current	A				8.8	12.1
33.7	32.4	36.5		Total Current	B				41.8	32.7
7.6	14.0	16.1		Long-Term Debt	L				14.3	15.6
.0	.2	.2		Deferred Taxes	E				.5	.2
7.5	6.8	16.9		All Other Non-Current					1.8	24.5
51.1	46.7	30.3		Net Worth					41.7	27.0
100.0	100.0	100.0		Total Liabilities & Net Worth					100.0	100.0
				INCOME DATA						
100.0	100.0	100.0		Net Sales					100.0	100.0
30.4	29.7	35.8		Gross Profit					38.5	31.1
22.2	23.3	31.9		Operating Expenses					37.1	24.8
8.3	6.4	3.9		Operating Profit					1.4	6.3
-.4	.9	2.4		All Other Expenses (net)					.2	3.9
8.7	5.5	1.4		Profit Before Taxes					1.3	2.4
				RATIOS						
3.6	4.5	3.4							5.3	2.5
2.5	2.5	1.7		Current					1.6	1.7
1.4	1.4	1.3							1.1	1.4
2.1	1.5	1.3							3.9	1.2
1.2	1.0	.5		Quick					.9	.5
.5	.6	.4							.3	.4
24 / 15.1	25 / 14.8	25 / 14.8							24 / 15.1	28 / 13.1
35 / 10.5	35 / 10.3	31 / 11.6		Sales/Receivables					32 / 11.5	33 / 11.2
52 / 7.0	45 / 8.2	37 / 9.8							36 / 10.2	46 / 7.9
50 / 7.3	46 / 8.0	60 / 6.1							42 / 8.6	72 / 5.1
81 / 4.5	74 / 4.9	87 / 4.2		Cost of Sales/Inventory					72 / 5.1	87 / 4.2
126 / 2.9	182 / 2.0	114 / 3.2							114 / 3.2	107 / 3.4
21 / 17.2	22 / 16.3	23 / 15.8							29 / 12.5	19 / 19.0
34 / 10.6	29 / 12.5	33 / 11.1		Cost of Sales/Payables					43 / 8.4	28 / 13.1
65 / 5.6	48 / 7.6	45 / 8.2							55 / 6.6	37 / 9.8
3.3	2.3	3.1							3.6	4.2
5.0	5.7	8.7		Sales/Working Capital					11.2	8.2
7.2	12.1	16.0							30.1	11.0
176.5	24.1	8.6							271.5	8.5
(20) 9.9	(30) 6.5	(49) 2.8		EBIT/Interest					(12) 2.9	(29) 1.9
5.8	3.3	.1							-8.8	.1
	15.8	7.3		Net Profit + Depr., Dep.,						2.7
(10) 6.2	(15) 1.1			Amort./Cur. Mat. L/T/D					(12) .1	
	2.9	-2.3								-2.3
.3	.3	.2							.0	.4
.4	.4	.8		Fixed/Worth					.1	1.3
.6	.8	-9.5							NM	-.1
.3	.5	1.0							.3	1.0
1.5	1.2	3.3		Debt/Worth					3.6	2.9
2.5	2.7	-8.5							-28.2	-4.1
51.4	36.6	33.4		% Profit Before Taxes/Tangible Net Worth						32.9
31.9	(32) 18.7	(39) 17.9							(20)	18.1
18.6	1.7	1.4								-2.5
26.4	21.4	12.2		% Profit Before Taxes/Total Assets					14.2	12.1
11.1	8.5	3.9							9.1	4.2
6.4	2.2	-4.5							-3.3	-4.5
43.6	30.6	63.0							999.8	51.7
11.7	11.7	20.4		Sales/Net Fixed Assets					71.0	11.8
4.4	5.0	5.3							14.8	3.7
2.5	3.2	2.6							3.8	2.5
1.6	2.0	1.9		Sales/Total Assets					2.5	1.7
1.3	1.2	1.3							1.7	1.3
.6	.5	.6								.6
(21) 1.4	(30) 1.6	(38) .9		% Depr., Dep., Amort./Sales					(27)	.9
3.1	3.4	2.1								1.6
	.8	1.3		% Officers', Directors' Owners' Comp/Sales						
(11) 1.4	(15) 2.3									
	3.9	16.4								
1127617M	2112112M	3993430M		Net Sales ($)		4139M	12077M	43143M	200325M	3733746M
718728M	1362907M	2517805M		Total Assets ($)		2088M	4654M	66136M	94238M	2350689M

© RMA 2024   M = $ thousand   MM = $ million
See Pages viii through xx for Explanation of Ratios and Data

MANUFACTURING—Perishable Prepared Food Manufacturing NAICS 311991

Current Data Sorted by Assets / Comparative Historical Data

							Type of Statement		
			4	1	3		Unqualified	5	3
		2	4	2			Reviewed	6	2
	1		2				Compiled	1	1
	2	2					Tax Returns	10	4
2		11	11	4	4		Other	26	25
	13 (4/1-9/30/23)		42 (10/1/23-3/31/24)					4/1/19-3/31/20	4/1/20-3/31/21
0-500M	500M-2MM	2-10MM	10-50MM	50-100MM	100-250MM			ALL	ALL
2	3	15	21	7	7		NUMBER OF STATEMENTS	48	35
%	%	%	%	%	%		ASSETS	%	%
		14.9	3.5				Cash & Equivalents	9.2	14.0
		17.3	16.9				Trade Receivables (net)	18.4	23.0
		16.9	18.5				Inventory	15.3	17.9
		2.3	2.0				All Other Current	1.5	.6
		51.4	40.8				Total Current	44.5	55.5
		30.4	40.7				Fixed Assets (net)	39.8	29.9
		3.1	5.4				Intangibles (net)	10.2	9.3
		15.1	13.1				All Other Non-Current	5.5	5.3
		100.0	100.0				Total	100.0	100.0
							LIABILITIES		
		5.6	7.7				Notes Payable-Short Term	6.8	11.7
		2.4	2.5				Cur. Mat.-L.T.D.	5.3	2.5
		20.8	16.2				Trade Payables	13.4	16.8
		.0	.1				Income Taxes Payable	.0	.1
		7.5	7.2				All Other Current	7.3	11.3
		36.2	33.6				Total Current	32.8	42.5
		34.4	19.1				Long-Term Debt	28.8	18.3
		.0	.0				Deferred Taxes	.3	.4
		16.2	16.3				All Other Non-Current	9.1	4.0
		13.1	31.0				Net Worth	28.9	34.8
		100.0	100.0				Total Liabilities & Net Worth	100.0	100.0
							INCOME DATA		
		100.0	100.0				Net Sales	100.0	100.0
		32.4	23.8				Gross Profit	30.9	30.3
		28.7	18.8				Operating Expenses	28.3	26.9
		3.7	4.9				Operating Profit	2.6	3.4
		.6	1.4				All Other Expenses (net)	1.2	.5
		3.1	3.5				Profit Before Taxes	1.4	2.9
							RATIOS		
		3.3	1.7					2.3	3.4
		1.4	1.3				Current	1.5	2.0
		.8	1.1					1.1	1.1
		2.9	1.0					1.4	2.1
		.5	.7				Quick	1.0	1.1
		.4	.5					.5	.7
		11 33.5	28 13.0					17 21.5	24 15.1
		25 14.4	33 11.1				Sales/Receivables	26 13.8	33 11.2
		40 9.1	43 8.5					39 9.4	41 8.8
		19 19.5	24 14.9					13 27.6	18 20.3
		28 13.1	40 9.2				Cost of Sales/Inventory	29 12.7	30 12.2
		61 6.0	65 5.6					51 7.2	49 7.5
		16 22.7	23 16.0					17 20.9	19 19.2
		26 14.3	36 10.1				Cost of Sales/Payables	24 15.5	28 13.2
		42 8.7	44 8.3					36 10.1	43 8.5
		7.0	10.9					8.1	7.3
		12.7	30.1				Sales/Working Capital	25.4	13.0
		-22.6	111.6					75.3	96.5
		11.7	13.8					13.9	21.0
		(14) 3.7	(20) 3.9				EBIT/Interest	(47) 4.4	(31) 10.7
		1.0	-.6					-2.2	.4
							Net Profit + Depr., Dep., Amort./Cur. Mat. L/T/D		
		.6	1.1					.6	.3
		4.3	1.8				Fixed/Worth	2.0	1.0
		-10.3	4.2					NM	3.0
		1.9	.9					1.1	.8
		7.7	2.4				Debt/Worth	2.7	2.1
		-16.2	9.2					NM	8.1
		154.2	56.9					55.5	90.8
		(10) 25.6	(18) 32.4				% Profit Before Taxes/Tangible Net Worth	(36) 23.5	(27) 39.4
		9.1	10.5					11.3	14.2
		15.4	19.4					15.5	19.8
		3.5	7.8				% Profit Before Taxes/Total Assets	8.1	10.8
		.2	-2.4					-6.1	2.4
		22.9	7.1					16.3	25.3
		8.5	4.5				Sales/Net Fixed Assets	7.4	11.7
		5.4	2.5					2.9	3.8
		3.1	2.7					3.5	3.6
		2.2	1.7				Sales/Total Assets	2.3	2.1
		1.5	1.1					1.5	1.5
		1.1	1.2					1.7	1.4
		(14) 2.6	(18) 2.2				% Depr., Dep., Amort./Sales	(39) 2.3	(27) 2.2
		5.2	3.7					4.2	3.7
								.9	1.2
							% Officers', Directors' Owners' Comp/Sales	(11) 2.8	(11) 1.8
								5.1	2.7
2740M	6866M	197532M	1164222M	801591M	2737365M		Net Sales ($)	3838029M	3415160M
602M	2824M	73251M	585632M	470476M	1239015M		Total Assets ($)	1989718M	1742775M

M = $ thousand   MM = $ million
See Pages viii through xx for Explanation of Ratios and Data

© RMA 2024

MANUFACTURING—Perishable Prepared Food Manufacturing NAICS 311991

Comparative Historical Data / Current Data Sorted by Sales

Comparative Historical					Current Data Sorted by Sales					
			Type of Statement							
4	8	8	Unqualified							8
5	6	8	Reviewed				1	1	1	6
4	2	3	Compiled			1	1	1	1	
2	5	4	Tax Returns		2	1	1	1	1	
25	30	32	Other	1	1	3	1	1	6	20
4/1/21-3/31/22 ALL	4/1/22-3/31/23 ALL	4/1/23-3/31/24 ALL		0-1MM	13 (4/1-9/30/23) 1-3MM	3-5MM	42 (10/1/23-3/31/24) 5-10MM	10-25MM		25MM & OVER
40	51	55	NUMBER OF STATEMENTS	1	3	4	4	9		34
%	%	%	ASSETS	%	%	%	%	%		%
12.6	10.4	8.3	Cash & Equivalents							5.0
17.0	19.1	15.3	Trade Receivables (net)							15.8
22.3	20.8	16.6	Inventory							18.4
2.9	3.0	4.4	All Other Current							2.8
54.8	53.4	44.5	Total Current							42.1
29.5	31.1	35.5	Fixed Assets (net)							38.3
9.2	7.9	7.0	Intangibles (net)							6.9
6.5	7.6	13.0	All Other Non-Current							12.7
100.0	100.0	100.0	Total							100.0
			LIABILITIES							
5.9	8.0	8.0	Notes Payable-Short Term							7.1
2.1	2.9	3.9	Cur. Mat.-L.T.D.							4.3
13.3	14.2	15.5	Trade Payables							17.8
.0	.1	.0	Income Taxes Payable							.1
9.0	8.6	8.6	All Other Current							10.1
30.3	33.8	36.0	Total Current							39.3
26.5	22.9	25.7	Long-Term Debt							19.4
.1	.1	.1	Deferred Taxes							.2
11.6	5.7	13.2	All Other Non-Current							9.9
31.4	37.5	25.0	Net Worth							31.2
100.0	100.0	100.0	Total Liabilities & Net Worth							100.0
			INCOME DATA							
100.0	100.0	100.0	Net Sales							100.0
33.5	26.4	27.7	Gross Profit							22.8
30.6	24.6	22.8	Operating Expenses							18.0
2.9	1.8	4.9	Operating Profit							4.8
-.7	.4	1.3	All Other Expenses (net)							1.2
3.6	1.4	3.6	Profit Before Taxes							3.6
			RATIOS							
3.8	2.9	2.1								1.7
2.3	1.7	1.3	Current							1.1
1.4	1.2	.8								.7
2.4	1.5	1.2								1.0
1.2	.8	.6	Quick							.6
.6	.5	.4								.3
20 17.9	17 21.2	19 19.6							20	18.7
28 13.2	27 13.4	29 12.6	Sales/Receivables						31	11.9
36 10.0	36 10.0	39 9.4							40	9.2
21 17.1	21 17.2	19 19.4							26	14.1
37 9.9	31 11.7	35 10.4	Cost of Sales/Inventory						40	9.2
73 5.0	81 4.5	63 5.8							64	5.7
13 27.4	11 33.8	20 18.3							24	15.3
27 13.5	25 14.8	30 12.3	Cost of Sales/Payables						33	11.2
47 7.8	41 9.0	42 8.7							45	8.1
4.8	6.1	7.5								12.5
7.0	12.3	19.4	Sales/Working Capital							34.9
18.3	34.7	-23.4								-22.3
27.9	19.5	10.3								17.3
(35) 8.8	(45) 4.9	(53) 3.5	EBIT/Interest						(33)	4.8
1.4	.2	.4								.8
		21.9	Net Profit + Depr., Dep.,							27.1
	(17) 4.1		Amort./Cur. Mat. L/T/D						(14)	4.6
		1.3								1.4
.3	.4	.8								.8
.9	1.0	1.8	Fixed/Worth							1.8
2.7	2.3	197.5								5.2
.7	.8	1.0								.9
1.7	1.8	5.6	Debt/Worth							3.3
9.6	8.9	-86.2								9.3
34.7	53.6	57.3	% Profit Before Taxes/Tangible							53.6
(32) 23.7	(43) 18.0	(41) 29.3	Net Worth						(28)	28.2
2.9	3.9	9.2								18.0
20.0	17.7	14.5	% Profit Before Taxes/Total							14.8
9.1	5.8	7.0	Assets							7.5
.0	-1.6	-1.7								.1
29.7	32.4	11.1								8.5
8.5	6.8	6.2	Sales/Net Fixed Assets							5.7
4.2	4.3	3.5								3.4
3.2	3.3	2.7								2.9
2.0	2.2	2.0	Sales/Total Assets							1.9
1.5	1.7	1.3								1.3
.9	1.2	1.2								1.1
(32) 2.0	(35) 2.2	(44) 2.5	% Depr., Dep., Amort./Sales						(28)	2.0
3.2	3.4	4.1								2.8
1.1	1.0	.7	% Officers', Directors'							
(10) 1.9	(14) 1.8	(10) 1.3	Owners' Comp/Sales							
4.1	3.3	3.1								
2188685M	4084852M	4910316M	Net Sales ($)	69M	5083M	14014M	27358M	146419M		4717373M
1234885M	2187710M	2371800M	Total Assets ($)	171M	1530M	8736M	29002M	74915M		2257446M

M = $ thousand   MM = $ million
See Pages viii through xx for Explanation of Ratios and Data

© RMA 2024

MANUFACTURING—All Other Miscellaneous Food Manufacturing NAICS 311999

Current Data Sorted by Assets | Comparative Historical Data

Type of Statement									
2			2	4	8	Unqualified		23	13
	2	6	9	3	1	Reviewed		18	10
	1	4				Compiled		5	2
3	5	4	2			Tax Returns		25	9
2	4	15	25	13	9	Other		88	63
	19 (4/1-9/30/23)		105 (10/1/23-3/31/24)					4/1/19-3/31/20	4/1/20-3/31/21
0-500M	500M-2MM	2-10MM	10-50MM	50-100MM	100-250MM			ALL	ALL
7	12	29	38	20	18	NUMBER OF STATEMENTS		159	97
%	%	%	%	%	%	ASSETS		%	%
	15.2	11.1	15.0	10.7	7.8	Cash & Equivalents		11.5	12.2
	48.7	28.1	16.9	13.0	16.6	Trade Receivables (net)		19.6	21.4
	9.9	24.5	25.0	24.0	30.5	Inventory		23.6	20.5
	5.0	1.6	2.2	5.3	1.9	All Other Current		2.5	2.2
	78.8	65.3	59.2	52.9	56.8	Total Current		57.2	56.3
	14.5	24.9	20.2	30.7	34.9	Fixed Assets (net)		29.0	29.5
	2.2	5.9	9.3	7.7	1.2	Intangibles (net)		9.0	8.9
	4.5	3.9	11.3	8.8	7.1	All Other Non-Current		4.8	5.5
	100.0	100.0	100.0	100.0	100.0	Total		100.0	100.0
						LIABILITIES			
	21.2	9.9	5.2	5.4	8.9	Notes Payable-Short Term		6.9	9.3
	2.7	2.7	1.3	4.0	4.3	Cur. Mat.-L.T.D.		5.4	2.5
	45.1	27.1	11.5	11.9	16.2	Trade Payables		16.4	16.4
	.0	.5	.2	.2	.2	Income Taxes Payable		.1	.4
	3.5	15.5	12.3	9.2	7.4	All Other Current		13.2	8.1
	72.4	55.8	30.5	30.7	36.9	Total Current		41.9	36.6
	12.0	24.3	11.3	27.2	16.2	Long-Term Debt		15.4	19.9
	.0	.1	.1	.5	1.3	Deferred Taxes		.3	.4
	6.1	11.1	9.2	5.7	6.8	All Other Non-Current		5.7	5.6
	9.6	8.7	48.9	35.9	38.7	Net Worth		36.7	37.4
	100.0	100.0	100.0	100.0	100.0	Total Liabilties & Net Worth		100.0	100.0
						INCOME DATA			
	100.0	100.0	100.0	100.0	100.0	Net Sales		100.0	100.0
	27.1	34.8	28.7	27.6	24.1	Gross Profit		33.7	32.3
	25.5	30.3	23.7	22.8	16.7	Operating Expenses		29.5	26.6
	1.6	4.5	5.0	4.8	7.4	Operating Profit		4.2	5.7
	.3	1.2	-.1	1.1	.8	All Other Expenses (net)		1.1	1.1
	1.3	3.4	5.1	3.7	6.6	Profit Before Taxes		3.1	4.7
						RATIOS			
	2.5	3.7	4.0	2.9	2.3	Current		2.6	2.8
	1.0	1.4	2.5	1.7	1.7			1.6	1.6
	.9	1.0	1.4	1.4	1.1			1.0	1.2
	2.0	1.5	2.5	1.4	1.0	Quick		1.8	1.5
	1.0	1.0	1.2	.7	.7			.7	.9
	.7	.4	.7	.4	.5			.4	.6
16	22.7	17	21.3	22	16.7	10	36.4	15	23.7	Sales/Receivables	19	19.5	19	19.4
28	12.9	24	15.3	33	11.0	24	15.4	34	10.6		29	12.7	27	13.6
31	11.6	45	8.2	42	8.7	36	10.1	44	8.3		38	9.5	40	9.1
0	UND	14	25.7	31	11.8	29	12.5	31	11.6	Cost of Sales/Inventory	22	16.5	24	15.1
4	83.1	51	7.2	58	6.3	78	4.7	85	4.3		57	6.4	49	7.5
16	22.9	101	3.6	85	4.3	111	3.3	114	3.2		99	3.7	79	4.6
13	28.5	14	25.7	11	31.9	18	20.7	19	19.6	Cost of Sales/Payables	16	22.2	16	22.6
35	10.4	22	16.9	26	14.1	29	12.6	29	12.6		29	12.7	26	14.0
50	7.3	56	6.5	39	9.3	37	9.9	39	9.3		43	8.4	38	9.7
	11.8	4.8	3.0	5.7	5.1	Sales/Working Capital		6.0	5.1
	-612.0	17.0	6.6	10.1	9.8			12.3	11.6
	-87.9	987.4	16.5	16.8	NM			-682.2	47.4
	14.4	24.9	57.0	8.5	53.7	EBIT/Interest		21.2	38.2
(10)	5.1	(23) 6.3	(27) 18.2	(18) 4.3	(17) 5.1		(137)	5.4	(82) 8.8
	-13.4	1.4	2.2	2.0	2.4			.8	.4
					8.7	Net Profit + Depr., Dep., Amort./Cur. Mat. L/T/D		8.4	12.0
				(10)	2.5		(34)	3.9	(14) 4.8
					.7			1.4	2.6
	.0	.2	.1	.3	.3	Fixed/Worth		.3	.4
	.8	.9	.4	1.0	1.1			.9	1.0
	UND	NM	1.0	NM	1.9			3.7	4.0
	1.2	.4	.2	.7	.7	Debt/Worth		.6	.7
	UND	2.4	1.0	2.3	1.6			1.7	1.9
	-13.0	NM	2.6	NM	3.4			7.9	19.3
		100.0	31.1	21.3	45.2	% Profit Before Taxes/Tangible Net Worth		52.4	62.8
	(22) 39.2	(34) 18.0	(15) 13.5	(17) 29.3		(130)	20.0	(79) 26.7
		8.6	2.6	4.0	12.5			7.2	.0
	33.6	21.2	18.2	9.9	14.5	% Profit Before Taxes/Total Assets		14.8	18.2
	11.6	6.4	7.4	6.1	8.4			7.3	9.1
	-5.1	1.6	.4	3.9	6.0			-.4	-1.2
	UND	34.1	26.6	14.0	18.5	Sales/Net Fixed Assets		25.5	25.4
	40.1	14.2	10.4	5.6	7.2			8.8	8.2
	11.8	5.1	4.9	4.0	2.7			4.7	3.8
	8.0	3.8	2.8	2.4	2.5	Sales/Total Assets		3.4	3.3
	4.0	2.5	1.8	1.8	1.7			2.2	2.1
	2.6	1.7	.9	1.1	1.5			1.4	1.3
		.7	.6	1.3	.5	% Depr., Dep., Amort./Sales		.8	1.0
	(18) 1.9	(33) 1.5	(18) 2.1	(17) 1.2		(117)	2.1	(67) 2.2
		4.7	3.1	3.5	2.2			3.7	5.0
			1.3			% Officers', Directors' Owners' Comp/Sales		.6	.7
		(10) 2.9					(38)	1.7	(19) 1.7
		7.4						4.1	5.7
6592M	95128M	571096M	1995294M	2852275M	6298088M	Net Sales ($)		15292060M	5719417M
1539M	15605M	138485M	932786M	1416361M	2551342M	Total Assets ($)		7771287M	3058010M

M = $ thousand   MM = $ million
See Pages viii through xx for Explanation of Ratios and Data

© RMA 2024

MANUFACTURING—All Other Miscellaneous Food Manufacturing NAICS 311999

Comparative Historical Data | Current Data Sorted by Sales

Comparative Historical Data						Current Data Sorted by Sales					
					Type of Statement						
	9		20		16	Unqualified	2				1	13
	5		18		21	Reviewed				4	3	14
	5		7		5	Compiled				1	4	
	8		10		14	Tax Returns	1	3	5	3	1	1
	49		93		68	Other	1	2	2	10	13	40
	4/1/21-3/31/22		4/1/22-3/31/23		4/1/23-3/31/24		0-1MM	19 (4/1-9/30/23) 1-3MM	3-5MM	105 (10/1/23-3/31/24) 5-10MM	10-25MM	25MM & OVER
	ALL 76		ALL 148		ALL 124	NUMBER OF STATEMENTS	4	5	7	18	22	68
	%		%		%	ASSETS	%	%	%	%	%	%
	14.2		13.3		12.9	Cash & Equivalents				17.2	14.3	10.5
	19.3		19.0		22.3	Trade Receivables (net)				24.9	23.6	21.2
	27.2		26.7		23.6	Inventory				14.7	24.3	26.1
	4.3		2.8		2.8	All Other Current				1.7	2.5	2.9
	65.0		61.8		61.6	Total Current				58.5	64.7	60.7
	26.4		26.3		24.8	Fixed Assets (net)				20.3	24.0	26.0
	3.7		5.3		5.9	Intangibles (net)				18.1	6.4	3.4
	5.0		6.6		7.7	All Other Non-Current				3.1	4.9	9.9
	100.0		100.0		100.0	Total				100.0	100.0	100.0
						LIABILITIES						
	9.7		9.6		9.4	Notes Payable-Short Term				11.7	11.9	6.5
	3.1		2.8		2.7	Cur. Mat.-L.T.D.				1.6	1.7	3.1
	14.3		16.5		19.6	Trade Payables				23.8	17.9	18.5
	.3		.1		.3	Income Taxes Payable				.0	.8	.2
	11.6		11.9		14.3	All Other Current				13.5	11.4	11.0
	38.9		40.9		46.3	Total Current				50.6	43.7	39.3
	19.7		19.9		17.9	Long-Term Debt				10.7	27.8	16.7
	.8		.3		.3	Deferred Taxes				.0	.1	.5
	7.9		7.5		9.2	All Other Non-Current				1.5	19.7	6.7
	32.7		31.4		26.3	Net Worth				37.3	8.7	36.7
	100.0		100.0		100.0	Total Liabilties & Net Worth				100.0	100.0	100.0
						INCOME DATA						
	100.0		100.0		100.0	Net Sales				100.0	100.0	100.0
	35.0		31.4		29.8	Gross Profit				36.8	37.4	23.5
	29.7		28.0		24.8	Operating Expenses				34.1	31.1	18.0
	5.3		3.4		5.0	Operating Profit				2.7	6.3	5.6
	-.6		.5		.6	All Other Expenses (net)				-.6	2.1	.6
	5.9		2.8		4.4	Profit Before Taxes				3.2	4.1	5.0
						RATIOS						
	4.5		3.2		3.0					6.8	3.2	3.0
	2.2		1.7		1.8	Current				2.0	1.9	1.8
	1.3		1.2		1.1					1.0	1.1	1.2
	2.8		1.9		1.8					3.0	2.4	1.6
	1.1		1.0		.9	Quick				1.1	1.1	.8
	.5		.4		.5					.9	.4	.5
21	17.8	17	21.6	17	21.7					21 17.2	19 18.8	16 22.9
31	11.8	28	12.9	28	13.0	Sales/Receivables				27 13.6	30 12.0	29 12.7
43	8.4	39	9.4	41	8.9					53 6.9	47 7.8	40 9.2
29	12.6	26	13.9	18	20.1					8 43.6	21 17.8	24 14.9
58	6.3	61	6.0	59	6.2	Cost of Sales/Inventory				69 5.3	54 6.8	64 5.7
104	3.5	111	3.3	91	4.0					85 4.3	94 3.9	91 4.0
13	27.9	14	26.1	15	24.9					17 22.0	14 25.5	16 23.4
28	13.1	27	13.7	26	13.9	Cost of Sales/Payables				26 14.1	33 11.2	25 14.5
50	7.3	47	7.7	41	8.8					59 6.2	61 6.0	38 9.7
	3.8		4.9		5.0					3.9	4.3	5.0
	8.1		10.5		10.2	Sales/Working Capital				9.1	10.0	9.8
	17.4		30.6		77.4					-770.3	85.6	35.3
	43.3		36.6		31.0					22.8	29.4	45.3
(63)	8.3	(123)	7.3	(97)	5.9	EBIT/Interest				(11) 3.0	(18) 6.7	(57) 5.9
	2.8		.5		2.2					-.1	1.0	2.4
			8.9		6.2	Net Profit + Depr., Dep.,						7.0
		(34)	4.8	(31)	3.2	Amort./Cur. Mat. L/T/D					(26)	3.3
			1.9		1.1							1.2
	.2		.2		.2					.2	.2	.2
	.6		.6		.7	Fixed/Worth				.7	.9	.5
	1.6		1.8		2.1					UND	2.9	1.8
	.3		.5		.5					.2	.7	.6
	1.7		1.5		1.8	Debt/Worth				2.8	1.8	1.7
	7.2		5.4		7.2					UND	6.6	5.9
	47.1		38.0		49.9	% Profit Before Taxes/Tangible				70.3	68.3	36.3
(65)	23.9	(124)	17.5	(100)	27.2	Net Worth				(14) 25.8	(18) 30.2	(56) 23.5
	7.7		2.4		8.1					2.6	4.7	8.3
	16.6		17.0		16.7	% Profit Before Taxes/Total				22.7	20.5	14.8
	9.3		7.1		7.4	Assets				3.0	13.1	7.3
	3.5		-.6		2.2					-.1	-.1	3.7
	44.4		26.9		29.0					30.4	26.5	36.1
	10.8		10.3		10.9	Sales/Net Fixed Assets				12.2	12.4	11.1
	3.9		4.8		4.5					3.9	5.1	4.5
	3.0		3.1		3.6					3.2	3.8	3.5
	1.9		2.0		2.2	Sales/Total Assets				1.9	2.3	2.2
	1.3		1.4		1.4					.8	1.5	1.5
	.7		.8		.8					.8	.9	.6
(58)	1.6	(111)	1.5	(94)	1.6	% Depr., Dep., Amort./Sales				(12) 1.9	(15) 1.4	(58) 1.5
	4.0		2.8		3.0					5.0	4.1	2.3
	1.1		1.9		1.5	% Officers', Directors'						.4
(20)	2.2	(28)	2.8	(26)	2.7	Owners' Comp/Sales					(11)	1.5
	6.8		5.3		6.4							2.4
	4815816M		12683840M		11818473M	Net Sales ($)	1217M	10627M	28893M	132816M	371119M	11273801M
	2528610M		6655498M		5056118M	Total Assets ($)	781M	5005M	12774M	111709M	205157M	4720692M

M = $ thousand   MM = $ million
See Pages viii through xx for Explanation of Ratios and Data

© RMA 2024

MANUFACTURING—Soft Drink Manufacturing NAICS 312111

Current Data Sorted by Assets | Comparative Historical Data

0-500M	500M-2MM	2-10MM	10-50MM	50-100MM	100-250MM	Type of Statement	4/1/19-3/31/20 ALL	4/1/20-3/31/21 ALL
						Unqualified	17	11
						Reviewed	4	
						Compiled	6	2
						Tax Returns	10	1
1	9		3	7	4	Other	33	19
		1	8	6	1			
		3	34		6			
1	1	5	12	13	11	NUMBER OF STATEMENTS	70	33
%	%	%	%	%	%	**ASSETS**	%	%
			20.4	16.7	11.6	Cash & Equivalents	9.7	16.1
			18.7	18.1	12.5	Trade Receivables (net)	15.8	12.7
			10.7	17.4	15.0	Inventory	13.2	11.9
			.9	3.6	3.0	All Other Current	2.7	3.0
			50.7	55.9	42.0	Total Current	41.3	43.7
			23.5	30.1	35.8	Fixed Assets (net)	36.6	36.6
			4.2	6.1	7.7	Intangibles (net)	13.4	13.8
			21.6	7.9	14.5	All Other Non-Current	8.6	5.9
			100.0	100.0	100.0	Total	100.0	100.0
						LIABILITIES		
			5.4	3.0	3.9	Notes Payable-Short Term	4.0	8.5
			5.4	2.7	1.0	Cur. Mat.-L.T.D.	4.3	4.5
			12.4	16.0	14.5	Trade Payables	14.6	12.7
			.2	.2	.5	Income Taxes Payable	.2	.4
			9.0	7.4	7.1	All Other Current	8.6	11.2
			32.4	29.3	26.9	Total Current	31.6	37.3
			10.1	16.5	13.6	Long-Term Debt	30.4	26.9
			.2	1.4	1.1	Deferred Taxes	1.3	.6
			2.8	2.9	5.2	All Other Non-Current	4.4	4.0
			54.5	50.0	53.3	Net Worth	32.3	31.1
			100.0	100.0	100.0	Total Liabilties & Net Worth	100.0	100.0
						INCOME DATA		
			100.0	100.0	100.0	Net Sales	100.0	100.0
			35.5	25.4	34.0	Gross Profit	32.9	38.6
			27.2	22.3	26.5	Operating Expenses	26.8	31.5
			8.3	3.0	7.4	Operating Profit	6.1	7.1
			-1.5	.4	-.5	All Other Expenses (net)	1.5	.6
			9.8	2.7	8.0	Profit Before Taxes	4.5	6.5
						RATIOS		
			3.4	3.0	2.2		2.1	2.7
			1.9	1.7	1.8	Current	1.4	1.4
			.9	1.4	1.1		.9	1.0
			3.0	1.5	1.3		1.5	2.1
			1.3	1.3	1.1	Quick	.8	.9
			.7	.8	.7		.5	.4
		20 18.3	20 18.4	19 19.1		Sales/Receivables	23 16.1	16 22.9
		28 13.0	24 15.0	23 15.9			28 13.0	26 13.9
		42 8.7	29 12.5	41 8.9			32 11.4	32 11.5
		13 28.7	13 27.2	19 19.0		Cost of Sales/Inventory	19 19.4	17 21.6
		20 18.3	22 16.5	28 13.2			25 14.8	25 14.4
		54 6.8	42 8.7	85 4.3			41 8.9	36 10.2
		16 22.2	18 20.3	18 20.4		Cost of Sales/Payables	23 16.2	18 19.8
		23 15.9	31 11.8	32 11.4			31 11.6	30 12.3
		31 11.6	43 8.5	47 7.7			42 8.7	49 7.5
			6.1	8.1	4.7	Sales/Working Capital	8.1	4.9
			9.8	13.0	10.8		23.3	11.1
			NM	17.5	64.1		-99.0	NM
				61.8	52.6	EBIT/Interest	15.4	28.7
			(11) 17.6	(10) 31.6			(63) 5.2	(30) 7.0
				2.3	3.5		1.7	1.9
						Net Profit + Depr., Dep., Amort./Cur. Mat. L/T/D	10.7	
							(14) 6.5	
							3.8	
			.1	.4	.6	Fixed/Worth	.6	.5
			.4	.7	.7		1.4	1.5
			1.6	1.0	.8		4.5	24.7
			.4	.4	.7	Debt/Worth	.8	.5
			.9	1.1	.7		1.7	2.4
			4.4	1.7	1.6		10.5	NM
			55.6	35.4	38.3	% Profit Before Taxes/Tangible Net Worth	44.6	56.2
			43.5	(12) 15.6	23.4		(58) 19.6	(25) 25.1
			15.4	5.2	17.6		7.6	5.0
			31.7	17.2	17.5	% Profit Before Taxes/Total Assets	10.6	15.2
			14.6	9.1	11.6		5.7	9.0
			8.1	1.9	4.2		2.2	4.4
			25.8	20.5	6.9	Sales/Net Fixed Assets	10.3	8.7
			12.6	8.1	5.9		5.8	6.0
			6.9	5.9	3.2		3.3	3.2
			2.7	3.4	2.2	Sales/Total Assets	2.9	2.3
			1.8	2.6	1.8		2.1	1.7
			1.5	2.0	1.0		1.3	1.3
			.2	1.5	1.3	% Depr., Dep., Amort./Sales	1.9	2.5
		(11)	1.0	(12) 2.4	(10) 1.5		(52) 3.1	(21) 3.9
			1.9	2.8	3.3		5.0	8.3
						% Officers', Directors' Owners' Comp/Sales		
635M	2505M	49454M	634561M	2360004M	3312438M	Net Sales ($)	11366613M	4855823M
147M	758M	25059M	290254M	927375M	1845488M	Total Assets ($)	5033451M	2437136M

© RMA 2024
M = $ thousand   MM = $ million
See Pages viii through xx for Explanation of Ratios and Data

MANUFACTURING—Soft Drink Manufacturing NAICS 312111

Comparative Historical Data

												Current Data Sorted by Sales					
	4		10		11	Type of Statement Unqualified											11
	7		4		6	Reviewed									3		3
	1		3			Compiled											
	3		1		2	Tax Returns									1		
	21		26		24	Other	1		1		1				3		18
	4/1/21- 3/31/22		4/1/22- 3/31/23		4/1/23- 3/31/24				9 (4/1-9/30/23)						34 (10/1/23-3/31/24)		
	ALL		ALL		ALL		0-1MM		1-3MM		3-5MM		5-10MM		10-25MM		25MM & OVER
	36		44		43	NUMBER OF STATEMENTS	1		2		1				7		32
	%		%		%	ASSETS	%		%		%		%		%		%
	11.4		14.9		15.3	Cash & Equivalents							D				16.4
	20.5		17.9		15.1	Trade Receivables (net)							A				17.3
	18.2		17.2		14.6	Inventory							T				14.8
	3.7		2.0		2.2	All Other Current							A				2.8
	53.9		51.9		47.1	Total Current											51.2
	30.6		27.7		31.9	Fixed Assets (net)							N				30.7
	7.8		9.4		5.3	Intangibles (net)							O				6.7
	7.7		11.0		15.7	All Other Non-Current							T				11.4
	100.0		100.0		100.0	Total											100.0
						LIABILITIES							A				
	5.0		2.9		4.7	Notes Payable-Short Term							V				4.2
	2.4		1.9		2.9	Cur. Mat.-L.T.D.							A				2.8
	14.5		15.5		13.4	Trade Payables							I				14.0
	.3		.0		.2	Income Taxes Payable							L				.3
	13.3		4.7		8.0	All Other Current							A				8.0
	35.5		25.0		29.2	Total Current							B				29.3
	25.6		23.9		22.7	Long-Term Debt							L				13.9
	.1		1.1		.8	Deferred Taxes							E				1.0
	4.7		4.9		3.6	All Other Non-Current											3.4
	34.1		45.1		43.7	Net Worth											52.4
	100.0		100.0		100.0	Total Liabilities & Net Worth											100.0
						INCOME DATA											
	100.0		100.0		100.0	Net Sales											100.0
	33.9		33.9		32.9	Gross Profit											30.2
	27.3		29.0		27.8	Operating Expenses											24.7
	6.6		4.9		5.0	Operating Profit											5.5
	-.5		.3		-.4	All Other Expenses (net)											-.7
	7.1		4.5		5.4	Profit Before Taxes											6.2
						RATIOS											
	3.0		3.4		2.4												2.7
	1.9		2.2		1.8	Current											1.8
	1.2		1.3		1.2												1.3
	2.2		2.6		1.6												1.5
	1.0		1.5		1.1	Quick											1.2
	.6		.7		.7												.7
23	15.7	21	17.3	19	19.7										20		18.7
32	11.4	29	12.5	24	15.5	Sales/Receivables									25		14.4
41	8.8	39	9.4	34	10.7										33		11.0
19	19.1	22	16.9	16	23.5										15		24.4
33	10.9	32	11.3	27	13.3	Cost of Sales/Inventory									21		17.5
63	5.8	66	5.5	49	7.4										43		8.5
19	19.2	16	22.9	18	20.4										18		20.5
28	13.0	30	12.1	29	12.7	Cost of Sales/Payables									28		13.2
43	8.5	52	7.0	38	9.7										37		9.8
	5.2		5.3		6.8												6.1
	11.1		8.5		13.0	Sales/Working Capital											12.1
	24.7		17.2		33.6												21.0
	37.9		41.4		52.3												52.3
(28)	16.3	(37)	13.7	(36)	20.8	EBIT/Interest									(28)		24.1
	1.3		3.1		2.5												3.8
					7.7	Net Profit + Depr., Dep.,											7.7
		(13)	5.2		Amort./Cur. Mat. L/T/D									(11)		5.2
					2.9												2.6
	.3		.2		.3												.4
	.6		.7		.7	Fixed/Worth											.7
	3.4		1.8		1.1												1.0
	.4		.4		.6												.5
	1.0		1.1		1.1	Debt/Worth											1.1
	6.6		4.7		1.9												1.6
	54.6		50.4		49.5												39.1
(28)	34.3	(38)	24.4	(40)	27.8	% Profit Before Taxes/Tangible Net Worth									(31)		27.6
	15.2		9.6		12.1												13.0
	29.8		22.8		20.2	% Profit Before Taxes/Total											19.7
	15.7		10.6		9.6	Assets											10.9
	2.4		3.0		3.9												7.1
	28.3		21.7		14.1												11.0
	8.6		8.7		7.9	Sales/Net Fixed Assets											7.3
	3.5		4.4		5.6												5.6
	3.1		2.9		3.0												2.9
	2.1		2.1		2.1	Sales/Total Assets											2.1
	1.4		1.6		1.6												1.8
	1.1		1.4		1.0												1.1
(26)	2.6	(35)	2.0	(37)	1.9	% Depr., Dep., Amort./Sales									(29)		1.9
	5.0		3.8		3.2												2.6
						% Officers', Directors' Owners' Comp/Sales											
	3879157M		4069538M		6359597M	Net Sales ($)	635M		5223M		4618M				116801M		6232320M
	2104616M		1953914M		3089081M	Total Assets ($)	147M		5251M		3203M				72595M		3007885M

© RMA 2024   M = $ thousand   MM = $ million
See Pages viii through xx for Explanation of Ratios and Data

MANUFACTURING—Breweries NAICS 312120

Current Data Sorted by Assets | Comparative Historical Data

				1			**Type of Statement**		
			2	6			Unqualified	6	6
			4				Reviewed	8	10
6	11		8				Compiled	8	4
8	19		27	10	1	1	Tax Returns	39	23
		6 (4/1-9/30/23)		98 (10/1/23-3/31/24)			Other	107	60
0-500M	500M-2MM	2-10MM	10-50MM	50-100MM	100-250MM			4/1/19-3/31/20	4/1/20-3/31/21
								ALL	ALL
14	30	41	17	1	1		**NUMBER OF STATEMENTS**	168	103
%	%	%	%	%	%		**ASSETS**	%	%
27.4	13.1	9.8	9.4				Cash & Equivalents	11.5	16.9
1.8	3.5	5.7	4.2				Trade Receivables (net)	5.1	4.8
7.5	16.5	15.0	14.1				Inventory	13.6	15.2
3.4	1.9	2.8	.4				All Other Current	2.0	3.4
40.1	35.1	33.4	28.0				Total Current	32.1	40.3
50.7	55.0	50.8	60.6				Fixed Assets (net)	57.9	51.4
5.2	3.6	10.9	.5				Intangibles (net)	5.3	3.5
4.0	6.4	5.0	10.9				All Other Non-Current	4.6	4.7
100.0	100.0	100.0	100.0				Total	100.0	100.0
							LIABILITIES		
4.4	4.6	7.1	1.5				Notes Payable-Short Term	6.6	6.8
4.6	3.0	2.2	5.6				Cur. Mat.-L.T.D.	4.1	4.1
6.8	4.3	7.5	4.5				Trade Payables	6.1	5.8
.0	.0	.3	.2				Income Taxes Payable	.0	.1
26.8	19.7	13.8	4.9				All Other Current	12.5	10.4
42.5	31.6	31.0	16.7				Total Current	29.3	27.2
69.2	37.5	43.7	30.3				Long-Term Debt	45.0	56.4
.0	.0	.0	.2				Deferred Taxes	.3	.1
19.1	8.5	16.0	7.6				All Other Non-Current	9.5	13.6
-30.8	22.3	9.4	45.3				Net Worth	15.8	2.7
100.0	100.0	100.0	100.0				Total Liabilities & Net Worth	100.0	100.0
							INCOME DATA		
100.0	100.0	100.0	100.0				Net Sales	100.0	100.0
65.3	60.8	52.0	42.1				Gross Profit	54.7	55.0
60.2	63.7	50.3	38.8				Operating Expenses	50.9	54.8
5.1	-2.9	1.7	3.2				Operating Profit	3.8	.1
.6	.5	3.9	1.6				All Other Expenses (net)	2.3	-.5
4.5	-3.4	-2.2	1.6				Profit Before Taxes	1.5	.7
							RATIOS		
3.0	4.2	2.8	2.7					2.5	3.3
1.5	1.3	1.5	2.1			Current		1.4	2.1
.6	.7	.8	.9					.8	.9
2.3	2.4	1.2	1.7					1.5	2.0
.8	.5	.6	.8			Quick		.6 (102)	.9
.4	.2	.3	.3					.3	.4
0 UND	0 UND	3 116.7	7 53.6					0 UND	1 276.4
0 UND	3 106.3	9 38.7	11 33.3			Sales/Receivables		8 47.0	7 54.1
3 107.7	8 47.3	21 17.6	18 20.4					18 19.8	17 21.3
0 UND	12 30.3	31 11.6	65 5.6					38 9.5	46 8.0
12 31.3	63 5.8	85 4.3	76 4.8			Cost of Sales/Inventory		63 5.8	81 4.5
41 8.8	118 3.1	135 2.7	101 3.6					99 3.7	114 3.2
0 UND	0 UND	11 34.6	16 22.6					0 UND	5 68.5
0 UND	4 99.6	31 11.8	22 16.6			Cost of Sales/Payables		19 19.4	20 18.4
5 72.9	22 16.8	55 6.6	28 13.0					43 8.5	35 10.3
8.2	9.0	7.5	6.0					7.0	4.7
25.3	33.1	15.4	7.3			Sales/Working Capital		18.0	8.4
-27.8	-16.6	-18.8	-36.4					-26.5	-88.2
20.3	17.8	4.0	3.6					9.2	10.3
(10) 1.6	(24) .3	(39) 1.8	(16) 1.6			EBIT/Interest		(154) 1.6	(94) 2.1
-1.6	-4.4	-2.3	-1.4					-1.4	-1.5
							Net Profit + Depr., Dep.,		2.9	
							Amort./Cur. Mat. L/T/D	(15)	.7	
									.5	
.6	.8	1.2	.8					1.0	1.2
NM	2.9	4.4	1.5			Fixed/Worth		2.3	3.3
-.6	-20.5	-11.2	3.1					-15.9	-3.4
.5	.4	1.4	.6					.9	1.4
NM	2.6	11.7	1.5			Debt/Worth		2.8	7.5
-2.0	-27.7	-10.0	3.3					-23.6	-8.0
	24.0	63.2	15.1			% Profit Before Taxes/Tangible		47.1	52.3
(20)	19.3	(24) 15.4	1.3			Net Worth	(121)	18.2	(67) 22.7
	-3.6	-5.5	-21.0					-7.9	-26.1
39.5	13.9	8.8	5.0			% Profit Before Taxes/Total		15.0	17.3
16.2	1.8	2.6	1.0			Assets		2.8	2.7
-6.5	-17.1	-10.2	-5.8					-7.7	-10.7
15.6	10.7	6.9	2.5					4.2	7.0
4.7	3.7	2.6	1.6			Sales/Net Fixed Assets		2.4	2.6
2.8	2.2	1.3	1.1					1.4	1.2
5.9	2.7	1.7	1.2					2.0	2.1
2.3	1.9	1.3	1.0			Sales/Total Assets		1.4	1.2
1.6	1.1	.9	.7					1.0	.8
	2.5	3.2	5.6					4.2	4.4
(20)	5.9	(24) 5.0	6.9			% Depr., Dep., Amort./Sales	(126)	6.4	(66) 7.5
	7.8	8.2	9.7					10.2	10.7
	2.5	6.4						3.2	2.8
(10)	4.8	(15) 7.1				% Officers', Directors'	(44)	5.2	(28) 6.2
	7.0	9.3				Owners' Comp/Sales		8.5	8.7
14832M	74267M	283437M	345099M	15512M	75340M		Net Sales ($)	3149358M	899038M
3529M	36678M	166885M	344705M	56697M	104250M		Total Assets ($)	1869848M	839665M

© RMA 2024

M = $ thousand MM = $ million
See Pages viii through xx for Explanation of Ratios and Data

MANUFACTURING—Breweries NAICS 312120

Comparative Historical Data | Current Data Sorted by Sales

					Type of Statement						
	5		5	1	Unqualified					1	
	5		5	8	Reviewed				3	3	2
	3		4	4	Compiled		1	1	2		
	26		28	25	Tax Returns	6	8	7	3	1	
	69		67	66	Other	10	19	10	11	10	6
	4/1/21-3/31/22 ALL		4/1/22-3/31/23 ALL	4/1/23-3/31/24 ALL		0-1MM	6 (4/1-9/30/23) 1-3MM	3-5MM	5-10MM	98 (10/1/23-3/31/24) 10-25MM	25MM & OVER
	108		109	104	NUMBER OF STATEMENTS	16	28	18	19	15	8
	%		%	%	ASSETS	%	%	%	%	%	%
	17.4		16.8	12.9	Cash & Equivalents	14.3	14.7	16.3	9.1	7.2	
	4.9		4.7	4.3	Trade Receivables (net)	1.5	2.0	5.3	6.0	6.1	
	14.3		16.5	14.8	Inventory	3.9	14.0	17.7	15.7	20.5	
	2.8		2.0	2.2	All Other Current	3.6	2.8	3.7	.6	.8	
	39.4		39.9	34.2	Total Current	23.2	33.4	43.0	31.5	34.6	
	50.3		50.2	53.3	Fixed Assets (net)	67.4	56.9	47.3	44.2	55.0	
	4.3		4.9	6.3	Intangibles (net)	6.4	3.5	5.2	17.1	.3	
	6.1		5.1	6.2	All Other Non-Current	3.0	6.1	4.6	7.2	10.1	
	100.0		100.0	100.0	Total	100.0	100.0	100.0	100.0	100.0	
					LIABILITIES						
	4.5		4.3	5.5	Notes Payable-Short Term	4.8	4.7	5.6	4.4	11.5	
	3.7		3.0	3.3	Cur. Mat.-L.T.D.	2.9	4.4	1.5	2.1	5.1	
	5.3		5.0	5.9	Trade Payables	1.4	1.8	12.2	8.4	6.2	
	.3		.2	.2	Income Taxes Payable	.0	.0	.0	.6	.2	
	8.2		10.5	15.6	All Other Current	17.0	20.8	20.2	13.9	5.1	
	22.0		23.0	30.5	Total Current	26.2	31.7	39.6	29.4	28.2	
	58.8		48.3	42.8	Long-Term Debt	66.7	41.8	34.9	39.5	44.7	
	.0		.0	.0	Deferred Taxes	.0	.0	.0	.0	.2	
	6.5		11.6	12.7	All Other Non-Current	2.8	13.2	19.6	15.7	15.4	
	12.7		17.1	14.1	Net Worth	4.4	13.2	5.9	15.4	11.5	
	100.0		100.0	100.0	Total Liabilities & Net Worth	100.0	100.0	100.0	100.0	100.0	
					INCOME DATA						
	100.0		100.0	100.0	Net Sales	100.0	100.0	100.0	100.0	100.0	
	55.9		55.6	54.5	Gross Profit	65.8	63.5	51.1	48.7	40.4	
	51.5		56.6	53.7	Operating Expenses	64.5	66.1	46.9	48.5	42.3	
	4.5		-.9	.8	Operating Profit	1.3	-2.5	4.2	.2	-1.9	
	-.8		.5	2.2	All Other Expenses (net)	2.0	1.8	1.6	4.3	2.5	
	5.3		-1.4	-1.4	Profit Before Taxes	-.8	-4.4	2.6	-4.1	-4.4	
					RATIOS						
	4.2		5.0	2.9		6.0	4.0	2.4	2.3	2.2	
	2.1		2.2	1.6	Current	1.8	1.3	1.5	1.5	1.4	
	1.2		1.3	.8		.5	.7	.7	.9	.8	
	2.4		2.9	1.6		5.8	1.2	1.5	1.2	1.2	
	1.0		1.0	.5	Quick	.8	.5	.4	.7	.4	
	.4		.4	.3		.4	.2	.2	.2	.3	
0	UND	0	999.8	0	908.6		0	UND	0	908.6	0	UND	7	50.1	6	57.0
8	47.1	8	43.6	6	57.6	Sales/Receivables	0	UND	4	86.9	6	61.8	15	24.8	15	25.0
22	16.6	18	20.7	15	24.3		0	UND	8	47.1	12	30.0	25	14.8	21	17.6
38	9.7	50	7.3	29	12.7		0	UND	41	8.8	5	79.4	34	10.6	58	6.3
72	5.1	79	4.6	69	5.3	Cost of Sales/Inventory	17	21.6	78	4.7	35	10.3	111	3.3	72	5.1
126	2.9	126	2.9	114	3.2		60	6.1	140	2.6	99	3.7	135	2.7	118	3.1
0	UND	2	207.1	0	UND		0	UND	0	UND	0	UND	26	13.9	16	23.3
16	22.3	22	16.7	19	19.6	Cost of Sales/Payables	0	UND	8	44.6	19	19.1	35	10.5	24	15.4
37	9.9	43	8.5	34	10.6		0	UND	25	14.8	47	7.8	57	6.4	31	11.6
	4.6		4.4	7.0		5.7	6.9	11.8	8.2	6.8	
	9.5		8.1	16.7	Sales/Working Capital	14.2	26.8	34.5	15.4	13.5	
	25.9		34.0	-23.3		-18.7	-15.5	-13.5	-50.7	-35.8	
	11.0		4.9	5.0		13.6	5.7	4.8	4.7	3.9	
(96)	3.2	(91)	.5	(91)	1.5	EBIT/Interest	(11)	-.2	(26)	.5	(14)	2.0	(18)	1.4	1.6
	.0		-3.3	-2.2		-3.4	-5.4	-1.8	-2.7	-1.5	
				3.0	Net Profit + Depr., Dep.,						
			(12)	1.4	Amort./Cur. Mat. L/T/D						
				.3							
	.9		.8	.9		.9	1.2	.7	.7	.9	
	2.3		2.3	2.6	Fixed/Worth	7.2	6.6	5.3	3.1	1.6	
	-10.3		-4.6	-15.2		-1.5	-5.7	-2.4	20.9	4.0	
	1.1		.9	.7		.6	1.2	.6	2.3	1.3	
	2.8		3.0	3.4	Debt/Worth	6.6	8.5	8.7	11.7	2.5	
	-21.0		-8.4	-20.9		-3.1	-9.6	-9.2	-25.8	4.5	
	58.1		40.0	35.0	% Profit Before Taxes/Tangible	23.8	74.7	23.8	6.5	
(77)	28.4	(74)	5.6	(70)	10.0	Net Worth	(17)	13.9	(11)	23.9	(12)	8.9	(13)	.4
	3.3		-23.2	-15.1			-10.1	9.6	-29.0	-33.5	
	17.4		9.8	13.1	% Profit Before Taxes/Total	25.7	8.5	22.3	6.7	5.6	
	7.4		-1.7	1.5	Assets	3.5	-1.2	5.8	-1.2	.3	
	-1.1		-13.2	-9.2		-14.5	-16.4	-4.9	-10.3	-7.0	
	7.4		5.8	7.8		5.0	4.8	11.7	6.7	4.0	
	3.0		2.8	2.5	Sales/Net Fixed Assets	1.6	2.3	5.6	2.9	1.6	
	1.3		1.5	1.4		.7	1.3	2.6	1.9	1.2	
	2.1		2.1	2.3		2.3	2.0	4.4	1.7	1.6	
	1.4		1.4	1.5	Sales/Total Assets	1.2	1.5	2.5	1.5	1.0	
	.9		.9	.9		.6	.8	1.3	.9	.6	
	3.1		3.1	3.9			4.8	1.1	4.1	4.5	
(72)	4.9	(78)	5.9	(70)	6.1	% Depr., Dep., Amort./Sales	(17)	6.7	(12)	3.2	(12)	6.0	(14)	6.8
	10.4		8.6	8.9			11.3	6.1	8.2	9.5	
	2.6		2.9	3.6	% Officers', Directors'		5.7				
(33)	3.8	(30)	5.6	(29)	6.5	Owners' Comp/Sales	(11)	7.6				
	9.3		10.3	9.0			9.6				
	794608M		1347735M	808487M	Net Sales ($)	8441M	59130M	72147M	125137M	224806M	318826M
	700472M		1567599M	712744M	Total Assets ($)	9367M	50067M	36918M	108793M	267564M	240035M

© RMA 2024   M = $ thousand   MM = $ million
See Pages viii through xx for Explanation of Ratios and Data

MANUFACTURING—Wineries NAICS 312130

Current Data Sorted by Assets | Comparative Historical Data

							Type of Statement				
				2	1	1	Unqualified		17		6
			1	6	1	1	Reviewed		22		7
			2	2			Compiled		10		4
2	7		6				Tax Returns		18		10
6	5		21	25	3	7	Other		124		42
	12 (4/1-9/30/23)			87 (10/1/23-3/31/24)					4/1/19-3/31/20 ALL		4/1/20-3/31/21 ALL
0-500M	500M-2MM		2-10MM	10-50MM	50-100MM	100-250MM	NUMBER OF STATEMENTS		191		69
8	12		30	35	5	9					
%	%		%	%	%	%	ASSETS		%		%
	10.6		8.6	2.8			Cash & Equivalents		5.3		13.0
	1.0		4.9	5.5			Trade Receivables (net)		7.6		5.6
	35.3		43.5	41.8			Inventory		45.2		41.9
	2.3		3.7	1.6			All Other Current		1.9		1.9
	49.2		60.7	51.7			Total Current		60.0		62.4
	46.0		32.9	37.1			Fixed Assets (net)		34.2		33.5
	2.8		.8	3.9			Intangibles (net)		3.2		1.3
	2.0		5.6	7.2			All Other Non-Current		2.6		2.8
	100.0		100.0	100.0			Total		100.0		100.0
							LIABILITIES				
	5.3		6.4	16.0			Notes Payable-Short Term		14.1		8.7
	.5		.6	1.5			Cur. Mat.-L.T.D.		2.4		2.3
	3.5		6.8	7.6			Trade Payables		7.7		6.7
	.0		.1	.0			Income Taxes Payable		.1		.2
	4.2		9.3	9.1			All Other Current		5.0		7.7
	13.5		23.2	34.3			Total Current		29.3		25.5
	41.0		19.6	24.6			Long-Term Debt		23.2		33.4
	.0		.0	.0			Deferred Taxes		.4		.1
	17.1		8.8	8.3			All Other Non-Current		7.4		13.1
	28.4		48.4	32.8			Net Worth		39.9		27.9
	100.0		100.0	100.0			Total Liabilities & Net Worth		100.0		100.0
							INCOME DATA				
	100.0		100.0	100.0			Net Sales		100.0		100.0
	76.7		61.7	52.0			Gross Profit		54.1		59.2
	72.6		56.0	50.3			Operating Expenses		43.1		50.6
	4.1		5.6	1.7			Operating Profit		11.0		8.6
	3.5		1.4	4.4			All Other Expenses (net)		3.4		2.0
	.5		4.2	-2.7			Profit Before Taxes		7.6		6.7
							RATIOS				
	13.1		10.4	2.7					4.9		6.7
	5.5		2.6	2.0			Current		2.5		3.4
	2.7		1.6	1.1					1.5		1.9
	4.2		.9	.4					.9		1.7
	.6		.3	.2			Quick		.4		.5
	.3		.1	.1					.2		.3
0	UND	1	435.1	9	41.7			10	37.6	3	145.8
0	UND	10	35.3	20	18.3		Sales/Receivables	30	12.3	16	22.3
6	62.4	35	10.3	33	11.1			49	7.5	35	10.4
0	UND	228	1.6	261	1.4			365	1.0	203	1.8
456	.8	608	.6	521	.7		Cost of Sales/Inventory	521	.7	456	.8
730	.5	1217	.3	730	.5			912	.4	912	.4
0	UND	8	48.3	41	8.9			27	13.3	11	31.8
6	60.1	68	5.4	70	5.2		Cost of Sales/Payables	61	6.0	44	8.3
50	7.3	126	2.9	111	3.3			111	3.3	101	3.6
	1.8		1.1	1.9					1.3		1.2
	3.2		2.3	3.2			Sales/Working Capital		2.2		2.1
	8.6		6.6	24.4					4.9		5.5
	12.1		13.7	9.4					10.2		15.7
(10)	3.6	(24)	2.3	(33)	.9		EBIT/Interest	(175)	3.4	(61)	4.7
	-.8		.5	-.1					1.1		1.2
				7.2					8.8		
			(10)	2.3			Net Profit + Depr., Dep., Amort./Cur. Mat. L/T/D	(35)	5.1		
				-.1					1.2		
	.2		.2	.5					.3		.4
	1.1		.6	1.2			Fixed/Worth		.8		1.0
	9.7		1.8	4.8					2.0		2.1
	.3		.3	.9					.5		.9
	2.0		1.6	1.3			Debt/Worth		1.5		1.4
	9.9		2.8	8.7					3.8		3.8
	47.4		19.4	13.8					31.2		45.6
(10)	26.4	(27)	8.6	(29)	1.8		% Profit Before Taxes/Tangible Net Worth	(173)	15.7	(57)	19.9
	2.7		-2.2	-11.6					1.5		2.9
	21.4		10.3	2.3					13.1		15.8
	9.6		3.6	-.9			% Profit Before Taxes/Total Assets		5.4		6.6
	-4.2		-.6	-6.0					.1		.3
	25.0		7.5	4.8					7.3		6.5
	7.3		2.4	1.9			Sales/Net Fixed Assets		2.5		2.6
	.9		1.1	.9					1.0		1.1
	1.6		1.2	.9					1.0		1.4
	1.2		.7	.7			Sales/Total Assets		.7		.8
	.6		.5	.4					.4		.4
			1.7	2.3					2.5		3.0
		(20)	2.5	(33)	4.9		% Depr., Dep., Amort./Sales	(142)	4.8	(42)	6.1
			3.3	9.9					8.3		10.0
									2.7		3.3
							% Officers', Directors' Owners' Comp/Sales	(30)	4.7	(13)	4.6
									7.8		6.4
6370M	23101M		114375M	716217M	156682M	849159M	Net Sales ($)		4305165M		816099M
2688M	17039M		153844M	855393M	334886M	1335885M	Total Assets ($)		6450740M		1157230M

© RMA 2024

M = $ thousand   MM = $ million
See Pages viii through xx for Explanation of Ratios and Data

MANUFACTURING—Wineries NAICS 312130

Comparative Historical Data | Current Data Sorted by Sales

				Type of Statement						
4		8	4	Unqualified					1	3
8		17	9	Reviewed		1	1	1	5	2
7		8	4	Compiled		1	1	1	2	
20		20	15	Tax Returns	5	4	3	3	6	
67		87	67	Other	8	13	8	10	18	10
4/1/21-		4/1/22-	4/1/23-			12 (4/1-9/30/23)		87 (10/1/23-3/31/24)		
3/31/22		3/31/23	3/31/24							
ALL		ALL	ALL		0-1MM	1-3MM	3-5MM	5-10MM	10-25MM	25MM & OVER
106		140	99	NUMBER OF STATEMENTS	13	17	13	15	26	15
%		%	%	**ASSETS**	%	%	%	%	%	%
9.1		7.7	6.8	Cash & Equivalents	13.8	6.5	11.2	8.4	2.6	3.2
6.3		4.8	4.5	Trade Receivables (net)	2.6	2.1	5.7	4.9	4.3	8.0
46.0		43.7	40.3	Inventory	26.7	48.0	52.5	32.9	42.0	37.2
3.4		3.2	2.5	All Other Current	2.3	3.6	4.8	1.5	1.1	3.1
64.8		59.4	54.2	Total Current	45.4	60.2	74.2	47.7	50.1	51.5
28.0		33.1	36.8	Fixed Assets (net)	48.5	33.5	22.7	42.5	39.5	32.3
2.7		1.7	2.7	Intangibles (net)	3.5	2.3	.6	1.6	3.4	4.3
4.5		5.8	6.2	All Other Non-Current	2.6	4.0	2.5	8.3	7.0	11.9
100.0		100.0	100.0	Total	100.0	100.0	100.0	100.0	100.0	100.0
				LIABILITIES						
13.7		17.1	10.6	Notes Payable-Short Term	3.3	10.6	7.9	11.7	15.4	10.1
1.8		1.6	1.1	Cur. Mat.-L.T.D.	.7	.5	.5	.8	2.1	1.5
8.8		6.1	6.0	Trade Payables	.7	4.6	6.5	9.0	6.1	8.8
.1		.1	.0	Income Taxes Payable	.0	.1	.0	.0	.0	.0
6.4		6.2	9.9	All Other Current	17.4	10.8	6.5	7.9	11.3	5.2
30.8		31.2	27.8	Total Current	22.2	26.6	21.4	29.3	34.9	25.6
23.8		25.7	25.7	Long-Term Debt	36.7	31.4	16.9	25.8	22.5	22.8
.2		.3	.0	Deferred Taxes	.0	.0	.0	.0	.1	.1
12.9		8.0	10.6	All Other Non-Current	4.5	21.6	1.2	8.8	13.2	8.7
32.2		34.8	35.9	Net Worth	36.6	20.4	60.5	36.1	29.2	42.7
100.0		100.0	100.0	Total Liabilities & Net Worth	100.0	100.0	100.0	100.0	100.0	100.0
				INCOME DATA						
100.0		100.0	100.0	Net Sales	100.0	100.0	100.0	100.0	100.0	100.0
57.2		61.0	59.5	Gross Profit	69.0	70.4	63.2	57.1	51.4	51.8
47.9		53.9	55.4	Operating Expenses	71.5	66.1	57.9	52.6	51.0	37.6
9.3		7.0	4.1	Operating Profit	-2.5	4.3	5.3	4.5	.4	14.3
.5		.9	3.1	All Other Expenses (net)	7.0	1.5	2.2	5.1	1.8	2.5
8.8		6.1	1.0	Profit Before Taxes	-9.5	2.8	3.2	-.6	-1.4	11.8
				RATIOS						
5.3		5.7	4.8		10.8	9.6	13.2	3.5	2.6	3.5
2.7		2.6	2.5	Current	2.9	4.7	6.2	2.0	2.1	2.0
1.5		1.3	1.5		1.7	2.0	1.6	1.0	1.1	1.6
1.6		.9	.8		4.3	.9	2.3	.9	.4	1.0
.5		.3	.3	Quick	.2	.4	.7	.3	.2	.4
.2		.1	.1		.2	.1	.2	.1	.1	.1
1	317.9	1 535.2	1 278.6		0 UND	0 UND	1 523.8	0 999.8	12 30.7	8 43.9
17	21.5	13 27.8	13 27.1	Sales/Receivables	0 UND	7 54.9	14 26.8	11 34.1	21 17.1	23 16.0
35	10.3	33 10.9	33 11.1		0 UND	17 21.5	31 11.7	39 9.3	33 11.2	38 9.6
261	1.4	261 1.4	281 1.3		0 UND	406 .9	332 1.1	15 23.8	304 1.2	215 1.7
406	.9	608 .6	521 .7	Cost of Sales/Inventory	406 .9	730 .5	608 .6	332 1.1	521 .7	521 .7
730	.5	912 .4	912 .4		912 .4	1217 .3	1825 .2	912 .4	912 .4	730 .5
8	47.8	8 48.2	24 15.1		0 UND	0 UND	11 33.2	24 15.1	44 8.3	38 9.7
46	8.0	51 7.1	56 6.5	Cost of Sales/Payables	0 UND	39 9.4	45 8.1	74 4.9	69 5.3	64 5.7
111	3.3	118 3.1	107 3.4		0 UND	146 2.5	101 3.6	130 2.8	101 3.6	101 3.6
	1.9	1.5	1.7		2.0	1.1	.8	1.2	1.8	1.9
	3.0	2.7	2.9	Sales/Working Capital	6.0	2.0	2.1	11.0	2.7	3.5
	6.1	6.7	9.6		11.8	7.8	3.3	139.5	15.8	4.3
	25.8	8.9	7.0		5.7	19.3		3.5	6.0	26.3
(94)	5.9	(125) 3.1	(86) 1.9	EBIT/Interest	(10) -.3	(15) 3.6		(13) -.1	(24) 1.2	3.4
	1.9	.6	-.1		-4.0	-.7			-.4	.0	.0
	11.7	4.1	7.0	Net Profit + Depr., Dep.,					7.1	
(15)	3.4	(23) 2.8	(20) 3.0	Amort./Cur. Mat. L/T/D				(11)	2.7	
	2.0	1.7	1.0						1.3	
	.3	.4	.3		.3	.2	.1	.3	.6	.4
	.7	.9	1.1	Fixed/Worth	1.5	.9	.3	1.4	1.2	.9
	3.1	2.1	3.7		5.9	NM	.8	-2.1	3.2	1.4
	.7	.8	.6		.5	1.0	.1	.4	.9	.7
	1.7	1.6	1.5	Debt/Worth	3.1	2.2	.6	1.5	1.7	1.2
	6.2	5.6	5.7		6.7	NM	2.0	-16.1	6.5	5.4
	56.5	32.7	22.8	% Profit Before Taxes/Tangible	84.1	29.4	18.9	28.8	7.4	43.7
(88)	27.3	(121) 11.9	(84) 6.0	Net Worth	(11) -3.9	(13) 18.3	(12) 5.6	(11) 8.3	(23) 1.8	(14) 12.1
	9.0	2.2	-4.9		-54.0	11.6	-1.1	-6.0	-20.7	-2.7
	20.5	11.1	9.5	% Profit Before Taxes/Total	26.8	12.5	13.0	13.9	2.3	11.1
	10.7	4.0	2.1	Assets	-2.5	5.6	2.4	2.6	.4	4.9
	1.5	-.4	-5.1		-16.2	-6.9	-.3	-7.2	-6.0	-.7
	16.5	10.9	8.6		22.1	14.3	13.1	8.9	2.8	9.4
	5.7	2.7	2.3	Sales/Net Fixed Assets	.6	2.4	6.8	3.0	1.7	4.0
	1.9	1.1	.9		.3	1.5	1.4	.9	.9	1.4
	1.5	1.2	1.2		2.1	1.3	1.4	1.8	.8	1.4
	1.0	.8	.8	Sales/Total Assets	.6	1.0	.9	.8	.6	.9
	.6	.4	.4		.3	.5	.5	.5	.4	.4
	.8	2.1	1.9				1.2	1.9	3.2	1.5
(65)	2.3	(101) 5.5	(74) 4.8	% Depr., Dep., Amort./Sales		(11) 1.8	(11) 2.6	(25) 5.6	(13) 4.9
	5.2	8.2	8.4				4.0	10.6	8.9	7.7
	1.6	2.8	2.2							
(35)	4.5	(29) 4.7	(16) 3.6	% Officers', Directors'						
	6.2	6.2	5.0	Owners' Comp/Sales						
2127418M		2859489M	1865904M	Net Sales ($)	8490M	32715M	48755M	110196M	416292M	1249456M
1756807M		3892206M	2699735M	Total Assets ($)	28805M	51226M	71518M	228455M	813895M	1505836M

© RMA 2024   M = $ thousand   MM = $ million
See Pages viii through xx for Explanation of Ratios and Data

MANUFACTURING—Distilleries NAICS 312140

Current Data Sorted by Assets						Type of Statement	Comparative Historical Data	
			1	1		Unqualified	3	3
			3			Reviewed	6	1
	1	3	1			Compiled	3	3
1	3		1			Tax Returns	8	1
4	5	9	12	3	1	Other	18	20
	4 (4/1-9/30/23)		45 (10/1/23-3/31/24)				4/1/19-3/31/20	4/1/20-3/31/21
0-500M	500M-2MM	2-10MM	10-50MM	50-100MM	100-250MM	NUMBER OF STATEMENTS	ALL	ALL
5	9	12	18	4	1		38	28
%	%	%	%	%	%	ASSETS	%	%
		1.1	3.8			Cash & Equivalents	12.6	12.4
		9.9	6.1			Trade Receivables (net)	9.7	9.2
		40.5	50.7			Inventory	35.5	38.6
		1.2	1.4			All Other Current	2.1	2.6
		52.6	62.0			Total Current	60.0	62.9
		32.4	23.9			Fixed Assets (net)	32.3	27.5
		7.9	3.4			Intangibles (net)	4.1	6.4
		7.1	10.7			All Other Non-Current	3.7	3.2
		100.0	100.0			Total	100.0	100.0
						LIABILITIES		
		14.3	15.7			Notes Payable-Short Term	17.7	12.2
		2.5	.8			Cur. Mat.-L.T.D.	2.9	.9
		5.5	6.4			Trade Payables	8.0	6.1
		.0	.1			Income Taxes Payable	.1	.3
		11.1	6.9			All Other Current	10.7	9.8
		33.4	30.0			Total Current	39.4	29.3
		27.9	17.1			Long-Term Debt	31.0	27.8
		.0	.0			Deferred Taxes	.0	.0
		11.9	5.5			All Other Non-Current	7.2	7.4
		26.8	47.5			Net Worth	22.4	35.6
		100.0	100.0			Total Liabilities & Net Worth	100.0	100.0
						INCOME DATA		
		100.0	100.0			Net Sales	100.0	100.0
		62.5	50.9			Gross Profit	53.8	54.6
		57.9	43.3			Operating Expenses	49.6	46.5
		4.6	7.7			Operating Profit	4.2	8.0
		5.3	2.4			All Other Expenses (net)	3.4	.4
		-.6	5.3			Profit Before Taxes	.8	7.6
						RATIOS		
		4.1	3.6				4.7	4.0
		1.3	2.0			Current	2.0	2.5
		1.1	1.6				1.1	1.5
		.8	1.1				1.8	1.3
		.3	.2			Quick	.7	.9
		.1	.1				.4	.5
		16 23.4	18 20.8				17 20.9	8 45.8
		24 14.9	32 11.5			Sales/Receivables	29 12.6	24 15.4
		45 8.1	51 7.2				46 7.9	36 10.1
		243 1.5	146 2.5				118 3.1	140 2.6
		365 1.0	730 .5			Cost of Sales/Inventory	261 1.4	281 1.3
		730 .5	1217 .3				521 .7	730 .5
		0 UND	21 17.3				14 25.2	0 UND
		38 9.5	55 6.6			Cost of Sales/Payables	47 7.8	31 11.6
		126 2.9	130 2.8				83 4.4	70 5.2
		1.8	1.7				1.9	2.5
		8.2	2.6			Sales/Working Capital	4.1	4.5
		33.5	7.8				20.7	7.6
		3.0	8.4				10.0	27.5
		1.3	(16) 2.4			EBIT/Interest	(33) 2.2	(22) 9.8
		-3.8	.1				-3.3	-1.5
						Net Profit + Depr., Dep., Amort./Cur. Mat. L/T/D		
		.2	.3				.3	.4
		1.1	.6			Fixed/Worth	1.0	.6
		NM	1.1				8.0	11.4
		1.1	.8				.7	.4
		2.6	1.3			Debt/Worth	2.0	1.2
		NM	2.0				29.3	24.3
			22.6				49.9	70.1
			6.0			% Profit Before Taxes/Tangible Net Worth	(30) 17.7	(24) 18.6
			-5.0				11.5	-9.2
		7.7	11.8				12.3	27.1
		2.0	5.2			% Profit Before Taxes/Total Assets	5.4	7.0
		-3.9	-1.2				-11.1	-5.4
		19.2	6.8				9.3	9.6
		5.3	3.7			Sales/Net Fixed Assets	4.0	4.2
		1.2	2.0				1.5	2.7
		1.2	1.2				1.5	1.6
		.8	.6			Sales/Total Assets	1.1	1.2
		.4	.5				.7	1.0
			1.8				1.6	.8
		(17)	4.0			% Depr., Dep., Amort./Sales	(34) 4.2	(19) 2.1
			5.7				6.6	5.1
						% Officers', Directors' Owners' Comp/Sales		
2256M	22049M	55307M	332102M	118135M	18631M	Net Sales ($)	1677160M	778786M
1122M	11431M	69879M	442150M	263638M	224618M	Total Assets ($)	1497009M	631302M

M = $ thousand   MM = $ million

MANUFACTURING—Distilleries NAICS 312140

Comparative Historical Data | Current Data Sorted by Sales

				Type of Statement						
1	1	2		Unqualified				1	1	
2	3	3		Reviewed				2	1	
1	5	5		Compiled		1				
5	8	5		Tax Returns	2	1	3	1		
22	26	34		Other	3	8	3	8	10	2
4/1/21-3/31/22 ALL	4/1/22-3/31/23 ALL	4/1/23-3/31/24 ALL			4 (4/1-9/30/23)			45 (10/1/23-3/31/24)		
31	43	49		NUMBER OF STATEMENTS	0-1MM 5	1-3MM 10	3-5MM 7	5-10MM 9	10-25MM 14	25MM & OVER 4
%	%	%		ASSETS	%	%	%	%	%	%
12.2	9.3	4.7		Cash & Equivalents		4.7			1.9	
6.8	8.1	7.9		Trade Receivables (net)		5.3			4.7	
35.3	44.7	42.9		Inventory		29.3			52.0	
.9	1.3	1.8		All Other Current		.6			1.4	
55.2	63.5	57.3		Total Current		39.9			60.0	
37.7	24.7	26.0		Fixed Assets (net)		47.4			23.2	
2.1	6.5	8.8		Intangibles (net)		5.5			12.8	
4.9	5.4	7.9		All Other Non-Current		7.2			3.9	
100.0	100.0	100.0		Total		100.0			100.0	
				LIABILITIES						
11.9	11.6	15.4		Notes Payable-Short Term		16.4			18.1	
1.4	1.2	1.1		Cur. Mat.-L.T.D.		.8			.6	
7.7	4.5	6.1		Trade Payables		2.1			4.2	
.4	.1	.2		Income Taxes Payable		.2			.2	
7.6	7.8	7.5		All Other Current		4.0			7.6	
28.9	25.1	30.2		Total Current		23.5			30.7	
36.6	36.5	32.2		Long-Term Debt		31.6			13.4	
.1	.0	.4		Deferred Taxes		.0			1.4	
11.8	9.0	6.8		All Other Non-Current		1.1			3.8	
22.7	29.3	30.4		Net Worth		43.8			50.7	
100.0	100.0	100.0		Total Liabilities & Net Worth		100.0			100.0	
				INCOME DATA						
100.0	100.0	100.0		Net Sales		100.0			100.0	
54.9	53.4	55.4		Gross Profit		60.5			49.1	
47.1	44.6	47.7		Operating Expenses		51.4			40.7	
7.8	8.8	7.7		Operating Profit		9.1			8.4	
.7	2.6	3.4		All Other Expenses (net)		5.9			1.0	
7.1	6.2	4.2		Profit Before Taxes		3.1			7.4	
				RATIOS						
5.8	5.9	4.6		Current		4.5			5.3	
2.5	3.4	1.7				1.5			2.1	
1.1	1.9	1.2				1.1			1.4	
1.8	2.2	1.3		Quick		1.7			1.4	
(30) .6	.6	.5				.8			.2	
.4	.2	.1				.1			.1	
5 71.2	13 27.5	8 46.5		Sales/Receivables	0 UND			6 64.3		
24 15.3	26 14.1	25 14.7			29 12.4			23 16.2		
39 9.4	51 7.1	45 8.1			40 9.2			51 7.2		
126 2.9	114 3.2	146 2.5		Cost of Sales/Inventory	0 UND			182 2.0		
228 1.6	332 1.1	365 1.0			228 1.6			912 .4		
365 1.0	730 .5	1217 .3			456 .8			1217 .3		
16 22.6	11 33.0	5 73.2		Cost of Sales/Payables	0 UND			15 24.5		
33 11.2	35 10.3	32 11.4			0 UND			47 7.7		
59 6.2	69 5.3	101 3.6			15 25.1			99 3.7		
2.4	1.6	1.8		Sales/Working Capital		2.5			1.7	
4.1	2.5	4.7				4.2			2.3	
25.6	4.5	13.8				NM			8.1	
16.8	52.0	7.8		EBIT/Interest		10.1			10.7	
(27) 7.7	(36) 8.5	(44) 2.1				2.1			(11) 5.6	
1.0	1.0	.3				.5			1.9	
				Net Profit + Depr., Dep., Amort./Cur. Mat. L/T/D						
.6	.0	.2		Fixed/Worth		.2			.2	
1.2	.5	.7				1.4			.5	
13.9	1.5	1.7				6.8			.9	
.7	.4	.9		Debt/Worth		.5			.8	
1.4	1.3	1.9				1.3			1.3	
16.9	3.3	7.8				6.5			NM	
63.4	36.2	40.7		% Profit Before Taxes/Tangible Net Worth					41.9	
(25) 20.2	(36) 17.5	(39) 8.7							(11) 18.1	
5.3	1.4	-3.4							5.0	
17.7	17.4	12.7		% Profit Before Taxes/Total Assets		16.5			13.8	
9.5	4.9	4.7				5.4			6.2	
.0	-1.3	-1.3				-1.6			3.0	
8.9	56.7	20.7		Sales/Net Fixed Assets		UND			5.9	
2.8	6.2	5.7				4.3			3.8	
1.1	1.8	2.0				.9			2.1	
1.5	1.4	1.4		Sales/Total Assets		1.4			1.0	
.9	.9	.8				.8			.5	
.7	.6	.5				.4			.4	
.8	1.4	1.2		% Depr., Dep., Amort./Sales					.4	
(21) 3.9	(30) 3.2	(34) 2.8							(13) 2.8	
6.2	5.1	6.1							4.9	
				% Officers', Directors', Owners' Comp/Sales						
486946M	571106M	548480M		Net Sales ($)	1619M	17709M	30211M	62516M	273153M	163272M
686379M	941221M	1012838M		Total Assets ($)	1928M	28516M	31713M	106278M	687977M	156426M

© RMA 2024   M = $ thousand   MM = $ million
See Pages viii through xx for Explanation of Ratios and Data

MANUFACTURING—Broadwoven Fabric Mills NAICS 313210

Current Data Sorted by Assets | Comparative Historical Data

						Type of Statement		
			1		2	Unqualified	4	
			1			Reviewed	5	4
			9	1		Compiled	1	
	1		3			Tax Returns	2	3
	2	6	9	2	5	Other	23	11
0-500M	8 (4/1-9/30/23) 500M-2MM	2-10MM	35 (10/1/23-3/31/24) 10-50MM	50-100MM	100-250MM		4/1/19-3/31/20 ALL	4/1/20-3/31/21 ALL
	3	8	22	3	7	NUMBER OF STATEMENTS	35	18
%	%	%	%	%	%	ASSETS	%	%
			12.8			Cash & Equivalents	7.5	17.5
			18.4			Trade Receivables (net)	20.6	17.4
D			28.7			Inventory	30.8	26.5
A			1.4			All Other Current	1.3	2.8
T			61.3			Total Current	60.2	64.1
A			22.0			Fixed Assets (net)	22.9	22.2
			2.7			Intangibles (net)	6.6	2.8
N			14.0			All Other Non-Current	10.3	10.9
O			100.0			Total	100.0	100.0
T						LIABILITIES		
			4.9			Notes Payable-Short Term	5.0	6.6
A			1.5			Cur. Mat.-L.T.D.	2.9	2.1
V			11.0			Trade Payables	12.5	8.2
A			.0			Income Taxes Payable	.1	.0
I			10.6			All Other Current	8.1	9.7
L			27.9			Total Current	28.7	26.6
A			9.9			Long-Term Debt	9.6	14.3
B			.5			Deferred Taxes	.8	.5
L			8.1			All Other Non-Current	4.7	8.2
E			53.5			Net Worth	56.2	50.4
			100.0			Total Liabilities & Net Worth	100.0	100.0
						INCOME DATA		
			100.0			Net Sales	100.0	100.0
			23.3			Gross Profit	21.6	30.6
			20.8			Operating Expenses	17.3	23.6
			2.5			Operating Profit	4.3	7.0
			-1.1			All Other Expenses (net)	.9	-.2
			3.6			Profit Before Taxes	3.4	7.2
						RATIOS		
			5.7				4.9	4.0
			4.0			Current	2.9	3.5
			1.7				1.3	1.9
			3.5				2.0	3.2
			2.2			Quick	1.6	1.8
			.5				.5	.8
		30	12.2				36 10.0	17 21.6
		38	9.5			Sales/Receivables	40 9.2	38 9.5
		59	6.2				51 7.2	55 6.6
		55	6.6				49 7.5	51 7.2
		111	3.3			Cost of Sales/Inventory	74 4.9	85 4.3
		152	2.4				122 3.0	130 2.8
		10	35.2				10 36.7	3 132.6
		16	22.8			Cost of Sales/Payables	19 19.5	19 19.1
		54	6.7				35 10.5	31 11.8
			2.1				3.3	2.5
			3.6			Sales/Working Capital	4.1	4.0
			7.3				9.5	6.1
			29.8				19.9	60.8
		(20)	5.6			EBIT/Interest	(33) 5.2	(15) 12.9
			-.2				-.1	1.2
						Net Profit + Depr., Dep., Amort./Cur. Mat. L/T/D		
			.2				.2	.3
			.3			Fixed/Worth	.4	.5
			1.2				1.0	1.2
			.2				.3	.3
			.5			Debt/Worth	.6	.4
			3.2				3.0	11.6
			18.9				28.2	28.0
		(20)	11.4			% Profit Before Taxes/Tangible Net Worth	(33) 7.4	(15) 16.8
			-.2				-7.2	6.7
			11.0				14.2	22.7
			3.4			% Profit Before Taxes/Total Assets	5.7	9.4
			-1.9				-3.4	3.4
			23.7				20.7	21.0
			7.3			Sales/Net Fixed Assets	8.5	5.7
			3.5				4.6	3.3
			1.8				2.1	2.2
			1.2			Sales/Total Assets	1.7	1.3
			.8				1.3	1.0
			.5				1.5	.7
		(19)	2.4			% Depr., Dep., Amort./Sales	(28) 2.1	(14) 3.3
			4.9				3.4	6.6
						% Officers', Directors' Owners' Comp/Sales		
	8387M	52312M	930966M	230779M	1607799M	Net Sales ($)	2205448M	555312M
	3318M	28124M	568226M	179819M	1092141M	Total Assets ($)	1497149M	437011M

M = $ thousand   MM = $ million
See Pages viii through xx for Explanation of Ratios and Data

© RMA 2024

MANUFACTURING—Broadwoven Fabric Mills NAICS 313210

Comparative Historical Data | Current Data Sorted by Sales

				Type of Statement						
2	3		5	Unqualified				1		4
4	6		10	Reviewed			1	1	6	2
2	3		3	Compiled					2	1
	1		1	Tax Returns				1		
16	21		24	Other		2	7	3	12	
4/1/21-	4/1/22-		4/1/23-			8 (4/1-9/30/23)		35 (10/1/23-3/31/24)		
3/31/22	3/31/23		3/31/24		0-1MM	1-3MM	3-5MM	5-10MM	10-25MM	25MM & OVER
ALL	ALL		ALL							
24	34		43	NUMBER OF STATEMENTS		2	1	10	11	19
%	%		%	ASSETS	%	%	%	%	%	%
13.5	8.7		12.3	Cash & Equivalents				17.7	14.0	8.1
24.8	17.3		17.2	Trade Receivables (net)	D			13.4	13.4	21.2
27.1	30.3		28.0	Inventory	A			27.5	23.5	28.8
.7	2.8		1.8	All Other Current	T			.6	1.8	2.8
66.1	59.0		59.3	Total Current	A			59.2	52.7	60.9
21.0	21.7		24.8	Fixed Assets (net)				35.4	17.3	26.7
4.5	9.0		7.2	Intangibles (net)	N			2.5	5.0	8.9
8.4	10.3		8.7	All Other Non-Current	O			2.9	25.0	3.5
100.0	100.0		100.0	Total	T			100.0	100.0	100.0
				LIABILITIES	A					
6.4	6.4		5.3	Notes Payable-Short Term	V			6.9	1.8	7.4
1.7	1.7		1.4	Cur. Mat.-L.T.D.	A			1.3	1.6	1.5
16.7	12.1		11.1	Trade Payables	I			8.4	5.7	13.4
.1	.1		.2	Income Taxes Payable	L			.0	.0	.4
8.2	8.1		10.4	All Other Current	A			8.9	11.9	8.7
33.0	28.4		28.4	Total Current	B			25.5	21.0	31.5
7.7	16.1		13.4	Long-Term Debt	L			13.9	8.6	15.2
1.2	.9		.9	Deferred Taxes	E			.1	.9	1.5
1.6	5.9		4.9	All Other Non-Current				.5	14.5	2.0
56.6	48.7		52.4	Net Worth				59.9	54.9	49.9
100.0	100.0		100.0	Total Liabilties & Net Worth				100.0	100.0	100.0
				INCOME DATA						
100.0	100.0		100.0	Net Sales				100.0	100.0	100.0
21.0	25.1		23.7	Gross Profit				19.8	31.9	18.0
14.7	20.0		19.2	Operating Expenses				19.4	26.6	12.0
6.4	5.1		4.5	Operating Profit				.4	5.4	6.0
-1.5	.9		-.3	All Other Expenses (net)				-.6	-1.8	.5
7.9	4.3		4.8	Profit Before Taxes				1.0	7.1	5.5
				RATIOS						
4.6	4.8		5.6					6.9	5.7	5.3
2.4	2.7		3.9	Current				4.9	3.9	3.4
1.8	1.7		1.5					1.1	1.8	1.4
2.3	2.4		2.9					3.1	4.2	2.7
1.5	1.1		1.7	Quick				2.5	1.7	1.5
.9	.7		.5					.9	.5	.5
41 9.0	21 17.1		30 12.2				0 UND	28 13.1	31 11.8	
59 6.2	38 9.7		38 9.5	Sales/Receivables			32 11.3	31 11.6	39 9.4	
72 5.1	54 6.7		50 7.3				43 8.5	66 5.5	57 6.4	
66 5.5	58 6.3		57 6.4				0 UND	87 4.2	43 8.5	
83 4.4	85 4.3		85 4.3	Cost of Sales/Inventory			79 4.6	111 3.3	63 5.8	
122 3.0	118 3.1		135 2.7				101 3.6	203 1.8	91 4.0	
19 19.5	10 35.6		12 31.3				10 36.4	15 24.6	11 34.1	
43 8.5	29 12.6		21 17.6	Cost of Sales/Payables			12 30.7	23 16.0	21 17.6	
64 5.7	54 6.8		48 7.6				18 20.8	64 5.7	41 9.0	
2.7	3.0		2.8					2.7	2.1	3.2
3.8	5.2		4.2	Sales/Working Capital				3.4	3.4	5.0
6.0	14.3		10.0					219.4	6.0	10.2
33.8	18.6		17.2					9.1	26.6	49.5
(17) 16.6	(28) 3.0		(39) 5.6	EBIT/Interest				1.8	(10) 5.6	(17) 6.7
6.8	-.6		.7					-15.0	2.3	1.4
				Net Profit + Depr., Dep., Amort./Cur. Mat. L/T/D						
.3	.3		.2					.3	.2	.3
.4	.4		.4	Fixed/Worth				.4	.3	.4
.8	4.8		1.4					2.3	1.2	7.2
.2	.2		.3					.1	.3	.3
.7	1.5		.9	Debt/Worth				.3	.4	1.0
1.8	9.0		5.6					4.8	2.9	8.9
39.1	39.7		20.3	% Profit Before Taxes/Tangible					19.7	21.1
(21) 9.9	(27) 16.2		(37) 12.4	Net Worth					12.4	(15) 16.0
3.4	-4.3		-1.6						3.7	2.9
21.0	17.7		13.2	% Profit Before Taxes/Total				7.9	10.6	14.1
7.4	4.7		3.9	Assets				.2	4.9	7.6
2.2	-2.5		-1.4					-9.0	2.7	-1.4
17.6	28.1		20.7					10.3	22.5	11.1
6.4	6.9		6.5	Sales/Net Fixed Assets				6.3	4.7	6.5
3.5	3.9		4.1					3.6	3.8	3.4
2.0	2.6		2.0					3.3	1.2	2.3
1.6	1.5		1.3	Sales/Total Assets				1.9	.8	1.5
1.0	1.1		.8					1.1	.6	1.1
1.7	.9		.1							.1
(22) 2.3	(23) 2.4		(33) 1.7	% Depr., Dep., Amort./Sales					(15) 2.4	
4.1	3.1		3.5							2.8
				% Officers', Directors' Owners' Comp/Sales						
2590288M	2064416M		2830243M	Net Sales ($)		3378M	4411M	69826M	172810M	2579818M
2071360M	1601111M		1871628M	Total Assets ($)		2116M	3328M	46951M	201319M	1617914M

© RMA 2024   M = $ thousand   MM = $ million
See Pages viii through xx for Explanation of Ratios and Data

MANUFACTURING—Textile and Fabric Finishing Mills NAICS 313310

Current Data Sorted by Assets | Comparative Historical Data

							Type of Statement				
			1		1	2	Unqualified		7		2
	1	1	2	6	1		Reviewed		11		4
		2	4				Compiled		4		
	2	2					Tax Returns		6		1
	2	4	4	1	2		Other		15		13
	2 (4/1-9/30/23)			29 (10/1/23-3/31/24)					4/1/19-3/31/20		4/1/20-3/31/21
0-500M	500M-2MM	2-10MM	10-50MM	50-100MM	100-250MM		NUMBER OF STATEMENTS		43 ALL		20 ALL
	5	9	10	3	4						
%	%	%	%	%	%		ASSETS		%		%
			8.6				Cash & Equivalents		8.9		16.6
			21.0				Trade Receivables (net)		25.8		19.4
			24.4				Inventory		38.3		32.1
DATA			2.8				All Other Current		1.7		3.2
NOT			56.8				Total Current		74.6		71.3
AVAILABLE			22.2				Fixed Assets (net)		18.4		17.4
			9.2				Intangibles (net)		1.6		7.7
			11.8				All Other Non-Current		5.8		3.6
			100.0				Total		100.0		100.0
							LIABILITIES				
			7.9				Notes Payable-Short Term		9.8		7.9
			1.0				Cur. Mat.-L.T.D.		7.6		4.0
			6.9				Trade Payables		19.5		14.4
			.1				Income Taxes Payable		.1		.3
			9.2				All Other Current		6.9		6.3
			25.1				Total Current		44.0		32.9
			14.1				Long-Term Debt		9.8		10.3
			.6				Deferred Taxes		.2		.6
			5.6				All Other Non-Current		14.2		5.7
			54.7				Net Worth		31.8		50.5
			100.0				Total Liabilities & Net Worth		100.0		100.0
							INCOME DATA				
			100.0				Net Sales		100.0		100.0
			25.5				Gross Profit		27.0		36.0
			21.2				Operating Expenses		24.2		32.8
			4.3				Operating Profit		2.8		3.2
			1.6				All Other Expenses (net)		.9		-.2
			2.7				Profit Before Taxes		2.0		3.4
							RATIOS				
			3.9						3.0		4.5
			2.7				Current		1.7		2.6
			1.7						1.2		1.6
			2.2						1.6		2.1
			1.1				Quick		.7		1.2
			.6						.3		.6
		41	9.0					24	15.1	25	14.5
		47	7.7				Sales/Receivables	42	8.6	38	9.5
		72	5.1					60	6.1	63	5.8
		43	8.5					58	6.3	25	14.6
		89	4.1				Cost of Sales/Inventory	78	4.7	101	3.6
		135	2.7					122	3.0	182	2.0
		10	37.8					28	13.2	23	15.9
		28	13.1				Cost of Sales/Payables	40	9.1	36	10.2
		32	11.3					55	6.6	62	5.9
			2.9						4.0		3.4
			3.6				Sales/Working Capital		8.2		4.3
			30.2						19.2		10.0
			9.4						5.9		66.4
			4.5				EBIT/Interest	(37)	2.4	(15)	9.4
			.0						-1.0		-.9
							Net Profit + Depr., Dep., Amort./Cur. Mat. L/T/D				
			.2						.1		.1
			.5				Fixed/Worth		.4		.3
			1.0						1.1		1.0
			.4						.7		.4
			.9				Debt/Worth		1.1		1.2
			2.1						3.5		2.4
			30.8						38.7		39.3
			9.3				% Profit Before Taxes/Tangible Net Worth	(40)	8.6	(18)	18.5
			-2.5						-3.7		2.8
			11.8						11.8		16.1
			4.5				% Profit Before Taxes/Total Assets		4.6		6.7
			-.9						-2.7		-1.9
			57.8						61.1		42.1
			4.1				Sales/Net Fixed Assets		20.0		14.5
			3.0						7.9		5.0
			1.8						2.9		2.6
			1.2				Sales/Total Assets		2.3		1.6
			.9						1.8		1.2
									.6		.7
							% Depr., Dep., Amort./Sales	(36)	1.1	(16)	2.0
									2.1		3.4
									1.4		
							% Officers', Directors' Owners' Comp/Sales	(11)	4.0		
									7.5		
	12093M	79954M	316410M	375600M	750606M		Net Sales ($)		2390382M		500950M
	4948M	48673M	269613M	166540M	871514M		Total Assets ($)		984464M		337076M

M = $ thousand   MM = $ million
See Pages viii through xx for Explanation of Ratios and Data

© RMA 2024

MANUFACTURING—Textile and Fabric Finishing Mills NAICS 313310

Comparative Historical Data | Current Data Sorted by Sales

				Type of Statement						
2	4	4		Unqualified					1	3
3	4	8		Reviewed			1		2	5
1	5	2		Compiled				2		
	3	4		Tax Returns				2	1	
10	23	13		Other	1	2	2	2	3	6
4/1/21-3/31/22 ALL	4/1/22-3/31/23 ALL	4/1/23-3/31/24 ALL			0-1MM	2 (4/1-9/30/23) 1-3MM	3-5MM	29 (10/1/23-3/31/24) 5-10MM	10-25MM	25MM & OVER
16	39	31	NUMBER OF STATEMENTS		1	3	6	7	14
%	%	%		ASSETS	%	%	%			%
12.8	15.1	14.9	Cash & Equivalents					D		8.3
24.9	22.8	19.5	Trade Receivables (net)					A		22.2
28.0	30.3	29.6	Inventory					T		23.8
1.3	3.5	1.5	All Other Current					A		1.3
66.9	71.8	65.4	Total Current							55.6
16.5	16.2	17.9	Fixed Assets (net)					N		20.7
8.3	4.7	7.8	Intangibles (net)					O		13.8
8.2	7.3	8.9	All Other Non-Current					T		9.9
100.0	100.0	100.0	Total							100.0
			LIABILITIES					A		
12.0	9.8	7.5	Notes Payable-Short Term					V		7.9
1.2	1.5	1.4	Cur. Mat.-L.T.D.					A		2.2
8.8	11.2	11.2	Trade Payables					I		7.2
.0	.2	.0	Income Taxes Payable					L		.1
5.0	7.9	7.9	All Other Current					A		11.6
27.0	30.6	28.1	Total Current					B		29.0
3.8	9.8	13.3	Long-Term Debt					L		15.4
.1	.2	.3	Deferred Taxes					E		.5
1.9	1.8	3.2	All Other Non-Current							4.3
67.2	57.5	55.2	Net Worth							50.8
100.0	100.0	100.0	Total Liabilities & Net Worth							100.0
			INCOME DATA							
100.0	100.0	100.0	Net Sales							100.0
29.3	29.8	30.8	Gross Profit							24.5
21.4	22.2	27.2	Operating Expenses							21.0
7.9	7.6	3.6	Operating Profit							3.5
-1.6	.3	1.2	All Other Expenses (net)							2.5
9.5	7.3	2.4	Profit Before Taxes							1.0
			RATIOS							
5.7	4.9	5.3								3.4
2.4	2.5	2.6	Current							2.1
1.6	1.7	1.6								1.4
4.0	3.0	3.2								1.9
1.2	1.3	1.0	Quick							1.0
.5	.7	.5								.5
26 14.3	27 13.3	24 15.4							33	11.0
43 8.4	40 9.2	35 10.3	Sales/Receivables						47	7.8
70 5.2	51 7.1	57 6.4							60	6.1
29 12.8	27 13.6	40 9.2							43	8.5
54 6.8	51 7.1	89 4.1	Cost of Sales/Inventory						89	4.1
96 3.8	130 2.8	130 2.8							118	3.1
10 35.7	16 23.3	12 30.0							14	25.7
25 14.6	23 15.9	24 15.4	Cost of Sales/Payables						22	16.4
38 9.5	40 9.2	33 11.1							30	12.2
2.9	3.6	2.5								3.0
4.5	4.4	3.9	Sales/Working Capital							6.2
9.3	8.5	8.4								30.3
46.8	94.6	10.1								9.0
(12) 15.7	(34) 11.2	(25) 2.9	EBIT/Interest							2.1
4.3	3.3	.6								-.4
			Net Profit + Depr., Dep., Amort./Cur. Mat. L/T/D							
.1	.0	.1								.2
.3	.2	.2	Fixed/Worth							.5
.4	.6	.8								1.7
.3	.4	.3								.4
.6	.7	.9	Debt/Worth							1.1
.9	1.5	2.6								5.5
47.6	40.3	32.3								34.9
20.1	(38) 14.0	(30) 11.9	% Profit Before Taxes/Tangible Net Worth						(13)	7.4
7.6	6.8	-.8								-3.8
30.8	30.0	14.3								10.0
9.7	7.9	5.0	% Profit Before Taxes/Total Assets							2.7
3.9	2.3	-.6								-3.0
54.1	166.0	47.3								48.6
21.7	33.8	9.0	Sales/Net Fixed Assets							5.8
5.4	5.3	3.4								2.8
2.3	2.6	2.2								1.9
1.6	1.9	1.2	Sales/Total Assets							1.1
1.2	1.4	1.0								.9
.4	.3	.6								
(14) 1.3	(26) 1.2	(22) 1.5	% Depr., Dep., Amort./Sales							
5.1	2.9	4.2								
		1.1	% Officers', Directors' Owners' Comp/Sales							
	(11)	5.3								
		7.1								
309481M	2176528M	1534663M	Net Sales ($)		980M	7639M	23865M		110044M	1392135M
230827M	1093325M	1361288M	Total Assets ($)		820M	3551M	22134M		77636M	1257147M

© RMA 2024
M = $ thousand   MM = $ million
See Pages viii through xx for Explanation of Ratios and Data

MANUFACTURING—Carpet and Rug Mills NAICS 314110

Current Data Sorted by Assets

		Type of Statement		
		Unqualified		
	2	1	1	Reviewed
		2		Compiled
	1	1		Tax Returns
1	1	1		Other
	2	6	7	7
0-500M	11 (4/1-9/30/23) 500M-2MM	2-10MM	21 (10/1/23-3/31/24) 10-50MM	50-100MM	100-250MM

0-500M	500M-2MM	2-10MM	10-50MM	50-100MM	100-250MM		Comparative Historical Data

Type of Statement
							6	4
						Unqualified	6	4
						Reviewed	1	2
						Compiled	4	2
						Tax Returns	1	2
						Other	16	10
							4/1/19-3/31/20 ALL	4/1/20-3/31/21 ALL
1	5	11	8	7		NUMBER OF STATEMENTS	28	20

%	%	%	%	%	%	ASSETS	%	%
			13.9			Cash & Equivalents	6.1	10.4
			13.2			Trade Receivables (net)	18.6	19.4
			32.4			Inventory	38.9	30.1
			8.9			All Other Current	1.6	2.1
			68.4			Total Current	65.1	62.0
			11.1			Fixed Assets (net)	17.2	20.0
			7.8			Intangibles (net)	12.6	13.8
			12.7			All Other Non-Current	5.1	4.2
			100.0			Total	100.0	100.0

DATA NOT AVAILABLE

LIABILITIES
			5.8			Notes Payable-Short Term	5.1	5.6
			2.7			Cur. Mat.-L.T.D.	2.5	2.9
			11.3			Trade Payables	20.0	20.5
			.0			Income Taxes Payable	.5	.0
			13.4			All Other Current	10.0	11.0
			33.2			Total Current	38.1	39.9
			21.6			Long-Term Debt	15.2	20.2
			.0			Deferred Taxes	.3	.7
			16.4			All Other Non-Current	6.0	9.5
			28.8			Net Worth	40.5	29.7
			100.0			Total Liabilities & Net Worth	100.0	100.0

INCOME DATA
			100.0			Net Sales	100.0	100.0
			35.8			Gross Profit	25.6	30.1
			29.6			Operating Expenses	21.9	26.4
			6.2			Operating Profit	3.6	3.7
			2.2			All Other Expenses (net)	1.2	.7
			4.0			Profit Before Taxes	2.4	3.1

RATIOS
			3.0				3.2	2.1
			2.5			Current	1.9	1.6
			1.4				1.3	1.3
			1.5				1.2	1.0
			.6			Quick	.7	.7
			.4				.4	.5
		16	22.8				20 18.0	29 12.6
		24	14.9			Sales/Receivables	34 10.6	39 9.3
		39	9.4				43 8.4	53 6.9
		65	5.6				65 5.6	47 7.8
		81	4.5			Cost of Sales/Inventory	96 3.8	111 3.3
		130	2.8				126 2.9	140 2.6
		18	20.2				23 15.7	23 16.2
		23	15.7			Cost of Sales/Payables	33 10.9	38 9.5
		35	10.4				57 6.4	66 5.5
			3.2				4.5	4.5
			4.0			Sales/Working Capital	7.7	6.1
			13.0				13.2	13.0
							7.8	8.9
						EBIT/Interest	3.5	(18) 3.1
							.9	-.4
						Net Profit + Depr., Dep., Amort./Cur. Mat. L/T/D		
			.2				.2	.3
			.4			Fixed/Worth	.5	.9
			-.2				1.6	NM
			.5				.7	1.4
			2.2			Debt/Worth	1.9	2.6
			-2.9				NM	NM
							30.2	39.5
						% Profit Before Taxes/Tangible Net Worth	(21) 8.8	(15) 16.7
							2.7	-5.6
			13.0				9.1	8.4
			9.2			% Profit Before Taxes/Total Assets	3.7	4.8
			4.6				-.1	-2.4
			27.9				55.3	45.3
			17.5			Sales/Net Fixed Assets	9.2	8.9
			13.8				5.7	5.2
			2.3				3.2	2.3
			1.8			Sales/Total Assets	1.9	1.4
			1.8				1.1	1.1
							.8	.6
						% Depr., Dep., Amort./Sales	(22) 1.7	(13) 1.0
							6.3	2.9
						% Officers', Directors' Owners' Comp/Sales		

| | 3371M | 54808M | 435634M | 1011256M | 2040268M | Net Sales ($) | 2348932M | 2054241M |
| | 1762M | 31213M | 252955M | 652642M | 1274440M | Total Assets ($) | 1651484M | 1536603M |

M = $ thousand   MM = $ million
See Pages viii through xx for Explanation of Ratios and Data

© RMA 2024

MANUFACTURING—Carpet and Rug Mills NAICS 314110

Comparative Historical Data | Current Data Sorted by Sales

						Type of Statement						
		3		4	2	Unqualified						2
		2		4	4	Reviewed						2
					1	Compiled						1
		3		2	3	Tax Returns				1	1	1
		9		10	22	Other		1	2		2	19
		4/1/21-3/31/22 ALL		4/1/22-3/31/23 ALL	4/1/23-3/31/24 ALL		0-1MM	11 (4/1-9/30/23) 1-3MM	3-5MM	21 (10/1/23-3/31/24) 5-10MM	10-25MM	25MM & OVER
		17		20	32	NUMBER OF STATEMENTS	2			2	3	25
		%		%	%	ASSETS	%	%	%	%	%	%
		11.0		4.9	9.2	Cash & Equivalents	D	D				5.9
		15.9		17.0	16.6	Trade Receivables (net)	A	A				15.9
		36.4		36.7	32.6	Inventory	T	T				34.3
		1.6		2.8	4.2	All Other Current	A	A				5.2
		64.9		61.4	62.5	Total Current						61.3
		20.4		20.8	20.5	Fixed Assets (net)	N	N				21.2
		11.3		8.2	5.8	Intangibles (net)	O	O				5.7
		3.3		9.6	11.1	All Other Non-Current	T	T				11.7
		100.0		100.0	100.0	Total						100.0
						LIABILITIES	A	A				
		6.6		5.1	6.1	Notes Payable-Short Term	V	V				4.2
		3.1		2.2	2.6	Cur. Mat.-L.T.D.	A	A				3.0
		10.7		14.0	10.3	Trade Payables	I	I				10.5
		.0		.1	.1	Income Taxes Payable	L	L				.2
		9.6		7.5	12.3	All Other Current	A	A				13.0
		30.0		28.9	31.5	Total Current	B	B				30.8
		25.4		14.9	23.3	Long-Term Debt	L	L				26.2
		.6		.4	.2	Deferred Taxes	E	E				.3
		3.1		16.6	12.3	All Other Non-Current						14.4
		41.0		39.3	32.7	Net Worth						28.3
		100.0		100.0	100.0	Total Liabilities & Net Worth						100.0
						INCOME DATA						
		100.0		100.0	100.0	Net Sales						100.0
		32.4		25.2	33.2	Gross Profit						31.6
		23.2		22.2	29.1	Operating Expenses						27.5
		9.2		3.0	4.1	Operating Profit						4.1
		-.7		.8	1.5	All Other Expenses (net)						1.7
		9.9		2.2	2.6	Profit Before Taxes						2.3
						RATIOS						
		3.7		3.9	3.0							2.9
		2.1		1.9	2.2	Current						2.2
		1.5		1.5	1.6							1.6
		2.3		1.6	1.5							1.1
		.7		.7	.7	Quick						.6
		.4		.3	.4							.4
19	19.2	22	16.8	21	17.6						21	17.3
32	11.3	38	9.7	37	9.9	Sales/Receivables					37	9.9
43	8.5	45	8.1	47	7.7						46	7.9
78	4.7	78	4.7	66	5.5						65	5.6
101	3.6	104	3.5	118	3.1	Cost of Sales/Inventory					130	2.8
146	2.5	174	2.1	146	2.5						140	2.6
15	24.1	19	18.9	19	18.8						20	18.7
31	11.8	42	8.6	31	11.8	Cost of Sales/Payables					29	12.7
42	8.7	56	6.5	46	8.0						42	8.7
		4.1		3.6	3.8							3.9
		5.8		5.0	5.1	Sales/Working Capital						5.2
		7.9		6.2	7.4							7.2
		22.4		69.1	4.6							4.8
(16)		7.7	(18)	3.3	(29) 2.0	EBIT/Interest					(24)	2.0
		3.0		-1.3	-.2							.4
					7.4	Net Profit + Depr., Dep.,						8.7
				(13)	1.9	Amort./Cur. Mat. L/T/D					(12)	2.4
					.4							.4
		.3		.1	.2							.4
		.7		.4	.7	Fixed/Worth						.9
		3.1		1.4	3.4							4.1
		1.0		.5	.9							1.0
		2.6		2.6	2.7	Debt/Worth						3.3
		6.0		4.8	6.4							10.4
		89.3		32.7	25.0	% Profit Before Taxes/Tangible						27.5
(14)		41.3	(17)	19.7	(27) 4.0	Net Worth					(20)	2.1
		11.7		-2.5	-9.6							-11.5
		23.2		12.2	12.9	% Profit Before Taxes/Total						12.9
		12.7		4.3	4.0	Assets						4.0
		5.6		-1.2	-1.6							-1.5
		21.6		45.5	19.6							17.6
		12.4		7.0	9.2	Sales/Net Fixed Assets						6.7
		5.6		3.7	4.6							4.6
		2.5		2.1	2.0							2.0
		1.7		1.5	1.7	Sales/Total Assets						1.8
		1.2		1.2	1.3							1.3
		.7		.9	.9							1.5
(15)		1.6	(17)	2.0	(28) 2.1	% Depr., Dep., Amort./Sales					(21)	2.3
		2.7		3.5	2.9							2.8
						% Officers', Directors' Owners' Comp/Sales						
		1511367M		2052798M	3545337M	Net Sales ($)		6425M	11499M		60801M	3466612M
		969494M		1516875M	2213012M	Total Assets ($)		8164M	10817M		30582M	2163449M

© RMA 2024 M = $ thousand MM = $ million
See Pages viii through xx for Explanation of Ratios and Data

MANUFACTURING—All Other Miscellaneous Textile Product Mills NAICS 314999

Current Data Sorted by Assets | Comparative Historical Data

						Type of Statement		
			2		1	Unqualified	9	1
		2	9			Reviewed	12	5
		4				Compiled	4	2
	1	1				Tax Returns	7	2
2	3	5	7	8		Other	35	20
	6 (4/1-9/30/23)		39 (10/1/23-3/31/24)				4/1/19-	4/1/20-
							3/31/20	3/31/21
0-500M	500M-2MM	2-10MM	10-50MM	50-100MM	100-250MM		ALL	ALL
2	4	12	18	8	1	NUMBER OF STATEMENTS	67	30
%	%	%	%	%	%	ASSETS	%	%
		12.4	12.0			Cash & Equivalents	10.4	14.5
		19.8	17.4			Trade Receivables (net)	20.8	18.7
		33.6	28.0			Inventory	34.2	26.2
		.5	2.2			All Other Current	3.3	3.0
		66.3	59.6			Total Current	68.8	62.4
		15.1	27.9			Fixed Assets (net)	19.1	25.2
		5.3	2.0			Intangibles (net)	6.6	5.0
		13.2	10.4			All Other Non-Current	5.5	7.4
		100.0	100.0			Total	100.0	100.0
						LIABILITIES		
		5.8	9.9			Notes Payable-Short Term	12.0	8.3
		3.8	2.4			Cur. Mat.-L.T.D.	1.8	1.4
		14.9	10.5			Trade Payables	13.5	13.7
		.2	.5			Income Taxes Payable	.0	.5
		9.8	7.3			All Other Current	10.4	10.6
		34.5	30.5			Total Current	37.7	34.4
		7.9	14.7			Long-Term Debt	9.7	16.7
		.0	1.1			Deferred Taxes	.5	.2
		8.4	2.1			All Other Non-Current	2.5	6.4
		49.3	51.7			Net Worth	49.6	42.2
		100.0	100.0			Total Liabilities & Net Worth	100.0	100.0
						INCOME DATA		
		100.0	100.0			Net Sales	100.0	100.0
		33.3	33.9			Gross Profit	37.4	31.7
		27.2	23.4			Operating Expenses	29.2	26.4
		6.1	10.4			Operating Profit	8.2	5.3
		.4	1.4			All Other Expenses (net)	1.0	-1.0
		5.7	9.1			Profit Before Taxes	7.2	6.3
						RATIOS		
		3.0	3.7				3.6	3.7
		1.9	1.9		Current	2.1	1.7
		1.2	1.4			1.2	1.1
		1.2	2.2				1.4	1.9
		.7	1.0			Quick	.9	.9
		.6	.6				.4	.6
		20 18.2	24 15.4				21 17.8	16 22.3
		35 10.3	43 8.5			Sales/Receivables	38 9.6	33 10.9
		41 8.9	57 6.4				56 6.5	49 7.4
		34 10.7	38 9.7				49 7.4	41 9.0
		78 4.7	85 4.3			Cost of Sales/Inventory	94 3.9	69 5.3
		135 2.7	140 2.6				159 2.3	126 2.9
		13 28.2	11 34.0				17 21.9	11 34.4
		35 10.3	18 20.8			Cost of Sales/Payables	29 12.6	29 12.7
		46 7.9	45 8.2				50 7.3	47 7.8
		3.0	2.6				2.9	3.5
		8.2	7.1			Sales/Working Capital	6.4	10.0
		30.0	15.9				22.6	34.4
		21.9	20.2				24.7	25.6
		(11) 4.7	(16) 6.9			EBIT/Interest	(56) 3.8	(25) 6.0
		3.1	2.9				.1	.1
							5.1	
						Net Profit + Depr., Dep.,	(10) 1.4	
						Amort./Cur. Mat. L/T/D	-1.1	
		.2	.3				.1	.3
		.3	.5			Fixed/Worth	.4	.7
		.7	1.0				1.1	1.3
		.4	.5				.4	.5
		1.1	.9			Debt/Worth	1.1	1.3
		4.5	2.0				6.1	4.2
		51.1	37.4				41.2	60.0
		(11) 17.0	19.6			% Profit Before Taxes/Tangible Net Worth	(60) 15.8	(26) 17.3
		5.6	11.3				4.2	1.5
		17.4	12.2				19.6	21.9
		7.6	8.3			% Profit Before Taxes/Total Assets	7.0	10.2
		3.2	5.4				.9	.7
		35.9	16.3				31.4	24.3
		16.5	5.3			Sales/Net Fixed Assets	13.4	11.2
		7.8	3.5				5.7	5.2
		2.8	2.4				2.8	2.8
		2.1	1.7			Sales/Total Assets	1.9	2.0
		1.6	1.1				1.3	1.2
		.7	.6				.7	1.1
		(11) 1.5	(16) 1.7			% Depr., Dep., Amort./Sales	(53) 1.7	(25) 2.1
		2.1	4.1				2.8	2.8
								1.1
						% Officers', Directors' Owners' Comp/Sales	(14) 1.9	
							3.1	
775M	22751M	165164M	721279M	818945M	341577M	Net Sales ($)	2514988M	1762237M
201M	6414M	78109M	435141M	541637M	197909M	Total Assets ($)	1588299M	1056284M

M = $ thousand   MM = $ million
See Pages viii through xx for Explanation of Ratios and Data

© RMA 2024

MANUFACTURING—All Other Miscellaneous Textile Product Mills NAICS 314999

Comparative Historical Data | Current Data Sorted by Sales

						Type of Statement						
		4		4	3	Unqualified						3
		6		3	11	Reviewed					4	7
		1		2	4	Compiled				1	3	
		5		2	2	Tax Returns		1		4	1	
		25		26	25	Other	2	6		39	7	12
		4/1/21-3/31/22		4/1/22-3/31/23	4/1/23-3/31/24		0-1MM	(4/1-9/30/23) 1-3MM	3-5MM	(10/1/23-3/31/24) 5-10MM	10-25MM	25MM & OVER
		ALL		ALL	ALL							
		41		37	45	NUMBER OF STATEMENTS	2	1		5	15	22
		%		%	%	ASSETS	%	%	%	%	%	%
		12.7		16.4	13.5	Cash & Equivalents					9.1	13.3
		21.6		21.3	20.5	Trade Receivables (net)			D		17.9	22.4
		28.4		31.9	29.2	Inventory			A		37.1	26.7
		1.8		4.1	1.9	All Other Current			T		.9	3.3
		64.5		73.7	65.1	Total Current			A		65.0	65.6
		21.4		16.3	18.3	Fixed Assets (net)					17.9	20.8
		8.5		4.2	3.5	Intangibles (net)			N		4.9	3.6
		5.6		5.8	13.1	All Other Non-Current			O		12.2	10.0
		100.0		100.0	100.0	Total			T		100.0	100.0
						LIABILITIES			A			
		9.6		9.3	7.3	Notes Payable-Short Term			V		7.6	9.7
		3.5		3.4	3.0	Cur. Mat.-L.T.D.			A		4.1	1.2
		14.4		12.1	13.6	Trade Payables			I		11.1	14.0
		.0		.1	.4	Income Taxes Payable			L		.1	.5
		8.5		12.9	9.5	All Other Current			A		8.3	10.3
		36.0		37.8	33.8	Total Current			B		31.2	35.6
		17.6		14.3	13.4	Long-Term Debt			L		9.8	11.8
		.6		.9	.5	Deferred Taxes			E		.0	1.1
		8.5		2.1	3.8	All Other Non-Current					7.1	2.1
		37.2		44.9	48.5	Net Worth					51.9	49.5
		100.0		100.0	100.0	Total Liabilities & Net Worth					100.0	100.0
						INCOME DATA						
		100.0		100.0	100.0	Net Sales					100.0	100.0
		33.5		32.7	32.7	Gross Profit					33.1	30.1
		25.4		25.2	24.8	Operating Expenses					25.0	21.9
		8.1		7.5	7.9	Operating Profit					8.2	8.2
		-.7		1.1	1.0	All Other Expenses (net)					.4	1.4
		8.8		6.4	6.9	Profit Before Taxes					7.8	6.8
						RATIOS						
		3.4		3.1	3.0						3.0	2.7
		2.0		2.0	2.0	Current					2.3	1.8
		1.2		1.6	1.4						1.4	1.4
		2.2		1.9	1.9						1.3	1.7
		.8		1.0	1.0	Quick					.7	1.1
		.5		.7	.7						.5	.7
14	26.0	21	17.0	22	16.5					23	16.0	24	15.4
43	8.5	41	9.0	38	9.5	Sales/Receivables				37	9.8	43	8.4
68	5.4	62	5.9	53	6.9					57	6.4	70	5.2
31	11.9	39	9.4	40	9.2					55	6.6	41	8.9
69	5.3	104	3.5	74	4.9	Cost of Sales/Inventory				126	2.9	65	5.6
146	2.5	135	2.7	126	2.9					243	1.5	122	3.0
14	25.9	13	28.4	12	31.1					11	34.7	14	25.6
30	12.1	29	12.4	26	14.1	Cost of Sales/Payables				24	15.4	27	13.3
44	8.3	50	7.3	50	7.3					39	9.4	76	4.8
	3.0		3.3		3.0						2.7		3.0
	5.4		4.7		7.5	Sales/Working Capital					4.6		7.1
	28.8		11.3		15.6						11.4		15.9
	73.8		23.5		16.5						13.5		24.6
(38)	17.6	(31)	9.0	(40)	5.2	EBIT/Interest				(14)	4.5	(18)	9.0
	4.4		5.2		3.0						3.1		2.4
					24.8	Net Profit + Depr., Dep.,							
				(11)	6.8	Amort./Cur. Mat. L/T/D							
					2.7								
	.2		.0		.2						.2		.3
	.4		.3		.3	Fixed/Worth					.3		.3
	2.1		.7		.7						.5		.8
	.6		.5		.5						.5		.6
	1.4		1.3		.9	Debt/Worth					.9		.9
	5.0		4.7		2.6						2.5		2.2
	44.5		46.6		39.3	% Profit Before Taxes/Tangible					24.3		41.0
(34)	24.9	(33)	22.3	(41)	17.3	Net Worth				(14)	17.5	(21)	17.2
	12.1		8.0		7.7						9.9		8.3
	20.5		17.4		14.6	% Profit Before Taxes/Total					14.7		13.9
	14.7		9.6		8.2	Assets					10.0		7.4
	5.0		4.0		4.6						3.9		4.3
	36.3		99.0		40.8						38.6		35.7
	12.8		19.7		11.8	Sales/Net Fixed Assets					12.6		9.1
	6.3		8.9		6.2						4.0		5.4
	2.4		2.5		2.7						2.5		2.1
	1.7		1.9		1.9	Sales/Total Assets					1.8		1.8
	1.3		1.4		1.2						1.0		1.2
	1.0		.7		.7						.7		.8
(33)	1.9	(22)	1.4	(32)	1.6	% Depr., Dep., Amort./Sales				(14)	1.6	(13)	1.5
	3.9		3.9		3.6						4.0		3.9
					.6	% Officers', Directors'							
			(10)		2.9	Owners' Comp/Sales							
					6.6								
	2029542M		2422327M		2070491M	Net Sales ($)	775M	2975M		33312M	226669M	1806760M
	1330533M		1523467M		1259411M	Total Assets ($)	201M	1211M		15603M	167324M	1075072M

© RMA 2024   M = $ thousand   MM = $ million
See Pages viii through xx for Explanation of Ratios and Data

MANUFACTURING—Cut and Sew Apparel Contractors NAICS 315210

Current Data Sorted by Assets

0-500M	500M-2MM	2-10MM	10-50MM	50-100MM	100-250MM		Comparative Historical Data	
	2	1 1 2 3	1 1 1 2 7	1 1 2 5	1 3 4	1 2 3	Type of Statement Unqualified Reviewed Compiled Tax Returns Other	4 5 4 6 12	2 2 1 2 11
		3 (4/1-9/30/23)		18 (10/1/23-3/31/24)				4/1/19- 3/31/20 ALL	4/1/20- 3/31/21 ALL
							NUMBER OF STATEMENTS	31	18
%	%	%	%	%	%		ASSETS	%	%
							Cash & Equivalents	12.1	20.6
							Trade Receivables (net)	23.7	27.5
D							Inventory	39.9	31.9
A							All Other Current	2.3	1.8
T							Total Current	78.0	81.7
A							Fixed Assets (net)	11.4	10.1
							Intangibles (net)	2.9	3.1
N							All Other Non-Current	7.7	5.1
O							Total	100.0	100.0
T							LIABILITIES		
							Notes Payable-Short Term	14.0	20.1
A							Cur. Mat.-L.T.D.	.9	.7
V							Trade Payables	11.8	9.6
A							Income Taxes Payable	.5	.0
I							All Other Current	5.7	9.8
L							Total Current	33.0	40.1
A							Long-Term Debt	4.6	8.5
B							Deferred Taxes	.2	.0
L							All Other Non-Current	5.5	3.1
E							Net Worth	56.8	48.3
							Total Liabilties & Net Worth	100.0	100.0
							INCOME DATA		
							Net Sales	100.0	100.0
							Gross Profit	39.4	37.6
							Operating Expenses	33.6	34.7
							Operating Profit	5.8	2.8
							All Other Expenses (net)	.1	-1.5
							Profit Before Taxes	5.7	4.3
							RATIOS		
								5.5	4.9
							Current	2.3	2.4
								1.9	1.6
								1.8	3.3
							Quick	1.1	1.2
								.6	.8
								24 15.4	21 17.1
							Sales/Receivables	34 10.6	29 12.4
								52 7.0	72 5.1
								52 7.0	44 8.3
							Cost of Sales/Inventory	126 2.9	70 5.2
								215 1.7	159 2.3
								10 36.1	0 UND
							Cost of Sales/Payables	28 13.2	22 16.8
								49 7.5	33 11.1
								2.7	2.8
							Sales/Working Capital	4.3	5.4
								9.0	7.1
								29.2	31.3
							EBIT/Interest	8.8 (16)	15.4
								2.6	3.3
							Net Profit + Depr., Dep., Amort./Cur. Mat. L/T/D		
								.0	.0
							Fixed/Worth	.1	.1
								.4	.4
								.4	.2
							Debt/Worth	.7	.8
								1.6	1.8
								40.8	37.6
							% Profit Before Taxes/Tangible Net Worth	(30) 18.5	(17) 22.1
								6.9	7.7
								22.6	19.2
							% Profit Before Taxes/Total Assets	10.9	11.2
								3.1	3.2
								93.8	99.8
							Sales/Net Fixed Assets	40.8	44.1
								13.2	15.3
								3.1	3.6
							Sales/Total Assets	2.1	2.2
								1.4	1.5
								.5	.4
							% Depr., Dep., Amort./Sales	(26) .7	(13) .6
								1.5	1.7
									.9	
							% Officers', Directors' Owners' Comp/Sales	(14) 1.8	
								7.2	
		4934M	107216M	254955M	514850M	628085M	Net Sales ($)	1448627M	932979M
		1424M	36535M	102158M	277275M	428888M	Total Assets ($)	714862M	484701M

© RMA 2024

M = $ thousand   MM = $ million
See Pages viii through xx for Explanation of Ratios and Data

MANUFACTURING—Cut and Sew Apparel Contractors NAICS 315210

Comparative Historical Data | Current Data Sorted by Sales

						Type of Statement						
			1		1	Unqualified				1	1	3
	4		3		4	Reviewed				1	1	1
	2		2		2	Compiled				1	1	
	3		2		2	Tax Returns			1	2	1	7
	16		15		12	Other	1	3 (4/1-9/30/23)	1	18 (10/1/23-3/31/24)		
	4/1/21-3/31/22 ALL		4/1/22-3/31/23 ALL		4/1/23-3/31/24 ALL		0-1MM	1-3MM	3-5MM	5-10MM	10-25MM	25MM & OVER
	25		23		21	NUMBER OF STATEMENTS	1	1	1	3	5	11
	%		%		%	ASSETS	%	%	%	%	%	%
	24.4		25.6		17.2	Cash & Equivalents						17.8
	23.1		23.3		22.2	Trade Receivables (net)		D				27.9
	32.0		33.3		32.5	Inventory		A				28.8
	2.4		1.6		4.2	All Other Current		T				2.7
	81.9		83.8		76.0	Total Current		A				77.1
	6.0		8.3		11.3	Fixed Assets (net)						10.8
	4.7		3.9		5.3	Intangibles (net)		N				5.1
	7.4		4.0		7.4	All Other Non-Current		O				7.0
	100.0		100.0		100.0	Total		T				100.0
						LIABILITIES		A				
	10.5		7.9		6.4	Notes Payable-Short Term		V				8.2
	2.9		1.7		.7	Cur. Mat.-L.T.D.		A				.8
	9.9		16.4		19.8	Trade Payables		I				19.4
	.2		.0		.0	Income Taxes Payable		L				.0
	6.4		11.2		10.5	All Other Current		A				9.4
	29.9		37.2		37.5	Total Current		B				37.9
	4.6		12.2		10.9	Long-Term Debt		L				10.5
	.0		.0		.0	Deferred Taxes		E				.0
	7.6		12.6		6.3	All Other Non-Current						9.3
	57.9		38.0		45.4	Net Worth						42.3
	100.0		100.0		100.0	Total Liabilities & Net Worth						100.0
						INCOME DATA						
	100.0		100.0		100.0	Net Sales						100.0
	43.1		37.9		36.1	Gross Profit						43.4
	36.2		31.7		28.8	Operating Expenses						31.2
	6.9		6.1		7.2	Operating Profit						12.2
	-2.4		.2		.6	All Other Expenses (net)						.9
	9.3		6.0		6.7	Profit Before Taxes						11.3
						RATIOS						
	6.1		4.6		3.2							3.1
	2.7		2.5		2.0	Current						1.9
	1.9		1.8		1.5							1.4
	3.8		2.4		1.8							2.0
	1.5		1.4		1.1	Quick						1.1
	.9		.9		.6							.9
16	22.6	18	20.2	10	37.9						10	35.7
37	9.9	34	10.7	34	10.7	Sales/Receivables					35	10.3
69	5.3	53	6.9	51	7.2						51	7.2
0	UND	37	9.9	35	10.5						56	6.5
83	4.4	65	5.6	104	3.5	Cost of Sales/Inventory					135	2.7
192	1.9	182	2.0	192	1.9						182	2.0
10	35.6	21	17.3	17	21.6						15	24.1
27	13.3	36	10.0	35	10.3	Cost of Sales/Payables					32	11.5
45	8.2	59	6.2	57	6.4						50	7.3
	2.3		3.3		3.1							3.1
	3.5		5.7		6.3	Sales/Working Capital						5.6
	6.0		12.8		9.3							9.8
	47.0		30.6		28.0							
(20)	21.1	(17)	11.7	(17)	9.7	EBIT/Interest						
	3.9		4.2		-.9							
						Net Profit + Depr., Dep., Amort./Cur. Mat. L/T/D						
	.0		.0		.0							.0
	.0		.1		.1	Fixed/Worth						.1
	.2		1.1		.7							.7
	.2		.4		.4							.4
	.6		1.2		1.6	Debt/Worth						1.6
	1.3		3.6		3.7							3.7
	62.2		78.7		71.4	% Profit Before Taxes/Tangible Net Worth						82.3
(24)	28.2	(22)	37.6	(19)	42.1						(10)	46.9
	8.6		7.4		21.0							34.8
	27.6		26.8		28.6							31.0
	12.3		19.2		18.4	% Profit Before Taxes/Total Assets						19.7
	5.1		3.7		3.3							8.8
	117.1		173.6		244.8							360.9
	76.5		53.0		60.1	Sales/Net Fixed Assets						60.2
	33.9		21.1		11.4							10.4
	2.6		3.5		3.4							3.2
	2.0		2.3		1.9	Sales/Total Assets						1.9
	1.0		1.8		1.4							1.8
	.4		.5		.4							
(17)	.6	(12)	.6	(13)	.7	% Depr., Dep., Amort./Sales						
	.9		1.6		1.2							
						% Officers', Directors' Owners' Comp/Sales						
	1367567M		1257050M		1510040M	Net Sales ($)	790M		4144M	24268M	76786M	1404052M
	754495M		729796M		846280M	Total Assets ($)	622M		802M	23700M	31154M	790002M

© RMA 2024   M = $ thousand   MM = $ million
See Pages viii through xx for Explanation of Ratios and Data

MANUFACTURING—Cut and Sew Apparel Manufacturing (except Contractors) NAICS 315250

Current Data Sorted by Assets | Comparative Historical Data

						Type of Statement				
				2	3	Unqualified		9		4
	1	5	13	2	1	Reviewed		22		18
		4	1			Compiled		2		2
1	2	1	1			Tax Returns		10		7
		13	16	3	4	Other		70		29
0-500M	7 (4/1-9/30/23) 500M-2MM	2-10MM	66 (10/1/23-3/31/24) 10-50MM	50-100MM	100-250MM			4/1/19-3/31/20 ALL		4/1/20-3/31/21 ALL
1	3	23	31	7	8	NUMBER OF STATEMENTS		113		60
%	%	%	%	%	%	ASSETS		%		%
		18.6	16.9			Cash & Equivalents		11.2		15.4
		22.3	15.9			Trade Receivables (net)		24.5		21.5
		29.8	38.8			Inventory		38.3		31.1
		6.8	7.0			All Other Current		5.2		8.5
		77.5	78.5			Total Current		79.2		76.4
		10.8	7.7			Fixed Assets (net)		8.4		9.8
		4.1	3.7			Intangibles (net)		8.7		7.7
		7.6	10.0			All Other Non-Current		3.7		6.0
		100.0	100.0			Total		100.0		100.0
						LIABILITIES				
		5.0	13.1			Notes Payable-Short Term		18.3		13.0
		.9	1.4			Cur. Mat.-L.T.D.		.8		2.9
		14.3	22.0			Trade Payables		20.5		22.9
		.1	.0			Income Taxes Payable		.1		.1
		9.2	9.5			All Other Current		9.3		9.9
		29.5	46.0			Total Current		48.9		48.8
		19.7	7.4			Long-Term Debt		7.4		14.0
		.0	.1			Deferred Taxes		.2		.0
		3.5	8.0			All Other Non-Current		3.0		3.0
		47.4	38.5			Net Worth		40.5		34.3
		100.0	100.0			Total Liabilities & Net Worth		100.0		100.0
						INCOME DATA				
		100.0	100.0			Net Sales		100.0		100.0
		41.3	35.6			Gross Profit		38.7		36.4
		35.9	30.4			Operating Expenses		35.2		35.0
		5.4	5.2			Operating Profit		3.5		1.3
		-.1	.8			All Other Expenses (net)		1.3		-.6
		5.5	4.3			Profit Before Taxes		2.3		1.9
						RATIOS				
		6.6	3.8					3.1		3.0
		3.4	1.7			Current		1.8		1.6
		1.7	1.2					1.1		1.1
		3.2	1.6					1.4		1.4
		1.8	.7			Quick		.8		.8
		.9	.3					.4		.5
		12 31.1	1 260.0				16	23.3	10	35.7
		35 10.3	27 13.6			Sales/Receivables	38	9.5	35	10.4
		62 5.9	56 6.5				53	6.9	61	6.0
		41 8.9	74 4.9				49	7.5	38	9.5
		79 4.6	130 2.8			Cost of Sales/Inventory	101	3.6	83	4.4
		146 2.5	192 1.9				174	2.1	182	2.0
		15 23.6	17 22.0				24	15.3	29	12.7
		31 11.9	42 8.7			Cost of Sales/Payables	40	9.1	52	7.0
		49 7.5	74 4.9				70	5.2	85	4.3
		2.8	2.3					4.4		3.0
		4.1	6.8			Sales/Working Capital		6.1		7.4
		9.0	25.3					26.6		49.3
		34.4	5.5					14.1		34.8
	(20)	9.1	(25) 2.8			EBIT/Interest	(99)	3.9	(56)	5.7
		2.1	1.4					.9		-.9
						Net Profit + Depr., Dep., Amort./Cur. Mat. L/T/D		4.6		7.0
							(19)	3.2	(12)	1.8
								1.1		-.5
		.0	.0					.0		.0
		.1	.1			Fixed/Worth		.2		.2
		.5	.8					.8		1.5
		.3	.6					.6		.8
		1.0	2.0			Debt/Worth		1.6		2.9
		9.7	6.2					7.4		13.2
		54.9	40.2					58.8		97.8
	(21)	23.4	(27) 16.8			% Profit Before Taxes/Tangible Net Worth	(97)	18.1	(49)	35.8
		8.2	10.3					2.7		-.2
		24.4	16.2					20.5		23.5
		14.3	6.1			% Profit Before Taxes/Total Assets		4.6		5.4
		1.4	1.5					.5		-3.6
		629.3	136.5					267.9		219.3
		37.2	45.8			Sales/Net Fixed Assets		63.7		57.4
		11.8	19.8					23.3		20.7
		2.9	2.8					3.4		2.6
		2.3	1.9			Sales/Total Assets		2.5		2.0
		1.6	1.2					1.5		1.3
		.2	.1					.2		.1
	(10)	.7	(19) .3			% Depr., Dep., Amort./Sales	(71)	.5	(40)	.5
		3.3	1.1					1.5		1.8
		1.4	.6					1.3		1.5
	(10)	2.7	(14) 2.0			% Officers', Directors' Owners' Comp/Sales	(42)	2.4	(21)	2.3
		4.8	2.9					4.5		3.8
377M	18965M	303172M	1386773M	893726M	1981752M	Net Sales ($)		4629432M		2504365M
234M	3283M	129223M	696472M	468511M	1339873M	Total Assets ($)		2876064M		1607174M

M = $ thousand   MM = $ million
See Pages viii through xx for Explanation of Ratios and Data

© RMA 2024

MANUFACTURING—Cut and Sew Apparel Manufacturing (except Contractors) NAICS 315250

Comparative Historical Data | Current Data Sorted by Sales

Comparative Historical Data						Type of Statement	Current Data Sorted by Sales					
		5		10	5	Unqualified						5
		8		25	22	Reviewed		1	1	2	4	14
		1		4	5	Compiled				1	4	
		6		4	3	Tax Returns				1	1	
		32		41	38	Other	1	1	2	5	9	20
		4/1/21-3/31/22		4/1/22-3/31/23	4/1/23-3/31/24		1	7 (4/1-9/30/23)			66 (10/1/23-3/31/24)	
		ALL		ALL	ALL		0-1MM	1-3MM	3-5MM	5-10MM	10-25MM	25MM & OVER
		52		84	73	NUMBER OF STATEMENTS	2	2	3	9	18	39
		%		%	%	ASSETS	%	%	%	%	%	%
		15.1		13.0	15.3	Cash & Equivalents					21.8	10.6
		18.1		21.3	20.0	Trade Receivables (net)					16.7	22.1
		38.2		41.0	34.2	Inventory					39.3	34.3
		6.8		5.4	6.0	All Other Current					2.4	6.9
		78.2		80.8	75.6	Total Current					80.2	73.9
		8.6		6.5	9.6	Fixed Assets (net)					8.6	7.9
		10.4		5.9	6.7	Intangibles (net)					2.0	10.2
		2.8		6.8	8.1	All Other Non-Current					9.3	8.0
		100.0		100.0	100.0	Total					100.0	100.0
						LIABILITIES						
		8.2		11.9	9.3	Notes Payable-Short Term					3.1	14.0
		3.9		2.0	2.1	Cur. Mat.-L.T.D.					.6	3.2
		16.9		17.9	18.4	Trade Payables					12.0	22.7
		.0		.1	.1	Income Taxes Payable					.0	.1
		8.0		10.5	9.0	All Other Current					10.3	7.9
		37.1		42.6	38.9	Total Current					26.1	48.1
		12.7		11.2	13.2	Long-Term Debt					12.5	10.1
		.0		.0	.0	Deferred Taxes					.0	.1
		2.0		4.8	6.3	All Other Non-Current					4.1	6.6
		48.2		41.5	41.5	Net Worth					57.3	35.2
		100.0		100.0	100.0	Total Liabilities & Net Worth					100.0	100.0
						INCOME DATA						
		100.0		100.0	100.0	Net Sales					100.0	100.0
		42.6		35.6	39.4	Gross Profit					38.8	38.1
		34.6		29.7	33.5	Operating Expenses					32.1	30.8
		8.0		5.9	5.9	Operating Profit					6.7	7.3
		-1.1		.3	.8	All Other Expenses (net)					.5	1.4
		9.1		5.6	5.1	Profit Before Taxes					6.2	5.9
						RATIOS						
		4.2		3.7	3.9						5.7	2.8
		2.5		2.2	2.4	Current					3.6	1.5
		1.3		1.4	1.3						2.6	1.2
		2.1		1.6	1.8						2.5	1.3
		.9		.8	1.0	Quick					1.4	.8
		.5		.4	.6						.9	.4
6		62.4	10	36.1	9	42.9					17	21.4	4	103.8
23		16.1	29	12.6	37	9.8	Sales/Receivables				34	10.6	40	9.2
55		6.6	56	6.5	60	6.1					46	7.9	62	5.9
64		5.7	54	6.8	54	6.8					81	4.5	52	7.0
126		2.9	114	3.2	118	3.1	Cost of Sales/Inventory				130	2.8	107	3.4
174		2.1	192	1.9	182	2.0					182	2.0	174	2.1
25		14.7	16	22.3	20	18.5					16	22.4	29	12.4
50		7.3	36	10.1	39	9.3	Cost of Sales/Payables				30	12.1	43	8.4
78		4.7	62	5.9	66	5.5					45	8.1	76	4.8
		3.0		3.1	2.7						2.5	4.3
		4.8		4.9	4.8	Sales/Working Capital					3.7	9.0
		12.3		10.9	15.1						4.8	25.7
		114.0		21.3	12.6						89.3	9.4
(44)		12.7	(68)	8.5	(63)	3.2	EBIT/Interest				(15)	6.6	(35)	3.2
		3.9		.8	1.5						1.0	1.9
				13.1	3.7	Net Profit + Depr., Dep.,						
	(16)		3.0	(12)	1.0	Amort./Cur. Mat. L/T/D						
				.7	.5							
		.0		.0	.0						.0	.0
		.1		.1	.1	Fixed/Worth					.1	.2
		.5		.4	1.3						.2	1.6
		.4		.6	.6						.4	.9
		1.7		1.4	1.6	Debt/Worth					.6	3.1
		4.1		3.9	9.9						1.6	22.3
		86.5		58.7	57.5	% Profit Before Taxes/Tangible					34.2	60.4
(45)		50.8	(77)	23.1	(63)	19.6	Net Worth				21.5	(31)	30.5
		18.5		4.4	5.6						1.7	10.4
		30.5		18.9	18.1	% Profit Before Taxes/Total					20.0	16.7
		14.7		9.0	6.4	Assets					9.6	7.5
		5.5		.8	1.4						1.3	3.0
		174.1		193.2	152.3						207.7	161.4
		55.0		73.8	39.3	Sales/Net Fixed Assets					37.7	44.0
		21.6		23.2	12.4						23.6	12.2
		2.7		3.0	2.7						2.6	2.9
		2.0		2.0	1.9	Sales/Total Assets					2.1	1.9
		1.2		1.5	1.4						1.1	1.5
		.3		.1	.2							.1
(30)		.6	(60)	.3	(44)	.5	% Depr., Dep., Amort./Sales					(27)	.3
		1.7		1.0	1.4							1.3
		.9		1.0	1.1	% Officers', Directors'						1.1
(18)		2.0	(27)	1.8	(26)	2.4	Owners' Comp/Sales					(11)	2.0
		3.1		3.1	3.8							2.6
		3237831M		5015093M	4584765M	Net Sales ($)	1353M	4926M	12394M	67740M	365503M	4132849M
		2031347M		2780109M	2637596M	Total Assets ($)	2614M	2721M	16302M	41086M	232166M	2342707M

© RMA 2024   M = $ thousand   MM = $ million
See Pages viii through xx for Explanation of Ratios and Data

MANUFACTURING—Apparel Accessories and Other Apparel Manufacturing NAICS 315990

Current Data Sorted by Assets

			Type of Statement		
			Unqualified		
		3	Reviewed		
	3	2	Compiled		
1	4	2	Tax Returns		
5	6	1			1
4	13	15	23	9	6
	19 (4/1-9/30/23)		89 (10/1/23-3/31/24)		
0-500M	500M-2MM	2-10MM	10-50MM	50-100MM	100-250MM

4	19	28	28	17	12	NUMBER OF STATEMENTS
%	%	%	%	%	%	ASSETS
	16.1	18.1	12.0	13.8	10.4	Cash & Equivalents
	21.1	22.5	17.7	17.3	15.6	Trade Receivables (net)
	29.8	25.6	36.8	28.8	26.0	Inventory
	2.6	2.0	5.4	5.0	5.9	All Other Current
	69.6	68.2	71.9	64.9	58.0	Total Current
	15.0	16.5	14.4	14.5	6.4	Fixed Assets (net)
	6.6	4.7	1.2	7.8	17.3	Intangibles (net)
	8.8	10.6	12.4	12.9	18.3	All Other Non-Current
	100.0	100.0	100.0	100.0	100.0	Total
						LIABILITIES
	13.1	11.0	12.6	2.7	10.7	Notes Payable-Short Term
	1.2	1.9	1.4	1.8	.5	Cur. Mat.-L.T.D.
	13.2	11.1	15.5	13.3	16.2	Trade Payables
	.0	.1	.2	.1	.1	Income Taxes Payable
	23.9	8.0	11.6	10.5	15.0	All Other Current
	51.4	32.2	41.2	28.4	42.3	Total Current
	20.9	15.4	15.9	13.9	8.0	Long-Term Debt
	.0	.0	.0	.3	.0	Deferred Taxes
	5.9	1.2	6.5	8.7	1.8	All Other Non-Current
	21.7	51.2	36.4	48.7	47.9	Net Worth
	100.0	100.0	100.0	100.0	100.0	Total Liabilities & Net Worth
						INCOME DATA
	100.0	100.0	100.0	100.0	100.0	Net Sales
	42.6	37.8	37.7	41.9	30.2	Gross Profit
	37.7	34.8	32.8	32.6	22.3	Operating Expenses
	4.9	3.1	4.8	9.3	7.9	Operating Profit
	.8	.6	.3	1.2	1.0	All Other Expenses (net)
	4.1	2.5	4.6	8.1	6.9	Profit Before Taxes
						RATIOS
	3.9	4.3	3.4	3.4	5.6	
	1.5	2.7	2.0	2.8	2.6	Current
	1.1	1.4	1.2	1.7	.8	
	3.6	2.8	1.7	1.8	1.7	
	.8	1.5	.9	.9	.8	Quick
	.4	.6	.5	.6	.3	
9 41.3	15 24.2	10 37.1	20 18.5	4 101.2		
22 16.8	30 12.3	29 12.5	40 9.1	38 9.7		Sales/Receivables
38 9.7	51 7.2	54 6.8	83 4.4	50 7.3		
8 45.0	36 10.1	55 6.6	76 4.8	34 10.7		
49 7.4	70 5.2	104 3.5	130 2.8	111 3.3		Cost of Sales/Inventory
91 4.0	122 3.0	215 1.7	159 2.3	166 2.2		
3 139.8	5 70.9	15 23.6	27 13.3	23 16.2		
13 27.2	21 17.8	27 13.3	64 5.7	38 9.7		Cost of Sales/Payables
31 11.7	45 8.1	62 5.9	78 4.7	53 6.9		
	5.7	3.3	4.5	2.5	2.8	
	8.8	6.0	6.9	3.5	4.6	Sales/Working Capital
	135.3	16.3	17.2	9.2	NM	
	33.2	22.0	19.1	36.3	253.1	
(15)	2.8	(23) 7.5	(22) 2.7	(14) 10.8	(10) 10.7	EBIT/Interest
	-2.7	1.0	-.3	2.2	2.6	
						Net Profit + Depr., Dep., Amort./Cur. Mat. L/T/D
	.1	.0	.1	.0	.1	
	.8	.2	.3	.2	.2	Fixed/Worth
	-2.3	.8	1.2	.8	UND	
	.5	.5	.5	.4	.3	
	3.3	.6	2.5	.9	.9	Debt/Worth
	-14.6	6.4	6.8	8.1	UND	
	66.5	36.9	45.6	37.1		
(12)	36.6	(24) 21.4	(26) 24.1	(15) 17.7		% Profit Before Taxes/Tangible Net Worth
	-13.6	2.1	-1.0	2.3		
	32.0	22.1	15.4	21.3	14.6	
	8.1	8.3	7.4	9.5	9.7	% Profit Before Taxes/Total Assets
	-5.2	.1	.9	2.4	6.2	
	108.0	134.2	93.7	56.7	448.7	
	33.1	26.2	27.4	11.5	21.7	Sales/Net Fixed Assets
	10.8	9.1	10.5	5.2	12.2	
	4.0	3.0	2.8	1.8	3.0	
	3.1	2.2	1.8	1.4	1.4	Sales/Total Assets
	2.6	1.5	1.6	1.2	1.1	
		.6	.3		.5	
	(20) 1.4	(20) .8	(11) 1.4			% Depr., Dep., Amort./Sales
		2.4	2.3	4.7		
	2.5					
(10)	3.6					% Officers', Directors', Owners' Comp/Sales
	5.0					
2946M	78537M	355205M	2403373M	1755711M	5718659M	Net Sales ($)
1037M	22109M	147471M	698268M	1134963M	1917038M	Total Assets ($)

Comparative Historical Data

12		10	
14		6	
6		3	
17		9	
63		37	
4/1/19-3/31/20		4/1/20-3/31/21	
ALL		ALL	
112		65	
%		%	
11.5		20.6	
20.1		20.0	
38.5		29.1	
4.1		4.3	
74.3		74.1	
12.6		11.9	
4.4		5.8	
8.7		8.2	
100.0		100.0	
13.4		14.0	
1.8		3.0	
12.9		17.3	
.1		.8	
15.8		14.8	
44.1		49.8	
13.2		12.9	
.1		.0	
5.3		6.9	
37.2		30.4	
100.0		100.0	
100.0		100.0	
37.3		36.4	
32.4		28.7	
4.9		7.7	
.9		-.3	
4.0		8.1	
3.3		2.8	
2.2		2.0	
1.3		1.1	
1.4		1.8	
.8		.9	
.4		.5	
8 43.9		12 30.3	
31 11.6		35 10.5	
49 7.4		54 6.7	
54 6.8		36 10.0	
96 3.8		96 3.8	
182 2.0		159 2.3	
13 27.3		12 29.6	
27 13.4		38 9.7	
42 8.7		66 5.5	
3.6		3.2	
5.6		5.9	
17.3		46.6	
15.2		40.3	
(99) 5.2		(56) 11.1	
1.3		3.0	
23.4		42.5	
(17) 4.3		(13) 9.4	
1.4		2.0	
.1		.1	
.2		.3	
.8		1.1	
.5		.8	
1.2		1.5	
6.3		11.6	
37.0		89.0	
(96) 17.0		(54) 39.0	
3.1		10.6	
19.7		23.9	
9.1		11.5	
1.7		3.0	
72.2		182.9	
31.3		25.4	
12.3		7.9	
3.0		2.7	
2.3		1.9	
1.6		1.4	
.5		.4	
(81) 1.1		(49) 1.2	
1.6		2.1	
1.9		.7	
(31) 2.5		(14) 1.6	
4.8		4.0	
6765003M		2840991M	
2801947M		1706515M	

M = $ thousand   MM = $ million
See Pages viii through xx for Explanation of Ratios and Data

© RMA 2024

MANUFACTURING—Apparel Accessories and Other Apparel Manufacturing NAICS 315990

Comparative Historical Data				Current Data Sorted by Sales					
			Type of Statement						
5	9	10	Unqualified						10
2	7	8	Reviewed		1		2	5	
4	3	8	Compiled				5	3	
10	13	12	Tax Returns	1	3	3	2	2	1
39	55	70	Other	3	9	6	11	35	
4/1/21-3/31/22 ALL	4/1/22-3/31/23 ALL	4/1/23-3/31/24 ALL			19 (4/1-9/30/23)		89 (10/1/23-3/31/24)		
				0-1MM	1-3MM	3-5MM	5-10MM	10-25MM	25MM & OVER
60	87	108	NUMBER OF STATEMENTS	4	12	9	9	20	54
%	%	%	ASSETS	%	%	%	%	%	%
16.7	16.3	14.2	Cash & Equivalents	20.0				16.6	12.8
23.1	22.6	19.2	Trade Receivables (net)	15.9				25.0	19.1
31.1	31.1	30.4	Inventory	27.2				32.1	31.0
3.6	3.8	3.8	All Other Current	.3				1.4	5.7
74.5	73.8	67.6	Total Current	63.5				75.2	68.6
13.8	11.7	14.2	Fixed Assets (net)	18.4				16.9	10.7
5.9	5.2	6.6	Intangibles (net)	4.0				2.7	6.6
5.8	9.2	11.6	All Other Non-Current	14.1				5.2	14.1
100.0	100.0	100.0	Total	100.0				100.0	100.0
			LIABILITIES						
7.3	13.1	12.5	Notes Payable-Short Term	21.8				10.8	9.5
1.1	2.0	1.7	Cur. Mat.-L.T.D.	2.8				1.0	1.2
15.8	13.9	13.3	Trade Payables	8.5				16.0	14.6
.5	.1	.1	Income Taxes Payable	.1				.0	.2
10.1	18.3	12.9	All Other Current	35.2				4.8	12.2
34.9	47.4	40.4	Total Current	68.4				32.5	37.7
18.9	16.1	16.6	Long-Term Debt	34.9				11.6	11.6
.0	.1	.1	Deferred Taxes	.0				.0	.1
6.2	3.1	4.6	All Other Non-Current	7.0				1.0	6.6
40.0	33.3	38.3	Net Worth	-10.4				54.9	43.9
100.0	100.0	100.0	Total Liabilities & Net Worth	100.0				100.0	100.0
			INCOME DATA						
100.0	100.0	100.0	Net Sales	100.0				100.0	100.0
33.3	39.6	38.4	Gross Profit	41.6				34.7	38.2
26.9	34.1	33.0	Operating Expenses	43.7				29.0	30.5
6.4	5.5	5.4	Operating Profit	-2.1				5.7	7.7
-1.0	.6	.7	All Other Expenses (net)	.0				-.2	.9
7.3	4.9	4.7	Profit Before Taxes	-2.1				5.9	6.8
			RATIOS						
4.5	4.5	3.6	Current	4.4				6.2	3.4
2.6	2.0	2.3		1.2				2.8	2.4
1.4	1.3	1.2		.9				1.3	1.4
2.5	1.8	1.9	Quick	2.5				2.8	1.8
1.2	1.0	.9		.8				1.2	.9
.6	.6	.5		.2				.8	.6
22 16.5	16 23.1	14 26.3	Sales/Receivables	2 168.6			11 33.0	15 24.7	
37 9.9	33 11.0	30 12.1		18 20.8			35 10.5	38 9.6	
61 6.0	54 6.7	51 7.2		48 7.6			73 5.0	55 6.6	
33 10.9	27 13.4	36 10.2	Cost of Sales/Inventory	27 13.6			34 10.8	54 6.7	
91 4.0	81 4.5	91 4.0		114 3.2			64 5.7	107 3.4	
140 2.6	182 2.0	159 2.3		261 1.4			114 3.2	174 2.1	
15 24.5	9 39.5	10 36.8	Cost of Sales/Payables	0 UND			6 60.8	17 21.0	
32 11.3	28 12.9	26 13.9		13 28.0			18 20.4	37 9.8	
50 7.3	55 6.6	59 6.2		140 2.6			55 6.6	65 5.6	
3.0	3.0	3.7	Sales/Working Capital	4.8				3.1	3.1
5.0	5.6	6.4		17.2				5.2	5.1
10.4	13.6	20.7		-52.9				16.3	15.5
79.5	34.5	22.0	EBIT/Interest					17.9	29.6
(46) 18.2	(76) 9.0	(87) 4.8					(15) 7.5	(44) 10.7	
4.7	2.5	.2						1.0	1.6
	24.6	26.8	Net Profit + Depr., Dep., Amort./Cur. Mat. L/T/D						
	(13) 8.8	(13) 1.5							
	2.9	.7							
.1	.0	.1	Fixed/Worth	.0				.1	.1
.2	.2	.2		NM				.2	.2
.6	.8	1.4		-1.6				.5	.9
.5	.4	.5	Debt/Worth	.4				.3	.5
1.6	1.4	1.2		NM				.5	1.1
4.7	7.0	10.0		-6.1				3.7	6.9
57.6	43.6	41.7	% Profit Before Taxes/Tangible Net Worth					34.6	42.6
(53) 32.1	(76) 26.5	(88) 22.3						(47) 22.1 25.0	
17.2	9.0	2.3						11.6	
22.1	19.3	20.9	% Profit Before Taxes/Total Assets	24.5				22.0	19.0
13.0	9.8	8.1		-.2				9.9	9.8
4.8	2.5	.3		-22.8				4.6	3.1
97.0	162.7	95.2	Sales/Net Fixed Assets	UND				123.9	94.6
27.5	37.6	25.9		11.2				23.4	28.4
10.9	11.8	10.5		8.7				8.0	10.5
2.7	3.0	3.1	Sales/Total Assets	3.3				3.0	2.7
2.2	2.1	1.9		2.3				2.2	1.7
1.5	1.4	1.4		.8				1.7	1.3
.4	.5	.4	% Depr., Dep., Amort./Sales					.2	.3
(38) .9	(44) 1.4	(69) 1.3					(15) 1.4	(37) 1.2	
1.8	2.7	2.6						2.0	2.6
1.7	2.2	1.4	% Officers', Directors' Owners' Comp/Sales						
(16) 3.5	(28) 3.8	(25) 3.3							
4.9	8.6	4.4							
4308619M	3589868M	10314431M	Net Sales ($)	2063M	26091M	37100M	58231M	342319M	9848627M
1940673M	2089392M	3920886M	Total Assets ($)	1236M	15508M	13567M	34974M	165939M	3689662M

© RMA 2024 M = $ thousand   MM = $ million
See Pages viii through xx for Explanation of Ratios and Data

MANUFACTURING—Other Leather and Allied Product Manufacturing   NAICS 316990

Current Data Sorted by Assets | Comparative Historical Data

							Type of Statement		
			1				Unqualified		
		1	1			1	Reviewed	6	2
		1		1			Compiled		1
1	2	1	4	5	2	1	Tax Returns	2	3
	5 (4/1-9/30/23)		17 (10/1/23-3/31/24)				Other	11	7
0-500M	500M-2MM	2-10MM	10-50MM	50-100MM	100-250MM			4/1/19- 3/31/20	4/1/20- 3/31/21
1	3	7	7	2	2		NUMBER OF STATEMENTS	ALL 19	ALL 14
%	%	%	%	%	%		ASSETS	%	%
							Cash & Equivalents	13.2	11.2
							Trade Receivables (net)	21.7	22.6
							Inventory	35.8	33.9
							All Other Current	2.6	1.2
							Total Current	73.2	68.9
							Fixed Assets (net)	12.5	11.8
							Intangibles (net)	6.1	13.1
							All Other Non-Current	8.2	6.3
							Total	100.0	100.0
							LIABILITIES		
							Notes Payable-Short Term	7.4	13.5
							Cur. Mat.-L.T.D.	5.6	1.0
							Trade Payables	15.5	12.6
							Income Taxes Payable	.3	.0
							All Other Current	16.7	21.9
							Total Current	45.6	48.9
							Long-Term Debt	12.4	17.4
							Deferred Taxes	.0	.3
							All Other Non-Current	.7	11.3
							Net Worth	41.3	22.0
							Total Liabilties & Net Worth	100.0	100.0
							INCOME DATA		
							Net Sales	100.0	100.0
							Gross Profit	39.4	39.8
							Operating Expenses	29.7	37.6
							Operating Profit	9.8	2.2
							All Other Expenses (net)	1.3	.1
							Profit Before Taxes	8.5	2.0
							RATIOS		
								3.7	5.4
							Current	1.9	2.4
								1.4	.9
								1.8	2.0
							Quick	1.1	.9
								.5	.5
								24 14.9	19 19.5
							Sales/Receivables	35 10.3	37 9.9
								40 9.2	63 5.8
								33 11.0	50 7.3
							Cost of Sales/Inventory	91 4.0	130 2.8
								159 2.3	203 1.8
								16 23.3	24 15.3
							Cost of Sales/Payables	34 10.6	42 8.7
								63 5.8	68 5.4
								3.8	2.7
							Sales/Working Capital	6.2	4.2
								18.9	-21.6
								22.9	23.2
							EBIT/Interest	(16) 8.9	8.7
								4.1	.3
							Net Profit + Depr., Dep., Amort./Cur. Mat. L/T/D		
								.0	.1
							Fixed/Worth	.2	.4
								.4	NM
								.5	.8
							Debt/Worth	.7	3.0
								3.0	NM
							% Profit Before Taxes/Tangible Net Worth	58.2	83.2
								(16) 33.1	(11) 26.0
								8.7	7.6
							% Profit Before Taxes/Total Assets	25.2	23.0
								14.1	8.8
								5.7	-1.9
								200.0	162.4
							Sales/Net Fixed Assets	25.3	23.4
								16.3	11.6
								2.6	2.3
							Sales/Total Assets	2.0	1.8
								1.8	1.2
								.4	1.1
							% Depr., Dep., Amort./Sales	(14) .6	(10) 2.1
								1.2	4.7
							% Officers', Directors' Owners' Comp/Sales		
1387M	9706M	67420M	523530M	119185M	424836M		Net Sales ($)	572689M	388153M
435M	4484M	41466M	211446M	153006M	313116M		Total Assets ($)	282963M	237785M

© RMA 2024   M = $ thousand   MM = $ million
See Pages viii through xx for Explanation of Ratios and Data

MANUFACTURING—Other Leather and Allied Product Manufacturing NAICS 316990

Comparative Historical Data | Current Data Sorted by Sales

				Type of Statement						
	1	1	2	Unqualified				1		1
	2	2	3	Reviewed			1		1	1
	2	1	1	Compiled					1	
	4	7	15	Tax Returns		2	1	1		1
	4/1/21-	4/1/22-	4/1/23-	Other		5 (4/1-9/30/23)	2	17 (10/1/23-3/31/24)	3	8
	3/31/22	3/31/23	3/31/24		0-1MM	1-3MM	3-5MM	5-10MM	10-25MM	25MM & OVER
	ALL	ALL	ALL	NUMBER OF STATEMENTS						
	9	11	22			2	2	2	5	10
	%	%	%	ASSETS	%	%	%	%	%	%
		9.5	13.1	Cash & Equivalents						11.4
		25.2	13.5	Trade Receivables (net)						17.5
		40.1	39.4	Inventory						37.6
		2.9	2.1	All Other Current	D					2.2
		77.6	68.1	Total Current	A					68.7
		3.8	9.4	Fixed Assets (net)	T					5.9
		.9	12.7	Intangibles (net)	A					14.3
		17.8	9.8	All Other Non-Current						11.0
		100.0	100.0	Total	N					100.0
				LIABILITIES	O					
		16.7	10.7	Notes Payable-Short Term	T					11.2
		.2	3.2	Cur. Mat.-L.T.D.						5.5
		25.5	12.7	Trade Payables	A					23.4
		.2	.5	Income Taxes Payable	V					.5
		20.9	10.8	All Other Current	A					15.7
		63.5	37.9	Total Current	I					56.2
		31.7	8.9	Long-Term Debt	L					10.5
		.0	.0	Deferred Taxes	A					.0
		1.5	5.4	All Other Non-Current	B					11.0
		3.3	47.8	Net Worth	L					22.2
		100.0	100.0	Total Liabilities & Net Worth	E					100.0
				INCOME DATA						
		100.0	100.0	Net Sales						100.0
		38.0	39.6	Gross Profit						40.7
		32.8	33.5	Operating Expenses						33.2
		5.1	6.0	Operating Profit						7.5
		1.8	2.4	All Other Expenses (net)						2.7
		3.3	3.6	Profit Before Taxes						4.8
				RATIOS						
		2.9	3.4							2.7
		1.8	2.5	Current						1.7
		.7	1.5							.7
		1.2	1.4							1.2
		.7	.9	Quick						.5
		.3	.2							.3
	6	60.3	11	34.3	Sales/Receivables				1	258.7
	38	9.6	22	16.3					38	9.6
	63	5.8	41	8.9					56	6.5
	51	7.2	78	4.7	Cost of Sales/Inventory				66	5.5
	83	4.4	130	2.8					130	2.8
	159	2.3	182	2.0					166	2.2
	7	54.6	6	60.6	Cost of Sales/Payables				32	11.5
	24	15.0	25	14.4					51	7.2
	30	12.3	53	6.9					73	5.0
		4.4		3.5	Sales/Working Capital					3.5
		8.5		5.2						7.6
		-15.2		256.9						-12.1
		31.5		10.7	EBIT/Interest					
		12.8	(19)	3.9						
		.2		-.1						
				Net Profit + Depr., Dep., Amort./Cur. Mat. L/T/D						
		.0		.1	Fixed/Worth					.0
		.1		.1						.2
		-3.1		.5						-5.9
		.5		.4	Debt/Worth					.7
		7.4		.8						17.3
		-4.4		12.0						-3.5
				48.4	% Profit Before Taxes/Tangible Net Worth					
			(18)	14.7						
				-1.4						
		23.3		18.5	% Profit Before Taxes/Total Assets					19.7
		6.1		7.4						9.8
		-1.5		-5.2						-.3
		999.8		93.3	Sales/Net Fixed Assets					388.5
		147.3		42.4						64.8
		23.4		11.0						14.4
		4.8		2.6	Sales/Total Assets					3.4
		2.2		1.7						1.7
		1.3		1.4						1.3
				.3	% Depr., Dep., Amort./Sales					
			(15)	.8						
				1.8						
					% Officers', Directors' Owners' Comp/Sales					
	385128M	607232M	1146064M	Net Sales ($)	4160M	11151M	16505M	62134M	1052114M
	188053M	372064M	723953M	Total Assets ($)	2257M	6144M	11283M	37495M	666774M

© RMA 2024   M = $ thousand   MM = $ million
See Pages viii through xx for Explanation of Ratios and Data

MANUFACTURING—Sawmills NAICS 321113

Current Data Sorted by Assets | Comparative Historical Data

						Type of Statement		
			3	1	1	Unqualified	15	6
	4	7	2	1	Reviewed	16	5
2	7	4	1	1	Compiled	11	5
1	1				Tax Returns	17	7
1	12	16	3	7	Other	53	38
1	15 (4/1-9/30/23)	61 (10/1/23-3/31/24)				4/1/19-3/31/20	4/1/20-3/31/21
0-500M	500M-2MM	2-10MM	10-50MM	50-100MM	100-250MM		ALL	ALL
1	4	24	30	7	10	NUMBER OF STATEMENTS	112	61
%	%	%	%	%	%	ASSETS	%	%
		5.5	9.3		10.6	Cash & Equivalents	7.3	11.2
		16.5	6.8		4.4	Trade Receivables (net)	9.7	9.3
		33.3	23.7		15.7	Inventory	25.9	21.7
		3.2	2.0		1.1	All Other Current	2.1	3.3
		58.6	41.8		31.8	Total Current	45.0	45.5
		30.4	45.6		45.2	Fixed Assets (net)	44.9	44.5
		3.0	4.0		4.4	Intangibles (net)	2.1	2.8
		8.0	8.7		18.6	All Other Non-Current	8.0	7.2
		100.0	100.0		100.0	Total	100.0	100.0
						LIABILITIES		
		10.1	5.9		5.0	Notes Payable-Short Term	10.0	7.0
		3.3	3.5		1.7	Cur. Mat.-L.T.D.	4.1	4.3
		7.7	3.1		3.5	Trade Payables	5.7	6.0
		.0	.0		.0	Income Taxes Payable	.1	.1
		8.0	4.9		1.9	All Other Current	7.0	8.0
		29.1	17.4		12.1	Total Current	26.8	25.3
		19.2	19.7		15.5	Long-Term Debt	20.7	24.0
		.1	.6		1.6	Deferred Taxes	.5	.4
		5.9	3.5		1.6	All Other Non-Current	4.8	3.7
		45.7	58.8		69.1	Net Worth	47.2	46.6
		100.0	100.0		100.0	Total Liabilities & Net Worth	100.0	100.0
						INCOME DATA		
		100.0	100.0		100.0	Net Sales	100.0	100.0
		24.0	15.2		13.3	Gross Profit	21.2	26.9
		18.0	14.6		15.4	Operating Expenses	18.3	18.3
		6.0	.6		-2.1	Operating Profit	2.9	8.7
		.7	.3		.4	All Other Expenses (net)	1.0	-.2
		5.4	.3		-2.5	Profit Before Taxes	1.9	8.9
						RATIOS		
		3.6	4.2		9.4		3.9	4.0
		2.5	2.7		4.4	Current	1.9	2.2
		1.1	1.7		1.1		1.1	1.4
		1.5	2.1		6.3		1.7	2.4
		.8	.9		1.4	Quick	.6	1.0
		.3	.4		.2		.3	.3
		10 38.2	11 33.2		9 40.9		11 31.8	13 27.4
		16 22.2	16 22.3		14 25.9	Sales/Receivables	18 20.7	19 19.6
		34 10.8	21 17.0		26 13.8		30 12.3	26 14.2
		35 10.4	43 8.4		48 7.6		38 9.5	38 9.6
		52 7.0	69 5.3		72 5.1	Cost of Sales/Inventory	69 5.3	61 6.0
		122 3.0	89 4.1		91 4.0		114 3.2	101 3.6
		6 64.0	5 74.6		3 108.1		5 78.4	8 44.8
		15 23.7	8 48.2		9 42.7	Cost of Sales/Payables	10 35.7	14 25.5
		26 14.3	12 29.2		23 15.8		23 16.2	26 14.3
		5.2	5.0		2.8		4.2	3.5
		9.3	6.2		5.5	Sales/Working Capital	7.8	7.9
		82.6	10.2		58.5		39.8	21.8
		35.9	9.7				8.5	30.0
		(23) 8.8	(27) 2.3			EBIT/Interest	(105) 2.5	(55) 8.6
		.3	-1.6				-.9	.3
							4.0	
						Net Profit + Depr., Dep., Amort./Cur. Mat. L/T/D	(12) 1.9	
							.7	
		.2	.4		.4		.5	.6
		.6	.8		.9	Fixed/Worth	1.0	.9
		1.7	1.4		1.2		1.8	1.8
		.3	.4		.1		.3	.4
		.9	.6		.4	Debt/Worth	1.2	1.0
		3.0	1.6		1.3		2.4	2.5
		55.0	18.7		5.3		22.7	56.2
		(20) 24.7	3.3		-1.6	% Profit Before Taxes/Tangible Net Worth	(105) 8.1	(56) 27.7
		4.4	-11.0		-16.7		-4.5	1.5
		23.7	10.6		3.2		9.2	31.3
		9.6	1.5		-1.5	% Profit Before Taxes/Total Assets	2.4	12.9
		-3.4	-5.3		-6.5		-3.7	-1.5
		32.2	6.1		3.1		7.3	6.9
		6.9	3.5		1.9	Sales/Net Fixed Assets	2.9	3.4
		3.4	2.3		1.6		2.0	2.2
		3.4	1.9		1.1		2.0	2.0
		2.3	1.4		.9	Sales/Total Assets	1.5	1.4
		1.3	1.0		.6		1.1	1.0
		1.2	2.6				2.5	2.9
		(19) 2.2	(29) 3.7			% Depr., Dep., Amort./Sales	(91) 3.8	(50) 3.8
		5.4	7.3				6.6	5.9
							.6	1.0
						% Officers', Directors' Owners' Comp/Sales	(19) 1.1	(12) 1.5
							2.1	3.2
1450M	18125M	333837M	994963M	645158M	1329999M	Net Sales ($)	5956800M	2942798M
310M	5377M	146273M	692434M	564203M	1529619M	Total Assets ($)	5352912M	2480058M

M = $ thousand   MM = $ million
See Pages viii through xx for Explanation of Ratios and Data

© RMA 2024

MANUFACTURING—Sawmills NAICS 321113

Comparative Historical Data / Current Data Sorted by Sales

				Type of Statement							
	6	10	5	Unqualified				1	4	5	
	9	8	14	Reviewed				3	7	9	
	6	12	15	Compiled			1	1		4	
	11	6	2	Tax Returns	1		2	1	13	19	
	39	41	40	Other		2	1	5			
	4/1/21-3/31/22 ALL	4/1/22-3/31/23 ALL	4/1/23-3/31/24 ALL			15 (4/1-9/30/23)		61 (10/1/23-3/31/24)			
					0-1MM	1-3MM	3-5MM	5-10MM	10-25MM	25MM & OVER	
	71	77	76	NUMBER OF STATEMENTS	1	3	1	10	24	37	
	%	%	%	ASSETS	%	%	%	%	%	%	
	13.4	12.1	9.5	Cash & Equivalents				7.6	8.5	10.5	
	10.2	9.1	10.3	Trade Receivables (net)				8.2	14.5	8.3	
	24.7	25.0	25.2	Inventory				39.1	26.5	23.2	
	3.2	2.1	2.1	All Other Current				1.3	3.2	1.8	
	51.4	48.3	47.2	Total Current				56.3	52.6	43.7	
	37.5	40.8	38.9	Fixed Assets (net)				29.6	39.3	39.6	
	3.5	1.5	3.5	Intangibles (net)				4.0	.5	3.7	
	7.7	9.4	10.3	All Other Non-Current				10.1	7.5	13.0	
	100.0	100.0	100.0	Total				100.0	100.0	100.0	
				LIABILITIES							
	7.8	5.6	6.8	Notes Payable-Short Term				13.6	7.8	4.5	
	1.9	2.7	3.0	Cur. Mat.-L.T.D.				3.8	3.6	2.0	
	6.1	5.8	5.5	Trade Payables				7.3	6.8	3.8	
	.1	.1	.0	Income Taxes Payable				.0	.0	.0	
	10.4	8.7	6.2	All Other Current				4.1	5.5	7.2	
	26.2	22.9	21.4	Total Current				28.8	23.8	17.6	
	22.5	20.2	19.5	Long-Term Debt				29.7	19.0	13.9	
	.5	.4	.5	Deferred Taxes				.0	.4	.7	
	2.1	5.0	4.9	All Other Non-Current				1.2	5.7	4.1	
	48.7	51.6	53.8	Net Worth				40.3	51.1	63.8	
	100.0	100.0	100.0	Total Liabilities & Net Worth				100.0	100.0	100.0	
				INCOME DATA							
	100.0	100.0	100.0	Net Sales				100.0	100.0	100.0	
	34.6	26.8	19.3	Gross Profit				25.4	16.6	16.6	
	19.4	15.9	17.5	Operating Expenses				19.6	14.5	15.9	
	15.1	10.8	1.8	Operating Profit				5.8	2.1	.7	
	-.5	1.2	.3	All Other Expenses (net)				.7	.5	.2	
	15.6	9.6	1.5	Profit Before Taxes				5.1	1.6	.5	
				RATIOS							
	5.1	6.3	4.3					5.0	3.6	6.5	
	3.1	2.8	2.6	Current				2.5	2.7	2.9	
	1.6	1.4	1.3					1.0	1.5	1.7	
	2.7	2.3	1.8					2.3	1.7	3.5	
	1.0	1.1	.9	Quick				.3	1.1	.9	
	.5	.4	.4					.1	.4	.4	
9	39.4	9 42.8	10 35.2		7	52.7	11	31.9	11	32.4	
15	24.6	14 26.1	17 22.1	Sales/Receivables	9	41.2	18	20.8	17	21.7	
27	13.3	24 15.4	24 15.2		20	18.6	26	14.0	25	14.7	
42	8.6	49 7.4	40 9.2		48	7.6	35	10.3	49	7.5	
61	6.0	63 5.8	60 6.1	Cost of Sales/Inventory	74	4.9	55	6.6	68	5.4	
101	3.6	91 4.0	91 4.0		215	1.7	91	4.0	87	4.2	
5	74.0	5 69.4	6 62.2		3	106.7	6	64.0	7	55.4	
11	32.3	10 36.8	10 36.5	Cost of Sales/Payables	10	36.2	9	42.6	10	37.1	
20	18.1	17 20.9	20 18.7		20	18.2	23	15.8	18	19.8	
	3.8	4.3	5.0					4.9	5.2	3.6	
	6.1	6.5	7.5	Sales/Working Capital				11.4	8.8	6.2	
	11.6	20.8	14.9					144.7	12.7	10.4	
	79.6	45.1	12.8						12.7	11.3	
(62)	18.7	(70) 13.6	(67) 2.6	EBIT/Interest				2.8	(31) 2.8	2.3	
	6.3	2.4	-1.6						-.4	-3.4	
		16.4	24.6	Net Profit + Depr., Dep.,							
		(15) 6.5	(11) 4.4	Amort./Cur. Mat. L/T/D							
		3.5	1.5								
	.4	.4	.3					.1	.3	.3	
	.6	.8	.7	Fixed/Worth				.7	.8	.7	
	1.5	1.4	1.5					-1.1	1.5	1.1	
	.3	.3	.3					.2	.5	.2	
	.7	.7	.7	Debt/Worth				.6	1.0	.6	
	2.0	2.4	2.1					-4.2	1.5	1.5	
	75.0	49.4	25.4	% Profit Before Taxes/Tangible					32.5	19.1	
(64)	45.4	(71) 25.9	(70) 4.7	Net Worth				(23)	10.6	4.5	
	17.6	8.0	-9.3						-9.1	-8.4	
	40.0	22.3	13.5	% Profit Before Taxes/Total				32.2	11.8	12.3	
	20.2	14.1	2.2	Assets				2.0	4.9	2.4	
	8.1	2.8	-5.1					-8.8	-4.1	-5.0	
	9.2	8.6	8.0					24.0	15.2	6.5	
	5.5	5.0	3.9	Sales/Net Fixed Assets				7.3	3.7	3.9	
	3.0	2.4	2.2					3.0	2.4	1.9	
	2.5	2.3	2.2					3.6	2.4	1.9	
	1.7	1.6	1.4	Sales/Total Assets				2.0	1.7	1.2	
	1.1	1.1	1.0					1.1	1.3	.9	
	1.9	1.8	2.0						1.6	2.4	
(56)	3.1	(63) 3.3	(61) 3.7	% Depr., Dep., Amort./Sales				(22)	4.0	(29) 3.5	
	4.6	5.9	6.4						7.6	5.6	
	1.1	.7	.9	% Officers', Directors'							
(18)	2.2	(12) 2.3	(17) 1.3	Owners' Comp/Sales							
	5.0	3.2	3.3								
	3585215M	4211039M	3323532M	Net Sales ($)	656M	6669M	4527M	79087M	392438M	2840155M	
	2582929M	3296646M	2938216M	Total Assets ($)	633M	13972M	4261M	48258M	226123M	2644969M	

M = $ thousand   MM = $ million
See Pages viii through xx for Explanation of Ratios and Data

© RMA 2024

MANUFACTURING—Hardwood Veneer and Plywood Manufacturing NAICS 321211

Current Data Sorted by Assets | Comparative Historical Data

							Type of Statement		
		3	6	1	2		Unqualified	4	4
		2	1				Reviewed	7	3
		5					Compiled	6	6
	2	4	5	5	2		Tax Returns	7	2
	6 (4/1-9/30/23)		32 (10/1/23-3/31/24)				Other	17	15
0-500M	500M-2MM	2-10MM	10-50MM	50-100MM	100-250MM			4/1/19-3/31/20 ALL	4/1/20-3/31/21 ALL
	2	14	12	6	4	NUMBER OF STATEMENTS		41	30
%	%	%	%	%	%	ASSETS		%	%
		12.6	3.1			Cash & Equivalents		8.0	11.2
		20.0	11.1			Trade Receivables (net)		16.4	17.3
		21.0	35.7			Inventory		35.1	27.1
DATA		.2	1.3			All Other Current		1.2	1.7
		53.8	51.2			Total Current		60.8	57.3
NOT		30.3	37.9			Fixed Assets (net)		27.9	28.4
		.0	1.8			Intangibles (net)		3.1	3.6
AVAILABLE		15.9	9.1			All Other Non-Current		8.2	10.8
		100.0	100.0			Total		100.0	100.0
						LIABILITIES			
		3.3	7.0			Notes Payable-Short Term		11.4	10.8
		2.2	5.0			Cur. Mat.-L.T.D.		2.5	2.3
		9.2	5.8			Trade Payables		7.7	7.3
		.5	.0			Income Taxes Payable		.0	.0
		6.2	8.5			All Other Current		8.5	10.2
		21.4	26.2			Total Current		30.1	30.6
		15.3	18.1			Long-Term Debt		14.0	17.1
		.0	1.4			Deferred Taxes		.1	.0
		14.1	2.0			All Other Non-Current		6.8	6.9
		49.2	52.3			Net Worth		49.0	45.3
		100.0	100.0			Total Liabilities & Net Worth		100.0	100.0
						INCOME DATA			
		100.0	100.0			Net Sales		100.0	100.0
		33.3	29.1			Gross Profit		23.2	25.7
		30.2	23.1			Operating Expenses		19.2	21.0
		3.1	6.1			Operating Profit		4.1	4.6
		.7	1.0			All Other Expenses (net)		.4	-1.8
		2.4	5.0			Profit Before Taxes		3.6	6.4
						RATIOS			
		3.9	7.0					5.4	3.4
		2.2	2.2			Current		2.3	2.4
		1.9	1.4					1.3	1.2
		3.1	1.5					1.8	2.1
		1.6	.8			Quick		.8	1.2
		.8	.3					.5	.4
		16 23.0	23 15.8					20 18.6	19 19.7
		25 14.4	26 14.0			Sales/Receivables		28 13.0	26 14.3
		50 7.3	40 9.2					40 9.2	33 10.9
		9 38.5	59 6.2					42 8.6	34 10.7
		58 6.3	99 3.7			Cost of Sales/Inventory		70 5.2	63 5.8
		66 5.5	228 1.6					152 2.4	96 3.8
		0 UND	7 54.1					6 62.9	6 58.4
		11 31.8	17 21.8			Cost of Sales/Payables		17 21.1	15 24.9
		18 19.8	31 11.6					24 15.2	30 12.1
		4.5	2.0					3.2	3.6
		7.7	6.0			Sales/Working Capital		7.4	6.3
		19.4	13.7					21.3	23.3
		20.2	21.6					7.9	14.9
		(10) 12.2	8.6			EBIT/Interest		(38) 3.3	(25) 5.0
		.9	.8					.4	1.4
						Net Profit + Depr., Dep., Amort./Cur. Mat. L/T/D			
		.2	.2					.3	.3
		.5	.5			Fixed/Worth		.6	.7
		1.0	1.3					1.3	1.5
		.2	.3					.5	.4
		.6	.8			Debt/Worth		.9	1.1
		1.9	1.7					2.0	3.1
		23.3	33.7					26.6	49.0
		(12) 13.8	(11) 21.6			% Profit Before Taxes/Tangible Net Worth		(37) 8.7	(26) 13.1
		1.8	.1					-2.1	.9
		12.2	17.1					11.5	18.7
		9.0	8.7			% Profit Before Taxes/Total Assets		4.9	4.4
		-.7	-1.7					-1.2	-.3
		41.0	21.6					25.7	13.3
		9.4	2.9			Sales/Net Fixed Assets		7.3	4.9
		4.7	2.2					3.8	3.8
		3.5	1.8					2.9	2.3
		2.2	1.5			Sales/Total Assets		2.0	2.1
		1.8	1.1					1.0	1.0
		.6	1.2					1.1	1.5
		(12) .9	2.3			% Depr., Dep., Amort./Sales		(34) 1.9	(26) 2.3
		4.3	3.1					3.1	3.7
						% Officers', Directors', Owners' Comp/Sales		.9	
								(14) 2.3	
								5.1	
5110M	160390M	386358M	703420M	1357364M		Net Sales ($)		2272383M	2070144M
2535M	61951M	285586M	347579M	866659M		Total Assets ($)		1349392M	1401179M

M = $ thousand   MM = $ million
See Pages viii through xx for Explanation of Ratios and Data

© RMA 2024

MANUFACTURING—Hardwood Veneer and Plywood Manufacturing NAICS 321211

Comparative Historical Data | Current Data Sorted by Sales

Comparative Historical Data					Current Data Sorted by Sales					
				Type of Statement						
3		2	3	Unqualified						3
2		1	9	Reviewed				1	1	7
6		3	3	Compiled				2	1	
1		4	5	Tax Returns				1	2	
11		13	18	Other		1		1	5	9
4/1/21-3/31/22 ALL		4/1/22-3/31/23 ALL	4/1/23-3/31/24 ALL		0-1MM	6 (4/1-9/30/23) 1-3MM	1 3-5MM	32 (10/1/23-3/31/24) 5-10MM	10-25MM	25MM & OVER
23		23	38	NUMBER OF STATEMENTS		3		6	9	19
%		%	%	ASSETS	%	%	%	%	%	%
13.0		7.1	6.8	Cash & Equivalents						2.9
19.9		11.8	15.0	Trade Receivables (net)						11.3
35.3		32.3	26.7	Inventory						31.7
1.6		1.8	.9	All Other Current						1.5
69.7		53.0	49.5	Total Current						47.5
22.3		34.9	39.2	Fixed Assets (net)						43.2
2.6		2.5	1.0	Intangibles (net)						1.2
5.4		9.6	10.4	All Other Non-Current						8.1
100.0		100.0	100.0	Total						100.0
				LIABILITIES						
8.5		3.7	7.5	Notes Payable-Short Term						8.0
2.2		2.1	3.0	Cur. Mat.-L.T.D.						3.8
6.2		6.9	9.7	Trade Payables						9.1
.0		.4	.2	Income Taxes Payable						.0
12.0		5.5	6.8	All Other Current						5.2
29.0		18.7	27.1	Total Current						26.1
9.6		18.8	16.9	Long-Term Debt						16.4
.0		.2	.4	Deferred Taxes						.6
7.8		4.3	8.7	All Other Non-Current						13.7
53.6		58.0	46.8	Net Worth						43.2
100.0		100.0	100.0	Total Liabilities & Net Worth						100.0
				INCOME DATA						
100.0		100.0	100.0	Net Sales						100.0
27.7		30.3	25.3	Gross Profit						18.7
20.5		20.2	23.8	Operating Expenses						18.3
7.2		10.1	1.5	Operating Profit						.4
-1.9		-.7	1.1	All Other Expenses (net)						1.3
9.1		10.8	.4	Profit Before Taxes						-.9
				RATIOS						
5.9		6.6	3.7							2.8
2.9		2.7	2.1	Current						2.0
1.4		1.7	1.1							1.1
2.4		2.5	1.6							.8
1.3		1.1	.8	Quick						.8
.6		.5	.4							.3
24 14.9	16	23.4	16 22.2						16	22.9
34 10.6	22	16.3	23 15.6	Sales/Receivables					23	15.8
45 8.1	39	9.3	39 9.3						36	10.0
46 8.0	54	6.8	30 12.1						33	10.9
79 4.6	81	4.5	60 6.1	Cost of Sales/Inventory					61	6.0
126 2.9	122	3.0	85 4.3						146	2.5
7 49.5	7	54.3	8 45.6						9	39.6
12 30.1	15	25.1	17 21.4	Cost of Sales/Payables					23	15.9
23 15.8	24	15.0	32 11.4						29	12.4
2.6		3.9	4.4							4.2
4.5		5.5	8.3	Sales/Working Capital						9.5
12.0		10.4	69.2							119.2
32.6		131.2	16.9							15.5
(18) 12.8	(21)	39.4	(34) 2.1	EBIT/Interest						.7
2.1		7.9	-3.0							-5.4
				Net Profit + Depr., Dep., Amort./Cur. Mat. L/T/D						
.2		.4	.2							.3
.4		.5	.7	Fixed/Worth						1.1
.9		1.1	1.8							2.0
.3		.3	.4							.6
.9		.7	.8	Debt/Worth						.9
1.6		1.6	2.1							2.4
56.1		50.7	22.4							17.9
(22) 27.7	(22)	27.7	(34) 6.1	% Profit Before Taxes/Tangible Net Worth					(18)	-5.6
13.6		14.0	-21.4							-34.8
25.8		35.4	11.7							10.0
20.4		17.1	1.1	% Profit Before Taxes/Total Assets						-2.2
5.0		6.2	-9.3							-12.7
41.2		10.3	14.3							13.3
8.2		5.4	4.6	Sales/Net Fixed Assets						3.4
5.0		2.4	2.9							2.9
2.3		2.2	2.3							2.3
1.9		1.6	1.9	Sales/Total Assets						1.8
1.4		1.3	1.4							1.3
.7		1.7	.6							.7
(17) 1.2	(17)	2.0	(33) 1.8	% Depr., Dep., Amort./Sales					(17)	1.8
2.1		3.2	3.1							3.0
			1.3							
	(12)		3.2	% Officers', Directors' Owners' Comp/Sales						
			4.0							
1804706M		2270918M	2612642M	Net Sales ($)		6890M	4225M	40891M	163818M	2396818M
998504M		1393871M	1564310M	Total Assets ($)		5011M	2267M	21465M	90127M	1445440M

M = $ thousand   MM = $ million
See Pages viii through xx for Explanation of Ratios and Data
© RMA 2024

MANUFACTURING—Wood Window and Door Manufacturing NAICS 321911

Current Data Sorted by Assets | Comparative Historical Data

						Type of Statement				
			2		1	Unqualified		2		2
		1	1	1		Reviewed		3		3
	1	5	2			Compiled		8		1
1	2	3				Tax Returns		9		8
	5 (4/1-9/30/23)	10	35 (10/1/23-3/31/24)	1		Other		33		24
0-500M	500M-2MM	2-10MM	10-50MM	50-100MM	100-250MM			4/1/19-3/31/20 ALL		4/1/20-3/31/21 ALL
1	3	19	14	2	1	NUMBER OF STATEMENTS		55		38
%	%	%	%	%	%	ASSETS		%		%
		23.0	15.8			Cash & Equivalents		12.4		19.4
		22.6	17.9			Trade Receivables (net)		20.2		17.4
		17.0	20.9			Inventory		25.7		20.9
		5.1	4.0			All Other Current		2.2		4.2
		67.7	58.6			Total Current		60.5		62.0
		18.7	23.7			Fixed Assets (net)		27.0		25.8
		3.2	10.4			Intangibles (net)		6.1		8.7
		10.3	7.3			All Other Non-Current		6.4		3.5
		100.0	100.0			Total		100.0		100.0
						LIABILITIES				
		3.0	2.1			Notes Payable-Short Term		10.1		9.3
		1.7	1.6			Cur. Mat.-L.T.D.		1.9		3.0
		10.0	6.6			Trade Payables		12.0		9.1
		.0	.4			Income Taxes Payable		.4		.0
		17.9	9.4			All Other Current		13.6		13.9
		32.6	20.1			Total Current		37.9		35.3
		14.9	12.6			Long-Term Debt		16.5		23.0
		.0	.1			Deferred Taxes		.0		.0
		4.9	6.5			All Other Non-Current		9.3		4.5
		47.6	60.6			Net Worth		36.3		37.2
		100.0	100.0			Total Liabilties & Net Worth		100.0		100.0
						INCOME DATA				
		100.0	100.0			Net Sales		100.0		100.0
		37.0	35.5			Gross Profit		34.2		35.1
		25.7	24.0			Operating Expenses		29.0		30.8
		11.3	11.5			Operating Profit		5.2		4.3
		-.3	.8			All Other Expenses (net)		.7		-.4
		11.6	10.7			Profit Before Taxes		4.5		4.7
						RATIOS				
		3.3	7.8					3.5		3.6
		1.9	2.3			Current		1.8		2.2
		1.5	1.3					1.2		1.3
		2.4	4.0					1.9		2.3
		1.4	1.5			Quick		.9		1.3
		.9	.6					.5		.6
		5 71.3	21 17.7				14	26.0	13	28.2
		40 9.2	29 12.6			Sales/Receivables	32	11.3	24	15.4
		72 5.1	42 8.7				45	8.2	36	10.1
		15 23.9	36 10.1				36	10.1	20	17.9
		41 8.8	54 6.8			Cost of Sales/Inventory	61	6.0	39	9.4
		74 4.9	76 4.8				85	4.3	60	6.1
		13 27.8	7 49.4				13	28.5	8	46.7
		23 15.7	15 23.7			Cost of Sales/Payables	20	18.2	17	21.0
		35 10.5	23 16.1				38	9.6	32	11.5
		2.6	3.6					5.1		5.2
		6.8	5.6			Sales/Working Capital		10.7		8.2
		11.6	16.2					24.3		20.2
		34.1	210.7					36.2		20.0
		(14) 11.1	(12) 31.1			EBIT/Interest	(47)	4.1	(33)	9.6
		6.3	3.0					1.5		1.3
						Net Profit + Depr., Dep., Amort./Cur. Mat. L/T/D				
		.2	.2					.3		.3
		.4	.4			Fixed/Worth		.7		.7
		.9	2.2					5.5		-3.8
		.7	.2					.5		.7
		1.3	.8			Debt/Worth		1.5		1.5
		2.4	2.7					10.8		-37.3
		89.7	55.2					54.0		59.8
		(16) 46.3	(12) 37.3			% Profit Before Taxes/Tangible Net Worth	(42)	26.4	(28)	39.0
		19.1	23.7					5.2		19.9
		39.7	37.3					21.8		29.8
		19.9	20.5			% Profit Before Taxes/Total Assets		6.9		12.8
		7.6	8.8					2.0		2.6
		29.5	28.1					19.2		25.7
		9.7	13.2			Sales/Net Fixed Assets		10.9		16.4
		7.3	3.8					6.5		5.5
		3.3	2.6					3.5		3.3
		2.0	1.9			Sales/Total Assets		2.6		2.5
		1.7	1.3					1.7		1.6
		1.2						1.0		1.0
		(13) 1.5				% Depr., Dep., Amort./Sales	(44)	1.8	(27)	2.1
		2.1						2.6		2.4
						% Officers', Directors' Owners' Comp/Sales		1.7		.5
							(15)	5.6	(14)	2.5
								13.7		6.9
925M	13386M	272567M	484091M	287523M	106699M	Net Sales ($)		2478269M		1256984M
230M	4453M	115711M	259593M	133815M	110418M	Total Assets ($)		1090212M		548910M

© RMA 2024

M = $ thousand   MM = $ million
See Pages viii through xx for Explanation of Ratios and Data

MANUFACTURING—Wood Window and Door Manufacturing NAICS 321911

Comparative Historical Data | Current Data Sorted by Sales

Comparative Historical Data				Type of Statement	Current Data Sorted by Sales					
2	5	3		Unqualified					1	2
5	7	3		Reviewed					1	2
5	6	8		Compiled			1	2	4	1
4	5	4		Tax Returns		1			3	
32	26	22		Other	1	1	3	3	5	10
4/1/21-3/31/22 ALL	4/1/22-3/31/23 ALL	4/1/23-3/31/24 ALL			0-1MM	5 (4/1-9/30/23) 1-3MM	3-5MM	35 (10/1/23-3/31/24) 5-10MM	10-25MM	25MM & OVER
48	49	40		NUMBER OF STATEMENTS	1	2	3	5	14	15
%	%	%		ASSETS	%	%	%	%	%	%
12.9	16.9	21.7		Cash & Equivalents					21.0	26.2
21.1	23.5	22.4		Trade Receivables (net)					21.2	20.4
28.4	27.9	17.6		Inventory					14.9	21.5
4.4	5.1	4.1		All Other Current					4.2	4.5
66.8	73.4	65.8		Total Current					61.3	72.5
22.1	18.7	20.5		Fixed Assets (net)					23.6	13.8
7.2	2.9	5.9		Intangibles (net)					1.4	9.6
3.8	4.9	7.9		All Other Non-Current					13.8	4.1
100.0	100.0	100.0		Total					100.0	100.0
				LIABILITIES						
6.2	7.3	2.5		Notes Payable-Short Term					3.4	.4
2.3	1.9	1.5		Cur. Mat.-L.T.D.					2.4	.9
9.2	9.0	8.9		Trade Payables					8.4	7.7
.0	.1	.2		Income Taxes Payable					.3	.1
14.2	15.6	13.2		All Other Current					7.9	19.0
31.8	33.9	26.3		Total Current					22.4	28.1
14.2	15.2	15.1		Long-Term Debt					15.6	4.9
.1	.1	.0		Deferred Taxes					.1	.0
7.7	1.9	4.6		All Other Non-Current					6.6	4.0
46.3	48.8	54.0		Net Worth					55.3	63.1
100.0	100.0	100.0		Total Liabilities & Net Worth					100.0	100.0
				INCOME DATA						
100.0	100.0	100.0		Net Sales					100.0	100.0
34.7	31.4	38.8		Gross Profit					35.9	36.2
27.0	21.7	27.4		Operating Expenses					24.7	23.1
7.7	9.6	11.4		Operating Profit					11.2	13.1
-.6	.3	.0		All Other Expenses (net)					-.9	.0
8.4	9.4	11.4		Profit Before Taxes					12.0	13.1
				RATIOS						
4.7	3.9	7.4							9.5	8.2
2.2	2.2	2.3		Current					2.1	3.4
1.7	1.4	1.5							1.5	1.5
2.2	2.4	4.3							5.5	4.8
1.2	1.2	1.6		Quick					1.5	1.7
.6	.7	.9							.9	.8
19 / 18.9	22 / 16.8	19 / 18.9							14 / 26.3	19 / 19.0
32 / 11.3	30 / 12.3	30 / 12.0		Sales/Receivables					37 / 9.8	23 / 15.7
42 / 8.7	41 / 8.9	61 / 6.0							49 / 7.5	41 / 9.0
39 / 9.4	36 / 10.2	29 / 12.8							23 / 15.9	34 / 10.8
66 / 5.5	66 / 5.5	49 / 7.5		Cost of Sales/Inventory					49 / 7.5	52 / 7.0
91 / 4.0	99 / 3.7	73 / 5.0							58 / 6.3	74 / 4.9
12 / 31.5	8 / 46.6	8 / 45.0							6 / 56.5	7 / 51.4
18 / 20.7	16 / 23.1	18 / 20.3		Cost of Sales/Payables					21 / 17.8	15 / 24.6
34 / 10.6	29 / 12.8	32 / 11.5							28 / 13.0	22 / 16.8
3.9	4.1	3.4							3.8	3.3
5.9	7.0	5.9		Sales/Working Capital					6.8	4.6
10.9	12.2	11.2							12.1	12.9
68.7	103.4	77.1							26.9	228.0
(40) 10.1	(39) 18.8	(30) 19.1		EBIT/Interest					(10) 11.1	(11) 80.5
2.9	5.3	6.8							7.6	29.1
				Net Profit + Depr., Dep., Amort./Cur. Mat. L/T/D						
.1	.1	.2							.1	.1
.6	.3	.4		Fixed/Worth					.4	.2
3.3	.9	1.4							.8	.6
.4	.4	.3							.1	.2
1.2	1.0	1.1		Debt/Worth					1.2	.8
8.2	3.2	2.1							1.6	1.8
61.8	71.0	69.5		% Profit Before Taxes/Tangible Net Worth					51.0	70.2
(38) 41.5	(45) 38.4	(35) 43.2							42.5	(12) 53.8
18.7	27.3	19.7							30.1	27.7
30.5	30.6	39.6		% Profit Before Taxes/Total Assets					39.6	46.5
16.4	19.6	20.5							20.5	34.0
6.1	10.9	10.6							9.6	18.0
31.1	56.6	28.3							36.0	41.7
12.8	16.7	10.1		Sales/Net Fixed Assets					9.5	24.7
6.4	8.0	5.7							5.4	10.1
3.3	3.1	3.1							2.6	3.3
2.2	2.3	2.0		Sales/Total Assets					1.8	2.5
1.4	1.8	1.6							1.6	1.9
.6	.9	1.2							1.2	
(32) 1.5	(36) 1.5	(25) 1.5		% Depr., Dep., Amort./Sales					(10) 1.7	
2.5	2.8	2.3							2.4	
1.1	1.2	1.0		% Officers', Directors', Owners' Comp/Sales						
(12) 4.1	(14) 1.9	(13) 1.9								
6.1	3.5	3.3								
1878250M	1930511M	1165191M		Net Sales ($)	925M	5715M	11067M	40209M	210129M	897146M
927713M	988604M	624220M		Total Assets ($)	230M	3663M	12633M	23941M	110514M	473239M

M = $ thousand   MM = $ million
See Pages viii through xx for Explanation of Ratios and Data

© RMA 2024

MANUFACTURING—Other Millwork (including Flooring) NAICS 321918

Current Data Sorted by Assets / Comparative Historical Data

							Type of Statement			
			1		1		Unqualified		4	2
		4	4				Reviewed		9	5
1		2		1			Compiled		3	
1	4	5	1				Tax Returns		8	5
4	9 (4/1-9/30/23)	9	10		3		Other		27	19
			46 (10/1/23-3/31/24)						4/1/19-3/31/20	4/1/20-3/31/21
0-500M	500M-2MM	2-10MM	10-50MM	50-100MM	100-250MM				ALL	ALL
6	8	20	16	1	4		NUMBER OF STATEMENTS		51	31
%	%	%	%	%	%		ASSETS		%	%
		10.1	11.0				Cash & Equivalents		5.5	18.1
		32.6	17.3				Trade Receivables (net)		25.7	24.3
		14.5	29.6				Inventory		27.0	23.1
		4.1	6.3				All Other Current		2.9	2.5
		61.4	64.2				Total Current		61.1	68.0
		25.2	25.0				Fixed Assets (net)		26.0	23.7
		5.4	3.8				Intangibles (net)		7.5	5.0
		8.1	7.1				All Other Non-Current		5.3	3.4
		100.0	100.0				Total		100.0	100.0
							LIABILITIES			
		4.3	6.8				Notes Payable-Short Term		15.1	6.4
		2.8	2.5				Cur. Mat.-L.T.D.		3.1	3.4
		10.6	9.5				Trade Payables		10.8	10.3
		.1	.1				Income Taxes Payable		.3	.0
		11.3	13.4				All Other Current		11.7	14.6
		29.2	32.3				Total Current		41.0	34.7
		18.5	9.8				Long-Term Debt		17.7	25.9
		.2	.0				Deferred Taxes		.4	.1
		5.8	17.8				All Other Non-Current		7.4	9.0
		46.2	40.0				Net Worth		33.6	30.3
		100.0	100.0				Total Liabilties & Net Worth		100.0	100.0
							INCOME DATA			
		100.0	100.0				Net Sales		100.0	100.0
		36.6	24.5				Gross Profit		30.9	30.1
		30.4	19.2				Operating Expenses		25.8	26.0
		6.2	5.3				Operating Profit		5.1	4.1
		.0	.7				All Other Expenses (net)		1.1	-1.5
		6.2	4.6				Profit Before Taxes		4.0	5.6
							RATIOS			
		3.1	2.9						3.0	4.5
		2.3	2.0				Current		1.6	2.7
		1.6	1.4						1.2	1.4
		2.6	1.6						1.5	2.7
		1.5	.7				Quick		.9	1.5
		1.1	.5						.4	.6
	21	17.7	20 18.5					17	21.3	18 20.0
	54	6.7	30 12.0				Sales/Receivables	32	11.3	40 9.2
	79	4.6	54 6.8					52	7.0	66 5.5
	0	UND	48 7.6					26	13.9	8 43.9
	26	14.2	111 3.3				Cost of Sales/Inventory	55	6.6	58 6.3
	46	8.0	140 2.6					96	3.8	91 4.0
	10	36.0	14 27.0					9	40.6	4 96.9
	23	15.7	22 16.3				Cost of Sales/Payables	18	19.8	19 19.6
	46	7.9	42 8.6					36	10.1	35 10.4
		3.7	3.1						5.3	3.6
		6.8	5.9				Sales/Working Capital		10.5	6.8
		9.3	9.2						35.4	10.2
		13.2	23.4						19.3	43.9
		6.8	(14) 7.5				EBIT/Interest	(47)	6.7	(29) 9.5
		1.7	1.5						2.7	2.0
							Net Profit + Depr., Dep., Amort./Cur. Mat. L/T/D			
		.2	.2						.3	.3
		.5	.5				Fixed/Worth		.6	.5
		1.7	.9						2.6	1.5
		.6	.4						.6	.7
		1.2	.7				Debt/Worth		1.5	1.5
		4.1	2.2						5.6	8.7
		53.6	19.7						46.5	57.7
		20.8	(14) 14.3				% Profit Before Taxes/Tangible Net Worth	(42)	27.1	(26) 37.7
		2.6	6.4						12.3	6.8
		16.6	12.7						20.7	27.9
		9.5	5.6				% Profit Before Taxes/Total Assets		9.3	11.0
		1.2	.8						3.5	1.2
		21.1	15.7						22.5	31.2
		9.3	9.1				Sales/Net Fixed Assets		11.9	9.9
		5.2	4.4						4.8	5.8
		2.9	2.4						3.4	3.0
		2.0	1.5				Sales/Total Assets		2.4	2.0
		1.4	1.2						1.7	1.7
		.6	1.2						.8	1.0
		(14) 1.6	(13) 1.9				% Depr., Dep., Amort./Sales	(40)	1.7	(24) 2.8
		3.1	2.8						3.7	3.5
									1.7	1.3
							% Officers', Directors' Owners' Comp/Sales	(13)	3.1	(11) 3.1
									4.8	5.6
13586M	34391M	245250M	519759M	162922M	903674M		Net Sales ($)		1461606M	1151185M
1976M	10003M	118257M	350919M	64520M	735785M		Total Assets ($)		740332M	467509M

© RMA 2024

M = $ thousand   MM = $ million
See Pages viii through xx for Explanation of Ratios and Data

MANUFACTURING—Other Millwork (including Flooring) NAICS 321918

Comparative Historical Data | Current Data Sorted by Sales

						Type of Statement						
		5		2		Unqualified				1	1	
	5	8		9		Reviewed				3	3	
	2	2		3		Compiled			1	3	2	
	3	10		11		Tax Returns		1	3	3	3	1
	34	23		30		Other	1	2	1	3	10	10
	4/1/21-3/31/22	4/1/22-3/31/23		4/1/23-3/31/24				9 (4/1-9/30/23)		46 (10/1/23-3/31/24)		
	ALL	ALL		ALL			0-1MM	1-3MM	3-5MM	5-10MM	10-25MM	25MM & OVER
	44	48		55	NUMBER OF STATEMENTS	1	7	4	9	19	15	
	%	%		%	ASSETS	%	%	%	%	%	%	
	16.5	13.9		12.6	Cash & Equivalents					9.7	7.9	
	20.9	23.4		27.3	Trade Receivables (net)					28.2	18.9	
	27.4	27.7		19.2	Inventory					20.7	25.1	
	4.0	5.5		4.7	All Other Current					4.8	6.0	
	68.8	70.5		63.8	Total Current					63.4	57.8	
	18.5	20.4		22.4	Fixed Assets (net)					23.1	25.9	
	7.3	2.4		6.6	Intangibles (net)					7.5	8.1	
	5.4	6.7		7.1	All Other Non-Current					6.0	8.2	
	100.0	100.0		100.0	Total					100.0	100.0	
					LIABILITIES							
	7.0	8.7		7.8	Notes Payable-Short Term					6.1	6.4	
	1.6	3.6		3.2	Cur. Mat.-L.T.D.					2.5	3.5	
	10.0	10.9		10.7	Trade Payables					11.2	10.4	
	.2	.1		.1	Income Taxes Payable					.1	.1	
	15.2	13.4		14.8	All Other Current					13.4	9.9	
	34.0	36.6		36.6	Total Current					33.3	30.2	
	15.7	16.2		22.5	Long-Term Debt					16.2	16.2	
	.5	.1		.2	Deferred Taxes					.2	.2	
	4.3	9.6		8.3	All Other Non-Current					4.4	20.3	
	45.5	37.4		32.3	Net Worth					45.9	33.0	
	100.0	100.0		100.0	Total Liabilities & Net Worth					100.0	100.0	
					INCOME DATA							
	100.0	100.0		100.0	Net Sales					100.0	100.0	
	31.9	28.5		34.0	Gross Profit					35.3	25.6	
	24.5	20.9		27.7	Operating Expenses					27.8	20.7	
	7.3	7.6		6.4	Operating Profit					7.5	4.9	
	-1.9	-.4		.4	All Other Expenses (net)					.3	1.2	
	9.2	8.0		6.0	Profit Before Taxes					7.2	3.8	
					RATIOS							
	4.2	3.9		3.5						2.6	2.8	
	2.2	2.4		2.2	Current					2.0	2.2	
	1.6	1.3		1.4						1.6	1.4	
	2.3	2.1		2.0						1.8	1.2	
	1.1	1.2		1.2	Quick					1.2	.9	
	.7	.5		.5						.5	.5	
15	25.0	15	23.9	19	19.4					23	15.9	19	19.4
27	13.4	26	14.0	41	8.9	Sales/Receivables				46	7.9	29	12.6
51	7.2	53	6.9	61	6.0					72	5.1	59	6.2
3	114.9	17	21.7	8	46.6					24	15.5	26	14.3
63	5.8	60	6.1	34	10.8	Cost of Sales/Inventory				38	9.5	78	4.7
107	3.4	122	3.0	111	3.3					111	3.3	135	2.7
8	44.1	6	64.3	10	37.9					14	26.9	15	24.4
18	19.8	18	20.7	21	17.4	Cost of Sales/Payables				27	13.7	23	16.1
35	10.3	41	8.9	40	9.2					68	5.4	40	9.2
	3.8		4.0		4.7						5.1	4.4	
	6.9		7.7		6.9	Sales/Working Capital					7.2	6.6	
	10.6		17.6		12.2						9.4	13.3	
	51.3		38.5		13.1						14.2	10.5	
(35)	19.4	(43)	9.6	(50)	5.9	EBIT/Interest					7.1	(13)	4.4
	5.3		2.2		1.4						1.4	1.2	
					14.7	Net Profit + Depr., Dep.,							
				(11)	5.5	Amort./Cur. Mat. L/T/D							
					2.6								
	.1		.2		.2						.3	.2	
	.3		.3		.5	Fixed/Worth					.5	.9	
	2.5		1.4		1.7						2.3	1.4	
	.3		.4		.5						.6	.5	
	1.0		1.4		1.5	Debt/Worth					1.2	1.6	
	5.5		6.9		8.8						7.0	5.1	
	79.4		64.9		72.3	% Profit Before Taxes/Tangible					140.2	19.1	
(38)	54.8	(42)	27.7	(48)	19.8	Net Worth				(18)	19.8	(13)	7.8
	18.4		14.2		5.0						5.0	2.8	
	28.4		27.5		19.6	% Profit Before Taxes/Total					16.8	10.5	
	20.9		14.1		8.5	Assets					11.6	5.5	
	10.2		2.4		1.0						1.0	.5	
	39.9		47.5		23.6						15.9	15.7	
	12.7		12.1		10.9	Sales/Net Fixed Assets					10.1	8.2	
	7.4		7.4		6.4						6.5	3.8	
	3.2		3.2		2.9						2.7	2.6	
	2.0		2.0		2.1	Sales/Total Assets					1.9	1.6	
	1.7		1.5		1.4						1.4	1.3	
	1.0		.8		.9						.5	1.2	
(32)	1.7	(37)	1.5	(35)	2.0	% Depr., Dep., Amort./Sales				(14)	1.5	(12)	2.2
	2.8		2.3		3.0						2.6	2.9	
	.3		1.1		1.5	% Officers', Directors'							
(10)	1.7	(15)	3.0	(17)	3.1	Owners' Comp/Sales							
	4.2		4.4		7.1								
	2369563M		1722786M		1879582M	Net Sales ($)	974M	13936M	17064M	68172M	304291M	1475145M	
	910799M		804201M		1281460M	Total Assets ($)	216M	4512M	7233M	32593M	178390M	1058516M	

© RMA 2024   M = $ thousand   MM = $ million
See Pages viii through xx for Explanation of Ratios and Data

MANUFACTURING—Wood Container and Pallet Manufacturing NAICS 321920

Current Data Sorted by Assets | Comparative Historical Data

Type of Statement									
			1	3		Unqualified		2	3
	1	1	7	1		Reviewed		8	7
		3				Compiled		3	3
	4	13				Tax Returns		22	10
	2	15	12	5	2	Other		52	29
	11 (4/1-9/30/23)		59 (10/1/23-3/31/24)					4/1/19- 3/31/20	4/1/20- 3/31/21
0-500M	500M-2MM	2-10MM	10-50MM	50-100MM	100-250MM			ALL	ALL
	7	32	20	9	2	NUMBER OF STATEMENTS		87	52
%	%	%	%	%	%	ASSETS		%	%
		19.1	9.7			Cash & Equivalents		8.2	11.3
		23.3	26.3			Trade Receivables (net)		32.8	31.6
		19.2	16.3			Inventory		16.9	15.9
		1.9	.7			All Other Current		1.4	1.9
		63.5	52.9			Total Current		59.3	60.8
		25.6	26.0			Fixed Assets (net)		24.7	24.5
		3.9	8.9			Intangibles (net)		7.0	7.1
		7.1	12.2			All Other Non-Current		9.0	7.6
		100.0	100.0			Total		100.0	100.0
						LIABILITIES			
		4.0	9.6			Notes Payable-Short Term		11.3	6.7
		2.3	2.5			Cur. Mat.-L.T.D.		3.5	4.5
		11.4	8.8			Trade Payables		14.0	10.2
		.3	.0			Income Taxes Payable		.1	.1
		3.7	5.3			All Other Current		6.3	6.5
		21.8	26.2			Total Current		35.2	28.0
		22.4	10.9			Long-Term Debt		16.3	14.7
		.0	.3			Deferred Taxes		.3	.4
		2.2	4.4			All Other Non-Current		4.0	5.1
		53.7	58.1			Net Worth		44.1	51.7
		100.0	100.0			Total Liabilities & Net Worth		100.0	100.0
						INCOME DATA			
		100.0	100.0			Net Sales		100.0	100.0
		35.7	24.0			Gross Profit		27.8	28.8
		26.7	16.6			Operating Expenses		22.4	22.7
		9.0	7.4			Operating Profit		5.3	6.2
		.3	1.4			All Other Expenses (net)		.4	-.9
		8.6	6.0			Profit Before Taxes		4.9	7.1
						RATIOS			
		11.4	3.3					3.4	6.0
		3.6	2.1			Current		1.8	2.5
		1.5	1.4					1.1	1.6
		8.7	2.1					2.2	4.2
		2.8	1.5			Quick		1.2	1.7
		.8	1.0					.7	1.0
	16	23.4	27	13.7			28	13.1	31	11.8
	29	12.7	36	10.2		Sales/Receivables	37	9.8	38	9.6
	38	9.6	49	7.4			45	8.2	45	8.1
	6	60.6	16	23.1			9	39.8	11	32.8
	29	12.7	29	12.4		Cost of Sales/Inventory	27	13.4	24	15.1
	53	6.9	48	7.6			46	7.9	52	7.0
	6	65.8	6	57.1			8	43.2	8	44.6
	15	24.3	14	26.0		Cost of Sales/Payables	19	18.9	14	25.2
	27	13.4	27	13.7			34	10.8	22	16.8
		4.3	6.2					8.0	5.6
		7.9	9.8			Sales/Working Capital		15.8	8.6
		20.0	21.7					66.3	16.4
		75.1	25.7					31.9	34.8
		(26) 8.3	(19) 7.2			EBIT/Interest	(73)	7.5	(46)	18.1
		4.2	5.1					2.5	3.3
						Net Profit + Depr., Dep., Amort./Cur. Mat. L/T/D		9.4	
							(13)	2.3	
								1.7	
		.1	.2					.2	.3
		.5	.6			Fixed/Worth		.5	.5
		1.2	1.0					1.1	.8
		.2	.3					.7	.5
		.9	.8			Debt/Worth		1.6	.9
		1.9	2.3					3.5	2.5
		58.1	52.2					67.3	48.2
		(28) 29.2	(19) 25.8			% Profit Before Taxes/Tangible Net Worth	(79)	26.7	(46)	31.7
		22.9	13.7					12.8	17.1
		32.3	18.7					30.7	26.7
		22.2	13.9			% Profit Before Taxes/Total Assets		10.7	17.9
		9.0	7.9					5.2	6.6
		72.8	25.3					44.7	31.2
		14.7	9.7			Sales/Net Fixed Assets		16.4	14.9
		7.5	5.9					6.8	7.4
		4.1	3.2					4.3	3.9
		2.8	2.4			Sales/Total Assets		2.8	2.7
		2.1	1.7					2.0	2.1
		.6	.6					.8	1.2
		(18) 1.8	(15) 1.5			% Depr., Dep., Amort./Sales	(58)	1.8	(36)	2.0
		3.9						2.9	2.8
		1.2						1.7	1.7
		(19) 1.8				% Officers', Directors' Owners' Comp/Sales	(34)	2.3	(17)	2.4
		5.0						4.9	5.1
	43397M	476368M	1288364M	1167606M	976797M	Net Sales ($)		3861750M	2190941M
	9792M	160462M	491313M	543613M	239092M	Total Assets ($)		1752886M	861180M

© RMA 2024

M = $ thousand MM = $ million
See Pages viii through xx for Explanation of Ratios and Data

MANUFACTURING—Wood Container and Pallet Manufacturing NAICS 321920

Comparative Historical Data | Current Data Sorted by Sales

				Type of Statement						
	6	7	4	Unqualified				1	4	
	6	3	10	Reviewed		1		1	8	
	11	17	3	Compiled				6	3	
	31	36	17	Tax Returns			2	7	8	1
			36	Other		2		9		18
	4/1/21-3/31/22	4/1/22-3/31/23	4/1/23-3/31/24			11 (4/1-9/30/23)		59 (10/1/23-3/31/24)		
	ALL	ALL	ALL		0-1MM	1-3MM	3-5MM	5-10MM	10-25MM	25MM & OVER
	54	63	70	NUMBER OF STATEMENTS		3	2	14	20	31
	%	%	%	ASSETS	%	%	%	%	%	%
	14.9	17.4	14.0	Cash & Equivalents	D			15.7	16.4	8.6
	35.2	29.6	26.6	Trade Receivables (net)	A			20.8	28.8	29.2
	19.2	20.3	16.5	Inventory	T			11.8	22.3	15.0
	1.6	1.6	1.2	All Other Current	A			1.9	1.7	.7
	71.0	69.0	58.2	Total Current				50.3	69.3	53.5
	20.2	22.1	27.8	Fixed Assets (net)	N			31.1	25.3	27.8
	4.5	3.3	5.5	Intangibles (net)	O			8.7	.6	7.8
	4.3	5.6	8.6	All Other Non-Current	T			9.9	4.8	10.9
	100.0	100.0	100.0	Total				100.0	100.0	100.0
				LIABILITIES	A					
	9.9	6.2	5.4	Notes Payable-Short Term	V			4.1	5.0	6.6
	2.5	2.6	2.8	Cur. Mat.-L.T.D.	A			3.2	2.1	2.8
	12.8	10.5	11.2	Trade Payables	I			15.5	10.9	10.8
	.1	.2	.2	Income Taxes Payable	L			.2	.4	.0
	5.6	5.5	5.2	All Other Current	A			7.6	2.5	6.1
	31.0	25.0	24.7	Total Current	B			30.6	20.9	26.4
	17.4	9.3	18.0	Long-Term Debt	L			41.2	10.4	11.5
	.5	.3	.3	Deferred Taxes	E			.0	.0	.7
	6.4	4.0	3.5	All Other Non-Current				1.5	3.0	5.2
	44.7	61.4	53.6	Net Worth				26.7	65.6	56.2
	100.0	100.0	100.0	Total Liabilties & Net Worth				100.0	100.0	100.0
				INCOME DATA						
	100.0	100.0	100.0	Net Sales				100.0	100.0	100.0
	27.5	32.6	29.5	Gross Profit				36.6	33.1	20.1
	19.9	21.9	21.7	Operating Expenses				29.5	24.1	13.3
	7.6	10.7	7.8	Operating Profit				7.0	9.1	6.8
	-1.7	-.1	.8	All Other Expenses (net)				1.0	.1	1.1
	9.3	10.7	7.1	Profit Before Taxes				6.0	9.0	5.7
				RATIOS						
	5.7	8.6	5.7					9.6	10.3	3.5
	2.3	3.7	2.4	Current				1.8	3.2	2.0
	1.6	1.9	1.4					.9	1.7	1.5
	4.0	5.3	3.8					8.1	6.3	2.1
	1.6	2.8	1.6	Quick				1.2	2.5	1.4
	.9	1.4	.9					.9	1.0	1.0
27	13.3	20	17.9	21	17.6			11	32.0	21	17.8	28	13.1

27	13.3	20	17.9	21	17.6	Sales/Receivables		11	32.0	21	17.8	28	13.1
41	8.9	30	12.0	31	11.6			21	17.1	29	12.4	35	10.3
53	6.9	40	9.2	41	9.0			34	10.8	40	9.2	47	7.8
12	29.9	11	33.1	10	35.8	Cost of Sales/Inventory		0	UND	19	19.0	12	31.3
27	13.5	27	13.7	28	12.9			7	52.0	36	10.1	25	14.6
44	8.3	48	7.6	46	7.9			45	8.2	72	5.1	37	9.9
8	45.2	5	70.3	7	49.1	Cost of Sales/Payables		7	55.6	7	49.3	8	48.1
15	24.6	14	26.8	14	26.0			21	17.2	14	26.0	13	27.6
30	12.2	21	17.0	27	13.3			42	8.6	30	12.3	22	16.7
	5.4		5.2		5.4	Sales/Working Capital			5.5		4.3		6.6
	8.2		8.4		9.6				22.0		7.5		10.6
	14.5		16.6		20.8				-314.4		13.7		20.0
	78.2		106.7		31.6	EBIT/Interest			33.0		120.9		30.3
(50)	23.4	(46)	39.2	(61)	8.4				5.8	(16)	17.1	(28)	8.7
	11.8		19.5		4.2				1.0		4.8		5.1
					10.4	Net Profit + Depr., Dep., Amort./Cur. Mat. L/T/D							17.4
		(17)	2.8							(14)			2.7
					1.2								1.3
	.2		.1		.2	Fixed/Worth			.8		.1		.3
	.4		.3		.6				4.7		.3		.6
	.8		.6		1.2				-.4		.8		1.0
	.5		.2		.4	Debt/Worth			1.5		.1		.4
	1.0		.5		.8				6.9		.7		.8
	3.0		1.5		2.2				-7.9		1.1		2.3
	94.5		83.8		51.8	% Profit Before Taxes/Tangible Net Worth			44.9				52.1
(50)	54.4	(60)	47.7	(63)	28.0				28.0	(30)			29.1
	27.3		27.3		18.8				22.9				14.5
	33.0		44.6		26.3	% Profit Before Taxes/Total Assets			27.6		32.2		19.9
	19.3		24.0		14.7				13.9		16.3		13.5
	11.1		17.2		7.8				.5		10.5		8.0
	36.6		76.7		35.3	Sales/Net Fixed Assets			79.5		24.6		27.2
	18.2		20.9		12.1				19.1		11.4		10.5
	8.9		11.5		5.8				5.3		7.3		5.7
	3.8		4.9		3.9	Sales/Total Assets			5.1		4.2		3.8
	3.1		3.6		2.7				2.5		2.8		2.7
	2.3		2.4		1.8				1.7		2.0		1.7
	1.0		.5		.6	% Depr., Dep., Amort./Sales					.6		.6
(37)	1.6	(46)	1.3	(47)	2.2					(14)	1.8	(25)	2.2
	2.3		2.6		3.8						3.3		3.5
	.9		.7		.9	% Officers', Directors' Owners' Comp/Sales					.9		
(25)	2.0	(34)	1.4	(25)	1.8					(11)	1.6		
	3.1		3.4		3.8						4.1		
	2410911M	2989288M	3952532M	Net Sales ($)		8556M	7940M	108807M	335408M	3491821M
	713172M	985344M	1444272M	Total Assets ($)		5428M	4315M	43802M	126846M	1263881M

© RMA 2024 M = $ thousand   MM = $ million
See Pages viii through xx for Explanation of Ratios and Data

MANUFACTURING—Prefabricated Wood Building Manufacturing NAICS 321992

Current Data Sorted by Assets | Comparative Historical Data

							Type of Statement				
		1		1	2		Unqualified		3		2
			1				Reviewed		3		3
1	2		1				Compiled		1		1
	3		7	7			Tax Returns		7		3
		3 (4/1-9/30/23)		28 (10/1/23-3/31/24)	5		Other		16		14
0-500M	500M-2MM	2-10MM	10-50MM	50-100MM	100-250MM				4/1/19-3/31/20		4/1/20-3/31/21
1	6	9	8	7			NUMBER OF STATEMENTS		ALL 30		ALL 23
%	%	%	%	%	%		ASSETS		%		%
						D	Cash & Equivalents		10.2		14.7
						A	Trade Receivables (net)		16.5		16.0
						T	Inventory		34.5		28.6
						A	All Other Current		2.2		1.4
							Total Current		63.3		60.6
						N	Fixed Assets (net)		28.2		22.8
						O	Intangibles (net)		3.5		6.0
						T	All Other Non-Current		5.0		10.6
							Total		100.0		100.0
						A	LIABILITIES				
						V	Notes Payable-Short Term		5.7		5.1
						A	Cur. Mat.-L.T.D.		4.1		1.7
						I	Trade Payables		10.1		8.1
						L	Income Taxes Payable		.3		.3
						A	All Other Current		16.5		17.7
						B	Total Current		36.7		33.0
						L	Long-Term Debt		15.1		16.3
						E	Deferred Taxes		.3		.0
							All Other Non-Current		3.5		6.1
							Net Worth		44.3		44.6
							Total Liabilities & Net Worth		100.0		100.0
							INCOME DATA				
							Net Sales		100.0		100.0
							Gross Profit		33.7		34.9
							Operating Expenses		25.5		26.1
							Operating Profit		8.2		8.8
							All Other Expenses (net)		.3		-1.0
							Profit Before Taxes		7.9		9.8
							RATIOS				
							Current		3.8		3.6
									1.7		2.5
									1.1		1.3
							Quick		1.5		1.8
									.8		1.0
									.3		.4
							Sales/Receivables	13	28.2	7	53.1
								22	16.7	25	14.6
								27	13.5	61	6.0
							Cost of Sales/Inventory	28	13.2	35	10.4
								68	5.4	64	5.7
								126	2.9	118	3.1
							Cost of Sales/Payables	9	40.1	8	47.0
								19	19.6	17	22.1
								33	10.9	28	13.0
							Sales/Working Capital		3.5		3.7
									12.7		5.6
									95.0		13.6
							EBIT/Interest		28.3		44.4
								(29)	9.2	(21)	23.8
									3.2		12.0
							Net Profit + Depr., Dep., Amort./Cur. Mat. L/T/D				
							Fixed/Worth		.3		.1
									.5		.4
									1.8		1.3
							Debt/Worth		.5		.5
									1.3		1.1
									2.8		3.2
							% Profit Before Taxes/Tangible Net Worth		52.3		54.3
								(27)	40.8	(21)	44.2
									18.5		24.7
							% Profit Before Taxes/Total Assets		26.1		32.2
									14.8		19.5
									6.1		8.1
							Sales/Net Fixed Assets		23.8		30.0
									9.8		11.5
									4.1		5.0
							Sales/Total Assets		3.0		2.8
									2.0		2.2
									1.4		1.2
							% Depr., Dep., Amort./Sales		1.0		.5
								(24)	1.7	(17)	1.3
									2.3		2.0
							% Officers', Directors' Owners' Comp/Sales				
1164M	32132M	130727M	361011M	1216432M			Net Sales ($)		1646792M		985105M
270M	7735M	51955M	171435M	481590M			Total Assets ($)		746883M		484450M

M = $ thousand   MM = $ million
See Pages viii through xx for Explanation of Ratios and Data

© RMA 2024

MANUFACTURING—Prefabricated Wood Building Manufacturing NAICS 321992

Comparative Historical Data | Current Data Sorted by Sales

Comparative Historical Data			Type of Statement	Current Data Sorted by Sales					
1	4	2	Unqualified					2	
1	3	2	Reviewed		1			1	
2	3	1	Compiled						1
1	4	4	Tax Returns	1		1	2		
22	15	22	Other	3			8	8	
4/1/21-3/31/22 ALL	4/1/22-3/31/23 ALL	4/1/23-3/31/24 ALL		0-1MM	3 (4/1-9/30/23) 1-3MM	3-5MM	28 (10/1/23-3/31/24) 5-10MM	10-25MM	25MM & OVER
27	29	31	NUMBER OF STATEMENTS	4		2	3	10	12
%	%	%	ASSETS	%	%	%	%	%	%
18.6	12.6	13.8	Cash & Equivalents					21.3	12.1
10.7	11.5	13.2	Trade Receivables (net)	D				11.6	8.2
30.9	39.5	41.5	Inventory	A				45.0	45.4
4.6	5.7	5.0	All Other Current	T				2.5	7.8
64.8	69.2	73.5	Total Current	A				80.4	73.6
23.1	19.1	14.2	Fixed Assets (net)					9.0	15.4
7.1	2.9	4.5	Intangibles (net)	N				1.8	6.2
5.0	8.7	7.7	All Other Non-Current	O				8.8	4.9
100.0	100.0	100.0	Total	T				100.0	100.0
			LIABILITIES	A					
5.6	5.8	7.4	Notes Payable-Short Term	V				.5	7.1
1.5	2.3	5.8	Cur. Mat.-L.T.D.	A				.3	1.6
10.0	9.1	10.4	Trade Payables	I				5.7	8.8
.3	.6	.0	Income Taxes Payable	L				.0	.0
20.5	19.6	19.8	All Other Current	A				16.4	19.2
37.9	37.4	43.4	Total Current	B				22.9	36.7
12.9	13.5	11.2	Long-Term Debt	L				1.3	10.6
.1	.1	.0	Deferred Taxes	E				.0	.0
6.8	5.6	1.4	All Other Non-Current					.0	3.6
42.3	43.5	44.0	Net Worth					75.8	49.1
100.0	100.0	100.0	Total Liabilities & Net Worth					100.0	100.0
			INCOME DATA						
100.0	100.0	100.0	Net Sales					100.0	100.0
34.0	29.5	37.2	Gross Profit					37.4	30.4
24.3	21.0	29.9	Operating Expenses					26.9	22.9
9.7	8.6	7.3	Operating Profit					10.5	7.5
-1.9	-.3	.1	All Other Expenses (net)					-.2	.1
11.6	8.8	7.2	Profit Before Taxes					10.7	7.4
			RATIOS						
3.8	3.5	9.6						170.7	4.1
2.0	2.2	2.0	Current					8.1	2.1
1.1	1.1	.9						1.5	1.3
1.7	1.0	2.2						35.7	1.3
1.0	.6	.7	Quick					2.0	.2
.2	.2	.2						1.0	.1
4 92.7	2 172.2	3 120.8		0 UND		3 114.9			
10 35.0	9 39.4	14 26.2	Sales/Receivables	10 35.1		9 41.7			
35 10.3	20 18.3	21 17.2		25 14.4		17 21.6			
31 11.9	34 10.7	39 9.3		44 8.3		37 9.8			
87 4.2	58 6.3	94 3.9	Cost of Sales/Inventory	140 2.6		99 3.7			
126 2.9	130 2.8	182 2.0		203 1.8		159 2.3			
9 41.5	7 49.2	7 49.3		0 UND		13 28.6			
19 19.6	11 33.0	16 22.2	Cost of Sales/Payables	15 24.6		16 23.0			
33 11.2	17 21.3	39 9.4		41 8.9		22 16.4			
4.1	4.9	3.5						2.2	3.8
6.7	12.0	10.4	Sales/Working Capital					4.0	8.0
53.6	33.2	-50.0						13.3	17.5
85.2	47.9	102.3						21.3	
(22) 28.0	(26) 19.6	(29) 20.5	EBIT/Interest					(11) 9.4	
2.2	7.6	5.2						6.0	
			Net Profit + Depr., Dep., Amort./Cur. Mat. L/T/D						
.3	.1	.0						.0	.1
.5	.3	.2	Fixed/Worth					.1	.3
3.2	1.3	.9						.3	.8
.5	.6	.1						.0	.5
1.9	1.5	1.1	Debt/Worth					.2	1.3
15.0	3.0	2.7						1.0	4.1
91.2	130.0	71.5						77.5	61.1
(22) 61.8	(27) 55.2	(27) 45.0	% Profit Before Taxes/Tangible Net Worth					27.8 (11)	53.5
17.5	25.9	20.4						14.5	28.5
36.7	47.2	22.8						50.2	22.4
19.8	18.3	14.7	% Profit Before Taxes/Total Assets					17.9	15.5
3.6	11.7	5.7						7.4	11.9
22.3	86.7	167.3						999.8	53.6
11.5	20.3	23.9	Sales/Net Fixed Assets					29.0	19.5
7.0	8.8	10.0						9.8	10.2
3.0	4.8	3.1						3.9	3.2
2.0	2.7	2.6	Sales/Total Assets					1.9	2.9
1.2	2.0	1.8						1.3	2.0
.4	.4	.4							.2
(20) 1.0	(17) 1.0	(19) .9	% Depr., Dep., Amort./Sales						.8
1.7	2.2	1.7							1.6
			% Officers', Directors' Owners' Comp/Sales						
1747403M	2613744M	1741466M	Net Sales ($)	7166M		7858M	23412M	166361M	1536669M
889898M	1084157M	712985M	Total Assets ($)	4039M		3019M	13335M	99877M	592715M

© RMA 2024   M = $ thousand   MM = $ million
See Pages viii through xx for Explanation of Ratios and Data

MANUFACTURING—All Other Miscellaneous Wood Product Manufacturing NAICS 321999

Current Data Sorted by Assets | Comparative Historical Data

						Type of Statement		
			1	4	3	2	Unqualified	8	5
			5	5	1		Reviewed	22	16
			3				Compiled	7	2
1	3		10		1		Tax Returns	39	12
3	3		18	15	5	2	Other	69	44
		10 (4/1-9/30/23)		72 (10/1/23-3/31/24)				4/1/19-3/31/20	4/1/20-3/31/21
0-500M	500M-2MM	2-10MM	10-50MM	50-100MM	100-250MM		ALL	ALL
1	6	37	24	10	4	NUMBER OF STATEMENTS	145	79
%	%	%	%	%	%	ASSETS	%	%
		16.6	7.7	7.0		Cash & Equivalents	9.6	13.1
		19.7	11.7	10.3		Trade Receivables (net)	21.0	17.8
		29.1	34.3	33.4		Inventory	28.0	26.9
		.9	4.4	1.7		All Other Current	1.8	2.3
		66.3	58.1	52.3		Total Current	60.3	60.0
		23.5	32.6	29.6		Fixed Assets (net)	28.8	31.4
		7.3	1.4	9.8		Intangibles (net)	4.7	4.2
		2.9	7.9	8.2		All Other Non-Current	6.2	4.4
		100.0	100.0	100.0		Total	100.0	100.0
						LIABILITIES		
		3.1	7.4	9.2		Notes Payable-Short Term	11.1	9.7
		2.0	2.6	2.8		Cur. Mat.-L.T.D.	3.1	3.9
		9.8	5.5	7.0		Trade Payables	10.9	9.2
		.0	.1	.1		Income Taxes Payable	.2	.2
		9.9	17.1	19.5		All Other Current	9.0	9.9
		24.7	32.7	38.6		Total Current	34.2	32.9
		15.2	17.9	18.1		Long-Term Debt	21.6	19.5
		.0	.2	.0		Deferred Taxes	.4	.6
		2.4	1.1	5.8		All Other Non-Current	6.9	7.2
		57.7	48.1	37.5		Net Worth	36.8	39.8
		100.0	100.0	100.0		Total Liabilities & Net Worth	100.0	100.0
						INCOME DATA		
		100.0	100.0	100.0		Net Sales	100.0	100.0
		37.2	28.5	26.2		Gross Profit	29.7	30.2
		29.7	21.7	21.1		Operating Expenses	23.5	23.0
		7.5	6.9	5.2		Operating Profit	6.1	7.1
		1.0	.7	1.2		All Other Expenses (net)	.6	-.3
		6.5	6.2	4.0		Profit Before Taxes	5.6	7.4
						RATIOS		
		8.5	3.4	2.7			3.3	4.0
		3.2	1.9	1.1		Current	2.0	2.2
		1.9	1.3	.8			1.4	1.3
		3.7	1.5	.5			1.7	2.2
		1.8	.5	.3		Quick	1.0	1.1
		.8	.2	.2			.4	.5
		19 19.3	18 20.6	5 68.4			14 25.2	16 22.7
		28 13.1	26 13.8	21 17.1		Sales/Receivables	30 12.1	28 12.9
		42 8.7	49 7.5	34 10.6			49 7.5	41 8.8
		39 9.4	45 8.2	62 5.9			26 14.1	26 14.0
		70 5.2	91 4.0	118 3.1		Cost of Sales/Inventory	57 6.4	69 5.3
		122 3.0	215 1.7	166 2.2			111 3.3	107 3.4
		8 47.4	9 39.4	9 42.8			8 46.8	10 36.0
		18 20.1	15 23.7	17 21.2		Cost of Sales/Payables	15 24.0	18 20.7
		34 10.8	29 12.4	38 9.6			32 11.4	29 12.5
		3.4	2.8	4.2			4.6	3.8
		5.4	4.5	19.9		Sales/Working Capital	7.4	8.0
		8.6	16.2	-10.7			17.7	22.0
		47.4	27.8				17.8	38.3
		(32) 12.2	(22) 6.0			EBIT/Interest	(127) 6.1	(68) 12.5
		2.1	1.2				1.3	2.4
						Net Profit + Depr., Dep.,	7.5	19.8
						Amort./Cur. Mat. L/T/D	(21) 3.7	(15) 5.7
							2.6	2.3
		.1	.2	.4			.2	.3
		.4	.6	1.2		Fixed/Worth	.7	.7
		.9	1.4	NM			1.9	2.9
		.3	.4	1.2			.5	.5
		.7	1.0	2.6		Debt/Worth	1.4	1.3
		1.6	2.7	NM			5.5	4.2
		40.9	36.2				44.8	67.0
		(34) 23.5	(21) 17.3			% Profit Before Taxes/Tangible Net Worth	(121) 21.5	(67) 34.1
		6.6	2.9				8.5	12.1
		28.5	19.3	12.4			18.4	24.2
		11.6	7.6	7.7		% Profit Before Taxes/Total Assets	8.7	13.1
		1.6	1.1	3.6			1.0	1.9
		64.9	12.4	12.7			25.6	17.2
		10.3	5.2	8.1		Sales/Net Fixed Assets	9.6	6.5
		4.1	2.2	3.7			4.5	3.2
		2.9	1.8	1.6			3.0	2.9
		1.9	1.5	1.4		Sales/Total Assets	1.9	1.7
		1.3	.8	1.0			1.5	1.3
		1.3	1.0				1.0	1.1
		(27) 3.2	(19) 2.4			% Depr., Dep., Amort./Sales	(123) 1.8	(66) 2.2
		4.3	3.7				4.0	4.4
		1.3					1.3	1.1
		(15) 2.1				% Officers', Directors' Owners' Comp/Sales	(55) 3.3	(21) 2.7
		3.2					5.1	4.8
877M	20885M	394194M	930017M	842947M	857324M	Net Sales ($)	5381248M	3003401M
272M	8632M	188530M	608941M	600396M	676748M	Total Assets ($)	3372386M	1919543M

M = $ thousand   MM = $ million
See Pages viii through xx for Explanation of Ratios and Data

© RMA 2024

MANUFACTURING—All Other Miscellaneous Wood Product Manufacturing NAICS 321999

Comparative Historical Data | Current Data Sorted by Sales

							Type of Statement							
	5		5		10		Unqualified				1	1	8	
	9		15		11		Reviewed			1	2	3	5	
	3		3		3		Compiled				1	2		
	17		13		15		Tax Returns			3	3	5	1	
	45		52		43		Other	2	1	2	8	18	14	
	4/1/21-3/31/22 ALL		4/1/22-3/31/23 ALL		4/1/23-3/31/24 ALL				10 (4/1-9/30/23)		72 (10/1/23-3/31/24)			
								0-1MM	1-3MM	3-5MM	5-10MM	10-25MM	25MM & OVER	
	79		88		82		NUMBER OF STATEMENTS	2	2	6	15	29	28	
	%		%		%		ASSETS	%	%	%	%	%	%	
	15.6		13.7		12.1		Cash & Equivalents				17.4	13.0	7.6	
	16.0		17.0		14.6		Trade Receivables (net)				16.9	18.7	12.3	
	27.4		26.1		30.2		Inventory				25.7	31.4	30.7	
	2.4		3.3		2.0		All Other Current				.8	3.3	1.7	
	61.5		60.1		58.8		Total Current				60.8	66.4	52.2	
	26.6		29.6		29.0		Fixed Assets (net)				33.3	22.9	32.5	
	6.2		5.1		6.8		Intangibles (net)				4.1	6.8	5.8	
	5.8		5.2		5.4		All Other Non-Current				1.8	3.9	9.5	
	100.0		100.0		100.0		Total				100.0	100.0	100.0	
							LIABILITIES							
	8.6		8.2		6.4		Notes Payable-Short Term				3.7	5.2	8.4	
	2.8		2.3		2.3		Cur. Mat.-L.T.D.				2.6	1.9	2.9	
	10.2		11.4		7.7		Trade Payables				5.5	11.3	6.4	
	.1		.1		.0		Income Taxes Payable				.0	.1	.1	
	11.1		10.3		13.4		All Other Current				11.2	9.4	13.7	
	32.8		32.2		29.9		Total Current				23.1	27.8	31.4	
	19.7		22.3		19.0		Long-Term Debt				21.5	12.2	18.9	
	.4		.1		.2		Deferred Taxes				.0	.0	.5	
	4.6		4.8		2.7		All Other Non-Current				.8	2.0	3.2	
	42.6		40.6		48.3		Net Worth				54.6	58.1	46.0	
	100.0		100.0		100.0		Total Liabilities & Net Worth				100.0	100.0	100.0	
							INCOME DATA							
	100.0		100.0		100.0		Net Sales				100.0	100.0	100.0	
	32.4		31.4		34.3		Gross Profit				37.7	34.4	26.1	
	24.4		24.1		27.0		Operating Expenses				27.1	27.8	18.9	
	8.0		7.4		7.3		Operating Profit				10.6	6.6	7.3	
	-1.3		.0		1.1		All Other Expenses (net)				1.2	1.0	1.0	
	9.3		7.3		6.2		Profit Before Taxes				9.5	5.6	6.3	
							RATIOS							
	3.7		3.5		4.3						10.8	4.6	3.3	
	2.1		2.3		2.2		Current				3.2	2.2	2.0	
	1.2		1.3		1.3						1.6	1.5	1.0	
	2.1		1.8		2.1						6.2	2.0	1.5	
	1.0	(87)	1.2		.7		Quick				2.8	.9	.6	
	.4		.5		.3						.7	.4	.2	
11	32.9	13	28.5	17	21.6					18	20.5	17 21.9	20 18.7	
21	17.0	26	13.8	25	14.5		Sales/Receivables			31	11.6	25 14.8	26 14.0	
45	8.1	50	7.3	35	10.3					45	8.1	36 10.1	35 10.5	
26	13.9	26	14.3	43	8.5					27	13.4	40 9.2	54 6.8	
68	5.4	58	6.3	74	4.9		Cost of Sales/Inventory			83	4.4	70 5.2	76 4.8	
99	3.7	107	3.4	140	2.6					130	2.8	118 3.1	146 2.5	
9	41.2	9	41.8	8	43.0					7	53.1	10 35.0	9 42.8	
19	19.1	18	19.9	17	22.1		Cost of Sales/Payables			18	20.1	23 15.9	15 23.9	
35	10.3	40	9.1	33	11.0					27	13.4	34 10.6	36 10.1	
	4.2		4.4		3.4						1.8	3.9	3.6	
	7.5		6.8		5.5		Sales/Working Capital				4.4	5.8	5.1	
	37.0		26.0		15.2						12.1	9.6	NM	
	50.3		24.6		29.0						42.9	48.8	14.7	
(69)	18.0	(76)	10.4	(71)	7.1		EBIT/Interest			(14)	13.9	(25) 11.3	(25) 5.0	
	4.5		3.4		1.4						3.2	1.1	3.2	
			7.9		36.2		Net Profit + Depr., Dep.,						63.7	
		(12)	5.1	(14)	4.1		Amort./Cur. Mat. L/T/D					(11)	7.6	
			2.6		2.6								3.0	
	.2		.4		.2						.3	.1	.3	
	.7		.6		.5		Fixed/Worth				.7	.4	.7	
	2.7		2.5		1.9						1.7	.7	3.0	
	.5		.5		.4						.1	.4	.5	
	1.5		1.4		1.1		Debt/Worth				1.4	.8	1.1	
	6.1		5.3		3.1						2.0	1.7	6.8	
	79.6		61.5		40.9		% Profit Before Taxes/Tangible				42.1	53.3	29.7	
(66)	39.9	(77)	30.8	(71)	22.0		Net Worth			(14)	33.0	(28) 23.5	(22) 18.0	
	26.5		14.4		4.6						11.6	.0	10.3	
	28.1		21.7		21.6		% Profit Before Taxes/Total				19.4	28.7	22.3	
	16.1		12.2		8.3		Assets				12.4	11.4	7.9	
	8.9		5.3		1.5						4.5	.2	3.7	
	26.3		18.7		17.3						7.2	86.6	12.4	
	9.1		8.9		7.6		Sales/Net Fixed Assets				3.7	16.4	7.4	
	4.3		3.7		3.5						2.9	4.1	2.9	
	2.8		2.8		2.4						1.9	3.1	1.8	
	1.9		2.0		1.6		Sales/Total Assets				1.3	2.1	1.5	
	1.2		1.3		1.1						1.0	1.5	1.2	
	.8		.9		1.4						3.3	.9	1.4	
(61)	2.0	(68)	2.0	(60)	2.8		% Depr., Dep., Amort./Sales			(11)	4.2	(21) 1.6	(22) 2.8	
	5.4		4.6		4.3						7.8	3.3	4.9	
	1.7		1.6		1.5		% Officers', Directors',							
(23)	2.8	(22)	2.7	(20)	2.2		Owners' Comp/Sales							
	5.7		7.0		4.0									
	3561120M		2960658M		3046244M		Net Sales ($)	1870M	4620M	22123M	107128M	452880M	2457623M	
	2242956M		1668816M		2083519M		Total Assets ($)	1679M	2927M	13007M	95419M	273454M	1697033M	

© RMA 2024   M = $ thousand   MM = $ million
See Pages viii through xx for Explanation of Ratios and Data

MANUFACTURING—Paper Mills NAICS 322120

Current Data Sorted by Assets

1						1
	1		1	1		
		1	1			
	1	2	2			
		2		4	2	7
0-500M	5 (4/1-9/30/23) 500M-2MM	2-10MM	20 (10/1/23-3/31/24) 10-50MM	50-100MM	100-250MM	
1	3	5	6	2	8	
%	%	%	%	%	%	

Comparative Historical Data

Type of Statement		
Unqualified	6	2
Reviewed	3	1
Compiled	1	1
Tax Returns	3	
Other	9	16
	4/1/19- 3/31/20 ALL	4/1/20- 3/31/21 ALL
NUMBER OF STATEMENTS	22	20

	%	%
ASSETS		
Cash & Equivalents	5.2	12.5
Trade Receivables (net)	21.2	20.5
Inventory	23.8	29.2
All Other Current	1.1	1.0
Total Current	51.4	63.3
Fixed Assets (net)	37.5	23.5
Intangibles (net)	1.9	5.3
All Other Non-Current	9.2	7.9
Total	100.0	100.0
LIABILITIES		
Notes Payable-Short Term	4.6	7.3
Cur. Mat.-L.T.D.	2.3	2.6
Trade Payables	16.5	16.1
Income Taxes Payable	.0	.0
All Other Current	6.8	5.7
Total Current	30.2	31.8
Long-Term Debt	20.9	20.0
Deferred Taxes	.6	.7
All Other Non-Current	8.8	6.8
Net Worth	39.6	40.8
Total Liabilities & Net Worth	100.0	100.0
INCOME DATA		
Net Sales	100.0	100.0
Gross Profit	18.9	22.1
Operating Expenses	13.8	19.4
Operating Profit	5.1	2.6
All Other Expenses (net)	1.5	1.0
Profit Before Taxes	3.7	1.6

RATIOS				
Current		2.7		4.7
		1.8		2.2
		1.1		1.2
Quick		1.4		2.3
		.8		1.3
		.5		.4
Sales/Receivables	23	16.0	23	15.9
	30	12.3	30	12.0
	41	8.8	49	7.4
Cost of Sales/Inventory	27	13.3	37	9.8
	34	10.7	70	5.2
	65	5.6	101	3.6
Cost of Sales/Payables	17	21.5	15	24.6
	28	12.9	26	14.0
	36	10.1	47	7.8
Sales/Working Capital		4.9		3.4
		11.5		6.6
		266.5		40.5
EBIT/Interest		9.6		11.3
	(21)	2.0	(14)	2.9
		1.1		.5
Net Profit + Depr., Dep., Amort./Cur. Mat. L/T/D				
Fixed/Worth		.3		.1
		1.3		.6
		3.1		3.0
Debt/Worth		.7		.6
		1.6		2.2
		5.6		7.6
% Profit Before Taxes/Tangible Net Worth		23.1		39.3
	(20)	9.4	(17)	22.7
		2.2		-2.6
% Profit Before Taxes/Total Assets		11.6		17.9
		3.8		2.7
		.6		-.3
Sales/Net Fixed Assets		33.5		59.8
		5.8		13.6
		2.1		2.8
Sales/Total Assets		3.3		3.7
		1.8		2.3
		1.2		1.1
% Depr., Dep., Amort./Sales		1.0		.5
	(20)	2.5	(16)	1.2
		4.0		3.4
% Officers', Directors' Owners' Comp/Sales				

| 32M | 16590M | 126833M | 287326M | 269351M | 1679370M | Net Sales ($) | 1960088M | 1738396M |
| 49M | 4933M | 28072M | 153024M | 144250M | 1384493M | Total Assets ($) | 1393775M | 1110011M |

© RMA 2024

M = $ thousand   MM = $ million
See Pages viii through xx for Explanation of Ratios and Data

MANUFACTURING—Paper Mills NAICS 322120

Comparative Historical Data / Current Data Sorted by Sales

							Type of Statement							
		2		5		2	Unqualified			1				1
		1		2		2	Reviewed				1			1
		1		1		2	Compiled						1	1
				1		3	Tax Returns					1		
		6		10		16	Other				1	2	1	14
		4/1/21-3/31/22 ALL		4/1/22-3/31/23 ALL		4/1/23-3/31/24 ALL		0-1MM	5 (4/1-9/30/23) 1-3MM	3-5MM	5-10MM	20 (10/1/23-3/31/24) 10-25MM		25MM & OVER
		10		19		25	NUMBER OF STATEMENTS		1		1	4	2	17
		%		%		%	ASSETS		%	%	%	%	%	%
		4.0		9.0		9.2	Cash & Equivalents							10.0
		21.5		16.4		19.3	Trade Receivables (net)							18.2
		16.2		29.6		24.8	Inventory			D				21.0
		.8		2.5		2.2	All Other Current			A				2.7
		42.4		57.6		55.5	Total Current			T				51.9
		31.8		31.2		30.1	Fixed Assets (net)			A				31.7
		21.9		2.2		6.4	Intangibles (net)							5.7
		3.9		9.0		8.0	All Other Non-Current			N				10.7
		100.0		100.0		100.0	Total			O				100.0
							LIABILITIES			T				
		2.1		5.7		7.3	Notes Payable-Short Term							4.3
		1.8		2.2		2.0	Cur. Mat.-L.T.D.			A				1.6
		18.7		10.7		12.0	Trade Payables			V				11.6
		.1		.0		.2	Income Taxes Payable			A				.3
		6.1		6.0		6.4	All Other Current			I				8.0
		28.7		24.6		28.0	Total Current			L				25.9
		28.3		21.0		10.6	Long-Term Debt			A				11.6
		1.1		1.2		1.3	Deferred Taxes			B				1.3
		3.8		4.6		5.1	All Other Non-Current			L				4.2
		38.0		48.7		55.0	Net Worth			E				56.9
		100.0		100.0		100.0	Total Liabilities & Net Worth							100.0
							INCOME DATA							
		100.0		100.0		100.0	Net Sales							100.0
		18.0		22.2		20.5	Gross Profit							17.7
		14.3		17.2		16.7	Operating Expenses							12.8
		3.7		5.0		3.8	Operating Profit							4.9
		1.7		-.4		1.1	All Other Expenses (net)							1.4
		1.9		5.5		2.7	Profit Before Taxes							3.5
							RATIOS							
		2.9		6.0		5.0								5.1
		1.6		2.5		1.9	Current							1.9
		.7		1.5		1.1								1.1
		1.7		1.6		2.8								3.2
		.8		1.3		.9	Quick							.7
		.3		.4		.5								.5
22	16.3		16	22.7	21	17.3							23	16.2
43	8.4		32	11.3	31	11.7	Sales/Receivables						35	10.4
51	7.1		45	8.1	42	8.6							42	8.6
27	13.6		33	10.9	35	10.5							29	12.6
40	9.2		72	5.1	53	6.9	Cost of Sales/Inventory						48	7.6
63	5.8		118	3.1	94	3.9							94	3.9
25	14.4		10	35.9	11	33.1							12	31.7
37	9.8		23	15.9	27	13.5	Cost of Sales/Payables						28	12.9
53	6.9		43	8.5	45	8.1							49	7.4
		6.1		4.0		4.7								3.6
		11.6		6.1		6.5	Sales/Working Capital							5.7
		-15.5		9.2		57.5								57.5
				43.0		24.6								34.6
		(17)		10.7	(20)	3.7	EBIT/Interest						(14)	3.8
				4.7		-.3								.8
							Net Profit + Depr., Dep., Amort./Cur. Mat. L/T/D							
		.6		.3		.2								.3
		3.2		.4		.5	Fixed/Worth							.7
		-1.5		.9		1.4								1.7
		.7		.4		.3								.2
		8.7		.9		.8	Debt/Worth							.4
		-4.2		1.4		2.2								3.0
				33.1		22.5	% Profit Before Taxes/Tangible Net Worth							22.5
		(18)		10.3	(24)	11.4							(16)	12.1
				7.6		-.9								1.3
		19.6		17.2		16.4								16.4
		5.4		7.5		5.9	% Profit Before Taxes/Total Assets							9.1
		-.8		2.2		-.6								-.3
		19.8		13.5		15.2								9.0
		10.1		6.4		5.7	Sales/Net Fixed Assets							5.0
		2.0		3.3		3.1								3.1
		2.5		3.0		2.8								2.2
		1.7		1.7		1.8	Sales/Total Assets							1.5
		.8		1.1		1.3								1.2
				.7		.7								.9
		(17)		2.1	(19)	2.6	% Depr., Dep., Amort./Sales						(13)	2.6
				3.1		4.0								3.6
							% Officers', Directors' Owners' Comp/Sales							
		1448590M		1920355M		2379502M	Net Sales ($)		32M		4705M	28957M	40729M	2305079M
		870702M		1266673M		1714821M	Total Assets ($)		49M		1624M	13885M	9539M	1689724M

M = $ thousand   MM = $ million

© RMA 2024

MANUFACTURING—Corrugated and Solid Fiber Box Manufacturing NAICS 322211

Current Data Sorted by Assets / Comparative Historical Data

			2	4	3	5	Type of Statement		
			2	5	2	1	Unqualified	19	6
	1	2	4	5			Reviewed	20	14
		1	7		1		Compiled	12	13
		1	6	25	8	10	Tax Returns	8	1
	22 (4/1-9/30/23)			73 (10/1/23-3/31/24)			Other	72	37
0-500M	500M-2MM	2-10MM	10-50MM	50-100MM	100-250MM			4/1/19-3/31/20 ALL	4/1/20-3/31/21 ALL
1	4	21	39	14	16		NUMBER OF STATEMENTS	131	71
%	%	%	%	%	%		ASSETS	%	%
		17.8	10.5	17.3	11.9		Cash & Equivalents	12.3	15.2
		26.8	22.0	18.3	17.0		Trade Receivables (net)	25.1	26.1
		20.6	15.5	10.3	8.9		Inventory	16.9	16.0
		.5	1.5	4.9	2.8		All Other Current	1.6	2.0
		65.7	49.4	50.8	40.5		Total Current	55.8	59.3
		23.9	36.1	27.8	35.9		Fixed Assets (net)	35.7	30.7
		6.3	3.3	9.5	8.1		Intangibles (net)	3.5	4.6
		4.1	11.2	12.0	15.4		All Other Non-Current	5.1	5.4
		100.0	100.0	100.0	100.0		Total	100.0	100.0
							LIABILITIES		
		2.7	3.3	.2	1.7		Notes Payable-Short Term	7.4	5.4
		2.9	4.6	2.0	2.0		Cur. Mat.-L.T.D.	3.2	3.3
		16.2	12.2	16.8	12.5		Trade Payables	12.5	15.2
		.0	.3	.1	.0		Income Taxes Payable	.1	.1
		7.4	7.2	4.5	7.9		All Other Current	6.4	7.1
		29.2	27.6	23.5	24.0		Total Current	29.6	31.1
		9.7	20.4	20.6	18.4		Long-Term Debt	17.6	17.4
		.1	.9	.0	.3		Deferred Taxes	.7	.4
		3.1	7.0	4.3	7.7		All Other Non-Current	2.7	4.1
		58.0	44.2	51.6	49.5		Net Worth	49.4	46.9
		100.0	100.0	100.0	100.0		Total Liabilities & Net Worth	100.0	100.0
							INCOME DATA		
		100.0	100.0	100.0	100.0		Net Sales	100.0	100.0
		27.6	20.8	21.9	22.2		Gross Profit	24.1	24.9
		20.1	15.0	17.9	12.7		Operating Expenses	18.3	20.2
		7.4	5.8	4.0	9.5		Operating Profit	5.8	4.7
		-.6	.5	-1.3	-.5		All Other Expenses (net)	.2	-.5
		8.0	5.4	5.3	10.0		Profit Before Taxes	5.7	5.1
							RATIOS		
		7.7	2.8	4.0	3.5			3.8	3.6
		2.3	1.7	2.7	1.6		Current	1.8	1.9
		1.5	1.3	1.4	1.4			1.3	1.2
		5.7	2.0	3.2	2.7			2.8	2.8
		1.4	.9	1.4	1.1		Quick	1.2	1.4
		1.0	.7	1.0	.8			.7	.9
		29 12.4	24 15.1	34 10.7	29 12.4			30 12.1	34 10.7
		34 10.6	36 10.0	40 9.2	35 10.5		Sales/Receivables	36 10.0	41 8.8
		40 9.2	45 8.1	42 8.7	48 7.6			46 8.0	49 7.4
		28 13.2	18 20.8	13 28.1	14 26.8			17 21.5	15 23.6
		38 9.7	26 14.1	20 18.0	18 19.8		Cost of Sales/Inventory	26 14.2	25 14.7
		45 8.1	51 7.1	33 10.9	40 9.2			50 7.3	44 8.3
		7 54.0	11 34.2	19 19.4	16 22.2			12 29.9	15 25.1
		21 17.4	20 18.0	25 14.8	28 13.1		Cost of Sales/Payables	21 17.8	21 17.3
		33 11.1	28 12.9	49 7.5	42 8.7			35 10.4	42 8.6
		4.3	4.7	4.0	5.0			5.6	4.6
		8.1	11.2	5.8	8.8		Sales/Working Capital	11.4	8.9
		22.0	36.3	18.2	25.0			29.3	28.4
		37.0	23.8	12.6	72.3			25.2	35.7
		(12) 11.6	(35) 11.2	(10) 3.4	(15) 17.6		EBIT/Interest	(118) 7.0	(64) 10.8
		4.8	3.2	.9	5.3			3.4	4.0
			7.7				Net Profit + Depr., Dep.,	8.7	7.3
			(12) 3.0				Amort./Cur. Mat. L/T/D	(43) 4.0	(19) 3.3
			.5					2.2	1.0
		.0	.5	.5	.5			.4	.4
		.5	1.0	.8	1.0		Fixed/Worth	.9	.6
		1.1	1.6	NM	1.4			1.5	1.4
		.1	.6	.4	.6			.5	.4
		.7	1.4	1.0	1.3		Debt/Worth	1.1	1.1
		1.4	2.6	NM	1.9			2.6	2.5
		58.6	55.9	22.4	57.7		% Profit Before Taxes/Tangible	44.5	42.1
		(19) 28.0	(36) 25.3	(11) 16.3	(15) 45.0		Net Worth	(122) 20.5	(65) 21.9
		16.5	8.8	3.9	18.2			7.5	9.4
		37.6	28.5	18.1	29.3		% Profit Before Taxes/Total	19.3	20.3
		16.0	13.6	5.8	19.3		Assets	10.4	10.6
		8.0	3.7	1.1	8.1			3.8	3.8
		256.4	10.9	19.0	6.1			13.3	14.3
		9.7	7.8	6.2	4.6		Sales/Net Fixed Assets	6.6	8.1
		7.9	4.0	3.8	3.8			4.2	5.0
		3.4	2.8	2.3	2.1			3.2	3.0
		2.8	2.3	1.6	1.8		Sales/Total Assets	2.4	2.3
		2.5	1.7	1.2	1.2			1.6	1.6
		.3	1.5	.8	1.5			1.5	.9
		(12) 1.2	(37) 2.1	(11) 2.1	(14) 2.4		% Depr., Dep., Amort./Sales	(115) 2.6	(61) 2.1
		1.8	3.3	3.8	3.6			3.6	3.6
		.6					% Officers', Directors'	.8	.8
		(10) 1.6					Owners' Comp/Sales	(32) 1.6	(17) 1.8
		5.0						3.0	3.6
148M	17338M	363112M	2659089M	1878632M	4382646M		Net Sales ($)	9491881M	4462857M
259M	5082M	121369M	1045962M	1085942M	2670379M		Total Assets ($)	5067887M	2586585M

© RMA 2024 M = $ thousand   MM = $ million
See Pages viii through xx for Explanation of Ratios and Data

MANUFACTURING—Corrugated and Solid Fiber Box Manufacturing NAICS 322211

Comparative Historical Data / Current Data Sorted by Sales

				Type of Statement							
8		7		14	Unqualified					1	13
14		14		10	Reviewed					4	6
10		9		12	Compiled	1		2		6	3
3		4		9	Tax Returns				3	2	4
32		40		50	Other		1			7	42
4/1/21-3/31/22 ALL		4/1/22-3/31/23 ALL		4/1/23-3/31/24 ALL			22 (4/1-9/30/23)			73 (10/1/23-3/31/24)	
						0-1MM	1-3MM	3-5MM	5-10MM	10-25MM	25MM & OVER
67		74		95	**NUMBER OF STATEMENTS**	1	1	2	3	20	68
%		%		%	**ASSETS**	%	%	%	%	%	%
13.5		12.1		14.4	Cash & Equivalents					13.9	13.0
26.6		25.2		21.7	Trade Receivables (net)					23.0	20.9
17.8		17.1		15.0	Inventory					21.1	12.8
2.3		3.6		2.5	All Other Current					.6	2.5
60.2		58.0		53.5	Total Current					58.6	49.2
29.0		31.2		30.9	Fixed Assets (net)					28.3	33.4
4.4		3.3		5.6	Intangibles (net)					9.0	4.9
6.5		7.6		10.1	All Other Non-Current					4.0	12.6
100.0		100.0		100.0	Total					100.0	100.0
					LIABILITIES						
4.9		6.3		2.6	Notes Payable-Short Term					4.4	1.8
2.4		2.6		3.1	Cur. Mat.-L.T.D.					3.4	3.3
15.2		18.8		13.5	Trade Payables					15.8	13.5
.3		.2		.1	Income Taxes Payable					.0	.2
6.3		7.3		7.1	All Other Current					6.2	7.2
29.1		35.2		26.6	Total Current					29.8	26.1
15.0		15.5		16.7	Long-Term Debt					11.5	19.3
.7		.4		.4	Deferred Taxes					.1	.6
3.3		3.9		5.5	All Other Non-Current					3.7	6.6
51.9		45.1		50.9	Net Worth					54.9	47.5
100.0		100.0		100.0	Total Liabilities & Net Worth					100.0	100.0
					INCOME DATA						
100.0		100.0		100.0	Net Sales					100.0	100.0
24.4		24.2		23.5	Gross Profit					26.1	21.3
16.2		17.1		16.4	Operating Expenses					19.9	14.8
8.2		7.1		7.1	Operating Profit					6.2	6.5
-1.9		-.2		-.2	All Other Expenses (net)					-.3	-.3
10.1		7.3		7.3	Profit Before Taxes					6.5	6.7
					RATIOS						
	3.6		3.4		3.6						5.1	3.6
	2.2		1.9		2.0	Current						2.0	1.9
	1.5		1.1		1.4						1.3	1.3
	2.8		2.6		2.6						3.0	2.3
	1.6		1.3		1.2	Quick						1.1	1.2
	.8		.7		.9						.9	.9
32	11.4	28	13.1	29	12.5					30	12.0	29	12.5
42	8.7	38	9.5	35	10.3	Sales/Receivables				35	10.5	35	10.3
48	7.6	47	7.8	43	8.5					42	8.6	43	8.5
20	17.9	16	23.5	17	21.1					29	12.4	15	24.5
32	11.3	25	14.7	29	12.7	Cost of Sales/Inventory				41	9.0	22	16.3
49	7.4	43	8.5	42	8.6					68	5.4	34	10.6
11	33.2	13	28.4	11	34.1					12	31.0	13	27.8
25	14.5	27	13.4	21	17.2	Cost of Sales/Payables				25	14.4	22	16.6
40	9.1	53	6.9	34	10.8					51	7.1	33	11.2
	3.9		5.1		4.7						4.5	4.8
	8.1		10.9		8.3	Sales/Working Capital					8.5	10.1
	15.2		46.6		25.9						26.2	29.0
	71.8		66.7		26.6						21.9	26.6
(55)	28.9	(65)	15.6	(75)	10.3	EBIT/Interest				(13)	6.2	(58)	13.3
	8.4		4.8		3.5						1.7	3.5
	28.9		14.6		8.1							9.3
(16)	9.6	(21)	6.1	(20)	4.1	Net Profit + Depr., Dep., Amort./Cur. Mat. L/T/D					(16)	4.6
	2.9		3.0		.8							1.5
	.3		.4		.4						.2	.5
	.6		.8		.8	Fixed/Worth					.7	.9
	1.3		1.3		1.3						1.4	1.4
	.4		.6		.5						.2	.5
	.8		1.0		1.1	Debt/Worth					1.0	1.2
	1.8		3.1		2.0						1.5	2.5
	51.1		58.4		53.2	% Profit Before Taxes/Tangible Net Worth					57.3	52.5
(60)	38.1	(65)	31.7	(86)	25.5					(18)	23.7	(61)	25.3
	25.3		18.0		13.6						13.6	12.9
	33.4		28.4		27.1	% Profit Before Taxes/Total Assets					23.0	27.1
	20.0		15.3		15.0						13.2	15.2
	13.4		6.9		5.8						6.4	4.2
	19.3		15.7		12.7						27.9	11.5
	9.1		8.0		7.4	Sales/Net Fixed Assets					8.4	6.2
	4.9		4.5		4.4						5.3	4.0
	3.1		3.1		2.8						3.1	2.7
	2.2		2.3		2.3	Sales/Total Assets					2.6	2.0
	1.6		1.6		1.6						1.9	1.6
	1.1		1.0		1.3						.9	1.4
(59)	1.9	(68)	1.7	(77)	2.0	% Depr., Dep., Amort./Sales				(12)	1.7	(61)	2.0
	3.1		3.1		3.1						2.4	3.3
	.7		.6		.8							.7
(16)	1.4	(15)	1.0	(22)	1.7	% Officers', Directors' Owners' Comp/Sales					(12)	1.6
	1.8		1.9		3.1							2.5
4813926M		5809579M		9300965M	Net Sales ($)	148M	2720M	8923M	20520M	331936M	8936718M
2553418M		2747568M		4928993M	Total Assets ($)	259M	1013M	2556M	7169M	159218M	4758778M

© RMA 2024   M = $ thousand   MM = $ million
See Pages viii through xx for Explanation of Ratios and Data

MANUFACTURING—Folding Paperboard Box Manufacturing NAICS 322212

Current Data Sorted by Assets | Comparative Historical Data

0-500M	500M-2MM	2-10MM	10-50MM	50-100MM	100-250MM	Type of Statement		4/1/19-3/31/20 ALL		4/1/20-3/31/21 ALL
			4	3	3	Unqualified		6		4
		2	2	1		Reviewed		8		3
	1	2				Compiled		2		2
		1				Tax Returns		4		1
	1		7	1	1	Other		21		16
	8 (4/1-9/30/23)		21 (10/1/23-3/31/24)			NUMBER OF STATEMENTS		41		26
2	2	5	13	5	4					
%	%	%	%	%	%	ASSETS		%		%
			7.9			Cash & Equivalents		7.1		14.8
D			14.3			Trade Receivables (net)		18.3		20.8
A			21.9			Inventory		20.6		19.7
T			3.5			All Other Current		1.7		3.2
A			47.5			Total Current		47.8		58.4
			39.2			Fixed Assets (net)		42.8		32.5
N			7.9			Intangibles (net)		2.8		3.7
O			5.3			All Other Non-Current		6.6		5.3
T			100.0			Total		100.0		100.0
A						LIABILITIES				
V			6.3			Notes Payable-Short Term		7.2		6.0
A			6.3			Cur. Mat.-L.T.D.		5.0		3.2
I			6.9			Trade Payables		12.5		11.5
L			.1			Income Taxes Payable		.3		.8
A			3.5			All Other Current		5.3		6.3
B			23.0			Total Current		30.3		27.8
L			14.5			Long-Term Debt		19.6		22.6
E			1.8			Deferred Taxes		1.1		1.1
			5.1			All Other Non-Current		2.4		4.7
			55.6			Net Worth		46.6		43.9
			100.0			Total Liabilities & Net Worth		100.0		100.0
						INCOME DATA				
			100.0			Net Sales		100.0		100.0
			22.7			Gross Profit		21.9		22.8
			16.2			Operating Expenses		17.8		16.7
			6.5			Operating Profit		4.0		6.1
			1.2			All Other Expenses (net)		1.0		-.7
			5.3			Profit Before Taxes		3.0		6.7
						RATIOS				
			4.9					2.6		4.5
			2.2			Current		1.7		1.9
			1.2					1.0		1.5
			2.2					1.5		3.0
			1.0			Quick		.8		1.1
			.4					.5		.7
		28	13.2				27	13.7	28	13.0
		33	10.9			Sales/Receivables	37	9.9	35	10.4
		43	8.4				42	8.6	46	8.0
		31	11.9				35	10.3	21	17.5
		51	7.1			Cost of Sales/Inventory	49	7.5	42	8.7
		122	3.0				69	5.3	74	4.9
		9	42.3				15	24.8	15	23.8
		17	21.2			Cost of Sales/Payables	26	14.2	21	17.3
		25	14.6				41	9.0	33	11.0
			3.2					6.1		4.1
			4.6			Sales/Working Capital		8.3		7.2
			38.2					-129.6		11.7
			8.0					15.9		17.5
		(12)	3.9			EBIT/Interest	(40)	4.1	(23)	9.4
			.9					1.0		4.2
						Net Profit + Depr., Dep., Amort./Cur. Mat. L/T/D		4.2		
							(15)	2.6		
								.5		
			.4					.5		.3
			.8			Fixed/Worth		1.1		.9
			1.7					1.8		1.9
			.4					.5		.5
			1.4			Debt/Worth		1.2		1.1
			2.0					2.2		3.5
			43.2					32.9		53.9
		(12)	21.3			% Profit Before Taxes/Tangible Net Worth	(38)	15.8	(24)	24.7
			4.1					-.8		7.8
			16.6					13.8		15.6
			9.2			% Profit Before Taxes/Total Assets		6.9		11.3
			.7					.0		4.5
			9.2					7.4		11.5
			4.1			Sales/Net Fixed Assets		4.4		6.2
			2.1					2.5		4.2
			1.9					2.3		2.6
			1.6			Sales/Total Assets		1.9		1.9
			1.1					1.4		1.5
			1.4					2.4		1.8
			4.5			% Depr., Dep., Amort./Sales	(33)	4.4	(22)	3.0
			6.1					5.3		4.2
						% Officers', Directors' Owners' Comp/Sales				
	7969M	64238M	562983M	515660M	759565M	Net Sales ($)		2454737M		1228939M
	2612M	27104M	378292M	347225M	460167M	Total Assets ($)		1410067M		630717M

© RMA 2024 M = $ thousand MM = $ million
See Pages viii through xx for Explanation of Ratios and Data

MANUFACTURING—Folding Paperboard Box Manufacturing NAICS 322212

Comparative Historical Data / Current Data Sorted by Sales

								Type of Statement									
		2		4		10		Unqualified								10	
		4		7		3		Reviewed								3	
		1		3		3		Compiled				1		2			
				1		2		Tax Returns						2			
		20		14		11		Other	1		1			2		7	
		4/1/21-		4/1/22-		4/1/23-					8 (4/1-9/30/23)			21 (10/1/23-3/31/24)			
		3/31/22		3/31/23		3/31/24											
		ALL		ALL		ALL			0-1MM		1-3MM	3-5MM	5-10MM	10-25MM		25MM & OVER	
		27		29		29		NUMBER OF STATEMENTS	1		1		1	6		20	
		%		%		%		ASSETS	%		%	%	%	%		%	
		9.9		5.5		11.3		Cash & Equivalents								10.5	
		20.4		17.6		16.5		Trade Receivables (net)				D				15.5	
		20.5		21.6		19.6		Inventory				A				19.6	
		2.3		4.5		2.5		All Other Current				T				3.1	
		53.0		49.2		49.8		Total Current				A				48.6	
		39.5		42.8		40.5		Fixed Assets (net)								39.1	
		2.4		2.9		3.9		Intangibles (net)				N				5.5	
		5.1		5.1		5.8		All Other Non-Current				O				6.8	
		100.0		100.0		100.0		Total				T				100.0	
								LIABILITIES				A					
		8.3		6.9		5.1		Notes Payable-Short Term				V				5.1	
		3.8		3.6		3.9		Cur. Mat.-L.T.D.				A				4.7	
		11.2		9.8		8.3		Trade Payables				I				7.2	
		.3		.4		.2		Income Taxes Payable				L				.3	
		5.1		4.7		4.2		All Other Current				A				4.5	
		28.6		25.4		21.8		Total Current				B				21.7	
		19.0		21.1		16.5		Long-Term Debt				L				13.6	
		1.3		1.5		1.6		Deferred Taxes				E				1.6	
		3.7		3.5		5.5		All Other Non-Current								5.2	
		47.4		48.5		54.6		Net Worth								57.9	
		100.0		100.0		100.0		Total Liabilities & Net Worth								100.0	
								INCOME DATA									
		100.0		100.0		100.0		Net Sales								100.0	
		19.4		23.4		25.9		Gross Profit								22.4	
		13.3		15.3		16.8		Operating Expenses								15.1	
		6.1		8.1		9.1		Operating Profit								7.3	
		-.7		.2		.7		All Other Expenses (net)								.6	
		6.8		7.9		8.4		Profit Before Taxes								6.7	
								RATIOS									
		3.6		3.1		5.0										5.0	
		1.8		2.1		3.0		Current								2.6	
		1.1		1.2		1.2										1.1	
		1.5		1.6		3.2										2.7	
		.9		.9		1.4		Quick								1.2	
		.6		.4		.5										.5	
32	11.3	28	13.2	23	16.0									28	13.2	
39	9.4	40	9.2	33	11.0		Sales/Receivables							36	10.1	
46	7.9	47	7.7	42	8.6									45	8.1	
35	10.5	28	12.9	30	12.3									32	11.5	
46	8.0	51	7.2	48	7.6		Cost of Sales/Inventory							49	7.5	
61	6.0	89	4.1	83	4.4									73	5.0	
13	28.2	11	33.4	9	38.7									10	38.4	
20	18.0	24	15.3	17	21.2		Cost of Sales/Payables							16	22.4	
47	7.7	33	11.0	34	10.7									26	14.0	
	4.4		4.7		3.0										3.0	
	8.0		6.8		5.6		Sales/Working Capital								5.1	
	83.3		31.4		41.2										51.7	
	48.9		25.9		38.2										43.7	
(26)	15.6	(25)	11.7	(26)	5.1		EBIT/Interest							(17)	5.8	
	6.3		3.5		.7										.7	
	11.9		7.4		12.3		Net Profit + Depr., Dep.,								13.3	
(10)	3.7	(15)	3.1	(12)	4.0		Amort./Cur. Mat. L/T/D							(10)	7.5	
	2.6		2.0		1.6										1.7	
	.4		.6		.3										.3	
	1.0		1.0		.8		Fixed/Worth								.8	
	1.9		1.9		1.8										1.7	
	.4		.5		.3										.3	
	1.8		1.1		.5		Debt/Worth								.5	
	2.6		2.4		2.8										2.4	
	51.0		41.8		35.3		% Profit Before Taxes/Tangible								35.3	
	26.3	(28)	26.8	(27)	18.9		Net Worth							(19)	20.0	
	16.1		12.2		3.5										3.5	
	19.1		19.9		18.2		% Profit Before Taxes/Total								18.3	
	13.3		12.7		9.2		Assets								9.6	
	8.0		5.3		.8										-.1	
	13.5		7.3		7.1										7.3	
	4.0		3.6		4.1		Sales/Net Fixed Assets								4.4	
	2.7		2.6		2.6										2.7	
	2.3		2.0		2.0										1.9	
	1.7		1.7		1.6		Sales/Total Assets								1.5	
	1.4		1.3		1.3										1.3	
	1.8		1.9		1.6										1.7	
(24)	3.8	(28)	4.1	(26)	4.0		% Depr., Dep., Amort./Sales								4.0	
	5.5		5.7		5.4										5.8	
							% Officers', Directors'									
							Owners' Comp/Sales									
	1790229M		1515036M		1910415M		Net Sales ($)	838M		1691M		6278M	100197M		1801411M	
	1008412M		941717M		1215400M		Total Assets ($)	2606M		898M		1714M	58516M		1151666M	

© RMA 2024

M = $ thousand   MM = $ million
See Pages viii through xx for Explanation of Ratios and Data

MANUFACTURING—Paper Bag and Coated and Treated Paper Manufacturing NAICS 322220

Current Data Sorted by Assets | Comparative Historical Data

0-500M	500M-2MM	2-10MM	10-50MM	50-100MM	100-250MM					
		1	2	1	1	Type of Statement				
		2	8			Unqualified		15		7
	1		3		1	Reviewed		12		7
1		2				Compiled		4		5
1		7	8	4	3	Tax Returns		11		2
5 (4/1-9/30/23)		42 (10/1/23-3/31/24)				Other		45		28
								4/1/19-3/31/20 ALL		4/1/20-3/31/21 ALL
3		12	22	6	4	NUMBER OF STATEMENTS		87		49
%	%	%	%	%	%	ASSETS		%		%
		15.0	5.9			Cash & Equivalents		8.3		12.9
D		26.2	18.6			Trade Receivables (net)		21.0		19.2
A		28.5	27.9			Inventory		24.5		22.2
T		.8	.7			All Other Current		2.2		2.3
A		70.4	53.2			Total Current		55.9		56.7
		18.2	33.7			Fixed Assets (net)		33.3		32.6
N		5.0	3.2			Intangibles (net)		6.5		4.9
O		6.3	9.9			All Other Non-Current		4.2		5.8
T		100.0	100.0			Total		100.0		100.0
A						LIABILITIES				
V		7.5	4.8			Notes Payable-Short Term		8.6		4.1
A		3.1	3.4			Cur. Mat.-L.T.D.		3.0		3.4
I		11.2	11.2			Trade Payables		9.4		9.3
L		.8	.0			Income Taxes Payable		.1		.2
A		10.2	6.5			All Other Current		6.6		7.7
B		32.9	25.8			Total Current		27.7		24.7
L		15.1	15.1			Long-Term Debt		14.6		16.9
E		.3	.6			Deferred Taxes		.6		.4
		3.6	6.5			All Other Non-Current		6.9		9.0
		48.2	52.0			Net Worth		50.3		49.0
		100.0	100.0			Total Liabilities & Net Worth		100.0		100.0
						INCOME DATA				
		100.0	100.0			Net Sales		100.0		100.0
		30.8	21.9			Gross Profit		24.5		29.3
		24.3	18.6			Operating Expenses		18.9		22.6
		6.5	3.4			Operating Profit		5.6		6.8
		.9	.5			All Other Expenses (net)		1.3		.3
		5.6	2.9			Profit Before Taxes		4.3		6.5
						RATIOS				
		6.7	4.5					3.7		5.4
		2.4	1.8			Current		2.1		3.0
		1.4	1.3					1.3		1.4
		4.6	2.7					2.1		2.9
		1.2	.9			Quick		1.0		1.6
		.8	.6					.6		.7
24		15.0	27 13.5				29	12.6	33	10.9
34		10.8	36 10.1			Sales/Receivables	38	9.6	39	9.4
51		7.1	43 8.4				47	7.8	48	7.6
27		13.7	50 7.3				42	8.6	47	7.7
56		6.5	64 5.7			Cost of Sales/Inventory	62	5.9	59	6.2
81		4.5	85 4.3				81	4.5	81	4.5
	8	46.1	15 24.0				10	37.6	10	36.9
	15	23.9	25 14.4			Cost of Sales/Payables	18	20.4	23	15.6
	26	14.3	38 9.6				36	10.1	42	8.6
		4.2	4.3					4.3		3.8
		5.9	7.6			Sales/Working Capital		7.1		5.1
		13.7	16.3					15.7		8.3
		20.0	28.1					28.6		74.8
	(10)	7.0	(21) 7.0			EBIT/Interest	(84)	4.5	(42)	9.1
		.7	.5					1.1		1.6
			11.5			Net Profit + Depr., Dep.,		14.2		
		(11)	2.8			Amort./Cur. Mat. L/T/D	(21)	3.0		
			1.6					1.2		
		.0	.4					.4		.3
		.3	.6			Fixed/Worth		.6		.6
		1.6	1.0					1.8		2.6
		.3	.5					.4		.3
		.8	.7			Debt/Worth		1.1		1.1
		4.8	1.8					2.6		3.5
		50.9	28.3					24.7		44.7
	(10)	19.1	(21) 15.1			% Profit Before Taxes/Tangible Net Worth	(77)	15.1	(43)	27.0
		4.0	.8					4.9		7.0
		27.4	16.8					14.8		24.2
		7.5	6.6			% Profit Before Taxes/Total Assets		6.1		11.0
		.0	-.2					.4		1.4
		168.3	10.2					10.5		12.0
		23.8	5.1			Sales/Net Fixed Assets		6.1		5.5
		6.6	3.8					3.3		3.2
		3.2	2.2					2.4		2.2
		2.5	1.9			Sales/Total Assets		1.8		1.5
		2.0	1.5					1.2		1.1
		.5	1.5					1.7		1.5
	(11)	1.2	1.9			% Depr., Dep., Amort./Sales	(82)	2.5	(46)	2.9
		3.5	4.6					4.0		4.6
						% Officers', Directors' Owners' Comp/Sales				
	9844M	166405M	877077M	583425M	786914M	Net Sales ($)		6309000M		2360980M
	5398M	67779M	486585M	490910M	660288M	Total Assets ($)		3958845M		1652730M

M = $ thousand   MM = $ million
See Pages viii through xx for Explanation of Ratios and Data

© RMA 2024

MANUFACTURING—Paper Bag and Coated and Treated Paper Manufacturing NAICS 322220

Comparative Historical Data | Current Data Sorted by Sales

							Type of Statement							
	7		5		5		Unqualified						2	3
	9		4		10		Reviewed						3	7
	6		8		5		Compiled				1			4
	3		6		4		Tax Returns						2	1
	19		19		23		Other		1			3		12
	4/1/21-3/31/22		4/1/22-3/31/23		4/1/23-3/31/24				1			7		
	ALL		ALL		ALL			0-1MM	5 (4/1-9/30/23)	3-5MM	5-10MM	42 (10/1/23-3/31/24)	10-25MM	25MM & OVER
	44		42		47		NUMBER OF STATEMENTS		1-3MM 2	1	3		14	27
	%		%		%		ASSETS	%	%	%	%	%	%	%
	12.2		12.1		8.3		Cash & Equivalents						10.0	7.9
	18.0		21.9		20.2		Trade Receivables (net)	D					19.6	20.0
	24.8		27.3		26.8		Inventory	A					30.0	26.7
	2.0		1.1		1.6		All Other Current	T					.4	2.3
	57.0		62.4		56.9		Total Current	A					59.9	57.0
	29.7		26.2		28.9		Fixed Assets (net)						29.0	26.4
	6.5		4.8		5.5		Intangibles (net)	N					4.8	6.7
	6.8		6.6		8.7		All Other Non-Current	O					6.3	10.0
	100.0		100.0		100.0		Total	T					100.0	100.0
							LIABILITIES	A						
	3.7		4.4		5.0		Notes Payable-Short Term	V					5.3	3.8
	4.7		5.1		3.9		Cur. Mat.-L.T.D.	A					3.2	3.5
	11.4		15.9		10.7		Trade Payables	I					9.2	11.2
	.1		.0		.2		Income Taxes Payable	L					.7	.0
	6.9		8.9		7.4		All Other Current	A					9.6	7.0
	26.7		34.4		27.3		Total Current	B					28.0	25.4
	26.0		13.2		17.0		Long-Term Debt	L					14.0	14.2
	.3		.4		.5		Deferred Taxes	E					1.1	.3
	7.6		4.2		6.2		All Other Non-Current						.8	7.9
	39.4		47.8		49.0		Net Worth						56.1	52.2
	100.0		100.0		100.0		Total Liabilities & Net Worth						100.0	100.0
							INCOME DATA							
	100.0		100.0		100.0		Net Sales						100.0	100.0
	27.7		25.3		26.2		Gross Profit						24.3	23.5
	19.2		17.4		21.5		Operating Expenses						20.3	18.4
	8.6		7.9		4.7		Operating Profit						4.0	5.1
	.9		.3		1.1		All Other Expenses (net)						.6	1.3
	7.7		7.7		3.6		Profit Before Taxes						3.4	3.8
							RATIOS							
	5.2		3.4		3.9								2.9	5.3
	2.9		2.1		2.1		Current						2.2	2.3
	1.4		1.3		1.4								1.4	1.4
	3.0		1.8		2.2								1.7	2.9
	1.5		1.2		1.0		Quick						.9	1.1
	.7		.5		.6								.6	.6
29	12.7	27	13.5	27	13.5							22	16.3	33	11.2
41	8.8	40	9.2	38	9.5		Sales/Receivables					28	12.9	42	8.7
47	7.7	49	7.5	45	8.1							39	9.3	50	7.3
53	6.9	41	9.0	53	6.9							42	8.7	60	6.1
62	5.9	70	5.2	68	5.4		Cost of Sales/Inventory					61	6.0	69	5.3
85	4.3	96	3.8	87	4.2							85	4.3	87	4.2
16	22.5	10	36.4	13	28.6							8	46.4	16	23.5
26	14.0	24	15.2	22	16.6		Cost of Sales/Payables					20	18.4	24	15.0
51	7.2	56	6.5	40	9.1							27	13.3	49	7.4
	3.6		4.0		4.1								5.2	3.5
	5.1		7.7		6.4		Sales/Working Capital						7.5	5.4
	13.5		17.6		14.6								13.2	13.0
	49.3		44.3		21.9								20.0	34.7
(41)	11.7	(36)	13.9	(42)	5.8		EBIT/Interest						8.6	(23)	4.6
	4.1		2.9		.3								.8	.3
	12.8				7.5		Net Profit + Depr., Dep.,						7.5
(12)	3.6			(18)	3.2		Amort./Cur. Mat. L/T/D						(14)	3.2
	.7				1.4									1.4
	.3		.2		.3								.2	.3
	.6		.4		.6		Fixed/Worth						.6	.6
	NM		1.5		1.4								1.0	1.0
	.4		.4		.5								.5	.5
	.9		1.1		.7		Debt/Worth						.7	.6
	NM		2.3		2.5								1.6	2.4
	51.4		42.6		28.1		% Profit Before Taxes/Tangible						24.1	38.2
(33)	30.2	(38)	24.0	(42)	15.0		Net Worth						14.5	(25)	16.5
	23.4		13.0		-.9								-.8	.5
	24.4		21.4		18.9		% Profit Before Taxes/Total						13.6	22.6
	15.5		14.8		6.1		Assets						7.2	6.1
	2.9		4.8		-.7								-.2	-.7
	12.9		20.9		12.0								47.5	9.8
	6.7		8.4		7.1		Sales/Net Fixed Assets						6.7	7.8
	3.8		5.1		3.7								3.7	4.1
	2.2		2.6		2.4								2.9	2.0
	1.9		2.1		1.8		Sales/Total Assets						2.2	1.7
	1.2		1.3		1.2								1.9	1.2
	2.0		.6		1.4								.6	1.5
(41)	3.1	(33)	2.1	(46)	2.2		% Depr., Dep., Amort./Sales					(13)	2.3	2.1
	4.8		4.5		4.8								5.0	4.6
			.7				% Officers', Directors'							
		(11)	2.0				Owners' Comp/Sales							
					2.6									
	2460480M		2218203M		2423665M		Net Sales ($)		5098M	4746M	22556M	254864M	2136401M
	1799927M		1354155M		1710960M		Total Assets ($)		3713M	1685M	14113M	130073M	1561376M

© RMA 2024   M = $ thousand   MM = $ million
See Pages viii through xx for Explanation of Ratios and Data

MANUFACTURING—Stationery Product Manufacturing NAICS 322230

Current Data Sorted by Assets | **Comparative Historical Data**

						Type of Statement		
			1	3	1	1	Unqualified	4	5
				3			Reviewed	2	1
			1				Compiled	2	1
							Tax Returns	2	1
	5 (4/1-9/30/23)		2	5 (10/1/23-3/31/24)	3	1	Other	10	7
0-500M	500M-2MM	2-10MM	10-50MM	50-100MM	100-250MM		4/1/19-3/31/20 ALL	4/1/20-3/31/21 ALL
		4	11	4	2	**NUMBER OF STATEMENTS**	20	15
%	%	%	%	%	%	**ASSETS**	%	%
			5.9			Cash & Equivalents	6.2	10.9
			22.0			Trade Receivables (net)	26.3	23.4
D	D		20.7			Inventory	24.3	27.1
A	A		2.0			All Other Current	2.1	2.3
T	T		50.7			Total Current	58.9	63.6
A	A		28.8			Fixed Assets (net)	28.2	27.9
			8.9			Intangibles (net)	7.5	5.5
N	N		11.6			All Other Non-Current	5.4	3.0
O	O		100.0			Total	100.0	100.0
T	T					**LIABILITIES**		
			2.1			Notes Payable-Short Term	13.9	9.8
A	A		3.1			Cur. Mat.-L.T.D.	3.5	4.0
V	V		10.0			Trade Payables	10.2	11.1
A	A		.1			Income Taxes Payable	.0	.0
I	I		6.5			All Other Current	10.5	13.7
L	L		21.8			Total Current	38.1	38.6
A	A		17.8			Long-Term Debt	21.3	20.3
B	B		1.0			Deferred Taxes	.8	.5
L	L		6.5			All Other Non-Current	10.4	7.5
E	E		52.9			Net Worth	29.5	33.2
			100.0			Total Liabilities & Net Worth	100.0	100.0
						INCOME DATA		
			100.0			Net Sales	100.0	100.0
			29.8			Gross Profit	29.9	21.5
			22.1			Operating Expenses	24.4	20.7
			7.7			Operating Profit	5.5	.8
			1.0			All Other Expenses (net)	.8	-.4
			6.7			Profit Before Taxes	4.7	1.2
						RATIOS		
			2.8				3.4	2.1
			2.2			Current	1.3	1.7
			2.0				1.1	1.3
			1.6				1.6	1.2
			1.3			Quick	.7	1.0
			.9				.6	.5
		32	11.5				34 10.6	17 21.0
		43	8.4			Sales/Receivables	40 9.1	39 9.4
		55	6.6				46 7.9	49 7.4
		36	10.1				32 11.4	31 11.6
		46	8.0			Cost of Sales/Inventory	47 7.8	46 7.9
		64	5.7				91 4.0	146 2.5
		12	30.8				16 23.1	10 37.4
		20	18.5			Cost of Sales/Payables	21 17.3	17 22.0
		51	7.2				31 11.6	27 13.5
			4.3				4.9	4.5
			6.4			Sales/Working Capital	17.2	8.5
			9.9				124.2	16.8
			30.6				5.6	5.3
			7.4			EBIT/Interest	(18) 3.6	(13) 3.4
			4.1				.4	.7
						Net Profit + Depr., Dep., Amort./Cur. Mat. L/T/D		
			.3				.6	.4
			.7			Fixed/Worth	1.5	.8
			.9				-6.1	-10.4
			.7				1.0	.9
			1.0			Debt/Worth	2.4	1.3
			1.8				-21.2	-40.0
			50.1				48.1	
		(10)	21.8			% Profit Before Taxes/Tangible Net Worth	(13) 5.7	
			5.7				-9.2	
			25.8				12.8	5.8
			10.0			% Profit Before Taxes/Total Assets	4.0	3.5
			4.2				.6	-.9
			16.4				18.7	15.1
			7.9			Sales/Net Fixed Assets	8.9	10.5
			4.6				5.4	5.5
			2.1				2.7	3.0
			1.8			Sales/Total Assets	2.2	2.2
			1.5				1.7	1.6
			1.5				1.2	1.4
		(10)	2.1			% Depr., Dep., Amort./Sales	(18) 2.4	(14) 2.1
			3.6				4.0	2.5
						% Officers', Directors' Owners' Comp/Sales		
		47836M	539778M	423118M	844006M	Net Sales ($)	1180477M	898351M
		30460M	274256M	247013M	330983M	Total Assets ($)	614053M	418703M

M = $ thousand   MM = $ million
See Pages viii through xx for Explanation of Ratios and Data

© RMA 2024

MANUFACTURING—Stationery Product Manufacturing NAICS 322230

Comparative Historical Data / Current Data Sorted by Sales

						Type of Statement						
		3		7	6	Unqualified					2	4
				2	3	Reviewed					1	2
				2		Compiled					1	
					1	Tax Returns						
		7		11	11	Other					1	9
		4/1/21-3/31/22		4/1/22-3/31/23	4/1/23-3/31/24			5 (4/1-9/30/23)			16 (10/1/23-3/31/24)	
		ALL		ALL	ALL		0-1MM	1-3MM	3-5MM	5-10MM	10-25MM	25MM & OVER
		10		22	21	NUMBER OF STATEMENTS			1		5	15
		%		%	%	ASSETS	%	%	%	%	%	%
		5.2		7.1	9.2	Cash & Equivalents	D	D		D		2.7
		21.8		24.2	21.3	Trade Receivables (net)	A	A		A		21.6
		22.7		27.7	25.8	Inventory	T	T		T		29.8
		3.0		3.7	2.1	All Other Current	A	A		A		2.4
		52.6		62.8	58.4	Total Current						56.5
		22.3		21.4	24.6	Fixed Assets (net)	N	N		N		28.3
		13.8		9.6	7.9	Intangibles (net)	O	O		O		9.6
		11.3		6.2	9.2	All Other Non-Current	T	T		T		5.6
		100.0		100.0	100.0	Total						100.0
						LIABILITIES	A	A		A		
		4.7		6.1	5.6	Notes Payable-Short Term	V	V		V		6.5
		6.6		2.9	2.4	Cur. Mat.-L.T.D.	A	A		A		3.2
		15.1		15.7	12.9	Trade Payables	I	I		I		12.0
		.0		.0	.1	Income Taxes Payable	L	L		L		.0
		7.8		7.8	7.2	All Other Current	A	A		A		7.8
		34.3		32.5	28.2	Total Current	B	B		B		29.6
		32.2		16.5	15.6	Long-Term Debt	L	L		L		19.6
		1.4		.7	.6	Deferred Taxes	E	E		E		.4
		5.4		3.4	8.3	All Other Non-Current						6.2
		26.8		46.9	47.2	Net Worth						44.2
		100.0		100.0	100.0	Total Liabilities & Net Worth						100.0
						INCOME DATA						
		100.0		100.0	100.0	Net Sales						100.0
		26.2		26.9	27.3	Gross Profit						23.1
		24.3		19.2	20.3	Operating Expenses						16.1
		1.9		7.8	7.0	Operating Profit						6.9
		.9		.4	1.2	All Other Expenses (net)						1.3
		1.0		7.3	5.8	Profit Before Taxes						5.6
						RATIOS						
		2.7		2.9	2.8							2.3
		1.4		1.9	2.0	Current						2.0
		1.1		1.4	1.6							1.5
		1.4		1.8	1.6							1.4
		.6		.9	1.0	Quick						1.0
		.5		.6	.6							.5
23	15.9		30	12.1	30	12.0					29	12.5
33	11.0		45	8.1	41	9.0	Sales/Receivables				41	9.0
42	8.6		53	6.9	56	6.5					54	6.8
28	13.2		46	8.0	37	9.8					38	9.5
45	8.2		61	6.0	54	6.8	Cost of Sales/Inventory				54	6.8
65	5.6		118	3.1	107	3.4					135	2.7
17	21.4		16	23.5	18	20.6					16	23.5
22	16.8		32	11.3	29	12.4	Cost of Sales/Payables				21	17.3
64	5.7		54	6.8	56	6.5					51	7.2
		5.6		4.0	3.9							4.3
		27.0		7.1	6.4	Sales/Working Capital						6.9
		43.9		11.3	9.7							9.9
		9.0		26.0	16.8							12.3
		1.8	(20)	15.4	(20) 6.0	EBIT/Interest						5.3
		-2.5		6.5	2.5							.7
						Net Profit + Depr., Dep., Amort./Cur. Mat. L/T/D						
		.3		.2	.3							.4
		2.7		.5	.7	Fixed/Worth						.9
		NM		1.1	1.0							3.5
		.9		.5	.7							.8
		6.2		1.2	1.4	Debt/Worth						1.6
		NM		4.3	2.1							6.3
				72.0	57.1							108.3
			(19)	30.7	(19) 23.3	% Profit Before Taxes/Tangible Net Worth					(13)	34.9
				12.1	5.3							-2.8
		19.4		20.9	16.7							17.6
		1.7		12.0	10.0	% Profit Before Taxes/Total Assets						11.9
		-3.0		5.7	2.3							-1.2
		26.7		16.4	15.8							12.4
		13.1		8.6	9.5	Sales/Net Fixed Assets						9.2
		7.4		5.2	4.8							4.7
		3.9		2.1	2.1							2.3
		2.1		1.8	1.8	Sales/Total Assets						2.0
		1.8		1.3	1.5							1.5
				.9	1.2							1.3
			(17)	1.7	(18) 1.8	% Depr., Dep., Amort./Sales					(13)	1.6
				3.6	2.7							2.9
						% Officers', Directors' Owners' Comp/Sales						
		581567M		1569682M	1854738M	Net Sales ($)		4203M		82226M		1768309M
		246315M		903375M	882712M	Total Assets ($)		2723M		53841M		826148M

M = $ thousand   MM = $ million
See Pages viii through xx for Explanation of Ratios and Data
© RMA 2024

MANUFACTURING—Sanitary Paper Product Manufacturing NAICS 322291

Current Data Sorted by Assets

0-500M	500M-2MM	2-10MM	10-50MM	50-100MM	100-250MM
	1	3	5 (10/1/23-3/31/24)	1	
	5 (4/1-9/30/23)		17 (10/1/23-3/31/24)	1	3
			5	7	
1					
%	%	%	%	%	%
1	1	3	6	9	3

DATA NOT AVAILABLE

Comparative Historical Data

	1	2
Type of Statement		
Unqualified	1	2
Reviewed	1	1
Compiled	1	1
Tax Returns	1	
Other	13	9
	4/1/19-3/31/20 ALL	4/1/20-3/31/21 ALL
NUMBER OF STATEMENTS	17	13
ASSETS	%	%
Cash & Equivalents	8.8	5.6
Trade Receivables (net)	29.0	21.8
Inventory	17.8	23.8
All Other Current	.5	2.7
Total Current	56.1	54.0
Fixed Assets (net)	35.9	36.4
Intangibles (net)	3.5	5.0
All Other Non-Current	4.5	4.7
Total	100.0	100.0
LIABILITIES		
Notes Payable-Short Term	3.3	5.7
Cur. Mat.-L.T.D.	2.8	6.5
Trade Payables	16.0	15.3
Income Taxes Payable	.0	.0
All Other Current	7.8	8.7
Total Current	29.8	36.2
Long-Term Debt	30.6	26.4
Deferred Taxes	.6	.8
All Other Non-Current	2.1	3.2
Net Worth	36.8	33.4
Total Liabilities & Net Worth	100.0	100.0
INCOME DATA		
Net Sales	100.0	100.0
Gross Profit	23.5	20.2
Operating Expenses	15.6	16.6
Operating Profit	7.9	3.6
All Other Expenses (net)	1.5	1.4
Profit Before Taxes	6.4	2.2
RATIOS		
Current	2.7	1.9
	1.8	1.7
	1.4	1.2
Quick	1.5	.9
	1.2	.7
	.9	.5
Sales/Receivables	32 11.3	32 11.4
	39 9.4	39 9.3
	69 5.3	49 7.4
Cost of Sales/Inventory	33 10.9	51 7.1
	56 6.5	65 5.6
	66 5.5	79 4.6
Cost of Sales/Payables	17 21.9	25 14.8
	25 14.7	33 11.1
	51 7.2	51 7.1
Sales/Working Capital	5.2	5.3
	7.1	8.6
	14.7	30.4
EBIT/Interest	14.3	6.5
	(15) 6.4	(12) .6
	3.4	-8.1
Net Profit + Depr., Dep., Amort./Cur. Mat. L/T/D		
Fixed/Worth	.3	.9
	1.0	1.4
	3.1	2.6
Debt/Worth	.9	1.3
	2.1	3.0
	5.3	5.0
% Profit Before Taxes/Tangible Net Worth	71.2	60.1
	33.0	14.2
	13.7	-26.4
% Profit Before Taxes/Total Assets	14.9	14.5
	9.5	1.2
	3.6	-6.5
Sales/Net Fixed Assets	20.2	8.0
	6.2	4.1
	1.9	3.2
Sales/Total Assets	2.5	2.0
	1.8	1.7
	1.0	1.2
% Depr., Dep., Amort./Sales	1.5	2.6
	(10) 2.3	(11) 3.8
	3.3	5.1
% Officers', Directors' Owners' Comp/Sales		

	500M-2MM	2-10MM	10-50MM	50-100MM	100-250MM		Historical 1	Historical 2
Net Sales ($)	1319M	31097M	294864M	874216M	768320M		1381488M	1063979M
Total Assets ($)	552M	10195M	167700M	658682M	660983M		996161M	825626M

M = $ thousand   MM = $ million
See Pages viii through xx for Explanation of Ratios and Data

© RMA 2024

MANUFACTURING—Sanitary Paper Product Manufacturing NAICS 322291

Comparative Historical Data

			Type of Statement						
		2	Unqualified						2
2	1	1	Reviewed						1
1	2	1	Compiled						
	2	1	Tax Returns						
6	6	18	Other						14
4/1/21-	4/1/22-	4/1/23-			5 (4/1-9/30/23)		17 (10/1/23-3/31/24)	3	
3/31/22	3/31/23	3/31/24							
ALL	ALL	ALL		0-1MM	1-3MM	3-5MM	5-10MM	10-25MM	25MM & OVER
9	11	22	NUMBER OF STATEMENTS	1			1	3	17
%	%	%	ASSETS	%	%	%	%	%	%
	8.5	7.1	Cash & Equivalents						3.7
	16.4	15.4	Trade Receivables (net)						15.6
	31.1	23.7	Inventory						21.9
	2.4	3.2	All Other Current						.8
	58.3	49.6	Total Current						42.0
	27.0	33.4	Fixed Assets (net)						39.5
	9.0	6.2	Intangibles (net)						7.0
	5.7	10.7	All Other Non-Current						11.4
	100.0	100.0	Total						100.0
			LIABILITIES						
	7.5	9.0	Notes Payable-Short Term						8.9
	5.6	8.0	Cur. Mat.-L.T.D.						10.0
	12.7	13.1	Trade Payables						11.0
	.0	.0	Income Taxes Payable						.0
	7.3	7.7	All Other Current						6.9
	33.1	37.8	Total Current						36.8
	17.4	27.0	Long-Term Debt						28.5
	.2	.0	Deferred Taxes						.0
	3.4	6.2	All Other Non-Current						7.8
	45.8	29.0	Net Worth						26.9
	100.0	100.0	Total Liabilties & Net Worth						100.0
			INCOME DATA						
	100.0	100.0	Net Sales						100.0
	21.2	26.2	Gross Profit						21.7
	19.5	21.5	Operating Expenses						18.1
	1.7	4.8	Operating Profit						3.6
	.6	2.3	All Other Expenses (net)						2.7
	1.1	2.5	Profit Before Taxes						.9
			RATIOS						
	2.8	2.5							2.3
	1.9	1.5	Current						1.4
	1.0	.6							.6
	1.2	1.3							1.0
	.6	.6	Quick						.6
	.3	.2							.2
25	14.5	23 15.6						33	11.1
28	12.9	34 10.6	Sales/Receivables					36	10.1
41	8.9	51 7.1						51	7.1
64	5.7	59 6.2						59	6.2
72	5.1	70 5.2	Cost of Sales/Inventory					70	5.2
91	4.0	89 4.1						89	4.1
22	16.3	25 14.8						25	14.8
33	10.9	38 9.6	Cost of Sales/Payables					38	9.5
49	7.5	47 7.7						47	7.7
	4.9	5.2							6.0
	7.2	9.3	Sales/Working Capital						10.1
	155.8	-7.7							-6.3
	13.3	8.0							5.2
(10)	2.3	2.2	EBIT/Interest						2.1
	-1.6	1.4							.7
		11.8	Net Profit + Depr., Dep.,						11.8
	(10)	1.0	Amort./Cur. Mat. L/T/D					(10)	1.0
		.3							.3
	.2	.4							.7
	1.1	1.6	Fixed/Worth						1.8
	2.1	20.5							37.8
	.8	1.3							1.8
	1.0	3.3	Debt/Worth						3.3
	4.1	52.0							55.2
	30.1	45.6	% Profit Before Taxes/Tangible						31.4
(10)	15.5	(18) 23.9	Net Worth					(14)	23.9
	-4.1	11.1							11.0
	15.7	9.2	% Profit Before Taxes/Total						7.2
	2.2	4.3	Assets						3.7
	-4.2	1.9							-2.3
	27.4	8.8							6.8
	4.4	4.6	Sales/Net Fixed Assets						3.8
	2.0	2.3							2.1
	2.8	2.2							1.8
	1.6	1.6	Sales/Total Assets						1.4
	1.0	1.2							1.1
		2.0							2.0
	(15)	2.6	% Depr., Dep., Amort./Sales					(14)	2.6
		2.7							2.7
			% Officers', Directors',						
			Owners' Comp/Sales						
831948M	944813M	1969816M	Net Sales ($)		1319M		6356M	46673M	1915468M
548739M	755934M	1498112M	Total Assets ($)		552M		2589M	19208M	1475763M

© RMA 2024   M = $ thousand   MM = $ million
See Pages viii through xx for Explanation of Ratios and Data

MANUFACTURING—All Other Converted Paper Product Manufacturing NAICS 322299

Current Data Sorted by Assets | Comparative Historical Data

0-500M	500M-2MM	2-10MM	10-50MM	50-100MM	100-250MM	Type of Statement		
		2	2		2	Unqualified	6	1
		1	6			Reviewed	12	3
		7	2		8	Compiled	3	1
	9 (4/1-9/30/23)	14	14	6		Tax Returns	7	4
			41 (10/1/23-3/31/24)			Other	30	19
							4/1/19-3/31/20	4/1/20-3/31/21
		10	24	6	10	NUMBER OF STATEMENTS	58 ALL	28 ALL
%	%	%	%	%	%	ASSETS	%	%
D	D	14.9	6.7		18.2	Cash & Equivalents	7.4	17.7
A	A	23.5	16.9		17.6	Trade Receivables (net)	26.1	18.7
T	T	29.1	29.7		16.8	Inventory	26.0	19.3
A	A	.2	1.0		2.4	All Other Current	1.0	1.0
		67.8	54.3		55.1	Total Current	60.4	56.8
N	N	21.1	24.5		20.9	Fixed Assets (net)	29.9	31.0
O	O	7.6	7.3		12.1	Intangibles (net)	6.1	8.4
T	T	3.6	13.9		11.9	All Other Non-Current	3.6	3.8
		100.0	100.0		100.0	Total	100.0	100.0
A	A					LIABILITIES		
V	V	2.6	5.1		.7	Notes Payable-Short Term	6.9	3.7
A	A	2.1	2.6		1.2	Cur. Mat.-L.T.D.	5.3	3.2
I	I	11.0	12.1		6.3	Trade Payables	18.5	11.0
L	L	.7	.0		.2	Income Taxes Payable	.0	.2
A	A	4.9	7.1		7.2	All Other Current	5.5	4.2
B	B	21.4	26.9		15.5	Total Current	36.3	22.4
L	L	20.3	17.5		29.8	Long-Term Debt	15.2	19.1
E	E	.0	.5		2.3	Deferred Taxes	.3	.3
		.3	10.2		34.4	All Other Non-Current	3.7	2.3
		58.0	44.9		18.0	Net Worth	44.6	56.0
		100.0	100.0		100.0	Total Liabilities & Net Worth	100.0	100.0
						INCOME DATA		
		100.0	100.0		100.0	Net Sales	100.0	100.0
		20.6	26.8		23.5	Gross Profit	22.6	27.8
		18.4	21.6		19.2	Operating Expenses	18.4	21.0
		2.2	5.1		4.3	Operating Profit	4.2	6.9
		.6	2.3		2.0	All Other Expenses (net)	.9	.1
		1.6	2.8		2.4	Profit Before Taxes	3.3	6.7
						RATIOS		
		5.0	4.3		5.7		3.0	5.0
		3.6	1.8		3.9	Current	1.7	2.6
		2.3	1.3		1.1		1.2	1.7
		3.4	1.7		3.6		1.9	2.8
		1.8	.9		2.9	Quick	1.0	1.8
		1.0	.6		.6		.5	1.0
		31 11.6	22 16.7	34 10.6		Sales/Receivables	25 14.7	23 16.1
		36 10.1	37 9.8	43 8.5			36 10.2	35 10.4
		55 6.6	50 7.3	59 6.2			45 8.2	46 7.9
		23 16.2	40 9.2	20 18.5		Cost of Sales/Inventory	37 9.9	25 14.8
		65 5.6	64 5.7	72 5.1			54 6.7	54 6.7
		126 2.9	146 2.5	81 4.5			76 4.8	72 5.1
		21 17.6	16 23.0	15 24.3		Cost of Sales/Payables	17 21.1	14 25.4
		28 13.0	26 14.1	22 16.9			26 13.8	23 16.1
		34 10.8	42 8.6	31 11.9			39 9.4	36 10.0
		2.5	3.1		2.6	Sales/Working Capital	5.0	3.3
		3.1	7.0		2.9		9.7	5.8
		8.5	19.1		NM		25.2	11.0
			27.8			EBIT/Interest	16.4	50.0
		(20)	4.5				(52) 5.9	(22) 6.9
			2.0				.9	-.5
						Net Profit + Depr., Dep., Amort./Cur. Mat. L/T/D	14.4	
							(15) 2.1	
							1.1	
		.1	.3		.3	Fixed/Worth	.3	.3
		.5	.6		.4		.7	.7
		.9	2.1		-.7		1.3	1.2
		.2	.4		.2	Debt/Worth	.5	.3
		.8	1.5		.4		1.3	1.3
		1.8	6.7		-2.6		5.2	2.4
			24.5			% Profit Before Taxes/Tangible Net Worth	36.5	55.9
		(22)	15.6				(50) 19.8	(27) 16.7
			6.5				4.8	.0
		28.4	11.9		12.4	% Profit Before Taxes/Total Assets	19.2	26.8
		1.6	6.5		8.1		7.8	11.5
		-8.0	1.3		1.6		-.4	.4
		21.1	23.2		10.7	Sales/Net Fixed Assets	19.8	11.5
		7.0	9.6		5.7		9.9	5.4
		6.2	3.9		4.6		4.7	3.3
		2.1	2.1		1.7	Sales/Total Assets	3.3	2.3
		1.8	1.5		1.5		2.3	1.8
		1.1	1.1		.6		1.5	1.2
			.6			% Depr., Dep., Amort./Sales	.6	1.7
		(19)	1.4				(53) 1.7	(23) 2.8
			4.3				3.1	4.7
						% Officers', Directors' Owners' Comp/Sales	.8	
							(11) 2.4	
							6.2	
		120737M	1021687M	724009M	2240840M	Net Sales ($)	3118366M	912221M
		64792M	606821M	461176M	1682028M	Total Assets ($)	1550195M	500947M

M = $ thousand MM = $ million
See Pages viii through xx for Explanation of Ratios and Data

© RMA 2024

MANUFACTURING—All Other Converted Paper Product Manufacturing NAICS 322299

Comparative Historical Data / Current Data Sorted by Sales

				Type of Statement						
	4	5	4	Unqualified					1	3
	5	8	8	Reviewed			1		2	5
	1	2		Compiled						1
	1	2	3	Tax Returns				2	2	
	30	26	35	Other				2	9	24
	4/1/21-3/31/22 ALL	4/1/22-3/31/23 ALL	4/1/23-3/31/24 ALL		9 (4/1-9/30/23) 0-1MM	1-3MM	3-5MM	5-10MM	41 (10/1/23-3/31/24) 10-25MM	25MM & OVER
	41	43	50	NUMBER OF STATEMENTS			1	4	12	33
	%	%	%	ASSETS	%	%	%	%	%	%
	11.6	6.3	10.6	Cash & Equivalents					9.7	9.4
	21.2	19.6	18.6	Trade Receivables (net)	D	D			18.5	19.2
	21.5	28.1	25.7	Inventory	A	A			21.3	27.8
	2.3	1.5	1.2	All Other Current	T	T			.5	1.6
	56.7	55.6	56.0	Total Current	A	A			50.0	57.9
	29.9	26.7	23.6	Fixed Assets (net)					23.5	24.0
	8.2	9.7	8.6	Intangibles (net)	N	N			11.9	6.2
	5.3	7.9	11.8	All Other Non-Current	O	O			14.6	11.9
	100.0	100.0	100.0	Total	T	T			100.0	100.0
				LIABILITIES	A	A				
	5.5	3.7	4.1	Notes Payable-Short Term	V	V			1.5	4.8
	3.6	3.0	2.2	Cur. Mat.-L.T.D.	A	A			2.9	2.2
	13.8	13.9	10.5	Trade Payables	I	I			8.2	11.8
	.1	.1	.2	Income Taxes Payable	L	L			.6	.1
	6.2	7.0	6.7	All Other Current	A	A			5.2	7.7
	29.2	27.7	23.6	Total Current	B	B			18.4	26.6
	18.4	19.4	19.8	Long-Term Debt	L	L			14.6	18.6
	.3	.0	.7	Deferred Taxes	E	E			1.0	.7
	3.9	3.8	14.2	All Other Non-Current					6.3	19.2
	48.2	49.0	41.7	Net Worth					59.7	34.9
	100.0	100.0	100.0	Total Liabilities & Net Worth					100.0	100.0
				INCOME DATA						
	100.0	100.0	100.0	Net Sales					100.0	100.0
	23.8	24.2	24.3	Gross Profit					32.2	22.2
	17.5	18.0	19.5	Operating Expenses					25.9	17.1
	6.3	6.1	4.8	Operating Profit					6.4	5.1
	-.6	2.2	1.6	All Other Expenses (net)					3.5	1.1
	7.0	3.9	3.1	Profit Before Taxes					2.8	4.0
				RATIOS						
	4.1	3.4	5.3						4.6	5.5
	1.9	1.9	2.6	Current					2.6	1.8
	1.2	1.3	1.3						1.5	1.0
	2.4	1.7	2.9						2.4	2.9
	1.1	.9	1.1	Quick					1.6	.9
	.6	.6	.6						.8	.6
29	12.4	24	15.4	31	11.6				28	13.0	32	11.4
37	9.8	37	9.8	37	9.8	Sales/Receivables			34	10.7	38	9.6
46	7.9	51	7.2	51	7.2				48	7.6	54	6.7
26	14.0	38	9.7	41	8.9				38	9.6	47	7.7
54	6.8	64	5.7	63	5.8	Cost of Sales/Inventory			65	5.6	63	5.8
79	4.6	104	3.5	99	3.7				101	3.6	94	3.9
16	22.3	17	21.8	15	24.2				4	102.5	19	18.9
29	12.4	31	11.9	26	14.1	Cost of Sales/Payables			21	17.7	25	14.5
44	8.3	47	7.7	39	9.3				29	12.4	46	7.9
	3.7		3.7		2.8					3.6		2.8
	8.4		7.5		4.9	Sales/Working Capital				6.6		6.3
	27.8		19.8		20.4					13.3		NM
	51.3		21.2		38.1							38.1
(36)	12.3	(39)	6.7	(43)	4.3	EBIT/Interest					(31)	5.6
	3.9		2.2		.7							2.1
			4.7		11.0	Net Profit + Depr., Dep.,						15.4
		(10)	3.3	(12)	4.4	Amort./Cur. Mat. L/T/D					(10)	3.5
			2.7		1.9							1.5
	.3		.3		.3					.1		.3
	.7		.7		.4	Fixed/Worth				.6		.4
	1.6		2.0		2.3					1.3		3.0
	.3		.3		.3					.2		.3
	1.3		1.5		1.0	Debt/Worth				.5		1.4
	3.2		4.5		5.6					1.7		7.8
	41.9		39.7		32.0	% Profit Before Taxes/Tangible				37.3		34.7
(37)	28.3	(37)	25.5	(43)	13.1	Net Worth			(10)	12.9	(29)	13.3
	11.8		6.6		4.2					4.0		7.7
	21.8		14.2		12.3	% Profit Before Taxes/Total				23.1		12.5
	13.3		6.7		6.6	Assets				5.1		7.8
	3.0		2.8		.0					-2.3		1.7
	12.2		14.1		18.5					36.4		18.1
	7.0		7.1		6.8	Sales/Net Fixed Assets				8.7		6.4
	4.1		4.3		4.6					4.4		4.6
	2.6		2.6		2.0					2.2		2.0
	1.9		2.0		1.5	Sales/Total Assets				1.9		1.5
	1.4		1.3		1.1					1.0		1.2
	1.3		.5		.6							.5
(36)	2.9	(32)	2.1	(39)	1.9	% Depr., Dep., Amort./Sales					(26)	1.9
	5.1		5.5		4.9							4.1
						% Officers', Directors'						
						Owners' Comp/Sales						
	2203099M	3162555M	4107273M	Net Sales ($)			4314M	31333M	202875M	3868751M
	1374956M	1837065M	2814817M	Total Assets ($)			3150M	31299M	155956M	2624412M

© RMA 2024 M = $ thousand MM = $ million
See Pages viii through xx for Explanation of Ratios and Data

MANUFACTURING—Commercial Printing (except Screen and Books) NAICS 323111

Current Data Sorted by Assets | Comparative Historical Data

							Type of Statement				
		1	3	8	9		Unqualified		35		22
	2	14	33	2			Reviewed		62		35
1	3	13	2				Compiled		48		22
9	11	27					Tax Returns		81		43
4	22	58	59	15	12		Other		261		157
	51 (4/1-9/30/23)		257 (10/1/23-3/31/24)						4/1/19-3/31/20		4/1/20-3/31/21
0-500M	500M-2MM	2-10MM	10-50MM	50-100MM	100-250MM				ALL		ALL
14	39	115	102	26	12		NUMBER OF STATEMENTS		487		279
%	%	%	%	%	%		ASSETS		%		%
29.5	28.0	18.8	13.2	8.8	9.8		Cash & Equivalents		12.4		19.6
30.3	29.0	22.3	23.0	16.1	20.8		Trade Receivables (net)		27.5		23.3
10.0	8.6	12.7	15.3	14.2	14.7		Inventory		11.3		10.8
2.8	1.1	4.6	2.6	7.7	1.7		All Other Current		2.2		2.2
72.6	66.7	58.4	54.1	46.8	46.9		Total Current		53.4		55.9
22.0	21.9	28.2	30.4	31.2	22.6		Fixed Assets (net)		33.1		30.4
3.1	4.2	5.2	5.9	12.0	13.3		Intangibles (net)		7.7		8.1
2.3	7.2	8.2	9.6	10.0	17.2		All Other Non-Current		5.8		5.6
100.0	100.0	100.0	100.0	100.0	100.0		Total		100.0		100.0
							LIABILITIES				
13.8	5.1	4.5	4.4	3.0	5.2		Notes Payable-Short Term		7.3		6.9
1.2	2.5	4.7	4.3	3.0	3.1		Cur. Mat.-L.T.D.		5.1		4.9
16.3	12.5	11.4	8.7	9.2	11.1		Trade Payables		14.6		11.2
.3	.2	.1	.2	.1	.6		Income Taxes Payable		.1		.1
15.3	17.0	8.1	11.8	8.1	13.1		All Other Current		10.9		8.7
46.8	37.2	28.7	29.5	23.5	33.1		Total Current		38.0		31.7
45.1	22.9	22.2	15.7	24.4	20.3		Long-Term Debt		23.8		28.6
.0	.0	.1	.5	1.3	.2		Deferred Taxes		.4		.2
7.0	2.8	3.4	9.4	4.6	8.9		All Other Non-Current		5.0		6.7
1.1	37.1	45.6	45.0	46.2	37.5		Net Worth		32.8		32.7
100.0	100.0	100.0	100.0	100.0	100.0		Total Liabilities & Net Worth		100.0		100.0
							INCOME DATA				
100.0	100.0	100.0	100.0	100.0	100.0		Net Sales		100.0		100.0
40.6	51.7	40.6	30.8	26.2	30.2		Gross Profit		36.5		37.7
36.5	42.7	35.9	25.5	20.0	23.3		Operating Expenses		32.0		34.0
4.1	9.1	4.8	5.4	6.2	6.8		Operating Profit		4.5		3.7
.2	.3	.4	.7	2.8	1.5		All Other Expenses (net)		.8		-1.1
3.9	8.8	4.4	4.7	3.4	5.3		Profit Before Taxes		3.7		4.8
							RATIOS				
6.6	5.1	3.2	3.0	3.3	2.9				2.5		3.2
1.6	2.4	2.3	1.9	2.0	1.8		Current		1.6		2.0
.9	1.0	1.5	1.3	1.5	.8				1.0		1.2
3.5	4.4	2.6	2.1	1.6	1.6				1.9		2.5
1.5	2.1	1.6	1.3	1.1	1.0		Quick		1.1		1.5
.8	.8	1.0	.8	.8	.5				.7		.9
0 UND	12 30.4	26 13.9	36 10.0	33 11.2	37 9.8			30	12.0	30	12.1
11 32.5	30 12.1	40 9.1	46 8.0	43 8.5	49 7.4		Sales/Receivables	42	8.7	42	8.6
24 15.1	41 8.9	51 7.2	59 6.2	55 6.6	54 6.7			56	6.5	54	6.7
0 UND	0 UND	9 38.7	23 15.7	31 11.8	28 13.1			9	39.8	10	38.3
0 UND	7 52.8	30 12.2	41 8.9	47 7.7	40 9.1		Cost of Sales/Inventory	24	15.5	27	13.6
23 15.9	35 10.5	53 6.9	68 5.4	58 6.3	59 6.2			39	9.3	45	8.1
0 UND	3 112.8	19 19.2	14 26.6	19 18.8	20 18.2			16	23.1	15	23.7
3 106.7	14 25.2	29 12.7	23 15.9	32 11.3	33 11.2		Cost of Sales/Payables	30	12.3	27	13.3
16 22.7	30 12.0	48 7.6	37 9.9	42 8.6	47 7.7			47	7.7	41	8.9
10.1	4.6	4.3	4.5	4.5	5.0				6.5		4.4
21.9	9.1	7.2	7.2	6.4	13.1		Sales/Working Capital		14.1		8.6
-121.7	-251.3	14.8	14.4	9.4	-11.1				-119.3		24.5
40.5	32.8	14.1	23.6	29.4	28.6				13.7		19.0
(10) 7.1	(28) 7.3	(107) 4.2	(94) 5.3	(25) 4.2	11.1		EBIT/Interest	(449)	3.9	(255)	5.6
-.3	2.4	-.4	2.3	1.2	2.5				1.0		.1
		8.2	8.3	8.2			Net Profit + Depr., Dep.,		4.4		5.4
	(17) 2.4	(29) 3.7	(12) 2.8				Amort./Cur. Mat. L/T/D	(103)	2.4	(40)	3.0
		1.2	1.6	1.3					1.3		.9
.2	.0	.2	.3	.4	.4				.5		.4
2.5	.4	.7	.7	1.2	.8		Fixed/Worth		1.1		1.1
-3.0	2.1	1.2	2.0	2.9	3.8				4.3		4.4
1.5	.4	.5	.6	.6	1.2				.7		.8
8.4	1.4	1.0	1.1	2.1	3.0		Debt/Worth		1.7		2.0
-5.5	10.9	3.1	3.1	6.8	11.2				9.0		12.4
237.4	75.3	47.6	34.1	37.9	55.8		% Profit Before Taxes/Tangible		45.1		55.8
(10) 43.1	(31) 51.4	(105) 11.7	(90) 16.8	(21) 18.6	(11) 27.8		Net Worth	(399)	20.5	(220)	24.0
-243.4	25.3	-1.1	5.2	14.4	9.5				2.8		2.5
80.3	41.3	18.8	13.5	13.3	13.1		% Profit Before Taxes/Total		15.8		19.0
21.2	21.9	4.9	7.5	7.4	10.3		Assets		5.9		8.1
-7.3	6.0	-1.1	1.9	-1.4	4.0				.2		-1.3
999.8	183.5	26.7	12.7	6.8	14.3				15.3		15.7
108.1	24.6	10.0	5.9	4.8	8.8		Sales/Net Fixed Assets		7.3		7.1
16.3	7.1	3.6	3.3	2.7	3.7				4.2		3.6
14.4	5.1	2.8	2.2	1.9	2.1				3.1		2.5
8.6	2.9	2.1	1.7	1.5	1.5		Sales/Total Assets		2.3		1.9
3.2	2.3	1.5	1.2	1.0	1.2				1.7		1.4
	.2	2.0	1.4	2.3					2.1		2.0
	(19) 1.5	(84) 3.3	(95) 2.9	(25) 3.6			% Depr., Dep., Amort./Sales	(390)	3.7	(216)	3.7
		5.4	4.5	4.6	5.8				5.5		5.6
	2.6	1.9	.6				% Officers', Directors'		1.7		1.9
	(17) 4.3	(56) 3.9	(19) 1.2				Owners' Comp/Sales	(198)	3.1	(108)	3.8
	5.4								6.0		
38232M	159121M	1298667M	3932463M	2398465M	2869525M		Net Sales ($)		14396132M		7167903M
3906M	43535M	611027M	2367250M	1711474M	1809838M		Total Assets ($)		7808954M		4861746M

© RMA 2024

M = $ thousand   MM = $ million
See Pages viii through xx for Explanation of Ratios and Data

MANUFACTURING—Commercial Printing (except Screen and Books) NAICS 323111

Comparative Historical Data / Current Data Sorted by Sales

				Type of Statement						
19	27		21	Unqualified			2	2	1	16
42	58		51	Reviewed			2	6	12	31
28	30		19	Compiled		1	3	7	5	2
50	63		47	Tax Returns	1	6	6	20	10	1
153	184		170	Other	4	9	16	28	39	75
4/1/21-3/31/22 ALL	4/1/22-3/31/23 ALL		4/1/23-3/31/24 ALL		3					
						51 (4/1-9/30/23)		257 (10/1/23-3/31/24)		
					0-1MM	1-3MM	3-5MM	5-10MM	10-25MM	25MM & OVER
292	362		308	NUMBER OF STATEMENTS	8	16	29	63	67	125
%	%		%	**ASSETS**	%	%	%	%	%	%
16.8	17.3		17.4	Cash & Equivalents		35.1	23.5	18.8	16.5	12.7
25.5	24.2		23.1	Trade Receivables (net)		23.5	20.6	26.6	21.6	22.9
12.9	15.6		13.1	Inventory		3.2	8.3	14.0	13.2	15.4
2.0	3.5		3.5	All Other Current		.1	2.6	2.8	4.5	4.0
57.3	60.6		57.3	Total Current		61.9	55.0	62.1	55.9	54.9
29.3	26.4		27.9	Fixed Assets (net)		19.8	33.0	26.5	26.9	28.9
6.8	6.2		6.1	Intangibles (net)		14.7	3.5	3.7	7.0	6.5
6.6	6.8		8.8	All Other Non-Current		3.5	8.5	7.7	10.2	9.6
100.0	100.0		100.0	Total		100.0	100.0	100.0	100.0	100.0
				LIABILITIES						
4.5	4.8		4.9	Notes Payable-Short Term		4.8	2.8	5.1	4.7	4.5
4.1	3.8		3.9	Cur. Mat.-L.T.D.		3.4	4.1	4.2	3.9	4.0
13.0	11.7		10.7	Trade Payables		6.6	9.5	11.3	13.1	10.1
.1	.2		.1	Income Taxes Payable		.5	.0	.0	.1	.2
10.7	11.1		11.0	All Other Current		24.4	9.6	7.6	12.3	10.8
32.5	31.6		30.6	Total Current		39.7	26.0	28.3	34.2	29.6
25.0	22.6		21.3	Long-Term Debt		29.4	28.1	21.3	19.3	18.0
.3	.4		.3	Deferred Taxes		.0	.0	.0	.2	.7
7.7	6.4		5.8	All Other Non-Current		4.6	2.7	2.4	7.0	7.9
34.5	39.0		42.0	Net Worth		26.3	43.1	48.0	39.4	43.9
100.0	100.0		100.0	Total Liabilities & Net Worth		100.0	100.0	100.0	100.0	100.0
				INCOME DATA						
100.0	100.0		100.0	Net Sales		100.0	100.0	100.0	100.0	100.0
38.3	37.8		37.2	Gross Profit		52.2	49.1	44.4	35.0	29.0
32.5	30.8		31.5	Operating Expenses		44.4	43.8	38.9	31.3	23.0
5.8	7.0		5.7	Operating Profit		7.8	5.3	5.4	3.8	6.0
-2.5	-.1		.7	All Other Expenses (net)		1.5	-.3	.2	.6	1.2
8.3	7.1		5.0	Profit Before Taxes		6.2	5.6	5.2	3.2	4.8
				RATIOS						
3.1	3.8		3.4			3.3	4.8	4.1	2.8	3.0
1.9	2.1		2.1	Current		1.8	2.6	2.5	2.1	1.9
1.2	1.3		1.4			.8	1.2	1.6	1.2	1.3
2.3	2.7		2.3			3.2	3.5	3.1	2.1	1.9
1.2	1.4		1.4	Quick		1.7	2.1	1.7	1.6	1.3
.9	.8		.8			.7	1.0	1.1	.7	.8
32 11.4	29 12.4	29	12.6		12 29.4	14 25.9	31 11.6	31 11.8	34 10.8	
45 8.2	41 8.8	41	8.9	Sales/Receivables	22 16.9	30 12.1	38 9.6	41 8.8	45 8.2	
57 6.4	55 6.6	53	6.9		52 7.0	43 8.5	55 6.6	56 6.5	54 6.7	
12 29.2	13 28.1	12	31.5		0 UND	0 UND	4 98.0	14 26.6	25 14.4	
32 11.3	40 9.1	33	11.0	Cost of Sales/Inventory	7 55.2	10 38.1	37 9.9	33 11.0	41 8.9	
54 6.7	65 5.6	56	6.5		13 27.6	36 10.1	54 6.7	54 6.7	60 6.1	
17 22.0	15 25.1	14	26.6		0 UND	4 90.1	16 23.1	18 19.8	15 23.6	
30 12.0	26 14.2	25	14.6	Cost of Sales/Payables	13 27.3	22 16.9	29 12.5	26 14.1	25 14.6	
46 7.9	43 8.5	40	9.1		32 11.5	51 7.1	49 7.5	43 8.4	38 9.5	
5.0	4.6		4.5			4.8	4.4	4.3	4.6	4.7
8.4	7.2		7.5	Sales/Working Capital		17.4	9.1	7.1	7.3	7.6
26.0	17.2		18.2			NM	NM	13.9	18.5	16.7
	28.9	28.5		20.4			24.8	14.8	20.0	24.1
(255) 11.3	(312) 10.7	(276)	5.9	EBIT/Interest		(25) 4.5	(57) 5.9	(60) 6.6	(119) 5.4	
3.9	3.3		1.2				.3	-.3	.7	2.0
	12.3	7.0		9.3	Net Profit + Depr., Dep.,		7.1			8.6	
(43) 5.4	(60) 3.2	(63)	3.4	Amort./Cur. Mat. L/T/D		(11) 2.0		(41) 3.6		
2.9	1.9		1.5					1.0		1.6
.4	.3		.2			.0	.2	.1	.2	.3
.9	.7		.7	Fixed/Worth		.5	.6	.6	.8	.7
2.1	2.0		2.0			14.3	3.4	1.1	2.5	2.0
.7	.6		.6			.7	.3	.5	.7	.6
1.7	1.4		1.2	Debt/Worth		3.4	1.2	.9	1.4	1.2
5.9	4.0		3.7			NM	7.0	2.9	5.2	3.3
77.5	56.8		49.9	% Profit Before Taxes/Tangible		223.3	74.4	50.7	38.1	40.7
(246) 40.5	(307) 30.3	(268)	18.7	Net Worth	(12) 61.9	(25) 31.1	(58) 17.7	(55) 11.7	(111) 18.6	
17.6	13.2		5.1			26.9	5.8	-.9	1.4	5.7
27.4	23.7		19.5	% Profit Before Taxes/Total		46.2	34.5	21.2	16.4	14.8
15.3	12.1		7.5	Assets		11.0	6.5	8.1	5.8	7.8
6.2	4.9		.8			-4.0	.9	-.8	-.5	2.5
18.3	20.7		21.0			135.0	27.6	43.6	23.5	13.3
7.4	8.7		7.8	Sales/Net Fixed Assets		26.9	9.9	11.0	7.3	6.5
3.9	4.6		3.5			7.9	4.0	3.4	3.5	3.3
2.7	2.9		2.7			4.3	4.0	2.9	2.8	2.2
2.0	2.0		2.0	Sales/Total Assets		2.8	2.5	2.2	2.0	1.7
1.5	1.5		1.3			2.2	1.7	1.4	1.3	1.3
1.9	1.5		1.5			1.2	1.1	1.8	1.6	
(218) 3.5	(278) 2.9	(239)	3.1	% Depr., Dep., Amort./Sales	(22) 2.0	(43) 3.3	(50) 3.4	(113) 2.9		
5.2	4.4		4.6				4.9	4.3	4.9	4.5
1.7	1.6		1.7			3.8	2.0	1.5	.7	
(110) 3.5	(141) 3.3	(103)	3.4	% Officers', Directors', Owners' Comp/Sales	(13) 5.5	(31) 3.9	(25) 2.2	(21) 1.5		
6.4	6.0		5.7			7.7	5.3	4.7	4.2	
8119726M	10361919M		10696473M	Net Sales ($)	5541M	28327M	115891M	475495M	1071528M	8999691M
4732395M	5937810M		6547030M	Total Assets ($)	3269M	16196M	52679M	244885M	721893M	5508108M

© RMA 2024   M = $ thousand   MM = $ million
See Pages viii through xx for Explanation of Ratios and Data

MANUFACTURING—Commercial Screen Printing NAICS 323113

Current Data Sorted by Assets | Comparative Historical Data

Type of Statement	0-500M	500M-2MM	2-10MM	10-50MM	50-100MM	100-250MM		4/1/19-3/31/20 ALL	4/1/20-3/31/21 ALL
Unqualified				4	1			2	1
Reviewed	1	1	2	2		1		3	6
Compiled	3	3	4	1				9	10
Tax Returns	2	6	17	19	1	2		10	5
Other		14 (4/1-9/30/23)		56 (10/1/23-3/31/24)				53	23
NUMBER OF STATEMENTS	6	10	23	26	2	3		77	45
	%	%	%	%	%	%	**ASSETS**	%	%
		20.4	18.6	12.4			Cash & Equivalents	14.0	21.5
		20.7	25.6	16.7			Trade Receivables (net)	23.4	21.7
		8.7	17.9	22.9			Inventory	17.2	16.5
		5.1	2.6	2.7			All Other Current	2.2	2.1
		54.9	64.8	54.8			Total Current	56.8	61.8
		30.7	25.0	23.7			Fixed Assets (net)	30.3	28.6
		5.5	4.2	6.3			Intangibles (net)	5.1	4.8
		8.9	6.0	15.2			All Other Non-Current	7.8	4.7
		100.0	100.0	100.0			Total	100.0	100.0
							LIABILITIES		
		17.5	10.3	4.2			Notes Payable-Short Term	9.9	8.8
		1.4	3.5	3.4			Cur. Mat.-L.T.D.	3.9	3.3
		6.2	17.6	14.8			Trade Payables	15.6	12.1
		.0	.2	.2			Income Taxes Payable	.1	.1
		24.4	10.2	15.8			All Other Current	12.4	9.7
		49.5	41.8	38.4			Total Current	41.9	33.9
		32.9	21.1	18.3			Long-Term Debt	19.9	30.6
		.0	.3	.0			Deferred Taxes	.3	.2
		.0	16.7	5.2			All Other Non-Current	8.2	10.2
		17.6	20.0	38.0			Net Worth	29.7	25.1
		100.0	100.0	100.0			Total Liabilities & Net Worth	100.0	100.0
							INCOME DATA		
		100.0	100.0	100.0			Net Sales	100.0	100.0
		60.3	36.7	36.6			Gross Profit	39.6	40.0
		56.7	29.9	29.5			Operating Expenses	34.7	36.6
		3.6	6.8	7.2			Operating Profit	4.9	3.5
		.7	-.2	1.5			All Other Expenses (net)	1.2	-1.7
		2.9	7.0	5.7			Profit Before Taxes	3.7	5.2
							RATIOS		
			3.6	2.9	2.5			2.5	3.7
			1.9	1.7	1.8		Current	1.7	2.1
			1.0	1.0	.8			1.0	1.2
			3.4	1.7	1.8			1.9	2.3
			1.6	1.2	.6		Quick	1.0	1.5
			.3	.6	.5			.6	.7
		0 UND	23 15.7	18 20.8				16 22.5	23 16.1
		19 18.8	38 9.5	25 14.6			Sales/Receivables	30 12.3	36 10.1
		39 9.4	57 6.4	43 8.5				48 7.6	51 7.2
		0 UND	20 18.2	29 12.7				4 100.1	5 80.1
		5 78.7	39 9.3	47 7.8			Cost of Sales/Inventory	26 14.0	37 9.8
		48 7.6	83 4.4	91 4.0				59 6.2	78 4.7
		0 UND	19 19.5	16 23.4				12 29.2	12 29.4
		1 454.9	27 13.5	23 16.2			Cost of Sales/Payables	27 13.3	22 16.9
		81 4.5	60 6.1	56 6.5				48 7.6	35 10.3
			10.4	4.4	3.7			7.0	3.7
			15.3	9.6	8.3		Sales/Working Capital	13.0	6.9
			NM	155.4	-17.1			-184.0	34.3
				18.2	29.9			20.7	31.0
				8.8 (23)	4.3		EBIT/Interest	(65) 4.7	(44) 8.3
				2.4	3.3			1.0	.9
								7.6	
							Net Profit + Depr., Dep., Amort./Cur. Mat. L/T/D	(13) 3.9	
								1.8	
			.5	.2	.2			.5	.5
			2.1	.4	.8		Fixed/Worth	1.0	.8
			-.7	4.7	3.9			25.0	2.3
			1.0	.8	.7			.6	.8
			3.1	1.6	1.0		Debt/Worth	1.8	1.5
			-4.0	6.1	11.7			45.3	6.5
				75.4	44.9			55.9	59.5
			(18) 40.4	(22) 23.2			% Profit Before Taxes/Tangible Net Worth	(59) 31.7	(37) 35.2
				15.0	6.8			7.4	11.8
			27.6	25.1	17.8			23.1	23.1
			7.5	12.5	7.4		% Profit Before Taxes/Total Assets	8.3	11.2
			.5	4.8	3.1			.7	-.2
			50.4	28.1	21.7			19.9	14.2
			9.8	11.6	10.2		Sales/Net Fixed Assets	9.7	8.3
			5.2	5.1	6.3			6.1	4.6
			6.2	3.2	2.9			3.9	3.1
			3.0	2.5	2.1		Sales/Total Assets	2.4	2.0
			1.7	1.5	1.6			2.0	1.6
				1.0	1.2			1.3	1.7
			(16) 1.7	(22) 2.3			% Depr., Dep., Amort./Sales	(64) 2.4	(39) 3.0
				2.7	5.4			4.0	4.3
				1.2				2.0	2.1
			(12) 2.4				% Officers', Directors' Owners' Comp/Sales	(28) 3.4	(17) 3.5
			4.3					5.3	9.5
	19196M	39700M	301103M	1151866M	196648M	491232M	Net Sales ($)	4863016M	562255M
	1612M	10276M	125700M	508815M	110023M	478364M	Total Assets ($)	1765927M	290810M

© RMA 2024 M = $ thousand   MM = $ million
See Pages viii through xx for Explanation of Ratios and Data

MANUFACTURING—Commercial Screen Printing NAICS 323113

Comparative Historical Data | Current Data Sorted by Sales

						Type of Statement						
			1			Unqualified					2	3
			4			Reviewed		2			3	2
			6			Compiled		1		3	3	1
			11			Tax Returns	1	1	1		1	1
			34			Other	2	4	4	6	11	20
			4/1/21-3/31/22 ALL	4/1/22-3/31/23 ALL	4/1/23-3/31/24 ALL		14 (4/1-9/30/23)			56 (10/1/23-3/31/24)		
							0-1MM	1-3MM	3-5MM	5-10MM	10-25MM	25MM & OVER
			56	55	70	NUMBER OF STATEMENTS	3	7	5	9	19	27
			%	%	%	ASSETS	%	%	%	%	%	%
			23.7	20.0	17.6	Cash & Equivalents					15.6	13.1
			23.9	19.2	20.2	Trade Receivables (net)					22.5	18.9
			14.5	17.2	18.4	Inventory					17.1	24.1
			2.6	2.6	3.4	All Other Current					4.9	3.5
			64.8	59.1	59.6	Total Current					60.1	59.6
			21.2	28.0	23.1	Fixed Assets (net)					29.3	18.0
			5.9	5.4	7.6	Intangibles (net)					5.4	8.5
			8.1	7.5	9.7	All Other Non-Current					5.2	13.9
			100.0	100.0	100.0	Total					100.0	100.0
						LIABILITIES						
			5.5	7.4	8.8	Notes Payable-Short Term					7.3	5.0
			2.5	3.9	3.8	Cur. Mat.-L.T.D.					4.0	3.1
			14.5	11.7	14.0	Trade Payables					13.4	16.9
			.7	.4	.2	Income Taxes Payable					.0	.3
			9.8	13.9	18.6	All Other Current					8.9	15.4
			33.0	37.4	45.4	Total Current					33.6	40.7
			30.6	31.4	21.9	Long-Term Debt					22.0	13.4
			.4	.1	.1	Deferred Taxes					.4	.0
			7.2	4.6	13.0	All Other Non-Current					7.8	6.2
			28.8	26.5	19.6	Net Worth					36.1	39.7
			100.0	100.0	100.0	Total Liabilities & Net Worth					100.0	100.0
						INCOME DATA						
			100.0	100.0	100.0	Net Sales					100.0	100.0
			40.2	41.3	40.8	Gross Profit					32.7	33.1
			31.2	34.0	34.5	Operating Expenses					26.4	27.9
			9.1	7.3	6.3	Operating Profit					6.3	5.2
			-2.2	.3	.5	All Other Expenses (net)					-.1	-.3
			11.3	7.0	5.8	Profit Before Taxes					6.4	5.5
						RATIOS						
			4.9	4.6	3.3						3.4	2.4
			2.1	2.2	1.8	Current					1.8	1.8
			1.3	1.4	.9						1.0	.8
			2.7	3.3	1.9						1.8	1.9
			1.6	1.4	1.0	Quick					1.3	.7
			.8	.7	.5						.6	.5
22	16.7	14	25.6	15	23.6						22 16.7	19 19.7
36	10.0	25	14.8	29	12.4	Sales/Receivables					35 10.5	29 12.6
54	6.8	42	8.6	47	7.8						46 7.9	49 7.4
2	175.3	4	89.2	19	19.5						20 18.2	26 13.9
32	11.4	38	9.7	40	9.2	Cost of Sales/Inventory					36 10.0	51 7.1
57	6.4	87	4.2	81	4.5						48 7.6	91 4.0
14	25.5	14	26.0	15	23.7						17 21.6	17 21.2
24	15.0	24	15.3	24	15.3	Cost of Sales/Payables					24 15.3	35 10.4
52	7.0	31	11.6	56	6.5						55 6.6	57 6.4
			3.8	3.9	4.9						4.3	4.2
			8.8	8.8	11.2	Sales/Working Capital					10.2	7.8
			24.3	20.3	-104.9						155.4	-34.6
			34.3	33.7	22.0						23.2	87.7
(43)	13.6	(47)	8.7	(64)	6.3	EBIT/Interest					8.8 (24)	5.8
			2.8	1.4	3.1						2.4	3.3
						123.1	Net Profit + Depr., Dep.,						
					(10)	5.0	Amort./Cur. Mat. L/T/D						
						2.5							
			.2	.2	.2						.2	.1
			.4	.7	.5	Fixed/Worth					1.0	.5
			1.9	2.5	5.0						2.2	3.2
			.6	.5	.7						.8	.6
			1.5	1.6	1.6	Debt/Worth					1.3	1.3
			4.8	8.1	NM						2.4	11.0
			97.9	58.4	61.8						55.6	73.2
(46)	55.3	(46)	34.8	(53)	34.0	% Profit Before Taxes/Tangible Net Worth					(15) 43.0	(23) 34.0
			15.1	12.8	9.9						8.1	7.1
			36.6	28.5	22.8						25.1	22.8
			17.6	16.1	10.3	% Profit Before Taxes/Total Assets					12.5	9.1
			4.6	2.5	3.1						2.6	3.2
			36.2	24.1	28.9						19.3	28.1
			13.8	10.9	12.3	Sales/Net Fixed Assets					7.1	15.6
			6.8	5.6	6.4						4.7	8.2
			3.4	3.4	3.6						3.0	3.2
			2.1	2.3	2.3	Sales/Total Assets					2.3	2.2
			1.8	1.7	1.6						1.5	1.7
			.8	1.2	1.0						.9	.9
(39)	2.3	(44)	2.3	(51)	1.8	% Depr., Dep., Amort./Sales					(17) 2.7	(23) 1.6
			3.5	4.0	3.6						3.7	2.6
			1.0	1.2	1.2							
(23)	2.8	(22)	3.0	(21)	3.0	% Officers', Directors', Owners' Comp/Sales						
			6.7	5.6	4.7							
			1541057M	1813655M	2199745M	Net Sales ($)	2429M	11740M	22030M	65266M	291142M	1807138M
			913160M	869575M	1234790M	Total Assets ($)	826M	18813M	8869M	25506M	150116M	1030660M

© RMA 2024   M = $ thousand   MM = $ million
See Pages viii through xx for Explanation of Ratios and Data

MANUFACTURING—Asphalt Paving Mixture and Block Manufacturing NAICS 324121

Current Data Sorted by Assets | **Comparative Historical Data**

							Type of Statement		
					1	3	Unqualified	11	6
				5	6		Reviewed	17	6
		1		7	1		Compiled	3	4
		6		3			Tax Returns	6	4
1	2	2					Other	37	24
	1	5	13	6	9			4/1/19-	4/1/20-
	19 (4/1-9/30/23)	6	58 (10/1/23-3/31/24)					3/31/20	3/31/21
0-500M	500M-2MM	2-10MM	10-50MM	50-100MM	100-250MM		NUMBER OF STATEMENTS	ALL 74	ALL 44
1	3	20	28	13	12				
%	%	%	%	%	%		ASSETS	%	%
		24.1	15.9	10.3	11.5		Cash & Equivalents	13.5	17.1
		23.0	24.0	26.7	18.0		Trade Receivables (net)	22.4	23.3
		8.2	8.8	9.4	16.0		Inventory	11.9	11.4
		3.8	3.0	3.8	5.5		All Other Current	2.1	2.4
		59.2	51.6	50.3	51.0		Total Current	49.9	54.3
		31.7	39.3	34.4	35.8		Fixed Assets (net)	39.4	36.6
		.9	1.4	6.4	5.4		Intangibles (net)	5.3	5.1
		8.1	7.8	8.9	7.8		All Other Non-Current	5.4	4.0
		100.0	100.0	100.0	100.0		Total	100.0	100.0
							LIABILITIES		
		1.1	2.6	1.7	2.9		Notes Payable-Short Term	3.9	3.9
		6.6	4.5	3.2	3.7		Cur. Mat.-L.T.D.	4.1	5.2
		5.8	8.6	10.0	7.7		Trade Payables	9.8	10.5
		.2	.0	.3	.3		Income Taxes Payable	.1	.1
		7.6	4.0	10.1	9.2		All Other Current	9.9	10.0
		21.4	19.7	25.3	23.7		Total Current	27.8	29.7
		24.1	22.4	14.7	13.7		Long-Term Debt	20.6	20.6
		.4	.4	.9	.3		Deferred Taxes	.3	.6
		2.3	1.7	5.4	1.8		All Other Non-Current	2.0	2.8
		51.8	55.8	53.7	60.5		Net Worth	49.3	46.4
		100.0	100.0	100.0	100.0		Total Liabilities & Net Worth	100.0	100.0
							INCOME DATA		
		100.0	100.0	100.0	100.0		Net Sales	100.0	100.0
		33.7	24.9	25.7	18.9		Gross Profit	23.3	29.8
		24.7	14.3	15.5	11.3		Operating Expenses	15.6	20.3
		9.0	10.6	10.2	7.5		Operating Profit	7.7	9.5
		.4	-.5	1.2	-.2		All Other Expenses (net)	.4	.1
		8.7	11.0	9.0	7.7		Profit Before Taxes	7.3	9.4
							RATIOS		
		6.1	3.8	2.6	2.8			3.2	4.2
		3.5	2.5	1.8	2.2		Current	1.8	1.8
		2.1	1.9	1.6	1.7			1.2	1.3
		4.8	3.1	2.0	1.9			2.5	3.1
		2.9	2.0	1.6	1.4		Quick	1.3	1.4
		1.4	1.4	.8	.6			.8	.8
		14 25.9	32 11.4	26 13.9	16 23.1			19 18.9	20 18.0
		31 11.6	50 7.3	60 6.1	50 7.3		Sales/Receivables	38 9.5	35 10.3
		58 6.3	68 5.4	94 3.9	64 5.7			60 6.1	54 6.7
		0 UND	9 39.4	0 UND	13 27.2			3 121.1	1 604.8
		7 55.3	17 21.1	24 14.9	42 8.6		Cost of Sales/Inventory	20 18.3	20 18.5
		34 10.7	27 13.4	65 5.6	89 4.1			46 8.0	51 7.2
		3 121.1	14 26.2	16 22.9	17 20.9			11 34.5	10 35.1
		10 37.5	24 15.4	28 13.1	23 15.6		Cost of Sales/Payables	19 19.2	22 16.9
		26 14.1	32 11.3	42 8.6	31 11.6			33 11.2	30 12.1
		3.7	3.0	5.1	3.5			5.0	4.6
		6.1	6.0	6.0	6.4		Sales/Working Capital	10.5	8.8
		12.3	8.8	11.6	9.0			22.5	16.1
		47.4	25.7	51.9	37.9			18.1	20.2
		(17) 11.8	(25) 12.3	21.2	11.4		EBIT/Interest	(69) 9.1	(37) 9.3
		4.6	6.3	9.3	4.5			4.2	4.1
			8.5					9.7	7.1
			(10) 4.4				Net Profit + Depr., Dep., Amort./Cur. Mat. L/T/D	(14) 6.5	(11) 3.4
			3.4					3.9	2.1
		.3	.4	.5	.4			.5	.5
		.5	.8	.7	.7		Fixed/Worth	.9	.9
		2.2	1.1	1.2	1.2			1.5	1.3
		.3	.3	.5	.3			.5	.5
		.6	.9	.9	.8		Debt/Worth	1.1	.9
		3.8	1.3	1.9	1.5			2.2	2.4
		57.6	46.3	52.1	28.4			44.2	53.3
	(19)	36.4	30.6	25.3	18.0		% Profit Before Taxes/Tangible Net Worth	(67) 22.5	(41) 33.3
		17.5	14.3	20.4	12.6			10.4	17.1
		32.1	23.9	22.3	15.0			17.6	25.7
		14.2	15.3	12.3	9.5		% Profit Before Taxes/Total Assets	11.8	16.6
		9.9	7.4	7.0	6.0			5.2	5.5
		19.0	6.7	7.4	5.7			9.6	9.6
		9.3	5.0	5.9	4.3		Sales/Net Fixed Assets	5.3	4.8
		5.0	2.7	3.5	3.3			3.0	3.2
		3.1	2.1	2.0	1.8			2.6	2.6
		2.5	1.7	1.6	1.4		Sales/Total Assets	1.8	1.8
		2.1	1.2	1.2	1.2			1.4	1.3
		.9	1.9	1.5				1.8	2.7
	(13)	1.9	(27) 3.3	3.3	3.1		% Depr., Dep., Amort./Sales	(61) 3.5	(36) 3.7
		4.8	5.9	4.7				4.8	6.4
								1.1	.7
							% Officers', Directors' Owners' Comp/Sales	(20) 2.6	(11) 2.5
								4.9	6.4
2528M	24952M	316331M	1099808M	1608854M	3102659M		Net Sales ($)	5162912M	2428340M
355M	4995M	124482M	619336M	952694M	2161777M		Total Assets ($)	2951415M	1410600M

© RMA 2024 M = $ thousand MM = $ million
See Pages viii through xx for Explanation of Ratios and Data

MANUFACTURING—Asphalt Paving Mixture and Block Manufacturing NAICS 324121

Comparative Historical Data | Current Data Sorted by Sales

				Type of Statement							
	6	12	15	Unqualified					3	12	
	14	17	14	Reviewed			2		7	5	
	3	4	5	Compiled					3	2	
	7	5	8	Tax Returns		1	3		3	1	
	21	38	35	Other	1		4		3	27	
	4/1/21-3/31/22 ALL	4/1/22-3/31/23 ALL	4/1/23-3/31/24 ALL		0-1MM	19 (4/1-9/30/23) 1-3MM	3-5MM	5-10MM	58 (10/1/23-3/31/24) 10-25MM	25MM & OVER	
	51	76	77	NUMBER OF STATEMENTS	1		1	9	19	47	
	%	%	%	ASSETS	%	%	%	%	%	%	
	17.4	17.4	16.4	Cash & Equivalents					28.1	11.9	
	22.5	19.5	22.8	Trade Receivables (net)	D				20.7	24.8	
	9.2	13.5	9.4	Inventory	A				7.6	11.5	
	4.5	3.9	3.6	All Other Current	T				2.1	4.2	
	53.5	54.3	52.3	Total Current	A				58.4	52.4	
	36.5	37.9	35.9	Fixed Assets (net)					34.7	37.2	
	4.0	1.9	2.7	Intangibles (net)	N				.8	4.0	
	6.0	5.8	9.1	All Other Non-Current	O				6.1	6.4	
	100.0	100.0	100.0	Total	T				100.0	100.0	
				LIABILITIES	A						
	4.7	4.2	3.0	Notes Payable-Short Term	V				2.0	2.6	
	4.1	5.1	4.5	Cur. Mat.-L.T.D.	A				6.4	4.1	
	10.7	9.5	8.1	Trade Payables	I				5.8	9.0	
	.1	.1	.2	Income Taxes Payable	L				.0	.3	
	7.1	5.5	6.8	All Other Current	A				6.3	8.0	
	26.6	24.5	22.6	Total Current	B				20.6	24.0	
	20.6	24.8	21.0	Long-Term Debt	L				29.8	18.8	
	.8	.4	.4	Deferred Taxes	E				.3	.5	
	3.3	3.2	2.4	All Other Non-Current					.9	2.8	
	48.7	47.1	53.6	Net Worth					48.5	53.8	
	100.0	100.0	100.0	Total Liabilities & Net Worth					100.0	100.0	
				INCOME DATA							
	100.0	100.0	100.0	Net Sales					100.0	100.0	
	23.5	23.4	27.1	Gross Profit					29.8	23.1	
	16.4	17.1	18.0	Operating Expenses					20.9	13.9	
	7.1	6.3	9.2	Operating Profit					8.9	9.2	
	-.2	-.1	.1	All Other Expenses (net)					.1	.2	
	7.4	6.4	9.1	Profit Before Taxes					8.8	8.9	
				RATIOS							
	3.8	3.8	3.6						5.0	2.8	
	2.2	2.6	2.4	Current					3.6	2.1	
	1.4	1.4	1.7						2.1	1.7	
	3.2	2.6	3.1						4.7	2.2	
	1.8	1.8	1.8	Quick					3.5	1.6	
	.8	.9	1.1						1.8	1.0	
22	16.3	15	24.3	26	14.2					17	21.2	26	13.9
39	9.4	33	10.9	43	8.4	Sales/Receivables				30	12.0	51	7.2
59	6.2	52	7.0	63	5.8					51	7.1	68	5.4
0	UND	3	111.0	3	121.9					0	32.0	11	27.0
8	43.4	15	24.1	16	23.1	Cost of Sales/Inventory				4	93.5	23	16.1
35	10.3	49	7.4	41	8.9					35	10.3	49	7.4
5	79.1	7	50.9	12	29.2					6	61.3	15	23.7
21	17.0	16	22.6	22	16.8	Cost of Sales/Payables				13	27.9	24	15.0
37	9.8	32	11.5	33	11.1					18	20.8	32	11.3
	4.7		4.2		4.0						2.9		4.6
	7.8		7.1		6.3	Sales/Working Capital					5.1		6.9
	16.9		15.5		11.1						7.5		9.6
	42.0		25.7		34.8						43.7		30.1
(46)	13.3	(69)	9.1	(71)	12.6	EBIT/Interest				(16)	7.5	(45)	12.6
	4.4		4.6		5.7						3.7		6.9
	6.8		6.5		11.6								16.7
(13)	2.2	(23)	4.0	(22)	4.3	Net Profit + Depr., Dep., Amort./Cur. Mat. L/T/D						(14)	5.1
	1.1		2.0		3.0								3.3
	.4		.4		.4						.3		.4
	.8		.7		.7	Fixed/Worth					.6		.7
	1.2		1.3		1.1						1.9		1.1
	.4		.4		.4						.2		.6
	.7		.8		.8	Debt/Worth					.5		.9
	2.6		2.3		1.5						11.6		1.4
	36.9		34.7		46.6						67.7		46.6
(45)	26.6	(69)	19.4	(75)	26.0	% Profit Before Taxes/Tangible Net Worth				(17)	22.2		29.2
	9.4		6.2		14.4						8.7		16.4
	25.5		18.1		23.1						33.4		20.5
	12.3		11.2		13.5	% Profit Before Taxes/Total Assets					12.8		14.0
	3.5		3.9		7.4						5.9		8.4
	12.2		10.2		10.0						14.3		6.7
	5.9		5.1		5.9	Sales/Net Fixed Assets					8.6		5.2
	3.1		3.5		3.5						6.0		3.4
	2.5		2.9		2.4						2.9		2.1
	2.0		2.0		1.9	Sales/Total Assets					2.2		1.7
	1.5		1.4		1.3						1.7		1.3
	1.7		1.9		1.6						1.3		1.9
(38)	3.9	(59)	3.2	(62)	3.1	% Depr., Dep., Amort./Sales				(16)	2.6	(39)	3.1
	6.0		5.3		4.7						5.7		4.5
	.8		1.1		1.1								.5
(17)	1.6	(28)	2.1	(22)	2.0	% Officers', Directors' Owners' Comp/Sales						(10)	1.4
	4.5		4.3		3.6								4.5
	2160791M		4751113M		6155132M	Net Sales ($)		2528M	3536M	63362M	323816M	5761890M	
	1236772M		2795412M		3863639M	Total Assets ($)		355M	7934M	54861M	159649M	3640840M	

© RMA 2024   M = $ thousand   MM = $ million
See Pages viii through xx for Explanation of Ratios and Data

MANUFACTURING—Petroleum Lubricating Oil and Grease Manufacturing NAICS 324191

Current Data Sorted by Assets

	0-500M	500M-2MM	2-10MM	10-50MM	50-100MM	100-250MM
Type of Statement						
Unqualified		2		2	1	1
Reviewed			1	1	2	1
Compiled			1	2		
Tax Returns		1	4	1		
Other		1		3	2	5
		6 (4/1-9/30/23)		24 (10/1/23-3/31/24)		
Number of Statements		3	6	9	5	7

(Current Data columns: DATA NOT AVAILABLE)

Comparative Historical Data

Type of Statement	4/1/19-3/31/20 ALL	4/1/20-3/31/21 ALL
Unqualified	4	4
Reviewed	6	6
Compiled	1	2
Tax Returns	3	1
Other	24	12
NUMBER OF STATEMENTS	**38**	**20**

ASSETS (%)
Cash & Equivalents	15.5	17.8
Trade Receivables (net)	23.5	21.0
Inventory	22.1	24.4
All Other Current	1.1	.8
Total Current	62.2	63.9
Fixed Assets (net)	26.4	21.2
Intangibles (net)	4.1	8.3
All Other Non-Current	7.2	6.6
Total	100.0	100.0

LIABILITIES
Notes Payable-Short Term	6.0	6.7
Cur. Mat.-L.T.D.	2.2	3.4
Trade Payables	12.2	12.6
Income Taxes Payable	.3	.0
All Other Current	8.4	4.7
Total Current	29.2	27.4
Long-Term Debt	16.7	19.4
Deferred Taxes	.4	.3
All Other Non-Current	4.3	4.2
Net Worth	49.4	48.7
Total Liabilities & Net Worth	100.0	100.0

INCOME DATA
Net Sales	100.0	100.0
Gross Profit	32.9	40.1
Operating Expenses	26.7	33.1
Operating Profit	6.2	7.0
All Other Expenses (net)	.8	-1.6
Profit Before Taxes	5.4	8.6

RATIOS
Current		3.6		4.2
		2.4		2.4
		1.3		1.9
Quick		2.4		2.7
		1.5		1.7
		.7		.9
Sales/Receivables	24	15.0	22	16.5
	33	11.2	33	11.2
	48	7.6	61	6.0
Cost of Sales/Inventory	26	13.8	38	9.6
	54	6.7	85	4.3
	104	3.5	130	2.8
Cost of Sales/Payables	16	22.2	24	15.4
	26	14.0	30	12.1
	41	8.9	48	7.6
Sales/Working Capital		3.6		2.7
		6.3		5.3
		29.2		11.3
EBIT/Interest		25.8		19.1
	(32)	8.0	(18)	10.3
		2.4		6.2
Net Profit + Depr., Dep., Amort./Cur. Mat. L/T/D				
Fixed/Worth		.2		.2
		.5		.5
		1.6		1.8
Debt/Worth		.4		.6
		1.3		1.4
		3.8		3.5
% Profit Before Taxes/Tangible Net Worth		45.9		61.1
	(37)	25.0	(18)	25.6
		10.7		20.0
% Profit Before Taxes/Total Assets		17.3		19.7
		11.0		13.6
		3.4		8.6
Sales/Net Fixed Assets		33.5		24.5
		12.4		10.2
		3.4		7.8
Sales/Total Assets		3.5		2.7
		1.9		2.0
		1.3		1.2
% Depr., Dep., Amort./Sales		.6		.6
	(32)	1.5	(16)	1.4
		3.6		3.7
% Officers', Directors' Owners' Comp/Sales		.9		
	(10)	2.4		
		5.5		

	500M-2MM	2-10MM	10-50MM	50-100MM	100-250MM		
Net Sales ($)	20482M	99060M	216714M	724149M	2078919M	3051903M	2331894M
Total Assets ($)	5636M	36111M	182452M	350202M	1296457M	1727609M	1242740M

M = $ thousand   MM = $ million
See Pages viii through xx for Explanation of Ratios and Data

© RMA 2024

MANUFACTURING—Petroleum Lubricating Oil and Grease Manufacturing NAICS 324191

Comparative Historical Data | Current Data Sorted by Sales

															Type of Statement											
		5			6			4							Unqualified											4
		3			2			6							Reviewed							2		1		3
		1			1			3							Compiled									3		
					3			2							Tax Returns											2
		4			10			15							Other		1					3		2		9
		4/1/21-3/31/22 ALL			4/1/22-3/31/23 ALL			4/1/23-3/31/24 ALL									0-1MM	6 (4/1-9/30/23) 1-3MM		3-5MM		5-10MM	24 (10/1/23-3/31/24) 10-25MM		25MM & OVER	
		15			22			30							NUMBER OF STATEMENTS		1					5		6		18
		%			%			%							ASSETS		%	%		%		%		%		%
		19.8			9.9			10.5							Cash & Equivalents											11.2
		15.1			20.4			21.6							Trade Receivables (net)		D	D								18.8
		34.0			27.8			27.2							Inventory		A	A								30.0
		1.2			3.0			2.8							All Other Current		T	T								3.3
		70.0			61.1			62.2							Total Current		A	A								63.4
		22.6			19.6			18.7							Fixed Assets (net)											17.9
		1.4			9.9			9.4							Intangibles (net)		N	N								8.6
		6.0			9.4			9.8							All Other Non-Current		O	O								10.0
		100.0			100.0			100.0							Total		T	T								100.0
															LIABILITIES											
		5.4			7.4			5.8							Notes Payable-Short Term		A	A								6.8
		3.6			2.9			1.6							Cur. Mat.-L.T.D.		V	V								1.7
		14.6			12.3			11.3							Trade Payables		A	A								9.7
		.1			.1			.9							Income Taxes Payable		I	I								.0
		8.2			3.9			7.5							All Other Current		L	L								7.0
		31.9			26.5			27.1							Total Current		A	A								25.2
		11.9			12.6			6.2							Long-Term Debt		B	B								8.9
		.4			.1			.3							Deferred Taxes		L	L								.5
		5.3			2.0			4.0							All Other Non-Current		E	E								3.8
		50.5			58.9			62.3							Net Worth											61.6
		100.0			100.0			100.0							Total Liabilties & Net Worth											100.0
															INCOME DATA											
		100.0			100.0			100.0							Net Sales											100.0
		32.9			25.6			30.8							Gross Profit											28.1
		25.3			19.3			24.7							Operating Expenses											20.4
		7.7			6.3			6.1							Operating Profit											7.7
		-1.0			1.0			-.3							All Other Expenses (net)											-.3
		8.6			5.3			6.4							Profit Before Taxes											8.0
															RATIOS											
		4.3			3.4			4.7																		5.6
		2.0			2.5			2.6							Current											2.6
		1.6			1.4			1.6																		1.6
		2.3			1.8			3.4																		4.1
		1.0			.8			1.1							Quick											1.1
		.6			.7			.5																		.5
16		22.2	30		12.0	32		11.3																27		13.3
31		11.6	34		10.7	38		9.7							Sales/Receivables									37		9.9
42		8.7	57		6.4	46		7.9																40		9.1
81		4.5	45		8.1	62		5.9																57		6.4
111		3.3	87		4.2	78		4.7							Cost of Sales/Inventory									78		4.7
130		2.8	107		3.4	101		3.6																101		3.6
19		19.6	11		33.6	15		24.4																12		29.7
34		10.7	21		17.0	27		13.7							Cost of Sales/Payables									20		18.5
57		6.4	47		7.7	34		10.7																30		12.1
		2.5			3.1			3.7																		4.3
		4.0			4.7			5.9							Sales/Working Capital											5.9
		9.5			8.0			9.4																		9.4
		92.7			35.1			67.9																		71.7
(12)		26.8	(18)		8.6	(25)		11.0							EBIT/Interest									(16)		11.2
		3.1			3.3			3.7																		3.6
															Net Profit + Depr., Dep., Amort./Cur. Mat. L/T/D											
		.1			.2			.2																		.2
		.4			.4			.4							Fixed/Worth											.4
		.7			1.0			.6																		.7
		.3			.5			.3																		.3
		1.1			1.0			.7							Debt/Worth											.9
		1.2			1.7			1.7																		1.9
		37.7			34.3			35.8																		35.8
(14)		20.2			20.0			19.0							% Profit Before Taxes/Tangible Net Worth											26.3
		8.8			6.0			6.2																		11.7
		25.6			16.0			20.7																		22.0
		11.5			8.5			9.3							% Profit Before Taxes/Total Assets											11.9
		3.5			2.8			2.7																		4.6
		24.6			17.2			22.1																		21.0
		11.0			11.6			13.6							Sales/Net Fixed Assets											14.0
		4.1			4.5			6.9																		9.9
		2.1			2.4			2.9																		2.8
		1.5			1.7			1.7							Sales/Total Assets											1.9
		1.2			1.1			1.3																		1.4
		.6			1.1			.5																		1.4
(13)		1.6	(19)		1.4	(25)		1.6							% Depr., Dep., Amort./Sales									(14)		1.7
		2.0			3.6			2.0																		1.9
															% Officers', Directors' Owners' Comp/Sales											
		1855252M			2553673M			3139324M							Net Sales ($)		912M					34925M		93931M		3009556M
		1196051M			1614927M			1870858M							Total Assets ($)		19185M					14574M		90595M		1746504M

© RMA 2024 M = $ thousand MM = $ million
See Pages viii through xx for Explanation of Ratios and Data

MANUFACTURING—Other Basic Inorganic Chemical Manufacturing NAICS 325180

Current Data Sorted by Assets | Comparative Historical Data

0-500M	500M-2MM	2-10MM	10-50MM	50-100MM	100-250MM	Type of Statement		4/1/19-3/31/20 ALL		4/1/20-3/31/21 ALL
			1		6	Unqualified		9		4
1		1	5	1	1	Reviewed		8		3
			1			Compiled		1		
			1			Tax Returns		5		1
1	1	2	10	6	15	Other		37		21
12 (4/1-9/30/23)			39 (10/1/23-3/31/24)			NUMBER OF STATEMENTS		60		29
1	1	3	17	7	22					
%	%	%	%	%	%	ASSETS		%		%
			14.5		12.2	Cash & Equivalents		7.2		12.0
			17.7		19.9	Trade Receivables (net)		19.2		20.0
			21.9		16.8	Inventory		21.2		20.3
			2.3		4.6	All Other Current		2.6		4.6
			56.3		53.5	Total Current		50.2		56.9
			22.3		32.2	Fixed Assets (net)		33.4		32.3
			2.5		4.5	Intangibles (net)		9.7		4.6
			18.9		9.7	All Other Non-Current		6.7		6.2
			100.0		100.0	Total		100.0		100.0
						LIABILITIES				
			2.6		4.1	Notes Payable-Short Term		5.9		11.9
			3.1		1.4	Cur. Mat.-L.T.D.		3.5		3.2
			10.5		7.6	Trade Payables		10.9		11.7
			.1		.1	Income Taxes Payable		.1		.0
			10.3		7.8	All Other Current		6.5		5.6
			26.6		20.9	Total Current		26.9		32.4
			5.6		21.5	Long-Term Debt		20.1		9.7
			.3		1.9	Deferred Taxes		1.1		.5
			8.7		5.1	All Other Non-Current		9.0		14.7
			58.8		50.6	Net Worth		42.8		42.7
			100.0		100.0	Total Liabilities & Net Worth		100.0		100.0
						INCOME DATA				
			100.0		100.0	Net Sales		100.0		100.0
			28.5		28.0	Gross Profit		29.6		29.4
			17.2		19.1	Operating Expenses		23.0		22.2
			11.3		8.8	Operating Profit		6.6		7.2
			-.3		.1	All Other Expenses (net)		2.0		-.6
			11.6		8.7	Profit Before Taxes		4.6		7.8
						RATIOS				
			3.9		4.6			2.9		3.4
			2.8		2.7	Current		1.9		2.0
			2.1		1.9			1.4		1.5
			2.4		3.1			1.4		2.2
			1.5		1.6	Quick		1.0		1.2
			1.0		1.0			.6		.8
		24	15.1	40	9.1		35	10.5	35	10.5
		39	9.3	54	6.7	Sales/Receivables	44	8.3	46	7.9
		49	7.4	61	6.0		57	6.4	54	6.7
		20	18.6	38	9.7		30	12.0	31	11.7
		74	4.9	52	7.0	Cost of Sales/Inventory	69	5.3	51	7.1
		87	4.2	74	4.9		107	3.4	85	4.3
		15	25.1	14	25.4		21	17.0	19	18.8
		26	14.1	26	13.9	Cost of Sales/Payables	33	10.9	32	11.5
		39	9.3	41	9.0		46	7.9	57	6.4
			3.9		3.3			4.1		2.9
			6.1		4.2	Sales/Working Capital		7.2		5.5
			11.8		6.3			15.5		12.3
			98.5		80.0			11.5		30.2
		(15)	32.8		6.1	EBIT/Interest	(56)	6.7	(25)	9.5
			9.7		3.1			2.1		4.0
						Net Profit + Depr., Dep., Amort./Cur. Mat. L/T/D		8.7		
							(17)	4.4		
								2.0		
			.2		.4			.3		.3
			.4		.6	Fixed/Worth		.8		.6
			.6		2.4			3.8		1.6
			.2		.3			.5		.4
			.5		.6	Debt/Worth		1.1		1.0
			1.7		6.1			9.2		3.6
			68.1		29.5			23.3		37.6
		(15)	29.4	(19)	13.6	% Profit Before Taxes/Tangible Net Worth	(49)	14.5	(24)	23.3
			16.7		5.7			8.2		10.6
			32.3		23.1			11.5		16.3
			14.2		13.2	% Profit Before Taxes/Total Assets		7.1		9.2
			10.2		3.2			2.7		4.8
			14.5		6.0			10.5		12.3
			9.5		4.5	Sales/Net Fixed Assets		5.6		6.5
			6.4		2.9			2.5		2.1
			2.2		1.7			2.1		2.3
			1.9		1.5	Sales/Total Assets		1.5		1.4
			1.5		.9			.9		.8
			.9		1.0			1.5		1.1
		(16)	2.3	(12)	1.9	% Depr., Dep., Amort./Sales	(52)	2.6	(25)	2.8
			3.1		3.6			4.9		4.5
						% Officers', Directors' Owners' Comp/Sales				
4435M	3906M	36404M	781873M	526620M	5414038M	Net Sales ($)		3206947M		1354229M
436M	946M	20744M	419590M	454016M	3913177M	Total Assets ($)		2663360M		1374957M

M = $ thousand   MM = $ million
See Pages viii through xx for Explanation of Ratios and Data

© RMA 2024

MANUFACTURING—Other Basic Inorganic Chemical Manufacturing NAICS 325180

Comparative Historical Data | Current Data Sorted by Sales

				Type of Statement							
	2	10	7	Unqualified							7
	5	6	6	Reviewed					3		3
	2	1	2	Compiled							2
		1	1	Tax Returns							1
	23	24	35	Other			2	1	3		29
	4/1/21-3/31/22	4/1/22-3/31/23	4/1/23-3/31/24		0-1MM	12 (4/1-9/30/23) 1-3MM	3-5MM	5-10MM	39 (10/1/23-3/31/24) 10-25MM		25MM & OVER
	ALL 32	ALL 42	ALL 51	NUMBER OF STATEMENTS			2	1	6		42
	%	%	%	ASSETS	%	%	%	%	%		%
	13.2	12.0	13.6	Cash & Equivalents	D	D					12.0
	18.4	20.1	18.9	Trade Receivables (net)	A	A					18.7
	27.7	27.0	20.1	Inventory	T	T					19.2
	1.8	3.8	3.8	All Other Current	A	A					3.4
	61.1	62.8	56.4	Total Current							53.3
	26.4	24.4	27.4	Fixed Assets (net)	N	N					30.4
	6.4	7.2	4.3	Intangibles (net)	O	O					4.8
	6.2	5.6	11.9	All Other Non-Current	T	T					11.5
	100.0	100.0	100.0	Total							100.0
				LIABILITIES	A	A					
	4.3	7.4	4.1	Notes Payable-Short Term	V	V					3.7
	2.0	2.7	2.1	Cur. Mat.-L.T.D.	A	A					2.0
	15.3	10.7	9.1	Trade Payables	I	I					8.7
	.1	.2	.1	Income Taxes Payable	L	L					.1
	8.6	7.9	8.2	All Other Current	A	A					5.9
	30.2	28.9	23.6	Total Current	B	B					20.5
	14.2	10.6	12.9	Long-Term Debt	L	L					15.2
	.7	.5	1.1	Deferred Taxes	E	E					1.2
	3.0	9.3	7.3	All Other Non-Current							5.6
	51.8	50.7	55.2	Net Worth							57.5
	100.0	100.0	100.0	Total Liabilties & Net Worth							100.0
				INCOME DATA							
	100.0	100.0	100.0	Net Sales							100.0
	28.5	29.6	27.9	Gross Profit							27.7
	20.9	22.6	19.1	Operating Expenses							18.6
	7.7	7.0	8.8	Operating Profit							9.1
	-.5	.9	.1	All Other Expenses (net)							.1
	8.1	6.1	8.7	Profit Before Taxes							9.0
				RATIOS							
	3.4	5.1	4.4								4.6
	2.6	2.6	2.7	Current							2.8
	1.5	1.6	2.1								2.2
	2.4	3.0	2.8								2.9
	1.3	1.3	1.5	Quick							1.6
	.6	.8	1.0								1.0
33	11.1	37	9.8	34	10.6					36	10.1
43	8.5	43	8.4	45	8.2	Sales/Receivables				45	8.1
62	5.9	51	7.1	57	6.4					59	6.2
42	8.7	42	8.7	38	9.6					40	9.2
76	4.8	78	4.7	68	5.4	Cost of Sales/Inventory				63	5.8
118	3.1	114	3.2	85	4.3					79	4.6
21	17.7	16	22.3	15	24.6					15	24.2
38	9.7	28	12.9	23	15.7	Cost of Sales/Payables				28	13.1
54	6.8	41	8.8	38	9.7					38	9.6
	3.3		2.8		3.5						3.3
	5.0		5.5		4.4	Sales/Working Capital					4.3
	12.2		9.1		8.1						7.7
	50.9		115.9		61.2						69.7
(27)	13.7	(37)	12.5	(47)	10.1	EBIT/Interest				(41)	11.2
	5.6		4.3		2.2						3.1
					23.3	Net Profit + Depr., Dep.,					18.1
				(15)	7.9	Amort./Cur. Mat. L/T/D				(13)	7.9
					4.3						5.5
	.2		.2		.2						.3
	.5		.4		.5	Fixed/Worth					.5
	1.3		1.1		1.2						1.3
	.2		.2		.3						.3
	1.1		.7		.6	Debt/Worth					.5
	2.2		2.4		2.4						2.1
	42.0		41.6		44.6	% Profit Before Taxes/Tangible					40.8
(27)	25.0	(37)	19.3	(46)	17.6	Net Worth				(39)	17.4
	11.9		7.8		5.7						5.7
	21.4		19.5		23.1	% Profit Before Taxes/Total					23.1
	11.0		9.2		13.7	Assets					13.7
	3.8		3.2		3.5						3.2
	15.7		13.0		13.1						9.8
	8.1		7.6		5.7	Sales/Net Fixed Assets					5.3
	3.1		4.0		3.5						3.1
	2.1		2.3		2.1						2.0
	1.6		1.7		1.6	Sales/Total Assets					1.6
	.9		1.0		1.0						.9
	.9		.9		1.0						1.3
(25)	1.8	(37)	2.1	(38)	2.2	% Depr., Dep., Amort./Sales				(31)	2.4
	3.0		3.2		3.2						3.2
						% Officers', Directors' Owners' Comp/Sales					
	1441664M		3723780M		6767276M	Net Sales ($)	8341M	9556M	114163M		6635216M
	1311079M		2242761M		4808909M	Total Assets ($)	1382M	8728M	77063M		4721736M

© RMA 2024   M = $ thousand   MM = $ million
See Pages viii through xx for Explanation of Ratios and Data

MANUFACTURING—All Other Basic Organic Chemical Manufacturing NAICS 325199

Current Data Sorted by Assets | Comparative Historical Data

0-500M	500M-2MM	2-10MM	10-50MM	50-100MM	100-250MM	Type of Statement	4/1/19-3/31/20 ALL	4/1/20-3/31/21 ALL
				2	5	Unqualified	11	4
			2	2	5	Reviewed	8	3
				1		Compiled	2	2
	2	3	13	6	7	Tax Returns	3	1
						Other		
	14 (4/1-9/30/23)		32 (10/1/23-3/31/24)				39	23
	2	5	16	11	12	NUMBER OF STATEMENTS	63	33
%	%	%	%	%	%	ASSETS	%	%
			15.1	3.8	7.4	Cash & Equivalents	9.4	11.6
D			19.6	16.3	16.2	Trade Receivables (net)	20.7	19.5
A			31.2	24.8	21.0	Inventory	25.0	26.4
T			3.0	4.3	3.3	All Other Current	2.6	4.1
A			68.9	49.2	47.9	Total Current	57.8	61.6
			20.6	36.1	34.9	Fixed Assets (net)	25.4	25.9
N			4.0	6.6	3.3	Intangibles (net)	10.7	7.7
O			6.5	8.1	13.8	All Other Non-Current	6.2	4.8
T			100.0	100.0	100.0	Total	100.0	100.0
A						LIABILITIES		
V			11.5	4.4	2.0	Notes Payable-Short Term	6.4	3.5
A			.9	3.0	2.1	Cur. Mat.-L.T.D.	2.4	2.7
I			16.0	12.5	8.4	Trade Payables	13.9	13.0
L			.1	.2	.2	Income Taxes Payable	.1	.1
A			9.6	6.2	11.7	All Other Current	9.5	5.6
B			38.0	26.2	24.5	Total Current	32.2	25.0
L			6.1	20.9	16.8	Long-Term Debt	16.1	17.1
E			.3	1.9	.7	Deferred Taxes	.4	.8
			2.9	7.2	5.1	All Other Non-Current	6.3	4.7
			52.7	43.8	53.0	Net Worth	44.9	52.5
			100.0	100.0	100.0	Total Liabilities & Net Worth	100.0	100.0
						INCOME DATA		
			100.0	100.0	100.0	Net Sales	100.0	100.0
			26.8	27.0	26.7	Gross Profit	34.4	35.1
			20.7	17.9	21.2	Operating Expenses	24.9	23.8
			6.1	9.1	5.5	Operating Profit	9.5	11.2
			-.1	-.1	.6	All Other Expenses (net)	1.8	.9
			6.2	9.2	4.8	Profit Before Taxes	7.7	10.4
						RATIOS		
			4.0	4.2	3.0		3.5	4.1
			1.7	2.0	2.2	Current	2.3	2.4
			1.3	1.3	1.3		1.3	1.6
			1.6	1.3	1.7		1.9	2.5
			1.0	1.0	1.0	Quick	1.1	1.4
			.6	.6	.4		.6	.7
		33 11.1	36 10.1	31 11.6			31 11.9	35 10.3
		49 7.5	38 9.6	46 7.9		Sales/Receivables	45 8.1	43 8.5
		56 6.5	52 7.0	56 6.5			56 6.5	51 7.1
		66 5.5	46 8.0	51 7.2			41 8.9	60 6.1
		81 4.5	70 5.2	62 5.9		Cost of Sales/Inventory	64 5.7	89 4.1
		118 3.1	118 3.1	94 3.9			122 3.0	130 2.8
		27 13.4	18 19.9	25 14.5			23 16.1	25 14.6
		31 11.8	31 11.9	30 12.1		Cost of Sales/Payables	34 10.8	34 10.8
		38 9.5	78 4.7	32 11.4			52 7.0	63 5.8
			2.7	3.7	3.6		3.4	3.3
			6.3	6.4	5.9	Sales/Working Capital	6.9	4.6
			12.3	18.7	24.0		12.7	8.7
			34.8	15.5	12.1		47.6	42.6
		(13) 7.8	(10) 8.9	(11) 8.2		EBIT/Interest	(53) 9.5	(28) 17.4
			4.5	3.2	1.7		3.8	5.7
						Net Profit + Depr., Dep.,	7.4	7.2
						Amort./Cur. Mat. L/T/D	(15) 4.5	(13) 5.2
							1.8	4.1
			.2	.2	.5		.2	.2
			.4	.8	.7	Fixed/Worth	.7	.6
			.7	2.5	.9		1.5	1.1
			.4	.6	.6		.3	.4
			.9	1.3	1.0	Debt/Worth	1.1	1.0
			2.0	2.1	1.4		2.9	2.7
			28.5	41.8	26.3		39.0	51.9
		(15) 17.7	(10) 15.0	(11) 15.3	% Profit Before Taxes/Tangible Net Worth	(51) 22.6	(29) 26.2
			7.0	5.2	3.0		10.5	17.7
			15.4	15.5	17.2		20.6	23.9
			13.2	12.0	7.5	% Profit Before Taxes/Total Assets	10.8	14.9
			4.7	1.9	1.3		5.9	9.1
			22.3	5.7	6.9		22.8	13.4
			12.6	5.2	5.2	Sales/Net Fixed Assets	7.8	5.8
			4.6	2.0	3.2		3.0	3.4
			2.4	1.9	2.0		2.2	2.1
			1.5	1.3	1.5	Sales/Total Assets	1.5	1.6
			1.2	.7	1.1		1.2	1.0
			.8	2.3			1.0	1.2
		(13) 1.7	(10) 3.5			% Depr., Dep., Amort./Sales	(48) 2.0	(31) 2.3
			3.0	4.6			4.2	4.7
						% Officers', Directors' Owners' Comp/Sales		
	4684M	72903M	782605M	1579076M	2581687M	Net Sales ($)	4754380M	2647523M
	3148M	34951M	431990M	809556M	1682751M	Total Assets ($)	3260802M	1570208M

M = $ thousand   MM = $ million
See Pages viii through xx for Explanation of Ratios and Data

© RMA 2024

MANUFACTURING—All Other Basic Organic Chemical Manufacturing NAICS 325199

Comparative Historical Data | Current Data Sorted by Sales

							Type of Statement						
		8		12		10	Unqualified						10
		2		3		2	Reviewed						2
		1		3		2	Compiled					2	
		1		1		1	Tax Returns					1	
		25		25		31	Other			2	1	3	25
		4/1/21-3/31/22 ALL		4/1/22-3/31/23 ALL		4/1/23-3/31/24 ALL		0-1MM	14 (4/1-9/30/23) 1-3MM	3-5MM	32 (10/1/23-3/31/24) 5-10MM	10-25MM	25MM & OVER
		37		44		46	NUMBER OF STATEMENTS		2		1	6	37
		%		%		%	ASSETS	%	%	%	%	%	%
		16.6		7.4		12.1	Cash & Equivalents	D		D			9.4
		19.6		18.6		18.2	Trade Receivables (net)	A		A			18.7
		24.8		29.8		25.8	Inventory	T		T			25.5
		2.5		3.9		3.2	All Other Current	A		A			3.2
		63.5		59.7		59.3	Total Current						56.9
		26.5		30.1		27.4	Fixed Assets (net)	N		N			29.1
		3.5		5.1		5.2	Intangibles (net)	O		O			4.8
		6.5		5.1		8.1	All Other Non-Current	T		T			9.2
		100.0		100.0		100.0	Total						100.0
							LIABILITIES	A		A			
		3.7		7.2		6.3	Notes Payable-Short Term	V		V			6.9
		2.0		1.8		2.0	Cur. Mat.-L.T.D.	A		A			1.8
		11.1		12.3		12.0	Trade Payables	I		I			12.8
		.2		.2		.1	Income Taxes Payable	L		L			.1
		9.1		9.1		11.6	All Other Current	A		A			9.7
		26.1		30.5		32.0	Total Current	B		B			31.3
		10.6		23.8		12.6	Long-Term Debt	L		L			13.0
		.8		.8		.7	Deferred Taxes	E		E			.9
		8.9		7.8		6.7	All Other Non-Current						5.1
		53.6		37.1		48.0	Net Worth						49.8
		100.0		100.0		100.0	Total Liabilities & Net Worth						100.0
							INCOME DATA						
		100.0		100.0		100.0	Net Sales						100.0
		34.1		30.4		30.6	Gross Profit						28.3
		21.7		20.6		23.0	Operating Expenses						21.7
		12.4		9.7		7.6	Operating Profit						6.5
		-.3		1.5		.0	All Other Expenses (net)						.1
		12.7		8.3		7.6	Profit Before Taxes						6.4
							RATIOS						
		5.5		3.2		4.1							3.4
		2.7		2.0		2.2	Current						1.9
		1.4		1.5		1.3							1.3
		2.9		1.7		1.9							1.5
		1.1		.8		1.0	Quick						1.0
		.6		.5		.6							.6
33	11.1	28	13.1	32	11.3						34	10.7
49	7.5	41	8.9	43	8.4	Sales/Receivables					44	8.3
62	5.9	61	6.0	55	6.6						57	6.4
56	6.5	50	7.3	51	7.2						52	7.0
91	4.0	87	4.2	72	5.1	Cost of Sales/Inventory					70	5.2
159	2.3	140	2.6	118	3.1						101	3.6
21	17.7	21	17.5	23	15.8						25	14.4
30	12.3	32	11.4	30	12.2	Cost of Sales/Payables					30	12.0
60	6.1	54	6.8	35	10.5						35	10.3
		2.6		3.4		3.1							3.5
		4.1		5.8		5.9	Sales/Working Capital						6.4
		9.7		11.4		12.9							13.6
		39.7		26.3		16.1							15.2
(27)	16.4	(38)	10.7	(36)	8.0	EBIT/Interest					(32)	7.3
		9.5		4.3		2.7							2.1
						11.2							11.2
				(15)	4.5	Net Profit + Depr., Dep., Amort./Cur. Mat. L/T/D					(15)	4.5
						2.0							2.0
		.2		.3		.2							.3
		.6		.7		.6	Fixed/Worth						.7
		1.2		6.4		.9							.9
		.3		.6		.5							.5
		1.1		1.4		1.0	Debt/Worth						1.1
		2.0		8.2		2.0							1.9
		63.2		42.7		38.3							30.6
(35)	33.8	(34)	19.6	(42)	16.6	% Profit Before Taxes/Tangible Net Worth					(34)	16.6
		23.3		13.9		5.2							4.3
		30.6		20.0		18.0							15.5
		17.8		11.6		10.9	% Profit Before Taxes/Total Assets						12.0
		10.2		6.8		1.9							1.9
		15.1		16.7		16.4							12.6
		6.7		5.6		6.4	Sales/Net Fixed Assets						5.7
		3.8		2.3		3.9							3.8
		1.9		2.2		2.1							2.2
		1.6		1.5		1.5	Sales/Total Assets						1.5
		1.1		.9		1.2							1.1
		1.2		1.3		1.3							1.6
(31)	1.8	(38)	2.5	(36)	2.4	% Depr., Dep., Amort./Sales					(29)	2.4
		3.1		5.2		3.5							3.7
							% Officers', Directors' Owners' Comp/Sales						
		2457449M		4346819M		5020955M	Net Sales ($)		4684M	6927M	94070M		4915274M
		1484690M		2854479M		2962396M	Total Assets ($)		3148M	4272M	69452M		2885524M

© RMA 2024 M = $ thousand MM = $ million
See Pages viii through xx for Explanation of Ratios and Data

MANUFACTURING—Plastics Material and Resin Manufacturing NAICS 325211

Current Data Sorted by Assets | Comparative Historical Data

							Type of Statement				
			2	6	2	3	Unqualified		7		3
			6	6	2		Reviewed		16		9
			5	2			Compiled		4		3
		3	1				Tax Returns		11		3
		2	13	19	5	10	Other		59		36
0-500M		13 (4/1-9/30/23)		74 (10/1/23-3/31/24)					4/1/19-3/31/20 ALL		4/1/20-3/31/21 ALL
		500M-2MM	2-10MM	10-50MM	50-100MM	100-250MM	NUMBER OF STATEMENTS		97		54
		5	27	33	9	13					
%		%	%	%	%	%	ASSETS		%		%
	D		14.4	13.3		11.6	Cash & Equivalents		13.7		15.6
	A		24.4	18.9		19.9	Trade Receivables (net)		22.3		20.9
	T		26.0	21.8		19.8	Inventory		22.0		21.6
	A		1.3	2.0		2.2	All Other Current		2.7		.7
			66.1	56.0		53.6	Total Current		60.7		58.8
	N		26.2	36.5		28.2	Fixed Assets (net)		29.2		30.7
	O		2.0	.9		11.3	Intangibles (net)		4.5		6.3
	T		5.7	6.6		7.0	All Other Non-Current		5.5		4.3
			100.0	100.0		100.0	Total		100.0		100.0
	A						LIABILITIES				
	V		6.1	5.3		4.9	Notes Payable-Short Term		12.0		6.2
	A		1.9	1.7		3.2	Cur. Mat.-L.T.D.		3.3		4.1
	I		16.3	10.7		15.4	Trade Payables		16.7		12.4
	L		.1	.0		.1	Income Taxes Payable		.5		.2
	A		6.8	10.5		4.3	All Other Current		11.3		6.4
	B		31.1	28.3		27.7	Total Current		43.8		29.2
	L		9.3	10.5		22.4	Long-Term Debt		17.8		21.5
	E		.0	1.0		1.6	Deferred Taxes		.4		.5
			2.4	5.7		7.4	All Other Non-Current		13.0		5.7
			57.2	54.6		40.8	Net Worth		24.9		43.1
			100.0	100.0		100.0	Total Liabilties & Net Worth		100.0		100.0
							INCOME DATA				
			100.0	100.0		100.0	Net Sales		100.0		100.0
			35.7	29.0		17.8	Gross Profit		29.2		30.4
			26.5	20.6		10.4	Operating Expenses		23.9		22.0
			9.2	8.4		7.4	Operating Profit		5.3		8.5
			.2	1.7		2.4	All Other Expenses (net)		1.2		.1
			8.9	6.7		5.1	Profit Before Taxes		4.1		8.4
							RATIOS				
			3.9	4.3		4.5			2.8		4.6
			2.1	2.6		1.7	Current		1.6		2.0
			1.4	1.1		1.2			1.1		1.2
			3.2	2.9		2.9			1.6		3.3
			1.3	1.3		1.0	Quick		.9		1.1
			.8	.5		.6			.5		.6
		23	15.9	30 12.2	36	10.1		32	11.5	27	13.3
		40	9.2	37 9.8	41	9.0	Sales/Receivables	40	9.2	40	9.2
		47	7.7	54 6.7	52	7.0		48	7.6	51	7.2
		39	9.3	37 9.9	31	11.7		26	14.0	35	10.4
		60	6.1	63 5.8	63	5.8	Cost of Sales/Inventory	59	6.2	62	5.9
		85	4.3	101 3.6	91	4.0		94	3.9	89	4.1
		15	24.7	16 23.0	16	22.5		20	18.5	21	17.2
		26	14.3	24 15.5	45	8.1	Cost of Sales/Payables	33	11.0	30	12.3
		44	8.3	41 9.0	54	6.7		54	6.7	45	8.2
			4.0	3.0		2.8			5.3		3.4
			6.5	4.7		6.5	Sales/Working Capital		10.9		5.6
			11.9	34.4		20.9			36.5		30.5
			31.8	49.4		17.7			13.8		31.8
		(18)	3.8	(29) 8.6	(11)	5.0	EBIT/Interest	(82)	5.6	(44)	9.6
			-1.7	1.1		-.2			1.2		2.4
				13.2			Net Profit + Depr., Dep.,		9.9		14.2
			(15)	8.0			Amort./Cur. Mat. L/T/D	(20)	3.4	(13)	6.3
				1.9					1.7		3.6
			.2	.4		.3			.4		.3
			.3	.6		.6	Fixed/Worth		.8		.8
			.8	1.1		NM			3.3		1.5
			.3	.3		.4			.6		.4
			.7	.8		1.7	Debt/Worth		1.6		1.6
			2.2	1.8		NM			7.5		3.0
			83.1	34.1		40.9			42.0		52.7
			34.6	(32) 14.2	(10)	26.7	% Profit Before Taxes/Tangible Net Worth	(80)	24.3	(49)	30.9
			-.4	2.4		13.2			6.5		7.9
			42.5	19.7		13.9			15.5		22.9
			10.9	8.7		7.9	% Profit Before Taxes/Total Assets		8.5		11.6
			-.2	.8		3.2			.7		2.9
			32.0	7.4		25.6			20.8		15.5
			13.6	4.0		7.2	Sales/Net Fixed Assets		7.2		5.3
			6.9	3.1		2.1			3.8		3.2
			2.9	2.0		2.2			2.9		2.7
			2.4	1.5		1.1	Sales/Total Assets		1.9		1.7
			1.6	1.2		.8			1.3		1.0
			1.1	1.9					1.1		1.4
		(21)	1.9	(30) 2.6			% Depr., Dep., Amort./Sales	(83)	2.7	(47)	2.8
			3.7	5.0					3.8		4.3
			.9						2.0		1.9
		(10)	3.0				% Officers', Directors' Owners' Comp/Sales	(21)	3.8	(15)	3.1
			6.7						7.6		5.8
		17333M	420897M	1358665M	957765M	3201603M	Net Sales ($)		5377512M		2937667M
		5928M	178538M	897804M	582110M	2192626M	Total Assets ($)		2525488M		2081991M

© RMA 2024 M = $ thousand MM = $ million
See Pages viii through xx for Explanation of Ratios and Data

MANUFACTURING—Plastics Material and Resin Manufacturing NAICS 325211

Comparative Historical Data / Current Data Sorted by Sales

						Type of Statement							
		8		13		13	Unqualified					2	11
		9		11		14	Reviewed		1		1	5	7
		4		8		7	Compiled				1	4	2
		2		8		4	Tax Returns			1	1	1	
		49		54		49	Other	2	2	1	6	7	33
		4/1/21-3/31/22		4/1/22-3/31/23		4/1/23-3/31/24			13 (4/1-9/30/23)			74 (10/1/23-3/31/24)	
		ALL		ALL		ALL		0-1MM	1-3MM	3-5MM	5-10MM	10-25MM	25MM & OVER
		72		94		87	NUMBER OF STATEMENTS	4	2	9	19	53	
		%		%		%	ASSETS	%	%	%	%	%	%
		9.5		9.1		13.1	Cash & Equivalents					14.9	12.1
		24.5		20.9		21.4	Trade Receivables (net)	D				23.8	20.3
		25.0		26.7		22.7	Inventory	A				24.6	23.7
		1.5		1.9		1.6	All Other Current	T				1.2	1.9
		60.5		58.6		58.9	Total Current	A				64.6	58.0
		29.7		31.5		31.7	Fixed Assets (net)					24.8	32.0
		4.7		5.9		3.5	Intangibles (net)	N				2.7	4.2
		5.1		4.1		5.9	All Other Non-Current	O				7.9	5.8
		100.0		100.0		100.0	Total	T				100.0	100.0
							LIABILITIES	A					
		7.5		7.4		5.1	Notes Payable-Short Term	V				6.5	5.2
		2.4		2.0		2.7	Cur. Mat.-L.T.D.	A				1.3	2.9
		13.3		12.9		14.0	Trade Payables	I				15.1	14.4
		.0		.1		.1	Income Taxes Payable	L				.1	.1
		4.6		6.9		8.1	All Other Current	A				9.0	8.7
		27.8		29.2		29.9	Total Current	B				31.9	31.3
		18.3		14.3		11.5	Long-Term Debt	L				7.9	11.9
		.3		.6		.7	Deferred Taxes	E				.0	1.1
		8.1		6.3		4.9	All Other Non-Current					1.6	6.7
		45.4		49.6		53.0	Net Worth					58.5	49.0
		100.0		100.0		100.0	Total Liabilities & Net Worth					100.0	100.0
							INCOME DATA						
		100.0		100.0		100.0	Net Sales					100.0	100.0
		30.3		26.9		29.2	Gross Profit					38.7	23.1
		22.1		18.7		21.5	Operating Expenses					26.9	17.6
		8.2		8.2		7.7	Operating Profit					11.8	5.5
		-1.6		-.2		1.2	All Other Expenses (net)					.6	1.4
		9.8		8.3		6.5	Profit Before Taxes					11.2	4.1
							RATIOS						
		3.6		3.4		3.9						3.3	3.9
		2.4		2.0		2.0	Current					2.0	1.9
		1.5		1.5		1.3						1.4	1.2
		2.3		2.0		2.7						2.7	2.5
		1.1		1.0		1.3	Quick					1.0	1.1
		.8		.6		.6						.6	.6
36	10.0		29	12.4	30	12.3					23	15.9	32	11.4
44	8.3		40	9.1	40	9.1	Sales/Receivables				41	8.8	39	9.4
59	6.2		54	6.8	53	6.9					54	6.8	52	7.0
39	9.4		42	8.7	35	10.3					41	8.8	40	9.2
68	5.4		69	5.3	62	5.9	Cost of Sales/Inventory				57	6.4	68	5.4
101	3.6		111	3.3	99	3.7					74	4.9	101	3.6
22	16.4		19	19.5	17	21.9					15	24.0	18	20.7
35	10.5		28	13.0	30	12.0	Cost of Sales/Payables				24	14.9	36	12.5
47	7.7		46	8.0	47	7.7					44	8.3	49	7.5
	3.5			4.0		3.5						4.0	3.1
	5.4			6.4		6.5	Sales/Working Capital					6.2	6.5
	14.7			14.7		17.1						34.3	30.2
	45.7			26.6		31.6						43.2	19.2
(61)	11.9		(84)	9.0	(71)	6.9	EBIT/Interest				(13)	6.9	(48)	6.9
	2.3			2.3		.8						1.4	.2
	15.2			8.1		12.3	Net Profit + Depr., Dep.,						12.0
(15)	11.8		(22)	5.0	(30)	5.7	Amort./Cur. Mat. L/T/D					(23)	4.8
	4.2			3.0		2.2							1.9
	.3			.3		.3						.2	.4
	.7			.7		.6	Fixed/Worth					.4	.6
	1.4			1.3		1.0						.8	1.4
	.5			.4		.3						.3	.3
	1.1			1.0		.8	Debt/Worth					.7	1.1
	4.1			2.5		2.3						1.9	2.5
	83.3			58.5		39.0	% Profit Before Taxes/Tangible					87.0	34.5
(62)	43.1		(86)	26.3	(81)	19.3	Net Worth					34.6	(47)	16.4
	14.9			9.3		3.2						12.6	2.3
	28.4			20.4		19.1	% Profit Before Taxes/Total					42.5	15.8
	13.1			9.4		9.0	Assets					11.3	7.9
	3.6			3.1		.6						6.6	-1.0
	18.1			13.8		15.8						32.0	12.6
	5.9			5.8		6.9	Sales/Net Fixed Assets					11.3	5.3
	3.9			3.2		3.1						6.9	2.8
	2.5			2.3		2.5						2.6	2.3
	1.8			1.8		1.8	Sales/Total Assets					2.3	1.5
	1.2			1.3		1.2						1.8	1.1
	1.3			1.8		1.6						1.1	1.4
(57)	2.4		(78)	3.0	(72)	2.5	% Depr., Dep., Amort./Sales				(16)	2.0	(43)	2.6
	4.0			3.7		4.4						2.6	4.0
	1.1			1.0		1.0	% Officers', Directors'						
(19)	1.5		(22)	1.7	(17)	2.7	Owners' Comp/Sales						
	3.3			2.2		6.1							
	4178357M			6671144M		5956263M	Net Sales ($)	8208M	9560M	70565M	335595M	5532335M
	2719025M			3765203M		3857006M	Total Assets ($)	20005M	5544M	43655M	157654M	3630148M

M = $ thousand MM = $ million
See Pages viii through xx for Explanation of Ratios and Data

© RMA 2024

MANUFACTURING—Fertilizer (Mixing Only) Manufacturing NAICS 325314

Current Data Sorted by Assets | Comparative Historical Data

						Type of Statement		
			2		1	Unqualified	3	3
		1	4		1	Reviewed	10	4
		1				Compiled	2	1
	2		1			Tax Returns	3	1
	1	1	10	1	4	Other	18	9
0-500M	7 (4/1-9/30/23) 500M-2MM	2-10MM	22 (10/1/23-3/31/24) 10-50MM	50-100MM	100-250MM		4/1/19-3/31/20 ALL	4/1/20-3/31/21 ALL
	3	3	16	1	6	NUMBER OF STATEMENTS	36	18
%	%	%	%	%	%	ASSETS	%	%
			7.2			Cash & Equivalents	8.4	12.2
DATA			15.9			Trade Receivables (net)	18.2	19.4
			28.9			Inventory	23.8	22.0
			1.4			All Other Current	1.5	3.5
NOT			53.4			Total Current	52.0	57.1
			34.8			Fixed Assets (net)	39.6	33.8
			4.8			Intangibles (net)	4.1	2.6
AVAILABLE			7.0			All Other Non-Current	4.3	6.5
			100.0			Total	100.0	100.0
						LIABILITIES		
			4.0			Notes Payable-Short Term	10.1	21.6
			2.8			Cur. Mat.-L.T.D.	4.4	4.7
			15.1			Trade Payables	12.5	14.2
			.4			Income Taxes Payable	.3	.1
			11.3			All Other Current	8.1	8.9
			33.5			Total Current	35.3	49.5
			8.4			Long-Term Debt	11.8	14.7
			1.1			Deferred Taxes	1.5	1.4
			4.4			All Other Non-Current	8.1	13.7
			52.6			Net Worth	43.3	20.7
			100.0			Total Liabilities & Net Worth	100.0	100.0
						INCOME DATA		
			100.0			Net Sales	100.0	100.0
			22.6			Gross Profit	32.8	30.4
			19.3			Operating Expenses	27.6	27.1
			3.3			Operating Profit	5.1	3.3
			-.7			All Other Expenses (net)	-.2	-.6
			4.1			Profit Before Taxes	5.3	3.9
						RATIOS		
			2.2				2.0	3.0
			1.8			Current	1.3	1.9
			1.4				1.2	1.1
			1.6				1.1	1.5
			.7			Quick	.8	1.0
			.5				.4	.5
		24	15.5				16 22.2	16 22.5
		36	10.2			Sales/Receivables	29 12.5	31 11.7
		50	7.3				43 8.5	48 7.6
		18	20.4				33 11.0	27 13.3
		69	5.3			Cost of Sales/Inventory	79 4.6	69 5.3
		101	3.6				111 3.3	87 4.2
		12	30.8				20 18.0	18 20.3
		20	18.5			Cost of Sales/Payables	31 11.6	24 15.5
		55	6.6				45 8.2	42 8.6
			6.0				6.3	4.8
			8.6			Sales/Working Capital	13.6	7.4
			12.4				32.2	NM
			9.6				14.1	20.4
			3.9			EBIT/Interest	(34) 6.1	12.0
			2.9				2.0	.9
						Net Profit + Depr., Dep., Amort./Cur. Mat. L/T/D		
			.4				.6	.5
			.7			Fixed/Worth	1.0	.7
			1.0				1.6	NM
			.6				.8	.7
			.8			Debt/Worth	1.2	1.5
			1.8				2.5	-14.2
			28.3				44.6	40.1
			10.0			% Profit Before Taxes/Tangible Net Worth	(34) 17.7	(13) 14.2
			7.5				9.2	11.1
			8.8				16.0	16.9
			5.4			% Profit Before Taxes/Total Assets	10.5	7.8
			3.6				2.6	-1.1
			10.5				10.2	11.2
			6.5			Sales/Net Fixed Assets	4.6	7.2
			1.6				2.7	2.8
			2.7				2.9	2.9
			1.8			Sales/Total Assets	1.5	2.1
			.9				1.2	1.2
			1.4				1.8	1.8
			3.0			% Depr., Dep., Amort./Sales	(33) 4.0	(17) 2.8
			5.0				6.3	5.8
						% Officers', Directors' Owners' Comp/Sales		
	15647M	29864M	603693M	304743M	2611690M	Net Sales ($)	1806769M	1055759M
	4113M	20244M	393859M	89847M	930796M	Total Assets ($)	1023512M	667112M

M = $ thousand   MM = $ million
See Pages viii through xx for Explanation of Ratios and Data

© RMA 2024

MANUFACTURING—Fertilizer (Mixing Only) Manufacturing NAICS 325314

Comparative Historical Data					Current Data Sorted by Sales					
3	4	3	Type of Statement Unqualified							3
4	4	6	Reviewed						2	4
1	1	1	Compiled					1		
	1	2	Tax Returns					2		
6	14	17	Other					1	3	13
4/1/21-3/31/22 ALL	4/1/22-3/31/23 ALL	4/1/23-3/31/24 ALL			0-1MM	7 (4/1-9/30/23) 1-3MM	3-5MM	22 (10/1/23-3/31/24) 5-10MM	10-25MM	25MM & OVER
14	24	29	NUMBER OF STATEMENTS					4	5	20
%	%	%	ASSETS		%	%	%	%	%	%
8.0	11.7	8.8	Cash & Equivalents		D	D	D			6.6
19.1	16.1	17.3	Trade Receivables (net)		A	A	A			19.5
25.6	24.0	25.6	Inventory		T	T	T			26.9
3.6	3.0	1.8	All Other Current		A	A	A			1.7
56.3	54.7	53.5	Total Current							54.7
34.3	29.4	27.3	Fixed Assets (net)		N	N	N			27.4
5.1	4.8	11.9	Intangibles (net)		O	O	O			13.8
4.3	11.1	7.4	All Other Non-Current		T	T	T			4.1
100.0	100.0	100.0	Total							100.0
			LIABILITIES		A	A	A			
3.4	1.7	4.5	Notes Payable-Short Term		V	V	V			4.8
2.4	4.2	1.8	Cur. Mat.-L.T.D.		A	A	A			1.7
10.6	11.6	15.6	Trade Payables		I	I	I			18.2
.1	.3	.2	Income Taxes Payable		L	L	L			.0
14.7	13.4	15.4	All Other Current		A	A	A			13.3
31.2	31.3	37.4	Total Current		B	B	B			38.0
15.2	13.0	8.1	Long-Term Debt		L	L	L			6.1
.8	.8	.7	Deferred Taxes		E	E	E			1.1
4.6	5.5	7.5	All Other Non-Current							9.7
48.3	49.5	46.2	Net Worth							45.2
100.0	100.0	100.0	Total Liabilities & Net Worth							100.0
			INCOME DATA							
100.0	100.0	100.0	Net Sales							100.0
31.3	24.4	23.1	Gross Profit							17.4
23.4	17.2	19.5	Operating Expenses							14.4
7.9	7.3	3.6	Operating Profit							3.1
-1.2	.5	-.6	All Other Expenses (net)							-.1
9.1	6.7	4.1	Profit Before Taxes							3.2
			RATIOS							
2.3	3.1	2.1								2.0
1.9	1.7	1.7	Current							1.6
1.5	1.2	1.1								1.1
1.5	1.5	1.6								1.5
.9	.9	.8	Quick							.7
.5	.4	.5								.5
22 16.8	13 28.3	18 20.7								24 15.5
29 12.6	23 16.2	30 12.2	Sales/Receivables							36 10.2
41 8.8	36 10.0	44 8.3								45 8.1
24 15.3	23 16.1	21 17.0								24 15.2
42 8.7	45 8.1	58 6.3	Cost of Sales/Inventory							60 6.1
99 3.7	78 4.7	81 4.5								74 4.9
10 36.3	9 39.9	12 31.3								13 29.0
28 12.9	22 16.7	24 15.4	Cost of Sales/Payables							24 15.1
37 9.9	34 10.7	52 7.0								51 7.2
6.0	7.6	7.1								7.0
10.0	9.9	10.0	Sales/Working Capital							9.5
13.7	24.9	51.3								60.4
50.0	27.1	10.4								5.9
21.1	(23) 14.6	(28) 4.3	EBIT/Interest							3.6
9.9	7.2	2.9								1.9
			Net Profit + Depr., Dep., Amort./Cur. Mat. L/T/D							
.4	.5	.4								.4
.7	.6	.7	Fixed/Worth							.9
1.2	1.2	2.2								2.4
.6	.7	.7								.7
1.4	1.1	1.1	Debt/Worth							1.2
2.9	2.4	4.6								5.8
67.1	71.9	42.1	% Profit Before Taxes/Tangible Net Worth							29.8
40.4	(23) 32.4	(24) 11.4							(16)	10.0
29.1	14.8	7.5								-.1
25.3	22.6	11.4	% Profit Before Taxes/Total Assets							12.7
18.7	15.3	7.6								6.7
7.6	8.8	3.8								1.5
13.1	22.1	15.8								12.0
7.4	9.7	8.3	Sales/Net Fixed Assets							9.2
3.5	2.8	4.5								2.8
2.9	3.4	3.0								3.0
1.8	2.3	2.3	Sales/Total Assets							2.6
1.5	1.4	1.4								1.3
2.4	.7	1.0								.6
(12) 3.1	(21) 2.2	(28) 2.7	% Depr., Dep., Amort./Sales							2.4
4.9	5.0	4.7								4.4
			% Officers', Directors' Owners' Comp/Sales							
1891520M	2629772M	3565637M	Net Sales ($)					23115M	83904M	3458618M
599642M	1018023M	1438859M	Total Assets ($)					8128M	77577M	1353154M

M = $ thousand   MM = $ million
See Pages viii through xx for Explanation of Ratios and Data
© RMA 2024

MANUFACTURING—Pesticide and Other Agricultural Chemical Manufacturing NAICS 325320

Current Data Sorted by Assets | Comparative Historical Data

0-500M	500M-2MM	2-10MM	10-50MM	50-100MM	100-250MM	Type of Statement	4/1/19-3/31/20 ALL	4/1/20-3/31/21 ALL
					1	Unqualified	8	1
			1			Reviewed	3	1
						Compiled	2	
			1			Tax Returns	3	1
	1	3	9	6	1	Other	12	4
	2 (4/1-9/30/23)		21 (10/1/23-3/31/24)					
	1	4	10	6	2	NUMBER OF STATEMENTS	28	7
%	%	%	%	%	%	ASSETS	%	%
			5.1			Cash & Equivalents	13.0	
			21.3			Trade Receivables (net)	19.4	
D			37.8			Inventory	28.8	
A			.9			All Other Current	4.6	
T			65.2			Total Current	65.8	
A			13.8			Fixed Assets (net)	25.3	
			12.7			Intangibles (net)	4.5	
N			8.4			All Other Non-Current	4.4	
O			100.0			Total	100.0	
T						LIABILITIES		
			11.2			Notes Payable-Short Term	8.8	
A			2.6			Cur. Mat.-L.T.D.	2.6	
V			25.4			Trade Payables	14.8	
A			.0			Income Taxes Payable	.2	
I			11.3			All Other Current	14.8	
L			50.4			Total Current	41.3	
A			18.4			Long-Term Debt	15.4	
B			.0			Deferred Taxes	1.1	
L			1.2			All Other Non-Current	4.8	
E			30.0			Net Worth	37.4	
			100.0			Total Liabilities & Net Worth	100.0	
						INCOME DATA		
			100.0			Net Sales	100.0	
			33.6			Gross Profit	36.5	
			25.1			Operating Expenses	31.4	
			8.5			Operating Profit	5.1	
			3.4			All Other Expenses (net)	.9	
			5.1			Profit Before Taxes	4.2	
						RATIOS		
			1.8				3.5	
			1.2			Current	2.0	
			.9				.9	
			.7				2.2	
			.6			Quick	1.0	
			.4				.4	
			0 UND				23 16.2	
			47 7.7			Sales/Receivables	46 7.9	
			57 6.4				68 5.4	
			74 4.9				53 6.9	
			107 3.4			Cost of Sales/Inventory	107 3.4	
			140 2.6				135 2.7	
			37 9.9				16 23.2	
			72 5.1			Cost of Sales/Payables	46 7.9	
			111 3.3				66 5.5	
			4.9				2.7	
			25.4			Sales/Working Capital	5.1	
			-57.9				-21.9	
			10.0				52.3	
			6.2			EBIT/Interest	(22) 2.4	
			4.6				-3.5	
						Net Profit + Depr., Dep., Amort./Cur. Mat. L/T/D	14.5	
							(10) 1.4	
							-12.7	
			.2				.1	
			.4			Fixed/Worth	.4	
			NM				2.4	
			1.0				.4	
			3.8			Debt/Worth	1.6	
			NM				9.2	
						% Profit Before Taxes/Tangible Net Worth	23.4	
							(25) 8.9	
							-5.6	
			17.7				13.9	
			13.3			% Profit Before Taxes/Total Assets	3.9	
			9.3				-4.8	
			34.2				21.0	
			12.4			Sales/Net Fixed Assets	6.6	
			6.6				3.9	
			2.4				1.9	
			1.8			Sales/Total Assets	1.6	
			1.1				1.1	
							1.0	
						% Depr., Dep., Amort./Sales	(20) 1.5	
							2.9	
						% Officers', Directors' Owners' Comp/Sales		
	4443M	25648M	435928M	380371M	263858M	Net Sales ($)	1202890M	452642M
	1265M	20732M	218677M	390025M	343679M	Total Assets ($)	1003265M	441897M

M = $ thousand   MM = $ million
See Pages viii through xx for Explanation of Ratios and Data

© RMA 2024

MANUFACTURING—Pesticide and Other Agricultural Chemical Manufacturing NAICS 325320

Comparative Historical Data | Current Data Sorted by Sales

					Type of Statement						
	2		2		1	Unqualified					1
	6		2		1	Reviewed					1
						Compiled					
	2		3		1	Tax Returns			1		
	13		11		20	Other		2		5	12
	4/1/21-		4/1/22-		4/1/23-			2 (4/1-9/30/23)	21 (10/1/23-3/31/24)		
	3/31/22		3/31/23		3/31/24		0-1MM	1-3MM	3-5MM	5-10MM	10-25MM	25MM & OVER
	ALL		ALL		ALL						
	23		18		23	NUMBER OF STATEMENTS			3	1	5	14
	%		%		%	ASSETS	%	%	%	%	%	%
	13.8		13.4		7.8	Cash & Equivalents	D	D				6.7
	22.0		12.0		17.7	Trade Receivables (net)	A	A				21.0
	32.4		36.5		33.1	Inventory	T	T				35.5
	3.6		8.1		2.9	All Other Current	A	A				2.6
	71.7		70.1		61.5	Total Current						65.8
	14.5		14.1		18.4	Fixed Assets (net)	N	N				17.0
	5.3		10.4		10.0	Intangibles (net)	O	O				7.5
	8.5		5.4		10.1	All Other Non-Current	T	T				9.7
	100.0		100.0		100.0	Total						100.0
						LIABILITIES	A	A				
	12.3		5.4		7.7	Notes Payable-Short Term	V	V				5.1
	3.4		2.2		2.6	Cur. Mat.-L.T.D.	A	A				1.2
	11.5		12.2		16.6	Trade Payables	I	I				18.2
	.1		.2		.0	Income Taxes Payable	L	L				.0
	9.0		11.1		12.1	All Other Current	A	A				16.2
	36.2		31.0		39.0	Total Current	B	B				40.7
	10.5		12.9		15.9	Long-Term Debt	L	L				9.1
	.5		.7		.0	Deferred Taxes	E	E				.0
	1.8		3.0		4.0	All Other Non-Current						6.4
	51.0		52.4		41.1	Net Worth						43.8
	100.0		100.0		100.0	Total Liabilities & Net Worth						100.0
						INCOME DATA						
	100.0		100.0		100.0	Net Sales						100.0
	35.7		34.6		31.8	Gross Profit						24.7
	23.4		24.0		25.7	Operating Expenses						19.0
	12.4		10.6		6.1	Operating Profit						5.7
	.2		-.6		1.4	All Other Expenses (net)						1.0
	12.2		11.2		4.8	Profit Before Taxes						4.7
						RATIOS						
	3.0		4.0		3.2							3.5
	1.8		2.5		1.5	Current						1.7
	1.4		1.6		1.1							1.1
	2.2		2.3		1.3							1.7
	.9		.9		.6	Quick						.6
	.5		.3		.5							.5
32	11.4	8	48.4	31	11.9						35	10.5
43	8.5	33	10.9	41	9.0	Sales/Receivables					47	7.7
68	5.4	53	6.9	58	6.3						61	6.0
33	10.9	49	7.4	64	5.7						63	5.8
101	3.6	114	3.2	107	3.4	Cost of Sales/Inventory					101	3.6
135	2.7	228	1.6	174	2.1						135	2.1
14	26.0	10	36.8	25	14.8						24	15.0
33	11.2	33	11.2	58	6.3	Cost of Sales/Payables					36	10.2
49	7.5	70	5.2	96	3.8						73	5.0
	3.0		2.5		3.0							3.1
	5.4		4.0		5.0	Sales/Working Capital						4.2
	10.3		6.5		43.6							34.6
	83.8		93.0		14.8							32.3
(18)	13.9	(15)	55.0	(22)	5.5	EBIT/Interest					(13)	5.9
	5.9		16.9		1.0							1.5
						Net Profit + Depr., Dep., Amort./Cur. Mat. L/T/D						
	.0		.1		.2							.1
	.4		.2		.4	Fixed/Worth						.3
	.6		.4		1.4							1.4
	.5		.4		.6							.9
	1.6		1.2		1.5	Debt/Worth						1.7
	2.7		2.1		5.9							5.7
	80.0		83.6		51.7	% Profit Before Taxes/Tangible Net Worth						49.6
(22)	50.7	(17)	35.8	(20)	18.4						(13)	11.0
	18.2		21.9		1.4							2.3
	33.2		28.0		16.1	% Profit Before Taxes/Total Assets						12.9
	17.8		16.9		7.7							7.2
	8.6		10.5		.2							1.0
	97.4		68.5		22.8							34.2
	20.3		18.3		9.7	Sales/Net Fixed Assets						11.1
	10.4		7.2		5.5							5.7
	2.6		1.8		2.4							2.4
	1.6		1.3		1.3	Sales/Total Assets						1.4
	1.3		1.0		.9							.8
	.9		.7		1.0							.6
(14)	1.6	(14)	.9	(18)	1.7	% Depr., Dep., Amort./Sales					(12)	1.7
	2.0		1.6		3.3							2.6
						% Officers', Directors' Owners' Comp/Sales						
	1093818M		1183685M		1110248M	Net Sales ($)			12322M	7575M	69077M	1021274M
	657641M		873097M		974378M	Total Assets ($)			9201M	8562M	56518M	900097M

© RMA 2024   M = $ thousand   MM = $ million
See Pages viii through xx for Explanation of Ratios and Data

MANUFACTURING—Medicinal and Botanical Manufacturing NAICS 325411

Current Data Sorted by Assets | Comparative Historical Data

0-500M	500M-2MM	2-10MM	10-50MM	50-100MM	100-250MM	Type of Statement		4/1/19-3/31/20		4/1/20-3/31/21
1	1	1	2	2		Unqualified		2		3
		2	5	1		Reviewed		10		
		2	3			Compiled				
	1	2	1			Tax Returns		5		3
		6	16	7	6	Other		46		16
1	1	11	27	10	6	**NUMBER OF STATEMENTS**		63 ALL		22 ALL
%	%	%	%	%	%	**ASSETS**		%		%
		18.8	12.2	11.9		Cash & Equivalents		12.4		21.2
		15.7	18.5	17.8		Trade Receivables (net)		16.3		13.0
		33.4	29.2	24.4		Inventory		29.2		26.6
		4.2	3.7	1.1		All Other Current		2.4		2.1
		72.0	63.6	55.3		Total Current		60.3		62.8
		21.5	24.4	24.8		Fixed Assets (net)		23.2		21.0
		2.0	6.4	12.9		Intangibles (net)		10.8		12.8
		4.5	5.6	7.1		All Other Non-Current		5.7		3.4
		100.0	100.0	100.0		Total		100.0		100.0
						LIABILITIES				
		6.7	6.2	6.7		Notes Payable-Short Term		5.6		4.1
		1.4	3.1	1.5		Cur. Mat.-L.T.D.		1.9		4.6
		18.1	10.0	7.1		Trade Payables		13.1		15.4
		.0	.3	.4		Income Taxes Payable		.1		.2
		18.5	6.2	11.9		All Other Current		10.4		8.4
		44.8	25.7	27.6		Total Current		31.2		32.7
		7.3	18.7	17.6		Long-Term Debt		12.5		25.1
		1.4	.7	.4		Deferred Taxes		1.0		.3
		1.9	8.7	10.1		All Other Non-Current		6.1		6.4
		44.6	46.1	44.3		Net Worth		49.2		35.6
		100.0	100.0	100.0		Total Liabilties & Net Worth		100.0		100.0
						INCOME DATA				
		100.0	100.0	100.0		Net Sales		100.0		100.0
		56.1	39.8	42.0		Gross Profit		42.9		45.6
		45.2	32.2	32.9		Operating Expenses		34.2		35.7
		10.9	7.7	9.0		Operating Profit		8.6		9.9
		.4	1.7	2.1		All Other Expenses (net)		1.2		1.6
		10.5	5.9	6.9		Profit Before Taxes		7.5		8.3
						RATIOS				
		6.0	4.1	2.6				2.9		3.6
		2.8	2.4	2.1		Current		2.1		2.2
		1.1	1.6	1.7				1.4		1.5
		4.9	2.2	1.5				1.7		2.0
		1.4	1.0	1.2		Quick		.9		1.2
		.2	.5	.5				.4		.6
		8 48.1	28 12.9	29 12.4			20	18.6	13	28.7
		32 11.5	39 9.4	51 7.2		Sales/Receivables	34	10.7	27	13.3
		40 9.1	60 6.1	58 6.3			43	8.4	49	7.5
		79 4.6	63 5.8	101 3.6			64	5.7	43	8.4
		111 3.3	122 3.0	159 2.3		Cost of Sales/Inventory	99	3.7	114	3.2
		182 2.0	192 1.9	261 1.4			166	2.2	146	2.5
		21 17.7	27 13.5	19 19.1			22	16.4	15	24.2
		51 7.1	39 9.3	34 10.6		Cost of Sales/Payables	44	8.3	32	11.5
		79 4.6	51 7.1	58 6.3			64	5.7	72	5.1
		2.6	2.9	3.2				3.6		3.5
		7.9	4.4	4.6		Sales/Working Capital		6.5		5.8
		48.1	7.1	6.8				18.3		17.4
			77.9	41.5				29.7		21.3
		(22)	3.1	6.9		EBIT/Interest	(55)	11.1	(18)	11.3
			1.3	.5				1.8		5.0
						Net Profit + Depr., Dep., Amort./Cur. Mat. L/T/D		7.0		
							(12)	4.7		
								2.1		
		.0	.2	.2				.2		.2
		.4	.5	.7		Fixed/Worth		.5		.7
		4.0	1.5	NM				1.4		NM
		.3	.4	.6				.5		1.0
		.5	1.1	1.6		Debt/Worth		1.1		3.3
		5.2	3.5	NM				5.6		-17.3
		140.1	46.3					49.1		126.8
	(10)	10.3	(22) 17.7			% Profit Before Taxes/Tangible Net Worth	(56)	32.0	(16)	47.2
		-32.1	.0					8.9		22.0
		50.3	30.4	15.5				23.0		35.8
		-4.2	5.2	8.3		% Profit Before Taxes/Total Assets		9.9		17.4
		-17.0	.9	-1.6				1.9		7.4
		250.8	16.1	15.5				27.3		68.1
		26.7	7.6	3.9		Sales/Net Fixed Assets		10.9		24.5
		2.4	4.0	2.1				4.3		3.4
		3.8	2.3	1.7				2.5		3.2
		1.7	1.5	1.0		Sales/Total Assets		1.9		1.8
		1.5	1.0	.8				1.1		1.2
			1.2	1.1				1.1		.8
		(22)	3.3	2.5		% Depr., Dep., Amort./Sales	(46)	1.9	(17)	1.6
			5.5	4.5				3.0		4.6
						% Officers', Directors' Owners' Comp/Sales				
630M	9259M	184001M	872906M	898135M	1016391M	Net Sales ($)		3448421M		1409784M
436M	1300M	72714M	598258M	733300M	1059502M	Total Assets ($)		2355198M		1170309M

© RMA 2024   M = $ thousand   MM = $ million
See Pages viii through xx for Explanation of Ratios and Data

MANUFACTURING—Medicinal and Botanical Manufacturing NAICS 325411

Comparative Historical Data | Current Data Sorted by Sales

						Type of Statement						
		5		4	4	Unqualified					2	2
		1		4	7	Reviewed					1	6
		1		3	5	Compiled					1	4
		4		1	4	Tax Returns	1	1			1	1
		20		29	36	Other		1		2	9	24
		4/1/21-3/31/22 ALL		4/1/22-3/31/23 ALL	4/1/23-3/31/24 ALL		0-1MM	12 (4/1-9/30/23) 1-3MM	3-5MM	44 (10/1/23-3/31/24) 5-10MM	10-25MM	25MM & OVER
		31		41	56	NUMBER OF STATEMENTS	1	2		2	14	37
		%		%	%	ASSETS	%	%	%	%	%	%
		17.4		16.3	14.2	Cash & Equivalents					10.1	13.9
		14.8		15.3	16.2	Trade Receivables (net)					12.0	19.3
		26.3		25.4	26.7	Inventory					39.5	24.2
		1.9		2.9	3.0	All Other Current					7.1	1.6
		60.4		59.9	60.1	Total Current					68.6	59.0
		20.0		23.8	25.5	Fixed Assets (net)					26.4	22.0
		16.3		10.5	8.6	Intangibles (net)					2.8	11.3
		3.3		5.7	5.7	All Other Non-Current					2.2	7.7
		100.0		100.0	100.0	Total					100.0	100.0
						LIABILITIES						
		3.8		5.8	5.8	Notes Payable-Short Term					11.2	3.9
		1.8		1.5	2.3	Cur. Mat.-L.T.D.					4.2	1.5
		10.0		9.2	10.4	Trade Payables					11.7	10.0
		.1		.1	.2	Income Taxes Payable					.4	.2
		7.9		11.9	9.7	All Other Current					15.4	8.0
		23.7		28.6	28.3	Total Current					42.8	23.6
		17.5		19.0	15.2	Long-Term Debt					17.7	13.1
		.3		.2	.7	Deferred Taxes					2.3	.2
		1.6		1.9	6.9	All Other Non-Current					4.4	8.4
		56.9		50.4	48.9	Net Worth					32.8	54.7
		100.0		100.0	100.0	Total Liabilities & Net Worth					100.0	100.0
						INCOME DATA						
		100.0		100.0	100.0	Net Sales					100.0	100.0
		43.9		43.2	43.6	Gross Profit					38.8	42.0
		32.8		37.3	35.4	Operating Expenses					39.0	31.1
		11.2		5.9	8.2	Operating Profit					-.1	10.9
		.2		.5	1.4	All Other Expenses (net)					2.1	1.0
		11.0		5.4	6.8	Profit Before Taxes					-2.3	10.0
						RATIOS						
		5.3		4.2	4.0						6.3	3.9
		2.2		2.3	2.4	Current					2.4	2.5
		1.7		1.4	1.6						.9	1.8
		3.3		2.0	2.1						1.5	2.2
		1.2		1.2	1.2	Quick					.5	1.4
		.7		.5	.5						.3	.8
24	15.5		17	21.2	24	15.0				17	21.6	27	13.6
33	11.1		32	11.5	38	9.7	Sales/Receivables				33	11.0	40	9.1
50	7.3		50	7.3	54	6.7					51	7.2	53	6.9
63	5.8		45	8.1	74	4.9				91	4.0	68	5.4
130	2.8		99	3.7	118	3.1	Cost of Sales/Inventory				192	1.9	101	3.6
174	2.1		192	1.9	192	1.9					304	1.2	152	2.4
22	16.9		16	22.9	21	17.0				26	13.9	21	17.4
38	9.6		30	12.3	39	9.4	Cost of Sales/Payables				50	7.3	31	11.9
61	6.0		51	7.1	53	6.9					55	6.6	49	7.4
		2.7		2.9	3.0						2.4	3.2
		4.7		4.9	4.5	Sales/Working Capital					3.3	4.9
		8.5		10.6	10.1						NM	8.0
		54.0		56.3	41.5						1.7	58.3
(20)	8.3		(31)	7.9	(46)	3.5	EBIT/Interest			(12)	-1.2	(31)	21.0
		2.2		-1.2	.2						-29.7	2.8
					6.5	Net Profit + Depr., Dep.,						6.5
				(15)	2.8	Amort./Cur. Mat. L/T/D					(11)	2.8
					.7							.9
		.1		.2	.2						.3	.2
		.4		.4	.5	Fixed/Worth					.6	.5
		2.6		1.1	1.5						NM	1.3
		.2		.3	.4						.5	.4
		1.2		.8	.9	Debt/Worth					2.1	.9
		5.9		2.3	3.6						NM	2.9
		73.5		36.6	43.7	% Profit Before Taxes/Tangible					18.2	60.3
(28)	26.8		(35)	8.1	(47)	17.2	Net Worth			(11)	-5.5	(32)	27.8
		13.7		-2.5	-5.5						-35.0	4.0
		23.0		25.5	25.1	% Profit Before Taxes/Total					4.3	28.0
		11.0		4.4	5.3	Assets					-6.3	10.8
		2.7		-4.0	-3.0						-20.2	1.1
		36.7		24.7	24.8						23.9	27.7
		10.8		8.8	6.3	Sales/Net Fixed Assets					5.7	9.6
		3.8		3.4	2.7						2.2	3.8
		2.6		2.5	2.1						1.7	2.3
		1.7		1.5	1.5	Sales/Total Assets					1.5	1.5
		.7		.9	.9						.7	.9
		.4		.7	1.2						3.1	.7
(23)	2.0		(34)	1.8	(46)	3.1	% Depr., Dep., Amort./Sales			(13)	4.1	(29)	2.8
		4.3		3.6	5.5						6.4	3.7
					1.7	% Officers', Directors'						
				(12)	2.7	Owners' Comp/Sales						
					5.4							
		1657506M		2658910M	2981322M	Net Sales ($)	630M	3398M		18889M	197581M	2760824M
		1057177M		1932354M	2465510M	Total Assets ($)	436M	5124M		24010M	189539M	2246401M

© RMA 2024 M = $ thousand MM = $ million
See Pages viii through xx for Explanation of Ratios and Data

MANUFACTURING—Pharmaceutical Preparation Manufacturing NAICS 325412

Current Data Sorted by Assets | Comparative Historical Data

						Type of Statement		
				2	8	Unqualified	19	9
			2	6		Reviewed	8	3
			6	1		Compiled	6	2
		2	2	1		Tax Returns	7	5
1	1	17	25	15	24	Other	85	48
	21	(4/1-9/30/23)	90	(10/1/23-3/31/24)			4/1/19-	4/1/20-
0-500M	500M-2MM	2-10MM	10-50MM	50-100MM	100-250MM		3/31/20	3/31/21
1	2	19	35	22	32	NUMBER OF STATEMENTS	ALL 125	ALL 67
%	%	%	%	%	%	ASSETS	%	%
		12.6	13.9	12.0	10.0	Cash & Equivalents	13.2	21.6
		26.4	19.3	15.3	17.3	Trade Receivables (net)	18.7	15.9
		27.5	25.5	19.9	15.0	Inventory	24.0	22.5
		4.7	3.8	2.3	2.8	All Other Current	2.4	1.6
		71.3	62.5	49.5	45.1	Total Current	58.3	61.5
		17.1	24.7	26.6	22.4	Fixed Assets (net)	23.4	17.4
		.0	3.6	14.1	24.8	Intangibles (net)	12.1	15.3
		11.6	9.2	9.8	7.8	All Other Non-Current	6.3	5.8
		100.0	100.0	100.0	100.0	Total	100.0	100.0
						LIABILITIES		
		4.8	8.6	2.6	2.1	Notes Payable-Short Term	9.1	4.2
		5.7	2.3	1.8	4.6	Cur. Mat.-L.T.D.	2.4	2.9
		22.6	14.4	9.1	8.2	Trade Payables	11.0	9.9
		.0	.0	.3	.1	Income Taxes Payable	.2	.2
		6.5	10.2	12.7	15.1	All Other Current	12.0	14.9
		39.6	35.6	26.5	30.0	Total Current	34.6	32.2
		20.0	11.6	23.1	27.9	Long-Term Debt	16.5	17.4
		.0	.0	.9	.3	Deferred Taxes	.5	.9
		12.1	5.9	2.3	7.4	All Other Non-Current	4.7	4.4
		28.3	46.9	47.1	34.4	Net Worth	43.5	45.2
		100.0	100.0	100.0	100.0	Total Liabilities & Net Worth	100.0	100.0
						INCOME DATA		
		100.0	100.0	100.0	100.0	Net Sales	100.0	100.0
		47.7	38.5	42.8	52.4	Gross Profit	43.7	50.2
		33.8	33.6	39.5	42.3	Operating Expenses	35.7	37.5
		13.9	4.9	3.4	10.1	Operating Profit	8.0	12.8
		1.4	.2	.7	4.6	All Other Expenses (net)	1.4	1.2
		12.4	4.6	2.6	5.5	Profit Before Taxes	6.6	11.5
						RATIOS		
		5.6	3.0	2.7	3.4		3.5	3.3
		2.6	1.9	1.9	1.9	Current	1.7	2.3
		1.5	1.3	1.3	1.0		1.2	1.3
		2.9	1.6	1.5	1.8		1.9	2.2
		1.0	1.0	1.0	.9	Quick	.9	1.4
		.7	.5	.7	.6		.5	.6
		18 20.4	24 15.3	35 10.4	32 11.5		28 12.9	29 12.8
		36 10.2	41 9.0	54 6.7	45 8.2	Sales/Receivables	42 8.6	46 7.9
		76 4.8	69 5.3	64 5.7	62 5.9		65 5.6	69 5.3
		35 10.5	54 6.8	83 4.4	76 4.8		51 7.2	68 5.4
		73 5.0	87 4.2	135 2.7	114 3.2	Cost of Sales/Inventory	91 4.0	126 2.9
		152 2.4	126 2.9	203 1.8	243 1.5		174 2.1	192 1.9
		6 63.8	15 24.8	28 13.1	37 9.8		25 14.7	20 18.1
		33 11.1	34 10.6	48 7.6	51 7.1	Cost of Sales/Payables	42 8.7	42 8.7
		52 7.0	57 6.4	69 5.3	70 5.2		70 5.2	79 4.6
		3.1	3.2	2.2	3.3		3.1	2.5
		5.3	6.8	5.4	4.3	Sales/Working Capital	7.2	5.3
		12.9	17.3	11.4	NM		33.6	13.4
		107.4	22.7	11.3	14.6		15.5	62.1
	(18)	8.6	(26) 3.2	(17) 2.0	(28) 5.2	EBIT/Interest	(101) 5.6	(52) 9.6
		-.1	.4	-1.6	.4		-.1	2.8
						Net Profit + Depr., Dep.,	22.7	20.8
						Amort./Cur. Mat. L/T/D	(30) 5.6 (15) 8.7	
							2.5	6.6
		.0	.3	.4	.3		.2	.1
		.2	.6	.7	.9	Fixed/Worth	.6	.5
		.6	1.1	1.7	NM		2.6	2.5
		.4	.4	.6	1.0		.4	.6
		1.0	1.4	1.2	3.1	Debt/Worth	1.2	1.2
		3.7	2.6	8.1	-2.3		4.3	-87.5
		84.9	28.2	38.3	77.5	% Profit Before Taxes/Tangible	47.8	57.6
	(17)	42.7	(31) 9.5	(19) 8.2	(20) 27.5	Net Worth	(99) 18.8	(50) 29.6
		-2.5	-2.3	-7.9	4.4		4.9	12.3
		65.5	22.3	9.3	17.5	% Profit Before Taxes/Total	20.7	23.8
		17.4	4.3	5.7	3.9	Assets	7.9	10.0
		-2.8	-1.8	-2.0	-3.0		-1.0	3.7
		949.3	64.7	9.4	38.2		21.3	47.0
		19.2	5.2	5.0	5.1	Sales/Net Fixed Assets	6.6	10.9
		7.2	3.0	2.1	3.0		3.6	4.8
		3.2	2.2	1.2	1.4		2.0	2.1
		2.4	1.6	.9	.9	Sales/Total Assets	1.4	1.1
		1.2	1.0	.7	.5		1.0	.8
		.6	.6	1.7	2.8		1.3	1.3
	(10)	2.9	(28) 2.1	(15) 3.0	(17) 3.0	% Depr., Dep., Amort./Sales	(96) 2.9	(42) 2.0
		3.7	4.2	7.4	3.9		4.5	4.7
							1.3	
						% Officers', Directors'	(15) 2.1	
						Owners' Comp/Sales	2.9	
1956M	29669M	261385M	1580615M	1581348M	5319525M	Net Sales ($)	8005926M	4666019M
233M	2522M	106230M	955309M	1431828M	4883039M	Total Assets ($)	6411208M	3896230M

M = $ thousand   MM = $ million
See Pages viii through xx for Explanation of Ratios and Data

© RMA 2024

MANUFACTURING—Pharmaceutical Preparation Manufacturing NAICS 325412

Comparative Historical Data			Type of Statement	Current Data Sorted by Sales						
7	15	15	Unqualified						1	14
5	9	7	Reviewed						2	5
2	4	3	Compiled					1	1	2
3	1	3	Tax Returns				1	2	2	
41	57	83	Other		2	1		6	10	64
4/1/21-3/31/22 ALL	4/1/22-3/31/23 ALL	4/1/23-3/31/24 ALL		0-1MM	21 (4/1-9/30/23) 1-3MM	3-5MM		5-10MM	90 (10/1/23-3/31/24) 10-25MM	25MM & OVER
58	86	111	NUMBER OF STATEMENTS		2	2		6	16	85
%	%	%	ASSETS	%	%	%		%	%	%
15.2	13.9	13.3	Cash & Equivalents	D					15.9	12.4
16.0	19.5	18.6	Trade Receivables (net)	A					15.6	19.0
22.6	25.5	21.9	Inventory	T					26.7	20.5
2.4	3.1	3.2	All Other Current	A					2.4	2.8
56.2	62.1	57.0	Total Current						60.6	54.7
20.1	21.2	22.8	Fixed Assets (net)	N					21.6	24.0
16.5	8.2	11.1	Intangibles (net)	O					9.2	12.7
7.1	8.5	9.1	All Other Non-Current	T					8.6	8.5
100.0	100.0	100.0	Total						100.0	100.0
			LIABILITIES	A						
5.5	7.6	4.7	Notes Payable-Short Term	V					5.1	4.5
2.2	2.3	3.4	Cur. Mat.-L.T.D.	A					2.6	3.0
12.5	12.4	12.7	Trade Payables	I					10.8	11.8
.0	.1	.1	Income Taxes Payable	L					.0	.1
12.2	11.4	11.3	All Other Current	A					10.5	12.0
32.5	33.9	32.3	Total Current	B					28.9	31.5
16.6	17.7	20.6	Long-Term Debt	L					12.4	19.9
.4	.6	.3	Deferred Taxes	E					.0	.4
11.0	3.9	6.5	All Other Non-Current						8.1	5.7
39.6	44.0	40.4	Net Worth						50.6	42.5
100.0	100.0	100.0	Total Liabilities & Net Worth						100.0	100.0
			INCOME DATA							
100.0	100.0	100.0	Net Sales						100.0	100.0
47.1	46.2	45.0	Gross Profit						44.1	43.8
39.2	37.8	37.3	Operating Expenses						37.1	35.9
7.9	8.5	7.7	Operating Profit						7.0	7.9
.2	1.3	1.8	All Other Expenses (net)						.2	2.0
7.7	7.2	5.9	Profit Before Taxes						6.8	5.9
			RATIOS							
3.5	3.6	3.6							5.0	2.7
2.0	1.9	2.0	Current						2.7	1.9
1.2	1.3	1.4							1.3	1.2
2.0	2.0	2.1							4.0	1.7
1.2	1.0	1.0	Quick						1.0	1.0
.5	.6	.6							.4	.6

29	12.8	25	14.6	23	15.6		Sales/Receivables					24	15.3	24	15.2
46	8.0	43	8.5	42	8.7							39	9.4	42	8.7
64	5.7	69	5.3	63	5.8							61	6.0	63	5.8
81	4.5	79	4.6	63	5.8		Cost of Sales/Inventory					65	5.6	63	5.8
126	2.9	122	3.0	101	3.6							89	4.1	101	3.6
182	2.0	192	1.9	159	2.3							281	1.3	152	2.4
31	11.9	24	15.5	22	16.9		Cost of Sales/Payables					7	51.8	23	15.8
50	7.3	43	8.5	46	8.0							38	9.6	47	7.8
101	3.6	79	4.6	59	6.2							79	4.6	56	6.5
	2.6		2.8		3.2		Sales/Working Capital						2.2		3.4
	5.7		4.7		5.7								5.3		6.3
	25.9		11.2		14.1								50.2		14.1
	25.5		31.7		16.1		EBIT/Interest						77.4		15.2
(53)	5.8	(75)	7.6	(91)	3.8							(12)	.9	(69)	4.9
	.1		1.1		.1								-9.6		.4
	15.0		11.2		9.5		Net Profit + Depr., Dep., Amort./Cur. Mat. L/T/D						10.2		10.2
(15)	3.8	(27)	3.2	(24)	2.1									(22)	2.5
	.5		1.6		.5										.8
	.2		.2		.2		Fixed/Worth						.2		.3
	.9		.6		.6								.5		.7
	-2.5		1.2		1.5								1.5		1.6
	.5		.5		.7		Debt/Worth						.3		.7
	2.1		1.3		1.4								1.4		1.4
	-8.0		4.8		4.3								5.2		6.3
	60.6		39.8		52.7		% Profit Before Taxes/Tangible Net Worth						106.3		51.1
(42)	25.7	(74)	18.6	(90)	14.3							(13)	16.0	(68)	14.7
	.1		5.5		-1.5								-8.9		1.9
	19.8		18.6		20.0		% Profit Before Taxes/Total Assets						59.7		19.6
	7.2		8.8		5.9								.1		6.3
	-1.2		.7		-2.2								-4.4		-1.1
	41.1		28.5		39.8		Sales/Net Fixed Assets						39.0		30.8
	8.1		8.2		6.7								7.1		6.2
	3.3		3.5		3.2								3.1		3.1
	1.5		2.0		2.1		Sales/Total Assets						3.2		2.0
	1.1		1.4		1.2								1.3		1.1
	.8		.9		.8								.6		.8
	1.5		1.1		1.5		% Depr., Dep., Amort./Sales								1.6
(41)	2.4	(66)	1.8	(71)	2.8									(57)	2.8
	4.7		5.8		4.1										4.0
	1.3		1.1		1.0		% Officers', Directors', Owners' Comp/Sales								
(11)	2.0	(17)	4.3	(10)	1.5										
	3.9		11.0		3.1										
	4273198M		7661650M		8774498M	Net Sales ($)		3943M	6240M	43771M			278943M		8441601M
	3976232M		5274691M		7379161M	Total Assets ($)		4487M	5877M	27974M			391915M		6948908M

© RMA 2024
M = $ thousand   MM = $ million
See Pages viii through xx for Explanation of Ratios and Data

MANUFACTURING—Paint and Coating Manufacturing NAICS 325510

Current Data Sorted by Assets | Comparative Historical Data

							Type of Statement				
		1		1	1	2	Unqualified		7		6
	1	1	3		2	1	Reviewed		15		7
	1	2	3				Compiled		6		1
2	2	4	2				Tax Returns		4		6
1	6	12	12	2	1		Other		34		35
0-500M	14 (4/1-9/30/23) 500M-2MM	2-10MM	48 (10/1/23-3/31/24) 10-50MM	50-100MM	100-250MM				4/1/19-3/31/20 ALL		4/1/20-3/31/21 ALL
3	10	19	21	5	4		NUMBER OF STATEMENTS		66		55
%	%	%	%	%	%		ASSETS		%		%
	14.0	9.1	12.6				Cash & Equivalents		11.9		19.9
	17.8	22.2	18.6				Trade Receivables (net)		22.5		19.9
	18.3	24.0	28.9				Inventory		25.0		23.7
	1.7	.4	5.5				All Other Current		3.1		1.7
	51.9	55.7	65.7				Total Current		62.5		65.1
	25.1	21.9	19.9				Fixed Assets (net)		21.9		20.9
	17.5	13.8	4.1				Intangibles (net)		7.0		3.6
	5.5	8.6	10.4				All Other Non-Current		8.7		10.4
	100.0	100.0	100.0				Total		100.0		100.0
							LIABILITIES				
	7.1	5.8	3.6				Notes Payable-Short Term		5.0		3.4
	5.6	2.8	1.0				Cur. Mat.-L.T.D.		3.6		5.2
	11.2	12.2	9.1				Trade Payables		18.0		10.0
	.0	.0	.4				Income Taxes Payable		.1		.2
	6.1	20.3	11.0				All Other Current		10.1		6.0
	30.0	41.1	25.2				Total Current		36.7		24.8
	22.6	21.0	9.1				Long-Term Debt		9.2		12.5
	.0	.3	.2				Deferred Taxes		.1		.6
	4.6	2.3	12.7				All Other Non-Current		11.2		9.8
	42.8	35.4	52.9				Net Worth		42.9		52.4
	100.0	100.0	100.0				Total Liabilities & Net Worth		100.0		100.0
							INCOME DATA				
	100.0	100.0	100.0				Net Sales		100.0		100.0
	42.4	41.7	36.0				Gross Profit		36.6		41.9
	31.2	36.1	24.9				Operating Expenses		30.2		34.3
	11.2	5.6	11.1				Operating Profit		6.4		7.6
	1.4	1.9	.7				All Other Expenses (net)		.8		-.8
	9.8	3.7	10.4				Profit Before Taxes		5.6		8.5
							RATIOS				
	2.7	3.2	4.3						4.6		5.7
	1.8	1.5	3.0				Current		2.4		3.0
	1.1	.7	2.0						1.6		1.5
	1.5	1.4	2.4						1.9		3.6
	1.0	.7	1.7				Quick		1.2		1.7
	.8	.4	.7						.7		.9
0	UND	20	18.1	28	12.9			27	13.3	25	14.5
27	13.5	44	8.3	36	10.1		Sales/Receivables	38	9.5	40	9.2
36	10.2	56	6.5	45	8.1			56	6.5	51	7.1
0	UND	4	97.5	56	6.5			30	12.2	36	10.0
27	13.6	47	7.8	81	4.5		Cost of Sales/Inventory	73	5.0	79	4.6
56	6.5	107	3.4	122	3.0			104	3.5	118	3.1
7	49.6	15	23.6	14	26.5			17	21.4	19	19.7
13	28.9	21	17.7	19	19.6		Cost of Sales/Payables	25	14.6	31	11.7
43	8.4	49	7.5	45	8.1			41	8.8	50	7.3
	9.8	5.0	3.2						3.8		3.0
	15.2	11.4	4.4				Sales/Working Capital		5.6		5.3
	68.8	-16.0	7.4						12.9		13.8
		40.9	143.2						30.5		71.0
	(18)	10.3	(15) 7.4				EBIT/Interest	(55)	4.7	(51)	17.9
		.1	3.1						1.6		4.7
							Net Profit + Depr., Dep.,		7.7		8.1
							Amort./Cur. Mat. L/T/D	(15)	2.4	(12)	4.6
									1.1		1.4
	.3	.2	.1						.1		.1
	.9	.7	.3				Fixed/Worth		.4		.3
	-213.8	-3.2	.5						1.6		1.0
	.6	.6	.3						.3		.4
	1.6	1.2	.7				Debt/Worth		1.3		.8
	-578.0	-19.5	2.7						2.7		2.2
		59.2	62.6						50.9		57.0
	(14)	36.8	(20) 29.5				% Profit Before Taxes/Tangible Net Worth	(59)	13.9	(52)	26.5
		.6	17.4						6.2		9.7
	47.1	24.8	25.4						17.0		27.4
	22.5	12.9	15.1				% Profit Before Taxes/Total Assets		6.5		10.4
	4.8	-3.2	6.8						.9		5.1
	55.0	24.4	33.4						23.3		42.8
	12.3	15.8	16.0				Sales/Net Fixed Assets		10.8		11.4
	8.5	3.8	5.2						5.7		5.7
	4.3	2.8	2.3						2.7		2.9
	3.1	1.9	2.0				Sales/Total Assets		1.8		1.7
	1.8	1.0	1.2						1.4		1.2
		.6	.7						.9		.8
	(10)	1.1	(19) 1.4				% Depr., Dep., Amort./Sales	(56)	1.8	(45)	1.3
		3.6	2.2						2.9		2.8
							% Officers', Directors'		1.5		2.8
							Owners' Comp/Sales	(12)	2.1	(15)	4.8
									2.6		8.9
7966M	40293M	229538M	1041425M	423925M	677087M		Net Sales ($)		2736340M		1913541M
1088M	13392M	102824M	587536M	298952M	542966M		Total Assets ($)		1853894M		1250129M

M = $ thousand   MM = $ million
See Pages viii through xx for Explanation of Ratios and Data

© RMA 2024

MANUFACTURING—Paint and Coating Manufacturing NAICS 325510

Comparative Historical Data

5 9 4 5 31 4/1/21- 3/31/22 ALL 54	4 6 4 8 31 4/1/22- 3/31/23 ALL 53	4 8 6 10 34 4/1/23- 3/31/24 ALL 62	Type of Statement Unqualified Reviewed Compiled Tax Returns Other NUMBER OF STATEMENTS

Current Data Sorted by Sales

		1 2 5	1 1 1 3 5	1 1 3 5	1 1 4	4 6 4 3 14
		14 (4/1-9/30/23)		48 (10/1/23-3/31/24)		
0-1MM	1-3MM	3-5MM	5-10MM	10-25MM	25MM & OVER
1	7	7	10	6	31

%	%	%		%	%	%	%	%	%
12.2	7.8	11.6	Cash & Equivalents				15.9		12.6
22.4	23.7	19.7	Trade Receivables (net)				22.2		19.9
29.9	31.9	25.1	Inventory				27.1		27.6
3.4	2.2	2.7	All Other Current				.1		4.5
67.9	65.6	59.1	Total Current				65.2		64.6
18.5	20.1	21.2	Fixed Assets (net)				28.9		19.4
7.5	8.4	11.9	Intangibles (net)				.1		7.2
6.1	5.9	7.9	All Other Non-Current				5.9		8.8
100.0	100.0	100.0	Total				100.0		100.0
			LIABILITIES						
8.6	6.6	4.7	Notes Payable-Short Term				4.4		2.7
2.9	1.7	2.5	Cur. Mat.-L.T.D.				2.9		1.2
12.1	12.8	12.1	Trade Payables				10.6		10.1
.2	.1	.1	Income Taxes Payable				.0		.3
7.4	12.0	12.2	All Other Current				13.7		9.2
31.2	33.3	31.6	Total Current				31.6		23.5
10.0	16.3	16.5	Long-Term Debt				15.3		9.3
.5	.4	.3	Deferred Taxes				.0		.4
6.4	7.7	9.7	All Other Non-Current				.3		11.5
51.9	42.4	42.0	Net Worth				52.8		55.2
100.0	100.0	100.0	Total Liabilties & Net Worth				100.0		100.0
			INCOME DATA						
100.0	100.0	100.0	Net Sales				100.0		100.0
38.2	36.6	38.3	Gross Profit				35.1		35.5
30.1	30.1	29.6	Operating Expenses				24.5		25.6
8.1	6.5	8.7	Operating Profit				10.6		9.9
-.7	.8	1.3	All Other Expenses (net)				-.5		.9
8.8	5.7	7.5	Profit Before Taxes				11.1		9.1
			RATIOS						
3.3	3.1	3.7	Current				3.0		4.3
2.4	2.3	2.6					1.8		3.4
1.6	1.5	1.4					1.4		2.5
1.6	1.7	2.0	Quick				1.6		2.4
1.1	1.0	1.1					1.0		1.7
.7	.5	.6					.9		.8
29 12.7	28 13.0	25 14.8	Sales/Receivables				0 UND	28 12.9
45 8.2	36 10.0	34 10.6					33 11.1	34 10.6
61 6.0	65 5.6	48 7.6					54 6.8	49 7.5
63 5.8	46 7.9	38 9.7	Cost of Sales/Inventory				9 39.2	59 6.2
101 3.6	94 3.9	69 5.3					39 9.4	94 3.9
140 2.6	152 2.4	118 3.1					114 3.2	130 2.8
22 16.9	18 20.6	13 28.7	Cost of Sales/Payables				10 37.3	15 25.0
34 10.8	31 11.7	21 17.7					17 22.0	19 19.6
55 6.6	50 7.3	43 8.4					23 15.7	43 8.4
3.4	4.0	3.6	Sales/Working Capital				4.7		2.7
4.9	6.0	6.6					11.9		4.4
8.5	9.4	18.2					20.9		6.0
40.4	23.2	44.3	EBIT/Interest				72.4		47.9
(49) 17.7	(46) 5.7	(54) 9.3					44.0	(24) 10.3
6.4	1.8	2.7					19.4		3.0
35.1		33.5	Net Profit + Depr., Dep., Amort./Cur. Mat. L/T/D						35.9
(14) 9.6	(12) 10.8							(10) 10.8
6.0	2.3								3.1
.2	.2	.2	Fixed/Worth				.1		.2
.4	.4	.5					.7		.3
.7	1.3	1.7					1.2		.7
.5	.5	.5	Debt/Worth				.6		.3
1.0	1.6	1.0					.8		.7
2.5	7.3	5.9					1.9		2.0
45.6	65.6	61.7	% Profit Before Taxes/Tangible Net Worth				180.2		44.9
(49) 28.4	(45) 28.2	(51) 32.1					40.9	(29) 25.1
13.2	11.2	15.7					17.8		15.2
22.8	17.3	25.1	% Profit Before Taxes/Total Assets				53.5		25.9
11.7	9.7	12.6					24.7		12.1
3.8	3.1	3.9					11.2		6.4
27.2	28.1	30.9	Sales/Net Fixed Assets				50.9		24.4
12.5	14.5	11.7					12.3		10.8
6.6	6.7	5.2					6.8		5.2
2.5	2.4	2.7	Sales/Total Assets				4.3		2.3
1.7	1.9	1.9					3.2		1.7
1.3	1.4	1.2					1.5		1.2
.9	.7	.7	% Depr., Dep., Amort./Sales						1.0
(47) 1.5	(42) 1.7	(43) 1.4						(27) 1.6
3.1	3.0	2.4							2.4
2.4	1.5	1.1	% Officers', Directors' Owners' Comp/Sales						
(12) 10.0	(10) 3.0	(14) 2.2							
16.3	4.5	3.8							
1805726M	1893582M	2420234M	Net Sales ($)	693M	14932M	27524M	69729M	97533M	2209823M
1192880M	1227107M	1546758M	Total Assets ($)	2156M	8237M	19934M	32049M	50882M	1433500M

© RMA 2024 M = $ thousand MM = $ million
See Pages viii through xx for Explanation of Ratios and Data

MANUFACTURING—Adhesive Manufacturing NAICS 325520

Current Data Sorted by Assets

						Type of Statement		Comparative Historical Data		
				3	3	Unqualified		6		6
		3	1	1	1	Reviewed		5		3
		3				Compiled		6		1
		2	1			Tax Returns		6		1
	5	6	3	2	1	Other		20		17
	3 (4/1-9/30/23)		32 (10/1/23-3/31/24)					4/1/19-3/31/20		4/1/20-3/31/21
0-500M	500M-2MM	2-10MM	10-50MM	50-100MM	100-250MM			ALL		ALL
	5	14	8	6	2	NUMBER OF STATEMENTS		43		28
%	%	%	%	%	%	ASSETS		%		%
		15.3				Cash & Equivalents		11.5		12.5
		24.8				Trade Receivables (net)		19.7		16.7
		35.5				Inventory		26.7		19.8
		.5				All Other Current		3.2		1.4
		76.1				Total Current		61.1		50.4
DATA NOT AVAILABLE		16.6				Fixed Assets (net)		26.0		27.1
		2.4				Intangibles (net)		9.7		15.3
		4.9				All Other Non-Current		3.2		7.2
		100.0				Total		100.0		100.0
						LIABILITIES				
		.9				Notes Payable-Short Term		6.8		3.9
		1.5				Cur. Mat.-L.T.D.		5.1		7.8
		14.6				Trade Payables		10.6		8.1
		.0				Income Taxes Payable		.2		.3
		7.7				All Other Current		8.7		14.4
		24.7				Total Current		31.3		34.5
		8.1				Long-Term Debt		12.2		16.7
		.0				Deferred Taxes		.5		.9
		3.6				All Other Non-Current		4.2		4.5
		63.7				Net Worth		51.8		43.4
		100.0				Total Liabilities & Net Worth		100.0		100.0
						INCOME DATA				
		100.0				Net Sales		100.0		100.0
		34.8				Gross Profit		32.8		38.4
		26.1				Operating Expenses		27.0		32.0
		8.6				Operating Profit		5.8		6.4
		-.5				All Other Expenses (net)		.5		1.0
		9.1				Profit Before Taxes		5.3		5.4
						RATIOS				
		8.9						4.4		4.0
		3.2				Current		2.0		2.0
		2.1						1.3		1.3
		5.1						1.9		3.1
		1.8				Quick		1.1		1.0
		.9						.5		.5
	27	13.6					28	12.9	34	10.6
	39	9.4				Sales/Receivables	37	9.9	45	8.2
	45	8.1					46	7.9	51	7.1
	69	5.3					49	7.5	52	7.0
	79	4.6				Cost of Sales/Inventory	65	5.6	70	5.2
	99	3.7					107	3.4	114	3.2
	11	33.0					17	21.2	19	19.0
	18	20.1				Cost of Sales/Payables	23	15.7	29	12.5
	40	9.2					40	9.2	38	9.6
		2.6						3.2		3.5
		4.8				Sales/Working Capital		7.2		5.9
		7.8						13.9		20.6
		58.3						15.7		30.0
		(12) 23.4				EBIT/Interest	(37)	5.4	(23)	8.7
		10.5						1.4		1.0
						Net Profit + Depr., Dep., Amort./Cur. Mat. L/T/D		3.4		14.3
							(11)	2.4	(11)	2.6
								1.2		1.7
		.0						.3		.4
		.2				Fixed/Worth		.7		1.0
		.5						1.4		3.4
		.2						.4		.4
		.6				Debt/Worth		1.0		1.5
		1.0						5.8		5.7
		50.4						30.9		42.8
		23.0				% Profit Before Taxes/Tangible Net Worth	(35)	14.1	(24)	25.0
		17.0						5.5		4.0
		29.8						14.5		17.3
		15.9				% Profit Before Taxes/Total Assets		8.1		8.7
		11.1						.5		.5
		104.5						11.7		16.3
		17.1				Sales/Net Fixed Assets		8.0		6.2
		6.6						4.3		2.9
		2.9						2.4		1.7
		2.2				Sales/Total Assets		1.9		1.4
		1.8						1.3		.9
		.7						1.0		1.7
		(12) 1.4				% Depr., Dep., Amort./Sales	(36)	1.7	(23)	2.8
		2.5						2.9		4.5
						% Officers', Directors' Owners' Comp/Sales		2.6		
							(10)	3.6		
								6.2		
	13303M	220582M	344083M	715502M	539113M	Net Sales ($)		1686411M		1190485M
	4718M	99021M	234045M	461864M	391447M	Total Assets ($)		1247910M		908816M

M = $ thousand   MM = $ million
See Pages viii through xx for Explanation of Ratios and Data

© RMA 2024

MANUFACTURING—Adhesive Manufacturing NAICS 325520

Comparative Historical Data | Current Data Sorted by Sales

						Type of Statement							
		3		5		6	Unqualified					1	5
		2		5		6	Reviewed					3	3
		3				3	Compiled				1	2	
		1		5		3	Tax Returns					2	1
		13		12		17	Other	1	2	1	1	7	5
		4/1/21-		4/1/22-		4/1/23-			3 (4/1-9/30/23)			32 (10/1/23-3/31/24)		
		3/31/22		3/31/23		3/31/24		0-1MM	1-3MM	3-5MM	5-10MM	10-25MM	25MM & OVER
		ALL		ALL		ALL							
		22		27		35	NUMBER OF STATEMENTS	1	2	1	2	15	14
		%		%		%	ASSETS	%	%	%	%	%	%
		10.8		9.5		11.4	Cash & Equivalents					12.8	11.6
		23.2		20.0		22.0	Trade Receivables (net)					24.3	20.7
		26.0		34.5		29.5	Inventory					33.8	19.7
		2.2		1.5		1.0	All Other Current					.5	1.6
		62.2		65.4		63.9	Total Current					71.4	53.7
		20.2		21.2		16.7	Fixed Assets (net)					14.8	19.5
		7.8		8.7		10.3	Intangibles (net)					9.3	13.3
		9.8		4.6		9.1	All Other Non-Current					4.6	13.4
		100.0		100.0		100.0	Total					100.0	100.0
							LIABILITIES						
		8.3		6.0		2.7	Notes Payable-Short Term					1.4	4.3
		3.1		2.1		2.0	Cur. Mat.-L.T.D.					1.2	3.0
		12.5		14.0		11.8	Trade Payables					13.9	9.8
		.3		.2		.3	Income Taxes Payable					.0	.8
		10.3		6.3		10.0	All Other Current					7.3	12.2
		34.5		28.6		26.9	Total Current					23.8	30.1
		18.1		13.5		8.4	Long-Term Debt					10.4	7.1
		1.0		.5		.5	Deferred Taxes					.3	1.0
		5.4		6.4		8.1	All Other Non-Current					8.3	5.2
		41.0		51.1		56.1	Net Worth					57.2	56.6
		100.0		100.0		100.0	Total Liabilities & Net Worth					100.0	100.0
							INCOME DATA						
		100.0		100.0		100.0	Net Sales					100.0	100.0
		32.6		31.2		34.1	Gross Profit					33.2	28.1
		26.0		26.0		28.5	Operating Expenses					26.7	22.9
		6.7		5.2		5.6	Operating Profit					6.5	5.3
		.7		.6		.5	All Other Expenses (net)					.8	.2
		5.9		4.6		5.1	Profit Before Taxes					5.7	5.1
							RATIOS						
		4.5		3.9		4.5						8.7	4.4
		2.0		2.6		2.5	Current					3.4	1.9
		1.1		1.4		1.6						1.7	1.2
		2.2		1.7		3.5						4.7	3.4
		1.1		1.0		1.1	Quick					1.9	1.1
		.5		.5		.6						.9	.6
30	12.3	29	12.5	27	13.5						32	11.5	30	12.3
41	8.9	40	9.1	43	8.4	Sales/Receivables					43	8.4	45	8.2
54	6.7	46	7.9	49	7.4						48	7.6	59	6.2
61	6.0	68	5.4	54	6.8						70	5.2	47	7.8
79	4.6	87	4.2	79	4.6	Cost of Sales/Inventory					81	4.5	61	6.0
104	3.5	135	2.7	94	3.9						94	3.9	85	4.3
23	15.9	18	20.2	13	27.3						12	31.4	16	23.4
32	11.3	34	10.7	22	16.5	Cost of Sales/Payables					18	20.2	24	15.5
47	7.7	54	6.7	39	9.3						38	9.6	40	9.1
	4.1		4.0		3.1						2.7	3.2
	5.8		5.3		5.2	Sales/Working Capital					5.2	5.2
	55.8		8.3		9.6						9.0	23.8
	41.9		33.1		34.0						54.5	21.7
(17)	16.1	(24)	6.4	(31)	10.6	EBIT/Interest					(13)	13.4	(12)	8.0
	7.2		1.3		.3						2.4	-.4
					16.9							
				(14)	4.5	Net Profit + Depr., Dep., Amort./Cur. Mat. L/T/D						
					.4							
	.2		.2		.1						.0	.3
	.7		.5		.3	Fixed/Worth					.3	.4
	1.7		1.0		.7						.6	1.0
	.3		.4		.3						.2	.4
	1.0		1.0		.7	Debt/Worth					.7	.8
	5.9		3.4		2.2						2.2	3.2
	41.6		44.4		47.4	% Profit Before Taxes/Tangible Net Worth					50.8	26.7
(18)	31.9	(24)	20.6	(31)	19.6						(13)	21.8	(13)	18.1
	23.7		4.2		9.0						16.2	-7.8
	19.3		19.6		20.8	% Profit Before Taxes/Total Assets					29.3	16.7
	16.1		6.3		11.2						14.0	10.1
	7.0		1.7		.2						6.3	-3.2
	22.5		50.4		28.3						88.3	12.6
	10.5		7.9		11.5	Sales/Net Fixed Assets					15.6	9.4
	4.4		4.9		6.4						6.7	4.4
	2.2		2.4		2.7						2.7	2.2
	1.8		1.8		1.9	Sales/Total Assets					2.2	1.5
	1.4		1.3		1.3						1.5	1.1
	1.2		.7		1.0						.8	.9
(19)	1.9	(24)	1.6	(29)	1.6	% Depr., Dep., Amort./Sales					(13)	1.4	(13)	1.9
	2.5		2.3		2.5						2.8	2.1
			1.9		1.8							
		(11)	3.2	(14)	3.6	% Officers', Directors' Owners' Comp/Sales						
			9.5		9.2							
	1175298M		1434147M		1832583M	Net Sales ($)	877M	3161M	4157M	12653M	252525M	1559210M
	757485M		821586M		1191095M	Total Assets ($)	681M	1329M	1523M	7786M	137628M	1042148M

M = $ thousand   MM = $ million

© RMA 2024

MANUFACTURING—Soap and Other Detergent Manufacturing NAICS 325611

Current Data Sorted by Assets

0-500M	500M-2MM	2-10MM	10-50MM	50-100MM	100-250MM	Type of Statement		
		1	1	1	3	Unqualified		
		1	3	1		Reviewed		
			1	1		Compiled		
		1	1			Tax Returns		
		13	7	7	1	Other		
5 (4/1-9/30/23)			38 (10/1/23-3/31/24)				4/1/19-3/31/20	4/1/20-3/31/21
		16	13	10	4	NUMBER OF STATEMENTS	37 ALL 55	17 ALL 20
%	%	%	%	%	%	**ASSETS**	%	%
		19.9	11.5	14.8		Cash & Equivalents	11.4	10.9
DATA	DATA	20.2	25.1	17.6		Trade Receivables (net)	24.3	23.2
		29.7	30.9	15.3		Inventory	28.2	25.9
		1.7	.6	6.2		All Other Current	1.9	2.0
NOT	NOT	71.5	68.0	53.9		Total Current	65.8	62.0
		14.7	14.5	25.3		Fixed Assets (net)	19.5	22.8
		1.8	5.1	15.4		Intangibles (net)	8.7	13.6
AVAILABLE	AVAILABLE	12.0	12.4	5.3		All Other Non-Current	6.0	1.7
		100.0	100.0	100.0		Total	100.0	100.0
						LIABILITIES		
		5.5	.9	6.1		Notes Payable-Short Term	10.0	4.6
		1.4	5.2	1.8		Cur. Mat.-L.T.D.	5.0	2.4
		10.6	13.6	8.1		Trade Payables	12.7	10.2
		.0	.0	1.7		Income Taxes Payable	.1	.5
		12.0	14.1	7.8		All Other Current	9.3	7.7
		29.5	33.8	25.4		Total Current	37.1	25.3
		23.8	10.6	13.6		Long-Term Debt	11.0	11.0
		.0	.0	.0		Deferred Taxes	.4	.1
		7.3	12.7	6.0		All Other Non-Current	8.0	4.9
		39.4	42.9	55.1		Net Worth	43.4	58.7
		100.0	100.0	100.0		Total Liabilities & Net Worth	100.0	100.0
						INCOME DATA		
		100.0	100.0	100.0		Net Sales	100.0	100.0
		48.6	32.3	38.5		Gross Profit	39.3	37.1
		46.0	25.2	29.9		Operating Expenses	34.0	25.0
		2.6	7.1	8.7		Operating Profit	5.3	12.2
		2.3	.4	2.5		All Other Expenses (net)	1.3	1.1
		.2	6.7	6.2		Profit Before Taxes	4.0	11.1
						RATIOS		
		6.8	3.5	4.3			2.8	3.9
		2.4	3.0	2.1		Current	2.1	2.3
		1.5	1.6	1.1			1.6	1.6
		3.7	1.6	2.7			1.7	2.7
		1.6	1.3	1.5		Quick	1.2	1.2
		.9	1.0	.5			.6	.8
		23 16.1	29 12.4	33 11.2			28 13.1	30 12.3
		29 12.7	40 9.1	43 8.5		Sales/Receivables	46 8.0	38 9.7
		45 8.1	52 7.0	46 8.0			55 6.6	49 7.5
		55 6.6	33 11.2	46 7.9			48 7.6	59 6.2
		79 4.6	72 5.1	56 6.5		Cost of Sales/Inventory	74 4.9	70 5.2
		182 2.0	94 3.9	72 5.1			122 3.0	111 3.3
		18 20.1	18 20.3	15 24.1			20 17.9	15 23.6
		30 12.2	33 11.2	27 13.5		Cost of Sales/Payables	35 10.3	28 13.0
		38 9.6	42 8.7	35 10.3			51 7.1	37 9.9
		3.0	4.2	3.0			4.6	2.9
		4.5	5.9	5.7		Sales/Working Capital	6.3	5.7
		12.2	10.2	NM			12.5	11.1
		16.3	52.2				35.2	69.8
		(12) 5.7	(11) 19.2			EBIT/Interest	(49) 5.8	(18) 15.0
		1.3	1.4				1.5	3.9
						Net Profit + Depr., Dep., Amort./Cur. Mat. L/T/D		
		.1	.2	.2			.1	.2
		.5	.3	.9		Fixed/Worth	.4	.6
		NM	.8	3.2			1.3	.7
		.5	.5	.4			.5	.5
		1.3	1.2	1.0		Debt/Worth	.9	.8
		NM	10.6	9.0			3.1	1.3
		38.1	45.9			% Profit Before Taxes/Tangible Net Worth	34.0	72.7
		(12) 11.3	(11) 32.3				(48) 20.8	(19) 45.8
		.3	7.5				9.2	15.8
		15.3	32.8	16.2		% Profit Before Taxes/Total Assets	16.3	32.8
		4.1	13.5	9.5			7.2	17.4
		-2.6	1.7	-.7			1.4	7.5
		39.2	107.4	20.9			56.4	32.6
		20.9	13.1	7.6		Sales/Net Fixed Assets	11.7	10.4
		9.8	7.4	2.7			6.5	5.2
		3.1	2.7	1.8			2.5	2.5
		2.0	2.1	1.5		Sales/Total Assets	2.0	1.9
		1.4	1.6	1.1			1.5	1.3
		.5	.3				1.1	.7
		(11) 1.5	(11) 1.2			% Depr., Dep., Amort./Sales	(38) 1.9	(17) 1.7
		2.8	1.6				2.5	2.3
						% Officers', Directors' Owners' Comp/Sales	1.4 (16) 2.7 5.2	
		213632M	665056M	1072137M	910237M	Net Sales ($)	2393188M	999986M
		87400M	280078M	721780M	716457M	Total Assets ($)	1529990M	595825M

M = $ thousand   MM = $ million
See Pages viii through xx for Explanation of Ratios and Data

© RMA 2024

MANUFACTURING—Soap and Other Detergent Manufacturing NAICS 325611

Comparative Historical Data | Current Data Sorted by Sales

Comparative Historical Data					Current Data Sorted by Sales					
6		4		6	**Type of Statement**				1	5
2		3		5	Unqualified				2	3
2		1		2	Reviewed					2
2		1		2	Compiled			1	1	
15		22		28	Tax Returns			3	1	16
4/1/21-3/31/22		4/1/22-3/31/23		4/1/23-3/31/24	Other	1	2		6	
ALL		ALL		ALL		5 (4/1-9/30/23)		38 (10/1/23-3/31/24)		
27		31		43	NUMBER OF STATEMENTS	0-1MM	1-3MM	3-5MM	5-10MM	10-25MM	25MM & OVER
						1	2	4	10	26
%		%		%	ASSETS	%	%	%	%	%	%
16.7		8.6		14.7	Cash & Equivalents					18.4	14.2
19.7		20.8		20.5	Trade Receivables (net)	D				20.0	21.5
26.3		28.3		25.2	Inventory	A				34.6	20.6
2.6		3.9		2.5	All Other Current	T				2.0	3.1
65.2		61.6		62.9	Total Current	A				75.1	59.3
21.9		22.2		18.6	Fixed Assets (net)	N				19.2	20.0
8.0		7.4		8.3	Intangibles (net)	O				1.9	12.6
4.9		8.7		10.2	All Other Non-Current	T				3.8	8.1
100.0		100.0		100.0	Total					100.0	100.0
					LIABILITIES	A					
6.5		7.2		3.9	Notes Payable-Short Term	V				3.1	3.8
2.9		1.8		2.8	Cur. Mat.-L.T.D.	A				.8	3.6
11.5		11.9		10.9	Trade Payables	I				9.2	11.8
.2		.3		.4	Income Taxes Payable	L				.0	.7
8.9		6.0		11.5	All Other Current	A				12.3	11.3
30.0		27.2		29.6	Total Current	B				25.4	31.2
12.8		15.9		18.7	Long-Term Debt	L				24.7	14.9
.1		.0		.1	Deferred Taxes	E				.0	.2
3.4		7.6		8.2	All Other Non-Current					8.2	4.8
53.7		49.3		43.4	Net Worth					41.6	48.9
100.0		100.0		100.0	Total Liabilities & Net Worth					100.0	100.0
					INCOME DATA						
100.0		100.0		100.0	Net Sales					100.0	100.0
38.4		38.6		39.2	Gross Profit					50.9	31.3
34.7		36.2		34.0	Operating Expenses					49.4	24.1
3.7		2.4		5.2	Operating Profit					1.6	7.2
-.5		.7		1.8	All Other Expenses (net)					1.1	1.5
4.2		1.6		3.5	Profit Before Taxes					.4	5.7
					RATIOS						
4.1		4.0		3.7						7.2	3.2
2.3		2.5		2.4	Current					3.6	1.9
1.5		1.5		1.4						2.4	1.2
2.5		2.4		1.8						3.4	1.7
1.1		.9		1.3	Quick					1.7	1.2
.6		.7		.7						1.1	.5
30	12.3	27	13.7	27	13.3					24	15.2	28	13.2
40	9.2	40	9.1	40	9.1	Sales/Receivables				36	10.0	40	9.1
51	7.2	56	6.5	47	7.8					48	7.6	46	8.0
58	6.3	54	6.7	48	7.6					78	4.7	33	11.1
85	4.3	74	4.9	70	5.2	Cost of Sales/Inventory				99	3.7	59	6.2
111	3.3	159	2.3	91	4.0					304	1.2	79	4.6
22	16.6	15	24.7	19	19.4					20	18.7	17	20.9
30	12.2	29	12.7	29	12.4	Cost of Sales/Payables				33	11.0	28	13.0
47	7.8	42	8.6	41	9.0					51	7.2	38	9.6
3.5		3.4		3.2						2.6	4.2
5.7		6.6		6.1	Sales/Working Capital					3.0	7.1
10.2		11.8		10.5						5.1	18.3
30.1		14.3		22.7							35.7
(22)	6.0	(25)	3.7	(34)	5.7	EBIT/Interest					(21)	14.2
.7		.4		1.4							1.5
					Net Profit + Depr., Dep., Amort./Cur. Mat. L/T/D						
.1		.3		.2						.2	.2
.6		.5		.6	Fixed/Worth					.6	.5
1.2		1.0		4.2						-4.3	3.2
.3		.6		.5						.5	.5
.7		.9		1.3	Debt/Worth					1.0	1.2
2.2		2.1		11.5						-46.6	10.6
28.4		29.4		40.6							46.9
(24)	15.7	(28)	7.4	(34)	13.8	% Profit Before Taxes/Tangible Net Worth					(22)	22.5
3.5		-7.0		3.0							3.1
14.9		11.7		19.8						11.9	31.7
6.5		3.0		8.7	% Profit Before Taxes/Total Assets					5.5	11.7
1.2		-2.9		1.1						-.9	1.8
24.1		15.1		37.1						19.6	46.5
13.7		10.9		12.8	Sales/Net Fixed Assets					9.8	12.2
4.4		6.3		5.7						6.1	4.9
2.3		2.5		2.4						2.1	2.5
1.8		1.8		1.8	Sales/Total Assets					1.8	1.8
1.3		1.3		1.3						1.5	1.3
1.0		.7		1.0							1.1
(22)	1.9	(25)	1.4	(31)	1.6	% Depr., Dep., Amort./Sales					(18)	1.6
2.3		1.9		2.6							2.2
					% Officers', Directors' Owners' Comp/Sales						
1439406M		2130036M		2861062M	Net Sales ($)	2771M	6374M	30502M	166904M	2654511M
831674M		1335436M		1805715M	Total Assets ($)	2105M	6489M	19325M	91984M	1685812M

© RMA 2024

M = $ thousand   MM = $ million

See Pages viii through xx for Explanation of Ratios and Data

MANUFACTURING—Polish and Other Sanitation Good Manufacturing NAICS 325612

Current Data Sorted by Assets | Comparative Historical Data

0-500M	500M-2MM	2-10MM	10-50MM	50-100MM	100-250MM	Type of Statement	4/1/19-3/31/20 ALL	4/1/20-3/31/21 ALL
			1			Unqualified	7	3
			4	1		Reviewed	4	
		1		1		Compiled	3	2
1	1	5	5	3	1	Tax Returns	5	4
			23 (10/1/23-3/31/24)			Other	16	13
	3 (4/1-9/30/23)							
1	1	7	10	6	1	NUMBER OF STATEMENTS	35	22
%	%	%	%	%	%	ASSETS	%	%
			12.1			Cash & Equivalents	10.7	13.8
			20.1			Trade Receivables (net)	24.6	27.3
			22.3			Inventory	26.1	27.5
			1.5			All Other Current	2.8	.7
			56.1			Total Current	64.2	69.4
			23.9			Fixed Assets (net)	23.4	16.5
			8.0			Intangibles (net)	5.0	12.0
			11.9			All Other Non-Current	7.3	2.0
			100.0			Total	100.0	100.0
						LIABILITIES		
			8.9			Notes Payable-Short Term	10.6	8.2
			3.0			Cur. Mat.-L.T.D.	2.4	2.3
			11.2			Trade Payables	12.5	12.9
			.0			Income Taxes Payable	.0	.1
			10.8			All Other Current	5.5	7.9
			33.9			Total Current	31.0	31.3
			10.4			Long-Term Debt	13.6	12.3
			.0			Deferred Taxes	.2	.4
			6.5			All Other Non-Current	3.5	5.0
			49.2			Net Worth	51.7	50.9
			100.0			Total Liabilities & Net Worth	100.0	100.0
						INCOME DATA		
			100.0			Net Sales	100.0	100.0
			35.6			Gross Profit	36.7	42.9
			29.7			Operating Expenses	28.1	29.0
			5.9			Operating Profit	8.5	13.8
			.1			All Other Expenses (net)	1.0	1.2
			5.7			Profit Before Taxes	7.5	12.6
						RATIOS		
			3.6				4.3	5.5
			1.6			Current	2.2	4.0
			1.1				1.5	1.3
			2.1				2.8	3.5
			.9			Quick	1.1	1.6
			.5				.6	.7
		32	11.5				26 14.3	34 10.8
		37	9.9			Sales/Receivables	42 8.7	47 7.8
		50	7.3				56 6.5	65 5.6
		59	6.2				35 10.4	55 6.6
		73	5.0			Cost of Sales/Inventory	66 5.5	91 4.0
		96	3.8				118 3.1	152 2.4
		22	16.8				20 17.9	11 34.0
		30	12.0			Cost of Sales/Payables	28 13.1	26 14.2
		43	8.4				48 7.6	49 7.4
			4.0				4.0	2.7
			11.9			Sales/Working Capital	6.3	4.2
			49.6				15.7	20.2
							18.1	79.7
						EBIT/Interest	(32) 6.0	(18) 23.6
							1.9	5.9
						Net Profit + Depr., Dep.,	31.1	
						Amort./Cur. Mat. L/T/D	(11) 2.3	
							1.3	
			.3				.1	.1
			.8			Fixed/Worth	.5	.3
			1.6				1.0	1.3
			.4				.5	.4
			1.6			Debt/Worth	1.1	.8
			3.3				2.5	3.6
							59.8	74.3
						% Profit Before Taxes/Tangible Net Worth	17.2	(19) 33.6
							9.3	21.4
			18.1				18.3	26.7
			8.4			% Profit Before Taxes/Total Assets	9.3	17.0
			5.0				2.2	10.0
			16.4				30.4	44.4
			9.7			Sales/Net Fixed Assets	8.9	18.1
			4.9				5.4	8.1
			2.3				2.8	2.4
			1.6			Sales/Total Assets	2.1	1.9
			1.2				1.5	1.5
			.5				.9	.6
			1.7			% Depr., Dep., Amort./Sales	(31) 1.9	(16) 1.4
			3.2				2.9	2.9
							2.4	
						% Officers', Directors' Owners' Comp/Sales	(10) 3.4	
							5.7	
527M	728M	96407M	372624M	560299M	319292M	Net Sales ($)	1935153M	869050M
212M	606M	40652M	208340M	397096M	181613M	Total Assets ($)	1093235M	460024M

M = $ thousand   MM = $ million
See Pages viii through xx for Explanation of Ratios and Data
© RMA 2024

MANUFACTURING—Polish and Other Sanitation Good Manufacturing NAICS 325612

Comparative Historical Data | Current Data Sorted by Sales

Comparative Historical Data			Type of Statement	Current Data Sorted by Sales					
2	4	2	Unqualified					1	2
6	4	6	Reviewed						5
1	1	1	Compiled						1
3	3	1	Tax Returns				1		
23	9	16	Other	2	1	1	1	1	10
4/1/21-3/31/22 ALL	4/1/22-3/31/23 ALL	4/1/23-3/31/24 ALL		0-1MM	3 (4/1-9/30/23) 1-3MM	3-5MM	23 (10/1/23-3/31/24) 5-10MM	10-25MM	25MM & OVER
35	21	26	NUMBER OF STATEMENTS	2	1	1	2	2	18
%	%	%	ASSETS	%	%	%	%	%	%
11.6	7.4	9.3	Cash & Equivalents						5.2
23.0	22.2	24.2	Trade Receivables (net)						22.8
29.0	30.1	18.3	Inventory						20.8
1.8	1.0	3.2	All Other Current						2.6
65.4	60.7	54.9	Total Current						51.4
18.1	19.7	21.6	Fixed Assets (net)						23.0
11.1	8.8	11.0	Intangibles (net)						12.3
5.4	10.7	12.4	All Other Non-Current						13.3
100.0	100.0	100.0	Total						100.0
			LIABILITIES						
6.3	8.6	10.1	Notes Payable-Short Term						10.2
2.2	1.3	2.9	Cur. Mat.-L.T.D.						2.7
14.3	10.7	10.3	Trade Payables						12.2
.0	.0	.0	Income Taxes Payable						.0
8.9	8.0	11.9	All Other Current						9.5
31.7	28.7	35.2	Total Current						34.6
17.0	17.0	12.9	Long-Term Debt						12.4
.2	.2	.3	Deferred Taxes						.2
3.9	6.7	7.1	All Other Non-Current						10.3
47.1	47.4	44.4	Net Worth						42.5
100.0	100.0	100.0	Total Liabilities & Net Worth						100.0
			INCOME DATA						
100.0	100.0	100.0	Net Sales						100.0
34.8	33.7	40.0	Gross Profit						33.4
27.9	27.6	30.9	Operating Expenses						26.9
6.9	6.0	9.0	Operating Profit						6.6
.2	.7	1.2	All Other Expenses (net)						.7
6.7	5.3	7.8	Profit Before Taxes						5.8
			RATIOS						
4.6	5.7	3.1							2.5
2.3	3.0	1.7	Current						1.7
1.5	1.5	1.0							1.1
2.7	2.7	1.7							1.0
1.7	1.2	.9	Quick						.9
.6	.8	.6							.6
23 15.9	36 10.1	29 12.7						29	12.7
41 8.8	43 8.4	37 9.8	Sales/Receivables					37	9.8
47 7.7	49 7.5	51 7.2						50	7.3
36 10.1	65 5.6	28 13.2						59	6.2
83 4.4	91 4.0	69 5.3	Cost of Sales/Inventory					69	5.3
118 3.1	159 2.3	89 4.1						85	4.3
18 20.7	21 17.7	19 19.6						22	16.8
26 13.9	27 13.6	29 12.8	Cost of Sales/Payables					29	12.8
35 10.4	37 9.9	38 9.7						38	9.7
3.2	2.4	4.3							5.4
5.3	3.9	11.3	Sales/Working Capital						11.3
20.6	15.6	436.1							50.9
81.9	49.9	10.9							11.7
(31) 19.1	(20) 6.4	(24) 5.4	EBIT/Interest						5.1
2.4	2.6	3.4							3.3
			Net Profit + Depr., Dep., Amort./Cur. Mat. L/T/D						
.1	.1	.1							.3
.4	.4	.5	Fixed/Worth						1.0
2.1	.9	1.4							1.6
.3	.4	.8							1.2
1.2	.9	1.5	Debt/Worth						1.9
5.2	5.0	3.8							3.9
43.8	43.1	57.0							62.0
(29) 23.3	(18) 20.4	(23) 18.1	% Profit Before Taxes/Tangible Net Worth					(16)	20.2
9.0	6.5	12.2							12.4
21.2	14.6	18.1							18.1
11.5	8.4	10.1	% Profit Before Taxes/Total Assets						9.0
4.6	2.1	5.4							4.0
62.6	56.4	37.3							30.3
18.5	9.6	12.9	Sales/Net Fixed Assets						10.0
6.9	5.5	5.7							5.5
2.7	2.2	2.3							2.3
2.1	1.6	1.7	Sales/Total Assets						1.8
1.1	1.2	1.2							1.3
.6	1.3	1.1							.9
(27) 1.2	(15) 1.9	(23) 1.5	% Depr., Dep., Amort./Sales					(17)	1.5
2.3	2.6	3.1							3.1
			% Officers', Directors' Owners' Comp/Sales						
2241435M	1404635M	1349877M	Net Sales ($)	1255M	1432M	4507M	16199M	28578M	1297906M
1405544M	882345M	828519M	Total Assets ($)	818M	9828M	3822M	7661M	21270M	785120M

© RMA 2024   M = $ thousand   MM = $ million
See Pages viii through xx for Explanation of Ratios and Data

MANUFACTURING—Toilet Preparation Manufacturing NAICS 325620

Current Data Sorted by Assets

Type of Statement	0-500M	500M-2MM	2-10MM	10-50MM	50-100MM	100-250MM
Unqualified				3	3	2
Reviewed			1	3	1	
Compiled			2	1		
Tax Returns	1	1	1		1	
Other			3	16	7	6
			11 (4/1-9/30/23)	41 (10/1/23-3/31/24)		
NUMBER OF STATEMENTS	1	1	7	23	12	8

Comparative Historical Data

	4/1/19-3/31/20 ALL	4/1/20-3/31/21 ALL
Unqualified	16	5
Reviewed	4	1
Compiled	3	
Tax Returns	4	3
Other	47	34
NUMBER OF STATEMENTS	74	43

Combined Data Table

0-500M %	500M-2MM %	2-10MM %	10-50MM %	50-100MM %	100-250MM %		Hist %	Hist %
						ASSETS		
			10.3	13.4		Cash & Equivalents	13.3	17.5
			19.0	18.4		Trade Receivables (net)	19.5	21.0
			36.2	28.4		Inventory	30.0	28.2
			1.9	1.1		All Other Current	4.0	3.8
			67.3	61.3		Total Current	66.7	70.5
			19.5	16.7		Fixed Assets (net)	18.3	11.3
			4.3	9.4		Intangibles (net)	7.6	13.3
			8.9	12.6		All Other Non-Current	7.4	4.9
			100.0	100.0		Total	100.0	100.0
						LIABILITIES		
			11.3	6.6		Notes Payable-Short Term	9.8	8.4
			4.4	2.1		Cur. Mat.-L.T.D.	1.7	4.8
			13.1	8.1		Trade Payables	14.9	9.3
			.1	.0		Income Taxes Payable	.5	.1
			9.8	6.5		All Other Current	10.4	9.3
			38.6	23.3		Total Current	37.4	31.8
			16.6	19.7		Long-Term Debt	11.8	16.8
			.1	.0		Deferred Taxes	.1	.2
			8.1	8.1		All Other Non-Current	4.4	5.3
			36.6	48.8		Net Worth	46.2	45.8
			100.0	100.0		Total Liabilities & Net Worth	100.0	100.0
						INCOME DATA		
			100.0	100.0		Net Sales	100.0	100.0
			46.3	33.5		Gross Profit	43.7	45.0
			40.9	21.1		Operating Expenses	36.5	34.2
			5.4	12.4		Operating Profit	7.2	10.8
			-.1	1.3		All Other Expenses (net)	1.2	1.8
			5.4	11.2		Profit Before Taxes	6.0	9.0
						RATIOS		
			2.5	3.6			3.4	3.6
			1.7	2.5		Current	1.9	2.4
			1.3	2.0			1.4	1.5
			1.5	2.5			2.0	2.2
			.6	1.1		Quick	.9	1.1
			.3	.8			.6	.7
		26 14.0	36 10.1			32 11.5	30 12.3	
		38 9.7	47 7.8		Sales/Receivables	42 8.7	41 9.0	
		51 7.1	61 6.0			58 6.3	54 6.7	
		74 4.9	68 5.4			73 5.0	68 5.4	
		126 2.9	101 3.6		Cost of Sales/Inventory	118 3.1	118 3.1	
		243 1.5	159 2.3			152 2.4	152 2.4	
		27 13.6	17 21.7			26 13.8	21 17.5	
		42 8.7	25 14.5		Cost of Sales/Payables	41 8.9	35 10.5	
		74 4.9	39 9.4			72 5.1	52 7.0	
			3.3	3.5			3.4	3.4
			7.0	4.3		Sales/Working Capital	5.7	5.0
			12.0	5.7			11.5	8.6
			25.0	81.9			29.0	50.6
			6.8	(11) 29.8		EBIT/Interest	(60) 9.1	(39) 14.5
			1.2	1.9			-.2	2.4
			5.3				32.0	
			(11) 2.6			Net Profit + Depr., Dep., Amort./Cur. Mat. L/T/D	(17) 6.1	
			1.0				1.9	
			.2	.2			.1	.1
			.7	.4		Fixed/Worth	.4	.4
			1.1	.7			1.2	1.0
			.7	.6			.5	.6
			1.8	1.5		Debt/Worth	1.1	1.5
			4.2	6.7			3.7	4.4
			63.1	150.4			53.7	76.1
			(20) 43.4	(11) 49.1		% Profit Before Taxes/Tangible Net Worth	(65) 28.5	(34) 47.2
			8.5	12.6			5.7	18.2
			20.3	29.7			22.1	33.4
			10.0	15.7		% Profit Before Taxes/Total Assets	10.8	13.0
			1.5	4.9			-2.1	2.1
			31.5	31.8			44.7	65.8
			13.9	16.2		Sales/Net Fixed Assets	10.6	28.1
			4.3	3.4			6.1	7.6
			2.4	2.2			2.2	2.3
			1.7	1.2		Sales/Total Assets	1.7	1.8
			1.3	1.0			1.3	1.3
			.6	1.2			.5	.7
			(16) .9	(11) 1.9		% Depr., Dep., Amort./Sales	(60) 1.7	(28) 1.5
			1.8	3.9			2.5	2.3
						% Officers', Directors' Owners' Comp/Sales	1.1	
							(14) 2.4	
							3.5	
279M	2756M	100621M	948264M	1306315M	1401200M	Net Sales ($)	5116874M	2913639M
241M	1278M	32951M	509557M	843653M	995588M	Total Assets ($)	3314381M	2000058M

M = $ thousand   MM = $ million
See Pages viii through xx for Explanation of Ratios and Data

© RMA 2024

MANUFACTURING—Toilet Preparation Manufacturing NAICS 325620

Comparative Historical Data | Current Data Sorted by Sales

				Type of Statement						
5	5	8		Unqualified					1	8
2	3	5		Reviewed				1	1	3
1	1	4		Compiled				1	1	2
2	4	3		Tax Returns				1	1	
29	28	32		Other	1	1	1	8	8	22
4/1/21-3/31/22	4/1/22-3/31/23	4/1/23-3/31/24				11 (4/1-9/30/23)			41 (10/1/23-3/31/24)	
ALL	ALL	ALL			0-1MM	1-3MM	3-5MM	5-10MM	10-25MM	25MM & OVER
39	41	52	NUMBER OF STATEMENTS	1	2	1	2	11	35	
%	%	%	ASSETS	%	%	%	%	%	%	
11.7	10.1	11.0	Cash & Equivalents					7.9	12.3	
19.6	21.6	19.4	Trade Receivables (net)					23.4	18.8	
26.7	30.8	30.1	Inventory					27.5	31.6	
1.4	3.1	2.1	All Other Current					3.3	1.3	
59.4	65.6	62.6	Total Current					62.1	63.9	
11.9	16.5	18.6	Fixed Assets (net)					19.5	19.1	
24.0	9.2	6.3	Intangibles (net)					1.2	6.8	
4.7	8.7	12.5	All Other Non-Current					17.3	10.2	
100.0	100.0	100.0	Total					100.0	100.0	
			LIABILITIES							
5.8	8.9	11.4	Notes Payable-Short Term					18.2	6.7	
5.7	2.8	2.8	Cur. Mat.-L.T.D.					2.0	3.3	
12.7	15.1	10.0	Trade Payables					12.7	10.1	
.1	.3	.3	Income Taxes Payable					.0	.4	
11.6	6.3	10.4	All Other Current					6.9	9.5	
35.9	33.4	34.9	Total Current					39.8	29.9	
16.5	17.6	15.8	Long-Term Debt					10.5	18.6	
.3	.2	.1	Deferred Taxes					.0	.1	
10.4	6.0	6.4	All Other Non-Current					8.3	5.0	
36.9	42.9	42.8	Net Worth					41.4	46.4	
100.0	100.0	100.0	Total Liabilities & Net Worth					100.0	100.0	
			INCOME DATA							
100.0	100.0	100.0	Net Sales					100.0	100.0	
43.9	37.7	42.9	Gross Profit					45.7	39.1	
35.4	34.5	36.2	Operating Expenses					43.2	28.4	
8.5	3.2	6.7	Operating Profit					2.5	10.6	
.4	1.8	.8	All Other Expenses (net)					-.8	1.9	
8.1	1.4	5.9	Profit Before Taxes					3.2	8.7	
			RATIOS							
3.2	3.6	2.7						2.1	2.9	
2.3	2.0	2.0	Current					1.6	2.3	
1.4	1.5	1.3						1.1	1.5	
1.7	1.7	1.7						1.7	1.7	
1.0	.9	.7	Quick					.7	.9	
.6	.5	.4						.3	.5	
25 14.7	33 11.0	26 13.9						27 13.6	28 13.0	
34 10.6	46 7.9	41 8.9	Sales/Receivables					36 10.1	45 8.2	
47 7.8	60 6.1	51 7.2						41 8.9	51 7.2	
34 10.6	58 6.3	65 5.6						15 24.7	76 4.8	
126 2.9	114 3.2	111 3.3	Cost of Sales/Inventory					65 5.6	114 3.2	
192 1.9	203 1.8	215 1.7						243 1.5	166 2.2	
21 17.8	20 18.2	19 19.4						10 38.1	22 16.7	
37 9.9	43 8.4	32 11.4	Cost of Sales/Payables					45 8.1	32 11.5	
62 5.9	79 4.6	51 7.1						74 4.9	42 8.6	
3.9	3.6	3.5						7.5	3.4	
6.0	5.3	5.7	Sales/Working Capital					8.3	5.3	
13.2	7.9	11.6						26.1	8.7	
69.6	31.3	47.8						54.0	46.2	
(35) 17.5	(38) 5.2	(48) 7.4	EBIT/Interest					6.8	(33) 8.8	
1.6	-1.0	1.5						1.5	2.1	
	20.5	11.8	Net Profit + Depr., Dep.,						11.8	
	(11) 7.5	(18) 3.6	Amort./Cur. Mat. L/T/D					(14)	4.5	
	2.5	2.1							2.5	
.2	.0	.2						.0	.2	
.5	.4	.5	Fixed/Worth					.7	.5	
-.3	1.2	1.1						1.1	.8	
.6	.8	.7						.6	.7	
1.9	1.7	1.4	Debt/Worth					1.4	1.3	
-3.4	4.9	4.1						3.8	3.9	
118.1	43.2	58.8	% Profit Before Taxes/Tangible					33.4	63.1	
(27) 45.4	(36) 15.4	(45) 27.4	Net Worth					(10) 13.1	(32) 37.9	
12.6	-9.6	11.2						3.4	12.6	
31.6	18.4	19.9	% Profit Before Taxes/Total					11.2	23.2	
13.3	5.0	9.4	Assets					8.0	13.7	
1.9	-4.7	2.1						1.9	2.9	
62.4	92.5	38.6						225.8	31.5	
24.3	12.2	12.1	Sales/Net Fixed Assets					15.6	12.0	
10.7	5.0	4.0						4.3	3.9	
2.9	2.1	2.4						5.6	2.3	
1.6	1.6	1.6	Sales/Total Assets					1.7	1.6	
1.1	1.2	1.2						1.3	1.2	
.4	.6	.7							.9	
(19) 1.2	(26) 1.6	(36) 1.5	% Depr., Dep., Amort./Sales					(25)	1.6	
3.0	3.4	2.9							2.8	
4.0	.8	.8	% Officers', Directors'							
(11) 4.8	(13) 1.8	(10) 3.3	Owners' Comp/Sales							
7.9	8.5	14.6								
1949825M	2125318M	3759435M	Net Sales ($)	279M	4170M	3143M	14295M	220285M	3517263M
1596578M	1511147M	2383268M	Total Assets ($)	241M	5232M	19260M	11346M	119312M	2227877M

© RMA 2024 M = $ thousand MM = $ million
See Pages viii through xx for Explanation of Ratios and Data

MANUFACTURING—All Other Miscellaneous Chemical Product and Preparation Manufacturing NAICS 325998

Current Data Sorted by Assets | Comparative Historical Data

							Type of Statement		
			2	7	3	3	Unqualified	12	9
			5	11	4		Reviewed	17	5
			3	3			Compiled	6	7
1	1		4				Tax Returns	16	8
1	3		11	22	12	11	Other	83	53
		20 (4/1-9/30/23)		87 (10/1/23-3/31/24)				4/1/19-3/31/20	4/1/20-3/31/21
0-500M	500M-2MM	2-10MM	10-50MM	50-100MM	100-250MM			ALL	ALL
2	4	25	43	19	14	NUMBER OF STATEMENTS	134	82
%	%	%	%	%	%	ASSETS	%	%
		13.9	10.5	9.8	15.0	Cash & Equivalents	11.0	13.9
		28.8	22.5	22.5	13.6	Trade Receivables (net)	23.8	23.1
		23.2	24.1	25.2	19.0	Inventory	26.4	24.5
		1.5	.7	6.5	2.0	All Other Current	2.5	3.7
		67.4	57.7	64.0	49.6	Total Current	63.8	65.3
		18.4	26.6	26.0	28.0	Fixed Assets (net)	23.1	20.9
		8.6	10.5	5.0	14.7	Intangibles (net)	8.1	8.8
		5.7	5.2	5.0	7.7	All Other Non-Current	5.0	5.0
		100.0	100.0	100.0	100.0	Total	100.0	100.0
						LIABILITIES		
		6.6	7.0	9.7	3.7	Notes Payable-Short Term	9.1	5.3
		1.7	3.5	1.5	.8	Cur. Mat.-L.T.D.	2.5	2.6
		13.2	10.8	13.4	9.0	Trade Payables	11.9	12.9
		1.0	.3	.1	.2	Income Taxes Payable	.3	.2
		12.6	7.4	7.7	4.8	All Other Current	8.1	9.0
		35.2	29.0	32.5	18.5	Total Current	31.9	30.1
		12.7	12.4	13.0	6.7	Long-Term Debt	9.5	12.6
		.0	.1	.3	.9	Deferred Taxes	.4	.3
		9.4	3.6	5.0	5.8	All Other Non-Current	11.2	9.1
		42.7	54.8	49.2	68.1	Net Worth	46.9	47.9
		100.0	100.0	100.0	100.0	Total Liabilities & Net Worth	100.0	100.0
						INCOME DATA		
		100.0	100.0	100.0	100.0	Net Sales	100.0	100.0
		40.9	33.6	23.8	29.1	Gross Profit	35.0	36.2
		34.4	25.3	15.4	19.9	Operating Expenses	28.5	29.7
		6.5	8.2	8.4	9.2	Operating Profit	6.5	6.5
		.0	.6	.5	-.5	All Other Expenses (net)	.7	-.3
		6.5	7.6	7.9	9.7	Profit Before Taxes	5.8	6.8
						RATIOS		
		3.5	4.4	5.2	3.9		3.6	4.1
		1.8	2.2	2.2	2.7	Current	2.1	2.2
		1.2	1.1	1.2	1.9		1.3	1.6
		2.4	2.9	2.5	2.6		2.2	2.1
		1.1	1.2	.9	1.5	Quick	1.0	1.2
		.8	.6	.5	.6		.6	.7
		30 12.1	33 11.2	41 8.8	27 13.4		33 10.9	29 12.5
		41 8.8	45 8.1	50 7.3	47 7.8	Sales/Receivables	44 8.3	49 7.5
		49 7.5	55 6.6	58 6.3	56 6.5		61 6.0	64 5.7
		31 11.7	46 7.9	51 7.1	46 8.0		45 8.2	50 7.3
		41 8.9	70 5.2	73 5.0	69 5.3	Cost of Sales/Inventory	70 5.2	78 4.7
		89 4.1	111 3.3	111 3.3	111 3.3		104 3.5	107 3.4
		19 19.1	23 16.1	18 20.1	28 13.1		20 18.6	21 17.2
		34 10.8	32 11.4	36 10.1	35 10.5	Cost of Sales/Payables	30 12.1	35 10.5
		46 8.0	43 8.4	66 5.5	54 6.7		46 8.0	49 7.4
		4.4	3.2	2.4	2.3		3.5	3.1
		11.3	5.6	4.6	3.1	Sales/Working Capital	6.4	5.1
		36.0	30.7	11.6	7.4		16.1	8.5
		65.0	37.3	85.4			27.5	28.4
		(21) 9.5	(39) 8.1	(16) 4.7		EBIT/Interest	(109) 6.3	(66) 8.6
		1.2	.9	.8			1.8	3.0
			23.9				11.1	9.3
			(16) 3.4			Net Profit + Depr., Dep., Amort./Cur. Mat. L/T/D	(33) 4.5	(17) 4.6
			1.1				2.5	2.5
		.2	.2	.3	.4		.2	.3
		.4	.6	.8	.6	Fixed/Worth	.5	.5
		1.9	1.3	1.4	.7		1.0	1.0
		.4	.3	.5	.2		.4	.4
		2.1	1.0	1.0	.7	Debt/Worth	1.1	1.6
		11.6	2.5	4.2	1.1		3.6	3.0
		128.8	33.1	46.6	31.2		46.0	62.0
		(21) 45.6	(39) 21.2	(17) 18.3	20.4	% Profit Before Taxes/Tangible Net Worth	(120) 25.1	(73) 26.3
		5.8	9.4	4.5	7.3		7.8	10.2
		37.1	19.6	17.3	14.0		18.8	25.1
		13.4	9.1	11.0	10.5	% Profit Before Taxes/Total Assets	8.4	10.6
		-.3	.1	-1.5	4.4		1.3	4.6
		39.0	18.2	10.7	11.0		27.9	29.1
		17.8	8.1	6.8	4.5	Sales/Net Fixed Assets	9.9	11.8
		8.6	3.6	3.1	2.6		5.1	4.7
		3.7	2.6	2.2	1.4		2.7	2.4
		2.5	1.7	1.6	1.3	Sales/Total Assets	1.8	1.6
		1.7	1.2	1.0	.9		1.2	1.1
		.4	.9	1.2	1.2		.8	1.1
		(18) 1.3	(42) 1.5	1.7	(11) 2.1	% Depr., Dep., Amort./Sales	(102) 1.8	(60) 2.1
		2.1	2.9	2.4	4.4		3.6	3.7
							1.6	2.2
						% Officers', Directors' Owners' Comp/Sales	(28) 2.9	(17) 3.4
							5.4	4.8
5740M	16162M	342779M	1918752M	1960916M	2664991M	Net Sales ($)	7243862M	2947884M
770M	5114M	130287M	1117070M	1210941M	2212013M	Total Assets ($)	4803376M	2167152M

© RMA 2024

M = $ thousand   MM = $ million
See Pages viii through xx for Explanation of Ratios and Data

MANUFACTURING—All Other Miscellaneous Chemical Product and Preparation Manufacturing NAICS 325998

Comparative Historical Data | Current Data Sorted by Sales

					Type of Statement						
		7	18	15	Unqualified				1	2	13
		5	10	20	Reviewed				1	7	12
		6	4	6	Compiled				2	2	3
		6	14	6	Tax Returns		2		2	1	1
		42	50	60	Other	3	2		8	7	40
		4/1/21-3/31/22	4/1/22-3/31/23	4/1/23-3/31/24		20 (4/1-9/30/23)			87 (10/1/23-3/31/24)		
		ALL	ALL	ALL		0-1MM	1-3MM	3-5MM	5-10MM	10-25MM	25MM & OVER
		66	96	107	NUMBER OF STATEMENTS		3	4	12	19	69
		%	%	%	ASSETS	%	%	%	%	%	%
		15.7	14.5	12.7	Cash & Equivalents				15.7	10.8	11.1
		24.8	24.7	23.9	Trade Receivables (net)	D			27.6	22.2	22.9
		23.0	26.6	22.6	Inventory	A			22.3	19.9	24.1
		2.9	2.0	2.1	All Other Current	T			.6	1.4	2.6
		66.4	67.8	61.3	Total Current	A			66.2	54.3	60.7
		18.7	19.6	24.2	Fixed Assets (net)				23.5	23.1	25.2
		9.7	7.0	9.2	Intangibles (net)	N			5.5	14.2	9.1
		5.2	5.6	5.3	All Other Non-Current	O			4.8	8.4	5.1
		100.0	100.0	100.0	Total	T			100.0	100.0	100.0
					LIABILITIES	A					
		7.0	6.9	6.6	Notes Payable-Short Term	V			6.6	3.9	7.6
		3.3	2.5	2.2	Cur. Mat.-L.T.D.	A			1.8	2.2	2.5
		14.9	14.1	11.3	Trade Payables	I			9.1	11.8	12.0
		.1	.2	.4	Income Taxes Payable	L			1.6	.3	.2
		6.1	7.4	8.1	All Other Current	A			7.5	12.3	7.5
		31.4	31.1	28.6	Total Current	B			26.7	30.6	29.9
		11.4	14.5	11.8	Long-Term Debt	L			22.2	12.7	9.2
		.2	.3	.2	Deferred Taxes	E			.0	.1	.3
		3.0	3.6	7.4	All Other Non-Current				5.2	11.8	4.1
		54.0	50.5	52.0	Net Worth				45.9	44.9	56.5
		100.0	100.0	100.0	Total Liabilities & Net Worth				100.0	100.0	100.0
					INCOME DATA						
		100.0	100.0	100.0	Net Sales				100.0	100.0	100.0
		37.9	33.2	33.8	Gross Profit				46.7	36.3	29.8
		27.5	25.8	25.7	Operating Expenses				39.6	28.2	21.5
		10.4	7.4	8.1	Operating Profit				7.1	8.1	8.3
		-.9	.2	.4	All Other Expenses (net)				-.2	.4	.3
		11.3	7.3	7.8	Profit Before Taxes				7.3	7.7	7.9
					RATIOS						
		3.9	4.0	4.4					4.6	3.3	4.2
		2.2	2.4	2.2	Current				2.7	1.8	2.2
		1.5	1.6	1.3					1.3	1.2	1.3
		2.6	2.6	2.9					3.4	2.1	2.8
		1.3	1.4	1.3	Quick				1.9	1.1	1.2
		.8	.6	.6					.9	.8	.5
29	12.7	30	12.3	33	11.2	Sales/Receivables			35	10.3	22	16.8	34	10.7
50	7.3	41	9.0	46	7.9				44	8.3	38	9.6	48	7.6
64	5.7	61	6.0	55	6.6				69	5.3	50	7.3	56	6.5
24	15.2	31	11.6	40	9.2	Cost of Sales/Inventory			36	10.2	36	10.0	45	8.2
64	5.7	79	4.6	63	5.8				65	5.6	60	6.1	64	5.7
107	3.4	114	3.2	104	3.5				126	2.9	91	4.0	111	3.3
26	13.9	20	18.0	21	17.5	Cost of Sales/Payables			23	15.8	23	15.8	23	16.1
38	9.7	30	12.3	33	11.0				34	10.8	31	11.7	33	10.9
59	6.2	46	8.0	47	7.8				49	7.5	37	9.8	49	7.4
		2.8	3.1	3.0	Sales/Working Capital				2.7	4.5	2.9
		5.2	5.6	6.4					7.4	9.2	5.6
		10.1	10.3	16.8					13.6	33.6	18.9
		34.5	42.1	44.2	EBIT/Interest				67.7	43.8	45.1
(48)	18.5	(69)	11.2	(88)	8.2			(11)	5.7	(15)	9.6	(57)	6.3
		5.5	1.7	1.6					-2.0	1.8	1.4
		11.2	13.7	15.6	Net Profit + Depr., Dep., Amort./Cur. Mat. L/T/D						19.7
(11)	9.0	(22)	4.1	(33)	6.6						(23)	7.1
		3.7	1.9	2.2							1.7
		.1	.1	.2	Fixed/Worth				.2	.2	.2
		.3	.3	.6					.7	.6	.6
		.8	.8	1.2					5.4	1.4	1.1
		.4	.3	.3	Debt/Worth				.3	1.0	.3
		.9	.8	1.0					1.3	1.3	.9
		3.1	4.1	2.7					12.6	3.9	2.0
		63.3	60.5	44.6	% Profit Before Taxes/Tangible Net Worth				54.0	104.1	36.7
(58)	34.1	(90)	23.9	(96)	23.8			(10)	21.7	(17)	39.4	(63)	21.2
		21.3	11.2	9.6					-25.1	8.0	10.3
		25.1	21.0	21.4	% Profit Before Taxes/Total Assets				22.1	25.1	19.6
		18.3	11.7	11.0					11.4	15.2	10.8
		8.6	5.4	2.5					-6.7	-1.1	3.3
		35.3	46.9	20.9	Sales/Net Fixed Assets				26.1	33.0	17.0
		11.7	12.6	9.2					9.4	13.8	8.3
		5.5	5.6	4.0					5.6	3.6	3.7
		2.3	2.7	2.6	Sales/Total Assets				2.5	3.2	2.6
		1.7	1.8	1.7					2.0	1.7	1.6
		1.3	1.3	1.2					1.5	1.2	1.2
		.7	.4	1.0	% Depr., Dep., Amort./Sales				.8	1.1	
(41)	2.4	(76)	1.3	(93)	1.6					(16)	1.4	(65)	1.7
		4.1	3.3	2.4						3.3	2.5
		.8	1.3	1.1	% Officers', Directors' Owners' Comp/Sales						
(17)	1.7	(18)	3.7	(18)	2.5						
		4.0	6.1	6.0							
		3251413M	6162273M	6909340M	Net Sales ($)		5966M	15224M	98879M	322870M	6466401M
		2015711M	3712241M	4676195M	Total Assets ($)		2176M	6963M	66703M	233738M	4366615M

© RMA 2024   M = $ thousand   MM = $ million
See Pages viii through xx for Explanation of Ratios and Data

MANUFACTURING—Plastics Bag and Pouch Manufacturing NAICS 326111

Current Data Sorted by Assets / Comparative Historical Data

						Type of Statement		
			4	1	3	Unqualified	1	8
		3	3			Reviewed	4	1
1	2	4	2			Compiled	6	5
	1	7	5	4	3	Tax Returns	8	4
		10 (4/1-9/30/23)		33 (10/1/23-3/31/24)		Other	34	26
0-500M	500M-2MM	2-10MM	10-50MM	50-100MM	100-250MM		4/1/19-3/31/20 ALL	4/1/20-3/31/21 ALL
1	3	14	14	5	6	NUMBER OF STATEMENTS	53	44
%	%	%	%	%	%	ASSETS	%	%
		19.0	14.4			Cash & Equivalents	6.3	18.1
		20.4	18.3			Trade Receivables (net)	23.6	20.2
		22.5	20.5			Inventory	27.3	19.7
		1.3	1.6			All Other Current	1.0	1.2
		63.2	54.9			Total Current	58.2	59.3
		20.0	31.0			Fixed Assets (net)	28.9	29.0
		4.4	5.0			Intangibles (net)	5.1	5.3
		12.3	9.0			All Other Non-Current	7.8	6.4
		100.0	100.0			Total	100.0	100.0
						LIABILITIES		
		1.5	3.3			Notes Payable-Short Term	10.0	5.3
		1.2	4.3			Cur. Mat.-L.T.D.	2.6	2.7
		9.9	8.1			Trade Payables	12.7	11.2
		.0	.5			Income Taxes Payable	.0	.0
		7.8	10.8			All Other Current	13.0	11.9
		20.4	26.9			Total Current	38.3	31.1
		16.3	15.8			Long-Term Debt	15.5	18.2
		.7	.1			Deferred Taxes	.2	.5
		.0	5.1			All Other Non-Current	4.9	2.7
		62.6	52.2			Net Worth	41.1	47.5
		100.0	100.0			Total Liabilities & Net Worth	100.0	100.0
						INCOME DATA		
		100.0	100.0			Net Sales	100.0	100.0
		38.7	21.4			Gross Profit	28.2	31.2
		29.8	17.4			Operating Expenses	20.7	23.2
		8.9	4.0			Operating Profit	7.5	8.1
		-.2	.5			All Other Expenses (net)	.8	.4
		9.1	3.5			Profit Before Taxes	6.6	7.7
						RATIOS		
		7.3	2.9				2.7	2.7
		3.7	2.1			Current	1.7	2.0
		1.9	1.5				1.2	1.4
		5.5	1.7				1.5	1.5
		1.9	1.1			Quick	.8	1.1
		.9	.8				.6	.7
		24 15.4	33 11.1				29 12.4	34 10.7
		37 9.9	36 10.1			Sales/Receivables	38 9.5	44 8.3
		46 8.0	47 7.8				49 7.5	54 6.8
		25 14.5	36 10.0				46 8.0	45 8.1
		53 6.9	49 7.4			Cost of Sales/Inventory	64 5.7	66 5.5
		74 4.9	89 4.1				85 4.3	81 4.5
		12 29.8	14 25.9				14 26.7	23 15.8
		21 17.1	19 18.8			Cost of Sales/Payables	26 14.0	33 10.9
		37 9.9	29 12.5				41 8.9	43 8.5
		3.4	5.5				4.7	4.4
		5.2	7.2			Sales/Working Capital	8.1	5.8
		31.8	13.3				26.2	14.7
			12.4				15.5	30.2
		(12)	3.0			EBIT/Interest	(47) 6.3	(34) 10.0
			-1.2				3.0	3.8
						Net Profit + Depr., Dep.,		12.4
						Amort./Cur. Mat. L/T/D	(10)	3.1
								2.3
		.1	.5				.2	.2
		.1	.7			Fixed/Worth	.8	.8
		.5	1.0				2.2	1.2
		.2	.4				.6	.6
		.3	1.1			Debt/Worth	1.5	1.0
		3.8	2.8				3.9	3.4
		48.7	31.9				41.6	53.9
	(13)	31.0	8.8			% Profit Before Taxes/Tangible Net Worth	(47) 21.3	(40) 23.2
		14.0	-6.5				4.5	14.2
		28.5	19.1				17.5	20.5
		18.7	4.3			% Profit Before Taxes/Total Assets	9.3	11.4
		1.5	-2.9				2.3	2.6
		82.9	35.4				29.7	22.3
		42.0	5.3			Sales/Net Fixed Assets	7.7	4.6
		3.0	3.3				3.1	3.0
		3.4	1.9				2.8	2.5
		2.1	1.7			Sales/Total Assets	2.0	1.6
		1.5	1.4				1.2	1.2
			1.9				.8	1.2
		(13)	4.6			% Depr., Dep., Amort./Sales	(34) 2.4	(27) 2.9
			5.4				3.8	4.3
						% Officers', Directors' Owners' Comp/Sales		
2325M	15716M	179963M	729969M	609102M	1027397M	Net Sales ($)	4027026M	3006027M
244M	4650M	72730M	410674M	366667M	839620M	Total Assets ($)	2966558M	2495031M

© RMA 2024   M = $ thousand   MM = $ million
See Pages viii through xx for Explanation of Ratios and Data

MANUFACTURING—Plastics Bag and Pouch Manufacturing NAICS 326111

Comparative Historical Data / Current Data Sorted by Sales

				Type of Statement						
6	10	8		Unqualified				1		8
2	5	3		Reviewed				3		2
5	1	5		Compiled				2	2	2
4	4	7		Tax Returns		1	1	2	2	1
22	20	20		Other		1	2	4	1	12
4/1/21-3/31/22 ALL	4/1/22-3/31/23 ALL	4/1/23-3/31/24 ALL			0-1MM	10 (4/1-9/30/23) 1-3MM	3-5MM	33 (10/1/23-3/31/24) 5-10MM	10-25MM	25MM & OVER
39	40	43		NUMBER OF STATEMENTS		2	3	6	7	25
%	%	%		ASSETS	%	%	%	%	%	%
14.2	10.5	13.4		Cash & Equivalents	D					6.9
24.7	23.5	18.6		Trade Receivables (net)	A					17.7
24.0	27.6	21.5		Inventory	T					23.9
.5	1.7	1.5		All Other Current	A					1.5
63.4	63.3	55.0		Total Current						50.0
27.9	24.7	27.1		Fixed Assets (net)	N					32.6
5.0	2.9	7.4		Intangibles (net)	O					6.9
3.8	9.1	10.5		All Other Non-Current	T					10.5
100.0	100.0	100.0		Total						100.0
				LIABILITIES	A					
5.7	8.3	3.5		Notes Payable-Short Term	V					4.8
16.3	1.7	2.9		Cur. Mat.-L.T.D.	A					3.5
11.5	12.6	8.3		Trade Payables	I					8.0
.0	.2	.2		Income Taxes Payable	L					.4
12.1	13.0	9.5		All Other Current	A					7.1
45.6	35.8	24.4		Total Current	B					23.8
20.9	16.9	17.0		Long-Term Debt	L					17.9
.2	.0	.3		Deferred Taxes	E					.0
1.6	5.8	3.4		All Other Non-Current						4.6
31.6	41.5	55.0		Net Worth						53.7
100.0	100.0	100.0		Total Liabilities & Net Worth						100.0
				INCOME DATA						
100.0	100.0	100.0		Net Sales						100.0
26.3	28.7	29.5		Gross Profit						23.5
19.8	22.7	23.2		Operating Expenses						18.3
6.5	6.0	6.2		Operating Profit						5.3
-.6	.6	.4		All Other Expenses (net)						.8
7.1	5.4	5.8		Profit Before Taxes						4.4
				RATIOS						
2.7	3.1	3.7								2.8
1.9	1.9	2.4		Current						2.0
1.3	1.2	1.5								1.5
1.7	1.9	2.2								1.3
.8	1.0	1.1		Quick						1.1
.6	.5	.7								.6
35 10.4	29 12.6	28 13.0								29 12.4
51 7.1	42 8.7	36 10.1		Sales/Receivables						36 10.1
60 6.1	50 7.3	47 7.8								49 7.4
46 8.0	48 7.6	38 9.7								41 8.9
68 5.4	64 5.7	51 7.1		Cost of Sales/Inventory						53 6.9
81 4.5	111 3.3	89 4.1								94 3.9
15 24.4	14 26.5	14 25.9								15 24.8
28 13.2	26 14.1	21 17.6		Cost of Sales/Payables						18 20.0
44 8.3	40 9.2	36 10.1								31 11.6
3.9	4.7	4.7								5.1
7.4	7.7	6.4		Sales/Working Capital						8.1
18.0	23.2	12.9								14.1
55.3	12.9	19.3								14.2
(35) 10.3	(33) 7.3	(34) 6.0		EBIT/Interest						(22) 5.2
5.4	2.2	1.5								1.8
		8.6		Net Profit + Depr., Dep.,						
	(11) 4.0			Amort./Cur. Mat. L/T/D						
		2.4								
.2	.1	.1								.4
.6	.6	.5		Fixed/Worth						.8
1.1	1.3	1.2								1.3
.7	.6	.3								.5
1.2	1.5	1.0		Debt/Worth						1.1
3.4	4.3	2.8								2.4
53.1	62.5	37.0								32.1
(36) 28.1	(38) 23.4	(41) 20.4		% Profit Before Taxes/Tangible Net Worth						17.5
13.5	7.1	5.5								5.5
22.1	19.0	19.8		% Profit Before Taxes/Total Assets						17.2
11.0	7.3	7.6								5.0
6.1	2.7	1.3								1.4
42.1	83.8	52.6								35.4
7.0	8.2	7.0		Sales/Net Fixed Assets						4.3
3.0	3.3	3.1								2.9
2.4	2.6	2.4								2.0
1.9	1.9	1.7		Sales/Total Assets						1.7
1.3	1.4	1.3								1.2
1.3	.4	.7								1.3
(26) 2.7	(28) 1.6	(32) 3.3		% Depr., Dep., Amort./Sales						(22) 4.0
5.0	4.2	5.3								5.3
		1.5		% Officers', Directors' Owners' Comp/Sales						
	(14) 2.2									
		4.6								
2160841M	1592710M	2564472M		Net Sales ($)		5227M	12951M	49231M	109441M	2387622M
1491491M	964988M	1694585M		Total Assets ($)		1953M	7818M	25644M	52782M	1606388M

© RMA 2024   M = $ thousand   MM = $ million
See Pages viii through xx for Explanation of Ratios and Data

MANUFACTURING—Plastics Packaging Film and Sheet (including Laminated) Manufacturing NAICS 326112

Current Data Sorted by Assets | Comparative Historical Data

						Type of Statement		
			1			Unqualified	11	7
			3	1		Reviewed	4	3
		1		1		Compiled	1	2
		5				Tax Returns		4
1	2	2	11	7	2	Other	5	21
	4 (4/1–9/30/23)		33 (10/1/23–3/31/24)				38 4/1/19–3/31/20	21 4/1/20–3/31/21
0-500M	500M-2MM	2-10MM	10-50MM	50-100MM	100-250MM		ALL	ALL
1	2	8	15	9	2	NUMBER OF STATEMENTS	59	37
%	%	%	%	%	%	ASSETS	%	%
			8.5			Cash & Equivalents	6.8	10.1
			19.6			Trade Receivables (net)	20.1	21.1
			28.5			Inventory	22.7	23.8
			3.2			All Other Current	2.1	1.3
			59.8			Total Current	51.6	56.3
			28.0			Fixed Assets (net)	34.3	35.1
			4.9			Intangibles (net)	8.7	5.0
			7.3			All Other Non-Current	5.4	3.6
			100.0			Total	100.0	100.0
						LIABILITIES		
			3.8			Notes Payable-Short Term	13.8	5.5
			5.0			Cur. Mat.-L.T.D.	3.0	3.9
			10.1			Trade Payables	13.8	13.9
			1.0			Income Taxes Payable	.2	.2
			6.4			All Other Current	7.5	18.9
			26.5			Total Current	38.2	42.4
			17.3			Long-Term Debt	21.2	22.0
			1.2			Deferred Taxes	.4	.5
			8.6			All Other Non-Current	6.2	3.5
			46.4			Net Worth	34.0	31.6
			100.0			Total Liabilities & Net Worth	100.0	100.0
						INCOME DATA		
			100.0			Net Sales	100.0	100.0
			22.9			Gross Profit	23.4	25.6
			17.4			Operating Expenses	19.1	20.0
			5.4			Operating Profit	4.4	5.6
			1.2			All Other Expenses (net)	.8	.2
			4.2			Profit Before Taxes	3.6	5.4
						RATIOS		
			4.1				2.0	2.4
			2.4			Current	1.4	1.9
			1.4				1.0	1.3
			1.5				1.1	1.2
			.8			Quick	.7	.9
			.5				.5	.6
		28	13.2				30 12.2	29 12.5
		41	9.0			Sales/Receivables	37 9.8	39 9.4
		53	6.9				54 6.7	47 7.7
		51	7.2				46 8.0	49 7.5
		65	5.6			Cost of Sales/Inventory	59 6.2	73 5.0
		122	3.0				79 4.6	89 4.1
		21	17.7				18 20.5	17 20.9
		27	13.7			Cost of Sales/Payables	29 12.4	30 12.2
		36	10.2				48 7.6	43 8.4
			2.5				7.2	6.2
			5.3			Sales/Working Capital	14.4	9.0
			11.8				-238.3	19.4
			12.8				12.7	30.4
		(14)	4.0			EBIT/Interest	(53) 3.4	(35) 11.7
			1.0				-.1	3.0
						Net Profit + Depr., Dep.,	9.1	5.7
						Amort./Cur. Mat. L/T/D	(12) 5.2	(13) 2.9
							1.7	1.2
			.3				.7	.7
			.6			Fixed/Worth	1.1	1.1
			1.6				-22.9	2.2
			.5				.8	.7
			1.7			Debt/Worth	3.0	1.9
			3.0				-65.8	4.5
			34.2				34.7	58.6
			6.5			% Profit Before Taxes/Tangible Net Worth	(44) 18.2	(31) 29.4
			.0				-1.3	17.7
			10.0				13.4	20.4
			4.1			% Profit Before Taxes/Total Assets	6.4	10.1
			.0				-1.7	4.6
			12.2				10.7	10.8
			7.0			Sales/Net Fixed Assets	4.8	5.4
			2.9				3.0	3.3
			2.3				2.4	2.5
			1.6			Sales/Total Assets	1.8	1.8
			1.3				1.1	1.2
			.9				1.4	1.5
			2.1			% Depr., Dep., Amort./Sales	(46) 3.0	(28) 3.3
			4.0				5.9	4.6
						% Officers', Directors' Owners' Comp/Sales	.9 (10) 3.3	
							4.6	
1795M	9186M	121846M	552071M	759929M	308436M	Net Sales ($)	4480424M	2478664M
421M	2970M	47637M	346927M	590246M	237871M	Total Assets ($)	3020873M	1762560M

M = $ thousand   MM = $ million
See Pages viii through xx for Explanation of Ratios and Data

© RMA 2024

MANUFACTURING—Plastics Packaging Film and Sheet (including Laminated) Manufacturing NAICS 326112

Comparative Historical Data / Current Data Sorted by Sales

				Type of Statement							
	5	1	1	Unqualified						1	1
	1	10	4	Reviewed					1	1	3
	2	2	2	Compiled					1	1	1
	3	4	5	Tax Returns					1	3	1
	22	26	25	Other			1	1	1	4	18
	4/1/21-3/31/22 ALL	4/1/22-3/31/23 ALL	4/1/23-3/31/24 ALL		0-1MM	1-3MM	4 (4/1-9/30/23)	3-5MM	5-10MM	33 (10/1/23-3/31/24) 10-25MM	25MM & OVER
	33	43	37	**NUMBER OF STATEMENTS**		1		1	2	9	24
	%	%	%	**ASSETS**	%	%	%	%	%	%	%
	8.1	7.8	10.4	Cash & Equivalents	D						10.9
	22.2	18.8	21.7	Trade Receivables (net)	A						20.0
	28.0	31.5	27.0	Inventory	T						23.7
	2.2	1.9	2.3	All Other Current	A						2.9
	60.5	60.0	61.4	Total Current							57.6
	26.6	31.7	26.0	Fixed Assets (net)	N						27.6
	8.4	4.2	5.8	Intangibles (net)	O						6.6
	4.4	4.1	6.7	All Other Non-Current	T						8.2
	100.0	100.0	100.0	Total							100.0
				LIABILITIES	A						
	6.8	4.9	3.2	Notes Payable-Short Term	V						3.0
	2.6	2.2	4.2	Cur. Mat.-L.T.D.	A						3.0
	12.3	12.2	10.9	Trade Payables	I						9.5
	.1	.3	.4	Income Taxes Payable	L						.7
	10.9	6.2	12.9	All Other Current	A						8.1
	32.7	25.8	31.5	Total Current	B						24.2
	17.8	20.1	19.0	Long-Term Debt	L						18.9
	.4	.5	.6	Deferred Taxes	E						.8
	5.8	3.2	5.6	All Other Non-Current							6.7
	43.3	50.3	43.4	Net Worth							49.4
	100.0	100.0	100.0	Total Liabilities & Net Worth							100.0
				INCOME DATA							
	100.0	100.0	100.0	Net Sales							100.0
	28.4	27.5	24.4	Gross Profit							26.1
	22.6	20.2	16.6	Operating Expenses							16.4
	5.8	7.3	7.8	Operating Profit							9.6
	-.9	.5	.9	All Other Expenses (net)							.7
	6.8	6.8	6.9	Profit Before Taxes							8.9
				RATIOS							
	2.7	4.0	4.0								5.1
	1.7	2.3	2.4	Current							2.0
	1.4	1.5	1.4								1.5
	1.3	1.5	2.2								2.7
	.8	1.1	1.0	Quick							1.1
	.7	.6	.6								.7
31	11.6	26	14.0	30	12.3					29	12.8
38	9.5	35	10.5	41	8.9	Sales/Receivables				41	8.9
43	8.4	46	7.9	53	6.9					51	7.2
51	7.1	49	7.4	49	7.4					51	7.1
68	5.4	69	5.3	65	5.6	Cost of Sales/Inventory				64	5.7
114	3.2	114	3.2	104	3.5					94	3.9
19	19.6	14	26.4	16	22.9					15	23.8
31	11.9	26	13.9	23	16.2	Cost of Sales/Payables				22	16.3
46	8.0	41	8.9	35	10.5					34	10.8
	5.0		4.0		3.0						2.8
	10.0		8.0		6.4	Sales/Working Capital					6.4
	16.7		12.7		12.4						11.6
	37.0		28.0		14.6						15.7
(30)	12.7	(37)	14.7	(33)	5.0	EBIT/Interest				(22)	5.7
	5.6		4.7		2.5						3.0
			24.4			Net Profit + Depr., Dep.,					
		(10)	4.5			Amort./Cur. Mat. L/T/D					
			2.2								
	.3		.3		.3						.3
	.9		.5		.5	Fixed/Worth					.6
	1.6		1.4		1.5						1.2
	.6		.4		.6						.4
	1.5		1.1		1.7	Debt/Worth					1.3
	6.5		2.2		2.8						2.5
	44.4		48.0		42.5						53.1
(29)	26.6	(41)	27.1	(34)	21.2	% Profit Before Taxes/Tangible Net Worth				(22)	27.3
	11.4		11.5		4.5						6.2
	18.8		20.4		17.1						33.9
	11.9		12.9		9.5	% Profit Before Taxes/Total Assets					9.8
	3.7		6.9		2.6						4.1
	23.4		17.5		20.0						12.1
	7.0		6.8		6.6	Sales/Net Fixed Assets					5.9
	3.8		3.5		4.0						3.7
	2.5		2.7		2.4						1.9
	2.0		1.9		1.6	Sales/Total Assets					1.5
	1.3		1.3		1.3						1.3
	1.4		1.0		.9						1.1
(26)	2.3	(35)	2.2	(31)	2.1	% Depr., Dep., Amort./Sales				(21)	3.0
	5.0		3.9		3.8						4.1
			1.9		1.0	% Officers', Directors', Owners' Comp/Sales					
		(16)	2.7	(11)	1.9						
			3.0		3.2						
	1807968M		1675320M		1753263M	Net Sales ($)		1795M	4179M	11456M	128255M	1607578M
	1207571M		1160036M		1226072M	Total Assets ($)		421M	1165M	4622M	94897M	1124967M

© RMA 2024 M = $ thousand   MM = $ million
See Pages viii through xx for Explanation of Ratios and Data

MANUFACTURING—Plastics Pipe and Pipe Fitting Manufacturing NAICS 326122

Current Data Sorted by Assets

0-500M	500M-2MM	2-10MM	10-50MM	50-100MM	100-250MM
	1		1	1	2
		1	6	1	
		1	1		
	1	6	1	1	5
	3 (4/1-9/30/23)		25 (10/1/23-3/31/24)		
1	1	8	9	3	7
%	%	%	%	%	%

Data Not Available

Comparative Historical Data

Type of Statement		
Unqualified	5	2
Reviewed	6	5
Compiled	5	4
Tax Returns	3	
Other	21	9
	4/1/19-3/31/20 ALL	4/1/20-3/31/21 ALL
NUMBER OF STATEMENTS	40	20
ASSETS	%	%
Cash & Equivalents	8.5	13.3
Trade Receivables (net)	24.8	22.2
Inventory	28.8	30.5
All Other Current	1.9	.6
Total Current	64.0	66.6
Fixed Assets (net)	29.5	23.7
Intangibles (net)	2.9	3.0
All Other Non-Current	3.6	6.7
Total	100.0	100.0
LIABILITIES		
Notes Payable-Short Term	8.5	6.0
Cur. Mat.-L.T.D.	2.5	2.9
Trade Payables	12.9	9.9
Income Taxes Payable	.4	.5
All Other Current	10.6	8.8
Total Current	34.9	28.2
Long-Term Debt	15.1	8.1
Deferred Taxes	.7	1.1
All Other Non-Current	7.1	4.2
Net Worth	42.1	58.5
Total Liabilities & Net Worth	100.0	100.0
INCOME DATA		
Net Sales	100.0	100.0
Gross Profit	30.1	30.7
Operating Expenses	22.8	21.3
Operating Profit	7.3	9.4
All Other Expenses (net)	.9	.0
Profit Before Taxes	6.4	9.4
RATIOS		
Current	3.3	3.6
	2.2	2.5
	1.2	1.9
Quick	1.8	2.6
	1.0	1.3
	.6	.7
Sales/Receivables	36 10.1	33 11.0
	44 8.3	51 7.1
	50 7.3	60 6.1
Cost of Sales/Inventory	53 6.9	55 6.6
	70 5.2	87 4.2
	101 3.6	182 2.0
Cost of Sales/Payables	12 30.5	11 31.9
	23 15.9	29 12.6
	45 8.2	42 8.6
Sales/Working Capital	3.7	2.5
	6.0	4.6
	32.7	7.8
EBIT/Interest	24.2	92.7
	(37) 6.9	(16) 22.3
	2.3	7.7
Net Profit + Depr., Dep., Amort./Cur. Mat. L/T/D	6.9	
	(12) 3.1	
	1.6	
Fixed/Worth	.4	.2
	.7	.4
	1.3	.6
Debt/Worth	.5	.4
	1.2	.9
	3.0	1.1
% Profit Before Taxes/Tangible Net Worth	34.0	38.1
	(33) 21.0	27.7
	11.3	7.3
% Profit Before Taxes/Total Assets	16.0	20.6
	9.8	12.6
	5.1	3.6
Sales/Net Fixed Assets	13.7	11.6
	6.7	6.0
	3.9	3.5
Sales/Total Assets	2.5	2.3
	1.8	1.5
	1.4	1.0
% Depr., Dep., Amort./Sales	1.7	1.6
	(38) 2.4	(19) 2.2
	3.6	3.6
% Officers', Directors', Owners' Comp/Sales	1.2	
	(10) 2.2	
	3.5	

| | 1068M | 102150M | 262176M | 313702M | 1287060M | Net Sales ($) | 2649281M | 1356113M |
| | 744M | 42349M | 205907M | 171340M | 1034401M | Total Assets ($) | 1550481M | 875881M |

M = $ thousand   MM = $ million

MANUFACTURING—Plastics Pipe and Pipe Fitting Manufacturing NAICS 326122

Comparative Historical Data / Current Data Sorted by Sales

					Type of Statement						
	2		2	4	Unqualified				1	1	3
	4		3	8	Reviewed				3	4	4
	3		2	2	Compiled					1	1
	1		1		Tax Returns						
	10		10	14	Other		1		4	2	7
	4/1/21-		4/1/22-	4/1/23-			3 (4/1-9/30/23)		25 (10/1/23-3/31/24)		
	3/31/22		3/31/23	3/31/24		0-1MM	1-3MM	3-5MM	5-10MM	10-25MM	25MM & OVER
	ALL		ALL	ALL			1		5	7	15
	20		18	28	NUMBER OF STATEMENTS						
	%		%	%	ASSETS	%	%	%	%	%	%
	11.0		15.9	17.4	Cash & Equivalents						19.2
	21.2		22.6	16.9	Trade Receivables (net)	D	D				18.4
	31.9		31.8	23.4	Inventory	A	A				21.3
	.3		2.0	1.1	All Other Current	T	T				1.3
	64.4		72.3	58.9	Total Current	A	A				60.1
	28.4		22.0	30.0	Fixed Assets (net)						34.0
	.7		2.6	4.7	Intangibles (net)	N	N				2.3
	6.5		3.1	6.4	All Other Non-Current	O	O				3.7
	100.0		100.0	100.0	Total	T	T				100.0
					LIABILITIES						
	2.7		2.4	7.6	Notes Payable-Short Term	A	A				1.9
	2.3		2.2	3.3	Cur. Mat.-L.T.D.	V	V				1.8
	11.1		11.8	9.3	Trade Payables	A	A				8.8
	.6		.5	1.0	Income Taxes Payable	I	I				1.8
	7.5		6.4	10.6	All Other Current	L	L				6.9
	24.2		23.5	31.8	Total Current	A	A				21.3
	8.4		10.8	7.7	Long-Term Debt	B	B				4.4
	.8		.7	.5	Deferred Taxes	L	L				.6
	3.3		1.9	3.3	All Other Non-Current	E	E				1.8
	63.3		63.1	56.6	Net Worth						71.8
	100.0		100.0	100.0	Total Liabilities & Net Worth						100.0
					INCOME DATA						
	100.0		100.0	100.0	Net Sales						100.0
	33.3		36.1	38.4	Gross Profit						39.0
	21.7		19.7	23.7	Operating Expenses						20.1
	11.6		16.4	14.6	Operating Profit						18.9
	-.3		.3	.7	All Other Expenses (net)						.4
	11.8		16.2	14.0	Profit Before Taxes						18.5
					RATIOS						
	5.1		5.7	4.0							4.0
	3.2		3.1	2.4	Current						2.9
	1.9		2.8	1.2							2.3
	2.8		3.9	2.2							2.1
	1.4		1.5	1.7	Quick						1.8
	.9		.9	.6							1.7
24	14.9	24	15.3	30	12.0					31	11.9
43	8.4	34	10.7	38	9.6	Sales/Receivables				36	10.1
62	5.9	47	7.7	49	7.4					53	6.9
74	4.9	43	8.5	53	6.9					51	7.2
91	4.0	65	5.6	74	4.9	Cost of Sales/Inventory				74	4.9
146	2.5	130	2.8	126	2.9					152	2.4
16	22.5	15	24.6	14	25.5					18	20.3
28	13.2	20	18.5	24	15.1	Cost of Sales/Payables				25	14.4
47	7.7	34	10.7	39	9.3					37	9.9
	2.9		3.2	2.6							2.6
	3.9		4.6	4.3	Sales/Working Capital						4.0
	6.4		5.6	16.4							6.0
	101.3		255.0	169.4							352.0
(18)	22.0	(16)	55.6	(27)	46.6	EBIT/Interest					107.6
	10.8		14.2	3.2							26.8
					Net Profit + Depr., Dep., Amort./Cur. Mat. L/T/D						
	.3		.2	.4							.4
	.4		.4	.6	Fixed/Worth						.4
	.6		.6	.9							.7
	.2		.2	.3							.2
	.5		.6	.5	Debt/Worth						.4
	1.2		.9	1.7							.6
	63.3		81.7	55.3							54.3
	37.1	(17)	57.2	(25)	36.9	% Profit Before Taxes/Tangible Net Worth					38.5
	15.4		25.6	22.0							23.1
	36.5		54.8	35.3							35.5
	17.5		27.1	16.8	% Profit Before Taxes/Total Assets						29.2
	11.4		13.0	7.6							16.2
	14.8		55.4	13.0							9.0
	5.3		10.0	4.8	Sales/Net Fixed Assets						4.5
	2.9		5.0	2.7							2.6
	2.7		3.0	1.9							1.7
	1.6		2.4	1.4	Sales/Total Assets						1.4
	1.0		1.7	1.2							1.2
	1.2		.9	1.4							1.6
(17)	2.8	(15)	1.7	(26)	2.7	% Depr., Dep., Amort./Sales					2.6
	3.8		2.1	5.4							4.3
					% Officers', Directors' Owners' Comp/Sales						
	1194493M		1522710M	1966156M	Net Sales ($)		1068M		39246M	119383M	1806459M
	827167M		741428M	1454741M	Total Assets ($)		744M		21365M	104031M	1328601M

© RMA 2024   M = $ thousand   MM = $ million
See Pages viii through xx for Explanation of Ratios and Data

MANUFACTURING—Polystyrene Foam Product Manufacturing NAICS 326140

Current Data Sorted by Assets

0-500M	500M-2MM	2-10MM	10-50MM	50-100MM	100-250MM
		1	1	2	2
		2			1
	1	2			
	8 (4/1-9/30/23)		15 (10/1/23-3/31/24)		4
	1	1	5		
2	6	6	2	7	

Comparative Historical Data

Type of Statement	4/1/19-3/31/20 ALL	4/1/20-3/31/21 ALL
Unqualified	4	1
Reviewed	2	1
Compiled	1	1
Tax Returns	4	1
Other	25	20
NUMBER OF STATEMENTS	36	24

	%	%		%	%
ASSETS					
Cash & Equivalents				11.9	22.5
Trade Receivables (net)				26.8	24.2
Inventory				18.3	18.7
All Other Current				2.5	.7
Total Current				59.5	66.1
Fixed Assets (net)				29.6	26.0
Intangibles (net)				3.9	2.5
All Other Non-Current				7.0	5.4
Total				100.0	100.0
LIABILITIES					
Notes Payable-Short Term				8.6	4.5
Cur. Mat.-L.T.D.				2.4	2.7
Trade Payables				14.2	13.9
Income Taxes Payable				.1	.2
All Other Current				8.4	6.3
Total Current				33.7	27.7
Long-Term Debt				18.4	23.4
Deferred Taxes				1.1	.7
All Other Non-Current				7.9	3.9
Net Worth				38.8	44.3
Total Liabilities & Net Worth				100.0	100.0
INCOME DATA					
Net Sales				100.0	100.0
Gross Profit				29.0	30.0
Operating Expenses				24.0	24.0
Operating Profit				5.0	6.1
All Other Expenses (net)				.9	-1.1
Profit Before Taxes				4.1	7.1
RATIOS					
Current				3.5 / 2.7 / 1.2	4.5 / 2.8 / 1.8
Quick				3.2 / 1.6 / .7	3.0 / 1.7 / 1.1
Sales/Receivables				30 / 12.2 / 37 / 9.8 / 46 / 8.0	33 / 11.1 / 40 / 9.1 / 48 / 7.6
Cost of Sales/Inventory				27 / 13.6 / 39 / 9.4 / 62 / 5.9	24 / 15.1 / 36 / 10.0 / 62 / 5.9
Cost of Sales/Payables				11 / 33.0 / 23 / 16.2 / 37 / 9.8	14 / 26.7 / 34 / 10.8 / 43 / 8.5
Sales/Working Capital				4.7 / 6.9 / 31.9	3.3 / 5.7 / 10.4
EBIT/Interest				43.2 / (31) 6.2 / 1.7	81.1 / (19) 28.5 / 12.5
Net Profit + Depr., Dep., Amort./Cur. Mat. L/T/D					
Fixed/Worth				.3 / .6 / 1.5	.3 / .4 / .9
Debt/Worth				.3 / .8 / 6.1	.4 / .8 / 1.6
% Profit Before Taxes/Tangible Net Worth				39.1 / (30) 26.6 / 8.2	47.5 / (22) 30.8 / 17.7
% Profit Before Taxes/Total Assets				22.1 / 11.4 / 1.6	20.2 / 18.8 / 5.6
Sales/Net Fixed Assets				15.6 / 6.8 / 4.6	21.2 / 9.5 / 5.0
Sales/Total Assets				2.6 / 2.2 / 1.7	2.9 / 1.8 / 1.6
% Depr., Dep., Amort./Sales				1.4 / (24) 2.3 / 3.1	1.4 / (18) 2.2 / 3.4
% Officers', Directors' Owners' Comp/Sales					
Net Sales ($)	15427M / 54435M / 141328M / 291204M / 1533302M			1544298M	855790M
Total Assets ($)	3381M / 26300M / 92580M / 134318M / 1090051M			770505M	447339M

M = $ thousand   MM = $ million

DATA NOT AVAILABLE (for 0-500M column)

© RMA 2024

MANUFACTURING—Polystyrene Foam Product Manufacturing NAICS 326140

Comparative Historical Data | Current Data Sorted by Sales

					Type of Statement						
	3	4		6	Unqualified				1	1	4
	2	1		3	Reviewed				1	1	1
	4	2		3	Compiled			1	2		
	1				Tax Returns						
	10	15		11	Other			1	3		7
	4/1/21-3/31/22 ALL	4/1/22-3/31/23 ALL		4/1/23-3/31/24 ALL			8 (4/1-9/30/23)		15 (10/1/23-3/31/24)		
	20	22		23	NUMBER OF STATEMENTS	0-1MM	1-3MM	3-5MM	5-10MM	10-25MM	25MM & OVER
							1	5	5	12
	%	%		%	ASSETS	%	%	%	%	%	%
	15.7	16.5		15.5	Cash & Equivalents	D	D				15.5
	26.2	24.9		19.1	Trade Receivables (net)	A	A				17.0
	21.6	29.2		22.2	Inventory	T	T				21.7
	1.9	1.3		1.7	All Other Current	A	A				2.3
	65.4	71.9		58.5	Total Current						56.6
	26.9	19.2		28.9	Fixed Assets (net)	N	N				29.5
	3.0	1.7		5.4	Intangibles (net)	O	O				2.8
	4.7	7.2		7.2	All Other Non-Current	T	T				11.1
	100.0	100.0		100.0	Total						100.0
					LIABILITIES	A	A				
	1.9	2.3		3.2	Notes Payable-Short Term	V	V				5.1
	2.5	1.3		1.7	Cur. Mat.-L.T.D.	A	A				2.4
	11.9	12.5		10.7	Trade Payables	I	I				10.4
	.2	.1		.0	Income Taxes Payable	L	L				.0
	3.9	6.5		5.0	All Other Current	A	A				7.9
	20.6	22.7		20.7	Total Current	B	B				25.8
	16.4	10.4		12.9	Long-Term Debt	L	L				14.0
	1.5	.7		.6	Deferred Taxes	E	E				.9
	3.8	4.8		3.8	All Other Non-Current						6.5
	57.8	61.4		62.0	Net Worth						52.7
	100.0	100.0		100.0	Total Liabilities & Net Worth						100.0
					INCOME DATA						
	100.0	100.0		100.0	Net Sales						100.0
	29.9	27.6		32.3	Gross Profit						29.0
	20.6	19.6		22.3	Operating Expenses						18.5
	9.3	8.1		10.0	Operating Profit						10.5
	-1.4	-.2		1.2	All Other Expenses (net)						2.5
	10.7	8.2		8.7	Profit Before Taxes						7.9
					RATIOS						
	4.4	4.8		5.5							3.6
	3.4	3.3		3.7	Current						2.0
	2.7	2.3		1.5							1.4
	3.1	3.5		4.0							2.2
	2.0	1.8		2.1	Quick						1.3
	1.4	1.1		.9							.7
34	10.8	23	15.6	30	12.0					31	11.9
36	10.1	38	9.5	39	9.3	Sales/Receivables				36	10.1
48	7.6	52	7.0	46	8.0					46	8.0
32	11.5	41	8.9	54	6.8					55	6.6
45	8.1	62	5.9	61	6.0	Cost of Sales/Inventory				65	5.6
68	5.4	79	4.6	78	4.7					74	4.9
15	24.0	14	26.9	19	19.6					23	15.7
24	15.5	25	14.4	31	11.8	Cost of Sales/Payables				36	10.2
35	10.5	33	11.0	38	9.6					42	8.7
	4.6	4.0		3.2							3.6
	5.3	5.6		5.2	Sales/Working Capital						7.3
	7.7	7.1		11.7							11.8
	81.7	180.9		58.6							15.4
(14)	32.0	(15) 15.0	(21)	9.5	EBIT/Interest					(11)	5.5
	11.4	3.1		5.2							-2.4
					Net Profit + Depr., Dep., Amort./Cur. Mat. L/T/D						
	.3	.1		.2							.3
	.4	.3		.5	Fixed/Worth						.7
	.8	.6		1.1							1.4
	.3	.2		.2							.4
	.6	.7		.7	Debt/Worth						1.3
	1.1	1.3		1.7							2.3
	56.5	50.1		52.6							51.2
(19)	37.8	28.4	(22)	33.0	% Profit Before Taxes/Tangible Net Worth						26.1
	24.8	13.7		3.4							-12.0
	30.2	40.8		41.5							37.6
	25.6	13.2		12.1	% Profit Before Taxes/Total Assets						11.2
	13.9	7.9		5.6							-4.1
	15.5	33.1		19.3							11.4
	10.4	12.4		7.9	Sales/Net Fixed Assets						5.4
	5.5	6.8		3.1							3.1
	3.3	3.4		2.3							2.1
	2.4	2.4		1.6	Sales/Total Assets						1.5
	1.7	1.5		1.2							1.2
	1.8	1.4		1.4							1.4
(16)	2.0	(13) 1.6	(18)	2.2	% Depr., Dep., Amort./Sales					(11)	2.3
	2.8	2.2		4.1							3.4
					% Officers', Directors' Owners' Comp/Sales						
	1699873M	1537774M		2035696M	Net Sales ($)		2852M		36586M	83322M	1912936M
	836470M	868539M		1346630M	Total Assets ($)		3883M		12343M	62071M	1268333M

© RMA 2024   M = $ thousand   MM = $ million
See Pages viii through xx for Explanation of Ratios and Data

MANUFACTURING—Urethane and Other Foam Product (except Polystyrene) Manufacturing NAICS 326150

Current Data Sorted by Assets | Comparative Historical Data

						Type of Statement		
		4				Unqualified	4	3
1	1	2	1			Reviewed	4	2
1	3					Compiled	2	3
	1					Tax Returns	2	3
3	6	3	1	3		Other	21	15
0-500M	6 (4/1-9/30/23) 500M-2MM	2-10MM	24 (10/1/23-3/31/24) 10-50MM	50-100MM	100-250MM		4/1/19-3/31/20 ALL	4/1/20-3/31/21 ALL
	5	11	9	2	3	NUMBER OF STATEMENTS	33	26
%	%	%	%	%	%	ASSETS	%	%
D		22.6				Cash & Equivalents	8.9	13.8
A		17.1				Trade Receivables (net)	29.7	25.1
T		15.0				Inventory	20.7	22.7
A		1.3				All Other Current	1.5	.9
		56.1				Total Current	60.8	62.5
N		23.4				Fixed Assets (net)	23.2	24.0
O		14.0				Intangibles (net)	7.0	6.8
T		6.5				All Other Non-Current	9.0	6.7
		100.0				Total	100.0	100.0
A						LIABILITIES		
V		2.1				Notes Payable-Short Term	7.3	7.5
A		1.6				Cur. Mat.-L.T.D.	1.5	1.8
I		10.3				Trade Payables	15.2	15.0
L		.1				Income Taxes Payable	.3	.2
A		10.4				All Other Current	7.5	6.2
B		24.5				Total Current	31.8	30.7
L		19.0				Long-Term Debt	8.2	17.2
E		.1				Deferred Taxes	.5	.1
		6.0				All Other Non-Current	4.1	7.4
		50.4				Net Worth	55.3	44.6
		100.0				Total Liabilties & Net Worth	100.0	100.0
						INCOME DATA		
		100.0				Net Sales	100.0	100.0
		35.3				Gross Profit	29.5	32.3
		26.1				Operating Expenses	22.5	24.8
		9.2				Operating Profit	7.0	7.6
		1.9				All Other Expenses (net)	.9	-.5
		7.4				Profit Before Taxes	6.1	8.1
						RATIOS		
		6.1					4.0	4.8
		2.1				Current	3.0	2.1
		1.3					1.6	1.4
		4.5					2.7	3.4
		1.3				Quick	1.8	1.3
		.7					.7	.8
	24	15.4					36 10.2	33 11.0
	31	11.9				Sales/Receivables	41 9.0	42 8.6
	38	9.5					49 7.4	55 6.6
	15	24.6					34 10.7	40 9.2
	39	9.3				Cost of Sales/Inventory	49 7.5	54 6.7
	94	3.9					65 5.6	79 4.6
	15	24.2					18 20.4	18 20.2
	22	16.3				Cost of Sales/Payables	27 13.4	32 11.4
	51	7.1					52 7.0	59 6.2
		2.5					4.7	4.8
		8.9				Sales/Working Capital	6.9	6.1
		22.6					12.0	12.8
							35.3	97.9
						EBIT/Interest	(26) 10.0	(23) 6.4
							4.3	3.9
						Net Profit + Depr., Dep., Amort./Cur. Mat. L/T/D		
		.2					.2	.3
		1.1				Fixed/Worth	.4	.5
		-2.0					.9	1.3
		.1					.3	.6
		2.0				Debt/Worth	.7	1.1
		-11.8					1.5	6.2
							46.2	105.9
						% Profit Before Taxes/Tangible Net Worth	(31) 27.1	(24) 48.1
							17.8	17.6
		25.0					21.8	22.7
		12.7				% Profit Before Taxes/Total Assets	12.7	15.2
		3.6					5.6	6.6
		110.0					24.6	33.3
		6.4				Sales/Net Fixed Assets	10.9	12.3
		5.3					4.9	5.5
		2.2					3.2	2.6
		1.9				Sales/Total Assets	2.3	2.0
		1.6					1.7	1.6
		.4					1.5	1.2
	(10)	2.0				% Depr., Dep., Amort./Sales	(25) 2.0	(20) 2.2
		3.3					3.4	3.2
						% Officers', Directors' Owners' Comp/Sales		
	19238M	127377M	381242M	283110M	776650M	Net Sales ($)	1613858M	999011M
	6907M	65056M	221625M	156571M	439263M	Total Assets ($)	1189834M	577961M

M = $ thousand   MM = $ million
See Pages viii through xx for Explanation of Ratios and Data

© RMA 2024

MANUFACTURING—Urethane and Other Foam Product (except Polystyrene) Manufacturing NAICS 326150

Comparative Historical Data			Type of Statement	Current Data Sorted by Sales					
2	4	4	Unqualified					1	3
3	4	5	Reviewed		1			1	3
1	2	4	Compiled	1	1		2		
2		1	Tax Returns			1			
14	10	16	Other		3	4	4	4	5
4/1/21-3/31/22 ALL	4/1/22-3/31/23 ALL	4/1/23-3/31/24 ALL		0-1MM	6 (4/1-9/30/23) 1-3MM	3-5MM	24 (10/1/23-3/31/24) 5-10MM	10-25MM	25MM & OVER
22	20	30	NUMBER OF STATEMENTS	1	5	5	8		11
%	%	%	ASSETS	%	%	%	%	%	%
14.2	14.7	18.5	Cash & Equivalents						11.2
25.5	23.6	18.6	Trade Receivables (net)	D					19.3
25.4	22.6	15.8	Inventory	A					19.1
2.6	3.3	1.5	All Other Current	T					2.0
67.6	64.3	54.5	Total Current	A					51.6
25.6	25.9	30.7	Fixed Assets (net)						34.8
2.0	2.9	7.5	Intangibles (net)	N					5.3
4.8	6.9	7.4	All Other Non-Current	O					8.3
100.0	100.0	100.0	Total	T					100.0
			LIABILITIES	A					
6.6	4.5	3.6	Notes Payable-Short Term	V					3.5
1.7	1.8	2.9	Cur. Mat.-L.T.D.	A					2.3
13.1	11.6	10.0	Trade Payables	I					11.1
.3	.3	.3	Income Taxes Payable	L					.3
8.9	7.8	7.1	All Other Current	A					6.5
30.6	26.0	23.8	Total Current	B					23.6
10.7	11.8	19.9	Long-Term Debt	L					17.6
.1	.0	.1	Deferred Taxes	E					.0
4.0	3.0	9.5	All Other Non-Current						3.8
54.5	59.2	46.8	Net Worth						55.1
100.0	100.0	100.0	Total Liabilties & Net Worth						100.0
			INCOME DATA						
100.0	100.0	100.0	Net Sales						100.0
28.2	29.7	34.2	Gross Profit						24.1
20.0	22.0	25.2	Operating Expenses						17.1
8.2	7.7	9.1	Operating Profit						7.0
-1.4	-.7	1.3	All Other Expenses (net)						.3
9.6	8.4	7.8	Profit Before Taxes						6.7
			RATIOS						
4.7	4.6	5.8							4.3
2.9	2.9	2.4	Current						2.3
1.3	1.6	1.3						1.9
3.2	2.7	3.5							2.4
1.3	1.5	1.7	Quick						1.4
.7	.7	.8							.9
36 10.0	28 12.9	26 13.8						37	9.9
45 8.1	41 8.8	37 9.9	Sales/Receivables					43	8.4
52 7.0	48 7.6	44 8.3						46	8.0
39 9.3	41 8.8	21 17.6						49	7.5
61 6.0	60 6.1	49 7.4	Cost of Sales/Inventory					50	7.3
87 4.2	79 4.6	74 4.9						55	6.6
19 19.3	21 17.8	15 24.4						15	25.1
27 13.3	29 12.7	24 15.0	Cost of Sales/Payables					29	12.6
47 7.7	31 11.6	50 7.3						50	7.3
3.4	4.1	3.4							4.5
5.9	5.3	5.3	Sales/Working Capital						5.4
14.5	11.3	29.4							7.7
	127.6	203.3	26.9						57.0
(18) 23.8	(18) 39.2	(24) 7.2	EBIT/Interest					(10)	11.7
10.8	5.2	3.6							4.2
			Net Profit + Depr., Dep., Amort./Cur. Mat. L/T/D						
.2	.2	.3							.4
.4	.3	.8	Fixed/Worth						.7
.7	.8	2.2							1.5
.3	.3	.2							.3
.8	.6	1.4	Debt/Worth						.5
2.8	2.0	4.5							3.1
66.5	43.6	36.2							31.5
39.0	25.9	(24) 25.6	% Profit Before Taxes/Tangible Net Worth					(10)	25.3
20.1	13.6	12.2							12.9
35.3	28.7	25.2							19.6
21.8	16.0	11.4	% Profit Before Taxes/Total Assets						8.0
10.8	5.2	5.5							5.6
22.1	14.6	12.3							9.0
8.3	9.4	7.2	Sales/Net Fixed Assets						6.9
4.5	5.0	3.6							2.6
2.8	2.8	2.4							2.1
2.2	2.1	1.9	Sales/Total Assets						1.7
1.4	1.4	1.5							1.4
1.4	1.3	.8							1.4
(17) 1.9	(16) 1.7	(26) 1.9	% Depr., Dep., Amort./Sales					(10)	2.3
3.7	2.4	2.9							3.6
			% Officers', Directors' Owners' Comp/Sales						
1200247M	1248369M	1587617M	Net Sales ($)		2184M	19965M	40013M	140595M	1384860M
660805M	598826M	889422M	Total Assets ($)		616M	12966M	20274M	77573M	777993M

© RMA 2024   M = $ thousand   MM = $ million
See Pages viii through xx for Explanation of Ratios and Data

MANUFACTURING—Plastics Bottle Manufacturing NAICS 326160

Current Data Sorted by Assets | **Comparative Historical Data**

							Type of Statement		
				3		2	Unqualified	2	1
			2		1		Reviewed		
		1					Compiled	1	
		1					Tax Returns	3	1
3		5		4	3		Other	1	2
	3 (4/1-9/30/23)		22 (10/1/23-3/31/24)					17	6
0-500M	500M-2MM	2-10MM	10-50MM	50-100MM	100-250MM			4/1/19-3/31/20 ALL	4/1/20-3/31/21 ALL
3	3	7	9	4	2		NUMBER OF STATEMENTS	24	10
%	%	%	%	%	%		ASSETS	%	%

							Cash & Equivalents	7.9	11.3
							Trade Receivables (net)	16.9	18.6
							Inventory	17.5	15.3
							All Other Current	1.7	1.0
							Total Current	44.0	46.2
							Fixed Assets (net)	44.7	38.0
							Intangibles (net)	10.5	6.2
							All Other Non-Current	.8	9.5
							Total	100.0	100.0
							LIABILITIES		
							Notes Payable-Short Term	8.9	6.6
							Cur. Mat.-L.T.D.	4.2	2.5
							Trade Payables	15.0	6.9
							Income Taxes Payable	.0	.0
							All Other Current	5.1	11.8
							Total Current	33.3	27.8
							Long-Term Debt	29.4	31.3
							Deferred Taxes	.7	.4
							All Other Non-Current	6.8	9.6
							Net Worth	29.8	30.5
							Total Liabilities & Net Worth	100.0	100.0
							INCOME DATA		
							Net Sales	100.0	100.0
							Gross Profit	31.6	38.0
							Operating Expenses	19.0	17.5
							Operating Profit	12.5	20.4
							All Other Expenses (net)	2.6	4.0
							Profit Before Taxes	9.9	16.5
							RATIOS		
							Current	3.2	2.7
								1.7	1.8
								.9	.9
							Quick	2.1	1.4
								1.1	1.0
								.4	.6
							Sales/Receivables	18 20.6	0 UND
								41 8.8	41 9.0
								51 7.1	58 6.3
							Cost of Sales/Inventory	26 13.8	0 UND
								38 9.7	38 9.5
								76 4.8	101 3.6
							Cost of Sales/Payables	20 18.2	0 UND
								29 12.6	19 19.6
								78 4.7	30 12.1
							Sales/Working Capital	5.5	5.3
								10.9	8.2
								-28.1	-753.0
							EBIT/Interest	12.5	
								(21) 5.1	
								2.1	
							Net Profit + Depr., Dep., Amort./Cur. Mat. L/T/D		
							Fixed/Worth	.8	.4
								1.8	.9
								-2.9	NM
							Debt/Worth	.7	.6
								1.5	1.6
								-5.4	NM
							% Profit Before Taxes/Tangible Net Worth	25.9	
								(15) 13.0	
								5.2	
							% Profit Before Taxes/Total Assets	16.3	19.5
								4.7	8.5
								3.5	4.2
							Sales/Net Fixed Assets	8.2	9.9
								3.7	6.8
								3.2	2.6
							Sales/Total Assets	2.2	2.4
								1.6	1.9
								1.3	.4
							% Depr., Dep., Amort./Sales	3.3	
								(16) 4.4	
								8.2	
							% Officers', Directors' Owners' Comp/Sales		
365M		102639M	223787M	323037M	608098M		Net Sales ($)	1696067M	406119M
376M		38943M	166686M	233679M	435639M		Total Assets ($)	1022204M	340809M

Data Not Available for 0-500M, 500M-2MM columns (rows 3, 3).

© RMA 2024   M = $ thousand   MM = $ million
See Pages viii through xx for Explanation of Ratios and Data

MANUFACTURING—Plastics Bottle Manufacturing NAICS 326160

Comparative Historical Data | Current Data Sorted by Sales

							Type of Statement						
		1		4		5	Unqualified				1		4
		1		1		3	Reviewed				2		1
		3		1		1	Compiled				1		
		10		9		15	Tax Returns				1		1
		4/1/21-3/31/22 ALL		4/1/22-3/31/23 ALL		4/1/23-3/31/24 ALL	Other	3	3 (4/1-9/30/23)		2 22 (10/1/23-3/31/24)		6
								0-1MM	1-3MM	3-5MM	5-10MM	10-25MM	25MM & OVER
		15		15		25	NUMBER OF STATEMENTS	3			2	9	11
		%		%		%	ASSETS	%	%	%	%	%	%
		10.6		10.9		8.4	Cash & Equivalents						9.0
		18.1		12.5		13.7	Trade Receivables (net)	D	D				11.1
		21.9		20.1		21.7	Inventory	A	A				21.5
		2.9		2.7		.7	All Other Current	T	T				1.0
		53.6		46.2		44.5	Total Current	A	A				42.6
		30.6		35.5		33.3	Fixed Assets (net)						29.6
		12.7		12.4		8.9	Intangibles (net)	N	N				10.0
		3.4		5.8		13.3	All Other Non-Current	O	O				17.8
		100.0		100.0		100.0	Total	T	T				100.0
							LIABILITIES	A	A				
		6.2		4.8		4.3	Notes Payable-Short Term	V	V				4.0
		2.6		5.1		3.2	Cur. Mat.-L.T.D.	A	A				3.9
		13.8		9.8		10.4	Trade Payables	I	I				9.9
		.1		.3		.4	Income Taxes Payable	L	L				.9
		10.6		8.6		8.8	All Other Current	A	A				10.4
		33.4		28.5		27.1	Total Current	B	B				29.1
		32.2		25.8		19.0	Long-Term Debt	L	L				16.0
		1.7		.4		.5	Deferred Taxes	E	E				.3
		2.5		6.9		13.5	All Other Non-Current						13.3
		30.3		38.3		40.0	Net Worth						41.3
		100.0		100.0		100.0	Total Liabilities & Net Worth						100.0
							INCOME DATA						
		100.0		100.0		100.0	Net Sales						100.0
		30.7		30.3		27.4	Gross Profit						17.6
		20.1		25.9		22.3	Operating Expenses						11.6
		10.6		4.4		5.1	Operating Profit						6.1
		.0		.8		1.3	All Other Expenses (net)						1.4
		10.6		3.7		3.8	Profit Before Taxes						4.6
							RATIOS						
		2.1		2.5		2.6							1.9
		1.3		1.6		1.7	Current						1.4
		1.1		1.2		1.3							1.3
		1.6		1.8		1.6							1.2
		.8		1.0		.9	Quick						.5
		.5		.3		.5							.4
13	28.0		13	27.8	18	20.2						5	74.8
36	10.1		24	15.0	34	10.6	Sales/Receivables					36	10.1
55	6.6		40	9.2	43	8.4						41	8.8
	29	12.6	29	12.8	39	9.4						39	9.3
	41	8.8	41	9.0	55	6.6	Cost of Sales/Inventory					49	7.4
	94	3.9	104	3.5	94	3.9						66	5.5
	21	17.0	17	21.3	15	24.4						16	22.9
	29	12.7	26	13.8	25	14.8	Cost of Sales/Payables					22	16.3
	62	5.9	38	9.6	38	9.5						32	11.4
		8.2		4.5		6.0							6.3
		12.0		14.0		11.6	Sales/Working Capital						12.2
		50.5		20.0		24.9							16.7
		19.6		13.7		21.5							23.1
(13)	6.4	(11)	2.6	(22)	3.1	EBIT/Interest					(10)	2.8
		3.0		-.4		1.4							1.8
							Net Profit + Depr., Dep., Amort./Cur. Mat. L/T/D						
		.4		.6		.6							.5
		2.2		2.0		1.0	Fixed/Worth						.9
		-3.2		-59.1		2.9							2.2
		1.3		1.1		.9							1.0
		3.9		3.0		2.5	Debt/Worth						2.6
		-10.6		-129.7		5.2							3.6
		104.6		26.3		34.7	% Profit Before Taxes/Tangible Net Worth						33.1
(10)	23.9	(11)	16.1	(21)	19.3							(10)	14.3
		2.7		-4.0		7.4							7.5
		20.5		15.4		15.0	% Profit Before Taxes/Total Assets						14.2
		9.1		1.9		3.9							2.9
		4.8		-1.9		1.4							1.6
		19.6		20.0		10.9							10.4
		5.5		3.8		5.4	Sales/Net Fixed Assets						5.4
		3.2		3.3		3.3							5.0
		2.4		2.0		2.4							2.3
		1.7		1.8		1.5	Sales/Total Assets						1.4
		1.2		1.3		1.1							1.3
		1.5		3.0		1.9							1.5
(10)	3.5	(10)	5.1	(19)	3.8	% Depr., Dep., Amort./Sales					(10)	2.6
		5.6		6.7		6.0							4.5
							% Officers', Directors' Owners' Comp/Sales						
		508539M		809762M		1257926M	Net Sales ($)	365M			14686M	146915M	1095960M
		382573M		620307M		875323M	Total Assets ($)	376M			13316M	106655M	754976M

© RMA 2024
M = $ thousand MM = $ million
See Pages viii through xx for Explanation of Ratios and Data

MANUFACTURING—All Other Plastics Product Manufacturing NAICS 326199

Current Data Sorted by Assets | Comparative Historical Data

							Type of Statement				
		4	15	6	16		Unqualified		49		31
		13	38	9	4		Reviewed		79		52
1	1	14	8	2			Compiled		30		26
1	9	11	3				Tax Returns		52		20
1	9	53	104	26	20		Other		269		175
	75 (4/1-9/30/23)		293 (10/1/23-3/31/24)						4/1/19-		4/1/20-
0-500M	500M-2MM	2-10MM	10-50MM	50-100MM	100-250MM				3/31/20		3/31/21
3	19	95	168	43	40		NUMBER OF STATEMENTS		ALL 479		ALL 304
%	%	%	%	%	%		ASSETS		%		%
	23.3	12.2	9.9	8.7	4.9		Cash & Equivalents		8.6		12.3
	22.8	21.8	20.4	15.2	16.1		Trade Receivables (net)		22.9		22.1
	21.3	25.9	22.8	17.7	18.5		Inventory		23.8		22.1
	2.6	3.0	2.0	1.4	4.3		All Other Current		2.3		2.0
	70.0	62.9	55.0	43.0	43.8		Total Current		57.7		58.5
	24.1	25.0	31.2	26.4	32.8		Fixed Assets (net)		30.9		30.2
	2.1	4.8	5.2	21.3	10.5		Intangibles (net)		6.0		5.6
	3.8	7.2	8.7	9.4	12.9		All Other Non-Current		5.5		5.7
	100.0	100.0	100.0	100.0	100.0		Total		100.0		100.0
							LIABILITIES				
	5.3	7.4	4.8	3.9	3.0		Notes Payable-Short Term		8.3		6.4
	9.2	2.3	3.4	4.7	2.0		Cur. Mat.-L.T.D.		3.6		4.8
	5.1	12.6	9.3	8.9	7.9		Trade Payables		12.4		12.5
	.1	.2	.2	.0	.1		Income Taxes Payable		.1		.1
	18.6	9.3	8.6	8.4	11.2		All Other Current		9.5		8.5
	38.3	31.8	26.4	25.9	24.2		Total Current		33.9		32.3
	26.9	21.9	15.3	19.8	19.7		Long-Term Debt		17.4		19.6
	.0	.2	.5	.8	1.1		Deferred Taxes		.3		.3
	8.7	4.8	7.5	8.2	6.6		All Other Non-Current		6.9		8.0
	26.2	41.3	50.3	45.3	48.4		Net Worth		41.4		39.8
	100.0	100.0	100.0	100.0	100.0		Total Liabilties & Net Worth		100.0		100.0
							INCOME DATA				
	100.0	100.0	100.0	100.0	100.0		Net Sales		100.0		100.0
	37.5	29.8	26.6	30.4	24.0		Gross Profit		27.4		27.1
	35.0	24.4	19.7	22.2	16.8		Operating Expenses		22.1		22.5
	2.6	5.4	6.9	8.2	7.2		Operating Profit		5.3		4.5
	.5	.8	1.4	2.7	1.3		All Other Expenses (net)		1.1		-.7
	2.1	4.6	5.5	5.5	5.9		Profit Before Taxes		4.1		5.2
							RATIOS				
		10.7	4.6	4.0	3.5	3.0			3.1		3.6
		2.5	2.4	2.1	1.8	1.9	Current		1.8		1.9
		1.4	1.4	1.4	1.3	1.4			1.3		1.3
		7.8	2.4	2.2	2.3	1.4			1.8		2.2
		1.4	1.1	1.2	1.1	1.1	Quick		1.0		1.1
		.9	.6	.7	.6	.6			.6		.7
	7	51.2	28	13.1	34	10.6	33	11.1	35	10.3			30	12.3	32	11.5
	24	15.1	38	9.5	45	8.1	42	8.6	45	8.1	Sales/Receivables	41	8.8	45	8.2
	45	8.2	55	6.6	57	6.4	57	6.4	56	6.5		55	6.6	61	6.0
	18	19.9	29	12.6	41	8.9	52	7.0	49	7.4		39	9.4	37	9.8
	29	12.5	66	5.5	64	5.7	89	4.1	63	5.8	Cost of Sales/Inventory	59	6.2	60	6.1
	126	2.9	104	3.5	99	3.7	107	3.4	104	3.5		87	4.2	89	4.1
	0	UND	10	36.6	14	25.6	19	19.5	18	19.8		17	21.0	17	21.2
	5	76.7	21	17.0	26	14.0	33	10.9	29	12.4	Cost of Sales/Payables	28	13.0	28	13.1
	14	25.7	45	8.2	36	10.1	57	6.4	40	9.2		42	8.7	45	8.2
		2.7		3.3		3.5		3.5		3.9			4.6		4.0
		7.7		6.0		5.9		6.6		6.3	Sales/Working Capital		8.3		6.8
		18.8		15.9		12.5		14.8		10.7			21.3		14.5
		19.8		17.8		20.2		18.2		31.6			15.4		18.9
	(16)	1.6	(86)	5.2	(151)	4.5	(39)	3.2	(38)	9.5	EBIT/Interest	(436)	5.0	(272)	6.2
		.4		1.2		1.1		.9		1.9			1.5		1.3
				8.3		7.4		5.4		9.9	Net Profit + Depr., Dep.,		7.3		8.0
		(16)	4.7	(60)	2.3	(13)	2.7	(11)	6.5	Amort./Cur. Mat. L/T/D	(121)	3.0	(65)	3.4
				1.1		1.0		1.1		2.0			1.4		1.6
		.1		.2		.4		.5		.5			.4		.4
		.2		.6		.6		1.2		.8	Fixed/Worth		.9		.9
		2.9		1.3		1.4		-.7		1.4			1.8		2.1
		.1		.4		.4		.6		.4			.6		.6
		.9		1.1		1.1		3.3		1.2	Debt/Worth		1.4		1.5
		-7.6		2.8		2.9		-4.4		4.7			3.7		3.7
		27.3		43.2		35.1		58.2		27.7			35.8		49.1
	(13)	4.8	(84)	18.4	(157)	18.8	(30)	23.9	(33)	15.5	% Profit Before Taxes/Tangible Net Worth	(417)	18.1	(264)	23.4
		-.5		.6		3.3		14.6		8.6			5.2		6.9
		18.5		18.2		17.5		16.5		12.4			15.4		18.3
		4.2		7.1		7.1		8.0		8.4	% Profit Before Taxes/Total Assets		7.1		8.2
		.0		.5		.1		-.4		1.7			.6		1.0
		117.1		20.5		8.8		19.8		6.4			12.0		11.5
		15.3		7.5		5.7		4.3		4.2	Sales/Net Fixed Assets		6.3		5.9
		4.6		4.6		3.1		2.9		2.5			3.7		3.3
		4.0		2.4		2.0		1.4		1.6			2.4		2.2
		2.1		2.0		1.6		1.1		1.2	Sales/Total Assets		1.9		1.6
		1.1		1.5		1.2		.8		.9			1.4		1.3
		.8		1.2		1.6		2.4		2.2			1.7		2.1
	(12)	1.6	(70)	2.4	(156)	2.8	(33)	3.6	(21)	3.5	% Depr., Dep., Amort./Sales	(387)	3.2	(248)	3.2
		4.3		3.9		4.3		6.3		5.0			4.9		4.8
				2.0		1.0							2.0		1.9
			(38)	3.8	(32)	1.9					% Officers', Directors' Owners' Comp/Sales	(118)	3.2	(80)	3.2
				7.1		3.1							5.5		6.7
2335M	69656M	954267M	6203532M	3788384M	7683456M	Net Sales ($)		24203097M		12472606M
430M	25942M	493583M	3958029M	3256046M	6302067M	Total Assets ($)		15442366M		8743415M

M = $ thousand   MM = $ million
See Pages viii through xx for Explanation of Ratios and Data

© RMA 2024

MANUFACTURING—All Other Plastics Product Manufacturing NAICS 326199

Comparative Historical Data | Current Data Sorted by Sales

Comparative Historical Data			Type of Statement	Current Data Sorted by Sales					
26	39	41	Unqualified			2	2	6	33
49	61	64	Reviewed		1	8	8	16	39
19	24	26	Compiled		1	1	7	8	9
21	36	24	Tax Returns	2	1	7	5	7	2
176	195	213	Other	1	10	6	28	49	119
4/1/21-3/31/22 ALL	4/1/22-3/31/23 ALL	4/1/23-3/31/24 ALL		75 (4/1-9/30/23)			293 (10/1/23-3/31/24)		
				0-1MM	1-3MM	3-5MM	5-10MM	10-25MM	25MM & OVER
291	355	368	NUMBER OF STATEMENTS	3	12	15	50	86	202
%	%	%	ASSETS	%	%	%	%	%	%
11.3	9.8	10.5	Cash & Equivalents	8.5	26.9	9.8	12.9	8.2	
22.4	22.1	19.8	Trade Receivables (net)	21.6	16.4	20.5	21.3	19.1	
24.6	25.6	22.7	Inventory	30.0	15.5	29.3	20.9	21.7	
2.3	2.5	2.5	All Other Current	4.4	2.0	1.6	2.2	2.9	
60.6	60.0	55.4	Total Current	64.4	60.7	61.2	57.3	51.8	
28.4	28.4	28.6	Fixed Assets (net)	24.7	25.0	28.2	27.9	29.9	
5.4	4.7	7.3	Intangibles (net)	6.8	1.9	4.6	7.7	8.4	
5.5	6.8	8.6	All Other Non-Current	4.0	12.4	6.0	7.1	9.9	
100.0	100.0	100.0	Total	100.0	100.0	100.0	100.0	100.0	
			LIABILITIES						
6.4	6.3	5.3	Notes Payable-Short Term	8.7	5.0	8.1	4.5	4.6	
2.5	2.9	3.4	Cur. Mat.-L.T.D.	2.0	1.7	5.5	2.6	3.5	
13.6	11.9	10.1	Trade Payables	4.1	7.8	13.5	10.0	9.2	
.1	.2	.2	Income Taxes Payable	.8	.2	.0	.1	.2	
7.7	8.1	9.6	All Other Current	27.0	8.0	10.7	8.1	9.3	
30.3	29.3	28.6	Total Current	42.6	22.6	37.9	25.3	26.7	
15.8	19.3	18.5	Long-Term Debt	21.7	27.2	26.9	16.4	16.7	
.5	.4	.5	Deferred Taxes	.4	.2	.1	.4	.6	
6.2	6.2	6.8	All Other Non-Current	2.4	9.4	6.8	6.0	7.3	
47.2	44.9	45.7	Net Worth	32.9	40.6	28.3	52.0	48.6	
100.0	100.0	100.0	Total Liabilities & Net Worth	100.0	100.0	100.0	100.0	100.0	
			INCOME DATA						
100.0	100.0	100.0	Net Sales	100.0	100.0	100.0	100.0	100.0	
27.5	27.5	28.0	Gross Profit	34.6	30.0	30.5	29.7	26.2	
20.9	21.0	21.6	Operating Expenses	38.3	24.6	25.4	23.6	18.6	
6.6	6.5	6.4	Operating Profit	-3.7	5.5	5.1	6.1	7.6	
-1.4	.3	1.3	All Other Expenses (net)	1.0	.4	1.0	1.9	1.3	
8.0	6.1	5.1	Profit Before Taxes	-4.8	5.0	4.1	4.2	6.3	
			RATIOS						
3.6	3.9	3.8	Current	2.7	9.8	4.0	4.7	3.5	
2.1	2.3	2.1		1.7	2.7	1.9	2.6	1.9	
1.4	1.5	1.3		1.1	2.0	1.2	1.5	1.3	
2.2	2.1	2.2	Quick	1.3	7.9	2.0	2.7	2.1	
1.2	1.2	1.1		.6	1.8	.8	1.5	1.1	
.7	.6	.6		.5	1.3	.5	.8	.6	
35 10.3	30 12.0	31 11.7	Sales/Receivables	20 18.1	7 51.2	25 14.7	34 10.7	33 11.0	
46 7.9	45 8.1	43 8.5		34 10.6	30 12.1	39 9.3	48 7.6	43 8.4	
61 6.0	58 6.3	55 6.6		96 3.8	45 8.1	52 7.0	59 6.2	55 6.6	
47 7.8	41 9.0	41 9.0	Cost of Sales/Inventory	54 6.8	21 17.5	43 8.5	30 12.3	45 8.1	
69 5.3	65 5.6	64 5.7		91 4.0	26 14.3	87 4.2	61 6.0	64 5.7	
94 3.9	107 3.4	101 3.6		174 2.1	46 7.9	146 2.5	89 4.1	99 3.7	
18 20.1	15 24.0	13 27.6	Cost of Sales/Payables	4 94.4	2 207.3	9 38.6	11 33.9	17 22.0	
32 11.4	26 14.3	26 14.1		9 41.4	15 25.0	24 15.5	24 15.1	27 13.4	
50 7.3	42 8.6	39 9.4		38 9.5	38 9.6	45 8.1	38 9.6	38 9.5	
3.6	3.7	3.5	Sales/Working Capital	2.8	2.7	3.3	3.5	3.8	
5.8	5.7	6.2		4.0	7.0	6.7	5.1	6.6	
11.8	11.4	13.6		38.7	12.4	21.9	11.9	13.0	
37.8	26.6	20.2	EBIT/Interest	5.5	23.1	20.6	23.9		
(255) 12.3	(314) 8.5	(331) 4.5		3.0	(45) 2.9	(77) 4.3	(185) 7.1		
3.8	2.2	1.1		1.0	1.3	-.1	1.5		
11.4	8.0	7.9	Net Profit + Depr., Dep., Amort./Cur. Mat. L/T/D	3.1	8.0	7.9			
(60) 4.6	(87) 3.7	(101) 2.6		(10) .9	(23) 3.1	(63) 2.6			
2.3	1.9	1.2		.1	.7	1.5			
.3	.3	.3	Fixed/Worth	.1	.2	.4	.3	.4	
.6	.6	.7		.4	.3	.8	.6	.7	
1.4	1.2	1.5		2.7	1.0	2.4	1.6	1.5	
.5	.4	.4	Debt/Worth	.6	.3	.6	.4	.5	
1.1	1.1	1.2		1.8	.8	1.6	.9	1.3	
2.8	2.7	3.9		NM	5.8	13.1	2.9	3.8	
43.3	41.5	36.9	% Profit Before Taxes/Tangible Net Worth	53.8	29.2	42.2	37.1		
(260) 24.9	(317) 24.7	(319) 18.6		(12) 4.9	(42) 10.7	(76) 19.9	(178) 20.4		
12.5	7.8	4.4		.1	-2.1	-1.6	8.3		
21.8	19.6	16.5	% Profit Before Taxes/Total Assets	9.8	14.2	13.5	20.3	17.0	
11.8	9.5	7.1		-2.7	4.2	4.9	5.9	8.1	
4.7	1.9	.1		-23.9	.0	.4	-2.0	1.7	
11.6	14.0	11.6	Sales/Net Fixed Assets	49.1	12.5	14.9	11.9	9.9	
6.2	6.7	5.8		11.4	9.9	6.6	5.9	5.5	
3.9	3.6	3.4		2.1	4.7	4.2	3.8	3.1	
2.2	2.3	2.1	Sales/Total Assets	2.4	2.2	2.4	2.2	1.9	
1.7	1.7	1.6		1.0	1.9	1.8	1.6	1.5	
1.2	1.3	1.1		.8	1.5	1.1	1.2	1.1	
1.8	1.4	1.6	% Depr., Dep., Amort./Sales	.5	1.5	1.9	1.6		
(245) 3.2	(283) 2.7	(293) 2.8		(11) 1.7	(40) 2.4	(66) 2.9	(168) 3.1		
4.8	4.2	4.5		4.8	4.2	4.9	4.5		
1.1	1.6	1.4	% Officers', Directors', Owners' Comp/Sales	1.9	1.5	.9			
(69) 2.3	(95) 2.5	(85) 2.7		(23) 3.2	(20) 3.2	(29) 1.8			
5.1	4.7	4.6		6.8	5.1	3.1			
14055927M	17538487M	18701630M	Net Sales ($)	1936M	22032M	61155M	365905M	1363132M	16887470M
9433143M	11358588M	14036097M	Total Assets ($)	890M	20498M	35015M	261766M	981729M	12736199M

© RMA 2024
M = $ thousand   MM = $ million
See Pages viii through xx for Explanation of Ratios and Data

MANUFACTURING—Rubber and Plastics Hoses and Belting Manufacturing NAICS 326220

Current Data Sorted by Assets | Comparative Historical Data

							Type of Statement		
		1				1	Unqualified	4	5
		1				1	Reviewed	4	3
	2	2	1				Compiled	1	
	1	2	2	7	2	3	Tax Returns	2	1
	5 (4/1-9/30/23)		19 (10/1/23-3/31/24)				Other	9	11
0-500M	500M-2MM	2-10MM	10-50MM	50-100MM	100-250MM			4/1/19-3/31/20	4/1/20-3/31/21
	3	7	7	2	5		NUMBER OF STATEMENTS	ALL 20	ALL 22
%	%	%	%	%	%		ASSETS	%	%
							Cash & Equivalents	6.3	13.9
							Trade Receivables (net)	20.8	25.1
							Inventory	37.0	37.3
							All Other Current	1.5	1.5
							Total Current	65.7	77.8
							Fixed Assets (net)	21.3	13.5
							Intangibles (net)	6.6	3.9
							All Other Non-Current	6.4	4.8
							Total	100.0	100.0
							LIABILITIES		
							Notes Payable-Short Term	9.7	7.6
							Cur. Mat.-L.T.D.	3.8	1.7
							Trade Payables	11.7	15.7
							Income Taxes Payable	.0	.3
							All Other Current	7.3	8.0
							Total Current	32.6	33.3
							Long-Term Debt	12.2	10.6
							Deferred Taxes	.7	.6
							All Other Non-Current	5.3	6.4
							Net Worth	49.2	49.1
							Total Liabilities & Net Worth	100.0	100.0
							INCOME DATA		
							Net Sales	100.0	100.0
							Gross Profit	27.2	34.4
							Operating Expenses	22.0	29.2
							Operating Profit	5.3	5.1
							All Other Expenses (net)	.6	-.1
							Profit Before Taxes	4.7	5.2
							RATIOS		
							Current	4.1	3.9
								2.3	2.8
								1.3	1.9
							Quick	1.7	2.0
								1.2	1.7
								.5	.6
						32	Sales/Receivables	11.3	36	10.2
						40		9.1	42	8.6
						50		7.3	63	5.8
						78	Cost of Sales/Inventory	4.7	69	5.3
						99		3.7	118	3.1
						135		2.7	174	2.1
						18	Cost of Sales/Payables	20.5	20	18.3
						26		14.3	33	10.9
						34		10.7	73	5.0
							Sales/Working Capital	4.1	3.0
								5.9	4.6
								10.1	6.5
							EBIT/Interest	38.4	41.7
						(18)		6.2	(18)	8.6
								1.5	3.5
							Net Profit + Depr., Dep., Amort./Cur. Mat. L/T/D		
							Fixed/Worth	.3	.1
								.6	.2
								1.1	.6
							Debt/Worth	.3	.4
								.9	.7
								4.5	3.2
							% Profit Before Taxes/Tangible Net Worth	20.9	35.9
						(17)		11.4	(20)	16.8
								7.5	9.6
							% Profit Before Taxes/Total Assets	11.1	16.8
								6.0	6.7
								1.8	2.4
							Sales/Net Fixed Assets	17.0	72.1
								11.8	13.9
								5.9	9.0
							Sales/Total Assets	2.2	2.3
								1.9	1.8
								1.7	1.6
							% Depr., Dep., Amort./Sales	1.2	.8
						(19)		2.1	(17)	1.2
								3.2	2.3
							% Officers', Directors' Owners' Comp/Sales		
	16396M	77138M	219921M	388058M	807202M		Net Sales ($)	1160069M	943916M
	3753M	33939M	135009M	169299M	611062M		Total Assets ($)	672982M	568039M

Data Not Available for 0-500M column.

M = $ thousand   MM = $ million
See Pages viii through xx for Explanation of Ratios and Data

© RMA 2024

MANUFACTURING—Rubber and Plastics Hoses and Belting Manufacturing NAICS 326220

Comparative Historical Data | Current Data Sorted by Sales

Comparative Historical Data			Type of Statement			Current Data Sorted by Sales			
3	5	2	Unqualified					1	1
2	2	2	Reviewed					1	1
4	4	2	Compiled				1	1	1
3	3	3	Tax Returns			1	1	1	1
13	14	15	Other			1	1	4	9
4/1/21-3/31/22 ALL	4/1/22-3/31/23 ALL	4/1/23-3/31/24 ALL		5 (4/1-9/30/23)				19 (10/1/23-3/31/24)	
				0-1MM	1-3MM	3-5MM	5-10MM	10-25MM	25MM & OVER
25	28	24	NUMBER OF STATEMENTS			2	3	8	11
%	%	%	ASSETS	%	%	%	%	%	%
6.9	4.9	8.2	Cash & Equivalents	D	D				8.1
27.9	27.0	27.1	Trade Receivables (net)	A	A				19.7
32.9	39.5	33.5	Inventory	T	T				33.8
3.2	1.9	2.7	All Other Current	A	A				4.5
70.8	73.3	71.5	Total Current						66.1
16.4	16.1	17.5	Fixed Assets (net)	N	N				20.7
2.4	4.1	4.5	Intangibles (net)	O	O				4.9
10.3	6.5	6.5	All Other Non-Current	T	T				8.2
100.0	100.0	100.0	Total						100.0
			LIABILITIES	A	A				
7.1	7.1	2.6	Notes Payable-Short Term	V	V				2.6
2.1	.9	1.4	Cur. Mat.-L.T.D.	A	A				1.2
18.9	16.5	19.4	Trade Payables	I	I				10.6
.1	.0	.2	Income Taxes Payable	L	L				.1
6.6	7.6	5.9	All Other Current	A	A				7.8
34.7	32.0	29.5	Total Current	B	B				22.3
12.0	12.2	7.5	Long-Term Debt	L	L				4.8
.5	.3	.4	Deferred Taxes	E	E				.2
5.9	5.1	2.3	All Other Non-Current						1.9
46.8	50.3	60.3	Net Worth						70.7
100.0	100.0	100.0	Total Liabilities & Net Worth						100.0
			INCOME DATA						
100.0	100.0	100.0	Net Sales						100.0
30.0	28.5	30.1	Gross Profit						28.7
23.4	22.6	22.3	Operating Expenses						19.6
6.6	6.0	7.8	Operating Profit						9.1
-1.0	.6	.3	All Other Expenses (net)						.1
7.6	5.4	7.5	Profit Before Taxes						9.0
			RATIOS						
3.2	3.9	3.8							5.4
2.6	2.4	2.6	Current						3.1
1.3	1.5	2.2							2.2
1.6	1.6	2.2							2.2
1.2	1.0	1.3	Quick						1.5
.6	.6	.9							.8
31 11.9	44 8.3	35 10.3						35	10.5
51 7.1	51 7.2	44 8.3	Sales/Receivables					43	8.5
76 4.8	66 5.5	62 5.9						61	6.0
60 6.1	53 6.9	51 7.1						69	5.3
101 3.6	111 3.3	101 3.6	Cost of Sales/Inventory					118	3.1
140 2.6	174 2.1	159 2.3						174	2.1
22 16.8	27 13.3	26 14.3						25	14.4
39 9.3	34 10.6	32 11.4	Cost of Sales/Payables					30	12.3
72 5.1	51 7.2	47 7.7						37	9.9
3.3	2.7	2.9							2.3
4.7	4.0	4.6	Sales/Working Capital						3.7
11.8	7.7	10.7							6.5
64.0	55.8	86.9							
(21) 27.0	(24) 17.0	(21) 14.2	EBIT/Interest						
7.5	3.2	5.5							
			Net Profit + Depr., Dep., Amort./Cur. Mat. L/T/D						
.1	.1	.1							.1
.4	.3	.3	Fixed/Worth						.3
.8	.6	.6							.6
.5	.4	.4							.2
.9	.9	.6	Debt/Worth						.5
3.3	1.9	1.1							.7
60.2	34.5	48.1							30.4
26.3	(25) 22.0	(23) 25.4	% Profit Before Taxes/Tangible Net Worth						25.4
13.4	11.2	8.1							8.9
20.9	17.9	24.4							23.1
12.2	12.5	11.1	% Profit Before Taxes/Total Assets						15.1
5.0	1.8	4.9							7.6
22.1	37.0	29.2							13.8
12.6	12.8	14.1	Sales/Net Fixed Assets						11.0
7.8	7.4	10.1							7.7
2.5	2.6	2.7							2.1
1.8	1.8	1.9	Sales/Total Assets						1.7
1.5	1.3	1.4							1.3
.8	1.0	.8							1.0
(20) 1.1	(20) 1.7	(20) 1.3	% Depr., Dep., Amort./Sales					(10)	1.6
2.2	2.4	2.8							3.1
			% Officers', Directors' Owners' Comp/Sales						
1078732M	1642857M	1508715M	Net Sales ($)			7933M	20229M	127078M	1353475M
618252M	998672M	953062M	Total Assets ($)			4812M	6326M	67448M	874476M

© RMA 2024
M = $ thousand   MM = $ million
See Pages viii through xx for Explanation of Ratios and Data

MANUFACTURING—All Other Rubber Product Manufacturing NAICS 326299

Current Data Sorted by Assets

							Comparative Historical Data	
						Type of Statement		
			1		2	Unqualified	7	4
		1	1		1	Reviewed	9	6
	1	1	3		1	Compiled	4	5
	3	3	8	5	3	Tax Returns	4	4
0-500M	8 (4/1-9/30/23) 500M-2MM	9 2-10MM	36 (10/1/23-3/31/24) 10-50MM	50-100MM	100-250MM	Other	31 4/1/19-3/31/20 ALL	20 4/1/20-3/31/21 ALL
	5	14	13	5	7	NUMBER OF STATEMENTS	55	39
%	%	%	%	%	%	ASSETS	%	%
D		11.6	14.2			Cash & Equivalents	9.6	16.9
A		23.5	22.6			Trade Receivables (net)	22.6	21.4
T		31.4	24.7			Inventory	27.9	22.8
A		.4	1.3			All Other Current	3.0	5.3
		67.0	62.8			Total Current	63.0	66.4
N		24.9	25.9			Fixed Assets (net)	28.0	23.3
O		3.1	1.8			Intangibles (net)	4.0	3.6
T		5.0	9.5			All Other Non-Current	4.9	6.7
		100.0	100.0			Total	100.0	100.0
A						LIABILITIES		
V		9.3	4.5			Notes Payable-Short Term	10.9	6.4
A		4.2	2.8			Cur. Mat.-L.T.D.	2.1	1.7
I		12.6	11.0			Trade Payables	11.5	11.6
L		.0	.7			Income Taxes Payable	.2	.1
A		6.2	9.6			All Other Current	11.3	13.4
B		32.3	28.5			Total Current	35.9	33.1
L		8.0	11.4			Long-Term Debt	13.0	16.6
E		.0	.4			Deferred Taxes	.4	.8
		1.0	6.8			All Other Non-Current	4.7	4.9
		58.6	52.9			Net Worth	46.0	44.5
		100.0	100.0			Total Liabilities & Net Worth	100.0	100.0
						INCOME DATA		
		100.0	100.0			Net Sales	100.0	100.0
		36.7	32.0			Gross Profit	32.5	27.9
		28.2	26.7			Operating Expenses	25.6	24.8
		8.5	5.3			Operating Profit	6.9	3.1
		1.3	-.7			All Other Expenses (net)	1.2	-1.1
		7.3	6.1			Profit Before Taxes	5.7	4.2
						RATIOS		
		4.8	4.2				3.4	4.6
		2.6	2.1			Current	2.0	2.1
		1.4	1.3				1.4	1.6
		3.1	2.5				2.1	2.7
		.9	1.3			Quick	1.0	1.2
		.5	.8				.5	.7
	23	15.8	35 10.5				24 14.9	35 10.4
	36	10.2	47 7.7			Sales/Receivables	44 8.3	49 7.5
	60	6.1	70 5.2				57 6.4	62 5.9
	39	9.4	41 9.0				33 11.2	32 11.4
	72	5.1	89 4.1			Cost of Sales/Inventory	65 5.6	59 6.2
	159	2.3	111 3.3				140 2.6	89 4.1
	15	23.6	16 22.9				19 19.5	16 22.5
	26	14.3	29 12.7			Cost of Sales/Payables	24 14.9	30 12.2
	49	7.4	34 10.7				43 8.5	52 7.0
		3.2	3.8				3.7	2.9
		6.3	4.1			Sales/Working Capital	6.6	4.7
		21.5	11.2				12.9	8.3
		34.0					26.1	19.7
	(11)	8.2				EBIT/Interest	(48) 8.3	(33) 12.2
		.2					2.2	3.2
						Net Profit + Depr., Dep.,	12.0	
						Amort./Cur. Mat. L/T/D	(13) 4.2	
							2.7	
		.1	.1				.3	.2
		.4	.4			Fixed/Worth	.5	.5
		.8	1.1				1.0	1.0
		.3	.3				.5	.4
		.9	1.1			Debt/Worth	1.4	1.0
		1.4	1.8				2.2	2.9
		71.4	40.0			% Profit Before Taxes/Tangible	35.3	38.4
		21.7	20.0			Net Worth	(52) 18.1	(36) 20.6
		5.7	9.4				5.4	3.2
		51.5	16.1			% Profit Before Taxes/Total	21.3	16.3
		13.8	9.1			Assets	8.7	9.5
		2.1	4.5				2.0	-1.4
		33.3	25.9				18.9	14.7
		8.5	8.1			Sales/Net Fixed Assets	7.5	6.7
		4.0	3.6				5.0	3.9
		3.2	2.0				2.7	2.1
		1.9	1.6			Sales/Total Assets	1.7	1.6
		1.4	1.2				1.3	1.2
		.1	.5				1.4	.7
	(13)	1.2	(11) 2.0			% Depr., Dep., Amort./Sales	(47) 2.0	(33) 2.0
		3.3	3.8				3.6	3.7
						% Officers', Directors'	2.0	3.8
						Owners' Comp/Sales	(17) 2.7	(12) 5.4
							8.7	7.1
	21142M	151681M	458331M	355979M	1246541M	Net Sales ($)	1782186M	1305187M
	6444M	72480M	285655M	332996M	1000680M	Total Assets ($)	1217674M	1003248M

© RMA 2024

M = $ thousand   MM = $ million
See Pages viii through xx for Explanation of Ratios and Data

MANUFACTURING—All Other Rubber Product Manufacturing NAICS 326299

Comparative Historical Data | Current Data Sorted by Sales

			Type of Statement						
5	5	6	Unqualified					2	6
3	3	3	Reviewed						1
2		3	Compiled						1
4	5	4	Tax Returns		1	1	1		1
20	22	28	Other		1	2	5	6	14
4/1/21-	4/1/22-	4/1/23-			8 (4/1-9/30/23)			36 (10/1/23-3/31/24)	
3/31/22	3/31/23	3/31/24							
ALL	ALL	ALL		0-1MM	1-3MM	3-5MM	5-10MM	10-25MM	25MM & OVER
34	35	44	NUMBER OF STATEMENTS	2	4	7	8	23	
%	%	%	ASSETS	%	%	%	%	%	%
13.8	10.3	13.3	Cash & Equivalents						16.9
18.1	20.1	22.5	Trade Receivables (net)	D					20.4
24.0	28.8	27.2	Inventory	A					23.2
4.0	2.3	1.1	All Other Current	T					1.1
59.8	61.5	64.1	Total Current	A					61.6
27.2	22.0	25.8	Fixed Assets (net)						25.2
5.5	11.4	2.8	Intangibles (net)	N					3.0
7.4	5.1	7.3	All Other Non-Current	O					10.1
100.0	100.0	100.0	Total	T					100.0
			LIABILITIES	A					
8.0	4.2	5.9	Notes Payable-Short Term	V					4.1
2.6	2.9	3.3	Cur. Mat.-L.T.D.	A					2.2
9.0	12.1	11.5	Trade Payables	I					10.5
.1	.2	.3	Income Taxes Payable	L					.5
11.9	8.3	9.4	All Other Current	A					10.7
31.5	27.6	30.3	Total Current	B					27.9
16.3	14.7	12.9	Long-Term Debt	L					9.6
.6	1.0	.3	Deferred Taxes	E					.5
1.6	3.9	6.2	All Other Non-Current						9.2
50.0	52.8	50.3	Net Worth						52.9
100.0	100.0	100.0	Total Liabilities & Net Worth						100.0
			INCOME DATA						
100.0	100.0	100.0	Net Sales						100.0
31.1	35.3	32.7	Gross Profit						30.1
25.8	26.4	26.6	Operating Expenses						23.8
5.4	8.8	6.1	Operating Profit						6.3
-.1	1.8	.5	All Other Expenses (net)						.1
5.5	7.1	5.6	Profit Before Taxes						6.2
			RATIOS						
5.0	4.4	3.7							3.6
2.2	2.3	2.1	Current						2.1
1.4	1.4	1.4							1.6
3.1	2.2	1.9							2.0
1.2	1.0	1.2	Quick						1.3
.6	.7	.7							.8
32 11.5	28 12.9	31 11.7						36	10.1
49 7.4	47 7.7	46 8.0	Sales/Receivables					47	7.8
55 6.6	61 6.0	65 5.6						69	5.3
55 6.6	49 7.4	40 9.2						38	9.5
76 4.8	72 5.1	85 4.3	Cost of Sales/Inventory					89	4.1
107 3.4	174 2.1	114 3.2						111	3.3
15 24.0	16 22.4	19 19.7						18	19.9
24 15.5	24 14.9	29 12.6	Cost of Sales/Payables					28	13.0
38 9.7	74 4.9	38 9.5						38	9.7
2.9	3.0	3.4							3.6
4.2	4.1	4.5	Sales/Working Capital						4.1
10.2	14.8	10.3							6.8
40.2	44.5	24.1							11.8
(23) 6.8	(26) 4.1	(35) 6.8	EBIT/Interest					(17)	6.8
2.6	-.3	2.2							1.5
		2.9	12.6	Net Profit + Depr., Dep.,					
	(12) 1.5	(14) 4.6	Amort./Cur. Mat. L/T/D						
		.6	1.2						
.3	.1	.2							.3
.5	.4	.5	Fixed/Worth						.5
1.0	1.8	1.1							.8
.3	.3	.4							.4
.9	1.2	1.1	Debt/Worth						1.0
2.4	4.4	1.8							1.8
38.2	44.2	61.2	% Profit Before Taxes/Tangible						40.1
(33) 22.2	(31) 11.7	(43) 17.0	Net Worth						17.9
9.8	-2.9	6.0							6.0
19.3	17.2	18.4	% Profit Before Taxes/Total						14.7
10.2	6.4	9.8	Assets						9.1
2.5	-2.4	3.5							3.9
15.3	37.9	16.3							15.8
6.0	10.9	8.2	Sales/Net Fixed Assets						4.8
3.3	3.8	3.8							3.7
1.9	2.1	2.3							1.9
1.4	1.4	1.5	Sales/Total Assets						1.5
1.0	1.1	1.2							1.1
1.0	.9	.5							.6
(27) 1.8	(26) 1.6	(34) 1.5	% Depr., Dep., Amort./Sales					(17)	1.6
4.0	4.0	3.6							3.1
		1.8	% Officers', Directors'						
	(10)	2.5	Owners' Comp/Sales						
		5.7							
1226227M	1215650M	2233674M	Net Sales ($)	4600M	14418M	50471M	137423M	2026762M	
1126749M	1007015M	1698255M	Total Assets ($)	2578M	7054M	28427M	118173M	1542023M	

© RMA 2024   M = $ thousand   MM = $ million
See Pages viii through xx for Explanation of Ratios and Data

MANUFACTURING—Glass Product Manufacturing Made of Purchased Glass NAICS 327215

Current Data Sorted by Assets | **Comparative Historical Data**

						Type of Statement		
					1	Unqualified	4	
		2	2	1		Reviewed	9	1
	1	3	1			Compiled	3	1
1	5	11	10	2	1	Tax Returns	7	4
	6 (4/1-9/30/23)		36 (10/1/23-3/31/24)			Other	26	18
0-500M	500M-2MM	2-10MM	10-50MM	50-100MM	100-250MM		4/1/19-3/31/20	4/1/20-3/31/21
1	6	16	14	3	2	NUMBER OF STATEMENTS	49 ALL	24 ALL
%	%	%	%	%	%	ASSETS	%	%
		18.5	11.4			Cash & Equivalents	11.8	12.6
		26.1	27.7			Trade Receivables (net)	23.9	20.5
		21.8	19.2			Inventory	18.8	15.3
		3.4	7.9			All Other Current	1.3	2.4
		69.8	66.2			Total Current	55.8	50.8
		20.8	28.5			Fixed Assets (net)	33.5	34.5
		3.5	.8			Intangibles (net)	4.4	7.2
		5.9	4.5			All Other Non-Current	6.4	7.5
		100.0	100.0			Total	100.0	100.0
						LIABILITIES		
		3.9	9.8			Notes Payable-Short Term	9.4	4.3
		2.1	1.9			Cur. Mat.-L.T.D.	4.2	5.1
		6.8	5.9			Trade Payables	9.9	7.6
		.1	.0			Income Taxes Payable	.0	.3
		7.5	6.2			All Other Current	13.2	14.8
		20.5	23.7			Total Current	36.7	32.1
		15.8	12.8			Long-Term Debt	18.6	25.9
		.0	.0			Deferred Taxes	.2	.0
		6.9	3.1			All Other Non-Current	7.4	7.7
		56.8	60.4			Net Worth	37.2	34.3
		100.0	100.0			Total Liabilities & Net Worth	100.0	100.0
						INCOME DATA		
		100.0	100.0			Net Sales	100.0	100.0
		40.8	34.0			Gross Profit	33.7	38.5
		30.1	24.5			Operating Expenses	27.6	33.4
		10.7	9.6			Operating Profit	6.1	5.1
		.5	.9			All Other Expenses (net)	1.3	.2
		10.2	8.7			Profit Before Taxes	4.8	5.0
						RATIOS		
		6.9	4.4				2.5	2.7
		4.5	2.8			Current	1.5	1.9
		2.2	1.8				1.1	1.2
		5.3	2.6				1.7	2.2
		2.5	1.6			Quick	.9	1.1
		1.2	1.1				.6	.5
		20 18.5	35 10.5				27 13.7	27 13.4
		39 9.4	57 6.4			Sales/Receivables	33 11.0	38 9.6
		50 7.3	73 5.0				44 8.3	56 6.5
		7 51.1	0 UND				21 17.5	22 16.3
		42 8.6	99 3.7			Cost of Sales/Inventory	32 11.4	52 7.0
		118 3.1	118 3.1				53 6.9	78 4.7
		8 44.8	8 46.2				11 34.5	16 22.7
		17 21.5	21 17.7			Cost of Sales/Payables	22 16.3	25 14.7
		25 14.4	25 14.7				31 11.6	37 9.9
		2.8	3.5				6.1	4.6
		4.5	4.6			Sales/Working Capital	12.9	7.1
		6.5	6.5				37.9	23.3
		32.3	81.0				31.9	22.3
		(12) 4.8	(12) 9.6			EBIT/Interest	(45) 6.9	(22) 4.8
		1.1	3.5				2.1	-.6
						Net Profit + Depr., Dep., Amort./Cur. Mat. L/T/D		
		.1	.1				.4	.4
		.3	.5			Fixed/Worth	.8	1.1
		.9	.9				1.9	NM
		.2	.4				.7	.6
		.5	.7			Debt/Worth	1.5	1.8
		5.0	1.2				3.2	NM
		61.5	48.4				52.3	34.9
		(13) 42.3	15.9			% Profit Before Taxes/Tangible Net Worth	(41) 27.9	(18) 21.0
		11.0	8.3				11.2	3.0
		40.3	31.2				24.2	15.5
		18.5	7.2			% Profit Before Taxes/Total Assets	10.1	6.7
		6.1	5.3				2.7	-2.1
		68.2	21.9				16.4	6.7
		14.4	6.2			Sales/Net Fixed Assets	6.6	4.7
		5.8	3.7				3.9	2.9
		2.5	2.2				2.6	2.0
		1.8	1.8			Sales/Total Assets	2.2	1.7
		1.7	1.4				1.7	1.3
			1.2				1.0	2.1
		(13)	2.1			% Depr., Dep., Amort./Sales	(43) 2.4	(21) 4.4
			2.8				5.4	5.7
						% Officers', Directors' Owners' Comp/Sales	.9	
							(20) 2.8	
							7.6	
2029M	18489M	166974M	532043M	277953M	221988M	Net Sales ($)	1531831M	1070849M
421M	5695M	83399M	310080M	191082M	289738M	Total Assets ($)	785477M	702955M

M = $ thousand   MM = $ million
See Pages viii through xx for Explanation of Ratios and Data

© RMA 2024

MANUFACTURING—Glass Product Manufacturing Made of Purchased Glass NAICS 327215

Comparative Historical Data | Current Data Sorted by Sales

				Type of Statement						
	1		1	Unqualified					3	1
4		7	5	Reviewed						2
2		3	1	Compiled						1
4		2	5	Tax Returns		2	1	1	1	
17		24	30	Other		4	4	1	8	13
4/1/21-		4/1/22-	4/1/23-			6 (4/1-9/30/23)			36 (10/1/23-3/31/24)	
3/31/22		3/31/23	3/31/24		0-1MM	1-3MM	3-5MM	5-10MM	10-25MM	25MM & OVER
ALL		ALL	ALL	NUMBER OF STATEMENTS						
28		36	42			6	5	2	12	17
%		%	%	ASSETS	%	%	%	%	%	%
13.7		10.5	13.4	Cash & Equivalents					19.8	10.7
21.8		24.9	26.9	Trade Receivables (net)	DATA				26.9	23.4
19.2		19.6	17.6	Inventory	NOT				16.0	17.2
2.9		4.0	4.4	All Other Current	AVAILABLE				6.1	4.9
57.6		59.1	62.3	Total Current					68.9	56.2
26.4		26.2	25.7	Fixed Assets (net)					25.5	33.8
6.8		9.8	6.5	Intangibles (net)					2.7	2.8
9.3		4.9	5.4	All Other Non-Current					3.0	7.2
100.0		100.0	100.0	Total					100.0	100.0
				LIABILITIES						
4.9		6.6	7.0	Notes Payable-Short Term					2.4	9.6
4.0		1.8	2.3	Cur. Mat.-L.T.D.					2.3	2.1
11.8		7.4	7.5	Trade Payables					5.6	5.9
.1		.2	.1	Income Taxes Payable					.2	.1
8.5		10.1	6.3	All Other Current					5.5	5.6
29.2		26.2	23.2	Total Current					16.0	23.3
21.9		19.8	18.5	Long-Term Debt					10.5	21.5
.6		.0	.0	Deferred Taxes					.0	.0
11.1		9.0	5.8	All Other Non-Current					1.8	3.3
37.2		45.0	52.6	Net Worth					71.7	51.9
100.0		100.0	100.0	Total Liabilities & Net Worth					100.0	100.0
				INCOME DATA						
100.0		100.0	100.0	Net Sales					100.0	100.0
29.6		35.1	37.0	Gross Profit					41.0	32.2
26.1		29.0	27.2	Operating Expenses					29.4	22.8
3.5		6.1	9.8	Operating Profit					11.6	9.4
-3.5		-.4	1.6	All Other Expenses (net)					-.7	3.6
7.0		6.5	8.2	Profit Before Taxes					12.3	5.9
				RATIOS						
	4.3		3.3		4.7					6.2	3.5
	2.6		2.6	Current	3.0					4.8	2.5
	1.3		1.6		1.6					4.0	1.6
	2.7		2.4		3.2					5.2	2.3
	2.0		1.5	Quick	1.5					2.9	1.4
	.7		.7		.9					1.6	.7
25	14.4	28	12.9	27	13.5				27	13.5	31	11.9
38	9.6	39	9.3	Sales/Receivables	41	9.0				41	9.0	54	6.8
50	7.3	64	5.7		69	5.3				66	5.5	73	5.0
16	22.8	1	639.1	6	63.2				3	144.8	23	15.8
34	10.6	42	8.6	Cost of Sales/Inventory	43	8.5				29	12.8	65	5.6
73	5.0	85	4.3		101	3.6				91	4.0	101	3.6
17	21.5	12	31.7	10	36.7				9	42.0	11	31.9
26	14.3	19	19.3	Cost of Sales/Payables	19	19.4				17	21.5	22	16.4
36	10.0	28	13.1		26	14.0				24	15.4	28	12.9
	4.1		3.8		3.8					2.6	4.3
	6.7		6.5	Sales/Working Capital	4.8					4.5	4.8
	20.8		13.0		9.6					6.5	7.0
	63.7		16.8		30.2						24.8
(26)	11.6	(30)	7.3	EBIT/Interest	(33)	6.5				(13)	6.5
	5.2		1.9		3.3						3.3
				Net Profit + Depr., Dep., Amort./Cur. Mat. L/T/D						
	.2		.1		.2					.1	.4
	.6		.6	Fixed/Worth	.6					.3	.7
	7.0		2.3		1.0					.6	.9
	.4		.4		.3					.2	.5
	1.2		1.4	Debt/Worth	.6					.3	.9
	11.0		4.4		4.2					.6	1.4
	62.9		39.2		52.3					52.3	42.0
(24)	32.1	(29)	25.2	% Profit Before Taxes/Tangible Net Worth	(34)	28.9			(11)	42.3	(16)	19.0
	13.6		8.4		10.3					7.2	10.0
	24.7		15.8		28.0					45.3	18.4
	15.8		9.3	% Profit Before Taxes/Total Assets	11.8					27.0	7.4
	4.5		3.0		5.4					6.4	4.6
	28.8		20.9		27.7					23.4	9.8
	9.4		9.3	Sales/Net Fixed Assets	9.6					10.6	4.1
	4.4		4.9		4.1					5.8	3.4
	2.7		2.4		2.6					2.6	2.1
	1.9		1.9	Sales/Total Assets	1.8					1.9	1.6
	1.5		1.6		1.5					1.8	1.3
	1.5		1.0		1.1						1.7
(22)	2.6	(28)	2.0	% Depr., Dep., Amort./Sales	(28)	2.1				(15)	2.7
	4.8		4.3		4.0						3.3
	1.0		1.1		1.1						
(12)	2.4	(13)	2.7	% Officers', Directors' Owners' Comp/Sales	(15)	2.5					
	3.7		4.1		4.7						
890569M		1155738M	1219476M	Net Sales ($)		13986M	21396M	14435M	180781M	988878M
493675M		701905M	880415M	Total Assets ($)		8260M	7278M	8280M	89904M	766693M

M = $ thousand   MM = $ million
See Pages viii through xx for Explanation of Ratios and Data
© RMA 2024

MANUFACTURING—Ready-Mix Concrete Manufacturing NAICS 327320

Current Data Sorted by Assets | Comparative Historical Data

						Type of Statement		
1			5	6	7	Unqualified	13	13
	1	3	17	6	1	Reviewed	37	19
		4	4			Compiled	12	11
			4	1		Tax Returns	16	7
1	3	17	33	17	3	Other	96	61
	21 (4/1-9/30/23)		113 (10/1/23-3/31/24)				4/1/19-3/31/20	4/1/20-3/31/21
0-500M	500M-2MM	2-10MM	10-50MM	50-100MM	100-250MM		ALL	ALL
2	4	28	59	30	11	NUMBER OF STATEMENTS	174	111
%	%	%	%	%	%	ASSETS	%	%
		17.9	13.8	9.6	11.8	Cash & Equivalents	10.0	12.7
		26.6	23.2	25.6	18.8	Trade Receivables (net)	23.4	22.1
		6.7	6.9	7.2	7.6	Inventory	8.0	7.4
		3.3	1.5	5.2	3.7	All Other Current	2.4	2.3
		54.6	45.4	47.6	41.9	Total Current	43.9	44.5
		34.6	45.9	44.6	42.3	Fixed Assets (net)	45.2	44.1
		5.6	3.5	3.7	10.7	Intangibles (net)	4.4	4.8
		5.2	5.1	4.1	5.2	All Other Non-Current	6.6	6.6
		100.0	100.0	100.0	100.0	Total	100.0	100.0
						LIABILITIES		
		.5	2.0	3.0	2.8	Notes Payable-Short Term	3.1	3.0
		3.6	5.8	4.9	3.7	Cur. Mat.-L.T.D.	5.6	5.6
		11.9	12.1	12.3	8.2	Trade Payables	13.5	12.1
		.3	.1	.2	.3	Income Taxes Payable	.1	.2
		6.8	4.9	8.6	7.1	All Other Current	7.3	6.8
		23.1	24.8	29.0	22.0	Total Current	29.6	27.7
		27.6	20.8	15.5	13.6	Long-Term Debt	21.4	25.6
		.0	.3	.0	1.8	Deferred Taxes	.6	.6
		2.8	3.4	3.2	9.6	All Other Non-Current	4.6	3.4
		46.5	50.6	52.3	53.0	Net Worth	43.8	42.7
		100.0	100.0	100.0	100.0	Total Liabilities & Net Worth	100.0	100.0
						INCOME DATA		
		100.0	100.0	100.0	100.0	Net Sales	100.0	100.0
		36.9	27.8	26.0	19.6	Gross Profit	28.0	26.1
		28.8	19.2	15.9	12.2	Operating Expenses	22.3	20.1
		8.1	8.6	10.1	7.5	Operating Profit	5.7	6.0
		-.4	.2	-.1	1.5	All Other Expenses (net)	.2	-.5
		8.4	8.4	10.2	6.0	Profit Before Taxes	5.5	6.5
						RATIOS		
		4.3	2.7	2.4	2.9		2.6	2.7
		2.8	1.6	1.7	2.3	Current	1.7	1.8
		1.9	1.3	1.3	1.1		1.1	1.2
		3.4	2.3	1.9	2.2		1.9	2.0
		2.2	1.3	1.2	1.7	Quick	1.2	1.4
		1.6	.9	.8	.9		.8	.9
		16 23.0	32 11.4	39 9.4	36 10.1		33 11.1	29 12.5
		33 11.1	45 8.2	51 7.2	49 7.4	Sales/Receivables	42 8.6	41 8.8
		54 6.8	58 6.3	63 5.8	54 6.7		56 6.5	55 6.6
		0 UND	6 58.0	5 78.5	0 UND		7 55.9	6 57.9
		6 61.2	20 18.3	16 23.4	18 20.8	Cost of Sales/Inventory	14 25.4	16 23.0
		28 13.1	28 12.9	25 14.4	59 6.2		38 9.5	34 10.8
		15 24.6	18 20.6	25 14.5	17 21.0		19 18.9	18 20.0
		18 20.5	26 14.2	33 10.9	27 13.7	Cost of Sales/Payables	30 12.3	29 12.6
		41 9.0	43 8.4	39 9.3	35 10.5		47 7.8	42 8.6
		4.1	5.6	6.7	4.9		5.9	5.8
		10.2	11.2	9.2	7.4	Sales/Working Capital	11.7	10.2
		21.3	26.2	17.6	30.2		76.9	34.2
		45.0	24.7	31.8	30.1		16.8	20.6
	(23)	12.2	(58) 10.4	(29) 14.2	10.6	EBIT/Interest	(168) 7.8	(106) 9.2
		3.9	5.6	8.5	2.8		2.9	4.4
			21.9				4.1	7.0
		(14)	4.7			Net Profit + Depr., Dep., Amort./Cur. Mat. L/T/D	(35) 2.5	(21) 2.5
			3.2				1.8	1.5
		.3	.5	.6	.6		.7	.7
		.8	1.1	1.0	.8	Fixed/Worth	1.1	1.1
		2.5	1.6	1.2	1.6		1.7	2.2
		.4	.6	.8	.4		.6	.6
		1.3	1.1	1.1	1.0	Debt/Worth	1.1	1.3
		10.1	1.8	1.4	1.8		2.6	3.2
		65.5	58.0	66.2	26.3		38.1	42.2
	(24)	37.0	31.1	27.7	(10) 18.0	% Profit Before Taxes/Tangible Net Worth	(159) 20.8	(101) 22.1
		12.9	19.1	20.2	12.4		7.7	14.8
		26.9	18.4	22.6	12.5		17.1	17.6
		14.8	13.9	14.1	7.9	% Profit Before Taxes/Total Assets	7.8	10.6
		3.4	8.8	9.5	4.9		2.7	4.5
		18.2	5.7	4.7	5.6		6.5	5.7
		7.2	3.8	4.0	3.6	Sales/Net Fixed Assets	3.9	3.9
		2.8	2.6	2.9	2.2		2.4	2.5
		2.8	2.3	2.2	1.7		2.4	2.1
		2.1	1.7	1.8	1.5	Sales/Total Assets	1.8	1.7
		1.2	1.4	1.4	.9		1.4	1.4
		2.2	2.5	2.3			2.8	3.0
	(17)	3.5	(52) 4.0	(25) 3.2		% Depr., Dep., Amort./Sales	(151) 4.7	(92) 5.1
		8.9	5.5	5.1			6.6	6.9
							1.0	1.3
						% Officers', Directors' Owners' Comp/Sales	(39) 1.4	(21) 1.6
							2.8	3.8
1669M	19585M	284259M	2972535M	3826962M	2337163M	Net Sales ($)	8643449M	7047658M
437M	6403M	125948M	1727376M	2146541M	1558088M	Total Assets ($)	5815697M	4463617M

© RMA 2024 M = $ thousand MM = $ million
See Pages viii through xx for Explanation of Ratios and Data

MANUFACTURING—Ready-Mix Concrete Manufacturing NAICS 327320

Comparative Historical Data | Current Data Sorted by Sales

						Type of Statement						
	9		19		19	Unqualified	1			3	5	18
	13		18		28	Reviewed				3	2	20
	11		17		8	Compiled		1		3	2	2
	8		8		5	Tax Returns				1	2	2
	60		85		74	Other		4	4	6	9	51
	4/1/21-3/31/22		4/1/22-3/31/23		4/1/23-3/31/24			21 (4/1-9/30/23)			113 (10/1/23-3/31/24)	
	ALL		ALL		ALL		0-1MM	1-3MM	3-5MM	5-10MM	10-25MM	25MM & OVER
	101		147		134	NUMBER OF STATEMENTS	1	4	5	13	18	93
	%		%		%	ASSETS	%	%	%	%	%	%
	15.8		13.4		13.4	Cash & Equivalents				16.8	19.8	11.5
	21.7		22.7		24.7	Trade Receivables (net)				37.8	18.0	25.3
	7.7		7.7		7.5	Inventory				7.3	9.5	6.5
	2.2		2.7		3.4	All Other Current				1.7	5.6	2.8
	47.3		46.5		49.1	Total Current				63.6	52.8	46.1
	42.9		42.6		41.6	Fixed Assets (net)				28.8	37.3	44.7
	4.4		3.5		4.5	Intangibles (net)				4.5	3.3	4.4
	5.3		7.4		4.8	All Other Non-Current				3.1	6.6	4.7
	100.0		100.0		100.0	Total				100.0	100.0	100.0
						LIABILITIES						
	2.0		3.4		2.1	Notes Payable-Short Term				2.3	.5	2.5
	4.6		5.5		4.8	Cur. Mat.-L.T.D.				1.3	4.8	5.6
	11.6		13.0		11.9	Trade Payables				16.8	8.8	12.5
	.1		.1		.2	Income Taxes Payable				.4	.2	.1
	7.1		7.0		6.9	All Other Current				9.5	6.6	6.3
	25.3		29.1		25.9	Total Current				30.3	20.9	27.0
	21.4		23.8		20.2	Long-Term Debt				20.4	22.0	18.8
	.6		.4		.3	Deferred Taxes				.0	.1	.4
	3.4		4.0		3.6	All Other Non-Current				1.0	3.6	3.8
	49.3		42.7		50.0	Net Worth				48.4	53.4	50.0
	100.0		100.0		100.0	Total Liabilities & Net Worth				100.0	100.0	100.0
						INCOME DATA						
	100.0		100.0		100.0	Net Sales				100.0	100.0	100.0
	28.2		28.3		28.8	Gross Profit				36.8	32.5	26.1
	22.3		22.2		20.2	Operating Expenses				32.0	23.0	17.2
	5.9		6.1		8.6	Operating Profit				4.8	9.6	9.0
	-.9		-.1		.1	All Other Expenses (net)				-.6	.8	.1
	6.8		6.2		8.5	Profit Before Taxes				5.4	8.8	8.8
						RATIOS						
	3.5		3.1		2.9					4.7	3.8	2.5
	1.9		1.9		1.9	Current				3.0	2.6	1.6
	1.3		1.2		1.3					1.4	1.6	1.2
	2.3		2.1		2.4					4.3	3.0	2.0
	1.6		1.4		1.5	Quick				2.6	1.6	1.3
	1.0		.9		.9					1.3	.9	.9
31	11.7	27	13.7	32	11.4		27	13.5	23	16.1	33	10.9
42	8.7	41	8.9	45	8.2	Sales/Receivables	73	5.0	34	10.8	46	7.9
55	6.6	54	6.7	59	6.2		101	3.6	45	8.1	59	6.2
6	58.4	4	87.3	4	81.8		0	UND	0	UND	5	77.1
15	24.6	13	28.8	16	22.7	Cost of Sales/Inventory	7	54.1	21	17.2	16	22.8
29	12.4	33	11.2	27	13.3		47	7.8	46	8.0	25	14.6
19	19.6	17	21.2	18	20.7		8	48.3	15	24.3	20	18.5
28	13.2	26	14.2	27	13.6	Cost of Sales/Payables	35	10.5	18	20.6	28	13.1
47	7.7	40	9.2	40	9.2		51	7.1	39	9.4	39	9.3
	4.6		5.7		5.3					3.4	5.1	6.4
	10.1		10.1		9.8	Sales/Working Capital				4.9	8.8	10.6
	19.9		31.3		23.3					NM	11.9	26.6
	24.9		23.7		28.7					41.6	23.9	28.7
(93)	12.4	(135)	8.5	(127)	11.7	EBIT/Interest	(12)	13.1	(16)	13.2	(91)	11.8
	6.3		2.3		5.7					-1.5	7.8	6.3
	12.7		6.5		9.5	Net Profit + Depr., Dep.,						10.3
(16)	3.7	(27)	3.2	(25)	4.5	Amort./Cur. Mat. L/T/D					(21)	4.6
	2.9		2.3		2.1							2.7
	.5		.6		.5					.1	.4	.6
	.9		1.0		1.0	Fixed/Worth				.4	.8	1.1
	1.5		1.8		1.6					1.7	1.6	1.6
	.5		.5		.5					.4	.4	.7
	1.0		1.0		1.1	Debt/Worth				.5	1.1	1.1
	1.8		2.2		1.8					5.2	1.7	1.7
	40.7		41.0		59.3	% Profit Before Taxes/Tangible				39.7	69.2	58.5
(95)	24.5	(134)	18.5	(128)	30.4	Net Worth			(12)	23.7	37.1	(91)	30.4
	11.4		8.4		17.7					-16.6	22.1	18.7
	20.6		18.7		20.7	% Profit Before Taxes/Total				24.3	38.8	20.4
	12.5		9.1		13.6	Assets				5.4	14.8	13.7
	5.9		3.4		7.9					-3.9	9.9	8.0
	7.2		7.4		7.2					43.1	11.2	5.8
	4.0		4.7		4.4	Sales/Net Fixed Assets				14.0	5.2	3.8
	2.4		2.7		2.6					4.1	3.9	2.6
	2.3		2.5		2.4					2.7	2.8	2.3
	1.7		1.9		1.7	Sales/Total Assets				2.2	2.0	1.7
	1.4		1.3		1.4					1.1	1.5	1.4
	3.0		2.6		2.3						2.0	2.3
(81)	4.9	(111)	4.3	(104)	3.6	% Depr., Dep., Amort./Sales				(14)	3.6	(75)	3.7
	7.5		5.6		5.5						6.1	5.3
	1.4		.9		.7	% Officers', Directors'						.5
(25)	2.0	(26)	1.7	(17)	1.3	Owners' Comp/Sales					(10)	1.1
	4.0		3.2		3.0							1.8
	5854797M		8408498M		9442173M	Net Sales ($)	58M	9730M	22275M	85528M	277374M	9047208M
	3811828M		5369356M		5564793M	Total Assets ($)	35M	14619M	21387M	91290M	149771M	5287691M

© RMA 2024 M = $ thousand MM = $ million
See Pages viii through xx for Explanation of Ratios and Data

MANUFACTURING—Concrete Block and Brick Manufacturing NAICS 327331

Current Data Sorted by Assets | Comparative Historical Data

0-500M	500M-2MM	2-10MM	10-50MM	50-100MM	100-250MM				4/1/19-3/31/20 ALL	4/1/20-3/31/21 ALL
		1	2	3		Type of Statement				
			3	1	1	Unqualified			6	3
		7	1			Reviewed			2	4
	5 (4/1-9/30/23)		25 (10/1/23-3/31/24)	2	1	Compiled			4	
						Tax Returns			8	1
						Other			18	12
1	1	10	11	6	2	NUMBER OF STATEMENTS			38	20
%	%	%	%	%	%	ASSETS			%	%
		19.7	15.0			Cash & Equivalents			11.6	17.6
D		13.9	14.7			Trade Receivables (net)			20.3	20.7
A		19.1	16.3			Inventory			23.8	17.1
T		2.0	1.8			All Other Current			2.5	4.5
A		54.7	47.8			Total Current			58.2	59.9
		23.5	39.1			Fixed Assets (net)			32.0	30.0
N		4.9	3.0			Intangibles (net)			4.4	1.3
O		16.9	10.1			All Other Non-Current			5.5	8.8
T		100.0	100.0			Total			100.0	100.0
A						LIABILITIES				
V		3.8	4.6			Notes Payable-Short Term			4.9	2.4
A		2.6	3.0			Cur. Mat.-L.T.D.			3.1	4.6
I		11.6	8.8			Trade Payables			12.9	11.1
L		.0	.0			Income Taxes Payable			.1	.0
A		4.9	4.1			All Other Current			7.3	7.7
B		22.8	20.6			Total Current			28.3	26.0
L		25.2	17.9			Long-Term Debt			23.2	28.2
E		.5	.6			Deferred Taxes			.8	.8
		17.5	.7			All Other Non-Current			5.0	7.9
		34.0	60.2			Net Worth			42.7	37.0
		100.0	100.0			Total Liabilities & Net Worth			100.0	100.0
						INCOME DATA				
		100.0	100.0			Net Sales			100.0	100.0
		47.7	34.6			Gross Profit			32.2	40.6
		31.5	29.6			Operating Expenses			25.7	31.5
		16.2	5.0			Operating Profit			6.5	9.1
		1.3	-.4			All Other Expenses (net)			.7	-.1
		14.9	5.5			Profit Before Taxes			5.7	9.2
						RATIOS				
		10.8	11.0						4.1	4.2
		2.9	2.0			Current			2.5	2.4
		2.3	1.2						1.5	1.8
		8.0	6.9						1.9	3.0
		2.3	1.0			Quick			1.2	1.6
		1.0	.4						.8	.9
		20 18.6	30 12.1				22	16.4	24	15.1
		26 14.0	37 9.8			Sales/Receivables	39	9.3	36	10.0
		36 10.0	64 5.7				48	7.6	55	6.6
		32 11.4	21 17.6				33	11.2	29	12.6
		59 6.2	54 6.7			Cost of Sales/Inventory	62	5.9	74	4.9
		81 4.5	174 2.1				135	2.7	104	3.5
		8 43.7	16 22.5				20	18.5	16	22.7
		27 13.4	41 8.9			Cost of Sales/Payables	30	12.1	28	13.2
		42 8.6	60 6.1				41	8.9	56	6.5
		3.2	1.5						3.1	3.2
		5.4	6.7			Sales/Working Capital			5.0	4.3
		8.8	24.4						14.2	8.6
			22.0						17.8	23.0
		(10)	10.9			EBIT/Interest	(34)	4.0	(16)	7.6
			.9						2.0	3.8
						Net Profit + Depr., Dep.,			6.3	
						Amort./Cur. Mat. L/T/D	(10)	2.8		
									2.2	
		.1	.5						.4	.4
		.6	.7			Fixed/Worth			.9	.6
		4.1	1.3						1.6	1.7
		.4	.3						.6	.5
		1.6	.8			Debt/Worth			1.4	1.1
		9.5	1.5						3.8	2.7
			48.2						48.1	55.5
			8.2			% Profit Before Taxes/Tangible Net Worth	(36)	20.4	(18)	25.9
			.7						8.0	13.7
		41.6	9.7						19.7	17.5
		15.6	3.4			% Profit Before Taxes/Total Assets			5.8	11.1
		3.0	.3						1.9	4.1
		22.4	5.0						11.2	16.7
		7.3	3.1			Sales/Net Fixed Assets			5.8	5.0
		5.2	1.5						2.7	2.6
		2.4	1.5						2.6	2.5
		1.7	1.2			Sales/Total Assets			1.7	1.4
		1.0	.7						1.1	1.0
									2.1	1.2
						% Depr., Dep., Amort./Sales	(31)	3.2	(15)	3.0
									4.4	4.4
									1.4	
						% Officers', Directors' Owners' Comp/Sales	(13)	2.5		
									3.7	
	4879M	99444M	361377M	690922M	282536M	Net Sales ($)			1517308M	816596M
	1101M	59941M	301611M	370519M	425534M	Total Assets ($)			1091114M	837346M

© RMA 2024

M = $ thousand   MM = $ million
See Pages viii through xx for Explanation of Ratios and Data

MANUFACTURING—Concrete Block and Brick Manufacturing NAICS 327331

Comparative Historical Data | Current Data Sorted by Sales

						Type of Statement							
				2		1		5		Unqualified							1		4
				3		4		7		Reviewed							2	1	4
				2		1		1		Compiled								1	
				1		4		1		Tax Returns							1		
				13		25		16		Other				1		2	6	6
				4/1/21-3/31/22		4/1/22-3/31/23		4/1/23-3/31/24				5 (4/1-9/30/23)				25 (10/1/23-3/31/24)		
				ALL		ALL		ALL			0-1MM	1-3MM	3-5MM	5-10MM	10-25MM	25MM & OVER
				21		35		30		NUMBER OF STATEMENTS		1	1	6	8	14
				%		%		%		ASSETS	%	%	%	%	%	%
				14.6		13.6		16.1		Cash & Equivalents	D					7.9
				26.1		19.4		14.4		Trade Receivables (net)	A					17.5
				20.8		22.5		17.5		Inventory	T					14.5
				.8		3.5		1.8		All Other Current	A					2.3
				62.3		59.0		49.8		Total Current						42.3
				27.6		31.0		33.8		Fixed Assets (net)	N					39.8
				5.4		3.4		4.4		Intangibles (net)	O					4.8
				4.6		6.6		12.0		All Other Non-Current	T					13.1
				100.0		100.0		100.0		Total						100.0
										LIABILITIES	A					
				6.8		6.4		5.4		Notes Payable-Short Term	V					6.0
				3.5		3.1		2.8		Cur. Mat.-L.T.D.	A					3.0
				17.3		11.8		9.3		Trade Payables	I					9.9
				.1		.0		.2		Income Taxes Payable	L					.5
				8.2		9.1		4.4		All Other Current	A					4.9
				35.9		30.4		22.2		Total Current	B					24.3
				19.3		26.9		18.5		Long-Term Debt	L					16.1
				.6		.3		.9		Deferred Taxes	E					1.7
				3.2		6.8		7.2		All Other Non-Current						2.8
				41.1		35.7		51.2		Net Worth						55.1
				100.0		100.0		100.0		Total Liabilities & Net Worth						100.0
										INCOME DATA						
				100.0		100.0		100.0		Net Sales						100.0
				33.7		35.1		37.5		Gross Profit						31.6
				25.4		26.4		27.4		Operating Expenses						24.1
				8.3		8.7		10.2		Operating Profit						7.5
				-.8		.8		.3		All Other Expenses (net)						.0
				9.2		8.0		9.8		Profit Before Taxes						7.5
										RATIOS						
				3.5		5.1		7.0								2.8
				2.1		2.7		2.6		Current						1.5
				1.3		1.0		1.3								1.2
				2.4		3.1		4.5								2.1
				1.2		1.5		1.8		Quick						.9
				.7		.4		.7								.6
24	15.0	24	15.3	26	14.3							33	11.1
46	7.9	35	10.5	35	10.3	Sales/Receivables						42	8.6
66	5.5	46	7.9	48	7.6							55	6.6
36	10.1	35	10.4	30	12.2							19	19.3
52	7.0	60	6.1	54	6.7	Cost of Sales/Inventory						54	6.7
87	4.2	99	3.7	94	3.9							91	4.0
22	16.9	16	22.8	16	23.2							20	18.4
38	9.6	26	13.8	32	11.3	Cost of Sales/Payables						36	10.2
59	6.2	57	6.4	43	8.4							44	8.3
				3.8		3.3		3.1								4.6
				7.7		7.0		6.3		Sales/Working Capital						14.6
				19.1		315.1		19.5								26.1
				22.6		22.8		24.4								35.7
(19)	10.7	(29)	6.6	(27)	9.5	EBIT/Interest					(13)	15.2
				5.0		2.0		1.8								1.2
										Net Profit + Depr., Dep., Amort./Cur. Mat. L/T/D						
				.4		.3		.5								.5
				.6		.6		.6		Fixed/Worth						.8
				1.7		1.7		1.3								1.4
				.5		.4		.3								.3
				1.4		.8		.9		Debt/Worth						.9
				3.5		3.5		1.8								2.0
				68.6		54.5		48.8								43.8
(19)	40.4	(30)	26.4	(29)	14.6	% Profit Before Taxes/Tangible Net Worth						16.2
				10.6		4.9		3.7								3.1
				27.7		25.2		26.2								23.1
				16.2		6.2		7.4		% Profit Before Taxes/Total Assets						5.6
				2.9		.9		2.3								1.0
				30.0		17.0		7.3								4.8
				5.6		6.4		4.5		Sales/Net Fixed Assets						3.9
				4.8		3.3		2.8								2.8
				2.7		2.6		2.1								2.0
				1.8		1.9		1.5		Sales/Total Assets						1.5
				1.2		1.1		1.0								1.1
				1.1		.9		1.0								3.1
(16)	3.0	(28)	2.3	(23)	3.5	% Depr., Dep., Amort./Sales					(12)	3.8
				4.0		4.7		6.1								5.7
										% Officers', Directors' Owners' Comp/Sales						
				876343M		1316794M		1439158M		Net Sales ($)		1606M	4879M	45838M	127594M	1259241M
				510551M		1054677M		1158706M		Total Assets ($)		2167M	1101M	34571M	111885M	1008982M

© RMA 2024 M = $ thousand   MM = $ million
See Pages viii through xx for Explanation of Ratios and Data

MANUFACTURING—Other Concrete Product Manufacturing NAICS 327390

Current Data Sorted by Assets | Comparative Historical Data

						Type of Statement		
		2	7	5	3	Unqualified	11	8
		2	8	3		Reviewed	15	9
		2		1		Compiled	7	6
1	5	5	1			Tax Returns	9	4
		18	15	5	2	Other	56	34
0-500M	15 (4/1-9/30/23) 500M-2MM	2-10MM	70 (10/1/23-3/31/24) 10-50MM	50-100MM	100-250MM		4/1/19-3/31/20 ALL	4/1/20-3/31/21 ALL
1	5	29	31	14	5	NUMBER OF STATEMENTS	98	61
%	%	%	%	%	%	ASSETS	%	%
		16.9	9.4	11.1		Cash & Equivalents	10.6	16.1
		27.5	25.7	25.4		Trade Receivables (net)	29.8	26.6
		10.7	16.5	7.8		Inventory	16.0	12.8
		3.5	6.3	2.3		All Other Current	3.0	3.5
		58.7	57.9	46.7		Total Current	59.3	58.9
		22.0	33.3	39.7		Fixed Assets (net)	30.4	31.4
		9.9	3.6	3.3		Intangibles (net)	4.5	5.8
		9.4	5.1	10.4		All Other Non-Current	5.7	3.8
		100.0	100.0	100.0		Total	100.0	100.0
						LIABILITIES		
		4.6	6.9	4.3		Notes Payable-Short Term	6.7	2.5
		2.7	3.1	3.7		Cur. Mat.-L.T.D.	4.3	3.2
		9.4	10.8	9.6		Trade Payables	13.3	9.8
		.2	.2	.0		Income Taxes Payable	.2	.2
		9.8	12.7	12.0		All Other Current	9.1	8.7
		26.8	33.8	29.7		Total Current	33.6	24.5
		22.1	16.3	18.1		Long-Term Debt	20.1	22.1
		.0	.2	.3		Deferred Taxes	.5	.4
		4.0	8.8	5.2		All Other Non-Current	3.3	5.2
		47.0	41.0	46.7		Net Worth	42.5	47.9
		100.0	100.0	100.0		Total Liabilties & Net Worth	100.0	100.0
						INCOME DATA		
		100.0	100.0	100.0		Net Sales	100.0	100.0
		37.3	32.9	30.2		Gross Profit	31.4	32.8
		24.3	22.7	19.0		Operating Expenses	24.5	23.7
		13.0	10.2	11.2		Operating Profit	6.8	9.0
		.3	.5	-.5		All Other Expenses (net)	.9	.2
		12.7	9.7	11.6		Profit Before Taxes	6.0	8.9
						RATIOS		
		4.1	2.4	2.8			3.0	5.4
		2.0	1.6	2.0		Current	1.9	2.5
		1.6	1.4	.9			1.3	1.6
		2.4	1.7	2.3			2.3	4.3
		1.7	1.1	1.3		Quick	1.3	1.7
		1.2	.7	.8			.7	1.1
	24	14.9	36 10.2	53 6.9			36 10.0	32 11.5
	42	8.6	60 6.1	74 4.9		Sales/Receivables	53 6.9	49 7.5
	66	5.5	68 5.4	111 3.3			73 5.0	70 5.2
	0	999.8	20 18.3	14 27.0			11 31.8	12 30.6
	17	21.0	50 7.3	22 16.3		Cost of Sales/Inventory	32 11.4	24 15.1
	58	6.3	126 2.9	79 4.6			68 5.4	62 5.9
	10	36.9	21 17.8	25 14.8			18 19.9	13 28.3
	20	18.3	33 11.1	36 10.1		Cost of Sales/Payables	33 11.2	23 15.9
	29	12.5	49 7.5	47 7.7			47 7.7	33 10.9
		4.1	4.8	3.5			4.8	3.5
		8.2	6.5	5.3		Sales/Working Capital	7.6	4.9
		15.6	14.4	-32.5			21.0	9.8
		63.8	24.0	33.5			20.7	36.8
		(26) 12.8	(26) 9.0	(13) 9.5		EBIT/Interest	(91) 6.3	(54) 10.2
		5.2	2.4	2.8			3.1	3.7
						Net Profit + Depr., Dep., Amort./Cur. Mat. L/T/D	7.3	
							(19) 2.7	
							1.9	
		.2	.5	.6			.3	.3
		.6	.7	.7		Fixed/Worth	.7	.7
		2.3	1.5	3.6			1.9	1.6
		.4	.7	.6			.5	.5
		1.4	1.3	1.0		Debt/Worth	1.5	1.4
		5.2	3.1	5.4			3.2	2.6
		122.2	65.3	67.5			44.3	50.6
		(24) 39.0	(28) 45.3	26.4		% Profit Before Taxes/Tangible Net Worth	(89) 24.8	(56) 31.9
		25.7	16.6	20.6			8.5	12.5
		37.7	28.2	18.4			18.2	28.1
		16.0	16.9	11.6		% Profit Before Taxes/Total Assets	9.6	12.8
		9.3	8.7	5.5			3.5	5.6
		17.8	9.6	4.1			16.1	17.9
		10.3	4.8	2.8		Sales/Net Fixed Assets	7.0	5.8
		6.3	3.4	1.6			3.8	3.0
		2.8	2.2	1.5			2.5	2.4
		2.0	1.6	1.2		Sales/Total Assets	2.0	1.7
		1.4	1.3	.7			1.4	1.1
		1.2	1.3	2.1			1.9	2.0
		(18) 2.7	(28) 2.7	3.6		% Depr., Dep., Amort./Sales	(81) 2.9	(44) 3.1
		4.3	4.7	6.0			4.6	5.3
						% Officers', Directors' Owners' Comp/Sales	1.4	1.0
							(24) 2.6	(13) 1.6
							4.3	5.0
2735M	11264M	309607M	1220263M	1108757M	949835M	Net Sales ($)	4137320M	2580479M
403M	6176M	148538M	755330M	959112M	1077932M	Total Assets ($)	2779200M	1812240M

© RMA 2024

M = $ thousand MM = $ million
See Pages viii through xx for Explanation of Ratios and Data

MANUFACTURING—Other Concrete Product Manufacturing NAICS 327390

Comparative Historical Data | Current Data Sorted by Sales

8		9		17	Type of Statement				1	2	14
9		16		13	Unqualified				1	5	7
8		8		3	Reviewed					2	1
3		14		12	Compiled				3	1
42		36		40	Tax Returns	5	2	1	4	15
					Other	1	5			
4/1/21-3/31/22		4/1/22-3/31/23		4/1/23-3/31/24		15 (4/1-9/30/23)			70 (10/1/23-3/31/24)		
ALL		ALL		ALL		0-1MM	1-3MM	3-5MM	5-10MM	10-25MM	25MM & OVER
70		83		85	NUMBER OF STATEMENTS	6	7	7	27	38
%		%		%	ASSETS	%	%	%	%	%	%
11.1		12.0		14.6	Cash & Equivalents					12.2	11.8
25.5		25.4		24.2	Trade Receivables (net)	DATA				27.9	26.3
12.3		14.6		12.6	Inventory	NOT				14.9	12.7
3.0		4.0		4.0	All Other Current	AVAILABLE				2.8	5.2
51.8		56.0		55.4	Total Current					57.8	56.0
31.4		30.8		30.3	Fixed Assets (net)					30.9	32.9
9.4		4.3		5.9	Intangibles (net)					4.8	3.1
7.3		8.9		8.4	All Other Non-Current					6.5	8.0
100.0		100.0		100.0	Total					100.0	100.0
					LIABILITIES						
2.9		5.7		4.9	Notes Payable-Short Term					5.3	5.0
3.5		3.0		3.7	Cur. Mat.-L.T.D.					2.1	3.2
12.6		12.6		10.8	Trade Payables					10.9	10.2
.1		.1		.2	Income Taxes Payable					.0	.3
8.8		10.3		11.1	All Other Current					10.6	12.1
27.9		31.7		30.7	Total Current					28.8	30.8
21.5		20.5		19.1	Long-Term Debt					15.8	14.4
.6		.3		.2	Deferred Taxes					.0	.5
3.9		4.4		5.8	All Other Non-Current					6.6	8.2
46.2		43.2		44.2	Net Worth					48.9	46.1
100.0		100.0		100.0	Total Liabilties & Net Worth					100.0	100.0
					INCOME DATA						
100.0		100.0		100.0	Net Sales					100.0	100.0
33.4		36.2		34.5	Gross Profit					34.3	29.4
24.5		27.6		23.4	Operating Expenses					23.6	18.0
8.9		8.6		11.1	Operating Profit					10.7	11.4
-.7		.8		.4	All Other Expenses (net)					.6	-.2
9.6		7.8		10.7	Profit Before Taxes					10.1	11.6
					RATIOS						
4.1		3.8		3.2						3.3	2.8
2.1		2.0		1.9	Current					1.9	2.1
1.3		1.4		1.3						1.6	1.2
2.7		2.4		2.1						2.0	2.1
1.2		1.3		1.4	Quick					1.5	1.3
.9		.7		.8						1.0	.8
34	10.6	26	14.2	30	12.0	Sales/Receivables				30	12.1	51	7.2
56	6.5	53	6.9	55	6.6					38	9.6	64	5.7
87	4.2	74	4.9	72	5.1					61	6.0	85	4.3
15	23.8	13	29.0	11	32.9	Cost of Sales/Inventory				3	134.8	16	22.6
33	10.9	34	10.8	29	12.4					36	10.0	32	11.4
70	5.2	65	5.6	85	4.3					114	3.2	79	4.6
16	23.3	12	30.0	14	25.6	Cost of Sales/Payables				13	27.4	23	15.6
32	11.4	30	12.1	30	12.3					26	13.8	33	10.9
55	6.6	53	6.9	46	7.9					46	7.9	46	7.9
3.5		4.0		4.2	Sales/Working Capital					4.4	3.9
6.7		6.7		6.7						6.6	5.3
15.5		14.1		15.2						13.6	14.8
28.9		41.5		26.3	EBIT/Interest					32.3	28.1
(64) 9.4	(73)	14.1	(74)	10.0					(22)	14.5	(35)	11.5
3.7		4.1		3.1						2.4	5.0
		13.4		8.7	Net Profit + Depr., Dep., Amort./Cur. Mat. L/T/D						
	(12)	4.3	(11)	6.7							
		2.8		2.4							
.4		.3		.4	Fixed/Worth					.2	.5
.9		.6		.7						.6	.7
2.1		1.4		1.6						1.0	1.1
.6		.4		.5	Debt/Worth					.5	.7
1.4		.9		1.1						.9	1.0
4.4		2.8		3.3						1.7	2.7
55.2		55.6		67.2	% Profit Before Taxes/Tangible Net Worth					61.6	70.8
(60) 30.0	(69)	27.6	(75)	33.2					(24)	27.6	(36)	44.0
14.1		10.5		18.0						8.0	22.8
20.8		23.9		26.2	% Profit Before Taxes/Total Assets					29.6	27.4
12.6		12.3		13.4						17.0	15.3
4.3		4.0		5.6						3.9	6.8
11.1		15.4		10.8	Sales/Net Fixed Assets					16.3	7.9
5.2		6.7		5.0						6.5	4.2
2.9		3.6		3.5						3.7	2.2
2.1		2.3		2.2	Sales/Total Assets					2.6	1.9
1.6		1.8		1.6						1.7	1.4
1.0		1.3		1.1						1.3	.9
2.1		1.5		1.4	% Depr., Dep., Amort./Sales					1.2	1.5
(52) 3.9	(60)	3.2	(68)	2.9					(22)	2.7	(34)	2.8
5.3		4.8		4.8						4.7	5.1
1.1		1.3		1.0	% Officers', Directors' Owners' Comp/Sales						
(11) 1.7	(16)	2.8	(16)	3.0							
2.8		5.4		6.9							
3216048M		2821886M		3602461M	Net Sales ($)	12081M	28611M	54778M	472519M	3034472M
2380156M		1935388M		2947491M	Total Assets ($)	6961M	21922M	30743M	316723M	2571142M

© RMA 2024 M = $ thousand MM = $ million
See Pages viii through xx for Explanation of Ratios and Data

MANUFACTURING—Cut Stone and Stone Product Manufacturing NAICS 327991

Current Data Sorted by Assets

							Type of Statement		Comparative Historical Data	
				3		1	Unqualified		3	4
			2	1			Reviewed		4	5
		1	3	1			Compiled		8	4
	1	2	6				Tax Returns		14	8
1	12	12	12	9	2	2	Other		43	39
1	3 (4/1-9/30/23)			56 (10/1/23-3/31/24)					4/1/19-3/31/20	4/1/20-3/31/21
0-500M	500M-2MM	2-10MM	10-50MM	50-100MM	100-250MM				ALL	ALL
2	15	23	14	2	3		NUMBER OF STATEMENTS		72	60
%	%	%	%	%	%		ASSETS		%	%
	12.4	16.0	7.7				Cash & Equivalents		11.2	17.0
	15.6	22.0	13.6				Trade Receivables (net)		19.5	16.2
	25.0	18.1	26.7				Inventory		27.3	28.6
	7.4	2.2	6.0				All Other Current		2.4	2.5
	60.4	58.2	54.1				Total Current		60.4	64.4
	29.4	25.7	21.0				Fixed Assets (net)		29.7	21.9
	5.9	6.8	13.9				Intangibles (net)		5.4	7.9
	4.3	9.4	11.0				All Other Non-Current		4.5	5.9
	100.0	100.0	100.0				Total		100.0	100.0
							LIABILITIES			
	6.2	2.0	2.8				Notes Payable-Short Term		10.3	5.4
	4.4	3.3	4.8				Cur. Mat.-L.T.D.		3.3	3.4
	20.3	10.3	9.8				Trade Payables		14.3	15.9
	.1	.1	.1				Income Taxes Payable		.1	.1
	12.5	6.7	16.1				All Other Current		10.3	11.5
	43.5	22.4	33.6				Total Current		38.3	36.2
	36.9	17.9	22.7				Long-Term Debt		21.6	19.1
	.0	.2	.1				Deferred Taxes		.0	.1
	12.1	3.5	9.6				All Other Non-Current		6.2	3.8
	7.5	55.9	34.0				Net Worth		33.8	40.7
	100.0	100.0	100.0				Total Liabilities & Net Worth		100.0	100.0
							INCOME DATA			
	100.0	100.0	100.0				Net Sales		100.0	100.0
	51.1	39.4	35.0				Gross Profit		43.2	40.3
	40.5	29.4	26.3				Operating Expenses		36.7	33.3
	10.6	10.0	8.6				Operating Profit		6.5	7.0
	.6	.1	.7				All Other Expenses (net)		1.2	-.4
	10.0	9.9	7.9				Profit Before Taxes		5.3	7.4
							RATIOS			
	2.3	6.1	2.6						2.9	3.0
	1.6	2.8	1.8			Current			1.8	1.9
	.9	1.8	1.0						1.1	1.3
	1.2	6.1	.9						1.4	1.7
	.8	1.5	.8			Quick			.7	1.0
	.3	1.0	.4						.4	.5
4	93.2	25 14.8	26 14.2					18	20.6	14 26.8
26	14.1	33 10.9	39 9.3				Sales/Receivables	31	11.7	30 12.2
39	9.3	49 7.5	56 6.5					51	7.2	43 8.5
1	333.7	15 25.0	42 8.6					31	11.8	33 11.1
45	8.1	42 8.7	81 4.5				Cost of Sales/Inventory	78	4.7	85 4.3
118	3.1	104 3.5	243 1.5					159	2.3	203 1.8
13	27.6	11 34.3	15 24.8					9	39.7	15 24.0
54	6.8	21 17.4	27 13.7				Cost of Sales/Payables	28	13.2	30 12.3
74	4.9	50 7.3	94 3.9					70	5.2	81 4.5
	6.7	5.4	3.2						4.5	3.8
	11.2	7.2	7.3				Sales/Working Capital		8.4	6.9
	-77.6	10.8	NM						64.6	15.6
	34.4	51.2	30.2						17.2	30.4
(14)	9.5	(21) 18.0	(13) 12.6				EBIT/Interest	(68)	6.0	(51) 15.6
	3.9	5.0	.1						1.9	5.6
							Net Profit + Depr., Dep., Amort./Cur. Mat. L/T/D			
	.3	.3	.2						.4	.2
	.6	.6	.8			Fixed/Worth			1.0	.6
	6.4	.8	NM						3.7	1.7
	1.6	.3	.7						1.0	.9
	5.6	.7	2.0			Debt/Worth			2.2	2.0
	13.1	2.4	NM						8.5	6.4
	162.6	61.8	59.1				% Profit Before Taxes/Tangible Net Worth		72.0	77.8
(12)	61.8	(22) 37.3	(11) 29.5					(61)	24.6	(53) 47.0
	17.8	20.7	7.5						7.5	22.6
	39.0	43.5	18.2				% Profit Before Taxes/Total Assets		17.3	23.9
	15.0	17.8	9.8						9.1	15.3
	7.2	9.4	-.7						1.5	5.1
	27.3	18.8	14.4						15.4	30.5
	18.7	10.9	5.5				Sales/Net Fixed Assets		9.6	10.4
	7.4	6.0	3.3						4.5	5.7
	4.4	3.2	1.6						3.2	2.5
	3.3	2.3	1.1				Sales/Total Assets		2.1	1.8
	1.4	1.5	.9						1.4	1.4
		1.5	1.5						.9	1.0
	(16)	2.8	(12) 3.1				% Depr., Dep., Amort./Sales	(47)	2.5	(40) 2.7
		3.8	7.7						3.7	4.7
		.7							2.0	1.8
	(11)	2.5					% Officers', Directors' Owners' Comp/Sales	(28)	3.2	(19) 3.7
		4.7							6.2	6.6
	2656M	55209M	268228M	354412M	161609M	749491M	Net Sales ($)		2374149M	1409234M
	628M	19639M	112344M	286179M	130403M	568526M	Total Assets ($)		753827M	983916M

© RMA 2024

M = $ thousand   MM = $ million
See Pages viii through xx for Explanation of Ratios and Data

MANUFACTURING—Cut Stone and Stone Product Manufacturing NAICS 327991

Comparative Historical Data | Current Data Sorted by Sales

							Type of Statement						
	6		2		4		Unqualified					2	2
	5		6		3		Reviewed					3	
	16		6		5		Compiled		1		1	3	
	30		16		9		Tax Returns	1	1		5	2	
	4/1/21-		46		38		Other	1	5	7	6	12	7
	3/31/22		4/1/22-		4/1/23-				3 (4/1-9/30/23)			56 (10/1/23-3/31/24)	
	ALL		3/31/23		3/31/24			0-1MM	1-3MM	3-5MM	5-10MM	10-25MM	25MM & OVER
	57		ALL 76		ALL 59		NUMBER OF STATEMENTS	2	7	7	12	22	9
	%		%		%		ASSETS	%	%	%	%	%	%
	15.2		11.6		12.9		Cash & Equivalents				13.0	12.3	
	17.9		18.5		18.2		Trade Receivables (net)				14.4	20.6	
	23.8		23.4		22.4		Inventory				15.5	21.7	
	2.5		5.4		4.9		All Other Current				6.1	4.3	
	59.4		58.9		58.4		Total Current				48.9	59.0	
	26.4		25.0		24.5		Fixed Assets (net)				31.8	22.9	
	7.8		7.7		8.3		Intangibles (net)				8.2	10.4	
	6.4		8.4		8.8		All Other Non-Current				11.0	7.8	
	100.0		100.0		100.0		Total				100.0	100.0	
							LIABILITIES						
	4.5		9.7		3.4		Notes Payable-Short Term				5.7	2.5	
	2.1		2.7		3.8		Cur. Mat.-L.T.D.				4.3	4.0	
	12.0		12.4		12.1		Trade Payables				14.6	10.8	
	.1		.1		.1		Income Taxes Payable				.0	.1	
	10.9		15.0		12.5		All Other Current				8.8	13.1	
	29.6		39.8		31.9		Total Current				33.5	30.5	
	21.1		22.8		24.2		Long-Term Debt				37.7	13.7	
	.1		.0		.2		Deferred Taxes				.2	.1	
	7.2		7.5		8.3		All Other Non-Current				19.4	5.1	
	42.0		29.9		35.5		Net Worth				9.2	50.6	
	100.0		100.0		100.0		Total Liabilities & Net Worth				100.0	100.0	
							INCOME DATA						
	100.0		100.0		100.0		Net Sales				100.0	100.0	
	41.1		39.9		40.7		Gross Profit				38.9	38.7	
	33.9		33.1		30.9		Operating Expenses				28.7	30.6	
	7.2		6.8		9.8		Operating Profit				10.2	8.1	
	-2.2		.1		.5		All Other Expenses (net)				1.3	-.1	
	9.4		6.7		9.3		Profit Before Taxes				8.9	8.2	
							RATIOS						
	3.5		2.9		3.0						6.4	3.0	
	1.9		1.8		2.1		Current				1.7	2.1	
	1.4		1.0		1.2						1.0	1.1	
	2.3		1.6		1.7						5.9	1.7	
	1.0		.9		1.0		Quick				1.1	1.0	
	.5		.4		.6						.2	.7	
15	23.9	13	28.1	15	24.6			0	UND			23	15.6
26	13.9	33	11.1	35	10.5		Sales/Receivables	19	19.3			37	9.8
41	8.8	47	7.8	50	7.3			51	7.1			56	6.5
21	17.0	4	90.2	23	15.9			4	84.9			27	13.3
63	5.8	73	5.0	66	5.5		Cost of Sales/Inventory	28	13.2			70	5.2
135	2.7	122	3.0	114	3.2			79	4.6			99	3.7
16	23.2	7	51.0	11	33.3			0	UND			17	22.0
28	13.1	29	12.5	25	14.8		Cost of Sales/Payables	24	14.9			22	16.4
52	7.0	55	6.6	54	6.8			59	6.2			47	7.8
	4.0		5.0		4.7						5.5	5.6	
	6.7		10.0		8.1		Sales/Working Capital				12.6	8.9	
	11.6		274.2		20.5						NM	22.2	
	43.0		26.7		37.6						17.4	55.0	
(50)	19.0	(63)	8.9	(53)	13.5		EBIT/Interest				8.0	(21) 18.0	
	6.8		2.0		4.1						3.9	3.4	
							Net Profit + Depr., Dep., Amort./Cur. Mat. L/T/D						
	.2		.3		.3						.4	.3	
	.7		.7		.6		Fixed/Worth				.9	.6	
	1.3		9.2		1.6						-1.4	.9	
	.6		.6		.6						.7	.5	
	1.2		2.4		1.7		Debt/Worth				3.6	.8	
	5.9		22.4		7.4						-4.3	2.8	
	69.8		73.1		73.2							68.3	
(47)	36.1	(59)	34.0	(50)	33.6		% Profit Before Taxes/Tangible Net Worth					(20) 37.0	
	17.5		11.6		16.9							19.8	
	25.8		23.3		34.0						34.4	36.0	
	13.1		9.5		14.8		% Profit Before Taxes/Total Assets				16.5	15.5	
	6.0		3.2		7.4						9.2	3.4	
	17.4		23.4		23.4						27.6	35.1	
	9.1		11.5		9.5		Sales/Net Fixed Assets				9.8	9.9	
	3.5		5.1		5.8						3.6	4.8	
	2.5		3.3		3.2						3.9	3.3	
	1.7		1.9		1.9		Sales/Total Assets				2.3	1.7	
	1.3		1.2		1.1						1.3	1.1	
	1.3		1.1		1.3							2.8	
(42)	3.1	(55)	2.0	(42)	2.9		% Depr., Dep., Amort./Sales					(15) 3.1	
	5.3		4.1		4.0							5.4	
	2.0		1.5		1.3								
(17)	3.0	(26)	2.6	(24)	3.0		% Officers', Directors' Owners' Comp/Sales						
	5.9		5.1		5.6								
	1031433M		1707607M		1591605M		Net Sales ($)	1457M	16160M	28137M	81623M	346277M	1117951M
	783071M		1180421M		1117719M		Total Assets ($)	1639M	11443M	9541M	46181M	205160M	843755M

M = $ thousand   MM = $ million
© RMA 2024
See Pages viii through xx for Explanation of Ratios and Data

MANUFACTURING—Iron and Steel Mills and Ferroalloy Manufacturing NAICS 331110

Current Data Sorted by Assets | Comparative Historical Data

0-500M	500M-2MM	2-10MM	10-50MM	50-100MM	100-250MM	Type of Statement		4/1/19-3/31/20 ALL	4/1/20-3/31/21 ALL
		2	3		6	Unqualified		7	4
	2	4	1	1		Reviewed		6	4
		5	1			Compiled		6	3
1	1	7	13		3	Tax Returns		7	3
	10 (4/1-9/30/23)		40 (10/1/23-3/31/24)			Other		24	11
1	3	18	18	1	9	NUMBER OF STATEMENTS		50	25
%	%	%	%	%	%	ASSETS		%	%
		12.9	7.5			Cash & Equivalents		9.8	10.7
		28.5	22.2			Trade Receivables (net)		27.0	30.0
		15.5	23.7			Inventory		21.0	22.1
		4.2	11.1			All Other Current		5.5	3.2
		61.1	64.5			Total Current		63.3	66.0
		25.0	24.6			Fixed Assets (net)		26.3	20.4
		4.6	1.3			Intangibles (net)		2.2	2.5
		9.3	9.7			All Other Non-Current		8.2	11.1
		100.0	100.0			Total		100.0	100.0
						LIABILITIES			
		7.5	9.0			Notes Payable-Short Term		15.7	10.1
		4.5	.8			Cur. Mat.-L.T.D.		2.7	2.3
		15.3	13.8			Trade Payables		15.9	14.1
		.1	.1			Income Taxes Payable		.1	.0
		9.4	11.6			All Other Current		8.8	14.8
		36.8	35.3			Total Current		43.2	41.4
		12.1	13.4			Long-Term Debt		15.4	16.9
		1.1	.8			Deferred Taxes		.3	.3
		7.8	6.0			All Other Non-Current		3.9	15.0
		42.1	44.4			Net Worth		37.2	26.5
		100.0	100.0			Total Liabilities & Net Worth		100.0	100.0
						INCOME DATA			
		100.0	100.0			Net Sales		100.0	100.0
		33.1	15.3			Gross Profit		24.8	26.3
		27.4	12.1			Operating Expenses		21.9	24.3
		5.7	3.2			Operating Profit		2.9	2.1
		.5	1.1			All Other Expenses (net)		.8	1.0
		5.2	2.1			Profit Before Taxes		2.1	1.1
						RATIOS			
		3.6	2.6					3.6	3.0
		2.1	2.0			Current		1.9	2.0
		1.1	1.4					1.2	1.1
		2.4	1.4					2.0	2.1
		1.0	.9			Quick		1.1	1.1
		.7	.5					.6	.4
		30 12.2	21 17.4				29	12.8	26 13.9
		46 7.9	36 10.2			Sales/Receivables	42	8.7	47 7.8
		66 5.5	59 6.2				66	5.5	70 5.2
		0 UND	8 44.3				9	39.6	14 26.3
		20 18.4	41 9.0			Cost of Sales/Inventory	33	11.2	38 9.6
		73 5.0	83 4.4				91	4.0	87 4.2
		19 19.4	14 26.1				16	22.5	17 21.2
		29 12.8	31 11.6			Cost of Sales/Payables	29	12.7	26 13.9
		62 5.9	53 6.9				41	8.8	59 6.2
		4.4	3.9					4.5	4.4
		8.6	6.6			Sales/Working Capital		7.2	7.0
		NM	23.5					21.5	70.1
		37.1	24.6					16.6	29.8
		(16) 9.3	(15) 6.1			EBIT/Interest	(45)	4.8	(22) 6.5
		1.9	.8					-.7	1.0
						Net Profit + Depr., Dep.,		9.8	
						Amort./Cur. Mat. L/T/D	(13)	3.9	
								1.8	
		.2	.3					.3	.1
		.5	.5			Fixed/Worth		.6	.6
		.9	1.3					1.2	10.0
		.5	.5					.5	.6
		1.5	1.2			Debt/Worth		1.3	1.6
		3.3	3.8					5.0	23.8
		60.0	33.4					50.4	57.8
		(16) 28.1	(16) 15.9			% Profit Before Taxes/Tangible Net Worth	(47)	14.2	(21) 26.5
		1.3	-8.9					-.7	9.1
		26.1	17.6					12.1	18.3
		8.7	6.8			% Profit Before Taxes/Total Assets		4.7	8.0
		.9	-2.2					-2.9	1.5
		155.4	24.7					30.9	50.1
		12.4	17.2			Sales/Net Fixed Assets		10.8	14.9
		3.6	3.4					4.5	6.8
		3.2	2.6					2.7	2.5
		1.8	1.8			Sales/Total Assets		2.0	2.0
		1.3	1.2					1.5	1.6
		.9	1.2					.6	.5
		(13) 2.0	(16) 2.1			% Depr., Dep., Amort./Sales	(41)	1.7	(20) 1.5
		3.6	3.5					3.7	2.8
						% Officers', Directors' Owners' Comp/Sales		1.0	
							(14)	2.8	
								5.6	
1052M	8249M	187280M	987788M	111450M	2882404M	Net Sales ($)		3881324M	1711275M
433M	4242M	85893M	415917M	54184M	1422672M	Total Assets ($)		2164391M	901392M

© RMA 2024

M = $ thousand   MM = $ million
See Pages viii through xx for Explanation of Ratios and Data

MANUFACTURING—Iron and Steel Mills and Ferroalloy Manufacturing NAICS 331110

Comparative Historical Data			Type of Statement	Current Data Sorted by Sales					
5	5	9	Unqualified				2		7
6	5	4	Reviewed			1	1		2
2	3	5	Compiled			2	3		1
3	3	7	Tax Returns		2	2			1
13	34	25	Other	2	1	3	4	3	14
4/1/21-3/31/22	4/1/22-3/31/23	4/1/23-3/31/24		0-1MM	10 (4/1-9/30/23)		40 (10/1/23-3/31/24)		
ALL	ALL	ALL			1-3MM	3-5MM	5-10MM	10-25MM	25MM & OVER
29	50	50	NUMBER OF STATEMENTS		3	5	8	9	25
%	%	%	**ASSETS**	%	%	%	%	%	%
15.2	11.7	10.4	Cash & Equivalents	D					7.1
24.4	25.9	25.7	Trade Receivables (net)	A					25.0
28.2	26.1	22.2	Inventory	T					28.9
3.6	2.6	6.8	All Other Current	A					8.7
71.4	66.2	65.1	Total Current						69.7
23.0	23.9	23.7	Fixed Assets (net)	N					21.3
.2	2.5	3.2	Intangibles (net)	O					2.1
5.1	7.4	8.1	All Other Non-Current	T					7.0
100.0	100.0	100.0	Total						100.0
			LIABILITIES	A					
9.6	10.0	8.7	Notes Payable-Short Term	V					11.1
1.7	3.8	2.7	Cur. Mat.-L.T.D.	A					1.8
13.3	15.3	14.1	Trade Payables	I					17.3
.2	.0	.1	Income Taxes Payable	L					.1
12.5	17.4	9.8	All Other Current	A					9.9
37.3	46.5	35.3	Total Current	B					40.2
13.5	13.8	16.9	Long-Term Debt	L					20.0
.3	.5	.7	Deferred Taxes	E					.5
2.1	4.4	5.9	All Other Non-Current						3.2
46.6	34.8	41.1	Net Worth						36.0
100.0	100.0	100.0	Total Liabilities & Net Worth						100.0
			INCOME DATA						
100.0	100.0	100.0	Net Sales						100.0
25.7	27.6	25.3	Gross Profit						17.1
18.9	21.5	19.9	Operating Expenses						11.5
6.8	6.1	5.3	Operating Profit						5.5
-2.0	.0	1.0	All Other Expenses (net)						1.2
8.9	6.1	4.3	Profit Before Taxes						4.3
			RATIOS						
4.4	2.6	3.6							2.8
2.0	1.6	1.9	Current						1.7
1.5	1.2	1.3							1.3
2.6	1.5	1.7							1.4
1.3	.9	1.0	Quick						.8
.6	.5	.6							.5
34 10.7	25 14.8	30 12.1						29	12.4
45 8.1	41 8.8	40 9.2	Sales/Receivables					37	9.8
58 6.3	83 4.4	65 5.6						54	6.7
21 17.6	22 16.6	11 32.9						24	15.0
70 5.2	72 5.1	34 10.6	Cost of Sales/Inventory					56	6.5
135 2.7	126 2.9	83 4.4						87	4.2
14 25.7	15 23.9	21 17.4						25	14.6
29 12.6	31 11.8	31 11.8	Cost of Sales/Payables					32	11.4
54 6.7	60 6.1	49 7.4						48	7.6
2.7	4.9	4.3							4.4
5.7	7.3	7.2	Sales/Working Capital						7.3
12.1	16.2	16.0							18.3
166.7	61.4	26.1							21.6
(25) 27.0	(41) 12.0	(42) 7.3	EBIT/Interest					(21)	6.1
3.8	2.1	1.5							1.2
		6.4	Net Profit + Depr., Dep.,						
		(10) 1.3	Amort./Cur. Mat. L/T/D						
		-.9							
.2	.2	.2							.2
.4	.5	.5	Fixed/Worth						.6
1.6	1.2	1.6							2.5
.3	.6	.5							.6
1.1	1.3	1.5	Debt/Worth						1.7
3.4	4.3	4.1							5.2
47.2	63.9	44.0	% Profit Before Taxes/Tangible						40.9
(25) 29.4	(40) 24.6	(44) 21.9	Net Worth					(21)	23.5
16.0	9.4	2.9							8.6
22.3	20.4	21.7	% Profit Before Taxes/Total						22.0
11.8	10.9	6.8	Assets						12.6
6.1	4.9	.9							.2
32.4	26.5	28.7							32.0
7.4	8.4	12.3	Sales/Net Fixed Assets						17.5
4.1	4.0	3.7							4.3
2.6	2.3	2.7							2.9
1.9	1.8	1.8	Sales/Total Assets						2.1
1.0	1.4	1.3							1.3
.9	.9	1.0							.6
(24) 1.4	(43) 1.7	(41) 1.9	% Depr., Dep., Amort./Sales					(21)	1.5
2.7	3.5	3.2							2.2
		.8	% Officers', Directors'						
		(15) 2.9	Owners' Comp/Sales						
		6.2							
3471361M	2402645M	4178223M	Net Sales ($)	4978M	21157M	60443M	145211M		3946434M
1367728M	1516182M	1983341M	Total Assets ($)	3539M	17397M	30442M	107204M		1824759M

© RMA 2024

M = $ thousand   MM = $ million

See Pages viii through xx for Explanation of Ratios and Data

MANUFACTURING—Iron and Steel Pipe and Tube Manufacturing from Purchased Steel NAICS 331210

Current Data Sorted by Assets | Comparative Historical Data

							Type of Statement				
			9	2	4		Unqualified		8		7
		4	9	2			Reviewed		8		6
		4	2		4		Compiled		4		3
		4	1				Tax Returns		5		6
3	3	16	17	6	9		Other		56		33
0-500M	16 (4/1-9/30/23) 500M-2MM	2-10MM	79 (10/1/23-3/31/24) 10-50MM	50-100MM	100-250MM				4/1/19-3/31/20 ALL		4/1/20-3/31/21 ALL
3	3	28	38	10	13		NUMBER OF STATEMENTS		81		55
%	%	%	%	%	%		ASSETS		%		%
		18.4	17.1	13.1	7.9		Cash & Equivalents		7.2		14.4
		32.4	22.3	20.7	19.4		Trade Receivables (net)		22.9		23.1
		21.5	21.3	29.1	33.5		Inventory		29.3		23.2
		2.1	2.4	4.0	1.6		All Other Current		1.8		2.9
		74.4	63.1	66.9	62.4		Total Current		61.2		63.7
		15.5	25.6	20.6	28.3		Fixed Assets (net)		26.2		26.5
		4.6	3.4	6.5	2.3		Intangibles (net)		6.4		5.4
		5.5	7.9	6.0	7.0		All Other Non-Current		6.2		4.4
		100.0	100.0	100.0	100.0		Total		100.0		100.0
							LIABILITIES				
		4.9	6.2	14.6	4.4		Notes Payable-Short Term		12.3		9.5
		2.3	2.1	5.7	1.5		Cur. Mat.-L.T.D.		2.2		2.4
		14.3	12.0	7.0	11.0		Trade Payables		13.6		11.3
		.0	.2	.0	.1		Income Taxes Payable		.2		.1
		10.8	12.9	6.9	12.8		All Other Current		8.5		9.1
		32.3	33.4	34.1	29.8		Total Current		36.7		32.4
		17.8	11.0	7.8	36.3		Long-Term Debt		14.0		16.1
		.2	.7	.0	.2		Deferred Taxes		.3		.4
		2.6	4.3	2.9	6.9		All Other Non-Current		6.6		7.0
		47.2	50.6	55.1	26.8		Net Worth		42.4		44.1
		100.0	100.0	100.0	100.0		Total Liabilities & Net Worth		100.0		100.0
							INCOME DATA				
		100.0	100.0	100.0	100.0		Net Sales		100.0		100.0
		30.7	25.2	27.1	14.1		Gross Profit		23.5		20.5
		21.9	15.4	11.9	8.8		Operating Expenses		19.6		17.1
		8.8	9.8	15.3	5.3		Operating Profit		3.9		3.4
		.4	-.1	2.6	1.6		All Other Expenses (net)		.6		-.8
		8.4	10.0	12.7	3.7		Profit Before Taxes		3.3		4.2
							RATIOS				
		5.3	3.3	3.5	2.7				2.8		4.0
		3.0	2.0	2.3	2.0		Current		1.8		2.0
		1.7	1.4	1.1	1.6				1.2		1.4
		3.8	2.3	1.8	1.1				1.8		3.0
		1.7	1.3	1.0	.9		Quick		.8		1.0
		.9	.8	.3	.6				.5		.6
		27 13.5	28 13.1	32 11.3	26 14.3				33 11.0		33 11.0
		41 8.8	38 9.7	46 8.0	38 9.6		Sales/Receivables		46 7.9		43 8.5
		78 4.7	54 6.8	64 5.7	57 6.4				54 6.8		59 6.2
		3 136.4	10 37.7	14 25.2	65 5.6				33 10.9		27 13.4
		37 9.9	46 7.9	43 8.4	91 4.0		Cost of Sales/Inventory		70 5.2		52 7.0
		101 3.6	83 4.4	203 1.8	159 2.3				126 2.9		85 4.3
		12 30.2	12 30.0	0 UND	16 22.2				11 33.6		11 34.5
		20 18.4	30 12.3	23 15.6	24 15.0		Cost of Sales/Payables		26 14.1		22 16.6
		54 6.7	40 9.1	29 12.4	41 8.8				47 7.8		35 10.3
		3.3	4.2	2.5	3.3				4.7		3.8
		6.2	6.1	5.0	4.1		Sales/Working Capital		7.0		4.9
		9.4	14.5	NM	8.0				19.6		15.5
		48.6	55.5		5.9				11.2		33.6
		(23) 13.7	(34) 32.5	(12) 2.3			EBIT/Interest	(72)	3.4	(50)	6.0
		3.0	9.5		1.1				-.6		1.3
			37.3						6.5		
			(11) 10.0				Net Profit + Depr., Dep., Amort./Cur. Mat. L/T/D	(15)	2.5		
			6.3						1.2		
		.1	.3	.0	.3				.3		.3
		.3	.4	.3	1.3		Fixed/Worth		.7		.5
		1.4	1.2	.8	NM				1.7		1.7
		.3	.4	.4	.8				.6		.5
		.7	1.2	.8	2.3		Debt/Worth		1.4		.9
		3.7	2.4	2.7	NM				6.3		4.7
		85.6	51.9	61.6	34.9				37.1		39.1
		(25) 21.0	(36) 31.7	27.8	(10) 17.7		% Profit Before Taxes/Tangible Net Worth	(72)	15.9	(47)	19.3
		11.6	13.8	2.5	3.1				-2.4		3.2
		29.1	25.5	36.5	11.8				12.9		17.7
		14.9	14.1	20.8	3.9		% Profit Before Taxes/Total Assets		4.0		5.8
		5.8	9.5	.7	.5				-1.7		1.6
		47.3	29.6	999.8	11.1				16.4		14.1
		23.7	8.5	16.2	5.1		Sales/Net Fixed Assets		7.8		8.4
		8.8	3.5	4.0	2.3				4.2		3.8
		3.2	2.4	1.9	1.9				2.3		2.5
		2.3	2.0	1.7	1.4		Sales/Total Assets		1.8		1.7
		1.4	1.3	1.3	1.1				1.3		1.2
		.5	.6		.7				1.1		1.6
		(22) 1.0	(33) 1.4	(11) 1.5			% Depr., Dep., Amort./Sales	(64)	2.1	(48)	2.2
		1.7	4.6		4.2				3.6		4.7
		1.1							1.6		
		(12) 1.8					% Officers', Directors' Owners' Comp/Sales	(20)	2.2		
		2.8							5.7		
4430M	8345M	328997M	1790963M	1205350M	3530074M		Net Sales ($)		4404224M		3891864M
667M	3911M	146265M	886946M	735093M	2258476M		Total Assets ($)		2713358M		2548840M

© RMA 2024

M = $ thousand MM = $ million
See Pages viii through xx for Explanation of Ratios and Data

MANUFACTURING—Iron and Steel Pipe and Tube Manufacturing from Purchased Steel NAICS 331210

Comparative Historical Data / Current Data Sorted by Sales

				Type of Statement						
	7	10	15	Unqualified					3	12
	3	9	15	Reviewed		1	2		2	10
	9	6	6	Compiled					5	1
	7	12	5	Tax Returns				2	3	
	37	50	54	Other	3		2	8	11	29
	4/1/21-3/31/22	4/1/22-3/31/23	4/1/23-3/31/24			16 (4/1-9/30/23)		79 (10/1/23-3/31/24)		
	ALL	ALL	ALL		0-1MM	1-3MM	3-5MM	5-10MM	10-25MM	25MM & OVER
	63	87	95	NUMBER OF STATEMENTS	3	1	3	12	24	52
	%	%	%	ASSETS	%	%	%	%	%	%
	16.2	15.3	15.6	Cash & Equivalents				19.2	17.8	13.9
	22.8	26.3	24.9	Trade Receivables (net)				35.7	22.6	23.6
	24.8	28.8	24.0	Inventory				13.5	22.6	26.9
	3.5	2.6	2.3	All Other Current				2.3	2.1	2.4
	67.3	73.1	66.8	Total Current				70.7	65.2	66.9
	22.7	20.3	21.9	Fixed Assets (net)				14.4	26.0	22.0
	5.2	2.2	4.4	Intangibles (net)				5.3	2.9	4.2
	4.9	4.4	6.8	All Other Non-Current				9.6	6.0	6.8
	100.0	100.0	100.0	Total				100.0	100.0	100.0
				LIABILITIES						
	8.5	7.6	6.5	Notes Payable-Short Term				3.9	4.1	7.6
	2.4	2.1	2.5	Cur. Mat.-L.T.D.				4.1	1.8	2.4
	10.5	13.3	12.1	Trade Payables				14.8	9.7	11.8
	.2	.3	.1	Income Taxes Payable				.0	.0	.2
	8.6	9.8	11.1	All Other Current				7.8	7.2	13.5
	30.2	33.1	32.3	Total Current				30.6	22.8	35.4
	17.4	17.7	18.3	Long-Term Debt				33.5	16.0	15.1
	.3	.2	.4	Deferred Taxes				.1	.2	.5
	4.7	3.5	4.2	All Other Non-Current				4.7	1.9	4.9
	47.3	45.4	44.8	Net Worth				31.1	59.0	44.1
	100.0	100.0	100.0	Total Liabilities & Net Worth				100.0	100.0	100.0
				INCOME DATA						
	100.0	100.0	100.0	Net Sales				100.0	100.0	100.0
	27.6	25.6	27.0	Gross Profit				34.2	31.7	21.1
	19.2	17.1	18.2	Operating Expenses				27.2	20.7	11.6
	8.4	8.5	8.8	Operating Profit				7.0	10.9	9.5
	-2.1	-.3	.7	All Other Expenses (net)				.5	-.6	1.1
	10.5	8.9	8.1	Profit Before Taxes				6.5	11.5	8.4
				RATIOS						
	4.2	4.3	3.8					4.9	6.9	2.9
	2.2	2.3	2.1	Current				2.1	3.2	2.1
	1.7	1.5	1.5					1.5	1.6	1.5
	2.7	2.6	2.4					2.6	3.9	1.6
	1.4	1.4	1.3	Quick				1.5	2.1	1.2
	.8	.6	.8					.9	1.0	.6
27	13.4	27	13.3	27	13.3			28	13.2	27	13.3	30	12.0
48	7.6	40	9.1	39	9.3	Sales/Receivables		45	8.1	35	10.4	40	9.1
68	5.4	57	6.4	58	6.3			104	3.5	55	6.6	57	6.4
16	22.6	23	16.0	12	30.7			0	UND	7	49.4	25	14.5
79	4.6	66	5.5	48	7.6	Cost of Sales/Inventory		4	100.7	43	8.5	58	6.3
122	3.0	130	2.8	107	3.4			63	5.8	107	3.4	111	3.3
11	32.1	10	37.7	13	28.0			12	30.2	10	35.3	14	26.5
26	14.1	24	15.5	25	14.6	Cost of Sales/Payables		26	13.9	23	16.2	25	14.8
45	8.1	40	9.1	41	9.0			61	6.0	44	8.3	38	9.6
	3.4		3.5		3.3				3.1		3.3		3.7
	4.5		6.0		5.8	Sales/Working Capital			5.5		5.6		5.9
	7.8		11.3		12.5				17.8		9.5		12.1
	47.2		52.0		43.8						37.4		49.1
(55)	14.4	(77)	18.1	(83)	13.0	EBIT/Interest			(21)	13.8	(47)	13.3
	6.5		5.1		2.5						10.2		2.1
	10.1		33.5		17.1	Net Profit + Depr., Dep.,							31.6
(13)	4.5	(15)	17.6	(22)	9.1	Amort./Cur. Mat. L/T/D					(16)	10.2
	1.6		1.3		4.8								6.1
	.2		.1		.1				.1		.1		.2
	.4		.3		.4	Fixed/Worth			.2		.4		.4
	.9		.9		1.4				NM		1.2		1.3
	.4		.4		.4				.2		.3		.6
	.9		1.1		1.0	Debt/Worth			.9		.5		1.2
	2.2		2.6		3.7				NM		1.7		3.7
	68.4		74.9		52.9	% Profit Before Taxes/Tangible					55.7		53.0
(57)	27.4	(78)	41.8	(84)	25.4	Net Worth			(23)	30.6	(47)	30.0
	15.3		14.1		10.9						16.2		9.9
	26.2		33.5		25.0	% Profit Before Taxes/Total			15.8		27.1		26.1
	12.9		15.6		12.9	Assets			9.5		14.3		12.7
	6.2		6.5		3.5				1.2		11.1		3.2
	26.6		71.8		36.3				47.3		34.3		29.4
	9.6		15.0		13.4	Sales/Net Fixed Assets			22.1		9.3		12.7
	5.5		5.5		5.1				9.4		3.8		5.0
	2.3		2.9		2.5				2.8		2.9		2.4
	1.7		2.0		1.9	Sales/Total Assets			2.3		1.7		1.9
	1.2		1.5		1.3				1.5		1.1		1.4
	.8		.6		.6						.6		.7
(48)	1.5	(60)	1.5	(77)	1.3	% Depr., Dep., Amort./Sales			(21)	1.2	(42)	1.2
	2.8		2.8		3.5						4.0		3.2
	.9		.6		.6	% Officers', Directors'					.8		
(13)	2.0	(19)	3.0	(21)	1.6	Owners' Comp/Sales				(11)	2.0		
	5.1		4.8		3.1						2.9		
3985914M		6840001M		6868159M		Net Sales ($)	1396M	1736M	11597M	84398M	398878M	6370154M
2737866M		3590915M		4031358M		Total Assets ($)	924M	1302M	8056M	41944M	255289M	3723843M

M = $ thousand   MM = $ million
See Pages viii through xx for Explanation of Ratios and Data

© RMA 2024

MANUFACTURING—Rolled Steel Shape Manufacturing NAICS 331221

Current Data Sorted by Assets | Comparative Historical Data

							Type of Statement		
			2	3	2	1	Unqualified	6	5
			2	3	2	1	Reviewed	8	3
			2				Compiled	3	2
		1	1				Tax Returns	3	2
		4	6	15	6	7	Other	27	17
		19 (4/1-9/30/23)		39 (10/1/23-3/31/24)				4/1/19-3/31/20	4/1/20-3/31/21
0-500M	500M-2MM	2-10MM	10-50MM	50-100MM	100-250MM			ALL	ALL
	5	13	21	10	9		NUMBER OF STATEMENTS	47	29
%	%	%	%	%	%		ASSETS	%	%
		15.4	11.3	1.3			Cash & Equivalents	9.6	10.8
D		27.6	25.5	17.8			Trade Receivables (net)	21.3	20.4
A		22.3	27.7	32.6			Inventory	30.0	26.8
T		.9	1.1	1.7			All Other Current	1.4	1.0
A		66.3	65.6	53.3			Total Current	62.4	58.9
		24.0	27.4	31.7			Fixed Assets (net)	25.1	30.2
N		3.4	1.6	5.8			Intangibles (net)	7.2	2.4
O		6.3	5.5	9.2			All Other Non-Current	5.3	8.5
T		100.0	100.0	100.0			Total	100.0	100.0
A							LIABILITIES		
V		2.2	5.3	12.4			Notes Payable-Short Term	8.7	5.4
A		3.4	2.7	2.9			Cur. Mat.-L.T.D.	2.8	3.4
I		12.5	12.2	9.2			Trade Payables	13.4	11.7
L		.1	.2	.0			Income Taxes Payable	.1	.0
A		12.7	14.6	7.0			All Other Current	6.7	11.9
B		31.0	35.0	31.6			Total Current	31.6	32.3
L		30.4	13.6	18.4			Long-Term Debt	17.3	20.1
E		.0	.1	.0			Deferred Taxes	.4	.1
		13.8	8.9	6.8			All Other Non-Current	4.8	4.1
		24.9	42.4	43.3			Net Worth	45.8	43.4
		100.0	100.0	100.0			Total Liabilities & Net Worth	100.0	100.0
							INCOME DATA		
		100.0	100.0	100.0			Net Sales	100.0	100.0
		31.9	23.8	19.8			Gross Profit	20.7	23.7
		30.1	18.5	11.5			Operating Expenses	15.5	19.3
		1.8	5.3	8.3			Operating Profit	5.2	4.4
		-1.5	2.5	3.3			All Other Expenses (net)	.9	-1.3
		3.3	2.8	5.0			Profit Before Taxes	4.3	5.7
							RATIOS		
		5.0	2.8	4.1				3.4	3.9
		2.9	1.9	1.3			Current	2.1	2.5
		1.7	1.5	1.1				1.4	1.3
		3.8	1.7	1.0				1.8	2.9
		1.8	.9	.5			Quick	1.0	1.0
		.7	.8	.5				.5	.6
	26	14.3	32	11.4	27	13.5		25	14.7	32	11.4
	38	9.5	43	8.5	37	9.8	Sales/Receivables	36	10.1	38	9.6
	66	5.5	66	5.5	59	6.2		51	7.1	50	7.3
	6	61.0	34	10.7	55	6.6		38	9.7	48	7.6
	49	7.4	59	6.2	68	5.4	Cost of Sales/Inventory	57	6.4	72	5.1
	76	4.8	94	3.9	126	2.9		111	3.3	87	4.2
	13	27.1	13	28.4	12	31.6		16	22.4	17	21.2
	26	14.0	17	21.4	27	13.6	Cost of Sales/Payables	25	14.7	25	14.7
	37	9.8	30	12.2	41	9.0		37	9.8	45	8.2
		3.8	4.5	3.3				4.7	3.8
		7.4	6.3	19.0			Sales/Working Capital	7.9	7.2
		11.2	10.2	NM				15.7	14.5
		25.8	43.8					14.3	38.6
	(11)	9.9	(20)	6.5			EBIT/Interest	(43)	7.1	(27)	11.9
		2.2	-.7					1.9	1.5
							Net Profit + Depr., Dep.,		9.3		10.5
							Amort./Cur. Mat. L/T/D	(16)	4.9	(10)	5.0
								2.3	1.7
		.3	.3	.3				.2	.4
		.6	.5	1.5			Fixed/Worth	.4	.5
		NM	.9	2.0				1.5	1.5
		.8	.4	.6				.6	.5
		1.2	1.2	2.1			Debt/Worth	1.0	1.1
		NM	2.8	4.7				3.3	5.0
		59.0	25.7	27.4			% Profit Before Taxes/Tangible	28.4	50.1
	(10)	42.4	(19)	17.3	20.0		Net Worth	(40)	13.8	(27)	15.7
		18.8	-21.8	16.8				7.4	5.0
		26.7	17.1	17.6			% Profit Before Taxes/Total	15.2	23.3
		15.2	7.4	6.6			Assets	6.6	6.8
		3.8	-6.9	3.1				2.0	1.8
		54.6	15.7	13.4				21.0	16.4
		14.7	10.7	5.2			Sales/Net Fixed Assets	10.4	6.4
		4.7	4.0	3.3				4.8	3.4
		3.5	2.6	2.2				3.2	2.4
		1.9	2.2	1.6			Sales/Total Assets	2.0	1.8
		1.6	1.5	1.4				1.5	1.3
		.2	.9					1.0	1.4
	(10)	1.6	(18)	2.5			% Depr., Dep., Amort./Sales	(40)	2.0	(28)	2.5
		4.5	3.6					2.8	4.6
							% Officers', Directors'		
							Owners' Comp/Sales		
	13033M	134197M	1062699M	1196985M	2860337M		Net Sales ($)	2650888M	1456367M
	6386M	55492M	522299M	694914M	1534457M		Total Assets ($)	1464418M	791084M

M = $ thousand MM = $ million
See Pages viii through xx for Explanation of Ratios and Data

© RMA 2024

MANUFACTURING—Rolled Steel Shape Manufacturing   NAICS 331221

Comparative Historical Data / Current Data Sorted by Sales

						Type of Statement							
		4		7		8	Unqualified					2	6
		3		5		8	Reviewed			1			7
				1		2	Compiled		1	1		1	
		2		3		2	Tax Returns		1		2	1	
		20		22		38	Other	1	1	1	4	7	23
		4/1/21-3/31/22 ALL		4/1/22-3/31/23 ALL		4/1/23-3/31/24 ALL		0-1MM	19 (4/1-9/30/23) 1-3MM	3-5MM	39 (10/1/23-3/31/24) 5-10MM	10-25MM	25MM & OVER
		29		38		58	NUMBER OF STATEMENTS	1	2	3	7	9	36
		%		%		%	ASSETS	%	%	%	%	%	%
		7.5		9.6		9.4	Cash & Equivalents						7.0
		24.0		23.8		23.2	Trade Receivables (net)						22.8
		30.3		27.2		27.5	Inventory						31.9
		3.3		1.6		1.5	All Other Current						1.6
		65.1		62.1		61.6	Total Current						63.3
		23.7		26.7		28.3	Fixed Assets (net)						25.3
		4.0		5.2		3.7	Intangibles (net)						4.0
		7.2		5.9		6.4	All Other Non-Current						7.4
		100.0		100.0		100.0	Total						100.0
							LIABILITIES						
		10.2		8.6		8.4	Notes Payable-Short Term						9.9
		3.6		2.0		3.1	Cur. Mat.-L.T.D.						2.0
		13.3		14.4		11.1	Trade Payables						11.7
		.2		.5		.1	Income Taxes Payable						.1
		7.7		7.9		14.4	All Other Current						11.1
		35.1		33.5		37.1	Total Current						34.8
		19.5		17.8		19.9	Long-Term Debt						13.5
		.1		.3		.1	Deferred Taxes						.1
		5.9		2.6		8.3	All Other Non-Current						8.1
		39.5		45.8		34.6	Net Worth						43.4
		100.0		100.0		100.0	Total Liabilities & Net Worth						100.0
							INCOME DATA						
		100.0		100.0		100.0	Net Sales						100.0
		22.5		20.3		24.4	Gross Profit						18.2
		14.8		12.9		19.5	Operating Expenses						11.9
		7.7		7.4		5.0	Operating Profit						6.3
		-1.4		.3		1.4	All Other Expenses (net)						2.1
		9.1		7.1		3.6	Profit Before Taxes						4.2
							RATIOS						
		3.0		3.6		3.3							3.1
		1.7		1.8		1.8	Current						1.7
		1.4		1.3		1.2							1.2
		1.8		1.6		1.5							1.4
		.8		1.0		.9	Quick						.9
		.6		.6		.5							.5
36	10.2	28	13.0	28	13.1		Sales/Receivables					28	13.0
44	8.3	36	10.2	39	9.3							40	9.1
56	6.5	48	7.6	64	5.7							62	5.9
42	8.6	25	14.4	35	10.4		Cost of Sales/Inventory					54	6.7
73	5.0	58	6.3	62	5.9							63	5.8
99	3.7	83	4.4	99	3.7							94	3.9
14	25.7	10	36.1	12	29.7		Cost of Sales/Payables					12	30.0
27	13.5	20	18.1	23	16.1							23	16.1
39	9.3	32	11.4	34	10.6							30	12.0
		4.8		3.8		4.6	Sales/Working Capital						4.5
		7.3		7.9		8.1							8.1
		12.3		15.9		21.2							21.0
		45.0		67.7		20.4	EBIT/Interest						21.8
	(27)	13.7	(35)	10.7	(53)	4.3						(34)	4.9
		3.2		6.0		1.2							1.7
				13.0		7.8	Net Profit + Depr., Dep., Amort./Cur. Mat. L/T/D						7.8
			(12)	5.7	(13)	2.8							(11)	2.6
				2.2		1.7							1.7
		.3		.2		.3	Fixed/Worth						.2
		.5		.7		.7							.6
		1.2		1.3		2.6							1.7
		.8		.4		.6	Debt/Worth						.5
		2.0		1.4		1.4							1.2
		3.9		3.4		5.9							3.8
		96.4		55.3		38.5	% Profit Before Taxes/Tangible Net Worth						27.4
	(26)	41.5	(34)	34.1	(50)	19.8						(34)	18.3
		20.6		18.3		10.6							9.7
		23.3		24.2		17.6	% Profit Before Taxes/Total Assets						15.6
		15.5		13.0		7.5							7.5
		6.3		6.1		1.8							2.2
		23.4		19.3		19.0	Sales/Net Fixed Assets						19.0
		10.4		9.6		7.7							8.8
		5.3		5.1		4.1							4.7
		2.6		2.8		2.5	Sales/Total Assets						2.5
		2.0		2.1		1.9							2.0
		1.2		1.7		1.5							1.5
		.4		.7		.9	% Depr., Dep., Amort./Sales						.8
	(25)	1.2	(34)	1.5	(47)	2.4						(29)	2.4
		2.6		2.9		3.9							3.6
						2.0	% Officers', Directors', Owners' Comp/Sales						
				(10)		3.1							
						3.6							
		2882168M		3807824M		5267251M	Net Sales ($)	595M	4523M	12310M	47920M	166062M	5035841M
		1103000M		1614016M		2813548M	Total Assets ($)	694M	2968M	5369M	26173M	96329M	2682015M

M = $ thousand   MM = $ million
See Pages viii through xx for Explanation of Ratios and Data

© RMA 2024

MANUFACTURING—Secondary Smelting and Alloying of Aluminum NAICS 331314

Current Data Sorted by Assets | Comparative Historical Data

Type of Statement						
			4		1	Unqualified
			3			Reviewed
						Compiled
						Tax Returns
			3	7	2	Other

0-500M	7 (4/1-9/30/23) 500M-2MM	2-10MM	13 (10/1/23-3/31/24) 10-50MM	50-100MM	100-250MM		Comparative Historical 6 4/1/19-3/31/20 ALL	3 4/1/20-3/31/21 ALL
			10	7	3	**NUMBER OF STATEMENTS**	8	6
%	%	%	%	%	%	**ASSETS**	%	%
			8.7			Cash & Equivalents		
			25.7			Trade Receivables (net)		
			23.0			Inventory		
			2.8			All Other Current		
			60.2			Total Current		
DATA NOT AVAILABLE	DATA NOT AVAILABLE	DATA NOT AVAILABLE	34.6			Fixed Assets (net)		
			.0			Intangibles (net)		
			5.1			All Other Non-Current		
			100.0			Total		
						LIABILITIES		
			9.2			Notes Payable-Short Term		
			4.5			Cur. Mat.-L.T.D.		
			9.2			Trade Payables		
			.0			Income Taxes Payable		
			8.1			All Other Current		
			31.0			Total Current		
			18.2			Long-Term Debt		
			.0			Deferred Taxes		
			11.2			All Other Non-Current		
			39.7			Net Worth		
			100.0			Total Liabilities & Net Worth		
						INCOME DATA		
			100.0			Net Sales		
			26.4			Gross Profit		
			16.1			Operating Expenses		
			10.4			Operating Profit		
			1.1			All Other Expenses (net)		
			9.3			Profit Before Taxes		
						RATIOS		
			5.0					
			1.7			Current		
			.9					
			2.2					
			.8			Quick		
			.8					
			39 9.3					
			46 7.9			Sales/Receivables		
			59 6.2					
			8 43.3					
			54 6.8			Cost of Sales/Inventory		
			76 4.8					
			15 24.3					
			26 13.9			Cost of Sales/Payables		
			29 12.5					
			3.0					
			6.9			Sales/Working Capital		
			-46.1					
						EBIT/Interest		
						Net Profit + Depr., Dep., Amort./Cur. Mat. L/T/D		
			.2					
			.5			Fixed/Worth		
			-75.9					
			.4					
			1.6			Debt/Worth		
			-102.5					
						% Profit Before Taxes/Tangible Net Worth		
			23.9					
			15.4			% Profit Before Taxes/Total Assets		
			7.8					
			20.2					
			8.9			Sales/Net Fixed Assets		
			2.3					
			2.2					
			1.9			Sales/Total Assets		
			1.7					
			.7					
			.8			% Depr., Dep., Amort./Sales		
			8.0					
						% Officers', Directors' Owners' Comp/Sales		
		588995M	1104137M	1290013M		Net Sales ($)	655765M	534702M
		308170M	548711M	528373M		Total Assets ($)	300113M	392472M

M = $ thousand   MM = $ million
See Pages viii through xx for Explanation of Ratios and Data

© RMA 2024

MANUFACTURING—Secondary Smelting and Alloying of Aluminum NAICS 331314

Comparative Historical Data | Current Data Sorted by Sales

Comparative Historical Data			Type of Statement	Current Data Sorted by Sales					
	2	5	Unqualified						5
		3	Reviewed						3
			Compiled						
7	6	12	Tax Returns						12
4/1/21-	4/1/22-	4/1/23-	Other						
3/31/22	3/31/23	3/31/24		7 (4/1-9/30/23)			13 (10/1/23-3/31/24)		
ALL	ALL	ALL		0-1MM	1-3MM	3-5MM	5-10MM	10-25MM	25MM & OVER
7	8	20	NUMBER OF STATEMENTS						20
%	%	%	ASSETS	%	%	%	%	%	%
		7.1	Cash & Equivalents	D	D	D	D	D	7.1
		21.2	Trade Receivables (net)	A	A	A	A	A	21.2
		26.8	Inventory	T	T	T	T	T	26.8
		1.5	All Other Current	A	A	A	A	A	1.5
		56.6	Total Current						56.6
		33.1	Fixed Assets (net)	N	N	N	N	N	33.1
		.9	Intangibles (net)	O	O	O	O	O	.9
		9.4	All Other Non-Current	T	T	T	T	T	9.4
		100.0	Total						100.0
			LIABILITIES	A	A	A	A	A	
		9.4	Notes Payable-Short Term	V	V	V	V	V	9.4
		3.4	Cur. Mat.-L.T.D.	A	A	A	A	A	3.4
		10.5	Trade Payables	I	I	I	I	I	10.5
		.1	Income Taxes Payable	L	L	L	L	L	.1
		6.2	All Other Current	A	A	A	A	A	6.2
		29.5	Total Current	B	B	B	B	B	29.5
		17.3	Long-Term Debt	L	L	L	L	L	17.3
		.0	Deferred Taxes	E	E	E	E	E	.0
		10.6	All Other Non-Current						10.6
		42.5	Net Worth						42.5
		100.0	Total Liabilties & Net Worth						100.0
			INCOME DATA						
		100.0	Net Sales						100.0
		19.6	Gross Profit						19.6
		11.8	Operating Expenses						11.8
		7.8	Operating Profit						7.8
		1.0	All Other Expenses (net)						1.0
		6.8	Profit Before Taxes						6.8
			RATIOS						
		2.6							2.6
		1.7	Current						1.7
		1.4							1.4
		1.5							1.5
		.8	Quick						.8
		.5							.5
	25	14.7						25	14.7
	38	9.5	Sales/Receivables					38	9.5
	49	7.4						49	7.4
	25	14.6						25	14.6
	57	6.4	Cost of Sales/Inventory					57	6.4
	85	4.3						85	4.3
	19	19.6						19	19.6
	25	14.7	Cost of Sales/Payables					25	14.7
	28	13.1						28	13.1
		4.8							4.8
		8.8	Sales/Working Capital						8.8
		12.6							12.6
		5.5							5.5
	(17)	4.3	EBIT/Interest					(17)	4.3
		3.1							3.1
			Net Profit + Depr., Dep., Amort./Cur. Mat. L/T/D						
		.3							.3
		.5	Fixed/Worth						.5
		1.5							1.5
		.6							.6
		1.7	Debt/Worth						1.7
		2.2							2.2
		26.2	% Profit Before Taxes/Tangible Net Worth						26.2
	(17)	20.4						(17)	20.4
		6.0							6.0
		19.7	% Profit Before Taxes/Total Assets						19.7
		8.4							8.4
		3.6							3.6
		18.7							18.7
		9.1	Sales/Net Fixed Assets						9.1
		2.6							2.6
		2.2							2.2
		1.9	Sales/Total Assets						1.9
		1.7							1.7
		.8							.8
	(18)	1.2	% Depr., Dep., Amort./Sales					(18)	1.2
		3.8							3.8
			% Officers', Directors' Owners' Comp/Sales						
482822M	1711974M	2983145M	Net Sales ($)						2983145M
253174M	532421M	1385254M	Total Assets ($)						1385254M

© RMA 2024 M = $ thousand   MM = $ million
See Pages viii through xx for Explanation of Ratios and Data

MANUFACTURING—Other Aluminum Rolling, Drawing, and Extruding NAICS 331318

Current Data Sorted by Assets | Comparative Historical Data

						Type of Statement		
			4	2	1	Unqualified	13	6
			2	2		Reviewed	6	5
		1	1			Compiled	2	2
	1	1	1			Tax Returns	6	
	4 (4/1-9/30/23)	3	5	9	2	Other	6	
			30 (10/1/23-3/31/24)				31	19
0-500M	500M-2MM	2-10MM	10-50MM	50-100MM	100-250MM		4/1/19-3/31/20	4/1/20-3/31/21
	1	5	12	13	3	NUMBER OF STATEMENTS	ALL 58	ALL 32
%	%	%	%	%	%	ASSETS	%	%
			15.0	8.7		Cash & Equivalents	6.7	11.8
	DATA		13.8	16.1		Trade Receivables (net)	22.1	21.7
			17.4	25.6		Inventory	22.0	21.8
	NOT		.4	2.3		All Other Current	1.2	1.8
			46.6	52.7		Total Current	52.1	57.1
	AVAILABLE		39.7	37.8		Fixed Assets (net)	38.5	34.6
			3.8	2.7		Intangibles (net)	5.7	5.4
			9.9	6.7		All Other Non-Current	3.8	2.9
			100.0	100.0		Total	100.0	100.0
						LIABILITIES		
			4.3	10.2		Notes Payable-Short Term	7.1	5.8
			1.6	3.7		Cur. Mat.-L.T.D.	2.2	3.4
			10.9	7.9		Trade Payables	12.3	11.4
			.1	.1		Income Taxes Payable	.1	.3
			3.6	5.7		All Other Current	8.9	10.3
			20.5	27.7		Total Current	30.6	31.2
			8.9	24.2		Long-Term Debt	18.8	16.6
			.3	.8		Deferred Taxes	.1	1.3
			12.0	2.7		All Other Non-Current	5.0	3.3
			58.2	44.7		Net Worth	45.6	47.6
			100.0	100.0		Total Liabilities & Net Worth	100.0	100.0
						INCOME DATA		
			100.0	100.0		Net Sales	100.0	100.0
			20.5	13.9		Gross Profit	20.8	20.4
			14.6	8.0		Operating Expenses	14.7	14.6
			5.9	5.9		Operating Profit	6.1	5.8
			.3	1.4		All Other Expenses (net)	.8	.2
			5.6	4.5		Profit Before Taxes	5.3	5.5
						RATIOS		
			5.2	3.4			2.8	3.1
			2.5	1.9		Current	1.8	2.2
			1.2	1.2			1.2	1.5
			3.8	2.8			1.6	1.8
			1.5	.9		Quick	.9	1.4
			.6	.4			.6	.8
			28 12.9	27 13.5			30 12.3	31 11.7
			34 10.8	31 11.6		Sales/Receivables	37 9.8	39 9.4
			45 8.2	49 7.5			47 7.7	45 8.2
			31 11.9	26 14.1			25 14.7	26 14.2
			63 5.8	53 6.9		Cost of Sales/Inventory	43 8.5	45 8.1
			85 4.3	126 2.9			70 5.2	79 4.6
			17 21.6	14 25.6			16 23.4	20 18.6
			28 13.0	19 19.6		Cost of Sales/Payables	24 15.3	26 14.1
			41 9.0	23 15.6			33 11.1	35 10.4
			2.4	4.1			4.7	5.0
			7.3	6.4		Sales/Working Capital	11.3	7.8
			62.4	33.2			26.0	12.9
				4.5			11.0	34.4
			(12) 2.8			EBIT/Interest	(52) 6.5	(29) 14.3
				1.2			2.1	4.5
						Net Profit + Depr., Dep.,	8.8	10.5
						Amort./Cur. Mat. L/T/D	(18) 5.7	(14) 5.6
							4.1	2.5
			.2	.5			.4	.4
			.8	.7		Fixed/Worth	.9	.7
			1.5	1.6			1.8	1.3
			.1	.9			.6	.7
			.4	1.1		Debt/Worth	1.1	1.0
			1.8	3.7			3.1	2.3
			18.1	27.5		% Profit Before Taxes/Tangible	41.8	50.1
			(10) 7.0	(12) 10.6		Net Worth	(51) 21.0	(29) 22.3
			3.5	2.7			6.1	9.7
			16.1	14.9		% Profit Before Taxes/Total	16.7	21.2
			5.8	4.9		Assets	9.2	10.7
			.2	.6			2.6	3.6
			9.2	8.2			10.2	13.1
			3.7	4.3		Sales/Net Fixed Assets	5.3	5.0
			2.6	3.1			3.2	2.7
			2.0	2.0			2.8	2.8
			1.5	1.7		Sales/Total Assets	2.0	1.7
			1.2	1.3			1.3	1.3
			1.9	2.1			1.8	2.0
			(11) 3.2	(11) 2.4		% Depr., Dep., Amort./Sales	(53) 2.7	(27) 2.8
			3.5	3.0			3.8	4.4
						% Officers', Directors' Owners' Comp/Sales		
	3574M	82045M	564721M	1558237M	1172901M	Net Sales ($)	4567152M	2491860M
	1413M	29941M	352593M	926090M	462872M	Total Assets ($)	2766269M	1576707M

M = $ thousand   MM = $ million
See Pages viii through xx for Explanation of Ratios and Data

© RMA 2024

MANUFACTURING—Other Aluminum Rolling, Drawing, and Extruding NAICS 331318

Comparative Historical Data			Type of Statement	Current Data Sorted by Sales					
			Unqualified					2	5
4	7	7	Reviewed						4
2	5	4	Compiled			1		1	
	1	1	Tax Returns		1		2	2	
18	3	3	Other			1	2	2	16
4/1/21-3/31/22	19 4/1/22-3/31/23	19 4/1/23-3/31/24		4 (4/1-9/30/23)			30 (10/1/23-3/31/24)		
ALL	ALL	ALL		0-1MM	1-3MM	3-5MM	5-10MM	10-25MM	25MM & OVER
24	35	34	NUMBER OF STATEMENTS			1	2	6	25
%	%	%	ASSETS	%	%	%	%	%	%
9.5	14.0	12.3	Cash & Equivalents	D	D				10.8
24.2	23.6	20.1	Trade Receivables (net)	A	A				16.2
25.7	22.3	20.8	Inventory	T	T				21.6
1.0	2.7	1.9	All Other Current	A	A				2.0
60.4	62.6	55.0	Total Current						50.6
33.2	27.0	34.6	Fixed Assets (net)	N	N				40.4
3.3	4.3	4.0	Intangibles (net)	O	O				3.6
3.1	6.0	6.3	All Other Non-Current	T	T				5.4
100.0	100.0	100.0	Total						100.0
			LIABILITIES	A	A				
5.8	6.4	7.7	Notes Payable-Short Term	V	V				7.0
1.7	2.1	2.2	Cur. Mat.-L.T.D.	A	A				2.4
15.3	11.7	10.1	Trade Payables	I	I				9.9
.6	.3	.1	Income Taxes Payable	L	L				.1
11.4	6.2	5.7	All Other Current	A	A				5.8
34.9	26.7	25.7	Total Current	B	B				25.3
18.4	13.7	13.9	Long-Term Debt	L	L				16.4
.6	.3	.4	Deferred Taxes	E	E				.5
1.5	3.2	6.0	All Other Non-Current						5.8
44.6	56.2	53.9	Net Worth						52.1
100.0	100.0	100.0	Total Liabilties & Net Worth						100.0
			INCOME DATA						
100.0	100.0	100.0	Net Sales						100.0
21.7	23.1	20.0	Gross Profit						14.5
13.7	15.8	13.9	Operating Expenses						8.5
8.0	7.2	6.1	Operating Profit						6.0
-1.6	.1	.8	All Other Expenses (net)						.9
9.6	7.1	5.3	Profit Before Taxes						5.1
			RATIOS						
3.3	3.8	3.4							3.3
1.7	2.6	2.4	Current						2.3
1.2	1.6	1.5							1.2
1.8	2.8	2.7							2.4
.9	1.7	1.5	Quick						1.0
.6	.8	.5							.5
39 9.4	23 15.8	29 12.7						27	13.6
45 8.2	42 8.7	34 10.7	Sales/Receivables					31	11.6
58 6.3	51 7.2	47 7.7						43	8.5
43 8.4	27 13.6	23 16.2						21	17.0
59 6.2	51 7.1	51 7.1	Cost of Sales/Inventory					41	8.9
91 4.0	68 5.4	83 4.4						78	4.7
27 13.5	14 26.8	15 24.3						13	27.4
34 10.8	26 13.9	21 17.2	Cost of Sales/Payables					20	18.0
49 7.4	30 12.1	30 12.2						29	12.8
5.7	3.8	3.8							4.7
8.8	7.2	6.5	Sales/Working Capital						7.9
14.6	13.9	13.3							34.3
66.1	35.0	26.4							25.4
(23) 21.0	(30) 17.6	(29) 4.5	EBIT/Interest					(22)	4.4
8.7	2.7	1.6							1.5
			Net Profit + Depr., Dep., Amort./Cur. Mat. L/T/D						
.6	.2	.4							.5
.8	.6	.7	Fixed/Worth						.7
1.6	1.0	1.3							1.5
.4	.3	.4							.4
1.3	.8	1.0	Debt/Worth						1.0
3.7	1.6	1.6							1.7
84.6	49.6	25.9							28.8
(22) 32.9	(31) 30.1	(31) 14.6	% Profit Before Taxes/Tangible Net Worth					(23)	14.6
17.6	9.8	5.9							5.0
23.6	29.7	16.4							17.5
17.3	18.5	8.2	% Profit Before Taxes/Total Assets						6.9
8.9	3.7	2.1							.9
10.4	19.4	10.1							8.6
6.3	9.6	5.6	Sales/Net Fixed Assets						4.5
3.2	5.5	3.1							3.1
2.5	2.9	2.2							2.2
1.9	2.3	1.9	Sales/Total Assets						1.8
1.3	1.5	1.4							1.4
1.3	1.3	1.9							1.9
(23) 1.8	(30) 1.7	(29) 3.0	% Depr., Dep., Amort./Sales					(22)	2.3
3.6	2.8	3.3							3.2
			% Officers', Directors' Owners' Comp/Sales						
1534147M	2919917M	3381478M	Net Sales ($)			3574M	13620M	113239M	3251045M
848019M	1265072M	1772909M	Total Assets ($)			1413M	6639M	88282M	1676575M

M = $ thousand   MM = $ million
See Pages viii through xx for Explanation of Ratios and Data

© RMA 2024

MANUFACTURING—Nonferrous Metal Die-Casting Foundries NAICS 331523

Current Data Sorted by Assets

0-500M	500M-2MM	2-10MM	10-50MM	50-100MM	100-250MM
	1	2	1 3 1	1	
	8 (4/1-9/30/23)	3	13 (10/1/23-3/31/24)	4	1
		1			
	1	6	8	5	1
%	%	%	%	%	%

Type of Statement (Current period 13 statements; 4/1/23-3/31/24):
- Unqualified: 1
- Reviewed: 3
- Compiled: 2+1 (see columns)
- Tax Returns: 1
- Other: 13

DATA NOT AVAILABLE (for all asset-size columns except as noted)

Comparative Historical Data

Type of Statement	4/1/19-3/31/20 ALL	4/1/20-3/31/21 ALL
Unqualified	5	4
Reviewed	5	4
Compiled	2	1
Tax Returns	4	1
Other	13	10
NUMBER OF STATEMENTS	**29**	**20**

ASSETS	%	%
Cash & Equivalents	6.3	13.4
Trade Receivables (net)	20.8	19.2
Inventory	20.1	17.0
All Other Current	2.0	1.9
Total Current	49.2	51.5
Fixed Assets (net)	43.3	41.1
Intangibles (net)	2.4	2.3
All Other Non-Current	5.1	5.1
Total	100.0	100.0

LIABILITIES		
Notes Payable-Short Term	7.2	6.1
Cur. Mat.-L.T.D.	2.3	3.6
Trade Payables	11.6	10.5
Income Taxes Payable	.3	.0
All Other Current	5.8	6.0
Total Current	27.1	26.2
Long-Term Debt	15.1	21.1
Deferred Taxes	1.0	1.3
All Other Non-Current	5.8	9.5
Net Worth	51.0	41.9
Total Liabilties & Net Worth	100.0	100.0

INCOME DATA		
Net Sales	100.0	100.0
Gross Profit	20.6	24.4
Operating Expenses	13.9	21.1
Operating Profit	6.7	3.3
All Other Expenses (net)	1.2	.4
Profit Before Taxes	5.5	3.0

RATIOS				
Current		2.7		3.5
		1.9		2.1
		1.2		1.4
Quick		1.5		2.2
		.9		1.3
		.6		.7
Sales/Receivables	36	10.0	37	9.9
	47	7.8	51	7.1
	62	5.9	60	6.1
Cost of Sales/Inventory	35	10.5	17	21.2
	51	7.1	49	7.4
	79	4.6	85	4.3
Cost of Sales/Payables	17	21.4	14	27.0
	29	12.8	30	12.2
	42	8.6	38	9.7
Sales/Working Capital		4.0		3.1
		7.4		5.7
		26.9		12.3
EBIT/Interest		16.7		17.8
	(26)	5.0	(18)	4.1
		2.0		.5
Net Profit + Depr., Dep., Amort./Cur. Mat. L/T/D				
Fixed/Worth		.5		.5
		.9		.9
		1.6		1.7
Debt/Worth		.5		.6
		1.1		1.3
		1.9		2.8
% Profit Before Taxes/Tangible Net Worth		28.6		32.0
	(28)	15.4	(18)	9.3
		7.3		1.0
% Profit Before Taxes/Total Assets		14.7		17.3
		6.8		5.2
		2.2		-.6
Sales/Net Fixed Assets		5.0		5.0
		3.4		3.5
		2.5		2.0
Sales/Total Assets		1.9		1.8
		1.6		1.3
		1.1		1.0
% Depr., Dep., Amort./Sales		2.8		1.8
	(24)	4.1	(16)	4.6
		5.2		6.1
% Officers', Directors', Owners' Comp/Sales				

| | 2201M | 66096M | 327425M | 366403M | 101073M | Net Sales ($) | 1745545M | 828059M |
| | 1014M | 33391M | 183798M | 319449M | 109129M | Total Assets ($) | 1407933M | 836882M |

M = $ thousand   MM = $ million
© RMA 2024

MANUFACTURING—Nonferrous Metal Die-Casting Foundries NAICS 331523

Comparative Historical Data | Current Data Sorted by Sales

						Type of Statement									
	4		4		2	Unqualified							1		1
	3		4		5	Reviewed							3		2
	3		3		2	Compiled						1			1
	1		1			Tax Returns									
	14		14		12	Other			1		1		3		6
	4/1/21-3/31/22		4/1/22-3/31/23		4/1/23-3/31/24				8 (4/1-9/30/23)				13 (10/1/23-3/31/24)		
	ALL		ALL		ALL		0-1MM	1-3MM	3-5MM		5-10MM	10-25MM		25MM & OVER	
	25		26		21	NUMBER OF STATEMENTS		1		2	1	7		10	
	%		%		%	ASSETS	%	%	%		%	%		%	
	16.0		7.6		8.9	Cash & Equivalents								7.0	
	23.5		23.5		22.0	Trade Receivables (net)								19.5	
	16.9		19.2		15.3	Inventory								14.6	
	1.4		2.8		1.6	All Other Current								2.2	
	57.9		53.1		47.8	Total Current								43.3	
	36.0		35.5		32.4	Fixed Assets (net)		DATA NOT AVAILABLE						37.5	
	.5		1.4		7.3	Intangibles (net)								9.2	
	5.6		9.9		12.5	All Other Non-Current								9.9	
	100.0		100.0		100.0	Total								100.0	
						LIABILITIES									
	6.7		7.6		1.7	Notes Payable-Short Term								3.1	
	4.4		3.2		3.0	Cur. Mat.-L.T.D.								2.7	
	9.9		12.3		9.2	Trade Payables								8.8	
	.0		.0		.0	Income Taxes Payable								.0	
	8.1		8.8		12.0	All Other Current								7.6	
	29.1		32.0		25.9	Total Current								22.2	
	13.8		16.9		13.3	Long-Term Debt								13.4	
	1.3		.9		1.6	Deferred Taxes								1.4	
	8.0		5.4		12.4	All Other Non-Current								22.1	
	47.8		44.8		46.8	Net Worth								41.0	
	100.0		100.0		100.0	Total Liabilities & Net Worth								100.0	
						INCOME DATA									
	100.0		100.0		100.0	Net Sales								100.0	
	28.9		20.9		26.4	Gross Profit								20.7	
	22.5		14.9		22.2	Operating Expenses								13.1	
	6.5		6.1		4.2	Operating Profit								7.6	
	-1.8		-.5		1.7	All Other Expenses (net)								3.5	
	8.3		6.5		2.4	Profit Before Taxes								4.0	
						RATIOS									
	3.8		2.1		3.1									2.9	
	1.9		1.7		1.9	Current								1.9	
	1.4		1.1		1.6									1.6	
	2.3		1.5		1.6									1.6	
	1.4		.9		1.2	Quick								1.2	
	.8		.6		.8									.9	
41	9.0	42	8.7	40	9.1								39	9.4	
53	6.9	58	6.3	46	7.9	Sales/Receivables							45	8.2	
78	4.7	68	5.4	55	6.6								51	7.2	
19	19.0	31	11.8	31	11.6								32	11.4	
51	7.2	52	7.0	43	8.4	Cost of Sales/Inventory							43	8.5	
94	3.9	68	5.4	61	6.0								54	6.8	
19	19.7	19	19.0	15	24.1								10	36.3	
36	10.0	36	10.1	23	15.9	Cost of Sales/Payables							23	16.0	
51	7.2	49	7.5	40	9.2								37	9.9	
	3.3		5.0		4.3									4.4	
	5.1		7.0		8.1	Sales/Working Capital								8.6	
	11.3		32.5		13.4									13.3	
	17.6		32.4		23.3									80.6	
(21)	7.7	(24)	6.6	(20)	4.6	EBIT/Interest								5.8	
	1.9		1.4		-.4									.3	
					3.2	Net Profit + Depr., Dep.,									
			(10)		.8	Amort./Cur. Mat. L/T/D									
					-4.2										
	.4		.4		.5									.6	
	.9		.9		.6	Fixed/Worth								1.1	
	1.4		1.7		1.9									NM	
	.6		.7		.7									.8	
	1.3		1.2		1.2	Debt/Worth								1.4	
	2.2		3.2		3.2									NM	
	30.0		31.8		31.3	% Profit Before Taxes/Tangible									
(24)	13.8		22.3	(19)	8.5	Net Worth									
	2.3		3.5		-26.2										
	18.8		22.1		13.2	% Profit Before Taxes/Total								19.6	
	5.3		7.2		4.4	Assets								3.8	
	1.1		1.3		-8.2									-3.5	
	7.9		7.6		8.1									5.8	
	4.6		4.5		5.5	Sales/Net Fixed Assets								3.8	
	2.0		2.7		3.5									3.2	
	1.9		2.0		2.2									2.1	
	1.3		1.5		1.7	Sales/Total Assets								1.4	
	1.0		1.2		1.1									1.0	
	2.5		1.9		1.7										
(21)	4.1	(20)	2.8	(16)	2.9	% Depr., Dep., Amort./Sales									
	6.6		4.5		4.1										
						% Officers', Directors' Owners' Comp/Sales									
	891764M		1250533M		863198M	Net Sales ($)		2201M	7588M		8611M	133744M		711054M	
	736096M		927730M		646781M	Total Assets ($)		1014M	4302M		8178M	138712M		494575M	

M = $ thousand   MM = $ million
See Pages viii through xx for Explanation of Ratios and Data
© RMA 2024

MANUFACTURING—Iron and Steel Forging NAICS 332111

Current Data Sorted by Assets | Comparative Historical Data

						Type of Statement			
			1	2		Unqualified		4	2
		3	12	1		Reviewed		8	6
		3	1			Compiled		5	1
	3					Tax Returns		4	4
	1	7	12	6	2	Other		29	27
	10 (4/1-9/30/23)		44 (10/1/23-3/31/24)					4/1/19-3/31/20	4/1/20-3/31/21
0-500M	500M-2MM	2-10MM	10-50MM	50-100MM	100-250MM			ALL	ALL
	4	13	26	9	2	NUMBER OF STATEMENTS		50	40
%	%	%	%	%	%	ASSETS		%	%
		8.3	10.6			Cash & Equivalents		8.3	11.6
		23.3	22.6			Trade Receivables (net)		22.3	19.0
D		30.7	25.3			Inventory		23.9	23.4
A		1.5	4.5			All Other Current		1.1	2.3
T		63.8	62.9			Total Current		55.6	56.3
A		25.6	25.5			Fixed Assets (net)		33.6	32.0
		5.6	4.5			Intangibles (net)		5.1	6.9
N		5.0	7.1			All Other Non-Current		5.7	4.7
O		100.0	100.0			Total		100.0	100.0
T						LIABILITIES			
		6.9	4.1			Notes Payable-Short Term		5.2	8.1
A		3.0	1.9			Cur. Mat.-L.T.D.		4.0	3.1
V		12.5	9.5			Trade Payables		11.2	9.5
A		.0	.2			Income Taxes Payable		.5	.0
I		4.0	9.9			All Other Current		7.2	7.6
L		26.4	25.6			Total Current		28.0	28.3
A		23.2	9.1			Long-Term Debt		15.3	24.5
B		.9	.1			Deferred Taxes		.6	.5
L		7.6	2.2			All Other Non-Current		7.1	2.9
E		41.9	63.0			Net Worth		49.0	43.8
		100.0	100.0			Total Liabilities & Net Worth		100.0	100.0
						INCOME DATA			
		100.0	100.0			Net Sales		100.0	100.0
		25.0	23.1			Gross Profit		25.2	23.4
		19.5	14.6			Operating Expenses		18.1	19.8
		5.6	8.6			Operating Profit		7.1	3.5
		.9	-.1			All Other Expenses (net)		.5	-.9
		4.7	8.7			Profit Before Taxes		6.6	4.5
						RATIOS			
		4.3	4.9					3.1	3.9
		2.9	2.3			Current		2.0	2.3
		2.0	1.4					1.3	1.3
		2.5	2.6					1.9	2.2
		1.5	1.3			Quick		1.0	1.4
		1.0	.6					.7	.5
	36	10.1	35 10.4				32	11.4	29 12.5
	49	7.4	49 7.4			Sales/Receivables	47	7.8	41 8.8
	55	6.6	73 5.0				64	5.7	55 6.6
	43	8.5	34 10.7				37	9.8	41 8.8
	81	4.5	65 5.6			Cost of Sales/Inventory	62	5.9	64 5.7
	122	3.0	146 2.5				99	3.7	104 3.5
	22	16.3	15 24.7				17	20.9	10 38.2
	27	13.4	28 13.2			Cost of Sales/Payables	29	12.4	22 16.6
	38	9.5	37 9.8				42	8.7	35 10.3
		3.7	2.8					3.9	3.0
		4.2	3.9			Sales/Working Capital		6.4	6.8
		10.9	8.4					17.5	18.3
		22.9	25.7					19.3	16.0
		4.3	(23) 13.3			EBIT/Interest	(46)	7.0	(36) 3.6
		2.5	5.0					2.0	-1.7
						Net Profit + Depr., Dep.,		13.0	
						Amort./Cur. Mat. L/T/D	(19)	4.0	
								1.1	
		.5	.2					.4	.4
		.6	.5			Fixed/Worth		.7	.8
		NM	.7					1.5	3.2
		.6	.3					.6	.6
		1.3	.5			Debt/Worth		1.0	1.2
		NM	1.5					2.4	5.6
		29.1	43.5					32.0	46.4
	(10)	11.2	19.2			% Profit Before Taxes/Tangible Net Worth	(45)	16.7	(34) 11.9
		7.6	7.4					7.9	-7.0
		15.9	24.5					17.0	18.6
		5.9	14.8			% Profit Before Taxes/Total Assets		7.4	5.4
		3.1	3.6					3.0	-4.2
		13.6	12.6					10.9	10.5
		5.4	5.5			Sales/Net Fixed Assets		4.5	4.6
		4.6	3.6					2.7	2.8
		2.2	2.2					2.0	2.4
		1.7	1.5			Sales/Total Assets		1.5	1.4
		1.4	1.1					1.3	1.0
		1.2	1.7					2.2	1.9
	(11)	2.6	(21) 2.8			% Depr., Dep., Amort./Sales	(46)	3.6	(36) 6.0
		4.2	3.9					5.4	7.7
						% Officers', Directors' Owners' Comp/Sales	(14)	2.2	
								2.9	
								4.6	
	14817M	123947M	734896M	1261506M	250117M	Net Sales ($)		2315228M	1614114M
	4020M	68161M	507619M	650070M	203435M	Total Assets ($)		1607886M	1363231M

M = $ thousand   MM = $ million
See Pages viii through xx for Explanation of Ratios and Data

© RMA 2024

MANUFACTURING—Iron and Steel Forging NAICS 332111

Comparative Historical Data & Current Data Sorted by Sales

Comparative Historical Data			Type of Statement	Current Data Sorted by Sales					
3	5	3	Unqualified					1	2
7	11	16	Reviewed				1	5	10
3	4	4	Compiled			1	2		1
3	4	3	Tax Returns		1	1	1	2	
19	20	28	Other	1		2	2	8	15
4/1/21-3/31/22 ALL	4/1/22-3/31/23 ALL	4/1/23-3/31/24 ALL		0-1MM	10 (4/1-9/30/23) 1-3MM	3-5MM	44 (10/1/23-3/31/24) 5-10MM	10-25MM	25MM & OVER
35	44	54	NUMBER OF STATEMENTS	1	1	4	6	14	28
%	%	%	ASSETS	%	%	%	%	%	%
10.2	10.9	11.6	Cash & Equivalents					10.3	10.0
24.2	23.2	21.9	Trade Receivables (net)					19.8	25.6
25.4	24.0	23.0	Inventory					24.9	22.2
2.2	3.7	2.9	All Other Current					1.9	4.1
62.1	61.8	59.5	Total Current					56.9	62.0
27.4	30.2	29.9	Fixed Assets (net)					27.4	29.8
7.1	3.8	4.1	Intangibles (net)					6.5	2.0
3.5	4.2	6.5	All Other Non-Current					9.2	6.3
100.0	100.0	100.0	Total					100.0	100.0
			LIABILITIES						
7.8	8.5	4.4	Notes Payable-Short Term					3.1	4.3
1.9	1.7	2.0	Cur. Mat.-L.T.D.					2.0	2.0
14.0	12.1	12.0	Trade Payables					6.7	14.6
.0	.0	.1	Income Taxes Payable					.0	.2
15.9	9.6	9.3	All Other Current					12.4	7.1
39.5	32.0	27.9	Total Current					24.2	28.3
13.6	10.7	13.2	Long-Term Debt					11.6	10.6
.1	.2	.3	Deferred Taxes					.7	.1
16.7	2.8	4.8	All Other Non-Current					3.3	4.2
30.0	54.3	53.8	Net Worth					60.2	56.9
100.0	100.0	100.0	Total Liabilities & Net Worth					100.0	100.0
			INCOME DATA						
100.0	100.0	100.0	Net Sales					100.0	100.0
25.1	24.4	25.1	Gross Profit					24.4	20.0
21.5	16.5	17.2	Operating Expenses					16.7	12.6
3.6	7.9	7.9	Operating Profit					7.7	7.4
-2.4	-.1	.3	All Other Expenses (net)					.2	.2
6.0	8.0	7.6	Profit Before Taxes					7.4	7.2
			RATIOS						
4.1	5.0	4.0	Current					5.1	3.8
1.8	1.8	2.3						2.5	2.2
1.2	1.2	1.4						1.4	1.6
2.7	2.5	2.2	Quick					2.8	2.1
1.1	1.1	1.4						1.4	1.3
.5	.6	.8						.6	.9
38 9.5	31 11.7	34 10.8	Sales/Receivables					38 9.5	38 9.7
51 7.2	49 7.4	46 7.9						49 7.5	46 7.9
78 4.7	64 5.7	59 6.2						61 6.0	69 5.3
32 11.4	32 11.5	31 11.9	Cost of Sales/Inventory					38 9.6	33 11.0
70 5.2	62 5.9	58 6.3						85 4.3	46 7.9
111 3.3	94 3.9	122 3.0						146 2.5	99 3.7
16 23.2	11 32.2	18 20.3	Cost of Sales/Payables					9 39.3	23 16.1
30 12.2	23 16.0	28 13.2						25 14.4	34 10.8
59 6.2	38 9.7	38 9.6						29 12.7	43 8.5
3.6	3.3	3.4	Sales/Working Capital					3.0	3.1
5.5	6.6	5.6						4.1	5.4
18.9	20.5	9.8						9.8	7.8
45.5	25.9	30.0	EBIT/Interest					33.3	23.0
(31) 13.4	(36) 11.3	(49) 9.6					(12) 8.8	(26) 10.4
3.3	4.7	3.8						3.8	4.1
		10.1	Net Profit + Depr., Dep., Amort./Cur. Mat. L/T/D						
	(11)	6.0							
		1.7							
.3	.3	.4	Fixed/Worth					.3	.4
.5	.5	.6						.6	.5
1.2	1.0	1.0						.8	.8
.5	.4	.4	Debt/Worth					.3	.4
1.2	.7	.7						.7	.5
4.8	1.5	2.2						2.0	1.9
66.2	36.9	39.4	% Profit Before Taxes/Tangible Net Worth					52.1	36.1
(29) 29.2	(41) 25.7	(49) 18.9						15.6	(27) 19.1
8.7	9.9	7.7						8.9	6.6
22.4	22.8	20.9	% Profit Before Taxes/Total Assets					15.7	23.9
11.6	10.6	12.4						10.0	12.4
4.6	3.6	3.6						5.5	2.8
17.7	15.5	9.8	Sales/Net Fixed Assets					8.1	11.6
7.0	6.5	5.3						4.8	5.7
3.7	3.3	3.9						3.8	3.6
2.1	2.4	2.4	Sales/Total Assets					1.7	2.6
1.6	1.9	1.6						1.3	1.6
1.1	1.1	1.2						.8	1.4
2.5	1.4	1.7	% Depr., Dep., Amort./Sales					2.0	1.7
(30) 3.9	(37) 2.2	(46) 2.7						(13) 2.9	(24) 3.0
6.4	4.4	4.3						4.8	4.5
	1.0	2.2	% Officers', Directors' Owners' Comp/Sales						
(11)	3.2 (12)	3.1							
	4.9	4.4							
1179678M	2034051M	2385283M	Net Sales ($)	653M	2479M	16943M	51313M	235521M	2078374M
849553M	1246182M	1433305M	Total Assets ($)	585M	682M	11981M	25100M	196887M	1198070M

M = $ thousand   MM = $ million
See Pages viii through xx for Explanation of Ratios and Data

© RMA 2024

MANUFACTURING—Metal Crown, Closure, and Other Metal Stamping (except Automotive) NAICS 332119

Current Data Sorted by Assets | Comparative Historical Data

						Type of Statement		
			2	3	2	Unqualified	9	2
		3	12	2		Reviewed	25	12
		6	2	2		Compiled	13	11
		5	1			Tax Returns	5	1
1	2	21	12	9	3	Other	67	40
	16 (4/1-9/30/23)		72 (10/1/23-3/31/24)				4/1/19-3/31/20	4/1/20-3/31/21
0-500M	500M-2MM	2-10MM	10-50MM	50-100MM	100-250MM		ALL	ALL
1	2	35	29	16	5	NUMBER OF STATEMENTS	119	66
%	%	%	%	%	%	ASSETS	%	%
		15.0	12.3	7.6		Cash & Equivalents	9.3	15.1
		23.2	20.7	15.7		Trade Receivables (net)	23.9	21.8
		25.0	24.2	19.0		Inventory	24.6	21.1
		1.4	1.1	.9		All Other Current	1.9	.9
		64.5	58.3	43.2		Total Current	59.7	58.9
		29.0	30.9	37.6		Fixed Assets (net)	32.1	30.7
		2.5	1.3	5.2		Intangibles (net)	1.7	4.6
		4.0	9.4	14.1		All Other Non-Current	6.5	5.8
		100.0	100.0	100.0		Total	100.0	100.0
						LIABILITIES		
		5.0	2.1	3.8		Notes Payable-Short Term	8.7	5.8
		2.5	2.7	3.6		Cur. Mat.-L.T.D.	3.1	3.3
		15.6	7.9	7.3		Trade Payables	13.9	10.6
		.2	.2	.0		Income Taxes Payable	.1	.1
		6.7	8.5	6.8		All Other Current	6.6	7.5
		30.0	21.4	21.5		Total Current	32.5	27.4
		15.3	9.3	19.7		Long-Term Debt	16.4	16.3
		.4	.4	1.2		Deferred Taxes	.4	.4
		8.2	6.1	9.0		All Other Non-Current	3.4	3.6
		46.0	62.8	48.6		Net Worth	47.4	52.4
		100.0	100.0	100.0		Total Liabilities & Net Worth	100.0	100.0
						INCOME DATA		
		100.0	100.0	100.0		Net Sales	100.0	100.0
		25.4	25.5	20.4		Gross Profit	21.9	22.5
		19.5	16.7	14.5		Operating Expenses	16.8	20.4
		5.9	8.8	5.8		Operating Profit	5.1	2.2
		.1	-.4	1.3		All Other Expenses (net)	.8	-1.0
		5.9	9.2	4.5		Profit Before Taxes	4.3	3.2
						RATIOS		
		5.8	4.9	3.9			3.6	3.6
		3.5	2.9	2.4		Current	1.9	2.4
		1.6	1.8	1.4			1.3	1.5
		4.2	3.4	2.8			1.9	2.3
		1.8	1.8	.9		Quick	1.0	1.5
		.9	.9	.5			.6	.9
		23 16.0	39 9.3	27 13.7			31 11.6	35 10.4
		40 9.1	47 7.7	49 7.5		Sales/Receivables	47 7.8	46 8.0
		49 7.4	68 5.4	60 6.1			62 5.9	63 5.8
		24 15.4	52 7.0	49 7.4			34 10.6	42 8.6
		57 6.4	76 4.8	61 6.0		Cost of Sales/Inventory	54 6.7	64 5.7
		89 4.1	107 3.4	78 4.7			87 4.2	83 4.4
		10 36.3	16 23.3	21 17.1			16 22.5	17 21.3
		25 14.8	23 15.8	26 13.8		Cost of Sales/Payables	27 13.6	27 13.7
		44 8.3	34 10.7	37 9.8			45 8.2	42 8.7
		2.9	2.7	2.9			4.1	3.6
		4.3	4.0	6.3		Sales/Working Capital	6.9	5.4
		11.4	9.9	11.5			15.9	11.3
		39.8	28.8	26.2			19.4	14.4
		(32) 10.9	(23) 13.8	(15) 8.1		EBIT/Interest	(111) 6.0	(61) 4.5
		3.1	2.2	.5			1.2	.6
						Net Profit + Depr., Dep.,	6.4	3.2
						Amort./Cur. Mat. L/T/D	(33) 3.3 (11) 1.6	
							1.1	.7
		.2	.3	.5			.4	.3
		.4	.5	.9		Fixed/Worth	.7	.6
		1.3	.9	1.9			1.3	1.3
		.3	.2	.5			.5	.4
		.7	.5	1.6		Debt/Worth	1.0	1.0
		2.5	1.1	3.3			2.6	2.3
		40.6	24.8	32.7		% Profit Before Taxes/Tangible	33.0	26.5
		(31) 24.3	17.8	15.9		Net Worth	(112) 14.5	(62) 11.0
		6.4	3.8	-.8			1.4	1.5
		20.3	18.8	13.4		% Profit Before Taxes/Total	15.0	13.2
		11.9	10.1	8.7		Assets	6.6	4.9
		3.6	1.7	.2			.3	-.1
		24.1	9.2	4.9			9.6	11.3
		7.5	4.2	3.7		Sales/Net Fixed Assets	5.8	5.5
		3.5	3.2	2.2			3.9	3.1
		2.9	1.9	1.8			2.4	2.0
		2.0	1.5	1.1		Sales/Total Assets	1.8	1.6
		1.4	1.2	1.0			1.5	1.3
		1.0	1.4	1.9			1.9	1.8
		(24) 1.9	(26) 2.9	(15) 3.8		% Depr., Dep., Amort./Sales	(111) 2.9	(56) 3.1
		3.0	4.3	5.7			4.3	5.0
		2.6				% Officers', Directors'	1.0	1.3
		(16) 3.6				Owners' Comp/Sales	(32) 2.1	(21) 2.9
		7.5					3.9	4.6
301M	4810M	435006M	1101253M	1381983M	1153647M	Net Sales ($)	4663407M	1965132M
369M	2724M	207291M	714292M	1102385M	737230M	Total Assets ($)	2863996M	1395568M

© RMA 2024   M = $ thousand   MM = $ million
See Pages viii through xx for Explanation of Ratios and Data

MANUFACTURING—Metal Crown, Closure, and Other Metal Stamping (except Automotive) NAICS 332119

Comparative Historical Data | Current Data Sorted by Sales

							Type of Statement						
	3		8		7		Unqualified						7
	14		12		17		Reviewed				1	6	10
	10		9		10		Compiled		1	1	1	5	3
	3		11		6		Tax Returns			1	3	2	5
	30		29		48		Other	1	1	3	8	17	18
	4/1/21-3/31/22 ALL		4/1/22-3/31/23 ALL		4/1/23-3/31/24 ALL					16 (4/1-9/30/23)		72 (10/1/23-3/31/24)	
								0-1MM	1-3MM	3-5MM	5-10MM	10-25MM	25MM & OVER
	60		69		88		NUMBER OF STATEMENTS	1	1	5	13	30	38
	%		%		%		ASSETS	%	%	%	%	%	%
	10.2		10.8		13.2		Cash & Equivalents				14.0	15.2	8.2
	26.2		22.4		20.7		Trade Receivables (net)				21.8	23.6	18.8
	27.5		26.3		23.2		Inventory				23.3	24.8	23.3
	1.3		1.5		1.1		All Other Current				.9	1.6	1.1
	65.2		61.0		58.3		Total Current				59.9	65.3	51.3
	27.9		26.0		31.1		Fixed Assets (net)				36.5	26.1	33.4
	3.1		3.6		3.0		Intangibles (net)				1.2	2.5	4.5
	3.8		9.4		7.6		All Other Non-Current				2.3	6.2	10.7
	100.0		100.0		100.0		Total				100.0	100.0	100.0
							LIABILITIES						
	5.5		7.7		5.3		Notes Payable-Short Term				.8	5.5	4.6
	2.6		4.2		2.8		Cur. Mat.-L.T.D.				3.1	2.1	3.4
	15.2		12.0		10.8		Trade Payables				11.5	15.0	8.7
	.2		.4		.1		Income Taxes Payable				.0	.2	.2
	8.4		6.1		7.7		All Other Current				3.0	9.2	8.4
	32.0		30.4		26.7		Total Current				18.4	32.0	25.2
	19.9		15.7		14.1		Long-Term Debt				18.0	10.1	14.3
	.3		.5		.5		Deferred Taxes				.4	.5	.7
	5.2		5.5		7.0		All Other Non-Current				18.7	2.7	7.7
	42.6		47.9		51.7		Net Worth				44.5	54.7	52.1
	100.0		100.0		100.0		Total Liabilities & Net Worth				100.0	100.0	100.0
							INCOME DATA						
	100.0		100.0		100.0		Net Sales				100.0	100.0	100.0
	24.9		24.4		24.4		Gross Profit				31.2	24.8	20.6
	17.7		16.9		17.9		Operating Expenses				21.9	19.0	13.5
	7.2		7.5		6.5		Operating Profit				9.3	5.8	7.1
	-2.9		-.4		.2		All Other Expenses (net)				1.5	-.7	.7
	10.0		8.0		6.3		Profit Before Taxes				7.8	6.5	6.3
							RATIOS						
	3.5		4.1		4.8						6.6	5.9	4.0
	2.1		2.3		2.7		Current				4.6	2.7	2.2
	1.5		1.5		1.4						2.4	1.3	1.3
	2.0		2.6		3.2						4.4	3.2	2.3
	1.1		1.3		1.5		Quick				3.6	1.7	.9
	.8		.7		.8						1.0	.8	.6
41	8.8	33	11.1	33	11.0			26	13.8	26	13.8	36	10.0
51	7.2	43	8.4	45	8.1	Sales/Receivables	40	9.1	47	7.8	46	8.0
66	5.5	56	6.5	54	6.7		70	5.2	57	6.4	54	6.7
45	8.2	39	9.3	40	9.1		38	9.6	25	14.6	47	7.7
74	4.9	63	5.8	66	5.5	Cost of Sales/Inventory	57	6.4	74	4.9	68	5.4
104	3.5	99	3.7	99	3.7		87	4.2	111	3.3	96	3.8
21	17.1	18	20.3	15	24.9		13	27.3	12	29.9	19	19.4
34	10.6	25	14.7	25	14.4	Cost of Sales/Payables	25	14.8	24	15.3	26	14.0
54	6.7	40	9.1	36	10.0		57	6.4	41	9.0	36	10.2
	3.8		3.8		3.0						2.3	3.2	3.3
	6.1		6.0		5.1	Sales/Working Capital				3.2	4.7	6.6
	9.5		11.3		10.9						9.1	17.5	11.5
	68.3		38.3		25.9						47.5	34.2	17.9
(58)	17.9	(67)	12.2	(76)	9.3	EBIT/Interest			(10)	6.2	(27) 14.8	(35) 8.1
	6.9		3.8		2.0						-10.7	3.6	1.7
	22.8		7.4		8.2	Net Profit + Depr., Dep.,						12.1
(14)	7.1	(19)	2.8	(25)	2.9	Amort./Cur. Mat. L/T/D					(16)	2.9
	3.8		1.3		1.8								1.8
	.3		.3		.3						.3	.1	.4
	.6		.6		.6	Fixed/Worth				.6	.4	.8
	1.4		1.0		1.2						2.6	1.0	1.2
	.5		.4		.3						.3	.2	.4
	1.1		1.2		.9	Debt/Worth				.8	.5	1.1
	3.1		2.5		2.0						4.3	1.6	2.4
	64.2		57.4		33.1	% Profit Before Taxes/Tangible				59.6	26.3	32.2
(55)	36.2	(63)	24.8	(83)	18.6	Net Worth			(12)	27.1	(27) 18.6	(37) 20.9
	22.8		15.2		6.1						-25.5	8.1	8.2
	29.2		20.7		17.3						24.1	18.2	16.1
	16.1		12.2		10.0	% Profit Before Taxes/Total Assets				11.9	10.3	8.9
	7.6		3.4		2.5						-9.2	5.9	2.4
	15.5		17.4		12.1						19.9	21.0	8.6
	6.7		8.1		5.1	Sales/Net Fixed Assets				3.4	7.4	4.6
	3.9		4.4		3.2						1.7	3.9	2.9
	2.3		2.4		2.1						2.2	3.0	1.9
	1.7		1.9		1.6	Sales/Total Assets				1.7	1.9	1.6
	1.4		1.4		1.2						1.0	1.2	1.1
	1.4		1.0		1.3							1.4	1.9
(53)	2.6	(59)	2.1	(70)	2.4	% Depr., Dep., Amort./Sales					(24) 2.4	(34) 2.7
	3.7		3.4		4.3							3.9	4.8
	1.0		1.3		1.7								2.7
(20)	3.0	(27)	2.5	(23)	3.2	% Officers', Directors' Owners' Comp/Sales					(11) 3.7	
	5.2		4.8		7.5							7.5	
	2538940M		2606165M		4077000M	Net Sales ($)	301M	1517M	20910M	100976M	518249M	3435047M
	1447746M		1452857M		2764291M	Total Assets ($)	369M	1556M	17039M	73358M	309457M	2362512M

© RMA 2024 M = $ thousand MM = $ million
See Pages viii through xx for Explanation of Ratios and Data

MANUFACTURING—Saw Blade and Handtool Manufacturing NAICS 332216

Current Data Sorted by Assets | | | | | **Comparative Historical Data**

						Type of Statement		
		2	4	1	1	Unqualified	9	3
	1					Reviewed	8	7
	1	2				Compiled	7	4
	1	5	7	1	1	Tax Returns	6	1
	5 (4/1-9/30/23)		22 (10/1/23-3/31/24)			Other	19	11
0-500M	500M-2MM	2-10MM	10-50MM	50-100MM	100-250MM		4/1/19-3/31/20	4/1/20-3/31/21
							ALL	ALL
	3	9	11	2	2	NUMBER OF STATEMENTS	49	26
%	%	%	%	%	%	ASSETS	%	%
			2.9			Cash & Equivalents	8.4	11.3
D			16.3			Trade Receivables (net)	18.2	18.6
A			36.9			Inventory	35.1	31.3
T			1.4			All Other Current	2.1	.9
A			57.4			Total Current	63.8	62.1
			27.8			Fixed Assets (net)	24.9	27.5
N			2.1			Intangibles (net)	6.1	4.2
O			12.7			All Other Non-Current	5.1	6.3
T			100.0			Total	100.0	100.0
						LIABILITIES		
A			14.0			Notes Payable-Short Term	6.3	5.0
V			3.5			Cur. Mat.-L.T.D.	2.3	2.6
A			13.4			Trade Payables	9.2	8.5
I			.1			Income Taxes Payable	.0	.1
L			7.5			All Other Current	6.9	8.3
A			38.4			Total Current	24.8	24.5
B			14.1			Long-Term Debt	13.9	21.5
L			.5			Deferred Taxes	.4	.0
E			12.7			All Other Non-Current	4.7	13.0
			34.3			Net Worth	56.3	41.0
			100.0			Total Liabilities & Net Worth	100.0	100.0
						INCOME DATA		
			100.0			Net Sales	100.0	100.0
			26.4			Gross Profit	32.7	28.5
			22.0			Operating Expenses	26.3	23.5
			4.4			Operating Profit	6.4	4.9
			1.6			All Other Expenses (net)	.7	-2.3
			2.8			Profit Before Taxes	5.6	7.3
						RATIOS		
			2.6				4.8	4.3
			2.2			Current	3.0	3.0
			1.1				1.7	1.6
			1.0				2.0	2.4
			.6			Quick	1.1	1.4
			.3				.7	.8
		35	10.4				33 11.2	33 10.9
		39	9.4			Sales/Receivables	39 9.4	41 9.0
		46	8.0				47 7.8	53 6.9
		68	5.4				72 5.1	60 6.1
		135	2.7			Cost of Sales/Inventory	107 3.4	85 4.3
		174	2.1				166 2.2	159 2.3
		23	16.1				14 25.7	18 20.0
		28	13.2			Cost of Sales/Payables	23 15.8	24 15.5
		66	5.5				37 9.8	32 11.3
			3.9				3.0	2.7
			6.4			Sales/Working Capital	4.3	3.5
			16.4				8.1	8.6
			8.0				23.2	27.0
			3.4			EBIT/Interest	(45) 6.6	(24) 11.2
			.3				2.2	1.6
								11.0
						Net Profit + Depr., Dep., Amort./Cur. Mat. L/T/D	(11) 7.7	
								1.0
			.3				.3	.3
			.7			Fixed/Worth	.4	.5
			1.8				.8	3.7
			.6				.3	.4
			2.0			Debt/Worth	.6	1.0
			8.6				1.6	10.4
						% Profit Before Taxes/Tangible Net Worth	28.6	35.2
							(45) 16.9	(22) 20.6
							5.6	9.2
			9.9				17.3	20.2
			2.0			% Profit Before Taxes/Total Assets	8.0	8.8
			-1.8				2.5	2.2
			18.4				12.0	10.6
			9.7			Sales/Net Fixed Assets	7.8	5.9
			2.5				4.3	4.1
			1.7				2.0	1.9
			1.4			Sales/Total Assets	1.6	1.5
			1.3				1.3	1.2
			.9				2.0	2.6
			1.9			% Depr., Dep., Amort./Sales	(45) 3.1	(23) 3.8
			3.5				4.4	4.6
						% Officers', Directors' Owners' Comp/Sales	1.9	
							(11) 3.5	
							4.5	
	4593M	98402M	260051M	178231M	524110M	Net Sales ($)	1693535M	875685M
	2885M	52953M	184189M	118979M	272866M	Total Assets ($)	1254563M	696699M

© RMA 2024   M = $ thousand   MM = $ million
See Pages viii through xx for Explanation of Ratios and Data

MANUFACTURING—Saw Blade and Handtool Manufacturing NAICS 332216

Comparative Historical Data

						Type of Statement
						Unqualified
	1		2			Reviewed
	7		9		8	Compiled
	1		1		1	Tax Returns
	2		1		3	Other
	16		19		15	
	4/1/21-3/31/22		4/1/22-3/23		4/1/23-3/31/24	
	ALL		ALL		ALL	
	27		32		27	NUMBER OF STATEMENTS
	%		%		%	**ASSETS**
	12.7		12.6		11.1	Cash & Equivalents
	18.9		19.7		16.5	Trade Receivables (net)
	31.0		33.7		32.7	Inventory
	2.5		3.6		1.3	All Other Current
	65.1		69.6		61.6	Total Current
	21.1		18.3		24.2	Fixed Assets (net)
	6.5		5.7		5.9	Intangibles (net)
	7.3		6.5		8.3	All Other Non-Current
	100.0		100.0		100.0	Total
						LIABILITIES
	4.7		5.5		6.9	Notes Payable-Short Term
	2.1		1.7		2.8	Cur. Mat.-L.T.D.
	10.4		7.8		9.9	Trade Payables
	.0		.1		.0	Income Taxes Payable
	8.5		12.0		8.4	All Other Current
	25.6		27.0		28.0	Total Current
	14.2		13.4		24.5	Long-Term Debt
	.2		.2		.3	Deferred Taxes
	8.1		7.6		8.9	All Other Non-Current
	51.9		51.8		38.3	Net Worth
	100.0		100.0		100.0	Total Liabilities & Net Worth
						INCOME DATA
	100.0		100.0		100.0	Net Sales
	34.2		30.3		34.2	Gross Profit
	26.7		24.9		28.5	Operating Expenses
	7.6		5.4		5.7	Operating Profit
	-3.2		.2		1.4	All Other Expenses (net)
	10.7		5.2		4.4	Profit Before Taxes
						RATIOS
	4.9		5.0		3.9	Current
	2.8		3.2		2.7	
	2.2		1.8		1.4	
	2.2		2.5		1.8	Quick
	1.3		1.2		1.0	
	.9		.6		.6	
33	11.1	33	11.2	28	12.9	Sales/Receivables
38	9.5	40	9.1	38	9.6	
51	7.2	54	6.8	43	8.5	
68	5.4	64	5.7	62	5.9	Cost of Sales/Inventory
107	3.4	122	3.0	96	3.8	
159	2.3	174	2.1	182	2.0	
17	21.4	13	27.7	15	24.3	Cost of Sales/Payables
26	14.0	20	18.2	26	13.8	
45	8.1	36	10.2	43	8.5	
	3.0		2.6		3.0	Sales/Working Capital
	3.7		3.5		4.5	
	6.8		6.8		10.9	
	74.9		21.4		8.0	EBIT/Interest
(25)	33.6	(27)	10.1	(23)	3.4	
	7.7		1.9		1.1	
			15.2			Net Profit + Depr., Dep., Amort./Cur. Mat. L/T/D
		(11)	4.2			
			1.0			
	.2		.1		.3	Fixed/Worth
	.5		.4		.6	
	.9		.7		1.8	
	.3		.3		.5	Debt/Worth
	1.0		.9		1.6	
	4.0		2.8		11.4	
	46.8		48.6		48.5	% Profit Before Taxes/Tangible Net Worth
(22)	21.5	(29)	20.4	(23)	14.8	
	14.4		5.8		3.0	
	24.7		16.7		14.2	% Profit Before Taxes/Total Assets
	14.9		10.0		4.9	
	10.3		2.1		.2	
	24.0		33.6		19.7	Sales/Net Fixed Assets
	7.4		9.1		9.7	
	4.9		4.8		3.4	
	1.9		1.9		2.0	Sales/Total Assets
	1.7		1.5		1.5	
	1.4		1.4		1.3	
	1.9		1.6		.9	% Depr., Dep., Amort./Sales
(23)	2.9	(27)	2.9	(24)	2.0	
	4.0		4.0		4.2	
						% Officers', Directors' Owners' Comp/Sales
	653711M		977225M		1065387M	Net Sales ($)
	441473M		719993M		631872M	Total Assets ($)

Current Data Sorted by Sales

			1		2	5
	1	1	3	1	7	4
	1	5 (4/1-9/30/23)		22 (10/1/23-3/31/24)		
0-1MM	1-3MM	3-5MM	5-10MM	10-25MM	25MM & OVER	
1		1	4	10	9	
%	%	%	%	%	%	
				4.5		Cash & Equivalents
				16.4		Trade Receivables (net)
				33.8		Inventory
				.8		All Other Current
				55.6		Total Current
				31.4		Fixed Assets (net)
				6.9		Intangibles (net)
				6.1		All Other Non-Current
				100.0		Total
				5.3		Notes Payable-Short Term
				4.6		Cur. Mat.-L.T.D.
				10.5		Trade Payables
				.1		Income Taxes Payable
				4.4		All Other Current
				24.9		Total Current
				26.4		Long-Term Debt
				.8		Deferred Taxes
				9.6		All Other Non-Current
				38.4		Net Worth
				100.0		Total Liab. & Net Worth
				100.0		Net Sales
				33.9		Gross Profit
				26.7		Operating Expenses
				7.2		Operating Profit
				1.3		All Other Expenses (net)
				5.9		Profit Before Taxes
				4.0		Current
				2.6		
				2.1		
				1.6		Quick
				.9		
				.5		
				31	11.7	Sales/Receivables
				42	8.7	
				50	7.3	
				64	5.7	Cost of Sales/Inventory
				89	4.1	
				215	1.7	
				16	23.2	Cost of Sales/Payables
				31	11.6	
				45	8.2	
				3.0		Sales/Working Capital
				5.2		
				10.0		
						EBIT/Interest
				.5		Fixed/Worth
				.9		
				NM		
				.6		Debt/Worth
				1.6		
				NM		
						% Profit Before Taxes/Tangible Net Worth
				19.6		% Profit Before Taxes/Total Assets
				8.3		
				.8		
				16.6		Sales/Net Fixed Assets
				8.7		
				2.3		
				2.1		Sales/Total Assets
				1.5		
				1.3		
				1.5		% Depr., Dep., Amort./Sales
				2.5		
				4.7		
979M	3614M	4393M	29637M	173020M	853744M	Net Sales ($)
1295M	1590M	3432M	21074M	112243M	492238M	Total Assets ($)

M = $ thousand   MM = $ million
See Pages viii through xx for Explanation of Ratios and Data

© RMA 2024

MANUFACTURING—Prefabricated Metal Building and Component Manufacturing NAICS 332311

Current Data Sorted by Assets | Comparative Historical Data

0-500M	500M-2MM	2-10MM	10-50MM	50-100MM	100-250MM	Type of Statement	4/1/19-3/31/20 ALL	4/1/20-3/31/21 ALL
		3	6	2	6	Unqualified	12	8
	2	3	8	1		Reviewed	10	5
1	2	14	1	1		Compiled	3	2
		11 (4/1-9/30/23)	15	5	4	Tax Returns	9	4
			62 (10/1/23-3/31/24)			Other	44	30
1	4	20	30	8	10	**NUMBER OF STATEMENTS**	78	49
%	%	%	%	%	%	**ASSETS**	%	%
		12.9	16.8		12.3	Cash & Equivalents	14.8	15.3
		41.3	29.1		19.3	Trade Receivables (net)	25.8	24.8
		15.8	16.7		24.2	Inventory	21.6	26.1
		3.7	7.8		4.1	All Other Current	5.0	4.9
		73.7	70.4		59.8	Total Current	67.2	71.1
		16.2	14.6		26.6	Fixed Assets (net)	26.2	21.8
		4.4	5.1		6.3	Intangibles (net)	2.6	1.8
		5.7	9.8		7.3	All Other Non-Current	4.1	5.3
		100.0	100.0		100.0	Total	100.0	100.0
						LIABILITIES		
		4.2	2.4		.7	Notes Payable-Short Term	4.4	5.1
		2.1	1.9		2.2	Cur. Mat.-L.T.D.	2.3	4.0
		15.6	12.1		8.9	Trade Payables	13.0	13.6
		.0	.1		.1	Income Taxes Payable	.3	.7
		15.3	19.6		14.9	All Other Current	17.3	14.6
		37.3	36.2		26.6	Total Current	37.2	38.0
		11.7	8.2		55.6	Long-Term Debt	18.5	19.3
		.0	.4		.2	Deferred Taxes	.3	.3
		4.6	16.6		7.8	All Other Non-Current	3.8	9.1
		46.4	38.6		9.7	Net Worth	40.2	33.3
		100.0	100.0		100.0	Total Liabilities & Net Worth	100.0	100.0
						INCOME DATA		
		100.0	100.0		100.0	Net Sales	100.0	100.0
		32.2	28.8		31.5	Gross Profit	31.2	28.4
		24.6	18.7		14.9	Operating Expenses	23.8	23.2
		7.6	10.1		16.6	Operating Profit	7.4	5.2
		.2	.4		.7	All Other Expenses (net)	.8	-.3
		7.4	9.7		15.8	Profit Before Taxes	6.6	5.6
						RATIOS		
		3.2	4.8		3.4		3.3	3.6
		2.1	2.3		2.2	Current	1.8	2.1
		1.6	1.3		1.5		1.3	1.5
		2.0	2.6		2.8		1.8	2.0
		1.5	1.4		.9	Quick	1.0	1.1
		1.0	.7		.6		.7	.6
		45 8.1	17 21.8		25 14.5		19 18.9	28 12.9
		60 6.1	39 9.4		30 12.3	Sales/Receivables	36 10.0	36 10.1
		94 3.9	94 3.9		54 6.7		56 6.5	51 7.1
		3 137.5	4 88.5		44 8.3		10 36.0	25 14.5
		17 22.1	26 13.9		57 6.4	Cost of Sales/Inventory	40 9.2	52 7.0
		68 5.4	78 4.7		79 4.6		76 4.8	89 4.1
		23 16.1	10 35.2		8 46.5		10 37.0	13 27.2
		36 10.2	29 12.5		23 15.8	Cost of Sales/Payables	22 16.7	27 13.3
		47 7.8	45 8.1		33 11.0		42 8.7	41 8.9
		4.3	3.2		4.0		5.1	4.2
		7.1	5.3		7.5	Sales/Working Capital	9.1	5.6
		9.4	19.0		10.8		17.5	17.4
		70.6	388.9				61.3	31.6
		(18) 15.4	(27) 24.0			EBIT/Interest	(71) 9.7	(42) 10.9
		4.0	7.6				3.5	2.3
							15.7	
						Net Profit + Depr., Dep., Amort./Cur. Mat. L/T/D	(11) 6.0	
							2.0	
		.1	.1		.5		.3	.3
		.3	.2		1.4	Fixed/Worth	.6	.6
		.8	.8		-.3		1.5	1.5
		.8	.4		.4		.6	.6
		1.5	.9		2.1	Debt/Worth	1.4	1.2
		2.2	4.3		-2.2		3.4	17.6
		71.1	56.7				67.7	61.0
		40.4	(26) 32.2			% Profit Before Taxes/Tangible Net Worth	(71) 28.9	(39) 29.9
		13.6	12.8				11.7	9.9
		31.8	26.2		41.1	% Profit Before Taxes/Total Assets	26.8	22.7
		12.6	19.1		27.9		11.1	11.9
		5.5	7.2		16.0		3.8	1.6
		72.4	26.1		14.1		19.8	30.9
		24.9	14.2		9.6	Sales/Net Fixed Assets	11.6	12.7
		10.2	8.1		6.3		6.4	6.7
		2.9	2.4		2.5		3.2	2.8
		2.1	2.0		2.1	Sales/Total Assets	2.6	2.3
		1.6	1.5		1.7		1.9	1.6
		.5	.6				1.1	.8
		(11) 1.9	(28) 1.0			% Depr., Dep., Amort./Sales	(60) 1.6	(38) 1.3
		5.3	1.6				2.4	2.1
							1.5	4.3
						% Officers', Directors' Owners' Comp/Sales	(21) 2.4	(10) 10.5
							4.5	15.6
1968M	16074M	250990M	1476653M	888656M	3676414M	Net Sales ($)	5409281M	3563121M
120M	5109M	111035M	798362M	575614M	1847941M	Total Assets ($)	2367919M	1421327M

M = $ thousand   MM = $ million
See Pages viii through xx for Explanation of Ratios and Data

© RMA 2024

MANUFACTURING—Prefabricated Metal Building and Component Manufacturing NAICS 332311

Comparative Historical Data | Current Data Sorted by Sales

						Type of Statement							
	7		5		14	Unqualified					4	14
	7		12		11	Reviewed		1				6
	3		4		4	Compiled			1			2
	6		4		4	Tax Returns	1			1	1	
	33		44		40	Other	1		1		14	21
	4/1/21-3/31/22		4/1/22-3/31/23		4/1/23-3/31/24							
	ALL		ALL		ALL			11 (4/1-9/30/23)			62 (10/1/23-3/31/24)	
	56		69		73	NUMBER OF STATEMENTS	0-1MM	1-3MM	3-5MM	5-10MM	10-25MM	25MM & OVER
							3	3	3	5	19	43
	%		%		%	ASSETS	%	%	%	%	%	%
	17.0		13.6		15.1	Cash & Equivalents					12.9	14.3
	24.3		29.2		29.2	Trade Receivables (net)					37.3	24.4
	24.9		22.9		19.1	Inventory					22.3	18.7
	4.8		4.5		5.4	All Other Current					3.9	7.0
	71.0		70.1		68.8	Total Current					76.4	64.4
	20.1		18.8		18.6	Fixed Assets (net)					14.1	21.0
	4.9		6.4		4.9	Intangibles (net)					2.9	5.1
	4.1		4.7		7.7	All Other Non-Current					6.6	9.5
	100.0		100.0		100.0	Total					100.0	100.0
						LIABILITIES						
	7.9		5.2		4.1	Notes Payable-Short Term					2.9	4.0
	1.5		1.6		1.9	Cur. Mat.-L.T.D.					2.4	2.1
	14.0		11.4		12.2	Trade Payables					13.0	10.6
	.5		.3		.1	Income Taxes Payable					.0	.1
	23.6		26.0		19.2	All Other Current					10.4	19.8
	47.6		44.5		37.3	Total Current					28.8	36.5
	15.1		19.1		17.3	Long-Term Debt					8.3	22.2
	.2		.2		.2	Deferred Taxes					.0	.3
	5.1		5.5		9.8	All Other Non-Current					4.7	13.8
	32.0		30.6		35.4	Net Worth					58.2	27.2
	100.0		100.0		100.0	Total Liabilities & Net Worth					100.0	100.0
						INCOME DATA						
	100.0		100.0		100.0	Net Sales					100.0	100.0
	27.5		27.5		30.4	Gross Profit					31.1	29.5
	21.6		20.2		19.9	Operating Expenses					24.8	17.0
	5.9		7.2		10.5	Operating Profit					6.3	12.5
	-1.1		.1		.4	All Other Expenses (net)					-.6	.9
	7.0		7.1		10.1	Profit Before Taxes					6.9	11.6
						RATIOS						
	3.1		3.0		3.3						6.0	3.1
	1.9		2.0		2.2	Current					2.5	2.0
	1.2		1.3		1.4						1.7	1.3
	1.8		1.9		2.1						3.8	1.9
	1.0		1.2		1.3	Quick					1.8	1.1
	.5		.5		.9						1.2	.6
23	15.9	27	13.3	25	14.6						35 10.5	25 14.7
39	9.4	49	7.5	45	8.1	Sales/Receivables					56 6.5	36 10.0
59	6.2	70	5.2	83	4.4						96 3.8	78 4.7
23	16.1	17	21.2	9	39.7						8 44.3	20 17.9
58	6.3	49	7.5	40	9.1	Cost of Sales/Inventory					46 8.0	47 7.7
89	4.1	83	4.4	81	4.5						107 3.4	81 4.5
13	27.6	11	33.4	13	27.5						15 24.8	16 23.4
25	14.4	26	14.3	29	12.5	Cost of Sales/Payables					35 10.4	28 13.2
45	8.1	40	9.2	42	8.7						39 9.4	41 8.9
	4.7		3.9		4.0						2.6	4.1
	7.5		6.0		6.5	Sales/Working Capital					5.5	6.3
	24.5		15.7		13.0						7.5	14.0
	140.0		66.6		70.6						66.0	48.7
(47)	24.5	(56)	12.5	(62)	14.1	EBIT/Interest					(16) 22.0	(37) 12.4
	8.3		3.6		5.3						5.4	4.5
			6.9		9.9	Net Profit + Depr., Dep.,						12.6
		(15)	5.1	(17)	6.5	Amort./Cur. Mat. L/T/D					(14) 7.2	
			2.8		2.1							2.4
	.2		.2		.1						.1	.2
	.5		.4		.4	Fixed/Worth					.2	.5
	NM		1.9		1.2						.4	1.9
	.5		.7		.5						.3	.6
	1.4		1.7		1.4	Debt/Worth					.9	1.4
	NM		4.8		2.6						1.8	4.3
	82.4		62.0		63.2	% Profit Before Taxes/Tangible					56.0	59.0
(42)	50.2	(55)	32.0	(64)	35.7	Net Worth					22.4	(35) 35.6
	17.7		18.2		16.0						9.3	20.9
	32.7		24.9		29.6	% Profit Before Taxes/Total					26.2	30.2
	15.2		11.7		17.4	Assets					10.9	19.5
	5.8		4.8		7.5						5.2	11.0
	42.0		31.7		26.6						82.3	22.5
	13.0		16.5		13.9	Sales/Net Fixed Assets					15.4	11.8
	6.6		7.5		7.4						8.0	7.0
	3.0		2.9		2.5						2.8	2.5
	2.2		1.9		2.0	Sales/Total Assets					2.0	2.0
	1.6		1.4		1.5						1.5	1.4
	.4		.5		.6						.9	.7
(44)	1.0	(54)	1.2	(55)	1.1	% Depr., Dep., Amort./Sales					(11) 1.3	(36) 1.0
	1.9		3.0		1.7						2.6	1.5
	.7		.5		1.1	% Officers', Directors'						
(13)	4.6	(17)	2.6	(17)	2.4	Owners' Comp/Sales						
	8.8		4.8		4.4							
	3468168M		4364262M		6310755M	Net Sales ($)	5562M	11625M	38471M	313959M	5941138M	
	1804623M		2337515M		3338181M	Total Assets ($)	1922M	6565M	15341M	183158M	3131195M	

M = $ thousand   MM = $ million
See Pages viii through xx for Explanation of Ratios and Data
© RMA 2024

MANUFACTURING—Fabricated Structural Metal Manufacturing NAICS 332312

Current Data Sorted by Assets | Comparative Historical Data

							Type of Statement				
		1	1	14	8	5	Unqualified		30		19
1		1	15	31	7	1	Reviewed		51		28
		2	12	5			Compiled		18		19
3		6	12	2			Tax Returns		32		14
3		16	41	59	20	7	Other		169		110
		39 (4/1-9/30/23)		233 (10/1/23-3/31/24)					4/1/19-3/31/20		4/1/20-3/31/21
0-500M	500M-2MM	2-10MM	10-50MM	50-100MM	100-250MM			ALL		ALL
7	25	81	111	35	13	NUMBER OF STATEMENTS	300		190

							ASSETS				
%	%	%	%	%	%			%		%
	19.8	16.3	9.9	12.2	13.1	Cash & Equivalents		10.0		13.8
	32.1	32.4	30.8	28.7	25.4	Trade Receivables (net)		33.0		28.6
	8.5	14.5	20.3	12.2	17.4	Inventory		17.5		16.5
	4.6	4.5	4.9	7.7	5.0	All Other Current		4.8		5.6
	65.0	67.7	65.9	60.8	60.9	Total Current		65.4		64.5
	27.0	21.3	24.2	24.4	18.5	Fixed Assets (net)		26.4		26.4
	4.3	3.7	3.9	6.2	8.3	Intangibles (net)		4.3		5.2
	3.7	7.3	6.0	8.6	12.4	All Other Non-Current		3.9		3.9
	100.0	100.0	100.0	100.0	100.0	Total		100.0		100.0

						LIABILITIES				
	9.7	4.9	7.0	3.6	4.7	Notes Payable-Short Term		9.5		9.1
	2.7	2.1	2.0	3.2	1.6	Cur. Mat.-L.T.D.		2.4		2.9
	16.2	12.5	11.0	11.7	13.9	Trade Payables		13.6		12.9
	.2	.1	.2	.2	.2	Income Taxes Payable		.1		.1
	15.2	14.8	15.2	17.0	10.0	All Other Current		16.1		14.0
	44.0	34.4	35.4	35.7	30.4	Total Current		41.5		39.1
	23.0	15.9	10.9	12.0	24.6	Long-Term Debt		16.4		19.4
	.0	.2	.1	.6	.2	Deferred Taxes		.3		.3
	10.9	5.6	4.1	10.9	18.9	All Other Non-Current		5.9		4.3
	22.0	43.9	49.5	40.8	26.0	Net Worth		35.9		36.9
	100.0	100.0	100.0	100.0	100.0	Total Liabilities & Net Worth		100.0		100.0

						INCOME DATA				
	100.0	100.0	100.0	100.0	100.0	Net Sales		100.0		100.0
	41.4	31.5	27.4	22.0	18.5	Gross Profit		27.3		25.3
	35.4	24.4	18.2	12.7	10.4	Operating Expenses		21.6		20.9
	6.0	7.1	9.3	9.3	8.0	Operating Profit		5.7		4.4
	.3	.2	.7	.1	1.4	All Other Expenses (net)		.8		-.9
	5.6	6.9	8.5	9.2	6.6	Profit Before Taxes		5.0		5.3

							RATIOS				
		4.9	4.0	3.1	3.2	2.7			3.0		3.2
		1.6	2.2	1.9	1.7	2.3	Current		1.7		1.9
		1.0	1.4	1.3	1.1	1.6			1.2		1.3
		3.9	2.7	1.9	2.2	2.0			2.1		2.2
		1.3	1.6	1.1	1.0	1.6	Quick		1.1		1.2
		.8	1.1	.7	.7	.8			.7		.7
	0	UND	35	10.4	40	9.2	45	8.2	32	11.4			36	10.0	33	11.0
	28	12.9	49	7.4	58	6.3	59	6.2	38	9.6	Sales/Receivables	54	6.7	50	7.3
	56	6.5	76	4.8	87	4.2	79	4.6	69	5.3		73	5.0	65	5.6
	0	UND	0	UND	18	20.6	8	46.0	15	23.7		7	53.2	6	62.1
	0	UND	20	18.5	47	7.8	22	16.3	45	8.2	Cost of Sales/Inventory	34	10.8	37	9.9
	32	11.5	69	5.3	99	3.7	66	5.5	73	5.0		70	5.2	73	5.0
	2	194.5	13	29.0	14	26.6	16	23.5	20	18.0		17	21.6	13	27.2
	21	17.8	24	15.3	29	12.8	26	13.8	33	11.0	Cost of Sales/Payables	28	13.2	28	13.2
	47	7.7	42	8.7	46	8.0	47	7.7	42	8.6		40	9.2	38	9.5
		5.2	3.5	4.0	3.9	4.8			4.2		4.0
		22.5	5.8	6.2	6.7	6.8	Sales/Working Capital		8.5		7.6
		-514.2	18.7	12.4	38.5	8.1			28.3		16.8
		27.8	60.4	29.9	31.5	21.2			18.8		25.4
	(22)	11.7	(65)	12.5	(98)	11.8	(31)	12.3	(11)	3.5	EBIT/Interest	(268)	6.6	(169)	10.3
		1.1	1.1	2.9	5.3	2.4			2.2		3.3
			12.5	20.3	8.6		Net Profit + Depr., Dep.,		10.1		8.5
		(10)	3.7	(22)	10.8	(16)	4.7		Amort./Cur. Mat. L/T/D	(57)	3.5	(31)	3.5
			1.4	2.9	1.7				1.6		2.2
		.3	.1	.3	.4	.3			.3		.3
		.9	.4	.5	.7	.7	Fixed/Worth		.7		.7
		-.8	1.0	.9	1.5	4.9			1.9		1.6
		.4	.5	.5	.5	.7			.7		.7
		2.3	1.2	1.1	1.9	1.9	Debt/Worth		1.5		1.3
		-5.9	2.8	2.0	6.0	30.4			4.1		4.5
		137.5	49.5	56.7	69.5	53.3	% Profit Before Taxes/Tangible		47.9		56.3
	(17)	58.6	(70)	24.4	(107)	28.3	(32)	46.0	(11)	31.8	Net Worth	(258)	23.3	(168)	28.8
		29.4	8.4	8.6	21.4	25.4			7.8		8.8
		44.0	25.1	23.4	23.1	20.1	% Profit Before Taxes/Total		18.0		21.7
		24.3	12.9	13.7	14.1	8.3	Assets		8.7		10.5
		3.8	2.0	3.0	7.2	2.0			2.4		3.9
		54.8	28.5	16.8	11.9	11.8			23.0		19.1
		20.1	9.3	8.2	7.9	9.5	Sales/Net Fixed Assets		9.5		8.6
		5.6	6.1	4.6	4.6	8.8			4.6		4.4
		5.1	2.6	2.2	2.0	2.4			2.7		2.5
		3.3	2.0	1.8	1.6	1.8	Sales/Total Assets		2.1		1.9
		2.0	1.4	1.3	1.3	1.4			1.5		1.4
		.8	1.0	.9	1.2	.9			1.1		1.2
	(14)	1.5	(51)	1.9	(98)	1.7	(34)	1.7		1.7	% Depr., Dep., Amort./Sales	(238)	2.1	(154)	2.2
		5.4	3.5	3.0	2.7	3.2			3.7		3.9
		1.6	1.7	.7			% Officers', Directors'		1.1		1.2
	(11)	4.1	(28)	2.7	(22)	1.3			Owners' Comp/Sales	(94)	2.3	(50)	2.2
		4.7	5.1	4.4					4.5		5.9
19829M	100310M	926377M	5008550M	4241116M	3604490M	Net Sales ($)	13236039M		8083406M
1955M	28276M	431152M	2520867M	2498014M	1915777M	Total Assets ($)	7146968M		4556653M

M = $ thousand   MM = $ million
See Pages viii through xx for Explanation of Ratios and Data

© RMA 2024

MANUFACTURING—Fabricated Structural Metal Manufacturing NAICS 332312

Comparative Historical Data

22		29		29	Type of Statement / Unqualified
35		51		55	Reviewed
19		19		19	Compiled
21		33		23	Tax Returns
117		130		146	Other
4/1/21-3/31/22 ALL		4/1/22-3/31/23 ALL		4/1/23-3/31/24 ALL	
214		262		272	NUMBER OF STATEMENTS

Current Data Sorted by Sales

	1		7	6	22
1				9	38
			6	9	4
1	3	4	11	3	1
1	10	12	20	35	68
39 (4/1-9/30/23)			233 (10/1/23-3/31/24)		
0-1MM	1-3MM	3-5MM	5-10MM	10-25MM	25MM & OVER
3	14	16	44	62	133

Combined Table

%	%	%		%	%	%	%	%	%
			ASSETS						
13.3	13.7	13.8	Cash & Equivalents	19.0	20.3	22.1	9.6	11.5	
30.6	32.3	30.1	Trade Receivables (net)	15.1	26.3	27.1	35.1	31.4	
18.3	18.4	16.0	Inventory	2.6	23.6	9.9	18.0	17.5	
5.3	5.8	5.0	All Other Current	6.5	1.0	3.3	5.2	6.0	
67.5	70.2	65.0	Total Current	43.1	71.3	62.3	67.9	66.4	
24.9	20.6	23.5	Fixed Assets (net)	36.6	19.4	22.2	22.8	23.1	
4.2	3.0	4.7	Intangibles (net)	11.7	3.3	6.1	4.3	3.9	
3.4	6.2	6.9	All Other Non-Current	8.5	6.0	9.4	5.1	6.6	
100.0	100.0	100.0	Total	100.0	100.0	100.0	100.0	100.0	
			LIABILITIES						
7.3	6.7	6.6	Notes Payable-Short Term	14.9	16.1	2.7	6.3	6.1	
3.1	2.3	2.3	Cur. Mat.-L.T.D.	4.0	1.4	1.6	2.3	2.4	
14.4	13.7	11.9	Trade Payables	10.1	9.6	10.5	11.2	13.4	
.1	.1	.1	Income Taxes Payable	.1	.2	.1	.1	.2	
12.1	13.1	14.9	All Other Current	10.4	9.5	14.8	17.9	14.9	
37.0	35.9	35.8	Total Current	39.5	36.8	29.6	37.8	36.9	
18.8	16.2	14.5	Long-Term Debt	29.1	17.4	22.1	12.2	11.4	
.4	.2	.2	Deferred Taxes	.0	.0	.1	.3	.2	
5.1	4.8	6.9	All Other Non-Current	3.6	19.2	5.4	5.5	6.8	
38.7	42.9	42.6	Net Worth	27.9	26.6	42.7	44.3	44.7	
100.0	100.0	100.0	Total Liabilities & Net Worth	100.0	100.0	100.0	100.0	100.0	
			INCOME DATA						
100.0	100.0	100.0	Net Sales	100.0	100.0	100.0	100.0	100.0	
27.0	27.9	29.6	Gross Profit	43.9	43.7	33.8	28.9	24.3	
21.7	21.0	21.2	Operating Expenses	39.7	33.2	27.4	21.3	15.1	
5.3	6.9	8.3	Operating Profit	4.2	10.5	6.4	7.7	9.2	
-1.4	.1	.5	All Other Expenses (net)	1.0	.9	-.3	.3	.7	
6.6	6.9	7.9	Profit Before Taxes	3.2	9.6	6.6	7.4	8.6	
			RATIOS						
3.4	3.9	3.4		5.1	5.4	4.4	3.5	2.6	
1.9	2.1	2.0	Current	1.0	2.3	2.9	2.1	1.8	
1.4	1.4	1.3		.4	1.1	1.3	1.3	1.3	
2.3	2.7	2.3		4.1	3.5	3.4	2.1	1.8	
1.2	1.3	1.3	Quick	.7	1.2	2.0	1.3	1.1	
.8	.8	.8		.2	.9	1.1	.7	.7	

37	9.9	35	10.3	34	10.7	Sales/Receivables	0	UND	21	17.6	24	14.9	45	8.2	38	9.5
52	7.0	55	6.6	51	7.1		15	24.2	40	9.1	43	8.5	66	5.5	54	6.7
78	4.7	79	4.6	79	4.6		38	9.6	62	5.9	64	5.7	91	4.0	74	4.9
9	42.7	4	91.4	5	80.4	Cost of Sales/Inventory	0	UND	0	UND	0	UND	3	119.9	10	35.9
37	9.8	38	9.5	31	11.6		0	UND	60	6.1	13	28.4	40	9.1	38	9.5
78	4.7	81	4.5	76	4.8		7	53.1	118	3.1	58	6.3	118	3.1	76	4.8
17	21.2	14	26.6	13	28.1	Cost of Sales/Payables	0	UND	10	37.6	9	39.8	13	27.7	16	23.2
30	12.2	27	13.3	26	14.0		18	20.3	21	17.8	21	17.3	27	13.6	30	12.0
49	7.4	45	8.1	43	8.5		60	6.1	27	13.4	35	10.3	43	8.5	47	7.8

3.9	3.6	4.0	Sales/Working Capital	4.7	2.3	3.1	3.5	4.9
6.9	6.0	6.6		NM	4.2	6.1	5.8	7.1
13.0	12.2	17.9		-8.1	32.9	33.3	14.7	13.5

	31.9		34.6		35.2	EBIT/Interest		88.0		51.8		31.2		37.0		35.2
(184)	12.2	(222)	13.7	(232)	11.8		(11)	11.0	(14)	11.5	(37)	7.5	(52)	10.3	(116)	12.2
	2.9		4.1		2.7			-3.7		-.7		.8		3.4		4.0

	16.2		10.0		15.6	Net Profit + Depr., Dep.,						12.9		18.7
(30)	6.8	(47)	5.4	(58)	5.2	Amort./Cur. Mat. L/T/D					(11)	6.3	(42)	5.2
	1.9		2.1		1.8							1.5		2.1

.3	.2	.3	Fixed/Worth	.4	.3	.2	.2	.3
.7	.4	.5		2.1	.5	.5	.5	.5
1.3	.9	1.1		-.7	NM	2.9	1.1	1.0
.7	.5	.5	Debt/Worth	.2	.7	.4	.6	.6
1.6	1.3	1.3		4.7	1.5	1.1	1.4	1.3
4.4	3.3	3.3		-4.0	NM	8.3	3.5	2.3

	54.5		54.7		58.8	% Profit Before Taxes/Tangible Net Worth		98.2		46.7		58.0		58.3
(191)	29.9	(247)	25.0	(241)	32.5			(12)	40.9	(36)	19.9	(56)	26.1	(126)	35.8
	10.1		9.3		13.2				21.8		1.4		10.5		17.4

20.4	22.7	24.9	% Profit Before Taxes/Total Assets	47.8	32.3	20.9	23.9	24.1
11.6	11.9	14.3		29.8	20.6	12.0	10.9	14.4
4.1	3.5	3.4		-21.7	1.3	.6	3.1	4.7
24.3	24.6	19.5	Sales/Net Fixed Assets	27.4	46.2	44.8	26.4	16.4
9.7	12.0	9.2		7.3	12.7	12.6	7.7	9.3
4.6	6.5	5.4		3.4	5.5	6.3	4.7	5.6
2.5	2.7	2.5	Sales/Total Assets	4.1	3.9	3.0	2.4	2.3
2.0	2.0	1.9		2.1	1.9	2.0	1.7	1.9
1.4	1.5	1.4		1.4	1.1	1.3	1.3	1.5

	1.1		.9		1.0	% Depr., Dep., Amort./Sales				1.3		1.1		1.0
(169)	1.8	(204)	1.7	(214)	1.7				(28)	2.7	(45)	1.6	(122)	1.7
	3.1		2.8		3.1					3.9		2.6		2.8
	1.4		1.1		1.2	% Officers', Directors', Owners' Comp/Sales					1.6		1.1		.9
(75)	2.7	(86)	2.7	(66)	2.9					(18)	3.0	(17)	2.0	(17)	1.2
	5.3		4.8		5.3						5.0		3.2		4.2

7601945M	12837832M	13900672M	Net Sales ($)	1365M	32112M	62020M	330373M	1017529M	12457273M
4511537M	6614813M	7396041M	Total Assets ($)	544M	14743M	37014M	185538M	675680M	6482522M

M = $ thousand   MM = $ million
See Pages viii through xx for Explanation of Ratios and Data

© RMA 2024

MANUFACTURING—Plate Work Manufacturing NAICS 332313

Current Data Sorted by Assets | Comparative Historical Data

						Type of Statement		
			2	2	2	Unqualified	7	5
	1		5			Reviewed	13	7
	4		1			Compiled	6	5
	3					Tax Returns	8	3
1	4		9	2		Other	28	23
	4 (4/1-9/30/23)		33 (10/1/23-3/31/24)				4/1/19-3/31/20	4/1/20-3/31/21
0-500M	500M-2MM	2-10MM	10-50MM	50-100MM	100-250MM		ALL	ALL
						NUMBER OF STATEMENTS	62	43
%	%	%	%	%	%	ASSETS	%	%
		24.8	7.3			Cash & Equivalents	13.3	16.7
		26.4	18.9			Trade Receivables (net)	24.3	21.2
		16.1	20.3			Inventory	18.8	18.3
		1.0	2.0			All Other Current	3.5	2.8
		68.2	48.5			Total Current	59.9	59.0
		25.8	41.2			Fixed Assets (net)	30.2	29.7
		1.7	3.3			Intangibles (net)	4.2	5.5
		4.2	7.0			All Other Non-Current	5.7	5.8
		100.0	100.0			Total	100.0	100.0
						LIABILITIES		
		6.4	5.2			Notes Payable-Short Term	7.2	6.0
		.7	4.0			Cur. Mat.-L.T.D.	2.8	3.9
		6.2	9.1			Trade Payables	11.6	9.3
		.1	.5			Income Taxes Payable	.1	.2
		12.3	13.3			All Other Current	12.1	9.0
		25.7	32.1			Total Current	33.8	28.4
		13.5	21.1			Long-Term Debt	15.1	20.4
		.0	.6			Deferred Taxes	.5	.4
		.1	3.1			All Other Non-Current	4.1	2.0
		60.7	43.1			Net Worth	46.6	48.9
		100.0	100.0			Total Liabilties & Net Worth	100.0	100.0
						INCOME DATA		
		100.0	100.0			Net Sales	100.0	100.0
		32.7	30.0			Gross Profit	28.5	26.6
		19.3	20.5			Operating Expenses	21.3	23.5
		13.4	9.5			Operating Profit	7.2	3.0
		.7	1.3			All Other Expenses (net)	.1	-1.1
		12.7	8.2			Profit Before Taxes	7.1	4.1
						RATIOS		
		14.6	2.2				3.5	3.5
		3.8	1.4			Current	2.0	2.0
		1.2	1.3				1.3	1.4
		9.1	1.5				2.8	2.7
		2.5	.9			Quick	1.2	1.3
		1.0	.3				.6	.8
		27 13.6	27 13.3				31 11.7	34 10.7
		35 10.5	38 9.6			Sales/Receivables	40 9.2	49 7.5
		66 5.5	64 5.7				54 6.7	69 5.3
		0 UND	24 15.1				14 26.6	28 13.0
		18 19.9	45 8.2			Cost of Sales/Inventory	39 9.4	46 7.9
		52 7.0	94 3.9				70 5.2	79 4.6
		5 73.1	10 38.2				13 28.5	13 28.7
		13 28.2	21 17.3			Cost of Sales/Payables	23 16.0	28 13.1
		17 21.6	43 8.5				33 10.9	48 7.6
		2.3	6.0				4.0	2.8
		5.6	13.3			Sales/Working Capital	7.9	6.2
		39.6	17.2				28.1	12.3
		384.0	31.8				24.1	14.7
		(10) 26.4	(14) 4.6			EBIT/Interest	(49) 7.1	(37) 4.2
		6.0	1.9				1.8	.3
						Net Profit + Depr., Dep.,	11.3	12.2
						Amort./Cur. Mat. L/T/D	(13) 5.7	(11) 3.0
							2.7	1.4
		.1	.5				.2	.2
		.5	.9			Fixed/Worth	.6	.6
		1.2	1.8				1.4	1.4
		.1	1.1				.4	.6
		.6	1.9			Debt/Worth	1.2	1.1
		3.2	2.3				2.8	2.3
		63.4	38.1				52.4	31.7
		(11) 30.4	21.9			% Profit Before Taxes/Tangible Net Worth	(58) 26.1	(41) 8.4
		12.7	8.2				11.6	-2.8
		40.8	16.3				25.6	16.0
		19.6	9.0			% Profit Before Taxes/Total Assets	11.0	2.6
		6.7	2.6				3.5	-1.9
		35.9	10.8				20.4	14.5
		10.1	3.6			Sales/Net Fixed Assets	7.8	5.3
		5.3	2.4				3.9	3.0
		2.8	1.9				2.8	2.2
		1.9	1.6			Sales/Total Assets	1.9	1.6
		1.4	1.0				1.4	.9
			1.2				1.6	1.5
		(16)	3.7			% Depr., Dep., Amort./Sales	(50) 2.8	(37) 2.6
			5.1				4.7	3.9
							1.2	.7
						% Officers', Directors' Owners' Comp/Sales	(17) 1.9	(11) 2.1
							5.5	5.0
	6496M	120769M	460412M	298253M	209381M	Net Sales ($)	1736324M	1245905M
	3629M	57621M	319244M	251592M	327934M	Total Assets ($)	1075992M	1028842M

M = $ thousand   MM = $ million
See Pages viii through xx for Explanation of Ratios and Data

© RMA 2024

MANUFACTURING—Plate Work Manufacturing NAICS 332313

Comparative Historical Data | Current Data Sorted by Sales

Comparative Historical Data			Type of Statement	Current Data Sorted by Sales					
3	6	6	Unqualified					1	5
5	6	6	Reviewed					4	2
3	3	5	Compiled				3	1	1
3	4	4	Tax Returns			1	3		
21	30	16	Other		1	1	2	4	8
4/1/21-3/31/22 ALL	4/1/22-3/31/23 ALL	4/1/23-3/31/24 ALL		0-1MM	4 (4/1-9/30/23) 1-3MM	3-5MM	33 (10/1/23-3/31/24) 5-10MM	10-25MM	25MM & OVER
35	49	37	NUMBER OF STATEMENTS	1	2	8	10	16	
%	%	%	ASSETS	%	%	%	%	%	%
15.9	16.7	16.2	Cash & Equivalents					7.8	11.7
26.4	24.5	20.5	Trade Receivables (net)					27.7	14.5
22.9	18.3	16.6	Inventory	DATA				12.2	18.0
3.6	5.0	4.2	All Other Current	NOT				1.1	8.4
68.8	64.4	57.4	Total Current	AVAILABLE				48.8	52.6
21.8	21.3	32.7	Fixed Assets (net)					40.7	32.5
4.2	7.0	3.7	Intangibles (net)					1.3	7.0
5.1	7.1	6.2	All Other Non-Current					9.2	7.8
100.0	100.0	100.0	Total					100.0	100.0
			LIABILITIES						
5.9	6.9	6.2	Notes Payable-Short Term					10.9	4.3
2.3	2.1	2.3	Cur. Mat.-L.T.D.					2.2	3.5
14.2	10.4	7.6	Trade Payables					6.4	10.6
.1	.3	.2	Income Taxes Payable					.5	.2
7.4	11.8	15.0	All Other Current					15.7	16.5
29.9	31.4	31.3	Total Current					35.8	35.1
19.0	14.7	17.7	Long-Term Debt					13.1	22.1
.4	.5	.3	Deferred Taxes					1.0	.1
3.5	5.4	2.9	All Other Non-Current					1.9	4.8
47.2	48.0	47.7	Net Worth					48.1	37.9
100.0	100.0	100.0	Total Liabilities & Net Worth					100.0	100.0
			INCOME DATA						
100.0	100.0	100.0	Net Sales					100.0	100.0
31.7	30.2	29.5	Gross Profit					33.5	23.9
25.0	22.8	19.2	Operating Expenses					24.0	15.9
6.8	7.5	10.3	Operating Profit					9.4	7.9
-2.6	-.1	.9	All Other Expenses (net)					1.3	.5
9.4	7.5	9.5	Profit Before Taxes					8.1	7.5
			RATIOS						
4.3	3.4	3.0						3.6	2.2
2.5	2.1	1.6	Current					1.2	1.5
1.5	1.4	1.3						.5	1.4
2.7	2.5	2.3						3.0	1.5
1.6	1.4	1.1	Quick					.9	.9
.8	.7	.5						.4	.3
37 9.8	31 11.8	29 12.4					36 10.0	23 16.2	
47 7.8	46 7.9	40 9.2	Sales/Receivables				50 7.3	38 9.7	
78 4.7	83 4.4	64 5.7					85 4.3	51 7.2	
10 36.9	9 40.6	5 79.9					0 UND	18 20.1	
54 6.7	29 12.5	29 12.5	Cost of Sales/Inventory				29 12.6	37 9.9	
111 3.3	94 3.9	81 4.5					55 6.6	91 4.0	
15 25.0	19 19.2	11 32.2					8 47.0	17 21.7	
33 11.1	31 11.7	17 21.3	Cost of Sales/Payables				15 25.1	27 13.6	
64 5.7	45 8.1	27 13.6					20 18.1	46 8.0	
2.6	2.8	3.1						4.0	3.7
5.5	5.5	7.7	Sales/Working Capital					31.8	7.9
9.7	12.0	17.6						-9.2	14.8
42.9	96.0	48.1							12.4
(30) 17.7	(43) 17.7	(30) 7.0	EBIT/Interest					(12) 3.8	
2.6	2.0	2.7							1.9
23.0	34.2	9.0	Net Profit + Depr., Dep.,						
(10) 12.7	(11) 7.4	(11) 1.5	Amort./Cur. Mat. L/T/D						
4.5	4.6	1.1							
.2	.2	.4						.4	.5
.6	.5	.7	Fixed/Worth					.7	.8
1.2	1.0	1.5						2.6	1.9
.4	.5	.4						.3	1.1
.9	1.4	1.2	Debt/Worth					1.5	2.0
2.7	2.3	2.3						2.3	7.2
64.0	57.4	39.9							39.9
(31) 25.1	(44) 25.9	(34) 21.7	% Profit Before Taxes/Tangible Net Worth					(14) 20.6	
10.7	3.3	10.7							5.7
22.3	24.5	18.7						20.1	13.7
11.8	12.4	9.4	% Profit Before Taxes/Total Assets					7.9	9.1
3.4	.1	3.4						2.6	2.5
24.4	29.1	11.9						9.6	8.0
7.2	8.0	5.1	Sales/Net Fixed Assets					7.3	4.5
5.1	3.9	3.0						2.5	3.0
2.4	2.2	2.0						2.9	1.9
1.8	1.8	1.6	Sales/Total Assets					1.8	1.3
1.4	1.1	1.1						.8	.9
.7	.8	1.1							1.2
(29) 1.6	(37) 1.8	(30) 2.3	% Depr., Dep., Amort./Sales					(15) 2.3	
2.7	3.4	4.1							4.0
2.4	1.3	1.4							
(10) 3.4	(15) 2.2	(10) 2.4	% Officers', Directors', Owners' Comp/Sales						
7.4	2.9	4.1							
1318656M	1611222M	1095311M	Net Sales ($)	2877M	7347M	63301M	169832M	851954M	
946009M	1328056M	960020M	Total Assets ($)	1885M	5439M	36653M	121847M	794196M	

© RMA 2024   M = $ thousand   MM = $ million
See Pages viii through xx for Explanation of Ratios and Data

MANUFACTURING—Metal Window and Door Manufacturing NAICS 332321

Current Data Sorted by Assets | Comparative Historical Data

							Type of Statement		
				5			Unqualified	9	5
			1	7			Reviewed	14	11
	1		2	1			Compiled	5	
2	1		1	2			Tax Returns	7	6
	2	6	14	9	5		Other	43	28
	6 (4/1-9/30/23)		52 (10/1/23-3/31/24)					4/1/19-3/31/20	4/1/20-3/31/21
0-500M	500M-2MM	2-10MM	10-50MM	50-100MM	100-250MM			ALL	ALL
2	4	9	29	9	5		NUMBER OF STATEMENTS	78	50
%	%	%	%	%	%		ASSETS	%	%
			16.4				Cash & Equivalents	11.9	22.0
			22.9				Trade Receivables (net)	26.5	24.9
			19.9				Inventory	23.3	21.2
			2.4				All Other Current	3.6	2.5
			61.6				Total Current	65.3	70.7
			21.2				Fixed Assets (net)	21.8	19.7
			6.3				Intangibles (net)	4.8	1.9
			10.9				All Other Non-Current	8.1	7.7
			100.0				Total	100.0	100.0
							LIABILITIES		
			3.0				Notes Payable-Short Term	5.6	4.4
			3.0				Cur. Mat.-L.T.D.	2.5	4.0
			8.2				Trade Payables	9.9	9.4
			.1				Income Taxes Payable	.0	.1
			22.9				All Other Current	14.5	14.1
			37.1				Total Current	32.5	32.0
			7.1				Long-Term Debt	13.0	16.2
			.2				Deferred Taxes	.2	.3
			5.1				All Other Non-Current	4.7	5.4
			50.5				Net Worth	49.6	46.1
			100.0				Total Liabilities & Net Worth	100.0	100.0
							INCOME DATA		
			100.0				Net Sales	100.0	100.0
			35.1				Gross Profit	33.1	35.5
			25.7				Operating Expenses	26.5	28.2
			9.4				Operating Profit	6.6	7.3
			.4				All Other Expenses (net)	.7	-.2
			9.0				Profit Before Taxes	5.9	7.5
							RATIOS		
			3.5					4.1	4.1
			2.2				Current	2.3	2.7
			1.1					1.3	1.4
			2.3					2.4	2.7
			1.2				Quick	1.2	1.7
			.6					.7	1.0
		29	12.6					25 14.8	24 14.9
		35	10.3				Sales/Receivables	36 10.0	45 8.1
		65	5.6					54 6.7	60 6.1
		29	12.7					35 10.4	27 13.5
		54	6.8				Cost of Sales/Inventory	54 6.8	46 7.9
		87	4.2					91 4.0	85 4.3
		9	40.8					11 34.6	8 44.3
		18	20.3				Cost of Sales/Payables	20 18.1	20 18.1
		33	11.2					40 9.1	45 8.1
			3.4					4.1	3.8
			6.7				Sales/Working Capital	6.3	4.9
			52.3					20.6	10.8
			116.2					31.8	48.5
		(26)	28.5				EBIT/Interest	(64) 8.9	(41) 13.2
			6.8					2.7	3.7
							Net Profit + Depr., Dep., Amort./Cur. Mat. L/T/D	18.6 (21) 4.9 2.4	
			.1					.2	.1
			.5				Fixed/Worth	.4	.3
			1.1					1.2	1.1
			.4					.3	.4
			.9				Debt/Worth	1.0	.9
			2.5					2.5	3.2
			46.6				% Profit Before Taxes/Tangible Net Worth	45.8	83.3
		(26)	24.2					(71) 28.3	(48) 42.3
			13.1					8.9	9.0
			29.0				% Profit Before Taxes/Total Assets	22.7	27.6
			14.2					11.9	15.4
			7.2					4.3	3.9
			19.0					34.4	35.6
			13.0				Sales/Net Fixed Assets	13.1	13.9
			5.7					5.5	8.4
			2.3					3.0	2.8
			1.9				Sales/Total Assets	2.1	2.0
			1.3					1.5	1.5
			1.0					.9	.7
		(24)	1.9				% Depr., Dep., Amort./Sales	(59) 1.4	(37) 1.3
			2.7					3.0	2.3
							% Officers', Directors' Owners' Comp/Sales	1.1 (20) 2.8 7.7	.9 (17) 3.0 6.2
7044M	14436M	128084M	1291095M	556211M	2080717M		Net Sales ($)	4761384M	1761339M
460M	3726M	50371M	679898M	510752M	956656M		Total Assets ($)	2282295M	944215M

© RMA 2024 M = $ thousand MM = $ million
See Pages viii through xx for Explanation of Ratios and Data

MANUFACTURING—Metal Window and Door Manufacturing NAICS 332321

Comparative Historical Data / Current Data Sorted by Sales

				Type of Statement						
	5	7	5	Unqualified					1	4
	8	11	8	Reviewed			1		1	7
	4	5	4	Compiled		1			2	1
	2	5	5	Tax Returns			1	1	1	1
	24	37	36	Other	1	1	2	8	24
	4/1/21-3/31/22 ALL	4/1/22-3/31/23 ALL	4/1/23-3/31/24 ALL		0-1MM	6 (4/1-9/30/23) 1-3MM	3-5MM	52 (10/1/23-3/31/24) 5-10MM	10-25MM	25MM & OVER
	43	65	58	NUMBER OF STATEMENTS	3	2	4	12	37
	%	%	%	ASSETS	%	%	%	%	%	%
	17.5	16.2	17.1	Cash & Equivalents	D				10.6	16.9
	24.0	22.3	21.2	Trade Receivables (net)	A				20.9	21.1
	26.8	22.4	19.2	Inventory	T				21.1	17.0
	3.2	5.7	2.9	All Other Current	A				3.1	2.7
	71.6	66.6	60.4	Total Current					55.7	57.8
	21.2	22.1	21.1	Fixed Assets (net)	N				23.7	21.7
	4.5	4.3	8.9	Intangibles (net)	O				7.1	10.0
	2.7	7.0	9.7	All Other Non-Current	T				13.6	10.5
	100.0	100.0	100.0	Total					100.0	100.0
				LIABILITIES	A					
	4.6	5.3	3.2	Notes Payable-Short Term	V				3.3	2.2
	3.2	2.1	2.5	Cur. Mat.-L.T.D.	A				4.0	2.3
	10.5	10.2	9.5	Trade Payables	I				11.2	8.2
	.2	.1	.1	Income Taxes Payable	L				.5	.0
	13.6	14.0	18.2	All Other Current	A				14.4	19.3
	32.1	31.8	33.5	Total Current	B				33.4	32.0
	15.5	21.5	15.9	Long-Term Debt	L				9.2	14.3
	.1	.2	.1	Deferred Taxes	E				.1	.2
	4.1	3.3	5.4	All Other Non-Current					7.0	6.2
	48.2	43.3	45.1	Net Worth					50.3	47.3
	100.0	100.0	100.0	Total Liabilities & Net Worth					100.0	100.0
				INCOME DATA						
	100.0	100.0	100.0	Net Sales					100.0	100.0
	33.8	33.7	35.9	Gross Profit					34.7	36.2
	28.1	23.6	26.3	Operating Expenses					26.4	26.2
	5.7	10.1	9.6	Operating Profit					8.3	9.9
	-2.7	.5	.8	All Other Expenses (net)					1.2	.5
	8.4	9.6	8.8	Profit Before Taxes					7.1	9.4
				RATIOS						
	3.9	3.9	3.3						3.3	3.2
	2.5	2.5	2.2	Current					1.7	2.2
	1.6	1.6	1.3						1.1	1.3
	2.7	2.4	2.0						1.8	2.0
	1.5	1.5	1.3	Quick					1.1	1.5
	.8	.7	.8						.6	.8
30	12.3	16	23.0	25	14.8				19	18.8	29	12.6
41	8.9	32	11.3	33	11.1	Sales/Receivables			29	12.4	35	10.3
64	5.7	65	5.6	64	5.7				68	5.4	65	5.6
36	10.0	28	13.2	29	12.8				22	16.9	33	11.0
66	5.5	52	7.0	54	6.8	Cost of Sales/Inventory			59	6.2	54	6.8
146	2.5	96	3.8	74	4.9				83	4.4	76	4.8
16	22.5	11	33.9	10	36.9				9	39.4	11	33.7
24	15.3	20	18.0	21	17.0	Cost of Sales/Payables			21	17.3	21	17.2
48	7.6	33	10.9	42	8.7				59	6.2	41	8.8
	3.2		3.4		3.8					6.7		3.5
	4.6		5.7		6.6	Sales/Working Capital				9.5		5.3
	7.8		12.9		21.9					28.4		22.6
	45.0		121.0		76.9					75.7		89.0
(35)	21.6	(53)	19.5	(50)	14.9	EBIT/Interest			(11)	18.2	(33)	16.6
	5.7		4.1		2.6					4.2		2.5
	15.7		27.2		22.4	Net Profit + Depr., Dep.,						22.4
(11)	4.2	(16)	8.5	(17)	5.6	Amort./Cur. Mat. L/T/D					(13)	5.6
	1.6		3.1		3.1							3.1
	.1		.2		.2					.3		.2
	.4		.5		.5	Fixed/Worth				.7		.5
	1.7		1.4		1.0					.9		1.1
	.4		.5		.5					.5		.5
	.9		1.1		1.1	Debt/Worth				.9		1.1
	4.1		4.0		3.9					1.8		3.9
	60.6		61.4		57.0	% Profit Before Taxes/Tangible				48.3		57.0
(38)	31.9	(59)	37.8	(49)	42.2	Net Worth			(10)	26.9	(33)	39.4
	12.7		20.0		16.4					13.1		16.4
	25.1		31.1		29.8	% Profit Before Taxes/Total				22.6		29.0
	11.0		18.7		18.6	Assets				14.0		15.1
	5.7		6.7		6.5					6.8		5.1
	22.2		31.9		23.2					22.0		19.8
	11.1		12.1		13.2	Sales/Net Fixed Assets				9.5		12.6
	5.0		5.0		6.4					6.0		5.4
	2.6		2.9		2.7					2.9		2.2
	1.9		1.8		1.9	Sales/Total Assets				2.1		1.8
	1.2		1.3		1.3					1.3		1.3
	1.1		1.0		1.0					.4		1.2
(34)	1.5	(45)	1.4	(41)	1.7	% Depr., Dep., Amort./Sales			(10)	1.0	(27)	2.1
	2.6		2.6		2.8					2.1		2.9
	1.7		.9		1.5	% Officers', Directors'						
(11)	3.6	(17)	1.4	(11)	2.4	Owners' Comp/Sales						
	5.2		4.7		3.0							
1357167M	2943908M	4077587M		Net Sales ($)		7289M	8950M	24327M	229043M	3807978M
768250M	1656543M	2201863M		Total Assets ($)		1527M	1484M	14625M	127817M	2056410M

© RMA 2024 M = $ thousand MM = $ million
See Pages viii through xx for Explanation of Ratios and Data

MANUFACTURING—Sheet Metal Work Manufacturing NAICS 332322

Current Data Sorted by Assets | **Comparative Historical Data**

							Type of Statement		
			1	3	3	4	Unqualified	8	9
	2		8	18			Reviewed	46	16
	1		6	7			Compiled	22	14
3	9		10	1			Tax Returns	30	19
3	7		36	33	9	7	Other	98	70
	38 (4/1-9/30/23)			133 (10/1/23-3/31/24)				4/1/19-3/31/20	4/1/20-3/31/21
0-500M	500M-2MM	2-10MM	10-50MM	50-100MM	100-250MM			ALL	ALL
6	19	61	62	12	11		NUMBER OF STATEMENTS	204	128
%	%	%	%	%	%		ASSETS	%	%
	21.5	16.9	14.9	15.8	12.3		Cash & Equivalents	13.1	19.9
	26.1	27.8	19.1	18.3	21.4		Trade Receivables (net)	28.3	25.0
	19.4	17.6	22.3	32.2	17.5		Inventory	21.3	19.7
	4.8	2.3	2.7	.9	3.0		All Other Current	2.7	1.7
	71.9	64.6	59.0	67.3	54.2		Total Current	65.4	66.2
	19.8	25.0	26.7	19.6	19.3		Fixed Assets (net)	24.9	25.7
	3.6	4.1	4.4	2.2	5.4		Intangibles (net)	4.6	4.0
	4.8	6.3	10.0	10.9	21.1		All Other Non-Current	5.0	4.1
	100.0	100.0	100.0	100.0	100.0		Total	100.0	100.0
							LIABILITIES		
	4.8	2.7	4.5	4.4	6.2		Notes Payable-Short Term	6.6	8.2
	3.5	3.5	2.6	1.7	2.1		Cur. Mat.-L.T.D.	3.8	4.3
	14.1	9.6	7.8	9.2	11.1		Trade Payables	13.7	9.7
	.0	.0	.6	.1	.0		Income Taxes Payable	.1	.0
	22.7	11.1	9.2	8.9	17.3		All Other Current	9.8	11.2
	45.2	26.9	24.7	24.3	36.7		Total Current	34.1	33.4
	16.8	18.6	13.8	8.2	26.2		Long-Term Debt	16.6	20.3
	.0	.2	.5	1.1	.2		Deferred Taxes	.5	.4
	4.9	6.5	4.3	7.3	12.6		All Other Non-Current	6.8	4.9
	33.1	47.8	56.7	59.1	24.4		Net Worth	42.0	40.9
	100.0	100.0	100.0	100.0	100.0		Total Liabilities & Net Worth	100.0	100.0
							INCOME DATA		
	100.0	100.0	100.0	100.0	100.0		Net Sales	100.0	100.0
	35.0	31.5	29.1	24.3	20.1		Gross Profit	30.1	32.8
	28.8	25.0	20.1	13.1	13.1		Operating Expenses	23.4	27.0
	6.1	6.5	9.0	11.2	7.0		Operating Profit	6.6	5.9
	-.6	.2	.0	.7	1.3		All Other Expenses (net)	.7	-1.1
	6.8	6.3	9.0	10.5	5.7		Profit Before Taxes	5.9	6.9
							RATIOS		
	6.4	4.7	6.0	3.7	2.3			3.8	4.5
	1.9	2.8	2.8	2.7	1.3		Current	2.1	2.3
	1.0	1.9	1.6	2.3	1.2			1.3	1.4
	6.3	3.2	4.2	2.4	1.7			2.7	3.6
	1.3	1.9	1.6	1.4	.8		Quick	1.4	1.6
	.4	1.1	.7	.7	.6			.7	.8
0 UND	31 11.9	30 12.1	27 13.6	40 9.2				30 12.2	26 14.2
32 11.3	47 7.7	42 8.6	30 12.2	47 7.8			Sales/Receivables	43 8.4	38 9.6
56 6.5	63 5.8	60 6.1	59 6.2	63 5.8				58 6.3	55 6.6
3 107.2	15 25.0	40 9.1	50 7.3	30 12.1				19 19.3	12 30.7
19 19.4	39 9.3	70 5.2	96 3.8	64 5.7			Cost of Sales/Inventory	46 7.9	46 8.0
44 8.3	68 5.4	91 4.0	114 3.2	96 3.8				78 4.7	87 4.2
0 UND	12 30.6	13 27.2	13 27.9	25 14.8				16 22.9	10 37.4
10 37.2	21 17.6	21 17.0	22 16.6	34 10.8			Cost of Sales/Payables	25 14.6	19 19.6
36 10.2	32 11.3	33 10.9	31 11.6	41 8.9				42 8.6	35 10.5
	6.5	3.7	2.8	3.0	3.9			4.0	3.4
	9.9	5.1	4.6	4.5	10.8		Sales/Working Capital	7.6	6.2
	-153.7	9.1	9.8	5.3	20.5			16.4	11.4
	42.1	24.0	80.0	74.4	25.9			24.3	21.5
(16)	10.8	(52) 6.1	(55) 13.8	(10) 17.9	(10) 6.0		EBIT/Interest	(177) 6.3	(106) 7.5
	1.9	2.6	4.0	3.5	1.5			2.1	2.1
		6.8	6.8				Net Profit + Depr., Dep.,	5.1	10.9
	(11)	3.3	(16) 2.6				Amort./Cur. Mat. L/T/D	(37) 2.7	(19) 4.5
		.6	1.2					1.3	1.9
	.1	.3	.2	.3	.5			.2	.2
	.6	.5	.5	.4	.6		Fixed/Worth	.6	.6
	2.4	.8	.9	.7	-1.9			1.3	1.3
	.7	.4	.3	.3	1.7			.4	.4
	1.8	1.0	.7	.6	3.0		Debt/Worth	1.2	1.3
	28.4	2.5	1.7	1.6	-13.0			3.5	3.5
	103.2	45.3	42.9	45.2			% Profit Before Taxes/Tangible	48.7	58.4
(15)	47.2	(54) 23.6	(59) 26.3	30.4			Net Worth	(178) 24.2	(117) 26.4
	19.5	2.1	11.4	19.1				5.3	7.4
	51.7	25.0	24.5	27.3	16.4		% Profit Before Taxes/Total	21.2	25.4
	23.5	9.5	11.7	18.8	8.7		Assets	10.1	11.1
	1.9	1.4	4.8	11.5	2.0			1.9	2.5
	81.5	24.5	14.9	12.8	10.6			22.0	26.2
	38.5	8.8	7.7	8.6	9.1		Sales/Net Fixed Assets	9.9	8.2
	13.2	4.9	3.8	6.4	4.8			4.9	4.8
	7.3	2.9	2.2	2.1	1.8			2.9	2.8
	3.3	2.1	1.6	1.8	1.5		Sales/Total Assets	2.2	2.0
	2.3	1.6	1.1	1.4	1.2			1.6	1.5
	.3	1.1	1.2	.8	1.5			1.1	1.2
(10)	1.9	(42) 2.5	(53) 2.2	1.6	(10) 2.2		% Depr., Dep., Amort./Sales	(169) 2.2	(99) 2.5
	2.8	3.8	3.9	2.7	4.8			4.1	4.2
	2.2		1.0					1.2	1.8
(11)	3.1	(28) 2.7	(15) 1.7				% Officers', Directors' Owners' Comp/Sales	(83) 2.7	(53) 3.8
	10.6	3.8	3.8					4.8	7.1
22631M	96038M	785805M	2287838M	1640619M	1869106M		Net Sales ($)	5417260M	3556239M
1930M	22157M	354984M	1364810M	904391M	1322792M		Total Assets ($)	3126759M	1847257M

M = $ thousand   MM = $ million
See Pages viii through xx for Explanation of Ratios and Data

© RMA 2024

MANUFACTURING—Sheet Metal Work Manufacturing NAICS 332322

Comparative Historical Data | Current Data Sorted by Sales

Comparative Historical Data			Type of Statement	Current Data Sorted by Sales						
10	13	11	Unqualified				1	1	10
18	34	28	Reviewed		1	1	7	6	13
16	19	14	Compiled		1	1	1	3	8
15	28	23	Tax Returns		2	5	7	8	1
51	90	95	Other		6	6	15	26	42
4/1/21-	4/1/22-	4/1/23-			38 (4/1-9/30/23)		133 (10/1/23-3/31/24)		
3/31/22	3/31/23	3/31/24		0-1MM	1-3MM	3-5MM	5-10MM	10-25MM	25MM & OVER
ALL	ALL	ALL	NUMBER OF STATEMENTS						
110	184	171			10	13	30	44	74
%	%	%	ASSETS	%	%	%	%	%	%
15.9	17.1	17.1	Cash & Equivalents		19.6	20.7	24.0	17.3	13.2
28.3	25.2	22.6	Trade Receivables (net)	D	28.1	15.9	25.5	25.8	20.0
19.7	20.6	20.4	Inventory	A	11.6	19.2	11.2	18.5	26.6
4.5	3.7	2.7	All Other Current	T	3.0	2.5	1.6	3.8	2.4
68.5	66.5	62.8	Total Current	A	62.3	58.3	62.3	65.4	62.2
23.5	24.4	24.7	Fixed Assets (net)		32.3	28.6	25.5	24.0	23.1
5.1	3.7	4.0	Intangibles (net)	N	3.1	6.4	4.1	3.1	4.1
2.9	5.5	8.6	All Other Non-Current	O	2.4	6.8	8.1	7.5	10.6
100.0	100.0	100.0	Total	T	100.0	100.0	100.0	100.0	100.0
			LIABILITIES	A					
4.0	4.7	4.2	Notes Payable-Short Term	V	4.7	5.5	2.6	1.8	6.0
2.3	3.3	3.0	Cur. Mat.-L.T.D.	A	2.7	4.2	3.4	2.5	2.9
12.5	9.4	9.3	Trade Payables	I	6.6	4.9	8.8	10.8	9.6
.1	.3	.3	Income Taxes Payable	L	.0	.0	.0	.4	.4
9.3	9.8	12.3	All Other Current	A	28.4	16.5	9.4	9.0	12.4
28.3	27.6	28.9	Total Current	B	42.4	31.0	24.2	24.5	31.2
17.3	18.8	17.0	Long-Term Debt	L	25.4	22.1	20.0	17.5	13.4
.5	.3	.4	Deferred Taxes	E	.0	.0	.2	.3	.6
3.6	4.4	5.8	All Other Non-Current		3.1	5.3	4.8	7.8	5.4
50.3	48.9	48.0	Net Worth		29.1	41.6	50.8	49.9	49.4
100.0	100.0	100.0	Total Liabilities & Net Worth		100.0	100.0	100.0	100.0	100.0
			INCOME DATA						
100.0	100.0	100.0	Net Sales		100.0	100.0	100.0	100.0	100.0
30.6	30.5	30.5	Gross Profit		41.1	39.1	34.8	29.5	26.3
23.5	22.7	22.6	Operating Expenses		37.7	30.6	27.7	22.0	17.5
7.1	7.7	7.8	Operating Profit		3.4	8.5	7.1	7.5	8.8
-2.8	.0	.1	All Other Expenses (net)		-.5	-.6	.2	-.2	.5
9.9	7.7	7.7	Profit Before Taxes		4.0	9.1	6.9	7.7	8.3
			RATIOS						
4.8	5.0	4.8			4.7	4.6	6.7	5.3	3.6
2.6	2.7	2.6	Current		1.8	2.2	3.1	3.1	2.3
1.8	1.6	1.5			1.0	1.1	1.8	2.0	1.3
3.5	3.2	3.2			4.1	3.9	5.7	4.0	2.2
1.7	1.7	1.6	Quick		1.6	1.2	2.4	2.3	1.0
1.0	.9	.7			.4	.4	1.3	1.3	.6
28 12.9	29 12.7	27 13.6		8 43.0	0 UND	31 11.7	29 12.4	27 13.7
44 8.3	43 8.5	42 8.7	Sales/Receivables	42 8.6	26 14.0	51 7.2	47 7.8	40 9.2
66 5.5	59 6.2	60 6.1		85 4.3	42 8.6	65 5.6	59 6.2	56 6.5
13 27.4	14 25.6	22 16.7		0 UND	0 UND	6 59.4	17 21.1	42 8.7
46 8.0	52 7.0	51 7.2	Cost of Sales/Inventory	12 29.4	44 8.3	40 9.2	36 10.0	70 5.2
81 4.5	83 4.4	81 4.5		74 4.9	54 6.7	70 5.2	74 4.9	99 3.7
14 25.5	11 34.4	11 32.6		8 47.1	0 UND	6 61.2	15 24.5	13 27.8
26 14.0	19 19.5	21 17.6	Cost of Sales/Payables	12 31.0	5 79.0	17 21.0	22 16.7	22 16.4
42 8.6	34 10.8	33 10.9		34 10.7	25 14.6	41 9.0	34 10.6	34 10.7
3.3	3.2	3.5			3.4	3.9	2.9	3.3	3.9
5.2	5.2	5.8	Sales/Working Capital		7.2	7.5	5.0	4.9	6.1
8.7	10.6	12.6			NM	NM	12.0	9.4	13.7
78.1	45.9	37.7			19.5	34.8	35.2	60.5
(97) 20.5	(167) 13.8	(149) 9.0	EBIT/Interest	(11) 9.9	(24) 8.0	(40) 5.3	(66) 12.8
6.5	3.3	3.1			2.6	3.1	.4	3.4
26.7	8.8	7.1	Net Profit + Depr., Dep.,					6.7
(20) 7.1	(39) 5.4	(37) 3.3	Amort./Cur. Mat. L/T/D				(27) 3.3
3.9	2.0	1.5						1.6
.2	.2	.3			.4	.4	.2	.3	.3
.4	.5	.5	Fixed/Worth		1.5	.6	.4	.5	.5
1.1	1.0	1.1			NM	1.7	1.4	.8	.9
.4	.4	.4			.5	.7	.3	.4	.4
1.0	1.0	.9	Debt/Worth		2.1	1.1	.8	.7	.9
2.5	2.4	3.0			NM	4.4	2.9	2.3	2.4
72.7	56.2	49.3	% Profit Before Taxes/Tangible		377.0	33.8	54.1	42.6
(102) 34.5	(168) 30.4	(153) 29.1	Net Worth		44.5	(26) 15.6	(38) 28.0	(68) 30.6
17.7	12.7	8.2			12.9	2.5	1.7	15.4
29.8	26.6	27.4	% Profit Before Taxes/Total		44.4	57.8	28.1	32.1	23.8
16.0	14.2	14.1	Assets		14.4	23.5	9.1	14.4	14.4
7.3	4.3	3.3			-3.5	3.5	1.2	.4	5.3
28.0	26.8	25.8			46.4	91.0	55.4	24.3	18.4
10.3	9.6	9.1	Sales/Net Fixed Assets		14.2	13.3	8.2	7.6	9.0
4.7	4.3	4.9			4.2	4.0	4.0	4.5	6.2
2.6	2.6	2.8			5.8	8.3	3.2	2.6	2.3
2.1	2.0	1.9	Sales/Total Assets		2.3	3.0	1.8	1.8	1.8
1.5	1.3	1.3			1.3	1.6	1.1	1.4	1.4
1.2	.8	1.2				1.5	1.1	1.1
(82) 2.1	(143) 2.0	(129) 2.2	% Depr., Dep., Amort./Sales	(18) 3.7	(36) 2.4	(65) 2.0
4.1	3.4	3.7				5.9	3.9	3.3
1.2	1.2	1.8				2.0	1.7
(42) 3.1	(72) 2.6	(57) 2.6	% Officers', Directors',	(19) 2.8	(19) 2.3
5.6	4.6	4.3	Owners' Comp/Sales			3.9	3.6
3563927M	5673130M	6702037M	Net Sales ($)	22400M	50393M	229157M	665984M	5734103M
1891414M	3244837M	3971064M	Total Assets ($)	11381M	19547M	159058M	389600M	3391478M

M = $ thousand   MM = $ million
See Pages viii through xx for Explanation of Ratios and Data
© RMA 2024

MANUFACTURING—Ornamental and Architectural Metal Work Manufacturing NAICS 332323

Current Data Sorted by Assets							Comparative Historical Data		
		1	1	1	1	Type of Statement		2	1
		4	10	1		Unqualified		11	6
		4				Reviewed		3	3
	1	2				Compiled		10	1
1	3	12	11	4	1	Tax Returns		38	31
	12 (4/1-9/30/23)		45 (10/1/23-3/31/24)			Other		4/1/19-	4/1/20-
0-500M	500M-2MM	2-10MM	10-50MM	50-100MM	100-250MM			3/31/20	3/31/21
1	4	22	22	6	2	NUMBER OF STATEMENTS		ALL 64	ALL 42
%	%	%	%	%	%	ASSETS		%	%
		16.6	15.2			Cash & Equivalents		14.9	16.2
		34.9	23.3			Trade Receivables (net)		30.6	35.1
		14.6	19.8			Inventory		16.5	17.9
		6.1	7.5			All Other Current		5.6	4.7
		72.2	65.8			Total Current		67.5	73.8
		17.8	21.7			Fixed Assets (net)		21.2	19.4
		1.4	3.3			Intangibles (net)		5.8	1.5
		8.5	9.1			All Other Non-Current		5.5	5.3
		100.0	100.0			Total		100.0	100.0
						LIABILITIES			
		5.0	1.6			Notes Payable-Short Term		8.9	9.6
		2.2	2.4			Cur. Mat.-L.T.D.		3.3	3.5
		9.1	8.9			Trade Payables		10.5	10.7
		.6	.0			Income Taxes Payable		.1	.3
		12.6	15.6			All Other Current		11.4	10.8
		29.5	28.5			Total Current		34.1	35.0
		13.6	13.8			Long-Term Debt		18.4	17.9
		.7	.3			Deferred Taxes		.4	.1
		4.9	8.4			All Other Non-Current		4.5	2.7
		51.3	49.0			Net Worth		42.6	44.3
		100.0	100.0			Total Liabilities & Net Worth		100.0	100.0
						INCOME DATA			
		100.0	100.0			Net Sales		100.0	100.0
		38.0	37.1			Gross Profit		35.8	37.2
		31.7	27.9			Operating Expenses		26.5	28.8
		6.3	9.2			Operating Profit		9.3	8.3
		-.3	-.1			All Other Expenses (net)		.4	-1.4
		6.6	9.3			Profit Before Taxes		8.9	9.8
						RATIOS			
		6.0	3.6					3.4	3.1
		2.4	2.3			Current		2.0	2.2
		1.6	1.6					1.4	1.6
		4.8	1.8					2.8	2.3
		1.7	1.5			Quick		1.3	1.5
		1.0	1.0					.7	1.0
		41 9.0	31 11.6				27	13.7	30 12.1
		61 6.0	56 6.5			Sales/Receivables	46	8.0	51 7.1
		81 4.5	89 4.1				81	4.5	91 4.0
		9 39.0	16 23.2				6	65.6	3 143.2
		46 8.0	73 5.0			Cost of Sales/Inventory	42	8.7	49 7.5
		89 4.1	135 2.7				74	4.9	79 4.6
		12 30.9	24 15.1				17	21.6	14 27.0
		21 17.0	30 12.2			Cost of Sales/Payables	28	13.0	24 15.5
		35 10.4	41 8.8				39	9.4	35 10.3
		3.5	3.1					4.2	4.0
		4.5	3.6			Sales/Working Capital		6.6	5.9
		8.2	7.1					13.7	8.5
		54.1	75.6					23.9	61.8
		(19) 6.1	(21) 12.9			EBIT/Interest	(56)	11.8	(36) 14.9
		1.8	4.6					3.4	6.0
						Net Profit + Depr., Dep.,		9.5	
						Amort./Cur. Mat. L/T/D	(14)	3.7	
								2.6	
		.2	.3					.2	.1
		.4	.4			Fixed/Worth		.5	.3
		.7	1.0					1.4	.7
		.3	.6					.4	.6
		.7	1.3			Debt/Worth		1.6	1.1
		3.4	2.9					3.8	2.0
		42.8	42.5					78.5	63.7
		(21) 22.5	(21) 31.2			% Profit Before Taxes/Tangible Net Worth	(58)	34.1	(41) 40.4
		4.2	15.4					15.6	18.2
		19.9	20.3					26.3	37.3
		9.8	9.1			% Profit Before Taxes/Total Assets		13.5	17.4
		1.8	6.2					5.7	7.2
		42.1	14.7					20.9	34.3
		9.1	9.5			Sales/Net Fixed Assets		11.9	14.0
		5.1	4.7					7.1	7.2
		2.3	1.9					2.6	2.8
		2.0	1.4			Sales/Total Assets		2.2	2.2
		1.5	1.2					1.7	1.7
		1.0	1.5					1.2	.6
		(18) 2.1	(21) 2.3			% Depr., Dep., Amort./Sales	(56)	1.6	(32) 1.1
		3.3	3.0					2.9	2.7
						% Officers', Directors' Owners' Comp/Sales		1.1	1.2
							(22)	2.5	(14) 2.7
								5.4	5.6
392M	17241M	265907M	703332M	592717M	637144M	Net Sales ($)		2695894M	1249610M
149M	6522M	137883M	499215M	376772M	327468M	Total Assets ($)		1435533M	651368M

© RMA 2024   M = $ thousand   MM = $ million
See Pages viii through xx for Explanation of Ratios and Data

MANUFACTURING—Ornamental and Architectural Metal Work Manufacturing   NAICS 332323

Comparative Historical Data | Current Data Sorted by Sales

												3
			3		3	**Type of Statement**						5
	1		15		15	Unqualified				2	8	
	11		4		4	Reviewed				2	2	
	6		6		3	Compiled			1	1	1	
	5		32		32	Tax Returns			3	4	11	13
	24					Other	1	12 (4/1-9/30/23)		45 (10/1/23-3/31/24)		
	4/1/21-		4/1/22-		4/1/23-							
	3/31/22		3/31/23		3/31/24		0-1MM	1-3MM	3-5MM	5-10MM	10-25MM	25MM & OVER
	ALL		ALL		ALL							
	47		60		57	NUMBER OF STATEMENTS	1	4	9	22	21	
	%		%		%	**ASSETS**	%	%	%	%	%	%
	15.8		12.3		15.0	Cash & Equivalents					14.1	14.1
	28.6		26.9		28.3	Trade Receivables (net)	D				36.1	19.2
	19.0		16.1		18.5	Inventory	A				14.6	25.4
	6.3		6.9		5.4	All Other Current	T				6.9	5.1
	69.7		62.2		67.3	Total Current	A				71.7	63.8
	20.4		26.6		22.2	Fixed Assets (net)					15.6	28.5
	4.8		3.1		2.3	Intangibles (net)	N				2.6	2.3
	5.1		8.1		8.3	All Other Non-Current	O				10.0	5.3
	100.0		100.0		100.0	Total	T				100.0	100.0
						LIABILITIES						
	6.1		5.8		4.7	Notes Payable-Short Term	A				4.1	4.7
	3.2		2.1		2.2	Cur. Mat.-L.T.D.	V				2.1	2.8
	9.5		10.2		9.1	Trade Payables	A				9.9	8.8
	.4		.2		.3	Income Taxes Payable	I				.6	.1
	15.1		13.7		13.1	All Other Current	L				16.7	12.6
	34.3		32.0		29.4	Total Current	A				33.2	29.0
	15.9		24.1		15.9	Long-Term Debt	B				13.4	21.8
	.2		.3		.4	Deferred Taxes	L				.4	.2
	3.3		8.0		5.7	All Other Non-Current	E				7.3	4.5
	46.5		35.6		48.6	Net Worth					45.6	44.5
	100.0		100.0		100.0	Total Liabilities & Net Worth					100.0	100.0
						INCOME DATA						
	100.0		100.0		100.0	Net Sales					100.0	100.0
	33.8		33.8		37.4	Gross Profit					35.9	34.4
	27.7		27.4		28.3	Operating Expenses					29.0	23.6
	6.1		6.4		9.1	Operating Profit					6.9	10.8
	-2.7		.4		-.1	All Other Expenses (net)					.0	.0
	8.8		6.1		9.2	Profit Before Taxes					6.9	10.8
						RATIOS						
	3.8		3.8		4.5						4.9	3.3
	2.2		2.3		2.2	Current					2.1	2.0
	1.5		1.0		1.5						1.5	1.5
	2.0		2.1		2.8						2.7	1.6
	1.4		1.3		1.4	Quick					1.4	1.3
	.9		.6		.9						1.0	.8
33	11.1	30	12.1	33	11.2					45	8.2	30	12.3
54	6.8	51	7.2	53	6.9	Sales/Receivables				65	5.6	41	8.8
76	4.8	69	5.3	78	4.7					87	4.2	72	5.1
4	86.5	3	104.3	12	30.4					9	42.7	42	8.7
54	6.7	38	9.5	64	5.7	Cost of Sales/Inventory				38	9.7	87	4.2
74	4.9	87	4.2	107	3.4					89	4.1	122	3.0
12	30.9	15	24.8	14	26.2					14	25.5	19	18.9
19	19.3	24	15.2	25	14.5	Cost of Sales/Payables				30	12.1	26	13.8
33	11.2	45	8.2	38	9.5					47	7.7	39	9.3
	3.9		4.0		3.2						3.3	3.1
	5.8		6.0		4.8	Sales/Working Capital					5.1	4.8
	11.5		50.5		11.1						9.1	11.3
	53.5		24.5		50.7						54.1	74.7
(41)	22.2	(52)	10.0	(50)	8.9	EBIT/Interest				(19)	7.1	13.3
	7.2		1.4		2.6						1.3	5.1
					16.3	Net Profit + Depr., Dep.,						
				(16)	7.9	Amort./Cur. Mat. L/T/D						
					2.4							
	.2		.2		.2						.2	.3
	.4		.7		.4	Fixed/Worth					.4	.7
	.9		3.2		1.1						.5	1.2
	.4		.5		.4						.5	.5
	.8		1.4		.9	Debt/Worth					1.4	1.3
	2.6		6.0		2.7						4.1	2.4
	68.2		61.3		48.4	% Profit Before Taxes/Tangible					49.1	44.3
(43)	39.0	(53)	22.1	(54)	25.1	Net Worth				(21)	27.2	(20)	19.5
	11.0		3.2		10.6						8.2	11.2
	33.3		25.2		21.3	% Profit Before Taxes/Total					23.2	23.1
	12.4		6.1		11.1	Assets					9.2	10.3
	3.5		.8		5.3						1.5	6.0
	21.4		18.4		20.5						32.7	13.4
	12.6		8.9		9.6	Sales/Net Fixed Assets					13.3	7.0
	6.6		4.0		4.6						6.4	3.4
	2.7		2.5		2.3						2.3	1.9
	2.2		2.0		1.9	Sales/Total Assets					2.0	1.5
	1.5		1.3		1.3						1.3	1.2
	.9		.9		1.1						1.0	1.5
(38)	1.4	(45)	1.5	(49)	2.3	% Depr., Dep., Amort./Sales				(18)	2.1	(19)	2.3
	3.0		3.2		3.0						3.0	3.0
	1.4		1.3		1.1							
(16)	3.6	(16)	2.9	(15)	3.0	% Officers', Directors'						
	5.4		6.5		4.8	Owners' Comp/Sales						
	1881336M		2827444M		2216733M	Net Sales ($)	392M		14909M	62082M	378585M	1760765M
	998480M		1589255M		1348009M	Total Assets ($)	149M		7131M	40147M	225602M	1074980M

© RMA 2024   M = $ thousand   MM = $ million
See Pages viii through xx for Explanation of Ratios and Data

MANUFACTURING—Metal Tank (Heavy Gauge) Manufacturing NAICS 332420

Current Data Sorted by Assets | Comparative Historical Data

							Type of Statement				
			2		1		Unqualified		7		3
		1	4	1			Reviewed		3		2
							Compiled		3		3
							Tax Returns		6		1
	1	2	7	4	3		Other		16		19
	7 (4/1-9/30/23)		19 (10/1/23-3/31/24)						4/1/19-3/31/20		4/1/20-3/31/21
0-500M	500M-2MM	2-10MM	10-50MM	50-100MM	100-250MM		NUMBER OF STATEMENTS		35 ALL		28 ALL
%	%	%	%	%	%		ASSETS		%		%
			11.3				Cash & Equivalents		11.5		15.4
			25.7				Trade Receivables (net)		24.8		23.5
			21.1				Inventory		21.5		17.8
			5.2				All Other Current		2.9		3.3
			63.2				Total Current		60.7		60.0
			21.3				Fixed Assets (net)		25.9		29.7
			6.7				Intangibles (net)		7.2		6.1
			8.7				All Other Non-Current		6.2		4.2
			100.0				Total		100.0		100.0
							LIABILITIES				
			5.0				Notes Payable-Short Term		6.8		3.6
			2.7				Cur. Mat.-L.T.D.		3.0		2.8
			13.5				Trade Payables		13.4		10.2
			.0				Income Taxes Payable		.1		.4
			18.2				All Other Current		19.7		17.0
			39.4				Total Current		42.9		34.0
			12.5				Long-Term Debt		16.6		21.1
			.1				Deferred Taxes		.3		.1
			4.0				All Other Non-Current		5.2		6.8
			44.1				Net Worth		35.0		38.1
			100.0				Total Liabilities & Net Worth		100.0		100.0
							INCOME DATA				
			100.0				Net Sales		100.0		100.0
			22.6				Gross Profit		24.8		31.8
			15.1				Operating Expenses		21.2		26.3
			7.5				Operating Profit		3.7		5.5
			1.2				All Other Expenses (net)		.3		-.7
			6.3				Profit Before Taxes		3.4		6.2
							RATIOS				
			2.5						2.4		3.8
			1.6				Current		1.7		2.0
			1.2						1.0		1.2
			1.5						2.0		2.6
			.9				Quick		.9		1.2
			.6						.5		.7
		31	11.6					37	9.9	23	15.9
		47	7.8				Sales/Receivables	46	7.9	35	10.3
		57	6.4					62	5.9	47	7.8
		1	257.3					18	20.6	7	51.7
		51	7.1				Cost of Sales/Inventory	56	6.5	41	9.0
		94	3.9					89	4.1	78	4.7
		19	19.7					16	22.7	11	31.9
		34	10.7				Cost of Sales/Payables	28	13.1	24	15.2
		49	7.4					40	9.1	39	9.4
			5.2						5.0		3.9
			6.9				Sales/Working Capital		7.6		6.5
			27.1						73.7		33.2
			65.9						52.1		56.4
			8.0				EBIT/Interest	(29)	4.9	(25)	7.9
			.4						2.5		1.6
							Net Profit + Depr., Dep., Amort./Cur. Mat. L/T/D				
			.3						.3		.4
			.6				Fixed/Worth		.6		.6
			1.3						1.0		1.9
			.6						.8		.8
			1.5				Debt/Worth		1.4		2.0
			5.4						6.5		5.2
			65.4						55.4		109.9
			37.9				% Profit Before Taxes/Tangible Net Worth	(31)	22.2	(25)	36.5
			-5.8						7.5		11.0
			27.4						13.1		26.9
			13.3				% Profit Before Taxes/Total Assets		9.1		10.0
			-2.6						1.6		1.5
			17.5						20.5		12.7
			11.6				Sales/Net Fixed Assets		7.2		7.1
			5.9						4.7		4.3
			2.5						2.2		2.2
			1.8				Sales/Total Assets		1.8		1.8
			1.3						1.4		1.5
			1.2						1.6		.8
		(12)	2.3				% Depr., Dep., Amort./Sales	(33)	2.2	(25)	1.9
			3.5						3.2		3.0
							% Officers', Directors' Owners' Comp/Sales				
	714M	35649M	693811M	573580M	2122607M		Net Sales ($)		1342783M		1164395M
	1080M	12034M	345906M	376444M	732486M		Total Assets ($)		790866M		676008M

Data Not Available (0-500M column)

M = $ thousand   MM = $ million
See Pages viii through xx for Explanation of Ratios and Data

© RMA 2024

MANUFACTURING—Metal Tank (Heavy Gauge) Manufacturing NAICS 332420

Comparative Historical Data | **Current Data Sorted by Sales**

			Type of Statement						
2	4	3	Unqualified					3	
5	1	6	Reviewed					1	5
1	1		Compiled						
11	3		Tax Returns						
	14	17	Other	1	7 (4/1-9/30/23)		1	1	14
4/1/21-3/31/22 ALL	4/1/22-3/31/23 ALL	4/1/23-3/31/24 ALL					19 (10/1/23-3/31/24)		
				0-1MM	1-3MM	3-5MM	5-10MM	10-25MM	25MM & OVER
NUMBER OF STATEMENTS									
19	23	26		1			1	2	22
%	%	%	**ASSETS**	%	%	%	%	%	%
10.8	11.6	9.7	Cash & Equivalents						10.4
26.6	26.4	29.0	Trade Receivables (net)		D	D			28.0
22.2	22.8	21.4	Inventory		A	A			21.0
4.0	6.1	5.2	All Other Current		T	T			5.9
63.6	67.0	65.3	Total Current		A	A			65.3
24.3	23.2	20.1	Fixed Assets (net)						18.5
7.6	5.4	6.4	Intangibles (net)		N	N			7.0
4.4	4.4	8.1	All Other Non-Current		O	O			9.2
100.0	100.0	100.0	Total		T	T			100.0
			LIABILITIES		A	A			
11.7	6.1	8.6	Notes Payable-Short Term		V	V			4.0
3.3	2.7	1.8	Cur. Mat.-L.T.D.		A	A			2.1
13.0	14.4	13.7	Trade Payables		I	I			13.8
.1	.2	.0	Income Taxes Payable		L	L			.1
14.0	23.3	22.6	All Other Current		A	A			24.3
42.0	46.7	46.7	Total Current		B	B			44.3
16.3	19.2	9.9	Long-Term Debt		L	L			11.4
.0	.2	.4	Deferred Taxes		E	E			.4
9.7	14.8	6.1	All Other Non-Current						6.0
32.0	19.1	37.0	Net Worth						37.8
100.0	100.0	100.0	Total Liabilities & Net Worth						100.0
			INCOME DATA						
100.0	100.0	100.0	Net Sales						100.0
26.2	25.7	24.2	Gross Profit						22.7
24.6	21.7	15.3	Operating Expenses						14.3
1.6	4.1	8.9	Operating Profit						8.4
-4.4	.7	1.0	All Other Expenses (net)						.9
6.1	3.4	7.8	Profit Before Taxes						7.5
			RATIOS						
2.4	2.4	2.4							2.4
1.7	1.3	1.5	Current						1.5
1.3	1.0	1.1							1.1
1.8	2.1	1.1							1.2
1.0	.7	.9	Quick						.9
.4	.5	.5							.6
26 14.1	38 9.6	30 12.0							32 11.4
59 6.2	47 7.7	48 7.6	Sales/Receivables						48 7.6
69 5.3	87 4.2	61 6.0							61 6.0
5 73.3	21 17.1	22 16.3							17 21.6
62 5.9	57 6.4	47 7.7	Cost of Sales/Inventory						50 7.3
99 3.7	104 3.5	91 4.0							99 3.7
18 20.8	26 14.3	20 18.2							23 16.2
28 13.1	35 10.3	31 11.7	Cost of Sales/Payables						33 11.0
38 9.7	54 6.7	46 7.9							49 7.4
5.1	3.3	5.3							4.8
6.0	8.8	10.9	Sales/Working Capital						10.9
12.4	304.1	40.4							38.8
117.3	21.0	34.0							35.6
(15) 13.3	9.0	(24) 6.9	EBIT/Interest						(21) 7.4
-3.6	-3.3	2.1							3.3
			Net Profit + Depr., Dep., Amort./Cur. Mat. L/T/D						
.3	.4	.2							.3
.6	.6	.5	Fixed/Worth						.5
5.4	-5.1	1.8							1.7
.6	1.3	.7							.7
1.5	2.3	1.9	Debt/Worth						2.0
28.0	-13.0	5.8							5.8
38.2	48.0	54.0							55.9
(15) 27.6	(16) 25.5	(22) 33.1	% Profit Before Taxes/Tangible Net Worth						(19) 34.3
4.1	6.2	7.6							9.7
21.1	20.8	23.0							24.3
9.2	9.0	10.8	% Profit Before Taxes/Total Assets						11.5
-3.9	-9.7	3.3							3.8
12.5	14.9	19.0							18.6
10.5	8.4	13.4	Sales/Net Fixed Assets						13.4
5.4	4.6	6.9							6.9
2.1	2.3	2.6							2.5
1.7	1.7	1.8	Sales/Total Assets						1.8
1.4	1.4	1.3							1.3
.9	1.4	1.1							1.1
(17) 2.2	(20) 2.2	(22) 1.7	% Depr., Dep., Amort./Sales						(20) 2.0
3.0	3.7	2.7							3.2
			% Officers', Directors' Owners' Comp/Sales						
421699M	877608M	3426361M	Net Sales ($)	714M			5889M	29760M	3389998M
241722M	618170M	1467950M	Total Assets ($)	1080M			2219M	9815M	1454836M

M = $ thousand   MM = $ million
See Pages viii through xx for Explanation of Ratios and Data
© RMA 2024

MANUFACTURING—Other Metal Container Manufacturing NAICS 332439

Current Data Sorted by Assets / Comparative Historical Data

0-500M	500M-2MM	2-10MM	10-50MM	50-100MM	100-250MM	Type of Statement		4/1/19-3/31/20 ALL		4/1/20-3/31/21 ALL
	1	3 1 1 7	2 3 1 5			Unqualified Reviewed Compiled Tax Returns Other		3 5 2 16		2 1 2 2 11
	2 6 (4/1-9/30/23)		22 (10/1/23-3/31/24)	2						
						NUMBER OF STATEMENTS		26		18
	3 %	12 %	11 %	%	%	**ASSETS**		%		%
D		25.6	11.8		D	Cash & Equivalents		15.0		16.2
A		12.4	18.2		A	Trade Receivables (net)		23.3		19.3
T		27.0	28.7		T	Inventory		25.7		24.8
A		6.9	.9		A	All Other Current		2.8		4.3
		71.9	59.4			Total Current		66.8		64.6
N		21.1	20.5		N	Fixed Assets (net)		24.1		25.1
O		.5	5.6		O	Intangibles (net)		3.8		5.2
T		6.5	14.5		T	All Other Non-Current		5.2		5.0
		100.0	100.0			Total		100.0		100.0
A					A	**LIABILITIES**				
V		7.1	5.4		V	Notes Payable-Short Term		8.7		9.8
A		2.5	3.6		A	Cur. Mat.-L.T.D.		1.9		3.8
I		8.7	11.1		I	Trade Payables		11.3		13.0
L		.0	.0		L	Income Taxes Payable		.8		.5
A		22.9	8.5		A	All Other Current		12.8		14.5
B		41.1	28.7		B	Total Current		35.5		41.5
L		10.8	6.7		L	Long-Term Debt		12.2		19.1
E		.0	.2		E	Deferred Taxes		.2		.8
		4.6	9.3			All Other Non-Current		13.8		2.8
		43.5	55.2			Net Worth		38.2		35.7
		100.0	100.0			Total Liabilities & Net Worth		100.0		100.0
						INCOME DATA				
		100.0	100.0			Net Sales		100.0		100.0
		37.6	29.8			Gross Profit		34.8		31.1
		26.6	27.4			Operating Expenses		26.5		27.8
		11.0	2.4			Operating Profit		8.2		3.4
		.2	.7			All Other Expenses (net)		1.8		-.5
		10.8	1.7			Profit Before Taxes		6.5		3.9
						RATIOS				
		3.3	5.5					4.1		2.5
		2.5	2.4			Current		2.4		1.8
		1.3	.7					1.5		1.2
		2.4	2.8					3.0		1.8
		1.3	.9			Quick		1.3		.9
		.5	.4					.7		.6
		6 57.5	26 13.9				30	12.0	26	14.0
		21 17.5	32 11.4			Sales/Receivables	39	9.3	33	11.1
		30 12.0	49 7.4				54	6.7	45	8.2
		24 15.4	51 7.2				33	11.0	35	10.3
		48 7.6	99 3.7			Cost of Sales/Inventory	52	7.0	73	5.0
		99 3.7	152 2.4				122	3.0	81	4.5
		12 30.8	15 24.1				11	33.1	15	24.3
		15 24.2	26 13.8			Cost of Sales/Payables	18	20.5	25	14.4
		19 19.0	37 9.8				33	11.2	41	8.9
		4.6	2.7					4.0		4.0
		7.3	3.9			Sales/Working Capital		5.9		7.3
		13.4	-11.1					14.2		27.6
								15.6		52.5
						EBIT/Interest	(16)	6.2	(17)	5.2
								1.4		1.5
						Net Profit + Depr., Dep., Amort./Cur. Mat. L/T/D				
		.2	.1					.2		.6
		.4	.3			Fixed/Worth		.5		.9
		.6	2.8					1.9		-2.0
		.4	.2					.3		.8
		1.6	.7			Debt/Worth		1.0		1.4
		2.3	3.4					5.6		-231.5
		62.1	19.7					33.1		26.2
	(11)	40.9	1.7			% Profit Before Taxes/Tangible Net Worth	(21)	19.6	(13)	11.3
		20.2	-110.1					10.4		5.1
		49.5	14.7					22.0		15.1
		17.2	1.6			% Profit Before Taxes/Total Assets		11.1		4.4
		9.8	-8.4					3.6		.9
		29.9	25.7					21.2		27.4
		13.7	9.5			Sales/Net Fixed Assets		8.7		12.3
		5.9	3.2					5.1		4.2
		3.2	2.0					2.5		2.6
		2.4	1.5			Sales/Total Assets		2.0		1.8
		1.5	1.1					1.7		1.4
		.7						.6		1.2
		.8				% Depr., Dep., Amort./Sales	(23)	1.1	(13)	2.4
		2.1						3.0		6.0
						% Officers', Directors' Owners' Comp/Sales				
	13601M	145179M	325331M	288427M		Net Sales ($)		837879M		512385M
	3797M	51533M	246995M	128351M		Total Assets ($)		429536M		305157M

M = $ thousand   MM = $ million
See Pages viii through xx for Explanation of Ratios and Data

© RMA 2024

MANUFACTURING—Other Metal Container Manufacturing NAICS 332439

Comparative Historical Data | Current Data Sorted by Sales

				Type of Statement						
	2	4	4	Unqualified				2	2	4
	3	4	6	Reviewed		1		1		2
		1	2	Compiled				1		1
	2	2	2	Tax Returns			2	5	3	4
	12	15	14	Other						
	4/1/21-3/31/22 ALL	4/1/22-3/31/23 ALL	4/1/23-3/31/24 ALL		0-1MM	6 (4/1-9/30/23) 1-3MM	3-5MM	22 (10/1/23-3/31/24) 5-10MM	10-25MM	25MM & OVER
	19	26	28	NUMBER OF STATEMENTS		1	2	9	5	11
	%	%	%	ASSETS	%	%	%	%	%	%
	23.1	14.0	19.6	Cash & Equivalents						18.5
	19.2	26.0	15.1	Trade Receivables (net)	D					16.9
	23.2	19.5	24.7	Inventory	A					24.1
	3.9	3.3	5.9	All Other Current	T					5.3
	69.4	62.8	65.4	Total Current	A					64.8
	19.6	24.9	22.7	Fixed Assets (net)						22.3
	7.0	4.2	2.5	Intangibles (net)	N					3.4
	4.0	8.1	9.5	All Other Non-Current	O					9.5
	100.0	100.0	100.0	Total	T					100.0
				LIABILITIES	A					
	6.1	3.9	5.2	Notes Payable-Short Term	V					3.1
	3.0	2.9	3.1	Cur. Mat.-L.T.D.	A					3.5
	16.9	11.3	9.4	Trade Payables	I					10.9
	.9	.2	.4	Income Taxes Payable	L					.0
	16.1	21.1	16.8	All Other Current	A					25.7
	42.9	39.4	34.8	Total Current	B					43.3
	13.9	15.6	8.7	Long-Term Debt	L					6.7
	.2	.7	.7	Deferred Taxes	E					.2
	6.7	6.4	6.5	All Other Non-Current						10.2
	36.4	37.9	49.3	Net Worth						39.6
	100.0	100.0	100.0	Total Liabilities & Net Worth						100.0
				INCOME DATA						
	100.0	100.0	100.0	Net Sales						100.0
	32.4	33.4	34.3	Gross Profit						28.0
	24.3	23.0	27.8	Operating Expenses						22.3
	8.1	10.4	6.4	Operating Profit						5.7
	-.4	.3	.5	All Other Expenses (net)						.7
	8.5	10.2	6.0	Profit Before Taxes						5.0
				RATIOS						
	5.3	2.8	5.4							5.5
	1.6	2.0	2.3	Current						1.7
	1.0	1.3	1.3							.7
	3.3	1.8	2.6							2.8
	1.1	1.3	1.1	Quick						.9
	.4	.6	.5							.4
30	12.1	30	12.0	15	24.2	Sales/Receivables				23	15.6
33	11.0	45	8.1	26	14.0					30	12.0
50	7.3	56	6.5	39	9.3					49	7.4
34	10.7	21	17.0	27	13.5	Cost of Sales/Inventory				40	9.2
54	6.8	53	6.9	54	6.7					58	6.3
74	4.9	73	5.0	104	3.5					126	2.9
26	14.1	11	32.6	12	31.6	Cost of Sales/Payables				15	24.1
42	8.7	24	15.5	17	21.0					26	13.8
64	5.7	39	9.4	27	13.6					37	9.8
	2.8	3.8	3.4	Sales/Working Capital						2.7
	5.6	7.7	7.7							12.1
	-123.0	16.7	22.8							-12.4
	32.8	65.5	32.3	EBIT/Interest						
(12)	13.9	(19) 12.1	(20) 7.7							
	4.2	3.8	-1.3							
				Net Profit + Depr., Dep., Amort./Cur. Mat. L/T/D						
	.4	.1	.2	Fixed/Worth						.1
	.7	.6	.3							.5
	243.0	2.4	1.1							11.1
	.5	.4	.4	Debt/Worth						.2
	1.6	.8	.7							.7
	999.8	4.9	2.3							34.9
	69.6	67.1	44.7	% Profit Before Taxes/Tangible Net Worth						
(15)	37.8	(22) 27.5	(26) 19.5							
	3.4	16.8	-1.6							
	24.8	36.7	29.6	% Profit Before Taxes/Total Assets						30.0
	11.2	14.6	11.8							9.4
	3.3	8.1	2.3							-4.7
	18.3	24.3	29.1	Sales/Net Fixed Assets						29.4
	13.6	10.3	11.4							9.5
	5.4	4.5	4.8							3.2
	2.5	2.4	2.4	Sales/Total Assets						2.4
	1.8	1.9	2.0							1.9
	1.4	1.2	1.4							1.1
	1.5	.6	.7	% Depr., Dep., Amort./Sales						.8
(11)	2.2	(22) 3.0	(26) 1.6						(10)	1.7
	4.4	4.5	3.1							4.4
				% Officers', Directors' Owners' Comp/Sales						
	666167M	956098M	772538M	Net Sales ($)		2712M	7695M	75252M	83882M	602997M
	425026M	617540M	430676M	Total Assets ($)		1801M	4549M	36133M	42209M	345984M

© RMA 2024 M = $ thousand MM = $ million
See Pages viii through xx for Explanation of Ratios and Data

MANUFACTURING—Hardware Manufacturing NAICS 332510

Current Data Sorted by Assets | Comparative Historical Data

						Type of Statement		
			1	1	1	Unqualified	8	6
		3	7			Reviewed	7	3
		3	3			Compiled	4	3
	2	1				Tax Returns	6	2
		5	9	2	3	Other	22	16
	12 (4/1-9/30/23)		29 (10/1/23-3/31/24)				4/1/19- 3/31/20	4/1/20- 3/31/21
0-500M	500M-2MM	2-10MM	10-50MM	50-100MM	100-250MM		ALL	ALL
	2	12	20	3	4	NUMBER OF STATEMENTS	47	30
%	%	%	%	%	%	ASSETS	%	%
		19.5	8.1			Cash & Equivalents	14.6	15.2
D		20.0	17.2			Trade Receivables (net)	19.4	20.5
A		35.5	37.6			Inventory	34.1	31.5
T		1.6	2.3			All Other Current	1.7	1.5
A		76.6	65.2			Total Current	69.8	68.8
		12.4	22.2			Fixed Assets (net)	22.7	23.7
N		7.4	4.2			Intangibles (net)	3.4	5.4
O		3.6	8.4			All Other Non-Current	4.1	2.1
T		100.0	100.0			Total	100.0	100.0
						LIABILITIES		
A		6.0	5.6			Notes Payable-Short Term	8.5	5.7
V		2.8	2.0			Cur. Mat.-L.T.D.	2.7	1.8
A		6.1	10.3			Trade Payables	9.2	8.0
I		.1	.6			Income Taxes Payable	.1	.1
L		6.9	6.2			All Other Current	7.3	6.1
A		21.9	24.8			Total Current	27.8	21.7
B		8.1	11.3			Long-Term Debt	11.0	14.5
L		.0	.1			Deferred Taxes	.1	.2
E		2.4	6.9			All Other Non-Current	13.5	3.0
		67.5	57.0			Net Worth	47.5	60.5
		100.0	100.0			Total Liabilities & Net Worth	100.0	100.0
						INCOME DATA		
		100.0	100.0			Net Sales	100.0	100.0
		38.9	37.1			Gross Profit	35.7	34.0
		28.8	27.4			Operating Expenses	27.5	25.8
		10.0	9.8			Operating Profit	8.2	8.2
		.1	.0			All Other Expenses (net)	.3	-.2
		9.9	9.8			Profit Before Taxes	7.8	8.4
						RATIOS		
		8.4	4.5				6.0	7.8
		2.8	3.1			Current	2.7	2.8
		2.2	1.9				1.7	1.9
		5.2	2.5				3.3	5.2
		1.5	.8			Quick	1.3	2.3
		.8					.6	1.0
	24	14.9	31	11.6			29	12.5	34	10.8
	38	9.5	39	9.3		Sales/Receivables	38	9.5	41	8.8
	61	6.0	54	6.7			50	7.3	49	7.5
	63	5.8	72	5.1			60	6.1	55	6.6
	87	4.2	152	2.4		Cost of Sales/Inventory	104	3.5	96	3.8
	182	2.0	261	1.4			152	2.4	152	2.4
	8	48.6	16	22.8			15	24.0	13	28.0
	15	23.9	29	12.4		Cost of Sales/Payables	26	14.1	19	19.0
	29	12.8	55	6.6			42	8.6	33	11.1
		2.2	2.2				3.4	2.6
		3.6	4.0			Sales/Working Capital	4.4	4.1
		5.6	5.1				11.0	6.5
		26.1	29.3				46.7	70.2
		(11) 14.7	(14) 7.5			EBIT/Interest	(40) 13.2	(24) 18.2
		5.3	4.0				4.3	6.0
						Net Profit + Depr., Dep., Amort./Cur. Mat. L/T/D		
		.0	.1				.2	.1
		.2	.4			Fixed/Worth	.3	.4
		.6	1.1				.8	.8
		.2	.3				.3	.2
		.6	.6			Debt/Worth	.7	.6
		.8	2.4				2.0	1.1
		40.7	54.6				32.7	38.5
		(11) 25.6	20.4			% Profit Before Taxes/Tangible Net Worth	(44) 23.9	(28) 21.7
		11.7	12.7				18.3	7.9
		26.4	19.4				25.8	19.4
		13.4	9.4			% Profit Before Taxes/Total Assets	12.3	11.6
		6.7	5.7				6.3	4.0
		70.7	15.8				32.9	26.0
		22.0	8.2			Sales/Net Fixed Assets	9.5	9.5
		10.2	4.3				4.0	4.2
		2.2	1.7				2.4	2.2
		1.8	1.3			Sales/Total Assets	1.7	1.7
		1.4	1.0				1.3	1.2
			1.1				1.1	1.8
			(17) 2.3			% Depr., Dep., Amort./Sales	(40) 2.0	(23) 2.6
			3.3				3.8	3.8
						% Officers', Directors' Owners' Comp/Sales	.8	.7
							(11) 1.6	(11) 2.9
							5.7	4.9
5492M	136604M	609859M	506641M	615259M		Net Sales ($)	1828807M	1321445M
2990M	73714M	400123M	233740M	645268M		Total Assets ($)	1220747M	805376M

M = $ thousand   MM = $ million
See Pages viii through xx for Explanation of Ratios and Data

© RMA 2024

MANUFACTURING—Hardware Manufacturing NAICS 332510

Comparative Historical Data / Current Data Sorted by Sales

					Type of Statement						
	5		2	3	Unqualified					1	2
	5		7	10	Reviewed				1	5	4
	1		2	6	Compiled					5	1
	1		4	3	Tax Returns		1		1		
	26		23	19	Other		1	1	3	4	11
	4/1/21-3/31/22 ALL		4/1/22-3/31/23 ALL	4/1/23-3/31/24 ALL		0-1MM	12 (4/1-9/30/23) 1-3MM	3-5MM	29 (10/1/23-3/31/24) 5-10MM	10-25MM	25MM & OVER
	38		38	41	NUMBER OF STATEMENTS		2	1	5	15	18
	%		%	%	ASSETS	%	%	%	%	%	%
	11.5		6.4	11.4	Cash & Equivalents	D				11.2	8.4
	17.4		20.7	17.9	Trade Receivables (net)	A				16.4	19.7
	33.6		38.3	37.2	Inventory	T				40.7	34.3
	2.2		2.1	2.0	All Other Current	A				.6	3.3
	64.8		67.5	68.5	Total Current					68.9	65.7
	19.7		21.7	17.4	Fixed Assets (net)	N				21.6	17.6
	6.1		6.5	6.9	Intangibles (net)	O				4.6	6.1
	9.4		4.2	7.2	All Other Non-Current	T				4.9	10.6
	100.0		100.0	100.0	Total					100.0	100.0
					LIABILITIES	A					
	7.2		10.9	6.3	Notes Payable-Short Term	V				6.2	7.6
	1.6		2.9	2.2	Cur. Mat.-L.T.D.	A				1.9	2.5
	11.5		11.5	9.6	Trade Payables	I				7.2	12.6
	.0		.1	.4	Income Taxes Payable	L				.1	.9
	10.5		5.0	6.8	All Other Current	A				4.5	8.4
	30.8		30.3	25.4	Total Current	B				19.9	32.0
	13.4		31.0	11.7	Long-Term Debt	L				9.8	12.5
	.2		.1	.1	Deferred Taxes	E				.0	.3
	6.0		4.2	4.8	All Other Non-Current					5.2	5.1
	49.5		34.4	58.0	Net Worth					65.1	50.2
	100.0		100.0	100.0	Total Liabilities & Net Worth					100.0	100.0
					INCOME DATA						
	100.0		100.0	100.0	Net Sales					100.0	100.0
	35.2		34.5	36.1	Gross Profit					35.5	33.4
	27.7		26.6	27.0	Operating Expenses					27.8	23.6
	7.5		7.8	9.1	Operating Profit					7.6	9.7
	-1.7		1.1	.2	All Other Expenses (net)					-.9	.7
	9.2		6.7	8.9	Profit Before Taxes					8.5	9.0
					RATIOS						
	3.7		3.8	5.1						6.9	3.6
	2.1		2.3	3.0	Current					3.1	2.0
	1.7		1.6	1.9						2.6	1.4
	2.3		1.7	2.4						3.9	1.5
	1.1		1.2	.8	Quick					1.0	.8
	.5		.5	.6						.6	.6
25	14.7	26	14.1	33	11.1					34	10.7	31	11.8
41	8.9	46	8.0	40	9.1	Sales/Receivables				41	8.8	39	9.4
52	7.0	58	6.3	46	7.9					59	6.2	46	8.0
60	6.1	81	4.5	76	4.8					83	4.4	74	4.9
89	4.1	118	3.1	111	3.3	Cost of Sales/Inventory				228	1.6	99	3.7
174	2.1	182	2.0	215	1.7					281	1.3	130	2.8
11	33.3	14	25.4	14	26.9					12	30.9	20	18.2
27	13.3	25	14.6	26	13.8	Cost of Sales/Payables				23	15.6	33	10.9
47	7.8	57	6.4	40	9.2					55	6.6	43	8.5
	2.9		2.8	2.3						1.9	3.8
	6.1		4.7	4.0	Sales/Working Capital					2.5	5.3
	10.4		7.2	5.5						4.1	11.9
	40.6		20.6	20.3						34.7	19.3
(31)	22.9	(32)	7.1	(32)	12.6	EBIT/Interest				(10)	11.1	(14)	15.2
	6.1		3.1	3.3						4.6	4.4
				58.5	Net Profit + Depr., Dep.,						
		(10)	11.5	Amort./Cur. Mat. L/T/D							
				3.8							
	.1		.2	.1						.2	.1
	.4		.5	.3	Fixed/Worth					.3	.4
	.9		1.0	.9						.7	1.3
	.6		.4	.3						.1	.4
	1.1		1.3	.7	Debt/Worth					.3	.9
	2.0		2.9	2.2						1.6	2.7
	49.5		58.8	41.2						25.6	64.2
(36)	25.4	(33)	25.6	(38)	21.6	% Profit Before Taxes/Tangible Net Worth				(16)	19.5	31.7
	11.5		10.6	10.8						10.3	17.9
	22.1		20.3	19.4						15.5	22.8
	13.9		11.3	9.6	% Profit Before Taxes/Total Assets					8.4	13.6
	5.7		4.9	5.7						5.4	8.1
	28.0		36.4	30.1						11.9	29.4
	13.1		11.1	11.4	Sales/Net Fixed Assets					10.1	15.2
	5.3		3.8	5.6						4.0	7.2
	2.6		1.9	1.9						1.7	2.7
	1.5		1.5	1.6	Sales/Total Assets					1.3	1.7
	1.3		1.2	1.1						1.0	1.3
	1.0		.7	1.1						1.4	.8
(26)	2.0	(29)	1.5	(33)	1.6	% Depr., Dep., Amort./Sales				(12)	2.7	(15)	1.3
	3.2		2.9	3.1						3.1	3.0
			1.0	.8	% Officers', Directors' Owners' Comp/Sales						
		(11)	1.5	(10)	1.4							
			3.5	1.6							
	1386589M		1778094M	1873855M	Net Sales ($)		4585M	3312M	37193M	249430M	1579335M
	856038M		1026677M	1355835M	Total Assets ($)		4616M	1612M	24655M	210759M	1114193M

M = $ thousand   MM = $ million
See Pages viii through xx for Explanation of Ratios and Data
© RMA 2024

MANUFACTURING—Spring Manufacturing NAICS 332613

Current Data Sorted by Assets | Comparative Historical Data

0-500M	500M-2MM	2-10MM	10-50MM	50-100MM	100-250MM		Type of Statement				
			1	2	1		Unqualified		1		
		1	1				Reviewed		4		4
	1	2					Compiled		3		1
		2	1				Tax Returns		6		3
		8	5	5	1		Other		13		9
	9 (4/1-9/30/23)		22 (10/1/23-3/31/24)						4/1/19-3/31/20		4/1/20-3/31/21
1	1	13	8	7	2		NUMBER OF STATEMENTS		26 ALL		18 ALL
%	%	%	%	%	%		**ASSETS**		%		%
		18.7					Cash & Equivalents		7.3		17.2
		28.3					Trade Receivables (net)		23.7		19.5
		25.8					Inventory		30.0		27.2
		.3					All Other Current		3.3		.2
		73.2					Total Current		64.4		64.0
		20.1					Fixed Assets (net)		25.0		24.5
		1.4					Intangibles (net)		6.4		4.9
		5.4					All Other Non-Current		4.2		6.6
		100.0					Total		100.0		100.0
							LIABILITIES				
		4.4					Notes Payable-Short Term		11.4		5.8
		.7					Cur. Mat.-L.T.D.		1.2		3.7
		15.3					Trade Payables		9.8		7.1
		.7					Income Taxes Payable		.2		.3
		6.6					All Other Current		4.9		6.8
		27.7					Total Current		27.6		23.6
		3.9					Long-Term Debt		13.3		14.9
		.6					Deferred Taxes		.2		.4
		1.3					All Other Non-Current		6.9		4.2
		66.6					Net Worth		52.0		56.9
		100.0					Total Liabilities & Net Worth		100.0		100.0
							INCOME DATA				
		100.0					Net Sales		100.0		100.0
		33.0					Gross Profit		29.6		28.4
		21.3					Operating Expenses		22.4		22.6
		11.7					Operating Profit		7.2		5.9
		.2					All Other Expenses (net)		1.0		-.3
		11.6					Profit Before Taxes		6.2		6.1
							RATIOS				
		7.2							5.9		8.2
		4.6					Current		2.3		3.1
		1.6							1.7		1.7
		5.5							2.1		6.0
		2.8					Quick		1.2		1.7
		.7							.5		.8
	33	11.1						34	10.8	24	15.3
	47	7.8					Sales/Receivables	46	8.0	47	7.7
	58	6.3						54	6.8	54	6.7
	44	8.3						56	6.5	45	8.1
	66	5.5					Cost of Sales/Inventory	78	4.7	72	5.1
	85	4.3						118	3.1	111	3.3
	9	40.9						14	26.0	2	150.9
	16	23.3					Cost of Sales/Payables	19	19.7	18	20.5
	42	8.7						33	11.0	30	12.1
		3.8							3.2		2.9
		4.3					Sales/Working Capital		5.4		4.8
		7.7							9.9		11.4
									15.9		41.0
							EBIT/Interest	(21)	5.5	(13)	4.0
									.5		-2.8
							Net Profit + Depr., Dep., Amort./Cur. Mat. L/T/D				
		.1							.2		.2
		.3					Fixed/Worth		.5		.4
		.6							.9		.8
		.1							.3		.3
		.3					Debt/Worth		.9		.6
		1.1							2.3		2.6
		54.2							47.5		23.0
		35.7					% Profit Before Taxes/Tangible Net Worth	(23)	11.8	(16)	11.1
		14.5							4.4		.0
		45.4							21.7		10.8
		29.1					% Profit Before Taxes/Total Assets		5.8		4.5
		8.0							1.8		-1.2
		24.6							16.7		19.9
		11.1					Sales/Net Fixed Assets		9.5		7.3
		7.7							4.2		3.7
		2.7							2.2		2.4
		2.1					Sales/Total Assets		1.9		1.6
		1.8							1.4		1.3
		1.8							1.4		1.0
	(11)	2.1					% Depr., Dep., Amort./Sales	(22)	2.2	(16)	3.7
		3.5							4.1		6.5
									1.3		
							% Officers', Directors' Owners' Comp/Sales	(10)	3.1		
									4.6		
	2445M	149798M	223966M	898752M	286323M		Net Sales ($)		833779M		564675M
	1434M	67561M	191621M	526225M	252666M		Total Assets ($)		624328M		369595M

© RMA 2024

M = $ thousand   MM = $ million
See Pages viii through xx for Explanation of Ratios and Data

MANUFACTURING—Spring Manufacturing NAICS 332613

Comparative Historical Data / Current Data Sorted by Sales

	2		1		4	**Type of Statement**							2	4
	3		3		2	Unqualified						2	2	
	1		1		3	Reviewed							2	1
	3		3		3	Compiled					1	2	8	8
	5		10		19	Tax Returns			1		2	2		
	4/1/21-		4/1/22-		4/1/23-	Other		9 (4/1-9/30/23)			22 (10/1/23-3/31/24)			
	3/31/22		3/31/23		3/31/24		0-1MM	1-3MM	3-5MM	5-10MM	10-25MM	25MM & OVER		
	ALL		ALL		ALL									
	14		18		31	**NUMBER OF STATEMENTS**		1	1	4	12	13		
	%		%		%	**ASSETS**	%	%	%	%	%	%		
	13.3		9.2		13.7	Cash & Equivalents	D				12.8	13.4		
	22.6		23.4		22.3	Trade Receivables (net)	A				26.7	16.6		
	28.5		30.9		29.9	Inventory	T				26.5	30.4		
	.3		3.0		1.4	All Other Current	A				.1	3.0		
	64.7		66.4		67.2	Total Current					66.1	63.5		
	26.7		25.7		22.6	Fixed Assets (net)	N				23.5	25.4		
	4.8		2.0		3.2	Intangibles (net)	O				4.5	2.6		
	3.8		5.8		6.9	All Other Non-Current	T				5.9	8.5		
	100.0		100.0		100.0	Total					100.0	100.0		
						LIABILITIES	A							
	7.4		6.8		3.6	Notes Payable-Short Term	V				8.8	.4		
	1.3		2.8		1.8	Cur. Mat.-L.T.D.	A				2.1	2.1		
	6.7		7.4		9.7	Trade Payables	I				14.9	4.8		
	.0		.1		.5	Income Taxes Payable	L				.2	.6		
	4.0		3.9		11.7	All Other Current	A				5.7	20.1		
	19.4		20.9		27.3	Total Current	B				31.7	28.1		
	9.3		6.0		10.1	Long-Term Debt	L				13.4	9.4		
	1.0		.6		.9	Deferred Taxes	E				1.0	1.3		
	8.4		4.7		7.0	All Other Non-Current					7.2	7.0		
	61.9		67.8		54.7	Net Worth					46.7	54.2		
	100.0		100.0		100.0	Total Liabilities & Net Worth					100.0	100.0		
						INCOME DATA								
	100.0		100.0		100.0	Net Sales					100.0	100.0		
	30.0		26.2		33.3	Gross Profit					27.7	33.4		
	22.9		22.4		25.8	Operating Expenses					20.0	29.1		
	7.1		3.8		7.5	Operating Profit					7.8	4.3		
	-2.5		-.8		1.5	All Other Expenses (net)					1.2	.2		
	9.6		4.5		6.0	Profit Before Taxes					6.6	4.1		
						RATIOS								
	13.1		8.0		5.7						4.6	5.6		
	2.9		3.2		3.5	Current					2.6	3.3		
	2.0		1.7		1.9						1.1	2.2		
	6.6		4.6		3.2						2.9	3.1		
	1.4		1.4		1.7	Quick					1.1	1.7		
	.9		.7		.7						.6	.9		
37	9.8	42	8.7	39	9.4						42	8.6	26	14.3
51	7.2	54	6.7	51	7.1	Sales/Receivables					51	7.2	52	7.0
59	6.2	64	5.7	61	6.0						66	5.5	61	6.0
49	7.4	66	5.5	53	6.9						45	8.2	54	6.7
91	4.0	94	3.9	83	4.4	Cost of Sales/Inventory					64	5.7	107	3.4
152	2.4	159	2.3	126	2.9						107	3.4	166	2.2
10	35.0	14	25.5	11	32.4						10	37.4	10	34.8
22	16.6	21	17.8	18	20.6	Cost of Sales/Payables					19	19.1	15	23.7
34	10.8	39	9.4	31	11.8						34	10.6	29	12.6
	2.3		1.9		2.6						4.1	2.1		
	3.9		3.8		4.3	Sales/Working Capital					4.7	2.9		
	6.4		6.2		6.6						NM	6.3		
	31.8		214.1		31.6						28.9	34.0		
(11)	9.4	(15)	9.5	(23)	2.2	EBIT/Interest				(10)	2.1	(10)	5.2	
	2.9		-1.1		-4.3						-.2	-5.1		
						Net Profit + Depr., Dep., Amort./Cur. Mat. L/T/D								
	.2		.2		.2						.3	.3		
	.5		.5		.5	Fixed/Worth					.5	.5		
	1.1		.7		.9						11.4	.9		
	.3		.2		.2						.3	.3		
	.8		.3		.5	Debt/Worth					1.2	.5		
	1.5		1.0		2.8						45.4	1.9		
	33.6		21.5		48.5						87.4	42.9		
	18.4		9.9	(28)	17.9	% Profit Before Taxes/Tangible Net Worth				(11)	17.5	(11)	10.4	
	9.8		-10.5		6.2						5.5	2.3		
	22.3		16.0		32.3						29.8	18.5		
	10.7		6.7		8.0	% Profit Before Taxes/Total Assets					6.3	6.3		
	4.7		-5.2		1.1						1.4	-2.8		
	13.4		12.4		11.6						11.2	10.1		
	4.8		5.0		7.8	Sales/Net Fixed Assets					7.7	4.6		
	3.5		3.1		4.6						5.4	3.1		
	2.2		2.0		2.2						2.6	2.0		
	1.5		1.5		1.8	Sales/Total Assets					1.9	1.6		
	1.2		1.0		1.3						1.4	.9		
	3.1		1.8		1.8						1.9	1.4		
(12)	4.2	(14)	3.2	(27)	3.3	% Depr., Dep., Amort./Sales				(11)	2.2	(11)	3.5	
	6.5		4.7		4.1						4.1	5.5		
						% Officers', Directors' Owners' Comp/Sales								
	610561M		637684M		1561284M	Net Sales ($)		2445M	4363M	33139M	185307M	1336030M		
	483190M		508486M		1039507M	Total Assets ($)		1434M	2459M	16319M	104628M	914667M		

© RMA 2024   M = $ thousand   MM = $ million
See Pages viii through xx for Explanation of Ratios and Data

MANUFACTURING—Other Fabricated Wire Product Manufacturing NAICS 332618

Current Data Sorted by Assets / Comparative Historical Data

							Type of Statement				
			4	1	1		Unqualified		13		3
		1	4	1			Reviewed		11		5
		2	1				Compiled		6		9
	1	2	1				Tax Returns		4		
1	5	10	11	1	6		Other		37		23
0-500M	6 (4/1-9/30/23) 500M-2MM	2-10MM	47 (10/1/23-3/31/24) 10-50MM	50-100MM	100-250MM				4/1/19-3/31/20 ALL		4/1/20-3/31/21 ALL
1	6	15	21	3	7		NUMBER OF STATEMENTS		71		40
%	%	%	%	%	%		ASSETS		%		%
		16.7	12.4				Cash & Equivalents		9.6		14.0
		24.3	22.5				Trade Receivables (net)		22.8		23.7
		29.2	35.8				Inventory		29.8		24.3
		1.7	1.8				All Other Current		2.2		2.1
		71.9	72.5				Total Current		64.4		64.2
		16.6	16.9				Fixed Assets (net)		23.8		20.0
		4.8	4.9				Intangibles (net)		7.5		7.1
		6.8	5.7				All Other Non-Current		4.3		8.8
		100.0	100.0				Total		100.0		100.0
							LIABILITIES				
		3.6	6.0				Notes Payable-Short Term		7.7		5.5
		.9	1.4				Cur. Mat.-L.T.D.		2.2		2.0
		20.4	14.4				Trade Payables		10.6		11.6
		.0	.1				Income Taxes Payable		.2		.1
		6.3	9.6				All Other Current		9.0		13.9
		31.2	31.5				Total Current		29.7		33.0
		10.3	15.4				Long-Term Debt		13.4		9.9
		1.4	.0				Deferred Taxes		.3		.1
		1.5	1.8				All Other Non-Current		6.9		5.1
		55.6	51.3				Net Worth		49.8		52.0
		100.0	100.0				Total Liabilities & Net Worth		100.0		100.0
							INCOME DATA				
		100.0	100.0				Net Sales		100.0		100.0
		30.5	25.5				Gross Profit		25.9		28.8
		23.0	17.6				Operating Expenses		19.8		23.2
		7.4	7.9				Operating Profit		6.2		5.6
		.5	.3				All Other Expenses (net)		1.1		1.4
		6.9	7.6				Profit Before Taxes		5.1		4.2
							RATIOS				
		5.0	4.6						4.0		3.4
		2.3	2.3				Current		2.3		2.4
		1.3	1.6						1.6		1.5
		3.1	2.3						1.9		2.3
		1.5	1.1				Quick		1.2		1.4
		1.1	.5						.7		.7
		24 15.4	28 12.9					33	10.9	36	10.1
		40 9.1	50 7.3				Sales/Receivables	40	9.2	45	8.1
		51 7.2	59 6.2					52	7.0	57	6.4
		43 8.5	56 6.5					41	8.9	40	9.2
		69 5.3	91 4.0				Cost of Sales/Inventory	76	4.8	65	5.6
		81 4.5	130 2.8					111	3.3	101	3.6
		24 15.3	12 31.3					13	27.4	11	31.9
		35 10.3	33 11.0				Cost of Sales/Payables	23	15.8	27	13.3
		51 7.2	49 7.5					38	9.7	46	7.9
		3.5	3.6						3.6		3.1
		5.9	4.6				Sales/Working Capital		5.4		5.9
		17.5	7.1						10.5		9.2
		74.6	76.4						17.3		18.8
		(11) 31.5	(19) 6.3				EBIT/Interest	(65)	5.1	(30)	5.5
		5.8	3.7						1.1		1.4
							Net Profit + Depr., Dep., Amort./Cur. Mat. L/T/D		3.1		
								(14)	2.1		
									1.1		
		.1	.1						.3		.3
		.2	.4				Fixed/Worth		.5		.4
		.9	.5						1.0		.8
		.3	.4						.6		.4
		1.1	.9				Debt/Worth		1.3		1.1
		2.9	2.3						2.8		3.4
		49.2	69.6						47.9		25.3
		34.2	(20) 28.9				% Profit Before Taxes/Tangible Net Worth	(65)	19.8	(36)	17.1
		17.5	10.9						.0		4.7
		25.6	23.7						19.8		13.8
		16.1	12.6				% Profit Before Taxes/Total Assets		6.9		7.6
		7.0	4.5						.2		1.3
		124.4	33.3						18.8		23.5
		12.4	11.3				Sales/Net Fixed Assets		8.6		9.6
		8.2	6.7						5.0		5.6
		2.4	2.2						2.6		2.3
		2.3	1.8				Sales/Total Assets		1.8		1.7
		1.9	1.5						1.4		1.2
			1.4						.9		.7
		(16)	1.8				% Depr., Dep., Amort./Sales	(58)	1.8	(29)	2.0
			2.3						3.1		4.2
									1.6		1.9
							% Officers', Directors' Owners' Comp/Sales	(23)	2.9	(16)	2.7
									8.6		3.4
139M	25146M	162345M	906493M	241499M	1257056M		Net Sales ($)		4727342M		1657381M
32M	6788M	71047M	499628M	222541M	1423472M		Total Assets ($)		2870860M		1156520M

M = $ thousand   MM = $ million
See Pages viii through xx for Explanation of Ratios and Data

© RMA 2024

MANUFACTURING—Other Fabricated Wire Product Manufacturing NAICS 332618

Comparative Historical Data / Current Data Sorted by Sales

Comparative Historical Data							Type of Statement						Current Data Sorted by Sales				
	3		6		6		Unqualified									1	5
	9		10		6		Reviewed									1	5
	7		4		4		Compiled					2				1	1
	2		3		3		Tax Returns							1		1	1
	19		28		34		Other	1		3		1		8		6	15
	4/1/21-3/31/22 ALL		4/1/22-3/31/23 ALL		4/1/23-3/31/24 ALL					6 (4/1-9/30/23)					47 (10/1/23-3/31/24)		
								0-1MM		1-3MM		3-5MM		5-10MM		10-25MM	25MM & OVER
	40		51		53		NUMBER OF STATEMENTS	1		3		3		9		10	27
	%		%		%		ASSETS	%		%		%		%		%	%
	9.7		11.7		16.4		Cash & Equivalents									21.7	10.8
	24.2		27.1		21.5		Trade Receivables (net)									22.4	18.4
	31.3		30.2		30.1		Inventory									34.1	30.6
	1.7		2.4		1.6		All Other Current									4.3	1.1
	66.9		71.5		69.6		Total Current									82.4	61.0
	23.6		18.4		16.1		Fixed Assets (net)									13.8	18.0
	4.2		5.3		7.5		Intangibles (net)									.6	11.9
	5.4		4.8		6.8		All Other Non-Current									3.3	9.1
	100.0		100.0		100.0		Total									100.0	100.0
							LIABILITIES										
	7.5		7.8		4.4		Notes Payable-Short Term									3.3	4.4
	1.9		2.2		1.4		Cur. Mat.-L.T.D.									1.5	2.0
	15.9		12.5		15.1		Trade Payables									27.7	9.7
	.6		.2		.0		Income Taxes Payable									.0	.1
	15.3		8.5		8.5		All Other Current									8.8	8.2
	41.2		31.1		29.5		Total Current									41.4	24.4
	12.1		14.3		14.5		Long-Term Debt									9.0	18.8
	.6		.1		.5		Deferred Taxes									.0	.1
	4.4		4.1		2.6		All Other Non-Current									2.6	3.2
	41.8		50.4		53.0		Net Worth									47.0	53.5
	100.0		100.0		100.0		Total Liabilities & Net Worth									100.0	100.0
							INCOME DATA										
	100.0		100.0		100.0		Net Sales									100.0	100.0
	31.5		25.6		30.9		Gross Profit									25.9	26.8
	23.7		17.9		22.9		Operating Expenses									19.8	17.3
	7.8		7.7		8.0		Operating Profit									6.2	9.4
	-1.3		.1		1.2		All Other Expenses (net)									-1.0	2.4
	9.1		7.6		6.8		Profit Before Taxes									7.1	7.1
							RATIOS										
	3.5		3.7		5.2		Current									4.0	5.2
	2.0		2.1		2.6											1.9	3.2
	1.2		1.6		1.6											1.5	1.8
	1.9		2.3		3.0		Quick									2.1	2.7
	.9		1.3		1.4											1.4	1.4
	.5		.7		.8											.4	.7
33	10.9	37	9.8	27	13.4		Sales/Receivables								24	15.5	32	11.4
46	7.9	46	7.9	41	8.8										41	8.9	43	8.4
55	6.6	56	6.5	53	6.9										54	6.8	54	6.7
46	8.0	54	6.8	51	7.2		Cost of Sales/Inventory								42	8.7	55	6.6
83	4.4	72	5.1	76	4.8										79	4.6	94	3.9
118	3.1	111	3.3	122	3.0										135	2.7	146	2.5
20	18.2	12	29.9	12	29.7		Cost of Sales/Payables								31	11.8	12	31.3
32	11.5	25	14.7	30	12.3										43	8.4	26	14.3
63	5.8	59	6.2	46	8.0										114	3.2	39	9.3
	4.2		3.5		3.4		Sales/Working Capital									3.4	2.7
	6.6		5.1		4.6											5.5	4.3
	28.7		8.1		7.7											10.9	5.6
	43.0		45.7		36.1		EBIT/Interest										40.1
(34)	11.0	(43)	10.5	(43)	8.2											(25)	6.3
	6.3		4.7		3.7												2.1
			20.7		12.2		Net Profit + Depr., Dep.,										10.2
		(12)	10.3	(13)	4.0		Amort./Cur. Mat. L/T/D									(11)	4.0
			6.4		.4												.7
	.3		.2		.1		Fixed/Worth									.0	.1
	.6		.4		.3											.3	.4
	1.7		.7		.7											.7	.8
	.5		.4		.4		Debt/Worth									.4	.4
	1.3		1.1		1.1											1.2	1.0
	2.8		2.7		2.9											2.6	4.0
	66.4		45.4		57.6		% Profit Before Taxes/Tangible									58.1	63.4
(33)	30.4	(47)	28.5	(51)	34.2		Net Worth									28.9	(25) 27.4
	18.3		15.6		10.4											16.7	7.7
	25.0		22.1		23.7		% Profit Before Taxes/Total									21.4	20.9
	15.4		12.6		11.3		Assets									11.7	9.7
	4.9		6.1		4.2											6.6	3.0
	24.2		36.2		51.3		Sales/Net Fixed Assets									172.6	30.6
	11.4		11.3		12.4											20.6	8.6
	5.6		7.5		6.2											8.2	5.0
	2.4		2.4		2.4		Sales/Total Assets									2.3	2.1
	1.9		1.9		1.9											2.0	1.6
	1.5		1.4		1.5											1.6	1.2
	.5		1.1		1.1		% Depr., Dep., Amort./Sales										1.4
(32)	1.8	(40)	1.9	(36)	1.7											(22)	1.9
	4.0		3.4		2.9												5.0
	1.1		1.2		.8		% Officers', Directors'										
(15)	2.8	(15)	2.4	(17)	1.7		Owners' Comp/Sales										
	3.6		4.0		3.7												
	1538009M		3508857M		2592678M		Net Sales ($)	139M		6003M		14143M		66378M		179759M	2326256M
	889847M		1974231M		2223508M		Total Assets ($)	32M		1666M		5911M		30311M		98529M	2087059M

M = $ thousand   MM = $ million
See Pages viii through xx for Explanation of Ratios and Data

© RMA 2024

MANUFACTURING—Machine Shops NAICS 332710

Current Data Sorted by Assets | Comparative Historical Data

							Type of Statement		
			2	10	3	3	Unqualified	15	14
	1	7	29	1		Reviewed	51	23
	4	26	10		1	Compiled	57	38
15	14	25				Tax Returns	88	54
8	27	91	47	10	5	Other	221	165
	75 (4/1-9/30/23)		264 (10/1/23-3/31/24)				4/1/19-3/31/20	4/1/20-3/31/21
0-500M	500M-2MM	2-10MM	10-50MM	50-100MM	100-250MM		ALL	ALL
23	46	151	96	14	9	NUMBER OF STATEMENTS	432	294
%	%	%	%	%	%	ASSETS	%	%
33.2	17.5	15.3	10.6	5.4		Cash & Equivalents	11.0	17.6
15.7	24.7	21.9	18.8	15.8		Trade Receivables (net)	23.3	20.1
2.3	8.6	17.6	24.0	23.8		Inventory	20.5	18.6
1.5	2.6	3.2	3.1	4.6		All Other Current	1.5	2.4
52.7	53.5	58.0	56.6	49.6		Total Current	56.2	58.7
42.6	37.8	30.6	32.0	25.0		Fixed Assets (net)	33.8	31.5
3.7	5.8	4.5	3.5	15.6		Intangibles (net)	4.3	4.6
1.0	3.0	6.9	7.9	9.8		All Other Non-Current	5.7	5.2
100.0	100.0	100.0	100.0	100.0		Total	100.0	100.0
						LIABILITIES		
14.7	6.3	6.1	4.6	5.0		Notes Payable-Short Term	8.0	7.9
5.5	5.9	5.0	3.5	4.5		Cur. Mat.-L.T.D.	5.5	4.4
7.7	10.5	9.1	8.0	7.6		Trade Payables	8.8	7.9
.8	.0	.0	.1	.0		Income Taxes Payable	.1	.1
7.0	19.6	7.0	9.2	9.3		All Other Current	6.9	8.0
35.6	42.4	27.3	25.4	26.5		Total Current	29.3	28.4
69.4	42.0	22.7	14.2	21.3		Long-Term Debt	25.8	27.2
.0	.1	.3	.6	.3		Deferred Taxes	.3	.3
4.9	4.8	4.2	9.2	11.6		All Other Non-Current	4.8	5.8
-9.9	10.7	45.5	50.6	40.3		Net Worth	39.7	38.2
100.0	100.0	100.0	100.0	100.0		Total Liabilities & Net Worth	100.0	100.0
						INCOME DATA		
100.0	100.0	100.0	100.0	100.0		Net Sales	100.0	100.0
54.8	46.7	36.8	25.8	22.3		Gross Profit	35.0	35.0
46.9	42.8	30.1	19.0	14.5		Operating Expenses	27.9	30.9
7.9	3.9	6.7	6.8	7.8		Operating Profit	7.1	4.1
1.2	1.1	.8	1.1	2.0		All Other Expenses (net)	1.1	-1.2
6.7	2.8	5.9	5.8	5.8		Profit Before Taxes	5.9	5.3
						RATIOS		
7.7	4.8	4.8	4.1	4.0			3.6	4.8
2.6	2.0	2.3	2.4	2.2		Current	2.0	2.4
1.0	.8	1.5	1.7	.9			1.3	1.5
6.6	3.9	3.3	2.4	2.1			2.4	2.9
2.1	1.3	1.6	1.1	.8		Quick	1.2	1.4
1.0	.5	.8	.6	.4			.6	.7
0 UND	16 22.5	30 12.3	35 10.3	33 11.2			31 11.9	30 12.2
0 UND	33 10.9	46 7.9	47 7.7	40 9.1		Sales/Receivables	45 8.1	44 8.3
26 13.8	54 6.8	62 5.9	64 5.7	61 6.0			58 6.3	60 6.1
0 UND	0 UND	7 50.1	41 8.8	49 7.5			17 22.1	14 26.9
0 UND	1 728.4	54 6.8	73 5.0	87 4.2		Cost of Sales/Inventory	52 7.0	55 6.6
0 UND	39 9.3	91 4.0	135 2.7	122 3.0			99 3.7	104 3.5
0 UND	1 410.1	12 31.4	12 29.9	20 18.7			11 32.4	9 38.5
0 UND	16 23.0	24 14.9	22 16.7	26 14.2		Cost of Sales/Payables	21 17.3	21 17.7
33 11.0	32 11.3	41 9.0	36 10.1	36 10.0			37 9.9	37 9.9
9.1	4.8	3.2	2.8	3.1			4.3	3.1
22.3	19.7	5.4	4.7	6.2		Sales/Working Capital	6.9	4.9
-528.0	-17.5	11.0	8.7	-73.1			17.6	12.5
23.3	19.0	24.2	27.3	43.2			15.4	23.2
(18) 7.4	(38) 1.4	(132) 5.8	(84) 5.7	3.8		EBIT/Interest	(408) 5.4	(277) 6.3
1.5	-1.5	1.8	.9	.8			1.9	.1
		9.7	5.8				6.7	5.6
	(16) 2.1	(28) 2.8			Net Profit + Depr., Dep., Amort./Cur. Mat. L/T/D	(82) 2.5	(45) 3.4
		.8	1.3				1.4	1.7
.1	.3	.3	.4	.7			.4	.4
1.0	1.5	.8	.6	1.7		Fixed/Worth	.9	.8
-3.0	-3.8	1.9	1.0	NM			2.1	2.9
.4	.5	.4	.4	1.5			.6	.6
12.5	2.7	1.1	.8	2.8		Debt/Worth	1.3	1.3
-4.2	-10.4	4.3	1.5	NM			4.3	6.7
194.1	67.6	37.6	29.4	44.1			44.2	49.6
(15) 85.1	(29) 35.1	(129) 16.2	(87) 16.6	(11) 31.4		% Profit Before Taxes/Tangible Net Worth	(371) 21.0	(243) 19.6
28.8	8.9	4.2	4.1	17.4			6.5	.0
54.7	29.5	16.7	15.9	17.0			19.3	19.8
20.7	7.8	7.7	7.1	7.8		% Profit Before Taxes/Total Assets	8.5	8.5
3.5	-8.1	1.4	.1	-.6			2.2	-1.9
248.4	18.5	13.2	7.1	8.6			11.4	12.4
14.6	8.3	6.0	4.8	6.1		Sales/Net Fixed Assets	5.9	5.5
4.1	4.3	3.4	2.9	4.6			3.2	3.2
9.3	3.6	2.1	1.7	1.6			2.5	2.1
5.4	2.4	1.6	1.4	1.3		Sales/Total Assets	1.7	1.5
3.4	1.9	1.2	1.0	.9			1.3	1.1
1.4	1.4	1.6	1.7	2.2			2.4	2.5
(11) 3.0	(29) 4.1	(108) 3.4	(88) 3.8	3.9		% Depr., Dep., Amort./Sales	(350) 4.3	(225) 4.5
6.3	7.7	5.9	6.6	5.8			6.4	6.7
5.9	2.9	1.7	.7				2.0	2.3
(13) 8.7	(22) 5.7	(74) 2.7	(20) 1.8			% Officers', Directors', Owners' Comp/Sales	(199) 3.9	(134) 4.8
10.2	7.6	4.8	4.0				7.4	9.0
30342M	164388M	1284725M	3096920M	1201113M	1490158M	Net Sales ($)	7550540M	4862962M
5893M	57151M	764382M	2114641M	914676M	1267973M	Total Assets ($)	4568374M	3509824M

© RMA 2024 M = $ thousand MM = $ million
See Pages viii through xx for Explanation of Ratios and Data

MANUFACTURING—Machine Shops NAICS 332710

Comparative Historical Data / Current Data Sorted by Sales

Comparative Historical Data			Type of Statement	Current Data Sorted by Sales					
11	13	18	Unqualified		1	1	3	13
22	40	38	Reviewed		1	2	22	13
35	41	41	Compiled	1	5	18	13	4
44	59	54	Tax Returns	9	15	6	15	9
195	206	188	Other	5	21	34	45	42	41
4/1/21-3/31/22 ALL	4/1/22-3/31/23 ALL	4/1/23-3/31/24 ALL		75 (4/1-9/30/23)			264 (10/1/23-3/31/24)		
				0-1MM	1-3MM	3-5MM	5-10MM	10-25MM	25MM & OVER
307	359	339	NUMBER OF STATEMENTS	14	38	46	81	89	71
%	%	%	ASSETS	%	%	%	%	%	%
15.4	13.8	14.8	Cash & Equivalents	27.4	24.0	14.9	14.3	14.3	8.6
23.0	22.7	20.5	Trade Receivables (net)	14.1	16.3	20.0	23.8	21.7	19.4
20.3	20.4	17.7	Inventory	.8	8.9	12.5	17.3	21.1	25.1
2.8	3.1	3.0	All Other Current	1.7	2.3	3.0	3.4	3.0	3.2
61.5	60.0	56.0	Total Current	44.1	51.6	50.3	58.8	60.1	56.3
30.6	30.3	32.5	Fixed Assets (net)	50.1	39.2	32.6	31.2	29.6	30.4
3.9	3.7	5.1	Intangibles (net)	2.8	6.5	11.7	2.9	2.7	6.0
4.0	6.0	6.4	All Other Non-Current	3.0	2.7	5.3	7.2	7.5	7.4
100.0	100.0	100.0	Total	100.0	100.0	100.0	100.0	100.0	100.0
			LIABILITIES						
6.2	5.3	6.1	Notes Payable-Short Term	15.6	7.2	7.7	6.6	4.9	3.5
4.7	4.8	4.7	Cur. Mat.-L.T.D.	8.9	4.8	5.4	5.9	3.7	3.0
10.4	9.0	8.8	Trade Payables	7.0	5.7	9.2	9.5	9.0	9.4
.1	.2	.1	Income Taxes Payable	1.3	.0	.0	.1	.1	.0
8.2	9.2	9.4	All Other Current	6.3	8.1	12.7	11.0	6.8	10.1
29.6	28.5	29.1	Total Current	39.1	25.8	35.1	33.1	24.4	26.2
23.2	22.9	25.8	Long-Term Debt	42.6	42.8	42.2	26.5	15.5	14.9
.3	.4	.4	Deferred Taxes	.0	.1	.0	.4	.5	.7
4.0	3.9	6.1	All Other Non-Current	11.5	2.2	6.6	4.5	3.2	12.4
43.0	44.3	38.6	Net Worth	6.8	29.1	16.2	35.4	56.4	45.8
100.0	100.0	100.0	Total Liabilities & Net Worth	100.0	100.0	100.0	100.0	100.0	100.0
			INCOME DATA						
100.0	100.0	100.0	Net Sales	100.0	100.0	100.0	100.0	100.0	100.0
36.3	35.6	35.2	Gross Profit	58.2	46.6	42.9	38.4	30.0	22.1
29.7	28.0	28.7	Operating Expenses	49.0	41.4	38.9	31.1	23.9	14.4
6.6	7.6	6.5	Operating Profit	9.2	5.2	4.0	7.3	6.1	7.7
-2.6	.0	1.0	All Other Expenses (net)	1.4	1.2	1.0	1.0	.5	1.3
9.2	7.5	5.5	Profit Before Taxes	7.7	3.9	3.0	6.3	5.6	6.4
			RATIOS						
4.4	4.3	4.5	Current	7.6	6.6	4.5	4.5	4.9	4.1
2.3	2.4	2.4		2.0	2.8	1.6	2.3	2.6	2.4
1.5	1.6	1.5		.3	1.2	.9	1.4	1.8	1.7
2.6	2.7	2.9	Quick	6.8	5.3	3.6	2.8	2.9	2.0
1.3	(358) 1.4	1.4		1.6	2.1	1.4	1.5	1.5	1.1
.7	.8	.7		.3	.7	.5	.7	.9	.6
33 11.0	33 10.9	27 13.4	Sales/Receivables	0 UND	7 55.2	15 24.0	29 12.4	35 10.3	31 11.7
47 7.8	46 8.0	43 8.4		0 UND	35 10.3	46 7.9	45 8.1	47 7.8	42 8.6
62 5.9	61 6.0	61 6.0		28 13.0	50 7.3	63 5.8	62 5.9	62 5.9	62 5.9
15 24.2	10 35.7	4 85.4	Cost of Sales/Inventory	0 UND	0 UND	0 UND	0 UND	31 11.6	43 8.5
63 5.8	60 6.1	48 7.6		0 UND	11 33.2	29 12.7	41 9.0	64 5.7	66 5.5
114 3.2	114 3.2	94 3.9		0 UND	52 7.0	85 4.3	96 3.8	101 3.6	126 2.9
15 23.7	12 31.0	10 35.6	Cost of Sales/Payables	0 UND	5 78.3	7 52.5	9 41.0	11 32.9	16 22.3
26 13.8	24 15.0	23 16.1		0 UND	16 23.0	28 13.0	24 15.4	21 17.4	29 12.8
46 7.9	38 9.7	36 10.0		46 8.0	29 12.8	39 9.3	45 8.1	35 10.5	36 10.1
3.2	3.4	3.2	Sales/Working Capital	5.7	4.0	3.1	3.4	2.8	3.2
5.4	5.5	5.9		28.1	9.1	9.0	6.2	4.5	5.0
11.3	11.1	15.7		-6.2	NM	-26.2	17.8	8.0	11.0
35.3	26.2	23.0	EBIT/Interest	21.5	17.1	8.3	28.7	30.0	24.1
(273) 11.3	(323) 8.8	(294) 5.3		(11) 4.5	(31) 3.2	(38) 2.6	(71) 5.9	(78) 6.7	(65) 6.3
2.8	2.7	.9		1.5	.0	-3.5	1.7	1.9	1.9
8.5	6.1	5.6	Net Profit + Depr., Dep., Amort./Cur. Mat. L/T/D					3.6	10.2
(43) 4.4	(63) 3.0	(57) 2.6					(18) 2.7	(26) 3.2
2.1	1.5	.9						1.1	1.2
.3	.3	.3	Fixed/Worth	.2	.3	.4	.3	.3	.4
.7	.7	.7		1.1	1.0	1.9	.8	.6	.7
1.5	1.4	2.1		-7.8	-255.3	-.8	3.3	1.0	1.2
.5	.5	.4	Debt/Worth	.5	.2	.6	.4	.3	.5
1.1	1.1	1.1		10.0	2.1	3.7	1.1	.8	1.0
3.2	3.0	4.5		-6.6	-92.0	-4.2	5.6	1.6	2.4
51.7	57.2	37.7	% Profit Before Taxes/Tangible Net Worth		64.7	54.2	43.9	27.4	33.5
(274) 29.6	(319) 26.3	(279) 18.3		(27) 26.0	(30) 16.9	(65) 16.5	(85) 16.6	(63) 23.9
13.2	7.5	4.5			5.9	-.9	3.8	4.0	9.9
27.0	25.3	17.5	% Profit Before Taxes/Total Assets	26.6	25.8	16.7	18.7	15.8	18.1
13.6	10.8	7.7		12.2	5.6	2.9	9.3	7.6	9.0
4.0	2.1	.0		4.4	-1.9	-6.1	.8	2.3	3.4
12.5	14.9	11.6	Sales/Net Fixed Assets	32.1	17.9	16.1	16.6	9.8	8.8
6.0	6.0	5.5		4.0	4.6	5.6	6.3	5.5	5.4
3.1	3.5	3.4		1.5	2.8	2.8	3.9	3.6	3.4
2.4	2.4	2.4	Sales/Total Assets	5.7	3.7	2.4	2.5	1.9	1.9
1.6	1.6	1.6		3.2	2.0	1.2	1.8	1.6	1.5
1.2	1.2	1.2		.9	1.2	1.1	1.2	1.2	1.1
2.0	2.1	1.6	% Depr., Dep., Amort./Sales		1.6	1.4	1.6	2.2	1.2
(227) 3.7	(257) 3.5	(253) 3.8		(24) 6.0	(29) 4.2	(58) 3.6	(75) 3.8	(59) 3.8
6.7	6.2	6.2			7.7	5.9	6.2	6.2	5.4
2.0	1.7	1.8	% Officers', Directors', Owners' Comp/Sales	7.3	4.4	2.4	2.0	1.0	
(129) 4.4	(136) 4.0	(130) 3.4		(10) 9.3	(19) 5.9	(19) 3.2	(40) 3.4	(35) 2.0	
6.5	5.9	6.4		10.8	8.4	7.0	5.9	4.0	
6180664M	7915800M	7267646M	Net Sales ($)	8435M	79300M	181174M	592540M	1434528M	4971669M
4271250M	4998323M	5124716M	Total Assets ($)	4916M	48365M	140813M	372857M	1032978M	3524787M

© RMA 2024
M = $ thousand MM = $ million
See Pages viii through xx for Explanation of Ratios and Data

MANUFACTURING—Precision Turned Product Manufacturing NAICS 332721

Current Data Sorted by Assets / Comparative Historical Data

	0-500M	500M-2MM	2-10MM	10-50MM	50-100MM	100-250MM	Type of Statement		4/1/19-3/31/20 ALL		4/1/20-3/31/21 ALL
	1	1	7	6	3	1	Unqualified		4		4
			4	6			Reviewed		21		9
	2	3	4	1			Compiled		9		4
	1	2	20	16	6	3	Tax Returns		8		7
			15 (4/1-9/30/23)	72 (10/1/23-3/31/24)			Other		48		38
	4	6	35	29	9	4	NUMBER OF STATEMENTS		90		62
	%	%	%	%	%	%	**ASSETS**		%		%
			12.2	6.1			Cash & Equivalents		8.3		13.4
			20.7	17.3			Trade Receivables (net)		19.9		19.3
			28.1	32.8			Inventory		23.0		19.9
			.6	2.1			All Other Current		1.5		1.9
			61.6	58.3			Total Current		52.8		54.4
			30.9	31.2			Fixed Assets (net)		35.4		35.1
			4.6	4.4			Intangibles (net)		6.2		6.3
			2.9	6.2			All Other Non-Current		5.6		4.0
			100.0	100.0			Total		100.0		100.0
							LIABILITIES				
			2.7	8.8			Notes Payable-Short Term		7.7		5.7
			4.3	3.9			Cur. Mat.-L.T.D.		6.8		5.0
			8.1	8.4			Trade Payables		8.9		8.7
			.0	.1			Income Taxes Payable		.1		.0
			7.9	5.0			All Other Current		6.3		7.0
			23.1	26.2			Total Current		29.7		26.4
			16.6	18.0			Long-Term Debt		23.9		28.7
			.6	.6			Deferred Taxes		1.0		.7
			6.7	7.6			All Other Non-Current		5.3		9.5
			53.0	47.7			Net Worth		40.0		34.8
			100.0	100.0			Total Liabilities & Net Worth		100.0		100.0
							INCOME DATA				
			100.0	100.0			Net Sales		100.0		100.0
			28.5	20.5			Gross Profit		28.4		32.1
			23.3	14.6			Operating Expenses		23.2		27.3
			5.2	5.9			Operating Profit		5.2		4.7
			1.0	2.0			All Other Expenses (net)		1.5		.2
			4.2	3.9			Profit Before Taxes		3.6		4.6
							RATIOS				
			6.4	4.2					3.4		3.5
			3.6	2.5		Current		2.1		2.1
			1.9	1.4					1.3		1.4
			3.8	1.9					2.0		2.3
			2.0	1.0		Quick		.9		1.2
			.8	.5					.6		.7
			30 12.1	30 12.3			Sales/Receivables	34	10.6	36	10.2
			49 7.5	49 7.5				49	7.4	50	7.3
			65 5.6	61 6.0				58	6.3	61	6.0
			60 6.1	89 4.1			Cost of Sales/Inventory	44	8.3	38	9.7
			89 4.1	118 3.1				73	5.0	74	4.9
			152 2.4	140 2.6				94	3.9	101	3.6
			12 29.4	15 24.2			Cost of Sales/Payables	17	20.9	14	25.5
			21 17.6	21 17.1				25	14.5	27	13.3
			37 9.8	36 10.2				38	9.7	47	7.8
			2.5	2.8					3.9		3.2
			4.2	4.7		Sales/Working Capital		6.8		4.8
			5.7	7.3					15.7		11.1
			27.3	7.2					9.6		11.5
		(32)	7.0	(26) 3.0		EBIT/Interest	(79)	4.0	(55)	2.3
			.8	-.9					.6		.3
							Net Profit + Depr., Dep.,		4.3		7.7
							Amort./Cur. Mat. L/T/D	(31)	1.6	(13)	1.4
									1.1		.2
			.3	.4					.5		.5
			.7	.8		Fixed/Worth		.8		1.0
			1.1	1.5					1.8		5.9
			.3	.7					.5		.6
			.8	1.2		Debt/Worth		1.2		2.0
			2.3	3.6					3.7		12.1
			24.0	42.2					27.3		32.6
		(33)	10.4	(28) 13.7		% Profit Before Taxes/Tangible Net Worth	(78)	14.4	(49)	14.5
			-.8	-8.3					6.6		-1.2
			14.0	15.9					11.6		11.5
			7.5	5.0		% Profit Before Taxes/Total Assets		6.2		5.2
			-.5	-3.4					-.8		-2.1
			7.9	6.5					8.7		7.6
			5.2	3.6		Sales/Net Fixed Assets		4.8		4.3
			3.0	2.6					2.6		3.0
			1.7	1.6					2.0		1.9
			1.5	1.3		Sales/Total Assets		1.5		1.4
			1.2	1.0					1.1		1.1
			1.6	2.7					2.9		2.7
		(29)	3.0	(26) 5.3		% Depr., Dep., Amort./Sales	(76)	4.0	(49)	4.5
			5.0	6.6					6.8		6.8
			1.7						2.1		2.9
		(14)	2.8			% Officers', Directors' Owners' Comp/Sales	(27)	2.6	(17)	4.7
			7.1						8.8		6.2
3127M	14601M	285494M	977180M	713547M	491624M	Net Sales ($)		3110254M		1321431M
1005M	7970M	197251M	767062M	579971M	583066M	Total Assets ($)		1776638M		1182308M

M = $ thousand MM = $ million
See Pages viii through xx for Explanation of Ratios and Data

© RMA 2024

MANUFACTURING—Precision Turned Product Manufacturing NAICS 332721

Comparative Historical Data | Current Data Sorted by Sales

Comparative Historical Data			Type of Statement	Current Data Sorted by Sales				
1	6	10	Unqualified			1	1	9
7	13	15	Reviewed	2	1	4	5	3
4	6	4	Compiled			3	1	
8	10	10	Tax Returns		2	2	2	
34	45	48	Other	1	4	8	11	22
4/1/21-3/31/22 ALL	4/1/22-3/31/23 ALL	4/1/23-3/31/24 ALL		1	2	4		
					15 (4/1-9/30/23)		72 (10/1/23-3/31/24)		
				0-1MM	1-3MM	3-5MM	5-10MM	10-25MM	25MM & OVER
54	80	87	NUMBER OF STATEMENTS	3	6	7	17	20	34
%	%	%	ASSETS	%	%	%	%	%	%
14.0	11.1	9.9	Cash & Equivalents				11.5	6.3	7.0
18.9	19.9	18.9	Trade Receivables (net)				19.7	23.5	17.9
22.8	26.9	29.9	Inventory				30.8	34.0	29.9
2.1	2.9	1.2	All Other Current				.6	.8	1.8
57.7	60.8	60.0	Total Current				62.6	64.6	56.6
33.3	30.4	29.5	Fixed Assets (net)				33.9	27.6	28.0
5.7	5.0	5.9	Intangibles (net)				2.2	2.6	9.0
3.3	3.8	4.7	All Other Non-Current				1.3	5.2	6.4
100.0	100.0	100.0	Total				100.0	100.0	100.0
			LIABILITIES						
4.6	4.3	6.2	Notes Payable-Short Term				.9	6.7	8.4
4.1	3.8	4.3	Cur. Mat.-L.T.D.				5.7	3.2	4.1
7.8	9.0	8.5	Trade Payables				7.1	9.7	10.3
.1	.1	.1	Income Taxes Payable				.0	.0	.2
7.8	8.7	7.7	All Other Current				8.4	3.7	8.4
24.3	25.9	26.8	Total Current				22.2	23.4	31.4
27.5	27.2	19.6	Long-Term Debt				13.8	18.3	16.0
.5	.4	.5	Deferred Taxes				.8	.6	.5
3.4	3.2	6.9	All Other Non-Current				3.7	4.1	9.5
44.2	43.3	46.2	Net Worth				59.6	53.6	42.7
100.0	100.0	100.0	Total Liabilities & Net Worth				100.0	100.0	100.0
			INCOME DATA						
100.0	100.0	100.0	Net Sales				100.0	100.0	100.0
35.7	32.6	27.3	Gross Profit				27.0	24.1	21.9
28.9	26.4	21.5	Operating Expenses				22.7	20.6	14.5
6.7	6.2	5.8	Operating Profit				4.4	3.5	7.4
-2.7	.2	1.5	All Other Expenses (net)				1.4	.9	1.9
9.4	6.0	4.3	Profit Before Taxes				2.9	2.6	5.5
			RATIOS						
3.7	5.3	4.5					7.5	4.6	3.7
2.1	2.7	2.5	Current				4.0	3.3	2.0
1.8	1.6	1.4					2.0	2.0	1.2
2.2	3.0	2.3					4.5	2.8	1.8
1.3	1.2	1.1	Quick				2.0	1.4	.8
.8	.7	.6					.8	.7	.4
33 11.0	35 10.5	33 11.2					34 10.8	37 9.8	34 10.6
47 7.8	48 7.6	49 7.5	Sales/Receivables				49 7.5	54 6.8	53 6.9
59 6.2	63 5.8	65 5.6					73 5.0	74 4.9	60 6.1
40 9.1	52 7.0	69 5.3					64 5.7	65 5.6	87 4.2
85 4.3	99 3.7	101 3.6	Cost of Sales/Inventory				99 3.7	99 3.7	101 3.6
130 2.8	159 2.3	152 2.4					166 2.2	174 2.1	126 2.9
23 16.2	19 19.1	14 25.4					12 31.0	15 23.9	17 21.9
29 12.4	29 12.5	21 17.1	Cost of Sales/Payables				19 19.4	28 13.2	28 13.1
39 9.4	45 8.2	43 8.4					27 13.7	43 8.4	62 5.9
2.8	2.4	2.8					2.2	2.7	3.2
4.7	4.3	4.6	Sales/Working Capital				2.5	4.1	5.5
7.0	8.2	8.5					6.1	5.0	10.4
21.6	19.9	17.1					27.1	15.6	24.6
(50) 12.9	(71) 5.1	(81) 4.6	EBIT/Interest				5.1	5.6	(31) 4.6
2.9	.3	.5					.8	-2.8	1.6
	11.6	12.4	Net Profit + Depr., Dep.,						14.5
(14)	5.2	(20) 2.3	Amort./Cur. Mat. L/T/D					(12) 2.3	
	3.0	.6							.6
.4	.3	.4					.3	.3	.4
.9	.9	.7	Fixed/Worth				.7	.5	.9
1.3	2.1	1.8					1.0	1.2	2.3
.5	.5	.5					.3	.3	.8
1.3	1.3	1.2	Debt/Worth				.5	.8	2.0
3.3	3.4	3.6					1.6	2.2	4.4
51.0	44.8	35.7					22.4	37.5	36.3
(47) 31.6	(68) 19.0	(76) 10.3	% Profit Before Taxes/Tangible Net Worth				10.4	10.1	(28) 16.9
11.7	1.3	-2.5					-.8	-13.4	1.6
23.2	18.1	13.7					14.4	13.5	12.2
12.5	8.1	5.8	% Profit Before Taxes/Total Assets				6.8	7.4	5.8
2.9	-1.0	-1.1					-.4	-5.4	1.0
8.7	7.9	10.1					6.8	8.5	11.0
4.7	5.8	5.1	Sales/Net Fixed Assets				5.2	4.7	5.0
2.7	3.0	2.8					2.4	3.7	2.8
1.8	1.8	1.7					1.7	1.9	1.5
1.4	1.4	1.3	Sales/Total Assets				1.3	1.6	1.3
1.0	1.0	1.1					1.1	1.2	1.0
3.2	2.8	1.7					1.9	2.0	1.7
(44) 4.9	(66) 4.0	(76) 3.7	% Depr., Dep., Amort./Sales			(15) 2.7	(18) 3.7	(31) 3.9
7.0	6.6	6.2					5.0	5.3	6.6
2.3	1.9	2.2	% Officers', Directors' Owners' Comp/Sales						
(21) 4.1	(31) 3.1	(28) 2.8							
6.1	5.8	8.3							
968504M	1494067M	2485573M	Net Sales ($)	876M	12349M	26347M	120769M	289361M	2035871M
834859M	1197206M	2136325M	Total Assets ($)	1037M	7800M	19799M	92667M	212030M	1802992M

© RMA 2024   M = $ thousand   MM = $ million
See Pages viii through xx for Explanation of Ratios and Data

MANUFACTURING—Bolt, Nut, Screw, Rivet, and Washer Manufacturing NAICS 332722

Current Data Sorted by Assets | **Comparative Historical Data**

						Type of Statement		
			2		5	Unqualified	5	7
		2	7	1		Reviewed	18	9
		3				Compiled	8	2
1	2	2	2			Tax Returns	8	2
	2	11	12	4	6	Other	31	28
	13 (4/1-9/30/23)		47 (10/1/23-3/31/24)				4/1/19-	4/1/20-
0-500M	500M-2MM	2-10MM	10-50MM	50-100MM	100-250MM		3/31/20	3/31/21
1	4	18	21	5	11	NUMBER OF STATEMENTS	ALL 70	ALL 48
%	%	%	%	%	%	ASSETS	%	%
		14.9	8.7		6.9	Cash & Equivalents	9.2	10.5
		19.9	18.7		18.7	Trade Receivables (net)	21.5	17.7
		23.9	33.4		29.8	Inventory	33.4	34.3
		.3	1.2		1.0	All Other Current	1.3	2.0
		59.1	62.0		56.3	Total Current	65.3	64.4
		28.4	26.5		30.2	Fixed Assets (net)	27.0	24.9
		3.8	4.7		9.4	Intangibles (net)	3.3	7.4
		8.8	6.8		4.1	All Other Non-Current	4.4	3.3
		100.0	100.0		100.0	Total	100.0	100.0
						LIABILITIES		
		7.1	5.8		1.1	Notes Payable-Short Term	9.5	8.0
		3.3	2.1		2.1	Cur. Mat.-L.T.D.	2.3	2.3
		9.0	7.1		8.2	Trade Payables	9.6	9.1
		.0	.2		.2	Income Taxes Payable	.1	.1
		4.5	7.4		13.1	All Other Current	6.1	8.0
		23.8	22.6		24.7	Total Current	27.7	27.5
		16.7	13.9		6.6	Long-Term Debt	11.2	13.5
		.0	.3		2.4	Deferred Taxes	.6	.8
		2.6	2.4		3.9	All Other Non-Current	5.8	3.6
		56.9	60.9		62.4	Net Worth	54.8	54.6
		100.0	100.0		100.0	Total Liabilities & Net Worth	100.0	100.0
						INCOME DATA		
		100.0	100.0		100.0	Net Sales	100.0	100.0
		36.7	29.2		26.1	Gross Profit	29.8	30.3
		25.3	21.8		14.5	Operating Expenses	21.9	26.3
		11.4	7.4		11.6	Operating Profit	7.8	3.9
		.1	.3		1.1	All Other Expenses (net)	.4	-.8
		11.3	7.1		10.4	Profit Before Taxes	7.4	4.7
						RATIOS		
		8.2	6.5		4.8		4.1	5.1
		3.3	3.0		2.2	Current	2.7	2.9
		1.5	1.9		1.7		1.7	1.9
		5.2	2.3		2.0		2.5	2.2
		1.8	1.1		1.2	Quick	1.2	1.4
		.8	.8		.6		.7	.7
	27	13.6	36	10.1	38	9.7		38	9.7	34	10.7
	42	8.7	45	8.1	45	8.1	Sales/Receivables	43	8.5	45	8.1
	51	7.2	63	5.8	48	7.6		52	7.0	62	5.9
	43	8.4	65	5.6	47	7.8		54	6.8	79	4.6
	74	4.9	140	2.6	111	3.3	Cost of Sales/Inventory	87	4.2	111	3.3
	135	2.7	166	2.2	182	2.0		130	2.8	166	2.2
	14	25.7	14	26.0	15	24.6		15	24.9	13	27.7
	31	11.6	19	18.8	18	19.9	Cost of Sales/Payables	26	13.8	28	13.1
	51	7.1	38	9.7	34	10.7		32	11.5	47	7.7
		3.6	2.8		3.0		3.3	2.7
		5.3	3.1		5.4	Sales/Working Capital	4.5	3.4
		10.1	4.4		9.0		8.2	5.4
		132.9	31.2				44.5	35.9
	(16)	7.6	(20)	9.0			EBIT/Interest	(64)	9.1	(42)	5.3
		2.2	1.7				2.7	.2
						Net Profit + Depr., Dep., Amort./Cur. Mat. L/T/D	9.3	7.2
							(21)	4.0	(12)	3.3
							3.0	1.3
		.1	.3		.4		.3	.2
		.5	.4		.7	Fixed/Worth	.4	.6
		.8	.9		.8		.9	.8
		.1	.2		.3		.4	.3
		.6	.5		.6	Debt/Worth	.7	.7
		2.5	1.2		1.1		1.9	2.0
		72.3	40.0		37.9		31.1	27.6
	(17)	15.9	(20)	14.9	(10)	26.0	% Profit Before Taxes/Tangible Net Worth	(65)	14.1	(41)	13.1
		3.1	4.4		13.7		5.9	.9
		46.1	22.4		23.0		18.9	13.8
		10.3	6.9		11.2	% Profit Before Taxes/Total Assets	7.9	5.8
		1.7	1.1		4.3		3.5	-.3
		21.6	7.5		14.7		15.4	13.8
		5.2	6.2		5.9	Sales/Net Fixed Assets	7.1	5.8
		3.0	3.0		2.8		3.5	3.2
		2.5	1.8		2.1		2.2	1.5
		1.6	1.3		1.5	Sales/Total Assets	1.6	1.3
		1.2	1.1		1.2		1.3	1.1
		1.1	1.5				1.5	1.3
	(13)	1.9	2.6			% Depr., Dep., Amort./Sales	(60)	2.5	(39)	2.9
		5.2	5.1				4.1	5.6
						% Officers', Directors' Owners' Comp/Sales	2.6	1.6
							(20)	4.6	(12)	6.3
							10.0	9.7
1187M	31343M	158547M	696059M	617702M	2709685M	Net Sales ($)	2394832M	1979537M
212M	5489M	86680M	500078M	360831M	1739856M	Total Assets ($)	1599109M	1580760M

M = $ thousand MM = $ million
See Pages viii through xx for Explanation of Ratios and Data

© RMA 2024

MANUFACTURING—Bolt, Nut, Screw, Rivet, and Washer Manufacturing NAICS 332722

Comparative Historical Data | Current Data Sorted by Sales

							Type of Statement						
	2		6		7		Unqualified				1	5	7
	7		7		10		Reviewed			1	2		4
	2		4		3		Compiled		1		2	1	
	8		8		5		Tax Returns	2		3	2		
	24		32		35		Other	1	3		4	10	17
	4/1/21-3/31/22 ALL		4/1/22-3/31/23 ALL		4/1/23-3/31/24 ALL			13 (4/1-9/30/23)			47 (10/1/23-3/31/24)		
	43		57		60	NUMBER OF STATEMENTS	0-1MM	1-3MM	3-5MM	5-10MM	10-25MM	25MM & OVER
								3	4	9	16	28
	%		%		%	ASSETS	%	%	%	%	%	%
	14.1		9.7		12.0	Cash & Equivalents	D				12.0	8.1
	19.7		22.1		20.8	Trade Receivables (net)	A				25.7	20.3
	34.4		31.7		27.6	Inventory	T				32.8	29.8
	.9		1.3		.8	All Other Current	A				1.4	.8
	69.1		64.8		61.2	Total Current					71.9	59.0
	20.1		25.3		27.4	Fixed Assets (net)	N				19.7	29.2
	8.0		6.4		4.6	Intangibles (net)	O				4.3	4.9
	2.9		3.5		6.7	All Other Non-Current	T				4.0	6.9
	100.0		100.0		100.0	Total					100.0	100.0
						LIABILITIES	A					
	6.1		5.0		4.4	Notes Payable-Short Term	V				4.4	3.3
	2.6		2.7		3.2	Cur. Mat.-L.T.D.	A				1.7	3.6
	10.6		12.6		9.6	Trade Payables	I				11.7	8.4
	.3		.0		.2	Income Taxes Payable	L				.2	.2
	6.7		5.9		7.2	All Other Current	A				3.2	9.9
	26.2		26.3		24.6	Total Current	B				21.3	25.5
	18.4		14.8		12.3	Long-Term Debt	L				8.4	10.6
	.4		.7		.6	Deferred Taxes	E				.0	1.2
	4.0		3.4		2.6	All Other Non-Current					.9	3.3
	50.9		54.8		60.0	Net Worth					69.3	59.3
	100.0		100.0		100.0	Total Liabilities & Net Worth					100.0	100.0
						INCOME DATA						
	100.0		100.0		100.0	Net Sales					100.0	100.0
	34.3		27.6		30.8	Gross Profit					34.5	26.5
	26.4		18.8		21.7	Operating Expenses					25.0	16.4
	7.8		8.9		9.0	Operating Profit					9.5	10.2
	-1.9		1.0		.4	All Other Expenses (net)					.4	.6
	9.8		7.9		8.6	Profit Before Taxes					9.1	9.6
						RATIOS						
	4.1		4.2		5.8						7.4	4.8
	3.1		2.6		2.9	Current					4.6	2.7
	2.0		1.8		1.7					2.5	1.7
	2.3		1.8		2.4						4.7	1.9
	1.2		1.2		1.3	Quick					2.0	1.1
	.7		.8		.8						.9	.7
38	9.6	38	9.6	34	10.6					34	10.6	43	8.5
51	7.2	46	7.9	45	8.1	Sales/Receivables				45	8.1	47	7.8
62	5.9	59	6.2	51	7.2					49	7.5	52	7.0
68	5.4	55	6.6	43	8.5					46	8.0	48	7.6
111	3.3	89	4.1	101	3.6	Cost of Sales/Inventory				118	3.1	107	3.4
174	2.1	140	2.6	152	2.4					152	2.4	159	2.3
17	21.6	14	25.5	15	24.5					17	21.6	15	24.5
36	10.1	33	10.9	24	15.0	Cost of Sales/Payables				24	15.3	23	15.9
55	6.6	47	7.7	40	9.1					39	9.3	38	9.5
	2.8		2.9		2.9						3.0	2.9
	3.9		4.1		4.2	Sales/Working Capital					3.8	4.0
	5.3		6.6		8.9						5.1	10.1
	88.4		32.5		28.6						69.6	16.8
(38)	17.5	(47)	11.2	(52)	8.0	EBIT/Interest				(14)	14.0	(24)	7.2
	6.9		3.1		2.1						1.5	2.1
			12.3		16.8							25.5
		(14)	5.0	(18)	5.9	Net Profit + Depr., Dep., Amort./Cur. Mat. L/T/D					(12)	5.9
			2.1		1.7							2.2
	.1		.3		.2						.1	.4
	.4		.5		.5	Fixed/Worth					.3	.6
	.9		.8		.8						.5	.8
	.3		.4		.2						.1	.3
	.8		.8		.6	Debt/Worth					.2	.6
	2.4		1.7		1.2						.9	1.2
	50.6		41.2		42.1						66.3	36.9
(37)	30.8	(51)	16.8	(57)	16.7	% Profit Before Taxes/Tangible Net Worth				(15)	17.3	(27)	19.4
	12.4		6.3		6.2						9.8	11.2
	26.9		22.9		25.5						52.9	22.9
	14.4		9.4		9.6	% Profit Before Taxes/Total Assets					12.8	10.9
	7.8		2.9		3.0						4.2	4.4
	30.1		20.5		15.1						30.5	12.1
	7.8		6.6		6.0	Sales/Net Fixed Assets					7.5	5.3
	4.6		3.8		3.1						5.5	3.1
	1.8		2.1		2.2						2.6	2.0
	1.5		1.6		1.5	Sales/Total Assets					1.8	1.5
	1.2		1.3		1.2						1.3	1.2
	1.2		1.5		1.1						.9	1.3
(32)	2.2	(45)	2.7	(51)	2.5	% Depr., Dep., Amort./Sales				(15)	1.7	(25)	2.5
	5.7		5.9		4.5						4.9	3.9
			2.5		2.2							
		(14)	3.9	(13)	4.2	% Officers', Directors', Owners' Comp/Sales						
			6.2		9.2							
	1553946M		3074888M		4214523M	Net Sales ($)		6386M	13538M	64389M	276656M	3853554M
	1189956M		1922615M		2693146M	Total Assets ($)		3293M	15228M	40803M	183736M	2450086M

© RMA 2024
M = $ thousand MM = $ million
See Pages viii through xx for Explanation of Ratios and Data

MANUFACTURING—Metal Heat Treating NAICS 332811

Current Data Sorted by Assets | Comparative Historical Data

						Type of Statement				
			6	1	1	Unqualified		8		2
		1				Reviewed		12		4
		3				Compiled		6		5
	2	1				Tax Returns		8		5
1		2	7	1	1	Other		10		13
	3 (4/1-9/30/23)		24 (10/1/23-3/31/24)					4/1/19-		4/1/20-
0-500M	500M-2MM	2-10MM	10-50MM	50-100MM	100-250MM			3/31/20		3/31/21
1	2	7	13	2	2	NUMBER OF STATEMENTS		44 ALL		29 ALL
%	%	%	%	%	%	ASSETS		%		%
			13.3			Cash & Equivalents		11.3		20.4
			12.5			Trade Receivables (net)		22.5		17.7
			2.9			Inventory		3.8		4.9
			4.0			All Other Current		3.0		1.7
			32.7			Total Current		40.7		44.7
			36.6			Fixed Assets (net)		47.7		44.7
			13.7			Intangibles (net)		6.0		3.8
			16.9			All Other Non-Current		5.7		6.8
			100.0			Total		100.0		100.0
						LIABILITIES				
			2.1			Notes Payable-Short Term		3.9		4.9
			4.0			Cur. Mat.-L.T.D.		4.8		4.5
			3.0			Trade Payables		7.2		8.6
			.0			Income Taxes Payable		.1		.0
			6.8			All Other Current		6.7		5.5
			15.9			Total Current		22.7		23.5
			16.8			Long-Term Debt		21.8		21.7
			.0			Deferred Taxes		.9		.0
			22.4			All Other Non-Current		7.0		5.8
			44.8			Net Worth		47.6		48.9
			100.0			Total Liabilities & Net Worth		100.0		100.0
						INCOME DATA				
			100.0			Net Sales		100.0		100.0
			43.8			Gross Profit		39.7		33.7
			34.2			Operating Expenses		31.1		34.4
			9.6			Operating Profit		8.6		-.6
			.5			All Other Expenses (net)		.8		-1.7
			9.1			Profit Before Taxes		7.8		1.0
						RATIOS				
			3.7					3.0		4.4
			2.5			Current		1.6		2.5
			1.5					1.0		1.5
			3.7					2.7		4.0
			1.5			Quick		1.4		2.5
			1.2					.8		1.3
			40 9.1				38	9.7	37	9.9
			50 7.3			Sales/Receivables	45	8.1	45	8.1
			66 5.5				63	5.8	62	5.9
			0 UND				0	UND	0	UND
			3 107.1			Cost of Sales/Inventory	2	226.6	5	70.0
			23 16.1				24	15.5	16	23.0
			10 37.0				10	35.4	10	35.0
			19 19.7			Cost of Sales/Payables	18	20.7	18	20.7
			26 13.9				24	15.2	24	14.9
			3.0					5.1		3.6
			4.7			Sales/Working Capital		16.2		7.3
			8.6					451.2		14.0
			119.8					30.2		19.7
		(12)	10.6			EBIT/Interest	(41)	10.7	(26)	7.0
			1.1					3.1		-1.0
						Net Profit + Depr., Dep., Amort./Cur. Mat. L/T/D				
			.5					.6		.6
			.8			Fixed/Worth		1.2		.8
			NM					2.0		1.6
			.6					.4		.4
			1.1			Debt/Worth		1.1		.9
			NM					2.6		1.9
			30.6					47.2		40.9
		(10)	16.5			% Profit Before Taxes/Tangible Net Worth	(38)	21.8	(25)	12.0
			5.2					12.2		-9.5
			13.0					23.2		16.1
			5.0			% Profit Before Taxes/Total Assets		14.4		6.1
			.6					2.6		-8.1
			4.3					6.9		8.1
			2.2			Sales/Net Fixed Assets		2.8		2.7
			1.3					1.9		1.5
			1.1					2.3		2.1
			.7			Sales/Total Assets		1.5		1.3
			.5					1.0		.8
			6.0					3.9		4.9
			7.7			% Depr., Dep., Amort./Sales	(40)	5.5	(26)	7.9
			12.5					8.7		14.1
								2.4		3.4
						% Officers', Directors', Owners' Comp/Sales	(19)	4.5	(11)	6.2
								6.9		7.0
949M	3985M	62212M	327516M	194419M	288917M	Net Sales ($)		802916M		492672M
425M	1969M	35811M	388611M	139410M	324394M	Total Assets ($)		664333M		456330M

M = $ thousand   MM = $ million
See Pages viii through xx for Explanation of Ratios and Data

© RMA 2024

MANUFACTURING—Metal Heat Treating NAICS 332811

Comparative Historical Data | Current Data Sorted by Sales

				Type of Statement						
8	3	8		Unqualified				2	2	4
6	5	1		Reviewed				1		
7	4	3		Compiled				2	1	
4	4	3		Tax Returns		2		1	5	
10	17	12		Other	1	1		1		5
4/1/21-3/31/22 ALL	4/1/22-3/31/23 ALL	4/1/23-3/31/24 ALL			0-1MM	3 (4/1-9/30/23) 1-3MM	3-5MM	24 (10/1/23-3/31/24) 5-10MM	10-25MM	25MM & OVER
35	33	27		NUMBER OF STATEMENTS	1	1		7	8	9
%	%	%		ASSETS	%	%	%	%	%	%
16.5	16.9	13.4		Cash & Equivalents						
17.7	20.4	16.6		Trade Receivables (net)			D			
8.5	16.9	5.6		Inventory			A			
1.6	2.6	2.1		All Other Current			T			
44.3	56.8	37.7		Total Current			A			
45.5	34.2	37.5		Fixed Assets (net)						
4.0	3.0	10.7		Intangibles (net)			N			
6.2	6.0	14.1		All Other Non-Current			O			
100.0	100.0	100.0		Total			T			
				LIABILITIES						
3.5	2.6	2.5		Notes Payable-Short Term			A			
4.4	2.6	4.8		Cur. Mat.-L.T.D.			V			
7.4	9.3	6.0		Trade Payables			A			
.1	.1	.0		Income Taxes Payable			I			
7.6	7.9	6.2		All Other Current			L			
23.0	22.5	19.6		Total Current			A			
20.0	17.0	19.3		Long-Term Debt			B			
.5	.2	.0		Deferred Taxes			L			
3.1	7.6	16.0		All Other Non-Current			E			
53.4	52.6	45.1		Net Worth						
100.0	100.0	100.0		Total Liabilties & Net Worth						
				INCOME DATA						
100.0	100.0	100.0		Net Sales						
38.1	32.5	41.8		Gross Profit						
34.2	25.8	34.2		Operating Expenses						
4.0	6.7	7.6		Operating Profit						
-3.7	-1.0	1.2		All Other Expenses (net)						
7.6	7.6	6.4		Profit Before Taxes						
				RATIOS						
3.9	5.4	4.2		Current						
2.6	3.9	2.3								
1.0	1.8	1.3								
3.6	5.0	4.2		Quick						
2.0	2.4	1.6								
.7	1.2	1.1								
40 9.1	36 10.1	36 10.1		Sales/Receivables						
56 6.5	45 8.1	46 7.9								
65 5.6	59 6.2	62 5.9								
0 UND	0 UND	0 UND		Cost of Sales/Inventory						
2 175.8	15 24.6	3 111.2								
47 7.8	79 4.6	24 14.9								
13 27.8	7 52.3	9 39.4		Cost of Sales/Payables						
23 16.0	18 20.2	16 22.2								
36 10.1	31 11.8	27 13.7								
2.5	3.0	3.4		Sales/Working Capital						
4.6	4.3	6.2								
149.9	7.9	16.6								
25.8	48.1	40.3		EBIT/Interest						
(31) 10.5	(26) 13.7	(25) 11.2								
1.8	3.9	.5								
				Net Profit + Depr., Dep., Amort./Cur. Mat. L/T/D						
.6	.3	.5		Fixed/Worth						
.9	.6	.8								
1.5	1.1	4.7								
.2	.3	.6		Debt/Worth						
.7	.6	1.1								
1.7	1.0	10.6								
36.9	31.1	31.8		% Profit Before Taxes/Tangible Net Worth						
(30) 19.4	(30) 14.8	(22) 16.9								
.1	4.9	5.2								
19.4	16.2	13.5		% Profit Before Taxes/Total Assets						
11.4	7.7	7.4								
1.4	4.4	-3.8								
5.5	13.7	5.7		Sales/Net Fixed Assets						
2.7	4.3	3.1								
1.6	2.4	1.8								
1.6	2.0	1.8		Sales/Total Assets						
1.2	1.3	1.2								
.9	1.1	.7								
3.3	1.2	3.9		% Depr., Dep., Amort./Sales						
(33) 7.4	(24) 4.3	(25) 6.6								
10.2	7.2	9.0								
1.8				% Officers', Directors' Owners' Comp/Sales						
(16) 4.1										
5.3										
757920M	905022M	877998M		Net Sales ($)	949M	3985M		54808M	138750M	679506M
688199M	637760M	890620M		Total Assets ($)	425M	1969M		59981M	172877M	655368M

M = $ thousand   MM = $ million

© RMA 2024
See Pages viii through xx for Explanation of Ratios and Data

MANUFACTURING—Metal Coating, Engraving (except Jewelry and Silverware), and Allied Services to Manufacturers   NAICS 332812

Current Data Sorted by Assets | Comparative Historical Data

							Type of Statement			
			5				Unqualified		5	2
	1	5	11	1	1		Reviewed		18	16
		5	1				Compiled		12	10
3	7	1			1		Tax Returns		13	5
1	15	14	10	5	3		Other		34	36
	8 (4/1-9/30/23)		84 (10/1/23-3/31/24)						4/1/19-	4/1/20-
0-500M	500M-2MM	2-10MM	10-50MM	50-100MM	100-250MM				3/31/20	3/31/21
4	23	25	27	6	7		NUMBER OF STATEMENTS		82 ALL	69 ALL
%	%	%	%	%	%		ASSETS		%	%
	17.1	17.0	11.5				Cash & Equivalents		14.1	16.9
	18.3	23.6	17.7				Trade Receivables (net)		25.1	21.6
	5.9	9.4	9.5				Inventory		11.1	10.1
	3.6	4.3	2.8				All Other Current		1.8	3.1
	44.9	54.3	41.4				Total Current		52.0	51.7
	28.8	26.6	37.8				Fixed Assets (net)		35.0	32.7
	8.7	6.1	7.6				Intangibles (net)		5.3	11.4
	17.7	13.0	13.3				All Other Non-Current		7.6	4.1
	100.0	100.0	100.0				Total		100.0	100.0
							LIABILITIES			
	4.9	3.5	3.7				Notes Payable-Short Term		5.0	5.9
	4.4	3.7	4.5				Cur. Mat.-L.T.D.		3.5	4.5
	8.3	11.2	7.5				Trade Payables		9.8	7.7
	.0	.3	.0				Income Taxes Payable		.2	.1
	20.3	7.3	8.2				All Other Current		9.9	7.2
	38.0	26.0	23.9				Total Current		28.3	25.5
	30.2	23.3	18.5				Long-Term Debt		19.5	18.6
	.0	.1	.0				Deferred Taxes		.8	.7
	4.7	12.7	9.6				All Other Non-Current		5.3	6.2
	27.0	37.9	48.0				Net Worth		46.1	49.0
	100.0	100.0	100.0				Total Liabilities & Net Worth		100.0	100.0
							INCOME DATA			
	100.0	100.0	100.0				Net Sales		100.0	100.0
	45.9	39.0	33.4				Gross Profit		38.8	33.2
	42.4	28.9	23.6				Operating Expenses		29.8	27.1
	3.5	10.1	9.7				Operating Profit		9.0	6.2
	2.0	.0	1.1				All Other Expenses (net)		1.5	-.4
	1.5	10.0	8.6				Profit Before Taxes		7.5	6.5
							RATIOS			
	7.2	5.4	2.7						3.9	4.1
	1.2	2.2	1.8			Current			2.1	2.2
	.7	1.4	1.0						1.2	1.3
	3.7	4.0	2.5						2.6	2.8
	1.0	1.7	1.3			Quick			1.4	1.7
	.4	1.0	.6						.8	.9
10	36.4	32	11.3	35	10.4			31	11.8	34	10.7
34	10.8	46	8.0	47	7.8		Sales/Receivables	41	8.9	47	7.8
48	7.6	51	7.2	57	6.4			57	6.4	69	5.3
0	UND	1	358.4	11	32.4			0	UND	12	31.1
10	36.4	22	16.4	29	12.8		Cost of Sales/Inventory	22	16.5	27	13.6
46	8.0	37	9.8	68	5.4			59	6.2	53	6.9
3	116.9	17	21.6	17	22.1			11	32.5	12	29.4
21	17.3	27	13.7	24	15.1		Cost of Sales/Payables	22	16.5	21	17.2
46	8.0	43	8.5	40	9.2			35	10.3	35	10.4
	5.6	3.7	4.8						4.8	3.6
	20.9	7.3	7.4			Sales/Working Capital			8.1	5.7
	-15.9	16.6	-142.4						45.0	20.3
	18.6	37.9	25.0						27.7	32.8
(20)	3.3	(24)	11.2	(26)	7.5		EBIT/Interest	(70)	8.2	(57)	7.0
	1.9	5.7	.6						3.6	.0
							Net Profit + Depr., Dep.,		4.3	14.7
							Amort./Cur. Mat. L/T/D	(14)	3.2	(13)	6.1
									1.3	2.5
	.1	.4	.4						.4	.4
	2.6	.7	.9			Fixed/Worth			.7	.8
	-1.1	NM	2.6						1.8	3.0
	.4	.4	.5						.4	.5
	4.5	1.2	1.1			Debt/Worth			.9	.9
	-5.8	NM	4.7						3.9	7.2
	44.7	47.2	58.1						57.9	47.2
(14)	25.2	(19)	37.8	(25)	31.7		% Profit Before Taxes/Tangible Net Worth	(71)	26.0	(58)	18.3
	10.4	20.7	6.5						10.4	1.2
	21.1	25.6	28.3						23.6	25.6
	4.6	18.0	13.0			% Profit Before Taxes/Total Assets			10.4	8.2
	.6	9.4	1.9						4.6	-2.3
	108.0	17.3	9.0						17.8	11.7
	12.1	6.9	3.5			Sales/Net Fixed Assets			5.9	5.5
	4.5	5.0	2.2						2.7	2.5
	3.0	2.7	1.9						2.8	2.2
	2.0	1.9	1.3			Sales/Total Assets			1.9	1.4
	1.3	1.5	.8						1.2	.9
	2.3	.9	1.7						1.3	1.4
(10)	4.1	(21)	2.7	(23)	3.4		% Depr., Dep., Amort./Sales	(66)	2.8	(61)	3.2
	6.6	4.2	11.7						4.5	5.2
							% Officers', Directors'		3.0	2.3
							Owners' Comp/Sales	(28)	4.0	(19)	4.3
									6.9	9.5
8355M	71670M	269104M	813979M	530510M	1065815M		Net Sales ($)		1686599M	1624154M
1366M	28824M	132617M	561692M	429908M	1007273M		Total Assets ($)		1251579M	1281422M

© RMA 2024

M = $ thousand   MM = $ million
See Pages viii through xx for Explanation of Ratios and Data

MANUFACTURING—Metal Coating, Engraving (except Jewelry and Silverware), and Allied Services to Manufacturers NAICS 332812

Comparative Historical Data | Current Data Sorted by Sales

Comparative Historical Data			Type of Statement	Current Data Sorted by Sales						
2	5	7	Unqualified					1	1	6
7	11	18	Reviewed		1	1	4	8	4	
6	10	7	Compiled			1		5	1	
8	15	12	Tax Returns		4	3	1	2	1	
30	29	48	Other	1	7	7	5	11	14	
4/1/21-3/31/22 ALL	4/1/22-3/31/23 ALL	4/1/23-3/31/24 ALL		4	8 (4/1-9/30/23)			84 (10/1/23-3/31/24)		
				0-1MM	1-3MM	3-5MM	5-10MM	10-25MM	25MM & OVER
53	70	92	NUMBER OF STATEMENTS	5	12	12	10	27	26
%	%	%	ASSETS	%	%	%	%	%	%
19.3	17.2	14.0	Cash & Equivalents		15.7	16.0	8.0	14.5	14.4
21.7	23.3	19.3	Trade Receivables (net)		16.4	21.3	17.2	20.8	21.1
9.9	12.2	9.4	Inventory		2.2	6.1	9.7	9.3	15.0
1.0	2.6	3.3	All Other Current		11.3	.6	2.2	2.5	2.5
51.8	55.3	46.0	Total Current		45.5	44.1	37.0	47.1	52.9
31.4	27.6	33.5	Fixed Assets (net)		31.3	31.6	43.0	29.4	35.3
10.5	9.0	8.3	Intangibles (net)		12.1	7.2	1.4	10.3	7.8
6.3	8.2	12.2	All Other Non-Current		11.2	17.2	18.7	13.1	4.0
100.0	100.0	100.0	Total		100.0	100.0	100.0	100.0	100.0
			LIABILITIES						
2.7	4.2	5.5	Notes Payable-Short Term		4.4	6.6	7.2	4.2	5.6
4.7	3.5	4.4	Cur. Mat.-L.T.D.		.6	6.1	4.3	5.3	3.6
7.8	7.7	8.6	Trade Payables		5.2	10.8	6.5	10.3	9.0
.0	.2	.1	Income Taxes Payable		.0	.0	.0	.3	.0
6.6	8.9	12.4	All Other Current		17.7	18.5	5.7	7.5	11.8
21.8	24.5	31.0	Total Current		28.0	42.0	23.7	27.6	30.1
23.5	21.9	23.9	Long-Term Debt		30.6	39.5	35.7	15.2	14.4
.2	.3	.2	Deferred Taxes		.0	.0	.0	.1	.5
6.9	6.2	8.5	All Other Non-Current		4.5	8.7	7.2	15.5	5.2
47.6	47.1	36.4	Net Worth		36.9	9.8	33.4	41.7	49.9
100.0	100.0	100.0	Total Liabilities & Net Worth		100.0	100.0	100.0	100.0	100.0
			INCOME DATA						
100.0	100.0	100.0	Net Sales		100.0	100.0	100.0	100.0	100.0
38.7	42.1	38.8	Gross Profit		52.9	47.3	39.3	35.0	27.9
29.1	32.1	31.6	Operating Expenses		46.1	40.0	30.3	27.7	18.6
9.6	10.0	7.2	Operating Profit		6.8	7.2	9.0	7.4	9.4
-.9	.6	1.1	All Other Expenses (net)		1.5	1.6	.6	.4	1.0
10.5	9.4	6.1	Profit Before Taxes		5.2	5.6	8.4	7.0	8.3
			RATIOS						
4.7	5.0	4.3			21.1	4.8	3.2	2.8	4.8
2.4	2.6	1.8	Current		4.2	1.8	1.2	1.8	1.9
1.5	1.4	1.0			1.5	.5	.9	1.3	1.1
4.1	3.9	2.7			7.1	4.0	2.1	2.4	2.8
1.9	1.9	1.2	Quick		2.4	1.5	.9	1.1	1.4
1.0	.9	.5			.4	.5	.6	.8	.5
29 12.6	28 13.2	29 12.7		3 135.7	27 13.4	27 13.7	34 10.6	38 9.7
40 9.1	42 8.7	45 8.2	Sales/Receivables	27 13.3	45 8.1	46 8.0	44 8.3	53 6.9
56 6.5	55 6.6	52 7.0		45 8.2	49 7.4	47 7.7	51 7.2	65 5.6
6 57.7	4 102.9	0 897.3		0 UND	0 UND	2 151.1	13 29.1	14 26.4
22 16.9	24 15.2	27 13.6	Cost of Sales/Inventory	0 UND	19 19.0	34 10.7	29 12.8	52 7.0
68 5.4	57 6.4	65 5.6		1 257.8	27 13.6	72 5.1	58 6.3	79 4.6
10 37.8	6 64.2	15 24.7		0 UND	1 429.4	15 23.7	17 21.7	16 22.8
16 22.5	18 20.3	24 15.0	Cost of Sales/Payables	17 22.0	24 15.0	17 21.8	27 13.7	25 14.7
26 14.3	33 11.0	42 8.7		48 7.6	48 7.6	41 8.9	42 8.7	43 8.4
3.8	3.3	4.9			2.8	7.1	5.0	6.6	4.0
5.6	5.9	10.0	Sales/Working Capital		6.4	16.0	36.8	9.5	6.5
18.7	17.1	UND			24.3	-20.5	-47.2	36.0	NM
59.0	40.6	23.8				13.9	13.2	27.9	37.2
(46) 12.2	(60) 12.2	(87) 7.3	EBIT/Interest			4.8	9.3	7.4	(25) 7.7
3.9	3.6	1.9				3.0	1.4	1.9	1.9
	21.3	54.7	Net Profit + Depr., Dep.,						
	(12) 5.1	(13) 5.8	Amort./Cur. Mat. L/T/D						
	2.6	2.6							
.4	.2	.4			.2	.9	.5	.4	.3
.7	.5	1.0	Fixed/Worth		1.0	-9.3	.9	.8	.9
20.8	2.1	NM			-1.5	-1.3	11.2	27.8	2.3
.5	.3	.5			.2	1.6	.5	.4	.5
1.0	.8	1.7	Debt/Worth		1.0	-22.0	1.7	1.2	1.1
54.2	2.9	NM			-4.6	-3.8	15.6	190.0	3.3
84.1	54.2	45.5						40.9	57.0
(41) 28.0	(56) 29.0	(69) 26.9	% Profit Before Taxes/Tangible Net Worth					(21) 24.8	(24) 32.5
14.4	10.1	10.9						7.7	9.1
27.6	31.7	21.6			21.9	23.6	24.2	19.8	28.2
19.2	14.8	10.1	% Profit Before Taxes/Total Assets		12.7	14.7	10.9	13.0	8.8
7.1	8.0	2.2			.8	3.2	1.3	1.9	3.2
13.3	26.5	15.0			46.9	30.3	9.7	17.6	11.2
5.8	7.9	5.7	Sales/Net Fixed Assets		7.4	6.5	5.7	6.9	3.7
3.2	3.8	2.8			3.0	5.2	1.6	3.0	2.4
2.3	3.0	2.5			2.6	3.2	2.3	2.8	1.9
1.7	1.9	1.7	Sales/Total Assets		1.5	2.5	1.6	1.7	1.6
1.2	1.1	1.0			1.1	1.5	.7	1.1	1.0
1.6	.5	1.7						1.0	1.0
(45) 3.0	(58) 2.2	(65) 3.4	% Depr., Dep., Amort./Sales					(22) 2.8	(21) 2.5
4.8	5.2	5.9						6.9	3.9
1.9	1.9	1.0						.3	
(18) 3.5	(19) 6.6	(23) 2.9	% Officers', Directors' Owners' Comp/Sales					(10) .9	
6.7	13.6	6.2						1.9	
1364257M	1468314M	2759433M	Net Sales ($)	3181M	21091M	54801M	77210M	405618M	2197532M
860632M	906704M	2161680M	Total Assets ($)	3217M	13727M	26019M	72405M	307656M	1738656M

© RMA 2024
M = $ thousand MM = $ million
See Pages viii through xx for Explanation of Ratios and Data

MANUFACTURING—Electroplating, Plating, Polishing, Anodizing, and Coloring NAICS 332813

Current Data Sorted by Assets									Comparative Historical Data	
							Type of Statement			
				2	1		Unqualified		3	2
	1	3	6	1			Reviewed		10	9
1	1	2	1				Compiled		7	3
2	8	12	11	1	2		Tax Returns		9	6
	5 (4/1-9/30/23)		50 (10/1/23-3/31/24)				Other		37	33
0-500M	500M-2MM	2-10MM	10-50MM	50-100MM	100-250MM				4/1/19-3/31/20 ALL	4/1/20-3/31/21 ALL
3	10	17	18	4	3		NUMBER OF STATEMENTS		66	53
%	%	%	%	%	%		ASSETS		%	%
	14.4	16.7	16.1				Cash & Equivalents		14.0	20.0
	18.8	24.0	14.0				Trade Receivables (net)		28.1	23.8
	6.9	7.1	13.1				Inventory		10.0	10.2
	8.4	1.4	1.3				All Other Current		2.4	1.7
	48.4	49.2	44.5				Total Current		54.5	55.6
	40.2	32.7	43.1				Fixed Assets (net)		34.2	35.8
	3.8	13.8	4.2				Intangibles (net)		5.6	4.3
	7.6	4.3	8.2				All Other Non-Current		5.7	4.4
	100.0	100.0	100.0				Total		100.0	100.0
							LIABILITIES			
	8.1	7.0	3.8				Notes Payable-Short Term		6.0	6.4
	2.0	3.4	4.1				Cur. Mat.-L.T.D.		3.7	2.3
	5.7	5.4	6.5				Trade Payables		8.3	7.2
	.5	2.2	.1				Income Taxes Payable		.1	.0
	5.8	10.4	4.9				All Other Current		7.8	9.9
	22.0	28.4	19.3				Total Current		25.9	25.9
	17.9	15.4	22.4				Long-Term Debt		24.9	17.9
	.0	.4	.4				Deferred Taxes		.5	.2
	7.5	10.0	3.1				All Other Non-Current		7.2	9.0
	52.6	45.7	54.8				Net Worth		41.5	46.9
	100.0	100.0	100.0				Total Liabilities & Net Worth		100.0	100.0
							INCOME DATA			
	100.0	100.0	100.0				Net Sales		100.0	100.0
	39.1	45.9	27.6				Gross Profit		35.2	31.1
	31.5	33.3	19.8				Operating Expenses		28.6	26.8
	7.6	12.7	7.8				Operating Profit		6.6	4.2
	.3	1.4	1.2				All Other Expenses (net)		1.0	-1.0
	7.3	11.3	6.5				Profit Before Taxes		5.6	5.2
							RATIOS			
	3.6	6.2	5.1						4.2	4.2
	2.6	2.9	3.0			Current			2.3	2.4
	1.2	1.1	1.2						1.3	1.6
	2.7	5.9	4.3						2.9	3.6
	1.3	2.4	1.3			Quick			1.5	1.8
	.8	.7	.6						.9	.9
18	20.0	29	12.8	26	14.3			38	9.6	39	9.3
27	13.4	42	8.6	39	9.4		Sales/Receivables	42	8.6	47	7.7
49	7.4	54	6.8	46	7.9			54	6.7	58	6.3
0	UND	0	UND	11	32.0			3	109.1	0	UND
8	47.2	8	43.2	35	10.3		Cost of Sales/Inventory	14	25.7	16	22.4
39	9.3	35	10.4	54	6.8			46	8.0	57	6.4
3	112.3	7	50.5	9	39.5			11	32.4	8	47.1
11	32.0	11	32.2	21	17.6		Cost of Sales/Payables	18	19.8	23	16.1
26	13.9	30	12.2	27	13.3			30	12.2	36	10.0
	4.8	5.0	3.7						5.2	3.3
	9.9	8.8	4.7			Sales/Working Capital			7.8	5.5
	65.7	47.4	24.1						22.6	12.5
		29.3	30.7						23.5	47.3
	(15)	17.1	(16) 12.1			EBIT/Interest		(56)	6.6	(42) 8.7
		3.4	.2						2.7	1.3
							Net Profit + Depr., Dep.,			6.2	
							Amort./Cur. Mat. L/T/D		(13)	3.5	
										2.9	
	.3	.6	.4						.3	.4
	.8	.8	.7			Fixed/Worth			.9	.8
	2.7	-5.7	2.5						2.3	2.1
	.3	.3	.2						.5	.3
	1.1	1.3	.7			Debt/Worth			1.3	.9
	4.4	-16.9	3.0						3.7	3.1
	113.6	101.5	24.5						52.9	45.4
	22.8	(12) 49.6	(17) 10.7			% Profit Before Taxes/Tangible Net Worth		(57)	22.5	(48) 18.2
	-1.8	21.2	-2.7						7.9	4.9
	29.6	47.7	20.7						24.6	17.6
	14.9	28.0	8.5			% Profit Before Taxes/Total Assets			11.4	9.9
	-.9	7.6	-1.3						4.1	.4
	18.1	11.1	6.3						18.3	10.2
	5.9	5.5	4.0			Sales/Net Fixed Assets			7.1	4.4
	2.8	3.3	2.2						2.9	2.7
	2.7	2.9	1.8						3.2	2.2
	2.0	2.1	1.4			Sales/Total Assets			2.0	1.6
	1.4	1.4	1.0						1.5	1.2
		1.8	2.2						1.6	2.1
	(16)	3.3	(17) 2.7			% Depr., Dep., Amort./Sales		(54)	3.1	(43) 3.7
		4.6	4.5						6.1	6.5
							% Officers', Directors'			2.2	1.9
							Owners' Comp/Sales		(23)	4.3	(12) 5.3
										6.7	11.3
5063M	25423M	215161M	547167M	311000M	677346M		Net Sales ($)		1418287M	912531M
1040M	11144M	102721M	390862M	250509M	333706M		Total Assets ($)		811739M	575314M

M = $ thousand   MM = $ million
See Pages viii through xx for Explanation of Ratios and Data

© RMA 2024

MANUFACTURING—Electroplating, Plating, Polishing, Anodizing, and Coloring NAICS 332813

Comparative Historical Data | Current Data Sorted by Sales

Comparative Historical Data			Type of Statement	Current Data Sorted by Sales					
5	3	3	Unqualified		1		2	2	3
3	11	11	Reviewed		1			3	6
5	4	4	Compiled		1				
17	3	1	Tax Returns						
4/1/21-	31	36	Other		7	4	5	11	9
3/31/22	4/1/22-	4/1/23-			5 (4/1-9/30/23)		50 (10/1/23-3/31/24)		
ALL	3/31/23	3/31/24		0-1MM	1-3MM	3-5MM	5-10MM	10-25MM	25MM & OVER
30	ALL 52	ALL 55	NUMBER OF STATEMENTS	10	4	7	16	18	
%	%	%	**ASSETS**	%	%	%	%	%	%
17.4	16.2	13.7	Cash & Equivalents		9.5			22.0	6.4
19.8	24.8	20.4	Trade Receivables (net)		25.5			22.7	16.5
10.0	11.2	11.3	Inventory		6.8			9.8	18.3
2.9	4.0	2.6	All Other Current		8.4			.7	1.6
50.1	56.1	48.0	Total Current	DATA	50.2			55.2	42.8
36.4	30.8	38.3	Fixed Assets (net)	NOT	37.0			31.3	47.7
5.9	7.1	7.2	Intangibles (net)	AVAILABLE	4.7			6.1	4.0
7.6	5.9	6.4	All Other Non-Current		8.1			7.5	5.6
100.0	100.0	100.0	Total		100.0			100.0	100.0
			LIABILITIES						
3.1	4.8	6.2	Notes Payable-Short Term		3.3			4.3	6.8
2.6	2.8	3.1	Cur. Mat.-L.T.D.		1.4			3.0	4.6
8.1	7.4	8.7	Trade Payables		18.5			5.6	8.8
.0	.0	.8	Income Taxes Payable		.5			2.4	.0
4.6	9.3	8.9	All Other Current		16.9			5.5	5.4
18.3	24.3	27.8	Total Current		40.6			20.8	25.6
34.1	16.7	17.5	Long-Term Debt		13.9			10.5	23.0
.0	.0	.4	Deferred Taxes		.0			.5	.7
3.7	4.8	8.1	All Other Non-Current		15.5			2.7	5.6
43.9	54.2	46.2	Net Worth		29.9			65.6	45.1
100.0	100.0	100.0	Total Liabilities & Net Worth		100.0			100.0	100.0
			INCOME DATA						
100.0	100.0	100.0	Net Sales		100.0			100.0	100.0
37.6	35.2	35.7	Gross Profit		42.9			35.0	25.8
31.7	25.1	27.1	Operating Expenses		37.3			24.5	18.2
5.8	10.1	8.6	Operating Profit		5.6			10.5	7.7
-3.5	.3	1.1	All Other Expenses (net)		.4			.8	1.4
9.3	9.8	7.5	Profit Before Taxes		5.2			9.6	6.2
			RATIOS						
7.0	5.4	4.0			3.1			7.2	3.5
3.6	2.8	2.6	Current		2.6			3.1	1.4
1.6	1.4	1.2			1.1			1.4	1.1
6.8	3.8	3.6			2.5			6.9	1.6
3.1	1.8	1.1	Quick		1.2			2.7	.7
.6	.9	.6			.4			.9	.6
28 13.1	34 10.6	27 13.6		21 17.5			28 12.9	29 12.7	
36 10.0	45 8.1	39 9.3	Sales/Receivables	30 12.1			40 9.2	39 9.3	
46 7.9	54 6.7	47 7.8		49 7.4			49 7.4	44 8.3	
0 UND	8 48.1	4 94.4		0 UND			4 103.2	30 12.1	
15 24.7	15 25.0	22 16.4	Cost of Sales/Inventory	5 75.7			11 34.0	44 8.3	
52 7.0	54 6.8	51 7.1		39 9.3			38 9.6	64 5.7	
6 60.8	11 33.9	8 43.7		0 UND			7 51.6	20 18.6	
19 18.8	19 19.3	19 18.8	Cost of Sales/Payables	18 19.8			9 38.8	24 16.4	
30 12.0	28 12.9	28 12.9		44 8.3			23 15.9	34 10.6	
3.7	3.4	4.3			4.8			4.1	4.3
7.3	5.6	8.8	Sales/Working Capital		11.0			6.3	13.8
10.9	15.7	33.9			NM			17.7	NM
70.0	75.8	29.3			73.0			73.0	48.0
(26) 13.0	(44) 13.9	(43) 10.7	EBIT/Interest		(13) 17.1		(17) 9.2		
1.5	1.8	.6			2.0				.6
	13.3	11.2	Net Profit + Depr., Dep.,						
	(12) 5.3	(14) 6.6	Amort./Cur. Mat. L/T/D						
	2.7	2.8							
.4	.3	.5			.4			.3	.6
.6	.6	.8	Fixed/Worth		.8			.6	.9
1.3	1.9	2.9			NM			.9	6.6
.2	.2	.3			.5			.2	.3
.9	.6	1.0	Debt/Worth		1.6			.7	1.3
1.7	3.5	4.6			NM			1.2	7.7
43.2	57.7	58.2	% Profit Before Taxes/Tangible					65.4	24.5
(27) 24.7	(45) 23.9	(47) 15.8	Net Worth					25.7	(17) 13.5
6.2	9.3	-1.7						10.4	-2.9
31.2	26.8	26.6	% Profit Before Taxes/Total		23.0			45.9	20.7
15.9	15.0	10.0	Assets		8.7			14.6	9.5
2.5	5.3	-.4			-2.0			6.9	-.6
15.3	11.1	8.8			28.9			11.5	6.2
5.4	6.4	5.4	Sales/Net Fixed Assets		7.6			6.4	4.0
2.7	4.0	2.9			2.8			5.0	1.9
2.4	2.4	2.4			4.0			2.9	2.0
1.6	1.9	1.8	Sales/Total Assets		2.0			2.1	1.6
1.2	1.4	1.3			1.4			1.4	1.3
1.6	1.2	1.6						2.1	1.6
(22) 4.1	(44) 2.3	(48) 2.6	% Depr., Dep., Amort./Sales				(14) 2.9	(16) 2.4	
7.4	4.4	4.2						4.8	3.4
3.3	3.3	3.5	% Officers', Directors',						
(11) 8.2	(13) 5.0	(12) 5.3	Owners' Comp/Sales						
17.6	9.2	6.5							
629982M	1483854M	1781160M	Net Sales ($)		17783M	14223M	54404M	284992M	1409758M
373204M	844320M	1089982M	Total Assets ($)		8484M	14560M	38161M	178447M	850330M

© RMA 2024
M = $ thousand   MM = $ million
See Pages viii through xx for Explanation of Ratios and Data

MANUFACTURING—Industrial Valve Manufacturing NAICS 332911

Current Data Sorted by Assets | Comparative Historical Data

						Type of Statement		
						Unqualified	9	3
			3	1		Reviewed	12	7
	2		7	2	1	Compiled	3	4
2	4	2	2	1		Tax Returns	17	8
	5	9	1			Other	51	35
	13 (4/1-9/30/23)		47 (10/1/23-3/31/24)				4/1/19-	4/1/20-
0-500M	500M-2MM	2-10MM	10-50MM	50-100MM	100-250MM		3/31/20	3/31/21
2	9	14	25	7	3	NUMBER OF STATEMENTS	92 ALL	57 ALL
%	%	%	%	%	%	ASSETS	%	%
		11.5	10.5			Cash & Equivalents	10.4	19.0
		19.0	18.9			Trade Receivables (net)	22.5	19.6
		36.0	33.6			Inventory	32.0	25.4
		1.3	4.9			All Other Current	2.4	5.1
		67.7	67.8			Total Current	67.2	69.1
		14.9	18.8			Fixed Assets (net)	19.6	19.2
		5.5	4.6			Intangibles (net)	8.3	5.6
		11.9	8.8			All Other Non-Current	4.9	6.1
		100.0	100.0			Total	100.0	100.0
						LIABILITIES		
		5.3	5.3			Notes Payable-Short Term	8.5	6.7
		2.3	1.5			Cur. Mat.-L.T.D.	3.7	5.3
		15.1	7.3			Trade Payables	12.7	11.1
		.1	.0			Income Taxes Payable	.3	.1
		11.7	8.7			All Other Current	9.9	10.2
		34.5	22.7			Total Current	35.1	33.4
		14.0	6.2			Long-Term Debt	14.7	19.2
		.3	.5			Deferred Taxes	.1	.1
		4.5	10.8			All Other Non-Current	11.3	10.4
		46.7	59.8			Net Worth	38.8	36.9
		100.0	100.0			Total Liabilities & Net Worth	100.0	100.0
						INCOME DATA		
		100.0	100.0			Net Sales	100.0	100.0
		34.1	36.7			Gross Profit	37.4	36.0
		27.5	26.4			Operating Expenses	29.5	31.6
		6.6	10.3			Operating Profit	7.9	4.4
		1.3	.1			All Other Expenses (net)	.9	-.8
		5.2	10.2			Profit Before Taxes	7.0	5.2
						RATIOS		
		5.5	4.6				3.8	4.3
		2.0	2.9			Current	2.3	2.8
		1.3	2.3				1.3	1.6
		2.7	2.4				1.8	2.4
		.8	1.0			Quick	1.0	1.5
		.5	.7				.6	.8
	15	24.7	35	10.3			33	11.0	27	13.7
	49	7.5	43	8.4		Sales/Receivables	42	8.7	41	8.9
	59	6.2	64	5.7			54	6.7	49	7.4
	58	6.3	89	4.1			54	6.7	32	11.5
	111	3.3	159	2.3		Cost of Sales/Inventory	104	3.5	79	4.6
	159	2.3	215	1.7			182	2.0	140	2.6
	24	15.3	17	22.0			15	23.7	8	43.6
	41	8.9	26	14.2		Cost of Sales/Payables	24	15.0	22	16.9
	56	6.5	54	6.8			46	7.9	51	7.1
		3.7	1.9				3.1	2.8
		5.3	2.9			Sales/Working Capital	4.8	4.7
		9.7	3.9				13.7	7.8
		34.1	73.8				24.6	20.3
		(12) 4.2	(22) 14.6			EBIT/Interest	(83) 8.4	(44) 3.7
		2.4	6.6				1.8	-.9
						Net Profit + Depr., Dep.,	6.4	
						Amort./Cur. Mat. L/T/D	(19) 2.4	
							1.0	
		.1	.1				.1	.1
		.4	.3			Fixed/Worth	.5	.3
		NM	.6				1.5	.9
		.3	.3				.4	.5
		1.0	.7			Debt/Worth	1.4	1.0
		NM	1.0				9.1	2.9
		19.1	39.2				55.7	48.7
		(11) 10.3	(24) 20.3			% Profit Before Taxes/Tangible Net Worth	(76) 25.5	(46) 22.2
		4.3	9.2				11.2	-3.6
		11.1	20.3				21.4	18.6
		4.7	11.1			% Profit Before Taxes/Total Assets	10.0	9.5
		2.6	5.6				3.1	-4.9
		35.9	25.3				32.2	51.8
		20.0	9.7			Sales/Net Fixed Assets	10.3	10.7
		7.2	4.2				5.1	4.9
		2.0	1.6				2.4	2.4
		1.7	1.2			Sales/Total Assets	1.7	1.6
		1.4	.9				1.1	1.1
		1.0	1.0				.9	1.0
		(11) 3.9	(23) 2.2			% Depr., Dep., Amort./Sales	(70) 2.1	(36) 3.0
		4.2	3.9				3.5	4.8
						% Officers', Directors'	1.9	1.9
						Owners' Comp/Sales	(23) 3.2	(18) 3.5
							6.5	4.9
8519M	35675M	142872M	714078M	636254M	451641M	Net Sales ($)	2036362M	1030930M
825M	9444M	78213M	539785M	472143M	680528M	Total Assets ($)	1594183M	793423M

M = $ thousand   MM = $ million
See Pages viii through xx for Explanation of Ratios and Data

© RMA 2024

MANUFACTURING—Industrial Valve Manufacturing NAICS 332911

Comparative Historical Data | Current Data Sorted by Sales

Comparative Historical Data					Current Data Sorted by Sales					
4	3	5	Type of Statement					2	3	
3	5	11	Unqualified					4	5	
2	7	4	Reviewed			2		1	2	
10	12	9	Compiled			1	4	2	1	
34	25	31	Tax Returns		2	1	3	6	10	10
4/1/21-	4/1/22-	4/1/23-	Other	1	13 (4/1-9/30/23)			47 (10/1/23-3/31/24)		
3/31/22	3/31/23	3/31/24		0-1MM	1-3MM	3-5MM	5-10MM	10-25MM	25MM & OVER	
ALL	ALL	ALL	NUMBER OF STATEMENTS	1	3	7	11	18	20	
53	52	60								
%	%	%	ASSETS	%	%	%	%	%	%	
16.8	10.7	15.5	Cash & Equivalents				9.8	9.6	12.1	
23.1	24.9	19.8	Trade Receivables (net)				29.9	17.9	18.1	
31.5	31.7	30.6	Inventory				26.4	38.1	33.0	
1.6	1.5	2.5	All Other Current				1.4	3.8	3.3	
72.9	68.8	68.3	Total Current				67.5	69.4	66.5	
15.5	18.0	17.6	Fixed Assets (net)				22.2	13.6	21.7	
6.1	7.8	5.7	Intangibles (net)				3.6	6.1	6.1	
5.5	5.4	8.3	All Other Non-Current				6.7	10.9	5.8	
100.0	100.0	100.0	Total				100.0	100.0	100.0	
			LIABILITIES							
5.0	6.7	5.2	Notes Payable-Short Term				4.5	4.7	6.7	
1.1	1.5	1.8	Cur. Mat.-L.T.D.				2.6	1.6	1.0	
10.4	13.5	9.2	Trade Payables				15.0	11.3	7.2	
.1	.2	.2	Income Taxes Payable				.1	.1	.6	
11.6	14.1	10.2	All Other Current				11.9	10.3	7.1	
28.2	35.9	26.6	Total Current				34.1	27.9	22.6	
15.4	14.4	13.0	Long-Term Debt				13.7	9.0	12.7	
.1	.1	.3	Deferred Taxes				.0	.0	.8	
4.0	3.2	6.2	All Other Non-Current				1.9	15.1	3.7	
52.3	46.4	53.9	Net Worth				50.3	48.0	60.3	
100.0	100.0	100.0	Total Liabilities & Net Worth				100.0	100.0	100.0	
			INCOME DATA							
100.0	100.0	100.0	Net Sales				100.0	100.0	100.0	
38.4	39.9	37.1	Gross Profit				34.9	36.1	37.0	
31.1	31.9	27.1	Operating Expenses				28.0	27.6	24.7	
7.2	8.0	9.9	Operating Profit				6.9	8.5	12.3	
-2.4	-.2	.5	All Other Expenses (net)				.1	.5	.8	
9.6	8.2	9.5	Profit Before Taxes				6.8	8.0	11.6	
			RATIOS							
5.8	5.2	5.4					3.7	4.5	5.3	
3.1	3.1	2.7	Current				2.0	2.6	2.8	
1.7	1.8	1.9					1.6	1.8	2.3	
3.6	2.9	2.8					2.4	2.1	2.7	
1.8	1.4	1.3	Quick				1.6	1.0	1.3	
.7	.7	.7					.7	.6	.7	
33 10.9	34 10.6	28 13.2					40 9.2	23 15.6	36 10.1	
47 7.7	50 7.3	43 8.5	Sales/Receivables				54 6.7	41 9.0	43 8.4	
55 6.6	70 5.2	59 6.2					62 5.9	64 5.7	54 6.7	
79 4.6	62 5.9	48 7.6					19 18.8	87 4.2	89 4.1	
130 2.8	114 3.2	130 2.8	Cost of Sales/Inventory				122 3.0	159 2.3	182 2.0	
174 2.1	215 1.7	182 2.0					146 2.5	243 1.5	228 1.6	
11 33.2	18 20.3	16 22.6					24 15.3	24 15.4	18 20.6	
25 14.5	29 12.8	26 13.8	Cost of Sales/Payables				43 8.5	32 11.5	26 14.2	
54 6.7	46 8.0	44 8.3					51 7.2	64 5.7	35 10.4	
2.7	2.5	2.3					3.0	1.8	2.2	
3.9	3.5	3.7	Sales/Working Capital				5.7	3.1	3.3	
5.7	7.2	5.8					11.6	5.9	4.2	
94.8	67.8	56.3					360.2	40.3	48.9	
(36) 19.1	(41) 12.3	(49) 12.8	EBIT/Interest				(10) 3.9	(15) 8.6	(16) 14.8	
3.2	2.1	3.6					2.5	3.9	2.8	
		30.4	Net Profit + Depr., Dep.,							
	(11)	10.3	Amort./Cur. Mat. L/T/D							
		3.5								
.1	.1	.1					.2	.1	.1	
.2	.4	.3	Fixed/Worth				.4	.2	.4	
.8	.8	1.0					1.0	1.1	.8	
.2	.3	.3					.3	.6	.3	
.8	.8	.8	Debt/Worth				1.0	.9	.7	
3.9	4.8	1.6					3.9	3.7	1.3	
51.7	43.2	41.7	% Profit Before Taxes/Tangible				72.4	27.0	45.1	
(45) 34.6	(45) 27.2	(51) 19.1	Net Worth				(10) 9.7	(15) 17.2	(18) 24.3	
14.6	5.0	9.5					4.4	7.3	13.2	
26.0	25.4	24.8	% Profit Before Taxes/Total				38.4	12.2	31.5	
16.6	10.4	10.9	Assets				5.1	8.2	12.1	
7.3	1.9	4.8					2.5	4.3	5.2	
32.3	49.6	32.3					31.5	27.7	22.7	
12.0	15.2	12.4	Sales/Net Fixed Assets				18.0	12.6	6.7	
6.6	4.1	5.6					2.5	6.4	4.1	
2.2	2.2	2.2					2.3	1.8	1.9	
1.6	1.6	1.5	Sales/Total Assets				1.5	1.3	1.3	
1.0	1.0	1.1					1.2	.9	1.0	
.9	1.1	1.0						.9	1.0	
(37) 1.7	(38) 2.3	(47) 2.1	% Depr., Dep., Amort./Sales				(16) 1.7	(17) 2.0		
3.0	3.6	3.9						3.0	3.8	
1.4	1.7	2.7	% Officers', Directors'							
(13) 3.9	(18) 3.5	(15) 4.3	Owners' Comp/Sales							
7.3	6.7	12.3								
1289866M	1275934M	1989039M	Net Sales ($)	893M	7439M	26900M	93338M	315940M	1544529M	
1113069M	1020648M	1780938M	Total Assets ($)	513M	2851M	9862M	68218M	262692M	1436802M	

M = $ thousand   MM = $ million

© RMA 2024 See Pages viii through xx for Explanation of Ratios and Data

MANUFACTURING—Fluid Power Valve and Hose Fitting Manufacturing NAICS 332912

Current Data Sorted by Assets | Comparative Historical Data

				Type of Statement		
				Unqualified	1	5
		1	6	Reviewed	9	5
	1	2	2	Compiled	2	2
	1	2	5	Tax Returns	5	
	6 (4/1-9/30/23)	14 (10/1/23-3/31/24)	1	Other	9	9
0-500M	500M-2MM	2-10MM	10-50MM	50-100MM	100-250MM	4/1/19-3/31/20 ALL	4/1/20-3/31/21 ALL

0-500M	500M-2MM	2-10MM	10-50MM	50-100MM	100-250MM		4/1/19-3/31/20 ALL	4/1/20-3/31/21 ALL
		2	13	1	1	NUMBER OF STATEMENTS	26	21
%	%	%	%	%	%	ASSETS	%	%
D			10.3			Cash & Equivalents	10.8	11.7
A			23.2			Trade Receivables (net)	23.9	23.3
T			38.5			Inventory	29.0	26.4
A			2.1			All Other Current	1.1	2.4
			74.1			Total Current	64.7	63.8
N			15.5			Fixed Assets (net)	18.0	21.2
O			7.8			Intangibles (net)	9.9	10.2
T			2.6			All Other Non-Current	7.4	4.9
			100.0			Total	100.0	100.0
A						LIABILITIES		
V			3.6			Notes Payable-Short Term	12.7	7.6
A			1.8			Cur. Mat.-L.T.D.	2.8	1.8
I			7.4			Trade Payables	12.2	11.1
L			.3			Income Taxes Payable	.1	.2
A			6.8			All Other Current	6.1	7.9
B			19.8			Total Current	33.9	28.5
L			8.6			Long-Term Debt	9.6	15.4
E			.1			Deferred Taxes	.1	.3
			9.7			All Other Non-Current	5.3	6.8
			61.8			Net Worth	51.0	49.0
			100.0			Total Liabilities & Net Worth	100.0	100.0
						INCOME DATA		
			100.0			Net Sales	100.0	100.0
			35.4			Gross Profit	35.1	33.4
			23.2			Operating Expenses	28.9	29.7
			12.2			Operating Profit	6.3	3.6
			.8			All Other Expenses (net)	.2	-1.1
			11.4			Profit Before Taxes	6.1	4.7
						RATIOS		
			6.8				4.3	3.4
			3.9			Current	2.2	2.5
			2.5				1.2	1.5
			2.9				1.9	2.2
			1.7			Quick	1.1	1.1
			.9				.5	.7
		38	9.5				30 12.2	37 9.8
		42	8.6			Sales/Receivables	40 9.1	43 8.5
		49	7.5				48 7.6	49 7.5
		78	4.7				46 8.0	51 7.1
		111	3.3			Cost of Sales/Inventory	64 5.7	63 5.8
		159	2.3				101 3.6	140 2.6
		14	26.1				18 20.0	18 20.3
		23	15.6			Cost of Sales/Payables	31 11.9	32 11.5
		30	12.0				46 7.9	39 9.4
			2.8				3.3	3.3
			3.7			Sales/Working Capital	6.0	5.0
			5.0				72.6	14.9
			63.5				17.9	37.7
		(11)	28.2			EBIT/Interest	(22) 4.5	(20) 13.0
			4.4				2.2	2.0
						Net Profit + Depr., Dep., Amort./Cur. Mat. L/T/D		
			.1				.1	.2
			.3			Fixed/Worth	.4	.5
			.5				1.4	1.0
			.2				.4	.4
			.7			Debt/Worth	1.1	.8
			1.3				8.1	1.4
			52.0				51.3	46.1
		(11)	31.3			% Profit Before Taxes/Tangible Net Worth	(23) 26.6	(19) 28.3
			18.0				3.4	14.8
			31.2				21.7	19.7
			19.6			% Profit Before Taxes/Total Assets	8.0	12.6
			11.1				1.1	3.7
			46.4				44.7	22.8
			10.7			Sales/Net Fixed Assets	14.2	9.8
			8.4				6.1	5.5
			2.5				2.6	2.4
			2.0			Sales/Total Assets	1.8	1.7
			1.3				1.4	1.4
			.5				.9	.9
		(12)	1.4			% Depr., Dep., Amort./Sales	(17) 1.9	(18) 2.2
			3.9				2.5	2.9
						% Officers', Directors' Owners' Comp/Sales		
	6290M	24859M	738414M	195697M	468724M	Net Sales ($)	1523822M	1562064M
	2488M	14444M	388314M	82977M	215141M	Total Assets ($)	883323M	986192M

© RMA 2024

M = $ thousand   MM = $ million
See Pages viii through xx for Explanation of Ratios and Data

MANUFACTURING—Fluid Power Valve and Hose Fitting Manufacturing NAICS 332912

Comparative Historical Data / Current Data Sorted by Sales

				Type of Statement						
	2	2		Unqualified					1	5
	6	9	6	Reviewed						2
	1	4	3	Compiled			2			
	16	5	2	Tax Returns		1		1	2	6
	4/1/21-	19	9	Other						
	3/31/22	4/1/22-	4/1/23-			6 (4/1-9/30/23)		14 (10/1/23-3/31/24)		
	ALL	3/31/23	3/31/24		0-1MM	1-3MM	3-5MM	5-10MM	10-25MM	25MM & OVER
	25	ALL 39	ALL 20	NUMBER OF STATEMENTS		1	2	1	3	13
	%	%	%	ASSETS	%	%	%	%	%	%
	12.1	12.4	11.6	Cash & Equivalents						10.0
	25.9	24.8	22.4	Trade Receivables (net)						27.6
	28.4	32.5	38.3	Inventory						40.2
	1.7	3.1	1.7	All Other Current	DATA					2.3
	68.1	72.9	74.0	Total Current	NOT					80.1
	22.4	16.5	15.7	Fixed Assets (net)	AVAILABLE					15.8
	5.8	7.3	7.2	Intangibles (net)						1.2
	3.7	3.2	3.2	All Other Non-Current						2.9
	100.0	100.0	100.0	Total						100.0
				LIABILITIES						
	25.6	10.9	5.0	Notes Payable-Short Term						3.6
	1.2	1.0	1.7	Cur. Mat.-L.T.D.						1.4
	11.6	10.6	8.6	Trade Payables						8.7
	.0	.1	.2	Income Taxes Payable						.4
	9.9	10.4	8.3	All Other Current						8.3
	48.2	33.1	23.8	Total Current						22.3
	9.4	10.7	7.8	Long-Term Debt						9.3
	.4	.1	.1	Deferred Taxes						.1
	1.6	6.2	6.4	All Other Non-Current						1.7
	40.4	50.0	62.0	Net Worth						66.6
	100.0	100.0	100.0	Total Liabilities & Net Worth						100.0
				INCOME DATA						
	100.0	100.0	100.0	Net Sales						100.0
	35.6	35.8	36.7	Gross Profit						31.9
	31.8	28.3	27.2	Operating Expenses						20.6
	3.9	7.5	9.5	Operating Profit						11.4
	-1.8	.2	.7	All Other Expenses (net)						.4
	5.7	7.3	8.8	Profit Before Taxes						10.9
				RATIOS						
	3.5	4.4	5.9							6.8
	1.9	2.5	3.3	Current						3.9
	1.6	1.6	2.2							2.5
	2.4	2.6	2.9							2.9
	1.0	.9	1.5	Quick						1.5
	.7	.7	.9							1.0
33	11.2	37 9.9	26 13.8						42	8.7
46	7.9	46 8.0	42 8.7	Sales/Receivables					43	8.4
51	7.1	54 6.7	49 7.4						52	7.0
51	7.1	53 6.9	66 5.5						68	5.4
74	4.9	91 4.0	111 3.3	Cost of Sales/Inventory					101	3.6
111	3.3	146 2.5	174 2.1						146	2.5
18	20.2	10 35.7	15 24.1						14	26.1
30	12.2	26 13.8	27 13.3	Cost of Sales/Payables					23	15.6
42	8.6	51 7.1	33 11.0						30	12.0
	4.5	3.0	2.9							2.8
	7.0	5.0	4.0	Sales/Working Capital						3.7
	10.7	8.8	5.8							4.8
	41.6	27.9	75.2							86.9
(20)	16.3	(32) 8.1	(17) 20.2	EBIT/Interest					(11)	40.3
	3.3	1.7	3.6							9.6
				Net Profit + Depr., Dep., Amort./Cur. Mat. L/T/D						
	.2	.1	.1							.1
	.4	.3	.2	Fixed/Worth						.2
	.8	.7	.5							.5
	.4	.4	.3							.2
	1.0	1.1	.6	Debt/Worth						.5
	1.4	1.9	1.4							1.0
	46.5	46.3	42.3	% Profit Before Taxes/Tangible Net Worth						52.4
(24)	24.5	(34) 22.3	(18) 25.2							31.3
	4.7	5.9	16.8							17.5
	22.9	21.1	24.1	% Profit Before Taxes/Total Assets						32.0
	10.1	11.3	15.7							20.6
	2.6	2.4	9.3							11.3
	29.9	57.9	38.9							48.9
	10.8	25.1	16.9	Sales/Net Fixed Assets						10.7
	6.9	9.0	9.0							9.1
	2.8	2.8	2.3							2.6
	2.0	1.8	2.0	Sales/Total Assets						2.1
	1.4	1.5	1.5							1.6
	1.1	.5	.7							.4
(18)	2.0	(28) 1.2	(19) 1.3	% Depr., Dep., Amort./Sales					(12)	1.2
	2.6	2.5	2.7							1.6
			1.0	% Officers', Directors' Owners' Comp/Sales						
		(11)	3.8							
			8.8							
	1392063M	1505368M	1433984M	Net Sales ($)	2753M	7991M	8651M	46032M	1368557M
	792781M	887960M	703364M	Total Assets ($)	1495M	4059M	5956M	33779M	658075M

© RMA 2024

M = $ thousand   MM = $ million
See Pages viii through xx for Explanation of Ratios and Data

MANUFACTURING—Other Metal Valve and Pipe Fitting Manufacturing NAICS 332919

Current Data Sorted by Assets | Comparative Historical Data

						Type of Statement		
		1	2	1		Unqualified	5	3
		3	4		1	Reviewed	6	3
		2	3			Compiled	5	1
1			1			Tax Returns	4	3
1	2	8	5	2	3	Other	25	24
	4 (4/1-9/30/23)		36 (10/1/23-3/31/24)				4/1/19-	4/1/20-
							3/31/20	3/31/21
0-500M	500M-2MM	2-10MM	10-50MM	50-100MM	100-250MM		ALL	ALL
2	2	14	15	3	4	NUMBER OF STATEMENTS	45	34
%	%	%	%	%	%	ASSETS	%	%
		22.6	10.1			Cash & Equivalents	14.8	14.5
		23.2	22.5			Trade Receivables (net)	23.8	20.2
		33.1	31.7			Inventory	31.2	35.0
		.4	1.2			All Other Current	1.1	2.1
		79.3	65.5			Total Current	70.9	71.8
		14.6	18.7			Fixed Assets (net)	20.5	19.7
		1.0	3.5			Intangibles (net)	4.6	4.7
		5.0	12.3			All Other Non-Current	3.9	3.8
		100.0	100.0			Total	100.0	100.0
						LIABILITIES		
		3.6	8.1			Notes Payable-Short Term	8.8	11.5
		1.9	1.7			Cur. Mat.-L.T.D.	2.8	3.3
		9.9	7.7			Trade Payables	11.7	12.6
		.0	.1			Income Taxes Payable	.2	.2
		7.0	10.5			All Other Current	10.2	11.3
		22.4	28.0			Total Current	33.7	38.8
		12.3	13.3			Long-Term Debt	12.1	19.9
		.1	.2			Deferred Taxes	.3	.2
		4.4	9.1			All Other Non-Current	6.4	8.2
		60.8	49.5			Net Worth	47.5	33.0
		100.0	100.0			Total Liabilities & Net Worth	100.0	100.0
						INCOME DATA		
		100.0	100.0			Net Sales	100.0	100.0
		40.0	33.0			Gross Profit	33.7	30.3
		27.2	23.2			Operating Expenses	26.3	26.5
		12.8	9.8			Operating Profit	7.4	3.8
		.4	.5			All Other Expenses (net)	.8	-1.0
		12.4	9.3			Profit Before Taxes	6.6	4.8
						RATIOS		
		17.7	4.1				3.9	4.6
		5.2	2.6			Current	2.3	2.2
		1.6	2.0				1.6	1.5
		9.8	1.8				2.6	2.3
		2.3	1.4			Quick	1.1	1.0
		1.0	.7				.7	.5
	27	13.5	28	13.1			35	10.4	31	11.7
	36	10.1	47	7.8		Sales/Receivables	45	8.1	41	8.9
	49	7.5	58	6.3			56	6.5	54	6.8
	53	6.9	64	5.7			44	8.3	56	6.5
	118	3.1	94	3.9		Cost of Sales/Inventory	87	4.2	96	3.8
	174	2.1	140	2.6			130	2.8	166	2.2
	12	31.2	12	30.1			17	20.9	19	19.0
	21	17.1	29	12.4		Cost of Sales/Payables	26	14.3	31	11.8
	41	8.9	35	10.4			37	9.8	45	8.2
		1.6	3.4				3.4	2.8
		3.2	4.7			Sales/Working Capital	4.6	4.5
		7.8	6.2				8.7	10.2
		28.2	29.3				26.5	26.7
	(11)	16.5	(14)	8.8		EBIT/Interest	(38)	4.9	(32)	5.6
		5.1	3.4				2.5	.7
						Net Profit + Depr., Dep., Amort./Cur. Mat. L/T/D		
		.1	.1				.2	.3
		.2	.2			Fixed/Worth	.4	.6
		.4	.7				.7	1.0
		.2	.6				.4	.9
		.5	1.2			Debt/Worth	1.0	1.8
		1.7	1.8				2.6	4.2
		69.3	41.2				75.2	46.7
		28.2	25.2		% Profit Before Taxes/Tangible Net Worth	(42)	16.2	(29)	17.6
		22.9	14.8			4.4	3.3
		28.6	22.2				19.8	16.0
		20.6	11.4		% Profit Before Taxes/Total Assets	7.3	6.1
		13.5	7.3			2.0	.2
		45.4	26.1				21.9	20.7
		16.2	16.6		Sales/Net Fixed Assets	9.7	8.9
		6.6	3.2			4.8	4.6
		2.7	2.2				2.7	2.2
		1.7	1.5		Sales/Total Assets	1.8	1.7
		1.2	1.2			1.4	1.3
		.9	1.0				.5	1.4
	(10)	2.7	(12)	2.8		% Depr., Dep., Amort./Sales	(40)	2.1	(27)	2.5
		3.3	3.7				3.7	4.7
							2.9	3.1
						% Officers', Directors' Owners' Comp/Sales	(12)	3.9	(11)	4.9
							8.9	8.8
3513M	5200M	171976M	625894M	346181M	1018686M	Net Sales ($)	1813337M	1372725M
678M	2010M	90103M	384956M	233321M	703845M	Total Assets ($)	1235454M	985608M

© RMA 2024   M = $ thousand   MM = $ million
See Pages viii through xx for Explanation of Ratios and Data

MANUFACTURING—Other Metal Valve and Pipe Fitting Manufacturing   NAICS 332919

Comparative Historical Data | Current Data Sorted by Sales

3		3		4	Type of Statement				1	3
2		3		8	Unqualified			2	4	1
4		2		5	Reviewed	1			1	4
2		2		2	Compiled			1		1
16		12		21	Tax Returns		1	2	4	10
4/1/21-3/31/22 ALL		4/1/22-3/31/23 ALL		4/1/23-3/31/24 ALL	Other	1	1	4 (4/1-9/30/23)		36 (10/1/23-3/31/24)
						0-1MM	1-3MM	3-5MM	5-10MM	10-25MM	25MM & OVER
27		22		40	NUMBER OF STATEMENTS	1	1	4	6	9	19
%		%		%	ASSETS	%	%	%	%	%	%
12.7		18.5		16.7	Cash & Equivalents						10.2
23.7		18.7		21.7	Trade Receivables (net)						23.0
35.2		33.5		31.5	Inventory						33.1
2.2		1.8		1.3	All Other Current						1.8
73.7		72.5		71.3	Total Current						68.2
17.2		20.4		16.2	Fixed Assets (net)						16.6
3.1		1.7		5.2	Intangibles (net)						6.4
6.0		5.4		7.3	All Other Non-Current						8.9
100.0		100.0		100.0	Total						100.0
					LIABILITIES						
7.5		2.8		6.7	Notes Payable-Short Term						5.9
1.7		1.6		2.0	Cur. Mat.-L.T.D.						2.1
10.2		12.3		8.9	Trade Payables						10.1
.5		.4		.1	Income Taxes Payable						.1
10.2		11.0		8.4	All Other Current						9.7
30.0		28.0		26.0	Total Current						27.8
16.9		19.4		17.5	Long-Term Debt						22.1
.2		.0		.2	Deferred Taxes						.4
4.4		6.1		10.8	All Other Non-Current						17.3
48.6		46.4		45.5	Net Worth						32.4
100.0		100.0		100.0	Total Liabilities & Net Worth						100.0
					INCOME DATA						
100.0		100.0		100.0	Net Sales						100.0
33.6		31.6		37.8	Gross Profit						31.4
27.1		23.6		25.5	Operating Expenses						19.9
6.6		8.0		12.3	Operating Profit						11.6
-1.5		.9		.6	All Other Expenses (net)						.9
8.0		7.1		11.8	Profit Before Taxes						10.6
					RATIOS						
	7.4		5.3		5.0							3.4
	2.9		2.9		3.0	Current						2.8
	1.5		2.0		2.0							2.0
	2.7		3.2		2.6							1.7
	1.0		1.4		1.5	Quick						1.4
	.8		.8		.8							.9
33	10.9	35	10.4	29	12.6					41	9.0
49	7.5	41	8.9	43	8.5	Sales/Receivables				47	7.8
72	5.1	52	7.0	55	6.6					57	6.4
68	5.4	89	4.1	58	6.3					64	5.7
122	3.0	126	2.9	114	3.2	Cost of Sales/Inventory				107	3.4
192	1.9	182	2.0	159	2.3					159	2.3
8	45.7	15	25.0	12	29.8					16	23.0
20	18.0	31	11.8	24	15.5	Cost of Sales/Payables				29	12.4
43	8.5	49	7.4	37	9.9					35	10.4
	2.4		2.2		2.6							3.1
	3.9		3.3		3.9	Sales/Working Capital						4.7
	8.7		6.5		6.2							6.2
	23.5		33.0		29.1							30.1
(25)	14.6	(19)	12.9	(34)	10.1	EBIT/Interest				(17)	9.1
	6.4		2.2		4.7							4.7
					11.4	Net Profit + Depr., Dep.,						
				(12)	5.5	Amort./Cur. Mat. L/T/D						
					3.7							
	.2		.2		.1							.2
	.3		.3		.2	Fixed/Worth						.3
	1.0		.7		.6							1.7
	.4		.5		.4							.7
	1.2		1.2		.8	Debt/Worth						1.3
	2.1		2.5		2.2							3.8
	45.6		40.0		58.5							71.4
(25)	21.6	(21)	20.7	(37)	30.1	% Profit Before Taxes/Tangible Net Worth				(17)	38.7
	13.8		3.4		21.2							21.1
	16.3		21.3		24.9							25.1
	10.7		11.3		16.9	% Profit Before Taxes/Total Assets						14.7
	6.1		2.0		9.2							7.7
	31.0		46.6		26.1							25.1
	11.5		8.7		13.1	Sales/Net Fixed Assets						12.5
	5.6		5.4		6.3							7.2
	2.3		2.0		2.3							2.2
	1.6		1.4		1.6	Sales/Total Assets						1.8
	1.2		1.2		1.2							1.3
	1.7		1.7		1.0							1.0
(19)	2.8	(16)	2.9	(31)	2.6	% Depr., Dep., Amort./Sales				(15)	1.3
	4.7		4.2		3.6							4.5
					2.9	% Officers', Directors'						
			(12)	4.6	Owners' Comp/Sales						
					9.3							
1227922M		1418057M		2171450M	Net Sales ($)	450M	2156M	12378M	52054M	158367M	1946045M
940689M		1029827M		1414913M	Total Assets ($)	383M	579M	6501M	39595M	103136M	1264719M

© RMA 2024   M = $ thousand   MM = $ million
See Pages viii through xx for Explanation of Ratios and Data

MANUFACTURING—Ball and Roller Bearing Manufacturing NAICS 332991

Current Data Sorted by Assets

0-500M	500M-2MM	2-10MM	10-50MM	50-100MM	100-250MM
1	4 (4/1-9/30/23)	1 2	4 16 (10/1/23-3/31/24)	8	1
1 %	%	3 %	7 %	8 %	1 %

Data Not Available (for columns 1-6)

Comparative Historical Data

	4/1/19-3/31/20 ALL	4/1/20-3/31/21 ALL
Type of Statement		
Unqualified	3	3
Reviewed	2	1
Compiled		
Tax Returns	2	
Other	5	3
NUMBER OF STATEMENTS	12	7
	%	%
ASSETS		
Cash & Equivalents	8.5	
Trade Receivables (net)	21.1	
Inventory	41.3	
All Other Current	2.8	
Total Current	73.8	
Fixed Assets (net)	20.7	
Intangibles (net)	.4	
All Other Non-Current	5.1	
Total	100.0	
LIABILITIES		
Notes Payable-Short Term	15.2	
Cur. Mat.-L.T.D.	1.7	
Trade Payables	13.0	
Income Taxes Payable	.1	
All Other Current	6.1	
Total Current	36.1	
Long-Term Debt	7.2	
Deferred Taxes	.7	
All Other Non-Current	7.0	
Net Worth	48.9	
Total Liabilities & Net Worth	100.0	
INCOME DATA		
Net Sales	100.0	
Gross Profit	29.3	
Operating Expenses	21.8	
Operating Profit	7.4	
All Other Expenses (net)	1.8	
Profit Before Taxes	5.6	
RATIOS		
Current	5.5	
	2.8	
	1.2	
Quick	2.4	
	.7	
	.4	
Sales/Receivables	42 8.6	
	54 6.7	
	65 5.6	
Cost of Sales/Inventory	79 4.6	
	166 2.2	
	228 1.6	
Cost of Sales/Payables	8 43.5	
	23 15.8	
	78 4.7	
Sales/Working Capital	1.7	
	2.5	
	11.9	
EBIT/Interest	18.2	
	(11) 2.8	
	.9	
Net Profit + Depr., Dep., Amort./Cur. Mat. L/T/D		
Fixed/Worth	.2	
	.5	
	.9	
Debt/Worth	.3	
	1.3	
	2.9	
% Profit Before Taxes/Tangible Net Worth	22.3	
	12.0	
	1.2	
% Profit Before Taxes/Total Assets	12.9	
	3.8	
	.5	
Sales/Net Fixed Assets	14.9	
	10.6	
	3.3	
Sales/Total Assets	1.7	
	1.1	
	1.0	
% Depr., Dep., Amort./Sales		
% Officers', Directors' Owners' Comp/Sales		

1401M		34464M	276037M	565679M	65290M	Net Sales ($)	295552M	215207M
245M		16172M	234644M	559812M	133839M	Total Assets ($)	283668M	224001M

M = $ thousand   MM = $ million
See Pages viii through xx for Explanation of Ratios and Data

© RMA 2024

MANUFACTURING—Ball and Roller Bearing Manufacturing NAICS 332991

Comparative Historical Data | Current Data Sorted by Sales

			Type of Statement						
		3	Unqualified						3
1			Reviewed						
1		2	Compiled	1			1	1	
4	6	15	Tax Returns	4 (4/1-9/30/23)			16 (10/1/23-3/31/24)		11
4/1/21-3/31/22 ALL	4/1/22-3/31/23 ALL	4/1/23-3/31/24 ALL	Other	0-1MM	1-3MM	3-5MM	5-10MM	10-25MM	25MM & OVER
6	6	20	NUMBER OF STATEMENTS	1			1	4	14
%	%	%	ASSETS	%	%	%	%	%	%
		10.3	Cash & Equivalents						7.4
		16.7	Trade Receivables (net)	D	D				14.6
		33.2	Inventory	A	A				32.5
		1.5	All Other Current	T	T				1.1
		61.7	Total Current	A	A				55.6
		23.9	Fixed Assets (net)						27.0
		5.3	Intangibles (net)	N	N				7.0
		9.0	All Other Non-Current	O	O				10.3
		100.0	Total	T	T				100.0
			LIABILITIES	A	A				
		2.1	Notes Payable-Short Term	V	V				1.6
		2.1	Cur. Mat.-L.T.D.	A	A				1.4
		9.6	Trade Payables	I	I				7.7
		.2	Income Taxes Payable	L	L				.2
		11.5	All Other Current	A	A				13.8
		25.5	Total Current	B	B				24.7
		7.9	Long-Term Debt	L	L				7.1
		.2	Deferred Taxes	E	E				.3
		9.7	All Other Non-Current						12.5
		56.7	Net Worth						55.3
		100.0	Total Liabilties & Net Worth						100.0
			INCOME DATA						
		100.0	Net Sales						100.0
		33.9	Gross Profit						30.7
		29.0	Operating Expenses						27.4
		4.9	Operating Profit						3.3
		.2	All Other Expenses (net)						.7
		4.6	Profit Before Taxes						2.6
			RATIOS						
		3.3							3.3
		2.5	Current						2.5
		2.0							1.8
		1.2							.9
		.9	Quick						.9
		.7							.7
	32	11.4						39	9.3
	51	7.1	Sales/Receivables					54	6.7
	63	5.8						64	5.7
	99	3.7						140	2.6
	166	2.2	Cost of Sales/Inventory					174	2.1
	192	1.9						203	1.8
	14	26.9						13	29.0
	29	12.4	Cost of Sales/Payables					24	15.0
	59	6.2						60	6.1
		3.0							2.9
		3.2	Sales/Working Capital						3.2
		5.3							5.3
		17.1							12.6
	(18)	9.5	EBIT/Interest					(13)	6.7
		-.3							-.4
			Net Profit + Depr., Dep., Amort./Cur. Mat. L/T/D						
		.3							.5
		.5	Fixed/Worth						.5
		.6							.7
		.5							.5
		.8	Debt/Worth						.9
		1.2							1.3
		37.5							19.9
	(19)	6.3	% Profit Before Taxes/Tangible Net Worth					(13)	5.5
		-3.1							-3.8
		20.3							11.9
		4.1	% Profit Before Taxes/Total Assets						3.1
		-1.9							-2.3
		12.2							4.7
		4.5	Sales/Net Fixed Assets						3.4
		3.2							2.9
		1.8							1.1
		1.1	Sales/Total Assets						1.0
		1.0							.9
		1.8							1.9
	(16)	2.6	% Depr., Dep., Amort./Sales					(12)	2.7
		4.5							4.7
			% Officers', Directors' Owners' Comp/Sales						
257432M	187698M	942871M	Net Sales ($)		1401M		7192M	65284M	868994M
192369M	165280M	944712M	Total Assets ($)		245M		2634M	45626M	896207M

© RMA 2024   M = $ thousand   MM = $ million
See Pages viii through xx for Explanation of Ratios and Data

MANUFACTURING—Small Arms, Ordnance, and Ordnance Accessories Manufacturing NAICS 332994

Current Data Sorted by Assets | Comparative Historical Data

						Type of Statement		
					2	Unqualified	10	1
			2	2		Reviewed	2	
	1		1			Compiled		2
4	3	6	7	4	4	Tax Returns	4	5
	6 (4/1-9/30/23)		30 (10/1/23-3/31/24)			Other	12	12
0-500M	500M-2MM	2-10MM	10-50MM	50-100MM	100-250MM		27 4/1/19-3/31/20 ALL	12 4/1/20-3/31/21 ALL
4	4	6	10	6	6	NUMBER OF STATEMENTS	43	20
%	%	%	%	%	%	ASSETS	%	%
			13.0			Cash & Equivalents	7.6	11.8
			12.1			Trade Receivables (net)	14.3	15.0
			25.2			Inventory	32.4	29.2
			6.0			All Other Current	3.2	5.6
			56.3			Total Current	57.5	61.6
			20.8			Fixed Assets (net)	24.9	24.5
			15.0			Intangibles (net)	10.7	7.0
			8.0			All Other Non-Current	6.9	6.9
			100.0			Total	100.0	100.0
						LIABILITIES		
			1.2			Notes Payable-Short Term	7.4	5.7
			6.8			Cur. Mat.-L.T.D.	5.6	1.7
			5.7			Trade Payables	11.3	11.5
			.2			Income Taxes Payable	.1	.1
			11.2			All Other Current	12.4	14.9
			25.0			Total Current	36.8	33.9
			18.3			Long-Term Debt	21.1	23.8
			1.1			Deferred Taxes	.4	.3
			2.9			All Other Non-Current	8.4	8.1
			52.7			Net Worth	33.2	34.0
			100.0			Total Liabilities & Net Worth	100.0	100.0
						INCOME DATA		
			100.0			Net Sales	100.0	100.0
			35.0			Gross Profit	34.2	44.7
			30.4			Operating Expenses	30.0	30.8
			4.6			Operating Profit	4.2	13.9
			1.9			All Other Expenses (net)	2.6	1.3
			2.7			Profit Before Taxes	1.6	12.6
						RATIOS		
			4.6				2.5	4.1
			2.3			Current	1.9	2.5
			1.5				1.2	1.5
			2.6				1.5	2.0
			.9			Quick	.6	1.2
			.6				.3	.6
			22 16.8				23 15.8	6 61.9
			37 9.8			Sales/Receivables	38 9.7	25 14.8
			44 8.3				51 7.1	54 6.7
			60 6.1				78 4.7	70 5.2
			107 3.4			Cost of Sales/Inventory	130 2.8	94 3.9
			182 2.0				182 2.0	140 2.6
			4 83.4				20 18.1	0 UND
			15 24.4			Cost of Sales/Payables	36 10.2	28 13.0
			39 9.3				51 7.2	55 6.6
			3.2				3.5	3.4
			5.1			Sales/Working Capital	6.4	5.2
			9.2				8.5	14.6
			18.0				8.5	100.9
			4.6			EBIT/Interest	(38) .4	(19) 7.0
			-3.5				-6.2	2.0
						Net Profit + Depr., Dep., Amort./Cur. Mat. L/T/D		
			.2				.4	.1
			.9			Fixed/Worth	1.1	1.2
			3.0				-2.2	8.8
			.4				1.2	.6
			1.6			Debt/Worth	2.8	3.3
			8.1				-51.1	16.2
						% Profit Before Taxes/Tangible Net Worth	56.0	126.1
							(31) 6.7	(16) 85.8
							-23.4	26.0
			12.3				17.5	42.9
			6.3			% Profit Before Taxes/Total Assets	-1.6	13.7
			-2.1				-8.4	6.5
			13.2				12.5	42.9
			6.9			Sales/Net Fixed Assets	6.8	9.7
			3.1				2.9	3.7
			1.7				1.8	2.8
			1.1			Sales/Total Assets	1.2	1.8
			.8				1.0	1.1
							1.8	2.0
						% Depr., Dep., Amort./Sales	(33) 4.5	(11) 2.8
							9.0	6.3
						% Officers', Directors' Owners' Comp/Sales		
7812M	9118M	30054M	295640M	660385M	1215604M	Net Sales ($)	2148099M	540083M
1603M	5676M	25896M	216081M	433978M	781896M	Total Assets ($)	1912780M	389296M

© RMA 2024   M = $ thousand   MM = $ million
See Pages viii through xx for Explanation of Ratios and Data

MANUFACTURING—Small Arms, Ordnance, and Ordnance Accessories Manufacturing NAICS 332994

Comparative Historical Data / Current Data Sorted by Sales

							Type of Statement							
		3		3		2	Unqualified							2
		3		3		4	Reviewed						1	3
		1		1			Compiled							
		5		4		2	Tax Returns		1			1	1	
		23		26		28	Other	1	6	4	3	4		10
		4/1/21-		4/1/22-		4/1/23-			6 (4/1-9/30/23)			30 (10/1/23-3/31/24)		
		3/31/22		3/31/23		3/31/24		0-1MM	1-3MM	3-5MM	5-10MM	10-25MM		25MM & OVER
		ALL		ALL		ALL	NUMBER OF STATEMENTS							
		35		37		36		1	7	4	3	6		15
		%		%		%	ASSETS	%	%	%	%	%		%
		13.8		13.7		11.8	Cash & Equivalents							7.2
		18.6		13.7		9.7	Trade Receivables (net)							13.9
		30.0		33.1		28.4	Inventory							35.0
		4.5		3.1		4.1	All Other Current							5.7
		66.8		63.6		54.0	Total Current							61.8
		21.6		22.7		25.2	Fixed Assets (net)							21.5
		6.8		5.7		7.8	Intangibles (net)							4.3
		4.8		8.0		13.0	All Other Non-Current							12.4
		100.0		100.0		100.0	Total							100.0
							LIABILITIES							
		2.7		3.5		6.0	Notes Payable-Short Term							3.5
		5.3		4.3		3.6	Cur. Mat.-L.T.D.							5.6
		14.4		9.9		6.4	Trade Payables							9.4
		.2		.1		.1	Income Taxes Payable							.0
		5.7		10.9		10.3	All Other Current							10.1
		28.2		28.6		26.3	Total Current							28.6
		23.4		20.7		22.5	Long-Term Debt							24.0
		.4		.3		.5	Deferred Taxes							.6
		5.6		2.5		8.5	All Other Non-Current							4.4
		42.4		47.9		42.2	Net Worth							42.4
		100.0		100.0		100.0	Total Liabilities & Net Worth							100.0
							INCOME DATA							
		100.0		100.0		100.0	Net Sales							100.0
		39.2		38.1		37.4	Gross Profit							24.9
		23.3		28.3		33.9	Operating Expenses							21.2
		15.8		9.8		3.6	Operating Profit							3.7
		.7		1.9		1.7	All Other Expenses (net)							1.7
		15.2		7.9		1.9	Profit Before Taxes							2.0
							RATIOS							
		3.9		3.8		2.8								2.8
		2.3		2.4		2.3	Current							2.3
		1.7		1.4		1.5								1.5
		1.6		1.4		1.2								1.0
		1.0		1.0		.8	Quick							.8
		.6		.5		.5								.5
21	17.0		15	23.9	9	41.0							24	15.4
32	11.3		32	11.3	23	15.7	Sales/Receivables						34	10.6
49	7.4		52	7.0	36	10.1							40	9.1
52	7.0		87	4.2	56	6.5							83	4.4
83	4.4		122	3.0	99	3.7	Cost of Sales/Inventory						118	3.1
146	2.5		243	1.5	140	2.6							140	2.6
20	18.4		21	17.5	4	82.9							11	32.1
34	10.6		33	11.0	15	24.4	Cost of Sales/Payables						28	12.9
51	7.1		53	6.9	40	9.2							40	9.2
		3.7		2.6		3.8								3.8
		5.5		4.2		5.1	Sales/Working Capital							4.6
		8.7		6.9		12.1								8.2
		119.5		39.0		20.2								21.1
(32)	16.1		(30)	7.6	(33)	3.7	EBIT/Interest							4.3
		7.0		1.6		-3.3								-.9
				42.0										
			(10)	7.4			Net Profit + Depr., Dep., Amort./Cur. Mat. L/T/D							
				2.1										
		.1		.2		.2								.2
		.7		.6		.7	Fixed/Worth							.7
		1.4		1.6		2.9								1.1
		.7		.6		.6								.8
		1.5		1.1		1.7	Debt/Worth							1.7
		8.5		3.3		6.0								2.8
		101.8		58.4		37.9								26.1
(31)	80.9		(32)	24.8	(29)	12.1	% Profit Before Taxes/Tangible Net Worth						(13)	12.1
		63.4		10.0		-12.6								-10.7
		43.7		22.0		14.1								8.1
		26.1		9.7		5.3	% Profit Before Taxes/Total Assets							5.4
		14.1		1.3		-7.0								-9.6
		55.4		22.2		17.1								17.1
		10.8		7.6		7.0	Sales/Net Fixed Assets							6.9
		5.0		3.1		3.0								3.6
		2.3		1.8		2.0								1.9
		1.9		1.3		1.5	Sales/Total Assets							1.6
		1.4		.9		1.0								1.4
		.5		1.3		1.1								.8
(26)	2.4		(25)	2.6	(20)	2.9	% Depr., Dep., Amort./Sales						(11)	1.4
		4.8		5.4		5.9								5.0
							% Officers', Directors' Owners' Comp/Sales							
		2696627M		2907791M		2218613M	Net Sales ($)	923M	13863M	16464M	23696M	96121M		2067546M
		1433989M		1971777M		1465130M	Total Assets ($)	425M	11081M	12638M	33524M	90835M		1316627M

© RMA 2024 M = $ thousand MM = $ million
See Pages viii through xx for Explanation of Ratios and Data

MANUFACTURING—Fabricated Pipe and Pipe Fitting Manufacturing NAICS 332996

Current Data Sorted by Assets

0-500M	500M-2MM	2-10MM	10-50MM	50-100MM	100-250MM		Comparative Historical Data	
						Type of Statement		
		1	3		1	Unqualified	5	5
		1	4			Reviewed	8	5
		2	2			Compiled	5	1
		1		1		Tax Returns	6	1
1	3	9	9		2	Other	31	11
0-500M	6 (4/1-9/30/23) 500M-2MM	2-10MM	34 (10/1/23-3/31/24) 10-50MM	50-100MM	100-250MM		4/1/19-3/31/20 ALL	4/1/20-3/31/21 ALL
1	3	14	18	1	3	NUMBER OF STATEMENTS	55	23
%	%	%	%	%	%	ASSETS	%	%
		10.2	13.4			Cash & Equivalents	12.9	18.6
		27.0	21.3			Trade Receivables (net)	22.4	21.0
		29.6	32.6			Inventory	25.4	23.4
		3.8	.6			All Other Current	2.4	2.3
		70.5	67.9			Total Current	63.1	65.3
		23.2	21.5			Fixed Assets (net)	24.5	22.7
		1.2	4.4			Intangibles (net)	5.4	3.9
		5.0	6.2			All Other Non-Current	7.0	8.1
		100.0	100.0			Total	100.0	100.0
						LIABILITIES		
		4.0	11.6			Notes Payable-Short Term	9.8	11.2
		3.4	2.7			Cur. Mat.-L.T.D.	1.9	5.2
		13.5	8.3			Trade Payables	10.7	8.2
		.4	.0			Income Taxes Payable	.2	.3
		9.7	12.8			All Other Current	11.5	8.1
		31.1	35.3			Total Current	34.1	32.9
		4.4	12.9			Long-Term Debt	11.5	22.7
		.3	.2			Deferred Taxes	.3	.5
		2.9	18.3			All Other Non-Current	3.2	14.6
		61.3	33.3			Net Worth	50.8	29.2
		100.0	100.0			Total Liabilities & Net Worth	100.0	100.0
						INCOME DATA		
		100.0	100.0			Net Sales	100.0	100.0
		35.9	32.2			Gross Profit	29.7	34.5
		27.1	22.1			Operating Expenses	23.4	28.5
		8.9	10.2			Operating Profit	6.2	6.1
		1.0	2.6			All Other Expenses (net)	1.1	.9
		7.9	7.6			Profit Before Taxes	5.1	5.1
						RATIOS		
		4.3	3.7				3.6	4.4
		2.5	2.7			Current	2.1	2.1
		1.9	1.2				1.4	1.5
		2.7	2.7				2.0	2.5
		1.2	1.3			Quick	1.1	1.1
		.8	.3				.6	.7
	38	9.7	36 10.0				35 10.4	33 11.1
	47	7.7	44 8.3			Sales/Receivables	47 7.8	60 6.1
	68	5.4	58 6.3				60 6.1	76 4.8
	38	9.7	48 7.6				48 7.6	31 11.6
	78	4.7	140 2.6			Cost of Sales/Inventory	74 4.9	83 4.4
	215	1.7	228 1.6				118 3.1	126 2.9
	21	17.8	19 19.7				16 22.8	11 34.5
	31	11.7	35 10.3			Cost of Sales/Payables	26 14.1	23 16.0
	54	6.8	46 8.0				45 8.1	46 7.9
		2.7	2.9				2.6	2.5
		5.0	4.1			Sales/Working Capital	6.0	4.4
		5.9	14.4				13.5	10.2
		97.5	30.8				21.2	20.4
		(12) 33.1	(17) 4.3			EBIT/Interest	(48) 6.4	(22) 5.5
		4.5	1.3				1.9	.0
						Net Profit + Depr., Dep.,	10.5	
						Amort./Cur. Mat. L/T/D	(13) 4.2	
							2.4	
		.1	.1				.2	.2
		.4	.6			Fixed/Worth	.5	.6
		.5	-4.3				1.0	1.2
		.3	.5				.3	.4
		.5	2.4			Debt/Worth	1.0	1.2
		1.4	-18.5				3.6	4.9
		44.3	53.0			% Profit Before Taxes/Tangible	39.7	25.6
		17.3	(13) 28.3			Net Worth	(51) 16.7	(19) 18.0
		2.8	10.6				1.4	6.4
		27.6	22.1			% Profit Before Taxes/Total	20.2	11.4
		10.6	7.6			Assets	5.6	8.3
		1.9	1.8				1.2	-3.6
		15.0	35.5				23.1	25.2
		9.1	6.9			Sales/Net Fixed Assets	9.5	10.4
		4.6	2.9				4.2	3.8
		2.4	1.8				2.4	2.3
		1.9	1.2			Sales/Total Assets	1.7	1.4
		1.0	1.0				1.1	1.0
		.6	1.0				.9	.7
		(12) 1.2	(17) 1.8			% Depr., Dep., Amort./Sales	(47) 2.3	(17) 2.0
		3.0	4.9				3.8	3.8
						% Officers', Directors',	.6	
						Owners' Comp/Sales	(16) 2.4	
							4.3	
495M	12634M	139780M	574853M	74917M	1215591M	Net Sales ($)	2219139M	1331265M
432M	5328M	79963M	435925M	80413M	647672M	Total Assets ($)	1720666M	1103436M

© RMA 2024 M = $ thousand MM = $ million
See Pages viii through xx for Explanation of Ratios and Data

MANUFACTURING—Fabricated Pipe and Pipe Fitting Manufacturing NAICS 332996

Comparative Historical Data | Current Data Sorted by Sales

						Type of Statement							
		3		3	5	Unqualified					3	1	2
		4		4	5	Reviewed				1	1	2	3
		2		2	5	Compiled				1	2	2	
		2		3	2	Tax Returns			1				
		16		23	23	Other	1	2	1	6	7		7
		4/1/21-3/31/22 ALL		4/1/22-3/31/23 ALL	4/1/23-3/31/24 ALL		0-1MM	6 (4/1-9/30/23) 1-3MM	3-5MM	5-10MM	34 (10/1/23-3/31/24) 10-25MM		25MM & OVER
		27		35	40	NUMBER OF STATEMENTS	1	2	1	8	13		14
		%		%	%	ASSETS	%	%	%	%	%		%
		15.4		14.5	13.6	Cash & Equivalents					14.9		15.5
		22.5		23.3	22.5	Trade Receivables (net)					20.7		23.3
		26.8		27.9	30.9	Inventory					33.0		33.8
		1.9		5.5	2.1	All Other Current					1.6		1.1
		66.5		71.2	69.1	Total Current					70.2		73.8
		24.4		18.7	22.6	Fixed Assets (net)					21.2		17.3
		5.3		4.3	2.4	Intangibles (net)					4.5		2.6
		3.8		5.8	5.8	All Other Non-Current					4.0		6.3
		100.0		100.0	100.0	Total					100.0		100.0
						LIABILITIES							
		9.4		16.0	9.0	Notes Payable-Short Term					9.0		12.4
		2.5		1.8	3.1	Cur. Mat.-L.T.D.					3.1		1.8
		9.8		11.7	10.0	Trade Payables					8.0		9.3
		.3		.1	.2	Income Taxes Payable					.4		.2
		9.7		14.7	11.3	All Other Current					10.5		13.4
		31.6		44.2	33.7	Total Current					31.0		37.1
		13.3		12.2	9.9	Long-Term Debt					9.4		11.9
		.2		.1	.2	Deferred Taxes					.3		.2
		4.1		4.3	9.7	All Other Non-Current					12.4		13.4
		50.8		39.2	46.5	Net Worth					46.9		37.4
		100.0		100.0	100.0	Total Liabilities & Net Worth					100.0		100.0
						INCOME DATA							
		100.0		100.0	100.0	Net Sales					100.0		100.0
		33.3		34.8	35.0	Gross Profit					35.6		30.7
		26.7		24.5	25.8	Operating Expenses					24.3		17.2
		6.6		10.2	9.2	Operating Profit					11.3		13.4
		-2.5		-.9	1.6	All Other Expenses (net)					2.6		1.7
		9.1		11.2	7.6	Profit Before Taxes					8.8		11.8
						RATIOS							
		4.1		3.3	3.5						5.2		3.7
		2.7		2.2	2.5	Current					2.6		1.9
		1.6		1.4	1.4						1.8		1.2
		2.7		1.6	2.3						3.3		2.7
		1.4		1.1	1.2	Quick					1.3		1.1
		.7		.5	.4						.9		.3
42	8.6		38	9.6	34	10.8					33	11.0	33	10.9
62	5.9		50	7.3	45	8.1	Sales/Receivables					44	8.3	41	8.9
74	4.9		61	6.0	59	6.2						52	7.0	69	5.3
69	5.3		40	9.2	40	9.1						61	6.0	52	7.0
94	3.9		83	4.4	87	4.2	Cost of Sales/Inventory					87	4.2	101	3.6
159	2.3		130	2.8	203	1.8						166	2.2	203	1.8
21	17.6		17	22.1	19	19.7						17	21.5	18	20.8
34	10.6		32	11.3	31	11.9	Cost of Sales/Payables					24	15.2	32	11.5
63	5.8		50	7.3	46	7.9						47	7.8	43	8.5
		2.0		2.7	2.9						3.0		2.9
		3.5		4.5	4.6	Sales/Working Capital					3.7		4.1
		8.3		8.7	9.2						9.9		10.2
		38.5		61.3	47.9						38.7		74.0
(22)	14.6		(31)	12.1	(36)	5.9	EBIT/Interest				(11)	11.3	(13)	8.7
		5.0		4.5	1.4						1.3		2.7
						Net Profit + Depr., Dep., Amort./Cur. Mat. L/T/D							
		.3		.1	.1						.2		.0
		.5		.5	.5	Fixed/Worth					.5		.2
		.8		.9	1.1						1.4		NM
		.4		.5	.4						.4		.5
		1.2		1.3	1.4	Debt/Worth					.8		1.6
		2.8		4.0	2.9						5.6		NM
		41.6		53.7	42.1						50.9		65.2
(26)	24.5		(30)	35.9	(35)	24.5	% Profit Before Taxes/Tangible Net Worth				(11)	29.2	(11)	35.2
		15.0		19.0	7.1						13.4		28.2
		17.8		24.6	22.8						27.3		30.3
		8.8		14.1	8.2	% Profit Before Taxes/Total Assets					13.0		17.4
		6.6		7.4	1.7						2.8		6.8
		17.6		49.5	29.0						12.6		144.9
		5.9		10.9	9.1	Sales/Net Fixed Assets					9.4		36.6
		2.9		4.1	3.5						5.5		3.0
		1.8		2.3	2.1						2.1		2.1
		1.4		1.5	1.4	Sales/Total Assets					1.4		1.3
		.9		1.1	1.0						1.0		1.0
		.6		.5	.7						.7		.2
(21)	1.7		(26)	1.7	(34)	1.6	% Depr., Dep., Amort./Sales					1.1	(12)	1.5
		4.2		3.2	4.7						3.8		4.5
						% Officers', Directors' Owners' Comp/Sales							
		1266270M		3100172M	2018270M	Net Sales ($)	495M	4107M	7361M	53395M	234437M		1718475M
		1168935M		2126190M	1249733M	Total Assets ($)	432M	4009M	3918M	37332M	179390M		1024652M

M = $ thousand   MM = $ million
See Pages viii through xx for Explanation of Ratios and Data
© RMA 2024

MANUFACTURING—All Other Miscellaneous Fabricated Metal Product Manufacturing NAICS 332999

Current Data Sorted by Assets | Comparative Historical Data

								Type of Statement				
			2		1	11	7	3	Unqualified		19	13
					9	22	4	1	Reviewed		37	24
			2		8	6			Compiled		27	21
		3	14		21	4			Tax Returns		75	47
		6	14		56	67	7	9	Other		167	116
			51 (4/1-9/30/23)			226 (10/1/23-3/31/24)					4/1/19-3/31/20 ALL	4/1/20-3/31/21 ALL
		0-500M	500M-2MM		2-10MM	10-50MM	50-100MM	100-250MM	NUMBER OF STATEMENTS		325	221
		9	32		95	110	18	13				
		%	%		%	%	%	%	ASSETS		%	%
			19.2		15.1	13.4	10.3	9.3	Cash & Equivalents		11.1	15.9
			22.6		21.9	19.6	19.1	24.9	Trade Receivables (net)		24.9	22.1
			20.3		24.7	25.7	23.5	22.6	Inventory		22.2	20.2
			1.6		2.3	2.4	2.5	2.8	All Other Current		3.0	3.4
			63.7		64.0	61.1	55.4	59.5	Total Current		61.2	61.6
			29.7		23.2	27.0	16.8	22.8	Fixed Assets (net)		27.7	28.5
			2.4		5.5	4.9	11.2	6.0	Intangibles (net)		5.6	5.2
			4.2		7.4	7.0	16.6	11.6	All Other Non-Current		5.4	4.7
			100.0		100.0	100.0	100.0	100.0	Total		100.0	100.0
									LIABILITIES			
			13.4		5.5	5.5	1.7	.6	Notes Payable-Short Term		9.3	8.9
			1.6		3.2	2.5	2.4	1.0	Cur. Mat.-L.T.D.		3.6	4.2
			7.5		10.3	9.8	10.4	10.6	Trade Payables		12.3	9.4
			.1		.1	.2	.2	.1	Income Taxes Payable		.1	.1
			10.4		9.3	8.7	9.1	11.3	All Other Current		11.1	9.5
			33.0		28.5	26.7	23.7	23.6	Total Current		36.4	32.2
			29.8		16.7	11.0	13.1	32.6	Long-Term Debt		19.7	22.6
			.0		.2	.4	1.6	.2	Deferred Taxes		.3	.3
			6.5		4.1	3.1	12.9	12.7	All Other Non-Current		5.1	5.8
			30.7		50.6	58.8	48.7	30.9	Net Worth		38.6	39.2
			100.0		100.0	100.0	100.0	100.0	Total Liabilities & Net Worth		100.0	100.0
									INCOME DATA			
			100.0		100.0	100.0	100.0	100.0	Net Sales		100.0	100.0
			42.7		38.0	29.2	24.7	32.4	Gross Profit		34.6	33.6
			33.1		29.9	20.8	15.6	18.6	Operating Expenses		27.8	28.9
			9.6		8.1	8.4	9.1	13.8	Operating Profit		6.8	4.6
			1.1		.5	.5	.6	.6	All Other Expenses (net)		.9	-1.8
			8.5		7.6	7.9	8.6	13.2	Profit Before Taxes		5.9	6.4
									RATIOS			
			9.7		4.5	5.0	4.3	2.7			3.6	4.0
			2.3		2.6	2.4	2.7	2.3	Current		2.0	2.4
			1.2		1.6	1.4	1.9	2.1			1.2	1.3
			6.4		3.8	2.9	2.1	1.5			2.1	2.7
			1.5		1.4	1.2	1.1	1.3	Quick		1.1	1.4
			.5		.8	.6	.8	1.1			.6	.7
	0	UND	25	14.4	34	10.6	29	12.5	43	8.4			29	12.8	30	12.0
	32	11.3	41	8.8	43	8.5	36	10.2	49	7.5	Sales/Receivables	40	9.1	42	8.6
	47	7.7	59	6.2	59	6.2	54	6.8	61	6.0		56	6.5	59	6.2
	0	UND	24	15.0	44	8.3	38	9.7	54	6.7		17	21.1	22	16.3
	15	24.0	70	5.2	89	4.1	66	5.5	72	5.1	Cost of Sales/Inventory	51	7.2	59	6.2
	81	4.5	111	3.3	146	2.5	118	3.1	83	4.4		99	3.7	94	3.9
	0	UND	13	27.9	16	23.0	20	18.1	21	17.0		13	28.4	12	30.3
	14	26.5	27	13.5	29	12.6	27	13.6	32	11.5	Cost of Sales/Payables	23	15.6	22	16.4
	35	10.3	42	8.7	41	9.0	41	8.8	41	9.0		42	8.7	40	9.2
				3.9		3.4	2.9	3.1	4.0			4.0	3.3
				8.0		5.2	4.6	4.8	4.8	Sales/Working Capital		7.7	5.8
				36.4		10.1	10.1	8.5	6.9			26.4	14.9
				12.0		33.7	52.3	54.9	111.9			18.3	25.2
		(23)		4.8	(84)	8.8	(89)	9.6	(16)	11.1	10.6	EBIT/Interest	(280)	5.4	(187)	8.8
				.9		3.2	2.2	2.5	7.9			1.7	1.7
							7.1					8.7	8.4
					(38)	3.2			Net Profit + Depr., Dep.,	(50)	3.6	(27)	3.4
							1.3			Amort./Cur. Mat. L/T/D		1.0	1.3
				.1		.2	.2	.2	.4			.3	.3
				.5		.4	.4	.4	.9	Fixed/Worth		.7	.6
				8.5		1.1	1.0	1.0	1.9			2.1	2.7
				.6		.3	.3	.6	.6			.5	.5
				1.5		1.0	.7	1.1	1.9	Debt/Worth		1.3	1.1
				-9.2		2.5	1.9	3.5	6.8			6.3	6.7
				65.1		51.1	33.8	54.0	66.4			47.5	51.5
		(22)		31.0	(84)	28.5	(108)	18.2	(16)	21.7	(12)	38.0	% Profit Before Taxes/Tangible Net Worth	(272)	26.4	(182)	24.8
				2.0		11.3	7.7	14.0	21.0			8.0	7.5
				31.8		25.5	18.9	28.2	34.4			22.5	23.6
				14.1		12.9	8.4	10.6	14.2	% Profit Before Taxes/Total Assets		10.3	10.7
				.5		4.8	3.0	6.5	7.5			2.1	1.7
				29.8		35.7	12.8	19.9	16.8			22.6	17.6
				11.5		10.3	6.1	10.0	7.2	Sales/Net Fixed Assets		8.9	7.5
				6.2		4.3	3.3	6.6	4.1			4.2	3.8
				4.1		2.5	1.8	2.0	2.0			2.8	2.4
				2.7		1.9	1.4	1.5	1.7	Sales/Total Assets		2.0	1.7
				1.9		1.3	1.1	1.0	1.3			1.4	1.2
				1.7		1.1	1.6	1.4	.7			1.2	1.1
		(16)		2.8	(68)	2.3	(97)	2.8	(16)	1.8	(11)	1.5	% Depr., Dep., Amort./Sales	(243)	2.3	(164)	2.8
				4.5		4.5	4.7	2.6	3.2			4.7	4.9
				2.4		2.1	.9					2.0	1.5
		(18)		4.2	(39)	4.3	(28)	1.3			% Officers', Directors' Owners' Comp/Sales	(136)	3.3	(79)	3.3
				6.4		5.4	2.8					5.1	6.0
		12583M		117051M		1020684M	3923364M	1963282M	3716721M	Net Sales ($)		12295711M	6546901M
		2478M		37960M		517005M	2576978M	1216334M	2140577M	Total Assets ($)		5866660M	4336801M

© RMA 2024 M = $ thousand MM = $ million
See Pages viii through xx for Explanation of Ratios and Data

MANUFACTURING—All Other Miscellaneous Fabricated Metal Product Manufacturing NAICS 332999

Comparative Historical Data / Current Data Sorted by Sales

				Type of Statement						
	17	28	24	Unqualified		1	1	1	4	17
	28	40	36	Reviewed		1		4	14	17
	20	17	16	Compiled			1	6	6	3
	49	60	42	Tax Returns	4	7	8	10	10	3
	146	147	159	Other	4	9	15	19	52	60
	4/1/21-3/31/22 ALL	4/1/22-3/31/23 ALL	4/1/23-3/31/24 ALL			51 (4/1-9/30/23)		226 (10/1/23-3/31/24)		
					0-1MM	1-3MM	3-5MM	5-10MM	10-25MM	25MM & OVER
	260	292	277	NUMBER OF STATEMENTS	8	18	25	40	86	100
	%	%	%	ASSETS	%	%	%	%	%	%
	14.1	14.2	15.0	Cash & Equivalents	20.9	21.4	14.9	13.3	12.7	
	23.5	23.0	20.9	Trade Receivables (net)	22.6	16.8	17.8	19.3	23.3	
	25.3	24.9	24.5	Inventory	20.1	17.6	23.5	25.4	26.6	
	2.4	2.6	2.2	All Other Current	1.1	1.6	3.4	2.2	2.2	
	65.3	64.7	62.6	Total Current	64.6	57.5	59.6	60.2	64.9	
	23.7	25.3	24.6	Fixed Assets (net)	25.7	24.9	28.0	28.7	20.6	
	4.9	4.3	5.2	Intangibles (net)	2.9	10.8	4.7	4.8	5.0	
	6.0	5.7	7.6	All Other Non-Current	6.8	6.8	7.8	6.2	9.5	
	100.0	100.0	100.0	Total	100.0	100.0	100.0	100.0	100.0	
				LIABILITIES						
	8.3	6.9	7.4	Notes Payable-Short Term	6.6	9.2	7.8	5.1	5.2	
	2.4	2.9	2.7	Cur. Mat.-L.T.D.	2.1	1.7	3.7	3.5	1.8	
	11.7	10.9	10.1	Trade Payables	9.5	5.2	8.1	10.0	11.4	
	.1	.2	.1	Income Taxes Payable	.2	.0	.1	.1	.2	
	9.4	10.4	9.3	All Other Current	12.0	6.3	7.9	9.9	9.5	
	31.9	31.4	29.6	Total Current	30.4	22.3	27.7	28.7	28.1	
	20.1	20.4	16.9	Long-Term Debt	22.9	24.2	24.0	14.5	12.5	
	.2	.2	.3	Deferred Taxes	.0	.0	.3	.3	.5	
	6.0	6.1	5.5	All Other Non-Current	13.9	.7	5.9	3.0	6.4	
	41.7	42.0	47.8	Net Worth	32.8	52.8	42.1	53.5	52.5	
	100.0	100.0	100.0	Total Liabilities & Net Worth	100.0	100.0	100.0	100.0	100.0	
				INCOME DATA						
	100.0	100.0	100.0	Net Sales	100.0	100.0	100.0	100.0	100.0	
	34.5	34.5	34.4	Gross Profit	48.1	43.5	39.3	32.2	28.1	
	27.0	26.1	25.8	Operating Expenses	39.9	34.4	32.5	24.8	18.3	
	7.5	8.4	8.5	Operating Profit	8.2	9.2	6.9	7.4	9.8	
	-2.4	.2	.6	All Other Expenses (net)	2.6	.3	-.1	.4	.7	
	9.9	8.3	7.9	Profit Before Taxes	5.6	8.9	6.9	7.0	9.1	
				RATIOS						
	4.5	3.9	4.7	Current	15.1	7.5	4.8	4.1	4.5	
	2.4	2.3	2.5		2.9	3.9	3.2	2.2	2.3	
	1.5	1.5	1.5		1.5	1.6	1.8	1.4	1.6	
	2.8	2.6	3.0	Quick	6.6	5.6	3.9	2.2	2.5	
	1.3	1.2	1.3		1.6	2.4	1.5	1.1	1.2	
	.7	.7	.7		.7	1.1	1.0	.6	.7	
33	11.1	27	13.4	29	12.4	Sales/Receivables	20	18.3	11	33.1	26	13.9	29	12.7	35	10.3
46	7.9	43	8.5	41	8.8		43	8.4	31	11.7	41	9.0	40	9.2	45	8.2
62	5.9	61	6.0	58	6.3		57	6.4	48	7.6	57	6.4	59	6.2	58	6.3
34	10.6	30	12.0	34	10.8	Cost of Sales/Inventory	0	UND	3	107.5	9	39.0	38	9.5	43	8.4
76	4.8	61	6.0	72	5.1		35	10.3	41	9.0	81	4.5	72	5.1	79	4.6
118	3.1	118	3.1	122	3.0		146	2.5	99	3.7	126	2.9	130	2.8	122	3.0
13	27.3	15	24.9	14	26.1	Cost of Sales/Payables	6	57.7	9	38.6	13	28.7	15	24.5	16	22.5
26	13.9	25	14.4	27	13.4		21	17.5	15	24.2	24	15.2	29	12.8	30	12.3
49	7.5	43	8.5	41	8.9		44	8.3	34	10.8	36	10.0	41	8.8	41	9.0
	3.2		3.4		3.3	Sales/Working Capital		3.3		3.3		3.2		3.6		3.2
	5.2		5.2		5.1			5.0		4.2		5.1		5.6		4.9
	9.1		13.4		10.6			12.3		17.0		9.0		14.7		8.7
	57.5		46.5		37.2	EBIT/Interest		8.8		22.0		26.5		36.2		75.1
(226)	16.5	(260)	10.6	(233)	8.9		(13)	4.5	(22)	10.0	(36)	9.3	(69)	7.0	(88)	10.9
	5.2		3.0		2.3			-.6		1.5		3.0		2.3		2.9
	17.2		11.8		7.1	Net Profit + Depr., Dep., Amort./Cur. Mat. L/T/D								9.9		7.6
(33)	6.0	(51)	3.8	(55)	2.9								(18)	3.6	(33)	2.9
	1.9		1.3		1.6									1.1		2.0
	.2		.2		.2	Fixed/Worth		.0		.2		.3		.2		.2
	.5		.5		.4			.4		.7		.5		.6		.4
	1.5		1.5		1.3			1.1		7.2		1.4		1.2		.9
	.5		.5		.3	Debt/Worth		.3		.2		.4		.3		.3
	1.2		1.2		1.0			1.2		1.1		1.1		.9		1.0
	4.6		3.9		2.8			-6.7		13.8		3.7		2.3		2.1
	70.2		57.2		48.1	% Profit Before Taxes/Tangible Net Worth		35.4		81.2		43.9		43.5		50.3
(224)	36.0	(252)	32.6	(247)	22.5		(13)	20.7	(21)	34.2	(32)	24.9	(81)	18.7	(96)	25.6
	17.9		15.1		9.0			-3.2		6.0		10.5		6.7		12.5
	32.4		26.2		24.8	% Profit Before Taxes/Total Assets		23.1		34.4		26.8		19.4		27.4
	14.7		15.3		11.1			11.2		16.2		13.5		9.0		12.4
	5.4		4.2		3.5			-1.1		3.1		2.0		3.9		4.6
	25.0		24.7		21.9	Sales/Net Fixed Assets		UND		22.3		25.0		20.5		18.8
	9.2		9.0		8.7			8.9		10.9		8.4		7.7		8.9
	4.0		4.5		4.3			5.3		4.0		3.8		3.3		5.6
	2.5		2.5		2.4	Sales/Total Assets		2.7		2.9		2.6		2.4		2.1
	1.8		1.8		1.6			2.0		1.5		1.6		1.6		1.7
	1.3		1.3		1.2			1.3		1.1		1.2		1.1		1.2
	1.1		1.2		1.4	% Depr., Dep., Amort./Sales				1.5		1.6		1.3		1.2
(183)	2.7	(221)	2.6	(210)	2.4				(19)	3.6	(28)	3.0	(66)	2.9	(89)	2.0
	5.4		4.9		4.4					6.4		6.7		5.1		3.1
	2.0		1.7		1.6	% Officers', Directors', Owners' Comp/Sales				2.5		2.2		1.0		.6
(83)	3.4	(109)	3.2	(91)	2.8				(13)	4.2	(18)	4.3	(29)	1.8	(17)	2.4
	4.8		5.7		5.2					5.6		4.9		3.2		3.5
	8484639M	9363227M	10753685M	Net Sales ($)	4468M	37767M	100550M	287833M	1374525M	8948542M
	5193396M	5403504M	6491332M	Total Assets ($)	3599M	22580M	74605M	188486M	950740M	5251322M

M = $ thousand   MM = $ million
See Pages viii through xx for Explanation of Ratios and Data

© RMA 2024

MANUFACTURING—Farm Machinery and Equipment Manufacturing NAICS 333111

Current Data Sorted by Assets | Comparative Historical Data

							Type of Statement				
1				6	4	4	Unqualified			9	5
	1		2	6	1	1	Reviewed			17	5
			3	1			Compiled			15	3
			4	2			Tax Returns			16	5
1	1		13	26	7	5	Other			71	27
	20 (4/1-9/30/23)			69 (10/1/23-3/31/24)						4/1/19-3/31/20	4/1/20-3/31/21
0-500M	500M-2MM	2-10MM	10-50MM	50-100MM	100-250MM					ALL	ALL
2	2	22	41	12	10		NUMBER OF STATEMENTS			128	45
%	%	%	%	%	%		ASSETS			%	%
		11.8	9.6	12.3	13.2		Cash & Equivalents			8.7	15.1
		12.6	13.0	10.5	10.8		Trade Receivables (net)			15.1	13.6
		51.0	41.9	42.1	50.8		Inventory			43.9	39.9
		4.5	1.9	2.1	1.1		All Other Current			2.2	2.5
		79.8	66.3	67.1	75.9		Total Current			69.8	71.0
		15.5	20.8	19.8	15.9		Fixed Assets (net)			19.5	15.5
		1.0	5.1	2.5	1.7		Intangibles (net)			6.1	6.6
		3.6	7.7	10.6	6.5		All Other Non-Current			4.6	6.9
		100.0	100.0	100.0	100.0		Total			100.0	100.0
							LIABILITIES				
		3.9	11.4	15.1	7.6		Notes Payable-Short Term			13.3	12.5
		1.6	2.7	.6	1.5		Cur. Mat.-L.T.D.			2.4	2.7
		9.8	9.7	7.8	8.2		Trade Payables			9.4	7.3
		.0	.3	.3	.1		Income Taxes Payable			.1	.0
		8.7	12.3	9.5	19.7		All Other Current			9.6	11.5
		24.0	36.4	33.4	37.1		Total Current			34.8	34.0
		26.7	11.2	7.4	4.2		Long-Term Debt			12.2	13.6
		.0	.7	.5	.4		Deferred Taxes			.3	.1
		1.6	5.2	6.6	12.7		All Other Non-Current			5.8	7.8
		47.7	46.5	52.1	45.6		Net Worth			46.9	44.5
		100.0	100.0	100.0	100.0		Total Liabilities & Net Worth			100.0	100.0
							INCOME DATA				
		100.0	100.0	100.0	100.0		Net Sales			100.0	100.0
		34.0	29.9	22.8	26.2		Gross Profit			27.0	26.8
		28.9	23.3	16.0	17.1		Operating Expenses			22.2	23.5
		5.1	6.7	6.8	9.2		Operating Profit			4.8	3.4
		-.5	1.1	.5	.2		All Other Expenses (net)			1.1	-.4
		5.5	5.6	6.3	9.0		Profit Before Taxes			3.7	3.8
							RATIOS				
		6.5	2.8	5.0	2.6					3.7	4.8
		4.3	2.0	1.9	2.1		Current			2.0	2.4
		2.2	1.3	1.1	1.6					1.4	1.3
		2.3	1.0	2.0	1.5					1.7	2.2
		.8	.5	.5	.5		Quick			.6	.9
		.4	.3	.2	.2					.3	.4
		13 28.4	20 18.6	18 20.5	9 41.3					20 18.2	24 15.4
		22 16.8	28 13.0	24 15.2	36 10.2		Sales/Receivables			33 11.0	33 11.0
		30 12.1	46 8.0	33 11.2	41 9.0					49 7.5	41 8.9
		68 5.4	89 4.1	96 3.8	140 2.6					85 4.3	83 4.4
		166 2.2	159 2.3	130 2.8	166 2.2		Cost of Sales/Inventory			140 2.6	146 2.5
		228 1.6	261 1.4	182 2.0	228 1.6					215 1.7	215 1.7
		12 30.3	14 26.5	12 30.2	10 34.9					12 30.6	11 32.0
		22 16.7	27 13.5	22 16.3	20 17.9		Cost of Sales/Payables			21 17.5	21 17.7
		62 5.9	47 7.8	38 9.5	39 9.3					38 9.5	33 11.1
		2.5	3.3	3.0	1.9					2.7	2.2
		2.9	4.0	5.4	3.4		Sales/Working Capital			4.2	4.6
		4.4	10.3	45.8	6.9					8.5	10.4
		29.1	25.6	31.5	19.0					17.1	30.9
		(21) 7.6	(37) 6.1	3.7	6.3		EBIT/Interest			(123) 4.9	(42) 6.2
		2.0	1.8	2.2	2.2					1.4	.9
				43.8			Net Profit + Depr., Dep.,			17.7	
			(14) 4.3				Amort./Cur. Mat. L/T/D			(25) 7.2	
			1.5							1.9	
		.1	.2	.1	.2					.2	.1
		.2	.4	.5	.4		Fixed/Worth			.4	.4
		.5	1.0	.9	.6					1.0	1.2
		.3	.6	.3	.9					.4	.3
		.6	1.2	1.4	1.4		Debt/Worth			1.0	1.1
		1.6	3.7	2.6	2.3					3.8	5.0
		32.1	29.6	17.2	45.8		% Profit Before Taxes/Tangible			28.3	28.2
		(21) 17.8	(39) 17.7	12.4	21.5		Net Worth			(119) 14.1	(40) 10.7
		3.7	7.6	7.1	6.7					2.3	4.1
		21.9	15.9	13.3	18.7		% Profit Before Taxes/Total			11.7	17.1
		10.3	8.5	5.6	10.5		Assets			6.0	4.4
		1.4	2.5	2.2	2.6					.7	.6
		37.6	17.6	20.5	15.1					23.1	28.3
		17.9	7.3	8.2	13.3		Sales/Net Fixed Assets			9.2	11.4
		12.4	4.2	5.1	4.9					4.4	4.8
		2.4	1.9	2.3	1.7					2.0	1.9
		1.9	1.4	1.6	1.3		Sales/Total Assets			1.4	1.3
		1.4	1.0	1.0	1.0					1.1	.9
		.7	1.6	.5						1.1	.8
		(14) 1.4	(34) 2.2	.9			% Depr., Dep., Amort./Sales			(105) 2.0	(32) 2.0
		2.4	3.5	2.2						3.0	3.2
			.3							.6	
			(11) .8				% Officers', Directors'			(37) 1.4	
			1.9				Owners' Comp/Sales			3.0	
1743M	4372M	224569M	1561052M	1245482M	2455918M		Net Sales ($)			6700875M	2458049M
529M	2273M	118480M	1056843M	791202M	1752695M		Total Assets ($)			4936043M	1881770M

M = $ thousand MM = $ million
See Pages viii through xx for Explanation of Ratios and Data

© RMA 2024

MANUFACTURING—Farm Machinery and Equipment Manufacturing NAICS 333111

Comparative Historical Data | Current Data Sorted by Sales

Comparative Historical Data			Type of Statement	Current Data Sorted by Sales					
3	7	15	Unqualified	1				1	13
11	11	11	Reviewed			1	1	2	7
3	5	4	Compiled				1	2	1
9	9	6	Tax Returns			1	2	3	7
34	51	53	Other	1	2		10	13	27
4/1/21-3/31/22 ALL	4/1/22-3/31/23 ALL	4/1/23-3/31/24 ALL		0-1MM	20 (4/1-9/30/23) 1-3MM	3-5MM	69 (10/1/23-3/31/24) 5-10MM	10-25MM	25MM & OVER
60	83	89	NUMBER OF STATEMENTS	2	2	2	14	21	48
%	%	%	ASSETS	%	%	%	%	%	%
10.8	11.1	10.8	Cash & Equivalents				7.0	9.7	13.0
12.4	17.1	12.2	Trade Receivables (net)				10.0	12.5	13.2
46.4	43.1	45.2	Inventory				53.8	46.9	42.1
3.5	3.1	2.4	All Other Current				2.0	3.5	2.1
73.2	74.4	70.6	Total Current				72.8	72.6	70.4
18.0	15.9	19.4	Fixed Assets (net)				15.2	18.8	18.8
4.5	5.2	3.2	Intangibles (net)				1.8	3.3	3.9
4.4	4.5	6.8	All Other Non-Current				10.2	5.3	6.9
100.0	100.0	100.0	Total				100.0	100.0	100.0
			LIABILITIES						
13.0	8.3	9.5	Notes Payable-Short Term				5.4	11.8	10.0
1.8	1.2	1.9	Cur. Mat.-L.T.D.				1.2	3.0	1.8
10.4	9.6	9.8	Trade Payables				17.7	6.6	8.0
.1	.3	.2	Income Taxes Payable				.0	.0	.4
14.8	10.6	12.0	All Other Current				11.9	5.8	14.9
40.1	30.0	33.4	Total Current				36.3	27.2	35.0
10.2	11.8	13.9	Long-Term Debt				30.2	12.8	8.7
.5	.3	.4	Deferred Taxes				.0	.4	.6
2.8	7.9	5.2	All Other Non-Current				2.3	1.9	8.0
46.4	50.1	47.0	Net Worth				31.2	57.7	47.6
100.0	100.0	100.0	Total Liabilities & Net Worth				100.0	100.0	100.0
			INCOME DATA						
100.0	100.0	100.0	Net Sales				100.0	100.0	100.0
26.9	28.2	29.7	Gross Profit				29.8	29.7	28.2
20.8	21.1	23.0	Operating Expenses				30.1	24.3	19.0
6.1	7.2	6.7	Operating Profit				-.3	5.4	9.2
-1.0	.0	.6	All Other Expenses (net)				-1.0	1.3	.6
7.1	7.2	6.0	Profit Before Taxes				.7	4.1	8.6
			RATIOS						
3.4	3.9	3.8	Current				4.0	7.1	3.2
2.1	2.6	2.1					2.3	2.2	2.1
1.3	1.8	1.5					1.4	1.6	1.3
1.2	2.1	1.3	Quick				.8	1.9	1.6
.5	1.0	.6					.4	.5	.6
.3	.4	.3					.1	.4	.3
10 35.3	22 16.9	18 20.8	Sales/Receivables				11 32.3	16 22.6	20 18.5
31 11.9	32 11.3	26 14.1					21 17.6	28 13.0	28 13.2
43 8.5	47 7.8	39 9.3					30 12.3	47 7.7	40 9.2
94 3.9	78 4.7	94 3.9	Cost of Sales/Inventory				114 3.2	104 3.5	89 4.1
114 3.2	118 3.1	152 2.4					203 1.8	174 2.1	130 2.8
166 2.2	215 1.7	243 1.5					332 1.1	261 1.4	203 1.8
14 26.4	9 39.6	13 28.1	Cost of Sales/Payables				14 26.9	13 28.9	12 30.2
24 15.3	23 16.2	26 14.2					28 12.9	27 13.7	19 19.0
40 9.2	38 9.6	47 7.7					78 4.7	41 8.9	39 9.3
3.4	2.5	2.8	Sales/Working Capital				2.4	2.6	3.2
5.3	3.6	3.7					3.4	3.2	4.3
10.2	5.5	8.5					6.2	5.0	13.6
55.8	29.8	25.6	EBIT/Interest				6.7	30.8	26.2
(55) 10.8	(73) 9.7	(83) 6.1					(13) 2.8	8.5	(44) 6.3
6.1	4.6	2.2					-3.0	2.2	2.3
	78.1	36.2	Net Profit + Depr., Dep., Amort./Cur. Mat. L/T/D						42.2
	(15) 8.1	(28) 4.3						(23) 6.0	
		5.4 1.8							2.5
.2	.1	.1	Fixed/Worth				.1	.1	.2
.4	.3	.3					.2	.3	.4
.7	.7	.7					.6	.7	1.0
.5	.6	.4	Debt/Worth				.3	.3	.5
1.2	1.0	1.0					1.3	.9	1.1
2.6	2.6	2.2					2.0	1.5	3.0
50.9	55.5	31.7	% Profit Before Taxes/Tangible Net Worth				21.3	20.1	42.0
(57) 26.6	(80) 26.2	(86) 17.6					(13) 4.4	17.4	(46) 22.5
13.4	6.4	6.5					-9.5	7.9	10.1
17.9	19.1	17.2	% Profit Before Taxes/Total Assets				9.4	13.9	20.1
11.4	9.3	8.6					1.9	8.3	12.7
5.0	3.5	2.1					-9.2	3.1	3.1
21.6	28.8	19.4	Sales/Net Fixed Assets				25.5	38.3	16.4
11.9	15.0	11.2					15.1	7.6	8.7
6.3	5.5	5.2					11.4	4.1	5.6
2.5	2.3	2.1	Sales/Total Assets				2.0	2.0	2.2
1.8	1.7	1.5					1.7	1.2	1.6
1.3	1.2	1.1					.7	1.1	1.2
1.0	.6	.9	% Depr., Dep., Amort./Sales				1.0	2.0	.8
(50) 1.8	(60) 1.3	(70) 1.8					(10) 1.8	(14) 3.4	(44) 1.7
2.9	2.3	2.9					2.9	3.9	2.3
.5	1.0	.4	% Officers', Directors', Owners' Comp/Sales					.3	
(23) 1.1	(16) 2.2	(20) 1.4						(11) .8	
3.0	3.4	3.0						1.6	
2866217M	5169737M	5493136M	Net Sales ($)	340M	3313M	7377M	103090M	348394M	5030622M
1803933M	3689966M	3722022M	Total Assets ($)	584M	5021M	3960M	112170M	275256M	3325031M

© RMA 2024   M = $ thousand   MM = $ million
See Pages viii through xx for Explanation of Ratios and Data

MANUFACTURING—Lawn and Garden Tractor and Home Lawn and Garden Equipment Manufacturing   NAICS 333112

Current Data Sorted by Assets | **Comparative Historical Data**

							Type of Statement				
			2	2	1		Unqualified		6		2
		2	3				Reviewed		3		1
		1	1				Compiled		2		
	1	1					Tax Returns		5		1
1	1	9	15	4	2		Other		17		8
0-500M	22 (4/1-9/30/23) 500M-2MM	2-10MM	24 (10/1/23-3/31/24) 10-50MM	50-100MM	100-250MM				4/1/19-3/31/20 ALL		4/1/20-3/31/21 ALL
1	2	13	21	6	3		NUMBER OF STATEMENTS		33		12
%	%	%	%	%	%		ASSETS		%		%
		5.1	7.4				Cash & Equivalents		10.0		9.3
		22.7	15.6				Trade Receivables (net)		17.3		14.8
		58.6	52.3				Inventory		43.9		44.0
		2.3	.8				All Other Current		2.7		2.7
		88.6	76.2				Total Current		73.9		70.9
		7.5	16.0				Fixed Assets (net)		16.5		18.7
		.8	.3				Intangibles (net)		5.5		7.9
		3.0	7.5				All Other Non-Current		4.2		2.5
		100.0	100.0				Total		100.0		100.0
							LIABILITIES				
		7.5	3.7				Notes Payable-Short Term		10.0		1.8
		.4	.6				Cur. Mat.-L.T.D.		1.1		3.7
		20.1	18.0				Trade Payables		13.9		17.5
		.0	.0				Income Taxes Payable		.1		.2
		10.7	8.8				All Other Current		11.0		9.6
		38.7	31.1				Total Current		36.1		32.7
		5.7	3.1				Long-Term Debt		17.4		15.4
		.0	.5				Deferred Taxes		.1		.3
		19.8	22.6				All Other Non-Current		4.1		13.9
		35.8	42.6				Net Worth		42.3		37.8
		100.0	100.0				Total Liabilities & Net Worth		100.0		100.0
							INCOME DATA				
		100.0	100.0				Net Sales		100.0		100.0
		28.4	26.0				Gross Profit		26.5		25.1
		30.2	20.9				Operating Expenses		22.2		18.7
		-1.8	5.1				Operating Profit		4.3		6.4
		1.2	.6				All Other Expenses (net)		1.1		1.4
		-3.0	4.5				Profit Before Taxes		3.2		5.0
							RATIOS				
		7.1	7.0						4.1		4.0
		2.6	2.7				Current		2.0		2.0
		1.3	1.6						1.4		1.6
		1.9	2.6						1.9		1.4
		1.4	.9				Quick		.7		.7
		.3	.6						.3		.5
		23 16.1	18 20.7					15	24.3	10	36.9
		35 10.5	37 9.9				Sales/Receivables	22	16.5	28	12.9
		51 7.1	58 6.3					59	6.2	58	6.3
		122 3.0	122 3.0					78	4.7	70	5.2
		146 2.5	159 2.3				Cost of Sales/Inventory	135	2.7	101	3.6
		203 1.8	215 1.7					152	2.4	152	2.4
		12 29.3	11 33.0					15	23.8	18	20.4
		23 15.7	27 13.6				Cost of Sales/Payables	23	15.7	33	11.0
		118 3.1	76 4.8					50	7.3	49	7.4
		2.5	2.6						3.0		3.8
		3.3	3.6				Sales/Working Capital		6.9		5.3
		24.5	7.0						12.3		10.4
		1.5	69.7						21.0		9.8
		-1.0	(17) 21.3				EBIT/Interest	(32)	3.7		5.9
		-2.4	2.7						1.0		1.7
							Net Profit + Depr., Dep., Amort./Cur. Mat. L/T/D				
		.0	.1						.2		.4
		.0	.2				Fixed/Worth		.5		.7
		.5	.6						1.0		-3.0
		.9	.5						.7		.8
		1.7	1.7				Debt/Worth		1.6		1.1
		3.6	2.9						2.6		-23.8
		3.6	29.4						18.7		
	(12)	-6.8	21.5				% Profit Before Taxes/Tangible Net Worth	(28)	9.3		
		-23.3	9.8						.5		
		1.0	13.2						8.2		10.6
		-4.2	7.6				% Profit Before Taxes/Total Assets		4.4		7.7
		-10.4	2.3						.1		4.2
		UND	39.1						43.5		21.7
		76.0	16.3				Sales/Net Fixed Assets		12.5		10.3
		20.8	5.0						5.6		6.0
		2.2	1.9						2.8		2.7
		1.9	1.7				Sales/Total Assets		1.7		2.0
		1.4	1.1						1.2		1.2
			.6						.7		1.1
		(17)	1.0				% Depr., Dep., Amort./Sales	(29)	1.4	(11)	2.3
			2.3						2.2		3.2
							% Officers', Directors' Owners' Comp/Sales				
420M	5149M	116107M	910250M	1029187M	904585M		Net Sales ($)		2763687M		1407920M
315M	2798M	68528M	553332M	471969M	519961M		Total Assets ($)		1444253M		767410M

M = $ thousand   MM = $ million
See Pages viii through xx for Explanation of Ratios and Data

© RMA 2024

MANUFACTURING—Lawn and Garden Tractor and Home Lawn and Garden Equipment Manufacturing NAICS 333112

Comparative Historical Data | Current Data Sorted by Sales

							Type of Statement											
			2		5		Unqualified							2		1		5
	1		2		5		Reviewed					1						2
					2		Compiled					1				1		1
	1		2		2		Tax Returns									1		
	21		19		32		Other		1			6			11		13	
	4/1/21-		4/1/22-		4/1/23-			0-1MM		22 (4/1-9/30/23)			24 (10/1/23-3/31/24)				
	3/31/22		3/31/23		3/31/24				1-3MM		3-5MM		5-10MM		10-25MM		25MM & OVER
	ALL		ALL		ALL												
	23		25		46		NUMBER OF STATEMENTS	1	2		1		8		13		21
	%		%		%		ASSETS	%	%		%		%		%		%
	20.1		13.5		6.0		Cash & Equivalents								4.2		6.1
	14.1		20.8		18.5		Trade Receivables (net)								12.2		19.9
	37.4		44.7		53.5		Inventory								53.5		48.5
	1.6		1.2		2.4		All Other Current								1.1		3.5
	73.2		80.2		80.4		Total Current								71.1		78.0
	14.8		15.0		12.3		Fixed Assets (net)								20.3		12.2
	3.7		.6		1.6		Intangibles (net)								.1		2.9
	8.3		4.1		5.8		All Other Non-Current								8.6		6.9
	100.0		100.0		100.0		Total								100.0		100.0
							LIABILITIES										
	6.1		7.6		5.2		Notes Payable-Short Term								1.0		6.3
	2.7		.7		.8		Cur. Mat.-L.T.D.								.3		1.5
	12.8		18.3		20.5		Trade Payables								11.4		23.8
	.1		.1		.0		Income Taxes Payable								.0		.0
	10.0		10.1		9.2		All Other Current								10.9		7.6
	31.7		36.7		35.7		Total Current								23.6		39.2
	23.1		12.3		8.3		Long-Term Debt								4.8		13.6
	.2		.4		.2		Deferred Taxes								.7		.1
	4.4		5.6		17.8		All Other Non-Current								37.2		8.6
	40.6		45.0		37.9		Net Worth								33.8		38.6
	100.0		100.0		100.0		Total Liabilities & Net Worth								100.0		100.0
							INCOME DATA										
	100.0		100.0		100.0		Net Sales								100.0		100.0
	31.9		24.6		27.4		Gross Profit								29.9		23.7
	17.2		17.8		22.4		Operating Expenses								29.8		16.9
	14.7		6.9		5.0		Operating Profit								.1		6.8
	-.8		.4		1.1		All Other Expenses (net)								.7		1.3
	15.4		6.4		4.0		Profit Before Taxes								-.6		5.5
							RATIOS										
	4.2		3.4		5.8										57.9		3.1
	2.6		2.4		2.8		Current								3.9		2.3
	1.5		1.7		1.5										2.1		1.6
	1.9		1.6		1.7										12.1		1.2
	1.0		1.0		1.0		Quick								1.1		.8
	.5		.6		.4										.4		.6
5	67.9	13	27.8	19	19.1									22	16.9	11	32.3
19	18.9	40	9.1	36	10.1		Sales/Receivables							34	10.7	37	9.9
40	9.2	49	7.5	51	7.2									58	6.3	47	7.7
56	6.5	63	5.8	118	3.1									146	2.5	63	5.8
76	4.8	94	3.9	146	2.5		Cost of Sales/Inventory							203	1.8	135	2.7
152	2.4	140	2.6	215	1.7									406	.9	166	2.2
18	20.2	18	20.3	15	25.0									4	93.2	24	15.2
30	12.0	30	12.0	30	12.3		Cost of Sales/Payables							23	15.6	40	9.2
46	7.9	49	7.5	69	5.3									32	11.4	76	4.8
	3.2		3.9		2.6										1.0		3.4
	5.3		4.5		3.6		Sales/Working Capital								3.3		4.4
	7.7		10.2		7.9										5.0		8.7
	127.6		76.8		55.3										42.5		107.0
(15)	26.9	(17)	10.2	(41)	4.1		EBIT/Interest						(11)	2.1	(19)	21.3
	9.2		3.2		.3										.4		4.1
					33.7												40.0
			(13)	24.8		Net Profit + Depr., Dep.,								(10)	16.8
					3.0		Amort./Cur. Mat. L/T/D										3.0
	.1		.1		.0										.1		.1
	.4		.3		.2		Fixed/Worth								.4		.3
	3.0		.6		1.1										2.8		.6
	.5		.7		.8										1.1		.7
	1.6		1.0		1.5		Debt/Worth								2.4		1.1
	27.5		3.2		5.0										6.7		2.9
	139.6		88.3		40.0		% Profit Before Taxes/Tangible							15.6		64.0
(19)	74.4		39.1	(42)	15.6		Net Worth							8.4	(18)	29.4
	19.8		5.8		-4.0										-12.9		22.3
	39.7		25.6		16.3		% Profit Before Taxes/Total								6.3		26.7
	24.5		18.7		6.7		Assets								1.8		14.1
	9.7		3.1		-2.1										-1.6		7.3
	24.4		56.9		78.6										40.3		94.1
	20.5		24.0		20.5		Sales/Net Fixed Assets								12.5		16.3
	12.3		16.7		11.2										1.8		10.6
	2.5		3.1		2.2										1.7		2.7
	1.9		2.5		1.7		Sales/Total Assets								1.5		1.8
	1.4		1.5		1.3										.6		1.4
	.7		.4		.6										.6		.2
(18)	1.1	(19)	.9	(33)	.7		% Depr., Dep., Amort./Sales						(11)	1.5	(19)	.7
	1.6		1.4		2.2										3.5		1.9
							% Officers', Directors' Owners' Comp/Sales										
	1417093M		1964005M		2965698M		Net Sales ($)	420M	4714M		3131M		64016M		241954M		2651463M
	822430M		882292M		1616903M		Total Assets ($)	315M	3561M		1426M		35980M		238790M		1336831M

M = $ thousand   MM = $ million
See Pages viii through xx for Explanation of Ratios and Data

© RMA 2024

MANUFACTURING—Construction Machinery Manufacturing NAICS 333120

Current Data Sorted by Assets | Comparative Historical Data

0-500M	500M-2MM	2-10MM	10-50MM	50-100MM	100-250MM	Type of Statement	4/1/19-3/31/20 ALL	4/1/20-3/31/21 ALL
		1	6	4	6	Unqualified	8	6
	1	2	8			Reviewed	10	6
	1	3	2		1	Compiled	7	4
	1	1				Tax Returns	6	1
	4	8	15	4	2	Other	51	34
	17 (4/1-9/30/23)		52 (10/1/23-3/31/24)					
DATA NOT AVAILABLE	6	15	31	8	9	**NUMBER OF STATEMENTS**	82	51
	%	%	%	%	%	**ASSETS**	%	%
		8.3	8.2			Cash & Equivalents	9.7	15.7
		11.3	19.1			Trade Receivables (net)	17.4	18.7
		38.0	32.5			Inventory	36.7	32.3
		1.8	8.5			All Other Current	4.1	3.2
		59.4	68.3			Total Current	67.9	70.0
		31.4	22.1			Fixed Assets (net)	21.9	19.3
		2.9	3.5			Intangibles (net)	4.9	5.3
		6.2	6.1			All Other Non-Current	5.4	5.4
		100.0	100.0			Total	100.0	100.0
						LIABILITIES		
		8.7	6.1			Notes Payable-Short Term	11.8	7.5
		2.5	2.7			Cur. Mat.-L.T.D.	2.7	2.0
		6.1	9.4			Trade Payables	10.2	10.4
		.1	.1			Income Taxes Payable	.1	.1
		8.2	14.3			All Other Current	13.1	15.2
		25.5	32.6			Total Current	37.9	35.3
		17.9	11.6			Long-Term Debt	8.4	11.8
		.0	.4			Deferred Taxes	.4	.6
		6.6	8.9			All Other Non-Current	5.2	8.3
		50.1	46.5			Net Worth	48.0	44.1
		100.0	100.0			Total Liabilities & Net Worth	100.0	100.0
						INCOME DATA		
		100.0	100.0			Net Sales	100.0	100.0
		33.8	28.5			Gross Profit	29.6	27.8
		27.2	20.1			Operating Expenses	22.7	22.5
		6.6	8.4			Operating Profit	6.9	5.3
		1.2	.8			All Other Expenses (net)	.3	-1.0
		5.4	7.6			Profit Before Taxes	6.6	6.3
						RATIOS		
		4.7	3.4				3.4	4.3
		2.9	2.2			Current	1.8	2.3
		1.7	1.5				1.3	1.4
		3.3	1.7				1.9	2.7
		.5	.9			Quick	.6	1.0
		.2	.6				.3	.6
		14 26.4	32 11.5				27 13.4	29 12.8
		23 15.9	42 8.6			Sales/Receivables	41 9.0	44 8.3
		41 8.8	74 4.9				53 6.9	61 6.0
		28 12.9	58 6.3				72 5.1	63 5.8
		85 4.3	122 3.0			Cost of Sales/Inventory	130 2.8	122 3.0
		203 1.8	215 1.7				174 2.1	174 2.1
		12 29.9	18 20.1				16 23.0	14 25.4
		16 22.7	27 13.3			Cost of Sales/Payables	27 13.6	28 12.9
		31 11.9	41 8.9				51 7.1	50 7.3
		2.7	2.4				3.0	2.3
		5.1	4.3			Sales/Working Capital	5.2	4.4
		11.6	6.0				14.5	10.6
		29.5	45.8				14.2	55.9
		(14) 10.3	(29) 9.6			EBIT/Interest	(67) 4.4	(46) 5.4
		3.4	4.3				1.4	2.1
						Net Profit + Depr., Dep., Amort./Cur. Mat. L/T/D	10.5	
							(21) 3.6	
							1.7	
		.3	.2				.2	.1
		.5	.5			Fixed/Worth	.4	.4
		1.5	1.3				1.1	1.4
		.3	.5				.5	.5
		.7	1.2			Debt/Worth	1.2	1.2
		3.3	3.7				3.2	3.6
		62.3	30.8				30.8	36.1
		(13) 16.9	(27) 21.3			% Profit Before Taxes/Tangible Net Worth	(76) 14.2	(44) 16.4
		11.8	10.1				5.4	2.9
		16.7	16.6				13.8	16.2
		12.2	9.9			% Profit Before Taxes/Total Assets	7.3	8.0
		-.4	5.3				1.2	1.4
		20.2	15.7				21.2	41.1
		6.0	6.5			Sales/Net Fixed Assets	10.1	11.3
		3.4	4.0				4.2	4.1
		2.4	1.8				1.9	2.1
		1.6	1.3			Sales/Total Assets	1.5	1.5
		.9	1.1				1.1	1.0
		.9	1.1				.9	.9
		(12) 2.4	(29) 2.6			% Depr., Dep., Amort./Sales	(66) 2.0	(37) 2.1
		3.1	4.1				3.3	4.2
						% Officers', Directors' Owners' Comp/Sales	.5	.9
							(13) 1.6	(13) 1.8
							6.3	6.7
	15056M	169726M	1087136M	678755M	2081942M	Net Sales ($)	4389998M	2064242M
	7495M	79709M	769094M	534146M	1563614M	Total Assets ($)	3504469M	1746485M

M = $ thousand   MM = $ million

MANUFACTURING—Construction Machinery Manufacturing NAICS 333120

Comparative Historical Data					Current Data Sorted by Sales					
7		8		17	Type of Statement				3	14
11		11		10	Unqualified				3	7
2		9		7	Reviewed	1	1	1	2	2
3		3		2	Compiled		1			
19		34		33	Tax Returns	1	4	1	3	8	16
4/1/21-3/31/22 ALL		4/1/22-3/31/23 ALL		4/1/23-3/31/24 ALL	Other					
						17 (4/1-9/30/23)			52 (10/1/23-3/31/24)	
						0-1MM	1-3MM	3-5MM	5-10MM	10-25MM	25MM & OVER
42		65		69	NUMBER OF STATEMENTS	1	6	3	4	16	39
%		%		%	**ASSETS**	%	%	%	%	%	%
14.8		12.9		10.6	Cash & Equivalents					10.7	10.0
17.6		19.8		15.0	Trade Receivables (net)					14.2	17.0
33.2		32.7		34.5	Inventory					38.6	33.2
3.4		4.4		5.0	All Other Current					2.7	7.1
69.0		69.7		65.1	Total Current					66.3	67.4
20.2		18.7		22.1	Fixed Assets (net)					23.7	19.3
7.3		6.5		5.1	Intangibles (net)					3.1	5.9
3.5		5.1		7.7	All Other Non-Current					6.9	7.4
100.0		100.0		100.0	Total					100.0	100.0
					LIABILITIES						
6.0		6.1		7.1	Notes Payable-Short Term					7.9	6.7
1.9		4.2		2.6	Cur. Mat.-L.T.D.					2.7	2.7
11.8		15.8		9.9	Trade Payables					7.2	9.7
.1		.2		.1	Income Taxes Payable					.1	.2
14.1		14.4		14.2	All Other Current					15.9	13.4
34.0		40.7		34.0	Total Current					33.7	32.7
10.1		12.1		13.7	Long-Term Debt					12.2	10.2
.3		.4		.3	Deferred Taxes					.0	.4
5.7		5.0		7.7	All Other Non-Current					3.8	10.0
49.9		41.8		44.4	Net Worth					50.3	46.6
100.0		100.0		100.0	Total Liabilities & Net Worth					100.0	100.0
					INCOME DATA						
100.0		100.0		100.0	Net Sales					100.0	100.0
30.6		29.7		29.6	Gross Profit					29.6	25.0
23.8		24.9		22.3	Operating Expenses					22.1	17.3
6.8		4.8		7.4	Operating Profit					7.5	7.7
-1.5		.0		.7	All Other Expenses (net)					1.0	.4
8.3		4.8		6.7	Profit Before Taxes					6.5	7.3
					RATIOS						
4.1		3.6		3.9						5.0	3.3
2.2		2.1		2.1	Current					2.2	1.9
1.6		1.6		1.4						1.4	1.4
1.9		2.2		1.7						2.0	1.7
.9		1.0		.7	Quick					.8	.7
.5		.4		.3						.3	.4
20	18.2	20	18.6	17	21.1					15	24.0	28	13.0
32	11.5	43	8.5	37	9.8	Sales/Receivables				33	10.9	41	9.0
59	6.2	60	6.1	52	7.0					65	5.6	54	6.7
72	5.1	56	6.5	59	6.2					66	5.5	58	6.3
135	2.7	114	3.2	130	2.8	Cost of Sales/Inventory				159	2.3	122	3.0
203	1.8	192	1.9	215	1.7					228	1.6	166	2.2
16	22.4	21	17.4	16	22.6					14	25.3	18	20.0
28	13.0	35	10.4	25	14.5	Cost of Sales/Payables				16	23.5	26	13.9
44	8.3	51	7.1	41	8.9					40	9.2	39	9.3
3.2		2.8		2.7						2.6	2.7
4.3		4.6		4.6	Sales/Working Capital					4.7	5.3
8.0		7.8		10.3						10.0	10.7
53.8		26.3		28.8						44.6	31.0
(34)	14.5	(50)	10.6	(61)	7.7	EBIT/Interest				5.7	(32)	9.3
2.7		1.5		2.8						1.8	3.9
				63.9		21.1							146.2
		(17)	6.0	(26)	5.9	Net Profit + Depr., Dep., Amort./Cur. Mat. L/T/D				(17)	8.8
				2.5		1.9							2.2
.2		.1		.2						.3	.2
.5		.4		.5	Fixed/Worth					.5	.5
1.0		.8		1.6						1.2	1.6
.5		.6		.5						.3	.7
1.3		1.2		1.3	Debt/Worth					1.1	1.3
3.3		4.1		4.3						3.6	8.2
36.3		41.3		31.5						34.3	30.0
(37)	23.3	(55)	17.8	(58)	18.8	% Profit Before Taxes/Tangible Net Worth				(15)	16.9	(34)	21.2
4.3		8.7		10.3						.4	11.8
17.0		14.8		14.2						16.5	14.0
10.3		8.5		9.9	% Profit Before Taxes/Total Assets					10.0	10.3
2.7		1.5		3.8						.9	5.9
22.3		24.2		17.2						14.2	17.5
8.0		9.5		7.2	Sales/Net Fixed Assets					5.4	7.7
4.5		4.7		4.7						3.6	5.4
1.9		2.2		1.8						2.2	1.8
1.5		1.5		1.4	Sales/Total Assets					1.3	1.4
1.1		1.0		1.0						.9	1.1
1.0		1.0		1.1						1.2	1.0
(34)	1.9	(47)	1.9	(59)	2.5	% Depr., Dep., Amort./Sales				(14)	2.4	(36)	2.4
3.1		2.9		3.3						3.8	3.9
1.2		.8		.9							
(10)	2.3	(15)	2.1	(10)	2.1	% Officers', Directors', Owners' Comp/Sales					
8.3		3.3		5.9							
2403609M		3036638M		4032615M	Net Sales ($)	411M	13828M	11455M	27830M	250453M	3728638M
1890282M		2407536M		2954058M	Total Assets ($)	734M	9681M	13281M	16499M	200892M	2712971M

© RMA 2024 M = $ thousand MM = $ million
See Pages viii through xx for Explanation of Ratios and Data

MANUFACTURING—Mining Machinery and Equipment Manufacturing NAICS 333131

Current Data Sorted by Assets

0-500M	7 (4/1-9/30/23) 500M-2MM	2-10MM	17 (10/1/23-3/31/24) 10-50MM	50-100MM	100-250MM	Type of Statement	Comparative Historical Data 17 4/1/19-3/31/20 ALL	3 4/1/20-3/31/21 ALL
			1	1		Unqualified	1	2
			1			Reviewed	1	1
		1	1			Compiled	1	1
		3	14	2	1	Tax Returns	2	
			17			Other	17	3
%	%	5 %	15 %	3 %	1 %	**NUMBER OF STATEMENTS**	22 %	7 %
						ASSETS		
D	D		6.3			Cash & Equivalents	13.1	
A	A		24.9			Trade Receivables (net)	17.3	
T	T		48.1			Inventory	38.9	
A	A		4.1			All Other Current	2.8	
			83.5			Total Current	72.1	
N	N		12.9			Fixed Assets (net)	19.5	
O	O		.8			Intangibles (net)	4.1	
T	T		2.9			All Other Non-Current	4.3	
			100.0			Total	100.0	
A	A					**LIABILITIES**		
V	V		6.6			Notes Payable-Short Term	7.3	
A	A		1.4			Cur. Mat.-L.T.D.	2.4	
I	I		14.0			Trade Payables	38.6	
L	L		.3			Income Taxes Payable	.1	
A	A		12.7			All Other Current	10.2	
B	B		34.9			Total Current	58.6	
L	L		15.5			Long-Term Debt	10.5	
E	E		.4			Deferred Taxes	.4	
			7.7			All Other Non-Current	7.7	
			41.5			Net Worth	22.7	
			100.0			Total Liabilities & Net Worth	100.0	
						INCOME DATA		
			100.0			Net Sales	100.0	
			28.8			Gross Profit	30.1	
			20.7			Operating Expenses	25.8	
			8.2			Operating Profit	4.3	
			.2			All Other Expenses (net)	.5	
			8.0			Profit Before Taxes	3.8	
						RATIOS		
			3.5				3.5	
			2.6			Current	2.2	
			1.9				1.2	
			1.4				1.5	
			1.0			Quick	.8	
			.7				.4	
		34	10.8				28	13.1
		47	7.8			Sales/Receivables	38	9.6
		60	6.1				52	7.0
		94	3.9				68	5.4
		152	2.4			Cost of Sales/Inventory	146	2.5
		215	1.7				182	2.0
		23	15.6				32	11.3
		32	11.4			Cost of Sales/Payables	46	7.9
		58	6.3				64	5.7
			2.4					2.7
			4.4			Sales/Working Capital		4.7
			5.3					27.1
			85.3					12.0
			(14) 11.3			EBIT/Interest	(20)	5.1
			3.3					2.8
						Net Profit + Depr., Dep., Amort./Cur. Mat. L/T/D		
			.1					.2
			.3			Fixed/Worth		.7
			.5					1.7
			.5					.5
			.8			Debt/Worth		1.9
			1.1					4.4
			61.9					46.4
			(14) 28.3			% Profit Before Taxes/Tangible Net Worth	(19)	25.0
			1.4					9.7
			30.4					14.0
			19.5			% Profit Before Taxes/Total Assets		5.8
			1.0					2.8
			65.2					33.7
			20.9			Sales/Net Fixed Assets		9.6
			6.2					4.8
			2.7					2.5
			1.6			Sales/Total Assets		1.4
			1.2					1.1
			.3					.9
			(14) 1.5			% Depr., Dep., Amort./Sales	(20)	2.2
			2.1					3.2
						% Officers', Directors', Owners' Comp/Sales		
		53654M	739461M	469119M	205179M	Net Sales ($)	1033142M	389942M
		25479M	407802M	239236M	120693M	Total Assets ($)	567287M	320430M

M = $ thousand   MM = $ million
See Pages viii through xx for Explanation of Ratios and Data

© RMA 2024

MANUFACTURING—Mining Machinery and Equipment Manufacturing NAICS 333131

Comparative Historical Data | Current Data Sorted by Sales

				Type of Statement						
	2	2	1	Unqualified						1
	4	1	1	Reviewed						1
		1	1	Compiled					1	
	2		1	Tax Returns				1	1	17
	15	15	20	Other		7 (4/1-9/30/23)		2	17 (10/1/23-3/31/24)	
	4/1/21-3/31/22 ALL	4/1/22-3/31/23 ALL	4/1/23-3/31/24 ALL		0-1MM	1-3MM	3-5MM	5-10MM	10-25MM	25MM & OVER
	23	19	24	NUMBER OF STATEMENTS				3	2	19
	%	%	%	ASSETS	%	%	%	%	%	%
	8.7	7.9	11.0	Cash & Equivalents						8.1
	23.4	28.0	24.8	Trade Receivables (net)	D	D	D			24.4
	29.6	39.6	38.7	Inventory	A	A	A			43.9
	4.1	2.8	3.7	All Other Current	T	T	T			4.3
	65.7	78.2	78.2	Total Current	A	A	A			80.7
	18.6	16.9	15.7	Fixed Assets (net)						12.1
	10.7	2.4	2.6	Intangibles (net)	N	N	N			2.9
	5.0	2.5	3.5	All Other Non-Current	O	O	O			4.3
	100.0	100.0	100.0	Total	T	T	T			100.0
				LIABILITIES						
	7.8	7.6	4.9	Notes Payable-Short Term	A	A	A			5.6
	3.8	1.0	3.9	Cur. Mat.-L.T.D.	V	V	V			4.5
	12.1	16.6	15.0	Trade Payables	A	A	A			15.4
	.7	.9	.9	Income Taxes Payable	I	I	I			.3
	17.8	14.8	10.0	All Other Current	L	L	L			11.9
	42.2	40.9	34.6	Total Current	A	A	A			37.6
	15.8	15.2	19.7	Long-Term Debt	B	B	B			19.5
	.6	.4	.3	Deferred Taxes	L	L	L			.4
	1.1	5.3	6.9	All Other Non-Current	E	E	E			8.0
	40.2	38.4	38.5	Net Worth						34.4
	100.0	100.0	100.0	Total Liabilities & Net Worth						100.0
				INCOME DATA						
	100.0	100.0	100.0	Net Sales						100.0
	30.5	36.7	30.2	Gross Profit						28.2
	27.7	28.5	21.1	Operating Expenses						19.8
	2.8	8.2	9.2	Operating Profit						8.4
	-.5	1.0	.6	All Other Expenses (net)						.7
	3.3	7.2	8.6	Profit Before Taxes						7.6
				RATIOS						
	2.7	4.3	4.0							3.5
	1.7	2.0	2.6	Current						2.6
	.9	1.4	1.8							1.7
	1.2	1.9	1.6							1.4
	.8	.9	1.1	Quick						.9
	.5	.6	.7							.5
46	7.9	42	8.7	35	10.3	Sales/Receivables			34	10.6
57	6.4	55	6.6	44	8.3				47	7.8
81	4.5	78	4.7	54	6.7				54	6.7
48	7.6	76	4.8	49	7.5	Cost of Sales/Inventory			94	3.9
122	3.0	130	2.8	101	3.6				107	3.4
182	2.0	174	2.1	166	2.2				174	2.1
19	18.9	30	12.2	18	19.9	Cost of Sales/Payables			22	16.5
34	10.6	42	8.6	28	13.1				32	11.4
57	6.4	79	4.6	54	6.7				58	6.3
	2.6	2.5	2.5	Sales/Working Capital						2.6
	7.1	5.8	4.5							4.4
	-42.8	7.1	8.1							7.3
	21.6	33.9	30.1							52.3
(20)	7.4	(18)	14.6	(22)	11.3	EBIT/Interest			(18)	9.9
	1.3	5.6	3.5							2.4
				Net Profit + Depr., Dep., Amort./Cur. Mat. L/T/D						
	.2	.2	.1							.1
	.5	.3	.4	Fixed/Worth						.3
	4.2	1.3	1.2							.7
	.6	.6	.6							.7
	1.6	1.4	1.0	Debt/Worth						.9
	20.8	6.1	3.3							15.5
	39.9	55.4	64.3	% Profit Before Taxes/Tangible Net Worth						63.0
(18)	20.3	(17)	37.8	(21)	42.0				(16)	35.8
	4.7	10.2	4.2							1.9
	11.3	22.4	30.4	% Profit Before Taxes/Total Assets						30.3
	4.0	8.8	22.8							19.5
	.8	3.9	3.1							1.0
	19.1	39.1	59.4	Sales/Net Fixed Assets						65.0
	11.5	16.2	16.3							20.9
	6.4	7.0	6.3							6.5
	1.8	2.2	2.7	Sales/Total Assets						2.7
	1.2	1.6	1.8							1.7
	1.0	1.3	1.5							1.5
	1.6	.4	.4	% Depr., Dep., Amort./Sales						.3
(19)	2.6	(16)	1.6	(22)	1.5				(18)	1.5
	4.7	2.9	2.6							2.3
				% Officers', Directors' Owners' Comp/Sales						
	921527M	797723M	1467413M	Net Sales ($)				24276M	29378M	1413759M
	698140M	464549M	793210M	Total Assets ($)				10904M	14575M	767731M

M = $ thousand   MM = $ million
See Pages viii through xx for Explanation of Ratios and Data

© RMA 2024

MANUFACTURING—Oil and Gas Field Machinery and Equipment Manufacturing NAICS 333132

Current Data Sorted by Assets

						Type of Statement		Comparative Historical Data		
				2		Unqualified		9		9
			2	1	2	Reviewed		7		4
		1	2	2		Compiled		6		3
	2	1				Tax Returns		3		1
1	2	11	17	7	9	Other		57		40
	7 (4/1-9/30/23)		53 (10/1/23-3/31/24)					4/1/19- 3/31/20		4/1/20- 3/31/21
0-500M	500M-2MM	2-10MM	10-50MM	50-100MM	100-250MM			ALL		ALL
1	4	13	21	10	11	NUMBER OF STATEMENTS		82		57
%	%	%	%	%	%	ASSETS		%		%
			14.6	6.3	3.6	6.7	Cash & Equivalents	7.6		13.5
			39.4	23.1	27.0	21.8	Trade Receivables (net)	22.0		16.8
			17.3	34.4	33.1	26.1	Inventory	28.4		23.2
			5.0	2.2	5.0	8.5	All Other Current	2.8		3.9
			76.2	66.0	68.7	63.2	Total Current	60.8		57.5
			18.3	21.7	13.9	20.7	Fixed Assets (net)	29.7		30.6
			.1	8.0	10.1	6.5	Intangibles (net)	4.9		5.5
			5.3	4.3	7.4	9.6	All Other Non-Current	4.5		6.4
			100.0	100.0	100.0	100.0	Total	100.0		100.0
							LIABILITIES			
			4.2	6.4	6.2	2.4	Notes Payable-Short Term	11.7		10.8
			5.6	1.9	2.5	1.6	Cur. Mat.-L.T.D.	2.0		2.0
			7.7	8.9	13.5	11.5	Trade Payables	11.8		9.0
			.9	.0	.0	.1	Income Taxes Payable	.2		.2
			11.3	10.7	12.2	13.8	All Other Current	10.5		9.6
			29.6	27.8	34.4	29.4	Total Current	36.2		31.6
			11.9	9.8	12.5	14.9	Long-Term Debt	23.1		24.9
			.0	.4	.1	.3	Deferred Taxes	.6		.4
			1.2	7.6	10.2	1.7	All Other Non-Current	3.9		2.8
			57.3	54.3	42.8	53.6	Net Worth	36.3		40.4
			100.0	100.0	100.0	100.0	Total Liabilties & Net Worth	100.0		100.0
							INCOME DATA			
			100.0	100.0	100.0	100.0	Net Sales	100.0		100.0
			49.1	37.2	26.9	30.5	Gross Profit	36.1		38.1
			33.9	24.7	18.7	18.7	Operating Expenses	28.9		37.8
			15.2	12.4	8.3	11.8	Operating Profit	7.2		.3
			.4	3.3	1.9	-1.0	All Other Expenses (net)	2.5		.5
			14.8	9.1	6.3	12.8	Profit Before Taxes	4.8		-.2
							RATIOS			
			6.8	5.5	3.3	3.3		3.5		3.7
			3.3	2.4	2.0	2.0	Current	2.3		2.1
			1.6	1.8	1.5	1.5		1.3		1.3
			4.8	2.4	1.3	1.3		1.8		1.9
			1.5	1.2	.9	1.2	Quick	.9		1.0
			1.0	.6	.7	.6		.5		.5
		41	8.8	34	10.7	48	7.6	55	6.6			38	9.5	36	10.1
		59	6.2	54	6.7	54	6.8	70	5.2	Sales/Receivables	53	6.9	53	6.9
		81	4.5	74	4.9	72	5.1	76	4.8		70	5.2	64	5.7
		0	UND	96	3.8	54	6.8	29	12.8		58	6.3	31	11.9
		37	9.9	166	2.2	111	3.3	135	2.7	Cost of Sales/Inventory	101	3.6	122	3.0
		166	2.2	243	1.5	135	2.7	203	1.8		203	1.8	203	1.8
		11	33.2	23	16.0	17	21.6	32	11.4		25	14.4	22	16.5
		16	23.4	36	10.1	36	10.0	38	9.5	Cost of Sales/Payables	35	10.5	36	10.1
		56	6.5	42	8.6	66	5.5	62	5.9		57	6.4	63	5.8
			2.4	2.0	3.2	1.3		2.7		1.8
			3.9	3.1	4.3	4.2	Sales/Working Capital	5.5		4.7
			12.0	5.3	NM	8.2		14.0		16.3
			122.3	43.0				20.2		8.2
			36.4	(19) 9.7			EBIT/Interest	(74) 6.2	(51)	2.2
			12.4	1.6				1.4		-1.5
							Net Profit + Depr., Dep., Amort./Cur. Mat. L/T/D	5.4		5.1
								(23) 3.4	(12)	2.4
								1.5		-.4
			.0	.2	.2	.2		.3		.2
			.1	.4	.4	.5	Fixed/Worth	.6		.7
			.5	1.0	NM	.8		1.2		1.4
			.3	.3	.8	.5		.5		.5
			.6	1.2	1.1	1.0	Debt/Worth	1.1		1.1
			2.0	2.4	NM	2.6		2.8		3.1
			88.7	50.5		61.9		43.3		11.9
			40.8	(19) 38.0		31.7	% Profit Before Taxes/Tangible Net Worth	(72) 18.0	(52)	4.2
			21.4	10.8		18.2		5.4		-10.6
			50.2	26.2	22.0	19.3		17.5		7.9
			18.9	17.1	7.7	13.3	% Profit Before Taxes/Total Assets	8.1		1.7
			12.7	3.3	1.8	9.3		1.0		-7.2
			146.5	12.6	29.0	9.0		11.3		13.0
			10.2	6.8	8.8	6.4	Sales/Net Fixed Assets	5.9		4.8
			6.7	3.6	6.9	4.3		3.0		2.1
			3.2	1.8	2.0	1.7		2.1		1.6
			2.0	1.3	1.5	1.2	Sales/Total Assets	1.5		1.1
			1.4	1.0	1.0	.8		.9		.6
				1.1				1.3		1.9
			(20)	2.3			% Depr., Dep., Amort./Sales	(64) 3.0	(40)	4.8
				9.2				5.8		9.0
							% Officers', Directors' Owners' Comp/Sales	1.4		
								(14) 3.6		
								7.9		
2894M	6041M	150086M	644261M	1141893M	2152072M	Net Sales ($)		4405984M		2150759M
36M	2823M	76916M	504983M	755192M	1769521M	Total Assets ($)		3365358M		2559860M

M = $ thousand   MM = $ million
See Pages viii through xx for Explanation of Ratios and Data

© RMA 2024

MANUFACTURING—Oil and Gas Field Machinery and Equipment Manufacturing NAICS 333132

Comparative Historical Data | Current Data Sorted by Sales

						Type of Statement							
		9		7		5	Unqualified						5
		6		6		4	Reviewed					1	3
		3		2		1	Compiled					1	
		2		2		3	Tax Returns		2		1		
		19		38		47	Other		3		5	11	27
		4/1/21-3/31/22 ALL		4/1/22-3/31/23 ALL		4/1/23-3/31/24 ALL		0-1MM	7 (4/1-9/30/23) 1-3MM	3-5MM	53 (10/1/23-3/31/24) 5-10MM	10-25MM	25MM & OVER
		39		55		60	NUMBER OF STATEMENTS		5	1	6	13	35
		%		%		%	ASSETS	%	%	%	%	%	%
		11.4		11.1		9.8	Cash & Equivalents					6.6	6.2
		24.0		25.1		25.4	Trade Receivables (net)					29.7	25.2
		21.5		23.7		28.5	Inventory	D				30.0	28.7
		6.9		5.1		4.3	All Other Current	A				2.2	5.3
		63.9		65.1		68.0	Total Current	T				68.4	65.4
		24.9		23.5		18.9	Fixed Assets (net)	A				21.3	19.3
		6.2		2.4		5.8	Intangibles (net)					4.4	8.1
		5.0		9.0		7.2	All Other Non-Current	N				5.9	7.2
		100.0		100.0		100.0	Total	O				100.0	100.0
							LIABILITIES	T					
		3.4		9.2		6.5	Notes Payable-Short Term					6.3	4.7
		1.4		1.6		2.6	Cur. Mat.-L.T.D.	A				5.9	2.1
		11.8		14.3		11.8	Trade Payables	V				8.3	11.3
		.0		.1		.2	Income Taxes Payable	A				.9	.0
		15.2		12.4		11.8	All Other Current	I				15.9	11.2
		31.9		37.7		33.0	Total Current	L				37.3	29.3
		11.8		13.9		14.5	Long-Term Debt	A				14.7	11.7
		.5		.2		.2	Deferred Taxes	B				.6	.2
		5.9		5.6		4.9	All Other Non-Current	L				9.3	4.6
		49.9		42.6		47.3	Net Worth	E				38.1	54.2
		100.0		100.0		100.0	Total Liabilities & Net Worth					100.0	100.0
							INCOME DATA						
		100.0		100.0		100.0	Net Sales					100.0	100.0
		31.9		35.0		37.6	Gross Profit					37.4	33.3
		29.0		26.2		24.6	Operating Expenses					29.3	21.3
		2.8		8.8		13.0	Operating Profit					8.1	12.0
		-1.2		1.0		1.6	All Other Expenses (net)					3.5	1.1
		4.0		7.8		11.4	Profit Before Taxes					4.6	10.9
							RATIOS						
		4.8		3.3		3.4						2.5	3.6
		2.1		1.9		2.2	Current					2.2	2.2
		1.4		1.2		1.5						1.5	1.6
		2.0		1.7		1.8						1.9	1.6
		1.1		1.1		1.2	Quick					.8	1.2
		.8		.5		.7						.4	.7
58	6.3	44	8.3	37	9.8						37	9.9	51	7.1
74	4.9	64	5.7	55	6.6	Sales/Receivables					54	6.7	60	6.1
99	3.7	87	4.2	74	4.9						65	5.6	76	4.8
9	38.5	7	48.9	30	12.1						1	331.1	55	6.6
130	2.8	76	4.8	126	2.9	Cost of Sales/Inventory					152	2.4	135	2.7
243	1.5	159	2.3	182	2.0						174	2.1	203	1.8
27	13.6	20	18.1	15	24.0						14	26.0	21	17.8
46	7.9	47	7.7	33	11.0	Cost of Sales/Payables					29	12.4	38	9.5
74	4.9	78	4.7	53	6.9						38	9.7	56	6.5
		1.2		2.7		2.2						2.5	2.2
		2.8		5.3		4.3	Sales/Working Capital					4.7	4.1
		7.6		17.3		9.9						15.0	6.6
		15.1		19.1		43.4						29.6	45.3
(34)	6.4	(47)	4.4	(54)	11.9	EBIT/Interest					7.1	(30)	9.7
		.8		1.5		3.9						1.4	3.8
		21.9				29.6	Net Profit + Depr., Dep.,					57.6	
(14)	6.1			(13)	9.8	Amort./Cur. Mat. L/T/D					(10)	10.0
		2.7				3.0						4.6
		.2		.2		.1						.1	.2
		.5		.5		.4	Fixed/Worth					.6	.4
		1.1		1.2		.8						1.4	.7
		.4		.6		.4						.8	.5
		1.0		1.4		1.1	Debt/Worth					1.9	.9
		3.1		4.4		2.7						4.0	2.0
		25.4		45.1		61.9						64.2	51.9
(37)	7.7	(49)	13.7	(54)	38.1	% Profit Before Taxes/Tangible Net Worth					(11)	23.9	(33)	37.7
		-.8		2.6		19.5						15.7	12.1
		9.0		21.1		29.3						27.6	22.3
		3.4		6.4		16.3	% Profit Before Taxes/Total Assets					10.1	13.3
		-1.4		.5		7.0						2.6	6.4
		12.5		24.7		16.8						63.0	11.8
		5.7		7.0		8.6	Sales/Net Fixed Assets					8.8	7.7
		1.7		3.1		4.5						3.0	4.3
		1.3		2.1		2.0						3.2	1.7
		.8		1.3		1.5	Sales/Total Assets					1.6	1.4
		.5		.9		1.1						1.3	1.1
		1.8		1.1		1.1						.6	1.3
(36)	3.1	(40)	2.3	(46)	2.3	% Depr., Dep., Amort./Sales					(12)	1.1	(29)	2.7
		5.0		4.4		4.4						4.3	4.6
							% Officers', Directors' Owners' Comp/Sales						
		1879479M		2369577M		4097247M	Net Sales ($)		8935M	4902M	47974M	231332M	3804104M
		2046668M		2056080M		3109471M	Total Assets ($)		2859M	2209M	36102M	172171M	2896130M

© RMA 2024   M = $ thousand   MM = $ million
See Pages viii through xx for Explanation of Ratios and Data

MANUFACTURING—Food Product Machinery Manufacturing NAICS 333241

Current Data Sorted by Assets | **Comparative Historical Data**

0-500M	500M-2MM	2-10MM	10-50MM	50-100MM	100-250MM		Type of Statement		4/1/19-3/31/20 ALL		4/1/20-3/31/21 ALL
							Unqualified		8		3
				7	2	1	Reviewed		10		6
			3				Compiled		3		1
		6	2				Tax Returns		14		2
	10 (4/1-9/30/23)	5	11	4	3		Other		24		17
		11	34 (10/1/23-3/31/24) 23	6	4		NUMBER OF STATEMENTS		59		29
%	%	%	%	%	%		ASSETS		%		%
D	D	14.8	19.4				Cash & Equivalents		15.7		18.7
A	A	18.2	22.7				Trade Receivables (net)		17.8		16.1
T	T	34.5	27.8				Inventory		27.4		24.8
A	A	3.7	3.7				All Other Current		2.6		2.3
		71.2	73.6				Total Current		63.6		61.8
N	N	14.3	14.0				Fixed Assets (net)		22.0		26.2
O	O	2.8	3.2				Intangibles (net)		5.1		3.0
T	T	11.7	9.1				All Other Non-Current		9.2		8.9
		100.0	100.0				Total		100.0		100.0
A	A						LIABILITIES				
V	V	10.0	5.2				Notes Payable-Short Term		5.3		4.6
A	A	2.6	2.2				Cur. Mat.-L.T.D.		2.3		3.0
I	I	33.6	11.3				Trade Payables		10.9		8.0
L	L	.7	.0				Income Taxes Payable		.4		.2
A	A	12.7	27.9				All Other Current		25.4		21.0
B	B	59.5	46.7				Total Current		44.2		36.8
L	L	8.6	13.9				Long-Term Debt		13.6		17.9
E	E	1.1	.0				Deferred Taxes		.3		.2
		7.8	1.1				All Other Non-Current		2.1		4.2
		22.9	38.3				Net Worth		39.8		40.9
		100.0	100.0				Total Liabilities & Net Worth		100.0		100.0
							INCOME DATA				
		100.0	100.0				Net Sales		100.0		100.0
		37.8	31.3				Gross Profit		36.5		32.8
		30.8	24.6				Operating Expenses		28.3		27.3
		6.9	6.8				Operating Profit		8.2		5.6
		1.5	.6				All Other Expenses (net)		1.0		.5
		5.4	6.1				Profit Before Taxes		7.2		5.1
							RATIOS				
		4.2	2.5						2.2		3.6
		2.0	1.4				Current		1.6		1.9
		.5	1.2						1.0		1.3
		2.0	1.4						1.5		2.0
		.7	.9				Quick		.9		1.2
		.5	.5						.4		.5
		13 28.2	24 15.2					20	18.1	23	15.6
		23 15.6	41 9.0				Sales/Receivables	35	10.3	32	11.3
		51 7.1	76 4.8					51	7.2	49	7.4
		19 19.2	31 11.8					41	8.8	26	14.3
		89 4.1	101 3.6				Cost of Sales/Inventory	94	3.9	91	4.0
		215 1.7	174 2.1					135	2.7	159	2.3
		20 18.4	14 25.2					14	26.3	13	28.5
		35 10.4	25 14.8				Cost of Sales/Payables	24	15.3	25	14.7
		107 3.4	38 9.7					41	8.9	35	10.4
		3.4	3.8						4.0		3.0
		5.6	6.9				Sales/Working Capital		6.9		5.5
		-9.1	17.0						999.8		NM
		56.3	38.3						50.0		34.1
		(10) 4.6	(19) 10.1				EBIT/Interest	(46)	8.9	(24)	6.7
		-.4	4.4						3.1		.2
							Net Profit + Depr., Dep., Amort./Cur. Mat. L/T/D		29.9		17.1
								(20)	9.3	(10)	4.7
									3.1		.6
		.1	.2						.2		.3
		.2	.4				Fixed/Worth		.5		.5
		.9	.6						1.1		2.4
		.7	.7						.7		.7
		1.9	1.7				Debt/Worth		1.0		1.2
		3.0	4.5						2.6		3.6
		67.7	43.0						42.2		36.4
		(10) 34.6	(22) 22.1				% Profit Before Taxes/Tangible Net Worth	(53)	19.1	(26)	18.9
		-.3	10.4						3.8		5.0
		28.4	20.1						21.5		13.8
		8.3	7.7				% Profit Before Taxes/Total Assets		9.4		9.4
		-.9	4.1						1.1		-.1
		78.6	31.6						25.9		16.1
		24.5	13.4				Sales/Net Fixed Assets		9.4		7.6
		14.0	7.3						3.8		4.0
		3.6	2.4						2.2		2.2
		2.1	1.5				Sales/Total Assets		1.5		1.6
		1.1	1.2						1.2		1.1
			.7						1.6		.9
		(21)	1.2				% Depr., Dep., Amort./Sales	(47)	2.4	(26)	2.7
			1.8						5.3		5.6
							% Officers', Directors' Owners' Comp/Sales		1.7		
								(15)	1.9		
									3.4		
		119161M	1090620M	553473M	1262780M		Net Sales ($)		3252874M		1352623M
		50808M	635217M	367155M	665255M		Total Assets ($)		2414049M		876081M

© RMA 2024

M = $ thousand   MM = $ million
See Pages viii through xx for Explanation of Ratios and Data

MANUFACTURING—Food Product Machinery Manufacturing NAICS 333241

Comparative Historical Data				Current Data Sorted by Sales						
			Type of Statement							
4	6	10	Unqualified							10
2	6	3	Reviewed							3
3	1		Compiled							
4	7	8	Tax Returns		1		1	5		1
18	21	23	Other		1		3	4		15
4/1/21-3/31/22	4/1/22-3/31/23	4/1/23-3/31/24		10 (4/1-9/30/23)				34 (10/1/23-3/31/24)			
ALL	ALL	ALL		0-1MM	1-3MM	3-5MM	5-10MM	10-25MM	25MM & OVER	
31	41	44	NUMBER OF STATEMENTS		2		4	9		29
%	%	%	ASSETS	%	%	%	%	%		%
21.3	19.4	15.3	Cash & Equivalents	D	D					15.0
19.5	21.9	21.2	Trade Receivables (net)	A	A					22.3
21.2	28.9	30.4	Inventory	T	T					29.7
7.3	5.0	4.2	All Other Current	A	A					3.9
69.4	75.2	71.1	Total Current							70.9
23.4	14.8	16.3	Fixed Assets (net)	N	N					18.3
3.1	5.6	3.3	Intangibles (net)	O	O					3.5
4.1	4.4	9.3	All Other Non-Current	T	T					7.4
100.0	100.0	100.0	Total							100.0
			LIABILITIES	A	A					
3.0	3.4	5.9	Notes Payable-Short Term	V	V					4.9
6.3	4.1	2.7	Cur. Mat.-L.T.D.	A	A					3.0
11.9	10.2	16.1	Trade Payables	I	I					11.1
.1	.3	.4	Income Taxes Payable	L	L					.3
23.1	25.0	22.9	All Other Current	A	A					24.3
44.3	43.0	47.9	Total Current	B	B					43.5
14.3	11.7	13.9	Long-Term Debt	L	L					16.0
.2	.3	.4	Deferred Taxes	E	E					.2
5.9	5.2	3.3	All Other Non-Current							2.1
35.3	39.8	34.4	Net Worth							38.2
100.0	100.0	100.0	Total Liabilties & Net Worth							100.0
			INCOME DATA							
100.0	100.0	100.0	Net Sales							100.0
35.9	31.6	31.8	Gross Profit							29.4
28.0	24.6	24.7	Operating Expenses							21.8
7.9	7.0	7.2	Operating Profit							7.6
-1.9	-.3	1.0	All Other Expenses (net)							.9
9.8	7.3	6.2	Profit Before Taxes							6.7
			RATIOS							
2.7	3.4	2.5								2.1
1.7	1.8	1.7	Current							1.6
1.2	1.3	1.2								1.3
1.8	1.8	1.4								1.3
.9	.9	.7	Quick							.7
.6	.6	.5								.5
31	11.8	32	11.4	24	15.5				28	12.9
43	8.5	49	7.5	37	9.8	Sales/Receivables			41	9.0
55	6.6	59	6.2	65	5.6				60	6.1
24	15.0	34	10.7	33	11.2				35	10.4
91	4.0	87	4.2	101	3.6	Cost of Sales/Inventory			104	3.5
152	2.4	159	2.3	174	2.1				166	2.2
17	21.2	16	22.2	15	24.4				14	25.2
33	10.9	27	13.4	24	15.0	Cost of Sales/Payables			24	15.3
48	7.6	41	8.8	38	9.5				38	9.7
3.3	2.9	3.5	Sales/Working Capital							3.5
5.8	5.1	6.8								6.8
9.2	10.9	16.6								16.2
121.8	48.0	29.6								33.5
(26) 19.9	(34) 17.5	(38) 8.2	EBIT/Interest						(25)	9.6
1.5	1.9	2.0								3.0
	17.3	27.8	Net Profit + Depr., Dep.,							16.3
(13) 11.9	(13) 5.6	Amort./Cur. Mat. L/T/D							(11)	5.6
	2.3	.5								.5
.2	.1	.2								.2
.5	.3	.4	Fixed/Worth							.5
6.0	1.5	.6								.7
.7	.5	.7								.8
1.6	1.6	1.7	Debt/Worth							1.7
14.2	5.8	3.7								4.0
67.1	48.8	47.6	% Profit Before Taxes/Tangible							46.7
(25) 32.9	(34) 31.1	(42) 26.4	Net Worth						(28)	30.1
15.2	14.8	11.6								14.4
26.2	21.2	20.1	% Profit Before Taxes/Total							19.4
15.3	12.5	10.0	Assets							12.3
1.0	3.7	4.2								4.5
18.0	30.1	28.6								20.8
10.3	13.0	13.3	Sales/Net Fixed Assets							10.9
2.9	7.7	7.4								6.8
2.0	2.5	2.5								2.4
1.2	1.5	1.6	Sales/Total Assets							1.7
1.0	1.2	1.2								1.3
1.2	1.0	.7								.7
(27) 2.2	(32) 1.4	(40) 1.2	% Depr., Dep., Amort./Sales						(28)	1.2
4.3	2.8	2.0								2.0
		1.5	% Officers', Directors'							
	(10) 2.8	Owners' Comp/Sales								
		4.9								
727775M	1972221M	3026034M	Net Sales ($)		4941M		33574M	141778M		2845741M
511810M	1311203M	1718435M	Total Assets ($)		4183M		22135M	77986M		1614131M

M = $ thousand   MM = $ million
See Pages viii through xx for Explanation of Ratios and Data

© RMA 2024

MANUFACTURING—All Other Industrial Machinery Manufacturing   NAICS 333248

Current Data Sorted by Assets | Comparative Historical Data

							Type of Statement				
			1	6	4	2	Unqualified		29		16
		3	19	2	1	Reviewed		35		27
		9	6		1	Compiled		17		6
	3	4	1			Tax Returns		29		12
1	7	21	38	22	17	Other		120		83
	36 (4/1-9/30/23)		132 (10/1/23-3/31/24)					4/1/19-3/31/20		4/1/20-3/31/21
0-500M	500M-2MM	2-10MM	10-50MM	50-100MM	100-250MM			ALL		ALL
1	10	38	70	28	21	NUMBER OF STATEMENTS		230		144
%	%	%	%	%	%	ASSETS		%		%
	21.2	15.1	13.5	13.8	12.8	Cash & Equivalents		12.6		16.5
	22.3	19.9	19.8	18.8	15.4	Trade Receivables (net)		22.8		20.4
	19.0	29.4	30.6	24.2	23.1	Inventory		27.4		24.3
	4.0	2.9	4.0	4.6	3.6	All Other Current		3.9		4.3
	66.5	67.4	67.8	61.4	54.9	Total Current		66.7		65.4
	19.9	15.8	18.3	21.5	18.9	Fixed Assets (net)		20.4		20.0
	5.6	9.0	5.5	7.7	12.8	Intangibles (net)		6.8		7.6
	8.0	7.8	8.5	9.4	13.4	All Other Non-Current		6.1		7.0
	100.0	100.0	100.0	100.0	100.0	Total		100.0		100.0
						LIABILITIES				
	20.6	5.7	3.4	3.5	3.1	Notes Payable-Short Term		7.7		5.4
	1.7	2.5	1.8	2.6	1.6	Cur. Mat.-L.T.D.		2.5		3.0
	13.4	9.2	8.1	6.9	7.6	Trade Payables		11.8		9.9
	1.3	.0	.2	.2	.1	Income Taxes Payable		.4		.2
	33.1	14.4	22.6	14.9	26.4	All Other Current		17.6		17.3
	70.0	31.8	36.1	28.2	38.8	Total Current		39.9		35.7
	2.7	14.3	7.3	11.0	13.3	Long-Term Debt		12.3		16.3
	.0	.1	.1	.0	.5	Deferred Taxes		.2		.4
	.1	7.7	3.9	11.9	4.9	All Other Non-Current		5.1		7.6
	27.3	46.1	52.6	49.0	42.5	Net Worth		42.4		40.1
	100.0	100.0	100.0	100.0	100.0	Total Liabilties & Net Worth		100.0		100.0
						INCOME DATA				
	100.0	100.0	100.0	100.0	100.0	Net Sales		100.0		100.0
	39.5	34.5	30.8	29.6	28.1	Gross Profit		33.8		33.5
	33.2	29.6	23.4	20.4	21.4	Operating Expenses		27.7		29.0
	6.3	4.9	7.4	9.2	6.7	Operating Profit		6.0		4.5
	-.5	.9	-.1	1.7	.8	All Other Expenses (net)		1.2		-.8
	6.7	4.0	7.5	7.5	5.9	Profit Before Taxes		4.9		5.3
						RATIOS				
	2.0	4.2	2.7	3.5	2.7			2.9		3.3
	1.2	2.4	1.9	2.2	1.5	Current		1.8		2.0
	.4	1.4	1.5	1.5	1.1			1.3		1.3
	1.7	2.2	1.6	1.8	1.0			1.6		1.8
	.7	1.1	1.0	1.4	.8	Quick		.9		1.1
	.2	.6	.5	.7	.5			.5		.6
1	278.2	26 14.1	32 11.5	33 11.1	41 8.9		30	12.2	33	10.9
41	8.9	38 9.6	50 7.3	57 6.4	50 7.3	Sales/Receivables	45	8.1	51	7.1
51	7.2	60 6.1	64 5.7	83 4.4	62 5.9		62	5.9	66	5.5
0	UND	30 12.2	60 6.1	38 9.5	72 5.1		39	9.3	42	8.6
20	18.6	87 4.2	114 3.2	94 3.9	107 3.4	Cost of Sales/Inventory	81	4.5	87	4.2
51	7.1	159 2.3	182 2.1	174 2.1	159 2.3		146	2.5	146	2.5
0	UND	11 32.7	13 27.7	14 25.2	24 14.9		15	24.7	14	26.2
37	9.9	22 16.5	23 15.6	25 14.5	30 12.2	Cost of Sales/Payables	27	13.4	27	13.7
55	6.6	42 8.6	38 9.7	40 9.1	48 7.6		47	7.8	48	7.6
	7.1	2.8	3.3	2.0	3.0			3.7		2.8
	55.0	5.5	4.4	4.2	8.6	Sales/Working Capital		6.5		4.4
	-3.9	10.1	6.9	12.0	17.2			15.6		9.3
		10.7	50.8	34.4	33.6			19.9		19.4
		(33) 3.7	(58) 10.9	(22) 7.1	(19) 9.1	EBIT/Interest	(190)	5.8	(124)	5.5
		.9	3.5	2.0	1.5			1.2		.6
			18.0			Net Profit + Depr., Dep.,		15.3		16.9
		(19) 11.0				Amort./Cur. Mat. L/T/D	(54)	3.7	(36)	4.6
			2.7					1.3		1.9
	.3	.1	.2	.2	.4			.2		.2
	.7	.3	.4	.4	.6	Fixed/Worth		.5		.4
	-2.1	1.1	.7	1.8	1.1			1.2		1.4
	.8	.5	.5	.5	.7			.5		.7
	1.7	1.0	.9	1.1	1.7	Debt/Worth		1.3		1.5
	-5.8	3.1	1.8	6.2	9.6			3.8		5.6
		42.7	38.0	30.6	32.9	% Profit Before Taxes/Tangible		38.6		45.0
		(33) 19.0	(67) 18.6	(26) 25.0	(17) 17.9	Net Worth	(200)	18.8	(127)	18.2
		3.1	3.1	17.6	5.6			4.2		4.5
	59.5	18.0	16.8	13.2	12.8	% Profit Before Taxes/Total		15.3		15.0
	7.6	6.2	9.2	9.6	5.2	Assets		6.6		6.7
	.8	.7	1.8	4.1	2.6			.3		-.2
	972.7	54.9	21.0	10.0	9.1			25.9		20.7
	15.1	19.7	11.4	7.9	5.0	Sales/Net Fixed Assets		10.6		8.3
	5.5	6.2	4.7	4.5	4.2			5.3		4.5
	3.8	2.5	1.8	1.6	1.4			2.2		1.9
	2.9	1.8	1.3	1.3	1.1	Sales/Total Assets		1.7		1.3
	1.7	1.2	1.1	.9	.7			1.1		.9
		.4	.5	1.5	1.8			1.0		1.2
		(31) 1.4	(64) 1.5	(27) 2.3	(19) 2.2	% Depr., Dep., Amort./Sales	(189)	2.0	(108)	2.3
		3.3	2.6	4.6	4.0			3.7		3.7
		2.0				% Officers', Directors'		1.6		1.5
		(12) 3.6				Owners' Comp/Sales	(55)	3.6	(25)	3.6
		4.7						6.9		6.7
631M	35884M	409595M	2366790M	2484983M	3211299M	Net Sales ($)		8014069M		5438016M
106M	12597M	231874M	1703861M	1978334M	3102196M	Total Assets ($)		5647091M		4773408M

© RMA 2024

M = $ thousand   MM = $ million
See Pages viii through xx for Explanation of Ratios and Data

MANUFACTURING—All Other Industrial Machinery Manufacturing NAICS 333248

Comparative Historical Data / Current Data Sorted by Sales

						Type of Statement							
		14		16		13	Unqualified					1	12
		18		18		25	Reviewed				1	12	12
		11		14		16	Compiled			1	6	4	5
		9		11		8	Tax Returns		2	1	2	3	2
		83		95		106	Other	1	5	4	5	26	65
		4/1/21-		4/1/22-		4/1/23-			36 (4/1-9/30/23)			132 (10/1/23-3/31/24)	
		3/31/22		3/31/23		3/31/24		0-1MM	1-3MM	3-5MM	5-10MM	10-25MM	25MM & OVER
		ALL		ALL		ALL							
		135		154		168	NUMBER OF STATEMENTS	1	7	7	13	46	94
		%		%		%	ASSETS	%	%	%	%	%	%
		16.8		15.6		14.3	Cash & Equivalents				14.1	16.0	13.0
		19.6		21.1		19.4	Trade Receivables (net)				17.3	17.0	20.6
		24.6		25.8		27.4	Inventory				33.1	29.6	26.7
		4.4		4.6		3.8	All Other Current				3.4	3.2	4.6
		65.5		67.1		64.9	Total Current				67.9	65.8	64.9
		20.0		19.2		18.5	Fixed Assets (net)				20.1	17.0	18.9
		8.3		7.3		7.6	Intangibles (net)				5.4	7.4	7.1
		6.2		6.4		9.0	All Other Non-Current				6.5	9.8	9.1
		100.0		100.0		100.0	Total				100.0	100.0	100.0
							LIABILITIES						
		6.4		5.3		5.5	Notes Payable-Short Term				12.1	3.5	3.4
		2.3		2.2		2.2	Cur. Mat.-L.T.D.				4.4	1.2	2.2
		10.1		9.8		8.4	Trade Payables				6.8	8.7	8.0
		.2		.1		.2	Income Taxes Payable				.1	.1	.2
		21.3		27.2		20.5	All Other Current				22.6	20.7	21.0
		40.3		44.7		36.8	Total Current				46.0	34.2	35.0
		15.0		12.8		10.8	Long-Term Debt				14.7	9.6	9.1
		.4		.4		.1	Deferred Taxes				.0	.1	.2
		5.2		4.3		5.9	All Other Non-Current				3.6	7.5	5.6
		39.2		37.8		46.3	Net Worth				35.7	48.7	50.2
		100.0		100.0		100.0	Total Liabilities & Net Worth				100.0	100.0	100.0
							INCOME DATA						
		100.0		100.0		100.0	Net Sales				100.0	100.0	100.0
		33.0		31.0		31.7	Gross Profit				37.3	35.4	28.3
		27.7		25.0		24.7	Operating Expenses				28.0	27.8	20.8
		5.3		6.0		7.0	Operating Profit				9.3	7.6	7.4
		-2.3		-.1		.5	All Other Expenses (net)				.7	.0	.7
		7.6		6.1		6.5	Profit Before Taxes				8.6	7.7	6.8
							RATIOS						
		2.8		2.5		2.9					5.0	3.5	2.6
		1.9		1.7		1.9	Current				1.7	2.0	1.9
		1.2		1.2		1.4					1.2	1.5	1.4
		1.7		1.4		1.7					2.5	2.0	1.5
		1.0		.9		1.0	Quick				1.0	1.2	1.0
		.6		.5		.6					.3	.6	.6
31	11.7		35	10.5	31	11.8					15	24.5	28	13.2	36	10.0
49	7.4		53	6.9	47	7.8	Sales/Receivables				36	10.2	36	10.2	53	6.9
72	5.1		68	5.4	63	5.8					42	8.7	52	7.0	70	5.2
39	9.4		47	7.8	47	7.8					14	25.5	66	5.5	51	7.2
87	4.2		96	3.8	99	3.7	Cost of Sales/Inventory				70	5.2	101	3.6	104	3.5
146	2.5		166	2.2	174	2.1					166	2.2	192	1.9	174	2.1
19	19.1		14	25.5	14	26.3					2	192.5	14	25.9	17	21.5
30	12.0		28	13.0	25	14.7	Cost of Sales/Payables				14	25.2	23	15.6	26	13.9
47	7.8		51	7.1	41	8.9					29	12.6	41	8.9	41	9.0
		2.9		3.2		3.1					3.6	3.1	3.2
		4.8		5.3		4.9	Sales/Working Capital				7.5	4.4	4.9
		13.3		13.6		9.9					47.0	8.6	9.9
		24.9		30.9		32.9					13.3	36.7	40.4
(103)	8.4	(125)	9.1	(141)	7.7	EBIT/Interest			(11)	9.1	(38)	5.9	(78)	9.2
		2.5		2.7		2.0					2.5	3.1	2.0
		27.5		7.8		16.3	Net Profit + Depr., Dep.,						12.3
(33)	15.4	(40)	3.1	(44)	3.8	Amort./Cur. Mat. L/T/D					(33)	3.0
		2.6		2.0		1.7							1.6
		.2		.2		.2					.1	.1	.2
		.5		.5		.4	Fixed/Worth				.6	.4	.4
		1.5		1.4		.9					4.4	.7	.8
		.7		.8		.6					.4	.7	.5
		1.4		1.6		1.1	Debt/Worth				1.1	1.1	1.1
		5.6		3.6		2.7					87.3	2.2	2.3
		55.9		39.2		38.2	% Profit Before Taxes/Tangible				102.0	44.2	34.9
(116)	27.9	(132)	20.1	(150)	21.4	Net Worth			(11)	31.3	(43)	25.4	(87)	21.5
		5.8		7.7		6.5					6.7	3.1	7.4
		19.9		15.8		15.7	% Profit Before Taxes/Total				37.8	18.7	13.4
		10.2		7.2		8.6	Assets				15.8	9.2	8.6
		2.6		2.0		2.1					2.7	1.8	3.0
		25.3		24.4		22.2					52.4	30.2	16.9
		9.2		8.5		9.5	Sales/Net Fixed Assets				20.6	14.8	8.3
		5.3		4.7		4.7					4.1	5.1	4.5
		1.9		1.8		1.9					2.9	2.1	1.7
		1.3		1.3		1.3	Sales/Total Assets				2.0	1.4	1.3
		1.0		1.1		1.1					1.3	1.1	1.1
		1.1		1.0		.9					1.0	.4	.9
(109)	1.9	(130)	1.9	(146)	1.9	% Depr., Dep., Amort./Sales			(10)	2.8	(40)	1.8	(87)	1.8
		3.4		3.0		3.2					4.7	3.3	2.8
		2.4		1.2		1.3	% Officers', Directors'						
(25)	3.6	(28)	3.8	(25)	3.6	Owners' Comp/Sales						
		8.1		8.2		4.6							
		4791147M		7536806M		8509182M	Net Sales ($)	631M	14045M	28804M	99639M	730297M	7635766M
		3931791M		6086869M		7028968M	Total Assets ($)	106M	8756M	28480M	59397M	546934M	6385295M

© RMA 2024 M = $ thousand MM = $ million
See Pages viii through xx for Explanation of Ratios and Data

MANUFACTURING—Commercial and Service Industry Machinery Manufacturing NAICS 333310

Current Data Sorted by Assets | Comparative Historical Data

	0-500M	500M-2MM	2-10MM	10-50MM	50-100MM	100-250MM	Type of Statement	4/1/19-3/31/20 ALL	4/1/20-3/31/21 ALL
			3	7	5	4	Unqualified	19	7
			2	10	4		Reviewed	13	8
			8	3			Compiled	7	8
		4	7	2			Tax Returns	15	10
	2	4	27	41	15	8	Other	98	62
		38 (4/1-9/30/23)		118 (10/1/23-3/31/24)			NUMBER OF STATEMENTS	152	95
	2	8	47	63	24	12			
	%	%	%	%	%	%	**ASSETS**	%	%
			14.0	11.7	8.2	8.2	Cash & Equivalents	11.2	19.4
			20.6	22.6	13.3	15.8	Trade Receivables (net)	24.5	18.8
			37.6	29.3	28.2	23.9	Inventory	27.0	28.8
			3.3	3.4	14.5	6.0	All Other Current	5.1	3.2
			75.5	67.0	64.1	54.0	Total Current	67.6	70.2
			8.8	18.1	16.9	19.8	Fixed Assets (net)	19.7	16.2
			3.1	6.5	8.9	22.4	Intangibles (net)	6.0	7.3
			12.7	8.5	10.1	3.9	All Other Non-Current	6.7	6.4
			100.0	100.0	100.0	100.0	Total	100.0	100.0
							LIABILITIES		
			4.7	5.6	3.0	1.7	Notes Payable-Short Term	7.8	5.4
			1.8	1.7	2.2	4.7	Cur. Mat.-L.T.D.	2.0	2.2
			12.8	11.5	8.8	9.8	Trade Payables	12.9	11.3
			1.1	.1	.7	.0	Income Taxes Payable	.1	.1
			11.0	14.8	17.0	13.8	All Other Current	17.4	17.5
			31.4	33.8	31.7	30.1	Total Current	40.2	36.5
			11.8	8.5	7.6	27.7	Long-Term Debt	16.2	12.7
			.0	.1	.3	.1	Deferred Taxes	.5	.4
			10.5	9.7	6.2	6.9	All Other Non-Current	5.1	7.1
			46.3	47.9	54.3	35.3	Net Worth	37.9	43.4
			100.0	100.0	100.0	100.0	Total Liabilities & Net Worth	100.0	100.0
							INCOME DATA		
			100.0	100.0	100.0	100.0	Net Sales	100.0	100.0
			39.1	33.4	34.9	36.9	Gross Profit	35.4	38.1
			31.9	25.9	26.7	32.3	Operating Expenses	29.0	32.1
			7.2	7.5	8.2	4.6	Operating Profit	6.4	6.0
			.0	.8	1.3	3.9	All Other Expenses (net)	.8	-.5
			7.2	6.8	6.9	.7	Profit Before Taxes	5.5	6.5
							RATIOS		
			4.4	3.0	4.1	2.3		3.1	4.0
			2.5	2.2	2.2	1.9	Current	1.8	2.2
			1.6	1.4	1.5	1.5		1.2	1.4
			2.4	1.7	1.0	1.3		1.6	2.0
			.9	1.1	.6	.7	Quick	.9	1.2
			.6	.6	.4	.5		.6	.6
			20 17.9	34 10.6	29 12.5	34 10.6		34 10.6	25 14.5
			31 11.6	51 7.1	40 9.1	46 7.9	Sales/Receivables	46 7.9	40 9.1
			54 6.8	74 4.9	69 5.3	58 6.3		68 5.4	61 6.0
			69 5.3	63 5.8	69 5.3	73 5.0		39 9.3	57 6.4
			118 3.1	122 3.0	122 3.0	104 3.5	Cost of Sales/Inventory	85 4.3	87 4.2
			182 2.0	159 2.3	203 1.8	174 2.1		140 2.6	152 2.4
			16 22.7	18 19.8	24 15.2	24 15.1		16 22.7	13 28.8
			31 11.8	35 10.5	46 7.9	46 8.0	Cost of Sales/Payables	31 11.6	29 12.7
			50 7.3	49 7.5	66 5.5	91 4.0		55 6.6	51 7.2
			3.1	3.1	2.4	3.7		3.6	2.8
			4.6	4.7	3.3	4.6	Sales/Working Capital	6.4	4.7
			9.4	8.9	5.2	6.8		22.1	10.0
			30.0	26.6	49.0	6.6		24.4	35.7
			(38) 8.9	(56) 9.1	(22) 9.0	(11) 2.0	EBIT/Interest	(126) 7.1	(73) 9.1
			3.1	2.3	.4	.7		2.6	1.9
				16.4	29.9			5.3	13.7
			(21) 8.4	(13) 1.2			Net Profit + Depr., Dep., Amort./Cur. Mat. L/T/D	(43) 3.5	(19) 9.4
			3.8	.2				.7	2.4
			.0	.1	.2	.4		.1	.1
			.2	.4	.3	6.5	Fixed/Worth	.4	.4
			.3	.8	.6	-.7		1.3	1.1
			.4	.6	.3	1.9		.7	.5
			1.4	1.1	.9	14.9	Debt/Worth	1.5	1.2
			2.8	2.7	2.5	-3.5		7.4	4.1
			46.8	47.8	32.5			47.7	50.4
			(45) 25.7	(60) 27.5	19.0		% Profit Before Taxes/Tangible Net Worth	(133) 22.0	(81) 18.8
			14.6	9.5	-.2			10.3	6.6
			20.7	21.4	19.0	14.2		18.2	20.8
			10.7	6.9	8.7	4.0	% Profit Before Taxes/Total Assets	8.4	7.4
			5.9	2.4	-.3	-1.7		2.2	1.8
			119.0	20.9	22.5	12.0		35.8	57.8
			26.5	9.9	8.6	6.4	Sales/Net Fixed Assets	12.6	17.2
			15.7	5.8	5.1	4.8		4.0	4.1
			2.8	2.0	1.3	1.7		2.3	2.2
			1.7	1.4	1.0	1.3	Sales/Total Assets	1.6	1.7
			1.5	1.1	.7	.9		1.2	1.1
			.4	1.0	.4			.8	.8
			(31) 1.1	(54) 1.6	(20) 1.4		% Depr., Dep., Amort./Sales	(117) 2.2	(72) 1.8
			1.5	3.6	5.9			3.9	3.3
			1.6					1.2	1.4
			(17) 3.5				% Officers', Directors', Owners' Comp/Sales	(35) 2.6	(27) 3.3
			5.2					3.7	5.3
	833M	27619M	529828M	2227351M	1702077M	2264820M	Net Sales ($)	6595108M	2912041M
	393M	9678M	258440M	1506950M	1603636M	1812459M	Total Assets ($)	4593304M	1849141M

© RMA 2024   M = $ thousand   MM = $ million
See Pages viii through xx for Explanation of Ratios and Data

MANUFACTURING—Commercial and Service Industry Machinery Manufacturing NAICS 333310

Comparative Historical Data | Current Data Sorted by Sales

Comparative Historical Data					Current Data Sorted by Sales						
				Type of Statement						
7	20	19		Unqualified					6	13
15	19	16		Reviewed					6	10
4	11	11		Compiled				2	3	2
6	7	13		Tax Returns	1	2	3	4	3	1
44	103	97		Other	3		3	14	22	55
4/1/21-3/31/22	4/1/22-3/31/23	4/1/23-3/31/24				38 (4/1-9/30/23)			118 (10/1/23-3/31/24)			
ALL	ALL	ALL			0-1MM	1-3MM	3-5MM	5-10MM	10-25MM	25MM & OVER
76	160	156		**NUMBER OF STATEMENTS**	4	2	8	21	40	81
%	%	%		**ASSETS**	%	%	%	%	%	%
15.3	13.4	11.9		Cash & Equivalents				17.7	13.6	9.7
21.8	19.7	19.8		Trade Receivables (net)				16.9	20.7	20.4
30.3	31.3	30.6		Inventory				31.2	34.6	29.3
5.6	6.2	5.1		All Other Current				1.5	3.8	6.9
73.0	70.6	67.5		Total Current				67.3	72.8	66.3
15.4	15.4	15.9		Fixed Assets (net)				13.2	12.3	17.6
6.8	8.0	7.3		Intangibles (net)				4.0	5.1	9.2
4.9	6.1	9.3		All Other Non-Current				15.6	9.8	6.9
100.0	100.0	100.0		Total				100.0	100.0	100.0
				LIABILITIES						
6.7	5.5	4.7		Notes Payable-Short Term				2.2	4.7	4.6
2.0	2.2	2.1		Cur. Mat.-L.T.D.				.7	1.7	2.6
8.9	12.2	11.7		Trade Payables				9.6	11.4	11.9
.3	.3	.8		Income Taxes Payable				.3	.1	.3
14.1	15.8	13.4		All Other Current				14.1	9.9	15.9
32.1	36.0	32.8		Total Current				27.0	27.8	35.3
16.5	14.9	11.7		Long-Term Debt				11.9	9.7	11.4
.3	.2	.1		Deferred Taxes				.0	.0	.2
5.7	8.0	8.6		All Other Non-Current				14.4	7.7	6.9
45.4	41.0	46.8		Net Worth				46.7	54.8	46.2
100.0	100.0	100.0		Total Liabilties & Net Worth				100.0	100.0	100.0
				INCOME DATA						
100.0	100.0	100.0		Net Sales				100.0	100.0	100.0
38.6	33.4	36.3		Gross Profit				39.7	37.9	32.6
29.7	27.6	29.2		Operating Expenses				32.6	29.8	25.3
8.8	5.8	7.1		Operating Profit				7.2	8.1	7.3
-1.7	.7	.8		All Other Expenses (net)				-.5	.1	1.5
10.5	5.2	6.2		Profit Before Taxes				7.6	8.0	5.9
				RATIOS						
4.5	3.8	3.4						9.5	3.7	2.9
2.3	2.0	2.1		Current				3.4	2.6	1.9
1.6	1.4	1.5						1.3	1.8	1.4
2.1	1.5	1.7						4.9	2.3	1.4
1.1	.9	.9		Quick				1.3	1.3	.9
.7	.5	.5						.4	.6	.5
31 11.7	24 15.2	28 13.1			20 18.2		24 15.4		33 11.0	
46 7.9	44 8.3	45 8.2		Sales/Receivables	37 9.9		42 8.6		49 7.5	
68 5.4	61 6.0	62 5.9			54 6.7		69 5.3		64 5.7	
59 6.2	50 7.3	63 5.8			61 6.0		72 5.1		64 5.7	
107 3.4	111 3.3	118 3.1		Cost of Sales/Inventory	122 3.0		135 2.7		114 3.2	
182 2.0	174 2.1	174 2.1			203 1.8		182 2.0		159 2.3	
18 20.0	16 22.7	18 20.1			12 29.9		18 20.0		22 16.7	
30 12.0	31 11.9	34 10.6		Cost of Sales/Payables	21 17.6		36 10.2		34 10.7	
45 8.1	51 7.1	51 7.1			48 7.6		48 7.6		59 6.2	
2.4	2.7	3.1						2.4	3.1	3.1
3.6	4.7	4.6		Sales/Working Capital				4.5	3.9	4.8
8.4	9.5	8.9						9.8	8.1	9.4
36.2	37.0	27.7						40.0	29.2	26.5
(62) 12.9	(135) 8.6	(135) 6.9		EBIT/Interest	(16) 12.5		(35) 8.9		(72) 6.7	
5.0	2.0	1.8						2.9	3.1	1.7
22.1	9.1	14.7		Net Profit + Depr., Dep.,						14.7
(16) 5.4	(31) 4.4	(44) 6.8		Amort./Cur. Mat. L/T/D					(32)	7.4
1.0	2.7	1.7								1.2
.1	.1	.1						.1	.1	.2
.3	.3	.3		Fixed/Worth				.3	.2	.4
.8	1.1	.8						.8	.3	.9
.4	.6	.5						.2	.4	.7
1.0	1.5	1.3		Debt/Worth				1.7	1.0	1.5
3.1	5.2	3.2						5.9	1.8	3.8
65.3	55.2	47.6		% Profit Before Taxes/Tangible				94.9	49.4	48.3
(69) 32.4	(138) 21.3	(144) 25.5		Net Worth	(20) 21.4		(28.3)		(73) 26.1	
13.4	4.4	8.4						9.8	9.5	11.4
24.5	17.5	19.7		% Profit Before Taxes/Total				20.0	21.8	20.0
14.9	7.0	9.2		Assets				12.6	10.0	9.4
5.3	.7	2.3						3.7	4.5	2.6
46.0	60.6	38.6						46.0	104.3	20.6
18.1	16.5	14.8		Sales/Net Fixed Assets				17.5	19.8	9.7
6.8	6.1	6.4						12.3	8.8	5.6
2.0	2.3	2.1						1.9	2.2	1.8
1.5	1.5	1.5		Sales/Total Assets				1.5	1.7	1.4
1.0	1.0	1.1						1.1	1.2	1.0
.7	.7	.8						1.0	1.0	.8
(61) 2.0	(109) 1.5	(115) 1.5		% Depr., Dep., Amort./Sales			(13) 1.1		(30) 1.7	(65) 1.4
3.8	3.5	2.7						2.2	3.7	2.7
1.5	.9	1.2		% Officers', Directors'						
(16) 3.4	(31) 2.6	(31) 2.6		Owners' Comp/Sales						
5.9	5.8	5.2								
2956970M	7920279M	6752528M		Net Sales ($)	2482M	4246M	32925M	157875M	642048M	5912952M
2028304M	5760934M	5191556M		Total Assets ($)	2054M	1640M	26442M	122399M	437325M	4601696M

© RMA 2024   M = $ thousand   MM = $ million
See Pages viii through xx for Explanation of Ratios and Data

MANUFACTURING—Industrial and Commercial Fan and Blower and Air Purification Equipment Manufacturing NAICS 333413

Current Data Sorted by Assets — **Comparative Historical Data**

							Type of Statement			
		1	2	2			Unqualified		4	6
	1	4	3				Reviewed		11	9
		2	4				Compiled		9	1
	2	3					Tax Returns		11	1
	4	10	13	3	1		Other		42	23
	8 (4/1-9/30/23)		47 (10/1/23-3/31/24)						4/1/19-3/31/20 ALL	4/1/20-3/31/21 ALL
0-500M	500M-2MM	2-10MM	10-50MM	50-100MM	100-250MM		NUMBER OF STATEMENTS		77	40
	7	20	22	5	1					
%	%	%	%	%	%		ASSETS		%	%
		16.6	15.7				Cash & Equivalents		12.2	19.1
D		30.0	24.8				Trade Receivables (net)		27.8	28.0
A		25.3	22.7				Inventory		23.2	18.5
T		3.2	3.1				All Other Current		2.9	3.3
A		75.0	66.4				Total Current		66.1	68.9
		14.9	18.2				Fixed Assets (net)		17.0	16.5
N		6.5	7.1				Intangibles (net)		9.2	12.5
O		3.7	8.3				All Other Non-Current		7.7	2.2
T		100.0	100.0				Total		100.0	100.0
							LIABILITIES			
A		5.6	2.4				Notes Payable-Short Term		18.2	4.9
V		2.0	2.2				Cur. Mat.-L.T.D.		2.1	2.9
A		13.3	8.8				Trade Payables		13.3	10.4
I		.3	.5				Income Taxes Payable		.3	.5
L		18.2	14.3				All Other Current		15.3	15.6
A		39.4	28.1				Total Current		49.1	34.2
B		7.9	8.7				Long-Term Debt		13.1	15.8
L		.3	.3				Deferred Taxes		.1	.4
E		6.3	4.7				All Other Non-Current		7.1	2.9
		46.2	58.3				Net Worth		30.5	46.7
		100.0	100.0				Total Liabilities & Net Worth		100.0	100.0
							INCOME DATA			
		100.0	100.0				Net Sales		100.0	100.0
		31.4	37.7				Gross Profit		34.6	35.3
		25.0	26.8				Operating Expenses		30.5	26.2
		6.3	10.9				Operating Profit		4.1	9.1
		.3	1.0				All Other Expenses (net)		.9	-.1
		6.1	9.9				Profit Before Taxes		3.2	9.1
							RATIOS			
		3.1	3.3						2.8	3.6
		2.5	2.4				Current		1.7	2.2
		1.6	2.1						1.3	1.8
		2.4	1.9						1.9	2.7
		1.5	1.5				Quick	(76)	.9	1.7
		.8	1.0						.7	.9
		35 10.4	32 11.3						36 10.0	44 8.3
		46 8.0	46 8.0				Sales/Receivables		52 7.0	54 6.8
		63 5.8	62 5.9						64 5.7	65 5.6
		28 13.2	43 8.4						28 13.0	23 16.0
		57 6.4	70 5.2				Cost of Sales/Inventory		54 6.8	63 5.8
		114 3.2	107 3.4						99 3.7	94 3.9
		16 23.1	12 29.4						20 18.5	13 29.0
		26 14.0	31 11.9				Cost of Sales/Payables		28 13.0	25 14.7
		43 8.4	45 8.1						53 6.9	45 8.2
		4.4	3.9						4.4	3.3
		5.9	5.5				Sales/Working Capital		8.2	4.8
		10.9	7.0						17.8	7.2
		105.2	66.7						18.7	38.5
	(19)	10.7	(20) 25.1				EBIT/Interest	(67)	5.3	(32) 14.4
		1.5	7.3						1.5	2.7
							Net Profit + Depr., Dep., Amort./Cur. Mat. L/T/D		7.4	82.4
								(17)	3.9	(12) 8.9
									.6	1.9
		.1	.2						.2	.2
		.3	.4				Fixed/Worth		.6	.5
		.6	.6						1.3	2.0
		.5	.3						.6	.5
		1.1	.6				Debt/Worth		1.5	1.1
		3.7	1.7						9.0	6.4
		54.1	48.9						44.2	50.6
	(17)	28.2	(20) 32.4				% Profit Before Taxes/Tangible Net Worth	(64)	18.0	(33) 32.4
		10.0	12.9						5.8	15.1
		24.9	26.3						16.2	18.5
		13.4	17.0				% Profit Before Taxes/Total Assets		6.1	10.8
		.7	7.2						.4	4.2
		112.1	33.2						61.0	54.8
		24.0	9.9				Sales/Net Fixed Assets		13.3	11.5
		7.9	5.4						6.4	5.3
		2.9	2.0						2.9	2.1
		2.2	1.8				Sales/Total Assets		1.8	1.7
		1.8	1.6						1.2	1.3
		.2	1.3						.7	1.4
	(15)	.8	(18) 1.8				% Depr., Dep., Amort./Sales	(54)	1.7	(27) 2.0
		2.3	3.1						2.8	4.4
							% Officers', Directors' Owners' Comp/Sales		1.4	.6
								(21)	3.0	(10) 1.4
									8.9	4.9
	40529M	280116M	820306M	373776M	292239M		Net Sales ($)		3136157M	2947632M
	11404M	121110M	478513M	339005M	183109M		Total Assets ($)		2153425M	1782980M

M = $ thousand   MM = $ million
See Pages viii through xx for Explanation of Ratios and Data

© RMA 2024

MANUFACTURING—Industrial and Commercial Fan and Blower and Air Purification Equipment Manufacturing NAICS 333413

Comparative Historical Data | Current Data Sorted by Sales

				Type of Statement						
	4	3	5	Unqualified					1	4
	8	7	8	Reviewed		1		3	1	3
	3	2	6	Compiled				2	3	3
	4	3	5	Tax Returns					3	
	25	38	31	Other	1	8	2	3	12	13
	4/1/21-3/31/22	4/1/22-3/31/23	4/1/23-3/31/24		0-1MM	(4/1-9/30/23) 1-3MM	3-5MM	47 (10/1/23-3/31/24) 5-10MM	10-25MM	25MM & OVER
	ALL	ALL	ALL							
	44	53	55	NUMBER OF STATEMENTS	1		3	8	20	23
	%	%	%	ASSETS	%	%	%	%	%	%
	17.6	13.0	16.5	Cash & Equivalents					20.3	11.2
	27.0	30.0	27.5	Trade Receivables (net)		D			25.7	24.8
	23.1	24.4	21.7	Inventory		A			22.6	21.2
	3.1	3.7	3.4	All Other Current		T			4.2	3.1
	70.8	71.2	69.0	Total Current		A			72.8	60.2
	15.1	14.4	14.9	Fixed Assets (net)					12.1	19.0
	8.1	7.3	9.8	Intangibles (net)		N			10.9	11.8
	6.0	7.1	6.2	All Other Non-Current		O			4.2	9.0
	100.0	100.0	100.0	Total		T			100.0	100.0
				LIABILITIES		A				
	3.6	7.0	3.7	Notes Payable-Short Term		V			5.6	3.1
	1.6	3.8	4.5	Cur. Mat.-L.T.D.		A			.8	8.8
	12.4	13.0	10.5	Trade Payables		I			12.6	7.8
	.4	.1	.4	Income Taxes Payable		L			.3	.5
	14.3	18.3	15.9	All Other Current		A			11.0	17.5
	32.3	42.1	35.0	Total Current		B			30.3	37.7
	24.6	13.8	9.9	Long-Term Debt		L			10.0	12.3
	.3	.2	.2	Deferred Taxes		E			.0	.3
	4.7	4.3	4.5	All Other Non-Current					5.1	3.4
	38.1	39.7	50.4	Net Worth					54.7	46.4
	100.0	100.0	100.0	Total Liabilties & Net Worth					100.0	100.0
				INCOME DATA						
	100.0	100.0	100.0	Net Sales					100.0	100.0
	39.8	36.8	38.1	Gross Profit					35.6	40.8
	30.0	31.0	28.3	Operating Expenses					25.9	31.8
	9.7	5.8	9.8	Operating Profit					9.7	8.9
	.7	-.1	2.3	All Other Expenses (net)					.8	5.1
	9.0	5.9	7.5	Profit Before Taxes					8.9	3.8
				RATIOS						
	4.7	3.1	3.2						3.8	2.8
	2.4	2.0	2.3	Current					2.5	2.1
	1.7	1.4	1.5						1.7	1.3
	3.0	1.8	2.3						2.9	1.6
	1.5	1.1	1.5	Quick					1.5	1.1
	1.0	.8	.9						.8	.9
34	10.7	41	8.9	35	10.5					31	11.7	35	10.5
46	8.0	54	6.8	45	8.1	Sales/Receivables				44	8.3	46	8.0
62	5.9	68	5.4	60	6.1					60	6.1	61	6.0
35	10.3	38	9.7	29	12.5					16	22.2	52	7.0
76	4.8	65	5.6	61	6.0	Cost of Sales/Inventory				54	6.7	69	5.3
96	3.8	104	3.5	99	3.7					130	2.8	99	3.7
20	18.2	19	18.9	15	23.7					13	28.5	13	28.5
30	12.3	29	12.4	27	13.7	Cost of Sales/Payables				27	13.5	27	13.7
49	7.4	59	6.2	44	8.3					46	7.9	44	8.3
	3.2		4.0		4.3						3.8		5.6
	4.9		6.3		6.2	Sales/Working Capital					5.4		6.5
	8.5		9.7		10.2						9.6		10.2
	38.3		63.2		65.5						78.5		63.3
(36)	10.2	(45)	8.9	(47)	17.5	EBIT/Interest				(17)	15.1	(21)	18.8
	2.5		4.2		5.7						2.1		6.5
					57.9	Net Profit + Depr., Dep.,							
			(13)	5.5	Amort./Cur. Mat. L/T/D								
					3.9								
	.1		.1		.1						.1		.3
	.5		.3		.4	Fixed/Worth					.3		.6
	1.5		1.2		.7						.6		1.1
	.5		.6		.4						.3		.5
	1.1		1.5		.9	Debt/Worth					1.1		.9
	5.4		2.9		2.6						2.5		2.4
	50.5		51.6		51.4	% Profit Before Taxes/Tangible					62.0		48.3
(35)	25.8	(43)	26.2	(46)	31.7	Net Worth				(17)	31.5	(19)	32.0
	11.0		16.2		17.2						13.1		16.5
	26.1		21.3		25.9	% Profit Before Taxes/Total					28.2		21.1
	12.5		9.0		14.8	Assets					16.4		13.3
	4.8		4.9		5.1						4.2		7.5
	55.9		89.9		59.8						133.1		32.9
	17.3		21.6		19.0	Sales/Net Fixed Assets					28.0		9.8
	5.8		6.8		7.3						10.4		5.2
	2.6		2.9		2.7						2.9		2.1
	1.8		1.9		1.9	Sales/Total Assets					2.1		1.8
	1.4		1.3		1.5						1.7		1.4
	.5		.5		.3						.3		1.3
(28)	1.2	(35)	1.4	(39)	1.6	% Depr., Dep., Amort./Sales				(16)	1.6	(17)	1.8
	3.6		2.1		2.8						2.4		2.9
	1.1		1.0		1.0	% Officers', Directors'							
(12)	4.1	(10)	2.3	(11)	2.9	Owners' Comp/Sales							
	8.2		3.3		4.8								
	2248082M	2109027M	1806966M	Net Sales ($)	438M		11379M	66269M	339660M	1389220M
	1450479M	1455574M	1133141M	Total Assets ($)	1474M		7110M	28716M	194298M	901543M

M = $ thousand   MM = $ million
See Pages viii through xx for Explanation of Ratios and Data
© RMA 2024

MANUFACTURING—Heating Equipment (except Warm Air Furnaces) Manufacturing NAICS 333414

Current Data Sorted by Assets | Comparative Historical Data

							Type of Statement				
				3	2		Unqualified		11		7
				4			Reviewed		5		1
		1		3			Compiled				2
	1	1	3				Tax Returns		4		3
	4 (4/1-9/30/23)		24 (10/1/23-3/31/24)	3	1		Other		19		13
0-500M	500M-2MM	2-10MM	10-50MM	50-100MM	100-250MM				4/1/19-3/31/20		4/1/20-3/31/21
	2	3	17	5	1		NUMBER OF STATEMENTS		ALL 39		ALL 26
%	%	%	%	%	%		ASSETS		%		%
			10.5				Cash & Equivalents		9.7		20.9
D			25.5				Trade Receivables (net)		21.6		22.6
A			25.4				Inventory		30.8		24.9
T			4.2				All Other Current		5.7		6.6
A			65.6				Total Current		67.9		75.0
			20.1				Fixed Assets (net)		16.6		13.4
N			5.5				Intangibles (net)		10.4		6.3
O			8.7				All Other Non-Current		5.2		5.2
T			100.0				Total		100.0		100.0
A							LIABILITIES				
V			.8				Notes Payable-Short Term		9.0		13.3
A			4.6				Cur. Mat.-L.T.D.		1.2		1.9
I			9.1				Trade Payables		12.1		13.6
L			.1				Income Taxes Payable		.4		.3
A			15.9				All Other Current		19.9		18.5
B			30.5				Total Current		42.7		47.6
L			12.2				Long-Term Debt		13.6		14.5
E			.0				Deferred Taxes		.6		.2
			6.9				All Other Non-Current		7.0		9.8
			50.3				Net Worth		36.1		27.9
			100.0				Total Liabilities & Net Worth		100.0		100.0
							INCOME DATA				
			100.0				Net Sales		100.0		100.0
			41.9				Gross Profit		34.2		36.6
			32.8				Operating Expenses		28.3		28.5
			9.1				Operating Profit		5.9		8.1
			.6				All Other Expenses (net)		1.5		-1.0
			8.6				Profit Before Taxes		4.4		9.1
							RATIOS				
			4.5						2.8		3.5
			2.4				Current		1.9		1.8
			1.4						1.2		1.3
			2.6						1.4		1.7
			1.4				Quick		.9		1.0
			.8						.5		.6
		31	11.7					30	12.1	31	11.7
		57	6.4				Sales/Receivables	42	8.6	45	8.2
		70	5.2					72	5.1	64	5.7
		62	5.9					57	6.4	30	12.2
		118	3.1				Cost of Sales/Inventory	99	3.7	91	4.0
		192	1.9					130	2.8	122	3.0
		16	22.5					14	25.8	16	22.8
		36	10.1				Cost of Sales/Payables	33	10.9	41	8.9
		47	7.7					49	7.4	52	7.0
			2.6						3.8		2.9
			4.3				Sales/Working Capital		5.7		4.9
			7.7						16.9		14.9
			59.5						13.1		40.4
		(13)	21.9				EBIT/Interest	(35)	4.5	(25)	21.3
			2.6						1.1		5.1
							Net Profit + Depr., Dep.,		5.8		
							Amort./Cur. Mat. L/T/D	(10)	3.7		
									2.1		
			.1						.2		.2
			.3				Fixed/Worth		.8		.4
			.7						53.9		1.2
			.5						.8		.7
			.9				Debt/Worth		2.3		2.3
			1.8						787.2		NM
			55.0				% Profit Before Taxes/Tangible		50.5		93.6
		(15)	31.4				Net Worth	(30)	26.2	(20)	53.2
			20.7						7.6		27.6
			22.4						17.9		30.0
			15.8				% Profit Before Taxes/Total Assets		4.6		16.2
			6.7						.3		4.7
			21.7						26.7		84.6
			13.9				Sales/Net Fixed Assets		10.0		13.8
			6.3						6.2		7.6
			2.1						2.6		2.2
			1.4				Sales/Total Assets		1.7		1.8
			1.2						1.1		1.2
			1.0						.8		.7
		(16)	1.5				% Depr., Dep., Amort./Sales	(29)	1.7	(17)	1.4
			3.3						2.3		2.7
							% Officers', Directors' Owners' Comp/Sales				
	7576M	32702M	579668M	485814M	104565M		Net Sales ($)		2954374M		1501399M
	2597M	17823M	390110M	361253M	105047M		Total Assets ($)		2010117M		1087261M

M = $ thousand   MM = $ million
See Pages viii through xx for Explanation of Ratios and Data

© RMA 2024

MANUFACTURING—Heating Equipment (except Warm Air Furnaces) Manufacturing NAICS 333414

Comparative Historical Data | Current Data Sorted by Sales

						Type of Statement							
		3		3		5	Unqualified			1		1	3
		3		2		4	Reviewed					1	3
				1		3	Compiled						3
		3		2		1	Tax Returns						
		14		18		15	Other		1	4		2	9
		4/1/21-3/31/22 ALL		4/1/22-3/31/23 ALL		4/1/23-3/31/24 ALL		0-1MM	4 (4/1-9/30/23) 1-3MM	3-5MM	24 (10/1/23-3/31/24) 5-10MM	10-25MM	25MM & OVER
		23		26		28	NUMBER OF STATEMENTS		1	1	4	4	18
		%		%		%	ASSETS	%	%	%	%	%	%
		14.6		9.8		12.4	Cash & Equivalents	D					13.4
		20.7		20.0		21.7	Trade Receivables (net)	A					24.1
		32.2		36.7		28.3	Inventory	T					29.0
		4.0		6.7		4.3	All Other Current	A					5.4
		71.5		73.2		66.8	Total Current						71.9
		9.8		11.5		18.1	Fixed Assets (net)	N					14.4
		9.7		3.5		4.7	Intangibles (net)	O					3.8
		9.1		11.8		10.4	All Other Non-Current	T					9.9
		100.0		100.0		100.0	Total						100.0
							LIABILITIES	A					
		8.1		6.2		2.9	Notes Payable-Short Term	V					2.5
		1.4		3.8		3.2	Cur. Mat.-L.T.D.	A					1.2
		9.2		9.0		10.6	Trade Payables	I					10.3
		.0		.2		.1	Income Taxes Payable	L					.1
		20.4		18.5		18.2	All Other Current	A					15.6
		39.1		37.9		35.0	Total Current	B					29.8
		15.2		8.1		16.2	Long-Term Debt	L					9.3
		.1		.4		.2	Deferred Taxes	E					.3
		8.0		7.7		11.4	All Other Non-Current						12.4
		37.6		46.0		37.2	Net Worth						48.1
		100.0		100.0		100.0	Total Liabilities & Net Worth						100.0
							INCOME DATA						
		100.0		100.0		100.0	Net Sales						100.0
		36.4		38.3		39.4	Gross Profit						36.7
		28.6		28.1		31.3	Operating Expenses						27.2
		7.8		10.2		8.1	Operating Profit						9.5
		-1.8		1.1		1.0	All Other Expenses (net)						.2
		9.6		9.1		7.1	Profit Before Taxes						9.3
							RATIOS						
		4.0		4.7		4.3							4.4
		2.0		2.2		2.2	Current						2.7
		1.2		1.3		1.3							1.9
		2.1		2.2		1.9							2.5
		1.1		.8		1.0	Quick						1.1
		.5		.6		.7							.9
26	13.9	30	12.3	29	12.6	Sales/Receivables					37	9.9
45	8.1	41	9.0	40	9.1						48	7.6
78	4.7	53	6.9	64	5.7						65	5.6
58	6.3	47	7.7	61	6.0	Cost of Sales/Inventory					61	6.0
94	3.9	122	3.0	122	3.0						107	3.4
159	2.3	192	1.9	174	2.1						152	2.4
14	25.8	9	39.5	15	25.1	Cost of Sales/Payables					13	28.3
29	12.6	26	13.8	36	10.0						35	10.5
47	7.7	51	7.1	54	6.7						49	7.4
		3.6		3.0		3.0	Sales/Working Capital						2.6
		6.4		4.6		4.6							3.6
		8.8		9.7		7.8							6.9
		87.7		163.8		34.1	EBIT/Interest						48.8
	(21)	22.2	(21)	20.1	(23)	7.7						(14)	15.9
		4.4		4.3		2.3							2.7
							Net Profit + Depr., Dep., Amort./Cur. Mat. L/T/D						
		.1		.1		.1	Fixed/Worth						.1
		.4		.2		.6							.3
		1.0		.4		1.5							.7
		.4		.3		.8	Debt/Worth						.6
		3.4		.9		1.7							1.0
		12.6		2.5		9.8							2.2
		94.6		49.1		54.1	% Profit Before Taxes/Tangible Net Worth						53.3
	(19)	48.9	(22)	31.1	(24)	31.5						(17)	31.4
		28.3		13.2		20.6							17.4
		41.8		26.2		21.7	% Profit Before Taxes/Total Assets						22.2
		17.4		12.3		13.8							15.0
		5.5		5.7		3.9							6.1
		66.3		85.8		32.7	Sales/Net Fixed Assets						30.6
		18.2		18.8		13.8							14.4
		8.9		9.8		6.3							6.3
		2.5		2.1		2.1	Sales/Total Assets						2.0
		1.7		1.8		1.4							1.7
		.9		1.5		1.2							1.3
		.6		.4		.8	% Depr., Dep., Amort./Sales						.9
	(15)	1.5	(17)	1.2	(24)	1.5						(16)	1.3
		2.6		2.5		3.1							2.7
							% Officers', Directors' Owners' Comp/Sales						
		1070129M		1595919M		1210325M	Net Sales ($)		1833M	3224M	31822M	65856M	1107590M
		765386M		978426M		876830M	Total Assets ($)		803M	21137M	32600M	62373M	759917M

M = $ thousand   MM = $ million
See Pages viii through xx for Explanation of Ratios and Data

© RMA 2024

MANUFACTURING—Air-Conditioning & Heating Equip. & Commercial & Industrial Refrigeration Equip. Manufacturing NAICS 333415

Current Data Sorted by Assets | Comparative Historical Data

							Type of Statement				
			1	2	2	5	Unqualified		13		8
		1	5	1		Reviewed		10		10	
		1	1			Compiled		6		5	
2	2	1	1			Tax Returns		9		2	
1	3	12	24	18	6	Other		53		33	
		23 (4/1-9/30/23)		67 (10/1/23-3/31/24)				4/1/19-3/31/20		4/1/20-3/31/21	
0-500M	500M-2MM	2-10MM	10-50MM	50-100MM	100-250MM			ALL		ALL	
4	5	16	33	21	11	NUMBER OF STATEMENTS		91		58	
%	%	%	%	%	%	**ASSETS**		%		%	
		14.9	19.3	6.1	6.9	Cash & Equivalents		11.6		14.0	
		33.8	26.0	20.9	14.2	Trade Receivables (net)		29.3		26.1	
		30.3	21.0	25.2	17.6	Inventory		25.7		22.8	
		6.3	12.1	24.0	3.0	All Other Current		3.8		2.4	
		85.3	78.4	76.2	41.7	Total Current		70.4		65.2	
		11.8	8.8	10.5	18.5	Fixed Assets (net)		14.4		19.6	
		.4	5.1	9.0	20.1	Intangibles (net)		10.2		9.4	
		2.4	7.7	4.3	19.8	All Other Non-Current		5.0		5.7	
		100.0	100.0	100.0	100.0	Total		100.0		100.0	
						LIABILITIES					
		6.5	1.2	5.8	5.9	Notes Payable-Short Term		8.8		8.6	
		2.2	1.2	1.1	2.5	Cur. Mat.-L.T.D.		1.5		4.8	
		14.0	12.7	16.8	7.1	Trade Payables		16.6		13.0	
		.3	.4	.1	.3	Income Taxes Payable		.1		.1	
		20.9	15.7	17.7	8.2	All Other Current		15.4		14.8	
		43.9	31.1	41.5	24.0	Total Current		42.4		41.3	
		3.7	6.5	6.2	19.3	Long-Term Debt		9.8		16.5	
		.0	.4	.0	.1	Deferred Taxes		.6		.0	
		19.4	10.5	3.5	11.8	All Other Non-Current		6.4		3.7	
		33.1	51.4	48.8	44.8	Net Worth		40.9		38.4	
		100.0	100.0	100.0	100.0	Total Liabilities & Net Worth		100.0		100.0	
						INCOME DATA					
		100.0	100.0	100.0	100.0	Net Sales		100.0		100.0	
		39.8	35.1	27.7	29.4	Gross Profit		29.7		29.9	
		28.8	19.9	12.8	16.5	Operating Expenses		23.5		24.5	
		11.0	15.2	14.8	12.9	Operating Profit		6.2		5.3	
		.1	.8	.2	1.7	All Other Expenses (net)		.6		-.1	
		10.9	14.5	14.7	11.2	Profit Before Taxes		5.6		5.4	
						RATIOS					
		5.5	4.5	2.0	3.3			2.5		2.9	
		1.7	2.7	1.7	1.6	Current		1.8		1.6	
		1.4	1.7	1.5	1.3			1.4		1.3	
		2.3	2.3	1.1	1.0			1.5		1.6	
		1.3	1.4	.5	.9	Quick		1.0		1.0	
		.5	1.0	.4	.6			.7		.7	
	28	13.1	33	11.2	23	15.7	33	10.9	Sales/Receivables	33	11.0	27	13.4
	41	8.8	49	7.5	26	14.1	35	10.5		43	8.5	40	9.1
	85	4.3	62	5.9	58	6.3	47	7.8		62	5.9	63	5.8
	10	36.7	30	12.0	33	11.2	38	9.5	Cost of Sales/Inventory	18	20.4	19	19.5
	68	5.4	78	4.7	55	6.6	59	6.2		57	6.4	51	7.1
	228	1.6	104	3.5	76	4.8	118	3.1		99	3.7	94	3.9
	10	36.1	19	19.3	25	14.6	17	21.4	Cost of Sales/Payables	19	18.9	15	24.3
	21	17.3	30	12.0	41	8.8	28	13.0		31	11.7	31	11.6
	59	6.2	49	7.4	68	5.4	34	10.7		49	7.4	41	8.9
		2.2	2.5	4.2	3.6	Sales/Working Capital		4.5		4.7	
		6.6	4.0	5.8	9.2			7.6		8.6	
		20.6	6.8	9.7	15.5			16.1		17.1	
		43.9	60.3	96.6	25.6	EBIT/Interest		34.5		31.8	
	(11)	17.8	(27)	45.9	(18)	45.8	8.3		(76)	6.1	(51)	7.7
		9.1	14.5	17.6	2.2			2.4		1.3	
						Net Profit + Depr., Dep., Amort./Cur. Mat. L/T/D		30.4		5.9	
							(17)	3.5	(13)	3.0	
								2.1		1.6	
		.1	.0	.0	.3	Fixed/Worth		.2		.2	
		.3	.1	.1	.6			.4		.6	
		.4	.4	.7	1.2			1.7		1.5	
		.5	.4	.9	.7	Debt/Worth		.6		.7	
		1.4	.8	1.3	2.7			1.4		2.3	
		2.4	1.7	1.8	4.2			6.6		9.8	
		80.3	60.0	88.1		% Profit Before Taxes/Tangible Net Worth		47.9		66.4	
	(15)	45.0	(29)	50.4	(19)	64.4			(76)	28.5	(47)	28.9
		30.3	25.6	42.3				13.9		9.1	
		31.6	38.1	36.8	19.4	% Profit Before Taxes/Total Assets		17.3		19.9	
		20.0	21.2	28.4	12.7			9.4		9.4	
		14.8	11.5	17.9	7.0			3.3		1.9	
		78.2	164.4	195.5	17.9	Sales/Net Fixed Assets		49.7		33.5	
		26.7	26.5	48.0	8.0			19.7		11.8	
		8.8	13.8	8.6	4.7			9.7		6.6	
		3.4	2.4	2.5	1.8	Sales/Total Assets		2.9		3.0	
		2.1	1.7	2.0	1.4			2.3		2.1	
		1.5	1.4	1.6	.6			1.6		1.5	
			.4	.4		% Depr., Dep., Amort./Sales		.5		.5	
		(24)	.9	(12)	1.9			(70)	1.2	(48)	1.4
			1.2	2.9				2.2		2.5	
						% Officers', Directors' Owners' Comp/Sales		1.1		.3	
							(19)	1.8	(15)	1.8	
								2.7		6.2	
9221M	18404M	254602M	1592307M	2530448M	2201911M	Net Sales ($)		6048765M		2966688M	
1553M	6444M	97628M	843300M	1329570M	1664196M	Total Assets ($)		3435525M		1857329M	

© RMA 2024 M = $ thousand MM = $ million
See Pages viii through xx for Explanation of Ratios and Data

MANUFACTURING—Air-Conditioning & Heating Equip. & Commercial & Industrial Refrigeration Equip. Manufacturing NAICS 333415

Comparative Historical Data | Current Data Sorted by Sales

	8		13		11	Type of Statement Unqualified		1		1		8
	9		13		7	Reviewed						7
	4		3		2	Compiled				1		1
	4		12		6	Tax Returns		1		1		1
	31		38		64	Other	1	4	2	13		44
	4/1/21-3/31/22 ALL		4/1/22-3/31/23 ALL		4/1/23-3/31/24 ALL		0-1MM	23 (4/1-9/30/23) 1-3MM	3-5MM	67 (10/1/23-3/31/24) 5-10MM 10-25MM		25MM & OVER
	56		79		90	NUMBER OF STATEMENTS	3	5	5	16		61
	%		%		%	ASSETS	%	%	%	%		%
	12.4		15.4		14.6	Cash & Equivalents				18.6		12.7
	30.1		28.6		24.9	Trade Receivables (net)		D		29.1		24.1
	23.8		25.5		23.8	Inventory		A		22.2		22.3
	6.1		5.9		11.9	All Other Current		T		8.4		13.4
	72.3		75.4		75.1	Total Current		A		78.3		72.5
	15.7		12.8		11.0	Fixed Assets (net)				13.9		10.6
	6.9		4.8		6.6	Intangibles (net)		N		4.1		8.4
	5.1		6.9		7.3	All Other Non-Current		O		3.6		8.6
	100.0		100.0		100.0	Total		T		100.0		100.0
						LIABILITIES		A				
	5.8		8.4		5.1	Notes Payable-Short Term		V		2.9		3.7
	1.6		1.3		1.9	Cur. Mat.-L.T.D.		A		2.9		1.3
	15.1		14.3		13.2	Trade Payables		I		8.4		14.1
	.0		.0		.3	Income Taxes Payable		L		.1		.4
	17.4		17.9		16.4	All Other Current		A		18.9		15.6
	39.9		41.8		36.9	Total Current		B		33.2		35.1
	9.2		14.6		9.5	Long-Term Debt		L		11.4		7.1
	.3		.0		.2	Deferred Taxes		E		.9		.0
	5.3		5.4		10.6	All Other Non-Current				5.6		7.8
	45.2		38.2		42.9	Net Worth				48.9		50.0
	100.0		100.0		100.0	Total Liabilities & Net Worth				100.0		100.0
						INCOME DATA						
	100.0		100.0		100.0	Net Sales				100.0		100.0
	26.8		32.0		34.5	Gross Profit				40.0		31.3
	23.4		25.1		21.5	Operating Expenses				28.5		16.5
	3.3		6.9		13.0	Operating Profit				11.5		14.8
	-1.9		.2		.7	All Other Expenses (net)				.7		.6
	5.2		6.7		12.4	Profit Before Taxes				10.8		14.2
						RATIOS						
	3.4		2.9		3.4					5.7		3.2
	1.8		1.7		1.8	Current				2.7		1.8
	1.4		1.4		1.5					1.5		1.6
	2.0		2.0		1.5					2.9		1.5
	1.1		1.1		1.0	Quick				1.4		.9
	.7		.6		.5					1.0		.5
34	10.8	32	11.4	25	14.4					43	8.5	25	14.5
51	7.1	45	8.1	38	9.6	Sales/Receivables				57	6.4	35	10.5
63	5.8	62	5.9	61	6.0					85	4.3	59	6.2
11	33.6	11	33.3	25	14.8					29	12.4	29	12.5
50	7.3	64	5.7	58	6.3	Cost of Sales/Inventory				81	4.5	56	6.5
99	3.7	122	3.0	107	3.4					107	3.4	96	3.8
15	24.3	18	19.9	18	20.6					13	28.8	22	16.3
30	12.0	31	11.7	29	12.5	Cost of Sales/Payables				21	17.0	31	11.7
44	8.3	49	7.5	51	7.2					47	7.7	49	7.4
	4.6		4.2		3.4					2.2		3.5
	8.0		7.0		5.5	Sales/Working Capital				4.7		5.5
	14.9		13.4		10.3					7.9		10.0
	137.7		41.8		56.3					29.3		65.6
(50)	23.0	(59)	9.1	(76)	26.5	EBIT/Interest				(10)	11.7	(54)	42.2
	.7		3.5		7.4					3.0		13.1
					7.1	Net Profit + Depr., Dep.,						
				(10)	5.3	Amort./Cur. Mat. L/T/D						
					3.2							
	.1		.1		.0					.1		.0
	.3		.3		.2	Fixed/Worth				.3		.2
	.8		.7		.7					.6		.6
	.5		.5		.6					.4		.5
	1.3		1.8		1.3	Debt/Worth				1.2		1.3
	2.9		3.9		2.7					2.4		2.4
	47.8		71.7		82.8					58.8		88.1
(48)	28.8	(74)	35.2	(78)	53.1	% Profit Before Taxes/Tangible Net Worth				(15)	34.7	(54)	57.7
	9.8		14.9		30.9					19.1		34.7
	25.1		24.9		33.6					29.7		38.6
	11.7		11.3		20.5	% Profit Before Taxes/Total Assets				15.8		24.6
	-.4		3.9		12.2					8.1		13.4
	59.6		74.1		103.5					47.5		161.2
	16.2		24.8		26.7	Sales/Net Fixed Assets				17.5		31.1
	8.2		10.7		8.9					7.3		9.0
	3.3		3.1		2.5					2.1		2.5
	2.2		2.1		1.9	Sales/Total Assets				1.6		1.9
	1.6		1.4		1.4					1.3		1.4
	.5		.4		.4					.3		.5
(44)	1.2	(55)	1.1	(57)	1.1	% Depr., Dep., Amort./Sales				(10)	1.1	(41)	1.1
	2.0		1.8		1.8					1.4		1.9
	.7		1.4		.7							
(12)	1.3	(19)	4.0	(18)	1.9	% Officers', Directors', Owners' Comp/Sales						
	2.6		7.5		7.6							
	2794272M		4389622M		6606893M	Net Sales ($)	1986M		17893M	38648M	243777M		6304589M
	1590355M		2611786M		3942691M	Total Assets ($)	1343M		7136M	21071M	151100M		3762041M

© RMA 2024   M = $ thousand   MM = $ million
See Pages viii through xx for Explanation of Ratios and Data

MANUFACTURING—Industrial Mold Manufacturing   NAICS 333511

Current Data Sorted by Assets | Comparative Historical Data

0-500M	500M-2MM	2-10MM	10-50MM	50-100MM	100-250MM	Type of Statement		
						Unqualified	3	5
			4	2		Reviewed	8	5
	2	1	1		1	Compiled	9	10
1	2	1				Tax Returns	9	6
	2	7	9	3	1	Other	34	21
	8 (4/1-9/30/23)		30 (10/1/23-3/31/24)				4/1/19-3/31/20 ALL	4/1/20-3/31/21 ALL
1	6	13	12	4	2	NUMBER OF STATEMENTS	63	47
%	%	%	%	%	%	ASSETS	%	%
		19.0	12.0			Cash & Equivalents	12.3	17.0
		20.2	17.8			Trade Receivables (net)	20.1	25.2
		19.6	12.9			Inventory	18.8	17.5
		7.2	5.3			All Other Current	2.7	2.6
		66.0	48.1			Total Current	53.9	62.4
		30.9	37.4			Fixed Assets (net)	33.2	26.8
		.9	3.8			Intangibles (net)	7.2	5.6
		2.2	10.8			All Other Non-Current	5.7	5.2
		100.0	100.0			Total	100.0	100.0
						LIABILITIES		
		6.0	3.7			Notes Payable-Short Term	7.2	9.3
		2.3	2.3			Cur. Mat.-L.T.D.	4.1	3.0
		8.0	6.4			Trade Payables	8.7	9.5
		.1	.2			Income Taxes Payable	.1	.1
		14.0	19.8			All Other Current	11.3	10.5
		30.4	32.4			Total Current	31.4	32.4
		9.1	14.8			Long-Term Debt	20.3	18.1
		.3	.0			Deferred Taxes	.9	.4
		3.3	5.6			All Other Non-Current	9.1	6.2
		56.9	47.2			Net Worth	38.3	42.9
		100.0	100.0			Total Liabilities & Net Worth	100.0	100.0
						INCOME DATA		
		100.0	100.0			Net Sales	100.0	100.0
		29.3	26.5			Gross Profit	25.6	31.0
		19.7	18.2			Operating Expenses	19.8	23.8
		9.6	8.3			Operating Profit	5.8	7.2
		-.2	-2.2			All Other Expenses (net)	1.3	-.1
		9.8	10.5			Profit Before Taxes	4.4	7.3
						RATIOS		
		5.7	4.0				2.8	3.2
		1.9	1.9			Current	1.7	2.1
		1.4	1.3				1.2	1.5
		3.6	2.5				1.9	2.3
		1.4	1.2			Quick	1.0	1.5
		.6	.6				.6	.7
	28	13.0	35 10.5				31 11.6	31 11.6
	40	9.2	56 6.5			Sales/Receivables	53 6.9	48 7.6
	61	6.0	78 4.7				70 5.2	76 4.8
	27	13.5	21 17.2				22 16.6	29 12.5
	69	5.3	46 7.9			Cost of Sales/Inventory	59 6.2	48 7.6
	122	3.0	89 4.1				87 4.2	83 4.4
	13	28.1	9 39.2				14 25.7	12 30.0
	22	16.3	28 13.1			Cost of Sales/Payables	26 14.0	24 15.4
	32	11.3	37 9.9				38 9.5	49 7.5
		2.6	2.7				3.8	3.6
		5.6	5.4			Sales/Working Capital	8.4	4.9
		12.2	15.9				23.3	10.9
		122.2	71.9				12.8	32.7
	(10)	29.9	(11) 11.6			EBIT/Interest	(57) 4.7	(42) 7.9
		1.0	7.1				1.8	1.0
						Net Profit + Depr., Dep., Amort./Cur. Mat. L/T/D	3.0	
							(12) 2.2	
							1.0	
		.3	.4				.4	.2
		.4	.7			Fixed/Worth	.9	.6
		1.8	1.1				2.5	1.3
		.2	.5				.6	.4
		.7	1.1			Debt/Worth	1.6	1.0
		2.1	2.5				4.8	4.4
		130.2	44.1				48.1	40.8
	(12)	15.0	(11) 29.2			% Profit Before Taxes/Tangible Net Worth	(54) 21.5	(41) 20.7
		2.6	9.3				8.3	5.7
		54.0	23.3				16.1	17.3
		5.3	10.8			% Profit Before Taxes/Total Assets	6.4	8.5
		-.4	6.3				1.3	.4
		16.5	6.5				9.2	17.1
		5.9	2.7			Sales/Net Fixed Assets	4.6	5.4
		3.5	2.2				2.8	3.4
		2.7	1.3				1.9	2.3
		2.1	1.1			Sales/Total Assets	1.3	1.5
		1.0	1.0				1.1	1.1
		1.7	3.2				2.3	2.0
	(11)	2.9	4.2			% Depr., Dep., Amort./Sales	(54) 4.6	(33) 3.7
		6.5	6.0				6.7	7.0
							1.4	1.9
						% Officers', Directors' Owners' Comp/Sales	(29) 4.0	(22) 3.1
							6.0	5.8
2551M	21146M	129765M	290909M	239100M	274707M	Net Sales ($)	2361713M	1154178M
197M	9689M	77248M	261364M	231338M	231641M	Total Assets ($)	1778176M	912354M

M = $ thousand   MM = $ million
See Pages viii through xx for Explanation of Ratios and Data

© RMA 2024

MANUFACTURING—Industrial Mold Manufacturing NAICS 333511

Comparative Historical Data | Current Data Sorted by Sales

Comparative Historical Data			Type of Statement	Current Data Sorted by Sales						
3	3	2	Unqualified						2
7	10	6	Reviewed		1	1	3	1	
3	7	4	Compiled		1	1	1	1	
8	10	4	Tax Returns	2		2			
28	23	22	Other	2	2	4	6	8	
4/1/21-3/31/22 ALL	4/1/22-3/31/23 ALL	4/1/23-3/31/24 ALL		0-1MM 8 (4/1-9/30/23)	1-3MM	3-5MM	5-10MM 30 (10/1/23-3/31/24)	10-25MM	25MM & OVER
49	53	38	NUMBER OF STATEMENTS	4	4	8	10	12
%	%	%	ASSETS	%	%	%	%	%	%
11.2	11.3	13.4	Cash & Equivalents					18.2	5.8
27.0	26.4	20.6	Trade Receivables (net)					22.5	19.6
21.3	17.9	16.7	Inventory	D				12.7	13.9
3.2	2.8	4.3	All Other Current	A				5.8	2.8
62.7	58.4	55.1	Total Current	T				59.3	42.2
25.8	29.9	30.9	Fixed Assets (net)	A				28.5	32.3
6.2	4.4	6.1	Intangibles (net)	N				1.8	16.4
5.3	7.2	7.9	All Other Non-Current	O				10.4	9.1
100.0	100.0	100.0	Total	T				100.0	100.0
			LIABILITIES	A					
5.9	7.9	9.9	Notes Payable-Short Term	V				1.2	12.5
2.8	3.1	2.8	Cur. Mat.-L.T.D.	A				2.5	2.3
11.2	8.8	7.8	Trade Payables	I				8.4	8.1
.1	.1	.2	Income Taxes Payable	L				.2	.3
9.8	12.7	14.7	All Other Current	A				25.3	8.8
29.8	32.6	35.4	Total Current	B				37.5	32.0
15.6	14.5	13.6	Long-Term Debt	L				10.4	17.0
.4	.3	1.9	Deferred Taxes	E				.1	.9
6.2	7.0	7.9	All Other Non-Current					3.7	15.9
48.0	45.6	41.1	Net Worth					48.3	34.1
100.0	100.0	100.0	Total Liabilities & Net Worth					100.0	100.0
			INCOME DATA						
100.0	100.0	100.0	Net Sales					100.0	100.0
26.9	27.1	26.2	Gross Profit					30.9	19.1
21.1	20.6	19.2	Operating Expenses					19.0	10.8
5.7	6.5	7.0	Operating Profit					12.0	8.3
-2.2	.8	.2	All Other Expenses (net)					-1.6	1.4
7.9	5.7	6.8	Profit Before Taxes					13.6	6.9
			RATIOS						
4.2	3.4	4.1						4.7	2.1
2.2	2.1	1.6	Current					2.0	1.4
1.3	1.3	1.0						1.3	.9
2.9	2.5	2.2						3.1	1.4
1.4	1.3	.9	Quick					1.4	.7
.7	.6	.6						.6	.6
43 8.4	35 10.5	34 10.7						35 10.4	43 8.4
61 6.0	54 6.8	52 7.0	Sales/Receivables					41 8.8	78 4.7
89 4.1	73 5.0	83 4.4						59 6.2	87 4.2
29 12.8	21 17.8	26 13.8						15 24.1	37 9.8
64 5.7	45 8.1	50 7.3	Cost of Sales/Inventory					41 9.0	51 7.2
96 3.8	89 4.1	89 4.1						72 5.1	89 4.1
16 22.7	11 33.2	12 31.5						11 32.6	16 22.4
31 11.7	21 17.5	26 14.1	Cost of Sales/Payables					28 12.9	32 11.4
46 7.9	40 9.2	38 9.7						42 8.7	41 9.0
3.1	3.7	4.7						2.1	5.4
5.9	6.3	6.7	Sales/Working Capital					5.5	15.9
9.4	33.2	NM						NM	-27.6
65.7	39.1	60.5							11.6
15.6	(44) 4.4	(34) 3.2	EBIT/Interest						7.4
2.5	1.2	-.2							.3
8.9		13.0	Net Profit + Depr., Dep.,						
(11) 4.8	(11) 1.8		Amort./Cur. Mat. L/T/D						
2.9		-2.1							
.2	.3	.4						.3	.6
.6	.6	.6	Fixed/Worth					.4	1.2
1.1	1.7	4.2						1.0	NM
.4	.5	.4						.4	.7
.9	1.0	1.6	Debt/Worth					.9	3.0
2.4	2.8	7.6						1.7	NM
47.1	36.9	57.2	% Profit Before Taxes/Tangible						
(41) 27.4	(43) 14.2	(32) 15.9	Net Worth						
15.4	3.4	-1.0							
22.7	25.2	15.1	% Profit Before Taxes/Total					40.4	14.0
10.4	6.8	6.4	Assets					22.3	8.8
2.5	1.1	-4.0						.8	-4.2
14.4	14.8	10.5						14.8	6.6
5.5	6.5	5.0	Sales/Net Fixed Assets					4.0	4.1
2.8	3.0	3.2						2.8	2.5
2.0	2.5	2.2						2.6	1.4
1.4	1.7	1.2	Sales/Total Assets					1.2	1.2
1.0	1.1	1.0						1.0	.9
1.8	1.4	1.8							2.3
(42) 4.5	(46) 3.4	(34) 3.7	% Depr., Dep., Amort./Sales						3.4
7.6	5.1	5.1							4.8
.9	1.9	1.2	% Officers', Directors'						
(20) 3.8	(21) 3.5	(19) 2.3	Owners' Comp/Sales						
9.2	6.8	5.3							
1480745M	1209125M	958178M	Net Sales ($)	8368M	17232M	60663M	175695M	696220M
1291452M	1038283M	811477M	Total Assets ($)	4421M	21321M	32611M	132516M	620608M

© RMA 2024 M = $ thousand MM = $ million
See Pages viii through xx for Explanation of Ratios and Data

MANUFACTURING—Special Die and Tool, Die Set, Jig, and Fixture Manufacturing NAICS 333514

Current Data Sorted by Assets | Comparative Historical Data

							Type of Statement				
			3	2	1		Unqualified		8		6
		8	6	1			Reviewed		27		19
1	3	13	3				Compiled		10		5
	4	4	1				Tax Returns		10		12
1	7	19	10	4	1		Other		65		39
0-500M	19 (4/1-9/30/23) 500M-2MM	2-10MM	73 (10/1/23-3/31/24) 10-50MM	50-100MM	100-250MM				4/1/19-3/31/20 ALL		4/1/20-3/31/21 ALL
2	14	44	23	6	3		NUMBER OF STATEMENTS		120		81
%	%	%	%	%	%		ASSETS		%		%
	12.1	13.6	12.7				Cash & Equivalents		10.0		14.2
	26.0	24.6	21.1				Trade Receivables (net)		23.9		23.0
	11.7	20.5	18.6				Inventory		18.5		16.7
	2.2	3.9	3.9				All Other Current		5.1		3.9
	52.0	62.6	56.4				Total Current		57.5		57.8
	32.0	26.1	32.2				Fixed Assets (net)		33.1		29.7
	5.3	3.2	5.5				Intangibles (net)		4.4		5.3
	10.7	8.2	5.9				All Other Non-Current		5.0		7.1
	100.0	100.0	100.0				Total		100.0		100.0
							LIABILITIES				
	8.1	3.1	6.2				Notes Payable-Short Term		8.3		8.5
	5.8	2.9	3.1				Cur. Mat.-L.T.D.		4.0		4.3
	8.9	7.8	7.1				Trade Payables		8.4		7.6
	.0	.1	.0				Income Taxes Payable		.1		.1
	8.4	8.1	11.7				All Other Current		7.9		8.2
	31.2	22.0	28.1				Total Current		28.7		28.6
	25.0	16.1	11.0				Long-Term Debt		19.3		18.5
	.0	.7	.4				Deferred Taxes		.3		.2
	1.8	5.8	10.3				All Other Non-Current		4.0		9.4
	42.1	55.4	50.2				Net Worth		47.7		43.4
	100.0	100.0	100.0				Total Liabilties & Net Worth		100.0		100.0
							INCOME DATA				
	100.0	100.0	100.0				Net Sales		100.0		100.0
	40.6	28.9	21.6				Gross Profit		29.6		28.0
	40.1	26.4	19.4				Operating Expenses		24.3		27.1
	.5	2.5	2.2				Operating Profit		5.3		.8
	1.1	.3	.7				All Other Expenses (net)		1.0		-2.0
	-.6	2.2	1.5				Profit Before Taxes		4.4		2.8
							RATIOS				
	4.0	5.2	5.7						3.6		4.3
	1.8	3.2	2.2			Current			2.1		1.9
	.9	2.2	1.4						1.4		1.3
	2.9	3.4	3.5						2.2		2.7
	1.2	1.9	1.3			Quick			1.1		1.3
	.6	1.1	.6						.6		.7
33	11.0	33	10.9	46	7.9			38	9.6	38	9.5
46	7.9	49	7.5	64	5.7		Sales/Receivables	54	6.8	55	6.6
68	5.4	76	4.8	85	4.3			70	5.2	83	4.4
0	UND	11	34.3	31	11.8			13	27.8	7	54.6
33	10.9	57	6.4	52	7.0		Cost of Sales/Inventory	46	7.9	49	7.5
72	5.1	111	3.3	122	3.0			94	3.9	101	3.6
10	35.0	10	34.8	14	26.1			13	28.8	13	28.2
27	13.4	20	18.2	23	16.1		Cost of Sales/Payables	21	17.1	25	14.7
43	8.4	34	10.8	36	10.2			36	10.0	38	9.7
	4.4	2.9	2.9						3.6		3.1
	10.8	3.7	4.6			Sales/Working Capital			5.8		5.0
	-124.1	7.3	9.2						11.3		11.5
	6.8	25.1	20.8						10.5		11.7
	.8	(41) 5.3	(22) 5.1			EBIT/Interest	(108)	3.8	(74)	3.3
	-3.2	.8	1.3						.3		.1
							Net Profit + Depr., Dep.,		6.0		5.7
							Amort./Cur. Mat. L/T/D	(25)	2.3	(14)	1.0
									.9		.3
	.3	.2	.4						.3		.3
	.8	.5	.7			Fixed/Worth			.7		.8
	7.9	.8	1.4						1.5		1.5
	.5	.4	.4						.4		.7
	1.3	.6	1.0			Debt/Worth			1.0		1.3
	15.6	1.6	3.5						2.4		3.1
	16.0	29.1	18.6			% Profit Before Taxes/Tangible		29.2		23.6
(12)	.4	(41) 11.8	(20) 7.9			Net Worth	(109)	10.2	(71)	6.8
	-68.7	-.2	2.0						1.4		-1.7
	4.8	15.3	8.9			% Profit Before Taxes/Total		10.4		11.6
	-.9	7.7	3.8			Assets			4.0		2.0
	-10.6	-.2	.7						-1.4		-1.4
	16.0	15.1	7.4						8.7		8.4
	5.4	6.5	4.7			Sales/Net Fixed Assets			5.0		5.2
	3.9	3.6	1.9						3.1		2.6
	2.4	1.9	1.5						2.2		1.8
	1.9	1.5	1.2			Sales/Total Assets			1.6		1.3
	1.5	1.2	.8						1.1		1.0
	1.6	2.1	2.0						2.5		2.6
(11)	5.4	(38) 2.8	(21) 3.7			% Depr., Dep., Amort./Sales	(101)	4.4	(67)	4.4
	6.9	5.5	4.9						6.1		6.9
		1.4					% Officers', Directors'		2.8		2.3
		(17) 3.1					Owners' Comp/Sales	(43)	4.1	(35)	4.1
		5.5							6.9		5.8
1103M	40071M	385012M	678970M	503252M	565531M		Net Sales ($)		3266525M		1520247M
348M	20370M	236789M	534979M	426630M	502673M		Total Assets ($)		2593482M		1389599M

M = $ thousand   MM = $ million
See Pages viii through xx for Explanation of Ratios and Data

© RMA 2024

MANUFACTURING—Special Die and Tool, Die Set, Jig, and Fixture Manufacturing   NAICS 333514

Comparative Historical Data | Current Data Sorted by Sales

												Type of Statement											
	2		5		6							Unqualified					5		7		6		
	12		17		15							Reviewed				4	7		5		3		
	7		12		20							Compiled			3	2	7		1		1		
	8		14		9							Tax Returns			3	4	3		12		8		
	38		38		42							Other		2	7	4	9		12		8		
	4/1/21-		4/1/22-		4/1/23-										19 (4/1-9/30/23)				73 (10/1/23-3/31/24)				
	3/31/22		3/31/23		3/31/24									0-1MM	1-3MM	3-5MM	5-10MM		10-25MM		25MM & OVER		
	ALL		ALL		ALL							NUMBER OF STATEMENTS											
	67		86		92									2	13	10	24		25		18		
	%		%		%							ASSETS		%	%	%	%		%		%		
	16.0		13.6		12.1							Cash & Equivalents			11.5	15.7	10.9		17.1		5.9		
	23.7		24.4		23.3							Trade Receivables (net)			22.3	26.2	22.0		23.6		24.4		
	21.6		18.3		19.0							Inventory			9.1	17.3	21.8		16.9		27.3		
	3.5		3.9		3.6							All Other Current			2.3	1.8	4.6		4.8		3.0		
	64.8		60.2		58.0							Total Current			45.1	61.0	59.4		62.4		60.6		
	25.7		27.2		29.1							Fixed Assets (net)			35.5	29.0	32.7		27.7		24.6		
	3.2		4.6		4.7							Intangibles (net)			4.7	5.7	3.0		4.1		5.2		
	6.4		8.1		8.2							All Other Non-Current			14.7	4.3	5.0		5.8		9.6		
	100.0		100.0		100.0							Total			100.0	100.0	100.0		100.0		100.0		
												LIABILITIES											
	5.2		4.7		5.1							Notes Payable-Short Term			11.3	3.5	2.8		2.3		8.8		
	3.1		3.6		3.5							Cur. Mat.-L.T.D.			6.5	4.1	2.5		2.8		3.7		
	9.0		7.9		8.3							Trade Payables			9.1	5.9	8.2		6.9		12.0		
	.1		.0		.0							Income Taxes Payable			.0	.0	.1		.0		.0		
	12.9		9.3		8.9							All Other Current			8.5	10.5	6.9		8.9		11.4		
	30.3		25.5		25.8							Total Current			35.5	24.0	20.5		20.8		35.8		
	16.0		15.7		17.8							Long-Term Debt			35.3	12.4	16.2		10.1		16.0		
	.3		.3		.5							Deferred Taxes			.0	.0	1.3		.3		.7		
	3.4		4.3		6.7							All Other Non-Current			4.6	.0	4.3		9.9		11.4		
	50.0		54.2		49.2							Net Worth			24.7	63.6	57.8		59.0		36.1		
	100.0		100.0		100.0							Total Liabilities & Net Worth			100.0	100.0	100.0		100.0		100.0		
												INCOME DATA											
	100.0		100.0		100.0							Net Sales			100.0	100.0	100.0		100.0		100.0		
	28.1		31.0		28.1							Gross Profit			37.4	33.3	30.7		23.8		19.8		
	22.7		24.0		25.9							Operating Expenses			39.7	27.1	30.0		20.5		16.4		
	5.4		7.0		2.1							Operating Profit			-2.2	6.2	.7		3.3		3.4		
	-4.6		-.2		.5							All Other Expenses (net)			1.6	-.7	.5		-.2		1.0		
	10.0		7.3		1.6							Profit Before Taxes			-3.9	7.0	.2		3.5		2.4		
												RATIOS											
	4.0		5.0		4.9										4.2	3.9	5.9		5.2		3.1		
	2.3		2.4		2.7							Current			1.0	2.9	2.9		3.4		1.6		
	1.4		1.6		1.3										.7	2.0	2.2		2.3		1.2		
	2.6		3.3		3.0										3.4	3.3	3.3		4.1		1.2		
	1.3		1.5		1.5							Quick			.7	1.5	1.9		2.2		.8		
	.9		.8		.8										.5	1.2	1.2		1.2		.6		
38	9.7	34	10.7	39	9.4								38	9.6	31	11.6	29	12.4	45	8.2	35	10.3	
52	7.0	49	7.5	51	7.2							Sales/Receivables	47	7.7	46	8.0	41	8.8	64	5.7	49	7.5	
72	5.1	74	4.9	76	4.8								72	5.1	64	5.7	74	4.9	78	4.7	78	4.7	
28	13.2	5	79.2	11	34.3								0	UND	36	10.1	6	58.7	3	129.1	37	9.8	
69	5.3	51	7.1	55	6.6							Cost of Sales/Inventory	29	12.5	60	6.1	52	7.0	52	7.0	79	4.6	
107	3.4	91	4.0	101	3.6								99	3.7	72	5.1	99	3.7	107	3.4	130	2.8	
11	33.1	10	35.9	13	28.2								13	27.3	9	41.7	8	43.1	15	24.7	21	17.8	
22	16.5	22	16.5	22	16.3							Cost of Sales/Payables	35	10.4	12	30.2	20	18.5	22	16.4	28	12.9	
40	9.1	38	9.5	36	10.0								63	5.8	24	15.5	41	9.0	29	12.4	59	6.2	
	2.7		3.0		3.0										6.4	2.7	2.7		2.9		3.2		
	4.8		5.4		4.6							Sales/Working Capital			87.5	4.3	4.6		3.4		8.7		
	10.1		8.5		9.9										-22.5	7.8	8.6		4.6		11.2		
	58.4		26.2		11.2										1.6		26.8		33.0		8.8		
(60)	19.1	(75)	8.0	(87)	3.4							EBIT/Interest			-1.6	(23)	5.1	(24)	6.4	(17)	3.1		
	7.1		1.9		-.3										-4.4		.9		2.2		.3		
	14.4		10.5		9.0							Net Profit + Depr., Dep.,										10.5		
(12)	4.0	(17)	2.1	(17)	2.0							Amort./Cur. Mat. L/T/D									(10)	2.0		
	2.1		1.5		1.2																1.3		
	.2		.2		.3										.5	.2	.3		.2		.4		
	.5		.6		.6							Fixed/Worth			1.7	.5	.7		.4		.6		
	.8		1.0		1.4										-1.8	.8	1.2		.7		2.6		
	.6		.3		.4										1.1	.4	.3		.4		.6		
	.9		.8		1.0							Debt/Worth			3.0	.5	.6		.6		2.5		
	1.7		1.9		3.6										-5.6	1.0	1.3		1.6		5.3		
	44.0		35.3		24.2											28.0	27.1		23.5		40.8		
(63)	29.5	(80)	15.8	(82)	8.0							% Profit Before Taxes/Tangible			11.8	(22)	7.3	(24)	9.3	(16)	9.0		
	14.0		5.3		-1.2							Net Worth			-2.6		-.5		1.9		-1.2		
	23.5		16.8		11.2							% Profit Before Taxes/Total			1.2	19.4	14.8		12.7		11.4		
	16.2		7.4		3.8							Assets			-6.4	6.4	5.0		4.2		4.3		
	7.4		1.8		-1.1										-14.0	-1.4	-.8		1.1		-1.1		
	11.2		13.8		10.6										7.1	38.7	9.9		11.3		9.0		
	6.4		6.2		5.5							Sales/Net Fixed Assets			4.9	5.2	6.0		5.0		5.8		
	3.8		3.1		3.2										3.1	2.6	3.6		2.1		4.4		
	2.0		2.1		1.9										2.0	2.1	2.4		1.7		1.7		
	1.4		1.4		1.4							Sales/Total Assets			1.6	1.5	1.6		1.2		1.4		
	1.2		1.1		1.1										1.0	1.3	1.1		.9		1.2		
	2.5		1.7		2.2										4.1		2.0		1.3		2.2		
(60)	3.3	(77)	3.0	(80)	3.6							% Depr., Dep., Amort./Sales	(12)	5.7	(22)	3.0	(23)	4.1	(15)	2.8		
	5.2		5.2		5.6										10.0		5.3		5.2		4.2		
	2.3		2.1		1.6							% Officers', Directors'					1.4		1.6				
(33)	4.2	(35)	4.1	(33)	3.7							Owners' Comp/Sales				(10)	2.3	(10)	2.8				
	5.2		6.3		6.6												10.5		5.0				
	1350340M		1647620M		2173939M							Net Sales ($)		484M	27435M	38389M	165658M		397485M		1544488M		
	1039547M		1333881M		1721789M							Total Assets ($)		8440M	20378M	27545M	115412M		357971M		1192043M		

© RMA 2024   M = $ thousand   MM = $ million
See Pages viii through xx for Explanation of Ratios and Data

MANUFACTURING—Cutting Tool and Machine Tool Accessory Manufacturing NAICS 333515

Current Data Sorted by Assets | Comparative Historical Data

0-500M	500M-2MM	2-10MM	10-50MM	50-100MM	100-250MM	Type of Statement	4/1/19-3/31/20 ALL	4/1/20-3/31/21 ALL
		1	2	1	1	Unqualified	7	5
		2	5			Reviewed	7	7
		6	1			Compiled	8	6
1	4	2				Tax Returns	14	4
1	6	10	12	3	1	Other	31	27
	13 (4/1-9/30/23)		46 (10/1/23-3/31/24)			NUMBER OF STATEMENTS	67	49
2	10	21	20	4	2			
%	%	%	%	%	%	**ASSETS**	%	%
	14.0	12.1	10.7			Cash & Equivalents	8.8	13.9
	33.7	22.3	17.6			Trade Receivables (net)	18.0	17.6
	24.3	27.2	41.6			Inventory	25.4	27.5
	2.0	2.6	1.3			All Other Current	1.8	2.3
	74.0	64.3	71.3			Total Current	54.0	61.4
	21.2	25.8	19.8			Fixed Assets (net)	29.9	24.2
	2.5	3.1	3.0			Intangibles (net)	8.0	9.5
	2.3	6.8	5.9			All Other Non-Current	8.2	4.9
	100.0	100.0	100.0			Total	100.0	100.0
						LIABILITIES		
	4.9	5.0	5.7			Notes Payable-Short Term	7.3	5.7
	3.2	3.9	2.9			Cur. Mat.-L.T.D.	2.9	3.5
	11.9	9.6	9.1			Trade Payables	7.7	6.0
	.0	.0	.1			Income Taxes Payable	.1	.1
	20.6	8.6	12.8			All Other Current	10.8	14.8
	40.5	27.1	30.7			Total Current	28.8	30.1
	20.8	14.6	8.9			Long-Term Debt	22.6	21.2
	.0	.6	.6			Deferred Taxes	.7	.7
	13.0	9.6	5.8			All Other Non-Current	4.8	4.3
	25.7	48.2	54.0			Net Worth	43.1	43.7
	100.0	100.0	100.0			Total Liabilities & Net Worth	100.0	100.0
						INCOME DATA		
	100.0	100.0	100.0			Net Sales	100.0	100.0
	49.3	37.0	34.7			Gross Profit	35.0	33.9
	44.7	35.3	25.3			Operating Expenses	29.3	31.8
	4.6	1.7	9.4			Operating Profit	5.7	2.2
	.4	.4	.7			All Other Expenses (net)	1.5	-.7
	4.2	1.3	8.7			Profit Before Taxes	4.2	2.9
						RATIOS		
	5.4	5.3	6.5				3.9	4.5
	3.4	2.6	4.5			Current	1.7	2.5
	1.1	1.5	1.4				1.1	1.5
	2.8	3.5	2.6				1.7	2.4
	1.6	1.2	1.7			Quick	.9	1.2
	.7	.8	.5				.5	.6
26	13.8	32	11.3	29	12.4		31	11.9	32	11.3
36	10.0	42	8.7	39	9.4	Sales/Receivables	43	8.4	44	8.3
68	5.4	70	5.2	51	7.2		54	6.7	59	6.2
14	25.8	22	16.4	101	3.6		39	9.4	52	7.0
53	6.9	91	4.0	166	2.2	Cost of Sales/Inventory	99	3.7	118	3.1
182	2.0	146	2.5	304	1.2		130	2.8	203	1.8
15	24.8	17	21.1	8	44.6		11	33.5	11	32.6
25	14.5	29	12.6	19	19.2	Cost of Sales/Payables	24	15.3	21	17.8
45	8.1	46	8.0	36	10.0		38	9.5	39	9.3
	4.0	2.4	2.3				3.3	2.8
	5.9	5.1	2.8			Sales/Working Capital	7.3	4.2
	NM	11.4	4.7				21.7	6.4
		7.8	42.8				14.3	10.5
	(15)	4.3	(13)	2.6		EBIT/Interest	(62)	3.5	(40)	3.5
		.7	1.5				1.1	-2.9
						Net Profit + Depr., Dep.,	8.6	2.9
						Amort./Cur. Mat. L/T/D	(14)	2.5	(10)	.9
							1.4	.1
	.1	.1	.1				.2	.1
	1.1	.5	.5			Fixed/Worth	.8	.7
	16.2	1.3	.8				10.2	1.5
	.6	.2	.2				.3	.4
	3.5	.8	.7			Debt/Worth	1.5	1.3
	NM	1.7	2.7				12.2	3.5
		22.5	29.4				39.9	34.4
	(19)	10.6	(19)	14.2		% Profit Before Taxes/Tangible Net Worth	(53)	15.4	(39)	7.4
		1.4	6.8				4.9	-12.1
	36.6	12.8	23.4				12.7	12.2
	2.4	5.6	5.8			% Profit Before Taxes/Total Assets	4.7	5.4
	-2.1	.2	1.4				.5	-5.0
	43.1	21.9	24.0				14.8	22.4
	30.1	6.6	8.7			Sales/Net Fixed Assets	6.2	5.8
	4.6	3.1	4.6				2.6	2.5
	3.2	2.0	1.8				2.0	1.7
	2.1	1.5	1.3			Sales/Total Assets	1.5	1.1
	1.7	1.2	.8				1.0	.9
		.6	1.1				1.8	1.8
	(15)	3.2	(17)	2.5		% Depr., Dep., Amort./Sales	(54)	3.7	(37)	5.3
		6.6	4.8				6.9	8.5
							4.5	3.5
						% Officers', Directors' Owners' Comp/Sales	(23)	7.6	(11)	6.0
							12.2	10.3
2827M	30193M	179917M	575200M	275538M	426972M	Net Sales ($)	2457328M	1064576M
629M	11646M	110854M	435314M	247755M	310742M	Total Assets ($)	1792116M	1169289M

M = $ thousand   MM = $ million
See Pages viii through xx for Explanation of Ratios and Data

© RMA 2024

MANUFACTURING—Cutting Tool and Machine Tool Accessory Manufacturing NAICS 333515

Comparative Historical Data / Current Data Sorted by Sales

				Type of Statement						
	2	4	5	Unqualified					1	4
	2	8	7	Reviewed				1	4	2
	7	8	7	Compiled			1	4	1	1
	8	5	7	Tax Returns		2	2	2		
	16	18	33	Other	1	7	1	8	7	10
	4/1/21-3/31/22 ALL	4/1/22-3/31/23 ALL	4/1/23-3/31/24 ALL		13 (4/1-9/30/23)			46 (10/1/23-3/31/24)		
					0-1MM	1-3MM	3-5MM	5-10MM	10-25MM	25MM & OVER
	35	43	59	**NUMBER OF STATEMENTS**	1	9	4	15	13	17
	%	%	%	**ASSETS**	%	%	%	%	%	%
	12.7	9.5	11.6	Cash & Equivalents				10.2	14.0	9.0
	20.6	21.6	22.2	Trade Receivables (net)				28.2	16.2	20.1
	29.8	34.5	32.3	Inventory				29.7	41.3	38.4
	1.3	3.0	2.0	All Other Current				2.5	.9	2.2
	64.4	68.6	68.1	Total Current				70.6	72.4	69.7
	23.9	22.5	23.6	Fixed Assets (net)				22.0	21.3	19.5
	7.1	4.0	2.8	Intangibles (net)				2.0	.0	3.6
	4.6	4.9	5.6	All Other Non-Current				5.4	6.3	7.2
	100.0	100.0	100.0	Total				100.0	100.0	100.0
				LIABILITIES						
	4.0	5.1	5.7	Notes Payable-Short Term				3.7	5.1	7.6
	3.3	2.5	3.4	Cur. Mat.-L.T.D.				3.1	4.4	2.9
	9.1	10.1	9.7	Trade Payables				11.0	8.5	10.6
	.1	.1	.1	Income Taxes Payable				.0	.2	.0
	6.0	14.3	12.0	All Other Current				13.2	9.6	12.3
	22.5	32.1	30.9	Total Current				31.0	27.8	33.5
	14.4	10.6	13.9	Long-Term Debt				6.5	12.8	4.0
	1.5	1.0	.5	Deferred Taxes				.8	.9	.2
	13.7	10.7	8.4	All Other Non-Current				1.9	11.2	7.3
	47.8	45.6	46.4	Net Worth				59.8	47.4	54.9
	100.0	100.0	100.0	Total Liabilities & Net Worth				100.0	100.0	100.0
				INCOME DATA						
	100.0	100.0	100.0	Net Sales				100.0	100.0	100.0
	34.8	32.4	38.2	Gross Profit				39.1	38.3	30.4
	31.6	27.7	32.8	Operating Expenses				33.3	30.3	21.6
	3.2	4.6	5.4	Operating Profit				5.8	8.1	8.8
	-3.0	.1	.4	All Other Expenses (net)				.1	.6	.3
	6.2	4.5	5.0	Profit Before Taxes				5.7	7.5	8.5
				RATIOS						
	5.2	5.2	5.5					5.5	6.7	5.4
	3.3	3.6	3.4	Current				3.8	4.4	3.2
	2.1	1.7	1.5					1.4	1.5	1.3
	2.6	2.2	2.4					3.2	2.4	2.6
	1.9	1.5	1.6	Quick				1.2	1.4	1.6
	1.0	.6	.6					.7	.7	.4
34	10.6	28	12.9	30	12.3	Sales/Receivables	31	11.9	28	13.2	33	11.1
42	8.7	42	8.7	38	9.6		51	7.1	33	11.0	45	8.1
61	6.0	69	5.3	57	6.4		64	5.7	42	8.7	49	7.4
56	6.5	49	7.5	53	6.9	Cost of Sales/Inventory	53	6.9	99	3.7	96	3.8
114	3.2	146	2.5	130	2.8		107	3.4	159	2.3	135	2.7
192	1.9	228	1.6	215	1.7		152	2.4	261	1.4	203	1.8
11	33.2	14	25.2	13	28.3	Cost of Sales/Payables	17	21.0	6	60.0	10	36.3
28	12.9	25	14.8	24	15.0		28	12.9	21	17.5	18	20.7
42	8.6	41	8.9	42	8.7		42	8.7	44	8.3	34	10.8
	2.0		2.5		2.4	Sales/Working Capital		2.4		2.1		2.8
	3.6		3.4		4.4			4.4		2.4		4.1
	10.5		5.9		10.7			8.6		6.4		15.1
	34.5		8.9		16.9	EBIT/Interest		33.3				86.0
(27)	8.5	(35)	5.4	(45)	3.8		(11)	6.2	(13)			10.1
	3.0		.8		1.2			1.4				1.7
					10.2	Net Profit + Depr., Dep., Amort./Cur. Mat. L/T/D						
			(13)		6.0							
					.7							
	.2		.1		.1	Fixed/Worth		.1		.1		.2
	.5		.5		.5			.4		.2		.5
	.9		1.0		1.1			.6		1.0		.7
	.3		.4		.3	Debt/Worth		.2		.5		.2
	.8		.9		.8			.6		.8		.6
	2.9		3.5		4.1			1.5		1.6		4.0
	48.9		34.9		25.6	% Profit Before Taxes/Tangible Net Worth		19.4		28.1		24.4
(30)	23.0	(39)	11.0	(54)	13.0		(14)	8.7	(12)	11.5	(16)	16.2
	8.5		.8		2.5			2.4		3.4		10.6
	27.4		18.0		14.7	% Profit Before Taxes/Total Assets		21.7		19.8		16.3
	13.3		5.1		4.6			5.6		6.9		9.3
	3.8		.3		1.2			1.2		1.6		2.2
	21.1		21.4		25.4	Sales/Net Fixed Assets		21.4		27.1		16.3
	6.0		6.9		6.7			6.6		17.8		6.7
	3.7		3.7		3.8			3.2		3.5		5.0
	2.4		2.0		2.1	Sales/Total Assets		2.4		2.0		1.9
	1.3		1.4		1.5			1.5		1.5		1.3
	1.1		1.0		1.1			1.2		.8		1.1
	1.6		.9		1.7	% Depr., Dep., Amort./Sales		.7		.4		1.7
(28)	5.0	(36)	3.6	(46)	2.5		(10)	2.5	(10)	3.9	(15)	2.1
	6.9		5.9		5.5			5.6		6.9		3.2
	2.8		3.8		3.9	% Officers', Directors', Owners' Comp/Sales						
(13)	8.4	(12)	5.5	(18)	5.3							
	11.2		9.8		8.3							
	554860M	923171M	1490647M	Net Sales ($)	890M	19176M	15799M	102876M	224457M	1127449M
	529534M	835513M	1116940M	Total Assets ($)	208M	14443M	12083M	78499M	179804M	831903M

© RMA 2024

M = $ thousand   MM = $ million

See Pages viii through xx for Explanation of Ratios and Data

MANUFACTURING—Machine Tool Manufacturing NAICS 333517

Current Data Sorted by Assets | Comparative Historical Data

0-500M	500M-2MM	2-10MM	10-50MM	50-100MM	100-250MM	Type of Statement		4/1/19-3/31/20 ALL		4/1/20-3/31/21 ALL
2	1	4	3	3	1	Unqualified		10		8
2	3	6	6	2		Reviewed		15		18
	4	2	2			Compiled		13		4
			2			Tax Returns		18		8
		14 (4/1-9/30/23)		5	2	Other		63		32
		15	13							
		58 (10/1/23-3/31/24)								
4	8	21	26	10	3	NUMBER OF STATEMENTS		119		70
%	%	%	%	%	%	ASSETS		%		%
		18.7	11.5	19.4		Cash & Equivalents		12.4		18.1
		21.5	21.2	15.3		Trade Receivables (net)		22.6		17.3
		21.1	25.5	22.9		Inventory		22.7		21.1
		2.4	6.7	5.6		All Other Current		3.8		4.8
		63.6	65.0	63.2		Total Current		61.6		61.2
		29.9	22.0	24.3		Fixed Assets (net)		26.0		27.6
		2.6	3.2	6.2		Intangibles (net)		5.9		6.5
		3.8	9.9	6.2		All Other Non-Current		6.5		4.6
		100.0	100.0	100.0		Total		100.0		100.0
						LIABILITIES				
		8.0	6.3	1.8		Notes Payable-Short Term		9.1		8.0
		4.3	1.7	.9		Cur. Mat.-L.T.D.		4.9		3.6
		7.4	9.6	9.0		Trade Payables		10.8		6.9
		.0	.1	.0		Income Taxes Payable		.1		.0
		5.8	21.7	26.3		All Other Current		11.0		12.0
		25.5	39.2	37.9		Total Current		35.9		30.5
		17.5	10.6	11.7		Long-Term Debt		19.7		20.4
		.5	.3	.7		Deferred Taxes		.4		.2
		6.0	11.2	10.7		All Other Non-Current		3.6		3.0
		50.6	38.7	39.0		Net Worth		40.4		45.8
		100.0	100.0	100.0		Total Liabilties & Net Worth		100.0		100.0
						INCOME DATA				
		100.0	100.0	100.0		Net Sales		100.0		100.0
		38.4	28.2	27.0		Gross Profit		33.0		34.2
		29.9	21.7	23.3		Operating Expenses		28.4		30.2
		8.4	6.5	3.7		Operating Profit		4.6		4.0
		1.5	.9	-.3		All Other Expenses (net)		.9		-2.4
		6.9	5.6	4.0		Profit Before Taxes		3.6		6.4
						RATIOS				
		8.1	3.2	5.7				3.4		5.8
		5.3	1.7	1.5		Current		1.9		2.9
		1.5	1.2	.9				1.2		1.5
		5.5	1.6	2.2				1.9		3.3
		3.2	.7	.8		Quick		1.0		1.6
		1.0	.5	.6				.6		.8
	33	10.9	41 8.9	52 7.0			30	12.0	34	10.6
	51	7.2	58 6.3	60 6.1		Sales/Receivables	44	8.3	47	7.7
	78	4.7	94 3.9	63 5.8			63	5.8	63	5.8
	7	55.7	36 10.1	42 8.6			20	17.9	26	14.0
	59	6.2	81 4.5	104 3.5		Cost of Sales/Inventory	58	6.3	73	5.0
	192	1.9	166 2.2	174 2.1			126	2.9	146	2.5
	7	49.5	16 23.0	21 17.2			16	23.4	10	37.1
	12	31.2	28 13.0	28 13.1		Cost of Sales/Payables	28	12.9	22	16.7
	35	10.3	45 8.1	62 5.9			42	8.6	38	9.6
		1.8	3.2	1.0				3.2		2.1
		4.9	5.7	7.1		Sales/Working Capital		7.1		4.0
		11.4	13.4	NM				20.3		9.2
		45.7	42.0					12.2		25.4
	(17)	4.5	(23) 5.3			EBIT/Interest	(106)	3.4	(54)	6.6
		.3	1.1					-.1		.8
						Net Profit + Depr., Dep.,		5.8		9.2
						Amort./Cur. Mat. L/T/D	(28)	2.7	(13)	4.3
								.7		1.8
		.3	.3	.2				.2		.2
		.7	.5	1.2		Fixed/Worth		.6		.5
		1.1	1.2	NM				2.2		1.3
		.2	.9	.3				.5		.3
		.6	2.3	3.1		Debt/Worth		1.3		.7
		5.3	5.4	NM				5.5		2.7
		94.7	42.6					36.3		35.5
	(19)	17.3	(24) 14.1			% Profit Before Taxes/Tangible Net Worth	(103)	14.8	(60)	15.3
		6.4	4.6					-.1		2.2
		25.6	12.4	10.3				13.4		17.5
		8.9	4.9	3.0		% Profit Before Taxes/Total Assets		5.3		7.6
		1.6	1.6	-3.3				-.5		1.1
		13.9	14.5	10.5				17.7		11.7
		5.5	7.1	4.8		Sales/Net Fixed Assets		8.2		6.0
		3.2	3.4	2.3				4.3		2.8
		2.0	1.6	1.2				2.4		1.9
		1.6	1.2	.8		Sales/Total Assets		1.7		1.2
		.9	1.0	.6				1.2		.9
		1.9	.9					1.4		2.0
	(11)	4.2	(21) 2.6			% Depr., Dep., Amort./Sales	(97)	3.0	(57)	3.3
		5.5	5.7					5.3		5.9
						% Officers', Directors' Owners' Comp/Sales		2.0		2.5
							(34)	4.0	(20)	4.1
								6.8		5.9
3525M	21932M	152217M	751775M	650475M	461793M	Net Sales ($)		3607361M		1956856M
665M	8049M	96650M	567718M	675466M	435890M	Total Assets ($)		2589558M		1555129M

M = $ thousand   MM = $ million
See Pages viii through xx for Explanation of Ratios and Data

© RMA 2024

MANUFACTURING—Machine Tool Manufacturing NAICS 333517

Comparative Historical Data | Current Data Sorted by Sales

Comparative Historical Data			Type of Statement	Current Data Sorted by Sales					
3	7	7	Unqualified				1	3	3
12	20	12	Reviewed		1		4	3	4
8	11	5	Compiled			2		3	
6	17	7	Tax Returns	2	1	2	2	1	1
41	46	41	Other	1	7	7	2	10	14
4/1/21-3/31/22 ALL	4/1/22-3/31/23 ALL	4/1/23-3/31/24 ALL		14 (4/1-9/30/23)			58 (10/1/23-3/31/24)		
				0-1MM	1-3MM	3-5MM	5-10MM	10-25MM	25MM & OVER
70	101	72	NUMBER OF STATEMENTS	3	9	11	7	20	22
%	%	%	ASSETS	%	%	%	%	%	%
19.0	15.3	14.9	Cash & Equivalents			14.7		16.2	10.4
19.5	21.3	20.9	Trade Receivables (net)			15.7		22.7	19.0
23.1	19.8	21.3	Inventory			19.9		23.0	23.7
3.8	4.3	4.5	All Other Current			1.1		3.7	6.5
65.4	60.7	61.6	Total Current			51.5		65.6	59.6
24.6	24.9	27.7	Fixed Assets (net)			36.6		27.1	23.5
4.6	7.3	4.6	Intangibles (net)			8.2		2.1	7.2
5.4	7.2	6.1	All Other Non-Current			3.7		5.2	9.8
100.0	100.0	100.0	Total			100.0		100.0	100.0
			LIABILITIES						
5.2	7.8	8.1	Notes Payable-Short Term			12.6		2.7	6.4
3.7	3.0	3.1	Cur. Mat.-L.T.D.			1.8		3.0	.9
9.3	10.0	16.6	Trade Payables			5.0		7.5	10.7
.1	.2	.0	Income Taxes Payable			.0		.1	.0
14.5	16.2	14.5	All Other Current			8.1		18.2	20.4
32.8	37.2	42.2	Total Current			27.5		31.4	38.2
14.2	18.4	17.8	Long-Term Debt			25.3		10.4	12.4
.2	.4	.4	Deferred Taxes			.2		.6	.6
2.4	4.5	8.5	All Other Non-Current			6.2		7.8	13.1
50.4	39.5	31.1	Net Worth			40.7		49.8	35.6
100.0	100.0	100.0	Total Liabilties & Net Worth			100.0		100.0	100.0
			INCOME DATA						
100.0	100.0	100.0	Net Sales			100.0		100.0	100.0
35.1	34.2	34.4	Gross Profit			38.1		32.1	27.1
28.6	28.0	28.2	Operating Expenses			31.7		26.1	21.3
6.5	6.2	6.1	Operating Profit			6.4		6.0	5.8
-3.0	.7	1.1	All Other Expenses (net)			1.8		.4	1.2
9.5	5.5	5.1	Profit Before Taxes			4.6		5.6	4.6
			RATIOS						
4.3	3.8	5.3				8.8		5.2	5.2
2.1	2.3	1.8	Current			3.7		1.8	1.6
1.3	1.4	1.2				.8		1.5	1.1
2.5	2.7	3.2				5.7		3.0	2.1
1.3	1.2	1.1	Quick			1.8		1.2	.8
.7	.6	.6				.6		.6	.6
29 12.4	35 10.3	38 9.5		2 208.0		41 9.0		39 9.3	
46 8.0	51 7.2	54 6.8	Sales/Receivables	44 8.3		52 7.0		61 6.0	
63 5.8	68 5.4	68 5.4		58 6.3		66 5.5		69 5.3	
32 11.4	17 21.1	21 17.1		0 UND		23 15.7		42 8.6	
73 5.0	68 5.4	64 5.7	Cost of Sales/Inventory	30 12.0		81 4.5		81 4.5	
146 2.5	118 3.1	146 2.5		182 2.0		174 2.1		146 2.5	
13 27.2	13 27.9	11 34.0		5 74.8		11 33.9		24 15.5	
22 16.7	29 12.7	27 13.7	Cost of Sales/Payables	9 40.9		16 23.5		29 12.5	
36 10.1	54 6.7	44 8.3		35 10.5		36 10.2		57 6.4	
2.6	3.2	2.8				2.4		2.5	3.5
5.3	5.2	5.7	Sales/Working Capital			5.0		4.7	6.9
13.7	13.8	25.5				-31.4		9.6	49.4
42.3	31.0	24.3						67.3	18.2
(56) 18.5	(82) 7.2	(60) 4.7	EBIT/Interest			(18) 14.9		(18) 3.6	
5.5	1.6	1.1						4.5	.9
40.7	11.5	41.8	Net Profit + Depr., Dep.,						
(12) 3.3	(27) 2.7	(16) 6.8	Amort./Cur. Mat. L/T/D						
1.2	1.7	.9							
.2	.2	.3				.2		.3	.3
.5	.5	.6	Fixed/Worth			.9		.5	.9
.9	1.7	2.3				20.7		.8	4.5
.3	.4	.3				.3		.4	1.0
.8	1.5	2.3	Debt/Worth			.9		1.0	4.1
2.6	7.3	8.7				22.6		2.7	12.6
46.5	39.8	54.4						44.0	40.6
(65) 27.7	(85) 23.3	(61) 16.2	% Profit Before Taxes/Tangible Net Worth					15.4 (18)	17.0
8.9	3.9	3.3						4.6	1.0
25.0	16.6	12.5				12.5		14.4	8.5
11.3	7.9	6.1	% Profit Before Taxes/Total Assets			3.2		6.4	3.5
2.9	1.7	.2				-2.4		2.3	-1.6
16.1	17.4	13.3				91.9		10.1	14.6
7.2	7.9	6.9	Sales/Net Fixed Assets			5.5		6.4	5.8
3.5	3.6	3.3				2.2		3.5	2.7
2.2	2.0	1.9				2.5		1.9	1.5
1.4	1.5	1.3	Sales/Total Assets			1.7		1.3	1.1
1.0	1.0	.9				.8		1.0	.9
1.4	1.2	1.6						1.9	1.0
(54) 2.8	(80) 2.8	(51) 3.4	% Depr., Dep., Amort./Sales				(14)	3.6 (18)	2.7
5.4	5.5	6.3						5.3	6.6
2.3	2.1	.9	% Officers', Directors'						
(23) 3.3	(22) 5.0	(23) 3.2	Owners' Comp/Sales						
11.4	8.4	6.4							
1916909M	3030916M	2041717M	Net Sales ($)	1807M	17825M	44516M	53917M	350989M	1572663M
1472074M	2565717M	1784438M	Total Assets ($)	532M	14756M	29626M	47514M	336048M	1355962M

M = $ thousand   MM = $ million
See Pages viii through xx for Explanation of Ratios and Data
© RMA 2024

MANUFACTURING—Rolling Mill and Other Metalworking Machinery Manufacturing NAICS 333519

Current Data Sorted by Assets | Comparative Historical Data

						Type of Statement		
			3	4	1	Unqualified	2	2
				2	1	Reviewed	7	8
		3	3	2		Compiled	6	4
1	1	1	8	9		Tax Returns	5	1
		6 (4/1-9/30/23)		37 (10/1/23-3/31/24)	4	Other	21	21
0-500M	500M-2MM	2-10MM	10-50MM	50-100MM	100-250MM		4/1/19-3/31/20 ALL	4/1/20-3/31/21 ALL
1	2	14	17	3	6	NUMBER OF STATEMENTS	41	36
%	%	%	%	%	%	ASSETS	%	%
		24.8	19.9			Cash & Equivalents	16.4	17.9
		23.1	19.5			Trade Receivables (net)	25.2	22.0
		16.9	25.0			Inventory	24.7	22.0
		6.1	5.0			All Other Current	4.6	5.1
		70.9	69.5			Total Current	70.9	67.1
		19.6	23.2			Fixed Assets (net)	15.9	17.4
		3.0	1.6			Intangibles (net)	7.0	5.1
		6.5	5.7			All Other Non-Current	6.2	10.4
		100.0	100.0			Total	100.0	100.0
						LIABILITIES		
		5.4	5.8			Notes Payable-Short Term	9.4	7.7
		2.0	1.6			Cur. Mat.-L.T.D.	1.4	2.4
		5.0	8.9			Trade Payables	10.5	8.8
		.1	.1			Income Taxes Payable	.2	.0
		17.0	24.0			All Other Current	19.4	15.4
		29.4	40.5			Total Current	40.9	34.4
		14.3	7.5			Long-Term Debt	11.7	15.6
		.0	.4			Deferred Taxes	.3	.3
		11.6	2.1			All Other Non-Current	8.9	10.8
		44.6	49.4			Net Worth	38.3	38.9
		100.0	100.0			Total Liabilities & Net Worth	100.0	100.0
						INCOME DATA		
		100.0	100.0			Net Sales	100.0	100.0
		43.4	32.1			Gross Profit	35.7	34.3
		33.8	23.9			Operating Expenses	30.2	31.1
		9.6	8.2			Operating Profit	5.5	3.2
		.6	-.7			All Other Expenses (net)	1.7	-1.2
		9.0	8.9			Profit Before Taxes	3.8	4.4
						RATIOS		
		4.6	2.3				3.9	4.1
		3.2	1.6			Current	2.2	2.1
		1.6	1.4				1.3	1.5
		2.9	1.6				2.6	2.2
		1.9	.9			Quick	1.2	1.2
		.7	.7				.6	.7
		33 11.2	20 18.6				33 11.2	35 10.3
		44 8.3	44 8.3			Sales/Receivables	43 8.4	44 8.3
		60 6.1	99 3.7				79 4.6	70 5.2
		9 42.1	72 5.1				28 13.0	24 15.1
		25 14.4	96 3.8			Cost of Sales/Inventory	70 5.2	57 6.4
		182 2.0	228 1.6				130 2.8	140 2.6
		6 57.4	14 26.1				17 21.9	11 33.6
		18 19.8	30 12.0			Cost of Sales/Payables	26 14.3	31 11.9
		27 13.7	50 7.3				44 8.3	43 8.4
		2.1	2.8				2.5	2.7
		3.9	4.0			Sales/Working Capital	4.8	5.0
		11.0	6.2				13.9	10.8
		16.0	32.2				19.3	37.9
		(10) 4.1	(14) 17.6			EBIT/Interest	(33) 7.5	(28) 8.0
		.8	6.5				.3	1.5
						Net Profit + Depr., Dep., Amort./Cur. Mat. L/T/D		
		.1	.1				.1	.1
		.6	.3			Fixed/Worth	.4	.4
		1.4	.7				.9	1.0
		.4	.4				.5	.5
		1.5	1.2			Debt/Worth	1.0	1.0
		3.1	2.3				4.1	3.5
		54.0	54.8				34.7	52.8
		(13) 10.8	21.3			% Profit Before Taxes/Tangible Net Worth	(34) 11.2	(33) 17.7
		2.1	14.3				.4	2.8
		19.8	15.4				13.6	15.4
		7.7	11.4			% Profit Before Taxes/Total Assets	5.3	7.3
		1.2	7.3				-.9	-.7
		70.1	76.6				33.9	35.9
		14.8	6.5			Sales/Net Fixed Assets	17.9	12.9
		4.3	2.5				8.3	6.2
		2.1	1.4				2.4	2.3
		1.5	1.1			Sales/Total Assets	1.6	1.8
		1.2	.8				1.1	1.3
		.5	.2				.5	.7
		(11) 1.6	(15) 1.6			% Depr., Dep., Amort./Sales	(32) 1.5	(27) 2.0
		3.8	6.2				3.3	3.9
						% Officers', Directors' Owners' Comp/Sales	2.2	1.9
							(17) 3.4	(12) 5.2
							5.9	6.9
1632M	14729M	118253M	431254M	262050M	1113076M	Net Sales ($)	789317M	796426M
154M	2815M	77146M	383547M	199673M	1055356M	Total Assets ($)	663700M	701436M

© RMA 2024   M = $ thousand   MM = $ million
See Pages viii through xx for Explanation of Ratios and Data

MANUFACTURING—Rolling Mill and Other Metalworking Machinery Manufacturing   NAICS 333519

Comparative Historical Data | Current Data Sorted by Sales

Comparative Historical Data					Current Data Sorted by Sales					
			Type of Statement							
2	2	8	Unqualified				2	3	3	
3	4	3	Reviewed					1	2	
2	4	2	Compiled				1		1	
4	2	5	Tax Returns			1	2	1		
14	23	25	Other		1	2	7	5	10	
4/1/21-	4/1/22-	4/1/23-				6 (4/1-9/30/23)		37 (10/1/23-3/31/24)		
3/31/22	3/31/23	3/31/24		0-1MM	1-3MM	3-5MM	5-10MM	10-25MM	25MM & OVER	
ALL	ALL	ALL								
25	35	43	**NUMBER OF STATEMENTS**		3	2	12	10	16	
%	%	%	**ASSETS**	%	%	%	%	%	%	
17.5	14.6	21.7	Cash & Equivalents				31.4	15.8	11.7	
20.3	19.7	19.8	Trade Receivables (net)	D			16.4	18.2	23.4	
25.8	24.1	21.0	Inventory	A			19.1	25.0	26.3	
6.6	7.8	7.9	All Other Current	T			7.2	3.7	11.3	
70.3	66.1	70.3	Total Current	A			74.1	62.8	72.7	
17.2	18.4	20.5	Fixed Assets (net)				17.4	30.1	16.5	
2.5	7.4	3.2	Intangibles (net)	N			3.0	2.9	4.6	
10.0	8.1	5.9	All Other Non-Current	O			5.5	4.2	6.2	
100.0	100.0	100.0	Total	T			100.0	100.0	100.0	
			LIABILITIES	A						
4.2	1.9	5.2	Notes Payable-Short Term	V			3.8	2.4	7.3	
1.9	1.9	1.6	Cur. Mat.-L.T.D.	A			1.5	2.5	1.3	
8.7	8.5	7.9	Trade Payables	I			2.2	12.4	8.9	
.1	.0	.1	Income Taxes Payable	L			.1	.0	.1	
22.7	23.0	21.9	All Other Current	A			20.0	19.4	27.5	
37.5	35.3	36.7	Total Current	B			27.6	36.8	45.1	
11.1	12.4	9.4	Long-Term Debt	L			11.6	17.5	5.0	
.2	.0	.3	Deferred Taxes	E			.0	.7	.4	
9.1	5.4	6.5	All Other Non-Current				12.6	2.2	5.6	
42.1	46.9	47.2	Net Worth				48.0	42.9	43.9	
100.0	100.0	100.0	Total Liabilities & Net Worth				100.0	100.0	100.0	
			INCOME DATA							
100.0	100.0	100.0	Net Sales				100.0	100.0	100.0	
31.8	35.9	36.4	Gross Profit				50.4	29.6	24.9	
26.1	26.8	27.9	Operating Expenses				41.1	20.5	15.4	
5.7	9.1	8.5	Operating Profit				9.2	9.0	9.5	
-2.2	1.5	.2	All Other Expenses (net)				.4	.5	1.1	
7.9	7.6	8.3	Profit Before Taxes				8.9	8.6	8.4	
			RATIOS							
2.8	3.1	3.8					4.6	2.2	2.2	
1.9	1.9	1.7	Current				3.6	1.8	1.5	
1.4	1.3	1.3					1.7	1.5	1.2	
1.6	1.6	2.3					3.3	1.8	1.0	
.9	.8	1.1	Quick				2.2	1.2	.9	
.4	.4	.5					.8	.5	.5	
29 12.4	23 16.0	21 17.2			14 26.8	20 17.9	31 11.7			
43 8.5	47 7.7	42 8.6	Sales/Receivables		38 9.5	35 10.3	53 6.9			
60 6.1	66 5.5	68 5.4			50 7.3	66 5.5	89 4.1			
37 9.9	23 15.9	21 17.8			11 34.1	39 9.3	60 6.1			
107 3.4	114 3.2	89 4.1	Cost of Sales/Inventory		101 3.6	76 4.8	96 3.8			
166 2.2	174 2.1	182 2.0			243 1.5	215 1.7	130 2.8			
14 26.8	20 17.9	13 27.6			5 67.2	24 15.4	16 22.2			
26 14.3	29 12.8	25 14.6	Cost of Sales/Payables		9 39.3	33 11.2	30 12.3			
42 8.6	51 7.2	39 9.3			25 14.7	61 6.0	47 7.8			
3.2	3.0	2.7					2.0	3.4	3.4	
4.3	5.4	4.3	Sales/Working Capital				3.0	4.6	6.0	
7.7	9.6	8.7					12.2	7.2	10.2	
57.8	34.8	32.2							44.9	
(21) 22.8	(32) 16.2	(34) 9.1	EBIT/Interest					(14) 16.5		
8.8	5.5	3.0							3.0	
			Net Profit + Depr., Dep., Amort./Cur. Mat. L/T/D							
.1	.1	.1					.1	.3	.2	
.4	.4	.5	Fixed/Worth				.4	.7	.4	
.9	.7	1.0					1.4	1.1	.5	
.6	.6	.5					.3	1.0	.8	
1.0	1.5	1.2	Debt/Worth				1.2	1.3	1.4	
2.4	2.3	2.5					3.1	3.0	2.3	
44.7	34.4	48.2					56.9	54.1	56.9	
(23) 21.8	(33) 20.8	(41) 21.2	% Profit Before Taxes/Tangible Net Worth			(11) 10.8	31.4	(15) 18.3		
6.9	4.8	8.7					3.6	16.0	13.6	
18.9	14.6	16.4					26.3	17.2	13.1	
10.2	9.5	8.3	% Profit Before Taxes/Total Assets				7.2	14.0	10.2	
4.1	2.6	4.5					2.2	8.1	6.6	
30.4	32.1	52.4					118.9	33.9	31.3	
13.0	8.1	7.3	Sales/Net Fixed Assets				33.8	3.8	7.8	
6.2	4.6	3.5					4.8	2.1	4.0	
2.3	1.9	1.9					2.0	1.6	1.9	
1.4	1.2	1.3	Sales/Total Assets				1.5	1.2	1.2	
.8	.7	.9					1.1	.8	.9	
.6	1.1	.4					.7		.2	
(18) 1.3	(25) 2.5	(34) 1.6	% Depr., Dep., Amort./Sales				3.4	(13) 1.2		
2.8	4.4	3.9					6.4		1.7	
		1.5								
	(11) 1.7	% Officers', Directors' Owners' Comp/Sales								
		5.3								
757649M	1465132M	1940994M	Net Sales ($)		5759M	8600M	89903M	188000M	1648732M	
677306M	1547929M	1718691M	Total Assets ($)		14468M	9566M	73310M	182676M	1438671M	

© RMA 2024   M = $ thousand   MM = $ million
See Pages viii through xx for Explanation of Ratios and Data

MANUFACTURING—Air and Gas Compressor Manufacturing   NAICS 333912

Current Data Sorted by Assets | Comparative Historical Data

							Type of Statement		
				5	2	3	Unqualified	5	5
		1		1			Reviewed	5	1
		2	1				Compiled		1
	1	1	1				Tax Returns	1	1
	1			2	4	5	Other	15	10
0-500M	5 (4/1-9/30/23) 500M-2MM	2-10MM	24 (10/1/23-3/31/24) 10-50MM	50-100MM	100-250MM			4/1/19-3/31/20 ALL	4/1/20-3/31/21 ALL
	2	5	8	6	8		NUMBER OF STATEMENTS	26	18
%	%	%	%	%	%		ASSETS	%	%
							Cash & Equivalents	8.9	10.8
							Trade Receivables (net)	23.3	18.5
							Inventory	25.2	27.2
							All Other Current	3.0	1.9
							Total Current	60.4	58.5
							Fixed Assets (net)	26.6	28.6
							Intangibles (net)	4.8	6.9
							All Other Non-Current	8.3	6.0
							Total	100.0	100.0
							LIABILITIES		
							Notes Payable-Short Term	8.1	6.9
							Cur. Mat.-L.T.D.	1.5	2.2
							Trade Payables	9.3	11.4
							Income Taxes Payable	.0	.0
							All Other Current	13.0	6.8
							Total Current	32.0	27.3
							Long-Term Debt	9.8	17.0
							Deferred Taxes	.2	.0
							All Other Non-Current	5.3	12.3
							Net Worth	52.6	43.4
							Total Liabilities & Net Worth	100.0	100.0
							INCOME DATA		
							Net Sales	100.0	100.0
							Gross Profit	36.7	33.7
							Operating Expenses	28.9	27.6
							Operating Profit	7.8	6.1
							All Other Expenses (net)	1.1	1.1
							Profit Before Taxes	6.7	5.0
							RATIOS		
							Current	3.5	4.3
								2.0	2.2
								1.3	1.5
							Quick	1.8	1.5
							(25)	.8	.9
								.6	.7
								34 / 10.7	27 / 13.7
							Sales/Receivables	61 / 6.0	41 / 8.9
								79 / 4.6	53 / 6.9
								52 / 7.0	53 / 6.9
							Cost of Sales/Inventory	101 / 3.6	111 / 3.3
								146 / 2.5	140 / 2.6
								16 / 23.4	14 / 25.8
							Cost of Sales/Payables	29 / 12.8	27 / 13.4
								45 / 8.2	38 / 9.6
								3.4	3.2
							Sales/Working Capital	4.9	5.2
								13.5	10.2
								26.5	19.9
							EBIT/Interest (23)	4.0	(16) 3.1
								1.5	-1.0
							Net Profit + Depr., Dep., Amort./Cur. Mat. L/T/D		
								.2	.3
							Fixed/Worth	.6	.8
								.8	1.9
								.4	.6
							Debt/Worth	1.2	1.4
								2.1	5.2
							% Profit Before Taxes/Tangible Net Worth	50.0	30.2
							(25)	19.5	(17) 10.2
								5.0	-10.0
							% Profit Before Taxes/Total Assets	20.2	15.4
								8.2	4.0
								2.3	-2.5
								14.7	63.6
							Sales/Net Fixed Assets	9.0	8.4
								4.1	2.5
								2.0	2.7
							Sales/Total Assets	1.5	1.6
								1.1	1.1
							% Depr., Dep., Amort./Sales	.7	.9
							(22)	1.5	(10) 2.1
								2.6	4.1
							% Officers', Directors' Owners' Comp/Sales		
7493M	53315M	336702M	751279M	990263M			Net Sales ($)	1174892M	688027M
2617M	35103M	208168M	442714M	1175570M			Total Assets ($)	1056701M	807559M

DATA NOT AVAILABLE (for 0-500M column)

M = $ thousand   MM = $ million
See Pages viii through xx for Explanation of Ratios and Data

© RMA 2024

MANUFACTURING—Air and Gas Compressor Manufacturing NAICS 333912

Comparative Historical Data | **Current Data Sorted by Sales**

Comparative Historical Data			Type of Statement	Current Data Sorted by Sales					
7	2	10	Unqualified					2	10
1	2	2	Reviewed				1	1	
1	2	2	Compiled			1		1	
2	2	2	Tax Returns			2			11
12	22	13	Other						
4/1/21-3/31/22 ALL	4/1/22-3/31/23 ALL	4/1/23-3/31/24 ALL		0-1MM	5 (4/1-9/30/23) 1-3MM	3-5MM	24 (10/1/23-3/31/24) 5-10MM	10-25MM	25MM & OVER
23	30	29	**NUMBER OF STATEMENTS**			3	1	4	21
%	%	%	**ASSETS**	%	%	%	%	%	%
9.2	13.0	5.9	Cash & Equivalents	D	D				5.3
26.9	22.7	19.2	Trade Receivables (net)	A	A				20.8
28.5	33.8	33.3	Inventory	T	T				28.9
3.7	3.2	2.7	All Other Current	A	A				2.8
68.3	72.7	61.1	Total Current						57.9
14.5	15.6	18.6	Fixed Assets (net)	N	N				18.6
11.5	8.2	16.4	Intangibles (net)	O	O				20.2
5.7	3.5	3.8	All Other Non-Current	T	T				3.4
100.0	100.0	100.0	Total						100.0
			LIABILITIES	A	A				
5.8	5.9	3.2	Notes Payable-Short Term	V	V				3.6
2.2	1.9	2.4	Cur. Mat.-L.T.D.	A	A				2.7
14.6	13.1	11.8	Trade Payables	I	I				7.8
.1	.4	.2	Income Taxes Payable	L	L				.1
14.7	11.9	14.9	All Other Current	A	A				12.1
37.3	33.2	32.5	Total Current	B	B				26.2
11.6	13.4	16.5	Long-Term Debt	L	L				13.9
.2	.2	.7	Deferred Taxes	E	E				.2
6.2	8.1	4.6	All Other Non-Current						1.8
44.7	45.1	45.7	Net Worth						57.9
100.0	100.0	100.0	Total Liabilities & Net Worth						100.0
			INCOME DATA						
100.0	100.0	100.0	Net Sales						100.0
30.7	34.4	36.6	Gross Profit						35.6
27.6	25.4	30.7	Operating Expenses						29.2
3.1	9.0	5.9	Operating Profit						6.5
-1.6	.8	1.9	All Other Expenses (net)						2.0
4.6	8.2	3.9	Profit Before Taxes						4.4
			RATIOS						
3.0	3.5	4.3							4.3
2.0	2.3	2.6	Current						2.6
1.5	1.5	1.6							1.7
1.4	1.5	1.9							1.9
1.1	1.1	1.0	Quick						1.0
.6	.7	.6							.7
41 9.0	36 10.1	36 10.0						38	9.7
56 6.5	52 7.0	51 7.1	Sales/Receivables					51	7.1
87 4.2	64 5.7	63 5.8						63	5.8
73 5.0	79 4.6	94 3.9						87	4.2
104 3.5	118 3.1	122 3.0	Cost of Sales/Inventory					107	3.4
126 2.9	174 2.1	174 2.1						174	2.1
22 16.5	13 28.1	14 25.5						14	25.5
44 8.3	30 12.0	26 13.9	Cost of Sales/Payables					25	14.7
59 6.2	43 8.5	52 7.0						45	8.1
2.9	3.1	3.0							3.6
4.8	4.4	4.1	Sales/Working Capital						4.1
9.2	7.6	5.9							5.7
90.4	34.9	23.8							25.4
(21) 7.4	(27) 13.7	(26) 5.1	EBIT/Interest					(20)	12.1
2.8	4.0	1.6							1.8
		14.6	Net Profit + Depr., Dep.,						17.6
	(16)	6.2	Amort./Cur. Mat. L/T/D					(14)	6.5
		1.3							1.4
.2	.1	.3							.3
.4	.5	.5	Fixed/Worth						.5
1.2	1.4	1.4							1.1
.8	.6	.5							.5
1.2	1.4	1.2	Debt/Worth						1.2
8.0	3.2	7.1							2.8
37.2	41.3	29.2							27.1
(19) 17.7	(25) 23.5	(24) 20.0	% Profit Before Taxes/Tangible Net Worth					(18)	18.5
4.9	15.2	15.4							15.5
18.1	22.5	15.8							13.2
6.5	11.5	7.7	% Profit Before Taxes/Total Assets						7.7
2.2	6.1	2.5							4.1
24.1	131.3	20.0							15.9
12.9	13.5	9.9	Sales/Net Fixed Assets						9.0
5.9	7.5	5.3							5.3
2.1	2.1	2.0							1.9
1.6	1.7	1.6	Sales/Total Assets						1.6
1.2	1.4	.8							.8
.8	.7	.4							.7
(15) 2.2	(16) 1.4	(23) 1.6	% Depr., Dep., Amort./Sales					(16)	1.8
3.0	1.9	2.1							2.0
			% Officers', Directors' Owners' Comp/Sales						
1199776M	1471926M	2139052M	Net Sales ($)	10590M	8868M		52606M		2066988M
1013307M	1092503M	1864172M	Total Assets ($)	7372M	2197M		41030M		1813573M

© RMA 2024   M = $ thousand   MM = $ million
See Pages viii through xx for Explanation of Ratios and Data

MANUFACTURING—Measuring, Dispensing, and Other Pumping Equipment Manufacturing NAICS 333914

Current Data Sorted by Assets | Comparative Historical Data

0-500M	500M-2MM	2-10MM	10-50MM	50-100MM	100-250MM	Type of Statement		
			1		2	Unqualified	3	4
		2	4			Reviewed	5	6
		2	2			Compiled	5	3
	1	2	2	1		Tax Returns	6	2
	3		15		3	Other	27	15
	6 (4/1-9/30/23)		35 (10/1/23-3/31/24)				4/1/19-3/31/20 ALL	4/1/20-3/31/21 ALL
	4	8	22	2	5	NUMBER OF STATEMENTS	46	30
%	%	%	%	%	%	**ASSETS**	%	%
D			10.8			Cash & Equivalents	11.3	16.2
A			22.7			Trade Receivables (net)	29.7	22.6
T			40.3			Inventory	31.5	30.4
A			1.9			All Other Current	2.3	4.3
			75.6			Total Current	74.8	73.5
N			14.4			Fixed Assets (net)	15.0	12.9
O			1.8			Intangibles (net)	6.0	6.5
T			8.2			All Other Non-Current	4.2	7.2
			100.0			Total	100.0	100.0
A						**LIABILITIES**		
V			3.2			Notes Payable-Short Term	14.2	2.5
A			.8			Cur. Mat.-L.T.D.	2.2	3.2
I			9.8			Trade Payables	14.3	12.6
L			.3			Income Taxes Payable	.1	.3
A			14.3			All Other Current	13.5	13.7
B			28.3			Total Current	44.3	32.4
L			5.6			Long-Term Debt	9.6	12.7
E			.2			Deferred Taxes	.4	.2
			2.7			All Other Non-Current	7.4	8.0
			63.1			Net Worth	38.3	46.8
			100.0			Total Liabilities & Net Worth	100.0	100.0
						INCOME DATA		
			100.0			Net Sales	100.0	100.0
			37.9			Gross Profit	37.2	41.1
			26.4			Operating Expenses	32.7	34.9
			11.6			Operating Profit	4.4	6.2
			.8			All Other Expenses (net)	.3	.2
			10.8			Profit Before Taxes	4.2	6.1
						RATIOS		
			5.4				3.0	3.8
			3.2			Current	1.9	2.2
			1.9				1.3	1.4
			2.7				1.7	2.0
			1.2			Quick	1.0	1.1
			.9				.6	.7
			41 8.9				38 9.7	36 10.0
			47 7.7			Sales/Receivables	51 7.1	47 7.8
			66 5.5				68 5.4	61 6.0
			107 3.4				59 6.2	69 5.3
			135 2.7			Cost of Sales/Inventory	87 4.2	118 3.1
			243 1.5				159 2.3	203 1.8
			20 18.0				22 16.9	20 17.9
			31 11.6			Cost of Sales/Payables	34 10.8	43 8.5
			47 7.8				51 7.2	51 7.2
			2.4				3.8	2.4
			3.3			Sales/Working Capital	6.1	3.7
			5.0				11.0	8.0
			178.5				22.3	14.2
		(19)	53.1			EBIT/Interest	(41) 7.5	(22) 6.7
			9.2				3.6	4.6
						Net Profit + Depr., Dep.,	9.9	8.2
						Amort./Cur. Mat. L/T/D	(15) 4.4	(10) 4.1
							1.6	1.5
			.1				.1	.1
			.2			Fixed/Worth	.4	.3
			.4				1.0	.7
			.3				.4	.7
			.4			Debt/Worth	1.9	1.6
			1.3				4.9	2.5
			44.0				46.9	31.2
			24.1			% Profit Before Taxes/Tangible Net Worth	(39) 24.4	(29) 21.8
			18.1				13.0	15.8
			23.7				16.7	15.2
			15.7			% Profit Before Taxes/Total Assets	9.3	8.8
			11.5				4.4	5.3
			33.2				47.0	32.4
			16.2			Sales/Net Fixed Assets	22.7	20.8
			5.7				6.4	5.9
			2.0				2.7	2.2
			1.5			Sales/Total Assets	1.9	1.7
			1.2				1.4	1.1
			.5				.9	.7
		(19)	1.3			% Depr., Dep., Amort./Sales	(29) 1.5	(24) 1.8
			2.5				2.9	3.4
							2.1	
						% Officers', Directors' Owners' Comp/Sales	(14) 4.8	
							9.7	
	11093M	99054M	862090M	202589M	621154M	Net Sales ($)	2044281M	798310M
	5664M	42366M	530583M	142889M	759643M	Total Assets ($)	1377874M	586084M

M = $ thousand   MM = $ million
See Pages viii through xx for Explanation of Ratios and Data

© RMA 2024

MANUFACTURING—Measuring, Dispensing, and Other Pumping Equipment Manufacturing NAICS 333914

Comparative Historical Data | Current Data Sorted by Sales

						Type of Statement							
		2		6	4	Unqualified						4	
		2		3	6	Reviewed					4	2	
		5		4	4	Compiled			1	1	2		
		7		4	3	Tax Returns				3			
		18		29	24	Other		3	1	1	2	18	
		4/1/21-3/31/22 ALL		4/1/22-3/31/23 ALL	4/1/23-3/31/24 ALL		0-1MM	6 (4/1-9/30/23) 1-3MM	3-5MM	35 (10/1/23-3/31/24) 5-10MM	10-25MM	25MM & OVER	
		34		46	41	NUMBER OF STATEMENTS		3	1	5	8	24	
		%		%	%	ASSETS	%	%	%	%	%	%	
		12.8		15.5	12.3	Cash & Equivalents						11.0	
		25.3		20.4	20.9	Trade Receivables (net)						22.7	
		32.5		31.3	35.9	Inventory	DATA					36.1	
		5.4		5.6	1.5	All Other Current	NOT					2.1	
		76.1		72.9	70.5	Total Current	AVAILABLE					71.8	
		13.8		16.7	17.0	Fixed Assets (net)						15.5	
		5.1		5.8	4.3	Intangibles (net)						4.9	
		5.0		4.6	8.2	All Other Non-Current						7.8	
		100.0		100.0	100.0	Total						100.0	
						LIABILITIES							
		4.1		5.5	2.8	Notes Payable-Short Term						3.4	
		2.9		1.1	2.1	Cur. Mat.-L.T.D.						1.2	
		16.2		13.6	12.4	Trade Payables						13.1	
		.0		.4	.4	Income Taxes Payable						.3	
		15.4		11.2	15.1	All Other Current						14.8	
		38.8		31.8	32.7	Total Current						32.8	
		10.4		11.3	8.1	Long-Term Debt						8.8	
		.3		.1	.3	Deferred Taxes						.3	
		7.7		6.1	7.9	All Other Non-Current						2.8	
		42.9		50.7	51.0	Net Worth						55.3	
		100.0		100.0	100.0	Total Liabilities & Net Worth						100.0	
						INCOME DATA							
		100.0		100.0	100.0	Net Sales						100.0	
		42.6		38.2	39.3	Gross Profit						35.8	
		35.3		30.4	29.8	Operating Expenses						26.6	
		7.3		7.8	9.5	Operating Profit						9.2	
		-1.6		.3	.9	All Other Expenses (net)						1.2	
		9.0		7.4	8.6	Profit Before Taxes						8.0	
						RATIOS							
		5.0		6.0	5.1							4.3	
		2.7		2.3	2.4	Current						2.1	
		1.3		1.6	1.6							1.6	
		2.5		2.5	2.4							2.1	
		1.5		1.1	1.1	Quick						1.2	
		.5		.5	.7							.9	
29	12.7		27	13.4	35	10.3						42	8.7
50	7.3		44	8.3	49	7.5	Sales/Receivables					52	7.0
73	5.0		57	6.4	68	5.4						69	5.3
66	5.5		52	7.0	85	4.3						87	4.2
126	2.9		118	3.1	122	3.0	Cost of Sales/Inventory					122	3.0
182	2.0		174	2.1	192	1.9						182	2.0
19	19.7		18	20.3	20	18.1						21	17.5
36	10.0		34	10.7	37	9.8	Cost of Sales/Payables					35	10.4
74	4.9		72	5.1	51	7.2						51	7.2
		2.9		2.7	2.5							2.5	
		4.2		4.3	4.6	Sales/Working Capital						5.0	
		13.7		9.8	6.4							6.1	
		50.7		21.0	120.9							178.5	
(25)	19.5		(33)	10.5	(33)	31.3	EBIT/Interest					(19)	53.1
		5.5		4.0	4.3							9.2	
				27.5	26.9	Net Profit + Depr., Dep.,							
			(12)	10.5	(12)	12.4	Amort./Cur. Mat. L/T/D						
				4.7	3.3								
		.2		.1	.1							.1	
		.4		.3	.3	Fixed/Worth						.3	
		1.0		.8	.6							.6	
		.4		.4	.3							.4	
		1.4		1.0	.8	Debt/Worth						.9	
		5.4		3.0	1.7							1.6	
		88.1		49.2	47.0	% Profit Before Taxes/Tangible						46.4	
(31)	33.4		(43)	19.3	(38)	23.9	Net Worth					(23)	24.4
		18.8		10.5	18.7							20.7	
		25.4		16.9	22.8	% Profit Before Taxes/Total						21.0	
		15.9		9.6	14.5	Assets						15.0	
		6.6		4.0	7.2							10.2	
		45.1		58.2	31.3							32.9	
		15.0		18.3	11.4	Sales/Net Fixed Assets						11.7	
		8.1		5.5	5.4							6.1	
		2.3		2.1	2.0							2.0	
		1.7		1.7	1.5	Sales/Total Assets						1.6	
		1.2		1.1	1.2							1.2	
		1.1		.8	.5							.5	
(25)	1.8		(35)	1.3	(32)	1.3	% Depr., Dep., Amort./Sales					(20)	1.1
		3.2		2.7	2.6							2.1	
		2.7				% Officers', Directors'							
(13)	4.0					Owners' Comp/Sales							
		8.7											
		756041M		1101851M	1795980M	Net Sales ($)		5748M	4053M	35836M	126584M	1623759M	
		460844M		795177M	1481145M	Total Assets ($)		3703M	2448M	22418M	94543M	1358033M	

M = $ thousand   MM = $ million

© RMA 2024

MANUFACTURING—Conveyor and Conveying Equipment Manufacturing NAICS 333922

Current Data Sorted by Assets | **Comparative Historical Data**

		2	1		3	**Type of Statement**		
		3	6	1		Unqualified	7	4
		1	3		1	Reviewed	14	3
1	1					Compiled	4	8
		8	13	4	6	Tax Returns	7	2
	10 (4/1-9/30/23)		44 (10/1/23-3/31/24)			Other	26	31
0-500M	500M-2MM	2-10MM	10-50MM	50-100MM	100-250MM		4/1/19-3/31/20	4/1/20-3/31/21
1	1	14	23	5	10	**NUMBER OF STATEMENTS**	58 ALL	48 ALL
%	%	%	%	%	%	**ASSETS**	%	%
		22.5	19.6		24.7	Cash & Equivalents	14.9	16.6
		22.7	23.1		21.4	Trade Receivables (net)	24.2	25.7
		16.6	18.7		11.7	Inventory	21.3	19.1
		15.9	5.6		8.0	All Other Current	6.1	4.9
		77.7	67.0		65.7	Total Current	66.5	66.2
		11.0	14.6		10.5	Fixed Assets (net)	19.6	17.3
		1.2	4.5		15.5	Intangibles (net)	6.8	9.9
		10.1	13.9		8.3	All Other Non-Current	7.1	6.6
		100.0	100.0		100.0	Total	100.0	100.0
						LIABILITIES		
		3.7	1.0		2.1	Notes Payable-Short Term	4.3	4.7
		1.0	1.6		1.1	Cur. Mat.-L.T.D.	2.0	3.5
		11.8	7.1		9.3	Trade Payables	9.3	10.4
		.4	.1		.3	Income Taxes Payable	.3	.3
		19.7	19.6		27.4	All Other Current	18.6	17.5
		36.6	29.3		40.2	Total Current	34.5	36.4
		4.2	7.0		10.0	Long-Term Debt	7.7	9.4
		.3	.4		.0	Deferred Taxes	.6	.3
		4.6	2.9		2.4	All Other Non-Current	3.8	4.6
		54.2	60.4		47.3	Net Worth	53.4	49.3
		100.0	100.0		100.0	Total Liabilities & Net Worth	100.0	100.0
						INCOME DATA		
		100.0	100.0		100.0	Net Sales	100.0	100.0
		32.7	37.9		30.4	Gross Profit	32.4	29.9
		27.0	24.2		23.0	Operating Expenses	26.9	26.4
		5.7	13.6		7.4	Operating Profit	5.5	3.5
		-.7	.3		1.4	All Other Expenses (net)	.8	-.9
		6.4	13.3		6.0	Profit Before Taxes	4.7	4.4
						RATIOS		
		4.2	7.4		2.4		4.7	3.0
		2.2	3.1		1.6	Current	2.0	1.9
		1.3	1.6		1.1		1.4	1.3
		1.5	3.5		1.4		2.4	2.1
		1.2	1.9		1.1	Quick	1.1	1.4
		1.0	1.1		.9		.6	.8
	32	11.5	43	8.4	29	12.6	37	9.9	42	8.7
	55	6.6	66	5.5	57	6.4	Sales/Receivables	47	7.7	54	6.7
	72	5.1	74	4.9	91	4.0		58	6.3	76	4.8
	1	302.3	39	9.4	28	13.0		32	11.3	24	14.9
	49	7.5	72	5.1	61	6.0	Cost of Sales/Inventory	72	5.1	59	6.2
	118	3.1	135	2.7	81	4.5		118	3.1	107	3.4
	5	71.6	12	29.3	27	13.3		14	27.0	16	23.5
	17	22.0	18	19.9	31	11.6	Cost of Sales/Payables	24	15.3	25	14.5
	57	6.4	31	11.7	59	6.2		42	8.7	49	7.5
		1.8		1.9		3.1			3.1		3.1
		3.1		2.8		4.4	Sales/Working Capital		5.3		6.1
		8.2		5.6		23.5			11.2		12.0
		52.7		53.9					40.2		30.2
	(10)	11.7	(16)	32.5			EBIT/Interest	(47)	17.7	(39)	11.9
		4.4		12.4					3.1		.6
							Net Profit + Depr., Dep.,		12.6		9.3
							Amort./Cur. Mat. L/T/D	(12)	5.5	(13)	2.5
									.9		1.6
		.1		.1		.2			.1		.2
		.2		.2		.4	Fixed/Worth		.4		.4
		.4		.4		NM			.7		.9
		.4		.3		1.1			.2		.4
		.9		.5		1.7	Debt/Worth		1.0		1.0
		2.5		2.7		NM			2.7		2.9
		24.2		52.0					37.4		35.3
		17.6	(22)	29.2			% Profit Before Taxes/Tangible Net Worth	(52)	17.2	(40)	20.5
		6.6		23.5					6.5		4.3
		10.8		29.2		14.8			20.5		19.0
		7.1		17.6		6.3	% Profit Before Taxes/Total Assets		6.6		7.9
		4.7		13.9		.9			1.9		.3
		65.7		40.5		20.5			26.0		29.7
		25.5		12.0		17.8	Sales/Net Fixed Assets		10.8		12.1
		8.7		6.8		10.2			5.4		5.7
		2.4		2.0		1.3			2.2		2.4
		1.5		1.3		1.0	Sales/Total Assets		1.7		1.6
		1.0		.9		.8			1.2		1.0
		.3		1.5					1.0		1.3
	(12)	1.3	(17)	1.7			% Depr., Dep., Amort./Sales	(49)	1.6	(40)	2.0
		2.1		2.7					3.8		3.3
									1.7		1.8
							% Officers', Directors' Owners' Comp/Sales	(18)	3.8	(12)	4.9
									4.9		6.4
2954M	4706M	120409M	842206M	371568M	2173713M	Net Sales ($)	1697046M	1905743M
462M	1444M	76500M	621652M	332087M	1815329M	Total Assets ($)	1228126M	1506110M

M = $ thousand MM = $ million
See Pages viii through xx for Explanation of Ratios and Data

© RMA 2024

MANUFACTURING—Conveyor and Conveying Equipment Manufacturing   NAICS 333922

Comparative Historical Data | Current Data Sorted by Sales

						Type of Statement						
		1		5	6	Unqualified			1	1	1	3
		8		8	10	Reviewed				1	5	4
		4		2	5	Compiled				1	1	3
		3		6	2	Tax Returns		1	1			
		31		31	31	Other			3			20
		4/1/21-		4/1/22-	4/1/23-			10 (4/1-9/30/23)		44 (10/1/23-3/31/24)		
		3/31/22		3/31/23	3/31/24		0-1MM	1-3MM	3-5MM	5-10MM	10-25MM	25MM & OVER
		ALL		ALL	ALL							
		47		52	54	NUMBER OF STATEMENTS		2	4	7	11	30
		%		%	%	ASSETS	%	%	%	%	%	%
		16.6		17.2	21.8	Cash & Equivalents					22.5	18.1
		22.9		23.7	22.0	Trade Receivables (net)					21.7	22.3
		22.6		26.6	16.5	Inventory					19.2	15.4
		8.9		6.1	11.2	All Other Current	DATA				1.8	13.5
		71.0		73.7	71.5	Total Current	NOT				65.3	69.3
		16.0		17.4	11.8	Fixed Assets (net)	AVAILABLE				8.7	13.6
		8.1		4.3	6.1	Intangibles (net)					6.9	7.8
		4.8		4.6	10.7	All Other Non-Current					19.1	9.3
		100.0		100.0	100.0	Total					100.0	100.0
						LIABILITIES						
		3.4		3.7	2.1	Notes Payable-Short Term					3.3	1.9
		1.9		2.4	1.7	Cur. Mat.-L.T.D.					1.7	2.2
		11.1		9.0	8.7	Trade Payables					6.3	10.8
		.2		.8	.2	Income Taxes Payable					.5	.1
		17.6		16.2	22.9	All Other Current					20.3	24.4
		34.2		32.1	35.6	Total Current					32.2	39.4
		8.5		10.9	6.9	Long-Term Debt					9.7	8.1
		.2		.6	.2	Deferred Taxes					.6	.1
		3.7		3.5	4.8	All Other Non-Current					4.3	4.9
		53.4		53.0	52.5	Net Worth					53.2	47.6
		100.0		100.0	100.0	Total Liabilities & Net Worth					100.0	100.0
						INCOME DATA						
		100.0		100.0	100.0	Net Sales					100.0	100.0
		28.1		34.8	34.8	Gross Profit					45.1	31.3
		23.2		27.9	25.3	Operating Expenses					35.3	20.6
		4.9		6.9	9.6	Operating Profit					9.7	10.8
		-2.1		-.9	.5	All Other Expenses (net)					.6	.9
		6.9		7.7	9.1	Profit Before Taxes					9.1	9.9
						RATIOS						
		4.5		6.8	4.1						8.0	3.4
		2.0		2.5	2.2	Current					2.1	1.9
		1.6		1.6	1.3						1.6	1.2
		2.9		3.1	2.2						3.5	2.0
		1.3		1.3	1.3	Quick					1.6	1.2
		.8		.8	1.0						1.1	.9
34	10.8	31	11.9	34	10.8					43	8.4	29	12.6
48	7.6	51	7.1	58	6.3	Sales/Receivables				63	5.8	55	6.6
72	5.1	65	5.6	74	4.9					87	4.2	73	5.0
31	11.8	41	8.8	18	20.1					70	5.2	17	21.3
69	5.3	78	4.7	70	5.2	Cost of Sales/Inventory				79	4.6	68	5.4
107	3.4	140	2.6	96	3.8					135	2.7	74	4.9
16	23.1	11	31.9	13	28.2					12	30.9	17	21.3
33	11.1	21	17.7	24	15.0	Cost of Sales/Payables				26	14.1	29	12.5
45	8.1	34	10.6	39	9.4					36	10.0	52	7.0
		2.7		2.3	2.1						1.8	2.5
		6.1		3.8	4.0	Sales/Working Capital					4.1	4.7
		9.3		7.8	7.4						10.9	21.2
		98.3		33.6	53.9							74.6
(40)	27.4	(38)	14.7	(40)	21.1	EBIT/Interest					(24)	21.7
		6.0		4.6	5.1							6.0
				15.2	14.7	Net Profit + Depr., Dep.,						
		(12)		3.6	(10) 4.6	Amort./Cur. Mat. L/T/D						
					1.5	1.6							
		.1		.1	.1						.1	.2
		.3		.2	.2	Fixed/Worth					.2	.3
		.6		.6	.4						.2	.5
		.4		.3	.4						.3	.4
		.8		.8	.8	Debt/Worth					.8	1.1
		2.6		2.0	3.1						3.0	4.8
		37.8		33.3	46.6						38.4	51.3
(41)	21.8	(48)	23.4	(49)	24.3	% Profit Before Taxes/Tangible Net Worth				(10)	27.0	(26)	28.0
		13.0		10.6	15.0						16.0	19.8
		18.7		21.9	19.4						22.2	19.7
		12.1		8.9	11.5	% Profit Before Taxes/Total Assets					13.9	13.6
		4.3		5.5	5.2						6.1	7.1
		39.5		43.5	40.6						40.9	22.9
		13.8		12.7	16.6	Sales/Net Fixed Assets					18.2	15.3
		6.0		5.6	8.0						9.1	7.5
		2.1		2.5	1.9						2.4	1.7
		1.4		1.5	1.3	Sales/Total Assets					1.3	1.2
		1.1		1.2	.9						.9	.9
		1.3		.8	.9						1.4	.9
(37)	1.9	(42)	1.5	(40)	1.6	% Depr., Dep., Amort./Sales				(10)	1.7	(19)	1.7
		2.8		2.3	2.3						2.7	2.8
		1.4		1.2	.8							
(11)	4.6	(18)	2.0	(12)	3.1	% Officers', Directors', Owners' Comp/Sales						
		6.4		4.9	4.6							
		2025061M		2186748M	3515556M	Net Sales ($)	5354M	15836M	50521M	189045M	3254800M
		1598726M		1649115M	2847474M	Total Assets ($)	2996M	22478M	32819M	172107M	2617074M

M = $ thousand   MM = $ million
See Pages viii through xx for Explanation of Ratios and Data

© RMA 2024

MANUFACTURING—Overhead Traveling Crane, Hoist, and Monorail System Manufacturing   NAICS 333923

Current Data Sorted by Assets | Comparative Historical Data

						Type of Statement		
			1	1	1	3	Unqualified	1	1
	1		1	2	1		Reviewed	1	1
			2				Compiled	2	2
1	4 (4/1-9/30/23)	2	5	7			Tax Returns		
				23 (10/1/23-3/31/24)			Other		
0-500M	500M-2MM	2-10MM	10-50MM	50-100MM	100-250MM		20 4/1/19-3/31/20 ALL	10 4/1/20-3/31/21 ALL
1		9	10	4	3	NUMBER OF STATEMENTS	24	14
%	%	%	%	%	%	ASSETS	%	%
			7.6			Cash & Equivalents	12.4	10.3
			28.5			Trade Receivables (net)	25.6	29.2
	DATA		29.2			Inventory	22.1	10.2
	NOT		2.5			All Other Current	2.4	8.8
	AVAILABLE		67.8			Total Current	62.5	58.5
			25.8			Fixed Assets (net)	23.8	26.4
			1.6			Intangibles (net)	6.3	10.7
			4.8			All Other Non-Current	7.4	4.4
			100.0			Total	100.0	100.0
						LIABILITIES		
			7.6			Notes Payable-Short Term	19.7	20.4
			5.6			Cur. Mat.-L.T.D.	5.1	3.6
			9.7			Trade Payables	11.3	11.2
			.0			Income Taxes Payable	.1	.0
			21.4			All Other Current	11.8	16.2
			44.3			Total Current	48.0	51.4
			18.1			Long-Term Debt	13.6	18.1
			.0			Deferred Taxes	.2	1.1
			3.3			All Other Non-Current	2.6	7.5
			34.2			Net Worth	35.6	21.9
			100.0			Total Liabilities & Net Worth	100.0	100.0
						INCOME DATA		
			100.0			Net Sales	100.0	100.0
			30.9			Gross Profit	39.0	33.6
			23.6			Operating Expenses	29.7	33.9
			7.4			Operating Profit	9.4	-.3
			1.9			All Other Expenses (net)	1.0	.0
			5.4			Profit Before Taxes	8.3	-.3
						RATIOS		
			2.4				4.4	2.8
			1.3			Current	1.4	1.4
			1.1				1.1	.6
			1.4				1.8	1.9
			.7			Quick	.9	.8
			.6				.5	.3
			40 9.2				35 10.3	41 8.8
			54 6.7			Sales/Receivables	48 7.6	60 6.1
			85 4.3				68 5.4	76 4.8
			64 5.7				7 51.8	0 UND
			76 4.8			Cost of Sales/Inventory	69 5.3	6 56.4
			114 3.2				126 2.9	74 4.9
			20 17.9				18 20.1	17 21.5
			26 14.2			Cost of Sales/Payables	27 13.7	26 14.0
			33 11.1				40 9.2	47 7.7
			4.2				3.4	4.1
			12.0			Sales/Working Capital	11.2	8.5
			22.3				47.8	-11.5
			18.6				28.4	53.9
			4.4			EBIT/Interest	(20) 4.9	(11) 1.3
			2.8				3.5	-3.9
						Net Profit + Depr., Dep., Amort./Cur. Mat. L/T/D		
			.4				.3	.2
			.6			Fixed/Worth	.8	.6
			1.1				2.0	-1.0
			1.4				.4	1.0
			1.9			Debt/Worth	1.9	2.8
			3.5				7.1	-3.4
			40.8				55.9	
			37.1			% Profit Before Taxes/Tangible Net Worth	(20) 25.2	
			21.3				11.7	
			13.4				16.1	18.9
			9.7			% Profit Before Taxes/Total Assets	10.6	4.1
			7.7				5.2	-5.6
			24.0				26.3	51.3
			9.2			Sales/Net Fixed Assets	14.7	16.1
			4.1				5.4	5.0
			2.2				2.5	2.1
			1.8			Sales/Total Assets	1.9	1.9
			1.7				1.2	1.1
							.9	.5
						% Depr., Dep., Amort./Sales	(17) 2.0	(10) 2.0
							3.1	16.9
						% Officers', Directors' Owners' Comp/Sales		
1313M		121137M	299485M	304956M	762440M	Net Sales ($)	1035490M	244313M
325M		61357M	162681M	263156M	590114M	Total Assets ($)	671393M	253526M

M = $ thousand   MM = $ million
See Pages viii through xx for Explanation of Ratios and Data

© RMA 2024

MANUFACTURING—Overhead Traveling Crane, Hoist, and Monorail System Manufacturing NAICS 333923

Comparative Historical Data | Current Data Sorted by Sales

						Type of Statement							
												1	4
		1		3		6	Unqualified				1	1	3
				2		4	Reviewed						
				2			Compiled					1	1
		1		2		2	Tax Returns			1	3	3	7
		14		15		15	Other						
		4/1/21-		4/1/22-		4/1/23-		0-1MM	1-3MM	3-5MM	5-10MM	10-25MM	25MM & OVER
		3/31/22		3/31/23		3/31/24		1 (4/1-9/30/23)			23 (10/1/23-3/31/24)		
		ALL		ALL		ALL			1	1	3	3	
		16		24		27	NUMBER OF STATEMENTS	1	1	4	6	15	
		%		%		%	ASSETS	%	%	%	%	%	%
		9.6		9.6		7.8	Cash & Equivalents						8.3
		23.6		12.7		24.3	Trade Receivables (net)	D					27.3
		17.7		29.9		28.6	Inventory	A					24.1
		8.4		6.6		4.3	All Other Current	T					7.5
		59.2		58.8		64.9	Total Current	A					67.1
		29.5		26.3		24.0	Fixed Assets (net)						22.0
		5.7		4.3		5.5	Intangibles (net)	N					4.4
		5.6		10.6		5.6	All Other Non-Current	O					6.5
		100.0		100.0		100.0	Total	T					100.0
							LIABILITIES						
		5.5		5.4		8.9	Notes Payable-Short Term	A					9.0
		2.0		2.6		3.0	Cur. Mat.-L.T.D.	V					4.2
		12.9		10.3		9.7	Trade Payables	A					9.4
		.1		.0		.0	Income Taxes Payable	I					.0
		25.4		17.8		22.3	All Other Current	L					28.0
		46.0		36.1		43.9	Total Current	A					50.7
		12.9		17.9		16.1	Long-Term Debt	B					13.3
		.0		.1		.4	Deferred Taxes	L					.8
		10.1		4.2		4.7	All Other Non-Current	E					5.1
		31.0		41.8		34.8	Net Worth						30.1
		100.0		100.0		100.0	Total Liabilities & Net Worth						100.0
							INCOME DATA						
		100.0		100.0		100.0	Net Sales						100.0
		39.8		39.2		36.0	Gross Profit						26.7
		30.4		33.5		27.9	Operating Expenses						19.7
		9.3		5.7		8.2	Operating Profit						7.1
		.1		-1.0		2.0	All Other Expenses (net)						2.2
		9.3		6.7		6.2	Profit Before Taxes						4.9
							RATIOS						
		2.4		3.2		2.7							2.7
		1.3		1.4		1.5	Current						1.2
		.7		1.0		1.1							1.1
		1.6		1.1		1.3							1.3
		.7		.8		.7	Quick						.7
		.4		.3		.5							.5
30	12.3	4	95.3	37	9.9							41	8.8
48	7.6	37	9.9	49	7.4	Sales/Receivables						49	7.4
72	5.1	58	6.3	73	5.0							78	4.7
0	UND	0	UND	59	6.2							57	6.4
35	10.3	99	3.7	83	4.4	Cost of Sales/Inventory						70	5.2
122	3.0	174	2.1	126	2.9							83	4.4
34	10.7	20	18.0	17	21.0							17	21.0
42	8.6	37	9.8	28	13.0	Cost of Sales/Payables						28	13.0
61	6.0	59	6.2	41	9.0							38	9.6
		4.3		2.4		3.8							4.2
		13.1		10.1		12.7	Sales/Working Capital						14.6
		-20.3		NM		21.9							23.4
		37.1		20.7		29.9							22.0
(13)	8.8	(16)	3.7	(25)	5.3	EBIT/Interest						(13)	4.8
		3.6		1.7		2.4							2.6
							Net Profit + Depr., Dep., Amort./Cur. Mat. L/T/D						
		.2		.1		.3							.4
		.7		.5		.6	Fixed/Worth						.7
		6.1		2.8		1.4							1.1
		1.1		.7		1.1							1.5
		2.0		1.7		2.2	Debt/Worth						2.5
		6.0		10.6		5.5							5.5
		80.2		34.5		46.1							41.8
(13)	29.2	(20)	14.5	(23)	35.4	% Profit Before Taxes/Tangible Net Worth						(13)	35.4
		7.8		6.0		17.7							19.8
		34.3		13.8		15.5							15.5
		8.0		5.8		9.8	% Profit Before Taxes/Total Assets						8.1
		2.7		1.9		4.9							4.9
		59.5		43.6		20.5							20.1
		9.1		6.7		11.7	Sales/Net Fixed Assets						11.7
		3.4		3.4		4.1							4.4
		2.3		2.6		2.0							2.0
		1.7		1.3		1.7	Sales/Total Assets						1.7
		.9		.9		1.2							1.2
		.8		1.1		.7							.8
(13)	1.9	(16)	2.7	(21)	1.3	% Depr., Dep., Amort./Sales						(12)	1.8
		4.5		8.8		2.6							2.4
							% Officers', Directors' Owners' Comp/Sales						
		414736M		858068M		1489331M	Net Sales ($)		1313M	3919M	28121M	112248M	1343730M
		383082M		712742M		1077633M	Total Assets ($)		325M	2307M	22531M	64008M	988462M

© RMA 2024   M = $ thousand   MM = $ million
See Pages viii through xx for Explanation of Ratios and Data

MANUFACTURING—Industrial Truck, Tractor, Trailer, and Stacker Machinery Manufacturing NAICS 333924

Current Data Sorted by Assets | Comparative Historical Data

0-500M	500M-2MM	2-10MM	10-50MM	50-100MM	100-250MM					
3	3	1 1 7 11 (4/1-9/30/23)	1 6 1 12 37 (10/1/23-3/31/24)	1 4	5	**Type of Statement** Unqualified Reviewed Compiled Tax Returns Other		4 4 5 12 25 4/1/19- 3/31/20 ALL		3 1 2 3 17 4/1/20- 3/31/21 ALL
3	5	10	20	5	5	**NUMBER OF STATEMENTS**		50		26
%	%	%	%	%	%	**ASSETS**		%		%
		18.5	12.3			Cash & Equivalents		7.2		10.0
		13.0	18.7			Trade Receivables (net)		19.6		24.5
		29.9	35.2			Inventory		40.9		41.1
		1.0	2.6			All Other Current		1.8		1.8
		62.4	68.8			Total Current		69.5		77.4
		24.4	23.2			Fixed Assets (net)		21.0		18.1
		8.8	3.3			Intangibles (net)		6.1		3.1
		4.4	4.7			All Other Non-Current		3.3		1.4
		100.0	100.0			Total		100.0		100.0
						LIABILITIES				
		17.1	8.1			Notes Payable-Short Term		17.3		17.2
		1.1	1.2			Cur. Mat.-L.T.D.		3.1		5.4
		6.8	10.0			Trade Payables		10.6		12.2
		.0	.1			Income Taxes Payable		.3		.0
		17.4	17.5			All Other Current		9.1		6.8
		42.4	36.8			Total Current		40.3		41.7
		12.7	16.7			Long-Term Debt		11.7		14.5
		.0	.5			Deferred Taxes		.5		.7
		2.9	7.9			All Other Non-Current		4.4		1.6
		42.0	38.0			Net Worth		43.2		41.6
		100.0	100.0			Total Liabilties & Net Worth		100.0		100.0
						INCOME DATA				
		100.0	100.0			Net Sales		100.0		100.0
		44.4	24.2			Gross Profit		28.3		26.8
		26.3	17.7			Operating Expenses		19.9		21.2
		18.1	6.5			Operating Profit		8.5		5.6
		3.6	1.0			All Other Expenses (net)		1.0		-.1
		14.4	5.5			Profit Before Taxes		7.4		5.7
						RATIOS				
		2.7	3.0					2.6		2.6
		1.6	1.9			Current		1.7		1.9
		1.1	1.5					1.2		1.4
		2.2	1.5					1.2		1.2
		.6	.9			Quick		.7		.9
		.2	.5					.3		.5
		0 UND	25 14.6				17	21.2	17	21.7
		26 13.8	40 9.1			Sales/Receivables	33	10.9	31	11.7
		38 9.5	46 7.9				54	6.8	57	6.4
		29 12.7	38 9.5				46	7.9	60	6.1
		99 3.7	114 3.2			Cost of Sales/Inventory	107	3.4	104	3.5
		203 1.8	182 2.0				192	1.9	159	2.3
		0 UND	8 43.3				11	32.9	8	45.1
		13 27.1	22 16.5			Cost of Sales/Payables	23	16.1	24	15.0
		29 12.4	38 9.5				39	9.4	40	9.2
		3.6	3.0					3.9		3.3
		6.6	5.1			Sales/Working Capital		5.9		5.0
		NM	10.3					15.4		8.3
			29.8					16.3		8.6
		(18)	7.6			EBIT/Interest	(47)	6.0	(25)	6.0
			3.7					2.3		2.9
						Net Profit + Depr., Dep., Amort./Cur. Mat. L/T/D				
		.1	.1					.1		.1
		.8	.5			Fixed/Worth		.5		.5
		NM	1.9					1.0		.8
		.6	1.1					.6		1.0
		1.2	2.0			Debt/Worth		1.5		1.5
		NM	3.3					2.7		2.3
			36.3					35.3		37.0
		(18)	24.6			% Profit Before Taxes/Tangible Net Worth	(45)	19.7	(25)	16.9
			7.2					7.8		6.9
		35.1	14.5					14.1		12.7
		17.3	7.0			% Profit Before Taxes/Total Assets		7.0		8.9
		11.0	3.7					2.5		2.8
		61.9	32.3					35.4		29.5
		18.4	8.4			Sales/Net Fixed Assets		15.9		18.2
		4.2	4.4					6.2		5.6
		2.6	1.9					2.4		2.3
		1.6	1.5			Sales/Total Assets		1.8		1.7
		1.0	1.1					1.2		1.1
			.6					1.4		1.3
		(14)	1.3			% Depr., Dep., Amort./Sales	(33)	1.8	(18)	2.1
			4.0					3.0		3.7
						% Officers', Directors' Owners' Comp/Sales		1.0		
							(10)	1.9		
								3.4		
3018M	38706M	85185M	708101M	629338M	1413526M	Net Sales ($)		2103229M		948162M
652M	6895M	46770M	425782M	378717M	819962M	Total Assets ($)		1609640M		579829M

© RMA 2024 M = $ thousand MM = $ million
See Pages viii through xx for Explanation of Ratios and Data

MANUFACTURING—Industrial Truck, Tractor, Trailer, and Stacker Machinery Manufacturing NAICS 333924

Comparative Historical Data | Current Data Sorted by Sales

						Type of Statement						
	3		5		3	Unqualified				1	1	1
	5		7		6	Reviewed					1	6
	6		6		2	Compiled				1	2	1
	3		2		3	Tax Returns					6	15
	18		21		34	Other	1	5	4	3		
	4/1/21-		4/1/22-		4/1/23-			(4/1-9/30/23)			37 (10/1/23-3/31/24)	
	3/31/22		3/31/23		3/31/24		0-1MM	1-3MM	3-5MM	5-10MM	10-25MM	25MM & OVER
	ALL		ALL		ALL	NUMBER OF STATEMENTS	1	5	5	4	10	23
	35		41		48							
	%		%		%	ASSETS	%	%	%	%	%	%
	9.5		8.3		15.3	Cash & Equivalents					31.8	5.8
	20.1		19.4		15.2	Trade Receivables (net)					14.2	17.8
	40.9		33.5		34.1	Inventory					26.8	34.9
	1.4		2.0		2.4	All Other Current					3.2	2.9
	71.9		63.2		67.1	Total Current					76.0	61.4
	18.9		25.4		21.7	Fixed Assets (net)					12.9	26.5
	4.5		7.2		4.2	Intangibles (net)					6.2	1.8
	4.7		4.2		7.0	All Other Non-Current					5.0	10.3
	100.0		100.0		100.0	Total					100.0	100.0
						LIABILITIES						
	16.0		12.2		12.9	Notes Payable-Short Term					3.2	10.0
	4.5		3.9		2.3	Cur. Mat.-L.T.D.					.6	3.0
	8.4		12.2		9.4	Trade Payables					9.2	12.4
	.2		.0		.3	Income Taxes Payable					.0	.5
	11.7		8.9		13.5	All Other Current					31.9	7.0
	40.9		37.1		38.4	Total Current					44.9	32.9
	14.8		18.9		16.3	Long-Term Debt					5.0	22.6
	1.0		.5		.5	Deferred Taxes					.0	1.0
	3.5		4.2		5.5	All Other Non-Current					3.1	6.5
	39.9		39.3		39.4	Net Worth					47.0	37.0
	100.0		100.0		100.0	Total Liabilities & Net Worth					100.0	100.0
						INCOME DATA						
	100.0		100.0		100.0	Net Sales					100.0	100.0
	32.8		29.0		29.3	Gross Profit					24.4	23.8
	27.5		20.1		20.8	Operating Expenses					15.1	16.9
	5.3		8.9		8.5	Operating Profit					9.3	7.0
	-1.4		1.7		1.2	All Other Expenses (net)					1.4	1.1
	6.7		7.2		7.2	Profit Before Taxes					7.9	5.9
						RATIOS						
	2.8		2.7		2.8						2.5	2.6
	1.8		1.5		1.8	Current					1.7	1.9
	1.3		1.3		1.4						1.4	1.5
	1.2		1.0		1.5						1.8	1.2
	.7		.7		.7	Quick					1.2	.7
	.3		.5		.4						.5	.4
17	21.8	30	12.0	14	25.3						18 20.6	21 17.3
36	10.2	47	7.7	31	11.6	Sales/Receivables					29 12.8	38 9.5
57	6.4	59	6.2	42	8.6						45 8.1	46 8.0
69	5.3	68	5.4	36	10.0						22 16.5	51 7.1
104	3.5	99	3.7	99	3.7	Cost of Sales/Inventory					35 10.3	94 3.9
140	2.6	146	2.5	166	2.2						192 1.9	140 2.6
11	33.3	17	21.9	7	48.9						5 80.1	19 19.3
20	17.9	30	12.0	20	18.6	Cost of Sales/Payables					9 40.1	26 14.0
27	13.4	45	8.2	34	10.6						49 7.4	41 9.0
	3.7		3.7		3.9						2.9	4.3
	6.1		6.3		6.4	Sales/Working Capital					5.2	6.6
	13.9		18.0		11.2						28.9	10.0
	25.1		21.0		19.6							12.8
(33)	9.4	(39)	6.6	(44)	6.6	EBIT/Interest						5.6
	3.5		2.0		2.8							3.0
					21.6							24.5
				(13)	4.5	Net Profit + Depr., Dep., Amort./Cur. Mat. L/T/D					(12)	4.4
					3.2							3.1
	.1		.3		.1						.1	.2
	.4		.7		.5	Fixed/Worth					.3	.5
	1.0		2.0		1.6						NM	1.3
	1.0		.9		.7						.6	1.1
	1.5		2.0		1.7	Debt/Worth					1.3	1.8
	3.0		4.2		3.6						NM	3.2
	40.5		42.7		53.2							36.3
(32)	29.1	(37)	23.2	(42)	29.8	% Profit Before Taxes/Tangible Net Worth					(22)	24.7
	15.0		10.7		16.4							15.8
	20.3		18.5		19.1						36.0	15.6
	9.7		7.9		11.4	% Profit Before Taxes/Total Assets					16.0	9.2
	5.3		1.8		4.6						1.0	5.0
	31.3		29.8		57.5						39.1	22.7
	16.1		7.5		16.7	Sales/Net Fixed Assets					23.8	7.6
	7.6		3.6		5.5						14.6	4.4
	2.4		2.1		2.3						3.8	2.0
	2.0		1.5		1.7	Sales/Total Assets					1.4	1.7
	1.3		1.3		1.3						1.1	1.5
	1.1		1.0		.5							.8
(22)	1.8	(31)	1.7	(31)	1.6	% Depr., Dep., Amort./Sales					(18)	1.7
	3.1		3.2		3.1							3.1
						% Officers', Directors' Owners' Comp/Sales						
	1589931M		2897908M		2877874M	Net Sales ($)	224M	9791M	19339M	30441M	176500M	2641579M
	866174M		1890422M		1678778M	Total Assets ($)	229M	12583M	8998M	26182M	108413M	1522373M

© RMA 2024 M = $ thousand MM = $ million
See Pages viii through xx for Explanation of Ratios and Data

MANUFACTURING—Welding and Soldering Equipment Manufacturing NAICS 333992

Current Data Sorted by Assets

0-500M	500M-2MM	2-10MM	10-50MM	50-100MM	100-250MM		Comparative Historical Data		
			1			Type of Statement			
		2	4			Unqualified		5	3
	1	2	1			Reviewed		3	2
		3				Compiled		7	2
2	4	6	12	2	1	Tax Returns		4	1
	8 (4/1-9/30/23)		33 (10/1/23-3/31/24)			Other		18	16
								4/1/19-	4/1/20-
								3/31/20	3/31/21
2	5	13	17	3	1	NUMBER OF STATEMENTS		ALL 37	ALL 24
%	%	%	%	%	%			%	%
						ASSETS			
		11.6	8.5			Cash & Equivalents		8.1	11.2
		24.5	21.3			Trade Receivables (net)		24.8	21.1
		29.3	34.6			Inventory		28.7	28.3
		5.3	2.4			All Other Current		3.5	3.9
		70.7	66.8			Total Current		65.1	64.4
		16.4	14.5			Fixed Assets (net)		23.9	21.0
		.8	10.4			Intangibles (net)		5.3	2.8
		12.2	8.3			All Other Non-Current		5.6	11.8
		100.0	100.0			Total		100.0	100.0
						LIABILITIES			
		7.6	7.1			Notes Payable-Short Term		9.0	7.0
		.7	.9			Cur. Mat.-L.T.D.		4.5	1.9
		9.5	9.6			Trade Payables		10.1	12.3
		.4	.1			Income Taxes Payable		.1	.3
		11.6	11.1			All Other Current		9.1	12.9
		29.8	28.7			Total Current		32.8	34.4
		18.0	5.2			Long-Term Debt		18.0	24.0
		.0	.7			Deferred Taxes		.6	1.0
		.6	12.5			All Other Non-Current		6.1	6.4
		51.6	52.9			Net Worth		42.5	34.1
		100.0	100.0			Total Liabilities & Net Worth		100.0	100.0
						INCOME DATA			
		100.0	100.0			Net Sales		100.0	100.0
		41.2	34.0			Gross Profit		34.9	33.1
		36.6	27.5			Operating Expenses		29.9	31.4
		4.6	6.5			Operating Profit		5.0	1.7
		-.2	1.9			All Other Expenses (net)		.8	-.8
		4.8	4.6			Profit Before Taxes		4.2	2.5
						RATIOS			
		5.0	3.8					3.8	4.0
		2.0	2.3			Current		2.4	2.1
		1.7	1.4					1.4	1.6
		2.2	1.9					2.5	1.9
		1.1	.9			Quick		1.2	.9
		.6	.7					.6	.7
		38 9.5	31 11.9					36 10.2	28 13.0
		51 7.1	40 9.2			Sales/Receivables		56 6.5	41 9.0
		63 5.8	58 6.3					74 4.9	56 6.5
		0 UND	66 5.5					38 9.6	39 9.4
		73 5.0	130 2.8			Cost of Sales/Inventory		99 3.7	85 4.3
		146 2.5	174 2.1					146 2.5	118 3.1
		3 138.1	12 30.5					13 27.7	10 36.5
		14 25.7	18 19.8			Cost of Sales/Payables		25 14.7	27 13.7
		43 8.4	32 11.4					45 8.2	57 6.4
		3.2	3.4					3.8	2.9
		4.7	4.9			Sales/Working Capital		5.2	4.5
		7.8	8.4					8.8	16.6
		42.5	33.9					11.6	22.7
		17.0	(16) 8.3			EBIT/Interest		(33) 4.3	(21) 9.3
		2.8	1.5					.7	-.7
						Net Profit + Depr., Dep., Amort./Cur. Mat. L/T/D			
		.1	.1					.2	.2
		.4	.3			Fixed/Worth		.4	.3
		.6	2.6					1.6	1.5
		.4	.3					.4	.3
		.8	.7			Debt/Worth		1.1	.9
		2.1	7.8					6.4	12.2
		75.0	36.9					32.3	32.7
		(12) 31.6	(15) 21.0			% Profit Before Taxes/Tangible Net Worth	(33)	15.6	(19) 14.4
		12.2	7.3					3.0	6.8
		26.0	16.3					11.3	12.9
		15.4	5.3			% Profit Before Taxes/Total Assets		5.9	6.6
		6.4	1.9					-.3	-5.2
		71.8	33.7					26.7	17.5
		13.0	13.4			Sales/Net Fixed Assets		10.4	11.2
		7.0	8.7					3.3	5.2
		3.5	2.2					2.2	2.4
		2.2	1.6			Sales/Total Assets		1.6	1.5
		1.2	1.2					1.1	1.1
			.6					.8	1.2
		(10)	.9			% Depr., Dep., Amort./Sales	(30)	2.2	(18) 1.6
			1.9					4.1	4.5
						% Officers', Directors', Owners' Comp/Sales		2.8	
							(12)	3.5	
								7.7	
352M	16246M	124297M	605768M	338523M	293960M	Net Sales ($)		807287M	553290M
386M	6394M	61584M	377581M	196965M	195332M	Total Assets ($)		634637M	428049M

M = $ thousand   MM = $ million
See Pages viii through xx for Explanation of Ratios and Data

© RMA 2024

MANUFACTURING—Welding and Soldering Equipment Manufacturing NAICS 333992

Comparative Historical Data | **Current Data Sorted by Sales**

Comparative Historical Data					Current Data Sorted by Sales					
3	3	1	Type of Statement						1	
2	6	6	Unqualified					3	2	
5	5	4	Reviewed			1	1	1	1	
2	2	3	Compiled		1	1	1	1		
16	23	27	Tax Returns		1	3	2	5	13	
4/1/21-3/31/22 ALL	4/1/22-3/31/23 ALL	4/1/23-3/31/24 ALL	Other	2	2					
				0-1MM	8 (4/1-9/30/23) 1-3MM	3-5MM	33 (10/1/23-3/31/24) 5-10MM	10-25MM	25MM & OVER	
28	39	41	NUMBER OF STATEMENTS	2	2	5	5	10	17	
%	%	%	ASSETS	%	%	%	%	%	%	
16.9	11.6	13.3	Cash & Equivalents					9.1	9.3	
19.6	27.6	24.0	Trade Receivables (net)					24.3	22.0	
28.5	20.8	26.1	Inventory					34.3	34.0	
3.6	5.0	3.8	All Other Current					4.2	3.6	
68.6	64.9	67.1	Total Current					71.8	68.8	
19.8	19.6	18.6	Fixed Assets (net)					13.8	14.5	
6.6	8.0	5.5	Intangibles (net)					8.1	7.7	
5.0	7.3	8.6	All Other Non-Current					6.3	9.0	
100.0	100.0	100.0	Total					100.0	100.0	
			LIABILITIES							
4.0	6.7	6.5	Notes Payable-Short Term					11.2	4.5	
2.8	3.0	1.3	Cur. Mat.-L.T.D.					.7	1.4	
7.7	10.8	8.9	Trade Payables					17.7	7.9	
.1	.1	.2	Income Taxes Payable					.1	.1	
11.1	12.7	11.0	All Other Current					11.4	12.4	
25.6	33.3	28.0	Total Current					41.2	26.2	
14.8	20.2	19.5	Long-Term Debt					6.3	5.9	
.2	.0	.3	Deferred Taxes					.0	.7	
9.7	5.1	7.5	All Other Non-Current					14.5	8.3	
49.7	41.2	44.7	Net Worth					38.1	58.9	
100.0	100.0	100.0	Total Liabilities & Net Worth					100.0	100.0	
			INCOME DATA							
100.0	100.0	100.0	Net Sales					100.0	100.0	
40.4	39.6	36.9	Gross Profit					37.6	28.2	
30.4	31.6	29.2	Operating Expenses					32.0	20.4	
10.0	8.0	7.6	Operating Profit					5.6	7.8	
-2.9	.4	.9	All Other Expenses (net)					2.4	.9	
12.9	7.5	6.7	Profit Before Taxes					3.2	7.0	
			RATIOS							
5.9	3.9	5.7						2.6	4.2	
2.8	2.4	2.3	Current					1.5	2.6	
1.9	1.3	1.5						1.2	1.9	
3.3	2.6	2.5						1.2	2.2	
2.0	1.2	1.1	Quick					.8	1.0	
.7	.8	.7						.5	.7	
12 30.3	30 12.0	30 12.0		28 12.9	30 12.0					
45 8.1	63 5.8	50 7.3	Sales/Receivables	49 7.4	39 9.3					
63 5.8	74 4.9	70 5.2		85 4.3	58 6.3					
22 16.6	0 UND	0 UND		0 UND	62 5.9					
79 4.6	37 9.8	74 4.9	Cost of Sales/Inventory	96 3.8	111 3.3					
166 2.2	146 2.5	146 2.5		166 2.2	140 2.6					
0 760.1	4 81.2	6 63.8		10 36.7	14 26.2					
23 15.8	24 14.9	16 22.7	Cost of Sales/Payables	30 12.3	18 19.8					
46 7.9	46 8.0	35 10.4		104 3.5	27 13.4					
3.1	2.9	3.4						6.0	3.1	
4.1	5.3	5.5	Sales/Working Capital					7.8	4.2	
7.7	15.7	8.1						10.1	6.5	
107.3	43.3	40.9						61.2	49.3	
(23) 29.0	(36) 21.1	(38) 9.6	EBIT/Interest					11.5	(15) 18.5	
9.2	3.1	2.4						1.2	2.2	
			Net Profit + Depr., Dep., Amort./Cur. Mat. L/T/D							
.2	.2	.2						.1	.1	
.3	.5	.4	Fixed/Worth					.5	.3	
1.2	1.3	1.8						2.3	1.0	
.2	.6	.4						.9	.3	
1.3	1.2	1.0	Debt/Worth					2.1	.5	
3.8	4.4	3.9						7.1	2.3	
68.5	72.7	45.4							40.0	
(26) 49.8	(33) 44.1	(34) 27.1	% Profit Before Taxes/Tangible Net Worth					(15) 23.5		
33.1	20.4	10.5						7.3		
32.9	26.4	24.9						22.5	19.9	
17.0	18.6	10.6	% Profit Before Taxes/Total Assets					10.7	9.2	
7.6	6.0	3.0						1.3	3.1	
34.6	32.1	31.6						103.9	33.7	
14.4	9.2	12.2	Sales/Net Fixed Assets					12.1	14.3	
6.8	5.7	7.4						7.6	9.6	
2.6	2.1	2.4						2.8	2.2	
1.9	1.7	1.6	Sales/Total Assets					1.7	1.6	
1.4	1.3	1.3						1.0	1.5	
1.0	.8	.6							.7	
(21) 2.0	(25) 1.9	(24) 1.5	% Depr., Dep., Amort./Sales					(10)	1.5	
2.7	3.2	2.8							2.0	
			% Officers', Directors' Owners' Comp/Sales							
620781M	1019940M	1379146M	Net Sales ($)	352M	3619M	20100M	37095M	146904M	1171076M	
398234M	757892M	838242M	Total Assets ($)	386M	1668M	9609M	22494M	106951M	697134M	

M = $ thousand   MM = $ million
See Pages viii through xx for Explanation of Ratios and Data

© RMA 2024

MANUFACTURING—Packaging Machinery Manufacturing NAICS 333993

Current Data Sorted by Assets | Comparative Historical Data

						Type of Statement		
			2	2		Unqualified	3	3
			3			Reviewed	5	7
						Compiled	2	2
		1				Tax Returns	8	3
	1	3	13	5	4	Other	22	15
	13 (4/1-9/30/23)		21 (10/1/23-3/31/24)				4/1/19-	4/1/20-
0-500M	500M-2MM	2-10MM	10-50MM	50-100MM	100-250MM		3/31/20	3/31/21
	1	4	18	7	4	NUMBER OF STATEMENTS	ALL 40	ALL 30
%	%	%	%	%	%	ASSETS	%	%
			8.5			Cash & Equivalents	15.8	18.7
D			18.0			Trade Receivables (net)	19.8	22.7
A			27.9			Inventory	26.7	28.9
T			4.3			All Other Current	3.6	2.9
A			58.8			Total Current	65.9	73.2
			13.4			Fixed Assets (net)	15.8	13.0
N			14.0			Intangibles (net)	12.6	9.5
O			13.8			All Other Non-Current	5.7	4.3
T			100.0			Total	100.0	100.0
A						LIABILITIES		
V			3.2			Notes Payable-Short Term	4.7	5.2
A			2.5			Cur. Mat.-L.T.D.	1.9	1.7
I			14.8			Trade Payables	11.9	15.1
L			.2			Income Taxes Payable	.1	.4
A			24.1			All Other Current	24.2	22.7
B			44.8			Total Current	42.8	45.2
L			21.3			Long-Term Debt	9.3	11.7
E			.0			Deferred Taxes	.2	.4
			2.8			All Other Non-Current	2.2	3.6
			31.1			Net Worth	45.5	39.2
			100.0			Total Liabilities & Net Worth	100.0	100.0
						INCOME DATA		
			100.0			Net Sales	100.0	100.0
			31.6			Gross Profit	34.5	30.9
			25.5			Operating Expenses	29.0	23.3
			6.1			Operating Profit	5.5	7.6
			1.9			All Other Expenses (net)	-.1	-.8
			4.2			Profit Before Taxes	5.6	8.4
						RATIOS		
			2.4				2.1	2.3
			1.6			Current	1.5	1.6
			.8				1.3	1.0
			1.1				1.3	1.6
			.5			Quick	.9	.9
			.3				.5	.4
			28 13.1				27 13.4	24 14.9
			39 9.4			Sales/Receivables	42 8.7	47 7.8
			49 7.4				58 6.3	68 5.4
			42 8.6				47 7.8	29 12.4
			79 4.6			Cost of Sales/Inventory	91 4.0	104 3.5
			152 2.4				122 3.0	140 2.6
			12 29.8				22 16.9	17 22.0
			36 10.2			Cost of Sales/Payables	29 12.8	27 13.3
			66 5.5				49 7.5	46 8.0
			4.0				4.2	3.3
			10.8			Sales/Working Capital	7.0	7.2
			-13.8				22.2	NM
			29.0				98.8	124.8
		(14)	6.5			EBIT/Interest	(28) 4.6	(25) 17.4
			1.1				1.2	2.7
						Net Profit + Depr., Dep., Amort./Cur. Mat. L/T/D		
			.1				.2	.1
			.2			Fixed/Worth	.3	.3
			-1.9				1.2	1.3
			.9				.8	1.0
			5.9			Debt/Worth	1.6	1.8
			-5.9				3.3	9.6
			83.7				51.1	90.5
		(12)	26.4			% Profit Before Taxes/Tangible Net Worth	(33) 24.4	(25) 42.9
			11.9				11.0	18.0
			18.1				17.6	23.7
			11.4			% Profit Before Taxes/Total Assets	10.3	11.1
			1.4				2.1	3.3
			50.7				32.1	50.1
			24.3			Sales/Net Fixed Assets	15.6	22.3
			6.8				7.8	10.3
			2.4				2.3	2.0
			1.8			Sales/Total Assets	1.7	1.6
			1.3				1.3	1.3
			.4				1.0	.8
		(17)	1.2			% Depr., Dep., Amort./Sales	(34) 1.5	(23) 1.3
			1.4				2.6	2.7
						% Officers', Directors' Owners' Comp/Sales		
6037M		47543M	821970M	582701M	1406623M	Net Sales ($)	2028199M	1363171M
1982M		18815M	477339M	437461M	807867M	Total Assets ($)	1443375M	870261M

© RMA 2024 M = $ thousand   MM = $ million
See Pages viii through xx for Explanation of Ratios and Data

MANUFACTURING—Packaging Machinery Manufacturing NAICS 333993

Comparative Historical Data | Current Data Sorted by Sales

			Type of Statement						
2	5	4	Unqualified				1	3	
4	4	3	Reviewed				1	2	
4	4		Compiled						
3	5	1	Tax Returns				1		
14	23	26	Other			3	3	20	
4/1/21-3/31/22 ALL	4/1/22-3/31/23 ALL	4/1/23-3/31/24 ALL		0-1MM	13 (4/1-9/30/23) 1-3MM	3-5MM	21 (10/1/23-3/31/24) 5-10MM	10-25MM	25MM & OVER
27	41	34	NUMBER OF STATEMENTS				3	6	25
%	%	%	**ASSETS**	%	%	%	%	%	%
17.8	16.5	9.2	Cash & Equivalents	D	D	D			10.2
24.1	22.6	21.3	Trade Receivables (net)	A	A	A			20.1
24.6	25.8	29.1	Inventory	T	T	T			26.1
4.6	5.1	3.4	All Other Current	A	A	A			3.9
71.0	69.9	63.1	Total Current						60.3
15.4	11.8	16.8	Fixed Assets (net)	N	N	N			19.3
9.6	9.5	10.0	Intangibles (net)	O	O	O			9.5
4.0	8.8	10.2	All Other Non-Current	T	T	T			10.9
100.0	100.0	100.0	Total						100.0
			LIABILITIES	A	A	A			
6.8	5.0	4.6	Notes Payable-Short Term	V	V	V			3.4
1.3	1.3	1.6	Cur. Mat.-L.T.D.	A	A	A			2.0
13.2	16.5	12.9	Trade Payables	I	I	I			13.5
1.1	1.2	.2	Income Taxes Payable	L	L	L			.1
24.3	24.5	26.7	All Other Current	A	A	A			26.0
46.7	48.6	46.1	Total Current	B	B	B			45.0
10.9	12.2	17.9	Long-Term Debt	L	L	L			19.2
.4	.2	.1	Deferred Taxes	E	E	E			.1
3.5	4.0	5.0	All Other Non-Current						3.6
38.5	35.1	30.9	Net Worth						32.1
100.0	100.0	100.0	Total Liabilites & Net Worth						100.0
			INCOME DATA						
100.0	100.0	100.0	Net Sales						100.0
34.3	31.1	36.8	Gross Profit						33.5
28.3	25.8	29.8	Operating Expenses						25.6
6.0	5.2	7.0	Operating Profit						7.8
-2.1	-.5	1.5	All Other Expenses (net)						.7
8.1	5.8	5.5	Profit Before Taxes						7.1
			RATIOS						
2.1	2.3	2.1	Current						2.0
1.8	1.5	1.5							1.5
1.1	1.0	1.0							1.1
1.3	1.3	1.2	Quick						1.1
.9	.7	.8							.8
.5	.5	.4							.4
30 12.3	33 11.2	33 11.2	Sales/Receivables						32 11.4
36 10.1	43 8.4	42 8.7							42 8.6
66 5.5	70 5.2	53 6.9							54 6.8
25 14.5	43 8.5	42 8.6	Cost of Sales/Inventory						41 8.8
61 6.0	78 4.7	101 3.6							70 5.2
152 2.4	140 2.6	166 2.2							146 2.5
15 25.0	18 20.4	19 19.2	Cost of Sales/Payables						14 26.0
24 15.0	34 10.6	35 10.5							26 14.3
61 6.0	61 6.0	56 6.5							62 5.9
5.0	4.7	4.5	Sales/Working Capital						4.7
7.1	7.4	9.9							10.5
34.5	142.0	137.0							71.3
130.8	55.1	58.9	EBIT/Interest						50.0
(20) 19.7	(30) 14.0	(29) 7.1						(21)	7.1
11.1	2.3	1.8							2.0
			Net Profit + Depr., Dep., Amort./Cur. Mat. L/T/D						
.1	.1	.1	Fixed/Worth						.2
.3	.3	.4							.3
1.0	1.1	-40.0							NM
1.0	1.0	.9	Debt/Worth						1.2
1.8	2.4	2.7							2.9
4.8	10.4	-101.9							NM
62.2	51.0	60.7	% Profit Before Taxes/Tangible Net Worth						68.7
(22) 40.3	(33) 34.1	(25) 23.3						(19)	23.3
25.3	11.4	12.3							12.1
21.5	16.7	18.1	% Profit Before Taxes/Total Assets						20.0
17.9	9.2	9.3							9.1
5.5	3.0	3.6							4.8
35.5	47.3	36.1	Sales/Net Fixed Assets						36.3
20.3	24.3	18.3							10.4
8.3	12.0	5.7							5.2
2.4	2.2	2.3	Sales/Total Assets						2.3
1.9	1.5	1.7							1.7
1.3	1.2	1.2							1.2
.9	.4	.6	% Depr., Dep., Amort./Sales						.6
(19) 1.1	(30) 1.0	(28) 1.2						(22)	1.2
2.5	1.9	2.1							2.3
			% Officers', Directors' Owners' Comp/Sales						
980815M	1854372M	2864874M	Net Sales ($)				21490M	107981M	2735403M
580063M	1286723M	1743464M	Total Assets ($)				8271M	84654M	1650539M

M = $ thousand   MM = $ million
See Pages viii through xx for Explanation of Ratios and Data

© RMA 2024

MANUFACTURING—Industrial Process Furnace and Oven Manufacturing NAICS 333994

Current Data Sorted by Assets | Comparative Historical Data

0-500M	500M-2MM	2-10MM	10-50MM	50-100MM	100-250MM	Type of Statement	4/1/19-3/31/20 ALL	4/1/20-3/31/21 ALL
			3		1	Unqualified	5	4
		2	1			Reviewed	3	1
	1	2				Compiled		
	6 (4/1-9/30/23)	1	9			Tax Returns	4	
			14 (10/1/23-3/31/24)			Other	14	9
	1	5	13		1	NUMBER OF STATEMENTS	26	14
%	%	%	%	%	%	ASSETS	%	%
			14.2			Cash & Equivalents	12.0	21.2
			23.1			Trade Receivables (net)	30.7	17.7
			19.4			Inventory	20.0	28.4
DATA	DATA	DATA	7.4	DATA	DATA	All Other Current	8.3	4.0
NOT	NOT	NOT	64.0	NOT	NOT	Total Current	71.1	71.3
AVAILABLE	AVAILABLE	AVAILABLE	21.8	AVAILABLE	AVAILABLE	Fixed Assets (net)	18.1	19.3
			.3			Intangibles (net)	3.9	4.3
			13.9			All Other Non-Current	7.0	5.2
			100.0			Total	100.0	100.0
						LIABILITIES		
			2.9			Notes Payable-Short Term	3.4	4.6
			2.7			Cur. Mat.-L.T.D.	3.5	2.9
			11.3			Trade Payables	14.6	8.6
			.1			Income Taxes Payable	.2	.3
			30.5			All Other Current	20.9	18.5
			47.5			Total Current	42.7	35.0
			14.6			Long-Term Debt	12.1	24.5
			6.5			Deferred Taxes	.2	.3
			6.5			All Other Non-Current	4.4	4.7
			24.8			Net Worth	40.5	35.6
			100.0			Total Liabilities & Net Worth	100.0	100.0
						INCOME DATA		
			100.0			Net Sales	100.0	100.0
			30.8			Gross Profit	30.0	32.5
			26.1			Operating Expenses	23.2	22.8
			4.7			Operating Profit	6.7	9.7
			.2			All Other Expenses (net)	1.3	7.1
			4.5			Profit Before Taxes	5.4	2.6
						RATIOS		
			2.1				2.3	3.6
			1.5			Current	1.7	2.0
			1.0				1.2	1.4
			1.5				1.5	2.0
			.9			Quick	1.0	1.2
			.6				.7	.8
		43	8.4				41 9.0	22 16.4
		65	5.6			Sales/Receivables	58 6.3	42 8.7
		72	5.1				81 4.5	52 7.0
		39	9.4				22 16.4	40 9.2
		46	8.0			Cost of Sales/Inventory	45 8.2	76 4.8
		130	2.8				94 3.9	118 3.1
		27	13.5				22 16.5	12 31.3
		44	8.3			Cost of Sales/Payables	36 10.1	23 15.6
		55	6.6				56 6.5	64 5.7
			4.8				3.8	3.2
			7.4			Sales/Working Capital	6.7	4.2
			NM				26.2	7.7
			14.8				23.0	13.2
			(11) 4.6			EBIT/Interest	(21) 4.2	(10) 6.0
			3.6				1.4	1.4
						Net Profit + Depr., Dep., Amort./Cur. Mat. L/T/D		
			.5				.1	.1
			.6			Fixed/Worth	.4	.7
			3.5				.7	2.0
			1.3				.7	.7
			1.7			Debt/Worth	1.9	2.7
			12.4				3.0	4.6
			58.5				51.8	36.6
			(11) 20.1			% Profit Before Taxes/Tangible Net Worth	(24) 20.8	(13) 33.3
			8.6				11.9	9.9
			10.5				18.1	16.4
			5.1			% Profit Before Taxes/Total Assets	7.4	7.2
			2.7				1.7	-1.3
			14.3				62.8	82.9
			5.6			Sales/Net Fixed Assets	16.8	8.5
			4.1				6.0	3.1
			2.0				2.9	2.2
			1.4			Sales/Total Assets	1.5	1.4
			1.2				1.2	1.1
			.5				.8	.5
			(12) 1.9			% Depr., Dep., Amort./Sales	(21) 1.8	(11) 1.3
			2.2				4.1	4.8
						% Officers', Directors' Owners' Comp/Sales		
	4381M	56614M	570713M		104565M	Net Sales ($)	1591428M	469229M
	1162M	26723M	392659M		105036M	Total Assets ($)	870252M	308118M

M = $ thousand   MM = $ million
See Pages viii through xx for Explanation of Ratios and Data

© RMA 2024

MANUFACTURING—Industrial Process Furnace and Oven Manufacturing NAICS 333994

Comparative Historical Data | Current Data Sorted by Sales

			Type of Statement						
	4	4	Unqualified					2	4
1	2	3	Reviewed						1
1			Compiled						
1	2	3	Tax Returns		3		2	2	
5	9	10	Other						6
4/1/21-3/31/22 ALL	4/1/22-3/31/23 ALL	4/1/23-3/31/24 ALL		0-1MM	6 (4/1-9/30/23) 1-3MM	3-5MM	14 (10/1/23-3/31/24) 5-10MM	10-25MM	25MM & OVER
9	17	20	NUMBER OF STATEMENTS			3	2	4	11
%	%	%	**ASSETS**	%	%	%	%	%	%
	16.5	17.9	Cash & Equivalents	D	D				21.5
	24.5	25.4	Trade Receivables (net)	A	A				24.7
	25.7	19.7	Inventory	T	T				15.0
	5.8	5.9	All Other Current	A	A				8.8
	72.5	68.9	Total Current						69.9
	12.8	15.8	Fixed Assets (net)	N	N				16.0
	8.6	4.5	Intangibles (net)	O	O				.5
	6.0	10.9	All Other Non-Current	T	T				13.5
	100.0	100.0	Total						100.0
			LIABILITIES	A	A				
	2.1	2.1	Notes Payable-Short Term	V	V				.1
	.9	3.1	Cur. Mat.-L.T.D.	A	A				2.0
	10.4	11.4	Trade Payables	I	I				10.0
	.2	.1	Income Taxes Payable	L	L				.1
	28.9	29.7	All Other Current	A	A				38.3
	42.5	46.2	Total Current	B	B				50.6
	16.0	15.7	Long-Term Debt	L	L				15.9
	.1	4.2	Deferred Taxes	E	E				7.5
	9.2	7.1	All Other Non-Current						7.0
	32.1	26.7	Net Worth						19.0
	100.0	100.0	Total Liabilities & Net Worth						100.0
			INCOME DATA						
	100.0	100.0	Net Sales						100.0
	30.6	34.7	Gross Profit						29.9
	26.8	28.8	Operating Expenses						25.7
	3.8	6.0	Operating Profit						4.2
	1.7	.7	All Other Expenses (net)						.3
	2.2	5.2	Profit Before Taxes						3.9
			RATIOS						
	3.5	2.2							2.1
	1.6	1.4	Current						1.5
	1.0	1.1							1.1
	1.6	1.5							1.5
	1.0	.9	Quick						.9
	.8	.6							.8
	43 8.5	38 9.7						38	9.6
	56 6.5	56 6.5	Sales/Receivables					58	6.3
	85 4.3	70 5.2						68	5.4
	38 9.5	27 13.6						23	16.1
	66 5.5	42 8.6	Cost of Sales/Inventory					43	8.5
	135 2.7	99 3.7						47	7.7
	24 15.4	26 14.1						25	14.5
	33 11.2	36 10.1	Cost of Sales/Payables					32	11.3
	51 7.2	52 7.0						45	8.1
	2.8	5.4							5.3
	5.2	8.1	Sales/Working Capital						7.4
	NM	27.4							24.3
	82.0	25.2							
(14)	14.5	(18) 5.3	EBIT/Interest						
	5.1	1.4							
			Net Profit + Depr., Dep., Amort./Cur. Mat. L/T/D						
	.1	.3							.5
	.4	.6	Fixed/Worth						.6
	3.6	5.0							.7
	.7	1.2							1.3
	4.2	2.5	Debt/Worth						3.2
	12.3	28.5							31.3
	117.8	73.9	% Profit Before Taxes/Tangible Net Worth						
(14)	53.4	(16) 23.0							
	8.5	6.8							
	17.5	15.1							11.0
	8.5	4.8	% Profit Before Taxes/Total Assets						7.4
	2.0	2.6							2.6
	114.8	43.2							14.5
	11.7	14.3	Sales/Net Fixed Assets						13.2
	5.7	5.2							5.4
	2.0	2.3							2.3
	1.3	1.4	Sales/Total Assets						1.4
	1.1	1.2							1.2
	.4	.6							.4
(13)	1.9	(16) 1.5	% Depr., Dep., Amort./Sales						.8
	2.4	2.2							2.0
			% Officers', Directors' Owners' Comp/Sales						
298661M	650372M	736273M	Net Sales ($)		12868M		15220M	81848M	626337M
150437M	397136M	525580M	Total Assets ($)		9204M		27856M	53939M	434581M

M = $ thousand   MM = $ million
See Pages viii through xx for Explanation of Ratios and Data
© RMA 2024

MANUFACTURING—All Other Miscellaneous General Purpose Machinery Manufacturing   NAICS 333998

Current Data Sorted by Assets / Comparative Historical Data

							Type of Statement				
			1	5			Unqualified			14	8
		1	9	12			Reviewed			17	7
	1	3	3	1	1		Compiled			12	8
	4	6	6				Tax Returns			21	13
3	18 (4/1-9/30/23)	24	24	30	2	5	Other			73	42
0-500M	500M-2MM	2-10MM	10-50MM	92 (10/1/23-3/31/24) 50-100MM		100-250MM				4/1/19-3/31/20	4/1/20-3/31/21
3	8	43	48	3	5		NUMBER OF STATEMENTS			137 ALL	78 ALL
%	%	%	%	%	%		ASSETS			%	%
		14.6	11.5				Cash & Equivalents			13.3	16.4
		25.2	20.2				Trade Receivables (net)			24.6	21.3
		23.9	28.3				Inventory			23.8	23.6
		5.5	2.6				All Other Current			3.5	5.9
		69.2	62.5				Total Current			65.2	67.2
		20.5	17.7				Fixed Assets (net)			20.1	22.5
		3.2	6.5				Intangibles (net)			7.4	5.5
		7.0	13.2				All Other Non-Current			7.3	4.8
		100.0	100.0				Total			100.0	100.0
							LIABILITIES				
		4.1	8.9				Notes Payable-Short Term			10.4	9.1
		2.0	2.4				Cur. Mat.-L.T.D.			3.2	4.9
		7.8	8.2				Trade Payables			11.8	9.8
		.7	.2				Income Taxes Payable			.1	.0
		12.1	14.4				All Other Current			14.0	9.6
		26.7	34.2				Total Current			39.5	33.5
		11.0	10.2				Long-Term Debt			15.6	18.1
		.1	.5				Deferred Taxes			.3	.5
		3.6	5.4				All Other Non-Current			4.5	4.5
		58.6	49.7				Net Worth			40.2	43.5
		100.0	100.0				Total Liabilities & Net Worth			100.0	100.0
							INCOME DATA				
		100.0	100.0				Net Sales			100.0	100.0
		38.5	34.6				Gross Profit			35.5	38.6
		29.9	23.5				Operating Expenses			29.6	32.4
		8.6	11.0				Operating Profit			6.0	6.2
		.2	.2				All Other Expenses (net)			1.5	-.5
		8.4	10.8				Profit Before Taxes			4.5	6.7
							RATIOS				
		5.7	3.2							3.7	4.0
		2.8	1.9				Current			2.1	2.0
		1.7	1.2							1.1	1.3
		4.0	1.7							2.3	2.2
		1.8	.9				Quick			1.0	1.2
		.8	.5							.5	.6
		35 10.4	39 9.4						27 13.4		31 11.8
		46 7.9	49 7.4				Sales/Receivables		44 8.3		43 8.5
		65 5.6	58 6.3						65 5.6		65 5.6
		30 12.2	46 8.0						16 22.4		31 11.6
		79 4.6	111 3.3				Cost of Sales/Inventory		62 5.9		76 4.8
		146 2.5	182 2.0						130 2.8		152 2.4
		9 41.2	17 22.1						14 26.5		19 19.4
		18 20.3	26 13.8				Cost of Sales/Payables		25 14.8		28 13.0
		45 8.1	40 9.1						46 8.0		51 7.2
		3.0	2.6							3.6	3.0
		4.3	6.0				Sales/Working Capital			6.4	4.5
		9.7	10.6							28.9	15.5
		26.8	49.7							23.3	21.8
		(27) 3.6	(37) 13.7				EBIT/Interest		(117)	7.2	(66) 8.2
		-.3	3.1							1.5	2.0
			67.5							9.8	6.3
		(13) 4.9					Net Profit + Depr., Dep., Amort./Cur. Mat. L/T/D		(30)	4.4	(22) 2.2
			3.5							1.0	1.5
		.1	.1							.2	.2
		.3	.3				Fixed/Worth			.5	.4
		.8	1.2							1.4	1.6
		.3	.4							.4	.6
		.6	.9				Debt/Worth			1.1	1.2
		1.3	5.4							9.7	4.7
		45.8	44.4							40.3	39.2
		(41) 24.0	(45) 19.3				% Profit Before Taxes/Tangible Net Worth		(111)	20.6	(69) 17.4
		3.5	10.3							5.9	9.0
		32.3	17.9							17.7	18.9
		12.5	9.6				% Profit Before Taxes/Total Assets			8.9	7.6
		1.0	3.2							.9	1.9
		32.3	27.0							32.0	25.4
		12.1	10.9				Sales/Net Fixed Assets			11.0	10.7
		5.5	5.5							5.4	4.8
		2.4	2.0							2.4	2.2
		1.8	1.3				Sales/Total Assets			1.8	1.5
		1.5	.9							1.2	1.1
		.6	.7							1.0	1.0
		(30) 1.8	(31) 1.7				% Depr., Dep., Amort./Sales		(101)	2.2	(58) 2.2
		4.4	3.0							3.9	3.7
		1.3	1.3							2.1	2.0
		(17) 2.9	(10) 2.3				% Officers', Directors', Owners' Comp/Sales		(51)	3.9	(28) 4.8
		4.1	5.3							6.5	9.7
2135M	32673M	429089M	1692917M	158247M	1784589M		Net Sales ($)			4900126M	2134179M
646M	8898M	237489M	1222578M	204809M	850006M		Total Assets ($)			3174550M	1744187M

© RMA 2024

M = $ thousand   MM = $ million
See Pages viii through xx for Explanation of Ratios and Data

MANUFACTURING—All Other Miscellaneous General Purpose Machinery Manufacturing NAICS 333998

Comparative Historical Data / Current Data Sorted by Sales

				Type of Statement				1	2	3	
	3	6	6	Unqualified				2	14	6	
	9	17	22	Reviewed			2	1	1	1	
	4	9	5	Compiled		1	1	6	1		
	12	16	9	Tax Returns		1	5	12	18	28	
	41	49	68	Other	2	3					
	4/1/21-3/31/22 ALL	4/1/22-3/31/23 ALL	4/1/23-3/31/24 ALL		0-1MM	18 (4/1-9/30/23) 1-3MM	3-5MM	92 (10/1/23-3/31/24) 5-10MM	10-25MM	25MM & OVER	
	69	97	110	**NUMBER OF STATEMENTS**	2	5	8	21	36	38	
	%	%	%	**ASSETS**	%	%	%	%	%	%	
	14.2	12.2	15.1	Cash & Equivalents				16.5	10.0	12.9	
	24.8	23.1	22.5	Trade Receivables (net)				25.4	20.3	23.2	
	22.4	25.1	24.2	Inventory				21.9	28.6	27.1	
	6.0	6.3	4.1	All Other Current				5.6	5.2	3.3	
	67.4	66.6	65.8	Total Current				69.5	64.1	66.6	
	19.0	16.8	18.4	Fixed Assets (net)				20.1	16.4	16.4	
	7.5	8.3	6.3	Intangibles (net)				3.6	6.0	8.1	
	6.1	8.3	9.4	All Other Non-Current				6.8	13.5	8.9	
	100.0	100.0	100.0	Total				100.0	100.0	100.0	
				LIABILITIES							
	5.5	7.4	7.3	Notes Payable-Short Term				4.1	3.5	11.5	
	4.5	2.3	2.0	Cur. Mat.-L.T.D.				2.5	2.0	1.9	
	14.6	10.1	9.5	Trade Payables				11.7	6.8	9.6	
	.1	.1	.3	Income Taxes Payable				.3	.7	.1	
	16.5	13.5	13.3	All Other Current				12.9	15.9	12.0	
	41.1	33.3	32.5	Total Current				31.6	28.8	35.2	
	17.3	15.1	11.7	Long-Term Debt				17.6	5.8	10.4	
	.1	.2	.3	Deferred Taxes				.0	.3	.5	
	3.5	10.8	5.4	All Other Non-Current				2.1	4.8	7.3	
	38.0	40.6	50.2	Net Worth				48.7	60.2	46.6	
	100.0	100.0	100.0	Total Liabilities & Net Worth				100.0	100.0	100.0	
				INCOME DATA							
	100.0	100.0	100.0	Net Sales				100.0	100.0	100.0	
	37.7	36.0	36.1	Gross Profit				41.4	35.3	30.5	
	33.7	29.3	26.7	Operating Expenses				25.7	28.2	22.0	
	4.0	6.8	9.4	Operating Profit				15.7	7.2	8.5	
	-1.0	.4	.1	All Other Expenses (net)				.5	-.4	-.2	
	5.0	6.4	9.3	Profit Before Taxes				15.2	7.6	8.7	
				RATIOS							
	4.4	4.2	5.2					8.4	4.2	3.4	
	2.4	2.3	2.4	Current				2.7	2.5	2.0	
	1.1	1.4	1.4					1.9	1.3	1.3	
	2.3	2.3	3.1					5.7	2.2	2.1	
	1.2	1.3	1.1	Quick				1.8	1.0	.9	
	.7	.6	.6					.5	.7	.6	
32	11.4	31	11.7	34	10.8			31	11.9	33	11.0	41	8.9
47	7.7	50	7.3	47	7.8	Sales/Receivables		37	9.8	49	7.4	49	7.5
66	5.5	76	4.8	59	6.2			56	6.5	70	5.2	57	6.4
19	19.2	23	15.7	16	22.4			6	64.3	51	7.2	43	8.5
74	4.9	79	4.6	81	4.5	Cost of Sales/Inventory		65	5.6	111	3.3	91	4.0
146	2.5	159	2.3	166	2.2			166	2.2	215	1.7	159	2.3
20	18.6	14	25.9	11	32.9			5	73.3	12	30.9	13	27.2
36	10.2	28	13.0	23	15.9	Cost of Sales/Payables		22	16.5	25	14.6	24	15.2
59	6.2	52	7.0	45	8.1			47	7.7	39	9.3	38	9.7
	3.5		2.7		3.0				2.5		3.0		3.0
	5.9		4.6		5.0	Sales/Working Capital			3.9		4.2		6.3
	40.1		8.9		10.6				8.5		9.2		16.9
	57.7		22.3		32.3				24.7		56.9		115.4
(53)	16.3	(80)	8.0	(80)	6.6	EBIT/Interest		(15)	2.4	(22)	10.7	(31)	7.5
	2.6		.9		1.3				.9		2.0		1.5
			43.2		35.1	Net Profit + Depr., Dep.,							109.5
		(21)	7.4	(18)	5.9	Amort./Cur. Mat. L/T/D						(10)	4.5
			1.0		2.8								2.1
	.2		.1		.1				.1		.1		.1
	.4		.3		.3	Fixed/Worth			.5		.2		.2
	2.2		1.8		1.2				.9		.7		1.3
	.4		.6		.4				.4		.2		.5
	1.6		1.3		.8	Debt/Worth			.7		.6		1.2
	7.9		11.3		4.3				1.6		2.1		7.4
	54.8		42.6		49.1	% Profit Before Taxes/Tangible			53.9		39.6		59.0
(55)	27.4	(77)	20.0	(100)	20.8	Net Worth		(18)	34.8	(34)	17.4	(36)	20.8
	8.2		6.8		7.7				3.6		5.4		13.4
	20.2		18.9		24.3	% Profit Before Taxes/Total			34.3		16.1		19.2
	10.9		8.4		11.6	Assets			18.6		9.2		12.4
	.8		2.2		3.0				1.0		3.1		3.7
	26.1		76.4		34.0				35.2		16.1		63.0
	12.1		14.2		12.7	Sales/Net Fixed Assets			12.8		9.9		16.7
	5.4		5.6		6.1				4.2		5.9		8.4
	2.4		2.1		2.4				2.4		1.8		2.3
	1.6		1.5		1.6	Sales/Total Assets			1.9		1.3		1.7
	1.2		1.1		1.2				1.3		.9		1.2
	.8		.7		.7				.8		.8		.7
(48)	1.7	(71)	1.6	(72)	1.7	% Depr., Dep., Amort./Sales		(13)	3.7	(25)	1.7	(25)	1.5
	3.8		3.9		3.5				5.1		3.0		2.7
	1.6		1.4		1.3				1.1				
(16)	2.8	(28)	2.8	(32)	2.7	% Officers', Directors', Owners' Comp/Sales		(14)	2.0				
	5.1		6.4		4.2				3.4				
	1910300M		2687712M		4099650M	Net Sales ($)	641M	10089M	32181M	162708M	535908M	3358123M
	1559680M		2163293M		2524426M	Total Assets ($)	296M	3314M	23183M	117549M	517241M	1862843M

© RMA 2024   M = $ thousand   MM = $ million
See Pages viii through xx for Explanation of Ratios and Data

MANUFACTURING—Electronic Computer Manufacturing NAICS 334111

Current Data Sorted by Assets | Comparative Historical Data

						Type of Statement		
				1	1	Unqualified	3	2
						Reviewed	4	1
	1	1				Compiled	1	
1	9 (4/1-9/30/23)	8	18	1	3	Tax Returns	5	1
0-500M	500M-2MM	2-10MM	26 (10/1/23-3/31/24) 10-50MM	50-100MM	100-250MM	Other	23	12
							4/1/19-3/31/20	4/1/20-3/31/21
1	1	9	19	1	4	NUMBER OF STATEMENTS	ALL 36	ALL 16
%	%	%	%	%	%	ASSETS	%	%
			25.6			Cash & Equivalents	15.5	20.7
			19.5			Trade Receivables (net)	23.4	17.1
			30.6			Inventory	30.9	25.4
			7.6			All Other Current	1.4	4.6
			83.3			Total Current	71.1	67.8
			4.6			Fixed Assets (net)	12.0	7.1
			9.8			Intangibles (net)	7.6	20.2
			2.4			All Other Non-Current	9.3	5.0
			100.0			Total	100.0	100.0
						LIABILITIES		
			2.1			Notes Payable-Short Term	8.8	5.5
			1.3			Cur. Mat.-L.T.D.	1.7	2.8
			17.1			Trade Payables	16.8	14.8
			.2			Income Taxes Payable	.2	.1
			13.7			All Other Current	22.9	15.0
			34.4			Total Current	50.5	38.2
			13.4			Long-Term Debt	10.8	23.7
			.0			Deferred Taxes	.1	1.1
			2.2			All Other Non-Current	7.5	9.1
			50.0			Net Worth	31.2	27.9
			100.0			Total Liabilities & Net Worth	100.0	100.0
						INCOME DATA		
			100.0			Net Sales	100.0	100.0
			34.5			Gross Profit	36.0	37.8
			27.0			Operating Expenses	34.0	30.7
			7.5			Operating Profit	2.0	7.1
			.9			All Other Expenses (net)	.4	1.6
			6.5			Profit Before Taxes	1.6	5.5
						RATIOS		
			3.0				3.1	2.1
			2.5			Current	1.8	1.8
			1.7				1.3	1.5
			2.0				1.7	1.5
			1.3			Quick	1.0	1.2
			.7				.6	.6
			17 22.1				21 17.0	21 17.6
			36 10.0			Sales/Receivables	47 7.8	33 10.9
			47 7.7				62 5.9	47 7.8
			22 16.7				31 11.6	24 15.1
			60 6.1			Cost of Sales/Inventory	91 4.0	76 4.8
			215 1.7				215 1.7	174 2.1
			10 35.0				22 16.8	32 11.3
			33 11.1			Cost of Sales/Payables	32 11.4	47 7.7
			59 6.2				72 5.1	69 5.3
			3.6				3.6	3.4
			6.2			Sales/Working Capital	5.2	6.5
			8.8				16.2	12.0
			98.6				50.1	23.4
			(17) 25.9			EBIT/Interest	(26) 4.7	(13) 11.6
			4.5				-2.4	.4
						Net Profit + Depr., Dep., Amort./Cur. Mat. L/T/D		
			.0				.1	.1
			.0			Fixed/Worth	.2	.8
			.3				1.6	-.9
			.5				.5	1.1
			.7			Debt/Worth	1.1	NM
			6.6				5.9	-6.7
			52.3				42.3	
			(15) 41.9			% Profit Before Taxes/Tangible Net Worth	(28) 12.6	
			16.4				-4.2	
			27.2				20.4	22.7
			23.5			% Profit Before Taxes/Total Assets	6.0	7.5
			8.9				-5.3	.5
			427.7				135.2	128.2
			164.2			Sales/Net Fixed Assets	26.0	50.6
			37.5				12.9	16.9
			5.4				2.9	2.3
			2.1			Sales/Total Assets	1.8	1.5
			1.1				1.1	1.0
								.3
						% Depr., Dep., Amort./Sales	(25) .9	
							2.7	
						% Officers', Directors' Owners' Comp/Sales		
2961M	12299M	175692M	943505M	65991M	946081M	Net Sales ($)	1319016M	699657M
283M	1597M	53275M	363744M	51515M	667016M	Total Assets ($)	880544M	446477M

© RMA 2024

M = $ thousand   MM = $ million
See Pages viii through xx for Explanation of Ratios and Data

MANUFACTURING—Electronic Computer Manufacturing NAICS 334111

Comparative Historical Data | Current Data Sorted by Sales

				Type of Statement						
				Unqualified						2
		1	2	Reviewed						
	1	1		Compiled						
1	2	1	2	Tax Returns						
2	25	31		Other	1		1	1		
17	4/1/22-	4/1/23-			1		5	6	19	
4/1/21-	3/31/23	3/31/24			9 (4/1-9/30/23)		26 (10/1/23-3/31/24)		
3/31/22	ALL	ALL			0-1MM	1-3MM	3-5MM	5-10MM	10-25MM	25MM & OVER
ALL										
20	30	35		NUMBER OF STATEMENTS		2		5	7	21
%	%	%		ASSETS	%	%	%	%	%	%
10.8	11.8	23.1		Cash & Equivalents						30.4
27.9	22.1	21.0		Trade Receivables (net)	D		D			18.2
27.1	38.5	29.7		Inventory	A		A			28.9
5.7	3.2	7.1		All Other Current	T		T			7.4
71.5	75.5	80.9		Total Current	A		A			85.0
7.8	7.8	6.0		Fixed Assets (net)						3.4
17.8	12.3	7.8		Intangibles (net)	N		N			9.5
2.9	4.4	5.3		All Other Non-Current	O		O			2.2
100.0	100.0	100.0		Total	T		T			100.0
				LIABILITIES	A		A			
7.5	6.5	3.8		Notes Payable-Short Term	V		V			1.4
5.3	1.3	1.1		Cur. Mat.-L.T.D.	A		A			1.0
24.1	19.8	19.7		Trade Payables	I		I			25.5
.1	.3	.1		Income Taxes Payable	L		L			.2
13.7	12.8	13.5		All Other Current	A		A			11.7
50.8	40.7	38.2		Total Current	B		B			39.9
13.9	12.2	9.8		Long-Term Debt	L		L			13.1
.0	.1	.0		Deferred Taxes	E		E			.0
6.1	4.5	2.0		All Other Non-Current						1.9
29.2	42.5	50.0		Net Worth						45.1
100.0	100.0	100.0		Total Liabilities & Net Worth						100.0
				INCOME DATA						
100.0	100.0	100.0		Net Sales						100.0
38.2	37.6	33.2		Gross Profit						25.2
34.5	32.8	26.9		Operating Expenses						21.2
3.8	4.8	6.3		Operating Profit						4.0
-1.2	1.0	.8		All Other Expenses (net)						1.1
4.9	3.8	5.5		Profit Before Taxes						3.0
				RATIOS						
2.4	2.6	3.0								3.0
1.6	1.8	2.4		Current						2.4
1.2	1.2	1.6								1.7
1.2	1.8	2.1								2.0
.8	.7	1.2		Quick						1.4
.5	.4	.6								.7
26 14.2	26 14.2	17 22.1							10	36.5
38 9.5	45 8.1	33 11.0		Sales/Receivables					27	13.4
59 6.2	69 5.3	59 6.2							45	8.2
23 15.6	34 10.7	21 17.8							20	18.7
52 7.0	104 3.5	60 6.1		Cost of Sales/Inventory					39	9.4
126 2.9	261 1.4	192 1.9							101	3.6
24 15.0	21 17.0	17 21.4							18	19.9
41 8.8	40 9.2	33 11.1		Cost of Sales/Payables					35	10.3
70 5.2	68 5.4	60 6.1							69	5.3
3.8	3.3	4.0								4.6
8.3	7.1	7.0		Sales/Working Capital						7.4
32.7	10.6	12.5								11.9
24.1	19.6	93.3								96.4
(16) 12.1	(22) 8.1	(29) 16.5		EBIT/Interest					(18)	17.1
.5	.6	1.8								.7
				Net Profit + Depr., Dep., Amort./Cur. Mat. L/T/D						
.1	.0	.0								.0
.4	.2	.1		Fixed/Worth						.1
-.6	1.3	.5								.5
1.4	.6	.5								.5
4.1	2.1	.8		Debt/Worth						1.0
-10.2	8.5	4.6								11.9
91.3	46.8	52.9								54.9
(14) 47.1	(25) 18.6	(30) 42.0		% Profit Before Taxes/Tangible Net Worth					(17)	43.2
8.2	11.2	14.3								14.2
19.5	17.6	27.2								27.4
9.8	6.8	17.3		% Profit Before Taxes/Total Assets						10.4
.3	1.8	2.8								-.3
77.7	148.1	420.2								486.4
38.3	40.8	86.5		Sales/Net Fixed Assets						96.3
16.5	15.5	28.4								39.0
3.9	2.8	5.4								6.6
2.2	1.9	2.1		Sales/Total Assets						2.7
1.1	.9	1.1								1.3
.1	.2	.1								
(13) .7	(16) .4	(16) .3		% Depr., Dep., Amort./Sales						
2.6	2.9	.7								
				% Officers', Directors' Owners' Comp/Sales						
1175343M	1490478M	2146529M		Net Sales ($)	4697M		40111M	122107M	1979614M	
690701M	715192M	1137430M		Total Assets ($)	7302M		31641M	76390M	1022097M	

M = $ thousand   MM = $ million
See Pages viii through xx for Explanation of Ratios and Data

© RMA 2024

MANUFACTURING—Computer Terminal and Other Computer Peripheral Equipment Manufacturing   NAICS 334118

Current Data Sorted by Assets | **Comparative Historical Data**

0-500M	1 (4/1-9/30/23) 500M-2MM	2-10MM	20 (10/1/23-3/31/24) 10-50MM	50-100MM	100-250MM		Type of Statement	4/1/19-3/31/20 ALL	4/1/20-3/31/21 ALL
	1	1	3		1		Unqualified	6	4
		1	1				Reviewed	2	1
							Compiled		
		6		1			Tax Returns	7	1
	1	8	20 (10/1/23-3/31/24) 7	1	3		Other	26	16
							NUMBER OF STATEMENTS	41	22
%	%	%	%	%	%		ASSETS	%	%

D						Cash & Equivalents	14.2	22.3
A						Trade Receivables (net)	23.8	24.2
T						Inventory	27.3	22.2
A						All Other Current	2.9	4.0
						Total Current	68.2	72.7
N						Fixed Assets (net)	8.1	7.2
O						Intangibles (net)	17.8	14.3
T						All Other Non-Current	5.8	5.8
						Total	100.0	100.0
A						LIABILITIES		
V						Notes Payable-Short Term	7.3	5.9
A						Cur. Mat.-L.T.D.	2.5	6.6
I						Trade Payables	14.9	15.8
L						Income Taxes Payable	.2	.3
A						All Other Current	12.8	11.0
B						Total Current	37.7	39.7
L						Long-Term Debt	10.9	14.1
E						Deferred Taxes	.2	.2
						All Other Non-Current	7.7	6.8
						Net Worth	43.4	39.1
						Total Liabilities & Net Worth	100.0	100.0
						INCOME DATA		
						Net Sales	100.0	100.0
						Gross Profit	38.6	39.0
						Operating Expenses	33.6	36.1
						Operating Profit	5.0	2.9
						All Other Expenses (net)	.6	-.4
						Profit Before Taxes	4.4	3.3
						RATIOS		
						Current	3.1 / 1.8 / 1.3	4.4 / 2.1 / 1.6
						Quick	1.9 / .9 / .7	3.0 / 1.4 / .7
						Sales/Receivables	37 9.8 / 46 7.9 / 59 6.2	40 9.1 / 52 7.0 / 68 5.4
						Cost of Sales/Inventory	45 8.1 / 76 4.8 / 152 2.4	32 11.5 / 87 4.2 / 130 2.8
						Cost of Sales/Payables	27 13.6 / 40 9.1 / 58 6.3	25 14.7 / 34 10.6 / 69 5.3
						Sales/Working Capital	3.4 / 7.5 / 21.5	3.1 / 3.9 / 10.1
						EBIT/Interest	33.0 / (36) 7.2 / 2.3	39.7 / (16) 3.7 / -.4
						Net Profit + Depr., Dep., Amort./Cur. Mat. L/T/D	27.9 / (10) 12.3 / 3.8	
						Fixed/Worth	.1 / .3 / 4.4	.1 / .1 / .5
						Debt/Worth	.6 / 2.4 / 76.0	.7 / 2.2 / 9.2
						% Profit Before Taxes/Tangible Net Worth	47.9 / (32) 20.9 / 11.1	38.7 / (18) 18.1 / -13.4
						% Profit Before Taxes/Total Assets	12.6 / 7.3 / 2.7	12.5 / 5.6 / -3.4
						Sales/Net Fixed Assets	96.3 / 39.1 / 15.4	176.3 / 35.8 / 11.6
						Sales/Total Assets	2.6 / 2.0 / 1.2	2.0 / 1.5 / 1.1
						% Depr., Dep., Amort./Sales	.6 / (21) 1.2 / 2.2	.2 / (11) 1.6 / 3.1
						% Officers', Directors' Owners' Comp/Sales		
6996M	117848M	211353M	75750M	507020M		Net Sales ($)	2595843M	1078346M
790M	51921M	149676M	60212M	543946M		Total Assets ($)	1491294M	827562M

M = $ thousand   MM = $ million
See Pages viii through xx for Explanation of Ratios and Data

© RMA 2024

MANUFACTURING—Computer Terminal and Other Computer Peripheral Equipment Manufacturing NAICS 334118

Comparative Historical Data / Current Data Sorted by Sales

							Type of Statement							
		4		3		5	Unqualified				1	2		2
				3		2	Reviewed				1	1		
						1	Compiled							
		1		1			Tax Returns							
		10		21		14	Other				4	1		9
		4/1/21-		4/1/22-		4/1/23-			1 (4/1-9/30/23)			20 (10/1/23-3/31/24)		
		3/31/22		3/31/23		3/31/24		0-1MM	1-3MM	3-5MM	5-10MM	10-25MM		25MM & OVER
		ALL		ALL		ALL								
		15		29		21	NUMBER OF STATEMENTS				6	4		11
		%		%		%	ASSETS	%	%	%	%	%		%
		15.5		12.1		12.4	Cash & Equivalents	D	D	D				9.7
		24.1		23.6		20.0	Trade Receivables (net)	A	A	A				17.9
		29.3		32.7		27.0	Inventory	T	T	T				20.5
		2.9		4.5		3.1	All Other Current	A	A	A				4.2
		71.8		72.9		62.5	Total Current							52.2
		6.5		11.5		15.6	Fixed Assets (net)	N	N	N				19.5
		10.8		9.1		8.6	Intangibles (net)	O	O	O				12.8
		10.8		6.5		13.2	All Other Non-Current	T	T	T				15.4
		100.0		100.0		100.0	Total							100.0
							LIABILITIES	A	A	A				
		4.9		4.3		4.2	Notes Payable-Short Term	V	V	V				2.8
		1.4		2.8		7.0	Cur. Mat.-L.T.D.	A	A	A				11.6
		12.8		18.3		11.2	Trade Payables	I	I	I				10.8
		.7		.2		.3	Income Taxes Payable	L	L	L				.5
		11.1		8.8		8.8	All Other Current	A	A	A				11.2
		31.0		34.3		31.4	Total Current	B	B	B				36.9
		13.3		8.4		14.1	Long-Term Debt	L	L	L				10.8
		.0		.0		.3	Deferred Taxes	E	E	E				.4
		13.9		12.6		13.5	All Other Non-Current							13.0
		41.8		44.5		40.7	Net Worth							38.9
		100.0		100.0		100.0	Total Liabilties & Net Worth							100.0
							INCOME DATA							
		100.0		100.0		100.0	Net Sales							100.0
		42.7		38.7		40.9	Gross Profit							40.3
		43.4		33.6		34.2	Operating Expenses							34.0
		-.7		5.1		6.7	Operating Profit							6.3
		-2.7		1.1		1.8	All Other Expenses (net)							1.5
		2.0		4.0		4.8	Profit Before Taxes							4.8
							RATIOS							
		3.6		3.6		3.4								2.7
		2.6		2.1		2.6	Current							2.1
		1.8		1.5		1.3								1.0
		1.7		2.1		2.3								1.2
		1.6		1.0		1.1	Quick							.9
		1.1		.7		.7								.6
34	10.7		31	11.6	30	12.1							29	12.4
43	8.4		51	7.1	39	9.3	Sales/Receivables						39	9.3
66	5.5		73	5.0	51	7.2							57	6.4
60	6.1		46	7.9	20	18.4							5	71.6
107	3.4		111	3.3	111	3.3	Cost of Sales/Inventory						50	7.3
228	1.6		215	1.7	174	2.1							174	2.1
22	16.5		25	14.4	25	14.6							27	13.3
31	11.8		42	8.6	36	10.1	Cost of Sales/Payables						38	9.7
56	6.5		83	4.4	45	8.2							47	7.8
		3.0		3.0		3.0								3.1
		4.0		4.3		4.2	Sales/Working Capital							8.1
		6.2		10.9		17.0								-62.0
		44.1		10.2		32.0								44.3
(14)	15.5	(20)		3.9	(19)	6.2	EBIT/Interest							7.2
		3.5		.3		3.1								3.1
				11.1			Net Profit + Depr., Dep.,							
			(10)	4.7			Amort./Cur. Mat. L/T/D							
				2.8										
		.1		.0		.1								.1
		.2		.2		.2	Fixed/Worth							.2
		.6		.6		1.8								2.5
		.7		.7		.6								.7
		1.5		1.5		1.9	Debt/Worth							1.9
		5.6		3.5		12.3								5.1
		70.3		54.5		61.5	% Profit Before Taxes/Tangible							
(13)	21.3	(27)		20.6	(18)	25.4	Net Worth							
		6.6		3.4		12.1								
		18.6		19.2		18.7	% Profit Before Taxes/Total							12.4
		8.1		7.1		10.3	Assets							6.3
		-8.1		1.4		3.9								4.6
		84.8		62.8		68.5								62.6
		31.1		30.3		22.6	Sales/Net Fixed Assets							10.4
		9.5		9.9		5.9								3.4
		2.4		2.5		2.3								2.6
		1.6		1.6		1.4	Sales/Total Assets							1.2
		1.1		1.1		1.1								1.0
				.2		.5								
			(18)	1.0	(14)	2.1	% Depr., Dep., Amort./Sales							
				3.5		3.9								
							% Officers', Directors'							
							Owners' Comp/Sales							
		529626M		1350198M		918967M	Net Sales ($)				50322M	75004M		793641M
		426732M		908154M		806545M	Total Assets ($)				29153M	47946M		729446M

© RMA 2024   M = $ thousand   MM = $ million
See Pages viii through xx for Explanation of Ratios and Data

MANUFACTURING—Radio and Television Broadcasting and Wireless Communications Equipment Manufacturing NAICS 334220

Current Data Sorted by Assets | Comparative Historical Data

0-500M	500M-2MM	2-10MM	10-50MM	50-100MM	100-250MM			4/1/19-3/31/20 ALL	4/1/20-3/31/21 ALL
			1			Type of Statement			
						Unqualified		12	10
						Reviewed		4	2
						Compiled			1
		1	3	1	1	Tax Returns			
	1	2	2			Other		3	
	2	8	10	3	4			24	20
5 (4/1-9/30/23)			35 (10/1/23-3/31/24)						
						NUMBER OF STATEMENTS		**43**	**33**
%	%	%	%	%	%			%	%
	3	12	16	4	5				
						ASSETS			
D		15.4	21.2			Cash & Equivalents		12.8	12.4
A		28.8	18.1			Trade Receivables (net)		17.7	16.8
T		37.3	28.5			Inventory		28.0	26.8
A		3.1	5.5			All Other Current		2.5	4.1
		84.6	73.3			Total Current		61.1	60.1
N		11.6	12.9			Fixed Assets (net)		13.2	16.5
O		.2	2.1			Intangibles (net)		15.2	17.6
T		3.6	11.7			All Other Non-Current		10.6	5.7
		100.0	100.0			Total		100.0	100.0
A						**LIABILITIES**			
V		9.9	5.0			Notes Payable-Short Term		7.3	10.3
A		2.4	.7			Cur. Mat.-L.T.D.		1.5	3.6
I		27.6	10.7			Trade Payables		12.6	10.3
L		.7	.0			Income Taxes Payable		.0	.0
A		11.1	13.5			All Other Current		8.8	13.6
B		51.7	30.0			Total Current		30.2	37.8
L		4.0	5.6			Long-Term Debt		15.5	29.4
E		.0	.8			Deferred Taxes		.2	.4
		5.7	10.7			All Other Non-Current		12.6	3.3
		38.6	52.9			Net Worth		41.5	29.2
		100.0	100.0			Total Liabilities & Net Worth		100.0	100.0
						INCOME DATA			
		100.0	100.0			Net Sales		100.0	100.0
		44.4	41.9			Gross Profit		41.1	43.9
		42.6	37.6			Operating Expenses		41.9	45.3
		1.8	4.3			Operating Profit		-.7	-1.4
		.8	1.3			All Other Expenses (net)		1.3	3.4
		.9	3.0			Profit Before Taxes		-2.1	-4.8
						RATIOS			
		2.3	8.6					3.9	2.6
		1.6	2.8			Current		2.3	1.7
		1.3	1.2					1.4	1.2
		1.2	5.8					1.9	1.6
		.9	1.2			Quick		1.1	1.0
		.6	.5					.7	.4
		19 18.9	33 10.9				29	12.8	26 14.2
		38 9.7	47 7.8			Sales/Receivables	42	8.7	46 7.9
		62 5.9	85 4.3				60	6.1	69 5.3
		18 20.3	76 4.8				52	7.0	62 5.9
		78 4.7	135 2.7			Cost of Sales/Inventory	118	3.1	107 3.4
		215 1.7	192 1.9				203	1.8	174 2.1
		25 14.7	18 20.6				29	12.8	28 12.9
		35 10.3	27 13.3			Cost of Sales/Payables	43	8.5	50 7.3
		107 3.4	62 5.9				64	5.7	79 4.6
		5.4	1.9					2.2	3.4
		8.0	3.8			Sales/Working Capital		4.3	4.8
		16.0	6.5					8.9	16.2
			49.6					23.3	19.6
		(10)	4.0			EBIT/Interest	(36)	1.5	(28) 1.4
			-5.0					-5.4	-3.7
						Net Profit + Depr., Dep., Amort./Cur. Mat. L/T/D			
		.0	.0					.1	.2
		.1	.2			Fixed/Worth		.2	.6
		.8	.6					-9.8	-.3
		.4	.2					.4	.5
		1.7	.9			Debt/Worth		.8	2.8
		105.8	5.9					-96.7	-4.5
		38.0	25.6					32.2	24.3
		(10) 15.1	(14) 13.9			% Profit Before Taxes/Tangible Net Worth	(32)	4.0	(22) 3.9
		-36.0	.7					-14.7	-8.7
		15.5	15.3					9.3	8.5
		3.1	8.9			% Profit Before Taxes/Total Assets		.3	.5
		-6.5	-.3					-9.0	-9.2
		391.2	63.4					35.8	36.1
		124.2	21.7			Sales/Net Fixed Assets		18.3	19.9
		14.4	6.5					10.5	9.3
		3.4	1.6					2.0	1.7
		2.4	1.3			Sales/Total Assets		1.4	1.2
		1.7	1.0					1.0	.8
			.3					.8	.7
		(12)	2.0			% Depr., Dep., Amort./Sales	(25)	1.6	(21) 1.8
			2.4					3.4	2.9
						% Officers', Directors' Owners' Comp/Sales			
	10288M	157287M	587689M	311551M	684377M	Net Sales ($)		1594721M	1815383M
	2558M	55718M	462045M	294064M	876616M	Total Assets ($)		1663639M	1840548M

M = $ thousand   MM = $ million
See Pages viii through xx for Explanation of Ratios and Data

© RMA 2024

MANUFACTURING—Radio and Television Broadcasting and Wireless Communications Equipment Manufacturing   NAICS 334220

Comparative Historical Data | Current Data Sorted by Sales

								Type of Statement												
		3		4		6		Unqualified									1		5	
		3		2				Reviewed												
		2				3		Compiled							1		2		1	
		3		2		4		Tax Returns					1		2		2			
		17		14		27		Other				2		4			5		15	
		4/1/21-3/31/22		4/1/22-3/31/23		4/1/23-3/31/24					5 (4/1-9/30/23)				35 (10/1/23-3/31/24)					
		ALL		ALL		ALL				0-1MM	1-3MM		3-5MM		5-10MM		10-25MM		25MM & OVER	
		28		24		40		NUMBER OF STATEMENTS			1		3		5		10		21	
		%		%		%		ASSETS		%	%		%		%		%		%	
		14.3		19.0		19.1		Cash & Equivalents									18.4		19.5	
		19.5		18.7		20.4		Trade Receivables (net)		D							26.0		16.8	
		31.1		36.7		27.8		Inventory		A							34.3		24.9	
		8.3		4.8		5.7		All Other Current		T							3.6		8.2	
		73.2		79.2		73.0		Total Current		A							82.3		69.5	
		9.5		8.4		11.6		Fixed Assets (net)									9.2		9.3	
		7.7		6.2		6.8		Intangibles (net)		N							.1		10.6	
		9.6		6.2		8.7		All Other Non-Current		O							8.3		10.6	
		100.0		100.0		100.0		Total		T							100.0		100.0	
								LIABILITIES		A										
		6.9		13.8		5.3		Notes Payable-Short Term		V							4.2		4.3	
		2.5		2.6		1.9		Cur. Mat.-L.T.D.		A							.1		1.7	
		13.4		8.8		15.1		Trade Payables		I							17.4		13.4	
		.0		.0		.2		Income Taxes Payable		L							.8		.1	
		15.9		12.7		12.9		All Other Current		A							9.4		13.3	
		38.7		37.8		35.5		Total Current		B							31.9		32.7	
		22.2		23.0		9.1		Long-Term Debt		L							1.4		11.7	
		.5		.3		.5		Deferred Taxes		E							.6		.7	
		8.4		7.8		7.8		All Other Non-Current									6.6		10.0	
		30.2		31.2		47.1		Net Worth									59.4		44.9	
		100.0		100.0		100.0		Total Liabilities & Net Worth									100.0		100.0	
								INCOME DATA												
		100.0		100.0		100.0		Net Sales									100.0		100.0	
		44.4		44.9		43.1		Gross Profit									41.4		37.8	
		38.6		37.4		39.8		Operating Expenses									34.0		33.3	
		5.8		7.4		3.2		Operating Profit									7.4		4.5	
		-.6		.6		1.7		All Other Expenses (net)									.7		2.2	
		6.5		6.8		1.5		Profit Before Taxes									6.8		2.3	
								RATIOS												
		2.8		7.3		4.4											11.2		4.2	
		1.9		2.5		1.9		Current									3.1		2.0	
		1.3		1.6		1.3											1.3		1.5	
		1.8		4.1		3.7											6.3		3.5	
		.9		1.2		.9		Quick									2.4		.8	
		.5		.7		.5											.8		.5	
31	11.8		25	14.6		31	11.6									34	10.8	31	11.9	
47	7.8		32	11.4		38	9.5	Sales/Receivables								44	8.3	38	9.6	
59	6.2		55	6.6		56	6.5									58	6.3	54	6.8	
62	5.9		91	4.0		51	7.2									60	6.1	73	5.0	
107	3.4		174	2.1		111	3.3	Cost of Sales/Inventory								122	3.0	111	3.3	
192	1.9		215	1.7		174	2.1									182	2.0	166	2.2	
26	14.1		10	36.2		18	20.6									22	16.9	21	17.0	
45	8.1		33	10.9		32	11.4	Cost of Sales/Payables								30	12.0	46	7.9	
87	4.2		62	5.9		78	4.7									41	8.8	78	4.7	
		3.4		2.2		2.7											1.8		2.5	
		4.2		3.2		4.8		Sales/Working Capital									5.2		3.8	
		9.9		8.8		9.8											15.9		5.9	
		100.0		21.9		28.4													35.4	
	(24)	18.0	(16)	6.4	(25)	1.5		EBIT/Interest									(14)		1.8	
		4.1		-.8		-5.8													-2.8	
								Net Profit + Depr., Dep., Amort./Cur. Mat. L/T/D												
		.1		.0		.0											.0		.1	
		.2		.1		.2		Fixed/Worth									.1		.3	
		NM		NM		.8											.4		1.1	
		.6		.2		.4											.2		.3	
		1.7		1.0		1.3		Debt/Worth									.4		1.8	
		NM		NM		7.3											2.0		9.5	
		83.9		37.1		27.0													26.7	
	(21)	37.2	(18)	17.0	(33)	10.9		% Profit Before Taxes/Tangible Net Worth									(17)		11.3	
		17.9		-.2		-15.4													-5.9	
		25.7		18.4		12.7											29.7		12.7	
		13.7		8.8		3.5		% Profit Before Taxes/Total Assets									13.1		3.6	
		2.2		-4.3		-5.2											3.2		-2.9	
		75.2		183.1		116.8											201.9		84.6	
		26.3		32.8		22.2		Sales/Net Fixed Assets									40.7		17.9	
		16.2		16.3		10.1											11.6		9.7	
		1.9		2.3		2.7											3.3		1.7	
		1.5		1.4		1.6		Sales/Total Assets									1.7		1.2	
		1.1		1.0		1.0											1.1		.8	
		.2		.2		.3													.3	
	(19)	1.6	(14)	.8	(23)	1.6		% Depr., Dep., Amort./Sales									(14)		2.2	
		2.7		1.8		2.4													2.8	
								% Officers', Directors' Owners' Comp/Sales												
		943809M		713314M		1751192M		Net Sales ($)			2953M		11948M		35538M		163376M		1537377M	
		750824M		553362M		1691001M		Total Assets ($)			812M		4557M		49612M		102800M		1533220M	

© RMA 2024   M = $ thousand   MM = $ million
See Pages viii through xx for Explanation of Ratios and Data

MANUFACTURING—Other Communications Equipment Manufacturing NAICS 334290

Current Data Sorted by Assets | Comparative Historical Data

Type of Statement							
			2			Unqualified	6	1
		1	1			Reviewed	2	3
		1				Compiled	2	1
		3				Tax Returns	9	1
		4	11	3	4	Other	27	10
0-500M	7 (4/1-9/30/23) 500M-2MM	2-10MM	23 (10/1/23-3/31/24) 10-50MM	50-100MM	100-250MM		4/1/19-3/31/20 ALL	4/1/20-3/31/21 ALL
		9	14	3	4	NUMBER OF STATEMENTS	46	16

%	%	%	%	%	%		%	%
						ASSETS		
D	D		17.4			Cash & Equivalents	11.9	18.7
A	A		20.9			Trade Receivables (net)	30.4	21.6
T	T		21.0			Inventory	29.0	24.9
A	A		5.6			All Other Current	2.8	2.8
			64.9			Total Current	74.1	68.0
N	N		14.1			Fixed Assets (net)	10.7	15.7
O	O		12.2			Intangibles (net)	9.3	9.4
T	T		8.9			All Other Non-Current	6.0	7.0
			100.0			Total	100.0	100.0
A	A					**LIABILITIES**		
V	V		2.5			Notes Payable-Short Term	8.2	2.3
A	A		1.4			Cur. Mat.-L.T.D.	2.4	5.5
I	I		10.2			Trade Payables	19.2	8.4
L	L		.4			Income Taxes Payable	.2	.3
A	A		15.4			All Other Current	11.4	9.2
B	B		29.9			Total Current	41.4	25.6
L	L		5.5			Long-Term Debt	9.3	8.7
E	E		.4			Deferred Taxes	.2	.3
			13.6			All Other Non-Current	6.6	8.4
			50.6			Net Worth	42.6	57.1
			100.0			Total Liabilities & Net Worth	100.0	100.0
						INCOME DATA		
			100.0			Net Sales	100.0	100.0
			44.4			Gross Profit	36.0	39.4
			30.3			Operating Expenses	29.9	31.4
			14.2			Operating Profit	6.1	8.0
			5.7			All Other Expenses (net)	1.2	1.3
			8.5			Profit Before Taxes	4.8	6.7
						RATIOS		
			5.8				2.9	6.6
			3.5			Current	1.9	3.4
			1.4				1.4	2.2
			3.6				2.2	4.2
			1.6			Quick	.9	2.0
			.5				.6	1.0
		25	14.7				37	9.8	33	11.0
		39	9.4			Sales/Receivables	49	7.4	39	9.3
		68	5.4				72	5.1	63	5.8
		8	45.3				49	7.5	52	7.0
		74	4.9			Cost of Sales/Inventory	85	4.3	83	4.4
		152	2.4				152	2.4	118	3.1
		11	32.1				21	17.0	13	28.5
		27	13.7			Cost of Sales/Payables	38	9.6	19	19.2
		68	5.4				60	6.1	43	8.4
			2.6				4.4	3.0
			4.7			Sales/Working Capital	6.6	4.0
			11.6				13.2	7.0
			27.9				21.1	103.6
		(11)	13.4			EBIT/Interest	(31)	5.1	(14)	24.9
			2.2				1.4	2.9
						Net Profit + Depr., Dep., Amort./Cur. Mat. L/T/D		
			.1				.1	.2
			.3			Fixed/Worth	.2	.3
			NM				.6	.5
			.2				.6	.3
			1.2			Debt/Worth	1.1	.7
			NM				3.8	1.2
			60.2				41.7	39.8
		(11)	38.9			% Profit Before Taxes/Tangible Net Worth	(41)	24.0	(14)	27.3
			13.0				11.6	7.4
			21.5				20.2	25.1
			12.9			% Profit Before Taxes/Total Assets	6.8	14.7
			1.9				2.1	2.4
			56.8				84.2	30.2
			22.9			Sales/Net Fixed Assets	33.5	13.6
			6.2				11.3	8.7
			2.7				3.0	3.0
			1.6			Sales/Total Assets	1.9	1.8
			.9				1.3	1.0
			.4				.7	1.1
		(10)	2.3			% Depr., Dep., Amort./Sales	(29)	1.3	(14)	1.7
			3.8				2.5	3.5
						% Officers', Directors' Owners' Comp/Sales		.9
							(10)	3.7		
							9.4	
		95768M	640660M	346315M	781290M	Net Sales ($)	2365701M	1122703M
		52394M	329555M	182676M	654743M	Total Assets ($)	1233289M	708625M

M = $ thousand   MM = $ million
See Pages viii through xx for Explanation of Ratios and Data

© RMA 2024

MANUFACTURING—Other Communications Equipment Manufacturing NAICS 334290

Comparative Historical Data | Current Data Sorted by Sales

				Type of Statement						
	1	1	2	Unqualified				1	1	
	1	3	1	Reviewed				1		
	1	3	2	Compiled					1	1
	1	1	3	Tax Returns				2	1	
	12	23	22	Other				2	6	14
	4/1/21-	4/1/22-	4/1/23-			7 (4/1-9/30/23)		23 (10/1/23-3/31/24)		
	3/31/22	3/31/23	3/31/24							
	ALL	ALL	ALL		0-1MM	1-3MM	3-5MM	5-10MM	10-25MM	25MM & OVER
	16	31	30	NUMBER OF STATEMENTS				6	9	15
	%	%	%	ASSETS	%	%	%	%	%	%
	16.2	12.9	19.9	Cash & Equivalents						19.9
	24.0	27.7	18.8	Trade Receivables (net)	D	D	D			19.7
	24.9	28.0	23.9	Inventory	A	A	A			24.6
	2.8	4.3	3.8	All Other Current	T	T	T			5.8
	68.0	73.0	66.4	Total Current	A	A	A			70.0
	12.6	10.9	10.4	Fixed Assets (net)						10.1
	14.2	6.6	13.1	Intangibles (net)	N	N	N			12.6
	5.2	9.4	10.1	All Other Non-Current	O	O	O			7.4
	100.0	100.0	100.0	Total	T	T	T			100.0
				LIABILITIES						
	3.6	7.6	2.6	Notes Payable-Short Term	A	A	A			2.6
	1.9	2.9	1.2	Cur. Mat.-L.T.D.	V	V	V			.5
	9.9	10.6	8.0	Trade Payables	A	A	A			10.6
	.1	.0	.2	Income Taxes Payable	I	I	I			.1
	32.7	11.3	11.5	All Other Current	L	L	L			12.4
	48.2	32.6	23.6	Total Current	A	A	A			26.3
	12.2	11.8	5.8	Long-Term Debt	B	B	B			4.7
	.1	.4	.2	Deferred Taxes	L	L	L			.4
	58.0	12.5	10.4	All Other Non-Current	E	E	E			7.7
	-18.4	42.8	60.0	Net Worth						60.9
	100.0	100.0	100.0	Total Liabilities & Net Worth						100.0
				INCOME DATA						
	100.0	100.0	100.0	Net Sales						100.0
	43.8	40.4	41.1	Gross Profit						44.0
	38.9	32.9	29.3	Operating Expenses						26.5
	4.9	7.4	11.8	Operating Profit						17.4
	-.8	1.6	3.2	All Other Expenses (net)						6.1
	5.6	5.8	8.6	Profit Before Taxes						11.3
				RATIOS						
	3.2	5.1	7.2							6.1
	2.0	2.5	3.9	Current						3.6
	1.2	1.3	1.7							1.7
	2.2	2.4	4.8							2.8
	.8	1.6	2.4	Quick						1.8
	.4	.5	1.0							1.1
37	9.9	36	10.1	25	14.4				11	31.8
46	7.9	55	6.6	41	9.0	Sales/Receivables			28	13.0
63	5.8	73	5.0	61	6.0				55	6.6
41	8.8	63	5.8	52	7.0				37	9.8
79	4.6	118	3.1	74	4.9	Cost of Sales/Inventory			70	5.2
140	2.6	174	2.1	146	2.5				261	1.4
19	19.6	17	20.9	13	27.5				17	21.4
31	11.6	34	10.6	25	14.6	Cost of Sales/Payables			30	12.2
46	8.0	48	7.6	51	7.1				51	7.2
	2.9		2.8		2.6					2.4
	6.4		3.7		3.7	Sales/Working Capital				3.8
	15.7		12.0		6.5					7.1
	88.0		41.7		40.1					44.2
(11)	5.7	(24)	8.7	(24)	14.0	EBIT/Interest			(11)	7.2
	1.7		.3		2.4					2.2
						Net Profit + Depr., Dep., Amort./Cur. Mat. L/T/D				
	.1		.1		.1					.1
	.3		.2		.2	Fixed/Worth				.2
	9.6		.7		.4					.4
	.5		.3		.2					.2
	4.2		1.0		.6	Debt/Worth				.9
	-192.2		4.9		2.5					2.2
	49.7		49.1		50.5					59.2
(11)	19.2	(24)	26.1	(26)	29.3	% Profit Before Taxes/Tangible Net Worth			(13)	24.1
	2.3		2.5		8.1					8.0
	22.6		24.6		21.4					21.4
	12.8		8.9		11.2	% Profit Before Taxes/Total Assets				11.2
	1.4		.0		2.6					5.6
	39.2		53.2		87.0					53.5
	16.4		25.6		27.8	Sales/Net Fixed Assets				23.4
	11.5		9.6		12.5					9.9
	2.5		2.4		2.2					2.9
	1.8		1.6		1.6	Sales/Total Assets				1.7
	1.1		1.2		1.0					1.0
	.9		1.5		.4					.4
(12)	1.6	(21)	2.4	(20)	1.8	% Depr., Dep., Amort./Sales			(10)	1.5
	2.6		3.5		3.2					3.4
						% Officers', Directors' Owners¹ Comp/Sales				
	563339M		1845570M		1864033M	Net Sales ($)			42661M	153824M	1667548M
	376813M		1246162M		1219368M	Total Assets ($)			37577M	120933M	1060858M

© RMA 2024   M = $ thousand   MM = $ million
See Pages viii through xx for Explanation of Ratios and Data

MANUFACTURING—Audio and Video Equipment Manufacturing NAICS 334310

Current Data Sorted by Assets | Comparative Historical Data

						Type of Statement		
			2	2	1	Unqualified	7	5
		1	1			Reviewed	8	1
		1	2			Compiled	3	2
1		8	16	7		Tax Returns	5	6
1	1	33 (10/1/23–3/31/24)				Other	29	18
0-500M	500M-2MM	2-10MM	10-50MM	50-100MM	100-250MM		4/1/19-3/31/20 ALL	4/1/20-3/31/21 ALL
2	1	10	21	9	1	NUMBER OF STATEMENTS	52	32
%	%	%	%	%	%	ASSETS	%	%
		13.9	6.9			Cash & Equivalents	11.9	14.0
		23.5	18.0			Trade Receivables (net)	23.2	19.1
		35.0	56.9			Inventory	38.7	38.5
		1.7	3.6			All Other Current	3.7	5.4
		74.0	85.4			Total Current	77.6	77.0
		11.0	8.5			Fixed Assets (net)	12.9	12.3
		3.9	2.9			Intangibles (net)	3.7	7.2
		11.0	3.2			All Other Non-Current	5.8	3.5
		100.0	100.0			Total	100.0	100.0
						LIABILITIES		
		5.2	17.1			Notes Payable-Short Term	13.3	10.2
		1.5	.6			Cur. Mat.-L.T.D.	1.2	1.0
		13.7	16.5			Trade Payables	20.5	10.4
		.0	.1			Income Taxes Payable	.1	.1
		21.3	7.7			All Other Current	14.8	13.1
		41.7	42.0			Total Current	49.8	34.9
		31.4	5.9			Long-Term Debt	9.7	19.1
		.0	.0			Deferred Taxes	.3	.0
		.6	3.9			All Other Non-Current	2.3	7.6
		26.3	48.2			Net Worth	37.9	38.4
		100.0	100.0			Total Liabilities & Net Worth	100.0	100.0
						INCOME DATA		
		100.0	100.0			Net Sales	100.0	100.0
		45.9	43.8			Gross Profit	40.0	41.9
		36.2	36.5			Operating Expenses	37.1	35.9
		9.7	7.3			Operating Profit	3.0	6.0
		.3	.2			All Other Expenses (net)	.8	.5
		9.4	7.0			Profit Before Taxes	2.2	5.5
						RATIOS		
		3.3	3.3				3.0	4.4
		2.2	2.0			Current	1.8	2.3
		1.2	1.7				1.2	1.6
		1.9	1.2				1.6	2.2
		.8	.4			Quick	.9	.9
		.5	.3				.4	.4
		27 13.5	30 12.3				27 13.3	15 24.2
		34 10.7	34 10.6			Sales/Receivables	40 9.2	36 10.2
		46 8.0	43 8.4				54 6.7	49 7.4
		17 21.8	83 4.4				65 5.6	65 5.6
		174 2.1	261 1.4			Cost of Sales/Inventory	118 3.1	146 2.5
		243 1.5	365 1.0				182 2.0	182 2.0
		6 64.8	45 8.1				19 19.0	11 32.9
		40 9.2	59 6.2			Cost of Sales/Payables	37 9.9	20 18.7
		91 4.0	79 4.6				64 5.7	51 7.1
		3.2	3.1				4.2	3.2
		5.5	3.6			Sales/Working Capital	6.5	4.6
		86.0	6.1				16.3	6.7
			15.8				28.6	54.2
		(19)	10.5			EBIT/Interest	(45) 5.4	(26) 7.9
			4.7				-.2	-8.8
						Net Profit + Depr., Dep., Amort./Cur. Mat. L/T/D	115.4	
							(10) 33.3	
							3.9	
		.0	.0				.1	.0
		.4	.1			Fixed/Worth	.2	.3
		NM	.3				.9	.9
		.9	.8				.5	.6
		2.7	1.1			Debt/Worth	1.3	1.4
		-11.1	1.4				6.2	40.0
			48.5				33.2	75.6
			33.7			% Profit Before Taxes/Tangible Net Worth	(43) 20.4	(25) 22.8
			14.2				7.2	.5
		29.8	18.4				15.5	40.3
		8.5	15.0			% Profit Before Taxes/Total Assets	6.3	9.1
		3.3	8.0				-3.7	-13.5
		422.0	117.1				59.5	137.9
		39.5	65.9			Sales/Net Fixed Assets	26.6	54.3
		12.1	22.8				11.1	11.9
		2.9	2.1				2.7	2.8
		2.4	1.5			Sales/Total Assets	2.0	1.9
		1.5	1.3				1.5	1.3
							.4	.5
						% Depr., Dep., Amort./Sales	(35) 1.2	(16) 1.1
							1.7	1.7
						% Officers', Directors' Owners' Comp/Sales		
8667M	7134M	119021M	936090M	1185434M	67472M	Net Sales ($)	2685011M	1020758M
525M	916M	54142M	529319M	687757M	190405M	Total Assets ($)	1601541M	582155M

M = $ thousand   MM = $ million
See Pages viii through xx for Explanation of Ratios and Data

© RMA 2024

MANUFACTURING—Audio and Video Equipment Manufacturing NAICS 334310

Comparative Historical Data | Current Data Sorted by Sales

						Type of Statement							
		1		2		5	Unqualified						5
				3		2	Reviewed					1	1
		1		3		3	Compiled				1	2	
		2		3		1	Tax Returns				1		
		21		22		33	Other		1	1	5	3	23
		4/1/21-3/31/22 ALL		4/1/22-3/31/23 ALL		4/1/23-3/31/24 ALL			11 (4/1-9/30/23)			33 (10/1/23-3/31/24)	
								0-1MM	1-3MM	3-5MM	5-10MM	10-25MM	25MM & OVER
		25		33		44	NUMBER OF STATEMENTS		1	1	7	6	29
		%		%		%	ASSETS	%	%	%	%	%	%
		19.4		16.5		11.1	Cash & Equivalents	D					10.1
		20.7		19.1		19.8	Trade Receivables (net)	A					19.1
		30.3		38.3		42.7	Inventory	T					48.1
		2.6		3.7		3.2	All Other Current	A					4.1
		73.1		77.6		76.8	Total Current						81.4
		13.8		8.8		9.0	Fixed Assets (net)	N					6.3
		9.0		7.5		6.3	Intangibles (net)	O					7.4
		4.2		6.2		7.8	All Other Non-Current	T					4.9
		100.0		100.0		100.0	Total						100.0
							LIABILITIES	A					
		4.7		8.4		11.5	Notes Payable-Short Term	V					11.9
		1.8		1.5		1.2	Cur. Mat.-L.T.D.	A					1.0
		13.4		11.8		17.3	Trade Payables	I					17.8
		.2		.7		.0	Income Taxes Payable	L					.1
		12.6		13.2		12.9	All Other Current	A					12.0
		32.7		35.5		42.9	Total Current	B					42.8
		16.3		27.7		18.6	Long-Term Debt	L					4.6
		.6		.5		.4	Deferred Taxes	E					.5
		2.7		2.5		3.7	All Other Non-Current						5.3
		47.7		33.7		34.4	Net Worth						46.8
		100.0		100.0		100.0	Total Liabilities & Net Worth						100.0
							INCOME DATA						
		100.0		100.0		100.0	Net Sales						100.0
		44.0		39.6		44.2	Gross Profit						43.4
		33.5		32.4		36.4	Operating Expenses						35.2
		10.4		7.2		7.7	Operating Profit						8.2
		-1.5		1.4		.7	All Other Expenses (net)						.7
		11.9		5.9		7.0	Profit Before Taxes						7.5
							RATIOS						
		3.1		3.9		2.5							2.3
		2.3		2.0		1.9	Current						1.9
		1.7		1.8		1.4							1.6
		2.0		1.9		1.3							1.1
		1.0		1.1		.6	Quick						.5
		.8		.5		.4							.3
20	18.7		21	17.8	29	12.8							30	12.3
31	11.8		33	11.0	34	10.6	Sales/Receivables						34	10.6
60	6.1		43	8.4	42	8.6							44	8.3
46	7.9		49	7.4	51	7.2							79	4.6
107	3.4		118	3.1	174	2.1	Cost of Sales/Inventory						215	1.7
152	2.4		215	1.7	304	1.2							332	1.1
22	16.5		11	32.6	33	11.0							46	8.0
36	10.2		37	9.9	58	6.3	Cost of Sales/Payables						61	6.0
65	5.6		50	7.3	76	4.8							73	5.0
		3.8		3.1		3.3							3.3
		5.1		4.9		4.1	Sales/Working Capital						4.0
		7.9		10.7		16.6							6.2
		160.7		9.6		16.2							17.2
(19)	28.1	(23)	3.4	(37)	9.7	EBIT/Interest						(24)	11.4
		7.8		.2		1.7							4.7
							Net Profit + Depr., Dep., Amort./Cur. Mat. L/T/D						
		.0		.0		.0							.0
		.2		.1		.1	Fixed/Worth						.1
		.8		.6		.5							.2
		.5		.6		.9							.8
		1.1		1.4		1.1	Debt/Worth						1.1
		2.3		31.3		4.7							1.9
		65.4		67.5		52.9							50.4
(23)	42.5	(27)	21.6	(36)	33.7	% Profit Before Taxes/Tangible Net Worth						(26)	34.7
		23.8		7.2		10.0							11.2
		34.0		22.9		20.1							20.8
		20.6		6.6		12.9	% Profit Before Taxes/Total Assets						16.2
		8.2		.3		3.6							3.9
		140.3		191.2		117.4							101.7
		31.0		77.8		58.4	Sales/Net Fixed Assets						63.2
		14.1		15.7		12.6							15.9
		2.6		2.5		2.7							2.1
		2.1		1.9		1.6	Sales/Total Assets						1.6
		1.4		1.4		1.3							1.3
		.5		.1		.3							.4
(16)	1.0	(20)	.6	(21)	1.3	% Depr., Dep., Amort./Sales						(14)	1.3
		2.7		1.7		1.6							1.5
							% Officers', Directors' Owners' Comp/Sales						
		1368833M		2105506M		2323818M	Net Sales ($)		1842M	4075M	50800M	92162M	2174939M
		876115M		1159176M		1463064M	Total Assets ($)		227M	2575M	33008M	51187M	1376067M

© RMA 2024   M = $ thousand   MM = $ million
See Pages viii through xx for Explanation of Ratios and Data

MANUFACTURING—Bare Printed Circuit Board Manufacturing NAICS 334412

Current Data Sorted by Assets

		Type of Statement	Comparative Historical Data	
		Unqualified	5	2
		Reviewed	8	3
		Compiled	3	2
		Tax Returns	4	2
	1	Other	22	13

1	4 (4/1–9/30/23)	8	13	19 (10/1/23–3/31/24)			4/1/19–3/31/20	4/1/20–3/31/21
0-500M	500M-2MM	2-10MM	10-50MM	50-100MM	100-250MM		ALL	ALL
1		8	13	1		NUMBER OF STATEMENTS	42	22
%	%	%	%	%	%		%	%

ASSETS

0-500M	500M-2MM	2-10MM	10-50MM	50-100MM	100-250MM		ALL	ALL
			12.0			Cash & Equivalents	11.5	7.7
	D		20.9		D	Trade Receivables (net)	32.6	28.8
	A		28.0		A	Inventory	26.3	34.3
	T		7.3		T	All Other Current	4.3	3.4
	A		68.2		A	Total Current	74.7	74.2
			11.2			Fixed Assets (net)	19.1	17.5
	N		5.3		N	Intangibles (net)	2.7	6.1
	O		15.3		O	All Other Non-Current	3.4	2.2
	T		100.0		T	Total	100.0	100.0

LIABILITIES

	A		9.9		A	Notes Payable-Short Term	6.5	7.5
	V		1.5		V	Cur. Mat.-L.T.D.	3.0	3.7
	A		11.8		A	Trade Payables	14.6	15.5
	I		.0		I	Income Taxes Payable	.1	.0
	L		13.6		L	All Other Current	9.9	7.6
	A		36.9		A	Total Current	34.1	34.4
	B		10.4		B	Long-Term Debt	11.4	14.3
	L		.0		L	Deferred Taxes	.2	.4
	E		10.2		E	All Other Non-Current	1.6	1.4
			42.5			Net Worth	52.7	49.4
			100.0			Total Liabilities & Net Worth	100.0	100.0

INCOME DATA

			100.0			Net Sales	100.0	100.0
			29.4			Gross Profit	27.9	27.7
			21.4			Operating Expenses	20.2	22.9
			8.0			Operating Profit	7.7	4.8
			2.8			All Other Expenses (net)	.5	-1.1
			5.1			Profit Before Taxes	7.2	5.8

RATIOS

			3.7			Current	3.0	3.0
			1.6				2.2	2.1
			1.5				1.7	1.6
			1.5			Quick	2.0	1.4
			.9				1.3	1.1
			.5				.8	.7
		45	8.2			Sales/Receivables	38 9.5	41 8.9
		54	6.7				51 7.2	47 7.8
		65	5.6				60 6.1	59 6.2
		76	4.8			Cost of Sales/Inventory	32 11.4	43 8.5
		101	3.6				45 8.1	89 4.1
		152	2.4				104 3.5	126 2.9
		19	19.3			Cost of Sales/Payables	18 20.3	22 16.3
		38	9.5				31 11.8	40 9.2
		74	4.9				47 7.8	51 7.2
			2.7			Sales/Working Capital	4.3	3.7
			4.0				5.7	5.8
			11.5				8.5	8.7
			11.2			EBIT/Interest	53.9	24.5
		(11)	4.4				(35) 11.7	(21) 8.1
			1.0				4.8	2.0
						Net Profit + Depr., Dep., Amort./Cur. Mat. L/T/D		
			.0			Fixed/Worth	.1	.1
			.2				.4	.4
			.9				.8	.8
			.5			Debt/Worth	.5	.7
			1.8				1.0	1.4
			NM				1.7	2.1
			44.4			% Profit Before Taxes/Tangible Net Worth	59.0	43.5
		(10)	12.7				33.2	27.2
			4.2				15.0	4.5
			13.7			% Profit Before Taxes/Total Assets	21.6	23.3
			3.3				15.8	8.1
			.3				5.9	1.6
			84.5			Sales/Net Fixed Assets	30.9	44.2
			19.8				14.7	11.7
			9.0				7.4	7.8
			1.5			Sales/Total Assets	2.9	2.6
			1.3				2.4	2.2
			1.0				1.8	1.5
						% Depr., Dep., Amort./Sales	1.0	1.5
							(33) 1.9	(17) 2.6
							3.0	4.2
						% Officers', Directors', Owners' Comp/Sales	1.4	
							(10) 2.9	
							5.1	
1693M		87006M	362801M	109944M		Net Sales ($)	1629480M	835155M
481M		46388M	287485M	76899M		Total Assets ($)	837115M	484742M

© RMA 2024

M = $ thousand   MM = $ million
See Pages viii through xx for Explanation of Ratios and Data

MANUFACTURING—Bare Printed Circuit Board Manufacturing   NAICS 334412

Comparative Historical Data | Current Data Sorted by Sales

					3		1	**Type of Statement**				1
		1			2			Unqualified				
		2			2			Reviewed				
		4			2			Compiled				
		14			13		22	Tax Returns				
		4/1/21-3/31/22 ALL			4/1/22-3/31/23 ALL		4/1/23-3/31/24 ALL	Other	0-1MM	1 4 (4/1-9/30/23) 1-3MM	3-5MM	2 5-10MM	13 19 (10/1/23-3/31/24) 10-25MM	6 25MM & OVER
		21			22		23	**NUMBER OF STATEMENTS**		1		2	13	7
		%			%		%	**ASSETS**	%	%	%	%	%	%
		10.8			14.3		12.5	Cash & Equivalents	D	D			14.9	
		29.1			25.8		24.0	Trade Receivables (net)	A	A			24.2	
		29.9			33.5		28.8	Inventory	T	T			29.8	
		1.7			3.6		5.2	All Other Current	A	A			6.2	
		71.5			77.2		70.5	Total Current					75.2	
		13.1			11.1		13.1	Fixed Assets (net)	N	N			15.8	
		9.5			6.2		4.4	Intangibles (net)	O	O			1.3	
		5.8			5.5		12.1	All Other Non-Current	T	T			7.8	
		100.0			100.0		100.0	Total					100.0	
								LIABILITIES	A	A				
		10.7			8.5		7.6	Notes Payable-Short Term	V	V			7.9	
		2.2			2.5		1.8	Cur. Mat.-L.T.D.	A	A			2.2	
		20.4			14.9		15.6	Trade Payables	I	I			16.6	
		.1			.0		.0	Income Taxes Payable	L	L			.0	
		5.2			8.4		14.4	All Other Current	A	A			15.4	
		38.6			34.2		39.4	Total Current	B	B			42.1	
		19.3			13.1		21.3	Long-Term Debt	L	L			28.6	
		.2			.0		.0	Deferred Taxes	E	E			.0	
		2.8			4.2		7.8	All Other Non-Current					4.4	
		39.1			48.4		31.5	Net Worth					24.8	
		100.0			100.0		100.0	Total Liabilties & Net Worth					100.0	
								INCOME DATA						
		100.0			100.0		100.0	Net Sales					100.0	
		29.9			32.1		31.1	Gross Profit					32.8	
		26.9			22.8		22.4	Operating Expenses					23.6	
		3.0			9.3		8.7	Operating Profit					9.2	
		-1.2			1.2		2.5	All Other Expenses (net)					2.3	
		4.2			8.1		6.2	Profit Before Taxes					6.9	
								RATIOS						
		2.6			4.4		3.1						3.9	
		2.2			2.1		1.6	Current					2.1	
		1.7			1.6		1.2						1.2	
		1.4			3.2		1.4						1.6	
		1.1			.8		.9	Quick					1.0	
		.7			.5		.5						.5	
36		10.2	33		10.9	45	8.1						38 9.7	
51		7.2	59		6.2	54	6.7	Sales/Receivables					51 7.1	
66		5.5	70		5.2	61	6.0						64 5.7	
15		24.7	62		5.9	54	6.7						33 11.1	
64		5.7	118		3.1	94	3.9	Cost of Sales/Inventory					135 2.7	
159		2.3	159		2.3	159	2.3						159 2.3	
26		14.1	22		16.7	21	17.5						16 22.9	
36		10.1	36		10.2	38	9.5	Cost of Sales/Payables					30 12.3	
57		6.4	62		5.9	72	5.1						118 3.1	
		4.3			3.0		3.3						2.7	
		5.8			4.6		5.4	Sales/Working Capital					4.4	
		9.1			6.4		16.2						18.4	
		23.6			28.3		11.1						11.2	
(19)		4.3	(20)		13.1	(18)	4.7	EBIT/Interest					(11) 6.8	
		2.8			3.8		1.1						1.6	
								Net Profit + Depr., Dep., Amort./Cur. Mat. L/T/D						
		.1			.1		.1						.1	
		.3			.2		.2	Fixed/Worth					.2	
		1.8			.9		1.1						NM	
		.8			.6		.5						.4	
		1.6			1.0		1.3	Debt/Worth					1.0	
		7.7			11.8		-27.1						-16.7	
		40.2			55.0		45.3	% Profit Before Taxes/Tangible Net Worth						
(18)		16.5	(18)		31.0	(17)	14.9							
		7.0			7.7		4.0							
		12.4			27.0		14.9	% Profit Before Taxes/Total Assets					20.8	
		6.2			11.0		6.2						6.2	
		2.2			2.4		.6						2.6	
		81.0			40.8		90.8						56.4	
		21.0			16.7		19.8	Sales/Net Fixed Assets					19.8	
		8.8			9.4		8.9						9.0	
		3.1			2.3		2.0						2.1	
		2.0			1.7		1.5	Sales/Total Assets					1.7	
		1.5			1.3		1.3						1.2	
		1.1			1.0		.9							
(14)		2.0	(16)		2.1	(16)	1.8	% Depr., Dep., Amort./Sales						
		3.9			3.0		4.7							
								% Officers', Directors' Owners' Comp/Sales						
		420889M			576889M		561444M	Net Sales ($)		1693M		10874M	196524M	352353M
		381099M			419402M		411253M	Total Assets ($)		481M		6396M	133636M	270740M

© RMA 2024   M = $ thousand   MM = $ million
See Pages viii through xx for Explanation of Ratios and Data

MANUFACTURING—Semiconductor and Related Device Manufacturing NAICS 334413

Current Data Sorted by Assets | Comparative Historical Data

0-500M	500M-2MM	2-10MM	10-50MM	50-100MM	100-250MM					
1	2	1	3			Type of Statement				
			1			Unqualified		11		4
						Reviewed		3		5
	2					Compiled				2
1	2	12	8	5		Tax Returns		6		3
	6 (4/1-9/30/23)		29 (10/1/23-3/31/24)			Other		33		17
								4/1/19-		4/1/20-
								3/31/20		3/31/21
1	4	12	10	8		NUMBER OF STATEMENTS		53 ALL		31 ALL
%	%	%	%	%	%	ASSETS		%		%
		11.6	11.9			Cash & Equivalents		18.3		18.9
		26.1	21.7		D	Trade Receivables (net)		22.8		27.0
		29.7	34.2		A	Inventory		24.3		23.5
		2.0	8.1		T	All Other Current		3.4		1.8
		69.3	76.0		A	Total Current		68.8		71.1
		13.9	13.7			Fixed Assets (net)		17.4		13.6
		6.4	2.3		N	Intangibles (net)		7.6		10.2
		10.4	8.1		O	All Other Non-Current		6.3		5.0
		100.0	100.0		T	Total		100.0		100.0
						LIABILITIES				
		6.2	2.8		A	Notes Payable-Short Term		4.5		7.0
		1.1	2.2		V	Cur. Mat.-L.T.D.		2.1		1.8
		5.7	8.2		A	Trade Payables		12.3		10.4
		.0	2.2		I	Income Taxes Payable		.1		.1
		7.4	22.7		L	All Other Current		17.3		14.0
		20.4	38.0		A	Total Current		36.4		33.4
		11.0	6.9		B	Long-Term Debt		9.2		11.8
		.0	.3		L	Deferred Taxes		.4		.5
		5.8	5.1		E	All Other Non-Current		4.4		11.5
		62.8	49.6			Net Worth		49.6		42.8
		100.0	100.0			Total Liabilties & Net Worth		100.0		100.0
						INCOME DATA				
		100.0	100.0			Net Sales		100.0		100.0
		53.9	33.5			Gross Profit		39.7		39.5
		40.9	23.0			Operating Expenses		32.2		30.1
		13.0	10.5			Operating Profit		7.5		9.4
		.3	1.2			All Other Expenses (net)		1.7		.3
		12.7	9.2			Profit Before Taxes		5.7		9.2
						RATIOS				
		5.5	4.3					3.4		4.7
		3.9	2.6			Current		2.1		2.5
		2.9	1.5					1.3		1.3
		4.5	1.6					2.3		3.1
		2.5	1.4			Quick		1.3		1.5
		1.1	.4					.7		.6
	33	11.0	38	9.7			36	10.0	32	11.4
	49	7.4	54	6.7		Sales/Receivables	50	7.3	54	6.7
	81	4.5	62	5.9			72	5.1	72	5.1
	35	10.4	62	5.9			49	7.4	49	7.4
	159	2.3	140	2.6		Cost of Sales/Inventory	104	3.5	99	3.7
	281	1.3	215	1.7			159	2.3	146	2.5
	12	29.7	7	51.9			18	20.6	14	25.6
	17	21.2	20	18.3		Cost of Sales/Payables	36	10.0	25	14.4
	60	6.1	61	6.0			61	6.0	46	7.9
		2.0	2.5					2.2		1.9
		3.1	4.0			Sales/Working Capital		5.0		4.4
		4.3	NM					10.9		11.7
								29.2		42.5
						EBIT/Interest	(41)	10.1	(27)	14.2
								2.2		1.0
						Net Profit + Depr., Dep., Amort./Cur. Mat. L/T/D				
		.0	.2					.1		.1
		.3	.2			Fixed/Worth		.3		.4
		.7	NM					1.5		2.8
		.3	.4					.4		.4
		.5	.8			Debt/Worth		1.1		1.6
		1.2	NM					3.6		15.5
		52.9						42.9		54.7
		20.3				% Profit Before Taxes/Tangible Net Worth	(46)	17.8	(25)	35.6
		.5						4.9		10.1
		20.6	21.0					15.2		29.5
		17.5	17.9			% Profit Before Taxes/Total Assets		6.6		9.1
		.3	5.1					1.4		1.2
		44.2	15.0					54.4		38.3
		9.8	12.0			Sales/Net Fixed Assets		13.1		11.7
		5.7	9.0					5.0		6.4
		1.9	1.7					2.2		2.5
		1.4	1.5			Sales/Total Assets		1.2		1.6
		1.1	1.1					1.0		.9
			1.5					.5		.6
			1.7			% Depr., Dep., Amort./Sales	(35)	2.0	(23)	1.8
			2.0					3.3		3.5
								1.3		
						% Officers', Directors' Owners' Comp/Sales	(10)	2.4		
								4.3		
1949M	12956M	119071M	313694M	519254M		Net Sales ($)		3413222M		959514M
486M	5247M	82100M	233769M	529761M		Total Assets ($)		2815564M		768738M

© RMA 2024

M = $ thousand   MM = $ million
See Pages viii through xx for Explanation of Ratios and Data

MANUFACTURING—Semiconductor and Related Device Manufacturing NAICS 334413

Comparative Historical Data / Current Data Sorted by Sales

				Type of Statement						
	1	3	4	Unqualified						4
	2		1	Reviewed						1
		2		Compiled						
	2	3	2	Tax Returns			1		1	
	15	27	28	Other		3		4	8	11
	4/1/21-3/31/22 ALL	4/1/22-3/31/23 ALL	4/1/23-3/31/24 ALL		0-1MM	6 (4/1-9/30/23) 1-3MM	3-5MM	29 (10/1/23-3/31/24) 5-10MM	10-25MM	25MM & OVER
	20	35	35	NUMBER OF STATEMENTS	4	4	2	5	8	16
	%	%	%	ASSETS	%	%	%	%	%	%
	28.0	17.2	11.9	Cash & Equivalents						12.6
	25.8	24.6	23.1	Trade Receivables (net)	D					17.9
	25.1	29.8	32.6	Inventory	A					36.3
	2.2	5.9	3.9	All Other Current	T					6.8
	81.0	77.6	71.5	Total Current	A					73.5
	8.7	12.6	14.7	Fixed Assets (net)						14.9
	7.7	4.5	4.2	Intangibles (net)	N					3.4
	2.5	5.3	9.6	All Other Non-Current	O					8.2
	100.0	100.0	100.0	Total	T					100.0
				LIABILITIES						
	5.4	5.7	4.2	Notes Payable-Short Term	A					1.6
	5.8	.8	1.2	Cur. Mat.-L.T.D.	V					1.3
	12.9	13.1	9.0	Trade Payables	A					8.8
	.3	.6	.6	Income Taxes Payable	I					1.0
	13.9	15.9	15.4	All Other Current	L					22.9
	38.3	36.1	30.5	Total Current	A					35.5
	12.0	16.2	13.3	Long-Term Debt	B					9.5
	.0	.0	.1	Deferred Taxes	L					.2
	3.7	3.9	6.4	All Other Non-Current	E					9.7
	46.0	43.9	49.7	Net Worth						45.0
	100.0	100.0	100.0	Total Liabilities & Net Worth						100.0
				INCOME DATA						
	100.0	100.0	100.0	Net Sales						100.0
	39.0	33.5	43.7	Gross Profit						32.2
	29.1	23.0	34.8	Operating Expenses						24.0
	9.9	10.5	8.9	Operating Profit						8.2
	-1.1	1.3	.7	All Other Expenses (net)						1.1
	11.0	9.2	8.2	Profit Before Taxes						7.1
				RATIOS						
	6.4	4.2	5.5							4.8
	2.6	2.5	3.3	Current						2.1
	1.5	1.6	1.6							1.4
	4.4	2.5	3.5							2.1
	1.9	1.3	1.5	Quick						1.1
	.7	.6	.7							.3
33	10.9	22	16.6	36	10.1				43	8.5
49	7.5	45	8.2	54	6.8	Sales/Receivables			56	6.5
64	5.7	60	6.1	81	4.5				66	5.5
37	9.8	35	10.4	54	6.7				65	5.6
79	4.6	99	3.7	146	2.5	Cost of Sales/Inventory			166	2.2
140	2.6	174	2.1	243	1.5				243	1.5
9	38.6	13	27.5	12	29.9				16	23.1
30	12.1	26	14.0	29	12.6	Cost of Sales/Payables			38	9.6
54	6.8	57	6.4	73	5.0				73	5.0
	2.4		3.1		2.1					1.6
	3.7		4.8		3.5	Sales/Working Capital				3.4
	6.3		8.7		4.7					4.6
	84.3		73.0		24.6					144.4
(17)	31.1	(29)	24.3	(24)	9.7	EBIT/Interest			(11)	3.6
	5.3		7.0		.7					.1
						Net Profit + Depr., Dep., Amort./Cur. Mat. L/T/D				
	.0		.0		.1					.2
	.1		.1		.3	Fixed/Worth				.2
	.4		.8		.8					NM
	.3		.4		.4					.3
	.7		.9		.7	Debt/Worth				1.2
	10.0		3.2		2.5					NM
	71.5		87.4		35.7					32.9
(16)	48.8	(31)	47.8	(29)	19.6	% Profit Before Taxes/Tangible Net Worth			(12)	19.5
	17.0		18.2		3.8					10.7
	43.0		34.4		19.7					18.2
	17.9		17.3		7.8	% Profit Before Taxes/Total Assets				7.5
	8.2		6.1		.6					.8
	250.8		131.0		22.1					16.8
	46.5		42.2		10.9	Sales/Net Fixed Assets				10.8
	7.9		8.8		6.1					6.6
	2.6		3.1		1.7					1.7
	1.8		1.8		1.3	Sales/Total Assets				1.0
	1.1		1.3		1.0					.8
	.2		.2		1.4					1.4
(11)	2.0	(25)	1.1	(26)	1.8	% Depr., Dep., Amort./Sales			(15)	1.8
	3.2		2.6		3.1					2.1
						% Officers', Directors', Owners' Comp/Sales				
	321038M		1525814M		966924M	Net Sales ($)	7992M	6635M	32489M	121208M	798600M
	212993M		787238M		851363M	Total Assets ($)	4507M	12191M	22251M	72760M	739654M

© RMA 2024
M = $ thousand   MM = $ million
See Pages viii through xx for Explanation of Ratios and Data

MANUFACTURING—Printed Circuit Assembly (Electronic Assembly) Manufacturing NAICS 334418

Current Data Sorted by Assets | Comparative Historical Data

						Type of Statement		
				3		Unqualified	5	3
				8	3	Reviewed	6	5
			2	2		Compiled	1	3
1			3		1	Tax Returns	6	2
		1	4	17	5	Other	29	17
	5 (4/1-9/30/23)			46 (10/1/23-3/31/24)			4/1/19-3/31/20	4/1/20-3/31/21
0-500M	500M-2MM	2-10MM	10-50MM	50-100MM	100-250MM		ALL	ALL
1	1	9	30	8	2	NUMBER OF STATEMENTS	47	30
%	%	%	%	%	%	ASSETS	%	%
			7.0			Cash & Equivalents	7.9	21.1
			21.1			Trade Receivables (net)	29.8	19.9
			37.6			Inventory	29.8	23.9
			7.3			All Other Current	3.7	3.2
			73.0			Total Current	71.3	68.1
			15.1			Fixed Assets (net)	17.0	21.4
			2.0			Intangibles (net)	5.8	2.8
			9.9			All Other Non-Current	5.8	7.7
			100.0			Total	100.0	100.0
						LIABILITIES		
			7.8			Notes Payable-Short Term	9.5	3.3
			1.2			Cur. Mat.-L.T.D.	2.1	2.8
			12.2			Trade Payables	14.7	11.0
			.1			Income Taxes Payable	.1	.7
			14.7			All Other Current	10.7	8.2
			36.0			Total Current	37.1	26.0
			10.3			Long-Term Debt	10.9	13.9
			.1			Deferred Taxes	.5	.2
			6.9			All Other Non-Current	3.5	3.2
			46.7			Net Worth	48.1	56.7
			100.0			Total Liabilities & Net Worth	100.0	100.0
						INCOME DATA		
			100.0			Net Sales	100.0	100.0
			25.7			Gross Profit	28.6	30.9
			21.0			Operating Expenses	21.7	25.0
			4.7			Operating Profit	7.0	5.9
			.6			All Other Expenses (net)	.7	-2.2
			4.1			Profit Before Taxes	6.2	8.1
						RATIOS		
			3.6				2.8	5.0
			2.5			Current	1.9	2.4
			1.7				1.5	1.7
			1.5				1.8	4.1
			.8			Quick	1.0	1.3
			.4				.7	.7
			39 9.4				40 9.2	36 10.2
			49 7.4			Sales/Receivables	48 7.6	45 8.1
			55 6.6				66 5.5	55 6.6
			81 4.5				31 11.6	28 12.9
			135 2.7			Cost of Sales/Inventory	72 5.1	79 4.6
			182 2.0				126 2.9	130 2.8
			20 18.1				22 16.5	8 44.8
			31 11.8			Cost of Sales/Payables	29 12.7	25 14.7
			55 6.6				53 6.9	54 6.8
			2.6				4.1	2.7
			3.5			Sales/Working Capital	5.8	4.5
			7.9				9.7	6.6
			46.9				41.5	38.3
			(28) 6.6			EBIT/Interest	(42) 10.5	(24) 9.8
			2.4				3.3	.1
							17.4	
						Net Profit + Depr., Dep., Amort./Cur. Mat. L/T/D	(16) 9.3	
							2.6	
			.1				.2	.2
			.3			Fixed/Worth	.4	.4
			.7				.6	.7
			.4				.6	.3
			.9			Debt/Worth	1.1	.7
			2.7				2.4	2.1
			31.2				44.6	33.1
			(28) 16.6			% Profit Before Taxes/Tangible Net Worth	(42) 23.4	(29) 20.0
			6.4				6.2	3.1
			12.7				22.2	18.3
			7.6			% Profit Before Taxes/Total Assets	10.1	8.7
			2.1				3.4	.2
			19.1				26.4	20.9
			10.5			Sales/Net Fixed Assets	12.3	9.0
			6.1				7.5	4.7
			1.9				2.6	2.1
			1.5			Sales/Total Assets	2.0	1.7
			1.1				1.5	1.1
			1.1				1.3	1.1
			(26) 1.9			% Depr., Dep., Amort./Sales	(39) 1.9	(26) 2.8
			2.8				3.3	4.2
							1.8	
						% Officers', Directors' Owners' Comp/Sales	(11) 2.4	
							5.4	
1486M	3714M	92884M	994213M	847835M	549830M	Net Sales ($)	2047329M	1149412M
444M	1991M	43813M	647163M	658107M	369241M	Total Assets ($)	1161265M	789203M

© RMA 2024

M = $ thousand   MM = $ million
See Pages viii through xx for Explanation of Ratios and Data

MANUFACTURING—Printed Circuit Assembly (Electronic Assembly) Manufacturing NAICS 334418

Comparative Historical Data								Current Data Sorted by Sales					
						Type of Statement							
	3		6		7	Unqualified				1	1	5	
	3		2		8	Reviewed					2	6	
			5		5	Compiled			1	2		2	
			1		3	Tax Returns				2	1		
	14		19		28	Other		1	1	1	12	14	
	4/1/21-3/31/22		4/1/22-3/31/23		4/1/23-3/31/24		0-1MM	5 (4/1-9/30/23) 1-3MM	3-5MM	46 (10/1/23-3/31/24) 5-10MM	10-25MM	25MM & OVER	
	ALL 20		ALL 33		ALL 51	NUMBER OF STATEMENTS		1	1	6	16	27	
	%		%		%	ASSETS	%	%	%	%	%	%	
	10.3		10.6		9.0	Cash & Equivalents					12.0	5.9	
	26.4		26.2		20.6	Trade Receivables (net)					17.1	24.5	
	34.4		39.0		35.3	Inventory					36.8	35.9	
	3.8		2.7		5.7	All Other Current					10.9	2.6	
	74.9		78.5		70.5	Total Current					76.8	68.9	
	14.0		12.3		15.3	Fixed Assets (net)					11.7	17.2	
	7.0		4.1		5.4	Intangibles (net)					1.6	7.2	
	4.1		5.1		8.8	All Other Non-Current					9.9	6.8	
	100.0		100.0		100.0	Total					100.0	100.0	
						LIABILITIES							
	10.2		10.8		7.1	Notes Payable-Short Term					7.0	6.4	
	1.4		3.6		3.2	Cur. Mat.-L.T.D.					1.0	2.5	
	16.0		13.8		11.4	Trade Payables					9.6	14.8	
	.0		.0		.1	Income Taxes Payable					.0	.1	
	7.3		11.6		13.8	All Other Current					14.0	12.6	
	34.9		39.8		35.6	Total Current					31.7	36.5	
	14.7		8.1		15.1	Long-Term Debt					12.1	12.6	
	.2		.0		.2	Deferred Taxes					.3	.3	
	4.5		3.1		7.6	All Other Non-Current					7.5	5.2	
	45.7		49.0		41.5	Net Worth					48.4	45.4	
	100.0		100.0		100.0	Total Liabilties & Net Worth					100.0	100.0	
						INCOME DATA							
	100.0		100.0		100.0	Net Sales					100.0	100.0	
	24.0		29.0		28.8	Gross Profit					31.0	25.3	
	20.0		22.7		24.7	Operating Expenses					27.3	20.7	
	4.1		6.3		4.0	Operating Profit					3.7	4.6	
	-1.1		.2		1.2	All Other Expenses (net)					1.4	1.2	
	5.2		6.1		2.8	Profit Before Taxes					2.2	3.4	
						RATIOS							
	3.8		3.2		3.3						4.1	3.3	
	2.4		2.2		2.3	Current					2.7	2.1	
	1.4		1.6		1.6						2.1	1.6	
	2.5		2.2		1.4						1.3	1.5	
	1.3		.8		.9	Quick					.9	.8	
	.4		.4		.4						.5	.5	
38	9.5	39	9.3	37	9.8						41	8.9	39	9.4
48	7.6	51	7.2	49	7.4	Sales/Receivables					47	7.7	53	6.9
58	6.3	63	5.8	55	6.6						53	6.9	72	5.1
54	6.7	66	5.5	79	4.6						107	3.4	74	4.9
101	3.6	140	2.6	122	3.0	Cost of Sales/Inventory					146	2.5	104	3.5
166	2.2	203	1.8	152	2.4						159	2.3	166	2.2
22	16.9	18	20.4	20	18.7						12	30.2	23	16.2
30	12.0	29	12.4	28	13.2	Cost of Sales/Payables					27	13.6	47	7.8
66	5.5	65	5.6	62	5.9						58	6.3	65	5.6
	3.2		3.4		2.8						2.3	3.6	
	4.4		4.4		3.8	Sales/Working Capital					2.8	4.7	
	10.3		8.2		10.8						3.7	10.8	
	194.7		51.5		12.2						60.3	11.4	
(17)	7.4	(28)	6.9	(47)	4.7	EBIT/Interest				(15)	4.0	(24)	5.4
	.5		2.0		.4						.1	.5	
					10.5	Net Profit + Depr., Dep.,						11.0	
			(17)		2.6	Amort./Cur. Mat. L/T/D					(15)	2.5	
					1.0							1.0	
	.1		.1		.2						.1	.2	
	.3		.3		.4	Fixed/Worth					.2	.5	
	.6		.6		1.2						.6	1.2	
	.4		.4		.5						.4	.6	
	1.1		1.0		1.1	Debt/Worth					.8	1.3	
	3.6		3.1		3.6						8.1	3.5	
	42.0		39.0		30.0	% Profit Before Taxes/Tangible					17.3	29.5	
(18)	30.8	(29)	30.1	(45)	15.6	Net Worth				(15)	7.9	(25)	16.6
	3.8		9.0		-.5						3.9	-9.2	
	24.9		24.5		13.8	% Profit Before Taxes/Total					11.2	13.8	
	9.5		10.1		6.0	Assets					5.1	7.3	
	.4		2.0		-2.0						-3.9	-2.0	
	33.8		44.4		21.4						39.8	16.8	
	15.8		17.2		10.6	Sales/Net Fixed Assets					10.4	10.6	
	7.2		7.8		6.2						6.0	5.5	
	2.3		2.5		2.0						1.8	1.9	
	1.7		1.6		1.6	Sales/Total Assets					1.3	1.6	
	1.3		1.3		1.2						1.0	1.2	
	1.1		.8		1.1						.6	1.3	
(17)	1.9	(27)	1.3	(42)	1.9	% Depr., Dep., Amort./Sales				(12)	1.5	(24)	2.1
	3.9		3.1		3.2						2.9	5.0	
						% Officers', Directors' Owners' Comp/Sales							
	1006723M		1034566M		2489962M	Net Sales ($)	1486M	3714M	43446M	293969M	2147347M	
	596993M		623933M		1720759M	Total Assets ($)	444M	1991M	29918M	237952M	1450454M	

M = $ thousand   MM = $ million
See Pages viii through xx for Explanation of Ratios and Data
© RMA 2024

(Data Not Available for 0-1MM, 1-3MM, 3-5MM, 5-10MM columns in assets/liabilities/income sections)

MANUFACTURING—Other Electronic Component Manufacturing NAICS 334419

Current Data Sorted by Assets | | Comparative Historical Data

							Type of Statement				
			2	7	3	2	Unqualified		11		6
			3	6	2		Reviewed		19		10
			3	1			Compiled		7		6
		1	7	1			Tax Returns		8		3
1	3		12	28	7	7	Other		50		40
	21 (4/1-9/30/23)			75 (10/1/23-3/31/24)					4/1/19- 3/31/20		4/1/20- 3/31/21
0-500M	500M-2MM	2-10MM	10-50MM	50-100MM	100-250MM				ALL		ALL
1	4	27	43	12	9		NUMBER OF STATEMENTS		95		65
%	%	%	%	%	%		ASSETS		%		%
		15.6	9.6	9.3			Cash & Equivalents		12.4		15.3
		22.1	23.8	23.2			Trade Receivables (net)		25.9		21.1
		33.1	34.9	27.7			Inventory		32.5		31.1
		1.5	3.6	4.5			All Other Current		2.2		1.2
		72.2	71.9	64.8			Total Current		72.9		68.7
		18.8	11.8	16.5			Fixed Assets (net)		15.9		18.7
		5.5	8.4	5.6			Intangibles (net)		6.1		7.4
		3.6	7.9	13.0			All Other Non-Current		5.1		5.2
		100.0	100.0	100.0			Total		100.0		100.0
							LIABILITIES				
		3.3	5.8	8.8			Notes Payable-Short Term		7.9		6.6
		2.5	3.2	1.8			Cur. Mat.-L.T.D.		1.7		3.3
		11.8	14.3	15.0			Trade Payables		14.1		10.3
		.0	.4	.5			Income Taxes Payable		.3		.4
		13.5	11.8	13.1			All Other Current		7.5		10.1
		31.2	35.6	39.2			Total Current		31.5		30.6
		11.3	9.2	7.1			Long-Term Debt		11.1		14.4
		.1	.0	.1			Deferred Taxes		.5		.6
		8.6	5.6	7.7			All Other Non-Current		3.5		5.2
		48.8	49.6	45.9			Net Worth		53.3		49.2
		100.0	100.0	100.0			Total Liabilities & Net Worth		100.0		100.0
							INCOME DATA				
		100.0	100.0	100.0			Net Sales		100.0		100.0
		38.2	32.3	22.3			Gross Profit		32.6		35.3
		27.2	25.2	17.5			Operating Expenses		24.3		29.4
		11.0	7.2	4.8			Operating Profit		8.3		5.9
		.0	.7	-.1			All Other Expenses (net)		.2		-1.2
		11.0	6.5	4.9			Profit Before Taxes		8.1		7.1
							RATIOS				
		5.0	4.0	2.7					4.6		3.9
		3.1	2.2	1.7			Current		2.7		2.6
		1.4	1.5	1.2					1.8		1.7
		3.0	1.7	1.3					2.4		2.6
		1.8	1.1	.8			Quick		1.3		1.2
		.5	.6	.5					.8		.7
		25 14.4	39 9.4	38 9.7				37	9.9	37	9.8
		40 9.2	47 7.8	54 6.8			Sales/Receivables	47	7.7	48	7.6
		54 6.8	61 6.0	85 4.3				59	6.2	58	6.3
		50 7.3	76 4.8	42 8.6				55	6.6	57	6.4
		99 3.7	135 2.7	135 2.7			Cost of Sales/Inventory	94	3.9	101	3.6
		166 2.2	166 2.2	166 2.2				152	2.4	159	2.3
		13 27.5	24 15.0	25 14.4				15	24.3	16	22.9
		20 18.0	39 9.3	53 6.9			Cost of Sales/Payables	30	12.3	29	12.5
		47 7.7	58 6.3	79 4.6				51	7.2	48	7.6
		3.2	2.8	3.3					2.9		2.7
		5.4	4.0	6.2			Sales/Working Capital		4.5		4.3
		11.3	9.4	19.9					7.3		7.3
		42.0	39.8	68.7					44.8		46.8
		(23) 12.5	(35) 9.3	(11) 4.4			EBIT/Interest	(79)	11.9	(60)	10.0
		4.4	2.0	.2					2.6		1.9
			8.4						12.8		10.1
			(10) 4.1				Net Profit + Depr., Dep., Amort./Cur. Mat. L/T/D	(29)	4.6	(21)	3.1
			2.2						2.8		1.1
		.1	.1	.2					.1		.2
		.4	.2	.4			Fixed/Worth		.3		.4
		1.2	.6	1.4					.6		.9
		.4	.6	.5					.3		.4
		1.0	1.3	1.4			Debt/Worth		.7		.8
		2.9	3.2	6.5					2.3		3.0
		81.3	55.7	28.4					45.6		47.5
		(24) 30.1	(40) 31.9	(11) 14.6			% Profit Before Taxes/Tangible Net Worth	(84)	25.7	(59)	20.5
		14.2	7.5	10.0					8.8		7.6
		37.5	20.3	11.3					20.3		18.8
		12.6	10.3	6.2			% Profit Before Taxes/Total Assets		12.3		8.4
		7.6	1.6	-1.6					3.9		2.4
		40.3	44.3	26.7					36.3		22.2
		8.9	18.5	12.4			Sales/Net Fixed Assets		14.4		9.1
		5.6	7.3	4.8					6.9		5.1
		2.6	2.3	1.7					2.4		2.4
		1.8	1.8	1.1			Sales/Total Assets		1.8		1.5
		1.5	1.1	.9					1.2		1.1
		.7	.6						.8		1.1
		(23) 1.8	(34) 1.3				% Depr., Dep., Amort./Sales	(74)	1.9	(58)	2.4
		4.0	2.9						3.3		4.2
									2.3		2.2
							% Officers', Directors' Owners' Comp/Sales	(21)	3.4	(16)	3.6
									6.9		7.3
149M	16941M	296581M	1689181M	1105053M	1703272M		Net Sales ($)		4008366M		1987268M
126M	4794M	149310M	1001580M	782090M	1346687M		Total Assets ($)		2882855M		1641547M

© RMA 2024

M = $ thousand   MM = $ million
See Pages viii through xx for Explanation of Ratios and Data

MANUFACTURING—Other Electronic Component Manufacturing NAICS 334419

Comparative Historical Data / Current Data Sorted by Sales

							Type of Statement							
		4		10		14	Unqualified				1	3	10	
		9		10		11	Reviewed				2	5	4	
		5		3		4	Compiled				1	2	1	
		10		5		9	Tax Returns			3	3	2	1	
		39		58		58	Other	2	1	2	4	15	34	
		4/1/21-3/31/22 ALL		4/1/22-3/31/23 ALL		4/1/23-3/31/24 ALL			21 (4/1-9/30/23)			75 (10/1/23-3/31/24)		
								0-1MM	1-3MM	3-5MM	5-10MM	10-25MM	25MM & OVER
		67		86		96	NUMBER OF STATEMENTS	2	1	5	11	27	50
		%		%		%	**ASSETS**	%	%	%	%	%	%
		18.8		14.3		11.6	Cash & Equivalents				10.6	12.9	10.5
		22.5		22.5		23.0	Trade Receivables (net)				19.7	22.9	24.1
		31.7		32.8		32.1	Inventory				41.3	30.4	31.0
		2.4		3.7		2.7	All Other Current				1.9	1.7	3.7
		75.4		73.4		69.5	Total Current				73.5	67.8	69.3
		13.3		14.3		14.4	Fixed Assets (net)				11.4	21.4	11.8
		8.0		6.5		8.7	Intangibles (net)				9.7	6.3	10.2
		3.3		5.8		7.4	All Other Non-Current				5.4	4.5	8.6
		100.0		100.0		100.0	Total				100.0	100.0	100.0
							LIABILITIES						
		6.5		5.7		6.1	Notes Payable-Short Term				4.2	5.1	7.4
		1.5		1.4		3.5	Cur. Mat.-L.T.D.				4.0	1.8	4.8
		11.7		13.1		13.1	Trade Payables				16.0	10.4	15.0
		.1		.3		.2	Income Taxes Payable				.0	.1	.4
		9.9		13.3		12.4	All Other Current				17.3	13.2	10.8
		29.6		33.8		35.3	Total Current				41.5	30.5	38.3
		8.1		14.3		9.9	Long-Term Debt				7.6	13.1	9.3
		.5		.1		.1	Deferred Taxes				.3	.0	.1
		5.8		5.6		6.3	All Other Non-Current				8.6	7.0	5.3
		56.1		46.2		48.4	Net Worth				41.9	49.3	47.0
		100.0		100.0		100.0	Total Liabilities & Net Worth				100.0	100.0	100.0
							INCOME DATA						
		100.0		100.0		100.0	Net Sales				100.0	100.0	100.0
		37.6		34.8		33.1	Gross Profit				32.7	34.8	31.2
		30.9		27.0		25.6	Operating Expenses				25.3	25.3	24.7
		6.8		7.8		7.5	Operating Profit				7.4	9.5	6.5
		-1.3		1.4		.7	All Other Expenses (net)				1.4	.1	1.1
		8.1		6.4		6.8	Profit Before Taxes				6.0	9.4	5.5
							RATIOS						
		5.7		4.9		3.8					3.9	5.0	3.0
		3.1		2.3		2.2	Current				2.2	3.1	1.8
		1.7		1.5		1.4					1.3	1.3	1.3
		3.3		2.3		1.9					1.8	2.7	1.4
		1.6		1.1		1.1	Quick				1.1	1.4	.9
		.8		.6		.6					.3	.9	.5
34	10.8		31	11.7	36	10.1		27	13.6	34	10.7	38	9.6
50	7.3		45	8.1	46	7.9	Sales/Receivables	38	9.5	43	8.5	49	7.5
66	5.5		63	5.8	68	5.4		65	5.6	57	6.4	72	5.1
66	5.5		68	5.4	63	5.8		94	3.9	46	7.9	60	6.1
111	3.3		135	2.7	118	3.1	Cost of Sales/Inventory	152	2.4	99	3.7	118	3.1
166	2.2		192	1.9	159	2.3		203	1.8	152	2.4	146	2.5
16	23.1		18	20.7	19	19.3		20	18.0	13	27.2	24	15.2
30	12.1		31	11.8	34	10.8	Cost of Sales/Payables	36	10.2	23	15.7	40	9.1
54	6.8		54	6.8	56	6.5		76	4.8	46	8.0	57	6.4
		2.3		2.2		3.0					3.2	2.7	3.3
		3.8		4.0		4.8	Sales/Working Capital				4.4	5.6	5.2
		6.8		7.4		11.1					10.5	11.5	13.0
		120.8		49.7		39.2						31.8	55.4
(53)	17.3		(70)	8.2	(81)	7.4	EBIT/Interest				(23)	13.1	(44)	6.9
		3.3		2.0		2.5						2.9	1.9
		29.4		9.7		12.7	Net Profit + Depr., Dep.,						22.0
(13)	10.3		(18)	5.1	(20)	5.7	Amort./Cur. Mat. L/T/D					(11)	8.3
		5.7		1.2		2.7							3.2
		.1		.1		.1					.2	.2	.1
		.3		.3		.3	Fixed/Worth				.4	.5	.3
		.5		.8		.9					3.7	1.4	.8
		.3		.4		.5					.6	.4	.7
		.6		1.1		1.2	Debt/Worth				1.0	1.1	1.4
		2.3		4.7		3.8					39.1	2.6	6.8
		56.0		48.3		51.1	% Profit Before Taxes/Tangible					44.8	57.8
(59)	25.5		(75)	24.9	(88)	26.0	Net Worth				(25)	30.1	(46)	24.3
		13.5		6.8		6.9						11.7	10.2
		28.6		19.5		20.8	% Profit Before Taxes/Total				32.6	26.6	15.8
		14.6		8.2		10.1	Assets				7.6	14.5	10.0
		2.1		3.0		3.0					3.3	6.1	2.7
		65.9		43.2		36.7					40.3	33.1	46.1
		16.9		13.7		13.7	Sales/Net Fixed Assets				18.5	7.9	18.0
		7.9		6.3		6.5					5.6	4.8	8.5
		2.5		2.3		2.4					2.5	2.4	2.4
		1.7		1.6		1.6	Sales/Total Assets				1.7	1.7	1.7
		1.1		1.1		1.1					.9	1.2	1.1
		.9		.5		.7						.7	.6
(43)	2.2		(63)	1.5	(73)	1.8	% Depr., Dep., Amort./Sales					(22)	2.6	(37)	1.3
		3.9		2.8		3.6						3.5	3.6
		2.4		1.2		1.4	% Officers', Directors'						
(17)	3.7		(16)	1.7	(18)	3.4	Owners' Comp/Sales						
		6.3		4.2		6.3							
		2618570M		4742533M		4811177M	Net Sales ($)	955M	1147M	19771M	82919M	434938M	4271447M
		1803779M		3140502M		3284587M	Total Assets ($)	887M	1088M	47182M	63218M	290585M	2881627M

© RMA 2024 M = $ thousand MM = $ million
See Pages viii through xx for Explanation of Ratios and Data

MANUFACTURING—Search, Detection, Navigation, Guidance, Aeronautical, and Nautical System and Instrument Manufacturing NAICS 334511

Current Data Sorted by Assets | Comparative Historical Data

						Type of Statement		
			3			Unqualified	6	3
			6			Reviewed	3	2
						Compiled		1
		2				Tax Returns	3	2
	6 (4/1-9/30/23)	3	11 25 (10/1/23-3/31/24)	2	4	Other	22	15
0-500M	500M-2MM	2-10MM	10-50MM	50-100MM	100-250MM		4/1/19-3/31/20 ALL	4/1/20-3/31/21 ALL
		5	20	2	4	NUMBER OF STATEMENTS	34	23
%	%	%	%	%	%	ASSETS	%	%
D	D		10.7			Cash & Equivalents	17.6	17.9
A	A		21.7			Trade Receivables (net)	23.8	19.1
T	T		30.6			Inventory	24.4	31.2
A	A		6.0			All Other Current	4.0	2.6
			69.1			Total Current	69.7	70.9
N	N		15.6			Fixed Assets (net)	13.1	16.1
O	O		5.7			Intangibles (net)	11.5	8.9
T	T		9.6			All Other Non-Current	5.6	4.1
			100.0			Total	100.0	100.0
A	A					LIABILITIES		
V	V		3.4			Notes Payable-Short Term	10.9	7.2
A	A		3.3			Cur. Mat.-L.T.D.	1.5	3.6
I	I		10.1			Trade Payables	12.9	10.9
L	L		.0			Income Taxes Payable	.1	.1
A	A		22.7			All Other Current	13.3	15.7
B	B		39.6			Total Current	38.6	37.5
L	L		5.8			Long-Term Debt	7.9	17.2
E	E		.2			Deferred Taxes	.1	.0
			9.4			All Other Non-Current	7.5	7.7
			45.0			Net Worth	45.8	37.5
			100.0			Total Liabilties & Net Worth	100.0	100.0
						INCOME DATA		
			100.0			Net Sales	100.0	100.0
			42.8			Gross Profit	39.2	35.7
			34.4			Operating Expenses	32.2	27.0
			8.4			Operating Profit	7.1	8.6
			.5			All Other Expenses (net)	.7	-.2
			7.9			Profit Before Taxes	6.3	8.9
						RATIOS		
			2.7				5.9	3.1
			2.1			Current	2.1	2.0
			1.2				1.3	1.1
			1.4				3.6	1.3
			.8			Quick	.9	.9
			.6				.6	.5
		35	10.3				36 10.0	27 13.5
		51	7.2			Sales/Receivables	47 7.7	52 7.0
		89	4.1				59 6.2	62 5.9
		87	4.2				12 31.2	34 10.6
		135	2.7			Cost of Sales/Inventory	73 5.0	76 4.8
		281	1.3				192 1.9	228 1.6
		21	17.3				11 32.0	19 19.5
		31	11.9			Cost of Sales/Payables	23 15.7	30 12.3
		54	6.8				49 7.4	49 7.5
			2.7				3.3	2.7
			3.8			Sales/Working Capital	5.7	6.7
			26.6				10.4	12.8
			73.0				13.9	25.7
		(16)	28.3			EBIT/Interest	(25) 6.2	(19) 5.6
			10.6				1.6	.3
			20.1			Net Profit + Depr., Dep.,		
		(11)	8.2			Amort./Cur. Mat. L/T/D		
			2.6					
			.1				.1	.1
			.3			Fixed/Worth	.2	.8
			1.5				NM	-4.6
			.6				.2	.9
			1.0			Debt/Worth	1.3	2.6
			5.2				-26.2	-11.8
			39.3				48.1	51.7
		(18)	17.9			% Profit Before Taxes/Tangible Net Worth	(25) 26.0	(16) 21.2
			7.8				5.2	2.6
			19.7				19.6	23.8
			10.6			% Profit Before Taxes/Total Assets	10.0	7.8
			6.1				.9	-.9
			24.5				43.8	40.8
			11.4			Sales/Net Fixed Assets	19.2	14.1
			7.2				8.0	7.4
			1.6				2.2	1.8
			1.1			Sales/Total Assets	1.5	1.4
			.9				1.1	1.2
			.8				.8	1.0
		(18)	1.7			% Depr., Dep., Amort./Sales	(23) 1.6	(15) 2.3
			3.3				3.2	4.2
						% Officers', Directors' Owners' Comp/Sales		
		49535M	683179M	136116M	496916M	Net Sales ($)	1159032M	594218M
		29282M	531904M	146515M	561736M	Total Assets ($)	931725M	495786M

M = $ thousand   MM = $ million
See Pages viii through xx for Explanation of Ratios and Data

© RMA 2024

MANUFACTURING—Search, Detection, Navigation, Guidance, Aeronautical, and Nautical System and Instrument Manufacturing NAICS 334511

Comparative Historical Data / Current Data Sorted by Sales

			Type of Statement						
2	4	3	Unqualified					1	2
4	3	6	Reviewed				2	2	2
	1		Compiled						
	2	2	Tax Returns				1	1	
11	18	20	Other				2	3	15
4/1/21-3/31/22 ALL	4/1/22-3/31/23 ALL	4/1/23-3/31/24 ALL		0-1MM	6 (4/1-9/30/23) 1-3MM	3-5MM	5-10MM	25 (10/1/23-3/31/24) 10-25MM	25MM & OVER
17	28	31	NUMBER OF STATEMENTS				5	7	19
%	%	%	**ASSETS**	%	%	%	%	%	%
21.5	20.0	10.2	Cash & Equivalents	D	D	D			9.1
22.7	19.6	19.9	Trade Receivables (net)	A	A	A			20.4
21.7	26.1	24.4	Inventory	T	T	T			24.2
3.0	6.7	7.4	All Other Current	A	A	A			9.5
68.9	72.3	61.9	Total Current						63.2
17.7	13.2	15.7	Fixed Assets (net)	N	N	N			9.4
8.3	7.5	13.5	Intangibles (net)	O	O	O			16.9
5.1	7.0	8.9	All Other Non-Current	T	T	T			10.5
100.0	100.0	100.0	Total						100.0
			LIABILITIES	A	A	A			
7.1	1.9	4.7	Notes Payable-Short Term	V	V	V			2.3
1.5	2.5	2.5	Cur. Mat.-L.T.D.	A	A	A			2.4
9.7	7.3	9.4	Trade Payables	I	I	I			11.9
.3	.2	.0	Income Taxes Payable	L	L	L			.0
18.6	12.6	18.2	All Other Current	A	A	A			21.7
37.3	24.5	34.9	Total Current	B	B	B			38.5
7.1	9.3	8.5	Long-Term Debt	L	L	L			7.4
.5	.3	.1	Deferred Taxes	E	E	E			.2
3.4	3.7	7.6	All Other Non-Current						9.8
51.8	62.1	48.8	Net Worth						44.1
100.0	100.0	100.0	Total Liabilities & Net Worth						100.0
			INCOME DATA						
100.0	100.0	100.0	Net Sales						100.0
39.9	41.6	42.5	Gross Profit						38.9
29.8	29.5	33.3	Operating Expenses						29.3
10.1	12.1	9.2	Operating Profit						9.6
-1.6	1.0	.8	All Other Expenses (net)						1.4
11.8	11.1	8.3	Profit Before Taxes						8.1
			RATIOS						
3.4	8.0	2.5							2.5
1.9	3.4	1.7	Current						1.7
1.3	1.7	1.3							1.5
2.3	4.3	1.4							1.4
1.2	1.5	.8	Quick						.6
.6	.7	.7							.5
31 / 11.6	34 / 10.6	35 / 10.4						36	10.0
47 / 7.8	46 / 7.9	49 / 7.5	Sales/Receivables					54	6.8
61 / 6.0	62 / 5.9	81 / 4.5						87	4.2
41 / 9.0	51 / 7.1	46 / 8.0						48	7.6
76 / 4.8	126 / 2.9	107 / 3.4	Cost of Sales/Inventory					96	3.8
166 / 2.2	166 / 2.2	182 / 2.0						174	2.1
12 / 31.0	9 / 40.5	17 / 21.9						21	17.6
30 / 12.2	29 / 12.4	32 / 11.4	Cost of Sales/Payables					41	8.9
41 / 8.9	41 / 9.0	56 / 6.5						57	6.4
3.0	2.2	2.8							3.3
3.8	3.2	5.0	Sales/Working Capital						5.1
8.5	6.0	12.6							6.4
57.3	100.6	67.3							62.3
(15) 9.4	(18) 28.1	(25) 22.7	EBIT/Interest					(13)	16.8
5.0	3.1	5.3							3.2
		11.2	Net Profit + Depr., Dep.,						
	(15)	5.2	Amort./Cur. Mat. L/T/D						
		2.7							
.2	.1	.1							.1
.4	.2	.4	Fixed/Worth						.3
.9	.6	1.5							3.6
.4	.2	.6							1.0
1.2	.5	1.2	Debt/Worth						1.4
2.9	1.6	5.5							29.1
56.6	45.3	37.5							38.5
(15) 26.3	(25) 23.5	(26) 23.7	% Profit Before Taxes/Tangible Net Worth					(15)	25.7
6.2	12.5	9.8							15.9
25.0	29.8	18.4							17.5
13.5	14.7	8.9	% Profit Before Taxes/Total Assets						10.1
3.1	3.8	5.6							5.5
33.3	34.5	34.6							30.1
9.5	14.2	11.9	Sales/Net Fixed Assets						16.4
3.9	7.5	7.1							9.0
2.2	1.9	1.6							1.6
1.4	1.6	1.2	Sales/Total Assets						1.2
1.1	1.1	.9							.8
.9	.8	1.0							.9
(13) 1.3	(20) 1.9	(27) 2.0	% Depr., Dep., Amort./Sales					(17)	2.0
2.8	3.4	4.2							3.7
			% Officers', Directors' Owners' Comp/Sales						
648373M	769912M	1365746M	Net Sales ($)				39191M	118410M	1208145M
457611M	633409M	1269437M	Total Assets ($)				38765M	87876M	1142796M

© RMA 2024 M = $ thousand MM = $ million
See Pages viii through xx for Explanation of Ratios and Data

MANUFACTURING—Instruments and Related Products Mfg. for Measuring, Displaying, & Controlling Industrial Process Variables NAICS 334513

Current Data Sorted by Assets | Comparative Historical Data

	0-500M	500M-2MM	2-10MM	10-50MM	50-100MM	100-250MM	Type of Statement		4/1/19-3/31/20 ALL		4/1/20-3/31/21 ALL
			1	2			Unqualified		8		5
			1	6			Reviewed		17		12
		1	4	2			Compiled		6		3
		1	3				Tax Returns		6		1
		3	1	24	4	2	Other		44		24
	8 (4/1-9/30/23)		8	53 (10/1/23-3/31/24)			NUMBER OF STATEMENTS		81		45
		5	16	34	4	2					
	%	%	%	%	%	%	**ASSETS**		%		%
			18.8	9.6			Cash & Equivalents		14.2		20.1
			28.5	18.7			Trade Receivables (net)		30.1		23.8
	DATA		32.4	33.4			Inventory		25.7		24.8
	NOT		1.9	2.8			All Other Current		3.2		3.4
	AVAILABLE		81.6	64.6			Total Current		73.2		72.1
			9.6	19.2			Fixed Assets (net)		14.4		16.6
			5.0	8.9			Intangibles (net)		5.3		5.2
			3.9	7.3			All Other Non-Current		7.1		6.1
			100.0	100.0			Total		100.0		100.0
							LIABILITIES				
			5.8	5.0			Notes Payable-Short Term		7.9		7.8
			1.2	2.4			Cur. Mat.-L.T.D.		2.3		2.8
			12.1	7.6			Trade Payables		12.3		9.9
			.2	.1			Income Taxes Payable		.2		.3
			18.7	14.2			All Other Current		14.6		14.6
			38.0	29.2			Total Current		37.2		35.3
			10.1	15.0			Long-Term Debt		8.5		9.9
			.1	.3			Deferred Taxes		.1		.2
			4.9	3.6			All Other Non-Current		8.4		5.3
			47.0	51.8			Net Worth		45.7		49.4
			100.0	100.0			Total Liabilities & Net Worth		100.0		100.0
							INCOME DATA				
			100.0	100.0			Net Sales		100.0		100.0
			39.2	40.7			Gross Profit		39.5		38.6
			33.3	32.3			Operating Expenses		33.0		33.3
			5.9	8.4			Operating Profit		6.5		5.4
			.3	1.8			All Other Expenses (net)		1.1		-1.5
			5.6	6.6			Profit Before Taxes		5.4		6.9
							RATIOS				
			3.0	4.1					4.0		4.1
			2.6	2.8		Current			2.2		2.4
			1.9	1.5					1.2		1.2
			2.1	1.9					2.2		2.5
			1.5	.9		Quick			1.3		1.3
			1.0	.6					.8		.7
		39	9.3	32	11.3			41	8.8	34	10.6
		46	7.9	51	7.2		Sales/Receivables	51	7.1	42	8.6
		73	5.0	66	5.5			70	5.2	64	5.7
		51	7.2	104	3.5			46	7.9	45	8.2
		94	3.9	152	2.4		Cost of Sales/Inventory	83	4.4	70	5.2
		203	1.8	192	1.9			146	2.5	166	2.2
		21	17.4	22	16.5			19	18.9	17	21.0
		28	13.1	32	11.5		Cost of Sales/Payables	34	10.8	30	12.3
		65	5.6	55	6.6			55	6.6	40	9.1
			3.0		2.1				3.0		2.5
			5.1		4.2		Sales/Working Capital		5.7		4.2
			6.5		7.7				13.2		18.1
			63.5		55.1				33.0		49.4
		(15)	6.1	(30)	8.9		EBIT/Interest	(68)	5.9	(41)	13.5
			1.7		2.0				2.0		4.9
									8.2		4.4
							Net Profit + Depr., Dep., Amort./Cur. Mat. L/T/D	(24)	3.6	(10)	1.4
									2.4		.6
			.0		.2				.1		.1
			.1		.4		Fixed/Worth		.3		.3
			.4		1.3				.7		.8
			.5		.4				.4		.4
			1.1		.8		Debt/Worth		1.1		1.1
			3.8		4.2				3.7		3.6
			45.8		29.3				39.5		53.4
		(15)	22.9	(28)	22.4		% Profit Before Taxes/Tangible Net Worth	(72)	12.9	(43)	18.7
			.9		10.8				2.8		6.0
			23.2		17.8				19.6		22.8
			8.9		9.3		% Profit Before Taxes/Total Assets		5.9		10.8
			1.1		3.1				1.8		3.0
			127.6		13.6				40.1		30.7
			59.3		9.6		Sales/Net Fixed Assets		15.9		12.3
			16.4		4.4				7.1		7.1
			2.0		1.6				2.4		2.1
			1.8		1.3		Sales/Total Assets		1.9		1.7
			1.6		.8				1.4		1.2
			.3		.9				.8		.9
		(13)	.5	(24)	1.6		% Depr., Dep., Amort./Sales	(59)	1.7	(39)	1.6
			1.4		2.4				2.9		3.0
									2.2		
							% Officers', Directors' Owners' Comp/Sales	(20)	4.6		
									9.5		
		16678M	172125M	1054172M	288367M	307473M	Net Sales ($)		3845793M		1435325M
		6232M	92103M	794322M	258200M	303626M	Total Assets ($)		2848259M		915636M

M = $ thousand   MM = $ million
See Pages viii through xx for Explanation of Ratios and Data

© RMA 2024

MANUFACTURING—Instruments and Related Products Mfg. for Measuring, Displaying, & Controlling Industrial Process Variables NAICS 334513

Comparative Historical Data | Current Data Sorted by Sales

					Type of Statement							
	1		5		2	Unqualified					1	1
	6		7		10	Reviewed			1		5	4
	3		6		6	Compiled		1	1		2	2
	3		5		2	Tax Returns		2		3		
	25		31		41	Other	1	2	2	2	20	15
	4/1/21-3/31/22 ALL		4/1/22-3/31/23 ALL		4/1/23-3/31/24 ALL		0-1MM	8 (4/1-9/30/23) 1-3MM	3-5MM	5-10MM	53 (10/1/23-3/31/24) 10-25MM	25MM & OVER
	38		54		61	NUMBER OF STATEMENTS		2	4	5	28	22
	%		%		%	ASSETS	%	%	%	%	%	%
	13.9		12.8		12.1	Cash & Equivalents					10.3	9.3
	26.1		25.3		22.4	Trade Receivables (net)	DATA NOT AVAILABLE				20.5	21.2
	27.8		29.2		31.4	Inventory					35.3	31.1
	4.0		3.9		2.8	All Other Current					2.4	4.3
	71.7		71.1		68.7	Total Current					68.6	65.9
	15.0		13.4		15.3	Fixed Assets (net)					15.5	19.8
	3.5		7.2		8.3	Intangibles (net)					7.8	7.1
	9.7		8.3		7.7	All Other Non-Current					8.1	7.2
	100.0		100.0		100.0	Total					100.0	100.0
						LIABILITIES						
	5.7		6.5		5.8	Notes Payable-Short Term					4.6	4.8
	1.6		2.5		1.8	Cur. Mat.-L.T.D.					1.7	2.3
	10.0		9.5		10.4	Trade Payables					9.0	7.7
	.2		.3		.1	Income Taxes Payable					.1	.2
	12.9		13.1		15.2	All Other Current					13.9	15.8
	30.4		31.9		33.3	Total Current					29.3	30.8
	8.8		10.6		13.5	Long-Term Debt					12.9	17.5
	.3		.3		.2	Deferred Taxes					.3	.1
	9.7		5.3		4.3	All Other Non-Current					4.6	4.3
	50.8		51.9		48.7	Net Worth					52.8	47.3
	100.0		100.0		100.0	Total Liabilities & Net Worth					100.0	100.0
						INCOME DATA						
	100.0		100.0		100.0	Net Sales					100.0	100.0
	37.5		41.5		40.0	Gross Profit					39.8	42.9
	33.2		33.8		33.0	Operating Expenses					31.7	34.2
	4.4		7.7		7.0	Operating Profit					8.1	8.7
	-2.6		.0		1.5	All Other Expenses (net)					2.0	1.5
	7.0		7.7		5.4	Profit Before Taxes					6.1	7.2
						RATIOS						
	5.1		4.2		3.5						3.7	3.8
	2.4		2.6		2.4	Current					2.6	2.5
	1.7		1.5		1.5						1.5	1.4
	2.8		2.6		1.9						1.8	1.9
	1.3		1.2		1.0	Quick					1.0	.9
	.9		.7		.6						.6	.6
38	9.6	43	8.5	38	9.5						38 9.5	37 9.8
46	8.0	61	6.0	50	7.3	Sales/Receivables					54 6.7	51 7.2
73	5.0	73	5.0	66	5.5						70 5.2	69 5.3
54	6.8	79	4.6	83	4.4						94 3.9	99 3.7
87	4.2	130	2.8	135	2.7	Cost of Sales/Inventory					159 2.3	140 2.6
159	2.3	203	1.8	182	2.0						215 1.7	192 1.9
17	21.6	21	17.6	23	16.1						23 15.9	22 16.4
29	12.5	33	10.9	35	10.4	Cost of Sales/Payables					41 8.8	32 11.5
42	8.7	54	6.7	57	6.4						62 5.9	42 8.6
	3.0		2.4		2.9						2.7	2.6
	3.8		3.6		4.8	Sales/Working Capital					3.7	4.4
	8.4		6.9		7.5						6.7	8.2
	50.8		44.5		40.6						35.5	106.8
(34)	25.9	(46)	11.1	(56)	5.8	EBIT/Interest					(26) 7.0	(19) 5.1
	5.2		2.7		1.1						1.4	2.5
	53.0		12.6		18.6	Net Profit + Depr., Dep.,						20.2
(11)	15.1	(14)	7.1	(15)	2.8	Amort./Cur. Mat. L/T/D					(10) 4.7	
	4.7		2.1		1.4							1.2
	.1		.1		.1						.1	.2
	.2		.3		.3	Fixed/Worth					.2	.5
	.6		.7		1.2						1.2	1.1
	.3		.4		.5						.4	.4
	.9		.8		1.0	Debt/Worth					.8	1.3
	2.1		3.7		4.2						3.8	4.2
	40.9		42.7		30.6	% Profit Before Taxes/Tangible					40.2	29.0
(35)	23.4	(49)	18.4	(52)	19.1	Net Worth					(25) 22.9	(19) 20.9
	10.4		7.0		4.6						9.8	4.1
	24.8		18.3		16.4	% Profit Before Taxes/Total					16.5	18.6
	11.8		8.0		6.6	Assets					9.8	9.6
	4.0		2.1		1.1						1.1	2.6
	49.0		26.1		39.5						25.3	14.6
	11.9		13.4		11.7	Sales/Net Fixed Assets					11.7	8.8
	6.9		7.0		6.7						6.0	5.7
	2.1		2.1		1.9						1.7	2.1
	1.8		1.6		1.5	Sales/Total Assets					1.4	1.4
	1.3		1.1		1.0						.8	1.0
	.8		.8		.5						.5	1.0
(33)	1.3	(41)	1.5	(46)	1.1	% Depr., Dep., Amort./Sales					(22) 1.1	(17) 1.5
	2.1		2.1		2.1						2.0	2.6
	1.4		2.7		1.8	% Officers', Directors'						
(10)	3.4	(13)	3.4	(10)	3.7	Owners' Comp/Sales						
	6.2		5.4		8.5							
	868217M		2014315M		1838815M	Net Sales ($)		4993M	15416M	32656M	463133M	1322617M
	572148M		1661047M		1454483M	Total Assets ($)		2801M	6465M	23612M	433009M	988596M

© RMA 2024   M = $ thousand   MM = $ million
See Pages viii through xx for Explanation of Ratios and Data

MANUFACTURING—Analytical Laboratory Instrument Manufacturing NAICS 334516

Current Data Sorted by Assets | Comparative Historical Data

							Type of Statement				
			2	2			Unqualified		6		2
		1	1				Reviewed		5		4
1		4	2				Compiled		3		3
		2					Tax Returns		1		1
	1	8		3			Other		17		10
	6 (4/1-9/30/23)		30 (10/1/23-3/31/24)						4/1/19-3/31/20		4/1/20-3/31/21
0-500M	500M-2MM	2-10MM	10-50MM	50-100MM	100-250MM				ALL		ALL
1	1	15	10	6	3		NUMBER OF STATEMENTS		32		20
%	%	%	%	%	%		ASSETS		%		%
		21.8	11.8				Cash & Equivalents		15.7		28.9
		29.5	18.9				Trade Receivables (net)		21.2		19.4
		24.7	33.6				Inventory		27.0		25.7
		.7	.5				All Other Current		3.5		3.7
		76.7	64.7				Total Current		67.4		77.7
		11.9	14.8				Fixed Assets (net)		14.8		12.5
		4.8	13.9				Intangibles (net)		10.5		5.7
		6.6	6.6				All Other Non-Current		7.3		4.1
		100.0	100.0				Total		100.0		100.0
							LIABILITIES				
		5.7	6.4				Notes Payable-Short Term		8.8		4.1
		.1	5.4				Cur. Mat.-L.T.D.		1.3		.4
		22.7	6.3				Trade Payables		7.8		4.9
		.1	.0				Income Taxes Payable		.3		.2
		10.0	13.1				All Other Current		17.5		16.0
		38.6	31.1				Total Current		35.7		25.6
		2.5	12.7				Long-Term Debt		9.0		7.5
		.0	1.3				Deferred Taxes		.3		.1
		1.0	2.2				All Other Non-Current		3.4		1.9
		57.9	52.6				Net Worth		51.5		64.9
		100.0	100.0				Total Liabilities & Net Worth		100.0		100.0
							INCOME DATA				
		100.0	100.0				Net Sales		100.0		100.0
		55.4	43.1				Gross Profit		54.9		46.0
		47.4	42.3				Operating Expenses		47.0		39.9
		8.0	.8				Operating Profit		7.9		6.1
		1.2	2.2				All Other Expenses (net)		.6		-.1
		6.9	-1.4				Profit Before Taxes		7.3		6.2
							RATIOS				
		5.1	4.1						4.4		9.4
		2.0	3.3				Current		2.2		3.6
		1.6	1.4						1.5		2.0
		2.4	2.0						2.1		8.1
		1.1	.9				Quick		1.3		2.1
		.8	.7						.8		1.2
		33 11.1	30 12.2					36	10.1	26	13.9
		42 8.7	50 7.3				Sales/Receivables	51	7.2	43	8.5
		65 5.6	87 4.2					61	6.0	68	5.4
		26 14.1	104 3.5					96	3.8	42	8.7
		78 4.7	192 1.9				Cost of Sales/Inventory	135	2.7	135	2.7
		182 2.0	304 1.2					215	1.7	192	1.9
		23 16.2	13 28.2					18	20.2	2	172.7
		28 13.0	30 12.2				Cost of Sales/Payables	29	12.7	10	34.8
		192 1.9	65 5.6					59	6.2	36	10.1
		3.0	2.1						2.1		2.2
		5.5	2.7				Sales/Working Capital		4.2		2.7
		9.9	NM						8.8		5.3
		190.7							28.6		
	(11)	9.8					EBIT/Interest	(23)	3.8		
		1.8							.4		
							Net Profit + Depr., Dep., Amort./Cur. Mat. L/T/D				
		.1	.3						.1		.0
		.2	.5				Fixed/Worth		.3		.1
		.3	-.2						1.0		.3
		.3	.2						.3		.1
		1.0	1.0				Debt/Worth		1.1		.4
		1.5	-3.7						2.9		.8
		49.4							48.6		41.8
		13.8					% Profit Before Taxes/Tangible Net Worth	(29)	24.5	(19)	19.7
		4.8							6.5		.4
		16.5	13.8						17.4		24.4
		12.1	3.8				% Profit Before Taxes/Total Assets		7.0		7.8
		3.5	-11.5						.1		.3
		100.1	31.3						39.1		168.4
		49.9	9.8				Sales/Net Fixed Assets		16.2		28.0
		5.1	3.9						5.3		8.1
		3.1	1.6						2.2		2.2
		2.0	1.2				Sales/Total Assets		1.5		1.6
		1.1	.9						1.0		1.4
		.2							.8		.5
	(12)	.8					% Depr., Dep., Amort./Sales	(23)	2.0	(15)	2.0
		1.8							3.8		5.6
							% Officers', Directors' Owners' Comp/Sales				
1035M	3983M	138814M	294074M	452837M	354656M		Net Sales ($)		1394730M		609068M
447M	1589M	78472M	253767M	445657M	391501M		Total Assets ($)		1220533M		407276M

M = $ thousand   MM = $ million
See Pages viii through xx for Explanation of Ratios and Data

© RMA 2024

MANUFACTURING—Analytical Laboratory Instrument Manufacturing NAICS 334516

Comparative Historical Data | Current Data Sorted by Sales

						Type of Statement						
		2		4		4	Unqualified				1	3
		4		4		2	Reviewed				1	1
				2		7	Compiled		2		1	1
		2		2		2	Tax Returns			2	1	
		12		13		21	Other			3	7	9
		4/1/21-3/31/22 ALL		4/1/22-3/31/23 ALL		4/1/23-3/31/24 ALL		0-1MM	6 (4/1-9/30/23) 1-3MM	3-5MM	30 (10/1/23-3/31/24) 5-10MM	10-25MM	25MM & OVER
		20		25		36	NUMBER OF STATEMENTS		2	2	7	11	14
		%		%		%	ASSETS	%	%	%	%	%	%
		20.7		16.4		17.6	Cash & Equivalents					9.9	12.4
		24.5		21.5		22.3	Trade Receivables (net)					28.5	16.3
		24.3		28.8		26.7	Inventory					33.2	26.5
		2.5		5.8		.8	All Other Current					1.1	1.1
		72.0		72.6		67.4	Total Current					72.7	56.3
		17.3		16.3		13.4	Fixed Assets (net)	DATA NOT AVAILABLE				9.9	17.8
		3.5		3.9		13.2	Intangibles (net)					14.1	19.6
		7.2		7.2		6.0	All Other Non-Current					3.3	6.3
		100.0		100.0		100.0	Total					100.0	100.0
							LIABILITIES						
		.3		1.4		4.8	Notes Payable-Short Term					5.4	3.1
		.5		2.7		1.8	Cur. Mat.-L.T.D.					4.2	1.0
		9.3		6.6		12.5	Trade Payables					18.9	5.6
		.0		.7		.0	Income Taxes Payable					.0	.0
		8.8		14.9		10.9	All Other Current					15.7	8.9
		19.0		26.2		29.9	Total Current					44.2	18.5
		4.4		6.3		10.7	Long-Term Debt					7.0	18.9
		.7		.3		.4	Deferred Taxes					.9	.4
		4.7		2.8		3.7	All Other Non-Current					2.9	7.2
		71.2		64.4		55.2	Net Worth					44.9	55.1
		100.0		100.0		100.0	Total Liabilities & Net Worth					100.0	100.0
							INCOME DATA						
		100.0		100.0		100.0	Net Sales					100.0	100.0
		54.6		49.9		50.1	Gross Profit					47.8	48.7
		39.1		38.1		44.1	Operating Expenses					48.6	41.0
		15.4		11.8		6.0	Operating Profit					-.8	7.8
		-1.8		.0		2.5	All Other Expenses (net)					1.8	3.8
		17.3		11.7		3.5	Profit Before Taxes					-2.6	4.0
							RATIOS						
		5.3		4.7		4.5						2.9	4.3
		3.5		3.4		2.4	Current					1.7	3.9
		3.0		2.0		1.7						1.3	2.2
		3.3		2.2		2.3						1.1	2.4
		2.2		1.4		1.2	Quick					.9	1.7
		1.8		1.2		.8						.8	.7
41	9.0	34	10.8	34	10.6		Sales/Receivables				42	8.7	47	7.8
50	7.3	49	7.5	48	7.6						44	8.3	57	6.4
73	5.0	72	5.1	65	5.6						68	5.4	66	5.5
76	4.8	81	4.5	78	4.7		Cost of Sales/Inventory				78	4.7	126	2.9
122	3.0	135	2.7	135	2.7						101	3.6	203	1.8
203	1.8	243	1.5	215	1.7						192	1.9	228	1.6
22	16.6	17	20.9	19	19.7		Cost of Sales/Payables				23	16.2	21	17.8
29	12.7	26	14.3	28	12.9						39	9.3	33	11.0
62	5.9	36	10.0	64	5.7						104	3.5	56	6.5
		2.1		2.3		2.4	Sales/Working Capital					2.6	2.3
		2.6		3.4		3.4						9.4	3.0
		3.6		4.2		6.8						13.8	4.2
				593.9		117.0	EBIT/Interest					75.6	156.0
		(17)		38.4	(28)	4.9						(10) 4.9	(12) 5.0
				3.6		.3						-.5	.0
							Net Profit + Depr., Dep., Amort./Cur. Mat. L/T/D						
		.1		.1		.1	Fixed/Worth					.1	.3
		.2		.3		.3						.2	.5
		.4		.5		2.5						-.2	-.3
		.2		.3		.2	Debt/Worth					.7	.2
		.4		.4		.9						1.4	.7
		.8		.8		18.7						-3.7	-3.4
		67.3		41.3		38.9	% Profit Before Taxes/Tangible Net Worth						32.4
		29.6	(23)	24.3	(29)	17.1						(10)	23.3
		13.3		7.1		7.4							15.5
		45.7		26.6		16.3	% Profit Before Taxes/Total Assets					16.5	16.6
		18.9		15.3		8.6						3.5	10.2
		10.6		4.2		-2.4						-9.0	-6.0
		30.9		28.8		50.2	Sales/Net Fixed Assets					150.1	11.4
		10.3		9.5		12.9						49.9	8.5
		4.6		5.2		5.1						13.1	4.7
		2.0		2.1		2.3	Sales/Total Assets					3.1	1.2
		1.3		1.5		1.2						1.7	1.1
		.9		1.0		.9						1.1	.7
		.7		1.1		.3	% Depr., Dep., Amort./Sales						
(18)	2.0	(19)	2.4	(22)	1.4								
		2.9		3.1		2.4								
							% Officers', Directors' Owners' Comp/Sales						
		1212233M		1120619M		1245399M	Net Sales ($)		3912M	8611M	55382M	156784M	1020710M
		1040299M		800916M		1171433M	Total Assets ($)		9189M	5619M	36656M	109865M	1010104M

© RMA 2024 M = $ thousand MM = $ million
See Pages viii through xx for Explanation of Ratios and Data

MANUFACTURING—Other Measuring and Controlling Device Manufacturing NAICS 334519

Current Data Sorted by Assets | Comparative Historical Data

						Type of Statement				
			4		2	Unqualified		6		5
		4	4		1	Reviewed		12		7
			1			Compiled		2		2
		3				Tax Returns		3		2
1	1	6	13	4	2	Other		38		22
	5 (4/1-9/30/23)		41 (10/1/23-3/31/24)					4/1/19-		4/1/20-
0-500M	500M-2MM	2-10MM	10-50MM	50-100MM	100-250MM			3/31/20		3/31/21
1	1	13	22	4	5	NUMBER OF STATEMENTS		61		38
								ALL		ALL
%	%	%	%	%	%	ASSETS		%		%
		10.5	10.3			Cash & Equivalents		15.7		19.4
		27.7	22.5			Trade Receivables (net)		27.8		23.5
		34.1	25.1			Inventory		26.8		22.3
		1.4	7.5			All Other Current		4.4		6.1
		73.7	65.4			Total Current		74.7		71.2
		10.4	14.2			Fixed Assets (net)		14.0		12.6
		11.1	7.2			Intangibles (net)		5.6		10.7
		4.8	13.2			All Other Non-Current		5.7		5.4
		100.0	100.0			Total		100.0		100.0
						LIABILITIES				
		11.1	3.1			Notes Payable-Short Term		6.1		8.3
		.6	4.2			Cur. Mat.-L.T.D.		1.6		1.4
		11.5	10.8			Trade Payables		9.7		8.6
		.6	.2			Income Taxes Payable		.3		.1
		21.3	15.1			All Other Current		15.6		10.9
		45.2	33.3			Total Current		33.4		29.2
		3.1	5.3			Long-Term Debt		7.1		11.5
		.0	.0			Deferred Taxes		.1		.2
		1.5	9.5			All Other Non-Current		4.2		5.7
		50.2	51.9			Net Worth		55.2		53.5
		100.0	100.0			Total Liabilties & Net Worth		100.0		100.0
						INCOME DATA				
		100.0	100.0			Net Sales		100.0		100.0
		43.8	35.1			Gross Profit		38.5		33.5
		39.6	27.1			Operating Expenses		33.2		28.4
		4.2	8.0			Operating Profit		5.3		5.1
		-.8	.5			All Other Expenses (net)		.2		-1.2
		5.0	7.4			Profit Before Taxes		5.2		6.3
						RATIOS				
		5.6	4.6					5.4		5.1
		2.3	2.5			Current		2.5		2.3
		1.4	1.1					1.6		1.6
		2.9	1.9					2.9		3.9
		.9	1.1			Quick		1.5		1.4
		.7	.6					.8		.8
		41 8.9	42 8.6				35	10.5	31	11.6
		46 8.0	61 6.0			Sales/Receivables	49	7.4	58	6.3
		69 5.3	87 4.2				72	5.1	99	3.7
		46 8.0	51 7.2				60	6.1	69	5.3
		114 3.2	130 2.8			Cost of Sales/Inventory	89	4.1	104	3.5
		174 2.1	215 1.7				140	2.6	159	2.3
		17 21.0	16 22.7				13	27.7	13	28.1
		40 9.1	33 11.1			Cost of Sales/Payables	24	15.3	26	14.0
		76 4.8	58 6.3				41	9.0	45	8.2
		2.9	1.7					2.3		2.2
		6.1	3.4			Sales/Working Capital		4.2		3.2
		14.5	15.8					8.1		4.9
		38.1	170.3					25.4		43.9
	(10)	10.5	(19) 6.2			EBIT/Interest	(44)	4.7	(30)	12.9
		.7	3.0					-.4		1.9
						Net Profit + Depr., Dep.,		16.5		
						Amort./Cur. Mat. L/T/D	(11)	1.6		
								-3.4		
		.1	.1					.1		.1
		.1	.2			Fixed/Worth		.2		.2
		.6	1.9					.5		.6
		.2	.5					.3		.4
		.9	.7			Debt/Worth		.6		.8
		3.2	9.8					2.4		3.0
		31.6	42.6			% Profit Before Taxes/Tangible		36.6		38.4
	(12)	21.2	(19) 23.5			Net Worth	(57)	12.9	(36)	14.0
		1.9	4.9					2.1		4.6
		19.1	14.9			% Profit Before Taxes/Total		15.5		16.1
		8.7	6.7			Assets		7.4		8.1
		1.8	2.6					1.7		2.0
		98.4	29.8					43.3		39.2
		30.0	12.2			Sales/Net Fixed Assets		21.1		19.2
		10.2	6.0					8.1		5.6
		2.8	1.4					2.5		1.9
		1.9	1.0			Sales/Total Assets		1.6		1.3
		1.2	.8					1.1		.8
		.3	.6					.8		.7
		(11) 1.1	(17) 1.7			% Depr., Dep., Amort./Sales	(47)	1.3	(29)	1.1
		1.4	4.2					2.6		3.3
						% Officers', Directors'		3.0		
						Owners' Comp/Sales	(14)	5.7		
								9.1		
976M	3045M	147564M	712317M	277320M	676835M	Net Sales ($)		1737195M		868960M
488M	924M	77389M	638017M	221788M	884009M	Total Assets ($)		1312114M		780303M

© RMA 2024
M = $ thousand   MM = $ million
See Pages viii through xx for Explanation of Ratios and Data

MANUFACTURING—Other Measuring and Controlling Device Manufacturing NAICS 334519

Comparative Historical Data / Current Data Sorted by Sales

								Type of Statement						
		7		6		6		Unqualified					1	5
		11		8		9		Reviewed					7	2
		1		5		1		Compiled					1	1
		4		5		4		Tax Returns			2		1	1
		14		23		26		Other	1	2	1	3	5	14
		4/1/21-3/31/22 ALL		4/1/22-3/31/23 ALL		4/1/23-3/31/24 ALL			0-1MM	1-3MM	5 (4/1-9/30/23) 3-5MM	5-10MM	41 (10/1/23-3/31/24) 10-25MM	25MM & OVER
		37		47		46		NUMBER OF STATEMENTS	1	2	3	4	13	23
		%		%		%		ASSETS	%	%	%	%	%	%
		16.4		12.2		10.3		Cash & Equivalents					14.4	8.3
		22.5		23.4		24.2		Trade Receivables (net)					35.6	19.4
		22.5		30.5		27.6		Inventory					28.6	26.9
		5.0		4.6		4.5		All Other Current					7.3	4.3
		66.3		70.7		66.5		Total Current					85.9	58.9
		14.2		14.5		16.2		Fixed Assets (net)					11.0	19.8
		15.5		7.3		8.4		Intangibles (net)					.2	8.0
		4.0		7.4		8.9		All Other Non-Current					2.9	13.3
		100.0		100.0		100.0		Total					100.0	100.0
								LIABILITIES						
		4.2		7.1		4.6		Notes Payable-Short Term					8.5	2.4
		2.6		1.8		2.7		Cur. Mat.-L.T.D.					.5	4.7
		6.0		12.2		11.5		Trade Payables					17.3	9.6
		.0		.4		.2		Income Taxes Payable					.0	.1
		16.0		16.8		16.8		All Other Current					18.1	17.4
		28.8		38.4		35.9		Total Current					44.5	34.3
		15.9		10.2		8.4		Long-Term Debt					3.2	10.0
		.0		.8		.0		Deferred Taxes					.0	.0
		9.8		5.9		7.4		All Other Non-Current					5.1	11.2
		45.5		44.8		48.2		Net Worth					47.2	44.6
		100.0		100.0		100.0		Total Liabilties & Net Worth					100.0	100.0
								INCOME DATA						
		100.0		100.0		100.0		Net Sales					100.0	100.0
		42.5		34.5		39.2		Gross Profit					32.6	38.9
		36.8		30.7		32.4		Operating Expenses					24.7	31.6
		5.7		3.7		6.8		Operating Profit					7.8	7.2
		.2		.3		.5		All Other Expenses (net)					-.1	1.1
		5.5		3.4		6.3		Profit Before Taxes					8.0	6.1
								RATIOS						
		4.5		4.3		4.7							4.9	4.6
		2.3		2.2		2.3		Current					1.7	2.3
		1.8		1.2		1.2							1.4	1.1
		2.4		2.2		2.3							2.8	1.9
		1.5		1.0		1.1		Quick					1.1	1.0
		.8		.6		.6							.8	.4
39	9.4	38	9.7	42	8.6							41	8.8	44	8.3
59	6.2	61	6.0	59	6.2		Sales/Receivables					57	6.4	62	5.9
85	4.3	76	4.8	89	4.1							122	3.0	85	4.3
27	13.7	66	5.5	54	6.8							13	28.8	94	3.9
99	3.7	122	3.0	122	3.0		Cost of Sales/Inventory					99	3.7	140	2.6
159	2.3	228	1.6	228	1.6							152	2.4	228	1.6
10	36.6	16	22.6	17	21.0							16	23.2	22	16.8
23	16.1	30	12.3	38	9.5		Cost of Sales/Payables					37	9.9	42	8.7
51	7.2	59	6.2	69	5.3							62	5.9	79	4.6
		2.3		2.5		2.2							1.9	1.8
		3.1		3.9		4.1		Sales/Working Capital					3.9	4.5
		4.9		15.5		11.6							12.1	40.4
		67.4		31.9		74.7							287.5	22.4
(26)	9.9	(41)	6.6	(40)	7.0		EBIT/Interest					(11)	15.6	(21)	5.0
		.4		1.4		1.6							4.9	1.7
						5.7		Net Profit + Depr., Dep.,						50.6
				(11)	2.6		Amort./Cur. Mat. L/T/D					(10)	3.6
						1.0								1.2
		.1		.1		.1							.0	.2
		.3		.2		.2		Fixed/Worth					.1	.5
		2.7		1.0		1.1							.4	4.0
		.4		.4		.5							.4	.5
		1.1		1.0		.8		Debt/Worth					1.1	.7
		5.9		11.4		3.5							3.2	14.2
		63.4		35.8		34.5		% Profit Before Taxes/Tangible					41.8	32.5
(30)	26.2	(39)	11.5	(41)	23.5		Net Worth					33.5	(20)	19.0
		.3		2.6		6.4							8.2	8.2
		21.2		14.3		15.7		% Profit Before Taxes/Total					22.9	13.4
		8.2		4.8		7.8		Assets					9.7	7.2
		-.1		.0		2.5							3.7	2.0
		51.4		60.1		31.3							140.6	14.2
		11.5		14.9		12.0		Sales/Net Fixed Assets					28.2	9.3
		6.6		5.7		5.3							6.2	3.9
		1.9		1.5		1.6							2.3	1.4
		1.3		1.3		1.2		Sales/Total Assets					1.5	1.0
		.7		.8		.9							1.0	.8
		.8		.6		.5							.2	1.4
(26)	1.2	(34)	1.7	(36)	1.5		% Depr., Dep., Amort./Sales					(11)	1.2	(18)	2.2
		2.7		2.9		3.3							2.2	4.0
								% Officers', Directors' Owners' Comp/Sales						
		1026975M		1738308M		1818057M		Net Sales ($)	976M	5880M	11867M	30486M	214793M	1554055M
		995003M		1599325M		1822615M		Total Assets ($)	488M	4454M	14478M	28937M	148100M	1626158M

© RMA 2024   M = $ thousand   MM = $ million
See Pages viii through xx for Explanation of Ratios and Data

MANUFACTURING—Commercial, Industrial, and Institutional Electric Lighting Fixture Manufacturing NAICS 335132

Current Data Sorted by Assets | Comparative Historical Data

0-500M	500M-2MM	2-10MM	10-50MM	50-100MM	100-250MM		Type of Statement		4/1/19-3/31/20 ALL		4/1/20-3/31/21 ALL
	1	4	4				Unqualified		6		5
		3	2				Reviewed		8		3
		2		1			Compiled		6		
	3	7	6	6	2		Tax Returns		2		4
	7 (4/1-9/30/23)		34 (10/1/23-3/31/24)				Other		32		17
4	4	16	12	7	2		NUMBER OF STATEMENTS		54		29
%	%	%	%	%	%		ASSETS		%		%
		12.3	12.2				Cash & Equivalents		12.3		14.0
		29.7	24.1				Trade Receivables (net)		27.6		22.2
		33.2	22.8				Inventory		34.2		33.1
		4.2	3.6				All Other Current		2.2		1.6
		79.3	62.7				Total Current		76.2		70.9
		11.2	15.0				Fixed Assets (net)		10.2		13.9
		7.4	12.3				Intangibles (net)		9.0		9.3
		2.0	10.0				All Other Non-Current		4.5		5.9
		100.0	100.0				Total		100.0		100.0
							LIABILITIES				
		5.9	11.8				Notes Payable-Short Term		7.7		17.1
		1.1	2.7				Cur. Mat.-L.T.D.		1.3		4.0
		13.3	10.8				Trade Payables		24.6		13.4
		.0	.2				Income Taxes Payable		.4		.0
		13.9	12.0				All Other Current		13.9		13.3
		34.3	37.3				Total Current		47.9		47.9
		7.5	8.6				Long-Term Debt		12.1		18.8
		.0	.1				Deferred Taxes		.1		.1
		7.0	8.9				All Other Non-Current		10.1		9.7
		51.3	45.0				Net Worth		29.9		23.6
		100.0	100.0				Total Liabilities & Net Worth		100.0		100.0
							INCOME DATA				
		100.0	100.0				Net Sales		100.0		100.0
		44.3	39.4				Gross Profit		42.0		37.1
		37.3	31.2				Operating Expenses		34.7		37.0
		7.1	8.1				Operating Profit		7.2		.1
		.8	.2				All Other Expenses (net)		1.3		-1.1
		6.2	7.9				Profit Before Taxes		6.0		1.2
							RATIOS				
		5.6	2.8						3.0		4.2
		2.9	2.0				Current		1.8		2.0
		1.4	1.0						1.3		1.6
		2.4	1.5						1.6		2.4
		1.3	.9				Quick		.9		1.0
		.8	.6						.6		.7
	33	11.2	34	10.7				27	13.7	29	12.4
	39	9.4	43	8.4			Sales/Receivables	41	9.0	45	8.1
	58	6.3	60	6.1				57	6.4	60	6.1
	5	72.5	19	19.5				56	6.5	58	6.3
	85	4.3	70	5.2			Cost of Sales/Inventory	91	4.0	91	4.0
	243	1.5	135	2.7				135	2.7	146	2.5
	20	18.2	21	17.5				21	17.0	17	21.9
	35	10.3	34	10.7			Cost of Sales/Payables	38	9.7	30	12.3
	56	6.5	52	7.0				72	5.1	46	8.0
		2.6	4.9						4.0		3.7
		5.5	6.6				Sales/Working Capital		6.7		5.7
		10.6	62.3						16.6		9.1
		108.7	34.8						28.2		24.6
		14.5	(11) 12.9				EBIT/Interest	(46)	4.4	(23)	.7
		1.8	1.1						-.7		-7.2
							Net Profit + Depr., Dep., Amort./Cur. Mat. L/T/D				
		.0	.1						.1		.1
		.2	.6				Fixed/Worth		.3		.3
		.8	NM						.7		.9
		.3	.6						.4		.5
		.7	1.9				Debt/Worth		1.8		1.3
		1.9	NM						30.3		5.2
		51.7							54.5		41.5
	(13)	16.8					% Profit Before Taxes/Tangible Net Worth	(42)	22.3	(24)	18.0
		3.6							.8		-16.0
		23.3	35.0						29.3		17.6
		10.5	18.4				% Profit Before Taxes/Total Assets		7.7		.5
		1.4	.3						-1.0		-5.2
		205.0	181.0						122.0		40.3
		25.1	21.0				Sales/Net Fixed Assets		34.0		18.6
		14.0	5.2						14.7		9.3
		3.1	2.3						2.8		2.5
		2.1	1.5				Sales/Total Assets		2.2		1.8
		1.4	1.4						1.6		1.4
									.7		.8
							% Depr., Dep., Amort./Sales	(33)	1.3	(21)	1.1
									1.7		2.8
									2.5		
							% Officers', Directors' Owners' Comp/Sales	(17)	6.1		
									9.9		
	8970M	161954M	501192M	635554M	514578M		Net Sales ($)		2204299M		1029135M
	4108M	79457M	271038M	437130M	260865M		Total Assets ($)		1305318M		545263M

(Data Not Available for 0-500M column)

M = $ thousand   MM = $ million
See Pages viii through xx for Explanation of Ratios and Data

© RMA 2024

MANUFACTURING—Commercial, Industrial, and Institutional Electric Lighting Fixture Manufacturing   NAICS 335132

Comparative Historical Data | Current Data Sorted by Sales

Comparative Historical Data						Type of Statement			Current Data Sorted by Sales				
	1		4		5	Unqualified							5
	4		5		6	Reviewed					2	4	
	2		8		4	Compiled				1	1	2	
	5		6		2	Tax Returns					2		
	23		27		24	Other		1	2	1	3	6	11
	4/1/21-		4/1/22-		4/1/23-					7 (4/1-9/30/23)		34 (10/1/23-3/31/24)	
	3/31/22		3/31/23		3/31/24			0-1MM	1-3MM	3-5MM	5-10MM	10-25MM	25MM & OVER
	ALL		ALL		ALL								
	35		50		41	NUMBER OF STATEMENTS		1	2	2	8	12	16
	%		%		%	ASSETS		%	%	%	%	%	%
	11.9		10.9		10.0	Cash & Equivalents						12.2	9.6
	23.6		25.9		28.3	Trade Receivables (net)						26.3	29.2
	36.8		32.4		27.8	Inventory						19.9	24.7
	2.4		3.9		6.0	All Other Current						5.0	6.2
	74.6		73.1		72.1	Total Current						63.4	69.6
	8.5		10.1		12.2	Fixed Assets (net)						21.7	8.8
	11.1		8.9		10.7	Intangibles (net)						10.3	15.4
	5.7		7.9		4.9	All Other Non-Current						4.7	6.2
	100.0		100.0		100.0	Total						100.0	100.0
						LIABILITIES							
	15.8		11.5		11.0	Notes Payable-Short Term						8.8	13.7
	2.0		3.6		1.6	Cur. Mat.-L.T.D.						2.5	1.8
	11.6		17.6		12.7	Trade Payables						12.7	12.1
	.0		.0		.1	Income Taxes Payable						.1	.1
	11.7		16.3		14.3	All Other Current						10.0	19.7
	41.0		49.1		39.6	Total Current						34.1	47.4
	16.8		15.7		11.5	Long-Term Debt						8.5	11.1
	.1		.2		.0	Deferred Taxes						.1	.0
	4.9		4.8		8.5	All Other Non-Current						5.1	9.7
	37.2		30.3		40.3	Net Worth						52.2	31.8
	100.0		100.0		100.0	Total Liabilities & Net Worth						100.0	100.0
						INCOME DATA							
	100.0		100.0		100.0	Net Sales						100.0	100.0
	41.8		39.5		41.6	Gross Profit						39.4	43.2
	42.8		34.2		33.8	Operating Expenses						33.9	31.6
	-1.0		5.3		7.9	Operating Profit						5.5	11.6
	-1.5		1.1		.7	All Other Expenses (net)						.4	1.4
	.5		4.2		7.1	Profit Before Taxes						5.1	10.2
						RATIOS							
	4.5		3.2		3.2							3.4	2.3
	1.8		1.7		2.1	Current						2.4	1.5
	1.2		1.1		1.2							1.3	1.0
	3.2		1.5		1.5							2.4	1.3
	.9		.8		1.1	Quick						1.5	.9
	.4		.5		.6							.6	.5
38	9.7	33	11.2	37	9.9						18	20.7	40	9.1
54	6.7	42	8.6	43	8.4	Sales/Receivables					40	9.2	54	6.7
79	4.6	56	6.5	72	5.1						53	6.9	89	4.1
85	4.3	52	7.0	19	18.8						5	75.0	21	17.2
126	2.9	104	3.5	89	4.1	Cost of Sales/Inventory					58	6.3	101	3.6
203	1.8	152	2.4	166	2.2						96	3.8	166	2.2
20	18.3	21	17.1	20	18.0						19	19.2	32	11.3
40	9.1	50	7.3	39	9.4	Cost of Sales/Payables					30	12.1	41	8.8
91	4.0	87	4.2	56	6.5						53	6.9	56	6.5
	2.5		3.3		3.4							4.6	4.8
	4.4		5.8		6.1	Sales/Working Capital						6.1	10.1
	12.4		38.2		32.2							36.2	NM
	43.8		46.0		40.2							55.2	28.3
(27)	9.2	(42)	13.3	(38)	9.0	EBIT/Interest						4.8	(14) 13.9
	-1.4		2.1		1.2							-2.6	1.2
			9.8			Net Profit + Depr., Dep.,							
		(10)	6.4			Amort./Cur. Mat. L/T/D							
			3.7										
	.1		.0		.1							.1	.2
	.3		.4		.5	Fixed/Worth						.7	NM
	2.1		NM		-1.7							.9	-.1
	.6		.5		.5							.3	1.0
	1.9		1.8		1.8	Debt/Worth						.8	NM
	68.9		-18.3		-16.0							3.1	-10.0
	46.0		77.1		61.9							40.1	
(28)	18.7	(35)	25.0	(28)	29.3	% Profit Before Taxes/Tangible Net Worth					(10)	16.3	
	-1.1		9.3		2.6							-.8	
	14.8		25.1		26.4	% Profit Before Taxes/Total Assets						22.0	35.0
	3.6		8.0		16.4							10.9	25.0
	-4.9		1.2		.5							-2.4	1.5
	68.3		149.9		142.2							119.4	143.5
	20.3		24.2		24.9	Sales/Net Fixed Assets						6.3	29.5
	10.5		10.3		9.2							4.0	10.5
	2.0		2.6		2.5							2.5	2.1
	1.5		2.0		1.8	Sales/Total Assets						1.8	1.6
	.9		1.3		1.4							1.5	1.4
	.8		.7		.5								.6
(24)	1.2	(35)	1.2	(26)	1.3	% Depr., Dep., Amort./Sales						(10) 1.0	
	1.5		2.0		1.8								1.4
	.9		2.5		1.1	% Officers', Directors' Owners' Comp/Sales							
(10)	2.8	(12)	4.3	(10)	2.4								
	10.2		8.1		4.2								
	1292375M		1257332M		1822248M	Net Sales ($)		911M	3648M	8700M	57304M	188988M	1562697M
	958813M		911831M		1052598M	Total Assets ($)		658M	1718M	5685M	33083M	104513M	906941M

© RMA 2024   M = $ thousand   MM = $ million
See Pages viii through xx for Explanation of Ratios and Data

MANUFACTURING—Power, Distribution, and Specialty Transformer Manufacturing NAICS 335311

Current Data Sorted by Assets | Comparative Historical Data

0-500M	500M-2MM	2-10MM	10-50MM	50-100MM	100-250MM	Type of Statement		4/1/19-3/31/20 ALL		4/1/20-3/31/21 ALL
				1	1	Unqualified		4		3
			5		2	Reviewed		6		4
						Compiled				1
1	1		4			Tax Returns		5		3
1	1	4	7	2	3	Other		17		9
4 (4/1-9/30/23)			28 (10/1/23-3/31/24)							
1	2	8	12	3	6	NUMBER OF STATEMENTS		32		20
%	%	%	%	%	%	**ASSETS**		%		%
			9.7			Cash & Equivalents		10.5		22.5
			27.9			Trade Receivables (net)		28.0		19.7
			33.8			Inventory		28.9		25.0
			.7			All Other Current		3.1		5.2
			72.1			Total Current		70.6		72.3
			19.6			Fixed Assets (net)		20.1		11.9
			5.3			Intangibles (net)		5.3		9.0
			3.0			All Other Non-Current		4.0		6.7
			100.0			Total		100.0		100.0
						LIABILITIES				
			4.8			Notes Payable-Short Term		10.9		7.7
			2.5			Cur. Mat.-L.T.D.		2.0		6.4
			19.4			Trade Payables		13.9		9.6
			.3			Income Taxes Payable		.1		.0
			16.8			All Other Current		9.8		15.5
			43.6			Total Current		36.8		39.1
			11.4			Long-Term Debt		10.9		11.2
			.2			Deferred Taxes		.5		.4
			3.5			All Other Non-Current		6.6		6.8
			41.3			Net Worth		45.2		42.5
			100.0			Total Liabilities & Net Worth		100.0		100.0
						INCOME DATA				
			100.0			Net Sales		100.0		100.0
			35.0			Gross Profit		27.9		36.0
			22.0			Operating Expenses		24.7		34.5
			13.0			Operating Profit		3.3		1.6
			.9			All Other Expenses (net)		.2		-1.1
			12.1			Profit Before Taxes		3.1		2.7
						RATIOS				
			3.8					3.1		5.0
			2.3			Current		2.2		2.8
			.9					1.3		1.5
			2.1					1.6		2.9
			1.2			Quick		1.2		1.5
			.5					.6		.6
		43	8.4				40	9.2	34	10.6
		60	6.1			Sales/Receivables	51	7.1	50	7.3
		72	5.1				61	6.0	60	6.1
		83	4.4				55	6.6	50	7.3
		91	4.0			Cost of Sales/Inventory	68	5.4	69	5.3
		152	2.4				99	3.7	130	2.8
		28	12.9				17	20.9	13	28.4
		34	10.7			Cost of Sales/Payables	26	14.1	25	14.4
		99	3.7				45	8.2	54	6.8
			2.6					4.2		3.4
			5.4			Sales/Working Capital		5.6		4.0
			-31.8					12.6		8.6
			62.4					16.0		9.0
		(11)	13.5			EBIT/Interest	(27)	6.4	(13)	3.0
			6.2					-.2		-2.5
						Net Profit + Depr., Dep., Amort./Cur. Mat. L/T/D				
			.3					.1		.1
			.7			Fixed/Worth		.4		.2
			-1.4					1.1		1.1
			.4					.4		.4
			1.0			Debt/Worth		1.1		1.1
			-10.2					5.0		NM
								29.0		21.4
						% Profit Before Taxes/Tangible Net Worth	(26)	17.4	(15)	10.4
								8.9		.0
			28.0					14.8		10.1
			18.6			% Profit Before Taxes/Total Assets		8.5		4.7
			11.6					-1.7		-1.2
			14.4					33.0		46.2
			10.7			Sales/Net Fixed Assets		8.6		16.7
			6.6					6.4		8.1
			2.1					2.6		2.5
			1.9			Sales/Total Assets		1.9		1.6
			1.5					1.4		.9
			.8					.7		.4
		(10)	1.6			% Depr., Dep., Amort./Sales	(26)	1.9	(13)	1.6
			2.3					3.5		4.0
						% Officers', Directors', Owners' Comp/Sales				
111M	4474M	168076M	496675M	285076M	1326709M	Net Sales ($)		1774260M		681512M
243M	3320M	42077M	279368M	163569M	739665M	Total Assets ($)		1064990M		590860M

© RMA 2024   M = $ thousand   MM = $ million
See Pages viii through xx for Explanation of Ratios and Data

MANUFACTURING—Power, Distribution, and Specialty Transformer Manufacturing NAICS 335311

Comparative Historical Data / Current Data Sorted by Sales

						Type of Statement						
	1		3		2	Unqualified						2
	3		6		7	Reviewed					1	6
			1			Compiled						
	1		1		6	Tax Returns	1	1		1	2	1
	8		13		17	Other		1		2	2	12
	4/1/21-3/31/22 ALL		4/1/22-3/31/23 ALL		4/1/23-3/31/24 ALL		0-1MM	1-3MM	4 (4/1-9/30/23) 3-5MM	5-10MM	28 (10/1/23-3/31/24) 10-25MM	25MM & OVER
	13		24		32	NUMBER OF STATEMENTS	1	2		3	5	21
	%		%		%	ASSETS	%	%	%	%	%	%
	6.9		13.3		15.2	Cash & Equivalents						15.2
	27.1		27.7		26.9	Trade Receivables (net)						27.6
	25.5		26.3		31.9	Inventory						31.5
	1.3		2.0		3.8	All Other Current			D			2.5
	60.8		69.4		77.9	Total Current			A			76.9
	14.0		15.4		12.2	Fixed Assets (net)			T			14.8
	16.0		7.6		7.4	Intangibles (net)			A			4.9
	9.2		7.6		2.6	All Other Non-Current						3.5
	100.0		100.0		100.0	Total			N			100.0
						LIABILITIES			O			
	4.0		5.0		4.3	Notes Payable-Short Term			T			4.6
	1.6		1.7		2.0	Cur. Mat.-L.T.D.						2.1
	10.4		12.7		17.0	Trade Payables			A			16.2
	.0		.0		.2	Income Taxes Payable			V			.1
	21.9		17.1		20.4	All Other Current			A			19.3
	37.8		36.5		44.0	Total Current			I			42.3
	15.5		8.9		14.1	Long-Term Debt			L			12.0
	.1		.3		.1	Deferred Taxes			A			.2
	2.0		3.5		3.5	All Other Non-Current			B			4.4
	44.6		50.8		38.3	Net Worth			L			41.1
	100.0		100.0		100.0	Total Liabilities & Net Worth			E			100.0
						INCOME DATA						
	100.0		100.0		100.0	Net Sales						100.0
	29.1		30.2		33.6	Gross Profit						33.4
	28.2		19.2		22.7	Operating Expenses						19.9
	1.0		10.9		11.0	Operating Profit						13.5
	.4		1.1		.4	All Other Expenses (net)						.4
	.6		9.9		10.6	Profit Before Taxes						13.2
						RATIOS						
	3.9		2.8		3.3							3.1
	2.4		2.1		1.9	Current						1.9
	1.5		1.4		1.0							1.2
	2.3		1.4		1.8							1.9
	1.2		1.1		1.1	Quick						.8
	.7		.9		.5							.5
42	8.6	46	8.0	36	10.0						45	8.2
57	6.4	59	6.2	53	6.9	Sales/Receivables					54	6.7
78	4.7	83	4.4	63	5.8						63	5.8
35	10.3	58	6.3	81	4.5						83	4.4
83	4.4	94	3.9	94	3.9	Cost of Sales/Inventory					91	4.0
107	3.4	122	3.0	159	2.3						122	3.0
15	24.3	22	16.6	21	17.2						20	18.0
35	10.4	34	10.8	33	10.9	Cost of Sales/Payables					36	10.2
54	6.8	48	7.6	51	7.1						49	7.4
	3.5		3.2		3.0							3.3
	5.0		4.9		6.1	Sales/Working Capital						6.2
	12.3		7.1		NM							NM
			22.0		60.9							74.3
		(19)	9.9	(27)	16.4	EBIT/Interest					(17)	13.5
			3.3		6.2							6.8
						Net Profit + Depr., Dep., Amort./Cur. Mat. L/T/D						
	.1		.2		.1							.1
	.5		.4		.5	Fixed/Worth						.5
	-.6		.8		NM							NM
	.5		.6		.5							.5
	1.5		1.2		2.6	Debt/Worth						1.7
	-9.7		2.0		-19.4							NM
			49.1		112.9							133.2
		(22)	33.5	(23)	53.2	% Profit Before Taxes/Tangible Net Worth					(16)	56.8
			12.2		19.3							17.7
	13.5		21.2		33.0							35.2
	5.0		12.9		17.3	% Profit Before Taxes/Total Assets						20.6
	-2.2		5.6		9.6							10.7
	30.0		39.7		112.9							53.3
	17.3		13.3		21.4	Sales/Net Fixed Assets						13.4
	7.3		5.2		10.3							9.0
	2.2		2.2		2.3							2.3
	1.5		1.7		1.9	Sales/Total Assets						2.0
	1.1		1.0		1.2							1.4
			.4		.6							.6
		(20)	1.2	(21)	.9	% Depr., Dep., Amort./Sales					(15)	.9
			2.8		2.3							2.3
						% Officers', Directors' Owners' Comp/Sales						
	773315M		1424514M		2281121M	Net Sales ($)	111M	4474M		22578M	95674M	2158284M
	643985M		1164142M		1228242M	Total Assets ($)	243M	3320M		17177M	46577M	1160925M

© RMA 2024   M = $ thousand   MM = $ million
See Pages viii through xx for Explanation of Ratios and Data

MANUFACTURING—Motor and Generator Manufacturing NAICS 335312

Current Data Sorted by Assets

						Type of Statement		
				2		Unqualified		
		2	3	2		Reviewed		
	2	2	2	1		Compiled		
	1	1	1	2		Tax Returns		
2	1	8	9	2	2	Other		
	10 (4/1-9/30/23)		31 (10/1/23-3/31/24)					
0-500M	500M-2MM	2-10MM	10-50MM	50-100MM	100-250MM	NUMBER OF STATEMENTS		
2	4	14	15	4	2			
%	%	%	%	%	%	ASSETS		
		12.4	10.2			Cash & Equivalents		
		26.6	18.6			Trade Receivables (net)		
		35.5	33.8			Inventory		
		6.5	2.4			All Other Current		
		81.0	64.9			Total Current		
		11.4	22.9			Fixed Assets (net)		
		3.4	3.3			Intangibles (net)		
		4.2	8.9			All Other Non-Current		
		100.0	100.0			Total		
						LIABILITIES		
		6.0	4.1			Notes Payable-Short Term		
		2.1	2.0			Cur. Mat.-L.T.D.		
		11.5	5.6			Trade Payables		
		.1	.0			Income Taxes Payable		
		25.9	20.0			All Other Current		
		45.6	31.7			Total Current		
		10.6	10.2			Long-Term Debt		
		.8	.3			Deferred Taxes		
		.0	1.4			All Other Non-Current		
		43.0	56.4			Net Worth		
		100.0	100.0			Total Liabilities & Net Worth		
						INCOME DATA		
		100.0	100.0			Net Sales		
		40.3	27.8			Gross Profit		
		33.5	23.5			Operating Expenses		
		6.9	4.4			Operating Profit		
		.1	.2			All Other Expenses (net)		
		6.8	4.1			Profit Before Taxes		
						RATIOS		
		5.4	2.7					
		2.1	2.1			Current		
		1.3	1.6					
		2.6	1.2					
		.8	1.0			Quick		
		.5	.6					
	26	14.2	20	18.6				
	47	7.7	40	9.1		Sales/Receivables		
	79	4.6	59	6.2				
	51	7.2	54	6.7				
	118	3.1	104	3.5		Cost of Sales/Inventory		
	203	1.8	146	2.5				
	13	28.5	3	125.5				
	30	12.2	21	17.4		Cost of Sales/Payables		
	63	5.8	29	12.4				
		2.9	3.2					
		5.1	5.1			Sales/Working Capital		
		25.0	6.0					
		63.1	138.2					
		13.4	(10)	18.0		EBIT/Interest		
		2.0	7.5					
						Net Profit + Depr., Dep., Amort./Cur. Mat. L/T/D		
		.1	.4					
		.4	.4			Fixed/Worth		
		NM	.6					
		.4	.5					
		1.1	.8			Debt/Worth		
		NM	1.4					
		52.3	24.8					
	(11)	21.5	22.3			% Profit Before Taxes/Tangible Net Worth		
		4.2	6.2					
		18.8	15.1					
		14.3	9.7			% Profit Before Taxes/Total Assets		
		2.1	3.4					
		111.5	10.2					
		27.1	8.4			Sales/Net Fixed Assets		
		10.0	5.4					
		2.5	2.0					
		1.9	1.6			Sales/Total Assets		
		1.4	1.1					
			.6					
			1.1			% Depr., Dep., Amort./Sales		
			1.7					
						% Officers', Directors' Owners' Comp/Sales		
5073M	8883M	166447M	740555M	284106M	290276M	Net Sales ($)		
416M	4879M	81915M	449499M	256771M	229402M	Total Assets ($)		

Comparative Historical Data

	3		3
	5		2
	2		
	4		2
	19		11
	4/1/19-3/31/20		4/1/20-3/31/21
	ALL		ALL
	33		18
	%		%
	7.0		14.6
	27.9		20.8
	34.4		30.9
	2.8		1.9
	72.2		68.1
	18.8		17.9
	3.9		9.3
	5.1		4.8
	100.0		100.0
	16.3		11.6
	2.4		4.6
	12.9		8.1
	.1		1.0
	13.2		9.6
	44.9		34.9
	11.3		6.7
	.2		.1
	3.3		9.1
	40.3		49.2
	100.0		100.0
	100.0		100.0
	27.2		31.4
	22.0		29.4
	5.2		2.0
	.6		-1.5
	4.5		3.6
	2.4		4.9
	1.7		2.4
	1.3		1.4
	1.6		3.0
	.8		1.5
	.4		.5
39	9.3	30	12.1
49	7.5	52	7.0
60	6.1	64	5.7
49	7.5	46	8.0
99	3.7	85	4.3
140	2.6	182	2.0
16	22.3	11	32.7
29	12.6	24	15.0
43	8.4	31	11.6
	4.6		3.1
	6.3		5.3
	13.2		7.8
	55.4		29.3
(32)	6.3	(15)	10.2
	1.7		-.4
	.2		.2
	.6		.4
	1.3		.6
	.7		.3
	1.7		.7
	4.1		4.6
	55.9		28.6
(29)	27.3	(15)	21.9
	4.7		10.8
	16.4		16.3
	7.5		9.8
	1.1		-4.4
	25.2		29.4
	11.6		11.2
	6.6		5.1
	2.6		2.1
	1.8		1.6
	1.5		1.2
	.3		1.3
(31)	1.3	(14)	1.6
	2.1		3.3
	1794790M		747309M
	966992M		514635M

© RMA 2024

M = $ thousand   MM = $ million
See Pages viii through xx for Explanation of Ratios and Data

MANUFACTURING—Motor and Generator Manufacturing NAICS 335312

Comparative Historical Data / Current Data Sorted by Sales

							Type of Statement							
		3		4		2	Unqualified					1	1	2
				3		5	Reviewed							3
				2		6	Compiled		2		1	2	2	1
		4		1		4	Tax Returns		1		1	2		
		11		16		24	Other		2	2	1	9		10
		4/1/21-		4/1/22-		4/1/23-			10 (4/1-9/30/23)			31 (10/1/23-3/31/24)		
		3/31/22		3/31/23		3/31/24		0-1MM	1-3MM	3-5MM	5-10MM	10-25MM	25MM & OVER
		ALL		ALL		ALL	NUMBER OF STATEMENTS							
		18		26		41		5	3	3	14	16
		%		%		%	ASSETS	%	%	%	%	%	%
		11.8		14.1		13.5	Cash & Equivalents					11.4	12.1
		29.7		28.4		22.6	Trade Receivables (net)	D				23.3	20.1
		27.0		28.3		32.6	Inventory	A				32.5	35.0
		8.5		4.8		3.4	All Other Current	T				3.5	1.9
		77.0		75.5		72.1	Total Current	A				70.7	69.0
		14.9		16.3		17.3	Fixed Assets (net)					17.5	23.1
		4.8		2.3		4.3	Intangibles (net)	N				6.1	1.2
		3.3		5.8		6.4	All Other Non-Current	O				5.8	6.6
		100.0		100.0		100.0	Total	T				100.0	100.0
							LIABILITIES	A					
		5.2		7.8		16.0	Notes Payable-Short Term	V				3.9	7.5
		.8		1.5		1.8	Cur. Mat.-L.T.D.	A				2.2	1.6
		17.4		12.5		7.5	Trade Payables	I				10.9	6.8
		.1		.1		.0	Income Taxes Payable	L				.1	.0
		19.9		13.8		21.7	All Other Current	A				24.8	22.8
		43.4		35.7		47.0	Total Current	B				41.9	38.8
		16.3		11.7		10.2	Long-Term Debt	L				9.5	11.2
		.2		.2		.4	Deferred Taxes	E				.8	.3
		6.0		5.4		1.8	All Other Non-Current					.0	3.3
		34.1		47.1		40.5	Net Worth					47.9	46.4
		100.0		100.0		100.0	Total Liabilties & Net Worth					100.0	100.0
							INCOME DATA						
		100.0		100.0		100.0	Net Sales					100.0	100.0
		33.3		33.6		31.7	Gross Profit					34.8	22.0
		27.2		29.8		26.2	Operating Expenses					32.3	17.2
		6.1		3.8		5.5	Operating Profit					2.6	4.8
		-.4		.3		.3	All Other Expenses (net)					.1	.6
		6.5		3.5		5.2	Profit Before Taxes					2.5	4.2
							RATIOS						
		3.9		3.6		3.5						4.7	2.4
		2.2		2.1		2.0	Current					2.1	1.7
		1.2		1.5		1.4						1.3	1.3
		1.6		1.6		1.5						2.1	1.0
		1.0		1.2		.8	Quick					1.0	.8
		.6		.7		.6						.5	.6
38	9.5	46	7.9	24	14.9						21	17.1	22	16.4
57	6.4	58	6.3	47	7.7	Sales/Receivables					37	9.8	47	7.8
81	4.5	74	4.9	72	5.1						60	6.1	65	5.6
19	18.9	46	7.9	54	6.8						49	7.5	66	5.5
89	4.1	81	4.5	104	3.5	Cost of Sales/Inventory					99	3.7	104	3.5
174	2.1	130	2.8	146	2.5						152	2.4	130	2.8
24	15.0	23	15.8	6	59.8						13	28.5	4	99.2
51	7.1	38	9.6	21	17.3	Cost of Sales/Payables					24	15.1	24	15.1
78	4.7	51	7.1	34	10.8						45	8.2	30	12.0
		3.2		3.2		3.1						3.0	4.8
		4.9		4.3		5.3	Sales/Working Capital					5.1	5.4
		11.6		8.4		9.5						25.0	10.3
		79.3		38.7		63.1						59.2	147.4
(17)	26.8	(22)	7.6	(34)	12.8	EBIT/Interest					15.6	(11)	9.0
		5.6		3.7		.1						5.8	.0
							Net Profit + Depr., Dep., Amort./Cur. Mat. L/T/D						
		.2		.1		.1						.2	.4
		.4		.3		.4	Fixed/Worth					.4	.4
		NM		.5		.8						.7	.7
		.5		.4		.5						.4	.6
		.8		1.1		1.3	Debt/Worth					.6	1.3
		NM		2.5		2.4						4.2	2.1
		33.1		35.8		31.5						44.9	24.3
(14)	29.6	(24)	19.0	(35)	21.5	% Profit Before Taxes/Tangible Net Worth					(12)	22.9	11.7
		16.3		5.4		3.2						1.2	-3.9
		18.1		13.7		15.5						16.9	11.0
		13.0		7.0		10.8	% Profit Before Taxes/Total Assets					14.3	4.9
		6.1		2.2		1.0						5.7	-1.5
		61.9		24.4		70.5						94.9	10.1
		11.0		11.3		10.3	Sales/Net Fixed Assets					10.6	8.5
		6.0		7.1		8.0						5.2	5.0
		2.5		2.3		2.1						2.5	2.0
		1.9		1.7		1.6	Sales/Total Assets					1.8	1.6
		1.0		1.3		1.2						1.2	1.3
		1.2		.8		.6						.8	.6
(12)	1.9	(19)	1.4	(29)	1.3	% Depr., Dep., Amort./Sales					(11)	1.3	(13)	1.1
		2.7		2.1		2.0						1.6	2.3
							% Officers', Directors' Owners' Comp/Sales						
		1073604M		1431574M		1495340M	Net Sales ($)		8078M	11931M	24389M	223947M	1226995M
		538750M		1003216M		1022882M	Total Assets ($)		8673M	5350M	19459M	144505M	844895M

© RMA 2024
M = $ thousand   MM = $ million
See Pages viii through xx for Explanation of Ratios and Data

MANUFACTURING—Switchgear and Switchboard Apparatus Manufacturing NAICS 335313

Current Data Sorted by Assets / Comparative Historical Data

0-500M	500M-2MM	2-10MM	10-50MM	50-100MM	100-250MM	Type of Statement	4/1/19-3/31/20 ALL	4/1/20-3/31/21 ALL
				2	3	Unqualified	3	3
		2				Reviewed	5	1
		4	1			Compiled	5	1
		4	4		2	Tax Returns	3	3
4 (4/1-9/30/23)			18 (10/1/23-3/31/24)			Other	12	9
		10	7		5	NUMBER OF STATEMENTS	28	17
%	%	%	%	%	%	ASSETS	%	%
D	D	15.4	D			Cash & Equivalents	10.4	14.4
A	A	30.0	A			Trade Receivables (net)	33.8	31.8
T	T	35.0	T			Inventory	24.9	23.8
A	A	.1	A			All Other Current	2.6	4.3
		80.4				Total Current	71.6	74.3
N	N	3.2	N			Fixed Assets (net)	14.5	12.9
O	O	6.6	O			Intangibles (net)	4.5	6.0
T	T	9.7	T			All Other Non-Current	9.4	6.8
		100.0				Total	100.0	100.0
A	A		A			LIABILITIES		
V	V	13.5	V			Notes Payable-Short Term	14.6	7.8
A	A	.1	A			Cur. Mat.-L.T.D.	1.7	3.5
I	I	10.3	I			Trade Payables	10.2	11.1
L	L	.0	L			Income Taxes Payable	.3	.9
A	A	19.3	A			All Other Current	22.2	8.6
B	B	43.3	B			Total Current	49.0	31.9
L	L	7.2	L			Long-Term Debt	6.5	12.5
E	E	.0	E			Deferred Taxes	.1	.1
		2.9				All Other Non-Current	5.6	6.2
		46.6				Net Worth	38.8	49.2
		100.0				Total Liabilties & Net Worth	100.0	100.0
						INCOME DATA		
		100.0				Net Sales	100.0	100.0
		30.9				Gross Profit	31.1	33.2
		19.2				Operating Expenses	25.3	28.9
		11.7				Operating Profit	5.8	4.3
		.3				All Other Expenses (net)	.7	-1.0
		11.5				Profit Before Taxes	5.1	5.3
						RATIOS		
		13.7					4.8	3.4
		4.1				Current	1.9	2.8
		1.5					1.2	1.9
		7.6					2.9	2.1
		2.3				Quick	1.3	1.4
		.7					.5	.9
		30 12.3					44 8.3	38 9.5
		47 7.8				Sales/Receivables	51 7.1	57 6.4
		61 6.0					66 5.5	65 5.6
		47 7.8					34 10.8	37 9.9
		99 3.7				Cost of Sales/Inventory	65 5.6	65 5.6
		159 2.3					89 4.1	76 4.8
		11 34.5					11 32.7	10 37.0
		19 19.4				Cost of Sales/Payables	22 16.8	30 12.3
		41 9.0					31 11.6	43 8.5
		3.2					4.0	3.2
		4.1				Sales/Working Capital	7.1	6.0
		NM					19.0	9.5
							17.5	13.5
						EBIT/Interest	(24) 6.9	(15) 9.3
							-2.7	1.8
						Net Profit + Depr., Dep., Amort./Cur. Mat. L/T/D		
		.0					.2	.1
		.0				Fixed/Worth	.3	.2
		NM					.9	1.2
		.2					.3	.4
		.6				Debt/Worth	1.2	.8
		NM					3.2	15.1
							65.5	37.6
						% Profit Before Taxes/Tangible Net Worth	(23) 24.4	(15) 19.8
							.7	-3.3
		46.4					22.7	18.3
		17.0				% Profit Before Taxes/Total Assets	13.3	10.7
		1.0					-6.2	-.4
		422.2					29.5	40.3
		86.7				Sales/Net Fixed Assets	16.0	25.1
		40.9					10.9	12.6
		2.5					2.5	3.2
		2.3				Sales/Total Assets	2.1	2.1
		1.3					1.8	1.6
							.5	.5
						% Depr., Dep., Amort./Sales	(24) .9	(12) .7
							1.4	.9
						% Officers', Directors' Owners' Comp/Sales		
		108767M	291038M		942667M	Net Sales ($)	997338M	752515M
		49348M	167228M		733241M	Total Assets ($)	501799M	455539M

M = $ thousand   MM = $ million
See Pages viii through xx for Explanation of Ratios and Data

© RMA 2024

MANUFACTURING—Switchgear and Switchboard Apparatus Manufacturing NAICS 335313

Comparative Historical Data | Current Data Sorted by Sales

							Type of Statement							
		2		4		3	Unqualified						2	3
		1		1		2	Reviewed					2	2	
				2		2	Compiled			1	2	2		
				2		5	Tax Returns			1	2			7
		8		16		10	Other		4 (4/1-9/30/23)			18 (10/1/23-3/31/24)		
		4/1/21-3/31/22		4/1/22-3/31/23		4/1/23-3/31/24		0-1MM	1-3MM	3-5MM	5-10MM	10-25MM	25MM & OVER	
		ALL		ALL		ALL								
		11		25		22	NUMBER OF STATEMENTS			2	4	6	10	
		%		%		%	ASSETS	%	%	%	%	%	%	
		13.8		20.3		15.2	Cash & Equivalents	D	D				11.5	
		28.0		29.2		26.5	Trade Receivables (net)	A	A				23.9	
		25.0		23.9		27.4	Inventory	T	T				27.1	
		3.7		3.8		1.1	All Other Current	A	A				1.9	
		70.4		77.2		70.2	Total Current						64.4	
		8.7		12.3		8.7	Fixed Assets (net)	N	N				10.7	
		15.7		5.2		6.8	Intangibles (net)	O	O				7.0	
		5.1		5.3		14.3	All Other Non-Current	T	T				17.9	
		100.0		100.0		100.0	Total						100.0	
							LIABILITIES	A	A					
		18.0		14.7		10.3	Notes Payable-Short Term	V	V				9.2	
		.8		.9		.4	Cur. Mat.-L.T.D.	A	A				.2	
		32.2		9.0		8.4	Trade Payables	I	I				7.3	
		.4		.5		.0	Income Taxes Payable	L	L				.0	
		18.2		17.5		18.3	All Other Current	A	A				20.2	
		69.6		42.6		37.3	Total Current	B	B				36.9	
		7.3		6.5		7.0	Long-Term Debt	L	L				7.3	
		.2		.0		.0	Deferred Taxes	E	E				.0	
		2.8		4.0		5.1	All Other Non-Current						5.4	
		20.1		46.8		50.6	Net Worth						50.3	
		100.0		100.0		100.0	Total Liabilities & Net Worth						100.0	
							INCOME DATA							
		100.0		100.0		100.0	Net Sales						100.0	
		33.4		33.2		35.9	Gross Profit						41.2	
		27.3		28.4		21.0	Operating Expenses						22.5	
		6.1		4.7		14.9	Operating Profit						18.7	
		-.5		-1.1		.2	All Other Expenses (net)						1.3	
		6.6		5.9		14.7	Profit Before Taxes						17.4	
							RATIOS							
		3.6		3.7		6.8							3.7	
		2.8		2.9		2.9	Current						2.3	
		.6		1.6		1.7							1.2	
		2.1		2.6		3.8							1.8	
		1.2		1.4		1.5	Quick						1.3	
		.4		.9		.8							.6	
42	8.6		45	8.1	46	7.9							42	8.7
51	7.2		60	6.1	58	6.3	Sales/Receivables						61	6.0
59	6.2		89	4.1	70	5.2							70	5.2
46	8.0		35	10.4	56	6.5							69	5.3
94	3.9		94	3.9	99	3.7	Cost of Sales/Inventory						104	3.5
114	3.2		122	3.0	152	2.4							140	2.6
20	17.9		17	22.1	13	28.5							11	32.6
26	13.9		30	12.1	28	13.0	Cost of Sales/Payables						30	12.2
69	5.3		52	7.0	41	8.9							41	8.9
		2.9		2.9		3.2							3.7	
		4.2		3.4		4.1	Sales/Working Capital						4.3	
		-4.1		5.4		6.1							14.6	
				125.3		365.9								
			(22)	17.6	(14)	21.4	EBIT/Interest							
				2.3		6.2								
							Net Profit + Depr., Dep., Amort./Cur. Mat. L/T/D							
		.1		.2		.0							.1	
		.4		.3		.2	Fixed/Worth						.2	
		-.3		.6		.7							.7	
		.5		.4		.4							.4	
		2.9		1.0		.6	Debt/Worth						1.3	
		-3.8		2.3		4.1							4.1	
				42.2		82.4	% Profit Before Taxes/Tangible Net Worth						101.2	
			(22)	21.4	(20)	52.2							60.2	
				4.6		31.8							39.4	
		22.6		18.8		34.5							36.3	
		17.6		8.5		19.8	% Profit Before Taxes/Total Assets						24.0	
		.3		1.8		8.0							7.0	
		44.7		33.6		85.0							26.2	
		22.0		12.3		24.2	Sales/Net Fixed Assets						15.5	
		11.4		10.0		13.5							12.9	
		1.7		2.0		2.4							2.2	
		1.5		1.5		1.6	Sales/Total Assets						1.6	
		1.2		1.2		1.2							1.2	
				.3		.4								
			(18)	1.5	(12)	.8	% Depr., Dep., Amort./Sales							
				2.2		1.8								
							% Officers', Directors' Owners' Comp/Sales							
		436777M		1198638M		1342472M	Net Sales ($)		8228M	31410M	96406M		1206428M	
		306173M		832509M		949817M	Total Assets ($)		5591M	15735M	68052M		860439M	

© RMA 2024
M = $ thousand   MM = $ million
See Pages viii through xx for Explanation of Ratios and Data

MANUFACTURING—Relay and Industrial Control Manufacturing NAICS 335314

Current Data Sorted by Assets | Comparative Historical Data

	0-500M	500M-2MM	2-10MM	10-50MM	50-100MM	100-250MM	Type of Statement		4/1/19-3/31/20 ALL		4/1/20-3/31/21 ALL
		2	4	1			Unqualified		1		1
			2	2		1	Reviewed		10		4
		2		2			Compiled		2		
		2	3	1			Tax Returns		6		2
				3	3	2	Other		14		11
		4 (4/1-9/30/23)		25 (10/1/23-3/31/24)							
		4	9	9	4	3	NUMBER OF STATEMENTS		33		18
	%	%	%	%	%	%	ASSETS		%		%
							Cash & Equivalents		14.6		16.4
							Trade Receivables (net)		26.3		23.1
							Inventory		28.3		25.2
							All Other Current		1.0		3.3
							Total Current		70.2		68.1
DATA NOT AVAILABLE							Fixed Assets (net)		14.3		14.3
							Intangibles (net)		9.9		11.1
							All Other Non-Current		5.6		6.6
							Total		100.0		100.0
							LIABILITIES				
							Notes Payable-Short Term		6.2		3.7
							Cur. Mat.-L.T.D.		1.3		3.2
							Trade Payables		9.4		10.9
							Income Taxes Payable		.2		.0
							All Other Current		8.2		7.4
							Total Current		25.3		25.2
							Long-Term Debt		8.2		19.6
							Deferred Taxes		.1		.2
							All Other Non-Current		3.7		14.9
							Net Worth		62.6		40.1
							Total Liabilities & Net Worth		100.0		100.0
							INCOME DATA				
							Net Sales		100.0		100.0
							Gross Profit		42.6		34.5
							Operating Expenses		33.4		26.6
							Operating Profit		9.2		7.9
							All Other Expenses (net)		.6		1.4
							Profit Before Taxes		8.6		6.5
							RATIOS				
							Current		5.2		6.4
									3.2		3.7
									1.9		1.7
							Quick		2.4		4.0
									1.6		2.3
									1.3		1.0
							Sales/Receivables	41	9.0	33	10.9
								49	7.5	58	6.3
								65	5.6	69	5.3
							Cost of Sales/Inventory	61	6.0	38	9.7
								114	3.2	114	3.2
								166	2.2	203	1.8
							Cost of Sales/Payables	11	31.9	10	36.8
								27	13.7	32	11.5
								38	9.7	62	5.9
							Sales/Working Capital		2.6		2.2
									4.2		3.3
									6.4		6.8
							EBIT/Interest		23.5		91.6
								(25)	9.9	(17)	3.2
									3.8		.8
							Net Profit + Depr., Dep., Amort./Cur. Mat. L/T/D				
							Fixed/Worth		.1		.1
									.2		.2
									.4		.4
							Debt/Worth		.3		.2
									.5		.5
									1.8		4.1
							% Profit Before Taxes/Tangible Net Worth		38.4		20.7
								(30)	18.5	(15)	9.2
									7.2		-.9
							% Profit Before Taxes/Total Assets		23.0		16.4
									8.5		6.7
									4.4		.1
							Sales/Net Fixed Assets		53.0		42.3
									17.1		18.5
									9.3		5.2
							Sales/Total Assets		2.4		2.2
									1.8		1.3
									1.1		.9
							% Depr., Dep., Amort./Sales		.8		.7
								(27)	1.7	(14)	1.7
									2.4		3.7
							% Officers', Directors' Owners' Comp/Sales		2.7		
								(11)	7.2		
									8.6		
		14151M	135004M	280442M	407034M	652330M	Net Sales ($)		599818M		428355M
		5373M	53618M	166578M	307670M	612735M	Total Assets ($)		515230M		432408M

M = $ thousand   MM = $ million
See Pages viii through xx for Explanation of Ratios and Data

© RMA 2024

MANUFACTURING—Relay and Industrial Control Manufacturing NAICS 335314

Comparative Historical Data | **Current Data Sorted by Sales**

							Type of Statement							
		2		2		2	Unqualified					1	1	1
		4		4		7	Reviewed				3	2	2	2
		1		2		4	Compiled				1	1	1	2
		1		3		3	Tax Returns			2				1
		14		14		13	Other		1	1		4		7
		4/1/21-3/31/22 ALL		4/1/22-3/31/23 ALL		4/1/23-3/31/24 ALL		0-1MM	4 (4/1-9/30/23) 1-3MM	3-5MM	25 (10/1/23-3/31/24) 5-10MM	10-25MM		25MM & OVER
		22		25		29	NUMBER OF STATEMENTS		1	3	4	8		13
		%		%		%	ASSETS	%	%	%	%	%		%
		15.5		11.5		14.4	Cash & Equivalents	D						7.5
		27.9		29.7		27.2	Trade Receivables (net)	A						26.0
		26.8		31.8		27.7	Inventory	T						32.0
		5.3		2.8		3.3	All Other Current	A						2.8
		75.5		75.8		72.5	Total Current							68.3
		14.2		13.4		12.8	Fixed Assets (net)	N						10.6
		7.8		3.6		6.2	Intangibles (net)	O						11.5
		2.6		7.2		8.4	All Other Non-Current	T						9.7
		100.0		100.0		100.0	Total							100.0
							LIABILITIES	A						
		3.8		7.2		5.0	Notes Payable-Short Term	V						5.3
		2.3		2.0		1.4	Cur. Mat.-L.T.D.	A						1.1
		12.3		15.5		9.7	Trade Payables	I						10.7
		.0		.3		.4	Income Taxes Payable	L						.7
		11.9		10.0		14.6	All Other Current	A						19.8
		30.3		35.0		31.0	Total Current	B						37.5
		13.0		12.9		10.7	Long-Term Debt	L						12.0
		.1		.0		.3	Deferred Taxes	E						.1
		4.1		7.1		9.0	All Other Non-Current							7.0
		52.5		45.0		48.9	Net Worth							43.4
		100.0		100.0		100.0	Total Liabilities & Net Worth							100.0
							INCOME DATA							
		100.0		100.0		100.0	Net Sales							100.0
		34.7		36.8		39.5	Gross Profit							36.2
		27.1		28.2		28.2	Operating Expenses							23.5
		7.6		8.6		11.4	Operating Profit							12.7
		-2.6		.9		1.3	All Other Expenses (net)							2.5
		10.2		7.6		10.0	Profit Before Taxes							10.2
							RATIOS							
		6.7		3.3		3.8								3.0
		2.5		2.1		2.5	Current							2.4
		1.9		1.5		1.7								1.3
		3.2		1.7		2.2								1.7
		1.6		1.2		1.3	Quick							1.2
		1.0		.9		.9								.5
39	9.3		47	7.8	36	10.2							40	9.1
54	6.7		57	6.4	52	7.0	Sales/Receivables						60	6.1
70	5.2		76	4.8	62	5.9							64	5.7
40	9.1		65	5.6	46	7.9							74	4.9
122	3.0		135	2.7	83	4.4	Cost of Sales/Inventory						111	3.3
166	2.2		159	2.3	174	2.1							192	1.9
14	25.3		36	10.1	15	24.5							22	16.9
29	12.6		46	8.0	26	13.8	Cost of Sales/Payables						35	10.3
54	6.8		62	5.9	54	6.8							63	5.8
		2.5		3.0		3.6								3.6
		3.9		4.4		4.4	Sales/Working Capital							4.2
		5.8		6.9		7.0								10.3
		46.9		80.9		60.3								37.2
(17)	10.9		(22)	5.3	(21)	4.8	EBIT/Interest						(10)	3.5
		1.5		1.3		1.3								-.1
							Net Profit + Depr., Dep., Amort./Cur. Mat. L/T/D							
		.1		.1		.1								.1
		.2		.2		.3	Fixed/Worth							.3
		.6		.9		.9								-.6
		.3		.7		.4								.5
		.9		1.2		1.0	Debt/Worth							1.4
		2.6		2.8		NM								-7.6
		74.4		57.1		74.5	% Profit Before Taxes/Tangible Net Worth							
(20)	31.8		(22)	15.1	(22)	35.1								
		7.0		1.2		9.7								
		25.1		20.4		34.5	% Profit Before Taxes/Total Assets							35.2
		14.4		6.7		11.0								6.9
		3.6		.4		2.6								-.3
		54.0		111.9		71.3								72.5
		19.3		25.5		20.3	Sales/Net Fixed Assets							18.8
		8.1		7.2		7.2								7.9
		2.3		2.4		2.4								2.3
		1.8		1.7		1.9	Sales/Total Assets							1.6
		1.5		1.1		1.2								1.0
		.4		.6		.5								
(20)	1.1		(14)	1.6	(21)	1.1	% Depr., Dep., Amort./Sales							
		2.3		2.7		2.0								
							% Officers', Directors' Owners' Comp/Sales							
		749947M		669262M		1488961M	Net Sales ($)		2652M	11499M	31317M	144466M		1299027M
		479987M		475448M		1145974M	Total Assets ($)		653M	4720M	17173M	79124M		1044304M

© RMA 2024 M = $ thousand MM = $ million
See Pages viii through xx for Explanation of Ratios and Data

MANUFACTURING—All Other Miscellaneous Electrical Equipment and Component Manufacturing NAICS 335999

Current Data Sorted by Assets | Comparative Historical Data

							Type of Statement		
			1	3	3	2	Unqualified	9	9
		1	6		1		Reviewed	15	4
		1					Compiled	5	2
		4					Tax Returns	16	7
1	2	21	17		9	6	Other	61	45
0-500M	500M-2MM	17 (4/1-9/30/23) 2-10MM	61 (10/1/23-3/31/24) 10-50MM		50-100MM	100-250MM		4/1/19-3/31/20 ALL	4/1/20-3/31/21 ALL
1	2	28	26		13	8	NUMBER OF STATEMENTS	106	67
%	%	%	%		%	%	ASSETS	%	%
		14.7	15.6		7.5		Cash & Equivalents	15.5	13.8
		21.1	19.5		21.3		Trade Receivables (net)	24.4	21.6
		39.1	34.9		41.0		Inventory	28.6	30.1
		1.3	3.1		2.1		All Other Current	3.1	3.9
		76.2	73.2		71.9		Total Current	71.5	69.3
		7.5	13.4		19.0		Fixed Assets (net)	15.9	15.1
		10.9	6.3		2.0		Intangibles (net)	8.3	9.9
		5.4	7.1		7.1		All Other Non-Current	4.3	5.7
		100.0	100.0		100.0		Total	100.0	100.0
							LIABILITIES		
		5.3	5.3		3.5		Notes Payable-Short Term	6.2	7.3
		1.0	1.1		1.0		Cur. Mat.-L.T.D.	2.3	2.3
		13.7	8.8		9.8		Trade Payables	11.7	10.0
		.1	.1		.2		Income Taxes Payable	.2	.1
		22.3	16.2		12.9		All Other Current	9.3	9.7
		42.3	31.5		27.4		Total Current	29.8	29.5
		6.1	12.0		3.8		Long-Term Debt	10.5	13.9
		.1	.2		.5		Deferred Taxes	.3	.5
		1.9	.7		6.4		All Other Non-Current	6.3	6.0
		49.7	55.5		61.9		Net Worth	53.2	50.1
		100.0	100.0		100.0		Total Liabilities & Net Worth	100.0	100.0
							INCOME DATA		
		100.0	100.0		100.0		Net Sales	100.0	100.0
		43.0	36.6		33.9		Gross Profit	38.3	39.7
		38.6	26.4		23.5		Operating Expenses	29.0	32.0
		4.4	10.2		10.4		Operating Profit	9.3	7.7
		.4	.9		-.3		All Other Expenses (net)	.9	.1
		4.0	9.3		10.7		Profit Before Taxes	8.4	7.6
							RATIOS		
		3.8	4.7		4.0			4.8	4.9
		1.9	2.4		2.8		Current	2.8	2.4
		1.2	1.6		2.0			1.8	1.6
		1.3	2.8		1.8			2.8	2.3
		1.0	1.2		1.2		Quick	1.4	1.1
		.4	.5		.6			.7	.6
	23	15.7	32	11.3	39	9.4		33 11.2	34 10.7
	40	9.2	48	7.6	47	7.8	Sales/Receivables	45 8.2	43 8.4
	53	6.9	72	5.1	55	6.6		59 6.2	55 6.6
	85	4.3	122	3.0	79	4.6		48 7.6	61 6.0
	126	2.9	159	2.3	135	2.7	Cost of Sales/Inventory	96 3.8	107 3.4
	281	1.3	228	1.6	203	1.8		135 2.7	159 2.3
	10	37.0	18	20.0	17	21.6		18 20.6	17 21.7
	26	14.1	30	12.1	20	17.9	Cost of Sales/Payables	32 11.5	26 13.8
	49	7.5	51	7.1	33	11.2		46 8.0	43 8.5
		3.5	2.0		2.4			2.9	2.8
		4.3	3.0		3.7		Sales/Working Capital	4.6	4.9
		27.8	5.2		5.8			7.7	7.7
		17.0	17.0		56.4			85.2	33.7
	(18)	3.3	(20)	10.4	(10)	19.3	EBIT/Interest	(83) 9.4	(60) 7.0
		-3.7	2.8		9.7			2.0	1.9
							Net Profit + Depr., Dep., Amort./Cur. Mat. L/T/D	7.5	5.1
								(22) 3.4	(13) 1.3
								2.2	-2.1
		.0	.1		.2			.1	.1
		.1	.2		.3		Fixed/Worth	.3	.3
		1.0	.5		.5			.7	.7
		.4	.3		.3			.3	.5
		1.1	.8		.6		Debt/Worth	.8	1.2
		3.7	2.4		1.2			3.2	2.7
		37.8	51.4		31.5			55.6	49.0
	(22)	25.3	(25)	20.2		25.9	% Profit Before Taxes/Tangible Net Worth	(93) 29.8	(59) 24.4
		-7.3	6.2		18.1			16.5	6.5
		22.2	17.8		20.6			26.5	23.6
		6.1	8.8		16.9		% Profit Before Taxes/Total Assets	14.6	10.3
		-4.9	2.9		9.5			4.3	2.2
		406.0	21.8		23.5			47.7	51.3
		63.0	14.4		9.4		Sales/Net Fixed Assets	14.1	17.1
		20.0	7.3		4.0			7.4	7.3
		2.4	1.5		2.2			2.5	2.1
		2.0	1.2		1.4		Sales/Total Assets	1.9	1.6
		1.1	1.0		1.0			1.4	1.1
		.3	.7		.9			.8	.7
	(14)	.9	(19)	1.3	(12)	1.3	% Depr., Dep., Amort./Sales	(80) 1.6	(50) 1.8
		4.1	2.0		1.8			3.1	3.4
							% Officers', Directors' Owners' Comp/Sales	1.5	1.2
								(25) 2.7	(21) 3.2
								5.5	6.6
402M	3621M	299200M	685904M		1453077M	1723874M	Net Sales ($)	4267934M	3021630M
199M	2133M	163075M	552159M		882411M	1304184M	Total Assets ($)	2936921M	2180938M

© RMA 2024   M = $ thousand   MM = $ million
See Pages viii through xx for Explanation of Ratios and Data

MANUFACTURING—All Other Miscellaneous Electrical Equipment and Component Manufacturing NAICS 335999

Comparative Historical Data | Current Data Sorted by Sales

				Type of Statement						
7	9	9		Unqualified				1	2	6
10	18	8		Reviewed				4	4	3
1	3	1		Compiled				1	1	
6	10	7		Tax Returns				2	2	
39	48	53		Other	1	2	2	10	19	22
4/1/21-3/31/22 ALL	4/1/22-3/31/23 ALL	4/1/23-3/31/24 ALL			17 (4/1-9/30/23)			61 (10/1/23-3/31/24)		
					0-1MM	1-3MM	3-5MM	5-10MM	10-25MM	25MM & OVER
63	88	78		NUMBER OF STATEMENTS	1	3	2	13	28	31
%	%	%		ASSETS	%	%	%	%	%	%
16.8	11.9	13.5		Cash & Equivalents				17.3	15.2	7.7
20.9	21.7	20.2		Trade Receivables (net)				19.5	20.3	21.1
29.7	36.5	35.1		Inventory				39.0	35.3	36.2
4.5	5.0	2.2		All Other Current				2.2	2.6	2.2
71.9	75.0	70.9		Total Current				78.0	73.4	67.2
15.8	13.1	14.1		Fixed Assets (net)				6.4	12.9	16.5
6.9	4.9	8.5		Intangibles (net)				10.7	8.9	7.7
5.4	7.0	6.5		All Other Non-Current				5.0	4.7	8.7
100.0	100.0	100.0		Total				100.0	100.0	100.0
				LIABILITIES						
6.6	7.7	4.4		Notes Payable-Short Term				5.4	5.5	3.6
1.9	2.1	1.4		Cur. Mat.-L.T.D.				1.4	1.1	1.1
10.7	15.3	10.7		Trade Payables				4.6	12.0	10.9
.1	.1	.2		Income Taxes Payable				.1	.1	.2
11.3	13.7	16.8		All Other Current				16.1	19.1	14.0
30.6	39.0	33.5		Total Current				27.7	37.8	29.8
14.8	11.7	9.3		Long-Term Debt				8.3	10.5	8.9
.2	.1	.2		Deferred Taxes				.2	.0	.5
11.9	3.0	2.5		All Other Non-Current				1.5	1.2	4.1
42.5	46.3	54.4		Net Worth				62.4	50.6	56.6
100.0	100.0	100.0		Total Liabilties & Net Worth				100.0	100.0	100.0
				INCOME DATA						
100.0	100.0	100.0		Net Sales				100.0	100.0	100.0
38.7	35.2	39.0		Gross Profit				52.2	36.3	34.3
29.5	26.3	30.9		Operating Expenses				44.1	30.4	24.2
9.2	9.0	8.1		Operating Profit				8.1	5.9	10.1
-1.9	.6	.5		All Other Expenses (net)				.7	.8	.4
11.1	8.4	7.5		Profit Before Taxes				7.4	5.1	9.7
				RATIOS						
5.5	4.0	4.0						7.0	3.6	3.9
2.4	2.0	2.3		Current				3.1	2.0	2.5
1.8	1.5	1.5						1.5	1.3	1.6
2.2	1.6	2.0						4.5	1.9	1.5
1.2	.9	1.0		Quick				1.1	1.0	.9
.7	.5	.5						.6	.5	.7
31 11.6	35 10.3	30 12.0			29 12.7		25 14.8	33 11.2		
45 8.1	47 7.7	46 7.9		Sales/Receivables	41 8.8		40 9.1	48 7.6		
55 6.6	57 6.4	62 5.9			65 5.6		59 6.2	69 5.3		
62 5.9	74 4.9	78 4.7			118 3.1		60 6.1	81 4.5		
114 3.2	130 2.8	140 2.6		Cost of Sales/Inventory	166 2.2		122 3.0	140 2.6		
166 2.2	228 1.6	203 1.8			365 1.0		203 1.8	203 1.8		
15 24.1	21 17.0	16 23.4			6 62.2		18 20.7	18 19.8		
31 11.6	34 10.6	25 14.6		Cost of Sales/Payables	15 24.2		27 13.4	25 14.5		
55 6.6	65 5.6	48 7.6			38 9.5		41 8.8	51 7.2		
2.7	2.9	2.6						1.9	2.8	2.4
4.0	4.7	4.0		Sales/Working Capital				3.6	4.1	4.0
6.3	7.9	7.6						4.3	10.6	5.9
58.4	27.9	22.4							17.4	32.8
(46) 16.9	(69) 9.5	(58) 9.5		EBIT/Interest				(23) 5.0	(25) 14.5	
4.4	2.1	1.2							2.4	2.8
26.4	13.2	19.5		Net Profit + Depr., Dep.,						
(12) 14.2	(17) 5.4	(15) 4.7		Amort./Cur. Mat. L/T/D						
2.4	3.4	1.4								
.1	.1	.1						.0	.1	.2
.4	.2	.2		Fixed/Worth				.0	.2	.3
1.0	.5	.6						.5	.9	.6
.5	.4	.4						.2	.5	.3
1.0	1.1	.8		Debt/Worth				.5	.9	.8
3.1	2.6	2.4						2.2	3.6	2.2
62.7	48.6	39.7						35.2	45.9	35.7
(52) 37.3	(79) 27.7	(69) 25.7		% Profit Before Taxes/Tangible Net Worth	(12) 26.3		(24) 15.6	(29) 26.0		
11.8	5.2	5.0						-11.8	4.1	14.4
30.1	23.3	20.1		% Profit Before Taxes/Total Assets				23.4	17.9	18.3
17.5	9.3	9.8						8.4	4.2	13.6
5.8	2.5	2.0						-7.1	1.0	6.1
82.9	62.2	59.7						336.0	56.1	18.9
18.2	16.4	16.5		Sales/Net Fixed Assets				86.9	19.6	9.1
5.9	9.0	7.3						11.6	11.8	5.3
2.2	2.1	2.0						2.0	2.4	1.9
1.6	1.6	1.4		Sales/Total Assets				1.2	1.5	1.4
1.2	1.1	1.0						1.1	1.0	1.1
.8	.6	.8							.5	1.0
(38) 1.9	(66) 1.1	(52) 1.3		% Depr., Dep., Amort./Sales				(18) 1.2	(25) 1.3	
6.2	1.8	2.2							2.2	2.0
1.0	1.0	.8		% Officers', Directors' Owners' Comp/Sales						
(16) 2.1	(20) 3.1	(13) 1.6								
4.6	5.9	8.7								
1637425M	3415389M	4166078M		Net Sales ($)	402M	6325M	8743M	93412M	476491M	3580705M
1223965M	2227572M	2904161M		Total Assets ($)	199M	5071M	9606M	77617M	322686M	2488982M

© RMA 2024 M = $ thousand   MM = $ million
See Pages viii through xx for Explanation of Ratios and Data

MANUFACTURING—Automobile and Light Duty Motor Vehicle Manufacturing NAICS 336110

Current Data Sorted by Assets | Comparative Historical Data

0-500M	500M-2MM	2-10MM	10-50MM	50-100MM	100-250MM		4/1/19-3/31/20 ALL	4/1/20-3/31/21 ALL
		1	1		2	Type of Statement		
		1	1			Unqualified	3	
	1	2	1	1		Reviewed	1	3
	1	1	5			Compiled	1	
7 (4/1-9/30/23)			23 (10/1/23-3/31/24)			Tax Returns	3	2
			11	2		Other	10	9
						NUMBER OF STATEMENTS	18	14
	2	9	14	3	2			
%	%	%	%	%	%	**ASSETS**	%	%
			12.0			Cash & Equivalents	7.4	11.2
			14.4			Trade Receivables (net)	19.1	19.2
DATA			39.3			Inventory	31.0	28.6
NOT			4.5			All Other Current	3.9	2.4
AVAILABLE			70.2			Total Current	61.5	61.4
			20.0			Fixed Assets (net)	21.8	21.1
			1.2			Intangibles (net)	12.0	14.9
			8.6			All Other Non-Current	4.8	2.5
			100.0			Total	100.0	100.0
						LIABILITIES		
			12.8			Notes Payable-Short Term	7.1	6.4
			2.2			Cur. Mat.-L.T.D.	4.2	5.2
			17.2			Trade Payables	17.6	14.2
			.5			Income Taxes Payable	.3	.2
			19.2			All Other Current	24.5	19.3
			51.9			Total Current	53.7	45.4
			9.1			Long-Term Debt	11.4	18.5
			.3			Deferred Taxes	1.5	.0
			2.5			All Other Non-Current	6.1	3.6
			36.2			Net Worth	27.3	32.5
			100.0			Total Liabilties & Net Worth	100.0	100.0
						INCOME DATA		
			100.0			Net Sales	100.0	100.0
			23.7			Gross Profit	19.7	27.1
			16.0			Operating Expenses	15.1	26.1
			7.7			Operating Profit	4.6	1.0
			.6			All Other Expenses (net)	2.1	-.7
			7.1			Profit Before Taxes	2.5	1.7
						RATIOS		
			2.0				2.1	3.0
			1.4			Current	1.3	1.4
			1.0				1.0	.9
			.9				.9	1.6
			.5			Quick	.6	.5
			.1				.2	.2
		2	227.3				14 26.5	10 35.3
		17	21.5			Sales/Receivables	30 12.0	38 9.7
		44	8.3				59 6.2	57 6.4
		46	7.9				34 10.7	35 10.4
		111	3.3			Cost of Sales/Inventory	72 5.1	66 5.5
		215	1.7				96 3.8	126 2.9
		12	30.3				20 18.4	23 15.8
		27	13.6			Cost of Sales/Payables	29 12.6	34 10.6
		50	7.3				54 6.7	59 6.2
			5.4				7.6	6.6
			9.8			Sales/Working Capital	15.4	10.9
			NM				NM	-14.9
			31.2				10.0	43.4
		(13)	10.5			EBIT/Interest	(14) 4.9	(11) 7.2
			7.5				2.6	-2.3
						Net Profit + Depr., Dep., Amort./Cur. Mat. L/T/D		
			.2				.3	.3
			.5			Fixed/Worth	1.0	2.3
			1.4				NM	114.2
			1.1				1.3	1.2
			2.2			Debt/Worth	3.9	6.2
			5.5				NM	358.1
			67.0				35.9	83.0
			38.3			% Profit Before Taxes/Tangible Net Worth	(14) 21.8	(12) 50.3
			18.4				9.0	-5.9
			14.8				10.4	22.1
			11.6			% Profit Before Taxes/Total Assets	6.7	12.4
			6.7				2.2	-6.1
			20.6				33.2	49.5
			13.9			Sales/Net Fixed Assets	15.3	5.2
			4.3				3.8	4.4
			2.2				3.3	2.9
			1.9			Sales/Total Assets	1.9	1.4
			1.4				1.1	.9
								1.1
						% Depr., Dep., Amort./Sales	(13) 1.8	
							5.2	
						% Officers', Directors' Owners' Comp/Sales		
	5222M	115308M	659753M	463857M	930971M	Net Sales ($)	1930659M	803535M
	2550M	53789M	381562M	230425M	336524M	Total Assets ($)	951988M	542778M

© RMA 2024

M = $ thousand   MM = $ million
See Pages viii through xx for Explanation of Ratios and Data

MANUFACTURING—Automobile and Light Duty Motor Vehicle Manufacturing NAICS 336110

Comparative Historical Data | Current Data Sorted by Sales

Comparative Historical Data			Type of Statement	Current Data Sorted by Sales					
3	4	4	Unqualified						4
2	1	2	Reviewed			1		1	1
	1	1	Compiled			1		1	
1	1	2	Tax Returns				1	2	
9	12	19	Other	1	7 (4/1-9/30/23)	1	2	4	12
4/1/21-3/31/22 ALL	4/1/22-3/31/23 ALL	4/1/23-3/31/24 ALL		0-1MM	1-3MM	3-5MM	23 (10/1/23-3/31/24) 5-10MM	10-25MM	25MM & OVER
15	19	30	NUMBER OF STATEMENTS	1		1	4	7	17
%	%	%	ASSETS	%	%	%	%	%	%
12.4	10.3	11.3	Cash & Equivalents						10.9
16.1	11.3	15.4	Trade Receivables (net)						14.7
31.4	33.4	30.3	Inventory						28.1
2.7	7.1	3.2	All Other Current		DATA				4.1
62.6	62.1	60.2	Total Current		NOT				57.9
26.1	23.1	26.0	Fixed Assets (net)		AVAILABLE				27.6
5.4	4.5	6.1	Intangibles (net)						5.3
5.9	10.2	7.7	All Other Non-Current						9.2
100.0	100.0	100.0	Total						100.0
			LIABILITIES						
19.9	19.3	8.4	Notes Payable-Short Term						7.8
2.2	1.6	2.7	Cur. Mat.-L.T.D.						2.9
11.0	14.1	14.7	Trade Payables						18.1
.0	.1	.2	Income Taxes Payable						.4
21.5	10.6	22.3	All Other Current						25.7
54.5	45.8	48.4	Total Current						55.0
13.4	14.9	14.1	Long-Term Debt						12.7
.6	.3	.1	Deferred Taxes						.3
2.8	4.2	15.5	All Other Non-Current						12.1
28.7	34.8	21.9	Net Worth						20.0
100.0	100.0	100.0	Total Liabilites & Net Worth						100.0
			INCOME DATA						
100.0	100.0	100.0	Net Sales						100.0
28.1	24.4	23.6	Gross Profit						22.4
21.1	17.6	18.6	Operating Expenses						16.5
7.0	6.7	4.9	Operating Profit						5.9
-1.8	-.5	.1	All Other Expenses (net)						1.1
8.8	7.2	4.8	Profit Before Taxes						4.8
			RATIOS						
2.7	2.9	2.0							1.5
1.2	1.2	1.2	Current						1.0
.6	.9	.7							.6
1.1	1.0	.8							.8
.4	.5	.5	Quick						.4
.2	.3	.3							.2
12 30.4	5 70.2	3 134.4						3	143.1
25 14.6	18 20.5	19 19.4	Sales/Receivables					15	23.7
39 9.3	46 8.0	47 7.8						52	7.0
44 8.3	45 8.1	25 14.4						26	13.8
66 5.5	56 6.5	58 6.3	Cost of Sales/Inventory					45	8.1
140 2.6	152 2.4	118 3.1						126	2.9
13 27.3	5 69.6	11 32.2						10	36.2
29 12.5	35 10.3	27 13.6	Cost of Sales/Payables					28	13.2
62 5.9	49 7.5	46 7.9						45	8.1
4.7	6.5	5.4							9.8
25.4	17.6	46.9	Sales/Working Capital						87.8
-5.9	-27.0	-13.7							-5.7
51.3	33.0	14.6							24.8
(14) 15.4	(15) 8.0	(29) 7.8	EBIT/Interest					(16)	8.9
3.4	3.8	.5							1.5
			Net Profit + Depr., Dep., Amort./Cur. Mat. L/T/D						
.2	.2	.3							.3
1.1	.6	.8	Fixed/Worth						1.1
8.5	5.6	6.0							5.7
.7	.9	1.2							1.2
5.2	2.3	2.9	Debt/Worth						4.5
10.6	8.2	33.7							14.6
139.2	93.9	82.4							74.1
(14) 67.0	(18) 37.6	(24) 30.6	% Profit Before Taxes/Tangible Net Worth					(15)	28.8
10.3	25.2	19.3							18.9
31.2	22.0	18.0							12.2
9.1	10.4	11.2	% Profit Before Taxes/Total Assets						10.2
4.2	4.6	-1.5							1.6
73.2	38.4	19.4							17.5
16.0	16.3	11.8	Sales/Net Fixed Assets						11.4
3.0	3.6	4.2							3.5
2.7	3.1	2.4							2.5
1.4	2.3	1.9	Sales/Total Assets						2.0
1.2	1.3	1.5							1.6
.4	.3	.9							
(10) 1.4	(11) 1.0	(18) 1.9	% Depr., Dep., Amort./Sales						
4.0	2.9	5.8							
			% Officers', Directors' Owners' Comp/Sales						
962887M	2208662M	2175111M	Net Sales ($)	835M	4387M	27925M	121376M	2020588M
685496M	1321618M	1004850M	Total Assets ($)	573M	1977M	19288M	58149M	924863M

M = $ thousand   MM = $ million

© RMA 2024
See Pages viii through xx for Explanation of Ratios and Data

MANUFACTURING—Motor Vehicle Body Manufacturing NAICS 336211

Current Data Sorted by Assets | Comparative Historical Data

Type of Statement								
						Unqualified	10	3
			4	2	2	Reviewed	9	5
		1	2	3		Compiled	1	1
		4				Tax Returns	9	5
1		9	9	1	3	Other	26	22
0-500M	8 (4/1-9/30/23) 500M-2MM	2-10MM	35 (10/1/23-3/31/24) 10-50MM	50-100MM	100-250MM		4/1/19-3/31/20 ALL	4/1/20-3/31/21 ALL
1		18	13	6	5	NUMBER OF STATEMENTS	55	36
%	%	%	%	%	%	ASSETS	%	%
		10.6	6.7			Cash & Equivalents	9.4	13.4
	D	19.3	16.4			Trade Receivables (net)	15.7	16.7
	A	45.9	38.8			Inventory	41.3	41.2
	T	.9	2.4			All Other Current	2.2	5.1
	A	76.6	64.4			Total Current	68.6	76.4
		12.5	21.1			Fixed Assets (net)	18.0	16.2
	N	2.7	11.7			Intangibles (net)	7.0	3.4
	O	8.1	2.9			All Other Non-Current	6.4	4.0
	T	100.0	100.0			Total	100.0	100.0
						LIABILITIES		
	A	9.4	8.9			Notes Payable-Short Term	15.7	9.1
	V	.7	.5			Cur. Mat.-L.T.D.	7.1	3.6
	A	14.8	11.6			Trade Payables	14.1	12.9
	I	.1	.0			Income Taxes Payable	.1	.2
	L	11.3	13.3			All Other Current	18.8	16.6
	A	36.4	34.3			Total Current	55.8	42.4
	B	15.6	9.9			Long-Term Debt	10.6	15.8
	L	.0	.2			Deferred Taxes	.0	.1
	E	6.3	4.0			All Other Non-Current	4.9	4.4
		41.8	51.5			Net Worth	28.6	37.3
		100.0	100.0			Total Liabilties & Net Worth	100.0	100.0
						INCOME DATA		
		100.0	100.0			Net Sales	100.0	100.0
		29.1	23.5			Gross Profit	22.1	23.1
		22.4	15.0			Operating Expenses	18.0	19.2
		6.8	8.5			Operating Profit	4.1	3.9
		1.2	.6			All Other Expenses (net)	1.0	-.6
		5.6	7.9			Profit Before Taxes	3.2	4.5
						RATIOS		
		5.7	2.9				2.6	3.2
		1.8	1.7			Current	1.4	1.9
		1.4	1.3				1.1	1.3
		3.2	1.1				1.1	1.3
		.8	.6			Quick	.5	.6
		.4	.4				.2	.4
		12 29.7	22 16.9				11 32.4	20 18.6
		26 14.2	24 15.4			Sales/Receivables	20 17.9	29 12.7
		43 8.4	49 7.4				44 8.3	40 9.1
		62 5.9	52 7.0				42 8.6	57 6.4
		107 3.4	96 3.8			Cost of Sales/Inventory	87 4.2	101 3.6
		135 2.7	135 2.7				122 3.0	130 2.8
		7 55.5	14 26.2				11 33.4	18 20.3
		24 15.5	21 17.7			Cost of Sales/Payables	24 15.4	27 13.5
		48 7.6	41 8.9				36 10.2	36 10.1
		4.7	4.0				5.0	3.8
		7.8	9.4			Sales/Working Capital	12.8	6.6
		11.0	14.1				27.0	9.7
		20.5	16.8				21.2	19.8
		(17) 5.4	5.9			EBIT/Interest	(51) 3.3	(32) 6.9
		1.9	4.6				1.9	2.7
						Net Profit + Depr., Dep.,		69.7
						Amort./Cur. Mat. L/T/D	(14) 5.3	
								1.1
		.1	.2				.1	.1
		.4	.5			Fixed/Worth	.5	.5
		2.8	.7				1.3	.9
		.2	.5				.6	.8
		1.8	1.8			Debt/Worth	1.8	1.6
		28.2	3.1				10.6	3.8
		89.9	91.8				31.3	54.9
		(15) 14.8	(12) 38.5			% Profit Before Taxes/Tangible Net Worth	(46) 18.8	(33) 32.8
		7.7	26.9				6.3	13.5
		29.5	22.2				16.0	17.9
		10.0	11.7			% Profit Before Taxes/Total Assets	5.1	10.2
		2.5	8.8				1.2	4.0
		85.7	36.7				81.9	74.2
		34.8	14.9			Sales/Net Fixed Assets	16.3	16.6
		8.7	4.5				7.8	6.1
		3.3	2.5				3.1	2.9
		2.2	1.8			Sales/Total Assets	2.2	2.0
		1.7	1.3				1.8	1.6
		.3	.5				.5	.3
		(11) .6	(10) 1.1			% Depr., Dep., Amort./Sales	(38) .9	(29) 1.1
		3.5	5.0				2.0	2.0
						% Officers', Directors' Owners' Comp/Sales	1.5	.7
							(13) 4.3	(10) 2.7
							5.4	5.4
1031M		262772M	672893M	911875M	1500912M	Net Sales ($)	3302697M	1853808M
104M		106677M	335046M	432158M	911411M	Total Assets ($)	1779407M	1211299M

M = $ thousand   MM = $ million
See Pages viii through xx for Explanation of Ratios and Data

© RMA 2024

MANUFACTURING—Motor Vehicle Body Manufacturing NAICS 336211

Comparative Historical Data / Current Data Sorted by Sales

								Type of Statement												
								Unqualified										2		4
	3		4		6			Reviewed										4		5
	6		8		9			Compiled								1				
			1		1			Tax Returns								1		2		1
	4		9		4			Other						1		2		7		13
	21		24		23						8 (4/1-9/30/23)				35 (10/1/23-3/31/24)				
	4/1/21-		4/1/22-		4/1/23-				0-1MM		1-3MM		3-5MM		5-10MM		10-25MM		25MM & OVER
	3/31/22		3/31/23		3/31/24															
	ALL		ALL		ALL															
	34		46		43			NUMBER OF STATEMENTS	1				4		15		23		
	%		%		%			ASSETS	%		%		%		%		%		%
	14.2		11.9		10.3			Cash & Equivalents									8.0		9.1
	16.3		14.4		16.3			Trade Receivables (net)	D		D						18.2		17.3
	42.0		43.0		43.1			Inventory	A		A						45.1		43.6
	2.2		2.3		2.2			All Other Current	T		T						1.0		3.4
	74.7		71.6		71.9			Total Current	A		A						72.3		73.4
	18.9		18.0		15.6			Fixed Assets (net)									18.9		11.8
	2.3		4.2		5.4			Intangibles (net)	N		N						1.7		7.9
	4.0		6.2		7.1			All Other Non-Current	O		O						7.1		6.9
	100.0		100.0		100.0			Total	T		T						100.0		100.0
								LIABILITIES											
	10.1		9.7		10.1			Notes Payable-Short Term	A		A						12.9		6.1
	2.3		1.6		.6			Cur. Mat.-L.T.D.	V		V						.5		.6
	13.1		10.9		14.5			Trade Payables	A		A						16.0		15.7
	.3		.4		.5			Income Taxes Payable	I		I						.1		.9
	13.4		12.0		11.7			All Other Current	L		L						11.1		12.5
	39.2		34.6		37.5			Total Current	A		A						40.6		35.8
	12.3		13.8		13.8			Long-Term Debt	B		B						17.6		9.5
	.1		.1		.1			Deferred Taxes	L		L						.0		.2
	5.3		5.8		5.4			All Other Non-Current	E		E						6.9		5.1
	43.1		45.6		43.3			Net Worth									34.9		49.4
	100.0		100.0		100.0			Total Liabilities & Net Worth									100.0		100.0
								INCOME DATA											
	100.0		100.0		100.0			Net Sales									100.0		100.0
	24.3		23.4		24.9			Gross Profit									28.0		21.0
	19.5		17.9		17.7			Operating Expenses									22.8		12.8
	4.8		5.5		7.2			Operating Profit									5.2		8.2
	-2.5		.0		.9			All Other Expenses (net)									.5		.9
	7.3		5.5		6.3			Profit Before Taxes									4.8		7.4
								RATIOS											
	4.2		4.3		3.2												3.2		2.8
	1.9		2.1		1.8			Current									1.6		2.2
	1.2		1.5		1.4												1.4		1.4
	1.4		1.6		1.4												1.2		1.3
	.8		.7		.6			Quick									.6		.6
	.4		.5		.4												.3		.4
25	14.7	17	21.6	15	23.9										11	33.4	22	16.7		
31	11.7	30	12.3	24	15.4			Sales/Receivables							29	12.5	24	15.4		
40	9.1	43	8.5	42	8.7										54	6.8	42	8.7		
69	5.3	68	5.4	60	6.1										81	4.5	60	6.1		
107	3.4	111	3.3	104	3.5			Cost of Sales/Inventory							118	3.1	96	3.8		
152	2.4	152	2.4	135	2.7										140	2.6	135	2.7		
11	32.9	9	40.4	12	29.6										10	34.9	20	18.3		
21	17.1	21	17.1	24	15.2			Cost of Sales/Payables							28	13.1	25	14.6		
49	7.5	41	8.8	55	6.6										60	6.1	57	6.4		
	3.6		3.4		3.9												4.7		3.9
	5.0		5.0		7.1			Sales/Working Capital									8.5		6.5
	19.1		9.1		13.3												13.3		13.7
	132.0		22.0		13.7												9.4		35.9
(31)	13.4	(42)	8.4	(41)	5.9			EBIT/Interest							(14)	4.6	(22)	6.8		
	7.6		1.7		3.2												2.0		5.1
								Net Profit + Depr., Dep., Amort./Cur. Mat. L/T/D											
	.1		.1		.1												.1		.1
	.5		.4		.4			Fixed/Worth									.7		.4
	.8		.8		.7												8.2		.5
	.4		.5		.4												.3		.5
	1.0		.8		1.8			Debt/Worth									2.0		1.6
	5.4		2.7		4.7												80.1		4.2
	42.4		31.7		77.4												77.3		77.4
(32)	25.3	(40)	14.2	(37)	32.1			% Profit Before Taxes/Tangible Net Worth							(12)	12.8	(21)	37.7		
	10.3		5.4		10.2												4.6		15.9
	22.3		15.0		18.8												12.8		25.6
	11.9		7.5		10.6			% Profit Before Taxes/Total Assets									7.5		12.2
	3.9		1.1		4.2												2.6		9.4
	31.1		54.8		55.4												69.0		46.9
	12.7		12.4		19.6			Sales/Net Fixed Assets									19.6		20.5
	5.8		6.3		7.8												6.2		11.2
	2.4		2.3		3.0												3.1		3.0
	1.9		1.6		1.9			Sales/Total Assets									2.1		1.9
	1.6		1.5		1.6												1.6		1.6
	.8		.8		.4														.5
(27)	1.4	(34)	1.6	(32)	.9			% Depr., Dep., Amort./Sales									(18)	.9		
	2.1		2.4		2.6														1.6
			.8		1.2			% Officers', Directors' Owners' Comp/Sales											
		(16)	2.1	(13)	3.2														
			5.9		7.6														
	1617174M		2826842M		3349483M			Net Sales ($)		1031M				30733M		229469M		3088250M		
	923515M		1694592M		1785396M			Total Assets ($)		104M				16720M		152668M		1615904M		

© RMA 2024   M = $ thousand   MM = $ million
See Pages viii through xx for Explanation of Ratios and Data

MANUFACTURING—Truck Trailer Manufacturing NAICS 336212

Current Data Sorted by Assets | Comparative Historical Data

							Type of Statement				
				3		3	Unqualified		9		6
		1		4		3	Reviewed		7		1
		2		4		1	Compiled		6		3
	3	2					Tax Returns		7		5
	3	10		29	5	10	Other		44		15
		26 (4/1-9/30/23)		57 (10/1/23-3/31/24)					4/1/19-3/31/20		4/1/20-3/31/21
0-500M	500M-2MM	2-10MM		10-50MM	50-100MM	100-250MM	NUMBER OF STATEMENTS		73 ALL		30 ALL
	6	15		40	8	14					
%	%	%		%	%	%	ASSETS		%		%
		14.2		14.0		6.6	Cash & Equivalents		15.1		18.0
		7.9		9.3		10.7	Trade Receivables (net)		14.1		14.2
D		51.4		41.1		25.7	Inventory		38.8		38.7
A		1.8		8.5		18.2	All Other Current		3.7		3.5
T		75.3		72.9		61.2	Total Current		71.6		74.4
A		17.3		17.7		32.4	Fixed Assets (net)		18.4		16.4
		.2		3.2		3.6	Intangibles (net)		6.3		2.7
N		7.2		6.2		2.8	All Other Non-Current		3.7		6.5
O		100.0		100.0		100.0	Total		100.0		100.0
T							LIABILITIES				
		15.1		6.1		13.8	Notes Payable-Short Term		6.0		7.2
A		1.2		.9		4.7	Cur. Mat.-L.T.D.		2.0		2.0
V		9.2		11.3		11.8	Trade Payables		11.3		10.9
A		.0		.3		.1	Income Taxes Payable		.2		.1
I		14.4		9.9		6.7	All Other Current		8.4		12.9
L		39.9		28.6		37.1	Total Current		28.0		33.1
A		13.0		12.3		16.1	Long-Term Debt		16.1		14.0
B		.0		.0		.1	Deferred Taxes		.1		.0
L		6.3		4.2		9.9	All Other Non-Current		10.4		22.2
E		40.8		54.9		36.7	Net Worth		45.3		30.7
		100.0		100.0		100.0	Total Liabilities & Net Worth		100.0		100.0
							INCOME DATA				
		100.0		100.0		100.0	Net Sales		100.0		100.0
		17.5		22.9		23.9	Gross Profit		21.9		21.6
		16.5		16.3		14.3	Operating Expenses		16.2		17.1
		1.0		6.7		9.6	Operating Profit		5.7		4.5
		.8		.0		1.5	All Other Expenses (net)		.8		-.7
		.2		6.7		8.1	Profit Before Taxes		4.9		5.3
							RATIOS				
		12.2		6.7		2.5			5.5		6.3
		2.9		2.7		1.4	Current		3.1		2.5
		1.1		1.8		1.2			1.5		1.5
		6.0		2.5		.8			2.2		2.8
		1.0		.5		.3	Quick		1.1		1.0
		.2		.2		.2			.5		.4
	0	UND	5	67.6	19	19.5		10	38.1	11	32.9
	8	46.3	13	28.5	23	16.0	Sales/Receivables	15	23.6	21	17.3
	22	16.6	21	17.2	32	11.4		31	11.7	34	10.8
	64	5.7	52	7.0	47	7.8		45	8.2	41	8.8
	87	4.2	81	4.5	63	5.8	Cost of Sales/Inventory	60	6.1	64	5.7
	111	3.3	111	3.3	99	3.7		101	3.6	104	3.5
	0	UND	7	52.2	20	18.5		8	44.1	8	48.6
	5	72.9	16	23.2	40	9.1	Cost of Sales/Payables	16	23.4	19	18.9
	21	17.7	28	13.1	48	7.6		27	13.3	30	12.1
		3.7		3.7		4.4			4.5		3.4
		7.2		5.1		6.3	Sales/Working Capital		6.5		5.8
		48.2		9.4		NM			11.0		11.7
		18.2		18.2		23.6			30.9		26.1
	(11)	2.8	(29)	6.2		4.8	EBIT/Interest	(59)	5.6	(24)	8.5
		-3.6		1.0		1.4			1.4		2.7
						9.4	Net Profit + Depr., Dep.,		21.6		
					(10)	2.0	Amort./Cur. Mat. L/T/D	(10)	2.5		
						.3			.6		
		.1		.1		.6			.2		.1
		.6		.3		1.0	Fixed/Worth		.4		.5
		3.0		.6		1.5			.9		4.7
		.2		.2		1.8			.3		.6
		1.1		.7		2.1	Debt/Worth		1.0		2.1
		15.6		4.0		3.9			3.1		15.3
		44.4		65.2		37.3			51.0		72.1
	(12)	13.1	(37)	32.0	(13)	25.0	% Profit Before Taxes/Tangible Net Worth	(61)	27.6	(24)	35.4
		-38.9		11.8		6.9			8.9		11.6
		13.1		31.0		14.9			25.5		25.7
		7.7		15.7		7.0	% Profit Before Taxes/Total Assets		12.8		10.4
		-16.7		3.8		1.9			2.3		4.5
		52.2		46.4		6.8			41.9		31.5
		19.4		15.3		4.0	Sales/Net Fixed Assets		14.1		16.5
		14.1		9.3		3.5			9.0		9.1
		3.3		3.1		2.0			3.7		3.3
		2.6		2.5		1.4	Sales/Total Assets		2.5		2.5
		1.6		1.7		1.2			1.9		1.9
		.8		.6		1.1			.6		.4
	(10)	1.0	(34)	1.0	(13)	1.7	% Depr., Dep., Amort./Sales	(55)	1.4	(22)	1.2
		4.7		2.0		2.6			2.1		1.5
							% Officers', Directors' Owners' Comp/Sales		.5		
								(19)	1.4		
									2.5		
	22702M	208398M		2445060M	901543M	3254485M	Net Sales ($)		4176321M		1577475M
	8264M	79005M		1038355M	666944M	2215983M	Total Assets ($)		2025328M		626474M

© RMA 2024 M = $ thousand   MM = $ million
See Pages viii through xx for Explanation of Ratios and Data

MANUFACTURING—Truck Trailer Manufacturing   NAICS 336212

Comparative Historical Data | Current Data Sorted by Sales

Comparative Historical Data			Type of Statement	Current Data Sorted by Sales						
5	5	9	Unqualified							9
6	6	5	Reviewed			1		1		4
3	4	7	Compiled			1		1	1	5
1	1	5	Tax Returns		2	2	1	3	6	45
31	26	57	Other		2					
4/1/21-3/31/22 ALL	4/1/22-3/31/23 ALL	4/1/23-3/31/24 ALL		0-1MM	26 (4/1-9/30/23) 1-3MM	3-5MM	5-10MM	57 (10/1/23-3/31/24) 10-25MM		25MM & OVER
48	42	83	NUMBER OF STATEMENTS		4	1	7	8		63
%	%	%	**ASSETS**	%	%	%	%	%		%
8.9	13.1	11.9	Cash & Equivalents							10.5
12.0	12.4	9.4	Trade Receivables (net)	D						9.1
39.7	39.4	39.0	Inventory	A						36.5
5.0	5.3	8.3	All Other Current	T						10.2
65.6	70.2	68.6	Total Current	A						66.3
19.4	16.4	20.1	Fixed Assets (net)							21.3
7.3	5.1	2.7	Intangibles (net)	N						3.4
7.7	8.2	8.6	All Other Non-Current	O						9.0
100.0	100.0	100.0	Total	T						100.0
			LIABILITIES	A						
7.9	10.3	9.1	Notes Payable-Short Term	V						9.1
1.8	.8	1.8	Cur. Mat.-L.T.D.	A						2.0
11.2	8.8	10.6	Trade Payables	I						11.1
.1	.5	.2	Income Taxes Payable	L						.2
8.9	11.3	10.8	All Other Current	A						10.0
29.9	31.8	32.5	Total Current	B						32.5
15.9	7.8	14.7	Long-Term Debt	L						15.1
.0	.1	.0	Deferred Taxes	E						.0
10.0	9.1	6.7	All Other Non-Current							6.8
44.2	51.2	46.0	Net Worth							45.6
100.0	100.0	100.0	Total Liabilities & Net Worth							100.0
			INCOME DATA							
100.0	100.0	100.0	Net Sales							100.0
20.8	21.7	23.1	Gross Profit							22.4
15.0	13.4	17.0	Operating Expenses							15.8
5.9	8.2	6.1	Operating Profit							6.6
-1.4	.1	.6	All Other Expenses (net)							.5
7.3	8.1	5.5	Profit Before Taxes							6.1
			RATIOS							
	4.4	5.7	5.4		Current					4.1
	2.0	2.9	2.2							2.0
	1.5	1.6	1.3							1.2
	1.3	2.8	2.4		Quick					1.9
	.7	.8	.4							.3
	.4	.4	.2							.2
11	32.7	3	126.6	6	61.9	Sales/Receivables			8	45.5
19	19.2	18	19.9	15	23.7				16	22.9
33	11.0	31	11.7	23	15.6				23	16.2
63	5.8	41	8.8	52	7.0	Cost of Sales/Inventory			51	7.2
83	4.4	65	5.6	87	4.2				76	4.8
130	2.8	104	3.5	118	3.1				104	3.5
11	33.6	4	95.0	7	54.9	Cost of Sales/Payables			11	33.3
22	16.6	14	26.1	17	21.3				21	17.7
38	9.6	25	14.8	34	10.6				39	9.4
	4.4		4.1		3.9	Sales/Working Capital				4.4
	6.3		5.4		6.0					6.5
	11.9		10.0		20.4					22.4
	40.7		50.4		17.8	EBIT/Interest				16.1
(40)	14.8	(33)	17.0	(66)	5.2				(52)	5.1
	6.2		6.7		1.1					1.2
					12.2	Net Profit + Depr., Dep., Amort./Cur. Mat. L/T/D				15.0
				(17)	3.8				(16)	3.3
					1.0					.8
	.2		.1		.1	Fixed/Worth				.2
	.6		.2		.5					.5
	2.4		.6		1.1					1.1
	.6		.3		.3	Debt/Worth				.4
	1.5		1.2		1.4					1.6
	6.2		2.1		5.2					5.2
	77.2		52.1		58.4	% Profit Before Taxes/Tangible Net Worth				61.5
(43)	41.5	(39)	34.7	(75)	29.5				(58)	30.8
	20.4		11.4		9.6					7.2
	26.7		29.0		25.2	% Profit Before Taxes/Total Assets				25.7
	14.0		14.7		9.5					10.0
	6.5		8.9		1.9					1.9
	27.1		63.2		36.3	Sales/Net Fixed Assets				28.2
	14.6		17.3		13.5					12.0
	7.2		10.6		4.5					4.0
	2.9		3.4		3.1	Sales/Total Assets				3.0
	2.2		2.5		2.2					2.2
	1.5		1.8		1.5					1.4
	.6		.7		.8	% Depr., Dep., Amort./Sales				.7
(41)	1.2	(35)	1.1	(66)	1.2				(55)	1.2
	2.1		1.5		2.5					2.5
					.2	% Officers', Directors', Owners' Comp/Sales				
				(16)	1.6					
					2.8					
	3771516M		5088233M		6832188M	Net Sales ($)	9765M	4005M	51254M	129046M	6638118M
	2010713M		2377558M		4008551M	Total Assets ($)	5786M	1122M	24235M	57510M	3919898M

© RMA 2024   M = $ thousand   MM = $ million
See Pages viii through xx for Explanation of Ratios and Data

MANUFACTURING—Travel Trailer and Camper Manufacturing NAICS 336214

Current Data Sorted by Assets | Comparative Historical Data

						Type of Statement		
			2			Unqualified	25	
		1	4		1	Reviewed	4	1
		2				Compiled	6	1
	1	3	1			Tax Returns	1	
1	3	7	16			Other	15	3
11 (4/1-9/30/23)	32 (10/1/23-3/31/24)					4/1/19-3/31/20	4/1/20-3/31/21
0-500M	500M-2MM	2-10MM	10-50MM	50-100MM	100-250MM	NUMBER OF STATEMENTS	ALL	ALL
1	4	13	23		2		51	5
%	%	%	%	%	%	ASSETS	%	%
		22.1	19.9			Cash & Equivalents	14.4	
		12.8	14.9			Trade Receivables (net)	16.4	
		42.5	39.8	D		Inventory	39.9	
		1.1	2.2	A		All Other Current	10.1	
		78.6	76.8	T		Total Current	80.9	
		13.9	14.9	A		Fixed Assets (net)	13.8	
		.5	5.1			Intangibles (net)	3.0	
		7.0	3.3	N		All Other Non-Current	2.4	
		100.0	100.0	O		Total	100.0	
				T		LIABILITIES		
		9.7	5.5			Notes Payable-Short Term	8.6	
		1.0	.7	A		Cur. Mat.-L.T.D.	.3	
		4.7	7.4	V		Trade Payables	16.9	
		.0	.0	A		Income Taxes Payable	.4	
		9.0	8.9	I		All Other Current	14.4	
		24.4	22.5	L		Total Current	40.5	
		6.3	11.3	A		Long-Term Debt	4.7	
		.0	.0	B		Deferred Taxes	.2	
		9.2	3.8	L		All Other Non-Current	14.7	
		60.1	62.4	E		Net Worth	39.9	
		100.0	100.0			Total Liabilities & Net Worth	100.0	
						INCOME DATA		
		100.0	100.0			Net Sales	100.0	
		22.3	19.9			Gross Profit	21.3	
		20.4	14.8			Operating Expenses	16.2	
		1.8	5.2			Operating Profit	5.1	
		-.4	-.3			All Other Expenses (net)	.3	
		2.2	5.5			Profit Before Taxes	4.8	
						RATIOS		
		12.0	9.0				5.3	
		8.0	4.2			Current	2.0	
		1.4	2.7				1.3	
		7.0	5.6				2.1	
		2.5	2.1			Quick	.6	
		.5	.3				.4	
		4 94.4	8 48.1				10 35.0	
		15 23.9	13 27.3			Sales/Receivables	21 17.2	
		25 14.4	27 13.3				32 11.4	
		22 16.3	35 10.3				42 8.7	
		96 3.8	68 5.4			Cost of Sales/Inventory	72 5.1	
		152 2.4	140 2.6				101 3.6	
		4 93.3	6 60.7				6 56.2	
		9 38.5	10 37.4			Cost of Sales/Payables	15 24.5	
		14 26.0	25 14.7				61 6.0	
		3.0	3.5				4.4	
		4.2	4.5			Sales/Working Capital	6.7	
		9.1	7.5				16.9	
		19.3	58.5				67.5	
		(11) 1.1	(18) 6.1			EBIT/Interest	(44) 20.8	
		-25.3	-2.5				3.2	
						Net Profit + Depr., Dep., Amort./Cur. Mat. L/T/D		
		.1	.1				.1	
		.4	.2			Fixed/Worth	.3	
		.5	.5				.5	
		.1	.3				.3	
		.3	.4			Debt/Worth	1.2	
		4.8	1.1				2.9	
		65.9	51.5				46.2	
		3.3	(21) 21.4			% Profit Before Taxes/Tangible Net Worth	(47) 26.3	
		-28.7	-4.3				10.5	
		40.1	38.6				19.5	
		.6	14.8			% Profit Before Taxes/Total Assets	12.0	
		-12.5	-2.8				4.3	
		24.7	45.8				90.9	
		17.6	20.7			Sales/Net Fixed Assets	20.9	
		12.6	10.7				11.0	
		3.2	3.3				3.6	
		2.1	2.3			Sales/Total Assets	2.8	
		1.5	1.8				2.1	
		.3	.2				.4	
		(11) .6	(21) .6			% Depr., Dep., Amort./Sales	(42) .7	
		.8	1.2				1.3	
		.7						
		(10) 1.6				% Officers', Directors' Owners' Comp/Sales		
		3.5						
2273M	23257M	174821M	1609119M		425672M	Net Sales ($)	5647210M	310201M
432M	5253M	75811M	571909M		276070M	Total Assets ($)	2621165M	167759M

© RMA 2024

M = $ thousand   MM = $ million
See Pages viii through xx for Explanation of Ratios and Data

MANUFACTURING—Travel Trailer and Camper Manufacturing NAICS 336214

Comparative Historical Data				Current Data Sorted by Sales						
3	5	2	Type of Statement Unqualified							2
1	1	6	Reviewed					1		5
1	1	2	Compiled					2		
1	2	5	Tax Returns		1	1	1	1		1
15	15	28	Other		1	2	1	9		15
4/1/21-3/31/22 ALL	4/1/22-3/31/23 ALL	4/1/23-3/31/24 ALL		0-1MM	11 (4/1-9/30/23) 1-3MM	3-5MM	5-10MM	32 (10/1/23-3/31/24) 10-25MM		25MM & OVER
21	24	43	NUMBER OF STATEMENTS		2	3	2	13		23
%	%	%	ASSETS	%	%	%	%	%		%
8.8	18.6	18.6	Cash & Equivalents	D				14.4		19.0
21.2	18.1	14.4	Trade Receivables (net)	A				9.7		16.6
45.3	34.4	41.7	Inventory	T				51.7		36.0
4.0	3.5	1.9	All Other Current	A				.7		2.3
79.3	74.6	76.6	Total Current					76.5		73.9
14.1	15.4	15.0	Fixed Assets (net)	N				12.6		18.8
3.2	4.9	4.0	Intangibles (net)	O				5.0		4.0
3.5	5.1	4.4	All Other Non-Current	T				5.8		3.4
100.0	100.0	100.0	Total					100.0		100.0
			LIABILITIES	A						
9.0	11.7	7.5	Notes Payable-Short Term	V				7.5		4.2
1.7	1.5	1.3	Cur. Mat.-L.T.D.	A				1.0		.8
8.3	8.6	7.5	Trade Payables	I				7.0		7.6
.0	.1	.0	Income Taxes Payable	L				.1		.0
16.4	14.2	9.7	All Other Current	A				9.0		9.1
35.4	36.1	26.0	Total Current	B				24.5		21.7
6.3	17.9	10.8	Long-Term Debt	L				5.8		14.9
.1	.8	.0	Deferred Taxes	E				.0		.0
.3	3.6	6.3	All Other Non-Current					10.4		4.3
58.0	41.6	56.9	Net Worth					59.3		59.2
100.0	100.0	100.0	Total Liabilities & Net Worth					100.0		100.0
			INCOME DATA							
100.0	100.0	100.0	Net Sales					100.0		100.0
25.6	21.8	21.8	Gross Profit					17.5		18.7
17.5	14.7	17.8	Operating Expenses					16.7		13.4
8.1	7.1	4.0	Operating Profit					.8		5.3
-1.5	-.9	-.2	All Other Expenses (net)					.5		-.2
9.7	8.0	4.3	Profit Before Taxes					.3		5.6
			RATIOS							
								11.9		5.7
4.6	3.1	9.0	Current					5.5		4.2
2.0	1.9	4.2						1.4		2.7
1.5	1.6	1.8								
1.2	2.0	3.1						4.1		3.1
.8	1.0	1.3	Quick					.9		2.1
.4	.4	.4						.4		.4
7 56.1	5 68.3	8 48.1					10 37.0		8 48.1
22 16.5	20 18.1	15 23.9	Sales/Receivables					15 23.9		14 25.7
51 7.1	35 10.4	27 13.3						23 15.6		27 13.5
45 8.2	42 8.7	35 10.3						87 4.2		31 11.6
83 4.4	73 5.0	70 5.2	Cost of Sales/Inventory					107 3.4		49 7.5
140 2.6	111 3.3	135 2.7						166 2.2		99 3.7
6 62.4	8 45.0	6 62.9						7 50.5		6 62.9
12 29.6	14 26.7	10 37.4	Cost of Sales/Payables					13 28.0		9 42.7
23 15.7	25 14.4	23 16.1						18 20.8		25 14.7
4.1	4.6	3.5						3.0		3.7
7.0	7.6	5.1	Sales/Working Capital					4.2		6.1
9.3	12.6	8.9						9.4		8.9
304.8	42.3	38.8								47.7
(18) 38.2	(21) 12.4	(33) 3.1	EBIT/Interest					(20) 11.3		
9.7	3.2	-3.6								-.8
			Net Profit + Depr., Dep., Amort./Cur. Mat. L/T/D							
.1	.1	.1						.1		.1
.2	.3	.4	Fixed/Worth					.4		.4
.4	3.8	.6						.6		.5
.4	.7	.2						.1		.3
.8	1.3	.5	Debt/Worth					.2		.6
1.4	6.5	4.1						5.5		1.1
64.3	70.3	53.8						19.5		66.2
(20) 32.5	(20) 41.2	(39) 21.4	% Profit Before Taxes/Tangible Net Worth					(12) -3.5	(21)	29.7
16.3	7.3	-10.3						-48.9		.1
40.8	45.7	35.6						15.1		46.0
16.8	11.7	10.7	% Profit Before Taxes/Total Assets					.6		17.2
8.3	2.5	-8.5						-12.5		-2.8
81.0	53.6	45.8						60.1		26.7
29.4	26.8	18.2	Sales/Net Fixed Assets					18.2		15.8
11.8	12.4	10.8						10.1		8.9
3.6	3.3	3.8						2.5		4.2
2.7	2.6	2.3	Sales/Total Assets					2.0		2.8
1.8	1.9	1.7						1.6		2.0
.2	.1	.3						.3		.3
(15) .2	(16) .2	(35) .6	% Depr., Dep., Amort./Sales					(12) .8	(20)	.6
.7	2.0	1.0						1.0		1.1
		.5	% Officers', Directors' Owners' Comp/Sales							
	(19)	1.4								
		4.3								
2194331M	2717792M	2235142M	Net Sales ($)	5110M	12709M		10641M	198557M		2008125M
829213M	1138561M	929475M	Total Assets ($)	1365M	12337M		5380M	108363M		802030M

© RMA 2024   M = $ thousand   MM = $ million
See Pages viii through xx for Explanation of Ratios and Data

MANUFACTURING—Motor Vehicle Gasoline Engine and Engine Parts Manufacturing NAICS 336310

Current Data Sorted by Assets | **Comparative Historical Data**

0-500M	5 (4/1-9/30/23) 500M-2MM	2-10MM	20 (10/1/23-3/31/24) 10-50MM	50-100MM	100-250MM	Type of Statement	4/1/19-3/31/20 ALL	4/1/20-3/31/21 ALL
1		5	2	1	2	Unqualified	5	3
1			1			Reviewed	3	1
			9	2	1	Compiled	5	1
	5		2			Tax Returns	2	1
			20			Other	20	9
2	5	5	12	3	3	NUMBER OF STATEMENTS	35	15
%	%	%	%	%	%	ASSETS	%	%
	D		4.3			Cash & Equivalents	9.9	11.4
	A		14.8			Trade Receivables (net)	16.8	14.8
	T		36.5			Inventory	35.5	32.0
	A		.5			All Other Current	3.6	4.0
			56.1			Total Current	65.7	62.2
	N		28.7			Fixed Assets (net)	23.7	20.4
	O		8.0			Intangibles (net)	6.2	12.5
	T		7.2			All Other Non-Current	4.4	5.0
			100.0			Total	100.0	100.0
	A					LIABILITIES		
	V		7.5			Notes Payable-Short Term	11.8	8.5
	A		3.1			Cur. Mat.-L.T.D.	1.7	2.6
	I		8.3			Trade Payables	11.9	8.9
	L		.0			Income Taxes Payable	.1	.1
	A		12.3			All Other Current	11.2	10.5
	B		31.2			Total Current	36.6	30.5
	L		15.0			Long-Term Debt	10.1	15.1
	E		.7			Deferred Taxes	.5	.5
			9.8			All Other Non-Current	6.4	5.7
			43.3			Net Worth	46.4	48.2
			100.0			Total Liabilities & Net Worth	100.0	100.0
						INCOME DATA		
			100.0			Net Sales	100.0	100.0
			29.6			Gross Profit	27.0	30.3
			23.4			Operating Expenses	19.8	22.9
			6.2			Operating Profit	7.2	7.4
			1.1			All Other Expenses (net)	1.2	-.3
			5.2			Profit Before Taxes	6.0	7.7
						RATIOS		
			3.2				2.4	3.6
			1.8			Current	1.8	2.9
			1.2				1.5	1.7
			1.0				1.2	1.4
			.7			Quick	.8	1.1
			.3				.4	.6
		15	23.6				19 19.7	15 23.8
		35	10.6			Sales/Receivables	36 10.2	36 10.0
		53	6.9				54 6.7	51 7.1
		76	4.8				57 6.4	91 4.0
		104	3.5			Cost of Sales/Inventory	94 3.9	111 3.3
		215	1.7				135 2.7	140 2.6
		9	40.4				11 33.0	26 14.0
		22	16.5			Cost of Sales/Payables	34 10.8	29 12.6
		35	10.5				45 8.1	40 9.1
			3.1				4.8	3.1
			6.4			Sales/Working Capital	6.2	4.2
			18.2				11.0	5.6
			11.2				19.1	61.9
		(11)	6.4			EBIT/Interest	(30) 8.0	(14) 13.5
			.5				2.4	-3.3
						Net Profit + Depr., Dep., Amort./Cur. Mat. L/T/D	15.8	
							(10) 8.0	
							2.5	
			.2				.3	.4
			.7			Fixed/Worth	.5	.5
			2.5				1.0	1.2
			.5				.7	.7
			1.9			Debt/Worth	1.2	1.3
			9.4				3.3	3.6
			85.2				39.9	42.8
		(11)	27.9			% Profit Before Taxes/Tangible Net Worth	(34) 20.3	(12) 20.4
			14.0				6.3	-.4
			11.4				12.6	20.2
			9.1			% Profit Before Taxes/Total Assets	8.2	13.3
			1.0				2.4	-.9
			12.3				29.6	15.1
			6.3			Sales/Net Fixed Assets	8.7	7.8
			5.1				4.8	4.6
			1.9				2.4	1.9
			1.5			Sales/Total Assets	1.7	1.7
			.8				1.2	.9
			.7				.5	1.2
		(10)	2.8			% Depr., Dep., Amort./Sales	(29) 1.8	(10) 1.9
			11.1				4.3	4.0
						% Officers', Directors' Owners' Comp/Sales		
2170M		33997M	404021M	230181M	555829M	Net Sales ($)	2749177M	1002151M
296M		17998M	262463M	181042M	523064M	Total Assets ($)	1918746M	827610M

© RMA 2024
M = $ thousand   MM = $ million
See Pages viii through xx for Explanation of Ratios and Data

MANUFACTURING—Motor Vehicle Gasoline Engine and Engine Parts Manufacturing NAICS 336310

Comparative Historical Data				Current Data Sorted by Sales						
1	3	5	Type of Statement						5
	4	1	Unqualified					1	
			Reviewed						
1	1	1	Compiled						
7	15	18	Tax Returns	1	2	2	2	5	7
4/1/21-	4/1/22-	4/1/23-	Other		5 (4/1-9/30/23)		20 (10/1/23-3/31/24)		
3/31/22	3/31/23	3/31/24		0-1MM	1-3MM	3-5MM	5-10MM	10-25MM	25MM & OVER
ALL	ALL	ALL							
8	23	25	NUMBER OF STATEMENTS	1	2	2	2	6	12
%	%	%	ASSETS	%	%	%	%	%	%
	4.8	5.3	Cash & Equivalents						3.8
	18.8	15.2	Trade Receivables (net)						15.7
	41.8	31.7	Inventory						36.2
	4.5	.9	All Other Current						.7
	69.8	53.1	Total Current						56.4
	20.3	29.5	Fixed Assets (net)						22.3
	6.4	10.9	Intangibles (net)						13.8
	3.4	6.4	All Other Non-Current						7.6
	100.0	100.0	Total						100.0
			LIABILITIES						
	9.6	11.8	Notes Payable-Short Term						5.5
	1.2	5.0	Cur. Mat.-L.T.D.						2.6
	15.2	8.9	Trade Payables						9.3
	.1	.0	Income Taxes Payable						.0
	17.5	16.2	All Other Current						16.3
	43.6	42.0	Total Current						33.7
	24.1	24.0	Long-Term Debt						12.8
	.3	.6	Deferred Taxes						.9
	6.5	7.9	All Other Non-Current						10.2
	25.5	25.5	Net Worth						42.4
	100.0	100.0	Total Liabilities & Net Worth						100.0
			INCOME DATA						
	100.0	100.0	Net Sales						100.0
	24.1	32.8	Gross Profit						27.1
	18.7	25.1	Operating Expenses						21.7
	5.5	7.7	Operating Profit						5.4
	.6	1.7	All Other Expenses (net)						2.2
	4.8	6.0	Profit Before Taxes						3.2
			RATIOS						
	2.5	3.0							2.6
	1.8	2.0	Current						2.0
	1.2	1.2							1.2
	.9	1.0							1.1
	.5	.6	Quick						.6
	.3	.3							.4
23	16.2	14	25.9					26	14.0
37	9.8	30	12.0	Sales/Receivables				38	9.6
56	6.5	48	7.6					49	7.5
59	6.2	69	5.3					91	4.0
111	3.3	114	3.2	Cost of Sales/Inventory				114	3.2
152	2.4	152	2.4					130	2.8
20	17.9	16	23.3					18	20.2
36	10.1	22	16.6	Cost of Sales/Payables				22	16.9
54	6.8	36	10.2					36	10.1
	3.4	3.7							4.1
	7.6	6.0	Sales/Working Capital						5.4
	25.0	22.0							18.2
	28.2	16.3							16.3
(19)	10.2	(24)	5.8	EBIT/Interest					6.5
	.9	1.8							1.2
			Net Profit + Depr., Dep., Amort./Cur. Mat. L/T/D						
	.1	.4							.5
	.3	.9	Fixed/Worth						.7
	2.5	NM							1.6
	.9	.5							.8
	1.6	2.0	Debt/Worth						2.1
	4.9	NM							5.9
	46.4	56.4	% Profit Before Taxes/Tangible Net Worth						39.6
(18)	21.6	(19)	27.9					(10)	24.4
	11.2	14.0							12.3
	14.8	12.9							10.6
	8.5	9.2	% Profit Before Taxes/Total Assets						8.8
	-2.9	5.3							.2
	95.4	12.5							8.7
	13.3	6.2	Sales/Net Fixed Assets						6.0
	4.1	4.2							5.0
	2.0	2.0							1.9
	1.6	1.4	Sales/Total Assets						1.5
	1.2	.9							1.1
	.7	2.1							2.5
(18)	1.9	(19)	3.1	% Depr., Dep., Amort./Sales					3.0
	4.1	6.8							3.7
			% Officers', Directors', Owners' Comp/Sales						
517875M	1393197M	1226198M	Net Sales ($)	714M	3032M	7708M	13469M	102072M	1099203M
340385M	966722M	984863M	Total Assets ($)	127M	3158M	14567M	8422M	83982M	874607M

© RMA 2024   M = $ thousand   MM = $ million
See Pages viii through xx for Explanation of Ratios and Data

MANUFACTURING—Motor Vehicle Electrical and Electronic Equipment Manufacturing NAICS 336320

Current Data Sorted by Assets

						Type of Statement		
			1		1	Unqualified		
				1		Reviewed		
1		2				Compiled		
	1	7	4	2	3	Tax Returns		
	3 (4/1-9/30/23)		20 (10/1/23-3/31/24)			Other		
0-500M	500M-2MM	2-10MM	10-50MM	50-100MM	100-250MM			
1	1	9	5	3	4	NUMBER OF STATEMENTS		
%	%	%	%	%	%			

Comparative Historical Data

Type of Statement		
Unqualified	4	4
Reviewed	3	
Compiled		
Tax Returns	2	2
Other	14	10
	4/1/19-3/31/20	4/1/20-3/31/21
	ALL	ALL
NUMBER OF STATEMENTS	23	16

	%	%
ASSETS		
Cash & Equivalents	8.4	7.6
Trade Receivables (net)	23.5	16.7
Inventory	28.1	31.1
All Other Current	1.4	1.6
Total Current	61.5	57.0
Fixed Assets (net)	17.6	18.7
Intangibles (net)	9.9	14.5
All Other Non-Current	11.1	9.8
Total	100.0	100.0
LIABILITIES		
Notes Payable-Short Term	9.4	11.3
Cur. Mat.-L.T.D.	1.2	2.5
Trade Payables	13.6	15.3
Income Taxes Payable	.2	.5
All Other Current	11.7	8.5
Total Current	36.1	38.1
Long-Term Debt	11.0	22.4
Deferred Taxes	.5	1.2
All Other Non-Current	5.4	1.4
Net Worth	46.9	37.0
Total Liabilities & Net Worth	100.0	100.0
INCOME DATA		
Net Sales	100.0	100.0
Gross Profit	28.1	32.4
Operating Expenses	25.2	29.1
Operating Profit	2.9	3.3
All Other Expenses (net)	.1	.8
Profit Before Taxes	2.8	2.4
RATIOS		
Current	3.1	3.4
	1.6	1.5
	1.2	.8
Quick	1.9	1.3
	.9	.6
	.5	.3
Sales/Receivables	43 / 8.4	27 / 13.5
	49 / 7.4	49 / 7.4
	54 / 6.7	70 / 5.2
Cost of Sales/Inventory	52 / 7.0	72 / 5.1
	89 / 4.1	94 / 3.9
	126 / 2.9	261 / 1.4
Cost of Sales/Payables	24 / 14.9	34 / 10.6
	40 / 9.2	45 / 8.1
	55 / 6.6	89 / 4.1
Sales/Working Capital	3.5	4.0
	8.4	7.2
	13.9	-10.0
EBIT/Interest	39.9	23.6
	(21) 3.3	3.9
	1.2	-1.3
Net Profit + Dep., Dep., Amort./Cur. Mat. L/T/D		
Fixed/Worth	.2	.3
	.4	.7
	1.0	NM
Debt/Worth	.5	1.1
	1.0	1.9
	7.5	NM
% Profit Before Taxes/Tangible Net Worth	28.4	58.3
	(20) 13.1	(12) 14.9
	3.1	-4.1
% Profit Before Taxes/Total Assets	9.7	19.7
	5.3	5.8
	.7	-4.9
Sales/Net Fixed Assets	28.5	23.7
	8.9	7.2
	6.4	4.0
Sales/Total Assets	2.2	2.2
	1.6	1.1
	1.2	.8
% Dep., Dep., Amort./Sales	1.0	1.2
	(19) 2.1	(11) 1.9
	3.1	5.9
% Officers', Directors', Owners' Comp/Sales		

0-500M	500M-2MM	2-10MM	10-50MM	50-100MM	100-250MM			
4068M	3619M	122372M	271375M	359842M	754658M	Net Sales ($)	1823772M	621704M
366M	1090M	55038M	142391M	220451M	568526M	Total Assets ($)	1175040M	567430M

M = $ thousand   MM = $ million

MANUFACTURING—Motor Vehicle Electrical and Electronic Equipment Manufacturing NAICS 336320

Comparative Historical Data | Current Data Sorted by Sales

				Type of Statement						2
2	5	2		Unqualified						1
1	3	1		Reviewed						
	1			Compiled						
4	1	3		Tax Returns			1	1	1	
6	12	17		Other		3 (4/1-9/30/23)	1	20 (10/1/23-3/31/24)	5	8
4/1/21-	4/1/22-	4/1/23-			0-1MM	1-3MM	3-5MM	5-10MM	10-25MM	25MM & OVER
3/31/22	3/31/23	3/31/24								
ALL	ALL	ALL								
13	22	23		NUMBER OF STATEMENTS			2	4	6	11
%	%	%		ASSETS	%	%	%	%	%	%
8.3	9.5	11.2		Cash & Equivalents						6.2
17.7	23.1	23.5		Trade Receivables (net)	D	D				23.6
36.5	41.1	32.0		Inventory	A	A				30.4
1.4	1.5	2.6		All Other Current	T	T				2.0
63.8	75.2	69.3		Total Current	A	A				62.1
19.1	14.9	14.5		Fixed Assets (net)						21.4
5.5	1.8	11.3		Intangibles (net)	N	N				8.7
11.6	8.0	4.9		All Other Non-Current	O	O				7.8
100.0	100.0	100.0		Total	T	T				100.0
				LIABILITIES						
12.0	11.3	9.2		Notes Payable-Short Term	A	A				10.5
2.3	1.1	1.1		Cur. Mat.-L.T.D.	V	V				1.9
14.6	19.4	16.5		Trade Payables	A	A				18.1
.1	.2	.1		Income Taxes Payable	I	I				.1
6.3	9.8	9.1		All Other Current	L	L				11.7
35.3	41.7	35.9		Total Current	A	A				42.4
20.9	10.9	12.9		Long-Term Debt	B	B				20.0
.4	.0	.1		Deferred Taxes	L	L				.2
7.4	3.8	6.1		All Other Non-Current	E	E				9.2
36.1	43.7	45.0		Net Worth						28.2
100.0	100.0	100.0		Total Liabilities & Net Worth						100.0
				INCOME DATA						
100.0	100.0	100.0		Net Sales						100.0
29.9	29.4	28.3		Gross Profit						25.7
25.9	24.0	21.3		Operating Expenses						18.8
4.0	5.4	6.9		Operating Profit						6.9
.3	-.1	.4		All Other Expenses (net)						.6
3.7	5.5	6.6		Profit Before Taxes						6.3
				RATIOS						
3.8	3.4	3.7								2.0
2.1	2.1	1.8		Current						1.3
1.0	1.2	1.2								1.0
1.4	1.5	1.5								1.2
1.2	.9	.9		Quick						.6
.3	.5	.5								.5
20 18.0	35 10.4	27 13.5							36	10.1
54 6.7	47 7.7	46 8.0		Sales/Receivables					58	6.3
61 6.0	58 6.3	58 6.3							62	5.9
78 4.7	79 4.6	65 5.6							69	5.3
101 3.6	99 3.7	96 3.8		Cost of Sales/Inventory					96	3.8
166 2.2	135 2.7	122 3.0							104	3.5
19 18.9	20 18.2	25 14.8							36	10.0
60 6.1	41 8.9	36 10.2		Cost of Sales/Payables					51	7.1
68 5.4	62 5.9	56 6.5							61	6.0
3.5	3.8	3.5								5.7
5.3	5.3	7.3		Sales/Working Capital						7.7
NM	15.2	26.8								94.9
16.4	14.2	25.6								
8.8	(17) 8.2	(19) 5.0		EBIT/Interest						
.7	3.1	1.7								
				Net Profit + Depr., Dep., Amort./Cur. Mat. L/T/D						
.1	.1	.1								.4
.6	.2	.4		Fixed/Worth						.9
NM	.9	-13.3								-5.0
.7	.7	.9								1.5
1.4	.8	1.5		Debt/Worth						1.9
NM	2.8	-45.5								-32.0
24.9	41.2	48.2		% Profit Before Taxes/Tangible Net Worth						
(10) 18.0	(20) 19.4	(17) 22.6								
-1.7	9.6	6.9								
12.4	20.3	25.6		% Profit Before Taxes/Total Assets						13.3
4.9	7.9	9.4								9.4
.2	3.1	2.3								2.3
29.1	46.3	64.2								23.4
9.6	23.0	23.4		Sales/Net Fixed Assets						10.5
5.2	7.6	7.4								4.4
2.0	2.3	2.5								2.1
1.3	1.9	2.0		Sales/Total Assets						1.5
1.1	1.5	1.4								1.0
		.7								
	(16) 1.1	(14) 1.0		% Depr., Dep., Amort./Sales						
		1.4								
		2.1								
				% Officers', Directors' Owners' Comp/Sales						
837744M	1240962M	1515934M		Net Sales ($)			7687M	34682M	104782M	1368783M
557592M	785062M	987862M		Total Assets ($)			1456M	17972M	57052M	911382M

M = $ thousand   MM = $ million
See Pages viii through xx for Explanation of Ratios and Data

© RMA 2024

MANUFACTURING—Motor Vehicle Seating and Interior Trim Manufacturing NAICS 336360

Current Data Sorted by Assets

0-500M	500M-2MM	2-10MM	10-50MM	50-100MM	100-250MM		Comparative Historical Data	
						Type of Statement		
			2	1	3	Unqualified	4	4
		1	2			Reviewed	6	4
						Compiled		
						Tax Returns	1	
	13 (4/1-9/30/23)	1	12 (10/1/23-3/31/24)	1	8	Other	27 4/1/19-3/31/20 ALL	10 4/1/20-3/31/21 ALL
		3	15	2	11	NUMBER OF STATEMENTS	38	18
%	%	%	%	%	%	ASSETS	%	%
			6.7		1.3	Cash & Equivalents	7.5	12.1
			30.9		25.5	Trade Receivables (net)	28.8	28.9
			24.4		22.2	Inventory	21.6	18.5
D	D		12.2		4.6	All Other Current	3.7	1.3
A	A		74.2		53.5	Total Current	61.5	60.8
T	T		19.7		23.7	Fixed Assets (net)	26.4	27.3
A	A		1.0		10.2	Intangibles (net)	6.2	.9
			5.1		12.7	All Other Non-Current	5.9	10.9
N	N		100.0		100.0	Total	100.0	100.0
O	O					LIABILITIES		
T	T		18.0		5.6	Notes Payable-Short Term	7.1	8.1
			2.3		2.2	Cur. Mat.-L.T.D.	2.4	3.4
A	A		12.5		21.1	Trade Payables	20.5	24.0
V	V		.1		.0	Income Taxes Payable	.0	.0
A	A		22.5		10.8	All Other Current	13.7	14.5
I	I		55.4		39.7	Total Current	43.7	50.2
L	L		12.3		20.2	Long-Term Debt	14.8	13.6
A	A		.0		.0	Deferred Taxes	.1	.2
B	B		8.0		11.0	All Other Non-Current	6.7	9.0
L	L		24.4		29.0	Net Worth	34.8	27.0
E	E		100.0		100.0	Total Liabilties & Net Worth	100.0	100.0
						INCOME DATA		
			100.0		100.0	Net Sales	100.0	100.0
			21.5		11.7	Gross Profit	17.0	15.3
			16.9		9.4	Operating Expenses	14.9	11.7
			4.6		2.3	Operating Profit	2.1	3.6
			2.7		.3	All Other Expenses (net)	2.0	1.0
			1.9		2.0	Profit Before Taxes	.1	2.6
						RATIOS		
			2.2		2.2		2.4	2.6
			1.4		1.2	Current	1.5	1.6
			1.0		1.0		1.0	.8
			1.2		.8		1.1	1.7
			.7		.7	Quick	.9	1.0
			.4		.7		.6	.5
			45 8.2		39 9.3		38 9.5	33 11.1
			56 6.5		43 8.5	Sales/Receivables	46 8.0	47 7.7
			64 5.7		50 7.3		54 6.8	63 5.8
			52 7.0		26 13.8		24 15.2	22 16.7
			68 5.4		47 7.8	Cost of Sales/Inventory	41 8.8	37 9.8
			79 4.6		57 6.4		58 6.3	69 5.3
			0 UND		34 10.7		26 14.2	24 15.0
			38 9.7		41 9.0	Cost of Sales/Payables	33 11.2	43 8.4
			63 5.8		47 7.7		55 6.6	54 6.7
			5.4		6.9		5.4	4.1
			10.5		21.6	Sales/Working Capital	12.4	9.3
			55.4		-999.8		-191.0	-10.4
			5.4		17.1		7.6	32.6
			(14) 2.8		7.1	EBIT/Interest	(35) 1.6	(16) 3.6
			.3		.7		-.7	-1.0
						Net Profit + Depr., Dep., Amort./Cur. Mat. L/T/D		
			.6		.6		.4	.5
			1.0		.7	Fixed/Worth	.9	1.3
			1.4		6.9		6.4	7.9
			1.4		1.0		.9	.7
			2.8		2.7	Debt/Worth	2.3	3.3
			14.2		24.4		19.6	21.0
			36.0				34.5	31.9
			(14) 18.6			% Profit Before Taxes/Tangible Net Worth	(31) 6.3	(15) 14.9
			-9.5				-5.3	-27.5
			9.3		11.2		8.6	13.1
			3.7		8.8	% Profit Before Taxes/Total Assets	1.9	3.1
			-2.1		-.6		-2.8	-4.6
			30.9		16.4		20.0	13.2
			9.9		7.6	Sales/Net Fixed Assets	8.6	6.8
			5.7		6.8		4.5	3.5
			2.3		2.5		2.5	2.1
			2.0		2.1	Sales/Total Assets	1.8	1.9
			1.3		2.0		1.6	1.3
			1.7				1.5	1.0
			(14) 1.8			% Depr., Dep., Amort./Sales	(29) 2.6	(13) 2.1
			3.2				3.6	3.0
						% Officers', Directors' Owners' Comp/Sales		
	34274M	723424M	242914M	3654340M		Net Sales ($)	7236811M	4167398M
	16749M	378730M	158957M	1725100M		Total Assets ($)	2797114M	1607431M

M = $ thousand   MM = $ million
See Pages viii through xx for Explanation of Ratios and Data

© RMA 2024

MANUFACTURING—Motor Vehicle Seating and Interior Trim Manufacturing NAICS 336360

Comparative Historical Data | Current Data Sorted by Sales

Comparative Historical Data					Current Data Sorted by Sales					
				Type of Statement						
1		3		5	Unqualified				4	5
5		2		4	Reviewed					
					Compiled					
					Tax Returns					
					Other					
10 4/1/21- 3/31/22 ALL		18 4/1/22- 3/31/23 ALL		22 4/1/23- 3/31/24 ALL		13 (4/1-9/30/23) 0-1MM	1-3MM	1 3-5MM	18 (10/1/23-3/31/24) 5-10MM	1 10-25MM	20 25MM & OVER
16		23		31	NUMBER OF STATEMENTS			1	5	25
%		%		%	ASSETS	%	%	%	%	%	%
10.2		3.5		5.2	Cash & Equivalents					2.8
27.6		25.6		26.9	Trade Receivables (net)	DATA	DATA	DATA	29.1
25.4		29.6		24.3	Inventory				24.6
5.6		8.0		7.5	All Other Current	NOT	NOT	NOT	8.1
68.7		66.6		64.0	Total Current				64.6
23.4		19.3		23.0	Fixed Assets (net)	AVAILABLE	AVAILABLE	AVAILABLE	20.9
1.0		3.1		4.4	Intangibles (net)				4.9
6.9		11.0		8.5	All Other Non-Current				9.6
100.0		100.0		100.0	Total				100.0
					LIABILITIES					
11.8		8.2		11.7	Notes Payable-Short Term				13.3
2.3		.8		2.2	Cur. Mat.-L.T.D.				2.5
19.1		20.6		15.0	Trade Payables				16.8
.0		.0		.0	Income Taxes Payable				.1
13.2		9.1		15.7	All Other Current				18.6
46.4		38.8		44.6	Total Current				51.3
13.2		12.3		16.4	Long-Term Debt				17.5
.0		.0		.0	Deferred Taxes				.0
7.2		9.8		9.2	All Other Non-Current				9.7
33.2		39.1		29.7	Net Worth				21.5
100.0		100.0		100.0	Total Liabilities & Net Worth				100.0
					INCOME DATA					
100.0		100.0		100.0	Net Sales				100.0
14.2		12.3		18.0	Gross Profit				17.2
13.1		9.2		14.4	Operating Expenses				13.4
1.1		3.1		3.6	Operating Profit				3.8
-2.3		-.2		1.3	All Other Expenses (net)				2.0
3.4		3.3		2.3	Profit Before Taxes				1.8
					RATIOS					
	3.3		2.5		2.2	Current					2.0
	1.7		2.1		1.5						1.2
	.8		1.4		1.1						1.0
	2.0		1.0		1.0	Quick					.8
	.7		.7		.7						.7
	.5		.5		.5						.5
41	8.9	35	10.5	39	9.3	Sales/Receivables				42	8.6
57	6.4	39	9.3	47	7.7					50	7.3
69	5.3	46	8.0	56	6.5					57	6.4
47	7.8	36	10.0	31	11.6	Cost of Sales/Inventory				36	10.0
57	6.4	59	6.2	57	6.4					57	6.4
83	4.4	68	5.4	74	4.9					72	5.1
26	14.3	31	11.8	19	19.5	Cost of Sales/Payables				24	15.2
45	8.2	41	8.9	38	9.7					41	9.0
53	6.9	48	7.6	48	7.6					51	7.2
	3.1		5.4		6.4	Sales/Working Capital					6.6
	7.4		6.1		10.0						17.7
	-49.5		10.9		45.5						NM
	17.4		19.5		14.0	EBIT/Interest					11.9
(13)	1.1	(22)	15.7	(30)	4.0						3.1
	-8.7		4.0		1.1						.6
					Net Profit + Depr., Dep., Amort./Cur. Mat. L/T/D					
	.3		.4		.6	Fixed/Worth					.6
	.6		.5		.9						1.0
	446.5		.7		1.6						3.1
	.5		1.2		1.0	Debt/Worth					1.4
	2.4		1.6		2.8						5.4
	756.7		2.6		15.1						20.4
	30.1		35.2		27.8	% Profit Before Taxes/Tangible Net Worth					32.1
(13)	8.0	(21)	24.8	(27)	18.4					(21)	21.3
	-19.6		16.8		9.8						-4.0
	13.6		13.8		10.1	% Profit Before Taxes/Total Assets					9.9
	.2		10.0		5.8						4.6
	-7.1		1.4		.3						-1.4
	15.4		16.3		22.3	Sales/Net Fixed Assets					22.3
	7.5		11.0		8.1						9.9
	4.5		7.8		5.7						6.8
	2.0		2.3		2.3	Sales/Total Assets					2.4
	1.8		2.1		2.1						2.1
	1.3		1.9		1.5						1.8
	.9		.9		1.2	% Depr., Dep., Amort./Sales					1.4
(15)	1.5	(18)	1.2	(23)	1.7					(17)	1.7
	3.3		1.3		3.0						1.8
					% Officers', Directors', Owners' Comp/Sales					
2771259M		5902788M		4654952M	Net Sales ($)		4274M		90769M	4559909M
1261297M		2611072M		2279536M	Total Assets ($)		2870M		61067M	2215599M

M = $ thousand   MM = $ million
See Pages viii through xx for Explanation of Ratios and Data
© RMA 2024

MANUFACTURING—Motor Vehicle Metal Stamping NAICS 336370

Current Data Sorted by Assets | Comparative Historical Data

							Type of Statement		
			2	1	3		Unqualified	6	4
		2	6	5			Reviewed	3	5
1		1	1				Compiled	4	2
	9 (4/1-9/30/23)	4	13	7	12		Tax Returns	4	
0-500M	500M-2MM	2-10MM	49 (10/1/23-3/31/24) 10-50MM	50-100MM	100-250MM		Other	40 4/1/19- 3/31/20 ALL	32 4/1/20- 3/31/21 ALL
1		7	22	13	15		NUMBER OF STATEMENTS	57	43
%	%	%	%	%	%		ASSETS	%	%
			5.7	6.1	4.2		Cash & Equivalents	3.7	8.0
			24.6	23.5	22.6		Trade Receivables (net)	25.6	23.1
	D		21.8	19.5	20.2		Inventory	20.7	17.1
	A		1.9	2.2	1.9		All Other Current	2.8	3.6
	T		54.1	51.2	48.9		Total Current	52.8	51.8
	A		33.6	35.3	34.5		Fixed Assets (net)	32.1	33.5
			3.4	1.9	5.2		Intangibles (net)	7.7	5.8
	N		9.0	11.6	11.4		All Other Non-Current	7.3	8.9
	O		100.0	100.0	100.0		Total	100.0	100.0
	T						LIABILITIES		
			8.6	6.7	8.0		Notes Payable-Short Term	10.8	10.7
	A		2.8	2.7	3.5		Cur. Mat.-L.T.D.	2.7	4.2
	V		16.5	17.0	15.1		Trade Payables	16.8	15.7
	A		.3	.0	.1		Income Taxes Payable	.1	.0
	I		7.5	9.8	11.6		All Other Current	7.2	8.6
	L		35.8	36.2	38.3		Total Current	37.6	39.3
	A		12.2	10.8	17.1		Long-Term Debt	15.6	20.8
	B		.1	1.2	.4		Deferred Taxes	.5	.3
	L		12.2	9.7	9.6		All Other Non-Current	8.3	9.8
	E		39.7	42.2	34.6		Net Worth	37.9	29.7
			100.0	100.0	100.0		Total Liabilities & Net Worth	100.0	100.0
							INCOME DATA		
			100.0	100.0	100.0		Net Sales	100.0	100.0
			17.2	12.5	14.8		Gross Profit	14.0	16.8
			14.5	8.4	10.3		Operating Expenses	13.0	15.9
			2.7	4.2	4.5		Operating Profit	1.0	.9
			.7	-.4	2.0		All Other Expenses (net)	1.2	1.7
			2.0	4.6	2.5		Profit Before Taxes	-.2	-.8
							RATIOS		
			2.6	3.1	2.5			2.7	2.4
			1.6	1.8	1.3		Current	1.4	1.2
			1.0	1.1	.8			1.0	1.0
			1.4	1.9	1.3			1.4	1.7
			.9	.8	.7		Quick	.7	.7
			.5	.5	.5			.5	.5
		37 9.8	42 8.7	47 7.8				46 7.9	43 8.5
		51 7.1	48 7.6	53 6.9		Sales/Receivables		57 6.4	66 5.5
		68 5.4	59 6.2	68 5.4				64 5.7	83 4.4
		36 10.0	34 10.8	44 8.3				31 11.9	37 9.9
		52 7.0	47 7.7	54 6.8		Cost of Sales/Inventory		50 7.3	51 7.2
		89 4.1	65 5.6	65 5.4				62 5.9	73 5.0
		22 16.8	20 18.0	31 11.7				26 14.0	32 11.3
		32 11.3	33 11.0	42 8.6		Cost of Sales/Payables		39 9.4	48 7.6
		44 8.3	51 7.1	54 6.7				56 6.5	64 5.7
			4.2	4.0	5.5			4.4	3.7
			11.2	8.5	16.8		Sales/Working Capital	14.5	11.7
			-94.4	NM	-13.4			NM	-55.0
			17.1	36.9	7.5			3.5	10.9
		(21)	3.2	13.1	(14) 3.6		EBIT/Interest	(55) 1.6	(38) 2.7
			1.0	1.2	1.1			-.6	-.5
							Net Profit + Depr., Dep.,	4.8	
							Amort./Cur. Mat. L/T/D	(12) 2.3	
								.7	
			.4	.5	.5			.6	.6
			1.1	.7	1.3		Fixed/Worth	1.0	1.1
			3.2	NM	2.7			2.8	UND
			.8	.3	1.0			1.0	.9
			1.4	.5	2.3		Debt/Worth	2.0	2.6
			7.1	NM	5.9			6.6	UND
			28.9	23.9	23.0		% Profit Before Taxes/Tangible	9.1	17.7
		(19)	9.3	(10) 15.9	(14) 13.2		Net Worth	(48) 4.3	(33) 8.6
			2.6	9.7	5.5			-8.2	.9
			9.9	12.8	9.2			3.9	5.9
			3.2	9.5	4.6		% Profit Before Taxes/Total Assets	1.6	1.0
			.2	-.2	.5			-2.7	-6.8
			14.1	8.0	9.0			8.6	7.8
			6.3	5.0	5.2		Sales/Net Fixed Assets	5.4	4.6
			3.9	3.5	2.3			3.4	2.9
			2.3	2.2	1.8			2.2	1.7
			1.8	1.7	1.5		Sales/Total Assets	1.7	1.3
			1.1	1.3	1.3			1.1	1.0
			2.0	2.3	2.3			1.5	2.7
		(21)	3.2	(12) 3.2	(10) 3.4		% Depr., Dep., Amort./Sales	(46) 2.6	(33) 4.4
			4.4	3.8	5.1			4.1	5.5
							% Officers', Directors' Owners' Comp/Sales		
579M		108693M	1058548M	1696959M	3222622M		Net Sales ($)	5395159M	3145541M
331M		48022M	599065M	963887M	2189232M		Total Assets ($)	3471479M	2376281M

© RMA 2024

M = $ thousand   MM = $ million
See Pages viii through xx for Explanation of Ratios and Data

MANUFACTURING—Motor Vehicle Metal Stamping NAICS 336370

Comparative Historical Data | Current Data Sorted by Sales

				Type of Statement						
	3	3	6	Unqualified				1	5	
	5	7	13	Reviewed				4	9	
	1		1	Compiled				1		
		3	2	Tax Returns	1			6	1	29
	30	31	36	Other				49		
	4/1/21-	4/1/22-	4/1/23-			9 (4/1-9/30/23)		(10/1/23-3/31/24)		
	3/31/22	3/31/23	3/31/24		0-1MM	1-3MM	3-5MM	5-10MM	10-25MM	25MM & OVER
	ALL	ALL	ALL							
	39	44	58	NUMBER OF STATEMENTS	1			1	12	44
	%	%	%	ASSETS	%	%	%	%	%	%
	5.3	8.4	5.7	Cash & Equivalents					6.2	4.7
	26.2	25.0	24.2	Trade Receivables (net)	D	D			20.9	24.7
	23.4	22.3	22.5	Inventory	A	A			30.0	21.2
	2.1	3.8	1.8	All Other Current	T	T			1.0	2.1
	57.1	59.6	54.2	Total Current	A	A			58.1	52.8
	33.0	31.4	32.4	Fixed Assets (net)					27.9	34.3
	3.4	3.4	3.2	Intangibles (net)	N	N			5.7	2.7
	6.6	5.6	10.2	All Other Non-Current	O	O			8.3	10.2
	100.0	100.0	100.0	Total	T	T			100.0	100.0
				LIABILITIES	A	A				
	8.6	12.4	7.9	Notes Payable-Short Term	V	V			7.9	8.3
	2.3	3.3	2.7	Cur. Mat.-L.T.D.	A	A			2.0	3.0
	19.1	18.1	16.2	Trade Payables	I	I			16.2	16.9
	.1	.1	.2	Income Taxes Payable	L	L			.0	.2
	7.6	10.0	8.8	All Other Current	A	A			8.2	9.2
	37.7	43.9	35.8	Total Current	B	B			34.2	37.5
	14.4	13.3	12.3	Long-Term Debt	L	L			4.7	14.4
	.8	.4	.4	Deferred Taxes	E	E			.0	.5
	12.1	5.4	10.0	All Other Non-Current					8.3	10.8
	35.0	36.9	41.6	Net Worth					52.8	36.7
	100.0	100.0	100.0	Total Liabilities & Net Worth					100.0	100.0
				INCOME DATA						
	100.0	100.0	100.0	Net Sales					100.0	100.0
	17.3	12.9	17.1	Gross Profit					18.4	14.6
	13.8	12.3	13.3	Operating Expenses					14.5	11.4
	3.5	.5	3.8	Operating Profit					4.0	3.3
	-1.8	.1	.8	All Other Expenses (net)					.4	.8
	5.2	.4	3.0	Profit Before Taxes					3.6	2.5
				RATIOS						
	2.1	2.5	2.8						2.3	2.8
	1.5	1.3	1.5	Current					1.5	1.3
	1.1	1.0	1.0						1.1	1.0
	1.3	1.3	1.5						1.3	1.5
	.8	.7	.8	Quick					.9	.7
	.5	.4	.5						.5	.5
51	7.1	38	9.5	39	9.4	Sales/Receivables			27	13.3	44	8.3
66	5.5	55	6.6	51	7.1				45	8.2	51	7.2
79	4.6	70	5.2	66	5.5				54	6.8	66	5.5
47	7.7	37	9.8	38	9.7	Cost of Sales/Inventory			52	7.0	35	10.4
64	5.7	53	6.9	54	6.7				76	4.8	48	7.6
96	3.8	66	5.5	76	4.8				101	3.6	69	5.3
41	8.9	27	13.6	25	14.6	Cost of Sales/Payables			17	22.0	27	13.7
54	6.7	37	9.9	34	10.8				32	11.3	39	9.4
78	4.7	56	6.5	48	7.6				49	7.5	49	7.5
	4.2		5.2		4.2	Sales/Working Capital				4.3		4.4
	8.3		11.9		9.6					9.8		12.3
	26.7		-110.2		-641.7					20.1		-151.8
	16.5		17.2		16.9	EBIT/Interest				12.5		23.5
(34)	6.6	(40)	2.1	(54)	2.9				(10)	1.6	(43)	3.2
	1.9		-1.6		.7					-2.4		.9
			13.3		14.6	Net Profit + Depr., Dep.,						13.4
		(14)	2.8	(21)	6.2	Amort./Cur. Mat. L/T/D					(18)	5.3
			1.1		1.4							1.4
	.5		.4		.4	Fixed/Worth				.2		.5
	1.0		.8		.7					.6		.9
	4.0		6.9		2.4					1.0		3.7
	.9		.8		.6	Debt/Worth				.6		.7
	1.7		1.6		1.4					1.0		1.8
	11.5		14.7		6.0					1.6		9.3
	34.6		19.3		23.4	% Profit Before Taxes/Tangible				19.5		23.9
(33)	17.8	(36)	5.5	(51)	11.6	Net Worth			(11)	6.8	(38)	13.6
	5.4		-1.7		3.6					-10.1		4.2
	15.5		6.6		9.9	% Profit Before Taxes/Total				8.9		9.8
	6.2		1.3		3.5	Assets				2.9		3.5
	2.1		-4.9		-.3					-3.8		-.1
	8.0		16.9		11.6	Sales/Net Fixed Assets				18.5		9.3
	4.5		6.3		6.0					10.5		5.1
	2.9		3.1		3.8					3.8		3.6
	1.6		2.2		2.3	Sales/Total Assets				2.7		2.3
	1.4		1.8		1.7					1.6		1.7
	1.2		1.3		1.3					1.1		1.3
	2.7		2.0		2.2	% Depr., Dep., Amort./Sales				1.9		2.3
(26)	3.3	(35)	2.7	(49)	3.2				(11)	2.7	(37)	3.2
	4.8		4.1		4.3					4.3		4.2
						% Officers', Directors', Owners' Comp/Sales						
	3628096M		3252616M		6087401M	Net Sales ($)	579M			7486M	217462M	5861874M
	2534339M		2093477M		3800537M	Total Assets ($)	331M			6272M	162610M	3631324M

M = $ thousand   MM = $ million

© RMA 2024

MANUFACTURING—Other Motor Vehicle Parts Manufacturing NAICS 336390

Current Data Sorted by Assets | Comparative Historical Data

							Type of Statement				
				7	9	14	Unqualified		31		19
			5	7	2	1	Reviewed		13		9
			2	2	1	2	Compiled		15		7
1	3		4	2			Tax Returns		8		6
1	2		12	31	11	28	Other		103		60
		24 (4/1-9/30/23)		121 (10/1/23-3/31/24)					4/1/19-		4/1/20-
0-500M	500M-2MM	2-10MM	10-50MM	50-100MM	100-250MM			3/31/20		3/31/21	
2	5	23	47	23	45	NUMBER OF STATEMENTS		ALL 170		ALL 101	
%	%	%	%	%	%	ASSETS		%		%	
		13.7	8.5	10.5	8.8	Cash & Equivalents		8.1		13.6	
		19.9	17.9	22.2	24.1	Trade Receivables (net)		20.2		19.8	
		33.3	28.2	21.5	27.4	Inventory		27.5		22.3	
		3.3	5.3	8.4	4.1	All Other Current		3.8		4.2	
		70.1	59.9	62.6	64.4	Total Current		59.7		59.8	
		14.5	26.2	19.9	25.6	Fixed Assets (net)		28.2		26.6	
		5.7	5.4	3.9	3.0	Intangibles (net)		6.0		5.7	
		9.7	8.5	13.5	7.0	All Other Non-Current		6.1		7.9	
		100.0	100.0	100.0	100.0	Total		100.0		100.0	
						LIABILITIES					
		8.0	7.0	5.5	6.4	Notes Payable-Short Term		8.5		8.8	
		1.3	1.7	2.0	6.3	Cur. Mat.-L.T.D.		4.0		2.9	
		13.6	14.2	13.8	18.2	Trade Payables		13.4		14.1	
		.3	.3	.1	.1	Income Taxes Payable		.2		.3	
		13.7	8.3	14.2	13.7	All Other Current		13.3		13.1	
		36.9	31.4	35.6	44.7	Total Current		39.4		39.3	
		12.3	13.9	8.7	11.7	Long-Term Debt		14.9		15.9	
		.4	.3	.3	.3	Deferred Taxes		.6		.5	
		10.8	7.2	6.5	8.9	All Other Non-Current		4.4		5.8	
		39.5	47.3	49.0	34.4	Net Worth		40.6		38.5	
		100.0	100.0	100.0	100.0	Total Liabilties & Net Worth		100.0		100.0	
						INCOME DATA					
		100.0	100.0	100.0	100.0	Net Sales		100.0		100.0	
		33.7	26.4	18.7	15.3	Gross Profit		27.0		23.0	
		27.5	18.1	10.6	10.5	Operating Expenses		21.8		17.0	
		6.2	8.3	8.1	4.8	Operating Profit		5.2		6.0	
		.8	.9	.9	.5	All Other Expenses (net)		1.0		-.3	
		5.3	7.4	7.1	4.3	Profit Before Taxes		4.2		6.3	
						RATIOS					
		4.5	3.2	3.1	1.7			2.8		3.1	
		2.5	2.1	1.9	1.5	Current		1.6		1.7	
		1.1	1.4	1.3	1.2			1.0		1.1	
		1.8	1.7	1.8	1.0			1.2		1.6	
		.9	.8	1.1	.7	Quick		.7		1.0	
		.6	.5	.5	.6			.4		.5	
		15 23.8	25 14.7	27 13.7	36 10.0		27	13.6	30	12.0	
		39 9.3	42 8.7	46 7.9	54 6.8	Sales/Receivables	39	9.3	49	7.4	
		61 6.0	54 6.8	54 6.7	61 6.0		52	7.0	65	5.6	
		41 8.9	43 8.4	26 14.0	33 11.0		29	12.6	30	12.1	
		96 3.8	68 5.4	43 8.5	76 4.8	Cost of Sales/Inventory	62	5.9	58	6.3	
		182 2.0	140 2.6	96 3.8	101 3.6		107	3.4	101	3.6	
		15 24.5	18 20.6	21 17.4	27 13.4		17	21.4	20	18.0	
		24 14.9	31 11.7	34 10.6	36 10.2	Cost of Sales/Payables	28	13.2	32	11.3	
		50 7.3	48 7.6	41 8.9	46 8.0		47	7.8	58	6.3	
		3.7	3.6	3.3	6.3			4.2		3.5	
		6.0	6.0	4.8	8.5	Sales/Working Capital		9.1		6.6	
		18.1	13.5	16.7	31.5			153.0		61.6	
		20.4	27.1	38.4	11.5			20.9		26.2	
	(19)	10.5	(41) 4.8	(19) 6.2	(39) 4.9	EBIT/Interest	(146)	3.5	(85)	4.6	
		1.1	2.5	2.6	1.9			.8		.9	
			16.6								
		(13)	2.4			Net Profit + Depr., Dep.,		6.3		6.8	
			1.3			Amort./Cur. Mat. L/T/D	(45)	2.3	(25)	3.2	
								.5		1.4	
		.0	.1	.2	.4			.3		.2	
		.2	.5	.4	.8	Fixed/Worth		.8		.6	
		.9	1.1	1.0	1.9			2.2		2.2	
		.3	.5	.5	1.3			.6		.7	
		1.3	1.4	1.0	1.7	Debt/Worth		1.7		1.5	
		4.3	3.4	2.2	4.8			4.7		5.5	
		67.4	34.6	35.6	25.9			35.1		35.3	
	(20)	27.9	(42) 17.8	(22) 22.0	(41) 12.7	% Profit Before Taxes/Tangible Net Worth	(147)	15.1	(89)	14.2	
		.7	12.7	10.2	3.1			1.8		.5	
		23.5	20.1	18.5	9.0			16.3		15.9	
		11.0	7.8	11.4	6.2	% Profit Before Taxes/Total Assets		4.9		4.5	
		.4	4.1	4.1	.6			.0		.1	
		670.0	33.3	11.4	15.6			21.8		18.9	
		31.6	6.5	9.5	8.7	Sales/Net Fixed Assets		7.1		6.4	
		6.5	3.5	6.2	3.9			3.8		3.8	
		2.9	2.0	2.7	2.3			2.5		2.0	
		1.9	1.7	1.8	1.6	Sales/Total Assets		1.9		1.5	
		1.5	1.2	1.1	1.2			1.2		1.0	
		.7	1.5	1.1	.5			1.2		1.1	
	(15)	2.3	(40) 2.3	2.1	(29) 2.1	% Depr., Dep., Amort./Sales	(142)	2.6	(81)	2.4	
		3.2	3.8	3.6	2.7			4.3		4.1	
						% Officers', Directors' Owners' Comp/Sales		2.5		1.2	
							(26)	3.7	(17)	2.5	
								5.9		4.6	
4167M	33470M	250862M	2055691M	3195445M	15244348M	Net Sales ($)		13735300M		8687157M	
724M	6572M	130888M	1256831M	1695219M	7615913M	Total Assets ($)		7901996M		5529225M	

© RMA 2024   M = $ thousand   MM = $ million
See Pages viii through xx for Explanation of Ratios and Data

MANUFACTURING—Other Motor Vehicle Parts Manufacturing NAICS 336390

Comparative Historical Data / **Current Data Sorted by Sales**

				Type of Statement						
	11	20	30	Unqualified				4	2	28
	11	12	15	Reviewed				2	2	9
	6	14	5	Compiled		3	2	2	2	3
	5	7	10	Tax Returns			1	3	1	1
	67	76	85	Other	1	24		4	17	62
	4/1/21-3/31/22 ALL	4/1/22-3/31/23 ALL	4/1/23-3/31/24 ALL		0-1MM	(4/1-9/30/23) 1-3MM	3-5MM	121 (10/1/23-3/31/24) 5-10MM	10-25MM	25MM & OVER
	100	129	145	**NUMBER OF STATEMENTS**	1	3	3	11	24	103
	%	%	%	**ASSETS**	%	%	%	%	%	%
	11.0	10.3	10.3	Cash & Equivalents				14.3	11.8	9.0
	20.5	20.1	20.9	Trade Receivables (net)				15.9	21.8	21.7
	30.6	29.4	28.1	Inventory				40.3	29.2	25.9
	3.6	4.7	4.9	All Other Current				2.5	4.1	5.6
	65.7	64.5	64.2	Total Current				73.0	67.0	62.3
	22.5	22.7	22.2	Fixed Assets (net)				11.7	19.3	24.7
	7.2	6.2	4.5	Intangibles (net)				7.6	2.5	4.3
	4.7	6.6	9.1	All Other Non-Current				7.7	11.2	8.6
	100.0	100.0	100.0	Total				100.0	100.0	100.0
				LIABILITIES						
	7.2	9.2	6.7	Notes Payable-Short Term				10.3	5.6	6.7
	3.1	2.7	3.2	Cur. Mat.-L.T.D.				1.4	1.2	3.8
	14.1	14.0	16.1	Trade Payables				15.3	13.5	16.3
	.1	.1	.3	Income Taxes Payable				.0	.0	.2
	13.8	10.9	11.6	All Other Current				12.5	11.7	12.0
	38.3	37.0	37.9	Total Current				39.6	32.1	39.1
	14.2	17.2	12.4	Long-Term Debt				10.3	13.6	10.9
	.5	.5	.3	Deferred Taxes				.1	.4	.3
	4.4	5.0	7.8	All Other Non-Current				1.9	11.7	8.1
	42.5	40.3	41.5	Net Worth				48.2	42.1	41.7
	100.0	100.0	100.0	Total Liabilities & Net Worth				100.0	100.0	100.0
				INCOME DATA						
	100.0	100.0	100.0	Net Sales				100.0	100.0	100.0
	27.2	24.8	23.9	Gross Profit				32.2	30.1	19.6
	21.3	19.0	17.1	Operating Expenses				24.9	21.9	13.1
	5.9	5.8	6.8	Operating Profit				7.3	8.2	6.5
	-1.1	.5	.8	All Other Expenses (net)				1.0	.6	.7
	6.9	5.3	6.0	Profit Before Taxes				6.3	7.5	5.8
				RATIOS						
	2.8	3.5	2.8					4.5	4.2	2.4
	2.0	1.9	1.6	Current				2.0	2.5	1.5
	1.5	1.2	1.3					1.1	1.3	1.3
	1.4	1.5	1.3					1.8	2.2	1.2
	.8	.9	.9	Quick				.9	1.2	.8
	.5	.5	.5					.2	.7	.5
24	15.2	26	13.8	25	14.7		3	114.0	15	23.6	31	11.9
42	8.7	41	9.0	46	7.9	Sales/Receivables	23	16.2	52	7.0	46	7.9
63	5.8	60	6.1	58	6.3		42	8.6	72	5.1	57	6.4
51	7.2	43	8.4	38	9.6		29	12.5	41	8.8	33	10.9
87	4.2	72	5.1	68	5.4	Cost of Sales/Inventory	99	3.7	55	6.6	58	6.3
122	3.0	130	2.8	104	3.5		146	2.5	203	1.8	96	3.8
20	18.0	17	22.0	19	18.8		17	21.6	15	24.0	21	17.4
34	10.8	28	13.1	31	11.6	Cost of Sales/Payables	25	14.8	25	14.8	33	11.1
58	6.3	49	7.5	45	8.2		50	7.3	38	9.5	44	8.3
	3.3		3.5		3.9			4.8		2.3		4.1
	5.9		7.1		7.7	Sales/Working Capital		8.4		4.7		8.2
	10.5		16.7		16.9			18.1		15.9		16.7
	62.2		15.3		22.5					34.0		18.9
(87)	14.6	(106)	5.8	(123)	5.0	EBIT/Interest		(20)		9.5	(88)	4.9
	1.2		1.1		2.3					2.1		2.3
	17.8		16.5		8.3	Net Profit + Depr., Dep.,						8.7
(24)	4.3	(43)	3.4	(33)	3.6	Amort./Cur. Mat. L/T/D				(28)		3.7
	1.4		1.2		1.3							1.7
	.2		.2		.2			.0		.0		.3
	.4		.5		.5	Fixed/Worth		.2		.2		.6
	1.5		1.5		1.1			.3		.9		1.2
	.6		.6		.7			.3		.4		.8
	1.4		1.3		1.6	Debt/Worth		1.8		.9		1.7
	3.7		5.4		3.7			4.0		3.2		3.5
	45.6		33.3		34.6			71.2		39.4		31.3
(87)	25.6	(107)	14.8	(130)	20.2	% Profit Before Taxes/Tangible Net Worth	(10)	28.9	(21)	20.3	(95)	18.0
	8.4		3.0		10.2			1.0		10.6		9.7
	19.2		14.5		18.2			30.7		23.4		15.4
	10.5		6.3		7.9	% Profit Before Taxes/Total Assets		10.3		10.1		7.2
	.9		.3		2.3			.4		1.1		2.3
	25.4		22.4		26.3			784.8		70.7		15.6
	11.0		8.1		9.3	Sales/Net Fixed Assets		39.0		14.9		8.1
	4.7		4.4		4.9			6.4		4.2		4.8
	2.2		2.3		2.3			3.8		2.0		2.3
	1.7		1.6		1.8	Sales/Total Assets		2.5		1.5		1.8
	1.2		1.2		1.3			1.6		1.3		1.2
	.8		1.0		1.1					1.5		1.1
(74)	1.9	(97)	2.4	(109)	2.2	% Depr., Dep., Amort./Sales			(18)	2.8	(82)	2.2
	3.5		4.3		3.5					4.3		3.3
	1.6		2.0		1.5	% Officers', Directors'						
(19)	2.6	(20)	3.2	(20)	2.5	Owners' Comp/Sales						
	4.2		5.5		5.2							
	7206974M		11040931M		20783983M	Net Sales ($)	947M	6083M	10523M	87011M	419676M	20259743M
	4968960M		7293814M		10706147M	Total Assets ($)	278M	4818M	6224M	42704M	416675M	10235448M

M = $ thousand   MM = $ million
See Pages viii through xx for Explanation of Ratios and Data

© RMA 2024

MANUFACTURING—Aircraft Manufacturing NAICS 336411

Current Data Sorted by Assets | Comparative Historical Data

						Type of Statement				
		1	2	2	1	Unqualified		4		2
1	1	1	1	1		Reviewed		3		3
		1	1			Compiled		2		
1	5	5	1			Tax Returns		2		4
5	12	7	4	1		Other		16		18
7 (4/1-9/30/23)			39 (10/1/23-3/31/24)					4/1/19-		4/1/20-
0-500M	500M-2MM	2-10MM	10-50MM	50-100MM	100-250MM			3/31/20		3/31/21
1	7	17	12	7	2	**NUMBER OF STATEMENTS**		ALL 27		ALL 27
%	%	%	%	%	%	**ASSETS**		%		%
		16.2	6.6			Cash & Equivalents		12.3		12.2
		20.6	17.4			Trade Receivables (net)		24.5		17.3
		25.5	37.7			Inventory		26.3		28.1
		2.8	6.4			All Other Current		3.0		4.9
		65.1	68.2			Total Current		66.0		62.5
		18.0	21.7			Fixed Assets (net)		20.9		24.6
		4.2	6.5			Intangibles (net)		7.4		7.4
		12.7	3.6			All Other Non-Current		5.6		5.5
		100.0	100.0			Total		100.0		100.0
						LIABILITIES				
		3.8	2.4			Notes Payable-Short Term		9.0		13.7
		2.3	2.5			Cur. Mat.-L.T.D.		3.3		3.3
		17.3	8.6			Trade Payables		11.2		6.3
		.1	.1			Income Taxes Payable		.4		.1
		19.1	23.7			All Other Current		10.4		17.3
		42.5	37.4			Total Current		34.3		40.6
		19.8	24.7			Long-Term Debt		24.4		22.1
		.3	.4			Deferred Taxes		.2		.4
		12.9	3.9			All Other Non-Current		2.6		10.1
		24.4	33.6			Net Worth		38.5		26.7
		100.0	100.0			Total Liabilities & Net Worth		100.0		100.0
						INCOME DATA				
		100.0	100.0			Net Sales		100.0		100.0
		38.5	28.0			Gross Profit		28.4		32.2
		33.4	27.5			Operating Expenses		23.4		26.9
		5.1	.5			Operating Profit		5.0		5.3
		1.0	2.2			All Other Expenses (net)		2.3		2.3
		4.1	-1.8			Profit Before Taxes		2.7		3.0
						RATIOS				
		2.8	4.6					4.4		4.5
		2.0	1.6			Current		2.1		2.2
		1.1	1.2					1.5		1.0
		1.9	2.0					2.7		2.1
		.8	.5			Quick		1.0		.8
		.5	.4					.6		.2
		26 14.0	27 13.4					32 11.5		17 21.9
		36 10.0	46 8.0			Sales/Receivables		44 8.3		43 8.4
		69 5.3	79 4.6					63 5.8		61 6.0
		0 UND	126 2.9					8 45.1		23 16.2
		85 4.3	215 1.7			Cost of Sales/Inventory		94 3.9		118 3.1
		140 2.6	243 1.5					182 2.0		215 1.7
		26 14.2	17 20.9					17 21.1		8 44.9
		43 8.5	21 17.2			Cost of Sales/Payables		28 13.0		21 17.0
		74 4.9	45 8.1					46 7.9		44 8.3
		3.0	2.2					2.3		2.4
		5.0	4.2			Sales/Working Capital		4.6		4.1
		32.6	8.9					12.2		-100.8
		30.0	18.6					21.0		9.8
	(14)	6.4	(11) 1.8			EBIT/Interest	(26)	7.6	(20)	4.4
		.0	-3.8					-1.3		1.3
						Net Profit + Depr., Dep., Amort./Cur. Mat. L/T/D				
		.2	.3					.2		.2
		1.0	.5			Fixed/Worth		.3		.6
		NM	2.9					-2.5		4.8
		.7	.5					.5		.7
		6.9	2.1			Debt/Worth		1.2		1.8
		NM	4.4					-24.0		9.5
		90.8	43.8					37.4		60.2
	(13)	16.3	(10) 9.0			% Profit Before Taxes/Tangible Net Worth	(20)	19.3	(22)	10.8
		.1	-8.6					-.7		-1.5
		12.7	14.4					17.8		12.0
		2.5	2.2			% Profit Before Taxes/Total Assets		3.0		5.7
		-10.5	-6.5					-2.8		.0
		133.8	8.4					26.9		18.7
		8.9	7.2			Sales/Net Fixed Assets		8.6		6.7
		4.4	3.0					4.9		2.7
		2.0	1.6					2.2		1.7
		1.7	1.2			Sales/Total Assets		1.5		1.2
		1.1	.7					1.0		.8
		.4	1.4					.5		1.5
	(10)	2.6	(11) 2.0			% Depr., Dep., Amort./Sales	(25)	2.3	(18)	3.5
		4.8	10.4					3.8		6.4
						% Officers', Directors' Owners' Comp/Sales				
305M	23991M	156170M	365752M	490115M	382455M	Net Sales ($)		1584010M		1029947M
371M	9106M	96620M	300167M	454973M	263011M	Total Assets ($)		1153581M		957413M

M = $ thousand   MM = $ million
See Pages viii through xx for Explanation of Ratios and Data

© RMA 2024

MANUFACTURING—Aircraft Manufacturing NAICS 336411

Comparative Historical Data / Current Data Sorted by Sales

						Type of Statement							
	6		8		5	Unqualified					1	1	4
	1				4	Reviewed	1	1			1	1	1
			2		1	Compiled				1			
	5		5		7	Tax Returns		1		3	2	1	1
	15		32		29	Other	2	3	2	5	7	7	10
	4/1/21-		4/1/22-		4/1/23-			7 (4/1-9/30/23)		39 (10/1/23-3/31/24)			
	3/31/22		3/31/23		3/31/24								
	ALL		ALL		ALL		0-1MM	1-3MM	3-5MM	5-10MM	10-25MM	25MM & OVER	
	27		47		46	NUMBER OF STATEMENTS	3	5	2	9	11	16	
	%		%		%	ASSETS	%	%	%	%	%	%	
	9.4		11.0		12.6	Cash & Equivalents					18.7	7.9	
	14.6		22.6		18.2	Trade Receivables (net)					19.9	19.5	
	28.1		26.8		28.0	Inventory					31.5	28.0	
	3.2		3.6		5.7	All Other Current					2.0	11.6	
	55.2		64.0		64.5	Total Current					72.1	67.0	
	29.0		17.1		21.9	Fixed Assets (net)					16.6	22.2	
	5.6		7.0		4.2	Intangibles (net)					4.5	2.6	
	10.1		11.9		9.4	All Other Non-Current					6.8	8.2	
	100.0		100.0		100.0	Total					100.0	100.0	
						LIABILITIES							
	5.2		7.0		6.5	Notes Payable-Short Term					3.9	3.7	
	3.1		2.4		3.2	Cur. Mat.-L.T.D.					2.2	2.9	
	8.7		11.3		11.4	Trade Payables					13.1	10.7	
	.0		.7		.1	Income Taxes Payable					.2	.1	
	15.7		13.6		18.4	All Other Current					15.7	28.2	
	32.7		35.0		39.6	Total Current					35.1	45.6	
	28.6		20.1		21.1	Long-Term Debt					21.5	24.5	
	.6		.3		.3	Deferred Taxes					.6	.0	
	8.0		6.6		10.0	All Other Non-Current					11.3	13.0	
	30.1		37.9		28.9	Net Worth					31.6	16.9	
	100.0		100.0		100.0	Total Liabilities & Net Worth					100.0	100.0	
						INCOME DATA							
	100.0		100.0		100.0	Net Sales					100.0	100.0	
	32.5		31.5		31.7	Gross Profit					27.0	26.1	
	27.3		26.2		29.2	Operating Expenses					28.4	19.2	
	5.2		5.2		2.5	Operating Profit					-1.4	6.9	
	.2		.4		1.8	All Other Expenses (net)					1.7	2.8	
	5.0		4.9		.7	Profit Before Taxes					-3.1	4.1	
						RATIOS							
	2.9		2.9		2.8						6.6	1.8	
	1.7		2.1		1.6	Current					2.3	1.4	
	1.3		1.3		1.2						1.2	1.2	
	1.2		1.6		1.4						2.8	.9	
	.5		1.2		.7	Quick					1.0	.6	
	.4		.5		.4						.7	.4	
8	45.8	27	13.7	25	14.4						24 15.1	26 14.2	
38	9.7	42	8.6	38	9.7	Sales/Receivables					34 10.8	51 7.2	
65	5.6	73	5.0	72	5.1						74 4.9	74 4.9	
21	17.5	22	16.3	19	18.8						14 26.1	43 8.5	
111	3.3	94	3.9	104	3.5	Cost of Sales/Inventory					130 2.8	99 3.7	
261	1.4	243	1.5	215	1.7						192 1.9	192 1.9	
16	23.0	15	23.9	18	20.8						21 17.7	18 20.2	
29	12.8	30	12.2	30	12.1	Cost of Sales/Payables					33 11.2	24 15.0	
46	8.0	54	6.8	58	6.3						58 6.3	49 7.5	
	2.9		3.2		3.1						2.0	4.1	
	4.7		4.8		4.7	Sales/Working Capital					3.7	5.6	
	20.7		25.0		26.9						26.2	17.9	
	28.6		41.5		14.2							9.1	
(24)	4.0	(40)	5.1	(39)	1.8	EBIT/Interest						1.8	
	.4		-.3		-1.4							.3	
					1.9	Net Profit + Depr., Dep.,							
			(11)		.5	Amort./Cur. Mat. L/T/D							
					.2								
	.3		.1		.3						.2	.3	
	.7		.3		.7	Fixed/Worth					.9	.5	
	1.9		1.6		7.4						-.5	3.7	
	.5		.8		.8						.2	1.6	
	2.1		1.9		2.5	Debt/Worth					6.9	4.0	
	4.6		5.8		29.1						-14.4	NM	
	38.8		41.0		44.4	% Profit Before Taxes/Tangible						39.6	
(22)	12.7	(39)	21.0	(36)	9.0	Net Worth					(12)	3.5	
	-.4		6.9		-5.2							-7.2	
	17.6		13.3		11.2	% Profit Before Taxes/Total					12.5	13.4	
	7.5		7.3		1.0	Assets					.0	1.4	
	-2.7		-1.8		-3.6						-17.5	-2.6	
	13.0		45.0		32.4						219.0	10.8	
	6.5		13.3		8.2	Sales/Net Fixed Assets					22.8	8.2	
	2.1		6.2		3.6						3.7	7.1	
	1.7		2.2		1.8						2.6	1.6	
	.9		1.4		1.3	Sales/Total Assets					2.0	1.3	
	.7		.8		.9						.7	1.2	
	1.6		.8		1.1							1.4	
(19)	3.1	(30)	1.6	(33)	2.6	% Depr., Dep., Amort./Sales					(13)	2.0	
	5.6		4.3		6.4							3.2	
			2.7		1.1	% Officers', Directors',							
		(12)	6.0	(10)	2.6	Owners' Comp/Sales							
			9.6		8.6								
	1538947M		2305951M		1418788M	Net Sales ($)	1437M	8162M	9630M	76303M	162483M	1160773M	
	1693601M		2231979M		1124248M	Total Assets ($)	2730M	9244M	5813M	59512M	131354M	915595M	

M = $ thousand   MM = $ million
See Pages viii through xx for Explanation of Ratios and Data

© RMA 2024

MANUFACTURING—Aircraft Engine and Engine Parts Manufacturing NAICS 336412

Current Data Sorted by Assets / Comparative Historical Data

							Type of Statement				
			4	2	4		Unqualified		6		1
		3	3				Reviewed		9		2
		4					Compiled		5		3
2	1	6	12	9	3		Tax Returns		8		1
	3						Other		39		17
	14 (4/1-9/30/23)		42 (10/1/23-3/31/24)						4/1/19-		4/1/20-
0-500M	500M-2MM	2-10MM	10-50MM	50-100MM	100-250MM				3/31/20		3/31/21
2	4	13	19	11	7		NUMBER OF STATEMENTS		ALL 67		ALL 24
%	%	%	%	%	%		ASSETS		%		%
		10.7	15.7	18.8			Cash & Equivalents		6.9		15.3
		22.4	14.3	15.6			Trade Receivables (net)		19.1		15.1
		35.9	32.1	28.2			Inventory		34.2		36.6
		.5	1.9	4.4			All Other Current		5.5		1.7
		69.5	64.0	67.1			Total Current		65.7		68.7
		20.1	20.9	17.1			Fixed Assets (net)		22.1		15.6
		5.9	8.9	12.1			Intangibles (net)		6.7		10.0
		4.5	6.2	3.7			All Other Non-Current		5.6		5.6
		100.0	100.0	100.0			Total		100.0		100.0
							LIABILITIES				
		6.1	6.9	5.2			Notes Payable-Short Term		16.3		7.5
		2.9	3.0	3.5			Cur. Mat.-L.T.D.		2.3		1.6
		9.5	9.9	7.7			Trade Payables		9.7		6.9
		.0	.0	.4			Income Taxes Payable		.3		.6
		17.2	18.2	12.6			All Other Current		10.5		6.9
		35.7	38.1	29.4			Total Current		39.0		23.5
		21.5	13.4	27.1			Long-Term Debt		18.9		18.5
		.0	.6	.4			Deferred Taxes		.4		.9
		.5	3.4	7.5			All Other Non-Current		5.8		13.8
		42.3	44.4	35.6			Net Worth		35.8		43.4
		100.0	100.0	100.0			Total Liabilities & Net Worth		100.0		100.0
							INCOME DATA				
		100.0	100.0	100.0			Net Sales		100.0		100.0
		38.1	38.0	48.8			Gross Profit		33.4		35.7
		31.2	28.0	22.0			Operating Expenses		23.7		28.2
		6.9	10.0	26.8			Operating Profit		9.7		7.5
		1.9	1.7	4.1			All Other Expenses (net)		3.4		3.2
		4.9	8.3	22.7			Profit Before Taxes		6.3		4.3
							RATIOS				
		3.5	2.6	5.0					4.2		5.1
		2.8	1.9	2.5			Current		2.3		3.0
		1.3	1.4	1.9					1.5		2.1
		2.6	1.2	2.3					1.5		2.4
		1.2	.8	1.1			Quick		.7		1.2
		.4	.4	.6					.4		.7
		27 13.7	35 10.3	42 8.7				34	10.7	29	12.7
		32 11.5	50 7.3	70 5.2		Sales/Receivables	50	7.3	45	8.1
		59 6.2	89 4.1	79 4.6			65	5.6	58	6.3
		30 12.1	101 3.6	146 2.5			85	4.3	99	3.7
		118 3.1	215 1.7	203 1.8		Cost of Sales/Inventory	146	2.5	174	2.1
		192 1.9	365 1.0	332 1.1			228	1.6	261	1.4
		13 28.8	24 15.2	31 11.6			21	17.7	16	22.7
		29 12.4	41 9.0	68 5.4		Cost of Sales/Payables	32	11.3	28	13.0
		43 8.5	87 4.2	89 4.1			53	6.9	34	10.8
		3.0	2.1	1.6					2.5		1.9
		8.4	3.6	2.0		Sales/Working Capital		3.5		2.6
		14.5	6.0	3.1					7.7		3.3
		6.0	12.2	33.2					18.1		21.2
	(11)	2.4	(17) 3.9	(10) 5.7		EBIT/Interest	(58)	3.9	(20)	4.1
		-1.1	.8	3.7				1.1		.7
							Net Profit + Depr., Dep.,		8.7		
							Amort./Cur. Mat. L/T/D	(17)	1.7		
									.9		
		.0	.4	.1					.2		.1
		.2	.5	.7		Fixed/Worth		.5		.3
		1.8	1.0	2.3					2.2		1.3
		.5	.7	.7					.5		.5
		1.8	1.5	1.6		Debt/Worth		1.1		.9
		4.0	2.5	6.5					6.1		3.7
		77.6	42.9						28.3		34.0
	(12)	4.4	(18) 20.4			% Profit Before Taxes/Tangible	(57)	13.7	(20)	10.2
		-.7	1.0			Net Worth		1.5		.1
		35.8	11.3	27.4					14.6		9.1
		.9	8.6	15.9		% Profit Before Taxes/Total Assets		4.8		3.4
		-3.1	.9	6.2					.6		-.9
		187.3	18.5	32.8					16.5		22.7
		11.2	4.2	10.6		Sales/Net Fixed Assets		8.9		8.6
		8.0	2.3	1.9					3.3		4.3
		2.6	1.2	1.1					1.8		1.4
		1.8	.8	.8		Sales/Total Assets		1.2		1.2
		1.3	.7	.5					.9		.9
			3.1	.8					.9		.4
		(13)	4.9	(10) 3.7		% Depr., Dep., Amort./Sales	(54)	1.9	(21)	2.4
			5.5	7.5					4.0		3.3
							% Officers', Directors'		2.1		
							Owners' Comp/Sales	(17)	3.0		
									8.3		
16138M	16195M	125757M	378804M	670909M	1257930M		Net Sales ($)		3135378M		1108503M
327M	4400M	63612M	414506M	801496M	1194057M		Total Assets ($)		2942334M		1043094M

© RMA 2024   M = $ thousand   MM = $ million
See Pages viii through xx for Explanation of Ratios and Data

MANUFACTURING—Aircraft Engine and Engine Parts Manufacturing NAICS 336412

Comparative Historical Data | Current Data Sorted by Sales

Comparative Historical Data						Current Data Sorted by Sales					
					Type of Statement					3	7
4		3		10	Unqualified					2	1
1		7		3	Reviewed				3		
5		1		3	Compiled			2	2	1	
1				5	Tax Returns	1		3	2	1	14
21		25		35	Other		14 (4/1-9/30/23)		42 (10/1/23-3/31/24)		
4/1/21-3/31/22		4/1/22-3/31/23		4/1/23-3/31/24		0-1MM	1-3MM	3-5MM	5-10MM	10-25MM	25MM & OVER
ALL		ALL		ALL							
32		36		56	NUMBER OF STATEMENTS	1		5	11	17	22
%		%		%	ASSETS	%	%	%	%	%	%
11.8		13.8		15.1	Cash & Equivalents				11.8	13.7	19.5
15.1		17.7		16.5	Trade Receivables (net)	D			17.2	16.0	19.4
42.1		34.2		32.3	Inventory	A			40.9	34.0	26.0
2.2		4.3		1.9	All Other Current	T			.7	1.8	3.2
71.2		69.9		65.9	Total Current	A			70.6	65.4	68.1
16.9		15.5		19.1	Fixed Assets (net)				13.8	22.7	15.4
7.4		7.8		8.8	Intangibles (net)	N			11.5	6.1	11.5
4.5		6.7		6.1	All Other Non-Current	O			4.1	5.8	5.0
100.0		100.0		100.0	Total	T			100.0	100.0	100.0
					LIABILITIES	A					
9.4		8.4		6.4	Notes Payable-Short Term	V			4.6	6.9	6.9
2.9		2.2		2.7	Cur. Mat.-L.T.D.	A			2.9	2.6	3.0
7.5		9.7		8.9	Trade Payables	I			10.0	6.6	10.9
.3		.1		.2	Income Taxes Payable	L			.0	.0	.2
11.0		10.5		21.5	All Other Current	A			17.2	36.4	14.4
31.2		30.9		39.6	Total Current	B			34.8	52.6	35.4
14.3		15.1		19.9	Long-Term Debt	L			25.9	13.9	20.2
.2		.2		.4	Deferred Taxes	E			.6	.3	.3
3.5		4.0		4.3	All Other Non-Current				1.6	4.1	4.9
50.8		49.9		35.8	Net Worth				37.1	29.2	39.2
100.0		100.0		100.0	Total Liabilties & Net Worth				100.0	100.0	100.0
					INCOME DATA						
100.0		100.0		100.0	Net Sales				100.0	100.0	100.0
38.2		34.6		39.7	Gross Profit				36.7	37.7	39.2
30.5		27.2		26.8	Operating Expenses				30.8	26.2	21.1
7.7		7.4		12.9	Operating Profit				6.0	11.5	18.1
-1.0		.7		2.4	All Other Expenses (net)				1.6	2.3	3.0
8.8		6.7		10.5	Profit Before Taxes				4.4	9.2	15.0
					RATIOS						
4.3		5.1		3.1					4.3	3.0	3.0
2.8		2.6		2.2	Current				2.7	2.2	2.3
1.6		1.4		1.4					1.3	1.2	1.4
1.6		2.8		1.9					3.0	1.6	2.2
.9		1.0		.9	Quick				.6	.6	.9
.5		.6		.4					.3	.3	.7
36	10.1	32	11.3	28	13.1			27	13.7	36	10.2	29	12.4
49	7.5	49	7.4	41	9.0	Sales/Receivables			32	11.5	62	5.9	54	6.7
65	5.6	79	4.6	74	4.9				50	7.3	91	4.0	79	4.6
159	2.3	78	4.7	104	3.5				62	5.9	101	3.6	104	3.5
261	1.4	166	2.2	166	2.2	Cost of Sales/Inventory			166	2.2	215	1.7	146	2.5
332	1.1	304	1.2	243	1.5				261	1.4	406	.9	215	1.7
17	21.3	16	23.4	23	16.2				15	24.2	16	22.6	29	12.4
33	11.2	32	11.4	37	9.8	Cost of Sales/Payables			36	10.1	42	8.7	37	9.9
54	6.7	68	5.4	78	4.7				43	8.4	96	3.8	76	4.8
1.7		1.9		2.3					2.1	2.2	2.0
2.4		2.8		3.6	Sales/Working Capital				7.1	3.4	3.6
5.2		5.4		8.7					10.9	14.5	6.2
11.9		5.6		11.9					22.6		11.1
(25)	5.9	(25)	1.7	(46)	4.0	EBIT/Interest			4.1	(17)	6.1
3.1		-2.7		1.4					1.9		2.0
				15.0	Net Profit + Depr., Dep.,						
		(12)		4.8	Amort./Cur. Mat. L/T/D						
				1.1							
.1		.0		.1					.0	.3	.1
.3		.2		.5	Fixed/Worth				.4	.5	.6
.8		.8		1.3					1.0	1.1	1.5
.5		.5		.7					1.1	.4	.7
.8		1.0		1.7	Debt/Worth				1.8	1.1	2.2
2.9		2.6		4.9					5.9	2.4	6.7
31.3		27.3		60.8	% Profit Before Taxes/Tangible				39.9		97.8
(29)	16.1	(32)	2.1	(48)	25.0	Net Worth			(15)	13.9	(19)	50.5
3.1		-3.7		2.0					1.1		25.6
12.4		15.2		22.3	% Profit Before Taxes/Total				8.6	13.4	22.9
7.8		1.9		8.8	Assets				.9	8.6	13.7
1.9		-1.8		.8					-5.4	.9	6.6
27.1		62.6		39.8					183.7	13.4	38.4
10.5		12.6		9.9	Sales/Net Fixed Assets				11.2	4.2	10.2
3.7		3.9		3.0					7.6	2.1	3.8
1.3		1.6		1.7					2.6	1.1	1.4
1.1		1.1		1.1	Sales/Total Assets				1.8	.8	1.2
.9		.7		.8					1.2	.7	.8
.7		.5		.8					2.2		1.0
(26)	2.2	(24)	4.0	(36)	2.8	% Depr., Dep., Amort./Sales			(13)	4.0	(14)	3.0
4.7		5.6		5.3					5.5		6.7
				1.6	% Officers', Directors'						
		(12)		3.8	Owners' Comp/Sales						
				9.9							
1324095M		1004393M		2465733M	Net Sales ($)	15M		17949M	81358M	278111M	2088300M
1365951M		1034657M		2478398M	Total Assets ($)	15M		11768M	72556M	388500M	2005559M

M = $ thousand   MM = $ million
See Pages viii through xx for Explanation of Ratios and Data

© RMA 2024

MANUFACTURING—Other Aircraft Parts and Auxiliary Equipment Manufacturing NAICS 336413

Current Data Sorted by Assets — **Comparative Historical Data**

						Type of Statement				
			7	4	4	Unqualified		13		4
		1	10	2		Reviewed		15		10
		1	1		1	Compiled		11		5
2	1	4				Tax Returns		9		3
	5	13	26	12		Other		68		47
	17 (4/1-9/30/23)		81 (10/1/23-3/31/24)		4			4/1/19-		4/1/20-
0-500M	500M-2MM	2-10MM	10-50MM	50-100MM	100-250MM			3/31/20		3/31/21
2	6	19	44	18	9	NUMBER OF STATEMENTS		ALL 116		ALL 69
%	%	%	%	%	%			%		%
						ASSETS				
		9.1	8.6	11.9		Cash & Equivalents		11.1		14.1
		22.7	17.1	12.1		Trade Receivables (net)		21.6		14.9
		44.3	40.3	28.6		Inventory		30.9		34.7
		1.3	3.3	6.7		All Other Current		2.9		2.8
		77.5	69.4	59.3		Total Current		66.4		66.5
		14.3	15.4	16.9		Fixed Assets (net)		22.1		20.3
		1.3	6.5	11.0		Intangibles (net)		6.9		6.6
		6.9	8.7	12.7		All Other Non-Current		4.5		6.7
		100.0	100.0	100.0		Total		100.0		100.0
						LIABILITIES				
		6.7	5.5	4.5		Notes Payable-Short Term		7.1		5.7
		2.5	2.9	2.1		Cur. Mat.-L.T.D.		3.5		5.3
		7.4	10.0	7.2		Trade Payables		9.9		7.5
		.4	.1	.2		Income Taxes Payable		.1		.1
		9.6	10.6	14.9		All Other Current		9.3		9.7
		26.5	29.1	28.8		Total Current		30.0		28.3
		13.3	11.8	16.3		Long-Term Debt		15.0		21.2
		.0	.7	.5		Deferred Taxes		.4		.3
		10.1	7.2	9.0		All Other Non-Current		7.5		8.8
		50.1	51.2	45.5		Net Worth		47.2		41.4
		100.0	100.0	100.0		Total Liabilities & Net Worth		100.0		100.0
						INCOME DATA				
		100.0	100.0	100.0		Net Sales		100.0		100.0
		36.8	28.8	32.5		Gross Profit		31.1		37.4
		31.7	24.3	21.8		Operating Expenses		23.6		31.5
		5.0	4.5	10.7		Operating Profit		7.6		5.8
		.0	1.4	1.7		All Other Expenses (net)		1.4		.6
		5.0	3.1	9.0		Profit Before Taxes		6.1		5.3
						RATIOS				
		5.9	3.6	3.8				4.6		4.8
		3.9	2.7	2.2		Current		2.6		2.4
		1.8	1.5	1.4				1.5		1.8
		2.9	1.6	1.7				2.2		2.2
		.9	.8	.9		Quick		1.1		1.2
		.6	.5	.3				.6		.5
		33 11.0	32 11.5	29 12.5				34 10.6	21	17.3
		49 7.5	44 8.3	45 8.2		Sales/Receivables		47 7.7	36	10.0
		62 5.9	54 6.8	58 6.3				62 5.9	53	6.9
		73 5.0	104 3.5	55 6.6				65 5.6	81	4.5
		182 2.0	152 2.4	140 2.6		Cost of Sales/Inventory		122 3.0	146	2.5
		281 1.3	215 1.7	261 1.4				182 2.0	243	1.5
		15 24.5	19 19.0	18 20.7				17 21.8	15	23.8
		29 12.7	35 10.5	30 12.3		Cost of Sales/Payables		28 13.1	25	14.6
		38 9.5	46 7.9	55 6.6				43 8.5	45	8.1
		2.1	2.1	1.8				2.7		2.2
		3.2	3.2	3.5		Sales/Working Capital		4.2		3.4
		4.8	5.6	6.0				8.2		6.3
		81.1	16.5	15.0				17.3		32.2
		(17) 3.9	(39) 3.2	(16) 5.6		EBIT/Interest		(98) 6.0	(62)	4.9
		-.1	-1.5	.5				1.6		.6
						Net Profit + Depr., Dep.,		5.0		5.7
						Amort./Cur. Mat. L/T/D	(30)	3.2	(13)	1.6
								1.5		-.1
		.0	.1	.1				.2		.1
		.2	.2	.7		Fixed/Worth		.5		.4
		.4	.8	52.6				1.3		2.0
		.2	.4	.9				.4		.5
		.5	1.2	1.7		Debt/Worth		1.1		1.2
		2.8	3.9	179.7				3.7		4.4
		40.6	29.4	37.0		% Profit Before Taxes/Tangible		43.5		45.2
	(17)	8.5	(40) 8.6	(15) 17.8		Net Worth	(103)	17.7	(58)	18.3
		1.8	-7.7	5.2				6.8		4.7
		27.5	12.6	13.1		% Profit Before Taxes/Total		16.6		15.6
		3.3	4.4	8.8		Assets		7.7		6.2
		-3.4	-5.1	-.6				1.2		.8
		122.1	75.3	34.5				24.3		31.9
		13.7	10.1	7.2		Sales/Net Fixed Assets		8.6		8.5
		7.2	4.7	3.5				3.8		4.1
		2.2	1.6	1.3				2.2		2.0
		1.8	1.2	1.1		Sales/Total Assets		1.4		1.4
		1.2	.9	.6				1.0		.8
		.3	.5	.6				1.0		.8
	(15)	1.2	(30) 2.2	(17) 1.8		% Depr., Dep., Amort./Sales	(94)	2.2	(59)	2.4
		2.8	4.8	6.2				5.2		5.5
						% Officers', Directors'		1.4		2.8
						Owners' Comp/Sales	(28)	3.0	(19)	4.9
								5.7		6.7
7225M	20154M	185873M	1172417M	1433377M	1566116M	Net Sales ($)		5376448M		2303648M
765M	8227M	110449M	956429M	1360977M	1333200M	Total Assets ($)		3743687M		1893236M

© RMA 2024
M = $ thousand MM = $ million
See Pages viii through xx for Explanation of Ratios and Data

MANUFACTURING—Other Aircraft Parts and Auxiliary Equipment Manufacturing NAICS 336413

Comparative Historical Data | Current Data Sorted by Sales

				Type of Statement						
	4	13	15	Unqualified				3	3	12
	6	17	13	Reviewed		1		5	5	7
	7	8	3	Compiled			1	1	1	1
	5	6	5	Tax Returns			1	1	1	
	34	62	62	Other		5	6	3	18	30
	4/1/21-3/31/22 ALL	4/1/22-3/31/23 ALL	4/1/23-3/31/24 ALL		0-1MM	17 (4/1-9/30/23) 1-3MM	3-5MM	81 (10/1/23-3/31/24) 5-10MM	10-25MM	25MM & OVER
	56	106	98	NUMBER OF STATEMENTS	6	17	8	6	28	50
	%	%	%	ASSETS	%	%	%	%	%	%
	14.1	9.6	11.1	Cash & Equivalents					10.7	8.9
	13.6	17.4	18.6	Trade Receivables (net)					21.1	15.6
	37.1	35.6	35.8	Inventory					41.3	35.2
	2.9	3.3	3.3	All Other Current					2.3	5.1
	67.7	65.9	68.8	Total Current					75.3	64.8
	20.9	19.9	15.5	Fixed Assets (net)		DATA NOT AVAILABLE			12.0	15.7
	7.7	9.1	7.3	Intangibles (net)					6.3	9.0
	3.7	5.0	8.5	All Other Non-Current					6.3	10.5
	100.0	100.0	100.0	Total					100.0	100.0
				LIABILITIES						
	7.0	5.4	5.6	Notes Payable-Short Term					6.0	6.6
	2.0	2.4	3.0	Cur. Mat.-L.T.D.					2.2	3.0
	5.6	8.9	10.1	Trade Payables					7.8	10.4
	.0	.1	.2	Income Taxes Payable					.2	.1
	16.6	11.5	11.4	All Other Current					10.0	13.5
	31.3	28.4	30.3	Total Current					26.1	33.6
	14.6	17.8	12.8	Long-Term Debt					10.6	12.2
	.3	.2	.4	Deferred Taxes					.7	.3
	11.5	9.0	7.9	All Other Non-Current					7.6	8.9
	42.4	44.6	48.5	Net Worth					55.0	45.0
	100.0	100.0	100.0	Total Liabilities & Net Worth					100.0	100.0
				INCOME DATA						
	100.0	100.0	100.0	Net Sales					100.0	100.0
	34.5	31.8	32.2	Gross Profit					28.2	29.2
	28.2	27.2	25.9	Operating Expenses					21.7	21.0
	6.3	4.5	6.3	Operating Profit					6.5	8.2
	-2.3	.8	1.4	All Other Expenses (net)					.6	2.0
	8.6	3.8	4.9	Profit Before Taxes					5.9	6.2
				RATIOS						
	4.5	4.7	4.4						4.3	3.2
	2.6	2.8	2.7	Current					3.2	2.2
	1.6	1.6	1.5						1.8	1.3
	2.6	2.3	1.9						2.0	1.5
	.9	.9	.8	Quick					.8	.8
	.5	.4	.5						.6	.3
23	15.6	26	14.3	32	11.3				35	10.4	31	11.6
38	9.6	45	8.2	44	8.3	Sales/Receivables			51	7.2	42	8.6
59	6.2	68	5.4	57	6.4				62	5.9	55	6.6
94	3.9	81	4.5	69	5.3				118	3.1	87	4.2
182	2.0	152	2.4	146	2.5	Cost of Sales/Inventory			166	2.2	146	2.5
261	1.4	243	1.5	228	1.6				243	1.5	203	1.8
12	31.1	15	25.0	18	20.2				12	29.9	21	17.2
21	17.0	30	12.3	32	11.4	Cost of Sales/Payables			32	11.5	37	9.9
33	10.9	46	8.0	47	7.7				38	9.5	51	7.2
	2.0		2.1		2.3					2.1		2.6
	3.1		3.5		3.7	Sales/Working Capital				2.9		4.6
	7.1		6.2		7.8					4.7		9.6
	34.1		11.7		16.7					19.7		14.5
(48)	7.5	(86)	3.7	(84)	3.5	EBIT/Interest			(23)	3.3	(45)	3.7
	1.9		.7		.0					-.8		.4
			17.4		6.8							7.2
		(17)	3.4	(17)	2.0	Net Profit + Depr., Dep., Amort./Cur. Mat. L/T/D					(11)	2.3
			.7		.9							1.1
	.2		.1		.1					.0		.1
	.4		.4		.3	Fixed/Worth				.2		.5
	1.4		1.3		1.2					.4		1.2
	.3		.4		.3					.3		.6
	1.2		1.4		1.3	Debt/Worth				.5		1.9
	3.3		3.5		5.0					1.9		5.6
	49.5		29.1		36.5	% Profit Before Taxes/Tangible Net Worth				41.6		35.2
(47)	23.5	(91)	13.2	(84)	13.6				(24)	9.0	(43)	17.8
	7.9		2.3		.3					.6		-2.2
	21.2		11.2		13.2	% Profit Before Taxes/Total Assets				15.3		12.6
	10.6		4.7		5.2					4.0		6.7
	2.3		.1		-1.7					-3.2		-1.2
	24.5		38.5		53.0					75.3		43.8
	7.9		7.8		10.0	Sales/Net Fixed Assets				14.3		7.4
	3.3		3.5		4.7					5.8		3.9
	1.7		1.8		1.9					1.8		1.7
	1.1		1.2		1.3	Sales/Total Assets				1.3		1.1
	.8		.8		.9					1.0		.9
	1.1		.6		.6					.1		.8
(43)	2.6	(78)	2.2	(71)	1.7	% Depr., Dep., Amort./Sales			(22)	.9	(36)	2.1
	7.7		6.7		3.9					4.0		4.2
	1.4		1.5		1.0							
(16)	4.5	(22)	3.0	(20)	3.0	% Officers', Directors' Owners' Comp/Sales						
	8.3		5.2		5.8							
	1182409M		3173341M		4385162M	Net Sales ($)	12557M	32265M	48854M	472443M	3819043M
	1261312M		3354217M		3770047M	Total Assets ($)	20463M	25254M	19313M	392733M	3312284M

© RMA 2024
M = $ thousand   MM = $ million
See Pages viii through xx for Explanation of Ratios and Data

MANUFACTURING—Ship Building and Repairing NAICS 336611

Current Data Sorted by Assets / Comparative Historical Data

0-500M	500M-2MM	2-10MM	10-50MM	50-100MM	100-250MM	Type of Statement	4/1/19-3/31/20 ALL	4/1/20-3/31/21 ALL
1		1	1	2	5	Unqualified	9	5
			1	2		Reviewed	4	1
2	1	1	2			Compiled	2	1
		1				Tax Returns		2
		9	6	9	5	Other	31	20
3	1	11	10	13	10	NUMBER OF STATEMENTS	46	29
%	%	%	%	%	%	**ASSETS**	%	%
		20.3	10.2	9.4	21.6	Cash & Equivalents	13.7	17.4
		32.7	15.3	15.7	15.4	Trade Receivables (net)	19.8	14.0
		8.6	4.8	9.4	5.6	Inventory	7.0	7.8
		1.1	14.9	12.4	14.1	All Other Current	11.2	14.6
		62.7	45.2	46.9	56.6	Total Current	51.7	53.7
		16.4	47.8	44.6	30.7	Fixed Assets (net)	39.9	39.8
		.6	2.2	1.3	2.7	Intangibles (net)	1.6	1.7
		20.3	4.8	7.1	9.9	All Other Non-Current	6.8	4.8
		100.0	100.0	100.0	100.0	Total	100.0	100.0
						LIABILITIES		
		14.2	18.2	6.2	1.2	Notes Payable-Short Term	5.7	9.5
		.6	3.8	2.2	1.6	Cur. Mat.-L.T.D.	4.5	2.5
		18.6	20.5	12.2	9.3	Trade Payables	10.6	8.7
		.0	.0	.0	.1	Income Taxes Payable	.2	.2
		40.8	24.9	10.7	16.6	All Other Current	14.2	18.8
		74.2	67.4	31.4	28.8	Total Current	35.2	39.8
		8.9	54.8	24.0	9.2	Long-Term Debt	16.7	14.8
		.0	.0	1.1	.7	Deferred Taxes	.6	.2
		6.2	5.9	8.7	3.2	All Other Non-Current	4.2	2.4
		10.7	-28.1	34.9	58.0	Net Worth	43.3	42.8
		100.0	100.0	100.0	100.0	Total Liabilities & Net Worth	100.0	100.0
						INCOME DATA		
		100.0	100.0	100.0	100.0	Net Sales	100.0	100.0
		21.8	29.3	16.3	18.4	Gross Profit	27.2	22.4
		21.5	25.5	16.3	13.0	Operating Expenses	21.5	20.6
		.4	3.8	.0	5.4	Operating Profit	5.7	1.8
		.3	.4	.3	-.6	All Other Expenses (net)	.7	-1.7
		.1	3.4	-.3	6.0	Profit Before Taxes	5.0	3.5
						RATIOS		
		2.0	2.4	2.7	3.6		2.5	3.3
		1.0	1.0	1.6	1.9	Current	1.7	1.1
		.8	.3	.6	1.5		1.1	.9
		1.5	1.2	1.7	1.9		1.6	1.7
		1.0	.3	.3	1.5	Quick	1.0	.8
		.7	.1	.2	.9		.5	.4
		23 16.2	16 22.7	17 21.8	27 13.3		15 24.5	10 37.1
		29 12.6	34 10.7	37 9.8	34 10.8	Sales/Receivables	28 13.1	31 11.8
		53 6.9	73 5.0	76 4.8	51 7.2		49 7.4	51 7.2
		0 UND	0 UND	0 UND	2 226.2		0 UND	0 UND
		0 UND	1 310.4	3 121.6	3 129.8	Cost of Sales/Inventory	3 121.6	3 110.2
		44 8.3	65 5.6	15 24.5	38 9.6		36 10.0	26 13.8
		11 31.8	9 38.8	24 15.0	18 20.3		15 24.0	11 33.9
		27 13.5	33 11.1	51 7.2	22 16.8	Cost of Sales/Payables	25 14.8	23 15.8
		61 6.0	63 5.8	87 4.2	35 10.5		46 8.0	37 9.9
		5.1	2.8	2.8	3.0		5.2	4.8
		101.6	-350.0	6.1	7.2	Sales/Working Capital	10.4	38.2
		-22.3	-4.5	-7.3	8.5		NM	-22.7
		23.4		9.1			26.3	17.8
		(10) 6.4		(12) .2		EBIT/Interest	(41) 8.3	(25) 3.2
		4.5			-3.7		.9	-11.1
						Net Profit + Depr., Dep., Amort./Cur. Mat. L/T/D		
		.1	1.1	.7	.3		.4	.5
		.8	4.2	1.4	.6	Fixed/Worth	.9	1.1
		1.7	-1.1	2.2	.9		2.0	1.7
		1.9	1.6	1.3	.4		.6	.8
		2.3	5.4	1.8	.7	Debt/Worth	1.3	1.4
		8.8	-2.4	3.5	1.1		3.6	3.0
		114.6		22.4	35.2		48.1	87.6
		(10) 44.6		-3.6	17.2	% Profit Before Taxes/Tangible Net Worth	18.5	(27) 20.1
		17.0		-23.0	11.1		.5	-13.9
		22.5	9.7	9.6	13.8		24.7	19.6
		11.4	2.5	-1.3	9.5	% Profit Before Taxes/Total Assets	7.6	3.1
		3.5	-26.5	-5.9	6.1		.2	-6.9
		51.5	7.7	4.5	7.6		9.1	7.5
		16.4	4.7	2.9	4.5	Sales/Net Fixed Assets	4.0	4.5
		11.3	1.3	1.0	2.8		2.3	2.4
		4.1	2.9	1.2	1.8		2.3	2.5
		3.5	1.2	.8	1.4	Sales/Total Assets	1.7	1.9
		1.7	.7	.8	1.0		1.1	1.1
				1.5			1.7	2.2
				4.5		% Depr., Dep., Amort./Sales	(37) 2.9	(24) 3.6
				5.7			4.2	5.4
						% Officers', Directors', Owners' Comp/Sales	1.4	
							(13) 2.6	
							4.8	
4214M	5561M	193792M	313926M	832625M	2227855M	Net Sales ($)	2730863M	1442153M
279M	1151M	60341M	224071M	884354M	1594843M	Total Assets ($)	1950428M	1152797M

M = $ thousand   MM = $ million
See Pages viii through xx for Explanation of Ratios and Data

© RMA 2024

MANUFACTURING—Ship Building and Repairing NAICS 336611

Comparative Historical Data | Current Data Sorted by Sales

					Type of Statement						
	4		11	8	Unqualified					1	7
	8		5	5	Reviewed	1				2	2
	3		1	2	Compiled						2
	7		1	4	Tax Returns		1	1	1	1	
	26		34	29	Other				3	6	20
	4/1/21-3/31/22 ALL		4/1/22-3/31/23 ALL	4/1/23-3/31/24 ALL		0-1MM	6 (4/1-9/30/23) 1-3MM	3-5MM	42 (10/1/23-3/31/24) 5-10MM	10-25MM	25MM & OVER
	48		52	48	NUMBER OF STATEMENTS	1	1	1	4	10	31
	%		%	%	ASSETS	%	%	%	%	%	%
	19.8		12.2	18.8	Cash & Equivalents					28.7	11.8
	19.3		19.3	19.0	Trade Receivables (net)					20.6	19.6
	7.7		7.5	7.1	Inventory					12.1	4.1
	9.7		12.6	9.8	All Other Current					7.4	12.6
	56.4		51.5	54.7	Total Current					68.9	48.1
	35.4		35.4	33.3	Fixed Assets (net)					17.1	40.7
	2.8		3.6	1.5	Intangibles (net)					.3	2.0
	5.3		9.6	10.5	All Other Non-Current					13.7	9.2
	100.0		100.0	100.0	Total					100.0	100.0
					LIABILITIES						
	7.7		5.5	9.2	Notes Payable-Short Term					7.9	10.0
	4.4		2.8	1.8	Cur. Mat.-L.T.D.					1.0	2.3
	11.3		13.1	15.7	Trade Payables					8.4	17.6
	.2		.0	.1	Income Taxes Payable					.0	.0
	16.3		14.2	21.9	All Other Current					47.3	14.2
	40.0		35.6	48.8	Total Current					64.7	44.1
	21.9		22.3	23.4	Long-Term Debt					11.2	27.4
	.5		.4	.4	Deferred Taxes					.0	.7
	3.7		4.3	5.7	All Other Non-Current					5.9	5.1
	33.9		37.4	21.7	Net Worth					18.2	22.6
	100.0		100.0	100.0	Total Liabilities & Net Worth					100.0	100.0
					INCOME DATA						
	100.0		100.0	100.0	Net Sales					100.0	100.0
	25.2		23.3	22.7	Gross Profit					28.8	16.8
	23.2		19.7	20.7	Operating Expenses					27.8	14.1
	1.9		3.6	2.0	Operating Profit					1.1	2.8
	-2.1		-.2	.1	All Other Expenses (net)					.4	.4
	4.1		3.8	2.0	Profit Before Taxes					.6	2.3
					RATIOS						
	3.0		2.7	2.7						2.5	2.7
	1.6		1.4	1.5	Current					1.7	1.5
	1.1		.9	.8						1.0	.7
	2.0		1.8	1.8						1.7	1.8
	1.0		.8	1.0	Quick					1.0	.9
	.6		.4	.3						.2	.3
19	19.3	18	20.4	20	18.4					15 24.3	26 14.2
39	9.4	39	9.3	35	10.4	Sales/Receivables				32 11.3	35 10.4
61	6.0	56	6.5	52	7.0					54 6.8	53 6.9
0	UND	0	UND	0	UND					0 UND	0 UND
3	125.2	3	136.1	2	150.9	Cost of Sales/Inventory				0 UND	3 127.9
33	10.9	47	7.8	41	9.0					140 2.6	54 54.0
14	25.7	19	19.3	15	25.1					8 48.0	21 17.4
28	13.1	34	10.8	31	11.9	Cost of Sales/Payables				18 20.4	33 11.1
42	8.6	68	5.4	63	5.8					44 8.3	76 4.8
	5.1		3.7		3.7					2.5	3.3
	10.8		13.0		11.3	Sales/Working Capital				9.1	8.3
	48.1		-49.8		-17.9					NM	-13.4
	25.2		21.1		10.2						11.8
(39)	7.0	(40)	3.6	(40)	3.7	EBIT/Interest				(29) 4.3	
	1.1		-3.0		-1.7						-1.2
			17.8			Net Profit + Depr., Dep.,					
		(10)	2.7			Amort./Cur. Mat. L/T/D					
			-2.2								
	.5		.4		.4					.1	.6
	1.0		.9		1.0	Fixed/Worth				.5	1.0
	4.0		2.8		2.2					NM	2.2
	.8		.6		.9					.6	.9
	1.8		1.7		1.9	Debt/Worth				2.1	1.7
	6.8		4.0		6.7					NM	4.2
	75.8		33.3		38.8	% Profit Before Taxes/Tangible					34.0
(41)	23.6	(43)	14.1	(42)	18.9	Net Worth				(29) 15.8	
	1.5		-1.7		-4.0						-4.5
	22.1		19.0		15.1	% Profit Before Taxes/Total				25.4	13.1
	5.7		5.8		6.4	Assets				9.9	6.3
	.1		-1.0		-3.3					-15.1	-2.0
	16.4		9.6		16.2					44.7	7.5
	4.7		4.5		6.0	Sales/Net Fixed Assets				18.6	3.7
	2.3		2.3		2.4					5.5	2.1
	2.6		2.0		2.5					3.6	2.0
	1.6		1.2		1.5	Sales/Total Assets				1.6	1.2
	1.1		.9		.9					1.0	.8
	1.8		1.7		1.3						1.6
(33)	3.5	(40)	3.2	(41)	2.5	% Depr., Dep., Amort./Sales				(30) 3.0	
	5.7		4.4		4.5						4.9
	1.1					% Officers', Directors'					
(10)	2.4					Owners' Comp/Sales					
	9.2										
	3120417M		3583998M		3577973M	Net Sales ($)	41M	1028M	3145M	26732M	145325M	3401702M
	2361871M		2718974M		2765039M	Total Assets ($)	21M	61M	197M	36143M	137977M	2590640M

© RMA 2024
M = $ thousand MM = $ million
See Pages viii through xx for Explanation of Ratios and Data

MANUFACTURING—Boat Building NAICS 336612

	Current Data Sorted by Assets						Type of Statement	Comparative Historical Data	
				9	7	1	Unqualified	19	7
		2	1	6			Reviewed	15	3
		1	6			1	Compiled	3	4
		2	2		7		Tax Returns	4	2
		4	13	73	41	15	Other		
	81 (4/1-9/30/23)			101 (10/1/23-3/31/24)				65 4/1/19-3/31/20	22 4/1/20-3/31/21
0-500M	500M-2MM	2-10MM	10-50MM	50-100MM	100-250MM			ALL	ALL
	7	22	88	49	16		NUMBER OF STATEMENTS	106	38
%	%	%	%	%	%		ASSETS	%	%
		22.9	15.8	20.8	18.5		Cash & Equivalents	14.8	17.8
D		9.5	8.6	9.3	10.5		Trade Receivables (net)	9.0	8.6
A		40.2	39.8	29.0	26.6		Inventory	36.7	31.8
T		2.0	9.5	6.9	4.5		All Other Current	3.6	3.0
A		74.5	73.7	66.0	60.1		Total Current	64.0	61.1
		19.9	18.7	19.1	14.5		Fixed Assets (net)	24.0	26.4
N		3.1	2.6	8.4	17.2		Intangibles (net)	6.5	7.3
O		2.5	5.1	6.6	8.1		All Other Non-Current	5.4	5.2
T		100.0	100.0	100.0	100.0		Total	100.0	100.0
							LIABILITIES		
A		2.8	2.7	2.9	1.5		Notes Payable-Short Term	6.4	5.1
V		.1	1.2	1.3	.4		Cur. Mat.-L.T.D.	2.0	3.3
A		15.0	14.0	6.9	8.2		Trade Payables	12.7	11.4
I		.1	.2	.1	.1		Income Taxes Payable	.2	.2
L		8.2	14.0	16.8	36.0		All Other Current	12.0	21.7
A		26.2	31.9	28.0	46.1		Total Current	33.3	41.8
B		7.9	7.8	8.8	13.8		Long-Term Debt	13.5	24.8
L		.0	.2	.0	.3		Deferred Taxes	.4	.6
E		9.0	4.4	11.2	5.5		All Other Non-Current	5.0	2.4
		56.9	55.6	51.9	34.3		Net Worth	47.7	30.4
		100.0	100.0	100.0	100.0		Total Liabilities & Net Worth	100.0	100.0
							INCOME DATA		
		100.0	100.0	100.0	100.0		Net Sales	100.0	100.0
		21.1	19.9	22.6	21.6		Gross Profit	22.0	22.7
		18.1	13.1	12.4	17.4		Operating Expenses	16.3	21.6
		2.9	6.8	10.1	4.2		Operating Profit	5.7	1.1
		.2	.1	.7	2.0		All Other Expenses (net)	.6	-.2
		2.7	6.7	9.5	2.2		Profit Before Taxes	5.1	1.3
							RATIOS		
		11.9	4.9	4.9	4.7			4.1	3.0
		3.7	2.5	2.7	1.5		Current	2.1	1.7
		2.0	1.6	1.5	.9			1.2	1.1
		5.4	1.5	3.1	2.9			1.4	1.3
		1.6	.8	.9	.7		Quick	.6	.7
		.3	.3	.3	.2			.3	.3
	1	245.5	4	87.6	4	81.9	9	41.6		3	140.5	5	68.8
	12	29.9	10	34.9	11	34.1	12	29.5	Sales/Receivables	8	46.3	10	37.5
	21	17.6	18	20.6	21	17.7	24	15.5		19	19.1	20	18.4
	26	13.8	49	7.4	51	7.1	65	5.6		35	10.4	34	10.6
	58	6.3	73	5.0	64	5.7	78	4.7	Cost of Sales/Inventory	64	5.7	64	5.7
	126	2.9	96	3.8	72	5.1	99	3.7		94	3.9	83	4.4
	8	43.8	9	38.8	7	50.5	11	34.6		10	36.9	9	42.5
	15	24.8	15	24.7	11	32.8	20	18.5	Cost of Sales/Payables	17	20.9	17	20.9
	33	11.0	31	11.6	29	12.4	38	9.7		31	11.7	34	10.7
		4.0	3.8	4.0	3.0			5.0	5.0
		7.5	6.3	6.7	6.9		Sales/Working Capital	8.5	10.7
		9.5	13.9	12.2	-48.8			27.4	71.7
		6.3	134.8	88.3	42.2			49.5	27.1
	(15)	4.0	(68)	24.2	(37)	29.4	(12)	.2	EBIT/Interest	(87)	10.6	(31)	6.0
		-.4	4.0	2.5	-2.3			3.4	1.3
			86.8					21.8	
			(12)	4.5			Net Profit + Depr., Dep., Amort./Cur. Mat. L/T/D	(14)	4.7	
			2.3					2.9	
		.2	.1	.2	.2			.2	.2
		.4	.4	.3	.8		Fixed/Worth	.5	.7
		.6	.6	15.2	-.6			1.7	3.6
		.2	.3	.3	.3			.4	.6
		1.0	.7	1.0	4.6		Debt/Worth	.9	1.6
		1.6	1.6	53.8	-3.1			6.1	13.3
		42.8	77.1	75.1				61.4	60.2
		19.6	(83)	41.1	(38)	54.6		% Profit Before Taxes/Tangible Net Worth	(88)	30.6	(30)	30.5
		.5	10.0	31.0				15.5	15.7
		19.6	35.6	43.6	20.3			28.2	22.8
		9.1	18.5	30.8	8.4		% Profit Before Taxes/Total Assets	13.9	12.3
		.5	6.4	8.8	-9.7			6.8	.4
		55.9	28.9	18.1	14.2			22.4	22.4
		19.9	18.0	15.5	9.6		Sales/Net Fixed Assets	13.0	9.6
		11.5	9.3	9.5	6.6			6.4	5.6
		4.2	3.5	2.9	1.8			3.5	3.5
		3.1	2.4	2.4	1.4		Sales/Total Assets	2.5	2.3
		2.0	1.9	1.7	.9			1.8	1.6
		.4	.6	.6	.7			.9	.8
	(19)	1.2	(79)	1.1	(44)	.7	(14)	1.4	% Depr., Dep., Amort./Sales	(82)	1.6	(25)	1.6
		1.6	1.8	1.2	2.2			2.4	2.7
								1.0	
							% Officers', Directors' Owners' Comp/Sales	(18)	2.2	
								4.4	
	46505M	327014M	6017041M	8967654M	3735046M		Net Sales ($)	8889839M	2621636M
	9046M	114387M	2160573M	3582381M	2548223M		Total Assets ($)	4083716M	1290649M

© RMA 2024

M = $ thousand   MM = $ million
See Pages viii through xx for Explanation of Ratios and Data

MANUFACTURING—Boat Building NAICS 336612

Comparative Historical Data / Current Data Sorted by Sales

Comparative Historical Data			Type of Statement	Current Data Sorted by Sales					
4	10	17	Unqualified				1	16	
5	8	7	Reviewed				7	7	
1	4	9	Compiled			1	1	1	
3	1	3	Tax Returns		1	1	7	1	
31	28	146	Other		1	2	8	15	121
4/1/21-3/31/22 ALL	4/1/22-3/31/23 ALL	4/1/23-3/31/24 ALL		0-1MM	1-3MM	3-5MM	5-10MM (4/1-9/30/23) 81	10-25MM (10/1/23-3/31/24) 101	25MM & OVER
44	51	182	NUMBER OF STATEMENTS		1	2	10	24	145
%	%	%	ASSETS	%	%	%	%	%	%
12.5	13.5	19.0	Cash & Equivalents				24.6	23.7	18.1
9.0	10.5	9.0	Trade Receivables (net)	DATA			10.2	9.5	8.8
40.1	35.8	35.1	Inventory				36.4	38.3	34.3
6.5	7.6	7.1	All Other Current	NOT			1.8	1.6	8.5
68.1	67.4	70.3	Total Current				72.9	73.1	69.8
23.0	21.8	18.7	Fixed Assets (net)				20.5	21.4	18.0
5.1	5.4	5.7	Intangibles (net)	AVAIL			6.0	1.9	6.3
3.8	5.3	5.4	All Other Non-Current				.6	3.6	6.0
100.0	100.0	100.0	Total	ABLE			100.0	100.0	100.0
			LIABILITIES						
8.9	6.5	2.9	Notes Payable-Short Term				5.7	2.3	2.5
.6	.6	1.0	Cur. Mat.-L.T.D.				.0	.9	1.1
13.1	12.7	11.7	Trade Payables				9.5	13.3	11.2
.1	.2	.1	Income Taxes Payable				.1	.2	.1
17.9	17.8	16.2	All Other Current				6.3	11.5	17.1
40.6	37.7	31.9	Total Current				21.6	28.2	32.0
10.1	7.8	8.4	Long-Term Debt				1.3	13.8	8.0
.3	.3	.1	Deferred Taxes				.1	.4	.1
9.7	7.7	6.8	All Other Non-Current				14.3	5.2	6.6
39.3	46.6	52.7	Net Worth				62.7	52.4	53.3
100.0	100.0	100.0	Total Liabilities & Net Worth				100.0	100.0	100.0
			INCOME DATA						
100.0	100.0	100.0	Net Sales				100.0	100.0	100.0
23.3	21.6	21.1	Gross Profit				24.2	20.6	20.7
16.5	16.1	14.2	Operating Expenses				21.7	16.4	13.0
6.8	5.6	6.9	Operating Profit				2.5	4.2	7.7
-1.4	-.2	.4	All Other Expenses (net)				-.2	-.1	.5
8.3	5.8	6.5	Profit Before Taxes				2.8	4.3	7.2
			RATIOS						
3.1	3.4	5.1					11.2	9.5	4.8
2.0	1.9	2.7	Current				5.2	3.7	2.5
1.2	1.3	1.5					2.1	1.7	1.4
1.1	1.2	2.4					8.3	5.5	1.8
.6	.7	.9	Quick				2.1	.9	.9
.2	.4	.3					.4	.3	.3
5 76.7	4 98.2	4 88.9		3 140.8	0 999.8				4 81.3
10 36.6	12 31.3	11 34.3	Sales/Receivables	9 41.6	11 32.5				11 34.2
20 18.6	22 16.3	18 19.9		23 16.0	21 17.5				18 20.7
47 7.7	44 8.3	47 7.8		8 43.5	34 10.6				50 7.3
70 5.2	64 5.7	68 5.4	Cost of Sales/Inventory	30 12.3	79 4.6				66 5.5
107 3.4	83 4.4	89 4.1		192 1.9	126 2.9				81 4.5
13 27.9	9 39.8	8 43.0		2 211.8	10 38.3				8 43.1
20 18.3	19 19.1	14 25.6	Cost of Sales/Payables	12 31.5	14 25.9				14 25.7
39 9.4	36 10.2	32 11.4		47 7.8	32 11.4				30 12.2
5.2	4.8	3.9					3.9	3.3	4.0
7.6	8.4	6.9	Sales/Working Capital				7.6	6.6	6.7
28.9	24.9	13.3					10.5	10.1	14.5
93.8	63.9	63.5						44.7	90.9
(33) 21.4	(38) 7.9	(139) 20.6	EBIT/Interest				(20) 4.5	(109) 27.8	
.9	1.0	1.7						.0	2.5
		86.8	Net Profit + Depr., Dep.,						
	(12)	4.5	Amort./Cur. Mat. L/T/D						
		2.3							
.3	.2	.2					.1	.3	.2
.6	.5	.4	Fixed/Worth				.3	.4	.3
3.3	3.1	.8					.6	.6	.8
.6	.4	.3					.1	.5	.3
1.0	.8	.8	Debt/Worth				.8	1.2	.6
15.2	18.9	2.1					3.2	1.5	2.2
81.0	76.4	71.7	% Profit Before Taxes/Tangible				81.7	39.2	73.8
(35) 52.8	(43) 44.8	(158) 41.1	Net Worth				2.8	(23) 18.2	(123) 47.5
13.5	13.2	13.0					-40.7	-.5	20.0
37.2	33.5	36.2	% Profit Before Taxes/Total				30.2	18.2	37.8
18.0	10.9	17.7	Assets				2.7	9.7	20.2
3.5	2.8	4.5					-5.2	-.1	6.9
19.5	20.6	26.2					43.6	21.9	23.9
13.0	14.4	15.8	Sales/Net Fixed Assets				27.1	15.4	15.8
6.7	7.7	9.3					10.7	6.6	9.4
3.3	3.7	3.3					4.7	4.1	3.2
2.4	2.5	2.4	Sales/Total Assets				3.2	2.1	2.4
2.0	1.9	1.8					1.6	1.7	1.7
.8	1.0	.6					.2	.7	.6
(38) 1.4	(45) 1.5	(161) 1.1	% Depr., Dep., Amort./Sales				(21) .7	(129) 1.2	1.0
2.7	2.0	1.5					1.3	2.2	1.5
		.6	% Officers', Directors'						
	(13)	1.3	Owners' Comp/Sales						
		3.0							
3400246M	4357132M	19093260M	Net Sales ($)	2665M	7171M	79479M	430017M	18573928M	
1209039M	1702238M	8414610M	Total Assets ($)	804M	2047M	30263M	212893M	8168603M	

© RMA 2024
M = $ thousand   MM = $ million
See Pages viii through xx for Explanation of Ratios and Data

MANUFACTURING—Motorcycle, Bicycle, and Parts Manufacturing NAICS 336991

Current Data Sorted by Assets | Comparative Historical Data

						Type of Statement				
			1	3	1	Unqualified		3		5
			1			Reviewed		1		3
			1			Compiled				1
2	2		3			Tax Returns		5		3
	14 (4/1-9/30/23)			15	6	4	Other		21	13
0-500M	500M-2MM	2-10MM		25 (10/1/23-3/31/24)					4/1/19-	4/1/20-
			10-50MM	50-100MM	100-250MM				3/31/20	3/31/21
2	2	6	18	7	4	NUMBER OF STATEMENTS			30 ALL	25 ALL
%	%	%	%	%	%				%	%
			4.2			ASSETS	Cash & Equivalents		13.4	19.3
			8.7				Trade Receivables (net)		13.0	16.3
			45.5				Inventory		49.4	39.2
			14.4				All Other Current		2.5	3.9
			72.9				Total Current		78.3	78.7
			12.4				Fixed Assets (net)		9.5	11.5
			8.5				Intangibles (net)		6.8	6.6
			6.3				All Other Non-Current		5.4	3.3
			100.0				Total		100.0	100.0
						LIABILITIES				
			16.2				Notes Payable-Short Term		15.3	9.9
			1.0				Cur. Mat.-L.T.D.		1.8	2.2
			8.8				Trade Payables		20.3	6.8
			.1				Income Taxes Payable		.5	.2
			14.7				All Other Current		14.9	15.4
			40.9				Total Current		52.8	34.5
			4.2				Long-Term Debt		10.8	14.3
			.1				Deferred Taxes		.0	.4
			7.7				All Other Non-Current		5.8	4.3
			47.1				Net Worth		30.6	46.5
			100.0				Total Liabilities & Net Worth		100.0	100.0
						INCOME DATA				
			100.0				Net Sales		100.0	100.0
			32.7				Gross Profit		35.4	35.7
			34.6				Operating Expenses		31.4	26.6
			-1.9				Operating Profit		4.1	9.1
			3.8				All Other Expenses (net)		1.0	-.2
			-5.7				Profit Before Taxes		3.1	9.3
						RATIOS				
			4.6				Current		3.1	5.3
			1.8						2.0	2.0
			1.2						1.0	1.4
			.9				Quick		1.2	1.6
			.2						.6	1.0
			.1						.3	.6
		7	49.9				Sales/Receivables	1	717.4	2 149.7
		17	21.5					28	12.9	31 11.8
		28	12.9					41	9.0	53 6.9
		126	2.9				Cost of Sales/Inventory	73	5.0	69 5.3
		281	1.3					126	2.9	99 3.7
		365	1.0					174	2.1	159 2.3
		10	35.6				Cost of Sales/Payables	7	52.0	0 UND
		35	10.4					36	10.1	12 31.5
		72	5.1					99	3.7	45 8.1
			2.0				Sales/Working Capital		4.0	3.1
			5.2						9.8	5.2
			9.3						137.9	12.0
			3.3				EBIT/Interest		18.0	43.8
		(15)	.0					(27)	4.7	(23) 17.4
			-2.0						1.2	6.9
							Net Profit + Depr., Dep., Amort./Cur. Mat. L/T/D			
			.0				Fixed/Worth		.0	.0
			.3						.2	.1
			1.5						1.6	.8
			.3				Debt/Worth		.7	.5
			1.7						2.0	1.4
			4.5						35.4	3.3
			6.7				% Profit Before Taxes/Tangible Net Worth		62.6	103.9
		(17)	-4.7					(24)	22.9	(23) 83.2
			-45.4						10.4	29.6
			2.9				% Profit Before Taxes/Total Assets		19.6	37.6
			-2.7						6.4	20.3
			-8.3						.3	11.5
			121.2				Sales/Net Fixed Assets		999.8	434.7
			26.4						73.5	43.4
			4.7						19.7	10.9
			1.7				Sales/Total Assets		3.0	2.6
			1.0						2.2	2.1
			.7						1.6	1.4
			.3				% Depr., Dep., Amort./Sales		.5	.3
		(16)	.6					(17)	1.2	(12) 2.1
			5.4						3.1	4.5
							% Officers', Directors', Owners' Comp/Sales		1.2	
								(10)	2.3	
									6.9	
3266M	3527M	66775M	648016M	1043667M	1562637M	Net Sales ($)			2235390M	482391M
666M	1733M	40473M	464355M	534277M	935579M	Total Assets ($)			749504M	274387M

© RMA 2024 M = $ thousand   MM = $ million
See Pages viii through xx for Explanation of Ratios and Data

MANUFACTURING—Motorcycle, Bicycle, and Parts Manufacturing   NAICS 336991

Comparative Historical Data | Current Data Sorted by Sales

Comparative Historical Data						Current Data Sorted by Sales					
1		2		5		**Type of Statement**					
1		3				Unqualified			2	1	2
1		1		1		Reviewed					
4		2		1		Compiled			1		
31		30		32		Tax Returns			3	1	20
						Other	4			5	
4/1/21-		4/1/22-		4/1/23-			14 (4/1-9/30/23)		25 (10/1/23-3/31/24)		
3/31/22		3/31/23		3/31/24			0-1MM	1-3MM	3-5MM	5-10MM	10-25MM	25MM & OVER
ALL		ALL		ALL		**NUMBER OF STATEMENTS**					
38		38		39			4	4	6	7	22
%		%		%		**ASSETS**	%	%	%	%	%
11.5		12.0		7.3		Cash & Equivalents					6.5
17.9		12.8		8.9		Trade Receivables (net)	D	D			12.0
46.5		47.0		48.9		Inventory	A	A			47.9
6.6		5.6		10.1		All Other Current	T	T			6.6
82.5		77.4		75.3		Total Current	A	A			73.1
8.7		10.2		9.5		Fixed Assets (net)					11.8
4.1		5.2		6.7		Intangibles (net)	N	N			3.5
4.8		7.1		8.5		All Other Non-Current	O	O			11.6
100.0		100.0		100.0		Total	T	T			100.0
						LIABILITIES					
11.0		10.2		15.3		Notes Payable-Short Term	A	A			11.9
.4		2.4		.9		Cur. Mat.-L.T.D.	V	V			.8
25.0		16.2		16.8		Trade Payables	A	A			10.1
.1		.4		.1		Income Taxes Payable	I	I			.1
8.7		12.8		18.6		All Other Current	L	L			23.3
45.1		42.0		51.8		Total Current	A	A			46.2
13.8		17.9		10.2		Long-Term Debt	B	B			4.0
.1		.1		.1		Deferred Taxes	L	L			.2
3.2		7.7		7.0		All Other Non-Current	E	E			6.5
37.9		32.3		31.0		Net Worth					43.1
100.0		100.0		100.0		Total Liabilities & Net Worth					100.0
						INCOME DATA					
100.0		100.0		100.0		Net Sales					100.0
35.3		31.0		28.4		Gross Profit					23.2
25.2		24.8		30.3		Operating Expenses					21.7
10.2		6.2		-1.9		Operating Profit					1.5
.6		.4		1.9		All Other Expenses (net)					1.4
9.5		5.8		-3.8		Profit Before Taxes					.1
						RATIOS					
4.4		3.6		4.6							2.8
2.8		1.9		1.8		Current					1.3
1.5		1.3		1.2							1.2
1.4		1.0		.6							.6
.7		.4		.2		Quick					.2
.3		.3		.1							.1
10	37.2	6	57.6	4	83.2					10	35.2
25	14.8	20	18.6	17	22.1	Sales/Receivables				24	15.1
41	9.0	29	12.8	28	13.0					30	12.2
68	5.4	65	5.6	96	3.8					85	4.3
126	2.9	118	3.1	146	2.5	Cost of Sales/Inventory				118	3.1
159	2.3	228	1.6	281	1.3					281	1.3
4	91.7	6	60.1	7	49.3					6	60.9
34	10.7	23	15.7	29	12.4	Cost of Sales/Payables				31	11.7
70	5.2	54	6.7	61	6.0					63	5.8
	3.6		3.8		2.9						4.0
	6.4		6.7		5.3	Sales/Working Capital					8.5
	10.9		11.3		13.3						13.6
	42.1		19.9		3.7						6.9
(26)	20.2	(29)	6.1	(26)	.5	EBIT/Interest				(13)	1.7
	9.0		1.1		-2.4						-.6
						Net Profit + Depr., Dep., Amort./Cur. Mat. L/T/D					
	.0		.0		.0						.0
	.2		.2		.1	Fixed/Worth					.2
	.5		3.1		1.4						1.0
	.4		.7		.6						.6
	1.0		2.4		1.7	Debt/Worth					2.2
	15.5		7.1		4.8						4.7
	83.9		77.2		14.7	% Profit Before Taxes/Tangible Net Worth					16.7
(31)	52.8	(30)	32.1	(34)	2.5						5.2
	23.2		8.6		-14.5						-12.3
	45.5		24.8		3.8	% Profit Before Taxes/Total Assets					9.0
	25.2		9.4		-.5						2.2
	12.8		1.4		-8.3						-4.3
	264.5		340.7		165.8						387.3
	38.1		37.6		82.3	Sales/Net Fixed Assets					42.0
	29.4		16.7		10.4						4.7
	3.0		2.7		2.4						2.5
	2.3		2.0		1.5	Sales/Total Assets					1.6
	1.8		1.4		.9						1.1
	.3		.4		.3						.2
(26)	.8	(23)	.9	(30)	.5	% Depr., Dep., Amort./Sales				(20)	.6
	1.4		1.5		1.7						5.0
						% Officers', Directors' Owners' Comp/Sales					
3374337M		4607953M		3327888M		Net Sales ($)	6793M		40834M	103073M	3177188M
1129774M		1703008M		1977083M		Total Assets ($)	2399M		71652M	90184M	1812848M

© RMA 2024   M = $ thousand   MM = $ million
See Pages viii through xx for Explanation of Ratios and Data

MANUFACTURING—All Other Transportation Equipment Manufacturing   NAICS 336999

Current Data Sorted by Assets

						Type of Statement
			2		1	Unqualified
			4	1		Reviewed
	1		1			Compiled
		4				Tax Returns
	2	11	22	11	4	Other
	23 (4/1-9/30/23)		42 (10/1/23-3/31/24)			
0-500M	500M-2MM	2-10MM	10-50MM	50-100MM	100-250MM	**NUMBER OF STATEMENTS**
	3	16	29	12	5	

Comparative Historical Data

4	5
4	1
8	1
12	3
26	11
4/1/19-3/31/20 ALL	4/1/20-3/31/21 ALL
54	21

0-500M	500M-2MM	2-10MM	10-50MM	50-100MM	100-250MM		4/1/19-3/31/20	4/1/20-3/31/21
%	%	%	%	%	%	**ASSETS**	%	%
		15.9	13.6	15.0		Cash & Equivalents	15.2	18.6
		10.4	17.1	9.2		Trade Receivables (net)	14.8	11.4
		48.3	41.3	39.7		Inventory	40.0	28.8
D		3.9	6.2	5.5		All Other Current	2.9	4.2
A		78.5	78.1	69.4		Total Current	72.9	63.0
T		20.7	11.4	13.2		Fixed Assets (net)	17.4	15.0
A		.6	5.4	2.3		Intangibles (net)	5.4	18.2
		.1	5.1	15.0		All Other Non-Current	4.4	3.7
N		100.0	100.0	100.0		Total	100.0	100.0
O						**LIABILITIES**		
T		10.4	6.5	8.4		Notes Payable-Short Term	11.0	6.1
		.5	3.1	1.3		Cur. Mat.-L.T.D.	1.7	7.2
A		19.3	8.3	10.1		Trade Payables	10.4	6.7
V		.1	.1	.4		Income Taxes Payable	.4	.5
A		7.7	9.7	10.4		All Other Current	13.2	11.9
I		37.9	27.6	30.6		Total Current	36.7	32.4
L		13.3	10.0	7.8		Long-Term Debt	11.5	22.9
A		.1	.1	.0		Deferred Taxes	.2	.2
B		3.6	5.9	18.2		All Other Non-Current	5.9	6.9
L		45.1	56.4	43.4		Net Worth	45.8	37.6
E		100.0	100.0	100.0		Total Liabilities & Net Worth	100.0	100.0
						INCOME DATA		
		100.0	100.0	100.0		Net Sales	100.0	100.0
		28.8	26.6	22.5		Gross Profit	31.6	29.9
		19.7	18.7	13.3		Operating Expenses	23.8	19.8
		9.1	7.9	9.3		Operating Profit	7.8	10.0
		.8	-.1	-.1		All Other Expenses (net)	.5	2.7
		8.3	8.1	9.3		Profit Before Taxes	7.2	7.3
						RATIOS		
		6.4	7.5	4.3			4.5	4.3
		3.0	2.8	2.4		Current	2.3	2.2
		1.3	1.9	1.4			1.3	1.5
		3.5	2.9	2.0			2.0	1.7
		.9	1.3	.8		Quick	.9	1.1
		.2	.5	.3			.4	.6
	4	102.5	18	20.4	6	57.2		10	35.5	16	22.5
	9	39.2	26	14.1	19	18.9	Sales/Receivables	23	16.0	30	12.1
	19	19.6	35	10.4	27	13.7		42	8.7	49	7.5
	51	7.1	65	5.6	50	7.3		47	7.7	59	6.2
	76	4.8	79	4.6	99	3.7	Cost of Sales/Inventory	73	5.0	101	3.6
	146	2.5	104	3.5	118	3.1		140	2.6	130	2.8
	9	38.9	8	45.7	14	25.2		15	25.0	10	35.2
	19	19.7	11	32.1	24	14.9	Cost of Sales/Payables	21	17.8	19	19.0
	45	8.1	26	13.8	38	9.7		32	11.5	39	9.3
		4.6		2.9		2.7			4.1		2.9
		6.2		4.5		6.3	Sales/Working Capital		5.8		4.1
		15.0		9.3		8.7			15.1		11.0
		32.0		31.0		21.9			60.4		89.5
	(13)	12.7	(26)	12.6	(11)	16.7	EBIT/Interest	(43)	8.4	(19)	3.4
		2.6		2.4		9.5			2.0		1.5
							Net Profit + Depr., Dep., Amort./Cur. Mat. L/T/D		
		.1	.1	.1			.1	.2
		.7	.1	.3		Fixed/Worth	.4	1.2
		1.0	.4	.7			1.0	-1.5
		.2	.3	1.2			.5	.5
		.8	1.0	1.8		Debt/Worth	1.3	4.4
		10.5	3.0	2.6			4.6	-11.8
		60.3	52.9	59.2			55.6	80.5
	(13)	49.9	34.4	49.2		% Profit Before Taxes/Tangible Net Worth	(50)	32.5	(14)	28.2
		35.1	15.6	45.2			11.3	16.3
		35.2	30.9	24.1			25.8	15.7
		16.1	17.9	19.2		% Profit Before Taxes/Total Assets	12.6	9.5
		11.9	3.9	11.1			2.9	1.1
		55.9	45.7	32.5			37.0	29.5
		15.8	32.7	12.7		Sales/Net Fixed Assets	20.7	12.7
		7.4	17.7	9.0			7.3	5.9
		3.7	2.9	2.1			3.6	1.9
		2.9	2.3	1.9		Sales/Total Assets	2.2	1.4
		2.2	1.8	1.8			1.5	.9
		.3	.3	.9			.7	.9
	(13)	.7	(19)	1.0	(10)	1.2	% Depr., Dep., Amort./Sales	(40)	1.2	(13)	2.2
		3.0	1.3	1.4			1.8	3.0
								1.5	
						% Officers', Directors' Owners' Comp/Sales	(15)	2.5	
							4.4	
	8695M	215696M	1457819M	1406387M	804090M	Net Sales ($)	1585912M	1214988M
	3261M	80946M	665351M	747960M	887735M	Total Assets ($)	1017481M	1011230M

© RMA 2024   M = $ thousand   MM = $ million
See Pages viii through xx for Explanation of Ratios and Data

MANUFACTURING—All Other Transportation Equipment Manufacturing NAICS 336999

Comparative Historical Data / Current Data Sorted by Sales

					Type of Statement							
	4		4		3	Unqualified					1	2
	6		9		5	Reviewed					1	5
			3		3	Compiled				1	1	1
	6		3		4	Tax Returns					4	
	27		28		50	Other	1		5	8	35	
	4/1/21-		4/1/22-		4/1/23-		23 (4/1-9/30/23)			42 (10/1/23-3/31/24)		
	3/31/22		3/31/23		3/31/24		0-1MM	1-3MM	3-5MM	5-10MM	10-25MM	25MM & OVER
	ALL		ALL		ALL	**NUMBER OF STATEMENTS**		2	1	5	14	43
	43		47		65							
	%		%		%	**ASSETS**	%	%	%	%	%	%
	13.2		10.7		15.1	Cash & Equivalents					13.6	16.0
	14.2		14.7		13.7	Trade Receivables (net)	D				9.5	14.6
	34.4		35.5		40.9	Inventory	A				45.0	39.1
	5.4		6.2		5.5	All Other Current	T				4.0	6.2
	67.2		67.1		75.2	Total Current	A				72.1	75.9
	16.2		12.8		13.6	Fixed Assets (net)					20.6	10.7
	12.9		11.1		5.6	Intangibles (net)	N				6.2	5.5
	3.8		8.7		5.5	All Other Non-Current	O				1.1	7.9
	100.0		100.0		100.0	Total	T				100.0	100.0
						LIABILITIES	A					
	6.4		5.0		7.2	Notes Payable-Short Term	V				6.4	6.6
	4.2		2.8		1.9	Cur. Mat.-L.T.D.	A				1.9	2.1
	9.8		9.0		11.4	Trade Payables	I				15.5	8.2
	.1		.2		.2	Income Taxes Payable	L				.1	.2
	10.8		14.1		10.3	All Other Current	A				8.7	11.6
	31.3		31.0		31.0	Total Current	B				32.6	28.7
	11.4		11.1		10.8	Long-Term Debt	L				18.5	8.3
	.4		.2		.1	Deferred Taxes	E				.1	.1
	5.7		10.6		7.3	All Other Non-Current					6.8	8.8
	51.2		46.9		50.8	Net Worth					42.0	54.1
	100.0		100.0		100.0	Total Liabilties & Net Worth					100.0	100.0
						INCOME DATA						
	100.0		100.0		100.0	Net Sales					100.0	100.0
	31.2		31.3		28.1	Gross Profit					30.5	25.6
	22.6		24.5		19.0	Operating Expenses					23.4	16.0
	8.6		6.7		9.0	Operating Profit					7.1	9.6
	-.1		.0		.2	All Other Expenses (net)					.2	.1
	8.6		6.7		8.8	Profit Before Taxes					6.9	9.5
						RATIOS						
	4.2		4.3		6.2						5.5	7.1
	2.0		2.4		2.6	Current					2.4	2.7
	1.6		1.6		1.7						1.4	1.7
	2.1		1.8		2.4						2.2	2.9
	1.0		.8		.9	Quick					1.0	1.0
	.7		.5		.5						.1	.5
16	23.2	12	30.1	9	42.1					5	76.6	14	26.2
29	12.7	33	11.0	19	18.9	Sales/Receivables				12	31.0	25	14.8
47	7.7	50	7.3	33	11.1					19	19.4	34	10.6
59	6.2	57	6.4	64	5.7					54	6.8	65	5.6
114	3.2	118	3.1	89	4.1	Cost of Sales/Inventory				73	5.0	89	4.1
152	2.4	152	2.4	118	3.1					111	3.3	107	3.4
11	31.9	11	33.8	10	36.2					10	37.9	10	36.2
26	13.9	25	14.4	17	21.1	Cost of Sales/Payables				16	22.5	15	24.1
42	8.6	50	7.3	34	10.6					43	8.4	29	12.5
	3.1		3.5		3.2						4.9	2.9
	5.2		4.7		5.6	Sales/Working Capital					6.2	4.5
	8.9		9.9		9.7						11.8	8.8
	123.9		38.3		27.9						21.1	48.2
(40)	13.1	(38)	8.3	(56)	12.9	EBIT/Interest				(12)	6.7	(38)	14.3
	3.5		2.8		3.3						1.8	5.2
			34.2			Net Profit + Depr., Dep.,						
		(10)	4.4			Amort./Cur. Mat. L/T/D						
			1.7									
	.1		.2		.1						.2	.1
	.4		.4		.3	Fixed/Worth					.7	.2
	1.2		1.4		.7						1.8	.5
	.4		.4		.4						.4	.4
	1.5		1.6		1.2	Debt/Worth					1.7	1.2
	5.1		13.7		3.2						8.4	2.6
	48.0		56.7		61.0	% Profit Before Taxes/Tangible					62.0	63.0
(38)	35.1	(40)	28.7	(61)	45.6	Net Worth				(12)	50.3	(42)	44.6
	10.9		5.1		25.3						26.1	23.0
	20.5		21.1		30.9	% Profit Before Taxes/Total					33.7	27.6
	13.2		6.0		17.7	Assets					12.8	18.2
	5.1		1.5		6.4						4.7	6.6
	37.8		30.9		47.3						50.9	42.6
	14.2		16.8		26.3	Sales/Net Fixed Assets					15.8	26.4
	6.3		9.6		9.6						6.5	10.2
	2.1		2.3		2.9						3.8	2.7
	1.5		1.8		2.2	Sales/Total Assets					2.9	2.1
	1.1		1.1		1.7						1.7	1.7
	.8		.7		.5						.3	.5
(31)	1.9	(35)	1.3	(47)	1.1	% Depr., Dep., Amort./Sales				(12)	.8	(32)	1.1
	3.3		2.6		1.4						4.1	1.3
	1.0		.7		1.7	% Officers', Directors'						
(12)	2.2	(11)	1.3		2.6	Owners' Comp/Sales						
	4.7				5.0							
	1818157M		2020629M		3892687M	Net Sales ($)		5405M	3290M	42145M	230425M	3611422M
	1501973M		1615640M		2385253M	Total Assets ($)		1641M	1620M	21547M	110779M	2249666M

© RMA 2024

M = $ thousand   MM = $ million
See Pages viii through xx for Explanation of Ratios and Data

MANUFACTURING—Wood Kitchen Cabinet and Countertop Manufacturing NAICS 337110

Current Data Sorted by Assets | Comparative Historical Data

							Type of Statement		
				4	2		Unqualified	3	3
			5	4	2		Reviewed	10	7
			3	2			Compiled	6	7
5	4		7	1			Tax Returns	28	19
7	16	21	17	5	2		Other	50	43
	7 (4/1-9/30/23)		100 (10/1/23-3/31/24)					4/1/19-	4/1/20-
0-500M	500M-2MM	2-10MM	10-50MM	50-100MM	100-250MM			3/31/20	3/31/21
12	20	36	28	9	2		NUMBER OF STATEMENTS	ALL 97	ALL 79
%	%	%	%	%	%		ASSETS	%	%
34.6	14.1	14.0	15.3				Cash & Equivalents	16.6	21.9
8.6	22.1	27.7	19.1				Trade Receivables (net)	21.9	21.6
13.2	16.0	17.1	21.1				Inventory	16.9	16.1
.5	8.3	2.8	2.6				All Other Current	2.3	3.8
56.9	60.5	61.6	58.1				Total Current	57.8	63.2
29.7	19.6	24.1	30.4				Fixed Assets (net)	31.9	25.2
5.5	4.2	6.1	4.8				Intangibles (net)	3.9	5.0
8.0	15.8	8.2	6.7				All Other Non-Current	6.4	6.6
100.0	100.0	100.0	100.0				Total	100.0	100.0
							LIABILITIES		
11.3	10.2	3.3	5.0				Notes Payable-Short Term	7.2	9.2
4.8	3.3	4.0	5.4				Cur. Mat.-L.T.D.	2.8	4.1
1.6	13.8	8.0	8.4				Trade Payables	9.4	9.7
.0	.0	.2	.5				Income Taxes Payable	.4	.1
27.4	21.6	14.0	15.9				All Other Current	15.2	17.9
45.1	48.9	29.5	35.2				Total Current	35.0	41.0
44.5	36.4	18.7	31.1				Long-Term Debt	22.2	22.2
.0	.0	.3	.6				Deferred Taxes	.2	.5
3.7	.5	3.5	13.0				All Other Non-Current	10.7	8.6
6.7	14.2	47.9	20.1				Net Worth	31.9	27.7
100.0	100.0	100.0	100.0				Total Liabilities & Net Worth	100.0	100.0
							INCOME DATA		
100.0	100.0	100.0	100.0				Net Sales	100.0	100.0
55.5	44.9	38.5	37.8				Gross Profit	34.7	36.9
40.6	38.7	28.5	27.9				Operating Expenses	28.3	30.7
14.9	6.2	10.0	9.8				Operating Profit	6.4	6.3
.9	.5	1.0	.9				All Other Expenses (net)	.4	-1.3
14.0	5.7	9.0	8.9				Profit Before Taxes	6.0	7.6
							RATIOS		
15.2	5.2	3.6	3.4					3.4	4.5
2.0	1.4	2.3	2.1			Current		1.9	2.1
.4	.6	1.3	1.0					1.1	1.3
15.2	1.9	2.4	2.1					2.5	2.7
1.6	.7	1.6	1.2			Quick		1.3	1.4
.1	.3	.7	.4					.6	.7
0 UND	10 38.2	21 17.6	10 35.2					14 25.9	16 22.5
2 206.3	21 17.7	39 9.3	20 18.5			Sales/Receivables		28 13.2	31 11.7
13 28.3	47 7.8	70 5.2	42 8.6					43 8.5	55 6.6
0 UND	0 UND	15 24.8	22 16.7					9 41.9	6 58.8
0 UND	10 35.7	30 12.2	35 10.3			Cost of Sales/Inventory		26 14.1	22 16.4
34 10.7	55 6.6	48 7.6	94 3.9					57 6.4	57 6.4
0 UND	0 UND	8 43.9	7 51.0					9 41.8	7 49.7
0 UND	25 14.5	15 24.8	14 25.4			Cost of Sales/Payables		15 23.7	15 23.7
5 80.2	44 8.3	25 14.6	39 9.4					28 13.2	33 11.0
4.7	5.1	4.4	3.9					5.3	4.6
27.1	17.2	6.7	9.9			Sales/Working Capital		11.4	9.7
-7.9	-11.5	16.9	113.3					79.3	24.4
	19.6	32.5	29.2					23.4	33.0
	(17) 4.0	(30) 14.5	(25) 7.0			EBIT/Interest		(85) 6.7	(60) 11.4
	.9	2.7	2.7					2.2	2.1
								18.3	
						Net Profit + Depr., Dep.,		(12) 5.4	
						Amort./Cur. Mat. L/T/D		1.5	
.2	.1	.2	.5					.3	.2
1.3	.7	.4	.9			Fixed/Worth		.7	.6
-.1	NM	1.7	3.0					NM	2.8
.4	.5	.5	.8					.4	.5
109.0	4.3	.9	2.0			Debt/Worth		1.4	1.6
-3.8	-9.2	9.8	7.7					NM	-22.4
	82.1	84.9	74.1					78.0	93.0
(13)	28.7 (32)	45.1 (23)	33.9			% Profit Before Taxes/Tangible Net Worth	(73)	29.6 (59)	38.4
	14.5	6.6	9.2					15.2	12.2
81.1	31.8	34.0	32.8					24.0	33.1
28.7	7.1	17.1	11.8			% Profit Before Taxes/Total Assets		12.0	16.8
4.6	2.3	3.4	3.0					3.3	2.8
461.6	58.7	21.6	11.2					23.1	41.2
30.7	23.2	10.6	7.8			Sales/Net Fixed Assets		10.3	11.5
9.5	11.8	6.2	4.8					5.0	5.0
7.6	4.1	2.9	2.9					3.5	3.4
4.0	3.4	2.1	2.0			Sales/Total Assets		2.5	2.4
2.3	1.6	1.6	1.3					1.7	1.7
	1.4	1.2	.6					1.1	1.0
(12)	1.9 (27)	1.9 (27)	1.6			% Depr., Dep., Amort./Sales	(84)	2.2 (57)	2.0
	3.6	3.2	3.1					3.1	3.0
		1.1						1.8	1.4
	(18)	2.2				% Officers', Directors' Owners' Comp/Sales	(46)	3.3 (28)	3.4
		4.5						5.9	6.7
17193M	71560M	406613M	1325875M	1096053M	467633M	Net Sales ($)		2387389M	1423156M
3364M	21549M	167598M	620000M	644512M	358060M	Total Assets ($)		1184445M	676446M

© RMA 2024

M = $ thousand   MM = $ million
See Pages viii through xx for Explanation of Ratios and Data

MANUFACTURING—Wood Kitchen Cabinet and Countertop Manufacturing NAICS 337110

Comparative Historical Data | Current Data Sorted by Sales

					Type of Statement						
	6		10	6	Unqualified				1	5	6
	3		8	11	Reviewed				2	2	5
	6		7	5	Compiled				2	2	1
	14		21	17	Tax Returns	2	5	3	4	3	
	54		60	68	Other	4	12	11	13	9	19
	4/1/21-3/31/22 ALL		4/1/22-3/31/23 ALL	4/1/23-3/31/24 ALL		7 (4/1-9/30/23)			100 (10/1/23-3/31/24)		
						0-1MM	1-3MM	3-5MM	5-10MM	10-25MM	25MM & OVER
	83		106	107	NUMBER OF STATEMENTS	6	17	14	20	19	31
	%		%	%	ASSETS	%	%	%	%	%	%
	14.8		17.1	16.8	Cash & Equivalents		13.9	12.1	13.8	15.5	15.5
	21.3		19.5	20.5	Trade Receivables (net)		12.8	28.8	26.0	20.9	20.5
	18.8		18.2	17.4	Inventory		14.0	20.9	11.7	24.6	18.6
	4.7		3.6	3.4	All Other Current		3.5	7.4	2.5	3.4	2.9
	59.5		58.3	58.2	Total Current		44.1	69.2	54.1	64.4	57.5
	28.7		28.0	26.2	Fixed Assets (net)		31.4	20.1	26.8	24.9	27.6
	7.1		6.4	6.3	Intangibles (net)		3.2	5.7	9.6	5.4	6.3
	4.7		7.3	9.3	All Other Non-Current		21.3	5.0	9.5	5.3	8.6
	100.0		100.0	100.0	Total		100.0	100.0	100.0	100.0	100.0
					LIABILITIES						
	7.4		9.2	5.6	Notes Payable-Short Term		10.7	9.2	5.0	4.3	3.4
	2.4		4.0	4.5	Cur. Mat.-L.T.D.		5.4	2.3	3.7	3.1	6.4
	9.5		9.3	8.2	Trade Payables		3.9	14.0	5.0	13.0	8.3
	.4		.5	.2	Income Taxes Payable		.3	.0	.0	.3	.3
	12.7		16.0	17.7	All Other Current		19.6	20.2	14.6	26.0	13.6
	32.4		38.9	36.3	Total Current		39.9	45.7	28.3	46.8	32.1
	29.4		25.4	28.5	Long-Term Debt		58.4	17.5	23.5	10.8	29.2
	.1		.4	.3	Deferred Taxes		.0	.0	.1	1.1	.4
	8.2		6.3	6.3	All Other Non-Current		.0	4.2	1.4	3.3	15.4
	29.8		29.0	28.6	Net Worth		1.6	32.6	46.6	38.0	22.8
	100.0		100.0	100.0	Total Liabilities & Net Worth		100.0	100.0	100.0	100.0	100.0
					INCOME DATA						
	100.0		100.0	100.0	Net Sales		100.0	100.0	100.0	100.0	100.0
	39.6		36.1	40.4	Gross Profit		51.9	41.9	43.7	36.1	31.4
	31.1		29.3	30.7	Operating Expenses		41.1	35.7	33.1	28.4	22.3
	8.5		6.8	9.7	Operating Profit		10.8	6.1	10.6	7.7	9.1
	-1.5		.0	1.0	All Other Expenses (net)		1.8	.9	1.2	.3	.9
	10.0		6.8	8.7	Profit Before Taxes		9.0	5.3	9.5	7.3	8.2
					RATIOS						
	3.8		4.1	3.6			4.4	2.5	4.4	3.6	2.9
	1.9		2.1	2.1	Current		1.3	1.8	2.4	2.1	2.2
	1.4		1.2	1.1			.3	1.1	1.1	1.3	1.2
	2.7		2.2	2.2			1.7	1.9	3.9	1.9	2.1
	1.2		1.3	1.3	Quick		.6	1.0	1.9	1.0	1.2
	.5		.5	.4			.2	.2	.6	.6	.6
13	27.9	7	51.5	9	39.1	0	UND	16	22.7	14	25.5	11	32.5	15	24.0
27	13.3	22	16.9	24	15.1	Sales/Receivables	10	35.7	46	7.9	54	6.8	29	12.4	24	15.1
45	8.1	39	9.3	48	7.6		26	14.3	61	6.0	73	5.0	39	9.4	42	8.7
13	28.0	6	62.9	8	43.9		0	UND	0	UND	0	UND	28	12.9	22	16.9
38	9.5	33	11.1	29	12.7	Cost of Sales/Inventory	4	102.5	28	13.0	26	14.2	41	9.0	30	12.1
70	5.2	56	6.5	55	6.6		47	7.8	114	3.2	45	8.1	107	3.4	48	7.6
9	41.8	7	50.9	6	63.9		0	UND	0	UND	2	162.5	8	43.6	8	45.4
18	20.6	16	23.0	13	27.6	Cost of Sales/Payables	6	60.5	25	14.8	14	26.2	18	20.2	12	30.2
34	10.6	27	13.4	28	13.2		28	13.0	63	5.8	28	13.2	26	14.1	30	12.3
	4.6		5.1	4.6			5.2	4.9	3.9	4.0	5.2
	8.6		8.6	8.4	Sales/Working Capital		122.0	11.2	5.3	8.4	10.4
	23.3		51.9	68.7			-9.0	70.7	142.3	17.3	31.2
	39.9		30.5	28.8			22.0	57.4	15.2	28.7	57.0
(69)	13.8	(86)	10.4	(91)	7.8	EBIT/Interest	(15)	2.5	(11)	8.3	(16)	7.2	(16)	22.0	(29)	15.2
	4.5		3.0	1.8			.7	2.4	2.4	2.4	3.8
	14.4		10.9	5.4							5.3
(11)	5.0	(16)	3.7	(16)	3.6	Net Profit + Depr., Dep., Amort./Cur. Mat. L/T/D					(12)	3.6
	3.6		.6	1.9							1.6
	.4		.3	.4			.5	.3	.2	.4	.5
	.9		.7	.9	Fixed/Worth		27.3	.5	.5	.6	1.0
	UND		NM	3.5			-.3	14.6	2.1	.9	15.9
	.6		.5	.6			.6	.6	.4	.6	.8
	2.0		1.5	2.1	Debt/Worth		215.5	2.7	1.5	.9	2.1
	UND		-41.1	57.9			-6.6	NM	9.9	2.7	57.9
	95.1		68.5	99.9			340.8	52.4	76.8	60.1	96.7
(63)	59.3	(79)	37.7	(84)	46.3	% Profit Before Taxes/Tangible Net Worth	(10)	105.9	(11)	28.7	(17)	31.8	(18)	47.0	(24)	53.8
	24.6		16.5	11.3			18.1	11.0	4.6	5.3	15.1
	34.4		29.4	33.0			36.0	20.0	33.7	32.4	34.5
	18.3		16.9	13.5	% Profit Before Taxes/Total Assets		9.1	7.0	16.8	19.1	15.0
	6.7		5.1	2.9			-.7	2.7	3.4	2.0	3.2
	21.6		29.4	24.2			69.3	43.2	20.3	21.4	12.0
	11.0		11.0	10.5	Sales/Net Fixed Assets		20.1	14.5	9.9	9.3	7.5
	6.4		5.5	5.7			9.9	9.0	5.4	5.2	5.7
	3.0		3.8	3.4			5.7	4.0	2.2	3.8	3.2
	2.4		2.4	2.0	Sales/Total Assets		3.4	3.1	1.9	2.5	2.0
	1.7		1.6	1.5			1.4	1.8	1.4	1.5	1.6
	1.2		1.1	1.2			1.0		1.6	1.2	.5
(62)	2.1	(76)	2.1	(80)	1.9	% Depr., Dep., Amort./Sales	(11)	2.3	(14)	2.0	(15)	2.7	(30)	1.6
	3.6		3.4	3.1			3.8	6.9	3.2	2.1
	1.1		1.3	1.2							
(27)	2.2	(37)	3.7	(34)	2.6	% Officers', Directors' Owners' Comp/Sales						
	4.1		6.1	5.5							
	2924052M		4667687M	3384927M	Net Sales ($)	3373M	33763M	53480M	141372M	341825M	2811114M
	1001244M		2009585M	1815083M	Total Assets ($)	1690M	21808M	25851M	149918M	162301M	1453515M

© RMA 2024
M = $ thousand   MM = $ million
See Pages viii through xx for Explanation of Ratios and Data

MANUFACTURING—Upholstered Household Furniture Manufacturing NAICS 337121

Current Data Sorted by Assets | Comparative Historical Data

0-500M	2 3 5 (4/1-9/30/23) 500M-2MM	2 3 6 11 2-10MM	6 2 1 8 48 (10/1/23-3/31/24) 10-50MM	2 1 1 6 10 50-100MM	2 2 8 10 100-250MM	Type of Statement			
						Unqualified		9	5
						Reviewed		11	4
						Compiled		5	1
						Tax Returns		1	2
						Other		24	18
								4/1/19- 3/31/20 ALL	4/1/20- 3/31/21 ALL
	5	11	17	10	10	NUMBER OF STATEMENTS		50	30
%	%	%	%	%	%	ASSETS		%	%
D			19.8	13.5	13.4	2.7	Cash & Equivalents	7.3	12.9
A			15.0	25.3	18.4	16.6	Trade Receivables (net)	23.7	23.9
T			36.8	30.9	31.2	17.7	Inventory	36.8	33.8
A			.9	2.2	1.2	14.5	All Other Current	4.5	4.3
			72.6	71.8	64.2	51.4	Total Current	72.4	74.9
N			21.5	15.8	30.3	20.2	Fixed Assets (net)	17.1	14.6
O			.2	1.2	3.1	17.3	Intangibles (net)	6.4	6.7
T			5.7	11.1	2.5	11.1	All Other Non-Current	4.2	3.7
			100.0	100.0	100.0	100.0	Total	100.0	100.0
A							LIABILITIES		
V			8.8	6.7	4.6	8.1	Notes Payable-Short Term	8.8	10.8
A			1.1	1.3	2.9	2.8	Cur. Mat.-L.T.D.	3.0	3.3
I			5.1	9.7	11.7	10.9	Trade Payables	14.1	13.2
L			.0	.0	.5	.1	Income Taxes Payable	.1	.3
A			9.0	12.7	11.2	12.5	All Other Current	15.4	16.1
B			24.0	30.5	30.9	34.3	Total Current	41.5	43.6
L			16.2	9.2	13.6	24.4	Long-Term Debt	9.2	15.1
E			.1	.0	.0	.0	Deferred Taxes	.0	.0
			15.7	13.1	5.3	10.6	All Other Non-Current	8.5	8.7
			44.1	47.3	50.3	30.7	Net Worth	40.9	32.6
			100.0	100.0	100.0	100.0	Total Liabilities & Net Worth	100.0	100.0
							INCOME DATA		
			100.0	100.0	100.0	100.0	Net Sales	100.0	100.0
			35.2	25.1	20.0	18.9	Gross Profit	25.7	30.9
			30.7	22.4	15.0	15.3	Operating Expenses	23.4	25.0
			4.5	2.7	5.0	3.6	Operating Profit	2.3	5.9
			-.3	.6	-1.1	.9	All Other Expenses (net)	.7	-.1
			4.7	2.2	6.1	2.7	Profit Before Taxes	1.5	6.0
							RATIOS		
			7.4	8.2	6.6	2.2		3.6	3.1
			5.8	2.9	2.2	1.5	Current	1.9	1.9
			2.1	1.3	1.6	.9		1.3	1.3
			5.6	5.0	2.5	.8		1.4	1.9
			3.5	2.1	1.1	.5	Quick	.7	.7
			.5	.4	.7	.4		.2	.4
		10 36.6	27 13.4	28 13.1	30 12.0		14 25.7	20 18.4
		26 14.2	38 9.6	33 11.0	37 9.9	Sales/Receivables	32 11.5	34 10.8
		43 8.4	52 7.0	40 9.1	42 8.7		47 7.7	56 6.5
		52 7.0	45 8.1	46 8.0	37 9.9		37 9.8	45 8.2
		58 6.3	72 5.1	65 5.6	46 8.0	Cost of Sales/Inventory	69 5.3	76 4.8
		166 2.2	135 2.7	85 4.3	65 5.6		101 3.6	114 3.2
		2 189.6	12 29.2	10 35.3	13 28.0		13 27.2	12 30.9
		15 24.5	17 21.0	19 19.2	28 12.9	Cost of Sales/Payables	24 15.0	25 14.6
		29 12.8	38 9.7	47 7.8	43 8.5		35 10.5	42 8.7
		3.1	2.8	5.3	5.6		4.9	4.2
		4.3	4.0	6.4	11.3	Sales/Working Capital	8.2	8.0
		6.9	13.1	14.5	-86.4		19.0	13.7
			9.3				16.1	21.2
			(15) 2.1			EBIT/Interest	(40) 4.0	(25) 6.3
			-1.9				1.7	1.0
						Net Profit + Depr., Dep., Amort./Cur. Mat. L/T/D		
		.2	.1	.3	.4		.1	.3
		.3	.3	.6	5.8	Fixed/Worth	.3	.6
		18.3	2.0	1.1	-1.5		NM	1.1
		.3	.2	.3	1.5		.6	.8
		.8	.7	.9	9.4	Debt/Worth	1.4	2.5
		26.4	8.6	1.9	-14.4		NM	6.6
			29.0				29.5	83.5
			(14) 10.4			% Profit Before Taxes/Tangible Net Worth	(38) 10.3	(26) 37.7
			-14.5				1.8	13.7
		19.6	12.4	28.4	13.0	% Profit Before Taxes/Total Assets	12.8	26.5
		5.8	4.9	8.2	5.2		3.7	9.5
		-.2	-5.8	3.9	-8.1		.8	1.3
		24.9	26.8	11.5	21.9		42.3	48.4
		14.8	12.9	6.2	8.7	Sales/Net Fixed Assets	22.7	21.6
		5.5	9.5	4.6	6.0		10.7	10.6
		2.5	2.3	2.6	2.3		3.5	3.0
		1.9	1.8	2.1	1.4	Sales/Total Assets	2.7	2.4
		1.4	1.4	1.7	1.2		1.9	1.6
			.5	.8			.4	.5
			(13) 1.0	1.2		% Depr., Dep., Amort./Sales	(39) .7	(22) .8
			1.5	2.2			1.5	2.2
						% Officers', Directors' Owners' Comp/Sales		
	29846M	110223M	682074M	1431417M	2414555M	Net Sales ($)	3153222M	3012547M
	5552M	58031M	356167M	687128M	1576003M	Total Assets ($)	1308714M	1422357M

M = $ thousand   MM = $ million
See Pages viii through xx for Explanation of Ratios and Data

© RMA 2024

MANUFACTURING—Upholstered Household Furniture Manufacturing NAICS 337121

Comparative Historical Data | Current Data Sorted by Sales

	3		8		8	**Type of Statement**				1	7
	2		4		5	Unqualified				1	4
			2		2	Reviewed			1	1	
	2		1		7	Compiled			3	1	
	16		22		31	Tax Returns		1	3	7	2
	4/1/21-3/31/22 ALL		4/1/22-3/31/23 ALL		4/1/23-3/31/24 ALL	Other	0-1MM	1-3MM	3-5MM	5-10MM	10-25MM	25MM & OVER
							5 (4/1-9/30/23)			48 (10/1/23-3/31/24)	
	23		37		53	**NUMBER OF STATEMENTS**		2	2	7	11	31
	%		%		%	**ASSETS**	%	%	%	%	%	%
	10.6		11.3		13.7	Cash & Equivalents					19.9	9.5
	23.6		20.8		21.1	Trade Receivables (net)	D				19.0	21.3
	38.1		32.7		27.9	Inventory	A				32.7	25.5
	1.8		5.2		4.1	All Other Current	T				1.9	6.1
	74.1		70.0		66.8	Total Current	A				73.5	62.4
	16.7		15.7		19.7	Fixed Assets (net)					15.7	21.5
	5.6		4.8		4.8	Intangibles (net)	N				2.8	7.2
	3.7		9.6		8.7	All Other Non-Current	O				8.0	8.9
	100.0		100.0		100.0	Total	T				100.0	100.0
						LIABILITIES						
	4.8		5.4		7.5	Notes Payable-Short Term	A				8.8	5.4
	2.7		1.7		1.8	Cur. Mat.-L.T.D.	V				.5	2.4
	20.7		12.6		9.3	Trade Payables	A				6.3	11.1
	.0		.0		.1	Income Taxes Payable	I				.0	.2
	17.6		10.9		11.8	All Other Current	L				13.2	12.7
	45.8		30.7		30.5	Total Current	A				28.8	31.8
	12.1		17.6		15.2	Long-Term Debt	B				5.6	16.5
	.0		.1		.0	Deferred Taxes	L				.1	
	5.8		4.9		11.7	All Other Non-Current	E				20.1	8.5
	36.2		46.7		42.5	Net Worth					45.4	43.2
	100.0		100.0		100.0	Total Liabilities & Net Worth					100.0	100.0
						INCOME DATA						
	100.0		100.0		100.0	Net Sales					100.0	100.0
	25.5		27.8		26.1	Gross Profit					24.9	22.2
	23.4		24.7		22.3	Operating Expenses					23.0	17.4
	2.2		3.1		3.9	Operating Profit					1.8	4.8
	-3.1		-.3		.2	All Other Expenses (net)					-.5	.1
	5.3		3.4		3.7	Profit Before Taxes					2.3	4.7
						RATIOS						
	3.0		5.5		7.1						9.7	6.5
	1.8		2.1		2.5	Current					2.9	1.9
	1.1		1.3		1.3						1.3	1.1
	1.3		2.8		4.6						5.6	3.1
	.8		.9		1.1	Quick					2.1	.9
	.4		.4		.5						.4	.5
12	30.3	19	19.3	25	14.4					23	15.9	27	13.3
33	11.0	33	10.9	34	10.6	Sales/Receivables				33	10.9	38	9.7
39	9.4	45	8.1	43	8.4					39	9.3	43	8.4
46	8.0	50	7.3	42	8.6					46	7.9	40	9.2
79	4.6	79	4.6	58	6.3	Cost of Sales/Inventory				130	2.8	54	6.7
135	2.7	130	2.8	99	3.7					152	2.4	72	5.1
13	28.9	12	31.0	10	37.7					13	27.2	12	30.9
31	11.7	24	15.4	16	22.8	Cost of Sales/Payables				15	24.2	23	15.8
54	6.7	36	10.0	34	10.6					19	19.3	46	7.9
	5.2		4.0		3.2						2.3	3.2
	8.7		7.1		6.1	Sales/Working Capital					3.6	7.5
	27.1		14.3		14.6						11.0	32.2
	85.9		23.6		26.6							51.6
(20)	9.6	(30)	7.8	(42)	3.1	EBIT/Interest					(25)	6.0
	1.5		.0		.0							.7
					4.2	Net Profit + Depr., Dep.,						
		(11)	3.2			Amort./Cur. Mat. L/T/D						
					.8							
	.2		.1		.2						.1	.2
	.7		.3		.5	Fixed/Worth					.3	.5
	2.2		1.1		5.8						2.4	5.8
	.6		.3		.3						.1	.3
	2.3		1.9		1.2	Debt/Worth					1.2	1.3
	11.5		3.9		18.8						52.2	11.2
	40.1		52.3		39.4							47.3
(20)	24.9	(34)	22.2	(42)	15.0	% Profit Before Taxes/Tangible Net Worth					(24)	20.2
	11.6		.4		-4.8							8.6
	21.2		15.3		16.9						19.6	16.9
	10.9		9.0		6.1	% Profit Before Taxes/Total Assets					.5	8.5
	1.4		-1.0		-2.0						-7.5	-1.8
	31.8		30.5		26.5						15.4	26.2
	15.0		17.8		11.7	Sales/Net Fixed Assets					13.5	11.0
	9.6		7.3		5.9						4.6	6.0
	3.9		3.2		2.5						2.3	2.3
	2.6		2.1		2.1	Sales/Total Assets					1.6	2.1
	1.6		1.5		1.4						1.2	1.4
	.5		.5		.6							.7
(19)	.8	(28)	.9	(37)	1.0	% Depr., Dep., Amort./Sales					(25)	1.0
	1.7		1.7		1.6							1.6
			1.9		1.5	% Officers', Directors'						
		(11)	2.3	(12)	3.4	Owners' Comp/Sales						
			4.2		4.0							
	1596586M		3095244M		4668115M	Net Sales ($)		5044M	6459M	49721M	201714M	4405177M
	752347M		1800227M		2682881M	Total Assets ($)		4413M	2441M	22205M	123876M	2529946M

© RMA 2024   M = $ thousand   MM = $ million
See Pages viii through xx for Explanation of Ratios and Data

MANUFACTURING—Household Furniture (except Wood and Upholstered) Manufacturing NAICS 337126

Current Data Sorted by Assets | Comparative Historical Data

0-500M	500M-2MM	2-10MM	10-50MM	50-100MM	100-250MM	Type of Statement		4/1/19-3/31/20 ALL	4/1/20-3/31/21 ALL
					1	Unqualified		1	2
						Reviewed		1	1
						Compiled		1	1
						Tax Returns		9	
1	3 (4/1-9/30/23)	8	17 (10/1/23-3/31/24)	3		Other		6	4
			6						
1	3	8	7	3	1	NUMBER OF STATEMENTS		18	8
%	%	%	%	%	%	ASSETS		%	%
						Cash & Equivalents		16.8	
						Trade Receivables (net)		20.7	
						Inventory		40.4	
						All Other Current		1.4	
						Total Current		79.3	
						Fixed Assets (net)		13.3	
						Intangibles (net)		.2	
						All Other Non-Current		7.2	
						Total		100.0	
						LIABILITIES			
						Notes Payable-Short Term		18.2	
						Cur. Mat.-L.T.D.		1.0	
						Trade Payables		21.7	
						Income Taxes Payable		.2	
						All Other Current		15.4	
						Total Current		56.4	
						Long-Term Debt		13.6	
						Deferred Taxes		.0	
						All Other Non-Current		19.4	
						Net Worth		10.6	
						Total Liabilities & Net Worth		100.0	
						INCOME DATA			
						Net Sales		100.0	
						Gross Profit		36.0	
						Operating Expenses		30.8	
						Operating Profit		5.2	
						All Other Expenses (net)		.2	
						Profit Before Taxes		5.0	
						RATIOS			
						Current		4.0	
								1.9	
								.9	
						Quick		2.4	
								.7	
								.4	
						Sales/Receivables	11	33.7	
							27	13.6	
							42	8.7	
						Cost of Sales/Inventory	43	8.5	
							89	4.1	
							159	2.3	
						Cost of Sales/Payables	8	47.6	
							34	10.8	
							47	7.7	
						Sales/Working Capital		2.4	
								9.4	
								-104.8	
						EBIT/Interest		140.5	
							(14)	5.5	
								1.7	
						Net Profit + Depr., Dep., Amort./Cur. Mat. L/T/D			
						Fixed/Worth		.0	
								.2	
								.9	
						Debt/Worth		.3	
								2.2	
								12.8	
						% Profit Before Taxes/Tangible Net Worth		90.8	
							(16)	24.1	
								4.0	
						% Profit Before Taxes/Total Assets		30.4	
								6.1	
								1.0	
						Sales/Net Fixed Assets		759.2	
								68.6	
								11.1	
						Sales/Total Assets		4.6	
								2.7	
								1.4	
						% Depr., Dep., Amort./Sales		.3	
							(14)	.7	
								1.4	
						% Officers', Directors' Owners' Comp/Sales		3.0	
							(10)	3.8	
								5.0	
6440M		117012M	273559M	204258M	306882M	Net Sales ($)		805540M	469377M
346M		45363M	168450M	185762M	214599M	Total Assets ($)		367691M	264622M

(Data Not Available for columns 0-500M through 500M-2MM for most rows)

M = $ thousand   MM = $ million
See Pages viii through xx for Explanation of Ratios and Data

© RMA 2024

MANUFACTURING—Household Furniture (except Wood and Upholstered) Manufacturing   NAICS 337126

Comparative Historical Data / **Current Data Sorted by Sales**

				Type of Statement						
		1		Unqualified						1
	2		1	Reviewed						
		3		Compiled					1	
	4	8	18	Tax Returns			1	2	5	10
	4/1/21-3/31/22 ALL	4/1/22-3/31/23 ALL	4/1/23-3/31/24 ALL	Other	3 (4/1-9/30/23)			17 (10/1/23-3/31/24)		
					0-1MM	1-3MM	3-5MM	5-10MM	10-25MM	25MM & OVER
	7	13	20	NUMBER OF STATEMENTS			1	3	5	11
	%	%	%	ASSETS	%	%	%	%	%	%
		24.4	15.9	Cash & Equivalents	D	D				13.0
		15.2	13.2	Trade Receivables (net)	A	A				16.7
		29.3	35.5	Inventory	T	T				36.3
		1.9	2.3	All Other Current	A	A				1.0
		70.8	66.9	Total Current						67.0
		19.0	16.7	Fixed Assets (net)	N	N				17.5
		4.3	8.9	Intangibles (net)	O	O				6.1
		5.9	7.5	All Other Non-Current	T	T				9.4
		100.0	100.0	Total						100.0
				LIABILITIES	A	A				
		11.0	4.6	Notes Payable-Short Term	V	V				5.9
		7.7	2.6	Cur. Mat.-L.T.D.	A	A				1.9
		28.4	8.4	Trade Payables	I	I				11.5
		.2	.1	Income Taxes Payable	L	L				.1
		14.8	13.8	All Other Current	A	A				13.2
		62.1	29.5	Total Current	B	B				32.6
		23.6	11.7	Long-Term Debt	L	L				13.8
		.2	.1	Deferred Taxes	E	E				.2
		48.9	44.4	All Other Non-Current						7.0
		-34.8	14.3	Net Worth						46.4
		100.0	100.0	Total Liabilities & Net Worth						100.0
				INCOME DATA						
		100.0	100.0	Net Sales						100.0
		38.1	37.9	Gross Profit						34.9
		27.8	28.8	Operating Expenses						25.6
		10.3	9.1	Operating Profit						9.3
		.5	1.4	All Other Expenses (net)						1.5
		9.8	7.7	Profit Before Taxes						7.8
				RATIOS						
		5.1	7.3							7.6
		2.4	2.8	Current						1.7
		1.2	1.3							1.1
		1.7	3.2							3.2
		.9	1.0	Quick						1.0
		.4	.4							.4
	5	76.0	13	28.1					18	20.3
	26	14.1	22	16.4	Sales/Receivables				34	10.8
	40	9.1	40	9.1					47	7.8
	0	UND	73	5.0					72	5.1
	83	4.4	126	2.9	Cost of Sales/Inventory				104	3.5
	261	1.4	243	1.5					243	1.5
	0	UND	9	38.5					17	21.3
	16	22.4	17	21.1	Cost of Sales/Payables				23	15.9
	47	7.8	35	10.5					43	8.4
		3.2	3.0							2.4
		5.2	5.5	Sales/Working Capital						6.7
		49.6	18.5							19.3
		45.8	17.3							
		(11) 17.5	(14) 9.2	EBIT/Interest						
		4.9	.9							
				Net Profit + Depr., Dep., Amort./Cur. Mat. L/T/D						
		.1	.1							.2
		.3	.3	Fixed/Worth						.4
		-.3	1.2							1.2
		.4	.2							.1
		5.7	1.9	Debt/Worth						2.2
		-2.3	12.2							8.1
			76.8							76.1
		(16)	36.4	% Profit Before Taxes/Tangible Net Worth					(10)	47.8
			4.2							-1.0
		39.3	32.7							34.3
		22.4	17.2	% Profit Before Taxes/Total Assets						17.5
		7.8	.0							-.6
		60.7	44.3							24.6
		22.5	18.6	Sales/Net Fixed Assets						13.2
		7.8	7.4							6.9
		3.1	2.5							2.4
		2.6	1.9	Sales/Total Assets						1.8
		1.2	1.4							1.3
			.5							
		(13)	1.5	% Depr., Dep., Amort./Sales						
			2.0							
				% Officers', Directors' Owners' Comp/Sales						
	315537M	545549M	908151M	Net Sales ($)			3319M	21718M	75156M	807958M
	93749M	383067M	614520M	Total Assets ($)			2404M	17550M	35483M	559083M

© RMA 2024   M = $ thousand   MM = $ million
See Pages viii through xx for Explanation of Ratios and Data

MANUFACTURING—Institutional Furniture Manufacturing NAICS 337127

Current Data Sorted by Assets | **Comparative Historical Data**

0-500M	500M-2MM	2-10MM	10-50MM	50-100MM	100-250MM			4/1/19-3/31/20 ALL		4/1/20-3/31/21 ALL
			4	3		**Type of Statement**				
			3	1		Unqualified		4		3
		1	2			Reviewed		9		4
	1	6			5	Compiled		3		5
1	8 (4/1-9/30/23)		32 (10/1/23-3/31/24)			Tax Returns		9		2
0	2	10	17	6	5	Other		32		14
						NUMBER OF STATEMENTS		57		28
%	%	%	%	%	%	**ASSETS**		%		%
	D	24.5	15.1			Cash & Equivalents		10.5		18.0
	A	15.8	22.2			Trade Receivables (net)		25.7		24.0
	T	32.0	24.7			Inventory		26.6		23.7
	A	.6	1.9			All Other Current		3.1		1.6
		72.9	63.9			Total Current		66.0		67.2
	N	19.6	18.2			Fixed Assets (net)		20.0		16.9
	O	1.4	5.1			Intangibles (net)		6.6		6.0
	T	6.1	12.8			All Other Non-Current		7.4		10.0
		100.0	100.0			Total		100.0		100.0
	A					**LIABILITIES**				
	V	1.7	5.2			Notes Payable-Short Term		11.7		6.0
	A	.4	1.7			Cur. Mat.-L.T.D.		2.1		5.3
	I	7.6	11.4			Trade Payables		14.9		10.0
	L	.0	.0			Income Taxes Payable		.1		.0
	A	13.3	17.4			All Other Current		11.0		12.3
	B	23.0	35.8			Total Current		39.9		33.7
	L	10.9	11.2			Long-Term Debt		11.4		12.1
	E	.0	.2			Deferred Taxes		.3		.4
		7.6	10.4			All Other Non-Current		3.0		7.8
		58.5	42.4			Net Worth		45.4		46.0
		100.0	100.0			Total Liabilties & Net Worth		100.0		100.0
						INCOME DATA				
		100.0	100.0			Net Sales		100.0		100.0
		36.0	32.0			Gross Profit		29.6		27.9
		27.3	25.3			Operating Expenses		24.5		27.2
		8.7	6.6			Operating Profit		5.1		.7
		-.3	.7			All Other Expenses (net)		.7		-2.9
		8.9	5.9			Profit Before Taxes		4.4		3.6
						RATIOS				
		7.9	3.8					2.8		6.4
		4.4	1.9			Current		1.7		2.2
		1.9	1.2					1.1		1.3
		4.5	2.6					1.7		3.5
		2.5	1.0			Quick		.9		1.3
		.8	.6					.5		.7
	15	24.6	24	14.9			25	14.7	26	14.3
	24	15.4	31	11.6		Sales/Receivables	37	9.8	38	9.5
	30	12.1	54	6.8			49	7.4	54	6.7
	31	11.7	41	8.9			35	10.4	37	9.8
	81	4.5	65	5.6		Cost of Sales/Inventory	59	6.2	55	6.6
	146	2.5	99	3.7			87	4.2	89	4.1
	2	225.0	14	26.8			13	27.6	9	38.6
	11	34.1	22	16.9		Cost of Sales/Payables	21	17.5	16	23.4
	17	21.3	35	10.3			34	10.8	29	12.6
		2.4	4.3					4.7		3.1
		4.1	6.4			Sales/Working Capital		8.4		5.4
		8.7	15.4					39.7		26.0
			22.1					22.9		20.7
		(15)	14.3			EBIT/Interest	(50)	6.6	(24)	2.9
			5.0					2.9		-.1
								6.4		
						Net Profit + Depr., Dep., Amort./Cur. Mat. L/T/D	(11)	3.5		
								.5		
		.1	.3					.2		.2
		.2	.5			Fixed/Worth		.4		.4
		.6	.7					1.3		.9
		.2	.7					.6		.4
		.6	1.1			Debt/Worth		1.4		1.0
		3.0	3.7					5.1		7.0
		54.8	50.1					37.6		48.6
		21.2	(15) 32.1			% Profit Before Taxes/Tangible Net Worth	(52)	19.6	(26)	3.3
		16.5	14.2					7.4		-6.2
		21.7	16.9					14.6		15.2
		12.0	8.4			% Profit Before Taxes/Total Assets		7.4		2.8
		8.2	4.9					2.5		-3.0
		204.0	21.7					37.4		59.7
		11.7	11.8			Sales/Net Fixed Assets		14.9		14.6
		5.0	7.0					7.4		7.0
		2.6	2.5					3.2		2.8
		1.9	1.9			Sales/Total Assets		2.2		2.1
		1.5	1.5					1.7		1.5
			1.0					.7		1.1
		(16)	1.7			% Depr., Dep., Amort./Sales	(45)	1.4	(22)	2.1
			2.6					2.1		3.4
								1.7		
						% Officers', Directors' Owners' Comp/Sales	(14)	3.5		
								8.6		
	5992M	141000M	765540M	649304M	1075389M	Net Sales ($)		3553224M		1123490M
	3303M	57822M	404776M	451569M	751081M	Total Assets ($)		1758678M		671304M

M = $ thousand   MM = $ million
See Pages viii through xx for Explanation of Ratios and Data

© RMA 2024

MANUFACTURING—Institutional Furniture Manufacturing NAICS 337127

Comparative Historical Data | **Current Data Sorted by Sales**

	3		5		7	Type of Statement									1	6
	5		10		5	Unqualified									2	3
	1		4		3	Reviewed									1	2
	4		4		3	Compiled								1	1	
	18		22		22	Tax Returns				1		2		2	2	15
	4/1/21-		4/1/22-		4/1/23-	Other				8 (4/1-9/30/23)				32 (10/1/23-3/31/24)		
	3/31/22		3/31/23		3/31/24		0-1MM		1-3MM		3-5MM		5-10MM		10-25MM	25MM & OVER
	ALL		ALL		ALL			1		3		3		7		26
	31		45		40	NUMBER OF STATEMENTS										
	%		%		%	ASSETS	%		%		%		%		%	%
	17.0		11.1		17.1	Cash & Equivalents										16.3
	20.5		25.1		19.7	Trade Receivables (net)		D								22.6
	23.9		26.7		24.5	Inventory		A								21.4
	2.2		2.5		3.7	All Other Current		T								5.4
	63.6		65.4		65.0	Total Current		A								65.7
	17.7		20.1		17.9	Fixed Assets (net)										16.9
	12.4		7.5		6.5	Intangibles (net)		N								5.8
	6.3		6.9		10.6	All Other Non-Current		O								11.6
	100.0		100.0		100.0	Total		T								100.0
						LIABILITIES		A								
	3.4		6.4		3.0	Notes Payable-Short Term		V								3.9
	1.7		1.9		1.1	Cur. Mat.-L.T.D.		A								1.2
	7.8		12.0		10.0	Trade Payables		I								11.0
	.0		.0		.0	Income Taxes Payable		L								.0
	13.8		13.1		15.0	All Other Current		A								14.9
	26.8		33.5		29.0	Total Current		B								31.1
	14.8		15.9		10.8	Long-Term Debt		L								9.8
	.2		.0		.2	Deferred Taxes		E								.2
	7.0		7.1		8.4	All Other Non-Current										9.9
	51.2		43.5		51.7	Net Worth										49.0
	100.0		100.0		100.0	Total Liabilities & Net Worth										100.0
						INCOME DATA										
	100.0		100.0		100.0	Net Sales										100.0
	29.0		28.3		33.3	Gross Profit										31.4
	24.6		23.3		25.3	Operating Expenses										23.8
	4.3		5.0		8.0	Operating Profit										7.6
	-2.9		.1		.7	All Other Expenses (net)										1.0
	7.2		4.8		7.3	Profit Before Taxes										6.7
						RATIOS										
	4.4		3.7		4.8											4.1
	2.4		2.2		2.3	Current										2.2
	1.7		1.5		1.7											1.7
	3.2		2.0		2.8											2.7
	1.1		1.1		1.3	Quick										1.3
	.8		.7		.8											.8
28	13.1	23	16.1	24	15.0										26	14.3
37	9.9	41	9.0	31	11.6	Sales/Receivables									33	11.0
57	6.4	70	5.2	54	6.8										64	5.7
42	8.7	43	8.5	43	8.5										41	8.9
79	4.6	72	5.1	68	5.4	Cost of Sales/Inventory									56	6.5
104	3.5	87	4.2	114	3.2										87	4.2
9	42.6	12	29.6	11	34.0										12	30.8
21	17.4	23	16.1	21	17.7	Cost of Sales/Payables									25	14.8
33	11.1	41	8.9	39	9.4										45	8.2
	2.9		3.7		3.0											3.7
	5.8		6.7		5.6	Sales/Working Capital										5.7
	8.3		11.8		8.8											8.9
	54.3		23.3		34.0											27.1
(29)	22.8	(38)	6.9	(36)	14.4	EBIT/Interest									(24)	11.2
	2.4		2.0		5.1											5.1
					19.8	Net Profit + Depr., Dep.,										20.3
				(14)	15.6	Amort./Cur. Mat. L/T/D									(11)	16.6
					5.6											5.8
	.2		.3		.2											.3
	.5		.5		.4	Fixed/Worth										.4
	.8		.9		.6											.5
	.4		.6		.4											.6
	.9		1.5		1.0	Debt/Worth										1.0
	4.6		3.7		2.7											2.5
	80.2		51.3		37.2	% Profit Before Taxes/Tangible										47.2
(27)	28.1	(41)	18.0	(36)	22.4	Net Worth									(24)	28.1
	8.0		5.2		13.2											15.3
	24.2		16.5		17.1	% Profit Before Taxes/Total										17.8
	13.3		7.0		10.1	Assets										9.5
	.8		1.3		5.6											5.2
	30.6		24.3		21.4											17.7
	12.3		11.4		10.1	Sales/Net Fixed Assets										10.9
	5.4		6.6		7.3											7.6
	2.1		2.6		2.3											2.4
	1.7		2.0		1.7	Sales/Total Assets										1.8
	1.3		1.6		1.5											1.4
	1.1		.8		1.1											1.1
(22)	1.9	(37)	1.4	(33)	1.7	% Depr., Dep., Amort./Sales									(24)	1.7
	2.4		2.3		2.2											2.0
			2.2			% Officers', Directors'										
		(10)	2.5			Owners' Comp/Sales										
			5.4													
	1699141M		1334158M		2637225M	Net Sales ($)		2373M		11723M		20150M		120216M		2482763M
	1137232M		725863M		1668551M	Total Assets ($)		1615M		6995M		14057M		78700M		1567184M

© RMA 2024 M = $ thousand   MM = $ million
See Pages viii through xx for Explanation of Ratios and Data

MANUFACTURING—Custom Architectural Woodwork and Millwork Manufacturing NAICS 337212

Current Data Sorted by Assets | Comparative Historical Data

							Type of Statement		
					1		Unqualified	1	
	1	5	6				Reviewed	10	3
		2	1				Compiled	1	
	1	2					Tax Returns	7	9
	3	9	9	3			Other	25	11
0-500M	1 (4/1-9/30/23) 500M-2MM	2-10MM	42 (10/1/23-3/31/24) 10-50MM	50-100MM	100-250MM			4/1/19- 3/31/20 ALL	4/1/20- 3/31/21 ALL
	5	18	16	4			NUMBER OF STATEMENTS	44	23
%	%	%	%	%	%		ASSETS	%	%
D		9.5	14.4		D		Cash & Equivalents	18.7	24.3
A		41.1	42.5		A		Trade Receivables (net)	36.1	26.3
T		8.5	6.9		T		Inventory	10.3	12.8
A		7.9	8.1		A		All Other Current	3.8	1.7
		66.9	71.8				Total Current	68.9	65.2
N		18.6	18.3		N		Fixed Assets (net)	17.9	27.2
O		5.8	1.6		O		Intangibles (net)	7.2	4.3
T		8.7	8.2		T		All Other Non-Current	6.0	3.3
		100.0	100.0				Total	100.0	100.0
A					A		LIABILITIES		
V		1.9	6.0		V		Notes Payable-Short Term	8.5	9.4
A		1.8	2.0		A		Cur. Mat.-L.T.D.	3.1	3.8
I		11.5	12.2		I		Trade Payables	10.6	7.4
L		.0	.0		L		Income Taxes Payable	.5	.1
A		15.3	15.8		A		All Other Current	17.8	13.5
B		30.6	36.0		B		Total Current	40.4	34.2
L		14.4	15.4		L		Long-Term Debt	15.0	35.0
E		.3	.1		E		Deferred Taxes	.3	.0
		6.1	7.1				All Other Non-Current	2.4	10.5
		48.6	41.5				Net Worth	41.9	20.3
		100.0	100.0				Total Liabilities & Net Worth	100.0	100.0
							INCOME DATA		
		100.0	100.0				Net Sales	100.0	100.0
		27.3	30.7				Gross Profit	36.5	36.9
		21.1	23.8				Operating Expenses	28.2	33.1
		6.2	6.9				Operating Profit	8.3	3.9
		.4	.6				All Other Expenses (net)	.5	.5
		5.8	6.3				Profit Before Taxes	7.8	3.4
							RATIOS		
		3.4	3.0					2.9	3.3
		2.4	2.1				Current	2.0	2.2
		1.6	1.5					1.4	1.2
		3.0	2.6					2.2	3.3
		1.9	1.8				Quick	1.6	1.5
		1.0	1.0					.9	.7
		43 8.4	65 5.6					27 13.4	9 38.5
		79 4.6	79 4.6				Sales/Receivables	51 7.2	40 9.2
		99 3.7	104 3.5					73 5.0	81 4.5
		6 63.8	2 235.6					0 UND	0 UND
		16 22.7	6 57.3				Cost of Sales/Inventory	7 55.2	14 26.6
		43 8.4	41 8.9					32 11.4	62 5.9
		15 23.6	16 23.0					9 40.1	5 73.0
		26 14.2	32 11.3				Cost of Sales/Payables	16 22.4	12 30.0
		42 8.6	52 7.0					33 11.2	25 14.7
		4.1	3.0					5.1	3.3
		5.9	4.1				Sales/Working Capital	7.3	5.9
		10.4	8.8					19.9	19.0
		22.7	34.8					36.2	11.9
	(12) 6.8	(14) 9.7				EBIT/Interest	(36) 6.5	(21) 1.3
		2.8	1.4					4.6	-2.5
							Net Profit + Depr., Dep., Amort./Cur. Mat. L/T/D		
		.1	.1					.2	.2
		.5	.5				Fixed/Worth	.5	1.5
		1.1	1.1					1.0	-1.6
		.5	1.0					.6	1.2
		1.0	1.4				Debt/Worth	1.2	3.5
		3.4	2.7					11.8	-5.9
		28.3	48.3					77.1	100.6
	(15) 17.2	(15) 17.8				% Profit Before Taxes/Tangible Net Worth	(37) 33.2	(16) 29.5
		6.3	10.8					14.8	-9.4
		15.5	20.6					37.4	17.7
		9.1	6.7				% Profit Before Taxes/Total Assets	14.7	2.9
		3.3	1.9					6.6	-3.6
		20.2	49.7					41.1	28.3
		14.6	20.7				Sales/Net Fixed Assets	17.2	16.0
		7.5	7.6					8.6	4.1
		2.5	2.3					3.4	3.1
		2.2	1.8				Sales/Total Assets	2.5	2.1
		1.7	1.2					2.0	1.2
		1.0	.7					.9	.9
	(15) 1.6	(13) .9				% Depr., Dep., Amort./Sales	(30) 1.3	(16) 1.8
		3.0	1.7					2.3	3.6
								2.5	3.7
							% Officers', Directors' Owners' Comp/Sales	(18) 5.1	(11) 6.8
								9.2	8.6
	17036M	243209M	404444M	450830M			Net Sales ($)	749880M	188854M
	4924M	120892M	225283M	331801M			Total Assets ($)	404939M	154252M

M = $ thousand   MM = $ million
See Pages viii through xx for Explanation of Ratios and Data

© RMA 2024

MANUFACTURING—Custom Architectural Woodwork and Millwork Manufacturing NAICS 337212

Comparative Historical Data | Current Data Sorted by Sales

					Type of Statement						
		1		1		1	Unqualified				1
	4		9		12		Reviewed			1	2	7	2
	1		3		3		Compiled					3	
	7		6		3		Tax Returns			2	1	1	
	15		19		24		Other		2	1	1	11	9
	4/1/21-3/31/22		4/1/22-3/31/23		4/1/23-3/31/24			1 (4/1-9/30/23)			42 (10/1/23-3/31/24)		
	ALL		ALL		ALL			0-1MM	1-3MM	3-5MM	5-10MM	10-25MM	25MM & OVER
	28		38		43	NUMBER OF STATEMENTS		2	4	3	22	12
	%		%		%	ASSETS	%	%	%	%	%	%
	16.7		15.1		12.2	Cash & Equivalents					14.8	4.2
	31.4		29.2		40.2	Trade Receivables (net)	D				41.6	42.8
	9.5		15.5		7.4	Inventory	A				7.0	8.8
	5.3		4.6		6.7	All Other Current	T				6.9	8.9
	62.9		64.5		66.4	Total Current	A				70.2	64.7
	28.1		24.9		17.8	Fixed Assets (net)					17.7	11.2
	3.4		5.1		6.7	Intangibles (net)	N				4.7	9.5
	5.6		5.6		9.1	All Other Non-Current	O				7.4	14.6
	100.0		100.0		100.0	Total	T				100.0	100.0
						LIABILITIES	A					
	2.8		4.5		4.1	Notes Payable-Short Term	V				2.3	6.6
	2.7		1.7		2.5	Cur. Mat.-L.T.D.	A				1.5	2.9
	11.3		9.4		11.1	Trade Payables	I				10.7	14.7
	.3		.1		.0	Income Taxes Payable	L				.0	.0
	16.3		12.2		15.8	All Other Current	A				15.6	21.2
	33.4		27.9		33.5	Total Current	B				30.0	45.4
	19.8		24.2		17.4	Long-Term Debt	L				13.4	15.2
	.1		.0		.3	Deferred Taxes	E				.2	.5
	6.8		1.9		9.6	All Other Non-Current					5.9	21.7
	39.8		46.0		39.3	Net Worth					50.5	17.2
	100.0		100.0		100.0	Total Liabilities & Net Worth					100.0	100.0
						INCOME DATA						
	100.0		100.0		100.0	Net Sales					100.0	100.0
	39.2		33.5		31.2	Gross Profit					30.8	22.3
	30.8		29.7		25.3	Operating Expenses					22.9	20.0
	8.4		3.9		5.9	Operating Profit					7.9	2.4
	-2.4		-.4		1.3	All Other Expenses (net)					.3	2.9
	10.8		4.3		4.6	Profit Before Taxes					7.6	-.5
						RATIOS						
	3.0		4.6		3.1						3.5	1.8
	1.9		2.9		2.0	Current					2.5	1.4
	1.4		1.4		1.4						1.7	1.0
	2.3		3.5		2.7						2.9	1.3
	1.5		2.0		1.7	Quick					2.0	.9
	.8		.9		.9						1.4	.8
25	14.7	28	12.9	57	6.4						43	8.4	63	5.8
63	5.8	55	6.6	78	4.7	Sales/Receivables					73	5.0	91	4.0
94	3.9	89	4.1	101	3.6						114	3.2	104	3.5
0	UND	4	82.5	4	84.2						5	79.1	3	142.8
12	31.7	20	17.9	15	24.3	Cost of Sales/Inventory					10	36.7	20	18.5
51	7.2	72	5.1	35	10.4						38	9.6	33	11.1
13	28.5	8	45.5	15	23.9						13	27.3	23	16.0
33	11.0	23	15.6	26	13.8	Cost of Sales/Payables					26	14.2	32	11.3
46	8.0	35	10.5	40	9.2						45	8.1	39	9.3
	4.1		3.8		3.7						3.5	7.0
	6.5		5.1		6.5	Sales/Working Capital					4.5	10.6
	16.7		13.0		11.1						8.4	115.4
	46.2		36.8		19.0						36.4	14.4
(26)	9.3	(31)	6.8	(35)	6.7	EBIT/Interest					(16) 13.0	(11) 1.4
	2.2		2.6		1.3						3.9	-.1
						Net Profit + Depr., Dep., Amort./Cur. Mat. L/T/D						
	.3		.2		.1						.1	.1
	.7		.6		.5	Fixed/Worth					.4	.9
	1.7		1.6		1.8						.7	-.2
	.8		.5		.6						.5	1.2
	1.6		1.0		1.5	Debt/Worth					1.0	3.4
	2.8		2.8		5.2						2.1	-3.9
	55.9		37.3		48.2						47.6	
(25)	40.2	(34)	14.4	(35)	21.1	% Profit Before Taxes/Tangible Net Worth					(20) 19.5	
	14.8		2.0		10.8						13.1	
	25.9		17.4		18.2	% Profit Before Taxes/Total Assets					18.6	9.3
	12.7		4.7		7.4						9.1	2.6
	2.6		.8		2.0						3.9	-8.0
	16.9		31.5		30.8						31.8	31.4
	8.4		10.5		16.0	Sales/Net Fixed Assets					15.7	21.4
	5.0		4.5		8.0						7.6	12.1
	2.7		2.7		2.5						2.4	2.5
	2.1		1.8		1.9	Sales/Total Assets					2.0	2.0
	1.6		1.3		1.5						1.6	1.2
	1.0		.8		.7						.7	
(19)	1.5	(29)	1.6	(31)	1.1	% Depr., Dep., Amort./Sales					(18) 1.1	
	3.3		3.1		2.0						1.8	
			1.8		1.5						1.4	
		(17)	2.8	(14)	3.4	% Officers', Directors', Owners' Comp/Sales					(11) 3.0	
			6.3		6.3						8.1	
	330983M		649813M		1115519M	Net Sales ($)		4020M	17985M	23725M	344514M	725275M
	193036M		389144M		682900M	Total Assets ($)		1799M	7786M	24142M	183335M	465838M

© RMA 2024   M = $ thousand   MM = $ million
See Pages viii through xx for Explanation of Ratios and Data

MANUFACTURING—Showcase, Partition, Shelving, and Locker Manufacturing NAICS 337215

Current Data Sorted by Assets | Comparative Historical Data

0-500M	500M-2MM	2-10MM	10-50MM	50-100MM	100-250MM	Type of Statement		4/1/19-3/31/20 ALL	4/1/20-3/31/21 ALL
			1			Unqualified		5	3
		3	4	2		Reviewed		10	7
		1	1			Compiled		2	2
	1	5				Tax Returns		6	3
	14	14	4	6		Other		29	11
	15 (4/1-9/30/23)		41 (10/1/23-3/31/24)						
	1	23	20	6	6	NUMBER OF STATEMENTS		52	26
%	%	%	%	%	%	ASSETS		%	%
		9.1	10.5			Cash & Equivalents		8.7	9.2
D		29.9	29.5			Trade Receivables (net)		28.5	28.7
A		32.7	23.4			Inventory		28.5	32.5
T		2.5	6.7			All Other Current		3.5	2.5
A		74.2	70.1			Total Current		69.3	72.9
		16.1	17.6			Fixed Assets (net)		19.1	17.2
N		1.2	4.2			Intangibles (net)		8.9	4.4
O		8.4	8.1			All Other Non-Current		2.7	5.5
T		100.0	100.0			Total		100.0	100.0
A						LIABILITIES			
V		7.9	9.4			Notes Payable-Short Term		13.2	19.7
A		2.3	3.2			Cur. Mat.-L.T.D.		5.4	3.0
I		14.2	11.8			Trade Payables		14.4	15.0
L		.0	.0			Income Taxes Payable		.2	.1
A		12.9	20.2			All Other Current		13.5	13.1
B		37.3	44.6			Total Current		46.6	51.0
L		12.2	8.3			Long-Term Debt		14.3	17.1
E		.1	.2			Deferred Taxes		.1	.1
		3.6	7.1			All Other Non-Current		13.1	21.1
		46.8	39.8			Net Worth		25.8	10.8
		100.0	100.0			Total Liabilities & Net Worth		100.0	100.0
						INCOME DATA			
		100.0	100.0			Net Sales		100.0	100.0
		34.1	35.3			Gross Profit		31.3	28.8
		30.5	28.3			Operating Expenses		27.8	29.7
		3.5	7.0			Operating Profit		3.4	-.9
		-.7	1.4			All Other Expenses (net)		1.2	-2.7
		4.3	5.6			Profit Before Taxes		2.2	1.9
						RATIOS			
		2.6	2.3					2.3	2.6
		2.2	1.9			Current		1.7	1.6
		1.6	1.1					1.1	1.3
		1.6	1.7					1.5	1.5
		1.0	.9			Quick		.9	.8
		.6	.4					.4	.6
		38 9.5	38 9.6				27 13.6		33 10.9
		54 6.7	59 6.2			Sales/Receivables	43 8.4		45 8.2
		66 5.5	70 5.2				65 5.6		73 5.0
		46 8.0	36 10.0				33 11.0		34 10.7
		74 4.9	72 5.1			Cost of Sales/Inventory	69 5.3		57 6.4
		166 2.2	83 4.4				94 3.9		118 3.1
		19 19.4	16 23.1				17 22.1		16 22.2
		32 11.3	32 11.4			Cost of Sales/Payables	26 14.0		29 12.7
		48 7.6	41 8.8				46 7.9		43 8.4
		4.5	4.3					5.3	4.3
		5.3	6.0			Sales/Working Capital		9.6	6.7
		7.8	30.4					24.1	14.2
		45.2	50.0					11.6	10.0
		(18) 10.4	(17) 10.6			EBIT/Interest	(50) 2.3		(23) 5.7
		1.1	.8					1.2	-5.2
						Net Profit + Depr., Dep., Amort./Cur. Mat. L/T/D			
		.1	.2					.3	.2
		.4	.5			Fixed/Worth		.7	.9
		.5	1.9					-2.8	1.8
		.6	.5					1.0	1.3
		1.0	1.3			Debt/Worth		1.9	2.3
		1.5	7.0					-21.6	8.2
		38.8	50.2					42.7	56.8
		(22) 17.1	(18) 27.6			% Profit Before Taxes/Tangible Net Worth	(38) 16.2		(21) 24.7
		3.8	5.9					1.7	-15.7
		22.6	21.7					12.2	19.9
		7.3	7.3			% Profit Before Taxes/Total Assets		4.1	5.8
		1.5	.1					.2	-6.9
		41.8	29.8					27.7	45.2
		13.0	11.1			Sales/Net Fixed Assets		14.0	18.8
		8.3	5.0					8.0	7.1
		2.4	2.3					2.8	2.9
		2.1	1.7			Sales/Total Assets		2.2	2.2
		1.9	1.4					1.7	1.8
		.4	.8					.9	.9
	(16)	1.0	(18) 1.9			% Depr., Dep., Amort./Sales	(47) 1.6		(21) 1.9
		1.9	4.1					2.3	2.8
		1.3						1.9	1.2
	(12)	3.1				% Officers', Directors' Owners' Comp/Sales	(20) 4.7		(12) 4.6
		4.6						6.3	6.4
	4672M	289340M	596596M	523932M	1002083M	Net Sales ($)		2270944M	591156M
	817M	137726M	354856M	424908M	859195M	Total Assets ($)		1294876M	362499M

© RMA 2024

M = $ thousand   MM = $ million
See Pages viii through xx for Explanation of Ratios and Data

MANUFACTURING—Showcase, Partition, Shelving, and Locker Manufacturing   NAICS 337215

Comparative Historical Data | Current Data Sorted by Sales

					Type of Statement						
		3		4		1	Unqualified							
		6		12		9	Reviewed			1	5		1
		4		2		2	Compiled			1	1		3
		4		6		6	Tax Returns		1	2	3		
		12		20		38	Other			7	11		20
		4/1/21-		4/1/22-		4/1/23-			15 (4/1-9/30/23)		41 (10/1/23-3/31/24)		
		3/31/22		3/31/23		3/31/24		0-1MM	1-3MM	3-5MM	5-10MM	10-25MM	25MM & OVER
		ALL		ALL		ALL	NUMBER OF STATEMENTS			1	11	20	24
		29		44		56							
		%		%		%	ASSETS	%	%	%	%	%	%
		10.4		10.1		10.1	Cash & Equivalents				12.1	7.0	10.9
		29.3		31.2		26.4	Trade Receivables (net)	DATA	DATA		26.9	30.5	23.9
		27.7		30.1		26.9	Inventory				29.0	33.0	21.0
		4.7		1.8		4.0	All Other Current				4.6	1.4	6.0
		72.0		73.3		67.4	Total Current	NOT	NOT		72.6	71.9	61.8
		18.6		14.1		15.0	Fixed Assets (net)				22.2	14.3	11.3
		2.9		6.2		9.0	Intangibles (net)	AVAILABLE	AVAILABLE		1.6	3.0	17.7
		6.5		6.4		8.6	All Other Non-Current				3.6	10.9	9.2
		100.0		100.0		100.0	Total				100.0	100.0	100.0
							LIABILITIES						
		9.1		8.9		7.9	Notes Payable-Short Term				10.3	8.1	6.8
		4.1		3.0		2.3	Cur. Mat.-L.T.D.				1.7	2.5	2.2
		15.4		15.9		12.2	Trade Payables				15.4	12.8	10.7
		.0		.1		.0	Income Taxes Payable				.0	.0	.1
		10.8		12.6		14.8	All Other Current				8.3	15.1	18.0
		39.4		40.4		37.3	Total Current				35.6	38.5	37.8
		16.4		12.4		14.5	Long-Term Debt				22.0	6.3	15.4
		.5		.3		.1	Deferred Taxes				.0	.3	.1
		1.6		2.7		8.2	All Other Non-Current				1.2	5.4	13.7
		42.0		44.1		39.8	Net Worth				41.1	49.5	33.0
		100.0		100.0		100.0	Total Liabilities & Net Worth				100.0	100.0	100.0
							INCOME DATA						
		100.0		100.0		100.0	Net Sales				100.0	100.0	100.0
		26.1		33.1		33.6	Gross Profit				38.0	30.6	33.3
		24.9		24.4		27.8	Operating Expenses				34.4	26.4	25.1
		1.2		8.7		5.8	Operating Profit				3.7	4.2	8.2
		-2.6		-1.0		1.3	All Other Expenses (net)				.8	-1.2	3.6
		3.8		9.7		4.5	Profit Before Taxes				2.9	5.4	4.6
							RATIOS						
		3.1		3.0		2.6					2.6	2.7	2.2
		2.0		1.9		1.8	Current				2.2	1.9	1.5
		1.4		1.2		1.4					1.7	1.5	1.2
		1.7		1.9		1.6					2.2	1.6	1.5
		1.1		1.0		.9	Quick				1.0	1.1	.8
		.6		.7		.6					.6	.5	.5
35	10.5	35	10.5	38	9.7				31	11.8	39	9.4	36	10.2
50	7.3	50	7.3	56	6.5	Sales/Receivables			41	9.0	58	6.3	59	6.2
68	5.4	69	5.3	66	5.5				66	5.5	68	5.4	65	5.6
38	9.7	40	9.2	40	9.1				36	10.0	57	6.4	41	9.0
69	5.3	72	5.1	78	4.7	Cost of Sales/Inventory			49	7.5	81	4.5	78	4.7
101	3.6	118	3.1	104	3.5				192	1.9	159	2.3	89	4.1
20	18.7	21	17.8	20	18.2				20	18.4	15	25.0	30	12.1
32	11.5	29	12.5	34	10.7	Cost of Sales/Payables			45	8.2	23	16.0	38	9.7
42	8.7	54	6.7	47	7.7				60	6.1	51	7.2	47	7.7
		3.6		4.1		4.5					4.1	4.6	4.4
		5.2		6.3		6.1	Sales/Working Capital				4.8	5.7	7.0
		13.6		14.4		11.7					8.8	7.6	17.0
		27.4		48.1		40.1						57.5	35.6
(26)	10.8	(38)	17.3	(47)	5.4	EBIT/Interest				(16)	26.9	(21)	3.1
		1.2		2.4		.5						4.6	.1
				34.2		30.1	Net Profit + Depr., Dep.,						
			(16)	5.4	(17)	4.2	Amort./Cur. Mat. L/T/D						
						2.7	.8						
		.1		.2		.1					.3	.1	.2
		.4		.3		.4	Fixed/Worth				.5	.4	.9
		1.0		.8		3.7					.9	.5	-.2
		.7		.5		.6					.8	.4	.8
		.9		1.3		1.4	Debt/Worth				1.0	1.0	4.0
		4.5		4.0		9.1					1.6	1.9	-3.5
		46.8		86.7		47.6	% Profit Before Taxes/Tangible				30.7	37.1	57.3
(26)	15.6	(37)	44.1	(44)	21.5	Net Worth			(10)	16.1	(19)	17.9	(15)	40.9
		1.5		20.8		5.1					-1.2	6.7	10.3
		13.7		25.1		19.7	% Profit Before Taxes/Total				11.0	23.6	18.9
		8.7		14.4		7.6	Assets				7.3	6.7	8.2
		.3		5.3		-.8					-4.6	1.9	-4.6
		67.1		46.9		39.5					25.2	39.5	41.0
		15.8		16.9		15.2	Sales/Net Fixed Assets				9.1	13.5	19.9
		5.1		9.9		7.7					6.3	8.0	8.5
		2.9		2.5		2.4					2.3	2.4	2.3
		2.2		2.3		1.9	Sales/Total Assets				2.1	2.0	1.4
		1.5		1.6		1.2					1.7	1.4	1.0
		.4		.6		.6					.4	.9
(22)	1.5	(34)	1.2	(39)	1.3	% Depr., Dep., Amort./Sales				(17)	.9	(15)	2.5
		2.5		2.6		3.5						1.5	4.1
		1.3		1.2		1.3	% Officers', Directors'						
(12)	4.4	(15)	3.3	(16)	3.1	Owners' Comp/Sales						
		6.8		6.3		5.2							
		1462368M		2427213M		2416623M	Net Sales ($)			4672M	86711M	363720M	1961520M
		979313M		1521154M		1777502M	Total Assets ($)			817M	43992M	208364M	1524329M

© RMA 2024   M = $ thousand   MM = $ million
See Pages viii through xx for Explanation of Ratios and Data

MANUFACTURING—Surgical and Medical Instrument Manufacturing NAICS 339112

Current Data Sorted by Assets | Comparative Historical Data

						Type of Statement		
			6	4	3	Unqualified	19	9
		1	3	1		Reviewed	10	5
		1				Compiled	3	3
	1	4	2			Tax Returns	15	4
	7	15	19	8	8	Other	66	39
0-500M	17 (4/1-9/30/23) 500M-2MM	2-10MM	66 (10/1/23-3/31/24) 10-50MM	50-100MM	100-250MM		4/1/19-3/31/20 ALL	4/1/20-3/31/21 ALL
	8	21	30	13	11	NUMBER OF STATEMENTS	113	60
%	%	%	%	%	%	ASSETS	%	%
D		19.0	14.3	5.9	11.5	Cash & Equivalents	15.0	16.0
A		21.6	20.2	19.3	11.5	Trade Receivables (net)	21.9	18.5
T		29.0	22.8	20.8	13.6	Inventory	25.1	20.8
A		4.5	3.7	1.2	1.2	All Other Current	2.0	2.7
		74.1	61.0	47.2	37.9	Total Current	64.0	58.0
N		5.2	17.4	28.2	14.1	Fixed Assets (net)	19.5	22.2
O		5.8	11.4	19.9	41.9	Intangibles (net)	11.0	14.0
T		15.0	10.2	4.7	6.1	All Other Non-Current	5.5	5.8
		100.0	100.0	100.0	100.0	Total	100.0	100.0
A						LIABILITIES		
V		4.3	2.0	4.3	.7	Notes Payable-Short Term	5.5	5.9
A		1.7	1.9	4.0	1.8	Cur. Mat.-L.T.D.	2.4	4.6
I		14.0	7.5	12.2	6.3	Trade Payables	9.3	8.0
L		.0	.1	.0	.4	Income Taxes Payable	.2	.4
A		12.4	14.9	5.3	9.5	All Other Current	12.1	12.3
B		32.4	26.3	25.8	18.7	Total Current	29.5	31.3
L		10.5	17.7	21.1	25.2	Long-Term Debt	16.2	25.1
E		.0	.1	.2	1.7	Deferred Taxes	.3	.6
		7.0	8.3	3.5	6.5	All Other Non-Current	4.6	4.3
		50.1	47.6	49.4	47.8	Net Worth	49.4	38.7
		100.0	100.0	100.0	100.0	Total Liabilities & Net Worth	100.0	100.0
						INCOME DATA		
		100.0	100.0	100.0	100.0	Net Sales	100.0	100.0
		45.6	50.5	39.2	45.3	Gross Profit	49.2	46.6
		38.5	39.0	31.0	38.7	Operating Expenses	38.3	38.9
		7.1	11.5	8.2	6.7	Operating Profit	10.9	7.7
		-.7	1.0	2.2	5.9	All Other Expenses (net)	1.1	.8
		7.8	10.5	6.0	.7	Profit Before Taxes	9.8	6.9
						RATIOS		
		4.5	4.4	2.2	3.6		4.4	4.9
		3.0	3.0	1.4	2.3	Current	2.4	2.1
		1.4	1.7	1.1	1.5		1.5	1.4
		3.1	2.4	1.0	1.8		2.8	3.1
		1.0	1.3	.8	1.2	Quick	1.2	1.2
		.6	.7	.6	.6		.7	.7
	28 12.9	42 8.7	37 9.9	39 9.4			35 10.4	36 10.0
	40 9.2	54 6.7	41 9.0	45 8.1		Sales/Receivables	46 7.9	46 8.0
	65 5.6	66 5.5	64 5.7	61 6.0			61 6.0	60 6.1
	33 11.1	68 5.4	74 4.9	101 3.6			63 5.8	53 6.9
	104 3.5	96 3.8	79 4.6	159 2.3		Cost of Sales/Inventory	96 3.8	85 4.3
	182 2.0	281 1.3	104 3.5	166 2.2			140 2.6	146 2.5
	23 15.8	24 15.4	32 11.4	30 12.0			16 23.3	13 29.0
	53 6.9	38 9.7	38 9.7	50 7.3		Cost of Sales/Payables	29 12.7	27 13.4
	87 4.2	87 4.2	76 4.8	70 5.2			51 7.2	54 6.8
		2.2	2.6	5.9	2.9		3.4	3.1
		3.7	3.7	7.0	3.3	Sales/Working Capital	5.4	5.0
		9.8	7.1	24.7	6.2		9.0	11.1
		16.7	17.5	11.0	4.3		46.6	22.3
	(12) 5.2	(20) 3.8	(12) 7.0	.8	EBIT/Interest	(91) 8.1	(47) 6.1
		1.5	-.4	2.9	.3		1.8	.9
						Net Profit + Depr., Dep., Amort./Cur. Mat. L/T/D	8.0	5.8
							(18) 2.9	(11) 3.9
							1.9	.9
		.0	.1	.5	.7		.1	.1
		.1	.4	.6	3.7	Fixed/Worth	.5	.7
		.2	1.7	NM	-.2		1.3	4.0
		.5	.5	.6	1.4		.3	.3
		1.3	1.1	1.1	9.4	Debt/Worth	.9	1.4
		2.3	9.6	NM	-2.1		3.2	11.8
		55.2	46.0	23.6			65.8	59.3
	(19)	25.8 (25)	22.7 (10)	14.9		% Profit Before Taxes/Tangible Net Worth	(99) 34.8	(48) 35.8
		.2	3.0	-32.0			11.4	9.6
		24.6	24.6	14.2	9.0		25.6	24.0
		7.7	9.4	9.2	-.8	% Profit Before Taxes/Total Assets	11.5	8.6
		.6	3.2	3.8	-2.1		2.8	1.9
		708.2	15.5	13.1	16.5		38.3	29.5
		35.6	9.7	6.0	6.9	Sales/Net Fixed Assets	12.4	8.5
		22.7	5.3	4.1	3.4		4.9	4.0
		1.9	1.9	2.1	1.0		2.3	2.1
		1.6	1.2	1.0	.8	Sales/Total Assets	1.7	1.5
		1.1	.7	.7	.4		1.1	1.1
			1.1				1.1	1.1
		(20)	3.1			% Depr., Dep., Amort./Sales	(83) 2.6	(42) 3.2
			6.3				4.6	7.9
						% Officers', Directors' Owners' Comp/Sales	2.0	2.2
							(25) 3.6	(10) 2.7
							5.6	6.7
	34333M	153746M	851497M	1089266M	1514198M	Net Sales ($)	4567713M	2351195M
	10529M	89759M	702236M	939191M	1858242M	Total Assets ($)	3634984M	2154194M

M = $ thousand   MM = $ million
See Pages viii through xx for Explanation of Ratios and Data

© RMA 2024

MANUFACTURING—Surgical and Medical Instrument Manufacturing NAICS 339112

Comparative Historical Data | Current Data Sorted by Sales

					Type of Statement						
	5		13	13	Unqualified					5	8
	5		5	5	Reviewed				1	1	4
	2		4	1	Compiled				1		
	4		9	7	Tax Returns		1		3	1	1
	56		59	57	Other	1	3	6	10	11	26
	4/1/21-		4/1/22-	4/1/23-			17 (4/1-9/30/23)			66 (10/1/23-3/31/24)	
	3/31/22		3/31/23	3/31/24		0-1MM	1-3MM	3-5MM	5-10MM	10-25MM	25MM & OVER
	ALL		ALL	ALL	NUMBER OF STATEMENTS						
	72		90	83		1	4	7	14	18	39
	%		%	%	ASSETS	%	%	%	%	%	%
	20.8		17.0	14.6	Cash & Equivalents				24.3	8.9	12.3
	20.5		20.6	19.5	Trade Receivables (net)				19.9	21.5	19.2
	22.0		22.9	22.2	Inventory				24.7	25.0	19.7
	2.1		4.7	3.6	All Other Current				5.3	2.8	2.6
	65.4		65.2	59.9	Total Current				74.1	58.1	53.7
	16.4		17.4	16.3	Fixed Assets (net)				9.6	12.9	20.3
	12.9		11.8	14.5	Intangibles (net)				7.0	17.7	19.1
	5.4		5.6	9.2	All Other Non-Current				9.2	11.3	6.9
	100.0		100.0	100.0	Total				100.0	100.0	100.0
					LIABILITIES						
	6.5		5.1	3.6	Notes Payable-Short Term				3.7	2.9	2.2
	2.6		1.5	2.2	Cur. Mat.-L.T.D.				2.4	2.1	2.3
	8.4		9.4	10.1	Trade Payables				11.7	9.4	9.7
	.2		.1	.1	Income Taxes Payable				.0	.0	.2
	8.9		10.6	11.9	All Other Current				6.9	11.6	13.4
	26.6		26.8	27.9	Total Current				24.6	26.1	27.8
	14.5		17.5	17.0	Long-Term Debt				13.4	19.0	18.8
	.3		.2	.3	Deferred Taxes				.0	.1	.6
	8.6		3.8	6.9	All Other Non-Current				3.4	3.6	7.8
	50.1		51.7	47.9	Net Worth				58.6	51.2	45.1
	100.0		100.0	100.0	Total Liabilties & Net Worth				100.0	100.0	100.0
					INCOME DATA						
	100.0		100.0	100.0	Net Sales				100.0	100.0	100.0
	46.5		46.3	47.5	Gross Profit				45.3	50.1	43.9
	38.1		36.6	38.7	Operating Expenses				37.5	44.0	33.1
	8.3		9.7	8.8	Operating Profit				7.8	6.1	10.8
	-.3		.1	1.3	All Other Expenses (net)				.5	.6	2.7
	8.6		9.6	7.4	Profit Before Taxes				7.3	5.5	8.1
					RATIOS						
	5.2		4.4	3.6					6.9	5.2	3.5
	2.7		2.7	2.5	Current				3.4	2.5	2.2
	1.7		1.7	1.4					1.5	1.5	1.3
	3.6		2.6	2.7					4.1	2.3	1.8
	1.5		1.5	1.1	Quick				2.3	1.1	1.1
	.9		.7	.7					.8	.6	.7
35	10.5	35	10.3	34	10.6				29	12.4	46	7.9	38	9.6
46	8.0	50	7.3	46	8.0	Sales/Receivables				37	9.9	57	6.4	45	8.1
61	6.0	64	5.7	64	5.7					63	5.8	78	4.7	62	5.9
63	5.8	61	6.0	64	5.7				8	46.5	78	4.7	72	5.1
83	4.4	91	4.0	96	3.8	Cost of Sales/Inventory				91	4.0	101	3.6	96	3.8
152	2.4	174	2.1	174	2.1					159	2.3	332	1.1	166	2.2
13	29.0	16	23.2	26	14.0				4	99.4	23	16.1	30	12.0
27	13.3	33	11.0	38	9.6	Cost of Sales/Payables				30	12.3	44	8.3	37	9.8
54	6.8	56	6.5	70	5.2					91	4.0	96	3.8	51	7.2
	2.4		2.8	2.8					2.7	2.6	3.3
	4.1		4.0	4.6	Sales/Working Capital				4.2	4.6	4.8
	6.6		7.8	9.8					10.1	8.6	13.8
	69.2		33.9	15.4					46.0	14.6	9.8
(60)	14.5	(71)	8.4	(63)	3.8	EBIT/Interest			(11)	9.8	(12)	2.8	(33)	3.8
	2.9		3.5	.5					1.0	-.4	.4
	11.3		18.9	3.4	Net Profit + Depr., Dep.,						
(15)	3.8	(14)	5.7	(10)	2.4	Amort./Cur. Mat. L/T/D									
	.8		2.9	1.5							
	.1		.1	.1					.0	.1	.2
	.3		.3	.4	Fixed/Worth				.1	.3	.7
	1.2		1.1	2.6					.7	NM	47.8
	.3		.4	.6					.4	.5	.7
	.8		.9	1.4	Debt/Worth				.9	1.9	1.4
	3.7		2.8	9.5					2.3	NM	76.1
	57.7		51.6	43.4					76.4	74.6	37.5
(57)	28.8	(75)	25.3	(66)	19.0	% Profit Before Taxes/Tangible Net Worth			(13)	26.1	(14)	16.4	(30)	18.8
	10.4		10.3	2.0					-.2	-1.8	9.1
	32.1		21.3	22.8	% Profit Before Taxes/Total Assets				28.1	20.9	18.2
	14.3		9.2	8.5					12.4	7.1	9.1
	3.0		4.0	1.2					.0	.8	-.8
	37.9		34.3	46.1					235.1	56.6	13.0
	11.3		12.1	11.7	Sales/Net Fixed Assets				46.2	10.8	6.9
	5.2		5.4	6.0					19.9	6.0	5.3
	2.1		2.0	1.9					2.1	1.6	1.9
	1.5		1.4	1.3	Sales/Total Assets				1.9	.9	1.1
	.8		.9	.8					1.5	.6	.8
	1.5		.8	1.3					.8	1.9
(45)	2.6	(53)	2.0	(46)	2.5	% Depr., Dep., Amort./Sales					(11)	3.1	(22)	3.6
	5.2		3.4	6.5						6.3	6.3
	1.4		1.7	1.7	% Officers', Directors'						
(20)	3.2	(19)	2.6	(10)	3.4	Owners' Comp/Sales									
	8.4		9.6	8.1							
2479363M		3057560M		3643040M	Net Sales ($)	980M	8484M	26705M	102307M	309255M	3195309M
2288270M		2571660M		3599957M	Total Assets ($)	861M	8923M	19953M	66425M	365476M	3138319M

© RMA 2024   M = $ thousand   MM = $ million
See Pages viii through xx for Explanation of Ratios and Data

MANUFACTURING—Surgical Appliance and Supplies Manufacturing NAICS 339113

Current Data Sorted by Assets | Comparative Historical Data

							Type of Statement		
			1	4	3	3	Unqualified	5	3
			3	8	1		Reviewed	12	5
			3				Compiled	3	1
		4	4				Tax Returns	11	9
	3	11	20	6	9		Other	48	32
	20 (4/1-9/30/23)		63 (10/1/23-3/31/24)					4/1/19-3/31/20	4/1/20-3/31/21
0-500M	500M-2MM	2-10MM	10-50MM	50-100MM	100-250MM		NUMBER OF STATEMENTS	ALL 79	ALL 50
	7	22	32	10	12		ASSETS		
%	%	%	%	%	%	%		%	%
D		14.6	8.2	2.9	18.4		Cash & Equivalents	10.0	12.9
A		21.8	20.2	10.1	16.0		Trade Receivables (net)	23.3	23.9
T		29.3	28.5	13.2	21.8		Inventory	28.3	29.1
A		1.8	2.8	1.3	4.1		All Other Current	2.5	1.7
		67.5	59.7	27.5	60.3		Total Current	64.2	67.7
N		16.7	14.9	13.4	14.2		Fixed Assets (net)	17.2	14.2
O		8.9	15.9	54.6	17.6		Intangibles (net)	12.9	12.5
T		6.9	9.6	4.5	7.9		All Other Non-Current	5.7	5.6
		100.0	100.0	100.0	100.0		Total	100.0	100.0
A							LIABILITIES		
V		6.2	6.1	7.0	2.4		Notes Payable-Short Term	7.8	6.1
A		2.7	2.2	2.5	1.6		Cur. Mat.-L.T.D.	2.1	1.7
I		12.8	10.5	3.5	5.9		Trade Payables	11.5	15.0
L		.1	.3	.0	.0		Income Taxes Payable	.1	.2
A		8.8	8.9	6.0	15.2		All Other Current	10.6	10.2
B		30.6	28.0	19.0	25.0		Total Current	32.1	33.3
L		12.0	8.3	16.8	22.4		Long-Term Debt	14.7	19.1
E		.0	.1	4.3	.2		Deferred Taxes	.3	.2
		2.7	7.4	12.8	12.4		All Other Non-Current	8.8	11.3
		54.7	56.2	47.0	39.9		Net Worth	44.0	36.1
		100.0	100.0	100.0	100.0		Total Liabilities & Net Worth	100.0	100.0
							INCOME DATA		
		100.0	100.0	100.0	100.0		Net Sales	100.0	100.0
		48.1	44.4	49.0	48.7		Gross Profit	45.7	43.8
		39.9	36.0	40.2	39.0		Operating Expenses	38.1	37.2
		8.1	8.4	8.8	9.7		Operating Profit	7.6	6.5
		.7	1.7	4.5	3.1		All Other Expenses (net)	.9	-.1
		7.4	6.7	4.3	6.6		Profit Before Taxes	6.7	6.6
							RATIOS		
		4.3	3.8	2.4	5.4			3.8	4.3
		2.6	2.2	1.3	3.3		Current	2.3	2.6
		1.4	1.5	.7	1.8			1.5	1.7
		3.1	1.8	1.3	3.0			2.0	2.7
		1.3	1.3	.5	1.7		Quick	1.0	1.4
		.4	.7	.3	.7			.7	.6
		24 15.2	38 9.5	43 8.4	38 9.7			33 10.9	32 11.5
		34 10.7	46 7.9	59 6.2	56 6.5		Sales/Receivables	43 8.4	43 8.5
		48 7.6	56 6.5	61 6.0	61 6.0			52 7.0	66 5.5
		40 9.2	63 5.8	76 4.8	111 3.3			63 5.8	63 5.8
		74 4.9	122 3.0	94 3.9	130 2.8		Cost of Sales/Inventory	101 3.6	107 3.4
		146 2.5	174 2.1	118 3.1	182 2.0			135 2.7	152 2.4
		21 17.6	21 17.6	24 15.0	27 13.4			17 20.9	20 18.0
		33 11.2	29 12.4	36 10.2	39 9.4		Cost of Sales/Payables	28 13.2	30 12.0
		54 6.7	47 7.7	65 5.6	60 6.1			54 6.8	64 5.7
		3.1	3.2	4.0	1.9			3.8	3.1
		5.6	4.7	NM	3.0		Sales/Working Capital	5.6	5.0
		12.8	12.3	-9.5	4.4			9.5	9.4
		84.6	27.7	10.5	14.4			32.8	47.8
	(17)	14.7	(26) 7.7	2.2	(11) 1.8		EBIT/Interest	(70) 7.4	(46) 11.3
		1.4	2.2	.7	1.0			2.3	2.0
							Net Profit + Depr., Dep.,	6.8	11.9
							Amort./Cur. Mat. L/T/D	(19) 3.5	(16) 5.4
								-.1	3.1
		.1	.1	1.0	.2			.2	.1
		.2	.4	-.4	.5		Fixed/Worth	.5	.4
		.6	.9	-.2	-.2			3.0	2.4
		.6	.4	1.7	.4			.6	.6
		1.1	1.1	-2.9	2.2		Debt/Worth	1.1	1.5
		1.9	3.6	-1.5	-6.1			13.4	13.1
		70.3	45.7				% Profit Before Taxes/Tangible	50.2	85.2
		32.5	(29) 23.5				Net Worth	(64) 25.2	(41) 32.5
		6.3	9.7					11.3	14.5
		31.4	15.8	8.3	7.5		% Profit Before Taxes/Total	21.5	17.3
		12.7	10.1	1.9	2.7		Assets	9.5	11.3
		2.8	3.2	-1.0	.1			2.8	2.9
		71.2	29.5	9.0	29.9			45.3	41.0
		14.9	14.4	6.7	9.1		Sales/Net Fixed Assets	16.9	20.3
		8.9	8.0	4.6	6.4			5.6	6.9
		2.8	1.8	.9	1.6			2.5	2.3
		2.0	1.5	.6	1.1		Sales/Total Assets	1.7	1.8
		1.6	1.3	.4	.8			1.3	1.2
		.5	.7					.9	1.4
	(10)	2.9	(28) 1.2				% Depr., Dep., Amort./Sales	(64) 1.8	(37) 2.0
		3.9	2.4					3.0	3.1
							% Officers', Directors'	1.0	1.5
							Owners' Comp/Sales	(20) 2.8	(12) 3.8
								5.4	6.4
	30374M	251941M	1074691M	460281M	2297246M		Net Sales ($)	2664143M	1799460M
	8750M	120192M	701744M	713620M	2010032M		Total Assets ($)	2214388M	1217028M

M = $ thousand   MM = $ million
See Pages viii through xx for Explanation of Ratios and Data

© RMA 2024

MANUFACTURING—Surgical Appliance and Supplies Manufacturing NAICS 339113

Comparative Historical Data | Current Data Sorted by Sales

Comparative Historical Data			Type of Statement	Current Data Sorted by Sales					
6	6	11	Unqualified				1	3	7
9	13	12	Reviewed				2	5	5
1	6	3	Compiled					3	
2	10	8	Tax Returns			1	5	1	
38	37	49	Other		1	3	4	11	29
4/1/21-3/31/22 ALL	4/1/22-3/31/23 ALL	4/1/23-3/31/24 ALL		0-1MM	1-3MM	3-5MM	5-10MM	10-25MM	25MM & OVER
					2		20 (4/1-9/30/23)	63 (10/1/23-3/31/24)	
56	72	83	NUMBER OF STATEMENTS		3	4	12	23	41
%	%	%	ASSETS	%	%	%	%	%	%
10.6	9.1	11.6	Cash & Equivalents	D			20.6	7.8	10.7
19.1	19.7	18.5	Trade Receivables (net)	A			20.8	22.8	16.5
27.4	28.5	27.1	Inventory	T			33.0	28.8	23.1
3.7	3.8	2.3	All Other Current	A			.3	2.9	2.5
60.9	61.1	59.5	Total Current				74.6	62.3	52.8
16.3	18.6	14.5	Fixed Assets (net)	N			16.8	12.5	16.6
15.2	11.7	17.8	Intangibles (net)	O			1.6	18.7	22.5
7.6	8.7	8.1	All Other Non-Current	T			7.0	6.4	8.2
100.0	100.0	100.0	Total				100.0	100.0	100.0
			LIABILITIES	A					
6.3	7.1	7.7	Notes Payable-Short Term	V			6.9	5.8	5.3
2.4	2.4	2.2	Cur. Mat.-L.T.D.	A			3.3	2.5	2.0
9.4	10.1	10.5	Trade Payables	I			6.9	14.5	7.9
.1	.2	.2	Income Taxes Payable	L			.2	.1	.2
9.2	9.7	10.3	All Other Current	A			13.4	6.8	11.1
27.5	29.4	30.8	Total Current	B			30.6	29.6	26.6
18.3	13.1	12.6	Long-Term Debt	L			10.0	12.1	12.7
.4	.5	.6	Deferred Taxes	E			.0	.1	1.1
8.4	7.7	7.1	All Other Non-Current				3.8	3.8	10.8
45.4	49.4	48.9	Net Worth				55.6	54.5	48.9
100.0	100.0	100.0	Total Liabilties & Net Worth				100.0	100.0	100.0
			INCOME DATA						
100.0	100.0	100.0	Net Sales				100.0	100.0	100.0
42.9	43.6	47.0	Gross Profit				51.7	40.2	47.3
37.1	36.2	38.9	Operating Expenses				44.8	31.8	38.6
5.8	7.4	8.2	Operating Profit				7.0	8.4	8.7
-.6	.0	1.7	All Other Expenses (net)				.2	1.5	2.5
6.3	7.4	6.4	Profit Before Taxes				6.8	6.9	6.2
			RATIOS						
3.6	3.3	3.7					9.0	3.7	3.8
2.4	2.3	2.2	Current				2.9	2.2	2.0
1.6	1.6	1.2					1.5	1.6	1.1
2.0	1.7	2.2					5.3	1.8	2.3
1.1	1.0	1.1	Quick				1.7	1.3	1.0
.6	.6	.5					.4	.7	.4
31 11.8	29 12.7	27 13.3					19 19.6	36 10.0	37 9.8
49 7.5	42 8.6	44 8.3	Sales/Receivables				37 9.8	46 7.9	48 7.6
54 6.7	59 6.2	57 6.4					54 6.7	61 6.0	57 6.4
54 6.7	57 6.4	68 5.4					37 9.9	41 9.0	79 4.6
94 3.9	107 3.4	104 3.5	Cost of Sales/Inventory				118 3.1	85 4.3	111 3.3
130 2.8	174 2.1	159 2.3					182 2.0	126 2.9	152 2.4
21 17.7	17 21.4	22 16.3					10 35.7	29 12.7	24 15.5
29 12.6	27 13.5	32 11.3	Cost of Sales/Payables				23 16.0	36 10.1	30 12.2
43 8.5	53 6.9	54 6.7					49 7.5	47 7.7	59 6.2
3.3	3.5	3.1					2.8	3.2	3.1
5.1	5.5	4.8	Sales/Working Capital				5.2	4.8	4.6
9.6	8.4	23.4					7.8	10.5	45.1
58.3	32.7	27.1					76.8	18.6	27.5
(50) 10.1	(59) 10.1	(71) 7.0	EBIT/Interest				(11) 12.5	(18) 5.9	(35) 5.2
1.0	3.7	1.6					.5	1.3	1.7
		17.5							20.4
8.0	6.6		Net Profit + Depr., Dep.,						
(18) 4.7	(25) 2.5	(20) 4.3	Amort./Cur. Mat. L/T/D					(17) 4.4	
2.0	1.1	.5							.5
.2	.1	.1					.1	.1	.2
.6	.5	.5	Fixed/Worth				.2	.4	.5
3.2	.9	1.9					.6	1.6	-1.4
.6	.5	.5					.3	.5	.4
1.4	1.3	1.5	Debt/Worth				.9	1.0	1.7
7.8	3.6	9.4					1.7	9.4	-8.5
55.2	41.2	56.9	% Profit Before Taxes/Tangible				56.2	78.9	38.6
(44) 24.2	(62) 28.7	(66) 23.7	Net Worth				23.2	(21) 29.8	(29) 20.5
6.7	8.4	9.0					-10.0	6.2	11.5
24.7	21.8	19.5	% Profit Before Taxes/Total				33.8	21.8	14.1
9.1	9.4	7.4	Assets				18.8	7.4	6.1
.3	2.1	2.0					-1.9	3.3	1.5
34.9	42.4	38.5					66.0	58.9	24.4
11.3	11.4	12.4	Sales/Net Fixed Assets				13.3	24.1	9.1
5.2	4.5	7.9					10.1	6.3	6.9
2.3	2.2	2.1					2.8	2.2	1.7
1.5	1.5	1.5	Sales/Total Assets				2.0	1.7	1.3
1.2	1.1	1.0					1.7	1.2	.9
1.0	1.0	.8						.6	1.0
(42) 1.9	(51) 2.1	(59) 1.6	% Depr., Dep., Amort./Sales					(16) 1.7	(35) 1.6
3.7	4.0	3.6						4.0	3.3
1.7	2.6	1.5	% Officers', Directors'						
(10) 2.9	(22) 4.6	(15) 3.0	Owners' Comp/Sales						
4.4	8.8	6.8							
2064935M	2115833M	4114533M	Net Sales ($)				6388M 18318M	89193M 418135M	3582499M
1766359M	1645135M	3554338M	Total Assets ($)				8556M 10823M	48678M 347243M	3139038M

© RMA 2024
M = $ thousand   MM = $ million
See Pages viii through xx for Explanation of Ratios and Data

MANUFACTURING—Dental Equipment and Supplies Manufacturing NAICS 339114

Current Data Sorted by Assets | Comparative Historical Data

						Type of Statement		
			1	1		Unqualified	3	2
		1	2			Reviewed	3	4
1	3					Compiled	1	2
	2					Tax Returns	1	2
	6 (4/1-9/30/23)	6	6	1	2	Other	17	13
0-500M	500M-2MM	2-10MM	10-50MM	50-100MM	100-250MM		4/1/19-3/31/20	4/1/20-3/31/21
1	5	7	8	2	2	NUMBER OF STATEMENTS	25 ALL	23 ALL
%	%	%	%	%	%	ASSETS	%	%
						Cash & Equivalents	12.4	22.7
						Trade Receivables (net)	23.7	18.5
						Inventory	30.2	27.8
						All Other Current	4.4	2.5
						Total Current	70.6	71.4
						Fixed Assets (net)	18.9	21.8
						Intangibles (net)	7.2	3.6
						All Other Non-Current	3.3	3.3
						Total	100.0	100.0
						LIABILITIES		
						Notes Payable-Short Term	6.7	4.4
						Cur. Mat.-L.T.D.	1.5	1.8
						Trade Payables	12.4	6.1
						Income Taxes Payable	.1	.0
						All Other Current	10.9	17.4
						Total Current	31.5	29.7
						Long-Term Debt	12.3	15.8
						Deferred Taxes	.5	.3
						All Other Non-Current	3.3	3.0
						Net Worth	52.4	51.2
						Total Liabilities & Net Worth	100.0	100.0
						INCOME DATA		
						Net Sales	100.0	100.0
						Gross Profit	42.7	47.1
						Operating Expenses	37.5	43.8
						Operating Profit	5.2	3.3
						All Other Expenses (net)	.3	-.7
						Profit Before Taxes	4.9	4.0
						RATIOS		
						Current	3.8	4.7
							2.1	2.9
							1.6	1.6
						Quick	2.1	2.5
							1.0	1.7
							.8	1.0
						Sales/Receivables	32 11.4	33 10.9
							37 9.8	41 8.8
							53 6.9	52 7.0
						Cost of Sales/Inventory	63 5.8	46 7.9
							87 4.2	91 4.0
							135 2.7	174 2.1
						Cost of Sales/Payables	17 21.5	13 28.1
							34 10.7	22 16.4
							49 7.5	35 10.5
						Sales/Working Capital	3.4	2.6
							5.6	4.3
							9.5	10.0
						EBIT/Interest	36.0	30.6
							(21) 8.5	(17) 8.4
							-.2	.6
						Net Profit + Depr., Dep., Amort./Cur. Mat. L/T/D		
						Fixed/Worth	.1	.1
							.3	.3
							.9	.8
						Debt/Worth	.3	.5
							.9	.8
							1.9	1.7
						% Profit Before Taxes/Tangible Net Worth	57.9	44.6
							(23) 16.0	(21) 23.9
							1.3	5.8
						% Profit Before Taxes/Total Assets	24.9	20.4
							8.1	9.5
							-.2	1.9
						Sales/Net Fixed Assets	42.0	26.1
							15.0	14.8
							5.7	4.3
						Sales/Total Assets	3.1	2.5
							2.1	1.8
							1.3	1.3
						% Depr., Dep., Amort./Sales	.8	.6
							(16) 2.4	(18) 2.4
							3.4	3.5
						% Officers', Directors' Owners' Comp/Sales		
555M	22923M	90412M	294567M	138523M	504795M	Net Sales ($)	1568564M	1462577M
167M	5357M	34696M	165521M	149307M	311338M	Total Assets ($)	990462M	820070M

© RMA 2024

M = $ thousand   MM = $ million
See Pages viii through xx for Explanation of Ratios and Data

MANUFACTURING—Dental Equipment and Supplies Manufacturing NAICS 339114

Comparative Historical Data | Current Data Sorted by Sales

						Type of Statement							
			1		1	Unqualified							1
	2		4		2	Reviewed							2
	2		1		1	Compiled							
	3		5		4	Tax Returns						1	
	15		12		17	Other	1	1	2	2	2	3	9
	4/1/21-		4/1/22-		4/1/23-				1	2	2		
	3/31/22		3/31/23		3/31/24			6 (4/1-9/30/23)			19 (10/1/23-3/31/24)		
	ALL		ALL		ALL		0-1MM	1-3MM	3-5MM	5-10MM	10-25MM	25MM & OVER	
	22		23		25	NUMBER OF STATEMENTS	1	2	4	2	4	12	
	%		%		%	ASSETS	%	%	%	%	%	%	
	20.3		18.3		13.0	Cash & Equivalents						10.1	
	20.2		21.3		20.7	Trade Receivables (net)						23.1	
	28.5		29.5		32.5	Inventory						27.2	
	2.5		2.6		1.4	All Other Current						1.1	
	71.5		71.6		67.6	Total Current						61.5	
	14.5		13.9		14.6	Fixed Assets (net)						16.9	
	8.8		9.4		9.9	Intangibles (net)						13.6	
	5.2		5.1		7.8	All Other Non-Current						8.1	
	100.0		100.0		100.0	Total						100.0	
						LIABILITIES							
	5.7		6.1		9.9	Notes Payable-Short Term						2.4	
	3.7		3.2		5.9	Cur. Mat.-L.T.D.						10.1	
	9.1		12.6		10.6	Trade Payables						10.4	
	.2		.1		.0	Income Taxes Payable						.1	
	14.9		9.5		9.6	All Other Current						14.4	
	33.6		31.6		36.0	Total Current						37.4	
	17.7		20.6		13.2	Long-Term Debt						9.3	
	.1		.2		.1	Deferred Taxes						.1	
	2.3		4.9		4.9	All Other Non-Current						6.5	
	46.3		42.7		45.9	Net Worth						46.8	
	100.0		100.0		100.0	Total Liabilities & Net Worth						100.0	
						INCOME DATA							
	100.0		100.0		100.0	Net Sales						100.0	
	48.7		47.0		47.5	Gross Profit						45.1	
	40.7		44.3		47.2	Operating Expenses						40.4	
	8.0		2.7		.3	Operating Profit						4.6	
	-2.6		1.1		2.1	All Other Expenses (net)						4.0	
	10.6		1.6		-1.9	Profit Before Taxes						.6	
						RATIOS							
	4.6		3.6		4.2							5.3	
	2.4		2.6		2.2	Current						2.1	
	1.7		1.4		1.3							1.2	
	2.8		1.9		2.3							2.4	
	1.4		1.0		1.1	Quick						1.2	
	.8		.7		.6							.5	
27	13.7	26	13.8	20	18.3							42	8.7
36	10.1	42	8.7	39	9.4	Sales/Receivables						47	7.7
45	8.2	49	7.4	49	7.5							50	7.3
29	12.7	61	6.0	62	5.9							72	5.1
104	3.5	107	3.4	111	3.3	Cost of Sales/Inventory						126	2.9
140	2.6	135	2.7	166	2.2							228	1.6
15	24.6	16	22.6	8	44.6							22	16.8
28	13.0	31	11.6	24	14.9	Cost of Sales/Payables						25	14.8
34	10.7	54	6.8	49	7.4							43	8.5
	3.9		3.8		3.4							2.4	
	5.6		5.4		5.3	Sales/Working Capital						6.7	
	9.8		10.2		13.4							43.7	
	93.5		23.5		10.9								
(16)	27.6	(19)	6.9	(15)	-.3	EBIT/Interest							
	7.4		-1.9		-15.5								
						Net Profit + Depr., Dep., Amort./Cur. Mat. L/T/D							
	.1		.2		.1							.1	
	.3		.5		.4	Fixed/Worth						.4	
	1.2		1.2		1.3							1.0	
	.3		.6		.6							.8	
	.8		1.5		1.2	Debt/Worth						1.3	
	2.7		5.9		4.5							1.7	
	60.2		62.6		32.4	% Profit Before Taxes/Tangible Net Worth						40.1	
(18)	41.3	(18)	21.4	(21)	11.1							(10)	20.5
	17.9		-16.4		-35.8							10.0	
	36.0		23.0		11.2	% Profit Before Taxes/Total Assets						17.8	
	19.2		9.2		1.5							7.7	
	6.9		-11.2		-13.8							.4	
	60.9		37.3		65.3							54.1	
	25.7		17.9		21.4	Sales/Net Fixed Assets						7.4	
	9.4		8.2		5.7							4.1	
	3.3		3.5		3.2							2.5	
	2.3		2.0		2.1	Sales/Total Assets						1.9	
	1.7		1.5		1.4							1.1	
	.6		.9		.7								
(16)	1.4	(14)	1.5	(15)	1.7	% Depr., Dep., Amort./Sales							
	2.9		2.1		2.5								
	1.9												
(10)	3.9					% Officers', Directors' Owners' Comp/Sales							
	5.1												
	887686M		866844M		1051775M	Net Sales ($)	555M	4592M	18759M	14202M	64188M	949479M	
	724390M		425632M		666386M	Total Assets ($)	167M	1109M	7460M	4853M	33601M	619196M	

© RMA 2024 M = $ thousand MM = $ million
See Pages viii through xx for Explanation of Ratios and Data

MANUFACTURING—Jewelry and Silverware Manufacturing NAICS 339910

Current Data Sorted by Assets

0-500M	500M-2MM	2-10MM	10-50MM	50-100MM	100-250MM		Comparative Historical Data	
						Type of Statement		
			4	1		Unqualified	7	1
		3	4			Reviewed	3	2
	1	3	1			Compiled	3	1
1	3	7	9			Tax Returns	14	8
1		6 (4/1-9/30/23)	32 (10/1/23-3/31/24)			Other	29	11
							4/1/19-3/31/20 ALL	4/1/20-3/31/21 ALL
2	4	13	18	1		**NUMBER OF STATEMENTS**	56	23
%	%	%	%	%	%	**ASSETS**	%	%
		26.9	11.9			Cash & Equivalents	9.8	16.7
		18.7	22.9			Trade Receivables (net)	21.8	14.8
		31.1	38.9			Inventory	37.2	40.6
		.6	1.7			All Other Current	1.9	2.4
		77.2	75.5			Total Current	70.6	74.6
		15.9	11.6			Fixed Assets (net)	17.6	18.4
		4.7	3.4			Intangibles (net)	6.1	2.6
		2.2	9.6			All Other Non-Current	5.7	4.5
		100.0	100.0			Total	100.0	100.0
						LIABILITIES		
		2.3	7.2			Notes Payable-Short Term	14.0	8.3
		.9	2.1			Cur. Mat.-L.T.D.	2.3	5.4
		5.5	15.6			Trade Payables	18.6	15.9
		.0	.0			Income Taxes Payable	.1	.1
		6.0	12.5			All Other Current	12.7	14.9
		14.7	37.4			Total Current	47.6	44.6
		15.9	6.7			Long-Term Debt	15.5	25.9
		.0	.0			Deferred Taxes	.2	.1
		1.7	5.5			All Other Non-Current	3.3	8.8
		67.8	50.4			Net Worth	33.4	20.7
		100.0	100.0			Total Liabilities & Net Worth	100.0	100.0
						INCOME DATA		
		100.0	100.0			Net Sales	100.0	100.0
		49.2	40.9			Gross Profit	40.3	38.8
		37.7	31.1			Operating Expenses	33.2	34.5
		11.4	9.8			Operating Profit	7.1	4.3
		.7	1.7			All Other Expenses (net)	1.3	-1.4
		10.7	8.1			Profit Before Taxes	5.7	5.7
						RATIOS		
		20.6	4.4				3.2	4.2
		5.4	1.9			Current	1.8	1.9
		3.4	1.6				1.1	1.6
		8.6	2.0				1.4	3.6
		3.9	.8			Quick	.6	.7
		1.9	.4				.4	.4
		3 129.3	26 14.1				9 39.6	7 49.1
		26 14.3	41 8.8			Sales/Receivables	29 12.6	25 14.4
		39 9.3	73 5.0				46 7.9	41 8.8
		30 12.1	85 4.3				28 13.0	41 8.8
		111 3.3	130 2.8			Cost of Sales/Inventory	94 3.9	104 3.5
		228 1.6	261 1.4				159 2.3	281 1.3
		5 68.7	24 15.0				12 30.7	10 35.2
		20 18.7	37 9.8			Cost of Sales/Payables	32 11.4	26 14.1
		41 9.0	73 5.0				50 7.3	41 8.9
		2.0	2.2				4.1	2.9
		3.7	6.0			Sales/Working Capital	7.8	5.4
		4.4	7.6				61.6	13.3
			74.5				16.5	49.9
		(16)	3.6			EBIT/Interest	(48) 4.3	(19) 5.0
			1.5				1.2	1.7
						Net Profit + Depr., Dep., Amort./Cur. Mat. L/T/D		
		.0	.0				.1	.1
		.2	.2			Fixed/Worth	.3	.3
		.5	.3				4.5	3.0
		.2	.6				.6	.4
		.4	1.0			Debt/Worth	1.2	1.2
		1.0	1.9				18.7	3.9
		42.0	62.3				41.8	55.6
		29.2	19.5			% Profit Before Taxes/Tangible Net Worth	(43) 16.9	(19) 10.8
		14.0	1.2				4.4	1.2
		26.9	19.3				22.0	23.9
		17.9	12.7			% Profit Before Taxes/Total Assets	5.3	5.7
		9.7	.6				.5	1.6
		84.0	55.5				61.3	30.7
		23.6	17.3			Sales/Net Fixed Assets	16.8	14.1
		6.8	8.0				8.5	6.7
		2.6	2.3				3.1	3.0
		1.7	1.5			Sales/Total Assets	2.3	1.7
		1.4	1.2				1.5	1.0
			.2				.5	.7
		(17)	.7			% Depr., Dep., Amort./Sales	(40) 1.2	(18) 2.1
			1.9				2.0	3.4
							2.3	2.3
						% Officers', Directors' Owners' Comp/Sales	(25) 3.2	(13) 3.7
							8.5	7.9
1014M	15577M	143474M	688933M	109876M		Net Sales ($)	1740278M	329922M
272M	5971M	66790M	378698M	99331M		Total Assets ($)	1087967M	182881M

© RMA 2024

M = $ thousand   MM = $ million
See Pages viii through xx for Explanation of Ratios and Data

MANUFACTURING—Jewelry and Silverware Manufacturing NAICS 339910

Comparative Historical Data / Current Data Sorted by Sales

						Type of Statement							
			5		5	Unqualified					2	3	
	2		7		4	Reviewed					2	2	
	2				3	Compiled			1	1	1		
	4		6		6	Tax Returns		1	2	2	1		
	14		17		20	Other	1	5	1	4		9	
	4/1/21-3/31/22 ALL		4/1/22-3/31/23 ALL		4/1/23-3/31/24 ALL		6 (4/1-9/30/23)			32 (10/1/23-3/31/24)			
							0-1MM	1-3MM	3-5MM	5-10MM	10-25MM	25MM & OVER	
	22		35		38	NUMBER OF STATEMENTS	2	8	4	10	14		
	%		%		%	ASSETS	%	%	%	%	%	%	
	19.4		15.9		15.7	Cash & Equivalents					21.3	8.8	
	16.3		19.5		21.9	Trade Receivables (net)		D			24.3	27.7	
	36.3		36.2		34.6	Inventory		A			26.4	41.9	
	.9		1.2		1.6	All Other Current		T			1.0	1.9	
	72.9		72.8		73.7	Total Current		A			73.0	80.3	
	12.5		12.5		13.2	Fixed Assets (net)					16.5	9.2	
	12.3		7.0		6.3	Intangibles (net)		N			5.3	3.9	
	2.3		7.7		6.5	All Other Non-Current		O			5.2	6.6	
	100.0		100.0		100.0	Total		T			100.0	100.0	
						LIABILITIES		A					
	7.1		11.7		8.3	Notes Payable-Short Term		V			6.3	8.3	
	1.3		2.4		2.7	Cur. Mat.-L.T.D.		A			3.3	1.3	
	6.4		10.3		11.1	Trade Payables		I			7.7	17.2	
	.1		.3		.0	Income Taxes Payable		L			.0	.0	
	24.0		12.8		11.5	All Other Current		A			10.7	11.8	
	38.8		37.5		33.5	Total Current		B			27.9	38.5	
	20.9		9.6		10.6	Long-Term Debt		L			13.4	5.4	
	.0		.0		.0	Deferred Taxes		E			.0	.0	
	3.8		12.0		5.8	All Other Non-Current					1.6	6.1	
	36.5		40.9		50.1	Net Worth					57.1	50.0	
	100.0		100.0		100.0	Total Liabilities & Net Worth					100.0	100.0	
						INCOME DATA							
	100.0		100.0		100.0	Net Sales					100.0	100.0	
	46.0		42.0		44.5	Gross Profit					48.0	39.5	
	33.7		31.9		35.3	Operating Expenses					38.1	29.7	
	12.4		10.1		9.2	Operating Profit					9.8	9.8	
	-.1		.6		.5	All Other Expenses (net)					1.3	.8	
	12.5		9.5		8.7	Profit Before Taxes					8.5	9.0	
						RATIOS							
	6.5		4.3		5.4						5.2	4.4	
	2.8		2.1		2.4	Current					3.1	1.8	
	1.8		1.4		1.6						2.0	1.6	
	3.0		2.6		3.2						4.2	2.0	
	1.1		.9		1.1	Quick					2.0	.7	
	.6		.5		.5						.7	.5	
8	46.1	6	62.8	16	22.8						8	48.6	26	14.1
26	14.2	31	11.9	40	9.1	Sales/Receivables					51	7.2	41	8.8
50	7.3	66	5.5	59	6.2						94	3.9	60	6.1
64	5.7	48	7.6	52	7.0						9	39.3	89	4.1
152	2.4	107	3.4	118	3.1	Cost of Sales/Inventory					49	7.5	130	2.8
228	1.6	203	1.8	203	1.8						261	1.4	174	2.1
12	31.4	14	26.1	16	22.9						19	19.7	21	17.6
21	17.3	27	13.6	29	12.8	Cost of Sales/Payables					33	10.9	30	12.0
37	9.8	41	8.8	52	7.0						55	6.6	81	4.5
	3.0		2.8		2.3						2.3	3.6	
	5.0		5.8		4.2	Sales/Working Capital					3.7	6.0	
	6.9		11.3		7.7						8.0	7.4	
	63.9		34.5		39.9							103.3	
(19)	16.5	(26)	10.9	(30)	4.8	EBIT/Interest						4.8	
	6.6		3.4		1.5							3.1	
						Net Profit + Depr., Dep., Amort./Cur. Mat. L/T/D							
	.1		.0		.0						.0	.1	
	.3		.3		.2	Fixed/Worth					.3	.2	
	4.4		1.0		.4						.6	.3	
	.5		.5		.4						.4	.7	
	1.6		1.3		1.0	Debt/Worth					.6	1.0	
	25.4		4.9		2.5						1.7	1.9	
	136.0		105.1		43.9						48.1	70.3	
(18)	58.0	(31)	48.7	(35)	24.7	% Profit Before Taxes/Tangible Net Worth					32.2	35.1	
	22.9		20.5		1.3						1.4	5.4	
	34.2		33.2		24.5						30.6	19.6	
	15.6		15.1		15.1	% Profit Before Taxes/Total Assets					16.4	14.7	
	9.3		5.1		.9						.8	3.7	
	75.7		74.1		84.4						62.3	84.4	
	27.3		18.5		17.8	Sales/Net Fixed Assets					11.3	17.8	
	7.4		8.7		7.5						6.4	13.1	
	2.6		2.5		2.5						2.4	2.6	
	1.9		1.8		1.7	Sales/Total Assets					1.4	2.2	
	1.5		1.2		1.3						1.1	1.4	
	.5		.4		.2							.1	
(10)	1.8	(24)	1.5	(28)	.8	% Depr., Dep., Amort./Sales					(13)	.7	
	3.6		3.4		2.2							1.9	
	2.3		1.3		.9								
(10)	4.5	(22)	2.5	(20)	2.3	% Officers', Directors' Owners' Comp/Sales							
	6.0		7.1		6.3								
	463381M		672137M		958874M	Net Sales ($)	1014M		33381M	30492M	158304M	735683M	
	301414M		446296M		551062M	Total Assets ($)	272M		19685M	23712M	106294M	401099M	

© RMA 2024 M = $ thousand MM = $ million
See Pages viii through xx for Explanation of Ratios and Data

MANUFACTURING—Sporting and Athletic Goods Manufacturing NAICS 339920

Current Data Sorted by Assets | **Comparative Historical Data**

						Type of Statement				
			1	5	4	3	Unqualified		12	6
				4			Reviewed		9	2
				2			Compiled		6	6
	1		3				Tax Returns		13	6
2	6		9	32	5	6	Other		53	30
	18 (4/1-9/30/23)			65 (10/1/23-3/31/24)					4/1/19-3/31/20	4/1/20-3/31/21
0-500M	500M-2MM	2-10MM	10-50MM	50-100MM	100-250MM		NUMBER OF STATEMENTS		ALL	ALL
2	7	13	43	9	9				93	50
%	%	%	%	%	%		ASSETS		%	%
		9.2	7.8				Cash & Equivalents		9.0	16.2
		19.2	16.3				Trade Receivables (net)		21.2	16.7
		36.9	41.9				Inventory		38.8	32.7
		5.0	4.2				All Other Current		2.5	1.6
		70.4	70.3				Total Current		71.6	67.1
		12.5	7.9				Fixed Assets (net)		11.6	12.8
		8.7	11.4				Intangibles (net)		14.0	15.2
		8.4	10.5				All Other Non-Current		2.9	4.8
		100.0	100.0				Total		100.0	100.0
							LIABILITIES			
		7.2	13.5				Notes Payable-Short Term		10.5	6.9
		6.2	2.6				Cur. Mat.-L.T.D.		1.8	1.3
		10.9	10.9				Trade Payables		13.7	9.5
		.0	.3				Income Taxes Payable		.3	.1
		13.8	12.3				All Other Current		8.2	7.9
		38.1	39.7				Total Current		34.6	25.7
		19.0	10.4				Long-Term Debt		13.0	20.6
		.0	.1				Deferred Taxes		.3	.2
		2.2	9.8				All Other Non-Current		5.9	8.4
		40.7	40.0				Net Worth		46.1	45.1
		100.0	100.0				Total Liabilities & Net Worth		100.0	100.0
							INCOME DATA			
		100.0	100.0				Net Sales		100.0	100.0
		37.3	39.4				Gross Profit		40.5	42.3
		33.4	30.8				Operating Expenses		33.3	34.5
		4.0	8.5				Operating Profit		7.1	7.7
		.5	3.8				All Other Expenses (net)		1.6	.1
		3.4	4.7				Profit Before Taxes		5.6	7.7
							RATIOS			
		2.8	3.6						3.5	4.9
		1.7	1.6				Current		2.5	3.3
		1.3	1.3						1.4	1.7
		1.0	1.4						1.7	2.5
		.6	.6				Quick		.9	1.3
		.2	.3						.5	.7
	8	44.4	19	19.6				29	12.6	21	17.4
	15	23.7	38	9.6			Sales/Receivables	46	8.0	37	9.8
	46	7.9	78	4.7				66	5.5	57	6.4
	68	5.4	152	2.4				91	4.0	79	4.6
	118	3.1	203	1.8			Cost of Sales/Inventory	152	2.4	126	2.9
	182	2.0	365	1.0				203	1.8	203	1.8
	9	41.1	19	18.8				21	17.4	9	41.1
	25	14.7	35	10.5			Cost of Sales/Payables	41	8.9	29	12.5
	46	8.0	99	3.7				66	5.5	55	6.6
		4.3	2.8						2.6	2.4
		7.7	3.8				Sales/Working Capital		4.4	3.6
		16.6	8.8						9.5	8.1
		24.3	12.9						22.6	76.5
		2.2	(40) 4.0				EBIT/Interest	(82)	4.6	(47)	8.3
		.6	1.8						1.5	1.9
							Net Profit + Depr., Dep.,		13.6	4.1
							Amort./Cur. Mat. L/T/D	(19) 3.3	(11) 2.7
									1.2	-3.7
		.1	.1						.1	.1
		.3	.3				Fixed/Worth		.3	.3
		NM	1.2						4.0	3.5
		.8	.8						.5	.5
		1.2	2.6				Debt/Worth		1.4	1.5
		NM	12.4						12.3	16.1
		54.0	36.8						44.7	91.8
	(10)	27.2	(36) 16.5				% Profit Before Taxes/Tangible Net Worth	(73)	21.7	(39)	42.1
		-2.9	5.9						9.8	6.8
		25.0	12.8						15.4	33.1
		4.7	6.3				% Profit Before Taxes/Total Assets		7.6	10.3
		-.8	1.9						1.8	2.1
		99.7	36.8						54.3	53.8
		39.8	16.5				Sales/Net Fixed Assets		22.5	19.5
		16.9	14.6						8.7	8.7
		3.2	1.3						2.1	2.5
		2.4	1.0				Sales/Total Assets		1.6	1.6
		1.0	.9						1.2	1.1
		.4	.6						.6	.6
	(11)	1.0	(33) 1.0				% Depr., Dep., Amort./Sales	(65)	1.8	(35)	1.5
		1.8	1.3						2.8	3.4
									1.7	1.9
							% Officers', Directors' Owners' Comp/Sales	(21)	3.4	(16)	3.3
									4.3	6.6
6157M	18915M	143021M	1453932M	914632M	1756827M		Net Sales ($)		4902209M	1809155M
828M	8939M	59272M	1198845M	626922M	1548649M		Total Assets ($)		3912350M	1672740M

M = $ thousand   MM = $ million
See Pages viii through xx for Explanation of Ratios and Data

© RMA 2024

MANUFACTURING—Sporting and Athletic Goods Manufacturing NAICS 339920

Comparative Historical Data | Current Data Sorted by Sales

								Type of Statement						
		5		12		13		Unqualified					1	10
		5		4		4		Reviewed					2	3
		1		2		2		Compiled					1	1
		6		1		4		Tax Returns					1	
		47		59		60		Other	1	4	3	4	11	37
		4/1/21-3/31/22 ALL		4/1/22-3/31/23 ALL		4/1/23-3/31/24 ALL			18 (4/1-9/30/23)			65 (10/1/23-3/31/24)		
									0-1MM	1-3MM	3-5MM	5-10MM	10-25MM	25MM & OVER
		64		78		83		NUMBER OF STATEMENTS	1	7	3	5	16	51
		%		%		%		ASSETS	%	%	%	%	%	%
		12.5		10.6		9.4		Cash & Equivalents					8.9	8.9
		19.6		18.4		16.7		Trade Receivables (net)					16.2	19.0
		35.7		37.9		39.4		Inventory					38.6	39.5
		4.9		5.1		4.1		All Other Current					5.1	3.4
		72.7		72.1		69.6		Total Current					68.7	70.8
		9.4		9.1		10.5		Fixed Assets (net)					7.6	10.3
		11.3		11.7		10.8		Intangibles (net)					16.7	9.2
		6.6		7.1		9.1		All Other Non-Current					7.1	9.7
		100.0		100.0		100.0		Total					100.0	100.0
								LIABILITIES						
		10.0		10.7		10.3		Notes Payable-Short Term					6.8	12.1
		2.1		1.5		2.5		Cur. Mat.-L.T.D.					1.7	2.3
		11.6		12.5		10.0		Trade Payables					8.7	11.6
		.2		.1		.4		Income Taxes Payable					.3	.6
		10.7		10.3		10.8		All Other Current					13.7	11.2
		34.6		35.2		34.1		Total Current					31.2	37.7
		22.6		12.6		14.5		Long-Term Debt					13.6	11.5
		.3		.2		.0		Deferred Taxes					.1	.0
		8.4		7.1		6.6		All Other Non-Current					9.0	6.7
		34.1		45.0		44.8		Net Worth					46.0	44.1
		100.0		100.0		100.0		Total Liabilities & Net Worth					100.0	100.0
								INCOME DATA						
		100.0		100.0		100.0		Net Sales					100.0	100.0
		36.8		37.0		38.9		Gross Profit					41.1	36.5
		31.0		31.2		31.4		Operating Expenses					34.0	27.5
		5.9		5.8		7.5		Operating Profit					7.2	9.0
		.2		.6		3.0		All Other Expenses (net)					5.5	2.6
		5.6		5.2		4.6		Profit Before Taxes					1.7	6.4
								RATIOS						
		4.2		4.2		5.2							11.0	4.2
		2.7		2.2		1.8		Current					2.1	1.7
		1.4		1.4		1.4							1.5	1.3
		2.0		1.7		2.1							4.1	2.0
		.9		.7		.6		Quick					.7	.6
		.5		.4		.3							.2	.4
28		13.0	25	14.8	17	21.4						8	47.4	29	12.5
44		8.3	40	9.2	39	9.4		Sales/Receivables				21	17.4	46	8.0
65		5.6	61	6.0	62	5.9						55	6.6	78	4.7
69		5.3	81	4.5	94	3.9						126	2.9	101	3.6
135		2.7	152	2.4	166	2.2		Cost of Sales/Inventory				215	1.7	174	2.1
166		2.2	215	1.7	304	1.2						365	1.0	304	1.2
12		29.5	20	18.6	17	21.4						9	41.9	19	18.8
31		11.8	36	10.1	27	13.3		Cost of Sales/Payables				26	13.9	35	10.5
56		6.5	68	5.4	64	5.7						42	8.7	85	4.3
		2.4		2.6		2.8							2.3	2.8
		3.8		4.4		4.4		Sales/Working Capital					4.0	3.7
		9.9		10.0		9.1							10.9	8.8
		32.5		46.7		14.0							35.6	10.4
(56)		9.8	(70)	6.2	(77)	2.7		EBIT/Interest				(14)	6.8	(49)	3.9
		2.9		1.5		.6							1.4	.9
		53.8		76.7		74.5		Net Profit + Depr., Dep.,						
(10)		20.8	(13)	12.6	(13)	2.4		Amort./Cur. Mat. L/T/D						
		1.2		2.5		-.7								
		.1		.1		.1							.0	.1
		.2		.3		.3		Fixed/Worth					.5	.3
		2.7		1.1		1.0							-.2	.7
		.6		.6		.5							.7	.4
		1.6		1.5		1.9		Debt/Worth					1.5	2.0
		18.2		10.4		8.8							-3.5	5.4
		43.9		60.3		47.0							47.4	40.7
(49)		22.3	(63)	17.5	(70)	16.5		% Profit Before Taxes/Tangible Net Worth				(10)	15.3	(47)	16.5
		8.8		4.9		-3.3							7.1	-2.2
		18.9		21.6		17.8		% Profit Before Taxes/Total Assets					19.1	17.7
		8.8		8.8		5.1							4.4	6.4
		2.6		.7		-.8							.3	.1
		64.0		75.0		39.8							75.7	33.8
		29.5		26.2		18.4		Sales/Net Fixed Assets					24.2	15.6
		13.2		11.1		12.2							10.5	9.5
		2.2		2.1		2.1							2.8	1.7
		1.5		1.6		1.2		Sales/Total Assets					.9	1.2
		1.2		1.1		.9							.8	1.0
		.7		.7		.6							.6	.6
(38)		1.0	(52)	1.1	(58)	1.1		% Depr., Dep., Amort./Sales				(10)	1.6	(39)	1.1
		2.6		2.0		1.7							2.6	1.4
		3.5		.3		.4								
(11)		5.1	(15)	.5	(16)	1.6		% Officers', Directors' Owners' Comp/Sales						
		6.5		2.7		4.4								
		3417271M		4091453M		4293484M		Net Sales ($)	947M	12310M	11355M	35812M	273641M	3959419M
		2260482M		3086672M		3443455M		Total Assets ($)	1868M	9395M	3346M	16070M	243883M	3168893M

© RMA 2024
M = $ thousand   MM = $ million
See Pages viii through xx for Explanation of Ratios and Data

MANUFACTURING—Sign Manufacturing NAICS 339950

Current Data Sorted by Assets | Comparative Historical Data

							Type of Statement		
		2	3	2	1		Unqualified	10	7
		7	7	2			Reviewed	17	6
		12	1				Compiled	6	4
4	8	5			1		Tax Returns	41	20
4	19	14	15	6	5		Other	90	50
	18 (4/1-9/30/23)		100 (10/1/23-3/31/24)					4/1/19-3/31/20	4/1/20-3/31/21
0-500M	500M-2MM	2-10MM	10-50MM	50-100MM	100-250MM		NUMBER OF STATEMENTS	164 ALL	87 ALL
8	27	40	26	10	7				
%	%	%	%	%	%		ASSETS	%	%
	33.0	17.5	7.9	16.2			Cash & Equivalents	14.3	24.7
	16.6	32.2	30.7	25.1			Trade Receivables (net)	28.1	27.3
	10.2	11.7	26.2	23.8			Inventory	14.2	11.3
	3.1	6.4	4.0	3.7			All Other Current	3.2	4.9
	62.8	67.8	68.8	68.8			Total Current	59.8	68.1
	18.3	19.8	15.1	9.5			Fixed Assets (net)	22.4	17.8
	9.2	3.4	8.5	17.3			Intangibles (net)	11.2	8.4
	9.7	9.0	7.5	4.3			All Other Non-Current	6.7	5.7
	100.0	100.0	100.0	100.0			Total	100.0	100.0
							LIABILITIES		
	10.0	5.3	7.1	13.1			Notes Payable-Short Term	9.7	9.1
	1.9	1.7	1.8	6.0			Cur. Mat.-L.T.D.	4.1	4.1
	5.1	10.3	11.6	8.0			Trade Payables	11.7	9.0
	.0	.6	.1	.0			Income Taxes Payable	.1	.0
	16.9	14.1	21.1	16.7			All Other Current	18.3	18.7
	34.0	32.0	41.7	43.7			Total Current	43.9	41.0
	16.6	18.2	15.3	9.2			Long-Term Debt	22.1	20.7
	.0	.0	.3	.0			Deferred Taxes	.1	.1
	.5	3.2	8.7	7.7			All Other Non-Current	6.5	3.1
	48.9	46.5	34.0	39.4			Net Worth	27.4	35.1
	100.0	100.0	100.0	100.0			Total Liabilities & Net Worth	100.0	100.0
							INCOME DATA		
	100.0	100.0	100.0	100.0			Net Sales	100.0	100.0
	60.8	40.5	31.0	23.4			Gross Profit	42.9	40.4
	53.7	33.5	22.8	18.5			Operating Expenses	38.0	37.8
	7.1	7.0	8.2	4.8			Operating Profit	4.9	2.7
	-1.4	.7	1.0	4.7			All Other Expenses (net)	1.0	-1.6
	8.4	6.3	7.2	.1			Profit Before Taxes	3.9	4.2
							RATIOS		
	3.6	4.2	2.2	2.6				2.3	3.3
	1.6	2.2	1.5	1.9			Current	1.4	1.6
	1.0	1.4	1.3	.8				1.0	1.1
	3.5	2.8	1.5	2.3				1.7	2.5
	1.1	1.7	.9	.8			Quick	1.0	1.2
	.8	1.1	.6	.4				.7	.8
0	UND	32	11.4	48	7.6	36	10.1	27	13.7	26	14.1
24	15.3	55	6.6	60	6.1	52	7.0	Sales/Receivables	42	8.6	48	7.6
36	10.2	70	5.2	74	4.9	72	5.1		63	5.8	72	5.1
0	UND	0	UND	18	19.9	0	UND		8	45.2	3	131.3
9	40.5	24	15.1	73	5.0	56	6.5	Cost of Sales/Inventory	32	11.4	17	21.4
57	6.4	54	6.7	118	3.1	114	3.2		64	5.7	48	7.6
0	UND	13	28.0	19	19.1	9	39.4		11	33.2	8	43.8
11	33.3	23	15.9	34	10.7	20	18.4	Cost of Sales/Payables	24	14.9	19	19.2
22	16.3	44	8.3	44	8.3	28	13.2		45	8.2	38	9.6
	4.3	4.4	5.5	3.2				6.2	5.1
	11.8	6.8	7.8	3.9			Sales/Working Capital	11.5	8.5
	-310.7	11.3	10.7	-23.8				-340.1	31.0
	41.7	76.4	33.2					14.7	23.6
(17)	8.8	(34)	11.9	(25)	7.2		EBIT/Interest	(155)	4.0	(74)	6.2
	1.5	3.1	1.9					1.0	.1
							Net Profit + Depr., Dep., Amort./Cur. Mat. L/T/D	11.4	13.7
								(22) 3.3	(11) 2.6
								1.2	.3
	.1	.1	.2	.1				.3	.1
	.4	.5	.4	.3			Fixed/Worth	1.0	.6
	-6.3	1.1	1.4	-.3				-5.7	2.5
	.2	.6	1.1	.7				1.0	.7
	.9	1.1	2.7	1.0			Debt/Worth	2.7	2.4
	-22.8	2.8	7.4	-4.2				-22.2	14.2
	93.6	65.5	56.1					65.6	66.3
(19)	34.7	(37)	33.9	(23)	26.0		% Profit Before Taxes/Tangible Net Worth	(119)	25.0	(69)	26.2
	1.8	6.4	12.8					4.8	8.1
	42.0	25.0	19.2	10.2				17.1	23.2
	14.5	16.9	6.9	4.9			% Profit Before Taxes/Total Assets	7.7	9.1
	1.9	2.0	3.3	-12.6				.1	-2.6
	133.4	43.0	35.9	121.6				42.8	65.1
	19.5	17.7	18.0	16.1			Sales/Net Fixed Assets	14.5	14.8
	10.6	6.0	8.0	9.0				6.9	7.4
	4.1	2.6	2.2	2.3				3.3	2.9
	2.6	2.2	1.9	1.2			Sales/Total Assets	2.3	2.0
	2.2	1.6	1.5	1.2				1.6	1.6
			1.1	1.0				1.0	1.1
		(25)	1.9	(19)	1.3		% Depr., Dep., Amort./Sales	(99)	1.8	(57)	1.8
			3.4	2.7				3.8	3.2
	2.1	1.2						2.3	2.3
(17)	3.5	(17)	2.0				% Officers', Directors' Owners' Comp/Sales	(60)	4.5	(35)	4.3
	5.4	5.2						7.3	11.6
8064M	99410M	449501M	1147962M	1169850M	1832146M		Net Sales ($)	4982512M	1582220M
3058M	31911M	209116M	622582M	713287M	1397471M		Total Assets ($)	2888957M	1001640M

M = $ thousand   MM = $ million
See Pages viii through xx for Explanation of Ratios and Data

© RMA 2024

MANUFACTURING—Sign Manufacturing NAICS 339950

Comparative Historical Data

								Current Data Sorted by Sales				
				Type of Statement								
7		7	8	Unqualified				1	1	1	5	
8		14	16	Reviewed					3	4	9	
6		5	13	Compiled				1	3	8	1	
14		18	18	Tax Returns	3	5	3	2	4	1		
51		74	63	Other	3	10	8	9	12	21		
4/1/21-		4/1/22-	4/1/23-			18 (4/1-9/30/23)			100 (10/1/23-3/31/24)			
3/31/22		3/31/23	3/31/24									
ALL		ALL	ALL		0-1MM	1-3MM	3-5MM	5-10MM	10-25MM	25MM & OVER		
86		118	118	**NUMBER OF STATEMENTS**	6	15	13	18	29	37		
%		%	%	**ASSETS**	%	%	%	%	%	%		
24.8		20.4	18.6	Cash & Equivalents	22.4	32.1	23.6	18.2	10.0			
23.2		22.2	25.5	Trade Receivables (net)	15.1	21.7	27.9	30.5	28.0			
14.8		16.3	14.7	Inventory	7.8	12.9	7.3	14.7	22.4			
5.3		5.6	5.5	All Other Current	3.3	5.0	7.3	4.9	7.1			
68.1		64.5	64.4	Total Current	48.6	71.7	66.2	68.3	67.5			
19.7		17.5	17.6	Fixed Assets (net)	17.6	20.6	21.4	15.7	14.0			
7.8		9.4	10.0	Intangibles (net)	21.3	3.7	2.8	4.5	13.0			
4.4		8.5	8.1	All Other Non-Current	12.5	3.9	9.7	11.5	5.5			
100.0		100.0	100.0	Total	100.0	100.0	100.0	100.0	100.0			
				LIABILITIES								
7.6		9.7	7.0	Notes Payable-Short Term	8.6	11.7	5.1	7.4	6.3			
3.9		2.8	2.3	Cur. Mat.-L.T.D.	3.3	.6	1.2	2.2	3.5			
10.4		8.3	9.3	Trade Payables	8.4	3.2	13.7	9.3	10.5			
.1		.3	.2	Income Taxes Payable	.0	1.1	.6	.0	.0			
19.0		19.2	18.9	All Other Current	22.9	14.6	11.4	17.0	22.9			
41.2		40.4	37.6	Total Current	43.1	31.2	32.0	35.8	43.2			
19.9		19.0	17.3	Long-Term Debt	24.9	16.4	19.2	15.0	17.6			
.1		.1	.1	Deferred Taxes	.0	.0	.0	.2	.2			
5.8		4.4	5.5	All Other Non-Current	13.2	3.6	1.7	5.5	5.8			
33.0		36.0	39.5	Net Worth	18.7	48.8	47.2	43.5	33.2			
100.0		100.0	100.0	Total Liabilities & Net Worth	100.0	100.0	100.0	100.0	100.0			
				INCOME DATA								
100.0		100.0	100.0	Net Sales	100.0	100.0	100.0	100.0	100.0			
40.7		41.5	43.4	Gross Profit	66.8	54.8	42.3	36.4	30.4			
36.6		36.3	35.9	Operating Expenses	57.1	46.0	36.8	29.7	22.3			
4.1		5.2	7.5	Operating Profit	9.7	8.8	5.5	6.7	8.0			
-2.4		-.2	1.0	All Other Expenses (net)	.1	-1.5	-.9	1.3	3.4			
6.5		5.4	6.5	Profit Before Taxes	9.6	10.3	6.4	5.4	4.6			
				RATIOS								
	3.6		3.4		3.2		Current	4.2	7.4	5.0	2.8	2.3
	1.8		1.7		1.8			1.1	2.9	2.1	1.8	1.5
	1.2		1.2		1.2			.8	1.6	1.1	1.3	1.3
	2.4		2.3		2.4		Quick	4.2	5.1	2.9	2.5	1.5
	1.1		1.1		1.2			.8	2.0	1.4	1.4	.8
	.6		.6		.7			.3	1.1	1.0	.7	.6
18	20.4	19	18.8	24	15.5		Sales/Receivables	0 UND	23 16.2	24 15.2	28 13.1	37 9.8
37	9.9	44	8.3	42	8.7			22 16.4	36 10.2	41 8.8	43 8.5	58 6.3
63	5.8	65	5.6	68	5.4			33 11.0	66 5.5	81 4.5	68 5.4	74 4.9
0	UND	4	86.7	0	UND		Cost of Sales/Inventory	0 UND	0 UND	0 UND	2 209.3	22 16.6
40	9.1	40	9.2	31	11.6			12 30.9	53 6.9	4 92.8	26 14.1	56 6.5
74	4.9	73	5.0	74	4.9			79 4.6	130 2.8	36 10.2	50 7.3	99 3.7
4	88.2	8	45.6	10	36.4		Cost of Sales/Payables	0 UND	0 UND	0 UND	12 29.7	17 21.8
23	15.7	23	15.6	22	16.9			13 27.7	11 33.3	28 12.9	20 18.1	26 14.1
37	9.9	41	9.0	39	9.3			43 8.4	17 21.1	74 4.9	38 9.6	40 9.1
	4.5		4.7		4.6		Sales/Working Capital	7.5	3.4	4.8	6.0	3.9
	7.0		8.0		7.9			41.7	4.1	11.3	8.4	7.3
	24.5		25.0		21.2			-26.8	9.1	32.5	10.8	14.2
	33.1		27.5		36.9		EBIT/Interest	114.2	38.7	59.2	59.6	25.1
(67)	9.8	(96)	6.4	(94)	7.5			(14) 11.2	(10) 14.5	(12) 5.0	(25) 7.2	(33) 3.5
	2.4		1.9		1.5			1.4	4.6	-.5	1.8	1.0
			15.2		9.7		Net Profit + Depr., Dep.,					
		(13)	7.7	(13)	3.6		Amort./Cur. Mat. L/T/D					
					2.3		.2					
	.2		.2		.1		Fixed/Worth	.1	.1	.1	.1	.2
	.5		.5		.5			-5.5	.4	.3	.5	.3
	3.5		5.6		4.2			-.4	.9	3.0	1.1	3.1
	.5		.5		.6		Debt/Worth	.2	.6	.3	.7	1.0
	2.1		2.1		1.5			-22.8	.9	1.0	1.3	2.4
	16.2		35.9		18.5			-2.9	2.1	8.2	3.8	31.6
	83.4		59.4		57.2		% Profit Before Taxes/Tangible	77.2	83.7	45.9	47.6	
(67)	41.2	(91)	33.3	(94)	26.1		Net Worth	(12) 35.0	(16) 46.3	(26) 30.8	(29) 21.7	
	12.2		10.0		6.5				12.0	5.8	4.9	10.7
	29.9		22.6		25.2		% Profit Before Taxes/Total	42.0	32.6	29.6	25.0	15.7
	11.1		11.1		10.2		Assets	14.5	23.9	12.9	12.0	5.4
	2.0		1.5		1.8			1.9	7.0	.8	1.5	.9
	34.5		37.7		45.9		Sales/Net Fixed Assets	163.6	54.0	81.3	42.0	46.2
	16.8		16.3		18.3			19.5	10.7	18.3	18.2	18.5
	6.7		7.9		7.4			10.0	4.2	6.4	7.1	9.4
	2.8		2.6		2.6		Sales/Total Assets	3.0	2.6	4.7	2.7	2.2
	2.2		2.0		2.1			2.4	2.2	2.2	2.3	1.9
	1.6		1.4		1.5			2.1	1.5	1.6	1.8	1.3
	1.1		1.0		1.0		% Depr., Dep., Amort./Sales			1.2	1.2	.8
(53)	2.0	(71)	1.6	(59)	1.9			(10) 2.2	(20) 2.0	(21) 1.1		
	3.3		2.7		3.2				4.3	3.1	1.8	
	2.1		2.1		1.3		% Officers', Directors'	2.2		.6		
(27)	5.6	(41)	3.8	(49)	2.6		Owners' Comp/Sales	(11) 3.0		(10) 1.8		
	8.0		6.8		5.4			4.1		2.5		
1918723M		3386175M		4706933M			Net Sales ($)	4103M	29635M	47826M	134420M	455468M	4035481M
1324399M		2290839M		2977425M			Total Assets ($)	2725M	12619M	26664M	64621M	218781M	2652015M

© RMA 2024
M = $ thousand   MM = $ million
See Pages viii through xx for Explanation of Ratios and Data

MANUFACTURING—Gasket, Packing, and Sealing Device Manufacturing NAICS 339991

Current Data Sorted by Assets

0-500M	500M-2MM	2-10MM	10-50MM	50-100MM	100-250MM		Type of Statement			
							Unqualified		3	3
		1	3				Reviewed		13	5
		2	2		4		Compiled		5	5
	1	8	1		1		Tax Returns		6	3
1	6 (4/1-9/30/23)		9 26 (10/1/23-3/31/24)				Other		14	8
									4/1/19-	4/1/20-
									3/31/20	3/31/21
		11	15		5		NUMBER OF STATEMENTS		ALL 41	ALL 24
%	%	%	%	%	%		ASSETS		%	%
		19.5	11.8				Cash & Equivalents		12.8	13.5
D		25.5	18.7	D			Trade Receivables (net)		28.9	25.2
A		30.1	24.0	A			Inventory		23.1	24.5
T		1.6	1.5	T			All Other Current		2.5	.8
A		76.7	56.0	A			Total Current		67.3	64.0
		17.1	24.1				Fixed Assets (net)		18.9	10.5
N		4.2	17.7	N			Intangibles (net)		9.7	16.6
O		2.0	2.2	O			All Other Non-Current		4.1	8.9
T		100.0	100.0	T			Total		100.0	100.0
A				A			LIABILITIES			
V		3.5	5.1	V			Notes Payable-Short Term		5.0	5.6
A		2.9	1.8	A			Cur. Mat.-L.T.D.		4.7	5.1
I		10.4	7.1	I			Trade Payables		12.1	9.2
L		1.7	.8	L			Income Taxes Payable		.1	.1
A		3.8	6.9	A			All Other Current		9.3	6.9
B		22.4	21.7	B			Total Current		31.2	27.0
L		15.7	6.1	L			Long-Term Debt		18.6	17.5
E		.5	1.2	E			Deferred Taxes		.9	.4
		2.3	.9				All Other Non-Current		5.6	5.1
		59.1	70.0				Net Worth		43.7	50.0
		100.0	100.0				Total Liabilties & Net Worth		100.0	100.0
							INCOME DATA			
		100.0	100.0				Net Sales		100.0	100.0
		45.2	35.1				Gross Profit		35.7	34.0
		31.0	22.7				Operating Expenses		29.3	27.6
		14.3	12.4				Operating Profit		6.4	6.4
		1.1	.4				All Other Expenses (net)		.9	1.1
		13.2	12.0				Profit Before Taxes		5.5	5.3
							RATIOS			
		7.4	5.5						3.8	5.3
		4.0	2.2				Current		2.6	2.6
		3.2	1.9						1.5	1.8
		3.4	2.9						2.3	3.1
		2.6	1.6				Quick		1.6	1.5
		.9	.8						.8	1.2
	33	11.2	40 9.2					35	10.4	29 12.7
	34	10.8	45 8.2				Sales/Receivables	46	8.0	42 8.6
	51	7.1	54 6.7					59	6.2	63 5.8
	94	3.9	51 7.2					32	11.4	39 9.3
	146	2.5	85 4.3				Cost of Sales/Inventory	54	6.7	70 5.2
	192	1.9	146 2.5					111	3.3	101 3.6
	5	66.8	16 23.1					18	20.8	15 24.3
	21	17.6	16 22.3				Cost of Sales/Payables	27	13.4	17 17.7
	111	3.3	45 8.1					38	9.7	33 11.2
		2.4	3.2						4.0	3.0
		2.8	4.4				Sales/Working Capital		4.9	4.2
		4.6	7.5						15.5	8.0
			35.7						23.6	16.0
		(12)	23.3				EBIT/Interest	(37)	4.8	(21) 5.9
			14.6						2.0	.0
							Net Profit + Depr., Dep.,		13.9	
							Amort./Cur. Mat. L/T/D	(11)	4.1	
									2.0	
		.1	.3						.2	.1
		.3	.4				Fixed/Worth		.5	.4
		.5	.6						8.7	NM
		.4	.4						.5	.6
		.5	.6				Debt/Worth		1.3	1.3
		1.0	.9						21.1	NM
		46.6	54.6						43.1	78.2
	(10)	26.5	23.0				% Profit Before Taxes/Tangible	(33)	27.1	(18) 29.9
		14.6	13.3				Net Worth		9.7	11.9
		25.5	20.9						17.6	19.4
		13.4	12.0				% Profit Before Taxes/Total		8.7	8.1
		7.6	9.1				Assets		2.6	.2
		23.1	11.7						40.0	79.7
		11.5	8.3				Sales/Net Fixed Assets		12.0	28.9
		6.2	4.0						6.6	7.6
		2.2	1.5						3.2	3.2
		1.6	1.5				Sales/Total Assets		1.8	2.2
		1.3	1.2						1.4	1.0
			1.9						1.1	.6
		(11)	2.8				% Depr., Dep., Amort./Sales	(29)	1.7	(17) 1.6
			3.0						2.8	4.2
									2.7	
							% Officers', Directors'	(19)	3.6	
							Owners' Comp/Sales		7.9	
	6921M	127597M	490337M	897212M			Net Sales ($)		1458457M	472942M
	1885M	57209M	333048M	854321M			Total Assets ($)		1014955M	430642M

M = $ thousand   MM = $ million
See Pages viii through xx for Explanation of Ratios and Data

© RMA 2024

MANUFACTURING—Gasket, Packing, and Sealing Device Manufacturing NAICS 339991

Comparative Historical Data / Current Data Sorted by Sales

Comparative Historical Data			Type of Statement	Current Data Sorted by Sales					
2	4	7	Unqualified				1	1	6
2	5	2	Reviewed					1	1
1		2	Compiled			1		1	
4	4	2	Tax Returns			1	4	5	
11	17	19	Other	1	1				8
4/1/21-3/31/22 ALL	4/1/22-3/31/23 ALL	4/1/23-3/31/24 ALL		6 (4/1-9/30/23)			26 (10/1/23-3/31/24)		
				0-1MM	1-3MM	3-5MM	5-10MM	10-25MM	25MM & OVER
20	30	32	NUMBER OF STATEMENTS	1	2	6	8		15
%	%	%	ASSETS	%	%	%	%	%	%
18.1	9.8	14.2	Cash & Equivalents						11.9
27.9	22.9	21.4	Trade Receivables (net)						19.3
19.6	28.1	25.0	Inventory						20.9
2.8	3.1	1.7	All Other Current						2.1
68.4	64.0	62.2	Total Current						54.3
17.1	23.7	20.5	Fixed Assets (net)						19.0
10.1	7.5	13.9	Intangibles (net)						22.0
4.5	4.8	3.5	All Other Non-Current						4.7
100.0	100.0	100.0	Total						100.0
			LIABILITIES						
4.6	5.6	3.8	Notes Payable-Short Term						.6
2.3	2.8	2.4	Cur. Mat.-L.T.D.						2.8
13.1	9.8	8.4	Trade Payables						7.7
.3	.1	1.0	Income Taxes Payable						.3
7.4	8.4	6.2	All Other Current						9.5
27.7	26.6	21.9	Total Current						20.9
17.4	15.5	12.0	Long-Term Debt						12.2
.7	.5	1.0	Deferred Taxes						1.6
3.6	4.1	2.2	All Other Non-Current						2.6
50.6	53.3	62.9	Net Worth						62.7
100.0	100.0	100.0	Total Liabilities & Net Worth						100.0
			INCOME DATA						
100.0	100.0	100.0	Net Sales						100.0
41.8	36.3	38.8	Gross Profit						33.9
29.6	27.2	26.5	Operating Expenses						22.2
12.3	9.0	12.3	Operating Profit						11.7
-.7	.7	.9	All Other Expenses (net)						1.0
12.9	8.3	11.3	Profit Before Taxes						10.7
			RATIOS						
5.2	4.7	5.4							3.6
2.5	3.1	3.2	Current						2.2
1.7	2.3	1.8							1.8
3.3	2.3	2.9							2.5
1.5	1.4	1.6	Quick						1.6
1.1	.9	.8							.8
32 11.4	32 11.5	33 10.9						38	9.6
45 8.1	45 8.1	45 8.2	Sales/Receivables					45	8.1
54 6.7	60 6.1	54 6.8						54	6.7
40 9.2	43 8.5	59 6.2						31	11.6
64 5.7	99 3.7	99 3.7	Cost of Sales/Inventory					81	4.5
104 3.5	130 2.8	152 2.4						140	2.6
23 16.2	16 22.7	16 23.2						16	23.0
38 9.6	21 17.4	22 16.9	Cost of Sales/Payables					25	14.4
57 6.4	35 10.5	40 9.2						40	9.2
3.8	3.2	2.8							3.2
4.6	4.5	4.4	Sales/Working Capital						5.5
7.8	9.3	6.9							8.0
51.5	106.5	40.0							50.7
(15) 13.5	(27) 22.1	(26) 19.3	EBIT/Interest					(13)	27.1
3.4	6.4	5.5							9.9
			Net Profit + Depr., Dep., Amort./Cur. Mat. L/T/D						
.1	.2	.2							.3
.4	.5	.4	Fixed/Worth						.4
1.3	1.3	.6							.6
.4	.4	.4							.5
1.4	.8	.7	Debt/Worth						.7
4.9	2.6	1.0							1.9
97.0	42.3	50.5	% Profit Before Taxes/Tangible Net Worth						66.6
(18) 43.7	(28) 30.1	(29) 24.8						(13)	32.7
27.0	15.0	14.2							17.7
59.2	21.2	21.9	% Profit Before Taxes/Total Assets						20.9
13.4	12.3	11.8							13.4
8.2	6.4	7.6							9.1
91.9	26.0	15.1							12.1
21.9	8.4	8.3	Sales/Net Fixed Assets						8.3
4.5	4.3	4.1							4.0
3.0	2.3	1.9							1.8
1.8	1.7	1.4	Sales/Total Assets						1.5
1.1	1.3	1.1							1.1
1.2	.7	1.8							1.5
(12) 2.5	(24) 1.8	(22) 2.6	% Depr., Dep., Amort./Sales					(11)	2.9
3.1	3.2	3.0							3.0
			% Officers', Directors' Owners' Comp/Sales						
584834M	1404624M	1522067M	Net Sales ($)	1134M	7747M	43413M	134445M		1335328M
410253M	852145M	1246463M	Total Assets ($)	4856M	5171M	25326M	100351M		1110759M

Data Not Available column applies to 0-1MM through 10-25MM ranges where noted.

© RMA 2024 M = $ thousand MM = $ million
See Pages viii through xx for Explanation of Ratios and Data

MANUFACTURING—Musical Instrument Manufacturing NAICS 339992

Current Data Sorted by Assets

0-500M	500M-2MM	2-10MM	10-50MM	50-100MM	100-250MM
1			1		1
			2		
1					
1		2	2		
	7 (4/1-9/30/23)	2	13 (10/1/23-3/31/24)	3	4
3	4	4	5	3	5
%	%	%	%	%	%

Comparative Historical Data

	4/1/19-3/31/20 ALL	4/1/20-3/31/21 ALL
Type of Statement		
Unqualified	2	
Reviewed	4	3
Compiled	1	
Tax Returns	5	
Other	9	5
NUMBER OF STATEMENTS	21	8
	%	%

	Current Data	Historical
ASSETS		
Cash & Equivalents		16.2
Trade Receivables (net)		14.2
Inventory		38.0
All Other Current		6.3
Total Current		74.5
Fixed Assets (net)		10.0
Intangibles (net)		8.2
All Other Non-Current		7.2
Total		100.0
LIABILITIES		
Notes Payable-Short Term		6.2
Cur. Mat.-L.T.D.		1.2
Trade Payables		7.8
Income Taxes Payable		.2
All Other Current		8.0
Total Current		23.3
Long-Term Debt		10.3
Deferred Taxes		.1
All Other Non-Current		6.7
Net Worth		59.6
Total Liabilities & Net Worth		100.0
INCOME DATA		
Net Sales		100.0
Gross Profit		36.9
Operating Expenses		29.9
Operating Profit		6.9
All Other Expenses (net)		-.4
Profit Before Taxes		7.3
RATIOS		
Current		5.9 / 4.1 / 2.4
Quick		3.1 / 1.5 / .8
Sales/Receivables		16 23.0 / 36 10.1 / 51 7.1
Cost of Sales/Inventory		104 3.5 / 166 2.2 / 215 1.7
Cost of Sales/Payables		18 20.8 / 26 13.9 / 41 9.0
Sales/Working Capital		1.6 / 2.2 / 5.3
EBIT/Interest		48.1 / (16) 6.6 / 2.7
Net Profit + Depr., Dep., Amort./Cur. Mat. L/T/D		
Fixed/Worth		.1 / .2 / .3
Debt/Worth		.2 / .6 / 3.7
% Profit Before Taxes/Tangible Net Worth		35.0 / (19) 15.2 / 1.1
% Profit Before Taxes/Total Assets		17.5 / 9.3 / .7
Sales/Net Fixed Assets		76.4 / 11.5 / 9.2
Sales/Total Assets		1.6 / 1.3 / 1.1
% Depr., Dep., Amort./Sales		.6 / (15) 2.9 / 3.3
% Officers', Directors' Owners' Comp/Sales		
Net Sales ($)	2131M / 17035M / 179454M / 263532M / 836032M	907285M / 265718M
Total Assets ($)	846M / 13614M / 135131M / 170606M / 1021949M	811014M / 384468M

M = $ thousand   MM = $ million
See Pages viii through xx for Explanation of Ratios and Data

© RMA 2024

MANUFACTURING—Musical Instrument Manufacturing NAICS 339992

Comparative Historical Data / Current Data Sorted by Sales

							Type of Statement							
		1					Unqualified	1				1	1	
		4		3			Reviewed						2	
		1		1		3	Compiled	1						
		2		2		1	Tax Returns			1				
		8		11		3	Other		1	1	1			9
		4/1/21-3/31/22 ALL		4/1/22-3/31/23 ALL		4/1/23-3/31/24 ALL		7 (4/1-9/30/23)			13 (10/1/23-3/31/24)			
							NUMBER OF STATEMENTS	0-1MM	1-3MM	3-5MM	5-10MM	10-25MM	25MM & OVER	
		16		17		20		2	2	2	1	1	12	
		%		%		%	ASSETS	%	%	%	%	%	%	
		23.1		14.8		16.8	Cash & Equivalents						8.0	
		12.2		9.5		11.5	Trade Receivables (net)						15.1	
		36.4		44.8		36.9	Inventory						35.8	
		3.6		2.5		3.2	All Other Current						2.2	
		75.3		71.5		68.3	Total Current						61.0	
		12.3		15.1		11.3	Fixed Assets (net)						14.2	
		5.0		4.0		3.3	Intangibles (net)						1.4	
		7.4		9.3		17.2	All Other Non-Current						23.4	
		100.0		100.0		100.0	Total						100.0	
							LIABILITIES							
		4.7		6.3		3.2	Notes Payable-Short Term						2.9	
		1.2		1.0		1.5	Cur. Mat.-L.T.D.						.4	
		10.6		5.9		5.7	Trade Payables						6.4	
		.3		.1		.5	Income Taxes Payable						.8	
		13.5		8.3		8.5	All Other Current						10.2	
		30.4		21.6		19.4	Total Current						20.7	
		7.1		10.7		11.8	Long-Term Debt						3.9	
		.0		.0		.0	Deferred Taxes						.0	
		8.1		5.3		17.2	All Other Non-Current						28.2	
		54.3		62.5		51.8	Net Worth						47.2	
		100.0		100.0		100.0	Total Liabilities & Net Worth						100.0	
							INCOME DATA							
		100.0		100.0		100.0	Net Sales						100.0	
		36.0		36.5		37.0	Gross Profit						36.2	
		29.8		31.4		27.5	Operating Expenses						26.5	
		6.2		5.2		9.5	Operating Profit						9.7	
		-2.4		-.4		.7	All Other Expenses (net)						.9	
		8.7		5.6		8.8	Profit Before Taxes						8.8	
							RATIOS							
		5.1		6.0		5.9							4.5	
		3.2		4.4		3.5	Current						2.8	
		2.1		2.4		2.3							2.2	
		2.2		2.2		2.9							2.0	
		1.3		1.6		1.3	Quick						1.0	
		.7		.6		.8							.8	
16	22.9	14	26.4	7	52.7							23	15.6	
29	12.4	25	14.7	26	14.1	Sales/Receivables						43	8.5	
45	8.2	46	8.0	49	7.5							55	6.6	
83	4.4	159	2.3	130	2.8							140	2.6	
166	2.2	192	1.9	174	2.1	Cost of Sales/Inventory						174	2.1	
228	1.6	243	1.5	203	1.8							203	1.8	
14	25.3	6	63.2	13	29.1							17	21.0	
30	12.1	22	16.6	23	15.9	Cost of Sales/Payables						26	14.0	
52	7.0	36	10.2	34	10.6							37	9.8	
		1.7		1.9		1.9							2.0	
		3.7		2.3		3.1	Sales/Working Capital						3.7	
		4.9		3.5		4.2							4.3	
		45.9		30.0		80.3							549.7	
	(14)	20.6	(14)	15.7	(17)	33.0	EBIT/Interest						41.7	
		9.0		3.3		2.2							7.5	
							Net Profit + Depr., Dep., Amort./Cur. Mat. L/T/D							
		.1		.1		.1							.1	
		.2		.2		.2	Fixed/Worth						.2	
		.8		.4		.4							.4	
		.4		.2		.3							.3	
		.7		.6		.6	Debt/Worth						.7	
		1.7		1.3		1.3							1.2	
		63.9		34.8		30.8							30.8	
	(15)	17.5	(16)	9.8	(19)	14.3	% Profit Before Taxes/Tangible Net Worth					(11)	14.4	
		9.8		3.4		7.8							10.8	
		17.5		10.6		18.7							18.7	
		8.5		6.8		7.7	% Profit Before Taxes/Total Assets						7.5	
		6.9		1.6		4.1							5.2	
		28.2		26.0		36.7							21.5	
		16.6		13.0		19.7	Sales/Net Fixed Assets						12.8	
		9.2		5.2		7.2							4.9	
		2.0		1.6		1.7							1.6	
		1.4		1.5		1.4	Sales/Total Assets						1.2	
		.9		.9		.9							.9	
		.5		.7		.7							.8	
	(12)	1.6	(14)	1.5	(17)	1.5	% Depr., Dep., Amort./Sales						1.5	
		3.0		3.3		3.1							3.1	
							% Officers', Directors' Owners' Comp/Sales							
		1129085M		966167M		1298184M	Net Sales ($)	510M	4314M	7885M	6457M	14669M	1264349M	
		950237M		889627M		1342146M	Total Assets ($)	455M	3382M	7698M	2925M	10101M	1317585M	

© RMA 2024   M = $ thousand   MM = $ million
See Pages viii through xx for Explanation of Ratios and Data

MANUFACTURING—All Other Miscellaneous Manufacturing NAICS 339999

Current Data Sorted by Assets | Comparative Historical Data

							Type of Statement		
		3	2	11	5	6	Unqualified	36	24
	1	2	4	10	3		Reviewed	39	16
	2	13	6	3			Compiled	34	18
	2	19	8	4			Tax Returns	64	37
			56	60	10	31	Other	204	118
		50 (4/1-9/30/23)		211 (10/1/23-3/31/24)				4/1/19- 3/31/20	4/1/20- 3/31/21
0-500M	500M-2MM	2-10MM	10-50MM	50-100MM	100-250MM			ALL	ALL
5	37	76	88	18	37		NUMBER OF STATEMENTS	377	213
%	%	%	%	%	%		ASSETS	%	%
	23.3	16.6	11.4	6.3	8.5		Cash & Equivalents	13.9	18.1
	18.6	20.8	20.5	19.2	15.8		Trade Receivables (net)	22.0	20.6
	23.9	28.0	26.0	28.9	22.3		Inventory	24.9	24.3
	3.9	3.8	4.4	10.7	8.2		All Other Current	3.0	2.5
	69.7	69.2	62.3	65.2	54.8		Total Current	63.8	65.6
	18.8	18.0	20.1	23.4	19.0		Fixed Assets (net)	23.3	22.7
	5.8	7.5	8.2	5.1	16.0		Intangibles (net)	7.0	6.5
	5.7	5.3	9.5	6.3	10.1		All Other Non-Current	5.9	5.1
	100.0	100.0	100.0	100.0	100.0		Total	100.0	100.0
							LIABILITIES		
	13.8	5.6	8.1	5.2	4.3		Notes Payable-Short Term	11.1	7.6
	2.9	2.0	2.4	1.6	1.6		Cur. Mat.-L.T.D.	2.5	2.6
	10.5	14.6	12.1	10.8	9.6		Trade Payables	12.9	13.5
	.0	.0	.1	.0	.2		Income Taxes Payable	.1	.2
	4.3	12.8	13.1	29.4	13.0		All Other Current	11.3	11.0
	31.4	34.9	35.8	47.0	28.6		Total Current	38.0	34.8
	24.3	14.9	13.5	15.6	14.8		Long-Term Debt	18.8	19.1
	.0	.1	.2	.2	.2		Deferred Taxes	.3	.2
	7.0	6.1	7.8	5.1	6.9		All Other Non-Current	4.9	4.6
	37.3	44.0	42.7	32.1	49.4		Net Worth	38.1	41.3
	100.0	100.0	100.0	100.0	100.0		Total Liabilties & Net Worth	100.0	100.0
							INCOME DATA		
	100.0	100.0	100.0	100.0	100.0		Net Sales	100.0	100.0
	50.2	37.9	34.1	28.1	28.5		Gross Profit	38.3	37.0
	43.8	33.0	25.8	19.1	22.4		Operating Expenses	30.8	29.5
	6.4	4.9	8.3	8.9	6.1		Operating Profit	7.6	7.5
	1.0	.2	1.2	.7	1.2		All Other Expenses (net)	1.3	-.9
	5.4	4.7	7.1	8.3	4.9		Profit Before Taxes	6.3	8.4
							RATIOS		
	8.1	4.7	3.0	2.0	3.5			3.6	4.0
	2.1	2.8	1.8	1.4	2.6	Current	2.0	2.0
	1.3	1.4	1.2	1.0	1.2		1.2	1.4
	6.9	2.8	1.4	1.0	1.6			2.1	2.3
	1.3	1.2	.9	.5	.8	Quick	1.0	1.1
	.5	.6	.5	.2	.5		.5	.6
3	108.8	15	24.3	32	11.5	19	18.8	23	15.7		22	16.6	23	16.0
26	14.0	34	10.8	44	8.3	40	9.1	46	8.0	Sales/Receivables	36	10.0	37	9.8
42	8.7	54	6.8	58	6.3	66	5.5	61	6.0		55	6.6	51	7.1
4	102.9	31	11.6	53	6.9	29	12.6	53	6.9		26	13.9	36	10.2
37	9.8	76	4.8	91	4.0	64	5.7	101	3.6	Cost of Sales/Inventory	69	5.3	70	5.2
104	3.5	126	2.9	140	2.6	122	3.0	126	2.9		122	3.0	118	3.1
0	UND	18	20.7	17	21.5	20	18.5	18	20.6		12	29.5	12	29.8
13	27.4	31	11.9	31	11.7	24	15.0	29	12.8	Cost of Sales/Payables	26	14.2	27	13.3
36	10.1	51	7.1	51	7.1	34	10.6	38	9.5		51	7.1	47	7.7
	3.8	3.6	4.4	6.0	2.6			4.0	3.8
	7.9	4.8	5.5	15.0	4.1	Sales/Working Capital	6.8	5.6
	41.5	14.5	19.0	NM	18.3		33.5	16.8
	13.6	21.6	19.3	44.5	39.4			23.7	32.5
(31)	5.5	(66)	6.2	(72)	6.6	(17)	19.2	(34)	5.6	EBIT/Interest	(329)	5.7	(185)	12.0
	.3	2.4	2.0	4.7	1.3		1.6	3.5
			41.0		27.2			10.7	23.6
		(22)	4.8		(15)	8.6	Net Profit + Depr., Dep., Amort./Cur. Mat. L/T/D	(72)	3.5	(35)	5.4
			2.2		3.4			1.6	2.6
	.0	.1	.1	.3	.2			.2	.2
	.2	.3	.4	.7	.4	Fixed/Worth	.6	.5
	2.3	1.4	1.2	1.7	1.5		1.8	1.6
	.4	.4	.7	1.0	.5			.5	.6
	1.2	1.0	1.7	1.9	1.5	Debt/Worth	1.5	1.4
	NM	6.8	5.2	11.1	3.3		6.9	4.1
	124.6	44.5	49.0	99.3	32.5			57.2	65.7
(28)	29.6	(63)	16.8	(76)	22.6	(16)	43.8	(33)	14.0	% Profit Before Taxes/Tangible Net Worth	(315)	22.3	(184)	34.4
	2.6	4.9	8.5	23.3	1.3		6.3	12.5
	29.6	15.8	15.5	28.6	9.3			21.0	26.9
	11.4	8.9	8.4	12.5	5.6	% Profit Before Taxes/Total Assets	8.2	12.8
	-1.2	2.6	2.7	5.8	.5		1.6	4.5
	557.0	138.0	31.8	15.9	11.4			37.0	35.2
	54.1	20.3	13.6	10.8	5.8	Sales/Net Fixed Assets	12.2	11.3
	8.8	6.1	4.5	5.7	4.2		5.3	4.4
	3.4	2.9	2.0	2.0	1.6			2.9	2.6
	2.8	1.9	1.5	1.8	1.2	Sales/Total Assets	2.0	1.8
	1.7	1.2	1.0	1.3	.7		1.4	1.3
	.4	.5	.5	.9	.8			.8	1.0
(17)	2.0	(44)	1.8	(71)	1.9	(17)	1.4	(33)	2.7	% Depr., Dep., Amort./Sales	(277)	2.0	(157)	2.3
	5.6	3.3	2.8	3.0	4.2		3.5	4.0
	3.2	1.4	1.2					1.6	1.7
(17)	4.8	(26)	2.9	(13)	1.9			% Officers', Directors' Owners' Comp/Sales	(111)	3.4	(60)	2.9
	7.3	4.9	4.2					5.9	4.9
5945M	124588M	847838M	3187814M	2516955M	8986505M		Net Sales ($)	15033140M	8657881M
1462M	45061M	394438M	2030389M	1349001M	5435520M		Total Assets ($)	9000942M	5403916M

M = $ thousand   MM = $ million
See Pages viii through xx for Explanation of Ratios and Data

© RMA 2024

MANUFACTURING—All Other Miscellaneous Manufacturing NAICS 339999

Comparative Historical Data / **Current Data Sorted by Sales**

						Type of Statement						
	18		21		24	Unqualified		1		1	3	19
	19		24		20	Reviewed		2	1	3	5	9
	18		15		12	Compiled		3	1	2	2	4
	32		31		27	Tax Returns	1	10	4	2	6	4
	134		148		178	Other	2	12	15	22	45	82
	4/1/21-3/31/22 ALL		4/1/22-3/31/23 ALL		4/1/23-3/31/24 ALL			50 (4/1-9/30/23)		211 (10/1/23-3/31/24)		
							0-1MM	1-3MM	3-5MM	5-10MM	10-25MM	25MM & OVER
	221		239		261	NUMBER OF STATEMENTS	3	28	21	30	61	118
	%		%		%	ASSETS	%	%	%	%	%	%
	18.6		11.9		14.0	Cash & Equivalents		27.7	14.9	14.8	15.4	9.6
	20.0		20.4		19.6	Trade Receivables (net)		12.0	17.3	21.9	18.8	21.3
	24.2		27.2		25.6	Inventory		14.5	31.1	24.7	29.6	26.0
	3.1		3.3		5.1	All Other Current		4.0	2.9	2.1	3.7	7.2
	66.0		62.9		64.2	Total Current		58.2	66.2	63.5	67.5	64.2
	20.5		19.2		19.1	Fixed Assets (net)		24.9	20.6	20.8	15.6	18.6
	8.0		10.6		9.0	Intangibles (net)		10.6	6.3	9.2	8.0	9.3
	5.5		7.3		7.7	All Other Non-Current		6.4	7.0	6.5	9.0	7.9
	100.0		100.0		100.0	Total		100.0	100.0	100.0	100.0	100.0
						LIABILITIES						
	7.0		9.0		7.5	Notes Payable-Short Term		11.3	6.7	5.9	6.3	7.5
	1.9		2.4		2.1	Cur. Mat.-L.T.D.		2.4	2.8	3.2	2.2	1.7
	11.8		12.9		12.1	Trade Payables		7.3	16.0	11.5	12.6	12.5
	.2		.2		.1	Income Taxes Payable		.0	.0	.0	.1	.1
	13.1		12.5		12.6	All Other Current		5.7	7.4	5.8	13.8	16.6
	34.1		36.9		34.4	Total Current		26.8	33.0	26.3	35.0	38.5
	16.9		19.5		15.9	Long-Term Debt		25.8	19.8	23.2	13.2	12.2
	.2		.1		.1	Deferred Taxes		.2	.0	.1	.1	.1
	5.7		6.6		6.7	All Other Non-Current		6.5	4.0	7.8	10.2	5.3
	43.1		36.8		42.9	Net Worth		40.7	43.2	42.5	41.5	43.8
	100.0		100.0		100.0	Total Liabilities & Net Worth		100.0	100.0	100.0	100.0	100.0
						INCOME DATA						
	100.0		100.0		100.0	Net Sales		100.0	100.0	100.0	100.0	100.0
	36.5		35.0		36.6	Gross Profit		51.4	41.3	43.4	37.1	29.3
	29.4		29.7		29.7	Operating Expenses		43.0	38.6	37.8	30.1	21.9
	7.1		5.3		6.9	Operating Profit		8.4	2.6	5.6	6.9	7.5
	-1.0		1.1		.9	All Other Expenses (net)		1.0	1.3	1.2	.9	.6
	8.1		4.2		6.0	Profit Before Taxes		7.5	1.4	4.4	6.0	6.9
						RATIOS						
	4.4		3.8		3.9			9.3	7.1	4.7	4.2	3.1
	2.4		2.1		2.1	Current		2.4	1.9	2.9	2.3	1.8
	1.3		1.3		1.2			1.3	1.1	1.8	1.2	1.2
	2.4		1.8		2.1			7.4	3.7	3.2	2.1	1.4
	1.2		1.0		1.0	Quick		1.4	.9	1.4	1.0	.8
	.7		.6		.5			.5	.5	.8	.6	.5
23	15.9	24	15.4	20	18.3		0	UND	16 23.1	19 19.4	15 24.7	28 13.0
41	8.8	40	9.1	40	9.2	Sales/Receivables	25 14.7	33 10.9	36 10.1	36 10.2	45 8.2
59	6.2	57	6.4	54	6.7		42 8.7	50 7.3	57 6.4	53 6.9	61 6.0
31	11.6	40	9.1	36	10.0		0 UND	38 9.6	32 11.4	60 6.1	46 7.9
76	4.8	81	4.5	78	4.7	Cost of Sales/Inventory	19 19.0	79 4.6	65 5.6	89 4.1	81 4.5
126	2.9	140	2.6	126	2.9		135 2.7	152 2.4	130 2.8	135 2.7	122 3.0
14	25.3	16	23.5	15	24.2		0 UND	11 31.8	15 24.4	18 20.5	18 20.4
29	12.8	30	12.1	28	13.0	Cost of Sales/Payables	11 34.3	29 12.8	28 13.2	31 11.9	29 12.7
48	7.6	51	7.2	45	8.2		30 12.0	61 6.0	52 7.0	47 7.8	43 8.5
	3.6		3.6		3.6			3.1	3.6	3.8	3.2	3.6
	5.1		5.4		5.4	Sales/Working Capital		4.5	6.2	4.8	5.6	5.5
	15.0		17.5		19.6			124.2	41.2	12.4	19.9	19.6
	45.0		31.8		22.0			10.5	12.0	15.4	21.7	37.5
(181)	15.3	(197)	7.4	(222)	6.4	EBIT/Interest	(18) 2.7	(20) 5.1	(26) 4.1	(53) 5.8	(103) 9.5
	3.3		1.5		2.0			-.1	.5	.9	1.4	3.0
	18.6		21.4		29.0	Net Profit + Depr., Dep.,						36.4
(37)	7.5	(43)	5.3	(51)	7.0	Amort./Cur. Mat. L/T/D					(41) 9.8
	3.7		2.3		2.8							3.3
	.2		.1		.1			.0	.1	.1	.0	.2
	.5		.4		.4	Fixed/Worth		.4	.5	.3	.3	.4
	1.5		3.4		1.4			5.5	1.5	3.3	1.5	1.2
	.4		.6		.5			.2	.3	.5	.4	.7
	1.3		1.7		1.5	Debt/Worth		1.6	1.2	1.7	1.5	1.6
	4.2		19.1		6.2			NM	14.4	NM	6.1	3.5
	66.2		53.9		47.4			87.5	48.4	45.6	44.1	49.7
(192)	34.3	(195)	23.8	(219)	21.8	% Profit Before Taxes/Tangible Net Worth	(21) 17.2	(18) 16.2	(23) 19.4	(49) 19.1	(106) 23.1
	13.0		7.4		8.1			3.6	-2.2	5.8	6.9	10.1
	26.3		18.0		18.0			27.0	21.7	16.7	16.3	19.1
	12.9		7.7		8.5	% Profit Before Taxes/Total Assets		9.0	7.0	8.4	8.6	8.4
	4.6		.8		2.4			-.2	-.8	.0	2.4	3.8
	34.6		39.7		56.1			122.8	59.0	146.6	139.8	33.1
	11.3		13.9		13.7	Sales/Net Fixed Assets		21.6	14.1	16.9	19.0	11.9
	5.5		5.5		5.0			3.2	5.6	5.5	7.5	5.0
	2.5		2.4		2.6			2.6	3.3	3.2	2.5	2.1
	1.8		1.7		1.7	Sales/Total Assets		1.7	2.3	1.8	1.8	1.6
	1.2		1.2		1.2			1.0	1.1	1.1	1.2	1.2
	.7		.7		.7			.4	.7	1.6	.9	.5
(162)	1.9	(173)	1.8	(184)	1.9	% Depr., Dep., Amort./Sales	(13) 1.8	(12) 2.3	(15) 3.0	(36) 2.0	(107) 1.6
	3.8		4.0		3.3			6.4	7.5	9.1	3.4	3.0
	2.2		1.1		1.7			4.5			1.6	1.2
(59)	4.3	(59)	2.9	(60)	3.5	% Officers', Directors' Owners' Comp/Sales	(12) 5.4			(18) 2.9	(14) 1.8
	7.0		5.9		6.1			9.1			4.9	5.3
	9502485M		11394481M		15669645M	Net Sales ($)	1798M	53945M	82827M	212127M	991413M	14327535M
	6148459M		7892625M		9255871M	Total Assets ($)	874M	46159M	56669M	134019M	686216M	8331934M

© RMA 2024 M = $ thousand   MM = $ million
See Pages viii through xx for Explanation of Ratios and Data

WHOLESALE TRADE

WHOLESALE—Automobile and Other Motor Vehicle Merchant Wholesalers NAICS 423110

Current Data Sorted by Assets

							Comparative Historical Data	
		1	8	4	7	Type of Statement		
		8	26	11	6	Unqualified	25	17
	2	13	12	1		Reviewed	32	23
1	4	23	6	2		Compiled	18	11
4	19	54	58	14	22	Tax Returns	29	12
	50 (4/1-9/30/23)		256 (10/1/23-3/31/24)			Other	134	68
0-500M	500M-2MM	2-10MM	10-50MM	50-100MM	100-250MM		4/1/19-3/31/20 ALL	4/1/20-3/31/21 ALL
5	25	99	110	32	35	NUMBER OF STATEMENTS	238	131
%	%	%	%	%	%	ASSETS	%	%
	23.1	15.7	13.5	11.3	11.8	Cash & Equivalents	11.0	18.7
	12.3	14.2	9.4	7.9	14.1	Trade Receivables (net)	13.5	13.0
	48.5	52.5	48.3	42.6	38.0	Inventory	47.1	38.8
	3.1	3.5	5.1	2.5	7.6	All Other Current	2.8	3.6
	86.9	85.9	76.3	64.3	71.4	Total Current	74.4	74.1
	7.6	7.2	12.5	15.7	13.0	Fixed Assets (net)	15.6	14.4
	3.2	4.0	4.7	8.0	5.3	Intangibles (net)	4.7	3.7
	2.4	2.9	6.5	12.0	10.3	All Other Non-Current	5.3	7.8
	100.0	100.0	100.0	100.0	100.0	Total	100.0	100.0
						LIABILITIES		
	10.2	10.4	15.1	21.4	16.7	Notes Payable-Short Term	27.2	21.5
	1.0	2.0	2.7	3.4	1.6	Cur. Mat.-L.T.D.	2.4	3.8
	23.3	30.4	19.4	15.0	17.1	Trade Payables	13.4	9.8
	.3	.1	.1	.1	.1	Income Taxes Payable	.0	.1
	7.1	8.6	11.8	10.0	14.2	All Other Current	9.5	10.6
	41.9	51.5	49.0	49.9	49.7	Total Current	52.6	45.8
	10.0	6.3	7.6	11.0	10.5	Long-Term Debt	11.0	13.7
	.0	.0	.2	.4	.3	Deferred Taxes	.3	.2
	5.0	4.2	4.5	4.0	4.4	All Other Non-Current	4.4	4.5
	43.1	37.9	38.7	34.7	35.1	Net Worth	31.7	35.8
	100.0	100.0	100.0	100.0	100.0	Total Liabilities & Net Worth	100.0	100.0
						INCOME DATA		
	100.0	100.0	100.0	100.0	100.0	Net Sales	100.0	100.0
	24.8	23.5	22.0	24.5	23.0	Gross Profit	21.0	23.8
	24.2	18.2	16.7	18.3	18.6	Operating Expenses	17.6	20.5
	.6	5.3	5.2	6.3	4.4	Operating Profit	3.4	3.3
	-.1	.9	.0	1.3	.3	All Other Expenses (net)	.1	-.5
	.7	4.4	5.2	5.0	4.1	Profit Before Taxes	3.3	3.8
						RATIOS		
	3.7	2.8	2.0	1.7	1.7		1.9	2.2
	2.0	1.7	1.5	1.2	1.2	Current	1.3	1.6
	1.5	1.2	1.3	1.0	1.1		1.1	1.2
	1.7	1.0	.8	.5	.6		.7	1.2
	.6	.6	.4	.3	.4	Quick	.4	.6
	.4	.2	.2	.1	.3		.2	.3
	0 UND	3 128.7	5 78.9	6 61.5	8 47.5		8 47.7	6 60.2
	6 64.2	14 26.6	11 32.3	14 25.6	15 24.2	Sales/Receivables	14 25.7	15 23.9
	25 14.4	30 12.0	22 16.7	30 12.1	35 10.5		29 12.7	33 10.9
	47 7.7	51 7.2	56 6.5	44 8.3	51 7.1		55 6.6	37 9.9
	104 3.5	85 4.3	94 3.9	83 4.4	64 5.7	Cost of Sales/Inventory	79 4.6	73 5.0
	152 2.4	140 2.6	166 2.2	122 3.0	94 3.9		114 3.2	118 3.1
	1 394.6	8 45.1	8 44.9	7 50.9	8 48.5		6 58.1	4 86.0
	37 9.8	31 11.7	21 17.6	18 20.2	12 29.6	Cost of Sales/Payables	12 31.1	10 37.8
	94 3.9	94 3.9	61 6.0	54 6.8	51 7.2		30 12.2	26 13.8
	3.0	4.6	6.0	9.5	8.5		6.9	4.7
	5.8	9.0	10.5	17.5	13.6	Sales/Working Capital	15.9	9.2
	15.4	19.6	16.0	137.1	30.0		51.8	22.1
	11.6	15.5	16.0	8.3	23.8		13.5	20.1
(19)	8.0	(89) 6.0	(92) 5.8	(30) 4.3	(29) 6.7	EBIT/Interest	(213) 4.7	(112) 6.4
	1.8	2.0	2.6	2.3	3.2		2.1	1.9
			26.9				8.2	7.3
		(16) 6.0				Net Profit + Depr., Dep., Amort./Cur. Mat. L/T/D	(28) 5.3	(13) 2.2
		2.8					1.4	1.0
	.0	.0	.1	.2	.1		.1	.1
	.0	.2	.2	.6	.3	Fixed/Worth	.4	.2
	.4	.4	.6	2.8	1.1		1.4	.9
	.9	.8	1.1	1.0	1.1		1.2	1.0
	1.5	2.0	2.2	2.7	2.9	Debt/Worth	2.7	2.3
	3.6	5.5	4.3	10.3	5.6		6.3	4.5
	50.5	60.2	48.3	66.2	51.6		39.3	40.6
(24)	32.5	(88) 26.3	(104) 33.1	(27) 22.7	(34) 34.3	% Profit Before Taxes/Tangible Net Worth	(215) 21.1	(123) 22.1
	1.6	11.5	17.9	17.2	22.6		11.5	8.0
	19.8	20.0	16.1	12.9	15.8		12.4	13.8
	10.1	9.4	10.2	7.9	8.8	% Profit Before Taxes/Total Assets	6.6	7.2
	-2.8	2.3	4.3	3.2	4.5		2.6	1.9
	999.8	300.3	102.0	58.7	101.6		123.6	163.7
	76.5	79.1	34.9	21.8	25.4	Sales/Net Fixed Assets	28.1	43.9
	25.7	33.6	10.7	5.2	10.6		9.6	7.9
	4.1	3.9	3.1	2.6	2.7		3.5	3.3
	2.7	2.7	2.1	1.6	2.0	Sales/Total Assets	2.4	2.4
	1.6	1.9	1.6	1.1	1.4		1.8	1.5
		.1	.2	.4	.3		.3	.2
	(54) .4	(91) .5	(30) .8	(26) .4		% Depr., Dep., Amort./Sales	(178) .7	(88) .8
		.8	1.3	3.3	1.2		1.7	2.5
	1.3	.4	.4				.5	.8
(13)	3.6	(39) 1.2	(31) .8			% Officers', Directors' Owners' Comp/Sales	(67) 1.0	(37) 1.4
	6.9	2.6	1.4				2.0	4.5
11118M	88267M	1683885M	6850850M	4941123M	14689138M	Net Sales ($)	22309037M	11346927M
1929M	29607M	503099M	2662256M	2314079M	5691929M	Total Assets ($)	10303510M	5260093M

M = $ thousand   MM = $ million
See Pages viii through xx for Explanation of Ratios and Data

© RMA 2024

WHOLESALE—Automobile and Other Motor Vehicle Merchant Wholesalers NAICS 423110

Comparative Historical Data / Current Data Sorted by Sales

					Type of Statement					1	18
	12		21	20	Unqualified				1	8	43
	27		24	51	Reviewed		2	2	1	9	14
	10		20	28	Compiled	2	3	2	6	14	9
	19		21	36	Tax Returns	3	8	13	26	39	82
	81		96	171	Other						
	4/1/21-3/31/22 ALL		4/1/22-3/31/23 ALL	4/1/23-3/31/24 ALL			50 (4/1-9/30/23)			256 (10/1/23-3/31/24)	
						0-1MM	1-3MM	3-5MM	5-10MM	10-25MM	25MM & OVER
	149		182	306	**NUMBER OF STATEMENTS**	7	11	17	34	71	166
	%		%	%	**ASSETS**	%	%	%	%	%	%
	17.8		16.5	14.8	Cash & Equivalents	23.0	19.9	20.7	14.2	12.7	
	13.1		12.1	11.5	Trade Receivables (net)	9.6	13.0	13.1	11.3	11.2	
	36.5		40.7	47.6	Inventory	48.2	48.6	43.4	49.1	48.2	
	4.6		2.8	4.4	All Other Current	.3	.7	5.3	5.1	4.3	
	72.0		72.1	78.3	Total Current	81.1	82.2	82.5	79.7	76.4	
	16.8		15.8	11.0	Fixed Assets (net)	12.8	9.0	5.7	10.7	11.9	
	2.7		3.6	4.8	Intangibles (net)	4.0	3.7	8.7	3.6	4.6	
	8.4		8.5	5.9	All Other Non-Current	2.0	5.1	3.0	6.0	7.0	
	100.0		100.0	100.0	Total	100.0	100.0	100.0	100.0	100.0	
					LIABILITIES						
	15.5		16.9	13.9	Notes Payable-Short Term	4.1	10.1	10.8	7.3	18.6	
	3.7		2.0	2.3	Cur. Mat.-L.T.D.	1.1	3.2	1.3	3.8	1.9	
	9.9		11.5	23.5	Trade Payables	39.3	23.5	27.1	24.7	20.6	
	.2		.1	.1	Income Taxes Payable	.0	.2	.3	.0	.1	
	12.1		12.2	10.3	All Other Current	6.1	8.2	13.3	7.5	11.7	
	41.5		42.6	50.0	Total Current	50.6	45.3	52.9	43.3	52.9	
	16.2		14.7	8.1	Long-Term Debt	11.9	10.1	10.1	7.5	7.7	
	.1		.2	.2	Deferred Taxes	.0	.0	.0	.1	.2	
	5.2		4.0	4.5	All Other Non-Current	2.7	1.9	4.7	4.0	4.3	
	37.0		38.5	37.2	Net Worth	34.9	42.8	32.2	45.1	34.9	
	100.0		100.0	100.0	Total Liabilities & Net Worth	100.0	100.0	100.0	100.0	100.0	
					INCOME DATA						
	100.0		100.0	100.0	Net Sales	100.0	100.0	100.0	100.0	100.0	
	24.7		25.0	23.5	Gross Profit	30.8	30.7	29.4	25.3	19.1	
	19.8		19.6	18.8	Operating Expenses	23.1	26.2	24.6	20.1	14.3	
	4.9		5.4	4.7	Operating Profit	7.8	4.5	4.8	5.2	4.8	
	-1.5		.0	.5	All Other Expenses (net)	4.4	.3	.4	.4	.3	
	6.4		5.4	4.2	Profit Before Taxes	3.4	4.2	4.4	4.9	4.5	
					RATIOS						
	2.5		2.6	2.2		5.4	2.6	2.9	3.0	1.8	
	1.6		1.6	1.5	Current	2.0	1.8	1.6	1.7	1.4	
	1.2		1.2	1.2		1.4	1.3	1.1	1.2	1.2	
	1.2		1.2	.9		4.1	1.3	1.1	1.3	.6	
	.7		.6	.5	Quick	.5	.6	.6	.6	.4	
	.4		.3	.2		.2	.3	.3	.2	.2	
5	78.3	3	109.7	4 86.0		0 UND	7 55.2	1 421.1	2 177.0	6 63.4	
13	27.3	11	33.5	12 29.9	Sales/Receivables	0 UND	15 24.1	17 21.6	11 33.8	11 31.8	
25	14.6	24	15.0	25 14.4		45 8.1	31 11.7	32 11.3	31 11.9	22 16.8	
34	10.7	38	9.7	51 7.1		18 20.5	72 5.1	49 7.4	49 7.5	51 7.1	
57	6.4	66	5.5	85 4.3	Cost of Sales/Inventory	89 4.1	126 2.9	111 3.3	89 4.1	74 4.9	
89	4.1	114	3.2	140 2.6		146 2.5	243 1.5	166 2.2	152 2.4	118 3.1	
4	93.8	2	170.2	8 48.5		0 UND	1 285.8	2 169.9	8 47.2	8 46.1	
13	27.5	11	32.4	24 15.4	Cost of Sales/Payables	25 14.8	50 7.3	50 7.3	29 12.4	16 23.1	
26	13.8	28	12.9	78 4.7		146 2.5	104 3.5	118 3.1	85 4.3	52 7.0	
	5.7		6.7	5.6		2.6	3.5	4.3	4.4	8.5	
	10.1		10.3	10.7	Sales/Working Capital	7.2	5.9	7.9	8.6	12.4	
	19.8		27.3	19.6		15.2	12.2	83.4	15.8	21.6	
	42.2		32.9	14.3		9.1	8.2	18.8	16.7		
(133)	15.0	(149)	15.2	(263) 5.8	EBIT/Interest	(16) 4.2	(32) 3.5	(58) 6.9	(147) 6.0		
	5.4		3.5	2.4		1.2	2.0	2.0	2.9		
	43.1		39.4	14.6	Net Profit + Depr., Dep.,				20.5		
(19)	6.8	(19)	4.7	(30) 5.3	Amort./Cur. Mat. L/T/D				(22) 6.5		
	2.2		2.1	1.5					1.9		
	.1		.0	.1		.0	.0	.0	.0	.1	
	.2		.2	.2	Fixed/Worth	.0	.2	.1	.2	.2	
	.9		.9	.7		.4	.4	1.7	.5	.7	
	.7		.9	1.0		.6	.7	1.3	.6	1.2	
	1.8		2.0	2.2	Debt/Worth	1.1	1.3	4.0	1.4	2.3	
	4.2		4.5	5.2		4.2	3.7	29.5	4.2	5.1	
	56.1		64.2	51.8	% Profit Before Taxes/Tangible		56.0	48.0	54.3	54.0	
(140)	35.1	(171)	36.3	(278) 31.8	Net Worth		29.5	(27) 24.5	(65) 23.0	(156) 34.2	
	18.5		16.0	15.2			3.9	15.3	6.8	20.3	
	20.7		22.0	16.8		14.9	17.9	17.4	20.3	15.9	
	11.9		11.1	9.2	% Profit Before Taxes/Total Assets	8.6	11.4	6.3	9.4	9.8	
	6.6		4.0	3.3		.0	1.2	2.3	2.1	4.7	
	116.9		134.5	141.3		UND	73.1	815.9	256.7	109.5	
	37.2		30.7	47.9	Sales/Net Fixed Assets	76.5	32.0	97.9	47.8	40.6	
	6.6		8.2	15.6		10.8	12.0	34.1	16.9	14.9	
	3.6		3.8	3.5		3.8	2.8	3.1	3.5	3.6	
	2.3		2.5	2.3	Sales/Total Assets	1.9	1.8	2.2	2.5	2.3	
	1.6		1.6	1.6		1.5	1.5	1.3	1.4	1.7	
	.3		.3	.2			.1	.2	.2		
(100)	.8	(116)	.7	(209) .5	% Depr., Dep., Amort./Sales		(11) .7	(46) .5	(139) .4		
	3.2		2.0	1.3			1.4	1.3	1.2		
	.6		.8	.3			1.0		.3		
(44)	1.4	(53)	1.2	(94) 1.0	% Officers', Directors', Owners' Comp/Sales		(11) 1.9	(27) 1.1	(40) .5		
	3.4		2.2	2.1			3.8	2.2	1.0		
	14430069M		20888587M	28264381M	Net Sales ($)	5169M	24043M	73370M	252485M	1162515M	26746799M
	6104584M		7720744M	11202899M	Total Assets ($)	5925M	12221M	45816M	180815M	792691M	10165431M

© RMA 2024   M = $ thousand   MM = $ million
See Pages viii through xx for Explanation of Ratios and Data

WHOLESALE—Motor Vehicle Supplies and New Parts Merchant Wholesalers NAICS 423120

Current Data Sorted by Assets | Comparative Historical Data

							Type of Statement				
	1		1	6	5	6	Unqualified		21		13
		2	7	18	2		Reviewed		33		14
1		9	30	13			Compiled		187		28
1		9	20	4			Tax Returns		39		15
		31	58	62	18	7	Other		146		90
		60 (4/1-9/30/23)		251 (10/1/23-3/31/24)					4/1/19-3/31/20		4/1/20-3/31/21
0-500M	500M-2MM	2-10MM	10-50MM	50-100MM	100-250MM		NUMBER OF STATEMENTS		ALL		ALL
3	51	116	103	25	13				426		160
%	%	%	%	%	%		ASSETS		%		%
	13.6	9.7	9.4	10.9	2.8		Cash & Equivalents		8.2		14.6
	14.0	17.0	18.2	13.2	11.4		Trade Receivables (net)		17.0		18.8
	54.6	53.8	47.6	34.5	36.7		Inventory		56.9		46.8
	4.4	3.8	2.4	3.3	1.3		All Other Current		1.9		2.0
	86.6	84.3	77.6	61.9	52.2		Total Current		84.0		82.2
	9.2	8.2	11.8	10.2	14.4		Fixed Assets (net)		9.1		9.9
	1.5	2.1	4.8	18.6	21.9		Intangibles (net)		3.1		4.6
	2.7	5.4	5.9	9.3	11.5		All Other Non-Current		3.7		3.3
	100.0	100.0	100.0	100.0	100.0		Total		100.0		100.0
							LIABILITIES				
	7.1	7.4	8.6	7.3	18.9		Notes Payable-Short Term		11.9		10.5
	1.4	1.3	1.2	1.4	2.4		Cur. Mat.-L.T.D.		.9		1.6
	14.5	18.6	16.1	16.1	12.1		Trade Payables		18.3		19.6
	.2	.2	.5	.1	.0		Income Taxes Payable		.1		.2
	7.7	6.5	8.3	10.4	11.5		All Other Current		6.9		10.7
	30.8	33.9	34.7	35.4	44.9		Total Current		38.2		42.6
	17.9	15.3	11.9	15.6	21.8		Long-Term Debt		14.3		12.4
	.0	.1	.1	.5	.8		Deferred Taxes		.1		.0
	4.8	5.2	6.3	7.2	9.1		All Other Non-Current		6.1		3.5
	46.5	45.5	47.0	41.3	23.4		Net Worth		41.3		41.5
	100.0	100.0	100.0	100.0	100.0		Total Liabilities & Net Worth		100.0		100.0
							INCOME DATA				
	100.0	100.0	100.0	100.0	100.0		Net Sales		100.0		100.0
	35.8	34.2	32.4	36.8	41.0		Gross Profit		33.2		31.3
	30.6	29.5	25.5	31.3	33.7		Operating Expenses		29.0		26.7
	5.2	4.7	7.0	5.5	7.3		Operating Profit		4.3		4.6
	.1	.2	.6	.9	3.6		All Other Expenses (net)		.6		-.5
	5.1	4.5	6.4	4.6	3.7		Profit Before Taxes		3.6		5.1
							RATIOS				
	5.0	4.3	3.6	3.8	1.5				3.9		3.6
	3.5	2.8	2.4	1.8	1.1		Current		2.6		2.1
	2.4	1.9	1.6	1.2	.9				1.6		1.4
	1.9	1.3	1.3	1.2	.6				1.1		1.3
	.9	.8	.7	.5	.5		Quick		.6		.8
	.6	.4	.4	.3	.1				.4		.5
17	21.0	18	20.6	21	17.3	16	22.2	18	20.8		
23	15.8	25	14.6	28	12.9	29	12.6	27	13.4	Sales/Receivables	20	18.4	20	18.7
31	11.8	35	10.4	42	8.6	43	8.5	36	10.1		27	13.5	29	12.7
											37	9.8	41	9.0
70	5.2	81	4.5	66	5.5	89	4.1	89	4.1		91	4.0	63	5.8
203	1.8	146	2.5	118	3.1	122	3.0	166	2.2	Cost of Sales/Inventory	166	2.2	107	3.4
281	1.3	228	1.6	215	1.7	203	1.8	215	1.7		243	1.5	182	2.0
26	14.0	22	16.3	22	16.5	31	11.7	26	14.1		25	14.5	22	16.5
40	9.2	50	7.3	43	8.5	47	7.8	47	7.7	Cost of Sales/Payables	45	8.1	36	10.0
56	6.5	68	5.4	63	5.8	65	5.6	91	4.0		65	5.6	65	5.6
	2.2	2.6	2.8	3.6	8.2				2.7		3.1
	2.8	3.7	4.9	5.1	26.0		Sales/Working Capital		4.1		5.1
	6.4	7.4	9.3	18.6	-33.0				8.8		8.9
	18.0	16.7	25.5	9.3	3.1				10.1		32.9
(45)	7.8	(104) 6.7	(92) 7.9	(20) 4.5	1.9		EBIT/Interest	(381)	4.1	(133)	8.7
	2.3	2.5	2.1	1.4	.9				1.8		2.3
		40.2	47.7	6.2			Net Profit + Depr., Dep., Amort./Cur. Mat. L/T/D		11.9		17.9
		(10) 2.8	(19) 3.4	(10) 3.9				(41)	4.0	(20)	5.8
		1.8	2.1	2.4					1.9		1.4
	.1	.0	.1	.1	.4				.1		.1
	.1	.1	.2	.2	1.2		Fixed/Worth		.2		.2
	.5	.3	.5	NM	2.1				.5		.5
	.4	.6	.5	1.0	3.6				.7		.6
	.8	1.1	1.1	2.0	8.3		Debt/Worth		1.6		1.5
	2.1	2.5	2.7	NM	NM				3.7		3.3
	33.1	32.5	40.0	37.5	36.0				31.5		37.4
(45)	16.1	(108) 17.3	(98) 20.9	(19) 14.0	(10) 20.1		% Profit Before Taxes/Tangible Net Worth	(400)	15.2	(144)	20.6
	6.4	10.3	8.8	6.6	-10.9				5.6		7.7
	17.2	16.0	21.3	11.7	9.6				11.2		16.9
	10.0	8.0	8.9	5.2	2.9		% Profit Before Taxes/Total Assets		5.5		8.4
	2.6	3.8	2.2	1.4	-1.0				1.7		2.0
	72.9	142.0	90.6	56.6	36.7				88.1		142.6
	38.5	41.1	31.8	21.1	12.9		Sales/Net Fixed Assets		36.9		33.9
	17.8	20.2	10.9	11.4	6.6				19.0		16.3
	3.1	2.7	2.4	1.7	1.5				2.7		2.9
	1.8	2.0	1.9	1.4	1.3		Sales/Total Assets		2.0		2.1
	1.4	1.5	1.5	1.1	1.0				1.5		1.5
	.6	.4	.2	.5					.4		.4
(38)	1.1	(88) .9	(85) .8	(20) 1.0			% Depr., Dep., Amort./Sales	(337)	.8	(114)	.8
	1.7	1.4	1.5	2.3					1.2		1.4
	2.4	1.0	.5						1.3		.8
(34)	3.6	(81) 1.6	(34) 1.0				% Officers', Directors', Owners' Comp/Sales	(231)	2.2	(48)	1.6
	5.1	2.9	2.1						3.8		3.4
2200M	161174M	1370180M	4629207M	2866397M	3073857M		Net Sales ($)		13842926M		6580317M
841M	60301M	617020M	2355551M	1884316M	2223022M		Total Assets ($)		6899942M		3416082M

M = $ thousand   MM = $ million
See Pages viii through xx for Explanation of Ratios and Data

© RMA 2024

WHOLESALE—Motor Vehicle Supplies and New Parts Merchant Wholesalers NAICS 423120

Comparative Historical Data | Current Data Sorted by Sales

Comparative Historical Data			Type of Statement	Current Data Sorted by Sales										
7	28	19	Unqualified	1		1	3	3	15
14	22	29	Reviewed				6	6	19
24	83	53	Compiled	2	8	5	6	23	9
20	34	34	Tax Returns	2	6	2	10	10	4
85	126	176	Other	2	24	10	25	36	79
4/1/21–3/31/22 ALL	4/1/22–3/31/23 ALL	4/1/23–3/31/24 ALL		60 (4/1–9/30/23)			251 (10/1/23–3/31/24)		
				0-1MM	1-3MM	3-5MM	5-10MM	10-25MM	25MM & OVER
150	293	311	NUMBER OF STATEMENTS	7	38	18	44	78	126
%	%	%	**ASSETS**	%	%	%	%	%	%
11.8	9.7	10.1	Cash & Equivalents	6.6	13.7	11.4	10.2	9.6
18.3	18.2	16.3	Trade Receivables (net)	12.9	17.3	14.0	16.4	18.3
48.5	51.7	49.5	Inventory	63.5	53.9	53.9	50.8	42.1
2.0	2.3	3.3	All Other Current	2.9	6.9	5.1	2.6	2.8
80.5	82.0	79.2	Total Current	85.9	91.9	84.5	80.0	72.7
10.7	9.7	9.9	Fixed Assets (net)	8.6	5.7	9.7	10.9	10.7
5.0	3.5	5.0	Intangibles (net)	1.8	1.4	1.3	3.3	9.2
3.8	4.8	5.9	All Other Non-Current	3.7	1.0	4.5	5.8	7.4
100.0	100.0	100.0	Total	100.0	100.0	100.0	100.0	100.0
			LIABILITIES						
10.1	10.1	8.2	Notes Payable-Short Term	5.3	8.1	10.5	7.6	8.6
1.2	1.4	1.3	Cur. Mat.-L.T.D.	.8	2.0	1.0	1.6	1.4
16.5	18.5	16.5	Trade Payables	13.5	18.5	18.0	16.5	16.9
.1	.1	.2	Income Taxes Payable	.1	.1	.2	.2	.4
8.0	6.6	8.0	All Other Current	6.9	5.3	3.8	8.4	9.7
35.9	36.7	34.3	Total Current	26.6	34.0	33.5	34.3	36.9
9.6	15.4	14.8	Long-Term Debt	16.8	13.6	19.4	16.5	12.0
.1	.1	.1	Deferred Taxes	.0	.1	.0	.2	.2
3.9	4.5	5.8	All Other Non-Current	5.6	4.3	6.1	3.9	7.4
50.5	43.3	44.9	Net Worth	51.0	48.1	41.0	45.1	43.5
100.0	100.0	100.0	Total Liabilities & Net Worth	100.0	100.0	100.0	100.0	100.0
			INCOME DATA						
100.0	100.0	100.0	Net Sales	100.0	100.0	100.0	100.0	100.0
31.0	31.5	34.4	Gross Profit	38.3	31.3	35.4	35.6	32.9
25.5	26.0	28.7	Operating Expenses	33.0	27.0	29.7	30.0	26.4
5.5	5.5	5.7	Operating Profit	5.3	4.2	5.7	5.5	6.4
-1.0	.3	.5	All Other Expenses (net)	.2	.0	.0	.5	.8
6.6	5.2	5.2	Profit Before Taxes	5.1	4.2	5.8	5.0	5.6
			RATIOS						
5.1	4.0	4.2		5.2	3.9	4.4	3.9	3.7
2.6	2.5	2.7	Current	4.0	3.3	2.9	2.6	2.1
1.6	1.5	1.6		2.7	2.1	2.0	1.6	1.4
2.1	1.4	1.3		1.2	1.5	1.6	1.2	1.3
.8	.7	.7	Quick	.8	.8	.7	.7	.7
.4	.4	.4		.5	.5	.4	.4	.4
20 / 18.4	19 / 19.1	19 / 19.7		20 / 18.6	20 / 18.4	14 / 26.9	18 / 20.0	20 / 18.3
30 / 12.2	30 / 12.1	26 / 14.1	Sales/Receivables	24 / 15.0	30 / 12.2	21 / 17.8	25 / 14.5	29 / 12.6
41 / 9.0	42 / 8.7	38 / 9.7		34 / 10.7	38 / 9.7	27 / 13.3	37 / 9.8	42 / 8.6
74 / 4.9	78 / 4.7	76 / 4.8		159 / 2.3	87 / 4.2	76 / 4.8	76 / 4.8	66 / 5.5
107 / 3.4	135 / 2.7	146 / 2.5	Cost of Sales/Inventory	243 / 1.5	203 / 1.8	166 / 2.2	130 / 2.8	104 / 3.5
182 / 2.0	228 / 1.6	228 / 1.6		304 / 1.2	243 / 1.5	261 / 1.4	228 / 1.6	182 / 2.0
16 / 22.4	24 / 14.9	24 / 15.1		35 / 10.3	49 / 7.4	21 / 17.1	16 / 23.1	24 / 15.2
35 / 10.3	51 / 7.2	46 / 8.0	Cost of Sales/Payables	47 / 7.8	54 / 6.7	44 / 8.3	45 / 8.2	43 / 8.5
58 / 6.3	72 / 5.1	63 / 5.8		64 / 5.7	73 / 5.0	78 / 4.7	64 / 5.7	62 / 5.9
3.0	2.8	2.7		1.9	2.0	2.6	2.9	3.5
4.9	4.1	4.2	Sales/Working Capital	2.5	2.7	3.8	4.2	6.0
10.5	8.7	8.9		3.9	4.1	6.5	11.4	11.6
62.9	19.7	18.2		18.1	10.3	18.8	15.1	24.0
(123) 15.4	(257) 8.1	(276) 6.3	EBIT/Interest	(36) 6.8	(15) 5.1	(42) 6.1	(70) 5.8	(108) 6.5
5.7	3.6	2.0		1.6	1.7	2.2	2.7	1.9
45.6	20.3	9.9					40.2	11.2
(16) 9.6	(43) 4.6	(47) 3.1	Net Profit + Depr., Dep., Amort./Cur. Mat. L/T/D				(10) 3.1	(29) 3.8
1.5	2.0	2.0					1.7	2.1
.0	.0	.1		.0	.0	.0	.1	.1
.1	.2	.2	Fixed/Worth	.1	.1	.1	.2	.2
.4	.4	.5		.3	.2	.3	.5	1.0
.4	.6	.5		.4	.5	.5	.6	.6
1.1	1.4	1.2	Debt/Worth	.7	1.0	1.3	1.1	1.7
2.7	3.1	3.4		2.2	1.8	3.2	2.8	6.0
48.0	36.0	35.3		24.9	28.5	40.0	36.1	41.7
(139) 26.7	(274) 22.2	(283) 17.6	% Profit Before Taxes/Tangible Net Worth	(35) 10.0	(17) 11.6	(41) 20.7	(71) 17.8	(112) 19.8
12.3	10.6	8.3		3.9	6.4	13.0	10.1	8.4
21.6	15.5	16.3		14.4	13.4	17.7	17.3	17.4
11.1	8.6	7.7	% Profit Before Taxes/Total Assets	5.4	5.4	9.6	8.7	7.0
4.2	3.6	2.5		1.1	2.6	4.5	3.7	2.0
151.6	112.0	99.2		80.4	272.1	149.0	85.6	80.3
43.4	35.2	33.0	Sales/Net Fixed Assets	29.1	36.5	40.3	36.1	31.8
17.6	15.5	15.2		16.0	23.6	16.5	15.8	11.3
3.0	2.6	2.5		1.9	1.9	2.7	2.9	2.5
2.2	1.9	1.9	Sales/Total Assets	1.7	1.6	2.0	2.0	1.9
1.6	1.4	1.4		1.3	1.3	1.4	1.6	1.3
.4	.4	.4		.6	.6	.3	.5	.3
(101) .9	(224) .9	(241) .9	% Depr., Dep., Amort./Sales	(32) .9	(14) 1.0	(34) .9	(59) 1.0	(100) .8
1.6	1.6	1.6		1.8	1.4	1.5	1.7	1.7
.7	1.3	1.0		2.6	1.0	1.2	.7	.4
(45) 1.7	(127) 2.3	(152) 1.8	% Officers', Directors' Owners' Comp/Sales	(29) 3.6	(12) 1.7	(32) 1.7	(52) 1.2	(26) 1.1
3.2	3.4	3.4		4.9	3.0	3.1	2.5	2.5
6969401M	14265025M	12103015M	Net Sales ($)	5252M	73485M	69479M	329114M	1262017M	10363668M
3754887M	7812107M	7141051M	Total Assets ($)	4770M	50073M	47007M	179643M	665812M	6193746M

© RMA 2024

M = $ thousand   MM = $ million
See Pages viii through xx for Explanation of Ratios and Data

WHOLESALE—Tire and Tube Merchant Wholesalers NAICS 423130

Current Data Sorted by Assets | Comparative Historical Data

0-500M	500M-2MM	2-10MM	10-50MM	50-100MM	100-250MM	Type of Statement	4/1/19-3/31/20 ALL	4/1/20-3/31/21 ALL
			2	3	6	Unqualified	11	6
		2	6	1	1	Reviewed	8	11
	1	3	5			Compiled	13	6
	1	4	1			Tax Returns	12	5
1	6	6	10	7	1	Other	46	21
8 (4/1-9/30/23)			52 (10/1/23-3/31/24)					
2	15	24	11	8		NUMBER OF STATEMENTS	90	49
%	%	%	%	%	%	ASSETS	%	%
		8.6	9.7	12.5		Cash & Equivalents	5.8	13.8
		28.7	26.7	19.0		Trade Receivables (net)	25.9	23.8
		36.1	43.1	37.2		Inventory	45.8	41.3
		6.5	1.9	2.9		All Other Current	2.4	2.2
		79.9	81.4	71.5		Total Current	79.8	81.1
		11.7	10.7	14.2		Fixed Assets (net)	11.4	10.2
		2.1	.3	2.5		Intangibles (net)	2.0	4.4
		6.3	7.7	11.8		All Other Non-Current	6.8	4.3
		100.0	100.0	100.0		Total	100.0	100.0
						LIABILITIES		
		10.6	9.8	3.1		Notes Payable-Short Term	14.0	10.9
		.7	.5	1.0		Cur. Mat.-L.T.D.	1.8	.8
		27.2	30.3	23.0		Trade Payables	27.5	28.8
		.0	.2	.1		Income Taxes Payable	.1	.0
		7.0	8.7	8.6		All Other Current	14.6	9.3
		45.6	49.5	35.8		Total Current	58.0	49.9
		12.0	8.1	6.4		Long-Term Debt	7.2	7.4
		.0	.2	.3		Deferred Taxes	.2	.1
		.1	5.5	6.4		All Other Non-Current	4.2	3.4
		42.3	36.8	51.1		Net Worth	30.3	39.2
		100.0	100.0	100.0		Total Liabilities & Net Worth	100.0	100.0
						INCOME DATA		
		100.0	100.0	100.0		Net Sales	100.0	100.0
		17.6	18.7	22.2		Gross Profit	20.7	22.5
		15.0	16.6	18.1		Operating Expenses	19.5	18.5
		2.6	2.1	4.1		Operating Profit	1.2	4.0
		.2	.2	-1.3		All Other Expenses (net)	.3	-.2
		2.3	1.9	5.4		Profit Before Taxes	1.0	4.2
						RATIOS		
		4.1	2.1	2.1			2.1	2.3
		2.2	1.6	1.8		Current	1.5	1.8
		1.1	1.2	1.6			1.1	1.3
		1.7	1.0	1.2			.9	1.1
		.9	.7	.8		Quick	.5	.7
		.3	.4	.3			.3	.4
		22 16.8	23 16.0	17 22.0			18 19.8	19 19.3
		33 11.0	30 12.2	20 18.6		Sales/Receivables	29 12.8	27 13.4
		40 9.1	58 6.3	52 7.0			48 7.6	39 9.4
		24 15.4	57 6.4	41 8.9			58 6.3	44 8.3
		53 6.9	72 5.1	96 3.8		Cost of Sales/Inventory	81 4.5	68 5.4
		76 4.8	104 3.5	114 3.2			107 3.4	101 3.6
		5 78.8	30 12.0	31 11.6			23 15.6	30 12.1
		33 10.9	55 6.6	41 8.9		Cost of Sales/Payables	47 7.8	39 9.4
		58 6.3	69 5.3	74 4.9			66 5.5	57 6.4
		5.8	6.1	4.9			6.4	6.0
		12.2	9.5	7.2		Sales/Working Capital	10.4	8.2
		79.5	20.7	8.1			41.0	17.7
		12.7	17.8	207.2			8.9	33.6
		(12) 5.5	(20) 2.6	(10) 10.9		EBIT/Interest	(80) 4.2	(45) 12.6
		3.1	.4	5.0			1.5	5.1
						Net Profit + Depr., Dep.,	9.0	11.5
						Amort./Cur. Mat. L/T/D	(26) 6.2	(11) 4.7
							2.2	2.5
		.0	.0	.2			.1	.1
		.2	.2	.2		Fixed/Worth	.3	.2
		1.0	.8	.3			.6	.7
		.6	.8	.8			1.1	.8
		2.3	2.6	1.1		Debt/Worth	2.1	1.5
		5.1	4.1	1.5			5.5	4.3
		49.4	26.8	25.8			34.3	45.5
		23.6	14.6	9.8		% Profit Before Taxes/Tangible Net Worth	(80) 15.4	(43) 21.7
		7.5	4.8	7.7			6.6	15.1
		11.1	11.5	17.3			9.2	16.1
		6.2	3.5	4.6		% Profit Before Taxes/Total Assets	5.0	8.9
		2.0	1.2	3.6			1.1	5.6
		813.5	144.4	27.7			67.2	87.9
		38.1	44.1	19.0		Sales/Net Fixed Assets	37.7	39.0
		15.5	17.8	11.6			14.8	15.5
		4.9	3.1	2.4			3.5	3.5
		3.2	2.6	2.3		Sales/Total Assets	2.6	3.1
		2.8	1.9	2.0			2.0	2.3
		.1	.2	.5			.4	.5
		(11) .8	(21) .6	.8		% Depr., Dep., Amort./Sales	(77) .8	(41) .7
		2.2	1.0	1.2			1.3	1.3
							.5	1.0
						% Officers', Directors' Owners' Comp/Sales	(27) .8	(12) 1.4
							1.7	1.7
	7617M	262789M	1489274M	1818309M	2303139M	Net Sales ($)	9908024M	5225422M
	3387M	78935M	570631M	839929M	1280371M	Total Assets ($)	3878528M	1857064M

M = $ thousand   MM = $ million
See Pages viii through xx for Explanation of Ratios and Data

© RMA 2024

WHOLESALE—Tire and Tube Merchant Wholesalers NAICS 423130

Comparative Historical Data / Current Data Sorted by Sales

				Type of Statement						
	8	9	11	Unqualified						11
	7	6	10	Reviewed						10
	8	6	8	Compiled				1	2	5
	2	10	6	Tax Returns					4	1
	29	34	25	Other		1		3	5	17
	4/1/21-3/31/22	4/1/22-3/31/23	4/1/23-3/31/24			8 (4/1-9/30/23)		52 (10/1/23-3/31/24)		
	ALL	ALL	ALL		0-1MM	1-3MM	3-5MM	5-10MM	10-25MM	25MM & OVER
	54	65	60	NUMBER OF STATEMENTS		1		4	11	44
	%	%	%	ASSETS	%	%	%	%	%	%
	10.6	7.1	10.2	Cash & Equivalents	D	D			7.3	11.2
	24.7	23.4	23.2	Trade Receivables (net)	A	A			25.4	23.2
	41.3	42.9	40.5	Inventory	T	T			43.6	39.5
	3.5	2.5	3.2	All Other Current	A	A			6.8	2.6
	80.1	75.9	77.1	Total Current					83.1	76.6
	13.4	12.1	11.4	Fixed Assets (net)	N	N			8.5	11.0
	1.5	2.6	1.4	Intangibles (net)	O	O			2.0	1.2
	5.0	9.4	10.1	All Other Non-Current	T	T			6.5	11.2
	100.0	100.0	100.0	Total					100.0	100.0
				LIABILITIES	A	A				
	5.3	9.5	8.5	Notes Payable-Short Term	V	V			9.7	6.8
	.8	1.0	.8	Cur. Mat.-L.T.D.	A	A			1.0	.8
	25.4	23.9	25.6	Trade Payables	I	I			35.5	25.4
	.1	.0	.2	Income Taxes Payable	L	L			.0	.3
	8.2	7.8	9.2	All Other Current	A	A			6.0	10.9
	39.6	42.2	44.4	Total Current	B	B			52.2	44.2
	6.1	9.0	8.2	Long-Term Debt	L	L			9.4	6.7
	.2	.1	.1	Deferred Taxes	E	E			.0	.2
	4.9	6.2	5.8	All Other Non-Current					.8	6.7
	49.2	42.5	41.6	Net Worth					37.7	42.3
	100.0	100.0	100.0	Total Liabilities & Net Worth					100.0	100.0
				INCOME DATA						
	100.0	100.0	100.0	Net Sales					100.0	100.0
	23.4	23.6	20.5	Gross Profit					17.1	20.1
	20.2	20.4	17.4	Operating Expenses					15.1	17.1
	3.2	3.2	3.0	Operating Profit					2.0	2.9
	-1.4	-.4	.0	All Other Expenses (net)					.1	-.2
	4.5	3.6	3.1	Profit Before Taxes					1.9	3.1
				RATIOS						
	4.3	2.4	2.3						4.1	2.2
	2.0	1.9	1.8	Current					1.3	1.8
	1.4	1.3	1.2						1.0	1.3
	2.2	1.2	1.2						1.3	1.1
	.9	.6	.7	Quick					.4	.7
	.5	.4	.3						.1	.4
21	17.1	17	21.4	19	19.0				19	19.2	20	18.4
30	12.3	27	13.4	29	12.4	Sales/Receivables			25	14.6	30	12.2
42	8.7	40	9.2	44	8.3				39	9.3	51	7.1
47	7.7	42	8.6	46	8.0				7	49.0	57	6.4
81	4.5	83	4.4	74	4.9	Cost of Sales/Inventory			53	6.9	78	4.7
126	2.9	122	3.0	107	3.4				104	3.5	111	3.3
14	26.5	23	15.7	18	20.1				16	23.3	27	13.4
35	10.3	39	9.4	43	8.4	Cost of Sales/Payables			44	8.3	49	7.5
62	5.9	57	6.4	65	5.6				76	4.8	69	5.3
	3.8		4.7		5.1					7.2		5.1
	6.6		7.3		8.2	Sales/Working Capital				12.4		7.9
	11.8		18.2		26.5					-146.8		17.0
	144.6		34.5		20.0							21.3
(46)	32.7	(55)	9.9	(50)	5.8	EBIT/Interest				(37)		5.8
	9.9		4.4		2.3							2.3
			14.1		23.4	Net Profit + Depr., Dep.,						
		(13)	6.9	(12)	4.1	Amort./Cur. Mat. L/T/D						
			3.1		-.5							
	.1		.1		.1					.0		.1
	.2		.2		.2	Fixed/Worth				.2		.2
	.4		.5		.5					1.0		.5
	.4		.7		.8					.6		.8
	1.1		1.7		1.5	Debt/Worth				3.3		1.4
	3.3		3.3		3.6					7.8		3.4
	47.5		35.4		31.8					54.1		23.0
	27.6	(64)	19.6		13.9	% Profit Before Taxes/Tangible Net Worth				32.7		12.6
	10.2		11.5		7.7					7.5		7.4
	17.2		13.4		12.0					11.1		12.0
	10.7		7.5		5.1	% Profit Before Taxes/Total Assets				6.2		4.5
	4.7		3.7		2.6					3.0		2.0
	53.0		62.9		63.2					999.8		60.1
	21.6		30.6		28.4	Sales/Net Fixed Assets				42.5		27.6
	10.8		15.3		15.9					29.0		17.2
	3.3		3.4		3.1					5.4		2.8
	2.6		2.6		2.4	Sales/Total Assets				3.4		2.3
	2.0		1.9		1.8					2.8		1.8
	.4		.4		.3							.4
(46)	.9	(60)	.7	(50)	.7	% Depr., Dep., Amort./Sales				(39)		.7
	1.3		1.2		1.1							1.0
	.4		.6		.5							
(11)	.7	(18)	1.0	(15)	.7	% Officers', Directors' Owners' Comp/Sales						
	2.1		2.7		1.5							
	4597458M		6044677M		5881128M	Net Sales ($)		2339M		26735M	204106M	5647948M
	1822277M		2467248M		2773253M	Total Assets ($)		1837M		12184M	60467M	2698765M

© RMA 2024   M = $ thousand   MM = $ million
See Pages viii through xx for Explanation of Ratios and Data

WHOLESALE—Motor Vehicle Parts (Used) Merchant Wholesalers NAICS 423140

Current Data Sorted by Assets

							Comparative Historical Data	
						Type of Statement		
			1			Unqualified		
		1	1			Reviewed	1	2
	1	1	5			Compiled	2	2
	2	5				Tax Returns	3	1
1	3 (4/1-9/30/23)		3		1	Other	10	8
0-500M	500M-2MM	2-10MM	19 (10/1/23-3/31/24) 10-50MM	50-100MM	100-250MM		4/1/19-3/31/20	4/1/20-3/31/21
1	4	11	5		1	**NUMBER OF STATEMENTS**	16 ALL	13 ALL
%	%	%	%	%	%	**ASSETS**	%	%
		19.4				Cash & Equivalents	11.0	9.0
		12.8				Trade Receivables (net)	15.5	16.4
		21.7	D			Inventory	43.8	46.4
		3.7	A			All Other Current	4.0	1.0
		57.5	T			Total Current	74.3	72.8
		31.2	A			Fixed Assets (net)	17.9	10.0
		1.1				Intangibles (net)	1.8	12.6
		10.3	N			All Other Non-Current	6.0	4.7
		100.0	O			Total	100.0	100.0
			T			**LIABILITIES**		
		2.6				Notes Payable-Short Term	11.9	7.7
		1.3	A			Cur. Mat.-L.T.D.	2.0	2.6
		4.6	V			Trade Payables	14.5	11.3
		.0	A			Income Taxes Payable	.6	.2
		5.0	I			All Other Current	17.4	13.5
		13.5	L			Total Current	46.4	35.2
		12.6	A			Long-Term Debt	14.0	18.9
		.0	B			Deferred Taxes	.6	.2
		.1	L			All Other Non-Current	5.7	1.7
		73.8	E			Net Worth	33.3	44.0
		100.0				Total Liabilites & Net Worth	100.0	100.0
						INCOME DATA		
		100.0				Net Sales	100.0	100.0
		46.9				Gross Profit	34.1	43.1
		36.6				Operating Expenses	30.7	37.4
		10.3				Operating Profit	3.3	5.8
		-.3				All Other Expenses (net)	.3	.2
		10.5				Profit Before Taxes	3.1	5.5
						RATIOS		
		20.2					4.0	5.9
		7.7				Current	1.5	3.1
		2.9					1.1	1.5
		10.7					1.5	1.6
		2.9				Quick	.5	1.1
		1.2					.2	.4
	3	116.2					4	88.2	14	25.4
	8	47.3				Sales/Receivables	15	24.0	19	19.4
	22	16.7					32	11.3	30	12.2
	15	23.7					31	11.6	81	4.5
	81	4.5				Cost of Sales/Inventory	96	3.8	111	3.3
	107	3.4					174	2.1	174	2.1
	2	237.0					3	121.8	0	UND
	6	65.2				Cost of Sales/Payables	16	23.2	17	21.2
	12	31.0					68	5.4	34	10.6
		2.2					4.7	3.0
		5.7				Sales/Working Capital	10.4	8.4
		9.7					32.2	14.2
		76.6					33.6	33.9
	(10)	50.7				EBIT/Interest	(13)	7.9	(12)	14.8
		11.3					2.3	2.3
						Net Profit + Depr., Dep., Amort./Cur. Mat. L/T/D		
		.1					.1	.1
		.3				Fixed/Worth	.4	.4
		.8					1.4	26.1
		.1					1.0	.9
		.1				Debt/Worth	2.0	1.9
		1.1					5.3	246.6
		36.0					60.1	82.1
		21.5				% Profit Before Taxes/Tangible Net Worth	(14)	24.3	(11)	21.7
		18.0					16.0	3.4
		22.5					17.6	20.5
		18.2				% Profit Before Taxes/Total Assets	12.6	10.7
		10.0					3.4	3.2
		88.0					43.8	64.1
		5.5				Sales/Net Fixed Assets	16.8	32.4
		2.3					9.0	18.6
		3.1					3.8	4.1
		1.8				Sales/Total Assets	3.1	2.2
		1.2					1.7	1.0
							.7	.5
						% Depr., Dep., Amort./Sales	(12)	.8	(11)	.7
							1.3	2.6
						% Officers', Directors', Owners' Comp/Sales		
1657M	20311M	135529M	192230M		192254M	Net Sales ($)	446368M	333908M
335M	4599M	57630M	82691M		142688M	Total Assets ($)	157166M	309204M

M = $ thousand   MM = $ million
See Pages viii through xx for Explanation of Ratios and Data

© RMA 2024

WHOLESALE—Motor Vehicle Parts (Used) Merchant Wholesalers NAICS 423140

Comparative Historical Data | **Current Data Sorted by Sales**

			Type of Statement						
	1	1	Unqualified				1	1	1
	1	3	Reviewed			2	1	1	1
1	3	6	Compiled		1	1	2	1	5
9	7	12	Tax Returns		2	3	3	1	
4/1/21-	4/1/22-	4/1/23-	Other		3 (4/1-9/30/23)			19 (10/1/23-3/31/24)	
3/31/22	3/31/23	3/31/24							
ALL	ALL	ALL		0-1MM	1-3MM	3-5MM	5-10MM	10-25MM	25MM & OVER
13	19	22	NUMBER OF STATEMENTS	3	3	3	6	2	8
%	%	%	ASSETS	%	%	%	%	%	%
12.1	17.5	17.8	Cash & Equivalents						
12.3	10.4	12.1	Trade Receivables (net)						
35.7	36.4	24.3	Inventory						
1.1	.9	4.2	All Other Current	D					
61.2	65.2	58.4	Total Current	A					
19.8	18.6	29.5	Fixed Assets (net)	T					
16.6	8.1	5.3	Intangibles (net)	A					
2.4	8.1	6.8	All Other Non-Current						
100.0	100.0	100.0	Total	N					
			LIABILITIES	O					
1.9	3.3	3.3	Notes Payable-Short Term	T					
1.1	.9	1.9	Cur. Mat.-L.T.D.						
5.0	4.8	5.3	Trade Payables	A					
.0	.5	.3	Income Taxes Payable	V					
3.8	6.4	11.2	All Other Current	A					
11.9	15.8	21.9	Total Current	I					
26.5	9.0	14.0	Long-Term Debt	L					
.0	.1	.1	Deferred Taxes	A					
4.0	11.3	6.5	All Other Non-Current	B					
57.5	63.8	57.5	Net Worth	L					
100.0	100.0	100.0	Total Liabilties & Net Worth	E					
			INCOME DATA						
100.0	100.0	100.0	Net Sales						
36.5	35.5	43.5	Gross Profit						
26.9	27.3	34.3	Operating Expenses						
9.6	8.1	9.2	Operating Profit						
.9	1.6	.7	All Other Expenses (net)						
8.7	6.6	8.6	Profit Before Taxes						
			RATIOS						
18.4	21.6	11.7							
4.6	5.9	4.0	Current						
3.1	2.9	1.7							
10.7	11.1	6.6							
2.2	2.3	1.6	Quick						
.9	.7	.8							
6 59.2	1 328.0	3 115.1							
14 26.9	13 28.3	7 52.4	Sales/Receivables						
25 14.6	20 18.3	24 15.3							
45 8.2	28 12.9	20 18.1							
83 4.4	85 4.3	73 5.0	Cost of Sales/Inventory						
146 2.5	104 3.5	85 4.3							
1 333.7	2 218.6	3 143.1							
11 32.3	4 93.8	7 53.1	Cost of Sales/Payables						
22 16.3	17 21.0	17 21.5							
3.0	2.4	4.4							
4.8	6.8	8.2	Sales/Working Capital						
9.8	10.1	12.8							
150.1	69.6	71.3							
42.8	(14) 13.9	(18) 18.8	EBIT/Interest						
3.3	.9	5.0							
			Net Profit + Depr., Dep., Amort./Cur. Mat. L/T/D						
.2	.1	.2							
.6	.4	.7	Fixed/Worth						
-.8	.8	1.8							
.3	.1	.1							
.8	.4	.8	Debt/Worth						
-5.8	1.6	5.8							
	40.4	60.7							
(16)	24.4 (20)	24.7	% Profit Before Taxes/Tangible Net Worth						
	4.0	10.2							
56.0	22.7	24.9							
16.5	10.3	15.8	% Profit Before Taxes/Total Assets						
4.0	-.3	3.6							
55.0	64.4	26.4							
18.2	21.1	12.5	Sales/Net Fixed Assets						
9.6	7.4	3.9							
3.1	4.7	3.6							
2.1	2.9	2.7	Sales/Total Assets						
1.4	1.3	1.5							
	.6	1.0							
(12)	1.0 (15)	1.9	% Depr., Dep., Amort./Sales						
	1.6	4.6							
			% Officers', Directors' Owners' Comp/Sales						
594177M	529393M	541981M	Net Sales ($)	6289M	13750M	41793M	36140M		444009M
488312M	398860M	287943M	Total Assets ($)	1632M	10321M	22349M	15793M		237848M

M = $ thousand   MM = $ million
See Pages viii through xx for Explanation of Ratios and Data

© RMA 2024

WHOLESALE—Furniture Merchant Wholesalers NAICS 423210

Current Data Sorted by Assets | Comparative Historical Data

						Type of Statement		
1			7	5	6	Unqualified	16	10
		13	18	2	3	Reviewed	40	22
		9	1			Compiled	15	9
3	8	10	1			Tax Returns	29	11
3	6	27	42	13	8	Other	116	83
	21 (4/1-9/30/23)		165 (10/1/23-3/31/24)				4/1/19-3/31/20	4/1/20-3/31/21
0-500M	500M-2MM	2-10MM	10-50MM	50-100MM	100-250MM	NUMBER OF STATEMENTS	ALL 216	ALL 135
7	14	59	69	20	17			
%	%	%	%	%	%	ASSETS	%	%
	20.5	18.3	9.8	3.7	1.1	Cash & Equivalents	9.5	16.3
	15.1	23.4	32.0	21.0	22.1	Trade Receivables (net)	35.7	30.3
	35.7	37.7	22.7	32.3	33.0	Inventory	33.9	29.6
	.1	5.8	6.6	6.5	5.4	All Other Current	4.6	3.4
	71.5	85.2	71.2	63.6	61.6	Total Current	83.7	79.5
	19.0	6.0	10.6	15.5	20.2	Fixed Assets (net)	7.9	9.8
	.4	1.8	5.7	3.1	4.0	Intangibles (net)	3.2	5.5
	9.2	6.9	12.5	17.8	14.2	All Other Non-Current	5.2	5.2
	100.0	100.0	100.0	100.0	100.0	Total	100.0	100.0
						LIABILITIES		
	2.6	7.6	8.2	10.1	7.7	Notes Payable-Short Term	14.4	9.6
	1.7	1.0	1.9	1.9	3.5	Cur. Mat.-L.T.D.	1.6	1.4
	21.5	16.3	14.9	8.5	14.2	Trade Payables	21.1	16.6
	.0	.0	.1	.1	.1	Income Taxes Payable	.1	.4
	24.7	21.9	24.4	14.6	19.3	All Other Current	17.1	20.9
	50.4	46.8	49.4	35.2	44.8	Total Current	54.2	48.9
	18.8	11.8	8.8	17.3	30.6	Long-Term Debt	8.0	13.8
	.0	.0	.1	.0	.3	Deferred Taxes	.1	.0
	.4	3.5	7.9	18.1	11.8	All Other Non-Current	5.9	11.4
	30.3	37.9	33.8	29.4	12.5	Net Worth	31.8	25.8
	100.0	100.0	100.0	100.0	100.0	Total Liabilities & Net Worth	100.0	100.0
						INCOME DATA		
	100.0	100.0	100.0	100.0	100.0	Net Sales	100.0	100.0
	45.5	35.6	28.5	30.7	29.2	Gross Profit	28.7	29.4
	39.0	29.0	24.2	29.2	26.4	Operating Expenses	24.1	25.8
	6.4	6.6	4.3	1.5	2.8	Operating Profit	4.6	3.6
	1.8	.1	.3	1.7	.2	All Other Expenses (net)	.5	-.4
	4.6	6.5	4.0	-.2	2.6	Profit Before Taxes	4.1	4.0
						RATIOS		
	18.3	3.1	1.8	2.7	1.7		2.5	3.1
	1.5	1.9	1.4	1.8	1.4	Current	1.5	1.8
	1.0	1.4	1.1	1.4	1.1		1.2	1.3
	4.9	1.9	1.2	1.5	.7		1.3	1.8
	1.0	.7	1.0	.8	.5	Quick	.8	1.1
	.4	.5	.5	.3	.3		.5	.7
0 UND	10 35.9	24 15.2	21 17.3	24 15.2			23 16.0	16 23.1
11 33.5	29 12.4	47 7.7	39 9.3	45 8.1		Sales/Receivables	39 9.3	36 10.2
28 12.9	58 6.3	68 5.4	65 5.6	53 6.9			58 6.3	55 6.6
20 18.7	21 17.7	14 26.7	25 14.6	43 8.4			20 18.3	19 19.2
83 4.4	73 5.0	32 11.3	146 2.5	101 3.6		Cost of Sales/Inventory	53 6.9	50 7.3
281 1.3	166 2.2	81 4.5	261 1.4	215 1.7			118 3.1	99 3.7
0 UND	10 34.8	17 21.5	13 28.0	26 14.2			16 22.8	11 34.7
19 19.6	23 15.7	25 14.8	21 17.4	34 10.6		Cost of Sales/Payables	26 13.8	22 16.4
87 4.2	56 6.5	43 8.5	27 13.7	51 7.2			46 7.9	41 9.0
	4.6	3.5	6.6	3.9	5.1		5.7	5.3
	8.9	6.4	13.2	5.8	11.3	Sales/Working Capital	10.6	8.6
	NM	17.0	71.6	11.1	39.7		28.7	18.7
		25.5	11.3	5.3	7.1		19.2	38.9
	(50)	7.9 (57)	6.5	3.7	4.7	EBIT/Interest	(183) 7.1	(114) 9.3
		1.3	2.5	-1.6	1.8		2.3	2.3
			7.1		5.4	Net Profit + Depr., Dep., Amort./Cur. Mat. L/T/D	41.1	14.6
		(16)	3.1	(14)	1.9		(34) 6.1	(11) 6.0
			.7		.4		2.3	1.5
	.0	.0	.1	.2	.6		.1	.1
	.2	.1	.3	.5	2.3	Fixed/Worth	.2	.2
	.4	.4	.8	1.1	-3.5		.7	1.0
	.3	.8	1.4	1.6	2.4		1.0	.8
	1.7	1.4	2.4	2.5	5.1	Debt/Worth	2.4	2.3
	17.7	4.8	4.6	6.2	-18.0		7.0	9.0
	43.1	90.9	60.5	56.0	35.1		58.7	63.2
(12)	37.3 (52)	24.4 (64)	27.1 (19)	10.1 (11)	13.4	% Profit Before Taxes/Tangible Net Worth	(184) 30.2	(109) 35.3
	14.0	4.1	7.4	-2.2	8.5		12.1	9.6
	22.8	30.1	12.5	10.8	8.5		16.9	22.6
	11.8	10.1	6.9	3.1	7.0	% Profit Before Taxes/Total Assets	9.5	9.3
	.4	1.0	2.6	-4.2	1.8		3.1	1.4
	UND	294.9	84.8	50.0	25.7		158.7	182.4
	50.9	69.2	38.5	14.9	13.2	Sales/Net Fixed Assets	70.0	62.6
	12.3	32.1	17.3	5.0	6.4		29.7	24.8
	4.4	3.4	3.2	2.4	2.7		3.8	4.0
	2.3	2.7	2.6	1.5	2.2	Sales/Total Assets	3.0	2.9
	1.0	1.9	1.9	.9	1.0		2.2	2.0
		.2	.3	.6	.5		.3	.2
	(41)	.4 (56)	.6 (19)	1.3 (15)	.9	% Depr., Dep., Amort./Sales	(156) .5	(90) .6
		.7	1.2	2.2	1.7		.8	1.0
		.8					.9	1.1
	(21)	1.5				% Officers', Directors' Owners' Comp/Sales	(59) 1.8	(22) 1.7
		2.5					2.9	3.4
15952M	46364M	939293M	3969710M	2299480M	5054520M	Net Sales ($)	12854800M	7974176M
1616M	16393M	341216M	1623719M	1396163M	2723020M	Total Assets ($)	5241496M	3170724M

© RMA 2024

M = $ thousand   MM = $ million
See Pages viii through xx for Explanation of Ratios and Data

WHOLESALE—Furniture Merchant Wholesalers NAICS 423210

Comparative Historical Data | Current Data Sorted by Sales

				Type of Statement						
	9	13	19	Unqualified				1	1	17
	22	30	36	Reviewed				3	11	22
	3	9	10	Compiled			1	1	7	1
	15	19	22	Tax Returns			3	4	6	1
	76	104	99	Other	3	5	3	4	6	1
	4/1/21-	4/1/22-	4/1/23-		3	3	4	5	20	64
	3/31/22	3/31/23	3/31/24		21 (4/1-9/30/23)			165 (10/1/23-3/31/24)		
	ALL	ALL	ALL		0-1MM	1-3MM	3-5MM	5-10MM	10-25MM	25MM & OVER
	125	175	186	NUMBER OF STATEMENTS	6	8	9	13	45	105
	%	%	%	ASSETS	%	%	%	%	%	%
	15.6	12.6	13.2	Cash & Equivalents				22.2	18.2	6.9
	25.1	24.6	24.9	Trade Receivables (net)				20.3	23.1	29.7
	34.9	34.4	30.9	Inventory				37.3	33.4	26.6
	6.6	6.4	6.1	All Other Current				1.7	6.0	6.9
	82.3	78.0	75.0	Total Current				81.5	80.7	70.0
	8.0	9.9	10.8	Fixed Assets (net)				2.1	8.5	12.7
	3.5	3.8	3.4	Intangibles (net)				4.7	2.7	4.3
	6.3	8.3	10.8	All Other Non-Current				11.6	8.1	13.0
	100.0	100.0	100.0	Total				100.0	100.0	100.0
				LIABILITIES						
	9.6	8.6	7.6	Notes Payable-Short Term				5.6	7.5	9.0
	1.2	1.5	1.7	Cur. Mat.-L.T.D.				2.2	.9	2.0
	16.5	15.6	15.9	Trade Payables				18.6	14.8	14.4
	.2	.1	.1	Income Taxes Payable				.0	.1	.1
	21.2	21.6	22.2	All Other Current				25.1	21.9	22.0
	48.8	47.5	47.5	Total Current				51.5	45.2	47.6
	7.7	13.3	13.7	Long-Term Debt				16.0	11.5	13.4
	.1	.0	.1	Deferred Taxes				.0	.1	.1
	5.8	5.5	9.5	All Other Non-Current				6.2	4.6	9.7
	37.7	33.6	29.3	Net Worth				26.3	38.6	29.3
	100.0	100.0	100.0	Total Liabilities & Net Worth				100.0	100.0	100.0
				INCOME DATA						
	100.0	100.0	100.0	Net Sales				100.0	100.0	100.0
	29.5	29.6	32.6	Gross Profit				40.6	35.1	28.4
	24.5	25.0	27.7	Operating Expenses				31.4	28.7	24.9
	5.0	4.6	4.9	Operating Profit				9.3	6.4	3.5
	-1.7	.2	.5	All Other Expenses (net)				.6	.1	.5
	6.7	4.4	4.4	Profit Before Taxes				8.7	6.3	2.9
				RATIOS						
	3.2	2.7	2.4					3.9	2.8	1.8
	1.8	1.7	1.6	Current				1.6	1.8	1.4
	1.3	1.2	1.2					.9	1.3	1.2
	1.5	1.3	1.4					1.3	1.8	1.1
	.9	.8	.8	Quick				.7	1.0	.7
	.5	.4	.5					.6	.5	.5
8	46.3	14	25.8	16	22.9			21	17.2	9	41.1	24	15.5
33	10.9	31	11.6	34	10.8	Sales/Receivables		38	9.6	29	12.7	45	8.2
57	6.4	55	6.6	58	6.3			60	6.1	49	7.4	61	6.0
25	14.4	24	15.2	18	20.8			0	UND	24	15.2	17	22.0
58	6.3	60	6.1	60	6.1	Cost of Sales/Inventory		70	5.2	79	4.6	55	6.6
118	3.1	146	2.5	140	2.6			174	2.1	140	2.6	122	3.0
10	36.1	11	32.5	12	29.8			27	13.3	10	36.7	17	21.4
23	16.0	24	15.4	24	14.9	Cost of Sales/Payables		54	6.8	19	19.7	25	14.6
48	7.6	46	7.9	45	8.2			59	6.2	54	6.7	36	10.2
	4.5		4.2		5.1				2.9		3.9		6.2
	7.5		8.0		9.6	Sales/Working Capital			5.9		6.4		10.8
	17.5		19.1		23.7				NM		17.1		22.4
	70.0		36.4		15.8				137.6		23.2		9.1
(97)	23.9	(131)	10.0	(157)	6.2	EBIT/Interest		(11)	7.4	(38)	7.2	(93)	5.2
	8.4		2.2		1.7				1.3		1.6		1.8
	24.7		11.1		8.6	Net Profit + Depr., Dep.,							6.6
(17)	6.2	(26)	4.0	(42)	2.2	Amort./Cur. Mat. L/T/D						(36)	2.1
	.9		1.4		.4								.4
	.0		.0		.1				.0		.0		.2
	.1		.2		.2	Fixed/Worth			.2		.1		.4
	.4		.6		.8				7.8		.3		1.1
	.6		.9		1.1				1.4		.8		1.6
	1.6		2.0		2.2	Debt/Worth			3.6		1.4		2.4
	3.5		5.4		5.9				674.2		4.6		5.8
	70.7		53.4		66.0				285.8		85.2		58.1
(112)	40.9	(151)	25.9	(162)	26.3	% Profit Before Taxes/Tangible Net Worth		(11)	20.0	(40)	26.3	(94)	26.3
	19.1		8.1		6.7				2.2		6.5		7.1
	31.3		21.7		18.4	% Profit Before Taxes/Total Assets			36.1		29.8		11.9
	15.3		9.6		7.5				10.2		10.1		6.8
	5.0		2.3		1.4				1.0		2.8		1.6
	133.9		203.0		166.8				368.1		289.4		67.5
	54.8		52.5		43.3	Sales/Net Fixed Assets			182.3		46.3		30.4
	24.2		19.9		17.5				56.0		22.1		12.4
	3.4		3.1		3.2				2.6		3.3		3.1
	2.6		2.4		2.4	Sales/Total Assets			2.0		2.5		2.5
	1.9		1.7		1.7				1.6		1.9		1.8
	.3		.3		.4						.2		.4
(85)	.7	(120)	.5	(137)	.6	% Depr., Dep., Amort./Sales				(30)	.4	(92)	.7
	1.1		.9		1.2						1.1		1.3
	1.1		1.0		.8						.8		.7
(30)	2.1	(36)	2.0	(43)	1.5	% Officers', Directors', Owners' Comp/Sales				(16)	1.5	(13)	1.0
	3.1		3.8		3.3						2.2		2.9
	5746416M		9909870M		12325319M	Net Sales ($)		3758M		15324M		36959M	110409M	748367M	11410502M
	2457491M		4677413M		6102127M	Total Assets ($)		5242M		3560M		17061M	62830M	342291M	5671143M

© RMA 2024   M = $ thousand   MM = $ million
See Pages viii through xx for Explanation of Ratios and Data

WHOLESALE—Home Furnishing Merchant Wholesalers NAICS 423220

Current Data Sorted by Assets

							Comparative Historical Data	
						Type of Statement		
			1	6	3	2	Unqualified	14	13
		2	3	21	4	1	Reviewed	25	11
	2	2	4	4			Compiled	18	11
2	2	4	7	1			Tax Returns	24	13
2	4	23	28	39	11	6	Other	121	69
0-500M	500M-2MM	23 (4/1-9/30/23) 2-10MM	130 (10/1/23-3/31/24) 10-50MM	50-100MM	100-250MM		4/1/19-3/31/20 ALL	4/1/20-3/31/21 ALL
4	8	43	71	18	9	**NUMBER OF STATEMENTS**	202	117
%	%	%	%	%	%	**ASSETS**	%	%
		18.7	12.0	9.4		Cash & Equivalents	9.3	14.8
		25.7	20.0	16.0		Trade Receivables (net)	24.1	25.1
		36.4	45.1	38.3		Inventory	44.8	39.9
		4.0	3.4	4.3		All Other Current	2.7	3.1
		84.8	80.5	68.0		Total Current	80.8	82.8
		4.6	9.0	11.2		Fixed Assets (net)	10.6	7.6
		1.6	1.9	9.1		Intangibles (net)	4.2	5.8
		9.1	8.6	11.7		All Other Non-Current	4.4	3.7
		100.0	100.0	100.0		Total	100.0	100.0
						LIABILITIES		
		13.7	13.1	9.4		Notes Payable-Short Term	16.8	12.8
		.5	2.5	1.9		Cur. Mat.-L.T.D.	1.1	1.6
		18.4	17.7	10.2		Trade Payables	20.0	19.0
		.0	.1	.3		Income Taxes Payable	.1	.1
		15.3	9.5	12.0		All Other Current	11.7	12.1
		47.9	42.9	33.8		Total Current	49.7	45.6
		3.0	12.3	10.3		Long-Term Debt	8.8	13.2
		.0	.1	.0		Deferred Taxes	.1	.1
		11.7	6.8	12.7		All Other Non-Current	7.8	8.1
		37.4	38.0	43.2		Net Worth	33.7	33.0
		100.0	100.0	100.0		Total Liabilities & Net Worth	100.0	100.0
						INCOME DATA		
		100.0	100.0	100.0		Net Sales	100.0	100.0
		37.3	38.0	38.8		Gross Profit	33.9	33.7
		31.9	33.3	32.1		Operating Expenses	29.1	29.9
		5.5	4.7	6.6		Operating Profit	4.8	3.8
		.5	.6	.9		All Other Expenses (net)	.7	.2
		5.0	4.1	5.8		Profit Before Taxes	4.1	3.6
						RATIOS		
		3.5	3.9	2.6			3.0	3.4
		2.0	1.7	2.2		Current	1.6	1.9
		1.2	1.3	1.6			1.2	1.3
		2.4	1.7	1.3			1.2	1.6
		1.0	.7	.7		Quick	.7	.9
		.4	.4	.4			.4	.5
		8 43.2	22 16.7	22 16.7			22 16.5	20 18.2
		29 12.8	37 9.8	27 13.4		Sales/Receivables	36 10.2	36 10.0
		65 5.6	52 7.0	45 8.2			51 7.1	68 5.4
		33 11.0	87 4.2	89 4.1			64 5.7	61 6.0
		81 4.5	140 2.6	111 3.3		Cost of Sales/Inventory	111 3.3	101 3.6
		159 2.3	243 1.5	203 1.8			166 2.2	159 2.3
		12 29.2	22 16.7	16 23.4			15 24.5	21 17.1
		37 9.8	40 9.2	37 9.9		Cost of Sales/Payables	33 11.0	38 9.6
		66 5.5	83 4.4	50 7.3			62 5.9	76 4.8
		3.9	3.7	3.0			4.5	3.9
		7.8	5.6	5.2		Sales/Working Capital	7.3	5.9
		15.9	13.6	9.9			17.9	12.2
		53.0	20.1	47.2			20.9	31.3
		(35) 4.9	(64) 3.8	(16) 6.3		EBIT/Interest	(173) 6.0	(102) 6.3
		-1.5	1.0	1.7			2.0	1.3
			14.5			Net Profit + Depr., Dep.,	28.5	17.7
		(18)	1.1			Amort./Cur. Mat. L/T/D	(32) 5.5	(18) 6.7
			-.3				1.1	2.6
		.0	.1	.1			.0	.0
		.1	.2	.3		Fixed/Worth	.2	.2
		.3	.6	NM			.8	.6
		.5	.6	.7			.7	.8
		1.1	1.9	1.2		Debt/Worth	2.1	2.3
		6.6	4.7	NM			6.2	7.1
		64.4	40.4	33.0			49.2	51.5
	(40)	29.4	(62) 18.4	(14) 16.8		% Profit Before Taxes/Tangible Net Worth	(171) 25.8	(95) 25.5
		6.5	7.1	9.6			9.7	7.9
		28.4	15.1	15.5			18.1	16.4
		10.9	6.1	7.7		% Profit Before Taxes/Total Assets	8.8	7.7
		1.6	.2	2.2			2.1	.8
		386.6	109.1	60.7			183.5	164.6
		127.3	30.2	15.5		Sales/Net Fixed Assets	49.0	54.3
		40.1	18.1	10.3			17.4	22.4
		3.3	2.8	2.4			3.3	3.0
		2.5	1.9	1.8		Sales/Total Assets	2.3	2.1
		1.9	1.5	1.0			1.7	1.5
		.1	.3	.4			.3	.3
	(22)	.2	(64) .5	(17) .6		% Depr., Dep., Amort./Sales	(144) .6	(82) .5
		.5	.9	1.6			1.1	1.2
		.7		.6			1.0	1.2
	(18)	1.9	(16) 2.1			% Officers', Directors' Owners' Comp/Sales	(70) 2.2	(28) 2.5
		4.1	4.0				4.3	5.1
3351M	86994M	680336M	3374790M	2307825M	2100891M	Net Sales ($)	11928210M	6669859M
1136M	12871M	252647M	1704770M	1302543M	1678638M	Total Assets ($)	5706736M	3549918M

© RMA 2024

M = $ thousand   MM = $ million
See Pages viii through xx for Explanation of Ratios and Data

WHOLESALE—Home Furnishing Merchant Wholesalers NAICS 423220

Comparative Historical Data / Current Data Sorted by Sales

						Type of Statement									
	10		21		12	Unqualified						1			11
	22		15		29	Reviewed						1		7	21
	3		9		10	Compiled						1		6	3
	8		16		12	Tax Returns			2		1	5		1	3
	67		90		90	Other		2	1		3	10		19	55
	4/1/21-		4/1/22-		4/1/23-				23 (4/1-9/30/23)			130 (10/1/23-3/31/24)			
	3/31/22		3/31/23		3/31/24			0-1MM	1-3MM		3-5MM	5-10MM		10-25MM	25MM & OVER
	ALL		ALL		ALL										
	110		151		153	**NUMBER OF STATEMENTS**		2	3		4	18		33	93
	%		%		%	**ASSETS**		%	%		%	%		%	%
	16.3		12.1		14.5	Cash & Equivalents						21.4		15.9	12.6
	21.8		19.4		20.4	Trade Receivables (net)						17.1		24.9	20.2
	37.2		43.1		40.0	Inventory						35.8		43.6	38.4
	3.8		4.2		3.6	All Other Current						8.5		1.7	3.6
	79.2		78.8		78.5	Total Current						82.8		86.1	74.9
	9.4		10.0		8.6	Fixed Assets (net)						6.1		5.4	10.5
	5.4		4.3		4.0	Intangibles (net)						1.7		2.9	5.0
	6.0		6.9		8.9	All Other Non-Current						9.4		5.6	9.6
	100.0		100.0		100.0	Total						100.0		100.0	100.0
						LIABILITIES									
	11.2		11.1		12.3	Notes Payable-Short Term						11.7		13.7	11.2
	1.5		2.1		1.7	Cur. Mat.-L.T.D.						.5		2.4	1.9
	17.0		19.5		17.4	Trade Payables						17.6		16.2	18.6
	.8		.1		.1	Income Taxes Payable						.0		.0	.2
	11.4		10.9		13.7	All Other Current						23.1		14.8	11.0
	42.0		43.7		45.3	Total Current						52.8		47.1	42.8
	12.7		13.4		10.7	Long-Term Debt						3.9		8.0	12.9
	.0		.1		.1	Deferred Taxes						.0		.0	.1
	7.0		6.5		9.0	All Other Non-Current						18.4		7.3	7.6
	38.3		36.4		34.9	Net Worth						24.9		37.6	36.5
	100.0		100.0		100.0	Total Liabilities & Net Worth						100.0		100.0	100.0
						INCOME DATA									
	100.0		100.0		100.0	Net Sales						100.0		100.0	100.0
	35.2		34.8		38.5	Gross Profit						42.8		38.5	36.8
	28.9		29.7		32.8	Operating Expenses						36.2		33.5	31.0
	6.3		5.2		5.7	Operating Profit						6.6		5.0	5.8
	-1.0		.6		.9	All Other Expenses (net)						.6		.8	.8
	7.3		4.6		4.9	Profit Before Taxes						6.0		4.2	5.0
						RATIOS									
	3.0		3.3		3.4							3.6		4.1	3.3
	1.7		1.8		1.8	Current						1.7		2.0	1.7
	1.4		1.4		1.3							1.2		1.3	1.3
	1.6		1.3		1.6							1.9		1.9	1.5
	.8		.6		.7	Quick						.9		.7	.7
	.5		.4		.4							.3		.4	.4
20	18.2	13	27.2	14	25.3						2	219.6	14	26.1	20	18.7
35	10.5	29	12.4	32	11.5	Sales/Receivables					22	16.5	43	8.5	33	11.0
51	7.1	46	7.9	52	7.0						40	9.2	69	5.3	51	7.1
47	7.8	61	6.0	63	5.8						0	UND	49	7.4	73	5.0
99	3.7	107	3.4	111	3.3	Cost of Sales/Inventory					89	4.1	118	3.1	104	3.5
166	2.2	182	2.0	192	1.9						174	2.1	304	1.2	166	2.2
12	29.2	16	22.6	20	18.2						7	53.0	17	21.9	22	16.9
38	9.7	38	9.6	39	9.4	Cost of Sales/Payables					28	12.9	40	9.1	39	9.4
64	5.7	74	4.9	68	5.4						66	5.5	74	4.9	68	5.4
	4.1		3.8		3.7							3.9		2.8	4.0
	6.7		6.4		6.3	Sales/Working Capital						9.0		4.4	6.3
	11.5		13.3		13.9							21.4		12.9	12.6
	42.7		27.3		42.0							80.5		10.6	42.8
(85)	17.9	(126)	8.4	(133)	4.6	EBIT/Interest					(15)	44.8	(28)	2.1	(81)	4.9
	4.9		1.3		1.1							-2.5		.1	1.2
	32.7		6.8		30.2	Net Profit + Depr., Dep.,									32.2
(17)	11.7	(20)	4.4	(33)	3.9	Amort./Cur. Mat. L/T/D							(28)	4.0
	6.4		1.6		.3										1.0
	.0		.0		.0							.0		.0	.1
	.1		.2		.2	Fixed/Worth						.0		.1	.3
	.5		.5		.7							.3		.7	.7
	.7		.7		.6							.5		.5	.6
	1.6		1.8		1.7	Debt/Worth						1.4		1.8	1.7
	3.9		5.0		8.2							18.1		8.1	7.3
	64.4		42.5		48.9							76.1		45.2	47.7
(97)	42.6	(129)	23.5	(129)	21.9	% Profit Before Taxes/Tangible					(15)	32.4	(30)	14.6	(76)	24.4
	25.1		9.6		7.8	Net Worth						7.7		2.3	11.3
	31.2		18.6		22.9							39.8		16.5	22.8
	16.5		8.9		7.7	% Profit Before Taxes/Total						16.2		4.5	8.6
	6.2		3.4		.8	Assets						-5.6		.2	1.8
	168.5		135.7		144.8							423.7		227.7	119.7
	53.1		52.9		41.4	Sales/Net Fixed Assets						122.1		46.5	30.2
	20.4		18.1		18.4							28.0		26.5	12.4
	3.1		3.1		2.9							3.7		2.7	3.0
	2.2		2.2		2.1	Sales/Total Assets						2.7		2.0	2.1
	1.6		1.5		1.5							1.7		1.2	1.5
	.3		.3		.2									.2	.2
(76)	.6	(99)	.5	(114)	.5	% Depr., Dep., Amort./Sales							(24)	.4	(78)	.5
	1.2		.9		1.0									1.0	1.1
	.9		.7		.9							2.4		.8	.3
(33)	1.3	(54)	1.5	(43)	1.9	% Officers', Directors'					(10)	4.2	(11)	1.9	(19)	1.2
	3.3		4.2		4.4	Owners' Comp/Sales						6.2		4.1	1.9
	6782351M		11497575M		8554187M	Net Sales ($)		1248M	4732M		19252M	140010M		579037M	7809908M
	3528495M		5836836M		4952605M	Total Assets ($)		461M	1785M		11765M	66139M		353759M	4518696M

M = $ thousand   MM = $ million
See Pages viii through xx for Explanation of Ratios and Data

© RMA 2024

WHOLESALE—Lumber, Plywood, Millwork, and Wood Panel Merchant Wholesalers   NAICS 423310

Current Data Sorted by Assets | Comparative Historical Data

							Type of Statement		
			3	14	9	5	Unqualified	34	28
			16	37	7	2	Reviewed	70	30
		3	21	9	2		Compiled	39	20
	1	7	21	2			Tax Returns	50	41
		19	50	55	24	12	Other	202	127
		53 (4/1-9/30/23)		266 (10/1/23-3/31/24)				4/1/19-3/31/20	4/1/20-3/31/21
	0-500M	500M-2MM	2-10MM	10-50MM	50-100MM	100-250MM		ALL	ALL
	1	29	111	117	42	19	NUMBER OF STATEMENTS	395	246
	%	%	%	%	%	%	ASSETS	%	%
		18.0	12.4	14.4	14.7	7.5	Cash & Equivalents	8.4	12.0
		36.6	26.8	20.6	18.3	20.8	Trade Receivables (net)	28.1	29.2
		29.4	36.1	36.1	30.2	37.1	Inventory	37.6	35.0
		1.0	2.8	2.7	3.0	5.5	All Other Current	2.4	2.6
		85.0	78.1	73.9	66.3	70.8	Total Current	76.5	78.8
		8.5	14.2	16.0	20.3	21.1	Fixed Assets (net)	14.7	13.2
		1.8	3.1	2.8	5.0	2.5	Intangibles (net)	3.6	3.2
		4.6	4.6	7.2	8.4	5.6	All Other Non-Current	5.2	4.9
		100.0	100.0	100.0	100.0	100.0	Total	100.0	100.0
							LIABILITIES		
		9.4	8.4	8.1	8.6	2.2	Notes Payable-Short Term	16.9	13.1
		.5	2.2	1.6	1.3	1.2	Cur. Mat.-L.T.D.	1.8	1.5
		18.9	11.7	9.3	8.6	9.7	Trade Payables	12.4	13.8
		.0	.1	.2	.1	.1	Income Taxes Payable	.1	.2
		6.0	10.4	10.4	10.0	6.6	All Other Current	9.0	10.5
		34.8	32.7	29.7	28.5	19.9	Total Current	40.2	39.1
		8.8	11.0	7.5	8.5	16.4	Long-Term Debt	8.8	11.8
		.0	.0	.3	.8	.3	Deferred Taxes	.2	.1
		2.1	3.6	4.6	8.3	3.8	All Other Non-Current	4.8	2.0
		54.3	52.7	58.0	53.9	59.6	Net Worth	45.9	46.8
		100.0	100.0	100.0	100.0	100.0	Total Liabilities & Net Worth	100.0	100.0
							INCOME DATA		
		100.0	100.0	100.0	100.0	100.0	Net Sales	100.0	100.0
		24.5	25.6	24.7	24.6	23.6	Gross Profit	22.3	22.4
		21.3	19.9	18.9	19.1	16.9	Operating Expenses	19.0	18.1
		3.2	5.7	5.7	5.5	6.8	Operating Profit	3.3	4.3
		-.2	.4	.5	.2	-.2	All Other Expenses (net)	.4	-.6
		3.4	5.3	5.2	5.3	6.9	Profit Before Taxes	2.9	4.8
							RATIOS		
		8.2	4.8	4.9	4.7	7.8		3.8	4.1
		2.8	2.9	2.8	2.8	4.1	Current	1.9	2.0
		1.6	1.6	1.7	1.7	2.6		1.4	1.5
		6.8	2.7	2.4	2.4	3.6		1.8	2.0
		1.8	1.4	1.2	1.2	1.2	Quick	.8	1.0
		.9	.6	.6	.6	.9		.5	.6
	15	24.8	18	20.0	18	20.3	19	19.3	23	16.1		20	17.9	21	17.7
	32	11.5	27	13.5	25	14.6	26	13.8	32	11.4	Sales/Receivables	29	12.6	31	11.8
	51	7.1	37	9.9	35	10.5	36	10.0	40	9.2		38	9.5	39	9.3
	2	149.8	25	14.4	33	11.0	40	9.2	54	6.8		33	11.0	29	12.4
	23	16.0	56	6.5	62	5.9	66	5.5	60	6.1	Cost of Sales/Inventory	56	6.5	58	6.3
	62	5.9	99	3.7	96	3.8	83	4.4	79	4.6		79	4.6	79	4.6
	4	90.7	6	58.6	7	49.9	12	29.8	11	33.7		7	48.8	8	43.7
	18	20.8	13	27.3	13	27.3	15	24.6	19	19.0	Cost of Sales/Payables	14	27.0	15	24.2
	37	9.8	25	14.8	21	17.5	22	16.9	22	16.8		24	15.2	24	14.9
		4.0	4.2	4.0	3.6	3.6		5.2	4.9
		6.9	7.3	6.3	4.9	5.1	Sales/Working Capital	9.4	8.3
		24.1	13.0	9.5	9.5	7.6		17.4	17.9
		60.9	31.6	57.7	56.8	112.2		14.8	44.5
	(24)	4.3	(97)	6.9	(93)	11.7	(38)	13.6	(18)	10.8	EBIT/Interest	(342)	4.9	(215)	12.5
		-.5	3.6	3.0	2.6	2.0		1.5	4.0
			15.2	30.5	17.7			12.9	17.5
			(18)	6.1	(26)	5.5	(15)	8.9		Net Profit + Depr., Dep., Amort./Cur. Mat. L/T/D	(84)	5.1	(42)	5.6
			4.1	1.9	1.8			2.0	3.0
		.0	.0	.1	.1	.3		.1	.0
		.1	.2	.2	.4	.4	Fixed/Worth	.3	.2
		.3	.5	.5	.6	.5		.6	.5
		.2	.3	.3	.5	.3		.5	.5
		.5	.9	.6	.8	.7	Debt/Worth	1.3	1.4
		1.4	2.3	1.4	1.9	1.7		3.1	2.6
		54.3	44.9	43.6	38.3	40.1		34.7	55.0
	(25)	21.9	(104)	28.0	(114)	24.6	(39)	23.4	20.0	% Profit Before Taxes/Tangible Net Worth	(364)	17.2	(234)	31.3
		1.9	11.7	10.6	13.8	6.6		5.6	12.4
		34.8	22.9	22.9	20.6	22.0		15.3	22.3
		9.6	10.9	12.6	13.4	12.4	% Profit Before Taxes/Total Assets	7.2	13.6
		-1.3	4.2	4.9	4.7	2.5		1.5	4.8
		801.9	172.5	58.0	44.3	18.4		89.8	207.5
		74.7	42.0	29.9	12.2	11.4	Sales/Net Fixed Assets	35.2	34.7
		27.8	14.8	10.2	5.3	7.9		12.8	14.0
		6.1	4.3	3.5	2.8	3.1		4.3	4.4
		3.6	3.1	2.6	2.1	2.4	Sales/Total Assets	3.1	3.1
		2.4	2.0	2.0	1.3	1.8		2.3	2.3
		.0	.3	.3	.3	.6		.4	.3
	(14)	.3	(82)	.6	(101)	.7	(37)	1.2	(17)	1.0	% Depr., Dep., Amort./Sales	(320)	.8	(187)	.7
		.6	1.2	1.3	1.7	1.4		1.3	1.3
			.9	.8				.9	1.3
		(46)	1.8	(28)	1.4			% Officers', Directors' Owners' Comp/Sales	(111)	1.6	(73)	2.0
			3.5	2.2				3.4	3.5
	719M	166271M	2010057M	7997905M	7144918M	6948514M	Net Sales ($)	29884629M	18287712M
	83M	35316M	600894M	2894763M	3109255M	2767018M	Total Assets ($)	10236367M	5913993M

© RMA 2024   M = $ thousand   MM = $ million
See Pages viii through xx for Explanation of Ratios and Data

WHOLESALE—Lumber, Plywood, Millwork, and Wood Panel Merchant Wholesalers NAICS 423310

Comparative Historical Data					Current Data Sorted by Sales					
26	34	31	**Type of Statement**					2	29	
42	47	62	Unqualified					10	50	
20	37	35	Reviewed		1	1	6	12	15	
32	39	31	Compiled	1	2	3	6	14	5	
121	176	160	Tax Returns	1	8	7	18	30	96	
4/1/21-3/31/22 ALL	4/1/22-3/31/23 ALL	4/1/23-3/31/24 ALL	Other	53 (4/1-9/30/23)			266 (10/1/23-3/31/24)			
				0-1MM	1-3MM	3-5MM	5-10MM	10-25MM	25MM & OVER	
241	333	319	NUMBER OF STATEMENTS	2	11	11	32	68	195	
%	%	%	**ASSETS**	%	%	%	%	%	%	
12.3	12.9	13.8	Cash & Equivalents	22.8	21.3	9.8	14.3	13.2		
30.0	25.2	23.9	Trade Receivables (net)	22.9	23.6	27.3	25.4	23.1		
35.1	37.3	34.7	Inventory	34.2	22.7	34.1	39.5	34.1		
1.7	2.7	2.8	All Other Current	1.0	.6	3.1	2.2	3.2		
79.0	78.1	75.1	Total Current	80.8	68.1	74.3	81.4	73.6		
12.8	12.7	15.7	Fixed Assets (net)	13.9	18.2	16.7	10.8	16.6		
3.0	3.4	3.1	Intangibles (net)	.8	7.2	3.4	2.7	3.1		
5.1	5.8	6.1	All Other Non-Current	4.4	6.4	5.6	5.1	6.6		
100.0	100.0	100.0	Total	100.0	100.0	100.0	100.0	100.0		
			LIABILITIES							
11.0	9.8	8.0	Notes Payable-Short Term	13.0	3.6	8.7	8.6	7.6		
1.5	1.2	1.6	Cur. Mat.-L.T.D.	.9	.4	2.0	1.2	1.9		
13.4	12.1	10.9	Trade Payables	13.8	18.0	14.9	11.8	9.5		
.3	.3	.1	Income Taxes Payable	.0	.0	.0	.1	.2		
10.7	10.3	9.7	All Other Current	6.9	10.7	7.4	7.8	10.8		
36.9	33.7	30.4	Total Current	34.6	32.8	33.1	29.5	30.0		
9.4	10.2	9.8	Long-Term Debt	7.2	18.7	15.4	8.2	8.4		
.2	.2	.2	Deferred Taxes	.0	.0	.0	.1	.4		
4.2	3.7	4.5	All Other Non-Current	4.4	2.2	2.3	3.7	5.2		
49.3	52.1	55.2	Net Worth	53.8	46.3	49.1	58.4	56.1		
100.0	100.0	100.0	Total Liabilities & Net Worth	100.0	100.0	100.0	100.0	100.0		
			INCOME DATA							
100.0	100.0	100.0	Net Sales	100.0	100.0	100.0	100.0	100.0		
23.0	24.5	24.9	Gross Profit	40.0	30.0	26.9	25.3	23.0		
17.4	17.9	19.3	Operating Expenses	31.9	21.7	22.2	20.1	17.7		
5.6	6.5	5.5	Operating Profit	8.0	8.3	4.8	5.2	5.3		
-1.1	.0	.3	All Other Expenses (net)	4.8	.0	1.0	-.3	.1		
6.7	6.5	5.2	Profit Before Taxes	3.2	8.3	3.8	5.4	5.2		
			RATIOS							
4.1	4.7	5.0		8.4	12.9	3.7	6.1	4.7		
2.3	2.5	2.9	Current	3.2	1.9	2.4	3.2	2.9		
1.5	1.6	1.7		2.0	1.0	1.5	1.9	1.7		
2.2	2.5	2.6		8.3	8.5	2.3	3.0	2.4		
1.1	1.2	1.3	Quick	2.0	1.0	1.2	1.6	1.2		
.6	.5	.7		.1	.8	.7	.6	.7		
20 18.2	15 23.7	18 20.1		5 67.0	13 28.6	21 17.5	16 22.3	18 19.8		
29 12.7	25 14.4	26 13.9	Sales/Receivables	37 9.8	37 9.9	30 12.3	27 13.5	25 14.7		
40 9.1	35 10.5	37 9.9		69 5.3	54 6.8	46 7.9	35 10.5	35 10.5		
29 12.7	30 12.0	30 12.2		0 UND	15 24.9	32 11.4	27 13.6	33 11.1		
53 6.9	57 6.4	60 6.1	Cost of Sales/Inventory	26 14.0	36 10.0	70 5.2	69 5.3	59 6.2		
87 4.2	91 4.0	89 4.1		332 1.1	60 6.1	104 3.5	122 3.0	79 4.6		
9 41.7	7 53.9	8 47.8		1 265.5	12 31.0	11 33.8	7 50.4	8 47.8		
17 21.3	13 27.3	14 25.6	Cost of Sales/Payables	20 18.6	22 16.8	23 15.8	16 22.2	13 28.5		
25 14.5	25 14.7	22 16.4		44 8.3	83 4.4	37 9.9	28 13.0	20 18.7		
5.2	4.6	4.0		2.1	3.6	4.3	3.6	4.2		
7.7	7.4	6.4	Sales/Working Capital	2.9	5.8	7.6	5.3	6.8		
14.9	14.9	11.4		4.3	697.6	13.2	8.9	11.6		
88.8	54.7	49.3				34.3	31.5	54.5		
(207) 23.5	(281) 18.4	(271) 9.8	EBIT/Interest	(29) 4.3	(58) 8.2	(168) 10.9				
9.7	7.6	2.8				2.2	2.9	3.0		
42.2	24.0	22.6	Net Profit + Depr., Dep.,				17.4	23.3		
(37) 10.4	(69) 11.5	(65) 6.3	Amort./Cur. Mat. L/T/D		(10) 6.1	(54) 7.6				
6.0	5.3	3.1					2.9	2.9		
.0	.1	.1		.0	.0	.0	.0	.1		
.2	.2	.2	Fixed/Worth	.1	.2	.2	.1	.2		
.5	.4	.5		.3	-11.4	1.3	.4	.5		
.4	.4	.3		.1	.1	.3	.3	.4		
1.0	1.0	.7	Debt/Worth	.4	1.3	1.3	.6	.7		
2.4	2.3	1.8		1.8	-22.1	4.3	1.8	1.6		
70.9	62.9	43.2	% Profit Before Taxes/Tangible			45.3	40.3	42.9		
(229) 43.2	(312) 40.7	(302) 24.8	Net Worth	(29) 24.0	(65) 21.7	(189) 25.3				
23.2	18.2	9.6				6.8	11.8	9.8		
28.8	29.8	22.8	% Profit Before Taxes/Total	21.2	33.2	17.6	21.0	22.9		
18.8	18.4	12.1	Assets	2.8	19.5	8.3	12.1	13.5		
11.4	9.2	4.2		-12.7	-5.2	2.6	4.0	4.9		
193.8	163.9	81.4		78.2	604.0	137.5	158.2	67.4		
36.8	40.0	28.1	Sales/Net Fixed Assets	42.1	18.3	28.2	39.5	25.3		
17.3	15.4	10.1		26.0	6.5	5.3	16.2	9.6		
4.4	4.2	3.7		3.2	3.8	3.6	3.7	3.8		
3.1	3.1	2.7	Sales/Total Assets	1.7	2.6	2.3	3.0	2.8		
2.2	2.3	2.0		1.4	1.4	1.6	1.9	2.0		
.2	.3	.3				.3	.4	.3		
(187) .6	(250) .6	(252) .7	% Depr., Dep., Amort./Sales		(25) .6	(46) .8	(170) .7			
1.1	1.0	1.4					1.3	1.4	1.4	
.9	.9	.9				2.1	.8	.8		
(77) 1.7	(126) 1.5	(95) 1.7	% Officers', Directors'	(11) 3.3	(37) 1.5	(40) 1.4				
3.4	3.1	3.2	Owners' Comp/Sales			4.3	2.9	2.3		
17282528M	25455934M	24268384M	Net Sales ($)	1062M	21292M	43664M	237407M	1088990M	22875969M	
5359589M	8530222M	9407329M	Total Assets ($)	2522M	25196M	22103M	105937M	452959M	8798612M	

M = $ thousand   MM = $ million
See Pages viii through xx for Explanation of Ratios and Data

© RMA 2024

WHOLESALE—Brick, Stone, and Related Construction Material Merchant Wholesalers NAICS 423320

Current Data Sorted by Assets | **Comparative Historical Data**

0-500M	500M-2MM	2-10MM	10-50MM	50-100MM	100-250MM		4/1/19-3/31/20 ALL	4/1/20-3/31/21 ALL
			4		3	Type of Statement		
		3	6		1	Unqualified	4	5
	1	9	2	3		Reviewed	25	9
1	3	6	5	1		Compiled	18	8
1	7	39	28		7	Tax Returns	23	9
	18 (4/1-9/30/23)		117 (10/1/23-3/31/24)	5		Other	88	53
2	11	57	45	9	11	NUMBER OF STATEMENTS	158	84
%	%	%	%	%	%	**ASSETS**	%	%
	28.7	12.0	13.4		9.5	Cash & Equivalents	10.2	16.5
	16.8	21.9	19.3		21.3	Trade Receivables (net)	22.8	20.6
	23.0	39.3	31.3		23.4	Inventory	32.4	27.2
	4.5	3.0	3.2		1.5	All Other Current	2.6	2.6
	73.0	76.1	67.2		55.8	Total Current	68.1	66.8
	18.7	12.2	24.2		31.8	Fixed Assets (net)	22.6	21.4
	6.2	2.2	2.3		7.1	Intangibles (net)	3.1	5.2
	2.1	9.4	6.3		5.3	All Other Non-Current	6.3	6.5
	100.0	100.0	100.0		100.0	Total	100.0	100.0
						LIABILITIES		
	4.8	8.2	7.9		3.1	Notes Payable-Short Term	11.0	4.4
	6.0	2.8	2.2		3.7	Cur. Mat.-L.T.D.	2.4	2.9
	7.2	18.6	12.3		15.7	Trade Payables	15.3	15.3
	.2	.0	.3		.2	Income Taxes Payable	.2	.1
	7.6	10.3	6.7		10.1	All Other Current	10.1	10.7
	25.9	39.9	29.5		32.8	Total Current	38.9	33.3
	8.3	14.1	12.8		21.1	Long-Term Debt	15.0	19.7
	.0	.2	.2		.7	Deferred Taxes	.3	.4
	1.7	4.4	4.0		7.0	All Other Non-Current	4.5	4.1
	64.1	41.4	53.5		38.4	Net Worth	41.3	42.5
	100.0	100.0	100.0		100.0	Total Liabilities & Net Worth	100.0	100.0
						INCOME DATA		
	100.0	100.0	100.0		100.0	Net Sales	100.0	100.0
	35.4	33.4	31.6		32.2	Gross Profit	33.7	33.9
	31.5	26.6	24.7		27.1	Operating Expenses	28.7	28.3
	3.9	6.8	6.9		5.1	Operating Profit	5.0	5.6
	-.2	1.0	.4		.7	All Other Expenses (net)	.7	-.3
	4.1	5.7	6.5		4.3	Profit Before Taxes	4.3	5.8
						RATIOS		
	6.2	3.2	3.7		2.6		3.0	3.8
	3.1	2.3	2.1		2.2	Current	2.1	2.4
	1.6	1.3	1.4		1.3		1.2	1.5
	3.4	2.0	2.2		1.8		1.7	2.0
	1.7	.8	1.1		1.2	Quick	.8	1.3
	1.0	.4	.6		.6		.4	.7
3	144.6	18 20.3	23 15.6		30 12.3		23 16.2	21 17.5
27	13.7	27 13.3	36 10.0		45 8.1	Sales/Receivables	32 11.3	33 11.2
36	10.2	50 7.3	53 6.9		46 7.9		54 6.7	48 7.6
0	UND	19 19.2	31 11.8		19 19.3		31 11.9	17 21.9
58	6.3	130 2.8	96 3.8		31 11.6	Cost of Sales/Inventory	65 5.6	56 6.5
114	3.2	203 1.8	192 1.9		104 3.5		140 2.6	122 3.0
0	UND	11 33.9	20 18.5		21 17.4		16 23.4	12 30.1
11	33.8	34 10.8	33 10.9		31 11.7	Cost of Sales/Payables	31 11.9	31 11.9
32	11.4	72 5.1	48 7.6		85 4.3		58 6.3	62 5.9
	3.6	3.7	2.5		5.6		4.4	3.4
	6.3	6.3	5.7		5.9	Sales/Working Capital	7.0	5.8
	61.1	15.3	11.8		18.5		18.8	11.0
		31.9	28.9		14.3		25.2	20.0
	(50)	9.0	(40) 6.7		(10) 9.8	EBIT/Interest	(141) 7.5	(68) 6.8
		2.2	2.6		1.5		2.4	1.6
			7.0			Net Profit + Depr., Dep.,	7.7	14.0
		(16)	5.0			Amort./Cur. Mat. L/T/D	(28) 3.3	(12) 2.9
			3.1				1.7	1.9
	.0	.0	.1		.4		.1	.1
	.2	.2	.4		.9	Fixed/Worth	.5	.6
	1.1	.8	1.0		1.4		1.1	1.3
	.2	.6	.5		.8		.6	.5
	.5	1.2	.9		1.0	Debt/Worth	1.3	1.2
	1.3	3.9	1.7		8.4		3.9	6.0
	73.4	55.7	36.1			% Profit Before Taxes/Tangible	41.9	41.7
	(10) 13.5	(51) 28.8	(43) 19.9			Net Worth	(139) 19.6	(69) 23.8
	1.2	14.1	10.1				7.1	11.1
	40.8	21.8	18.5		14.2	% Profit Before Taxes/Total	17.0	16.1
	7.3	9.7	9.7		11.3	Assets	7.4	9.5
	-2.9	4.0	3.6		2.3		2.1	2.5
	76.3	80.6	40.0		37.4		46.6	42.3
	22.6	30.6	9.5		4.6	Sales/Net Fixed Assets	19.9	17.9
	12.3	11.0	4.0		3.2		5.2	6.0
	4.9	2.9	2.2		2.0		2.9	2.8
	2.7	2.1	1.6		1.9	Sales/Total Assets	2.2	1.9
	2.1	1.5	1.3		1.4		1.3	1.3
		.4	.7				.6	.4
	(29)	.9	(36) 1.7			% Depr., Dep., Amort./Sales	(114) 1.4	(56) 1.3
		2.9	3.0				3.4	3.5
		.9	.3			% Officers', Directors'	.8	1.0
	(18)	1.8	(15) 1.3			Owners' Comp/Sales	(47) 1.8	(27) 2.3
		2.8	2.6				3.9	6.4
15647M	47909M	661253M	1815400M	1015757M	3275428M	Net Sales ($)	5958711M	3495593M
252M	13457M	311555M	993393M	612463M	1582208M	Total Assets ($)	3158435M	2099442M

© RMA 2024   M = $ thousand   MM = $ million
See Pages viii through xx for Explanation of Ratios and Data

WHOLESALE—Brick, Stone, and Related Construction Material Merchant Wholesalers NAICS 423320

Comparative Historical Data | Current Data Sorted by Sales

				Type of Statement						
3	8	7		Unqualified				1	2	7
15	19	13		Reviewed			1	4	7	10
9	12	13		Compiled		1	2	6	3	1
7	21	15		Tax Returns		2	5	6	3	2
52	98	87		Other	2	5	8	18	27	34
4/1/21-3/31/22 ALL	4/1/22-3/31/23 ALL	4/1/23-3/31/24 ALL			3			117 (10/1/23-3/31/24)		
					0-1MM	1-3MM	3-5MM	5-10MM	10-25MM	25MM & OVER
86	158	135		NUMBER OF STATEMENTS	5	5	8	29	39	54
%	%	%		ASSETS	%	%	%	%	%	%
13.5	11.3	14.0		Cash & Equivalents				14.8	13.0	12.6
23.0	21.6	19.8		Trade Receivables (net)	DATA NOT AVAILABLE			15.7	23.3	21.2
31.6	36.2	33.3		Inventory				34.3	37.3	27.4
2.1	3.6	3.1		All Other Current				6.9	2.4	2.1
70.2	72.6	70.3		Total Current				71.7	76.1	63.2
18.6	18.5	19.5		Fixed Assets (net)				16.2	14.4	26.9
4.8	3.0	3.1		Intangibles (net)				2.8	.9	3.8
6.5	5.9	7.1		All Other Non-Current				9.3	8.6	6.1
100.0	100.0	100.0		Total				100.0	100.0	100.0
				LIABILITIES						
8.1	7.9	7.3		Notes Payable-Short Term				4.7	7.9	7.1
1.7	2.7	2.9		Cur. Mat.-L.T.D.				3.0	1.8	3.0
15.3	20.8	15.1		Trade Payables				19.0	13.8	13.6
.1	.1	.1		Income Taxes Payable				.1	.0	.3
9.5	8.0	9.9		All Other Current				16.3	9.8	7.7
34.7	39.5	35.3		Total Current				43.2	33.3	31.7
13.6	14.8	14.1		Long-Term Debt				10.4	13.9	16.5
.4	.2	.2		Deferred Taxes				.3	.1	.3
3.9	3.9	4.2		All Other Non-Current				5.9	3.2	5.0
47.5	41.6	46.2		Net Worth				40.2	49.5	46.5
100.0	100.0	100.0		Total Liabilities & Net Worth				100.0	100.0	100.0
				INCOME DATA						
100.0	100.0	100.0		Net Sales				100.0	100.0	100.0
34.9	33.5	32.8		Gross Profit				33.1	36.1	29.3
26.4	25.5	26.4		Operating Expenses				26.2	28.9	23.2
8.5	7.9	6.3		Operating Profit				6.9	7.2	6.1
-1.0	.4	.6		All Other Expenses (net)				.1	1.2	.2
9.6	7.5	5.8		Profit Before Taxes				6.8	6.0	5.9
				RATIOS						
3.0	3.1	3.1		Current				3.2	6.1	2.7
2.4	2.0	2.2						2.3	2.6	2.1
1.6	1.3	1.4						1.1	1.7	1.5
1.9	1.5	1.9		Quick				1.3	2.9	1.8
1.2	.7	1.0						.6	1.0	1.1
.7	.4	.5						.3	.6	.6
23 15.6	19 19.0	20 18.1		Sales/Receivables	5 75.0	21 17.5	26 14.0			
37 9.8	35 10.4	33 11.1			19 19.2	35 10.3	38 9.6			
57 6.4	53 6.9	47 7.7			37 9.8	52 7.0	47 7.7			
20 17.9	25 14.7	19 19.1		Cost of Sales/Inventory	0 UND	20 18.7	27 13.7			
73 5.0	101 3.6	91 4.0			99 3.7	122 3.0	73 5.0			
146 2.5	203 1.8	182 2.0			203 1.8	203 1.8	111 3.3			
20 18.4	21 17.6	17 21.9		Cost of Sales/Payables	9 39.5	14 25.2	17 21.3			
35 10.5	38 9.6	30 12.3			25 14.5	33 10.9	28 13.1			
72 5.1	81 4.5	55 6.6			74 4.9	55 6.6	48 7.6			
3.3	3.5	3.6		Sales/Working Capital				3.9	2.7	5.0
4.8	6.2	5.9						7.6	4.9	6.8
11.9	12.7	15.6						39.5	11.5	12.2
70.3	50.9	28.9		EBIT/Interest				44.6	57.0	23.9
(75) 16.7	(128) 14.3	(116) 8.8			(21) 17.4	(35) 8.8	(50) 8.8			
7.2	4.7	2.3						2.6	1.8	2.9
	9.7	7.0		Net Profit + Depr., Dep., Amort./Cur. Mat. L/T/D						6.9
	(22) 5.1	(27) 3.9							(20) 3.8	
	2.5	2.6								2.6
.1	.0	.1		Fixed/Worth				.1	.0	.2
.3	.2	.3						.3	.1	.7
1.0	.9	1.0						1.2	.9	1.0
.5	.6	.5		Debt/Worth				.6	.3	.7
1.2	1.3	1.0						1.4	.8	1.0
2.7	4.6	2.7						6.1	2.7	2.0
58.5	65.3	48.0		% Profit Before Taxes/Tangible Net Worth				57.3	49.1	40.0
(78) 33.0	(144) 31.6	(122) 23.7					(25) 26.0	(36) 22.9	(50) 23.9	
18.5	15.4	10.4						10.3	10.2	13.5
26.2	23.3	19.6		% Profit Before Taxes/Total Assets				32.1	21.1	18.9
13.4	13.4	9.7						9.0	12.9	10.1
6.6	4.7	3.7						4.6	2.8	4.5
81.0	122.6	61.3		Sales/Net Fixed Assets				70.7	130.9	33.5
24.8	24.9	17.7						22.6	31.8	8.1
5.7	6.3	6.6						8.0	7.7	3.7
2.7	2.7	2.6		Sales/Total Assets				3.5	2.6	2.4
1.8	1.8	1.9						1.8	2.0	1.9
1.3	1.3	1.4						1.2	1.3	1.5
.6	.7	.6		% Depr., Dep., Amort./Sales				.5	.2	.8
(58) 1.2	(90) 1.7	(87) 1.7					(17) 2.0	(21) .7	(45) 1.8	
3.7	3.5	3.4						3.5	2.9	4.1
.8	1.1	.7		% Officers', Directors', Owners' Comp/Sales					.6	.5
(27) 2.0	(41) 1.6	(42) 1.7						(12) 1.5	(17) 1.3	
5.1	3.2	2.9							2.7	2.2
2909293M	6743059M	6831394M		Net Sales ($)	11480M	32322M	221561M	590347M	5975684M	
1749576M	3714174M	3513328M		Total Assets ($)	5838M	19112M	132212M	344509M	3011657M	

© RMA 2024 M = $ thousand MM = $ million
See Pages viii through xx for Explanation of Ratios and Data

WHOLESALE—Roofing, Siding, and Insulation Material Merchant Wholesalers NAICS 423330

Current Data Sorted by Assets | Comparative Historical Data

							Type of Statement		
			1	2	1	1	Unqualified	6	3
			4	4	1		Reviewed	9	6
		2	2	3			Compiled	7	2
	3	2	14	12			Tax Returns	10	9
1	3	10 (4/1-9/30/23)		48 (10/1/23-3/31/24)	2	6	Other	40	33
0-500M	500M-2MM	2-10MM	10-50MM	50-100MM	100-250MM			4/1/19-3/31/20	4/1/20-3/31/21
1	6	19	21	4	7		NUMBER OF STATEMENTS	72 ALL	53 ALL
%	%	%	%	%	%		ASSETS	%	%
		12.2	16.5				Cash & Equivalents	10.5	17.5
		35.9	19.2				Trade Receivables (net)	27.9	27.7
		36.7	29.2				Inventory	36.1	30.7
		2.8	2.7				All Other Current	1.6	2.4
		87.6	67.6				Total Current	76.0	78.3
		9.6	21.4				Fixed Assets (net)	14.0	13.3
		1.1	3.3				Intangibles (net)	1.9	2.8
		1.8	7.7				All Other Non-Current	8.0	5.6
		100.0	100.0				Total	100.0	100.0
							LIABILITIES		
		8.9	5.6				Notes Payable-Short Term	11.3	7.9
		1.1	2.6				Cur. Mat.-L.T.D.	2.1	1.3
		20.5	14.2				Trade Payables	18.9	17.2
		.7	.0				Income Taxes Payable	.1	.1
		8.4	7.7				All Other Current	14.5	10.8
		39.6	30.2				Total Current	47.0	37.4
		14.0	8.5				Long-Term Debt	9.9	14.1
		.0	.0				Deferred Taxes	.1	.0
		2.7	2.9				All Other Non-Current	2.0	1.9
		43.7	58.4				Net Worth	41.1	46.6
		100.0	100.0				Total Liabilities & Net Worth	100.0	100.0
							INCOME DATA		
		100.0	100.0				Net Sales	100.0	100.0
		31.0	33.5				Gross Profit	26.0	27.8
		25.3	23.7				Operating Expenses	21.7	21.5
		5.7	9.7				Operating Profit	4.4	6.2
		-.4	.2				All Other Expenses (net)	.1	-.2
		6.1	9.5				Profit Before Taxes	4.3	6.4
							RATIOS		
		4.5	5.1					3.2	3.7
		2.6	3.1				Current	2.0	2.1
		1.6	1.5					1.2	1.4
		2.2	2.8					1.7	2.0
		1.3	1.2				Quick	1.0	1.4
		.8	.8					.5	.7
		22 16.3	18 20.5					23 16.2	22 16.6
		43 8.5	29 12.8				Sales/Receivables	36 10.2	32 11.5
		65 5.6	43 8.4					49 7.4	43 8.4
		42 8.6	62 5.9					45 8.1	31 11.8
		69 5.3	85 4.3				Cost of Sales/Inventory	60 6.1	54 6.7
		79 4.6	107 3.4					89 4.1	81 4.5
		15 25.0	19 19.6					16 22.5	16 22.9
		31 11.6	26 14.3				Cost of Sales/Payables	31 11.9	24 14.9
		45 8.1	39 9.3					42 8.7	35 10.3
		4.1	2.9					4.7	4.4
		5.5	4.8				Sales/Working Capital	8.8	8.1
		8.4	10.4					21.3	14.8
		17.9	114.6					22.9	65.2
		(18) 11.1	(16) 9.5				EBIT/Interest	(65) 8.8	(43) 27.6
		5.6	4.7					3.1	10.8
							Net Profit + Depr., Dep., Amort./Cur. Mat. L/T/D	9.9	
								(17) 2.4	
								1.9	
		.0	.2					.1	.1
		.2	.3				Fixed/Worth	.2	.2
		.8	.7					.5	.6
		.3	.2					.5	.5
		1.3	.8				Debt/Worth	1.1	1.0
		3.3	2.1					2.8	2.6
		44.6	52.4					36.7	56.3
		(17) 27.8	34.1				% Profit Before Taxes/Tangible Net Worth	(68) 19.7	(49) 38.5
		12.5	16.6					6.7	19.6
		30.7	29.2					16.4	24.6
		12.8	13.5				% Profit Before Taxes/Total Assets	7.3	17.5
		6.0	4.5					2.7	9.4
		167.5	22.5					82.4	85.3
		60.6	13.0				Sales/Net Fixed Assets	26.3	30.9
		10.5	6.0					13.9	13.4
		3.3	2.8					3.5	3.9
		2.9	2.1				Sales/Total Assets	2.5	2.8
		2.2	1.5					1.9	2.2
		.3	1.0					.4	.7
		(11) .9	(15) 1.7				% Depr., Dep., Amort./Sales	(54) .8	(32) 1.1
		1.6	2.7					1.5	1.8
							% Officers', Directors', Owners' Comp/Sales	1.3	1.6
								(29) 2.2	(19) 3.0
								4.6	7.3
782M	25923M	320221M	872531M	633177M	3000898M		Net Sales ($)	6745235M	5072881M
217M	7209M	116481M	402888M	296952M	1211478M		Total Assets ($)	2558198M	2025846M

M = $ thousand   MM = $ million
See Pages viii through xx for Explanation of Ratios and Data

© RMA 2024

WHOLESALE—Roofing, Siding, and Insulation Material Merchant Wholesalers NAICS 423330

Comparative Historical Data | Current Data Sorted by Sales

						Type of Statement						
	7		4		5	Unqualified					2	5
	2		8		3	Reviewed					3	3
	2		3		5	Compiled				2	1	2
	6		3		5	Tax Returns	1	2		4	15	1
	27		38		38	Other	1					16
	4/1/21-3/31/22 ALL		4/1/22-3/31/23 ALL		4/1/23-3/31/24 ALL		0-1MM	10 (4/1-9/30/23) 1-3MM	3-5MM	48 (10/1/23-3/31/24) 5-10MM	10-25MM	25MM & OVER
	44		56		58	NUMBER OF STATEMENTS	2	2		6	21	27
	%		%		%	ASSETS	%	%	%	%	%	%
	12.0		16.7		14.9	Cash & Equivalents					14.6	14.4
	26.6		23.1		24.9	Trade Receivables (net)			D		32.3	23.2
	34.5		36.6		29.8	Inventory			A		29.1	31.9
	6.5		3.2		2.7	All Other Current			T		3.3	2.3
	79.6		79.6		72.4	Total Current			A		79.3	71.8
	10.9		11.2		17.6	Fixed Assets (net)					12.0	18.0
	4.8		4.1		4.4	Intangibles (net)			N		2.7	3.6
	4.8		5.0		5.6	All Other Non-Current			O		6.0	6.7
	100.0		100.0		100.0	Total			T		100.0	100.0
						LIABILITIES			A			
	10.4		9.5		8.5	Notes Payable-Short Term			V		9.8	5.2
	1.2		1.1		1.6	Cur. Mat.-L.T.D.			A		1.2	2.1
	19.3		18.1		17.3	Trade Payables			I		18.5	18.8
	.1		.1		.2	Income Taxes Payable			L		.4	.0
	8.4		7.9		8.6	All Other Current			A		10.3	6.2
	39.3		36.7		36.2	Total Current			B		40.2	32.4
	12.7		10.4		15.5	Long-Term Debt			L		11.7	9.3
	.0		.0		.1	Deferred Taxes			E		.0	.1
	4.1		3.2		3.2	All Other Non-Current					3.3	4.2
	43.8		49.7		45.1	Net Worth					44.7	53.9
	100.0		100.0		100.0	Total Liabilties & Net Worth					100.0	100.0
						INCOME DATA						
	100.0		100.0		100.0	Net Sales					100.0	100.0
	28.3		28.5		31.9	Gross Profit					35.4	27.6
	19.3		18.6		24.2	Operating Expenses					27.4	19.3
	9.0		9.9		7.7	Operating Profit					8.0	8.2
	.1		.4		.0	All Other Expenses (net)					.1	-.2
	8.9		9.5		7.7	Profit Before Taxes					7.9	8.4
						RATIOS						
	4.0		4.0		4.2						4.3	3.6
	2.2		2.6		2.4	Current					2.0	2.5
	1.4		1.8		1.4						1.5	1.4
	1.6		2.0		2.2						2.9	2.0
	1.1		1.1		1.3	Quick					1.1	1.3
	.7		.7		.8						.8	.8
25	14.6	20	18.5	18	20.3					22	16.8	21	17.2
39	9.4	35	10.4	32	11.4	Sales/Receivables				48	7.6	29	12.5
55	6.6	42	8.6	50	7.3					70	5.2	50	7.3
40	9.1	49	7.4	38	9.7					47	7.7	38	9.5
66	5.5	69	5.3	69	5.3	Cost of Sales/Inventory				69	5.3	70	5.2
96	3.8	99	3.7	94	3.9					83	4.4	91	4.0
19	19.7	17	21.5	16	22.8					17	21.7	21	17.7
37	9.8	27	13.3	29	12.7	Cost of Sales/Payables				31	11.6	36	10.2
53	6.9	44	8.3	45	8.1					52	7.0	46	8.0
	4.2		4.2		3.4						2.8	4.5
	6.6		5.5		6.0	Sales/Working Capital					5.5	6.1
	11.3		10.7		13.6						9.9	12.9
	77.7		181.6		67.3						21.2	110.5
(38)	26.2	(43)	50.6	(47)	9.7	EBIT/Interest				(18)	11.7	(22)	8.2
	6.0		7.7		4.4						5.3	4.8
						Net Profit + Depr., Dep., Amort./Cur. Mat. L/T/D						
	.1		.1		.1						.1	.2
	.3		.2		.3	Fixed/Worth					.2	.3
	.8		.4		.9						1.0	.7
	.5		.4		.4						.3	.4
	1.3		.8		1.3	Debt/Worth					1.3	1.0
	4.3		2.4		3.0						3.5	2.3
	73.0		80.6		46.1	% Profit Before Taxes/Tangible Net Worth					42.7	49.3
(38)	49.1	(51)	49.8	(52)	29.5					(19)	29.1	34.1
	31.2		31.8		15.5						20.2	17.5
	36.5		36.9		29.0	% Profit Before Taxes/Total Assets					28.6	31.4
	20.9		23.4		12.6						13.5	12.4
	9.5		12.2		4.8						5.3	7.8
	64.7		75.2		59.7						72.1	24.1
	29.6		29.1		15.9	Sales/Net Fixed Assets					21.4	15.2
	14.8		14.2		9.0						8.4	11.0
	3.3		3.4		3.2						3.2	3.0
	2.6		2.6		2.3	Sales/Total Assets					2.2	2.4
	1.9		2.1		1.7						1.5	2.0
	.6		.3		.4						.3	.6
(35)	1.1	(43)	.8	(39)	1.2	% Depr., Dep., Amort./Sales				(14)	1.0	(21)	1.2
	1.6		1.4		1.9						3.0	1.7
	.6		.7		.8	% Officers', Directors' Owners' Comp/Sales						
(10)	1.2	(16)	1.6	(22)	1.8							
	3.8		3.9		3.7							
	5869038M		6569994M		4853532M	Net Sales ($)	1694M	4970M		40008M	354041M	4452819M
	2236262M		2490611M		2035225M	Total Assets ($)	1631M	2572M		12304M	182895M	1835823M

M = $ thousand   MM = $ million
See Pages viii through xx for Explanation of Ratios and Data

© RMA 2024

WHOLESALE—Other Construction Material Merchant Wholesalers NAICS 423390

Current Data Sorted by Assets | Comparative Historical Data

0-500M	500M-2MM	2-10MM	10-50MM	50-100MM	100-250MM	Type of Statement		4/1/19-3/31/20 ALL	4/1/20-3/31/21 ALL
2	1	4	2	1	4	Unqualified		5	2
	2	6	15	2	1	Reviewed		17	17
	9	7	2	1		Compiled		16	9
	27 (4/1-9/30/23)	21	25	8	2	Tax Returns		24	8
			90 (10/1/23-3/31/24)			Other		83	53
2	12	38	46	12	7	**NUMBER OF STATEMENTS**		145	89
%	%	%	%	%	%	**ASSETS**		%	%
	27.2	14.8	18.0	5.4		Cash & Equivalents		13.0	19.9
	21.3	29.6	28.6	32.9		Trade Receivables (net)		29.2	25.7
	22.7	30.3	27.6	23.7		Inventory		27.9	26.4
	2.4	2.1	4.1	1.8		All Other Current		3.1	2.0
	73.6	76.7	78.3	63.9		Total Current		73.2	74.0
	2.0	11.6	14.6	21.0		Fixed Assets (net)		16.6	15.2
	14.3	5.5	1.2	7.8		Intangibles (net)		4.9	6.9
	10.1	6.2	5.9	7.3		All Other Non-Current		5.3	3.8
	100.0	100.0	100.0	100.0		Total		100.0	100.0
						LIABILITIES			
	1.4	4.5	8.4	15.0		Notes Payable-Short Term		8.9	5.8
	1.6	3.2	1.8	5.5		Cur. Mat.-L.T.D.		3.1	1.9
	14.6	12.9	11.6	11.4		Trade Payables		17.9	13.5
	.4	.3	.2	.2		Income Taxes Payable		.1	.2
	24.8	12.7	11.7	12.2		All Other Current		9.3	8.9
	42.9	33.7	33.7	44.3		Total Current		39.3	30.3
	8.6	11.9	6.1	13.0		Long-Term Debt		12.4	15.1
	.0	.2	.6	.5		Deferred Taxes		.2	.2
	.6	4.0	5.1	5.8		All Other Non-Current		4.8	2.4
	47.9	50.2	54.6	36.4		Net Worth		43.3	52.0
	100.0	100.0	100.0	100.0		Total Liabilities & Net Worth		100.0	100.0
						INCOME DATA			
	100.0	100.0	100.0	100.0		Net Sales		100.0	100.0
	33.1	30.9	30.2	26.8		Gross Profit		31.8	32.4
	27.0	23.2	21.5	23.1		Operating Expenses		27.0	24.8
	6.1	7.7	8.7	3.6		Operating Profit		4.8	7.6
	-1.8	.7	.6	1.5		All Other Expenses (net)		.5	-.2
	7.9	7.0	8.1	2.1		Profit Before Taxes		4.3	7.8
						RATIOS			
	3.5	3.9	5.0	2.5				3.4	5.0
	1.6	2.4	2.8	1.7		Current		2.2	2.8
	1.3	1.6	1.5	1.2				1.2	1.7
	1.5	2.5	3.0	1.4				1.9	3.3
	1.2	1.5	1.4	1.0		Quick		1.1	1.8
	.7	.7	.8	.4				.6	1.0
19	18.8	21 17.4	29 12.7	37 9.9			23	16.0	24 14.9
36	10.2	31 11.6	45 8.2	60 6.1		Sales/Receivables	36	10.0	34 10.6
38	9.5	49 7.5	73 5.0	78 4.7			52	7.0	55 6.6
3	129.5	14 25.7	29 12.8	33 10.9			17	21.2	32 11.5
51	7.2	43 8.5	46 7.9	56 6.5		Cost of Sales/Inventory	47	7.7	51 7.1
79	4.6	96 3.8	126 2.9	79 4.6			94	3.9	89 4.1
10	38.0	9 40.1	12 31.0	16 22.8			15	24.9	12 31.2
19	19.0	16 22.9	27 13.3	22 16.9		Cost of Sales/Payables	25	14.8	21 17.1
32	11.4	34 10.8	36 10.0	37 9.8			42	8.6	39 9.3
	4.4	5.0	3.3	5.9				4.9	3.8
	10.3	7.0	4.7	8.4		Sales/Working Capital		7.3	5.7
	19.5	10.3	9.9	30.7				25.8	8.3
		56.0	65.3	7.3				29.6	54.7
	(31)	13.2 (38)	10.6 (11)	5.0		EBIT/Interest	(121)	7.4 (65)	14.9
		3.4	3.1	1.8				2.5	5.1
						Net Profit + Depr., Dep.,		8.3	11.1
						Amort./Cur. Mat. L/T/D	(19)	6.0 (18)	7.3
								2.6	3.4
	.0	.0	.1	.2				.1	.1
	.0	.2	.1	.8		Fixed/Worth		.2	.2
	.2	1.0	.5	1.7				.9	.7
	.8	.6	.2	.9				.5	.4
	1.1	.9	.7	1.7		Debt/Worth		1.3	.8
	2.8	5.0	2.6	4.8				3.7	2.4
	76.8	57.7	46.0	37.0				52.3	50.2
(11)	42.9 (35)	31.6 (44)	32.4 (10)	19.2		% Profit Before Taxes/Tangible	(131)	26.8 (84)	29.7
	5.6	15.0	17.9	15.4		Net Worth		11.5	14.2
	20.4	29.3	32.2	13.5				20.2	21.7
	18.9	14.6	15.5	9.3		% Profit Before Taxes/Total		10.8	12.8
	7.0	5.4	5.3	3.1		Assets		3.5	7.8
	UND	167.8	98.8	36.1				132.6	80.5
	559.3	31.2	23.9	16.3		Sales/Net Fixed Assets		32.8	26.5
	69.3	16.0	8.0	4.2				12.2	9.0
	3.3	3.6	2.8	2.3				3.6	3.2
	2.2	2.6	2.1	2.0		Sales/Total Assets		2.8	2.4
	1.2	1.9	1.4	1.7				1.7	1.7
		.4	.5					.4	.7
	(25)	.8 (33)	.8			% Depr., Dep., Amort./Sales	(102)	.9 (64)	1.1
		2.3	1.6					2.5	2.0
		1.1	.7					1.0	1.1
	(17)	3.3 (15)	1.5			% Officers', Directors'	(52)	2.4 (35)	2.1
		5.9	2.8			Owners' Comp/Sales		4.5	4.7
3830M	28977M	561443M	2405290M	1919978M	2331520M	Net Sales ($)		5466329M	3333078M
577M	12296M	205233M	1122901M	935005M	1134464M	Total Assets ($)		2209932M	1633529M

M = $ thousand MM = $ million
See Pages viii through xx for Explanation of Ratios and Data

© RMA 2024

WHOLESALE—Other Construction Material Merchant Wholesalers NAICS 423390

Comparative Historical Data | Current Data Sorted by Sales

Comparative Historical Data			Type of Statement	Current Data Sorted by Sales					
3	8	7	Unqualified				1	1	6
12	22	22	Reviewed		1		2	7	15
4	16	10	Compiled		1		1	3	4
9	14	11	Tax Returns	1	1		1	8	
43	67	67	Other	8	6	6	6	11	36
4/1/21-3/31/22 ALL	4/1/22-3/31/23 ALL	4/1/23-3/31/24 ALL		27 (4/1-9/30/23)			90 (10/1/23-3/31/24)		
				0-1MM	1-3MM	3-5MM	5-10MM	10-25MM	25MM & OVER
71	127	117	NUMBER OF STATEMENTS	1	10	6	9	30	61
%	%	%	ASSETS	%	%	%	%	%	%
13.1	13.4	16.5	Cash & Equivalents		34.1			15.2	12.9
31.0	29.0	27.9	Trade Receivables (net)		19.7			27.8	32.1
30.7	28.9	27.3	Inventory		13.3			32.3	27.3
2.4	3.9	3.0	All Other Current		2.4			3.1	3.0
77.2	75.2	74.7	Total Current		69.4			78.4	75.3
15.4	12.0	13.4	Fixed Assets (net)		7.7			11.8	14.2
4.2	6.6	4.9	Intangibles (net)		16.0			4.4	3.2
3.2	6.3	7.1	All Other Non-Current		6.9			5.4	7.3
100.0	100.0	100.0	Total		100.0			100.0	100.0
			LIABILITIES						
7.0	8.3	6.7	Notes Payable-Short Term		1.8			7.6	8.2
1.6	1.5	2.6	Cur. Mat.-L.T.D.		1.9			1.3	2.6
15.4	16.9	12.1	Trade Payables		13.2			12.5	12.3
.3	.4	.3	Income Taxes Payable		.2			.4	.2
10.3	11.8	13.1	All Other Current		14.8			12.6	10.2
34.6	38.8	34.7	Total Current		31.9			34.4	33.5
12.6	11.5	9.3	Long-Term Debt		.0			11.5	7.9
.3	.3	.3	Deferred Taxes		.0			.6	.3
2.4	5.7	4.5	All Other Non-Current		.0			2.1	5.8
50.1	43.8	51.1	Net Worth		68.1			51.4	52.4
100.0	100.0	100.0	Total Liabilities & Net Worth		100.0			100.0	100.0
			INCOME DATA						
100.0	100.0	100.0	Net Sales		100.0			100.0	100.0
27.8	28.2	30.4	Gross Profit		30.5			27.8	29.4
20.3	22.2	22.7	Operating Expenses		21.7			22.2	21.2
7.4	6.1	7.7	Operating Profit		8.8			5.5	8.1
-1.4	-.3	.5	All Other Expenses (net)		-2.2			1.1	.5
8.9	6.3	7.2	Profit Before Taxes		11.0			4.4	7.6
			RATIOS						
4.5	3.2	4.2	Current		16.2			5.0	4.2
2.2	2.0	2.3			1.7			2.6	2.4
1.5	1.4	1.5			1.4			1.8	1.5
2.2	2.0	2.4	Quick		14.4			2.5	2.4
1.1	1.1	1.4			1.4			1.5	1.4
.7	.5	.8			.9			.7	.8
25 14.6	25 14.4	26 14.2	Sales/Receivables	0 UND	30 12.2			24 15.5	30 12.1
38 9.6	38 9.6	38 9.5			41 8.9			33 10.9	46 7.9
56 6.5	65 5.6	61 6.0						63 5.8	65 5.6
24 15.0	27 13.4	21 17.2	Cost of Sales/Inventory	0 UND	33 11.2			21 17.5	33 11.0
58 6.3	57 6.4	47 7.7			57 6.4			63 5.8	45 8.2
104 3.5	111 3.3	96 3.8						114 3.2	83 4.4
14 25.7	14 27.0	12 31.4	Cost of Sales/Payables	0 UND	13 28.9			9 39.2	14 26.1
23 15.6	23 15.7	21 17.8			32 11.4			18 20.6	25 14.6
37 9.9	47 7.8	35 10.4						43 8.5	34 10.7
4.3	5.0	4.2	Sales/Working Capital		4.9			4.5	4.1
5.9	7.4	6.2			10.4			6.3	6.0
12.8	13.8	10.4			11.7			9.9	10.0
130.7	56.4	50.2	EBIT/Interest					25.7	82.0
(58) 25.8	(112) 12.2	(96) 10.1					(27) 9.8	(52) 10.4
7.5	3.6	3.2						1.2	3.9
	12.6	12.8	Net Profit + Depr., Dep., Amort./Cur. Mat. L/T/D						11.9
(19) 4.5	(15) 4.5							(10) 4.0	
	2.9	.9							1.8
.1	.1	.0	Fixed/Worth		.0			.0	.1
.2	.2	.2			.0			.1	.2
.7	.6	.7			.1			.6	.7
.4	.6	.4	Debt/Worth		.2			.4	.4
.9	1.3	.9			1.0			.8	.8
3.5	4.0	2.9			1.1			3.1	2.4
68.6	55.1	57.0	% Profit Before Taxes/Tangible Net Worth		84.1			42.2	47.9
(65) 47.7	(110) 30.7	(109) 31.6			71.0			(27) 24.4	(58) 31.2
27.1	14.5	17.4			33.7			6.8	19.4
30.3	25.8	28.3	% Profit Before Taxes/Total Assets		46.1			24.1	29.0
18.2	13.7	14.6			19.4			12.1	15.0
10.7	3.9	5.5			16.2			2.0	6.3
77.8	93.2	115.2	Sales/Net Fixed Assets		UND			143.4	94.8
28.7	34.5	31.5			109.2			29.1	22.7
12.4	13.3	10.1			63.1			10.9	9.5
3.3	3.4	3.1	Sales/Total Assets		3.6			3.6	3.0
2.5	2.3	2.3			2.6			2.5	2.3
2.1	1.8	1.6			1.3			1.8	1.7
.6	.3	.5	% Depr., Dep., Amort./Sales					.5	.5
(56) .9	(90) .7	(77) .8						(22) .7	(46) .9
1.3	1.2	1.6						1.4	1.5
.6	1.0	1.1	% Officers', Directors', Owners' Comp/Sales					1.5	.5
(24) 1.5	(38) 1.9	(38) 2.4						(17) 3.3	(13) .8
3.1	3.1	6.2						5.9	2.2
3309049M	7105596M	7251038M	Net Sales ($)	941M	17989M	25579M	66415M	475339M	6664775M
1463582M	3109387M	3410476M	Total Assets ($)	1035M	7954M	27214M	36626M	262236M	3075411M

M = $ thousand   MM = $ million
See Pages viii through xx for Explanation of Ratios and Data

© RMA 2024

WHOLESALE—Office Equipment Merchant Wholesalers NAICS 423420

Current Data Sorted by Assets | Comparative Historical Data

							Type of Statement				
		2	1	2			Unqualified		5		4
	1	2	7	1			Reviewed		11		9
	1	3					Compiled		9		6
		6	1				Tax Returns		6		8
1	3	14	12	8	4		Other		52		33
	18 (4/1-9/30/23)		51 (10/1/23-3/31/24)						4/1/19-3/31/20 ALL		4/1/20-3/31/21 ALL
0-500M	500M-2MM	2-10MM	10-50MM	50-100MM	100-250MM		NUMBER OF STATEMENTS		83		60
1	5	27	21	11	4						
%	%	%	%	%	%		ASSETS		%		%
		13.9	9.9	12.5			Cash & Equivalents		15.1		19.8
		31.8	28.9	14.1			Trade Receivables (net)		28.0		21.8
		29.7	16.1	18.8			Inventory		25.6		26.7
		3.5	4.9	4.5			All Other Current		3.8		3.2
		78.8	59.8	50.0			Total Current		72.5		71.6
		10.2	6.3	5.3			Fixed Assets (net)		14.6		12.9
		4.7	16.8	27.3			Intangibles (net)		6.8		8.7
		6.3	17.1	17.5			All Other Non-Current		6.1		6.9
		100.0	100.0	100.0			Total		100.0		100.0
							LIABILITIES				
		10.5	6.7	.8			Notes Payable-Short Term		8.3		5.0
		1.9	3.1	1.9			Cur. Mat.-L.T.D.		3.1		3.5
		20.9	9.6	8.2			Trade Payables		16.5		14.5
		.2	.0	.0			Income Taxes Payable		.1		.0
		8.7	18.2	14.9			All Other Current		16.5		15.3
		42.3	37.7	25.7			Total Current		44.5		38.4
		9.5	14.1	12.5			Long-Term Debt		14.7		19.9
		.1	.1	.2			Deferred Taxes		.2		.2
		3.7	15.6	7.9			All Other Non-Current		5.6		7.7
		44.4	32.5	53.7			Net Worth		35.0		33.9
		100.0	100.0	100.0			Total Liabilties & Net Worth		100.0		100.0
							INCOME DATA				
		100.0	100.0	100.0			Net Sales		100.0		100.0
		38.7	39.8	39.1			Gross Profit		39.6		45.3
		37.2	34.4	32.8			Operating Expenses		32.7		39.6
		1.4	5.4	6.3			Operating Profit		6.9		5.7
		.3	1.8	1.8			All Other Expenses (net)		1.5		-1.0
		1.2	3.6	4.4			Profit Before Taxes		5.4		6.7
							RATIOS				
		4.4	2.0	2.8					2.3		3.0
		1.6	1.4	1.6			Current		1.7		2.0
		1.4	1.3	1.2					1.3		1.4
		3.0	1.2	.9					1.5		1.7
		1.2	1.0	.9			Quick		1.0		1.1
		.5	.8	.7					.7		.7
		24 15.1	32 11.3	27 13.7				21	17.4	21	17.8
		32 11.5	42 8.6	29 12.4			Sales/Receivables	30	12.1	30	12.1
		51 7.1	62 5.9	32 11.3				42	8.6	41	8.9
		21 17.7	11 32.0	30 12.3				23	15.9	37	9.8
		66 5.5	51 7.2	49 7.5			Cost of Sales/Inventory	48	7.6	68	5.4
		111 3.3	78 4.7	79 4.6				78	4.7	107	3.4
		15 25.1	9 40.6	18 20.0				15	24.9	15	23.8
		36 10.0	21 17.4	24 15.5			Cost of Sales/Payables	24	15.0	24	15.0
		96 3.8	46 7.9	32 11.4				39	9.4	41	9.0
		3.9	6.6	5.0					6.0		4.5
		7.8	12.1	17.0			Sales/Working Capital		10.9		7.1
		16.1	20.4	48.8					18.3		14.1
		27.4	18.3						35.9		40.3
	(22)	4.8	(19) 4.6				EBIT/Interest	(70)	9.3	(53)	16.2
		1.2	.4						3.7		3.6
							Net Profit + Depr., Dep., Amort./Cur. Mat. L/T/D				
		.0	.1	.0					.1		.1
		.0	.3	.2			Fixed/Worth		.3		.3
		.7	-.9	-.7					1.0		1.3
		.5	1.3	.8					.7		.9
		1.8	6.7	1.7			Debt/Worth		1.5		1.9
		4.8	-58.4	-8.2					4.3		4.7
		41.4	75.3						64.9		80.9
	(25)	28.3	(15) 35.9				% Profit Before Taxes/Tangible Net Worth	(71)	31.5	(51)	36.8
		3.2	6.3						14.1		11.4
		23.9	12.7	14.2					19.8		26.8
		12.2	5.0	4.1			% Profit Before Taxes/Total Assets		9.0		12.3
		2.2	-1.7	-.1					4.9		4.8
		463.0	278.8	172.4					103.2		80.4
		181.7	69.3	32.9			Sales/Net Fixed Assets		39.0		38.4
		44.3	27.0	23.5					12.3		14.6
		3.8	2.6	2.3					4.0		3.2
		2.7	2.0	1.6			Sales/Total Assets		2.9		2.4
		1.7	1.7	1.4					1.9		1.7
		.4	.2						.5		.6
	(17)	.5	(13) .8				% Depr., Dep., Amort./Sales	(52)	.8	(34)	1.1
		1.8	1.5						3.0		3.0
							% Officers', Directors' Owners' Comp/Sales		1.0		.9
								(25)	3.0	(17)	2.6
									7.7		5.3
1170M	30796M	444516M	950296M	1498340M	805066M		Net Sales ($)		3942659M		2497696M
69M	7090M	158215M	451031M	871583M	693178M		Total Assets ($)		1835493M		1264257M

© RMA 2024

M = $ thousand   MM = $ million
See Pages viii through xx for Explanation of Ratios and Data

WHOLESALE—Office Equipment Merchant Wholesalers NAICS 423420

Comparative Historical Data / Current Data Sorted by Sales

				Type of Statement						
3	6	5		Unqualified				1	3	4
6	10	11		Reviewed				3	3	8
7	4	4		Compiled			1			
8	8	7		Tax Returns				5	12	2
34	47	42		Other		1	1			20
4/1/21-3/31/22 ALL	4/1/22-3/31/23 ALL	4/1/23-3/31/24 ALL			0-1MM	18 (4/1-9/30/23) 1-3MM	3-5MM	51 (10/1/23-3/31/24) 5-10MM	10-25MM	25MM & OVER
58	75	69		NUMBER OF STATEMENTS		1	2	13	19	34
%	%	%		ASSETS	%	%	%	%	%	%
19.3	12.9	12.6		Cash & Equivalents	D			16.0	11.8	11.7
19.8	22.7	25.4		Trade Receivables (net)	A			22.5	27.3	27.1
24.7	29.7	22.5		Inventory	T			21.7	32.4	18.1
4.1	4.4	5.0		All Other Current	A			4.2	4.7	4.6
68.0	69.6	65.6		Total Current				64.3	76.3	61.5
10.7	7.9	8.0		Fixed Assets (net)	N			15.5	4.5	6.0
9.2	11.5	11.8		Intangibles (net)	O			2.0	14.5	15.2
12.2	10.9	14.6		All Other Non-Current	T			18.2	4.7	17.4
100.0	100.0	100.0		Total				100.0	100.0	100.0
				LIABILITIES	A					
4.1	7.9	7.6		Notes Payable-Short Term	V			2.5	12.0	6.6
2.6	2.3	2.2		Cur. Mat.-L.T.D.	A			2.1	2.2	2.4
11.3	13.6	13.8		Trade Payables	I			18.8	16.6	11.3
.1	.1	.1		Income Taxes Payable	L			.0	.3	.0
13.6	12.3	12.9		All Other Current	A			9.6	13.2	14.6
31.8	36.2	36.5		Total Current	B			33.0	44.2	34.9
17.4	14.3	12.3		Long-Term Debt	L			18.0	6.2	12.8
.2	.1	.1		Deferred Taxes	E			.0	.1	.1
8.3	8.0	16.0		All Other Non-Current				1.5	9.7	8.9
42.3	41.4	35.1		Net Worth				47.5	39.8	43.3
100.0	100.0	100.0		Total Liabilities & Net Worth				100.0	100.0	100.0
				INCOME DATA						
100.0	100.0	100.0		Net Sales				100.0	100.0	100.0
44.2	42.6	41.1		Gross Profit				50.8	44.3	34.6
39.3	38.8	37.2		Operating Expenses				45.2	44.2	29.7
4.9	3.8	3.9		Operating Profit				5.6	.1	4.9
-1.3	-.1	.7		All Other Expenses (net)				.2	1.0	.5
6.3	3.9	3.2		Profit Before Taxes				5.4	-.9	4.4
				RATIOS						
3.7	3.4	2.8						6.3	2.1	2.7
1.9	2.0	1.6		Current				1.9	1.5	1.6
1.5	1.3	1.3						.9	1.4	1.3
2.1	2.2	1.4						4.0	1.3	1.3
1.2	.9	1.0		Quick				1.2	.9	1.0
.6	.6	.6						.5	.5	.8
25 14.6	25 14.5	24 14.9			17 21.1	26 14.2	29 12.5
33 11.1	31 11.6	32 11.5		Sales/Receivables	24 15.1	30 12.0	34 10.8
48 7.6	41 8.8	51 7.1			40 9.2	81 4.5	51 7.1
51 7.2	41 8.8	21 17.0			10 38.1	49 7.4	12 31.5
79 4.6	78 4.7	51 7.2		Cost of Sales/Inventory	47 7.7	81 4.5	48 7.6
114 3.2	118 3.1	96 3.8			111 3.3	140 2.6	81 4.5
19 19.6	16 23.4	13 27.4			20 18.2	8 43.1	13 28.5
30 12.0	28 13.2	27 13.3		Cost of Sales/Payables	38 9.7	27 13.3	24 15.3
49 7.4	46 8.0	55 6.6			114 3.2	101 3.6	37 9.8
3.8	4.1	4.7						4.2	4.2	5.0
6.5	7.3	9.9		Sales/Working Capital				10.4	7.4	13.6
11.8	17.6	20.3						-109.5	12.6	22.9
40.5	23.6	18.3						79.2	16.9	26.9
(47) 15.5	(61) 4.7	(59) 4.7		EBIT/Interest	(11) 9.0	(16) 2.2	(29) 4.7
3.4	.8	.7						3.6	-6.3	1.7
				Net Profit + Depr., Dep., Amort./Cur. Mat. L/T/D						
.1	.1	.0						.0	.0	.0
.2	.2	.1		Fixed/Worth				.1	.1	.1
.8	.8	1.1						2.5	1.4	.8
.6	.6	.8						.4	1.3	.7
1.6	1.6	2.0		Debt/Worth				.9	4.3	1.9
5.4	8.2	7.0						5.5	6.8	7.7
64.6	49.8	59.3		% Profit Before Taxes/Tangible Net Worth				84.7	49.5	66.3
(50) 35.4	(60) 18.6	(57) 28.3			(12) 32.7	(15) 17.5	(28) 28.6
11.8	-.4	2.6						6.2	-119.2	4.8
23.8	17.0	21.3		% Profit Before Taxes/Total Assets				34.6	22.7	19.2
11.9	6.7	7.3						12.9	5.3	7.3
4.0	.4	.1						5.1	-10.0	1.5
169.1	148.1	197.2						583.4	405.8	174.5
34.5	55.5	82.7		Sales/Net Fixed Assets				131.8	181.1	45.1
12.9	23.6	27.0						6.0	91.6	25.6
2.7	3.1	3.1						3.6	2.7	2.7
1.9	2.3	2.3		Sales/Total Assets				2.8	2.3	2.1
1.2	1.8	1.5						1.8	1.1	1.5
.2	.3	.4						.2		.4
(39) .5	(43) .7	(41) .5		% Depr., Dep., Amort./Sales			(13) .4	(19) .7
3.3	1.9	1.8							.7	2.7
2.3	.7	1.7		% Officers', Directors', Owners' Comp/Sales						
(18) 4.7	(14) 3.5	(12) 2.6								
9.0	5.5	4.8								
2234525M	3931553M	3730184M		Net Sales ($)	1170M	7899M	95552M	301497M	3324066M
1362506M	2043378M	2181166M		Total Assets ($)	69M	13371M	40792M	179336M	1947598M

M = $ thousand MM = $ million
See Pages viii through xx for Explanation of Ratios and Data

© RMA 2024

WHOLESALE—Computer and Computer Peripheral Equipment and Software Merchant Wholesalers NAICS 423430

Current Data Sorted by Assets / Comparative Historical Data

							Type of Statement		
		1	4	8	2	2	Unqualified	25	6
		2	5	11	1		Reviewed	14	4
	1	4	3	1			Compiled	6	6
1	14	44	34		9	20	Tax Returns	18	3
	30 (4/1-9/30/23)			140 (10/1/23-3/31/24)			Other	123	56
0-500M	500M-2MM	2-10MM	10-50MM	50-100MM	100-250MM			4/1/19-3/31/20 ALL	4/1/20-3/31/21 ALL
2	21	59	54	12	22		NUMBER OF STATEMENTS	186	75
%	%	%	%	%	%		ASSETS	%	%
	23.6	17.6	19.9	11.6	12.0		Cash & Equivalents	15.1	21.8
	42.1	36.1	32.8	34.3	25.1		Trade Receivables (net)	38.3	37.1
	22.9	30.5	15.2	12.9	11.9		Inventory	20.1	19.2
	.3	2.5	5.7	5.0	5.8		All Other Current	6.9	3.3
	88.9	86.7	73.5	63.8	54.8		Total Current	80.3	81.4
	4.5	4.3	6.5	7.5	3.9		Fixed Assets (net)	7.0	5.5
	1.6	4.2	11.8	13.9	35.9		Intangibles (net)	5.8	6.1
	5.0	4.8	8.2	14.8	5.4		All Other Non-Current	6.9	7.0
	100.0	100.0	100.0	100.0	100.0		Total	100.0	100.0
							LIABILITIES		
	3.1	9.3	4.2	8.8	1.7		Notes Payable-Short Term	10.2	8.6
	.7	.8	2.4	2.4	.7		Cur. Mat.-L.T.D.	1.6	2.0
	29.0	23.6	22.8	23.8	18.6		Trade Payables	29.0	24.5
	.1	.1	.1	.4	.0		Income Taxes Payable	.3	.2
	14.0	15.6	18.7	16.2	14.9		All Other Current	14.0	17.4
	46.9	49.4	48.2	51.6	36.0		Total Current	55.2	52.7
	6.9	5.8	6.7	9.1	23.7		Long-Term Debt	7.5	9.8
	.0	.0	.0	.0	.0		Deferred Taxes	.1	.1
	4.0	3.1	6.2	10.9	14.8		All Other Non-Current	6.2	9.0
	42.3	41.7	39.0	28.3	25.5		Net Worth	31.0	28.4
	100.0	100.0	100.0	100.0	100.0		Total Liabilities & Net Worth	100.0	100.0
							INCOME DATA		
	100.0	100.0	100.0	100.0	100.0		Net Sales	100.0	100.0
	28.8	28.9	34.2	25.2	26.4		Gross Profit	29.5	31.0
	19.5	25.3	28.0	20.3	24.3		Operating Expenses	25.9	26.3
	9.3	3.6	6.2	4.9	2.1		Operating Profit	3.6	4.7
	.1	.2	.4	.4	3.3		All Other Expenses (net)	.6	.2
	9.1	3.4	5.8	4.4	-1.3		Profit Before Taxes	3.0	4.5
							RATIOS		
	2.7	2.7	2.7	1.6	2.5			2.2	2.7
	2.2	1.9	1.5	1.2	1.8		Current	1.5	1.6
	1.5	1.3	1.1	1.0	1.2			1.1	1.0
	2.5	1.7	1.7	1.3	1.3			1.4	1.9
	1.6	1.2	1.2	.9	1.0		Quick	1.0	1.1
	.6	.7	.7	.7	.8			.6	.7
13	29.0	24	15.5	34	10.6	32	11.3	22	16.5			26	13.8	24	15.3
33	11.2	33	11.1	45	8.2	42	8.6	49	7.4		Sales/Receivables	43	8.5	43	8.4
41	9.0	47	7.8	56	6.5	69	5.3	66	5.5			59	6.2	60	6.1
0	UND	3	119.8	0	UND	2	211.7	21	17.2			1	250.1	3	136.8
5	68.9	36	10.2	14	26.2	13	28.5	35	10.3		Cost of Sales/Inventory	17	21.5	22	16.6
62	5.9	91	4.0	53	6.9	37	9.8	47	7.8			51	7.2	62	5.9
13	27.6	17	22.1	21	17.7	16	23.0	18	20.8			20	18.3	14	25.5
30	12.3	27	13.6	38	9.7	33	10.9	39	9.3		Cost of Sales/Payables	41	9.0	40	9.1
43	8.5	47	7.8	54	6.7	74	4.9	55	6.6			69	5.3	60	6.1
	7.6	5.7	5.2	8.7	7.3			7.4	6.1
	11.0	9.2	10.6	30.4	8.4		Sales/Working Capital	13.7	10.2
	26.4	20.7	40.4	174.8	23.1			40.0	425.5
	999.8	52.5	120.3	20.5	5.2			46.3	41.7
(18)	8.1	(47)	5.7	(46)	14.0	(11)	5.9	(20)	.0		EBIT/Interest	(148)	9.2	(54)	16.5
	2.1	2.1	1.0	3.5	-.3			3.0	4.0
							Net Profit + Depr., Dep., Amort./Cur. Mat. L/T/D		30.3
								(12)	3.3
									1.1
	.0	.0	.0	.1	.2			.0	.0
	.0	.0	.1	.3	-.1		Fixed/Worth	.1	.1
	.4	.3	.6	NM	-.1			.8	1.8
	.7	.6	1.0	2.5	2.3			1.0	.8
	.9	1.4	1.9	6.0	-2.5		Debt/Worth	2.2	2.3
	3.3	5.2	14.1	NM	-2.1			7.8	40.6
	261.7	53.3	57.1					66.3	80.3
(18)	103.5	(52)	16.9	(45)	27.0						% Profit Before Taxes/Tangible Net Worth	(159)	31.0	(58)	37.0
	19.7	5.6	14.5					13.3	19.9
	109.4	18.9	20.9	10.2	8.4			18.0	21.0
	18.7	5.7	9.9	6.0	-4.6		% Profit Before Taxes/Total Assets	7.9	12.6
	1.3	1.7	.6	4.8	-6.9			2.9	3.4
	UND	323.6	299.2	195.9	56.9			618.9	999.8
	UND	145.3	75.3	103.0	42.9		Sales/Net Fixed Assets	97.9	142.6
	99.4	49.7	31.7	9.3	36.5			32.6	31.5
	6.4	5.6	3.9	3.7	2.7			4.5	4.8
	5.1	3.4	2.6	2.9	1.5		Sales/Total Assets	3.4	3.1
	3.6	2.4	1.5	1.5	1.3			2.0	1.8
		.3	.1					.1	.1
		(37)	.3	(36)	.4						% Depr., Dep., Amort./Sales	(116)	.3	(46)	.5
		.5	1.1					1.2	1.1
			.6					.8	.7
		(10)	1.1				% Officers', Directors' Owners' Comp/Sales	(33)	2.1	(17)	1.6
			3.6					5.7	7.4
4828M	160568M	1195870M	3797152M	2331871M	6513710M		Net Sales ($)	18530103M	8436665M
846M	28809M	314068M	1243146M	893131M	3415172M		Total Assets ($)	5722472M	2521998M

© RMA 2024

M = $ thousand MM = $ million
See Pages viii through xx for Explanation of Ratios and Data

WHOLESALE—Computer and Computer Peripheral Equipment and Software Merchant Wholesalers NAICS 423430

Comparative Historical Data / Current Data Sorted by Sales

5	13	16	**Type of Statement**				1	1	2	3	9
7	9	18	Unqualified					1	1	3	13
3	10	6	Reviewed						1	2	2
5	6	8	Compiled					1	1	4	1
47	82	122	Tax Returns				2	1	10	44	62
4/1/21-3/31/22 ALL	4/1/22-3/31/23 ALL	4/1/23-3/31/24 ALL	Other				3	3			
				0-1MM	1-3MM	3-5MM	5-10MM	10-25MM	25MM & OVER		
				30 (4/1-9/30/23)			140 (10/1/23-3/31/24)				
67	120	170	**NUMBER OF STATEMENTS**		6	7	14	56	87		
%	%	%	**ASSETS**	%	%	%	%	%	%		
21.9	20.9	18.7	Cash & Equivalents				28.5	16.9	16.7		
37.0	29.7	34.0	Trade Receivables (net)	D			39.6	37.2	32.8		
18.9	21.0	20.7	Inventory	A			14.2	29.1	16.0		
4.1	4.1	3.8	All Other Current	T			.9	3.6	4.9		
82.0	75.6	77.2	Total Current	A			83.1	86.9	70.4		
5.4	4.0	5.1	Fixed Assets (net)				5.4	3.7	5.9		
7.4	14.1	11.0	Intangibles (net)	N			6.6	5.3	16.0		
5.3	6.3	6.6	All Other Non-Current	O			4.9	4.0	7.7		
100.0	100.0	100.0	Total	T			100.0	100.0	100.0		
			LIABILITIES	A							
8.7	7.9	5.8	Notes Payable-Short Term	V			1.1	8.7	5.1		
1.6	1.3	1.4	Cur. Mat.-L.T.D.	A			3.1	.8	1.4		
25.9	21.8	23.2	Trade Payables	I			23.2	26.6	22.6		
.2	.5	.1	Income Taxes Payable	L			.1	.1	.2		
13.5	17.1	16.6	All Other Current	A			13.6	16.2	17.2		
49.8	48.6	47.1	Total Current	B			41.1	52.3	46.4		
7.3	11.4	8.7	Long-Term Debt	L			12.9	4.4	11.0		
.1	.1	.0	Deferred Taxes	E			.0	.0	.0		
4.7	7.0	6.2	All Other Non-Current				.2	3.0	8.8		
38.0	33.0	38.0	Net Worth				45.8	40.3	33.8		
100.0	100.0	100.0	Total Liabilities & Net Worth				100.0	100.0	100.0		
			INCOME DATA								
100.0	100.0	100.0	Net Sales				100.0	100.0	100.0		
30.2	31.4	30.1	Gross Profit				39.3	30.4	26.5		
22.2	25.1	24.8	Operating Expenses				27.1	25.5	22.3		
8.0	6.3	5.3	Operating Profit				12.2	4.9	4.2		
-.4	1.0	.7	All Other Expenses (net)				.3	.3	1.1		
8.3	5.3	4.6	Profit Before Taxes				11.9	4.6	3.1		
			RATIOS								
2.6	2.8	2.6					2.5	2.7	2.6		
1.6	1.7	1.7	Current				2.2	1.8	1.6		
1.2	1.2	1.2					1.5	1.3	1.1		
1.7	1.8	1.7					2.5	1.6	1.4		
1.1	1.0	1.2	Quick				1.9	1.1	1.1		
.6	.6	.7					1.1	.6	.7		
29 12.4	20 18.0	26 14.2					23 16.1	29 12.8	26 14.0		
47 7.7	36 10.0	39 9.4	Sales/Receivables				35 10.5	36 10.1	43 8.4		
64 5.7	54 6.7	53 6.9					47 7.7	48 7.6	56 6.5		
2 184.1	1 405.8	1 401.1					0 UND	1 344.8	2 147.1		
17 21.0	35 10.5	24 15.4	Cost of Sales/Inventory				0 UND	35 10.3	22 16.3		
76 4.8	66 5.5	53 6.9					52 7.0	101 3.6	41 8.8		
24 15.1	13 28.1	18 20.8					7 49.6	19 19.1	16 23.2		
45 8.1	26 14.0	30 12.0	Cost of Sales/Payables				31 11.8	28 13.1	32 11.5		
65 5.6	51 7.2	51 7.1					47 7.8	52 7.0	51 7.1		
5.0	5.0	6.4					7.6	6.3	7.3		
8.9	9.9	9.5	Sales/Working Capital				10.4	9.2	11.6		
26.5	27.9	29.4					11.7	24.6	44.8		
151.3	52.8	69.5					999.8	128.3	34.5		
(50) 28.6	(92) 11.5	(142) 6.1	EBIT/Interest				(10) 516.4	(50) 8.6	(74) 4.7		
5.7	1.3	1.1					2.5	4.5	.2		
19.7	9.5	11.3	Net Profit + Depr., Dep.,						12.6		
(10) 5.6	(12) 6.0	(18) 3.2	Amort./Cur. Mat. L/T/D					(13) 5.0		
1.6	1.0	.4							.5		
.0	.0	.0					.0	.0	.0		
.1	.1	.1	Fixed/Worth				.0	.1	.2		
.3	5.1	1.8					.8	.4	-.8		
.9	1.1	.8					.7	.7	1.1		
2.0	3.1	1.8	Debt/Worth				1.1	1.5	3.6		
5.1	-33.3	19.3					2.4	6.7	-17.6		
107.2	106.4	79.2					234.0	83.7	53.4		
(57) 54.8	(89) 49.7	(133) 28.6	% Profit Before Taxes/Tangible Net Worth				(12) 98.6	(49) 21.7	(61) 29.6		
25.4	24.8	8.6					18.1	5.7	14.1		
42.5	25.4	19.3					93.8	21.1	15.0		
15.0	10.4	6.4	% Profit Before Taxes/Total Assets				24.1	5.8	6.1		
7.1	1.7	.7					2.7	3.0	-.8		
999.8	734.9	468.1					UND	336.7	269.1		
134.3	128.8	99.2	Sales/Net Fixed Assets				283.7	170.3	61.5		
46.5	49.0	40.8					42.9	48.7	38.4		
4.2	4.4	4.9					5.2	5.6	4.2		
2.9	2.5	3.1	Sales/Total Assets				4.5	3.2	2.9		
2.0	1.5	1.6					2.3	2.1	1.5		
.1	.1	.2						.3	.1		
(37) .5	(52) .3	(95) .4	% Depr., Dep., Amort./Sales				(34) .4	(49) .3		
1.4	.8	.9						.7	1.3		
.7								.9	.2		
(12) 1.1	(22) 2.0	(28) 1.6	% Officers', Directors' Owners' Comp/Sales				(10) 1.8	(11) .8		
2.2	6.3	6.9						4.4	1.6		
6284888M	12700414M	14003999M	Net Sales ($)		14107M	30565M	103144M	972830M	12883353M		
2321360M	5943419M	5895172M	Total Assets ($)		13146M	13012M	44474M	353676M	5470864M		

© RMA 2024
M = $ thousand MM = $ million
See Pages viii through xx for Explanation of Ratios and Data

WHOLESALE—Other Commercial Equipment Merchant Wholesalers NAICS 423440

Current Data Sorted by Assets | Comparative Historical Data

0-500M	500M-2MM	2-10MM	10-50MM	50-100MM	100-250MM	Type of Statement	4/1/19-3/31/20	4/1/20-3/31/21
			1		1	Unqualified	6	8
		4	9	2	1	Reviewed	19	17
		4	2			Compiled	14	5
1	1	10				Tax Returns	23	15
	6	14	13	4	4	Other	73	49
1	8 (4/1-9/30/23)	32	69 (10/1/23-3/31/24) 25	6	6	NUMBER OF STATEMENTS	135 ALL	94 ALL
1	7							
%	%	%	%	%	%	ASSETS	%	%
		14.1	7.1			Cash & Equivalents	10.9	18.2
		25.0	28.9			Trade Receivables (net)	26.9	20.5
		37.6	38.5			Inventory	35.3	34.5
		4.2	1.7			All Other Current	2.2	3.2
		81.0	76.2			Total Current	75.2	76.5
		9.3	15.9			Fixed Assets (net)	13.0	10.2
		1.9	1.2			Intangibles (net)	5.6	9.0
		7.8	6.7			All Other Non-Current	6.1	4.4
		100.0	100.0			Total	100.0	100.0
						LIABILITIES		
		8.2	19.0			Notes Payable-Short Term	15.8	11.1
		1.5	2.2			Cur. Mat.-L.T.D.	2.0	1.6
		12.3	14.5			Trade Payables	17.1	12.9
		.3	.0			Income Taxes Payable	.4	.4
		15.8	15.2			All Other Current	12.6	13.0
		38.1	50.9			Total Current	47.9	39.0
		7.7	14.3			Long-Term Debt	10.8	12.0
		.2	.2			Deferred Taxes	.2	.2
		2.0	6.8			All Other Non-Current	6.9	3.7
		52.0	27.7			Net Worth	34.2	45.0
		100.0	100.0			Total Liabilities & Net Worth	100.0	100.0
						INCOME DATA		
		100.0	100.0			Net Sales	100.0	100.0
		29.5	25.4			Gross Profit	30.3	32.5
		24.2	20.9			Operating Expenses	24.5	27.2
		5.3	4.5			Operating Profit	5.9	5.3
		-.1	.3			All Other Expenses (net)	.5	-.7
		5.4	4.2			Profit Before Taxes	5.3	6.0
						RATIOS		
		3.0	2.1				2.5	3.9
		1.9	1.4			Current	1.6	2.0
		1.7	1.2				1.2	1.4
		1.4	1.0				1.4	1.9
		1.0	.8			Quick	.7	1.2
		.7	.3				.4	.6
		18 20.3	34 10.8				17 21.3	14 25.3
		34 10.8	42 8.6			Sales/Receivables	35 10.5	34 10.6
		47 7.8	65 5.6				52 7.0	46 7.9
		36 10.1	43 8.4				28 13.1	46 8.0
		60 6.1	89 4.1			Cost of Sales/Inventory	73 5.0	79 4.6
		107 3.4	146 2.5				111 3.3	126 2.9
		13 28.0	18 20.2				16 23.5	11 33.9
		19 18.8	30 12.1			Cost of Sales/Payables	25 14.8	23 15.9
		33 11.0	47 7.7				44 8.3	39 9.4
		4.2	4.5				5.8	3.8
		6.6	10.6			Sales/Working Capital	9.4	6.2
		12.0	20.0				24.4	15.7
		65.5	7.3				15.7	33.0
		(29) 12.4	(23) 4.2			EBIT/Interest	(118) 4.7	(79) 7.7
		4.6	2.4				2.6	2.6
						Net Profit + Depr., Dep.,	12.2	19.1
						Amort./Cur. Mat. L/T/D	(23) 5.5	(16) 4.5
							1.4	1.6
		.0	.3				.1	.1
		.2	.5			Fixed/Worth	.3	.2
		.2	1.0				.9	.9
		.6	1.0				.9	.6
		.9	2.4			Debt/Worth	1.8	1.6
		1.7	9.2				4.2	7.2
		45.6	61.1				52.0	55.3
		(30) 22.2	(24) 22.9			% Profit Before Taxes/Tangible Net Worth	(117) 23.1	(82) 25.0
		8.4	7.9				7.8	12.8
		25.7	11.1				19.6	18.9
		9.8	6.2			% Profit Before Taxes/Total Assets	7.0	10.5
		2.9	3.2				2.6	3.0
		144.3	53.0				114.1	81.0
		31.9	18.1			Sales/Net Fixed Assets	40.9	34.8
		21.4	9.4				17.5	16.8
		3.8	2.6				3.7	2.9
		2.7	2.0			Sales/Total Assets	2.8	2.2
		2.1	1.7				2.1	1.6
		.5	.7				.3	.4
		(21) .8	(18) 1.0			% Depr., Dep., Amort./Sales	(98) .8	(62) .8
		1.6	2.4				1.8	1.5
		1.5					1.2	1.1
		(16) 3.0				% Officers', Directors', Owners' Comp/Sales	(54) 2.5	(30) 2.7
		5.6					4.1	6.0
1913M	23612M	545382M	1114593M	626359M	1924677M	Net Sales ($)	6439869M	4419533M
434M	7242M	178291M	587366M	396946M	895257M	Total Assets ($)	2992086M	2142087M

M = $ thousand   MM = $ million
See Pages viii through xx for Explanation of Ratios and Data

© RMA 2024

WHOLESALE—Other Commercial Equipment Merchant Wholesalers NAICS 423440

Comparative Historical Data / Current Data Sorted by Sales

4	8	2	**Type of Statement**					2	4	2
14	14	16	Unqualified				1			11
6	9	6	Reviewed						4	2
13	8	12	Compiled					2	7	2
41	59	41	Tax Returns		1			5	9	20
			Other	3	1	3				
4/1/21-3/31/22	4/1/22-3/31/23	4/1/23-3/31/24			8 (4/1-9/30/23)			69 (10/1/23-3/31/24)		
ALL	ALL	ALL		0-1MM	1-3MM	3-5MM	5-10MM	10-25MM		25MM & OVER
78	98	77	**NUMBER OF STATEMENTS**	3	2	3	8	24		37
%	%	%	**ASSETS**	%	%	%	%	%		%
16.0	11.6	12.5	Cash & Equivalents					14.2		9.0
24.1	23.3	24.6	Trade Receivables (net)					25.6		28.9
32.9	38.0	35.2	Inventory					38.3		34.8
5.1	4.7	3.6	All Other Current					2.4		2.8
78.1	77.5	76.0	Total Current					80.4		75.5
9.7	11.2	13.6	Fixed Assets (net)					11.7		14.1
5.9	6.0	3.5	Intangibles (net)					2.8		2.6
6.3	5.3	6.9	All Other Non-Current					5.1		7.8
100.0	100.0	100.0	Total					100.0		100.0
			LIABILITIES							
9.7	10.6	11.4	Notes Payable-Short Term					6.8		13.5
1.9	2.9	2.0	Cur. Mat.-L.T.D.					1.4		2.3
13.7	13.2	13.7	Trade Payables					16.3		12.5
.2	.2	.2	Income Taxes Payable					.2		.2
15.4	16.0	15.9	All Other Current					13.1		17.3
40.8	42.9	43.3	Total Current					37.7		45.7
11.8	16.3	11.3	Long-Term Debt					6.1		14.0
.1	.2	.2	Deferred Taxes					.4		.1
5.8	5.7	4.5	All Other Non-Current					3.5		5.3
41.5	34.9	40.8	Net Worth					52.3		34.8
100.0	100.0	100.0	Total Liabilities & Net Worth					100.0		100.0
			INCOME DATA							
100.0	100.0	100.0	Net Sales					100.0		100.0
28.3	31.0	29.5	Gross Profit					28.5		26.4
22.6	24.4	23.3	Operating Expenses					22.2		21.9
5.7	6.6	6.3	Operating Profit					6.3		4.5
-1.7	.2	.3	All Other Expenses (net)					.1		.5
7.4	6.4	5.9	Profit Before Taxes					6.2		4.0
			RATIOS							
3.4	3.3	2.9						2.9		3.0
2.0	2.0	1.9	Current					1.9		1.4
1.4	1.4	1.3						1.7		1.2
1.9	1.5	1.3						1.3		1.4
.9	(97) .9	.9	Quick					.9		.9
.5	.5	.5						.6		.5
19 19.1	18 20.6	20 18.5						27 13.6	25	14.5
38 9.5	34 10.6	38 9.7	Sales/Receivables					36 10.1	41	8.8
49 7.4	49 7.5	52 7.0						47 7.7	55	6.6
35 10.4	46 8.0	35 10.5						38 9.6	30	12.1
70 5.2	94 3.9	70 5.2	Cost of Sales/Inventory					73 5.0	59	6.2
104 3.5	140 2.6	135 2.7						118 3.1	135	2.7
12 30.8	13 27.6	15 24.8						19 19.4	13	28.9
21 17.4	22 16.4	26 14.0	Cost of Sales/Payables					31 11.7	21	17.3
34 10.6	45 8.2	38 9.6						45 8.1	35	10.3
4.2	4.1	4.5						4.1		5.6
7.3	6.5	7.5	Sales/Working Capital					5.8		12.9
14.9	13.9	17.3						8.8		22.1
111.8	33.4	24.1						63.6		21.1
(66) 13.2	(79) 10.8	(68) 6.4	EBIT/Interest					(22) 12.2	(34)	5.5
5.5	3.8	2.5						6.7		2.4
11.2		37.4	Net Profit + Depr., Dep.,							
(11) 6.6		(10) 10.8	Amort./Cur. Mat. L/T/D							
3.7		4.3								
.1	.1	.1						.1		.1
.2	.2	.3	Fixed/Worth					.2		.3
.7	1.1	.7						.3		.8
.7	.6	.7						.7		.9
1.2	1.6	1.8	Debt/Worth					.9		2.0
3.6	9.3	4.7						1.7		8.1
58.7	54.0	47.1						41.8		48.6
(67) 36.2	(81) 27.6	(71) 25.6	% Profit Before Taxes/Tangible Net Worth					(23) 22.9	(36)	29.0
20.9	16.3	15.3						16.7		16.1
21.5	21.3	17.6						19.1		14.3
14.7	10.5	8.2	% Profit Before Taxes/Total Assets					10.5		7.1
6.7	5.0	3.2						5.9		3.3
114.0	116.0	86.3						134.5		72.2
43.0	39.1	28.0	Sales/Net Fixed Assets					31.8		21.9
17.8	21.9	11.7						14.2		11.4
3.2	3.2	3.1						3.3		3.1
2.3	2.3	2.3	Sales/Total Assets					2.3		2.2
1.7	1.7	1.7						2.0		1.8
.3	.3	.5						.7		.4
(56) .7	(67) .6	(52) .7	% Depr., Dep., Amort./Sales					(18) 1.1	(28)	.6
1.3	1.1	1.9						2.1		1.6
1.2	1.4	.8						1.3		.2
(28) 2.1	(31) 2.0	(28) 2.2	% Officers', Directors' Owners' Comp/Sales					(12) 3.0	(10)	.7
5.3	3.8	5.6						5.4		2.3
4647465M	6052620M	4236536M	Net Sales ($)	1516M	4891M	13299M	53342M	414890M		3748598M
2242753M	2556263M	2065536M	Total Assets ($)	3395M	1890M	10100M	26802M	197720M		1825629M

M = $ thousand   MM = $ million
See Pages viii through xx for Explanation of Ratios and Data

© RMA 2024

WHOLESALE—Medical, Dental, and Hospital Equipment and Supplies Merchant Wholesalers NAICS 423450

Current Data Sorted by Assets | Comparative Historical Data

							Type of Statement		
			4	11	8	7	Unqualified	24	14
			1	17	1	1	Reviewed	29	14
			10	2			Compiled	20	13
4	6		12	3			Tax Returns	32	17
3	16		45	50	13	19	Other	130	95
	40 (4/1-9/30/23)			193 (10/1/23-3/31/24)				4/1/19-3/31/20	4/1/20-3/31/21
0-500M	500M-2MM	2-10MM	10-50MM	50-100MM	100-250MM		NUMBER OF STATEMENTS	235 ALL	153 ALL
7	22	72	83	22	27				
%	%	%	%	%	%		ASSETS	%	%
	18.7	15.4	10.0	10.6	8.8		Cash & Equivalents	13.7	17.0
	22.9	28.8	27.7	21.1	18.4		Trade Receivables (net)	28.9	28.4
	30.4	29.3	30.8	25.9	15.7		Inventory	26.8	24.9
	4.5	4.6	3.0	2.3	2.7		All Other Current	3.0	3.0
	76.5	78.0	71.4	59.8	45.5		Total Current	72.3	73.3
	7.8	10.3	13.7	15.7	25.7		Fixed Assets (net)	11.7	10.4
	2.4	3.4	7.1	18.2	18.8		Intangibles (net)	8.6	9.1
	13.4	8.3	7.9	6.2	10.0		All Other Non-Current	7.3	7.2
	100.0	100.0	100.0	100.0	100.0		Total	100.0	100.0
							LIABILITIES		
	14.2	8.0	9.5	3.3	3.5		Notes Payable-Short Term	13.9	11.0
	2.9	1.8	3.7	2.9	2.9		Cur. Mat.-L.T.D.	2.0	2.3
	10.9	15.3	19.4	12.9	12.2		Trade Payables	18.9	16.7
	.0	.4	.1	.1	.1		Income Taxes Payable	.1	.2
	34.8	10.2	13.1	9.5	11.0		All Other Current	11.3	12.9
	62.8	35.7	45.7	28.7	29.7		Total Current	46.2	43.1
	9.6	6.0	12.4	30.4	31.2		Long-Term Debt	11.8	15.5
	.0	.0	.6	.2	.3		Deferred Taxes	.3	.2
	6.9	3.3	5.3	17.1	4.4		All Other Non-Current	4.9	6.2
	20.7	55.0	36.0	23.5	34.3		Net Worth	36.8	35.1
	100.0	100.0	100.0	100.0	100.0		Total Liabilities & Net Worth	100.0	100.0
							INCOME DATA		
	100.0	100.0	100.0	100.0	100.0		Net Sales	100.0	100.0
	50.3	47.9	41.6	43.5	50.2		Gross Profit	40.3	39.7
	48.7	38.1	33.0	36.4	38.5		Operating Expenses	34.4	33.7
	1.6	9.8	8.6	7.1	11.7		Operating Profit	5.8	6.0
	.8	.2	1.8	2.3	4.8		All Other Expenses (net)	.8	-.3
	.8	9.6	6.8	4.8	6.9		Profit Before Taxes	5.0	6.3
							RATIOS		
	3.2	4.6	2.9	4.3	2.0			2.9	3.3
	2.1	2.4	1.6	2.1	1.5		Current	1.8	1.9
	1.1	1.4	1.1	1.6	1.2			1.2	1.3
	1.6	2.7	1.1	1.6	1.2			1.8	1.9
	1.0	1.3	.8	1.2	.9		Quick	.9	1.1
	.6	.6	.6	.9	.6			.6	.6
6	63.7	27	13.5	33	11.1	41	9.0	38	9.5			27	13.5	26	14.2
24	15.4	38	9.7	47	7.7	45	8.2	45	8.2	Sales/Receivables	42	8.7	41	9.0
60	6.1	58	6.3	66	5.5	57	6.4	54	6.7		55	6.6	58	6.3
2	188.9	29	12.5	52	7.0	41	9.0	45	8.1		25	14.4	25	14.8
38	9.6	70	5.2	87	4.2	83	4.4	83	4.4	Cost of Sales/Inventory	56	6.5	56	6.5
152	2.4	135	2.7	174	2.1	166	2.2	140	2.6		101	3.6	104	3.5
2	154.3	19	19.3	26	14.2	27	13.4	27	13.5		17	22.1	12	29.4
30	12.1	34	10.8	48	7.6	46	8.0	40	9.1	Cost of Sales/Payables	34	10.6	32	11.4
46	8.0	66	5.5	81	4.5	68	5.4	96	3.8		61	6.0	64	5.7
	3.4	3.2	3.9	3.1	7.0			4.5	4.6
	13.1	5.8	8.8	5.1	11.7		Sales/Working Capital	10.1	8.0
	90.5	12.9	46.3	9.7	29.1			33.1	18.8
	40.0		57.9		18.1		14.7		15.1				21.8		39.5
(15)	5.8	(52)	15.8	(71)	5.6	(21)	5.0	(26)	5.3	EBIT/Interest	(189)	8.0	(128)	12.4
	-1.9		4.5		1.0		-.4		.6			1.4		3.6
					13.4								31.0		12.6
			(18)		1.8					Net Profit + Depr., Dep., Amort./Cur. Mat. L/T/D	(34)	6.8	(25)	5.4
					.7							1.5		1.6
	.0	.0	.1	.2	.3			.1	.0
	.1	.1	.4	.5	2.1		Fixed/Worth	.3	.2
	.4	.3	1.9	-5.0	-4.0			1.4	.9
	.3	.4	.6	.8	1.5			.7	.8
	1.0	.7	2.1	4.7	4.1		Debt/Worth	2.0	1.8
	NM	2.1	10.7	-19.3	-10.2			7.5	5.5
	55.1		63.1		70.4		54.0		68.3				61.3		78.5
(17)	27.3	(69)	40.2	(70)	27.0	(15)	25.7	(19)	46.1	% Profit Before Taxes/Tangible Net Worth	(196)	27.5	(124)	34.6
	12.8		15.6		3.3		-28.7		13.0			8.9		13.8
	22.3	33.8	19.5	18.2	14.7			20.5	27.8
	12.7	17.7	8.3	12.2	7.8		% Profit Before Taxes/Total Assets	8.3	12.4
	-.5	5.0	.3	-5.5	-.8			.8	3.7
	811.4	425.5	101.6	70.6	47.1			190.5	267.7
	139.1	99.6	28.7	12.8	12.4		Sales/Net Fixed Assets	52.9	54.1
	23.2	20.9	8.4	7.4	2.7			16.3	18.0
	7.0	3.4	2.7	1.9	2.3			3.7	3.6
	2.6	2.5	1.9	1.6	1.0		Sales/Total Assets	2.6	2.4
	1.6	1.6	1.3	.9	.7			1.6	1.6
	.2	.2	.4	.5	.2			.3	.3
(11)	.5	(38)	.4	(62)	.8	(13)	1.2	(11)	1.0	% Depr., Dep., Amort./Sales	(147)	.6	(89)	.7
	1.5	1.5	2.3	4.4	3.4			1.8	1.9
	1.6	1.6	1.0					2.1	2.1
(16)	2.9	(19)	3.4	(12)	1.2					% Officers', Directors' Owners' Comp/Sales	(65)	4.1	(37)	3.3
	8.2	5.0	2.0					7.7	6.3
10203M	117871M	983608M	4487717M	2168618M	5493890M		Net Sales ($)	12964073M	8056897M
1162M	29402M	357433M	1980792M	1481355M	3829298M		Total Assets ($)	6671119M	4234319M

© RMA 2024
M = $ thousand MM = $ million
See Pages viii through xx for Explanation of Ratios and Data

WHOLESALE—Medical, Dental, and Hospital Equipment and Supplies Merchant Wholesalers NAICS 423450

Comparative Historical Data | Current Data Sorted by Sales

			Type of Statement						
16	27	30	Unqualified				3	3	24
14	18	20	Reviewed					5	15
7	8	12	Compiled			2	5	3	2
10	20	25	Tax Returns	2	4	7	5	5	2
96	137	146	Other	4	8	8	15	36	75
4/1/21-	4/1/22-	4/1/23-		40 (4/1-9/30/23)			193 (10/1/23-3/31/24)		
3/31/22	3/31/23	3/31/24							
ALL	ALL	ALL		0-1MM	1-3MM	3-5MM	5-10MM	10-25MM	25MM & OVER
143	210	233	NUMBER OF STATEMENTS	6	12	17	28	52	118
%	%	%	**ASSETS**	%	%	%	%	%	%
19.5	11.4	12.9	Cash & Equivalents	24.2	9.8	11.1	15.9	10.6	
22.7	25.5	25.3	Trade Receivables (net)	18.9	23.4	21.4	27.3	26.3	
27.0	29.8	27.4	Inventory	24.4	27.0	37.1	26.2	27.0	
3.2	3.4	3.7	All Other Current	6.3	1.4	3.4	5.0	2.9	
72.3	70.1	69.2	Total Current	73.8	61.6	73.0	74.4	66.8	
13.2	12.7	13.9	Fixed Assets (net)	8.5	17.2	13.8	13.3	14.8	
7.4	9.0	8.1	Intangibles (net)	4.0	9.4	2.6	4.6	11.1	
7.1	8.1	8.9	All Other Non-Current	13.8	11.8	10.6	7.7	7.3	
100.0	100.0	100.0	Total	100.0	100.0	100.0	100.0	100.0	
			LIABILITIES						
8.9	9.7	9.6	Notes Payable-Short Term	7.2	18.4	9.8	9.3	6.7	
2.1	2.4	2.9	Cur. Mat.-L.T.D.	2.7	1.3	1.3	4.4	3.0	
13.8	17.8	15.3	Trade Payables	7.0	8.6	15.6	14.9	17.9	
.1	.1	.2	Income Taxes Payable	.0	.0	.0	.0	.3	
10.5	9.7	16.7	All Other Current	9.5	37.9	9.6	18.6	12.0	
35.3	39.7	44.7	Total Current	26.4	66.2	36.4	47.2	39.9	
14.0	14.0	13.8	Long-Term Debt	11.6	9.4	11.0	10.7	17.2	
.2	.3	.3	Deferred Taxes	.0	.0	.0	.1	.5	
4.7	5.1	5.7	All Other Non-Current	8.3	5.2	4.6	2.1	7.4	
45.8	40.9	35.5	Net Worth	53.7	19.2	48.0	39.9	35.0	
100.0	100.0	100.0	Total Liabilities & Net Worth	100.0	100.0	100.0	100.0	100.0	
			INCOME DATA						
100.0	100.0	100.0	Net Sales	100.0	100.0	100.0	100.0	100.0	
43.7	42.1	46.1	Gross Profit	61.2	55.1	50.2	49.0	40.0	
35.0	35.4	37.3	Operating Expenses	52.2	47.1	39.6	40.5	31.6	
8.7	6.7	8.8	Operating Profit	9.0	8.0	10.6	8.5	8.4	
-.7	.6	1.6	All Other Expenses (net)	-.1	.4	2.4	1.3	1.8	
9.4	6.1	7.2	Profit Before Taxes	9.1	7.6	8.3	7.2	6.6	
			RATIOS						
4.6	3.1	3.2	Current	9.0	4.1	4.6	3.5	2.7	
2.3	1.8	1.8		2.5	2.0	2.3	2.2	1.7	
1.4	1.2	1.2		2.3	1.2	1.2	1.2	1.2	
2.7	1.7	1.8	Quick	6.0	2.8	1.8	2.6	1.3	
1.3	.9	1.0		1.5	.8	1.2	1.0	.9	
.7	.5	.6		1.0	.4	.4	.7	.6	
20 18.0	27 13.5	29 12.7	Sales/Receivables	19 19.3	13 27.8	15 24.7	29 12.7	34 10.7	
36 10.2	39 9.4	43 8.5		36 10.2	48 7.6	35 10.3	41 8.9	45 8.2	
52 7.0	54 6.7	61 6.0		94 3.9	73 5.0	58 6.3	66 5.5	56 6.5	
26 14.0	41 9.0	32 11.4	Cost of Sales/Inventory	19 19.3	18 20.4	24 14.9	30 12.3	41 9.0	
70 5.2	83 4.4	78 4.7		73 5.0	81 4.5	91 4.0	89 4.1	78 4.7	
114 3.2	146 2.5	152 2.4		304 1.2	215 1.7	159 2.3	215 1.7	140 2.6	
12 29.3	21 17.6	21 17.7	Cost of Sales/Payables	0 UND	8 46.8	23 15.7	14 26.4	26 14.3	
33 11.1	39 9.4	38 9.5		39 9.3	31 11.7	43 8.5	40 9.1	41 8.9	
62 5.9	73 5.0	70 5.2		61 6.0	49 7.5	91 4.0	73 5.0	69 5.3	
3.8	4.1	3.8	Sales/Working Capital	1.8	2.2	3.2	3.8	4.4	
6.9	7.2	8.4		2.8	4.7	7.2	8.4	9.2	
21.1	23.6	22.9		10.0	49.4	24.4	21.3	25.6	
38.3	40.6	29.1	EBIT/Interest	31.1		29.5	77.4	19.0	
(112) 15.6	(179) 8.7	(190) 6.5		(16) 6.8	(20) 14.7	(38) 9.9	(105) 5.9		
5.2	1.6	1.5		1.3	2.3	1.7	1.2		
10.6	11.6	14.0	Net Profit + Depr., Dep., Amort./Cur. Mat. L/T/D					20.6	
(23) 5.6	(28) 3.9	(33) 3.5						(25) 4.1	
1.6	2.3	1.4						1.4	
.0	.0	.0	Fixed/Worth	.0	.0	.0	.0	.1	
.2	.2	.2		.1	.1	.2	.1	.4	
.6	1.1	1.1		.1	.8	1.1	.7	3.5	
.4	.5	.6	Debt/Worth	.3	.4	.3	.4	.8	
1.1	1.7	1.7		.5	1.2	.9	.9	2.7	
3.4	6.4	6.0		.9	3.0	4.2	3.9	16.6	
71.7	62.7	63.6	% Profit Before Taxes/Tangible Net Worth	43.3	50.3	67.2	66.3	65.1	
(123) 39.7	(175) 28.6	(194) 33.3		(11) 15.5	(14) 26.5	(24) 39.3	(48) 29.2	(94) 38.5	
16.7	7.9	12.9		.1	9.0	12.3	14.7	12.9	
34.5	24.4	22.4	% Profit Before Taxes/Total Assets	26.3	17.8	35.5	24.5	20.3	
16.5	9.8	11.6		11.3	9.1	12.7	13.8	10.0	
6.6	1.4	2.0		.9	.7	3.3	3.7	1.4	
198.3	164.0	186.5	Sales/Net Fixed Assets	UND	UND	233.2	179.9	124.3	
49.2	49.7	44.2		40.5	40.5	48.2	56.7	33.1	
12.1	12.5	10.4		24.7	8.3	18.0	6.4	9.0	
3.4	3.1	3.0	Sales/Total Assets	2.4	2.3	3.1	3.0	3.0	
2.3	2.1	2.0		1.6	1.6	2.5	2.1	2.0	
1.7	1.2	1.2		.8	1.1	1.6	1.4	1.2	
.4	.2	.2	% Depr., Dep., Amort./Sales		.2	.2	.2	.2	
(93) .7	(131) .7	(136) .7			(19) .6	(37) .7	(69) .8		
2.0	1.4	2.0			2.3	3.2	1.8		
1.6	1.6	1.4	% Officers', Directors', Owners' Comp/Sales		2.5		1.4	.9	
(38) 4.0	(53) 3.0	(51) 2.9		(10) 3.3		(12) 1.8	(11) 1.2		
9.0	4.9	5.5		7.7		3.8	2.2		
5789475M	11161225M	13261907M	Net Sales ($)	3514M	26287M	67695M	213787M	874931M	12075693M
3273668M	6524631M	7679442M	Total Assets ($)	2557M	19895M	44911M	121859M	494874M	6995346M

© RMA 2024 M = $ thousand MM = $ million
See Pages viii through xx for Explanation of Ratios and Data

WHOLESALE—Other Professional Equipment and Supplies Merchant Wholesalers NAICS 423490

Current Data Sorted by Assets | Comparative Historical Data

0-500M	500M-2MM	2-10MM	10-50MM	50-100MM	100-250MM	Type of Statement	4/1/19-3/31/20 ALL	4/1/20-3/31/21 ALL
		11 (4/1-9/30/23)	65 (10/1/23-3/31/24)			Unqualified	5	1
1	3	18	39	1	1	Reviewed	13	4
1	4	6	14	3	1	Compiled	3	7
2	8	15	30	4	2	Tax Returns	3	4
		30	30			Other	40	32
						NUMBER OF STATEMENTS	64	48
%	%	%	%	%	%	**ASSETS**	%	%
		17.0	13.1			Cash & Equivalents	12.5	17.6
		27.6	23.8			Trade Receivables (net)	34.2	28.2
		32.8	29.6			Inventory	31.1	25.1
		1.1	3.9			All Other Current	2.4	4.8
		78.5	70.4			Total Current	80.2	75.7
		9.0	11.4			Fixed Assets (net)	6.6	10.2
		6.9	7.8			Intangibles (net)	7.8	10.3
		5.6	10.4			All Other Non-Current	5.3	3.8
		100.0	100.0			Total	100.0	100.0
						LIABILITIES		
		7.6	4.7			Notes Payable-Short Term	12.0	10.8
		1.4	4.0			Cur. Mat.-L.T.D.	2.6	2.1
		12.7	18.1			Trade Payables	26.3	19.4
		.1	.4			Income Taxes Payable	.1	.6
		16.6	13.5			All Other Current	15.8	20.5
		38.4	40.7			Total Current	56.8	53.4
		5.9	11.0			Long-Term Debt	7.1	10.4
		.0	.0			Deferred Taxes	.1	.0
		4.3	16.1			All Other Non-Current	2.7	5.2
		51.5	32.2			Net Worth	33.4	31.0
		100.0	100.0			Total Liabilities & Net Worth	100.0	100.0
						INCOME DATA		
		100.0	100.0			Net Sales	100.0	100.0
		33.6	29.3			Gross Profit	32.0	34.2
		27.7	24.5			Operating Expenses	28.1	28.5
		5.8	4.8			Operating Profit	3.9	5.7
		.2	.4			All Other Expenses (net)	1.0	-.4
		5.7	4.4			Profit Before Taxes	2.9	6.1
						RATIOS		
		3.7	2.4				2.4	3.8
		2.0	2.1			Current	1.5	2.3
		1.6	1.3				1.3	1.2
		1.9	1.4				1.4	2.2
		1.2	.9			Quick	.9	1.2
		.6	.6				.4	.6
		26 14.2	24 15.5				23 15.7	18 20.3
		44 8.3	38 9.7			Sales/Receivables	41 8.8	41 8.9
		59 6.2	53 6.9				53 6.9	60 6.1
		35 10.4	33 11.1				13 29.1	15 23.8
		57 6.4	74 4.9			Cost of Sales/Inventory	52 7.0	46 7.9
		104 3.5	130 2.8				130 2.8	104 3.5
		10 36.1	21 17.2				22 16.6	21 17.7
		26 13.8	29 12.4			Cost of Sales/Payables	34 10.8	33 11.0
		43 8.4	49 7.5				54 6.7	47 7.7
		3.6	4.9				6.7	3.9
		6.0	6.4			Sales/Working Capital	10.4	8.0
		9.4	18.3				24.4	30.0
		57.8	41.0				32.9	54.2
		(22) 5.0	(25) 8.7			EBIT/Interest	(52) 8.1	(37) 15.5
		2.5	2.8				2.5	3.2
						Net Profit + Depr., Dep., Amort./Cur. Mat. L/T/D	10.5	
							(11) 4.2	
							1.6	
		.0	.1				.0	.0
		.1	.2			Fixed/Worth	.1	.2
		.3	.8				.5	.6
		.4	.7				.7	.4
		.9	1.7			Debt/Worth	1.7	1.1
		1.8	4.3				6.7	9.4
		39.2	45.9				51.1	73.0
		(28) 12.8	(27) 31.5			% Profit Before Taxes/Tangible Net Worth	(54) 29.5	(40) 45.9
		5.2	17.6				13.9	11.9
		18.6	17.7				16.3	27.1
		4.7	10.7			% Profit Before Taxes/Total Assets	8.6	13.0
		1.9	3.4				2.0	3.1
		137.4	111.0				297.0	265.8
		55.6	20.8			Sales/Net Fixed Assets	76.2	61.0
		13.4	13.5				30.5	18.1
		3.1	3.1				4.4	3.8
		2.2	2.0			Sales/Total Assets	3.2	2.8
		1.8	1.4				1.9	1.8
		.6	.5				.3	.2
		(16) 1.0	(23) 1.0			% Depr., Dep., Amort./Sales	(36) .4	(26) .8
		3.3	2.0				1.5	1.9
		1.8					.9	.7
		(10) 3.6				% Officers', Directors' Owners' Comp/Sales	(14) 1.8	(15) 2.5
		5.9					5.2	5.2
865M	45346M	402496M	1803011M	457493M	333284M	Net Sales ($)	3722300M	1304116M
142M	11545M	163487M	749018M	279521M	225192M	Total Assets ($)	1578505M	530085M

© RMA 2024 M = $ thousand   MM = $ million
See Pages viii through xx for Explanation of Ratios and Data

WHOLESALE—Other Professional Equipment and Supplies Merchant Wholesalers   NAICS 423490

Comparative Historical Data / Current Data Sorted by Sales

															4
												1		1	9
1		2		4		Type of Statement						7		2	4
4		5		11		Unqualified						2		4	
5		11		13		Reviewed					2	2		4	
9		9		10		Compiled	1		1		2	6		12	16
18		30		38		Tax Returns	1		1		2				
4/1/21-3/31/22 ALL		4/1/22-3/31/23 ALL		4/1/23-3/31/24 ALL		Other	0-1MM	11 (4/1-9/30/23) 1-3MM		3-5MM		65 (10/1/23-3/31/24) 5-10MM		10-25MM	25MM & OVER
37		57		76		NUMBER OF STATEMENTS	2		2		4	16		19	33
%		%		%		ASSETS	%		%		%	%		%	%
17.9		14.9		16.0		Cash & Equivalents						15.3		14.5	12.2
35.2		31.7		27.0		Trade Receivables (net)						32.0		23.2	24.6
25.6		31.2		30.0		Inventory						25.3		32.5	33.0
4.2		4.0		2.4		All Other Current						1.9		1.2	3.8
83.0		81.9		75.4		Total Current						74.4		71.4	73.6
10.1		7.2		10.5		Fixed Assets (net)						8.9		12.0	12.6
3.9		4.5		6.8		Intangibles (net)						8.7		9.0	5.6
3.1		6.4		7.3		All Other Non-Current						8.0		7.7	8.1
100.0		100.0		100.0		Total						100.0		100.0	100.0
						LIABILITIES									
14.1		7.7		6.1		Notes Payable-Short Term						5.1		5.4	6.6
1.5		1.6		2.2		Cur. Mat.-L.T.D.						.9		1.7	3.6
22.0		20.2		16.2		Trade Payables						12.8		11.7	17.8
.2		.7		.2		Income Taxes Payable						.0		.2	.4
14.0		13.8		15.4		All Other Current						13.6		24.2	12.2
51.7		44.0		40.0		Total Current						32.3		43.2	40.7
7.1		8.0		7.9		Long-Term Debt						4.5		7.1	11.9
.1		.0		.1		Deferred Taxes						.0		.0	.3
3.4		4.8		8.3		All Other Non-Current						6.3		3.9	13.6
37.7		43.1		43.7		Net Worth						56.9		45.8	33.5
100.0		100.0		100.0		Total Liabilties & Net Worth						100.0		100.0	100.0
						INCOME DATA									
100.0		100.0		100.0		Net Sales						100.0		100.0	100.0
30.9		32.5		32.5		Gross Profit						33.8		33.7	29.9
28.6		28.0		26.8		Operating Expenses						30.6		30.3	23.4
2.2		4.5		5.7		Operating Profit						3.2		3.3	6.5
-1.2		.6		.3		All Other Expenses (net)						-.5		.2	.7
3.5		4.0		5.4		Profit Before Taxes						3.7		3.2	5.9
						RATIOS									
	2.8		4.2		3.0								3.5	2.6	2.5
	1.9		2.1		2.0	Current							2.5	2.1	1.9
	1.3		1.5		1.5								1.8	1.3	1.4
	1.6		2.3		1.6								1.9	1.7	1.3
	1.1		1.1		1.1	Quick							1.2	1.1	.9
	.7		.6		.6								1.1	.5	.6
33	10.9	29	12.7	24	15.5							30	12.3	18	20.5	26	14.1
45	8.2	47	7.8	41	8.9	Sales/Receivables						53	6.9	40	9.1	37	9.9
53	6.9	63	5.8	56	6.5							76	4.8	53	6.9	51	7.1
14	26.6	23	15.7	27	13.4							29	12.7	27	13.7	38	9.7
34	10.6	72	5.1	62	5.9	Cost of Sales/Inventory						78	4.7	70	5.2	78	4.7
111	3.3	146	2.5	126	2.9							101	3.6	140	2.6	140	2.6
16	22.4	14	26.6	16	22.2							8	45.9	9	38.7	24	15.2
38	9.6	30	12.3	28	13.0	Cost of Sales/Payables						29	12.7	26	13.8	28	12.9
52	7.0	59	6.2	49	7.5							49	7.4	35	10.3	45	8.1
	3.8		3.3		4.0								3.3	5.3	5.0
	8.0		6.3		6.3	Sales/Working Capital							4.7	7.0	6.3
	13.5		17.7		12.8								6.8	18.3	14.1
	81.7		57.2		42.1								23.6	114.4	34.2
(26)	20.5	(42)	12.3	(59)	7.0	EBIT/Interest						(12)	6.3	(16)	12.1	(28)	9.3
	5.6		2.3		3.1								.3	3.1	3.8
					8.1	Net Profit + Depr., Dep.,									
			(10)	4.7	Amort./Cur. Mat. L/T/D									
					1.9										
	.0		.0		.0								.0	.1	.1
	.1		.1		.2	Fixed/Worth							.2	.2	.2
	.3		.3		.5								.3	.5	.8
	.7		.4		.5								.5	.5	.7
	1.5		1.0		1.1	Debt/Worth							.7	1.2	1.4
	5.0		5.2		2.5								1.6	3.4	3.0
	50.4		40.5		46.2	% Profit Before Taxes/Tangible							39.2	37.6	48.1
(32)	26.3	(48)	26.2	(70)	24.7	Net Worth							9.1	(17) 15.4	(30) 32.1
	7.6		14.5		9.6								.5	9.4	21.0
	23.6		19.5		19.1	% Profit Before Taxes/Total							14.2	13.2	20.5
	10.2		9.5		7.7	Assets							3.5	3.8	11.9
	3.5		3.7		2.9								.1	1.6	6.5
	968.1		337.2		130.3								348.1	75.6	113.5
	83.5		62.4		37.3	Sales/Net Fixed Assets							41.2	33.7	19.8
	15.4		22.0		13.1								12.8	13.6	9.7
	3.7		3.5		3.3								2.7	3.5	3.2
	2.9		2.5		2.2	Sales/Total Assets							1.9	2.1	2.2
	1.9		1.6		1.7								1.4	1.7	1.7
	.2		.2		.5									.5	.5
(22)	.6	(35)	.7	(49)	.9	% Depr., Dep., Amort./Sales							(12) .8	(26) .8
	1.5		1.4		2.2									1.7	2.1
	1.2		.7		.6	% Officers', Directors'									
(17)	3.4	(18)	2.7	(21)	3.0	Owners' Comp/Sales									
	7.4		4.6		3.9										
1401692M		1460267M		3042495M		Net Sales ($)	865M		4581M		17010M	113185M		317927M	2588927M
522903M		627443M		1428905M		Total Assets ($)	142M		4736M		7348M	66502M		155232M	1194945M

© RMA 2024   M = $ thousand   MM = $ million
See Pages viii through xx for Explanation of Ratios and Data

WHOLESALE—Metal Service Centers and Other Metal Merchant Wholesalers NAICS 423510

Current Data Sorted by Assets | **Comparative Historical Data**

0-500M	500M-2MM	2-10MM	10-50MM	50-100MM	100-250MM	Type of Statement	4/1/19-3/31/20 ALL	4/1/20-3/31/21 ALL
		2	25	17	17	Unqualified	49	37
		14	40	7	2	Reviewed	52	50
	3	22	11	1		Compiled	35	30
3	8	14	4	1		Tax Returns	37	19
2	11	48	80	27	42	Other	244	142
	75 (4/1-9/30/23)		326 (10/1/23-3/31/24)					
5	22	100	160	53	61	NUMBER OF STATEMENTS	417	278
%	%	%	%	%	%	**ASSETS**	%	%
	16.1	11.3	10.7	5.5	6.1	Cash & Equivalents	7.1	9.7
	24.3	28.4	23.6	25.1	22.9	Trade Receivables (net)	26.8	27.5
	20.9	39.5	38.7	39.0	44.9	Inventory	42.2	38.4
	5.2	2.3	2.5	2.3	3.3	All Other Current	1.9	2.7
	66.5	81.5	75.5	71.9	77.2	Total Current	78.0	78.2
	20.6	10.6	16.3	17.2	14.3	Fixed Assets (net)	14.5	14.1
	6.7	2.1	2.0	4.0	3.3	Intangibles (net)	3.0	3.0
	6.3	5.8	6.2	6.9	5.2	All Other Non-Current	4.5	4.6
	100.0	100.0	100.0	100.0	100.0	Total	100.0	100.0
						LIABILITIES		
	10.5	7.7	11.0	19.7	10.8	Notes Payable-Short Term	17.2	15.9
	.4	1.2	1.7	3.2	.9	Cur. Mat.-L.T.D.	1.5	1.8
	15.2	16.3	15.6	13.3	14.1	Trade Payables	15.7	16.7
	.0	.2	.2	.2	.1	Income Taxes Payable	.1	.2
	9.9	10.3	7.3	8.5	9.0	All Other Current	6.5	8.4
	36.0	35.7	35.8	44.8	34.9	Total Current	41.1	43.0
	20.7	8.6	10.0	14.2	15.9	Long-Term Debt	10.3	12.4
	.0	.4	.2	.3	.1	Deferred Taxes	.4	.2
	5.0	8.2	3.9	4.7	3.0	All Other Non-Current	4.9	4.9
	38.3	47.2	50.1	36.0	46.1	Net Worth	43.2	39.5
	100.0	100.0	100.0	100.0	100.0	Total Liabilities & Net Worth	100.0	100.0
						INCOME DATA		
	100.0	100.0	100.0	100.0	100.0	Net Sales	100.0	100.0
	29.2	25.3	21.8	17.6	15.9	Gross Profit	20.0	20.5
	26.1	18.8	14.8	11.2	9.8	Operating Expenses	16.1	17.3
	3.2	6.5	6.9	6.4	6.0	Operating Profit	3.9	3.1
	.0	.3	.6	.9	.5	All Other Expenses (net)	.8	-.1
	3.1	6.3	6.3	5.4	5.5	Profit Before Taxes	3.1	3.3
						RATIOS		
	6.0	5.6	3.9	3.3	4.9		3.7	3.7
	2.1	3.2	2.2	1.4	2.5	Current	2.0	2.0
	1.3	1.6	1.5	1.0	1.4		1.3	1.3
	2.3	2.7	2.0	1.4	1.7		1.5	1.8
	1.2	1.2	.9	.6	.9	Quick	.8	.9
	.7	.7	.6	.4	.6		.5	.5
7	48.7	23 15.8	26 14.1	26 14.3	31 11.8		28 13.1	32 11.5
19	19.4	33 11.1	36 10.2	38 9.6	36 10.2	Sales/Receivables	36 10.1	42 8.6
30	12.2	46 8.0	42 8.7	54 6.8	41 8.9		50 7.3	55 6.6
6	59.3	33 10.9	41 8.9	39 9.3	57 6.4		46 8.0	42 8.7
24	15.4	61 6.0	73 5.0	72 5.1	78 4.7	Cost of Sales/Inventory	78 4.7	76 4.8
58	6.3	99 3.7	130 2.8	130 2.8	126 2.9		122 3.0	135 2.7
5	80.8	13 28.8	15 24.2	12 29.9	15 24.4		14 27.0	15 24.0
17	21.0	20 18.1	23 15.8	25 14.6	24 15.0	Cost of Sales/Payables	23 15.7	29 12.5
31	11.6	31 11.6	40 9.1	33 11.1	37 9.8		37 9.8	43 8.5
	8.1	3.6	3.4	4.1	3.3		4.0	3.4
	15.0	5.7	5.9	7.3	5.9	Sales/Working Capital	6.7	5.9
	222.5	11.4	11.9	286.5	12.3		15.0	15.6
	19.8	43.4	23.5	12.0	16.4		9.8	18.1
(18)	1.1	(86) 11.5	(140) 6.8	(51) 5.0	(57) 7.0	EBIT/Interest	(376) 3.8	(252) 5.4
	-3.9	4.2	2.9	2.8	2.3		1.1	1.2
		51.2	14.5	28.6	24.1	Net Profit + Depr., Dep.,	12.3	9.1
		(17) 5.7	(46) 5.9	(22) 4.5	(15) 6.1	Amort./Cur. Mat. L/T/D	(76) 4.8	(52) 3.7
		2.4	2.2	1.7	3.0		1.4	1.2
	.0	.0	.0	.1	.0		.0	.0
	.3	.1	.2	.4	.2	Fixed/Worth	.2	.3
	1.5	.3	.7	2.0	.6		.8	.8
	1.0	.3	.4	.7	.6		.5	.6
	1.5	1.0	1.0	2.6	1.1	Debt/Worth	1.4	1.4
	3.5	2.7	2.5	14.0	3.5		3.5	4.3
	73.1	49.3	40.7	84.4	36.1		31.3	35.0
(19)	14.4	(91) 26.3	(155) 24.8	(46) 25.7	(58) 20.8	% Profit Before Taxes/Tangible Net Worth	(382) 14.8	(246) 18.0
	-7.9	11.3	12.2	17.5	12.3		3.1	4.7
	22.3	25.5	18.5	18.7	16.3		12.4	14.1
	3.1	14.0	11.4	10.9	9.8	% Profit Before Taxes/Total Assets	5.5	6.2
	-12.9	5.7	4.4	4.3	3.1		.5	.6
	999.8	470.6	139.7	67.9	197.5		228.9	169.4
	38.4	52.5	23.7	17.2	24.4	Sales/Net Fixed Assets	32.0	23.3
	12.5	15.0	7.1	7.0	8.5		9.9	8.5
	6.4	3.9	3.0	2.6	2.9		3.2	2.9
	4.0	2.9	2.2	2.2	2.0	Sales/Total Assets	2.3	2.1
	2.2	1.8	1.4	1.5	1.5		1.8	1.5
		.2	.3	.3	.1		.3	.3
	(59)	.8	(127) .7	(48) .9	(52) .6	% Depr., Dep., Amort./Sales	(322) .8	(221) .9
		1.7	1.9	1.5	1.3		1.6	2.1
		1.4	.4				.9	1.2
	(39)	2.2	(37) 1.0			% Officers', Directors' Owners' Comp/Sales	(101) 1.7	(74) 2.2
		6.7	2.6				3.6	5.0
19244M	129827M	1869573M	9954079M	8722438M	24458711M	Net Sales ($)	33030419M	20532988M
1957M	23554M	581537M	3952504M	3699792M	9557045M	Total Assets ($)	14357030M	9700190M

© RMA 2024   M = $ thousand   MM = $ million
See Pages viii through xx for Explanation of Ratios and Data

WHOLESALE—Metal Service Centers and Other Metal Merchant Wholesalers   NAICS 423510

Comparative Historical Data | Current Data Sorted by Sales

				Type of Statement						
	33	53	61	Unqualified				3	14	58
	42	53	63	Reviewed			1	14	14	48
	27	25	37	Compiled		1	6	14	8	16
	29	33	30	Tax Returns		4	6	8	8	8
	158	162	210	Other	1	7	7	18	40	137
	4/1/21-3/31/22 ALL	4/1/22-3/31/23 ALL	4/1/23-3/31/24 ALL		75 (4/1-9/30/23)			326 (10/1/23-3/31/24)		
					0-1MM	1-3MM	3-5MM	5-10MM	10-25MM	25MM & OVER
	289	326	401	NUMBER OF STATEMENTS	1	11	12	31	79	267
	%	%	%	ASSETS	%	%	%	%	%	%
	10.7	10.0	9.8	Cash & Equivalents		10.7	16.3	10.7	11.8	8.7
	29.6	24.9	24.8	Trade Receivables (net)		16.2	23.7	22.2	23.0	26.1
	39.2	40.7	38.8	Inventory		25.6	32.6	28.1	41.9	40.0
	3.0	3.0	2.7	All Other Current		6.4	.9	5.2	2.1	2.5
	82.4	78.6	76.0	Total Current		59.0	73.5	66.2	78.7	77.3
	10.5	13.0	15.0	Fixed Assets (net)		19.2	19.1	17.6	14.2	14.7
	2.1	2.6	2.7	Intangibles (net)		13.9	3.9	2.8	2.2	2.4
	4.9	5.9	6.2	All Other Non-Current		7.9	3.6	13.3	4.9	5.6
	100.0	100.0	100.0	Total		100.0	100.0	100.0	100.0	100.0
				LIABILITIES						
	12.5	12.5	11.5	Notes Payable-Short Term		12.4	2.7	12.1	8.5	12.6
	2.2	1.5	1.6	Cur. Mat.-L.T.D.		1.8	1.0	1.7	1.3	1.7
	17.7	14.7	15.1	Trade Payables		9.2	11.6	12.7	13.5	16.3
	.3	.2	.2	Income Taxes Payable		.1	.0	.0	.1	.2
	8.4	10.0	8.5	All Other Current		10.3	9.1	7.3	7.4	9.0
	41.0	38.9	36.9	Total Current		33.8	24.3	33.9	30.8	39.7
	8.0	9.3	11.8	Long-Term Debt		15.8	23.4	11.0	12.6	11.0
	.3	.3	.2	Deferred Taxes		.0	.0	.6	.3	.2
	3.9	4.2	5.0	All Other Non-Current		.7	15.8	7.9	3.6	4.8
	46.8	47.2	46.1	Net Worth		49.7	36.4	46.6	52.7	44.4
	100.0	100.0	100.0	Total Liabilities & Net Worth		100.0	100.0	100.0	100.0	100.0
				INCOME DATA						
	100.0	100.0	100.0	Net Sales		100.0	100.0	100.0	100.0	100.0
	24.0	22.9	21.7	Gross Profit		42.4	27.7	30.1	25.9	18.3
	15.6	14.8	15.4	Operating Expenses		39.4	26.4	23.1	18.8	12.0
	8.4	8.2	6.4	Operating Profit		3.0	1.3	7.0	7.1	6.3
	-.6	.1	.5	All Other Expenses (net)		.2	.7	.0	.4	.6
	9.0	8.1	5.9	Profit Before Taxes		2.7	.6	7.0	6.7	5.6
				RATIOS						
	3.5	3.8	4.4			4.8	13.5	5.8	6.0	3.6
	2.1	2.1	2.3	Current		2.2	5.7	2.6	3.0	2.1
	1.4	1.4	1.4			.9	2.0	1.6	1.7	1.3
	1.9	1.9	2.1			2.1	8.3	2.7	2.6	1.7
	1.0	.9	1.0	Quick		1.6	1.8	1.3	1.1	.8
	.5	.5	.6			.5	.8	.5	.7	.5
30	12.3	21	17.5	25	14.6		15	24.3	23	16.2	15	23.9	23	16.0	26	13.9
42	8.6	32	11.3	34	10.6	Sales/Receivables	18	20.7	30	12.0	31	11.7	36	10.1	35	10.4
54	6.7	50	7.3	43	8.4		26	14.3	35	10.5	50	7.3	46	7.9	42	8.6
38	9.6	34	10.8	37	9.9		38	9.6	16	22.2	5	68.4	49	7.4	38	9.7
81	4.5	70	5.2	68	5.4	Cost of Sales/Inventory	55	6.6	54	6.7	33	11.1	89	4.1	66	5.5
130	2.8	135	2.7	118	3.1		83	4.4	166	2.2	101	3.6	182	2.0	107	3.4
14	26.6	11	33.5	13	27.6		17	21.2	4	88.6	3	111.3	12	31.2	15	24.5
28	13.1	22	16.5	22	16.8	Cost of Sales/Payables	21	17.3	16	22.7	18	20.8	21	17.6	23	15.8
45	8.2	35	10.5	35	10.4		31	11.7	36	10.0	34	10.7	40	9.2	35	10.3
	3.5		4.0		3.6			2.9		2.8		3.6		2.7		3.9
	6.1		6.8		6.2	Sales/Working Capital		11.6		4.9		6.7		4.6		6.7
	11.9		14.3		15.4			-118.6		9.4		20.4		8.4		16.3
	77.4		57.0		20.8					13.8		52.8		38.3		18.1
(246)	26.4	(287)	15.0	(356)	6.7	EBIT/Interest		2.0	(24)	9.4	(70)	8.2	(242)	6.7
	9.5		6.9		2.8			-3.3		3.4		2.9		2.9
	25.2		21.8		17.6	Net Profit + Depr., Dep.,						11.6		18.9
(48)	9.8	(70)	9.0	(101)	5.9	Amort./Cur. Mat. L/T/D					(20)	4.3	(78)	5.9
	1.7		5.2		2.3								1.9		2.5
	.0		.0		.0			.1		.1		.0		.0		.0
	.1		.2		.2	Fixed/Worth		.5		.2		.2		.2		.2
	.5		.5		.7			8.8		35.1		.5		.5		.7
	.4		.5		.4			.2		.3		.4		.3		.5
	1.2		1.2		1.2	Debt/Worth		1.3		1.8		1.3		1.0		1.2
	3.0		2.7		3.4			10.4		NM		2.5		2.5		3.7
	72.8		62.7		43.1	% Profit Before Taxes/Tangible				68.0		40.3		44.1
(268)	46.7	(307)	39.0	(374)	23.7	Net Worth			(29)	31.7	(77)	20.1	(249)	25.0
	25.3		25.2		12.1							14.5		9.2		14.2
	33.1		28.1		19.9	% Profit Before Taxes/Total		10.6		18.0		24.8		23.6		19.0
	19.0		17.0		11.0	Assets		-1.8		1.3		14.2		10.1		11.4
	10.0		7.9		4.1			-4.3		-21.2		5.4		4.2		4.5
	305.2		260.2		190.1			121.0		88.5		114.7		135.9		224.0
	46.8		41.3		31.5	Sales/Net Fixed Assets		10.7		31.9		31.8		35.1		30.6
	14.4		12.5		8.9			7.5		10.1		6.8		9.0		9.9
	3.2		3.5		3.4			3.4		4.5		3.8		3.3		3.3
	2.4		2.6		2.4	Sales/Total Assets		2.5		1.9		2.5		2.1		2.4
	1.7		1.8		1.6			1.8		1.5		1.7		1.3		1.8
	.2		.2		.2							.8		.4		.2
(202)	.6	(246)	.6	(296)	.8	% Depr., Dep., Amort./Sales			(17)	1.7	(52)	1.0	(218)	.7
	1.3		1.2		1.6							3.4		1.8		1.4
	.9		.8		.5	% Officers', Directors'						1.7		1.3		.4
(80)	1.5	(86)	1.8	(91)	1.7	Owners' Comp/Sales			(12)	2.2	(26)	2.1	(46)	.9
	3.9		3.9		3.5							6.6		4.9		2.5
	23043111M	30697615M	45153872M	Net Sales ($)	339M	19714M	47459M	241636M	1427370M	43417354M
	9131130M	12697111M	17816389M	Total Assets ($)	502M	9956M	21820M	134812M	791619M	16857680M

© RMA 2024   M = $ thousand   MM = $ million
See Pages viii through xx for Explanation of Ratios and Data

WHOLESALE—Electrical Apparatus and Equipment, Wiring Supplies, and Related Equipment Merchant Wholesalers NAICS 423610

Current Data Sorted by Assets | Comparative Historical Data

							Type of Statement		
				3	6	7	Unqualified	33	21
		16	21	8	2	Reviewed	57	38
	2	14	3		1	Compiled	27	18
2	3	19	5			Tax Returns	56	25
3	5	46	61	15	24	Other	206	121
	47 (4/1-9/30/23)		219 (10/1/23-3/31/24)				4/1/19-3/31/20	4/1/20-3/31/21
0-500M	500M-2MM	2-10MM	10-50MM	50-100MM	100-250MM		ALL	ALL
5	10	95	93	29	34	NUMBER OF STATEMENTS	379	223
%	%	%	%	%	%	ASSETS	%	%
	27.6	16.4	9.6	3.9	6.2	Cash & Equivalents	9.2	13.6
	42.5	31.0	27.9	34.4	28.5	Trade Receivables (net)	35.9	33.9
	17.4	33.1	33.6	32.3	25.6	Inventory	32.8	31.3
	1.0	4.0	2.0	4.9	5.9	All Other Current	3.1	2.7
	88.5	84.4	73.2	75.5	66.2	Total Current	80.9	81.4
	4.6	6.7	12.4	9.8	10.5	Fixed Assets (net)	9.9	8.8
	2.7	2.9	7.7	8.2	12.1	Intangibles (net)	4.3	5.8
	4.2	5.9	6.7	6.5	11.2	All Other Non-Current	4.9	4.1
	100.0	100.0	100.0	100.0	100.0	Total	100.0	100.0
						LIABILITIES		
	3.9	5.6	7.2	18.7	7.5	Notes Payable-Short Term	15.6	11.3
	.1	1.2	1.7	1.1	2.2	Cur. Mat.-L.T.D.	1.6	1.3
	21.9	21.4	17.5	17.6	16.3	Trade Payables	21.5	20.2
	.0	.0	.1	.0	.2	Income Taxes Payable	.1	.5
	13.5	9.1	10.7	10.5	13.8	All Other Current	10.2	10.0
	39.4	37.4	37.1	47.9	39.9	Total Current	49.0	43.2
	2.3	8.5	7.6	10.9	14.3	Long-Term Debt	7.8	9.6
	.0	.2	.2	.1	.3	Deferred Taxes	.2	.2
	.7	6.0	6.8	4.9	8.2	All Other Non-Current	4.4	4.7
	57.7	48.0	48.3	36.2	37.3	Net Worth	38.7	42.4
	100.0	100.0	100.0	100.0	100.0	Total Liabilities & Net Worth	100.0	100.0
						INCOME DATA		
	100.0	100.0	100.0	100.0	100.0	Net Sales	100.0	100.0
	29.2	31.6	29.3	29.6	26.7	Gross Profit	30.2	28.3
	24.7	26.0	21.8	21.8	21.6	Operating Expenses	25.5	23.5
	4.6	5.6	7.5	7.8	5.1	Operating Profit	4.7	4.7
	.1	.2	.2	.9	1.9	All Other Expenses (net)	.4	-.5
	4.4	5.4	7.3	6.9	3.2	Profit Before Taxes	4.3	5.2
						RATIOS		
	4.0	4.3	3.9	2.4	2.5		2.9	3.2
	2.4	2.5	2.1	1.6	1.8	Current	1.7	2.2
	1.5	1.6	1.4	1.3	1.2		1.3	1.4
	3.3	2.2	1.8	1.2	1.4		1.5	1.9
	1.8	1.5	1.1	.8	.9	Quick	.9	1.1
	1.0	.8	.6	.5	.6		.7	.8
29	12.7	27	13.6	32	11.3	44	8.3	36	10.0		33	11.0	36	10.0
60	6.1	40	9.1	44	8.3	54	6.8	51	7.2	Sales/Receivables	46	7.9	49	7.5
73	5.0	58	6.3	59	6.2	64	5.7	60	6.1		63	5.8	60	6.1
5	69.2	35	10.5	45	8.1	28	12.9	41	9.0		33	11.0	31	11.9
18	20.1	76	4.8	70	5.2	76	4.8	62	5.9	Cost of Sales/Inventory	55	6.6	55	6.6
91	4.0	111	3.3	130	2.8	146	2.5	96	3.8		89	4.1	104	3.5
18	19.9	21	17.5	21	17.6	36	10.1	30	12.1		24	15.2	20	18.3
25	14.6	33	11.1	30	12.3	41	8.8	37	9.9	Cost of Sales/Payables	34	10.7	32	11.5
42	8.7	54	6.7	46	7.9	47	7.8	49	7.5		51	7.2	46	8.0
	3.7		3.1		3.4		4.8		4.8			4.8		3.8
	7.0		5.0		6.1		7.0		7.0	Sales/Working Capital		7.8		6.2
	10.5		10.0		11.8		11.5		19.3			17.6		12.2
			45.7		30.4		20.4		25.3			19.1		39.7
	(73)		8.5	(82)	10.6	(27)	9.7	(31)	10.5	EBIT/Interest	(318)	7.1	(187)	11.2
			4.0		5.2		2.8		1.6			2.9		3.9
			19.4		14.3		38.0		36.9			10.3		8.8
	(12)		7.8	(21)	6.4	(10)	7.5	(11)	1.3	Net Profit + Depr., Dep., Amort./Cur. Mat. L/T/D	(82)	5.5	(39)	3.7
			2.0		3.3		1.8		.5			1.5		1.3
	.0		.0		.1		.1		.1			.1		.0
	.0		.1		.2		.2		.2	Fixed/Worth		.2		.1
	.0		.3		.7		.5		2.8			.5		.5
	.3		.4		.5		1.3		1.0			.7		.6
	.6		.9		1.2		1.8		2.1	Debt/Worth		1.6		1.3
	1.8		2.5		2.9		4.6		8.1			3.8		3.7
	43.7		46.0		44.2		52.8		49.6			44.5		49.6
	7.3	(89)	21.8	(81)	27.0	(26)	38.0	(30)	35.1	% Profit Before Taxes/Tangible Net Worth	(351)	23.1	(200)	25.9
	-6.8		8.7		16.8		17.5		25.1			9.5		12.2
	15.6		18.6		21.4		19.2		16.4			15.7		18.9
	5.2		9.9		11.8		11.1		8.2	% Profit Before Taxes/Total Assets		7.6		9.1
	-4.5		4.4		7.2		4.3		2.6			2.9		3.7
	UND		192.7		97.1		79.6		86.7			134.4		186.6
	UND		79.7		40.2		35.1		35.5	Sales/Net Fixed Assets		49.2		49.9
	207.2		32.7		9.0		12.2		11.5			23.1		21.6
	5.4		3.5		3.1		2.7		2.5			3.5		3.2
	2.7		2.4		2.2		2.0		2.1	Sales/Total Assets		2.8		2.5
	2.3		1.7		1.4		1.6		1.5			2.1		1.8
			.1		.3		.2		.3			.2		.2
		(51)	.3	(78)	.6	(24)	.4	(29)	.7	% Depr., Dep., Amort./Sales	(287)	.5	(172)	.4
			.6		1.6		1.2		.9			.9		.9
			1.6		1.1							1.1		.9
		(37)	2.8	(24)	1.6					% Officers', Directors' Owners' Comp/Sales	(108)	2.1	(57)	1.7
			6.1		2.6							4.4		4.3
19761M	49824M	1329925M	4981225M	4039158M	10122722M	Net Sales ($)	26319925M	16849840M
1021M	14687M	517460M	2225905M	1937634M	5222286M	Total Assets ($)	10428357M	7148360M

© RMA 2024

M = $ thousand   MM = $ million
See Pages viii through xx for Explanation of Ratios and Data

WHOLESALE—Electrical Apparatus and Equipment, Wiring Supplies, and Related Equipment Merchant Wholesalers NAICS 423610

Comparative Historical Data / Current Data Sorted by Sales

Comparative Historical Data					Current Data Sorted by Sales					
			Type of Statement							
10	16	16	Unqualified					3	16	16
41	47	47	Reviewed				1	4	12	27
21	23	20	Compiled				1	4	12	3
27	41	29	Tax Returns		1	1	3	5	14	5
154	157	154	Other		1	5	3	15	35	95
4/1/21-3/31/22 ALL	4/1/22-3/31/23 ALL	4/1/23-3/31/24 ALL			47 (4/1-9/30/23)			219 (10/1/23-3/31/24)		
					0-1MM	1-3MM	3-5MM	5-10MM	10-25MM	25MM & OVER
253	284	266	NUMBER OF STATEMENTS		2	7	7	27	77	146
%	%	%	ASSETS		%	%	%	%	%	%
12.2	14.2	12.0	Cash & Equivalents					19.0	17.4	7.3
32.4	29.7	30.5	Trade Receivables (net)					27.2	30.3	30.9
33.6	32.7	31.3	Inventory					32.1	30.1	32.5
2.3	3.3	3.5	All Other Current					3.5	3.4	3.3
80.5	80.0	77.4	Total Current					81.8	81.2	74.0
8.6	9.6	9.6	Fixed Assets (net)					8.7	9.2	10.0
5.8	4.5	6.3	Intangibles (net)					1.7	4.3	8.4
5.1	5.9	6.8	All Other Non-Current					7.9	5.4	7.6
100.0	100.0	100.0	Total					100.0	100.0	100.0
			LIABILITIES							
9.7	9.2	9.3	Notes Payable-Short Term					6.1	5.2	9.8
1.9	.9	1.4	Cur. Mat.-L.T.D.					.5	.8	1.9
21.0	18.1	19.1	Trade Payables					14.8	19.0	19.0
.1	.2	.1	Income Taxes Payable					.0	.1	.1
10.1	11.4	10.6	All Other Current					8.7	9.6	11.3
42.8	39.7	40.5	Total Current					30.1	34.7	42.1
10.9	11.1	8.8	Long-Term Debt					6.6	7.2	10.5
.2	.1	.2	Deferred Taxes					.4	.1	.2
3.4	4.9	6.1	All Other Non-Current					2.4	4.3	7.6
42.7	44.2	44.4	Net Worth					60.5	53.8	39.6
100.0	100.0	100.0	Total Liabilties & Net Worth					100.0	100.0	100.0
			INCOME DATA							
100.0	100.0	100.0	Net Sales					100.0	100.0	100.0
30.9	32.4	30.4	Gross Profit					35.2	31.6	27.5
24.4	24.7	24.0	Operating Expenses					29.9	23.9	21.6
6.4	7.7	6.4	Operating Profit					5.3	7.7	6.0
-1.0	.4	.5	All Other Expenses (net)					.2	.3	.7
7.4	7.3	5.9	Profit Before Taxes					5.1	7.4	5.3
			RATIOS							
2.9	3.7	3.4						4.9	4.2	2.6
2.0	2.2	2.1	Current					3.1	2.7	1.8
1.4	1.5	1.5						1.9	1.8	1.4
1.7	2.1	1.8						2.4	2.3	1.4
1.1	1.1	1.2	Quick					1.8	1.6	.9
.7	.7	.7						.9	.8	.6
34 10.7	28 12.9	31 11.9			23 15.8	28 13.1	35 10.5			
49 7.4	45 8.1	46 8.0	Sales/Receivables		42 8.7	44 8.3	47 7.7			
62 5.9	61 6.0	60 6.1			63 5.8	66 5.5	58 6.3			
41 8.8	38 9.6	36 10.2			15 23.6	26 14.2	41 8.9			
70 5.2	70 5.2	69 5.3	Cost of Sales/Inventory		99 3.7	74 4.9	63 5.8			
104 3.5	118 3.1	114 3.2			130 2.8	114 3.2	111 3.3			
24 15.5	21 17.5	23 15.6			19 19.5	19 19.3	27 13.5			
35 10.3	33 10.9	34 10.6	Cost of Sales/Payables		27 13.5	32 11.5	36 10.2			
52 7.0	53 6.9	50 7.3			54 6.8	51 7.1	47 7.8			
4.3	3.7	3.8						2.8	2.9	4.8
6.7	5.8	6.2	Sales/Working Capital					3.9	4.4	7.2
12.0	11.2	11.6						8.2	9.1	13.0
64.9	70.8	28.5						68.8	51.5	25.0
(207) 22.2	(227) 19.8	(221) 9.5	EBIT/Interest		(19) 11.1	(59) 10.6	(132) 9.6			
9.8	7.4	3.8						4.0	4.7	3.6
23.2	19.8	17.0	Net Profit + Depr., Dep.,						18.6	14.7
(44) 8.7	(40) 7.8	(54) 6.6	Amort./Cur. Mat. L/T/D				(13) 12.8	(37) 5.0		
2.7	2.7	1.5							6.5	1.4
.0	.0	.0						.0	.0	.1
.2	.1	.1	Fixed/Worth					.1	.1	.2
.4	.5	.5						.2	.4	.7
.6	.5	.5						.3	.4	.7
1.2	1.2	1.2	Debt/Worth					.6	.7	1.7
3.9	3.0	2.9						1.3	1.9	4.0
57.8	54.1	46.1						21.3	53.7	49.5
(224) 34.0	(253) 33.5	(240) 26.8	% Profit Before Taxes/Tangible Net Worth		(26) 12.4	(73) 26.3	(127) 31.5			
20.0	17.9	12.9						4.0	11.2	18.0
22.6	23.2	19.5	% Profit Before Taxes/Total Assets					16.3	21.2	19.7
13.4	13.7	10.3						6.0	13.1	10.5
7.3	5.9	5.0						2.6	6.2	6.2
162.7	191.7	128.0						268.2	163.2	99.8
54.1	52.5	51.0	Sales/Net Fixed Assets					99.4	61.1	45.0
22.2	17.9	17.6						29.9	20.7	13.5
3.2	3.0	3.1						2.9	3.4	3.1
2.5	2.3	2.3	Sales/Total Assets					2.2	2.2	2.3
1.8	1.7	1.6						1.7	1.4	1.8
.3	.2	.2						.1	.2	.3
(177) .5	(192) .4	(187) .4	% Depr., Dep., Amort./Sales		(11) .4	(50) .4	(119) .4			
1.2	1.0	1.1						.7	1.4	1.1
1.3	1.0	1.3	% Officers', Directors' Owners' Comp/Sales					1.6	1.2	1.1
(59) 2.9	(94) 2.1	(77) 2.4			(14) 3.7	(25) 2.3	(31) 1.6			
6.5	3.6	4.1						6.1	3.0	2.9
17731383M	20514693M	20542615M	Net Sales ($)		621M	16662M	25210M	189738M	1263981M	19046403M
7473166M	9755974M	9918993M	Total Assets ($)		132M	13879M	19745M	87766M	688441M	9109030M

© RMA 2024   M = $ thousand   MM = $ million
See Pages viii through xx for Explanation of Ratios and Data

WHOLESALE—Household Appliances, Electric Housewares, and Consumer Electronics Merchant Wholesalers NAICS 423620

Current Data Sorted by Assets | Comparative Historical Data

							Type of Statement		
			1	2	3		Unqualified	2	3
	1	3	13	1			Reviewed	12	6
		5	2				Compiled	9	4
2	4	3					Tax Returns	12	5
	3	20	42	7	16		Other	65	34
	40 (4/1-9/30/23)		88 (10/1/23-3/31/24)					4/1/19- 3/31/20	4/1/20- 3/31/21
0-500M	500M-2MM	2-10MM	10-50MM	50-100MM	100-250MM			ALL	ALL
2	8	31	58	10	19		NUMBER OF STATEMENTS	100	52
%	%	%	%	%	%		ASSETS	%	%
		13.5	12.1	4.9	23.6		Cash & Equivalents	11.9	13.6
		26.3	22.9	33.7	17.6		Trade Receivables (net)	26.6	26.5
		40.0	43.2	33.9	36.7		Inventory	38.2	38.6
		3.4	2.5	3.8	2.5		All Other Current	2.6	2.6
		83.1	80.7	76.4	80.4		Total Current	79.3	81.3
		9.3	9.3	8.1	9.1		Fixed Assets (net)	9.5	6.3
		4.8	3.3	5.8	1.4		Intangibles (net)	6.3	7.6
		2.9	6.7	9.7	9.1		All Other Non-Current	4.9	4.8
		100.0	100.0	100.0	100.0		Total	100.0	100.0
							LIABILITIES		
		11.2	12.9	14.0	2.8		Notes Payable-Short Term	13.4	10.3
		.3	.7	1.4	.7		Cur. Mat.-L.T.D.	.9	1.2
		22.4	18.8	13.1	12.5		Trade Payables	24.5	23.1
		.5	.1	.1	1.5		Income Taxes Payable	.2	.1
		8.6	9.1	12.7	35.6		All Other Current	9.6	7.2
		43.0	41.6	41.4	53.3		Total Current	48.5	41.9
		7.8	6.5	20.7	2.0		Long-Term Debt	9.3	14.6
		.1	.1	.0	.0		Deferred Taxes	.1	.0
		.4	3.9	6.3	5.6		All Other Non-Current	4.6	3.2
		48.6	47.9	31.6	39.1		Net Worth	37.5	40.4
		100.0	100.0	100.0	100.0		Total Liabilities & Net Worth	100.0	100.0
							INCOME DATA		
		100.0	100.0	100.0	100.0		Net Sales	100.0	100.0
		26.2	22.7	25.1	14.0		Gross Profit	26.5	25.4
		25.0	18.3	20.9	11.5		Operating Expenses	22.3	19.2
		1.2	4.4	4.3	2.5		Operating Profit	4.2	6.2
		-.3	.4	1.4	-.4		All Other Expenses (net)	.8	.0
		1.5	4.0	2.8	2.8		Profit Before Taxes	3.4	6.2
							RATIOS		
		3.2	3.2	3.1	2.6			2.5	3.0
		1.9	1.9	1.8	1.8		Current	1.7	2.0
		1.2	1.4	1.4	.9			1.2	1.4
		2.4	1.3	1.5	1.6			1.3	1.7
		.8	.8	.9	.8		Quick	.7	1.0
		.6	.5	.5	.5			.5	.5
	14	26.7	18	19.8	22	16.4	13	28.2		17	21.9	16	23.0

14	26.7	18	19.8	22	16.4	13	28.2	Sales/Receivables	17	21.9	16	23.0
31	11.6	27	13.6	58	6.3	23	15.7		27	13.7	28	13.0
54	6.8	42	8.7	69	5.3	41	8.8		44	8.3	49	7.4
17	21.0	44	8.3	27	13.4	32	11.3	Cost of Sales/Inventory	34	10.6	37	9.9
70	5.2	83	4.4	37	9.9	42	8.6		65	5.6	70	5.2
126	2.9	114	3.2	261	1.4	91	4.0		96	3.8	107	3.4
15	25.0	12	29.4	9	38.7	10	37.7	Cost of Sales/Payables	18	20.3	21	17.5
30	12.0	24	15.5	16	23.3	19	18.9		37	9.9	40	9.1
53	6.9	51	7.2	31	11.8	34	10.7		60	6.1	60	6.1

5.1	4.9	2.6	5.5			6.2	4.4
7.4	6.8	9.9	6.4	Sales/Working Capital	9.3	8.4
24.1	14.7	17.1	-74.5		22.3	14.3
45.6	51.8		19.6		23.6	32.1
(21) 2.8	(43) 3.9	(14) 6.4	EBIT/Interest	(87) 8.0	(45) 14.1
-.3	1.4		1.5		2.2	3.5
	192.6				9.6	
	(10) 71.0			Net Profit + Depr., Dep., Amort./Cur. Mat. L/T/D	(14) 3.4	
	4.6				.5	
.0	.0	.0	.0		.0	.0
.1	.1	.2	.1	Fixed/Worth	.1	.1
.4	.4	NM	1.7		.8	.6
.5	.6	.8	.6		.7	.8
1.1	1.2	2.2	.9	Debt/Worth	2.1	1.9
2.5	2.9	NM	12.1		5.8	4.0
30.5	38.1		20.1		63.0	65.5
(29) 11.0	(55) 17.2		10.3	% Profit Before Taxes/Tangible Net Worth	(90) 29.7	(44) 35.9
-2.7	6.0		.0		11.5	25.7
14.6	18.2	12.2	9.9		18.2	24.5
4.7	6.4	4.0	2.6	% Profit Before Taxes/Total Assets	7.7	15.3
-2.9	1.7	-.7	.0		3.0	6.7
427.9	418.0	152.1	204.8		245.7	882.5
92.1	138.2	132.8	71.1	Sales/Net Fixed Assets	63.5	116.9
21.5	20.9	27.0	34.5		25.9	47.0
3.9	3.7	3.5	3.4		4.1	3.4
3.0	2.7	2.3	2.7	Sales/Total Assets	3.2	2.6
1.8	1.9	1.4	2.2		2.2	2.0
.1	.1		.1		.1	.1
(16) .3	(44) .3	(18) .2	% Depr., Dep., Amort./Sales	(70) .4	(23) .3
.7	.8		.6		.8	.8
1.1	.2				.5	.3
(11) 3.6	(16) .6			% Officers', Directors', Owners' Comp/Sales	(34) 1.4	(15) 1.0
5.6	1.4				3.5	7.0

| 4052M | 126763M | 610216M | 3645414M | 1635266M | 7902892M | Net Sales ($) | 8220336M | 3947834M |
| 458M | 9698M | 191477M | 1316911M | 634338M | 2796797M | Total Assets ($) | 3444781M | 1650913M |

© RMA 2024

M = $ thousand   MM = $ million
See Pages viii through xx for Explanation of Ratios and Data

WHOLESALE—Household Appliances, Electric Housewares, and Consumer Electronics Merchant Wholesalers NAICS 423620

Comparative Historical Data | Current Data Sorted by Sales

Comparative Historical Data					Current Data Sorted by Sales					
4	7	6	**Type of Statement**							
7	13	18	Unqualified					1	4	6
3	5	7	Reviewed				2	3	13	
8	7	9	Compiled		1	3	3		2	
37	55	88	Tax Returns	1	1	2	3	16	1	
			Other						66	
4/1/21-3/31/22 ALL	4/1/22-3/31/23 ALL	4/1/23-3/31/24 ALL			40 (4/1-9/30/23)			88 (10/1/23-3/31/24)		
				0-1MM	1-3MM	3-5MM	5-10MM	10-25MM	25MM & OVER	
59	87	128	**NUMBER OF STATEMENTS**	1	3	5	8	23	88	
%	%	%	**ASSETS**	%	%	%	%	%	%	
17.9	13.6	14.7	Cash & Equivalents					8.5	14.9	
23.5	23.7	23.3	Trade Receivables (net)					21.2	24.7	
37.4	39.2	39.5	Inventory					44.2	39.7	
3.4	3.0	2.9	All Other Current					5.3	2.4	
82.2	79.3	80.4	Total Current					79.2	81.6	
6.6	8.3	8.8	Fixed Assets (net)					10.0	8.3	
6.2	6.1	3.9	Intangibles (net)					6.8	3.1	
5.1	6.2	6.9	All Other Non-Current					4.1	7.0	
100.0	100.0	100.0	Total					100.0	100.0	
			LIABILITIES							
5.3	10.1	11.3	Notes Payable-Short Term					8.2	11.1	
1.4	1.0	1.9	Cur. Mat.-L.T.D.					.2	.8	
18.3	18.2	18.3	Trade Payables					22.0	18.4	
.3	.2	.4	Income Taxes Payable					.7	.4	
15.1	16.7	14.2	All Other Current					10.4	14.8	
40.2	46.4	46.2	Total Current					41.5	45.6	
6.4	7.5	7.4	Long-Term Debt					9.0	6.3	
.1	.1	.1	Deferred Taxes					.0	.1	
1.7	5.8	3.2	All Other Non-Current					1.3	4.3	
51.5	40.3	43.1	Net Worth					48.2	43.7	
100.0	100.0	100.0	Total Liabilties & Net Worth					100.0	100.0	
			INCOME DATA							
100.0	100.0	100.0	Net Sales					100.0	100.0	
27.9	25.9	22.9	Gross Profit					26.1	19.6	
20.4	22.0	19.5	Operating Expenses					24.6	15.8	
7.5	3.8	3.3	Operating Profit					1.5	3.8	
-.5	.3	.2	All Other Expenses (net)					-.2	.4	
8.0	3.6	3.1	Profit Before Taxes					1.6	3.4	
			RATIOS							
3.6	3.0	3.0	Current					3.5	2.9	
2.1	1.8	1.9						1.8	1.9	
1.5	1.2	1.2						1.2	1.3	
1.9	1.3	1.6	Quick					1.1	1.6	
1.2	.8	.8						.7	.9	
.6	.5	.5						.6	.5	
13 28.5	17 21.1	14 26.8	Sales/Receivables					16 22.4	14 26.3	
28 13.1	28 13.0	26 13.9						33 11.0	26 14.0	
56 6.5	50 7.3	48 7.6						54 6.8	47 7.8	
34 10.7	32 11.5	33 11.2	Cost of Sales/Inventory					62 5.9	32 11.5	
65 5.6	73 5.0	70 5.2						89 4.1	63 5.8	
135 2.7	122 3.0	114 3.2						140 2.6	107 3.4	
12 30.4	9 39.6	12 29.6	Cost of Sales/Payables					18 20.6	12 29.6	
31 11.6	26 13.9	22 16.6						39 9.3	22 16.6	
47 7.8	47 7.7	44 8.3						58 6.3	41 8.8	
4.0	5.3	5.0	Sales/Working Capital					2.7	5.7	
6.6	8.8	7.3						6.1	8.3	
14.0	32.4	18.8						32.9	17.9	
147.3	47.3	22.1	EBIT/Interest					54.3	27.2	
(45) 34.8	(64) 12.3	(91) 4.0						(17) 5.0	(66) 4.1	
6.6	1.9	1.4						1.6	1.4	
	28.0	99.6	Net Profit + Depr., Dep., Amort./Cur. Mat. L/T/D						163.5	
	(10) 9.1	(15) 30.9						(12) 31.0		
	-2.3	5.1							5.9	
.0	.0	.0	Fixed/Worth					.0	.0	
.1	.2	.1						.2	.1	
.4	.7	.4						.5	.4	
.5	.7	.6	Debt/Worth					.7	.6	
1.0	1.9	1.2						1.3	1.2	
2.5	5.9	3.6						2.5	3.6	
59.4	41.3	37.9	% Profit Before Taxes/Tangible Net Worth					13.1	39.1	
(52) 40.4	(76) 20.7	(119) 14.9						(21) 6.0	(83) 18.4	
22.1	7.3	3.6						-.9	5.1	
34.0	16.8	14.5	% Profit Before Taxes/Total Assets					5.5	15.9	
16.2	7.1	5.2						2.2	6.7	
7.9	2.1	1.1						-2.9	1.1	
595.3	635.3	419.0	Sales/Net Fixed Assets					395.4	414.3	
152.5	95.9	93.9						92.1	118.0	
27.7	18.2	24.7						10.7	27.6	
3.9	3.6	3.8	Sales/Total Assets					3.2	4.0	
2.6	2.7	2.8						2.2	2.9	
1.8	1.8	2.1						1.7	2.2	
.1	.1	.1	% Depr., Dep., Amort./Sales					.2	.1	
(39) .2	(55) .2	(88) .2						(11) .4	(68) .2	
.7	.8	.7						1.4	.6	
.5	.5	.4	% Officers', Directors' Owners' Comp/Sales						.3	
(18) 1.0	(21) 1.5	(35) 1.1							(20) .6	
5.2	3.0	2.4							1.4	
5215793M	6058707M	13924603M	Net Sales ($)	567M	7104M	18949M	58127M	404127M	13435729M	
1797984M	2447070M	4949679M	Total Assets ($)	271M	7483M	5543M	23666M	200364M	4712352M	

© RMA 2024   M = $ thousand   MM = $ million
See Pages viii through xx for Explanation of Ratios and Data

WHOLESALE—Other Electronic Parts and Equipment Merchant Wholesalers NAICS 423690

Current Data Sorted by Assets

								Comparative Historical Data	
							Type of Statement		
		3	8	4	8	7	Unqualified	20	11
		2	7	16	1		Reviewed	34	16
	2	3	10	5			Compiled	16	11
2	4	8	39	3	12	10	Tax Returns	31	9
4		30 (4/1-9/30/23)		26			Other	113	67
				148 (10/1/23-3/31/24)				4/1/19-	4/1/20-
0-500M	500M-2MM	2-10MM	10-50MM	50-100MM	100-250MM			3/31/20	3/31/21
6	16	64	54	21	17		NUMBER OF STATEMENTS	214 ALL	114 ALL
%	%	%	%	%	%		ASSETS	%	%
		15.5	13.6	11.1	12.2	17.4	Cash & Equivalents	13.0	13.3
		30.8	26.8	31.0	22.6	24.1	Trade Receivables (net)	32.8	29.1
		41.5	36.9	32.1	22.4	32.7	Inventory	33.1	35.4
		3.0	5.2	5.1	1.8	6.9	All Other Current	3.2	2.8
		90.8	82.4	79.4	59.0	81.0	Total Current	82.0	80.7
		1.9	7.6	8.5	12.1	8.9	Fixed Assets (net)	7.6	8.1
		2.2	3.8	3.0	9.1	6.5	Intangibles (net)	5.7	6.0
		5.2	6.2	9.2	19.8	3.6	All Other Non-Current	4.8	5.3
		100.0	100.0	100.0	100.0	100.0	Total	100.0	100.0
							LIABILITIES		
		7.5	8.8	11.4	6.8	2.5	Notes Payable-Short Term	10.8	11.8
		2.1	1.7	1.0	1.3	5.2	Cur. Mat.-L.T.D.	1.8	1.6
		31.1	18.7	18.8	17.0	28.1	Trade Payables	24.1	21.0
		.0	.1	.0	.3	.1	Income Taxes Payable	.1	.1
		3.9	8.8	11.0	9.4	18.3	All Other Current	12.3	9.9
		44.5	38.0	42.2	34.7	54.2	Total Current	49.1	44.4
		6.4	13.4	6.2	16.0	9.1	Long-Term Debt	7.9	8.7
		.0	.0	.1	.4	.6	Deferred Taxes	.1	.1
		12.4	6.0	3.9	9.9	2.3	All Other Non-Current	6.6	4.5
		36.7	42.6	47.7	39.0	33.8	Net Worth	36.3	42.2
		100.0	100.0	100.0	100.0	100.0	Total Liabilties & Net Worth	100.0	100.0
							INCOME DATA		
		100.0	100.0	100.0	100.0	100.0	Net Sales	100.0	100.0
		30.7	34.6	26.7	30.7	24.0	Gross Profit	28.0	28.2
		33.7	27.8	19.8	23.8	18.5	Operating Expenses	23.4	24.3
		-2.9	6.8	6.9	6.9	5.5	Operating Profit	4.5	3.9
		-.5	.4	.3	3.2	.8	All Other Expenses (net)	.7	-.3
		-2.5	6.4	6.6	3.7	4.7	Profit Before Taxes	3.9	4.2
							RATIOS		
		6.3	5.6	3.4	2.4	3.4		3.2	3.5
		2.1	2.3	2.0	1.4	2.1	Current	1.8	1.9
		1.4	1.4	1.4	1.3	1.0		1.2	1.3
		4.7	2.3	1.9	1.7	1.4		1.6	1.7
		1.1	1.0	1.1	.8	1.2	Quick	1.0	1.0
		.5	.6	.5	.6	.6		.6	.6
	18	19.8	26 13.9	30 12.3	33 10.9	38 9.6		27 13.7	27 13.5
	24	15.2	38 9.7	42 8.7	42 8.7	51 7.1	Sales/Receivables	41 8.9	44 8.3
	43	8.4	56 6.5	64 5.7	48 7.6	62 5.9		56 6.5	58 6.3
	14	26.7	40 9.1	23 16.0	26 13.9	36 10.1		26 14.3	33 11.1
	87	4.2	91 4.0	57 6.4	55 6.6	65 5.6	Cost of Sales/Inventory	54 6.7	74 4.9
	122	3.0	135 2.7	104 3.5	101 3.6	146 2.5		111 3.3	118 3.1
	12	30.1	18 20.1	20 18.6	20 18.1	25 14.4		18 20.7	24 15.1
	24	15.0	33 11.1	31 11.6	34 10.6	34 10.7	Cost of Sales/Payables	35 10.3	40 9.2
	91	4.0	57 6.4	49 7.5	78 4.7	76 4.8		58 6.3	59 6.2
		5.1	3.0	3.7	4.3	3.2		4.7	3.2
		9.9	5.9	6.6	8.4	7.7	Sales/Working Capital	8.8	7.1
		14.6	12.8	18.8	24.1	128.4		29.3	22.5
		69.3	31.6	37.1	5.4	737.1		29.0	33.0
	(13)	5.9	(50) 4.8	(45) 8.4	(19) 3.3	(12) 13.2	EBIT/Interest	(166) 6.9	(96) 8.9
		-1.9	1.8	3.2	1.6	.6		2.1	2.3
				52.0				9.6	16.7
			(13)	6.0			Net Profit + Depr., Dep., Amort./Cur. Mat. L/T/D	(25) 4.3	(24) 4.9
				2.4				.9	1.7
		.0	.0	.0	.1	.1		.0	.0
		.0	.1	.1	.2	.2	Fixed/Worth	.1	.1
		.1	.3	.3	1.4	4.3		.8	.6
		.4	.5	.5	.7	.5		.6	.5
		1.7	1.1	1.1	2.4	9.3	Debt/Worth	1.9	1.6
		7.2	4.8	2.8	5.9	29.2		8.9	4.3
		71.0	61.3	45.8	34.5	54.6	% Profit Before Taxes/Tangible Net Worth	49.4	57.1
	(14)	18.4	(56) 27.5	(51) 24.7	(18) 21.7	(15) 22.4		(181) 24.1	(97) 22.5
		1.3	11.8	11.0	6.5	5.7		10.5	9.3
		35.6	24.1	21.6	10.7	11.4	% Profit Before Taxes/Total Assets	18.3	18.8
		4.1	10.4	9.2	5.8	7.4		8.9	8.4
		-14.1	3.1	3.7	2.0	-1.2		1.9	1.3
		UND	999.8	317.1	80.1	136.9		302.2	337.9
		710.5	86.7	59.2	22.1	23.2	Sales/Net Fixed Assets	84.6	71.9
		171.5	21.2	21.7	13.4	13.5		29.5	21.7
		5.5	3.0	3.1	3.1	3.2		4.0	3.4
		3.3	2.4	2.4	1.5	2.0	Sales/Total Assets	2.7	2.3
		2.5	1.9	1.6	.9	1.0		1.9	1.6
			.2	.2	.2	.1		.1	.1
		(30)	.5 (40)	.4 (17)	.7 (10)	1.1	% Depr., Dep., Amort./Sales	(138) .4	(71) .5
			1.1	.8	1.3	1.7		.8	1.2
			1.8	.3				1.0	1.3
		(23)	2.9 (10)	1.0			% Officers', Directors' Owners' Comp/Sales	(57) 1.8	(33) 3.2
			4.3	3.6				3.7	7.9
8762M	97962M	940936M	3471640M	2618839M	7199380M		Net Sales ($)	17497975M	7874389M
1962M	22032M	365191M	1242449M	1393902M	2754284M		Total Assets ($)	7181240M	3494139M

© RMA 2024

M = $ thousand   MM = $ million
See Pages viii through xx for Explanation of Ratios and Data

WHOLESALE—Other Electronic Parts and Equipment Merchant Wholesalers NAICS 423690

Comparative Historical Data / Current Data Sorted by Sales

					Type of Statement					1	18	
	11		14		19	Unqualified			1	2	7	16
	10		20		28	Reviewed	1	1	1	1	7	4
	6		12		14	Compiled			2	1	7	2
	10		14		18	Tax Returns	1	1	3	5	6	47
	70		87		99	Other	1	3	5	14	29	
	4/1/21-3/31/22 ALL		4/1/22-3/31/23 ALL		4/1/23-3/31/24 ALL		30 (4/1-9/30/23)			148 (10/1/23-3/31/24)		
							0-1MM	1-3MM	3-5MM	5-10MM	10-25MM	25MM & OVER
	107		147		178	**NUMBER OF STATEMENTS**	3	5	11	22	50	87
	%		%		%	**ASSETS**	%	%	%	%	%	%
	16.5		14.4		13.6	Cash & Equivalents			18.8	15.0	12.7	12.3
	31.3		28.8		27.2	Trade Receivables (net)			28.6	22.1	31.5	27.4
	30.8		36.6		32.9	Inventory			42.4	32.2	34.5	31.4
	2.9		3.1		4.8	All Other Current			2.4	2.6	4.4	5.8
	81.5		82.8		78.5	Total Current			92.3	71.9	83.1	76.8
	8.1		7.6		8.0	Fixed Assets (net)			1.9	12.7	5.8	9.0
	4.8		3.3		4.4	Intangibles (net)			1.8	6.5	4.4	4.2
	5.5		6.3		9.1	All Other Non-Current			4.1	8.9	6.8	10.0
	100.0		100.0		100.0	Total			100.0	100.0	100.0	100.0
						LIABILITIES						
	10.9		11.1		8.8	Notes Payable-Short Term			7.9	7.6	7.7	9.5
	1.5		1.3		1.9	Cur. Mat.-L.T.D.			2.0	1.4	2.0	1.8
	21.1		20.8		20.1	Trade Payables			27.0	19.8	15.7	21.4
	.2		.1		.1	Income Taxes Payable			.0	.0	.1	.1
	8.9		9.4		10.2	All Other Current			6.8	12.3	8.8	11.3
	42.6		42.7		41.1	Total Current			43.8	41.1	34.2	44.1
	9.9		11.5		11.4	Long-Term Debt			13.9	20.3	8.3	9.2
	.1		.2		.1	Deferred Taxes			.0	.0	.1	.2
	4.7		4.4		6.0	All Other Non-Current			12.9	4.6	6.4	4.6
	42.7		41.1		41.4	Net Worth			29.5	34.0	51.1	41.8
	100.0		100.0		100.0	Total Liabilities & Net Worth			100.0	100.0	100.0	100.0
						INCOME DATA						
	100.0		100.0		100.0	Net Sales			100.0	100.0	100.0	100.0
	28.9		26.5		30.9	Gross Profit			40.3	38.5	33.0	25.5
	22.6		20.7		25.2	Operating Expenses			37.6	30.2	27.2	19.3
	6.3		5.9		5.7	Operating Profit			2.7	8.3	5.8	6.1
	-.8		.0		.9	All Other Expenses (net)			-.7	.3	.2	1.2
	7.1		5.8		4.8	Profit Before Taxes			3.4	8.0	5.6	5.0
						RATIOS						
	3.6		3.5		3.5				14.4	2.6	6.1	2.9
	2.0		2.0		2.0	Current			2.1	1.9	2.4	1.9
	1.4		1.4		1.3				1.3	1.4	1.6	1.3
	1.9		1.8		1.9				5.5	1.7	2.9	1.5
	1.0		1.0		1.0	Quick			1.5	.8	1.3	.9
	.7		.5		.6				.5	.4	.7	.5
18	19.8	22	16.8	25	14.5		20	18.0	20	18.4	32	11.3	29	12.6
39	9.3	38	9.6	40	9.2	Sales/Receivables	27	13.3	28	12.9	47	7.8	39	9.4
59	6.2	55	6.6	56	6.5		68	5.4	45	8.2	64	5.7	52	7.0
15	24.8	21	17.0	31	11.9		19	19.4	29	12.6	38	9.6	29	12.6
47	7.8	62	5.9	73	5.0	Cost of Sales/Inventory	118	3.1	89	4.1	87	4.2	57	6.4
79	4.6	126	2.9	118	3.1		182	2.0	146	2.5	146	2.5	96	3.8
18	20.6	13	27.3	19	19.6		8	47.5	23	16.0	17	22.1	20	18.4
35	10.3	31	11.9	33	11.2	Cost of Sales/Payables	73	5.0	39	9.3	29	12.4	32	11.3
55	6.6	57	6.4	59	6.2		96	3.8	64	5.7	49	7.4	52	7.0
	3.7		4.3		3.6				2.3	3.0	2.9	4.2
	9.2		7.2		7.1	Sales/Working Capital			10.5	7.2	5.0	8.1
	15.6		13.6		17.0				14.6	18.1	10.4	24.5
	87.8		60.4		29.2					42.9	30.3	28.0
(87)	31.3	(117)	10.8	(143)	4.9	EBIT/Interest			(17)	3.4	(39)	5.0	(73)	4.9
	8.5		4.6		1.8					1.2	1.8	2.0
	58.3		14.4		16.1	Net Profit + Depr., Dep.,						16.1
(13)	7.9	(18)	6.1	(27)	4.4	Amort./Cur. Mat. L/T/D						(19)	3.8
	5.1		2.0		1.9							1.9
	.0		.0		.0				.0	.0	.0	.0
	.1		.1		.1	Fixed/Worth			.0	.3	.1	.1
	.3		.3		.4				.0	.9	.2	.4
	.6		.7		.5				.3	.5	.4	.5
	1.7		1.5		1.5	Debt/Worth			3.4	1.3	1.0	1.7
	4.2		4.8		4.9				8.4	NM	2.6	5.2
	91.7		79.6		51.3	% Profit Before Taxes/Tangible			65.2	83.0	38.2	50.4
(96)	50.3	(134)	32.3	(158)	24.5	Net Worth	(10)	38.1	(17)	40.3	(46)	19.8	(80)	24.5
	22.8		16.3		9.0				7.0	6.4	9.8	10.3
	27.1		20.6		19.8	% Profit Before Taxes/Total			38.4	26.7	23.5	15.9
	17.3		10.7		8.2	Assets			7.9	10.1	10.3	8.0
	6.7		4.1		2.7				.5	.9	3.0	3.2
	417.0		575.2		520.0				UND	458.0	999.8	206.9
	85.7		77.6		66.7	Sales/Net Fixed Assets			595.5	40.0	111.2	40.9
	29.4		26.7		19.7				65.3	6.1	27.9	18.4
	4.0		4.0		3.2				3.5	3.2	3.0	3.5
	2.7		2.7		2.4	Sales/Total Assets			2.4	2.1	2.4	2.4
	1.8		1.7		1.6				1.8	1.2	1.7	1.5
	.1		.1		.2					.2	.2	.2
(61)	.3	(92)	.4	(106)	.4	% Depr., Dep., Amort./Sales			(12)	.5	(26)	.5	(62)	.4
	.9		.9		1.1					2.0	.9	1.1
	1.0		1.0		1.1	% Officers', Directors'					1.5	.3
(31)	2.7	(38)	1.8	(47)	2.8	Owners' Comp/Sales					(17)	2.9	(12)	.8
	5.5		4.5		4.3						5.4	2.5
	10731431M		13665673M		14337519M	Net Sales ($)	1428M	8997M	43142M	151242M	826924M	13305786M
	3748846M		4930269M		5779820M	Total Assets ($)	1205M	3083M	18251M	83862M	407267M	5266152M

© RMA 2024   M = $ thousand   MM = $ million
See Pages viii through xx for Explanation of Ratios and Data

WHOLESALE—Hardware Merchant Wholesalers NAICS 423710

Current Data Sorted by Assets

							Type of Statement		Comparative Historical Data	
				4	4	2	Unqualified		6	8
			6	17	3	1	Reviewed		23	11
		1	13	4			Compiled		23	13
		6	10	2			Tax Returns		28	18
		3	19	19	9	11	Other		87	56
		23 (4/1-9/30/23)		111 (10/1/23-3/31/24)					4/1/19-3/31/20	4/1/20-3/31/21
0-500M	500M-2MM	2-10MM	10-50MM	50-100MM	100-250MM		NUMBER OF STATEMENTS		ALL 167	ALL 106
	10	48	46	16	14					
%	%	%	%	%	%		ASSETS		%	%
D	12.8	16.8	10.6	5.1	10.1		Cash & Equivalents		9.2	12.1
A	25.3	26.5	27.3	24.7	22.9		Trade Receivables (net)		26.9	23.9
T	39.5	41.4	37.7	33.8	30.9		Inventory		42.1	41.5
A	4.7	1.6	3.6	3.0	2.8		All Other Current		2.0	2.1
	82.3	86.3	79.2	66.7	66.8		Total Current		80.3	79.6
N	4.9	5.4	9.5	8.7	13.2		Fixed Assets (net)		10.3	9.2
O	3.9	1.9	5.2	11.6	7.7		Intangibles (net)		4.5	7.0
T	8.9	6.4	6.2	13.0	12.3		All Other Non-Current		4.9	4.1
	100.0	100.0	100.0	100.0	100.0		Total		100.0	100.0
A							LIABILITIES			
V	6.0	11.1	8.9	9.5	7.0		Notes Payable-Short Term		12.8	10.7
A	4.3	1.4	3.1	1.1	2.3		Cur. Mat.-L.T.D.		1.6	1.9
I	22.8	15.2	11.9	12.3	11.6		Trade Payables		17.1	14.7
L	.0	.0	.2	.0	.3		Income Taxes Payable		.1	.2
A	2.2	8.0	8.3	9.3	10.6		All Other Current		7.1	7.9
B	35.4	35.7	32.5	32.1	31.7		Total Current		38.8	35.3
L	12.5	9.4	10.4	15.0	10.2		Long-Term Debt		10.0	11.8
E	.0	.0	.1	.2	.0		Deferred Taxes		.2	.0
	4.6	5.0	7.5	10.8	11.1		All Other Non-Current		4.7	6.3
	47.5	49.9	49.6	41.8	46.9		Net Worth		46.4	46.5
	100.0	100.0	100.0	100.0	100.0		Total Liabilities & Net Worth		100.0	100.0
							INCOME DATA			
	100.0	100.0	100.0	100.0	100.0		Net Sales		100.0	100.0
	31.6	35.6	37.8	31.7	29.1		Gross Profit		33.1	33.8
	28.7	27.3	27.6	25.9	21.9		Operating Expenses		27.0	27.7
	2.9	8.3	10.2	5.8	7.2		Operating Profit		6.0	6.1
	-.1	.4	.8	1.4	1.3		All Other Expenses (net)		.7	-.4
	3.0	8.0	9.4	4.4	5.9		Profit Before Taxes		5.4	6.4
							RATIOS			
	9.0	6.3	4.7	3.5	3.3				3.6	3.8
	2.5	2.8	2.6	2.1	2.3		Current		2.4	2.3
	1.7	1.6	1.7	1.1	1.4				1.5	1.7
	2.2	2.9	2.9	1.5	2.0				1.7	1.8
	1.2	1.4	1.3	1.0	1.0		Quick		1.0	1.0
	.6	.6	.6	.6	.8				.6	.6
3 108.1	19 19.5	38 9.5	42 8.6	32 11.3					29 12.7	25 14.4
23 15.6	37 9.9	49 7.4	59 6.2	42 8.7			Sales/Receivables		37 9.9	35 10.5
32 11.4	54 6.7	57 6.4	69 5.3	58 6.3					49 7.4	48 7.6
9 39.2	51 7.2	54 6.7	33 11.0	81 4.5					58 6.3	61 6.0
57 6.4	94 3.9	107 3.4	94 3.9	104 3.5			Cost of Sales/Inventory		101 3.6	99 3.7
166 2.2	126 2.9	192 1.9	203 1.8	122 3.0					146 2.5	152 2.4
4 83.4	6 56.8	21 17.4	28 13.0	29 12.8					15 23.7	11 32.6
25 14.5	21 17.8	29 12.5	32 11.5	33 11.2			Cost of Sales/Payables		32 11.3	31 11.8
36 10.1	40 9.1	49 7.4	56 6.5	44 8.3					49 7.4	47 7.7
	3.8	3.1	3.2	3.4	3.0				3.8	3.4
	7.8	5.0	4.0	6.1	4.6		Sales/Working Capital		5.6	5.3
	14.9	9.3	6.8	25.3	7.8				9.8	9.3
		76.2	112.5	38.1	105.9				19.0	36.8
	(38)	12.2	(42) 17.7	(15) 5.5	(13) 10.0		EBIT/Interest		(147) 7.6	(99) 13.7
		2.9	3.8	.1	3.5				2.5	4.8
			48.4				Net Profit + Depr., Dep.,		14.5	30.1
		(11)	12.4				Amort./Cur. Mat. L/T/D	(30)	3.6	(15) 7.6
			7.3						1.7	4.3
	.0	.0	.1	.1	.1				.1	.0
	.1	.1	.1	.4	.2		Fixed/Worth		.2	.1
	.3	.2	.4	1.8	1.1				.5	.5
	.4	.3	.3	.5	.7				.5	.5
	1.2	.8	1.1	2.5	1.2		Debt/Worth		1.2	1.1
	4.0	2.7	1.8	15.4	3.8				3.2	2.5
		56.3	44.2	26.7	33.1		% Profit Before Taxes/Tangible		44.3	47.6
	(45)	32.4	(40) 30.7	(13) 15.3	(13) 22.7		Net Worth	(148)	26.0	(94) 29.9
		9.3	17.3	-39.3	16.6				11.5	13.3
	24.5	35.2	23.9	13.7	12.8		% Profit Before Taxes/Total		19.0	21.4
	15.8	19.1	17.7	8.3	11.1		Assets		9.7	12.5
	-1.4	2.3	6.6	-5.2	4.0				3.5	4.9
	999.8	203.0	80.4	57.0	30.8				107.3	140.7
	98.3	59.3	40.1	18.8	16.4		Sales/Net Fixed Assets		43.6	42.9
	40.3	21.9	17.0	11.2	8.7				17.1	20.4
	5.2	3.6	2.3	2.0	1.8				2.9	3.0
	3.8	2.7	1.9	1.4	1.7		Sales/Total Assets		2.3	2.3
	1.9	1.7	1.6	1.2	1.3				1.8	1.7
		.2	.2	.4	.7				.4	.4
	(33)	.6	(41) .5	(12) 1.5	(11) .9		% Depr., Dep., Amort./Sales	(127)	.7	(77) .8
		1.0	1.1	3.5	3.3				1.1	1.2
		2.3	.8				% Officers', Directors'		1.6	1.3
	(20)	3.9	(16) 1.7				Owners' Comp/Sales	(60)	3.1	(39) 3.2
		5.8	3.0						5.6	5.3
	40480M	666468M	1964190M	1964524M	3059857M		Net Sales ($)		6679638M	3501475M
	10886M	246704M	1007660M	1275014M	2032694M		Total Assets ($)		3137005M	1818045M

M = $ thousand   MM = $ million
See Pages viii through xx for Explanation of Ratios and Data

© RMA 2024

WHOLESALE—Hardware Merchant Wholesalers NAICS 423710

Comparative Historical Data | Current Data Sorted by Sales

				Type of Statement						
10	10	10		Unqualified						10
13	21	27		Reviewed			1	4	4	18
17	19	18		Compiled			5	7	7	6
18	16	18		Tax Returns		3	3	5	7	
51	52	61		Other	1	1	3	7	9	40
4/1/21-3/31/22 ALL	4/1/22-3/31/23 ALL	4/1/23-3/31/24 ALL				23 (4/1-9/30/23)			111 (10/1/23-3/31/24)	
					0-1MM	1-3MM	3-5MM	5-10MM	10-25MM	25MM & OVER
109	118	134		NUMBER OF STATEMENTS	1	4	7	21	27	74
%	%	%		ASSETS	%	%	%	%	%	%
10.8	9.3	12.3		Cash & Equivalents				19.1	10.5	9.2
28.8	25.8	26.1		Trade Receivables (net)				26.3	25.7	28.9
42.0	45.9	38.0		Inventory				32.6	47.9	34.4
2.1	2.6	2.8		All Other Current				1.3	2.3	3.3
83.6	83.7	79.2		Total Current				79.3	86.4	75.9
6.8	7.5	8.0		Fixed Assets (net)				8.4	7.0	8.9
5.2	4.3	5.0		Intangibles (net)				2.8	2.2	6.9
4.3	4.5	7.9		All Other Non-Current				9.4	4.5	8.3
100.0	100.0	100.0		Total				100.0	100.0	100.0
				LIABILITIES						
10.2	10.3	9.4		Notes Payable-Short Term				9.5	11.0	8.8
1.1	1.7	2.3		Cur. Mat.-L.T.D.				.7	2.2	2.2
16.8	16.6	13.9		Trade Payables				16.5	12.3	12.7
.2	.1	.1		Income Taxes Payable				.0	.0	.2
9.0	9.0	8.1		All Other Current				5.2	8.8	9.2
37.3	37.8	33.7		Total Current				31.9	34.4	33.2
10.0	9.7	10.7		Long-Term Debt				13.2	6.6	10.6
.1	.0	.1		Deferred Taxes				.0	.0	.1
3.8	3.6	7.1		All Other Non-Current				11.7	1.5	8.9
48.8	48.9	48.3		Net Worth				43.2	57.6	47.3
100.0	100.0	100.0		Total Liabilities & Net Worth				100.0	100.0	100.0
				INCOME DATA						
100.0	100.0	100.0		Net Sales				100.0	100.0	100.0
32.9	30.5	34.9		Gross Profit				39.9	35.5	33.9
27.1	23.4	26.8		Operating Expenses				28.5	27.4	25.7
5.8	7.1	8.1		Operating Profit				11.5	8.1	8.2
-1.4	-.2	.7		All Other Expenses (net)				.5	.1	1.0
7.2	7.3	7.4		Profit Before Taxes				10.9	8.0	7.2
				RATIOS						
4.0	3.5	4.6						6.9	4.7	4.1
2.5	2.3	2.6		Current				2.7	3.0	2.3
1.7	1.5	1.6						1.9	1.6	1.7
1.9	1.6	2.2						3.4	2.0	2.0
1.2	.9	1.2		Quick				1.6	1.2	1.1
.7	.5	.6						.9	.6	.7
29 12.7	23 16.0	26 13.9					24 15.2	22 16.4	38 9.7	
40 9.1	39 9.3	42 8.6		Sales/Receivables			38 9.5	33 11.2	48 7.6	
54 6.8	52 7.0	57 6.4					48 7.6	52 7.0	64 5.7	
54 6.7	68 5.4	50 7.3					40 9.1	68 5.4	48 7.6	
91 4.0	114 3.2	96 3.8		Cost of Sales/Inventory			114 3.2	96 3.8	91 4.0	
152 2.4	166 2.2	159 2.3					182 2.0	192 1.9	135 2.7	
16 22.9	16 22.3	17 21.7					16 22.5	11 32.5	21 17.1	
32 11.3	31 11.8	29 12.8		Cost of Sales/Payables			23 15.7	28 13.1	30 12.1	
54 6.7	52 7.0	41 8.8					47 7.8	33 10.9	44 8.3	
3.3	3.1	3.2						2.8	3.1	3.4
5.0	6.0	4.8		Sales/Working Capital				3.8	5.0	5.0
8.5	9.1	8.9						8.9	11.1	8.4
53.8	56.7	70.2						103.3	60.1	78.2
(97) 19.5	(102) 14.7	(117) 11.2		EBIT/Interest		(15) 8.2	(24) 20.9	(68) 12.1		
7.8	4.3	2.9						2.6	2.5	3.6
85.0	33.5	50.5		Net Profit + Depr., Dep.,						79.6
(13) 18.5	(16) 5.9	(27) 11.2		Amort./Cur. Mat. L/T/D					(18) 18.5	
3.6	.4	1.3								1.4
.0	.0	.0						.0	.0	.1
.1	.1	.1		Fixed/Worth				.1	.1	.2
.3	.3	.3						.2	.2	.5
.4	.4	.4						.4	.3	.5
1.0	1.2	1.1		Debt/Worth				.7	1.0	1.1
2.3	3.2	3.1						3.7	1.4	3.6
52.2	47.5	44.6		% Profit Before Taxes/Tangible				57.4	40.0	42.6
(99) 31.3	(110) 27.4	(120) 28.2		Net Worth		(17) 44.2	(64) 27.5			
16.9	9.3	13.5						12.4	4.2	16.4
21.4	25.5	24.7		% Profit Before Taxes/Total				34.2	32.1	21.9
13.7	13.2	13.6		Assets				17.7	17.7	12.7
8.8	4.4	4.9						6.7	1.5	6.0
117.9	239.4	112.2						116.2	792.0	74.8
47.6	61.0	41.0		Sales/Net Fixed Assets				29.7	76.6	35.1
26.9	23.7	17.3						20.0	20.9	15.1
3.2	3.1	2.8						2.9	3.8	2.6
2.3	2.1	1.9		Sales/Total Assets				2.1	2.7	1.9
1.8	1.6	1.6						1.6	1.7	1.6
.3	.3	.3						.4	.2	.3
(85) .6	(73) .5	(101) .7		% Depr., Dep., Amort./Sales		(14) .8	(19) .6	(63) .7		
1.0	1.1	1.3						1.4	1.3	1.1
1.0	1.7	1.4		% Officers', Directors'				3.1	1.6	.9
(39) 3.9	(39) 3.1	(42) 3.1		Owners' Comp/Sales		(10) 4.4	(13) 3.0	(14) 1.7		
5.7	4.1	5.3						5.2	6.2	2.5
4147883M	5101551M	7695519M		Net Sales ($)	671M	7295M	28336M	159591M	463462M	7036164M
1908782M	2580537M	4572958M		Total Assets ($)	2993M	10419M	16092M	87458M	207152M	4248844M

© RMA 2024 M = $ thousand MM = $ million
See Pages viii through xx for Explanation of Ratios and Data

WHOLESALE—Plumbing and Heating Equipment and Supplies (Hydronics) Merchant Wholesalers NAICS 423720

Current Data Sorted by Assets | Comparative Historical Data

							Type of Statement		
				7	5	4	Unqualified	18	10
		8	20	4	1	Reviewed	41	24
		10	8	1		Compiled	18	9
1	6	10	3			Tax Returns	26	10
2	11	38	41	22	7	Other	103	59
	40 (4/1-9/30/23)		169 (10/1/23-3/31/24)				4/1/19-3/31/20	4/1/20-3/31/21
0-500M	500M-2MM	2-10MM	10-50MM	50-100MM	100-250MM		ALL	ALL
3	17	66	79	32	12	NUMBER OF STATEMENTS	206	112
%	%	%	%	%	%	ASSETS	%	%
	24.3	18.3	11.9	9.3	3.9	Cash & Equivalents	7.5	14.1
	24.7	28.2	26.7	22.0	21.6	Trade Receivables (net)	29.6	27.5
	26.9	33.8	39.2	34.5	34.1	Inventory	40.1	39.6
	1.1	1.7	2.7	2.8	5.5	All Other Current	2.1	2.3
	76.9	81.9	80.5	68.6	65.0	Total Current	79.3	83.5
	11.4	9.5	12.2	11.1	18.3	Fixed Assets (net)	12.0	9.1
	5.8	4.6	2.3	8.6	6.4	Intangibles (net)	3.7	3.4
	5.9	3.9	5.0	11.8	10.3	All Other Non-Current	5.0	3.9
	100.0	100.0	100.0	100.0	100.0	Total	100.0	100.0
						LIABILITIES		
	13.6	6.7	7.8	9.8	3.6	Notes Payable-Short Term	14.1	12.5
	1.5	3.4	1.4	2.7	2.3	Cur. Mat.-L.T.D.	1.2	2.3
	22.2	16.6	15.8	10.2	14.5	Trade Payables	18.7	18.2
	.1	.2	.2	.5	.6	Income Taxes Payable	.1	.2
	17.1	10.5	10.0	11.1	8.1	All Other Current	10.1	8.6
	54.5	37.3	35.2	34.3	29.1	Total Current	44.2	41.9
	18.5	8.1	8.7	7.8	14.4	Long-Term Debt	9.2	10.6
	.0	.5	.1	.3	.2	Deferred Taxes	.2	.1
	1.2	2.0	4.8	10.6	14.0	All Other Non-Current	4.7	4.2
	25.8	52.0	51.3	47.0	42.3	Net Worth	41.7	43.2
	100.0	100.0	100.0	100.0	100.0	Total Liabilities & Net Worth	100.0	100.0
						INCOME DATA		
	100.0	100.0	100.0	100.0	100.0	Net Sales	100.0	100.0
	31.8	31.4	30.2	27.3	27.2	Gross Profit	30.5	29.7
	29.8	25.1	23.5	20.8	23.2	Operating Expenses	26.3	24.9
	2.0	6.3	6.6	6.5	4.0	Operating Profit	4.1	4.8
	.1	-.8	-.2	-.5	-1.6	All Other Expenses (net)	.2	-.8
	1.8	7.1	6.9	7.0	5.6	Profit Before Taxes	4.0	5.6
						RATIOS		
	8.5	5.0	3.6	2.6	3.0		3.0	3.1
	2.7	2.5	2.4	2.2	2.0	Current	2.0	2.1
	1.2	1.4	1.8	1.6	1.7		1.4	1.5
	3.3	3.1	1.9	1.3	1.3		1.4	1.8
	1.3	1.3	1.1	.8	.7	Quick	.8	1.0
	.6	.6	.6	.6	.6		.5	.6
	4 95.0	27 13.4	33 11.2	31 11.7	28 13.1		29 12.6	28 13.1
	25 14.7	35 10.4	42 8.7	41 8.8	32 11.4	Sales/Receivables	39 9.4	38 9.5
	52 7.0	48 7.6	48 7.6	46 7.9	40 9.1		50 7.3	49 7.5
	0 UND	38 9.5	66 5.5	60 6.1	59 6.2		52 7.0	49 7.5
	19 19.7	81 4.5	91 4.0	91 4.0	72 5.1	Cost of Sales/Inventory	83 4.4	79 4.6
	104 3.5	130 2.8	135 2.7	140 2.6	101 3.6		114 3.2	114 3.2
	7 51.4	16 23.2	23 16.2	18 20.8	25 14.7		21 17.5	22 16.5
	15 24.1	27 13.5	31 11.7	24 15.0	33 11.0	Cost of Sales/Payables	34 10.8	34 10.8
	30 12.3	42 8.6	41 8.9	33 11.1	38 9.6		46 7.9	54 6.8
	2.2	3.4	3.4	4.1	5.0		4.6	4.1
	6.1	6.0	4.9	5.8	6.8	Sales/Working Capital	6.8	6.2
	83.8	10.0	8.2	10.6	10.9		13.8	10.8
	25.0	84.0	57.1	19.4	15.3		16.6	54.7
(11)	1.0	(56) 16.2	(66) 17.9	(29) 8.7	10.7	EBIT/Interest	(185) 7.0	(96) 12.7
	-2.8	3.8	3.7	5.0	7.1		2.4	3.3
		71.8	74.2	12.0			14.4	24.4
		(12) 3.4	(21) 9.1	(16) 5.9		Net Profit + Depr., Dep., Amort./Cur. Mat. L/T/D	(49) 4.9	(28) 9.6
		.3	3.6	1.9			3.1	2.7
	.0	.0	.1	.1	.2		.1	.0
	.1	.1	.2	.3	.5	Fixed/Worth	.2	.2
	1.7	.4	.4	.7	.6		.5	.5
	.2	.3	.4	.6	1.0		.6	.7
	1.4	.8	.9	1.3	2.3	Debt/Worth	1.4	1.2
	7.8	1.9	2.2	2.9	2.9		3.1	3.1
	21.3	51.8	46.1	41.5	48.1	% Profit Before Taxes/Tangible Net Worth	37.5	54.5
(15)	2.1	(59) 27.4	(77) 24.2	(29) 31.2	22.1		(182) 20.0	(101) 27.3
	-15.2	12.8	12.7	19.1	18.3		10.0	14.3
	13.9	27.5	21.9	16.8	16.6	% Profit Before Taxes/Total Assets	15.3	23.4
	.9	11.8	15.0	10.7	8.2		8.7	11.7
	-6.7	4.3	5.2	6.4	4.6		2.5	4.7
	585.0	182.8	92.1	39.6	23.9	Sales/Net Fixed Assets	91.0	104.4
	74.4	41.7	39.0	17.2	19.0		35.8	50.9
	30.3	12.6	14.3	12.6	7.9		15.3	20.6
	6.1	3.3	2.8	2.4	2.4	Sales/Total Assets	3.3	3.1
	3.1	2.4	2.3	2.0	2.1		2.6	2.4
	1.7	1.7	1.7	1.4	2.1		2.1	2.0
		.3	.3	.5	.6	% Depr., Dep., Amort./Sales	.4	.3
		(48) .5	(63) .5	(29) .7	(11) .8		(166) .7	(87) .6
		.9	.9	1.0	1.3		1.0	1.0
		1.5	.5			% Officers', Directors' Owners' Comp/Sales	1.4	1.4
		(23) 2.3	(25) 1.1				(75) 2.6	(45) 2.4
		7.9	3.6				5.8	5.0
8024M	160496M	962050M	4189392M	4473936M	3875464M	Net Sales ($)	13241690M	6149363M
1083M	24917M	377243M	1830588M	2376239M	1722700M	Total Assets ($)	5567282M	2828399M

M = $ thousand   MM = $ million
See Pages viii through xx for Explanation of Ratios and Data

© RMA 2024

WHOLESALE—Plumbing and Heating Equipment and Supplies (Hydronics) Merchant Wholesalers NAICS 423720

Comparative Historical Data | **Current Data Sorted by Sales**

						Type of Statement							
		6		12	16	Unqualified					1	1	15
		18		26	33	Reviewed				1	9	9	23
		13		21	19	Compiled			1	2	2	8	7
		14		15	20	Tax Returns			8	3	6	7	3
		65		83	121	Other		1	8	7	8	33	65
		4/1/21-3/31/22 ALL		4/1/22-3/31/23 ALL	4/1/23-3/31/24 ALL		0-1MM	1-3MM	40 (4/1-9/30/23) 3-5MM	5-10MM	169 (10/1/23-3/31/24) 10-25MM		25MM & OVER
		116		157	209	**NUMBER OF STATEMENTS**	9	13	16	58	113		
		%		%	%	**ASSETS**	%	%	%	%	%	%	
		13.4		10.5	14.5	Cash & Equivalents			29.6	15.3	18.1	9.6	
		26.3		25.4	25.8	Trade Receivables (net)	DATA		20.4	29.2	24.1	27.2	
		39.2		39.8	35.1	Inventory	NOT		24.6	25.1	35.2	37.9	
		1.8		2.8	2.5	All Other Current	AVAILABLE		.5	1.5	2.1	3.0	
		80.8		78.5	77.9	Total Current			75.0	71.2	79.6	77.6	
		10.2		8.2	11.6	Fixed Assets (net)			14.3	19.2	12.6	10.1	
		4.6		7.3	4.5	Intangibles (net)			10.1	4.9	2.5	4.6	
		4.4		6.0	6.0	All Other Non-Current			.5	4.7	5.4	7.6	
		100.0		100.0	100.0	Total			100.0	100.0	100.0	100.0	
						LIABILITIES							
		9.7		8.1	8.1	Notes Payable-Short Term			.5	3.1	5.8	10.7	
		1.9		1.9	2.3	Cur. Mat.-L.T.D.			.7	4.8	3.0	1.8	
		15.9		15.0	15.4	Trade Payables			10.8	15.6	15.8	16.6	
		.1		.2	.3	Income Taxes Payable			.1	.2	.1	.4	
		8.7		10.6	12.3	All Other Current			8.2	22.3	10.0	10.1	
		36.3		35.8	38.4	Total Current			20.4	46.0	34.7	39.7	
		7.9		10.6	9.4	Long-Term Debt			7.6	25.1	9.9	7.9	
		.3		.2	.2	Deferred Taxes			.0	.2	.5	.2	
		3.4		3.8	5.1	All Other Non-Current			.8	3.2	1.8	7.6	
		52.1		49.7	46.8	Net Worth			71.3	25.4	53.1	44.6	
		100.0		100.0	100.0	Total Liabilities & Net Worth			100.0	100.0	100.0	100.0	
						INCOME DATA							
		100.0		100.0	100.0	Net Sales			100.0	100.0	100.0	100.0	
		32.0		33.3	30.4	Gross Profit			33.0	31.6	33.5	28.1	
		25.8		25.5	24.5	Operating Expenses			32.3	25.5	26.4	21.9	
		6.2		7.7	5.9	Operating Profit			.8	6.2	7.1	6.2	
		-1.2		-.1	-.5	All Other Expenses (net)			-2.3	.6	-.5	-.3	
		7.4		7.9	6.4	Profit Before Taxes			3.0	5.6	7.7	6.4	
						RATIOS							
		4.1		3.5	3.7	Current			8.6	3.5	4.3	3.0	
		2.3		2.2	2.4				4.5	1.5	2.6	2.3	
		1.6		1.6	1.5				2.7	1.1	1.4	1.6	
		2.3		1.7	2.1	Quick			5.6	2.9	2.7	1.7	
		1.0		1.0	1.0				3.1	.9	1.3	.9	
		.6		.6	.6				1.4	.5	.6	.6	
29	12.5	26	13.9	28	13.0	Sales/Receivables	27	13.5	33	11.2	25	14.4	32	11.5
38	9.5	35	10.3	39	9.4		43	8.5	46	7.9	33	10.9	41	9.0
49	7.5	47	7.7	47	7.7		55	6.6	70	5.2	44	8.3	47	7.7
54	6.7	54	6.7	46	7.9	Cost of Sales/Inventory	0	UND	6	63.2	42	8.6	58	6.3
87	4.2	79	4.6	83	4.4		99	3.7	34	10.7	94	3.9	81	4.5
122	3.0	126	2.9	126	2.9		126	2.9	146	2.5	140	2.6	114	3.2
22	16.9	19	19.2	17	21.0	Cost of Sales/Payables	14	26.5	5	79.2	16	23.2	22	16.5
30	12.3	29	12.7	28	13.2		19	19.7	28	13.2	27	13.4	29	12.4
41	8.8	39	9.3	38	9.6		31	11.8	40	9.2	44	8.3	38	9.6
	3.8		4.2		3.7	Sales/Working Capital		2.2		4.6		3.4		4.1
	5.2		5.6		5.6			3.2		9.0		5.7		5.7
	8.0		10.2		10.0			6.1		95.6		9.7		9.9
	95.8		63.7		52.4	EBIT/Interest				20.0		56.8		55.0
(98)	21.2	(126)	20.0	(176)	11.8			(14)	6.4	(49)	17.8	(100)	11.7
	7.8		6.9		3.5					1.6		5.9		3.7
	33.7		32.4		41.3	Net Profit + Depr., Dep., Amort./Cur. Mat. L/T/D				20.8		41.5	
(20)	7.8	(39)	9.4	(55)	6.1					(12)	2.2	(38)	8.1
	3.8		4.0		2.0							.6		3.4
	.1		.1		.1	Fixed/Worth			.1		.3		.0		.1
	.2		.1		.2				.2		.6		.1		.2
	.4		.3		.5				.2		NM		.4		.5
	.4		.5		.4	Debt/Worth			.1		.8		.4		.6
	1.0		1.0		1.0				.2		1.8		.8		1.1
	1.9		2.2		2.4				1.2		NM		1.7		2.7
	53.6		56.7		45.9	% Profit Before Taxes/Tangible Net Worth			17.9		42.7		51.8		47.3
(109)	31.7	(143)	35.4	(193)	24.1			(12)	3.1	(12)	20.6	(55)	22.1	(107)	29.1
	18.2		20.5		12.1				-15.6		2.2		15.0		17.8
	27.0		28.2		20.8	% Profit Before Taxes/Total Assets			13.4		13.4		27.0		20.8
	15.7		17.2		11.2				1.5		9.0		12.6		12.3
	8.9		7.0		4.7				-6.7		.7		5.3		5.2
	79.4		106.7		101.4	Sales/Net Fixed Assets			71.4		91.3		213.1		70.6
	32.9		45.7		33.3				13.6		12.7		40.9		31.9
	17.9		24.2		13.2				11.8		5.8		12.3		14.1
	3.0		3.2		2.9	Sales/Total Assets			2.8		3.4		3.3		2.8
	2.5		2.5		2.3				1.8		2.3		2.4		2.3
	1.9		1.9		1.7				1.4		1.4		1.5		1.9
	.4		.2		.3	% Depr., Dep., Amort./Sales			.2		.2		.3		.3
(90)	.6	(121)	.5	(160)	.6		(10)	.5	(12)	.6	(40)	.5	(93)	.7
	1.0		.9		.9				.8		1.0		.9		1.0
	.9		1.1		1.1	% Officers', Directors' Owners' Comp/Sales							1.3		.6
(42)	2.9	(50)	1.9	(58)	2.3							(19)	2.0	(24)	1.4
	6.1		3.4		5.8								5.0		3.7
7360399M		10204201M		13669362M		Net Sales ($)	20251M	52019M	115761M	955740M	12525591M		
3425456M		4418195M		6332770M		Total Assets ($)	13926M	34899M	57645M	497245M	5729055M		

M = $ thousand   MM = $ million
See Pages viii through xx for Explanation of Ratios and Data

© RMA 2024

WHOLESALE—Warm Air Heating and Air-Conditioning Equipment and Supplies Merchant Wholesalers NAICS 423730

Current Data Sorted by Assets | Comparative Historical Data

							Type of Statement		
							Unqualified	16	11
				9	6	8	Reviewed	30	21
		7	15	3		Compiled	19	14
	1	7	5		1	Tax Returns	24	10
	1	5	3			Other	76	48
1	5	17	30	12	9		4/1/19-	4/1/20-
	26 (4/1-9/30/23)		119 (10/1/23-3/31/24)				3/31/20	3/31/21
0-500M	500M-2MM	2-10MM	10-50MM	50-100MM	100-250MM	NUMBER OF STATEMENTS	ALL	ALL
1	7	36	62	21	18		165	104
%	%	%	%	%	%	ASSETS	%	%
		13.5	12.6	4.2	6.7	Cash & Equivalents	7.8	11.7
		37.7	23.7	23.4	31.3	Trade Receivables (net)	39.0	34.6
		33.2	40.2	44.9	28.0	Inventory	36.3	36.3
		1.9	1.6	4.5	4.7	All Other Current	2.3	1.8
		86.3	78.0	77.0	70.7	Total Current	85.5	84.5
		6.0	9.7	11.4	9.8	Fixed Assets (net)	7.8	7.2
		2.8	4.7	2.9	11.6	Intangibles (net)	2.3	3.7
		4.8	7.6	8.6	7.9	All Other Non-Current	4.4	4.6
		100.0	100.0	100.0	100.0	Total	100.0	100.0
						LIABILITIES		
		5.7	7.7	11.3	8.2	Notes Payable-Short Term	13.4	11.6
		1.1	.7	1.2	2.7	Cur. Mat.-L.T.D.	1.6	2.0
		23.1	18.9	13.2	13.5	Trade Payables	22.7	25.0
		.2	.1	.1	.0	Income Taxes Payable	.1	.2
		14.3	10.0	14.6	20.8	All Other Current	10.7	12.1
		44.4	37.4	40.5	45.3	Total Current	48.7	51.0
		4.0	6.8	15.7	6.0	Long-Term Debt	7.1	9.9
		.2	.1	.1	.2	Deferred Taxes	.1	.1
		6.9	5.8	7.1	7.0	All Other Non-Current	3.5	3.1
		44.4	49.9	36.6	41.5	Net Worth	40.7	36.0
		100.0	100.0	100.0	100.0	Total Liabilities & Net Worth	100.0	100.0
						INCOME DATA		
		100.0	100.0	100.0	100.0	Net Sales	100.0	100.0
		29.5	27.9	27.4	27.6	Gross Profit	27.6	27.8
		22.9	20.9	21.6	22.4	Operating Expenses	23.5	23.4
		6.6	7.0	5.8	5.2	Operating Profit	4.2	4.4
		-.2	.5	.0	.9	All Other Expenses (net)	.0	-.6
		6.8	6.5	5.8	4.3	Profit Before Taxes	4.2	5.0
						RATIOS		
		3.0	3.9	3.4	2.2		2.8	2.8
		1.9	2.1	2.4	1.7	Current	1.8	1.7
		1.5	1.5	1.1	1.3		1.3	1.2
		1.9	1.8	1.0	1.2		1.4	1.4
		1.2	.9	.8	.9	Quick	.9	.9
		.6	.5	.4	.6		.6	.5
		27 13.5	26 13.8	28 13.2	34 10.8		31 11.7	27 13.3
		37 9.8	34 10.6	35 10.5	46 8.0	Sales/Receivables	43 8.4	38 9.7
		52 7.0	44 8.3	42 8.6	74 4.9		60 6.1	53 6.9
		10 35.0	69 5.3	73 5.0	18 20.7		19 19.4	24 15.3
		49 7.4	96 3.8	96 3.8	81 4.5	Cost of Sales/Inventory	72 5.1	76 4.8
		140 2.6	140 2.6	126 2.9	111 3.3		101 3.6	104 3.5
		21 17.0	16 22.6	16 22.8	20 18.4		20 18.0	22 16.6
		36 10.1	37 9.9	25 14.7	26 13.9	Cost of Sales/Payables	31 11.6	34 10.6
		44 8.3	55 6.6	39 9.3	49 7.5		51 7.2	60 6.1
		4.4	3.8	4.2	5.6		5.1	4.9
		7.7	5.3	5.6	7.4	Sales/Working Capital	8.5	8.0
		12.5	9.6	31.1	12.9		15.2	21.3
		70.5	113.7	17.2	43.8		32.2	35.3
		(30) 27.8	(53) 15.1	(19) 4.1	(17) 8.7	EBIT/Interest	(147) 10.0	(93) 14.2
		5.0	2.7	1.5	3.2		3.5	4.2
					63.5		11.9	20.0
				(10) 27.0	Net Profit + Depr., Dep., Amort./Cur. Mat. L/T/D	(34) 5.3	(25) 6.1
					3.9		2.4	1.4
		.0	.0	.1	.1		.1	.1
		.1	.2	.3	.3	Fixed/Worth	.2	.2
		.2	.4	.8	.7		.4	.5
		.6	.5	.7	1.0		.7	1.1
		1.6	1.3	3.0	1.9	Debt/Worth	1.4	2.2
		2.8	2.1	5.9	5.3		3.6	4.7
		81.3	40.2	51.9	46.4		51.9	63.7
		(34) 37.5	(60) 25.3	28.8	(16) 24.1	% Profit Before Taxes/Tangible Net Worth	(155) 24.3	(94) 28.7
		16.8	11.5	11.8	10.5		13.1	12.2
		34.7	23.6	23.9	12.9		19.2	20.3
		15.0	14.1	10.6	8.3	% Profit Before Taxes/Total Assets	10.3	11.5
		7.2	3.9	2.2	3.6		4.5	4.0
		205.4	111.8	133.9	84.3		117.4	130.1
		104.5	42.7	29.8	19.4	Sales/Net Fixed Assets	53.8	52.2
		45.2	10.8	11.3	12.7		29.3	30.0
		4.1	2.7	2.8	2.7		3.6	3.4
		3.1	2.2	2.2	2.1	Sales/Total Assets	2.9	2.9
		2.3	1.7	2.0	1.8		2.4	2.4
		.2	.2	.2	.2		.3	.2
		(24) .3	(49) .4	(20) .4	(17) .7	% Depr., Dep., Amort./Sales	(133) .5	(86) .4
		1.0	.9	.8	1.1		.8	.9
		.9	.2				.8	1.2
		(14) 2.1	(15) .7			% Officers', Directors' Owners' Comp/Sales	(51) 1.6	(27) 1.7
		5.5	2.5				2.8	3.7
16397M	34829M	653198M	3559021M	3429016M	5986043M	Net Sales ($)	10878360M	7088003M
200M	9326M	198249M	1618979M	1467175M	2811605M	Total Assets ($)	3825927M	2768902M

M = $ thousand   MM = $ million
See Pages viii through xx for Explanation of Ratios and Data

© RMA 2024

WHOLESALE—Warm Air Heating and Air-Conditioning Equipment and Supplies Merchant Wholesalers NAICS 423730

Comparative Historical Data | Current Data Sorted by Sales

Comparative Historical Data			Type of Statement	Current Data Sorted by Sales					
13	18	23	Unqualified				1	22	
12	19	25	Reviewed			4	4	17	
9	15	14	Compiled			1	3	10	
10	13	9	Tax Returns		1	1	4	3	
49	67	74	Other	2	3	2	16	51	
4/1/21-3/31/22 ALL	4/1/22-3/31/23 ALL	4/1/23-3/31/24 ALL		0-1MM	26 (4/1-9/30/23) 1-3MM	3-5MM	119 (10/1/23-3/31/24) 5-10MM 10-25MM		25MM & OVER
93	132	145	NUMBER OF STATEMENTS	3	3	8	28	103	
%	%	%	ASSETS	%	%	%	%	%	%
9.2	8.4	11.7	Cash & Equivalents					15.4	10.0
36.4	35.7	28.7	Trade Receivables (net)					30.7	28.2
36.8	31.9	36.2	Inventory	DATA				35.1	37.5
2.3	3.8	2.6	All Other Current	NOT				2.6	2.7
84.7	79.9	79.1	Total Current	AVAILABLE				83.8	78.2
7.5	7.4	9.1	Fixed Assets (net)					6.0	9.7
4.2	6.5	4.7	Intangibles (net)					5.9	4.4
3.6	6.1	7.0	All Other Non-Current					4.2	7.7
100.0	100.0	100.0	Total					100.0	100.0
			LIABILITIES						
11.6	9.5	9.0	Notes Payable-Short Term					8.4	8.4
1.5	1.7	1.2	Cur. Mat.-L.T.D.					1.5	1.1
22.8	20.7	18.3	Trade Payables					20.7	18.2
.2	.2	.1	Income Taxes Payable					.3	.1
12.4	14.3	13.4	All Other Current					10.5	14.0
48.6	46.5	42.0	Total Current					41.4	41.7
6.8	13.1	7.4	Long-Term Debt					4.4	8.0
.2	.2	.1	Deferred Taxes					.1	.1
5.4	5.3	6.1	All Other Non-Current					8.6	5.7
39.0	35.0	44.3	Net Worth					45.4	44.5
100.0	100.0	100.0	Total Liabilities & Net Worth					100.0	100.0
			INCOME DATA						
100.0	100.0	100.0	Net Sales					100.0	100.0
28.1	29.9	28.2	Gross Profit					29.8	27.2
21.5	22.8	21.8	Operating Expenses					21.7	21.3
6.5	7.1	6.5	Operating Profit					8.2	5.9
-.4	.2	.3	All Other Expenses (net)					.3	.3
6.9	6.9	6.2	Profit Before Taxes					7.9	5.7
			RATIOS						
2.9	2.7	3.3						4.2	3.2
1.7	1.8	2.0	Current					2.1	1.9
1.3	1.3	1.4						1.5	1.4
1.5	1.5	1.6						2.0	1.4
1.0	1.0	1.0	Quick					1.5	.9
.5	.5	.5						.6	.5
30 12.2	30 12.0	27 13.3					22 16.5	28 13.1	
41 8.8	40 9.2	36 10.2	Sales/Receivables				35 10.3	37 9.9	
51 7.1	62 5.9	47 7.7					54 6.8	44 8.3	
15 24.8	10 36.7	29 12.6					19 19.4	45 8.2	
69 5.3	65 5.6	89 4.1	Cost of Sales/Inventory				99 3.7	89 4.1	
111 3.3	126 2.9	130 2.8					166 2.2	126 2.9	
18 20.6	21 17.8	18 20.8					18 20.6	20 18.7	
34 10.8	34 10.8	32 11.5	Cost of Sales/Payables				35 10.4	33 11.0	
50 7.3	53 6.9	48 7.6					52 7.0	48 7.6	
5.3	4.5	4.2						3.4	4.3
8.1	6.8	6.2	Sales/Working Capital					5.4	6.6
16.4	16.3	11.0						10.1	11.2
72.5	79.6	70.8						106.3	68.9
(79) 22.7	(122) 26.8	(125) 12.7	EBIT/Interest				(21) 36.5	(93) 12.7	
8.5	10.3	3.1						4.6	3.2
48.2	12.9	28.8	Net Profit + Depr., Dep.,						32.1
(14) 8.1	(34) 7.3	(33) 8.7	Amort./Cur. Mat. L/T/D					(28) 10.8	
5.6	2.5	2.1							3.4
.1	.1	.1						.0	.1
.1	.2	.2	Fixed/Worth					.1	.2
.4	.4	.4						.3	.5
.7	.8	.6						.5	.7
1.7	2.0	1.4	Debt/Worth					1.7	1.4
4.0	4.2	3.1						3.0	3.2
87.3	82.3	53.1	% Profit Before Taxes/Tangible					66.5	50.1
(84) 44.0	(121) 42.3	(137) 26.4	Net Worth				(25) 30.7	(100) 26.4	
28.1	25.4	13.3						19.3	12.7
27.5	22.4	26.8	% Profit Before Taxes/Total					33.4	24.5
20.1	15.2	13.3	Assets					15.5	11.5
10.8	8.6	4.6						8.7	4.5
152.0	159.3	154.3						202.9	146.2
61.5	65.0	49.6	Sales/Net Fixed Assets					96.8	40.6
32.3	26.6	15.1						30.3	12.1
3.7	3.3	3.0						3.5	3.0
3.0	2.5	2.3	Sales/Total Assets					2.7	2.3
2.6	1.9	1.9						1.7	1.9
.2	.2	.2						.2	.2
(79) .4	(103) .4	(112) .4	% Depr., Dep., Amort./Sales				(18) .5	(88) .4	
.7	.8	.9						1.1	.9
.9	.6	.7	% Officers', Directors'						.3
(19) 1.4	(37) 1.0	(36) 1.7	Owners' Comp/Sales					(19) 1.2	
4.2	3.4	4.0							2.5
7741582M	11784996M	13678504M	Net Sales ($)	7153M	12315M	63662M	456934M	13138440M	
2766169M	5254439M	6105534M	Total Assets ($)	4066M	5144M	28661M	228856M	5838807M	

© RMA 2024   M = $ thousand   MM = $ million
See Pages viii through xx for Explanation of Ratios and Data

WHOLESALE—Refrigeration Equipment and Supplies Merchant Wholesalers NAICS 423740

Current Data Sorted by Assets | Comparative Historical Data

						Type of Statement		
				2		Unqualified	8	3
		4	9	2		Reviewed	14	6
		3	2	1		Compiled	7	2
	1	1	1			Tax Returns	8	2
1	1	9	5		2	Other	21	12
	6 (4/1-9/30/23)		41 (10/1/23-3/31/24)				4/1/19- 3/31/20	4/1/20- 3/31/21
0-500M	500M-2MM	2-10MM	10-50MM	50-100MM	100-250MM		ALL	ALL
1	2	17	17	8	2	NUMBER OF STATEMENTS	58	25
%	%	%	%	%	%	ASSETS	%	%
		6.2	13.1			Cash & Equivalents	10.5	19.9
		34.0	30.3			Trade Receivables (net)	25.1	17.4
		30.6	34.2			Inventory	38.1	37.3
		8.3	2.2			All Other Current	2.4	1.8
		79.1	79.9			Total Current	76.0	76.5
		15.1	12.6			Fixed Assets (net)	13.6	9.0
		1.0	2.4			Intangibles (net)	4.6	11.0
		4.8	5.1			All Other Non-Current	5.8	3.5
		100.0	100.0			Total	100.0	100.0
						LIABILITIES		
		6.2	3.3			Notes Payable-Short Term	13.9	8.3
		.2	.9			Cur. Mat.-L.T.D.	1.8	1.9
		21.6	16.6			Trade Payables	18.2	13.4
		.1	.1			Income Taxes Payable	.1	.0
		15.6	14.8			All Other Current	9.5	10.6
		43.7	35.8			Total Current	43.5	34.2
		3.0	5.2			Long-Term Debt	10.6	13.2
		.0	.0			Deferred Taxes	.2	.1
		5.1	.9			All Other Non-Current	4.9	7.8
		48.1	58.1			Net Worth	40.8	44.6
		100.0	100.0			Total Liabilties & Net Worth	100.0	100.0
						INCOME DATA		
		100.0	100.0			Net Sales	100.0	100.0
		29.5	26.2			Gross Profit	25.9	29.5
		26.7	19.1			Operating Expenses	21.9	23.2
		2.8	7.1			Operating Profit	4.0	6.2
		-.2	-.4			All Other Expenses (net)	.1	-.5
		3.0	7.5			Profit Before Taxes	3.9	6.8
						RATIOS		
		2.9	3.2				2.5	5.7
		1.9	2.0			Current	1.7	2.1
		1.4	1.7				1.4	1.4
		1.9	1.8				1.4	3.3
	(16)	1.0	1.4			Quick	.7	.9
		.6	.8				.4	.5
		19 19.2	27 13.7				20 18.4	19 18.8
		33 11.0	38 9.6			Sales/Receivables	29 12.8	30 12.1
		53 6.9	66 5.5				41 8.9	41 8.9
		5 67.7	27 13.3				26 14.1	37 9.8
		41 8.8	59 6.2			Cost of Sales/Inventory	62 5.9	81 4.5
		111 3.3	99 3.7				99 3.7	166 2.2
		7 51.7	15 23.7				12 30.5	9 38.5
		30 12.3	25 14.4			Cost of Sales/Payables	21 17.1	20 18.2
		41 8.9	51 7.1				51 7.2	59 6.2
		5.9	3.6				5.2	3.3
		10.4	5.2			Sales/Working Capital	8.1	6.1
		13.1	8.5				15.3	10.1
		45.5	81.6				32.1	157.0
	(16)	7.3	(14) 50.4			EBIT/Interest	(52) 5.7	(22) 12.9
		3.1	11.2				2.8	1.8
						Net Profit + Depr., Dep., Amort./Cur. Mat. L/T/D	11.0	
							(13) 5.3	
							3.6	
		.0	.1				.1	.1
		.2	.2			Fixed/Worth	.2	.2
		.6	.3				.6	1.2
		.6	.5				.8	.4
		1.1	.6			Debt/Worth	1.5	1.4
		1.9	1.4				3.2	13.1
		46.0	39.3				38.2	57.7
	(16)	8.0	23.2			% Profit Before Taxes/Tangible Net Worth	(51) 24.1	(20) 28.0
		.4	18.4				10.4	14.8
		22.6	21.4				17.6	20.1
		4.8	13.6			% Profit Before Taxes/Total Assets	9.2	11.2
		.4	10.5				3.7	2.5
		300.7	46.8				89.0	97.9
		59.9	28.6			Sales/Net Fixed Assets	31.7	40.4
		9.4	17.3				16.1	16.0
		4.1	2.8				3.8	3.0
		3.0	2.2			Sales/Total Assets	2.7	2.0
		2.3	1.7				2.0	1.5
		.3	.3				.4	.4
	(14)	1.1	(16) .6			% Depr., Dep., Amort./Sales	(48) .8	(20) .8
		2.0	1.2				1.7	2.6
						% Officers', Directors' Owners' Comp/Sales	.5	
							(20) 2.1	
							5.3	
2019M	6360M	247794M	899184M	1076834M	513261M	Net Sales ($)	2608175M	875565M
458M	2146M	81111M	401045M	595036M	306903M	Total Assets ($)	1118863M	529683M

© RMA 2024

M = $ thousand   MM = $ million
See Pages viii through xx for Explanation of Ratios and Data

WHOLESALE—Refrigeration Equipment and Supplies Merchant Wholesalers NAICS 423740

Comparative Historical Data | Current Data Sorted by Sales

Comparative Historical Data					Current Data Sorted by Sales					
				Type of Statement						
	1	2	2	Unqualified						2
	6	9	15	Reviewed					6	9
		6	6	Compiled					3	3
	1	1	3	Tax Returns			1	1		1
	16	19	21	Other		2		5	3	11
	4/1/21-3/31/22	4/1/22-3/31/23	4/1/23-3/31/24		0-1MM	6 (4/1-9/30/23) 1-3MM	3-5MM	41 (10/1/23-3/31/24) 5-10MM	10-25MM	25MM & OVER
	ALL 24	ALL 37	ALL 47	NUMBER OF STATEMENTS		2	1	6	12	26
	%	%	%	ASSETS	%	%	%	%	%	%
	14.8	13.3	9.1	Cash & Equivalents	D				8.0	8.3
	18.5	25.0	32.3	Trade Receivables (net)	A				35.8	31.5
	33.3	37.8	28.9	Inventory	T				32.8	29.6
	9.9	2.2	4.4	All Other Current	A				3.8	3.0
	76.6	78.3	74.8	Total Current					80.5	72.4
	13.1	14.4	13.7	Fixed Assets (net)	N				13.6	13.9
	6.3	3.3	4.9	Intangibles (net)	O				.9	6.4
	4.0	4.0	6.6	All Other Non-Current	T				5.0	7.3
	100.0	100.0	100.0	Total					100.0	100.0
				LIABILITIES	A					
	6.1	6.9	6.2	Notes Payable-Short Term	V				6.2	5.5
	3.0	1.3	.9	Cur. Mat.-L.T.D.	A				.3	1.2
	11.0	17.6	18.3	Trade Payables	I				19.9	17.7
	.1	.4	.0	Income Taxes Payable	L				.0	.0
	17.5	10.0	16.9	All Other Current	A				18.8	16.5
	37.6	36.2	42.3	Total Current	B				45.3	40.9
	21.8	11.2	7.1	Long-Term Debt	L				4.1	8.8
	.1	.2	.0	Deferred Taxes	E				.1	.0
	3.5	3.2	3.5	All Other Non-Current					6.1	2.9
	37.0	49.3	47.0	Net Worth					44.5	47.4
	100.0	100.0	100.0	Total Liabilties & Net Worth					100.0	100.0
				INCOME DATA						
	100.0	100.0	100.0	Net Sales					100.0	100.0
	26.1	24.8	27.8	Gross Profit					30.1	23.0
	21.7	18.5	22.2	Operating Expenses					26.4	17.3
	4.4	6.3	5.6	Operating Profit					3.7	5.6
	-1.8	-.1	.2	All Other Expenses (net)					.2	.0
	6.2	6.5	5.4	Profit Before Taxes					3.5	5.7
				RATIOS						
	3.3	3.3	2.4						2.0	2.8
	2.2	2.1	1.8	Current					1.9	1.9
	1.6	1.6	1.4						1.5	1.3
	1.6	2.1	1.7						1.8	1.7
	.9	.9	1.0	Quick					.8	1.1
	.6	.5	.6						.6	.5
13	28.0	25 14.8	29 12.5					24	14.9	33 10.9
30	12.0	32 11.3	41 9.0	Sales/Receivables				34	10.8	42 8.7
45	8.1	49 7.5	64 5.7					69	5.3	73 5.0
19	19.0	35 10.5	15 25.1					0	832.1	20 18.3
83	4.4	83 4.4	54 6.8	Cost of Sales/Inventory				41	9.0	56 6.5
146	2.5	140 2.6	91 4.0					135	2.7	91 4.0
14	26.4	16 23.0	19 19.5					13	27.3	20 18.3
24	15.1	28 13.0	28 13.1	Cost of Sales/Payables				33	11.0	27 13.7
38	9.6	39 9.4	46 7.9					42	8.7	53 6.9
	3.4	4.1	4.9						4.7	4.8
	6.8	5.6	8.3	Sales/Working Capital					10.0	5.5
	10.5	8.9	12.8						10.9	12.9
	73.0	65.3	46.2						35.4	59.9
(22)	12.8	(31) 18.5	(43) 10.9	EBIT/Interest					7.1	(23) 17.0
	3.8	6.0	3.7						1.6	4.8
			99.4	Net Profit + Depr., Dep.,						
			(12) 31.1	Amort./Cur. Mat. L/T/D						
			4.6							
	.2	.1	.1						.0	.1
	.2	.2	.2	Fixed/Worth					.3	.2
	.5	.5	.7						.6	1.3
	.6	.6	.6						.7	.5
	1.1	1.0	1.2	Debt/Worth					1.1	1.2
	3.3	2.4	3.1						1.7	5.2
	54.7	59.8	53.5	% Profit Before Taxes/Tangible					39.8	51.3
(20)	28.1	(35) 24.6	(42) 21.3	Net Worth				(11)	11.6	(22) 23.2
	18.1	11.5	9.3						.1	15.9
	17.8	21.4	20.7	% Profit Before Taxes/Total					21.7	15.8
	9.0	12.2	10.7	Assets					5.8	11.0
	6.3	5.4	2.6						.3	5.3
	46.9	99.3	154.1						579.5	100.9
	20.9	23.6	33.7	Sales/Net Fixed Assets					44.2	31.1
	11.3	13.8	13.6						9.0	17.4
	3.7	3.4	3.1						4.0	2.8
	2.3	2.2	2.5	Sales/Total Assets					3.0	2.3
	1.4	1.7	1.9						2.1	1.5
	.5	.3	.3						.3	.3
(21)	.8	(29) .7	(38) .9	% Depr., Dep., Amort./Sales				(10)	1.0	(22) .6
	1.5	1.7	1.7						1.6	2.2
			.8	% Officers', Directors'						
		(12)	2.5	Owners' Comp/Sales						
			5.7							
	1368973M	2076514M	2745452M	Net Sales ($)		3839M	4540M	49038M	212731M	2475304M
	767476M	1073759M	1386699M	Total Assets ($)		1136M	1468M	18048M	83158M	1282889M

© RMA 2024 M = $ thousand   MM = $ million
See Pages viii through xx for Explanation of Ratios and Data

WHOLESALE—Construction and Mining (except Oil Well) Machinery and Equipment Merchant Wholesalers NAICS 423810

Current Data Sorted by Assets | Comparative Historical Data

					9	7	21	**Type of Statement**			
			12		50	12	4	Unqualified		70	29
		1	14		20	1	2	Reviewed		78	43
	1	4	13		6			Compiled		62	18
	4	8	55		131	59	66	Tax Returns		72	19
		147 (4/1-9/30/23)			353 (10/1/23-3/31/24)			Other		321	91
	0-500M	500M-2MM	2-10MM		10-50MM	50-100MM	100-250MM			4/1/19-3/31/20 ALL	4/1/20-3/31/21 ALL
	5	13	94		216	79	93	**NUMBER OF STATEMENTS**		603	200
	%	%	%		%	%	%	**ASSETS**		%	%
		12.5	12.3		8.1	7.3	3.7	Cash & Equivalents		8.0	12.0
		22.7	12.2		10.3	10.5	11.1	Trade Receivables (net)		13.1	13.8
		43.3	56.5		56.2	51.2	46.3	Inventory		55.7	49.5
		.7	1.6		1.6	1.7	1.5	All Other Current		2.0	3.0
		79.1	82.6		76.2	70.7	62.7	Total Current		78.8	78.3
		12.0	12.5		17.1	19.5	26.1	Fixed Assets (net)		16.5	16.4
		4.9	1.8		2.2	5.0	5.6	Intangibles (net)		2.8	2.0
		4.0	3.1		4.5	4.9	5.6	All Other Non-Current		1.9	3.3
		100.0	100.0		100.0	100.0	100.0	Total		100.0	100.0
								LIABILITIES			
		12.0	24.1		32.7	32.6	26.6	Notes Payable-Short Term		32.2	24.2
		.9	3.1		2.7	3.3	4.7	Cur. Mat.-L.T.D.		3.9	6.5
		12.9	14.4		8.6	8.3	7.8	Trade Payables		8.9	9.1
		.0	.1		.1	.1	.3	Income Taxes Payable		.1	.4
		8.0	6.2		5.8	6.1	7.0	All Other Current		6.2	7.4
		33.8	48.1		50.0	50.5	46.3	Total Current		51.3	47.5
		2.8	11.1		9.3	11.7	21.7	Long-Term Debt		10.9	11.5
		.7	.1		.5	.8	.8	Deferred Taxes		.8	1.0
		5.4	3.0		3.2	4.1	4.1	All Other Non-Current		3.5	3.5
		57.3	37.7		36.9	32.8	27.0	Net Worth		33.5	36.5
		100.0	100.0		100.0	100.0	100.0	Total Liabilities & Net Worth		100.0	100.0
								INCOME DATA			
		100.0	100.0		100.0	100.0	100.0	Net Sales		100.0	100.0
		37.3	26.4		25.6	24.1	24.7	Gross Profit		25.0	26.9
		32.0	21.0		20.4	19.1	19.6	Operating Expenses		20.0	22.6
		5.3	5.3		5.2	5.0	5.1	Operating Profit		5.0	4.3
		.2	-.4		.1	1.3	2.2	All Other Expenses (net)		.6	-.2
		5.1	5.7		5.0	3.7	2.9	Profit Before Taxes		4.3	4.5
								RATIOS			
			8.1	3.2		2.1	1.8	1.9		2.1	2.6
			2.5	1.7		1.4	1.3	1.4	Current		1.5	1.7
			1.7	1.3		1.2	1.1	1.1		1.2	1.3
			3.4	1.3		.7	.5	.5		.7	1.0
			.9	.4		.3	.3	.3	Quick		.3	.5
			.4	.2		.2	.2	.2		.2	.3
	5	75.6	6	60.8	10	36.7	15	23.6	22	16.9			15	24.5	20	18.0
	38	9.5	18	20.7	23	16.2	24	15.1	32	11.4	Sales/Receivables	27	13.7	33	11.2
	54	6.8	36	10.0	33	10.9	36	10.1	43	8.5		41	8.8	47	7.7
	5	67.3	94	3.9	114	3.2	107	3.4	118	3.1		111	3.3	94	3.9
	122	3.0	159	2.3	174	2.1	159	2.3	182	2.0	Cost of Sales/Inventory	174	2.1	166	2.2
	152	2.4	228	1.6	228	1.6	261	1.4	243	1.5		261	1.4	261	1.4
	3	129.9	6	61.6	7	51.4	11	34.1	13	28.4		7	50.3	9	40.3
	23	15.6	18	20.3	15	23.6	19	19.7	20	18.0	Cost of Sales/Payables	17	21.5	20	18.2
	36	10.0	50	7.3	31	11.7	36	10.2	41	9.0		35	10.5	41	9.0
			3.1	3.0		4.1	4.0	3.9			3.6	2.9
			4.3	6.0		6.5	7.4	7.9	Sales/Working Capital		6.2	4.8
			15.0	10.4		15.8	33.6	22.3			13.7	8.9
				26.0		16.5		14.0		8.0				10.1		16.1
			(85)	6.7	(207)	6.0	(78)	4.0	(91)	2.6	EBIT/Interest	(568)	3.8	(184)	5.3
				1.9		2.0		1.6		1.5			1.8		2.2
						8.1		9.3		13.2	Net Profit + Depr., Dep.,			9.8		8.5
				(62)		2.8	(19)	3.1	(23)	3.0	Amort./Cur. Mat. L/T/D	(90)	4.2	(26)	3.9
						1.4		1.8		1.9				1.4		1.0
		.0	.0		.1	.1	.3			.1	.1
		.2	.2		.3	.6	1.1	Fixed/Worth		.3	.2
		.4	.6		.9	1.4	3.1			1.0	.7
		.2	.6		1.1	1.3	2.0			1.2	.9
		.9	1.6		1.9	2.9	3.5	Debt/Worth		2.3	1.7
		2.1	4.1		4.1	4.7	6.2			4.3	3.4
			49.3	36.9		33.2	31.7	27.8	% Profit Before Taxes/Tangible		31.0	31.9
		(12)	16.7	(87)	26.1	(209)	21.8	(72)	20.3	(81)	18.4	Net Worth	(569)	17.7	(190)	16.5
			-9.5	10.6		8.2	9.7	9.5			7.2	7.3
			29.2	15.4		12.0	9.4	7.2	% Profit Before Taxes/Total		10.2	10.3
			5.7	7.5		6.4	4.7	4.2	Assets		4.9	6.2
			-2.6	2.3		2.3	1.5	1.6			1.8	2.5
			UND	175.4		41.6	34.4	24.1			49.7	58.2
			32.9	35.8		18.0	13.9	7.2	Sales/Net Fixed Assets		22.5	23.2
			14.3	13.2		6.1	5.5	2.7			7.3	7.1
			2.8	2.3		2.0	1.8	1.6			2.0	1.9
			2.3	1.8		1.6	1.4	1.3	Sales/Total Assets		1.5	1.4
			1.8	1.3		1.1	1.1	1.0			1.1	1.0
				.2		.6	.8	.7			.6	.8
			(47)	1.0	(162)	1.2	(58)	1.3	(48)	1.1	% Depr., Dep., Amort./Sales	(345)	1.3	(103)	1.5
				3.0		4.6	2.2	2.4			4.1	6.4
				1.3		.3		.5			.7	.8
			(30)	1.7	(61)	.8	(14)	.9		% Officers', Directors'	(144)	1.4	(50)	2.1
				3.6		1.8		2.5	Owners' Comp/Sales		2.6	4.3
5986M	35257M	994151M	8609877M	8095025M	20599205M	Net Sales ($)	35102102M	12747334M
1750M	15276M	516800M	5468028M	5555701M	15532389M	Total Assets ($)	25947186M	9721231M

© RMA 2024

M = $ thousand   MM = $ million
See Pages viii through xx for Explanation of Ratios and Data

WHOLESALE—Construction and Mining (except Oil Well) Machinery and Equipment Merchant Wholesalers NAICS 423810

Comparative Historical Data | Current Data Sorted by Sales

							Type of Statement						
	27		38		37		Unqualified					3	34
	42		49		78		Reviewed		1	4	5	15	53
	12		23		38		Compiled	1		3	4	12	18
	20		18		24		Tax Returns	1	4	2	6	4	7
	129		157		323		Other	4	5	12	21	67	214
	4/1/21-3/31/22		4/1/22-3/31/23		4/1/23-3/31/24				147 (4/1-9/30/23)		353 (10/1/23-3/31/24)		
	ALL		ALL		ALL			0-1MM	1-3MM	3-5MM	5-10MM	10-25MM	25MM & OVER
	230		285		500		NUMBER OF STATEMENTS	6	10	21	36	101	326
	%		%		%		ASSETS	%	%	%	%	%	%
	11.2		10.9		8.1		Cash & Equivalents	19.9	7.4	9.8	9.4	6.9	
	13.4		13.5		11.4		Trade Receivables (net)	20.7	12.6	11.0	10.5	11.2	
	47.5		49.4		53.1		Inventory	47.8	49.7	60.2	52.5	53.3	
	2.4		2.4		1.6		All Other Current	.4	.9	2.1	1.9	1.5	
	74.4		76.2		74.2		Total Current	88.9	70.7	83.1	74.3	73.0	
	18.2		15.9		18.1		Fixed Assets (net)	5.1	21.6	12.8	19.4	18.4	
	3.4		2.8		3.3		Intangibles (net)	1.9	3.8	.9	2.8	3.6	
	4.0		5.1		4.4		All Other Non-Current	4.1	3.9	3.3	3.6	5.0	
	100.0		100.0		100.0		Total	100.0	100.0	100.0	100.0	100.0	
							LIABILITIES						
	22.2		20.9		29.3		Notes Payable-Short Term	16.6	15.5	30.0	26.3	31.6	
	4.1		3.6		3.2		Cur. Mat.-L.T.D.	1.5	3.6	3.4	3.7	3.1	
	8.8		10.1		9.7		Trade Payables	9.1	9.5	10.5	11.1	9.1	
	.2		.2		.1		Income Taxes Payable	.0	.0	.1	.1	.2	
	6.8		8.6		6.3		All Other Current	9.2	4.7	6.8	5.2	6.5	
	42.2		43.4		48.6		Total Current	36.4	33.3	50.8	46.4	50.5	
	13.5		10.4		12.1		Long-Term Debt	6.7	16.4	13.7	11.5	12.1	
	1.0		.8		.6		Deferred Taxes	.0	.2	.2	.4	.7	
	2.1		4.1		3.5		All Other Non-Current	1.5	8.8	3.4	2.2	3.7	
	41.2		41.3		35.2		Net Worth	55.4	41.2	31.9	39.4	33.1	
	100.0		100.0		100.0		Total Liabilities & Net Worth	100.0	100.0	100.0	100.0	100.0	
							INCOME DATA						
	100.0		100.0		100.0		Net Sales	100.0	100.0	100.0	100.0	100.0	
	26.9		26.5		25.8		Gross Profit	31.9	34.3	25.6	27.2	24.1	
	21.8		20.3		20.7		Operating Expenses	28.4	27.7	22.2	20.9	19.2	
	5.1		6.1		5.1		Operating Profit	3.5	6.7	3.4	6.3	4.9	
	-1.0		-.3		.6		All Other Expenses (net)	.9	-.7	-.3	.5	.8	
	6.1		6.5		4.5		Profit Before Taxes	2.6	7.4	3.7	5.8	4.1	
							RATIOS						
	2.8		2.7		2.2			10.5	5.4	3.6	2.0	2.1	
	1.7		1.8		1.5		Current	2.3	1.9	1.8	1.5	1.4	
	1.2		1.3		1.2			1.7	1.3	1.3	1.2	1.1	
	1.1		1.0		.7			8.4	1.7	1.4	.7	.6	
	.6		.5		.3		Quick	.7	.5	.5	.3	.3	
	.2		.3		.2			.3	.3	.2	.2	.2	
14	26.9	15	25.1	12	29.8			3	114.7	5	75.6	5	79.1	10	35.7	14	25.5
26	13.8	25	14.8	24	15.2		Sales/Receivables	29	12.5	33	10.9	33	11.0	22	16.4	24	15.1
42	8.7	38	9.6	37	9.8			55	6.6	46	7.9	39	9.3	34	10.6	37	9.9
78	4.7	89	4.1	107	3.4			33	11.2	73	5.0	130	2.8	104	3.5	107	3.4
126	2.9	135	2.7	174	2.1		Cost of Sales/Inventory	101	3.6	174	2.1	174	2.1	182	2.0	166	2.2
192	1.9	215	1.7	228	1.6			203	1.8	281	1.3	243	1.5	228	1.6	228	1.6
9	41.3	10	35.5	8	46.7			0	UND	7	50.1	5	78.3	7	54.5	9	39.4
18	20.8	21	17.2	17	21.1		Cost of Sales/Payables	9	40.8	23	15.6	18	20.7	17	21.1	17	21.4
36	10.2	37	9.8	36	10.1			39	9.4	38	9.7	59	6.2	39	9.3	34	10.6
	3.6		3.3		3.8			1.9	3.0	2.3	3.7	4.2	
	5.4		5.3		6.5		Sales/Working Capital	4.6	4.3	4.9	6.6	7.3	
	14.0		10.5		15.9			10.4	9.4	8.1	16.4	16.6	
	24.3		27.2		15.8				26.9	14.4	23.2	13.9	
(216)	8.3	(259)	10.0	(472)	4.6		EBIT/Interest	(18)	4.6	(31)	3.1	(97)	6.7	(315)	4.5
	3.6		4.0		1.7				1.2	1.6	1.9	1.8	
	7.6		8.0		10.4						7.6	10.3	
(38)	3.1	(43)	3.9	(115)	3.0		Net Profit + Depr., Dep., Amort./Cur. Mat. L/T/D			(21)	2.8	(84)	3.0
	1.8		1.8		1.6						1.0	1.7	
	.1		.1		.1			.0	.1	.1	.1	.1	
	.2		.2		.4		Fixed/Worth	.1	.3	.2	.3	.4	
	1.1		.7		1.3			.3	1.7	1.0	1.0	1.4	
	.8		.8		1.2			.2	.7	.6	1.1	1.3	
	1.7		1.6		2.2		Debt/Worth	1.0	1.7	1.9	1.9	2.6	
	3.5		3.3		4.7			2.7	4.8	4.0	3.3	4.9	
	41.4		40.0		32.8		% Profit Before Taxes/Tangible Net Worth		39.5	31.3	34.8	33.4	
(214)	25.8	(272)	26.9	(465)	21.3			(20)	26.3	(32)	16.8	(97)	22.5	(303)	21.3
	11.3		14.2		9.2				7.6	6.8	7.0	10.3	
	15.2		15.3		11.2		% Profit Before Taxes/Total Assets	7.5	17.4	11.6	14.4	10.6	
	9.3		10.1		5.8			3.8	5.3	3.6	6.4	5.9	
	4.5		4.8		1.9			-1.4	1.1	1.9	2.1	2.1	
	47.5		53.6		42.8			UND	43.3	120.9	59.2	39.2	
	23.7		21.3		17.9		Sales/Net Fixed Assets	UND	19.2	23.1	17.1	17.3	
	7.0		8.7		5.3			16.2	2.9	9.5	4.5	5.3	
	2.3		2.3		2.0			3.5	2.2	2.2	2.2	2.0	
	1.6		1.6		1.5		Sales/Total Assets	2.6	1.5	1.4	1.5	1.5	
	1.2		1.2		1.1			.8	.8	1.0	1.0	1.1	
	.7		.7		.6				.2	.2	.5	.6	
(151)	1.4	(169)	1.4	(323)	1.2		% Depr., Dep., Amort./Sales	(12)	2.9	(21)	1.0	(69)	1.5	(218)	1.2
	4.2		4.0		2.9				4.8	2.7	7.7	2.4	
	.9		.8		.5					1.3	.8	.3	
(49)	2.3	(66)	2.4	(114)	1.2		% Officers', Directors', Owners' Comp/Sales		(10)	1.6	(24)	2.3	(69)	.7
	3.8		4.0		2.2					3.6	3.2	1.3	
14104568M		19826802M		38339501M			Net Sales ($)	3747M	18947M	85113M	269346M	1737632M	36224716M
9505334M		12689819M		27089944M			Total Assets ($)	8698M	13343M	74207M	217154M	1356938M	25419604M

M = $ thousand MM = $ million
See Pages viii through xx for Explanation of Ratios and Data

© RMA 2024

WHOLESALE—Farm and Garden Machinery and Equipment Merchant Wholesalers NAICS 423820

Current Data Sorted by Assets | **Comparative Historical Data**

							Type of Statement				
			1	5	16	19	Unqualified		40		17
			6	30	10		Reviewed		53		21
		1	30	21	3		Compiled		43		14
1		6	5	14			Tax Returns		39		16
3	6	14	92	122	59	50	Other		212		90
2	14	159 (4/1-9/30/23)		350 (10/1/23-3/31/24)					4/1/19-3/31/20		4/1/20-3/31/21
0-500M	500M-2MM	2-10MM	10-50MM	50-100MM	100-250MM				ALL		ALL
6	20	134	192	88	69		NUMBER OF STATEMENTS		387		158
%	%	%	%	%	%		ASSETS		%		%
	13.2	9.0	7.4	4.4	3.4		Cash & Equivalents		7.5		10.2
	7.3	6.9	8.9	10.7	8.0		Trade Receivables (net)		11.4		11.5
	54.4	64.1	68.1	69.5	64.9		Inventory		63.2		59.5
	2.2	3.8	1.9	1.2	4.0		All Other Current		1.9		1.7
	77.2	83.8	86.3	85.8	80.3		Total Current		84.1		82.9
	17.9	10.7	7.9	8.9	8.7		Fixed Assets (net)		11.1		10.7
	3.6	2.8	1.5	1.0	4.0		Intangibles (net)		2.0		2.6
	1.4	2.7	4.3	4.2	7.1		All Other Non-Current		2.8		3.7
	100.0	100.0	100.0	100.0	100.0		Total		100.0		100.0
							LIABILITIES				
	7.6	16.6	20.2	16.3	24.2		Notes Payable-Short Term		28.8		20.7
	.2	1.6	1.4	.8	3.0		Cur. Mat.-L.T.D.		2.0		3.0
	35.4	28.8	25.1	33.8	19.0		Trade Payables		14.2		14.2
	.1	.1	.1	.0	.0		Income Taxes Payable		.1		.1
	5.7	4.7	6.9	6.1	8.8		All Other Current		8.6		9.1
	48.9	51.8	53.7	57.0	55.0		Total Current		53.7		47.1
	8.4	8.2	6.7	6.1	7.7		Long-Term Debt		8.6		10.2
	.0	.1	.3	.1	.2		Deferred Taxes		.2		.4
	1.6	2.8	4.4	4.8	6.8		All Other Non-Current		3.1		4.3
	41.0	37.0	34.9	31.9	30.3		Net Worth		34.5		38.0
	100.0	100.0	100.0	100.0	100.0		Total Liabilities & Net Worth		100.0		100.0
							INCOME DATA				
	100.0	100.0	100.0	100.0	100.0		Net Sales		100.0		100.0
	25.6	23.6	21.3	20.7	17.7		Gross Profit		24.5		21.1
	20.7	19.0	17.6	16.4	14.6		Operating Expenses		20.4		17.3
	5.0	4.5	3.7	4.2	3.1		Operating Profit		4.1		3.7
	2.3	.4	.2	.4	.7		All Other Expenses (net)		.6		-.2
	2.6	4.1	3.5	3.8	2.3		Profit Before Taxes		3.5		4.0
							RATIOS				
	7.8	2.1	2.1	1.8	1.8				2.1		2.6
	1.8	1.5	1.5	1.5	1.4		Current		1.5		1.6
	1.3	1.3	1.3	1.2	1.2				1.3		1.4
	2.7	.6	.6	.4	.3				.7		.8
	.4	.2	.2	.3	.2		Quick	(386)	.3		.4
	.2	.1	.1	.1	.1				.1		.2
0	864.8	3	107.2	5	74.8	6	60.3	4	81.8				6	63.4	6	59.3
6	60.9	9	42.6	11	32.0	19	19.3	12	29.6	Sales/Receivables	14	25.6	15	24.9
19	19.7	15	23.7	30	12.0	34	10.7	29	12.7		31	11.7	32	11.3
62	5.9	101	3.6	135	2.7	152	2.4	146	2.5		104	3.5	87	4.2
104	3.5	152	2.4	182	2.0	182	2.0	174	2.1	Cost of Sales/Inventory	152	2.4	126	2.9
174	2.1	243	1.5	261	1.4	215	1.7	203	1.8		215	1.7	166	2.2
2	221.4	9	40.8	10	37.0	21	17.2	10	36.8		6	60.4	6	63.1
70	5.2	33	11.2	44	8.3	94	3.9	30	12.1	Cost of Sales/Payables	18	19.9	18	20.2
146	2.5	111	3.3	118	3.1	146	2.5	83	4.4		47	7.7	42	8.6
	3.9	4.4	3.9	4.7	5.5				4.4		4.2
	8.7	6.8	5.8	6.5	9.0		Sales/Working Capital		7.0		7.0
	13.7	12.4	8.6	9.7	11.7				12.0		10.2
	26.4	17.9	17.5	17.7	12.1				9.7		16.8
(18)	5.3	(121)	5.2	(174)	6.3	(83)	4.8	(68)	4.3	EBIT/Interest	(357)	4.0	(148)	7.8
	1.5	2.8	3.3	2.0	1.6				1.8		3.4
		19.5	18.3	26.5	13.5		Net Profit + Depr., Dep.,		14.0		8.2
		(18)	3.1	(30)	9.3	(15)	5.9	(14)	4.6	Amort./Cur. Mat. L/T/D	(63)	4.1	(29)	2.4
		1.8	.9	2.9	3.7				1.4		1.0
	.1	.1	.1	.1	.1				.1		.1
	.3	.2	.2	.2	.3		Fixed/Worth		.2		.2
	2.0	.8	.4	.4	.6				.6		.5
	.3	1.2	1.0	1.6	1.7				1.1		1.0
	2.5	2.2	2.2	2.1	2.9		Debt/Worth		2.3		1.8
	8.2	3.8	3.4	4.0	4.7				4.4		3.5
	77.1	37.9	28.4	33.4	35.7		% Profit Before Taxes/Tangible		31.1		34.5
(17)	31.1	(128)	18.9	(186)	17.5	(87)	22.3	(67)	23.4	Net Worth	(360)	15.8	(147)	19.2
	14.4	10.0	9.0	10.1	10.7				7.3		9.3
	27.7	11.3	9.9	11.8	10.7		% Profit Before Taxes/Total		10.1		12.8
	11.6	6.6	6.2	6.2	4.9		Assets		5.1		7.3
	.6	3.3	2.4	2.1	1.9				1.7		3.4
	124.1	133.3	77.3	56.5	68.6				74.9		77.9
	36.3	36.9	30.6	30.7	34.2		Sales/Net Fixed Assets		36.6		37.8
	12.7	12.5	14.7	15.7	13.6				13.5		16.2
	3.3	2.6	2.2	2.0	2.1				2.6		2.8
	2.6	2.0	1.7	1.7	1.7		Sales/Total Assets		2.0		2.2
	1.5	1.4	1.4	1.5	1.3				1.5		1.6
		.3	.5	.4	.3				.4		.4
	(80)	.7	(156)	.7	(78)	.6	(61)	.6	% Depr., Dep., Amort./Sales	(296)	.7	(128)	.7
		1.5	1.1	.9	1.0				1.3		1.2
		.7	.6	.7					.6		.9
	(54)	1.1	(67)	1.0	(21)	1.1		% Officers', Directors', Owners' Comp/Sales	(134)	1.4	(47)	1.6
		2.1	1.9	1.1					3.1		3.2
9581M	64799M	1600050M	7813541M	10702817M	18921679M		Net Sales ($)		23045558M		13111193M
1867M	23628M	760977M	4466952M	6021050M	10834762M		Total Assets ($)		11737767M		5760662M

© RMA 2024 M = $ thousand MM = $ million
See Pages viii through xx for Explanation of Ratios and Data

WHOLESALE—Farm and Garden Machinery and Equipment Merchant Wholesalers NAICS 423820

Comparative Historical Data / Current Data Sorted by Sales

						Type of Statement											
	23		39		41	Unqualified											41
	28		31		46	Reviewed							1		13		32
	18		36		55	Compiled					3		10		25		16
	21		30		28	Tax Returns			1		5		3		6		10
	143		159		339	Other		3	3		16		31		80		200
	4/1/21-3/31/22 ALL		4/1/22-3/31/23 ALL		4/1/23-3/31/24 ALL				159 (4/1-9/30/23)				350 (10/1/23-3/31/24)				
								0-1MM	1-3MM		3-5MM		5-10MM		10-25MM		25MM & OVER
	233		295		509	NUMBER OF STATEMENTS		4	13		24		45		124		299
	%		%		%	ASSETS		%	%		%		%		%		%
	11.5		9.3		7.1	Cash & Equivalents		15.3	11.9		7.9		8.6				5.7
	13.4		11.3		8.5	Trade Receivables (net)		8.5	4.3		6.5		6.7				10.0
	55.6		57.9		66.1	Inventory		39.7	56.3		69.0		69.0				66.5
	2.0		2.0		2.6	All Other Current		7.6	8.5		3.4		1.2				2.4
	82.6		80.4		84.3	Total Current		71.0	81.0		86.8		85.5				84.6
	10.9		11.3		9.4	Fixed Assets (net)		27.0	14.5		7.3		9.1				8.3
	2.4		3.3		2.2	Intangibles (net)		.4	3.5		4.3		1.9				2.0
	4.2		4.9		4.1	All Other Non-Current		1.6	1.0		1.5		3.5				5.1
	100.0		100.0		100.0	Total		100.0	100.0		100.0		100.0				100.0
						LIABILITIES											
	16.7		20.1		18.8	Notes Payable-Short Term		15.3	10.8		14.6		20.0				19.7
	2.0		1.5		1.5	Cur. Mat.-L.T.D.		.5	.7		2.0		1.8				1.4
	16.5		16.4		27.0	Trade Payables		30.1	32.4		28.2		27.1				26.0
	.2		.2		.1	Income Taxes Payable		.0	.0		.1		.1				.1
	10.2		10.2		6.3	All Other Current		5.9	6.4		3.0		6.0				7.0
	45.6		48.2		53.7	Total Current		51.8	50.3		47.9		55.0				54.1
	7.1		7.9		7.2	Long-Term Debt		12.8	9.0		8.3		7.7				6.5
	.2		.3		.2	Deferred Taxes		.0	.0		.1		.2				.2
	4.2		4.2		4.2	All Other Non-Current		2.7	5.1		2.1		1.8				5.6
	42.9		39.4		34.6	Net Worth		32.7	35.6		41.6		35.2				33.7
	100.0		100.0		100.0	Total Liabilities & Net Worth		100.0	100.0		100.0		100.0				100.0
						INCOME DATA											
	100.0		100.0		100.0	Net Sales		100.0	100.0		100.0		100.0				100.0
	21.2		21.9		21.5	Gross Profit		32.5	30.8		24.3		21.6				19.8
	16.0		16.9		17.5	Operating Expenses		20.6	26.9		20.4		17.9				16.0
	5.1		5.0		3.9	Operating Profit		11.8	3.8		3.9		3.8				3.8
	-.8		-.4		.4	All Other Expenses (net)		.9	.1		.9		.1				.4
	5.9		5.4		3.5	Profit Before Taxes		10.9	3.7		3.0		3.7				3.4
						RATIOS											
	2.7		2.2		2.0			6.3	4.6		3.4		1.9				2.0
	1.9		1.6		1.5	Current		1.3	1.4		1.5		1.4				1.5
	1.5		1.3		1.3			.7	1.2		1.4		1.3				1.3
	1.0		.7		.6			1.9	.7		.7		.5				.6
	.5		.3		.2	Quick		.3	.2		.2		.2				.2
	.2		.2		.1			.2	.1		.1		.1				.1
6	65.4	5	74.9	5	79.5		0	UND	1	350.9	5	69.8	4	85.6	5		72.5
13	28.5	12	29.2	11	33.6	Sales/Receivables	6	65.1	5	73.1	11	32.2	9	42.2	13		27.4
31	11.7	30	12.0	27	13.4		24	15.5	17	21.0	17	21.1	16	23.0	31		11.7
72	5.1	87	4.2	126	2.9		0	UND	76	4.8	111	3.3	126	2.9	130		2.8
101	3.6	130	2.8	174	2.1	Cost of Sales/Inventory	152	2.4	261	1.4	192	1.9	182	2.0	166		2.2
146	2.5	174	2.1	228	1.6		304	1.2	406	.9	304	1.2	261	1.4	215		1.7
6	58.5	7	52.1	10	37.5		0	UND	2	219.6	7	55.3	9	40.5	12		31.6
17	21.3	18	20.4	44	8.3	Cost of Sales/Payables	61	6.0	87	4.2	46	7.9	43	8.5	38		9.5
46	8.0	56	6.5	122	3.0		114	3.2	281	1.3	182	2.0	118	3.1	114		3.2
	4.5		4.5		4.5			2.9	3.6		3.6		4.4				4.6
	6.8		6.9		6.5	Sales/Working Capital		10.0	5.9		5.3		6.6				6.5
	11.7		11.7		10.3			-17.2	13.6		8.2		11.1				10.2
	50.3		38.3		17.3			26.4	47.1		12.4		17.4				17.7
(210)	19.2	(267)	14.4	(468)	5.3	EBIT/Interest	(10)	5.3	(21)	4.2	(42)	3.3	(113)	5.7	(279)		5.9
	6.1		5.7		2.7			1.1	1.2		2.1		3.1				2.8
	17.8		22.3		18.1	Net Profit + Depr., Dep.,								23.1				17.9
(39)	8.3	(42)	7.1	(77)	6.2	Amort./Cur. Mat. L/T/D							(21)	6.2	(50)		6.2
	3.6		2.4		2.3									1.0				3.4
	.1		.1		.1			.1	.1		.0		.1				.1
	.2		.2		.2	Fixed/Worth		.8	.3		.2		.2				.2
	.4		.5		.5			41.6	.8		.4		.6				.4
	.7		.9		1.2			.7	1.1		1.2		1.1				1.3
	1.4		1.6		2.3	Debt/Worth		3.0	2.9		1.9		2.4				2.2
	2.6		3.2		4.1			53.4	10.0		2.8		3.4				4.0
	49.1		45.1		33.4	% Profit Before Taxes/Tangible		88.9	35.6		35.0		26.9				34.0
(218)	29.8	(280)	29.2	(490)	20.0	Net Worth	(11)	63.8	(22)	21.2		13.1	(118)	16.9	(292)		22.0
	19.7		16.6		9.6			13.5	2.9		7.2		10.4				10.2
	19.5		17.0		10.8	% Profit Before Taxes/Total		27.7	14.9		10.7		9.5				10.8
	12.7		10.6		6.2	Assets		5.2	4.9		5.6		6.2				6.6
	7.2		5.0		2.4			-2.5	.3		2.6		2.6				2.6
	81.8		73.1		81.3			179.8	117.8		163.0		88.8				72.5
	40.4		33.1		32.1	Sales/Net Fixed Assets		14.4	31.0		31.3		32.3				34.5
	18.5		14.4		13.8			3.4	12.5		12.6		11.0				15.6
	3.4		2.8		2.3			3.8	2.5		2.5		2.3				2.3
	2.7		2.2		1.8	Sales/Total Assets		2.1	1.1		1.8		1.7				1.8
	1.8		1.6		1.4			1.1	.9		1.2		1.3				1.5
	.4		.4		.4				.5		.5		.4				.4
(182)	.6	(225)	.7	(383)	.6	% Depr., Dep., Amort./Sales			(12)	1.3	(21)	1.4	(91)	.6	(257)		.6
	1.1		1.1		1.1					10.6		2.9		1.2			.9
			.5		.6							.7		.6			.4
(57)	1.3	(81)	.9	(158)	1.0	% Officers', Directors' Owners' Comp/Sales			(15)	2.1	(57)	.8	(73)			1.1
	2.3		2.3		2.1							2.8		1.6			1.7
	22847976M		26813668M		39112467M	Net Sales ($)		1310M	23359M		92653M		330860M		2006604M			36657681M
	8765557M		12827802M		22109236M	Total Assets ($)		2013M	15867M		80570M		245909M		1325212M			20439665M

© RMA 2024 M = $ thousand MM = $ million
See Pages viii through xx for Explanation of Ratios and Data

WHOLESALE—Industrial Machinery and Equipment Merchant Wholesalers NAICS 423830

Current Data Sorted by Assets | Comparative Historical Data

Type of Statement								
			4	28	22	27	Unqualified	73	63

	0-500M	500M-2MM	2-10MM	10-50MM	50-100MM	100-250MM		4/1/19-3/31/20 ALL	4/1/20-3/31/21 ALL
Unqualified		1	4	28	22	27		73	63
Reviewed		5	36	98	19	7		158	94
Compiled	1	22	51	36	1			84	62
Tax Returns	3	31	29	12				172	60
Other	3		134	180	77	47		479	297
		179 (4/1-9/30/23)		695 (10/1/23-3/31/24)					
NUMBER OF STATEMENTS	7	59	254	354	119	81		966	576

ASSETS (%)

	0-500M	500M-2MM	2-10MM	10-50MM	50-100MM	100-250MM		ALL	ALL
Cash & Equivalents		30.2	15.8	11.2	7.0	6.0		10.3	15.1
Trade Receivables (net)		20.9	27.8	22.6	20.0	16.6		25.8	23.9
Inventory		25.8	35.5	38.6	38.6	39.9		38.8	35.9
All Other Current		3.8	2.4	2.9	2.9	5.4		2.5	2.3
Total Current		80.8	81.5	75.2	68.5	67.9		77.4	77.3
Fixed Assets (net)		10.3	10.5	13.9	16.5	17.2		14.1	13.8
Intangibles (net)		4.6	2.8	3.8	5.0	8.7		3.8	4.4
All Other Non-Current		4.3	5.2	7.1	10.0	6.3		4.7	4.5
Total		100.0	100.0	100.0	100.0	100.0		100.0	100.0

LIABILITIES

Notes Payable-Short Term		8.2	8.9	13.2	17.2	14.8		15.5	14.1
Cur. Mat.-L.T.D.		2.3	2.1	2.5	3.8	2.7		2.9	3.1
Trade Payables		18.2	16.0	13.6	9.7	12.6		15.3	12.8
Income Taxes Payable		.2	.3	.2	.1	.1		.2	.2
All Other Current		10.9	12.1	13.3	11.4	12.1		11.0	11.1
Total Current		39.8	39.5	42.9	42.2	42.3		44.9	41.3
Long-Term Debt		9.8	7.5	9.6	12.9	13.4		9.7	11.4
Deferred Taxes		.0	.2	.4	.9	.6		.4	.6
All Other Non-Current		3.8	4.2	4.3	7.5	5.9		4.7	6.0
Net Worth		46.6	48.7	42.7	36.5	37.8		40.2	40.7
Total Liabilities & Net Worth		100.0	100.0	100.0	100.0	100.0		100.0	100.0

INCOME DATA

Net Sales		100.0	100.0	100.0	100.0	100.0		100.0	100.0
Gross Profit		41.2	31.9	30.1	29.4	29.0		29.9	31.1
Operating Expenses		35.0	25.9	23.1	22.1	21.6		24.8	26.7
Operating Profit		6.2	6.0	7.0	7.2	7.3		5.1	4.4
All Other Expenses (net)		-.5	-.2	.3	1.0	1.1		.4	-.6
Profit Before Taxes		6.7	6.2	6.7	6.2	6.2		4.7	5.0

RATIOS

Current		4.9	3.9	2.7	2.1	2.2		2.8	3.3
		2.6	2.2	1.7	1.6	1.5		1.8	1.9
		1.4	1.4	1.3	1.3	1.2		1.3	1.3
Quick		3.0	2.2	1.5	1.1	.9		1.5	1.9
		1.8	1.2	.8	.7	.5		.8	.9
		.5	.7	.4	.3	.3		.4	.5
Sales/Receivables	0	999.8	25 14.8	27 13.4	29 12.5	26 14.0		27 13.3	28 13.2
	23	15.8	39 9.3	42 8.7	41 8.8	42 8.7		39 9.4	40 9.2
	40	9.2	53 6.9	54 6.8	52 7.0	53 6.9		51 7.2	53 6.9
Cost of Sales/Inventory	3	145.5	34 10.7	60 6.1	69 5.3	79 4.6		42 8.6	42 8.7
	41	8.9	81 4.5	111 3.3	107 3.4	118 3.1		79 4.6	89 4.1
	91	4.0	130 2.8	174 2.1	174 2.1	203 1.8		152 2.4	152 2.4
Cost of Sales/Payables	0	UND	12 31.4	14 25.7	12 31.6	19 19.0		14 26.0	13 28.2
	22	16.4	27 13.5	27 13.5	23 16.1	33 11.1		26 13.8	24 15.0
	53	6.9	49 7.5	51 7.1	42 8.6	50 7.3		43 8.5	41 9.0
Sales/Working Capital		4.0	3.6	3.6	4.0	3.4		4.4	3.5
		8.9	6.1	6.1	6.8	6.2		7.3	5.9
		24.4	10.9	12.5	11.9	17.0		14.9	11.8
EBIT/Interest		28.8	51.5	26.7	24.0	19.4		19.9	21.8
	(38)	4.9	(207) 12.1	(310) 9.6	(113) 7.7	(77) 5.6	(844)	6.0	(497) 7.6
		2.4	3.1	3.4	3.2	2.2		2.5	2.2
Net Profit + Depr., Dep., Amort./Cur. Mat. L/T/D			9.3	14.0	11.8	72.0		9.2	12.7
			(30) 4.2	(80) 5.3	(31) 4.4	(16) 4.5	(160)	3.2	(82) 3.3
			2.3	2.1	1.5	2.4		1.3	1.3
Fixed/Worth		.0	.0	.1	.1	.2		.1	.1
		.1	.1	.2	.3	.5		.3	.2
		.5	.4	.6	1.3	1.3		.8	.7
Debt/Worth		.4	.4	.7	.9	1.2		.7	.6
		.8	1.1	1.5	2.0	2.3		1.7	1.5
		3.3	2.8	3.1	4.3	5.3		3.8	3.5
% Profit Before Taxes/Tangible Net Worth		82.4	53.3	41.8	45.4	38.7		38.6	39.0
	(50)	28.9	(239) 29.0	(338) 25.9	(109) 29.8	(70) 25.1	(891)	19.9	(532) 20.1
		9.8	11.6	13.2	16.9	18.3		9.5	5.2
% Profit Before Taxes/Total Assets		29.8	21.8	16.9	15.8	12.9		14.7	15.8
		11.7	12.2	10.1	8.8	7.1		7.4	7.3
		2.3	4.2	4.6	5.1	4.3		3.0	1.7
Sales/Net Fixed Assets		716.6	130.3	63.3	43.8	36.6		80.2	76.4
		111.3	46.1	24.4	16.4	15.6		28.8	29.5
		22.4	17.2	9.5	6.7	6.1		10.4	9.6
Sales/Total Assets		4.8	3.1	2.2	2.0	1.8		3.1	2.7
		3.4	2.4	1.7	1.5	1.5		2.1	2.0
		2.0	1.7	1.3	1.3	1.0		1.5	1.4
% Depr., Dep., Amort./Sales		.1	.2	.4	.6	.5		.5	.5
	(28)	.6	(165) .6	(279) .8	(88) 1.2	(49) 1.3	(672)	1.0	(365) 1.2
		1.6	1.4	2.1	3.6	2.8		2.4	3.0
% Officers', Directors', Owners' Comp/Sales		2.2	1.4	.6				1.3	1.1
	(29)	3.9	(102) 2.6	(82) 1.2			(279)	2.7	(158) 2.4
		8.4	4.1	2.7				5.1	5.2
Net Sales ($)	7375M	258876M	3513887M	15682514M	14763710M	19896724M		48146806M	25960133M
Total Assets ($)	2151M	69881M	1418816M	8486496M	8455721M	13272172M		25075883M	15284463M

M = $ thousand   MM = $ million
See Pages viii through xx for Explanation of Ratios and Data

© RMA 2024

WHOLESALE—Industrial Machinery and Equipment Merchant Wholesalers NAICS 423830

Comparative Historical Data | Current Data Sorted by Sales

				Type of Statement						
44	85		81	Unqualified				9		72
110	134		161	Reviewed		1		45		106
55	84		94	Compiled		2	4	17	43	27
55	73		66	Tax Returns	3	7	10	19	20	7
319	417		472	Other	3	18	24	51	105	271
4/1/21-3/31/22 ALL	4/1/22-3/31/23 ALL		4/1/23-3/31/24 ALL		179 (4/1-9/30/23)			695 (10/1/23-3/31/24)		
					0-1MM	1-3MM	3-5MM	5-10MM	10-25MM	25MM & OVER
583	793		874	NUMBER OF STATEMENTS	7	28	38	96	222	483
%	%		%	ASSETS	%	%	%	%	%	%
14.8	13.4		12.9	Cash & Equivalents		25.6	24.4	15.9	16.1	8.9
25.3	24.5		23.0	Trade Receivables (net)		17.6	18.5	22.0	26.5	22.5
34.1	36.8		36.9	Inventory		25.6	35.9	35.8	34.9	38.8
3.2	4.1		3.0	All Other Current		1.4	3.2	3.7	2.5	3.1
77.4	78.8		75.8	Total Current		70.2	82.0	77.5	80.1	73.3
13.7	11.9		13.3	Fixed Assets (net)		14.2	11.3	12.7	11.5	14.4
3.8	3.7		4.2	Intangibles (net)		7.8	.7	3.7	2.8	4.9
5.1	5.6		6.7	All Other Non-Current		7.8	6.0	6.1	5.5	7.3
100.0	100.0		100.0	Total		100.0	100.0	100.0	100.0	100.0
				LIABILITIES						
10.8	11.0		12.3	Notes Payable-Short Term		8.3	10.7	9.4	9.0	14.8
3.0	2.3		2.6	Cur. Mat.-L.T.D.		1.6	1.7	1.7	2.7	2.9
13.1	14.2		14.1	Trade Payables		17.0	15.6	14.2	14.9	13.4
.2	.3		.2	Income Taxes Payable		1.3	.1	.2	.2	.2
12.2	13.2		12.5	All Other Current		10.5	12.4	13.7	13.1	12.1
39.2	40.9		41.7	Total Current		38.6	40.5	39.2	39.8	43.3
10.3	10.5		10.1	Long-Term Debt		12.8	10.3	8.9	8.3	10.6
.5	.4		.4	Deferred Taxes		.0	.0	.1	.3	.6
4.4	3.9		4.9	All Other Non-Current		2.1	3.9	5.3	3.9	5.4
45.5	44.2		43.0	Net Worth		46.5	45.3	46.6	47.7	40.1
100.0	100.0		100.0	Total Liabilities & Net Worth		100.0	100.0	100.0	100.0	100.0
				INCOME DATA						
100.0	100.0		100.0	Net Sales		100.0	100.0	100.0	100.0	100.0
30.8	31.2		31.2	Gross Profit		38.6	35.5	36.3	32.6	28.5
25.3	24.6		24.5	Operating Expenses		36.3	28.4	29.8	25.6	21.7
5.6	6.6		6.6	Operating Profit		2.3	7.1	6.5	7.0	6.8
-1.7	-.2		.3	All Other Expenses (net)		.3	.2	-.4	-.1	.6
7.2	6.8		6.3	Profit Before Taxes		2.0	6.9	7.0	7.1	6.2
				RATIOS						
3.5	3.3		3.0			4.8	8.0	4.5	3.6	2.4
2.0	2.0		1.8	Current		1.7	3.0	2.2	2.1	1.6
1.5	1.4		1.3			1.1	1.4	1.3	1.4	1.3
1.9	1.7		1.7			2.6	2.7	2.6	2.1	1.2
1.1	.9		.8	Quick		1.1	1.3	1.2	1.1	.7
.6	.5		.4			.5	.5	.4	.6	.4
29 12.8	27 13.6	24	15.1		4 82.8	10 35.1	24 15.3	24 14.9	28 13.2	
43 8.5	41 9.0	40	9.2	Sales/Receivables	36 10.0	24 15.5	37 9.8	41 8.9	41 8.8	
58 6.3	55 6.6	53	6.9		59 6.2	40 9.2	53 6.9	58 6.3	52 7.0	
39 9.4	46 7.9	49	7.4		31 11.8	32 11.4	40 9.1	37 9.8	61 6.0	
78 4.7	91 4.0	94	3.9	Cost of Sales/Inventory	101 3.6	83 4.4	99 3.7	87 4.2	104 3.5	
135 2.7	152 2.4	159	2.3		203 1.8	166 2.2	174 2.1	159 2.3	159 2.3	
14 26.7	14 25.8	13	29.0		8 43.6	5 71.4	9 38.9	12 29.5	13 27.8	
25 14.5	28 13.0	27	13.5	Cost of Sales/Payables	44 8.3	24 15.2	30 12.3	26 13.8	27 13.6	
42 8.6	47 7.8	49	7.5		101 3.6	52 7.0	65 5.6	49 7.4	45 8.1	
3.6	3.4		3.7			2.1	3.3	2.9	3.4	4.1
5.5	5.6		6.2	Sales/Working Capital		4.0	5.7	5.8	5.8	6.8
10.3	10.3		12.3			42.8	9.9	12.8	10.7	13.3
44.3	45.1		29.0			11.2	41.9	33.8	38.6	26.4
(496) 15.7	(658) 15.0	(750)	9.0	EBIT/Interest	(15) 3.3	(30) 13.3	(77) 9.1	(180) 10.4	(444) 8.7	
6.2	5.2		3.0			-.2	1.7	1.7	3.3	3.4
15.4	14.5		12.7	Net Profit + Depr., Dep.,				10.6	17.8	
(75) 6.8	(140) 6.1	(161)	4.8	Amort./Cur. Mat. L/T/D				(31) 6.7	(117) 4.6	
3.1	2.1		2.0					2.8	1.8	
.1	.1		.1			.0	.0	.0	.1	.1
.2	.2		.2	Fixed/Worth		.1	.1	.2	.2	.3
.6	.5		.6			1.2	.5	.6	.5	.8
.5	.6		.6			.6	.3	.4	.5	.9
1.3	1.2		1.5	Debt/Worth		1.7	.8	1.1	1.1	1.8
3.1	2.9		3.4			3.9	1.6	5.1	2.9	3.5
54.9	49.1		45.6			32.0	50.6	47.3	50.5	45.0
(540) 29.6	(746) 28.7	(810)	27.4	% Profit Before Taxes/Tangible Net Worth	(25) 10.6	(32) 23.2	(88) 29.9	(209) 26.3	(451) 28.3	
15.9	13.8		13.5			-2.9	10.0	13.5	11.9	16.7
21.6	21.4		18.4			11.7	22.6	19.1	20.8	17.0
12.3	11.7		10.0	% Profit Before Taxes/Total Assets		3.2	14.3	8.7	10.7	10.1
6.3	5.2		4.5			-2.1	3.7	2.6	5.0	5.0
74.5	90.8		84.7			117.7	959.3	117.0	104.0	56.5
26.7	32.2		27.2	Sales/Net Fixed Assets		36.8	105.6	43.2	37.3	23.3
10.6	12.1		10.1			10.5	25.8	11.6	14.6	9.0
2.8	2.7		2.7			2.1	4.3	3.0	2.9	2.3
2.1	2.1		1.9	Sales/Total Assets		1.4	2.5	1.9	2.1	1.8
1.5	1.4		1.3			.8	1.5	1.2	1.4	1.3
.5	.4		.4			.3	.1	.2	.3	.4
(394) 1.1	(511) .8	(612)	.8	% Depr., Dep., Amort./Sales	(19) .7	(16) .5	(56) .8	(157) .7	(360) .9	
2.5	1.7		2.0			2.9	1.0	1.9	1.7	2.4
1.2	1.1		.9			5.0	1.6	2.0	1.2	.5
(151) 2.2	(219) 2.1	(230)	2.0	% Officers', Directors', Owners' Comp/Sales	(10) 7.7	(19) 3.3	(44) 3.2	(77) 2.0	(78) .9	
4.1	4.5		3.7			10.5	5.5	6.0	3.6	2.1
26723759M	44281190M		54123086M	Net Sales ($)	5102M	56662M	157301M	711864M	3726036M	49466121M
15187946M	25256146M		31705237M	Total Assets ($)	4339M	76139M	72532M	493832M	2076662M	28981733M

© RMA 2024
M = $ thousand   MM = $ million
See Pages viii through xx for Explanation of Ratios and Data

WHOLESALE—Industrial Supplies Merchant Wholesalers   NAICS 423840

Current Data Sorted by Assets | Comparative Historical Data

							Type of Statement		
		1	3	14	10	5	Unqualified	28	21
			8	22	6		Reviewed	53	27
		7	23	11			Compiled	31	22
	3	5	25	6			Tax Returns	33	23
	2	12	43	43	15	22	Other	190	119
		50 (4/1-9/30/23)		236 (10/1/23-3/31/24)				4/1/19-3/31/20	4/1/20-3/31/21
0-500M	500M-2MM	2-10MM	10-50MM	50-100MM	100-250MM			ALL	ALL
							NUMBER OF STATEMENTS		
5	25	102	96	31	27			335	212
%	%	%	%	%	%		ASSETS	%	%
	13.3	13.1	11.0	4.4	5.4		Cash & Equivalents	7.5	11.8
	26.7	31.7	27.0	29.0	24.5		Trade Receivables (net)	29.6	28.1
	35.3	33.8	33.9	34.7	32.1		Inventory	37.9	34.5
	.6	2.2	3.5	2.6	2.7		All Other Current	2.3	2.0
	75.8	80.8	75.4	70.7	64.8		Total Current	77.2	76.5
	15.8	9.2	10.4	14.2	11.4		Fixed Assets (net)	13.0	12.0
	3.6	3.7	6.2	6.0	12.0		Intangibles (net)	4.9	6.3
	4.8	6.2	8.0	9.0	11.8		All Other Non-Current	4.9	5.3
	100.0	100.0	100.0	100.0	100.0		Total	100.0	100.0
							LIABILITIES		
	3.6	7.6	7.2	9.7	13.9		Notes Payable-Short Term	13.0	9.3
	18.0	1.4	1.4	1.2	.9		Cur. Mat.-L.T.D.	1.7	2.5
	15.0	18.0	12.5	16.1	11.7		Trade Payables	17.2	16.1
	.0	.2	.3	.1	.1		Income Taxes Payable	.2	.1
	16.8	10.5	11.8	13.6	13.7		All Other Current	8.0	8.4
	53.5	37.7	33.2	40.7	40.2		Total Current	40.1	36.4
	12.5	6.3	9.6	8.6	8.4		Long-Term Debt	11.0	13.9
	.0	.3	.2	.9	.2		Deferred Taxes	.2	.1
	1.4	4.7	5.4	5.4	13.6		All Other Non-Current	4.1	4.1
	32.7	51.0	51.7	44.4	37.5		Net Worth	44.6	45.5
	100.0	100.0	100.0	100.0	100.0		Total Liabilities & Net Worth	100.0	100.0
							INCOME DATA		
	100.0	100.0	100.0	100.0	100.0		Net Sales	100.0	100.0
	33.6	33.1	32.4	28.0	36.0		Gross Profit	30.2	30.1
	29.2	25.5	25.1	22.9	29.7		Operating Expenses	25.5	26.4
	4.4	7.6	7.2	5.0	6.3		Operating Profit	4.7	3.8
	.7	.0	.4	.4	1.5		All Other Expenses (net)	.3	-.4
	3.7	7.6	6.9	4.6	4.8		Profit Before Taxes	4.4	4.2
							RATIOS		
	7.5	4.0	3.9	3.4	2.6			3.2	3.9
	2.9	2.4	2.4	1.7	1.7		Current	2.0	2.4
	.8	1.5	1.7	1.2	1.3			1.4	1.6
	5.2	2.4	1.9	1.6	1.4			1.6	2.0
	1.4	1.3	1.1	.8	.8		Quick	1.0	1.2
	.4	.7	.7	.6	.6			.6	.7
24	15.1	30	12.2	33	11.0	39	9.3	44	8.3			32	11.3	32	11.4
33	10.9	41	9.0	46	8.0	47	7.8	48	7.6		Sales/Receivables	42	8.6	42	8.7
47	7.8	54	6.7	62	5.9	53	6.9	54	6.7			52	7.0	56	6.5
52	7.0	32	11.3	54	6.7	42	8.6	62	5.9			47	7.7	43	8.4
79	4.6	65	5.6	99	3.7	74	4.9	111	3.3		Cost of Sales/Inventory	74	4.9	72	5.1
111	3.3	140	2.6	146	2.5	89	4.1	215	1.7			135	2.7	135	2.7
7	50.1	15	24.4	15	24.2	24	15.4	22	16.7			18	20.0	16	22.4
20	18.0	28	13.2	29	12.7	35	10.5	31	11.7		Cost of Sales/Payables	31	11.6	27	13.3
35	10.3	45	8.2	41	8.8	45	8.2	58	6.3			48	7.6	46	8.0
	2.5	3.7	3.2	4.5	3.8			4.1	3.6
	6.6	6.7	5.0	7.4	5.4		Sales/Working Capital	6.6	5.4
	-64.9	11.9	8.7	16.6	12.5			12.3	10.9
	18.7	82.5	27.3	44.2	39.1			22.3	34.4
(19)	3.8	(79) 17.1	(71) 9.5	(28) 10.1	(26) 2.9		EBIT/Interest	(295) 7.8	(195) 9.8
	-.2	4.7	3.7	4.6	1.9			2.9	2.8
		8.3	28.3	7.3				11.2	12.4
	(11)	3.8	(23) 5.1	(13) 4.3			Net Profit + Depr., Dep., Amort./Cur. Mat. L/T/D	(62) 4.3	(40) 3.3
		1.3	2.3	3.6				1.4	.7
	.0	.0	.1	.1	.1			.1	.1
	.1	.1	.2	.3	.7		Fixed/Worth	.2	.2
	-.9	.4	.5	.6	-.6			.7	.7
	.2	.3	.4	.4	.5			.6	.5
	1.1	.9	.9	2.4	3.1		Debt/Worth	1.3	1.2
	-3.8	2.2	2.7	3.1	-10.4			3.1	3.1
	36.2	55.3	46.8	38.1	29.5			43.0	42.1
(17)	15.9	(93) 33.7	(86) 23.6	(29) 28.2	(17) 22.4		% Profit Before Taxes/Tangible Net Worth	(307) 21.7	(189) 23.1
	8.3	16.2	13.5	15.6	9.0			10.6	8.7
	20.1	26.1	19.4	14.2	13.7			16.0	18.0
	8.1	14.2	10.9	8.8	7.0		% Profit Before Taxes/Total Assets	8.9	9.6
	-6.6	6.4	5.8	6.2	2.1			3.4	2.5
	UND	234.4	85.8	51.7	55.5			98.3	88.1
	56.6	57.6	31.8	24.8	31.0		Sales/Net Fixed Assets	31.2	32.2
	10.6	22.1	12.5	10.3	14.8			11.5	12.4
	3.4	3.8	2.5	2.8	2.0			3.3	3.2
	2.1	2.7	2.1	2.3	1.8		Sales/Total Assets	2.5	2.2
	1.5	2.1	1.5	1.5	1.2			1.7	1.6
	.2	.2	.5	.4	.4			.3	.4
(13)	1.0	(65) .6	(74) .9	(29) .5	(18) 1.4		% Depr., Dep., Amort./Sales	(253) .8	(146) .9
	1.7	1.2	1.5	1.3	2.6			1.5	1.7
	3.9	1.1	1.1					1.0	1.3
(11)	5.6	(41) 2.2	(18) 1.8				% Officers', Directors' Owners' Comp/Sales	(93) 2.3	(60) 2.4
	11.3	3.8	2.7					4.0	6.5
6341M	78254M	1503397M	4668539M	5202339M	7876525M		Net Sales ($)	18412967M	9682022M
946M	30570M	540083M	2291952M	2223893M	4762683M		Total Assets ($)	8541442M	5037258M

© RMA 2024

M = $ thousand   MM = $ million
See Pages viii through xx for Explanation of Ratios and Data

WHOLESALE—Industrial Supplies Merchant Wholesalers NAICS 423840

Comparative Historical Data

			Type of Statement
18	22	33	Unqualified
31	44	36	Reviewed
30	34	41	Compiled
23	30	39	Tax Returns
104	133	137	Other
4/1/21-3/31/22 ALL	4/1/22-3/31/23 ALL	4/1/23-3/31/24 ALL	
206	263	286	NUMBER OF STATEMENTS

Current Data Sorted by Sales

	1		1	4	27
			2	11	23
	3	2	3	23	10
2	4	4	4	18	7
2	11	6	16	28	74
	50 (4/1-9/30/23)		236 (10/1/23-3/31/24)		
0-1MM	1-3MM	3-5MM	5-10MM	10-25MM	25MM & OVER
4	19	12	26	84	141

Combined Table

Hist %	Hist %	Hist %	Category	%	%	%	%	%	%
			ASSETS						
11.1	10.1	10.9	Cash & Equivalents	14.8	10.8	21.1	12.4	7.4	
29.9	29.7	28.2	Trade Receivables (net)		16.1	26.9	28.7	30.4	29.2
35.7	37.7	33.9	Inventory		32.6	36.9	30.7	35.5	33.1
2.5	2.6	2.6	All Other Current		.6	1.4	5.3	2.2	2.7
79.2	80.1	75.6	Total Current		64.0	76.0	85.8	80.6	72.5
10.7	10.4	11.1	Fixed Assets (net)		26.6	6.5	6.4	10.1	10.7
4.6	4.8	5.5	Intangibles (net)		3.5	2.7	4.5	3.3	7.7
5.5	4.6	7.8	All Other Non-Current		5.8	14.7	3.3	6.1	9.1
100.0	100.0	100.0	Total		100.0	100.0	100.0	100.0	100.0
			LIABILITIES						
7.6	8.0	8.3	Notes Payable-Short Term		2.7	4.9	4.0	8.3	9.4
1.5	1.5	3.5	Cur. Mat.-L.T.D.		22.4	.1	1.2	1.8	1.2
16.1	16.0	14.8	Trade Payables		10.9	10.6	12.3	16.8	15.2
.2	.1	.2	Income Taxes Payable		.0	.0	.2	.3	.1
7.8	9.0	12.3	All Other Current		24.6	6.3	6.7	11.6	12.4
33.2	34.6	39.0	Total Current		60.6	21.9	24.4	38.9	38.3
9.4	10.4	8.7	Long-Term Debt		17.4	5.9	4.7	7.7	9.1
.2	.3	.3	Deferred Taxes		.0	.0	.3	.3	.3
3.7	4.0	5.8	All Other Non-Current		.2	16.1	.5	3.8	7.4
53.4	50.8	46.2	Net Worth		21.8	56.1	70.1	49.4	44.9
100.0	100.0	100.0	Total Liabilities & Net Worth		100.0	100.0	100.0	100.0	100.0
			INCOME DATA						
100.0	100.0	100.0	Net Sales		100.0	100.0	100.0	100.0	100.0
30.8	30.7	32.5	Gross Profit		38.8	37.3	39.3	31.8	30.6
25.2	23.9	25.8	Operating Expenses		34.4	29.3	27.0	24.9	24.6
5.7	6.7	6.7	Operating Profit		4.5	8.0	12.3	6.9	6.0
-1.5	-.1	.4	All Other Expenses (net)		1.0	.2	-.7	-.2	.8
7.2	6.8	6.4	Profit Before Taxes		3.4	7.8	13.0	7.1	5.2
			RATIOS						
3.8	4.0	3.9			9.7	10.7	12.3	3.8	3.1
2.5	2.4	2.3	Current		2.4	4.9	3.6	2.2	2.0
1.8	1.6	1.5			.3	1.7	2.4	1.5	1.4
2.1	2.0	1.9			7.1	4.7	5.7	1.9	1.7
1.3	1.2	1.1	Quick		1.0	2.5	2.2	1.2	.9
.8	.7	.7			.2	.6	1.4	.8	.7
34 10.7	33 11.1	32 11.5		12 29.6	33 11.1	29 12.5	30 12.2	35 10.3	
45 8.1	45 8.2	43 8.4	Sales/Receivables	24 15.0	43 8.5	46 7.9	39 9.4	47 7.8	
54 6.8	61 6.0	55 6.6		41 8.8	53 6.9	60 6.1	54 6.7	55 6.6	
47 7.8	43 8.4	45 8.1		59 6.2	58 6.3	46 7.9	40 9.2	48 7.6	
72 5.1	79 4.6	78 4.7	Cost of Sales/Inventory	83 4.4	111 3.3	89 4.1	74 4.9	74 4.9	
126 2.9	140 2.6	135 2.7		146 2.5	215 1.7	146 2.5	135 2.7	122 3.0	
19 19.2	17 22.1	16 23.3		0 UND	19 19.4	8 44.3	15 24.0	19 19.1	
30 12.3	30 12.1	29 12.8	Cost of Sales/Payables	12 30.9	21 17.2	24 15.0	29 12.4	31 11.8	
46 7.9	49 7.5	42 8.7		33 11.0	40 9.2	44 8.3	42 8.7	43 8.4	
3.6	3.4	3.7			1.9	2.1	2.0	3.7	4.0
5.3	5.3	5.9	Sales/Working Capital		15.6	3.8	3.4	5.8	7.0
9.4	8.9	12.1			-1.4	12.2	5.9	11.3	11.9
78.0	55.6	41.5			16.5		464.3	45.3	37.2
(174) 25.4	(217) 15.5	(225) 9.9	EBIT/Interest	(12) .3		(17) 80.0	(67) 16.1	(119) 7.9	
7.7	5.0	3.0			-.3		5.6	5.0	2.7
13.4	21.7	20.4	Net Profit + Depr., Dep.,					18.7	18.5
(38) 5.1	(41) 4.7	(53) 4.9	Amort./Cur. Mat. L/T/D				(14) 4.4	(37) 4.7	
3.2	2.1	2.2						1.8	2.3
.1	.0	.1			.1	.0	.0	.0	.1
.2	.1	.2	Fixed/Worth		2.6	.1	.1	.1	.2
.4	.4	.7			-.9	.6	.2	.4	.8
.4	.4	.4			.2	.1	.1	.4	.6
.8	1.0	1.1	Debt/Worth		2.0	.5	.4	.9	1.4
2.0	2.4	3.3			-2.6	2.4	1.1	2.8	3.6
50.8	48.1	48.0	% Profit Before Taxes/Tangible		37.0	61.1	48.4	49.2	46.6
(192) 27.6	(243) 27.9	(245) 27.6	Net Worth	(12) 16.9	(11) 25.2	(25) 18.9	(77) 32.8	(118) 25.8	
14.6	10.9	14.3			4.4	10.7	8.1	15.8	14.7
25.7	24.6	21.3	% Profit Before Taxes/Total		15.9	23.7	27.0	25.0	18.7
14.3	12.1	11.1	Assets		6.6	15.1	15.8	13.7	9.6
7.1	4.7	4.9			-6.9	6.0	6.5	7.6	4.8
97.2	136.7	118.6			56.6	UND	215.6	150.2	72.0
39.6	40.4	37.0	Sales/Net Fixed Assets		20.8	64.6	87.0	40.9	32.9
13.6	13.5	14.4			2.2	26.1	15.6	14.2	14.9
3.2	3.1	3.1			3.1	2.7	3.0	3.4	2.8
2.5	2.3	2.3	Sales/Total Assets		1.8	1.7	2.4	2.3	2.3
1.7	1.6	1.6			1.3	1.4	1.5	2.0	1.6
.4	.2	.3			.9		.2	.2	.4
(158) .8	(197) .7	(202) .7	% Depr., Dep., Amort./Sales	(11) 1.7		(14) .9	(59) .6	(109) .7	
1.6	1.2	1.4			1.7		2.0	1.1	1.5
1.6	1.1	1.2					1.1	1.3	.9
(57) 2.6	(76) 2.1	(74) 2.4	% Officers', Directors' Owners' Comp/Sales		(10) 2.4	(31) 2.3	(20) 1.2		
4.6	3.9	4.1					4.8	3.7	2.5
9377964M	12706974M	19335395M	Net Sales ($)	2843M	36440M	50464M	182923M	1430191M	17632534M
4354019M	6807132M	9850127M	Total Assets ($)	2710M	20525M	27120M	128771M	622139M	9048862M

© RMA 2024
M = $ thousand MM = $ million
See Pages viii through xx for Explanation of Ratios and Data

WHOLESALE—Service Establishment Equipment and Supplies Merchant Wholesalers NAICS 423850

Current Data Sorted by Assets

				1			Type of Statement	Comparative Historical Data	
		7	5	1			Unqualified	2	5
	2	6	3				Reviewed	19	12
3	3	4	1				Compiled	10	9
	7	19	15	3	2		Tax Returns	20	12
	19 (4/1-9/30/23)		63 (10/1/23-3/31/24)				Other	58	38
0-500M	500M-2MM	2-10MM	10-50MM	50-100MM	100-250MM			4/1/19-3/31/20 ALL	4/1/20-3/31/21 ALL
3	12	36	24	5	2		NUMBER OF STATEMENTS	109	76
%	%	%	%	%	%		ASSETS	%	%
	26.0	16.8	13.7				Cash & Equivalents	9.7	17.5
	11.0	26.9	26.0				Trade Receivables (net)	30.9	23.6
	39.6	34.5	33.7				Inventory	34.1	32.9
	4.5	2.3	2.9				All Other Current	3.6	2.5
	81.1	80.5	76.4				Total Current	78.3	76.4
	3.1	12.4	10.9				Fixed Assets (net)	10.4	10.5
	3.9	2.6	5.0				Intangibles (net)	6.6	7.9
	11.9	4.5	7.7				All Other Non-Current	4.7	5.2
	100.0	100.0	100.0				Total	100.0	100.0
							LIABILITIES		
	8.1	5.3	11.4				Notes Payable-Short Term	11.3	11.3
	1.6	5.0	3.0				Cur. Mat.-L.T.D.	2.0	2.6
	15.4	21.4	12.3				Trade Payables	17.2	12.6
	.0	.2	.1				Income Taxes Payable	.3	.0
	9.0	10.1	15.0				All Other Current	14.1	11.1
	34.0	41.9	41.8				Total Current	44.9	37.6
	9.1	13.3	7.2				Long-Term Debt	15.1	12.9
	.1	.1	.1				Deferred Taxes	.1	.1
	10.1	1.7	5.3				All Other Non-Current	6.9	2.5
	46.8	43.1	45.5				Net Worth	33.0	47.0
	100.0	100.0	100.0				Total Liabilties & Net Worth	100.0	100.0
							INCOME DATA		
	100.0	100.0	100.0				Net Sales	100.0	100.0
	38.5	34.2	32.7				Gross Profit	32.9	32.9
	29.6	28.6	25.9				Operating Expenses	28.5	27.5
	8.9	5.6	6.9				Operating Profit	4.4	5.4
	-.1	.1	-.6				All Other Expenses (net)	.2	-1.1
	9.0	5.5	7.4				Profit Before Taxes	4.2	6.5
							RATIOS		
	4.0	3.4	6.1					3.2	4.5
	2.5	2.6	1.7			Current		1.8	2.1
	1.5	1.3	1.2					1.3	1.4
	1.9	2.1	3.3					1.5	2.5
	1.2	1.4	1.1			Quick	(108)	1.0	1.1
	.3	.6	.5					.6	.7
0	UND	21	17.5	28	13.2			25	14.6	18	20.0
3	126.7	33	11.2	34	10.8		Sales/Receivables	36	10.2	29	12.4
22	16.6	43	8.4	52	7.0			51	7.2	49	7.4
28	12.9	40	9.2	45	8.2			32	11.3	36	10.1
46	7.9	63	5.8	74	4.9		Cost of Sales/Inventory	60	6.1	61	6.0
135	2.7	104	3.5	118	3.1			101	3.6	101	3.6
0	UND	21	17.2	11	32.2			16	22.4	11	34.2
21	17.1	39	9.4	25	14.8		Cost of Sales/Payables	29	12.6	21	17.4
35	10.4	55	6.6	43	8.5			43	8.4	36	10.2
	5.7	4.1	3.1					4.6	4.0
	10.0	6.6	4.9			Sales/Working Capital		8.4	7.5
	13.2	20.9	14.8					18.6	13.5
		37.7	60.6					17.0	40.7
		(30)	8.2	(20)	10.8		EBIT/Interest	(87)	5.7	(56)	6.4
		2.0	1.8					2.1	2.1
								34.3	
							Net Profit + Depr., Dep., Amort./Cur. Mat. L/T/D	(14)	5.7	
								2.1	
	.0	.1	.1					.1	.1
	.0	.1	.2			Fixed/Worth		.2	.2
	.3	1.3	.9					.7	.8
	.4	.5	.4					1.0	.4
	.8	1.5	1.9			Debt/Worth		2.4	1.4
	2.0	5.2	6.8					4.7	6.3
	77.9	67.3	35.6					45.9	63.7
(11)	45.0	(33)	27.7	22.9			% Profit Before Taxes/Tangible Net Worth	(95)	25.6	(66)	32.8
	40.4	6.6	5.0					11.9	13.0
	37.4	22.2	18.6					19.1	27.4
	25.3	10.7	9.6			% Profit Before Taxes/Total Assets		8.4	11.0
	15.3	3.1	1.2					2.5	3.1
	UND	99.0	70.1					118.8	157.7
	485.7	42.5	23.3			Sales/Net Fixed Assets		55.8	48.4
	104.3	19.1	10.6					22.6	20.3
	5.5	3.7	2.8					3.9	3.4
	4.0	2.9	1.9			Sales/Total Assets		2.9	2.6
	2.5	2.2	1.4					1.9	1.9
		.3	.4					.4	.3
		(22)	.7	(20)	.9		% Depr., Dep., Amort./Sales	(79)	.7	(49)	.7
		1.8	1.9					1.2	1.6
			1.1					1.4	1.4
		(13)	1.6			% Officers', Directors' Owners' Comp/Sales	(46)	2.5	(31)	2.8
			2.3					4.5	5.9
8846M	67229M	497168M	997928M	834459M	688091M		Net Sales ($)	4552827M	2968397M
823M	16574M	174495M	516647M	349526M	361055M		Total Assets ($)	1868151M	1438860M

M = $ thousand MM = $ million
See Pages viii through xx for Explanation of Ratios and Data

© RMA 2024

WHOLESALE—Service Establishment Equipment and Supplies Merchant Wholesalers NAICS 423850

Comparative Historical Data / Current Data Sorted by Sales

Comparative Historical Data						Current Data Sorted by Sales					
				Type of Statement							
	4	8	1	Unqualified							1
	14	14	13	Reviewed			1		1	4	7
	5	8	11	Compiled					5	5	1
	8	9	11	Tax Returns	1	2	2	3	3	3	
	28	42	46	Other	1	1	3	8	15	18	
	4/1/21-3/31/22	4/1/22-3/31/23	4/1/23-3/31/24			19 (4/1-9/30/23)			63 (10/1/23-3/31/24)		
	ALL	ALL	ALL		0-1MM	1-3MM	3-5MM	5-10MM	10-25MM	25MM & OVER
	59	81	82	**NUMBER OF STATEMENTS**	2	4	5	17	27	27
	%	%	%	**ASSETS**	%	%	%	%	%	%
	15.3	12.5	17.6	Cash & Equivalents				19.7	16.5	14.6
	23.8	28.6	24.1	Trade Receivables (net)				23.1	27.8	25.6
	34.1	32.4	34.2	Inventory				34.2	37.1	31.3
	3.5	4.0	3.2	All Other Current				3.5	3.4	2.9
	76.7	77.5	79.1	Total Current				80.5	84.9	74.4
	10.3	9.3	9.9	Fixed Assets (net)				11.7	8.0	10.9
	7.8	7.4	3.9	Intangibles (net)				1.8	2.0	6.4
	5.1	5.8	7.1	All Other Non-Current				6.0	5.1	8.2
	100.0	100.0	100.0	Total				100.0	100.0	100.0
				LIABILITIES						
	10.4	8.7	7.6	Notes Payable-Short Term				6.0	6.0	11.2
	2.0	2.9	3.4	Cur. Mat.-L.T.D.				2.4	7.3	1.2
	16.8	20.6	17.1	Trade Payables				14.9	22.9	14.4
	.1	.3	.1	Income Taxes Payable				.0	.2	.1
	11.5	13.2	11.4	All Other Current				17.2	9.3	11.7
	40.8	45.8	39.6	Total Current				40.6	45.8	38.6
	10.7	14.4	11.0	Long-Term Debt				19.7	8.6	7.5
	.0	.1	.1	Deferred Taxes				.1	.0	.2
	14.4	3.3	5.0	All Other Non-Current				2.9	2.8	5.9
	34.2	36.5	44.4	Net Worth				36.7	42.8	47.8
	100.0	100.0	100.0	Total Liabilities & Net Worth				100.0	100.0	100.0
				INCOME DATA						
	100.0	100.0	100.0	Net Sales				100.0	100.0	100.0
	29.4	33.0	34.5	Gross Profit				38.1	31.5	29.8
	25.0	28.3	28.3	Operating Expenses				30.2	26.4	24.7
	4.4	4.7	6.2	Operating Profit				7.9	5.1	5.1
	-1.0	.5	-.1	All Other Expenses (net)				-.1	-.1	-.1
	5.3	4.2	6.3	Profit Before Taxes				8.0	5.3	5.2
				RATIOS						
	3.1	2.8	4.0					4.2	3.1	5.8
	2.0	1.7	2.2	Current				1.8	2.1	1.7
	1.4	1.3	1.4					1.6	1.4	1.2
	1.6	1.6	2.3					1.8	1.6	2.7
	1.0	.9	1.2	Quick				1.3	1.1	1.0
	.7	.6	.5					.5	.5	.5
13	29.0	28	13.0	19	18.9				9	38.9	22	16.4	29	12.6
33	11.1	39	9.4	31	11.8	Sales/Receivables			21	17.5	31	11.9	35	10.3
46	8.0	53	6.9	43	8.4				41	8.8	43	8.4	44	8.3
31	11.6	31	11.9	44	8.3				20	18.6	45	8.1	45	8.2
57	6.4	62	5.9	65	5.6	Cost of Sales/Inventory			74	4.9	55	6.6	69	5.3
99	3.7	140	2.6	104	3.5				104	3.5	94	3.9	85	4.3
13	28.6	19	19.2	12	29.3				11	32.7	19	19.1	11	31.9
26	14.1	34	10.8	31	11.9	Cost of Sales/Payables			24	15.0	38	9.5	29	12.7
43	8.4	62	5.9	47	7.7				41	9.0	60	6.1	40	9.2
	4.2		4.6		3.8	Sales/Working Capital				3.6		4.6		3.8
	7.7		7.6		6.8					7.5		6.6		8.2
	15.2		19.4		13.6					24.1		12.2		15.1
	74.1		49.2		43.7					79.7		47.1		19.2
(45)	20.9	(68)	9.7	(67)	8.9	EBIT/Interest			(14)	25.5	(24)	11.1	(23)	4.9
	7.0		4.0		2.5					3.6		3.6		1.8
			23.2		9.2	Net Profit + Depr., Dep.,								
		(13)	5.3	(11)	4.6	Amort./Cur. Mat. L/T/D								
			2.2		1.0									
	.0		.1		.0					.1		.0		.1
	.2		.2		.1	Fixed/Worth				.1		.1		.3
	.4		.7		.6					1.7		.6		.5
	.5		.9		.5					.9		.5		.5
	1.4		2.3		1.6	Debt/Worth				2.0		1.3		1.7
	6.2		8.0		4.7					5.6		4.6		3.6
	57.7		54.3		47.2	% Profit Before Taxes/Tangible				121.5		67.3		31.9
(48)	33.5	(71)	26.8	(78)	26.3	Net Worth			(16)	42.7	(25)	34.5		22.6
	14.8		10.9		7.3					13.7		9.9		4.6
	26.5		21.1		21.3	% Profit Before Taxes/Total				28.2		29.0		17.5
	14.3		7.6		11.0	Assets				21.7		11.0		8.0
	5.4		2.7		2.9					5.8		3.2		1.6
	129.3		140.0		142.4					128.3		165.9		63.5
	62.1		53.5		47.2	Sales/Net Fixed Assets				59.3		46.7		28.8
	26.7		22.3		18.6					17.8		21.0		13.1
	3.7		3.6		3.4					4.4		3.8		3.0
	2.8		2.5		2.8	Sales/Total Assets				3.0		3.0		2.6
	2.0		1.8		1.8					2.0		2.1		1.8
	.3		.3		.3							.3		.4
(39)	.5	(61)	.6	(52)	.7	% Depr., Dep., Amort./Sales					(18)	.7	(22)	.8
	1.2		1.2		1.5							1.8		1.1
	1.7		1.0		1.3	% Officers', Directors'						1.2		
(19)	2.5	(28)	2.0	(27)	1.7	Owners' Comp/Sales					(10)	1.6		
	5.5		4.3		3.9							3.0		
	2615679M		3036514M		3093721M	Net Sales ($)	930M	7601M	18184M	128954M	450580M	2487472M
	1188703M		1502725M		1419120M	Total Assets ($)	970M	10109M	5947M	64322M	185394M	1152378M

© RMA 2024
M = $ thousand   MM = $ million
See Pages viii through xx for Explanation of Ratios and Data

WHOLESALE—Transportation Equipment and Supplies (except Motor Vehicle) Merchant Wholesalers NAICS 423860

Current Data Sorted by Assets | **Comparative Historical Data**

							Type of Statement				
			4	1	4		Unqualified		15	4	
		2	7	3	1		Reviewed		8	6	
		4	2				Compiled		10	6	
3	3	5	2				Tax Returns		14	7	
	5	18	14	26	6	4	Other		48	35	
		18 (4/1-9/30/23)		78 (10/1/23-3/31/24)					4/1/19-3/31/20	4/1/20-3/31/21	
0-500M	500M-2MM	2-10MM	10-50MM	50-100MM	100-250MM				ALL	ALL	
3	8	25	41	10	9		NUMBER OF STATEMENTS		95	58	
%	%	%	%	%	%		ASSETS		%	%	
		10.4	15.9	9.2			Cash & Equivalents		10.0	17.8	
		23.1	15.3	12.4			Trade Receivables (net)		21.9	17.0	
		36.0	38.1	43.8			Inventory		40.4	36.9	
		.9	2.0	4.9			All Other Current		3.0	2.2	
		70.3	71.3	70.3			Total Current		75.3	74.0	
		17.1	16.3	16.7			Fixed Assets (net)		14.2	14.7	
		3.2	7.3	2.1			Intangibles (net)		5.2	5.5	
		9.4	5.1	10.8			All Other Non-Current		5.3	5.8	
		100.0	100.0	100.0			Total		100.0	100.0	
							LIABILITIES				
		12.5	9.3	16.6			Notes Payable-Short Term		11.1	18.2	
		3.7	2.8	1.7			Cur. Mat.-L.T.D.		2.8	2.9	
		19.2	12.1	7.3			Trade Payables		15.1	13.0	
		.0	.0	.0			Income Taxes Payable		.2	.1	
		6.8	10.6	11.4			All Other Current		9.2	8.4	
		42.2	34.9	37.0			Total Current		38.3	42.6	
		17.5	10.0	16.0			Long-Term Debt		15.6	18.0	
		.3	.1	.4			Deferred Taxes		.4	.1	
		3.2	4.1	7.3			All Other Non-Current		4.0	4.2	
		36.8	50.9	39.2			Net Worth		41.8	35.0	
		100.0	100.0	100.0			Total Liabilities & Net Worth		100.0	100.0	
							INCOME DATA				
		100.0	100.0	100.0			Net Sales		100.0	100.0	
		32.2	30.8	39.6			Gross Profit		28.7	34.1	
		24.3	21.0	22.5			Operating Expenses		21.5	29.0	
		7.9	9.8	17.2			Operating Profit		7.2	5.1	
		.3	.8	-.1			All Other Expenses (net)		1.2	.2	
		7.6	9.0	17.2			Profit Before Taxes		6.0	5.0	
							RATIOS				
		3.2	5.4	5.0					3.3	4.5	
		1.8	1.9	2.5			Current		1.9	2.1	
		1.0	1.4	1.1					1.4	1.1	
		1.4	1.6	2.2					1.4	1.8	
		.7	.7	.5			Quick		.7	.9	
		.4	.4	.2					.4	.4	
		18 19.9	15 24.4	17 21.0					18 20.5	10 36.1	
		31 11.7	36 10.1	41 8.8			Sales/Receivables		37 9.8	32 11.3	
		62 5.9	49 7.5	72 5.1					51 7.1	57 6.4	
		27 13.7	52 7.0	69 5.3					49 7.4	33 11.1	
		81 4.5	89 4.1	111 3.3			Cost of Sales/Inventory		89 4.1	122 3.0	
		126 2.9	174 2.1	730 .5					174 2.1	228 1.6	
		21 17.3	20 18.6	17 21.2					16 23.3	18 19.8	
		29 12.5	29 12.7	32 11.3			Cost of Sales/Payables		32 11.3	29 12.6	
		52 7.0	49 7.5	64 5.7					48 7.6	56 6.5	
		4.0	2.3	1.1					3.5	2.3	
		7.0	4.5	4.1			Sales/Working Capital		6.6	5.3	
		NM	14.0	NM					14.0	35.6	
		21.2	26.8						25.4	13.4	
		(24) 7.8	(34) 8.4				EBIT/Interest	(83)	7.2	(48) 4.7	
		1.8	2.4						2.7	1.9	
							Net Profit + Depr., Dep., Amort./Cur. Mat. L/T/D		12.7		
								(14)	3.4		
									.7		
		.0	.0	.1					.0	.1	
		.2	.2	.2			Fixed/Worth		.2	.2	
		1.5	1.0	1.2					.9	1.4	
		.8	.4	.8					.9	.6	
		1.6	1.2	2.1			Debt/Worth		1.5	2.1	
		4.9	2.4	5.6					3.2	9.4	
		53.0	44.6	84.7					50.1	41.1	
		(21) 27.3	(38) 29.1	38.5			% Profit Before Taxes/Tangible Net Worth	(86)	27.0	(49) 21.8	
		12.0	13.9	24.7					14.0	3.9	
		26.3	19.2	31.1					20.8	17.0	
		10.1	14.0	11.3			% Profit Before Taxes/Total Assets		9.6	7.5	
		2.4	4.6	5.6					2.8	1.0	
		212.2	145.7	56.6					146.4	113.8	
		41.2	24.2	10.9			Sales/Net Fixed Assets		31.5	25.0	
		6.9	6.6	2.6					11.2	8.9	
		2.9	2.3	2.3					3.3	2.5	
		2.2	1.7	1.3			Sales/Total Assets		2.1	1.7	
		1.5	1.1	.7					1.2	1.0	
		.2	.4						.3	.5	
		(20) .5	(29) 1.0				% Depr., Dep., Amort./Sales	(75)	.8	(36) .9	
		2.0	2.3						2.5	3.1	
		1.2							.9	1.8	
		(12) 2.1					% Officers', Directors' Owners' Comp/Sales	(29)	2.6	(16) 4.0	
		3.4							4.1	6.3	
4188M	37239M	361879M	1911256M	1025502M	1906870M		Net Sales ($)		3382545M	1887988M	
612M	10323M	148207M	1100951M	734337M	1491053M		Total Assets ($)		2092021M	1148819M	

© RMA 2024   M = $ thousand   MM = $ million
See Pages viii through xx for Explanation of Ratios and Data

WHOLESALE—Transportation Equipment and Supplies (except Motor Vehicle) Merchant Wholesalers NAICS 423860

Comparative Historical Data / Current Data Sorted by Sales

				Type of Statement							
	2	7	9	Unqualified						3	9
	9	10	13	Reviewed						1	10
	7	9	6	Compiled			1		1	1	3
	10	10	13	Tax Returns				3	3	4	1
	43	48	55	Other	2	1		5	6	10	32
	4/1/21-3/31/22 ALL	4/1/22-3/31/23 ALL	4/1/23-3/31/24 ALL			18 (4/1-9/30/23)			78 (10/1/23-3/31/24)		
					0-1MM	1-3MM	3-5MM	5-10MM			25MM & OVER
	71	84	96	NUMBER OF STATEMENTS	3	2	8	10	18	55
	%	%	%	ASSETS	%	%	%	%	%	%
	17.8	16.7	13.5	Cash & Equivalents				10.1	9.0	12.5
	17.6	15.7	18.7	Trade Receivables (net)				14.0	26.1	17.5
	39.6	40.4	37.6	Inventory				43.6	40.4	39.7
	2.8	4.2	2.4	All Other Current				.1	1.2	3.7
	77.7	76.9	72.1	Total Current				67.9	76.7	73.3
	14.8	13.7	16.2	Fixed Assets (net)				15.9	11.2	14.6
	3.9	4.7	4.9	Intangibles (net)				3.2	8.2	4.3
	3.6	4.8	6.7	All Other Non-Current				13.0	3.9	7.7
	100.0	100.0	100.0	Total				100.0	100.0	100.0
				LIABILITIES						
	12.2	11.0	12.7	Notes Payable-Short Term				11.2	8.9	15.6
	2.5	2.1	2.5	Cur. Mat.-L.T.D.				8.1	1.3	2.0
	12.6	13.0	15.6	Trade Payables				23.6	12.5	13.5
	.2	.1	.1	Income Taxes Payable				.1	.1	.1
	16.3	12.6	14.9	All Other Current				7.8	9.2	10.0
	43.8	38.8	45.8	Total Current				50.8	32.1	41.2
	12.8	14.6	12.8	Long-Term Debt				21.2	10.6	10.8
	.4	.2	.2	Deferred Taxes				.0	.0	.2
	2.6	6.9	3.9	All Other Non-Current				1.4	6.4	4.2
	40.3	39.5	37.3	Net Worth				26.6	50.9	43.6
	100.0	100.0	100.0	Total Liabilities & Net Worth				100.0	100.0	100.0
				INCOME DATA						
	100.0	100.0	100.0	Net Sales				100.0	100.0	100.0
	32.3	35.0	31.9	Gross Profit				36.7	34.1	28.3
	26.5	26.3	22.5	Operating Expenses				29.8	24.9	17.9
	5.9	8.8	9.5	Operating Profit				6.9	9.2	10.4
	-.5	.2	.6	All Other Expenses (net)				1.1	-.9	.7
	6.3	8.6	8.8	Profit Before Taxes				5.8	10.1	9.8
				RATIOS						
	4.0	4.8	3.5					1.9	6.6	3.6
	2.1	2.6	1.8	Current				1.3	2.9	1.8
	1.4	1.4	1.1					.5	2.0	1.2
	1.7	2.1	1.4					.7	1.9	1.3
	.9	.9	.6	Quick				.3	1.3	.6
	.4	.3	.4					.2	.8	.4
20	18.6	16	22.5	19	19.4			0	UND	27	13.4	20	18.6
43	8.5	31	11.9	35	10.3	Sales/Receivables	25	14.5	42	8.7	36	10.0
63	5.8	42	8.6	60	6.1		33	11.0	72	5.1	51	7.2
64	5.7	58	6.3	46	8.0		68	5.4	39	9.3	51	7.1
126	2.9	135	2.7	94	3.9	Cost of Sales/Inventory	111	3.3	122	3.0	94	3.9
243	1.5	228	1.6	174	2.1		215	1.7	159	2.3	203	1.8
16	23.4	11	34.0	19	18.8		36	10.2	23	15.8	19	19.4
34	10.8	34	10.6	32	11.4	Cost of Sales/Payables	43	8.4	28	13.1	32	11.4
65	5.6	58	6.3	50	7.3		104	3.5	58	6.3	49	7.4
	2.4		2.3		3.3			6.4		3.1		3.0
	3.8		4.2		6.9	Sales/Working Capital		8.1		4.0		6.9
	10.4		10.8		30.1			-8.6		7.7		19.6
	26.3		33.8		14.3					41.1		13.4
(61)	5.7	(68)	9.6	(83)	7.4	EBIT/Interest		(15)		11.7	(47)	7.6
	2.9		3.4		2.1					2.5		2.4
						Net Profit + Depr., Dep., Amort./Cur. Mat. L/T/D						
	.0		.0		.0			.0		.0		.1
	.2		.2		.2	Fixed/Worth		.3		.2		.2
	.7		.9		1.1			NM		.5		1.0
	.5		.5		.8			1.5		.4		.8
	1.4		1.5		1.8	Debt/Worth		3.4		.8		1.7
	3.0		3.9		5.4			NM		2.1		4.1
	47.9		44.6		57.7	% Profit Before Taxes/Tangible Net Worth				56.3		67.1
(63)	24.0	(71)	24.4	(83)	30.2			(16)		31.4	(53)	30.2
	10.1		12.3		12.5					24.9		14.6
	19.0		24.1		22.2	% Profit Before Taxes/Total Assets		18.7		23.7		22.2
	10.0		10.2		11.7			6.0		16.0		12.6
	1.8		4.5		3.3			2.6		3.7		5.1
	381.6		157.2		180.7			261.6		164.1		121.8
	24.4		26.4		29.8	Sales/Net Fixed Assets		83.0		29.7		24.2
	6.0		10.1		6.6			6.5		5.9		6.9
	2.5		2.6		2.6			2.8		2.6		2.3
	1.5		1.7		1.7	Sales/Total Assets		2.3		1.6		1.7
	1.0		1.1		1.2			1.6		1.2		1.2
	.5		.3		.4					.2		.4
(49)	1.2	(50)	.8	(67)	1.0	% Depr., Dep., Amort./Sales		(17)		.6	(37)	.8
	3.4		2.5		2.1					1.8		1.8
	2.1		1.3		1.1							
(21)	3.3	(23)	2.6	(27)	2.2	% Officers', Directors', Owners' Comp/Sales						
	5.9		4.5		3.1							
	1932899M	3156645M	5246934M	Net Sales ($)	1733M	3605M	33494M	73710M	314864M	4819528M
	1363350M	2247820M	3485483M	Total Assets ($)	1121M	3267M	56193M	48217M	257457M	3119228M

M = $ thousand   MM = $ million
See Pages viii through xx for Explanation of Ratios and Data
© RMA 2024

WHOLESALE—Sporting and Recreational Goods and Supplies Merchant Wholesalers NAICS 423910

Current Data Sorted by Assets | Comparative Historical Data

						Type of Statement		
	1		6	5	6	Unqualified	21	8
1		4	10		1	Reviewed	28	20
		3	2			Compiled	13	4
2	5	10	3			Tax Returns	34	17
6	8	30	34	11	19	Other	132	92
	26 (4/1-9/30/23)		141 (10/1/23-3/31/24)				4/1/19-3/31/20	4/1/20-3/31/21
0-500M	500M-2MM	2-10MM	10-50MM	50-100MM	100-250MM		ALL	ALL
9	14	47	55	16	26	NUMBER OF STATEMENTS	228	141
%	%	%	%	%	%	ASSETS	%	%
	20.6	14.5	10.9	9.1	7.5	Cash & Equivalents	10.1	17.9
	15.6	15.8	15.6	20.9	22.1	Trade Receivables (net)	22.8	23.3
	50.6	49.3	47.0	48.8	40.1	Inventory	45.4	35.9
	1.0	2.3	5.2	2.4	1.6	All Other Current	3.1	3.6
	87.8	81.9	78.7	81.2	71.3	Total Current	81.4	80.7
	5.9	9.1	9.8	8.0	8.3	Fixed Assets (net)	9.6	8.2
	3.9	3.9	5.8	6.5	14.4	Intangibles (net)	5.3	7.2
	2.4	5.1	5.8	4.3	6.0	All Other Non-Current	3.8	3.9
	100.0	100.0	100.0	100.0	100.0	Total	100.0	100.0
						LIABILITIES		
	15.9	5.8	12.7	11.0	15.6	Notes Payable-Short Term	13.6	12.1
	.5	1.2	1.5	1.6	2.8	Cur. Mat.-L.T.D.	1.2	1.5
	14.1	15.4	15.4	23.9	10.9	Trade Payables	17.9	17.4
	.0	.0	.1	.2	.1	Income Taxes Payable	.1	.2
	6.6	12.9	15.2	8.9	7.2	All Other Current	10.6	11.5
	37.0	35.3	44.9	45.6	36.6	Total Current	43.4	42.8
	16.2	12.0	9.4	11.6	13.5	Long-Term Debt	9.6	17.7
	.0	.2	.0	.2	.3	Deferred Taxes	.1	.1
	7.6	6.4	10.9	1.7	7.7	All Other Non-Current	6.0	7.3
	39.3	46.1	34.7	40.9	41.8	Net Worth	40.9	32.2
	100.0	100.0	100.0	100.0	100.0	Total Liabilities & Net Worth	100.0	100.0
						INCOME DATA		
	100.0	100.0	100.0	100.0	100.0	Net Sales	100.0	100.0
	37.3	41.0	35.1	29.1	26.7	Gross Profit	32.9	35.5
	31.9	33.4	31.6	24.5	23.6	Operating Expenses	27.7	28.5
	5.4	7.5	3.4	4.6	3.1	Operating Profit	5.2	7.1
	.3	.6	1.3	2.8	3.6	All Other Expenses (net)	.9	-.3
	5.1	6.9	2.2	1.9	-.6	Profit Before Taxes	4.3	7.3
						RATIOS		
	5.3	5.3	3.6	4.0	3.8		3.3	4.0
	2.5	2.5	1.9	1.7	1.8	Current	1.9	2.2
	1.7	1.7	1.1	1.3	1.4		1.3	1.3
	2.0	2.2	1.2	1.3	1.4		1.3	1.9
	.9	.9	.5	.7	.7	Quick	.7	1.0
	.5	.4	.3	.3	.3		.4	.6
0	UND	7	50.2	13	27.4	23	15.8	25	14.7		18	20.5	12	29.5
12	31.5	18	20.6	33	11.2	46	8.0	38	9.5	Sales/Receivables	36	10.2	32	11.3
19	19.2	40	9.2	51	7.2	74	4.9	68	5.4		52	7.0	63	5.8
26	14.0	66	5.5	94	3.9	118	3.1	83	4.4		79	4.6	46	8.0
55	6.6	159	2.3	166	2.2	146	2.5	114	3.2	Cost of Sales/Inventory	122	3.0	94	3.9
122	3.0	281	1.3	261	1.4	215	1.7	192	1.9		174	2.1	152	2.4
0	UND	8	46.6	14	27.0	23	15.9	18	20.5		12	30.8	13	28.5
4	91.0	37	9.8	32	11.3	39	9.3	24	15.1	Cost of Sales/Payables	32	11.3	32	11.4
29	12.4	66	5.5	68	5.4	152	2.4	57	6.4		64	5.7	62	5.9
	3.8	3.0	3.0	2.8	3.5		3.6	3.1
	7.2	4.7	5.9	4.5	5.0	Sales/Working Capital	5.6	5.8
	17.9	6.6	21.0	9.3	8.6		12.8	14.1
	21.7	33.2	28.5	31.1	4.8		18.4	46.1
(12)	9.7	(38)	9.4	(50)	2.0	(15)	2.6	(24)	1.5	EBIT/Interest	(202)	5.2	(125)	14.1
	2.2	2.0	-1.8	-.1	-.4		1.4	4.4
						Net Profit + Depr., Dep., Amort./Cur. Mat. L/T/D	11.2	18.2
							(35) 2.4	(13) 6.0
							.6	1.6
	.0	.0	.1	.0	.1		.0	.0
	.1	.1	.3	.1	.1	Fixed/Worth	.2	.2
	.3	.2	2.3	.8	-3.4		.6	.8
	.4	.6	.7	.8	.4		.6	.7
	1.7	1.0	2.0	2.2	2.2	Debt/Worth	1.5	2.1
	4.7	2.1	13.9	5.5	-9.4		4.6	13.6
	154.9	66.6	46.0	30.0	24.8		38.3	85.8
(12)	38.1	(42) 42.7	(44) 6.9	(15) 14.2	(19) 16.5	% Profit Before Taxes/Tangible Net Worth	(196) 18.0	(113) 50.3
	14.5	7.8	-30.4	-.7	5.4		4.4	26.7
	41.3	29.0	17.1	18.2	11.7		16.1	27.3
	12.5	15.3	2.8	2.9	1.8	% Profit Before Taxes/Total Assets	6.3	14.1
	4.9	3.1	-7.6	-1.1	-7.4		1.0	5.8
	565.3	196.2	120.2	288.0	105.8		125.6	157.4
	142.7	64.2	41.2	72.1	33.6	Sales/Net Fixed Assets	42.2	56.7
	56.1	18.9	11.2	10.5	11.0		15.1	23.0
	5.9	3.3	2.3	2.0	2.0		2.8	3.1
	4.1	2.0	1.7	1.8	1.5	Sales/Total Assets	2.1	2.2
	2.9	1.2	1.4	1.4	.9		1.5	1.5
			.3	.4	.3	.1		.3	.2
	(21) .8	(41) .8	(12) .6	(17) .5	% Depr., Dep., Amort./Sales	(164) .6	(82) .6
	1.7	1.6	1.6	1.0		1.3	1.1
			1.1				1.6	1.5
	(19) 1.7					% Officers', Directors' Owners' Comp/Sales	(65) 2.7	(37) 2.8
	2.6						5.2	6.2
20660M	76900M	585593M	2208952M	1935426M	6779844M	Net Sales ($)	11390843M	8684353M
2299M	16488M	242515M	1218481M	1137248M	4225041M	Total Assets ($)	6473585M	4173580M

M = $ thousand   MM = $ million
See Pages viii through xx for Explanation of Ratios and Data
© RMA 2024

WHOLESALE—Sporting and Recreational Goods and Supplies Merchant Wholesalers NAICS 423910

Comparative Historical Data			Type of Statement	Current Data Sorted by Sales					
16	19	18	Unqualified		1			1	16
21	28	16	Reviewed	1			2	7	6
8	9	5	Compiled					5	
27	25	20	Tax Returns	1	1	2	5	7	4
111	100	108	Other	2	7	10	11	21	57
4/1/21-3/31/22 ALL	4/1/22-3/31/23 ALL	4/1/23-3/31/24 ALL		26 (4/1-9/30/23)			141 (10/1/23-3/31/24)		
				0-1MM	1-3MM	3-5MM	5-10MM	10-25MM	25MM & OVER
183	181	167	NUMBER OF STATEMENTS	4	9	12	18	41	83
%	%	%	ASSETS	%	%	%	%	%	%
15.4	10.3	12.7	Cash & Equivalents			22.8	12.4	13.6	10.2
19.8	17.4	17.2	Trade Receivables (net)			15.1	12.9	15.1	19.9
44.6	51.0	46.8	Inventory			42.1	53.0	47.6	45.4
2.2	2.7	3.2	All Other Current			5.6	3.0	3.9	2.8
82.0	81.4	79.9	Total Current			85.6	81.2	80.2	78.3
8.3	7.9	8.8	Fixed Assets (net)			7.3	8.6	8.9	8.3
5.7	5.6	6.2	Intangibles (net)			4.8	7.3	4.7	7.6
4.0	5.1	5.1	All Other Non-Current			2.4	2.9	6.2	5.7
100.0	100.0	100.0	Total			100.0	100.0	100.0	100.0
			LIABILITIES						
9.9	13.5	11.5	Notes Payable-Short Term			14.2	7.8	9.1	12.8
.9	1.5	1.7	Cur. Mat.-L.T.D.			1.3	.4	2.1	1.6
17.6	17.6	15.2	Trade Payables			10.1	14.9	16.4	15.8
.3	.1	.1	Income Taxes Payable			.0	.0	.0	.1
10.4	9.3	11.7	All Other Current			15.0	7.2	12.6	12.1
39.1	42.1	40.1	Total Current			40.6	30.3	40.2	42.4
11.5	15.0	11.8	Long-Term Debt			5.7	13.8	9.1	11.6
.0	.1	.1	Deferred Taxes			.0	.1	.0	.1
7.2	5.8	7.7	All Other Non-Current			3.3	12.1	4.6	8.6
42.2	37.0	40.3	Net Worth			50.3	43.7	46.1	37.2
100.0	100.0	100.0	Total Liabilities & Net Worth			100.0	100.0	100.0	100.0
			INCOME DATA						
100.0	100.0	100.0	Net Sales			100.0	100.0	100.0	100.0
32.8	33.0	35.3	Gross Profit			43.7	38.6	37.6	31.3
24.6	27.7	30.5	Operating Expenses			38.6	33.3	34.4	25.8
8.2	5.2	4.8	Operating Profit			5.1	5.4	3.2	5.5
-.3	.7	1.5	All Other Expenses (net)			.6	.7	1.3	1.9
8.5	4.5	3.2	Profit Before Taxes			4.5	4.7	1.9	3.6
			RATIOS						
4.1	3.6	4.5				4.9	6.1	3.8	4.1
2.3	2.2	2.2	Current			2.3	3.4	2.2	1.8
1.5	1.3	1.3				1.4	1.7	1.5	1.3
2.0	1.4	1.6				3.0	1.9	1.8	1.4
.9 (180)	.6	.7	Quick			.9	.9	.8	.6
.5	.3	.3				.5	.3	.2	.3
10 37.7	8 43.3	9 38.9		3 137.0	1 297.2	13 28.3	16 22.3		
29 12.6	24 15.1	26 13.9	Sales/Receivables	18 20.1	19 19.2	18 20.6	33 11.0		
49 7.5	47 7.8	49 7.5		69 5.3	39 9.3	45 8.1	51 7.1		
61 6.0	76 4.8	73 5.0		46 7.9	44 8.3	79 4.6	87 4.2		
104 3.5	140 2.6	146 2.5	Cost of Sales/Inventory	146 2.5	192 1.9	182 2.0	118 3.1		
159 2.3	228 1.6	228 1.6		281 1.3	456 .8	304 1.2	192 1.9		
10 35.9	13 29.1	12 29.4		0 UND	4 103.3	9 38.9	14 25.4		
30 12.2	32 11.3	29 12.5	Cost of Sales/Payables	32 11.5	40 9.2	37 9.9	29 12.6		
60 6.1	74 4.9	62 5.9		118 3.1	64 5.7	68 5.4	56 6.5		
3.1	3.0	3.2				2.2	2.2	2.6	3.5
5.7	5.1	5.2	Sales/Working Capital			5.7	4.3	5.0	5.3
11.7	10.5	9.8				20.6	7.2	7.7	12.1
69.8	31.7	26.8				25.4	22.9	22.5	53.2
(151) 24.5	(156) 6.8	(145) 3.6	EBIT/Interest	(10) 1.0	(14) 11.2	(34) 2.4	(77) 4.0		
5.2	1.8	-.1				-1.1	2.8	-3.1	.5
32.5	18.2	4.2	Net Profit + Depr., Dep.,						5.6
(16) 12.7	(25) 3.7	(23) 1.7	Amort./Cur. Mat. L/T/D					(19)	2.5
6.7	1.6	.1							.4
.0	.0	.0				.0	.0	.0	.0
.1	.1	.1	Fixed/Worth			.1	.2	.1	.2
.6	.4	.8				.5	.3	.6	1.0
.5	.6	.6				.4	.7	.5	.6
1.2	1.6	1.7	Debt/Worth			.9	2.0	1.1	2.1
6.5	5.4	5.7				1.8	3.5	7.4	11.6
74.8	53.0	54.3	% Profit Before Taxes/Tangible			54.3	150.3	54.4	46.0
(157) 43.5	(152) 25.4	(140) 21.8	Net Worth	(10) 21.8	(17) 23.2	(37) 13.9	(66) 18.5		
23.8		.6				-1.4	5.6	-14.0	4.3
31.7	22.7	22.3				25.7	28.9	23.3	20.7
18.4	9.4	6.6	% Profit Before Taxes/Total Assets			7.6	9.1	6.5	6.3
7.3	1.4	-2.0				-4.6	3.2	-7.6	-1.8
189.4	259.5	199.5				183.8	562.0	125.7	178.6
56.3	64.1	51.4	Sales/Net Fixed Assets			50.0	86.9	46.3	41.2
26.5	17.8	17.7				19.4	18.7	15.1	12.1
3.2	2.9	2.9				4.8	4.0	3.0	2.6
2.3	1.9	1.9	Sales/Total Assets			1.6	1.7	1.9	1.9
1.6	1.4	1.2				1.1	1.0	1.0	1.5
.2	.2	.3				.3	.5	.3		
(117) .5	(115) .5	(100) .6	% Depr., Dep., Amort./Sales	(10) 1.1	(21) .8	(59) .6				
1.1	1.1	1.3				2.5	1.5	1.1		
1.2	1.2	1.2						1.0	.4
(55) 2.2	(44) 2.3	(41) 2.4	% Officers', Directors' Owners' Comp/Sales			(11) 1.6	(11) 1.3		
4.7	4.9	3.5						2.6	1.5
12367195M	11870969M	11607375M	Net Sales ($)	2188M	19598M	50402M	122236M	651625M	10761326M
5025086M	6135688M	6842072M	Total Assets ($)	1072M	10972M	29543M	71796M	480804M	6247885M

M = $ thousand   MM = $ million
See Pages viii through xx for Explanation of Ratios and Data
© RMA 2024

WHOLESALE—Toy and Hobby Goods and Supplies Merchant Wholesalers NAICS 423920

Current Data Sorted by Assets

							Type of Statement		
			2	1	3		Unqualified		
		2	2	1			Reviewed		
	1	4	5				Compiled		
1	1	4	2				Tax Returns		
2	6	11	20	3	5		Other		
	20 (4/1-9/30/23)		56 (10/1/23-3/31/24)						
0-500M	500M-2MM	2-10MM	10-50MM	50-100MM	100-250MM				
3	8	21	31	5	8	NUMBER OF STATEMENTS			

Comparative Historical Data

5	2	
11	6	
11	4	
10	9	
34	22	
4/1/19-	4/1/20-	
3/31/20	3/31/21	
ALL	ALL	
71	43	

0-500M	500M-2MM	2-10MM	10-50MM	50-100MM	100-250MM		4/1/19-3/31/20 ALL	4/1/20-3/31/21 ALL
%	%	%	%	%	%	**ASSETS**	%	%
		13.5	13.0			Cash & Equivalents	14.7	24.6
		15.2	17.1			Trade Receivables (net)	23.1	22.9
		42.5	41.0			Inventory	38.3	35.9
		1.7	6.0			All Other Current	3.3	1.1
		73.0	77.1			Total Current	79.4	84.5
		13.0	8.6			Fixed Assets (net)	8.6	9.0
		3.6	3.5			Intangibles (net)	7.2	3.3
		10.4	10.8			All Other Non-Current	4.7	3.2
		100.0	100.0			Total	100.0	100.0
						LIABILITIES		
		9.0	5.6			Notes Payable-Short Term	14.8	10.0
		3.5	2.2			Cur. Mat.-L.T.D.	1.1	.9
		7.3	8.2			Trade Payables	17.1	13.9
		.0	.3			Income Taxes Payable	.0	.2
		11.2	17.7			All Other Current	8.7	7.1
		31.1	34.0			Total Current	41.8	32.0
		15.9	10.0			Long-Term Debt	7.7	14.2
		.0	.1			Deferred Taxes	.1	.1
		10.3	8.1			All Other Non-Current	4.0	4.7
		42.6	47.8			Net Worth	46.4	48.9
		100.0	100.0			Total Liabilities & Net Worth	100.0	100.0
						INCOME DATA		
		100.0	100.0			Net Sales	100.0	100.0
		44.2	44.6			Gross Profit	35.3	36.4
		33.7	37.2			Operating Expenses	29.7	28.3
		10.5	7.4			Operating Profit	5.6	8.1
		3.1	1.3			All Other Expenses (net)	1.6	.6
		7.4	6.1			Profit Before Taxes	4.1	7.5
						RATIOS		
		7.0	3.9				4.0	6.2
		3.6	2.7			Current	2.2	2.6
		1.5	1.8				1.3	1.8
		2.3	1.7				1.8	2.6
		1.0	1.1			Quick	.9	1.4
		.3	.5				.5	.8
	0	UND	15	24.6			15	23.8	9	41.4
	25	14.6	35	10.4		Sales/Receivables	37	9.8	41	8.9
	60	6.1	61	6.0			70	5.2	62	5.9
	94	3.9	107	3.4			59	6.2	51	7.1
	215	1.7	174	2.1		Cost of Sales/Inventory	111	3.3	79	4.6
	332	1.1	261	1.4			203	1.8	140	2.6
	0	853.5	15	24.9			19	19.7	6	58.8
	19	19.6	28	13.1		Cost of Sales/Payables	37	9.9	28	13.1
	76	4.8	49	7.5			55	6.6	50	7.3
			1.8	2.2				2.9	3.3
			3.0	3.5		Sales/Working Capital	5.1	4.5
			7.4	5.7			9.6	7.1
			12.3	11.3			23.1	31.3
		(17)	2.6	(25)	5.5		EBIT/Interest	(63)	6.2	(37)	11.4
			2.0	2.2			1.5	1.8
						Net Profit + Depr., Dep., Amort./Cur. Mat. L/T/D		
			.0	.0			.0	.0
			.1	.1		Fixed/Worth	.1	.1
			2.3	.4			.4	.3
			.3	.4			.5	.5
			1.8	1.1		Debt/Worth	1.4	1.1
			5.2	1.9			4.1	2.1
			39.8	24.3			59.2	67.2
		(18)	13.8	(28)	14.8		% Profit Before Taxes/Tangible Net Worth	(64)	22.5	(39)	39.1
			6.0	5.4			6.0	19.1
			19.6	18.1			19.6	29.3
			6.0	7.9		% Profit Before Taxes/Total Assets	7.7	18.3
			1.3	2.2			1.5	5.1
			145.8	90.8			290.2	445.3
			46.8	36.8		Sales/Net Fixed Assets	66.3	46.1
			8.0	13.8			19.5	18.0
			2.2	2.2			2.5	2.9
			1.2	1.4		Sales/Total Assets	2.0	2.0
			.7	1.0			1.4	1.6
			.5	.4			.2	.2
		(16)	.7	(21)	.8		% Depr., Dep., Amort./Sales	(49)	.6	(26)	.7
			2.8	2.0			1.4	1.3
						% Officers', Directors' Owners' Comp/Sales	1.3	.6
							(21)	3.6	(17)	2.6
							6.4	5.1
1965M	26351M	136892M	1183991M	368469M	3385888M	Net Sales ($)	3731571M	2380168M
592M	8596M	105780M	762634M	374742M	1244526M	Total Assets ($)	1899516M	1002640M

M = $ thousand   MM = $ million
See Pages viii through xx for Explanation of Ratios and Data
© RMA 2024

WHOLESALE—Toy and Hobby Goods and Supplies Merchant Wholesalers NAICS 423920

Comparative Historical Data | Current Data Sorted by Sales

Comparative Historical Data				Type of Statement	Current Data Sorted by Sales					
4	9	6		Unqualified				1	1	6
4	8	5		Reviewed				1	5	2
3	4	10		Compiled		1	2	1	2	1
7	11	8		Tax Returns	1		1	2	2	2
30	33	47		Other	4	4	4	7	6	22
4/1/21-3/31/22 ALL	4/1/22-3/31/23 ALL	4/1/23-3/31/24 ALL			0-1MM	20 (4/1-9/30/23) 1-3MM	3-5MM	56 (10/1/23-3/31/24) 5-10MM	10-25MM	25MM & OVER
48	65	76		NUMBER OF STATEMENTS	5	5	8	11	14	33
%	%	%		ASSETS	%	%	%	%	%	%
18.1	11.2	13.0		Cash & Equivalents				14.2	10.7	9.8
21.6	22.6	18.1		Trade Receivables (net)				17.1	16.9	21.5
38.3	43.8	40.9		Inventory				48.5	40.3	39.8
1.4	2.7	3.4		All Other Current				2.2	8.5	3.1
79.4	80.3	75.4		Total Current				81.9	76.4	74.1
11.7	8.5	9.7		Fixed Assets (net)				8.0	9.7	7.9
3.5	3.8	5.6		Intangibles (net)				.1	1.9	9.4
5.3	7.3	9.3		All Other Non-Current				10.0	11.9	8.7
100.0	100.0	100.0		Total				100.0	100.0	100.0
				LIABILITIES						
9.8	12.4	8.7		Notes Payable-Short Term				13.7	5.5	9.0
1.9	2.1	3.0		Cur. Mat.-L.T.D.				4.2	1.9	4.1
17.9	16.8	10.1		Trade Payables				7.5	5.4	13.4
.1	.0	.2		Income Taxes Payable				.0	.0	.3
10.0	7.4	13.0		All Other Current				10.7	20.3	11.8
39.6	38.6	35.0		Total Current				36.1	33.1	38.6
13.6	8.7	12.9		Long-Term Debt				10.6	14.5	11.4
.0	.0	.1		Deferred Taxes				.0	.0	.1
4.6	3.2	10.0		All Other Non-Current				7.6	8.7	8.7
42.2	49.5	42.2		Net Worth				45.7	43.7	41.2
100.0	100.0	100.0		Total Liabilties & Net Worth				100.0	100.0	100.0
				INCOME DATA						
100.0	100.0	100.0		Net Sales				100.0	100.0	100.0
36.7	40.0	42.6		Gross Profit				47.4	49.5	38.1
25.1	32.7	34.9		Operating Expenses				37.8	42.0	31.8
11.6	7.3	7.8		Operating Profit				9.6	7.4	6.4
-.1	1.0	2.0		All Other Expenses (net)				1.8	2.2	1.7
11.8	6.3	5.8		Profit Before Taxes				7.8	5.3	4.7
				RATIOS						
3.3	3.7	5.5						10.3	8.8	3.4
2.2	2.4	2.4		Current				2.8	2.6	2.1
1.4	1.6	1.4						1.4	1.6	1.2
1.9	1.5	2.0						3.8	2.3	1.3
.8	.8	1.0		Quick				.6	1.2	.8
.6	.5	.4						.4	.3	.5

9	38.9	10	36.9	4	82.2					3	136.2	17	21.9	14	25.9	
28	12.9	36	10.1	29	12.7	Sales/Receivables				43	8.4	32	11.3	31	11.7	
63	5.8	68	5.4	62	5.9					85	4.3	65	5.6	66	5.5	
61	6.0	79	4.6	89	4.1					146	2.5	122	3.0	87	4.2	
126	2.9	159	2.3	159	2.3	Cost of Sales/Inventory				261	1.4	332	1.1	114	3.2	
166	2.2	261	1.4	281	1.3					304	1.2	406	.9	182	2.0	
21	17.8	10	35.5	10	36.5					0	934.6	8	45.3	22	16.6	
41	8.8	34	10.6	29	12.6	Cost of Sales/Payables				21	17.4	19	19.4	41	8.9	
62	5.9	61	6.0	58	6.3					74	4.9	41	9.0	57	6.4	

3.2	2.8	2.2	Sales/Working Capital	2.2 / 1.8 / 3.4
5.3	4.6	3.9		3.3 / 3.3 / 5.2
9.9	9.1	7.7		7.0 / 6.9 / 21.4

133.0	36.7	12.1		EBIT/Interest			10.2	10.7	10.9
(43) 29.9	(52) 5.7	(60) 4.0				(10) 3.3	(12) 4.2	(27) 3.8
9.5	2.3	1.9					2.0	2.2	.7

		38.6	Net Profit + Depr., Dep., Amort./Cur. Mat. L/T/D
	(10)	4.1	
		.2	

.0	.0	.0	Fixed/Worth	.0	.0	.1
.1	.1	.1		.1	.1	.1
.6	.3	1.1		4.0	.7	4.2
.5	.4	.5	Debt/Worth	.2	.6	.7
1.0	.9	1.3		1.6	1.7	1.1
3.9	4.1	5.2		5.3	3.0	8.8

93.8	71.4	46.9	% Profit Before Taxes/Tangible Net Worth		33.8		47.7
(42) 54.9	(59) 25.1	(63) 17.2			(13) 14.9	(26)	18.7
24.5	7.7	8.3			10.6		9.3

39.6	23.1	22.4	% Profit Before Taxes/Total Assets	30.4	10.9	24.1
26.3	10.2	7.8		11.5	5.4	9.1
8.5	1.9	1.8		2.0	2.6	-.4

367.3	232.7	207.9	Sales/Net Fixed Assets	999.8	83.8	99.2
57.1	54.5	47.9		110.8	28.4	44.4
13.4	20.9	16.6		28.0	8.2	19.3

2.8	2.9	2.6	Sales/Total Assets	2.2	1.6	2.9
2.0	1.9	1.4		1.7	1.1	1.7
1.4	1.2	1.0		1.1	.8	1.2

	.2		.2	.2	% Depr., Dep., Amort./Sales	.4	.2
(30)	.5	(42)	.6	(50) .8		(10) .9	(24) .7
	1.5		1.9	2.1		1.9	2.0

	1.7		1.0	1.3	% Officers', Directors' Owners' Comp/Sales
(16)	2.9	(20)	4.3	(23) 2.7	
	5.4		5.9	7.1	

4764016M	4707830M	5103556M	Net Sales ($)	2423M	9402M	30827M	76554M	233665M	4750685M
1999012M	1985729M	2496870M	Total Assets ($)	7407M	19220M	18966M	55364M	212808M	2183105M

© RMA 2024   M = $ thousand   MM = $ million
See Pages viii through xx for Explanation of Ratios and Data

WHOLESALE—Recyclable Material Merchant Wholesalers NAICS 423930

Current Data Sorted by Assets | Comparative Historical Data

							Type of Statement		
		2	10	7	6		Unqualified	16	15
	1	12	24	3	1		Reviewed	45	19
	3	11	3	1			Compiled	22	14
3	9	11	6		1		Tax Returns	34	20
2	21	53	52	32	12		Other	183	114
	46 (4/1-9/30/23)		240 (10/1/23-3/31/24)					4/1/19-	4/1/20-
0-500M	500M-2MM	2-10MM	10-50MM	50-100MM	100-250MM		NUMBER OF STATEMENTS	3/31/20 ALL	3/31/21 ALL
5	34	89	95	43	20			300	182
%	%	%	%	%	%		ASSETS	%	%
	24.4	11.1	8.2	5.7	8.4		Cash & Equivalents	9.6	14.0
	15.2	26.5	26.6	34.0	26.9		Trade Receivables (net)	24.0	21.3
	9.3	17.4	19.0	15.6	19.2		Inventory	18.7	16.6
	1.8	1.3	2.7	2.5	5.6		All Other Current	2.4	2.7
	50.7	56.3	56.6	57.7	60.2		Total Current	54.7	54.7
	37.6	32.7	31.8	19.3	29.4		Fixed Assets (net)	33.6	31.6
	4.2	1.3	4.4	11.0	3.6		Intangibles (net)	3.8	5.9
	7.5	9.7	7.2	12.0	6.8		All Other Non-Current	7.9	7.9
	100.0	100.0	100.0	100.0	100.0		Total	100.0	100.0
							LIABILITIES		
	9.6	6.8	9.1	7.9	6.5		Notes Payable-Short Term	11.6	9.7
	5.0	3.8	2.6	2.4	1.7		Cur. Mat.-L.T.D.	3.7	3.3
	8.6	15.9	15.0	17.3	15.2		Trade Payables	13.8	13.3
	.0	.0	.0	.1	.0		Income Taxes Payable	.0	.1
	5.7	5.9	7.8	5.8	5.9		All Other Current	9.1	7.7
	28.8	32.4	34.6	33.5	29.3		Total Current	38.2	34.1
	32.8	17.7	13.1	16.1	11.0		Long-Term Debt	20.8	22.0
	.0	.2	.4	.1	.3		Deferred Taxes	.3	.1
	15.3	5.1	11.3	4.0	6.2		All Other Non-Current	6.9	7.3
	23.1	44.7	40.6	46.3	53.1		Net Worth	33.7	36.5
	100.0	100.0	100.0	100.0	100.0		Total Liabilities & Net Worth	100.0	100.0
							INCOME DATA		
	100.0	100.0	100.0	100.0	100.0		Net Sales	100.0	100.0
	32.3	27.8	21.5	16.5	14.5		Gross Profit	25.2	28.8
	27.6	23.9	18.1	14.3	12.6		Operating Expenses	21.4	23.7
	4.7	3.8	3.3	2.1	1.9		Operating Profit	3.8	5.1
	.3	.3	.6	-.1	-1.2		All Other Expenses (net)	.8	-.2
	4.4	3.6	2.7	2.2	3.0		Profit Before Taxes	3.0	5.2
							RATIOS		
	7.6	4.8	2.5	2.7	3.0			2.9	3.3
	1.6	2.0	1.7	1.9	2.1		Current	1.5	1.6
	.7	1.1	1.1	1.3	1.6			1.0	1.1
	4.7	2.4	1.6	2.0	2.1			1.6	1.9
	1.3	1.2	1.1	1.2	1.3		Quick	.9 (181)	1.0
	.6	.7	.6	.7	.9			.5	.6
0 UND	8 47.9	21 17.3	37 9.8	26 13.9				13 28.2	8 44.2
8 43.2	29 12.7	35 10.4	41 8.8	41 8.8			Sales/Receivables	29 12.6	31 11.7
34 10.7	43 8.5	46 7.9	47 7.8	51 7.2				43 8.5	47 7.8
0 UND	2 167.2	12 29.4	7 54.6	14 26.3				7 49.9	8 44.6
5 67.2	14 26.4	28 13.0	20 18.0	26 13.8			Cost of Sales/Inventory	24 15.1	24 15.4
20 18.7	45 8.1	51 7.1	47 7.7	34 10.8				49 7.5	48 7.6
0 UND	4 103.4	9 42.5	21 17.0	22 16.9				8 44.2	4 104.2
7 50.2	22 16.7	22 16.6	26 13.9	27 13.6			Cost of Sales/Payables	18 20.1	20 18.3
24 15.1	40 9.1	30 12.0	35 10.4	34 10.8				32 11.5	33 11.0
	9.1	8.2	7.7	6.7	6.5			8.0	7.5
	16.1	15.6	13.2	10.9	7.4		Sales/Working Capital	20.7	16.1
	-137.8	62.9	47.8	32.1	12.7			-999.8	46.8
	32.5	21.8	13.2	14.6	25.7			10.9	18.2
(25) 6.5	(82) 7.3	(86) 5.1	(33) 3.1	(17) 6.7			EBIT/Interest	(277) 3.3	(164) 7.3
	-.8	2.4	1.2	.7	2.5			.6	1.6
			6.7					6.7	9.7
			(22) 2.8				Net Profit + Depr., Dep., Amort./Cur. Mat. L/T/D	(47) 1.6	(19) 2.3
			1.3					.8	.5
	.3	.3	.3	.2	.3			.3	.3
	1.4	.6	.8	.4	.6		Fixed/Worth	.9	.8
	NM	1.3	1.4	1.3	1.2			2.5	3.1
	.6	.5	.6	.4	.5			.6	.7
	1.4	1.3	1.3	1.5	.9		Debt/Worth	1.7	1.7
	NM	3.3	4.6	3.2	1.9			6.9	5.8
	105.9	44.4	28.2	21.9	29.4			35.4	60.3
(26) 38.6	(84) 20.1	(87) 16.2	(36) 15.8	17.3			% Profit Before Taxes/Tangible Net Worth	(248) 15.0	(152) 25.7
	4.0	7.3	3.5	1.7	9.3			1.5	6.4
	50.9	19.2	14.5	13.4	10.7			13.1	20.9
	16.4	8.1	6.2	5.4	8.4		% Profit Before Taxes/Total Assets	5.1	9.0
	-1.6	2.5	.5	-1.6	2.4			-1.0	1.1
	69.7	52.5	31.3	42.5	20.2			34.1	30.1
	11.1	11.9	8.4	11.5	12.3		Sales/Net Fixed Assets	9.4	9.1
	5.5	4.2	4.0	8.5	4.2			3.9	4.6
	6.0	5.4	3.7	3.5	3.4			4.5	4.3
	3.6	3.6	2.3	2.5	2.5		Sales/Total Assets	2.7	2.5
	2.4	1.9	1.7	2.2	1.7			1.6	1.7
	1.3	.7	.7	.3	.5			.7	.7
(13) 2.1	(62) 2.2	(83) 2.0	(26) 1.4	(12) 1.1			% Depr., Dep., Amort./Sales	(232) 1.9	(137) 1.9
	5.9	4.5	4.0	2.5	4.4			4.5	4.1
	1.2	.6	.4					.7	.8
(13) 2.3	(27) 1.6	(21) 1.5					% Officers', Directors' Owners' Comp/Sales	(84) 2.1	(46) 1.8
	4.0	3.1	3.2					3.6	4.7
13953M	211986M	1748638M	6332874M	8762078M	11057659M		Net Sales ($)	16902959M	11585144M
1364M	39620M	454374M	2171794M	3018560M	3150949M		Total Assets ($)	6793103M	4872325M

© RMA 2024 M = $ thousand MM = $ million
See Pages viii through xx for Explanation of Ratios and Data

WHOLESALE—Recyclable Material Merchant Wholesalers NAICS 423930

Comparative Historical Data / Current Data Sorted by Sales

				Type of Statement						
	11	33	25	Unqualified				3	3	22
	30	39	41	Reviewed		1	1	6	5	28
	16	27	18	Compiled				4	8	6
	22	32	30	Tax Returns		3	3	8	11	4
	125	163	172	Other	1	13	12	10	34	103
	4/1/21-3/31/22 ALL	4/1/22-3/31/23 ALL	4/1/23-3/31/24 ALL		46 (4/1-9/30/23)			240 (10/1/23-3/31/24)		
					0-1MM	1-3MM	3-5MM	5-10MM	10-25MM	25MM & OVER
	204	294	286	NUMBER OF STATEMENTS	1	17	16	28	61	163
	%	%	%	ASSETS	%	%	%	%	%	%
	12.9	13.0	11.4	Cash & Equivalents		16.0	12.5	20.7	15.5	7.7
	28.0	25.4	25.9	Trade Receivables (net)		16.6	11.8	17.2	20.3	32.0
	17.4	17.0	16.5	Inventory		7.3	15.2	11.5	16.0	18.8
	2.6	3.4	2.3	All Other Current		.6	.4	2.5	1.1	3.1
	61.0	58.9	56.2	Total Current		40.4	39.9	52.0	52.9	61.6
	28.3	28.4	30.5	Fixed Assets (net)		51.4	55.6	28.3	35.5	24.5
	3.3	3.9	4.4	Intangibles (net)		2.6	.6	1.0	2.7	6.0
	7.5	8.8	8.8	All Other Non-Current		5.5	3.9	18.8	8.9	7.9
	100.0	100.0	100.0	Total		100.0	100.0	100.0	100.0	100.0
				LIABILITIES						
	9.1	7.4	8.1	Notes Payable-Short Term		4.5	3.0	12.5	6.8	8.7
	3.2	4.4	3.2	Cur. Mat.-L.T.D.		4.5	3.8	4.4	5.4	2.1
	13.3	13.7	14.6	Trade Payables		6.6	8.5	11.4	11.2	18.0
	.1	.2	.0	Income Taxes Payable		.0	.0	.0	.0	.0
	7.0	6.7	6.6	All Other Current		10.8	2.9	6.2	5.8	7.0
	32.8	32.3	32.6	Total Current		26.5	18.2	34.5	29.2	35.7
	20.1	21.3	19.7	Long-Term Debt		77.4	28.9	17.2	19.1	13.6
	.2	.1	.2	Deferred Taxes		.0	.0	.4	.3	.2
	6.7	7.1	8.2	All Other Non-Current		28.5	10.5	3.2	6.0	7.6
	40.3	39.2	39.3	Net Worth		-32.5	42.4	44.7	45.4	42.9
	100.0	100.0	100.0	Total Liabilities & Net Worth		100.0	100.0	100.0	100.0	100.0
				INCOME DATA						
	100.0	100.0	100.0	Net Sales		100.0	100.0	100.0	100.0	100.0
	26.5	26.5	23.9	Gross Profit		37.8	40.5	34.3	30.5	16.5
	18.6	20.4	20.4	Operating Expenses		32.5	36.1	30.2	26.3	13.6
	7.8	6.2	3.4	Operating Profit		5.3	4.4	4.1	4.1	2.9
	-.5	.1	.2	All Other Expenses (net)		1.8	.0	-.3	.3	.2
	8.3	6.1	3.2	Profit Before Taxes		3.5	4.4	4.4	3.8	2.7
				RATIOS						
	3.6	3.5	3.2			3.4	8.3	5.2	5.5	2.9
	1.9	1.9	1.8	Current		1.4	2.3	1.5	1.8	1.9
	1.3	1.3	1.1			.6	.9	.8	1.1	1.2
	2.4	2.3	2.2			3.1	3.4	2.9	2.8	2.0
	1.3	1.2	1.2	Quick		.8	1.1	1.1	1.4	1.2
	.8	.7	.7			.4	.5	.6	.8	.7
14	26.1	12	30.3	14	25.2		4	81.3	0	999.8	7	49.6	5	73.6	23	16.2
34	10.7	26	13.9	34	10.8	Sales/Receivables	34	10.8	28	13.2	30	12.1	27	13.7	38	9.5
49	7.5	39	9.3	45	8.1		50	7.3	40	9.2	43	8.4	42	8.7	46	7.9
6	57.8	6	61.4	5	75.9		0	UND	6	63.1	0	UND	2	150.6	9	42.5
19	19.3	18	19.9	19	18.9	Cost of Sales/Inventory	0	UND	29	12.6	6	60.1	22	16.9	22	16.8
43	8.5	43	8.5	44	8.3		17	20.9	89	4.1	27	13.4	63	5.8	36	10.1
5	74.1	5	66.7	7	54.1		0	UND	0	UND	1	341.2	4	103.4	11	33.9
21	17.7	17	21.8	23	16.2	Cost of Sales/Payables	18	19.9	24	14.9	19	18.8	18	20.1	24	15.3
34	10.8	31	11.8	34	10.8		36	10.1	49	7.5	44	8.3	30	12.2	33	11.0
	6.5		7.2		7.0			7.5		4.6		7.6		7.4		7.3
	11.9		13.9		12.9	Sales/Working Capital		18.8		7.5		19.2		13.8		12.5
	30.1		39.2		49.8			-25.9		NM		-22.8		55.0		40.2
	58.4		32.6		18.6			10.2		31.4		23.4		24.9		17.5
(188)	19.6	(256)	11.5	(246)	5.7	EBIT/Interest	(14)	3.7		4.1	(22)	4.6	(54)	7.0	(140)	5.7
	6.7		4.0		1.3			-1.0		-1.1		.3		2.1		1.6
	22.0		19.6		7.9											5.9
(21)	10.1	(41)	7.1	(37)	3.5	Net Profit + Depr., Dep., Amort./Cur. Mat. L/T/D									(27)	3.7
	4.5		2.9		1.4											1.4
	.2		.2		.3			.9		.6		.2		.4		.3
	.6		.6		.6	Fixed/Worth		2.9		1.1		.6		.9		.6
	1.2		1.4		1.5			-.3		NM		1.9		1.7		1.2
	.6		.6		.5			.8		.3		.5		.5		.5
	1.4		1.4		1.3	Debt/Worth		2.5		1.1		.9		1.4		1.4
	3.2		3.0		3.4			-2.4		NM		2.4		3.4		3.3
	78.1		60.8		39.7			33.7		68.2		38.9		80.5		30.6
(188)	43.4	(268)	34.7	(255)	17.9	% Profit Before Taxes/Tangible Net Worth	(12)	17.9	(12)	23.2	(24)	15.0	(56)	23.9	(150)	17.7
	23.7		13.5		4.4			-15.3		-2.4		2.1		3.9		6.6
	31.0		26.5		16.8			22.9		17.7		15.1		26.7		15.4
	18.7		12.0		7.4	% Profit Before Taxes/Total Assets		9.9		9.6		7.2		11.6		6.2
	8.6		4.9		.8			-3.8		-4.1		.4		1.9		1.4
	58.5		56.4		44.8			11.1		7.2		67.1		23.6		56.3
	13.5		13.9		11.2	Sales/Net Fixed Assets		4.7		3.9		10.1		9.6		14.5
	5.7		5.7		5.0			2.5		1.5		4.1		4.1		7.3
	4.5		5.2		4.4			3.4		3.4		4.6		5.2		4.4
	3.1		3.2		2.8	Sales/Total Assets		2.3		1.9		2.7		3.4		2.9
	2.0		2.1		1.9			1.7		.9		1.7		1.5		2.1
	.5		.5		.7							1.4		1.1		.5
(149)	1.4	(217)	1.3	(198)	1.9	% Depr., Dep., Amort./Sales			(17)	3.6	(43)	2.4	(119)	1.2
	3.2		2.6		4.0							5.5		5.0		2.6
	.6		.6		.6					1.6		.6		.3
(62)	2.1	(74)	2.0	(65)	1.8	% Officers', Directors' Owners' Comp/Sales			(11)	2.3	(17)	2.2	(28)	.8
	3.1		3.5		3.1							4.0		3.9		2.1
	17902930M	28457797M	28127188M	Net Sales ($)	429M	39149M	68844M	204071M	978963M	26835732M
	6015697M	8420726M	8836661M	Total Assets ($)	491M	19741M	63425M	87032M	480725M	8185247M

© RMA 2024   M = $ thousand   MM = $ million
See Pages viii through xx for Explanation of Ratios and Data

WHOLESALE—Jewelry, Watch, Precious Stone, and Precious Metal Merchant Wholesalers NAICS 423940

Current Data Sorted by Assets | Comparative Historical Data

							Type of Statement		
			3		2		Unqualified	1	3
		1	4	1	1		Reviewed	10	4
	1	7	1				Compiled	7	4
	5	7					Tax Returns	13	10
3	6	15	12	3	5		Other	47	22
	17 (4/1-9/30/23)		53 (10/1/23-3/31/24)					4/1/19-3/31/20	4/1/20-3/31/21
0-500M	500M-2MM	2-10MM	10-50MM	50-100MM	100-250MM			ALL	ALL
3	12	23	20	4	8		NUMBER OF STATEMENTS	78	43
%	%	%	%	%	%		ASSETS	%	%
	11.4	12.8	8.8				Cash & Equivalents	9.8	18.4
	19.5	26.8	19.7				Trade Receivables (net)	25.0	18.2
	49.2	48.3	58.2				Inventory	47.1	46.7
	6.8	4.1	3.0				All Other Current	2.5	3.4
	86.9	91.9	89.7				Total Current	84.4	86.7
	10.9	2.7	5.1				Fixed Assets (net)	9.2	5.1
	.3	.7	1.2				Intangibles (net)	1.8	3.5
	1.9	4.7	4.0				All Other Non-Current	4.5	4.5
	100.0	100.0	100.0				Total	100.0	100.0
							LIABILITIES		
	8.5	8.3	12.6				Notes Payable-Short Term	12.5	14.5
	1.1	.5	2.2				Cur. Mat.-L.T.D.	.7	.5
	17.0	20.4	16.6				Trade Payables	17.5	13.4
	.4	.2	.0				Income Taxes Payable	.0	.4
	12.5	5.9	8.9				All Other Current	10.5	7.8
	39.5	35.3	40.3				Total Current	41.2	36.5
	8.0	10.2	4.9				Long-Term Debt	10.4	6.9
	.0	.0	.0				Deferred Taxes	.0	.0
	7.3	4.3	2.7				All Other Non-Current	7.0	10.3
	45.2	50.2	52.1				Net Worth	41.4	46.2
	100.0	100.0	100.0				Total Liabilities & Net Worth	100.0	100.0
							INCOME DATA		
	100.0	100.0	100.0				Net Sales	100.0	100.0
	41.4	34.0	20.9				Gross Profit	27.4	28.0
	31.2	27.9	15.2				Operating Expenses	23.7	23.8
	10.3	6.1	5.7				Operating Profit	3.8	4.2
	1.1	.2	.1				All Other Expenses (net)	.6	-.2
	9.2	5.9	5.6				Profit Before Taxes	3.2	4.4
							RATIOS		
	5.8	4.1	3.9					3.8	5.8
	1.9	2.9	2.1			Current		2.2	2.4
	1.4	1.9	1.6					1.4	1.4
	.8	2.1	1.1					1.5	2.3
	.6	1.1	.8			Quick		.8	1.1
	.3	.8	.4					.4	.5
0	UND	16	22.8	2	167.5			8	44.8	2	147.1
11	31.8	50	7.3	33	11.0		Sales/Receivables	35	10.3	23	15.6
35	10.5	69	5.3	54	6.7			69	5.3	59	6.2
29	12.4	34	10.6	24	15.1			29	12.8	23	16.2
87	4.2	130	2.8	111	3.3		Cost of Sales/Inventory	79	4.6	122	3.0
203	1.8	261	1.4	243	1.5			192	1.9	192	1.9
0	UND	19	18.9	2	209.7			3	112.9	1	579.0
8	46.7	50	7.3	16	23.1		Cost of Sales/Payables	33	11.0	17	21.9
68	5.4	72	5.1	70	5.2			74	4.9	83	4.4
	4.0	2.5	2.0					3.8	2.1
	5.5	3.3	8.0			Sales/Working Capital		6.5	5.2
	20.0	6.3	21.0					18.7	18.0
		15.1	47.0					12.4	30.0
	(18)	7.7	(19)	13.2			EBIT/Interest	(66)	4.3	(32)	6.5
		2.3	5.6					1.4	1.2
							Net Profit + Depr., Dep., Amort./Cur. Mat. L/T/D		
	.0	.0	.0					.0	.0
	.0	.0	.0			Fixed/Worth		.1	.0
	.5	.1	.1					.4	.2
	.3	.5	.3					.6	.4
	1.7	1.0	1.1			Debt/Worth		1.3	1.0
	3.5	2.4	2.0					3.6	4.9
	50.8	44.9	76.1			% Profit Before Taxes/Tangible Net Worth		31.1	54.2
	14.7	(22)	16.5	(19)	21.2			(70)	15.0	(38)	15.9
	-1.6	10.4	11.4					3.3	1.0
	32.7	19.9	28.3					12.9	14.0
	8.5	8.6	13.2			% Profit Before Taxes/Total Assets		4.9	6.2
	-1.0	4.7	4.6					.9	.3
	873.4	999.8	999.8					999.8	999.8
	187.9	176.7	298.9			Sales/Net Fixed Assets		85.9	122.5
	43.7	42.7	37.5					21.1	33.5
	4.2	3.8	8.5					4.3	4.1
	2.9	2.0	2.7			Sales/Total Assets		2.4	2.1
	1.9	1.5	1.3					1.3	1.3
		.1	.0					.1	.0
	(11)	.2	(13)	.1			% Depr., Dep., Amort./Sales	(45)	.3	(25)	.2
		.8	.5					.9	.6
		1.8						.7	.6
	(12)	4.0					% Officers', Directors' Owners' Comp/Sales	(32)	1.7	(16)	1.5
		4.8						5.4	3.1
7424M	45555M	316515M	3647088M	681309M	3457680M		Net Sales ($)	13313182M	7687813M
1294M	14516M	110396M	482248M	266087M	1526945M		Total Assets ($)	2258005M	691588M

M = $ thousand   MM = $ million
See Pages viii through xx for Explanation of Ratios and Data

© RMA 2024

WHOLESALE—Jewelry, Watch, Precious Stone, and Precious Metal Merchant Wholesalers NAICS 423940

Comparative Historical Data | Current Data Sorted by Sales

				Type of Statement						
2	3	5		Unqualified				1	1	5
5	10	7		Reviewed			1			5
7	6	2		Compiled			2	1		1
3	13	12		Tax Returns	1	3	1	3	2	1
15	33	44		Other		7		8	9	19
4/1/21-3/31/22 ALL	4/1/22-3/31/23 ALL	4/1/23-3/31/24 ALL				17 (4/1-9/30/23)		53 (10/1/23-3/31/24)		
					0-1MM	1-3MM	3-5MM	5-10MM	10-25MM	25MM & OVER
32	65	70		NUMBER OF STATEMENTS	1	10	4	12	12	31
%	%	%		ASSETS	%	%	%	%	%	%
12.3	15.7	10.4		Cash & Equivalents		11.8		12.6	13.8	7.8
15.9	14.9	20.3		Trade Receivables (net)		10.8		25.5	28.4	17.9
54.4	50.8	53.0		Inventory		50.4		51.3	45.2	56.1
3.7	2.1	4.7		All Other Current		7.4		.2	6.9	5.2
86.4	83.4	88.4		Total Current		80.4		89.5	94.4	87.0
5.9	5.3	6.0		Fixed Assets (net)		14.1		6.0	1.7	5.4
1.1	3.0	1.0		Intangibles (net)		1.2		.5	.3	1.6
6.7	8.3	4.7		All Other Non-Current		4.3		4.0	3.7	6.1
100.0	100.0	100.0		Total		100.0		100.0	100.0	100.0
				LIABILITIES						
11.5	12.2	9.7		Notes Payable-Short Term		6.8		10.9	5.2	12.1
1.6	1.8	1.1		Cur. Mat.-L.T.D.		1.7		1.0	1.1	1.1
20.3	16.0	17.1		Trade Payables		8.8		19.4	23.2	16.2
.2	.1	.3		Income Taxes Payable		.1		.4	.3	.4
16.1	9.2	11.4		All Other Current		19.3		5.9	1.1	16.5
49.7	39.3	39.6		Total Current		36.7		37.7	30.9	46.3
5.3	11.9	8.2		Long-Term Debt		9.1		9.6	11.3	6.0
.0	.0	.0		Deferred Taxes		.0		.0	.0	.0
25.5	12.7	4.8		All Other Non-Current		.0		.9	7.3	5.0
19.5	36.1	47.4		Net Worth		54.2		51.7	50.5	42.7
100.0	100.0	100.0		Total Liabilities & Net Worth		100.0		100.0	100.0	100.0
				INCOME DATA						
100.0	100.0	100.0		Net Sales		100.0		100.0	100.0	100.0
23.7	28.9	30.2		Gross Profit		52.0		40.9	25.9	22.1
19.0	22.8	23.8		Operating Expenses		42.3		29.9	21.1	17.2
4.7	6.1	6.3		Operating Profit		9.7		10.9	4.7	4.9
-.5	.5	.3		All Other Expenses (net)		-.6		1.2	.1	.2
5.2	5.6	6.0		Profit Before Taxes		10.4		9.7	4.6	4.7
				RATIOS						
5.5	4.4	3.8				4.4		3.2	7.3	3.2
1.6	2.3	2.4		Current		2.0		2.6	3.6	1.8
1.1	1.4	1.5				1.3		1.6	2.2	1.3
1.2	1.6	1.2				1.0		1.6	2.5	.9
.7	.7	.8		Quick		.7		.9	1.2	.5
.4	.3	.4				.2		.6	1.0	.3
0 UND	0 750.1	2 182.5			0 UND	17 21.2	2 170.5	2 174.9		
16 23.3	9 40.2	25 14.7		Sales/Receivables	0 UND	38 9.7	47 7.7	20 18.6		
46 7.9	40 9.1	53 6.9			45 8.2	91 4.0	62 5.9	49 7.5		
23 15.6	26 14.0	34 10.6			45 8.2	38 9.5	24 15.4	31 11.6		
114 3.2	99 3.7	104 3.5		Cost of Sales/Inventory	215 1.7	146 2.5	118 3.1	99 3.7		
166 2.2	261 1.4	243 1.5			730 .5	281 1.3	228 1.6	203 1.8		
3 122.0	3 128.0	4 82.5			0 UND	22 16.8	16 22.6	3 106.6		
17 21.3	21 17.1	26 13.9		Cost of Sales/Payables	26 13.8	52 7.0	28 13.2	23 15.7		
72 5.1	53 6.9	72 5.1			114 3.2	79 4.6	62 5.9	78 4.7		
4.0	2.5	2.5				2.4		2.7	2.1	3.0
10.9	8.1	4.7		Sales/Working Capital		4.0		4.1	3.0	9.9
95.9	23.6	18.9				12.0		11.2	8.3	34.0
91.0	50.5	18.5							22.2	19.7
(27) 27.7	(52) 17.9	(59) 7.6		EBIT/Interest				(10) 10.9	(29) 7.4	
9.4	4.5	3.2							3.0	4.6
				Net Profit + Depr., Dep., Amort./Cur. Mat. L/T/D						
.0	.0	.0				.0		.0	.0	.0
.0	.1	.0		Fixed/Worth		.0		.1	.0	.1
.5	.2	.1				.3		.1	.1	.1
.9	.6	.4				.3		.4	.4	.7
1.9	1.3	1.3		Debt/Worth		1.2		1.3	1.1	1.4
6.7	3.6	2.4				2.2		2.2	2.7	2.5
101.0	48.7	49.8				43.6		53.9	21.2	66.6
(27) 42.1	(59) 26.2	(66) 18.5		% Profit Before Taxes/Tangible Net Worth		14.5		24.0	(11) 13.6	(28) 22.8
18.1	10.6	9.9				2.9		8.4	7.8	14.0
27.7	23.1	19.8				21.4		33.9	15.3	30.1
13.1	9.5	9.6		% Profit Before Taxes/Total Assets		9.2		10.3	7.5	11.7
4.5	4.5	4.1				.8		3.0	5.2	4.7
UND	999.8	999.8				UND		863.6	UND	999.8
199.3	147.8	136.6		Sales/Net Fixed Assets		93.7		62.7	431.7	100.8
35.5	32.9	34.0				14.9		31.2	153.0	30.5
5.3	5.0	4.2				3.4		4.4	4.4	6.4
2.5	2.1	2.3		Sales/Total Assets		1.9		2.0	2.0	2.6
1.7	1.3	1.4				1.0		1.6	1.5	1.7
.1	.1	.1								.1
(19) .2	(33) .5	(41) .2		% Depr., Dep., Amort./Sales					(21) .3	
.5	.9	.7								.7
.4	.4	.8								
(12) 2.4	(25) 1.6	(31) 2.5		% Officers', Directors' Owners' Comp/Sales						
4.6	3.4	4.9								
2952717M	5995531M	8155571M		Net Sales ($)	905M	18975M	15801M	89380M	179533M	7850977M
491274M	1288972M	2401486M		Total Assets ($)	1074M	18212M	7627M	51670M	85473M	2237430M

© RMA 2024

M = $ thousand   MM = $ million
See Pages viii through xx for Explanation of Ratios and Data

WHOLESALE—Other Miscellaneous Durable Goods Merchant Wholesalers NAICS 423990

Current Data Sorted by Assets | Comparative Historical Data

							Type of Statement		
		1	6	4	5		Unqualified	26	16
		8	18	2	1		Reviewed	38	27
	1	17	6	2	1		Compiled	24	20
5	24	36	6	1			Tax Returns	124	77
9	32	111	63	17	20		Other	267	171
	60 (4/1-9/30/23)		333 (10/1/23-3/31/24)					4/1/19-3/31/20	4/1/20-3/31/21
0-500M	500M-2MM	2-10MM	10-50MM	50-100MM	100-250MM		NUMBER OF STATEMENTS	ALL	ALL
14	57	173	99	24	26			479	311
%	%	%	%	%	%		ASSETS	%	%
29.8	19.1	13.5	10.2	8.1	6.0		Cash & Equivalents	11.0	17.2
12.2	25.9	24.7	21.5	21.6	21.6		Trade Receivables (net)	27.1	22.3
31.3	26.8	37.3	37.3	40.5	39.2		Inventory	37.6	34.0
2.6	6.0	2.3	3.7	2.7	6.0		All Other Current	2.4	4.7
75.8	77.9	77.9	72.7	72.9	72.7		Total Current	78.2	78.2
11.7	11.2	10.6	11.7	6.8	7.7		Fixed Assets (net)	10.6	10.4
5.6	4.1	4.4	7.5	8.5	8.5		Intangibles (net)	5.9	6.6
6.9	6.8	7.2	8.2	11.8	11.0		All Other Non-Current	5.4	4.8
100.0	100.0	100.0	100.0	100.0	100.0		Total	100.0	100.0
							LIABILITIES		
21.3	11.4	9.3	6.7	10.7	5.7		Notes Payable-Short Term	12.9	9.3
.4	1.3	2.1	1.6	1.2	2.7		Cur. Mat.-L.T.D.	2.0	2.4
11.3	17.6	17.5	19.0	18.3	9.3		Trade Payables	21.0	18.2
.0	.1	.1	.1	.1	.0		Income Taxes Payable	.1	.2
30.9	10.6	10.9	7.9	12.2	16.0		All Other Current	10.4	9.3
63.9	41.0	40.0	35.3	42.5	33.7		Total Current	46.4	39.4
11.4	11.4	14.3	10.0	8.4	13.0		Long-Term Debt	10.5	15.1
.0	.0	.0	.1	.3	.2		Deferred Taxes	.1	.1
8.1	8.0	3.6	6.6	8.0	7.0		All Other Non-Current	6.1	5.8
16.4	39.5	42.1	48.0	40.7	46.1		Net Worth	37.0	39.6
100.0	100.0	100.0	100.0	100.0	100.0		Total Liabilities & Net Worth	100.0	100.0
							INCOME DATA		
100.0	100.0	100.0	100.0	100.0	100.0		Net Sales	100.0	100.0
43.1	35.9	34.1	33.1	28.3	31.0		Gross Profit	33.2	33.9
37.7	31.1	28.3	26.9	25.3	27.9		Operating Expenses	27.9	26.6
5.4	4.7	5.7	6.2	3.0	3.1		Operating Profit	5.2	7.3
.4	.3	.2	.7	1.7	-.3		All Other Expenses (net)	.8	-.4
5.0	4.5	5.5	5.5	1.4	3.4		Profit Before Taxes	4.4	7.6
							RATIOS		
3.5	5.1	3.5	3.6	3.7	2.9			3.0	4.1
1.2	2.1	2.2	2.1	1.7	2.2	Current		1.8	2.2
.7	1.3	1.5	1.3	1.2	1.6			1.2	1.4
3.5	3.7	1.9	1.9	1.2	1.1			1.5	2.1
.7	1.1	1.0	.9	.6	.8	Quick		.8	1.1
.1	.6	.5	.5	.5	.5		(478)	(310)	
									.5	.5
0 UND	12 31.7	17 22.0	25 14.5	24 15.4	38 9.5			18 20.4	13 28.9
0 UND	22 16.6	32 11.5	38 9.7	43 8.5	50 7.3	Sales/Receivables		36 10.1	30 12.2
24 15.3	41 8.8	46 7.9	52 7.0	61 6.0	56 6.5			54 6.8	49 7.5
0 UND	3 104.3	39 9.4	59 6.2	72 5.1	101 3.6			38 9.5	27 13.4
16 22.3	28 13.2	79 4.6	101 3.6	122 3.0	135 2.7	Cost of Sales/Inventory		78 4.7	73 5.0
68 5.4	114 3.2	130 2.8	203 1.8	182 2.0	159 2.3			146 2.5	126 2.9
0 UND	2 224.2	12 30.3	20 18.5	16 23.0	18 20.0			14 25.3	13 28.6
0 UND	17 21.9	25 14.5	38 9.6	38 9.6	30 12.0	Cost of Sales/Payables		32 11.4	31 11.9
38 9.6	38 9.7	48 7.6	70 5.2	65 5.6	39 9.3			61 6.0	54 6.8
14.5	4.5	3.8	3.0	2.9	3.3			4.3	3.7
UND	9.0	6.5	6.0	6.8	4.2	Sales/Working Capital		8.0	6.7
-78.3	37.2	15.2	11.7	22.0	5.8			24.0	15.0
	22.8	32.7	18.8	7.0	16.8			25.8	47.0
(39)	5.0	(142) 8.5	(87) 6.8	(21) 3.9	4.2	EBIT/Interest	(397)	6.9	(248) 11.0
	-3.4	3.1	2.0	-1.2	.3			1.9	3.4
		27.9	13.7					13.5	14.9
	(17)	6.1	(15) 10.8			Net Profit + Depr., Dep., Amort./Cur. Mat. L/T/D	(47)	3.0	(16) 4.3
		2.3	4.6					1.6	1.2
.0	.0	.0	.0	.1	.1			.0	.0
.2	.1	.1	.2	.1	.1	Fixed/Worth		.2	.2
-2.8	.6	.6	.8	.6	.4			.7	.8
.5	.3	.5	.6	.7	.8			.7	.6
UND	1.7	1.1	1.2	2.1	1.7	Debt/Worth		1.8	1.7
-3.8	10.2	3.2	4.1	9.1	2.2			6.7	8.0
	83.2	54.7	46.2	70.2	23.5			57.8	82.9
(47)	29.7	(150) 25.5	(88) 21.0	(22) 25.1	(24) 9.3	% Profit Before Taxes/Tangible Net Worth	(412)	28.2	(258) 41.1
	-4.6	10.5	8.0	5.4	-6.1			7.8	13.4
96.0	34.8	25.2	18.7	11.8	12.9			19.4	28.9
17.0	9.9	11.3	7.9	7.7	5.1	% Profit Before Taxes/Total Assets		8.3	15.1
.0	-3.3	4.5	2.9	-3.0	-1.9			2.1	3.8
UND	774.4	285.9	101.8	146.6	58.6			210.4	384.5
575.5	98.9	65.6	32.2	30.7	43.8	Sales/Net Fixed Assets		51.8	62.5
27.9	27.7	17.6	10.9	16.0	7.9			20.7	22.9
12.3	5.9	3.6	2.5	2.1	2.1			3.7	3.4
5.7	3.2	2.6	1.8	1.6	1.5	Sales/Total Assets		2.4	2.3
3.4	2.3	1.7	1.3	1.3	1.3			1.7	1.7
	.1	.2	.2	.3	.3			.2	.3
(26)	.4	(103) .4	(72) .7	(17) .7	(24) .5	% Depr., Dep., Amort./Sales	(298)	.6	(173) .6
	1.7	1.1	1.3	1.4	1.7			1.4	1.5
	1.7	1.0	.8					1.2	1.2
(32)	2.7	(69) 2.3	(31) 1.4			% Officers', Directors' Owners' Comp/Sales	(174)	2.3	(107) 2.7
	6.1	4.2	2.2					4.9	5.7
31358M	317885M	2726139M	4362555M	2917246M	6432270M	Net Sales ($)		22115602M	16802403M
3675M	73569M	920407M	2224166M	1715733M	3904606M	Total Assets ($)		9181603M	5229658M

M = $ thousand   MM = $ million
See Pages viii through xx for Explanation of Ratios and Data

© RMA 2024

WHOLESALE—Other Miscellaneous Durable Goods Merchant Wholesalers NAICS 423990

Comparative Historical Data | Current Data Sorted by Sales

Comparative Historical Data					Current Data Sorted by Sales					
			Type of Statement							
16	28	16	Unqualified			1		3	12	
25	28	29	Reviewed				4	5	20	
22	35	25	Compiled			1	3	12	9	
77	105	71	Tax Returns		2	14	8	24	15	8
174	218	252	Other		7	19	12	41	75	98
4/1/21-3/31/22 ALL	4/1/22-3/31/23 ALL	4/1/23-3/31/24 ALL			60 (4/1-9/30/23)			333 (10/1/23-3/31/24)		
					0-1MM	1-3MM	3-5MM	5-10MM	10-25MM	25MM & OVER
314	414	393	**NUMBER OF STATEMENTS**		9	33	22	72	110	147
%	%	%	**ASSETS**		%	%	%	%	%	%
15.3	15.0	13.3	Cash & Equivalents			18.6	19.7	14.3	13.5	10.4
22.5	23.5	23.2	Trade Receivables (net)			19.4	17.6	24.8	24.0	24.6
37.4	36.6	35.9	Inventory			31.2	32.5	35.8	36.1	37.9
4.4	4.4	3.4	All Other Current			2.3	5.3	3.1	2.7	3.7
79.5	79.6	75.8	Total Current			71.4	75.1	77.9	76.3	76.6
9.6	9.6	10.6	Fixed Assets (net)			13.8	14.1	11.4	10.6	9.3
5.1	3.9	5.7	Intangibles (net)			4.8	.9	6.0	6.4	5.2
5.8	6.9	7.9	All Other Non-Current			10.0	9.9	4.6	6.7	8.9
100.0	100.0	100.0	Total			100.0	100.0	100.0	100.0	100.0
			LIABILITIES							
9.4	9.1	9.2	Notes Payable-Short Term			8.8	16.7	9.4	8.3	8.2
1.5	1.6	1.8	Cur. Mat.-L.T.D.			.9	1.7	3.2	1.1	1.9
19.0	17.8	17.2	Trade Payables			15.6	10.3	16.4	17.2	19.6
.4	.1	.1	Income Taxes Payable			.1	.2	.0	.1	.1
11.3	10.3	11.2	All Other Current			14.8	14.9	7.6	9.9	12.3
41.7	39.0	39.5	Total Current			40.2	43.7	36.6	36.7	42.1
10.2	11.0	12.2	Long-Term Debt			12.1	14.7	16.8	11.6	9.8
.1	.1	.1	Deferred Taxes			.0	.0	.0	.1	.1
6.1	5.7	5.7	All Other Non-Current			5.9	16.0	3.0	3.8	6.9
42.0	44.3	42.5	Net Worth			41.9	25.6	43.6	47.8	41.2
100.0	100.0	100.0	Total Liabilities & Net Worth			100.0	100.0	100.0	100.0	100.0
			INCOME DATA							
100.0	100.0	100.0	Net Sales			100.0	100.0	100.0	100.0	100.0
31.8	32.4	33.9	Gross Profit			39.4	45.5	35.9	33.0	29.7
24.9	26.3	28.5	Operating Expenses			34.8	39.2	31.6	26.6	24.8
6.8	6.0	5.3	Operating Profit			4.6	6.3	4.3	6.4	4.9
-.6	-.2	.4	All Other Expenses (net)			.5	.7	.4	.3	.4
7.4	6.2	4.9	Profit Before Taxes			4.1	5.6	3.9	6.1	4.6
			RATIOS							
3.8	4.2	3.6	Current			6.0	3.6	3.5	4.0	3.4
2.2	2.1	2.2				2.2	2.3	2.3	2.2	2.0
1.4	1.4	1.4				1.0	1.4	1.5	1.6	1.3
1.9	2.2	1.9	Quick			3.9	2.4	2.0	2.0	1.6
.9	1.0	1.0				1.0	.8	1.0	1.1	.8
.5	.5	.5				.5	.2	.5	.6	.5
15 24.0	15 23.6	19 19.7	Sales/Receivables		12 31.5	0 UND	14 25.2	22 16.7	24 15.5	
34 10.7	33 11.0	32 11.3			28 12.9	27 13.4	31 11.9	32 11.4	38 9.6	
51 7.1	53 6.9	49 7.5			45 8.1	49 7.5	50 7.3	43 8.4	52 7.0	
35 10.3	26 14.2	39 9.4	Cost of Sales/Inventory		0 UND	2 161.4	35 10.4	45 8.2	46 8.0	
81 4.5	74 4.9	85 4.3			61 6.0	35 10.4	94 3.9	85 4.3	85 4.3	
146 2.5	152 2.4	146 2.5			182 2.0	228 1.6	140 2.6	140 2.6	152 2.4	
12 30.1	9 38.8	12 30.1	Cost of Sales/Payables		4 93.4	0 UND	12 31.1	12 29.5	16 22.3	
29 12.6	27 13.5	27 13.6			24 15.2	16 22.6	25 14.6	25 14.6	32 11.5	
59 6.2	54 6.8	49 7.5			55 6.6	37 9.8	45 8.2	49 7.5	50 7.3	
3.7	3.9	3.7	Sales/Working Capital			2.3	3.5	3.7	3.8	3.7
6.6	6.5	6.6				5.1	8.5	5.7	6.4	7.2
15.0	15.4	16.5				NM	26.9	16.7	13.0	15.7
49.2	38.2	22.8	EBIT/Interest			8.0	14.1	18.6	54.4	22.3
(242) 16.6	(307) 12.0	(321) 6.5			(19) 3.8	(14) 3.7	(61) 5.5	(89) 10.5	(132) 6.5	
6.3	4.0	2.1				-2.0	-3.7	1.9	3.6	2.3
19.8	12.9	13.7	Net Profit + Depr., Dep., Amort./Cur. Mat. L/T/D						38.0	13.3
(27) 6.0	(35) 5.2	(47) 7.1						(11) 12.2	(29) 7.1	
2.7	2.2	2.3							2.7	2.5
.0	.0	.0	Fixed/Worth			.0	.0	.0	.0	.0
.1	.1	.1				.1	.2	.1	.2	.1
.5	.5	.7				2.4	3.4	.4	.7	.5
.5	.5	.6	Debt/Worth			.2	.4	.7	.5	.7
1.3	1.3	1.3				1.7	1.5	1.1	1.2	1.5
4.1	3.4	4.4				NM	NM	4.4	3.3	4.1
80.9	71.1	55.2	% Profit Before Taxes/Tangible Net Worth			45.6	62.6	39.6	63.4	53.7
(277) 40.1	(376) 32.7	(338) 22.9			(25) 6.6	(17) 26.9	(59) 17.7	(98) 35.0	(133) 22.0	
16.4	11.0	8.1				-4.6	8.1	5.7	12.0	9.7
27.9	25.1	22.0	% Profit Before Taxes/Total Assets			16.9	41.9	16.7	27.5	18.7
15.7	12.3	9.6				4.5	11.7	7.0	15.4	8.6
5.4	3.6	2.9				-3.7	-.8	2.9	5.1	3.3
409.5	377.8	236.6	Sales/Net Fixed Assets			395.9	579.1	427.8	208.8	150.9
67.3	67.9	54.6				75.7	48.9	55.0	54.0	51.2
20.1	24.4	16.4				15.3	11.7	16.0	15.2	17.7
3.4	3.6	3.4	Sales/Total Assets			3.5	6.1	3.2	3.5	3.3
2.3	2.3	2.3				2.5	2.6	2.4	2.4	2.1
1.6	1.6	1.5				1.2	1.4	1.6	1.7	1.5
.2	.2	.2	% Depr., Dep., Amort./Sales			.2		.2	.1	.3
(178) .6	(237) .5	(244) .5			(13) .4		(48) .6	(67) .4	(107) .6	
1.3	1.3	1.4				1.9		1.7	.9	1.3
1.4	1.0	1.0	% Officers', Directors', Owners' Comp/Sales			2.5	2.3	1.4	.9	.6
(103) 2.4	(147) 2.2	(140) 2.1			(18) 5.0	(11) 3.4	(33) 2.1	(45) 1.7	(33) 1.1	
4.2	4.3	3.5				9.5	6.2	4.0	3.0	1.9
13692532M	16047959M	16787453M	Net Sales ($)		3730M	78635M	84491M	536866M	1886351M	14197380M
6211894M	7835434M	8842156M	Total Assets ($)		11180M	56901M	39043M	255816M	975866M	7503350M

M = $ thousand   MM = $ million

© RMA 2024
See Pages viii through xx for Explanation of Ratios and Data

WHOLESALE—Printing and Writing Paper Merchant Wholesalers NAICS 424110

Current Data Sorted by Assets | Comparative Historical Data

						Type of Statement		
			3	2	1	Unqualified	2	1
	2		2	1		Reviewed	4	2
1						Compiled	3	5
1						Tax Returns	5	3
4	10		14	2	2	Other	31	20
	14 (4/1-9/30/23)		31 (10/1/23-3/31/24)				4/1/19-3/31/20	4/1/20-3/31/21
0-500M	500M-2MM	2-10MM	10-50MM	50-100MM	100-250MM		ALL	ALL
6		12	19	5	3	NUMBER OF STATEMENTS	45	31
%	%	%	%	%	%	ASSETS	%	%
		6.0	8.3			Cash & Equivalents	9.1	10.7
D		41.7	24.6			Trade Receivables (net)	35.5	33.3
A		32.4	29.6			Inventory	29.7	24.9
T		1.8	.9			All Other Current	2.2	1.4
A		81.9	63.4			Total Current	76.6	70.3
		10.6	22.9			Fixed Assets (net)	11.1	17.5
N		.1	4.1			Intangibles (net)	6.9	6.9
O		7.4	9.6			All Other Non-Current	5.5	5.2
T		100.0	100.0			Total	100.0	100.0
						LIABILITIES		
A		8.6	5.7			Notes Payable-Short Term	22.4	14.1
V		3.7	1.9			Cur. Mat.-L.T.D.	3.4	1.9
A		40.3	8.9			Trade Payables	21.8	21.8
I		.4	.0			Income Taxes Payable	.1	.1
L		11.2	6.2			All Other Current	6.9	7.9
A		64.2	22.7			Total Current	54.6	45.6
B		13.0	7.9			Long-Term Debt	8.7	15.9
L		.0	.0			Deferred Taxes	.1	.0
E		3.1	3.7			All Other Non-Current	1.1	6.9
		19.7	65.6			Net Worth	35.6	31.5
		100.0	100.0			Total Liabilities & Net Worth	100.0	100.0
						INCOME DATA		
		100.0	100.0			Net Sales	100.0	100.0
		27.4	21.3			Gross Profit	21.0	28.1
		24.3	17.2			Operating Expenses	18.3	25.9
		3.1	4.0			Operating Profit	2.7	2.1
		.7	1.4			All Other Expenses (net)	.6	-1.3
		2.4	2.6			Profit Before Taxes	2.1	3.4
						RATIOS		
		3.8	4.1				2.9	2.7
		1.8	3.4			Current	1.9	1.6
		1.5	1.7				1.1	1.3
		2.4	2.1				2.1	1.5
		1.4	1.7			Quick	.9	1.0
		.4	.9				.5	.7
	20	18.6	21 17.5				24 15.3	31 11.9
	35	10.5	29 12.6			Sales/Receivables	34 10.6	38 9.5
	52	7.0	46 7.9				47 7.8	49 7.5
	2	173.7	36 10.2				24 15.2	20 18.5
	38	9.6	49 7.5			Cost of Sales/Inventory	40 9.1	38 9.5
	85	4.3	62 5.9				62 5.9	58 6.3
	11	33.9	7 53.9				13 28.4	18 20.5
	24	15.2	17 21.1			Cost of Sales/Payables	23 15.9	33 11.0
	43	8.4	29 12.8				35 10.4	42 8.7
		7.5	5.8				5.4	6.7
		11.7	6.8			Sales/Working Capital	10.7	10.2
		21.4	10.6				87.1	17.3
		23.5	17.5				12.9	11.4
		5.7	11.0			EBIT/Interest	(38) 5.9	(28) 7.1
		1.9	.7				.8	2.0
			48.6			Net Profit + Depr., Dep.,		
		(10)	19.3			Amort./Cur. Mat. L/T/D		
			3.9					
		.0	.3				.0	.1
		.1	.3			Fixed/Worth	.2	.2
		1.4	.6				1.3	3.2
		.6	.2				.6	1.0
		1.5	.4			Debt/Worth	2.5	2.3
		3.5	1.3				17.9	12.0
		40.0	24.1				25.9	54.9
	(10)	17.7	(18) 16.0			% Profit Before Taxes/Tangible Net Worth	(36) 12.7	(25) 18.1
		9.6	-1.1				1.7	2.4
		22.7	16.3				12.0	15.3
		10.0	8.8			% Profit Before Taxes/Total Assets	7.1	6.8
		2.2	-2.5				.1	1.2
		346.4	20.1				290.1	109.2
		89.0	14.5			Sales/Net Fixed Assets	75.4	44.6
		31.6	9.6				25.2	9.6
		5.8	3.3				5.3	4.4
		4.1	2.9			Sales/Total Assets	3.6	3.3
		2.8	1.7				2.2	2.0
			.1				.2	.1
		(16)	.3			% Depr., Dep., Amort./Sales	(31) .4	(23) .6
			2.9				.7	3.8
							.8	1.5
						% Officers', Directors' Owners' Comp/Sales	(17) 1.6	(12) 2.9
							3.3	4.4
	27191M	277216M	930344M	742140M	1258134M	Net Sales ($)	4636093M	2632102M
	9182M	59049M	376575M	378365M	510304M	Total Assets ($)	1492197M	776113M

M = $ thousand   MM = $ million
See Pages viii through xx for Explanation of Ratios and Data

© RMA 2024

WHOLESALE—Printing and Writing Paper Merchant Wholesalers NAICS 424110

Comparative Historical Data | Current Data Sorted by Sales

				Type of Statement							
	1	2	6	Unqualified						1	5
	2	2	3	Reviewed							3
	3	3	3	Compiled					2	1	
	2	7	1	Tax Returns					1		
	18	15	32	Other		1	2	2	4		23
	4/1/21-3/31/22 ALL	4/1/22-3/31/23 ALL	4/1/23-3/31/24 ALL		0-1MM	14 (4/1-9/30/23) 1-3MM	3-5MM	31 (10/1/23-3/31/24) 5-10MM	10-25MM		25MM & OVER
	26	29	45	NUMBER OF STATEMENTS		1	2	5	6		31
	%	%	%	ASSETS	%	%	%	%	%		%
	12.0	7.8	9.8	Cash & Equivalents	D						9.9
	43.1	31.6	27.5	Trade Receivables (net)	A						28.9
	25.0	39.7	30.1	Inventory	T						29.9
	1.8	2.1	2.0	All Other Current	A						2.2
	81.9	81.1	69.4	Total Current							70.9
	11.2	10.0	14.6	Fixed Assets (net)	N						16.7
	2.1	5.2	4.0	Intangibles (net)	O						1.4
	4.9	3.7	12.0	All Other Non-Current	T						11.0
	100.0	100.0	100.0	Total							100.0
				LIABILITIES	A						
	17.1	12.2	6.2	Notes Payable-Short Term	V						7.9
	1.9	1.5	2.2	Cur. Mat.-L.T.D.	A						1.2
	26.3	21.0	17.6	Trade Payables	I						19.6
	.2	.0	.1	Income Taxes Payable	L						.1
	9.4	6.6	8.1	All Other Current	A						9.5
	54.9	41.4	34.4	Total Current	B						38.4
	8.4	9.8	8.1	Long-Term Debt	L						5.2
	.1	.1	.0	Deferred Taxes	E						.1
	3.0	5.8	4.7	All Other Non-Current							4.8
	33.6	42.9	52.8	Net Worth							51.6
	100.0	100.0	100.0	Total Liabilities & Net Worth							100.0
				INCOME DATA							
	100.0	100.0	100.0	Net Sales							100.0
	24.1	25.6	25.4	Gross Profit							20.5
	19.8	21.8	20.8	Operating Expenses							17.3
	4.3	3.8	4.6	Operating Profit							3.2
	-1.8	-.4	.6	All Other Expenses (net)							.3
	6.1	4.2	4.0	Profit Before Taxes							2.8
				RATIOS							
	4.3	3.6	4.2								4.0
	2.1	2.3	3.3	Current							3.3
	1.1	1.4	1.6								1.5
	2.4	1.7	2.3								2.1
	1.3	.9	1.5	Quick							1.5
	.9	.7	.7								.6
22	16.8	24	15.3	20	18.5	Sales/Receivables				21	17.5
42	8.6	35	10.5	30	12.3					30	12.3
59	6.2	45	8.1	47	7.7					47	7.8
15	24.5	30	12.2	34	10.8	Cost of Sales/Inventory				34	10.6
27	13.5	51	7.1	46	7.9					44	8.3
61	6.0	107	3.4	76	4.8					70	5.2
19	18.8	13	27.9	9	42.7	Cost of Sales/Payables				8	43.8
30	12.2	25	14.5	21	17.1					20	18.3
49	7.4	38	9.6	28	12.9					26	14.0
	5.6		4.2		5.1	Sales/Working Capital					5.4
	9.0		8.3		7.2						6.8
	30.5		20.5		14.6						16.4
	36.9		38.4		21.4	EBIT/Interest					19.4
(19)	15.0	(26)	10.9	(41)	10.7					(29)	11.0
	8.0		2.4		2.0						2.6
					48.6	Net Profit + Depr., Dep., Amort./Cur. Mat. L/T/D					49.0
		(14)	25.8							(13)	26.3
					7.0						6.0
	.0		.1		.1	Fixed/Worth					.1
	.1		.1		.2						.3
	.5		.5		.4						.4
	.4		.7		.3	Debt/Worth					.3
	1.3		1.8		.7						.6
	4.1		2.8		1.6						1.5
	87.0		54.1		33.5	% Profit Before Taxes/Tangible Net Worth					24.4
(24)	35.0	(27)	30.2	(42)	19.3					(30)	14.5
	15.7		15.4		7.8						4.5
	22.9		24.4		20.8	% Profit Before Taxes/Total Assets					16.0
	13.6		11.1		10.6						9.0
	5.2		3.6		2.6						2.8
	999.8		276.6		75.7	Sales/Net Fixed Assets					58.7
	113.1		67.8		29.9						14.9
	15.2		30.0		11.7						10.3
	4.8		4.6		3.5	Sales/Total Assets					3.5
	2.8		3.2		2.9						2.9
	2.1		2.1		2.0						1.7
	.3		.2		.1	% Depr., Dep., Amort./Sales					.1
(15)	.7	(19)	.6	(30)	.4					(24)	.4
	2.4		1.5		.9						1.1
	1.2				.7	% Officers', Directors', Owners' Comp/Sales					
(10)	2.4			(12)	1.3						
	12.4				5.3						
	1461994M		1844137M		3235025M	Net Sales ($)		1940M	6697M	34010M	83717M	3108661M
	531696M		653580M		1333475M	Total Assets ($)		1323M	2073M	12629M	39674M	1277776M

© RMA 2024 M = $ thousand   MM = $ million
See Pages viii through xx for Explanation of Ratios and Data

WHOLESALE—Stationery and Office Supplies Merchant Wholesalers NAICS 424120

Current Data Sorted by Assets | Comparative Historical Data

						Type of Statement		
			3		1	Unqualified	8	1
		5	5			Reviewed	11	6
		2				Compiled	5	3
		2				Tax Returns	17	3
3	2	13	8	6	2	Other	38	22
0-500M	10 (4/1-9/30/23) 500M-2MM	2-10MM	42 (10/1/23-3/31/24) 10-50MM	50-100MM	100-250MM		4/1/19-3/31/20 ALL	4/1/20-3/31/21 ALL
3	2	22	16	6	3	NUMBER OF STATEMENTS	79	35
%	%	%	%	%	%	ASSETS	%	%
		13.4	4.1			Cash & Equivalents	10.0	18.1
		31.5	38.6			Trade Receivables (net)	34.3	27.4
		30.0	23.0			Inventory	25.6	20.9
		3.9	3.6			All Other Current	5.0	3.4
		78.7	69.3			Total Current	75.0	69.8
		10.4	14.1			Fixed Assets (net)	12.8	15.9
		5.3	4.7			Intangibles (net)	6.6	5.9
		5.6	11.8			All Other Non-Current	5.6	8.4
		100.0	100.0			Total	100.0	100.0
						LIABILITIES		
		9.2	11.7			Notes Payable-Short Term	17.7	21.5
		1.5	1.5			Cur. Mat.-L.T.D.	1.8	2.9
		18.9	17.9			Trade Payables	21.8	16.6
		.1	.1			Income Taxes Payable	.0	.0
		9.3	12.1			All Other Current	13.0	11.1
		39.0	43.3			Total Current	54.3	52.0
		9.1	6.7			Long-Term Debt	9.1	19.8
		.0	.1			Deferred Taxes	.2	.3
		6.9	6.9			All Other Non-Current	5.2	4.6
		44.9	43.0			Net Worth	31.2	23.2
		100.0	100.0			Total Liabilties & Net Worth	100.0	100.0
						INCOME DATA		
		100.0	100.0			Net Sales	100.0	100.0
		33.8	26.5			Gross Profit	32.2	34.0
		30.9	24.7			Operating Expenses	29.7	30.9
		2.9	1.8			Operating Profit	2.5	3.0
		.3	.1			All Other Expenses (net)	.8	-.3
		2.6	1.7			Profit Before Taxes	1.7	3.4
						RATIOS		
		3.9	2.6				2.1	3.2
		2.1	2.0			Current	1.5	1.6
		1.3	1.1				.9	1.2
		2.2	1.4				1.3	2.7
		1.0	1.1			Quick	.8	1.0
		.6	.7				.5	.7
		26 14.2	32 11.5				27 13.5	21 17.5
		35 10.3	38 9.6			Sales/Receivables	36 10.2	33 10.9
		52 7.0	61 6.0				53 6.9	43 8.4
		11 34.4	23 16.1				12 29.5	12 29.7
		42 8.7	41 8.8			Cost of Sales/Inventory	42 8.7	42 8.6
		111 3.3	89 4.1				81 4.5	79 4.6
		13 27.3	13 29.0				16 22.4	13 27.7
		24 15.2	24 14.9			Cost of Sales/Payables	31 11.6	24 15.0
		53 6.9	47 7.7				49 7.5	33 10.9
		5.0	6.0				6.0	5.3
		7.2	6.9			Sales/Working Capital	13.1	8.1
		18.2	67.8				-96.1	41.4
		19.5	13.1				9.3	27.2
	(19)	3.7	(14) 2.6			EBIT/Interest	(72) 2.9	(32) 7.1
		1.3	.7				.7	-.9
							11.2	
						Net Profit + Depr., Dep., Amort./Cur. Mat. L/T/D	(15) 3.4	
							-.1	
		.0	.1				.1	.0
		.1	.3			Fixed/Worth	.4	.4
		2.6	.7				3.6	1.9
		.5	.6				1.0	.6
		.9	1.5			Debt/Worth	2.4	1.9
		8.3	7.7				25.2	15.5
		49.1	32.8				38.0	54.9
	(18)	24.1	(15) 7.9			% Profit Before Taxes/Tangible Net Worth	(61) 15.8	(28) 29.2
		-.1	.5				3.6	-2.2
		19.8	9.1				10.1	20.7
		7.5	3.6			% Profit Before Taxes/Total Assets	4.2	7.1
		.2	.2				.0	-1.7
		684.7	151.4				172.4	142.7
		73.6	36.0			Sales/Net Fixed Assets	49.2	40.4
		28.3	12.2				17.7	10.0
		3.8	3.3				4.4	4.4
		3.1	2.4			Sales/Total Assets	3.0	2.6
		2.4	1.9				2.2	1.7
		.2	.1				.3	.4
	(13)	.6	(14) .8			% Depr., Dep., Amort./Sales	(59) .6	(23) 1.5
		1.4	1.5				1.4	3.7
			1.1				1.0	
	(10)		1.5			% Officers', Directors' Owners' Comp/Sales	(25) 3.7	
			2.9				6.7	
5741M	7311M	364149M	1233547M	1245711M	1472411M	Net Sales ($)	5833945M	1813666M
720M	1947M	112479M	425568M	470259M	544982M	Total Assets ($)	1859802M	583109M

M = $ thousand MM = $ million
See Pages viii through xx for Explanation of Ratios and Data

© RMA 2024

WHOLESALE—Stationery and Office Supplies Merchant Wholesalers NAICS 424120

Comparative Historical Data / Current Data Sorted by Sales

							Type of Statement						
		2		5		4	Unqualified					3	4
		6		4		10	Reviewed				1	2	6
				3		2	Compiled						1
		4		3		2	Tax Returns				1	9	16
		20		23		34	Other	2	2	1	4		
		4/1/21-3/31/22		4/1/22-3/31/23		4/1/23-3/31/24			10 (4/1-9/30/23)			42 (10/1/23-3/31/24)	
		ALL		ALL		ALL		0-1MM	1-3MM	3-5MM	5-10MM	10-25MM	25MM & OVER
		32		38		52	NUMBER OF STATEMENTS	2	2	1	6	14	27
		%		%		%	ASSETS	%	%	%	%	%	%
		13.3		10.4		12.0	Cash & Equivalents					14.6	3.8
		35.1		33.9		34.5	Trade Receivables (net)					24.6	41.0
		23.2		30.8		25.1	Inventory					33.0	23.8
		3.6		3.8		3.8	All Other Current					4.5	4.3
		75.2		78.9		75.4	Total Current					76.6	72.9
		10.7		8.4		11.4	Fixed Assets (net)					11.1	10.7
		5.9		5.3		4.7	Intangibles (net)					7.5	5.1
		8.2		7.5		8.4	All Other Non-Current					4.8	11.3
		100.0		100.0		100.0	Total					100.0	100.0
							LIABILITIES						
		11.4		12.7		14.0	Notes Payable-Short Term					7.1	16.4
		.9		4.8		1.4	Cur. Mat.-L.T.D.					2.0	1.4
		19.5		15.9		16.3	Trade Payables					12.5	19.6
		.2		.1		.1	Income Taxes Payable					.2	.1
		12.5		13.0		10.1	All Other Current					9.8	12.5
		44.4		46.5		42.1	Total Current					31.6	50.0
		10.2		8.0		7.6	Long-Term Debt					7.9	5.5
		.0		.2		.0	Deferred Taxes					.0	.0
		4.5		8.9		6.3	All Other Non-Current					8.3	7.2
		40.9		36.4		43.9	Net Worth					52.1	37.3
		100.0		100.0		100.0	Total Liabilities & Net Worth					100.0	100.0
							INCOME DATA						
		100.0		100.0		100.0	Net Sales					100.0	100.0
		31.2		29.5		33.0	Gross Profit					36.9	26.9
		26.3		26.0		29.6	Operating Expenses					31.6	24.3
		4.8		3.5		3.4	Operating Profit					5.4	2.6
		-1.3		.9		.3	All Other Expenses (net)					.2	.3
		6.1		2.6		3.1	Profit Before Taxes					5.1	2.3
							RATIOS						
		3.5		2.9		2.7						4.1	2.2
		2.0		1.9		2.0	Current					2.8	1.5
		1.2		1.3		1.2						1.8	1.1
		2.3		1.6		1.7						2.8	1.3
		1.1		1.0		.9	Quick					.9	.9
		.7		.6		.7						.6	.7
26	14.1		28	13.1	30	12.3					14	25.8	32	11.4
36	10.0		44	8.3	38	9.7	Sales/Receivables				31	11.9	42	8.6
53	6.9		59	6.2	56	6.5					35	10.5	69	5.3
14	26.8		15	24.5	18	20.4					17	21.5	23	16.1
45	8.1		52	7.0	41	8.8	Cost of Sales/Inventory				69	5.3	41	8.8
76	4.8		118	3.1	118	3.1					126	2.9	140	2.6
12	30.1		13	29.1	13	29.0					12	31.2	17	22.1
23	16.0		19	19.0	23	15.9	Cost of Sales/Payables				18	20.3	23	15.7
51	7.2		46	8.0	42	8.6					33	10.9	54	6.8
		3.6		4.6		5.0						5.0	5.1
		8.3		8.8		7.2	Sales/Working Capital					6.4	9.5
		39.3		21.7		29.2						8.9	110.0
		46.8		22.4		13.3						39.0	10.6
(25)	16.8	(25)	8.9	(47)	3.8	EBIT/Interest				(13)	8.4	(25)	3.8
		6.1		-.8		1.4						2.9	1.5
							Net Profit + Depr., Dep., Amort./Cur. Mat. L/T/D						
		.0		.0		.0						.0	.1
		.2		.1		.2	Fixed/Worth					.1	.2
		1.1		.3		.6						1.0	.5
		.5		.7		.6						.3	.8
		1.7		1.8		.9	Debt/Worth					.7	2.3
		3.2		4.1		4.6						6.5	9.3
		71.5		55.6		42.9						56.5	37.2
(28)	31.6	(31)	22.8	(47)	21.2	% Profit Before Taxes/Tangible Net Worth				(12)	38.1	(24)	20.5
		5.2		10.3		5.5						9.0	6.7
		24.8		20.2		13.3						33.4	9.5
		14.1		10.0		7.5	% Profit Before Taxes/Total Assets					9.7	4.7
		1.3		.4		1.1						4.3	1.6
		435.2		876.4		643.8						740.9	183.7
		65.3		73.7		42.4	Sales/Net Fixed Assets					56.2	40.4
		12.0		34.0		14.3						16.2	13.8
		4.3		4.2		3.7						3.7	3.5
		2.9		2.9		2.9	Sales/Total Assets					3.1	2.4
		1.7		2.0		1.9						2.4	1.9
		.4		.3		.2							.1
(17)	.7	(22)	.5	(35)	.6	% Depr., Dep., Amort./Sales					(23)	.6
		2.7		1.4		1.4							1.1
				.5		1.2	% Officers', Directors' Owners' Comp/Sales						
			(11)	1.3	(14)	2.3							
				3.0		4.0							
		2477995M		3183101M		4328870M	Net Sales ($)	1456M	5209M	3935M	46635M	248060M	4023575M
		844664M		1213264M		1555955M	Total Assets ($)	1017M	378M	2605M	17772M	87144M	1447039M

© RMA 2024

M = $ thousand   MM = $ million

See Pages viii through xx for Explanation of Ratios and Data

WHOLESALE—Industrial and Personal Service Paper Merchant Wholesalers NAICS 424130

Current Data Sorted by Assets | **Comparative Historical Data**

						Type of Statement		
		2		2	2	Unqualified	8	5
		2	10	3	2	Reviewed	20	13
		4				Compiled	4	3
1	3	6				Tax Returns	15	9
	2	14	13	5	3	Other	45	31
	22 (4/1-9/30/23)		52 (10/1/23-3/31/24)				4/1/19- 3/31/20 ALL	4/1/20- 3/31/21 ALL
0-500M	500M-2MM	2-10MM	10-50MM	50-100MM	100-250MM	NUMBER OF STATEMENTS	92	61
1	5	28	23	10	7			
%	%	%	%	%	%	ASSETS	%	%
		16.3	9.4	9.8		Cash & Equivalents	6.7	9.6
		27.6	31.8	32.1		Trade Receivables (net)	34.3	30.5
		37.2	27.7	28.9		Inventory	32.6	36.1
		1.5	2.2	3.1		All Other Current	3.8	2.1
		82.7	71.1	73.8		Total Current	77.5	78.3
		9.0	8.4	9.5		Fixed Assets (net)	11.3	12.3
		1.7	2.5	4.6		Intangibles (net)	6.4	4.4
		6.6	18.0	12.0		All Other Non-Current	4.8	5.0
		100.0	100.0	100.0		Total	100.0	100.0
						LIABILITIES		
		5.9	6.0	9.3		Notes Payable-Short Term	15.3	13.2
		.6	1.0	.7		Cur. Mat.-L.T.D.	1.6	2.7
		19.1	19.3	15.1		Trade Payables	21.8	22.5
		.0	.2	.0		Income Taxes Payable	.1	.2
		8.3	8.6	20.7		All Other Current	8.8	9.6
		33.8	35.2	45.8		Total Current	47.7	48.1
		12.5	4.3	4.6		Long-Term Debt	10.9	15.8
		.0	.4	.2		Deferred Taxes	.1	.2
		5.0	14.0	5.8		All Other Non-Current	5.9	6.2
		48.7	46.2	43.6		Net Worth	35.4	29.6
		100.0	100.0	100.0		Total Liabilities & Net Worth	100.0	100.0
						INCOME DATA		
		100.0	100.0	100.0		Net Sales	100.0	100.0
		26.8	24.3	23.4		Gross Profit	23.8	26.1
		21.9	20.3	18.3		Operating Expenses	20.8	22.8
		4.9	4.1	5.1		Operating Profit	3.0	3.3
		-.1	.1	-.9		All Other Expenses (net)	.0	-.2
		5.0	4.0	6.0		Profit Before Taxes	3.0	3.5
						RATIOS		
		4.9	3.8	3.2			2.3	2.6
		2.6	2.7	2.0		Current	1.6	1.6
		1.8	1.4	1.1			1.2	1.2
		2.5	1.9	2.3			1.5	1.5
		1.4	1.1	.9		Quick	.9	.8
		.7	.9	.5			.6	.5
		16 22.2	27 13.4	30 12.0			31 11.8	30 12.3
		29 12.7	39 9.3	35 10.5		Sales/Receivables	36 10.0	36 10.1
		49 7.5	51 7.2	45 8.2			44 8.3	43 8.5
		29 12.8	33 11.1	17 21.7			28 13.0	35 10.4
		47 7.8	40 9.1	49 7.5		Cost of Sales/Inventory	42 8.6	50 7.3
		94 3.9	83 4.4	96 3.8			68 5.4	87 4.2
		11 33.2	14 26.7	11 33.7			16 23.2	21 17.5
		22 16.5	26 14.1	24 15.4		Cost of Sales/Payables	27 13.4	33 11.0
		40 9.2	34 10.8	32 11.3			41 8.8	50 7.3
		4.1	4.4	4.4			7.5	6.1
		7.1	6.4	11.1		Sales/Working Capital	12.0	9.4
		12.7	14.1	22.7			22.5	29.4
		30.4	28.4				15.9	34.2
		(21) 10.0	(20) 12.6			EBIT/Interest	(81) 4.8	(58) 6.7
		4.6	5.5				2.2	3.6
						Net Profit + Depr., Dep., Amort./Cur. Mat. L/T/D	8.4	13.6
							(20) 4.9	(11) 6.5
							3.0	1.5
		.0	.0	.0			.1	.1
		.1	.1	.1		Fixed/Worth	.3	.3
		.2	.2	.6			.7	.9
		.5	.6	.4			.9	1.1
		1.2	1.3	1.1		Debt/Worth	2.3	2.6
		2.2	2.7	6.7			5.9	6.4
		64.1	37.2				38.4	61.1
		(25) 28.6	24.3			% Profit Before Taxes/Tangible Net Worth	(78) 23.9	(50) 27.0
		19.4	7.4				6.4	8.3
		25.7	14.8	29.5			16.0	15.9
		13.1	8.9	15.2		% Profit Before Taxes/Total Assets	7.5	10.3
		7.6	5.6	9.2			2.2	3.4
		747.3	237.1	960.6			192.7	123.5
		117.4	73.8	87.0		Sales/Net Fixed Assets	49.3	41.9
		22.7	15.1	18.0			15.2	18.9
		4.5	4.0	4.2			4.2	3.8
		3.4	2.8	2.9		Sales/Total Assets	3.5	3.2
		2.3	2.0	2.1			2.0	2.4
		.2	.2				.2	.2
		(13) .4	(15) .5			% Depr., Dep., Amort./Sales	(63) .6	(44) .6
		1.4	1.1				1.1	1.3
		1.2					.9	.8
		(11) 1.7				% Officers', Directors' Owners' Comp/Sales	(29) 2.2	(25) 1.7
		4.0					3.6	3.8
1015M	35105M	529877M	1771722M	2158615M	2741352M	Net Sales ($)	8131465M	4920501M
79M	7286M	161621M	604464M	667042M	1125108M	Total Assets ($)	2939984M	1742749M

M = $ thousand   MM = $ million
See Pages viii through xx for Explanation of Ratios and Data

© RMA 2024

WHOLESALE—Industrial and Personal Service Paper Merchant Wholesalers NAICS 424130

Comparative Historical Data / Current Data Sorted by Sales

			Type of Statement						
4	2	6	Unqualified				1	2	5
15	12	17	Reviewed					3	15
2	7	4	Compiled		1				
9	11	10	Tax Returns		1	1	2	4	2
21	37	37	Other	1	3	3	1	11	22
4/1/21-3/31/22 ALL	4/1/22-3/31/23 ALL	4/1/23-3/31/24 ALL		0-1MM	22 (4/1-9/30/23) 1-3MM	3-5MM	52 (10/1/23-3/31/24) 5-10MM	10-25MM	25MM & OVER
51	69	74	NUMBER OF STATEMENTS	1	5	4	20	44	
%	%	%	ASSETS	%	%	%	%	%	%
8.6	10.1	12.4	Cash & Equivalents					16.7	8.3
35.2	34.9	29.1	Trade Receivables (net)					23.9	31.7
32.2	35.2	33.7	Inventory					39.5	31.7
3.1	2.4	2.1	All Other Current	DATA NOT AVAILABLE				1.7	2.4
79.2	82.5	77.3	Total Current					81.9	74.1
14.5	9.3	9.1	Fixed Assets (net)					6.3	9.3
2.0	2.3	2.2	Intangibles (net)					1.4	2.6
4.3	5.9	11.4	All Other Non-Current					10.5	14.0
100.0	100.0	100.0	Total					100.0	100.0
			LIABILITIES						
8.4	7.4	7.2	Notes Payable-Short Term					7.4	6.8
1.6	1.1	1.1	Cur. Mat.-L.T.D.					.9	1.3
21.3	25.8	17.5	Trade Payables					15.4	18.6
.0	.1	.1	Income Taxes Payable					.0	.1
9.7	9.4	9.8	All Other Current					10.2	11.3
41.0	43.8	35.6	Total Current					33.9	38.1
9.6	9.8	10.1	Long-Term Debt					9.7	7.8
.1	.1	.2	Deferred Taxes					.3	.1
2.5	3.6	9.3	All Other Non-Current					7.6	10.2
46.9	42.8	44.8	Net Worth					48.5	43.8
100.0	100.0	100.0	Total Liabilties & Net Worth					100.0	100.0
			INCOME DATA						
100.0	100.0	100.0	Net Sales					100.0	100.0
25.1	23.0	25.1	Gross Profit					28.2	22.7
20.5	18.4	20.4	Operating Expenses					22.0	19.1
4.6	4.7	4.7	Operating Profit					6.2	3.6
-1.7	-.5	-.1	All Other Expenses (net)					.3	.0
6.3	5.2	4.8	Profit Before Taxes					5.9	3.6
			RATIOS						
3.4	3.1	3.9						4.1	3.1
1.9	1.9	2.5	Current					3.1	2.2
1.4	1.3	1.6						1.8	1.4
1.7	1.7	2.1						2.5	1.8
1.1	1.0	1.1	Quick					1.3	1.1
.7	.7	.7						.6	.7
29 12.5	25 14.7	23 16.0					15 24.5	26 14.0	
39 9.3	35 10.4	35 10.5	Sales/Receivables				32 11.3	34 10.7	
51 7.1	45 8.2	49 7.5					47 7.7	47 7.8	
32 11.4	27 13.4	31 11.8					32 11.3	28 12.9	
49 7.5	47 7.8	46 7.9	Cost of Sales/Inventory				43 8.5	46 7.9	
76 4.8	66 5.5	94 3.9					94 3.9	87 4.2	
15 23.8	17 20.9	12 30.6					7 49.4	14 26.3	
27 13.7	30 12.1	25 14.7	Cost of Sales/Payables				20 18.2	24 14.9	
48 7.6	47 7.8	36 10.0					32 11.4	35 10.5	
5.7	6.2	4.3						4.5	4.8
8.0	10.3	7.6	Sales/Working Capital					5.8	8.6
18.3	21.9	14.2						14.5	15.6
88.4	70.5	27.5						90.7	26.7
(43) 39.6	(53) 19.8	(60) 11.8	EBIT/Interest				(15) 10.4	(39) 12.3	
9.4	9.1	3.9						7.3	2.3
16.4		264.9							290.9
(12) 8.8		(15) 6.1	Net Profit + Depr., Dep., Amort./Cur. Mat. L/T/D					(12) 10.5	
3.3		1.6							1.8
.1	.0	.0						.0	.1
.2	.1	.1	Fixed/Worth					.1	.1
.4	.3	.3						.2	.4
.5	.7	.7						.4	.7
1.0	1.2	1.1	Debt/Worth					1.1	1.1
2.9	3.4	2.7						2.2	2.7
59.7	59.1	39.4						72.9	36.7
(50) 36.5	(65) 36.6	(68) 25.2	% Profit Before Taxes/Tangible Net Worth				(18) 36.3	(42) 24.5	
21.4	22.3	16.3						20.2	11.3
24.5	23.5	24.5						30.6	18.6
15.3	14.7	13.2	% Profit Before Taxes/Total Assets					15.2	11.0
8.1	8.2	6.3						8.6	3.3
100.7	675.9	644.7						999.8	232.1
39.9	107.9	75.9	Sales/Net Fixed Assets					187.0	68.9
11.7	23.6	18.4						30.4	18.3
3.9	4.7	4.1						4.2	4.3
3.3	3.4	3.1	Sales/Total Assets					2.8	3.3
2.2	2.7	2.2						2.2	2.1
.3	.1	.2							.2
(37) .6	(43) .4	(44) .6	% Depr., Dep., Amort./Sales					(31) .4	
1.5	.9	1.1							.9
.6	.8	.7							.5
(24) 1.6	(24) 1.6	(28) 1.4	% Officers', Directors', Owners' Comp/Sales					(15) .9	
3.6	3.0	2.0							1.6
4004380M	5725440M	7237686M	Net Sales ($)	1015M	20616M	36243M	356380M	6823432M	
1444155M	1812301M	2565600M	Total Assets ($)	79M	18688M	10841M	125235M	2410757M	

M = $ thousand   MM = $ million

© RMA 2024

WHOLESALE—Drugs and Druggists' Sundries Merchant Wholesalers NAICS 424210

Current Data Sorted by Assets | **Comparative Historical Data**

0-500M	500M-2MM	2-10MM	10-50MM	50-100MM	100-250MM	Type of Statement	4/1/19-3/31/20 ALL	4/1/20-3/31/21 ALL
	1	3	7	6	6	Unqualified	29	14
	6	2	8	1		Reviewed	8	3
	6	5	2	2		Compiled	10	5
			2	1		Tax Returns	15	10
		27	38	8	7	Other	91	59
27 (4/1-9/30/23)			109 (10/1/23-3/31/24)			NUMBER OF STATEMENTS	153	91
	13	37	57	16	13	ASSETS		
	%	%	%	%	%		%	%
DATA NOT AVAILABLE	26.7	14.3	14.4	9.0	10.3	Cash & Equivalents	13.7	17.4
	14.3	27.7	27.3	22.6	33.4	Trade Receivables (net)	29.5	27.5
	15.5	32.3	30.6	24.7	18.5	Inventory	32.0	31.9
	9.2	3.6	3.7	4.0	3.4	All Other Current	3.5	2.2
	65.8	77.9	76.0	60.3	65.6	Total Current	78.7	78.9
	6.6	12.6	9.7	12.8	6.9	Fixed Assets (net)	7.8	7.8
	15.2	4.9	6.1	20.9	23.3	Intangibles (net)	7.5	8.1
	12.4	4.5	8.2	5.9	4.1	All Other Non-Current	6.0	5.2
	100.0	100.0	100.0	100.0	100.0	Total	100.0	100.0
						LIABILITIES		
	13.3	9.1	6.3	4.0	3.6	Notes Payable-Short Term	11.2	9.8
	1.6	1.3	4.2	2.0	2.0	Cur. Mat.-L.T.D.	1.8	2.3
	9.5	16.9	24.5	19.1	24.8	Trade Payables	23.4	23.7
	.0	.0	.2	.6	.1	Income Taxes Payable	.2	.2
	6.7	15.2	10.2	10.7	13.1	All Other Current	11.0	9.7
	31.1	42.5	45.4	36.4	43.5	Total Current	47.6	45.5
	20.6	7.5	28.6	14.2	21.5	Long-Term Debt	8.9	14.5
	.0	.1	.1	.4	.0	Deferred Taxes	.1	.1
	4.1	6.4	6.6	11.2	4.5	All Other Non-Current	5.0	4.1
	44.2	43.6	19.4	37.8	30.4	Net Worth	38.5	35.8
	100.0	100.0	100.0	100.0	100.0	Total Liabilities & Net Worth	100.0	100.0
						INCOME DATA		
	100.0	100.0	100.0	100.0	100.0	Net Sales	100.0	100.0
	32.9	39.6	33.3	32.5	23.2	Gross Profit	32.4	34.9
	26.7	32.2	26.4	25.5	20.2	Operating Expenses	26.3	26.8
	6.3	7.3	6.9	6.9	3.0	Operating Profit	6.0	8.1
	-.4	.2	.6	2.7	1.8	All Other Expenses (net)	.8	.2
	6.6	7.1	6.3	4.3	1.2	Profit Before Taxes	5.2	7.8
						RATIOS		
	7.1	2.8	2.4	2.2	2.3	Current	3.3	3.2
	4.2	1.9	1.9	1.7	1.6		1.7	1.8
	1.3	1.4	1.2	1.1	1.0		1.1	1.2
	4.1	1.8	1.3	1.1	1.2	Quick	1.7	1.9
	2.3	1.0	1.0	.7	1.0		1.0	1.0
	.7	.6	.6	.5	.8		.6	.6
	0 UND	13 27.1	16 23.0	25 14.5	22 16.6	Sales/Receivables	23 15.8	16 22.4
	7 50.8	40 9.2	40 9.2	38 9.6	32 11.3		40 9.2	35 10.4
	21 17.8	59 6.2	53 6.9	70 5.2	51 7.1		57 6.4	51 7.2
	0 UND	20 18.0	28 13.0	46 7.9	6 59.1	Cost of Sales/Inventory	26 13.9	17 21.2
	12 31.6	55 6.6	81 4.5	79 4.6	26 14.2		73 5.0	68 5.4
	43 8.5	166 2.2	135 2.7	126 2.9	59 6.2		126 2.9	122 3.0
	0 UND	17 21.5	29 12.6	27 13.7	12 31.1	Cost of Sales/Payables	18 20.5	22 16.6
	3 108.0	33 11.2	43 8.4	41 8.9	32 11.5		42 8.7	41 9.0
	17 21.4	57 6.4	57 6.4	94 3.9	36 10.2		78 4.7	60 6.1
	10.2	3.4	4.2	5.2	6.1	Sales/Working Capital	4.0	4.5
	11.1	8.0	8.0	7.1	18.9		8.8	9.3
	NM	15.7	26.6	45.6	441.2		37.3	24.5
		15.9	23.5	75.0	15.5	EBIT/Interest	29.1	58.8
	(27) 7.4	(49) 11.5	(12) 14.2	(11) 1.9		(119) 5.8	(65) 16.5
	-1.8	2.1	1.2	-1.5		1.6	3.5
			15.2			Net Profit + Depr., Dep., Amort./Cur. Mat. L/T/D	39.8	54.2
		(13) 6.6					(21) 7.3	(10) 14.5
		1.9					1.1	2.7
	.0	.0	.1	.3	.1	Fixed/Worth	.0	.0
	.1	.1	.2	.8	1.3		.1	.1
	NM	.6	.9	-.4	-.8		.6	.8
	.6	.6	.8	.9	1.3	Debt/Worth	.6	.7
	1.5	1.4	1.5	2.4	15.6		2.0	1.6
	-5.1	4.1	6.7	-7.1	-2.8		8.2	7.6
		85.6	52.3	84.9		% Profit Before Taxes/Tangible Net Worth	59.7	97.4
	(33) 26.9	(48) 21.5	(10) 33.0			(128) 27.3	(73) 40.3
	4.8	8.5	10.0			7.8	14.7
	42.0	29.7	20.4	19.6	12.7	% Profit Before Taxes/Total Assets	22.1	38.1
	32.7	8.1	9.5	10.0	3.1		8.2	15.9
	11.5	1.3	2.6	-3.9	-5.5		.5	3.0
	UND	243.4	134.0	58.1	126.5	Sales/Net Fixed Assets	415.4	604.2
	447.3	46.7	47.8	26.5	69.5		82.7	85.8
	58.8	7.2	12.1	12.8	28.0		24.1	30.2
	8.0	3.5	3.4	2.8	5.3	Sales/Total Assets	3.6	4.4
	5.0	2.5	2.2	1.5	2.9		2.3	2.7
	3.5	1.6	1.7	1.3	.9		1.6	1.7
		.1	.2	.2		% Depr., Dep., Amort./Sales	.2	.1
	(17) .4	(42) .5	(11) 1.0			(96) .3	(55) .3
	1.4	1.2	2.7			1.0	1.0
						% Officers', Directors' Owners' Comp/Sales	1.0	1.3
							(28) 2.2	(22) 2.7
							5.7	6.4
	68559M	512507M	4094809M	2246282M	6355102M	Net Sales ($)	11833869M	9161443M
	11237M	193203M	1413603M	1080823M	2075028M	Total Assets ($)	4685260M	3203712M

M = $ thousand   MM = $ million
See Pages viii through xx for Explanation of Ratios and Data

© RMA 2024

WHOLESALE—Drugs and Druggists' Sundries Merchant Wholesalers NAICS 424210

Comparative Historical Data					Current Data Sorted by Sales					
				Type of Statement						
13		23	19	Unqualified				1	5	19
7		14	12	Reviewed				1	1	7
6		7	6	Compiled			1	3	1	3
13		16	13	Tax Returns	1		4	1	4	1
54		74	86	Other		3		11	17	51
4/1/21-		4/1/22-	4/1/23-			27 (4/1-9/30/23)		109 (10/1/23-3/31/24)		
3/31/22		3/31/23	3/31/24							
ALL		ALL	ALL		0-1MM	1-3MM	3-5MM	5-10MM	10-25MM	25MM & OVER
93		134	136	NUMBER OF STATEMENTS	1	3	9	15	27	81
%		%	%	**ASSETS**	%	%	%	%	%	%
15.5		15.5	14.5	Cash & Equivalents				11.9	15.0	13.0
25.6		26.9	26.2	Trade Receivables (net)				22.1	23.1	28.6
31.8		31.4	27.8	Inventory				37.8	31.7	26.1
3.2		3.7	4.2	All Other Current				2.9	4.8	3.8
76.1		77.5	72.7	Total Current				74.8	74.6	71.4
9.5		8.5	10.3	Fixed Assets (net)				9.7	13.3	9.5
11.0		7.6	10.0	Intangibles (net)				12.3	2.0	12.6
3.5		6.3	7.0	All Other Non-Current				3.2	10.2	6.4
100.0		100.0	100.0	Total				100.0	100.0	100.0
				LIABILITIES						
11.7		9.6	7.2	Notes Payable-Short Term				13.4	9.0	4.8
1.5		3.3	2.7	Cur. Mat.-L.T.D.				.5	4.5	2.7
20.9		23.6	20.4	Trade Payables				13.5	14.4	25.4
.1		.2	.2	Income Taxes Payable				.0	.0	.3
10.2		9.2	11.5	All Other Current				14.8	9.7	11.4
44.4		45.9	42.0	Total Current				42.2	37.6	44.5
15.5		10.5	19.7	Long-Term Debt				20.1	7.0	25.8
.2		.1	.1	Deferred Taxes				.0	.1	.1
8.5		5.0	6.6	All Other Non-Current				4.5	5.5	7.6
31.4		38.6	31.5	Net Worth				33.3	49.8	22.0
100.0		100.0	100.0	Total Liabilities & Net Worth				100.0	100.0	100.0
				INCOME DATA						
100.0		100.0	100.0	Net Sales				100.0	100.0	100.0
34.6		33.3	33.9	Gross Profit				35.5	40.8	29.7
27.3		25.7	27.3	Operating Expenses				27.5	35.1	23.8
7.2		7.6	6.6	Operating Profit				8.0	5.8	5.9
.4		.6	.8	All Other Expenses (net)				.1	.3	1.2
6.8		7.0	5.8	Profit Before Taxes				7.9	5.5	4.8
				RATIOS						
3.1		2.7	2.7					4.7	2.8	2.3
1.8		1.7	1.9	Current				2.4	1.9	1.7
1.2		1.3	1.3					1.3	1.4	1.2
1.7		1.7	1.4					2.3	1.6	1.3
.9		.9	.9	Quick				.9	1.2	.9
.5		.5	.6					.5	.7	.6
15	24.3	21	17.3	16	23.5		12	31.3	7	51.6	17	20.9
32	11.4	38	9.5	34	10.6	Sales/Receivables	40	9.1	33	10.9	35	10.5
62	5.9	51	7.1	53	6.9		63	5.8	54	6.7	51	7.1
38	9.7	20	17.9	19	18.9		26	14.2	21	17.6	19	19.7
79	4.6	59	6.2	57	6.4	Cost of Sales/Inventory	114	3.2	79	4.6	59	6.2
135	2.7	111	3.3	126	2.9		166	2.2	192	1.9	104	3.5
20	18.6	24	15.1	21	17.4		5	79.7	12	30.5	27	13.6
38	9.6	38	9.7	36	10.2	Cost of Sales/Payables	25	14.8	34	10.7	38	9.6
70	5.2	70	5.2	56	6.5		52	7.0	62	5.9	54	6.7
4.0		4.6	4.7					2.8	4.1	5.1
8.8		8.2	8.7	Sales/Working Capital				8.0	8.7	8.7
24.8		23.2	25.3					25.2	15.4	39.0
42.9		47.5	24.4						18.7	29.3
(71)	7.6	(95)	10.2	(108)	9.3	EBIT/Interest			(22)	8.1	(68)	11.4
.8		1.8	2.0						1.6	2.0
		34.7	17.0	Net Profit + Depr., Dep.,						18.4
		(24)	6.6	(24)	5.9	Amort./Cur. Mat. L/T/D					(19)	6.6
		1.9	1.7							2.3
.0		.0	.0					.0	.1	.1
.3		.2	.3	Fixed/Worth				.1	.2	.4
1.7		.7	1.3					2.5	.4	-4.0
.9		.7	.8					1.4	.6	.9
2.6		1.8	1.7	Debt/Worth				3.6	1.0	2.1
-14.3		7.2	12.5					28.7	1.9	-21.9
71.2		73.9	74.9	% Profit Before Taxes/Tangible				161.2	62.0	75.7
(67)	36.1	(117)	34.1	(108)	27.3	Net Worth	(12)	32.9	(26)	19.6	(59)	26.2
14.1		12.7	9.5					10.8	8.1	12.2
27.1		25.6	25.2	% Profit Before Taxes/Total				24.7	37.7	19.8
12.7		12.0	9.6	Assets				8.7	7.2	9.2
.2		1.6	1.6					1.4	2.3	.9
412.1		428.8	188.9					999.8	139.0	127.5
79.0		72.1	49.4	Sales/Net Fixed Assets				270.9	28.2	47.8
16.0		18.3	12.9					6.9	11.8	15.5
3.7		4.0	3.8					2.9	3.7	3.7
1.9		2.5	2.4	Sales/Total Assets				2.4	2.5	2.3
1.3		1.5	1.6					1.1	1.7	1.7
.2		.2	.2						.1	.2
(60)	.5	(78)	.4	(83)	.5	% Depr., Dep., Amort./Sales			(17)	.5	(57)	.4
1.4		1.1	1.2						1.6	1.2
1.2		.6	.7	% Officers', Directors'						
(29)	3.3	(31)	1.6	(21)	1.5	Owners' Comp/Sales					
6.1		4.8	3.6							
8724996M		9893264M	13277259M	Net Sales ($)	959M	5987M	35761M	111769M	481035M	12641748M
3733573M		3797017M	4773894M	Total Assets ($)	686M	9485M	15536M	63384M	242338M	4442465M

© RMA 2024

M = $ thousand   MM = $ million

See Pages viii through xx for Explanation of Ratios and Data

WHOLESALE—Piece Goods, Notions, and Other Dry Goods Merchant Wholesalers NAICS 424310

Current Data Sorted by Assets

						Type of Statement		
			2	1		Unqualified		
		4	11	1		Reviewed		
		6				Compiled		
2	3	4				Tax Returns		
3	4	10	22	4	1	Other		
	9 (4/1-9/30/23)		69 (10/1/23-3/31/24)					
0-500M	500M-2MM	2-10MM	10-50MM	50-100MM	100-250MM			
5	7	24	35	6	1	NUMBER OF STATEMENTS		

Comparative Historical Data

2		4	
11		7	
10		6	
9		12	
54		30	
4/1/19-		4/1/20-	
3/31/20		3/31/21	
ALL		ALL	
86		59	

%	%	%	%	%	%		%	%
						ASSETS		
		12.7	15.3			Cash & Equivalents	11.3	14.7
		24.8	23.7			Trade Receivables (net)	26.0	25.1
		42.5	32.4			Inventory	42.3	39.1
		3.4	4.4			All Other Current	3.7	4.1
		83.4	75.9			Total Current	83.3	83.0
		5.1	9.2			Fixed Assets (net)	8.4	6.4
		3.6	6.3			Intangibles (net)	4.1	5.4
		7.8	8.6			All Other Non-Current	4.3	5.2
		100.0	100.0			Total	100.0	100.0
						LIABILITIES		
		12.8	8.9			Notes Payable-Short Term	10.2	10.6
		1.6	.9			Cur. Mat.-L.T.D.	1.0	2.5
		20.0	17.1			Trade Payables	22.5	17.9
		.0	.0			Income Taxes Payable	.1	.0
		6.8	7.3			All Other Current	8.8	6.3
		41.2	34.2			Total Current	42.5	37.4
		13.3	15.1			Long-Term Debt	6.9	9.8
		.0	.0			Deferred Taxes	.0	.3
		8.0	8.0			All Other Non-Current	6.3	4.3
		37.5	42.7			Net Worth	44.3	48.2
		100.0	100.0			Total Liabilities & Net Worth	100.0	100.0
						INCOME DATA		
		100.0	100.0			Net Sales	100.0	100.0
		35.7	28.0			Gross Profit	30.3	33.2
		31.3	23.0			Operating Expenses	26.3	28.2
		4.3	5.0			Operating Profit	3.9	5.0
		1.1	1.1			All Other Expenses (net)	1.0	-.3
		3.2	3.9			Profit Before Taxes	3.0	5.3
						RATIOS		
		3.3	4.7				3.9	4.2
		2.2	2.1			Current	1.9	2.1
		1.5	1.5				1.4	1.5
		1.5	3.4				1.9	2.0
		.9	1.0			Quick	.8	1.0
		.4	.5				.5	.6
		11 32.8	22 16.7				23 16.0	16 23.1
		40 9.1	40 9.2			Sales/Receivables	34 10.8	38 9.5
		59 6.2	59 6.2				52 7.0	53 6.9
		61 6.0	36 10.1				41 8.8	58 6.3
		99 3.7	73 5.0			Cost of Sales/Inventory	107 3.4	99 3.7
		215 1.7	130 2.8				146 2.5	174 2.1
		18 20.0	16 23.3				14 25.8	12 30.1
		41 8.8	30 12.3			Cost of Sales/Payables	34 10.8	30 12.1
		70 5.2	49 7.5				65 5.6	61 6.0
		3.3	3.0				3.6	3.1
		5.2	4.4			Sales/Working Capital	6.0	4.7
		9.4	9.7				13.4	8.9
		15.9	18.6				18.9	33.2
		(21) 8.4	(31) 4.8			EBIT/Interest	(71) 4.7	(54) 7.8
		.7	2.1				1.7	1.2
						Net Profit + Depr., Dep., Amort./Cur. Mat. L/T/D		
		.0	.0				.0	.0
		.1	.1			Fixed/Worth	.1	.1
		.4	.6				.5	.3
		.8	.7				.6	.4
		1.6	1.4			Debt/Worth	1.5	1.2
		3.1	2.9				3.4	3.4
		50.9	26.2			% Profit Before Taxes/Tangible Net Worth	38.5	46.0
		(21) 18.0	(32) 14.8				(78) 15.9	(54) 21.2
		6.0	8.4				5.9	6.2
		12.6	14.0			% Profit Before Taxes/Total Assets	16.9	26.3
		6.1	7.0				6.7	9.3
		-2.6	4.0				1.5	.8
		821.9	801.3				245.1	999.8
		125.9	58.2			Sales/Net Fixed Assets	85.5	107.0
		25.3	11.4				25.5	26.5
		3.2	2.6				3.6	3.0
		2.4	1.8			Sales/Total Assets	2.3	2.1
		1.8	1.4				1.7	1.7
		.2	.2				.2	.2
		(14) .4	(22) .6			% Depr., Dep., Amort./Sales	(56) .5	(35) .6
		.9	1.4				1.1	1.1
		1.6					1.1	2.2
		(13) 4.7				% Officers', Directors' Owners' Comp/Sales	(32) 2.0	(26) 4.1
		5.1					6.3	10.3
13639M	31822M	246579M	1649146M	605204M	93138M	Net Sales ($)	2732724M	1377004M
1550M	11537M	109367M	821133M	380723M	194684M	Total Assets ($)	1422720M	727727M

© RMA 2024
M = $ thousand   MM = $ million
See Pages viii through xx for Explanation of Ratios and Data

WHOLESALE—Piece Goods, Notions, and Other Dry Goods Merchant Wholesalers NAICS 424310

Comparative Historical Data | Current Data Sorted by Sales

Comparative Historical Data					Current Data Sorted by Sales					
				Type of Statement						
4	2	3		Unqualified				2	4	3
6	16	16		Reviewed			1	3	3	9
8	6	6		Compiled	1	1	1	4	2	
36	10	9		Tax Returns	3	9 (4/1-9/30/23)	3	69 (10/1/23-3/31/24)		24
4/1/21-3/31/22 ALL	4/1/22-3/31/23 ALL	4/1/23-3/31/24 ALL		Other	0-1MM	1-3MM	3-5MM	5-10MM	10-25MM	25MM & OVER
54	77	78		NUMBER OF STATEMENTS	4	2	6	14	16	36
%	%	%		ASSETS	%	%	%	%	%	%
16.2	15.8	14.4		Cash & Equivalents				9.3	13.4	17.4
25.3	23.2	22.6		Trade Receivables (net)				26.2	27.3	22.6
37.9	41.6	38.4		Inventory				45.2	40.5	28.4
3.6	2.6	3.4		All Other Current				1.1	2.6	4.1
83.0	83.2	78.7		Total Current				81.8	83.8	72.6
5.9	8.2	7.6		Fixed Assets (net)				7.3	7.2	8.2
3.2	3.2	6.1		Intangibles (net)				2.6	5.2	9.4
7.9	5.5	7.6		All Other Non-Current				8.4	3.8	9.8
100.0	100.0	100.0		Total				100.0	100.0	100.0
				LIABILITIES						
9.6	13.7	10.2		Notes Payable-Short Term				19.9	8.9	7.8
.6	.9	1.0		Cur. Mat.-L.T.D.				1.0	.4	.9
18.0	17.6	16.2		Trade Payables				16.0	20.5	15.9
.2	.1	.0		Income Taxes Payable				.0	.0	.0
8.9	6.1	7.0		All Other Current				9.0	4.6	7.2
37.3	38.5	34.5		Total Current				45.9	34.3	31.8
7.8	8.8	14.0		Long-Term Debt				13.4	10.2	15.7
.0	.0	.0		Deferred Taxes				.0	.0	.0
6.4	7.3	8.1		All Other Non-Current				7.2	6.0	7.5
48.5	45.5	43.5		Net Worth				33.5	49.4	44.9
100.0	100.0	100.0		Total Liabilties & Net Worth				100.0	100.0	100.0
				INCOME DATA						
100.0	100.0	100.0		Net Sales				100.0	100.0	100.0
31.9	32.3	33.8		Gross Profit				38.2	32.5	29.3
24.8	27.3	28.7		Operating Expenses				35.1	25.6	23.9
7.1	5.0	5.1		Operating Profit				3.1	6.8	5.4
.2	-.4	1.2		All Other Expenses (net)				.9	.9	1.5
7.0	5.5	3.9		Profit Before Taxes				2.1	6.0	4.0
				RATIOS						
5.6	3.9	5.0						2.8	4.0	7.0
2.4	2.1	2.3		Current				2.0	2.9	2.0
1.5	1.4	1.5						1.4	1.7	1.4
3.1	1.7	3.0						1.3	3.1	3.8
1.2	1.0	1.0		Quick				.9	.8	1.1
.7	.5	.6						.4	.5	.7
19 19.0	23 15.6	19 19.0						13 27.5	5 69.3	27 13.6
38 9.7	34 10.6	36 10.1		Sales/Receivables				39 9.3	51 7.1	39 9.4
61 6.0	55 6.6	58 6.3						60 6.1	69 5.3	56 6.5
44 8.3	52 7.0	51 7.2						59 6.2	32 11.3	44 8.3
87 4.2	104 3.5	94 3.9		Cost of Sales/Inventory				89 4.1	99 3.7	78 4.7
146 2.5	182 2.0	182 2.0						228 1.6	228 1.6	122 3.0
6 58.0	14 26.5	14 27.0						8 48.0	21 17.8	16 23.2
30 12.0	35 10.5	32 11.3		Cost of Sales/Payables				35 10.3	47 7.8	29 12.8
51 7.1	57 6.4	52 7.0						79 4.6	65 5.6	41 9.0
3.0	2.8	3.0						3.9	3.2	3.0
5.7	5.2	4.7		Sales/Working Capital				5.2	4.7	5.0
10.4	11.4	9.5						18.6	8.0	10.1
67.8	41.2	18.2						23.9	38.2	22.2
(41) 14.0	(60) 8.5	(65) 4.9		EBIT/Interest			(13) 5.3	(14) 10.5	(30) 4.8
5.4	3.4	2.0						.6	2.8	1.1
		12.6		Net Profit + Depr., Dep.,						
	(10) 7.4			Amort./Cur. Mat. L/T/D						
		1.6								
.0	.0	.0						.0	.0	.0
.0	.1	.1		Fixed/Worth				.1	.1	.1
.1	.3	.4						NM	.3	1.0
.5	.4	.6						.7	.7	.4
1.1	1.4	1.4		Debt/Worth				1.7	1.3	1.6
2.3	3.1	2.9						NM	2.2	4.4
57.7	44.1	34.2						36.6	50.0	28.7
(53) 35.2	(70) 22.1	(68) 16.9		% Profit Before Taxes/Tangible Net Worth		(11) 14.7		24.0	(31) 16.2	
15.2	8.3	11.3						8.0	14.3	9.6
25.1	17.6	14.5						11.6	21.7	14.2
15.2	9.3	7.1		% Profit Before Taxes/Total Assets				6.4	10.2	7.7
4.6	3.2	3.1						-7.9	5.2	2.2
999.8	999.8	708.4						944.3	790.2	265.9
138.6	70.3	107.2		Sales/Net Fixed Assets				299.0	104.0	62.4
27.4	16.5	19.8						19.8	22.9	14.8
3.1	3.3	2.9						3.3	3.3	2.7
2.0	2.1	2.0		Sales/Total Assets				2.8	2.1	1.9
1.5	1.5	1.6						1.9	1.7	1.3
.1	.2	.2							.3	.2
(27) .4	(45) .6	(45) .6		% Depr., Dep., Amort./Sales				(11) .5	(22) .6	
.9	1.0	1.0							.8	1.6
1.2	1.3	1.5								
(25) 3.3	(34) 2.9	(26) 4.2		% Officers', Directors' Owners' Comp/Sales						
5.8	5.4	6.2								
1482229M	2629103M	2639528M		Net Sales ($)	2361M	2576M	24747M	107383M	284141M	2218320M
595600M	1355221M	1518994M		Total Assets ($)	1803M	3905M	13174M	47647M	142085M	1310380M

© RMA 2024   M = $ thousand   MM = $ million
See Pages viii through xx for Explanation of Ratios and Data

WHOLESALE—Footwear Merchant Wholesalers NAICS 424340

Current Data Sorted by Assets | Comparative Historical Data

0-500M	500M-2MM	2-10MM	10-50MM	50-100MM	100-250MM	Type of Statement				
		1	1			Unqualified		5		1
	1	4	7	1		Reviewed		11		8
	1	1				Compiled		3		2
	2	2	1			Tax Returns		8		3
	7 (4/1-9/30/23)	3	8	2	2	Other		28		17
			30 (10/1/23-3/31/24)					4/1/19-3/31/20 ALL		4/1/20-3/31/21 ALL
	4	10	17	4	2	NUMBER OF STATEMENTS		55		31
%	%	%	%	%	%	ASSETS		%		%
		11.9	8.8			Cash & Equivalents		11.8		14.2
		21.9	21.7			Trade Receivables (net)		27.9		24.9
DATA		43.5	37.6			Inventory		41.5		39.8
		6.7	9.5			All Other Current		3.9		8.6
NOT		84.0	77.5			Total Current		85.2		87.5
		13.7	5.3			Fixed Assets (net)		7.3		4.2
		.6	6.0			Intangibles (net)		2.1		3.6
AVAILABLE		1.8	11.1			All Other Non-Current		5.4		4.7
		100.0	100.0			Total		100.0		100.0
						LIABILITIES				
		16.5	10.0			Notes Payable-Short Term		15.9		15.3
		.7	1.2			Cur. Mat.-L.T.D.		.5		2.7
		15.6	25.4			Trade Payables		18.5		18.3
		.0	.0			Income Taxes Payable		.1		.1
		14.8	8.3			All Other Current		10.6		12.2
		47.6	44.9			Total Current		45.6		48.4
		7.1	2.9			Long-Term Debt		4.8		3.6
		.0	.0			Deferred Taxes		.1		.0
		.0	10.2			All Other Non-Current		10.1		13.7
		45.4	41.9			Net Worth		39.5		34.3
		100.0	100.0			Total Liabilities & Net Worth		100.0		100.0
						INCOME DATA				
		100.0	100.0			Net Sales		100.0		100.0
		32.5	35.9			Gross Profit		35.2		34.1
		26.5	32.7			Operating Expenses		29.4		30.3
		6.0	3.2			Operating Profit		5.8		3.7
		.4	-.9			All Other Expenses (net)		.8		.0
		5.7	4.1			Profit Before Taxes		5.0		3.7
						RATIOS				
		3.4	4.7					3.6		3.5
		1.8	1.5			Current		2.0		1.8
		1.4	1.1					1.3		1.5
		1.0	2.0					1.8		1.3
		.5	.6			Quick		.8		.8
		.4	.3					.5		.6
		0 UND	25 14.5					25 14.5	28	13.0
		36 10.0	40 9.1			Sales/Receivables		41 8.8	42	8.7
		43 8.4	70 5.2					62 5.9	70	5.2
		38 9.7	55 6.6					78 4.7	79	4.6
		152 2.4	159 2.3			Cost of Sales/Inventory		118 3.1	146	2.5
		228 1.6	228 1.6					182 2.0	174	2.1
		8 47.8	22 16.8					16 22.2	15	24.1
		29 12.6	57 6.4			Cost of Sales/Payables		35 10.3	38	9.7
		45 8.1	118 3.1					63 5.8	62	5.9
		2.9	2.4					2.7		2.8
		7.2	6.5			Sales/Working Capital		6.4		4.6
		16.9	33.0					12.8		8.7
			34.5					20.4		18.2
		(15) 2.3				EBIT/Interest	(44)	4.7	(26)	5.1
			1.3					.8		1.3
						Net Profit + Depr., Dep., Amort./Cur. Mat. L/T/D				
		.0	.0					.0		.0
		.2	.2			Fixed/Worth		.1		.1
		.6	.7					.3		.2
		.6	.5					.4		.9
		1.2	2.0			Debt/Worth		1.3		1.8
		2.2	8.1					5.0		5.9
		45.7	41.2					36.3		32.6
		27.6	(16) 13.5			% Profit Before Taxes/Tangible Net Worth	(49)	18.3	(27)	14.9
		-.2	5.2					3.4		.6
		25.0	14.6					16.8		14.9
		15.0	3.6			% Profit Before Taxes/Total Assets		7.2		7.8
		-.5	.9					-.2		.3
		402.5	178.3					382.3		411.8
		43.1	37.5			Sales/Net Fixed Assets		65.7		102.2
		5.7	16.3					27.2		32.0
		4.5	1.9					2.9		2.3
		1.9	1.6			Sales/Total Assets		2.0		2.0
		1.3	1.3					1.5		1.3
			.4					.1		.1
		(12)	.5			% Depr., Dep., Amort./Sales	(40)	.4	(22)	.2
			1.3					.9		.6
						% Officers', Directors' Owners' Comp/Sales		.8		
							(22)	3.2		
								4.8		
	15375M	151730M	648766M	554659M	314223M	Net Sales ($)		2359172M		1380977M
	4759M	55258M	369017M	267793M	265773M	Total Assets ($)		1213345M		656164M

M = $ thousand   MMM = $ million
See Pages viii through xx for Explanation of Ratios and Data

© RMA 2024

WHOLESALE—Footwear Merchant Wholesalers NAICS 424340

Comparative Historical Data / Current Data Sorted by Sales

						Type of Statement							
		2		3		2	Unqualified					2	2
		1		5		13	Reviewed				2	4	7
		2		4		2	Compiled			1	1	1	1
		1		6		3	Tax Returns		1	1	1	6	
		20		17		17	Other		1	1	2		7
		4/1/21-		4/1/22-		4/1/23-		0-1MM	1-3MM	3-5MM	5-10MM	10-25MM	25MM & OVER
		3/31/22		3/31/23		3/31/24		7 (4/1-9/30/23)			30 (10/1/23-3/31/24)		
		ALL		ALL		ALL							
		26		35		37	NUMBER OF STATEMENTS		2	2	5	11	17
		%		%		%	ASSETS	%	%	%	%	%	%
		12.0		17.2		12.0	Cash & Equivalents					11.1	13.4
		24.7		20.5		22.2	Trade Receivables (net)					23.0	23.7
		40.4		44.3		39.7	Inventory					39.3	35.8
		6.2		2.7		7.2	All Other Current	D				9.0	5.6
		83.3		84.7		81.1	Total Current	A				82.4	78.5
		5.2		4.9		8.2	Fixed Assets (net)	T				5.5	6.8
		6.8		4.2		4.3	Intangibles (net)	A				4.0	6.8
		4.7		6.2		6.4	All Other Non-Current					8.1	7.9
		100.0		100.0		100.0	Total	N				100.0	100.0
							LIABILITIES	O					
		11.7		10.5		11.2	Notes Payable-Short Term	T				12.0	12.3
		.5		2.0		1.0	Cur. Mat.-L.T.D.					1.4	.9
		28.5		20.3		21.8	Trade Payables	A				21.5	24.6
		.2		.4		.0	Income Taxes Payable	V				.0	.0
		14.9		7.2		9.4	All Other Current	A				8.6	7.9
		55.8		40.4		43.4	Total Current	I				43.6	45.7
		4.9		17.7		10.9	Long-Term Debt	L				2.6	15.3
		.3		.0		.0	Deferred Taxes	A				.0	.0
		6.6		13.1		8.8	All Other Non-Current	B				8.0	13.4
		32.4		28.8		36.9	Net Worth	L				45.8	25.7
		100.0		100.0		100.0	Total Liabilities & Net Worth	E				100.0	100.0
							INCOME DATA						
		100.0		100.0		100.0	Net Sales					100.0	100.0
		34.0		31.6		34.1	Gross Profit					35.0	31.3
		27.6		27.3		30.0	Operating Expenses					31.6	27.4
		6.4		4.3		4.1	Operating Profit					3.4	3.9
		-.7		.5		.3	All Other Expenses (net)					-2.1	1.4
		7.2		3.7		3.9	Profit Before Taxes					5.5	2.5
							RATIOS						
		2.3		5.6		3.4						6.7	2.5
		1.6		2.1		1.8	Current					2.5	1.7
		1.2		1.4		1.3						1.1	1.3
		1.3		2.1		1.4						2.9	1.2
		.7		1.0		.7	Quick					.8	.8
		.4		.4		.4						.5	.3
27	13.4	14	25.5	19	19.2						28	13.2	19	19.0
48	7.6	34	10.7	40	9.1	Sales/Receivables					42	8.7	41	8.9
63	5.8	54	6.7	53	6.9						53	6.9	66	5.5
87	4.2	43	8.4	41	8.8						41	9.0	29	12.8
130	2.8	166	2.2	159	2.3	Cost of Sales/Inventory					152	2.4	114	3.2
166	2.2	281	1.3	203	1.8						174	2.1	203	1.8
38	9.6	9	41.0	19	18.8						18	19.8	17	21.3
73	5.0	44	8.3	35	10.4	Cost of Sales/Payables					31	11.8	45	8.2
104	3.5	81	4.5	78	4.7						94	3.9	94	3.9
	4.2		2.3		2.9						2.1	4.3
	6.0		5.3		6.2	Sales/Working Capital					3.4	6.6
	17.9		10.9		12.4						28.0	11.4
	35.3		27.0		11.3						54.6	9.1
(23)	16.4	(28)	8.3	(33)	3.3	EBIT/Interest					(10)	9.2	(15)	1.7
	1.9		-.2		1.2						2.1	1.1
						Net Profit + Depr., Dep., Amort./Cur. Mat. L/T/D						
	.0		.0		.0						.0	.1
	.1		.1		.2	Fixed/Worth					.1	.2
	1.7		.6		.6						.4	.9
	1.2		.9		.6						.2	.8
	2.1		2.0		1.6	Debt/Worth					1.8	1.8
	NM		21.1		5.7						3.8	10.0
	58.5		60.2		40.6						40.6	63.4
(20)	41.2	(30)	28.0	(34)	13.5	% Profit Before Taxes/Tangible Net Worth					(10)	22.2	(15)	10.9
	24.5		8.4		3.2						10.0	2.3
	24.5		21.6		16.1						15.7	15.2
	12.1		5.2		4.8	% Profit Before Taxes/Total Assets					9.5	3.1
	4.0		-1.3		.8						2.0	.8
	263.9		536.7		195.4						203.3	231.3
	139.9		104.1		37.5	Sales/Net Fixed Assets					66.1	27.5
	30.7		23.3		15.3						16.3	13.8
	2.4		2.6		2.9						1.9	3.1
	1.8		1.7		1.7	Sales/Total Assets					1.6	1.7
	1.3		1.3		1.3						1.2	1.3
	.1		.1		.1							.3
(13)	.2	(18)	.4	(26)	.5	% Depr., Dep., Amort./Sales					(11)	.8
	.7		.6		1.3							2.0
					.8							
		(13)	2.8	(13)	2.7	% Officers', Directors' Owners' Comp/Sales						
			6.7		6.4							
	1260657M		1445422M		1684753M	Net Sales ($)		3650M	7410M	40261M	222080M	1411352M
	749475M		851245M		962600M	Total Assets ($)		1509M	3394M	25617M	139274M	792806M

M = $ thousand   MM = $ million
See Pages viii through xx for Explanation of Ratios and Data

© RMA 2024

WHOLESALE—Clothing and Clothing Accessories Merchant Wholesalers NAICS 424350

Current Data Sorted by Assets | **Comparative Historical Data**

							Type of Statement		
		2	6	4	7		Unqualified	14	9
	5	13	12	4			Reviewed	40	16
	3	4	6				Compiled	9	7
1	5	8	2				Tax Returns	25	11
1	8	33	36	12	6		Other	157	52
	29 (4/1-9/30/23)		149 (10/1/23-3/31/24)					4/1/19-3/31/20	4/1/20-3/31/21
0-500M	500M-2MM	2-10MM	10-50MM	50-100MM	100-250MM		NUMBER OF STATEMENTS	ALL 245	ALL 95
2	21	60	62	20	13				
%	%	%	%	%	%		**ASSETS**	%	%
	18.4	17.5	12.6	5.1	9.2		Cash & Equivalents	10.5	17.1
	13.4	19.8	25.2	17.6	28.3		Trade Receivables (net)	30.4	20.5
	38.8	43.5	43.7	48.0	22.8		Inventory	39.6	40.7
	10.4	4.0	4.1	8.5	2.5		All Other Current	5.0	7.9
	81.0	84.9	85.6	79.2	62.8		Total Current	85.6	86.2
	7.3	5.8	4.6	5.0	8.3		Fixed Assets (net)	5.3	5.7
	2.5	4.0	1.5	5.6	8.4		Intangibles (net)	3.5	4.0
	9.1	5.3	8.3	10.2	20.4		All Other Non-Current	5.7	4.0
	100.0	100.0	100.0	100.0	100.0		Total	100.0	100.0
							LIABILITIES		
	7.3	8.9	10.8	16.6	14.6		Notes Payable-Short Term	18.0	12.3
	.6	1.3	3.0	5.2	1.6		Cur. Mat.-L.T.D.	1.1	1.5
	13.8	23.1	24.9	27.1	17.5		Trade Payables	23.5	21.0
	.0	.3	.1	.0	.0		Income Taxes Payable	.1	.1
	34.2	10.6	6.3	6.3	12.9		All Other Current	11.2	11.6
	56.0	44.1	45.1	55.2	46.6		Total Current	53.9	46.5
	27.9	10.1	7.5	8.1	15.0		Long-Term Debt	5.7	10.5
	.0	.0	.0	.0	.0		Deferred Taxes	.0	.0
	4.6	4.6	8.3	15.0	15.1		All Other Non-Current	7.5	10.1
	11.5	41.2	39.1	21.7	23.4		Net Worth	32.9	32.8
	100.0	100.0	100.0	100.0	100.0		Total Liabilities & Net Worth	100.0	100.0
							INCOME DATA		
	100.0	100.0	100.0	100.0	100.0		Net Sales	100.0	100.0
	40.6	39.1	35.0	37.2	44.2		Gross Profit	34.8	36.8
	37.2	32.3	28.2	30.9	33.5		Operating Expenses	29.8	31.4
	3.4	6.8	6.8	6.3	10.7		Operating Profit	5.0	5.4
	-.1	.8	.9	1.1	2.4		All Other Expenses (net)	1.0	.1
	3.5	6.0	5.9	5.1	8.3		Profit Before Taxes	4.0	5.3
							RATIOS		
	8.6	3.5	3.6	2.5	2.2			2.7	4.4
	3.2	2.2	2.0	1.4	1.1		Current	1.7	2.0
	1.3	1.2	1.2	1.1	.9			1.2	1.4
	4.1	2.3	1.5	.7	1.3			1.4	1.6
	.8	.9	.8	.5	.7		Quick	.7	.7
	.1	.4	.4	.1	.3			.5	.4
	0 UND	3 104.6	19 18.9	0 786.5	6 64.2			22 16.4	10 37.3
	3 141.9	23 16.1	40 9.2	32 11.3	36 10.2		Sales/Receivables	43 8.5	31 11.7
	25 14.6	41 8.8	70 5.2	52 7.0	83 4.4			68 5.4	61 6.0
	18 20.7	43 8.4	59 6.2	87 4.2	33 11.0			53 6.9	55 6.6
	70 5.2	104 3.5	130 2.8	126 2.9	104 3.5		Cost of Sales/Inventory	94 3.9	111 3.3
	152 2.4	159 2.3	192 1.9	281 1.3	146 2.5			152 2.4	215 1.7
	0 UND	16 23.0	22 16.9	39 9.4	23 15.8			16 22.4	12 29.9
	12 29.2	41 9.0	49 7.4	61 6.0	46 8.0		Cost of Sales/Payables	36 10.1	45 8.2
	43 8.5	64 5.7	85 4.3	114 3.2	99 3.7			64 5.7	94 3.9
	2.9	3.4	2.9	3.3	5.7			3.8	2.7
	5.8	6.1	5.7	13.0	14.2		Sales/Working Capital	7.9	4.5
	38.8	16.4	18.5	38.2	-240.3			21.6	11.7
	12.1	30.1	20.9	4.7	15.9			17.3	21.0
(13)	4.7	(55) 4.4	(58) 7.7	(17) 3.5	(12) 9.7		EBIT/Interest	(200) 4.6	(79) 7.8
	1.1	1.1	2.0	1.2	.7			1.6	.8
							Net Profit + Depr., Dep., Amort./Cur. Mat. L/T/D	40.1	16.9
								(25) 3.4	(11) 1.4
								.9	-.8
	.0	.0	.0	.0	.0			.0	.0
	.1	.1	.1	.1	.4		Fixed/Worth	.1	.1
	1.6	.4	.3	.6	1.8			.4	.5
	.4	.4	.5	.9	1.2			.7	.6
	2.6	1.5	1.4	8.9	12.2		Debt/Worth	1.8	2.0
	NM	9.6	5.9	89.8	51.9			6.6	5.0
	67.5	60.5	58.2	151.5	391.0		% Profit Before Taxes/Tangible Net Worth	53.3	61.2
(16)	33.4	(53) 24.9	(52) 25.8	(16) 37.6	(11) 126.2			(207) 26.7	(80) 25.3
	15.6	4.4	14.4	9.6	25.9			6.6	7.0
	18.6	33.0	19.5	14.6	34.2		% Profit Before Taxes/Total Assets	20.7	30.2
	11.4	9.0	11.0	7.3	18.3			8.1	7.8
	2.1	.2	3.4	2.7	3.3			1.3	.2
	744.2	534.8	664.2	458.9	680.9			468.5	379.6
	196.5	140.6	89.3	115.9	42.7		Sales/Net Fixed Assets	126.4	107.4
	57.0	58.2	35.3	19.5	9.3			46.0	39.0
	4.1	3.5	3.0	2.7	2.5			3.2	2.9
	3.0	2.7	2.3	1.7	1.9		Sales/Total Assets	2.4	2.1
	2.2	1.9	1.3	1.4	1.3			1.8	1.3
	.1	.1	.1	.1				.1	.1
(10)	.2	(32) .2	(39) .3	(12) .3			% Depr., Dep., Amort./Sales	(152) .3	(57) .4
	.6	.9	.7	.6				.8	.9
	2.4	1.2	.5					1.3	1.5
(13)	3.6	(20) 3.1	(14) .9				% Officers', Directors' Owners' Comp/Sales	(66) 2.5	(28) 2.3
	8.5	4.7	2.5					3.9	5.4
12728M	93742M	818487M	3529980M	2678295M	3666117M		Net Sales ($)	13625929M	4403096M
564M	24597M	310552M	1457386M	1405274M	1901485M		Total Assets ($)	6330364M	2080195M

M = $ thousand MM = $ million
See Pages viii through xx for Explanation of Ratios and Data

© RMA 2024

WHOLESALE—Clothing and Clothing Accessories Merchant Wholesalers NAICS 424350

Comparative Historical Data / Current Data Sorted by Sales

Comparative Historical Data			Type of Statement	Current Data Sorted by Sales					
10	23	19	Unqualified				1	3	15
10	38	34	Reviewed		1	2	6	12	13
4	8	13	Compiled		1	2	1	4	5
10	15	16	Tax Returns	1	1	2	7	3	1
53	103	96	Other	1	3	3	14	23	52
4/1/21-3/31/22 ALL	4/1/22-3/31/23 ALL	4/1/23-3/31/24 ALL		0-1MM	29 (4/1-9/30/23) 1-3MM	3-5MM	149 (10/1/23-3/31/24) 5-10MM	10-25MM	25MM & OVER
87	187	178	NUMBER OF STATEMENTS	2	7	9	29	45	86
%	%	%	ASSETS	%	%	%	%	%	%
14.8	12.3	14.0	Cash & Equivalents				21.3	14.3	10.3
26.9	22.0	21.1	Trade Receivables (net)				17.8	21.8	23.6
36.0	44.5	41.5	Inventory				38.6	44.3	42.0
5.6	5.9	5.5	All Other Current				5.4	6.3	4.7
83.2	84.6	82.0	Total Current				83.2	86.8	80.6
5.3	5.9	6.1	Fixed Assets (net)				4.0	6.2	5.1
3.9	3.1	3.4	Intangibles (net)				6.6	2.1	3.4
7.7	6.4	8.4	All Other Non-Current				6.2	4.9	10.8
100.0	100.0	100.0	Total				100.0	100.0	100.0
			LIABILITIES						
12.1	14.5	10.6	Notes Payable-Short Term				8.9	9.6	12.4
.9	2.3	2.2	Cur. Mat.-L.T.D.				1.1	.9	3.6
21.1	20.7	22.4	Trade Payables				23.5	17.4	26.7
.0	.0	.1	Income Taxes Payable				.4	.1	.1
8.6	13.4	11.6	All Other Current				18.9	6.1	7.8
42.7	50.8	46.9	Total Current				52.8	34.0	50.5
11.6	10.7	12.1	Long-Term Debt				12.0	9.1	9.8
.1	.0	.0	Deferred Taxes				.0	.0	.0
6.9	4.5	9.2	All Other Non-Current				5.6	3.8	11.2
38.7	34.0	31.8	Net Worth				29.5	53.0	28.5
100.0	100.0	100.0	Total Liabilities & Net Worth				100.0	100.0	100.0
			INCOME DATA						
100.0	100.0	100.0	Net Sales				100.0	100.0	100.0
36.4	35.5	37.8	Gross Profit				40.1	36.8	36.8
29.0	28.6	31.2	Operating Expenses				35.8	28.3	29.7
7.4	6.8	6.6	Operating Profit				4.3	8.5	7.1
.1	.7	.9	All Other Expenses (net)				.7	.9	1.2
7.3	6.2	5.7	Profit Before Taxes				3.5	7.6	5.9
			RATIOS						
3.4	3.1	3.6	Current				3.2	5.9	2.6
2.2	1.8	2.0					2.0	3.0	1.6
1.3	1.2	1.2					1.1	1.8	1.1
1.8	1.2	1.6	Quick				2.5	2.6	1.2
.9	.7	.8					.9	1.0	.6
.6	.3	.4					.3	.5	.3
15 25.0	9 40.3	3 124.4	Sales/Receivables				3 123.3	3 107.5	5 79.2
46 7.9	33 11.0	30 12.3					27 13.7	36 10.0	33 11.0
73 5.0	58 6.3	53 6.9					63 5.8	58 6.3	51 7.2
52 7.0	53 6.9	50 7.3	Cost of Sales/Inventory				29 12.8	54 6.7	55 6.6
107 3.4	111 3.3	111 3.3					94 3.9	135 2.7	111 3.3
182 2.0	182 2.0	182 2.0					152 2.4	215 1.7	174 2.1
26 14.2	19 19.0	19 19.5	Cost of Sales/Payables				13 27.4	5 70.9	34 10.8
43 8.4	34 10.7	42 8.7					46 7.9	21 17.4	54 6.8
76 4.8	64 5.7	74 4.9					87 4.2	49 7.4	91 4.0
3.0	3.8	3.3	Sales/Working Capital				3.2	2.2	4.7
5.2	7.2	6.9					5.9	4.1	9.2
10.6	18.0	22.1					32.9	14.9	43.7
61.7	25.8	18.3	EBIT/Interest				22.8	25.6	15.9
(70) 12.5	(156) 7.9	(157) 5.3				(25)	3.3	(42) 7.9	(78) 4.7
2.4	2.5	1.5					.2	1.8	1.9
	11.5	9.1	Net Profit + Depr., Dep.,						15.6
(23) 3.9	(23) 2.6		Amort./Cur. Mat. L/T/D					(19) 2.3	
	.4	.2							.1
.0	.0	.0	Fixed/Worth				.0	.0	.0
.1	.1	.1					.0	.0	.1
.5	.4	.5					.2	.3	.7
.7	.8	.6	Debt/Worth				.5	.3	.8
1.6	2.0	2.0					4.5	.7	3.2
7.4	9.2	15.6					15.8	3.7	35.2
65.0	82.1	87.3	% Profit Before Taxes/Tangible Net Worth				53.6	50.0	128.6
(73) 33.2	(160) 37.8	(148) 30.4				(23)	18.9	(43) 20.4	(69) 50.1
13.4	17.6	11.6					.3	7.4	18.8
28.3	28.6	23.2	% Profit Before Taxes/Total Assets				17.8	26.4	23.2
14.5	11.5	10.3					7.2	11.6	11.0
4.2	3.9	1.5					-1.3	3.0	3.0
449.4	436.2	577.7	Sales/Net Fixed Assets				999.8	434.4	568.9
122.4	104.7	115.7					315.5	86.3	103.8
26.4	32.8	38.1					66.4	32.2	25.4
2.8	3.3	3.2	Sales/Total Assets				3.5	3.3	3.1
1.9	2.4	2.4					2.5	2.3	2.5
1.5	1.4	1.5					1.8	1.3	1.6
.1	.1	.1	% Depr., Dep., Amort./Sales				.1	.1	.1
(50) .5	(102) .3	(101) .3				(12)	.2	(28) .4	(53) .3
1.0	.7	.7					.9	.8	.7
1.2	1.7	.9	% Officers', Directors', Owners' Comp/Sales				2.1	.8	.5
(23) 2.8	(45) 3.2	(49) 2.6				(13)	3.7	(11) 3.2	(14) .9
5.0	5.2	4.3					6.8	4.0	2.4
4360601M	12375705M	10799349M	Net Sales ($)	1843M	11633M	35864M	212296M	746721M	9790992M
2291971M	5514444M	5099858M	Total Assets ($)	2524M	4890M	16825M	104821M	397633M	4573165M

M = $ thousand   MM = $ million
See Pages viii through xx for Explanation of Ratios and Data
© RMA 2024

WHOLESALE—General Line Grocery Merchant Wholesalers NAICS 424410

Current Data Sorted by Assets

								Comparative Historical Data	
							Type of Statement		
				7	1	8	Unqualified	25	23
		2	7	15	3		Reviewed	24	16
			12	6			Compiled	17	7
5		12	13	1			Tax Returns	31	9
3		8	26	56	14	10	Other	121	69
		44 (4/1-9/30/23)		165 (10/1/23-3/31/24)				4/1/19-	4/1/20-
0-500M	500M-2MM	2-10MM	10-50MM	50-100MM	100-250MM			3/31/20	3/31/21
8	22	58	85	18	18		**NUMBER OF STATEMENTS**	218 ALL	124 ALL
%	%	%	%	%	%		**ASSETS**	%	%
	12.0	13.8	10.5	13.0	11.1		Cash & Equivalents	9.5	14.3
	27.3	31.5	29.0	26.2	24.0		Trade Receivables (net)	32.4	25.1
	27.1	30.6	30.5	24.2	21.9		Inventory	31.3	28.9
	1.8	3.5	3.3	2.0	5.2		All Other Current	2.2	2.6
	68.1	79.3	73.4	65.4	62.1		Total Current	75.3	70.8
	9.0	10.0	13.8	18.9	20.9		Fixed Assets (net)	14.7	19.5
	14.0	5.8	4.7	6.7	9.2		Intangibles (net)	4.4	4.8
	8.9	4.8	8.1	9.0	7.8		All Other Non-Current	5.6	4.9
	100.0	100.0	100.0	100.0	100.0		Total	100.0	100.0
							LIABILITIES		
	7.7	8.1	10.3	8.5	3.7		Notes Payable-Short Term	12.1	9.5
	1.1	1.1	1.5	3.1	3.3		Cur. Mat.-L.T.D.	1.6	2.5
	16.1	24.0	21.0	17.3	17.3		Trade Payables	23.2	18.7
	.0	.1	.1	.0	.0		Income Taxes Payable	.1	.2
	13.8	7.7	7.5	9.4	7.1		All Other Current	9.0	9.3
	38.8	41.0	40.5	38.4	31.4		Total Current	46.0	40.1
	29.4	12.2	9.4	18.4	14.1		Long-Term Debt	9.6	14.2
	.0	.0	.5	.0	.8		Deferred Taxes	.2	.3
	5.6	1.9	5.6	5.2	9.3		All Other Non-Current	3.5	3.4
	26.3	44.8	44.0	38.0	44.4		Net Worth	40.7	42.0
	100.0	100.0	100.0	100.0	100.0		Total Liabilities & Net Worth	100.0	100.0
							INCOME DATA		
	100.0	100.0	100.0	100.0	100.0		Net Sales	100.0	100.0
	23.4	18.6	25.5	17.8	16.3		Gross Profit	16.9	19.8
	18.8	15.7	20.1	15.5	12.7		Operating Expenses	14.4	16.4
	4.7	2.9	5.4	2.3	3.6		Operating Profit	2.4	3.4
	1.6	-.5	.5	.6	.1		All Other Expenses (net)	.1	.0
	3.1	3.4	4.9	1.7	3.5		Profit Before Taxes	2.4	3.4
							RATIOS		
	18.9	3.5	2.9	4.0	2.7			2.8	3.7
	2.0	2.0	2.1	2.1	2.0		Current	1.6	1.8
	1.1	1.4	1.3	1.2	1.3			1.1	1.2
	9.8	2.4	1.8	2.3	1.9			1.6	1.9
	1.2	1.1	1.0	1.3	1.1		Quick	.9	1.0
	.5	.7	.7	.5	.7			.5	.6
0 UND	16 23.3	21 17.1	14 25.3	15 25.0				14 25.2	12 31.6
8 47.9	25 14.8	32 11.4	24 15.5	25 14.5			Sales/Receivables	24 15.4	19 19.2
26 14.0	45 8.2	41 8.8	38 9.7	30 12.3				35 10.5	30 12.3
3 104.8	16 22.9	25 14.6	17 21.9	17 21.3				15 25.1	14 25.4
17 21.6	30 12.0	41 8.8	25 14.7	20 18.3			Cost of Sales/Inventory	24 15.0	23 15.9
47 7.8	53 6.9	69 5.3	63 5.8	29 12.5				44 8.3	43 8.4
0 UND	11 34.0	14 25.2	14 25.8	15 24.7				12 31.3	8 43.9
10 36.8	20 18.4	27 13.3	23 15.6	17 21.6			Cost of Sales/Payables	18 20.0	16 23.0
24 14.9	42 8.7	45 8.2	27 13.5	21 17.0				30 12.3	25 14.4
	6.1	6.0	6.5	4.6	8.9			9.0	7.7
	20.1	11.0	8.9	16.1	14.9		Sales/Working Capital	19.1	15.2
	209.3	25.0	23.1	55.3	26.1			60.6	47.0
	9.2	29.7	36.7	45.0	84.3			13.9	29.0
(18) 3.5	(51) 7.7	(72) 9.1	(15) 5.2	(17) 7.6			EBIT/Interest	(175) 4.7	(109) 9.1
	1.1	3.3	4.0	-.5	2.7			1.9	3.2
			22.7				Net Profit + Depr., Dep.,	13.9	3.6
		(18) 9.4					Amort./Cur. Mat. L/T/D	(38) 2.9	(16) 2.1
			2.1					1.4	1.1
	.0	.0	.0	.2	.4			.1	.1
	.1	.1	.3	.4	.8		Fixed/Worth	.2	.5
	-1.6	.6	.7	2.2	1.4			1.0	1.2
	.7	.4	.7	.4	.6			.7	.6
	2.5	1.4	1.3	2.7	2.4		Debt/Worth	1.7	1.6
	-7.5	3.7	3.5	10.6	5.8			4.7	3.8
	75.3	59.8	62.8	47.6	45.6		% Profit Before Taxes/Tangible	41.1	63.8
(15) 30.2	(51) 29.2	(80) 33.4	(15) 38.4	(16) 25.9			Net Worth	(198) 17.6	(112) 27.4
	5.7	11.0	17.7	14.5	17.3			6.8	9.8
	17.6	21.9	22.2	17.5	16.8			15.9	19.3
	9.1	9.9	15.2	7.8	9.4		% Profit Before Taxes/Total Assets	6.0	10.2
	6.1	3.3	5.7	.3	4.4			2.3	3.8
	UND	636.5	420.5	61.0	63.9			238.4	165.3
	279.7	106.0	36.0	38.7	22.9		Sales/Net Fixed Assets	68.4	37.9
	50.3	29.0	15.4	10.4	13.3			19.8	15.3
	10.7	5.6	4.5	5.6	5.8			6.6	6.6
	4.7	4.2	3.3	3.2	3.7		Sales/Total Assets	5.0	4.4
	2.7	2.7	2.4	2.0	2.9			3.2	2.9
		.1	.3	.2	.3			.2	.3
	(32) .3	(59) .5	(16) .5	(14) .6			% Depr., Dep., Amort./Sales	(169) .4	(82) .5
		.8	.9	1.3	.8			.9	1.0
	1.0	.6	.4					.4	.6
(13) 1.8	(24) 1.2	(22) .5					% Officers', Directors' Owners' Comp/Sales	(60) 1.2	(34) 1.4
	4.2	1.9	1.0					2.5	2.9
20225M	167469M	1395374M	7040772M	5299844M	12131328M		Net Sales ($)	31503786M	20319195M
2477M	27083M	314231M	2060149M	1275815M	3060613M		Total Assets ($)	6196859M	3968907M

© RMA 2024

M = $ thousand   MM = $ million
See Pages viii through xx for Explanation of Ratios and Data

WHOLESALE—General Line Grocery Merchant Wholesalers NAICS 424410

Comparative Historical Data / Current Data Sorted by Sales

				Type of Statement						
	13	18	16	Unqualified				1	5	16
	12	17	27	Reviewed				7	22	
	10	14	18	Compiled				1	10	
	20	31	31	Tax Returns	3	3	2	8	14	1
	78	89	117	Other	2	4	2	10	12	87
	4/1/21-3/31/22 ALL	4/1/22-3/31/23 ALL	4/1/23-3/31/24 ALL		0-1MM	44 (4/1-9/30/23) 1-3MM	3-5MM	5-10MM	165 (10/1/23-3/31/24) 10-25MM	25MM & OVER
				NUMBER OF STATEMENTS	5	7	4	19	38	136
	%	%	%	ASSETS	%	%	%	%	%	%
	15.2	14.9	12.6	Cash & Equivalents				15.3	13.8	11.5
	27.2	27.9	28.2	Trade Receivables (net)				28.5	28.5	29.8
	29.8	30.6	29.2	Inventory				30.3	30.0	28.8
	2.6	3.8	3.1	All Other Current				5.8	2.3	3.2
	74.8	77.3	73.2	Total Current				79.9	74.5	73.3
	15.0	13.0	13.0	Fixed Assets (net)				6.9	11.4	14.4
	3.9	4.5	6.5	Intangibles (net)				9.6	6.1	5.3
	6.3	5.2	7.3	All Other Non-Current				3.5	7.9	7.0
	100.0	100.0	100.0	Total				100.0	100.0	100.0
				LIABILITIES						
	10.5	9.3	8.6	Notes Payable-Short Term				10.0	5.9	9.4
	2.5	1.6	1.6	Cur. Mat.-L.T.D.				.0	1.5	1.8
	19.5	23.0	21.0	Trade Payables				18.8	23.9	21.7
	.0	.1	.1	Income Taxes Payable				.0	.2	.1
	8.9	6.4	8.8	All Other Current				6.9	6.3	8.2
	41.4	40.4	40.2	Total Current				35.7	37.9	41.2
	10.3	11.1	13.7	Long-Term Debt				17.6	13.6	10.3
	.2	.1	.3	Deferred Taxes				.0	.4	.3
	4.3	4.1	4.7	All Other Non-Current				4.9	1.6	5.8
	43.8	44.2	41.3	Net Worth				41.8	46.5	42.3
	100.0	100.0	100.0	Total Liabilities & Net Worth				100.0	100.0	100.0
				INCOME DATA						
	100.0	100.0	100.0	Net Sales				100.0	100.0	100.0
	20.3	19.5	22.1	Gross Profit				23.4	20.9	21.1
	16.9	16.3	18.0	Operating Expenses				19.1	17.4	17.0
	3.5	3.3	4.1	Operating Profit				4.2	3.5	4.1
	-.5	-.1	.3	All Other Expenses (net)				.3	-.4	.3
	3.9	3.4	3.8	Profit Before Taxes				3.9	3.9	3.8
				RATIOS						
	3.5	3.9	3.2					15.3	3.8	2.8
	2.0	2.0	2.0	Current				3.5	2.0	1.9
	1.3	1.4	1.3					1.4	1.5	1.3
	2.2	2.2	2.1					5.7	2.6	1.6
	1.0	1.0	1.1	Quick				1.6	1.2	1.0
	.6	.6	.6					.9	.7	.7
11	32.5	13	28.1	16	23.2	Sales/Receivables		16	22.9	13	28.2	19	19.3
20	18.0	23	15.8	25	14.6			41	8.8	23	15.7	27	13.7
32	11.5	33	11.0	40	9.1			60	6.1	38	9.5	39	9.3
16	23.0	16	22.9	17	21.3	Cost of Sales/Inventory		23	15.9	13	27.3	18	19.9
24	14.9	29	12.7	33	11.1			57	6.4	28	13.0	33	11.1
47	7.8	51	7.2	65	5.6			94	3.9	51	7.2	63	5.8
8	44.9	10	36.3	13	27.8	Cost of Sales/Payables		3	133.3	14	25.8	14	26.7
16	23.4	19	19.5	20	18.2			18	20.6	23	15.6	22	16.7
30	12.2	35	10.3	38	9.6			40	9.1	43	8.5	37	9.9
	7.7		6.9		6.4	Sales/Working Capital			3.3		5.8		7.3
	14.9		13.8		10.6				5.5		12.8		11.2
	32.3		28.7		26.5				10.5		27.6		26.6
	63.0		51.6		31.4	EBIT/Interest			34.6		43.1		41.3
(112)	17.9	(141)	14.3	(177)	7.6			(17)	7.2	(33)	6.5	(116)	8.4
	5.4		3.3		3.1				3.6		3.2		3.6
	16.9		36.3		25.5	Net Profit + Depr., Dep., Amort./Cur. Mat. L/T/D							24.4
(21)	5.2	(34)	3.9	(34)	6.2							(32)	5.5
	1.1		2.0		1.7								1.7
	.0		.0		.0	Fixed/Worth			.0		.0		.0
	.2		.1		.2				.1		.1		.3
	.8		.7		.9				.5		.6		1.0
	.6		.4		.6	Debt/Worth			.4		.5		.6
	1.4		1.3		1.6				2.2		1.4		1.5
	3.5		3.3		4.4				26.2		3.7		3.7
	63.2		55.4		59.8	% Profit Before Taxes/Tangible Net Worth			77.4		59.8		57.2
(122)	34.3	(151)	33.5	(182)	31.8			(16)	29.2	(34)	28.8	(123)	33.5
	15.2		14.1		14.9				7.9		12.2		17.7
	25.0		24.0		21.3	% Profit Before Taxes/Total Assets			16.1		16.7		22.0
	13.2		12.5		10.7				10.2		9.5		13.1
	6.1		4.4		4.3				4.4		3.1		4.7
	230.6		387.2		438.0	Sales/Net Fixed Assets			999.8		776.3		287.7
	63.8		82.4		52.2				120.8		101.7		43.2
	20.4		28.0		18.9				43.0		26.2		16.7
	6.3		6.1		5.4	Sales/Total Assets			4.6		6.3		5.2
	4.6		4.1		3.6				2.7		4.2		3.6
	3.0		2.8		2.6				2.1		2.4		2.7
	.2		.1		.2	% Depr., Dep., Amort./Sales					.1		.2
(95)	.5	(111)	.4	(132)	.5					(19)	.4	(98)	.5
	.8		.8		1.0						.8		.9
	.5		.6		.5	% Officers', Directors' Owners' Comp/Sales					1.1		.3
(39)	1.2	(48)	1.0	(64)	1.0			(11)	1.8	(20)	1.3	(27)	.5
	2.4		2.2		2.1				2.5		2.0		.9
	17947684M		23929106M		26055012M	Net Sales ($)	2721M	12817M	16979M	140881M	660511M	25221103M
	3742024M		5598260M		6740368M	Total Assets ($)	2677M	4910M	3120M	57666M	217834M	6454161M

© RMA 2024 M = $ thousand MM = $ million
See Pages viii through xx for Explanation of Ratios and Data

WHOLESALE—Packaged Frozen Food Merchant Wholesalers NAICS 424420

Current Data Sorted by Assets | Comparative Historical Data

							Type of Statement				
		1		2	2	2	Unqualified		10		6
			2	4			Reviewed		12		6
		1	3	5			Compiled		11		4
		2					Tax Returns		9		4
	1	6	11	22	6	6	Other		51		40
	12 (4/1-9/30/23)			64 (10/1/23-3/31/24)					4/1/19-3/31/20		4/1/20-3/31/21
0-500M	500M-2MM	2-10MM	10-50MM	50-100MM	100-250MM				ALL		ALL
1	10	16	33	8	8		NUMBER OF STATEMENTS		93		60
%	%	%	%	%	%		ASSETS		%		%
	15.6	8.7	11.6				Cash & Equivalents		8.4		11.5
	44.8	28.8	33.2				Trade Receivables (net)		36.4		31.6
	17.6	33.6	31.4				Inventory		31.0		32.7
	1.2	2.1	2.2				All Other Current		3.1		2.1
	79.1	73.3	78.4				Total Current		78.9		77.9
	6.8	14.5	13.6				Fixed Assets (net)		15.2		13.6
	5.1	4.9	1.5				Intangibles (net)		2.6		5.4
	9.0	7.3	6.5				All Other Non-Current		3.4		3.1
	100.0	100.0	100.0				Total		100.0		100.0
							LIABILITIES				
	13.0	5.8	10.6				Notes Payable-Short Term		16.9		14.7
	.0	1.2	1.4				Cur. Mat.-L.T.D.		2.0		2.7
	33.7	20.9	20.8				Trade Payables		23.6		21.9
	.0	.1	.4				Income Taxes Payable		.1		.0
	10.1	6.9	8.1				All Other Current		8.8		8.5
	56.8	34.9	41.4				Total Current		51.3		47.8
	11.7	15.3	8.9				Long-Term Debt		10.8		15.7
	.0	.3	.0				Deferred Taxes		.1		.2
	1.4	1.9	1.5				All Other Non-Current		4.2		4.3
	30.1	47.6	48.2				Net Worth		33.5		31.8
	100.0	100.0	100.0				Total Liabilities & Net Worth		100.0		100.0
							INCOME DATA				
	100.0	100.0	100.0				Net Sales		100.0		100.0
	20.9	20.3	17.1				Gross Profit		15.8		19.9
	16.0	18.0	11.3				Operating Expenses		12.9		16.4
	4.9	2.4	5.8				Operating Profit		2.9		3.5
	.4	-.6	.4				All Other Expenses (net)		.4		.0
	4.5	3.0	5.4				Profit Before Taxes		2.5		3.4
							RATIOS				
		3.0	4.5	3.3					2.3		2.7
		1.6	2.1	1.9			Current		1.6		1.8
		.8	1.4	1.3					1.1		1.2
		1.8	2.3	1.9					1.5		1.8
		1.2	1.0	.9			Quick		.8		1.0
		.4	.5	.6					.5		.5
13	29.0	14	25.7	15	24.5			18	20.5	14	25.6
19	18.9	26	14.3	31	11.7		Sales/Receivables	28	13.1	29	12.5
47	7.8	37	9.8	39	9.4			40	9.1	40	9.2
4	92.3	21	17.8	20	18.1			17	21.6	17	21.3
6	65.8	31	11.9	34	10.6		Cost of Sales/Inventory	28	13.1	33	11.2
26	14.0	61	6.0	49	7.5			49	7.5	66	5.5
11	33.6	6	61.8	11	33.8			12	31.1	12	29.7
17	22.0	21	17.8	20	17.9		Cost of Sales/Payables	19	19.2	21	17.1
34	10.7	33	11.0	33	10.9			32	11.4	30	12.3
	8.8	6.2	7.1						8.6		7.5
	32.5	12.1	10.0				Sales/Working Capital		17.4		14.8
	-93.9	27.7	19.6						54.2		28.2
	133.5	24.2	46.3						17.6		19.6
	3.5	(11) 8.9	(30) 15.0				EBIT/Interest	(83)	6.8	(51)	9.0
	-2.4	3.0	3.5						2.2		3.9
			30.3								
		(10)	8.6				Net Profit + Depr., Dep., Amort./Cur. Mat. L/T/D				
			4.3								
	.0	.0	.0						.0		.0
	.1	.0	.3				Fixed/Worth		.3		.3
	NM	.8	.6						1.0		1.4
	1.0	.3	.5						1.0		.9
	4.8	1.1	1.2				Debt/Worth		2.6		2.1
	NM	6.2	3.2						7.3		10.1
		33.5	53.7						56.8		77.1
	(14)	20.5	28.2				% Profit Before Taxes/Tangible Net Worth	(80)	26.6	(53)	29.6
		8.9	16.2						8.7		13.5
	31.2	16.0	24.4						20.3		19.0
	14.8	5.5	15.6				% Profit Before Taxes/Total Assets		7.4		9.6
	-4.0	1.8	6.2						2.1		4.9
	UND	UND	310.6						654.6		456.1
	340.6	599.2	49.4				Sales/Net Fixed Assets		75.0		99.1
	61.3	25.5	17.3						15.4		21.3
	10.5	7.1	6.1						6.5		5.8
	7.2	4.2	3.9				Sales/Total Assets		4.2		3.7
	4.9	2.3	2.6						2.7		2.6
			.1						.1		.1
		(28)	.3				% Depr., Dep., Amort./Sales	(63)	.4	(37)	.5
			.8						.9		1.1
									.8		.9
							% Officers', Directors' Owners' Comp/Sales	(29)	1.2	(23)	1.6
									2.0		3.6
1857M	74428M	398981M	3224920M	1951525M	2902307M		Net Sales ($)		11650188M		6203854M
318M	10696M	89687M	769547M	521404M	1261764M		Total Assets ($)		2904057M		1762621M

© RMA 2024

M = $ thousand   MM = $ million
See Pages viii through xx for Explanation of Ratios and Data

WHOLESALE—Packaged Frozen Food Merchant Wholesalers NAICS 424420

Comparative Historical Data | **Current Data Sorted by Sales**

						Type of Statement						
	3		9		7	Unqualified						6
	7		6		6	Reviewed				2		4
	4		5		6	Compiled			1	1		5
	4		9		5	Tax Returns					3	2
	26		39		52	Other		1	1	6	7	37
	4/1/21-3/31/22 ALL		4/1/22-3/31/23 ALL		4/1/23-3/31/24 ALL			12 (4/1-9/30/23)			64 (10/1/23-3/31/24)	
							0-1MM	1-3MM	3-5MM	5-10MM	10-25MM	25MM & OVER
	44		68		76	NUMBER OF STATEMENTS		1	2	9	10	54
	%		%		%	ASSETS	%	%	%	%	%	%
	17.5		10.3		10.7	Cash & Equivalents					15.6	9.4
	29.0		31.8		31.4	Trade Receivables (net)	D				29.2	30.7
	31.5		31.9		29.1	Inventory	A				30.6	31.7
	2.3		2.8		3.1	All Other Current	T				.8	2.5
	80.3		76.7		74.3	Total Current	A				76.1	74.3
	10.9		11.9		14.4	Fixed Assets (net)					7.7	15.5
	3.7		5.1		3.6	Intangibles (net)	N				6.7	2.8
	5.1		6.4		7.7	All Other Non-Current	O				9.4	7.4
	100.0		100.0		100.0	Total	T				100.0	100.0
						LIABILITIES	A					
	10.8		11.9		10.7	Notes Payable-Short Term	V				4.2	11.8
	1.6		2.3		1.3	Cur. Mat.-L.T.D.	A				1.8	1.3
	22.9		23.5		21.4	Trade Payables	I				24.5	20.1
	.2		.2		.2	Income Taxes Payable	L				.1	.3
	7.6		6.6		7.6	All Other Current	A				12.1	7.1
	43.1		44.4		41.2	Total Current	B				42.7	40.7
	12.1		12.5		13.6	Long-Term Debt	L				9.1	13.3
	.0		.0		.1	Deferred Taxes	E				.6	.0
	2.1		2.3		3.2	All Other Non-Current					.0	4.3
	42.5		40.7		41.9	Net Worth					47.7	41.8
	100.0		100.0		100.0	Total Liabilties & Net Worth					100.0	100.0
						INCOME DATA						
	100.0		100.0		100.0	Net Sales					100.0	100.0
	19.4		16.2		18.6	Gross Profit					19.0	17.5
	15.7		12.7		13.9	Operating Expenses					15.4	12.5
	3.7		3.5		4.8	Operating Profit					3.6	4.9
	-.4		.3		.4	All Other Expenses (net)					.5	.6
	4.0		3.2		4.4	Profit Before Taxes					3.1	4.4
						RATIOS						
	3.0		2.8		3.1						3.9	2.8
	2.0		1.6		1.8	Current					1.5	1.8
	1.5		1.3		1.2						1.1	1.2
	2.0		1.7		1.8						1.9	1.6
	1.0		.9		.9	Quick					1.0	.9
	.7		.6		.6						.6	.6
16	22.7	15	25.0	15	25.0						17 21.3	15 25.0
24	15.4	30	12.1	27	13.5	Sales/Receivables					25 14.7	27 13.4
38	9.5	37	9.8	37	9.8						33 11.1	37 9.9
15	23.8	19	19.1	17	21.3						12 31.2	21 17.2
27	13.6	30	12.1	30	12.1	Cost of Sales/Inventory					34 10.7	33 11.2
51	7.1	47	7.8	53	6.9						56 6.5	54 6.7
12	30.7	15	25.1	12	31.2						4 85.0	13 28.9
22	16.9	22	16.3	21	17.4	Cost of Sales/Payables					25 14.5	21 17.4
27	13.7	35	10.5	32	11.3						45 8.2	31 11.6
	6.9		8.5		6.6						4.8	7.7
	11.2		13.6		13.2	Sales/Working Capital					15.3	13.5
	18.7		27.3		35.2						78.5	28.4
	41.5		27.6		31.8							32.0
(34)	13.0	(59)	9.0	(67)	8.5	EBIT/Interest					(49) 8.5	8.5
	4.9		2.8		2.3							2.3
			26.4		50.9	Net Profit + Depr., Dep.,						42.6
		(18)	12.7	(19)	9.8	Amort./Cur. Mat. L/T/D					(16) 8.6	8.6
			4.9		3.6							3.8
	.0		.0		.0						.0	.1
	.1		.3		.3	Fixed/Worth					.0	.3
	.5		.8		.8						.4	.8
	.5		.6		.6						.5	.6
	1.3		1.6		1.6	Debt/Worth					2.1	1.6
	3.8		4.1		5.0						6.1	4.0
	67.2		59.9		56.3	% Profit Before Taxes/Tangible					101.9	54.5
(40)	33.2	(61)	28.5	(71)	28.2	Net Worth					24.0	(51) 31.4
	15.9		11.1		15.1						7.3	16.5
	26.4		17.3		22.3	% Profit Before Taxes/Total					17.0	22.2
	12.5		9.6		11.7	Assets					8.1	11.7
	5.4		3.1		3.5						.7	4.2
	303.4		436.1		569.3						UND	302.5
	79.5		59.2		64.3	Sales/Net Fixed Assets					UND	40.8
	29.7		20.9		16.7						106.3	13.7
	5.6		5.1		6.3						7.1	6.0
	3.4		4.0		3.9	Sales/Total Assets					2.7	3.9
	2.6		2.8		2.4						2.3	2.4
	.2		.1		.1							.1
(28)	.3	(47)	.4	(51)	.4	% Depr., Dep., Amort./Sales					(44)	.4
	.9		.8		.9							.9
	.4		.4		.9							
(16)	1.2	(20)	1.0	(18)	1.7	% Officers', Directors' Owners' Comp/Sales						
	2.8		2.5		3.1							
	5429850M		9293489M		8554018M	Net Sales ($)		1857M	9297M	66692M	169301M	8306871M
	1635648M		2555736M		2653416M	Total Assets ($)		318M	2168M	17930M	53097M	2579903M

© RMA 2024   M = $ thousand   MM = $ million
See Pages viii through xx for Explanation of Ratios and Data

WHOLESALE—Dairy Product (except Dried or Canned) Merchant Wholesalers NAICS 424430

Current Data Sorted by Assets | Comparative Historical Data

						Type of Statement		
		1	4	1	1	Unqualified	12	3
	1	1	1			Reviewed	8	1
		1	1			Compiled	7	3
	1					Tax Returns	5	
	11 (4/1-9/30/23)	5	13 (10/1/23-3/31/24)	11	2	Other	26	18
0-500M	500M-2MM	2-10MM	10-50MM	50-100MM	100-250MM		4/1/19-3/31/20 ALL	4/1/20-3/31/21 ALL
						NUMBER OF STATEMENTS	58	25
%	2 %	8 %	19 %	12 %	3 %	ASSETS	%	%
			11.1	6.1		Cash & Equivalents	11.2	13.6
D			32.5	29.3		Trade Receivables (net)	33.8	27.6
A			24.9	21.1		Inventory	23.3	24.1
T			2.5	1.1		All Other Current	3.2	4.8
A			71.0	57.6		Total Current	71.5	70.1
			21.2	17.9		Fixed Assets (net)	18.2	18.4
N			1.5	12.0		Intangibles (net)	5.2	3.7
O			6.4	12.5		All Other Non-Current	5.2	7.8
T			100.0	100.0		Total	100.0	100.0
						LIABILITIES		
A			11.2	11.2		Notes Payable-Short Term	14.9	9.4
V			3.7	2.0		Cur. Mat.-L.T.D.	2.0	3.0
A			27.8	20.5		Trade Payables	27.5	28.3
I			.5	.0		Income Taxes Payable	.1	.2
L			9.2	14.0		All Other Current	10.1	7.5
A			52.4	47.7		Total Current	54.6	48.4
B			11.1	11.9		Long-Term Debt	12.2	19.2
L			.0	.0		Deferred Taxes	.2	.1
E			3.1	5.2		All Other Non-Current	7.5	4.0
			33.5	35.2		Net Worth	25.6	28.2
			100.0	100.0		Total Liabilities & Net Worth	100.0	100.0
						INCOME DATA		
			100.0	100.0		Net Sales	100.0	100.0
			17.3	19.0		Gross Profit	17.8	18.1
			11.8	15.7		Operating Expenses	16.9	15.2
			5.5	3.3		Operating Profit	.9	2.9
			1.0	.5		All Other Expenses (net)	.1	.0
			4.5	2.9		Profit Before Taxes	.8	2.9
						RATIOS		
			1.6	1.4			1.8	3.4
			1.4	1.2		Current	1.3	1.2
			1.2	1.0			1.0	1.0
			1.1	.9			1.4	1.5
			.7	.7		Quick	.8	1.0
			.5	.6			.5	.5
		21 17.7	19 19.7				18 20.5	17 21.8
		26 13.8	22 16.3			Sales/Receivables	24 15.1	21 17.6
		38 9.6	30 12.2				30 12.0	27 13.5
		13 28.8	6 59.9				7 53.5	5 69.0
		34 10.7	10 37.3			Cost of Sales/Inventory	18 20.2	15 24.7
		60 6.1	53 6.9				31 11.7	60 6.1
		15 24.1	10 36.0				14 26.9	14 25.7
		25 14.4	29 12.4			Cost of Sales/Payables	21 17.2	23 15.6
		33 11.1	35 10.5				30 12.0	33 10.9
			11.3	28.3			17.2	8.8
			16.6	71.2		Sales/Working Capital	46.0	42.1
			51.8	192.4			468.7	597.2
			27.7	20.1			13.5	11.3
		(17)	6.6 (11)	9.3		EBIT/Interest	(45) 5.2	(18) 4.8
			4.5	3.2			.3	-.1
						Net Profit + Depr., Dep.,	12.1	
						Amort./Cur. Mat. L/T/D	(16) 3.6	
							2.4	
			.1	.0			.2	.0
			.6	.6		Fixed/Worth	.6	.6
			1.1	1.5			2.2	3.8
			1.3	1.6			1.2	.7
			2.0	3.0		Debt/Worth	2.8	3.1
			4.0	6.8			19.6	NM
			43.1	71.1		% Profit Before Taxes/Tangible	46.9	49.3
		(18)	35.9 (11)	42.7		Net Worth	(45) 22.4	(19) 17.8
			24.9	3.8			2.1	-3.2
			20.5	16.8			14.9	12.6
			12.0	11.1		% Profit Before Taxes/Total Assets	5.8	4.1
			5.6	1.7			-1.4	-1.1
			186.0	912.7			288.2	548.2
			22.3	38.4		Sales/Net Fixed Assets	41.4	44.2
			5.5	20.1			12.5	10.2
			7.3	6.1			8.0	7.0
			3.3	3.8		Sales/Total Assets	5.4	4.6
			2.2	2.6			3.6	2.7
			.1	.2			.2	.1
		(16)	.2 (10)	.9		% Depr., Dep., Amort./Sales	(45) .7	(19) .6
			.8	1.2			1.6	1.6
						% Officers', Directors'	.6	
						Owners' Comp/Sales	(15) 1.1	
							2.5	
18119M	315625M	1838838M	3636770M	2254891M		Net Sales ($)	6921272M	2376008M
2699M	55043M	486200M	836425M	423365M		Total Assets ($)	1542774M	545136M

M = $ thousand   MM = $ million
See Pages viii through xx for Explanation of Ratios and Data

© RMA 2024

WHOLESALE—Dairy Product (except Dried or Canned) Merchant Wholesalers NAICS 424430

Comparative Historical Data / Current Data Sorted by Sales

			Type of Statement						
3	7	7	Unqualified						7
3	3	3	Reviewed					1	2
4	6	3	Compiled				1	1	1
6	2	2	Tax Returns			1			
10	20	32	Other		1				29
4/1/21-3/31/22 ALL	4/1/22-3/31/23 ALL	4/1/23-3/31/24 ALL		0-1MM	11 (4/1-9/30/23) 1-3MM	3-5MM	5-10MM	33 (10/1/23-3/31/24) 10-25MM	25MM & OVER
26	38	44	NUMBER OF STATEMENTS			1	1	3	39
%	%	%	ASSETS	%	%	%	%	%	%
15.4	9.0	10.5	Cash & Equivalents						8.7
26.2	29.8	33.0	Trade Receivables (net)	D	D				31.9
17.1	26.8	23.3	Inventory	A	A				24.1
2.0	4.3	2.0	All Other Current	T	T				1.6
60.7	70.0	68.7	Total Current	A	A				66.3
21.7	16.1	18.2	Fixed Assets (net)						19.3
6.3	4.2	4.9	Intangibles (net)	N	N				5.5
11.4	9.7	8.2	All Other Non-Current	O	O				8.8
100.0	100.0	100.0	Total	T	T				100.0
			LIABILITIES						
7.3	5.7	10.7	Notes Payable-Short Term	A	A				10.7
4.9	3.0	2.7	Cur. Mat.-L.T.D.	V	V				2.8
21.1	23.2	25.3	Trade Payables	A	A				24.5
.3	.1	.2	Income Taxes Payable	I	I				.2
7.7	10.3	11.8	All Other Current	L	L				12.7
41.2	42.3	50.7	Total Current	A	A				50.9
17.9	16.3	11.5	Long-Term Debt	B	B				12.1
.1	.0	.0	Deferred Taxes	L	L				.0
2.6	4.7	4.1	All Other Non-Current	E	E				4.6
38.2	36.7	33.7	Net Worth						32.4
100.0	100.0	100.0	Total Liabilities & Net Worth						100.0
			INCOME DATA						
100.0	100.0	100.0	Net Sales						100.0
27.4	22.3	18.7	Gross Profit						18.2
23.9	19.7	14.6	Operating Expenses						14.0
3.5	2.6	4.1	Operating Profit						4.2
-.9	-.8	.5	All Other Expenses (net)						.6
4.4	3.4	3.6	Profit Before Taxes						3.5
			RATIOS						
2.9	2.4	1.6							1.6
1.3	1.5	1.3	Current						1.3
1.0	1.1	1.1							1.1
2.2	1.3	1.0							1.0
1.0	.8	.8	Quick						.7
.7	.7	.6							.5
13 27.2	11 32.1	19 19.7						18	20.1
23 15.6	19 19.2	25 14.5	Sales/Receivables					24	15.4
29 12.5	28 13.2	33 11.0						32	11.5
4 84.4	7 52.1	8 47.6						8	43.4
12 31.0	24 15.0	21 17.5	Cost of Sales/Inventory					22	16.5
27 13.7	36 10.1	56 6.5						56	6.5
9 39.3	10 37.3	13 29.1						12	30.2
26 14.3	21 17.5	26 13.9	Cost of Sales/Payables					26	14.3
31 11.7	30 12.3	33 11.1						32	11.3
9.7	12.2	12.7							14.5
34.7	23.4	27.2	Sales/Working Capital						30.5
843.2	131.8	91.5							135.8
36.9	36.8	16.6							19.2
(25) 16.1	(33) 15.9	(39) 6.6	EBIT/Interest					(36)	7.3
3.3	5.6	3.6							4.3
		10.4	Net Profit + Depr., Dep.,						8.7
	(15) 4.9	Amort./Cur. Mat. L/T/D					(14)	4.9
		4.1							3.9
.2	.1	.1							.1
.6	.4	.6	Fixed/Worth						.6
7.9	1.0	1.2							1.3
.5	.8	1.3							1.4
2.3	2.7	2.1	Debt/Worth						2.4
18.9	7.1	4.9							5.1
47.2	115.5	67.6	% Profit Before Taxes/Tangible						77.3
(21) 22.7	(35) 43.7	(41) 38.2	Net Worth					(36)	39.5
8.7	12.9	19.9							28.3
20.3	26.5	20.2	% Profit Before Taxes/Total						19.5
8.0	15.1	12.9	Assets						13.0
2.0	4.4	4.8							5.6
68.0	249.0	231.6							186.0
24.3	59.3	39.5	Sales/Net Fixed Assets						36.5
13.5	19.9	11.6							10.7
5.7	7.9	6.7							6.9
4.5	5.4	4.5	Sales/Total Assets						4.3
3.7	3.7	2.6							2.6
.5	.1	.1							.1
(20) .8	(25) .5	(34) .3	% Depr., Dep., Amort./Sales					(32)	.3
1.7	1.5	1.2							1.2
.6	.4	.3							.1
(11) 3.2	(15) 1.4	(14) 1.1	% Officers', Directors'					(11)	.5
7.0	2.7	1.2	Owners' Comp/Sales						1.1
1810975M	3729240M	8064243M	Net Sales ($)		4004M	6643M	56237M		7997359M
452728M	807943M	1803732M	Total Assets ($)		819M	13011M	12300M		1777602M

© RMA 2024
M = $ thousand   MM = $ million
See Pages viii through xx for Explanation of Ratios and Data

WHOLESALE—Poultry and Poultry Product Merchant Wholesalers NAICS 424440

Current Data Sorted by Assets | Comparative Historical Data

						Type of Statement				
		2	4	1	1	Unqualified		4		
		1	1		1	Reviewed		3		4
		3	1			Compiled		1		
		4	3	3	1	Tax Returns		5		3
	7 (4/1-9/30/23)					Other		24		15
0-500M	500M-2MM	2-10MM	10-50MM	50-100MM	100-250MM			4/1/19-3/31/20 ALL		4/1/20-3/31/21 ALL
		10	9	4	3	NUMBER OF STATEMENTS		37		22
%	%	%	%	%	%	ASSETS		%		%
		24.0				Cash & Equivalents		8.7		15.0
		40.8				Trade Receivables (net)		42.0		35.6
D	D	18.7				Inventory		25.5		23.6
A	A	.3				All Other Current		3.3		1.4
T	T	83.8				Total Current		79.5		75.5
A	A	7.3				Fixed Assets (net)		11.6		14.3
		4.6				Intangibles (net)		2.5		2.3
N	N	4.3				All Other Non-Current		6.4		7.9
O	O	100.0				Total		100.0		100.0
T	T					LIABILITIES				
		6.1				Notes Payable-Short Term		16.9		8.8
A	A	.4				Cur. Mat.-L.T.D.		.8		1.7
V	V	27.5				Trade Payables		25.6		20.1
A	A	.3				Income Taxes Payable		.1		.0
I	I	10.8				All Other Current		10.2		18.5
L	L	45.1				Total Current		53.5		49.1
A	A	1.5				Long-Term Debt		9.3		7.7
B	B	1.0				Deferred Taxes		.0		.0
L	L	4.8				All Other Non-Current		.6		.8
E	E	47.6				Net Worth		36.6		42.4
		100.0				Total Liabilities & Net Worth		100.0		100.0
						INCOME DATA				
		100.0				Net Sales		100.0		100.0
		14.2				Gross Profit		12.9		15.2
		11.5				Operating Expenses		10.9		12.1
		2.7				Operating Profit		2.0		3.0
		-1.4				All Other Expenses (net)		.1		.0
		4.1				Profit Before Taxes		1.9		3.0
						RATIOS				
		3.8						2.3		2.4
		2.3				Current		1.4		1.5
		1.0						1.1		1.1
		3.1						1.2		1.7
		2.0				Quick		.9		1.0
		.8						.6		.7
	8	45.0					13	28.6	16	23.1
	18	20.4				Sales/Receivables	21	17.4	23	16.2
	26	13.8					33	10.9	29	12.5
	2	187.2					4	86.7	6	62.6
	5	72.2				Cost of Sales/Inventory	12	29.4	16	23.3
	14	25.3					32	11.4	26	14.1
	6	57.1					8	45.3	8	46.6
	14	26.7				Cost of Sales/Payables	14	26.7	14	25.5
	18	20.2					23	16.0	23	15.6
		10.8						13.4		11.9
		17.4				Sales/Working Capital		25.5		22.8
		NM						79.2		81.8
								30.4		55.1
						EBIT/Interest	(34)	5.4	(20)	21.5
								2.2		5.6
						Net Profit + Depr., Dep., Amort./Cur. Mat. L/T/D				
		.0						.0		.0
		.1				Fixed/Worth		.1		.1
		1.8						.6		.6
		.3						.6		.8
		.8				Debt/Worth		2.3		1.7
		16.7						4.8		3.0
						% Profit Before Taxes/Tangible Net Worth		40.8		64.2
							(35)	18.3		31.3
								5.5		11.3
		41.5						13.3		20.9
		18.2				% Profit Before Taxes/Total Assets		7.0		10.7
		2.0						1.9		3.0
		999.8						999.8		999.8
		298.1				Sales/Net Fixed Assets		202.1		625.6
		63.0						42.3		22.3
		9.7						9.4		7.6
		8.8				Sales/Total Assets		5.6		5.6
		5.8						3.9		3.1
								.0		.0
						% Depr., Dep., Amort./Sales	(26)	.2	(15)	.3
								1.0		1.3
								.2		
						% Officers', Directors', Owners' Comp/Sales	(10)	1.1		
								2.8		
	445703M	2030625M	1226105M	1710706M		Net Sales ($)		5074274M		2495487M
	54782M	253829M	280067M	417051M		Total Assets ($)		992580M		482751M

M = $ thousand   MM = $ million
See Pages viii through xx for Explanation of Ratios and Data

© RMA 2024

WHOLESALE—Poultry and Poultry Product Merchant Wholesalers NAICS 424440

Comparative Historical Data | Current Data Sorted by Sales

							Type of Statement							
							Unqualified							6
		1			4		Reviewed					1		3
		1			4		Compiled							1
		1			4		Tax Returns							4
		2			6		Other					1		10
		11			11				7 (4/1-9/30/23)				19 (10/1/23-3/31/24)	
	4/1/21-3/31/22		4/1/22-3/31/23		4/1/23-3/31/24									
	ALL 15		ALL 28		ALL 26		NUMBER OF STATEMENTS	0-1MM	1-3MM	3-5MM	5-10MM	10-25MM 2	25MM & OVER 24
	%		%		%		ASSETS	%	%	%	%	%	%
	13.7		12.9		17.9		Cash & Equivalents	D	D	D	D		18.6
	38.6		39.0		38.9		Trade Receivables (net)	A	A	A	A		39.9
	21.4		20.5		16.5		Inventory	T	T	T	T		13.4
	1.7		2.0		2.9		All Other Current	A	A	A	A		3.1
	75.4		74.4		76.2		Total Current						74.9
	10.6		16.5		13.5		Fixed Assets (net)	N	N	N	N		14.1
	7.0		3.1		2.7		Intangibles (net)	O	O	O	O		2.8
	7.1		6.1		7.6		All Other Non-Current	T	T	T	T		8.2
	100.0		100.0		100.0		Total						100.0
							LIABILITIES	A	A	A	A		
	9.5		12.6		8.8		Notes Payable-Short Term	V	V	V	V		8.7
	2.5		1.8		.9		Cur. Mat.-L.T.D.	A	A	A	A		1.0
	19.8		26.2		25.9		Trade Payables	I	I	I	I		23.1
	.0		.0		.1		Income Taxes Payable	L	L	L	L		.1
	16.0		7.0		14.0		All Other Current	A	A	A	A		14.8
	47.8		46.7		49.8		Total Current	B	B	B	B		47.7
	14.9		11.7		5.2		Long-Term Debt	L	L	L	L		5.3
	.0		.9		.4		Deferred Taxes	E	E	E	E		.4
	1.6		4.0		4.6		All Other Non-Current						3.6
	35.6		35.8		40.0		Net Worth						43.0
	100.0		100.0		100.0		Total Liabilities & Net Worth						100.0
							INCOME DATA						
	100.0		100.0		100.0		Net Sales						100.0
	13.7		11.1		12.1		Gross Profit						11.2
	11.5		9.7		9.8		Operating Expenses						8.9
	2.1		1.4		2.3		Operating Profit						2.3
	.9		.0		-.2		All Other Expenses (net)						-.3
	1.3		1.4		2.5		Profit Before Taxes						2.6
							RATIOS						
	2.9		2.0		2.1								2.0
	1.6		1.4		1.5		Current						1.5
	1.2		1.1		1.1								1.2
	1.8		1.5		1.8								1.8
	1.0		.9		1.0		Quick						1.1
	.7		.8		.8								.9
14	25.8	12	29.3	14	26.6							14	25.8
26	13.9	21	17.2	18	20.1		Sales/Receivables					19	18.8
47	7.8	40	9.1	26	13.8							27	13.3
7	52.9	1	287.8	4	91.6							3	109.4
12	31.0	11	32.1	7	55.5		Cost of Sales/Inventory					6	59.4
26	14.0	27	13.4	14	26.6							12	30.0
7	50.2	6	61.3	9	39.8							9	39.8
14	26.7	13	29.0	14	26.7		Cost of Sales/Payables					13	27.7
24	15.0	32	11.3	19	19.1							17	21.7
	7.8		18.8		15.5								16.6
	28.6		33.0		28.4		Sales/Working Capital						28.4
	49.1		82.3		90.2								53.6
	248.6		36.4		77.2								80.0
(14)	40.0	(25)	13.6	(25)	14.4		EBIT/Interest					(23)	24.0
	11.0		3.2		5.9								6.3
							Net Profit + Depr., Dep., Amort./Cur. Mat. L/T/D						
	.0		.0		.0								.0
	.2		.2		.4		Fixed/Worth						.3
	3.2		.8		.6								.6
	.6		1.1		.8								.8
	1.5		2.2		1.6		Debt/Worth						1.2
	57.5		5.9		4.7								3.5
	56.2		57.5		87.2		% Profit Before Taxes/Tangible Net Worth						74.7
(12)	35.2	(27)	24.2	(25)	34.5								33.6
	26.6		6.0		18.4								18.0
	24.0		14.9		21.4		% Profit Before Taxes/Total Assets						23.7
	16.3		5.0		9.0								9.0
	3.1		.8		6.5								7.1
	999.8		695.8		496.4								600.8
	141.8		137.1		98.3		Sales/Net Fixed Assets						98.3
	39.2		28.7		31.6								28.4
	6.9		8.1		9.3								9.6
	5.5		5.1		6.9		Sales/Total Assets						6.9
	3.6		3.7		4.6								4.4
	.0		.1		.1								.1
(10)	.2	(20)	.3	(20)	.4		% Depr., Dep., Amort./Sales					(18)	.4
	1.0		1.0		.9								1.1
					.6								.4
		(14)	1.3	(10)	1.6		% Officers', Directors' Owners' Comp/Sales						
					1.7								2.6
	2205353M		4867864M		5413139M		Net Sales ($)					39860M	5373279M
	453770M		1001879M		1005729M		Total Assets ($)					5727M	1000002M

M = $ thousand   MM = $ million
See Pages viii through xx for Explanation of Ratios and Data

© RMA 2024

WHOLESALE—Confectionery Merchant Wholesalers NAICS 424450

Current Data Sorted by Assets | Comparative Historical Data

						Type of Statement		
			2		1	Unqualified	1	2
		2	3	1		Reviewed	12	4
		2	1	1		Compiled	3	3
	1	2	1			Tax Returns	7	3
	3	6	9	1		Other	24	19
	9 (4/1-9/30/23)		27 (10/1/23-3/31/24)				4/1/19-3/31/20	4/1/20-3/31/21
0-500M	500M-2MM	2-10MM	10-50MM	50-100MM	100-250MM		ALL	ALL
	4	12	16	3	1	NUMBER OF STATEMENTS	47	31
%	%	%	%	%	%	ASSETS	%	%
D		7.3	6.7			Cash & Equivalents	8.5	10.1
A		22.1	22.1			Trade Receivables (net)	28.1	22.6
T		41.6	38.3			Inventory	31.8	33.1
A		4.2	.3			All Other Current	2.7	4.7
		75.1	67.4			Total Current	71.2	70.5
N		17.1	13.8			Fixed Assets (net)	18.7	19.8
O		2.2	5.5			Intangibles (net)	4.2	6.9
T		5.6	13.2			All Other Non-Current	5.9	2.8
		100.0	100.0			Total	100.0	100.0
A						LIABILITIES		
V		11.2	11.8			Notes Payable-Short Term	12.4	13.7
A		1.6	1.6			Cur. Mat.-L.T.D.	2.4	2.5
I		28.4	21.7			Trade Payables	27.0	20.6
L		.1	.0			Income Taxes Payable	.1	.0
A		8.1	11.6			All Other Current	5.5	10.6
B		49.4	46.7			Total Current	47.4	47.4
L		15.7	8.7			Long-Term Debt	16.9	19.7
E		.3	.1			Deferred Taxes	.2	.1
		1.6	11.8			All Other Non-Current	.7	4.8
		33.0	32.7			Net Worth	34.7	28.1
		100.0	100.0			Total Liabilties & Net Worth	100.0	100.0
						INCOME DATA		
		100.0	100.0			Net Sales	100.0	100.0
		27.2	21.2			Gross Profit	22.1	24.3
		24.4	17.1			Operating Expenses	18.6	22.4
		2.7	4.1			Operating Profit	3.5	1.9
		-.6	.7			All Other Expenses (net)	.7	1.4
		3.4	3.4			Profit Before Taxes	2.8	.5
						RATIOS		
		3.4	1.7				2.3	2.3
		1.6	1.3			Current	1.6	1.3
		.9	1.1				1.1	1.2
		1.0	1.0				1.2	1.3
		.5	.5			Quick	.8	.7
		.4	.3				.5	.4
	13	27.6	24 15.3				19 18.9	17 21.5
	24	15.3	34 10.8			Sales/Receivables	32 11.4	29 12.7
	31	11.7	41 9.0				43 8.4	38 9.5
	35	10.5	37 9.8				25 14.4	27 13.4
	46	8.0	81 4.5			Cost of Sales/Inventory	40 9.1	45 8.2
	107	3.4	101 3.6				68 5.4	70 5.2
	12	29.7	23 15.6				17 21.6	11 33.0
	28	13.1	38 9.7			Cost of Sales/Payables	29 12.8	30 12.2
	58	6.3	64 5.7				44 8.3	55 6.6
		5.5	7.3				8.4	8.7
		16.5	21.1			Sales/Working Capital	13.1	15.3
		NM	77.7				34.3	32.5
		9.7	14.4				10.0	12.5
		5.6	(15) 2.9			EBIT/Interest	(40) 4.2	(25) 3.1
		2.5	1.4				1.6	.7
						Net Profit + Depr., Dep.,		8.8
						Amort./Cur. Mat. L/T/D	(12) 5.6	
							2.6	
		.1	.1				.1	.4
		.6	.4			Fixed/Worth	.4	.8
		1.7	7.1				1.2	5.7
		.7	1.3				.6	.7
		2.3	3.9			Debt/Worth	2.6	2.5
		14.8	19.3				5.5	22.9
		88.1	73.2				48.4	45.3
	(10)	24.6	(14) 15.1			% Profit Before Taxes/Tangible Net Worth	(43) 21.2	(24) 19.4
		13.1	10.2				8.7	5.6
		13.7	15.8				12.2	16.5
		6.3	5.9			% Profit Before Taxes/Total Assets	5.1	6.4
		2.5	1.1				1.9	-.4
		208.7	110.9				160.9	65.5
		37.2	35.9			Sales/Net Fixed Assets	30.8	21.2
		7.3	10.8				9.6	9.6
		5.4	2.7				4.6	4.4
		3.3	2.4			Sales/Total Assets	3.1	3.0
		2.1	2.0				2.1	2.2
			.1				.4	.6
		(15)	.5			% Depr., Dep., Amort./Sales	(38) 1.1	(20) 1.2
			.9				2.1	1.9
						% Officers', Directors' Owners' Comp/Sales	.6	
							(19) 1.2	
							1.7	
18942M	220112M	1065153M	728358M	379237M		Net Sales ($)	3324696M	2035560M
5436M	58174M	395081M	191073M	120439M		Total Assets ($)	1292425M	855640M

M = $ thousand   MM = $ million
See Pages viii through xx for Explanation of Ratios and Data
© RMA 2024

WHOLESALE—Confectionery Merchant Wholesalers   NAICS 424450

Comparative Historical Data | Current Data Sorted by Sales

				Type of Statement						
	4	4	3	Unqualified						3
	6	9	6	Reviewed						6
	2	3	4	Compiled					3	1
	4	6	4	Tax Returns			1	1	1	1
	13	21	19	Other		1	6	2	10
	4/1/21-	4/1/22-	4/1/23-							
	3/31/22	3/31/23	3/31/24		0-1MM	1-3MM	3-5MM	5-10MM	10-25MM	25MM & OVER
	ALL	ALL	ALL		9 (4/1-9/30/23)			27 (10/1/23-3/31/24)		
	29	43	36	NUMBER OF STATEMENTS		1	1	7	6	21
	%	%	%	ASSETS	%	%	%	%	%	%
	9.2	9.3	7.1	Cash & Equivalents						6.7
	25.3	24.4	24.2	Trade Receivables (net)						20.9
	35.8	36.5	36.9	Inventory						42.7
	1.8	2.3	1.7	All Other Current						.9
	72.1	72.6	69.8	Total Current	DATA NOT AVAILABLE					71.2
	15.1	20.1	16.4	Fixed Assets (net)						13.7
	10.4	1.0	3.8	Intangibles (net)						2.1
	2.4	6.4	9.9	All Other Non-Current						13.0
	100.0	100.0	100.0	Total						100.0
				LIABILITIES						
	17.1	10.4	11.9	Notes Payable-Short Term						10.8
	2.5	1.4	1.4	Cur. Mat.-L.T.D.						1.1
	19.7	20.8	25.2	Trade Payables						21.8
	.0	.0	.1	Income Taxes Payable						.1
	10.9	10.1	11.0	All Other Current						11.6
	50.2	42.8	49.6	Total Current						45.3
	13.9	14.0	17.8	Long-Term Debt						9.1
	.0	.1	.1	Deferred Taxes						.0
	14.8	9.9	13.6	All Other Non-Current						10.8
	21.2	33.2	18.9	Net Worth						34.7
	100.0	100.0	100.0	Total Liabilities & Net Worth						100.0
				INCOME DATA						
	100.0	100.0	100.0	Net Sales						100.0
	22.3	24.8	23.7	Gross Profit						21.5
	21.0	19.8	19.3	Operating Expenses						16.7
	1.2	5.0	4.5	Operating Profit						4.8
	-1.1	.5	.6	All Other Expenses (net)						.7
	2.3	4.5	3.9	Profit Before Taxes						4.1
				RATIOS						
	2.3	3.0	2.5	Current						2.5
	1.4	1.8	1.4							1.4
	1.2	1.3	1.1							1.2
	1.2	1.5	1.0	Quick						1.0
	.6	.7	.5							.4
	.5	.4	.4							.3
20	18.5	12 30.2	18 20.0	Sales/Receivables					15	24.7
31	11.9	27 13.7	29 12.5						23	15.8
38	9.6	39 9.3	37 9.8						36	10.2
31	11.7	24 15.4	34 10.6	Cost of Sales/Inventory					34	10.6
49	7.4	51 7.1	53 6.9						74	4.9
81	4.5	96 3.8	101 3.6						99	3.7
15	23.7	16 22.4	15 23.9	Cost of Sales/Payables					14	26.3
30	12.1	25 14.4	31 11.9						26	14.2
47	7.8	53 6.9	58 6.3						41	8.8
	7.9	6.8	8.6	Sales/Working Capital						9.1
	14.5	10.8	17.0							17.5
	22.5	17.3	77.7							25.0
	18.9	24.9	13.2	EBIT/Interest						14.7
(24)	10.5	(33) 7.8	(34) 4.4						(19)	6.9
	.0	2.1	1.9							2.2
		9.0		Net Profit + Depr., Dep., Amort./Cur. Mat. L/T/D						
		(11) 4.3								
		-1.0								
	.1	.1	.1	Fixed/Worth						.1
	.4	.5	.4							.4
	24.8	.9	1.7							.8
	.9	.5	.9	Debt/Worth						1.0
	2.6	1.7	2.5							2.5
	NM	3.8	14.8							5.1
	43.5	47.8	84.1	% Profit Before Taxes/Tangible Net Worth						105.9
(22)	28.7	(40) 22.6	(30) 25.5						(20)	25.5
	10.8	11.5	11.3							12.0
	17.1	21.9	17.4	% Profit Before Taxes/Total Assets						20.3
	9.2	11.0	6.7							6.9
	-1.1	3.2	2.1							4.0
	145.2	286.7	195.6	Sales/Net Fixed Assets						117.7
	31.2	23.5	32.7							30.8
	10.7	7.9	10.6							14.1
	4.3	4.6	4.1	Sales/Total Assets						4.0
	3.4	2.8	2.6							2.7
	2.1	2.1	2.1							2.2
	.3	.2	.2	% Depr., Dep., Amort./Sales						.2
(22)	.8	(32) 1.0	(26) .5							.5
	1.9	1.8	.9							1.0
	.6	.4		% Officers', Directors' Owners' Comp/Sales						
(12)	2.2	(16) 1.9								
	6.2	2.4								
	2511568M	2539243M	2411802M	Net Sales ($)	2890M	4060M	52742M	116872M	2235238M	
	1009608M	959075M	770203M	Total Assets ($)	1323M	1012M	25780M	41967M	700121M	

M = $ thousand   MM = $ million
See Pages viii through xx for Explanation of Ratios and Data

© RMA 2024

WHOLESALE—Fish and Seafood Merchant Wholesalers NAICS 424460

Current Data Sorted by Assets | Comparative Historical Data

						Type of Statement		
			5	5	3	Unqualified	19	10
		6	10			Reviewed	14	10
		7	2	1		Compiled	14	8
3	2	4	1			Tax Returns	15	2
1	4	20	23	8	4	Other	93	51
0-500M	500M-2MM	15 (4/1-9/30/23) 2-10MM	94 (10/1/23-3/31/24) 10-50MM	50-100MM	100-250MM	NUMBER OF STATEMENTS	4/1/19-3/31/20 ALL 155	4/1/20-3/31/21 ALL 81
%	%	%	%	%	%	ASSETS	%	%
		12.0	6.8	4.3		Cash & Equivalents	6.9	8.6
		31.0	27.7	29.4		Trade Receivables (net)	28.8	29.9
		30.3	41.1	50.0		Inventory	40.7	40.0
		.8	1.6	1.3		All Other Current	3.3	2.6
		74.1	77.1	85.0		Total Current	79.6	81.1
		17.4	11.5	6.8		Fixed Assets (net)	10.7	11.4
		4.2	4.4	5.4		Intangibles (net)	2.1	3.3
		4.3	6.9	2.9		All Other Non-Current	7.6	4.1
		100.0	100.0	100.0		Total	100.0	100.0
						LIABILITIES		
		12.4	18.0	18.4		Notes Payable-Short Term	25.5	16.7
		1.6	1.1	.7		Cur. Mat.-L.T.D.	2.0	1.7
		25.0	21.8	16.6		Trade Payables	20.9	19.9
		.0	.0	.0		Income Taxes Payable	.1	.1
		4.0	7.0	23.9		All Other Current	6.0	7.1
		43.1	47.9	59.6		Total Current	54.6	45.4
		17.4	13.5	6.0		Long-Term Debt	6.2	11.2
		.0	.0	.0		Deferred Taxes	.3	.2
		5.3	5.0	16.2		All Other Non-Current	5.3	7.9
		34.2	33.5	18.2		Net Worth	33.7	35.3
		100.0	100.0	100.0		Total Liabilities & Net Worth	100.0	100.0
						INCOME DATA		
		100.0	100.0	100.0		Net Sales	100.0	100.0
		17.2	11.7	10.5		Gross Profit	12.8	13.5
		16.2	9.7	8.6		Operating Expenses	10.6	11.1
		1.0	2.1	1.9		Operating Profit	2.2	2.4
		.9	.8	.5		All Other Expenses (net)	.3	.2
		.2	1.3	1.4		Profit Before Taxes	1.8	2.2
						RATIOS		
		2.7	2.2	2.4			2.1	3.2
		1.9	1.6	1.3		Current	1.4	1.8
		1.2	1.2	1.1			1.2	1.3
		1.6	1.1	.9			.9	1.5
		.9	.8	.6		Quick	.6	.8
		.6	.5	.3			.4	.5
		18 20.1	24 15.0	26 14.1			23 16.1	23 15.9
		30 12.2	29 12.4	29 12.5		Sales/Receivables	31 11.6	31 11.8
		39 9.3	41 10.0	35 10.4			39 9.3	41 8.8
		11 32.8	26 13.9	31 11.6			29 12.6	30 12.3
		27 13.4	47 7.8	60 6.1		Cost of Sales/Inventory	57 6.4	54 6.8
		65 5.6	87 4.2	89 4.1			83 4.4	76 4.8
		17 21.4	15 24.0	9 39.9			12 31.5	9 38.6
		25 14.7	24 14.9	16 22.5		Cost of Sales/Payables	23 16.1	20 18.2
		39 9.4	36 10.0	33 11.0			36 10.1	33 11.1
		6.4	7.2	5.7			7.6	6.5
		12.8	14.8	24.9		Sales/Working Capital	15.1	10.5
		36.0	24.6	NM			33.7	17.5
		15.1	10.1	6.6			6.7	13.1
		(34) 4.8	(39) 2.9	(12) 2.6		EBIT/Interest	(137) 3.3	(72) 5.0
		1.6	1.0	.8			1.4	1.7
						Net Profit + Depr., Dep., Amort./Cur. Mat. L/T/D	9.8	9.0
							(27) 3.0	(18) 4.0
							.8	2.0
		.1	.0	.0			.0	.0
		.3	.1	.0		Fixed/Worth	.1	.2
		1.0	.7	-.7			.6	.6
		.7	1.1	1.4			1.1	1.2
		1.5	1.9	5.0		Debt/Worth	2.5	2.2
		2.6	9.0	-27.0			4.2	4.0
		34.4	35.5	35.9			36.4	58.3
		(32) 16.1	(37) 15.9	(10) 18.7		% Profit Before Taxes/Tangible Net Worth	(148) 14.0	(76) 16.2
		4.1	2.5	3.7			4.5	2.6
		12.1	11.9	11.2			9.8	14.6
		5.3	4.3	1.0		% Profit Before Taxes/Total Assets	3.8	5.6
		1.3	.2	-1.5			.9	.8
		236.9	999.8	999.8			808.9	470.0
		36.4	170.5	840.7		Sales/Net Fixed Assets	118.2	76.3
		16.8	23.9	99.7			24.6	20.3
		5.5	4.8	4.0			4.4	4.5
		4.0	2.8	3.1		Sales/Total Assets	3.2	3.4
		2.4	2.1	2.7			2.3	2.5
		.3	.1	.0			.1	.1
		(23) .8	(29) .2	(10) .0		% Depr., Dep., Amort./Sales	(110) .3	(59) .3
		1.5	.9	.3			1.1	.9
		.8					.8	.3
		(18) 1.7	(12) .9			% Officers', Directors' Owners' Comp/Sales	(41) 1.1	(25) 1.2
		2.2	1.3				2.6	2.8
4354M	34813M	777345M	2838236M	3739294M	3086480M	Net Sales ($)	14480234M	8534079M
530M	6998M	191441M	905487M	1055223M	1016699M	Total Assets ($)	5337469M	2741990M

© RMA 2024 M = $ thousand MM = $ million
See Pages viii through xx for Explanation of Ratios and Data

WHOLESALE—Fish and Seafood Merchant Wholesalers NAICS 424460

Comparative Historical Data | Current Data Sorted by Sales

Comparative Historical Data					Current Data Sorted by Sales						
				Type of Statement							
7		17	13	Unqualified							13
6		11	16	Reviewed						5	11
8		11	10	Compiled			1		1	3	5
12		10	10	Tax Returns		1	3		1	2	3
34		51	60	Other	1		2	1	5	10	41
4/1/21-		4/1/22-	4/1/23-		**0-1MM**	**15 (4/1-9/30/23)**		**3-5MM**	**94 (10/1/23-3/31/24)**		
3/31/22		3/31/23	3/31/24				**1-3MM**		**5-10MM**	**10-25MM**	**25MM & OVER**
ALL		ALL	ALL								
67		100	109	**NUMBER OF STATEMENTS**	2		6	1	7	20	73
%		%	%	**ASSETS**	%		%	%	%	%	%
14.7		8.5	9.9	Cash & Equivalents						11.4	8.0
31.8		29.3	27.8	Trade Receivables (net)						29.1	29.8
33.9		43.3	36.7	Inventory						29.3	40.9
1.3		1.6	1.4	All Other Current						1.0	1.5
81.7		82.6	75.7	Total Current						70.8	80.2
10.2		9.9	13.8	Fixed Assets (net)						20.1	10.0
2.8		1.7	5.3	Intangibles (net)						4.5	4.2
5.2		5.8	5.2	All Other Non-Current						4.6	5.6
100.0		100.0	100.0	Total						100.0	100.0
				LIABILITIES							
16.7		15.5	16.0	Notes Payable-Short Term						8.9	17.6
.7		1.3	1.3	Cur. Mat.-L.T.D.						1.9	1.0
23.6		21.0	20.6	Trade Payables						24.7	21.5
.2		.2	.1	Income Taxes Payable						.0	.1
6.3		7.1	8.7	All Other Current						5.6	10.1
47.5		45.1	46.7	Total Current						41.1	50.3
8.5		14.1	15.1	Long-Term Debt						18.0	10.6
.2		.1	.0	Deferred Taxes						.1	.0
6.0		4.3	9.1	All Other Non-Current						7.5	6.6
37.8		36.5	29.1	Net Worth						33.3	32.5
100.0		100.0	100.0	Total Liabilities & Net Worth						100.0	100.0
				INCOME DATA							
100.0		100.0	100.0	Net Sales						100.0	100.0
16.0		14.4	14.8	Gross Profit						17.8	11.5
11.9		10.9	12.8	Operating Expenses						16.0	9.2
4.1		3.5	2.0	Operating Profit						1.8	2.3
-.5		.2	.7	All Other Expenses (net)						.0	.6
4.6		3.3	1.2	Profit Before Taxes						1.8	1.7
				RATIOS							
2.5		2.6	2.5	Current						2.9	2.3
1.6		1.8	1.7							2.1	1.6
1.3		1.4	1.2							1.0	1.2
1.5		1.4	1.4	Quick						1.6	1.2
1.0		.7	.8							.8	.8
.6		.5	.5							.6	.5
18	19.8	19	19.7	23	16.0	Sales/Receivables				16	22.4	24	15.0
32	11.3	27	13.7	29	12.4					29	12.5	29	12.4
43	8.4	36	10.0	37	9.9					33	11.1	38	9.7
12	30.8	20	18.4	20	18.6	Cost of Sales/Inventory				11	34.0	21	17.1
29	12.8	51	7.2	42	8.7					29	12.8	45	8.2
64	5.7	94	3.9	87	4.2					65	5.6	87	4.2
12	31.4	10	35.3	12	29.5	Cost of Sales/Payables				15	24.3	13	28.6
23	16.2	20	18.4	22	16.9					26	14.2	21	17.3
33	11.0	29	12.4	35	10.3					41	8.8	33	11.0
	7.7		6.3		7.5	Sales/Working Capital					5.7		7.8
	13.3		9.6		13.4						9.5		14.8
	21.7		22.8		26.3						-375.7		24.6
	46.0		21.5		11.5	EBIT/Interest					14.8		11.5
(60)	22.7	(92)	8.8	(101)	4.4				(19)	8.9	(67)	2.9
	8.1		3.5		1.3						2.8		1.2
	48.4		11.7		20.2	Net Profit + Depr., Dep.,							23.9
(10)	10.6	(13)	4.8	(16)	2.7	Amort./Cur. Mat. L/T/D						(14)	2.8
	1.9		3.3		.8								.6
	.0		.0		.0	Fixed/Worth					.2		.0
	.1		.1		.2						.6		.1
	.5		.4		.8						3.1		.6
	1.0		.9		1.0	Debt/Worth					.7		1.1
	2.0		2.0		1.8						1.4		1.9
	3.5		4.0		7.3						14.0		7.3
	76.4		55.3		38.3	% Profit Before Taxes/Tangible Net Worth					30.9		36.7
(65)	45.9	(96)	31.0	(92)	19.3					(16)	13.7	(64)	19.3
	23.9		13.3		3.9						5.8		3.9
	27.2		17.2		14.0	% Profit Before Taxes/Total Assets					10.8		12.6
	17.1		9.9		5.2						5.2		4.7
	7.1		3.5		.7						1.3		.6
	999.8		999.8		999.8	Sales/Net Fixed Assets					106.7		999.8
	223.3		166.7		97.7						30.6		170.5
	30.0		36.0		19.4						13.7		25.3
	5.5		5.1		5.0	Sales/Total Assets					5.3		5.0
	4.0		3.7		3.6						3.9		3.4
	2.8		2.4		2.4						2.4		2.5
	.0		.1		.1	% Depr., Dep., Amort./Sales					.7		.0
(47)	.2	(64)	.2	(72)	.4					(13)	1.2	(53)	.2
	.7		.7		1.0						1.6		
	.6		.6		.6	% Officers', Directors' Owners' Comp/Sales							.2
(29)	1.0	(31)	1.2	(37)	1.4							(22)	.8
	2.3		3.6		2.0								1.4
6218082M		10854649M	10480522M	Net Sales ($)	676M		11806M	3521M	51437M	326076M	10087006M
1876823M		3373916M	3176378M	Total Assets ($)	148M		12259M	1057M	13748M	93635M	3055531M

M = $ thousand   MM = $ million
See Pages viii through xx for Explanation of Ratios and Data

© RMA 2024

WHOLESALE—Meat and Meat Product Merchant Wholesalers NAICS 424470

Current Data Sorted by Assets | Comparative Historical Data

						Type of Statement				
			1	3	6	Unqualified		10		6
		5	7	1		Reviewed		27		9
	1	8	2			Compiled		19		3
	8	7	1			Tax Returns		18		6
3	3	17	24	18	5	Other		70		56
	26 (4/1-9/30/23)		94 (10/1/23-3/31/24)					4/1/19-3/31/20		4/1/20-3/31/21
0-500M	500M-2MM	2-10MM	10-50MM	50-100MM	100-250MM			ALL		ALL
3	12	37	35	22	11	NUMBER OF STATEMENTS		144		80
%	%	%	%	%	%	ASSETS		%		%
	23.5	18.0	14.5	3.4	1.1	Cash & Equivalents		6.8		14.1
	39.7	36.4	35.6	25.7	21.2	Trade Receivables (net)		36.2		32.6
	23.5	20.0	22.5	36.9	33.2	Inventory		24.8		23.7
	3.3	1.8	1.8	1.8	4.6	All Other Current		2.4		2.2
	90.0	76.1	74.5	67.9	60.1	Total Current		70.3		72.7
	7.7	13.4	14.6	15.9	15.9	Fixed Assets (net)		19.7		18.2
	.0	7.2	4.6	10.8	17.3	Intangibles (net)		6.0		6.7
	2.3	3.3	6.3	5.5	6.8	All Other Non-Current		4.1		2.4
	100.0	100.0	100.0	100.0	100.0	Total		100.0		100.0
						LIABILITIES				
	3.1	8.1	11.6	14.3	25.4	Notes Payable-Short Term		20.7		13.9
	.7	1.5	1.4	1.7	2.0	Cur. Mat.-L.T.D.		2.5		3.3
	26.6	17.7	21.8	11.5	12.1	Trade Payables		20.4		17.1
	.4	.2	.1	.0	.0	Income Taxes Payable		.1		.0
	9.0	7.1	7.1	5.4	9.3	All Other Current		6.7		6.9
	39.7	34.6	42.0	32.9	48.8	Total Current		50.4		41.1
	9.1	10.2	10.2	8.3	13.2	Long-Term Debt		10.4		15.0
	.0	.1	.1	.1	.4	Deferred Taxes		.2		.3
	1.2	.7	3.1	5.4	5.2	All Other Non-Current		2.6		2.9
	50.0	54.3	44.6	53.3	32.4	Net Worth		36.4		40.7
	100.0	100.0	100.0	100.0	100.0	Total Liabilities & Net Worth		100.0		100.0
						INCOME DATA				
	100.0	100.0	100.0	100.0	100.0	Net Sales		100.0		100.0
	21.8	17.1	12.9	12.9	12.6	Gross Profit		15.1		15.6
	19.7	13.3	10.2	9.9	12.9	Operating Expenses		12.8		12.8
	2.0	3.8	2.7	2.9	-.3	Operating Profit		2.3		2.7
	-.1	.2	.0	1.3	1.8	All Other Expenses (net)		.5		-.2
	2.1	3.5	2.7	1.7	-2.1	Profit Before Taxes		1.9		2.9
						RATIOS				
	3.9	3.7	3.3	2.6	1.8			2.2		2.5
	1.9	2.3	1.6	2.2	1.1	Current		1.4		1.7
	1.8	1.6	1.3	1.7	.9			1.1		1.3
	3.4	2.8	2.4	1.3	.8			1.5		1.7
	1.8	1.4	1.0	.8	.4	Quick		.8		1.2
	.8	1.0	.7	.6	.2			.5		.8
8	44.5	12	29.3	17	20.9	17	21.7	15	24.6			16	22.3	13	27.6
13	27.7	21	17.6	25	14.7	19	19.5	18	20.2	Sales/Receivables		21	17.3	21	17.7
22	16.4	27	13.5	31	11.8	26	14.3	20	18.0			29	12.7	32	11.3
0	UND	6	59.3	8	44.3	20	18.0	12	31.7			7	53.7	10	37.1
6	62.1	13	28.1	20	18.1	38	9.5	29	12.6	Cost of Sales/Inventory		18	20.1	18	20.8
19	19.4	30	12.1	34	10.6	54	6.8	41	8.8			35	10.3	32	11.4
1	351.7	7	54.2	10	37.7	9	38.9	6	60.3			8	47.4	9	41.7
16	22.6	14	25.3	17	22.1	10	37.5	14	26.6	Cost of Sales/Payables		14	26.6	12	29.7
28	13.2	20	18.5	24	15.4	12	29.9	24	14.9			23	16.2	19	19.4
	8.7		9.5		9.9		9.8		15.9				13.2		10.0
	20.2		15.4		17.9		11.4		26.9	Sales/Working Capital			26.6		16.1
	40.6		22.7		39.4		15.5		-69.2				71.7		33.6
			79.6		21.9		11.8		8.2				13.7		32.3
		(31)	14.3	(29)	10.3	(21)	10.6		3.3	EBIT/Interest		(133)	4.1	(74)	10.2
			4.2		2.9		2.8		1.8				2.0		2.8
										Net Profit + Depr., Dep.,			11.3		9.8
										Amort./Cur. Mat. L/T/D		(35)	3.9	(15)	3.4
													1.8		2.3
	.0		.0		.0		.3		.0				.1		.1
	.1		.1		.4		.3		.5	Fixed/Worth			.5		.3
	.4		.4		.7		1.1		2.8				1.3		1.3
	.3		.4		.8		.5		1.1				.9		.9
	1.2		.9		1.6		.9		5.4	Debt/Worth			2.3		1.7
	2.1		1.8		2.8		3.9		10.4				5.9		3.5
	27.0		78.5		60.1		35.7						46.8		62.4
(11)	22.2	(34)	26.4	(34)	26.7	(19)	21.5			% Profit Before Taxes/Tangible Net Worth		(133)	28.3	(72)	32.0
	13.7		9.5		10.7		19.5						8.0		16.9
	21.5		35.3		18.1		16.2		8.4				14.2		23.9
	13.5		15.0		9.8		12.0		6.5	% Profit Before Taxes/Total Assets			6.7		13.2
	5.3		4.9		3.3		6.9		3.9				2.0		4.2
	UND		687.2		763.4		59.7		999.8				330.2		682.9
	281.9		157.5		87.0		24.6		27.2	Sales/Net Fixed Assets			39.5		46.0
	57.2		28.5		11.8		21.7		4.6				13.5		12.1
	12.1		7.5		7.3		5.3		5.6				7.1		7.7
	9.6		5.4		4.9		4.6		5.0	Sales/Total Assets			5.0		5.2
	5.7		3.6		3.2		3.7		1.5				3.3		3.0
			.1		.1		.8						.1		.1
		(20)	.5	(26)	.5	(16)	1.1			% Depr., Dep., Amort./Sales		(106)	.6	(60)	.6
			1.0		1.7		1.2						1.4		1.2
			.6		.4								.7		.8
		(13)	.9	(10)	.7					% Officers', Directors' Owners' Comp/Sales		(44)	1.2	(18)	1.4
			1.3		1.1								1.6		3.0
3275M	151775M	1329849M	4369048M	6576688M	6596239M	Net Sales ($)		18873076M		12420640M
465M	15594M	206998M	764386M	1415936M	1672097M	Total Assets ($)		4019301M		2491799M

© RMA 2024
M = $ thousand   MM = $ million
See Pages viii through xx for Explanation of Ratios and Data

WHOLESALE—Meat and Meat Product Merchant Wholesalers NAICS 424470

Comparative Historical Data | Current Data Sorted by Sales

Comparative Historical Data						Current Data Sorted by Sales					
				Type of Statement							
8		12		10	Unqualified					1	9
6		17		13	Reviewed					3	10
7		9		11	Compiled					3	8
7		16		16	Tax Returns		1	1	2	8	4
52		59		70	Other	1	26	2	94	8	56
4/1/21-3/31/22 ALL		4/1/22-3/31/23 ALL		4/1/23-3/31/24 ALL		0-1MM	(4/1-9/30/23) 1-3MM	3-5MM	(10/1/23-3/31/24) 5-10MM	10-25MM	25MM & OVER
80		113		120	NUMBER OF STATEMENTS	1	3	1	5	23	87
%		%		%		%	%	%	%	%	%
				ASSETS							
13.9		13.5		14.1	Cash & Equivalents					20.4	10.9
32.8		32.3		32.5	Trade Receivables (net)					31.9	33.5
25.4		23.3		25.4	Inventory					15.1	28.2
1.7		1.6		2.2	All Other Current					1.2	2.7
73.9		70.7		74.2	Total Current					68.7	75.3
17.5		17.3		13.9	Fixed Assets (net)					17.0	13.3
5.3		7.9		7.1	Intangibles (net)					12.1	5.9
3.3		4.1		4.7	All Other Non-Current					2.3	5.6
100.0		100.0		100.0	Total					100.0	100.0
				LIABILITIES							
10.6		9.2		11.3	Notes Payable-Short Term					3.1	13.9
2.1		2.0		1.5	Cur. Mat.-L.T.D.					1.5	1.5
18.7		18.2		18.1	Trade Payables					20.9	17.4
.2		.1		.1	Income Taxes Payable					.1	.1
5.8		7.8		7.1	All Other Current					4.5	7.4
37.4		37.2		38.1	Total Current					30.0	40.4
15.0		15.0		10.4	Long-Term Debt					11.2	8.5
.2		.1		.1	Deferred Taxes					.0	.1
2.2		2.8		2.7	All Other Non-Current					.9	3.5
45.3		44.9		48.7	Net Worth					57.9	47.4
100.0		100.0		100.0	Total Liabilities & Net Worth					100.0	100.0
				INCOME DATA							
100.0		100.0		100.0	Net Sales					100.0	100.0
16.6		17.1		15.3	Gross Profit					18.6	13.4
12.0		14.0		12.2	Operating Expenses					15.0	10.8
4.7		3.0		3.0	Operating Profit					3.6	2.6
-.3		.3		.5	All Other Expenses (net)					.8	.4
4.9		2.7		2.5	Profit Before Taxes					2.8	2.1
				RATIOS							
4.0		3.4		3.0						3.4	2.9
1.9		1.9		1.9	Current					2.0	1.8
1.4		1.3		1.4						1.7	1.4
2.7		2.1		2.1						3.1	1.9
1.3		1.2		1.1	Quick					1.6	1.0
.8		.8		.7						1.2	.6
14	25.9	12	31.0	15	24.6					12	30.5	16	22.3
20	17.9	18	20.0	20	18.4	Sales/Receivables				21	17.6	20	18.0
28	13.1	26	14.0	27	13.5					47	7.8	27	13.6
7	56.1	7	55.1	7	52.1					1	493.8	9	38.9
17	21.8	17	21.6	21	17.5	Cost of Sales/Inventory				13	27.9	23	15.9
35	10.5	29	12.5	36	10.0					26	14.2	38	9.5
6	60.6	5	68.5	8	46.5					12	31.0	7	48.9
14	26.3	12	31.5	13	27.9	Cost of Sales/Payables				17	21.1	12	30.5
22	16.6	19	19.2	20	18.2					25	14.7	19	19.2
	8.9		11.1		10.2						7.5		10.4
	15.6		19.5		15.8	Sales/Working Capital					11.9		16.4
	32.2		43.7		28.1						21.4		28.1
	45.5		49.0		22.4						42.2		20.3
(67)	19.5	(88)	12.6	(101)	10.0	EBIT/Interest				(17)	18.0	(77)	9.7
	7.0		3.0		3.3						4.5		2.7
			22.9		11.6	Net Profit + Depr., Dep.,							11.6
		(23)	5.9	(20)	5.1	Amort./Cur. Mat. L/T/D						(16)	5.1
			2.4		2.9								2.7
	.1		.0		.0						.0		.0
	.2		.2		.3	Fixed/Worth					.3		.3
	.9		1.0		.6						.7		.6
	.7		.6		.5						.4		.5
	1.4		1.3		1.2	Debt/Worth					.8		1.3
	2.9		4.3		2.8						2.2		3.0
	76.5		68.2		61.7	% Profit Before Taxes/Tangible					56.0		61.3
(74)	49.1	(99)	33.0	(110)	23.4	Net Worth				(21)	22.2	(81)	23.2
	24.6		14.8		13.6						12.9		14.7
	30.7		28.2		20.0	% Profit Before Taxes/Total					22.5		19.0
	17.0		14.5		11.3	Assets					13.4		11.0
	7.9		4.4		5.2						5.5		4.9
	221.8		584.1		689.0						999.8		723.7
	51.8		59.5		63.0	Sales/Net Fixed Assets					121.8		48.3
	15.2		19.3		22.0						20.5		22.0
	8.1		8.4		7.4						5.7		7.5
	5.6		5.6		5.3	Sales/Total Assets					5.3		5.2
	3.4		3.2		3.4						2.9		3.8
	.1		.1		.1								.1
(57)	.6	(70)	.4	(74)	.7	% Depr., Dep., Amort./Sales						(59)	.8
	1.0		1.0		1.3								1.3
	.9		.5		.5	% Officers', Directors'					.7		.3
(22)	1.3	(39)	.9	(30)	.9	Owners' Comp/Sales				(10)	1.2	(18)	.7
	2.1		2.1		2.1						2.3		1.3
16581869M		17685907M		19026874M	Net Sales ($)	302M	5694M	4132M	38001M	402523M	18576222M
3111307M		3328609M		4075476M	Total Assets ($)	144M	1673M	800M	7397M	167749M	3897713M

M = $ thousand   MM = $ million
See Pages viii through xx for Explanation of Ratios and Data

© RMA 2024

WHOLESALE—Fresh Fruit and Vegetable Merchant Wholesalers NAICS 424480

Current Data Sorted by Assets | Comparative Historical Data

	0-500M	500M-2MM	2-10MM	10-50MM	50-100MM	100-250MM	Type of Statement		4/1/19-3/31/20 ALL		4/1/20-3/31/21 ALL
		2	1	9	4	2	Unqualified		18		11
		4	2	11	2		Reviewed		25		9
		6	14	6			Compiled		24		12
	3	6	8		10		Tax Returns		28		11
			24	44		8	Other		121		61
		31 (4/1-9/30/23)		129 (10/1/23-3/31/24)							
	3	12	49	70	16	10	NUMBER OF STATEMENTS		216		104
	%	%	%	%	%	%	ASSETS		%		%
		15.7	13.9	9.3	7.5	9.7	Cash & Equivalents		14.4		18.3
		38.9	47.4	39.9	30.1	24.7	Trade Receivables (net)		38.9		34.2
		16.2	10.4	12.6	7.8	5.9	Inventory		9.8		10.1
		4.4	4.4	7.9	7.5	3.6	All Other Current		4.9		2.7
		75.2	76.1	69.6	52.9	43.8	Total Current		67.9		65.2
		15.4	14.5	15.3	18.4	33.3	Fixed Assets (net)		20.6		22.1
		1.1	1.9	5.7	16.4	9.3	Intangibles (net)		3.9		6.0
		8.2	7.4	9.3	12.3	13.5	All Other Non-Current		7.6		6.8
		100.0	100.0	100.0	100.0	100.0	Total		100.0		100.0
							LIABILITIES				
		4.6	9.9	7.5	5.8	3.7	Notes Payable-Short Term		8.6		7.5
		1.6	1.2	1.8	2.4	2.4	Cur. Mat.-L.T.D.		1.9		1.6
		50.8	28.0	29.0	18.5	19.1	Trade Payables		31.3		24.7
		.2	.0	.1	.5	.0	Income Taxes Payable		.0		.1
		3.4	15.1	15.1	22.9	6.6	All Other Current		11.4		11.4
		60.6	54.2	53.5	50.0	31.8	Total Current		53.3		45.3
		10.8	10.6	7.8	8.4	10.4	Long-Term Debt		12.1		16.0
		.0	.1	.1	.3	.0	Deferred Taxes		.2		.4
		.1	4.8	5.7	3.7	2.9	All Other Non-Current		7.8		4.1
		28.5	30.2	32.9	37.6	54.9	Net Worth		26.5		34.1
		100.0	100.0	100.0	100.0	100.0	Total Liabilities & Net Worth		100.0		100.0
							INCOME DATA				
		100.0	100.0	100.0	100.0	100.0	Net Sales		100.0		100.0
		17.1	16.4	17.1	13.2	15.8	Gross Profit		19.4		16.6
		14.2	14.3	14.1	7.7	13.7	Operating Expenses		16.6		15.5
		2.9	2.0	3.0	5.5	2.1	Operating Profit		2.8		1.1
		.6	.3	-.2	.0	.3	All Other Expenses (net)		.7		-.3
		2.3	1.7	3.2	5.5	1.8	Profit Before Taxes		2.2		1.4
							RATIOS				
		2.4	2.3	2.0	1.7	1.6			1.8		2.5
		1.4	1.5	1.4	1.1	1.4	Current		1.3		1.5
		.8	1.1	1.0	.9	1.3			1.0		1.1
		1.4	2.1	1.5	1.2	1.3			1.4		1.8
		1.0	1.3	.9	.7	1.1	Quick		1.0		1.2
		.5	.9	.6	.5	1.0			.7		.9
	13	28.9	20	18.7	23	15.9	19	18.9	21	17.8			19	19.2	16	22.3
	19	19.0	32	11.5	29	12.5	26	14.1	24	14.9	Sales/Receivables	27	13.5	23	16.0
	30	12.1	43	8.4	36	10.2	35	10.5	34	10.8		38	9.6	31	11.7
	0	778.4	2	237.5	4	87.5	6	62.3	5	66.8		1	576.5	3	113.5
	5	70.2	6	57.5	7	50.2	8	47.7	7	49.8	Cost of Sales/Inventory	5	67.3	6	60.2
	16	22.2	21	17.8	14	25.7	13	27.2	11	32.7		11	32.1	13	27.5
	15	24.4	8	48.2	17	21.1	13	28.2	17	20.9		17	21.7	12	29.6
	30	12.2	18	20.8	23	15.6	22	16.3	23	16.2	Cost of Sales/Payables	27	13.6	20	18.2
	60	6.1	35	10.3	38	9.6	28	13.1	28	12.9		40	9.1	34	10.8
		15.8		9.3		14.4		12.5		14.5				15.6		11.9
		27.8		21.8		26.5		104.3		33.7	Sales/Working Capital		40.1		22.8
		-51.9		65.4		NM		-47.6		48.1			999.8		115.1
				21.2		48.4		19.8		20.2				22.6		32.1
			(40)	8.2	(60)	8.6	(15)	4.2		17.6	EBIT/Interest	(184)	6.5	(91)	9.6
				2.7		3.9		.4		-11.1				2.4		1.3
						43.4								9.8		23.8
					(13)	16.7					Net Profit + Depr., Dep., Amort./Cur. Mat. L/T/D	(30)	3.7	(21)	3.5
						4.0								1.9		-1.2
				.1		.0		.1		.4	.4			.1		.1
				.7		.3		.4		.8	.8	Fixed/Worth		.6		.7
				4.4		.8		1.1		2.2	1.2			1.7		1.7
				.7				1.1		1.5	.6			1.2		.9
				2.9		2.1		2.3		2.4	1.2	Debt/Worth		2.4		1.6
				27.6		5.6		8.9		14.9	1.4			8.9		7.6
				83.7		45.6		64.7		45.1	25.5			48.9		57.0
		(10)	41.7	(42)	18.7	(59)	30.0	(14)	8.6	22.9	% Profit Before Taxes/Tangible Net Worth	(189)	23.1	(82)	26.9
			1.8		7.9		14.7		-3.6	-6.5			6.9		10.9
				22.5		14.7		16.9		11.9	12.9			13.8		19.4
				8.9		7.9		9.4		4.1	10.0	% Profit Before Taxes/Total Assets		5.9		9.0
				1.7		2.4		4.4		-1.0	-3.6			1.7		.7
				479.4		392.6		326.5		29.2	18.0			174.1		104.3
				102.0		88.1		77.1		22.4	8.5	Sales/Net Fixed Assets		39.2		36.4
				26.4		27.3		18.5		15.3	7.5			13.3		10.9
				9.7		7.2		6.2		4.7	4.1			7.2		7.1
				6.8		5.0		4.8		4.0	3.0	Sales/Total Assets		5.0		4.6
				3.7		3.4		3.2		2.5	2.5			3.1		3.2
						.2		.1		.5				.2		.2
					(32)	.5	(50)	.6		.7		% Depr., Dep., Amort./Sales	(146)	.7	(84)	.7
						.7		1.1		1.6				1.3		1.4
						.8		.3						.5		.5
					(22)	1.1	(17)	.6				% Officers', Directors' Owners' Comp/Sales	(70)	1.1	(33)	1.2
						2.2		1.2						1.7		1.9
	13020M		132155M		1489719M		7172646M		4523713M	4684227M	Net Sales ($)		19842955M		11945967M
	724M		18237M		273331M		1520919M		1162077M	1565323M	Total Assets ($)		5178508M		3263420M

© RMA 2024

M = $ thousand   MM = $ million
See Pages viii through xx for Explanation of Ratios and Data

WHOLESALE—Fresh Fruit and Vegetable Merchant Wholesalers NAICS 424480

Comparative Historical Data | Current Data Sorted by Sales

Comparative Historical Data			Type of Statement	Current Data Sorted by Sales					
8	9	16	Unqualified						16
10	20	15	Reviewed		1		1	9	13
14	22	22	Compiled			2	4	11
11	14	12	Tax Returns	1		1	4	6
55	91	95	Other	2	2	4	11	76
4/1/21-3/31/22 ALL	4/1/22-3/31/23 ALL	4/1/23-3/31/24 ALL		31 (4/1-9/30/23)			129 (10/1/23-3/31/24)		
				0-1MM	1-3MM	3-5MM	5-10MM	10-25MM	25MM & OVER
98	156	160	NUMBER OF STATEMENTS	3	3	7	25	122
%	%	%	ASSETS	%	%	%	%	%	%
17.3	15.0	11.7	Cash & Equivalents	DATA NOT AVAILABLE				8.9	11.1
36.2	40.0	39.5	Trade Receivables (net)					45.2	40.0
9.1	10.4	11.1	Inventory					13.7	10.6
3.4	5.3	6.1	All Other Current					5.7	6.0
66.0	70.7	68.4	Total Current					73.5	67.8
21.9	16.3	16.5	Fixed Assets (net)					17.1	16.4
3.9	3.9	5.4	Intangibles (net)					1.2	6.8
8.2	9.2	9.7	All Other Non-Current					8.1	9.0
100.0	100.0	100.0	Total					100.0	100.0
			LIABILITIES						
7.2	8.7	7.6	Notes Payable-Short Term					10.4	6.9
1.6	1.3	1.7	Cur. Mat.-L.T.D.					1.6	1.7
24.4	26.5	28.3	Trade Payables					30.4	27.9
.1	.1	.1	Income Taxes Payable					.1	.1
10.2	10.8	14.4	All Other Current					19.2	14.3
43.5	47.4	52.0	Total Current					61.7	50.8
14.2	10.7	9.7	Long-Term Debt					12.4	8.1
.4	.1	.1	Deferred Taxes					.3	.1
3.9	4.8	4.5	All Other Non-Current					.5	5.8
38.0	36.9	33.6	Net Worth					25.1	35.2
100.0	100.0	100.0	Total Liabilities & Net Worth					100.0	100.0
			INCOME DATA						
100.0	100.0	100.0	Net Sales					100.0	100.0
20.3	18.4	16.6	Gross Profit					19.8	15.1
18.0	15.3	13.6	Operating Expenses					17.8	12.2
2.3	3.1	2.9	Operating Profit					2.0	2.9
-.7	-.2	.1	All Other Expenses (net)					.4	.0
3.0	3.2	2.9	Profit Before Taxes					1.6	3.0
			RATIOS						
2.4	2.3	2.0	Current					2.4	1.9
1.5	1.5	1.4						1.4	1.4
1.1	1.1	1.0						.8	1.0
2.0	1.9	1.5	Quick					1.6	1.5
1.3	1.2	1.1						1.2	1.0
.9	.8	.7						.7	.7
20 18.2	21 17.6	19 19.0	Sales/Receivables				20 18.7	20 18.4
28 13.1	29 12.7	28 12.9					33 10.9	28 12.9
39 9.4	38 9.7	36 10.0					69 5.3	34 10.6
2 157.4	2 164.7	3 112.5	Cost of Sales/Inventory				2 160.3	4 92.0
7 55.6	6 57.3	7 50.5					9 38.6	7 50.5
12 29.6	12 29.9	13 28.1					27 13.6	12 30.7
10 35.1	10 35.1	13 27.4	Cost of Sales/Payables				11 33.8	15 24.8
23 16.0	22 16.9	23 16.1					20 17.9	23 16.1
37 9.8	33 10.9	37 9.9					42 8.7	32 11.4
10.4	12.1	13.7	Sales/Working Capital					8.9	14.5
20.3	22.6	29.2						20.8	30.3
66.2	75.2	684.2						-61.3	171.3
54.3	36.9	23.5	EBIT/Interest					28.0	22.8
(84) 14.1	(125) 12.5	(135) 8.1				(20) 5.2	(105) 9.6
2.9	3.4	2.8						2.9	2.7
27.0	13.1	23.9	Net Profit + Depr., Dep., Amort./Cur. Mat. L/T/D						27.0
(14) 3.4	(35) 5.8	(26) 9.0						(22) 9.2
1.7	3.1	2.1							2.1
.1	.1	.1	Fixed/Worth					.1	.1
.5	.4	.5						.5	.5
1.3	.9	1.1						2.2	1.0
.8	.8	1.0	Debt/Worth					.7	1.1
1.5	1.7	2.1						2.4	2.0
3.0	4.5	6.5						14.6	5.9
60.6	59.9	50.2	% Profit Before Taxes/Tangible Net Worth					19.1	51.1
(85) 28.6	(139) 26.9	(137) 24.6					(21) 15.0	(105) 26.2
11.2	7.3	7.4						-3.7	7.4
23.8	19.0	15.8	% Profit Before Taxes/Total Assets					11.4	16.1
10.4	10.0	8.4						7.7	9.4
3.2	2.4	2.5						.4	2.6
148.7	289.4	328.6	Sales/Net Fixed Assets					254.2	306.6
30.9	55.0	53.2						73.2	46.7
9.8	17.0	18.1						10.6	18.4
6.8	6.6	6.7	Sales/Total Assets					6.8	6.6
4.5	4.7	4.7						3.9	4.8
2.7	3.1	3.2						2.6	3.3
.2	.2	.2	% Depr., Dep., Amort./Sales					.2	.2
(75) .8	(113) .6	(109) .6					(17) .4	(88) .6
1.6	1.2	1.2						1.9	1.1
.6	.3	.3	% Officers', Directors', Owners' Comp/Sales					1.0	.3
(42) 1.3	(56) .9	(46) 1.0					(14) 1.3	(28) .6
2.5	2.1	1.9						2.4	1.3
7957009M	15225862M	18015480M	Net Sales ($)	7381M	12261M	49755M	461359M	17484724M
2231842M	3726249M	4540611M	Total Assets ($)	4588M	4734M	10458M	152118M	4368713M

M = $ thousand   MM = $ million
See Pages viii through xx for Explanation of Ratios and Data
© RMA 2024

WHOLESALE—Other Grocery and Related Products Merchant Wholesalers NAICS 424490

Current Data Sorted by Assets | **Comparative Historical Data**

							Type of Statement				
		1	2	6	4	12	Unqualified		42		24
	1	2	9	22	1	4	Reviewed		34		18
	2	11	14	6		1	Compiled		24		11
	3	12	20	3	1		Tax Returns		39		16
		55 (4/1-9/30/23)	37	58	24	8	Other		167		114
				209 (10/1/23-3/31/24)					4/1/19-3/31/20		4/1/20-3/31/21
0-500M	500M-2MM	2-10MM	10-50MM	50-100MM	100-250MM			ALL		ALL	
6	26	82	95	30	25	NUMBER OF STATEMENTS		306		183	
%	%	%	%	%	%	**ASSETS**		%		%	
	18.8	14.7	11.6	11.0	6.5	Cash & Equivalents		9.0		11.9	
	23.9	29.1	24.3	35.0	22.9	Trade Receivables (net)		28.8		26.7	
	34.1	33.0	32.2	27.2	28.0	Inventory		31.5		32.6	
	4.4	2.7	3.6	3.1	3.3	All Other Current		2.8		2.3	
	81.3	79.6	71.7	76.2	60.6	Total Current		72.1		73.5	
	10.6	9.8	16.5	14.3	18.5	Fixed Assets (net)		18.3		17.8	
	6.3	3.1	4.4	4.4	7.8	Intangibles (net)		4.3		4.4	
	1.9	7.6	7.4	5.1	13.1	All Other Non-Current		5.3		4.4	
	100.0	100.0	100.0	100.0	100.0	Total		100.0		100.0	
						LIABILITIES					
	5.4	7.7	9.7	8.6	5.4	Notes Payable-Short Term		12.2		11.1	
	1.9	1.0	1.4	1.2	2.3	Cur. Mat.-L.T.D.		2.2		2.3	
	18.4	19.9	19.3	21.0	15.2	Trade Payables		22.1		20.0	
	.0	.2	.1	.0	.1	Income Taxes Payable		.0		.1	
	6.7	12.3	11.3	12.9	9.8	All Other Current		10.1		8.9	
	32.5	41.0	41.8	43.7	32.7	Total Current		46.6		42.3	
	17.1	11.7	10.5	8.0	20.8	Long-Term Debt		12.0		16.7	
	.0	.2	.2	.2	.5	Deferred Taxes		.3		.2	
	6.6	5.0	7.9	8.9	7.5	All Other Non-Current		6.6		3.7	
	43.8	42.1	39.6	39.2	38.5	Net Worth		34.5		37.1	
	100.0	100.0	100.0	100.0	100.0	Total Liabilities & Net Worth		100.0		100.0	
						INCOME DATA					
	100.0	100.0	100.0	100.0	100.0	Net Sales		100.0		100.0	
	27.5	24.2	23.0	16.0	15.9	Gross Profit		23.3		23.8	
	24.9	19.7	18.0	11.6	11.9	Operating Expenses		20.7		20.1	
	2.7	4.4	5.0	4.3	3.9	Operating Profit		2.7		3.7	
	.3	.5	.7	-.1	1.0	All Other Expenses (net)		.5		-.1	
	2.3	3.9	4.2	4.4	2.9	Profit Before Taxes		2.1		3.8	
						RATIOS					
	6.6	3.4	2.8	3.5	2.8			2.6		3.1	
	3.0	1.9	1.8	1.8	1.9	Current		1.5		1.9	
	1.3	1.4	1.2	1.1	1.4			1.1		1.2	
	4.1	1.9	1.4	1.9	1.4			1.4		1.5	
	1.4	1.1	.8	1.0	.9	Quick		.8		.9	
	.4	.7	.5	.7	.6			.5		.6	
7	55.9	15 23.8	18 20.7	27 13.6	26 14.1		19	19.6	18	19.9	
16	22.5	25 14.5	29 12.5	33 11.1	37 9.9	Sales/Receivables	28	13.1	28	13.1	
41	8.8	34 10.6	38 9.6	46 7.9	45 8.1		40	9.1	40	9.2	
8	43.6	16 23.4	25 14.7	33 11.0	31 11.8		22	16.4	22	16.8	
41	8.8	38 9.6	45 8.1	45 8.2	41 8.8	Cost of Sales/Inventory	39	9.4	47	7.7	
87	4.2	69 5.3	74 4.9	73 5.0	72 5.1		68	5.4	85	4.3	
0	UND	10 35.6	17 22.1	12 30.8	15 24.0		14	26.9	14	25.7	
11	32.6	21 17.0	24 15.2	18 20.7	31 11.8	Cost of Sales/Payables	25	14.5	25	14.8	
45	8.1	32 11.4	42 8.7	30 12.2	46 7.9		42	8.7	41	9.0	
	3.8	6.9	5.3	4.4	5.8			7.1		6.0	
	11.8	10.9	11.9	11.1	10.6	Sales/Working Capital		14.3		11.2	
	38.3	21.8	35.1	66.7	15.3			51.0		32.3	
	29.5	36.1	30.6	150.3	8.8			16.9		27.1	
(20)	5.7	(67) 10.8	(82) 8.2	(27) 16.7	(24) 4.4	EBIT/Interest	(267)	5.7	(156)	12.1	
	1.3	2.3	3.3	3.3	.9			2.0		3.3	
			56.3	40.9				11.9		14.5	
		(20) 13.5	(11) 3.8			Net Profit + Depr., Dep., Amort./Cur. Mat. L/T/D	(66)	5.5	(39)	3.8	
			1.8	3.4				2.3		.8	
	.0	.0	.1	.0	.2			.1		.1	
	.2	.1	.3	.2	.5	Fixed/Worth		.3		.4	
	.9	.6	.8	1.1	.9			1.4		1.2	
	.4	.5	.6	.8	1.1			.7		.8	
	1.4	1.2	1.5	3.2	2.1	Debt/Worth		1.9		1.7	
	7.3	3.7	3.3	7.4	4.4			6.3		3.8	
	41.1	57.3	51.6	44.1	33.6			46.2		68.5	
(22)	11.6	(72) 33.2	(86) 28.9	(29) 31.4	(23) 18.7	% Profit Before Taxes/Tangible Net Worth	(268)	23.2	(163)	27.5	
	1.1	10.0	16.1	19.6	9.5			8.7		14.1	
	20.2	25.9	19.6	20.1	10.2			16.1		19.2	
	8.7	14.0	10.6	11.2	4.9	% Profit Before Taxes/Total Assets		6.4		10.5	
	.8	3.2	3.8	5.4	-.5			1.9		3.4	
	999.8	702.0	118.3	999.8	24.5			173.0		175.2	
	168.1	106.4	30.3	250.6	16.2	Sales/Net Fixed Assets		36.6		36.8	
	56.3	39.1	13.5	12.7	7.7			11.4		10.3	
	8.9	5.9	3.9	3.8	3.1			5.0		4.8	
	3.2	4.3	2.8	2.7	2.4	Sales/Total Assets		3.2		3.1	
	1.9	2.5	1.9	2.2	1.7			2.1		2.0	
		.1	.2	.0	.1			.2		.2	
	(41)	.4	(76) .5	(27) .1	(21) .7	% Depr., Dep., Amort./Sales	(229)	.7	(124)	.7	
		1.1	1.1	.9	1.7			1.5		1.7	
	1.0	.8	.2					.6		.5	
(14)	2.8	(33) 1.5	(24) .6			% Officers', Directors' Owners' Comp/Sales	(83)	1.4	(55)	1.2	
	5.0	2.4	1.6					3.1		3.2	
9979M	176211M	1808919M	6998533M	7937317M	9734906M	Net Sales ($)		34603293M		24148051M	
1516M	32327M	445990M	2292785M	1996780M	3934584M	Total Assets ($)		9539193M		6080970M	

© RMA 2024   M = $ thousand   MM = $ million
See Pages viii through xx for Explanation of Ratios and Data

WHOLESALE—Other Grocery and Related Products Merchant Wholesalers NAICS 424490

Comparative Historical Data | Current Data Sorted by Sales

22	34	25	**Type of Statement**				1		24
18	38	36	Unqualified				7	7	29
7	21	24	Reviewed				1	11	10
21	36	37	Compiled	1	1	4	4	11	11
80	144	142	Tax Returns	2	5	3	7	28	96
4/1/21-3/31/22	4/1/22-3/31/23	4/1/23-3/31/24	Other		55 (4/1-9/30/23)		209 (10/1/23-3/31/24)		
ALL	ALL	ALL		0-1MM	1-3MM	3-5MM	5-10MM	10-25MM	25MM & OVER
148	273	264	**NUMBER OF STATEMENTS**	3	14	7	13	57	170
%	%	%	**ASSETS**	%	%	%	%	%	%
12.5	11.5	13.2	Cash & Equivalents	13.9	15.2		14.9		11.3
26.8	27.2	27.0	Trade Receivables (net)	9.3	26.0		28.7		27.8
31.9	33.2	31.5	Inventory	45.2	31.7		31.7		30.6
2.7	2.7	3.2	All Other Current	5.7	1.9		3.6		3.2
73.8	74.7	74.9	Total Current	74.1	74.9		78.9		72.9
14.9	14.7	13.6	Fixed Assets (net)	14.9	9.5		11.2		14.8
5.6	4.3	4.4	Intangibles (net)	9.6	8.1		3.2		4.3
5.7	6.3	7.1	All Other Non-Current	1.4	7.5		6.7		8.0
100.0	100.0	100.0	Total	100.0	100.0		100.0		100.0
			LIABILITIES						
11.1	11.8	8.1	Notes Payable-Short Term	9.9	13.7		6.6		8.0
1.5	2.9	1.4	Cur. Mat.-L.T.D.	3.3	2.4		1.0		1.3
20.7	21.2	19.8	Trade Payables	12.8	18.4		18.1		20.2
.2	.2	.1	Income Taxes Payable	.2	.2		.1		.1
10.5	9.4	11.1	All Other Current	8.8	8.3		13.8		11.0
44.0	45.5	40.5	Total Current	34.9	42.9		39.5		40.6
13.0	13.4	12.0	Long-Term Debt	16.8	31.4		10.7		10.8
.1	.2	.2	Deferred Taxes	.0	.0		.2		.2
3.0	4.6	6.9	All Other Non-Current	1.2	2.0		4.2		8.4
40.0	36.3	40.4	Net Worth	47.1	23.7		45.4		40.0
100.0	100.0	100.0	Total Liabilities & Net Worth	100.0	100.0		100.0		100.0
			INCOME DATA						
100.0	100.0	100.0	Net Sales	100.0	100.0		100.0		100.0
21.8	23.0	22.5	Gross Profit	32.3	29.5		24.7		19.9
18.0	18.4	18.2	Operating Expenses	29.5	25.9		20.5		15.2
3.7	4.6	4.3	Operating Profit	2.8	3.6		4.2		4.7
-.4	.1	.6	All Other Expenses (net)	2.4	1.2		.2		.5
4.1	4.6	3.7	Profit Before Taxes	.5	2.4		3.9		4.2
			RATIOS						
2.9	2.9	3.2		6.1	3.2		3.5		2.9
1.8	1.8	1.9	Current	2.0	2.7		1.9		1.8
1.2	1.3	1.2		1.1	1.5		1.4		1.2
1.6	1.7	1.7		1.9	1.8		2.0		1.5
.9	.9	1.0	Quick	.4	1.3		1.1		1.0
.6	.5	.6		.2	.6		.7		.6
17 21.5	16 22.7	17 21.3		0 UND	15 25.1		15 23.6		20 18.3
26 14.3	27 13.7	29 12.8	Sales/Receivables	15 23.7	32 11.3		27 13.6		29 12.6
38 9.5	40 9.1	40 9.2		47 7.8	43 8.4		45 8.1		38 9.6
20 18.2	20 18.5	22 16.4		31 11.9	15 24.3		15 24.8		23 15.6
37 9.8	40 9.1	41 8.9	Cost of Sales/Inventory	70 5.2	87 4.2		42 8.6		40 9.1
68 5.4	78 4.7	73 5.0		304 1.2	126 2.9		78 4.7		63 5.8
13 27.3	12 29.8	12 31.4		0 UND	11 32.6		10 35.8		13 28.1
23 15.9	23 16.2	22 16.4	Cost of Sales/Payables	28 13.1	33 10.9		20 18.2		22 16.4
35 10.5	40 9.2	38 9.5		64 5.7	49 7.5		29 12.5		37 9.8
6.8	6.0	5.5		1.9	3.9		6.8		6.1
11.0	12.0	11.5	Sales/Working Capital	6.5	11.3		10.4		12.0
43.7	28.6	27.6		52.1	23.4		18.7		33.4
50.9	48.1	33.4		12.7	24.9		26.3		50.8
(125) 12.0	(229) 11.9	(223) 8.8	EBIT/Interest	(10) .5	7.7	(47)	10.2	(147)	8.9
4.6	3.6	2.7		-.6	.8		3.1		3.2
24.6	29.4	41.4	Net Profit + Depr., Dep.,						46.7
(19) 10.4	(51) 10.6	(43) 6.1	Amort./Cur. Mat. L/T/D					(38)	5.6
5.1	3.2	2.3							2.1
.0	.0	.0		.0	.0		.0		.0
.3	.2	.2	Fixed/Worth	.0	.2		.2		.3
1.0	1.0	.9		5.3	NM		.5		.9
.8	.7	.6		.3	.9		.6		.6
1.6	1.5	1.6	Debt/Worth	1.6	1.6		1.0		1.8
4.5	5.5	4.3		10.1	NM		2.4		4.4
55.6	58.2	51.9	% Profit Before Taxes/Tangible	18.5	104.6		50.0		52.3
(136) 30.8	(235) 31.2	(237) 29.4	Net Worth	(12) 2.2	(10) 44.0	(51)	23.0	(156)	30.5
16.3	15.9	12.0		-17.0	9.5		8.6		16.3
21.1	21.2	20.7	% Profit Before Taxes/Total	10.0	30.8		20.7		20.3
10.8	12.4	10.5	Assets	1.3	10.9		11.2		11.3
5.6	4.7	3.6		-5.1	-.2		3.4		4.6
459.1	399.8	434.4		UND	UND		327.9		308.5
59.9	55.6	61.7	Sales/Net Fixed Assets	238.1	151.4		83.8		36.0
12.9	13.4	15.5		16.0	39.4		26.8		14.9
5.6	5.0	4.7		2.9	6.6		5.2		4.5
3.5	3.3	3.0	Sales/Total Assets	1.5	2.4		3.7		3.0
2.2	2.1	2.1		1.0	1.9		2.3		2.2
.1	.2	.1					.2		.1
(99) .5	(176) .5	(171) .5	% Depr., Dep., Amort./Sales			(28)	.6	(135)	.5
1.3	1.2	1.1					1.6		1.0
.4	.4	.5					.7		.2
(40) 1.0	(81) .9	(80) 1.0	% Officers', Directors'			(28)	1.5	(38)	.5
3.3	2.6	2.4	Owners' Comp/Sales				2.2		1.4
18624072M	25632540M	26665865M	Net Sales ($)	1954M	27912M	26452M	93001M	1001820M	25514726M
5355815M	8058906M	8703982M	Total Assets ($)	559M	17933M	8801M	39834M	361821M	8275034M

© RMA 2024 M = $ thousand MM = $ million
See Pages viii through xx for Explanation of Ratios and Data

WHOLESALE—Grain and Field Bean Merchant Wholesalers NAICS 424510

Current Data Sorted by Assets | Comparative Historical Data

							Type of Statement				
			4	4	9	14	Unqualified		46		16
			4	11			Reviewed		31		13
			3				Compiled		6		1
1	2		2				Tax Returns		10		4
1	5		14	19	5	9	Other		73		42
0-500M	500M-2MM	54 (4/1-9/30/23) 2-10MM		53 (10/1/23-3/31/24) 10-50MM	50-100MM	100-250MM			4/1/19-3/31/20 ALL		4/1/20-3/31/21 ALL
2	7		27	34	14	23	NUMBER OF STATEMENTS		166		76
%	%		%	%	%	%	ASSETS		%		%
			17.1	14.5	6.5	14.7	Cash & Equivalents		9.0		11.9
			22.9	18.9	24.0	10.2	Trade Receivables (net)		17.1		16.3
			28.2	33.3	31.1	31.9	Inventory		35.3		35.6
			8.9	2.7	10.1	6.4	All Other Current		4.9		4.7
			77.1	69.4	71.7	63.2	Total Current		66.3		68.5
			17.0	23.7	23.1	27.8	Fixed Assets (net)		25.8		25.5
			1.3	1.5	.3	2.9	Intangibles (net)		1.8		1.1
			4.6	5.4	4.8	6.1	All Other Non-Current		6.1		4.9
			100.0	100.0	100.0	100.0	Total		100.0		100.0
							LIABILITIES				
			9.1	8.7	15.1	6.1	Notes Payable-Short Term		16.8		12.6
			1.6	1.8	1.5	1.1	Cur. Mat.-L.T.D.		1.9		2.3
			19.0	20.5	26.4	18.5	Trade Payables		15.8		20.2
			.3	.1	.0	.1	Income Taxes Payable		.2		.1
			11.5	15.0	14.9	13.1	All Other Current		12.9		13.6
			41.5	46.0	57.9	38.9	Total Current		47.6		48.8
			5.7	8.8	13.3	9.6	Long-Term Debt		10.1		10.2
			.8	.7	.3	1.1	Deferred Taxes		1.2		.5
			3.3	3.4	1.1	2.3	All Other Non-Current		2.1		2.0
			48.7	41.1	27.4	48.0	Net Worth		39.0		38.5
			100.0	100.0	100.0	100.0	Total Liabilties & Net Worth		100.0		100.0
							INCOME DATA				
			100.0	100.0	100.0	100.0	Net Sales		100.0		100.0
			11.2	12.0	9.3	8.2	Gross Profit		12.7		12.9
			8.6	9.1	7.6	6.6	Operating Expenses		10.4		10.6
			2.6	2.9	1.7	1.6	Operating Profit		2.3		2.3
			.0	.4	.3	.0	All Other Expenses (net)		.3		-.3
			2.7	2.4	1.4	1.6	Profit Before Taxes		1.9		2.6
							RATIOS				
			2.5	1.9	1.4	1.8			1.8		1.8
			1.7	1.4	1.2	1.4	Current		1.4		1.3
			1.2	1.3	1.1	1.2			1.2		1.1
			2.2	1.1	.7	1.1			.9		.9
			.8	.7	.6	.6	Quick		.4		.5
			.4	.3	.3	.3			.2		.3
		8	45.1	8	44.8	8	45.9	6	60.5	Sales/Receivables	8	46.7	8	43.9
		21	17.5	14	26.5	23	16.0	12	31.3		17	21.1	17	21.1
		30	12.1	33	10.9	48	7.6	17	21.6		36	10.1	34	10.8
		7	50.1	21	17.6	17	21.9	24	15.4	Cost of Sales/Inventory	29	12.8	21	17.2
		24	15.4	35	10.5	26	14.0	43	8.5		58	6.3	65	5.6
		63	5.8	94	3.9	85	4.3	68	5.4		114	3.2	114	3.2
		5	72.5	9	38.9	12	30.7	9	42.9	Cost of Sales/Payables	7	49.9	10	36.5
		10	35.8	20	18.5	19	19.4	19	19.2		19	18.9	22	16.6
		31	11.8	52	7.0	59	6.2	30	12.3		34	10.8	51	7.2
			6.1		7.7		16.0		7.4	Sales/Working Capital		8.1		6.9
			12.6		11.8		23.1		14.6			16.1		14.8
			21.1		25.7		104.3		41.0			30.4		32.4
			25.5		10.4		5.6		4.8	EBIT/Interest		6.5		13.4
		(21)	4.3	(32)	3.7		2.4	(22)	3.5		(159)	2.3	(71)	2.9
			1.0		1.6		1.6		1.7			1.2		1.3
										Net Profit + Depr., Dep., Amort./Cur. Mat. L/T/D		8.9		3.6
											(49)	3.1	(15)	2.3
												1.4		1.2
			.1		.1		.1		.5	Fixed/Worth		.3		.3
			.3		.5		.8		.7			.6		.8
			.8		1.0		1.4		1.1			1.1		1.2
			.6		.8		1.5		.7	Debt/Worth		.9		.9
			1.1		1.5		3.3		1.2			1.6		1.7
			2.6		2.2		5.7		2.8			3.2		3.5
			35.2		19.6		42.7		16.6	% Profit Before Taxes/Tangible Net Worth		13.4		20.0
			12.3	(33)	10.2		15.1		9.5		(161)	6.8	(74)	7.3
			1.9		4.1		6.3		4.1			1.8		2.3
			13.2		10.2		8.8		6.7	% Profit Before Taxes/Total Assets		6.2		7.0
			4.3		5.7		3.4		4.8			2.4		3.3
			.5		1.6		1.6		2.2			.5		.5
			120.9		41.3		249.8		23.0	Sales/Net Fixed Assets		29.1		26.9
			27.7		11.2		13.8		11.0			10.4		10.4
			16.3		7.0		6.1		7.5			5.4		5.4
			5.5		4.2		6.9		4.1	Sales/Total Assets		3.3		3.6
			4.0		2.7		3.4		2.8			2.3		2.2
			2.0		1.5		1.5		2.3			1.6		1.7
			.2		.6		.1		.5	% Depr., Dep., Amort./Sales		.7		.8
		(23)	.8	(30)	1.1	(13)	.7	(21)	1.0		(154)	1.4	(68)	1.4
			1.1		2.0		1.8		1.6			2.3		2.3
										% Officers', Directors' Owners' Comp/Sales		.4		.2
											(33)	.9	(13)	.8
												2.8		1.8
1481M	52831M		648045M	2250101M	4981616M	12470281M	Net Sales ($)		21774279M		9195055M
618M	9256M		166583M	745193M	1090053M	3633982M	Total Assets ($)		7950921M		3215561M

M = $ thousand   MM = $ million
See Pages viii through xx for Explanation of Ratios and Data

© RMA 2024

WHOLESALE—Grain and Field Bean Merchant Wholesalers NAICS 424510

Comparative Historical Data | Current Data Sorted by Sales

					Type of Statement							
	29		29	31	Unqualified					1	2	30
	16		17	15	Reviewed					2	13
	1		3	3	Compiled				1	1	1
	7		6	5	Tax Returns	1		1	3		
	55		56	53	Other	2	1	1	3	15	31
	4/1/21-3/31/22		4/1/22-3/31/23	4/1/23-3/31/24			54 (4/1-9/30/23)			53 (10/1/23-3/31/24)	
	ALL		ALL	ALL		0-1MM	1-3MM	3-5MM	5-10MM	10-25MM	25MM & OVER
	108		111	107	NUMBER OF STATEMENTS	3	1	2	7	19	75
	%		%	%	ASSETS	%	%	%	%	%	%
	8.6		11.6	15.9	Cash & Equivalents					24.3	13.3
	14.9		19.1	18.6	Trade Receivables (net)					13.6	19.0
	38.8		36.8	30.2	Inventory					30.9	30.3
	6.3		5.7	5.9	All Other Current					5.7	6.1
	68.6		73.2	70.6	Total Current					74.5	68.8
	24.7		20.6	21.9	Fixed Assets (net)					16.7	24.7
	1.4		1.3	1.5	Intangibles (net)					3.9	1.1
	5.2		4.9	6.1	All Other Non-Current					4.9	5.4
	100.0		100.0	100.0	Total					100.0	100.0
					LIABILITIES						
	14.9		15.9	9.5	Notes Payable-Short Term					13.9	8.3
	1.4		1.7	1.5	Cur. Mat.-L.T.D.					2.4	1.4
	17.7		21.4	20.2	Trade Payables					23.4	20.6
	.0		.1	.1	Income Taxes Payable					.3	.1
	14.4		13.5	12.8	All Other Current					6.8	14.6
	48.4		52.7	44.0	Total Current					46.8	45.0
	9.2		10.7	8.6	Long-Term Debt					10.9	8.8
	1.1		.8	.7	Deferred Taxes					.4	.9
	1.7		1.9	2.8	All Other Non-Current					3.4	3.4
	39.5		34.0	43.8	Net Worth					41.1	41.9
	100.0		100.0	100.0	Total Liabilities & Net Worth					100.0	100.0
					INCOME DATA						
	100.0		100.0	100.0	Net Sales					100.0	100.0
	10.8		10.7	12.0	Gross Profit					16.5	8.8
	8.8		8.5	9.6	Operating Expenses					11.7	7.1
	2.0		2.2	2.4	Operating Profit					4.8	1.7
	-.5		.2	.3	All Other Expenses (net)					1.3	.0
	2.5		2.1	2.1	Profit Before Taxes					3.4	1.7
					RATIOS						
	1.8		1.7	2.0						2.3	1.9
	1.4		1.3	1.4	Current					1.6	1.4
	1.2		1.2	1.2						1.2	1.2
	.7		1.0	1.2						1.8	1.1
	.4		.4	.6	Quick					.5	.6
	.2		.3	.4						.2	.4
7	55.0	8	46.4	7	50.9					4	102.1	7	50.9
16	22.2	15	23.7	14	25.2	Sales/Receivables				12	31.5	14	26.8
35	10.3	32	11.3	30	12.1					27	13.5	30	12.3
37	9.9	25	14.7	15	23.7					5	77.4	16	22.3
65	5.6	52	7.0	33	11.2	Cost of Sales/Inventory				49	7.4	30	12.1
99	3.7	101	3.6	78	4.7					152	2.4	63	5.8
9	42.6	8	46.8	7	49.3					5	77.6	9	42.6
21	17.8	20	17.9	18	20.0	Cost of Sales/Payables				15	23.8	18	20.0
47	7.8	41	9.0	36	10.2					111	3.3	32	11.4
	8.0		7.8	7.5						5.2	8.9
	13.0		14.0	13.8	Sales/Working Capital					12.6	15.5
	34.3		36.5	29.2						21.1	33.5
	10.3		10.5	7.5						7.5	6.8
(94)	4.4	(99)	3.0	(96)	3.4	EBIT/Interest				(17)	3.1	(71)	3.4
	1.9		1.1	1.5						1.3	1.5
	7.6		5.0	7.8	Net Profit + Depr., Dep.,						8.7
(29)	4.7	(26)	2.9	(24)	4.2	Amort./Cur. Mat. L/T/D					(21)	4.4
	2.6		1.2	1.7							1.8
	.3		.2	.1						.1	.2
	.8		.6	.5	Fixed/Worth					.4	.7
	1.2		1.1	1.0						.7	1.1
	1.0		1.2	.7						.7	.8
	1.7		2.1	1.3	Debt/Worth					1.3	1.5
	3.4		4.8	2.8						2.6	3.1
	22.1		24.7	22.1	% Profit Before Taxes/Tangible					34.5	21.6
(103)	10.6	(105)	8.5	(105)	10.9	Net Worth				(18)	14.0	10.9
	4.5		.6	4.1						2.0	4.1
	8.4		10.2	9.2	% Profit Before Taxes/Total					10.4	8.4
	3.9		2.9	4.5	Assets					4.3	4.6
	1.6		.3	1.4						.5	1.7
	21.7		44.3	37.1						162.7	30.5
	9.8		17.3	16.4	Sales/Net Fixed Assets					21.6	14.1
	6.3		7.4	7.7						8.5	7.6
	3.6		4.6	4.6						4.4	4.8
	2.5		2.8	3.1	Sales/Total Assets					2.8	3.4
	1.6		1.7	1.9						1.2	2.2
	.7		.4	.5						.3	.5
(96)	1.2	(95)	1.0	(92)	.9	% Depr., Dep., Amort./Sales				(16)	1.0	(68)	.9
	1.9		1.6	1.4						3.1	1.4
	.7		.3	.5							
(21)	1.3	(21)	.8	(20)	.8	% Officers', Directors'					
	2.5		2.2	2.1	Owners' Comp/Sales						
	18800234M		18583879M	20404355M	Net Sales ($)	2365M	1435M	7142M	59503M	321783M	20012127M
	5940743M		5800219M	5645685M	Total Assets ($)	1470M	1415M	7837M	25523M	150835M	5458605M

© RMA 2024 M = $ thousand   MM = $ million
See Pages viii through xx for Explanation of Ratios and Data

WHOLESALE—Other Farm Product Raw Material Merchant Wholesalers NAICS 424590

Current Data Sorted by Assets | Comparative Historical Data

						Type of Statement		
			1	6	2	2 Unqualified	11	4
			1	6		Reviewed	16	6
		1	1	2		Compiled	12	6
	1		3			Tax Returns	15	4
2		3	23			Other	51	36
1	20 (4/1-9/30/23)		53 (10/1/23-3/31/24)	6	4		4/1/19-	4/1/20-
0-500M	500M-2MM	2-10MM	10-50MM	50-100MM	100-250MM		3/31/20 ALL	3/31/21 ALL
3	4	29	23	8	6	NUMBER OF STATEMENTS	105	56
%	%	%	%	%	%	ASSETS	%	%
		11.6	6.4			Cash & Equivalents	10.2	13.3
		23.8	30.4			Trade Receivables (net)	27.4	24.4
		49.7	29.8			Inventory	28.7	30.6
		.6	6.3			All Other Current	5.7	3.0
		85.6	72.8			Total Current	72.0	71.3
		8.7	19.7			Fixed Assets (net)	19.7	18.4
		1.5	3.4			Intangibles (net)	1.6	2.4
		4.1	4.1			All Other Non-Current	6.6	7.9
		100.0	100.0			Total	100.0	100.0
						LIABILITIES		
		8.9	8.9			Notes Payable-Short Term	14.7	8.7
		1.0	3.2			Cur. Mat.-L.T.D.	1.5	1.5
		23.6	28.0			Trade Payables	21.0	22.8
		.1	.1			Income Taxes Payable	.1	.1
		12.6	9.8			All Other Current	12.2	5.8
		46.2	50.0			Total Current	49.6	39.0
		6.1	12.0			Long-Term Debt	7.7	8.1
		.0	.4			Deferred Taxes	.2	.1
		3.4	3.7			All Other Non-Current	6.7	6.5
		44.3	33.9			Net Worth	35.8	46.3
		100.0	100.0			Total Liabilties & Net Worth	100.0	100.0
						INCOME DATA		
		100.0	100.0			Net Sales	100.0	100.0
		26.6	16.8			Gross Profit	19.1	20.5
		22.5	13.5			Operating Expenses	15.7	17.3
		4.1	3.3			Operating Profit	3.4	3.2
		.5	.5			All Other Expenses (net)	1.0	.6
		3.6	2.8			Profit Before Taxes	2.4	2.6
						RATIOS		
		4.1	2.8				2.3	3.3
		2.5	1.5			Current	1.4	1.8
		1.3	1.1				1.0	1.2
		1.2	1.1				1.3	2.3
		.8	.9			Quick	.8 (55)	.9
		.3	.5				.5	.4
		18 20.8	29 12.4				15 24.1	6 58.7
		24 15.2	40 9.1			Sales/Receivables	31 11.7	26 13.8
		38 9.7	60 6.1				46 7.9	42 8.6
		22 16.6	14 25.5				8 46.9	7 55.0
		146 2.5	46 7.9			Cost of Sales/Inventory	42 8.6	51 7.1
		228 1.6	101 3.6				89 4.1	107 3.4
		4 99.8	20 18.0				5 72.6	11 32.0
		16 23.0	37 9.8			Cost of Sales/Payables	19 19.3	31 11.8
		50 7.3	54 6.7				45 8.1	51 7.1
		2.5	5.3				5.8	5.4
		6.0	11.9			Sales/Working Capital	12.6	10.0
		17.2	37.2				118.6	27.6
		14.3	9.5				14.5	31.5
		(26) 3.4	(22) 3.2			EBIT/Interest	(88) 4.5	(46) 5.7
		2.5	.3				1.7	1.5
						Net Profit + Depr., Dep.,	10.0	
						Amort./Cur. Mat. L/T/D	(17) 2.1	
							1.1	
		.0	.1				.1	.0
		.0	.6			Fixed/Worth	.3	.3
		.4	1.4				1.2	.8
		.5	1.0				.8	.4
		.7	2.1			Debt/Worth	2.0	1.1
		2.4	5.0				5.3	4.2
		40.6	33.9			% Profit Before Taxes/Tangible	38.2	34.0
		(25) 15.8	(19) 26.5			Net Worth	(97) 19.0	(52) 21.5
		7.9	.5				6.1	5.8
		17.0	15.6			% Profit Before Taxes/Total	11.3	16.1
		6.6	6.3			Assets	5.6	6.8
		3.8	-1.0				1.5	.5
		239.0	71.6				219.3	131.4
		180.0	14.5			Sales/Net Fixed Assets	27.7	37.0
		25.4	7.8				9.0	8.3
		3.3	3.3				4.7	4.2
		2.1	2.1			Sales/Total Assets	2.6	2.4
		1.6	1.8				1.6	1.5
		.0	.2				.2	.3
		(18) .1	(18) 1.1			% Depr., Dep., Amort./Sales	(81) .5	(39) .6
		.3	1.8				1.8	2.1
		.5					.5	.8
		(11) .8				% Officers', Directors'	(32) .7	(15) 1.3
		1.0				Owners' Comp/Sales	2.1	2.4
887M	32606M	420813M	1398148M	1159389M	1530984M	Net Sales ($)	10467051M	2826399M
209M	5470M	168123M	499097M	551481M	861720M	Total Assets ($)	3752686M	1008708M

M = $ thousand   MM = $ million
See Pages viii through xx for Explanation of Ratios and Data

© RMA 2024

WHOLESALE—Other Farm Product Raw Material Merchant Wholesalers NAICS 424590

Comparative Historical Data / Current Data Sorted by Sales

Comparative Historical Data						Current Data Sorted by Sales					
3		11		11	Type of Statement					1	10
4		10		7	Unqualified			1	1	1	5
8		7		4	Reviewed		1		1	1	2
8		5		5	Compiled				1	2	
31		42		46	Tax Returns	2		1		21	20
4/1/21-		4/1/22-		4/1/23-	Other	1	20 (4/1-9/30/23)	1	3	53 (10/1/23-3/31/24)	
3/31/22		3/31/23		3/31/24		0-1MM	1-3MM	3-5MM	5-10MM	10-25MM	25MM & OVER
ALL		ALL		ALL	NUMBER OF STATEMENTS						
54		75		73		3	1	2	4	26	37
%		%		%	ASSETS	%	%	%	%	%	%
14.3		12.1		10.4	Cash & Equivalents					10.6	6.6
28.2		29.6		27.0	Trade Receivables (net)					26.2	31.3
25.7		29.1		36.6	Inventory					43.3	32.5
3.9		4.6		4.8	All Other Current					1.1	5.8
72.0		75.4		78.9	Total Current					81.3	76.1
20.7		14.1		12.9	Fixed Assets (net)					12.3	15.0
1.1		2.7		2.5	Intangibles (net)					1.6	2.7
6.0		7.8		5.6	All Other Non-Current					4.8	6.1
100.0		100.0		100.0	Total					100.0	100.0
					LIABILITIES						
15.6		12.7		12.4	Notes Payable-Short Term					8.1	14.5
3.0		1.6		2.4	Cur. Mat.-L.T.D.					2.5	2.4
21.5		23.7		22.7	Trade Payables					22.8	26.2
.4		.1		.1	Income Taxes Payable					.1	.1
15.3		8.8		10.4	All Other Current					9.9	8.8
55.8		47.0		47.9	Total Current					43.3	52.0
9.3		9.6		9.6	Long-Term Debt					7.4	9.8
.1		.1		.1	Deferred Taxes					.0	.3
1.9		5.0		3.1	All Other Non-Current					3.6	2.6
32.9		38.3		39.2	Net Worth					45.8	35.4
100.0		100.0		100.0	Total Liabilities & Net Worth					100.0	100.0
					INCOME DATA						
100.0		100.0		100.0	Net Sales					100.0	100.0
22.7		20.5		22.3	Gross Profit					22.1	16.9
20.3		16.6		18.6	Operating Expenses					18.9	13.8
2.4		4.0		3.8	Operating Profit					3.2	3.1
-.4		.6		.5	All Other Expenses (net)					.5	.7
2.8		3.4		3.2	Profit Before Taxes					2.7	2.4
					RATIOS						
2.3		2.8		3.0						4.5	2.3
1.2		1.6		1.6	Current					2.6	1.6
1.0		1.2		1.2						1.3	1.2
1.2		1.4		1.2						1.4	1.2
.8		1.0		.8	Quick					.8	.8
.4		.5		.4						.4	.5
18 20.1	17	21.5	21	17.0						20 18.2	30 12.3
34 10.7	35	10.5	34	10.8	Sales/Receivables					25 14.7	41 8.8
52 7.0	63	5.8	56	6.5						37 9.8	72 5.1
6 56.3	15	24.9	20	18.7						19 19.4	26 13.8
41 9.0	49	7.4	70	5.2	Cost of Sales/Inventory					70 5.2	59 6.2
81 4.5	111	3.3	146	2.5						215 1.7	101 3.6
9 40.8	12	30.8	7	53.4						3 108.8	19 19.4
28 13.2	28	13.1	26	14.2	Cost of Sales/Payables					15 23.6	37 9.8
68 5.4	59	6.2	50	7.3						49 7.5	54 6.8
7.0		4.9		4.1						2.5	4.3
16.7		10.8		10.0	Sales/Working Capital					6.3	11.7
NM		27.0		23.1						24.2	25.3
25.2		26.0		9.5						14.3	5.3
(42) 7.8	(63)	6.7	(63)	2.8	EBIT/Interest					(22) 2.9	(35) 2.6
2.2		-.7		1.6						2.0	1.1
		10.2		4.7							5.2
	(14)	3.8	(13)	1.9	Net Profit + Depr., Dep.,					(12) 1.7	
		1.4		-1.1	Amort./Cur. Mat. L/T/D						-1.2
.1		.0		.0						.0	.2
.5		.3		.3	Fixed/Worth					.1	.4
1.6		.8		.9						1.0	1.1
.6		.7		.7						.4	1.0
2.0		1.6		1.5	Debt/Worth					.7	2.0
4.9		4.1		3.7						3.1	4.4
50.1		39.6		33.9	% Profit Before Taxes/Tangible					39.8	31.3
(46) 21.7	(69)	21.9	(63)	17.0	Net Worth					(23) 15.8	(32) 12.4
9.2		3.2		7.6						7.9	.3
18.2		16.7		15.6	% Profit Before Taxes/Total					16.7	9.8
6.9		6.5		5.9	Assets					7.1	4.2
1.9		-.5		1.8						3.5	.0
119.1		230.5		229.1						222.9	116.4
18.6		31.2		46.2	Sales/Net Fixed Assets					137.4	14.9
8.3		10.0		10.2						13.3	9.1
4.4		3.8		3.3						3.2	3.3
2.5		2.3		2.1	Sales/Total Assets					2.1	2.1
1.9		1.7		1.6						1.7	1.5
.3		.3		.1						.0	.3
(38) 1.1	(51)	.7	(51)	.3	% Depr., Dep., Amort./Sales					(17) .1	(29) .9
2.5		2.0		1.2						.4	1.5
.4		.3		.5	% Officers', Directors'					.5	
(13) .8	(24)	1.0	(17)	.8	Owners' Comp/Sales					(10) .8	
5.3		2.1		1.5						1.0	
2774629M		4646680M		4542827M	Net Sales ($)	887M	1802M	8591M	34006M	369538M	4128003M
1248966M		1824222M		2086100M	Total Assets ($)	209M	5821M	3162M	17929M	154796M	1904183M

M = $ thousand   MM = $ million
See Pages viii through xx for Explanation of Ratios and Data

© RMA 2024

WHOLESALE—Plastics Materials and Basic Forms and Shapes Merchant Wholesalers NAICS 424610

Current Data Sorted by Assets / Comparative Historical Data

0-500M	500M-2MM	2-10MM	10-50MM	50-100MM	100-250MM		4/1/19-3/31/20 ALL	4/1/20-3/31/21 ALL
1	2	4	4			Type of Statement		
		3	6			Unqualified	6	8
		5	1			Reviewed	15	6
		3	1	2	2	Compiled	5	7
1	2	5	18			Tax Returns	7	8
		9 (4/1-9/30/23)	49 (10/1/23-3/31/24)			Other	43	22
1	6	17	30	2	2	**NUMBER OF STATEMENTS**	76	51
%	%	%	%	%	%	**ASSETS**	%	%
		14.9	9.1			Cash & Equivalents	8.3	14.7
		38.7	33.7			Trade Receivables (net)	36.1	33.4
		30.0	27.8			Inventory	33.3	31.5
		2.4	2.5			All Other Current	3.5	1.3
		86.1	73.0			Total Current	81.2	81.0
		5.9	14.6			Fixed Assets (net)	8.7	9.3
		5.9	3.5			Intangibles (net)	6.6	4.7
		2.1	8.9			All Other Non-Current	3.5	5.1
		100.0	100.0			Total	100.0	100.0
						LIABILITIES		
		5.5	9.7			Notes Payable-Short Term	16.1	10.5
		.3	1.9			Cur. Mat.-L.T.D.	1.4	2.1
		24.8	14.1			Trade Payables	26.4	19.5
		.3	.2			Income Taxes Payable	.1	.2
		5.6	5.8			All Other Current	8.2	5.8
		36.5	31.7			Total Current	52.1	38.1
		13.7	6.5			Long-Term Debt	7.7	10.0
		.1	.3			Deferred Taxes	.2	.1
		3.0	7.1			All Other Non-Current	6.4	6.8
		46.7	54.4			Net Worth	33.6	45.0
		100.0	100.0			Total Liabilties & Net Worth	100.0	100.0
						INCOME DATA		
		100.0	100.0			Net Sales	100.0	100.0
		25.1	21.6			Gross Profit	22.5	26.8
		20.5	16.1			Operating Expenses	18.5	21.3
		4.7	5.5			Operating Profit	4.0	5.5
		.1	.7			All Other Expenses (net)	.6	-.3
		4.6	4.8			Profit Before Taxes	3.3	5.8
						RATIOS		
		10.0	4.5				2.6	3.5
		2.3	2.7			Current	1.5	2.1
		1.4	1.6				1.2	1.7
		5.1	2.9				1.3	2.3
		1.6	1.5			Quick	.8	1.3
		.9	.8				.5	.9
		36 10.0	35 10.3				32 11.4	30 12.2
		44 8.3	46 8.0			Sales/Receivables	42 8.7	41 8.9
		47 7.8	60 6.1				51 7.1	59 6.2
		26 13.9	23 15.6				28 13.2	24 14.9
		49 7.5	61 6.0			Cost of Sales/Inventory	61 6.0	64 5.7
		81 4.5	114 3.2				81 4.5	89 4.1
		22 16.4	15 25.1				22 16.7	20 18.6
		36 10.0	22 16.8			Cost of Sales/Payables	33 11.1	30 12.1
		49 7.5	40 9.2				49 7.5	45 8.2
		3.6	3.2				5.8	3.7
		4.9	5.4			Sales/Working Capital	10.5	6.4
		15.1	8.2				28.6	12.8
		28.9	68.9				25.8	45.7
		(11) 9.4	(28) 8.7			EBIT/Interest	(67) 7.5	(40) 11.8
		2.6	1.9				2.4	3.8
			11.4			Net Profit + Depr., Dep.,	11.1	23.8
			(10) 6.5			Amort./Cur. Mat. L/T/D	(13) 7.7	(10) 5.5
			1.3				4.6	1.6
		.0	.0				.0	.0
		.0	.2			Fixed/Worth	.1	.2
		.5	.5				.7	.5
		.4	.4				.8	.5
		1.4	.7			Debt/Worth	2.1	1.0
		3.1	1.5				7.2	3.4
		63.6	32.2			% Profit Before Taxes/Tangible	46.7	59.4
		(15) 33.4	(29) 21.1			Net Worth	(65) 29.0	(45) 30.3
		7.6	7.8				10.0	15.8
		20.3	17.1			% Profit Before Taxes/Total	15.6	20.3
		12.7	9.6			Assets	9.2	13.7
		8.0	3.5				2.6	5.2
		999.8	119.8				999.8	531.0
		161.4	39.1			Sales/Net Fixed Assets	96.9	70.2
		28.1	7.7				26.2	13.9
		3.7	3.1				4.1	3.3
		3.0	2.2			Sales/Total Assets	3.0	2.8
		2.1	1.3				1.9	2.0
			.1				.1	.2
		(25)	.6			% Depr., Dep., Amort./Sales	(51) .4	(30) .9
			1.7				1.1	1.9
		1.1				% Officers', Directors'	.4	.6
		(13) 2.1				Owners' Comp/Sales	(22) 1.8	(19) 1.9
		2.7					4.5	5.4
1397M	35798M	272730M	1545574M	435198M	776777M	Net Sales ($)	6605316M	2310900M
224M	7805M	81705M	648698M	142463M	383078M	Total Assets ($)	2368230M	1045021M

© RMA 2024

M = $ thousand   MM = $ million
See Pages viii through xx for Explanation of Ratios and Data

WHOLESALE—Plastics Materials and Basic Forms and Shapes Merchant Wholesalers NAICS 424610

Comparative Historical Data | Current Data Sorted by Sales

Comparative Historical Data						Type of Statement	Current Data Sorted by Sales					
	2		5		4	Unqualified						4
	8		8		10	Reviewed					7	3
	2		5		5	Compiled				1	3	1
	8		9		9	Tax Returns			1	4	2	1
	20		29		30	Other	1	1	3	3	6	17
	4/1/21-		4/1/22-		4/1/23-				9 (4/1-9/30/23)		49 (10/1/23-3/31/24)	
	3/31/22		3/31/23		3/31/24		0-1MM	1-3MM	3-5MM	5-10MM	10-25MM	25MM & OVER
	ALL		ALL		ALL	NUMBER OF STATEMENTS						
	40		56		58		1	1	4	8	18	26
	%		%		%	**ASSETS**	%	%	%	%	%	%
	12.8		13.2		12.8	Cash & Equivalents					9.9	10.1
	37.4		34.4		32.9	Trade Receivables (net)					23.0	44.8
	32.3		28.0		28.5	Inventory					34.1	24.5
	1.6		4.2		2.2	All Other Current					1.5	2.3
	84.2		79.8		76.4	Total Current					68.5	81.6
	9.0		12.0		11.9	Fixed Assets (net)					17.6	6.6
	2.0		1.9		5.3	Intangibles (net)					9.6	1.7
	4.8		6.3		6.4	All Other Non-Current					4.4	10.1
	100.0		100.0		100.0	Total					100.0	100.0
						LIABILITIES						
	15.8		10.0		8.5	Notes Payable-Short Term					5.9	11.1
	1.2		.6		1.6	Cur. Mat.-L.T.D.					1.1	1.6
	22.9		19.8		17.1	Trade Payables					14.5	19.6
	.1		.1		.2	Income Taxes Payable					.4	.1
	6.3		7.3		6.6	All Other Current					3.6	7.6
	46.3		37.8		34.1	Total Current					25.5	40.1
	7.7		9.2		11.2	Long-Term Debt					14.0	2.5
	.1		.1		.2	Deferred Taxes					.4	.1
	3.6		6.0		5.7	All Other Non-Current					6.9	5.5
	42.3		46.9		48.8	Net Worth					53.1	51.8
	100.0		100.0		100.0	Total Liabilities & Net Worth					100.0	100.0
						INCOME DATA						
	100.0		100.0		100.0	Net Sales					100.0	100.0
	22.4		25.4		24.7	Gross Profit					24.3	18.8
	16.4		18.6		19.9	Operating Expenses					19.2	13.3
	6.0		6.8		4.8	Operating Profit					5.1	5.5
	-1.1		-.7		.7	All Other Expenses (net)					1.0	.4
	7.1		7.5		4.1	Profit Before Taxes					4.0	5.1
						RATIOS						
	3.0		5.8		4.5						6.3	3.4
	1.6		2.2		2.4	Current					3.3	2.1
	1.3		1.4		1.5						1.8	1.5
	1.5		2.7		2.9						3.9	2.3
	1.0		1.3		1.5	Quick					1.1	1.5
	.7		.8		.8						.7	.9
33	11.1	24	14.9	33	11.1						30 12.0	38 9.7
44	8.3	37	9.9	44	8.3	Sales/Receivables					38 9.6	49 7.4
60	6.1	52	7.0	57	6.4						47 7.8	63 5.8
22	16.8	23	16.0	24	15.5						36 10.2	16 22.5
50	7.3	43	8.4	51	7.2	Cost of Sales/Inventory					78 4.7	30 12.0
87	4.2	83	4.4	91	4.0						140 2.6	85 4.3
22	16.7	17	21.5	15	25.1						9 41.3	15 24.0
33	10.9	26	14.1	26	13.9	Cost of Sales/Payables					33 11.2	22 16.8
47	7.7	44	8.3	40	9.2						39 9.3	39 9.4
	4.6		3.8		3.7						3.0	5.0
	8.5		6.2		5.4	Sales/Working Capital					4.1	6.9
	15.6		14.8		12.1						8.1	11.8
	57.0		55.1		37.7						9.5	64.1
(32)	21.8	(44)	15.8	(46)	8.8	EBIT/Interest				(14)	4.5	(25) 18.4
	9.0		5.3		2.0						2.0	4.5
			41.5		18.4	Net Profit + Depr., Dep.,						
		(11)	10.9	(14)	9.2	Amort./Cur. Mat. L/T/D						
			5.0		2.6							
	.0		.0		.0						.0	.0
	.1		.1		.1	Fixed/Worth					.3	.1
	.4		.4		.5						.9	.2
	.5		.5		.5						.3	.5
	1.5		1.3		1.0	Debt/Worth					1.1	.9
	3.3		2.6		2.2						3.7	1.8
	61.3		55.2		39.0	% Profit Before Taxes/Tangible					32.6	40.9
(39)	41.7	(53)	33.6	(53)	23.5	Net Worth				(16)	18.8	27.9
	28.8		15.5		7.9						7.7	11.5
	26.9		25.4		17.8	% Profit Before Taxes/Total					11.8	21.7
	17.6		13.2		10.4	Assets					9.0	13.3
	9.1		7.6		3.9						4.1	6.2
	999.8		999.8		439.2						254.9	999.8
	111.8		82.3		47.0	Sales/Net Fixed Assets					33.3	52.7
	23.3		18.3		13.9						5.3	28.6
	4.1		3.5		3.5						3.6	3.6
	2.7		2.7		2.6	Sales/Total Assets					2.0	2.8
	2.2		1.9		1.7						1.0	2.0
	.3		.0		.1						.1	.1
(24)	.6	(37)	.5	(42)	.6	% Depr., Dep., Amort./Sales				(15)	.4	(20) .3
	1.1		1.9		1.4						3.7	1.0
	.8		2.0		1.0	% Officers', Directors'						
(14)	2.2	(14)	2.6	(26)	2.1	Owners' Comp/Sales						
	4.8		5.1		3.3							
	2354994M		3546160M		3067474M	Net Sales ($)	664M	1397M	15212M	64978M	299679M	2685544M
	803140M		1301605M		1263973M	Total Assets ($)	874M	224M	8041M	22720M	176025M	1056089M

© RMA 2024   M = $ thousand   MM = $ million
See Pages viii through xx for Explanation of Ratios and Data

WHOLESALE—Other Chemical and Allied Products Merchant Wholesalers NAICS 424690

Current Data Sorted by Assets | Comparative Historical Data

							Type of Statement		
		2	12	6	9		Unqualified	27	12
	1	11	20	4	2		Reviewed	44	21
	2	13	6				Compiled	21	15
3	5	11	4				Tax Returns	23	12
	6		49	67	17	16	Other	149	109
	39 (4/1-9/30/23)			227 (10/1/23-3/31/24)				4/1/19-3/31/20	4/1/20-3/31/21
0-500M	500M-2MM	2-10MM	10-50MM	50-100MM	100-250MM			ALL	ALL
3	14	86	109	27	27		NUMBER OF STATEMENTS	264	169
%	%	%	%	%	%		ASSETS	%	%
	25.9	15.3	11.9	8.2	11.1		Cash & Equivalents	10.9	13.6
	29.7	31.4	30.4	25.8	22.0		Trade Receivables (net)	32.4	31.2
	25.8	29.7	30.6	27.2	20.2		Inventory	29.7	25.6
	1.1	1.7	2.6	3.4	2.1		All Other Current	2.2	2.5
	82.5	78.1	75.5	64.5	55.4		Total Current	75.2	72.8
	9.6	10.8	14.5	18.4	25.6		Fixed Assets (net)	14.6	15.3
	1.5	4.7	3.9	8.3	12.9		Intangibles (net)	4.2	5.1
	6.4	6.4	6.1	8.9	6.1		All Other Non-Current	6.0	6.8
	100.0	100.0	100.0	100.0	100.0		Total	100.0	100.0
							LIABILITIES		
	11.2	7.7	8.6	3.3	4.6		Notes Payable-Short Term	13.3	8.4
	3.9	2.8	1.8	2.7	1.8		Cur. Mat.-L.T.D.	1.7	2.0
	28.6	21.5	16.5	15.3	11.3		Trade Payables	19.9	19.2
	.2	.1	.2	.0	.2		Income Taxes Payable	.1	.1
	4.3	7.8	6.6	11.4	10.7		All Other Current	8.5	8.0
	48.2	39.9	33.6	32.7	28.5		Total Current	43.6	37.7
	7.7	9.3	10.1	17.4	15.0		Long-Term Debt	10.9	14.6
	.0	.1	.3	.4	1.6		Deferred Taxes	.4	.4
	.0	5.7	3.8	3.2	5.7		All Other Non-Current	4.0	4.8
	44.0	45.0	52.2	46.3	49.1		Net Worth	41.1	42.6
	100.0	100.0	100.0	100.0	100.0		Total Liabilities & Net Worth	100.0	100.0
							INCOME DATA		
	100.0	100.0	100.0	100.0	100.0		Net Sales	100.0	100.0
	25.4	29.4	24.9	21.6	31.5		Gross Profit	27.5	29.3
	18.4	23.2	18.6	16.5	22.9		Operating Expenses	22.5	23.4
	7.0	6.3	6.3	5.1	8.7		Operating Profit	5.0	6.0
	-.2	.3	.4	.5	1.9		All Other Expenses (net)	.4	-.2
	7.2	6.0	5.9	4.6	6.8		Profit Before Taxes	4.6	6.2
							RATIOS		
		3.8	3.6	4.0	3.2	3.7		3.0	3.5
		1.7	2.1	2.5	1.8	2.1	Current	1.7	2.1
		1.3	1.4	1.5	1.3	1.2		1.3	1.5
		1.8	2.5	2.5	1.5	1.9		1.8	2.0
		1.2	1.3	1.4	.9	1.1	Quick	1.0	1.3
		.7	.6	.7	.6	.8		.7	.8
	15	25.0	27	13.4	36	10.1	29	12.6	26	13.8			31	11.6	32	11.3
	26	14.1	36	10.1	44	8.3	47	7.8	41	8.9	Sales/Receivables	40	9.2	44	8.3
	49	7.4	50	7.3	51	7.1	61	6.0	51	7.2		51	7.2	55	6.6
	0	UND	20	18.4	35	10.5	34	10.6	29	12.8		27	13.3	26	14.2
	14	25.5	58	6.3	58	6.3	65	5.6	47	7.7	Cost of Sales/Inventory	49	7.4	47	7.8
	96	3.8	96	3.8	89	4.1	96	3.8	85	4.3		87	4.2	79	4.6
	11	31.9	21	17.1	18	20.0	21	17.8	15	23.8		19	19.7	21	17.3
	21	17.2	32	11.3	29	12.5	29	12.4	24	15.1	Cost of Sales/Payables	30	12.2	33	11.2
	38	9.5	49	7.4	41	8.9	41	8.8	43	8.5		45	8.2	51	7.1
		5.4		3.8		3.9		3.5		3.5			5.1		4.5
		20.9		9.0		5.3		6.8		7.2	Sales/Working Capital		8.9		7.4
		32.8		15.9		9.9		22.3		29.8			20.1		14.9
		48.1		38.0		34.8		18.5		63.4			25.6		32.6
	(12)	14.2	(68)	8.6	(92)	13.8	(24)	6.1	(24)	10.0	EBIT/Interest	(234)	7.0	(137)	12.7
		2.1		3.7		2.9		2.7		3.6			2.5		4.5
				123.6		58.3		29.3					13.8		16.5
			(12)	16.1	(31)	14.3	(14)	6.8			Net Profit + Depr., Dep., Amort./Cur. Mat. L/T/D	(49)	5.1	(29)	7.4
				4.5		3.2		2.8					2.2		3.0
		.0		.0		.0		.2		.1			.0		.0
		.1		.1		.1		.3		.4	Fixed/Worth		.2		.2
		.8		.6		.5		.9		1.7			.7		.7
		.9		.6		.4		.6		.4			.6		.5
		1.4		1.5		.8		1.4		1.2	Debt/Worth		1.5		1.2
		2.8		3.6		1.8		6.1		7.9			4.1		3.4
		88.6		71.4		44.2		37.3		50.4			50.9		54.7
	(13)	36.6	(78)	27.7	(103)	22.7	(25)	26.0	(22)	30.7	% Profit Before Taxes/Tangible Net Worth	(241)	23.2	(159)	30.2
		4.2		13.5		9.5		13.1		21.6			8.9		12.4
		30.4		23.9		20.2		13.7		16.1			18.4		21.2
		16.8		12.4		11.2		6.5		10.7	% Profit Before Taxes/Total Assets		7.9		10.2
		.2		4.9		3.9		3.6		7.8			2.4		4.6
		UND		999.8		161.9		44.7		149.5			384.0		247.4
		140.8		111.1		32.7		11.3		10.7	Sales/Net Fixed Assets		41.0		37.3
		31.3		12.7		10.4		5.6		4.0			9.7		8.3
		8.2		4.0		3.0		3.0		2.3			3.7		3.3
		5.4		2.6		2.4		1.7		1.8	Sales/Total Assets		2.7		2.4
		1.6		1.8		1.7		1.2		1.2			1.9		1.8
				.1		.2		.3		.3			.2		.2
			(53)	.4	(82)	.6	(25)	1.4	(15)	1.0	% Depr., Dep., Amort./Sales	(179)	1.0	(102)	.8
				2.2		1.4		2.7		2.3			2.6		2.7
				1.5		.9							1.3		1.5
			(24)	2.2	(25)	2.1					% Officers', Directors' Owners' Comp/Sales	(68)	2.9	(40)	2.8
				4.1		3.8							6.2		5.7
2154M	97602M	1524096M	6242962M	4246316M	8337149M		Net Sales ($)	20831723M	10794477M
649M	15927M	510307M	2582912M	1925556M	4571085M		Total Assets ($)	7000693M	4564122M

© RMA 2024 M = $ thousand   MM = $ million
See Pages viii through xx for Explanation of Ratios and Data

WHOLESALE—Other Chemical and Allied Products Merchant Wholesalers NAICS 424690

Comparative Historical Data / Current Data Sorted by Sales

						Type of Statement						
		14		25	29	Unqualified				1	1	27
		30		31	38	Reviewed				1	7	30
		20		24	21	Compiled		2		2	11	6
		16		15	23	Tax Returns		2	1	8	5	4
		92		128	155	Other	3	2	9	9	35	99
		4/1/21-3/31/22		4/1/22-3/31/23	4/1/23-3/31/24			39 (4/1-9/30/23)			227 (10/1/23-3/31/24)	
		ALL		ALL	ALL		0-1MM	1-3MM	3-5MM	5-10MM	10-25MM	25MM & OVER
		172		223	266	NUMBER OF STATEMENTS	3	7	10	21	59	166
		%		%	%	ASSETS	%	%	%	%	%	%
		10.8		10.9	13.5	Cash & Equivalents			18.2	18.1	13.7	12.3
		31.3		31.2	29.3	Trade Receivables (net)			18.5	24.9	31.4	30.4
		29.8		31.5	28.7	Inventory			22.9	28.0	33.6	27.1
		2.1		1.7	2.2	All Other Current			.5	.6	2.5	2.5
		74.0		75.3	73.8	Total Current			60.2	71.6	81.1	72.2
		15.7		14.5	14.4	Fixed Assets (net)			18.0	14.8	11.2	15.6
		4.8		4.8	5.3	Intangibles (net)			15.3	5.4	1.4	6.0
		5.5		5.3	6.4	All Other Non-Current			6.5	8.2	6.2	6.3
		100.0		100.0	100.0	Total			100.0	100.0	100.0	100.0
						LIABILITIES						
		10.0		11.5	7.6	Notes Payable-Short Term			10.6	4.3	8.7	7.1
		2.2		2.3	2.3	Cur. Mat.-L.T.D.			8.0	3.8	1.5	1.8
		19.8		18.9	18.3	Trade Payables			19.8	30.1	17.8	17.2
		.1		.2	.2	Income Taxes Payable			.0	.1	.1	.2
		9.9		9.2	8.0	All Other Current			2.5	4.8	8.3	8.5
		42.1		42.2	36.3	Total Current			40.8	43.0	36.5	34.8
		12.8		11.2	12.6	Long-Term Debt			13.8	11.9	6.5	12.0
		.4		.3	.4	Deferred Taxes			.0	.3	.3	.4
		4.2		4.3	4.3	All Other Non-Current			1.2	6.1	4.3	4.5
		40.5		42.0	46.5	Net Worth			44.2	38.7	52.4	48.3
		100.0		100.0	100.0	Total Liabilities & Net Worth			100.0	100.0	100.0	100.0
						INCOME DATA						
		100.0		100.0	100.0	Net Sales			100.0	100.0	100.0	100.0
		28.8		27.2	26.8	Gross Profit			40.7	32.5	30.3	23.4
		22.4		21.1	20.6	Operating Expenses			32.0	28.0	24.0	17.2
		6.4		6.1	6.2	Operating Profit			8.7	4.5	6.2	6.2
		-.8		-.1	.5	All Other Expenses (net)			.0	1.1	.0	.6
		7.1		6.2	5.7	Profit Before Taxes			8.7	3.4	6.2	5.6
						RATIOS						
		2.9		3.4	3.7				7.3	5.1	4.4	3.7
		1.9		2.0	2.2	Current			1.3	1.9	2.5	2.2
		1.3		1.3	1.4				1.1	1.2	1.7	1.4
		1.8		2.0	2.3				2.4	2.6	3.0	2.1
		1.0		1.1	1.2	Quick			1.1	1.0	1.5	1.1
		.6		.6	.7				.5	.5	.8	.7
32	11.3	29	12.5	30	12.0		21	17.1	18	19.9	33	11.1	31	11.6
44	8.3	41	9.0	41	8.9	Sales/Receivables	26	14.2	36	10.1	40	9.1	42	8.7
55	6.6	49	7.4	51	7.1		44	8.3	63	5.8	53	6.9	51	7.1
33	11.1	27	13.4	26	14.1		13	27.5	8	48.6	45	8.1	25	14.8
55	6.6	55	6.6	57	6.4	Cost of Sales/Inventory	51	7.1	96	3.8	69	5.3	47	7.7
96	3.8	91	4.0	91	4.0		243	1.5	152	2.4	101	3.6	76	4.8
21	17.4	16	22.2	19	19.4		14	26.4	36	10.2	22	16.7	18	20.2
32	11.4	27	13.6	29	12.6	Cost of Sales/Payables	28	13.2	48	7.6	34	10.8	27	13.6
47	7.8	42	8.6	43	8.5		66	5.5	118	3.1	45	8.1	38	9.6
	5.0		4.7		3.9					7.4		2.7		3.1		4.2
	8.3		8.0		7.0	Sales/Working Capital				23.3		5.8		4.9		7.8
	15.6		19.1		16.6					32.1		76.3		10.2		16.6
	43.3		37.1		32.8						5.3		43.2		31.5
(147)	16.7	(192)	13.5	(222)	9.7	EBIT/Interest			(15)	4.3	(49)	14.5	(141)	9.8
	6.9		5.4		3.1						1.4		4.8		3.0
	20.8		18.9		32.0	Net Profit + Depr., Dep.,										52.1
(26)	6.1	(48)	6.7	(64)	10.6	Amort./Cur. Mat. L/T/D									(53)	14.3
	3.9		2.6		3.2											3.3
	.0		.0		.0					.1		.0		.0		.0
	.2		.2		.2	Fixed/Worth				.7		.2		.1		.2
	.8		.7		.6					1.1		1.5		.3		.6
	.5		.6		.5					.9		1.0		.3		.5
	1.4		1.5		1.1	Debt/Worth				3.3		2.0		.8		1.0
	3.7		3.1		3.0					4.4		3.5		1.9		2.8
	61.6		66.9		49.3	% Profit Before Taxes/Tangible				25.2		42.0		52.7
(155)	33.9	(207)	33.2	(242)	26.0	Net Worth			(17)	9.6	(55)	19.4	(153)	27.8
	19.3		15.8		11.8						5.6		11.3		14.3
	20.8		23.2		20.3	% Profit Before Taxes/Total				25.5		14.3		20.7		20.1
	12.9		13.7		11.1	Assets				15.9		4.4		10.8		11.0
	6.7		5.6		4.1					8.9		1.0		5.7		4.1
	376.7		485.7		285.1					202.1		447.2		656.9		240.6
	32.1		50.7		38.4	Sales/Net Fixed Assets				16.0		35.2		72.8		37.7
	8.7		10.5		9.7					8.0		5.8		11.1		9.4
	3.3		3.7		3.4					5.4		2.7		3.4		3.4
	2.5		2.7		2.4	Sales/Total Assets				1.9		1.7		2.3		2.6
	1.9		1.9		1.6					.8		1.2		1.7		1.7
	.2		.1		.2						.3		.1		.2
(115)	.9	(138)	.8	(182)	.6	% Depr., Dep., Amort./Sales			(13)	1.3	(43)	.7	(117)	.5
	2.4		1.9		1.8						7.1		1.4		1.6
	1.3		.9		1.3	% Officers', Directors'						1.4		.6
(40)	2.5	(51)	2.2	(64)	2.4	Owners' Comp/Sales					(18)	2.0	(29)	1.5
	4.7		2.9		4.2										3.2		3.5
	12225762M		18976443M		20450279M	Net Sales ($)	1462M	14407M	41241M	159809M	1035614M	19197746M
	4510883M		6799468M		9606436M	Total Assets ($)	1929M	10077M	36181M	101085M	475159M	8982005M

© RMA 2024   M = $ thousand   MM = $ million
See Pages viii through xx for Explanation of Ratios and Data

WHOLESALE—Petroleum Bulk Stations and Terminals NAICS 424710

Current Data Sorted by Assets / Comparative Historical Data

							Type of Statement		
			1	4	5		Unqualified	8	8
		1	3	3	1		Reviewed	16	6
	2	1	4		1		Compiled	15	5
	2	3					Tax Returns	15	3
	1	6	15	5	9		Other	44	29
	27 (4/1-9/30/23)		40 (10/1/23-3/31/24)					4/1/19-3/31/20	4/1/20-3/31/21
0-500M	500M-2MM	2-10MM	10-50MM	50-100MM	100-250MM		NUMBER OF STATEMENTS	ALL 98	ALL 51
5		11	23	12	16				
%	%	%	%	%	%	ASSETS		%	%
		24.2	18.0	11.5	4.0	Cash & Equivalents		11.4	14.5
D		25.2	26.1	18.4	21.5	Trade Receivables (net)		26.6	20.2
A		12.5	7.9	17.0	12.0	Inventory		14.7	14.6
T		3.1	5.8	4.6	2.8	All Other Current		3.5	2.7
A		64.9	57.8	51.5	40.3	Total Current		56.1	52.0
		20.8	27.2	37.4	43.3	Fixed Assets (net)		31.8	32.8
N		2.6	7.1	6.5	9.7	Intangibles (net)		3.3	4.5
O		11.7	8.0	4.5	6.7	All Other Non-Current		8.7	10.6
T		100.0	100.0	100.0	100.0	Total		100.0	100.0
A						LIABILITIES			
V		1.5	4.5	2.3	4.3	Notes Payable-Short Term		13.6	3.1
A		.4	2.1	2.9	3.9	Cur. Mat.-L.T.D.		2.3	3.1
I		18.7	18.9	12.4	8.8	Trade Payables		17.5	15.7
L		.0	.1	.0	.1	Income Taxes Payable		.2	.1
A		7.0	12.2	10.1	7.3	All Other Current		7.7	8.5
B		27.7	37.8	27.6	24.3	Total Current		41.4	30.5
L		10.4	10.3	11.1	22.0	Long-Term Debt		15.2	20.1
E		.2	.9	1.3	1.5	Deferred Taxes		.4	.5
		.9	3.7	3.7	5.5	All Other Non-Current		7.6	4.8
		60.8	47.2	56.3	46.7	Net Worth		35.4	44.0
		100.0	100.0	100.0	100.0	Total Liabilities & Net Worth		100.0	100.0
						INCOME DATA			
		100.0	100.0	100.0	100.0	Net Sales		100.0	100.0
		12.9	14.9	18.7	26.0	Gross Profit		16.4	22.0
		10.9	12.5	15.1	21.2	Operating Expenses		15.0	19.8
		2.1	2.4	3.6	4.8	Operating Profit		1.4	2.1
		-.3	-.3	1.0	1.8	All Other Expenses (net)		.2	-.1
		2.4	2.7	2.6	3.0	Profit Before Taxes		1.3	2.2
						RATIOS			
		2.9	1.9	2.7	2.5			2.3	2.2
		1.9	1.4	1.9	1.7	Current		1.4	1.7
		1.7	1.2	1.3	1.1			1.1	1.2
		2.5	1.4	1.7	1.5			1.6	1.6
		1.6	1.1	1.3	1.0	Quick		1.0	1.0
		1.1	.9	.5	.7			.7	.7
	4	83.1	10	36.7	10	34.8	12	30.2		7	52.0	8	44.3
	14	27.0	13	27.6	12	30.6	20	18.1	Sales/Receivables	13	27.6	14	25.4
	25	14.7	21	17.3	19	19.2	38	9.7		22	16.4	24	15.5
	2	151.8	2	164.2	6	61.3	5	75.1		3	111.9	4	91.2
	4	92.5	5	80.0	12	31.0	12	29.4	Cost of Sales/Inventory	8	45.2	10	35.8
	18	20.2	12	30.6	46	7.9	45	8.1		16	22.5	31	11.8
	5	72.6	9	40.2	7	49.0	3	105.5		8	48.6	8	44.3
	8	47.8	12	29.7	11	31.9	9	38.9	Cost of Sales/Payables	10	35.5	12	30.0
	20	18.3	16	22.9	16	22.2	15	24.8		15	25.1	22	16.8
		8.8	19.6	13.4	11.3			15.6	11.3
		17.7	31.9	25.0	23.4	Sales/Working Capital		38.5	18.9
		80.8	88.3	56.4	NM			318.9	117.4
			17.5	54.9	11.0			12.5	12.6
		(22)	11.7	9.4	5.7	EBIT/Interest	(92)	5.6	(43)	6.5
			3.7	4.9	2.2			2.4	2.9
						Net Profit + Depr., Dep.,		7.7	
						Amort./Cur. Mat. L/T/D	(19)	3.2	
								1.9	
		.1	.4	.4	.6			.4	.4
		.2	.7	.8	1.0	Fixed/Worth		.7	.9
		.3	1.3	1.3	1.8			1.6	1.5
		.4	.7	.5	.7			.7	.8
		.6	1.4	.6	1.4	Debt/Worth		1.7	1.6
		.9	3.4	1.8	2.4			3.9	3.1
		38.2	44.6	30.5	57.8	% Profit Before Taxes/Tangible		43.0	40.4
	(10)	15.8	23.9	15.3	(15)	28.9	Net Worth	(87)	21.0	(50)	21.5
		10.1	9.3	11.7	8.8			9.3	10.1
		15.6	18.6	10.4	14.6	% Profit Before Taxes/Total		13.5	15.8
		9.1	8.9	8.6	6.2	Assets		6.9	8.9
		6.9	4.7	5.0	2.4			2.5	3.2
		194.5	53.9	34.2	27.2			53.6	39.6
		46.9	32.0	15.3	8.2	Sales/Net Fixed Assets		20.7	15.6
		17.4	8.8	4.1	2.7			9.9	5.6
		10.0	8.1	9.4	5.7			9.4	5.8
		4.9	5.7	5.6	3.4	Sales/Total Assets		6.2	4.3
		3.6	3.3	1.5	1.5			3.5	2.5
		.1	.6	.5	.6			.5	.4
		.8	(20)	.9	.7	(10)	1.7	% Depr., Dep., Amort./Sales	(85)	.9	(42)	1.1
		1.8	1.4	5.7	5.2			1.7	2.2
						% Officers', Directors'		.2	.2
						Owners' Comp/Sales	(33)	.4	(17)	.3
								1.2	2.3
	19986M	559097M	3357899M	4949475M	8698727M	Net Sales ($)	13036044M	5982735M
	5985M	71702M	554274M	835248M	2409155M	Total Assets ($)	2282057M	1877577M

M = $ thousand   MM = $ million
See Pages viii through xx for Explanation of Ratios and Data

© RMA 2024

WHOLESALE—Petroleum Bulk Stations and Terminals NAICS 424710

Comparative Historical Data / Current Data Sorted by Sales

	6		5		10	Type of Statement					10
	7		16		8	Unqualified					8
	7		7		8	Reviewed					6
	9		7		5	Compiled				2	3
	22		36		36	Tax Returns		1	1		3
	4/1/21-		4/1/22-		4/1/23-	Other		1		2	3	30
	3/31/22		3/31/23		3/31/24			27 (4/1-9/30/23)		40 (10/1/23-3/31/24)		
	ALL		ALL		ALL		0-1MM	1-3MM	3-5MM	5-10MM	10-25MM	25MM & OVER
	51		71		67	NUMBER OF STATEMENTS		2	1	4	3	57
	%		%		%	ASSETS	%	%	%	%	%	%
	11.7		14.2		13.7	Cash & Equivalents	D					14.2
	27.2		23.1		22.8	Trade Receivables (net)	A					24.6
	13.7		14.6		11.7	Inventory	T					11.0
	3.1		4.1		5.1	All Other Current	A					4.5
	55.7		56.0		53.3	Total Current						54.2
	34.0		29.5		32.8	Fixed Assets (net)	N					30.4
	4.0		5.0		6.3	Intangibles (net)	O					7.4
	6.2		9.5		7.6	All Other Non-Current	T					8.0
	100.0		100.0		100.0	Total						100.0
						LIABILITIES	A					
	7.1		5.8		3.4	Notes Payable-Short Term	V					3.5
	2.9		2.4		3.0	Cur. Mat.-L.T.D.	A					2.4
	16.4		17.0		14.6	Trade Payables	I					15.5
	.3		.3		.0	Income Taxes Payable	L					.0
	7.0		7.2		10.4	All Other Current	A					10.2
	33.6		32.7		31.4	Total Current	B					31.7
	16.1		15.9		20.0	Long-Term Debt	L					14.5
	1.0		.8		.9	Deferred Taxes	E					.7
	3.2		7.9		5.1	All Other Non-Current						3.7
	46.1		42.7		42.6	Net Worth						49.3
	100.0		100.0		100.0	Total Liabilities & Net Worth						100.0
						INCOME DATA						
	100.0		100.0		100.0	Net Sales						100.0
	19.6		17.9		19.2	Gross Profit						16.9
	15.7		14.8		16.2	Operating Expenses						13.3
	4.0		3.0		3.1	Operating Profit						3.6
	-1.1		-.1		.2	All Other Expenses (net)						.4
	5.0		3.1		2.9	Profit Before Taxes						3.3
						RATIOS						
	2.3		2.1		2.3							2.3
	1.7		1.6		1.7	Current						1.7
	1.2		1.2		1.3							1.3
	1.6		1.5		1.6							1.6
	1.2		1.1		1.2	Quick						1.2
	.8		.7		.7							.8
10	35.4	7	49.5	10	36.0						10	35.7
19	19.1	12	30.0	14	25.2	Sales/Receivables					14	25.2
31	11.7	22	16.9	23	15.9						23	16.1
2	157.4	4	94.6	4	92.5						4	97.5
11	32.0	7	52.7	7	50.5	Cost of Sales/Inventory					7	52.3
35	10.3	22	16.4	20	18.5						17	21.8
10	35.1	6	58.6	7	50.2						7	50.0
14	25.2	10	37.2	10	37.4	Cost of Sales/Payables					10	37.4
21	17.4	18	20.7	16	22.7						16	23.1
	9.2		14.9		13.0							13.7
	19.5		28.7		25.1	Sales/Working Capital						25.4
	85.2		71.5		80.8							63.2
	29.3		29.8		18.8							19.8
(43)	7.6	(64)	12.7	(62)	8.3	EBIT/Interest					(54)	9.8
	3.8		5.3		3.7							3.7
	7.1		14.4		9.4	Net Profit + Depr., Dep.,						11.0
(10)	2.9	(19)	4.6	(22)	4.2	Amort./Cur. Mat. L/T/D					(19)	4.3
	1.4		2.2		2.1							2.1
	.3		.3		.3							.3
	.9		.7		.7	Fixed/Worth						.7
	1.7		1.4		1.4							1.3
	.5		.7		.6							.6
	1.3		1.3		1.2	Debt/Worth						1.2
	3.1		2.8		2.5							2.5
	47.3		55.5		39.4	% Profit Before Taxes/Tangible						44.3
	30.8	(66)	31.4	(62)	20.9	Net Worth					(55)	23.9
	15.8		17.0		10.8							12.2
	16.3		20.4		16.1	% Profit Before Taxes/Total						15.5
	9.2		12.1		9.1	Assets						8.9
	4.6		4.7		4.8							4.8
	37.4		48.8		46.9							49.0
	15.4		24.2		22.4	Sales/Net Fixed Assets						25.5
	6.1		7.7		6.8							7.2
	7.8		8.8		8.0							8.1
	4.1		6.1		4.6	Sales/Total Assets						4.9
	2.1		3.2		2.8							3.0
	.6		.5		.6							.5
(46)	1.0	(59)	.9	(57)	.9	% Depr., Dep., Amort./Sales					(48)	.8
	3.4		1.5		2.1							1.8
	.3		.2		.2	% Officers', Directors'						.2
(24)	.7	(24)	.5	(15)	.5	Owners' Comp/Sales					(13)	.5
	1.6		.7		.9							.9
	4442039M		17779226M		17585184M	Net Sales ($)		2635M	3504M	29412M	61841M	17487792M
	1595729M		3434161M		3876364M	Total Assets ($)		2942M	578M	21858M	124297M	3726689M

© RMA 2024   M = $ thousand   MM = $ million
See Pages viii through xx for Explanation of Ratios and Data

WHOLESALE—Petroleum and Petroleum Products Merchant Wholesalers (except Bulk Stations and Terminals) NAICS 424720

Current Data Sorted by Assets

Type of Statement	0-500M	500M-2MM	2-10MM	10-50MM	50-100MM	100-250MM
Unqualified	1	1	4	9	10	22
Reviewed	1	1	8	34	8	3
Compiled		2	15	10	1	1
Tax Returns	5	6	13	3		
Other	3	10	40	72	32	31
		87 (4/1-9/30/23)		258 (10/1/23-3/31/24)		
NUMBER OF STATEMENTS	9	20	80	128	51	57

Comparative Historical Data

Type of Statement	4/1/19-3/31/20 ALL	4/1/20-3/31/21 ALL
Unqualified	49	44
Reviewed	84	53
Compiled	37	21
Tax Returns	45	9
Other	233	144
NUMBER OF STATEMENTS	448	271

	0-500M %	500M-2MM %	2-10MM %	10-50MM %	50-100MM %	100-250MM %	ASSETS	Hist1 %	Hist2 %
		27.8	22.9	13.8	11.2	3.9	Cash & Equivalents	12.8	14.7
		26.1	28.3	31.0	22.7	29.2	Trade Receivables (net)	27.6	25.1
		10.3	14.0	12.9	14.5	14.8	Inventory	13.5	11.9
		5.0	2.0	3.6	3.8	5.2	All Other Current	3.6	4.5
		69.1	67.2	61.3	52.3	53.0	Total Current	57.5	56.3
		16.7	19.2	26.0	32.5	30.8	Fixed Assets (net)	27.8	29.5
		6.1	3.4	4.7	3.1	6.3	Intangibles (net)	4.7	5.1
		8.1	10.3	8.0	12.1	9.9	All Other Non-Current	10.1	9.2
		100.0	100.0	100.0	100.0	100.0	Total	100.0	100.0
							LIABILITIES		
		7.7	5.5	6.6	2.7	7.6	Notes Payable-Short Term	7.6	6.1
		1.6	1.8	2.7	1.5	2.5	Cur. Mat.-L.T.D.	3.0	3.2
		19.6	19.8	22.5	19.7	18.6	Trade Payables	20.6	20.6
		.0	.1	.1	.3	.1	Income Taxes Payable	.1	.2
		11.5	6.7	7.9	9.5	11.7	All Other Current	7.9	8.1
		40.4	33.9	39.8	33.8	40.6	Total Current	39.2	38.2
		14.1	10.8	11.8	10.6	13.9	Long-Term Debt	14.5	14.7
		.0	.3	.7	.5	.3	Deferred Taxes	.5	.8
		2.7	3.2	4.2	4.5	5.9	All Other Non-Current	4.6	4.7
		42.9	51.8	43.6	50.6	39.4	Net Worth	41.1	41.7
		100.0	100.0	100.0	100.0	100.0	Total Liabilities & Net Worth	100.0	100.0
							INCOME DATA		
		100.0	100.0	100.0	100.0	100.0	Net Sales	100.0	100.0
		26.2	16.6	11.5	11.2	11.3	Gross Profit	12.3	14.5
		23.4	13.1	9.6	8.9	8.6	Operating Expenses	10.5	12.4
		2.9	3.5	1.9	2.3	2.7	Operating Profit	1.8	2.1
		.2	-.2	-.2	-.5	-.2	All Other Expenses (net)	-.2	-.4
		2.7	3.7	2.1	2.8	2.9	Profit Before Taxes	1.9	2.5
							RATIOS		
		3.6	3.6	2.2	2.3	1.8		2.2	2.3
		1.7	2.0	1.5	1.5	1.3	Current	1.5	1.4
		1.0	1.2	1.2	1.1	1.1		1.0	1.1
		3.3	2.5	1.6	1.4	1.1		1.6	1.6
		1.1	1.5	1.2	1.0	.9	Quick	1.0	1.0
		.6	1.0	.7	.6	.6		.6	.7
0	UND	7	49.9	9	39.0	7	49.0	11	32.8				
6	57.8	17	21.9	17	21.2	12	30.6	19	19.1	Sales/Receivables	7	49.8	9	39.6
17	21.0	22	16.8	27	13.7	21	17.4	29	12.4		16	23.5	16	22.8
											28	13.2	27	13.6
0	UND	1	447.9	1	514.0	3	138.1	5	77.7		2	169.1	2	178.6
2	217.3	6	60.6	7	55.0	9	41.0	8	45.2	Cost of Sales/Inventory	6	57.0	7	53.2
10	36.4	17	21.9	21	17.5	16	23.3	19	18.9		15	24.1	18	20.7
4	89.8	7	54.1	8	44.6	8	46.3	10	38.3		7	48.9	10	38.2
9	40.6	10	35.1	12	30.7	11	32.1	13	27.2	Cost of Sales/Payables	12	31.6	15	24.9
17	21.0	18	20.1	19	19.0	15	24.7	18	20.0		19	19.0	23	15.7
		15.3	9.7	14.5	15.7	21.2		17.2	14.1
		24.4	23.0	31.5	37.4	50.9	Sales/Working Capital	38.4	31.9
		NM	60.2	143.2	189.5	128.4		999.8	176.7
		7.2	37.0	34.4	68.7	18.1		19.1	16.0
(14)		3.7	(64)	11.6	(120)	10.0	(42)	21.4	(56)	5.4	EBIT/Interest	(400)	6.5	(238)	7.8
		.1	1.7	3.7	8.4	3.8		2.6	3.0
				17.4	13.7	21.5		8.9	5.7
			(27)	6.3	(14)	3.9	(15)	6.0	Net Profit + Depr., Dep., Amort./Cur. Mat. L/T/D	(96)	3.1	(56)	3.7
				1.9	2.7	3.3		1.8	2.0
		.0	.1	.2	.4	.6		.2	.2
		.3	.3	.7	.8	1.1	Fixed/Worth	.7	.8
		.9	.9	1.3	1.1	1.6		1.4	1.6
		.6	.4	.7	.6	1.3		.7	.7
		1.3	1.1	1.6	.9	2.4	Debt/Worth	1.6	1.6
		4.4	2.3	2.5	1.7	3.4		3.4	3.6
		76.0	43.7	35.2	34.3	37.9		34.5	38.4
(19)		26.0	(75)	23.0	(123)	20.9	27.3	(53)	29.1	% Profit Before Taxes/Tangible Net Worth	(423)	21.2	(254)	22.6
		-1.1	7.2	12.0	20.8	19.6		9.2	10.0
		21.1	20.0	15.1	17.1	14.2		13.0	15.3
		13.0	10.4	8.6	12.9	8.5	% Profit Before Taxes/Total Assets	6.7	8.0
		.4	2.8	3.8	7.8	4.6		2.9	2.9
		837.9	224.4	91.5	63.8	36.3		76.1	57.1
		81.3	45.0	26.6	22.3	17.5	Sales/Net Fixed Assets	25.5	17.5
		29.9	17.2	11.5	8.9	9.1		11.4	7.9
		9.1	9.6	8.9	8.5	7.8		9.1	7.1
		6.2	5.8	5.9	5.6	5.4	Sales/Total Assets	6.0	4.5
		4.5	3.2	4.0	3.7	3.3		3.7	3.0
		.0	.2	.3	.4	.3		.3	.5
(11)		.3	(56)	.7	(111)	.8	(46)	.8	(47)	.7	% Depr., Dep., Amort./Sales	(361)	.8	(211)	1.1
		1.2	1.3	1.4	1.3	1.1		1.4	1.9
			.3	.1		.0		.2	.2
		(33)	.9	(29)	.3	(11)	.0	% Officers', Directors' Owners' Comp/Sales	(110)	.6	(59)	.6
			2.3	.7		.0		1.2	1.1
16781M	224505M	3732444M	21288115M	23290190M	54326027M	Net Sales ($)	98769182M	54093428M
3050M	23091M	502978M	3218380M	3420905M	8810046M	Total Assets ($)	16554508M	11055092M

© RMA 2024

M = $ thousand   MM = $ million
See Pages viii through xx for Explanation of Ratios and Data

WHOLESALE—Petroleum and Petroleum Products Merchant Wholesalers (except Bulk Stations and Terminals) NAICS 424720

Comparative Historical Data | Current Data Sorted by Sales

				Type of Statement						
	33	44	47	Unqualified				1		45
	44	59	54	Reviewed	1				3	51
	23	21	29	Compiled				1	3	25
	23	21	27	Tax Returns	2	4	5	3	4	9
	156	153	188	Other		5	4	8	13	158
	4/1/21-3/31/22 ALL	4/1/22-3/31/23 ALL	4/1/23-3/31/24 ALL		87 (4/1-9/30/23)			258 (10/1/23-3/31/24)		
					0-1MM	1-3MM	3-5MM	5-10MM	10-25MM	25MM & OVER
	279	298	345	NUMBER OF STATEMENTS	3	9	9	13	23	288
	%	%	%	ASSETS	%	%	%	%	%	%
	13.8	15.9	15.0	Cash & Equivalents				13.1	23.2	13.7
	31.1	31.4	28.6	Trade Receivables (net)				32.5	18.5	30.0
	13.1	11.8	13.5	Inventory				25.0	13.8	13.2
	3.4	3.9	3.5	All Other Current				.6	1.3	3.9
	61.4	63.1	60.6	Total Current				71.3	56.8	60.7
	26.0	24.2	25.4	Fixed Assets (net)				13.4	25.8	26.0
	4.3	4.2	4.4	Intangibles (net)				5.3	3.0	4.4
	8.3	8.6	9.5	All Other Non-Current				10.1	14.3	8.8
	100.0	100.0	100.0	Total				100.0	100.0	100.0
				LIABILITIES						
	7.4	5.4	6.4	Notes Payable-Short Term				10.5	5.2	5.9
	2.2	2.2	2.2	Cur. Mat.-L.T.D.				1.0	2.3	2.2
	24.6	22.6	20.7	Trade Payables				18.9	11.1	21.9
	.1	.2	.1	Income Taxes Payable				.0	.0	.2
	8.0	9.0	9.4	All Other Current				1.4	5.2	9.1
	42.3	39.4	38.9	Total Current				31.8	23.8	39.3
	12.3	13.3	12.1	Long-Term Debt				7.8	18.8	10.8
	.6	.6	.4	Deferred Taxes				.0	.7	.5
	3.5	4.0	4.1	All Other Non-Current				2.2	4.4	4.1
	41.2	42.6	44.5	Net Worth				58.2	52.2	45.4
	100.0	100.0	100.0	Total Liabilities & Net Worth				100.0	100.0	100.0
				INCOME DATA						
	100.0	100.0	100.0	Net Sales				100.0	100.0	100.0
	13.4	12.3	14.2	Gross Profit				22.2	22.0	10.6
	11.3	9.9	11.9	Operating Expenses				15.1	17.7	8.6
	2.0	2.4	2.3	Operating Profit				7.1	4.3	2.0
	-.8	-.4	-.2	All Other Expenses (net)				-.3	.0	-.3
	2.8	2.7	2.5	Profit Before Taxes				7.4	4.3	2.2
				RATIOS						
	2.0	2.4	2.5					4.6	3.5	2.3
	1.4	1.5	1.5	Current				2.3	2.6	1.5
	1.1	1.2	1.1					1.4	1.5	1.1
	1.6	1.8	1.7					2.7	3.0	1.6
	1.0	1.2	1.1	Quick				1.5	1.7	1.1
	.7	.8	.7					.8	.6	.7
10	35.1	8	45.7	8	45.0			4	104.1	3	104.3	9	40.0
20	17.9	17	21.7	16	22.8	Sales/Receivables			27	13.7	17	20.9	16	23.4
33	11.0	26	13.8	26	13.8			40	9.1	24	15.2	26	13.9
2	172.6	1	393.6	1	259.8			0	UND	0	UND	1	257.6
7	49.6	6	65.0	7	54.7	Cost of Sales/Inventory			17	21.8	4	92.1	7	54.7
19	19.5	15	23.7	18	20.7			30	12.1	17	21.1	16	22.3
11	34.6	7	49.8	8	46.6			7	49.3	6	60.1	8	46.3
16	23.0	11	32.7	11	32.1	Cost of Sales/Payables			16	22.9	10	36.9	11	32.2
28	13.2	20	18.1	18	20.0			40	9.1	17	21.3	18	20.7
	13.6		14.8		13.8				4.8		9.3		15.6
	34.0		33.5		32.1	Sales/Working Capital				10.9		16.4		36.7
	274.0		91.4		140.6				48.5		24.3		147.2
	34.3		29.9		31.2				84.5		45.5		31.2
(238)	14.1	(258)	13.8	(301)	8.7	EBIT/Interest		(10)	28.0	(19)	3.7	(257)	9.7
	5.2		6.5		3.4				1.8		1.0		4.0
	8.0		11.3		14.2	Net Profit + Depr., Dep.,							15.0
(47)	5.2	(65)	5.3	(66)	6.2	Amort./Cur. Mat. L/T/D						(62)	6.2
	2.5		3.0		3.4								3.2
	.2		.1		.2				.0		.0		.2
	.6		.6		.6	Fixed/Worth				.1		.4		.7
	1.3		1.2		1.3				.7		1.5		1.2
	.9		.7		.6				.2		.3		.6
	1.6		1.5		1.4	Debt/Worth				1.0		.7		1.4
	3.2		2.7		2.9				1.9		3.4		2.7
	46.2		48.9		37.3				47.7		51.8		35.7
(264)	27.4	(283)	28.3	(326)	24.4	% Profit Before Taxes/Tangible Net Worth		(12)	34.0	(22)	24.2	(278)	24.6
	13.5		16.0		13.0				15.0		2.4		13.8
	16.4		19.1		16.6				33.6		25.6		16.2
	10.0		11.5		9.5	% Profit Before Taxes/Total Assets			19.6		7.4		9.5
	4.7		5.5		4.3				6.3		.9		4.6
	89.3		187.7		91.2				UND		79.6		90.5
	23.7		36.0		27.7	Sales/Net Fixed Assets			50.6		21.0		27.0
	10.4		13.3		11.1				39.3		6.3		11.5
	7.5		9.7		8.8				6.6		5.4		9.4
	5.2		6.2		5.7	Sales/Total Assets			4.2		3.7		6.2
	3.1		3.8		3.8				1.4		2.2		4.3
	.4		.3		.3						.9		.2
(220)	.9	(238)	.7	(276)	.7	% Depr., Dep., Amort./Sales				(15)	1.3	(240)	.7
	1.6		1.2		1.3						1.7		1.2
	.2		.2		.1						.8		.1
(75)		(80)	.5	(88)	.5	% Officers', Directors', Owners' Comp/Sales				(14)	1.7	(61)	.2
	2.3		1.3		2.0						2.3		.6
	63060797M		79100855M		102878062M	Net Sales ($)		794M	18827M	33181M	98236M	371555M	102355469M
	11978999M		12515434M		15978450M	Total Assets ($)		2076M	8161M	19272M	36547M	131572M	15780822M

© RMA 2024   M = $ thousand   MM = $ million
See Pages viii through xx for Explanation of Ratios and Data

WHOLESALE—Beer and Ale Merchant Wholesalers NAICS 424810

Current Data Sorted by Assets | Comparative Historical Data

	0-500M	500M-2MM	2-10MM	10-50MM	50-100MM	100-250MM	Type of Statement	4/1/19-3/31/20 ALL	4/1/20-3/31/21 ALL
			1	16	16	13	Unqualified	61	21
			4	19	7	1	Reviewed	36	23
		3	8	3	1		Compiled	24	17
		3	8				Tax Returns	30	12
		1	10	38	27	20	Other	161	74
	33 (4/1-9/30/23)			166 (10/1/23-3/31/24)					
	7		31	76	51	34	NUMBER OF STATEMENTS	312	147
	%	%	%	%	%	%	ASSETS	%	%
			17.9	12.1	8.0	5.4	Cash & Equivalents	8.7	14.9
D			7.3	6.8	6.1	3.4	Trade Receivables (net)	7.2	8.6
A			32.1	18.3	15.1	9.1	Inventory	20.7	20.1
T			4.2	4.2	1.7	1.8	All Other Current	2.2	2.2
A			61.4	41.4	30.9	19.7	Total Current	38.7	45.9
			14.5	14.8	15.3	13.6	Fixed Assets (net)	17.4	14.4
N			14.9	31.9	42.0	55.4	Intangibles (net)	36.0	31.8
O			9.1	11.8	11.9	11.3	All Other Non-Current	7.9	7.9
T			100.0	100.0	100.0	100.0	Total	100.0	100.0
A							LIABILITIES		
V			4.0	2.8	3.8	1.3	Notes Payable-Short Term	4.5	4.0
A			2.4	2.2	2.6	1.7	Cur. Mat.-L.T.D.	2.9	2.7
I			13.1	8.3	7.2	5.2	Trade Payables	9.1	9.3
L			.3	.1	.1	.2	Income Taxes Payable	.1	.1
A			11.7	8.4	6.1	3.3	All Other Current	9.7	11.5
B			31.6	21.9	19.8	11.6	Total Current	26.2	27.6
L			16.2	14.4	20.0	30.1	Long-Term Debt	26.3	23.7
E			.0	.2	.4	.3	Deferred Taxes	.3	.1
			.9	5.7	6.3	5.4	All Other Non-Current	4.8	6.8
			51.4	57.7	53.5	52.6	Net Worth	42.3	41.8
			100.0	100.0	100.0	100.0	Total Liabilities & Net Worth	100.0	100.0
							INCOME DATA		
			100.0	100.0	100.0	100.0	Net Sales	100.0	100.0
			29.3	27.1	27.1	27.3	Gross Profit	27.3	26.8
			25.4	22.6	22.4	20.2	Operating Expenses	22.8	21.6
			3.9	4.6	4.7	7.1	Operating Profit	4.5	5.2
			.0	.2	.1	.3	All Other Expenses (net)	.5	-.2
			4.0	4.4	4.6	6.7	Profit Before Taxes	3.9	5.4
							RATIOS		
			4.0	3.4	2.6	2.1		2.8	3.5
			2.0	2.1	1.7	1.5	Current	1.8	1.9
			1.4	1.2	1.2	1.3		1.2	1.2
			1.6	1.3	1.2	1.2		1.2	2.0
			.6	.8	.6	.4	Quick	.6	.9
			.4	.4	.3	.3		.3	.5
		1	249.1	3 137.0	3 114.0	4 86.1		3 132.3	2 178.4
		4	96.2	5 68.0	6 56.6	6 65.1	Sales/Receivables	5 69.2	5 79.1
		12	30.7	12 30.0	21 17.3	7 55.7		16 22.3	19 19.6
		32	11.5	27 13.3	28 13.1	21 17.1		27 13.7	23 16.2
		37	9.8	34 10.6	34 10.8	28 13.1	Cost of Sales/Inventory	33 11.2	28 13.1
		48	7.6	42 8.7	41 8.9	39 9.4		39 9.4	35 10.3
		9	40.1	9 42.1	10 37.6	12 31.6		9 39.1	7 51.9
		16	22.4	14 26.2	18 20.8	19 19.7	Cost of Sales/Payables	15 24.8	13 27.9
		25	14.6	22 16.9	25 14.7	23 16.0		20 18.6	19 19.3
			7.1	8.4	10.9	16.5		11.5	7.9
			14.2	14.4	20.6	23.4	Sales/Working Capital	21.4	15.5
			32.5	45.2	75.8	41.7		70.7	50.0
			16.2	32.1	51.4	18.1		18.1	30.3
		(23)	10.5	(66) 10.1	(45) 5.9	(33) 5.6	EBIT/Interest	(277) 7.0	(123) 12.7
			2.5	3.9	2.4	3.8		3.4	5.5
				10.0	24.0			6.1	14.5
			(15) 2.8	(12) 5.9		Net Profit + Depr., Dep., Amort./Cur. Mat. L/T/D	(34) 2.8	(20) 4.8
				1.2	1.7			1.3	2.9
			.1	.2	.4	.6		.3	.2
			.4	.5	1.9	-4.5	Fixed/Worth	1.6	.8
			2.1	3.9	-.4	-.3		-.6	-.9
			.3	.3	.8	2.6		.8	.6
			1.1	1.1	6.2	-13.9	Debt/Worth	3.9	2.0
			8.0	8.2	-2.5	-2.2		-3.0	-3.9
			106.1	59.5	85.9	129.4	% Profit Before Taxes/Tangible Net Worth	64.2	70.5
		(27)	40.4	(60) 24.8	(33) 36.9	(14) 38.6		(184) 34.0	(94) 38.7
			6.9	14.5	21.0	32.0		18.0	22.3
			28.8	15.1	15.2	13.5		16.0	20.6
			16.1	10.3	8.8	8.6	% Profit Before Taxes/Total Assets	9.1	14.0
			1.2	4.6	3.0	6.4		4.7	8.3
			94.8	47.1	31.6	24.4		46.2	68.2
			38.7	21.4	16.0	12.3	Sales/Net Fixed Assets	21.6	25.4
			18.2	12.8	9.6	8.6		9.2	12.2
			5.3	3.2	2.7	1.8		3.6	4.0
			3.9	2.5	1.9	1.4	Sales/Total Assets	2.4	2.6
			2.4	1.7	1.4	1.1		1.6	1.9
			.7	.7	.7	.6		.8	.7
		(23)	.9	(64) 1.0	(45) 1.0	(31) 1.2	% Depr., Dep., Amort./Sales	(265) 1.1	(118) 1.0
			1.1	1.6	1.6	1.4		1.6	1.4
			1.3	.8				.9	1.0
		(13)	2.2	(15) 1.2			% Officers', Directors' Owners' Comp/Sales	(63) 1.3	(39) 1.7
			3.1	6.3				2.7	3.1
	53085M	654805M	5348493M	7624871M	7268608M		Net Sales ($)	27633883M	12152025M
	10485M	169509M	2094636M	3535934M	5010477M		Total Assets ($)	14067777M	5654747M

M = $ thousand   MM = $ million
See Pages viii through xx for Explanation of Ratios and Data

© RMA 2024

WHOLESALE—Beer and Ale Merchant Wholesalers NAICS 424810

Comparative Historical Data | Current Data Sorted by Sales

						Type of Statement						
	22		43		46	Unqualified					1	45
	17		36		31	Reviewed					5	26
	15		13		15	Compiled			1	2	4	8
	14		11		11	Tax Returns			2	4	3	2
	74		71		96	Other			1	2	10	83
	4/1/21-		4/1/22-		4/1/23-							
	3/31/22		3/31/23		3/31/24		33 (4/1-9/30/23)				166 (10/1/23-3/31/24)	
	ALL		ALL		ALL		0-1MM	1-3MM	3-5MM	5-10MM	10-25MM	25MM & OVER
	142		174		199	NUMBER OF STATEMENTS			4	8	23	164
	%		%		%	ASSETS	%	%	%	%	%	%
	14.4		12.0		11.0	Cash & Equivalents					8.9	10.8
	6.8		6.9		6.1	Trade Receivables (net)					4.4	6.2
	20.7		21.3		18.8	Inventory					28.4	16.7
	2.2		2.3		3.1	All Other Current	DATA NOT AVAILABLE	DATA NOT AVAILABLE			1.6	2.9
	44.1		42.5		38.9	Total Current					43.3	36.6
	18.2		17.4		15.0	Fixed Assets (net)					14.0	14.7
	30.3		30.6		35.0	Intangibles (net)					34.2	36.8
	7.5		9.5		11.1	All Other Non-Current					8.5	11.9
	100.0		100.0		100.0	Total					100.0	100.0
						LIABILITIES						
	2.5		3.7		3.2	Notes Payable-Short Term					7.2	2.7
	2.4		2.2		2.3	Cur. Mat.-L.T.D.					2.4	2.2
	9.3		9.4		8.2	Trade Payables					9.3	8.1
	.1		.1		.1	Income Taxes Payable					.4	.1
	7.0		9.1		7.3	All Other Current					4.8	7.2
	21.3		24.5		21.1	Total Current					24.0	20.3
	25.2		19.4		19.1	Long-Term Debt					15.8	19.6
	.2		.3		.2	Deferred Taxes					.0	.3
	7.5		6.7		5.3	All Other Non-Current					3.9	5.6
	45.8		49.1		54.3	Net Worth					56.3	54.2
	100.0		100.0		100.0	Total Liabilities & Net Worth					100.0	100.0
						INCOME DATA						
	100.0		100.0		100.0	Net Sales					100.0	100.0
	27.7		27.7		27.4	Gross Profit					26.3	27.0
	21.5		22.8		22.6	Operating Expenses					22.3	21.8
	6.2		4.9		4.8	Operating Profit					4.0	5.2
	-.8		-.1		.1	All Other Expenses (net)					.1	.2
	6.9		5.0		4.7	Profit Before Taxes					3.9	5.0
						RATIOS						
	4.4		3.1		3.1						3.5	2.9
	2.1		2.0		1.9	Current					2.0	1.8
	1.4		1.3		1.3						1.3	1.2
	2.0		1.6		1.3						1.1	1.3
	1.0		.7		.6	Quick					.5	.7
	.5		.3		.3						.2	.3
2	166.0	2	155.9	3	134.9						1 354.5	3 115.0
5	77.8	5	79.4	6	65.3	Sales/Receivables					3 132.3	6 63.1
12	29.9	12	29.7	12	29.9						6 59.9	12 29.4
23	15.7	29	12.6	27	13.5						33 11.0	26 13.9
30	12.3	34	10.7	34	10.6	Cost of Sales/Inventory					37 9.9	34 10.8
37	9.9	41	8.9	42	8.7						42 8.6	41 9.0
6	56.3	8	47.9	9	39.5						2 196.0	10 37.1
12	30.6	14	26.6	16	22.8	Cost of Sales/Payables					16 23.3	16 22.7
18	20.3	19	19.5	23	16.0						20 18.2	23 16.1
	8.8		9.4		9.2						11.3	9.6
	15.2		16.0		18.5	Sales/Working Capital					18.5	19.2
	34.7		36.0		42.7						35.0	49.5
	55.0		36.9		32.0						45.0	31.7
(116)	17.9	(148)	13.3	(174)	8.3	EBIT/Interest					(20) 8.9	(143) 8.1
	8.3		6.2		3.5						1.4	3.8
	10.1		10.4		15.3	Net Profit + Depr., Dep.,						15.8
(21)	4.6	(31)	4.8	(39)	4.9	Amort./Cur. Mat. L/T/D						(36) 6.3
	2.8		2.9		2.1							2.0
	.2		.3		.2						.2	.2
	.7		.8		.8	Fixed/Worth					.8	1.0
	-1.7		-5.1		-1.8						9.2	-1.2
	.5		.5		.5						.3	.5
	2.2		2.0		2.5	Debt/Worth					1.8	3.0
	-5.8		-7.9		-8.6						18.1	-4.7
	90.3		84.1		66.3	% Profit Before Taxes/Tangible					106.1	67.6
(98)	53.1	(128)	40.5	(140)	34.8	Net Worth					(19) 40.8	(111) 36.0
	33.4		20.4		16.6						15.8	18.2
	26.6		19.7		16.2	% Profit Before Taxes/Total					19.9	16.1
	16.5		12.1		9.8	Assets					11.0	9.9
	11.1		7.5		4.4						1.2	5.2
	48.2		46.8		46.9						51.7	43.0
	23.3		20.6		20.3	Sales/Net Fixed Assets					22.0	19.9
	9.8		8.5		10.5						12.2	10.5
	4.0		3.6		3.3						5.5	3.1
	2.7		2.4		2.2	Sales/Total Assets					2.9	2.2
	1.9		1.7		1.5						1.6	1.5
	.7		.7		.7						.7	.7
(113)	1.0	(138)	1.0	(169)	1.0	% Depr., Dep., Amort./Sales					(19) 1.0	(140) 1.0
	1.4		1.6		1.5						1.4	1.5
	1.0		.8		.8	% Officers', Directors',					1.0	.8
(33)	1.4	(40)	1.2	(39)	1.5	Owners' Comp/Sales					(10) 2.0	(23) 1.3
	3.0		2.0		3.4						2.9	3.4
	11888999M		15771056M		20949862M	Net Sales ($)			15933M	58538M	398847M	20476544M
	5563827M		7697683M		10821041M	Total Assets ($)			8328M	28988M	200566M	10583159M

M = $ thousand   MM = $ million
See Pages viii through xx for Explanation of Ratios and Data
© RMA 2024

WHOLESALE—Wine and Distilled Alcoholic Beverage Merchant Wholesalers NAICS 424820

Current Data Sorted by Assets | Comparative Historical Data

							Type of Statement		
		1	1	5	7	4	Unqualified	13	11
		1	9	2	2		Reviewed	14	8
		2	2	2	1	1	Compiled	11	7
	1	3	2				Tax Returns	24	4
1	4	20	20	7	8		Other	95	34
	25 (4/1-9/30/23)			77 (10/1/23-3/31/24)				4/1/19-	4/1/20-
0-500M	500M-2MM	2-10MM	10-50MM	50-100MM	100-250MM			3/31/20	3/31/21
								ALL	ALL
1	6	27	38	17	13		NUMBER OF STATEMENTS	157	64
%	%	%	%	%	%		ASSETS	%	%
		11.9	11.0	6.1	6.0		Cash & Equivalents	6.7	12.3
		19.3	21.0	12.0	14.3		Trade Receivables (net)	22.0	19.2
		50.3	40.0	28.4	38.8		Inventory	41.1	37.2
		3.7	3.0	1.5	5.4		All Other Current	4.3	3.1
		85.2	75.0	48.0	64.5		Total Current	74.1	71.8
		8.0	11.5	18.6	11.5		Fixed Assets (net)	10.9	10.7
		2.4	7.1	20.5	18.6		Intangibles (net)	8.3	10.6
		4.4	6.4	12.8	5.4		All Other Non-Current	6.6	6.9
		100.0	100.0	100.0	100.0		Total	100.0	100.0
							LIABILITIES		
		9.2	5.8	8.0	4.7		Notes Payable-Short Term	13.7	8.7
		.9	2.7	5.1	.8		Cur. Mat.-L.T.D.	1.5	1.3
		18.3	24.2	15.8	14.3		Trade Payables	24.5	20.0
		.0	.0	.0	.2		Income Taxes Payable	.1	.1
		7.4	8.7	7.2	13.5		All Other Current	7.9	8.8
		35.8	41.4	36.0	33.5		Total Current	47.7	39.0
		15.9	11.8	15.9	26.0		Long-Term Debt	13.4	13.4
		.0	.1	.2	1.1		Deferred Taxes	.2	.3
		3.4	4.0	6.6	6.0		All Other Non-Current	5.9	6.4
		44.9	42.8	41.3	33.4		Net Worth	32.8	40.9
		100.0	100.0	100.0	100.0		Total Liabilities & Net Worth	100.0	100.0
							INCOME DATA		
		100.0	100.0	100.0	100.0		Net Sales	100.0	100.0
		35.2	29.3	27.6	25.9		Gross Profit	28.9	28.2
		27.5	25.3	25.8	19.5		Operating Expenses	24.2	22.3
		7.7	3.9	1.7	6.5		Operating Profit	4.7	5.9
		1.1	.5	1.3	1.3		All Other Expenses (net)	.6	-.6
		6.7	3.4	.4	5.2		Profit Before Taxes	4.1	6.5
							RATIOS		
		4.4	2.5	2.0	4.6			2.3	3.0
		2.8	1.7	1.5	2.8		Current	1.6	2.2
		1.7	1.4	1.0	1.3			1.2	1.4
		1.6	1.1	.8	1.8			1.0	1.4
		.9	.7	.5	.8		Quick	.6	.9
		.5	.5	.3	.4			.4	.4
	4	103.2	12	29.4	4	96.6	17	21.2		12	31.4	9	42.7
	29	12.7	36	10.2	16	22.4	32	11.5	Sales/Receivables	33	11.2	27	13.6
	58	6.3	48	7.6	28	12.9	41	9.0		46	8.0	42	8.6
	76	4.8	56	6.5	38	9.6	51	7.1		41	8.9	39	9.3
	111	3.3	83	4.4	43	8.5	111	3.3	Cost of Sales/Inventory	74	4.9	65	5.6
	192	1.9	118	3.1	89	4.1	261	1.4		114	3.2	99	3.7
	8	43.0	24	15.4	18	20.6	23	15.9		21	17.5	16	22.3
	41	9.0	47	7.7	23	16.1	35	10.3	Cost of Sales/Payables	34	10.6	31	11.7
	68	5.4	69	5.3	32	11.5	46	7.9		65	5.6	59	6.2
		3.0		5.7		11.3		2.9			5.8		4.4
		4.6		7.6		14.1		5.6	Sales/Working Capital		10.9		8.2
		7.8		11.6		-166.8		25.4			28.7		24.3
		22.7		21.9		31.4		8.9			15.4		37.1
	(26)	8.6	(30)	7.1	(15)	2.3		3.8	EBIT/Interest	(138)	5.7	(50)	13.7
		2.5		3.0		-1.3		1.8			2.2		4.6
									Net Profit + Depr., Dep.,		17.6		
									Amort./Cur. Mat. L/T/D	(24)	3.4		
											2.2		
		.0		.0		.1		.3			.0		.0
		.1		.1		1.0		.9	Fixed/Worth		.2		.2
		.4		.7		-5.0		NM			.7		.7
		.6		.9		1.0		1.4			1.0		.8
		1.4		1.6		2.2		6.4	Debt/Worth		2.1		1.8
		2.6		2.3		-63.7		NM			8.2		6.1
		52.1		42.1		44.5		68.3	% Profit Before Taxes/Tangible		47.8		69.0
	(25)	23.4	(34)	20.7	(12)	17.2	(10)	35.1	Net Worth	(134)	25.2	(55)	40.0
		13.9		9.7		7.3		7.5			10.7		23.7
		15.2		17.5		12.4		12.2	% Profit Before Taxes/Total		16.8		23.5
		12.5		8.0		2.7		5.6	Assets		7.2		12.3
		5.3		3.7		-4.7		2.5			2.1		6.4
		369.1		157.7		91.7		141.9			244.0		217.9
		78.4		53.7		21.2		21.5	Sales/Net Fixed Assets		69.0		57.2
		28.8		19.7		6.8		8.0			17.7		13.9
		2.9		3.2		3.2		2.0			3.4		3.4
		2.4		2.8		2.1		1.6	Sales/Total Assets		2.6		2.6
		1.7		1.8		1.6		.9			1.8		1.6
		.1		.2		.5		.2			.2		.2
	(12)	.3	(28)	.5	(16)	.7	(12)	.6	% Depr., Dep., Amort./Sales	(109)	.5	(45)	.5
		.7		1.0		1.4		1.1			1.0		1.5
											1.0		1.3
									% Officers', Directors'	(36)	2.1	(18)	2.1
									Owners' Comp/Sales		4.3		3.7
456M	18295M	392566M	2476696M	2919791M	4170671M		Net Sales ($)	30824641M	5405270M
430M	6053M	150031M	1009546M	1224304M	2372800M		Total Assets ($)	6970381M	2451420M

© RMA 2024   M = $ thousand   MM = $ million
See Pages viii through xx for Explanation of Ratios and Data

WHOLESALE—Wine and Distilled Alcoholic Beverage Merchant Wholesalers NAICS 424820

Comparative Historical Data | Current Data Sorted by Sales

Comparative Historical Data					Current Data Sorted by Sales						
				Type of Statement							
11		14		18	Unqualified		1			1	16
9		12		12	Reviewed					1	11
3		9		6	Compiled			2		2	4
7		14		6	Tax Returns				1	1	2
37		63		60	Other	3	1	4	6	11	35
4/1/21-3/31/22		4/1/22-3/31/23		4/1/23-3/31/24		25 (4/1-9/30/23)				77 (10/1/23-3/31/24)	
ALL		ALL		ALL		0-1MM	1-3MM	3-5MM	5-10MM	10-25MM	25MM & OVER
67		112		102	**NUMBER OF STATEMENTS**	3	2	5	8	16	68
%		%		%	**ASSETS**	%	%	%	%	%	%
10.9		10.0		10.5	Cash & Equivalents					17.7	8.8
17.8		20.9		17.7	Trade Receivables (net)					19.2	17.9
37.2		42.8		39.2	Inventory					40.3	38.2
3.0		2.9		3.2	All Other Current					5.5	3.1
68.9		76.7		70.7	Total Current					82.7	68.1
12.7		10.1		13.2	Fixed Assets (net)					12.8	11.7
10.6		5.6		9.3	Intangibles (net)					1.2	12.7
7.8		7.6		6.9	All Other Non-Current					3.3	7.6
100.0		100.0		100.0	Total					100.0	100.0
				LIABILITIES							
7.7		8.6		7.0	Notes Payable-Short Term					7.6	6.3
1.5		1.8		2.3	Cur. Mat.-L.T.D.					.6	3.0
18.1		20.8		20.1	Trade Payables					19.0	20.4
.2		.0		.0	Income Taxes Payable					.0	.0
8.4		7.8		8.4	All Other Current					10.9	8.0
35.8		39.2		37.8	Total Current					38.1	37.8
11.7		15.3		16.3	Long-Term Debt					11.2	16.2
.3		.1		.2	Deferred Taxes					.0	.3
5.1		6.1		4.5	All Other Non-Current					5.3	4.8
47.1		39.3		41.2	Net Worth					45.4	40.8
100.0		100.0		100.0	Total Liabilities & Net Worth					100.0	100.0
				INCOME DATA							
100.0		100.0		100.0	Net Sales					100.0	100.0
31.1		29.6		31.2	Gross Profit					30.5	27.2
23.2		24.2		26.2	Operating Expenses					25.6	23.2
7.9		5.3		5.0	Operating Profit					4.9	4.0
-.2		.7		.9	All Other Expenses (net)					.4	.6
8.1		4.6		4.1	Profit Before Taxes					4.5	3.5
				RATIOS							
	2.8		3.4		3.2	Current					4.4	2.8
	2.1		2.0		1.9						2.6	1.8
	1.5		1.4		1.4						1.6	1.4
	1.3		1.3		1.2	Quick					1.9	1.1
	.8		.8		.7						1.1	.7
	.6		.5		.5						.6	.4
6	58.4	7	53.5	9	41.3	Sales/Receivables				2	165.8	11	32.8
26	14.3	33	10.9	27	13.6					14	26.1	27	13.6
41	9.0	51	7.2	46	8.0					54	6.7	42	8.7
40	9.1	46	8.0	44	8.3	Cost of Sales/Inventory				59	6.2	43	8.5
62	5.9	87	4.2	85	4.3					89	4.1	72	5.1
111	3.3	135	2.7	140	2.6					118	3.1	114	3.2
20	18.6	20	18.7	21	17.7	Cost of Sales/Payables				15	24.7	21	17.7
30	12.1	35	10.4	36	10.0					39	9.3	30	12.2
52	7.0	62	5.9	64	5.7					62	5.9	61	6.0
	4.5		4.2		4.1	Sales/Working Capital					4.1	5.8
	8.5		7.1		7.5						5.8	8.7
	16.1		16.5		15.7						12.1	16.7
	79.4		39.8		21.7	EBIT/Interest					41.3	20.7
(61)	23.8	(102)	12.1	(88)	5.5					(14)	13.6	(60)	4.6
	8.8		3.6		1.8						4.7	1.8
	24.6		35.2		6.5	Net Profit + Depr., Dep., Amort./Cur. Mat. L/T/D						6.5
(15)	8.5	(23)	5.2	(17)	3.4						(17)	3.4
	4.1		1.8		1.7							1.7
	.0		.0		.1	Fixed/Worth					.0	.1
	.2		.1		.3						.1	.3
	.7		.5		1.0						.5	1.1
	.6		.7		.9	Debt/Worth					.6	1.0
	1.3		1.9		1.7						1.5	1.7
	2.7		4.1		4.2						2.1	8.5
	63.6		50.8		43.4	% Profit Before Taxes/Tangible Net Worth					35.6	43.3
(58)	37.1	(100)	25.3	(87)	20.8					(15)	18.4	(56)	22.2
	16.5		9.1		11.0						13.1	10.1
	23.3		21.0		15.9	% Profit Before Taxes/Total Assets					14.6	16.1
	16.2		10.6		7.2						10.8	6.8
	7.7		2.1		2.2						5.6	2.2
	152.1		406.8		156.8	Sales/Net Fixed Assets					517.8	145.7
	37.4		74.4		39.4						72.2	38.7
	11.3		16.7		11.5						12.5	12.9
	3.3		3.2		3.1	Sales/Total Assets					2.9	3.2
	2.5		2.4		2.3						2.4	2.4
	1.5		1.6		1.6						2.0	1.7
	.4		.2		.2	% Depr., Dep., Amort./Sales						.2
(47)	.8	(73)	.5	(72)	.6						(56)	.6
	1.1		1.0		1.1							1.1
	.6		.5		.7	% Officers', Directors', Owners' Comp/Sales						.7
(13)	2.0	(27)	2.1	(17)	1.7						(12)	1.7
	4.3		3.0		3.2							2.3
6482938M		9731019M		9978475M	Net Sales ($)	1725M	2843M	19496M	53029M	259026M	9642356M
2540663M		3672383M		4763164M	Total Assets ($)	3879M	1283M	36881M	28146M	126512M	4566463M

M = $ thousand   MM = $ million

© RMA 2024

See Pages viii through xx for Explanation of Ratios and Data

WHOLESALE—Farm Supplies Merchant Wholesalers NAICS 424910

Current Data Sorted by Assets

		3	11	7	5	Type of Statement		
	2	3	12	2	1	Unqualified	48	20
	1	11	5			Reviewed	39	15
	6	5	4			Compiled	23	11
1	9	19	26	12	13	Tax Returns	45	19
						Other	100	52

0-500M	500M-2MM	2-10MM	10-50MM	50-100MM	100-250MM		4/1/19-3/31/20 ALL	4/1/20-3/31/21 ALL
1	52 (4/1-9/30/23)	41	106 (10/1/23-3/31/24) 58	21	19	NUMBER OF STATEMENTS	255	117
%	18 %	%	%	%	%	ASSETS	%	%
	10.8	10.7	8.5	6.8	5.4	Cash & Equivalents	8.3	10.1
	19.1	27.6	19.9	20.6	19.4	Trade Receivables (net)	21.1	19.1
	27.9	37.4	36.9	35.7	32.6	Inventory	37.7	37.5
	.2	2.2	3.1	4.2	7.7	All Other Current	4.5	3.2
	58.0	78.0	68.4	67.2	65.1	Total Current	71.6	69.9
	27.8	14.0	21.9	19.1	21.2	Fixed Assets (net)	18.5	19.7
	2.3	1.4	2.3	5.7	1.2	Intangibles (net)	3.9	4.3
	12.0	6.6	7.4	8.1	12.5	All Other Non-Current	6.0	6.1
	100.0	100.0	100.0	100.0	100.0	Total	100.0	100.0
						LIABILITIES		
	7.1	12.0	10.6	12.7	8.8	Notes Payable-Short Term	14.9	11.2
	2.1	2.2	1.6	2.8	2.2	Cur. Mat.-L.T.D.	1.8	2.4
	12.0	22.1	17.0	14.1	15.5	Trade Payables	17.3	16.5
	.1	.0	.1	.2	.4	Income Taxes Payable	.1	.1
	7.8	7.7	12.0	16.2	13.0	All Other Current	11.3	8.7
	29.1	44.1	41.4	45.9	39.9	Total Current	45.3	38.9
	35.5	8.6	9.2	7.7	7.6	Long-Term Debt	9.0	12.2
	.1	.2	.5	.9	.3	Deferred Taxes	.4	.4
	1.5	1.6	3.4	5.1	6.5	All Other Non-Current	5.6	5.3
	33.8	45.4	45.5	40.4	45.8	Net Worth	39.7	43.2
	100.0	100.0	100.0	100.0	100.0	Total Liabilities & Net Worth	100.0	100.0
						INCOME DATA		
	100.0	100.0	100.0	100.0	100.0	Net Sales	100.0	100.0
	30.0	23.7	21.6	22.2	17.5	Gross Profit	23.3	25.0
	21.3	20.6	16.5	18.8	13.3	Operating Expenses	20.6	21.4
	8.7	3.1	5.0	3.4	4.2	Operating Profit	2.6	3.6
	.9	.3	-.3	.8	-.2	All Other Expenses (net)	.0	-.3
	7.8	2.8	5.3	2.6	4.4	Profit Before Taxes	2.7	3.9
						RATIOS		
	2.8	3.0	2.8	2.4	2.6		2.3	2.8
	2.3	1.9	1.5	1.6	1.8	Current	1.5	1.8
	1.6	1.4	1.2	1.1	1.2		1.2	1.3
	1.8	1.6	1.4	1.0	1.0		1.2	1.4
	1.3	1.0	.6	.6	.6	Quick	.6	.7
	.6	.3	.3	.3	.5		.3	.3
	0 UND	14 26.1	13 27.5	17 21.3	21 17.2		15 24.7	13 28.2
	19 18.9	23 15.7	26 13.9	35 10.3	32 11.5	Sales/Receivables	28 12.9	29 12.7
	41 8.8	44 8.3	46 7.9	46 7.9	48 7.6		51 7.1	47 7.8
	6 56.4	21 17.0	43 8.5	41 9.0	34 10.8		42 8.6	48 7.6
	32 11.3	69 5.3	85 4.3	101 3.6	63 5.8	Cost of Sales/Inventory	81 4.5	85 4.3
	87 4.2	135 2.7	166 2.2	130 2.8	111 3.3		159 2.3	146 2.5
	0 UND	13 27.2	15 25.1	22 16.3	17 21.4		12 31.1	11 33.6
	11 34.3	26 13.8	28 13.8	31 11.6	23 16.0	Cost of Sales/Payables	28 13.0	32 11.5
	56 6.5	53 6.9	47 7.8	47 7.7	43 8.4		56 6.5	55 6.6
	7.7	4.8	4.7	6.3	6.0		4.4	4.8
	9.9	8.8	8.8	9.1	9.2	Sales/Working Capital	9.1	7.9
	27.3	17.2	19.8	62.3	18.3		20.6	15.4
	11.5	16.1	25.0	20.7	12.2		10.9	19.5
	(15) 4.8	(34) 3.5	(54) 5.2	(20) 3.4	5.1	EBIT/Interest	(230) 4.3	(106) 6.5
	1.4	1.2	2.1	1.6	2.6		1.4	2.4
			13.2			Net Profit + Depr., Dep.,	6.7	9.0
		(13) 4.8				Amort./Cur. Mat. L/T/D	(50) 3.7 (18) 4.3	
			3.3				1.6	2.9
	.2	.0	.2	.2	.3		.2	.1
	.7	.1	.5	.4	.4	Fixed/Worth	.4	.5
	-740.4	.6	.8	7.9	.7		.8	.8
	.5	.7	.6	.7	.4		.7	.6
	1.0	1.1	1.2	1.2	1.3	Debt/Worth	1.6	1.4
	-752.6	2.4	2.6	22.3	3.2		3.8	3.4
	50.1	39.1	28.1	25.1	24.9	% Profit Before Taxes/Tangible	27.2	37.8
(13)	29.4	(38) 13.2	(55) 13.8	(17) 13.8	17.6	Net Worth	(235) 13.1 (108) 16.9	
	5.8	5.4	7.2	9.1	9.8		4.0	7.3
	26.8	21.3	12.9	11.9	13.5		10.1	13.2
	16.3	5.9	7.0	5.3	7.0	% Profit Before Taxes/Total Assets	4.6	7.2
	2.4	1.0	3.1	2.2	4.1		1.0	2.7
	156.2	748.0	41.0	18.6	24.1		53.6	66.0
	24.9	66.8	9.9	13.3	9.8	Sales/Net Fixed Assets	13.9	13.8
	4.8	11.8	5.2	7.3	6.4		6.3	5.7
	4.8	3.6	2.7	2.7	3.1		2.9	2.8
	2.9	2.5	1.9	2.0	2.0	Sales/Total Assets	2.0	1.9
	1.6	1.9	1.3	1.5	1.5		1.3	1.5
	.5	.3	.6	.9	.9		.7	.6
(11)	.9	(23) 1.4	(51) 1.3	(20) 1.5	(17) 1.1	% Depr., Dep., Amort./Sales	(199) 1.4 (91) 1.5	
	2.7	3.9	2.3	1.8	1.5		2.4	2.7
			.5				.8	.9
		(20) 1.0				% Officers', Directors' Owners' Comp/Sales	(65) 1.7 (31) 1.1	
			2.3				3.2	3.4
1601M	78076M	876259M	3375672M	3384059M	6663044M	Net Sales ($)	14004619M	6911458M
278M	22599M	205906M	1539439M	1488744M	2883789M	Total Assets ($)	7645690M	3755009M

M = $ thousand MM = $ million
See Pages viii through xx for Explanation of Ratios and Data

© RMA 2024

WHOLESALE—Farm Supplies Merchant Wholesalers NAICS 424910

Comparative Historical Data / Current Data Sorted by Sales

						Type of Statement						
		25		31	26	Unqualified				2	4	20
		14		27	20	Reviewed			1	3	4	12
		10		23	17	Compiled				5	4	7
		25		25	15	Tax Returns		1	2	3	5	3
		68		77	80	Other		2	2	10	11	49
		4/1/21-3/31/22 ALL		4/1/22-3/31/23 ALL	4/1/23-3/31/24 ALL		1	5	4			
							0-1MM	52 (4/1-9/30/23) 1-3MM	3-5MM	106 (10/1/23-3/31/24) 5-10MM	10-25MM	25MM & OVER
		142		183	158	NUMBER OF STATEMENTS	1	8	7	23	28	91
		%		%	%	ASSETS	%	%	%	%	%	%
		10.4		10.9	8.7	Cash & Equivalents				9.7	10.0	7.8
		21.1		20.4	21.9	Trade Receivables (net)				23.4	20.6	22.8
		33.8		38.7	35.4	Inventory				38.8	42.6	33.9
		3.4		3.4	3.2	All Other Current				2.5	1.7	4.4
		68.7		73.4	69.2	Total Current				74.4	74.9	68.9
		20.1		17.4	19.9	Fixed Assets (net)				18.9	15.5	19.5
		3.7		2.7	2.4	Intangibles (net)				1.6	1.3	3.0
		7.5		6.5	8.5	All Other Non-Current				5.1	8.3	8.6
		100.0		100.0	100.0	Total				100.0	100.0	100.0
						LIABILITIES						
		14.2		12.0	10.8	Notes Payable-Short Term				13.2	12.5	10.3
		2.3		2.6	2.0	Cur. Mat.-L.T.D.				3.4	2.1	1.9
		15.9		15.5	17.3	Trade Payables				16.3	19.6	17.7
		.0		.2	.1	Income Taxes Payable				.1	.0	.2
		8.9		13.5	11.0	All Other Current				7.2	9.5	13.2
		41.4		43.7	41.2	Total Current				40.1	43.7	43.2
		11.4		11.4	11.6	Long-Term Debt				17.5	10.6	7.9
		.3		.3	.4	Deferred Taxes				.1	.5	.5
		4.2		2.8	3.3	All Other Non-Current				2.7	1.3	4.3
		42.7		41.9	43.5	Net Worth				39.5	43.9	44.0
		100.0		100.0	100.0	Total Liabilities & Net Worth				100.0	100.0	100.0
						INCOME DATA						
		100.0		100.0	100.0	Net Sales				100.0	100.0	100.0
		26.2		23.0	22.7	Gross Profit				29.9	23.6	18.7
		21.0		18.6	18.0	Operating Expenses				26.8	18.3	14.8
		5.2		4.4	4.6	Operating Profit				3.1	5.2	3.9
		-.9		-.2	.2	All Other Expenses (net)				.3	.0	.0
		6.2		4.7	4.5	Profit Before Taxes				2.8	5.2	3.9
						RATIOS						
		2.5		2.8	2.7					3.1	2.5	2.8
		1.6		1.7	1.7	Current				1.9	1.9	1.6
		1.2		1.3	1.3					1.3	1.4	1.2
		1.4		1.4	1.4					2.0	1.4	1.2
		.7		.7	.7	Quick				.9	.7	.7
		.4		.4	.3					.4	.2	.4
14	25.7		10	35.5	13	27.3				20	18.4	11	34.0	14	25.5
26	13.8		24	14.9	26	14.0	Sales/Receivables				34	10.8	22	16.9	29	12.7
50	7.3		45	8.2	43	8.4					72	5.1	39	9.4	42	8.6
31	11.7		31	11.8	33	11.1					53	6.9	39	9.3	33	11.1
69	5.3		78	4.7	69	5.3	Cost of Sales/Inventory				101	3.6	78	4.7	62	5.9
130	2.8		152	2.4	126	2.9					228	1.6	166	2.2	114	3.2
14	26.6		12	31.2	14	25.4					14	26.3	15	24.3	14	25.4
27	13.6		22	16.5	25	14.7	Cost of Sales/Payables				31	11.8	28	13.2	23	15.6
45	8.1		39	9.3	50	7.3					68	5.4	57	6.4	43	8.4
		5.1		5.1	5.4					2.8	4.7	6.2
		9.5		8.8	9.1	Sales/Working Capital				5.6	8.9	9.4
		24.2		18.3	19.8					8.8	13.7	25.6
		32.3		27.1	16.4					5.8	16.0	27.4
(122)	10.0		(163)	9.2	(143)	4.3	EBIT/Interest			(18)	2.4	(25)	4.8	(87)	5.1
		3.1		3.0	1.8					.7	1.0	2.4
		25.2		14.6	10.4	Net Profit + Depr., Dep.,						15.7
(20)	7.0		(36)	5.7	(32)	4.0	Amort./Cur. Mat. L/T/D						(19)	4.3
		2.9		2.7	1.8							1.9
		.1		.1	.1					.0	.0	.2
		.4		.4	.4	Fixed/Worth				.3	.2	.4
		.9		.8	.9					1.1	.8	.9
		.5		.7	.6					.7	.7	.6
		1.4		1.3	1.2	Debt/Worth				1.0	1.0	1.3
		3.2		3.3	2.8					5.1	2.4	2.8
		41.8		47.6	31.0	% Profit Before Taxes/Tangible				24.6	34.8	31.8
(129)	19.7		(170)	21.2	(143)	15.4	Net Worth			(21)	6.3	(26)	13.4	(84)	16.6
		7.6		10.0	6.8					.6	4.4	9.4
		15.3		16.4	15.0	% Profit Before Taxes/Total				9.5	18.4	14.4
		8.5		9.4	7.0	Assets				3.2	4.5	7.0
		2.8		2.7	1.9					-.1	.5	3.6
		90.2		120.1	96.6					125.6	134.5	57.3
		15.6		16.5	13.8	Sales/Net Fixed Assets				21.1	28.8	12.8
		5.8		8.4	6.3					4.0	7.4	7.1
		2.9		3.2	3.2					2.6	3.8	3.2
		2.0		2.1	2.1	Sales/Total Assets				1.9	2.4	2.1
		1.4		1.6	1.5					1.1	1.6	1.6
		.6		.5	.6					.5	.7	.4
(104)	1.4		(143)	1.1	(122)	1.3	% Depr., Dep., Amort./Sales			(17)	2.2	(17)	1.5	(80)	1.1
		3.4		2.0	2.1					4.3	2.7	1.7
		.7		.7	.6							.4
(38)	1.4		(49)	1.6	(41)	1.6	% Officers', Directors'					(20)	.6
		3.9		4.9	3.1	Owners' Comp/Sales						2.7
		9481677M		15473139M	14378711M	Net Sales ($)	902M	17431M	26687M	169212M	438656M	13725823M
		4249664M		6794585M	6140755M	Total Assets ($)	1366M	9164M	11476M	140489M	226775M	5751485M

M = $ thousand   MM = $ million
See Pages viii through xx for Explanation of Ratios and Data

© RMA 2024

WHOLESALE—Flower, Nursery Stock, and Florists' Supplies Merchant Wholesalers NAICS 424930

Current Data Sorted by Assets | Comparative Historical Data

						Type of Statement				
						Unqualified				
		1	2			Reviewed		4		1
		7	1			Compiled		13		8
	1	6	1			Tax Returns		5		8
	4	3			1	Other		15		5
3	2	12	12	6	1			36		16
	15 (4/1-9/30/23)		48 (10/1/23-3/31/24)					4/1/19-		4/1/20-
0-500M	500M-2MM	2-10MM	10-50MM	50-100MM	100-250MM			3/31/20		3/31/21
3	7	29	16	6	2	NUMBER OF STATEMENTS		73 ALL		38 ALL
%	%	%	%	%	%	ASSETS		%		%
		22.2	15.7			Cash & Equivalents		14.2		21.4
		19.8	19.5			Trade Receivables (net)		25.0		20.2
		23.7	24.7			Inventory		23.3		22.5
		2.1	2.9			All Other Current		2.9		1.6
		67.8	62.8			Total Current		65.5		65.6
		13.2	20.1			Fixed Assets (net)		21.7		19.1
		6.9	3.3			Intangibles (net)		4.0		8.0
		12.2	13.8			All Other Non-Current		8.8		7.2
		100.0	100.0			Total		100.0		100.0
						LIABILITIES				
		6.7	11.2			Notes Payable-Short Term		9.0		5.6
		2.1	1.2			Cur. Mat.-L.T.D.		2.8		1.6
		13.5	24.6			Trade Payables		18.8		16.0
		.2	.0			Income Taxes Payable		.1		.3
		8.5	6.2			All Other Current		7.8		7.9
		31.0	43.3			Total Current		38.5		31.4
		10.1	12.3			Long-Term Debt		10.3		16.2
		.1	.5			Deferred Taxes		.3		.7
		6.6	8.4			All Other Non-Current		7.1		4.6
		52.2	35.5			Net Worth		43.9		47.0
		100.0	100.0			Total Liabilities & Net Worth		100.0		100.0
						INCOME DATA				
		100.0	100.0			Net Sales		100.0		100.0
		38.1	29.5			Gross Profit		33.7		32.1
		31.0	25.6			Operating Expenses		31.2		27.1
		7.0	3.8			Operating Profit		2.4		5.0
		-.1	.2			All Other Expenses (net)		.5		-.9
		7.1	3.6			Profit Before Taxes		2.0		5.9
						RATIOS				
		3.5	2.4					3.1		4.3
		2.7	1.2			Current		1.6		2.3
		1.4	1.1					1.1		1.3
		2.3	1.0					1.9		2.7
		1.3	.8			Quick		1.0		1.4
		.6	.3					.5		.7
		12 29.5	23 15.9				14	26.9	16	23.0
		22 16.3	33 11.2			Sales/Receivables	29	12.8	27	13.7
		32 11.5	40 9.2				40	9.2	41	9.0
		0 UND	24 14.9				5	74.3	15	25.1
		30 12.2	76 4.8			Cost of Sales/Inventory	23	15.7	41	8.9
		159 2.3	104 3.5				140	2.6	114	3.2
		11 32.9	16 23.1				7	53.8	6	59.8
		23 15.7	46 8.0			Cost of Sales/Payables	24	15.3	26	14.3
		38 9.6	69 5.3				47	7.7	46	8.0
		5.6	6.7					5.0		4.2
		7.6	11.4			Sales/Working Capital		15.7		8.1
		25.5	37.3					71.0		33.4
		52.4	39.9					13.6		43.0
		(24) 7.6	(13) 2.2			EBIT/Interest	(62)	3.4	(35)	11.4
		2.4	.5					1.2		3.7
						Net Profit + Depr., Dep.,		11.6		
						Amort./Cur. Mat. L/T/D	(13)	2.1		
								.3		
		.0	.1					.1		.1
		.2	.6			Fixed/Worth		.6		.4
		.9	1.2					1.2		1.2
		.4	.9					.4		.4
		1.3	2.3			Debt/Worth		1.3		1.2
		1.8	5.2					3.8		3.1
		44.5	60.4					36.7		62.9
	(26) 27.5	(15) 20.8				% Profit Before Taxes/Tangible	(66)	14.7	(36)	28.6
		10.7	2.4			Net Worth		2.4		7.7
		34.2	13.3					14.8		20.0
		14.3	8.0			% Profit Before Taxes/Total		4.8		10.4
		3.8	-.4			Assets		.7		3.2
		181.0	107.4					82.1		87.1
		53.3	13.6			Sales/Net Fixed Assets		24.9		20.9
		13.2	6.7					6.9		7.9
		4.3	2.7					5.0		3.9
		3.1	1.8			Sales/Total Assets		2.6		2.7
		1.9	1.3					1.5		1.7
		.1	.8					.4		.5
	(21) .5	(12) 1.0			% Depr., Dep., Amort./Sales	(55)	.9	(31)	.8
		1.4	3.8					1.6		1.5
		.9						1.2		1.6
	(15) 1.8				% Officers', Directors'	(23)	3.5	(11)	2.5
		2.6				Owners' Comp/Sales		8.1		6.8
2306M	36415M	630517M	680394M	1053058M	973753M	Net Sales ($)		2997521M		1334151M
567M	9784M	156721M	329164M	392014M	249571M	Total Assets ($)		1282481M		563901M

© RMA 2024

M = $ thousand   MM = $ million
See Pages viii through xx for Explanation of Ratios and Data

WHOLESALE—Flower, Nursery Stock, and Florists' Supplies Merchant Wholesalers NAICS 424930

Comparative Historical Data | Current Data Sorted by Sales

				Type of Statement						
1	3	4		Unqualified				1	2	3
6	14	8		Reviewed				3	3	3
4	7	8		Compiled	1		1	3	1	2
5	8	7		Tax Returns	1	1	1	3		2
16	35	36		Other	2	2	1	2	10	19
4/1/21-3/31/22 ALL	4/1/22-3/31/23 ALL	4/1/23-3/31/24 ALL			0-1MM	15 (4/1-9/30/23) 1-3MM	3-5MM	48 (10/1/23-3/31/24) 5-10MM	10-25MM	25MM & OVER
32	67	63		NUMBER OF STATEMENTS	2	4	3	11	14	29
%	%	%		ASSETS	%	%	%	%	%	%
16.0	15.2	20.2		Cash & Equivalents				32.3	19.5	17.0
22.7	18.6	18.5		Trade Receivables (net)				9.8	15.3	25.2
22.0	29.2	23.7		Inventory				36.5	17.0	18.4
5.4	3.9	2.3		All Other Current				.0	3.8	1.7
66.0	66.8	64.6		Total Current				78.6	55.7	62.3
22.8	18.1	15.2		Fixed Assets (net)				10.1	17.0	17.6
4.7	5.7	7.9		Intangibles (net)				6.4	11.3	7.1
6.4	9.3	12.3		All Other Non-Current				4.9	16.0	13.0
100.0	100.0	100.0		Total				100.0	100.0	100.0
				LIABILITIES						
11.4	8.2	6.8		Notes Payable-Short Term				10.2	8.2	6.5
1.7	2.0	1.8		Cur. Mat.-L.T.D.				1.6	3.2	1.3
15.6	16.5	16.1		Trade Payables				7.9	14.2	22.8
.2	.4	.1		Income Taxes Payable				.4	.1	.0
6.6	7.1	7.2		All Other Current				6.8	7.4	7.8
35.5	34.3	32.0		Total Current				26.9	33.0	38.4
22.6	16.5	14.5		Long-Term Debt				10.0	12.9	10.2
.4	.7	.2		Deferred Taxes				.0	.5	.1
5.4	4.2	6.6		All Other Non-Current				5.0	12.0	6.7
36.1	44.3	46.7		Net Worth				58.2	41.6	44.7
100.0	100.0	100.0		Total Liabilities & Net Worth				100.0	100.0	100.0
				INCOME DATA						
100.0	100.0	100.0		Net Sales				100.0	100.0	100.0
32.1	37.1	36.3		Gross Profit				44.8	39.2	28.1
24.7	31.2	30.9		Operating Expenses				38.5	32.9	24.3
7.4	5.9	5.3		Operating Profit				6.3	6.3	3.8
-.4	.0	.1		All Other Expenses (net)				-.7	-.5	.2
7.8	5.8	5.2		Profit Before Taxes				7.0	6.9	3.6
				RATIOS						
4.3	3.5	3.5						6.9	2.7	3.2
2.3	2.1	2.0		Current				3.1	1.9	1.5
1.2	1.4	1.2						1.5	1.1	1.1
2.5	1.9	2.3						2.5	1.6	2.3
1.1	1.0	1.0		Quick				1.7	1.0	.9
.7	.4	.6						.6	.6	.5
8 48.0	8 45.5	10 35.0			0 999.8			11 31.8	15 25.1	
26 14.1	24 15.1	23 15.6		Sales/Receivables	18 20.8			18 20.4	26 13.8	
37 9.8	36 10.1	34 10.7			30 12.3			36 10.1	37 9.8	
16 22.3	10 36.7	12 30.9			17 21.3			0 UND	6 62.0	
42 8.6	68 5.4	33 11.0		Cost of Sales/Inventory	60 6.1			27 13.3	31 11.6	
76 4.8	166 2.2	99 3.7			215 1.7			47 7.7	85 4.3	
10 38.2	14 25.4	12 30.2			7 52.1			11 33.9	14 25.9	
22 16.7	27 13.6	28 13.0		Cost of Sales/Payables	16 22.4			26 14.3	33 11.1	
41 9.0	54 6.8	45 8.1			36 10.0			40 9.2	49 7.4	
	4.8	4.2	5.6					3.9	6.3	7.1
9.0	6.9	7.9		Sales/Working Capital				6.1	12.4	14.5
30.3	21.3	32.4						7.9	178.6	80.5
43.7	43.8	48.9						92.8	50.3	
(27) 17.6	(56) 14.2	(50) 7.6		EBIT/Interest				(13) 15.1	(21) 14.9	
6.4	5.3	2.0						4.2	.5	
	17.6	11.6		Net Profit + Depr., Dep.,						
(19) 6.3	(10) 5.2		Amort./Cur. Mat. L/T/D						
	1.9	1.5								
.1	.1	.1						.0	.1	.1
.4	.4	.4		Fixed/Worth				.1	.7	.6
1.5	1.4	1.2						.4	NM	1.3
.7	.5	.4						.3	.7	.4
1.3	1.3	1.4		Debt/Worth				.5	1.5	2.0
3.5	5.2	5.6						3.6	NM	5.5
74.9	47.1	60.7						62.9	60.9	60.8
(28) 35.3	(61) 23.8	(56) 26.3		% Profit Before Taxes/Tangible Net Worth				28.1	(11) 24.0	(26) 23.5
21.6	15.2	8.7						13.6	3.9	7.5
33.2	20.2	24.4						32.6	30.4	21.3
15.8	11.5	10.5		% Profit Before Taxes/Total Assets				13.7	13.1	8.8
8.5	5.2	2.8						3.6	4.5	.7
131.2	83.5	120.5						267.3	64.8	187.0
26.6	18.2	25.8		Sales/Net Fixed Assets				53.3	22.6	19.8
6.0	7.0	10.4						12.8	12.1	7.2
4.4	3.8	4.3						3.8	4.3	4.4
2.7	2.4	2.6		Sales/Total Assets				2.3	2.6	2.7
1.9	1.5	1.8						1.9	1.3	1.7
.2	.3	.3							.4	.3
(22) .8	(53) 1.2	(43) .9		% Depr., Dep., Amort./Sales				(11) .7	(21) 1.0	
1.8	1.8	1.6							1.6	1.9
.7	.9	1.0		% Officers', Directors' Owners' Comp/Sales						
(10) 1.6	(17) 2.4	(25) 2.1								
3.4	5.7	5.0								
1376058M	3689803M	3376443M		Net Sales ($)	404M	7308M	10208M	87894M	204858M	3065771M
490547M	1529626M	1137821M		Total Assets ($)	172M	8924M	3897M	34243M	92990M	997595M

M = $ thousand   MM = $ million
See Pages viii through xx for Explanation of Ratios and Data

© RMA 2024

WHOLESALE—Tobacco Product and Electronic Cigarette Merchant Wholesalers NAICS 424940

Current Data Sorted by Assets | Comparative Historical Data

0-500M	500M-2MM	2-10MM	10-50MM	50-100MM	100-250MM			4/1/19-3/31/20 ALL		4/1/20-3/31/21 ALL
1	3	3 4 6 8 (4/1-9/30/23)	1 4 2 2 12 56 (10/1/23-3/31/24)	1 1 5	3 4	**Type of Statement** Unqualified Reviewed Compiled Tax Returns Other		9 12 4 10 26		3 8 3 9 25
1	9	19	21	7	7	**NUMBER OF STATEMENTS**		61		48
%	%	%	%	%	%			%		%
						ASSETS				
		21.8	10.1			Cash & Equivalents		12.0		14.9
		25.6	29.9			Trade Receivables (net)		27.6		24.5
		40.9	37.1			Inventory		39.8		41.1
		.2	1.6			All Other Current		1.9		3.3
		88.4	78.8			Total Current		81.3		83.8
		6.2	12.9			Fixed Assets (net)		9.0		8.1
		.1	1.6			Intangibles (net)		1.9		2.6
		5.3	6.7			All Other Non-Current		7.7		5.5
		100.0	100.0			Total		100.0		100.0
						LIABILITIES				
		6.2	17.3			Notes Payable-Short Term		13.7		18.7
		.8	1.9			Cur. Mat.-L.T.D.		1.7		1.9
		19.9	12.8			Trade Payables		14.6		12.9
		.0	.1			Income Taxes Payable		.1		.1
		7.7	5.6			All Other Current		10.6		8.7
		34.6	37.7			Total Current		40.6		42.3
		10.2	5.5			Long-Term Debt		11.1		9.9
		.0	.1			Deferred Taxes		.3		.3
		.7	5.8			All Other Non-Current		3.3		3.0
		54.5	51.0			Net Worth		44.6		44.5
		100.0	100.0			Total Liabilities & Net Worth		100.0		100.0
						INCOME DATA				
		100.0	100.0			Net Sales		100.0		100.0
		8.7	10.1			Gross Profit		12.8		10.6
		6.9	7.7			Operating Expenses		10.4		7.3
		1.9	2.4			Operating Profit		2.3		3.3
		.2	-.4			All Other Expenses (net)		.1		-.1
		1.7	2.8			Profit Before Taxes		2.3		3.4
						RATIOS				
		5.3	3.7					4.1		3.3
		2.7	2.1			Current		1.9		2.0
		1.6	1.4					1.3		1.4
		2.8	1.9					2.0		1.8
		2.2	1.3			Quick		.8		.9
		.8	.6					.6		.5
		5 66.6	8 43.0					5 73.6	7	50.4
		9 41.1	11 32.9			Sales/Receivables		12 30.5	11	33.4
		18 20.4	17 21.9					18 20.7	15	24.5
		9 38.6	9 39.4					12 31.7	11	34.2
		19 19.4	17 21.0			Cost of Sales/Inventory		17 21.8	20	18.1
		42 8.6	41 9.0					37 9.8	38	9.7
		3 120.5	2 162.1					2 150.1	2	151.1
		6 58.5	5 74.4			Cost of Sales/Payables		5 68.9	6	63.8
		15 23.9	13 28.6					10 35.9	13	28.1
		9.9	12.1					11.5		14.3
		18.6	26.3			Sales/Working Capital		21.9		22.8
		38.8	32.0					48.6		41.8
		36.3	34.7					14.9		63.0
	(15)	5.5	5.6			EBIT/Interest	(51)	4.5	(43)	11.1
		1.7	2.7					2.9		4.2
						Net Profit + Depr., Dep., Amort./Cur. Mat. L/T/D				
		.0	.1					.0		.0
		.1	.2			Fixed/Worth		.2		.1
		.2	.6					.4		.3
		.3	.4					.6		.7
		.6	1.1			Debt/Worth		1.3		1.4
		2.4	1.8					2.9		2.2
		33.6	33.7			% Profit Before Taxes/Tangible		34.7		56.5
		25.8	16.1			Net Worth	(60)	18.9	(47)	28.3
		6.1	5.6					7.0		12.5
		19.5	13.3					13.9		20.9
		8.3	8.0			% Profit Before Taxes/Total Assets		6.6		10.7
		4.6	1.9					2.7		4.7
		999.8	442.7					422.2		954.5
		149.4	126.6			Sales/Net Fixed Assets		149.0		185.7
		106.6	24.2					63.5		51.9
		18.0	11.6					10.9		11.2
		8.9	8.6			Sales/Total Assets		8.9		8.2
		5.0	4.3					5.9		5.7
		.0	.1					.1		.1
	(11)	.1	(17) .2			% Depr., Dep., Amort./Sales	(44)	.2	(35)	.2
		.2	.5					.4		.3
		.2						.2		.2
	(11)	.3				% Officers', Directors' Owners' Comp/Sales	(22)	.5	(12)	.5
		.4						.9		1.1
253M	106024M	895095M	3609858M	2686151M	4855653M	Net Sales ($)		11945280M		10834057M
49M	12173M	100444M	466597M	539686M	1076349M	Total Assets ($)		1552735M		1402747M

M = $ thousand   MM = $ million
See Pages viii through xx for Explanation of Ratios and Data

© RMA 2024

WHOLESALE—Tobacco Product and Electronic Cigarette Merchant Wholesalers NAICS 424940

Comparative Historical Data | Current Data Sorted by Sales

						Type of Statement							
		5		4	5	Unqualified							5
		9		11	8	Reviewed							8
		3		5	6	Compiled							6
		5		8	12	Tax Returns			1		3		7
		20		25	33	Other		1	3		1	3	26
		4/1/21-3/31/22 ALL		4/1/22-3/31/23 ALL	4/1/23-3/31/24 ALL		0-1MM	8 (4/1-9/30/23) 1-3MM	3-5MM	56 (10/1/23-3/31/24) 5-10MM	10-25MM	25MM & OVER
		42		53	64	NUMBER OF STATEMENTS	1	4	4		4	3	52
		%		%	%	ASSETS	%	%	%		%	%	%
		10.6		12.8	15.6	Cash & Equivalents							14.5
		22.3		21.3	24.0	Trade Receivables (net)	D						25.1
		46.2		41.9	39.3	Inventory	A						40.4
		3.6		3.1	1.1	All Other Current	T						1.1
		82.8		79.1	79.9	Total Current	A						81.1
		9.8		9.4	8.8	Fixed Assets (net)							9.5
		3.2		2.6	3.5	Intangibles (net)	N						2.4
		4.2		8.9	7.8	All Other Non-Current	O						6.9
		100.0		100.0	100.0	Total	T						100.0
						LIABILITIES	A						
		13.6		12.2	14.0	Notes Payable-Short Term	V						13.1
		.7		.7	1.1	Cur. Mat.-L.T.D.	A						1.3
		12.4		12.6	14.0	Trade Payables	I						14.7
		.1		.0	.0	Income Taxes Payable	L						.0
		11.6		7.3	6.8	All Other Current	A						6.4
		38.4		32.9	36.0	Total Current	B						35.4
		8.4		12.1	10.1	Long-Term Debt	L						11.7
		.2		.3	.1	Deferred Taxes	E						.1
		4.0		3.3	3.8	All Other Non-Current							3.4
		48.9		51.6	49.9	Net Worth							49.4
		100.0		100.0	100.0	Total Liabilties & Net Worth							100.0
						INCOME DATA							
		100.0		100.0	100.0	Net Sales							100.0
		11.5		14.5	13.1	Gross Profit							10.0
		7.9		10.1	10.6	Operating Expenses							7.8
		3.6		4.4	2.5	Operating Profit							2.2
		.0		-.1	.1	All Other Expenses (net)							.3
		3.6		4.5	2.5	Profit Before Taxes							1.9
						RATIOS							
		3.2		5.1	4.8								4.2
		2.1		2.6	2.3	Current							2.3
		1.5		1.6	1.4								1.5
		1.3		2.3	2.6								2.6
		.7		.9	1.0	Quick							1.0
		.5		.5	.5								.6
8	48.1	6	57.7	7	52.5							8	46.7
11	33.2	11	31.8	10	36.5	Sales/Receivables						10	36.4
16	23.0	17	21.7	16	23.4							16	23.4
15	24.5	15	24.1	12	29.4							10	37.2
22	16.3	22	16.7	23	15.8	Cost of Sales/Inventory						21	17.8
39	9.3	61	6.0	47	7.8							42	8.7
3	129.5	2	163.5	3	121.9							3	121.9
6	59.5	6	64.4	6	59.0	Cost of Sales/Payables						6	64.8
11	32.3	24	15.3	13	27.6							11	33.4
		8.4		6.0	8.9								11.5
		20.4		14.4	21.7	Sales/Working Capital							23.8
		34.7		29.8	32.7								31.3
		55.1		40.1	18.2								20.2
(33)	10.8	(44)	12.9	(57)	4.6	EBIT/Interest						(46)	5.0
		4.2		5.1	2.5								2.4
						Net Profit + Depr., Dep., Amort./Cur. Mat. L/T/D							
		.0		.0	.0								.0
		.1		.1	.2	Fixed/Worth							.2
		.3		.5	.5								.5
		.5		.4	.4								.4
		1.4		1.1	1.4	Debt/Worth							1.4
		2.0		2.4	2.5								2.5
		43.0		44.8	32.1								33.8
(40)	25.8	(52)	22.2	(60)	18.2	% Profit Before Taxes/Tangible Net Worth						(50)	20.6
		8.5		11.5	6.5								6.8
		19.3		20.4	15.2								15.1
		9.3		11.3	8.5	% Profit Before Taxes/Total Assets							8.5
		3.6		4.4	2.5								2.4
		547.9		789.0	842.0								534.0
		183.5		135.3	137.7	Sales/Net Fixed Assets							132.7
		47.4		33.1	42.3								42.3
		11.5		9.8	11.2								11.7
		7.8		7.0	6.9	Sales/Total Assets							7.9
		2.7		2.6	3.4								5.1
		.1		.1	.1								.1
(31)	.1	(34)	.2	(44)	.2	% Depr., Dep., Amort./Sales						(38)	.2
		.2		.6	.3								.3
		.2		.2	.2								.1
(11)	.7	(21)	.3	(26)	.4	% Officers', Directors' Owners' Comp/Sales						(20)	.3
		3.4		1.2	1.6								.4
		7593139M		9650812M	12153034M	Net Sales ($)	253M	14870M	22871M		69933M	12045107M
		1084727M		1564184M	2195298M	Total Assets ($)	49M	5133M	7313M		41295M	2141508M

M = $ thousand   MM = $ million
See Pages viii through xx for Explanation of Ratios and Data

© RMA 2024

WHOLESALE—Other Miscellaneous Nondurable Goods Merchant Wholesalers NAICS 424990

Current Data Sorted by Assets | **Comparative Historical Data**

							Type of Statement		
		1	13	4	3		Unqualified	23	14
		10	15	2	1		Reviewed	26	26
	3	13	3		1		Compiled	27	13
3	22	18	8				Tax Returns	83	36
7	24	71	51	18	6		Other	208	125
	44 (4/1-9/30/23)		253 (10/1/23-3/31/24)					4/1/19-3/31/20	4/1/20-3/31/21
0-500M	500M-2MM	2-10MM	10-50MM	50-100MM	100-250MM			ALL	ALL
10	49	113	90	24	11		NUMBER OF STATEMENTS	367	214
%	%	%	%	%	%		ASSETS	%	%
30.7	23.5	15.0	10.2	8.8	4.1		Cash & Equivalents	11.2	15.2
22.7	17.0	27.1	22.0	21.2	19.6		Trade Receivables (net)	27.1	27.5
13.7	30.0	31.6	34.1	41.4	27.9		Inventory	36.1	31.8
6.1	4.9	3.5	5.3	4.1	3.0		All Other Current	3.5	3.3
73.2	75.4	77.3	71.7	75.5	54.6		Total Current	77.9	77.8
13.1	11.1	11.4	13.6	11.4	15.6		Fixed Assets (net)	10.9	11.7
2.6	5.5	4.3	6.2	2.1	10.6		Intangibles (net)	4.7	5.2
11.1	8.0	7.0	8.5	11.0	19.2		All Other Non-Current	6.5	5.3
100.0	100.0	100.0	100.0	100.0	100.0		Total	100.0	100.0
							LIABILITIES		
3.5	6.8	8.1	8.3	14.7	8.6		Notes Payable-Short Term	12.6	10.9
3.4	2.0	1.2	2.5	1.0	1.4		Cur. Mat.-L.T.D.	1.5	1.8
17.2	20.8	19.3	17.8	18.9	11.2		Trade Payables	21.3	19.0
.0	.8	.1	.0	.0	.0		Income Taxes Payable	.1	.3
13.1	14.8	10.5	7.9	10.3	10.5		All Other Current	10.6	11.4
37.1	45.3	39.2	36.5	45.0	31.7		Total Current	46.0	43.4
14.2	19.2	12.8	9.6	5.2	16.9		Long-Term Debt	9.5	12.4
.0	.0	.1	.1	.1	.1		Deferred Taxes	.2	.2
52.7	6.7	2.2	8.5	9.6	9.3		All Other Non-Current	5.5	6.0
-3.2	28.8	45.7	45.2	40.2	42.0		Net Worth	38.8	37.9
100.0	100.0	100.0	100.0	100.0	100.0		Total Liabilities & Net Worth	100.0	100.0
							INCOME DATA		
100.0	100.0	100.0	100.0	100.0	100.0		Net Sales	100.0	100.0
46.6	34.8	29.5	35.0	26.8	22.3		Gross Profit	31.1	32.2
35.1	30.3	23.2	28.2	25.0	21.0		Operating Expenses	25.6	26.3
11.5	4.6	6.4	6.7	1.7	1.3		Operating Profit	5.4	5.9
.4	.3	.6	.8	.5	1.8		All Other Expenses (net)	.4	-.2
11.1	4.2	5.7	5.9	1.2	-.5		Profit Before Taxes	5.1	6.1
							RATIOS		
9.3	6.0	3.9	4.0	3.9	2.5			3.2	3.9
2.6	1.9	2.2	2.1	1.7	1.7		Current	1.9	1.9
.8	1.0	1.5	1.3	1.1	1.4			1.3	1.3
8.2	2.2	2.3	1.7	1.6	.9			1.5	2.0
1.4	.9	1.2	.8	.6	.8		Quick	.9	1.1
.5	.5	.7	.5	.4	.4			.5	.6
0 UND	1 538.8	20 18.1	26 14.1	23 15.6	12 29.6			20 18.6	22 16.9
9 39.4	12 30.9	34 10.7	41 8.8	39 9.4	33 11.1		Sales/Receivables	35 10.4	36 10.2
31 11.8	27 13.3	54 6.8	51 7.2	52 7.0	46 8.0			51 7.1	56 6.5
0 UND	9 41.5	19 18.9	46 8.0	74 4.9	22 16.5			34 10.6	27 13.5
6 59.9	38 9.5	59 6.2	99 3.7	118 3.1	41 9.0		Cost of Sales/Inventory	68 5.4	62 5.9
62 5.9	91 4.0	101 3.6	192 1.9	166 2.2	174 2.1			122 3.0	126 2.9
0 UND	6 58.5	16 22.2	16 22.2	27 13.7	17 21.6			12 29.3	15 24.9
0 UND	21 17.6	27 13.4	36 10.1	44 8.3	26 14.3		Cost of Sales/Payables	31 11.7	31 11.8
30 12.0	52 7.0	55 6.6	66 5.5	60 6.1	45 8.1			55 6.6	56 6.5
7.1	5.7	4.2	3.2	2.3	4.5			4.5	3.9
23.0	10.7	6.7	4.7	9.1	11.7		Sales/Working Capital	8.4	7.3
-114.5	NM	12.6	13.8	20.1	15.1			21.2	16.2
	23.7	28.4	14.3	4.4	16.6			22.5	45.1
(31)	7.3 (92)	6.0 (79)	5.4 (19)	2.4 (10)	1.4		EBIT/Interest	(294) 6.2 (176)	10.2
	.9	2.3	1.9	.3	-.2			2.7	2.2
			7.5	10.7				22.6	32.4
		(23)	5.2 (10)	5.3			Net Profit + Depr., Dep., Amort./Cur. Mat. L/T/D	(41) 7.2 (17)	10.6
			.8	1.7				2.6	2.3
.0	.0	.0	.1	.1	.1			.0	.0
.0	.1	.1	.4	.2	.9		Fixed/Worth	.1	.2
.8	1.3	.4	.8	.6	4.3			.6	.8
.2	.5	.4	.5	.5	.7			.6	.6
1.5	2.0	1.2	1.7	2.1	2.1		Debt/Worth	1.7	1.6
NM	18.8	3.0	4.5	5.8	35.0			5.0	3.8
	102.0	56.5	52.6	25.5				52.0	60.7
(40)	32.8 (105)	29.0 (83)	23.0	4.6		% Profit Before Taxes/Tangible Net Worth	(327) 25.8 (189)	32.1
	18.2	10.7	6.5	-7.1				10.0	10.6
104.5	25.5	23.9	18.4	9.6	9.5			19.0	26.5
67.3	14.1	11.6	9.5	1.9	1.8		% Profit Before Taxes/Total Assets	9.2	11.8
25.2	2.9	3.9	1.5	-1.9	-4.0			3.4	2.6
UND	UND	402.8	95.9	76.7	66.8			309.5	235.6
UND	109.1	120.1	22.8	32.3	24.7		Sales/Net Fixed Assets	59.9	50.6
39.6	25.2	16.8	10.1	7.7	4.0			19.2	15.0
12.9	5.3	3.8	2.3	2.5	3.0			3.8	3.7
7.0	3.4	2.6	1.9	2.0	1.8		Sales/Total Assets	2.6	2.5
4.3	2.4	1.6	1.2	1.5	1.3			1.8	1.7
	.9	.1	.2	.2				.2	.2
	1.6 (62)	.6 (71)	.6 (21)	.8		% Depr., Dep., Amort./Sales	(228) .5 (126)	.6
	2.5	1.3	1.5	1.7				1.3	1.8
	.8	1.1	.8					1.1	1.1
(25)	2.6 (49)	1.9 (23)	1.6			% Officers', Directors' Owners' Comp/Sales	(141) 2.2 (72)	2.0
	4.1	3.9	1.8					4.9	5.0
19724M	241837M	1662526M	3956724M	3372448M	4120741M		Net Sales ($)	15661878M	11156317M
2406M	60776M	606876M	2011698M	1669497M	1773847M		Total Assets ($)	6153204M	4769333M

© RMA 2024   M = $ thousand   MM = $ million
See Pages viii through xx for Explanation of Ratios and Data

WHOLESALE—Other Miscellaneous Nondurable Goods Merchant Wholesalers NAICS 424990

Comparative Historical Data / Current Data Sorted by Sales

					Type of Statement											
	10		25		21		Unqualified				1		2		2	19
	24		42		28		Reviewed								9	16
	20		20		20		Compiled			2			3		9	6
	38		61		51		Tax Returns			11	8		15		11	6
	116		172		177		Other	2		17	9		30		48	71
	4/1/21-3/31/22 ALL		4/1/22-3/31/23 ALL		4/1/23-3/31/24 ALL					44 (4/1-9/30/23)			253 (10/1/23-3/31/24)			
	208		320		297		NUMBER OF STATEMENTS	0-1MM		1-3MM	3-5MM		5-10MM		10-25MM	25MM & OVER
								2		30	18		50		79	118
	%		%		%		ASSETS	%		%	%		%		%	%
	15.7		13.6		14.6		Cash & Equivalents			23.6	20.4		18.9		10.9	12.0
	24.6		23.9		23.0		Trade Receivables (net)			15.5	17.3		22.6		26.1	23.8
	35.2		35.7		32.1		Inventory			17.7	40.0		28.7		36.4	33.4
	3.7		3.9		4.4		All Other Current			9.9	2.2		2.2		4.2	4.4
	79.2		77.2		74.2		Total Current			66.6	79.8		72.4		77.6	73.7
	9.8		12.9		12.3		Fixed Assets (net)			18.9	5.8		13.3		11.2	11.9
	4.8		3.9		5.1		Intangibles (net)			5.2	6.4		5.6		4.9	4.6
	6.2		6.0		8.5		All Other Non-Current			9.3	8.1		8.7		6.2	9.8
	100.0		100.0		100.0		Total			100.0	100.0		100.0		100.0	100.0
							LIABILITIES									
	11.2		10.1		8.3		Notes Payable-Short Term			5.0	6.5		6.2		8.5	10.4
	1.4		2.1		1.8		Cur. Mat.-L.T.D.			1.5	.5		2.1		1.4	2.2
	19.2		18.3		18.7		Trade Payables			20.1	13.1		19.9		21.2	17.2
	.2		.2		.2		Income Taxes Payable			.1	.1		.7		.1	.1
	12.3		11.5		10.5		All Other Current			15.0	25.9		9.3		8.4	8.8
	44.4		42.2		39.5		Total Current			41.7	46.1		38.3		39.6	38.6
	11.4		11.1		12.5		Long-Term Debt			21.5	9.7		18.1		9.9	10.1
	.0		.3		.1		Deferred Taxes			.0	.0		.0		.2	.1
	4.6		4.0		7.4		All Other Non-Current			25.7	1.7		2.5		5.0	7.3
	39.6		42.4		40.5		Net Worth			11.1	42.5		41.1		45.3	43.9
	100.0		100.0		100.0		Total Liabilties & Net Worth			100.0	100.0		100.0		100.0	100.0
							INCOME DATA									
	100.0		100.0		100.0		Net Sales			100.0	100.0		100.0		100.0	100.0
	34.2		31.4		32.1		Gross Profit			45.8	39.6		31.9		30.4	28.4
	28.1		25.2		26.3		Operating Expenses			36.1	35.4		25.2		26.1	22.9
	6.2		6.2		5.8		Operating Profit			9.7	4.2		6.8		4.3	5.5
	-.7		.2		.7		All Other Expenses (net)			1.8	1.2		.2		.5	.6
	6.8		6.0		5.1		Profit Before Taxes			7.8	3.0		6.6		3.7	4.8
							RATIOS									
	4.3		3.9		4.0					8.4	6.8		5.3		3.8	3.3
	2.1		2.0		2.1		Current			1.6	3.4		2.1		2.2	1.9
	1.3		1.3		1.3					.8	2.2		1.3		1.4	1.3
	2.1		1.7		2.0					3.3	6.1		3.1		1.8	1.7
	1.0		.9		1.0		Quick			.7	1.6		1.1		1.1	.8
	.6		.5		.5					.4	.7		.7		.5	.5
18	19.8	17	22.1	16	22.4			7	55.7	0	UND	8	45.3	20	18.1	24	15.5
32	11.5	29	12.4	33	11.1		Sales/Receivables	17	21.4	22	16.7	30	12.0	32	11.4	38	9.6
49	7.5	45	8.1	50	7.3			40	9.1	39	9.4	51	7.2	56	6.5	49	7.5
33	11.2	24	15.1	26	14.0			0	UND	0	UND	14	27.0	35	10.5	39	9.3
66	5.5	65	5.6	70	5.2		Cost of Sales/Inventory	45	8.1	91	4.0	45	8.1	79	4.6	81	4.5
146	2.5	130	2.8	135	2.7			140	2.6	192	1.9	104	3.5	114	3.2	146	2.5
12	29.9	11	31.8	16	23.2			0	UND	15	23.8	14	26.4	19	19.4	17	21.8
29	12.8	25	14.5	29	12.7		Cost of Sales/Payables	14	26.7	23	16.2	32	11.4	28	13.0	30	12.3
51	7.1	51	7.1	57	6.4			87	4.2	42	8.6	63	5.8	62	5.9	48	7.6
	3.7		3.9		3.8				4.0		3.8		4.1		3.8	3.5
	6.7		7.7		7.2		Sales/Working Capital		7.6		4.9		6.8		7.1	8.3
	16.5		17.2		18.1				-55.9		6.4		24.0		14.9	15.3
	65.6		39.1		17.8				21.8		12.4		28.4		17.8	16.6
(158)	15.9	(251)	9.4	(237)	5.4		EBIT/Interest	(21)	6.9	(10)	3.6	(40)	9.8	(66)	4.2	(99)	5.6
	5.5		3.0		1.8				2.5		-3.2		2.4		1.6	1.8
	7.7		12.6		8.2		Net Profit + Depr., Dep.,								7.7	8.6
(19)	4.5	(35)	6.4	(41)	3.8		Amort./Cur. Mat. L/T/D							(12)	2.1	(27)	5.4
	2.3		2.1		.9										-.1	2.0
	.0		.0		.0				.0		.0		.0		.0	.1
	.1		.1		.2		Fixed/Worth		.4		.0		.1		.2	.2
	.5		.6		.7				3.4		.1		1.3		.6	.7
	.5		.5		.5				.4		.3		.3		.6	.5
	1.2		1.4		1.4		Debt/Worth		2.3		.6		1.5		1.2	1.7
	4.4		4.0		4.5				41.0		1.1		4.5		4.5	4.5
	58.0		56.7		58.1				153.4		43.4		56.9		56.7	52.3
(184)	30.4	(295)	27.0	(269)	24.5		% Profit Before Taxes/Tangible Net Worth	(24)	33.8	(16)	17.5	(43)	30.8	(74)	21.2	(110)	23.0
	15.6		9.9		6.3				18.3		7.0		15.6		2.7	5.2
	25.4		25.2		20.8				24.9		30.2		26.7		21.0	19.0
	12.0		11.1		10.0		% Profit Before Taxes/Total Assets		9.8		14.8		14.5		7.2	9.6
	5.4		3.4		1.8				2.5		2.4		6.4		1.5	1.5
	270.2		354.0		273.7				UND		UND		346.6		379.3	104.0
	74.2		56.8		48.6		Sales/Net Fixed Assets		40.5		249.6		106.7		80.9	30.9
	21.8		14.7		15.0				7.7		61.8		21.9		11.3	13.4
	3.6		3.9		3.5				4.5		3.5		4.4		3.7	3.1
	2.5		2.5		2.3		Sales/Total Assets		2.2		2.5		2.5		2.5	2.1
	1.6		1.7		1.6				1.0		1.7		1.7		1.4	1.6
	.2		.2		.2				1.0		.3		.1		.2
(118)	.6	(187)	.6	(184)	.7		% Depr., Dep., Amort./Sales	(12)	2.4			(24)	.8	(53)	.6	(90)	.6
	1.3		1.3		1.6				4.1				1.9		1.4	1.2
	1.2		.9		.9				3.9				1.1		.7	.6
(72)	2.8	(108)	1.7	(103)	1.8		% Officers', Directors' Owners' Comp/Sales	(10)	4.2			(28)	2.2	(31)	1.5	(26)	1.2
	4.7		3.3		3.9				15.5				4.3		3.6	1.8
	10281209M		12075311M		13374000M		Net Sales ($)		292M		64179M		73933M		348208M		1312129M	11575259M
	3842090M		5300955M		6125100M		Total Assets ($)		141M		73446M		33772M		153882M		678242M	5185617M

M = $ thousand   MM = $ million
See Pages viii through xx for Explanation of Ratios and Data

© RMA 2024

WHOLESALE—Wholesale Trade Agents and Brokers NAICS 425120

Current Data Sorted by Assets

							Type of Statement	Comparative Historical Data	
		1	3				Unqualified	6	7
		5	8	1	1		Reviewed	22	9
1	1	8	7	1			Compiled	20	9
4	9	14	2				Tax Returns	36	16
6	13	40	21	2	3		Other	90	56
	17 (4/1-9/30/23)		134 (10/1/23-3/31/24)					4/1/19-3/31/20	4/1/20-3/31/21
0-500M	500M-2MM	2-10MM	10-50MM	50-100MM	100-250MM		NUMBER OF STATEMENTS	ALL 174	ALL 97
11	23	68	41	4	4				
%	%	%	%	%	%		ASSETS	%	%
62.6	29.1	14.8	13.6				Cash & Equivalents	16.1	19.3
.6	19.2	31.0	35.1				Trade Receivables (net)	38.1	35.3
22.2	21.5	27.4	19.5				Inventory	25.7	22.5
1.4	5.2	4.4	8.3				All Other Current	2.3	3.7
86.8	75.1	77.6	76.5				Total Current	82.2	80.7
10.9	7.6	10.1	9.8				Fixed Assets (net)	7.2	8.4
1.1	6.4	4.4	6.6				Intangibles (net)	5.1	4.9
1.2	10.8	7.9	7.0				All Other Non-Current	5.5	6.0
100.0	100.0	100.0	100.0				Total	100.0	100.0
							LIABILITIES		
10.8	12.9	9.0	6.4				Notes Payable-Short Term	11.9	12.1
3.9	4.4	1.0	2.0				Cur. Mat.-L.T.D.	1.7	2.5
8.7	23.1	24.2	25.8				Trade Payables	24.3	24.2
.0	.0	.1	.2				Income Taxes Payable	.1	1.0
25.5	8.6	9.2	9.1				All Other Current	14.1	13.2
49.0	48.9	43.4	43.5				Total Current	52.1	52.9
27.5	11.5	15.6	6.9				Long-Term Debt	8.3	11.3
.0	.0	.0	.0				Deferred Taxes	.1	.0
.9	3.3	4.7	4.4				All Other Non-Current	7.1	3.2
22.6	36.3	36.3	45.2				Net Worth	32.4	32.5
100.0	100.0	100.0	100.0				Total Liabilities & Net Worth	100.0	100.0
							INCOME DATA		
100.0	100.0	100.0	100.0				Net Sales	100.0	100.0
47.1	30.7	24.1	22.0				Gross Profit	26.3	29.8
34.2	22.4	19.1	15.3				Operating Expenses	21.8	22.3
12.9	8.3	4.9	6.7				Operating Profit	4.5	7.5
.5	.0	.2	.1				All Other Expenses (net)	.6	.2
12.4	8.3	4.7	6.5				Profit Before Taxes	3.9	7.3
							RATIOS		
15.6	3.8	3.6	2.5					2.6	3.1
3.9	1.5	1.7	1.7				Current	1.6	1.4
1.1	1.1	1.2	1.3					1.2	1.1
9.7	1.7	1.9	2.0					1.9	2.1
3.7	1.0	1.0	1.1				Quick	1.0	1.0
.6	.5	.6	.6					.6	.7
0 UND	0 UND	7 48.8	20 18.5					18 20.7	11 33.7
0 UND	8 46.4	25 14.8	34 10.6				Sales/Receivables	35 10.5	33 11.1
0 999.8	31 11.8	41 8.9	54 6.7					52 7.0	53 6.9
0 UND	0 UND	4 99.3	1 293.1					1 287.0	0 UND
12 29.6	12 29.3	27 13.3	12 30.1				Cost of Sales/Inventory	25 14.6	23 16.1
34 10.8	66 5.5	68 5.4	47 7.8					81 4.5	66 5.5
0 UND	0 UND	3 105.0	10 34.9					8 47.8	7 49.1
8 44.0	15 23.6	24 15.0	27 13.5				Cost of Sales/Payables	23 16.2	24 15.0
15 24.3	42 8.7	38 9.5	47 7.7					49 7.4	47 7.7
4.1	6.4	5.1	5.1					5.7	5.9
9.3	14.9	15.8	10.4				Sales/Working Capital	13.3	13.3
168.2	248.7	55.3	26.3					53.7	174.8
		28.9	34.8	93.4				28.2	72.0
	(16) 10.8	(60) 9.4	(35) 16.6				EBIT/Interest	(128) 6.6	(74) 16.7
		2.8	3.2	3.1				2.7	5.2
							Net Profit + Depr., Dep.,		12.1
							Amort./Cur. Mat. L/T/D	(16) 5.2	
									3.0
.0	.0	.0	.0					.0	.0
.0	.0	.1	.1				Fixed/Worth	.1	.1
.4	.6	.7	.7					.6	1.1
.1	.4	.8	.5					.8	.8
1.7	1.7	2.1	1.5				Debt/Worth	1.9	2.3
5.9	9.0	5.7	9.1					6.1	20.7
	182.4	66.1	66.4					67.9	76.6
	(21) 65.7	(61) 43.0	(37) 29.0				% Profit Before Taxes/Tangible Net Worth	(149) 31.4	(76) 39.1
	16.6	20.4	10.5					13.7	21.7
116.8	57.8	21.6	23.1					19.4	30.6
31.2	22.7	13.9	10.1				% Profit Before Taxes/Total Assets	10.1	15.2
12.6	2.9	4.6	3.7					3.6	5.9
UND	UND	581.8	999.8					999.8	999.8
201.5	250.5	118.3	155.0				Sales/Net Fixed Assets	156.4	148.8
35.9	68.8	29.8	21.2					37.1	32.0
14.2	7.4	6.4	5.0					5.5	5.4
7.1	3.9	3.3	2.7				Sales/Total Assets	3.2	3.4
1.6	2.5	2.2	1.6					2.1	1.9
		.0	.0					.1	.2
	(34) .4	(26) .3					% Depr., Dep., Amort./Sales	(93) .3	(47) .4
		1.1	.8					.9	1.2
	1.7	1.1						.8	1.1
	(11) 3.7	(31) 2.2					% Officers', Directors' Owners' Comp/Sales	(57) 1.8	(31) 2.0
	5.6	3.6						3.6	4.7
25996M	210235M	1419916M	3674155M	1040097M	2401550M		Net Sales ($)	8998809M	7775647M
3316M	26481M	327914M	851325M	303286M	716533M		Total Assets ($)	2374984M	1949734M

M = $ thousand   MM = $ million
See Pages viii through xx for Explanation of Ratios and Data

© RMA 2024

WHOLESALE—Wholesale Trade Agents and Brokers NAICS 425120

Comparative Historical Data				Current Data Sorted by Sales						
			Type of Statement						
10	10	6	Unqualified				3	3	
15	15	14	Reviewed			1	3	10	
12	21	17	Compiled	1		1	10	5	
30	35	29	Tax Returns	2	4	4	6	11	2
63	89	85	Other	2	8	3	17	18	37
4/1/21-	4/1/22-	4/1/23-			17 (4/1-9/30/23)		134 (10/1/23-3/31/24)		
3/31/22	3/31/23	3/31/24		0-1MM	1-3MM	3-5MM	5-10MM	10-25MM	25MM & OVER
ALL	ALL	ALL	**NUMBER OF STATEMENTS**						
130	170	151		5	12	7	25	45	57
%	%	%	**ASSETS**	%	%	%	%	%	%
17.7	20.1	20.0	Cash & Equivalents	33.6	14.9		16.8	16.6	
37.2	29.1	27.9	Trade Receivables (net)	9.4	29.5		30.8	33.9	
23.5	22.0	23.7	Inventory	18.7	26.6		24.4	23.6	
3.6	7.6	6.3	All Other Current	2.5	4.9		4.7	8.4	
82.1	78.8	77.8	Total Current	64.1	76.0		76.7	82.5	
9.4	9.5	9.6	Fixed Assets (net)	12.0	11.4		10.2	7.5	
3.6	4.9	4.9	Intangibles (net)	9.2	4.6		4.2	3.5	
4.9	6.8	7.7	All Other Non-Current	14.7	8.0		8.9	6.5	
100.0	100.0	100.0	Total	100.0	100.0		100.0	100.0	
			LIABILITIES						
12.0	10.0	8.8	Notes Payable-Short Term	13.0	14.0		5.2	9.2	
2.2	1.0	2.4	Cur. Mat.-L.T.D.	.3	3.9		1.0	2.8	
24.3	21.5	23.1	Trade Payables	7.4	21.9		26.5	26.3	
.2	.0	.1	Income Taxes Payable	.0	.0		.1	.1	
10.5	10.9	11.4	All Other Current	12.9	9.9		9.5	12.3	
49.3	43.5	45.8	Total Current	33.6	49.7		42.4	50.8	
11.2	13.9	13.4	Long-Term Debt	16.8	9.1		14.8	6.7	
.0	.0	.0	Deferred Taxes	.0	.0		.0	.0	
6.9	6.0	4.9	All Other Non-Current	6.9	7.8		1.9	5.9	
32.6	36.6	36.0	Net Worth	42.8	33.4		41.0	36.6	
100.0	100.0	100.0	Total Liabilities & Net Worth	100.0	100.0		100.0	100.0	
			INCOME DATA						
100.0	100.0	100.0	Net Sales	100.0	100.0		100.0	100.0	
28.9	30.0	26.7	Gross Profit	51.9	28.8		26.6	15.9	
20.9	23.0	20.1	Operating Expenses	42.7	22.7		20.0	11.5	
8.1	7.1	6.6	Operating Profit	9.2	6.1		6.5	4.4	
-.4	.5	.2	All Other Expenses (net)	1.0	.1		.3	.1	
8.5	6.6	6.4	Profit Before Taxes	8.3	6.0		6.2	4.3	
			RATIOS						
2.9	3.8	3.3		6.6	4.2		3.7	2.4	
1.9	1.9	1.7	Current	1.3	1.5		1.8	1.6	
1.2	1.2	1.2		.8	1.0		1.3	1.2	
1.9	2.3	2.0		3.3	2.5		1.9	1.6	
1.1	1.2	1.1	Quick	1.0	.9		1.3	1.0	
.7	.6	.6		.6	.3		.8	.5	
14 26.6	2 221.5	5 66.5		0 UND	2 205.7	20 18.5	9 39.4		
33 10.9	28 13.2	24 15.2	Sales/Receivables	3 131.2	33 10.9	35 10.5	21 17.0		
61 6.0	47 7.7	41 9.0		28 12.9	60 6.1	47 7.7	36 10.0		
0 UND	0 UND	0 999.8		0 UND	7 52.7	3 111.7	0 UND		
17 22.1	19 19.0	18 20.0	Cost of Sales/Inventory	18 20.8	17 21.2	25 14.5	18 20.0		
69 5.3	72 5.1	65 5.6		135 2.7	69 5.3	85 4.3	45 8.1		
8 44.6	5 74.7	5 69.6		0 UND	0 UND	14 25.6	7 50.9		
23 15.6	21 17.5	22 16.8	Cost of Sales/Payables	11 32.5	25 14.8	28 13.0	19 18.8		
49 7.4	49 7.4	42 8.7		29 12.5	56 6.5	63 5.8	37 9.9		
5.3	4.7	5.2		4.1	4.6		4.2	9.1	
10.8	12.5	13.1	Sales/Working Capital	11.6	11.7		11.0	18.3	
27.5	49.8	38.7		-70.0	138.9		20.3	44.4	
59.1	38.5	50.9			33.9		97.4	51.4	
(99) 20.7	(124) 14.3	(124) 10.3	EBIT/Interest	(20) 4.6	(40) 9.9	(47) 12.4			
7.4	4.1	3.3			2.3		4.4	3.2	
37.2	49.4		Net Profit + Depr., Dep.,						
(12) 7.7	(14) 14.8		Amort./Cur. Mat. L/T/D						
2.8	1.6								
.0	.0	.0		.0	.0		.0	.0	
.1	.1	.1	Fixed/Worth	.1	.2		.1	.0	
.5	.5	.6		1.4	.6		1.1	.4	
.7	.7	.7		.4	.9		.6	.7	
1.7	1.9	1.8	Debt/Worth	2.0	2.4		1.6	1.5	
6.8	6.4	6.3		5.5	6.0		6.4	8.8	
125.1	97.2	69.6	% Profit Before Taxes/Tangible	83.3	198.5		68.2	65.9	
(114) 60.0	(154) 47.8	(133) 43.0	Net Worth	(10) 40.5	(24) 56.5	(39) 32.7	(51) 46.9		
30.8	21.2	15.2		9.9	19.7		12.3	18.3	
36.2	32.2	25.8	% Profit Before Taxes/Total	29.0	26.7		21.8	25.7	
19.2	15.4	14.2	Assets	14.1	13.6		11.7	15.4	
9.0	4.6	4.5		1.7	2.9		4.8	5.2	
999.8	999.8	999.8		386.9	480.2		946.1	999.8	
144.2	115.1	152.7	Sales/Net Fixed Assets	92.1	99.8		94.3	232.7	
31.2	26.5	30.1		6.6	20.4		17.0	71.6	
6.3	6.4	6.4		3.0	5.1		4.9	8.3	
3.4	3.2	3.3	Sales/Total Assets	2.5	2.7		2.6	5.0	
2.3	2.0	2.0		1.3	1.8		1.5	2.7	
.1	.1	.0			.1		.1	.0	
(67) .3	(82) .3	(76) .3	% Depr., Dep., Amort./Sales	(12) .1	(26) .6	(33) .1			
.6	1.1	1.1			.5		1.9	.4	
.8	.7	1.0			1.2		.8	.4	
(42) 1.8	(60) 2.0	(58) 2.2	% Officers', Directors'	(12) 2.7	(20) 1.7	(13) .7			
3.9	4.5	4.2	Owners' Comp/Sales		3.6		3.9	2.3	
7495618M	9865491M	8771949M	Net Sales ($)	2406M	23779M	29113M	176905M	745063M	7794683M
1761332M	2744370M	2228855M	Total Assets ($)	1603M	12680M	8240M	69347M	373298M	1763687M

© RMA 2024   M = $ thousand   MM = $ million
See Pages viii through xx for Explanation of Ratios and Data

TEXT—KEY WORD INDEX OF INDUSTRIES APPEARING IN THE STATEMENT STUDIES

STATEMENT STUDIES KEY WORD INDEX

A complete description of each industry category listed below begins on page 31.

A

Adhesive Manufacturing, 332-333, mfg
Administration of Education Programs, 1358-1359, pub admin
Administration of General Economic Programs, 1366-1367, pub admin
Administration of Housing Programs, 1362-1363, pub admin
Administration of Public Health Programs, 1360-1361, pub admin
Administration of Urban Planning and Community and Rural Development, 1364-1365, pub admin
Administrative Management and General Management Consulting Services, 1022-1023, prof serv
Advertising Agencies, 1042-1043, prof serv
Air and Gas Compressor Manufacturing, 468-469, mfg
Air-Conditioning and Warm Air Heating Equipment and Commercial and Industrial Refrigeration Equipment Manufacturing, 456-457, mfg
Aircraft Engine and Engine Parts Manufacturing, 544-545, mfg
Aircraft Manufacturing, 542-543, mfg
All Other Amusement and Recreation Industries, 1254-1255, ent
All Other Automotive Repair and Maintenance, 1296-1297, other
All Other Basic Organic Chemical Manufacturing, 318-319, mfg
All Other Business Support Services, 1082-1083, Admin
All Other Consumer Goods Rental, 968-969, R/E
All Other Converted Paper Product Manufacturing, 306-307, mfg
All Other General Merchandise Retailers, 760-761, rtl
All Other Health and Personal Care Retailers, 768-769, rtl
All Other Home Furnishings Retailers, 756-757, rtl
All Other Industrial Machinery Manufacturing, 448-449, mfg
All Other Insurance Related Activities, 930-931, fin
All Other Legal Services, 986-987, prof serv
All Other Miscellaneous Ambulatory Health Care Services, 1188-1189, HC
All Other Miscellaneous Chemical Product and Preparation Manufacturing, 340-341, mfg
All Other Miscellaneous Crop Farming, 100-101, ag
All Other Miscellaneous Electrical Equipment and Component Manufacturing, 522-523, mfg
All Other Miscellaneous Fabricated Metal Product Manufacturing, 434-435, mfg
All Other Miscellaneous Food Manufacturing, 254-255, mfg
All Other Miscellaneous General Purpose Machinery Manufacturing, 484-485, mfg
All Other Miscellaneous Manufacturing, 584-585, mfg
All Other Miscellaneous Retailers, 794-795, rtl
All Other Miscellaneous Schools and Instruction, 1144-1145, edu
All Other Miscellaneous Textile Product Mills, 270-271, mfg
All Other Miscellaneous Waste Management Services, 1126-1127, Admin
All Other Miscellaneous Wood Product Manufacturing, 292-293, mfg
All Other Outpatient Care Centers, 1176-1177, HC
All Other Personal Services, 1320-1321, other
All Other Plastics Product Manufacturing, 354-355, mfg
All Other Professional, Scientific, and Technical Services, 1056-1057, prof serv
All Other Rubber Product Manufacturing, 358-359, mfg
All Other Specialty Food Retailers, 748-749, rtl
All Other Specialty Trade Contractors, 216-217, cons-g
All Other Specialty Trade Contractors, 1389, cons-%
All Other Support Activities for Transportation, 848-849, trans
All Other Support Services, 1108-1109, Admin
All Other Telecommunications, 886-887, info
All Other Transit and Ground Passenger Transportation, 824-825, trans
All Other Transportation Equipment Manufacturing, 554-555, mfg
All Other Travel Arrangement and Reservation Services, 1088-1089, Admin
All Other Traveler Accommodation, 1264-1265, rest/lodg
Ambulance Services, 1184-1185, HC
Amusement and Theme Parks, 1238-1239, ent
Analytical Laboratory Instrument Manufacturing, 508-509, mfg
Animal (except Poultry) Slaughtering, 236-237, mfg
Apparel Accessories and Other Apparel Manufacturing, 276-277, mfg
Apple Orchards, 92-93, ag
Architectural Services, 996-997, prof serv
Asphalt Paving Mixture and Block Manufacturing, 312-313, mfg
Assisted Living Facilities for the Elderly, 1204-1205, HC
Audio and Video Equipment Manufacturing, 494-495, mfg
Automobile and Light Duty Motor Vehicle Manufacturing, 524-525, mfg
Automobile and Other Motor Vehicle Merchant Wholesalers, 588-589, wsle
Automotive Body, Paint, and Interior Repair and Maintenance, 1290-1291, other
Automotive Oil Change and Lubrication Shops, 1292-1293, other
Automotive Parts and Accessories Retailers, 726-727, rtl

B

Baked Goods Retailers, 746-747, rtl
Ball and Roller Bearing Manufacturing, 428-429, mfg
Bare Printed Circuit Board Manufacturing, 496-497, mfg
Beauty Salons, 1304-1305, other
Bed-and-Breakfast Inns, 1262-1263, rest/lodg
Beef Cattle Ranching and Farming, 102-103, ag
Beer and Ale Merchant Wholesalers, 700-701, wsle
Beer, Wine, and Liquor Retailers, 750-751, rtl
Blood and Organ Banks, 1186-1187, HC
Boat Building, 550-551, mfg
Boat Dealers, 722-723, rtl
Bolt, Nut, Screw, Rivet, and Washer Manufacturing, 414-415, mfg
Book Publishers, 870-871, info
Bowling Centers, 1252-1253, ent
Breweries, 258-259, mfg
Brick, Stone, and Related Construction Material Merchant Wholesalers, 602-603, wsle
Broadwoven Fabric Mills, 264-265, mfg
Business Associations, 1336-1337, other

C

Car Washes, 1294-1295, other
Carpet and Rug Mills, 268-269, mfg
Carpet and Upholstery Cleaning Services, 1100-1101, Admin
Casino Hotels, 1260-1261, rest/lodg
Casinos (except Casino Hotels), 1240-1241, ent
Caterers, 1274-1275, rest/lodg
Cattle Feedlots, 104-105, ag
Charter Bus Industry, 822-823, trans
Cheese Manufacturing, 232-233, mfg
Child and Youth Services, 1208-1209, HC
Child Care Services, 1222-1223, HC
Civic and Social Organizations, 1334-1335, other
Clothing and Clothing Accessories Merchant Wholesalers, 668-669, wsle
Clothing and Clothing Accessories Retailers, 776-777, rtl
Coffee and Tea Manufacturing, 248-249, mfg
Coin-Operated Laundries and Drycleaners, 1310-1311, other
Collection Agencies, 1080-1081, Admin
Colleges, Universities, and Professional Schools, 1132-1133, edu
Commercial Air, Rail, and Water Transportation Equipment Rental and Leasing, 972-973, R/E
Commercial and Industrial Machinery and Equipment (except Automotive and Electronic) Repair and Maintenance, 1300-1301, other
Commercial and Institutional Building Construction, 168-169, cons-g
Commercial and Institutional Building Construction, 1375, cons-%
Commercial and Service Industry Machinery Manufacturing, 450-451, mfg
Commercial Bakeries, 244-245, mfg
Commercial Printing (except Screen and Books), 308-309, mfg
Commercial Screen Printing, 310-311, mfg
Commercial, Industrial, and Institutional Electric Lighting Fixture Manufacturing, 512-513, mfg
Community Food Services, 1214-1215, HC
Computer and Computer Peripheral Equipment and Software Merchant Wholesalers, 610-611, wsle
Computer Facilities Management Services, 1018-1019, prof serv
Computer Systems Design Services, 1016-1017, prof serv
Computer Terminal and Other Computer Peripheral Equipment Manufacturing, 488-489, mfg
Computing Infrastructure Providers, Data Processing, Web Hosting, and Related Services, 888-889, info
Concrete Block and Brick Manufacturing, 364-365, mfg
Confectionery Merchant Wholesalers, 678-679, wsle
Construction and Mining (except Oil Well) Machinery and Equipment Merchant Wholesalers, 634-635, wsle
Construction Machinery Manufacturing, 440-441, mfg
Construction Sand and Gravel Mining, 134-135, mng
Construction, Mining, and Forestry Machinery and Equipment Rental and Leasing, 974-975, R/E
Consumer Electronics and Appliances Rental, 962-963, R/E
Consumer Lending, 896-897, fin
Continuing Care Retirement Communities, 1202-1203, HC
Convenience Retailers, 742-743, rtl
Convention and Trade Show Organizers, 1106-1107, Admin
Conveyor and Conveying Equipment Manufacturing, 472-473, mfg
Corporate, Subsidiary, and Regional Managing Offices, 1062-1063, mgmt
Corrugated and Solid Fiber Box Manufacturing, 296-297, mfg
Cosmetics, Beauty Supplies, and Perfume Retailers, 764-765, rtl
Cotton Ginning, 112-113, ag

STATEMENT STUDIES KEY WORD INDEX

A complete description of each industry category listed below begins on page 31.

Couriers and Express Delivery Services, 850-851, trans
Crude Petroleum Extraction, 126-127, mng
Crushed and Broken Limestone Mining and Quarrying, 130-131, mng
Custom Architectural Woodwork and Millwork Manufacturing, 564-565, mfg
Custom Computer Programming Services, 1014-1015, prof serv
Cut and Sew Apparel Contractors, 272-273, mfg
Cut and Sew Apparel Manufacturing (except Contractors), 274-275, mfg
Cut Stone and Stone Product Manufacturing, 368-369, mfg
Cutting Tool and Machine Tool Accessory Manufacturing, 462-463, mfg

D

Dairy Cattle and Milk Production, 106-107, ag
Dairy Product (except Dried or Canned) Merchant Wholesalers, 674-675, wsle
Deep Sea Freight Transportation, 804-805, trans
Dental Equipment and Supplies Manufacturing, 572-573, mfg
Diagnostic Imaging Centers, 1180-1181, HC
Direct Health and Medical Insurance Carriers, 918-919, fin
Direct Mail Advertising, 1048-1049, prof serv
Direct Property and Casualty Insurance Carriers, 920-921, fin
Distilleries, 262-263, mfg
Dog and Cat Food Manufacturing, 220-221, mfg
Drilling Oil and Gas Wells, 136-137, mng
Drinking Places (Alcoholic Beverages), 1276-1277, rest/lodg
Drugs and Druggists' Sundries Merchant Wholesalers, 662-663, wsle
Drycleaning and Laundry Services (except Coin-Operated), 1312-1313, other
Drywall and Insulation Contractors, 202-203, cons-g
Drywall and Insulation Contractors, 1386, cons-%

E

Educational Support Services, 1146-1147, edu
Electric Power Distribution, 150-151, util
Electrical Apparatus and Equipment, Wiring Supplies, and Related Equipment Merchant Wholesalers, 620-621, wsle
Electrical Contractors and Other Wiring Installation Contractors, 196-197, cons-g
Electrical Contractors and Other Wiring Installation Contractors, 1384, cons-%
Electronic and Precision Equipment Repair and Maintenance, 1298-1299, other
Electronic Computer Manufacturing, 486-487, mfg
Electronics and Appliance Retailers, 758-759, rtl
Electroplating, Plating, Polishing, Anodizing, and Coloring, 420-421, mfg
Elementary and Secondary Schools, 1130-1131, edu
Employment Placement Agencies, 1070-1071, Admin
Engineering Services, 1000-1001, prof serv
Environment, Conservation and Wildlife Organizations, 1330-1331, other
Environmental Consulting Services, 1032-1033, prof serv
Executive and Legislative Offices, Combined, 1352-1353, pub admin
Executive Offices, 1346-1347, pub admin
Executive Search Services, 1072-1073, Admin
Exterminating and Pest Control Services, 1094-1095, Admin

F

Fabricated Pipe and Pipe Fitting Manufacturing, 432-433, mfg
Fabricated Structural Metal Manufacturing, 390-391, mfg
Facilities Support Services, 1068-1069, Admin
Farm and Garden Machinery and Equipment Merchant Wholesalers, 636-637, wsle
Farm Machinery and Equipment Manufacturing, 436-437, mfg
Farm Management Services, 118-119, ag
Farm Product Warehousing and Storage, 858-859, trans
Farm Supplies Merchant Wholesalers, 704-705, wsle
Fertilizer (Mixing Only) Manufacturing, 322-323, mfg
Financial Transactions Processing, Reserve, and Clearinghouse Activities, 904-905, fin
Fine Arts Schools, 1140-1141, edu
Finish Carpentry Contractors, 210-211, cons-g
Fire Protection, 1356-1357, pub admin
Fish and Seafood Merchant Wholesalers, 680-681, wsle
Fitness and Recreational Sports Centers, 1250-1251, ent
Flight Training, 1136-1137, edu
Floor Covering Retailers, 754-755, rtl
Flooring Contractors, 206-207, cons-g
Flooring Contractors, 1387, cons-%
Flour Milling, 224-225, mfg
Flower, Nursery Stock, and Florists' Supplies Merchant Wholesalers, 706-707, wsle
Fluid Milk Manufacturing, 230-231, mfg
Fluid Power Valve and Hose Fitting Manufacturing, 424-425, mfg
Folding Paperboard Box Manufacturing, 298-299, mfg
Food (Health) Supplement Retailers, 766-767, rtl
Food Product Machinery Manufacturing, 446-447, mfg
Food Service Contractors, 1272-1273, rest/lodg
Footwear Merchant Wholesalers, 666-667, wsle
Fossil Fuel Electric Power Generation, 142-143, util
Framing Contractors, 186-187, cons-g
Freestanding Ambulatory Surgical and Emergency Centers, 1174-1175, HC
Freight Transportation Arrangement, 844-845, trans
Fresh Fruit and Vegetable Merchant Wholesalers, 684-685, wsle
Frozen Specialty Food Manufacturing, 226-227, mfg
Fruit and Vegetable Canning, 228-229, mfg
Fuel Dealers, 774-775, rtl
Full-Service Restaurants, 1278-1279, rest/lodg
Funeral Homes and Funeral Services, 1308-1309, other
Furniture Merchant Wholesalers, 596-597, wsle
Furniture Retailers, 752-753, rtl

G

Gasket, Packing, and Sealing Device Manufacturing, 580-581, mfg
Gasoline Stations with Convenience Stores, 770-771, rtl
General Automotive Repair, 1286-1287, other
General Freight Trucking, Local, 808-809, trans
General Freight Trucking, Long-Distance, Less Than Truckload, 812-813, trans
General Freight Trucking, Long-Distance, Truckload, 810-811, trans
General Line Grocery Merchant Wholesalers, 670-671, wsle
General Medical and Surgical Hospitals, 1190-1191, HC
General Rental Centers, 970-971, R/E
General Warehousing and Storage, 854-855, trans
Gift, Novelty, and Souvenir Retailers, 788-789, rtl
Glass and Glazing Contractors, 190-191, cons-g
Glass and Glazing Contractors, 1382, cons-%
Glass Product Manufacturing Made of Purchased Glass, 360-361, mfg
Golf Courses and Country Clubs, 1244-1245, ent
Grain and Field Bean Merchant Wholesalers, 688-689, wsle
Grantmaking Foundations, 1324-1325, other
Grape Vineyards, 94-95, ag
Graphic Design Services, 1010-1011, prof serv

H

Hardware Manufacturing, 404-405, mfg
Hardware Merchant Wholesalers, 626-627, wsle
Hardware Retailers, 732-733, rtl
Hardwood Veneer and Plywood Manufacturing, 282-283, mfg
Hazardous Waste Treatment and Disposal, 1114-1115, Admin
Heating Equipment (except Warm Air Furnaces) Manufacturing, 454-455, mfg
Highway, Street, and Bridge Construction, 178-179, cons-g
Highway, Street, and Bridge Construction, 1378, cons-%
HMO Medical Centers, 1170-1171, HC
Home Centers, 730-731, rtl
Home Furnishing Merchant Wholesalers, 598-599, wsle
Home Health Care Services, 1182-1183, HC
Home Health Equipment Rental, 964-965, R/E
Hotels (except Casino Hotels) and Motels, 1258-1259, rest/lodg
Household Appliances, Electric Housewares, and Consumer Electronics Merchant Wholesalers, 622-623, wsle
Household Furniture (except Wood and Upholstered) Manufacturing, 560-561, mfg
Human Resources Consulting Services, 1024-1025, prof serv

I

Ice Cream and Frozen Dessert Manufacturing, 234-235, mfg
Independent Artists, Writers, and Performers, 1232-1233, ent
Indoor and Outdoor Display Advertising, 1046-1047, prof serv
Industrial and Commercial Fan and Blower and Air Purification Equipment Manufacturing, 452-453, mfg
Industrial and Personal Service Paper Merchant Wholesalers, 660-661, wsle
Industrial Building Construction, 166-167, cons-g
Industrial Building Construction, 1374, cons-%
Industrial Design Services, 1008-1009, prof serv
Industrial Machinery and Equipment Merchant Wholesalers, 638-639, wsle
Industrial Mold Manufacturing, 458-459, mfg
Industrial Process Furnace and Oven Manufacturing, 482-483, mfg
Industrial Supplies Merchant Wholesalers, 640-641, wsle
Industrial Truck, Tractor, Trailer, and Stacker Machinery Manufacturing, 476-477, mfg
Industrial Valve Manufacturing, 422-423, mfg
Inland Water Freight Transportation, 806-807, trans
Institutional Furniture Manufacturing, 562-563, mfg

STATEMENT STUDIES KEY WORD INDEX

A complete description of each industry category listed below begins on page 31.

Instruments and Related Products Manufacturing for Measuring, Displaying, and Controlling Industrial Process Variables, 506-507, mfg
Insurance Agencies and Brokerages, 926-927, fin
Interior Design Services, 1006-1007, prof serv
International, Secondary Market, and All Other Nondepository Credit Intermediation, 900-901, fin
Investment Banking and Securities Intermediation, 908-909, fin
Iron and Steel Forging, 382-383, mfg
Iron and Steel Mills and Ferroalloy Manufacturing, 370-371, mfg
Iron and Steel Pipe and Tube Manufacturing from Purchased Steel, 372-373, mfg

J

Janitorial Services, 1096-1097, Admin
Jewelry and Silverware Manufacturing, 574-575, mfg
Jewelry Retailers, 780-781, rtl
Jewelry, Watch, Precious Stone, and Precious Metal Merchant Wholesalers, 652-653, wsle

K

Kidney Dialysis Centers, 1172-1173, HC

L

Labor Unions and Similar Labor Organizations, 1340-1341, other
Land Subdivision, 176-177, cons-g
Landscape Architectural Services, 998-999, prof serv
Landscaping Services, 1098-1099, Admin
Lawn and Garden Tractor and Home Lawn and Garden Equipment Manufacturing, 438-439, mfg
Legislative Bodies, 1348-1349, pub admin
Lessors of Miniwarehouses and Self-Storage Units, 944-945, R/E
Lessors of Nonfinancial Intangible Assets (except Copyrighted Works), 980-981, R/E
Lessors of Nonresidential Buildings (except Miniwarehouses), 942-943, R/E
Lessors of Other Real Estate Property, 946-947, R/E
Lessors of Residential Buildings and Dwellings, 940-941, R/E
Limited-Service Restaurants, 1280-1281, rest/lodg
Linen Supply, 1314-1315, other
Local Messengers and Local Delivery, 852-853, trans
Logging, 110-111, ag
Lumber, Plywood, Millwork, and Wood Panel Merchant Wholesalers, 600-601, wsle

M

Machine Shops, 410-411, mfg
Machine Tool Manufacturing, 464-465, mfg
Marinas, 1248-1249, ent
Marine Cargo Handling, 834-835, trans
Marketing Consulting Services, 1026-1027, prof serv
Marketing Research and Public Opinion Polling, 1052-1053, prof serv
Masonry Contractors, 188-189, cons-g
Materials Recovery Facilities, 1122-1123, Admin
Measuring, Dispensing, and Other Pumping Equipment Manufacturing, 470-471, mfg
Meat and Meat Product Merchant Wholesalers, 682-683, wsle
Meat Processed from Carcasses, 238-239, mfg
Meat Retailers, 744-745, rtl
Media Streaming Distribution Services, Social Networks, and Other Media Networks and Content Providers, 878-879, info
Medical Laboratories, 1178-1179, HC

Medical, Dental, and Hospital Equipment and Supplies Merchant Wholesalers, 614-615, wsle
Medicinal and Botanical Manufacturing, 326-327, mfg
Metal Coating, Engraving (except Jewelry and Silverware), and Allied Services to Manufacturers, 418-419, mfg
Metal Crown, Closure, and Other Metal Stamping (except Automotive), 384-385, mfg
Metal Heat Treating, 416-417, mfg
Metal Service Centers and Other Metal Merchant Wholesalers, 618-619, wsle
Metal Tank (Heavy Gauge) Manufacturing, 400-401, mfg
Metal Window and Door Manufacturing, 394-395, mfg
Mining Machinery and Equipment Manufacturing, 442-443, mfg
Miscellaneous Financial Investment Activities, 916-917, fin
Miscellaneous Intermediation, 910-911, fin
Mortgage and Nonmortgage Loan Brokers, 902-903, fin
Motion Picture and Video Production, 864-865, info
Motion Picture Theaters (except Drive-Ins), 866-867, info
Motor and Generator Manufacturing, 516-517, mfg
Motor Vehicle Body Manufacturing, 526-527, mfg
Motor Vehicle Electrical and Electronic Equipment Manufacturing, 534-535, mfg
Motor Vehicle Gasoline Engine and Engine Parts Manufacturing, 532-533, mfg
Motor Vehicle Metal Stamping, 538-539, mfg
Motor Vehicle Parts (Used) Merchant Wholesalers, 594-595, wsle
Motor Vehicle Seating and Interior Trim Manufacturing, 536-537, mfg
Motor Vehicle Supplies and New Parts Merchant Wholesalers, 590-591, wsle
Motor Vehicle Towing, 840-841, trans
Motorcycle, ATV, and All Other Motor Vehicle Dealers, 724-725, rtl
Motorcycle, Bicycle, and Parts Manufacturing, 552-553, mfg
Museums, 1234-1235, ent
Music Publishers, 868-869, info
Musical Instrument and Supplies Retailers, 784-785, rtl
Musical Instrument Manufacturing, 582-583, mfg

N

Natural Gas Distribution, 152-153, util
Natural Gas Extraction, 128-129, mng
Navigational Services to Shipping, 836-837, trans
New Car Dealers, 716-717, rtl
New Housing For-Sale Builders, 162-163, cons-g
New Housing For-Sale Builders, 1372, cons-%
New Multifamily Housing Construction (except For-Sale Builders), 160-161, cons-g
New Multifamily Housing Construction (except For-Sale Builders), 1371, cons-%
New Single-Family Housing Construction (except For-Sale Builders), 158-159, cons-g
New Single-Family Housing Construction (except For-Sale Builders), 1370, cons-%
Nonferrous Metal Die-Casting Foundries, 380-381, mfg
Nonresidential Property Managers, 952-953, R/E
Nonscheduled Chartered Passenger Air Transportation, 800-801, trans
Nursery and Tree Production, 98-99, ag
Nursery, Garden Center, and Farm Supply Retailers, 738-739, rtl

Nursing Care Facilities (Skilled Nursing Facilities), 1196-1197, HC

O

Office Administrative Services, 1066-1067, Admin
Office Equipment Merchant Wholesalers, 608-609, wsle
Office Machinery and Equipment Rental and Leasing, 976-977, R/E
Office Supplies and Stationery Retailers, 786-787, rtl
Offices of All Other Miscellaneous Health Practitioners, 1166-1167, HC
Offices of Certified Public Accountants, 988-989, prof serv
Offices of Chiropractors, 1156-1157, HC
Offices of Dentists, 1154-1155, HC
Offices of Lawyers, 984-985, prof serv
Offices of Mental Health Practitioners (except Physicians), 1160-1161, HC
Offices of Optometrists, 1158-1159, HC
Offices of Other Holding Companies, 1060-1061, mgmt
Offices of Physical, Occupational and Speech Therapists, and Audiologists, 1162-1163, HC
Offices of Physicians (except Mental Health Specialists), 1150-1151, HC
Offices of Physicians, Mental Health Specialists, 1152-1153, HC
Offices of Podiatrists, 1164-1165, HC
Offices of Real Estate Agents and Brokers, 948-949, R/E
Oil and Gas Field Machinery and Equipment Manufacturing, 444-445, mfg
Oil and Gas Pipeline and Related Structures Construction, 172-173, cons-g
Open-End Investment Funds, 932-933, fin
Ornamental and Architectural Metal Work Manufacturing, 398-399, mfg
Other Accounting Services, 994-995, prof serv
Other Activities Related to Credit Intermediation, 906-907, fin
Other Activities Related to Real Estate, 954-955, R/E
Other Aircraft Parts and Auxiliary Equipment Manufacturing, 546-547, mfg
Other Airport Operations, 826-827, trans
Other Aluminum Rolling, Drawing, and Extruding, 378-379, mfg
Other Animal Food Manufacturing, 222-223, mfg
Other Basic Inorganic Chemical Manufacturing, 316-317, mfg
Other Building Equipment Contractors, 200-201, cons-g
Other Building Finishing Contractors, 212-213, cons-g
Other Building Material Dealers, 734-735, rtl
Other Chemical and Allied Products Merchant Wholesalers, 694-695, wsle
Other Commercial and Industrial Machinery and Equipment Rental and Leasing, 978-979, R/E
Other Commercial Equipment Merchant Wholesalers, 612-613, wsle
Other Communications Equipment Manufacturing, 492-493, mfg
Other Community Housing Services, 1218-1219, HC
Other Computer Related Services, 1020-1021, prof serv
Other Concrete Product Manufacturing, 366-367, mfg
Other Construction Material Merchant Wholesalers, 606-607, wsle
Other Crushed and Broken Stone Mining and Quarrying, 132-133, mng
Other Direct Insurance (except Life, Health, and Medical) Carriers, 922-923, fin
Other Electric Power Generation, 148-149, util

STATEMENT STUDIES KEY WORD INDEX
A complete description of each industry category listed below begins on page 31.

Other Electronic Component Manufacturing, 502-503, mfg
Other Electronic Parts and Equipment Merchant Wholesalers, 624-625, wsle
Other Fabricated Wire Product Manufacturing, 408-409, mfg
Other Farm Product Raw Material Merchant Wholesalers, 690-691, wsle
Other Financial Vehicles, 936-937, fin
Other Foundation, Structure, and Building Exterior Contractors, 194-195, cons-g
Other Gambling Industries, 1242-1243, ent
Other Gasoline Stations, 772-773, rtl
Other General Government Support, 1354-1355, pub admin
Other Grantmaking and Giving Services, 1328-1329, other
Other Grocery and Related Products Merchant Wholesalers, 686-687, wsle
Other Heavy and Civil Engineering Construction, 180-181, cons-g
Other Heavy and Civil Engineering Construction, 1379, cons-%
Other Individual and Family Services, 1212-1213, HC
Other Leather and Allied Product Manufacturing, 278-279, mfg
Other Management Consulting Services, 1030-1031, prof serv
Other Measuring and Controlling Device Manufacturing, 510-511, mfg
Other Metal Container Manufacturing, 402-403, mfg
Other Metal Valve and Pipe Fitting Manufacturing, 426-427, mfg
Other Millwork (including Flooring), 286-287, mfg
Other Miscellaneous Durable Goods Merchant Wholesalers, 654-655, wsle
Other Miscellaneous Nondurable Goods Merchant Wholesalers, 710-711, wsle
Other Motor Vehicle Parts Manufacturing, 540-541, mfg
Other Nonhazardous Waste Treatment and Disposal, 1118-1119, Admin
Other Nonscheduled Air Transportation, 802-803, trans
Other Personal and Household Goods Repair and Maintenance, 1302-1303, other
Other Personal Care Services, 1306-1307, other
Other Professional Equipment and Supplies Merchant Wholesalers, 616-617, wsle
Other Residential Care Facilities, 1206-1207, HC
Other Scientific and Technical Consulting Services, 1034-1035, prof serv
Other Services Related to Advertising, 1050-1051, prof serv
Other Services to Buildings and Dwellings, 1102-1103, Admin
Other Similar Organizations (except Business, Professional, Labor, and Political Organizations), 1342-1343, other
Other Snack Food Manufacturing, 246-247, mfg
Other Social Advocacy Organizations, 1332-1333, other
Other Specialized Design Services, 1012-1013, prof serv
Other Support Activities for Air Transportation, 828-829, trans
Other Support Activities for Road Transportation, 842-843, trans
Other Support Activities for Water Transportation, 838-839, trans
Other Technical and Trade Schools, 1138-1139, edu
Other Vegetable (except Potato) and Melon Farming, 90-91, ag
Other Warehousing and Storage, 860-861, trans
Other Waste Collection, 1112-1113, Admin

Outdoor Power Equipment Retailers, 736-737, rtl
Outpatient Mental Health and Substance Abuse Centers, 1168-1169, HC
Overhead Traveling Crane, Hoist, and Monorail System Manufacturing, 474-475, mfg

P

Packaged Frozen Food Merchant Wholesalers, 672-673, wsle
Packaging and Labeling Services, 1104-1105, Admin
Packaging Machinery Manufacturing, 480-481, mfg
Packing and Crating, 846-847, trans
Paint and Coating Manufacturing, 330-331, mfg
Painting and Wall Covering Contractors, 204-205, cons-g
Paper Bag and Coated and Treated Paper Manufacturing, 300-301, mfg
Paper Mills, 294-295, mfg
Parking Lots and Garages, 1318-1319, other
Passenger Car Leasing, 958-959, R/E
Passenger Car Rental, 956-957, R/E
Payroll Services, 992-993, prof serv
Perishable Prepared Food Manufacturing, 252-253, mfg
Pesticide and Other Agricultural Chemical Manufacturing, 324-325, mfg
Pet and Pet Supplies Retailers, 792-793, rtl
Pet Care (except Veterinary) Services, 1316-1317, other
Petroleum and Petroleum Products Merchant Wholesalers (except Bulk Stations and Terminals), 698-699, wsle
Petroleum Bulk Stations and Terminals, 696-697, wsle
Petroleum Lubricating Oil and Grease Manufacturing, 314-315, mfg
Pharmaceutical Preparation Manufacturing, 328-329, mfg
Pharmacies and Drug Retailers, 762-763, rtl
Pharmacy Benefit Management and Other Third Party Administration of Insurance and Pension Funds, 928-929, fin
Piece Goods, Notions, and Other Dry Goods Merchant Wholesalers, 664-665, wsle
Plastics Bag and Pouch Manufacturing, 342-343, mfg
Plastics Bottle Manufacturing, 352-353, mfg
Plastics Material and Resin Manufacturing, 320-321, mfg
Plastics Materials and Basic Forms and Shapes Merchant Wholesalers, 692-693, wsle
Plastics Packaging Film and Sheet (including Laminated) Manufacturing, 344-345, mfg
Plastics Pipe and Pipe Fitting Manufacturing, 346-347, mfg
Plate Work Manufacturing, 392-393, mfg
Plumbing and Heating Equipment and Supplies (Hydronics) Merchant Wholesalers, 628-629, wsle
Plumbing, Heating, and Air-Conditioning Contractors, 198-199, cons-g
Plumbing, Heating, and Air-Conditioning Contractors, 1385, cons-%
Polish and Other Sanitation Good Manufacturing, 336-337, mfg
Polystyrene Foam Product Manufacturing, 348-349, mfg
Port and Harbor Operations, 832-833, trans
Portfolio Management and Investment Advice, 912-913, fin
Postharvest Crop Activities (except Cotton Ginning), 116-117, ag
Potato Farming, 88-89, ag
Poultry and Poultry Product Merchant Wholesalers, 676-677, wsle
Poured Concrete Foundation and Structure Contractors, 182-183, cons-g

Poured Concrete Foundation and Structure Contractors, 1380, cons-%
Power and Communication Line and Related Structures Construction, 174-175, cons-g
Power and Communication Line and Related Structures Construction, 1377, cons-%
Power, Distribution, and Specialty Transformer Manufacturing, 514-515, mfg
Precision Turned Product Manufacturing, 412-413, mfg
Prefabricated Metal Building and Component Manufacturing, 388-389, mfg
Prefabricated Wood Building Manufacturing, 290-291, mfg
Printed Circuit Assembly (Electronic Assembly) Manufacturing, 500-501, mfg
Printing and Writing Paper Merchant Wholesalers, 656-657, wsle
Process, Physical Distribution, and Logistics Consulting Services, 1028-1029, prof serv
Professional and Management Development Training, 1134-1135, edu
Professional Employer Organizations, 1076-1077, Admin
Professional Organizations, 1338-1339, other
Promoters of Performing Arts, Sports, and Similar Events with Facilities, 1230-1231, ent
Psychiatric and Substance Abuse Hospitals, 1192-1193, HC
Public Finance Activities, 1350-1351, pub admin
Public Relations Agencies, 1044-1045, prof serv

R

Radio and Television Broadcasting and Wireless Communications Equipment Manufacturing, 490-491, mfg
Radio Broadcasting Stations, 874-875, info
Ready-Mix Concrete Manufacturing, 362-363, mfg
Real Estate Credit, 898-899, fin
Recreational and Vacation Camps (except Campgrounds), 1268-1269, rest/lodg
Recreational Goods Rental, 966-967, R/E
Recreational Vehicle Dealers, 720-721, rtl
Recyclable Material Merchant Wholesalers, 650-651, wsle
Refrigerated Warehousing and Storage, 856-857, trans
Refrigeration Equipment and Supplies Merchant Wholesalers, 632-633, wsle
Reinsurance Carriers, 924-925, fin
Relay and Industrial Control Manufacturing, 520-521, mfg
Religious Organizations, 1322-1323, other
Remediation Services, 1120-1121, Admin
Research and Development in Biotechnology (except Nanobiotechnology), 1036-1037, prof serv
Research and Development in the Physical, Engineering, and Life Sciences (except Nanotechnology and Biotechnology), 1038-1039, prof serv
Research and Development in the Social Sciences and Humanities, 1040-1041, prof serv
Residential Intellectual and Developmental Disability Facilities, 1198-1199, HC
Residential Mental Health and Substance Abuse Facilities, 1200-1201, HC
Residential Property Managers, 950-951, R/E
Residential Remodelers, 164-165, cons-g
Residential Remodelers, 1373, cons-%
Retail Bakeries, 242-243, mfg
Rolled Steel Shape Manufacturing, 374-375, mfg
Rolling Mill and Other Metalworking Machinery Manufacturing, 466-467, mfg
Roofing Contractors, 192-193, cons-g
Roofing Contractors, 1383, cons-%
Roofing, Siding, and Insulation Material Merchant Wholesalers, 604-605, wsle

STATEMENT STUDIES KEY WORD INDEX

A complete description of each industry category listed below begins on page 31.

Rooming and Boarding Houses, Dormitories, and Workers' Camps, 1270-1271, rest/lodg
Rubber and Plastics Hoses and Belting Manufacturing, 356-357, mfg
RV (Recreational Vehicle) Parks and Campgrounds, 1266-1267, rest/lodg

S

Sales Financing, 894-895, fin
Sanitary Paper Product Manufacturing, 304-305, mfg
Saw Blade and Handtool Manufacturing, 386-387, mfg
Sawmills, 280-281, mfg
Scheduled Passenger Air Transportation, 798-799, trans
School and Employee Bus Transportation, 820-821, trans
Seafood Product Preparation and Packaging, 240-241, mfg
Search, Detection, Navigation, Guidance, Aeronautical, and Nautical System and Instrument Manufacturing, 504-505, mfg
Secondary Smelting and Alloying of Aluminum, 376-377, mfg
Security Guards and Patrol Services, 1090-1091, Admin
Security Systems Services (except Locksmiths), 1092-1093, Admin
Semiconductor and Related Device Manufacturing, 498-499, mfg
Septic Tank and Related Services, 1124-1125, Admin
Service Establishment Equipment and Supplies Merchant Wholesalers, 642-643, wsle
Services for the Elderly and Persons with Disabilities, 1210-1211, HC
Sheet Metal Work Manufacturing, 396-397, mfg
Ship Building and Repairing, 548-549, mfg
Shoe Retailers, 778-779, rtl
Showcase, Partition, Shelving, and Locker Manufacturing, 566-567, mfg
Sign Manufacturing, 578-579, mfg
Site Preparation Contractors, 214-215, cons-g
Site Preparation Contractors, 1388, cons-%
Skiing Facilities, 1246-1247, ent
Small Arms, Ordnance, and Ordnance Accessories Manufacturing, 430-431, mfg
Snack and Nonalcoholic Beverage Bars, 1282-1283, rest/lodg
Soap and Other Detergent Manufacturing, 334-335, mfg
Soft Drink Manufacturing, 256-257, mfg
Software Publishers, 872-873, info
Soil Preparation, Planting, and Cultivating, 114-115, ag
Solar Electric Power Generation, 144-145, util
Solid Waste Collection, 1110-1111, Admin
Solid Waste Landfill, 1116-1117, Admin
Soybean Farming, 86-87, ag
Special Die and Tool, Die Set, Jig, and Fixture Manufacturing, 460-461, mfg
Specialized Automotive Repair, 1288-1289, other
Specialized Freight (except Used Goods) Trucking, Local, 816-817, trans
Specialized Freight (except Used Goods) Trucking, Long-Distance, 818-819, trans
Specialty (except Psychiatric and Substance Abuse) Hospitals, 1194-1195, HC
Spice and Extract Manufacturing, 250-251, mfg
Sporting and Athletic Goods Manufacturing, 576-577, mfg
Sporting and Recreational Goods and Supplies Merchant Wholesalers, 646-647, wsle
Sporting Goods Retailers, 782-783, rtl
Sports and Recreation Instruction, 1142-1143, edu
Sports Teams and Clubs, 1228-1229, ent
Spring Manufacturing, 406-407, mfg
Stationery and Office Supplies Merchant Wholesalers, 658-659, wsle
Stationery Product Manufacturing, 302-303, mfg
Structural Steel and Precast Concrete Contractors, 184-185, cons-g
Structural Steel and Precast Concrete Contractors, 1381, cons-%
Supermarkets and Other Grocery Retailers (except Convenience Retailers), 740-741, rtl
Support Activities for Animal Production, 120-121, ag
Support Activities for Forestry, 122-123, ag
Support Activities for Oil and Gas Operations, 138-139, mng
Support Activities for Rail Transportation, 830-831, trans
Surgical and Medical Instrument Manufacturing, 568-569, mfg
Surgical Appliance and Supplies Manufacturing, 570-571, mfg
Surveying and Mapping (except Geophysical) Services, 1002-1003, prof serv
Switchgear and Switchboard Apparatus Manufacturing, 518-519, mfg

T

Tax Preparation Services, 990-991, prof serv
Telecommunications Resellers, 884-885, info
Telemarketing Bureaus and Other Contact Centers, 1078-1079, Admin
Television Broadcasting Stations, 876-877, info
Temporary Help Services, 1074-1075, Admin
Temporary Shelters, 1216-1217, HC
Testing Laboratories and Services, 1004-1005, prof serv
Textile and Fabric Finishing Mills, 266-267, mfg
Theater Companies and Dinner Theaters, 1226-1227, ent
Tile and Terrazzo Contractors, 208-209, cons-g
Timber Tract Operations, 108-109, ag
Tire and Tube Merchant Wholesalers, 592-593, wsle
Tire Dealers, 728-729, rtl
Tobacco Product and Electronic Cigarette Merchant Wholesalers, 708-709, wsle
Toilet Preparation Manufacturing, 338-339, mfg
Tour Operators, 1086-1087, Admin
Toy and Hobby Goods and Supplies Merchant Wholesalers, 648-649, wsle
Transportation Equipment and Supplies (except Motor Vehicle) Merchant Wholesalers, 644-645, wsle
Travel Agencies, 1084-1085, Admin
Travel Trailer and Camper Manufacturing, 530-531, mfg
Tree Nut Farming, 96-97, ag
Truck Trailer Manufacturing, 528-529, mfg
Truck, Utility Trailer, and RV (Recreational Vehicle) Rental and Leasing, 960-961, R/E
Trust, Fiduciary, and Custody Activities, 914-915, fin
Trusts, Estates, and Agency Accounts, 934-935, fin

U

Upholstered Household Furniture Manufacturing, 558-559, mfg
Urethane and Other Foam Product (except Polystyrene) Manufacturing, 350-351, mfg
Used Car Dealers, 718-719, rtl
Used Household and Office Goods Moving, 814-815, trans
Used Merchandise Retailers, 790-791, rtl

V

Veterinary Services, 1054-1055, prof serv
Vocational Rehabilitation Services, 1220-1221, HC
Voluntary Health Organizations, 1326-1327, other

W

Warm Air Heating and Air-Conditioning Equipment and Supplies Merchant Wholesalers, 630-631, wsle
Water and Sewer Line and Related Structures Construction, 170-171, cons-g
Water and Sewer Line and Related Structures Construction, 1376, cons-%
Water Supply and Irrigation Systems, 154-155, util
Web Search Portals and All Other Information Services, 890-891, info
Welding and Soldering Equipment Manufacturing, 478-479, mfg
Wholesale Trade Agents and Brokers, 712-713, wsle
Wind Electric Power Generation, 146-147, util
Wine and Distilled Alcoholic Beverage Merchant Wholesalers, 702-703, wsle
Wineries, 260-261, mfg
Wired Telecommunications Carriers, 880-881, info
Wireless Telecommunications Carriers (except Satellite), 882-883, info
Wood Container and Pallet Manufacturing, 288-289, mfg
Wood Kitchen Cabinet and Countertop Manufacturing, 556-557, mfg
Wood Window and Door Manufacturing, 284-285, mfg

Z

Zoos and Botanical Gardens, 1236-1237, ent